W9-BZK-484

The Norton Anthology of Western Philosophy

After Kant

THE INTERPRETIVE TRADITION

The Norton Anthology of Western Philosophy
Richard Schacht, *General Editor*
PROFESSOR OF PHILOSOPHY AND JUBILEE PROFESSOR
OF LIBERAL ARTS AND SCIENCES, EMERITUS
UNIVERSITY OF ILLINOIS AT URBANA-CHAMPAIGN

The Norton Anthology of Western Philosophy

After Kant

THE INTERPRETIVE TRADITION

Volume Editor:

Richard Schacht

PROFESSOR OF PHILOSOPHY AND JUBILEE PROFESSOR
OF LIBERAL ARTS AND SCIENCES, EMERITUS
UNIVERSITY OF ILLINOIS AT URBANA-CHAMPAIGN

with the assistance of
Matthew Rukgaber

W · W · NORTON & COMPANY · New York · London

W. W. Norton & Company has been independent since its founding in 1923, when William Warder Norton and Mary D. Herter Norton first published lectures delivered at the People's Institute, the adult education division of New York City's Cooper Union. The firm soon expanded its program beyond the Institute, publishing books by celebrated academics from America and abroad. By midcentury, the two major pillars of Norton's publishing program—trade books and college texts—were firmly established. In the 1950s, the Norton family transferred control of the company to its employees, and today—with a staff of four hundred and a comparable number of trade, college, and professional titles published each year—W. W. Norton & Company stands as the largest and oldest publishing house owned wholly by its employees.

Editors: Ken Barton, Peter Simon, Allen Clawson
Project Editor: Jennifer Barnhardt
Manuscript Editor: Alice Falk
Associate Editor: Quynh Do
Assistant Editors: Shannon Jilek, Gerra Goff, and Conor Sullivan
Managing Editor, College: Marian Johnson
Managing Editor, College Digital Media: Kim Yi
Production Manager: Sean Mintus
Media Editor: Erica Wnek
Marketing Manager, Philosophy: Michael Moss
Design Director: Rubina Yeh
Designer: Jo Anne Metsch
Permissions Manager: Megan Jackson
Composition: Westchester
Manufacturing: LSC

Permission to use copyrighted material is included on page A-117.

ISBN: 978-0-393-97468-3 (pbk.)

W. W. Norton & Company, Inc., 500 Fifth Avenue, New York,
NY 10110-0017
wwnorton.com

W. W. Norton & Company Ltd., 15 Carlisle Street, London W1D 3BS

1 2 3 4 5 6 7 8 9 0

Contents

III. PHENOMENOLOGIES: CONSCIOUSNESS AND HUMAN EXISTENCE

IV. CROSS-CURRENTS: RETHINKING HUMAN REALITY AND POSSIBILITY

Preface

This volume deals with a part of the history of Western philosophy after Kant. Western philosophy, as almost anyone picking up this volume will know, has a history that began with the pre-Christian Greeks and Romans. It continued (after a fashion) in the European Middle Ages as a ward of Christian theology, and then underwent a renascence in the Renaissance, recovering its autonomy and commencing what is commonly referred to as its "modern" (or "early modern") period. That period is generally considered to have begun with such late Renaissance thinkers as René Descartes and Thomas Hobbes in the first half of the seventeenth century, and to have culminated impressively in the "critical philosophy" of Immanuel Kant toward the end of the eighteenth century. It featured the emergence and development of the very different traditions of "empiricism" and "rationalism" and their synthesizing supersession in Kant's "critiques" of the various forms of reason and judgment. Kant thought nothing of importance remained for philosophy to do.

The history of philosophy did not end with Kant, but philosophy after him certainly did change. The period that ended with him was followed by another, during which philosophy went in different directions that undoubtedly would have astonished (and perhaps distressed) him, and yet became even more interesting in many ways than it had been previously. This post-Kantian era—which may or may not turn out in the eyes of posterity to have ended in the late twentieth century—is sometimes referred to as philosophy's "recent modern" period. It was a period during which two quite different traditions emerged and developed, one of which became what has come to be known as "analytic philosophy," while the other became a kind of adventuresome contest of modes and avenues of interpretation. They are explored in the two After Kant volumes of this anthology of Western philosophy: the present volume, The Interpretive Tradition, and its companion volume, The Analytic Tradition.

These two volumes provide selective introductions to these somewhat parallel (and, for much of the twentieth century, antagonistic) post-Kantian traditions in the history of philosophy, and to thinkers who figured prominently in them. The two developments are sometimes identified geographically as "Anglo-American" and "Continental" because although both had European origins, one relocated to the Anglo-American part of the world (in the 1930s), while the other remained centered in Continental Europe for much of the twentieth century. But it is both possible and more appropriate to designate them differently and more informatively, in the above manner—in terms broadly indicative of the differing basic characters and preoccupations of the developments themselves. Thus the former is commonly referred to as "analytic" philosophy, or philosophy as it has been pursued in the "analytic" tradition, in which primacy has been accorded to various sorts of *analysis*.

That tradition's geographically-identified "other" and longtime rival may contrastingly but comparably be thought of as a tradition in which philosophy has had a more *interpretive* character. Its characterization as a contest of "interpretations" is to be understood rather broadly. This term's virtue is its suggestiveness as a flexible but meaningful rubric that can be used to embrace diverse attempts at *sense-making comprehension and assessment*, addressing many sorts of matters and issues (mostly relating to human reality and possibility) about which there are no clear and decisive decision procedures—including the problem of what to make of these competing ways of thinking themselves. And in this "contest," convincing *case-making* pro and con—rather than rigorous proof, straightforward analysis, or factual determination—is the name of the game.

This volume is an introduction to a broad range of thinkers who have figured significantly in this philosophical tradition, from Kant's immediate successors—most notably Hegel and Marx—through the generations of Kierkegaard and Nietzsche, and of Heidegger and Sartre, to that of Michel Foucault and Jürgen Habermas (and to a few others at each end). This is as much of the interpretive tradition as can reasonably be regarded at this point as a part of the history of modern Western philosophy. Special attention is given to a relatively small number of figures who were of particular importance in the development of this tradition (Hegel, Nietzsche, and Heidegger in particular). The thinkers to be encountered are presented in four broad groupings. These groupings, and the resultant division of the volume into four parts, reflect some of the affinities and differences among them. Other groupings are possible, however, and may better suit particular courses or interests. Instructors and individual readers alike are encouraged to bring together figures from different parts of the volume as may suit their purposes and interests.

Anyone familiar with figures and developments in this tradition is likely to find some favorites missing here. Even anthologies as substantial as this one are finite, and choices had to be made. Instructors may well want to integrate other figures—and other texts by included figures—into their courses on developments in this tradition. There is a lot here, however; and the contents of this volume should be largely sufficient to enable readers to become broadly acquainted with this extraordinarily rich and interesting part of modern philosophy. It is hoped and expected that many readers will want to read more deeply in authors whose writings included here inspire their interest. Time will tell which of them continue to seem to be of importance, and which others will come to seem deserving of inclusion with them—or in their places.

The interpretive tradition is a tradition that originated and largely developed in Continental Europe (hence the label "Continental"), and in a period during much of which the leading lights in most disciplines (philosophy included) were predominantly male and of European descent. That is inevitably reflected in the demographics of this volume, the primary focus of which is upon key figures in the first two centuries of this tradition. An effort has been made, however, to make the volume more inclusive than a standard list of choices would be by attempting to identify notable figures from other demographics during that time-frame whose thought and work may reasonably be considered to be both associated with the interpretive tradition and of sufficient quality and significance to warrant their inclusion. (This is an advantage of construing this tradition as broadly "interpretive," which readily allows for its compass to be conceived as extending beyond its "Continental" originators and mainstays to others with links to them and whose thought has a similarly and relatedly interpretive character.) Hence the inclusion of W. E. B. Du Bois and Frantz Fanon; of Mary Wollstonecraft (as well as John Stuart Mill and Ralph Waldo Emerson—other non-Continental interpretive kindred spirits); of Hannah Arendt and Simone Weil (as well as Simone de Beauvoir); and of several contemporary figures differently but plausibly associated with strands of this tradition as it is configured here, Judith Butler and Martha Nussbaum among them.

While the four groupings in this volume are not the only ones possible, there are good reasons for them. The first two parts divide philosophers in the interpretive tradition between Kant and Husserl (and the beginning of the phenomenological movement) in a way that is both roughly chronological and philosophically meaningful. Part I is devoted primarily to variations on the philosophical "idealisms" that were inspired by combining Kant's "transcendental idealism" with his insistence on the irreducibility of moral reality to sensible reality. Part II presents a number of figures who reacted against these "idealisms" and approached and interpreted human reality quite differently, as something whose character and distinctiveness are owed to its development as a form of *life*. Their approaches may in contrast be characterized, very broadly and loosely, as "naturalisms."

Part III features twentieth-century thinkers from Husserl onward who, reacting against this "naturalistic" turn, gave interpretive priority to "first-person" experiential perspectives over others, often under the label "phenomenology." It includes some associated with "existential philosophy" (the philosophy of human "existing") and the "existentialism" derived from it, as well as others who were very differently-minded—including Husserl himself. The fourth and final part introduces a number of thinkers who have gone in other directions—and who have little more in common than a dissatisfaction with (or even an aversion to) what might be called the "phenomenological turn" encountered in the previous part. They include representatives of such other significant developments as philosophical anthropology, poststructuralism, hermeneutics, and various sorts of critical (social, race, and gender) theory.

———

Two basic uses for this volume are envisioned. One, of course, is in courses in the history of philosophy after Kant. But it may also be used as a resource by individuals in philosophy and other disciplines, and also by readers more generally, who are interested in (or may simply be curious about) some of these figures and developments and wish to become better acquainted with them. The interpretive tradition features many daunting thinkers and works; and without help both in finding key texts and in understanding them, few readers are likely to get very far. With this volume as a guide and resource, interested readers can actually explore it on their own. And since few potential readers—even in philosophy—are likely to have taken courses on very many of these figures and developments, even the more knowledgeable among them should find this volume a very useful resource. It is sure to fill many gaps in the personal libraries of students in philosophy, and in any other discipline to which the history of recent modern philosophy is relevant.

Most philosophy departments have one or more faculty members who can easily teach a survey course in the history of philosophy from Descartes to Kant. This frequently does not extend to the post-Kantian interpretive tradition, even though student interest in some of its leading figures is often high. This volume is designed to be of assistance to instructors whose familiarity with this tradition is limited but who are nonetheless confronted with the challenges of teaching courses in it, as well as to supply those who know their way around with a rich array of textual assets and assistance for their students.

The contents of this volume greatly exceed what could be covered (or even reasonably assigned) in a one-semester course. Such coverage, even if selective, would require a two-semester course or sequence (for which its four-part division makes it well suited). A one-semester survey of the whole period could be devised that would pass over many of the less prominent figures and deal only with some selections from major figures, while encouraging students to take note of and sample the rest. But other types of courses in this general area are also possible (and popular) that can be variously structured, not just chronologically but also by developments that span both centuries (for example, existential philosophy). The volume is designed to work well in any such course—and it has the advantage of being able to serve as the single primary text in a variety of them that might be offered (and taken) successively.

The amount of material included from the various figures varies greatly. In a fair number of cases one or two relatively brief selections must suffice, offering simply a sample of the sort of work for which they deserve recognition and attention. For major figures, on the other hand, enough of their work has been provided—selected with an eye to (relative) accessibility as well as to significance and interest—that instructors who wish to do so can devote considerable attention to them individually, and can construct whole courses around relatively small numbers of them with few if any supplementary texts. Other figures fall in between, with selections more modest in number and length but still sufficient to provide a good introduction to their thought.

For some authors, such as Schopenhauer, Heidegger, and Sartre, the volume includes substantial portions of the particular major works that are their primary claims to enduring importance (along with samplings of their other writings). For others, such as Hegel and Nietzsche, no one or two of whose writings stand clearly above the rest in that respect, selections from a variety of different works are offered in an attempt to provide a more suitable introduction to their thought. Excerpts have been made with a view to enabling readers to get a good sense of the works from which they are taken, and of what it is about them (and in them) that matters. Instructors can also select from the selections, using those that they find work best for them and their students, within the time they choose to devote to the figures in question. Individual readers can do the same.

Hegel is a special case, owing not only to his special place and importance in the interpretive tradition but also to the problems presented by the character and variety of his texts and terminology. This volume offers a solution to what has long been a challenge for anyone who undertakes to introduce Hegel to those who are new to him—or anyone attempting to become acquainted with him on their own: the challenge of text selection, since none of his major writings by themselves works very well for this purpose. The approach taken here involves making use of Hegel's own introductions to his various lecture series (in which he communicates his thought most clearly and accessibly) as well as judiciously selected and topically arranged excerpts from his *Encyclopedia* (itself written as a kind of textbook to accompany his core series of lecture courses) and from accompanying lecture notes, paired with corresponding excerpts from his *Phenomenology of Spirit* and *Philosophy of Right*. In these ways readers are introduced to the range (and power) of Hegel's thinking; and his own explanations and elaborations are employed to make his thought optimally comprehensible and teachable—in the very way he himself (to great acclaim) led his own students and wider audiences into it. (Instructors and readers can decide for themselves how much and which of the extensive array of these selections they wish to avail themselves of; for they are intended to enable those who are so inclined to proceed well beyond the level of simply making Hegel's philosophical acquaintance.)

———————

Each of the four parts of this volume has its own introduction, presenting the developments and figures that will be encountered in it. A good deal more about each figure is conveyed in the headnote that precedes each author's selection or group of selections, and sometimes in footnotes to the selections. Readers are strongly encouraged to avail themselves of all explanatory material; for there is often much about the figures, and in and about the selections, that is helpful to know and that needs explaining. The footnotes as well as the headnotes are often interpretive as well as factual, and so are not beyond dispute. They are intended to begin discussion of the texts rather than to end it; and their discussion should itself serve both to enhance the comprehension of the selections and to heighten interest in them.

Headnotes begin with brief introductions to the featured figures, followed by biographical information, discussion of their thinking and significance, and some remarks about the selections that follow. Bibliographical sections for each figure are to be found in the back of the volume (along with general bibliographies). They provide information both about writings by them available in English or English translation and about the secondary literature on them that is available in English. (This extensive bibliographical information is another feature that makes the volume a valuable resource for advanced graduate students and faculty in philosophy and in kindred disciplines who are interested in these figures. It also provides an indication of the extent to which the various figures have [or have not] received attention in the English-speaking world.)

English-speaking readers often have difficulty with many of the European-language names to be encountered here. (The pronunciation of my own name illustrates the problem; "shocked" is acceptable—for non-Germans—but that needs telling.) Learning to pronounce these philosophers' names properly is almost as important as learning to spell them properly (when writing about them). Unless the proper pronunciation of a name is completely obvious (for example, "Marx"), pronunciation guidance is offered near the beginning of each headnote. Such assistance is also provided for the pronunciation of a number of Hegel's (and some other German writers') key terms in German, which are often shown in their selections. Readers are urged to think of the German terms when encountering the English terms commonly (but often oddly or misleadingly) used to translate them; and to be able to do so, knowing how they are pronounced helps.

Keeping key German (or French) terms in mind is desirable because translating them—not only in Hegel's writings but in those of many of the other figures in the interpretive tradition as well—is a tricky business. It sometimes happens that there are no exact or even close counterparts in English to the terms' standard use in the original languages, let alone to the special meanings they have been given or usages they have acquired in the writings of Hegel and others. In some cases there are no counterparts at all that are not confusing or misleading, particularly when the meanings of the English terms originally chosen have themselves changed in the course of the decades (or even century or more) since some translations were made. And there are also cases in which the word choices of translators are simply perplexing, or have interpretive consequences that are problematic. Sometimes, therefore, it arguably would have been better to leave key terms untranslated in the text and to explain them in footnotes—as some translators themselves have done. Where this has been possible and has seemed to me to be advisable, I have replaced misleading or questionable translation choices with their (mainly German) originals. Where for copyright reasons this has not been possible but arguably would have been desirable, I have inserted the original terms in brackets following the translators' choices of English terms, to remind readers of the terms actually used on those occasions, and of any special points of meaning that may have been noted.

———

This volume is intended to serve as a kind of guide into and through the fascinating but rocky and often bewildering terrain of the interpretive tradition in philosophy after Kant. The landscape is sufficiently strange and daunting upon first encounter that such a guide is needed to assist newcomers in learning their way around in it. I certainly needed such guidance myself in my student days. I had the good fortune to be at the right places at the right times to receive it—first from Paul Tillich at Harvard (as an undergraduate), then from Walter Kaufmann at Princeton (as a graduate student), and subsequently from the excellent philosophy faculty at Tübingen University in Germany (during two lengthy stays there early in my career)—Otto Bollnow, Ernst Bloch, Walter Schultz, Helmut Fahrenbach, and Frithjof Rodi in particular. Those were only beginnings; but they were essential ones toward enabling me to become such a guide myself, both for students and for others.

What I and others seeking to provide that guidance have long needed but lacked has been a volume like this one, to be able both to use in courses and to recommend to anyone interested—a volume bringing together a substantial array of suitably introduced selections and excerpts from key texts (in English or English translation) of thinkers who have figured significantly in this tradition. That is the resource this volume is intended to be. Differing approaches have been taken to the selection of texts by the various interpretive tradition figures included. Their mix is what I believe to be the best way of introducing this tradition and these figures to readers who do not yet know them well—and of enabling such readers to gain a fuller sense of the dimensions, contours, and major themes of the thought of the more prominent figures among them. The latter objective, as I have pursued it, has involved taking a "key parts" (rather than "single portion" or "short work") approach to the work of these figures. That is one of the forms of assistance a good guide is needed to provide. But it should go without saying that, after benefiting from it, readers in whom interest has been kindled by the gathered parts should go to their sources (and further texts, and secondary sources) to see them in full context, and take their studies to the next level.

————

I dedicate this volume to my grandchildren, Madison, Kayley, Noelle, and Wade, in the fond hope that they may one day come to know and take an interest in what it's all about—but with just as much love even if they don't.

Acknowledgments

This project, embracing both "After Kant" volumes, would have been long and difficult under the best of circumstances—and the circumstances have instead been trying, in multiple respects. It seemed for a time, for example, that permissions issues relating to available translations of selections would prove an insurmountable roadblock. (Happily, ways of resolving most of these problems were eventually found. While not always ideal, they did make it possible to include the desired—often substantial—portions of various key texts in English translation.) And events seemed to conspire to compound delays. I want to express my great gratitude to Peter Simon and his colleagues at Norton, whose enduring belief in and commitment to the project have been inspiring, and whose forbearance has been as remarkable as it was crucial.

I also want to thank my first editor for this project at Norton, Allen Clawson, whose early contributions to it were vital. He and his Norton colleague Roby Harrington recruited me as general editor of the project quite some time ago, for which I was and remain very grateful. I am further grateful for his responsiveness, as we worked together to evolve the anthology concept initially formulated by him and Norton into a multivolume project appropriate to the history of Western philosophy and to the reality of how its teaching is generally structured. My gratitude to him extends to his support as I proceeded to develop the plan for this specific volume, which I was to edit. It was Peter Simon, however, who took over the project once the basic volume plans were set; and I couldn't have hoped for a better working relationship than I have had with him over the intervening years, through thick and thin. I am greatly indebted to his successor Ken Barton, to their assistants—Quynh Do, Conor Sullivan, Gerra Goff, and Shannon Jilek—and (with special thanks) to Project Editor Jennifer Barnhardt, for their labors in this volume's production; and I am in awe of the editing abilities, efforts, and contributions of Alice Falk. I am further grateful to their colleagues Sean Mintus (Production Manager), Michael Moss (Marketing Manager), and Megan Jackson (Permissions Manager) for their various important contributions to the project.

My thanks also go to Jim Conant, for agreeing to undertake the editing of the companion post-Kantian volume, and for his subsequent recruitment of Jay Elliot to collaborate with him in that task. Conant was my first choice for that role, both because I considered him ideal for it and because he is a philosophical kindred spirit. For the successful pairing of the two volumes, it was just as important that he appreciate the tradition with which my volume deals as it was that I appreciate the tradition covered by his. I am deeply gratified by the outcome of our collaboration, and I value the working (as well as philosophical and personal) relationship that has seen us through the long march this project has been. Elliot's contributions have been crucial to its successful completion.

While developing the plan for this volume I benefitted from discussing it with a good many colleagues who share my interest in the post-Kantian interpretive tradition—and who teach courses dealing with figures and developments in it. I was gratified by their support for the idea of such a volume and for my proposed approach. I subsequently have been even more gratified by the enthusiasm of those with whom I have shared its developing table of contents (whom I would like to thank collectively for their helpful feedback)—and to whom I apologize for making them wait so long for the volume itself to become available for their use!

I wish in conclusion to express my enormous appreciation to Matthew Rukgaber, whose assistance with this volume has been extraordinary. That assistance began quite some time ago, when he was a graduate student in my department and I was in need of a research assistant; and it evolved markedly as he completed his graduate program and entered into the life of the profession. First and foremost a Kant scholar, he proved also to be an invaluable comrade-in-arms for me in navigating the post-Kantian seas of this volume. In addition to having done much of the biographical research and even more of the bibliographical research for it, he deserves primary credit for the substantive portions of a number of the headnotes as well (in particular, those for Deleuze and Guattari, Derrida, Lyotard, Foucault, Lévinas, Fanon, Butler, Gadamer, and Ricoeur); his own interests and knowledge were so well suited to these tasks that I found the drafts he prepared hard to improve on. All of this (and more) was assistance at the highest of levels, amply warranting its recognition on the title page.

The Norton Anthology of Western Philosophy

After Kant

THE INTERPRETIVE TRADITION

General Introduction

I

The two-century period spanned by this volume was one of enormous change in the Western world on both sides of the Atlantic. At the time of the publication of its first selection (by IMMANUEL KANT, in 1784), France was still a monarchy and the United States was still a "confederation" with no constitution or president. It was the age of Haydn and Mozart in music; German-speaking Europe's greatest writer, Johann Wolfgang von Goethe, was only beginning to make his literary reputation; and the recent publication of Kant's revolutionary *Critique of Pure Reason* (1781) had made him the newly dominant figure on the philosophical scene.

The close of the eighteenth century and the dawning of the post-Kantian era were rocked by the French Revolution, after which France no longer had a king (but did have Napoleon, who assumed power in a coup). The United States had a national government along with its first president and a constitution (one that allowed slavery), and Beethoven had just written his first symphony. East of France there was no "Germany," but rather a thousand-year-old collection of states called the "Holy Roman Empire of the German People," containing a traditionally strong Austria and an ascendant Prussia in the east, and a large number of smaller principalities in the south and west.

It was a very different world. In 1800 the United States extended only as far west as the Mississippi River, and most of its mere 5 million people (nearly 1 million of whom were slaves) lived on or near the Atlantic Coast. The combined population of Great Britain was 10.5 million, while that of the German states was 25 million. In North America Canada was British, the southwest and west (plus Florida) were Spanish, and the middle of the continent from the Mississippi to the Rockies was French. The Industrial Revolution was just beginning in Europe, where monarchs and aristocracies were dominant politically and economically. Transportation was by foot, horse or carriage, and water. Wood, coal, animal fat, and whale oil were the only sources of heat and light. Institutional religion was widespread and very powerful in public and intellectual life, particularly in Europe, where in some places religious orthodoxy was a requirement of academic appointment. France was the most powerful nation-state in Europe and was about to conquer the continent under Napoleon, while the German states, although politically backward and militarily and economically weak, were at the forefront of an explosion of artistic, musical, literary, and intellectual development.

By 1860, sixty years later, the United States had tripled in size, extending beyond the Mississippi River all the way to the Pacific Ocean. Its population

1

had risen to 31 million (4 million of whom were slaves). A civil war was about to begin that would result in casualties in unheard-of numbers, the abolition of slavery, the preservation of the union, and the assassination of a president, Abraham Lincoln. Russia's serfs would soon be emancipated, two years before Lincoln emancipated America's slaves. Great Britain, with a population of only 23 million, had become the world's greatest maritime power, with an empire that had recently come to include India. The Napoleonic era had come and gone, destroying the Holy Roman Empire in the process. In its place an Austrian empire had emerged centered on Vienna, and a confederation of northern and western German states had been formed. The German Confederation would in 1871 become a unified and Prussia-dominated German *Reich* (empire), with Berlin as its capital and with a population of 38 million.

The Industrial Revolution was in high gear, fueling the complex dynamic of capitalism, nationalism, and imperialism that was reshaping the political and economic contours of the West and the world, even though monarchs and aristocrats remained in nominal control. The railroad and steamship were revolutionizing transportation, while other technologies were beginning to revolutionize communication (notably, the telegraph) and warfare. Composers such as Schumann and Wagner were revolutionizing music, and literature was flourishing not only in Britain and Continental Europe but even in America. The influence of religion in cultural and social life on both sides of the Atlantic remained strong, despite the lessening of its institutional power. The sciences were surging ahead in many new areas. Charles Darwin had just published *On the Origin of Species* (1859), but its impact had not yet begun to be felt.

In another sixty years, by 1920, the Western world had been transformed again, even more dramatically. It had just undergone the incredible devastation of the First World War, which had pitted the two German-speaking empires against the rest of Europe's nations (and, at the end, the United States as well). Millions of the young men of Europe had died, spelling the beginning of the end of Europe's global dominance—and, within Europe, of the era of monarchs and aristocracies. One of Europe's great empires (the Austro-Hungarian) had ceased to exist; another (the Russian) was overthrown and radically transformed in the revolution that gave birth to the Soviet Union; and a third (the German) had been differently transformed into an ill-fated and short-lived democracy (the Weimar Republic). The catastrophe then called the Great War ended in a way that sowed the seeds of the economic and the political disasters of the Great Depression and contributed to the rise of Fascism (in Italy) and Nazism (under Hitler in Germany).

America had been drawn unwillingly into the fray, but it emerged as a potential rival to the traditional European powers, with a relatively unscathed and rapidly growing population and with dramatically increasing economic strength. Its population had grown to 105 million (surpassing the combined total of Germany's 60 million and Great Britain's 44 million). The automobile, truck, airplane, electric light, telephone, radio, and cinema were transforming social, cultural, and economic life throughout the Western world, and new technologies were giving rise to new industries. The sciences, multiplying and developing at an extraordinary rate, were coming to rival religion in popular as well as academic thinking. Europe continued to be the cultural and intellectual center it had been before the war, but political storm clouds were gathering. Popular culture was coming to challenge and even eclipse the forms of music, arts, and literature that were being cultivated among the cultural elite, contributing to their marginalization.

The world of 1980, sixty more years later (and more or less the time of the most recent selections in this volume), was astonishingly transfigured yet again. The First World War was the beginning of the end of the world as the nineteenth century had known it; but no one could have imagined what was to come. That war was said to have been fought to "make the world safe for democracy," and was thought to have been "the war to end all wars." Nothing could have been further from the truth. The shape of the Western world was profoundly altered by the revolutionary transformation of the Russian empire into a "Marxist" Soviet Union, global economic collapse (beginning with hyperinflation in Germany and the stock market crash of 1929 in the United States), the rise and spread of political radicalism (fascism and Nazism on the right, communism on the left), another and even more catastrophic world war, the horror of the Holocaust, the first use of nuclear weapons, the emergence of the Soviet Union under Stalin as a new "superpower" intent on rivalry with the United States and committed to "world revolution," the dawning of the age of possible thermonuclear war, and a "cold war" that made such a world-ending real war a constant danger. Germany, which under Hitler and the Nazis had become a monstrosity whose actions resulted in tens of millions of deaths and had threatened the very survival of Western civilization, was greatly reduced in size, divided (although eventually reunified), and essentially eliminated as a major military power (as was Japan, its ally in the Second World War). Britain and France, while emerging victorious from the war, ceased to be major powers. Caught in the middle in the confrontation between the United States and the Soviet Union, Europe was in effect divided by an "iron curtain" that split Eastern from Western Europe and ran between the two Germanys.

These multiple traumas cast long and dark shadows over intellectual and spiritual life during these generations and beyond them—in Europe, in the societies of the two superpowers, and in much of the rest of the world. Since 1980 these shadows have largely receded. The cold war is now a thing of the past. The Soviet Union (and its empire in Eastern Europe) no longer exists, and Europe is no longer divided. New technologies—particularly those related to electronics and bioengineering—have powerfully transformed life. New challenges and perils have emerged, and much else has changed. But the world of 1980—in contrast to that of 1920—is at least recognizably similar to our own. (For much more information relating events in the history of the past several centuries to the figures and writings featured here, see the Timeline in the back of this volume.)

The philosopher G. W. F. HEGEL (who looms large in the "interpretive tradition," and therefore in this volume) said many famous things, one of which is "Philosophy is its age comprehended in thought." If he was on to something here, then the philosophical developments comprehended in this volume—which were primarily European in their geography—must stand in some relation of this sort to significant features of these two centuries of recent Western (and primarily European) history. If the phrase "its age" is construed broadly enough to mean something like "the character, fundamental convictions, problems, and preoccupations of the society and culture in which it occurs," there may well be something to Hegel's observation. But he was not saying that all philosophy is of purely regional and momentary significance, in the manner of the editorial pages of a newspaper. On the contrary: he believed and maintained that the human spirit (no less than the human body) not merely changes but develops and matures, moving toward the full realization of its true nature—and that the same applies to philosophy, as one of the human spirit's most important expressions.

Hegel's suggestion was that the philosophy associated with a particular part of human history reflects where the human spirit is at that historical juncture, in the course of its unfolding human-spiritual development. That kind of philosophy will reflect not just the contingencies and limitations of its age but also its level of attained sophistication in its comprehension of ourselves and our world. What is of greatest significance in any philosophy, according to Hegel, is what it captures and expresses of that which its age is contributing to the self-realization of the human spirit—even though philosophy always has been and always will be a human endeavor, carried on in particular human-historical circumstances (which make "its age" *its* age). In reflecting upon the selections that follow, readers should be mindful of both sides of this thought (at least as a guiding idea) and make allowances for the influences of the differences of the "ages" out of which they speak to us from our own.

Pursuing this thought a step further: while the philosophical tradition under consideration here is a part of the larger "Western" intellectual-historical tradition that most readers of this volume are likely either to share or to know, the branch (or cluster of branches) after Kant on which it centers differs markedly from its predominantly English-speaking ones. Its geographical heartland has been the continent of Europe—for which reason it is often referred to as "Continental philosophy." Its primary languages have been German and French; and, more to the present point, the historical experience of Continental Europe during this period not only has been enormously diverse internally but also has been radically different even from that of Great Britain, let alone that of the United States.

As the foregoing sketch has recalled, from the French Revolution onward the European Continent has been the site of numerous revolutions, crises, social and political upheavals and nightmares, human catastrophes and horrors, and devastating wars that have shaken its foundations and torn it apart time and again. It has also had to deal with a profusion of linguistic, national, and ethnic traditions, histories, and identities existing in close proximity. If there is anything to Hegel's observation, therefore, it is not surprising that differences in philosophical sensibility have developed in the recent history of Western philosophy—even in the same areas at different periods—that take some getting used to, thus posing challenges for those encountering them for the first time. These challenges can be surmounted; but doing so is not easy, in part because of this complexity.

Another challenge has to do with the need to have some sense of the relevant philosophical background of the developments to be considered in this volume. The next two sections provide some of that background.

II

"Modern philosophy" is generally understood to mean (Western) philosophy from René Descartes (1596–1650) and Thomas Hobbes (1588–1679) through David Hume (1711–1776) and Immanuel Kant, ending around 1800. This is because that tradition *was* "modern" philosophy *for Hegel* (writing in the first quarter of the nineteenth century). Hegel was largely responsible for the idea of "the history of philosophy" as a significant part of philosophy itself—and his influence was so great that the label became permanent. But what happened after Kant? That is the story of this volume and its companion, *The Analytic Tradition*.

Kant himself thought that there was not much left for philosophy to do other than refine and extend the system of thought he had established. A part of philosophy after him continued in the spirit of Hume and of Kant's "critiques" of theoretical and practical knowledge and rationality. By the last quarter of the nineteenth century Kant's view regained currency among the "Neo-Kantians," who by the turn of the century became the new academic-philosophical establishment in central Europe, and it gave impetus to the development of the like-minded "analytical" movement in British philosophy. But that was by no means the whole story. Other post-Kantians took a different part of Kant as their inspiration and point of departure, and their efforts blossomed into one of the most remarkable and fascinating arrays of adventuresome thought in the history of philosophy. While commonly referred to as "Continental philosophy" (as has already been noted), that geographical designation is less apt than the characterization chosen here to designate it: the "interpretive tradition."

This distinction is somewhat misleading, since both "analytical" and "interpretive" thinking are in evidence in both cases. Yet because of the difference in their emphases, the paired expressions capture (or at least suggest) a readily available and intelligible way of identifying these palpably divergent clusters of philosophical developments after Kant.

The difference may be vague; but for too much of the twentieth century it was deeply felt by partisans on both sides of the divide, going beyond mutual incomprehension to disdain and hostility. It will be all to the good if philosophy in the twenty-first century can outgrow the division and render the distinction merely a historically dated rubric. As a way of illuminating the history of philosophy after Kant to make its differing stories comprehensible, however, it remains useful. In particular, the terms "analytical" and "interpretive" are apt and helpful in that they convey something of the differing sorts of philosophical aspiration and sensibility that have long characterized the two traditions.

There are, of course, many different sorts of "analysis," and many different sorts of "interpretation" (and "reinterpretation"). But the developments associated with the interpretive tradition were in some measure first prompted and then characterized by a strong sense on the part of many of those included in this volume that a kind of thinking venturing beyond the analytical and rigorously argumentative (and the mathematical or scientific) is needed to do justice to the richness, interconnectedness, and depth of much of human reality, life, and experience, as well as to the normative and evaluative issues that arise regarding them. These issues include questions relating to our significance (if any) in the larger scheme of things, individually and collectively (as "humankind"), to the quality of life, and to human development and self-realization.

What made such issues and questions seem so pressing after Kant was that Kant himself had made it legitimate to raise and pursue them—independently of all religious tradition and authority, but without surrendering them to the natural sciences—and yet he did so in a manner that his successors found unconvincing, unsatisfactory, and even untenable. If neither religion nor science nor Kant had the last word with respect to the comprehension of human reality, possibility, and worth, how are these matters better to be conceived, pursued, and understood? The interpretive tradition might be thought of as a profusion of attempts to respond to this challenge, at once drawing on, reacting to, and competing with Kant and each other. All agreed that in his "critical" philosophy, Kant had set limits on what could be settled by natural-scientific and similarly modeled forms of inquiry. It was further agreed that far from imposing the same limits on philosophy, he had shown how it could and should be liberated from the authority of the sciences when it came to the things that matter most, and should be empowered to bring other sorts of considerations to bear upon them. But Kant's successors soon found themselves in considerable disagreement over how best to proceed in this brave new world of postreligious, postmetaphysical, postrationalist, postempiricist, and even post-"critical" interpretive philosophy.

For many of those who found themselves drawn to the alternative analytical tradition, the results were so alien to their philosophical sensibilities that they dismissed them as the productions of a kind of philosophical "dark age" from which it was best simply to avert one's eyes (and attempt to shield the eyes of one's students, lest they be corrupted). For many others, however, at each step of the way and still today, the results were experienced as liberating, exciting, and promising, offering the hope of a kind of philosophical thinking that has more to offer in terms of human self-understanding—and of self-realization—than is to be found elsewhere in the history of philosophy both before and after Kant (as well as in Kant himself).

Kant had conceived of himself as achieving not only a grand synthesis and culminating systematic development of what was best and most important in the empiricist and rationalist traditions in modern philosophy from Descartes to Hume, but also a "Copernican revolution" in our conception of the relation between mind and world. The original revolution launched by Copernicus (1473–1543) reversed the traditional understanding of the heavens, arguing that the earth revolved around the sun rather than being at the center in the arrangement of things. Kant's version reversed the traditional picture of the relationship between the basic *features of the world of experience* and the basic *structures of the mind* that cognizes that world, according primacy to the latter rather than the former. This Kantian "Copernican revolution"—and the accompanying problematization of the natural sciences' claim to have the last word in all things—was indeed important to many subsequent philosophers, for whom it was one of their points of departure. It was the basis of what Kant called his "transcendental idealism," which ascribed "ideality" or mind-relatedness to all of the basic features of the world of experience.

There was another revolution that was no less earth-shaking for many of Kant's immediate successors: the French Revolution of 1789. It and its aftermath shook European culture and society to their foundations. Some Europeans were inspired by its ideals, while others were traumatized by the "reign of terror" into which it descended and by the Napoleonic era that followed. There were other revolutionary changes occurring as well, whose impact was no less profound. One was the development of the sciences—physical, biological, and social—and their increasing autonomy in relation to religion, to philosophy, and to each other. The result was a confusing profusion of new ways of thinking about life and the world that challenged traditional ones.

Another change was the decline of the sway and unquestioning acceptance of traditional Christian thought, particularly in its biblical-literalist forms, resulting in a growing desire for something more sophisticated and persuasive that might take its place among those who now had to rethink the many matters concerning which it had long been deemed authoritative. On another front, a combination of industrial, economic, demographic, and social-structural revolutions was producing increasingly dramatic changes in the circumstances and character of people's lives across much of Europe, raising questions relating to the quality of life in newly vivid ways.

It seemed to a number of thinkers after Kant that problems and issues were being raised that not only called for philosophical consideration (with implications for the agenda of philosophy) but were going to require new ways of philosophical thinking and proceeding if philosophers were to have any chance of doing justice to them and contributing significantly to their treatment. The interpretive tradition is characterized most fundamentally and comprehensively by this general sense of the matter—and by the great diversity of the attempts made to meet the challenge.

III

The primary preoccupation of "classical modern" philosophers from Descartes onward, prior to Hume and Kant, was with questions pertaining to the nature of reality—generally understood to mean the world in which we find ourselves and the things of which it consists; our own selves, insofar as we are more than such things; and the God to whom we and the world were taken to owe our existence—and to the nature of the knowledge we may have of this reality and its constituent elements. Many philosopher-theologians in the late Middle Ages held the view that the world is *there*, created and existing independently of us and our perceptual access to it. We exist *in* this world but are not entirely part and parcel *of* it, by virtue of being endowed with souls or minds having the capacity to perceive and come to know it. We perceive it more or less as it is; it has (or the things that constitute it have) the kinds of qualities we perceive, provided that our organs and faculty of perception are generally operating properly and that the conditions for perceiving are normal. (This is sometimes called "naïve realism.")

Philosophers such as Descartes and John Locke (1632–1704) felt that there were certain difficulties in this position. In particular, they held that it must be modified to distinguish between "primary" and "secondary" qualities. On this view—which might be characterized as a qualified (or "sophisticated") realism—the world is still there, existing independently of us and our perceptual experience; but the things of which it consists, considered as they are in themselves, have only *some* of the kinds of qualities that we perceive: in particular, extension, size, shape, mass, number, and motion or rest (the primary qualities). Other qualities commonly associated with them—for example, color, heat, sound, taste—cannot strictly speaking and *as experienced* be attributed to things (and are therefore secondary); they instead occur in our perceptual experience as the result of the action upon our senses of certain imperceptible configurations of things' primary qualities. Things exist independently of us, and cause us to perceive secondary as well as primary qualities; but they themselves have only primary qualities, while the secondary qualities they appear to have are brought about as much by our senses as by the things perceived.

Later philosophers, such as George Berkeley (1685–1753) and David Hume, took a further step away from the thesis of naïve realism. Indeed, they rejected *any* sort of "realism" as a defensible and coherent philosophical position with respect to the objects of our perceptual experience and to anything that might be supposed to occasion them. They argued that we have no better reason to attribute the so-called primary qualities to things existing independently of our perceptual experience than we have to attribute the secondary qualities to them. Our experience of the former is not significantly different from our experience of the latter; and since the latter cannot plausibly be said to exist independently of our perceptual experience, there is no good reason to suppose that the former can, either.

This reasoning, however, raises doubts about the fundamental thesis of realism—the thesis, namely, that the thing-world we tend to take for granted exists independently of us and our perceptual experience. For if none of the qualities of the things we perceive can be attributed to things existing independently of us, it follows that we do not encounter such things in experience at all. And if this is so, an unsettling question arises: What evidence do we actually have that there *are* things existing independently of our consciousness? There is, of course, a phenomenal world—that is, the "world" of our experience, consisting of the totality of those of our perceptions that can be integrated with one another in accordance with the laws or principles of association, consistency, and the like. But *this* world cannot be *known* to exist—indeed, it cannot even be *conceived* to exist—except in relation to our consciousness. It therefore cannot be that world existing independently of our perceptual experience of which the realists speak.

Nor is this all. Berkeley and Hume further maintain that we can say nothing at all about what might lie *beyond* the realm of possible perceptual experience. We can never know the nature or existence of something we have never experienced; therefore, we cannot in principle know what lies beyond our perceptual experience—beyond the contents or objects of consciousness, plus consciousness itself in its various modes—or even if anything does. Indeed, the very idea of something of which we can never even in principle have any experience is virtually meaningless.

Moreover, a consequence of this empiricist critique of realism is that all of the "knowledge" we *can* have pertaining to the phenomena we *do* experience can only be inductive—that is, based on generalization from the experience of similar particular instances. And since induction from a limited set of particular instances can never render certain a general proposition ranging over all possible similar instances, we can never establish the truth of such propositions as "Every event has a cause." Such universal propositions can never be established by experience (a posteriori); they can only be formulated by reasoning independently or in advance of relevant experience (a priori), or at least by going beyond what is given in experience. But they therefore cannot be supposed to yield or constitute knowledge *of the world*, even if the world is conceived in terms of our perceptual experience and its contents; for only perceptual experience itself can tell us anything about it.

Descartes, at the dawn of modern philosophy, had hoped that by starting with a systematic suspension of belief in everything that could possibly be doubted, he would be able to erect an edifice of knowledge that would be completely certain. Moreover (as luck would have it), it would accord with the basic ideas of the world, man, God, and morality adhered to by traditionally Christian philosophers and theologians, and for that matter with ordinary common sense as well. By the time of Hume, these hopes seemed to have been dashed, from first to last. In Hume's hands Descartes' systematic doubt, applied more rigorously than it had been by Descartes himself, led to skepticism with regard to the nature and existence of everything except the actual contents of perceptual experience—and in particular, with regard to the nature and existence of the three objects of traditional metaphysics: the world, the soul, and God. It also led to the view that the concepts of traditional metaphysics are meaningless, to the denial of freedom of the will and of the idea of any sort of immortality, and to a kind of conventionalism in ethics.

Confronted with this situation, Kant was profoundly disturbed. He was convinced, among other things, (1) that we have more knowledge (for example, of the validity of such propositions as "Every event has a cause") than Hume was willing to allow; (2) that at least some of the central concepts of traditional metaphysics are not completely meaningless; (3) that far from being mere groundless superstition, belief in God, the soul, and immortality, in something like the way they have been traditionally conceived in the Western religious and philosophical traditions, is in fact reasonable even if not demonstrable; and (4) that moral duty and responsibility are real, as is our freedom of will with respect to them. His problem, therefore, was to show how these various propositions can all be true—to show, indeed, that they actually *are* true—even though Hume's basic criticisms of realism (and rationalism) are sound.

Consider first our perceptual experience. Kant maintains that there are three elements of it that must be distinguished, rather than only one (sensible qualities or "impressions") to which Hume had thought all experience ultimately must be reduced. They are, first, those sensible qualities; second, the two basic *forms* under which all such qualities are experienced—namely, the forms of space and time; and third, the *categories* under which these qualities are arranged and ordered in our experience. The sensible qualities constitute the *content* of perceptual experience, while the forms of space and time and the categories constitute its *formal* elements. Both, according to Kant, are indispensable, for without the latter as well as the former, experience as we know it would be impossible.

Having reached this point, Kant was confronted by the question of how these various elements of experience are to be accounted for, and by the more specific question of what contribution the mind makes to the occurrences of each of them. His answers bring him close to the "idealism" of his successors. Historically considered, they make its emergence quite understandable—and perhaps almost inevitable. First, with regard to the sensible content or qualities of our experience: Kant agrees with earlier critics of realism who maintained that none of these qualities can be attributed to things in themselves, because of the various ways in which they can be shown to be conditioned by our faculties of sense. It does seem to him, however, that their *occurrence* must have some sort of "ground," and that it not only possible but reasonable to have the idea that if there are "appearances," then there must be something underlying them that thereby "appears" in them. Thus the idea of some sort of "thing in itself" is not meaningless, though we cannot attribute any of the sensible qualities of our perceptual experience to whatever that might be.

The same also holds, according to Kant, for the forms of space and time. For experience shows us only that these forms of perceptual experience have application *within* the realm of perceptual experience; no logical or a priori reasoning can establish the conclusion or even the meaningfulness of the idea that they have any application beyond it, to what is "in itself." Kant accepts the argument of empiricism that we cannot legitimately extend *beyond* the bounds of perceptual experience the employment of notions that have been determined to have application only *within* it. Indeed, he goes further, maintaining that the necessity and universality of certain kinds of propositions of mathematics and natural science (whose validity he considers to be beyond dispute) presuppose that the forms of space and time are inseparable from the very nature of perceptual experience, and so have a reality that is strictly phenomenal. He thus concludes that it must be *the mind itself* that supplies our sensibility with the forms of space and time. In short: these forms are a contribution of the mind—rather than of the nature of things in themselves or of the world in itself—to our experience.

The same is also the case, Kant argues, with respect to the categories. They likewise cannot be known or even supposed to be features of things in themselves that are simply mirrored in our experience. Rather, there must be certain structures in the mind, in accordance with which the sensible contents of our experience are arranged, that account for their always being so arranged in our experience. Categories such as unity, plurality, substantiality, and cause and effect may legitimately be applied only to the phenomena we experience and not to things in themselves or the world in itself; for there is neither any experiential ground nor any a priori reason to extend their application further, and there is no way even to make sense of the idea of extricating them meaningfully from the domain of perceptual experience.

Indeed, Kant maintains that it is *only if* these categories are conceived as the mind's contributions to experience that the necessary and universal validity of a proposition like "Every event has a cause" can be understood. And he regards it as a virtually conclusive point in favor of his position that propositions of this sort clearly *are* necessarily and universally valid. His reasoning, reduced to its barest essentials, goes something like this: "These propositions are necessarily and universally valid for all possible perceptual experience. For them to have this strict sort of validity, the categories would have to be contributions of the understanding to experience. Thus the mind must be constituted in such a way that it does structure experience in this manner."

This is an instance of what has come to be known since Kant as a "transcendental argument." And if his premises are sound, his reasoning must be granted to have considerable force.

In short, we cannot (according to Kant) conceive of experience except in terms of the forms of space and time and the categories; but it is because the mind operates as it does, rather than because of what things in themselves are (or the world in itself is) actually like, that we experience things as ordered in space and time and as conforming to the categories. Consequently, while something or other transcending our perceptual experience must exist and be supposed to be its ground, Kant agrees with the critics of realism that we can have no knowledge of what it is or might be like. He is thus a realist himself, but only in a very limited sense; for while he does preserve a kind of role for the idea of the "in itself" of things, he contends that the entire phenomenal world—which is the whole world of our perceptual experience, and which Kant quite appropriately identifies as "nature"—is ordered, structured, and colored (and so supplied with the kinds of features it has for us) by faculties of the mind. All possible empirical and theoretical knowledge (including scientific knowledge) thus pertains only to the phenomenal world, for Kant, and reflects not the natures of things in themselves but the nature of the mind.

So Kant says that the mind "prescribes its laws to nature," rather than discovering laws of a nature that exists independently of it. Nature, as we experience and come to know it, has the forms and laws it does because the mind is responsible for the very forms and laws that structure it. This is Kant's "Copernican revolution," mentioned above. The mind, according to this "revolutionary" turning of the tables, is far from being merely a sort of passive mirror of nature: it actually plays a very active and extensive role in generating experience. But these activities of the mind obviously are not the sorts of mental activities of which we are or can be *self-conscious* (as are our various particular thoughts, decisions, choices, and the like), and that are or even can be *deliberate*. Rather, they are the operations of what might be thought of as the *basic structures* of the mind, which are the same in all of us and do their work before our thoughts and perceptions emerge into consciousness.

The question then arises: since "the mind" is not *identical* with the self-conscious, living, individual selves that we all are or take ourselves to be, how do you and I and human beings generally fit into Kant's general scheme? The mind obviously is not part of the phenomenal world, which it orders and organizes. For this reason, it may be referred to as the "transcendental ego"—a dimension of mentality that transcends the kinds of subjectivity and objectivity that occur within experience. But what about individual human beings, who (ourselves included) occur in experience as *part of* the phenomenal world? Are they (or we) simply on a par with other phenomenal objects? If so, then it would follow that we would have no reason to regard ourselves as free moral agents; for, according to Kant, all events in the phenomenal world are connected with all other events of a purely "natural" sort in accordance with the principle of causality. If we are purely natural entities, then we too must be completely determined causally in our actions.

But this, Kant contends, is not the case. He maintains that, first, his reflections on the role of the mind in experience establish at least the logical *possibility* that we are not *merely* or entirely natural entities, and we to some extent transcend the natural or phenomenal world; and that, second, there are good—if not logically conclusive—reasons for supposing that we *do* transcend the natural world, and that we *have* a sort of freedom of the will that renders us moral agents responsible for our decisions and choices. As has already been observed, Kant leaves room for the idea of something "in itself" that transcends and grounds phenomenal reality. That idea may be supposed to apply to our own reality, as well as to that of objects of our experience—and its application to our own reality is particularly significant. For it implies that it is at least possible that even if our phenomenal or experiential selves are part and parcel of the causally determined natural world, our transcendent or "noumenal" selves (our "selves in themselves") are *not* causally determined.

But to make this point is not to establish that we *are* free, at least in any very significant sense. And no such conclusion can be demonstrated by any line of pure a priori reasoning based on considerations of the nature of the soul; for any such proof always presupposes some abstract definition—here, of the soul—that cannot be decisively shown to be applicable to reality (and, more specifically, to human reality). What then is it that leads Kant to conclude that we actually *are* free? In the absence of a theoretical proof (or even of the possibility of a theoretical proof) one way or the other, Kant turns to practical experience and finds in our *consciousness of moral duty* a kind of "practical proof" or indication of our freedom. For duty presupposes the ability to act either in accordance with it or contrary to it. In short, duty presupposes freedom—at least regarding the matters that one's duty concerns. If I have a clear awareness of such obligation, therefore, I have good reason to regard myself as free. (So Kant in effect argues, "ought implies can"—even though it also implies "might not.") This argument does not establish my freedom for theoretical purposes; but it does warrant this conclusion for practical purposes—especially since Kant has shown to his satisfaction that our freedom cannot be ruled out on theoretical grounds, and so is theoretically *possible*.

Next, on metaphysical concepts: Hume had argued that all of our genuine ideas derive ultimately from sense impressions and consist either of simple copies of those impressions or of complex groupings of such simple copies. A term is meaningful, on his view, if and only if it is associated with an idea whose derivation from impressions of sense can be explained or demonstrated. It thus followed for Hume that if one can produce no such impressions in connection with the use of some such term, the term conveys no actual genuine idea; it is being used meaninglessly, and so must be presumed to signify nothing. This, he had contended, is precisely the case for most metaphysical terms. They do not designate genuine ideas or concepts at all, because they fail to pass the test—that is, his test—of meaningfulness. Consequently, it had seemed to him that all metaphysical talk of such things as substance, the necessary connection of events called causes and effects of each other, God, and the human soul must end, or at any rate must be acknowledged to be fundamentally meaningless, strictly speaking (that is, according to strict—empiricist—philosophical standards).

Kant rejects this conclusion—even while granting to Hume that these and similar terms do not refer to any simple sense impression or complex of such impressions—because he rejects Hume's empiricist criterion of meaningfulness. There are at least two basic types of designating concepts, he holds, that do not refer to simple or complex perceptual contents but nonetheless are meaningful even strictly speaking, according to the revised standards of meaningfulness he proposes and employs, and may legitimately be employed philosophically—subject to certain restrictions. These are the "categories" of the analytic faculty of "understanding" and the "ideas" of the synthesizing faculty of "reason." Concepts such as substance and cause-and-effect connection are examples of the former, while the concepts of God and the soul are examples of the latter. These and certain other concepts like them may legitimately be employed, according to Kant, because they have a legitimate and even indispensable use in analyzing and systematically exploring our experience. And they are meaningful, he contends, precisely because they have these legitimate, recognizable, and important uses.

Kant does agree with Hume to this extent: he holds that we have no reason to suppose, on strictly theoretical grounds, that these concepts do or do not have any application to things in themselves—that there is an "entity in itself" corresponding to the term "God," for example, or others corresponding to the term "soul." And he grants that if the concepts that Hume had termed meaningless are thought to name or refer to metaphysical things or other such entities in themselves, then they are indeed—from a theoretical standpoint—incoherent and meaningless. They derive, he contends, from the functioning of the understanding, on the one hand, and from that of reason, on the other, which warrants no inferences with respect to what might lie beyond or ground experience (in addition to the mind); and they may legitimately (theoretically speaking) be used only in connection with our experience, and only because of how the mind shapes our experience.

But properly understood and employed, these concepts for Kant are both meaningful and useful. The error of traditional metaphysics, he maintains, was not in employing terms that do not denote sensible particulars or complexes of them. Rather, it was in regarding the "ideas" of reason as terms denoting particulars of another sort—non-sensible, metaphysical entities—and in thinking that the "categories" of the understanding can legitimately be applied to them. On his view, these categories have application only to the phenomenal world of experience; while the ideas of reason—such as "God" and the "soul"—serve as useful ("regulative") *guides* in our attempts to achieve a unified comprehension of the phenomena we experience.

In saying this, Kant is by no means *denying* the existence of any sort of God or the existence and immortality of some version of the soul. He might seem to be a skeptic like Hume, from what has been said above, and from the devastating criticism to which he subjects the traditional theoretical attempted "proofs" of the existence of God and of the soul (as something capable of independence from the body and of immortality). But he is not. He is careful to point out that what he says about the theoretical status of the ideas of reason in no way implies anything about what does or does not exist beyond the realm of phenomena and in the realm of "noumena," or things in themselves. And he further maintains that on "practical" (and more specifically morality-related) rather than purely theoretical grounds, there are compelling reasons for holding both that there is a God and that the soul exists and is immortal.

Kant's argument in support of this conclusion is as surprising as it is unusual. In brief: he holds that the moral law in part tells one to act so that one will be deserving of happiness. Happiness, therefore, ought to be proportionate to morality. But it plainly is not proportionate to morality in this life. A future state of existence of some sort, in which things will be set right, thus must be postulated;

and such a postulation presupposes both the immortality (or at any rate non-mortality) of the soul and the reality of a being sufficiently knowledgeable and good and powerful to set them right—that is, a divine being who might reasonably be called "God." To some, this may not seem to be a very compelling line of reasoning; but Kant deemed it sufficient to render the acceptance of certain basic propositions about God and the soul at least more reasonable than not.

Kant thus believed himself to have met the various challenges posed by Humean skepticism, to have shown (in a general way, at any rate) what it is possible to know and reasonable to suppose beyond the limits Hume seemed to have set on human thought and philosophical inquiry; and to have done so in a manner that essentially settled these matters once and for all, to the extent that they admit of settlement. Subsequent philosophers (FICHTE, SCHELLING, and Hegel among them) were persuaded of the soundness of some parts of his position—in particular, his new Copernican revolution and his insistence on human freedom—but found others unsatisfactory or even objectionable. The development of their own positions, and those of many others after them, may best be understood in light of what they did and did not find acceptable and convincing in Kant.

IV

Hume and Kant were already post-Christian thinkers, who represent quite different ways of positioning themselves to think beyond Christian theology in their philosophical endeavors; but they were very much concerned with one of the problems that loomed large for philosophers in the interpretive tradition after Kant. It might be called *the problem of religion*—including (but not restricted to) *the problem of Christianity*. For most of them the traditional Judeo-Christian worldview, based on a literalistic reading of the Bible, could no longer be taken for granted and accepted at face value. Indeed, for most of them (as for most Enlightenment and post-Enlightenment philosophers) it could not even be taken seriously as a contender or pretender, where the truth about ourselves and the world is concerned, and where rational argument—or at least the making of a plausible and compelling case—is supposed to prevail. To many, therefore, some sort of radical revision of traditional thinking with respect to the status of religious belief and tenets of faith (not to mention religious practices) seemed necessary.

But what sort of revision should that be? And what are the consequences of any particular such proposed revision, where matters of self-interpretation, meaning, value, and morality are concerned? Concerns of these sorts were felt to be pressing by Hume and Kant, who came to quite different conclusions. The same was true of their successors in the interpretive tradition, who likewise differed greatly in their solutions and prescriptions. These concerns remain with us today—for example, in the heated debate that continues to surround such questions as "Can we be good (or moral) without God?" and "Can life be meaningful if there is no God?" Enlightenment challenges to religious "superstition" were already beginning to provoke such questions and concerns, despite the reluctance of many in polite philosophical society to raise them openly and bluntly until well into the nineteenth century.

An obvious special and important version of this problem is *the problem of God*—that is, the problem of what to do with the idea of "God," if neither the powerful personal God of the Bible and traditional Judeo-Christianity nor one of the more austere versions of God conceived by earlier modern philosophers such as Descartes and Kant could continue to be affirmed as a kind of supreme being existing above and beyond this life and world. Some in the interpretive tradition (KIERKEGAARD in particular) persisted in affirming one or another such candidate as the true and real referent of the term, while others (such as MARX and NIETZSCHE) contented themselves with simply rejecting the idea of anything of the kind, turning their attention instead to the diagnosis of what might dispose people to some such faith.

For many, however, a third option remained open and beckoned: to give the idea of God a new and different lease on life by recasting it in a manner that (by their lights) endowed it with modified but attractive significance—sometimes even suggesting that this was what earlier philosophers had been groping for. Still others might be seen as overtly setting aside or letting go of the "God-idea" while using different language to give expression to what in effect are alternative versions of something like it. In short: during much of the past two centuries the interpretive tradition might be said to have been haunted by the God-idea, which for many was as difficult to reject entirely as it was impossible to accept at traditional religious or metaphysical face value.

A quite different problem in this tradition has been what might be called *the problem of science*. One part of it relates to the sciences that are among or are related or akin to the *natural* sciences. In the absence of any sort of divine or metaphysical transcendent reality beyond this life and this world, is there anything in or about them—and about or related to human reality in particular—that is not to be explained and comprehended in the manner in which merely natural phenomena are dealt with by these disciplines? The relation between these disciplines and philosophy is another aspect of this problem. It is made all the more interesting and complicated by the fact that the German term *Wissenschaft* (usually translated as "science") has long been used by German thinkers to refer not only to the natural and social sciences but also to other cognitive disciplines, from mathematics to history to philosophy itself. Indeed, for philosophers as diverse as Kant, Hegel, and HUSSERL, philosophy (if properly pursued) is considered to be the paradigmatic and master *Wissenschaft*.

A host of more specific problems that were in the air as the post-Kantian interpretive tradition began and developed may usefully be noted and kept in mind as readers encounter the succession of thinkers and writings brought together in this volume. The problems themselves evolved in the course of the two centuries separating the first and last selections, and each could be discussed at considerable length. Here a relatively brief mention will have to suffice, enabling them to be seen together as significant elements of the intellectual-historical context in which this tradition emerged, by which it was influenced in many ways, and to whose further development it in turn contributed.

The problem of the Enlightenment. The eighteenth-century Enlightenment was characterized by the emancipation of European thought from subservience to social, cultural, and (above all) religious traditions and authorities, as well as by the emergence of an optimistic confidence in the ability of human rationality both to comprehend and to master the world, society, and human life, bringing clarity and order to them in the service of human happiness. Their mysteries were to be banished, their secrets uncovered, and their needless defects remedied through the development and use of the power of reason, thereby ending the long tyranny of superstition and ignorance and ushering in a new age of "enlightened" and autonomous human maturity and flourishing. The spirit of the Enlightenment was the animating dream of the French Revolution, as it also was of the American transformation of independence from England into a new experiment in democratic and constitutional self-government. Rude awakenings soon followed, however, most vividly in post-revolutionary France; and naïve confidence in human rationality quickly gave way to skepticism and doubt regarding its powers in other matters as well, both theoretical and practical. (This might be considered the first major "crisis of modernity.") The moral of the story was uncertain, but the need for a reassessment of Enlightenment ideals and ambitions was clear.

The problem of Romanticism. The Romantic movement, which developed in reaction to the rationalism of the Enlightenment, had already emerged in the last decades of the eighteenth century and was in full bloom in all areas of intellectual and cultural life as the nineteenth century began. It accentuated and celebrated the nonrational dimensions of human nature and experience, and it somewhat paradoxically valorized both individuality and various forms of human unity (notably love) and community (from the aesthetic to the political). The modest achievements and satisfactions of rationality paled in comparison with the power of the feelings and emotions; and there was great demand for ways to intensify and express them—not only in their traditional religious guises but also in other areas of life, cultural as well as personal. Literature, music, and other arts underwent extraordinary transformations, displaying a virtual explosion of creative vitality; and creativity itself was accorded the highest of honors, supplanting rationality as the supposed epitome of human attainment and worth. For many, the cult of emotion and feeling became a kind of new religion—a locus of meaning intertwined with that of artistic creativity, and the primary focus of that creativity. Yet here again, reservations soon began to be felt, as the excesses of Romanticism began to suggest its limitations and even dangers. Like Enlightenment rationalism, Romanticism was on to something important—but was missing something important as well.

The problem of materialism. The idea that there is nothing more to reality than matter in motion, in accordance with causally deterministic laws of nature, had great appeal for many in the eighteenth century (and ever since). It was widely taken to be the logical consequence of abandoning the ideas of God and the soul as immaterial entities that exist above and beyond or are connected with but separable from the "extended substances" or material entities of which the world apart from them was supposed to consist. For many others who agreed that these ideas are untenable, however, this was a matter of great concern; for while materialism with respect to nature seemed neither objectionable nor implausible, its extension to include the whole of human reality and possibility seemed as threatening and demeaning as it was difficult to resist. The idea of "man as machine," popularized by materialists like Julien Offray de La Mettrie (1709–1751), was considered "enlightened," sensible, and sophisticated by some; but it was repellent to others—not only the religiously minded but also many, no less "enlightened" and sophisticated, for whom it did not begin to do justice to our sense of ourselves and the richness of human experience. Kant attempted to develop an account of human reality that would be a plausible posttraditional alternative to deterministic mechanistic materialism, appealing to his conception of morality. His attempt inspired others in the interpretive tradition to tackle the problem in ways that were less problematic than they took Kant's morality-based strategy to be.

The problem of morality. Morality in the Western world has long been closely bound up with religion, and more specifically with Judeo-Christian religiousness, in which its normative force and content have often been considered to be (quite properly and effectively) grounded. Kant was not the first to attempt to develop a moral philosophy that had no such religious grounding. His account of morality was by far the most impressive, however, and he even turned the tables by offering it as the only philosophically legitimate basis for any sort of philosophically respectable religiousness. Other philosophers sought to provide accounts of morality that appealed to various sorts of social and psychological considerations. The questions of how to think about morality and of what sorts of force and content it can and should have in human life were thereby vividly raised. Kant's answers were problematic; few others that had been proposed seemed deserving of serious consideration; and so the entire topic appeared to be in need of fundamental rethinking.

The problem of life. The term "life" here refers to the phenomenon of biological reality—that is, to life as a biological phenomenon in its many different forms, of which ours as human beings is an instance. Strange as it may seem, it was only as traditional religious and metaphysical ways of thinking waned and the novelty of mechanistic materialism began to fade that *life*—as a kind of reality to which the languages of both "mind" (or "reason") and "matter in motion" (or "mechanism") seem ill-suited—came into focus, and began to receive scientific and philosophical attention in its own right. The concept of "life" attracted a great deal of interest, because it seemed perfectly positioned to serve as an alternative to the concept of "mechanism" and the idea of "matter-in-motion materialism," and to provide a way out of and around the duality and dichotomy of the mental and the physical. By the beginning of the nineteenth century, in central Europe it had already become the conceptual centerpiece of a new *Naturphilosophie* (philosophy of nature), which by the century's end evolved into a *Lebensphilosophie* (philosophy of life) concerned with historical as well as biological life forms and dimensions of human life. The interpretation of "life" was something that many philosophers in the interpretive tradition have not been prepared to leave entirely to life scientists in the various biological disciplines, and they have sought to contribute to it.

The problem of humanity. This problem is closely associated with the previous one, as has just been indicated, but its more specific focus makes a difference. Human life—human nature, human existence, human reality— may fairly be said to have become the central concern of the post-Kantian interpretive tradition virtually from the outset. Kant himself had helped to initiate this "anthropological turn" at the end of his long career with the publication of a book titled *Anthropology* (1798), in which he asserted that the question "What is man?" sums up and embraces the other most important questions of philosophy ("What can I know? What ought I do? What may I hope?"). The reinterpretation of human reality was a task of great urgency and importance. As the influence of traditional religious and metaphysical ways of thinking waned, the focus of philosophical attention turned to "this life in this world," and our fundamental identity came to be reconceptualized as "human beings" sharing a common identity that extends beyond simply that of our biological species. The idea of "man" (*der Mensch* in German, *l'homme* in French), as a master concept that could be used in the collective singular to refer to and speak significantly about human beings generally, was discovered (or, as MICHEL FOUCAULT would have it, invented); and the question of what can and should (and cannot and should not) be said about human reality generally, human flourishing, and *genuinely human* existing in partial contrast to both—has been perhaps the most contested question in the interpretive tradition.

The problem of spirituality. One of the issues in dispute with respect to human reality, as its postreligious and postmetaphysical reinterpretation began, was whether it was possible or even important for humanity to continue to be understood in terms of some version of the idea of "spirit" (*Geist* in German) or "spirituality." The question took on new meaning and interest among those for whom this idea no longer designated an immaterial entity conjoined to but capable of existing independently of the body (such as the Christian "soul" or the Cartesian "thinking substance"), but who thought it nonetheless can and should be retained as a way of calling attention to something significant about human reality or possibility. Most of those who will be encountered in the first part of this volume strongly held this position, as did many (though by no means all) of those in the other three parts—even though many of them preferred to use different terminology than that of *Geist* or "spirituality" to refer to that about our humanity that cannot be adequately characterized in the language of the life sciences.

The problem of rationality. The idea that human beings are not simply a particular species of animal but a type of living creature (ours) that is distinguished from others by its capacity for *rationality* is as old as philosophy itself. It was taken to be beyond dispute by Aristotle (384–322 B.C.E.), who conceived of and even defined man as the "rational animal," and by many others after him, as well as by Socrates (469–399 B.C.E.) and Plato (ca. 427–ca. 347 B.C.E.) before him. The status of human rationality in relation to our various other capacities and activities (biological, psychological, and social), as well as its relation to whatever the fundamental nature and structure of reality may be, took on new significance when it could no longer be taken for granted that these issues were settled by the assumption of our fundamental and distinctive kinship to "the divine" (whether as conceived by the Greeks or as conceived in the Judeo-Christian tradition). Moreover, the very nature of rationality was soon called into question and reconsidered, even by some (like Hegel) who seemingly agreed with Kant about its significance and applicability to practical as well as theoretical matters but made something quite different of it than Kant had. Others after Hegel departed still further from the conception of it that one finds in Kant (or in subsequent refinements associated with developments in analytical philosophy of science and philosophical logic), even to the point of taking rationality to be merely a psychological or historical phenomenon, whose powers and authoritativeness were therefore problematic. There are few matters over which the interpretive tradition has been divided more deeply and significantly.

The problem of individuality. Another aspect of human reality that requires reinterpretation and reassessment, when no longer conceived in the context of Judeo-Christian beliefs about the soul or personal identity of each human being, is that of human individuality. If individuality beyond the level of mere biological distinctness and particularity is a human possibility with developmental preconditions and requirements (rather than a divinely bestowed or metaphysically grounded reality possessed by all), both its nature and its significance in relation to other human possibilities have to be reconsidered. The same applies to different types of individuality, in relation to each other as well as to such other possibilities that may be either impersonal or only contingently related to them. As the interpretive tradition has shown, this is an especially rich topic that can generate great differences—differences that can have significant consequences, as normative and evaluative considerations are conjoined with them.

The problem of community. This problem is a kind of opposite number to the problem of individuality, and the remark just made equally applies to it. There are many sorts of more-than-merely-biological community that are humanly possible on interpersonal, social, institutional, linguistic, cultural, and even intellectual levels. Moreover, at least some of them may be humanly crucial, in the sense that human reality in which any and all forms of such community were absent would be a virtual impossibility, as anything more than a biological possibility. Such an existence could not be considered human in any real sense. "Community" here refers not merely to groups of people interacting but to groups having a measure of common identity and a shared way of life that undergird and channel their action and interaction. Community and individuality are often considered to be opposed to each other; but while their relative importance has been a matter of intense debate in the interpretive tradition, their interdependence has also received a great deal of attention. The concern with the quality of human life that pervades this tradition from its outset has been articulated and pursued in the context of a growing awareness of the crucial importance to the character of human life of the kinds of community that develop and prevail in it.

The problem of culture. The focus of this related issue is on what might be called the cultural fabric of the life of human communities—the various ways of generating, sustaining, developing, and communicating the shared meanings that are the substance of the common identities associated with them. Shared traditions, values, norms, beliefs, aspirations, practices, and variants of languages, religions, myths, legends, and pastimes are examples of cultural elements that perform these functions and contribute to this dimension of human reality. Culture in this broad sense had of course always been present; but a new or heightened awareness of it was one of the developments of intellectual life in the nineteenth century that figured importantly in the interpretive tradition, and one of the developments to which that philosophical tradition itself contributed. It includes the arts but embraces much more—all of which has become a focus of social-scientific as well as philosophical interest. It is something quite distinct from cognitive and psychological phenomena and from theoretical and practical rationality. The recognition of the need to take seriously and do justice to the phenomenon (and phenomena) of human culture, and to its significance for the understanding of human reality, was one of the primary drivers of the interpretive turn in philosophy after Kant.

The problem of art. The arts are a cluster of cases within the general domain of human culture. Hume and Kant already recognized that in the inventory of forms of human experience and activity, they required special attention as transformations of natural capacities in directions that are governed by neither theoretically nor practically rational considerations. After Kant they came to be of even greater interest—not surprisingly, in view of the incredible flowering of artistic genius in all of the arts that began in the late eighteenth century and increased dramatically in the century that followed. The arts were hotbeds of creativity, in which the human spirit developed and unleashed a very different set of powers from those employed in cognitive pursuits, moral life, and the conduct of social affairs. Doing justice to the arts and to artistic creativity became a challenge and mandate to those seeking to reinterpret human reality and possibility. Yet it was by no means obvious what to say about them (beyond what Kant had already said) and what their significance is for human culture and human life more generally. These are questions that drew the attention of many in the interpretive tradition, and their disputes are among the most interesting in that tradition.

The problem of society. There is more to human community than interpersonal interactions, culture, and the arts. Beyond and beneath and all around them are also social structures, institutions, and practices. As thinkers in the interpretive tradition became increasingly aware, these vary from time to time and place to place, affecting the character and quality of human life differently but no less significantly than do cultural configurations. They became the focus of a number of social sciences that emerged in the course of the nineteenth and twentieth centuries and gradually separated themselves from philosophy. One of the great achievements of the interpretive tradition was to bring them to attention as another significant part of the fabric of human reality that, like cultural formations, transcends human individuality as well as human-biological and psychological determinations. They figured prominently in Hegel's conception of "objective spirituality," and even more fundamentally in Marx's analysis of human reality. Their philosophical consideration has loomed large in this tradition ever since, and is an important complement and supplement to their social-scientific study and treatment.

The problem of language. The relation between language and thought, experience, and their objects had been discussed by philosophers and others prior to Kant; but like most philosophers before him, Kant did not seem to consider this relation to be of particular importance, his strong interest in different types and uses of "ideas" and "concepts" notwithstanding. Even during his lifetime, however, language was coming to attract a great deal of attention. Linguistic differences and the development of languages were studied with growing sophistication and interest, exhibited in the great dictionary projects that were begun and in the emergence of philology as a major discipline. This new fascination with language was soon reflected in the thinking of a number of figures in the interpretive tradition, for whom such questions as what could and could not be expressed or adequately articulated in language (of one sort or another), and to what extent language either distorts or contributes to the constitution of objects of experience, became matters of considerable importance. The implications of recognizing the developmental, contingent, and basically social-functional characteristics of human languages became further matters of debate, significantly complicating the consideration of these questions.

The problem of history. Language is a historical phenomenon. This fact affects its comprehension and the understanding of anything done by means of it. These observations are specific instances of the more general recognition that human reality itself is something that has "come to be," not only biologically but also historically. That recognition in turn raises the more fundamental question of what it means for our understanding and assessment of everything about human reality beyond the biological level that has a historical character. Further questions arise because it cannot be assumed that anything about ourselves that has come about historically warrants characterization as "development" in any evaluatively significant sense. Coming to terms with the historicality of human reality can arguably be called the "master problem" of post-Kantian thought. It includes such questions as whether there is or can be anything about it that has any sort of more-than-merely-historical significance, and how the character of this historicality relates to what might be called both the animality and the spirituality of human reality. The interpretive tradition has had much to do both with the growing awareness of this problem in its many dimensions and with the exploration of possible ways of reckoning with it, ranging from attempting to discern some grand unfolding scheme in it to denying anything and everything of the kind.

The problem of identities. In many respects, as already noted above, human reality is not monolithic. In addition to individual differences, various kinds of shared but differing human identity have been ascribed to human beings—as pervasively even if not universally or timelessly real—by figures in the interpretive tradition as they have attempted to flesh out their accounts of human reality. Such identity differences, which arise from circumstances beyond our control, can be changed only with difficulty if at all. And they are taken to matter—both philosophically and humanly—because they can and do translate into real differences, both positive and negative, in the character and quality of human lives. Having (or acquiring) such identities may be virtually inescapable, and needing or being disposed to want them (or being susceptible to their imposition) may even be a part of the human condition; but no particular one of them is even partially definitive of being a human being at all, either generally or genuinely. They all have developmental histories and social and cultural dimensions, and so are more than merely biological, even though many of them relate in various ways to the sort of living creature that human beings are, and to certain of our differing physical traits. Thinkers in the interpretive tradition have made much of a considerable number of them, ranging from Hegel's (racially tinged) language- and "spirit"-sharing "peoples" (*Völker*)—and DU BOIS's (rather similarly conceived) "races"—to Marx's "classes," BEAUVOIR's and JUDITH BUTLER's "sexes" and "genders," Nietzsche's differing human "types," HEIDEGGER's heritage-sharing historical cohorts, and CASSIRER's and Foucault's denizens of differing cultural worlds. Questions of what to make of—and do about—such shared (but differing) and contingent (but not easily alterable) human identities, and about the human possibilities that are at stake, are among the most interesting of the many that have been contested in the interpretive tradition.

The problem of knowledge. It is hardly surprising that many philosophers after Kant considered it necessary to reconsider the problem of the nature and possibility of knowledge in the broader context of the other issues mentioned above. Knowledge, insofar as it is meaningful for us to think and speak of it, is the kind (or kinds) of knowledge *of which we are capable*, or can conceive of becoming capable; and this would seem to make it problematic to discuss knowledge in abstraction from at least some of these issues, even if ideas we may have with respect to them can be held only provisionally, pending the outcome of reflection on its nature and limits. One of the lessons learned in the course of the earlier history of philosophy is that questions of metaphysics cannot be properly addressed without first settling questions pertaining to knowledge in a way that establishes our competence to answer them. But the interpretive tradition has been concerned with the very possibility of properly addressing and settling questions regarding knowledge without taking into account a good many things about ourselves and the world in which we find ourselves and our cognitive capacities. This complicates the problem of knowledge—and the question of how to proceed in philosophy—considerably.

The problem of philosophy. One of the reasons for including this in the list of problems with which philosophers after Kant found themselves confronted has just been given. Another reason is much more fundamental. Some philosophers after Kant were content to continue to focus primarily on the kinds of questions to which Hume and Kant had maintained that philosophy should restrict itself, and to deal with such questions much as they had done—or, in any event, with questions and in ways developing out of theirs. But others found themselves wanting to think and talk about a broad range of other questions as well (or instead), requiring different approaches: for example, questions pertaining to "quality of life," to matters of value and meaning, and to the comprehension of human reality, possibility, self-realization, and the idea of genuinely human existence. The interpretive tradition was the result.

One of the remarks made most frequently about developments in the interpretive tradition by critics—those in other strands of that tradition as well as in the analytic tradition—is "That's not philosophy." But that sort of comment obviously begs the question, by assuming that it is already settled what does and does not count. The question of whether something "is philosophy" has been much discussed (and often heatedly debated) by some in the interpretive tradition, while being of no concern to others, who simply wrote as they chose to write and left it to others to decide what to make of their writings. It may well be a question to which there is and can be no definitive answer. But even if the only real answer is that "philosophy" is ultimately a matter of what is done by those who develop and extend the larger tradition of thought to which they were responding and reacting, the interpretive tradition has contributed enormously and richly not only to its history but to the kind of intellectual adventure that it has been, has become, and can continue to be.

The nature of philosophy—what it can and should be or include, and how it can and perhaps should be best pursued—has been contested throughout its history; and that contest has continued during the past two centuries, both between the analytical and interpretive traditions and within each of them. The best answer may simply be "All of the above." But aversion to the idea of allowing philosophy to become a game anyone can play in any way one wants, and thus to cease to be anything worth taking seriously as an intellectually conscientious activity devoted to the pursuit of comprehension, has been a powerful deterrent to accepting that answer; and so the dispute over this last problem has long been both an important and a lively one, to say the least, within as well as beyond the interpretive tradition.

Prologue

IMMANUEL KANT
(1724 – 1804)

The history of Western philosophy after Kant is just that: philosophy "after Kant"— in Kant's shadow, inspired by Kant, in response to Kant, in reaction to Kant. Kant's influence upon later thinkers and developments was and continues to be so profound that one cannot even imagine what the subsequent history of philosophy would have been like had he never appeared on the scene. It therefore will be helpful to begin this volume with a few brief selections from Kant himself that are indicative of some of the ways in which he set the stage and the agenda for those who followed him, particularly in Europe in the first half-century after his death in 1804. These selections do not begin to do justice to Kant's thought; but they highlight aspects of it that were among the most significant of his successors' points of departure.

Immanuel Kant (best pronounced like "want," though the British rhyme it with the American "can't") lived his entire life in what is now the Russian Baltic city of Kaliningrad. In his time it was the East Prussian city of Königsberg, on the far northeastern edge of German-speaking Europe. He was the first great modern philosopher to hold a professorship in philosophy—at the University of Königsberg, where he had received his own philosophical education (1740–46). He began his teaching career there in 1755, and attracted little notice for many years; but by the time he retired in 1796 he was the dominant figure in European philosophy—even though the work that made him famous, *Critique of Pure Reason*, was not published until 1781.

During the fifteen years after that volume appeared, Kant published a remarkable number of books and essays in many areas of philosophy while continuing to lecture on a wide range of subjects, not only in philosophy but also in mathematics and the sciences. It was his conviction, by the end of his career, that he had at long last given philosophy the status of a mature cognitive discipline, had settled the basic questions about the nature and limits of human knowledge and morality, and had said as much as can rationally and justifiably be said with respect to the large and important questions that have preoccupied philosophers and religious thinkers from time immemorial, concerning such matters as God, the soul, immortality, and human worth and significance. His work was so comprehensive, formidable, and impressive that he was widely taken to be right—or at any rate, to have shown the way to philosophers of the future, who could not but be his heirs, and would have to begin by reckoning with him.

The heart of Kant's philosophy is his three "critiques": his critical analyses and assessments of the various types of reasoning and judgment of which the human mind is capable that seemed to him to set us apart from all mere animals. One is theoretical reasoning and the kinds of knowledge it is capable of yielding, either aided by or independently of experience. Another is practical reasoning and the kinds of moral norms it is capable of establishing for rational agents. And the third is judgments of quality of various sorts, which have a very different character and basis than do either of the first two forms of rationality. Kant sought to establish once and for all what we can and cannot reasonably aspire to know or establish—as philosophers, scientists, or simply human beings—with respect to ourselves and the reality with which we find ourselves confronted, how such knowledge can best be pursued, and what may meaningfully and reasonably be said and thought about matters lying beyond its bounds.

So his *Critique of Pure Reason* was followed by his *Critique of Practical Reason* (1788), and then by his *Critique of Judgment* (1790). He subsequently wrote a book on the kind of religion he deemed defensible and desirable, *Religion within the Limits of Reason Alone* (1793); and, shortly after his retirement, he published several books based on his popular courses of lectures, including one dealing with our human nature: his *Anthropology in Pragmatic Perspective* (1798). This list of titles reflects the general conception of philosophy that he expresses in his *Logic* (1800):

> Philosophy is the idea of a perfect wisdom that shows us the ultimate ends of human reason. . . . [It] is the cognitive discipline of relating all knowledge and *uses* of reason to the ultimate *end* of human reason, to which, as the supreme end, all others are subordinated, and in which they must be joined into unity. The field of philosophy in this cosmopolitan sense may be summed up in the following questions:
>
> 1) What can I know? [*Was kann ich wissen?*]
> 2) What ought I do? [*Was soll ich tun?*]
> 3) What may I hope? [*Was darf ich hoffen?*]
> 4) What is man? [*Was ist der Mensch?*]

The first question is answered by *metaphysics*, the second by *morality*, the third by *religion*, and the fourth by *anthropology*. At bottom all this could be reckoned to be anthropology, because the first three questions are related to the last.

This is a conception of philosophy that places our own existence—our nature, capacities, and prospects—at the center of its focus, in ways that are reflected in the preoccupations of Kant's successors. Indeed, his suggestion that the first three questions are all related to the fourth, under which they may therefore be subsumed, anticipates a central theme amplified in the post-Kantian interpretive tradition: that the central task of philosophy is the interpretation of our attained and attainable human reality, which in turn has major implications for the answers to be given to the other main questions of philosophy.

As his predecessor David Hume (1711–1776) was in Britain, Kant was a leading figure in and spokesman for the Enlightenment in German-speaking Europe. His philosophical enterprise is one of the great contributions to the development of this fundamentally humanistic and optimistic movement in the last half of the eighteenth century, with its resolute declaration of independence from all religious authority, as well as its faith in the power of rational analysis and assessment to guide us to the best answers we can get to all questions, practical as well as theoretical—even in matters previously supposed to be the special province of religion. The first selection below, an essay written in 1784 on what Kant takes "enlightenment" most importantly to mean and to require, displays these convictions. (It also displays his concern to convince the authorities that, properly understood, it posed no threat to the existing monarchical political order, and so could and should be tolerated.)

The other two selections together show aspects of Kant's thinking that are very much at variance with the spirit of Hume, and of many other Enlightenment figures as well—and that were tremendously exciting to some of Kant's successors, while giving others pause. In the first of them, from the 1787 second edition of his *Critique of Pure Reason*, Kant discusses the profound implications of his analysis of the limits of theoretical rationality—and of natural-scientific thinking in particular—for the great questions of religion, morality, and our self-understanding. He takes himself to have established that scientific inquiry does not and cannot have the last word regarding any of these matters, and that the door is open for a philosophically sophisticated thinker to embrace conclusions pertaining to them that have no scientific basis—*if* there are other sorts of sound reasons for doing so that are differently warranted and defensible. In the final short selection, from the conclusion of his *Critique of Practical Reason*, Kant makes it equally clear that he believes there are indeed grounds for some such conclusions, and indicates where they are to be found: namely, in our moral experience. Together, these two selections display those aspects of his thinking that legitimized, inspired, and showed the way to the flow-

ering of philosophical interpretation in the next generation, under the banner of "idealism."

The third selection highlights an assumption that is of crucial importance for Kant, the acceptance or rejection of which had major consequences for his successors. Kant supposes that there is something about morality that makes it completely different from anything material or otherwise contingently empirical and causally explainable. He considers morality to have a kind of reality that neither is nor can have developed out of anything merely natural. Yet we are at least capable of being responsive to it: and this, for Kant, warrants the supposition that we too have something about us that is not merely part and parcel of the mundane world of natural processes and causal relations—our human psychological and social reality included. The philosophical and human stakes are very high here; and working out the interpretive implications of either accepting or modifying or rejecting Kant's position on the matter was one of the first and most important challenges that confronted his heirs.

What is Enlightenment?

Enlightenment is man's release from his self-incurred tutelage. Tutelage is man's inability to make use of his understanding without direction from another. Self-incurred is this tutelage when its cause lies not in lack of reason but in lack of resolution and courage to use it without direction from another. *Sapere aude!*[1] "Have courage to use your own reason!"—that is the motto of enlightenment.

Laziness and cowardice are the reasons why so great a portion of mankind, after nature has long since discharged them from external direction (*naturaliter maiorennes*),[2] nevertheless remains under lifelong tutelage, and why it is so easy for others to set themselves up as their guardians. It is so easy not to be of age. If I have a book which understands for me, a pastor who has a conscience for me, a physician who decides my diet, and so forth, I need not trouble myself. I need not think, if I can only pay—others will readily undertake the irksome work for me.

That the step to competence is held to be very dangerous by the far greater portion of mankind (and by the entire fair sex)—quite apart from its being

1. Dare to know! (Latin); from the Roman poet Horace, *Epistles* 1.2.40 (ca. 20 B.C.E.).

2. Those who have come of age through the course of nature (Latin).

arduous—is seen to by those guardians who have so kindly assumed superintendence over them.[3] After the guardians have first made their domestic cattle dumb and have made sure that these placid creatures will not dare take a single step without the harness of the cart to which they are confined, the guardians then show them the danger which threatens if they try to go alone. Actually, however, this danger is not so great, for by falling a few times they would finally learn to walk alone. But an example of this failure makes them timid and ordinarily frightens them away from all further trials.

For any single individual to work himself out of the life under tutelage which has become almost his nature is very difficult. He has come to be fond of this state, and he is for the present really incapable of making use of his reason, for no one has ever let him try it out. Statutes and formulas, those mechanical tools of the rational employment or rather misemployment of his natural gifts, are the fetters of an everlasting tutelage. Whoever throws them off makes only an uncertain leap over the narrowest ditch because he is not accustomed to that kind of free motion. Therefore, there are only few who have succeeded by their own exercise of mind both in freeing themselves from incompetence and in achieving a steady pace.

But that the public should enlighten itself is more possible; indeed, if only freedom is granted, enlightenment is almost sure to follow. For there will always be some independent thinkers, even among the established guardians of the great masses, who, after throwing off the yoke of tutelage from their own shoulders, will disseminate the spirit of the rational appreciation of both their own worth and every man's vocation for thinking for himself. But be it noted that the public, which has first been brought under this yoke by their guardians, forces the guardians themselves to remain bound when it is incited to do so by some of the guardians who are themselves capable of some enlightenment—so harmful is it to implant prejudices, for they later take vengeance on their cultivators or on their descendants. Thus the public can only slowly attain enlightenment. Perhaps a fall of personal despotism or of avaricious or tyrannical oppression may be accomplished by revolution, but never a true reform in ways of thinking. Rather, new prejudices will serve as well as old ones to harness the great unthinking masses.

For this enlightenment, however, nothing is required but freedom, and indeed the most harmless freedom of all, which alone should be called by this name. It is the freedom to make public use of one's reason at every point. But I hear on all sides, "Do not argue!" The officer says: "Do not argue but drill!" The tax-collector: "Do not argue but pay!" The cleric: "Do not argue but believe!" Only one prince in the world[4] says, "Argue as much as you will, and about what you will, but obey!" Everywhere there is restriction on freedom.

Which restriction is an obstacle to enlightenment, and which is not an obstacle but a promoter of it? I answer: The public use of one's reason must always be free, and it alone can bring about enlightenment among men. The private use of reason, on the other hand, may often be very narrowly restricted without particularly hindering the progress of enlightenment. By the public use

---

3. That is, these self-appointed guardians see to it that most people believe that thinking for oneself is dangerous.

4. Kant is referring to his own sovereign, Frederick the Great (1712–1786).

of one's reason I understand the use which a person makes of it as a scholar before the reading public. Private use I call that which one may make of it in a particular civil post or office which is intrusted to him.[5] Many affairs which are conducted in the interest of the community require a certain mechanism through which some members of the community must passively conduct themselves with an artificial unanimity, so that the government may direct them to public ends, or at least prevent them from destroying those ends. Here argument is certainly not allowed—one must obey. But so far as a part of the mechanism regards himself at the same time as a member of the whole community or of a society of world citizens, and thus in the role of a scholar who addresses the public (in the proper sense of the word) through his writings, he certainly can argue without hurting the affairs for which he is in part responsible as a passive member. Thus it would be ruinous for an officer in service to debate about the suitability or utility of a command given to him by his superior; he must obey. But the right to make remarks on errors in the military service and to lay them before the public for judgment cannot equitably be refused him as a scholar. The citizen cannot refuse to pay the taxes imposed on him; indeed, an impudent complaint at those levied on him can be punished as a scandal (as it could occasion general refractoriness). But the same person nevertheless does not act contrary to his duty as a citizen when, as a scholar, he publicly expresses his thoughts on the inappropriateness or even the injustice of these levies. Similarly a clergyman is obligated to make his sermon to his pupils in catechism and his congregation conform to the symbol of the church which he serves, for he has been accepted on this condition. But as a scholar he has complete freedom, even the calling, to communicate to the public all his carefully tested and well-meaning thoughts on that which is erroneous in the symbol and to make suggestions for the better organization of the religious body and church. In doing this, there is nothing that could be laid as a burden on his conscience. For what he teaches as a consequence of his office as a representative of the church, this he considers something about which he has no freedom to teach according to his own lights; it is something which he is appointed to propound at the dictation of and in the name of another. He will say, "Our church teaches this or that; those are the proofs which it adduces." He thus extracts all practical uses for his congregation from statutes to which he himself would not subscribe with full conviction but to the enunciation of which he can very well pledge himself because it is not impossible that truth lies hidden in them, and, in any case, there is at least nothing in them contradictory to inner religion. For if he believed he had found such in them, he could not conscientiously discharge the duties of his office; he would have to give it up. The use, therefore, which an appointed teacher makes of his reason before his congregation is merely private, because this congregation is only a domestic one (even if it be a large gathering); with respect to it, as a priest, he is not free, nor can he be free, because he carries out the orders of another. But as a scholar, whose writings speak to his public, the world, the clergyman in the public use of his reason enjoys an unlimited freedom to

5. Kant is using the expression "private use" here in a rather unusual way, to mean not privately *personal* uses of reason but rather *restricted* uses of it, subject to the obligations associated with one's particular official duties and responsibilities. He is using the expression "public use," on the other hand, to mean something like "intellectual use" in inquiry and debate, whether undertaken as scholar or as citizen.

use his own reason and to speak in his own person. That the guardians of the people (in spiritual things) should themselves be incompetent is an absurdity which amounts to the eternalization of absurdities.

But would not a society of clergymen, perhaps a church conference or a venerable classis (as they call themselves among the Dutch), be justified in obligating itself by oath to a certain unchangeable symbol in order to enjoy an unceasing guardianship over each of its members and thereby over the people as a whole, and even to make it eternal? I answer that this is altogether impossible. Such a contract, made to shut off all further enlightenment from the human race, is absolutely null and void even if confirmed by the supreme power, by parliaments, and by the most ceremonious of peace treaties. An age cannot bind itself and ordain to put the succeeding one into such a condition that it cannot extend its (at best very occasional) knowledge, purify itself of errors, and progress in general enlightenment. That would be a crime against human nature, the proper destination of which lies precisely in this progress; and the descendants would be fully justified in rejecting those decrees as having been made in an unwarranted and malicious manner.

The touchstone of everything that can be concluded as a law for a people lies in the question whether the people could have imposed such a law on itself. Now such a religious compact might be possible for a short and definitely limited time, as it were, in expectation of a better. One might let every citizen, and especially the clergyman, in the role of scholar, make his comments freely and publicly, i.e., through writing, on the erroneous aspects of the present institution. The newly introduced order might last until insight into the nature of these things had become so general and widely approved that through uniting their voices (even if not unanimously) they could bring a proposal to the throne to take those congregations under protection which had united into a changed religious organization according to their better ideas, without, however, hindering others who wish to remain in the order. But to unite in a permanent religious institution which is not to be subject to doubt before the public even in the lifetime of one man, and thereby to make a period of time fruitless in the progress of mankind toward improvement, thus working to the disadvantage of posterity—that is absolutely forbidden. For himself (and only for a short time) a man can postpone enlightenment in what he ought to know, but to renounce it for himself and even more to renounce it for posterity is to injure and trample on the rights of mankind.

And what a people may not decree for itself can even less be decreed for them by a monarch, for his lawgiving authority rests on his uniting the general public will in his own. If he only sees to it that all true or alleged improvement stands together with civil order, he can leave it to his subjects to do what they find necessary for their spiritual welfare. This is not his concern, though it is incumbent on him to prevent one of them from violently hindering another in determining and promoting this welfare to the best of his ability. To meddle in these matters lowers his own majesty, since by the writings in which his subjects seek to present their views he may evaluate his own governance. He can do this when, with deepest understanding, he lays upon himself the reproach, *Caesar non est supra grammaticos.*[6] Far more does he injure his own majesty

---

6. Caesar [the ruler] is not above the grammarians (Latin).

when he degrades his supreme power by supporting the ecclesiastical despotism of some tyrants in his state over his other subjects.

If we are asked, "Do we now live in an *enlightened age?*" the answer is, "No," but we do live in an *age of enlightenment*. As things now stand, much is lacking which prevents men from being, or easily becoming, capable of correctly using their own reason in religious matters with assurance and free from outside direction. But, on the other hand, we have clear indications that the field has now been opened wherein men may freely deal with these things and that the obstacles to general enlightenment or the release from self-imposed tutelage are gradually being reduced. In this respect, this is the age of enlightenment, or the century of Frederick.[7]

A prince who does not find it unworthy of himself to say that he holds it to be his duty to prescribe nothing to men in religious matters but to give them complete freedom while renouncing the haughty name of *tolerance*, is himself enlightened and deserves to be esteemed by the grateful world and posterity as the first, at least from the side of government, who divested the human race of its tutelage and left each man free to make use of his reason in matters of conscience. Under him venerable ecclesiastics are allowed, in the role of scholars, and without infringing on their official duties, freely to submit for public testing their judgments and views which here and there diverge from the established symbol. And an even greater freedom is enjoyed by those who are restricted by no official duties. This spirit of freedom spreads beyond this land, even to those in which it must struggle with external obstacles erected by a government which misunderstands its own interest. For an example gives evidence to such a government that in freedom there is not the least cause for concern about public peace and the stability of the community. Men work themselves gradually out of barbarity if only intentional artifices are not made to hold them in it.

I have placed the main point of enlightenment—the escape of men from their self-incurred tutelage—chiefly in matters of religion because our rulers have no interest in playing the guardian with respect to the arts and sciences and also because religious incompetence is not only the most harmful but also the most degrading of all. But the manner of thinking of the head of a state who favors religious enlightenment goes further, and he sees that there is no danger to his lawgiving in allowing his subjects to make public use of their reason and to publish their thoughts on a better formulation of his legislation and even their open-minded criticisms of the laws already made. Of this we have a shining example wherein no monarch is superior to him whom we honor.

But only one who is himself enlightened, is not afraid of shadows, and has a numerous and well-disciplined army to assure public peace can say: "Argue as much as you will, and about what you will, only obey!" A republic could not dare say such a thing. Here is shown a strange and unexpected trend in human affairs in which almost everything, looked at in the large, is paradoxical. A greater degree of civil freedom appears advantageous to the freedom of mind of the people, and yet it places inescapable limitations upon it; a lower

---

7. Frederick the Great (1712–1786), king of Prussia (1740–86) during its emergence as a European power. Kant's sovereign when this essay was written, he was at once an autocrat and a champion of Enlightenment values.

degree of civil freedom, on the contrary, provides the mind with room for each man to extend himself to his full capacity. As nature has uncovered from under this hard shell the seed for which she most tenderly cares—the propensity and vocation to free thinking—this gradually works back upon the character of the people, who thereby gradually become capable of managing freedom; finally, it affects the principles of government, which finds it to its advantage to treat men, who are now more than machines, in accordance with their dignity.[8]

I. KANT

KÖNIGSBERG, PRUSSIA
September 30, 1784

SOURCE: From Immanuel Kant, *Critique of Practical Reason and Other Writings in Moral Philosophy*, ed. and trans. Lewis White Beck (Chicago: University of Chicago Press, 1949), pp. 286–92. Originally published as "Was ist Aufklarung?" (1784), an essay written in response to a call for discussions of this topic.

From Critique of Pure Reason

From *Preface to the Second Edition*

* * *

But, it will be asked, what sort of a treasure is this that we propose to bequeath to posterity? What is the value of the metaphysics that is alleged to be thus purified by criticism and established once for all? On a cursory view of the present work it may seem that its results are merely *negative*, warning us that we must never venture with speculative reason beyond the limits of experience. Such is in fact its primary use. But such teaching at once acquires a *positive* value when we recognise that the principles with which speculative reason ventures out beyond its proper limits do not in effect *extend* the employment of reason, but, as we find on closer scrutiny, inevitably *narrow* it. These principles properly belong [not to reason but] to sensibility,[1] and when thus employed they threaten to make the bounds of sensibility coextensive with the real, and so to supplant reason in its pure (practical) employment.[2] So far, therefore, as our Critique limits speculative reason, it is indeed *negative*; but since it thereby removes an obstacle which stands in the way of the employment of practical reason, nay threatens to destroy it, it has in reality a *positive* and very important use. At least this is so, immediately we are convinced that there is an absolutely necessary *practical* employment of pure reason—the

8. Today I read in the *Büschingsche Wöchentliche Nachrichten* [*Büsching's Weekly News*] for September 13 an announcement of the *Berlinische Monatsschrift* [*Berlin Monthly*] for this month, which cites the answer to the same question by Herr Mendelssohn. But this issue has not yet come to me; if it had, I would have held back the present essay, which is now put forth only in order to see how much agreement in thought can be brought about by chance [Kant's note]. The reference is to Moses Mendelssohn (1729–1786), German philosopher and critic.

1. That is, experience by means of our senses.

2. By "practical reason" or "reason in its pure (practical) employment" Kant means *moral* reasoning.

moral—in which it inevitably goes beyond the limits of sensibility. Though [practical] reason, in thus proceeding, requires no assistance from speculative reason, it must yet be assured against its opposition, that reason may not be brought into conflict with itself. To deny that the service which the Critique renders is *positive* in character, would thus be like saying that the police are of no positive benefit, inasmuch as their main business is merely to prevent the violence of which citizens stand in mutual fear, in order that each may pursue his vocation in peace and security. That space and time are only forms of sensible intuition,[3] and so only conditions of the existence of things as appearances; that, moreover, we have no concepts of understanding, and consequently no elements for the knowledge of things, save in so far as intuition can be given corresponding to these concepts; and that we can therefore have no knowledge of any object as thing in itself, but only in so far as it is an object of sensible intuition, that is, an appearance—all this is proved in the analytical part of the Critique. Thus it does indeed follow that all possible speculative knowledge of reason is limited to mere objects of *experience*. But our further contention must also be duly borne in mind, namely, that though we cannot *know* these objects as things in themselves, we must yet be in position at least to *think* them as things in themselves; otherwise we should be landed in the absurd conclusion that there can be appearance without anything that appears. Now let us suppose that the distinction, which our Critique has shown to be necessary, between things as objects of experience and those same things as things in themselves, had not been made. In that case all things in general, as far as they are efficient causes, would be determined by the principle of causality, and consequently by the mechanism of nature. I could not, therefore, without palpable contradiction, say of one and the same being, for instance the human soul, that its will is free and yet is subject to natural necessity, that is, is not free. For I have taken the soul in both propositions *in one and the same sense*, namely as a thing in general, that is, as a thing[4] in itself; and save by means of a preceding critique, could not have done otherwise. But if our Critique is not in error in teaching that the object is to be taken *in a twofold sense,* namely as appearance and as thing in itself; if the deduction of the concepts of understanding is valid, and the principle of causality therefore applies only to things taken in the former sense, namely, in so far as they are objects of experience—these same objects, taken in the other sense, not being subject to the principle—then there is no contradiction in supposing that one and the same will is, in the appearance, that is, in its visible acts, necessarily subject to the law of nature, and so far *not free*, while yet, as belonging to a thing in itself, it is not subject to that law, and is therefore *free*. My soul, viewed from the latter standpoint, cannot indeed be known by means of speculative reason (and still less through empirical observation); and freedom as a property of a being to which I attribute effects in the sensible world, is therefore also not knowable in any such fashion. For I should then have to know such a being as determined in its existence, and yet as not determined in time—which is impossible, since I cannot support my concept by any intuition. But though I cannot *know*, I can yet *think* freedom: that is to say, the representation of it is at least not self-contradictory provided due

3. That is, sense perception.   4. That is, a "something" (*Sache*).

account be taken of our critical distinction between the two modes of representation, the sensible and the intellectual, and of the resulting limitation of the pure concepts of understanding and of the principles which flow from them.

If we grant that morality necessarily presupposes freedom (in the strictest sense) as a property of our will; if, that is to say, we grant that it yields practical principles—original principles, proper to our reason—as *a priori data* of reason, and that this would be absolutely impossible save on the assumption of freedom; and if at the same time we grant that speculative reason has proved that such freedom does not allow of being thought, then the former supposition—that made on behalf of morality—would have to give way to this other contention, the opposite of which involves a palpable contradiction. For since it is only on the assumption of freedom that the negation of morality contains any contradiction, freedom, and with it morality, would have to yield to the mechanism of nature.

Morality does not, indeed, require that freedom should be understood, but only that it should not contradict itself, and so should at least allow of being thought, and that as thus thought it should place no obstacle in the way of a free act (viewed in another relation) likewise conforming to the mechanism of nature. The doctrine of morality and the doctrine of nature may each, therefore, make good its position. This, however, is only possible in so far as criticism has previously established our unavoidable ignorance of things in themselves, and has limited all that we can theoretically *know* to mere appearances.

This discussion as to the positive advantage of critical principles of pure reason can be similarly developed in regard to the concept of *God* and of the *simple*[5] *nature* of our *soul*; but for the sake of brevity such further discussion may be omitted. [From what has already been said, it is evident that] even the *assumption*—as made on behalf of the necessary practical employment of my reason—of *God, freedom*, and *immortality* is not permissible unless at the same time speculative reason be deprived of its pretensions to transcendent insight.[6] For in order to arrive at such insight it must make use of principles which, in fact, extend only to objects of possible experience, and which, if also applied to what cannot be an object of experience, always really change this into an appearance, thus rendering all *practical extension* of pure reason impossible. I have therefore found it necessary to deny *knowledge*, in order to make room for *faith*.[7] The dogmatism of metaphysics, that is, the preconception that it is possible to make headway in metaphysics without a previous criticism of pure reason, is the source of all that unbelief,[8] always very dogmatic, which wars against morality.

Though it may not, then, be very difficult to leave to posterity the bequest of a systematic metaphysic, constructed in conformity with a critique of pure

---

5. Indivisible.
6. That is, insight into the nature of things in themselves apart from our experience of them.
7. "Faith" translates *Glaube*, perhaps better rendered here as "belief" to avoid its identification with traditional religious faith. "Deny": here, "deny the pretension of"—that is, "restrict" or "curtail." While

Kant's restriction of (scientific) knowledge to the realm of the empirical makes (or leaves) room for the legitimacy of *Glaube* (belief) in the reality of God, the soul, and immortality, his critique of theoretical reason is not meant to leave the door open to any and all forms (and leaps) of religious faith.
8. That is, skepticism (*Unglaube*).

reason, yet such a gift is not to be valued lightly. For not only will reason be enabled to follow the secure path of a science,[9] instead of, as hitherto, groping at random, without circumspection or self-criticism; our enquiring youth will also be in a position to spend their time more profitably than in the ordinary dogmatism by which they are so early and so greatly encouraged to indulge in easy speculation about things of which they understand nothing, and into which neither they nor anyone else will ever have any insight—encouraged, indeed, to invent new ideas and opinions, while neglecting the study of the better-established sciences.[1] But, above all, there is the inestimable benefit, that all objections to morality and religion will be for ever silenced, and this in Socratic fashion, namely, by the clearest proof of the ignorance of the objectors. There has always existed in the world, and there will always continue to exist, some kind of metaphysics, and with it the dialectic that is natural to pure reason. It is therefore the first and most important task of philosophy to deprive metaphysics, once and for all, of its injurious influence, by attacking its errors at their very source.

* * *

SOURCE: From Immanuel Kant, *Critique of Pure Reason*, trans. Norman Kemp Smith (1929; reprint, London: Macmillan; New York: St. Martin's Press, 1961), pp. 26–30. The second edition of *Kritik der reinen Vernunft* was published in 1787; the first edition, in 1781. All bracketed additions are the translator's.

From Critique of Practical Reason

From *Conclusion*

Two things fill the mind with ever new and increasing wonder and awe, the oftener and the more steadily we reflect on them: the starry heavens above me and the moral law within me. I do not merely conjecture them and seek them as though obscured in darkness or in the transcendent region beyond my horizon: I see them before me, and I associate them directly with the consciousness of my own existence. The heavens begin at the place I occupy in the external world of sense, and broaden the connection in which I stand into an unbounded magnitude of worlds beyond worlds and systems of systems and into the limitless times of their periodic motion, their beginning and their duration. The latter begins at my invisible self, my personality, and exhibits me in a world which has true infinity but which is comprehensible only to the understanding[1]—a world with which I recognize myself as existing in a universal and necessary (and not, as in the first case, merely contingent) connection, and thereby also in connection with all those visible worlds. The former view of a countless multitude of worlds annihilates, as it were, my importance as an *animal creature*, which must give back to the planet (a mere speck in the

9. That is, "the secure path of a mature cognitive discipline" (*Wissenschaft*).
1. That is, cognitive disciplines (*Wissenschaften*).
1. That is, a capacity for comprehension that is distinct from the capacity for the kind of cognition associated with logical and scientific thinking but is rational in its own way.

universe) the matter from which it came, the matter which is for a little time provided with vital force, we know not how. The latter, on the contrary, infinitely raises my worth as that of an *intelligence* by my personality, in which the moral law reveals a life independent of all animality and even of the whole world of sense—at least so far as it may be inferred from the final destination assigned to my existence by this law, a destination which is not restricted to the conditions and boundaries of this life but reaches into the infinite.

* * *

SOURCE: From Immanuel Kant, *Critique of Practical Reason*, trans. Lewis White Beck, 3rd ed. (New York: Macmillan, 1993), p. 169. Originally published in 1788 as *Kritik der praktischen Vernunft*.

Part I

Idealisms: Spirituality and Reality

The first major development in philosophy after KANT was actually initiated by Kant himself, who provided both the name and the impetus for it. Kant had called his philosophical position "transcendental idealism," and that rubric—or at any rate, the label "idealism"—was embraced by many of his immediate successors, to whom the first part of this volume is largely devoted. Kant's idealism was by no means the "subjective idealism" of George Berkeley (1685–1753)—summed up in the slogan "to be is to be perceived (or to be a perceiver)"—as Kant was at pains to insist; but while he considered himself an "empirical realist," for whom the existence of a spatiotemporal material world external to ourselves was a reality, he also rejected the metaphysical "realism" that would grant the status of "things in themselves" (i.e., actual independent reality) to the objects encountered in the world of experience. Those objects, like the spatiotemporal world of experience investigated by the sciences more generally (or, as Kant puts it, "everything [perceived] in space and time, and therefore all objects of any [such] experience possible to us"), "are *nothing but appearances*—that is, *mere representations* which, in the manner in which they are represented, *as extended beings* or as series of alterations, *have no independent existence* outside our thoughts" (*Critique of Pure Reason* [1781]; emphasis added).

Kant's transcendental idealism thus asserts the "ideality" or mind-relatedness of everything about the world of (perceptual) experience. It thereby grants *objective but not absolute* reality to the objects of experience—the whole world of "nature" both as we experience it and as natural scientists investigate it. Indeed, it extends this significant but limited status to the very possibility of something being an "object" to which such "categories" as "unity," "plurality," "individuality," and "cause and effect" can apply, and even to the very "forms" of space and time. It also rules out applying *these* notions to "things in themselves," and renders problematic even talking about that which "appears" (when "appearance" occurs in experience) as "things": that is, the world as a *plurality* of *individual objects* that are *causally related*, either to each other or to the contents of our experience.

Moreover, Kant's version of idealism rules out the possibility of any sort of theoretical (scientific or metaphysical) "knowledge"—strictly speaking—of the "in-itself," or of whatever it is that "grounds" experience and thus the whole spatiotemporal world of experience. But it *does* license the "thought" of such a "ground" that transcends or underlies experience and that makes an "appearance" in what "appears" in our experience—even while insisting that its reality can be neither established nor even comprehended by theoretical reason. And Kant also allowed that certain sorts of experience other than perceptual experience—in particular, *moral* experience—could warrant certain "practical" conclusions going beyond the limits of scientific and logical rationality and shedding some light on this "ground" and our own more-than-merely-phenomenal reality.

The idealisms of Kant's immediate successors were their attempts to press ahead with the project of such a transcendental idealism, in ways they considered to be possible and similarly warranted. They took Kant's version as their point of departure, modifying it where they thought that to be necessary and extending it where they believed that to be possible. The results were quite remarkable. Kant himself lived long enough to see some of them; and his *Opus Postumum* (his unfinished final work, edited and published posthumously) would seem to indicate that he was taking them seriously. In any event, the "interpretive tradition" may be said to have originated in Kant's successors' acceptance of the limitations to which Kant had contended that analytical-theoretical (and in particular, natural-scientific) rationality was subject, together with his apparent legitimation of "speculative" philosophical thinking about matters transcending them if such thinking was properly conducted—that is, guided by and employing a broader sort of rationality better suited to that different terrain. Kant's reflections along these lines had been governed by and largely restricted to the kinds of thinking he associated with moral experience and reasoning, and with aesthetic and related forms of judgment; but his successors saw no good reason either to follow closely and narrowly in his footsteps or to accept these restrictions.

Post-Kantian idealism—sometimes referred to as "absolute idealism" or (for linguistic reasons) as "German idealism"—was a series of attempts both to revisit and revise the account Kant had given of the character and structure of the world of experience, and to develop the idea of its ground much more fully and very differently than Kant had. Like Kant, these idealists are deserving of that name not because they were "idealistic" in the ordinary sense of the term (even though some were), or because they denied the existence of things like chairs and tables and stars and planets and human bodies and the world in which we live. Rather, it is because they held that reality at this level of description is not ultimate or fundamental, that there is more to our own reality than can be captured in such terms, and that the fundamental nature of the reality in which it is all ultimately grounded is not itself something merely "material" or physical, or even dynamic in the way that energies and forces in nature are dynamic.

It was not uncommon for these thinkers to adopt a religious manner of speaking at times and to call this ultimate reality "God." For the most part, however, they conceived of it not as some sort of anthropomorphically modeled Supreme Being existing above and beyond this world, but rather as a power or principle manifesting itself in life and the world (and most particularly in ourselves) that has a fundamental reality to which our own higher spirituality as well as our basic vitality has an essential affinity, and that may appropriately be characterized as "divine." Their various versions of this divine ultimate ground of all reality may for the most part bear little conceptual resemblance to the God of traditional Judeo-Christianity; but for them this was what the "God-idea" comes to when philosophically interpreted—and for them, being able to preserve this much of it with a clear philosophical conscience was a triumph over the bleakness of a thoroughly materialistic worldview. For at least one among them, however (namely, SCHOPENHAUER), this ultimate reality was far from divine; indeed, it might better be characterized as *demonic*.

This first part of the volume has been given the subheading "Spirituality and Reality" to convey this general character of the idealisms represented in it. The thinkers to be encountered here, like Kant before them, are intent upon doing what they believed to be interpretive justice to what it is about human reality— and, for many, about reality more generally as well—that transcends the merely material and natural, and that must be conceived and comprehended quite differently from everything that is merely material and natural. Traditional Western religious thought—with its talk of a transcendent God and immortal immaterial souls—was for many (with the radical exception of KIERKEGAARD) outmoded if taken literally; but it was on to something important—something that it was one of philosophy's most crucial tasks to illuminate and communicate. (Schopenhauer took this to be true not of Western religious thought but of Buddhism.) And for a number of them, the language of "spirit" and "spirituality" seemed particularly apt for this purpose.

Later thinkers as diverse as WILHELM DILTHEY, EDMUND HUSSERL, MAX SCHELER, and even MARTIN HEIDEGGER and MICHEL FOUCAULT could also be grouped and read together with figures included in this part of the volume, as their kindred spirits in some significant respects. On the other hand, FRIEDRICH SCHILLER's interpretation of human reality and possibility could be considered an anticipation of the "naturalisms" that will be encountered in the next part of the volume. Kierkegaard's could (also) be reckoned among the (existential) "phenomenologies" (in the third part). And the differences between the figures (and idealisms) in this first part are at least as significant as their similarities. But these complications are a part of what makes the interpretive tradition so rich and interesting.

This introduction (like the introductions to the other parts) will conclude with a few preliminary remarks about the various thinkers who will be encountered here, providing a kind of preview that may be especially helpful to those who are making their first acquaintance with them, or who know them only by general reputation or popular caricature. Their great predecessor Immanuel Kant (1724–1804), introduced and briefly excerpted in the prologue, was the culminating figure in the history of classical modern philosophy, about whom much has already been said above. He is deserving of mention again here because, as has been noted, he called his philosophy a "transcendental idealism," thereby making the term "idealism" both readily available to his immediate successors and respectable for them to use. In his hands it implied no commitment regarding the ultimate character of reality, which for him was unknowable and inaccessible to human reason. His use of it to set limits on the authoritativeness of theoretical (and more specifically scientific) rationality, however, was temptingly suggestive to his successors, of whom the figures to be encountered here are salient cases in point.

Friedrich Schiller (1759–1805) was one of German-speaking Europe's literary giants, best known for his dramatic and poetic efforts; but he also was a historian and a philosopher. Like virtually everyone else in philosophy in the decades around the turn of the century, he considered himself a Kantian; but in his attempts to interpret Kant's thought and its significance he could not help developing ideas of his own—with respect to human nature, development, and flourishing—that were highly influential among his readers at the time and later. An inspiration to many who were looking for a new direction beyond Kant, he is an excellent figure with whom to begin the survey of the interpretive tradition that was already emerging in the last years of Kant's lifetime.

JOHANN GOTTLIEB FICHTE (1762–1814) also considered himself a Kantian—but a Kantian who (unlike Kant himself) had the courage of Kant's convictions, and was prepared to carry Kant's philosophical "Copernican revolution" through to (what Fichte took to be) its truly radical conclusions. His "absolute idealism" dispensed completely with the idea of any sort of "thing-in-itself" other than the spiritual principle he called "absolute ego"—which was no "thing" or entity at all. The excerpts from Kant's critiques in the prologue show the thinking in Kant that inspired Fichte's leap of philosophical "faith" beyond Kant and into the more radical position that is on display in the two selections from his writings.

FRIEDRICH SCHELLING (1775–1854), a brilliant young philosopher who burst upon the scene in rivalry with Fichte, was also eager to develop Kant's transcendental idealism into an absolute idealism. His version of it placed less weight than Fichte's had on morality, however, emphasizing initially the interpretation of nature and subsequently his attempt to develop a historically developmental philosophy of the freedom of the human spirit. In this latter respect he was closer to his friend and fellow university student G. W. F. Hegel, who was slower to attract attention but eventually eclipsed him. (Schelling had the good fortune to outlive Hegel by many years, and toward the end of his long life attained new celebrity as a kind of post-Hegelian proto-existentialist.) Schelling was more than a transitional figure between Fichte and Hegel (as Hegel critically portrayed him); for in his idealist period, the kind of metaphysical idealism that so appealed to "transcendentalists" found its most extreme expression in his writings. (It thereby also provided Hegel with a convenient foil in his telling of the then-recent history of modern philosophy, as he sought to recast the project and profile of absolute idealism.)

Georg Wilhelm Friedrich Hegel (1770–1831) is the towering figure who gave the interpretive tradition its initial shape and weight, and whose long shadow has accompanied it ever since. His extraordinary importance in it (and in the history of modern philosophy more generally) explains the extensiveness of the selections from him in this volume. Hegel's version of absolute idealism is one of the most impressive accomplishments in the history of philosophy.

It was dominant in German-speaking Europe at the time of Hegel's death, and in the nineteenth and early twentieth centuries it was the foundation of powerful and long-lasting Hegelian movements in British and American philosophy, as well as in Germany and elsewhere in Europe. It also figured importantly in the later history of philosophy on both sides of the English Channel as that *against* which Schopenhauer, MARX, Kierkegaard, and many later philosophers in the interpretive as well as the analytic traditions strongly reacted and rebelled.

In short: to understand the history of philosophy after Kant, one needs to have at least some understanding of Hegel. Yet understanding (and teaching) Hegel is very difficult, both because of his manner of thought and expression and because none of his works provides either a succinct and self-contained statement or a comprehensive and comprehensible overview of his philosophy. An attempt has been made here to assemble and organize an extensive array of excerpts from various of his writings and lectures that should make it possible to understand him in the full range of his thought—and, with the help of the notes commenting on them, to make his thought comprehensible and bring it to life. The heart of Hegel's seemingly abstract and artificial philosophical system is his philosophy of *Geist* (spirit)—that is, of everything in and about human life and experience that is more than merely biological. If properly understood, it is concretely and richly meaningful. All of the selections relate to it in one way or another, and all are intended to help illuminate it.

RALPH WALDO EMERSON (1803–1882) nicely exemplifies the influence of the foregoing figures—in some cases directly, in others through their British enthusiasts and interpreters—on philosophical thinking in the English-speaking world in the second quarter of the nineteenth century. Emerson's "Transcendentalism" was inspired by his encounters with these sources, as he (along with many others at the time) sought an uplifting spiritualistic alternative to the traditional Christianity that he was no longer able to embrace as the literal truth about ourselves and the world. At the same time, with an eclecticism for which he makes no apology, Emerson also celebrates individuality in a way that is closer to the spirit of Schiller and the Romantics than to that of the "absolute idealists." Emerson was no academic philosopher, but he was the most interesting and influential philosophical voice of the newly emerging America in his time. It is a voice that resonated strongly to a philosophical tradition very different from that of Hume.

Søren Kierkegaard (1813–1855) is not usually considered a philosophical "idealist," and indeed in the twentieth century he provided the impetus to the emergence of existential philosophy, with which he is quite appropriately associated. He was scornful of Hegel's kind and version of idealism; yet he could be considered a kind of idealist as well, at least insofar as he insisted that the "truth" of human selfhood is irreducible to anything objective about human reality. He therefore is included here and should be read in conjunction with Hegel, as well as with his existential-philosophical kindred spirits (in some respects) in the third part of this volume. He made much of the question of "what it means to exist as a human being"; and it was his emphasis on individual human first-person-singular "*existing*," conceived in terms of its "subjective" rather than objective dimensions, that gave existential philosophy its central theme and agenda. He thus gave powerful expression to a very different sort of spirituality than that associated with any of the (other) idealisms represented here.

Kierkegaard also (and relatedly) was passionately committed to an intensely Christian religiousness, in vehement opposition to Hegel's assimilation of religion in general and Christianity in particular to his kind of philosophy. He might be seen as making common cause with Kant, who likewise sought to give the ideas of God, the soul, and immortality a new lease on life, through his "critique" of theoretical reason that enabled him to set limits on the "knowable" that "made room for faith." But Kierkegaard goes further, appealing to a kind of "leap of faith" that Kant would have found appalling, owing to his emphasis on the "absurdity" of its central ideas. Yet for him, absurdity is *required* for it to be a leap of *faith*—not only beyond but actually contrary to all rationality. The stakes, he argued, could not be higher; for such a leap alone is proof against despair and the dark victory of Schopenhauerian pessimism.

In conclusion: it is notoriously difficult to avoid confusion and misunderstanding about what is meant by "idealism" in the context of this first major development in the post-Kantian interpretive tradition. One might think of what is going on here in the following general way. Suppose we take Kant as our point of departure (as many of Kant's successors did), and feel impelled to attempt to go a step farther than he did—to speculate about the ground of the entire world of experience and all that transpires in it of which he speaks. After all, Kant himself did so to some extent (and thereby legitimized doing so), in his reflections on what moral experience suggests and would seem to require with respect to the ideas of God and the soul and freedom. What we come up with will certainly not be (or be on a par with) the kind of knowledge that Kant associates with scientific thought and other forms of analytical and theoretical reasoning. Yet it could turn out to be appropriately considered *another sort* of comprehension, attained by a different use of reason—a use akin to one or both of those that Kant himself associates with practical rationality and with judgment, and does not hesitate to employ. It might, for example, be another sort of comprehension on a par with his own postulates concerning the soul, freedom, and God in the context of his moral philosophy, and also in his suggestively titled *Religion within the Limits of Reason Alone* (1793).

If it is taken for granted that Kant has established the "ideality" or mind-relatedness of the conditions of the possibility of anything being an object, including space and time, then that ground presumably will have to be something other than a spatiotemporal entity of any kind; for nothing internal to the world of experience can be its ground. If its ground must be something non-spatiotemporal and other than any sort of object (and thus nothing in or about "nature"), the only possible alternative would seem to be some sort of ultimate *subject*-like reality or principle that is capable of activating and expressing itself in the form of the world of experience. Kant had spoken of a "transcendental ego" in this connection. Other such terms, such as "spirit" and "will," were pressed into service as well. The burning question became something like this: What principle of this sort is at the bottom or heart of all things, expressing itself in us and in the world of experience, if it is nothing merely "natural" and yet is also inadequately expressed in traditional religious language? That, in effect, is the basic question in the post-Kantian contest of idealisms and associated reinterpretations of human reality.

FRIEDRICH SCHILLER
(1759 – 1805)

Schiller was one of Germany's greatest writers, and one of the greatest contributors to modern European intellectual and literary history. He was not a philosopher by training, and is known and revered primarily as a poet and playwright; but he was a writer and thinker of many talents, with many interests, and philosophy was one of them. (History was another.) And there is perhaps no better introduction to the history of European philosophy after IMMANUEL KANT than his *Letters on the Aesthetic Education of Man*, begun in 1793 (to an interested Danish prince) in a series of twenty-six installments written over a two-year period, and then published together in 1795. In these essays Schiller sounded many of the concerns and gave initial expression to many of the critical and constructive ideas that would reverberate through philosophy throughout the next century—and that remain alive, well, important, and engaging in our own time. Here human reality and possibility, the character of life in the modern world, genuine humanity, and the means to its attainment are his central topics. He considered himself a Kantian, and tried to present and express himself as such; but his own thinking carried him beyond Kant, in ways that inspired generations of young philosophers for whom Kant was only the beginning and not the end of modern philosophy.

Johann Christoph Friedrich Schiller ("SHILL-er") was born in 1759 in a small town near Stuttgart in what is now southwestern Germany. (He became "von Schiller" upon being ennobled in 1802.) He was the only brother of ten sisters. Thanks to his precocious academic abilities, he was accepted into the newly established Karlsschule (a military academy) in Stuttgart in 1773. His father was a military doctor, who wanted him to become a minister. He began by liking that idea; but his interests turned in the direction first of law and then for a time (not surprisingly) of medicine. However, at the Karlsschule he became acquainted with the writings of the great literary figures of the day, which sparked his interest in the ideals of both classical Greek civilization and the contemporary European Enlightenment. He also developed and pursued philosophical interests. He had great gifts as a writer, as well as a deep and lively intelligence. These interests and abilities came together very early on, in a play he wrote while still at the academy: *The Robbers* (1781). It was a spectacular success and made him an instant literary sensation, but its daring politics got him into trouble with the conservative political authorities.

Upon leaving the academy Schiller initially followed in his father's footsteps, obtaining a position as a military doctor (at the age of 21); but his political difficulties prompted him to flee to a more liberally minded principality in the southeastern part of Germany, and he settled in Weimar in 1787. During this period he continued to write plays and poetry, began to write on culture and the arts, and also developed historical interests. His pursuit of these interests somehow won him an appointment in 1789 as a professor of history at the University of Jena—at that time one of the leading universities in central Europe. He taught there for ten years, and during the last half of that span he had both JOHANN FICHTE and FRIEDRICH SCHELLING as colleagues. It was during this period that he wrote his popular *Letters on the Aesthetic Education of Man* (excerpted below), as well as a good deal of history, while ceasing to write poetry and drama for a time.

By 1799 Schiller had tired of academic life. He relinquished his position at Jena and returned to Weimar, where he resumed his literary efforts in the company of Johann Wilhelm von Goethe and his circle. Together they made Weimar the literary and intellectual center of German-speaking Europe. His health soon failed, however, and he died of tuberculosis in 1805, at the age of only 45. His career was as astonishing as it was brief; and he is revered today, together with Goethe, as the greatest of the great figures in the pantheon of the golden age of German literature. (Goethe, ten years his senior, outlived him by twenty-seven years and also died in Weimar. They are entombed together there.)

Schiller was profoundly influenced philosophically by Kant, and more specifically by Kant's moral and aesthetic philosophy. In his theoretical writings, he tried to be true to what he took to be the spirit of Kant's thought, with its emphasis on the kinds of rationality—moral as well as theoretical—of which we are capable. Yet he also was greatly impressed by the example of Goethe, who not only was German-speaking Europe's greatest writer but also seemed to Schiller—and to many others—to exemplify both the diversity and the harmonious unity of many different sorts of human excellence, and to stand as a paradigm of the ideal of humanity. Schiller was acutely aware of the importance of culture and the arts both in the kind of humanity Goethe represented and in his own life, and he became convinced that nurturing our capacity for aesthetic experience and activity was the key to the cultivation and attainment of that human ideal. Schiller's series of letters displays the development of his thinking, as his efforts to apply Kantian ideas and principles to the critical assessment of human life in the emerging modern Western world morph into a reinterpretation of human reality and ideality that departs significantly from Kant's. For Kant our capacity for practical (moral) and theoretical rationality is the cornerstone of human dignity and worth. For Schiller the key to genuine humanity is the cultivation of our aesthetic sensibility and creative powers, incorporating but also transcending both elements of that double capacity.

Schiller's central concern in the *Letters* is with the quality of human life—and therefore also with the character of human reality, both as it could and should be and as it actually is. He is convinced that it makes good and important sense to talk about what he calls "the ideal man," or the human ideal, as well as about the way human life is in the modern world. And it further seems clear to him that there is a great disparity between "is" and "should be" that needs to be overcome.

Schiller conceives of human reality as something that has a developmental history. He assumes that its actual character can and does change in the course of history, and that such change can be either for the better or for the worse—sometimes for the worse in the short run in ways that may set the stage for change for the better in the longer run. And he holds that the conditions that prevail in human societies have a great deal to do with the character and quality of human life, also for the better or for the worse. So he offers an early severe critique of the dehumanizing effects of certain aspects of the kind of society that was taking shape in his time, anticipating many other subsequent criticisms of it before the Industrial Revolution had even gotten up a good head of steam. He was acutely aware that there is more to the quality of human life than its material conditions; and he was concerned above all with what, beyond material improvement, is required for the enhancement of its quality.

Whether for philosophical reasons or for reasons relating to his artistic and historical sensibility, Schiller makes it very clear that his concern is with ourselves as *human*, and with human reality conceived in terms of human *life* as real flesh-and-blood, socially and culturally existing, historically situated human beings do live it and might be able to live it. For him, our humanity has at least as much to do with our attained and attainable spirituality as it does with our existence as a type of living creature—and our spirituality is inseparable from our living human reality. His understanding of that reality is neither metaphysical nor theological—and yet it also is not merely materialistic or naturalistic. He avoids such debates, preferring to try to focus attention on ourselves in a way that is true to his vivid poetic-dramatic sense of the human.

The human ideal, for Schiller, is a kind of humanity in which not only the merely natural but also the opposite one-sidedness and inadequacy of the purely rational has been transcended. It is a condition in which the cultivation of both our natural and our rational powers has been undertaken in a manner that overcomes their opposition and achieves their harmonious integration. He considers "the aesthetic education of man" to be essential at two stages of this complex developmental process. Its powers are needed initially (and here he follows Kant) to assist in the liberation of humanity from the tyranny of nature, breaking its grip upon us and enabling our rational powers to come into play. And subsequently (now going beyond Kant), its powers are needed again to assist in a further liberation of humanity from the opposite tyranny of rules and principles. It does (or can) accomplish this by showing the way to a kind of experience and activity that has the character of what he calls "play," in which both our rational and natural powers are engaged, equally essentially and harmoniously, in activity that is expressive and enjoyable for its own sake rather than as a means to any extrinsic end.

Schiller's *Letters*, written as Kant's dominance of European philosophy was about to end and the nineteenth century was about to dawn, admirably and powerfully marks the transformation of philosophical interests and concerns that was beginning, and it may well have helped to spark the developments that made the emergence of the post-Kantian interpretive tradition one of the most remarkable chapters in the history of philosophy.

From On the Aesthetic Education of Man, in a Series of Letters

From *Letter I*

By your permission I lay before you,[1] in a series of letters, the results of my researches upon beauty and art. I am keenly sensible of the importance as well as of the charm and dignity of this undertaking. I shall treat a subject which is closely connected with the better portion of our happiness and not far removed from the moral nobility of human nature. I shall plead this cause of the Beautiful before a heart by which her whole power is felt and exercised,

1. The Danish prince Friedrich Christian of Schleswig-Holstein-Augustenborg (1765–1814), a patron to whom Schiller began writing these letters in 1793.

and which will take upon itself the most difficult part of my task in an investigation where one is compelled to appeal as frequently to feelings as to principles.

That which I would beg of you as a favor, you generously impose upon me as a duty; and, when I solely consult my inclination, you impute to me a service. The liberty of action you prescribe is rather a necessity for me than a constraint. Little exercised in formal rules, I shall scarcely incur the risk of sinning against good taste by any undue use of them; my ideas, drawn from within myself rather than from reading or from an intimate experience with the world, will not disown their origin; they would rather incur any reproach than that of a sectarian bias, and would prefer to succumb by their innate feebleness than sustain themselves by borrowed authority and external support.

In truth, I will not keep back from you that the assertions which follow rest chiefly upon Kantian principles; but if in the course of these researches you should be reminded of any special school of philosophy, ascribe it to my incapacity, not to those principles. * * *

With regard to the ideas which predominate in the practical part of Kant's system, only philosophers disagree, whilst mankind, I am confident of proving, have never done so. If stripped of their technical shape, they will appear as the verdict of reason pronounced from time immemorial by common consent, and as facts of the moral instinct which nature, in its wisdom, has given to man in order to serve as guide and teacher until his enlightened intelligence gives him maturity. But this very technical shape which renders truth visible to the understanding conceals it from the feelings; for, unhappily, understanding begins by destroying the object of the inner sense before it can appropriate the object. Like the chemist, the philosopher finds synthesis only by analysis, or the spontaneous work of nature only through the torture of art. Thus, in order to detain the fleeting apparition, he must enchain it in the fetters of rule, dissect its fair proportions into abstract notions, and preserve its living spirit in a fleshless skeleton of words. Is it surprising that natural feeling should not recognise itself in such a copy, and if in the report of the analyst the truth appears as paradox?

*　*　*

Letter III

Man is not better treated by nature in his beginnings than its other works are; so long as he is unable to act for himself as an independent intelligence, it acts for him. But the very fact that constitutes him a man is that he does not remain stationary, where nature has placed him, that he can pass with his reason, retracing the steps nature had made him anticipate, that he can convert the work of necessity into one of free solution, and transform physical necessity into a moral law.

When man is raised from his slumber in the senses, he feels that he is a man, he surveys his surroundings, and finds that he is in a state.[2] He was

2. That is, in a human society with some sort of political structure and organization.

introduced into this state, by the power of circumstances, before he could freely select his own position. But as a moral being he cannot possibly rest satisfied with a political condition forced upon him by necessity, and only calculated for that condition; and it would be unfortunate if this did satisfy him. In many cases man shakes off this blind law of necessity by his free spontaneous action, of which among many others we have an instance, in his ennobling by beauty and suppressing by moral influence the powerful impulse implanted in him by nature in the passion of love. Thus, when arrived at maturity, he recovers his childhood by an artificial process, he founds a state of nature in his ideas, not given him by any experience, but established by the necessary laws and conditions of his reason, and he attributes to this ideal condition an object, an aim, of which he was not cognizant in the actual reality of nature. He gives himself a choice of which he was not capable before, and sets to work just as if he were beginning anew, and were exchanging his original state of dependence for one of complete independence, doing this with complete insight and of his free decision. However artfully and firmly blind impulse may have established its political outcome, and although it may strive to maintain itself with great arrogance and encompass itself with a halo of veneration, he is justified in regarding his political subjection as completely fictitious. For the work of blind powers possesses no authority before which freedom need bow, and all must be made to adapt itself to the highest end which reason has set up in his personality. It is in this wise that a mature people is justified in transforming its natural condition into an ethical [*sittlich*] one.[3]

Now the term "natural condition" can be applied to every political body which owes its establishment originally to forces and not to laws, and such a state contradicts the moral nature of man, because lawfulness can alone have authority over this. At the same time this natural condition is quite sufficient for the physical man, who gives himself laws only in order to get rid of brute force. Moreover, the physical man is *real*, while the moral man is *problematical*.[4] Therefore when reason suppresses the natural condition, as it must if it wishes to replace that condition with its own, it weighs the real physical man against the problematical moral man, it weighs the existence of society against a possible, though morally necessary, ideal of society. It takes from man something which he really possesses, and without which he possesses nothing, and refers him to something as a substitute that he ought to possess and might possess; and if reason had relied too exclusively on that substitute, it might—in order to secure him a state of humanity he lacks (and can lack without injury to his life)—rob him even of the means of animal existence which is the first necessary condition of his human reality. Before he had opportunity to hold firm to the law with his will, reason would have withdrawn from his feet the ladder of nature.

The great point is therefore to reconcile these two considerations: to prevent physical society from ceasing for a moment *in time*, while the moral society is being formed *in idea*; in other words, to prevent its existence from being

---

3. The German term Schiller uses here is *Sittlichkeit*. Often translated as "morality," it is better translated as "the ethical" or "ethicality." The terms "moral" and "morality" are best reserved to render the German *moralisch* and *Moralität*, which Schiller (like KANT before him and HEGEL after) also uses. For the same reason, it is best to translate *sittlich* as "ethical" rather than as "moral."
4. That is, uncertain—what is problematic may or may not become a reality.

placed in jeopardy, for the sake of the moral dignity of man. When the mechanic has to mend a watch, he lets the wheels run down; but the living watchworks of the state have to be repaired while they act, and a wheel has to be exchanged for another during its revolutions. Accordingly props must be sought to support society and keep it going while it is made independent of the natural condition from which it is to be emancipated.

This prop is not found in the natural character of man, who, being selfish and violent, directs his energies rather toward the destruction than toward the preservation of society. Nor is it found in his ethical character, which has to be formed, which can never be worked upon or counted on with certainty by the lawgiver, because it is free and unobservable. It would seem therefore that another measure must be adopted. It would seem that the physical character of the arbitrary must be separated from moral freedom; that it is incumbent to make the former harmonize with the laws and the latter dependent on impressions; it would be expedient to remove the former still farther from matter and to bring the latter somewhat more near to it; in short, to produce a third character related to both the physical and the moral, paving the way to a transition from the sway of mere force to that of law, without preventing the proper development of the moral character, but serving rather as an anticipation in the realm of the senses of invisible ethicality [*Sittlichkeit*].

Letter IV

Thus much is certain. It is only when a third character, as previously suggested, has preponderance that a revolution in a state according to moral principles can be free from injurious consequences; nor can anything else secure its endurance. In proposing or setting up a moral state, the moral law is relied upon as a real power, and free will is drawn into the realm of causes, where all hangs together mutually with stringent necessity and rigidity. But we know that the condition of the human will always remains contingent, and that physical and moral necessity coincide only in the Absolute Being. Accordingly if one wishes to be able to depend on the ethical conduct of man as on natural results, this conduct must *become* nature, and he must be led by disposition to such a course of action as can only result from having an ethical character. But the will of man is perfectly free between inclination and duty, and no physical necessity ought to enter as a sharer in this magisterial personality. If therefore he is to retain this power of solution, and yet become a reliable link in the causal concatenation of forces, this can only be effected when the operations of both these impulses are presented quite equally in the world of appearances. It is only possible when, with every difference of form, the matter of man's volition remains the same, when all his impulses agreeing with his reason are sufficient to have the value of a universal legislation.

It may be urged that every individual man carries, within himself, at least in his adaptation and destination, a purely ideal man. The great problem of his existence is to bring all the incessant changes of his outer life into conformity with the unchanging unity of this ideal. This pure ideal man, which makes itself known more or less clearly in every subject, is represented by the state, which is the objective and, so to speak, canonical form in which the manifold differences of the subjects strive to unite. Now two ways can be conceived in which man *in time* can agree with man *in idea*,[5] and there are also two ways in which the state can maintain itself in individuals. One of these ways is when the pure ideal man is imposed upon the empirical man, and the state suppresses the individual; while the other is when the individual *becomes* the state, and existing man is *ennobled* into ideal man.

I admit that in a one-sided estimate from the point of view of morality this difference vanishes, for the reason is satisfied if its law prevails unconditionally. But in a complete anthropological assessment, in which the form is considered together with the substance, and a living feeling has a voice, the difference will become far more evident. No doubt reason demands unity, and nature variety, and both legislations take man in hand. The law of the former is stamped upon him by an incorruptible consciousness, that of the latter by an ineradicable feeling. Consequently it will always be a sign of an education[6] that is still deficient when ethical character can be maintained only through the sacrifice of the natural; and a political administration will always be very imperfect when it is able to bring about unity only by suppressing variety. The state ought to respect not only the objective and generic but also the subjective and specific in individuals; and while expanding the invisible realm of the ethical, it must not impoverish the realm of appearance.[7]

When the mechanical artist places his hand on the formless block, to give it a form according to his intention, he has no scruples about doing violence to it. For the nature on which he works does not deserve any respect in itself, and he does not value the whole for its parts, but the parts on account of the whole. When the fine artist sets his hand to the same block, he has no scruples about doing violence to it either; he only avoids displaying this violence. He does not respect the matter in which he works, any more than the mechanical artist; but he seeks, by an apparent consideration for it, to deceive the eye which takes this matter under its protection. The political and educating artist follows a very different course, while making man at once his material and his end. In this case the aim or end meets in the material, and it is only because the whole serves the parts that the parts adapt themselves to the end. The political artist has to treat his material man with a very different kind of respect from that shown by the artist of fine art to his work. He must spare man's peculiarity and personality, not to produce a deceptive effect on the senses, but objectively and out of consideration for his inner being.

But the state is an organization which fashions itself through itself and for itself, and for this reason it can be realized only when the parts have been aligned with the idea of the whole. The state serves as a representative of pure ideal and objective humanity in the breast of its citizens. Accordingly it will have to observe the same relation to its citizens as they stand in to it, and it will do justice to their subjective humanity only to the degree that that humanity is elevated into an objective existence. If the internal man is one with himself, he will be able to preserve his peculiarity, even in the greatest generalization

---

5. That is, two ways in which it is possible for existing human beings ("man in time") to be brought—or to try to come—into accord with the ideal of genuine humanity ("man in idea").

6. A translation of *Bildung*: education in the broadly developmental (rather than formal) sense.
7. That is, the material dimension of human reality.

of his conduct,[8] and the state will only become the exponent of his refined instinct, the clearer formulation of his internal legislation. But if the subjective man is in conflict with the objective and contradicts him in the character of the people, so that only the oppression of the former can give the victory to the latter, then the state will take up the severe aspect of the law against the citizen, and in order not to fall a sacrifice, it will have to crush under foot such a hostile individuality, without any compromise.

Now man can be opposed to himself in a twofold manner: either as a savage, when his feelings rule over his principles; or as a barbarian,[9] when his principles destroy his feelings. The savage despises art, and acknowledges nature as his despotic ruler; the barbarian laughs at nature, and dishonors it, but he often proceeds in a more contemptible way than the savage, to be the slave of his senses. The cultivated man makes of nature his friend, and honors its friendship, while only bridling its caprice.

Consequently, when reason brings its moral unity into physical society, it must not injure the manifold in nature. When nature strives to maintain its manifold character in the moral structure of society, this must not create any breach in moral unity; the victorious form is equally remote from uniformity and confusion. Therefore, totality of character must be found in the people which is capable and worthy to exchange the state of necessity for that of freedom.

Letter V

Does the present age—do current events—present this character? I direct my attention at once to the most prominent object in this vast structure.

It is true that the consideration of opinion is fallen, caprice is unnerved, and, although still armed with power, receives no longer any respect. Man has awaked from his long lethargy and self-deception, and he demands with impressive unanimity to be restored to his imperishable rights. But he does not only demand them; he rises on all sides to seize by force what, in his opinion, has been unjustly wrested from him. The edifice of the natural state is tottering, its foundations shake, and a physical possibility seems at length granted to place law on the throne, to honor man at length as an end, and to make true freedom the basis of political union. Vain hope! The moral possibility is lacking, and the occasion for generosity is met by an unresponsive race.

Man paints himself in his actions, and what is the form depicted in the drama of the present time? On the one hand, he is seen running wild, on the other in a state of lethargy: the two extremest stages of human degeneracy, and both seen in one and the same period.

In the lower larger masses, coarse, lawless impulses come to view, breaking loose when the bonds of civil order are burst asunder, and hastening with unbridled fury to satisfy their savage instinct. Objective humanity may have had cause to complain of the state; yet subjective man must honor its institu-

---

8. That is, even when his conduct must conform to general norms or rules.
9. That is, the sort of (religious or moral) zealot who (unlike the "savage") does have and act in accordance with "principles," but whose principles are fanatical convictions, leading to radical harshness that is heedless of feeling (and so, in a sense, is "barbaric").

tions. Ought he to be blamed because he lost sight of the dignity of human nature, so long as he was concerned in preserving his existence? Can we blame him that he proceeded to separate by the force of gravity, to fasten by the force of cohesion, at a time when there could be no thought of building or raising up? The extinction of the state contains its justification. Society set free, instead of hastening upward into organic life, collapses into its elements.

On the other hand, the civilized classes give us the still more repulsive sight of lethargy, and of a depravity of character which is the more revolting because it roots in culture. I forget who of the older or more recent philosophers makes the remark that the nobler is the more revolting in its destruction. The remark applies with truth to the world of morals. The child of nature, when he breaks loose, becomes a madman; but the art scholar, when he breaks loose, becomes a debased character. The enlightenment of the understanding, on which the more refined classes pride themselves with some ground, shows on the whole so little of an ennobling influence on the mind that it seems rather to confirm corruption by its maxims. We deny nature in its legitimate field and feel its tyranny in the moral sphere, and while resisting its impressions, we receive our principles from it. While the affected decency of our manners does not even grant to nature a pardonable influence in the initial stage, our materialistic system of morals allows nature the deciding vote in the last and essential stage of deliberation.

Egotism has founded its system in the very bosom of a refined society, and without developing even a sociable character, we feel all the contagions and miseries of society. We subject our free judgment to its despotic opinions, our feelings to its bizarre customs, and our will to its seductions. We only maintain our caprice against its holy rights. The man of the world has his heart contracted by a proud self-complacency, while that of the man of nature often beats in sympathy; and every man seeks for nothing more than to save his wretched property from the general destruction, as it were from some great conflagration. It is conceived that the only way to find a shelter against the aberrations of sentiment is by completely forgoing its indulgence, and mockery, which is often a useful chastener of mysticism, slanders in the same breath the noblest aspirations. Culture, far from giving us freedom, only develops, as it advances, new necessities; the fetters of the physical close more tightly around us, so that the fear of loss quenches even the ardent impulse toward improvement, and the maxims of passive obedience are held to be the highest wisdom of life. Thus the spirit of the time is seen to waver between perversion and savagery, between what is unnatural and mere nature, between superstition and moral unbelief, and it is often nothing but the equilibrium of evils that sets bounds to it.

From *Letter VI*

Have I gone too far in this portrait of our times? I do not anticipate this stricture, but rather another—that I have proved too much by it. You will tell me that the picture I have presented resembles the humanity of our day, but it also characterizes all peoples that have attained the same degree of culture, because all, without exception, have fallen off from nature by the abuse of reason, before they can return to it through reason.

But if we bestow some serious attention to the character of our times, we shall be astonished at the contrast between the present and the previous form of humanity, especially that of Greece. We are justified in claiming the reputation of culture and refinement, when contrasted with a purely natural state of society, but not so comparing ourselves with the Grecian nature. For the latter was combined with all the charms of art and with all the dignity of wisdom, without, however, as with us, becoming a victim to these influences. The Greeks put us to shame not only by their simplicity, which is foreign to our age; they are at the same time our rivals, nay, frequently our models, in those very points of superiority from which we seek comfort when regretting the unnatural character of our manners. We see that remarkable people uniting at once fullness of form and fullness of substance, both philosophizing and creating, both tender and energetic, uniting a youthful fancy to the virility of reason in a glorious humanity.

At that time, in that beautiful awakening of the powers of the spirit,[1] the senses and the spirit had no distinctly separated domains; no division had yet torn them asunder, leading them to partition in a hostile attitude, and to mark off their limits with precision. Poetry had not yet become the adversary of wit, nor had speculation abused itself by passing into quibbling. In cases of necessity both poetry and wit could exchange parts, because they both honored truth only in their special way. However high might be the flight of reason, it drew matter in a loving spirit after it, and, while sharply and stiffly defining it, never mutilated what it touched. To be sure, the Greeks displaced human nature, and recast it on a magnified scale in the glorious circle of their gods; but they did this not by sundering human nature into pieces, but by giving it fresh configurations, for the whole of human nature was not lacking in any of the gods.

How different is the course followed by us moderns! We also displace and magnify individuals to form the image of the species, but we do this in a fragmentary way, not by altered combinations, so that it is necessary to gather up from different individuals the elements that form the species in its totality. It would almost appear as if the powers of spirit express themselves with us in real life or empirically as separately as the psychologist distinguishes them in the representation. For we see not only individual subjects, but whole classes of men, uphold their capacities only in part, while the rest of their faculties scarcely show a germ of activity, as in the case of the stunted growth of plants.

I do not overlook the advantages to which the present-day human race, regarded as a unity and in the balance of considerations, may lay claim to superiority over what is best in the ancient world; but it is obliged to engage in the contest as a compact mass, and measure itself as a whole against a whole. Who among the moderns could step forth, man against man, and strive with an Athenian for the prize of higher humanity?

1. "Spirit," here and later, translates the German word *Geist*, which has a broader meaning than "mind," the English term often used to render it. "Mind" is suggestive of a much narrower range of human capacities and processes, and more aptly fits Schiller's *Gemut* (here so translated). *Geist* for Schiller does not have the traditional religious connotation of something supernatural, along the lines of "the soul" as something distinct from the body; it is a word for everything about ourselves that is more than merely physical and biological.

Whence comes this disadvantageous relation of individuals coupled with great advantages of the race? Why could the individual Greek be considered representative of his time? and why can no modern dare to offer himself as such? Because all-uniting nature imparted its forms to the Greek, and an all-dividing understanding gives our forms to us.

It was culture itself that gave these wounds to modern humanity. The inner unity of human nature was broken, and a destructive contest divided its harmonious forces directly; on the one hand, an enlarged experience and a more distinct thinking necessitated a sharper separation of the sciences, while on the other hand, the more complicated machinery of states necessitated a stricter sundering of ranks and occupations. Intuitive and speculative forms of understanding took up a hostile stance toward each other in opposite fields, whose borders were guarded with jealousy and distrust; and by thus limiting understanding's operation in one way or another to a narrow sphere, men have created a master within themselves tending not infrequently to subdue and oppress all the other faculties. While on the one hand a luxuriant imagination creates ravages in the plantations that have cost the intelligence so much labor, on the other hand a spirit of abstraction suffocates the fire that might have warmed the heart and inflamed the imagination.

This breakdown, commenced by art and learning in the inner man, was carried out to fullness and finished by the spirit of innovation in government. It was, no doubt, reasonable to expect that the simple organization of the primitive republics should survive the quaintness of primitive manners and of the relations of antiquity. But, instead of rising to a higher and nobler degree of animal life, this organization degenerated into a common and coarse mechanism. The polyp-like nature of the Greek states, in which each individual enjoyed an independent life, and could, in cases of necessity, become a separate whole and unit unto himself, gave way to an ingenious mechanism, whence, from the splitting up into numberless parts, there results a mechanical life in the combination.

Then there was a rupture between the state and the church, between laws and customs; enjoyment was separated from labor, the means from the end, the effort from the reward. Man himself, eternally chained down to a little fragment of the whole, only forms a kind of fragment; having nothing in his ears but the monotonous sound of the perpetually revolving wheel, he never develops the harmony of his being; and instead of imprinting the seal of humanity on his being, he ends by being nothing more than the living impress of the craft to which he devotes himself, of the science that he cultivates. This very partial and paltry relation, linking the isolated members to the whole, does not depend on forms that are given spontaneously; for how could a complicated machine, which shuns the light, confide itself to the free will of man? This relation is rather dictated, with a rigorous strictness, by a regulation in which free intelligence is chained down. The dead letter takes the place of a living meaning, and a practiced memory becomes a safer guide than genius and feeling.

If the community or state measures man by his function, only asking of its citizens memory, or the intelligence of a craftsman, or mechanical skill, we cannot be surprised that the other faculties of the mind are neglected, in favor of the exclusive cultivation of the one that brings in honor and profit. So also if it is indifferent about character, caring only about knowledge, or if, to promote the spirit of order and lawful behavior, it tolerates the greatest darkening of understanding, it must result that individuals lose in breadth what they gain in depth in the exercise of special aptitudes. We are aware, no doubt, that a powerful genius does not shut up its activity within the limits of its functions; but mediocre talents consume in the craft that is their lot the whole of their feeble energy[.] * * *

It is thus that concrete individual life is extinguished, in order that the abstract whole may continue its miserable life, and the state remains forever a stranger to its citizens, because feeling does not discover it anywhere. The governing authorities find themselves compelled to classify, and thereby simplify, the multiplicity of citizens, and to know humanity only in a representative form and at second hand. Accordingly they end by entirely losing sight of humanity, and by confounding it with a simple artificial creation of the understanding, while on their part the subject classes cannot help receiving coldly laws that address themselves so little to their personality. At length society, weary of having a burden that the state takes so little trouble to lighten, falls to pieces and is broken up—a destiny that has long since attended most European states. They are dissolved in what may be called a moral "state of nature," in which public authority is only one function more, hated and deceived by those who think it necessary, respected only by those who can do without it.

Thus compressed between two forces, within and without, could humanity follow any other course than that which it has taken? The speculative spirit, pursuing imperishable goods in the sphere of ideas, must needs have become a stranger to the world of sense, and lose sight of matter for the sake of form. On the other hand, the spirit of civic life,[2] shut up in a monotonous circle of objects, and even there restricted by regulations, was led to lose sight of the life and liberty of the whole, while becoming impoverished at the same time in its own sphere. Just as the speculative spirit was tempted to model the real after the intelligible, and to raise the subjective laws of its imagination into laws constituting the existence of things, so the civic spirit rushed into the opposite extreme, wished to make a particular and fragmentary experience the measure of all observation, and to apply without exception to all affairs the rules of its own particular craft. The speculative spirit had necessarily to become the prey of a vain subtlety, the civic spirit of a narrow pedantry; for the former was placed too high to see the individual, and the latter too low to survey the whole.

But the disadvantage of this spiritual direction was not confined to knowledge and creativity; it extended to action and feeling. We know that the sensibility of the mind depends, as to degree, on the liveliness of the imagination, and for extent, on its richness. Now the predominance of the faculty of analysis must necessarily deprive the imagination of its warmth and energy, and a restricted sphere of objects must diminish its wealth. It is for this reason that the abstract thinker has very often a cold heart, because he analyzes impressions, which move the mind only by their combination or totality; on the other hand, the man of business, the statesman, has very often a narrow

---

2. In German, *der Geschaftsgeist* (the spirituality of the civically minded person), here opposed to   *der spekulative Geist* (speculative or intellectual spirituality).

heart, because shut up in the narrow circle of his employment, his imagination can neither expand nor adapt itself to another manner of viewing things.

My subject has led me naturally to place in relief the distressing tendency of the character of our own times to show the sources of the evil, without its being my province to point out the compensations offered by nature. I will readily admit to you that although this splitting up of their being was unfavorable for individuals, it was the only road open for the progress of the race. The point at which we see humanity arrived among the Greeks was undoubtedly a maximum; it could neither stop there nor rise higher. It could not stop there, for the attainments of the intellect already achieved compelled it to break with feeling and intuition, and to strive for clarity of knowledge. Nor could it rise any higher; for it is only in a determinate measure that clarity can be reconciled with a certain degree of abundance and of warmth. The Greeks had attained this measure, and to continue their progress in culture, they, as we, were obliged to renounce the totality of their being, and to pursue truth along different and separate roads.

There was no other way to develop the manifold aptitudes of man than to bring them in opposition with one another. This antagonism of forces is the great instrument of culture, but it is only an instrument; for as long as this antagonism lasts, man is only on the road to culture. It is only because these special forces are isolated in man, and because they take it upon themselves to lay down the law exclusively, that they enter into strife with the truth of things, and impel common sense, which generally adheres imperturbably to external phenomena, to attempt to delve into the essence of things. While pure understanding usurps authority in the world of sense, and empiricism attempts to subject this intellect to the conditions of experience, these two rival directions arrive at the highest possible development, and exhaust the whole extent of their sphere. While on the one hand imagination, by its tyranny, ventures to destroy the order of the world, it forces reason, on the other side, to rise up to the supreme sources of knowledge, and to invoke against this predominance of fancy the help of the law of necessity.

Through one-sidedness in the use of his powers, the individual is fatally led to error; but the species is led to truth. It is only by gathering up all the energy of our spirit in a single focus, and concentrating a single force in our being, that we give in some sort wings to this isolated force, and that we extend it creatively far beyond the limits that nature seems to have imposed upon it. If it be certain that all human individuals taken together would never have arrived, with the visual power given them by nature, to see a satellite of Jupiter, discovered by the telescope of the astronomer, it is just as well established that the human understanding never would have produced the analysis of the infinite, or the critique of pure reason, if in particular branches, destined for this mission, reason had not applied itself to special researches, and if, after having, as it were, freed itself from all matter, it had not by the most powerful abstraction given to the spiritual eye of man the force necessary, in order to look into the absolute. But the question is whether a spirit thus absorbed in pure reason and intuition will be able to emancipate itself from the rigorous fetters of logic, to take the free action of poetry, and seize the individuality of things with a faithful and eager sense. Here nature imposes even on the most universal genius a limit it cannot pass, and truth will make martyrs as long as philosophy is reduced to making its principal occupation the search for arms against errors.

But whatever may be the final profit for the totality of the world of this distinct and special perfecting of the human faculties, it cannot be denied that the individuals affected suffer under the curse of this world-goal. I grant that the exercises of the gymnasium form athletic bodies; but beauty is developed only by the free and equal play of the limbs. In the same way the tension of the isolated spiritual forces may make extraordinary men; but it is only the well-tempered equilibrium of these forces that can produce happy and complete human beings. And in what relation should we be placed with past and future ages if the perfecting of human nature made such a sacrifice indispensable? In that case we will have been the slaves of humanity, we will have expended our energies in servile work for it during some thousands of years, and we will have the shameful brand of this slavery stamped on our humiliated, mutilated nature—all in order that future generations, in a happy leisure, may be able to devote themselves to the enjoyment of their moral health, and the free development of their humanity.

But can it be true that man has to neglect himself for any end whatever? Can nature snatch from us, for any end whatever, the perfection which is prescribed to us by the aim of reason? It must be false that the perfecting of particular faculties renders the sacrifice of their totality necessary; and even if the law of nature had imperiously this tendency, we must be able to recover this totality in our nature that art has destroyed, through a higher art.

From *Letter X*

Convinced by my preceding letters, you agree with me on this point, that man can depart from his destination by two opposite roads, that our epoch is actually moving on these two false roads, and that it has become the prey, in one case, of coarseness, and elsewhere of exhaustion and depravity. It is the beautiful that must bring it back from this twofold departure. But how can the cultivation of the fine arts remedy, at the same time, these opposite defects, and unite in itself two contradictory qualities? Can it bind nature in the savage, and set it free in the barbarian? Can it at once tighten a spring and loose it, and if it cannot produce this double effect, how will it be reasonable to expect from it so important a result as the education of man?

* * *

From *Letter XI*

* * *

Considered in itself and independently of all sensuous matter, man's personality is nothing but the capacity for a possible infinite expression, and so long as there is neither intuition nor feeling, it is nothing more than a form, an empty power. Considered in itself, and independently of all spontaneous activity of the spirit, sensuousness can make only a material man; without it, it is a pure form; but it cannot in any way establish a union between matter and itself. So long as man feels, wishes, and acts only under the influence of desire, he is nothing more than the world, if by this word we point out only the formless contents of time. Without doubt, it is only his sensuousness that makes his strength pass into efficacious acts, but it is his personality alone that makes this activity his own. Thus, that he may not only be world,[3] he must give form to matter, and in order not to be a mere form, he must give reality to the capacity that he bears in him. He gives matter to form by creating time, and by opposing the immutable to change, the diversity of the world to the eternal unity of the Ego. He gives a form to matter by again suppressing time, by maintaining permanence in change, and by placing the diversity of the world under the unity of the Ego.

Now from this source issue for man two opposite exigencies, the two fundamental laws of sensuous-rational nature. The first has for its object absolute reality; it must make a world of what is only form, manifest all that in it is only a force. The second law has for its object absolute formality; it must destroy in him all that is only world, and carry out harmony in all changes. In other words, he must manifest all that is internal, and give form to all that is external. Considered in its most lofty accomplishment, this twofold labor brings us back to the idea of humanity which was my starting point.

Letter XII

This twofold labor or task, which consists in making the necessary pass into reality in us and in making out of us reality subject to the law of necessity, is urged upon us as a duty by two opposing forces, which are justly styled drives or impulses,[4] because they impel us to realize their object. The first of these impulses, which I shall call the "sensuous" impulse, issues from the physical existence of man, or from sensuous nature; and it is this impulse that tends to enclose him in the limits of time and to make of him a material being. I do not say to give him matter, for to do that a certain free activity of the personality would be necessary, which, receiving matter, distinguishes it from the Ego, or what is permanent. By matter I only understand in this place the change or reality that fills time. Consequently the impulse requires that there should be change, and that time should contain something. This simply filled state of time is named sensation, and it is only in this state that physical existence manifests itself.

As all that is in time is successive, it follows by that fact alone that something is: all the remainder is excluded. When one note on an instrument is touched, among all those that it virtually offers, this note alone is real. When man is actually modified, the infinite possibility of all his modifications is limited to this single mode of existence. Thus, then, the exclusive action of sensuous impulse has for its necessary consequence the narrowest limitation. In this state man is only a unity of magnitude, a complete moment in time; or, to speak more correctly, *he* is not, for his personality is suppressed as long as sensation holds sway over him and carries time along with it.

This impulse extends its domains over the entire sphere of the finite in man, and as form is revealed only in matter, and the absolute by means of its limits,

---

3. That is, be a mere part or piece or function of the material world.
4. The German term *Triebe*, commonly translated "drives" and understood biologically or psycho-logically. It is translated here as "impulses," because Schiller conceives of such *Triebe* as tendencies of the human spirit.

the total manifestation of human nature is connected on a close analysis with the sensuous impulse. But though it is only this impulse that awakens and develops what exists virtually in man, it is nevertheless this very impulse which renders his perfection impossible. It binds down to the world of sense by indestructible ties the spirit that tends higher and it calls abstraction, which had its free development in the sphere of the infinite, back to the confines of the present. Thought undoubtedly can escape it for a moment, and a firm will victoriously resists its exigencies; but repressed nature soon resumes her rights to give an imperious reality to our existence, to give it contents, substance, knowledge, and an aim for our activity.

The second impulse, which may be called the "form" or formal impulse, issues from the absolute existence of man, or from his rational nature, and works to set free and harmonize the diversity of its manifestations, and to maintain personality notwithstanding all its changes of condition. As this personality, being an absolute and indivisible unity, can never be in contradiction with itself (since we are always ourselves), this impulsion, which tends to maintain personality, can never demand in one time anything but what it demands and requires for always. It therefore decides for always what it decides now, and orders now what it orders for always. Hence it embraces the whole series of times, or what comes to the same thing, it suppresses time and change. It wishes the real to be necessary and eternal, and it wishes the eternal and the necessary to be real; in other terms, it tends to truth and justice.

Whereas the sensuous impulse produces only accidents, the formal impulse provides laws—laws for every judgment when it is a question of knowledge, laws for every will when it is a question of action. Whether, therefore, we recognize an object or conceive an objective value to a state of the subject, whether we act in virtue of knowledge or make of the objective the determining principle of our state; in both cases we withdraw this state from the jurisdiction of time, and we attribute to it reality for all men and for all time, that is, universality and necessity. Feeling can only say: "That is true for this subject and at this moment," and there may come another moment, another subject, which withdraws the affirmation from the actual feeling. But when once thought pronounces and says: "That is," it decides for always and ever, and the validity of its decision is guaranteed by the personality itself, which defies all change. Inclination can only say: "That is good for your individuality and present necessity"; but the changing current of affairs will sweep them away, and what you ardently desire today will form the object of your aversion tomorrow. But when the moral feeling says: "That ought to be," it decides for always. If you confess the truth because it is the truth, and if you practice justice because it is justice, you have made of a particular case the law of all possible cases, and treated one moment of your life as eternity.

Accordingly, when the formal impulse holds sway and the pure object acts in us, being attains its highest expansion, all barriers disappear, and from the unity of magnitude in which man was enclosed by a narrow sensuousness, he rises to the unity of idea, which embraces and keeps subject the entire sphere of phenomena. During this operation we are no longer in time, but time is in us with its infinite succession. We are no longer individuals but a species; the judgment of all spirits is expressed by our own, and the choice of all hearts is represented by our own act.

Letter XIV

We have been brought to the idea of such a correlation between the two impulses that the action of the one establishes and limits at the same time the action of the other, and that each of them, taken in isolation, arrives at its highest manifestation just because the other is active.

No doubt this correlation of the two impulses is simply a problem advanced by reason, and which man will only be able to solve in the perfection of his being. It is, in the strictest signification of the expression, *the idea of his humanity [Menschheit]*. Accordingly, it is an infinite to which he can approach nearer and nearer in the course of time, but without ever reaching it. "He ought not to aim at form to the injury of reality, nor to reality to the detriment of the form. He must rather seek the absolute being by means of a determinate being, and the determinate being by means of an infinite being. He must set the world before him because he is a person, and he must be a person because he has the world before him. He must feel because he has a consciousness of himself, and he must have a consciousness of himself because he feels."

It is only in conformity with this idea that one is man[5] in the full sense of the word; but he cannot be convinced of this so long as he gives himself over exclusively to one of these two impulses, or only satisfies them one after the other. For as long as he only feels, his absolute personality and existence remain a mystery to him, and as long as he only thinks, his condition or existence in time escapes him. But if there were cases in which he could have at once this twofold experience in which he would have the consciousness of his freedom and the feeling of his existence together, in which he would simultaneously feel as matter and know himself as spirit—in such cases, and in such only, would he have a complete apprehension of his humanity, and the object that would procure him this apprehension would be a symbol of his accomplished destiny, and consequently serve to express the infinite to him—since this destination can only be fulfilled in the fullness of time.

Presuming that cases of this kind could present themselves in experience, they would awake in him a new impulse, which, precisely because the two other impulses would cooperate in it, would be opposed to each of them taken in isolation, and might therefore rightly count as a new impulse. The sensuous impulse requires that there should be change, that time should have contents; the formal impulse requires that time should be superseded,[6] that there should be no change. Consequently, the impulse in which both of the others act in concert—allow me simply to call it the *play impulse*, until I explain the expression—the play impulse would have as its object to supersede time in time, to reconcile the state of transition or becoming with absolute being, change with identity.

The sensuous impulse wants to become determined, it wants to receive an object; the formal instinct wants to determine itself, it wants to produce an object. Therefore the play impulse will endeavor to receive as it would itself have produced, and to produce as it aspires to receive.

5. That is, human (*Mensch*).
6. "Superseded" translates *aufgehoben*, the past tense of *aufheben* (noun, *Aufhebung*), a remarkable term that can mean either to cancel, to preserve, or to transcend—or, commonly, something that has elements of all three at once, as it often does for Schiller (and for Hegel after him).

The sensuous impulse excludes from its subject all autonomy and freedom; the formal impulse excludes all dependence and passivity. But the exclusion of freedom is physical necessity; the exclusion of passivity is moral necessity. Thus the two impulses subjugate the mind: the former to the laws of nature, the latter to the laws of reason. Thus the play impulse, in which the other two impulses are interactive, will impel the mind at once morally and physically. Hence, as it suppresses all that is contingent, it will also suppress all coercion, and will set man free physically and morally. When we welcome with effusion someone who deserves our contempt, we feel painfully that nature is constrained. When we have a hostile feeling against a person who commands our esteem, we feel painfully the constraint of reason. But if this person inspires us with interest, and also wins our esteem, the constraint of feeling vanishes together with the constraint of reason, and we begin to love him, that is to say, to play, simultaneously with our inclination and our esteem.

Moreover, as the sensuous impulse controls us physically, and the formal impulse morally, the former makes our formal constitution contingent, and the latter makes our material constitution contingent, that is to say, there is contingency in the agreement of our happiness with our perfection, and reciprocally. The play impulse, in which both act in concert, will render both our formal and our material constitution contingent; accordingly, our perfection and our happiness in like manner. And on the other hand, exactly because it makes both of them contingent, and because the contingent disappears with necessity, it will suppress this contingency in both, and will thus give form to matter and reality to form. In proportion that it will lessen the dynamic influence of feeling and passion, it will place them in harmony with rational ideas, and by taking from the laws of reason their moral constraint, it will reconcile them with the interest of the senses.

Letter XV

I approach continually nearer to the end to which I lead you, by a path offering few attractions. Be pleased to follow me a few steps further, and a large horizon will open up to you and a delightful prospect will reward you for the labor of the way.

The object of sensuous impulse, expressed in a universal conception, is named Life in the widest construal: a conception that expresses all material existence and all that is immediately present to the senses. The object of the formal impulse, expressed in a universal conception, is called shape or Form, as well in an exact as in an inexact acceptation; a conception that embraces all formal qualities of things and all relations of the same to the thinking powers. The object of the play impulse, represented in a general statement, may therefore bear the name of *living form*; a term that serves to describe all aesthetic qualities of phenomena, and what people style, in the widest sense, *beauty*.

Beauty is neither extended to the whole field of all living things nor merely enclosed in this field. A marble block, though it is and remains lifeless, can nevertheless become a living form by the architect and sculptor. A man, though he lives and has a form, is far from being a living form on that account. For this to be the case, it is necessary that his form should be life, and that his life should be a form. As long as we only think of his form, it is lifeless, a mere abstraction; as long as we only feel his life, it is without form, a mere impression. It is only when his form lives in our feeling, and his life in our understanding, that he is living form; and this will everywhere be the case where we judge him to be beautiful.

But the genesis of beauty is by no means explained when we know how to point out the component parts, which in their combination produce beauty. For to this end it would be necessary to comprehend that combination itself, which continues to defy our exploration, as is generally the case in all interaction between the finite and the infinite. Reason, on transcendental grounds,[7] makes the following demand: There shall be a communion between the formal impulse and the material impulse—that is, there shall be a play impulse—because it is only in the unity of reality with the form, of the accidental with the necessary, of the passive state with freedom, that the conception of humanity is completed. Reason is obliged to make this demand, because her nature impels her to completeness and to the removal of all bounds; while every exclusive activity of one or the other impulse leaves human nature incomplete and places a limit in it. Accordingly, as soon as reason issues the mandate, "a [genuine] humanity shall exist," it proclaims at the same time the law, "there shall be a beauty." Experience can tell us whether there is beauty, and we shall know it as soon as it has taught us whether [such] humanity can exist. But neither reason nor experience can tell us how beauty can be, and how humanity is possible.

We know that man is neither exclusively matter nor exclusively spirit. Accordingly, beauty, as the consummation of humanity, can neither be exclusively mere life, as has been asserted by sharp-sighted observers, who kept too close to the testimony of experience, and to which the taste of the time would gladly degrade it; nor can beauty be merely form, as has been judged by speculative sophists, who departed too far from experience, and by philosophic artists, who were led too much by the necessity of art in explaining beauty. It is rather the common object of both impulses—that is, of the play impulse.

The use of language completely justifies this name, as it is wont to qualify with the word "play" what is neither subjectively nor objectively accidental, and yet does not impose necessity either externally or internally. As the mind in the intuition of the beautiful finds itself in a happy medium between law and necessity, it is, because it divides itself between both, emancipated from the pressure of both. The formal impulse and the material impulse are equally earnest in their demands, because one relates cognitively to things in their reality and the other to their necessity; because in action the first is directed to the preservation of life, the second to the safeguarding of dignity, and therefore both to truth and perfection. But life comes to be of more indifference when dignity is involved with it, and duty no longer coerces when inclination attracts. In like manner the mind takes in the reality of things, material truth, more freely and tranquilly as soon as it encounters formal truth, the law of necessity; nor does the mind find itself strung by abstraction as soon as immediate intuition can accompany it. In one word, when the mind comes into communion with ideas, all reality loses its seriousness because it becomes small;

7. That is, for reasons relating to the nature of reason itself.

and as it comes in contact with feeling, necessity parts also with its serious-ness because it is easy.

But perhaps the objection has for some time occurred to you: Is not the beautiful degraded by taking it to be mere play? And is it not reduced to the level of frivolous objects which have for ages passed under that name? Does it not contradict the conception of the reason and the dignity of beauty, which is definitely regarded as an instrument of culture, to confine it to the work of being mere play? And does it not contradict the empirical conception of play, which is consistent with the absence of all taste, to restrict it entirely to beauty?

But what is meant by "mere play," when we know that in all conditions of humanity it is precisely play, and *only* play, which makes man complete and develops simultaneously his twofold nature? What you style limitation, accord-ing to your representation of the matter, I name *enlargement*, according to my views, which I have justified by arguments. Consequently, I should have said exactly the reverse: man is *merely* serious with the agreeable, with the good, and with the perfect, but he *plays* with beauty.

In saying this we must not indeed think of the games that are in vogue in real life, and which commonly refer only to our material state. But in real life we should also seek in vain for the beauty of which we are here speaking. Actu-ally existing beauty is worthy of the actually existing play impulse; but through the ideal of beauty, which is established by reason, an ideal of the play-impulse is also presented, which man ought to have before his eyes in all his playing.

Therefore, no error will ever be incurred if we seek the ideal of beauty on the same road on which we satisfy our play-impulse. We can immediately understand why the ideal form of a Venus, of a Juno, and of an Apollo,[8] is to be sought not at Rome, but in Greece, if we contrast the Greek population, delighting in the bloodless athletic contests of boxing, racing, and intellec-tual rivalry at Olympia,[9] with the Roman people gloating over the agony of a gladiator. Now reason says that the beautiful must not only be life and form, but a living form, that is, beauty, inasmuch as it dictates to man the twofold law of absolute formality and absolute reality. Reason thereby also proclaims: man shall only *play* with beauty, and he shall play with *beauty alone*.[1]

For, to speak out once for all, man only plays when in the full meaning of the word he is a man, and *he is only completely a man when he plays*.[2] This proposition, which at this moment perhaps appears paradoxical, will receive a great and deep meaning if we have advanced far enough to apply it to the twofold seriousness of duty and of destiny. I promise you that the whole edi-fice of aesthetic art and the still more difficult art of life will be supported by this principle. But this proposition is unexpected only in science; long ago it lived and worked in art and in the feeling of the Greeks, her most accomplished masters—only they transferred to Olympus what ought to have been preserved

---

8. Three major deities in the classical pantheon: Venus (the Greek Aphrodite), goddess of love; Juno (the Greek Hera), queen of the Olympian gods and goddess of marriage; and Apollo, god of the arts (who was considered the ideal of mature male beauty).
9. The site on Greece's Peloponnese of the qua-drennial Olympic Games, held there for more than a thousand years (776 B.C.E.–ca. 400 C.E.) as
part of a religious festival; it included poetry as well as athletic competitions.
1. That is, "play" is the only appropriate thing to do with beauty, and beauty is the only truly appropri-ate thing with which to "play."
2. That is, (true) "playing" requires that one be fully and truly human, and one is only fully and truly human when one (truly) "plays."

on earth.[3] Influenced by the truth of this principle, they effaced from the brow of their gods the earnestness and labor which furrow the brows of mortals, and also the hollow lust that smoothes the empty face. They set free the ever serene from the chains of every purpose, of every duty, of every care, and they made indolence and indifference the envied condition of the godlike race; merely human appellations for the freest and highest form of existence. The material pressure of natural laws as well as the spiritual pressure of moral laws lost itself in its higher idea of necessity, which embraced at the same time both worlds, and out of the union of these two necessities issued true freedom.

Inspired by this spirit, the Greeks also effaced from the features of their ideal, together with desire or inclination, all traces of volition—or, better still, they made both unrecognizable, because they knew how to wed them both in the closest alliance. It is neither charm nor dignity which speaks from the glorious face of the Juno Ludovici;[4] it is neither of these—for it is both at once. While the female god challenges our veneration, the godlike woman at the same times kindles our love. But while in ecstasy we give ourselves up to the heavenly beauty, the heavenly self-repose takes us aback in awe. The whole form rests and dwells in itself—a fully complete creation in itself— and as if she were out of space, without advance or resistance; it shows no force contending with force, no opening through which time could break in. Irresistibly carried away and attracted by her womanly charm, yet kept at a distance by her godly dignity, we also find ourselves at length in the state of the greatest repose, and the result is a wonderful emotion for which the understanding has no concept and language no name.

Letter XX

That freedom is an active and not a passive principle results from its very conception; but that freedom itself should be an effect of nature (taking this word in its widest sense), and not the work of man, and therefore that it can be favored or thwarted by natural means, is the necessary consequence of the preceding discussion. It begins only when man is complete, and when these two fundamental impulses have been developed. It will then be lacking as long as he is incomplete, and while one of these impulses is excluded, and it will be reestablished by all that gives back to man his completeness.

Thus it is possible, with regard both to the entire species and to the individual, to recognize the moment when man is yet incomplete, and when one of the two impulses acts exclusively in him. We know that man begins with mere life, to end with form; that he initially is more of an individual than a person, and that he starts from the limited or finite to approach the infinite. The sensuous impulse arises therefore before the rational impulse, because sensation precedes consciousness; and in this priority of sensuous impulse we find the crux of the history of the whole of human freedom.

There is a moment, in fact, when the impulse of life, not yet opposed to the

3. That is, they projected into their mythology of the gods on Mount Olympus what they ought to have attributed to humanity here below.
4. A colossal Roman marble head (ca. 1st c. c.e.), much admired by Goethe, which in the 17th century was collected by Cardinal Ludovico Ludovisi, in Rome.

impulse of form, acts as nature and as necessity; when the sensuous is a power because man has not yet [truly] begun;[5] for even in man there can be no other power than his will. But in the condition of thought, to which man ought to ascend, reason will be a power, and moral or logical necessity will take the place of physical necessity. Sensuous power must then be annihilated before the law which must govern it can be established. It is not enough that something shall begin which as yet was not; something which already was must first end. Man cannot pass immediately from sensuousness to thought. He must step backwards, for it is only when one determination is suppressed that the contrary determination can take place.

Consequently, in order to exchange passivity for self-initiated activity,[6] and passive for active determination, he must be momentarily free from all determination, and must traverse a state of pure determinability. He has then to return in some degree to that state of pure negative indetermination in which he was before his senses were affected by anything. But this state was absolutely empty of all contents, and now the question is to reconcile an equal determination and a determinability equally without limit, with the greatest possible fullness, because from this situation something positive must immediately follow. The determination which man received by sensation must be preserved, because he must not lose reality; but at the same time, insofar as it is limiting, it should be superseded, because a determinability without limitation is to be attained. The task then consists in removing the determination of the mode of existence, and yet at the same time in preserving it—which is possible only in one way: *by opposing another to it.* The two sides of a balance are in equilibrium when empty; they are also in equilibrium when their contents are of equal weight.

Thus, to pass from sensation to thought, the mind must pass through an intermediate state, in which sensibility and reason are simultaneously active. In this way they mutually cancel their determinant power, and by their antagonism produce a negation. This intermediate state, in which the mind is neither physically nor morally constrained, and yet is in both ways active, merits essentially the name of a *free* state; and if we call the condition of sensuous determination *physical*, and the condition of rational determination *logical or moral*, that intermediate condition of real and active determination should be called the *aesthetic*.

Letter XXI

I have remarked in the beginning of the foregoing letter that there is a twofold condition of determinability and a twofold condition of determination. I now can clarify this proposition.

The mind can be determined—is determinable—only in as far as it is not determined; it is, however, determinable also, in as far as it is not exclusively

---

5. That is, because the process of becoming genuinely human has not yet begun.
6. "Self-initiated activity" translates the German coinage *Selbsttätigkeit*, hereafter rendered more literally as "self-activity." Schiller intends this expression to capture the Kantian idea of "auton-

omy" or action in accordance with a law of one's own. It is set against *Leiden* (here translated as "passivity"), which can mean "suffering" but here (as often in the philosophical literature) refers to acting in response to external compulsion or influence, rather than autonomously.

determined; that is, if it is not confined in its determination. The former is only a lack of determination—it is without limits, because it is without reality; but the latter, the aesthetic determinability, has no limits, because it unites all reality.

The mind is determined, inasmuch as it is only limited; but it is also determined because it limits itself of its own absolute capacity. It finds itself in the former position when it feels, in the second when it thinks. Accordingly the aesthetic constitution is in relation to determinability what thought is in relation to determination. The latter is a negative from internal infinite completeness, the former a limitation from internal infinite power. When feeling and thought come into contact in a single point, the mind is determined in both conditions, the man becomes something and exists—either as individual or person—by exclusion; in other cases these two faculties stand infinitely apart. Just in the same manner, the aesthetic determinability comes in contact with the mere lack of determination in a single point, by excluding every distinct determined existence, by thus being in all other points nothing and all, and hence by being infinitely different. Therefore, if the latter, in the absence of determination from deficiency, is represented as an empty infiniteness, the aesthetic freedom of determination, which forms the proper counterpart to the former, can be considered, as a completed infiniteness—a representation which exactly agrees with the ideas advanced in the previous investigations.

Man therefore achieves *nothing* in the aesthetic state, if attention is focused on single results rather than on the whole faculty, and if we consider only the lack of every special determination. We must therefore do justice to those who assert the beautiful, and the disposition in which it places the mind, to be entirely indifferent and unprofitable in relation to *knowledge* and *feeling*. They are perfectly right; for it is certain that beauty yields no single distinct result, either for the understanding or for the will; it does not carry out a single intellectual or moral object; it discovers no truth, does not help us to fulfill a single duty, and, in a word, is equally unfit to found the character or to clear the head. Accordingly, the personal worth of a man, or his dignity, as far as this can depend only on himself, remains entirely undetermined by aesthetic culture, and nothing further is attained than that, *as far as nature is concerned*, it is made possible for him to make of himself what he will; that the freedom to be what he ought to be is restored perfectly to him.

But by this, something infinite is attained. For as soon as we remember that freedom is taken from man by the one-sided compulsion of nature in feeling, and by the exclusive legislation of the reason in thinking, we must consider the capacity restored to him by the aesthetic disposition, as the highest of all gifts, as the gift of humanity. To be sure, man possesses this capacity for humanity prior to every definite determination in which he may be placed. But as a matter of fact, he loses it with every determined condition into which he may come, and if he is to pass over to an opposite condition, humanity must be in every case restored to him through aesthetic life.

It is therefore not only poetically licensed but also philosophically correct, when beauty is called our "second creator." Nor is this inconsistent with the fact that it only makes it possible for us to attain and realize humanity, leaving this to our free will. For in this it acts in common with our original creator, nature, which has imparted to us nothing further than this capacity for humanity, but leaves the use of it to our own determination of will.

From *Letter XXII*

While the aesthetic disposition of the mind must be looked upon in one respect as nothing, therefore—that is, when we confine our view to separate and determined operations—it must be looked upon in another respect as a state of the highest reality, in as far as we attend to the absence of all limits and the sum of powers which are commonly active in it. Accordingly we cannot say that those are wrong who consider the aesthetic state to be the most fruitful in relation to knowledge and morality. They are perfectly right, for a state of mind which comprises the whole of humanity in itself must of necessity include in itself also—necessarily and potentially—every separate expression of it. Again, a disposition of mind that removes all limitation from the totality of human nature must also disassociate it from any specific expression of that nature. Precisely because its "aesthetic disposition" does not exclusively shelter any separate function of humanity, it is favorable to all without distinction; nor does it favor any particular functions, precisely because it is the foundation of the possibility of all. All other exercises give to the mind some special aptitude, but for that very reason give it some definite limits; only the aesthetical leads him to the unlimited. Every other condition in which we can live refers us to a previous condition, and requires for its solution a following condition; only the aesthetic is a complete whole in itself, for it unites in itself all conditions of its source and of its duration. Here alone we feel ourselves swept out of time, and our humanity expresses itself with purity and integrity as if it had not yet received any impression or interruption from the operation of external powers.

That which flatters our senses in immediate sensation opens our weak and volatile spirit to every impression, but makes us in the same degree less apt for exertion. That which stretches our thinking power and encourages abstract conceptions strengthens our mind for every kind of challenge, but hardens it also in the same proportion, and deprives us of sensitivity in the same degree as it helps us to greater self-activity. For this very reason, one as well as the other brings us at length to exhaustion, because matter cannot long do without the shaping, constructive force, and the force cannot do without the constructible material. But on the other hand, if we have given ourselves over to the enjoyment of genuine beauty, we are at such a moment and to that extent master of our passive and active powers, and we can turn with equal ease from grave to gay, from rest to movement, from submission to resistance, to abstract thinking and intuition.

This high equanimity and freedom of spirit, united with power and elasticity, is the disposition in which a true work of art ought to leave us, and there is no better test of true aesthetic excellence.

* * *

Letter XXIII

I take up the thread of my researches, which I broke off only to apply the principles I laid down to practical art and the appreciation of its works.

The transition from the passivity of sensuousness to the activity of thought and of will can be effected only by the intermediary state of aesthetic freedom; and though in itself this state decides nothing respecting our opinions and our sentiments, and therefore leaves our intellectual and moral value entirely problematical, it is nonetheless the necessary condition without which we should never attain to insight or conviction. In a word, there is no other way to make a reasonable being out of a sensuous man than by making him first aesthetic.

But, you might object: Is this mediation absolutely indispensable? Could not truth and duty, one or the other, in themselves and by themselves, find access to the sensuous man? To this I reply: Not only is it possible, but it is absolutely necessary that they owe solely to themselves their determining force, and nothing would be more contradictory to our preceding affirmations than to appear to defend the contrary opinion. It has been expressly proved that the beautiful furnishes no result, either for the comprehension or for the will; that it mingles with no operations, either of thought or of resolution; and that it confers this double power without determining anything with regard to the real exercise of this power. Here all external help disappears, and the pure logical form, the concept, must speak immediately to the intelligence, as the pure moral form, the law, must speak immediately to the will.

But for them to be able to do so, and for there to be pure form generally for sensuous man, I maintain, must be rendered possible by the aesthetic disposition of the mind. Truth is not a thing which can be received from without like reality or the visible existence of objects. It is the thinking force, in its own freedom and activity, which produces it, and it is just this freedom proper to it, this freedom which we seek in vain in sensuous man. The sensuous man is already determined physically, and thenceforth he has no longer his free determinability; he must necessarily first enter into possession of this lost determinability before he can exchange the passive for an active determination. Therefore, in order to recover it, he must either lose the passive determination that he had, or he should already contain within himself the active determination to which he should transition. If he were merely to lose passive determination, he would thereby lose with it the possibility of an active determination, because thought needs a body, and form can only be realized through matter. He must therefore contain already in himself the active determination that he may be at once both actively and passively determined, that is to say, he must become aesthetic.

Consequently, by the aesthetic disposition of the soul the proper activity of reason is already revealed in the sphere of sensuousness, the power of sense is already broken within its own boundaries, and the ennobling of physical man has been carried far enough that spiritual man has only to develop himself according to the laws of freedom. The transition from an aesthetic state to a logical and moral state (from the beautiful to truth and duty) is then infinitely more easy than the transition from the physical state to the aesthetic state (from mere blind life to form). This is a transition that man can accomplish through his mere freedom, since he has only to take possession of himself rather than to produce himself, and has only to unify rather than broaden his nature. Having attained to the aesthetic disposition, man will give to his judgments and to his actions a universal value as soon as he desires it. This passage from brute nature to beauty, in which an entirely new faculty would awaken in him, nature would render easier, and his will has no power over a disposition which, we know, itself gives birth to the will. To bring the aesthetic man to insight and to elevated sentiments, he requires nothing more than important occasions; to obtain the same thing from the sensuous man, his nature must at first be changed. To make of the former a hero and sage, it is often only necessary to meet with a grand situation (which calls immediately upon the faculty of the will), while the latter would have a long way to go.

One of the most important tasks of culture, then, is to submit man to form, even in a purely physical life, and to render it aesthetic as far as the domain of the beautiful can be extended, for it is only in the aesthetic state, and not in the physical state, that the moral state can be developed. If in each particular case man ought to possess the power to make his judgment and his will the judgment of the entire species;[7] if he ought to find in each limited existence the transition to an infinite existence; if, lastly, he ought from every dependent situation to take his flight to rise to autonomy and to freedom, it must be observed that at no moment is he only individual and does he solely obey the law of nature. To be able and ready to raise himself from the narrow circle of the ends of nature to rational ends, in the sphere of the former man must already have practice in the second; and he must have pursued his physical vocation[8] with a certain freedom of spirit—that is to say, in accordance with the laws of the beautiful.

And that he can do without thwarting in the least degree his physical requirements. The demands of nature upon him focus only upon *what* he does—upon the substance of his acts; but the ends of nature in no degree determine *how* he acts, the form of his actions. On the other hand, the demands of reason have to do strictly with the form of his activity. Thus, inasmuch as the moral vocation of man requires that he be purely moral, that he manifest absolute self-activity, it is a matter of indifference to his physical vocation whether it is purely physical, and whether he acts in a manner entirely passive. Hence with regard to this latter vocation, it entirely depends on him to fulfill it solely as a sensuous being and natural force (as a force which acts only as it diminishes) or, at the same time, as absolute force, as a rational being. To which of these does his dignity best correspond? Of this there can be no question. It is as disgraceful and contemptible for him to do under sensuous impulsion that which he ought to have determined solely by the motive of duty, as it is noble and honorable for him to incline toward conformity with laws, harmony, independence, where the common man only satisfies a legitimate want. In a word, in the domain of truth and morality, sensuousness must determine nothing; but in the sphere of happiness, form may find a place, and the impulse of play may prevail.

Thus then, in the indifferent sphere of physical life, man ought to already commence his moral life; his self-activity ought already to begin in his pas-

---

7. A reference to one of the primary formulations of Kant's "categorical imperative" (the basic principle of his moral philosophy and kind of morality).

8. "Vocation" translates the German term *Bestimmung*, which can also mean "constitution," "determinate mode of existence," "purpose," "mission," and "calling." FICHTE uses it similarly in the title of his contemporaneous book *The Vocation of Man* (*Die Bestimmung des Menschen*, 1800), excerpted below.

sivity, and his rational freedom even within the limits of sense; he ought already begin to impose the law of his will upon his inclinations; he ought—if you will permit me the expression—to carry into the domain of matter the war against matter, in order to be relieved of having to combat this redoubtable enemy upon the sacred ground of freedom; he ought to learn to have nobler desires, not to be forced to have sublime volitions. This is achieved through aesthetic culture, which submits to the laws of the beautiful, in which neither the laws of nature nor those of reason suffer, which does not force the will of man, and which by the form it gives to exterior life already opens up internal life.

From *Letter XXIV*

Accordingly three different moments or stages of development can be distinguished, which the individual man, as well as the whole race, must of necessity traverse in a determinate order if they are to fulfill the circle of their vocation. No doubt, the separate periods can be lengthened or shortened, through accidental causes which are inherent either in the influence of external things or under the free caprice of men; but neither of them can be overstepped, and the order of their sequence cannot be inverted either by nature or by the will. Man in his *physical* state is subject to the power of nature alone; he defeats this power in the *aesthetic* state; and he masters it in the *moral*.

What is man before beauty liberates him from free pleasure, and the serenity of form tames down the savageness of life? Eternally uniform in his aims, eternally changing in his judgments, self-seeking without being himself, unfettered without being free, a slave without serving any rule. In this period, the world is to him only fate, not yet an object; all has existence for him only in as far as it procures existence to him; a thing that neither seeks from nor gives to him is nonexistent. Every appearance comes before him separate and cut off, just as he finds himself in the series of beings. All that is, is to him through the decree of the moment; every change is to him an entirely fresh creation, because [preoccupied] with the necessary *within* him, the necessary *external to him* is missed, which binds together all the changing forms in the universe, and which upholds the law on the theater of events even as the individual departs. It is in vain that nature lets the rich variety of her forms pass before him; he sees in her glorious fullness nothing but his prey, in her power and greatness nothing but his enemy. Either he encounters objects, and wishes to draw them to himself in desire, or the objects press in a destructive manner upon him, and he thrusts them away in dismay and terror. In both cases his relation to the world of sense is immediate contact; and perpetually anxious owing to its pressure, restless and plagued by imperious wants, he finds no rest except in exhaustion, and no limits save in depleted desire.

* * *

Ignorant of his own human dignity, he is far removed from honoring it in others, and conscious of his own savage greed, he fears it in every creature that he sees like himself. He never sees others in himself, only himself in others, and human society, instead of enlarging him to the race, only shuts him up continually closer in his individuality. Thus limited, he wanders through his sunless life, till favoring nature rolls away the load of matter from his darkened senses, reflection separates him from things, and objects show themselves at length in the afterglow of consciousness.

It is true we cannot point out this state of rude nature as we have here portrayed it in any definite people and age. It is only an idea, but an idea with which experience agrees most closely in special features. It may be said that man was never in this animal condition, but he has not, on the other hand, ever entirely escaped from it. Even in the rudest subjects, unmistakable traces of rational freedom can be found, and even in the most cultivated, features are not wanting that remind us of that dismal natural condition. It is possible for man, at one and the same time, to unite the highest and the lowest in his nature; and if his *dignity* depends on a strict separation of one from the other, his *happiness* depends on a skillful removal of this separation. The culture which is to bring his dignity into agreement with his happiness will therefore have to provide for the greatest purity of these two principles in their most intimate combination.

The first appearance of reason in man thus is not yet the beginning of his humanity. This is first determined by his freedom, and reason begins by making his sensuous dependence boundless—a phenomenon that seems to me not to have been sufficiently elucidated, considering its importance and universality. We know that reason makes itself known to man by the demand for the absolute—the self—dependent and necessary. But as this demand of reason cannot be satisfied in any separate or single state of his physical life, he is obliged to leave the physical entirely and to rise from a limited reality to ideas. But although the true meaning of that demand of reason is to withdraw him from the limits of time and to lead him up from the world of sense to an ideal world, yet this same demand, by a misunderstanding (and one that is hardly to be avoided in this age so prone to sensuousness), can steer man to physical life, and, instead of making him independent, can plunge him into the most terrible slavery.

And this is what in fact happens. Man raised on the wings of imagination leaves the narrow limits of the present, in which mere animality is confined, in order to press forward into an unlimited future. But while the limitless is unfolded to his dazed imagination, his heart has not ceased to live in the particular, and to serve the moment. The impulse toward the absolute seizes him suddenly in the midst of his animality; and as in this stupid condition all his efforts aim only at the material and temporal and are limited by his individuality, instead of abstracting from that individuality he is merely prompted by that demand of reason to project it into the infinite. He is led to seek not form but inexhaustible matter, and not the unchangeable but rather everlasting change and an absolute securing of his temporal existence. The same impulse which, directed to his thought and action, ought to lead to truth and morality, yet now directed to his passion and emotional state, produces nothing but unlimited desire and absolute want. The first fruits, therefore, that he reaps in the world of spirits are cares and fear—both operations of the reason: not of sensuousness, but of a reason that mistakes its object and applies its categorical imperative to matter.

All unconditional systems of happiness are fruits of this tree, whether they have for their object the present day or the whole of life, or what does not make them any more respectable, the whole of eternity, for their object. An unlimited duration of existence and of well-being is only an ideal of the desires, amounting merely to a demand made by an animality questing for the absolute. Man, therefore, without gaining anything for his humanity by a rational expression of this sort, loses the happy limitation of the animal, over which he now only possesses the unenviable superiority of losing the present in his striving for the distant, yet without seeking in the limitless future anything but the present.

But even if reason does not go astray in its object, or err in the question, sensuousness will continue to falsify the answer for a long time. As soon as man has begun to use his understanding and to link together phenomena in relations of cause and effect, reason, in accordance with its nature, presses on toward an absolute linkage and an unconditional ground. In order merely to be able to put forward this demand, man must already have stepped beyond the sensuous; but the sensuous uses this very demand to bring back the fugitive.

This would be the point at which one might be expected to abandon entirely the world of sense in order to take flight into the realm of ideas; for the intelligence remains eternally shut up in the finite and in the contingent, and does not cease putting questions without reaching the last link of the chain. But as the type of man with whom we are concerned is not yet capable of such an abstraction, and does not find it in the sphere of sensuous knowledge, and because he does not look for it in pure reason, he will seek for it below in the region of sentiment, and will appear to find it. No doubt the sensuous shows him nothing that has its foundation in itself, and that legislates for itself, but it shows him something that does not care for foundation or law; therefore thus not being able to quiet the intelligence by showing it a final cause, he reduces it to silence by the conception which desires no cause; and being incapable of understanding the sublime necessity of reason, he keeps to the blind constraint of matter. As sensuousness knows no other end than its interest, and is determined by nothing except blind chance, it makes the former the motive of its actions, and the latter the master of the world.

Even the divine part in man, the moral law, cannot avoid this perversion in its first manifestation in the sensuous. As this moral law only prohibits and combats in man the interest of sensuous egotism, it must appear to him as something strange until he has come to consider this self-love as the stranger, and the voice of reason as his true self. Therefore he confines himself to feeling the fetters which the latter imposes on him, without having the consciousness of the infinite emancipation which it procures for him. Without suspecting in himself the dignity of lawgiver, he experiences only the constraint and the impotent revolt of a subject fretting under the yoke, because in this experience the sensuous impulse precedes the moral impulse; he gives to the law of necessity a beginning in him, a positive origin; and by the most unfortunate of all mistakes he converts the immutable and the eternal in himself into a transitory accident. He persuades himself to regard the notions of the just and the unjust as statutes which have been introduced by a will, and not as having in themselves an eternal value.

Just as in the explanation of certain natural phenomena he goes beyond nature and seeks out of it what can only be found in it, in its own laws, so also in the explanation of moral phenomena he goes beyond reason and makes light of his humanity, seeking a god in this way. It is not surprising that a religion which he has purchased at the cost of his humanity shows itself worthy of this origin, and that he only considers as absolute and eternally binding laws that have never been binding from all eternity. He has placed himself in relation not with a holy being, but rather only with a powerful one. Therefore the spirit of his religion, of the homage that he gives to God, is a fear that abases him, and not a veneration that elevates him in his own esteem.

These different aberrations by which man departs from the ideal of his vocation cannot all take place at the same time, because several stages have to be passed through in the transition from thoughtlessness to error, and from the absence of will to corruption of the will. Yet these stages are all, without exception, the consequence of his physical condition, because in all the life-impulse dominates the form-impulse. Now, it may be either that reason has not yet spoken in man, and the physical reigns over him with a blind necessity, or that reason is not sufficiently purified of the sensuous, and the moral is still subject to the physical. In both cases the only principle that has a real power over him is a material principle, and man, at least as regards his fundamental tendency, is a sensuous being. The only difference is that in the former case he is an animal without reason, and in the second case a rational animal. But he ought to be neither one nor the other: he ought to be *man* [*Mensch*]. Nature ought not to rule him exclusively; and reason should not rule him conditionally. The two legislations ought to be completely independent from each other and nonetheless completely in accord.

SOURCE: Friedrich Schiller, *Letters upon the Æsthetical Education of Man*, in *Essays Æsthetical and Philosophical*, vol. 6 of Bohn's Standard Library of Schiller's Works (1875; reprint, London: G. Bell and Sons, 1910), as revised by Richard Schacht. Except where otherwise indicated, German words in brackets are the terminology used in the German original, inserted by the editor in addition to their renderings in the translation. Originally published in 1794, as *Über die ästhetische Erziehung des Menschen, in einer Reihe von Briefen*. The 26 "letters" in which the book consists were written and published separately over a period of several years prior to their publication together under this title.

JOHANN GOTTLIEB FICHTE
(1762 – 1814)

Fichte played a major role in the direction taken by German philosophy after KANT, helping to transform "idealism" as Kant had construed it (as a "transcendental" but metaphysically noncommittal view of the status of consciousness in relation to the experiential features of its various objects) into a far more robust and metaphysically adventuresome way of thinking that came to be called "absolute idealism." Fichte considered himself to be a follower of Kant, but truer to what he took to be the basic insights of Kant than Kant himself had been—with the courage of his Kantian convictions that he thought Kant had lacked—in the elaboration of his radicalized version of Kantianism. He is often regarded mainly as a transitional figure between Kant and HEGEL, but that view of him both understates and distorts his philosophical significance and interest. The position he staked out was fundamentally more extreme than Hegel's, and his kind of idealism was much more appealing than Hegel's to those who were looking for an exhilarating "spiritualistic" replacement for traditional Christianity. It was Fichte, far more than either Kant or Hegel, who provided the inspiration for such developments as American Transcendentalism (see, e.g., the selections by EMERSON, below).

Johann Gottlieb Fichte ("FIK-teh") was born in 1762 in Rammenau, Saxony, in what is now the eastern part of Germany. He received his early education at Schulpforta, the same distinguished school emphasizing the study of languages and literatures that FRIEDRICH NIETZSCHE would later attend. Fichte's interests turned to philosophy during his university years, and his reading of Kant's *Critique of Pure Reason* (1781) and subsequent writings on moral philosophy inspired his passionate commitment to the revolutionary philosophical program he took Kant to be pursuing. Seeking to carry that program forward, in 1792 Fichte anonymously published his first book, on religion (*Attempt at a Critique of All Revelation*), which was akin in spirit and intention to Kant's *Religion within the Limits of Reason Alone* (1793). In it he contended that traditional forms of religiousness have contributed to human moral development but leave much to be desired, and he called for their supersession by a form of spirituality and moral maturity grounded in a more rigorous Kantian philosophical outlook.

Fichte's book received considerable attention and was widely supposed to have been written by Kant himself. When Fichte's authorship was revealed, he became an instant philosophical celebrity. In 1793, at the age of 31—very young, by the standards of the time—he was appointed to a professorship at the University of Jena. (FRIEDRICH SCHILLER happened to be a professor of history there, and became his colleague and friend.) Though he was a popular lecturer at first, sentiment turned against him, both because he was so abrasive and zealous and because he was deemed to be pantheistic or even atheistic, since his idea of "God" was nothing like the personal God of Christianity.

The charge of atheism led to Fichte's dismissal from his position at Jena in 1799. He subsequently taught for a time at Erlangen, and then in 1810 was called to a professorship at the new University of Berlin, where remarkably (in view of his personality) he was named rector in 1811. His temperamental unsuitability to that leadership role quickly became obvious, and he returned to the faculty in 1812. He died just two years later, at the height of his fame—ironically an indirect victim of a war he championed. An enthusiastic supporter of the French Revolution, he became a strident opponent of Napoleon's imperialism and an impassioned advocate of German nationalism in opposition to it (as may be seen in his 1807–08 *Addresses to the German Nation*); and his wife, who was a nurse tending the wounded during the Prussian struggle with Napoleon, transmitted typhus to him.

Fichte's fundamental philosophical interests were not metaphysical or epistemological but "practical," relating to matters of morality and value and to the foundations of human dignity and worth. Like Kant, however, his first major work—*Science of Knowledge* (Wissenschaftslehre, 1794)—was an extended treatment of knowledge and of the knowing subject and its objects. (Its title might more aptly be translated as *Theory of Knowledge*.) It culminated in his reinterpretation of the reality of which we are a part, which he construed in a manner permitting him to make bold claims regarding the kind of spirituality associated with God and the soul (as he reinterpreted them). He then turned to an elaboration of his moral philosophy in several volumes on "natural right" and ethics, followed by *The Vocation of Man* (1800)—an artfully constructed and rhetorically powerful three-essay exposition of his thinking intended to make it accessible to a wider readership.

Always a radical and vehement opponent of materialism, Fichte became a staunch proponent of a form of idealism in which ultimate reality is accorded to a form of spirituality he called "Absolute Ego." He conceived of it as no mere particular conscious subject or collection of such "egos," but rather as the immaterial principle grounding all particular subjects (and objects) of experience. This view of reality cannot be proven or con-firmed by any form of theoretical reason; but as Kant had observed, it cannot be ruled out, either—and it can be warranted in a "practical" way by the indisputable reality of moral duty, which would be inconceivable if there were no spirituality independent of materiality. This is Fichte's version of the kind of philosophical "faith" or "belief" (*Glaube*) for which Kant had proclaimed his *Critique of Pure Reason* to have "made room" (in its second edition introduction, included above). *Glaube* in this context has nothing to do with a groundless "leap of faith" or unreflective embrace of some religious way of thinking. What both Kant and Fichte had in mind was the considered acceptance of something as true that goes beyond the bounds of what can be settled logically or scientifically, but that is warranted by good reasons of a different sort.

The first of the readings, from Fichte's *Science of Knowledge*, provides an introduction to his philosophical system, in which he attempts to radicalize and thereby complete Kant's philosophical "Copernican revolution" (according to which the world takes its cues from the mind's fundamental nature rather than the other way around). In the second selection—the concluding part of his *The Vocation of Man*—Fichte passionately advocates and elaborates on his philosophical "faith," for which Kant himself prepared the way in the ringing remarks with which he concluded his *Critique of Practical Reason* (included above). To read that conclusion and then turn to this second selection is to see very clearly where Fichte is coming from—and where he went.

From Science of Knowledge [*Wissenschaftslehre*]

First Introduction

1

Attend to yourself: turn your attention away from everything that surrounds you and towards your inner life; this is the first demand that philosophy makes of its disciple. Our concern is not with anything that lies outside you, but only with yourself.

Even the most cursory introspection will reveal to anyone a remarkable difference between the various immediate modifications of his consciousness, or what we may also call his presentations.[1] Some of them appear to us as completely dependent on our freedom, but it is impossible for us to believe that there is anything answering to them outside us, independently of our activity. Our imagination and will appear to us to be free. Others of our presentations [*Vorstellungen*] we refer to a reality which we take to be established independently of us, as to their model; and we find ourselves limited in determining these presentations by the condition that they must correspond to this reality. In regard to the content of cognition, we do not consider ourselves free. In brief, we may say that some of our presentations [*Vorstellungen*] are accompanied by the feeling of freedom, others by the feeling of necessity.

The question, "Why are the presentations which depend on freedom determined [*bestimmt*] precisely as they are, and not otherwise?" cannot reasonably arise, because in postulating that they depend on freedom all application of the concept of "wherefore" is rejected; they are so because I have so determined [*bestimmt*] them, and if I had determined them otherwise, they would be otherwise.

But the question, "What is the source of the system of presentations which are accompanied by the feeling of necessity, and of this feeling of necessity itself?" is one that is surely worthy of reflection. It is the task of philosophy to provide an answer to this question, and in my opinion nothing is philosophy save the science [*Wissenschaft*] which performs this task. The system of presentations accompanied by the feeling of necessity is also called *experience*, both internal and external. Philosophy, in other words, must therefore furnish the ground of all experience.

Only three objections may be brought against the above. A person might deny that presentations occur in consciousness which are accompanied by the feeling of necessity and referred to a reality which is taken to be determined without our assistance. Such a person would either deny against his better knowledge or be differently constituted from other people; if so, there would actually be nothing there for him to deny, and no denial, and we could disregard his objection without further ado. Secondly, someone might say that the question thus raised is completely unanswerable, for we are, and must remain, in insurmountable ignorance on this issue. It is quite unnecessary to discuss arguments and counterarguments with such a person. He is best refuted by providing the actual answer to the question, and then nothing remains for him to do but to examine our attempt and to indicate where and why it does not appear to him sufficient. Finally, someone might lay claim to the name and maintain that philosophy is entirely different from what has been indicated, or that it is something over and above this. It would be easy to show him that precisely what I have set forth has from the earliest been considered to be philosophy by all competent exponents, that everything he might wish

---

1. "Presentations" translates the German *Vorstellungen* (normally translated "representations"): the way in which various matters are experienced, whatever or however they might be independently of how they figure in experience. "Modifications": a translation of *Bestimmungen*, perhaps better rendered as "determinations." In Fichte's book *Die Bestimmung des Menschen*, commonly translated as *The Vocation of Man*, it has the sense of an essential "calling"—that which our essential nature as *Menschen* (humans) "determines" that we ought to strive to achieve or become.

to pass off as such has a different name already, and that if this word is to designate anything specific, it must designate precisely this science.

However, since we are not inclined to engage in this essentially fruitless controversy about a word, we have ourselves long ago surrendered this name and called the science[2] which is expressly committed to solving the problem indicated, *the Science of Knowledge*.[3]

2

One can ask for a reason only in the case of something judged to be contingent, viz., where it is assumed that it could also have been otherwise, and yet is not a matter of determination through freedom; and it is precisely the fact that he inquires as to its ground that makes it, for the inquirer, contingent. The task of seeking the ground of something contingent means: to exhibit some other thing whose properties reveal why, of all the manifold determinations that the explicandum[4] might have had, it actually has just those that it does. By virtue of its mere notion, the ground falls outside what it grounds; both ground and grounded are, as such, opposed and yet linked to each other, so that the former explains the latter.

Now philosophy must discover the ground of all experience;[5] thus its object necessarily lies outside all experience. This proposition holds good of all philosophy, and really did hold universally until the time of the Kantians and their facts of consciousness, and thus of inner experience.

There can be no objection at all to the proposition here established: for the premise of our argument is the mere analysis of our proposed concept of philosophy, and it is from this that our conclusion follows. Should someone say perhaps that the concept of ground ought to be explained in some other way, we certainly cannot prevent him from thinking what he likes in using this expression: however, it is our right to declare that under the above description of philosophy *we* wish nothing to be understood beyond what has been said. If this meaning be not accepted, the possibility of philosophy in our sense would accordingly have to be denied; and we have already attended to that alternative above.

3

A finite rational being has nothing beyond experience; it is this that comprises the entire staple of his thought. The philosopher is necessarily in the same position; it seems, therefore, incomprehensible how he could raise himself above experience.

2. Better translated as "cognitive discipline" (*Wissenschaft*).
3. Again, *Wissenschaftslehre*, "Theory of Knowledge": that is, the philosophical analysis of knowledge (*Wissen*) and its pursuit or attainment (*Wissenschaft*).
4. A word or an expression whose meaning must be explicated.
5. A clear distinction from the position of KANT, who had taken "the ground of all experience" (*den Grund aller Erfahrung*) to be some "thing-in-itself" that may be "thought" and must be "supposed" but about which nothing more than that can be known or even conceived by theoretical rationality. Fichte is here proclaiming the attempt to comprehend the "ground" or basis of the world of experience to be a legitimate and major task of philosophy after all, rather than one that philosophy can and should abandon as being beyond the limits of our intellectual powers and competence (as Kant had argued).

But he is able to abstract; that is, he can separate what is conjoined in experience through the freedom of thought. *The thing*, which must be determined independently of our freedom and to which our knowledge must conform, and *the intelligence*, which must know, are in experience inseparably connected. The philosopher can leave one of the two out of consideration, and he has then abstracted from experience and raised himself above it. If he leaves out the former, he retains an intelligence in itself, that is, abstracted from its relation to experience, as a basis for explaining experience; if he leaves out the latter, he retains a thing-in-itself, that is, abstracted from the fact that it occurs in experience, as a similar basis of explanation. The first method of procedure is called *idealism*, the second *dogmatism*.[6]

The present discussion should have convinced anyone that these two are the only philosophical systems possible. According to the former system, the presentations accompanied by the feeling of necessity are products of the intelligence which must be presupposed in their explanation; according to the latter, they are products of a thing-in-itself which must be assumed to precede them.

Should someone wish to deny this proposition, he would have to prove either that there is a way, other than that of abstraction, by which to rise above experience, or that the consciousness of experience consists of more constituents than the two mentioned.

Now in regard to the first system, it will indeed become clear later on that what is to rank as intelligence is not something produced merely by abstraction, but under a different predicate really has its place in consciousness; it will nonetheless emerge, however, that the consciousness thereof is conditioned by an abstraction, of a kind that is, of course, natural to man.

It is not at all denied that a person might fuse together a whole from fragments of these heterogeneous systems, or that idle work of this nature has in fact very often been done: but it is denied that, given a consistent procedure, there are any other systems possible besides these two.

4

Between the objects—we shall call the explanatory ground of experience that a philosophy establishes *the object of that philosophy*, since only through and for the latter does it appear to exist—between the object of *idealism* and that of *dogmatism*, there is, in respect of their relation to consciousness in general, a remarkable difference. Everything of which I am conscious is an object of consciousness. Such an object may stand in three relations to the subject. The object appears either as having first been created by the presentation [*Vorstellung*] of the intellect, or as existing without the aid of the intellect; and, in the latter case, either as determined in its nature, as well, or as present merely in its existence, while its essence is determinable by the free intellect.

The first relation amounts to a mere inventing, with or without an aim, the second to an object of experience, the third to a single object only, as we shall demonstrate forthwith.

---

6. That is, "idealism" for Fichte asserts the primacy of "intelligence," or some sort of spirituality, while "dogmatism" asserts the "dogma" of the primacy of some sort of nonmental and nonspiritual thing-in-itself (usually conceived materialistically).

I can freely determine myself to think this or that; for example, the thing-in-itself of the dogmatic philosophers. If I now abstract from what is thought and observe only myself, I become to myself in this object the content of a specific presentation. That I appear to myself to be determined precisely so and not otherwise, as thinking, and as thinking, of all possible thoughts, the thing-in-itself, should in my opinion depend on my self-determination: I have freely made myself into such an object. But I have not made myself as it is in itself; on the contrary, I am compelled to presuppose myself as that which is to be determined by self-determination. I myself, however, am an object for myself whose nature depends, under certain conditions, on the intellect alone, but whose existence must always be presupposed.

Now the object of idealism is precisely this self-in-itself.[7] The object of this system, therefore, actually occurs as something real in consciousness, not as a *thing-in-itself,* whereby idealism would cease to be what it is and would transform itself into dogmatism, but as a *self-in-itself;* not as an object of experience, for it is not determined but will only be determined by me, and without this determination is nothing, and does not even exist; but as something that is raised above all experience.[8]

By contrast, the object of dogmatism belongs to those of the first group, which are produced solely by free thought; the thing-in-itself is a pure invention and has no reality whatever. It does not occur in experience: for the system of experience is nothing other than thinking accompanied by the feeling of necessity, and not even the dogmatist, who like any other philosopher must exhibit its ground, can pass it off as anything else. The dogmatist wants, indeed, to assure to that thing reality, that is, the necessity of being thought as the ground of all experience, and will do it if he proves that experience can really be explained by means of it, and cannot be explained without it; but that is the very question at issue, and what has to be proved should not be presupposed.

Thus the object of idealism has this advantage over the object of dogmatism, that it may be demonstrated, not as the ground of the explanation of experience, which would be contradictory and would turn this system itself into a part of experience, but still in general in consciousness; whereas the latter object cannot be looked upon as anything other than a pure invention, which expects its conversion into reality only from the success of the system.

This is adduced only to promote clear insight into the differences between the two systems, and not in order to infer from it something against dogmatism. That the object of every philosophy, as the ground of the explanation of experience, must lie outside experience, is demanded simply by the nature of philosophy, and is far from proving a disadvantage to a system. We have not as yet found the reasons why this object should furthermore occur in a special manner in consciousness.

Should somebody be unable to convince himself of what has just been asserted, then, since this is only a passing remark, his conviction as to the whole is not yet made impossible thereby. Nevertheless, in accordance with

7. I have avoided this expression until now, in order not to engender the idea of a self as a *thing-in-itself.* My caution was in vain: for this reason I now abandon it, for I do not see whom I should need to protect [Fichte's note].

8. This is a fairly clear statement of Fichte's form of idealism: there *is* something "in itself," beyond all experience and *Vorstellungen* (presentations, representations)—but it is no material-object-like "*thing*-in-itself." Rather, it must be supposed to have the character of something that is more on the order of a "subject" or "self."

my plan, I shall consider possible objections even here. One could deny the claim that there is immediate self-consciousness involved in a free action of the spirit.[9] We would only have to remind such a person once more of the conditions of self-consciousness we have detailed. This self-consciousness does not force itself into being and is not its own source; one must really act freely and then abstract from objects and concentrate only upon oneself. No one can be compelled to do this, and even if he pretends to, one can never know if he proceeds correctly and in the requisite way. In a word, this consciousness cannot be demonstrated to anyone; each person must freely create it in himself. One could only object to the second assertion, viz., that the thing-in-itself is a sheer invention, by reason of having misunderstood it. We would refer such a person to the above description of the origin of this concept.

5

Neither of these two systems can directly refute its opposite, for their quarrel is about the first principle, which admits of no derivation from anything beyond it; each of the two, if only its first principle is granted, refutes that of the other; each denies everything in its opposite, and they have no point at all in common from which they could arrive at mutual understanding and unity. Even if they appear to agree about the words in a sentence, each takes them in a different sense.[1]

First of all, idealism cannot refute dogmatism. As we have seen, the former, indeed, has this advantage over the latter, that it is able to exhibit the presence in consciousness of the freely acting intellect, which is the basis of its explanation of experience. This fact, as such, even the dogmatist must concede, for otherwise he disqualifies himself from any further discussion with the idealist; but through a valid inference from his principle he converts it into appearance and illusion, and thereby renders it unfit to serve as an explanation of anything else, since in his philosophy it cannot even validate itself. According to him, everything that appears in our consciousness, along with our presumed determinations through freedom and the very belief that we are free, is the product of a thing-in-itself.[2] This latter belief is evoked in us by the operation of the thing, and the determinations which we deduce from our freedom are brought about by the same cause: but this we do not know, and hence we attribute them to no cause, and thus to freedom. Every consistent dogmatist is necessarily a fatalist: he does not deny the fact of consciousness

9. Fichte is here appealing to what he takes to be an awareness we do or may have—as spiritual, conscious beings (*Geist*)—that we are capable of "free action" and that a kind of "immediate self-consciousness" is presupposed by such action and is a part of it.
1. This is why *Kant* has not been understood and the Science of Knowledge has not found favor and is not soon likely to do so. The Kantian system and the Science of Knowledge are, in the usual vague sense of the word, but in the precise sense just specified, idealistic; the modern philosophers, however, are one and all *dogmatists*, and firmly determined to remain so. *Kant* has been tolerated only because it was possible to make him into a dogmatist; the Science of Knowledge, which does not admit of such a

transformation, is necessarily intolerable to these sages. The rapid diffusion of *Kantian* philosophy, once understood—as best it has been—is a proof not of the profundity, but of the shallowness of the age. In part, in its current form, it is the most fantastic abortion that has ever been produced by the human imagination, and it reflects little credit on the perspicacity of its defenders that they do not recognize this: in part, it is easy to prove that it has recommended itself only because people have thereby thought to rid themselves of all serious speculation and to provide themselves with a royal charter to go on cultivating their beloved, superficial empiricism [Fichte's note].
2. That is, the product of some sort of material thing(-in-itself).

that we consider ourselves free, for that would be contrary to reason; but he demonstrates, on the basis of his principle, the falsity of this belief. —He completely denies the independence of the self upon which the idealist relies, and construes the self merely as a product of things, an accident of the world; the consistent dogmatist is necessarily also a materialist. He could be refuted only on the basis of the postulate of the freedom and independence of the self; but it is precisely this that he denies.

The dogmatist is no less incapable of refuting the idealist.

The thing-in-itself, which is the fundamental principle of the dogmatist, is nothing and has no reality, as even its exponents must concede, apart from what it is alleged to acquire through the circumstance that experience can be explained only on its basis. The idealist destroys this proof by explaining experience in another way: thus he denies precisely what the dogmatist relies on. The thing-in-itself becomes completely chimerical; there no longer appears to be any reason at all to assume one; and with this the entire edifice of dogmatism collapses.[3]

From what has been said the absolute incompatibility of the two systems appears at once, in that what follows from one of them annihilates the conclusions of the other; hence their fusion necessarily leads to inconsistency. Wherever it is attempted, the parts do not mesh, and at some juncture an immense hiatus ensues. Whoever would wish to take issue with what has just been asserted would have to demonstrate the possibility of such a combination, which presupposes a continued passage from matter to spirit or its reverse, or what is the same, a continued passage from necessity to freedom.

So far as we can yet see, from the speculative point of view the two systems appear to be of equal value: they cannot coexist, but neither one can make any headway against the other. In this light, it is interesting to ask what might motivate the person who sees this—and it is easy enough to see—to prefer one of the systems over the other, and how it is that skepticism, as the total surrender of the attempt to solve the problem presented, does not become universal.

The dispute between the idealist and the dogmatist is, in reality, about whether the independence of the thing should be sacrificed to the independence of the self or, conversely, the independence of the self to that of the thing. What is it, then, that motivates a reasonable man to declare his preference for one over the other?

From the given vantage point, which a person must necessarily adopt if he is to be counted a philosopher, and to which one comes sooner or later, even without meaning to, in the course of reflection the philosopher finds nothing but *that he must present himself as free*[4] and that there are determinate things outside him. It is impossible for a person to rest content with this thought; the thought of a mere presentation is only a half-thought, the fragment of a thought; something must be superadded which corresponds to the presentation independently of the presenting. In other words, the presentation cannot exist for itself alone: it is something only when conjoined with something

---

3. Fichte's "idealism" thus rests upon and springs from his rejection of the idea of (materialistically conceived) "things in themselves."

4. A better translation would be "he must experience and conceive of himself (*er sich vorstellen müsse*) as free."

else, and for itself it is nothing. It is precisely this necessity of thought which drives us on from that standpoint to the question, "What is the ground of presentations?" or, what comes to the very same, "What is it that corresponds thereto?"

Now the presentation [*Vorstellung*] of the independence of the self, and that of the thing, can assuredly coexist, but not the independence of both. Only one of them can be the first, the initiatory, the independent one: the second, by virtue of being second, necessarily becomes dependent on the first, with which it is to be conjoined.

Now which of the two should be taken as primary? Reason provides no principle of choice; for we deal here not with the addition of a link in the chain of reasoning, which is all that rational grounds extend to, but with the beginning of the whole chain, which, as an absolutely primary act, depends solely upon the freedom of thought. Hence the choice is governed by caprice, and since even a capricious decision must have some source, it is governed by *inclination* and *interest*. The ultimate basis of the difference between idealists and dogmatists is thus the difference of their interests.

The highest interest and the ground of all others is self-interest. This is also true of the philosopher. The desire not to lose, but to maintain and assert himself in the rational process, is the interest which invisibly governs all his thought. Now there are two levels of humanity, and before the second level is reached by everyone in the progress of our species, two major types of man. Some, who have not yet raised themselves to full consciousness of their freedom and absolute independence, find themselves only in the presentation [*Vorstellung*] of thing[s],[5] they have only that dispersed self-consciousness which attaches to objects, and has to be gleaned from their multiplicity. Their image is reflected back at them only by things, as by a mirror; if these were taken from them, their self would be lost as well; for the sake of their self they cannot give up the belief in the independence of things, for they themselves exist only if things do. Everything they are, they have really become through the external world. Whoever is in fact a product of things, will never see himself as anything else; and he will be right so long as he speaks only of himself and of others like him. The principle of the dogmatists is belief in things for the sake of the self: indirect belief therefore, in their own scattered self sustained only by objects.[6]

The man who becomes conscious of his self-sufficiency and independence of everything that is outside himself, however—and this can be achieved only by making oneself into something independently of everything else—does not need things for the support of himself, and cannot use them, because they destroy that self-sufficiency, and convert it into mere appearance. The self which he possesses, and which is the subject of his interest, annuls this belief in things; he believes in his independence out of inclination, he embraces it with feeling. His belief in himself is direct.[7]

5. That is, find themselves only in the way things are perceptually experienced.
6. Fichte's point here is that if the self is relationally constituted, and if the only relations of which one's experience consists are perceptual relations to objects (and relations to other people that are of a similar nature), then one's self will amount to nothing more than one can be in the context of such relations.
7. Here Fichte sketches the basis of an account of a different and far more significant sort of humanly attainable selfhood.

This interest also explains the emotions which usually enter into the defense of philosophical systems. The attack on his system in fact exposes the dogmatist to the danger of losing his self; yet he is not armed against this attack, because there is something within him that sides with the attacker; hence he defends himself with passion and animosity. By contrast, the idealist cannot readily refrain from regarding the dogmatist with a certain contempt, for the latter can tell him nothing save what he has long since known and already discarded as erroneous; for one reaches idealism, if not through dogmatism itself, at least through the inclination thereto. The dogmatist flies into a passion, distorts, and would persecute if he had the power: the idealist is cool and in danger of deriding the dogmatist.

What sort of philosophy one chooses depends, therefore, on what sort of man one is,[8] for a philosophical system is not a dead piece of furniture that we can reject or accept as we wish; it is rather a thing animated by the soul of the person who holds it. A person indolent by nature or dulled and distorted by mental servitude, learned luxury, and vanity will never raise himself to the level of idealism.

We can show the dogmatist the inadequacy and incoherence of his system, of which we shall speak in a moment: we can bewilder and harass him from all sides; but we cannot convince him, because he is incapable of calmly receiving and coolly assessing a theory which he absolutely cannot endure. If idealism should prove to be the only true philosophy, it is necessary to be born, raised, and self-educated as a philosopher: but one cannot be made so by human contrivance. Our science expects few converts, therefore, among those *already formed*; if it may have any hopes at all, they are set, rather, upon the young whose innate power has not yet foundered in the indolence of our age.

6

But dogmatism is completely unable to explain what it must, and this demonstrates its untenability.

It must explain the fact of presentation,[9] and undertakes to render it intelligible on the basis of the influence of the thing-in-itself. Now it must not deny what our immediate consciousness tells us about presentation. —What, then, does it say about presentation? It is not my intention here to conceptualize what can only be intuited internally, nor to treat exhaustively of that to whose discussion a large part of the Science of Knowledge [*Wissenschaftslehre*] is dedicated. I merely wish to recall what everybody who has taken just one good look into himself must have discovered long ago.

The intellect [*Intelligenz*] as such *observes itself*; and this self-observation is directed immediately upon its every feature. The nature of intelligence [*Intelligenz*] consists in this *immediate* unity of being and seeing. What is in it, and what it is in general, it is *for itself*; and it is that, *qua* intellect, only in so far as it is that for itself. I think of this or that object: what, then, does this involve, and how, then, do I appear to myself in this thinking? In no other way than

8. This is one of Fichte's most famous pronouncements. It should be understood in the light of the immediately preceding discussion.

9. That is, the fact of perceptual experience (*Vorstellung*).

this: when the object is a merely imaginary one, I create certain determinations in myself; when the object is to be something real, these determinations are present without my aid: *and I observe that creation and this being.*[1] They are in me only in so far as I observe them: seeing and being are inseparably united. —A thing, to be sure, is supposed to have a diversity of features, but as soon as the question arises: "*For whom,* then, is it to have them?" no one who understands the words will answer: "For itself"; for we must still subjoin in thought an intellect *for* which it exists. The intellect is, by contrast, necessarily what it is for itself, and requires nothing subjoined to it in thought. By being posited as intellect, that for which it exists is already posited with it. In the intellect, therefore—to speak figuratively—there is a double series, of being and of seeing, of the real and of the ideal; and its essence consists in the inseparability of these two (it is synthetic); while the thing has only a single series, that of the real (a mere being posited). Intellect and thing are thus exact opposites:[2] they inhabit two worlds[3] between which there is no bridge.

It is by the principle of causality that dogmatism wishes to explain this constitution of intellect in general, as well as its particular determinations: it is to be an effect and the second member in the series.

But the principle of causality holds of a single *real* series, not of a double one. The power of the cause is transferred to something else that lies outside it, opposed to it, and creates a being therein and nothing more; a being for a possible intellect outside it and not for the being itself. If you endow the object acted upon with mechanical power only, it will transfer the received impulse to its neighbor, and thus the motion originating in the first member may proceed through a whole series, however long you wish to make it; but nowhere in it will you find a member which reacts upon itself. Or if you endow the object acted upon with the highest quality you can give to a thing, that of sensitivity, so that it governs itself on its own account and in accordance with the laws of its own nature, not according to the law given it by its cause, as in the series of mere mechanism, then it certainly reacts back upon the stimulus, and the determining ground of its being in this action lies not in the cause, but only in the requirement to be something at all; yet it is and remains a bare, simple being: a being for a possible intellect outside of itself. You cannot lay hold of the intellect if you do not subjoin it in thought as a primary absolute,[4] whose connection with that being independent of it may be difficult for you to explain. —The series is simple, and after your explanation it remains so, and what was to be explained is not explained at all. The dogmatists were supposed to demonstrate the passage from being to presentation [*Vorstellung*]; this they do not, and cannot, do; for their principle contains only the ground of a being, but not that of presentation, which is the exact opposite of being. They take an enormous leap into a world quite alien to their principle.

They seek to conceal this leap in a variety of ways. Strictly—and that is the procedure of consistent dogmatism, which becomes materialism at

---

1. That is, "that bringing forth, this [kind of] reality" (*jenem Hervorbringen, diesem Sein*).
2. That is, "are thus precisely juxtaposed/contrasted" (*sind also geradezu entgegengesetzt*).
3. That is, "they lie in two worlds" (*sie liegen in zwei Welten*). Compare Kant's "two worlds" in the con-

clusion of his *Critique of Practical Reason* (1788; above).
4. That is, you cannot grasp intelligence (*die Intelligenz*) if you do not comprehend it as something primary and absolute (*ein Erstes, ein Absolutes*).

once[5]—the soul should not be a thing at all, and should be nothing whatever but a product, simply the result of the interaction of things among themselves.

But by this means there arises something in the things only, and never anything apart from them, unless an intellect, which observes things, is supplied in thought. The analogies the dogmatists present to make their system intelligible—that of harmony, for example, which arises out of the concord of several instruments—actually make its irrationality apparent. The concord and the harmony are not in the instruments; they are only in the mind of the listener who unifies the manifold in himself; and unless such a listener is supplied, they are nothing at all.

And yet, who is to prevent the dogmatist from assuming a soul as one of the things-in-themselves? This would then belong among the postulates he assumes for the solution of the problem, and only so is the principle of the action of things on the soul applicable, for in materialism there is only an interaction among things whereby thought is supposed to be produced. In order to make the inconceivable thinkable, he has sought to postulate the active thing, or the soul, or both, to be such that through their action presentations could result. The *acting thing* was to be such that its actions could become presentations, much like *God* in *Berkeley's*[6] system (which is a dogmatic, and not at all an idealistic one). This leaves us no better off; we understand only mechanical action, and it is absolutely impossible for us to think of any other; the above proposal, therefore, consists of mere words without any sense. Or again, the soul is to be such that every action upon it becomes a presentation. But with this we fare exactly as with the previous principle: we simply cannot understand it.

This is the course dogmatism takes everywhere and in every form in which it appears. In the immense hiatus left to it between things and presentations, it inserts some empty words instead of an explanation. To be sure, these words can be memorized and repeated, but nobody at all has ever had, nor ever will have, a thought connected to them. For if one tries to conceive distinctly *how* the above occurs, the whole notion vanishes in an empty froth.

Thus dogmatism can only repeat its principle, and then reiterate it under various guises; it can state it, and then state it again; but it cannot get from this to the explanandum,[7] and deduce the latter. Yet philosophy consists precisely of this deduction. Hence dogmatism, even from the speculative viewpoint, is no philosophy at all, but merely an impotent claim and assurance. Idealism is left as the only possible philosophy.[8]

What is here established has nothing to do with the objections of the reader, for there is absolutely nothing to be said against the latter; its concern is, rather, with the absolute incapacity of many to understand it. Nobody who even understands the words can deny that all causation is mechanical and that no presentation [*Vorstellung*] comes about through mechanism. But this is pre-

---

5. Here Fichte makes it clear that when he talks about "dogmatism," he is thinking of (dogmatic) *materialism* (in German, *Materialismus*).
6. George Berkeley (1685–1753), Anglo-Irish bishop and philosopher; he argued that to be is to be perceived or to be a perceiver, and that God is the cause of sensory ideas.
7. The word or expression whose meaning must be explained.
8. Fichte takes this radical conclusion to follow from the recognition of the untenability of (materialistic) "dogmatism."

cisely where the difficulty lies. A grasp of the nature of intelligence as depicted, upon which our entire refutation of dogmatism is founded,[9] presupposes a degree of independence and freedom of mind. Now many people have progressed no further in their thinking than to grasp the simple sequence of the mechanism of nature; so it is very natural that presentations [*Vorstellungen*], if they wish to think of them, should also fall for them in this series, the only one that has entered their minds. The presentation [*Die Vorstellung*] becomes for them a kind of thing: a singular confusion, of which we find traces in the most famous of philosophical authors. Dogmatism is enough for such men; there is no hiatus for them, because for them the opposing world does not even exist. —Hence the dogmatist cannot be refuted by the argument we have given, however clear it may be; for it cannot be brought home to him, since he lacks the power to grasp its premise.

The manner in which we deal here with dogmatism also offends against the indulgent logic of our age, which, though uncommonly widespread in every period, has only in our own been raised to the level of a maxim expressed in words: one need not be so strict in reasoning, proofs are not to be taken so rigorously in philosophy as they are, say, in mathematics. Whenever thinkers of this type observe even a couple of links in the chain of reasoning, and catch sight of the rule of inference, they at once supply the remainder pell-mell by imagination, without further investigation of what it consists of. If an Alexander[1] perforce tells them: Everything is determined by natural necessity: our presentations are dependent upon the disposition of things and our will upon the nature of our presentations; hence all our volitions are determined by natural necessity and our belief in free will is an illusion; they find this wonderfully intelligible and clear, and go off convinced and amazed at the brilliance of this demonstration, in spite of the fact that there is no sense to it. I beg to observe that the Science of Knowledge neither proceeds from nor counts upon this indulgent logic. If even a single member of the long chain that it must establish be not rigorously joined to the next, it will have proved nothing whatever.

7

As already stated above, idealism explains the determinations of consciousness on the basis of the activity of the intellect.[2] The intellect, for it, is only active and absolute, never passive; it is not passive because it is postulated to be first and highest, preceded by nothing which could account for a passivity therein. For the same reason, it also has no *being* proper, no subsistence, for this is the result of an interaction and there is nothing either present or assumed with which the intellect could be set to interact. The intellect, for idealism, is an *act*, and absolutely nothing more; we should not even call it an *active* something, for this expression refers to something subsistent in which activity inheres. But idealism has no reason to assume such a thing, since it is not included in its principle and everything else must first be deduced. Now out

---

9. This is a crucial point: Fichte here makes it clear that his fundamental case against materialism and for idealism rests on the persuasiveness of his construal of the nature of intelligence (*Intelligenz*).
1. Alexander the Great (356–323 B.C.E.), the Macedonian king and conqueror, has traditionally been viewed as interested in philosophy (chiefly because Aristotle at one point was his teacher).
2. That is, "intelligence" (*Intelligenz*).

of the activity of this intellect we must deduce *specific* presentations: of a world, of a material, spatially located world existing without our aid, etc., which notoriously occur in consciousness. But a determinate cannot be deduced from an indeterminate: the grounding principle, which is the rule of all deduction, is inapplicable here. Hence this primordial action of the intellect must needs be a determinate one, and, since the intellect is itself the highest ground of explanation, an action determined by the intellect and its nature, and not by something outside it. The presupposition of idealism will, therefore, be as follows: the intellect acts, but owing to its nature, it can act only in a certain fashion. If we think of this necessary way of acting in abstraction from the action itself, we shall call it, most appropriately, the law of action: hence there are necessary laws of the intellect. —This, then, also renders immediately intelligible the feeling of necessity that accompanies specific presentations: for here the intellect does not register some external impression, but feels in this action the limits of its own being. So far as idealism makes this one and only rationally determined and genuinely explanatory assumption, that the intellect has necessary laws, it is called critical, or also transcendental idealism. A transcendent idealism would be a system that deduced determinate presentations from the free and totally lawless action of the intellect; a completely contradictory hypothesis, for surely, as has just been remarked, the principle of grounding is inapplicable to such an action.

As surely as they are to be grounded in the unitary being of the intellect, the intellect's assumed laws of operation themselves constitute a system.[3] This means that the fact that the intellect operates in just such a way under this specific condition can be further explained by the fact that it has a definite mode of operation under a condition in general; and the latter in turn may be explained on the basis of a single fundamental law: the intellect gives its laws to itself in the course of its operation; and this legislation itself occurs through a higher necessary action, or presentation. The law of causality, for example, is not a primordial law, but is merely one of several ways of connecting the manifold, and can be deduced from the fundamental law of this connection: and the law of this connection of the manifold, along with the manifold itself, can again be deduced from higher laws.

In accordance with this remark, critical idealism itself can now proceed in two different ways. On the one hand, it may really deduce the system of the necessary modes of operation, and with it concurrently the objective presentations [*Vorstellungen*] created thereby, from the fundamental laws of the intellect, and so allow the whole compass of our presentations to come gradually into being before the eyes of its readers or listeners. On the other hand, it may conceive these laws as already and immediately applied to objects, that is, as applied somewhere, upon their lowest level (at which stage they are called categories), and then maintain that it is by means of them that objects are ordered and determined.

Now how can the critical philosopher of the latter sort, who does not deduce the accepted laws of the intellect from the nature thereof, obtain even a mere material knowledge of them—the knowledge that they are precisely these, viz., the laws of substantiality and causality? For I will not yet

---

3. Here Fichte anticipates HEGEL's claim to the same effect on the part of "reason."

burden him with the question of how he knows that they are mere immanent laws of the intellect. They are the laws that are applied directly to objects: and he can have formed them only by abstraction from these objects, and hence only from experience. It avails nothing if he borrows them in some roundabout way from logic; for logic itself has arisen for him no otherwise than by abstraction from objects, and he merely does indirectly what, if done directly, would too obviously catch our eyes. Hence he can in no way confirm that his postulated laws of thought are really laws of thought, really nothing but immanent laws of the intellect. The dogmatist maintains against him that they are universal properties of things grounded in the nature of the latter, and it is past seeing why we should give more credence to the unproved assertion of the one than to the unproved assertion of the other. —This method yields no knowledge that the intellect must act precisely thus, nor why it must do so. In order to promote such understanding, something would have to be set forth in the premises that is the unique possession of the intellect, and those laws of thought would have to be deduced from these premises before our very eyes.

It is especially difficult to see how, according to this method, the object itself arises; for, even if we grant the critical philosopher his unproved postulate, it explains nothing beyond the *dispositions* and *relations* of the thing; that, for example, it is in space, that it manifests itself in time, that its accidents must be related to something substantial, and so on. But whence comes that which has these relations and dispositions; whence the stuff that is organized in these forms? It is in this stuff that dogmatism takes refuge, and you have merely made a bad situation worse.

We know well enough that the thing comes into being surely through an action in accord with these laws, that it is nothing else but the *totality of these relations unified by the imagination,* and that all these relations together constitute the thing; the object is surely the original synthesis of all these concepts. Form and matter are not separate items; the totality of form is the matter, and it is through analysis that we first obtain individual forms. But the critical philosopher who follows the present method can only assure us of this; and it is in fact a mystery how he knows it himself, if indeed he does. So long as the thing is not made to arise as a whole in front of the thinker's eyes, dogmatism is not hounded to its last refuge. But this is possible only by dealing with the intellect in its total, and not in its partial, conformity to law.

Such an idealism is, therefore, unproved and unprovable. It has no other weapon against dogmatism save the assurance that it is right; and against the higher, perfected critical philosophy, nothing save impotent rage and the assertion that one can go no further, the assurance that beyond it there is no more ground, that from there one becomes unintelligible to *it,* and the like; all of which means nothing whatever.

Finally, in such a system only those laws are established whereby the purely subsumptive faculty of judgment determines the objects of external experience alone. But this is by far the smallest part of the system of reason. Since it lacks insight into the whole procedure of reason, this halfhearted critical philosophy gropes around in the sphere of practical reason and reflective judgment just as blindly as the mere imitator and copies out, just as artlessly, expressions totally unintelligible to it.

In another place[4] I have already set forth in full clarity the methods of the perfected transcendental idealism established by the Science of Knowledge. I cannot explain how people could have failed to understand that exposition; at any rate, it is asserted that some have not understood it.

I am forced, therefore, to repeat what has been said before, and warn that in this science everything turns on the understanding thereof.

This idealism proceeds from a single fundamental principle of reason, which it demonstrates directly in consciousness. In so doing it proceeds as follows. It calls upon the listener or reader to think a certain concept freely; were he to do so, he would find himself obliged to proceed in a certain way. We must distinguish two things here: the required mode of thinking—this is accomplished through freedom, and whoever does not achieve it with us will see nothing of what the Science of Knowledge reveals—and the necessary manner in which it is to be accomplished, which latter is not dependent on the will, being grounded in the nature of the intellect; it is something *necessary*, which emerges, however, only in and upon the occurrence of a free action; something *found*, though its discovery is conditioned by freedom.

So far idealism demonstrates its claims in our immediate consciousness. But that the above necessity is the fundamental law of all reason, that from it one can deduce the whole system of our necessary presentations—not only of a world whose objects are determined by the subsuming and reflective judgment, but also of ourselves as free practical beings under laws—this is a mere hypothesis. Idealism must prove this hypothesis by an actual deduction, and this precisely is its proper task.

In so doing it proceeds in the following fashion. *It shows that what is first set up as fundamental principle and directly demonstrated in consciousness, is impossible unless something else occurs along with it, and that this something else is impossible unless a third something also takes place, and so on until the conditions of what was first exhibited are completely exhausted, and this latter is, with respect to its possibility, fully intelligible.* Its course is an unbroken progression from conditioned to condition; each condition becomes, in turn, a conditioned whose condition must be sought out.

If the hypothesis of idealism is correct and the reasoning in the deduction is valid, the system of all necessary presentations or the entirety of experience (this identity is established not in philosophy but only beyond it) must emerge as the final result, as the totality of the conditions of the original premise.

Now idealism does not keep this experience, as the antecedently known goal at which it must arrive, constantly in mind; in its method it knows nothing of experience and takes no account of it at all; it proceeds from its starting point in accordance with its rule, unconcerned about what will emerge in the end. It has been given the right angle from which to draw its straight line; does it then still need a point to draw it to? In my opinion, all the points on its line are given along with it. Suppose that you are given a certain number. You surmise it to be the product of certain factors. Your task then is simply to seek out, by the rule well known to you, the product of these factors. Whether or not it agrees with the given number will turn out later, once you have the product. The given number is the entirety of experience; the factors are the prin-

4. A short manifesto, *Concerning the Concept of the Wissenschaftslehre (Über den Begriff der Wissenschaftslehre*, 1794; 2nd ed., 1798).

ciple demonstrated in consciousness and the laws of thought; the multiplication is the activity of philosophizing. Those who advise you always to keep an eye on experience when you philosophize are recommending that you change the factors a bit and multiply falsely on occasion, so that the numbers you get may, after all, match: a procedure as dishonest as it is superficial.

To the extent that these final results of idealism are viewed as such, as consequences of reasoning, they constitute the a priori in the human mind; and to the extent that they are regarded, where reasoning and experience really agree, as given in experience, they are called a posteriori. For a completed idealism the a priori and the a posteriori are by no means twofold, but perfectly unitary; they are merely two points of view, to be distinguished solely by the mode of our approach. Philosophy anticipates the entirety of experience and *thinks* it only as necessary, and to that extent it is, by comparison with real experience, a priori. To the extent that it is regarded as given, the number is a posteriori; the same number is a priori insofar as it is derived as a product of the factors. Anyone who thinks otherwise, simply does not know what he is talking about.

A philosophy whose results do not agree with experience is surely false, for it has not fulfilled its promise to deduce the entirety of experience and to explain it on the basis of the necessary action of the intellect. Either the hypothesis of transcendental idealism is, therefore, completely false, or it has merely been wrongly handled in the particular version which fails to perform its task. Since the demand for an explanation of experience is surely founded in human reason; since no reasonable man will accept that reason can impose a demand whose satisfaction is absolutely impossible; since there are only two roads to its satisfaction, that of dogmatism and that of transcendental idealism, and it can be proved without further ado that the former cannot fulfill its promise; for these reasons, the resolute thinker will always prefer the latter, holding that the hypothesis as such is completely right and that error has occurred only in the reasoning; nor will any vain attempt deter him from trying again, until finally success is achieved.

The course of this idealism runs, as can be seen, from something that occurs in consciousness, albeit only as the result of a free act of thought, to the entirety of experience. What lies between these two is its proper field. This latter is not a fact of consciousness and does not lie within the compass of experience; how could anything that did so ever be called philosophy, when philosophy has to exhibit the ground of experience, and the ground lies necessarily outside of what it grounds. It is something brought forth by means of free but law-governed thought. —This will become entirely clear as soon as we take a closer look at the fundamental assertion of idealism.

The absolutely postulated is impossible, so idealism shows, without the condition of a second something, this second without a third, and so on; that is, of all that it establishes nothing is possible alone, and it is only in conjunction with them all that each individual item is possible. Hence, by its own admission, only the whole occurs in consciousness, and this totality is in fact experience. Idealism seeks a closer acquaintance with this whole, and so must analyze it, and this not by a blind groping, but according to the definite rule of composition, so that it may see the whole take form under its eyes. It can do this because it can abstract; because in free thought it is surely able to grasp the individual alone. For not only the necessity of presentations, but also their freedom is present in consciousness: and this freedom, again, can proceed either lawfully or capriciously. The whole is given to it from the standpoint of necessary consciousness; it discovers it, just as it discovers itself. The series created by the unification of this whole emerges only through freedom. Whoever performs this act of freedom will come to be aware of it, and lay out, as it were, a new field in his consciousness: for one who does not perform it, that which the act conditions does not exist at all. —The chemist synthesizes a body, say a certain metal, from its elements. The ordinary man sees the metal familiar to him; the chemist, the union of these specific elements. Do they then see different things? I should think not! They see the same thing, though in different ways. What the chemist sees is the a priori, for he sees the individual elements: what the common man sees is the a posteriori, for he sees the whole. —But there is this difference here: the chemist must first analyze the whole before he can compound it, since he is dealing with an object whose rule of composition he cannot know prior to the analysis; but the philosopher can synthesize without prior analysis, because he already knows the rule that governs his object, reason.

No reality other than that of necessary thought falls, therefore, within the compass of philosophy, given that one wishes to think about the ground of experience at all. Philosophy maintains that the intellect can be thought only as active, and active only in this particular way. This reality is completely adequate for it; since it follows from philosophy that there is in fact no other.

It is the complete critical idealism here described that the Science of Knowledge intends to establish. What has just been said contains the concept of this former, and I shall entertain no objections to it, for no one can know better than I what I propose to do. Proofs of the impossibility of a project that will be accomplished, and in part already is so, are simply ridiculous. One has only to attend to the course of the argument, and examine whether or not it fulfills its promise.

SOURCE: Johann Gottlieb Fichte, *Science of Knowledge (Wissenschaftslehre) with the First and Second Introductions*, ed. and trans. Peter Heath and John Lachs (New York: Appleton-Century-Crofts, 1970), pp. 6–28. Except where otherwise indicated, German words in brackets are the terminology used in the German original, inserted by the editor in addition to their renderings in the translation. Originally published as *Grundlage der gesamten Wissenschaftslehre* (1794/95; published with two new introductions, 1797). This English title, though standard, is a misleading translation of Fichte's German. In his time, and well into the twentieth century, *Wissenschaft* was understood to mean cognitive inquiry or knowledge (*Wissen*) rigorously pursued. *Lehre*, which can mean "teaching" or "doctrine," has the meaning of something like "theory" or "system" when used as it is in Fichte's title, which thus has the sense of (systematic) *Theory of Knowledge*.

From The Vocation [*Bestimmung*] of Man

From *Book III. Faith.*

* * *

There is within me an impulse to absolute, independent self-activity.[1] Nothing is more insupportable to me, than to be merely by another, for another,

---

1. That is, a drive (*ein Trieb*) to absolute, independent *Selbsttätigkeit*—literally "self-activity," by which Fichte means "self-*directed* [and so autonomous] activity." The idea of autonomy, or lawfulness that is truly *self*-determined, had been a very central and crucial one for KANT; and, under the banner of *Selbsttätigkeit*, it remained so for Fichte and HEGEL—and for MARX as well.

and through another; I must be something for myself and by myself alone. This impulse I feel along with the perception of my own existence, it is inseparably united to my consciousness of myself.

I explain this feeling to myself by reflection; and, as it were, add to this blind impulse the power of sight by means of thought. According to this impulse I must act as an absolutely independent being:—thus I understand and translate the impulse. I must be independent. Who am I? Subject and object in one,—the conscious being and that of which I am conscious, gifted with intuitive knowledge and myself revealed in that intuition, the thinking mind and myself the object of the thought—inseparable, and ever present to each other. As both, must I be what I am, absolutely by myself alone;—by myself originate conceptions,—by myself produce a condition of things lying beyond these conceptions. But how is the latter possible? With nothing I cannot connect any being whatsoever; from nothing there can never arise something; my objective thought is necessarily meditative only. But any being which is connected with another being becomes thereby dependent;—it is no longer a primary, original, and genetic, but only a secondary and derived being. I am constrained to connect myself with something;—with another being I cannot connect myself without losing that independence which is the condition of my own existence.[2]

My conception and origination of *a purpose*, however, is, by its very nature, absolutely free,—producing something out of nothing. With such a conception I must connect my activity, in order that it may be possible to regard it as free, and as proceeding absolutely from myself alone.

*   *   *

I feel within me an impulse and an effort towards outward activity;[3] this appears to be true, and to be the only truth belonging to the matter. Since it is I who feel this impulse, and since I cannot pass beyond myself, either with my whole consciousness, or in particular with my capacity of sensation,—since this *I* itself is the last point at which I am conscious of this impulse, it certainly appears to me as an impulse founded in myself, to an activity also founded in myself. Might it not be however that this impulse, although unperceived by me, is in reality the impulse of a foreign power invisible to me, and that notion of independence merely a delusion, arising from my sphere of vision being limited to myself alone? I have no reason to assume this, but just as little reason to deny it. I must confess that I absolutely know nothing, and can know nothing, about it.

*   *   *

What unity and completeness does this view present!—what dignity does it confer on human nature! Our thought is not founded on itself alone, independently of our impulses and affections;[4]—man does not consist of two independent and separate elements; he is absolutely one. All our thought is

---

2. As he does so often, the translator has greatly embellished Fichte's original text here, thereby obscuring what he is actually saying—which is quite important. Fichte simply asserted: "*Anknüpfen* muß ich; an ein *Sein* kann ich nicht anknüpften." That is: "*Connect* I must; [but] with a *being* I cannot connect."
3. That is, "a drive and striving outwardly" (*ein Trieb und Streben weiter hinaus*).
4. That is, "our drives and inclinations" (*unseren Trieben und Neigungen*).

founded on our impulses;—as a man's affections are, so is his knowledge. These impulses[5] compel us to a certain mode of thought only so long as we do not perceive the constraint; the constraint vanishes the moment it is perceived; and it is then no longer the impulse by itself, but we ourselves, according to our impulse, who form our own system of thought.

But I shall open my eyes; shall learn thoroughly to know myself; shall recognise that constraint;—this is my vocation.[6] I shall thus, and under that supposition I shall necessarily, form my own mode of thought. Then I shall stand absolutely independent, thoroughly equipt and perfected through my own act and deed. The primitive source of all my other thought and of my life itself, that from which everything proceeds which can have an existence in me, for me, or through me, the innermost spirit of my spirit,[7]—is no longer a foreign power, but it is, in the strictest possible sense, the product of my own will. I am wholly my own creation.[8] I might have followed blindly the leading of my spiritual [geistig] nature. But I would not be a work of Nature but of myself, and I have become so even by means of this resolution. By endless subtleties I might have made the natural conviction of my own mind dark and doubtful. But I have accepted it with freedom, simply because I resolved to accept it. I have chosen the system which I have now adopted with settled purpose and deliberation from among other possible modes of thought, because I have recognised in it the only one consistent with my dignity and my vocation. With freedom and consciousness I have returned to the point at which Nature had left me. I accept that which she announces;—but I do not accept it because I must; I believe it because I will.[9]

* * *

There is but one point towards which I have unceasingly to direct all my attention,—namely, what I *ought to do*, and how I may best fulfil the obligation. All my thoughts must have a bearing on my actions, and must be capable of being considered as means, however remote, to this end; otherwise they are an idle and aimless show, a mere waste of time and strength, the perversion of a noble power which is entrusted to me for a very different end.

I dare hope, I dare surely promise myself, to follow out this undertaking with good results. The Nature on which I have to act is not a foreign element, called into existence without reference to me, into which I cannot penetrate. It is moulded by my own laws of thought, and must be in harmony with them; it must be thoroughly transparent, knowable and penetrable to me, even to its inmost recesses. In all its phenomena it expresses nothing but the connexions and relations of my own being to myself; and as surely as I may hope to know myself, so surely may I expect to comprehend it. Let me seek only that which I ought to seek, and I shall find; let me ask only that which I ought to ask, and I shall receive an answer.

---

5. That is, "this drive" (*dieser Trieb*).
6. That is, "my mission [essential task, destiny]" (*meine Bestimmung*).
7. That is, "spirit of my spirit" (*Geist meines Geistes*); the translator has added "innermost."

8. In Fichte's German, "Ich bin durchaus mein eigenes Geschöpf."
9. That is, "I believe it because I choose to do so" (*ich glaube es, weil ich will*).

I.

That voice within my soul in which I believe,[1] and on account of which I believe in every other thing to which I attach credence, does not command me merely to act *in general*. This is impossible; all these general principles are formed only through my own voluntary observation and reflection, applied to many individual facts; but never in themselves express any fact whatever. This voice of my conscience announces to me precisely what I ought to do, and what leave undone, in every particular situation of life; it accompanies me, if I will but listen to it with attention, through all the events of my life, and never refuses me its reward where I am called upon to act. It carries with it immediate conviction, and irresistibly compels my assent to its behests:—it is impossible for me to contend against it.

To listen to it, to obey it honestly and unreservedly, without fear or equivocation,—this is my true vocation,[2] the whole end and purpose of my existence. My life ceases to be an empty play without truth or significance. There is something that must absolutely be done for its own sake alone;—that which conscience demands of me in this particular situation of life it is mine to do, for this only I am here;—to know it, I have understanding; to perform it, I have power. Through this edict of conscience alone, truth and reality are introduced into my conceptions. I cannot refuse them my attention and my obedience without thereby surrendering the very purpose of my existence.

Hence I cannot withhold my belief from the reality which they announce, without at the same time renouncing my vocation. It is absolutely true, without farther proof or confirmation,—nay, it is the first truth, and the foundation of all other truth and certainty, that this voice must be obeyed; and therefore everything becomes to me true and certain, the truth and certainty of which is assumed in the possibility of such obedience.

There appear before me in space, certain phenomena to which I transfer the idea of myself;—I conceive of them as beings like myself. Speculation, when carried out to its last results, has indeed taught me, or would teach me, that these supposed rational beings out of myself are but the products of my own presentative power; that, according to certain laws of my thought, I am compelled to represent out of myself my conception of myself; and that, according to the same laws, I can transfer this conception only to certain definite intuitions. But the voice of my conscience thus speaks:—"Whatever these beings may be in and for themselves, thou shalt act towards them as self-existent, free, substantive beings, wholly independent of thee. Assume it as already known, that they can give a purpose to their own being wholly by themselves, and quite independently of thee; never interrupt the accomplishment of this purpose, but rather further it to the utmost of thy power. Honour their freedom, lovingly take up their purposes as if they were thine own."[3] Thus ought I to act:—by this course of action *ought* all my thought to be guided,—nay, it *shall* and *must* necessarily be so, if I have resolved to obey the voice of my conscience. Hence I shall always regard these beings as in possession of

1. Better translated: "That voice in myself (*in meinem Inneren*), which I believe."
2. In German, *Bestimmung*; on that term, see the source note to this text.
3. This thought is echoed by SARTRE in "Existentialism Is a Humanism" (1946; see below).

an existence for themselves wholly independent of mine, as capable of forming and carrying out their own purposes;—from this point of view, I shall never be able to conceive of them otherwise, and my previous speculations regarding them shall vanish like an empty dream.

* * *

In short, there is for me absolutely no such thing as an existence which has no relation to myself, and which I contemplate merely for the sake of contemplating it;—whatever has an existence for me, has it only through its relation to my own being. But there is, in the highest sense, only one relation to me possible, all others are but subordinate forms of this:—my vocation to moral activity. My world is the object and sphere of my duties,[4] and absolutely nothing more; there is no other world for me, and no other qualities of my world than what are implied in this;—my whole united capacity, all finite capacity, is insufficient to comprehend any other. Whatever possesses an existence for me, can bring its existence and reality into contact with me only through this relation, and only through this relation do I comprehend it:—for any other existence than this I have no organ whatever.

* * *

* * * From this necessity of action proceeds the consciousness of the actual world; and not the reverse way, from the consciousness of the actual world the necessity of action:—this, not that, is the first; the former is derived from the latter. We do not act because we know, but we know because we are called upon to act:—the practical reason is the root of all reason. The laws of action for rational beings are *immediately certain*; their world is certain only through that previous certainty. We cannot deny these laws without plunging the world, and ourselves with it, into absolute annihilation;—we raise ourselves from this abyss, and maintain ourselves above it, solely by our moral activity.

II.

* * *

I say, it is the law which commands me to act that of itself assigns an end to my action; the same inward power that compels me to think that I ought to act thus, compels me also to believe that from my action some result will arise; it opens to my spiritual vision a prospect into another world,—which is really a world, a state, namely, and not an action,—but another and better world than that which is present to the physical eye; it constrains me to aspire after this better world, to embrace it with every power, to long for its realization, to live only in it, and in it alone find satisfaction. The law itself is my guarantee for the certain attainment of this end. The same resolution by which I devote my whole thought and life to the fulfillment of this law, and determine to see nothing beyond it, brings with it the indestructible conviction that the promise it implies is likewise true and certain, and renders it impossible for

---

4. This is one of Fichte's fundamental ideas and claims: the true and ultimate significance—and therefore the essential nature—of the world in which I find myself, as far as I am and should be concerned, is to provide me (and other moral agents) with a setting for moral action.

me even to conceive the possibility of the opposite. As I live in obedience to it, so do I live also in the contemplation of its end,—in that better world which it promises to me.[5]

———————

Even in the mere consideration of the world as it is, apart from this law, there arises within me the wish, the desire,—no, not the mere desire, but the absolute demand for a better world. I cast a glance on the present relations of men towards each other and towards Nature; on the feebleness of their powers, the strength of their desires and passions. A voice within me proclaims with irresistible conviction—"It is impossible that it can remain thus; it must become different and better."

I cannot think of the present state of humanity as that in which it is destined to remain; I am absolutely unable to conceive of this as its complete and final vocation. Then, indeed, were all a dream and a delusion; and it would not be worth the trouble to have lived, and played out this ever-repeated game, which tends to nothing and signifies nothing. Only in so far as I can regard this state as the means towards a better, as the transition point to a higher and more perfect state, has it any value in my eyes;—not for its own sake, but for the sake of that better world for which it prepares the way, can I support it, esteem it, and joyfully perform my part in it. My mind can accept no place in the present, nor rest in it even for a moment; my whole being flows onward, incessantly and irresistibly, towards that future and better state of things.

Shall I eat and drink only that I may hunger and thirst and eat and drink again, till the grave which is open beneath my feet shall swallow me up and I myself become the food of worms? Shall I beget beings like myself, that they too may eat and drink and die, and leave behind them beings like themselves to do the same that I have done? To what purpose this ever-revolving circle, this ceaseless and unvarying round, in which all things appear only to pass away, and pass away only that they may re-appear as they were before;—this monster continually devouring itself that it may again bring itself forth, and bringing itself forth only that it may again devour itself?[6]

This can never be the vocation of my being, and of all being. There must be something which is because it has come into existence; and endures, and cannot come anew, having once become such as it is. And this abiding existence must be produced amid the vicissitudes of the transitory and perishable, maintain itself there, and be borne onwards, pure and inviolate, upon the waves of time.

* * *

* * * [M]an must resolve either to renounce his freedom altogether, and patiently to become a mere passive wheel in the great machine of the universe, or else to employ it for good. In soil thus prepared, good will easily

5. Here and in what follows, Fichte picks up on and elaborates what he takes to follow from Kant's conclusion to the *Critique of Practical Reason* (1788; see above), expressing the vision and conviction that is at the heart of American Transcendentalism (of which EMERSON is a classic proponent).

6. This is the vision from which KIERKEGAARD recoils, motivating his "leap of faith," and which prompts SCHOPENHAUER to his radical condemnation of life and of the "will to live."

prosper.[7] When men shall no longer be divided by selfish purposes, nor their powers exhausted in struggles with each other, nothing will remain for them but to direct their united strength against the one common enemy which still remains unsubdued,—resisting, uncultivated nature. No longer estranged from each other by private ends, they will necessarily combine for this common object; and thus there arises a body, everywhere animated by the same spirit and the same love. Every misfortune to the individual, since it can no longer be a gain to any other individual, is a misfortune to the whole, and to each individual member of the whole; and is felt with the same pain, and remedied with the same activity, by every member;—every step in advance made by one man is a step in advance made by the whole race. Here, where the petty, narrow self of mere individual personality is merged in the more comprehensive unity of the social constitution, each man truly loves every other as himself,—as a member of this greater *self* which now claims all his love, and of which he himself is no more than a member, capable of participating only in a common gain or in a common loss. The strife of evil against good is here abolished, for here no evil can intrude. The strife of the good among themselves for the sake of good, disappears, now that they find it easy to love good for its own sake alone and not because they are its authors; now that it has become of all-importance to them that the truth should really be discovered, that the useful action should be done,—but not at all by whom this may be accomplished. Here each individual is at all times ready to join his strength to that of others, to make it subordinate to that of others; and whoever, according to the judgment of all, is most capable of accomplishing the greatest amount of good, will be supported by all, and his success rejoiced in by all with an equal joy.

This is the purpose of our earthly life, which reason sets before us, and for the infallible attainment of which she is our pledge and security. This is not an object given to us only that we may strive after it for the mere purpose of exercising our powers on something great, the real existence of which we may perhaps be compelled to abandon to doubt;—it shall, it must be realized; there must be a time in which it shall be accomplished, as surely as there is a sensible world and a race of reasonable beings existent in time with respect to which nothing earnest and rational is conceivable besides this purpose, and whose existence becomes intelligible only through this purpose. Unless all human life be metamorphosed into a mere theatrical display for the gratification of some malignant spirit, who has implanted in poor humanity this inextinguishable longing for the imperishable only to amuse himself with its ceaseless pursuit of that which it can never overtake,—its ever-repeated efforts, Ixion-like,[8] to embrace that which still eludes its grasp,—its restless hurrying onward in an ever-recurring circle,—only to mock its earnest aspirations with an empty, insipid farce;—unless the wise man, seeing through this mockery, and feeling an irrepressible disgust at continuing to play his part in it, is to

---

7. Here Fichte articulates the basic version and principles of his normative political philosophy. One can hear clear echoes of it—and of what follows—in Marx.

8. In Greek mythology, Ixion was punished by being bound on an ever-rolling fiery wheel. The figure punished by having food and drink always elude his grasp was Tantalus.

cast life indignantly from him and make the moment of his awakening to reason also that of his physical death;—unless these things are so this purpose most assuredly must be attained.—Yes! it is attainable *in life*, and *through life*, for Reason commands me to live:—it is attainable, for I am.

III.

But when this end shall have been attained, and humanity shall at length stand at this point, what is there then to do? Upon earth there is no higher state than this;—the generation which has once reached it, can no more than abide there, steadfastly maintain its position, die, and leave behind it descendants who shall do the like, and who will again leave behind them descendants to follow in their footsteps. Humanity would thus stand still upon her path; and therefore her earthly end cannot be her highest end. This earthly end is conceivable, attainable, and finite. Even although we consider all preceding generations as means for the production of the last complete one, we do not thereby escape the question of earnest reason,—to what end then is this last one? Since a Human Race has appeared upon earth, its existence there must certainly be in accordance with, and not contrary to, reason;[9] and it must attain all the development which it is possible for it to attain on earth. But why should such a race have an existence at all,—why may it not as well have remained in the womb of chaos? Reason is not for the sake of existence, but existence for the sake of reason.[1] An existence which does not of itself satisfy reason and solve all her questions, cannot by possibility be the true being.

* * *

But, as a reasonable being, before whom a purpose must be set solely by its own will and determination, it is impossible for me to act without a motive and without an end. If this obedience is to be recognised by me as a reasonable service,—if the voice which demands this obedience be really that of the creative reason within me, and not a mere fanciful enthusiasm, invented by my own imagination, or communicated to me somehow from without,—this obedience must have some consequences, must serve some end. It is evident that it does not serve the purpose of the world of sense;—there must, therefore, be a super-sensual [*übersinnlich*] world, whose purposes it does promote.[2]

* * *

And now the Eternal World rises before me more brightly, and the fundamental law of its order stands clearly and distinctly apparent to my mental vision. In this world, *will* alone, as it lies concealed from mortal eye in the secret obscurities of the soul, is the first link in a chain of consequences that stretches through the whole invisible realms of spirit; as, in the physical world, *action*—a certain movement of matter—is the first link in a material chain

---

9. Here Fichte shows himself to be in accord with the conviction—commonly associated with and attributed to Hegel—that there is a deep rationality in the heart of things, active in nature and history.
1. A secularized version of the classical Christian-theological view that the divine nature is rational and that divinity's rationality is not for the sake of existence, but rather existence is for the sake of (the realization of) the divine nature and its essential rationality.
2. Another echo of Kant's conclusion to his *Critique of Practical Reason*, with which Fichte engages throughout this passage.

that runs through the whole system of nature. The will is the efficient, living principle of the world of reason, as motion is the efficient, living principle of the world of sense. I stand in the centre of two entirely opposite worlds:—a visible world, in which action is the only moving power; and an invisible and absolutely incomprehensible world, in which will is the ruling principle. I am one of the primitive forces of both these worlds. My will embraces both.[3] This will is, in itself, a constituent element of the super-sensual world; for as I move it by my successive resolutions, I move and change something in that world, and my activity thus extends itself throughout the whole, and gives birth to new and ever-enduring results which henceforward possess a real existence and need not again to be produced. This will may break forth in a material act,—and this act belongs to the world of sense and does there that which pertains to a material act to do.

It is not necessary that I should first be severed from the terrestrial world before I can obtain admission into the celestial one;—I am and live in it even now, far more truly than in the terrestrial; even now it is my only sure foundation, and the eternal life on the possession of which I have already entered is the only ground why I should still prolong this earthly one. That which we call heaven does not lie beyond the grave; it is even here diffused around us, and its light arises in every pure heart. My will is mine, and it is the only thing that is wholly mine and entirely dependent on myself; and through it I have already become a citizen of the realm of freedom and of pure spiritual activity. * * *

In short, I do not pursue the earthly purpose for its own sake alone, or as a final aim; but only because my true final aim, obedience to the law of conscience, does not present itself to me in this world in any other shape than as the advancement of this end. I may not cease to pursue it, unless I were to deny the law of duty, or unless that law were to manifest itself to me, in this life, in some other shape than as a commandment to promote this purpose in my own place;—I shall actually cease to pursue it in another life in which that commandment shall have set before me some other purpose wholly incomprehensible to me here. In this life, I must *will* to promote it, because I must obey; whether it be *actually* promoted by the deed that follows my will thus fittingly directed is not my care; I am responsible only for the will, but not for the result. Previous to the actual deed, I can never resign this purpose; the deed, when it is completed, I may resign, and repeat it, or improve it. Thus do I live and labour, even here, in my most essential nature and in my nearest purposes, only for the other world, and my activity for it is the only thing of which I am completely certain;—in the world of sense I labour only for the sake of the other, and only because I cannot work for the other without at least *willing* to work for it.

* * *

* * * The present is the commencement of our existence; the endowments requisite for its purpose, and a firm footing in it, have been freely bestowed on us:—the future is the continuation of this existence, and in it we must acquire for ourselves a commencement, and a definite standing-point.

* * *

---

3. A significant modification of Kant, giving primacy to "will" over both theoretical and practical rationality.

This, then, is my whole sublime vocation, my true nature. I am a member of two orders:—the one purely spiritual, in which I rule by my will alone; the other sensuous, in which I operate by my deed. The whole end of reason is pure activity, absolutely by itself alone, having no need of any instrument out of itself,—independence of everything which is not reason,—absolute freedom. The will is the living principle of reason,—is itself reason, when purely and simply apprehended; that reason is active by itself alone, means, that pure will, merely as such, lives and rules. It is only the Infinite Reason that lives immediately and wholly in this purely spiritual order. The finite reason,—which does not of itself constitute the world of reason, but is only one of its many members,—lives necessarily at the same time in a sensuous order; that is to say, in one which presents to it another object, beyond a purely spiritual activity:—a material object, to be promoted by instruments and powers which indeed stand under the immediate dominion of the will, but whose activity is also conditioned by their own natural laws. Yet as surely as reason is reason, must the will operate absolutely by itself, and independently of the natural laws by which the material action is determined;—and hence the sensuous life of every finite being points towards a higher, into which the will, by itself alone, may open the way, and of which it may acquire possession,—a possession which indeed we must again sensuously conceive of as a state, and not as a mere will.

These two orders,—the purely spiritual [geistig] and the sensuous, the latter consisting possibly of an innumerable series of particular lives,—have existed since the first moment of the development of an active reason within me, and still proceed parallel to each other. The latter order is only a phenomenon for myself, and for those with whom I am associated in this life; the former alone gives it significance, purpose, and value. I am immortal, imperishable, eternal, as soon as I form the resolution to obey the laws of reason; I do not need to become so. The super-sensual [übersinnlich] world is no future world; it is now present; it can at no point of finite existence be more present than at another; not more present after an existence of myriads of lives than at this moment.[4] My sensuous existence may, in future, assume other forms, but these are just as little the true life, as its present form. By that resolution I lay hold on eternity, and cast off this earthly life and all other forms of sensuous life which may yet lie before me in futurity, and place myself far above them. I become the sole source of my own being and its phenomena, and, henceforth, unconditioned by anything without me, I have life in myself. My will, which is directed by no foreign agency in the order of the super-sensual world, but by myself alone, is this source of true life, and of eternity.

* * *

IV.

* * *

There is nothing real, lasting, imperishable in me, but these two elements:—the voice of conscience, and my free obedience. By the first, the spiritual world

4. Another Kantian theme that becomes a fundamental tenet of Emerson's Transcendentalism via Fichte (not Hegel).

bows down to me, and embraces me as one of its members; by the second I raise myself into this world, apprehend it, and re-act upon it. That Infinite Will is the mediator between it and me; for it itself is the original source of both this world and me. This is the one True and Imperishable for which my soul yearns even from its inmost depths; all else is mere appearance, ever vanishing, and ever returning in a new semblance.[5]

This Will unites me with itself; it also unites me with all finite beings like myself, and is the common mediator between us all. This is the great mystery of the invisible world, and its fundamental law, in so far as it is a *world or system of many individual wills:—the union, and direct reciprocal action, of many separate and independent wills;* a mystery which already lies clearly before every eye in the present life, without attracting the notice of any one, or being regarded as in any way wonderful. The voice of conscience, which imposes on each his particular duty, is the light-beam on which we come forth from the bosom of the Infinite, and assume our place as particular individual beings; it fixes the limits of our personality; it is thus the true original element of our nature, the foundation and material of all our life. The absolute freedom of the will, which we bring down with us from the Infinite into the world of Time, is the principle of this our life. I act:—and, the sensible intuition through which alone I become a personal intelligence being supposed, it is easy to conceive how I must necessarily know of this my action,—I know it, because it is I myself who act;—it is easy to conceive how, by means of this sensible intuition, my spiritual act appears to me as a fact in a world of sense; and how, on the other hand, by the same sensualization, the law of duty which, in itself, is a purely spiritual law, should appear to me as the command to such an action;—it is easy to conceive, how an actually present world should appear to me as the condition of this action, and, in part, as the consequence and product of it. Thus far I remain within myself and upon my own territory; everything here, which has an existence for me, unfolds itself purely and solely from myself; I see everywhere only myself, and no true existence outside of me.

* * *

Man is not a product of the world of sense, and the end of his existence cannot be attained in it. His vocation transcends Time and Space, and everything that pertains to sense. What he is, and to what he is to train himself, that he must know;—as his vocation is a lofty one, he must be able to raise his thoughts above all the limitations of sense. He must accomplish it:—where his being finds its home, there his thoughts too seek their dwelling-place; and the truly human mode of thought, that which alone is worthy of him, that in which his whole spiritual strength is manifested, is that whereby he raises himself above those limitations, whereby all that pertains to sense vanishes into nothing,—into a mere reflection, in mortal eyes, of the One, Self-existent Infinite.

* * *

---

5. This is what remains, for Fichte, of the idea of God in the aftermath of its Kantian-philosophical demythologization and demystification.

My entire complete vocation I cannot comprehend; what I shall be here-after transcends all my thoughts. A part of that vocation is concealed from me; it is visible only to One, to the Father of Spirits, to whose care it is committed. I know only that it is sure, and that it is eternal and glorious like [its source]. But that part of it which is confided to myself, I know, and know it thoroughly, for it is the root of all my other knowledge. I know assuredly, in every moment of my life, what I ought to do; and this is my whole vocation in so far as it depends on me. From this point, since my knowledge does not reach beyond it, I shall not depart; I shall not desire to know aught beyond this; I shall take my stand upon this central point, and firmly root myself here. To this shall all my thoughts and endeavours, my whole powers, be directed; my whole existence shall be interwoven with it.

I ought, as far as in me lies, to cultivate my understanding and to acquire knowledge;—but only with the purpose of preparing thereby within me a larger field and wider sphere of duty. I ought to desire to have much;—in order that much may be required of me. I ought to exercise my powers and capacities in every possible way;—but only in order to render myself a more serviceable and fitting instrument of duty, for until the commandment shall have been realized in the outward world, by means of my whole personality, I am answerable for it to my conscience. I ought to exhibit in myself, as far as I am able, humanity in all its completeness;—not for the mere sake of humanity, which in itself has not the slightest worth, but in order that virtue, which alone has worth in itself, may be exhibited in its highest perfection in human nature.[6] I ought to regard myself, body and soul, with all that is in me or that belongs to me, only as a means of duty; and only be solicitous to fulfil that, and to make myself able to fulfil it, as far as in me lies.

* * *

In this point of view I become a new creature, and my whole relations to the existing world are changed. The ties by which my mind was formerly united to this world, and by whose secret guidance I followed all its movements, are for ever sundered, and I stand free, calm and immovable, a universe to myself. No longer through my affections, but by my eye alone, do I apprehend outward objects and am connected with them; and this eye itself is purified by freedom, and looks through error and deformity to the True and Beautiful, as upon the unruffled surface of water shapes are more purely mirrored in a milder light.

My mind is for ever closed against embarrassment and perplexity, against uncertainty, doubt, and anxiety;—my heart, against grief, repentance and desire. There is but one thing that I may know,—namely, what I ought to do; and this I always know infallibly. Concerning all else I know nothing, and know that I know nothing. I firmly root myself in this my ignorance, and refrain from harassing myself with conjectures concerning that of which I know nothing. No occurrence in this world can affect me either with joy or sorrow; calm and unmoved I look down upon all things, for I know that I cannot explain a single event, nor comprehend its connexion with that which alone concerns

---

6. This radical but very Kantian sentence shows how far Fichte (like Kant) is from most versions of "humanism."

me. All that happens belongs to the plan of the Eternal World, and is good in its place: this much I know;—what in this plan is pure gain, what is only a means for the removal of some existing evil, what therefore ought to afford me more or less satisfaction, I know not. In that world all things prosper;—this satisfies me, and in this belief I stand fast as a rock;—but what in that world is merely the germ, what the blossom, and what the fruit itself, I know not.

The only matter in which I can be concerned is the progress of reason and morality in the world of reasonable beings; and this only for its own sake,—for the sake of this progress. Whether I or some one else be the instrument of this progress, whether it be my deed or that of another which prospers or is prevented, is of no importance to me. I regard myself merely as one of the instruments for carrying out the purpose of reason; I respect, love, or feel an interest in myself only as such an instrument, and desire the successful issue of my deed only in so far as it promotes this purpose. In like manner, I regard all the events of this world only with reference to this one purpose; whether they proceed from me or from others, whether they relate directly to me or to others. My breast is steeled against annoyance on account of personal offences and vexations, or exultation in personal merit; for my whole personality has disappeared in the contemplation of the purpose of my being.

* * *

The world on which but now I gazed with wonder passes away from before me and sinks from my sight. With all the fulness of life, order, and increase which I beheld in it, it is yet but the curtain by which a world infinitely more perfect is concealed from me, and the germ from which that other shall develop itself. My FAITH [GLAUBE] looks behind this veil, and cherishes and animates this germ. It sees nothing definite, but it expects more than it can conceive here below, more than it will ever be able to conceive in all time.

———

Thus do I live, thus am I, and thus am I unchangeable, firm, and completed for all Eternity;—for this is no existence assumed from without,—it is my own, true, essential Life and Being [Sein und Wesen].

SOURCE: Johann Gottlieb Fichte, The Vocation of Man, trans. William Smith, 3rd ed. (LaSalle, Ill.: Open Court Publishing, 1916), pp. 95–97, 102–9, 111–15, 126–37, 139–42, 153–54, 163, 165–68, 176. Translation modified by the editor. Except where otherwise indicated, German words in brackets are the terminology used in the German original, inserted by the editor in addition to their renderings in the translation; and unbracketed German words are the original terminology, substituted in place of their renderings in the translation by the editor for reasons given in notes and in the Hegel glossary (p. 144). Originally published in 1800 as Die Bestimmung des Menschen. The title is better translated as The Mission of Man (i.e., of humanity), or perhaps even as The Destiny of Man.

FRIEDRICH SCHELLING
(1775 – 1854)

Schelling was a phenomenon. He began his university studies at Tübingen at the age of 16, published his first book (on FICHTE) while still a student in his teens, earned a theology degree at 20, was appointed professor of philosophy at the University of Jena at the astonishingly early age of 23, wrote a flurry of books before the age of 35—and then never published another book for the remaining forty-five years of his long and very active life, while nonetheless maintaining a high reputation and attaining something like cult status. In less than twenty years, at the beginning of his career, he moved with startling speed through a series of stages in his philosophical development, prompting HEGEL to remark that he "carried on his philosophical development in public, signaling each new stage with a new treatise." Beginning as a follower of Fichte, he next developed his own version of "absolute idealism"—emphasizing the "philosophy of nature"—in rivalry with Fichte's (and also with Hegel's). He then shifted his standpoint and attention to a different way of conceiving of the relation between nature and knowledge that he called the "philosophy of identity."

Schelling ceased publishing at that point; but there was more to come, as he turned in a vaguely religious and mystical but also somewhat existential direction. There at last his philosophical journey ended, though he continued to carry on philosophically in a very public manner through four decades of lecturing—the way he chose to share this long final stage of his thinking. But it is as a leading representative of the "absolute idealist" movement between KANT and Hegel that he is best known today and had the most influence. Had it not been for Hegel, who eclipsed him in life and continued to do so in death, he would be known today as its culminating exponent. He was a remarkably complex and protean figure,

however, whose thought defies simple classification.

Like SCHILLER and Hegel, Friedrich Wilhelm Joseph Schelling ("SHELL-ing") was born in what is now southwestern Germany, in the duchy (state) of Würtemberg, in 1775. He thus was sixteen years younger than Schiller, thirteen years younger than Fichte, and five years younger than Hegel—all of whom he came to know personally as colleagues at Jena. His father, a chaplain as well as a professor of oriental studies at Tübingen University, was in a position to help the 16-year-old Schelling obtain permission to enter the university and be admitted to its Protestant residential college. There he met and roomed with Hegel and Hölderlin. While he had initially been inclined toward theology and the ministry, he soon came to share their interest in philosophy and fascination with the Greeks. He obtained a degree in theology; but by the time he did so, he was already preoccupied with Kant and Fichte. He had even begun publishing on Fichte, whose thought excited and inspired him.

By the age of 20 Schelling not only had written a book on Fichte but had also published another, setting forth his own rather Fichtean thinking, on the self (the *Ich*) as a central philosophical principle. His writings brought him to Fichte's attention and attracted wider attention as well. Publishing at a rapid rate during the next few years, he obtained his first academic appointment at Jena in 1798—where his mentor Fichte (as well as Schiller) also happened to be teaching. Fichte was dismissed from the faculty (on charges of atheism) and departed in 1799, however; and the two also parted company philosophically, as Schelling's thinking began to diverge significantly from Fichte's.

Happily for Schelling, his good friend Hegel was appointed to the philosophy faculty at Jena in 1800 (at Schelling's initiative), in the aftermath of Fichte's departure. They resumed their close personal and philosophical relationship, and even edited a journal together. Though Hegel was five years older, he was virtually unknown, whereas Schelling already had a major reputation and thus in effect was the senior partner. At Jena Schelling came under the spell of Goethe and Schiller in nearby Weimar, which their celebrity had made the center of German Romanticism. Their influence on his thinking contributed to his disaffection with the austerity and moralistic rigor of Fichte's thought. That influence also began to drive a wedge between him and Hegel, whose Romanticism was considerably more moderate than Schelling's was coming to be.

Schelling's involvement with the Romantics also had a very personal aspect, in the form of the close attachment he formed with the Romantic poet and scholar August Schlegel and his wife Caroline. He might have married their young daughter, had she not died of dysentery in 1800. It was Caroline whom he really loved, however, and the feeling was mutual. Schlegel eventually agreed to a divorce to enable her and Schelling to marry, which they did in 1803. (Yet all three remained friends.) Caroline was the love of his life and his inspiration; and her untimely death in 1809 may well have had much to do with the abrupt ending of his publishing shortly thereafter. Three years later he married a close friend of hers, Pauline Gotter.

Schelling left Jena for a position at Würzburg in 1803, and then took a position at Munich in 1806, where for the most part he remained until 1841. When Hegel's first major work, the *Phenomenology of Spirit* (1807), was published, Schelling took offense at the treatment of his thinking in it. They became increasingly estranged, and their rivalry grew. Schelling was completely eclipsed by Hegel in the 1820s. Yet after Hegel's death in 1831, he once again began to come into vogue, in part owing to the mystery surrounding the possible direction of his

thinking—a mystery only heightened by his refusal to publish. In 1841 he was made a member of the Berlin Academy (as well as Prussian privy counselor!), and he lectured at the university there until 1845.

Schelling's Berlin lectures drew an audience from far and wide (remarkably including both SØREN KIERKEGAARD and FRIEDRICH ENGELS, and even the Russian anarchist Mikhail Bakunin). It was eagerly expected that he would at last set forth the new philosophy that would both supersede his own earlier thinking and provide a major challenge and alternative to Hegelianism. For many, his lectures— which focused centrally on religion and mythology—were a disappointment; but the originality and significance of his later thought continue to be debated. He ceased lecturing publicly in 1845 after an unsuccessful lawsuit against an academic enemy who had published some of his lectures. He lived the last years of his life in Bad Ragatz in Switzerland, where he died in 1854.

Schelling's later thought revolves around the general idea that philosophical rationality, even at its systematic best, is incapable of answering the question of the meaningfulness of existence. Religion and myth, he maintained, are the keys to understanding and finding that meaning. For the Romantics authentic feeling and emotion (rather than rationality) were the touchstones not only of beauty but also of goodness and truth, and so of all of the kinds of meaning that matter most; and in view of his lifelong Romantic inclinations, it is not at all surprising that Schelling's later thought took this turn. Indeed, the surprise is the very different character of his earlier thinking, which accorded ultimate primacy to at least a very generalized conception of rationality. Schelling's version of philosophical "idealism" might be thought of as an attempt to recast its fundamental principle of the rationality of both thought and reality to render it more hospitable to a Romantic sensibility without abandoning it. This is the phase of his thought that set the stage in important ways for Hegel, who was much more influenced by it than he was by Fichte's version of idealism but who reacted in different ways against both.

Like Fichte, Schelling took it to be the case that Kant had established that the contents of perceptual experience and all objects making up the world of observable nature and material reality cannot be considered "things in themselves" with an absolute and unconditioned existence. Nature is certainly real, but it cannot be considered *absolutely* real. And the same is true of our subjective consciousness. Consciousness and objects of consciousness exist only in relation to each other, and thus have only a conditioned reality. Yet Schelling considered it necessarily to be the case that they must have an ultimate ground in some sort of absolute reality, beyond all subjectivity and all objectivity. And he maintained that this ground must be nothing other than absoluteness itself, or the most absolute of all principles: the idea of "pure identity," or "A = A." But to express itself as all of reality, this pure identity cannot be merely static: it must also be pure activity.

This idea, for Schelling, is the "absolute idea," which is "independent of subjectivity and objectivity" and which subsumes and grounds all possible distinctions, such as "thought and being," "subject and object," and "matter and form." It is no "thing" or "being" at all; and yet it is the most real of all realities, because it is their ultimate ground and is itself groundless, depending on nothing else. Or as he also puts it in the first selection below, "the absolute-ideal is also the absolute-real." It might be thought of as the active "self" of all reality—no particular "self" (*Ich*), but rather (as Fichte had called it) "the absolute *Ich*" (usually translated as "ego").

Further: since identity is the absolute self-relation ("A = A" means that "A" is identical to itself), and since Schelling takes the essence of *Geist* (best translated as "spirit") to be precisely the idea of self-expressing self-relatedness that becomes explicit (or active, developing self-relatedness), the "absolute idea" may also be conceived as the essential nature

of "absolute *Geist*," and vice versa. The whole of reality may thus be thought of as the self-realizing development of this seemingly abstract but actually richly expressive absolute principle. Indeed, since "A = A" might be considered the ultimate correspondence, it can also be considered the absolute and ultimate truth, and making it explicit may be thought of as "the absolute act of cognition," or "absolute knowing."

In this way Schelling believed that he had provided the basis for a new philosophy that would be capable of comprehending everything about the world and ourselves that there is to know about them. In its elaboration he sought to provide a reinterpretation of the status of nature, as well as of human consciousness, cognition, and spirituality, that would display not just their fundamental features but also their fundamental relatedness. By "nature" he means "the all-inclusive world of experience," even though it is also "a world outside of us." His "philosophy of nature" is not meant to compete with or replace the natural sciences, but rather is intended to provide an account of how the very possibility, the actual existence, and the fundamental character of nature are to be understood. And it more specifically is meant to deal with the question of the relation of nature to consciousness and cognition, to *Geist*, and the "absolute-ideal." Nature is the correlate of consciousness, the object of cognition, the counterpart of *Geist*, and the initial but boundlessly rich creative expression of the "absolute-ideal" of "pure identity" that is also "pure activity."

Schelling thus attaches greater significance to nature than had either Kant or Fichte, in a manner strongly reminiscent of Spinoza, whose philosophical reputation he helped to rehabilitate. But Schelling's emphasis on activity as well as identity, and on the creatively developmental expressive character of the spirit animating life and the world, sets him well apart from Spinoza. It reflects the Romanticism of Schelling's thinking, which would have been deeply alien to

Spinoza (and to Descartes, Hume, and Kant as well).

The first of the following selections shows how Schelling attempts to set forth and explain this conception of reality. In the second he deals more explicitly with our relation to and place in it. The expressiveness of nature pales, for him, in comparison with that of which humanity is capable. Schelling casts his discussion here in terms of "human freedom"; but the kind of "freedom" he has in mind has more to do with our capacity for self-transformation and self-realization through creative activity than with mere unfettered choice, "free will," or self-mastery. Indeed, he considers "the true conception of freedom" to have been "lacking in all modern systems" prior to "the discovery of Idealism." In this context he also explicitly distinguishes himself from Spinoza (while availing himself as freely as Spinoza does of the term "God,"

but appropriating it—as does Spinoza—for his own philosophical purposes).

Schelling associates genuine freedom with "the possibility of good and evil"; its key, for him, is the spirituality of human reality and the Kantian recognition that we have an "intelligible essence" or fundamental dimension of our reality that is "outside of all causal connections as it is outside or beyond all time." (Recall the conclusion to Kant's *Critique of Practical Reason*.) But Schelling takes this idea further, in a manner that at once recalls Spinoza and anticipates Hegel, maintaining that "only that is free which acts according to the laws of its own inner being and is not determined by anything else either within it or outside it." This conception of freedom—as true self-determination, in accordance with "the laws of [our] own inner being"—became one of the central themes and points of controversy in the interpretive tradition.

From Ideas for a Philosophy of Nature

From *Introduction*

What philosophy is as such cannot just be answered immediately. If it were so easy to agree about a definite concept of philosophy, one would only need to analyse this concept to see oneself at once in possession of a philosophy of universal validity. The point is this: Philosophy is not something with which our mind, without its own agency, is originally and by nature imbued. It is throughout a work of freedom. It is for each only what he has himself made it; and therefore the idea of philosophy is also only the result of philosophy itself, which, as an infinite science [*eine unendliche Wissenschaft*], is at the same time the science of itself.

Instead, therefore, of prescribing an arbitrary concept of philosophy in general or of the Philosophy of Nature in particular, in order thereafter to resolve it into its parts, I shall endeavor to let such a concept itself first *come into being*[1] before the eyes of the reader.

Meanwhile, as one must, after all, have some starting point, I shall provisionally presuppose that a Philosophy of Nature *ought* to deduce the possibility of Nature, that is of the all-inclusive world of experience,[2] from first

1. That is, "arise" (*entstehen*).
2. "Nature" for Schelling is "the all-inclusive world of experience (*Erfahrungswelt*)," rather than the world as it might be conceived independently of our (or any other creature's) experience, and as

such also encompasses more than just the world of phenomena investigated by the "natural sciences." (The translators' use of "she" to refer to Nature reflects the grammatical gender of the German noun *Natur*.)

principles. But I shall not deal with this concept analytically, or presuppose that it is correct and derive consequences from it, but before all else I shall investigate whether reality belongs to it as such, and whether it expresses anything that admits of *development*.

ON THE PROBLEMS WHICH A PHILOSOPHY OF NATURE HAS TO SOLVE

Whoever is absorbed in research into Nature, and in the sheer enjoyment of her abundance, does not ask whether Nature and experience be possible. It is enough that she is there for him; he has made her real by his very *act*,[3] and the question of what is possible is raised only by one who believes that he does not hold the reality in his *hand*. Whole epochs have been spent in research into Nature, and yet one does not weary of it. Some have devoted their entire lives to this avocation and have not ceased to pray to the veiled goddess. Great spirits have lived in their own world, untroubled about the principles of their discoveries; and what is the whole reputation of the shrewdest doubter against the life of a man who has carried a world in his head and the whole of Nature in his imagination?

How a world outside us, how a Nature and with it experience,[4] is possible— these are questions for which we have *philosophy* to thank; or rather, *with* these questions philosophy came to be. Prior to them mankind had lived in a (philosophical) state of nature.[5] At that time man was still at one with himself and the world about him. In obscure recollection this condition still floats before even the most wayward thinker. Many never lose it and would be happy in themselves, if the fateful example did not lead them astray; for Nature releases nobody willingly from her tutelage, and there are no *native* sons of freedom. Nor would it be conceivable how man should ever have forsaken that condition, if we did not know that his spirit [*Geist*], whose element is *freedom*, strives to make *itself* free, to disentangle itself from the fetters of Nature and her guardianship, and must abandon itself to the uncertain fate of its own powers, in order one day to return, as victor and by its own merit, to that position in which, unaware of itself, it spent the childhood of its reason.

As soon as man sets himself in opposition to the external world (how he does so we shall consider later), the first step to philosophy has been taken. With that separation, reflection [*Reflexion*] first begins; he separates from now on what Nature had always united, separates the object from the intuition,[6] the concept from the image, finally (in that he becomes his own *object*) himself from himself.

But this separation is only *means*, not *end*. For the essence of man is action.[7] But the less he reflects upon himself, the more active he is. His noblest activity is that which is not aware of itself. As soon as he makes himself object, the *whole* man no longer acts; he has suspended one part of his activity so as

3. Schelling is talking about the "world of experience," which (as KANT had convinced him) is as it is owing to the way in which we—that is, our minds—have structured our experience.
4. Here Schelling shows that he assimilates Nature conceived as "a world outside us" (but still considered as it is experienced) to what he above calls "the all-inclusive world of experience."
5. That is, in a state of naïve innocence.
6. That is, appearance (*Anschauung*).
7. Perhaps better translated as "the nature [true being, fundamental reality] of man [humans] is action" (*das Wesen des Menschen ist Handeln*).

to be able to reflect upon the other. Man is not born to waste his mental power in conflict against the fantasy of an imaginary world, but to exert all his powers upon a world which has influence upon him, lets him feel its forces, and upon which he can react. Between him and the world, therefore, no rift must be established; contact and reciprocal action must be possible between the two, for only so does man become man. Originally in man there is an absolute equilibrium of forces and of consciousness. But he can upset this equilibrium through freedom, in order to reestablish it through freedom. But only in equilibrium of forces is there health.

Mere reflection, therefore, is a spiritual sickness in mankind, the more so where it imposes itself in domination over the whole man, and kills at the root what in germ is his highest being, his spiritual life [*sein geistiges Leben*], which issues only from Identity. It is an evil which accompanies man into life itself, and distorts all his intuition even for the more familiar objects of consideration. But its preoccupation with dissection does not extend only to the phenomenal world; so far as it separates the spiritual principle from this, it fills the intellectual world with chimeras, against which, because they lie beyond all reason, it is not even possible to fight. It makes that separation between man and the world permanent, because it treats the latter as a thing in itself, which neither intuition nor imagination, neither understanding nor reason, can reach.

In contrast to this stands the true philosophy, which regards reflection as such merely as a means. Philosophy *must* presuppose that original divorce, because without it we should have no need to philosophize.

* * *

But now beyond and above Nature, in the ordinary notion of it, nothing higher is acknowledged than mind [*Geist*].[8] However, if we now want to conceive the Life-force as a spiritual principle, then we totally abolish that concept in so doing. For *force* means what, at least as a *principle*, we can put at the apex of natural science, and what, although not itself presentable, yet, in the *way it works*, is definable by physical laws. But how mind [*Geist*] can act physically we have not the slightest idea; for that reason also, a mental [*geistig*] principle cannot be called *Life-force*, an expression by which one always at least suggests the hope of allowing that principle to work according to physical laws.

But if we forgo, as we are then compelled to do, this concept (of a Life-force), we are now obliged to take refuge in a completely antithetical system, in which at once mind [*Geist*] and matter stand opposed to each other, regardless of the fact that we now understand how mind affects matter as little as we could previously understand how matter affects mind.

Mind [*Geist*] considered as the principle of life [*Leben*], is called *soul* [*Seele*]. I shall not repeat the objections that have long since been brought against the philosophy of the dualists. It has hitherto been contested for the most part from principles which had as little content as the contested system itself. We do not ask how in general a connection is possible between soul and body

---

8. "Mind" is a common but misleading translation of *Geist*, a term central to the interpretive tradition after Kant (with different meanings for different figures). "Spirit" comes closer to capturing its richness. *Geist* is best left untranslated.

(a question to which one is not entitled, because the questioner himself does not understand it) but rather—what one can understand and must answer—how the idea of such a connection has arisen *in us*. That I think, imagine, will, and that this thinking, etc., can so little be a result of my body, that on the contrary the latter only becomes *my* body through these capacities to think and to will, I know full well. Let it meanwhile be permitted, moreover, for the sake of speculation, to distinguish the principle of motion from the moved, the soul from the body, despite the fact that as soon as the talk is of action we completely forget this distinction. Now with all these assumptions, at least this much is obvious, that if there is in me life and soul, the last as something distinct from the body, I can become aware of either only through *immediate* experience. That I *am* (think, will, etc.) is something that I must know, if I know anything at all. Thus I understand how an idea of my own being and life arises in me, because if I understand anything whatsoever, I must understand this. Also, because I am immediately aware of my own being, the inference to a soul in me, even if the conclusion should be false, at least rests on *one* indubitable premise, that I *am, live, imagine, will*.

But how do I now come to transfer *being, life,* etc., to things *outside* me? For just as soon as this happens, my immediate knowledge is converted into *mediate*. But now I maintain that there can be only an *immediate* knowledge of being and life, and that what *is* and *lives* only is and lives insofar as it first and foremost exists *for itself*, is aware of its life through being alive. Suppose, then, that there appears to me in my perception an organic being, freely self-moving, then I certainly know that this being *exists*, that it is *for me*, but not that it *exists for itself* and *in itself*. For life can as little be represented outside life as consciousness outside consciousness. So even an empirical conviction that something lives outside me is absolutely impossible. For the Idealist can say that your representing to yourself organized, free, self-moving bodies can just as well belong simply to the necessary peculiarities of your faculty of representation; and even the philosophy which bestows life on everything external to me does not permit the idea of this life outside me to come into me from *outside*.

But if this idea arises only *in me*, how can I be persuaded that anything corresponds to it outside me? It is also obvious that I am persuaded of a life and self-existence outside me only *practically*. I must in practice be *compelled* to acknowledge beings outside me, who are like me. If I were not compelled to enter into the company of people [*Menschen*], outside me and into all the practical relationships associated with that; if I did not know that beings, who resemble me in external shape and appearance, have no *more* reason to acknowledge freedom and mentality[9] in me than I have to acknowledge the same in them; in fine, if I were not aware that my moral existence only acquires purpose and direction through the existence of other moral beings outside me, then left to mere speculation, I could of course doubt whether humanity [*Menschheit*] dwelt behind each face and freedom within each breast. All this is confirmed by our commonest judgements. Only of beings external to me, who put themselves on an equal footing with me in life, between whom and myself giving and receiving, doing and suffering, are fully reciprocal, do I

9. That is, spirituality (*Geistigkeit*).

acknowledge that they are spiritual [*geistig*] in character. On the other hand, if the rather curious question is brought up, whether animals also have souls, a person of common sense is at once taken aback, because, with the affirmation of that, he would consider himself committed to something he cannot immediately know.

If in the end we go back to the original source of the dualistic belief, that a soul [*Seele*] distinct from the body dwells at least in *me*, then what is it in me which itself in turn judges that I consist of body and soul, and what is this I [*Ich*] which is supposed to consist of body and soul? Here, clearly, there is something still higher, which, freely and independently of the body, gives the body a soul, conceives body and soul together, and does not itself enter into this union—a higher principle, as it seems, in which body and soul are themselves again identical.

Finally, if we persist in this dualism, we now have close at hand the antithesis from which we began: mind [*Geist*] and matter. For the same incomprehensibility, as to how connection is possible between matter and mind, continues to oppress us. One can conceal from oneself the finality of this antithesis by deceptions of all kinds, can insert between mind and matter any number of physical intermediaries, which come to be ever more and more tenuous. But sometime, somewhere, a point must surely come where mind and matter are one, or where the great leap we have so long sought to avoid becomes inevitable; and in this all theories are alike.

Whether I allow animal spirits, electrical fluids, or types of gas to suffuse or fill the nerves, and thereby to propagate impressions from outside into the sensorium, or whether I pursue the soul into the uttermost (and still more problematical) humours of the brain (a project which at least has the merit of having done the *uttermost*) is, with respect to the *matter in hand*, altogether indifferent. It is clear that our critique has come full circle, but not that we have become in any degree wiser than we were to begin with, about that antithesis from which we started. We leave behind man [*den Menschen*], as evidently the most devious problem of all philosophy, and our critique ends here in the same extremity with which it began.

If, finally, we gather up Nature into a single Whole, *mechanism*, that is, a regressive series of causes and effects, and *purposiveness*, that is, independence of mechanism, simultaneity of causes and effects, stand confronting each other. If we unite these two extremes, the idea arises in us of a purposiveness of the whole; Nature becomes a circle which returns into itself, a self-enclosed system. The series of causes and effects ceases entirely, and there arises a reciprocal connection of *means* and *end*; neither could the individual become *real* without the whole, nor the whole without the individual.

Now this absolute purposiveness of the whole of Nature is an Idea [*Idee*], which we do not think arbitrarily, but *necessarily*. We feel ourselves forced to relate every individual to such a purposiveness of the whole; where we find something in Nature that seems purposeless or quite contrary to purpose, we believe the whole scheme of things to be torn apart, or do not rest until the apparent refractoriness to purpose is converted to purposiveness from another viewpoint. It is therefore a necessary maxim of the reflective reason, to presuppose everywhere in Nature a connection by end and means. And although we do not transform this maxim into a constitutive law, we still follow it so steadfastly and so naïvely that we openly assume that Nature will, as it were, voluntarily come to meet our endeavour to discover absolute purposiveness in her. Similarly, we proceed with complete confidence in the agreement of Nature with the maxims of our reflective reason, from special subordinate laws to general higher laws; nor do we cease to assume *a priori*, even of phenomena which still stand isolated in the series of our perceptions, that *they* too are interconnected through some common principle. And we only believe in a Nature external to us where we discern multiplicity of effects and unity of means.

What then is that secret bond which couples our mind [*Geist*] to Nature, or that hidden organ through which Nature speaks to our mind or our mind to Nature? We grant you in advance all your explanations of how such a purposive Nature has come to be actual *outside us*. For to explain this purposiveness by the fact that a divine intelligence is its author is not to philosophize, but to propound pious opinions. By that you have explained to us virtually nothing; for we require to know, not how such a Nature arose outside us, but how even the very *idea* of such a Nature has got *into us*; not merely how we have, say, arbitrarily generated it, but how and why it originally and *necessarily* underlies everything that our race has ever thought about Nature. For the existence of such a Nature *outside me* is still far from explaining the existence of such a Nature *in me*; for if you assume that a predetermined harmony occurs between the two, indeed that is just the object of our question. Or if you maintain that we simply *impose* such an idea on Nature, then no inkling of what Nature is and ought to be for us has ever entered your soul. For what we want is not that Nature should coincide with the laws of our mind *by chance* (as if through some *third* intermediary), but that *she herself*, necessarily and originally, should not only *express*, but *even realize*, the laws of our mind [*unseres Geistes*], and that she is, and is called, Nature only insofar as she does so.

Nature should be mind [*Geist*] made visible, mind [*Geist*] the invisible Nature.[1] Here then, in the absolute identity of mind *in us* and Nature *outside us*, the problem of the possibility of a Nature external to us must be resolved. The final goal of our further research is, therefore, this idea of Nature; if we succeed in attaining this, we can also be certain to have dealt satisfactorily with that problem.

———

These are the main problems, whose solution is to be the purpose of this essay.

But this essay does not begin *from above* (with the establishment of principles), but *from below* (with experimental findings and the testing of previous systems).

Only when I have reached the goal which I have set myself will it be permissible for me to retrace in reverse the course which has been run.

---

1. A very important sentence. In the original, "Die Natur soll der sichtbare Geist, der Geist die unsichtbare Natur sein."

Supplement to the Introduction: Exposition of the General Idea of Philosophy as Such, and of the Philosophy of Nature in Particular, as a Necessary and Integral Part of It

Against the empirical realism, which, before Kant, had become a general system of thought and was even dominant in philosophy, in consequence of the necessity with which every one-sidedness immediately calls up another opposed to it, only an equally empirical idealism could at first arise and be accredited. In Kant himself, of course, it was not so fully elaborated in its entire empirical character as it appeared among his followers, but it was, in germ, implicit in his writings. Those who had not laid empiricism aside, before they encountered him, would also not have acquired it through him. It remained quite the same, only translated into another, idealistic-sounding language, and returned in an altered form all the more obstinately the more certainly those, who had taken it in this form from Kant, were persuaded that they had in every respect freed themselves from it and risen superior to it. That the determinations of things by and for the understanding in no way bear upon things *in themselves*, this they accepted; meanwhile, these things-in-themselves still had the same relation to the conscious mind as had previously been ascribed to empirical things, the relation of affecting, of cause and effect. The foregoing Introduction is in part directed against empirical realism in itself, in part against that absurd combination of the crudest empiricism with a kind of idealism, which had developed out of the Kantian school.

Both are in certain measure smitten with their own weapons. Against the first, those concepts and ways of thinking, which it uses itself, as derived from experience, are exploited only inasmuch as it is shown that they are degenerate and misused ideas. Against the second, all that was needed was the eviction of the first contradiction which lies at the base, and which on particular occasions returns only the more strikingly and more glaringly.

In the present supplement[2] what has been done, therefore, is to set out in more positive fashion the idea of philosophy in itself, and that of the Philosophy of Nature especially, as the one necessary aspect of the whole of this science [*Wissenschaft*].

The first step to philosophy, and the condition without which it cannot even be entered, is the insight that the absolute-ideal is also the absolute-real[3] and that without this there is only sensible and conditioned, but no absolute and unconditioned, reality. Those upon whom the absolute-ideal has not yet dawned as the absolute-real can be driven to the point of this insight in various ways, but it can be proved only indirectly, not directly, since it is actually the ground and principle of all demonstration.

We shall indicate one of the possible ways to raise a person to this insight. Philosophy is an absolute science [*Wissenschaft*]; for what can be extracted

---

2. Added to the second edition of 1803.
3. The fundamental principle of "absolute idealism": what is "absolutely real" is the "absolutely ideal" (*das absolute-Ideale auch das absolute Reale ist*), rather than the merely material. Its comprehension (as Schelling goes on to explain) is philosophy conceived as "absolute knowing," or knowledge of what is "absolute"—which (as he contends) is the "absolute-ideal" itself.

from the conflicting concepts, as universally agreed, is that, far from borrowing the principles of its knowledge from another science, it also has (among other subjects, at least) knowledge as its object, and so cannot itself in turn be a subordinate science. It follows immediately from this formal definition of philosophy as a science [*Wissenschaft*], which, if it exists, cannot be of a conditioned kind, that it can also know its objects, whatever they may be, not in a conditioned but only in an unconditioned and absolute way, and thus also know only the absolute of these objects themselves. Against every possible definition of philosophy, whereby it has as its object any contingency, particularity or conditionality, it could be shown that this contingency or particularity has already been pre-empted by one of the other, supposedly or actually existing, sciences. If, therefore, philosophy, in order to know in an absolute way, can only know of the absolute, and if this absolute stands open to her only through knowing itself, then it is clear that the first idea of philosophy already rests on the tacit presupposition of a possible indifference between absolute knowing and the absolute itself, and consequently on the fact that the absolute-ideal is the absolute-real.

This argument has in no way proved anything as to the reality of this idea, which also, as said, being the ground of all evidence, can only prove itself. Our inference is merely hypothetical: If philosophy exists, then that is its necessary presupposition. An opponent can now deny either the hypothesis or the validity of the argument. Either he will do the first in a scientific manner, and thus will hardly be able to accomplish it otherwise than by himself embarking upon a science of knowledge, that is, upon philosophy. In order to meet him, we must await him in this attempt, but may be convinced in advance that whatever he may bring forward for such a purpose will certainly be fundamental principles, which we could contest with adequate reasons, so that, although we may be unable to persuade him, since he can only give himself the initial insight, he is also unable to bring forward the least thing by which he would not expose striking weaknesses to us. Or again, he will simply assure us in general, without any scientific [*wissenschaftlich*] grounds at all, that he does not and is not disposed to admit philosophy as a science. This we are by no means to grant, since without philosophy he cannot know at all that there is no philosophy, and only his knowledge interests us. This question, therefore, he must allow others to settle among themselves; he himself forgoes any opinion on the matter.

The other alternative is that he denies the correctness of the argument. This could happen, according to the above account, only if he puts forward another conception of philosophy, on the strength of which a conditioned knowledge would be possible in it. There is nothing to prevent him from calling something of the sort philosophy, even if it were empirical psychology; but the place of the absolute science and the inquiry into it will only remain more certain, since it is self-evident that the misuse of a word indicating something, in which it is given the meaning of lesser things, cannot abolish the thing itself. Also, whoever possesses philosophy can be perfectly convinced in advance that whatever conception of philosophy might be brought forward, other than that of the absolute science [*Wissenschaft*], he would always and unfailingly be able to prove that that conception, so far from being that of philosophy, is not even that of a science at all.

In a word, the insight, that the absolute-ideal is the absolute-real, is the condition for any higher scientific attitude [*Wissenschaftlichkeit*], not only in philosophy, but also in geometry and the whole of mathematics. The same indifference of the real and ideal, which the mathematical sciences assume in a subordinate sense, thus makes philosophy valid in itself, only in the highest and most universal meaning, once all relation to the sensible has been removed from her. Upon it rests that authenticity [*Evidenz*][4] which is peculiar to the higher sciences. Only on this basis, where nothing but absolute ideality is demanded for absolute reality, can the geometer ascribe absolute reality to his construction, which is nevertheless an ideal one, and assert that what is valid of this construction as form is also eternally and necessarily valid of the object.

If anybody wishes to remind the philosopher, on the other hand, that that absolute-ideal is once again only *for him* and only *his thinking*, as empirical idealism especially can as a rule bring nothing against Spinoza[5] except only that he erred in not reflecting again upon his own thought, wherein he would then undoubtedly have realized that his system, after all, is again just a product of *his* thinking, then we bid such a one, for his part, just to heed the quite simple consideration that indeed this very reflection, by which he makes this thinking *his* thinking, and consequently subjective, is again only *his* reflection, and thus a merely subjective affair, so that here one subjectivity is corrected and removed by another. As he will not be able to deny that, so he must concede that this absolute-ideal is therefore in itself neither a subjective nor an objective, neither his own nor anyone else's thinking, but just absolute thinking.

In the whole of the following exposition we presuppose this acknowledgement of the indifference between the absolute-ideal and the absolute-real, which itself is an absolute, and we must assure everybody that, if he conceives or requires yet another absolute besides that, not only can we not help him to any knowledge of it, but also in our own knowledge of the absolute could not possibly become intelligible to him.

We have to proceed from this idea of the *absolute-ideal*; we define it as *absolute knowing*, the absolute act of cognition.

An absolute knowing is not one in which subjective and objective are united as opposites, but one in which the entire subjective is the entire objective, and *vice versa*. The absolute identity of subjective and objective as the principle of philosophy has been understood in part merely negatively (as mere non-difference) and in part as the mere conjunction of two intrinsic opposites in another, which was here to be the absolute, and partly it is still so understood. The intention was, rather, that subjective and objective, each also considered on its own, should be one, not merely in a union accidental, or at least alien, to them. In general, in this characterization of the highest idea of subjective and objective, it should be not presupposed, but rather indicated, that both, whether opposed or combined, are simply to be conceived from out of that identity alone.

---

4. That is, evidentness.
5. Benedict (Baruch) de Spinoza (1632–1677), Dutch philosopher, for whom "God" and "Nature" were two designations of one and the same fundamental and all-encompassing reality or "substance," of which thought and extension were simply two different "attributes."

The absolute, as perhaps everybody will automatically admit who has thought it over at all, is necessarily *pure identity*; it is just absoluteness and nothing else, and absoluteness *per se* is equal only to itself; but it does indeed also belong to the idea of that, that this pure identity, independent of subjectivity and objectivity, *as this*, and without ceasing to be so in one or the other, is itself matter and form, subject and object. This follows from the fact that only the absolute is the absolute-ideal, and *vice versa*.[6]

That equal and pure absoluteness, that equal identity in the subjective and objective, was what we have defined in this characterization as the identity, *the equal essence* of subjective and objective. Subjective and objective are, according to this explanation, not one, as opposites are, for with this we should just admit them as such; rather, it is a subjectivity and objectivity only *insofar as* that pure absoluteness, which in itself must be independent of both and can be neither the one nor the other, introduces itself, for itself and through itself, into both as the equal absoluteness.

We have to demonstrate the necessity of this self-differentiation of the undivided absoluteness into subject and object still more precisely.

The absolute is an eternal act of cognition, which is itself matter and form, a producing in which, in eternal fashion, it converts itself in its totality as Idea, as sheer identity, into the real, into the form, and conversely, in equally eternal fashion, resolves itself as form, and to that extent as object, into the essence [*das Wesen*] or subject. Simply in order to make this relationship clear to oneself (for in itself there is no transition here), let the absolute be thought of, to start with, purely as matter, as pure identity, as sheer absoluteness; now since its essence is a producing and it can take the form only out of itself, yet is itself pure identity, so the form too must be *this identity*, and thus essence and form in it must be *one and the same*, namely, the equal pure absoluteness.

At that moment (if we may so call it) at which it is mere matter or essence, the absolute would be pure subjectivity, enclosed and hidden in itself. In that it makes its own essence into form, that whole subjectivity in its absoluteness becomes objectivity, just as in the resumption and transformation of form into essence, the whole objectivity, in its absoluteness, becomes subjectivity.

Here there is no before and no after, no exit of the absolute out of itself or transition to action. *It is itself* this eternal activity, *since it belongs to its Idea* that *immediately through its concept it should also be, that its essence should also be form for it, and the form essence.*

In the absolute act of cognition we have provisionally distinguished two actions, that in which it delivers its subjectivity and infinity entirely into objectivity and finitude, up to the essential unity of the latter with the former, and that in which, in its objectivity or form, it again resolves itself into essence. Since it is not subject, not object, but only the identical essence of both, it cannot, as absolute act of cognition, be here the pure subject or there the pure object, and as subject (where it resolves the form into essence) and as object (where it moulds the essence into form), it is always only the pure absoluteness, the whole identity. Any difference which can take place here is not the absoluteness itself, which remains the same, but only in the fact that in the one act, as essence, it is changed undivided into form, and in the other, as

6. A succinct statement of what Schelling means by "absolute idealism."

form, is changed undivided into essence, and so fashions itself eternally into unity with itself.

In the absolute itself these two unities are not distinguished. One might be tempted now to define the absolute itself in turn as the unity of these two unities, but to speak precisely, it is not that, since, as the unity of both, it can be recognized and defined only insofar as these are distinguished, which is precisely not the situation here. It is therefore just *the absolute* without further determination. In this absoluteness and in the eternal act, it is utterly one, and yet, in this unity, again immediately a totality of the three unities, namely, that in which the essence is absolutely shaped into form, that in which the form is absolutely shaped into essence, and that in which both these absolutenesses are again one absoluteness.

The absolute produces nothing out of itself except itself, thus again an absolute; each of the three unities is the whole absolute act of cognition, and, as essence or identity, itself becomes form again, just as does the absolute itself. In each of the three unities, seen from its formal side, there is a special feature, for example, that in it the infinite is embodied in the finite, or *vice versa*, but this special character does not remove the absoluteness, nor is it removed by itself, although in the absoluteness where the form is fashioned in complete equality to the essence, and is itself essence, this special character is not distinguished.

What we have designated here as unities are the same as what others have understood under the terms *Ideas*[7] or *monads*,[8] although the true meaning of these concepts has long since been lost. Every idea is a particular, which as such is absolute; absoluteness is always one, just as is the subject-object character of this absoluteness in its own identity; only *the manner*, in which the absoluteness is subject-object in the Idea, makes the difference.

The Ideas are nothing other than syntheses, in which the absolute identity of universal and particular (of essence and form), so far as this identity is itself again universal, is combined with the particular form; and precisely because this particular form is again equated to the absolute form or essence, there can be no individual thing in these Ideas. Only insofar as one of the unities, which again in the absolute itself are as one, conceives itself, its essence, its identity, as mere form, and accordingly as relative difference, does it symbolize itself through individual actual things. The individualized thing is only one moment of the eternal act of transformation of the essence into the form; for this reason the form is distinguished as particular, for example as the embodiment of the infinite into the finite; but that which becomes objective through this form is still only the absolute unity itself. Since, however, all moments and degrees of the absolute embodiment (for instance, of essence into form) lie at once in the absolute form, and since in everything which appears to us as particular the universal or essence is absolutely taken up in

7. In German, *Ideen*: not particular thoughts that might pass through someone's head, but rather certain very basic formal structures that Schelling supposes to be fundamental to all thought and reality. In appropriating the term in this way, Schelling intended to be true to Kant, who had used this term in a technical sense to refer to certain basic "guiding ideas" of reason and thought but had warned against taking them to refer to existing realities.

8. A term originating in Greek philosophy but particularly associated with Gottfried Wilhelm Leibniz (1646–1716), who applied it to the basic substances that are immaterial but make up all of reality.

the Idea, so nothing in itself has either finitely or truly arisen; it has been expressed, rather, in absolute and eternal fashion, in the unity in which it was conceived.

Things-in-themselves are therefore the Ideas in the eternal act of cognition, and since ideas in the absolute are themselves in turn one Idea, so all things, likewise, are truly and intrinsically one essence, namely that of pure absoluteness in the form of subject-object identification, and even in appearance, where absolute unity becomes objective only through particular form, for example, through individual actual things, all difference between these is still not essential or qualitative, but merely an inessential and quantitative difference, resting on the degree of embodiment of the infinite into the finite.

With respect to the last-mentioned, the following law is to be noted: that insofar as the infinite is embodied into a finite, the latter, as finite, is itself again embodied into the infinite, and that both these unities, with respect to that essence, are again one unity.

The absolute, in the eternal cognitive act, expands itself into the particular, merely so that, in the absolute embodiment of its infinity into the finite itself, it may take back the latter into itself, and in it both are one act. Thus where the one moment of this act, for example, the expansion of the unity into multiplicity, becomes *as such* objective, there the other moment, the resumption of the finite into the infinite, must likewise become objective, just as that which corresponds to the act as it is in itself—where, namely, the one (expansion of the infinite into the finite) is immediately the other also (re-embodiment of the finite into the infinite)—and each in particular become distinguishable.

We see that in this manner just as that eternal knowing permits knowledge of itself in distinguishability, and out of the night of its essence delivers itself into daylight, the three unities immediately emerge from it as particular.

The first, as these differentiate, is Nature, which, as objectification of the infinite in the finite, immediately changes again into the other in the absolute, as the latter changes into it; and the other is the ideal world; and the third becomes distinguished as such where the particular unity of each one, in both of them, in that it becomes absolute for itself, at the same time resolves itself and changes into the other.

But just because of Nature and the ideal world each contains a point of absoluteness, where both opposites flow together, each must again, if it is to be distinguished as the *particular* unity, contain the three unities distinguishably in itself; in this distinguishability and subordination under one unity, we call them *potencies*, so that this general type of appearance necessarily repeats itself also in the particular, and as the same and equivalent in the real and the ideal worlds.

By the foregoing we have led the reader so far that in general he might demand in the first place an intuition of the world in which alone there is philosophy; an intuition, that is, of the absolute world, as also of the scientific form in which it necessarily presents itself. We needed the general idea of philosophy itself in order to present the Philosophy of Nature as the one necessary and integrative aspect of the whole of this science. Philosophy is the science [*Wissenschaft*] of the absolute, but as the absolute in its eternal activity necessarily grasps two sides in one, one real and the other ideal, so philosophy, seen in its formal aspect, necessarily has to divide itself in accordance with the two sides, although its essence consists just in seeing both sides as one in the absolute act of cognition.

The real side of the eternal act is revealed in Nature; Nature in itself, or eternal Nature, is just mind [Geist] born into objectivity, the essence [Wesen] of God introduced into form, save only that in Him this introducing immediately grasps the other unity. Phenomenal nature, on the other hand, is the embodiment of essence in form appearing as such or in particularity, and hence is eternal Nature, so far as it takes on itself for a body, and so presents itself through itself as particular form. Nature, so far as it appears as Nature, that is, as this *particular* unity, is accordingly as such already *external* to the absolute, not Nature as the absolute act of cognition itself (*Natura naturans*), but Nature as the mere body or symbol thereof (*Natura naturata*).[9] In the absolute, it exists with the opposed unity, which is that of the ideal world, as one unity, but just for that reason the absolute contains neither Nature as Nature nor ideal world as ideal world, but both are as one world.

If we therefore define philosophy as a whole according to that wherein it surveys and presents everything, namely the absolute act of cognition, of which even Nature is again only one side, the Idea of all ideas, then it is Idealism. Idealism is and remains, therefore, the whole of philosophy, and only under itself does the latter again comprehend realism and idealism, save that the first absolute Idealism is not to be confused with this other, which is of a merely relative kind.

In eternal Nature the absolute becomes, for itself in its absoluteness (which is sheer identity), a particular, a being, but in phenomenal nature only the particular form is known as particular, the absolute veils itself here in what is other than it is in its absoluteness, in a finite, a being, which is its symbol, and as such, like every symbol, takes on a life independent of that which it means. In the ideal world it lays the veil aside, as it were, and appears even as that which it is, as ideal, as act of cognition, but, on the other hand, in such a way that it leaves the other side behind and only contains the one, that of reresolution of the finitude in infinitude, of the particular in the essence.

This aspect, in which the absolute appears in the phenomenal ideal without change into an other, has given occasion for this relative-ideal to be granted a priority over the real, and for a merely relative idealism to be set up as the absolute philosophy itself. The system of the *Wissenschaftslehre*[1] is unmistakably of this kind.

The whole from which the Philosophy of Nature issues is *absolute* Idealism. The Philosophy of Nature does not take precedence over Idealism, nor is it in any way opposed to it so far as it is absolute, but certainly is opposed, so far as it is relative idealism, and accordingly grasps only the one side of the absolute act of cognition, which, without the other, is unthinkable.

In order to fulfill our purpose completely, we still have to mention in particular something of the inner relationships and structure of the Philosophy of Nature as a whole. It has already been recalled that the particular unity,

9. Two Latin phrases, literally "Nature naturing" (or nature doing its thing) and "Nature natured" (or nature as it has come to be), respectively; the distinction they draw was particularly important to Spinoza.

1. The title of FICHTE's main work, to which Schelling is here referring; see the source note to *Science of Knowledge*, p. 88.

just because it is this, also again comprehends, in itself and for itself, all unities. So too with Nature. These unities, each of which signifies a definite degree of embodiment of the infinite into the finite, are represented in three potencies of Nature-philosophy. The first unity, which in embodying the infinite into the finite is itself again this embodiment, presents itself as a whole through the *universal structure of the world*, individually through the series of bodies. The other unity, of the reverse embodiment of the particular into the universal or essence, expresses itself, though always in subordination to the real unity which is predominant in Nature, in *universal mechanism*, where the universal or essence issues as *light*, the particular as *bodies*, in accordance with all dynamical determinations. Finally, the absolute integration into one, or indifferencing, of both unities, yet still in the real, is expressed by *organism*, which is therefore once more the *in-itself* of the first two unities (though considered, not as synthesis, but as primary), and the perfect mirror-image of the absolute in Nature and for Nature.

But even here, where the embodiment of the infinite into the finite reaches the point of absolute indifferencing, it immediately resolves itself again into its opposite and therewith into the aether of absolute ideality, so that with the perfectly real image of the absolute in the real world, the most perfect organism, the completely *ideal* image, also immediately enters, as reason, although even this again only for the *real* world; and here, in the real world, the two sides of the absolute act of cognition show themselves as archetype and ectype[2] of each other, just as they do in the absolute; reason symbolizing itself in the organism, just as the absolute act of cognition does in eternal Nature; and the organism transfigured into absolute ideality in reason, just as Nature is transfigured in the eternal resumption of the finite into the infinite.

The exposition of the same potencies and relationships for the ideal side, where they return, the same as to essence, although altered as to form, lies here outside our province.

If one considers the Philosophy of Nature on its philosophical side, of which the present work, in its first version, still contained only remote premonitions, confused by the subordinate concepts of a merely relative idealism, then up to the present time it is the most fully worked out endeavour to set forth the theory of Ideas and the identity of Nature with the world of Ideas. In Leibniz this exalted view had at last been revived, but it remained in great part, even with him, and still more so with his successors, confined merely to the most generalized doctrines, moreover quite uncomprehended by them, and not developed scientifically even by him, there being no attempt to apprehend the universe genuinely by means of this view or to make it universally and objectively valid. What had not perhaps for long been so much as suspected, or at best been considered impossible, namely the complete presentation of the mental [*geistig*] world in the laws and forms of the phenomena, and thus, conversely, the complete apprehension of these laws and forms from the mental world, has in part been actually achieved already by the Philosophy of Nature, while in part it is on the way to doing so.

As perhaps the most evident example, we cite the construction that it gives

---

2. A copy from an original; an instantiation in the world of external reality (as opposed to its ideal archetype).

for the universal laws of motion of the heavenly bodies, a construction of which one would perhaps not have believed that the germ of it already lay in Plato's theory of Ideas[3] and the monadology of Leibniz.

Considered from the side of the speculative knowledge of Nature as such, or as speculative physics, there has been nothing like the Philosophy of Nature before, unless one were to count here the mechanical physics of le Sage,[4] which, like all atomistic theories, is a tissue of empirical fictions and arbitrary assumptions devoid of any philosophy. What antiquity provided, of a somewhat more closely related kind, has for the most part been lost. After the blind and mindless type of natural research, which has generally established itself since the corruption of philosophy by Bacon and of physics by Boyle and Newton,[5] with the Philosophy of Nature a higher knowledge of Nature begins; a new instrument for the intuiting and conceiving of Nature is taking shape. Whoever has raised himself to the standpoint of Nature-philosophy, and is in possession of the intuition it calls for and the method it employs, will hardly be able to refrain from admitting that it puts one in a position to solve, with assurance and necessity, precisely those problems which have seemed impenetrable to previous nature research, *although admittedly in an area quite other than that where their solution had been sought.*

What distinguishes the Philosophy of Nature from all that have hitherto been called *theories* of natural phenomena, is that the latter concluded to the grounds from the phenomena, arranged causes according to effects, in order subsequently to derive the latter from the former. Apart from the everlasting circle in which those fruitless endeavours revolve, theories of this sort could still, even on reaching their peak, establish only a possibility that such is the case, but never the necessity. The common pronouncements against theories of this kind, which empiricists constantly denounce, while they can never suppress their inclination toward them, are what even now one hears brought against the Philosophy of Nature. In the Philosophy of Nature, explanations take place as little as they do in mathematics; it proceeds from principles certain in themselves, without any direction prescribed to it, as it were, by the phenomena. Its direction lies in itself, and the more faithful it remains to this, the more certainly do the phenomena step of their own accord into that place in which alone they can be seen as necessary, and this place in the system is the only explanation of them that there is.

Within this necessity, in the universal coherence of the system and in the type which flows from the essence of the absolute and the Ideas themselves for Nature as a whole and in detail, we see comprised the phenomena, not only of universal Nature, about which only hypotheses were previously known, but equally simply and surely the phenomena of the organic world as well, whose relationships have always been counted among the most deeply hidden and forever unknowable. What still remained over for the most pregnant hypotheses, the possibility of accepting or not accepting them, here falls away altogether. For one who has but grasped the coherence as such, and has himself

3. For the Greek philosopher Plato (ca. 427–ca. 347 B.C.E.), the fundamental, timeless universals or types of which worldly objects are (imperfect) copies.
4. Georges-Louis Lesage (1724–1804), Genevan physicist.
5. Three British thinkers: Sir Francis Bacon (1561–1626), Robert Boyle (1627–1691), and Sir Isaac Newton (1642–1727).

reached the standpoint of the whole, all doubt is likewise removed; he perceives that the phenomena can only be thus, and so must also exist as they are presented in this context: In a word, he possesses the objects through their form.

We conclude with some considerations about the higher relation of the Philosophy of Nature to modern times and to the modern world in general.

Spinoza has lain unrecognized for over a hundred years. The view of his philosophy as a mere theory of objectivity did not allow the true absolute to be perceived in it. The definiteness with which he recognized subject-objectivity as the necessary and eternal character of absoluteness shows the high destiny implicit in his philosophy, whose full development was reserved to a later age. Yet in him there is still a want of any scientifically observable transition from the first definition of substance to the great first principle of his doctrine: quod quidquid ab infinito intellectu percipi potest tanquam substantiae essentiam constituens, id omne ad *unicam tantum substantiam* pertinet, et consequenter, *quod substantia cogitans et substantia extensa una eademque est substantia*, quae jam sub hoc jam sub illo attributo comprehenditur.[6] The scientific knowledge of this identity, whose absence in Spinoza subjected his teaching to the misunderstandings of a former day, was bound to be the beginning of a reawakening of philosophy itself.

Fichte's philosophy was the first to restore validity to the universal form of subject-objectivity, as the one and all of philosophy; but the more it developed, the more it seemed to restrict that very identity, again as a special feature, to the subjective consciousness; yet as absolute and in itself, to make it the *object* of an endless *task*, an absolute *demand*, and in this way after extracting all substance from speculation, to abandon it as just empty froth, while proceeding, on the other hand, like the Kantian theory, to reconnect absoluteness with the deepest subjectivity, through action and faith.

Philosophy has higher demands to fulfil, and is called upon to lead mankind, which, whether in faith or unbelief, has long enough lived unworthily and unsatisfied, at last to vision. The character of the whole modern era is idealistic; its dominant spirit, the return to inwardness. The ideal world presses mightily towards the light, but is still held back by the fact that Nature has withdrawn as a mystery. The very secrets which the ideal harbours cannot truly become objective save in proclaiming the mystery of Nature. The still-unknown deities, which the ideal world is preparing, cannot emerge as such until they can seize possession of Nature. After all *finite* forms have been struck down, and there is nothing more in the wide world to unite mankind but collective intuition, it can only be the contemplation of absolute identity in the fullest objective totality that afresh, and in the final development to religion, unites them forever.

SOURCE: From Friedrich Wilhelm Joseph von Schelling, *Ideas for a Philosophy of Nature as Introduction to the Study of This Science, 1797*, trans. Errol E. Harris and Peter Heath (Cambridge: Cambridge University Press, 1988), pp. 9–11, 38–55. Originally published in 1797 as *Ideen zu einer Philosophie der Natur*. Except where otherwise indicated, German words in brackets are the terminology used in the German original, inserted by the editor in addition to their renderings in the translation.

6. "That whatsoever can be perceived by the infinite intellect as constituting the essence of substance, belongs altogether only to one substance: consequently, substance thinking and substance extended are one and the same substance, comprehended now through one attribute, now through the other" (Spinoza, *Ethics* [trans. R. H. M. Elwes], II, Prop. VII, Note) [translator's note].

From Of Human Freedom

Philosophical investigations into the nature of human freedom may, in part, concern themselves with the correct conception of the term; for though the feeling of freedom is ingrained in every individual, the fact itself is by no means so near to the surface that merely to express it in words would not require more than common clarity and depth of perception. In part such investigations may be concerned with the relation of this concept to a whole systematic world view. But here, as indeed everywhere, these two sides of the investigation coincide, since no conception can be defined in isolation and depends for its systematic completion on the demonstration of its connections with the whole. This is especially the case in the conception of freedom, for if it has any reality at all it cannot be a merely subordinate or incidental conception but must be one of the dominant central points of the system. To be sure, according to an ancient but by no means forgotten tradition, the idea of freedom is said to be entirely inconsistent with the idea of system, and every philosophy which makes claim to unity and completeness is said to end in denying freedom. * * *

* * * Much as may be adduced from a merely historic consideration of previous systems in support of the contention that freedom and systematic unity are incompatible, we have nowhere found arguments derived from the nature of reason and knowledge themselves. Hence it seems that the connection between the concept of freedom and a total world view will always remain the subject of an inevitable problem which, if it is not solved, will leave the concept of freedom ambiguous and philosophy, indeed, totally without value. For this great problem alone constitutes the unconscious and invisible mainspring of all striving for knowledge from the lowest to the highest. Without the contradiction of necessity and freedom[1] not only philosophy but every nobler ambition of the spirit [*Geist*] would sink to that death which is peculiar to those sciences in which that contradiction serves no function. To withdraw from the conflict by foreswearing reason looks more like flight than victory. Another person would have the same right to turn his back on freedom in order to throw himself into the arms of reason and necessity, without there being any cause for self-congratulation on either side.

* * * Most people, if they were honest, would have to admit that in terms of their ideas individual freedom seems to be in contradiction to almost all attributes of a Highest Being, omnipotence for instance. In maintaining freedom, a power which by its nature is unconditioned is asserted to exist alongside of and outside the divine power, which in terms of their ideas is inconceivable. As the sun outshines all the other celestial lights in the firmament, so, but to a greater degree, infinite power extinguishes all finite power. Absolute causal power in one being leaves nothing but unconditional passivity for all the rest. Thus there follows the dependence of all earthly creatures

---

1. Or rather, the *apparent* "contradiction of necessity and freedom"—which KANT (see selections above) had sought to resolve in a way that gave both their due and that showed how a profoundly significant conception of human freedom could be rendered consistent with the acknowledg-ment that nature is a realm in which "necessity" prevails. Schelling here is making common cause with Kant, though he does so initially by arguing for the compatibility of human freedom with divine omnipotence.

upon God, their very persistence being nothing but a constantly renewed creation in which the finite being is produced not as something generic and undetermined but as this particular individual with such and such thoughts, desires and actions and no others. To say that God restrains his omnipotence so that man can act, or that he permits freedom, explains nothing; for if God withdrew his power for an instant, man would cease to be. Since freedom is unthinkable in contradistinction to omnipotence, is there any other escape from this argument than by placing man and his freedom in the divine being, by saying that man exists not outside God but in God, and that man's activity itself belongs to God's life? From this very point of view mystics and religious temperaments in all ages have come to believe in the unity of man with God, a belief which seems to appeal to our inmost feelings as much as, or even more than, it does to reason and speculation.

* * *

To proceed[:] if the denial of freedom, not of individuality, should now be declared to be the essential characteristic of pantheism, then a multitude of systems would come under this heading which are otherwise essentially differentiated from it. For the true conception of freedom[2] was lacking in all modern systems, that of Leibniz as well as that of Spinoza,[3] until the discovery of Idealism.[4] And the sort of freedom which many among us have conceived, even those boasting of the liveliest sense thereof, a freedom, namely, consisting of the mere mastery of intelligence over senses and passions, could be deduced from Spinoza himself without difficulty, indeed quite easily and with superior decisiveness. Thus it seems that the denial or affirmation of freedom in general is based on something quite other than the acceptance or nonacceptance of pantheism, the immanence of things in God. For if, at the first glance, it seems that freedom, unable to maintain itself in opposition to God, is here submerged in identity, it may be said that this apparent result is merely the consequence of an imperfect and empty conception of the law of identity. This principle does not express a unity which, revolving in the indifferent circle of sameness, would get us nowhere and remain meaningless and lifeless. The unity of this law is of an intrinsically creative kind. * * *

We attain a much loftier point of view by regarding the divine Being itself, the very idea of which would be completely incompatible with a result which was not a living creation,—that is, the positing of something autonomous. God is not a God of the dead but of the living. It is incomprehensible that an all-perfect Being could rejoice in even the most perfect mechanism possible. No matter how one pictures to oneself the procession of creatures from God, it can never be a mechanical production, no mere construction or setting up, in which the construct is naught in itself. Just as certainly, it cannot be an emanation in which that which has flowed forth remains the same as its source,

2. The history of philosophy in the interpretive tradition from Kant onward can aptly be characterized as a long argument about the nature of "the true conception of freedom" and its relative worth and significance in relation to other conceptions of freedom and human values.
3. Benedict (Baruch) de Spinoza (1632–1677), Dutch philosopher. Gottfried Wilhelm Leibniz

(1646–1716), German philosopher and mathematician.
4. That is, Kantian "transcendental idealism," which denies ultimacy to spatiotemporal reality, and thus to the pretensions of the natural sciences to have the last word with respect to the whole of reality (our own included), while granting them authority regarding all natural phenomena.

thus lacking individuality and independence. The procession of things from God is God's self-revelation. But God can only reveal himself in creatures who resemble him, in free, self-activating beings for whose existence there is no reason save God, but who are as God is. * * *

* * * It will always remain a striking circumstance in the history of German intellectual development, that at any time the assertion could be made: The system which merges (as it was understood) God with all things, creatures with the creator, and makes all subordinate to blind, irrational necessity, is the only possible system of reason and the only one capable of being developed by pure reason. In order to comprehend this we must recall the dominant spirit of an earlier age. At that time all minds had fallen victim to the mechanistic trend of thought which attained the pinnacle of its nefariousness in French atheism. In Germany, too, one began to regard and expound this type of thought as the only true and genuine philosophy. Meanwhile, as the native German temperament could never assimilate the consequences of this view, there at first appeared that conflict of mind and heart which is so typical of philosophical literature in recent times. One abhorred the consequences of this mode of thinking, without being able to free oneself from its cause or to rise to a better way. There was the wish to voice these consequences; and as the German spirit could grasp this mechanistic philosophy only in its (supposedly) highest expression, the terrible truth was uttered in this way: All philosophy, absolutely all, which is based on pure reason alone, is, or will become, Spinozism.[5] All men were now warned of the abyss; it was clearly laid bare before all eyes. The only remedy which still seemed possible was seized; only that bold utterance could bring on the crisis; it alone could frighten Germans away from this ruinous philosophy and lead them back to the Heart, to inwardness of feeling and to faith. Nowadays, as this type of thought has long since ceased to be and the higher light of Idealism shines for us, this same declaration would neither be comprehensible to a like extent nor promise the same results.

Here, then, once and for all our definite opinion about Spinozism! This system is not fatalism because it lets things be conceived in God; for as we have shown, pantheism does not make formal freedom, at least, impossible. Spinoza must then be a fatalist for another reason, entirely independent of this. The error of his system is by no means due to the fact that he posits all *things in God*, but to the fact that they are *things [Dinge]*—to the abstract conception of the world and its creatures, indeed of eternal Substance itself, which is also a thing for him. Thus his arguments against freedom are altogether deterministic, and in no wise pantheistic. He treats the will, too, as a thing, and then proves, very naturally, that in every case of its operation it must be determined by some other thing, which in turn is determined by another, and so forth endlessly. Hence the lifelessness of his system, the harshness of its form, the bareness of its concepts and expressions, the relentless austerity of its definitions; this admirably in accord with the abstract outlook. Thence also, quite consistently, his mechanistic view of nature. Or can one doubt that even

---

5. By "Spinozism" Schelling means Spinoza's position that "God" and "nature" are two words for the same ultimate reality, "nature" is the whole of that reality (as is "God"), and the entirety of "nature" is governed by a rational necessity (which may also be conceived as the divine nature).

a dynamic conception of nature must necessarily bring about an essential change in the basic views of Spinozism? If the doctrine that all things are conceived in God is the basis of the entire system, it must at least first be vitalized and severed from abstractness before it can become the principle of a system of reason. How general and vague is the expression, that the eternal beings are modes or consequences of God; what a chasm there is here, needing to be filled in; what questions remain to be answered! Spinozism in its rigidity could be regarded like Pygmalion's statue,[6] needing to be given a soul through the warm breath of love: but this comparison is imperfect, as Spinozism more closely resembles a work of art which has been sketched only in its most general outlines and in which, if it were endowed with a soul, one would still notice how many features were lacking or incompleted. It could more readily be compared to the most ancient likenesses of the divinities, which seemed all the more mysterious the fewer the features of individual lifelikeness apparent in them. In a word, it is a onesidedly realistic system, and although this expression sounds less damning than 'pantheism,' it nevertheless describes the peculiar nature of this system far more correctly, and is, moreover, not now used for the first time. It would be tedious to repeat the many explanations concerning this point which are to be found in the author's earliest writings. The expressed intention of his efforts was a mutual interpenetration of realism and idealism. Spinoza's fundamental concept, spiritualized by the principle of idealism (and changed at one essential point) was given a vital basis through the more elevated way of regarding nature, and through the recognized unity of what is dynamic with what is spiritual and emotional. From this there developed a Philosophy of Nature, which as a mere physics could indeed stand by itself, but which was always regarded, with respect to the whole of philosophy, as merely one of its parts (that is, its real part) and which would permit of being raised into a genuine system of reason only by first being completed by an ideal part wherein freedom is sovereign. In this freedom, it was declared, the final intensifying act was to be found through which the whole of nature found its transfiguration in feeling, in intelligence, and, ultimately, in will.—In the final and highest instance there is no other Being than Will. Will is primordial Being, and all predicates apply to it alone—groundlessness, eternity, independence of time, self-affirmation! All philosophy strives only to find this highest expression.

It is to this point that Idealism has raised philosophy, up to our time; and only at this point are we really able to take up the investigation of our subject, since it could by no means be our purpose to take account of all those difficulties which can be raised (and have already been raised) against the concept of freedom on the basis of the one-sidedly realistic or dogmatic system. However, high as we have been placed in this respect by Idealism, and certain as it is that we owe to it the first formally perfect concept of freedom, Idealism itself is, after all, nothing less than a finished system. And as soon as we seek to enter into the doctrine of freedom in greater detail and exactitude, it nonetheless leaves us helpless. * * *

6. In the story told in Ovid's *Metamorphoses* (ca. 10 c.e.), Pygmalion fashioned an ivory sculpture of a woman, fell in love with it, and, after he prayed to the goddess of love, brought it to life with his kiss.

For idealism supplies only the most general conception of freedom, and a merely formal one. But the real and vital conception of freedom is that it is a possibility of good and evil.

This is the point of profoundest difficulty in the whole doctrine [*Lehre*] of freedom, which has always been felt and which applies not only to this or that system, but, more or less, to all. To be sure it applies most strikingly to the concept of immanence, for either real evil is admitted, in which case it is unavoidable to include evil itself in infinite Substance or in the Primal Will, and thus totally disrupt the conception of an all-perfect Being; or the reality of evil must in some way or other be denied, in which case the real conception of freedom disappears at the same time.

* * *

* * * Idealism, if it is not grounded in a vital realism, will become just as empty and attenuated a system as the Leibnizian, Spinozistic or any other dogmatic philosophy. The whole of modern European philosophy since its inception (through Descartes[7]) has this common deficiency—that nature does not exist for it and that it lacks a living basis. On this account Spinoza's realism is as abstract as the idealism of Leibniz. Idealism is the soul of philosophy; realism is its body; only the two together constitute a living whole. Realism can never furnish the first principles, but it must be the basis and the instrument by which idealism realizes itself and takes on flesh and blood. If a philosophy lacks this vital basis, usually a sign that the ideal principle was but weak from the outset, it then loses itself in those systems whose attenuated concepts of *a-se-ity*,[8] modality, etc., stand in the sharpest contrast to the vital power and fullness of reality. On the other hand, where the ideal principle really operates to a high degree but cannot discover a reconciling and mediating basis, it gives birth to a dreary and fanatic enthusiasm which breaks forth in self-mutilation or—as in the case of the priests of the Phrygian goddess[9]—in self-emasculation, which in philosophy is accomplished by the renunciation of reason and science [*Wissenschaft*].

* * *

* * * Following the eternal act of self-revelation, the world as we now behold it, is all rule, order and form; but the unruly[1] lies ever in the depths as though it might again break through, and order and form nowhere appear to have been original, but it seems as though what had initially been unruly had been brought to order. This is the incomprehensible basis of reality in things, the irreducible remainder which cannot be resolved into reason by the greatest

7. René Descartes (1596–1650), French mathematician and philosopher. Schelling's point here is that his radical distinction between mind and matter (as thinking and extended substances), and his relegation of everything that is not the former to the latter category, bequeathed an ontological dualism to modern philosophy that rendered it oblivious to living nature.
8. The quality or state of not depending on anything else for coming into existence and continuing to exist.
9. Cybele, Great Mother of the Gods, whose worship arose in Asia Minor (Phrygia) and was adopted by the Greeks by the 5th century B.C.E.; the male followers of her cult sometimes castrated themselves.
1. That is, "the ruleless" (*das Regellose*); subject to no rules or laws.

exertion but always remains in the depths. Out of this which is unreasonable, reason[2] in the true sense is born. * * *

All birth is a birth out of darkness into light: the seed must be buried in the earth and die in darkness in order that the lovelier creature of light should rise and unfold itself in the rays of the sun. Man is formed in his mother's womb; and only out of the darkness of unreason (out of feeling, out of longing, the sublime mother of understanding) grow clear thoughts. We must imagine the primal longing in this way—turning towards reason, indeed, though not yet recognizing it, just as we longingly desire unknown, nameless excellence. This primal longing moves in anticipation like a surging, billowing sea, similar to the 'matter' of Plato,[3] following some dark, uncertain law, incapable in itself of forming anything that can endure. But there is born in God himself an inward, imaginative response, corresponding to this longing, which is the first stirring of divine Being in its still dark depths. Through this response, God sees himself in his own image, since his imagination can have no other object than himself. This image is the first in which God, viewed absolutely, is realized, though only in himself; it is in the beginning in God, and is the God-begotten God himself. This image is at one and the same time, reason— the logic of that longing, and the eternal Spirit [Geist] which feels within it the Logos[4] and the everlasting longing. This Spirit, moved by that Love which it itself is, utters the Word which then becomes creative and omnipotent Will combining reason and longing, and which informs nature, at first unruly, as its own element or instrument. The first effect of reason in nature is the separation of forces, which is the only way in which reason can unfold and develop the unity which had necessarily but unconsciously existed within nature, as in a seed. Just as in man there comes to light, when in the dark longing to create something, thoughts separate out of the chaotic confusion of thinking in which all are connected but each prevents the other from coming forth— so the unity appears which contains all within it and which had lain hidden in the depths. Or it is as in the case of the plant which escapes the dark fetters of gravity only as it unfolds and spreads its powers, developing its hidden unity as its substance becomes differentiated. For since this Being [of primal nature][5] is nothing else than the eternal basis of God's existence, it must contain within itself, though locked away, God's essence, as a light of life shining in the dark depths. But longing, roused by reason, now strives to preserve this light shining within it, and returns unto itself so that a basis of being might ever remain. * * *

It can readily be seen that in the tension of longing necessary to bring things completely to birth the innermost nexus of the forces can only be released in a graded evolution, and at every stage in the division of forces there is developed out of nature a new being whose soul must be all the more perfect the

---

2. "Reason" here translates *Verstand*, while "this which is unreasonable" translates *Verstandlosen*. A better translation of this sentence would be "It is out of this irrationality that genuine rationality (i.e., rational *structure*) is born," reserving "reason" to translate *Vernunft* (a term used elsewhere by Schelling, as well as by Kant and HEGEL).
3. Greek philosopher (ca. 427–ca. 347 B.C.E.);

what endured, in his view, were the eternal forms or ideas.
4. Literally, "Word" (Greek): in some ancient Greek philosophy, divine reason as the ordering principle in the universe; in Christian thought, the creative word of God, identified in John 1 with Jesus (the Word made flesh).
5. Translator's brackets.

more differentiatedly it contains what was left undifferentiated in the others. It is the task of a complete philosophy of nature to show how each successive process more closely approaches the essence of nature, until in the highest division of forces the innermost center is disclosed. For our present purpose only the following is essential. Every being which has arisen in nature in the manner indicated, contains a double principle which, however, is at bottom one and the same regarded from the two possible aspects. The first principle is the one by which they are separated from God or wherein they exist in the mere basis of things. But as an original unity exists between that which is in the basis, and what is prefigured in understanding, the second principle, which by its own nature is dark, is at the same time the very one which is revealed in light, and the two are one in every natural object, though only to a certain extent. For the process of creation consists only in an inner transmutation, or revelation in light of what was originally the principle of darkness since understanding or the light which occurs in nature is actually only searching in the depths for that light which is akin to it and is turned inward. The principle of darkness, insofar as it was drawn from the depths and is dark, is the self-will of creatures, but self-will, insofar as it has not yet risen to complete unity with light, as the principle of understanding cannot grasp it and is mere craving or desire, that is blind will. This self-will of creatures stands opposed to reason as universal will, and the latter makes use of the former and subordinates it to itself as a mere tool. But this will becomes one whole with the primal will or reason when, in the progressive transformation and division of all forces, there is totally revealed in light the inmost and deepest point of original darkness, in One Being. The will of this One Being, to the extent to which it is individual, is also a particular will, though in itself or as the center of all other particular wills it is one with the primal will or reason. This elevation of the most abysmal center into light,[6] occurs in no creatures visible to us except in man. In man there exists the whole power of the principle of darkness and, in him too, the whole force of light. In him there are both centers—the deepest pit[7] and the highest heaven. Man's will is the seed—concealed in eternal longing—of God,[8] present as yet only in the depths,—the divine light of life locked in the deeps which God divined when he determined to will nature. Only in him (in man) did God love the world,—and it was this very image of God which was grasped in its center by longing when it opposed itself to light. By reason of the fact that man takes his rise from the depths (that he is a creature) he contains a principle relatively independent of God. But just because this very principle is transfigured in light—without therefore ceasing to be basically dark—something higher, the *spirit* [*Geist*], arises in man. For the eternal spirit pronounces[9] unity, or the Word, in nature. But the (real) Word, pronounced, exists only in the unity of light and darkness (vowel and consonant). Now these two principles do indeed exist in all things, but without complete consonance because of the inadequacy of that which has been raised from the depths. Only in man, then, is the Word completely articulate, which in all other creatures was held back and left unfinished. But in the articulate

---

6. More accurately, "This raising of the very deepest center into the light."
7. That is, "the deepest depths" (*der tieftste Abgrund*).

8. "The seed (*Keim*) of God"—that is, the kernel of the divine.
9. That is, expresses.

word the spirit reveals itself, that is God as existing, in act. Now inasmuch as the soul [*die Seele*] is the living identity of both principles, it is spirit [*Geist*]; and spirit is in God. If, now, the identity of both principles were just as indissoluble in man as in God, then there would be no difference—that is, God as spirit would not be revealed. Therefore that unity which is indissoluble in God must be dissoluble in man—and this constitutes the possibility of good and evil.

* * *

* * * The birth of spirit [*Geist*] is the realm of history, as the birth of light is the realm of nature. The same stages of creation which exist in the latter are also in the former; and the one is the symbol and explanation of the other. The identical principle which was the basis of the first creation is here again the germ and seed, only in a higher form, from which a higher world is developed.

* * *

It was, indeed, Idealism which first raised the doctrine of freedom into that realm in which it alone can be understood. In consequence of it the intelligible essence of everything, and particularly of man, is outside of all causal connections as it is outside or beyond all time. Therefore it can never be determined by anything which preceded, since it itself rather takes precedence over all else which is or develops within it, not in time but in terms of its concept as an absolute unity whose totality and completeness must ever be actual in order that a specific act or determination may be possible in it. For we are expressing the Kantian conception not exactly in his words but in just such a way as, we believe, it must be expressed in order to be understood. But if this conception is accepted then the following too seems to have been correctly inferred. Free activity follows immediately from the intelligible nature of man. But it is necessarily an activity of determinate character; for instance—to refer to what is nearest at hand—it must be a good or bad activity. However there is no transition from the absolutely undetermined to the determined. The notion that an intelligible being could determine itself from sheer and utter indetermination without any reason, leads back to the above mentioned system of the equilibrium of choice. In order to be able to determine itself it would have to be already determined in itself; not indeed from the outside, since this would be in contradiction to its nature, nor from within by any merely accidental or empirical necessity, since all this (psychological as well as physical) is subordinate to it. But it would have to be determined by its own essence, that is by its own nature. This essence is no indefinite generality but definitely the intelligible essence of this specific human being. The saying, *determinatio est negatio*,[1] does not in any way apply to this sort of determination, since this is itself one with the reality and concept of this essence, thus really being the essential element in the essence. The intelligible being, therefore, insofar as it acts absolutely and with full freedom, can as certainly only act according to its own inner nature. Or the activity can follow from its inner nature only

1. Determination is negation (Latin), a statement made by Spinoza in a letter of 1674, and which Hegel soon would not only embrace but underscore as a general principle, proclaiming: "*All determination is negation*."

in accordance with the law of identity, and with absolute necessity which is also the only absolute freedom. For only that is free which acts according to the laws of its own inner being and is not determined by anything else either within it or outside it.[2]

* * *

But in a way far more definite than this general sense, these truths have an immediate relation to man. In original creation, as has been shown, man is an undetermined entity (which may be mythologically presented as a condition antecedent to this life, a state of innocence and of initial bliss). He alone can determine himself. But this determination [Entscheidung] cannot occur in time; it occurs outside of time altogether and hence it coincides with the first creation even though as an act differentiated from it. Man, even though born in time, is nonetheless a creature of creation's beginning (the centrum). The act which determines [bestimmt] man's life in time does not itself belong in time but in eternity. Moreover it does not precede life in time but occurs throughout time (untouched by it) as an act eternal by its own nature. Through it man's life extends to the beginning of creation, since by means of it he is also more than creature, free and himself eternal beginning. Though this idea may seem beyond the grasp of common ways of thought, there is in every man a feeling which is in accord with it, as if each man felt that he had been what he is from all eternity, and had in no sense only come to be so in time.

* * *

* * * True freedom is in accord with a holy necessity, of a sort which we feel in essential knowledge when heart and spirit, bound only by their own law, freely affirm that which is necessary. If evil consists in strife between the two principles, then the good can only consist in their complete accord. And the tie which unites the two must be divine, since they are one not in a conditional way but completely and unconditionally. The relation of the two is not to be conceived as optional morality or one derived from self-determination. The last concept presupposed that they were not, in themselves, one; but how can they become one if they are not? Besides it leads back to the inconsistent system of the equilibrium of choices. The relation of the two principles is that the dark principle (selfhood) is bound to the light.

* * *

* * * For we have sufficiently shown that all natural creatures have a mere being in the depths or in the initial longing which has not yet achieved unity with understanding, that they are thus mere peripheral entities in relation to God. Only man is in God, and through this very being-in-God is capable of freedom. He alone is a central being and therefore should also remain in the center. In him all things are created, just as it is also only through man that God accepts nature and ties it to him. Nature is the first, or old, Testament, since things are still outside the center and therefore under the law. Man is the beginning of the new covenant through whom, as mediator, since he himself is connected with God, God (the last division being attained) also accepts

2. This is Schelling's basic definition of freedom—deriving from Kant (and, even more fundamentally, from Spinoza) and anticipating Hegel.

nature and takes it to *him*. Man is thus the redeemer of nature towards whom all its archetypes strive. The Word which is fulfilled in man exists in nature as a dark, prophetic (still incompletely spoken) Word.

* * *

These considerations lead us back to our point of departure. A system which contradicts the most sacred sentiments and feelings and moral consciousness can, at least in these characteristics, never be called a system of reason, but rather of unreason. On the contrary, a system in which reason fulfilled itself, would have to unite all the demands of the spirit as of the heart, of the most conscientious feeling as of the strictest understanding. The polemic against reason and science does indeed permit a kind of distinguished generality which circumvents precise concepts, so that we can more easily guess its purposes than its exact meaning. Moreover we fear that even if we fathomed it, we would not reach anything extraordinary. For however highly we place reason, we still do not believe, for example, that anyone can through pure reason become virtuous or a hero or any kind of great man, nor even—in the well known phrase—that the human race can be propagated by it. Only in personality is there life; and all personality rests on a dark foundation which must, to be sure, also be the foundation of knowledge. But only reason can bring forth what is contained in these depths, hidden and merely potential, and elevate it to actuality. This can occur only through distinction, that is through science and dialectic. And we are convinced that they alone will grasp and bring to eternal knowledge that system which has been present more often than we realize, but which has always again escaped, which has hovered before all of us but has never yet been entirely apprehended by anyone. As in life we actually trust only vigorous reason, and miss all true tenderness in those especially who always expose their feelings to our gaze, so too, where we are considering truth and knowledge, selfhood which has merely reached the point of feelings cannot win our confidence. The emotions are glorious when they stay in the depths, but not when they come forth into the day and wish to become of the essence and to rule. * * * The nexus[3] of our personality is the spirit [*Geist*], and if the active combination of both principles can alone be creative and productive, then inspiration [*Begeisterung*] in the actual sense is the effective principle of every productive or creative art or science.[4]

* * *

SOURCE: From *Philosophical Inquiries into the Nature of Human Freedom: A Translation of F. W. J. Schelling's "Philosophische Untersuchungen über das Wesen der menschlichen Freiheit und die damit zusammenhängenden Gegenstände,"* trans. James Gutmann (La Salle, Ill.: Open Court Press, 1936), pp. 7, 9–11, 17–24, 26, 30–31, 34–39, 54–55, 61–64, 70–71, 92, 95–96. Except where otherwise indicated, German words in brackets are the terminology used in the German original, inserted by the editor in addition to their renderings in the translation. This work (whose title is more fully translated "Philosophical Investigations into the Nature of Human Freedom and Related Matters") was first published in 1809.

3. Literally, "the bond" (*das Band*), or the unifying principle.
4. *Begeisterung* is better rendered "spiritualization" (infusion by *Geist* or spirituality). Schelling's point here is that the emotions require spiritualization if they are to be creative and productive, either cognitively or artistically, and that all creative and productive activity requires and is driven by that active combination of feeling and rationality that is *Geist*.

GEORG WILHELM FRIEDRICH HEGEL
(1770 – 1831)

KANT towered over the classical modern philosophical tradition that preceded him. Hegel loomed large over the interpretive tradition that began in earnest with him. After Kant opened the door to it, SCHILLER, FICHTE, and SCHELLING had ventured through that door and begun to explore the possibilities it presented. Hegel, following close behind, soon eclipsed them, laying claim to the entire territory and erecting a kind of philosophical Valhalla—his all-encompassing "system"—that in short order became one of the wonders of the philosophical world, overshadowing even Kant's "critical philosophy." By the time of his untimely death (at the age of 61), Hegel had replaced Kant as the dominant philosophical figure and force of the day in German-speaking Europe. His influence quickly spread throughout the rest of Europe and into England and North America as well. He dominated philosophy—both academically and more popularly and broadly—for nearly a century, through both the following he inspired and the opposition his system and kind of thinking provoked; and versions of elements of his thought have continued to figure importantly in philosophical and wider intellectual debates.

Georg Wilhelm Friedrich Hegel ("HAY-gel"), the oldest of three children of a revenue officer, was born in 1770 (as was Beethoven), in the southwestern German city of Stuttgart. He had a comfortable childhood and good early education, developing broad literary and intellectual interests. He entered the illustrious university at Tübingen in 1788, as a student in the Protestant seminary, where he soon met and came to live with the precocious Schelling and the gifted young poet Friedrich Hölderlin. The three students shared a love of literature, history, philosophy, and the Greeks, as well as an enthusiasm for the ideals of the French Enlightenment and French Revolution. Hegel soon abandoned his initial thoughts of preparing for the ministry, gravitating instead (like Schelling) toward philosophy. His philosophical development did not match the meteoric rise of Schelling; but he took advantage of the flowering of many areas of academic, intellectual, and artistic life in central Europe to absorb a wealth of knowledge and culture that he would eventually put to good effect. He was attracted both by the long tradition of rationalism in modern European philosophy—a tradition that culminated in one way in Kant and in another in the advances of natural science and Enlightenment thinking—and by the Romanticism that was emerging all around him, in many areas of intellectual and artistic life, in opposition to these developments.

After five years at Tübingen Hegel received a theological degree. For a time he supported himself by working privately as a tutor to the children of wealthy families, first in the Swiss city of Berne (1793–96) and then (with the help of Hölderlin) in Frankfurt (1797–1801), while continuing his self-education and writing on topics related to his religious and philosophical interests. In 1801, aided by Schelling—already a professor at the university at Jena—Hegel obtained a much more modest position at Jena as an unsalaried lecturer. It was there that he published his first monograph, *The Difference between Fichte's and Schelling's Systems of Philosophy* (aligning himself with Schelling), and established and co-edited a journal with Schelling. Then, after Schelling's departure in 1803, he began working on his first—and perhaps his greatest—book, *The Phenomenology of Spirit* [*Geist*]. With the support of Goethe he was promoted to a professorial rank in 1805, but he remained unsalaried.

Hegel hoped that the *Phenomenology* would gain him a salaried appointment; but just as he was finishing it, Napoleon arrived with his army. The defeat of the German states' forces in the Battle of Jena in late 1806 ended the rather amorphous political entity known as the Holy Roman Empire. It also plunged the university at Jena into financial crisis, requiring Hegel to seek employment elsewhere. His *Phenomenology* was published, but in the turmoil of the time it went largely unnoticed. To make matters worse, Hegel found himself with an illegitimate son in early 1807, in consequence of an affair with his landlady. In desperate straits, he left Jena (and this personal complication) behind, for a position as editor of a newspaper in the town of Bamberg.

A year later Hegel was able to resume his academic career and began to enjoy more financial security, as in October 1808 he obtained an appointment as teacher and headmaster at an advanced secondary school in Nuremberg (Nürnberg). There he met Marie von Tucher, whom he married in 1811; and by 1814 he and his wife had two sons. While in Nuremberg he published his second major work, the three-volume *Science* [Wissenschaft] *of Logic* (1812–16). He also developed the idea and first version of what subsequently became his *Encyclopedia of the Philosophical Sciences*. It was initially intended to serve as an outline to aid students attending his lectures. (It thus was structured and worded rather simply and concisely, with numbered short paragraphs, to facilitate comprehension—in marked contrast to his *Phenomenology*, which is of legendary difficulty.)

The publication of his *Logic* finally enabled Hegel in 1816 to obtain a professorship in philosophy, at Heidelberg University—at the age of 46. (A year later, with his wife's consent, Hegel's illegitimate 10-year-old son was taken into their household after the boy's mother died.) While in Heidelberg, Hegel also published the first edition of his *Encyclopedia*. He remained there for only two years, however, accepting an offer in 1818 to take up the professorship in philosophy

at Berlin previously held by Fichte, which had been vacant since Fichte's death in 1814. At Berlin Hegel flourished, in the university as well as in the discipline. He even was appointed rector—the university's highest academic-administrative officer—in 1830. But just a year later, at the height of his fame and influence, he was dead, falling victim to a cholera epidemic that swept through the city.

Hegel's prominence was not earned by copious publication. Beyond a revised edition of his *Encyclopedia*, he published only one new book, *Philosophy of Right* (1821), during his thirteen years at Berlin. Like the *Encyclopedia*, moreover, it was mainly intended to be used in connection with his lectures there. These lectures, attended by large audiences that were by no means limited to students, were major intellectual events that drew attention throughout German-speaking Europe and even abroad. In them Hegel masterfully surveyed not only the topics covered in his published expositions of his famous "system" of philosophy (his philosophical "logic," his philosophy of nature, and his philosophy of spirit [*Geist*] and of "right" or normativity), but also the history of philosophy and the philosophy of history, of religion, and of art.

Many volumes of Hegel's lectures were published after his death, thanks to the note-taking skills and dedication of those present. Their notes (as well as material from Hegel's own lecture notes) were added to later editions of Hegel's works, providing elaborations that greatly help the reader comprehend and appreciate his thought. The entire "Hegel phenomenon"—his remarkable influence during the last dozen years of his life and long after his death, throughout the Western philosophical and intellectual world—owes much to this unique combination of ways in which he expressed his thinking and to the kinds of texts that resulted. It is in the material drawn from his lectures that Hegel's thought comes most vividly to life.

Kant and Hegel were both extraordinarily audacious, not only in their aspirations but also in their convictions of the significance of their philosophical accomplishments. Kant thought that he had established once and for all the nature and limits of theoretical and practical reason and judgment, settling the main questions that needed to be asked and answered with respect to all of the main areas and topics of traditional philosophical (and theological) inquiry. Hegel went even further, supposing himself to have superseded Kant (as well as Fichte and Schelling) and indeed to have attained something Hume and Kant had thought to be humanly impossible: "absolute knowledge" of the fundamental nature and general character of reality—knowledge that is "absolute" in both its form and its content. He deemed the philosophical system he developed to be all-encompassing and definitive with respect to everything of which it is meaningful and philosophically significant to speak. And he undertook to transform the understanding of philosophy itself, along with all other forms of inquiry, experience, and activity, by showing how they all fit into our human-spiritual development toward full genuine self-realization and "absolute knowing."

Kant had thought that his kind of philosophical thinking, of the sort that is on display in his three critiques, was philosophy at its best and at its limits. Hegel thought that Kant's "critical philosophy," admirable as it might be, was inadequate to the most important tasks of philosophy. In its place, or beyond it, he advocated a kind of thinking he (like Kant, but who had traditional metaphysics in mind) called "speculative." It might also (and perhaps better) be called "interpretive." One response to Kant over the past two centuries has been to emphasize the kinds of analytical, theoretical, and critical inquiry that he considered to be possible and needful within the domains of philosophical inquiry legitimized. Another, while not neglecting these matters, has been to consider how best to rethink and pursue various kinds of questions regarding ourselves and the world that are

important but seem to call for a different sort of treatment.

One way of characterizing this difference is to say that the latter response, unlike the former, focuses on the interpretation and reinterpretation of matters that such rigorous forms of inquiry do not and cannot settle. In reflecting on this situation, Hegel distinguished between the kind of thinking he calls "understanding" (*Verstand*) and what he calls "reason" (*Vernunft*), more broadly understood. He attempted to pursue a kind of interpretive philosophical inquiry through the employment of such a broadened ("speculative") form of reason, which he believed would make possible a deeper comprehension of ourselves and the reality of which we are a part than that yielded by the kinds of inquiry to which Kant had thought the scope of knowledge had to be restricted. Properly conducted, Hegel contended that such thought could be deserving (and perhaps even most deserving) of the name of "knowledge," whereas Kant had relegated it to the more problematic status of a sort of philosophical "faith" or "belief" (*Glaube*) for which he claimed simply to have "made room" (by limiting the scope and authority of theoretical and scientific rationality).

Hegel thus championed "the interpretive turn" in philosophy after Kant; and he inaugurated it by advancing one of the grandest and most audacious reinterpretations of ourselves and the world that is to be found in the history of philosophy. Its boldness is both mitigated and heightened by his claim that it is heir to all of the ways of thinking and experiencing—philosophical, scientific, artistic, and religious, as well as ordinary and practical—that have emerged and developed in the course of human cultural and intellectual history. For Hegel, it appreciates and respects them, even as it also supersedes them all. Some philosophers have taken themselves to be right, and their rivals all to be wrong. Hegel saw not rivals but rather participants in a common enterprise wherever he looked, whether in the history of religion, art, and science or in the history of philosophy. His strategy was to interpret them accordingly, emphasizing what they grasped as well as the limitations of their grasp of it. One of his favorite terms and concepts is *Aufhebung*, which can mean "cancellation" or "negation," but also "preservation" and "transformation." In Hegel's hands it frequently means all three things at once. In this threefold sense, he saw his philosophy as the *Aufhebung* of all previous forms of thought. It made provision for the conceptions of knowledge, meaning, value, and normativity associated with them, while considering what sense can be given to the idea of subjective, objective, and "absolute" forms of each of these conceptions.

Hegel thus was a synthesizer and also an astonishingly original interpreter on a grand scale, inspired in both respects by Aristotle's example. He sought to reinterpret all of reality in a way that would show its fundamental interconnectedness, drawing on and yet transcending previous efforts on the part of both philosophical and religious thinkers to grasp its nature and significance. He also attempted to overcome a host of bifurcations that make a certain amount of sense as distinctions but distort and mislead when taken to represent radically different realities: for example, the divine and the mundane, the mental and the physical, the natural and the rational, the temporal and the eternal, the finite and the infinite, the particular and the general, the individual and the social, the subjective and the objective, and the religious and the philosophical. Indeed, in his early monograph on Fichte and Schelling, he pointed to the tendency of our thinking to generate and become ensnared in such dichotomies as the fundamental source of "the need for philosophy"—or rather, for *his kind* of philosophically synthesizing reinterpretation, since it is philosophical thinking, too, that contributes to the problem (even if it thereby also sets the stage for further advances in philosophical sophistication and comprehension).

But Hegel was responding to another, even more contemporary and urgent source of "the need for philosophy"—and more specifically for his kind of philosophy. For many in his time, neither the Judeo-Christian religious tradition nor radically secular, materialistic, and rationalistic Enlightenment thought seemed to provide the literal and whole truth about life and the world; and neither classical modern philosophical empiricism nor rationalism—nor even Kant's "critical" response to them—were satisfactory substitutes. They felt a need for something more intellectually compelling than traditional religious thought but more capable than any of the alternatives to it of providing an intellectually and emotionally satisfying way to fill the void left by its rejection. Hegel's philosophy, resonating with the entire Western religious, intellectual, and cultural tradition while positioning itself beyond that tradition as its more sophisticated culmination, met that need admirably. It assigned such a lofty and glorious place in the larger scheme of things to the kind of humanity then emerging in the modern Western world (in which its audience could see itself) that many could feel that the gain in meaningfulness more than compensated for what was being lost with the waning of religious literalism.

Like Spinoza (1632–1677), Hegel attempted to reinterpret the divine and the natural as fundamentally one—along with the historical. He does make extensive use of religious language, speaking often of "God"; but even as he embraces the language and imagery of religion (particularly Christianity), and while proclaiming the fundamental unity of religion and philosophy, he contends that philosophical thinking alone is capable of getting truth into proper conceptual form: religious ideas and symbols are to be superseded by refined and purified philosophical concepts. The consequences of this transformation, as Hegel proceeds with it, are profound—for the ideas of "God" and "*Geist*," and for virtually every other religious idea that Hegel affirms, appropriates, and recasts. Hegel's God turns out to be immanent rather than transcendent, having no sort of existence or reality above and beyond the existence and reality of nature, history, and the kinds of consciousness, activity, and spirituality of which we are capable. It is these forms of existence and reality in which the divine nature (which is the essential nature of all reality) expresses and manifests itself, and attains its self-realization. That is the culminating thought of Hegel's monumental *Phenomenology*, in which he positions his kind of philosophy to be not religion's opponent but its ally—and its successor, having the last word with respect to the sort of meaning and significance that the ideas of religion are to be accorded.

Hegel makes so much of "reason" (*Vernunft*) that he is often viewed as a kind of post-Kantian philosophical "rationalist," in the tradition of Leibniz (1646–1716) and Spinoza. In fact, however, he conceives of reason so broadly that it applies not only to formal systems of thought and calculation but also to natural and social reality—not only to the timeless but also to temporal and historical phenomena that reflect structured and structuring developments of various sorts. He famously maintains that "reason rules the world," not only at the level of the laws of nature but also with respect to everything historical, social, and spiritual. Yet he conceives of their "rational" determinations in a way that leaves inventiveness not only possible at all levels but required for the concrete realization of the basic structures involved.

Hegel's "absolute" has the fundamental character of "substance"—conceived as the underlying rational essential structure of all reality and developmental possibility. But it also has the equally fundamental character of "subject," conceived as the disposition to activity that gives expression—and ultimately brings self-knowledge—to that structure. He chooses the term and idea of *Geist* to characterize not only human reality but also the larger reality of which ours is a part, when our reality—and thereby that larger reality along with it—begins to show its true more-than-merely-biological colors. And this expression is ideally suited to recognize and emphasize its essential creativity as well as rationality. In this way Hegel gives both rationalism and romanticism their due, in a synthesis far richer than was offered by any other interpretation on the scene.

Geist, as Hegel conceives of it, refers to everything about human reality that is more than merely natural—and more than merely psychological and interpersonal as well, insofar as those dimensions of our reality can come into play independently of social structure. With the advent of social structure, and of such social-structural phenomena as language, norms, rules, laws, institutions, and practices, human reality began to restructure itself, as human experience and activity came to be mediated by socially objective phenomena that we ourselves (collectively speaking) create. Human reality has proceeded by these means to diversify itself into groups sharing forms of life that they have elaborated in the course of their histories, giving rise to what Hegel calls "peoples" (*Völker*); each such *Volk* has a distinctive shared identity and type of spiritual character that he calls its *Volksgeist*. He further suggests that it makes sense to speak of the human spirit more generally and comprehensively, as it develops in the course of human history through the emergence and interactions of such peoples and their cultures, societies and institutions. This *Weltgeist* ("world spirit") is relatively abstract in relation to the concrete reality of the various human traditions and communities in which we all live our lives and obtain our human identities; but it is what ultimately matters most about them—and us.

What is genuinely "individual" in human reality, for Hegel, is a subset of humanity that has become an autonomously existing unitary and functioning whole—not the single human being, but rather humanity at this level of general-and-yet-particular sociocultural (or *Volk*) identity. Single human beings have very limited identities, if they are abstracted from everything deriving from their *Volk*-identities. The account and interpretation Hegel offers of ourselves thus emphasize the "general" (*allgemein*) dimension and elements of our identities, which have their own sort of "particular" (*einzeln*) character (at the level at which the Germans, for example, differ from the French)—even though he also makes provision for personal identity *within* cultural identity, as mere biological and psychological particularity is transformed into distinct human personality. It is at the level of the *Volk* and its "objective spirituality"—and only at that level, for Hegel—that humanity becomes truly and significantly free, or *self-determining*. So he contends that to act in a manner that is truly free, one must conduct oneself in ways according with the norms of the life of one's people.

Hegel does not ignore the kinds of freedom and self-determination that are possible only on a particular human level, but he considers them far less important than those made possible by the sort of normativity that characterizes the "objective-spiritual" dimension of human reality, through which alone human life is emancipated from the dominion of naturalistic determination. He associates a still higher conception of freedom and self-determination with the attainment of the kind of "absolute spirituality"— transcending the limitations and particularity of specific peoples and their cultures and societies—that artistic, religious, scientific, and philosophical experience and activity make possible and constitute. Through their more truly "universal" forms of meaning, significance, and truth, an individual's identity is raised to the level of what is "absolute" about the reality of which we are a part.

Reality, for Hegel, thus does not consist merely in the world of nature and of material and biological phenomena. It also—and very importantly—includes the phenomena of *Geist*—the forms of subjective, objective, and absolute spirituality that have come into existence as human life has come to be characterized by the wealth of kinds of experience and activity that constitute our societies, cultures, institutions, and practices, as well as arts, religions, sciences, and other interpretive and cognitive disciplines. And it is only with the emergence and maturation of these forms of objective and absolute spirituality that the reality of which we are a part shows what it has in itself to become, achieves the full realization of its inherent possibilities, and so attains what Hegel calls full "actuality." The *merely real* does not amount to much—except insofar as it serves to make possible the development of the *fully actual*. And the same may be said of the *merely essential*. It too amounts to nothing of any significance until the possibilities it delineates are concretely realized.

Hegel's philosophy bears the rather strange and misleading label of "absolute idealism" because he attributes the highest, truest, and most complete kind of reality to this sort of *full actuality*, with respect to the realized essential constitution of the world of which we are a part: and that constitution turns out to have a complex structure generated by its own internal "logic," which guides its self-realization. The difference between mere reality and full actuality is what Hegel calls the "ideality" of the latter— by which he means that it adequately embodies its essential content. He uses the term *Idee* (plural, *Ideen*) in a special sense, to convey something more substantial than the mere structural "concept" (*Begriff*) of some sort of thing (whether a work of art, a state, or a human being): specifically, it is applied to that *Begriff* as it is *instantiated* in some specific way or other—or as he puts it, it signifies "the union of *Begriff* and objectivity." By *Idee*, therefore, he means the very opposite of something that exists merely "in principle," or in someone's thought or imagination. It applies only to actual, fully developed instances of the kind of phenomenon in question.

Kant had made much of the importance of what he called "regulative ideas"

(*Ideen*) of reason, which reason generates in order to guide itself in its inquiries (much as we speak of "guiding ideas"). Hegel adapts this usage to his own related but different purposes. "Reason," in his writing, refers most fundamentally to the rational structure and dynamic of the world's inherent nature; and *Idee* refers to what might be thought of as reason's guiding prescription to realize that structure's various provisions: namely, by their becoming objectified or instantiated in the appropriate sorts of ways, and by actually achieving such concrete existence in some particular way that accords fully and adequately with the *Begriff* in question. So, for example, a state is an *actual* state only if it really is in all essential respects the sort of thing that a state ought to be—a true or genuine state, and not just a "real" one that may leave much to be desired; and in such a state the *Idee* of the state has *come true*. The "absolute *Idee*" takes this way of thinking to be the way to do the best possible interpretive justice to the whole of reality (our own human reality included), as an all-encompassing totality of natural, historical, and spiritual reality from and within which everything derives its meaning and significance.

Our own significance, for Hegel, must be reinterpreted in light of the significance of human—and, more specifically, of human-spiritual—reality in this larger scheme of things. What matters about us is neither our physical existence nor even our existence as a particular biological species (in aggregate or as the ephemeral individuals we are). Anthropologically speaking, human life does have features that the existence of other types of creatures lacks, and that are of some interest; but much more important is the spiritual reality that has developed in the course of human history, in the forms of "objective spirituality" that various peoples have developed at the level of social and cultural life, and of "absolute spirituality" that they have gone on to develop by way of their arts, religions, and cognitive pursuits.

The story of human history, as Hegel conceives and presents it, is the story of the emergence and development in the world of human-spiritual *freedom*, socially and intellectually as well as personally understood. It is also the story of the enrichment of human-spiritual reality, through the forms of creative expressiveness that have become humanly possible at the levels of personal, cultural, artistic, and intellectual life. And it is further the story of the development of knowledge of ourselves and our world, by way of the emergence and refinement of manifold cognitive disciplines, culminating in the sort of interpretive comprehension that is philosophy at its best (that is, Hegel's kind of philosophy), which Hegel characterizes finally as "*Geist* knowing itself as *Geist*."

It is these kinds of themes, rather than metaphysical or epistemological questions concerning the status, knowability, or meaningfulness of "things in themselves" pursued independently of them, that are at the heart of Hegel's kind of idealism. And with respect to such questions, Hegel's position is far from the "subjective idealism" of Berkeley (1685–1753), for whom "to be is to be perceived (or to be a perceiver)." The following comments from the introduction to his *Philosophy of Nature* (included in the excerpts below) should be borne in mind in this connection:

> Philosophical, true idealism consists in nothing else but [maintaining] that the truth about things is that as immediately [perceived] single, i.e. sensuous things, they are only a show, an appearance [*Schein*]. Of a metaphysics prevalent today which maintains that we cannot know things because they are absolutely shut [i.e., inaccessible] to us, it might be said that not even the animals are so stupid as these metaphysicians; for they go after things, seize and consume them. . . . Intelligence familiarizes itself with things, not of course in their sensuous existence, but by thinking them and positing their content in itself;

and in, so to speak, adding form, universality [*Allgemeinheit*, "generality"], to [this] practical ideality. . . . This universal [*allgemein*] aspect of things is not something subjective, something belonging to us: rather is it, in contrast to the transient phenomenon, the noumenon, the true, objective, actual nature of things themselves, like the Platonic Ideas, which are not somewhere afar off in the beyond, but exist in individual things as their substantial genera [i.e., types].

It is an important part of Hegel's thinking that reality is incomplete or incompletely actualized unless and until its essential nature not only is fully objectified but also comprehended in thought that is itself concretely real. (In his view, this position was aptly anticipated and symbolically expressed in the religious conception that self-knowledge is a part of God's nature and perfection, and knowledge of God is an essential element of our own highest purpose.) It is only when natural and historical development is capped off by the emergence of "*Geist* knowing itself as *Geist*," and the natural and historical development of which this emergence is the culmination is comprehended, that the "truth" of reality is *fully realized*, for Hegel, in the double sense of that expression. So, for example, the reality of nature is incomplete until its reality comes to include the knowledge of itself that we call the natural sciences. Through the appearance and development of these disciplines, the reality that expresses itself as nature comes to know those aspects of itself.

But for Hegel the "truth" of nature remains incomplete until the historical, social, and cultural *Geist* for which it sets the stage has emerged, superseding it. The reality of *Geist* likewise is incomplete until its reality comes to include the knowing of itself that in German goes by the name of the *Geisteswissenschaften* (the historical, social, and cultural disciplines). Through the appearance and development of the knowledge of objective-spiritual reality, that reality comes to know itself, and the reality that expresses itself in these phenomena comes to know that much more of itself.

But the "truth" of *Geist* itself remains incomplete, for Hegel, until the forms of "absolute" spirituality (knowledge and expression) for which sociocultural "objective" spirituality sets the stage have emerged and fully developed, superseding the limitations of sociocultural particularity. And through the appearance and development of the forms of absolute spirituality (culminating in Hegel's kind of philosophy and Hegelian "absolute knowing"), the whole reality of which we are a part comes to know itself, as well as to give essentially complete objective expression to its inherent conceptual structure that Hegel calls its *Begriff* or "concept"; in this way it attains full "actuality," having actually become what it truly is. That, for Hegel, is what "the Absolute" is—and is the only "absolute" reality there is. So he also calls it "the True" (*das Wahre*)—with the provision that it is not actually the True until it has "come true," or become what it "in truth" is. (All of this helps to make sense of his use of the term *Idee* to characterize the most complete sort of reality, and his use of the expression "absolute *Idee*" to refer to the whole of it.)

Hegel's reality is a reality of structures, relations, processes, and activities. The only "substances" it truly involves are these structures themselves (which is all that remains for him of "things in themselves") and the various ways in which it is possible for them to be objectified. His reality is also a reality of "becoming" and development, rather than of any sort of fixed and immutable being. Or rather: the only thing in or about it that is fixed and immutable is the *Begriff* (or Hegelian-logical "concept") that is its essential structural nature, which is what it is and as it is timelessly and of its own internal necessity. But even that structure is held to have a kind of developmental dynamic, in terms of its unfolding "logic," which generates the whole of that structure by way of a "logical" version of the "dialectic" that Hegel considers to characterize natural and historical phenomena as well.

In Hegelian "dialectical" development, concepts and states of affairs turn into or give rise to their own opposites, and the resulting relations of opposition and tension engender something different yet again; the cycle continues, in a context of increasing relational and interactive complexity. One version of this dialectic, at the conceptual level, is to be found in Hegel's "Logic," in the first part of his *Encyclopedia*. Another, at the experiential level, is to be found in his *Phenomenology*. Further versions are encountered not only in the two other parts of his *Encyclopedia*, which set forth his "philosophy of nature" and his "philosophy of *Geist*," but also in his lectures on the philosophy of history and the history of philosophy. In all of them, development is a central theme; and in all of them, Hegel advances a conception of development that emphasizes its dialectical rather than mechanistically causal nature.

Hegel's thinking with respect to value and normativity reflects his conviction that what matters most in this life and world—indeed, what matters absolutely—is the emergence and full development of *Geist*. That is the grand narrative that he elaborates in the *Phenomenology*, and it is also the central theme of his *Encyclopedia*, his *Philosophy of Right*, and his lectures. Nature matters because it is a precondition of the existence of *Geist*; and humanity matters because it is only in our kind of existence that subjective, objective, and absolute spirituality (as well as the animal vitality upon which they depend and build) can and do become a reality. Hegel does not maintain that the capacity for all such spirituality is necessarily limited to our species alone in the universe, and indeed he makes the species-neutral concept of *Geist*—rather than "man" (*der Mensch*) or "humanity" (*die Menschheit*) per se—his central category. What is essential is the kinds of experience and activity in question, rather than the biological species of the creatures capable of them.

The logic of Hegel's reinterpretation and argument has further consequences. Peoples and individuals alike *matter more* than creatures incapable of these forms of spirituality owing precisely to their capacity for them, and—just as important—*only to the extent* that they attain them in their own lives or contribute to their realization and development. Our human capacity for attaining spirituality already sets us apart from all mere animals, and gives human beings generally a worth and dignity that they lack; but for Hegel "*Geist* is what it does," and is nothing real apart from the forms of experience and activity in question.

Similarly, while Hegel makes much of the point that we now know that all human beings, by virtue of their common human-spiritual essential nature, are "free" in a profoundly important sense, he also stresses that human beings differ importantly—both as peoples and as individuals—in the extent to which and respects in which they develop the capacities that freedom represents. Their significance is thus a function of the actuality of their spirituality. It follows that a people or society in which all three forms of spirituality are cultivated, developed, and harmoniously flourishing is more significant—both "world-historically," in contributing our collective human-spiritual self-realization, and also intrinsically, as an instance of human-spiritual reality—than peoples or societies in which such flourishing is not occurring. And the same holds with respect to individual human beings.

It is the function and responsibility of Hegel's "state" (by which he means a broad range of a society's institutions as well as its governmental authority) to strive to ensure not only that the basic needs of its citizens can be met but also that the conditions exist for the cultivation and attainment of all three forms of spirituality. The emergence and development of such states are essential to human-spiritual self-realization for Hegel, and so are of the greatest importance. And Hegel's conception of that self-realization is also his conception of the best sort of life that it is possible for a human being to live.

Subjective (and intersubjective) spirituality presupposes but transcends biological vitality and the various forms of consciousness that are associated with the ability to function in the kind of environment in which human beings exist. It involves the transformation of the *particularity* that is characteristic of all human existence into *personality*, with forms of self-consciousness and subjectivity that are mediated and enriched by meanings arising out of one's interactions with things and others. *Objective* spirituality involves the transformation of the implicit *generality* of patterns in ways of doing things that is characteristic of existence in groups into the more explicit sociality that is mediated by *rules* associated with practices and institutions—requiring that the scope given to subjective spirituality as well as to more basic forms of behavior be curtailed. *Absolute* spirituality involves the development of ways of thought, experience, and activity with a more generalizable sort of meaning and significance, requiring the curtailment and supersession of the authority accorded to objective spirituality to settle matters of meaning and truth.

In short: for Hegel, full human-spiritual self-realization involves the cultivation of *personality*, within the context of attained *social identity*—associated with self-conscious, intelligent, and committed *participation* in the institutions of one's society and the life of one's culture—and accompanied by the achievement of a sophisticated *comprehension* of oneself and the larger reality of which one is a part. It is all of these things at once; and he believes that while it has not always been possible, and is not everywhere possible even now, it has come to be humanly possible in the kind of society that was coming into existence in his own time. The nature of that kind of society is the topic of his *Philosophy of Right*; and its emergence is the centerpiece of the story in his *Philosophy of History*.

Another way to think of these three types of spirituality is as three different types or levels of identity, selfhood, and self-realization associated with three different types of expression, rationality, and creativity—all of which are more than merely vital or biological affairs, even though human existence at the biological level is their point of departure and presupposition. All of them involve the supersession or transformation of the sorts of particularity and generality that are characteristic of human beings as a type of living creature, and of the kinds of laws, imperatives, and impulses associated with merely natural existence and biological functioning. *Subjective* spirituality, as has already been observed, involves the development of discretely self-centered forms of experience and activity and the attainment of personality, and thus of the kind of personal identity that features awareness of one's distinctness and separateness from others. It is not purely inward, however, for it also involves outward expression, in interactions with others, and objective expression, centering on the possession, use, and transformation of *things*. The kind of rationality associated with it is instrumental rationality, relating to such interactions and activities. And the kind of creativity it involves is of the sort manifested in the diversity of human personalities as they develop distinctively and express themselves in self-directed ways.

Objective spirituality involves the attainment of social identity—the identity and selfhood derived from belonging to a normatively structured society to which one is committed and with which one identifies. Its institutions and practices are objective human-spiritual realities, and participation in them enables one to transcend both the bonds of the natural and the ephemerality and particularity of the personal. One thereby achieves a more meaningful kind of self-determination, since one's conduct is guided by the historically engendered *norms* of the social and cultural "substance" of the life *of one's own people* rather than by laws of nature or contingencies of one's particular circumstances. And since conducting oneself in accordance with well-developed sets of such norms is precisely what Hegel takes rationality in the context of social life to require and amount to concretely, this is a further (and higher) form of self-realization as well; for by such conduct one realizes one's capacity for practical rationality, or action in accordance with rules. This, together with the structures themselves that Hegel supposes to be necessary features of well-turned-out societies, is the kind of "rationality" associated with objective spirituality; its creativity is manifested in the diversity of the forms of life of different peoples, and of the ways in which the same structures within a given society can and must be realized. (For a useful analogy, consider a game, like chess, that is highly structured—in ways that themselves exemplify human-spiritual creativity—and yet permits and even encourages considerable creativity in how it is played.)

Finally, *absolute* spirituality involves the attainment of an identity transcending the limitations and particular characteristics of the objective as well as subjective spirituality of those attaining it, through forms of experience and activity that bring one into relation with the most general of kinds of truth, meaning, and significance. It is the identity and selfhood of *the knower*, in the various modes of such comprehension that Hegel associates with art, religion, and scientific and philosophical thinking at their best. Each of these forms of experience and activity enables a person to enter into a *knowing* relation to something fundamental and important about reality that also is or can be an identification relation. They have other sorts of meaning and significance in human life and culture as well; but it is their "absolute" significance that matters here. For Hegel, each of them both reveals and constitutes something fundamental and important about reality and actuality. And to the extent that we engage in them

and incorporate them into what we are, *we* are incorporated into *them*. The result is a higher-level version of the kind of "twofold actuality" Hegel speaks of while discussing "objective spirituality," in which "social substance" has real existence and human lives have that sort of substantiality.

Absolute spirituality involves the sorts of rationality that are appropriate to the forms of comprehension they involve; but even here, creativity is both possible and necessary in its realization. This is obvious in the case of art, whose various forms are endless variations on the theme of the endowment of sensuous existence with significance and of significance with sensuous form. This artistic activity is one of the ways of both expressing and realizing the truth of *Geist*—and thereby also of the reality of which *Geist* is the fulfillment. But for Hegel another way of both expressing and realizing the truth of *Geist* is to be found in religion, in which religious representations (imagery and symbolism) perform the same sort of function on a deeper and richer level, mediating and making possible a more adequate comprehension and attainment of this truth. It too requires creativity, in the development of these symbolic forms. And the same point applies even in cases of scientific and philosophical thinking, which require more than pure and abstract rationality as they proceed with their projects of explanation and conceptualization, even if the presentation of their results (as, for example, in Hegel's *Logic*) may not show it.

Hegel emphasizes the importance of what he calls "the state" more than almost any other major philosopher since Plato and Aristotle, going so far as to say that it is "the march of God on earth." He accords such importance to it not as an end in itself, but rather because he considers it to be the indispensable means to the existence, development, and full realization of *Geist*, at all levels. This is the very reason for his grandly figurative characterization of the state. What is "divine," for Hegel, is nothing other than *Geist*; and the "state" is the sort of context that the actualization and flourishing of *Geist* "on earth"—that is, in the real world—requires.

"The state," as Hegel conceives of it, is the totality of institutions that make legal, economic, cultural, social, and intellectual life possible, as well as the set of political institutions that enables them to exist and operate. It even constitutes the setting within which the institution of the *family* can flourish and make its contributions to human-spiritual life, and within which the institutional conditions of the development of the various forms of *absolute*-spiritual life are established and maintained. Because it is at once the objective expression and (as it were) the infrastructure and exoskeleton of the life and "spirit" of a particular people (*Volksgeist*), it will tend to reflect something of that people's specific collective personality; but it is a state *at all* only if it performs at least the basic functions that the survival of a people requires—and is a *genuine* state only to the extent that it performs the full set of functions necessary for them to attain full human-spiritual self-realization.

Hegel's "philosophy of right" focuses on a topic that is central to the understanding both of such a state and of such self-realization: the various sorts of "right"—that is, "rightness" and normativity—they involve. He contrasts the abstractly objective rightness of legality and positive law with the subjectively intense but indeterminate rightness of "morality" and "conscience," and then distinguishes the rightness associated with what he calls "ethical life" or "ethicality" (*Sittlichkeit*) from both of them. This kind of rightness has the concrete determinateness of the customs (*Sitte*) out of which the norms of ethicality develop; but it also has the subjective conviction of commitment to the normative totality or form of life of which particular such norms are a part. They supply conscience with the "objective" content appropriate for one who identifies with such an ethical community and substance.

Raising the question of "what one ought to do," normatively speaking, *outside of* any such context is meaningless for Hegel; for it is only in such contexts that there are norms to which such questions can have reference. The fundamental principle of morality—to do "the right thing" and to promote "the good"—thus remains as abstractly and emptily subjective as the basic principle of legality remains abstractly and emptily formal until supplied with concrete content. And for Hegel such content can come only out of the historical process through which human communities develop forms of life and values overlaying natural inclination with alternate determinations that give creative expression, form, and reality to their nascent cultural identity.

———

The following selections are intended to make Hegel's thinking on a broad range of the matters with which he was concerned as accessible and intelligible as possible. Drawn from both his published writings and his lectures, they are arranged strategically rather than chronologically. The most obvious departure from chronological ordering is in the placement of the excerpts from his first major book, *Phenomenology of Geist*, which have been integrated among corresponding selections from his other writings to aid readers (and especially readers who are new to Hegel) in understanding them. His introduction to his *Encyclopedia*, on the other hand, is actually intended by Hegel to acquaint readers with his approach to philosophy and to his thought—as do his famous preface and introduction to his *Phenomenology*, his introductions to the three parts of the *Encyclopedia*, and his introductions to his lectures on the history of philosophy and the philosophy of history. These, therefore, are placed first.

They are followed by selections from Hegel's writings and lectures relating to the central topic of his entire philosophy: *Geist* (best translated as "spirit"; see the glossary below). The organization of the excerpts follows that used by Hegel in his systematic works, which distinguish three basic types or dimensions of human-spiritual reality: "subjective," "objective," and "absolute." He discusses each of them in both his *Phenomenology* and the third part of his *Encyclopedia*, his *Philosophy of Geist*. In the case of "objective" *Geist*, the relevant passages from those works are supplemented by extensive selections from his *Philosophy of Right*. (When he wrote the *Phenomenology* his thinking on moral, social, ethical, political and legal philosophy was relatively underdeveloped in relation to other aspects of his thought. In later years he devoted far more attention to normative matters, which culminated in the *Philosophy of Right*.) In the case of "absolute" *Geist*, they are supplemented by portions of the introductions to his lectures on the philosophy of art and of religion (which, together with science and philosophy, make up the domain of that type of spirituality).

Many of the translations drawn on here were done a century or more ago, during the time of Hegel's greatest popularity in Great Britain and North America. There are better recent translations of some of these works (notably *Phenomenology* and the *Philosophy of Right*), which were not available for the extensive use desired in this anthology. Where permissible, the editor has updated the older versions and improved their style and accuracy.

There is one problem that no such changes could solve: a number of Hegel's key German-language terms have no English translations that capture what he means by them sufficiently well to convey that distinctive meaning and to avoid contributing to their misunderstanding. The problem is worsened by inconsistencies among translations and even within single translations in the inadequate English words chosen to render them. The best solution is to leave these key words untranslated, incorporating them into our own philosophical vocabulary as Hegelian terms with Hegelian meanings. Where this has not been possible in the following selections, the Hegelian terms have been inserted in

brackets or footnotes as reminders to the reader to recall the specific Hegelian meanings of the inadequate English-language terms in these texts.

In both sorts of cases, explanatory notes have been provided to assist the reader in coming to understand not just their dictionary meanings but their meanings for Hegel and what Hegel is saying when he uses them. Their strangeness should soon fade, and their growing familiarity should aid the reader in understanding them and in better understanding Hegel. A glossary of the main terms in question is given at the end of this introduction, providing brief explanatory and explicatory comments, as well as guidance in German pronunciation.

———

Philosophy, for Hegel, is (or at any rate still can and should be) the attempt to think through and answer its Big Questions as clearly, objectively, fully, and deeply as possible—questions about the fundamental nature of reality, about the nature and significance (if any) of our own human reality in the larger scheme of things, and about how we might best and most meaningfully live our lives. These are questions he believes can be rightly answered by philosophy—more specifically, by his kind of philosophy—better than they can be in any other way, even though various religious as well as other philosophical ways of answering them turn out to have been on the right track. He believed that philosophy, rightly pursued, can enable us to achieve a sound fundamental and essentially complete comprehension of our own reality and the larger reality of which we are a part, to reconcile ourselves with and accept these realities, and to attain practical wisdom concerning the living of life.

Hegel's general answer to the Big Questions is that there is a Big Story, and that we figure importantly in it. It has to do with what is going on in the world of nature and history in which we find ourselves. It is the story of that reality—our reality—as it unfolds and shows its true colors, becoming what it has in it to become. And the heart of the story is what may aptly be called its Big Idea, because that is precisely what he calls it: "the Idea," *die Idee*—a term that is best left untranslated, because it has a very special meaning for him (see the glossary below). And the Big Story is the realization of that *Idee*, which "comes true" in nature and history, as natural reality comes to be supplemented and superseded by the various forms of spiritual activity he calls "subjective," "objective," and "absolute," culminating in a form of knowing he characterizes as "absolute." In such absolute knowing (or knowledge), as we attain a fundamental comprehension of the nature of reality, that reality (of which we are a part) attains comprehension of itself.

But what is Hegel's *Idee*? In a word: it is his philosophical appropriation and reconceptualization of what is expressed in Christian religious language as "the Word [*Logos*] made flesh," the Divine become incarnate. Hegel's *Idee* is what might be called the principle of *reason* (or rational structure) *objectified*—of self-objectifying (and thereby self-realizing) rationality. The abstract, merely "logical" *Idee* is simply *this principle*; but the actual *Idee* is this principle "come true," finding full and adequate expression in real existence (natural, historical, and spiritual).

The Greek term *Logos* had been used to refer to the fundamental structure of various types of reality and of reality itself, and Hegel's "Logic" reflects that philosophical origin. The three parts of his "Logic" are concerned with various categories of *Sein* ("being" or "be-ing"), *Wesen* ("essence" or "what-ness"), and *Begriff* ("concept" or "essence" structurally articulated). Hegel's *Idee* points beyond the abstractions of this charting of the fundamental categorical and structural features of both thought and reality to their real-world manifestation—to what he calls "the union of *Begriff* and objectivity": essence that has attained existence, and existence that has come to accord with essence.

Nature and history are the results of that manifestation, in which what Hegel calls logic or the *logos* of reality acquires embodiment, and (in religious imagery or "representation") this divine nature is made flesh and becomes incarnate. It thereby moves toward self-realization, in the manifold actuality described in Hegel's "Philosophy of Nature" and "Philosophy of *Geist*"—*Geist* (exemplified by our human spirituality) being that sort of reality in which this self-realization (in both senses of this expression) is most fully and completely achieved. And that development and achievement prove to be the Big Story: reality coming to be what it had and has in it to become—with our role (and that of the institutions required for our spirituality to be attained and sustained) turning out to be a very significant one. Essentially or "logically" speaking, nothing has changed, because its basic structure is the same at the end (developmentally speaking) as it was at the beginning. But existentially or "realistically" speaking, the difference is very great indeed: all the difference in the world.

———

Understanding Hegel is not easy. The strangeness of both his language and that of many of his translators compounds the challenge posed by the strangeness of his thought. But the effort that is required to understand him is well worth making—not only because of his profound influence on the subsequent history of modern philosophy, through the opposition as well as the admiration that his thought inspired, but also because of its genuine interest. Even if one concludes that his "system" is a remarkable but fundamentally untenable interpretation of our human reality and the world in which we find ourselves, there is much to be said for looking at many of the matters he discusses in a Hegelian way.

As many philosophers after Hegel have long recognized, the stakes here are very high. Hegel makes a grand attempt to justify—by way of a philosophical interpretation rather than an appeal to religious authority—the accordance of special importance to humanity and of superiority to the kind of society, civilization, and intellectual life that was emerging in his time in the Western world, to which much of modern humanity has come to aspire. If no such interpretive strategy can be carried out plausibly and convincingly, the consequences are profound. And that, for many of Hegel's successors in the interpretive tradition, is precisely the situation in which we find ourselves. Hegel, however, would beg to differ. In this vital contest of interpretations, some version of his scheme of things—or at any rate, of his scheme of human reality—remains a formidable and fascinating contender.

SHORT GLOSSARY OF
PROBLEMATIC HEGELIAN TERMS

allgemein ("AHL-geh-mine," adjective), **Allgemeine** (noun), **Allgemeinheit** (noun): literally "common(ness) to all." Usually translated as "universal" and "universality"; it can have this sense, but in Hegel's usage it often means something less comprehensive, applying (for example) throughout some domain but only within that domain. (For example, the rules of a game or the laws of a country are *general* in form but not "universal" in the ways that the rules of logic or the laws of nature are supposed to be.) Least misleading translation in Hegel: "general." But since they can have either of these sets and sorts of meaning for him, depending on the context in which he is using them, these terms are best left untranslated.

aufheben ("OWF-hay-ben," verb), **aufgehoben** ("OWF-geh-HO-ben," past tense), **Aufhebung** ("owf-HAY-boong [as in 'book']," noun): can mean "cancel" (negate), "preserve," or "transcend." In Hegel's usage it often means all three things at once. Best translation (to try to capture all three meanings): "supersede," "supersession."

Begriff ("be-GRIFF," noun): from the verb *begreifen* ("be-GRIFE-en"), "to grasp, comprehend." Formerly often translated

in the Hegel literature as "notion," sometimes as "conception" and "idea." For Hegel it means not merely the way in which something happens to be conceived, but rather the properly conceived general (essential) nature of something structurally elaborated with respect to its specific type-character and the prerequisites of its realization: e.g., the true and structurally elaborated nature of freedom, a work of art, a state. Best translated as "concept"; but better left untranslated.

Bildung ("BILD-oong," noun): from the verb *bilden*, which can mean "to form," "to shape," or "to educate." Formerly often translated as "culture." Best translation in Hegel's usage: "education," understood in the sense not of "instruction" but rather of "formation" or "cultivation." Better left untranslated.

Gedanke ("geh-DANK-eh," noun). Generally (and appropriately) translated as "thought"; but Hegel often (and importantly) uses this term not to refer to what goes on in the conscious experience of particular thinking subjects, but rather to refer to objective (or even absolute) thought-*content*, of which few such subjects may ever become even dimly aware. So also he often uses "reason" (and "rationality") to refer both (and identically) to the essential structural content of "thought" and to that of reality—as when he states that "reason rules the world."

Geist ("gaist" [rhymes with "Christ"], noun), **geistig** (adjective). Often translated as "mind" (and "mental"), which is sometimes appropriate; but Hegel uses the language of *Geist* much more broadly. It refers not only to psychological and cognitive phenomena (things that go on "in the head") but also to artistic and religious experience and activity, language, social and cultural institutions, economic and political life, and everything else in and about human reality that has a historical-developmental character, as well as to forms of meaning and significance that transcend the plane of the merely natural (both physical and biological). Least misleading translation: "spirit" (and "spiritual"), though its religious overtones are wholly inappropriate. For Hegel, *Geist* is no nonphysical substance or entity, has no existence apart from the spatiotemporal phenomena in which it is realized, and is nothing at all apart from the activities or processes of which it consists. Best left untranslated.

Idealität ("ee-day-ahl-ih-TATE," noun). Generally and reasonably translated as "ideality," but easily misunderstood, since for Hegel it means not "unreality" but the very opposite: something like what he means by **Wirklichkeit** (actuality), and so the best sort of reality. Hegel uses the term to call attention to the meaning-ladenness (or coming to be meaning-laden) of the various forms of objectivity we encounter in our experience—but also to the objectivity-dependence (or objectification requirement) of the various forms of meaning that we and the world have it in our natures to make come true. So, in speaking of the "ideality" of the body, he is calling attention to what is not merely physical about it—namely, its animation and involvement in spiritually significant forms of experience and activity; in speaking of the "ideality" of the soul (*Seele*), he is underscoring its requirement of and inseparability from embodiment.

Idee ("ee-DAY," noun), **Ideen** ("ee-DAY-en," plural). Often translated as "idea," since that translation so readily suggests itself, but best left untranslated, because for Hegel it has a very special and important meaning that is nothing like what is generally understood by its English cognate. He uses it (abstractly) to convey the principle of "the union of *Begriff* and objectivity," as well as (more properly and appropriately) in connection with the actual existence of instances of such *Begriff*-actualization—that is, of *structure realized* (which is what Hegel means by "actuality"). *Idee* in Hegelian usage differs from *Begriff* because it refers to realization or manifestation of what is only structurally articulated in the *Begriff*, and to what it means and requires for the latter to "come true," or attain real existence and full actuality. See his explana-

tion in the selection below from *The Wissenschaft of Logic* (§§213–15).

Recht (almost rhymes with "wrecked," noun). Commonly translated in ordinary German contexts as "law," and in Hegelian texts as "right," but better translated (or thought of) as "rightness," and understood as referring to different types of norms and normativity (Hegel distinguishes between "legal," "moral," and "ethical" rightness).

Sittlichkeit ("ZITT-lich-kite," noun), **sittlich** (adjective). Sometimes translated as "morality," thereby blurring the important Hegelian distinction between *Sittlichkeit* and *Moralität* (for which that translation is appropriate); often (and better) translated as "ethical life." But best translated in Hegel as "ethicality," understood to mean "being-ethical" (parallel to the understanding of "morality" as meaning "being-moral"). *Sittlichkeit* (ethicality), for Hegel, is properly understood to be a development and refinement of action in accordance with "customs" (*Sitte*) of one's society: there is and can be no *Sittlichkeit* in abstraction from everything *sittlich* (custom-based). *Moralität*, on the other hand, can and does abstract from both the legal and the *sittlich*, but does so at the cost of losing all nonproblematic concrete content: the deliverances of "conscience" are dubious (owing to the problematic character of their origins), and those of pure practical reason are emptily formal. Where normativity is concerned, therefore, there is nothing substantively "higher" than *Sittlichkeit* to which appeal can be made. Above it is only the development of the *Weltgeist* or human spirit in the course of *Weltgeschichte* (world history), which for Hegel is "the *Weltgericht*" (the world's supreme court), and beyond that only the essential nature of *Geist* itself.

Staat ("shtaht," noun). Appropriately translated as "state"; but as Hegel uses the term it refers to the totality of a society's institutions (e.g., legal, economic, educational, and welfare-related) that undergird, structure, facilitate, and enhance life in that society, rather than just to its political and military structure and leadership. A *Staat* is a "true" or "genuine" one only if it fosters the full human-spiritual self-realization of its citizens.

Volk ("folk," noun). Often translated as "nation," but better translated as "people" (as in "the Germans are a people very different from the French," or "the peoples of Europe"). Hegel uses this term to refer to populations sharing a cultural identity (values, way of life, traditions), sensibility, and dispositions differing from those of other such historically engendered subsets of humankind near and far, as well as a sense of themselves as a community; often (but not always) they have a common language, religion, history, and political organization.

Volksgeist ("FOLKS-gaist," noun). Sometimes translated (very inadequately) as "national mind," but what is meant is the animating spirit of a people (**Volk**), reflecting the distinctive character of their culture as well as the general self-realizing dynamic of their culture or "social substance." Best left untranslated.

Vorstellung ("FOR-shtell-oong," noun). Variously translated as "idea," "conception," "mental image," and "representation." Hegel uses the term to refer (often rather condescendingly) to what he considers to be mere visualizations or crude depictions of the matters under consideration—what commonly comes to mind, for example, when something like "chair," "animal," "man," "life," "the state," "God" or "freedom" is mentioned—in contrast to the more refined conception or thought (**Gedanke**) of the thing that might be yielded by analytical reflection or scientific inquiry, and to the corresponding proper philosophical concept (**Begriff**) of that sort of thing (if there is or can be or should be one), to both of which it is philosophically inferior. Best translated as "image" or "representation" (the way we ordinarily "represent" something to ourselves, as we ordinarily tend to think of it or picture it).

Wahrheit ("VAR-hite," noun). Always translated as "truth," but for Hegel generally something more important than mere correctness: "Truth" with a capital "T." In what he calls its "philosophical sense," it conveys the idea not merely of the correspondence of something said with what is the case but of the accordance of the reality of something with its essential nature (e.g., a state is not a "true" state unless it is as a state ought to be), or of something being the realization of the potentiality of something antecedent to it (e.g., an oak tree is the "truth" of an acorn—it is what an acorn has it in it to become, and by its nature should become).

Weltgeist ("VELT-gaist," noun). "World spirit"—the same general kind of animating dynamic as that of a **Volksgeist**, but reflecting both the basic circumstances and characteristics of human existence and the nature of the human spirit more generally. It operates at the level of world history (*Weltgeschichte*) and the interactions of peoples, and enables the human spirit to transcend the limitations of particular cultures and peoples in the cultivation of its capacity for "absolute" forms of spirituality beyond their beginnings in particular cultures.

Wirklichkeit ("VIRK-lich-kite," noun), **wirklich** (adjective). Often translated as "reality" and "real," but better translated as "actuality" and "actual" because Hegel uses these terms to signify something quite different from *Realität* (reality) and *real* (real). The latter signify the mere existence of something, whereas the former signify that something exists in a manner that is in full and complete accord with its nature or true concept (**Begriff**).

Wissenschaft ("VIS-sen-shahft," noun), **wissenschaftlich** (adjective). Usually translated as "science" and "scientific"; but Hegel uses these terms to characterize any cognitive discipline, including philosophy (he divides the "philosophical sciences" into what he calls "logic," philosophy of nature, and philosophy of *Geist*). Indeed, he considers philosophy to be both very different from the natural sciences and a paradigmatic *Wissenschaft* or group of related *Wissenschaften*. Better translated by the more comprehensive term "discipline," or left untranslated.

Introductions

On Philosophy

From The Encyclopedia of the Philosophical Sciences [*Wissenschaften*]

From *Introduction*

1.] Philosophy misses an advantage enjoyed by the other sciences.[1] It cannot like them rest the existence of its objects on the natural admissions of consciousness, nor can it assume that its method of cognition, either for starting or for continuing, is one already accepted. The objects of philosophy, it is true, are upon the whole the same as those of religion. In both the object is Truth, in that supreme sense in which God and God only is the Truth. Both in like manner go on to treat of the finite worlds of Nature and the human *Geist*,[2] with their relation to each other and to their truth in God. Some *acquaintance* with its objects, therefore, philosophy may and even must presume— and a certain interest in them to boot, were it for no other reason than this: that in point of time consciousness makes general *images*[3] of objects, long before it makes *Begriffe*[4] of them, and that it is only through these mental images, and by recourse to them, that the thinking *Geist* rises to know and comprehend *thinkingly*.

But with the rise of this thinking study of things, it soon becomes evident that thought will be satisfied with nothing short of showing the *necessity* of its facts, of demonstrating the existence of its objects, as well as their nature and qualities. Our original acquaintance with them is thus discovered to be inadequate. We can assume nothing, and assert nothing dogmatically; nor can we accept the assertions and assumptions of others. And yet we must make a beginning: and a beginning, as primary and underived, makes an assumption, or rather is an assumption. It seems as if it were impossible to make a beginning at all.

2.] This *thinking study of things* may serve, in a general way, as a description of philosophy. But the description is too wide. If it be correct to say, that thought makes the distinction between man and the lower animals, then everything human is human for the sole and simple reason that it is due to the operation of thought. Philosophy, on the other hand, is a peculiar mode of thinking—a mode in which thinking becomes knowledge, and knowledge through *Begriffe*. However great therefore may be the identity and essential unity of the two modes of thought, the philosophic mode gets to be different from the more general thought which acts in all that is human, in all that

---

1. That is, disciplines (*Wissenschaften*).
2. Wallace, like many translators, renders *Geist* as "mind," which misleadingly connotes intellectual and psychological phenomena, while Hegel is referring to everything in human life beyond the merely biological. See the Hegel glossary, p. 144.
3. That is, representations (*Vorstellungen*).

4. An important term in Hegel's system—his technical term for the true objective nature or essential structural character of some type or aspect of reality (e.g., work of art, state, life, *Geist*, freedom). Often translated as "concept"; sometimes as "notion." Best left untranslated. See *Begriff* in the Hegel glossary, p. 144.

gives humanity its distinctive character. And this difference connects itself with the fact that the strictly human and thought-induced phenomena of consciousness do not originally appear in the form of a thought, but as a feeling, a perception [*Anschauung*], or mental image [*Vorstellung*]—all of which aspects must be distinguished from the form of thought [*Denken*] proper.

According to an old preconceived idea, which has passed into a trivial proposition, it is thought which marks the man off from the animals. Yet trivial as this old belief may seem, it must, strangely enough, be recalled to mind in presence of certain preconceived ideas of the present day. These ideas would put feeling and thought so far apart as to make them opposites, and would represent them as so antagonistic, that feeling, particularly religious feeling, is supposed to be contaminated, perverted, and even annihilated by thought. They also emphatically hold that religion and piety grow out of, and rest upon something else, and not on thought. But those who make this separation forget meanwhile that only man has the capacity for religion, and that animals no more have religion than they have law and morality.

Those who insist on this separation of religion from thinking usually have before their minds the sort of thought that may be styled *after-thought*.[5] They mean 'reflective' thinking, which has to deal with thoughts as thoughts, and brings them into consciousness. Slackness to perceive and keep in view this distinction which philosophy definitely draws in respect of thinking is the source of the crudest objections and reproaches against philosophy. Man— and that just because it is his nature to think—is the only being that possesses law, religion, and morality. In these spheres of human life, therefore, thinking, under the guise of feeling, faith, or generalised image, has not been inactive: its action and its productions are there present and therein contained. But it is one thing to have such feelings and generalised images that have been moulded and permeated by thought, and another thing to have thoughts about them. The thoughts, to which after-thought [*Nachdenken*] upon those modes of consciousness gives rise, are what is comprised under reflection, general reasoning, and the like, as well as under philosophy itself.

The neglect of this distinction between thought in general and the reflective thought of philosophy has also led to another and more frequent misunderstanding. Reflection of this kind has been often maintained to be the condition, or even the only way, of attaining a consciousness and certitude of the Eternal and True. The (now somewhat antiquated) metaphysical proofs of God's existence, for example, have been treated, as if a knowledge of them and a conviction of their truth were the only and essential means of producing a belief and conviction that there is a God. Such a doctrine would find its parallel, if we said that eating was impossible before we had acquired a knowledge of the chemical, botanical, and zoological characters of our food; and that we must delay digestion till we had finished the study of anatomy and physiology. Were it so, these sciences in their field, like philosophy in its, would gain greatly in point of utility; in fact, their utility would rise to the height of absolute and universal indispensableness. Or rather, instead of being indispensable, they would not exist at all.[6]

3.] The *Content*, of whatever kind it be, with which our consciousness is taken up, is what constitutes the qualitative character of our feelings, per-

---

5. That is, contemplation (*Nachdenken*).   6. Because we would not be able to survive.

ceptions, fancies, and ideas; of our aims and duties; and of our thoughts and concepts. From this point of view, feeling, perception, &c. are the *forms* assumed by these contents. The contents remain one and the same, whether they are felt, seen, represented, or willed, and whether they are merely felt, or felt with an admixture of thoughts, or merely and simply thought. In any one of these forms, or in the admixture of several, the contents confront consciousness, or are its *object*. But when they are thus objects of consciousness, the modes of the several forms ally themselves with the contents; and each form of them appears in consequence to give rise to a special object. Thus what is the same at bottom, may look like a different sort of fact.

The several modes of feeling, perception, desire, and will, so far as we are *aware* of them, are in general called representations [*Vorstellungen*];[7] and it may be roughly said, that philosophy puts thoughts, categories, or, in more precise language, adequate *Begriffe*, in the place of the generalised images we ordinarily call ideas. *Vorstellungen* such as these may be regarded as the metaphors of thoughts and notions. But to have these *Vorstellungen* does not imply that we appreciate their intellectual significance, the thoughts and concepts to which they correspond. Conversely, it is one thing to have thoughts and concepts, and another to know what impressions, perceptions, and feelings correspond to them.

This difference will to some extent explain what people call the unintelligibility of philosophy. Their difficulty lies partly in an incapacity—which in itself is nothing but want of habit—for abstract thinking; *i.e.* in an inability to get hold of pure thoughts and move about in them. In our ordinary state of mind, the thoughts are clothed upon and made one with the sensuous or spiritual material of the hour; and in contemplation, reflection, and general reasoning, we introduce a blend of thoughts into feelings, percepts, and *Vorstellungen*. (Thus, in propositions where the subject-matter is due to the senses—e.g. 'This leaf is green'—we have such categories introduced as being and individuality.) But it is a very different thing to make the thoughts pure and simple our object.

But their complaint that philosophy is unintelligible is as much due to another reason; and that is an impatient wish to have before them as a *Vorstellung* that which is in consciousness as a thought or concept. When people are asked to apprehend some concept, they often complain that they do not know what they have to think. But the fact is that in a concept there is nothing further to be thought than the concept itself. What the phrase reveals, is a hankering after *Vorstellungen* with which we are already familiar. The mind, denied the use of its familiar ideas, feels the ground where it once stood firm and at home taken away from beneath it, and, when transported into the region of pure thought, cannot tell where in the world it is.

One consequence of this weakness is that authors, preachers, and orators are found most intelligible, when they speak of things which their readers or hearers already know by rote—things which the latter are conversant with, and which require no explanation.

4.] The philosopher then has to reckon with popular modes of thought, and with the objects of religion. In dealing with the ordinary modes of

7. Because Hegel has a low opinion of the philosophical worth of *Vorstellungen* and a high opinion of *Ideen*, it is very confusing to translate the for-mer as "ideas" (as Wallace did here). See *Idee* and *Vorstellung* in the Hegel glossary, p. 144.

consciousness, he will first of all, as we saw, have to prove and almost to awaken the need for his peculiar method of knowledge. In dealing with the objects of religion, and with truth as a whole, he will have to show that philosophy is capable of apprehending them from its own resources; and should a difference from religious conceptions come to light, he will have to justify the points in which it diverges.

5.] To give the reader a preliminary explanation of the distinction thus made, and to let him see at the same moment that the real import of our consciousness is retained, and even for the first time put in its proper light, when translated into the form of thought and concept, it may be well to recall another of these old unreasoned beliefs. And that is the conviction that to get at the truth of any object or event, even of feelings, perceptions, opinions, and *Vorstellungen*, we must *think it over* [nachdenken]. Now in any case to think things over is at least to transform feelings, *Vorstellungen*, &c. into thoughts.

Nature has given everyone a faculty of thought. But thought is all that philosophy claims as the form proper to her business: and thus the inadequate view which ignores the distinction stated in § 3, leads to a new delusion, the reverse of the complaint previously mentioned about the unintelligibility of philosophy. In other words, this *Wissenschaft* must often submit to the slight of hearing even people who have never taken any trouble with it, talking as if they thoroughly understood all about it. With no preparation beyond an ordinary education they do not hesitate, especially under the influence of religious sentiment, to philosophise and to criticise philosophy. Everybody allows that to know any other *Wissenschaft* you must have first studied it, and that you can only claim to express a judgment upon it in virtue of such knowledge. Everybody allows that to make a shoe you must have learned and practised the craft of the shoemaker, though every man has a model in his own foot, and possesses in his hands the natural endowments for the operations required. For philosophy alone, it seems to be imagined, such study, care, and application are not in the least requisite.

This comfortable view of what is required for a philosopher has recently received legitimation through the theory of immediate or intuitive knowledge.

6.] So much for the form of philosophical knowledge. It is no less desirable, on the other hand, that philosophy should understand that its content is no other than *Wirklichkeit*, that core of truth which, originally produced and producing itself within the precincts of living *Geist*, has become the world—the inward and outward world of consciousness [*Welt des Bewusstseins*]. At first we become aware of these contents in what we call Experience [*Erfahrung*]. But even Experience, as it surveys the wide range of inward and outward existence [*Dasein*], has sense enough to distinguish the mere appearance [*Erscheinung*], which is transient and meaningless, from what in itself really deserves the name of *Wirklichkeit*. As it is only in form that philosophy is distinguished from other modes of attaining an acquaintance with this same content, it must necessarily be in agreement with actuality and experience. In fact, this agreement may be viewed as at least an extrinsic means of testing the truth of a philosophy. Similarly it may be held the highest and final aim of philosophic *Wissenschaft* to bring about, through the ascertainment of this agreement, a reconciliation of the self-conscious reason with *existing* reason [*seiende* Vernunft]—in other words, with actuality [*Wirklichkeit*].[8]

In the preface to my *Philosophy of Right* are found the propositions:

> *Was vernünftig ist, das ist wirklich, und*
> *was wirklich ist, das ist vernünftig.*[9]

These simple statements have given rise to expressions of surprise and hostility, even in quarters where it would be reckoned an insult to presume absence of philosophy, and still more of religion. Religion at least need not be brought in evidence; its doctrines of the divine government of the world affirm these propositions too decidedly. For their philosophic sense, we must pre-suppose intelligence enough to know, not only that God is *wirklich*,[1] that he is the most actual,[2] that he alone is truly *wirklich*; but also, as regards the logical bearings of the question, that existence is in part mere appearance, and only in part *Wirklichkeit*. In common life, any freak of fancy, any error, evil and everything of the nature of evil, as well as every degenerate and transitory existence whatever, gets in a casual way the name of *Wirklichkeit*. But even our ordinary feelings are enough to forbid a casual (fortuitous) existence getting the emphatic name of something *wirklich*; for by fortuitous we mean an existence which has no greater value than that of something possible, which could as well not be as be. As for the term *Wirklichkeit*, these critics would have done well to consider the sense in which I employ it. In a detailed Logic I had treated amongst other things of *Wirklichkeit*, and accurately distinguished it not only from the fortuitous, which, after all, has existence, but even from the cognate categories of existence and the other modifications of being.

The *Wirklichkeit* of the rational stands opposed by the popular fancy that Ideas [*Ideen*] and ideals [*Ideale*] are nothing but chimeras, and philosophy a mere system of such phantasms. It is also opposed by the very different fancy that Ideas and ideals are something far too excellent to have *Wirklichkeit*, or something too impotent to procure it for themselves. This divorce between idea and *Wirklichkeit* is especially dear to the analytic understanding which looks upon its own abstractions, dreams though they are, as something true and real, and prides itself on the imperative 'ought,' which it takes especial pleasure in prescribing even on the field of politics. As if the world had waited on it to learn how it ought to be, and was not! For, if it were as it ought to be, what would come of the precocious wisdom of that 'ought'? When understanding turns this 'ought' against trivial external and transitory objects, against social regulations or conditions, which very likely possess a great relative importance for a certain time and special circles, it may often be right. In such a case the intelligent observer may meet much that fails to satisfy the general requirements of right; for who is not acute enough to see a great deal in his own surroundings which is really far from being as it ought to be? But such

8. This term is best translated as "actuality"; but for Hegel it has a special meaning. See the discussion of *Wirklichkeit* (and *wirklich*) in the glossary, p. 144.
9. That is, "What is rational is actual, and what is actual is rational." Less cryptically put: it is the full development (attainment, realization) of the sort of rational character (structure) appropriate to a thing of some kind that makes it not merely a *real* thing of

that kind but a truly *actual* one. Thus, for Hegel, what distinguishes the "actual" from the merely "real" is its complete embodiment of the appropriate sort of "rationality."
1. Hegel's frequent use of this religious language indicates nothing about what he takes its philosophical meaning and content to be.
2. The *Wirklichste*; the supreme actuality.

acuteness is mistaken in the conceit that, when it examines these objects and pronounces what they ought to be, it is dealing with questions of philosophic *Wissenschaft.* The concern of philosophy is with the Idea [*der Idee*][3]—which is not so impotent as merely to have a right or an obligation to exist without actually existing, and which is the *Wirklichkeit* of which those objects, social regulations and conditions, are only the superficial outside.

7.] Thus reflection—thinking things over—in a general way involves the principle (which also means the beginning) of philosophy. And when the reflective spirit arose again in its independence in modern times, after the epoch of the Lutheran Reformation,[4] it did not, as in its beginnings among the Greeks, stand merely aloof, in a world of its own, but at once turned its energies also upon the apparently illimitable material of the phenomenal world. In this way the name philosophy came to be applied to all those branches of knowledge that are engaged in ascertaining the standard and the general[5] in the ocean of empirical individualities, as well as in ascertaining the Necessary element, or Laws, to be found in the apparent disorder of the endless masses of the fortuitous. It thus appears that modern philosophy derives its materials from our own personal observations and perceptions of the external and internal world, from nature as well as from the mind and heart of man, when both stand in the immediate presence of the observer.

This principle of Experience carries with it the unspeakably important condition that, in order to accept and believe any fact, we must be in contact with it; or, in more exact terms, that we must find the fact united and combined with the certainty of our own selves. We must be in touch with our subject-matter, whether it be by means of our external senses, or, else, by our profounder spirit and our intimate self-consciousness. —This principle is the same as that which has in the present day been termed faith, immediate knowledge, the revelation in the outward world, and, above all, in our own heart.

Those *Wissenschaften,* which thus got the name of philosophy, we call *empirical* sciences, for the reason that they take their departure from experience. Still the essential results which they aim at and provide, are laws, general propositions, a theory—the thoughts of what is found existing. On this ground the Newtonian physics[6] was called Natural Philosophy. * * *

8.] In its own field this empirical knowledge may at first give satisfaction; but in two ways it is seen to come short. In the first place there is another circle of objects which it does not embrace. These are Freedom, *Geist,* and God. They belong to a different sphere, not because it can be said that they have nothing to do with experience; for though they are certainly not experiences of the senses, it is quite an identical proposition to say that whatever is in consciousness is experienced. The real ground for assigning them to

---

3. This term is very important for Hegel, but it is used by him in a way that diverges so greatly from the ordinary English meaning of "idea" that it is best left untranslated wherever possible to indicate that it is to be understood in Hegel's technical sense. Very briefly put: Hegel uses the term *Begriff* (concept) to refer to rational structure (of some sort or another), and he uses the term *Idee* to refer to such structure conceived as realized or objectified. See both terms in the Hegel glossary, p. 144.
4. The 16th-century religious movement that resulted in schism within the Roman Catholic Church and the new Protestant traditions, led in part by the German theologian Martin Luther (1483–1546).
5. The *Allgemeine.* The adjective *allgemein* and the nouns formed from it are commonly translated as "universal," "the universal," and "universality"; but some more limited form of "generality" is often what is meant. See the Hegel glossary, p. 144.
6. That is, the three laws of motion first set forth by the English physicist Sir Isaac Newton (1642–1727).

another field of cognition is that in their scope and *content* these objects evidently show themselves as infinite.

* * *

9.] * * * The relation of speculative *Wissenschaft* to the other disciplines [*Wissenschaften*] may be stated in the following terms. It does not in the least neglect the empirical facts contained in the several *Wissenschaften* but recognises and adopts them: it appreciates and applies towards its own structure what is general [*Allgemeine*] in these *Wissenschaften*, their laws and classifications: but besides all this, into the categories of *Wissenschaft* it introduces, and gives currency to, other categories. The difference, looked at in this way, is only a change of categories. Speculative Logic contains all previous Logic and Metaphysics: it preserves the same forms of thought, the same laws and objects—while at the same time remodelling and expanding them with wider categories.

From *Begriff* in the speculative sense we should distinguish what is ordinarily called a *Begriff*. The phrase, that no *Begriff* can ever comprehend the Infinite, a phrase which has been repeated over and over again till it has grown axiomatic, is based upon this narrow estimate of what is meant by '*Begriffe*.'

10.] This thought, which is proposed as the instrument of philosophic knowledge, itself calls for further explanation. We must understand in what way it possesses necessity or cogency: and when it claims to be equal to the task of apprehending the absolute objects (God, *Geist*, Freedom), that claim must be substantiated. Such an explanation, however, is itself a lesson in philosophy, and properly falls within the scope of the science itself. A preliminary attempt to make matters plain would only be unphilosophical, and consist of a tissue of assumptions, assertions, and inferential pros and cons, *i.e.* of dogmatism without cogency, as against which there would be an equal right of counter-dogmatism.

A main line of argument in the Critical Philosophy [of Kant] bids us pause before proceeding to inquire into God or into the true being of things, and tells us first of all to examine the faculty of cognition and see whether it is equal to such an effort. We ought, says Kant, to become acquainted with the instrument, before we undertake the work for which it is to be employed;[7] for if the instrument be insufficient, all our trouble will be spent in vain. The plausibility of this suggestion has won for it general assent and admiration; the result of which has been to withdraw cognition from an interest in its objects and absorption in the study of them, and to direct it back upon itself; and so turn it to a question of form. Unless we wish to be deceived by words, it is easy to see what this amounts to. In the case of other instruments, we can try and criticise them in other ways than by setting about the special work for which they are destined. But the examination of knowledge can only be carried out by an act of knowledge. To examine this so-called instrument is the same thing as to know it. But to seek to know before we know is as absurd as the [supposedly] wise resolution of Scholasticus, not to venture into the water until he had learned to swim.[8]

* * *

7. An effort undertaken in KANT's *Critique of Pure Reason* (1781).
8. A story that appears in a collection of tales about a pedant (*scholasticus*), traditionally attributed to the Greek Stoic philosopher Hierocles (active 117–138 C.E.).

11.] The special conditions which call for the existence of philosophy may be described as follows. *Geist*, when it is sentient or perceptive, finds its object in something sensuous; when it imagines, in a picture or image; when it wills, in an aim or end. But in contrast to—or it may be only in distinction from—these forms of its existence and of its objects, *Geist* has also to gratify the cravings of its highest and most inward life. That innermost self is thought. Thus *Geist* renders thought its object. In the best meaning of the phrase, it comes to itself; for thought is its principle, and its very unadulterated self. But while thus occupied, thought entangles itself in contradictions, *i.e.* loses itself in the hard-and-fast non-identity of its thoughts, and so, instead of reaching itself, is caught and held in its counterpart. This result, to which honest but narrow thinking leads the mere understanding, is resisted by the loftier craving of which we have spoken. That craving expresses the perseverance of thought, which continues true to itself, even in this conscious loss of its native rest and independence, 'that it may overcome' and work out in itself the solution of its own contradictions.

To see that thought in its very nature is dialectical, and that, as understanding, it must fall into contradiction—the negative of itself, will form one of the main lessons of logic. When thought grows hopeless of ever achieving, by its own means, the solution of the contradiction which it has by its own action brought upon itself, it turns back to those solutions of the question with which *Geist* had learned to pacify itself in some of its other modes and forms. Unfortunately, however, the retreat of thought has led it, as Plato[9] noticed even in his time, to a very uncalled-for hatred of reason (misology); and it then takes up against its own endeavours that hostile attitude of which an example is seen in the doctrine that 'immediate' knowledge, as it is called, is the exclusive form in which we become cognisant of truth.

12.] The rise of philosophy is due to these cravings of thought. Its point of departure is Experience; including under that name both our immediate consciousness and the inductions from it. Awakened, as it were, by this stimulus, thought is vitally characterised by raising itself above the natural state of *Geist*, above the senses and inferences from the senses into its own unadulterated element, and by assuming, accordingly, at first a stand-aloof and negative attitude towards the point from which it started. Through this state of antagonism to the phenomena of sense its first satisfaction is found in itself, in the idea of the *allgemein* essence of these phenomena: an idea (the Absolute, or God) which may be more or less abstract. Meanwhile, on the other hand, the empirical sciences exert a stimulus to overcome the form in which their varied contents are presented, and to elevate these contents to the rank of necessity. For these contents have the aspect of a vast conglomerate, one thing coming side by side with another, as if they were merely given and presented—as in short devoid of all essential or necessary connexion. In consequence of this stimulus thought is dragged out of its unrealised *Allgemeinheit* and its fancied or merely possible satisfaction, and impelled onwards to a development from itself. On one hand this development only means that thought incorporates the contents of *Wissenschaft*, in all their speciality of

9. Greek philosopher (ca. 427–ca. 347 B.C.E.).

detail as submitted. On the other it makes these contents imitate the action of the original creative thought, and present the aspect of a free evolution determined by the logic of the matter itself.

On the relation between 'immediacy' and 'mediation' in consciousness we shall speak later, expressly and with more detail. Here it may be sufficient to premise that, though the two 'moments' or factors present themselves as distinct, still neither of them can be absent, nor can one exist apart from the other. Thus the knowledge of God, as of everything supersensible [*übersinnlich*], is in its true character an exaltation above sensations or perceptions: it consequently involves a negative attitude to the initial data of sense, and to that extent implies mediation. For to mediate is to take something as a beginning and to go onward to a second thing; so that the existence of this second thing depends on our having reached it from something else contradistinguished from it. In spite of this, the knowledge of God is no mere sequel, dependent on the empirical phase of consciousness: in fact, its independence is essentially secured through this negation and exaltation. —No doubt, if we attach an unfair prominence to the fact of mediation, and represent it as implying a state of conditionedness, it may be said—not that the remark would mean much—that philosophy owes its origin to experience (to the *a posteriori*). (As a matter of fact, thinking is always the negation of what we have immediately before us.) With as much truth however we may be said to owe eating to the means of nourishment, so long as we can have no eating without them. If we take this view, eating is certainly represented as ungrateful: it devours that to which it owes itself. Thinking, upon this view of its action, is equally ungrateful.

But there is also an *a priori* aspect of thought, where by a mediation, not made by anything external but by a reflection into self, we have that immediacy which is universality, the self-satisfaction of thought which is so much at home with itself that it feels an indifference to descend to particulars, and in that way to the development of its own nature. It is thus also with religion, which, whether it be rude or elaborate, whether it be invested with scientific precision of detail or confined to the simple faith of the heart, possesses, throughout, the same intensive nature of contentment and felicity. But if thought never gets further than the *Allgemeinheit* of ideas, as was perforce the case in the first philosophies (when the Eleatics never got beyond Being, or Heraclitus[1] beyond Becoming), it is justly open to the charge of formalism. Even in a more advanced phase of philosophy, we may often find a doctrine which has mastered merely certain abstract propositions or formulae, such as, 'In the absolute all is one,' 'Subject and object are identical'—and only repeating the same thing when it comes to particulars. With respect to this first period of thought, the period of abstract *Allgemeinheit*, we may safely say that experience is the real source of *development* in philosophy. For, firstly, the empirical disciplines do not stop short at the mere observation of the individual features of a phenomenon. By the aid of thought, they are able to meet philosophy with materials prepared for it, in the shape of

---

1. Greek philosopher (active ca. 500 B.C.E.); he believed that the world (made of fire) is constantly changing. The Eleatics, based in a Greek colony in southern Italy (5th c. B.C.E.), believed that what exists is single, indivisible, and unchanging.

allgemein determinations, *i.e.* laws, and classifications of the phenomena. When this is done, the particular facts which they contain are ready to be received into philosophy. This, secondly, implies a certain compulsion on thought itself to proceed to these concrete specific truths. The reception of these contents, now that thought has removed their immediacy and made them cease to be mere data, forms at the same time a development of thought out of itself. Philosophy, then, owes its development to the empirical disciplines. In return it gives their contents what is so vital to them, the *freedom* of thought (that is, an *a priori* character) and the *warrant* of *necessity*, in place of dependence on the evidence of facts merely, that they were so found and so experienced. The fact as experienced thus becomes an illustration and a reflection of the original and completely self-supporting activity of thought.

13.] Viewed in the particulars of its external history, the origin and development of philosophy is the history of this discipline. The stages in the evolution of the *Idee*[2] there seem to follow each other by accident, and to present merely a number of different and unconnected principles, which the several systems of philosophy carry out in their own way. But it is not so. For these thousands of years the same Architect has directed the work: and that Architect is the one living *Geist* whose nature is to think, to bring to self-consciousness what it is, and, with its being thus set as object before it, to be at the same time raised above it, and so to reach a higher stage of its own being. The different systems which the history of philosophy presents are therefore not irreconcilable with unity. We may either say, that it is one philosophy at different degrees of maturity: or that the particular principle, which is the groundwork of each system, is but a branch of one and the same universe of thought. In philosophy the latest birth of time is the result of all the systems that have preceded it, and must include their principles; and so, if, on other grounds, it deserve[s] the title of philosophy, [it] will be the fullest, most comprehensive, and most adequate system of all.

The spectacle of so many and so various systems of philosophy suggests the necessity of defining more exactly the relation of the *Allgemeine* and the particular. When the *Allgemeine* is made a mere form and co-ordinated with the particular, as if it were on the same level, it sinks into a particular itself. Even common sense in every-day matters is above the absurdity of setting the *Allgemeine beside* the particulars. Would any one, who wished for fruit, reject cherries, pears, and grapes, on the ground that they were cherries, pears, or grapes, and not fruit? But when philosophy is in question, the excuse of many is that philosophies are so different, and none of them is *the* philosophy— that each is only *a* philosophy. Such a plea is assumed to justify any amount of contempt for philosophy. And yet cherries too are fruit. Often, too, a system, of which the principle is the *Allgemeine*, is put on a level with another of which the principle is something particular, and with theories which deny the existence of philosophy altogether. Such systems are said to be only different views of philosophy. With equal justice, light and darkness might be styled different kinds of light.

---

2. That is, the evolution of the comprehension of the fundamental nature of reality as *Idee* (i.e., as self-realizing rationality).

14.] The same evolution of thought that is exhibited in the history of philosophy is presented in the System of Philosophy itself—freed, however, from historical externality, and purely in the element of thought. Free and genuine thought is intrinsically concrete—and so it is *Idee*; and when it is viewed in the whole of its universality, it is *the Idee*, or the Absolute. Its *Wissenschaft* must form a system. For the truth is concrete; that is, whilst it gives a bond and principle of unity, it also possesses an internal source of development. Truth, then, is only possible as a totality of thought; and the freedom of the whole, as well as the necessity of the several sub-divisions, which it implies, are only possible when these are discriminated and defined.

Unless it is systematic, philosophy cannot be *wissenschaftlich*. Unsystematic philosophising can only be expected to give expression to personal peculiarities, and has no principle for the regulation of its contents. Apart from their interdependence and organic union, the truths of philosophy are valueless, and must then be treated as baseless hypotheses or subjective convictions. Yet many philosophical treatises confine themselves to such an exposition of the opinions and sentiments of the author.

The term *system* is often misunderstood. It does not denote a philosophy, the principle of which is narrow and to be distinguished from others. On the contrary, a genuine philosophy makes it a principle to include every particular principle.

15.] Each of the parts of philosophy is a philosophical whole, a circle rounded and complete in itself. In each of these parts, however, the philosophical *Idee* is found in a particular specificality or medium. The single circle, because it is a real totality, bursts through the limits imposed by its special medium, and gives rise to a wider circle. The whole of philosophy in this way resembles a circle of circles. The *Idee* appears in each single circle, but, at the same time, the whole *Idee* is constituted by the system of these peculiar phases, and each is a necessary member of the organisation.

16.] In the form of an Encyclopaedia, the *Wissenschaft* has no room for a detailed exposition of particulars, and must be limited to setting forth the commencement of the special *Wissenschaften* and the *Begriffe* of cardinal importance in them.

How much of the particular parts is requisite to constitute a particular branch of knowledge is so far indeterminate, that the part, if it is to be something true, must be not an isolated member merely, but itself an organic whole. The entire field of philosophy therefore really forms a single *Wissenschaft*; but it may also be viewed as a whole composed of several particular *Wissenschaften*.

The encyclopaedia of philosophy must not be confounded with ordinary encyclopaedias. An ordinary encyclopaedia does not pretend to be more than an aggregation of *Wissenschaften* regulated by no principle, and merely as experience offers them. Sometimes it even includes what merely bear the name of *Wissenschaften*, while they are nothing more than a collection of bits of information. In an aggregate like this, the several branches of knowledge owe their place in the encyclopaedia to extrinsic reasons, and their unity is therefore artificial: they are *arranged*, but we cannot say they form a *system*. For the same reason, especially as the materials to be combined also depend upon no one rule or principle, the arrangement is at best an experiment, and will always exhibit inequalities.

An encyclopaedia of philosophy excludes three kinds of partial *Wissenschaft*. I. It excludes mere aggregates of bits of information. Philology in its *prima facie* aspect belongs to this class. II. It rejects the quasi-*Wissenschaften*, which are founded on an act of arbitrary will alone, such as Heraldry. *Wissenschaften* of this sort are entirely *positive*.[3] III. In another class of *Wissenschaften*, also styled positive, but which have a rational basis and a rational beginning, philosophy claims that portion as its own, while the positive features remain the property of the *Wissenschaften* themselves.

The positive element in the last class of *Wissenschaften* is of different sorts. (I) Their commencement, though rational at bottom, yields to the influence of fortuitousness, when they have to bring their universal truth into contact with actual facts and the single phenomena of experience. In this region of chance and change, the adequate concept of *Wissenschaft* must yield its place to reasons or grounds of explanation. Thus, *e.g.* in the *Wissenschaft* of jurisprudence, or in the system of direct and indirect taxation, it is necessary to have certain points precisely and definitively settled which lie beyond the absolute lines laid down by the pure *Begriff*.[4] A certain latitude of settlement accordingly is left: and each point may be determined in one way on one principle, in another way on another, and admits of no definitive certainty. Similarly the *Idee* of Nature, when parcelled out in detail, is dissipated into contingencies. Natural history, geography, and medicine stumble upon descriptions of existence, upon kinds and distinctions, which are not determined by reason, but by sport and adventitious incidents. Even history comes under the same category. The *Idee* is its essence and inner nature; but, as it appears, everything is under contingency and in the field of voluntary action. (II) These *Wissenschaften* are positive also in failing to recognise the finite nature of what they predicate, and to point out how these categories and their whole sphere pass into a higher. They assume their statements to possess an authority beyond appeal. Here the fault lies in the finitude of the form, as in the previous instance it lay in the matter. (III) In close sequel to this, such *Wissenschaften* are positive in consequence of the inadequate grounds on which their conclusions rest: based as these are on detached and casual inference, upon feeling, faith, and authority, and, generally speaking, upon the deliverances of inward and outward perception. Under this head we must also class the philosophy which proposes to build upon 'anthropology,' facts of consciousness, inward sense or outward experience. It may happen, however, that 'empirical' is an epithet applicable only to the form of scientific exposition; whilst intuitive sagacity has arranged what are mere phenomena, according to the essential sequence of the *Begriff*. In such a case the contrasts between the varied and numerous phenomena brought together serve to eliminate the external and accidental circumstances of their conditions, and the *Allgemeine* thus comes clearly into view. Guided by such an intuition, experimental physics will present the rational *Wissenschaft* of Nature—as history will present the *Wissenschaft* of human affairs and actions—in an external picture, which mirrors the philosophic *Begriff*.

---

3. That is, posited (as in "positive law"): stipulated or determined by choice or decision (rather than from some sort of necessity).

4. More literally, "beyond the in-and-of-itself-determinateness of the concept" (*ausser dem An-und-für-sich-Bestimmtsein des Begriffes*).

17.] It may seem as if philosophy, in order to start on its course, had, like the rest of the *Wissenschaften*, to begin with a subjective presupposition. The various *Wissenschaften* postulate their respective objects, such as space, number, or whatever it be; and it might be supposed that philosophy had also to postulate the existence of thought. But the two cases are not exactly parallel. It is by the free act of thought that it occupies a point of view, in which it is for its own self, and thus gives itself an object of its own production. Nor is this all. The very point of view, which originally is taken on its own evidence only, must in the course of the *Wissenschaft* be converted to a result—the ultimate result in which philosophy returns into itself and reaches the point with which it began. In this manner philosophy exhibits the appearance of a circle which closes with itself, and has no beginning in the same way as the other *Wissenschaften* have. To speak of a beginning of philosophy has a meaning only in relation to a person who proposes to commence the study, and not in relation to the discipline as *Wissenschaft*. The same thing may be thus expressed. The concept of *Wissenschaft*—the concept therefore with which we start—which, for the very reason that it is preliminary, implies a separation between the thought which is our object and the subject philosophising which is, as it were, external to the former, must be grasped and comprehended by the discipline itself. This is in short the one single aim, action, and goal of philosophy—to arrive at the *Begriff* of its *Begriff*,[5] and thus secure its return and its satisfaction.

18.] As the whole *Wissenschaft*, and only the whole, can exhibit what the *Idee* is, it is impossible to give a preliminary general *Vorstellung* of a philosophy.[6] Nor can a division of philosophy into its parts be intelligible, except in connexion with the system. A preliminary division, like the limited conception from which it comes, can only be an anticipation. But the *Idee* turns out to be thought [*Denken*][7] which is completely identical with itself—and not identical simply in the abstract, but also in its action of setting itself over against itself, so as to gain a being of its own, and yet of being in full possession of itself while it is in this other. Thus philosophy is subdivided into three parts:

I. Logic, the *Wissenschaft* of the *Idee* in and for itself.

II. The Philosophy of Nature: the *Wissenschaft* of the *Idee* in its otherness.

III. The Philosophy of *Geist*: the *Wissenschaft* of the *Idee* come back to itself out of that otherness.

As observed in § 15, the differences between the several philosophical disciplines are only aspects or specialisations of the *Idee* itself, which alone is what is exhibited in these different media. In Nature it is not something other than the *Idee* that is to be discerned; but it is in the form of relinquishment [*Entäußerung*].[8] In *Geist* it takes the form of being for-itself [*für sich sein*] and of becoming in- and for-itself [*an und für sich*

---

5. That is, to arrive at the fully and properly articulated *Begriff* (concept) of what is under consideration—namely, the concept of philosophy (as the ultimate *Wissenschaft*).

6. That is, of a philosophy so conceived, as the kind of *Wissenschaft* that Hegel has been discussing.

7. By "thought" (*Denken*) Hegel here means not subjective thinking but rather thought conceived independently of any particular thinker, and thus

the fundamental rational structure of reality—which, as he goes on to say, realizes itself by giving itself expression (in nature and history).

8. That is, the form the *Idee* takes in nature involves externalizing (*Äusserung*) itself (i.e., its essential nature, the ultimate *Begriff*) in objective particular and finite imperfect existence, which requires and means relinquishing or giving up the purity and clarity of its rational structure.

werdend].[9] Every such form in which the *Idee* is expressed is at the same time a passing or fleeting stage: and hence each of these subdivisions has not only to know its contents as an object which has being for the time, but also in the same act to expound how these contents pass into their higher circle. To represent the relation between them as a division, therefore, leads to misconception; for it co-ordinates the several parts or disciplines one beside another, as if they had no innate development, but were, like so many species, really and radically distinct.

SOURCE: From *The Logic of Hegel, Translated from "The Encyclopaedia of the Philosophical Sciences,"* trans. William Wallace, 2nd ed., rev. and augmented (Oxford: Oxford University Press, 1892), 3–14, 16–29 (translation modified by the editor). Except where otherwise indicated, German words in brackets are the terminology used in the German original, inserted by the editor in addition to their renderings in the translation; and unbracketed German words are the original terminology, substituted in place of their renderings in the translation by the editor for reasons given in notes and in the Hegel glossary (p. 144). While not intended by Hegel to be taken as an introduction simply to the first part of his 3-volume *Encyclopedia of the Philosophical Sciences* (*Encyklopädie der philosophischen Wissenschaften im Grundrisse*), this introduction was so presented by Wallace as the first chapter in his translation of *Die Wissenschaft der Logik* (3rd ed., 1830).

This text not only is a good introduction to Hegel's *Encyclopedia*, thought, and system but also situates him in relation to the history of modern philosophy prior to him (as he saw it) in a way that is very helpful in understanding his general philosophical project. The term "encyclopedia" in the work's general title should be understood as "comprehensive systematic exposition." *Wissenschaft*, commonly translated (by Wallace and many others) as "science," should be understood as "cognitive discipline" (as in various academic disciplines that all pursue knowledge or understanding, but inquire into different matters by differing methods). To prevent confusion with the natural sciences, this term will often be translated in the following selections as "discipline" or left in German. And "logic" here (as was traditional in philosophy through the 19th century but ceased to be after its formalization in the early 20th century by GOTTLOB FREGE and BERTRAND RUSSELL) refers to the basic structures and laws of thought and reality. Thus Hegel is introducing not only his version of the part of philosophy that (in his view) deals or should deal with these fundamental matters, but also his own comprehensive systematic treatment of the ways in which these structures and laws are reflected in the realms of Nature and *Geist* (Spirit).

On Philosophy and "Phenomenology"

From Phenomenology of *Geist*

From *Preface*

In the case of a philosophical work it seems not only superfluous, but, in view of the nature of the subject, even inappropriate and inexpedient to begin, as writers usually do, with a preface explaining the end the author had in mind, the circumstances which gave rise to the work, and the relation in which the writer takes it to stand to other treatises on the same subject, written by his predecessors or his contemporaries. For whatever it might be suitable to state about philosophy in a preface—say, an historical sketch of the main drift and point of view, the general content and results, a string of desultory assertions

---

9. That is, the form the *Idee* takes in *Geist* involves both self-consciousness and development toward a kind of self-consciousness in which adequacy to what it is "in itself" (i.e., essentially) is attained.

and assurances about truth—this cannot be accepted as the form and manner in which to expound philosophical truth.

Moreover, because philosophy has its being essentially in the element of *Allgemeinheit*,[1] which encloses the particular within it, the end or final result seems, in the case of philosophy more than in that of other *Wissenschaften*,[2] to have absolutely expressed the complete fact itself in its very nature, for which the mere process of bringing it to light would seem, properly speaking, to have no essential significance. On the other hand, in the general idea of e.g. anatomy—the knowledge of the parts of the body regarded as lifeless—we are quite sure we do not possess the objective concrete fact, the actual content of the science, but must, over and above, be concerned with particulars. Further, in the case of such a collection of items of knowledge, which has no real right to the name of science, any talk about purpose and such-like *Allgemeinheiten* is not commonly very different in manner from the descriptive and superficial way in which the contents of the science—these nerves and muscles, etc.—are themselves spoken of. In philosophy, on the other hand, it would at once be felt incongruous were such a method made use of and yet shown by philosophy itself to be incapable of grasping the truth.

In the same way too by determining the relation which a philosophical work professes to have to other treatises on the same subject, an extraneous interest is introduced, and obscurity is thrown over the point at issue in the knowledge of the truth. The more the ordinary mind takes the opposition between true and false to be fixed, the more is it accustomed to expect either agreement or contradiction with a given philosophical system, and only to see the one or the other in any explanation about such a system. It does not conceive the diversity of philosophical systems as the progressive evolution of truth; rather, it sees only contradiction in that variety. The bud disappears when the blossom breaks through, and we might say that the former is refuted by the latter; in the same way when the fruit comes, the blossom may be explained to be a false form of the plant's existence, for the fruit appears as its true nature in place of the blossom. These stages are not merely differentiated; they supplant one another as being incompatible with one another. But the ceaseless activity of their own inherent nature makes them at the same time moments of an organic unity, where they not merely do not contradict one another, but where one is as necessary as the other; and this equal necessity of all moments constitutes from the outset the life of the whole. But contradiction in the case of a philosophical system is not usually conceived in this way; and again, the mind perceiving the contradiction does not commonly know how to relieve it or keep it free of onesidedness, or to recognise in what seems conflicting and inherently antagonistic the presence of mutually necessary moments.

The demand for such explanations, as also the attempts to satisfy this demand, very easily pass for the essential business philosophy has to undertake. Where could the inmost truth of a philosophical work be found better

1. Literally, "common to all"; often better translated as "generality" rather than as "universality." See the Hegel glossary, p. 144.
2. Literally, something like "knowledge business" or "knowledge work." The translation "science" is often appropriate, but for Hegel as for many other German philosophers the term should be understood more broadly to mean something like "cognitive inquiry" or "cognitive discipline" (depending on the context), rather than being conceived on the model of the natural sciences. Hegel considers his kind of philosophy to be paradigmatic of *Wissenschaft*, and its broader sense should be kept in mind whenever "science," "scientific," etc. appear here. See the Hegel glossary, p. 144.

expressed than in its purposes and results? and in what way could these be more definitely known than through their distinction from what is produced during the same period by others working in the same field? If, however, such procedure is to pass for more than the beginning of knowledge, if it is to pass for actually knowing what a philosophical system is, then we must, in point of fact, look on it as a device for avoiding the real business at issue, an attempt to combine the appearance of being in earnest and taking trouble about the subject with an actual neglect of the subject altogether. For the real subject-matter is not exhausted in its purpose, but in working the matter out; nor is the mere result attained the concrete whole itself, but the result along with the process of arriving at it. The purpose by itself is a lifeless *Allgemeine*, just as the general drift is a bare activity in a certain direction, which is still without its concrete realisation; and the naked result is the corpse of the system which has left its guiding tendency behind it. Similarly, the distinctive difference of anything is rather the boundary, the limit, of the subject; it is found at that point where the matter stops, or it is what the matter is *not*. To trouble oneself in this fashion with the purpose and results, or again with the differences, the positions taken up and judgments passed by one thinker and another, is therefore an easier task than perhaps it seems. For instead of laying hold of the matter itself, a procedure of that kind is all the while away from the subject altogether. Instead of dwelling within it and becoming absorbed by it, knowledge of that sort is always grasping at something else; such knowledge, instead of keeping to the subject-matter and giving itself up to it, never gets away from itself. The easiest thing of all is to pass judgments on what has a solid substantial content; it is more difficult to grasp it, and most of all difficult to do both together and produce the systematic exposition of it.

The beginning of *Bildung*[3] and of the struggle to get out of the unbroken immediacy of naïve psychical life has always to be made by acquiring knowledge of *allgemein* principles and points of view, by striving, in the first instance, to work up simply to the *thought* of the subject-matter in general, not forgetting at the same time to give reasons for supporting it or refuting it, to apprehend the concrete riches and fullness contained in its various determinate qualities, and to know how to furnish a coherent, orderly account of it and a responsible judgment upon it. This beginning of *Bildung* will, however, very soon make way for the earnestness of actual life in all its fullness, which leads to a living experience of the subject-matter itself; and when, in addition, conceptual thought strenuously[4] penetrates to the very depths of its meaning, such knowledge and style of judgment will be relegated to their due place in everyday thought and conversation.

The systematic development of truth in *wissenschaftlich* form can alone be the true shape in which truth exists.[5] To help to bring philosophy nearer to

---

3. That is, "education" in the broad sense of cultural and intellectual development. See the Hegel glossary, p. 144.
4. Hegel's famous phrase is: "der Ernst des Begriffs"—that is, "the seriousness of the 'concept,'" the hard work of replacing ordinary, religious, and even natural-scientific ways of thinking and images or representations (or *Vorstellungen*)

with philosophically refined and sophisticated "concepts" (*Begriffe*), the essential structures of the phenomena under consideration. *Begriff* is a very important technical Hegelian term, best left untranslated. See the Hegel glossary, p. 144.
5. More accurately, "The true form in which the truth exists can only be the *wissenschaftlich* system of it"—that is, of "the truth" itself.

the form of *Wissenschaft*—that goal where it can lay aside the name of *love* of knowledge and be actual *knowing*—that is what I have set before me. The inner necessity that knowledge should be *Wissenschaft* lies in its very nature; and the adequate and sufficient reason for this is simply and solely the systematic exposition of philosophy itself. The external necessity, however, so far as this is apprehended in an *allgemein* way, and apart from the accident of the personal element and the particular occasioning influences affecting the individual, is the same as the internal: it lies in the form and shape in which the process of time presents the existence of its moments.[6] To show that the time has come to raise philosophy to the level of *wissenschaftlich* system would, therefore, be the only true justification of the attempts which aim at proving that philosophy must assume this character; because the temporal process would thus bring out and lay bare the necessity of it, nay, more, would at the same time be carrying out that very aim itself.

When we state the true form of truth to be its *wissenschaftlich* character—or, what is the same thing, when it is maintained that truth finds the medium of its existence in *Begriffe* alone—I know that this seems to contradict an idea with all its consequences which makes great pretensions and has gained widespread acceptance and conviction at the present time. A word of explanation concerning this contradiction seems, therefore, not out of place, even though at this stage it can amount to no more than a dogmatic assurance exactly like the view we are opposing. If, that is to say, truth exists merely in what, or rather exists merely *as* what, is called at one time intuition, at another immediate knowledge of the Absolute, religion, Being—not being in the centre of divine love, but the very Being of this centre, of the Absolute itself—from that point of view it is rather the opposite of the *Begriff* form which would be required for systematic philosophical exposition. The Absolute would not be grasped in conceptual form [*begriffen*], but felt, intuited; it is not its *Begriff*, but the feeling of it and intuition of it that are to have the say and find expression.

If we consider the appearance of a claim like this in its more general setting, and look at it from the level which self-conscious *Geist* at present occupies, we shall find that self-consciousness has got beyond the substantial fullness of life, which it used to carry on in the element of thought—beyond this naïve immediacy of belief, beyond the satisfaction and security arising from the sense of certainty which conscious life possessed regarding its reconciliation with ultimate reality wherever present, whether inner or outer. Self-conscious *Geist* has not merely passed beyond that to the opposite extreme of insubstantial reflection of self into self, but beyond this too. It has not merely lost its essential and concrete life, it is also conscious of this loss and of the transitory finitude characteristic of its content. Turning away from the husks it has to feed on, and confessing that it lies in wickedness and sin, it reviles itself for so doing, and now desires from philosophy not so much to bring it to a knowledge of what it is, as to obtain once again through philosophy the restoration of that comfortably solid and substantial mode of existence it has lost. Philosophy is thus expected not so much to meet this want by opening up the compact solidity of substantial existence and bringing this to the light

6. That is, its various aspects, dimensions, or elements (*Momente*).

and level of self-consciousness, and not so much to get chaotic conscious life brought back to the orderly ways of thought and the simple unity of the *Begriff*, as to run together what thought has divided asunder, suppress the notion with its distinctions, and restore the *feeling* of existence. What it wants from philosophy is not so much *insight* as *edification*. The beautiful, the holy, the eternal, religion, love—these are the bait required to awaken the desire to bite: not the *Begriff*, but ecstasy; not the march of cold necessity in the subject-matter, but ferment and enthusiasm—these are to be the ways by which the wealth of the concrete substance is to be stored and spread out to view.[7]

With this demand there goes the strenuous effort, almost perfervidly zealous in its activity, to rescue mankind from being sunken in what is sensuous, vulgar, and of fleeting importance, and to raise men's eyes to the stars; as if men had quite forgotten the divine, and were on the verge of finding satisfaction, like worms, in mud and water. Time was when man had a heaven, decked and fitted out with endless wealth of thoughts and pictures. The significance of all that lay in the thread of light by which it was attached to heaven; instead of dwelling in the present as it is here and now, the eye glided away over the present to the Divine—away, so to say, to a present that lies beyond. The mind's gaze had to be directed under compulsion to what is earthly, and kept fixed there; and it has needed a long time to introduce that clearness, which only celestial realities had, into the crassness and confusion shrouding the sense of things earthly, and to make attention to the immediate present as such—which was called Experience—of interest and of value. Now we have apparently the need for the opposite of all this; man's mind and interest are so deeply rooted in the earthly that we require a like power to get them raised above that level. His spirit [*Geist*] shows such poverty of nature that it seems to long for the mere pitiful feeling of the divine in the abstract, and to get refreshment from that, like a wanderer in the desert craving for the merest mouthful of water. By the little which can thus satisfy the needs of the human spirit [*Geist*] we can measure the extent of its loss.

This easy contentment in receiving, or stinginess in giving, does not suit the character of *Wissenschaft*. The man who only seeks edification, who wants to envelop in mist the manifold diversity of his earthly existence and thought, and craves after the vague enjoyment of this vague and indeterminate Divinity—he may look where he likes to find this: he will easily find for himself the means to get something he can rave over and puff himself up with. But philosophy must beware of the wish to be edifying.[8]

Still less must this kind of contentment, which holds science in contempt, take upon itself to claim that raving obscurantism of this sort is something higher than *Wissenschaft*. These apocalyptic utterances pretend to occupy the very centre and the deepest depths; they look askance at all definiteness and preciseness (ὅρος)[9] of meaning; and they deliberately hold back from conceptual thinking and the constraining necessities of thought, as being the sort of reflection which, they say, can only feel at home in the sphere of finitude. But

---

7. Here, as elsewhere in the preface, Hegel is lamenting and scorning the Romantic movement that was gaining force in the early 19th century.
8. Hegel saw himself instead as attempting to give philosophy the rigor appropriate to the kind of *Wissenschaft* it is (or ought to be).
9. Literally, "boundary" (Greek, *horos*).

just as there is a breadth which is emptiness, there is a depth which is empty too: as we may have an extension of substance which overflows into finite multiplicity without the power of keeping the manifold together, in the same way we may have an insubstantial intensity which, keeping itself in as mere force without actual expression, is no better than superficiality. The force of *Geist* is only as great as its expression; its depth only as deep as its power to expand and lose itself when spending and giving out its substance. Moreover, when this unreflective emotional knowledge makes a pretext of having immersed its own very self in the depths of the absolute Being, and of philosophising in all holiness and truth, it hides from itself the fact that instead of devotion to God, it rather, by this contempt for all measurable precision and definiteness, simply confirms in its own case the fortuitous character of its content, and on the other endows God with its own caprice. When such minds commit themselves to the unrestrained ferment of sheer emotion, they think that, by putting a veil over self-consciousness, and surrendering all understanding, they are thus God's beloved ones to whom He gives His wisdom in sleep. This is the reason, too, that in point of fact what they do conceive and bring forth in sleep is dreams.

For the rest it is not difficult to see that our epoch is a birth-time, and a period of transition. The spirit [*Geist*] has broken with the world as it has hitherto existed, and with the old ways of thinking [*Vorstellens*],[1] and is of a mind to let them all sink into the depths of the past and to set about its own transformation. It is indeed never at rest, but carried along the stream of progress ever onward. But it is here as in the case of the birth of a child; after a long period of nutrition in silence, the continuity of the gradual growth in size, of quantitative change, is suddenly cut short by the first breath drawn—there is a break in the process, a qualitative change—and the child is born. In like manner the spirit of the time growing slowly and quietly ripe for the new form it is to assume [*der sich bildende Geist*],[2] loosens one fragment after another of the structure of its previous world. That it is tottering to its fall is indicated only by symptoms here and there. Frivolity and again ennui, which are spreading in the established order of things, the undefined foreboding of something unknown—all these are hints foretelling that there is something else approaching. This gradual crumbling to pieces, which did not alter the general look and aspect of the whole, is interrupted by the sunrise, which, in a flash and at a single stroke, brings into view the form and structure of the new world.[3]

But this new world is perfectly realised just as little as the new-born child; and it is essential to bear this in mind. It comes on the stage to begin with in its immediacy, in its bare *Begriff*. A building is not finished when its foundation is laid; and just as little is the attainment of a general *Begriff* of a whole the whole itself. When we want to see an oak with all its vigour of trunk, its spreading branches, and mass of foliage, we are not satisfied to be shown an acorn instead. In the same way *Wissenschaft*, the crowning glory of a spiritual

1. See *Vorstellung* in the Hegel glossary, p. 144.
2. More accurately, "the self-shaping *Geist*." See *Bildung* in the Hegel glossary at the end of the introductory headnote.
3. A reference to the French Revolution (1787–99)

and the subsequent transformation of Europe under Napoleon Bonaparte (1769–1821), who became emperor of the French and, when *Phenomenology* was published in 1807, was gaining control of much of continental Europe.

[*geistig*] world, is not found complete in its initial stages. The beginning of the new *Geist* is the outcome of an extensive transformation of manifold forms of spiritual culture; it is the reward which comes after a chequered and devious course of development, and after much struggle and effort. It is a whole which, after running its course and laying bare all its content, returns again to itself; it is the resultant abstract *Begriff* of the whole. But the actual realisation of this abstract whole is only found when those previous shapes and forms, which are now reduced to ideal moments of the whole, are developed anew again, but developed and shaped within this new medium, and with the meaning they have thereby acquired.

While the new world makes its first appearance merely in general outline, merely as a whole lying concealed and hidden within a bare abstraction, the wealth of the bygone life, on the other hand, is still consciously present in recollection. Consciousness misses in the new form the detailed expanse of content; but still more the developed expression of form by which distinctions are definitely determined and arranged in their precise relations. Without this last feature *Wissenschaft* has no general intelligibility, and has the appearance of being an esoteric possession of a few individuals—an esoteric possession, because in the first instance it is only the essential principle or *Begriff* of *Wissenschaft*, only its inner nature that is to be found; and a possession of few individuals, because, at its first appearance, its content is not elaborated and expanded in detail, and thus its existence is turned into something particular. Only what is perfectly determinate in form is at the same time exoteric, comprehensible, and capable of being learned and possessed by everybody. Intelligibility is the form in which *Wissenschaft* is offered to everyone, and is the open road to it made plain for all. To reach rational knowledge by our intelligence is the just demand of the mind [*Bewusstsein*] which comes to *Wissenschaft*. For intelligence [*Verstand*] is thinking, pure activity of the self in general; and what is intelligible [*Verständige*] is something already familiar [*Bekannte*] and common to the *Wissenschaft* and the *unwissenschaftlich* mind alike, enabling the latter to enter the domain of *Wissenschaft*.

Wissenschaft, at its commencement, when as yet it has neither got as far as detailed completeness nor perfection of form, is exposed to blame on that account. But to suppose this blame to attach to its essential nature would be as unjust as it is inadmissible not to be ready to recognise the demand for that further development in fuller detail. In the contrast and opposition between these two aspects (the initial and the developed stages of *Wissenschaft*) seems to lie the critical knot which *wissenschaftlich Bildung* at present struggles to loosen, and about which it is so far not very clear. One side parades the wealth of its material and the intelligibility of its ideas; the other pours contempt at any rate on the latter, and makes a parade of the immediate intuitive rationality and divine quality of its content. Although the first is reduced to silence—perhaps by the inner force of truth alone, perhaps, too, by the noisy bluster of the other side[4]—and though having regard to the reason and nature of the case it did feel overborne, yet it does not therefore feel satisfied as regards those demands for greater development; for those demands are just, but still unfulfilled. Its silence is due only in part to the victory of the other side; it is

4. SCHELLING and his followers, a frequent target of Hegel's criticism.

half due to that weariness and indifference which are usually the consequence when expectations are being constantly awakened by promises which are not followed up by performance.

The other side no doubt at times makes an easy enough matter of getting a vast expanse of content. They haul in a lot of material—already familiar and arranged in order; and since they are concerned more especially about what is exceptional, strange, and curious, they seem all the more to be in possession of the rest, which knowledge in its own way was finished and done with, as well as to have control over what was unregulated and disorderly. Hence everything appears brought within the compass of the Absolute *Idee*, which seems thus to be recognised in everything, and to have succeeded in becoming a system *in extenso*[5] of *wissenschaftlich* knowledge. But if we look more closely at this expanded system we find that it has not been reached by one and the same principle taking shape in diverse ways; it is the shapeless repetition of one and the same idea, which is applied in an external fashion to different material, the wearisome reiteration of it keeping up the semblance of diversity. The *Idee*, which by itself is no doubt the truth, really never gets any farther than just where it began, as long as the development of it consists in nothing else than such a repetition of the same formula. If the knowing subject carries round everywhere the one inert abstract form, taking up in external fashion whatever material comes his way, and dipping it into this element, then this comes about as near to fulfilling what is wanted—viz. a self-origination of the wealth of detail, and a self-determining distinction of shapes and forms—as any chance fancies about the content in question. It is rather a monotonous formalism, which only comes by distinction in the matter it has to deal with, because this is already prepared and well known.

This monotonousness and abstract *Allgemeinheit* are maintained to be the Absolute. This formalism insists that to be dissatisfied therewith argues an incapacity to grasp the standpoint of the Absolute, and keep a firm hold on it. If it was once the case that the bare possibility of thinking of something in some other fashion was sufficient to refute a given idea, and the naked possibility, the bare general thought, possessed and passed for the entire substantive value of actual knowledge; we find here similarly all the value ascribed to the *allgemein Idee* in this bare form without concrete realisation; and we see here, too, the style and method of speculative contemplation identified with dissipating and resolving what is determinate and distinct, or rather with hurling it down, without more ado and without any justification, into the abyss of vacuity. To consider any specific fact as it is in the Absolute, consists here in nothing else than saying about it that, while it is now doubtless spoken of as something specific, yet in the Absolute, in the abstract identity $A = A$, there is no such thing at all, for everything is there all one. To pit this single assertion, that "in the Absolute all is one," against the organised whole of determinate and complete knowledge, or of knowledge which at least aims at and demands complete development—to give out its Absolute as the night in which, as we say, all cows are black—that is the very *naïveté* of vacuous knowledge.

The formalism which has been deprecated and despised by recent philosophy,

5. At length (Latin); that is, an elaborated system.

and which has arisen once more in philosophy itself, will not disappear from *Wissenschaft*, even though its inadequacy is known and felt, till the knowledge of absolute reality has become quite clear as to what its own true nature consists in. Having in mind that the general idea of what is to be done, if it precedes the attempt to carry it out, facilitates the comprehension of this process, it is worth while to indicate here some rough idea of it, with the hope at the same time that this will give us the opportunity to set aside certain forms whose habitual presence is a hindrance in the way of speculative knowledge.

In my view—a view which the developed exposition of the system itself can alone justify—everything depends on grasping and expressing the ultimately True [*das Wahre*] not [only] as Substance but as Subject as well. At the same time we must note that concrete substantiality implicates and involves the *Allgemeine* or the immediacy of knowledge itself, as well as the immediacy which is being, or immediacy *qua* object *for* knowledge. If the generation which heard God spoken of as the One Substance[6] was shocked and revolted by such a characterisation of his nature, the reason lay partly in the instinctive feeling that in such a conception self-consciousness was simply submerged, and not preserved. But partly, again, the opposite position,[7] which maintains thinking to be merely subjective thinking, abstract *Allgemeinheit* as such, is exactly the same bare uniformity, is undifferentiated, unmoved substantiality. And even if, in the third place, thought combines with itself the being of substance, and conceives immediacy or intuition [*Anschauung*] as thinking, it is still a question whether this intellectual intuition does not fall back into that inert, abstract simplicity,[8] and exhibit and expound reality itself in an unreal manner.

The living substance, further, is that being which is truly subject, or, what is the same thing, is truly realised and *wirklich* solely in the process of positing itself, or in mediating with its own self its transitions from one state or position to the opposite.[9] As subject it is pure and simple negativity,[1] and just on that account a process of splitting up what is simple and undifferentiated, a process of duplicating and setting factors in opposition, which [process] in turn is the negation of this indifferent diversity and of the opposition of factors it entails. *Das Wahre* is merely this process of reinstating self-identity, of reflecting into its own self in and from its other, and is not an original and primal unity as such, not an immediate unity as such. It is the process of its own becoming, the circle which presupposes its end or its purpose, and has its end for its beginning; it becomes concrete and actual only by being carried out, and by the end it involves.

---

6. That is, by the Dutch philosopher Benedict (Baruch) de Spinoza (1632–1677). He conceived of "God" or "Nature" (different names for the same and sole ultimate reality) as the single all-inclusive "substance" that is the whole of reality, of which thought and matter are simply two different "attributes."
7. Held by FICHTE.
8. Of Schelling.

9. That is, for Hegel "the Absolute" (and also *Geist*) as "subject" is not any sort of metaphysical *entity* but rather a self-expressive and self-realizing *activity*.
1. The opposite or absence of "positivity," which is the sort of existence that a thing or object is paradigmatically taken to have—fixed, definite, and specifically determinate in its features or properties. A "subject" thus is real but precisely *not* in that sort of ("positive") way.

The life of God and divine intelligence, then, can, if we like, be spoken of as love disporting[2] with itself; but this idea falls into edification, and even sinks into insipidity, if it lacks the seriousness, the suffering, the patience, and the labour of the negative.[3] *Per se* the divine life is no doubt undisturbed identity and oneness with itself, which feels no anxiety over otherness and estrangement, and none over the surmounting of this estrangement. But this "per se" is abstract *Allgemeinheit*, where we abstract from its real nature, which consists in its being objective to itself, conscious of itself on its own account [*für sich zu sein*]; and where consequently we neglect altogether the self-movement which is the formal character of its activity. If the form is declared to correspond to the essence, it is just for that reason a misunderstanding to suppose that knowledge can be content with the "per se," essence [*Wesen*], but can do without form, that the absolute principle, or absolute intuition, makes the carrying out of the former, or the development of the latter, needless. Precisely because form is as necessary to essence as essence to it, absolute reality must not be conceived of and expressed as essence [*Wesen*] alone, i.e. as immediate substance, or as pure self-intuition of the Divine, but as form also, and with the entire wealth of the developed form. Only then is it grasped and expressed as really actual.[4]

Das Wahre is the whole. The whole, however, is merely the essential nature [*Wesen*] reaching its completeness through the process of its own development. Of the Absolute it must be said that it is essentially a result, that only at the end is it what it is in very truth; and just in that consists its nature, which is to be actual, subject, or self-becoming, self-development.[5] Should it appear contradictory to say that the Absolute has to be conceived essentially as a result, a little consideration will set this appearance of contradiction in its true light. The beginning, the principle, or the Absolute, as at first or immediately expressed, is merely the universal.[6] If we say "all animals," that does not pass for zoology; for the same reason we see at once that the words absolute, divine, eternal, and so on do not express what is implied in them; and only mere words like these, in point of fact, express intuition as the immediate. Whatever is more than a word like that, even the mere transition to a proposition, is a form of mediation, contains a process towards another state from which we must return once more. It is this process of mediation, however, that is rejected with horror, as if absolute knowledge were being surrendered when more is made of mediation than merely the assertion that it is nothing absolute, and does not exist in the Absolute.

This horrified rejection of mediation, however, arises as a fact from want of acquaintance with its nature, and with the nature of absolute knowledge

2. Playing.
3. That is, the "seriousness, suffering, patience, and work" of negating (or refusing to be satisfied and to stop) with any particular "positive" sort of self-expression, self-objectification, and self-realization until finally a form of self-realization is attained that is fully adequate to the essential nature (or "substance") of the self-realizing "subject."
4. These two sentences clarify a number of Hegel's key terms. "Form" means "existing form" (i.e., determinate existence of one sort or another); "substance" means "essence"; "absolute reality" or

"the Divine" means "essence" that has determinate existence ("form")—and indeed "the entire wealth of developed form [determinate existence]." And that, in turn, is what Hegel means by "actuality" or the truly and fully "actual."
5. This sentence sums up what Hegel means by "the Absolute" (*das Absolut*).
6. That is, "the general" (*das Allgemeine*); see the Hegel glossary at the end of the introductory headnote. Often the terms in this family are better understood as meaning "general" rather than "universal," but neither rendering gets Hegel's use exactly right; they therefore are best left untranslated.

itself. For mediating is nothing but self-identity working itself out through an active self-directed process; or, in other words, it is reflection into self, the aspect in which the ego is for itself, objective to itself.[7] It is pure negativity, or, reduced to its utmost abstraction, the process of bare and simple becoming. The ego, or becoming in general, this process of mediating, is, because of its being simple, just immediacy coming to be, and is immediacy itself. We misconceive therefore the nature of reason if we exclude reflection or mediation from ultimate truth, and do not take it to be a positive moment of the Absolute. It is reflection which constitutes truth the final result, and yet at the same time does away with the contrast between result and the process of arriving at it. For this process is likewise simple, and therefore not distinct from the form of truth, which consists in appearing as simple in the result; it is indeed just this restoration and return to simplicity. While the embryo is certainly, in itself, implicitly a human being, it is not so explicitly, it does not take itself to be a human being [*für sich*]; it is only the latter in the form of developed and cultivated reason, which has made itself to be what it is implicitly. Its actual reality is first found here. But this result arrived at is itself simple immediacy; for it is self-conscious freedom, which is at one with itself, and has not set aside the opposition it involves and left it there, but has made its account with it and become reconciled to it.

What has been said may also be expressed by saying that reason is purposive activity. Extolling so-called nature at the expense of thought misunderstood, and more especially the rejection of external purposiveness, have brought the idea of purpose in general into disrepute. All the same, in the sense in which Aristotle, too, characterises nature as purposive activity,[8] purpose is the immediate, the undisturbed, the unmoved which is self-moving; as such it is subject. Its power of moving, taken abstractly, is its existence for itself, or pure negativity. The result is the same as the beginning solely because the beginning is purpose. Stated otherwise, what is actual and concrete is the same as its inner principle or notion simply because the immediate *qua* purpose contains within it the self or pure actuality. The realised purpose, or concrete actuality, is movement and process of development. But this very unrest is the self; and it is one and the same with that immediacy and simplicity characteristic of the beginning just for the reason that it is the result, and has returned upon itself—while this latter again is just the self, and the self is self-referring and self-relating identity and simplicity.

When thinking of the Absolute as subject, men have made use of statements like 'God is the eternal,' the 'moral order of the world,' or 'love,' etc. In such propositions ultimate truth is just barely stated to be Subject, but not set forth as the process of reflectively mediating itself within itself. In a proposition of that kind we begin with the word God. By itself this is a meaningless sound, a mere name; the predicate says afterwards *what* it is, gives it content and meaning: the empty beginning becomes real knowledge only when we thus get to the end of the statement. So far as that goes, why not speak alone of

---

7. "Mediation" (*Vermittlung*), for Hegel, is the key to all *geistig* (subjective-, objective-, and absolute-spiritual) development and self-realization but has no content of its own. The process of setting up and going through an intermediary of some sort often enriches and develops (as well as complicates) the reality in question.

8. The Greek philosopher Aristotle (384–322 B.C.E.) contends in his *Physics* and elsewhere that nature is inherently purposive.

the eternal, of the moral order of the world, etc., or, like the ancients, of pure *Begriffe* such as being, the one, etc., i.e. of what gives the meaning without adding the meaningless sound at all? But this word just indicates that it is not a being or essence or *Allgemeine* in general that is put forward, but something reflected into self, a subject. Yet at the same time this acceptance of the Absolute as Subject is merely anticipated, not really affirmed. The subject is taken to be a fixed point, and to it as their support the predicates are attached, by a process falling within the individual knowing about it, but not looked upon as belonging to the point of attachment itself; only by such a process, however, could the content be presented as subject. Constituted as it is, this process cannot belong to the subject; but when that point of support is fixed to start with, this process cannot be otherwise constituted, it can only be external. The anticipation that the Absolute is subject is therefore not merely not the actuality of this *Begriff*, but even makes that impossible. For it makes the *Begriff* out to be a static point, while its actual reality is self-movement.

Among the many consequences that follow from what has been said, it is of importance to emphasise this, that knowledge is only real and can only be set forth fully in the form of *Wissenschaft*, in the form of system; and further, that a so-called fundamental proposition or first principle of philosophy, even if it is true, is yet none the less false just because and in so far as it is merely a fundamental proposition, merely a first principle. It is for that reason easily refuted. The refutation consists in bringing out its defective character; and it *is* defective because it is merely the *Allgemeine*, merely a principle, the beginning. If the refutation is complete and thorough, it is derived and developed from the nature of the principle itself, and not accomplished by bringing in from elsewhere other counter assurances and chance fancies. It would be strictly the development of the principle, and thus the completion of its deficiency, were it not that it misunderstands its own purport by taking account solely of the negative aspect of what it seeks to do, and is not conscious of the positive character of its process and result. The really positive working out of the beginning is at the same time just as much the very reverse—it is a negative attitude towards the principle we start from, negative, that is to say, of its one-sided form, which consists in being primarily immediate, a mere purpose. It may therefore be regarded as a refutation of what constitutes the basis of the system; but more correctly it should be looked at as a demonstration that the *basis* or principle of the system is in point of fact merely its *beginning*.

That the truth is only realised in the form of system, that substance is essentially subject, is expressed in the *Vorstellung* which characterizes the Absolute as *Geist*—the grandest *Begriff* of all, and one which is due to modern times and its religion. The *Geistige* alone is the *Wirkliche*. It is the inner being of the world, that which essentially is, and is *per se*; it assumes objective, determinate form, and enters into relations with itself—it is externality (otherness), and exists for self; yet, in this determination, and in its otherness, it is still one with itself—it is self-contained and self-complete, in itself and for itself at once. This self-containedness, however, is first something known by us, it is implicit in its nature [*an sich*]; it is *geistig* substance. It has to become self-contained *for itself*, on its own account; it must be knowledge of the *Geistige* and knowledge of itself as *Geist*. This means, it must be presented to itself as an object, but at the same time straightway supersede [*aufheben*][9] this objective form; it must be its own object in which it finds itself reflected. So far as its *geistig* content is produced by its own activity, it is only *we* [the thinkers] who know *Geist* to be for itself, to be objective to itself; but in so far as *Geist* knows itself to be for itself, then this self-production, the pure *Begriff*, is the sphere and element in which its objectification takes effect, and where it gets its existential form. In this way it is in its existence aware of itself as an object in which its own self is reflected. *Geist* which, when thus developed, knows itself to be *Geist* is *Wissenschaft*, which is its realisation, and the realm [*Reich*] it sets up for itself in its own native element.[1]

A self having knowledge purely of itself in the absolute antithesis of itself, this pure ether as such, is the very soil where *Wissenschaft* flourishes, is knowledge in *allgemein* form. The beginning of philosophy presupposes or demands from consciousness that it should feel at home in this element. But this element only attains its perfect meaning and acquires transparency through the process of gradually developing it. It is pure *Geistigkeit* as the *Allgemeine*, which assumes the shape of simple immediacy; and this simple element, existing as such, is the soil of *Wissenschaft*, is thinking, and can be only in *Geist*. Because this medium, this immediacy of *Geist*, is the substantial nature of *Geist* in general, it is the transfigured essence, reflection which itself is simple, which is aware of itself as immediacy; it is being, which is reflection into itself. *Wissenschaft* on its side requires the individual self-consciousness to have risen into this high ether in order to be able to live with it, and in it, and really to feel alive there.

Conversely the individual has the right to demand that *Wissenschaft* shall hold the ladder to help him to get at least as far as this position, shall show him that he has in himself this ground to stand on. His right rests on his absolute independence, which he knows he possesses in every type and phase of knowledge; for in every phase, whether recognised by *Wissenschaft* or not, and whatever be the content, his right as an individual is the absolute and final form, i.e. he is the immediate certainty of self, and thereby is unconditioned being, were this expression preferred. If the position taken up by consciousness[2]—that of knowing about objective things as opposed to itself, and about itself as opposed to them—is held by *Wissenschaft* to be the very opposite of this position: if, when in knowing it keeps within itself and never gets beyond itself, *Wissenschaft* holds this state to be rather the loss of *Geist* altogether—then, on the other hand, the element in which *Wissenschaft* consists is looked at by consciousness as a remote and distant region, in which

---

9. The form used here in the German text is *aufgehobener*; see *Aufhebung* in the Hegel glossary, p. 144.
1. That is, in pure *Begriffe* (structurally articulated objective "concepts").
2. "Bewusstsein": here, ordinary consciousness—

but also (elsewhere) the consciousness associated by Hegel with natural-scientific inquiry and the sort of philosophical thinking that remains stuck at the level of merely analytical "understanding" (*Verstand*) as sharply distinguished from "reason" (*Vernunft*).

consciousness is no longer in possession of itself. Each of these two sides takes the other to be the perversion of the truth. For the naïve [*natürlichen*] consciousness to give itself up completely and straight away to *Wissenschaft* is to make an attempt, induced by some unknown influence, all at once to walk on its head. The compulsion to take up this attitude and move about in this position is a constraining force it is urged to fall in with, without ever being prepared for it and with no apparent necessity for doing so.

Whatever *Wissenschaft per se* may be, in its relation to naïve immediate self-conscious life it presents the appearance of being a reversal of the latter; or, again, because naïve self-consciousness finds the principle of its reality in the certainty of itself, *Wissenschaft* bears the character of unreality, since consciousness 'for itself' is a state quite outside of it. *Wissenschaft* has for that reason to combine that other element of self-certainty with its own, or rather to show that the other element belongs to itself, and how it does so. When devoid of that sort of reality, *Wissenschaft* is merely content *qua* something implicit or potential [*an sich*]; purpose which at the start is no more than something internal; not *Geist*, but at first merely *geistig* substance. This implicit moment [*Ansich*] has to find external expression, and become objective on its own account. This means nothing else than that this moment has to establish self-consciousness as one with itself.

It is this process by which *Wissenschaft* in general comes about, this gradual development of knowing, that is set forth here in the *Phenomenology of Geist*. Knowing, as it is found at the start, *Geist* in its immediate and primitive stage, is without the essential nature of *Geist*, is *sense-consciousness*. To become genuine knowledge, or produce the element of which *Wissenschaft* consists—the pure *Begriff* of *Wissenschaft* itself—a long and laborious journey must be undertaken. This process towards *Wissenschaft*, as regards the content it will bring to light and the forms it will assume in the course of its progress, will not be what is primarily imagined by leading the *unwissenschaftlich* consciousness up to the level of *Wissenschaft*: it will be something different, too, from establishing and laying the foundations of *Wissenschaft*; and in any event something else than the sort of ecstatic enthusiasm which starts straight off with absolute knowledge, as if shot out of a pistol, and makes short work of other points of view simply by explaining that it is to take no notice of them.

The task of conducting the individual from his *unwissenschaftlich* standpoint to that of *Wissenschaft* had to be taken in its general sense; we had to contemplate the *Bildung* of the *allgemein*[3] individual, of self-conscious *Geist*. As to the relation between these two [the particular and general individual], every moment, as it gains concrete form and its own proper shape and appearance, finds a place in the life of the *allgemein* individual. The particular individual is incomplete *Geist*, a concrete shape in whose existence, taken as a whole, one determinate characteristic predominates, while the others are found only in blurred outline. In that *Geist* which stands higher than another,[4] the lower concrete form of existence has sunk into an obscure moment;[5] what was once substantial objective fact [*die Sache selbst*] is now

3. That is, (general).
4. That is, in an instance of a form of *Geist* that has developed beyond its lower level.

5. That is, the superseded level or stage remains as an element of the transformed constitution of the form of *Geist* that has developed out of it.

only a single trace: its definite shape has been veiled, and become simply a piece of shading. The individual, whose substance is *Geist* at the higher level, passes through these past forms, much in the way that one who takes up a higher *Wissenschaft* goes through those preparatory forms of knowledge, which he has long since made his own, in order to call up their content before him; he brings back the recollection of them without stopping to fix his interest upon them.

The particular individual, so far as content is concerned, has also to go through the stages through which the *allgemein Geist* has passed, but as shapes once assumed by *Geist* and now laid aside, as stages of a road which has been worked over and levelled out. Hence it is that, in the case of various kinds of knowledge, we find that what in former days occupied the energies of those of mature *Geist* sinks to the level of information, exercises, and even pastimes for children; and in this educational progress we can see the history of the world's *Bildung* delineated in faint outline. This bygone mode of existence has already become an acquired possession of the *allgemein Geist*, which constitutes the substance of the individual, and furnishes his apparently external inorganic nature.[6] In this respect *Bildung*, regarded from the side of the individual, consists in his acquiring what lies at his hand ready for him, in making its inorganic nature organic to himself, and taking possession of it for himself. Looked at, however, from the side of *allgemein Geist qua* general *geistig* substance, *Bildung* means nothing else than that this substance gives itself its own self-consciousness, brings about its own inherent process and its own reflection into self.

Wissenschaft lays before us the morphogenetic process of this *Bildung* in all its detailed fullness and necessity, and at the same time shows it to be something that has already sunk into *Geist* as a moment of its being and possession. The goal to be reached is insight on the part of *Geist* into what knowing is. Impatience asks for the impossible, wants to reach the goal without the means of getting there. The length of the journey has to be borne with, for every moment is necessary; and again we must halt at every stage, for each is itself a complete individual form, and is fully and finally considered only so far as its determinate character is taken and dealt with as a rounded and concrete whole, or only so far as the whole is looked at in the light of the special and peculiar character which this determination gives it. Because the substance of the individual, and indeed the *Weltgeist*, has had the patience to go through these forms in the long stretch of time's extent, and to take upon itself the prodigious labour of the world's history, where it bodied forth in each form the entire content of itself, which each is capable of grasping; and because by nothing less could that all-pervading *Geist* ever manage to become conscious of what itself is—for that reason, the individual, in the nature

---

6. That is, the content or substance of the historically developed general *Geist* not only of one's own people (*Volk*) but also of "the world" (humanity as a whole) also constitutes "the substance of the individual," though it may seem to be something "external" and even alien. The entire content of *Geist* comes historically to exist as peoples create it. As cultural-*geistig* objective content, it provides human beings with a second, supra-organic nature that is the medium of their own *geistig* existence and self-realization. They have no other substantial reality, either within themselves or beyond this life and this world.

of the case, cannot expect by less toil to grasp what its own substance contains.

All the same, its task has meanwhile been made much lighter, because this has historically been implicitly [*an sich*] accomplished, the content is one where reality has already given place to spiritual possibilities, where immediacy has been overcome and brought under the control of reflection, the various forms and shapes have been already reduced to their intellectual abbreviations, to determinations of thought [*Gedankenbestimmung*] pure and simple. Being now something *thought*, the content is the possession of the substance of *Geist*; existence no longer has to be changed into the form of what is inherent and implicit [*Ansichseins*], but only the implicit—no longer merely something primitive, nor lying hidden within existence, but already present as a recollection—into the form of what is explicit, of what is objective to self [*Fürsichseins*].

We have to state more exactly the way this is done. At the point at which we here take up this movement, we are spared, in connection with the whole, the supersession of the stage of mere existence. This process has already taken place. What is still to be done and needs a higher kind of transformation is to go beyond the forms as represented [*Vorstellung*] and made familiar [*Bekanntschaft*]. By that previous negative process, existence, having been withdrawn into the substance of *Geist*, is, in the first instance, transferred to the element of the self only in an immediate way. The possession the self has thereby acquired, has still the same character of uncomprehended immediacy—of passive indifference—which existence itself had; existence has in this way merely passed into the form of mere *Vorstellung*. At the same time, by so doing, it is something familiar to us, something "well-known," something which existent *Geist* has finished and done with, and hence takes no more to do with and no further interest in. While the activity that is done with the existent is itself merely the process of the particular *Geist* that is not yet comprehending itself, on the other hand, *knowledge* is directed against this *Vorstellung* which has hereby arisen, against this "being-familiar" and "well-known"; it is an action of the *allgemein* self [*Selbst*], the concern of *thought*.

Generally speaking, the "familiar" [*Bekannte*] is not comprehended [*Erkannt*] merely by virtue of being "familiar." When engaged in the process of knowing, it is the commonest form of self-deception—and a deception of other people as well—to assume something to be familiar, and give assent to it on that very account. Knowledge of that sort, with all its talk, never amounts to anything, but has no idea that this is the case. Subject and object, and so on—God, nature, understanding, sensibility, etc.—are uncritically presupposed as familiar and something significant, and become fixed points from which to start and to which to return. The process of knowing flits between these secure points, and in consequence goes on merely along the surface. Apprehending and demonstrating consist similarly in seeing whether every one finds what is said corresponding to his idea too, whether it is familiar and seems to him so and so or not.

Analysis of a *Vorstellung*, as it used to be carried out, did anyhow consist in nothing else than doing away with its character of familiarity. To break up a representation into its ultimate elements [*Elemente*] means returning upon its aspects [*Momente*], which at least do not have the form of the *Vorstellung* as picked up, but are the immediate property of the self. Doubtless this analysis only arrives at thoughts which are themselves known elements, fixed inert determinations. But what is thus broken up into parts, this unreal entity, is itself an essential aspect; for just because the concrete fact is self-divided, and turns into unreality, it is something self-moving, self-active. The action of separating the elements is the exercise of the force of Understanding [*Verstand*], the most astonishing and greatest of all powers, or rather the absolute power. The circle, which is self-enclosed and at rest, and, being a substance, holds its own aspects, is an immediate condition, the immediate, continuous relation of elements with their unity, and hence arouses no sense of wonderment.

But that an accident as such, when cut loose from its containing circumference—that what is bound and held by something else and actual only by being connected with it—should get an existence all its own, gain freedom and independence on its own account: this is the portentous power of the negative; it is the energy of thought, of pure ego. Death, as we may call that unreality, is the most terrible thing, and to keep and hold fast what is dead demands the greatest force of all. Beauty, powerless and helpless, hates understanding, because the latter exacts from it what it cannot perform.

But the life of *Geist* is not one that shuns death, and keeps clear of destruction; it endures its death and in death maintains its being. It only wins to its truth when it finds itself in utter desolation. It is this mighty power, not by being a positive which turns away from the negative, as when we say of anything it is nothing or it is false, and, being then done with it, pass off to something else; on the contrary, *Geist* is this power only by looking the negative in the face, and dwelling with it. This dwelling beside it is the magic power that converts the negative into being. That power is just what we spoke of above as "subject," which by giving determinateness a place in its substance, cancels abstract immediacy, i.e. immediacy which merely *is*, and, by so doing, becomes true substance, becomes being or immediacy that does not have mediation outside it, but is this mediation itself.

This process of making what is represented [*das Vorgestellte*] a possession of pure self-consciousness, of raising it to the level of *Allgemeinheit*, is merely one aspect of *Bildung*, which is not yet completed. The manner of study in ancient times is distinct from that of the modern world, in that the former consisted in the cultivation and perfecting [*Durchbildung*] of the natural mind [*Bewusstsein*]. Testing life carefully at all points, philosophising about everything it came across, the former created an experience permeated through and through by *Allgemeinheit*. In modern times, however, an individual finds the abstract form ready made. In straining to grasp it and make it his own, he rather strives to bring forward the inner meaning alone, without any process of mediation; the production of the *Allgemeine* is abridged, instead of its arising out of the manifold detail of concrete existence. Hence nowadays the task before us consists not so much in getting the individual beyond the level of sensuous immediacy, and making him a substance that thinks and is grasped in terms of thought, but rather the very opposite: it consists in actualising the *Allgemeine*, and giving it spiritual vitality, by the *Aufhebung* of fixed and determinate thoughts. But it is much more difficult to make fixed and definite thoughts fuse with one another and form a continuous whole than to bring sensuous existence into this state.

The reason lies in what was said before. Thought determinations get their substance and the element of their existence from the ego, the power of the negative, or pure reality; while determinations of sense find this in impotent abstract immediacy, in mere being as such. Thoughts become fluent and interfuse, when thinking pure and simple, this inner immediacy, knows itself as an aspect [ein Moment], when pure certainty of self abstracts from itself. It does not "abstract" in the sense of getting away from itself and setting itself on one side, but of surrendering the fixed quality of its self-affirmation, and giving up both the fixity of the purely concrete—which is the ego as contrasted with the variety of its content—and the fixity of all those distinctions [the various thought-functions, principles, etc.] which are present in the element of pure thought and share that absoluteness of the ego. In virtue of this process pure thoughts become Begriffe, and are then what they are in truth, self-moving functions, circles, are what their substance consists in, geistig essentialities [Wesenheiten].

This movement of pure essentialities constitutes the nature of Wissenschaftlichkeit in general. Looked at as the concatenation of their content, this movement is the necessitated development and expansion of that content into an organic systematic whole. By this movement, too, the road which leads to the Begriff of knowledge becomes itself likewise a necessary and complete evolving process [Werden]. This preparatory stage thus ceases to consist of casual philosophical reflections, referring to objects here and there, to processes and thoughts of the undeveloped consciousness as chance may direct; and it does not try to establish the truth by miscellaneous ratiocinations, inferences, and consequences drawn from circumscribed thoughts. The road to Wissenschaft, by the very movement of the Begriff itself, will compass the entire objective world of conscious life in its rational necessity.

Further, a systematic exposition like this constitutes the first part of Wissenschaft, because the positive existence of Geist, qua primary and ultimate, is nothing but the immediate aspect of Geist; the beginning, but not yet its return to itself. The characteristic feature distinguishing this part of Wissenschaft [phenomenology] from the others is the element of positive immediate existence. The mention of this distinction leads us to discuss certain established ideas that usually come to notice in this connection.

The immediate existence of Geist, consciousness [Bewusstsein], has two aspects—cognition and objectivity, which is opposed to or negative of the subjective function of knowing. Since it is in the medium of consciousness that Geist is developed and brings out its various moments, this opposition between the forms of consciousness is found at each stage in the development of Geist, and all the various aspects appear as modes or forms [Gestalten] of consciousness. The Wissenschaft of the course of this development is the Wissenschaft of the experience through which consciousness passes; the substance and its process are considered as the object of consciousness. Consciousness knows and comprehends nothing but what falls within its experience; for what is found in experience is only geistig substance, and, moreover, object of its self. Geist, however, becomes object, for it consists in the process of becoming an other to itself, i.e. an object for its own self, and in transcending this otherness. And "experience" is what this very process is called, by which the element that is immediate, unexperienced, i.e. abstract—whether it be in the form of sense or of a bare thought—makes itself alien [*sich entfremdet*], and then comes back to itself from this state of estrangement,[7] and by so doing is at length set forth in its concrete nature and real truth, and becomes too a possession of consciousness.

The dissimilarity which obtains in consciousness between the ego and the substance constituting its object is their inner distinction, the factor of negativity in general. We may regard it as the defect of both opposites, but it is their very soul, their moving spirit. It was on this account that certain thinkers long ago[8] took "the void" to be the principle of movement, when they conceived the moving principle to be the negative element, though they had not as yet thought of it as self. While this negative factor appears in the first instance as a dissimilarity, as an inequality, between ego and object, it is just as much the inequality of the substance with itself. What seems to take place outside it, to be an activity directed against it, is its own doing, its own activity; and substance shows that it is in reality subject. When it has brought this out completely, *Geist* has made its existence adequate to and one with its essential nature. *Geist* is object to itself just as it *is*, and the abstract element of immediacy, of the separation between knowing and the truth, is overcome. Being is entirely mediated; it is a substantial content, that is likewise directly in the possession of the ego, has the character of self, is *Begriff*. With the attainment of this the *Phenomenology of Geist* concludes. What *Geist* prepares for itself by the argument of the *Phenomenology* is the element of true knowledge. In this element the aspects or "moments" of *Geist* are now set out in the form of thought pure and simple, which knows its object to be itself. They no longer involve the opposition between being and knowing; they remain within the undivided simplicity of the knowing function. They are the truth in the form of truth; and their diversity is merely diversity of the content of truth. The process by which they are developed into an organically connected whole is Logic and Speculative Philosophy.

* * *

Philosophy does not deal with a determination [*Bestimmung*] that is nonessential, but with a determination so far as it is an essential factor. The abstract or unreal is not its element and content, but rather the *Wirkliche*, what is self-establishing, has life within itself, existence in its very *Begriff*. It is the process that creates its own moments in its course, and goes through them all; and the whole of this movement constitutes its positive content and its truth. This movement thus includes within it the negative factor as well—the element which would be named "falsity" if it could be considered one from which we had to abstract. The element that disappears has rather to be looked at as itself essential, not in the sense of being something fixed, that has to be cut off from truth and allowed to lie outside it (heaven knows where); just as

---

7. That is, "(self-)alienation" (*Entfremdung*). This is the first explicit mention in Hegel's writings of this idea, which was to have great prominence both in MARX's early writings and in later philosophical and social theory and criticism.
8. The atomists of ancient Greece, such as Democritus (ca. 460–ca. 370 B.C.E.).

similarly the truth is not to be held to stand on the other side as an immovable lifeless positive element.

Appearance [*Erscheinung*] is the process of arising into being and passing away again—a process that itself does not arise and does not pass away, but is *per se*, and constitutes reality and the life-movement of truth. In this way truth is the bacchanalian revel, in which no member [*Glied*] is not intoxicated; and because each no sooner gets detached than it *eo ipso*[9] collapses straightway, the revel is just as much a state of transparent unbroken calm. Judged by that movement, the particular shapes which *Geist* assumes do not indeed subsist any more than do determinate thoughts; but they are, all the same, as much positive and necessary moments, as negative and transitory. In the entirety of the movement, taken as an unbroken quiescent whole, that which gets distinctness in the course of its process and secures specific existence is preserved in the form of a self-recollection, in which existence is self-knowledge, and self-knowledge, again, is immediate existence.

* * *

What has been said can be expressed in a formal manner by saying that the nature of judgment or the proposition in general, which involves the distinction of subject and predicate, is subverted and destroyed by the speculative judgment; and the identical proposition, which the former becomes [by uniting subject and predicate], implies the rejection and repudiation of the above relation between subject and predicate. This conflict between the form of a proposition in general and the unity of the *Begriff* which destroys that form is similar to what we find between metre and accent in the case of rhythm. Rhythm is the result of what hovers between and unites both. So in the case of the speculative or philosophical judgment: the identity of subject and predicate is not intended to destroy their distinction, as expressed in propositional form; their unity is to appear as a harmony of the elements. The form of the judgment is the way the specific sense appears, or is made manifest: it is the accent which differentiates the content of its meaning. The predicate expresses the substance, and the subject itself falls within the *Allgemeine*, which is the unity wherein that accent dies away.

To explain what has been said by examples, let us take the proposition "God is Being." The predicate is "being": it has substantive significance, and thus absorbs the meaning of the subject within it. "Being" is meant to be here not predicate but the essential nature. Thereby, "God" seems to cease to be what he was when the proposition was put forward, viz. a fixed subject. Thinking [i.e. ordinary reflection], instead of getting any farther with the transition from subject to predicate, in reality finds its activity checked through the loss of the subject, and is thrown back on the thought of the subject because it misses this subject. Or again, since the predicate has itself been pronounced to be a subject—to be *the* being, to be the essential reality, which exhausts the nature of the subject—thinking finds the subject directly present in the predicate too: and now, instead of having, in the predicate, gone into *itself*, and preserved the freedom characteristic of ratiocination, it is absorbed in the content all the while (or, at any rate, is required to be so).

9. By that fact alone (Latin).

Similarly, when it is said: "the *Wirkliche* is the *Allgemeine*," the *Wirkliche*, *qua* subject, disappears into its predicate. The *Allgemeine* is not only meant to have the significance of a predicate, as if the proposition stated that the *Wirkliche* is *allgemein*; it is meant to express the essential nature of the *Wirkliche*. Thinking therefore loses that fixed objective basis which it had in the subject, just as much as in the predicate it is thrown back on the subject, and therein returns not into itself but into the subject underlying the content.

This unaccustomed restraint imposed upon thought is for the most part the cause of the complaints made regarding the unintelligibility of philosophical writings, when otherwise the individual has in him the requisite cultivation [*Bildung*] for understanding them. In what has been said we see the reason for the definite objection often made against them, that a good deal has to be read repeatedly before it can be understood—an accusation which is meant to imply something objectionable in the extreme, and one which if granted to be sound admits of no further reply. It is obvious from the above what is the state of the case here. The philosophical proposition [*Satz*], being a proposition, evokes the accepted view of the usual relation of subject and predicate, and suggests the idea of the customary procedure which takes place in knowledge. Its philosophical content destroys this way of proceeding and the ordinary view taken of this process. The common view discovers that the statement is intended in another sense than it is thinking of, and this correction of its opinion compels knowledge to recur to the proposition and take it now in some other sense.

* * *

Introduction

It is natural to suppose that, before philosophy enters upon its subject proper—namely, the actual knowing [*Erkennen*] of what truly is—it is necessary to come first to an understanding concerning knowledge, which is looked upon as the instrument by which to take possession of the Absolute, or as the means through which to get a sight of it. The precaution seems legitimate, partly because there are various kinds of knowledge [*Erkenntnis*], among which one might be better adapted than another for the attainment of our purpose—and thus a wrong choice is possible: partly, again, because knowing is a faculty of a definite kind and with a determinate range, without the more precise determination of its nature and limits we might take hold on clouds of error instead of the heaven of truth.

This apprehensiveness is sure to pass even into the conviction that the whole enterprise which sets out to secure for consciousness by means of knowledge what exists *per se* is in its very nature absurd; and that between knowledge and the Absolute there lies a boundary which completely cuts off the one from the other. For if knowledge is the instrument by which to get possession of absolute Reality, the suggestion immediately occurs that the application of an instrument to anything does *not* leave it as it is for itself, but rather entails in the process and has in view a moulding and alteration of it. Or, again, if knowledge is not an instrument which we actively employ, but a kind of passive medium through which the light of the truth reaches us, then here, too, we do not receive it as it is in itself, but as it is through and in this medium. In either case we employ a means which immediately brings about the very opposite of its own end; or, rather, the absurdity lies in making use of any means at all. It seems indeed open to us to find in the knowledge of the way in which the *instrument* operates, a remedy for this parlous state; for thereby it becomes possible to remove from the result the part which, in our idea of the Absolute received through that instrument, belongs to the instrument, and thus to get the truth in its purity.

But this improvement would, as a matter of fact, only bring us back to the point where we were before. If we take away again from a definitely formed thing that which the instrument has done in the shaping of it, then the thing (in this case the Absolute) stands before us once more just as it was previous to all this trouble, which, as we now see, was superfluous. If the Absolute were only to be brought on the whole nearer to us by this agency, without any change being wrought in it, like a bird caught by a limestick,[1] it would certainly scorn a trick of that sort, if it were not in its very nature, and did it not wish to be, with us from the start. For a trick is what knowledge in such a case would be, since by all its busy toil and trouble it gives itself the air of doing something quite different from bringing about a relation that is merely immediate, and so a waste of time to establish. Or, again, if the examination of knowledge, which we represent as a medium, makes us acquainted with the law of its refraction, it is likewise useless to eliminate this examination from the result. For knowledge is not the divergence of the ray, but the ray itself by which the truth comes in contact with us; and if this be removed, the bare direction or the empty place would alone be indicated.

Meanwhile, if the fear of falling into error introduces an element of distrust into *Wissenschaft*, which without any scruples of that sort goes to work and actually does know, it is not easy to understand why, conversely, a distrust should not be placed in this very distrust, and why we should not take care lest the fear of error is not just the initial error. As a matter of fact, this fear presupposes something—indeed a great deal—as truth, and supports its scruples and consequences on what should itself be examined beforehand to see whether it is truth. It starts with ideas of knowledge as an instrument, and as a medium, and presupposes a distinction of ourselves from this knowledge. More especially, it takes for granted that the Absolute stands on one side, and that knowledge on the other side—by itself and cut off from the Absolute—is still something real; in other words, that knowledge, which, by being outside the Absolute, is certainly also outside truth, is nevertheless true—a position which, while calling itself fear of error, makes itself known rather as fear of the truth.

This conclusion comes from the fact that the Absolute alone is true or that the True is alone absolute. It may be set aside by making the distinction that a knowledge which does not indeed know the Absolute (as *Wissenschaft* wants to do) is none the less true too; and that knowledge in general, though it may possibly be incapable of grasping the Absolute, can still be capable of truth of another kind. But we shall see as we proceed that random talk like this leads in the long run to a confused distinction between an *absolute* truth and a truth

---

1. A stick smeared with birdlime, an adhesive substance used to capture small birds.

of some other sort, and that "absolute," "knowledge," and so on, are words which presuppose a meaning that has first to be got at.

With suchlike useless *Vorstellungen* and expressions about knowledge—as an instrument to take hold of the Absolute, or as a medium through which we have a glimpse of truth, and so on (external relations to which all these ideas of a knowledge which is divided from the Absolute and an Absolute divided from knowledge in the last resort lead)—we need not concern ourselves. Nor need we trouble about the evasive pretexts which create the incapacity of *Wissenschaft* out of the presupposition of such relations, in order at once to be rid of the toil of *Wissenschaft*, and to assume the air of serious and zealous effort about it. Instead of being troubled with giving answers to all these, they may be straightway rejected as adventitious and arbitrary ideas; and the use which is here made of words like "absolute," "knowledge," as also "objective" and "subjective," and innumerable others, whose meaning is assumed to be familiar to everyone, might well be regarded as so much deception. For to proclaim that their significance is universally familiar, and that every one indeed possesses their notion, rather looks like an attempt to dispense with the only important matter—which is just to provide this *Begriff*. With better right, on the contrary, we might spare ourselves the trouble of taking any notice at all of such ideas and ways of talking which would have the effect of warding off *Wissenschaft* altogether; for they make a mere empty show of knowledge which at once vanishes when *Wissenschaft* comes on the scene.

But *Wissenschaft*, in the very fact that it comes on the scene, is itself a phenomenon; its "coming on the scene" is not yet *itself* carried out in all the length and breadth of its truth. In this regard, it is a matter of indifference whether we consider that *Wissenschaft* is the phenomenon because it makes its appearance alongside another kind of knowledge, or call that other untrue knowledge its process of appearing. *Wissenschaft*, however, must liberate itself from this phenomenality, and it can only do so by turning against it. For *Wissenschaft* cannot simply reject a form of knowledge which is not true, and treat this as a common view of things, and then assure us that itself is an entirely different kind of knowledge, and holds the other to be of no account at all; nor can it appeal to the fact that in this other there are presages of a better. By giving that assurance it would declare its force and value to lie in its bare existence; but the untrue knowledge appeals likewise to the fact that it *is*, and assures us that to it *Wissenschaft* is nothing.

One barren assurance, however, is of just as much value as another. Still less can *Wissenschaft* appeal to the presages of a better, which are to be found present in untrue knowledge and are there pointing the way towards *Wissenschaft*; for it would, on the one hand, be appealing again in the same way to a merely existent fact—and, on the other, it would be appealing to itself, to the way in which it exists in untrue knowledge, i.e. to a bad form of its own existence, to its appearance, rather than to its real and true nature [*an und für sich*]. For this reason we shall here undertake the exposition of *appearing knowledge* [*erscheinenden Wissen*].[2]

2. That is, the general topic of *Phenomenology of Geist* is "appearing knowledge," or "knowledge as it makes its appearance": "knowing" as a developing phenomenon and paradigmatic series of forms of *geistige* (human-spiritual) reality, practical and social as well as theoretical and *wissenschaftlich*.

Now because this exposition has for its object only "appearing knowledge," the exposition itself seems not to be *Wissenschaft*—free, self-moving in the shape proper to itself—but may, from this point of view, be taken as the pathway of the natural consciousness which is pressing forward to true knowledge. Or it can be regarded as the path of the soul, which is traversing the series of its own forms of embodiment, like stages appointed for it by its own nature, that it may possess the clearness of *Geist* when, through the complete experience of its own self, it arrives at the knowledge of what it is in itself.

Natural consciousness will prove itself to be only knowledge in principle or not real knowledge. Since, however, it immediately takes itself to be real and genuine knowledge, this pathway has a negative significance for it; what is a realisation of the *Begriff* of knowledge means for it rather the ruin and overthrow of itself; for on this road it loses its own truth. Because of that, the road can be looked on as the path of doubt, or more properly a highway of despair. For what happens there is not what is usually understood by doubting, a jostling against this or that supposed truth, the outcome of which is again a disappearance in due course of the doubt and a return to the former truth, so that at the end the matter is taken as it was before. On the contrary, that pathway is the conscious insight into the untruth of appearing [or apparent] knowledge, for which that is the most real which is after all only the unrealised *Begriff*. On that account, too, this thoroughgoing scepticism is not what doubtless earnest zeal for truth and *Wissenschaft* fancies it has equipped itself with in order to be ready to deal with them,—viz.: the *resolve*, in *Wissenschaft*, not to deliver itself over to the thoughts of others on their mere authority, but to examine everything for itself, and only follow its own conviction, or, still better, to produce everything itself and hold only its own act for true.

The series of shapes, which consciousness traverses on this road, is rather the detailed history of the *Bildung* of consciousness itself up to the level of science. That resolve presents this *Bildung* in the simple form of an intended purpose, as immediately finished and complete, as having taken place. This pathway, on the other hand, is, as opposed to this abstract intention, or untruth, the actual carrying out of that process of development. To follow one's own conviction is certainly more than to hand oneself over to authority; but by the conversion of opinion held on authority into opinion held out of personal conviction, the content of what is held is not necessarily altered, and truth has not thereby taken the place of error. If we stick to a system of opinion and prejudice resting on the authority of others, or upon personal conviction, the one differs from the other merely in the conceit which animates the latter. Scepticism, directed to the whole compass of phenomenal consciousness, on the contrary, makes *Geist* for the first time qualified to test what truth is; since it brings about a despair regarding what are called natural views, thoughts, and opinions, which it is a matter of indifference to call personal or belonging to others, and with which the consciousness, that proceeds straight away to criticise and test, is still filled and hampered, thus being, as a matter of fact, incapable of what it wants to undertake.

The completeness of the forms of unreal consciousness will be brought about precisely through the necessity of the advance and the necessity of their connection with one another. To make this comprehensible we may remark, by way of preliminary, that the exposition of untrue consciousness in its untruth is not a merely negative process. Such a one-sided view of it is what the natural consciousness generally adopts; and a knowledge, which makes this one-sidedness its essence, is one of those shapes assumed by incomplete consciousness which falls into the course of the inquiry itself and will come before us there. For this view is scepticism, which always sees in the result only pure nothingness, and abstracts from the fact that this nothing is determinate, is the nothing of *that out of which* it comes as a result. Nothing, however, is only, in fact, the true result, when taken as the nothing of what it comes from; it is thus itself a determinate nothing, and has a *content*. The scepticism which ends with the abstraction "nothing" or "emptiness" can advance from this not a step farther, but must wait and see whether there is possibly anything new offered, and what that is—in order to cast it into the same abysmal void. When once, on the other hand, the result is apprehended, as it truly is, as *determinate* negation, a new form has thereby immediately arisen; and in the negation the transition is made by which the progress through the complete succession of forms comes about of itself.

The goal, however, is fixed for knowledge just as necessarily as the succession in the process. The terminus is at that point where knowledge is no longer compelled to go beyond itself, where it finds its own self, and the *Begriff* corresponds to the object and the object to the *Begriff*.[3] The progress towards this goal consequently is without a halt and at no earlier stage is satisfaction to be found. That which is confined to a life of nature is unable of itself to go beyond its immediate existence; but by something other than itself it is forced beyond that; and to be thus wrenched out of its setting is its death. Consciousness, however, is to itself its own *Begriff*; thereby it immediately transcends what is limited, and, since this latter belongs to it, consciousness transcends its own self. Along with the particular there is at the same time set up the "beyond," were this only *beside* what is limited, as in the case of spatial intuition. Consciousness, therefore, suffers this violence at its own hands; it destroys its own limited satisfaction. At the feeling of this violence, anxiety for the truth may well withdraw, and struggle to preserve for itself that which is in danger of being lost. But it can find no rest. Should that anxious fearfulness wish to remain always in unthinking indolence, thought will agitate the thoughtlessness, its restlessness will disturb that indolence. Or let it take its stand as a form of sentimentality which assures us it finds everything good in its kind, and this assurance likewise will suffer violence at the hands of reason, which finds something *not* good just because and in so far as it is a *kind*. Or, again, fear of the truth may conceal itself from itself and others behind the pretext that precisely burning zeal for the very truth makes it so difficult, nay impossible, to find any other truth except that of which alone vanity is capable—that of being ever so much cleverer than any ideas, which one gets from oneself or others, could make possible. This sort of conceit which understands how to belittle every truth and turn away from it back into itself, and gloats over this its own private understanding, which always knows how to dissipate every possible thought, and to find, instead of all the content, merely

---

3. This is Hegel's definition of both "actuality" (*Wirklichkeit*) and the most important kind of "truth" (*Wahrheit*). It also sets the terms for both self-realization (as the attainment of this correspondence) and self-alienation (the loss of such correspondence).

the barren Ego—this is a satisfaction which must be left to itself; for it flees the *Allgemeine* and seeks only an isolated existence on its own account [*Fürsichsein*].[4]

―――

As the foregoing has been stated, provisionally and in general, concerning the manner and the necessity of the process of the inquiry, it may also be of further service to make some observations regarding the method of carrying this out. This exposition, viewed as a process of relating *Wissenschaft* to phenomenal knowledge, and as an inquiry and critical examination into the reality of knowing, does not seem able to be effected without some presupposition which is laid down as an ultimate criterion. For an examination consists in applying an accepted standard, and, on the final agreement or disagreement therewith of what is tested, deciding whether the latter is right or wrong; and the standard in general—and *Wissenschaft* as well, were this to be the criterion—is thereby accepted as the essence or inherently real [*Ansich*]. But here, where *Wissenschaft* first appears on the scene, neither it nor any sort of standard has justified itself as the essence or ultimate reality; and without this no examination seems able to be carried out.

This contradiction and the removal of it will become more definite if, to begin with, we call to mind the abstract determinations of knowledge and of truth as they are found in consciousness. Consciousness, we find, *distinguishes* from itself something, to which at the same time it *relates* itself. Or, to use the current expression, there is something *for* consciousness; and the determinate form of this process of relating, or of there being something for a consciousness, is knowledge. But from this being-for-another we distinguish being-in-itself or *per se*; what is related to knowledge is likewise distinguished from it, and posited as also existing outside this relation; the aspect of being *per se* or in-itself is called Truth. What really lies in these determinations does not further concern us here; for since the object of our inquiry is appearing knowledge [*erscheinende Wissen*],[5] its determinations are also taken up, in the first instance, as they are immediately offered to us. And they are offered to us very much in the way we have just stated.

If now our inquiry deals with the truth of knowledge, it appears that we are inquiring what knowing is in itself. But in this inquiry knowledge is *our* object, it is *for us*; and the essential nature [*Ansich*] of knowledge, were this to come to light, would be rather its being *for us*: what we should assert to be its essence would rather be, not the truth of knowledge, but only our knowledge of it. The essence or the criterion would lie in us, and what was to be compared with this standard, and decided upon as a result of this comparison, would not necessarily have to recognise that criterion.

But the nature of the object which we are examining surmounts this separation, or semblance of separation, and presupposition. Consciousness furnishes its own criterion in itself, and the inquiry will thereby be a comparison of itself with its own self; for the distinction just made falls inside itself. In

―――

4. This paragraph summarizes the sections of the *Phenomenology*—"Unhappy Consciousness" and "Self-Alienated *Geist*"—in which Hegel deals with several types of self-alienation.

5. That is, knowledge as it makes its appearance or arises, in the various forms it takes in different experiential contexts and at various stages in the development of *Geist*.

consciousness there is one element *for* an other, or, in general, consciousness implicates the specific character of the moment of knowledge. At the same time this "other" is to consciousness not merely *for it*, but also outside this relation, or has a being in itself, i.e. there is the moment of truth. Thus in what consciousness inside itself declares to be the essence or truth we have the standard which itself sets up, and by which we are to measure its knowledge. Suppose we call knowledge the *Begriff*, and the essence or truth "being" or the object, then the examination consists in seeing whether the *Begriff* corresponds with the object. But if we call the inner nature of the object, or what it is in itself, the *Begriff*, and, on the other side, understand by object the *Begriff qua* object, i.e. the way the *Begriff* is *for* an other, then the examination consists in our seeing whether the object corresponds to its own *Begriff*. It is clear, of course, that both of these processes are the same. The essential fact, however, to be borne in mind throughout the whole inquiry is that both these moments—*Begriff* and object, "being-for-another" and "being-in-itself"—themselves fall within that knowledge which we are examining. Consequently we do not require to bring standards with us, nor to apply *our* fancies and thoughts in the inquiry; and just by our leaving these aside we are enabled to treat and discuss the subject as it actually is in itself and for itself, as it is in its complete reality.

But it is not only in this respect that, since *Begriff* and object—the criterion and what is to be tested—are ready to hand in consciousness itself, any addition of ours is superfluous. We are also spared the trouble of comparing these two and of making an examination of them in the strict sense of the term; so that in this respect, too, since consciousness tests and examines itself, all we are left to do is simply and solely to look on. For consciousness is, on the one hand, consciousness of the object, and on the other, is consciousness of itself; consciousness of what to it is true, and consciousness of its knowledge of that truth. Since both are for the same consciousness, it is itself their comparison; it is the same consciousness that decides and knows whether its knowledge of the object corresponds with this object or not.

The object, it is true, appears only to be in such a way for consciousness as consciousness knows it. Consciousness does not seem able (so to speak) to *get behind it* as it is (not for consciousness, but in itself), and consequently seems also unable to test knowledge by it. But just because consciousness has, in general, knowledge of an object, there is already present the distinction that the inherent nature—what the object is in itself—is one thing to consciousness, while knowledge—or the being of the object *for* consciousness—is another moment. Upon this distinction, which is present as a fact, the examination turns. Should both, when thus compared, not correspond, consciousness seems bound to alter its knowledge, in order to make it fit the object. But in the alteration of the knowledge, the object itself also, in point of fact, is altered; for the knowledge which existed was essentially a knowledge of the object; with change in the knowledge, the object also becomes different, since it belonged essentially to this knowledge. Hence consciousness comes to find that what formerly to it was the essence is not what is *per se*, or what was *per se* was only *per se for consciousness*. Since, then, in the case of its object consciousness finds its knowledge not corresponding with this object, the object likewise fails to hold out; or the standard for examining is altered when that whose criterion this standard was to be does not hold its ground in the course of the examination; and the examination is not only an examination of knowledge, but also of the criterion used in the process.

This dialectic process which consciousness executes on itself—on its knowledge as well as on its object—in the sense that out of it the new and true object arises, is precisely what is termed Experience [*Erfahrung*]. In this connection, there is a moment in the process just mentioned which should be brought into more decided prominence, and by which a new light is cast on the *wissenschaftlich* aspect of the following exposition. Consciousness knows something; this something is the essence or what is *per se*. This object, however, is also the *per se*, the inherent reality, *for consciousness*. Hence comes the ambiguity of this truth. Consciousness, as we see, has now two objects; one is the first *per se*, the second is the existence *for consciousness* of this *per se*. The last object appears at first sight to be merely the reflection of consciousness into itself, i.e. an idea not of an object, but solely of its knowledge of that first object. But, as was already indicated, by that very process the first object is altered; it ceases to be what is *per se*, and becomes consciously something which is *per se* only *for consciousness*. Consequently, then, what this real *per se* is for consciousness is truth: which, however, means that this is the essential reality, or the object which consciousness has. This new object contains the nothingness of the first; the new object is the *experience* concerning that first object.

In this treatment of the course of experience, there is an element in virtue of which it does not seem to be in agreement with what is ordinarily understood by "experience." The transition from the first object and the knowledge of it to the other object, in regard to which we say we have had experience, was so stated that the knowledge of the first object, the existence *for consciousness* of the first *ens*[6] *per se*, is itself to be the second object. But it usually seems that we learn by experience the untruth of our first *Begriff* by appealing to some other object which we may happen to find casually and externally; so that, in general, what we have is merely the bare and simple apprehension of what is in and for itself. On the view above given, however, the new object is seen to have come about by a transformation [*Umkehrung*] of consciousness itself. This way of looking at the matter is *our* doing, what *we* contribute; by its means the series of experiences through which consciousness passes is elevated into a *wissenschaflich* sequence, but this is not the case for the consciousness we contemplate and consider. We have here, however, the same sort of circumstance, again, of which we spoke a short time ago when dealing with the relation of this exposition to scepticism, viz. that the result which at any time comes about in the case of an untrue mode of knowledge cannot possibly collapse into an empty nothing, but must necessarily be taken as the negation of that of which it is a result—a result which contains what truth the preceding mode of knowledge has in it. What we have here is presented to us in this form:—since what at first appeared as object is reduced, when it passes into consciousness, to what knowledge takes it to be, and the ultimate entity, the real in itself, becomes what this entity *per se* is *for consciousness*; this latter is the new object, whereupon there appears also a new mode or embodiment of consciousness, of which the essence is something other than

---

6. Being (Latin); that is, the first being or object. This is the translator's Latin. Hegel does not actually say "of the first being *per se*"; he says simply "*des ersten Ansich*"—that is, "of the first in-itself," meaning what he has just referred to as the "*ersten Gegenstand*" (the "first object"), considered as it is "*an sich*" ("in itself").

that of the preceding mode. It is this circumstance which carries forward the whole succession of the modes or attitudes of consciousness in their own necessity. It is only this necessity, this origination of the new object—which offers itself to consciousness without consciousness knowing how it comes by it—that to us, who watch the process, is to be seen going on (so to speak) behind its back. Thereby there enters into its process a moment of being *per se* or of being for us, which is not expressly presented to that consciousness which is in the grip of experience itself. The *content*, however, of what we see arising, exists for it, and we lay hold of and comprehend merely its formal character, i.e. its *bare* origination; *for it*, what has thus arisen has merely the character of object, while, *for us*, it appears at the same time as a process and coming into being.

In virtue of that necessity this pathway to *Wissenschaft* is itself *eo ipso Wissenschaft* and is, moreover, as regards its content, *Wissenschaft* of the Experience of Consciousness.

The experience which consciousness has concerning itself can, by its essential principle, embrace nothing less than the entire system of consciousness, the whole realm of the truth of *Geist*, and in such wise that the moments of truth are set forth in the specific and peculiar character they here possess— i.e. not as abstract pure moments, but as they are for consciousness, or as consciousness itself appears in its relation to them, and in virtue of which they are moments of the whole, are *forms of consciousness* [*Gestalten des Bewusstsein*]. In pressing forward to its true form of existence, consciousness will come to a point at which it lays aside its semblance of being hampered with what is foreign to it, with what is only for it and exists as an other; it will reach a position where its appearance accords with its essence, where, in consequence, its exposition coincides with just this very point, this very stage of the *Wissenschaft* proper of *Geist*. And, finally, when it grasps this its own essence, it will indicate the nature of absolute knowledge itself.

SOURCE: From G. W. F. Hegel, *The Phenomenology of Mind*, trans. J. B. Baillie (London: Swan Sonnenschein; New York: Macmillan, 1910), 1:1–35, 43–44, 60–63, 73–89 (translation modified by the editor). Except where otherwise indicated, German words in brackets are the terminology used in the German original, inserted by the editor in addition to their renderings in the translation; and unbracketed German words are the original terminology, substituted in place of their renderings in the translation by the editor for reasons given in notes and in the Hegel glossary (p. 144). The changes in this translation improve its accuracy, sometimes by rephrasing but more often in terminology. For example, Baillie uses "mind" (and related terms like "mental") to render Hegel's term *Geist*, which instead is here usually left in the original German. (On the meaning of *Geist*, see the Hegel glossary at the end of the introductory headnote.) *Phänomenologie des Geistes* was first published in 1807.

On Philosophical "Logic"

From The *Wissenschaft* of Logic (Encyclopedia, part 1)

From *Preliminaries* [Vorbegriff]

19.] Logic is the *Wissenschaft* of the pure *Idee*;[1] pure, that is, because the *Idee* is in the abstract medium of Thought.

1. On *Wissenschaft* and *Idee*, see the Hegel glossary, p. 144.

This definition, and the others which occur in these introductory outlines, are derived from a survey of the whole system, to which accordingly they are subsequent. The same comment applies to all prefatory remarks whatever about philosophy.

Logic might have been defined as the *Wissenschaft* of thought, and of its determinations and laws. But thought as such constitutes only the general determinateness or element in which the *Idee* is logical. If we identify the *Idee* with thought, thought must not be taken in the sense of something formal, but in the sense of the self-developing totality of its own determinations and laws. These laws are the work of thought itself, and not a fact which it finds and must submit to.

From different points of view, Logic is either the hardest or the easiest of the disciplines. Logic is hard, because it has to deal not with perceptions, nor, like geometry, with abstract representations of the sensible, but with pure abstractions; and because it demands a force and facility of withdrawing into pure thought, of keeping firm hold on it, and of moving in such an element. Logic is easy, because its facts are nothing but our own thought and its familiar forms or terms: and these are the acmè of simplicity, the a b c of everything else. They are also what we are best acquainted with: such as, 'Is' and 'Is not': quality and magnitude: being potential and being actual: one, many, and so on. But such an acquaintance only adds to the difficulties of the study; for while, on the one hand, we naturally think it is not worth our trouble to occupy ourselves any longer with things so familiar, on the other hand, the problem is to become acquainted with them in a new way, quite opposite to that in which we know them already.

The utility of Logic is a matter which concerns its bearings upon the student, and the training it may give for other purposes. This logical training consists in the exercise in thinking which the student has to go through (this discipline is the thinking of thinking): and in the fact that he stores his head with thoughts, in their native unalloyed character. It is true that Logic, being the absolute form of truth, and another name for the very truth itself, is something more than merely useful. Yet if what is noblest, most liberal and most independent is also most useful, Logic has some claim to the latter character. Its utility must then be estimated at another rate than exercise in thought for the sake of the exercise.

(Add. I)[2] The first question is: What is the object of our discipline? The simplest and most intelligible answer to this question is that Truth is the object of Logic. Truth is a noble word, and the thing is nobler still. So long as man is sound at heart and in spirit, the search for truth must awake all the enthusiasm of his nature. But immediately there steps in the objection—Are *we* able to know truth? There seems to be a disproportion between finite beings like ourselves and the truth which is absolute: and doubts suggest themselves whether there is any bridge between the finite and the infinite. God is truth: how shall we know him? Such an undertaking appears to stand in contradiction with the graces of lowliness and humility.—Others who ask whether we

---

2. These paragraphs introduced with "Add." are the *Zusätze* (additions) compiled after Hegel's death from lecture notes (mainly those of his students but sometimes his own). They cannot be given the same weight as text that he himself published; but they are nonetheless valuable elaborations of his thinking, and are generally considered to be reliable.

can know the truth have a different purpose. They want to justify themselves in living on contented with their petty, finite aims. And humility of this stamp is a poor thing.

But the time is past when people asked: How shall I, a poor worm of the dust, be able to know the truth? And in its stead we find vanity and conceit: people claim, without any trouble on their part, to breathe the very atmosphere of truth. The young have been flattered into the belief that they possess a natural birthright of moral and religious truth. And in the same strain, those of riper years are declared to be sunk, petrified, ossified in falsehood. Youth, say these teachers, sees the bright light of dawn: but the older generation lies in the slough and mire of the common day. They admit that the special disciplines are something that certainly ought to be cultivated, but merely as the means to satisfy the needs of outer life. In all this it is not humility which holds back from the knowledge and study of the truth, but a conviction that we are already in full possession of it. And no doubt the young carry with them the hopes of their elder compeers; on them rests the advance of the world and *Wissenschaft*. But these hopes are set upon the young, only on the condition that, instead of remaining as they are, they undertake the stern labour of *Geist*.

This modesty in truth-seeking has still another phase: and that is the genteel indifference to truth, as we see it in Pilate's conversation with Christ. Pilate asked 'What is truth?'[3] with the air of a man who had settled accounts with everything long ago, and concluded that nothing particularly matters:— he meant much the same as Solomon when he says: 'All is vanity.'[4] When it comes to this, nothing is left but self-conceit.

The knowledge of the truth meets an additional obstacle in timidity. A slothful mind finds it natural to say: 'Don't let it be supposed that we mean to be in earnest with our philosophy. We shall be glad *inter alia*[5] to study Logic: but Logic must be sure to leave us as we were before.' People have a feeling that, if thinking passes the ordinary range of our ideas and impressions, it cannot but be on the evil road. They seem to be trusting themselves to a sea on which they will be tossed to and fro by the waves of thought, till at length they again reach the sandbank of this temporal scene, as utterly poor as when they left it. What comes of such a view, we see in the world. It is possible within these limits to gain varied information and many accomplishments, to become a master of official routine, and to be trained for special purposes. But it is quite another thing to educate the spirit for the higher life and to devote our energies to its service. In our own day it may be hoped a longing for something better has sprung up among the young, so that they will not be contented with the mere straw of outer knowledge.

(Add. 2) It is universally agreed that thought is the object of Logic. But of thought our estimate may be very low, or it may be very high. On one hand, people say: 'It is *only* a thought.' In their view thought is subjective, arbitrary and accidental—distinguished from the thing itself, from the true and the real. On the other hand, a very high estimate may be formed of thought—

---

3. John 18:38; to Pontius Pilate (d. ca. 36 C.E.), the governor of Judaea, whom Hegel takes to be expressing indifference to the truth of the matter of Jesus's guilt.

4. Ecclesiastes 1:2; the book is traditionally attributed to Solomon (r. 968–928 B.C.E.), king of Israel. 5. Among other things (Latin).

when thought alone is held adequate to attain the highest of all things, the nature of God, of which the senses can tell us nothing. God is spirit [*Geist*], it is said, and must be worshipped in spirit and in truth. But the merely felt and sensible, we admit, is not the *geistig*; its heart of hearts is in thought; and only *Geist* can know *Geist*. And though it is true that *Geist* can demean itself as feeling and sense—as is the case in religion, the mere feeling, as a mode of consciousness, is one thing, and its contents another. Feeling, as feeling, is the general form of the sensuous nature which we have in common with the brutes. This form, viz. feeling, may possibly seize and appropriate the full organic truth: but the form has no real congruity with its contents. The form of feeling is the lowest in which *geistig* content can be expressed. This content, God himself, exists in proper truth, only in thought and as thought. If this be so, therefore, thought, far from being a mere thought, is the highest and, in strict accuracy, the sole mode of apprehending the eternal and absolute.

As of thought, so also of the *Wissenschaft* of thought, a very high or a very low opinion may be formed. Any man, it is supposed, can think without Logic, as he can digest without studying physiology. If he have studied Logic, he thinks afterwards as he did before, perhaps more methodically, but with little alteration. If this were all, and if Logic did no more than make men acquainted with the action of thought as the faculty of comparison and classification, it would produce nothing which had not been done quite as well before. And in point of fact Logic hitherto had no other idea of its duty than this. Yet to be well-informed about thought, even as a mere activity of the subject-mind, is honourable and interesting for man. It is in knowing what he is and what he does, that man is distinguished from the animals. But we may take the higher estimate of thought—as what alone can get really in touch with the supreme and true. In that case, Logic as the *Wissenschaft* of thought occupies a high ground. If the *Wissenschaft* of Logic then considers thought in its action and its productions (and thought being no resultless energy produces thoughts and the particular thought required), the theme of Logic is in general the supersensible world [*die übersinnliche Welt*], and to deal with that theme is to dwell for a while in that world. Mathematics is concerned with the abstractions of time and space. But these are still the object of sense, although the sensible is abstract and idealised. Thought bids adieu even to this last and abstract sensible: it asserts its own native independence, renounces the field of the external and internal sense, and puts away the interests and inclinations of the individual. When Logic takes this ground, it is a higher discipline than we are in the habit of supposing.

* * *

20.] If we take our *primâ facie* impression of thought, we find on examination first (*a*) that, in its usual subjective acceptation, thought is one out of many *geistig* activities or faculties, co-ordinate with such others as sensation, perception, imagination, desire, volition, and the like. The product of this activity, the form or character peculiar to thought, is the *Allgemeine* or, generally speaking, the abstract. Thought, regarded as an *activity*, may be accordingly described as the *active*—and, indeed, the *self*-activating— *Allgemeine*, since the deed, its product, is the *Allgemeine* once more.

Thought conceived as a *subject* (agent) is a thinker, and the subject existing as a thinker is simply denoted by the term 'I.'[6]

The propositions giving an account of thought in this and subsequent sections are not offered as mere assertions or opinions of mine on the matter. But in these preliminary chapters any deduction or proof would be impossible, and the statements may be taken as matters in evidence. In other words, every man, when he thinks and considers his thoughts, will discover by the experience of his consciousness that they possess the character of *Allgemeinheit* as well as the other aspects of thought to be afterwards enumerated. We assume of course that his powers of attention and abstraction have undergone a previous training, enabling him to observe correctly the evidence of his consciousness and his representations [*Vorstellungen*].

This introductory exposition has already alluded to the distinction between Sense, Representation, and Thought. As the distinction is of capital importance for understanding the nature and kinds of knowledge, it will help to explain matters if we here call attention to it. For the explanation of *Sense* [*das Sinnliche*], the readiest method certainly is to refer to its external source— the organs of sense. But to name the organ does not help much to explain what is apprehended by it. The real distinction between sense and thought lies in this—that the essential feature of the sensible is particularity [*Einzelheit*], and as the particular (which, reduced to its simplest terms, is the atom) is also a member of a group, sensible existence presents a number of mutually exclusive units—of units, to speak in more definite and abstract formulae, which exist next to, and after, one another. *Vorstellung*[7] works with content from the same sensuous source, but having the characteristics of being in *me* and therefore *mine*; and of *Allgemeinheit*, relatedness to self, and *simplicity*. Nor is sense the only source of *Vorstellungen*. There are *Vorstellungen* constituted by materials emanating from self-conscious thought, such as those of law, morality, religion, and even of thought itself; and it requires some effort to detect wherein lies the difference between such *Vorstellungen* and thoughts having the same import. For it is a thought of which such *Vorstellung* is the vehicle, and there is no lack of the form of *Allgemeinheit*, without which no content could be in me, or be a *Vorstellung* at all. Yet here also the peculiarity of *Vorstellung*, generally speaking, consists in the isolation of its contents. True it is that, for example, law and legal provisions do not exist in a sensible space, mutually excluding one another. Nor as regards time, though they appear to some extent in succession, are their contents themselves conceived as affected by time, or as transient and changeable in it. The limitation of *Vorstellung* lies deeper. These ideas, though implicitly possessing the organic unity of *Geist*, stand isolated here and there on the broad terrain of *Vorstellung*, with its inward and abstract *Allgemeinheit*. Thus cut adrift, each is simple, unrelated: Right, Duty, God. *Vorstellung* in these circumstances either rests satisfied with declaring that Right is Right, God is

---

6. That is, "thought" conceived as thinking *subject* is a thinker, the "I" or ego (*Ich*) that thinks. "Thought" conceived as *activity* is fundamentally a matter of the production and use of general forms, such as words with general meanings. And "thought" conceived as *object*, or as what it is or can be *about*, is that which can be articulated by means of such (general) forms. "Thought" most broadly and objectively conceived, for Hegel, is that about reality—its general structural features— that can be so articulated. These structures are thus both the proper ultimate *objects of* thought and thought's *own* general structural features.
7. That is, images and image formation.

God: or in a higher grade of *Bildung*, it proceeds to enunciate the attributes; as, for instance, God is the Creator of the world, omniscient, almighty, &c. In this way several isolated, simple predicates are strung together: but in spite of the link supplied by their subject, the predicates never get beyond mere contiguity. In this point *Vorstellung* coincides with Understanding [*Verstand*]: the only distinction being that the latter introduces relations of *Allgemeine* and particular, of cause and effect, &c., and in this way supplies a necessary connexion to the isolated instances of *Vorstellung*, while still leaving them merely side by side in its vague domain, connected only by a bare 'and.'

The difference between *Vorstellung* and thought is of special importance, because philosophy may be said to do nothing but transform *Vorstellungen* into thoughts—though it works the further transformation of a mere thought into a *Begriff*.

Sensibility has been characterised by the attributes of particularity and mutual externality to each other of its contents. It is well to remember that these very attributes of sense are thoughts and general terms. It will be shown in the Logic that thought (and the general) is not a mere opposite of sense: it lets nothing escape it, but, outflanking its other, is at once that other and itself. Now language is the work of thought: and hence nothing can be expressed in it that is not *allgemein*. What I alone mean [*meine*] is mine [*mein*]: it belongs to me—this particular individual. But language expresses nothing but the *allgemein*; and so I cannot say what I alone *mean*.[8] And the unutterable— feeling or sensation—far from being the highest truth, is the most unimport- ant and untrue. If I say 'the *particular*,' 'this particular,' 'here,' 'now,' all these are *Allgemeinheiten*. Everything and anything is a particular [*ein Einzelnes*], a 'this,' and if it be sensible, is here and now. Similarly when I say, 'I,' I *mean* my single self to the exclusion of all others: but what I *say*, viz. 'I,' is just every 'I,' which in like manner excludes all others from itself. In an awkward expres- sion which Kant used, he said that I *accompany* all my *Vorstellungen*[9]— sensations too, desires, actions, &c. 'I' is something completely general [*das an und für sich Allgemeines*]—as is communality, though that is an external form of *Allgemeinheit*.[1] All other men have it in common with me to be 'I': just as it is common to all my sensations and conceptions to be mine. But 'I,' in the abstract, as such, is the mere act of self-concentration or self-relation, in which we make abstraction from all *Vorstellung* and feeling, from every state of mind and every peculiarity of nature, talent, and experience. To this extent, 'I' is the existence of a wholly *abstract* generality, a principle of abstract free- dom. Hence thought, viewed as a subject, is what is expressed by the word 'I': and since I am at the same time in all my sensations, *Vorstellungen*, and states of consciousness, thought is everywhere present, and is a category that runs through all these modifications.

* * *

8. Hegel is playing on the similar-sounding words *meinen* (to think, mean, intend, suppose) and *mein* (my, mine).
9. KANT, *Critique of Pure Reason* (2nd ed., 1787), B 131–32.
1. Hegel is playing on the literal meaning of *allge-*

mein (all-common, common to all) to make the point that while I may use the term "I" (*Ich*) to refer uniquely to myself, the term itself is no less a *general* term than its seeming opposite, the term *Gemeinschaftlichkeit* (communality).

22.] * * * In common life we reflect, without particularly reminding ourselves that this is the process of arriving at the truth, and we think without hesitation, and in the firm belief that thought coincides with thing. And this belief is of the greatest importance. It marks the diseased state of the age when we see it adopt the despairing creed that our knowledge is only subjective, and that beyond this subjective we cannot go. Whereas, rightly understood, truth is objective, and ought so to regulate the conviction of every one, that the conviction of the individual is stamped as wrong when it does not agree with this rule. Modern views, on the contrary, put great value on the mere fact of conviction, and hold that to be convinced is good for its own sake, whatever be the burden of our conviction—there being no standard by which we can measure its truth.

We said above that, according to the old belief, it was the characteristic right of the mind to know the truth. If this be so, it also implies that everything we know both of outward and inward nature, in one word, the objective world, is in its own self the same as it is in thought, and that to think is to bring out the truth of our object, be it what it may. The business of philosophy is only to bring into explicit consciousness what the world in all ages has believed about thought. Philosophy therefore advances nothing new; and our present discussion has led us to a conclusion which agrees with the natural belief of mankind.

23.] (d) Since the true nature of things is brought to light in reflection, and since it is no less true that this thinking is *my* act, then this is an accomplishment of *my* Geist, in its character of thinking subject—mine through my simple *Allgemeinheit* as an 'I' on its own—or, my freedom.

'Think for yourself' is a phrase which people often use as if it had some special significance.[2] The fact is, no man can think for another, any more than he can eat or drink for him: and the expression is a pleonasm.[3] To think is in fact *ipso facto* to be free, for thought as the action of the *Allgemeine* is an abstract relating of self to self, where, being at ease with ourselves and undistracted by subjectivity, our consciousness is, in the matter of its contents, focused entirely on the matter at hand and its characteristics. If this be admitted, and if we apply the term humility or modesty to an attitude where our subjectivity is not allowed to interfere by act or quality, it is easy to appreciate the question touching the humility or modesty and pride of philosophy. For in point of contents, thought is only true in proportion as it immerses itself in the matter at hand [*die Sache*]; and in point of form it is no particular state or act of the subject, but rather that attitude of consciousness where the abstract self, freed from all the special limitations to which its ordinary states or qualities are liable, restricts itself to that *allgemein* mode of action in which it is identical with all individuals. In these circumstances philosophy may be acquitted of the charge of pride. And when Aristotle[4] summons one to rise to

---

2. An apparent reference to Kant's "What Is Enlightenment?" (1784); see above.
3. That is, a pointless truism.
4. Greek philosopher (384–322 B.C.E.). Hegel presumably has in mind here Aristotle's discussion of "greatness of soul" (*megalopsychia*) in his Nichomachean Ethics 4.3. Hegel's point is that in a philosopher, to think highly of philosophical thinking is not merely self-regarding "pride" (*Hochmut*). And he is suggesting that Aristotle's praise of the self-assurance or "dignity" (*Würdigkeit*, better translated as "worthiness") of those with "greatness of soul" is properly directed at the loftiness of the thinking rather than at a specific thinker.

the dignity of that attitude, the dignity he seeks is won by letting go of all our individual opinions and prejudices, and submitting to the sway of the matter at hand.

24.] With these explanations and qualifications, thoughts may be termed Objective Thoughts—among which are also to be included the forms which are more especially discussed in the common logic, where they are usually treated as forms of conscious thought only. *Logic* therefore coincides with *Metaphysics*, the *Wissenschaft* of *things* grasped *in thoughts*—thoughts accredited able to express the *essential reality of things*.

An exposition of the relation in which such forms as notion, judgment, and syllogism stand to others, such as causality, is a matter for the discipline itself. But this much is evident beforehand. If thought tries to form a *Begriff*[5] of things, this *Begriff* (as well as its proximate phases, the judgment and syllogism) cannot be composed of articles and relations which are alien and irrelevant to the things. Reflection [*Nachdenken*], it was said above, leads to the *Allgemeine* of things—which is itself one of the constituent factors of a *Begriff*. To say that Reason or Understanding is in the world is equivalent in its import to the phrase 'Objective Thought.' The latter phrase however has the inconvenience, that thought is usually confined to express what belongs to *Geist* or consciousness only, while 'objective' is a term applied, at least primarily, only to the non-mental.[6]

(Add. I) To speak of thought or objective thought as the heart and soul of the world may seem to be ascribing consciousness to the things of nature. We feel a certain repugnance against making thought the inward function of things, especially as we speak of thought as marking the divergence of man from nature. It would be necessary, therefore, if we use the term thought at all, to speak of nature as the system of unconscious thought, or, to use Schelling's expression, a petrified intelligence. And in order to prevent misconception, thought-form or thought-type should be substituted for the ambiguous term thought.

From what has been said the principles of logic are to be sought in a system of thought-types or fundamental categories, in which the opposition between subjective and objective, in its usual sense, vanishes. The signification thus attached to thought and its characteristic forms may be illustrated by the ancient saying that 'νοῦς governs the world,'[7] or by our own phrase that 'Reason is in the world': which means that Reason is the soul of the world it inhabits, its immanent principle, its most proper and inward nature, its *Allgemeine*. Another illustration is offered by the circumstance that in speaking of some definite animal we say it is (an) animal. Now, the *animal as such* cannot be shown; nothing can be pointed out excepting some particular animal. '*The* animal' does not exist: that is merely the general nature of the particular animals, whilst each existing animal is a more concretely defined and particularised thing. But to be an animal—the law of kind which is the *Allgemeine* in this case—is the property of the particular animal, and constitutes its definite essence. Take away from the dog its animality, and it becomes impossible

5. That is, a "genuine concept"; see the Hegel glossary, p. 144.
6. In the original, *Ungeistigem*—that is, things that do not have the character of *Geist*. That is a

restriction of the term "objective" that Hegel rejects.
7. A saying of the Greek philosopher Anaxagoras (ca. 500–ca. 428 B.C.E.); the Greek word *nous* means "mind" or "reason."

to say what it is. All things have a permanent inward nature, as well as an outward existence. They live and die, arise and pass away; but their essentiality and *Allgemeinheit* is the type; and this means much more than something *common* to them all.

If thought is the constitutive substance of external things, it is also the general substance of what is spiritual. In all human perception thought is present; so too thought is the *Allgemeine* in all the acts of conception and recollection; in short, in every mental [*geistig*] activity, in willing, wishing and the like. All of them are only further specialisations of thought. When it is presented in this light, thought has a different part to play from what it has if we speak of a faculty of thought, one among a crowd of other faculties, such as perception, conception and will, with which it stands on the same level. When it is seen to be the true *Allgemeine* of everything natural and also everything *geistig*, it extends its scope far beyond all these *geistig* activities, and becomes the basis of everything.

From this view of thought, in its objective meaning (as νοῦς), we may next pass to consider the subjective sense of the term. We say first, Man [*der Mensch*] is a being that thinks; but we also say at the same time, Man is a being that perceives and wills. Man is a thinker, and is *Allgemeine*; but he is a thinker only because the *Allgemeine* is something *for* him.[8] The animal too is in itself *Allgemeine*; yet what there is *for* it is not the *Allgemeine*, but rather only the particular. The animal sees something particular—for instance, its food, or a man. For the animal all this never goes beyond the particular thing. Similarly, sensation has to do with nothing but particulars such as *this* pain or *this* sweet taste. Nature does not bring its νοῦς into consciousness: it is man who first makes himself double so as to be an *Allgemeine* for an *Allgemeine*.[9] This first happens when man knows that he is 'I'. By the term 'I' I mean myself, a single and altogether determinate person. And yet I really utter nothing peculiar to myself, for every one else is 'I'; and when I call myself 'I,' though I indubitably mean the single person myself, I express something entirely *Allgemeine*. 'I,' therefore, is mere being-for-self, in which everything particular is superseded; it is as it were the ultimate and unanalysable point of consciousness.

We may say 'I' and thought are the same, or, more definitely, 'I' is thought as a thinker. What I have in my consciousness, is for me. 'I' is the empty space or receptacle for anything and everything: for which everything is and which stores up everything in itself. Every man is a whole world of *Vorstellungen*, that lie buried in the night of the 'I.' It follows that the 'I' is the *Allgemeine* in which we leave aside all that is particular, and in which at the same time all the particulars have a latent existence. In other words, it is not a mere abstract *Allgemeinheit* and nothing more, but the *Allgemeinheit* that contains everything in itself. Commonly we use the word 'I' without attaching much importance to it, nor is it an object of study except to philosophical analysis. In the 'I' we have thought before us in its utter purity. While the animal cannot say 'I,' man can, because it is his nature to think. Now in the 'I' there are a variety of contents, derived both from within and from without, and according to the nature of these contents our state may be described as

8. That is, something of which he is aware. In other words, man is a thinker only because he is able to be aware of the *allgemein*, the "general" (e.g., "man"), rather than just the merely particular.

9. That is, to apprehend things as instances of general types (e.g., "food") in relation to himself as instance of a general type distinct from other general types.

perception, or conception, or reminiscence. But in all of them the 'I' is found: or in them all thought is present. Man, therefore, is always thinking, even when he only perceives: if he observes anything, he always observes it as something general, fixes on a single point which he places in relief, thus withdrawing his attention from other points, and takes it as abstract and general, even if only formally *allgemein*.

In the case of our ordinary conceptions, two things may happen. Either the contents are moulded by thought, but not the form; or, the form belongs to thought and not the contents. In using such terms, for instance, as anger, rose, hope, I am speaking of things which I have learnt in the way of sensation, but I express these contents in an *allgemein* mode, that is, in the form of thought. I have left out much that is particular and given the contents in their generality: but still the contents remain sense-derived. On the other hand, when I imagine[1] God, the content is undeniably a product of pure thought, but the form still retains the sensuous limitations which it has as I find it immediately present in myself. In these generalised images the content is not merely and simply sensible, as it is in a visual inspection; but either the content is sensuous and the form appertains to thought, or *vice versâ*. In the first case the material is given to us, and our thought supplies the form: in the second case the content which has its source in thought is by means of the form turned into a something given, which accordingly reaches the mind from without.

(Add. 2) Logic is the study of thought pure and simple, or of the pure thought-forms. In the ordinary sense of the term, by thought we generally represent to ourselves something more than simple and unmixed thought; we mean some thought, the material of which is from experience. Whereas in logic a thought is understood to include nothing else but what depends on thinking and what thinking has brought into existence. It is in these circumstances that thoughts are *pure* thoughts. *Der Geist* is then in its own home-element and therefore free: for freedom means that the other thing with which you deal is a second self—so that you never leave your own ground but give the law to yourself. In the impulses or appetites the beginning is from something else, from something which we feel to be external. In this case then we speak of dependence. For freedom it is necessary that we should feel no presence of something else which is not ourselves. The natural man, whose motions follow the rule only of his appetites, is not his own master. Be he as self-willed as he may, the constituents of his will and opinion are not his own, and his freedom is merely formal. But when we *think*, we renounce our selfish and particular being, sink ourselves in the thing, allow thought to follow its own course, and—if we add anything of our own, we think ill.

If in pursuance of the foregoing remarks we consider Logic to be the system of the pure types of thought, we find that the other philosophical *Wissenschaften*, the Philosophy of Nature and the Philosophy of *Geist*,[2] take the place, as it were, of an Applied Logic, and that Logic is the soul which animates them both. Their problem in that case is only to recognise the logical forms under the shapes they assume in Nature and *Geist*—shapes which are only a particular mode of expression for the forms of pure thought. * * *

1. That is, form an image of (*vorstellen*).   2. The other two parts of the *Encyclopedia*.

Physics also teaches us to know the *Allgemeine*, the essence [*Wesen*] [in Nature]: and the only difference between it and the Philosophy of Nature is that the latter brings to consciousness the proper [*wahrhaft*] forms of the *Begriff* in the physical world.

It will now be understood that Logic is the all-animating *Geist* of all the *Wissenschaften*, and its categories the *geistig* hierarchy. They are the heart and centre of things: and yet at the same time they are always on our lips, and, apparently at least, perfectly familiar objects. But things thus familiar are usually the greatest strangers. Being, for example, is a category of pure thought: but to make 'Is' an object of investigation never occurs to us. Common fancy puts the Absolute far away in a world beyond. The Absolute is rather something entirely present to us, which as thinkers we must, (though without express consciousness of it) always carry with us and always use.[3] Language is the main depository of these determinations of thought [*Denkbestimmungen*]; and one use of the grammatical instruction which children receive is unconsciously to turn their attention to distinctions of thought.

Logic is usually said to be concerned with forms [*Formen*] *only* and to derive the material for them from elsewhere. But this 'only,' which assumes that the logical thoughts [*logischen Gedanken*] are nothing in comparison with the rest of the contents, is not the word to use about them. They are the ultimate ground of everything.[4] Everything else rather is an 'only' compared with these thoughts.

To take an interest in such pure determinations [*Bestimmungen*] pre-supposes in the inquirer a higher level of *Bildung* than ordinary; and to study them in themselves and for their own sake signifies in addition that these determinations must be deduced out of thought itself, and their truth or reality examined by the light of their own laws. We do not assume them as data from without, and then define them or exhibit their value and authority by comparing them with the shape they take in our minds. If we thus acted, we should proceed from observation and experience, and should, for instance, say we habitually employ the term 'force' in such a case, and such a meaning. A definition like that would be called correct, if it agreed with the conception of its object present in our ordinary state of mind. The defect of this empirical method is that a notion is not defined as it is in and for itself, but in terms of something assumed, which is then used as a criterion and standard of correctness. No such test need be applied: we have merely to let the living determinations justify themselves.

To ask if a category is true or not must sound strange to the ordinary mind: for a category apparently becomes true only when it is applied to a given object, and apart from this application it would seem meaningless to inquire into its truth. But this is the very question on which everything turns. We must however in the first place understand clearly what we mean by Truth. In common life truth means the agreement of an object with our representation of it. We thus pre-suppose an object to which our representation must conform. In the philosophical sense of the word, on the other hand, truth may be described, in general abstract terms, as the agreement of a thought-content with itself. This meaning is quite different from the one given above. At the same time

---

3. That is, instead of being something above and beyond ourselves and the world of which we are a part, "the Absolute" is present to us in the very thought that pervades our thinking experience— for the fundamental essential nature of thought is also the fundamental essential nature of reality.
4. Literally, the "forms" or "thoughts" (or "thought-forms") with which Hegel is dealing in his "Logic" are said to be "the in-and-for-itself existing ground [*der an und für sich seiende Grund*] of everything."

the deeper and philosophical meaning of truth can be partially traced even in the ordinary usage of language. Thus we speak of a true friend; by which we mean a friend whose manner of conduct accords with the *Begriff* of friendship. In the same way we speak of a true work of Art. Untrue in this sense means the same as "bad" or self-discordant.[5] In this sense a "bad state"[6] is an untrue state; and badness and untruth may be said to consist in the contradiction subsisting between the function or *Begriff* and the existence of the object. Of such a "bad" object we may form a correct *Vorstellung*, but the import of such *Vorstellungen* is inherently false. Of these correctnesses, which are at the same time untruths, we may have many in our heads.—God alone is the complete harmony of *Begriff* and reality. All finite things involve an untruth: they have a *Begriff* and an existence, but their existence does not meet the requirements of the *Begriff*. For this reason they must perish, and then the incompatibility between their *Begriff* and their existence becomes manifest. It is in the species that the particular animal has its *Begriff*: and the species liberates itself from this particularity by death.

The study of truth, or, as it is here explained to mean, self-agreement,[7] constitutes the proper problem of logic. In our every-day mind we are never troubled with questions about the truth of the forms of thought.—We may also express the problem of logic by saying that it examines the determinations of thought touching their capability to capture truth. And the question comes to this: What are the forms of the infinite, and what are the forms of the finite? Usually no suspicion attaches to the finite determinations of thought; they are allowed to pass unquestioned. But it is from thinking and acting in accordance with finite categories that all deception originates.

(Add. 3) Truth may be ascertained in various ways, each of which however is no more than a form.[8] Experience [*Erfahrung*] is the first of these methods. But experience is only a form: it has no intrinsic value of its own. For in experience everything depends upon the sensibility [*Sinn*] we bring to bear upon actuality. A great sensibility is great in its experience, and in the motley play of phenomena at once perceives the point of real significance. The *Idee* is present and actual, not something (as it were) over the hill and far away. The genius of a Goethe,[9] for example, looking into nature or history, has great experiences, catches sight of the living principle, and gives expression to it. A second method of apprehending the truth is Reflection [*Reflexion*], which determines it by conceptual relations. But in these two modes the absolute truth has not yet found its appropriate form. The most perfect method of knowledge proceeds in the pure form of thought [*Denken*]: and here man proceeds in a manner of complete freedom.[1]

* * *

* * * Man in so far as he is *Geist* is not the creature of nature: and when he behaves as such, and follows the cravings of appetite, he *chooses* to be so. The natural wickedness of man is therefore unlike the natural life of animals.

---

5. That is, "shabby, or at odds with itself" (*schlecht, in sich selbst angemessen*): not measuring up to the way it is supposed to be (its nature).
6. That is, a very deficient state; a sorry excuse for a state; a pathetic (instance of a) state.
7. Literally, "agreement [of something] with itself" (*Übereinstimmung mit sich selbst*).

8. That is, is only a kind of way of going about ascertaining truth.
9. Johann Wolfgang von Goethe (1749–1832), a scientist as well as the preeminent German literary figure of the time.
1. That is, unhindered by anything external to the nature of thought itself.

A mere natural life may be more exactly defined by saying that the natural man as such is a particular creature; for nature in every part is in the bonds of particularization. Thus when man wills to be a creature of nature, he wills particularity [*Einzelheit*]. Yet against the impulsive and appetitive action associated with this natural particularity, there enters the law or *allgemein* principle. This law may either be an external force, or have the form of divine authority. So long as he continues in his natural state, man is in bondage to the law.[2] It is true that among the dispositions and feelings of man, there are social or benevolent inclinations, love, sympathy, and others, reaching beyond his selfish isolation. But so long as these tendencies are instinctive,[3] their implicitly *allgemein* content is vitiated by the subjective form which always allows free play to self-seeking and random action.

25.] The term 'Objective Thoughts' [*objektiven Gedanken*] indicates the *truth* [*Wahrheit*]—the truth which is to be the absolute *object* of philosophy, and not merely the *goal* at which it aims. But the very expression cannot fail to suggest an opposition, to characterise and appreciate which is the main motive of the philosophical attitude of the present time, and which forms the real problem of the question about truth and our means of ascertaining it. If the thought-determinations are vitiated by a fixed antithesis, *i.e.* if they are only of a finite character, they are unsuitable for the self-centred universe of truth, and truth cannot enter into thought. Thought that can produce only limited and partial categories and proceed by their means is what, in the stricter sense of the word, is termed Understanding [*Verstand*]. The finitude, further, of these categories lies in two points. Firstly, they are only subjective, and the contrast to the objective permanently clings to them. Secondly, they are always of restricted content, and so persist in contrast to one another and still more to the Absolute. In order more fully to explain the position and import here attributed to logic, the attitudes in which thought is supposed to stand to objectivity will next be examined by way of further introduction.

In my *Phenomenology of Geist*, which on that account was at its publication described as the first part of the System of Philosophy, the method adopted was to begin with the first and simplest phase of *Geist*, immediate consciousness, and to show how that stage gradually of necessity worked onward to the philosophical point of view, the necessity of that view being proved by the process. But in these circumstances it was impossible to restrict the quest to the mere form of consciousness. For the stage of philosophical knowledge is the richest in material and organisation, and therefore, as it came before us in the shape of a result, it pre-supposed the existence of the concrete formations of consciousness, such as morality, the ethical, art and religion. In the development of consciousness, which at first sight appears limited to the point of form merely, there is thus at the same time included the development of the matter or of the objects discussed in the special branches of philosophy. But the latter process must, so to speak, go on 'behind the back' of consciousness, since those facts are the essential nucleus which is raised into consciousness. The exposition accordingly is rendered more intricate, because so much that

2. That is, as long as man continues in his natural state, the law is experienced as bondage because it is experienced as restrictive and alien external constraint.

3. Literally, "immediate" (*unmittelbar*); these are things one simply feels, without the involvement (mediation) of thought.

properly belongs to the concrete branches is prematurely dragged into the introduction. The survey which follows in the present work has the even greater inconvenience of being only historical and inferential in its method. But it tries especially to show how the questions men have proposed, outside academic circles, on the nature of knowledge, belief, and the like—questions which they imagine to have no connexion with abstract thoughts—are really reducible to simple thought-determinations, which only receive their proper treatment in Logic.

From *The Idee*[4]

213.] The *Idee* is truth in itself and for itself—the absolute unity of *Begriff* and objectivity. Its 'ideal' content is nothing but the *Begriff* in its determinations [*Bestimmungen*]; its 'real' content is only the expression [*Darstellung*] which the *Begriff* gives itself in the form of external existence, whilst yet, by enclosing this shape in its ideality, it keeps it in its power, and so preserves itself in it.

The definition, which declares the Absolute to be the *Idee*, is itself absolute. All former definitions come back to this. The *Idee* is the Truth: for Truth is objectivity corresponding to *Begriff*:—not of course the correspondence of external things with my *Vorstellungen*—for these are only *correct Vorstellungen* held by *me*, the individual person. In the *Idee* we have nothing to do with the individual, nor with representations, nor with external things. And yet, again, everything *wirklich*, in so far as it is true, is the *Idee*, and has its truth by and in virtue of the *Idee* alone. Every particular being is some aspect [*Seite*] of the *Idee*: for which, therefore, yet other actualities are needed, which in their turn appear to have a self-subsistence of their own. It is only in them all together and in their relation that the *Begriff* is realised [*realisiert*]. The particular by itself does not correspond to its *Begriff*. It is this limitation of its existence which constitutes its finitude and its downfall.

The *Idee* itself is not to be taken as an idea of something or other, any more than the *Begriff* is to be taken as merely a specific concept. The Absolute is the *allgemein* and one *Idee*, which, as *urteilend*,[5] articulates itself into the

4. The following sections of the *Logic* open the final part of its concluding division, "The Theory of Rational Structure" ("Die Lehre vom Begriff": literally, "The Doctrine of the Concept"). Hegel's term *Idee* is left untranslated for reasons explained in the glossary at the end of the introductory headnote.
5. This participle (*urteilend*) and the corresponding noun (*Urteil*) in the next sentence should not have their usual translations here, because of the way Hegel is playing on their literal sense to suggest a different meaning that is completely obscured and lost when those ordinary translations are used. *Urteil* normally means (and is appropriately translated as) "judgment"; *urteilend* would ordinarily be translated as "judging." But the prefix *ur-* means "primordial," *Teil* means "part," *teilen* means "to divide" or "to separate," and *teilend* means "separating" or "dividing"; and what Hegel appears to be doing is using the terms *Urteil* and *urteilend* to convey the idea of a primordial division or separa-

tion within the *Idee* that results in the articulation of the one general simple *Idee* into a "system" of interconnected but distinct specific *Ideen* (the plural of *Idee*). The most appropriate and simplest translation of the phrase "as *urteilend*" would therefore be not "as judging" (which would make no good and comprehensible Hegelian sense), but rather "as primordially dividing." Hegel's point is that division into a system of more specific *Ideen* is as fundamental to the one "absolute *Idee*" as is its underlying unity and generality (*Allgemeinheit*). Hegel may also be drawing on the archaic but powerful association of *Teil* with "portion" in the sense of "lot" or "fate" or "destiny," thereby suggesting that the relinquishment of abstract and undifferentiated purity in favor of differentiation and actualization is somehow the inescapable intrinsic fate or destiny—the "*Ur-Teil*"—of the *Idee*. It differentiated and objectified itself because it had to, out of some inner necessity.

system of specific *Ideen*; which after all are constrained by their nature to come back to the one *Idee* where their truth lies. It is out of this process that the *Idee*—initially only the one *allgemein substance*—in its developed and genuine actuality is to be as *subject*, and so as *Geist*.

Because it has no *existence* for starting-point and *point d'appui*, the *Idee* is frequently treated as a mere logical form. Such a view must be relegated to those theories that ascribe so-called reality and genuine *Wirklichkeit* to the existent thing and other determinations, and that have not yet penetrated as far as the *Idee*. It is no less false to imagine the *Idee* to be mere abstraction. It is abstract certainly, in so far as everything untrue is consumed in it: but in its own self it is essentially concrete, because it is the free *Begriff* determining and giving reality to itself. It would be an abstract form only if the *Begriff*, which is its principle, were construed as an abstract unity, rather than as it is—as the negative return into itself, and as subjectivity.[6]

(Add.) Truth is at first taken to mean that I *know* how something *is*. This is truth, however, only in reference to consciousness; it is formal truth, bare correctness. Truth in the deeper sense consists in the identity between objectivity and the *Begriff*. It is in this deeper sense of truth that we speak of a 'true state,' or of a 'true work of art.' These objects are 'true' if they are as they ought to be, *i.e.* if their reality corresponds to their *Begriff*. When thus viewed, to be untrue means much the same as to be 'bad.'[7] A 'bad man' is an 'untrue man,' a man who does not behave as his *Begriff* or his vocation [*Bestimmung*][8] requires. Nothing however can subsist, if it be *wholly* devoid of identity between its *Begriff* and reality. Even 'bad' and untrue things have being, in so far as their reality still, somehow, conforms to their *Begriff*. Whatever is thoroughly bad or contrary to its *Begriff* is for that very reason on the way to ruin. It is by the *Begriff* alone that the things in the world have their subsistence; or, as it is expressed in the language of religious conception, things are what they are, only in virtue of the divine and thereby creative thought [*Gedanken*] which dwells within them.

When we hear the *Idee* spoken of, we need not imagine something far away beyond this mortal sphere. The *Idee* is rather something completely present, and it is found, however confused and degenerated, in every consciousness. We conceive the world to ourselves as a great totality which is created by God, and so created that in it God has manifested himself to us. We regard the world also as ruled by Divine Providence: implying that the scattered and divided parts of the world are continually brought back, and made conformable, to the unity from which they have issued. The purpose of philosophy has always been the intellectual ascertainment of the *Idee*; and everything deserving the name of philosophy has constantly been based on the conscious-

---

6. That is, the *Idee* is no mere abstract form, because the *Begriff* is no mere abstract unity. It involves (1) a "negating" process (its identity with itself is sacrificed for the sake of its attainment of articulation and realization, and then is regained with a difference, as its realization comes to accord fully with that articulation) and (2) the mediation of subjectivity (knowing and willing consciousness).

7. "Bad" (*schlecht*) is here to be understood evalu-

atively but not moralistically.

8. Here translated "vocation" (as in the title of FICH-TE's book *The Vocation of Man* [1800]; see source note to that work, above), the same term (in the plural) is used by Hegel for differently articulated "determinations" of the *Idee*, associated with different specific *Begriffe* (logical "concepts" or structures). Hegel—like Fichte and others before him—saw our general essential nature as having not only descriptive but also normative significance.

ness of an absolute unity—where the understanding [*Verstand*][9] sees and accepts only separation.

It is too late now to ask for proof that the *Idee* is the truth. The proof of that is contained in the whole deduction and development of thought up to this point. The *Idee* is the result of this course of dialectic. Not that it is to be supposed that the *Idee* is mediate only, *i.e.* mediated through something else than itself. It is rather its own result, and being so, is no less immediate than mediate. The stages hitherto considered, viz. those of Being and Essence, as well as those of *Begriff* and of Objectivity, are not, when so distinguished, something permanent, resting upon themselves. They have proved to be dialectical; and their only truth is that they are dynamic elements of the *Idee*.

214.] The *Idee* may be described in many ways. It may be called reason (and this is the proper philosophical signification of reason); subject-object; the unity of the ideal and the real, of the finite and the infinite, of soul and body; the possibility which has its *Wirklichkeit* in its own self; that of which the nature can be thought only as existent, &c. All these descriptions apply, because the *Idee* contains all the relations of understanding, but contains them in their infinite self-return and self-identity.

It is easy work for the understanding to show that everything said of the *Idee* is self-contradictory. But that can quite as well be countered, or rather in the *Idee* the counter is actually made. And this work, which is the work of reason, is certainly not so easy as that of the understanding. Understanding may demonstrate that the *Idee* is self-contradictory: because the subjective is subjective only and is always confronted by the objective—because being is different from *Begriff* and therefore cannot be picked out of it—because the finite is finite only, the exact antithesis of the infinite, and therefore not identical with it; and so on with every term of the description. The reverse of all this however is the doctrine of Logic. Logic shows that the subjective which is to be subjective only, the finite which would be finite only, the infinite which would be infinite only, and so on, have no truth, but contradict themselves, and pass over into their opposites. Hence this transition, and the unity in which the extremes are merged and become factors, each with a merely reflected existence, reveals itself as their truth.

The understanding, when it addresses itself to deal with the *Idee*, commits a double misunderstanding. It takes *first* the extremes of the *Idee* (however they may be expressed, so long as they are in their unity), not as they are understood when stamped with this concrete unity, but as if they remained abstractions outside of it. It no less mistakes the relation between them, even when it has been expressly stated. Thus, for example, it overlooks even the nature of the copula in the judgment, which affirms that the particular, or subject, is after all not particular, but general. But, in the *second* place, the understanding believes *its* 'reflection'—that the self-identical *Idee* contains its own negative, or contains contradiction—to be an external reflection which does not lie within the *Idee* itself. But the reflection is really no peculiar cleverness of the understanding. The *Idee* itself is the dialectic which for ever divides

---

9. For Hegel, *Verstand* is a kind of analytical thinking that specializes in making distinctions and determining correctness; for more truly philosophical thinking that grasps underlying unities and more significant forms of truth and meaning, *Vernunft* (reason) is required.

and distinguishes the self-identical from the differentiated, the subjective from the objective, the finite from the infinite, soul from body. Only on these terms is it an eternal creation, eternal vitality, and eternal spirit. But while it thus passes or rather translates itself into the abstract understanding, it for ever remains reason [*Vernunft*]. The *Idee* is the dialectic which again makes this mass of understanding and diversity comprehend its finite nature and the pseudo-independence in its productions, and which brings the diversity back to unity. Since this double movement is not separate or distinct in time, nor indeed in any other way—otherwise it would be only a repetition of the abstract understanding—the *Idee* is the eternal vision of itself in the other—*Begriff* which in its objectivity *has* carried out *itself*—object which is inward design, essential subjectivity.

The different modes of apprehending the *Idee* as unity of ideal and real, of finite and infinite, of identity and difference, &c. are more or less formal. They designate some one stage of the *specific Begriff*. Only the *Begriff* itself, however, is free and the genuine *Allgemeine*: in the *Idee*, therefore, the specific character of the *Begriff* is only the *Begriff* itself—an objectivity, viz. into which it, being the *Allgemeine*, continues itself, and in which it has only its own character, the total character. The *Idee* is the infinite judgment, of which the terms are severally the independent totality; and in which, as each grows to the fulness of its own nature, it has thereby at the same time passed into the other. None of the other specific *Begriffe* exhibits this totality complete on both its sides as the *Begriff* itself and objectivity.

215.] The *Idee* is essentially a process, because its identity is the absolute and free identity of the *Begriff* only in so far as it is absolute negativity, and for that reason dialectical. It is the course of movement in which the *Begriff*, as the *Allgemeinheit* that is particular, gives itself the character of objectivity and of the antithesis thereto; and this externality which has the *Begriff* for its substance, finds its way back to subjectivity through its immanent dialectic.

As the *Idee* is (*a*) a process, it follows that such an expression for the Absolute as *unity* of thought and being, of finite and infinite, &c. is false; for unity expresses an abstract and merely quiescent identity. As the *Idee* is (*b*) subjectivity, it follows that the expression is equally false on another account. That unity of which it speaks expresses a merely virtual or underlying presence of the genuine unity. The infinite would thus seem to be merely *neutralised* by the finite, the subjective by the objective, thought by being. But in the negative unity of the *Idee* the infinite overlaps and includes the finite, thought overlaps being, subjectivity overlaps objectivity. The unity of the *Idee* is thought, infinity, and subjectivity, and is in consequence to be essentially distinguished from the *Idee* as *substance*, just as this overlapping subjectivity, thought, or infinity is to be distinguished from the one-sided subjectivity, one-sided thought, one-sided infinity to which it descends in judging and defining.

(Add.) The *Idee* as a process runs through three stages in its development. The first form of the *Idee* is Life: that is, the *Idee* in the form of immediacy. The second form is that of mediation or differentiation; and this is the *Idee* in the form of Knowledge, which appears under the double aspect of the Theoretical and Practical *Idee*. The process of knowledge eventuates in the restoration of the unity enriched by difference. This gives the third form of the *Idee*, the Absolute *Idee*: which last stage of the logical *Idee* shows itself to be at the same time the true first,[1] and to be through itself alone.

* * *

SOURCE: From *The Logic of Hegel, Translated from "The Encyclopaedia of the Philosophical Sciences,"* trans. William Wallace, 2nd ed., rev. and augmented (Oxford: Oxford University Press, 1892), 30–39, 44–53, 57–59, 352–58 (translation modified by the editor). Except where otherwise indicated, German words in brackets are the terminology used in the German original, inserted by the editor in addition to their renderings in the translation; and unbracketed German words are the original terminology, substituted in place of their renderings in the translation by the editor for reasons given in notes and in the Hegel glossary (p. 144). The "preliminaries" is the chapter Hegel titled "Vorbegriff" (literally, "preliminary concept"), which introduces and provides a preliminary characterization and sketch of what he means by "logic" (the fundamental structures of thought and reality) and of the volume's contents.

On Nature

From Philosophy of Nature

(Encyclopedia, part 2)

From *Introduction*

Zusatz. It can be said perhaps that in our time, philosophy does not enjoy any special favour and liking. At least, it is no longer recognized, as it was formerly, that the study of philosophy must constitute the indispensable introduction and foundation for all further scientific [*wissenschaftlich*] education and professional study. But this much may be assumed *without hesitation* as correct, that the *Philosophy of Nature* in particular is in considerable disfavour. I do not intend to deal at length with the extent to which this prejudice against the Philosophy of Nature in particular, is justified; and yet I cannot altogether pass it over. What is seldom absent from a period of great intellectual ferment has, of course, happened in connection with the *idea of the Philosophy of Nature* as recently expounded. It can be said that in the first satisfaction afforded by its discovery, this idea met with crude treatment at unskilled hands, instead of being cultivated by thinking Reason; and it has been brought low not so much by its opponents as by its friends.[1]

* * *

FROM WAYS OF CONSIDERING NATURE

In order to find the Notion [*Begriff*] *of the Philosophy of Nature*, we must *first* of all indicate the Notion of the knowledge of Nature in general, and *secondly*, develop the *distinction between physics and the Philosophy of Nature*.

---

1. That is, this final stage in the process of the development of the *Idee* turns out to have fundamental priority, "logically" speaking, and to owe its nature and reality to itself alone.

1. An allusion to SCHELLING, criticized by name later in this paragraph (in a sentence omitted from the selection): "It is on account of such charlatanism that the Philosophy of Nature, especially Schelling's, has become discredited."

What is Nature? We propose to answer this general question by reference to the knowledge of Nature and the Philosophy of Nature. Nature confronts us as a riddle and a problem, whose solution both attracts and repels us: attracts us, because Spirit [*Geist*] is presaged in Nature; repels us, because Nature seems an alien existence, in which Spirit [*Geist*] does not find itself. That is why Aristotle said that philosophy started from wonder.[2] We start to perceive, we collect facts about the manifold formations and laws of Nature; this procedure, on its own account, runs on into endless detail in all directions, and just because no end can be perceived in it, this method does not satisfy us. And in all this wealth of knowledge the question can again arise, or perhaps come to us for the first time: What is Nature? It remains a problem. * * *

* * * Our approach to Nature is partly practical and partly theoretical. An examination of the theoretical approach will reveal a contradiction which, thirdly, will lead us to our standpoint; to resolve the contradiction we must incorporate what is peculiar to the practical approach, and by this means practical and theoretical will be united and integrated into a totality.

§ 245.] In man's *practical* approach to Nature, the latter is, for him, something immediate and external; and he himself is an external and therefore sensuous individual, although in relation to natural objects, he correctly regards himself as *end*. A consideration of Nature according to this relationship yields the standpoint of *finite* teleology (§ 205). In this, we find the correct presupposition that Nature does not itself contain the absolute, final end (§§ 207–11). But if this way of considering the matter starts from particular, *finite* ends, on the one hand it makes them into presuppositions whose contingent content may in itself be even insignificant and trivial. On the other hand, the end-relationship demands for itself a deeper mode of treatment than that appropriate to external and finite relationships, namely, the mode of treatment of the Notion [*Begriff*] which in its own general [*allgemein*] nature is immanent and therefore is immanent in Nature as such.

* * *

§ 246.] What is now called *physics* was formerly called *natural philosophy*, and it is also a *theoretical*, and indeed a *thinking* consideration of Nature; but, on the one hand, it does not start from determinations which are external to Nature, like those ends already mentioned; and secondly, it is directed to a knowledge of the *universal* aspect [*Allgemeinen*] of Nature, a universal [*Allgemeine*] which is also *determined* within itself—directed to a knowledge of forces, laws and genera, whose content must not be a simple aggregate, but arranged in orders and classes, must present itself as an organism. As the Philosophy of Nature is a *comprehending* [*begreifend*] treatment, it has as its object the same universal [*Allgemeine*], but *explicitly*, and it considers this universal in its *own immanent necessity* in accordance with the self-determination of the Notion [*Begriff*].

REMARK

The relation of philosophy to the empirical sciences [*Wissenschaften*] was discussed in the general introduction [to the *Encyclopaedia*].[3] Not only must phi-

2. See *Metaphysics* 928b by the Greek philosopher Aristotle (384–322 B.C.E.).

3. See the first Hegel selection, above.

losophy be in agreement with our empirical knowledge of Nature, but the *origin* and *formation* of the Philosophy of Nature presupposes and is conditioned by empirical physics. However, the course of a science's origin and the preliminaries of its construction are one thing, while the science itself is another. In the latter, the former can no longer appear as the foundation of the science; here, the foundation must be the necessity of the Notion [*Begriff*].

It has already been mentioned that, in the progress of philosophical knowledge, we must not only give an account of the object *as determined by its Notion*, but we must also name the *empirical* appearance corresponding to it, and we must show that the appearance does, in fact, correspond to its Notion. However, this is not an appeal to experience in regard to the necessity of the content. Even less admissible is an appeal to what is called *intuition* [*Anschauung*], which is usually nothing but a fanciful and sometimes fantastic exercise of the imagination on the lines of *analogies*, which may be more or less significant, and which impress determinations and schemata on objects only *externally* (§ 231, Remark).

Zusatz. In the theoretical approach to Nature (α) the first point is that we stand back from natural objects, leaving them as they are and adjusting ourselves to them. Here, we start from our sense-knowledge of Nature. However, if physics were based solely on perceptions, and perceptions were nothing more than the evidence of the senses, then the physical act would consist only in seeing, hearing, smelling, etc., and animals, too, would in this way be physicists. But what sees, hears, etc., is a spirit, a thinker. Now if we said that, in our theoretical approach to Nature, we left things free, this applied only partly to the outer senses, for these are themselves partly theoretical and partly practical (§ 358); it is only our ideational faculty [*Vorstellen*],[4] our intelligence, that has this free relationship to things. We can, of course, consider things practically, as means; but then knowing is itself only a means, not an end in itself. (β) The second bearing of things on us is that things acquire the character of universality [*Allgemeinheit*] for us or that we transform them into universals [*Allgemeinheiten*]. The more thought enters into our representation [*Vorstellen*] of things, the less do they retain their naturalness, their singularity and immediacy. The wealth of natural forms, in all their infinitely manifold configuration, is impoverished by the all-pervading power of thought, their vernal life and glowing colours die and fade away. The rustle of Nature's life is silenced in the stillness of thought; her abundant life, wearing a thousand wonderful and delightful shapes, shrivels into arid forms and shapeless generalities resembling a murky northern fog. (γ) These two characteristics are not only opposed to the two practical ones, but we also find that the theoretical approach is self-contradictory, for it seems to bring about the direct opposite of what it intends; for we want to know the Nature that really is, not something that is not. But instead of leaving Nature as she is, and taking her as she is in truth, instead of simply perceiving her, we make her into something quite different. In thinking things, we transform them into something universal; but things are singular and the Lion as Such does not exist. We give them the form of something subjective, of something produced by us

---

4. That is, our representational faculty, or ability to form general representations or mental images of things (e.g., of the Lion as Such; see below).

and belonging to us, and belonging to us in our specifically human character: for natural objects do not think, and are not presentations [*Vorstellungen*] or thoughts. But according to the second characteristic of the theoretical approach referred to above, it is precisely this inversion which does take place; in fact, it might seem that what we are beginning is made impossible for us at the outset. The theoretical approach begins with the arrest of appetite, is disinterested, lets things exist and go on just as they are; with this attitude to Nature, we have straightway established a duality of object and subject and their separation, something here and something yonder. Our intention, however, is rather to grasp, to comprehend Nature, to make her ours, so that she is not something alien and yonder. Here, then, comes the difficulty: How do we, as subjects, come into contact with objects? If we venture to bridge this gulf and mislead ourselves along that line and so think this Nature, we make Nature, which is an Other than we are, into an Other than she is. Both theoretical approaches are also directly opposed to each other: we transform things into universals [*Allgemeinen*], or make them our own, and yet as natural objects they are supposed to have a free, self-subsistent being. This, therefore, is the point with which we are concerned in regard to the nature of cognition—this is the interest of philosophy.

* * *

The difficulty arising from the one-sided assumption of the theoretical consciousness, that natural objects confront us as permanent and impenetrable objects, is directly negatived[5] by the practical approach which acts on the absolutely idealistic belief that individual things are nothing in themselves. The defect of appetite, from the side of its relationship to things, is not that it is realistic towards them, but that it is all too idealistic. Philosophical, true idealism consists in nothing else but laying down that the truth about things is that as such immediately single, i.e. sensuous things, they are only a show, an appearance [*Schein*].[6] Of a metaphysics prevalent today which maintains that we cannot know things because they are absolutely shut to us, it might be said that not even the animals are so stupid as these metaphysicians; for they go after things, seize and consume them. The same thing is laid down in the second aspect of the theoretical approach referred to above, namely, that we think natural objects. Intelligence familiarizes itself with things, not of course in their sensuous existence, but by thinking them and positing their content in itself; and in, so to speak, adding form, universality [*Allgemeinheit*], to the practical ideality which, by itself, is only negativity, it gives an affirmative character to the negativity of the singular. This universal [*allgemein*] aspect of things is not something subjective, something belonging to us: rather is it, in contrast to the transient phenomenon, the noumenon, the true, objective, actual nature of things themselves, like the Platonic Ideas,[7] which are not somewhere afar off in the beyond, but exist in individual things as their substantial genera.

5. That is, negated, refuted, disproved, shown to be incorrect (*widerlegt*).
6. A very important sentence; and what follows (especially the final sentence of the paragraph) is a very helpful elaboration of that characterization of "philosophical, true idealism" (*der philosophische wahrhafte Idealismus*)—that is, of Hegel's kind of "idealism."

7. In the dialogues of the Greek philosopher Plato (ca. 427–ca. 347 B.C.E.), the Forms or Ideas are fundamental, timeless universals, in which objects in the natural world (their less than perfect copies) participate or share.

* * *

The Philosophy of Nature takes up the material which physics has prepared for it empirically, at the point to which physics has brought it, and reconstitutes it, so that experience is not its final warrant and base. Physics must therefore work into the hands of philosophy, in order that the latter may translate into the Notion [*Begriff*][8] the abstract universal [*Allgemeine*] transmitted to it, by showing how this universal, as an intrinsically necessary whole, proceeds from the Notion [*Begriff*]. The philosophical way of putting the facts is no mere whim, once in a way to walk on one's head for a change, after having walked for a long while on one's legs, or once in a way to see our everyday face bedaubed with paint: no, it is because the method of physics does not satisfy the Notion,[9] that we have to go further.

What distinguishes the Philosophy of Nature from physics is, more precisely, the kind of metaphysics used by them both; for metaphysics is nothing else but the entire range of the universal [*allgemein*] determinations of thought, as it were, the diamond net into which everything is brought and thereby first made intelligible. Every educated consciousness[1] has its metaphysics, an instinctive way of thinking,[2] the absolute power within us of which we become master only when we make it in turn the object of our knowledge. Philosophy in general has, as philosophy, other categories than those of the ordinary consciousness: all education [*Bildung*] reduces to the distinction of categories. All revolutions, in the sciences [*Wissenschaften*] no less than in world history, originate solely from the fact that spirit [*Geist*], in order to understand and comprehend itself with a view to possessing itself, has changed its categories, comprehending itself more truly, more deeply, more intimately, and more in unity with itself. Now the inadequacy of the thought-determinations used in physics can be traced to two points which are closely bound up with each other. (α) The universal [*Allgemeine*] of physics is abstract or only formal; its determination is not immanent in it and it does not pass over into particularity. (β) The determinate content falls for that very reason outside the universal; and so is split into fragments, into parts which are isolated and detached from each other, devoid of any necessary connection, and it is just this which stamps it as only finite. * * *

Spirit [*Geist*] cannot remain at this stage of thinking in terms of detached, unrelated concepts [*Verstandesreflexion*] and there are two ways in which it can advance beyond it. (α) The naïve mind (*der unbefangene Geist*), when it vividly contemplates Nature, as in the suggestive examples we often come across in Goethe,[3] feels the life and the universal [*allgemein*] relationship in Nature; it divines that the universe is an organic whole and a totality pervaded

8. That is, translate into the appropriate fundamental and refined conceptuality.
9. That is, does not satisfy the philosophical requirement of appropriate fundamental and refined conceptuality, articulating in rigorous concepts the relevant structures and relations. Even though it is authoritative at its level of (re-)description of natural phenomena, physics is not philosophically definitive.
1. That is, every cultivated, developed, and refined type of consciousness (e.g., the natural-scientific,

mathematical, or legal mentality).
2. That is, a way of thinking that has become instinct-like (*instinktartige*), or second nature, to those who have become proficient in it.
3. Johann Wolfgang von Goethe (1749–1832), a scientist as well as the preeminent German literary figure of the time; Hegel has just quoted from his drama *Faust: Part One* (1808) and later in this passage (also omitted here) quotes his *On Morphology* (1820).

by Reason, and it also feels in single forms of life an intimate oneness with itself; but even if we put together all those ingredients of the flower the result is still not a flower. And so, in the Philosophy of Nature, people have fallen back on intuition [*Anschauung*] and set it above reflective thought; but this is a mistake, for one cannot philosophize out of intuition. (β) What is intuited must also be thought, the isolated parts must be brought back by thought to simple universality;[4] this thought unity is the Notion [*Begriff*], which contains the specific differences, but as an immanent self-moving unity. The determinations of philosophical universality are not indifferent; it is the universality which fulfils itself, and which, in its diamantine identity, also contains difference.

The true infinite is the unity of itself and the finite; and this, now, is the category of philosophy and so, too, of the Philosophy of Nature. If genera and forces are the inner side of Nature, the universal, in face of which the outer and individual is only transient, then still a third stage is demanded, namely, the inner side of the inner side, and this, according to what has been said, would be the unity of the universal and the particular. * * *

In grasping this inner side, the one-sidedness of the theoretical and practical approaches is transcended, and at the same time each side receives its due. The former contains a universality [*Allgemeinheit*] without determinateness, the latter an individuality without a universal; the cognition which comprehends [*begreifendes Erkennen*] is the middle term in which universality does not remain on *this* side, in *me*, over against the individuality[5] of the objects: on the contrary, while it stands in a negative relation to things and assimilates them to itself, it equally finds individuality in them and does not encroach upon their independence, or interfere with their free self-determination. The cognition which comprehends is thus the unity of the theoretical and practical approaches: the negation of individuality [*Einzelheit*] is, as negation of the negative, the affirmative universality which gives permanence to its determinations; for the true individuality [*Einzelheit*] is at the same time within itself a universality [*Allgemeinheit*].

* * * This, now, is the specific character and the goal of the Philosophy of Nature, that Spirit [*Geist*] finds in Nature its own essence, i.e. the Notion [*Begriff*], finds its counterpart in her. The study of Nature is thus the liberation of Spirit [*Geist*] in her, for Spirit is present in her in so far as it is in relation, not with an Other, but with itself. This is also the liberation of Nature; implicitly she is Reason, but it is through Spirit that Reason as such first emerges from Nature into existence. Spirit has the certainty which Adam had when he looked on Eve: 'This is flesh of my flesh, and bone of my bone.'[6] Thus Nature is the bride which Spirit [*Geist*] weds. But is this certainty also truth? Since the inner being of Nature is none other than the universal [*Allgemeine*], then in our thoughts of this inner being we are at home with ourselves. Truth in its subjective meaning is the agreement of thought [*Vorstellung*] with the object: in its objective meaning, truth is the agreement of the object with its own self, the correspondence of its reality with its Notion [*Begriff*]. The Ego in its essence is the Notion [*Begriff*], which is equal to itself and pervades all things,

---

4. That is, generality or univerality. (See the Hegel Glossary, p. 144.)

5. That is, particularity (*Einzelheit*).

6. See Genesis 2:23.

and which, because it retains the mastery over the particular differences, is the universal which returns into itself. This Notion [*Begriff*] is directly the true Idea [*Idee*], the divine Idea of the universe which alone is the Actual [*Wirkliche*].

* * *

§ 249.] Nature is to be regarded as a *system of stages* [*Stufen*], one arising necessarily from the other and being the proximate truth of the stage from which it results: but it is not generated *naturally* out of the other but only in the inner Idea [*Idee*] which constitutes the ground of Nature. *Metamorphosis* pertains only to the Notion [*Begriff*] as such, since only *its* alteration is development. But in Nature, the Notion [*Begriff*] is partly only something inward, partly existent only as a living individual: *existent* metamorphosis, therefore, is limited to this individual alone.

REMARK

It has been an inept conception of ancient and also recent Philosophy of Nature to regard the progression and transition of one natural form and sphere into a higher as an outwardly-actual production which, however, to be made *clearer*, is relegated to the *obscurity* of the past. It is precisely externality which is characteristic of Nature, that is, differences are allowed to fall apart and to appear as indifferent to each other: the dialectical Notion [*Begriff*] which leads forward the *stages*, is the inner side of them. A thinking consideration must reject such nebulous, at bottom, sensuous ideas, as in particular the so-called *origination*, for example, of plants and animals from water, and then the *origination* of the more highly developed animal organisms from the lower, and so on.[7]

* * *

§ 251.] Nature is, in itself, a living Whole. The movement through its stages is more precisely this: that the Idea [*Idee*] *posits* itself as that which it is *in itself*; or what is the same thing, that it returns *into itself* out of its immediacy and externality which is *death*, in order to be, first a *living creature*, but further, to sublate [*aufhebe*] this determinateness also in which it is only Life, and to give itself an existence as Spirit [*Geist*], which is the truth and the final goal of Nature and the genuine actuality of the Idea [*Idee*].

* * *

SOURCE: From *Hegel's Philosophy of Nature: Being Part Two of the "Encyclopaedia of the Philosophical Sciences"* (1830), trans. A. V. Miller (Oxford: Clarendon Press, 1970), pp. 1, 3–13, 20, 24. Except where otherwise indicated, German words in brackets are the terminology used in the German original, inserted by the editor in addition to their renderings in the translation. Originally published as *Naturphilosophie*, in *Enzyklopädie der philosophischen Wissenschaften*, this translation of the 1959 edition includes the *Zusätze* or "additions" (marked *Zusatz*) that were incorporated into the work in 1847; they were compiled after Hegel's death from lecture notes (both his students' and his own).

7. That is, Hegel rejects the idea of biological evolution occurring in nature, his emphasis upon "development" notwithstanding.

On the History of Philosophy

From Lectures on the History of Philosophy

From *Introduction*

* * *

What the history of Philosophy shows us is a succession of noble minds, a gallery of heroes of thought, who, by the power of Reason, have penetrated into the being of things, of nature and of *Geist*, into the Being of God, and have won for us by their labours the highest treasure, the treasure of reasoned knowledge.

The events and actions of this history are therefore such that personality and individual character do not enter to any large degree into its content and matter. In this respect the history of Philosophy contrasts with political history, in which the individual, according to the peculiarity of his disposition, talents, affections, the strength or weakness of his character, and in general, according to that through which he is this individual, is the subject of actions and events. In Philosophy, the less deserts and merits are accorded to the particular individual, the better is the history; and the more it deals with thought as free, with the *allgemein* character of man as man, the more this thought, which is devoid of special characteristic, is itself shown to be the producing subject.

The acts of thought appear at first to be a matter of history, and, therefore, things of the past, and outside our real existence. But in reality we are what we are historically [*geschichtlich*]:[1] or, more accurately, as in the history of Thought, what has passed away is only one side, so in the present, what we have as a permanent possession is essentially bound up with our place in history. The possession of self-conscious reason, which belongs to us of the present world, did not arise suddenly, nor did it grow only from the soil of the present. This possession must be regarded as previously present, as an inheritance, and as the result of labour—the labour of all past generations of men. Just as the arts, of outward life, the accumulated skill and invention, the customs and arrangements of social and political life, are the result of the thought, care, and needs, of the want and the misery, of the ingenuity, the plans and achievements of those who preceded us in history, so, likewise, in *Wissenschaft*, and specially in Philosophy, do we owe what we are to the tradition which, as Herder[2] has put it, like a holy chain, runs through all that was transient, and has therefore passed away. Thus has been preserved and transmitted to us what antiquity produced.

But this tradition is not only a housekeeper who simply guards faithfully that which she has received, and thus delivers it unchanged to posterity, just as the course of nature in the infinite change and activity of its forms ever remains constant to its original laws and makes no step in advance. Such tradition is no

---

1. This is one of Hegel's most important principles, which he applies to the understanding of virtually everything human—philosophy included. He uses the term *Geist* for everything to which it applies.
2. Johann Gottfried Herder (1744–1803), a German philosopher and contemporary of KANT, whom Hegel greatly admired for his emphasis on the importance of history, language, and culture for our self-understanding.

motionless statue, but is alive, and swells like a mighty river, which increases in size the further it advances from its source. The content of this tradition is that which the *geistig* world has brought forth, and the *allgemein Geist*[3] does not remain stationary. But it is just the *allgemein Geist* with which we have to do. It may certainly be the case with a single nation that its culture, art, science—its *geistig* activities as a whole—are at a standstill. This appears, perhaps, to be the case with the Chinese, for example, who may have been as far advanced in every respect two thousand years ago as now. But the spirit of the world [*Geist der Welt*] does not sink into this rest of indifference; this follows from its very nature, for its *life* is *activity*. This activity presupposes a material already present, on which it acts, and which it does not merely augment by the addition of new matter, but completely fashions and transforms. Thus that which each generation has produced in *Wissenschaft* and in intellectual activity is an heirloom to which all the past generations have added their savings, a temple in which all races of men thankfully and cheerfully deposit that which rendered aid to them through life, and which they had won from the depths of Nature and of *Geist*. To receive this inheritance is also to enter upon its use. It constitutes the soul of each successive generation, the intellectual substance of the time; its principles, prejudices, and possessions; and this legacy is reduced to material which becomes metamorphosed by *Geist*. In this manner that which is received is changed, and the material worked upon is both enriched and preserved at the same time.

This is the function of our own and of every age: to grasp the knowledge which is already existing, to make it our own, and in so doing to develop it still further and to raise it to a higher level. In thus appropriating it to ourselves we make it into something different from what it was before. We start with an already existing *geistig* world which is transformed in our appropriation of it; and Philosophy can only arise in connection with previous Philosophy, from which of necessity it has arisen. The course of history does not show us the Becoming of things foreign to us, but the Becoming of ourselves and of our own knowledge.

The ideas and questions which may be present to our mind regarding the character and ends of the history of Philosophy depend on the nature of the relationship here given. In this lies the explanation of the fact that the study of the history of Philosophy is an introduction to Philosophy itself. The guiding principles for the formation of this history are given in this fact, the further discussion of which must thus be the main object of this introduction. We must also, however, keep in mind, as being of fundamental importance, the conception of the aim of Philosophy. And since, as already mentioned, the systematic exposition of this conception cannot here find a place, such discussion as we can now undertake can only propose to deal with the subject provisionally and not to give a thorough and conclusive account of the nature of the Becoming of Philosophy.

This Becoming is not merely a passive movement, as we suppose movements such as those of the sun and moon to be. It is no mere movement in the unresisting medium of space and time. What we must represent to ourselves

---

3. On *allgemein* and its variants (often misleadingly translated as "universal") and *Geist* (often misleadingly translated as "mind"), see the Hegel glossary, p. 144.

is the activity of free thought; we have to present the history of the world of thought as it has arisen and produced itself.

There is an old tradition that it is the faculty of thought which separates men from beasts; and to this tradition we shall adhere. In accordance with this, what man has, as being nobler than a beast, he has through thinking. Everything which is human, however it may appear, is so only because the thought contained in it is at work and has been at work in it. But thought, although it is thus the essential, substantial, and effectual, has many other elements. We must, however, consider it best when Thought does not pursue anything else, but is occupied only with itself—with what is noblest—when it has sought and found itself. The history which we have before us is the history of Thought finding itself, and it is the case with Thought that it only finds itself in producing itself; indeed, that it only exists and is actual in finding itself. These productions are the philosophic systems; and the series of discoveries on which Thought sets out in order to discover itself, forms a work which has lasted twenty-five hundred years.

If the Thought which is essentially Thought is in and for itself and eternal, and that which is true is contained in Thought alone, how, then, does this *geistig* world come to have a history? In history what appears is transient, has disappeared in the night of the past and is no more. But true, necessary thought—and it is only with such that we have to do—is capable of no change. The question here raised constitutes one of those matters first to be brought under our consideration.

But in the second place, there are also many most important things outside of Philosophy, which are yet the work of Thought, and which are left unconsidered. Such are Religion, Political History, forms of Government, and the Arts and *Wissenschaften*. The question arises as to how these operations differ from the subject under consideration, and how they are related in history? As regards these two points of view, it is desirable to show in what sense the history of Philosophy is here taken, in order to see clearly what we are about.

Moreover, in the third place, we must first take a general survey before we descend to particulars, else the whole is not seen for the mere details—the wood is not seen for the trees, nor Philosophy for mere philosophies. We require to have a general idea of the nature and aim of the whole in order to know what to look for. Just as we first desire to obtain a general idea of a country, which we should no longer see in going into detail, so we desire to see the relation which single philosophies bear to the whole; for in reality, the high value of the particular parts lies in their relation to the whole. This is nowhere more the case than with Philosophy, and also with its history. In the case of a history, indeed, the establishment of the *Allgemeine* seems to be less needful than in the case of one of the *Wissenschaften* proper. For history seems at first to be a succession of chance events, in which each fact stands isolated by itself, which has Time alone as a connecting-link. But even in political history we are not satisfied with this. We surmise and discern in it that essential connection in which the individual events have their place and relation to an end or aim, and in this way obtain significance. For the significant in history is its relation to and connection with something general [*Allgemeine*]. To discern that *Allgemeine* is thus to apprehend its significance.

* * *

FROM THE CONCEPT OF THE HISTORY OF PHILOSOPHY

* * *

EXPLANATORY REMARKS ON THE DIVERSITY IN PHILOSOPHIES

Certainly the fact is sufficiently well established that there are and have been different philosophies. The Truth, however, is one; and the instinct of reason maintains this irradicable intuition or belief. It is said that only one philosophy can be true, and, because philosophies are different, it is concluded that all others must be erroneous. But, in fact, each one in turn gives every assurance, evidence and proof of being the one and true Philosophy. This is a common mode of reasoning and is what seems in truth to be the view of sober thought. As regards the sober nature of the word at issue—thought—we can tell from everyday experience that if we fast we feel hunger either at once or very soon. But sober thought always has the fortunate power of not resulting in hunger and desire, but of being and remaining as it is, content. Hence the thought expressed in such an utterance reveals the fact that it is dead understanding; for it is only death which fasts and yet rests satisfied. But neither physical nor *geistig* life remains content with mere abstention; as desire it presses on through hunger and through thirst towards Truth, towards knowledge itself. It presses on to satisfy this desire and does not allow itself to feast and find sufficiency in a reflection such as this.

As to this reflection, the next thing to be said of it is that however different the philosophies have been, they had a common bond in that they were Philosophy. Thus whoever may have studied or become acquainted with a philosophy, of whatever kind, provided only that it is such, has thereby become acquainted with Philosophy. That delusive mode of reasoning which takes notice of diversity alone, and from doubt of or aversion to the particular form in which something general finds its expression will not grasp or even acknowledge it, I have elsewhere likened to an invalid advised by the doctor to eat fruit, and who has cherries, plums or grapes, before him, but who pedantically refuses to take anything because no part of what is offered him is *fruit*— some of it being cherries, and the rest plums or grapes.[4]

But it is really important to have a deeper insight into the bearings of this diversity in the systems of Philosophy. Truth and Philosophy, understood philosophically, make such diversity appear in another light from that of abstract opposition between Truth and Error. The explanation of how this comes about will reveal to us the significance of the whole history of Philosophy. We must make it conceivable that the diversity and number of philosophies not only does not prejudice Philosophy itself, that is to say the possibility of a philosophy, but that such diversity is, and has been, absolutely necessary to the existence of a *Wissenschaft* of Philosophy, and that it is essential to it.

This makes it easy to us to comprehend the aim of Philosophy, which is in thought and in conception to grasp the Truth. It is not merely to discover that nothing can be known, or that temporal, finite truth (which also is an untruth) can alone be known, and not the actual Truth. Further, we find that in the

---

4. See the introduction to *The Wissenschaft of Logic*, part 1 of Hegel's *Encyclopedia* (3rd ed., 1830), §13 (the first selection, above).

history of Philosophy we are dealing with Philosophy itself. The occurrences within that history are not mere adventures, and contain no more romance than does the history of the world. They are not a mere collection of chance events, of expeditions of wandering knights, each going about, fighting, struggling purposelessly, leaving no results to show for all his efforts. Nor is it so that one thing has been thought out here, another there, at will; in the activity of thinking *Geist* there is real connection, and what there takes place is rational. It is with this belief in the *Weltgeist* that we must proceed to history, and in particular to the history of Philosophy.

EXPLANATORY REMARKS UPON THE DEFINITION OF THE HISTORY OF PHILOSOPHY

The above statement, that the Truth is only one, is still abstract and formal. In the deeper sense it is our starting point. But the aim of Philosophy is to know this one Truth as the immediate source from which all else proceeds—both all the laws of nature and all the manifestations of life and consciousness of which they are mere reflections—and to trace these laws and manifestations (in ways apparently contrary) back to that single source, and from that source to comprehend them, which is to understand their derivation. Thus what is most essential is to know that the single truth is not merely a solitary, empty thought, but one determined within itself. To obtain this knowledge we must enter into some abstract *Begriffe* which, as such, are quite general and dry, and which are the two principles of *Development* and of the *Concrete*. We could, indeed, embrace the whole in the single principle of development; if this were clear, all else would result and follow of its own accord. The product of thinking [*Denken*] is thought [*Gedachtes*]. Thought [*Gedanke*] is, however, still formal. Somewhat more defined it becomes *Begriff*; and finally, *Idee* is Thought in its totality, implicitly and explicitly determined. Thus the *Idee*, and it alone, is the True [*das Wahre*].[5] Now it is essentially in the nature of the *Idee* to develop, and only through development to arrive at comprehension of itself, or to become what it is. That the *Idee* should have to make itself what it is may seem like a contradiction; for it may be supposed that it simply is what it is.

THE CONCEPT OF DEVELOPMENT

The idea of development is well known, but it is the special task of Philosophy to investigate such matters as were formerly taken to be known. What is dealt with or made use of without consideration, as an aid to daily life, is certainly uncomprehended to man unless he be informed in Philosophy. The further discussion of this idea belongs to the *Wissenschaft* of Logic.[6]

In order to comprehend what development is, two different states (so to speak) must be distinguished. The first is what is known as capacity, power,

---

5. "Spirit" (*Geist*), "Concept" (*Begriff*), "Idea" (*Idee*), and even "Truth" (*Wahrheit*) are all terms to which Hegel gives special meanings, related to but also differing from their ordinary and usual philosophical meanings (both in German and in English). See the Hegel glossary, p. 144.

6. In Hegel's sense of the term "logic," as set forth in the first part of his *Encyclopedia* (see selections above).

or what I call being-in-itself (*potentia*, δύναμις[7]); the second principle is that of being-for-itself, actuality (*actus*, ἐνέργεια[8]). If we say, for example, that man is by nature rational, we would mean that he has reason only inherently or in germ. In this sense, reason, understanding, imagination, will, are possessed from birth or even from the mother's womb. But while the child only has capacities or the real possibility of reason, it is just the same as if he had no reason; reason does not yet exist in him since he cannot yet do anything rational, and has no rational consciousness. Thus what man is at first implicitly, becomes explicit, and it is the same with reason. If, then, man has actuality in that respect, he is actually rational.—And now we come to reason [*Vernunft*].

What is the real meaning of this word? That which is *in itself*[9] must become an object to mankind, must arrive at consciousness, thus becoming *for* man.[1] What has become an object to him is the same as what he is "in himself"; through the "becoming objective" of this implicit being, man first becomes "for himself"; he is made double, and yet persists and is not changed into another. For example, man is thinking, and thus he thinks out thoughts. In this way it is in thought alone that thought is object; reason produces what is rational: reason is its own object. The fact that thought may also descend to what is devoid of reason is a consideration involving wider issues, which do not concern us here. But even though man, who "in himself" is rational, does not at first seem to have got further on since he became rational "for himself"— what is implicit having merely persisted—the difference is quite enormous: no new content has been produced, and yet this form of "being *for* self" makes all the difference.

The whole variation in world history is founded on this difference. This alone explains how, since all mankind is naturally rational, and freedom is the hypothesis on which this reason rests, slavery yet has been, and in part still is, maintained by many peoples, and men have remained contented under it. The only distinction between the Africans and the Asiatics on the one hand, and the Greeks, Romans, and moderns on the other,[2] is that the latter know (and it is explicit for them) that they are free, but the others are so without knowing that they are, and thus without existing as being free. This constitutes the enormous difference in their condition. All knowledge, and learning, *Wissenschaft*, and even commerce have no other object than to draw out what is inward or implicit and thus to become objective.

Because that which is implicit comes into existence, it certainly passes into change, yet it remains one and the same, for the whole process is dominated by it. The plant, for example, does not lose itself in mere indefinite change. From the germ much is produced when at first nothing was to be seen; but the whole of what is brought forth, if not developed, is yet hidden and ideally contained within itself. The principle of this projection into existence is that the germ cannot remain merely implicit, but is impelled towards development,

---

7. "Power" or "potentiality" in Latin and Greek (*dynamis*).
8. "Actuality" in Latin and Greek (*energeia*).
9. In Hegel, "in itself" (*an sich*) means "implicitly," "essentially," or sometimes "potentially."
1. In Hegel, "for itself" (*für sich*)—here, "for man"—indicates that something that was formerly

merely implicit has become explicit, or an object of awareness (though not necessarily fully and adequately realized, in both senses of that term).
2. That is, as Hegel supposed that the former continue to be, and the latter to have been or to have come to be.

since it presents the contradiction of being only implicit and yet not desiring so to be. But this coming without itself has an end in view; its completion fully reached, and its previously determined end is the fruit or produce of the germ, which causes a return to the first condition. The germ will produce itself alone and manifest what is contained in it, so that it then may return to itself once more thus to renew the unity from which it started. With nature it certainly is true that the subject which commenced and the matter which forms the end are two separate units, as in the case of seed and fruit. The doubling process has apparently the effect of separating into two things that which in content is the same. Thus in animal life the parent and the young are different individuals although their nature is the same.

In the case of *Geist* it is otherwise: it is consciousness and therefore it is free,[3] uniting in itself the beginning and the end. As with the germ in nature, *Geist* indeed resolves itself back into unity after constituting itself another. But what is "in itself" becomes "for *Geist*" and thus arrives at being "for itself."[4] The fruit and seed latently contained within the original germ on the other hand, do not become "for it" but "for us" alone, while in the case of *Geist* both factors not only are implicitly the same in character, but there is a being "for the other" and at the same time a being "for self." That for which the "other" is, is the same as that "other"; and thus only *Geist* is at home with itself in its "other." The development of *Geist* lies in the fact that its going forth and separation constitutes its coming to itself.[5]

This being-at-home-with-self, or coming-to-self of *Geist* may be described as its complete and highest end: it is this alone that it desires and nothing else. Everything that from eternity has happened in heaven and earth, the life of God and all the deeds of time simply are the struggles for *Geist* to know itself, to make itself objective to itself, to find itself, be for itself, and finally unite itself to itself; it is alienated and divided, but only so as to be able thus to find itself and return to itself. Only in this manner does *Geist* attain its freedom,[6] for that is free which is not bound to or dependent on another. True self-possession and satisfaction are only to be found in this, and in nothing else but Thought[7] does *Geist* attain this freedom. In sense-perception, for instance, and in feeling, I find myself confined and am not free; but I am free when I have a consciousness of this my feeling. Man has particular ends and interests even in will; I am free indeed when this is mine. Such ends, however, always contain "another," or something which constitutes for me "another," such as desire and impulse. It is in Thought alone that all foreign matter disappears from view, and that *Geist* is absolutely free. All interest which is contained in the *Idee* and in Philosophy is expressed in it.

---

3. That is, self-determining.
4. That is, in the case of things of the human spirit (such as social, cultural, artistic, and intellectual phenomena), what is "in itself" (i.e., merely potential) becomes "for *Geist*" (i.e., an object of awareness) as the human spirit engages in such experience and activity, and so arrives at "being for itself" (i.e., an actual and recognized realization of that potential).
5. That is, *Geist* develops by expressing its potentialities and thereby realizing them—a process that involves producing things other than itself, which it may experience as "other" and alien before it learns to identify with them and find its self-realization in and through them.
6. That is, its true self-determination.
7. That is, in nothing else but the kinds of meaning and significance that *Geist* engenders and with which it imbues the contents of its experience and activity.

THE CONCEPT OF THE CONCRETE

As to development, it may be asked, what does develop and what forms the absolute content? Development is considered in the light of a formal process in action and as destitute of content. But the act has no other end but activity, and through this activity the general character of the content is already fixed. For being-in-self and being-for-self are the moments present in action; but the act is the retention of these diverse elements within itself. The act thus is really one, and it is just this unity of differences which is the concrete. Not only is the act concrete, but also the implicit, which stands to action in the relation of initiating subject; and, finally, the product is just as concrete as the action or as the initiating subject. Development in process likewise forms the content, the *Idee* itself; for this we must have the one element and then the other: both combined will form a unity as third, because the one in the other is at home with—and not without—itself. Thus the *Idee* is in its content concrete within itself, and this in two ways: first it is concrete potentially, and then it is its interest that what is "in itself" should be there "for it."

It is a common prejudice that the *Wissenschaft* of Philosophy deals only with abstractions and empty generalities, and that on the other hand it is sense-perception, our empirical self-consciousness, natural instinct, and the feelings of every-day life that lie in the region of the concrete and the determinate. As a matter of fact, Philosophy is in the region of thought, and has therefore to deal with the general [*Allgemeinheiten*]; its content is abstract, but only with respect to form and element. In itself the *Idee* is really concrete, for it is the union of the different determinations. It is here that knowledge by way of reason [*Vernunft*] differs from mere knowledge by way of the understanding [*Verstand*], and it is the business of Philosophy, as opposed to understanding, to show that the True, the *Idee*, does not consist in empty generalities [*Allgemeinheiten*] but in something general [*Allgemeinen*] that is within itself the particular and the determinate. If the True were abstract, it would be untrue. Healthy human reason goes out towards what is concrete; the reflection of the understanding comes first as abstract and untrue, correct in theory only, and amongst other things unpractical. Philosophy is what is most antagonistic to abstraction, and it leads back to the concrete.

If we unite the concept of the concrete with that of development we have the movement of the concrete. Since the implicit is already concrete within itself, and we only set forth what is implicitly there, the new form which now looks different and which was formerly shut up in the original unity, is merely distinguished. The concrete must become for itself or explicit; as implicit or potential it is only differentiated within itself, not as yet explicitly set forth, but still in a state of unity. The concrete is thus simple, and yet at the same time differentiated. This, its inward contradiction, which is indeed the impelling force in development, brings distinction into being. But thus, too, its right to be taken back and reinstated extends beyond the difference; for its truth is only to be found in unity. Life—both that which is in Nature and that which is of the *Idee*, of *Geist* within itself—is thus manifested. Were the *Idee* abstract, it would simply be the highest conceivable existence, and that would be all that could be said of it; but such a God is the product of the understanding of modern times. What is true is rather found in movement—in a process, however, in which there is rest. Difference, while it lasts, is but a temporary condition, preparing the way for unity, full and concrete.

We may now proceed to give examples of sensuous things, which will help us further to explain this concept of the concrete. Although the flower has many qualities, such as smell, taste, form, colour, &c., yet it is one. None of these qualities could be absent in the particular leaf or flower: each particular part of the leaf shares alike all the qualities of the leaf entire. Gold similarly contains in every particle all its qualities unseparated and entire. It is frequently allowed with sensuous things that such varied elements may be joined together, but in the conceptual, differentiation supposedly involves opposition. We do not dispute the fact, or think it contradictory, that the smell and taste of the flower, although otherwise opposed, are yet clearly in one subject; nor do we place the one against the other. But the [abstract] understanding and its mode of thought find everything of a different kind, placed in conjunction, to be incompatible. Matter, for example, is complex and coherent, or space is continuous and uninterrupted. Likewise we may take separate points in space and break up matter, dividing it ever further into infinity. It then is said that matter consists of atoms and points, and hence is not continuous. Therefore we have here the two determinations of continuity and of definite points, which understanding regards as mutually exclusive, combined in one. It is said that matter must be clearly either continuous or divisible into points, but in reality it has both these qualities.

Or when we say of man that he has freedom, [abstract] understanding at once brings up the other quality, which in this case is necessity, saying, that if *Geist* is free it is not in subjection to necessity, and, inversely, if its will and thought are determined through necessity, it is not free—the one, they say, excludes the other. The distinctions here are regarded as exclusive, and not as forming something concrete. But that which is true, *Geist*, is concrete, and its attributes are freedom and necessity. Similarly the higher point of view is that *Geist* is free in its necessity, and finds its freedom in it alone, since its necessity rests on its freedom. But it is more difficult for us to show the unity here than in the case of natural objects. Freedom can, however, be also abstract freedom without necessity—but such false freedom is self-will, and for that reason it is self-opposed, unconsciously limited, and an imaginary freedom which is free in form alone.

The fruit of development, which comes third, is a result of movement; but while in this respect it is merely the result of one stage in development, and is last in this stage, it is both the starting point and the first in order in another such stage. Goethe[8] somewhere truly says, "That which is formed ever resolves itself back into its elements." Matter—which as developed has form—constitutes once more the material for a new form. *Geist* again takes as its object and applies its activity to the *Begriff* in which in going within itself, it has comprehended itself, which it is in form and being, and which has just been separated from it anew. The application of thought to this supplies it with the form and determination of thought. This action thus further forms the previously formed, gives it additional determinations, makes it more deter-

---

8. Johann Wolfgang von Goethe (1749–1832), a scientist as well as the preeminent German literary figure of the time.

minate in itself, further developed and more profound. As concrete, this activity is a succession of processes in development which must be represented not as a straight line drawn out into vague infinity, but as a circle returning within itself, which, as periphery, has very many circles, and whose whole is a large number of processes in development turning back within themselves.

PHILOSOPHY AS THE APPREHENSION OF THE DEVELOPMENT OF THE CONCRETE

Having thus generally explained the nature of the Concrete, I now add as regards its import, that the True thus determined within itself is impelled towards development. It is only the living and *Geistige* which internally bestirs and develops itself. Thus the *Idee* as concrete in itself, and self-developing, is an organic system and a totality which contains a multitude of stages and of moments in development. Philosophy has now become for itself the apprehension of this development, and as comprehending Thought, is itself this development in Thought. The more progress made in this development, the more perfect is the Philosophy.

This development goes no further out than into externality, but the "going out of itself" of development also is a going inwards. That is to say, the *allgemeine Idee* continues to remain at the foundation and still is the all-embracing and unchangeable. While in Philosophy the going out of the *Idee* in the course of its development is not a change, a becoming "another," but really is a "going within itself," a self-immersion, the progress forward makes the *Idee* which was previously general and undetermined, determined within itself. Further development of the *Idee* or its further determination is the same thing exactly. Depth seems to signify intensiveness, but in this case the most extensive is also the most intensive. The more intensive *Geist* is, the more extensive it is, and hence the larger is its embrace. Extension as development is not dispersion or falling asunder, but a uniting bond which is the more powerful and intense as the expanse of that embraced is greater in extent and richer. In such a case what is greater is the strength of opposition and of separation; and the greater power overcomes the greater separation.

These are the abstract propositions regarding the nature of the *Idee* and of its development, and thus within it Philosophy in its developed state is constituted: it is one *Idee* in its totality and in all its individual parts, like one life in a living being, one pulse throbs throughout all its members. All the parts represented in it, and their systematization, emanate from the one *Idee*; all these particulars are but the mirrors and copies of this one life, and have their actuality only in this unity. Their differences and their various qualities are only the expression of the *Idee* and the form contained within it. Thus the *Idee* is the central point, which is also the periphery, the source of light, which in all its expansion does not come without itself, but remains present and immanent within itself. Thus it is both the system of necessity and its own necessity, which also constitutes its freedom.

* * *

FROM THE RELATION OF PHILOSOPHY TO OTHER DEPARTMENTS OF KNOWLEDGE

* * *

PHILOSOPHY AS THE THOUGHT OF ITS TIME

It is not the case that, in various epochs, philosophizing in general simply goes on. Rather, there is a definite Philosophy which arises among a people [*Volk*], and the definite character of the standpoint of thought is the same character which permeates all the other historical aspects of the spirit of the people [*Volksgeist*], which is most intimately related to them, and which constitutes their foundation. The particular form of a Philosophy is thus contemporaneous with a particular constitution of the *Volk* amongst whom it makes its appearance, with their institutions and forms of government, their morality, their social life and the capabilities, customs and enjoyments of the same; also with their attempts and achievements in art and science, with their religions, warfares and external relationships; likewise with the decadence of the States in which this particular principle and form had maintained its supremacy, and with the origination and progress of new States in which a higher principle finds its manifestation and development. *Geist* in each case has elaborated and expanded in the whole domain of its manifold nature the principle of the particular stage of self-consciousness to which it has attained. Thus the *Geist* of a *Volk* in its richness is an organization, and, like a Cathedral, is divided into numerous vaults, passages, pillars and vestibules, all of which have proceeded out of one whole and are directed to one end. Philosophy is one form of these many aspects. And which is it? It is the fullest blossom, the *Begriff* of *Geist* in its entire form, the consciousness and spiritual essence of the whole situation, the spirit of the time [*Zeitgeist*] as thinking *Geist* present to itself. The multifarious whole is reflected in it as in the single focus, in the *Begriff* which knows itself.

The Philosophy which is essential within Christianity could not be found in Rome, for all the various forms of the whole are only the expression of one and the same determinate character. Hence political history, forms of government, art and religion are not related to Philosophy as its causes, nor, on the other hand, is Philosophy the ground of their existence—one and all have the same common root, the spirit of the time [*Geist der Zeit*]. It is one determinate existence, one determinate character which permeates all sides and manifests itself in politics and in all else as in different elements; it is a condition which hangs together in all its parts, and the various parts of which contain nothing which is really inconsistent, however diverse and accidental they may appear to be, and however much they may seem to contradict one another. This particular stage is the product of the one preceding. But to show how the *Geist* of a particular time moulds its whole actuality and destiny in accordance with its principle, to show this whole edifice in its conception, is far from us—for that would be the object of the whole philosophic world-history. Those forms alone concern us which express the principle of *Geist* in a spiritual element related to Philosophy.

This is the position of Philosophy amongst its varying forms, from which it follows that it is entirely identical with its time. But if Philosophy does not stand above its time in content, it does so in form, because, as the thought and knowledge of that which is the substantial spirit of its time, it makes that spirit its object. In as far as Philosophy is in the spirit of its time, philosophy is its determinate worldly content—although as knowledge, Philosophy is above it, since it deals with it in the relation of object. But this is in form alone, for Philosophy really has no other content. This knowledge itself undoubtedly is the actuality of *Geist*, the self-knowledge of *Geist* which previously was not present: thus the formal difference is also a real and actual difference. Through knowledge, *Geist* makes manifest a distinction between knowledge and that which is; this knowledge is thus what produces a new form of development. The new forms at first are only special modes of knowledge, and it is thus that a new Philosophy is produced: yet since it already is a wider kind of *Geist*, it is the inward birth-place of the *Geist* which will later attain actual form.

* * *

SOURCE: Georg Wilhelm Friedrich Hegel, *Lectures on the History of Philosophy*, trans. E. S. Haldane, vol. 1 (London: Kegan Paul, Trench, Trübner, 1892), pp. 1–6, 17–28, 53–55 (translation modified by the editor). Except where otherwise indicated, German words in brackets are the terminology used in the German original, inserted by the editor in addition to their renderings in the translation; and unbracketed German words are the original terminology, substituted in place of their renderings in the translation by the editor for reasons given in notes and in the Hegel glossary (p. 144). Originally edited and published after Hegel's death as *Vorlesungen über die Geschichte der Philosophie* (1833–36), drawn from the lecture notes of his Berlin students and supplemented by his own lecture notes.

On History and *Geist*

From Lectures on the Philosophy of History

From *Introduction*

* * *

The only thought [*Gedanke*] which philosophy brings with it to the contemplation of history is the simple conception of *reason* [*Vernunft*]—that reason rules the world; that the history of the world, therefore, proceeds in a rational manner.[1] This conviction and intuition is a hypothesis in the domain of history as such. In that of philosophy it is no hypothesis. It is there proved by speculative cognition, that reason—and this term may here suffice us, without going into the relation and connection to God—is *substance*, as well as *infinite power*; its own *infinite material* underlying all the natural and spiritual life which it originates, as also the *infinite form*—that which sets this material in motion. On the one hand, reason is the ultimate *substance* by which and in which all reality has its being and subsistence. On the other hand, it is the *infinite power* [*Macht*] of the universe; since reason is not so powerless as to be incapable of producing anything but a mere ideal, a mere intention—having its place outside reality, nobody knows where; something separate and abstract, in the heads of certain human beings. It is *the infinite content*, all essentiality [*Wesenheit*] and truth. It is its own material which it commits to its own active energy to work up; not needing, as finite action

---

1. That is, in a manner that turns out to have a fundamentally rational (*vernünftig*) character.

does, the conditions of an external material of given means from which it may obtain its support, and the objects of its activity. It supplies its own nourishment, and is the object of its own operations. While it is exclusively its own basis of existence, and absolute final aim, it is also the energizing power realizing this aim; developing it not only in the phenomena of the natural, but also of the *geistig* universe. That this *"Idee"*[2] or "reason" is the *true*, the *eternal*, the simply *powerful*; that it reveals itself in the world, and that in that world nothing else is revealed but this and its honor and glory—is the thesis which, as we have said, has been proved in philosophy,[3] and is here regarded as presupposed.

In those of my hearers who are not acquainted with philosophy, I may fairly presume, at least, the existence of a *belief* in reason, a desire, a thirst for acquaintance with it, in entering upon this course of lectures. It is, in fact, the wish for rational insight, for *knowledge*, not the ambition to amass a mere collection of information, that should be presupposed in every case as possessing the mind of the learner in the study of *Wissenschaft*.[4] If the *Idee* of reason and comprehension are not brought to the study of world history, one should at least have the firm, unconquerable faith that reason *does* exist there; and that the world of intelligence and conscious volition is not abandoned to chance, but must show itself in the light of the self-comprehending *Idee*.

Yet I am not obliged to make any such preliminary demand upon your faith. What I have said thus provisionally, and what I shall have further to say, is, even in reference to *our Wissenschaft*, not to be regarded as hypothetical, but as a summary view of the whole, the *result of the investigation* we are about to pursue—a result which happens to be known to *me*, because I already am acquainted with the whole of it.[5] It is only an inference from world history that its development has been a rational process; that the history in question has constituted the rational necessary course of the *Weltgeist*[6]—that *Geist* whose nature is always one and the same, but which unfolds this its one nature in the phenomena of the world's existence. This must, as before stated, present itself as the ultimate *result* of history.

* * *

The inquiry into the *vocation* [*Bestimmung*][7] of reason—as far as it is considered in reference to the world—is identical with the question, *what is the ultimate aim* [*Endzweck*] *of the world?* And the expression implies that that *aim* is destined to be realized. Two points of consideration suggest themselves: first, the *import* of this aim—its abstract definition; and secondly, its *realization*.[8]

2. A technical term for Hegel, which does not carry the usual meaning of "idea" in English: it is not simply the *Begriff* ("concept" or essential character) of something, but that *Begriff* considered as objectified or realized. It thus is used by Hegel to refer to what might be called "the principle of the objectification of the essential." See the Hegel glossary, p. 144.
3. That is, it has been argued by Hegel in his "Logic."
4. That is, cognitive inquiry, whether natural-scientific, social and historical, or philosophical. See the Hegel glossary, p. 144.
5. More literally, "because I already know it all" (*weil ich bereits das Ganze kenne*).
6. Literally, "world spirit": the impetus that Hegel believes to be at work in the world that brings its essential nature to full expression and realization. It is not something apart from the world that creates

or controls it, but rather is something about it that animates all that transpires within it (at least at a general level), both in nature and in history, as it becomes in reality what it is intrinsically.
7. Here translated "vocation" (as in the title of FICHTE's book *The Vocation of Man* [1800]; see source note to that work, above), the same term (in the plural) is used by Hegel for differently articulated "determinations" of the *Idee*, associated with different specific *Begriffe* (logical "concepts" or structures); it can also mean "purpose," "calling," "task," or even "destiny." For Hegel here (as for Fichte), it is meant to convey something like all of these things at once.
8. Its *Verwirklichung*—that is, what its actualization would or must involve, and the form its actualization would need to take.

It must be observed at the outset that the phenomenon we investigate— world history—takes place on *geistig* terrain. The term *"world"* includes both physical and psychical [*psychische*] nature. Physical nature also plays its part in the world's history, and attention will have to be paid to the fundamental natural relations thus involved. But *Geist*,[9] and the course of its development, is our substantial object. Our task does not require us to contemplate nature as a rational system in itself—though in its own proper domain it proves itself such—but simply in its relation to *Geist*. On the stage on which we are observing it—world history—*Geist* displays itself in its most concrete reality. Notwithstanding this (or rather for the very purpose of comprehending the <u>allgemein</u> principles which this, its form of *concrete reality*, embodies) we must premise some abstract characteristics of the *nature of Geist*. Such an explanation, however, cannot be given here under any other form than that of bare assertion. The present is not the occasion for unfolding the *Idee* of *Geist* speculatively; for whatever has a place in an Introduction, must, as already observed, be taken as simply historical; something assumed as having been explained and proved elsewhere; or whose demonstration awaits the sequel of the *Wissenschaft* of history itself.

We have therefore to mention here:

(1.) The abstract characteristics of the nature of *Geist*.
(2.) What means *Geist* uses in order to realize its *Idee*.
(3.) Lastly, we must consider the shape which the complete realization of *Geist* assumes—the state.[1]

(1.) The nature of *Geist* may be understood by a glance at its direct opposite—*matter*. As the essence of matter is gravity, so, on the other hand, we may affirm that the substance, the essence of *Geist* is freedom. All will readily assent to the doctrine that *Geist*, among other properties, is also endowed with freedom; but philosophy teaches that all the qualities of *Geist* exist only through freedom; that all are but means for attaining freedom; that all seek and produce this and this alone.

It is a result of speculative philosophy that freedom is the sole truth of *Geist*. Matter possesses gravity in virtue of its tendency toward a central point. It is essentially composite; consisting of parts that *exclude* each other. It seeks its unity; and therefore exhibits itself as self-destructive, as verging toward its opposite [an indivisible point]. If it could attain this, it would be matter no longer, it would have perished. It strives after the realization of its *Idee*; for in unity it exists *ideally*. *Geist*, on the contrary, may be defined as that which has its centre in itself. It has not a unity outside itself, but has already found it; it exists *in* and *with itself*. Matter has its essence out of itself; *Geist* is *self-contained existence* [*Bei-sich-selbst-sein*]. Now this is freedom, exactly.[2] For if I am dependent, my being is referred to something else which I am not; I cannot

---

9. On this crucial term, see the Hegel glossary, p. 144.
1. That is, the type of socially, politically, and culturally institutionalized, integrated, and individuated phenomenon that is exemplified by modern Germany, France, and many other such "states"

that are more than just political entities.
2. That is, *Bei-sich-selbst-sein* (literally, "being-by-itself") entails "being determined by nothing other than itself," which means "being self-determined" (for Hegel, the essence of freedom).

exist independently of something external. I am free, on the contrary, when my existence depends upon myself. This self-contained existence of Geist is none other than self-consciousness—consciousness of one's own being.

Two things must be distinguished in consciousness; first, the fact that I know; secondly, what I know. In self-consciousness these are merged in one; for Geist knows itself. It involves an appreciation of its own nature, as also an energy enabling it to realize itself; to make itself actually that which it is potentially. According to this abstract definition it may be said of world history that it is the exhibition of Geist in the process of working out the knowledge of that which it is potentially.[3] And as the germ bears in itself the whole nature of the tree, and the taste and form of its fruits, so do the first traces of Geist virtually contain the whole of that History.

The Orientals have not attained the knowledge that Geist—or man as such—is free; and because they do not know this, they are not free. They only know that one is free. But on this very account, the freedom of that one is only caprice; ferocity—brutal recklessness of passion, or a mildness and tameness of the desires, which is itself only an accident of nature—mere caprice like the former. That one is therefore only a despot; not a free man. The consciousness of freedom first arose among the Greeks, and therefore they were free; but they, and the Romans likewise, knew only that some are free—not man as such. Even Plato and Aristotle[4] did not know this. The Greeks, therefore, had slaves; and their whole life and the maintenance of their splendid freedom was implicated with the institution of slavery: a fact, moreover, which made that freedom on the one hand only an accidental, transient and limited growth; on the other hand, constituted it a rigorous thraldom of the human.[5] The Germanic nations,[6] under the influence of Christianity, were the first to attain the consciousness, that man as man [der Mensch als Mensch] is free: that it is the freedom of Geist which constitutes its true nature [eigenste Natur].

This consciousness arose first in religion, the inmost region of Geist; but introducing the principle into the various relations of the actual world involved a more extensive problem than its simple implantation—a problem whose solution and application require a severe and lengthened process of cultural development [Bildung]. In proof of this, we may note that slavery did not cease immediately on the reception of Christianity. Still less did freedom predominate in states; or did governments and constitutions adopt a rational organization, or recognize freedom as their basis. That application of the principle to political relations—the thorough molding and interpenetration of the constitution of society by it—is a process identical with history itself. I have already directed attention to the distinction here involved, between a principle as such, and its application; i.e. its introduction and carrying out in the actual phenomena of Geist and life. This is a point of fundamental impor-

---

3. That is, world history may be conceived as the "self-realization" of Geist, in the twofold sense of coming to be in reality what it essentially is and coming to comprehend itself accordingly.
4. The two Greek philosophers with the greatest influence on Western thought; Aristotle (384–322 B.C.E.) was a student of Plato (ca. 427–ca. 347 B.C.E.).

5. For emphasis, Hegel here uses both Germanic and Latinate terms for "the human" (des Menschlichen, des Humanen).
6. The nations and peoples of northwestern Europe, whom Hegel wishes to distinguish not only from the Greeks, Romans, and latter-day southern European Latin peoples but also from the Slavic peoples to the east and the Celtic peoples to the west.

tance in our *Wissenschaft*, and one which must be constantly respected as essential. And in the same way as this distinction has attracted attention in view of the *Christian* principle of the self-consciousness of freedom, it also shows itself as an essential one, in view of the principle of freedom *generally*. World history is the progress of the consciousness of freedom[7]—a progress whose development according to the necessity of its nature it is our business to investigate.

The general statement given above, of the various grades in the consciousness of freedom—and which we applied in the first instance to the fact that the Eastern nations knew only that *one* is free, the Greek and Roman world only that *some* are free, while *we* know that all men absolutely (man *as man*) are free—supplies us with the natural division of world history, and suggests the mode of its discussion. This is remarked, however, only incidentally and anticipatively; some other ideas must be first explained.

The nature and task [*Bestimmung*] of the *geistig* world, and—since this is the *substantial world*,[8] while the physical remains subordinate to it, or, in the language of speculation, has no "truth" *as against* the *geistig*—the *ultimate aim* [*Endzweck*] *of the world at large*, we allege to be the *consciousness* of its own freedom on the part of *Geist*, and *ipso facto*, the *actuality* of that freedom. But it has never been more clearly known and felt than in modern times that this term "freedom," without further qualification, is an indefinite and incalculable ambiguous term; and that while that which it represents is the highest attainment, it is liable to an infinity of misunderstandings, confusions and errors, and to become the occasion for all imaginable excesses. Yet, for the present, we must content ourselves with the term itself without further definition. Attention was also directed to the importance of the infinite difference between a principle in the abstract, and its realization in the concrete. In the process before us, the essential nature of freedom—which involves in it absolute necessity—is to be displayed as coming to a consciousness of itself (for it is in its very nature self-consciousness) and thereby realizing its existence. Itself is its own object of attainment, and the sole aim of *Geist*. This result it is, at which the process of world history has been continually aiming; and to which the sacrifices that have ever and anon been laid on the vast altar of the earth, through the long lapse of ages, have been offered. This is the only aim that sees itself realized and fulfilled; the only pole of repose amid the ceaseless change of events and conditions, and the sole efficient principle that pervades them. This final aim is God's purpose with the world; but God is the most perfect [*Vollkommenste*], and can, therefore, will nothing other than himself—his own will. The nature of his will—that is, his nature itself— is what we here call the *Idee* of freedom, translating the language of religion into that of thought. The question, then, which we may next put, is: What means does this principle of freedom use for its realization? This is the second point we have to consider.

(2.) The question of the *means* by which freedom develops itself to a world leads us to the spectacle [*Erscheinung*] of history itself. Although freedom is initially an undeveloped concept, the means it uses are external and apparent

---

7. That is, the progression of both the development of freedom and its comprehension.

8. That is, the world *that matters*, to which significance attaches.

[*Erscheinende*], presenting themselves in history to our eyes. A first glance at history convinces us that the actions of men proceed from their needs, their passions, their characters and talents, and impresses us with the belief that such needs, passions and interests are the sole springs of action—the efficient agents in this scene of activity. Among these may, perhaps, be discerned general aims such as benevolence or noble patriotism; but such virtues and general views are insignificant compared with the real world and its doings. We may perhaps see the determinations of reason actualized in those who adopt such aims, and within the sphere of their influence; but they bear only a trifling proportion to the mass of the human race, and the extent of that influence is limited accordingly.

Passions, private aims, and the satisfaction of selfish desires are, on the other hand, most effective springs of action. Their power lies in the fact that they respect none of the limitations which justice and morality would impose on them; and that these natural impulses have a more direct influence over man than the artificial and tedious discipline that tends to order and self-restraint, law and morality. When we look at this display of passions, and the consequences of their violence; the unreason which is associated not only with them, but even (rather we might say *especially*) with *good* designs and righteous aims; when we see the evil, the vice, the ruin that has befallen the most flourishing kingdoms which the mind of man ever created; we can scarce avoid being filled with sorrow at this universal taint of corruption. And since this decay is not the work of mere nature, but of the human will, a moral imbitterment, a revolt of the good spirit (if it have a place within us) may well be the result of our reflections. Without rhetorical exaggeration, a simply truthful combination of the miseries that have overwhelmed the noblest of nations and polities, and the finest exemplars of private virtue, forms a picture of most fearful aspect, and excites emotions of the profoundest and most hopeless sadness, counterbalanced by no consolatory result. We endure in beholding it a *geistig* torment, allowing no defence or escape but the consideration that what has happened could not be otherwise, and that it is a fatality which no intervention could alter. And at last we draw back from the intolerable disgust with which these sorrowful reflections threaten us into the more agreeable environment of our individual life—the present formed by our private aims and interests. In short we retreat into the selfishness that stands on the quiet shore, and from it enjoys in safety the distant spectacle of chaotic destruction.

But even regarding history as the slaughter-bench upon which the happiness of peoples, the wisdom of states, and the virtue of individuals have been victimized, the question involuntarily arises of the purpose or ultimate end to which these enormous sacrifices have been offered. From this point the investigation usually proceeds to that which we have made the general commencement of our inquiry. Starting from this we pointed out those phenomena which made up a picture so suggestive of gloomy emotions and thoughtful reflections—as *the very field* which we, for our part, regard as exhibiting only the means for realizing what we assert to be the essential destiny—the absolute aim, or—which comes to the same thing—the true *result* of world history. We have all along purposely eschewed "moral reflections" as a method of rising from the scene of historical specialities to the general principles which they embody. Besides, it is not the interest of such sentimentalities really to rise above those depressing emotions, and to solve the enigmas of providence which the considerations that occasioned them present. It is essential to their character to find a gloomy satisfaction in the empty and fruitless sublimities of that negative result. We return then to the point of view which we have adopted, observing that the successive steps [*Momente*] of the analysis to which it will lead us, will also yield the conditions requisite for answering the inquiries suggested by the spectacle that history unfolds.

The *first* remark we have to make, and which—though already presented more than once, cannot be too often repeated when the occasion seems to call for it—is that what we call *principle, aim, determination* [*Bestimmung*], or the nature and concept of *Geist*, is something merely *allgemein* and abstract. Principle (and so also basic tenet, law) is something inner, which *as such*—however true in itself—is not completely real. Aims, principles, etc., as we tend to think of them, have a place in our thoughts, but not yet in the sphere of reality. That which exists in itself only is a possibility, a potentiality, but has not yet emerged into actuality. A *second* element must be introduced in order to produce actuality—viz. actuation, realization; and whose motive power is the will—the activity of man in the widest sense. It is only by this activity that any *Begriff* as well as any intrinsic determination [*Bestimmung*] is realized, actualized; for of themselves they are powerless. The motive power that puts them in effect and existence is the need, instinct, inclination, and passion of man. That some intention of mine should be developed into act and existence, may be my earnest desire: I wish to assert my personality in connection with it; I wish to be satisfied by its execution. If I am to exert myself for any object, it must in some way or other be *my* object.[9] In the accomplishment of such or such designs I must at the same time find *my* satisfaction; although the purpose for which I exert myself includes a complication of results, many of which have no interest for me. This is the absolute right of the agent subject—to find *itself* satisfied in its activity and labor. If men[1] are to interest themselves in anything, they must (so to speak) have part of their existence involved in it; and find their self-feeling [*Selbstgefühl*] gratified by its attainment.

Here a mistake must be avoided. We intend blame, and justly impute it as a fault, when we say of an individual that he is "interested" (in taking part in such or such transactions), that is, seeks only his private advantage. In reprehending this we find fault with him for furthering his personal aims without any regard to a more comprehensive end, of which he takes advantage to promote his own interest, or which he even sacrifices with this view. But he who is actively engaged in some matter is not simply "interested," but interested *in that object itself.* Language faithfully expresses this distinction. Thus nothing happens, nothing is accomplished, unless the individuals concerned seek their own satisfaction in the issue. They are particular human beings; that is, they have special needs, instincts, and interests generally, peculiar to themselves. Among these needs are not only such as we usually call necessities—the stimuli of individual desire and volition—but also those connected with their own views and convictions, or at any rate opinions, if

9. That is, I must in some way identify with it, and see it as *my* objective.

1. That is, humans (*Menschen*).

the promptings of reflection, understanding, and reason have been awakened. In these cases people demand, if they are to exert themselves in any direction, that the object should commend itself to them; that in point of opinion—whether as to its goodness, justice, advantage, profit—they should be able to "enter into it" [*dabei sein*]. This is a consideration of especial importance in our age, when people are less than formerly influenced by reliance on others, and by authority; when, on the contrary, they devote their activities to a cause on the ground of their own understanding, their independent conviction and opinion.

Thus we assert that nothing has been accomplished without interest on the part of the actors; and—if interest be called a passion [*Leidenschaft*] inasmuch as the whole individuality, to the neglect of all other actual or possible interests and claims, is devoted to an object with every fibre of volition, concentrating all its desires and powers upon it—we may affirm absolutely that *nothing great in the world* has been accomplished without *passion*.[2] Two elements, therefore, enter into the object of our investigation; the first the *Idee*, the second the complex of human passions; the one the warp, the other the woof of the vast tapestry of world history. The concrete mean and union of the two is ethical freedom [*sittliche Freiheit*][3] in a state.

We have spoken of the *Idee* of freedom as the nature of *Geist*, and the absolute goal of history. Passion tends to be regarded as a thing of sinister aspect, as more or less immoral. One is supposed to have no passions. Passion, it is true, is not quite the suitable word for what I wish to express. I mean here nothing more than human activity as resulting from private interests—special, or if you will, self-seeking designs—with this qualification: that the whole energy of will and character is devoted to their attainment; and that other interests (which would in themselves constitute attractive aims), or rather all things else, are sacrificed to them. The object in question is so bound up with one's will that it entirely fills out its determinateness, and is inseparable from it. It has become the very essence of his volition. For a person is a specific existence—not "man" [*Mensch*] in general (a term to which no real existence corresponds), but a particular human being.[4]

The term "character" likewise expresses this determinateness of will and intelligence. But *character* comprehends all peculiarities whatever; the way in which a person conducts himself in private relations, etc., and is not limited to his idiosyncrasy in its practical and active phase. I shall, therefore, use the term "passion," understanding thereby the particular bent of character, as far as the determinations of volition are not limited to private interest, but supply the impelling and actuating force for common endeavor. Passion is in the first instance the *subjective*, and therefore the *formal* side of energy, will, and activity—leaving the object or aim still undetermined. And there is a similar relation of formality to reality in merely individual conviction, individual views, individual conscience. It is always a question of essential importance, what is the purport of my conviction, what the object of my passion, in deciding whether the one or the other is of a true and substantial nature. Conversely, if it is so, it will inevitably attain actual existence and be realized.

2. An important qualification of Hegel's assertion that "reason rules the world," showing one of the things that it should *not* be taken to mean.
3. That is, at the level of "objective *Geist*" or social and cultural life, self-determination in accordance with the norms of the society and culture of one's *Volk*.
4. This important point, which Hegel was said by Kierkegaard to have forgotten, is thus one of which he was well aware (see p. 427 below).

From this comment on the second essential element in the historical embodiment of an aim, we infer—glancing at the institution of the state in passing—that a state is then well constituted and internally powerful, when the private interest of its citizens is one with the common interest of the state; when the one finds its gratification and realization in the other—a proposition in itself very important. But in a state many institutions must be adopted, much political machinery invented, accompanied by appropriate political arrangements—necessitating long struggles of the understanding before what is really appropriate can be discovered, and involving, moreover, contentions with private interest and passions, and a tedious discipline of these latter, in order to bring about the desired harmony. The epoch in which a state attains this harmonious condition marks the period of its bloom, its virtue, its vigor, and its prosperity.

But the history of mankind does not begin with a *conscious* aim of any kind, as it is the case with the particular circles into which form themselves for set purposes. The mere social instinct implies a conscious purpose of security for life and property; and when society has been constituted, this purpose becomes more comprehensive. World history begins with its general aim—the realization of the *Idee* of *Geist*—only in an *implicit* form [*an sich*], that is, as nature; a hidden, most profoundly hidden, unconscious instinct. The whole process of history (as already observed) is directed to rendering this unconscious impulse a conscious one. Thus appearing in the form of merely natural existence, natural will—that which has been called the subjective side (physical craving, instinct, passion, private interest, as also opinion and subjective conception) spontaneously makes its appearance at the very commencement. This vast array of volitions, interests and activities constitute the instruments and means of the *Weltgeist* for attaining its object—bringing it to consciousness, and realizing it. And this aim is none other than *finding itself*, coming to itself, and contemplating itself, in concrete actuality.

But that those manifestations of vitality on the part of individuals and peoples, in which they seek and satisfy their own purposes, are, at the same time, the means and instruments of something higher and broader of which they know nothing—which they realize unconsciously—might be made a matter of question. Or rather: it has been questioned, and in every variety of form denied, decried and criticized as mere dreaming and "philosophy." But on this point I announced my view at the very outset, and asserted our hypothesis—which, however, will appear in the sequel, in the form of a legitimate inference—and our belief, that reason rules the world, and has consequently governed its history. In relation to this independently *allgemein* and substantial existence, all else is subordinate, subservient, and the means for its development. The union of the *Allgemeine* with the particular, the subjective, and that this alone is truth, is speculative, and is treated in this general form in Logic. But in the process of world history itself (as still incomplete), the abstract final aim of history is not yet made the distinct object of desire and interest. While these limited sentiments are still unconscious of the purpose they are fulfilling, the *allgemein* principle is implicit in them, and is realizing itself through them. The question also assumes the form of the union of *freedom* and *necessity*; the latent abstract process of *Geist* being regarded as *necessity*, while that which exhibits itself in the conscious will of men, as their interest, belongs to the domain of *freedom*. As the metaphysical connection (*i.e.* the connection in the *Idee*) of these forms of thought belongs to Logic, it would be out of place to analyze it here. Only the chief and cardinal points shall be mentioned [in what follows].

Philosophy shows that the *Idee* advances to an infinite antithesis; that, viz., between the *Idee* in its free, general form—in which it exists unto itself [*bei sich*]—and the contrasted form of abstract introversion, reflection on itself, which is formal existence-for-self, personality, formal freedom, such as belongs to *Geist* only. The general *Idee* exists thus as the substantial totality of things on the one hand, and as the abstract essence of free volition on the other. This reflection into itself is individual self-consciousness—the polar opposite of the *Idee* in its general form, and therefore existing in absolute limitation. This polar opposite is consequently limitation, particularization, for the *allgemein* absolute; it is the side of its *existence* [*Dasein*]; the sphere of its formal reality, the sphere of the reverence paid to God.

To comprehend the absolute connection of the antithesis is the profound task of metaphysics. This limitation originates all forms of particularity of whatever kind. The formal volition [of which we have spoken] wills itself; desires to make its own personality valid in all that it purposes and does: even the pious individual wishes to be saved and happy. This pole of the antithesis, existing for itself, is—in contrast with the absolute general reality [*allgemeinen Wesen*]—something particular [*ein Besonderes*], taking cognizance of particularity only, and willing that alone. In short it plays its part in the region of mere phenomena. This is the sphere of particular purposes, in effecting which individuals exert themselves on behalf of their individuality—give it full play and objective realization. This is also the sphere of happiness and its opposite. He is happy who finds his condition suited to his special character, will, and fancy, and so enjoys himself in that condition. World history is not the theatre of happiness. Periods of happiness are blank pages in it, for they are periods of harmony—periods when the antithesis is in abeyance. Reflection on self—the freedom above described—is abstractly defined as the formal element of the activity of the absolute *Idee*. The realizing *activity* of which we have spoken is the middle term of the "syllogism," one of whose extremes is the general essence, the *Idee*, which reposes in the depth [*Schacht*] of *Geist*; and the other, the complex of external things, is objective matter. That activity is the medium that translates the general and inner into objectivity.

* * *

* * * These contingencies realize themselves in history: they involve a general principle of a different order from that on which depends the *permanence* of a people or a state. This principle is an essential phase in the development of the *creating Idee*, of Truth, striving and pressing toward [consciousness of] itself. Historical men—*world-historical individuals*—are those in whose aim such a general principle lies.

* * * Such are all great historical men—whose own particular aims involve those large issues which are the will of the *Weltgeist*. They may be called heroes, inasmuch as they have derived their purposes and their calling [*Beruf*] not from the calm, regular course of things, sanctioned by the existing order, but from a source the content of which is concealed and has not attained to present existence—from that inner *Geist* still hidden beneath the surface, which, impinging on the outer world as on a shell, bursts it in pieces, because it is another kernel than that which belonged to the shell in question. They are men, therefore, who appear to draw the impulse of their life from themselves; and whose deeds have produced a condition of things and a complex of historical relations which appear to be only *their* interest, and *their* work.

Such individuals had no consciousness of the general *Idee* they were unfolding, while prosecuting those aims of theirs; on the contrary, they were practical, political men. But at the same time they were thinking men who had an insight into the requirements of the time and that for which *the time had come* [*was an der Zeit ist*]. This was the very truth for their age, for their world; the species next in order, so to speak, and which was already formed in the womb of time. It was theirs to know this nascent principle; the necessary, directly sequent step in progress, which their world was to take; to make this their aim, and to expend their energy in promoting it. World-historical men—the heroes of an epoch—must, therefore, be recognized as its clear-sighted ones; *their* deeds, *their* words are the best of that time. Great men have formed purposes to satisfy themselves, not others. Whatever prudent designs and counsels they might have learned from others, would be the more limited and inconsistent features in their career; for it was they who best understood affairs; from whom *others* learned, and approved—or at least acquiesced in—their policy. For that *Geist* which had taken this fresh step in history is the inmost soul of all individuals, but in a state of unconsciousness which the great men in question aroused. Their fellows, therefore, follow these soul-leaders; for they feel the irresistible power of their own inner *Geist* thus embodied.

If we go on to cast a look at the fate of these world-historical persons, whose calling it was to be the agents of the *Weltgeist*, we shall find it to have been no happy one. They attained no calm enjoyment; their whole life was labor and trouble; their whole nature was naught else but their master-passion. When their object is attained they fall off like empty hulls from the kernel. They die early, like Alexander; they are murdered, like Cæsar; transported to St. Helena, like Napoleon.[5] This fearful consolation—that historical men have not enjoyed what is called happiness, and of which only private life (and this may be passed under very various external circumstances) is capable—this consolation those may draw from history, who stand in need of it; and it is craved by envy—vexed at what is great and transcendent—striving, therefore, to depreciate it, and to find some flaw in it. Thus in modern times it has been demonstrated *ad nauseam* that princes are generally unhappy on their thrones—in consideration of which the possession of a throne is tolerated, and men acquiesce in the fact that not themselves but the personages in question are its occupants. (The free man, we may observe, is not envious, but gladly recognizes what is great and exalted, and rejoices that it exists.)

---

5. Three of the most prominent figures of ancient and modern history: Alexander the Great (356–323 B.C.E.), who unified Greece and conquered much of Asia; Julius Caesar (100–44 B.C.E.), great Roman general whose victory in a civil war ended the Roman Republic and who soon thereafter was assassinated by a group of nobles; and Napoleon Bonaparte (1769–1821), who became emperor of the French and, before his defeat and forced abdication and exile in 1815, gained control of much of continental Europe.

It is in the light of those common elements which, constitute the interest and therefore the passions of individuals, that these historical men are to be regarded. They are *great* men, because they willed and accomplished something great—not a mere fancy, a mere intention, but something right and necessary. * * *

A world-historical individual is not so unwise as to indulge a variety of wishes to divide his regards. He is devoted to *one* goal, regardless of all else. It is even possible that such men may treat other great, even sacred interests, inconsiderately—conduct which indeed invites moral reprehension. But so mighty a form must trample down many an innocent flower—crush to pieces many an object in its path.

The special interest of passion is thus inseparable from the active development of a general principle: for it is from the special and determinate and from its negation that the *Allgemeine* results. Particularity contends with its like, and some loss is involved in the issue. It is not the *allgemein Idee* that is implicated in opposition and combat, and that is exposed to danger. That remains in the background, untouched and uninjured. This may be called the *cunning of reason*[6]—that it sets the passions to work for itself, while that which develops its existence through such impulsion pays the penalty, and suffers loss. For it is *phenomenal* being that is so treated, and of this, part is of no value, part is positive and real. The particular is for the most part of too trifling value as compared with the general: individuals are sacrificed and abandoned. The *Idee* pays the penalty of determinate existence and of corruptibility, not from itself, but from the passions of individuals.

We might tolerate the idea that individuals, their desires and the gratification of them, are thus sacrificed, and their happiness given up to the rule of chance, to which it belongs; and that, as a general rule, individuals come under the category of means to an ulterior end. Yet there is one aspect of them[7] which we should hesitate to regard in that subordinate light, even in relation to the highest; since it is absolutely no subordinate element, but exists in them as inherently eternal and divine. I mean *morality, ethics, religion*. Even when speaking of the realization of the great ideal aim by means of individuals, the *subjective* element in them—their interest and that of their cravings and impulses, their views and judgments, though exhibited as the merely formal side of their existence—was spoken of as having an infinite right to be satisfied. The first idea that presents itself in speaking of *means* is that of something external to the object, and having no share in the object itself. But merely natural things—even the commonest lifeless objects—used as means, must be of such a kind as adapts them to their purpose; they must possess something in common with it. Human beings least of all sustain the bare external relation of mere means to the great ideal aim. Not only do they, in the very act of realizing it, make it the occasion of satisfying personal desires, whose purport is diverse from that aim. They further share in that ideal aim itself, and are for that very reason objects of their own existence—not merely *formally*, as the world of living beings generally is, whose individual existence is

---

6. "Die List der Vernunft," a famous figure of speech; its point is that irrational impulses may figure significantly in the realization of funda- mentally rational ends (e.g., the goal of reproduction is served by passions).

7. That is, of ourselves.

essentially subordinate to that of man, and is properly utilized as an instrument. Human beings [*Menschen*], on the contrary, are objects of existence[8] to themselves, as regards the intrinsic import of the aim in question. To this order belongs that in them which we would exclude from the category of mere means—morality, ethics, religion. That is to say, man is an object of existence in himself only in virtue of the Divine that is in him—that which was designated at the outset as *reason*; which, in view of its activity and power of self-determination, was called *freedom*. And we affirm—without entering at present on the proof of the assertion—that religion, morality, etc., have their foundation and source in that principle, and so are essentially elevated above all alien necessity and chance. And here we must remark that individuals, to the extent of their freedom, are responsible for the depravation and enfeeblement of ethicality [*Sittlichkeit*] and religion. This is the seal of the absolute and sublime destiny of man—that he knows what is good and what is evil; that he is able to will either good or evil—in one word, that he can be responsible [*kann Schuld haben*], responsibility not only for evil, but for good; and not only concerning this or that particular matter, and all that happens *ab extrâ*,[9] but *also* the good and evil attaching to his individual freedom.

* * *

(3.) The third point to be analyzed is, therefore—what is the object to be realized by these means; *i.e.* what is the form it assumes in the realm of reality. We have spoken of *means*; but in the carrying out of a subjective, limited aim, we have also to take into consideration the element of a *material*, either already present or which has to be procured. Thus the question would arise: What is the material in which the rational final aim [*vernünftige Endzweck*] is to be attained? The [initial] answer would be the subject itself, human desires, subjectivity generally. In human knowledge and volition, as its material element, reason attains positive existence. We have considered subjective volition where it has an object which is the truth and essence of a reality; viz. where it constitutes a great world-historical passion. As a subjective will, occupied with limited passions, it is dependent, and can gratify its desires only within the limits of this dependence.

But the subjective will has also a substantial life—a reality—in which it moves in the region of *essential* being, and has the essential itself as the object of its existence. This essential being is the union of the *subjective* with the *rational* will: it is the ethical whole [*das sittliche Ganze*], the *state*, which is that form of reality in which the individual has and enjoys his freedom—but on the condition of his recognizing, believing in and willing that which is common to the whole. And this must not be understood as if the subjective will of the social unit attained its gratification and enjoyment through that common will; as if this were a means provided for its benefit; as if the individual, in his relations to other individuals, thus limited his freedom, in order that this universal limitation—the mutual constraint of all—might secure a small space of freedom for each. Rather, we affirm, ethical life, the state, and law, and they alone, are the positive reality and completion of freedom. Freedom

8. That is, they matter.   9. From without or outside (Latin).

as such[1] is mere caprice, which finds its exercise in the sphere of particular and limited desires.

Subjective volition, passion, is the activating, the realizing. The *Idee* is the inwardly impelling. The state is actually existing, realized ethical life. For it is the unity of the general, essential will with that of the individual; and this is ethicality [*Sittlichkeit*].[2] The individual living in this unity has an ethical life [*sittliche Leben*] and possesses a value that consists in this substantiality alone.[3] Sophocles in his *Antigone* says, "The divine commands are not of yesterday, nor of to-day; no, they have an infinite existence, and no one could say whence they came."[4] The laws of *Sittlichkeit* are not accidental, but are the essentially rational. It is the very object of the state that what is essential in the practical activity of men, and in their dispositions, should be duly recognized; that it should have a manifest existence, and maintain its position.

It is the absolute interest of reason that this ethical whole should exist: and herein lies the justification and merit of heroes who have founded states— however rudimentary these may have been. In the history of the world, only those peoples can come under our notice which form a state. For it must be understood that the state is the realization of freedom, *i.e.* of the absolute final aim [*Endzweck*], and that it exists for its own sake. It must further be understood that all the worth which the human being possesses, all *geistig* actuality, he possesses only through the state. For his *geistig* actuality consists in this: that his own essence—reason—is objectively present to him, that it possesses objective immediate existence for him. Thus only is he fully conscious; thus only is he a partaker of ethicality [*Sittlichkeit*]—of a just and ethical social and political life. For truth is the unity of the general [*allgemein*] and subjective will; and the *Allgemeine* is to be found in the state, in its laws, its *allgemein* and rational arrangements. The state is the divine *Idee* as it exists on earth.

We have in it, therefore, the object of history in a more definite shape than before; that in which freedom obtains objectivity, and lives in the enjoyment of this objectivity. For law is the objectivity of *Geist*; volition in its true form. Only that will which obeys law, is free; for it obeys itself—it is independent and so free. When the state or country constitutes a community of existence; when the subjective will of man submits to laws—the contradiction between "freedom" and "necessity" vanishes. The rational has necessary existence, as being the reality and substance of things, and we are free in recognizing it as law, and following it as the substance of our own being. The objective and the subjective will are then reconciled, and present one identical homogeneous whole. For the ethicality [*Sittlichkeit*] of the state is not of that moral [*moralische*], inward kind in which one's own conviction holds sway. This latter is rather in accordance with the modern time, while the true, original ethicality is based on the principle of abiding by one's duty. An Athenian citizen did what was required of him, as it were from instinct: but if I reflect on the

---

1. "*Die* Freiheit": that is, freedom abstracted and separated from legal, ethical, and political norms.
2. That is, living, thinking, experiencing, and acting in accordance with the norms (the refined forms of the *Sitte*, or customs and rules) of one's community and society.

3. That is, the substantiality and significance of embodying the norms and values of one's "people"—their normative "substance" (its cultural content, personality, and identity).
4. See *Antigone* (ca. 441 B.C.E.), lines 453–57, by the Greek dramatist Sophocles (ca. 496–406 B.C.E.).

object of my activity, I must have the consciousness that my will has been called into exercise. But ethicality is duty—substantial right—a "*second* nature," as it has been justly called; for the *first* nature of man is his primary merely animal existence.

* * *

Summing up what has been said of the state: the vitality of the state in individuals may be called ethicality [*Sittlichkeit*]. The state, its laws, its arrangements, constitute the rights of its members; its natural features, its mountains, air, and waters, are *their* country, their fatherland, their outward material property; the history of this state, *their* deeds; what their ancestors have produced belongs to them and lives in their memory. All is their possession, just as they are possessed by it; for it constitutes their substance, their being. It fills their minds; and their will is the will of these laws, and of this fatherland. It is this *geistig* totality which thus constitutes *one* being, the *Geist* of *one* people [*Volk*]. To it the individual members belong; each [one] is the son of his people, and at the same time—in as far as the state to which he belongs is undergoing development—the son of his time. None remains behind it, still less advances beyond it. This *geistig* reality is his; he is a representative of it; it is that in which he originated, and in which he lives. Among the Athenians the word Athens had a double import—suggesting primarily a complex of political institutions, but no less, in the second place, that Goddess[5] who represented the *Geist* of the people and its unity.

This *Geist* of a people is a *determinate* and particular *Geist*, and is, as just stated, further modified by the degree of its historical development. This *Geist*, then, constitutes the basis and substance of those other forms of its consciousness which have been noted. For *Geist* in its self-consciousness must become an object of contemplation to itself, and objectivity involves, in the first instance, the rise of differences which make up a total of distinct spheres of objective *Geist*; in the same way as the soul [*Seele*] exists only as the complex of its faculties, which in their form of concentration in a simple unity produce that soul. It is thus *one* individuality which, in its essentiality, is represented, revered, and enjoyed as God in *religion*; which is exhibited as form and appearance in *art*; and which is comprehended and grasped as thought [*als Gedanken*][6] in *philosophy*.

In virtue of the original identity of their essence, purport, and object, these various forms are inseparably united with the *Geist* of the state. Only in connection with some particular religion can some particular political constitution exist; just as in such or such a state there can only be such or such a philosophy or type of art.

Further: each particular *Volksgeist* is to be treated as only one individual in the process of world history. For that history is the exhibition of the divine, absolute development of *Geist* in its highest forms—that succession of stages

5. That is, Athena (*Athēnē*); "Athens" in Greek is *Athēnai*, the plural of her name.
6. That is, the ultimate "individuality," the essential nature of which is *represented* (*vorgestellt*) in religious imagery as "God," and is *exhibited* (*dargestellt*) in the medium of art as significant form (*Bild*), is ultimately comprehended (*erkannt*) and grasped (*begriffen*) philosophically as "thought" (*Gedanke*) in the objective and ultimate sense (i.e., as the objective and ultimate thought-content: the *Begriff* or fundamental rational self-realizing structure of all reality).

by which it attains its truth and consciousness of itself. The forms which these stages assume are the characteristic world historical *Volksgeister*—the peculiar tenor of their ethical life, of their government, their art, religion, and science. To realize these stages is the boundless impulse of the *Weltgeist*, the goal of its irresistible urging; for this division into organic members, and the full development of each, is its *Idee*. World history is exclusively occupied with showing how *Geist* comes to a recognition and adoption of the truth: the dawn of knowledge appears; it begins to discover salient principles, and at last it arrives at full consciousness.

Having, therefore, learned the abstract characteristics of the nature of *Geist*, the means which it uses to realize its *Idee*, and the shape assumed by it in its complete realization in phenomenal existence—namely, the state—nothing further remains for this introductory section to contemplate but the following:

The course of world history. The mutations which history presents have been long characterized, in a general way, as an advance to something better, more perfect. The changes that take place in nature—how infinitely manifold soever they may be—exhibit only a perpetually self-repeating cycle; in nature there happens "nothing new under the sun," and the manifold play of its phenomena induces a feeling of boredom; only in those changes which take place in the region of *Geist* does anything new arise. This manifestation of the *Geistige* in man is indicative of an altogether different nature [*Bestimmung*] from that of merely natural objects—in which we find always one and the same stable character, to which all change reverts—namely, a *real* capacity for change, and that for the better—an impulse of *perfectibility*.[7] This principle, which reduces change itself under a law, has met with an unfavorable reception from religions—such as the Catholic—and from states claiming as their just right a stereotyped, or at least a stable position. If the mutability of worldly things in general—political constitutions, for instance—is conceded, either religion (as the religion of *truth*) is absolutely excepted, or the difficulty escaped by ascribing changes, revolutions, and abrogations of immaculate theories and institutions, to accidents or imprudence—but principally to the levity and evil passions of man. The principle of perfectibility indeed is almost as indefinite a term as mutability in general; it is without scope or goal, and has no standard by which to estimate the changes in question: the improved, more perfect, state of things toward which it professedly tends is altogether undetermined.

The principle of *development* involves also the existence of a latent germ of being—a capacity or potentiality striving to realize itself. This formal conception finds actual existence in *Geist*, which has world history for its theatre, its possession, and the sphere of its realization. It is not of such a nature as to be tossed to and fro amid the superficial play of accidents, but is rather the absolute arbiter of things; entirely unmoved by contingencies, which, indeed, it applies and manages for its own purposes. Development, however, is also a property of organized natural objects. Their existence presents itself, not as an exclusively dependent one, subjected to external changes, but

---

7. It is a characteristic of the *geistig* not only to be capable of change but to have an impetus to change toward more closely approximating the ideal or essential nature of the thing in question. (As an abstract principle, however, Hegel finds "perfectibility" to be vacuous.)

as one which expands itself in virtue of an internal unchangeable principle—a simple essence, whose existence in germ[8] is primarily simple—but which subsequently develops a variety of parts, that become involved with other objects, and consequently live through a continuous process of changes—a process, nevertheless, that results in the very contrary of change, and is even transformed into a preservation of the organic principle, and the form embodying it. Thus the organized *Individuum* produces itself; it expands itself *actually* to what it was always *potentially*.

So *Geist* is only that which it attains by its own efforts; it makes itself *actually* what it always was *potentially*. The development of natural organisms takes place in a direct, unopposed, unhindered manner. Between the *Idee* and its realization—the essential constitution of the original germ and the conformity to it of the existence derived from it—no disturbing influence can intrude. But in the case of *Geist* it is quite otherwise. Its realization is mediated by consciousness and will. These very faculties are, in the first instance, sunk in their primary *merely* natural life; the first object and goal of their striving is the realization of their merely natural destiny. But since it is *Geist* that animates its existence, it is possessed of vast attractions and displays great power and richness. Thus *Geist* is at war with itself; it has to overcome itself as its most formidable obstacle. That development which in the sphere of nature is a peaceful growth is, in that of *Geist*, a severe, a mighty conflict with itself. What *Geist* really strives for is the realization of its own *Begriff*; but in doing so, it hides that goal from its own vision, and is proud and well satisfied in this alienation from itself [*Entfremdung seiner selbst*].[9]

Its development, therefore, does not present the harmless tranquillity of mere growth, as does that of organic life, but a stern reluctant working against itself. It exhibits, moreover, not the mere formal conception of development, but the attainment of a definite result. The goal of attainment we determined at the outset: it is *Geist*, and in accordance with its essential nature, the *Begriff* of freedom. This is the fundamental object, and therefore also the leading principle of the development—that whereby it receives meaning and importance (as in the Roman history, Rome is the object—consequently that which directs our consideration of the facts related); as, conversely, the phenomena of the process have resulted from this principle alone, and possess a sense and meaning only in relation to it. There are many considerable periods in history in which this development seems to have been interrupted—in which, we might rather say, the whole enormous gain of previous cultural *Bildung* appears to have been entirely lost; after which, unhappily, a new commencement has been necessary, made in the hope of recovering—by the assistance of some remains saved from the wreckage of a former civilization, and by dint of a renewed incalculable expenditure of strength and time—one of the regions which had been an ancient possession of that civilization. We behold also *continued* processes of growth; structures and systems of *Bildung* in particular spheres, rich in kind, and well developed in every direction. The merely formal and indeterminate view of development in general can neither assign

---

8. That is, initially in rudimentary form (like the initial existence of an oak tree in the form of an acorn).

9. That is, its "self-alienation," or the disparity between its essential nature and its actual existence. This is one of the most important of Hegel's several conceptions of "alienation" (*Entfremdung*)—a concept whose later history was very rich.

superiority to one form of advance over another, nor render comprehensible the object of that decay of older periods of growth; but must regard such occurrences—or, to speak more particularly, the retrogressions they exhibit—as external contingencies, and can only judge of particular modes of development from indeterminate points of view, which—since the development, as such, is all in all—are relative and not absolute goals of attainment.

World history exhibits the *gradation* in the development of that principle whose substantial content is the consciousness of freedom. The analysis of the successive grades, in their abstract form, belongs to logic; in their concrete aspect, to the philosophy of *Geist*. Here it is sufficient to state that the first step in the process presents that immersion of *Geist* in nature which has been already referred to, while the second shows it as advancing to the consciousness of its freedom. But this initial separation from nature is imperfect and partial, since it is derived immediately from the merely natural state, is consequently related to it, and is still encumbered with it as an essentially connected element. The third step is elevation from this still limited and special form of freedom to its pure *Allgemeinheit*, in the self-consciousness and self-feeling of the very nature of *Geistigkeit*. These grades are the basic principles of the general process.

* * *

World history—as has already been asserted—displays the development of the consciousness of freedom on the part of *Geist*, and of the consequent realization of that freedom. This development implies a gradation—a series of increasingly adequate expressions or manifestations of freedom, which result from its *Idee*. The logical and (still more prominently) *dialectical* nature of the *Idee* in general, is set forth in [my] *Logic*: viz. that it is self-determined—that it assumes successive forms which it successively transcends; and by this very process of transcending its earlier stages, gains an affirmative, and, in fact, a richer and more concrete shape. This necessity of its nature, and the necessary series of pure abstract forms which the *Idee* successively assumes—is established there. Here we need adopt only one of its results, viz. that every step in the process, as differing from any other, has its determinate peculiar principle. In history this principle is determinateness of *Geist*—the particularity of a *Volksgeist*. It is within the limitations of this determinateness that a *Volksgeist* concretely expresses every aspect of its consciousness and will—the whole cycle of its realization. Its religion, its polity, its ethics, its legislation, and even its science, art, and technical ability all bear its stamp. These special characteristics spring from a general character—the specific principle that characterizes a *Volk*.

* * *

It is the concrete *Geist* of a *Volk* that we have distinctly to recognize, and since it is *Geist* it can only be comprehended spiritually, that is, by thought. It is this alone which takes the lead in all the deeds and tendencies of that *Volk*, and which is occupied in realizing itself—in satisfying its ideal and becoming self-conscious—for its great task is self-production. But for *Geist*, the highest attainment is self-knowledge; an advance not only to the *intuition*, but to the *thought*—the clear conception—of itself. This it must and is also destined to accomplish; but the accomplishment is at the same time its dissolution, and the rise of another *Geist*, another world-historical *Volk*, another epoch of world history. This transition and connection leads us to the connection of the whole—the idea of world history as such—which we have now to consider more closely, and of which we have to give an account.

History in general is therefore the development of *Geist* in *time*, as nature is the development of the *Idee* in *space*.

* * *

SOURCE: From G. F. W. Hegel, *Lectures on the Philosophy of History*, trans. J. Sibree (1857; reprint, New York: P. F. Cother and Son, 1902), pp. 52–54, 60–73, 76–81, 85–88, 102–7, 115–16, 125 (translation modified by the editor). Except where otherwise indicated, German words in brackets are the terminology used in the German original, inserted by the editor in addition to their renderings in the translation; and unbracketed German words are the original terminology, substituted in place of their renderings in the translation by the editor for reasons given in notes and in the Hegel glossary (p. 144). Like Hegel's other lectures, these were published after his death, compiled from the lecture notes of his students supplemented by his own lecture notes. This translation is based on the second edition of *Vorlesungen über die Philosophie der Geschichte* (1840).

On *Geist*

From Philosophy of Mind [*Geist*]

(Encyclopedia, part 3)

From *Introduction*

§ 377.] The knowledge of mind [*Geist*][1] is the highest and hardest, just because it is the most 'concrete' of sciences [*Wissenschaften*].[2] The significance of that 'absolute' commandment, *Know thyself*—whether we look at it in itself or under the historical circumstances of its first utterance[3]—is not to promote mere self-knowledge in respect of the *particular* capacities, character, propensities, and foibles of the single self. The knowledge it commands means that of man's genuine reality—of what is essentially and ultimately true and real[4]—of mind [*Geist*] as the true and essential being. Equally little is it the purport of mental philosophy[5] to teach what is called *knowledge of men*—the knowledge whose aim is to detect the *peculiarities*, passions, and foibles of other men, and lay bare what are called the recesses of the human heart. Information of this kind is, for one thing, meaningless, unless on the assumption that we know the universal [*Allgemeine*][6]—man as man, and, that always must be, as mind [*Geist*]. And

---

1. Wallace, like many other translators (including here Miller, who follows him for the sake of consistency), renders Hegel's term *Geist* as "mind." But "mind" in English does not begin to convey the broader meaning of the German word as Hegel appropriates and uses it: it encompasses virtually everything that goes on in human life, experience and activity beyond the merely biological and individual psychological level, including everything social, cultural, political, legal, artistic, religious, intellectual, and otherwise linguistic (see the Hegel glossary at the end of the introductory headnote). For this reason *Geist* and *geistig* have frequently been inserted to remind the reader of the rich special terminology he is using.

2. That is, cognitive disciplines (*Wissenschaften*). See the Hegel glossary, p. 144.
3. "Know thyself" (*gnōthi seauton*) was a Greek maxim carved into the temple of Apollo at Delphi (4th c. B.C.E.), home of the god's oracle.
4. More literally, "knowledge of what is fundamentally true with respect to man [human reality] as of what is fundamentally true in and of itself" (*Erkenntnis des Wahrhaften des Menschen wie des Wahrhaften an und für sich*).
5. That is, of the philosophy of *Geist* (*die Philosophie des Geistes*).
6. That is, the general; here, the fundamental general character of human reality. See the Hegel glossary, p. 144.

for another, being only engaged with casual, insignificant, and *untrue* aspects of mental life,[7] it fails to reach the underlying essence of them all—mind [*Geist*] itself.

Zusatz. The difficulty of the philosophical cognition of mind [*Geist*] consists in the fact that in this we are no longer dealing with the comparatively abstract, simple logical Idea [*Idee*],[8] but with the most concrete, most developed form achieved by the Idea [*Idee*], in its self-actualization. Even finite or subjective mind [*Geist*], not only absolute mind [*Geist*], must be grasped as an actualization of the Idea. The treatment of mind [*Geist*] is only truly philosophical when it cognizes the Notion [*Begriff*] of mind [*Geist*] in its living development and actualization, which simply means, when it comprehends mind as a type of the absolute Idea. But it belongs to the nature of mind to cognize its Notion [*Begriff*]. Consequently, the summons to the Greeks of the Delphic Apollo, *Know thyself*, does not have the meaning of a law externally imposed on the human mind by an alien power; on the contrary, the god who impels to self-knowledge is none other than the absolute law of mind [*Geist*] itself. Mind is, therefore, in its every act only apprehending itself, and the aim of all genuine science [*Wissenschaften*] is just this, that mind shall recognize itself in everything in heaven and on earth. An out-and-out Other simply does not exist for mind. Even the oriental does not wholly lose himself in the object of his worship; but the Greeks were the first to grasp expressly as mind what they opposed to themselves as the Divine, although even they did not attain, either in philosophy or in religion, to a knowledge of the absolute infinitude of mind; therefore with the Greeks the relation of the human mind to the Divine is still not one of absolute freedom. It was Christianity, by its doctrine of the Incarnation and of the presence of the Holy Spirit in the community of believers, that first gave to human consciousness a perfectly free relationship to the infinite and thereby made possible the comprehensive knowledge of mind in its absolute infinitude.

Henceforth, such a knowledge alone merits the name of a philosophical treatment. Self-knowledge in the usual trivial meaning of an inquiry into the foibles and faults of the single self has interest and importance only for the individual, not for philosophy; but even in relation to the individual, the more the focus of interest is shifted from the general intellectual [*geistig*] and moral nature of man,[9] and the more the inquiry, disregarding duties and the genuine content of the will, degenerates into a self-complacent absorption of the individual in the idiosyncrasies so dear to him, the less is the value of that self-knowledge. The same is true of the so-called knowledge of *human nature* which likewise is directed to the peculiarities of individual minds. This knowledge is, of course, useful and necessary in the conduct of life, especially in bad political conditions where right and morality have given place to the self-will, whims and caprice of individuals, in the field of

7. "Des Geistigen": that is, the various sorts of reality that have the character of *Geist*.
8. A technical term for Hegel, which does not carry the usual meaning of "idea" in English: it is not simply the *Begriff* ("concept" or essential character) of something, but that *Begriff* considered as objectified or realized. It thus is used by Hegel to refer to

what might be called "the principle of the objectification of the essential." See the Hegel glossary, p. 144.
9. In the German, "die Erkenntnis der allgemeinen intellektuellen und moralischen Natur des Menschen."

intrigues where characters do not rely on the nature of the matter in hand but hold their own by cunningly exploiting the peculiarities of others and seeking by this means to attain their arbitrary ends. For philosophy, however, this knowledge of human nature is devoid of interest in so far as it is incapable of rising above the consideration of contingent particularities to the understanding of the characters of great men, by which alone the true nature of man in its serene purity is brought to view. But this knowledge of human nature can even be harmful for philosophy if, as happens in the so-called pragmatic treatment of history, through failure to appreciate the substantial character of world-historical individuals and to see that great deeds can only be carried out by great characters, the supposedly clever attempt is made to trace back the greatest events in history to the accidental idiosyncrasies of those heroes, to their presumed petty aims, propensities, and passions. In such a procedure history, which is ruled by divine Providence, is reduced to a play of meaningless activity and contingent happenings.

§ 378.] Pneumatology, or, as it was also called, Rational Psychology, has been already alluded to in the Introduction to the *Logic*[1] as an *abstract* and generalizing metaphysic of the subject. *Empirical* (or inductive) psychology, on the other hand, deals with the 'concrete' mind; and, after the revival of the sciences when observation and experience had been made the distinctive methods for the study of concrete reality, such psychology was worked on the same lines as other sciences. In this way it came about that the metaphysical theory was kept outside the inductive science, and so prevented from getting any concrete embodiment or detail: whilst at the same time the inductive science clung to the conventional commonsense metaphysic, with its analysis into forces, various activities, etc., and rejected any attempt at a 'speculative' treatment.

The books of Aristotle on the Soul,[2] along with his discussions on its special aspects and states, are for this reason still by far the most admirable, perhaps even the sole, work of philosophical value on this topic. The main aim of a philosophy of mind [*Geist*] can only be to reintroduce unity of idea and principle into the theory of mind [*Geist*], and so reinterpret the lesson of those Aristotelian books.

Zusatz. Genuinely speculative philosophy, which excludes the mode of treatment discussed in the previous Paragraph which is directed to the unessential, isolated, empirical phenomena of mind, also excludes the precisely opposite mode of so-called Rational Psychology or Pneumatology, which is concerned only with abstractly universal [*allgemein*] determinations, with the supposedly unmanifested essence, the 'in-itself' of mind. For speculative philosophy may not take its subject-matter from picture-thinking [*Vorstellung*] as a *datum*, nor may it determine such given material merely by categories of the abstractive intellect (*Verstand*) as the said psychology did when it posed the question whether mind or soul is simple and immaterial, whether it is substance. In these questions mind was treated as a thing; for these categories were regarded,

---

1. That is, the introduction to *The Wissenschaft of Logic*, part 1 of Hegel's *Encyclopedia* (see the first selection, above).

2. The 3-book work *On the Soul* or *De Anima* (its Latin title), by the Greek philosopher Aristotle (384–322 B.C.E.).

in the general manner of the abstractive intellect, as inert, fixed; as such, they are incapable of expressing the nature of mind. Mind [*Geist*] is not an inert being but, on the contrary, absolutely restless being, pure activity, the negating or ideality of every fixed category of the abstractive intellect; not abstractly simple but, in its simplicity, at the same time a distinguishing of itself from itself; not an essence that is already finished and complete before its manifestation, keeping itself aloof behind its host of appearances, but an essence which is truly actual only through the specific forms of its necessary self-manifestation; and it is not, as that psychology supposed, a soul-thing only externally connected with the body, but is inwardly bound to the latter by the unity of the Notion [*Begriff*].

* * *

§ 379.] Even our own sense of mind's *living* unity naturally protests against any attempt to break it up into different faculties, forces, or, what comes to the same thing, activities, conceived as independent of each other. But the craving for a *comprehension* of the unity is still further stimulated, as we soon come across distinctions between mental [*geistig*] freedom and mental determinism [its becoming determinate], antitheses between free *psychic* agency and the corporeity that lies external to it, whilst we equally note the intimate interdependence of the one upon the other. In modern times especially the phenomena of *animal magnetism* have given, even in experience, a lively and visible confirmation of the underlying unity of soul [*Seele*] and of the power of its 'ideality.'[3] Before these facts, the rigid distinctions of practical common sense are struck with confusion; and the necessity of a 'speculative' examination[4] with a view to the removal of difficulties is more directly forced upon the student.

Zusatz. * * * In contrast to the empirical sciences, where the material as given by experience is taken up from outside and is ordered and brought into context in accordance with an already established general rule, speculative thinking has to demonstrate each of its objects and the explication of them, in their absolute necessity. This is effected by deriving each particular Notion [*Begriff*] from the self-originating and self-actualizing universal Notion [*allgemein Begriff*] or the logical Idea. Philosophy must therefore comprehend mind as a necessary development of the eternal Idea and must let the science of mind [*Wissenschaft vom Geiste*], as constituted by its particular parts, unfold itself entirely from its Notion. Just as in the living organism generally, everything is already contained, in an ideal manner, in the germ and is brought forth by the germ itself, not by an alien power, so too must all the particular forms of living mind grow out of its Notion as from their germ. In so doing, our thinking, which is actuated by

---

3. "Idealität": that is, the fundamental disposition of our psychological nature to develop toward *geistig* self-realization (see n. 4, p. 248, and the Hegel glossary at the end of the introductory headnote.). "Animal magnetism": a force, according to an 18th-century theory, that influences human beings via an invisible fluid found in the body and throughout the universe.

4. That is, a Hegelian-philosophical consideration of the matter (*speculative Betrachtung*). Hegel calls his kind of philosophical thinking "speculative" to distinguish it from the merely analytical kind of thinking that is the specialty and primary method of what he calls the "understanding" (*Verstand*); it is not unconstrained imaginative thinking but rather a more interpretive reasoning that has its own sort of rigor and discipline.

the Notion [*Begriff*], remains for the object, which likewise is actuated by the Notion, absolutely immanent; we merely look on, as it were, at the object's own development, not altering it by importing into it our own subjective ideas and fancies. The Notion [*Begriff*] does not require any external stimulus for its actualization; it embraces the contradiction of simplicity and difference, and therefore its own restless nature impels it to actualize itself, to unfold into actuality the difference which, in the Notion itself, is present only in an ideal manner, that is to say, in the contradictory form of differencelessness, and by this removal of its simplicity as of a defect, a one-sidedness, to make itself actually that whole, of which to begin with it contained only the possibility.

But the Notion [*Begriff*] is no less independent of our caprice in the conclusion of its development than it is in the beginning and in the course of it. In a merely ratiocinative mode of treatment the conclusion, to be sure, appears more or less arbitrary; in philosophical science [*Wissenschaft*], on the contrary, the Notion itself sets a limit to its self-development by giving itself an actuality that is perfectly adequate to it. Already in the living being we see this self-limitation of the Notion. The germ of the plant, this sensuously present Notion, closes its development with an actuality like itself, with the production of the seed. The same is true of mind [*Geist*]; its development, too, has achieved its goal when the Notion of mind [*Geist*] has completely actualized itself or, what is the same thing, when mind has attained to complete consciousness of its Notion. But this contraction of beginning and end into one, this coming of the Notion to its own self in its actualization, appears in mind in a yet more complete form than in the merely living being; for whereas in the latter, the seed produced is not identical with the seed from which it came, in self-knowing mind the product is one and the same as that which produces it.

Only when we contemplate mind [*Geist*] in this process of the self-actualization of its Notion, do we know it in its truth (for truth means precisely agreement of the Notion with its actuality). In its immediacy, mind is not yet true, has not yet made its Notion objective to it, has not yet transformed what confronts it in immediate guise into something which it has posited, has not yet transformed its actuality into one which is adequate to its Notion. The entire development of mind [*Geist*] is nothing else but the raising of itself to its truth, and the so-called psychic forces have no other meaning than to be the stages of this ascent. By this self-differentiation, this self-transformation, and the bringing back of its differences to the unity of its Notion, mind as a true being is also a living, organic, systematic being; and only by knowing this its nature is the science [*Wissenschaft*] of mind likewise true, living, organic, systematic: predicates bestowable neither on rational nor empirical psychology, for the former makes mind into a dead essence [*toten Wesen*] divorced from its actualization, while the latter kills the living mind by tearing it asunder into a manifold of independent forces which neither derive from the Notion nor are held together by it.

* * *

§ 380.] The 'concrete' nature of mind involves for the observer the peculiar difficulty that the several grades and special types which develop its intelligible unity in detail are not left standing as so many separate existences confronting its more advanced aspects. It is otherwise in external nature. There, matter and movement, for example, have a manifestation all their own— it is the solar system; and similarly the *differentiae* of sense-perception have a sort of earlier existence in the properties of *bodies*, and still more independently in the four elements.[5] The species and grades of mental [*geistig*] evolution on the contrary, lose their separate existence and become factors, states, and features in the higher grades of development. As a consequence of this, a lower and more abstract aspect of mind betrays the presence in it, even to experience, of a higher grade. Under the guise of sensation, for example, we may find the very highest mental [*geistig*] life as its modification or its embodiment. And so sensation, which is but a mere form and vehicle, may to the superficial glance seem to be the proper seat and, as it were, the source of those moral [*Sittliche*] and religious principles with which it is charged; and the moral [*Sittliche*] and religious principles thus modified may seem to call for treatment as species of sensation. But at the same time, when lower grades of mental life are under examination, it becomes necessary, if we desire to point to actual cases of them in experience, to direct attention to more advanced grades for which they are mere forms. In this way subjects will be treated of by anticipation which properly belong to later stages of development (e.g. in dealing with natural awaking from sleep we speak by anticipation of consciousness, or in dealing with mental derangement we must speak of intellect).

FROM WHAT MIND IS [*BEGRIFF DES GEISTES*]

§ 381.] From our point of view mind [*Geist*] has for its *presupposition* Nature, of which it is the truth,[6] and for that reason its *absolute prius*.[7] In this its truth Nature is vanished, and mind has resulted as the Idea entered on possession of itself. Here the subject and object of the Idea are one—either is the intelligent unity, the Notion.[8] This identity is *absolute negativity*—for whereas in Nature the intelligent unity has its objectivity perfect but externalized, this self-externalization has been nullified [*aufgehoben*] and the unity in that way been made one and the same with itself. Thus at the same time it *is* this identity only so far as it is a return out of nature.

Zusatz. We have already stated, in the *Zusatz* to § 379, that the Notion of mind is the self-knowing, actual Idea [*Idee*]. Philosophy has to demonstrate the necessity of this Notion, as of all its other Notions [*Begriffe*], which means that philosophy must cognize it as the result of the development of the universal Notion [*allgemein Begriff*] or of the logical Idea. But in this development, mind is preceded not only by the logical Idea but also by external Nature. For the cognition already contained in the simple *logical* Idea[9] is only the Notion

5. Earth, air, fire, and water (which, according to ancient Greek theory, were the constituents of everything).

6. *Geist* is the "truth" of nature in the sense that it is what nature has it in itself to become, somewhat as the oak tree is the "truth" or self-realization of the acorn, or as a mature and fully developed human being is the "truth" of the fetus and newborn.

7. Precondition (literally, "something that precedes"; Latin).

8. Better translated: "With the emergence of *Geist*,

nature vanishes [recedes into the background] and *Geist* comes forth as the *Idee* that has attained presence to itself, the *object* as well as the *subject* of which is the *Begriff*."

9. "The simple *logical Idee*," or the *Idee* as a logical structure, in contrast to "the self-knowing, actual *Idee*" (which is actually existing *Geist* knowing itself as *Geist*), is only what we might call the logical-conceptual essential blueprint of that culminating form of reality.

of cognition thought *by us*, not cognition existing on its own account, not actual mind [*Geist*] but merely its possibility. Actual mind [*Geist*] which, in the science of mind [*Wissenschaft* of *Geist*] is alone our subject-matter, has external Nature for its proximate, and the logical Idea for its first, presupposition. The Philosophy of Nature, and indirectly Logic, must have, therefore, as its final outcome the proof of the necessity of the Notion of mind [*Begriff* of *Geist*]. The science of mind, on its part, has to authenticate this Notion by its development and actualization. Accordingly, what we say here assertorically[1] about mind [*Geist*], at the beginning of our treatment of it, can only be scientifically proved by philosophy in its entirety. All we can do at the outset is to elucidate the Notion of mind [*Geist*] for ordinary thinking.

In order to establish what this Notion is, we must indicate the determinateness by which the Idea has being as mind [*Geist*]. But every determinateness is a determinateness only counter to another determinateness; to that of mind [*Geist*] in general is opposed, in the first instance, that of Nature; the former can, therefore, only be grasped simultaneously with the latter. We must designate as the distinctive determinateness of the Notion of mind, *ideality*, that is, the reduction of the Idea's otherness to a *moment*, the process of returning— and the accomplished return—into itself of the Idea from its Other; whereas the distinctive feature of the logical Idea is immediate, simple being-within-self, but for Nature it is the self-externality of the Idea. A more detailed development of what was said in passing in the *Zusatz* to § 379 about the logical Idea would involve too wide a digression here; more necessary at this point is an elucidation of what has been assigned as characteristic of external Nature, for it is to the latter, as we have already remarked, that mind [*Geist*] is proximately related.

External Nature, too, like mind [*Geist*], is rational, divine, a representation of the Idea. But in Nature, the Idea appears in the element of asunderness, is external not only to mind but also to itself, precisely because it is external to that actual, self-existent inwardness which constitutes the essential nature of mind. This Notion of Nature which was already enunciated by the Greeks and quite familiar to them, is in complete agreement with our ordinary idea of Nature. We know that natural things are spatial and temporal, that in Nature one thing exists alongside another, that one thing follows another, in brief, that in Nature all things are mutually external, *ad infinitum*; further, that matter, this universal basis of every existent form in Nature, not merely offers resistance to *us*, exists apart from mind but holds itself asunder against its own self, divides itself into concrete points, into material atoms, of which it is composed. The differences into which the Notion of Nature unfolds itself are more or less mutually independent existences; true, through their original unity they stand in mutual connection, so that none can be comprehended without the others; but this connection is in a greater or less degree external to them. We rightly say, therefore, that not freedom but necessity reigns in Nature; for this latter in its strictest meaning is precisely the merely internal, and for that reason also merely external, connection of mutually independent existences.

* * *

1. By affirming or asserting that something is.

* * * Even in the most perfect form to which Nature raises itself, in animal life,[2] the Notion does not attain to an actuality resembling its soul-like nature, to complete victory over the externality and finitude of its existence. This is first achieved in mind, which, just by winning this victory, *distinguishes itself* from Nature[3] so that this distinguishing is not merely the act of an *external* reflection about the nature of mind [*Geist*].

This triumph over externality which belongs to the Notion of mind is what we have called the ideality[4] of mind. Every activity of mind is nothing but a distinct mode of reducing what is external to the inwardness which mind [*Geist*] itself is, and it is only by this reduction, by this idealization or assimilation, of what is external that it becomes and is mind.

If we consider mind more closely, we find that its primary and simplest determination is the 'I' [*Ich*]. The 'I' is something perfectly simple, universal [*allgemein*].[5] When we say 'I', we mean, to be sure, an individual [*ein Einzelnes*]; but since everyone is 'I', when we say 'I', we only say something quite universal [*allgemein*]. The universality of the 'I' enables it to abstract from everything, even from its life. But mind is not merely this abstractly simple being equivalent to light, which was how it was considered when the simplicity of the soul in contrast to the composite nature of the body was under discussion; on the contrary, mind in spite of its simplicity is distinguished within itself; for the 'I' sets itself over against itself, makes itself its own object and returns from this difference, which is, of course, only abstract, not yet concrete, into unity with itself. This being-with-itself of the 'I' in its difference from itself is the 'I's infinitude or ideality. But this ideality is first authenticated in the relation of the 'I' to the infinitely manifold material confronting it. This material, in being seized by the 'I', is at the same time poisoned[6] and transfigured by the latter's universality; it loses its isolated, independent existence and receives a spiritual [*geistig*] one. So far, therefore, is mind from being forced out of its simplicity, its being-with-itself, by the endless multiplicity of its images and ideas [*Vorstellungen*],[7] into a spatial asunderness, that, on the contrary, its simple self, in undimmed clarity, pervades this multiplicity through and through and does not let it reach an independent existence.

But mind [*Geist*] is not satisfied, as *finite* mind, with transposing things by its own ideational activity into its own interior space and thus stripping them of their externality in a manner which is still external; on the contrary, as *religious* consciousness, it pierces through the seemingly absolute independence of things to the one, infinite power of God operative in them and holding all

---

2. That is, biological sexual reproduction; it is "the most perfect form to which Nature raises itself, in animal life," because it is the closest Nature is able to come to a supersession (*Aufhebung*—see the Hegel glossary, p. 144.) of finitude (i.e., the limitation of biological death).

3. That is, *Geist* sets itself apart from all that is merely natural, and from the merely natural form of reality, by attaining a form of experience and activity in which "the externality and finitude of its existence" are overcome. The word translated in this sentence as "victory" (*Überwindung*) would be better translated as "overcoming," "surpassing," or "supersession" (like *Aufhebung*).

4. "Idealität." Hegel's discussion of what he means

by the "ideality of *Geist*" in this passage sheds light on both his conception of *Geist* and his kind of "idealism." *Geist* as activity, he suggests, just *is* the self-developing ongoing dialectic of internalization and externalization, which proceeds until all forms of externality or objectivity have been internalized, and all forms of externality or objectivity have been discovered to be expressions of the dynamic self-realizing rationality that is the essential substantive nature of *Geist* itself.

5. That is, general.

6. That is, deprived of its status (its "life") as something entirely external and alien to the "I" (*Ich*).

7. That is, representations.

together; and as *philosophical* thinking, it consummates this idealization of things by discerning the specific mode in which the eternal Idea forming their common principle is represented in them. By this cognition, the idealistic nature of mind, which is already operative in finite mind, attains its completed, concretest shape, and becomes the actual Idea [*Idee*] which perfectly apprehends itself and hence becomes absolute mind [*Geist*]. Already in finite mind, ideality has the meaning of a movement returning into its beginning, by which mind, moving onward from its undifferentiated stage, its first position, to an Other, to the negation of that position, and by means of the negation of this negation returning to itself, demonstrates itself to be absolute negativity, infinite self-affirmation; and we have to consider finite mind, conformably to this its nature, first, in its immediate unity with Nature, then in its opposition to it, and lastly, in a unity which contains that opposition as overcome [*aufgehoben*] and is mediated by it. Grasped in this manner, finite mind is known as totality, as Idea, and moreover as the Idea which is for itself, which returns to itself out of that opposition and is actual. But in finite mind there is only the beginning of this return which is consummated only in absolute mind [*Geist*]; for only in this does the Idea apprehend itself in a form which is neither merely the one-sided form of Notion [*Begriff*] or subjectivity, nor merely the equally one-sided form of objectivity or actuality, but is the perfect unity of these its distinct moments, that is, in its absolute truth.

* * *

So much for the distinctive determinatenesses of external Nature and mind [*Geist*] as such. The explicated difference at the same time provides an indication of the relation in which Nature and mind [*Geist*] stand to each other. Since this relation is often misunderstood, this is the appropriate place in which to elucidate it. We have said that mind [*Geist*] negates the externality of Nature, assimilates Nature to itself and thereby idealizes it. In finite mind which places Nature outside of it, this idealization has a one-sided shape; here the activity of our willing, as of our thinking, is confronted by an external material which is indifferent to the alteration which we impose on it and suffers quite passively the idealization which thus falls to its lot.[8]

But a different relationship obtains with the mind [*Geist*] that makes world-history. In this case, there no longer stands, on the one side, an activity external to the object, and on the other side, a merely passive object: but the spiritual [*geistig*] activity is directed to an object which is active in itself, an object which has spontaneously worked itself up into the result to be brought about by that activity, so that in the activity and in the object, one and the same content is present. Thus, for example, the people [*Volk*] and the time which were moulded by the activity of Alexander and Caesar[9] as *their* object, on their own part, qualified themselves for the deeds to be performed by these individuals;

8. When Hegel says that *Geist* "negates the externality of Nature, assimilates Nature to itself and thereby idealizes it," he has in mind nothing more dramatic or mysterious than what we do when we transform nature to suit our practical purposes, or conceptualize nature to suit our theoretical purposes.

9. Two world-historical figures, conventionally taken to be the greatest generals of antiquity: Alexander the Great (356–323 B.C.E.), who unified Greece and conquered much of Asia, and Julius Caesar (100–44 B.C.E.), whose victory in a civil war ended the Roman Republic.

it is no less true that the time created these men as that it was created by them; they were as much the instruments of the mind or spirit [*Geist*] of their time and their people [*Volk*], as conversely, their people [*Volk*] served these heroes as an instrument for the accomplishment of their deeds.

Similar to the relationship just delineated is the manner in which the philosophizing mind [*Geist*] relates itself to external Nature. That is to say, philosophical thinking knows that Nature is idealized not merely by us, that Nature's asunderness is not an absolutely insuperable barrier for Nature itself, for its Notion [*Begriff*]; but that the eternal Idea immanent in Nature or, what is the same thing, the essence of mind [*Geist*] itself at work within Nature brings about the idealization, the triumph over the asunderness, because this form of mind's existence conflicts with the inwardness of its essence. Therefore philosophy has, as it were, only to watch how Nature itself overcomes its externality, how it takes back what is self-external into the centre of the Idea, or causes this centre to show forth in the external, how it liberates the Notion concealed in Nature from the covering of externality and thereby overcomes external necessity. This transition from necessity to freedom is not a simple transition but a progression through many stages, whose exposition constitutes the Philosophy of Nature. At the highest stage of this triumph over asunderness, in feeling, the essence of mind [*Geist*] which is held captive in Nature attains to an incipient being-for-self and begins to be free. By this being-for-self which is itself still burdened with the form of individuality [*Einzelheit*] and externality, consequently also with unfreedom, Nature is driven onwards beyond itself to mind [*Geist*] as such, that is, to mind which, by thinking, is in the form of universality, of self-existent, actually free mind.

But it is already evident from our preceding exposition that the procession[1] of mind [*Geist*] from Nature must not be understood as if Nature were the absolutely immediate and the *prius*, and the original positing agent, mind, on the contrary, were only something posited by Nature; rather is it Nature which is posited by mind [*Geist*], and the latter is the absolute *prius*. Mind which exists in and for itself is not the mere result of Nature, but is in truth its own result; it brings forth itself from the presuppositions which it makes for itself, from the logical Idea and external Nature, and is as much the truth of the one as of the other, i.e. is the true form of mind which is only internal, and of the mind [*Geist*] which is only external, to itself mind.[2] The illusory appearance which makes mind seem to be mediated by an Other is removed by mind itself, since this has, so to speak, the sovereign ingratitude of ridding itself of, of mediatizing, that by which it appears to be mediated, of reducing it to something dependent solely on mind and in this way making itself completely self-subsistent.

From what has been said, it already follows that the transition from Nature to mind [*Geist*] is not a transition to an out-and-out Other, but is only a coming-

---

1. That is, the "coming forth" or "emergence" (*her-vorgehen*).
2. That is, *Geist*, not nature, is the "absolute *prius*" or what is absolutely prior to all particular existence in the sense that Geist's essence—the rational structure that Hegel calls the *Begriff*—is also nature's essence, of which nature's reality is the "external" manifestation. Yet *Geist* has no *real* existence prior to and apart from all nature and history, through which alone it attains *reality* and may attain full *actuality*.

to-itself of mind out of its self-externality in Nature. But equally, the differentia of Nature and mind [*Geist*] is not abolished by this transition, for mind does not proceed in a natural manner from Nature. When it was said in § 222 that the death of the merely immediate, individual form of life is the procession of mind [*Geist*], this procession is not 'according to the flesh' but spiritual [*geistig*], is not to be understood as a natural procession but as a development of the Notion [*Begriff*]: for in the Notion, the one-sidedness of the genus which fails properly to actualize itself, proving itself in death to be rather the negative power opposed to that actuality, and also the opposite one-sidedness of the animal existence which is tied to individuality, these are both overcome in the individuality which is in and for itself universal or, what is the same thing, in the universal which exists for itself in a universal mode, which universal is mind.

Nature as such in its inwardizing of itself does not attain to this being-for-self, to the consciousness of itself; the animal, the most perfect form of this inwardization, represents only the non-spiritual dialectic of transition from one single sensation filling its whole soul to another single sensation which equally exclusively dominates it; it is man [*der Mensch*] who first raises himself above the singleness of sensation to the universality of thought, to self-knowledge, to the grasp of his subjectivity, of his 'I' in a word, it is only man who is thinking mind [*Geist*] and by this, and by this alone, is essentially distinguished from Nature. What belongs to Nature as such lies at the back of mind; it is true that mind has within itself the entire filling of Nature, but in mind the determinations of Nature exist in a radically different manner from their existence in external Nature.

§ 382.] For this reason the essential, but formally essential, feature of mind [*Geist*] is Liberty[3]: i.e. it is the Notion's absolute negativity or self-identity. Considered as this formal aspect, it *may* withdraw itself from everything external and from its own externality, its very existence; it can thus submit to infinite *pain*, the negation of its individual immediacy: in other words, it can keep itself affirmative in this negativity and possess its own identity. All this is possible so long as it is considered in its abstract self-contained universality.

Zusatz. The substance of mind is freedom i.e. the absence of dependence on an Other, the relating of self to self.[4] Mind is the actualized Notion which is for itself and has itself for object. Its truth and its freedom alike consist in this unity of Notion and objectivity present in it. The truth, as Christ said, makes mind free;[5] freedom makes it true. But the freedom of mind is not merely an absence of dependence on an Other won outside of the Other, but won in it; attains actuality not by fleeing from the Other but by overcoming it.[6] Mind can step out of its abstract, self-existent universality, out of its simple self-relation, can posit within itself a determinate, actual difference,

---

3. That is, freedom (*Freiheit*).
4. This characterization is the basis of Hegel's conception of true "freedom" as genuine self-determination, in the sense of determination by or in accordance with that which one essentially or most truly is.

5. See John 8:32: "and you will know the truth, and the truth will make you free" (RSV).
6. That is, by an overcoming (*Überwindung*) of the relation—or apparent relation—of "otherness" between itself and the other.

something other than the simple 'I', and hence a negative; and this relation to the Other is, for mind, not merely possible but necessary, because it is through the Other and by the triumph over [*Aufhebung* of] it, that mind [*Geist*] comes to authenticate itself and to be in fact what it ought to be according to its Notion [*Begriff*], namely, the ideality of the external, the Idea which returns to itself out of its otherness; or, expressed more abstractly, the self-differentiating universality which in its difference is at home with itself and for itself. The Other, the negative, contradiction, disunity, therefore also belongs to the nature of mind [*Geist*]. * * * This power over every content present in it forms the basis of the freedom of mind. But in its immediacy, mind is free only implicitly, in principle or potentially, not yet in actuality; actual freedom does not therefore belong to mind in its immediacy but has to be brought into being by mind's own activity. It is thus as the creator of its freedom that we have to consider mind [*Geist*] in philosophy. The entire development of the Notion of mind [*Geist*] represents only mind's freeing of itself from all its existential forms which do not accord with its Notion: a liberation which is brought about by the transformation of these forms into an actuality perfectly adequate to the Notion of mind [*Geist*].

§ 383.] This universality [*Allgemeinheit*] is also its determinate sphere of being. Having a being of its own, the universal is self-particularizing, whilst it still remains self-identical. Hence the special mode of spiritual being is '*manifestation*'. Mind [*Geist*] is not some one mode or meaning which finds utterance or externality only in a form distinct from itself: it does not manifest or reveal *something*, but its very mode and meaning is this revelation. And thus in its mere possibility mind is at the same moment an infinite, 'absolute', *actuality*.

Zusatz. Earlier on, we placed the differentia of mind in *ideality*, in the abolition of the otherness of the Idea. If, now, in § 383 above, 'manifestation' is assigned as the determinateness of mind [*Geist*], this is not a new, not a second, determination of mind, but only a development of the determination discussed earlier. For by getting rid of its otherness, the logical Idea, or mind which is only in itself, becomes for itself, in other words, becomes manifest to itself. Mind which is for itself, or mind as such—in distinction from mind which does not know itself and is manifest only to us, which is poured out into the asunderness of Nature and only ideally present therein—is, therefore, that which manifests itself not merely to an Other but to itself; or, what amounts to the same thing, is that which accomplishes its manifestation in its own element, not in an alien material. This determination belongs to mind [*Geist*] as such; it holds true therefore of mind not only in so far as this relates itself simply to itself and is an 'I' having itself for object, but also in so far as mind steps out of its abstract, self-existent universality, posits within itself a specific distinction, something other than itself; for mind does not lose itself in this Other, but, on the contrary, preserves and actualizes itself therein, impresses it with mind's own inner nature, converts the Other into an existence corresponding to it, and therefore by this triumph over[7] the Other, over the specific, actual difference, attains to concrete being-for-self, becomes defi-

---

7. That is, supersession of (*Aufhebung*).

nitely manifest to itself. In the Other, therefore, mind [Geist] manifests only itself, its own nature; but this consists in self-manifestation. The manifestation of itself to itself is therefore itself the content of mind and not, as it were, only a form externally added to the content; consequently mind, by its manifestation, does not manifest a content different from its form, but manifests its form which expresses the entire content of mind [Geist], namely, its self-manifestation.[8] In mind, therefore, form and content are identical with each other. Admittedly, manifestation is usually thought of as an empty form to which must still be added a content from elsewhere; and by content is understood a being-within-self which remains within itself, and by form, on the other hand, the external mode of the relation of the content to something else. But in speculative logic it is demonstrated that, in truth, the content is not merely something which is and remains within itself, but something which spontaneously enters into relation with something else; just as, conversely, in truth, the form must be grasped not merely as something dependent on and external to the content, but rather as that which makes the content into a content, into a being-within-self, into something distinct from something else. The true content contains, therefore, form within itself, and the true form is its own content. But we have to know mind as this true content and as this true form.

* * *

Just as mind [Geist] represents the unity of form and content, so too is it the unity of possibility and actuality. We understand by the possible as such, that which is still inward, that which has not yet come to utterance, to manifestation. But now we have seen that mind as such only is, in so far as it manifests itself to itself.[9] Actuality, which consists just in mind's manifestation, belongs therefore to its Notion. In finite mind the Notion of mind does not, of course, reach its absolute actualization; but absolute mind [Geist] is the absolute unity of actuality and the Notion or possibility of mind.

§ 384.] *Revelation*,[1] taken to mean the revelation of the *abstract* Idea, is an unmediated transition to Nature which *comes* to be. As mind is free, its manifestation is to *set forth* Nature as *its* world; but because it is reflection, it, in thus setting forth its world, at the same time *presupposes* the world as a nature independently existing. In the intellectual sphere[2] to reveal is thus to create a world as its being—a being in which the mind procures the *affirmation* and *truth* of its freedom.[3]

---

8. Hegel's very important point here is analogous to the idea that what *art* is fundamentally all about is *creativity*—not the creation of this or that particular "work of art," but simply *creating* (though that necessarily requires creating something specific, and amounts to nothing real except insofar as this occurs).

9. That is, Geist as such exists only in and through the manifestation or expression of itself. It is no existing thing or reality of any kind apart from some such sort of expressive activity.

1. A translation of Offenbarung, the term previously rendered as "manifestation." This section is therefore a continuation of the discussion of the same topic.

2. That is, where concepts are concerned (im Begriffe).

3. Hegel here is saying that when Geist begins to "manifest" (offenbaren, here translated "reveal") itself by way of concepts, its self-manifestation in concepts is their creation as its being (Sein)—that is, as a kind of being or world of its own, in which it is able to affirm its essential freedom and make that freedom come true.

The Absolute is mind (spirit) [*Geist*]—this is the supreme definition of the Absolute. To find this definition and to grasp its meaning and burden was,[4] we may say, the ultimate purpose of all education [*Bildung*] and all philosophy: it was the point to which turned the impulse of all religion and science: and it is this impulse that must explain the history of the world. The word 'Mind' [*Geist*]—and some glimpse of its meaning—was found at an early period: and the spirituality of God is the lesson of Christianity. It remains for philosophy in its own element of intelligible unity to get hold of what was thus given as a mental image [*Vorstellung*], and what implicitly is the ultimate reality; and that problem is not genuinely, and by rational methods, solved so long as liberty[5] and intelligible unity is not the theme and the soul of philosophy.

Zusatz. Self-manifestation is a determination belonging to mind [*Geist*] as such; but it has three distinct forms. The first mode in which mind [*Geist*], as [only][6] in itself or as the logical Idea manifests itself, consists in the direct release [*Umschlagen*] of the Idea into the immediacy of external and particularized existence. This release is the coming-to-be of Nature.[7] Nature, too, is a posited existence; but its positedness has the form of immediacy, of a being outside of the Idea. This form contradicts the inwardness of the self-positing Idea which brings forth itself from its presuppositions. The Idea, or mind [*Geist*] implicit, slumbering in Nature, overcomes, therefore, the externality, separateness, and immediacy, creates for itself an existence conformable to its inwardness and universality [*Allgemeinheit*] and thereby becomes mind which is reflected into itself and is for itself, self-conscious and awakened mind or mind [*Geist*] as such.

This gives the second form of mind's manifestation. On this level, mind [*Geist*], which is no longer poured out into the asunderness of Nature but exists for itself and is manifest to itself, opposes itself to unconscious Nature which just as much conceals mind as manifests it. Mind converts Nature into an object confronting it, reflects on it, takes back the externality of Nature into its own inwardness, idealizes Nature and thus in its object becomes for itself. But this first being-for-self of mind is itself still immediate, abstract, not absolute; the self-externality of mind [*Geist*] is not absolutely overcome by it. The awakening mind does not yet discern here its unity with the mind [*Geist*] concealed and implicit in Nature, to which it stands, therefore, in an external relation, does not appear as all in all, but only as one side of the relation; it is true that in its relation to the Other it is also reflected into itself and so is self-consciousness, but yet it lets this unity of consciousness and self-consciousness still exist as a unity that remains so external, empty and superficial that in it self-consciousness and consciousness still fall asunder; and

---

4. That is, has been (in the course of the history of philosophy leading up to Hegel).
5. That is, freedom (*Freiheit*).
6. Translator's brackets.
7. Hegel nowhere gives an account of just how this *Umschlagen* is to be understood. In the next sentence he refers to nature as "something posited" (*ein Gesetztes*); but that is only another figure of speech. It is a kind of Hegelian-logical necessity that the "logical *Idee*" should manifest itself in the

form of a world of nature in order to be able further to find eventual full actualization; but it is far from clear how that sort of necessity could have a real result of this character and magnitude. Hegel's position would appear to be simply that the existence of the world of nature shows it to be so— and that is all that can or need be said. See also the discussion of the inner necessity of the actualization of the *Idee* in n. 3, p. 201.

mind, despite its self-communion is at the same time in communion not with itself but with an Other, and its unity with mind implicitly present and active in the Other does not as yet become *for* mind. Here, mind [*Geist*] posits Nature as a reflectedness-into-self, as *its* world, strips Nature of its form of otherness and converts the Other confronting it into something it has itself posited; but, at the same time, this Other still remains independent of mind, something immediately given, not posited but only presupposed by mind, as something, therefore, the positing of which is antecedent to reflective thought. Hence from this standpoint the positedness of Nature by mind is not yet absolute but is effected only in the reflective consciousness; Nature is, therefore, not yet comprehended as existing only through infinite mind [*Geist*] as its creation. Here, consequently, mind still has in Nature a limitation and just by this limitation is finite mind.

Now this limitation is removed by absolute knowledge, which is the third and supreme manifestation of mind [*Geist*]. On this level there vanishes, on the one hand, the dualism of a self-subsistent Nature or of mind poured out into asunderness, and, on the other hand, the merely incipient self-awareness of mind which, however, does not yet comprehend its unity with the former. Absolute mind [*Geist*] knows that it posits being itself, that it is itself the creator of its Other, of Nature and finite mind, so that this Other loses all semblance of independence in face of mind, ceases altogether to be a limitation for mind, and appears only as a means whereby mind attains to absolute being-for-self, to the absolute unity of what it is in itself and what it is for itself, of its Notion and its actuality.

The highest definition of the Absolute is that it is not merely mind [*Geist*] in general but that it is mind which is absolutely manifest to itself, self-conscious, infinitely creative mind [*Geist*], which we have just characterized as the third form of its manifestation. Just as in philosophy we progress from the imperfect forms of mind's manifestation delineated above to the highest form of its manifestation, so, too, world-history exhibits a series of conceptions of the Eternal, the last of which first shows forth the Notion of absolute mind [*Geist*]. The oriental religions, and the Hebrew, too, stop short at the still abstract concept of God and of mind [*Geist*] (as is done even by the Enlightenment which wants to know only of God the Father); for God the Father, by himself, is the God who is shut up within himself, the abstract god, therefore not yet the spiritual [*geistig*], not yet the true God. In the Greek religion God did, indeed, begin to be manifest in a definite manner. The representation of the Greek gods had beauty for its law, Nature raised to the level of mind. The Beautiful does not remain something abstractly ideal, but in its ideality is at once perfectly determinate, individualized. The Greek gods are, however, at first only representations for sensuous intuition or for picture-thinking, they are not yet grasped in thought. But the medium of sense can only exhibit the totality of mind as an asunderness, as a circle of independent, mental or spiritual [*geistig*] shapes; the unity embracing all these shapes remains, therefore, a wholly indeterminate, alien power over against the gods. It is in the Christian religion that the immanently differentiated *one* nature of God, the totality of the divine mind in the form of unity, has first been manifested. This content, presented in the guise of picture-thinking [*Vorstellung*], has to be raised by philosophy into the form of the Notion [*Begriff*] or of absolute knowledge which, as we have said, is the highest manifestation of that content.

FROM SUBDIVISION

§ 385.] The development of mind [*Geist*] is in three stages:

(1) In the form of self-relation: within it it has the *ideal* totality of the Idea—i.e. it has before it all that its Notion contains: its being is to be self-contained and free. This is *Mind Subjective* [*subjektiver Geist*].

(2) In the form of *reality* [*Realität*]: realized, i.e. in a *world* produced and to be produced by it: in this world freedom presents itself under the shape of necessity. This is *Mind Objective* [*objektiver Geist*].

(3) In that unity of mind [*Geist*] as objectivity and of mind as ideality and concept [*Begriff*], which essentially and actually is and for ever produces itself, mind in its absolute truth. This is *Mind Absolute* [*der absolute Geist*].

Zusatz. Mind [*Geist*] is always Idea; but to begin with it is only the Notion of the Idea, or the Idea in its indeterminateness, in the most abstract mode of reality, in other words, in the mode of being. In the beginning we have only the quite universal, undeveloped determination of mind, not yet mind in its particular aspect; this we obtain only when we pass from one thing to something else: for the particular contains a One and an Other; but it is just at the beginning that we have not yet made this transition. The reality of mind is, therefore, to begin with still a quite universal [*allgemein*], not particularized reality: the development of this reality will be completed only by the entire Philosophy of Mind [*Geist*]. The still quite abstract, immediate reality is, however, the natural, the unspiritual. This is the reason why the child is still in the grip of natural life, has only natural impulses, is not actually but only potentially or notionally[8] a rational being. Accordingly, we must characterize the first reality of mind as the most inappropriate for mind [*Geist*], simply because it is still an abstract, immediate reality in the natural sphere; but the true reality must be defined as the totality of the developed moments of the Notion which remains the soul, the unity of these moments.[9] In this development of its reality, the Notion's progress is prescribed by necessity, for the form of immediacy, of indeterminateness, which its reality has at first is in contradiction with it; that which in mind appears to be immediately present is not truly immediate, but is intrinsically something posited, mediated. Mind is impelled by this contradiction to rid itself of its own presupposition in the guise of immediacy, of otherness. It is by doing this that it first comes to itself, first emerges *as* mind [*Geist*]. Consequently, we cannot begin with mind as such, but must start from its most inappropriate reality. Mind, it is true, is already mind [*Geist*] at the outset, but it does not yet know that it is. It is not mind [*Geist*] itself that, at the outset, has already grasped its Notion: it is only we who contemplate it who know its Notion. That mind comes to a knowledge of what it is, this constitutes its realization. Mind [*Geist*] is essentially only

8. "Dem Begriff nach": that is, only potentially or essentially, in principle, in accordance with its *Begriff* (as a human being).
9. "The soul" (*die Seele*) is a term and idea retained by Hegel, but it refers only to the unity of the various "moments" or aspects of *Geist* (it does not name an entity of any sort that each of us has or truly is, and that might be capable of separate existence).

what it knows itself to be. At first, it is only potentially mind [*Geist*]; its becoming-for-itself makes it an actuality. But it becomes for itself only by particularizing, determining itself, making itself into its own presupposition, into the Other of itself, first relating itself to this Other as to its immediacy, but making itself free of this Other *qua* Other. As long as mind stands related to itself as to an Other, it is only *subjective* mind [*Geist*], originating in Nature and at first itself natural mind. But the entire activity of subjective mind is directed to grasping itself as its own self, proving itself to be the ideality of its immediate reality. When it has attained to a being-for-self, then it is no longer merely subjective, but *objective* mind [*Geist*]. Whereas subjective mind on account of its connection with an Other is still unfree or, what is the same thing, is free only in principle, in objective mind [*Geist*] there comes into existence freedom, mind's knowledge of itself as free. Mind that is objective is a person [*Person*], and as such has a reality of its freedom in property; for in property, the thing is posited as what it is, namely, something lacking a subsistence of its own, something which essentially has the significance of being only the reality of the free will of a person, and for that reason, of being for any other person inviolable. Here we see a subjective mind that knows itself to be free, and, at the same time, an external reality of this freedom; here, therefore, mind attains to a being-for-self, the objectivity of mind receives its due. Thus mind [*Geist*] has emerged from the form of mere subjectivity. But the full realization of that freedom which in property is still incomplete, still [only][1] formal, the consummation of the realization of the Notion of objective mind [*Geist*], is achieved only in the State [well-ordered polity], in which mind develops its freedom into a world posited by mind itself, into the ethical world.[2] Yet mind [*Geist*] must pass beyond this level too. The defect of this objectivity of mind consists in its being only posited. Mind must again freely let go the world, what mind [*Geist*] has posited must at the same time be grasped as having an immediate being. This happens on the third level of mind [*Geist*], the standpoint of absolute mind [*Geist*], i.e. of art, religion, and philosophy.

* * *

SOURCE: *Hegel's Philosophy of Mind: Being Part Three of the "Encyclopaedia of the Philosophical Sciences" (1830)*, trans. William Wallace and A. V. Miller (Oxford: Clarendon Press, 1971), pp. 1–9, 11–22. Except where otherwise indicated, German words in brackets are the terminology used in the German original, inserted by the editor in addition to their renderings in the translation. This edition adds to Wallace's 1894 translation of the 1830 *Philosophie des Geistes*, part 3 of *Enzyklopädie der philosophischen Wissenschaften*, Miller's translation of the *Zusätze* or "additions" (marked *Zusatz*) that were incorporated into the work in 1845; they were compiled after Hegel's death from lecture notes (both his students' and his own).

1. Translator's brackets.
2. "Sittlichen Welt": that is, the realm that begins as the customs (*Sitte*) of a people and develops into the various forms of normativity that constitute and structure "ethical life" or "ethicality" for that people. As such they have a real and significant "objective" reality in the life of the people and their institutions. Because they are only the contingent rules creatively established or "posited" by that particular people (*Volk*), however, they have only a limited sort of *Allgemeinheit* (generality or universality).

Subjective *Geist*

On Subjective (and Intersubjective) *Geist*

From Philosophy of Mind [*Geist*]

From *Section One. Mind* [Geist] *Subjective*

[INTRODUCTION]

§ 387.] Mind [*Geist*], on the ideal stage of its development,[1] is mind as *cognitive*.[2] Cognition, however, being taken here not as a merely logical category of the Idea [*Idee*] (§ 223), but in the sense appropriate to the *concrete* mind.

Subjective mind [*Geist*] is:

(A) Immediate or implicit: a soul—in *Nature*—the object treated by *Anthropology*.[3]

(B) Mediate or explicit: still as identical reflection into itself and into other things: mind [*Geist*] in correlation or particularization: consciousness—the object treated by the *Phenomenology of Mind* [*Geist*].[4]

(C) *Mind* [*Geist*] defining itself in itself, as an independent subject—the object treated by *Psychology*.[5]

In the *Soul* is the *awaking* of *Consciousness*:[6] Consciousness sets itself up as Reason, awaking at one bound to the sense of its rationality: and this Reason by its activity emancipates itself to objectivity and the consciousness of its intelligent unity.

For an intelligible unity or principle of comprehension each modification it presents is an advance of *development*: and so in mind [*Geist*] every character under which it appears is a stage in a process of specification and development, a step forward towards its goal, in order to make itself into, and to realize in itself, what it implicitly is. Each step, again, is itself such a process, and its product is that what mind [*Geist*] was implicitly at the beginning (and so for the observer) it is *for itself*—for the special form, viz. which mind has in that step.[7] The ordinary method of psychology is to narrate what mind or soul [*Seele*] is, what happens to it, what it does. The soul is presupposed as a ready-made agent, which displays such features as its acts and utterances, from which we can learn what it is, what sort of faculties and powers it

---

1. Better translated: "Spirit, developing itself in its ideality" (*Der Geist, in seiner Idealität sich entwickelnd*): that is, spirit, as it begins to develop in the direction of more fully and adequately realizing its essential nature.

2. That is, knowing (*erkennend*).

3. "Subjective *Geist*," in its merely implicit, immediate (unselfconscious) form, is what might be called "soul" (*Seele*), or "natural *Geist*" (*Naturgeist*), and is the subject matter of Hegel's version of a philosophical "anthropology."

4. A narrow use of the term "phenomenology" to designate the analysis of forms of consciousness and self-consciousness considered as forms of experience of particular conscious subjects (not a reference to Hegel's book of this title).

5. "Subjective *Geist*," in the final stage of its development, is *Geist* "determining itself within itself" (*der sich in sich bestimmende Geist*), as a subject "for itself," or more directly conscious of itself (*als Subjekt für sich*), and is the subject matter of Hegel's version of a philosophical "psychology."

6. That is, in the stage or form of what Hegel is calling "soul," consciousness (*Bewusstsein*) may be said to "awaken."

7. That is, each developmental step involves the kind of process described in the sentence—and as a result, some aspect of *Geist* that initially characterized it only potentially or implicitly (and of which only we as philosophical observers are retrospectively aware) emerges and becomes something of which the developing subject is aware.

possesses—all without being aware that the act and utterance of what the soul is really invests it with that character in our conception and makes it reach a higher stage of being than it explicitly had before.

We must, however, distinguish and keep apart from the progress here to be studied what we call education [*Bildung*] and instruction. The sphere of education is the individuals only: and its aim is to bring the universal mind [*allgemeine Geist*] to exist in them. But in the philosophic theory of mind [*Geist*], mind is studied as self-instruction and self-education in very essence; and its acts and utterances are stages in the process which brings it forward to itself, links it in unity with itself, and so makes it actual mind [*Geist*].

Zusatz. In § 385[8] we distinguished the three main forms of mind [*Geist*]: subjective, objective, and absolute mind [*Geist*], and also pointed out the necessity of the progress from the first to the second and from this to the third. We called the first form of mind [*Geist*] we have to consider *subjective* mind [*Geist*] because here mind is still in its undeveloped Notion [*Begriff*], has not as yet made its Notion an object for itself. But in this its subjectivity mind is at the same time objective, has an immediate reality by overcoming which it first becomes for itself, attains to a grasp of its Notion, of its subjectivity. We could therefore just as well say that mind is, to begin with, objective and has to become subjective, as conversely, that it is first subjective and has to make itself objective. Consequently, we must not regard the difference between subjective and objective mind as fixed. Even at the beginning, we have to grasp mind [*Geist*] not as mere Notion, as something merely subjective, but as Idea, as a unity of subjectivity and objectivity, and any progress from this beginning is a movement away from and beyond the first, simple subjectivity of mind, a progress in the development of its reality or objectivity. This development brings forth a succession of shapes;[9] these, it is true, must be specified empirically, but in the philosophical treatment cannot remain externally juxtaposed, but must be known as the corresponding expression of a necessary series of specific Notions, and they are of interest to philosophy only in so far as they express such a series of Notions.[1] However, at first, we can only assert what the different forms of subjective mind are; their necessity will emerge only from the specific development of subjective mind.

The three main forms of subjective mind [*Geist*] are: (1) Soul, (2) Consciousness, and (3) Mind [*Geist*] as such. As soul, mind [*Geist*] has the form of abstract universality, as consciousness, that of particularization, and as explicitly for itself, that of individuality [*Einzelheit*]. This is how subjective mind in its development represents the development of the Notion. The reason why, in the above Paragraph, the names Anthropology, Phenomenology, and Psychology have been given to the parts of the science [*Wissenschaft*] corresponding to these three forms of subjective mind, will become evident from a more detailed, provisional statement of the contents of the science of subjective mind.

We must begin our treatment with immediate mind; but this is natural mind, *soul*. To suppose that we begin with the mere Notion of mind [*Geist*]

8. See previous selection, pp. 256–57.
9. That is, "forms" (*Gestaltungen*).

1. That is, as a "necessary series."

would be a mistake; for as we have already said, mind [*Geist*] is always Idea, therefore realized Notion. But at the beginning, the Notion [*Begriff*] of mind [*Geist*] cannot as yet have the mediated reality which it receives in abstract thought; true, at the beginning, its reality, too, must already be an abstract one, only thus does it correspond to the ideality of mind; but it is necessarily a reality that is still unmediated, not yet posited, consequently a simply affirmative reality given by Nature and external to mind. We must start, therefore, from mind which is still in the grip of Nature and connected with its corporeity, mind which is not as yet in communion with itself, not yet free. This—if we may so express it—basis of man [*Grundlage des Menschen*] is the subject-matter of Anthropology. In this part of the science of subjective mind, the Notion of mind[2] is only in us who think it, not as yet in the object itself; the object of our treatment here is formed by the, at first, merely immediate Notion of mind, mind [*Geist*] which has not as yet grasped its Notion and is still external to itself.

The first stage in Anthropology is the qualitatively determined soul which is tied to its natural forms (racial differences, for example, belong here). Out of this immediate oneness with its natural aspect, soul enters into opposition and conflict with it (this embraces the states of insanity and somnambulism). The outcome of this conflict is the triumph of the soul over its corporeity, the process of reducing, and the accomplished reduction of, this corporeity to a sign, to the representation of the soul. The ideality of the soul thus becomes apparent in its corporeity and this reality of mind is posited as ideal but in a still corporeal mode.

In Phenomenology, the soul, by the negation of its corporeity, raises itself to purely ideal self-identity, becomes *consciousness*, becomes 'I', is for itself over against its Other. But this first being-for-self of mind is still conditioned by the Other from which it proceeds. The 'I' is still perfectly empty, a quite abstract subjectivity which posits the whole content of immediate mind outside of it and relates itself to it as to a world already in existence. Thus what was at first only *our* object,[3] does indeed become an object for mind itself, but the 'I' does not as yet know that what confronts it is natural mind itself. Therefore, the 'I', in spite of its being-for-self, is at the same time still not for itself, for it is only in relation to an Other, to something given. The freedom of the 'I' is consequently only an abstract, conditioned, relative freedom. True, mind here is no longer immersed in Nature but reflected into itself and in a relation to Nature, but it only *appears*, stands only in a relation to actuality, is not yet *actual* mind. Therefore, we call the part of the science [*Wissenschaft*] in which this form of mind is treated, Phenomenology. But now the 'I', in reflecting itself out of its relation-to-other into itself, becomes *self-consciousness*. In this form, the 'I' at first knows itself only as the empty, unfulfilled 'I', and all concrete content as something other than it. Here the

2. That is, the explicitly contemplated *Begriff* of *Geist*.
3. That is, what at first was only recognized and conceived by the philosophical observer to be "an object" (or various objects) to which *Geist* in its "natural," prereflective mode of existence is relating. Hegel frequently uses this philosophical "voice" to say something *about* the kind of experience he is exploring, which is very different from the way that things *in* that kind of experience are experienced and conceptualized (which he also attempts to express in the same text). This can be confusing and misleading.

activity of the 'I' consists in filling the void of its abstract subjectivity, in building objectivity into itself but, on the other hand, in making subjectivity objective. In this way, self-consciousness overcomes the one-sidedness of its subjectivity, breaks away from its particularity, from its opposition to objectivity, and attains to the universality [*Allgemeinheit*] which embraces both sides and represents within itself the immanent unity of itself with consciousness; for the content of mind here becomes an objective content as in consciousness, and at the same time, as in self-consciousness, a subjective content. This universal self-consciousness is, in itself or for us, Reason; but it is only in the third part of the science of subjective mind[4] that Reason becomes objective to itself.

This third part, Psychology, treats of mind as such, mind which, in the object, is only *self*-related, is occupied only with its own determinations, mind which grasps its own Notion.[5] Thus mind comes to its truth; for the unity of subjectivity and objectivity which, in mere soul, is still immediate, still abstract, is now, after the resolution of the opposition arising in consciousness between these determinations, restored as a mediated unity; and the Idea of mind,[6] leaving behind it its contradictory form of simple Notion and the equally contradictory separation of its moments, attains, therefore, to a mediated unity and accordingly to true actuality. In this shape, mind is Reason which is explicitly for itself. Mind and Reason stand in a similar relation to each other as body and its heaviness, as will and freedom. Reason forms the substantial nature of mind; it is only another expression for Truth or the Idea which constitutes the essence of mind; but it is only mind as such that knows that its nature is Reason and Truth. Mind which embraces both sides, subjectivity and objectivity, now posits itself first in the form of subjectivity: as such it is Intelligence; secondly, in the form of objectivity: as such it is Will. Intelligence, which is itself at first without content, sets aside its form of subjectivity which does not conform to the Notion of mind, by applying to the objective content confronting it which is still burdened with the form of an isolated *datum*, the absolute standard of Reason, clothes this content with rationality, informs it with the Idea, transforms it into a concrete universal, and thus receives it into itself. Intelligence thereby reaches the stage where what it knows is no abstraction but the objective Notion, and where, on the other hand, the object loses its character of 'givenness' and acquires the shape of a content belonging to mind itself. But intelligence, in becoming aware that it is itself the source of its content, becomes practical mind [*Geist*] which sets only itself for its goal, becomes *will* which, unlike intelligence, does not begin with an isolated object externally given, but with something it knows to be its own. Then, reflecting itself into itself out of this content of impulses, tendencies, it relates the content to a universal;[7] and lastly, it raises itself to the willing of

---

4. That is, the third part of Hegel's philosophical analysis of "subjective *Geist*."
5. At this stage *Geist* grasps (begins to recognize) its own essential nature.
6. That is, the *existing reality* of *Geist* that now is

verging on "true actuality" or full self-realization; its existence is coming into accordance with its essential nature.
7. That is, something general (*ein Allgemeine*).

the universal in and for itself, of freedom, of its Notion.[8] Having reached this goal, mind has just as much returned to its beginning, to self-unity, as it has progressed to absolute, truly immanently determined self-unity, to a unity in which the determinations are determinations not of Nature but of the Notion.[9]

FROM A. ANTHROPOLOGY: THE SOUL

§ 388.] Mind [*Geist*] *came into* being as the truth of Nature.[1] But not merely is it, as such a result, to be held the true and real first of what went before: this becoming or transition bears in the sphere of the Notion the special meaning of '*free judgement*'.[2] Mind, thus come into being, means therefore that Nature in its own self realizes its untruth and sets itself aside:[3] it means that mind [*Geist*] presupposes itself no longer as the universality [*Allgemein-heit*] which in corporal individuality is always self-externalized, but as a universality which in its concretion and totality is one and simple. At such a stage it is not yet mind, but *soul*.

§ 389.] The soul is no separate immaterial entity. Wherever there is Nature, the soul is its universal [*allgemein*] immaterialism, its simple 'ideal' life. Soul is the *substance* or 'absolute' basis of all the particularizing and individualizing of mind [*Geist*]: it is in the soul that mind finds the material on which its character is wrought, and the soul remains the pervading, identical ideality of it all. But as it is still conceived thus abstractly, the soul is only the *sleep* of mind [*Geist*]—the passive νοῦς[4] of Aristotle, which is potentially all things.

The question of the immateriality of the soul has no interest, except where, on the one hand, matter is regarded as something *true*, and mind conceived as a *thing*, on the other. But in modern times even the physicists have found matters grow thinner in their hands: they have come upon *imponderable* matters, like heat, light, etc., to which they might perhaps add space and time. These 'imponderables', which have lost the property (peculiar to matter) of gravity and, in a sense, even the capacity of offering resistance, have still, however, a sensible existence and outness of part to part; whereas the '*vital*' *matter*, which may also be found enumerated among them, not merely lacks

---

8. That is, *Geist* finally raises itself to the willing of freedom itself (by which Hegel means true self-conscious self-determination), which is its *Begriff* and essential nature, and which is not merely something general (like "happiness" or "well-being"), but rather is the supreme general or "universal" principle (*das Allgemeine*) "in and for itself"—that is, as an actual self-conscious reality.
9. That is, its determinations are now supplied not by Nature but rather by the very nature or *Begriff* of *Geist* itself, which is freedom (conceived as actual self-conscious rational self-determination).
1. "Der Geist ist als die Wahrheit der Natur geworden". That is, it is as the "truth" of Nature—as that which Nature had it within its essential nature to become—that *Geist* has emerged or come to be.
2. That is, the "coming to be" of *Geist* out of Nature may be thought of in a very fundamental (but also extended) sense as involving a "judging" or "passing of judgment"—and a "free" or "self-determined" one at that (rather than one imposed externally).

See n. 5, p. 201, and n. 7, p. 254, above.
3. That is, *Geist*'s "coming to be" out of Nature thus has the meaning that Nature in effect passes a negative judgment on itself by revealing its inadequacy: its own essential nature can never be adequately manifested and expressed in the mere externalities of natural spatiotemporal existence and processes. It can never be "true to itself" as long as it remains mere Nature (hence its "untruth"), and so it *supersedes* itself (*sich aufhebt*, here inadequately translated as "sets itself aside") by way of the emergence or "coming into being" and "becoming" of *Geist* out of mere "life"—initially in the form of what Hegel calls "soul" (*Seele*).
4. A Greek word (*nous*) usually translated as "mind." Hegel considers *nous* to be a receptive form of mentality surpassed by fully active and actual *Geist*. In *On the Soul* 3.5, the Greek philosopher Aristotle (384–322 B.C.E.) wrote that *nous* has both active and passive senses, and its passive sense "is such because it becomes all things."

gravity, but even every other aspect of existence which might lead us to treat it as material. The fact is that in the Idea of Life the self-externalism of nature is *implicitly* at an end: subjectivity is the very substance and conception of life—with this proviso, however, that its existence or objectivity is still at the same time forfeited to the sway of self-externalism. It is otherwise with mind [*Geist*]. There, in the intelligible unity which exists as freedom, as absolute negativity, and not as the immediate or natural individual, the object or the reality of the intelligible unity is the unity itself; and so the self-externalism, which is the fundamental feature of matter, has been completely dissipated and transmuted into [*Allgemeinheit*] or the subjective ideality of the conceptual unity. Mind [*Geist*] is the existent truth of matter—the truth that matter itself has no truth.[5]

* * *

§ 395.] (3) The soul is further de-universalized [*vereinzelt*][6] into the individualized subject. But this subjectivity is here only considered as a differentiation and singling out of the modes which nature gives; we find it as the special temperament, talent, character, physiognomy, or other disposition and idiosyncrasy, of families or single individuals.

Zusatz. As we have seen, mind or spirit in Nature [*Naturgeist*] at first falls asunder into the *general* differences of the races of mankind, and reaches in the national minds or spirits [*Volksgeistern*] a difference which has the form of a *particularization*. The third stage is that mind in Nature goes on to separate itself into *individuals*, and as individual soul opposes itself to itself. But the opposition arising here is not as yet the opposition which belongs to the essence of consciousness. The singularity or individuality of the soul comes into account here in anthropology only as a natural determinateness.

Now first of all we must remark that it is in the individual soul that the sphere of contingency begins, for only the universal [*Allgemeine*] is the necessary. Individual souls are distinguished from one another by an infinite number of contingent modifications. But this infinity belongs to the spurious kind of infinite. One should not therefore rate the peculiarities of people[7] too highly.

* * *

THE ACTUAL SOUL [*DIE WIRKLICHE SEELE*]

§ 411.] The Soul, when its corporeity has been moulded and made thoroughly its own, finds itself there a *single* subject; and the corporeity is an externality which stands as a predicate, in being related to which, it is related to itself. This externality, in other words, represents not itself, but the soul, of which it is the *sign*. In this identity of interior and exterior, the latter subject to the former, the soul is *actual*: in its corporeity it has its free shape, in which it *feels itself* and makes *itself felt*, and which as the Soul's work of art has *human* pathognomic and physiognomic expression.[8]

---

5. That is, the "truth" of "matter," like the "truth" of "Nature," is the realization of that which it has it in it to become. As mere "matter," therefore, matter is far from being that "truth," and so in that sense "has [or is] no truth."
6. That is, particularized.

7. That is, humans (*Menschen*).
8. That is, expression of signs of passions or feelings ("pathognomic") and of temperament and character ("physiognomic," usually through facial features).

Under the head of human expression are included,[9] for example, the upright figure in general, and the formation of the limbs, especially the hand, as the absolute instrument, of the mouth—laughter, weeping, etc., and the note of mentality [*geistige Ton*] diffused over the whole, which at once announces the body as the externality of a higher nature. This note is so slight, indefinite, and inexpressible a modification, because the figure in its externality is something immediate and natural, and can therefore only be an indefinite and quite imperfect sign for the mind, unable to represent it in its actual universality. Seen from the animal world, the human figure is the supreme phase in which mind [*Geist*] makes an appearance. But for mind it is only its first appearance, while language is its perfect expression. And the human figure, though the proximate phase of mind's existence, is at the same time in its physiognomic and pathognomic quality something contingent to it.

*   *   *

§ 412.] Implicitly the soul shows the untruth and unreality of matter; for the soul, in its concentrated self, cuts itself off from its immediate being, placing the latter over against it as a corporeity incapable of offering resistance to its moulding influence. The soul, thus setting in opposition its being to its (conscious) self, absorbing it, and making it its own, has lost the meaning of mere soul, or the 'immediacy' of mind. The actual soul with its sensation and its concrete self-feeling turned into habit [*Gewohnheit*], has implicitly realised the 'ideality' of its qualities; in this externality it has recollected and inwardized itself, and is infinite self-relation. This free universality thus made explicit shows the soul awaking to the higher stage of the ego, or abstract universality, in so far as it is *for* the abstract universality. In this way it gains the position of thinker and subject—specially a subject of the judgement in which the ego excludes from itself the sum total of its merely natural features as an object, a world external to it—but with such respect to that object that in it it is immediately reflected into itself. Thus soul rises to become *Consciousness* [*Bewusstsein*].

*   *   *

By this reflection-into-self, mind [*Geist*] consummates its liberation from the form of mere being, gives itself the form of essence [*Wesen*] and becomes 'I'. It is true that the soul, in so far as it is subjectivity or selfhood, is already *in itself*, or *implicitly*, 'I'. But the *actuality* of the 'I' involves more than the soul's immediate, natural subjectivity; for the 'I' is this universal [*allgemein*], simple being that in truth exists only when it has itself for object, when it has become the being-for-self of the simple in the simple, the relation of the universal to the universal. The self-related universal exists nowhere save in the 'I'. In external Nature, as was already stated in the introduction to the doctrine of subjective mind, the universal only attains the highest manifestation of its power by destruction of the individual existence, hence does not attain to an actual being-for-self. The natural soul too is, in the first instance, only the real possibility of this being-for-self. Only in the 'I' does this possibility become an actuality. Therefore, in the 'I' a waking ensues of a higher

9. That is, "Human expression [*menschlichen Ausdruck*] includes . . ."

kind than the natural waking which is confined to the mere sensation of single things; for the 'I' is the lightning which pierces through the natural soul and consumes its natural being. In the 'I', therefore, the ideality of natural being, and so the essence of the soul, becomes *for* the soul.

It is to this goal that the whole anthropological development presses forward. Looking back over it we shall recall how the *human* soul, in contrast to the animal soul which remains sunk in the singleness and limitation of sensation, has raised itself above the limited content of what is felt or sensed, a content which is in contradiction with its inherently infinite nature, has transformed this content into an ideal moment, and particularly in habit has made it into something universal [*allgemein*], inwardized, and total, into a being; and also how by this very act it has filled the initially empty space of its inwardness with a content appropriate to its universality, has placed the being of the content within itself, just as, on the other hand, it has transformed its body into the likeness of its ideality, of its freedom, and thus has reached the stage where it exists in the 'I' as the self-related, individually determined universal, a self-existent, abstract totality freed from corporeity. Whereas in the sphere of the merely feeling soul the self is manifested in the shape of the genius[1] as a power acting only externally and at the same time only internally on the existent individuality, at the stage of the soul's development now reached, the self as already shown has actualized itself in the soul's outer existence, in its bodily nature, and, conversely, has given a being to itself; so that now the self or the 'I' beholds itself in its Other and is this intuiting of itself.

From B. Phenomenology of Mind [*Geist*]: Consciousness

§ 413.] Consciousness constitutes the reflected or correlational grade[2] of mind: the grade of mind as *appearance*. Ego[3] is infinite self-relation of mind, but as subjective or as self-certainty. The immediate identity of the natural soul has been raised to this pure 'ideal' self-identity; and what the former *contained* is for this self-subsistent reflection set forth as an *object*. The pure abstract freedom of mind lets go from it its specific qualities—the soul's natural life—to an equal freedom as an independent *object*. It is of this latter, as external to it, that the *ego* is in the first instance aware (conscious), and as such it is Consciousness. Ego, as this absolute negativity, is implicitly the identity in the otherness: the *ego* is itself that other and stretches over the object (as if that object were implicitly cancelled)—it is one side of the relationship and the whole relationship—the light, which manifests itself and something else too.

Zusatz. As we remarked in the *Zusatz* to the previous Paragraph, the 'I' must be grasped as the individually determined universal which, in its determinateness, in its difference, relates itself to itself alone. This already implies that the 'I' is immediately *negative* self-relation, consequently the unmediated opposite of its universality [*Allgemeinheit*] which is abstracted from every determinateness, an individuality which is, therefore, equally abstract and

---

1. That is, "in the form of distinctive ability" (*in der Gestalt des Genius*).

2. That is, "level" (*Stufe*).

3. That is, "I" (*Ich*).

simple. It is not only *we* who reflect on it who thus differentiate the 'I' into its opposed moments, but it is the 'I' itself which, in virtue of its immanently universal, hence self-differentiated, individuality, is this distinguishing of itself from itself; for as self-relating, its exclusive individuality excludes itself from itself, i.e. from individuality, and thereby makes itself into its own opposite, an opposite with which it is immediately united; that is, it makes itself into a universality. But the determination of abstractly universal [*allgemein*] individuality essentially belonging to the 'I' constitutes its *being*. I and my being are therefore inseparably united; the difference of my being from me is a difference that is none. On the one hand we must, of course, distinguish *being* which is absolutely immediate, indeterminate, undifferentiated, from *thought* which is self-differentiating and—by the reduction of difference to a moment— self-mediating, that is, from the 'I'; yet, on the other hand, being is identical with thought, since the latter returns from every mediation to immediacy, from all its self-differentiation to serene unity with itself. The 'I' is, therefore, being or has being as a moment within it. When I set this being as an Other over against me and at the same time as identical with me, I am Knowing [*Wissen*] and have the absolute certainty [*Gewissheit*] of my being. This certainty must not be regarded—as happens from the standpoint of mere mental representation [*Vorstellung*]—as a kind of property of the 'I', as a determination *in* its nature; on the contrary, it is to be grasped as the very nature of the 'I', for this cannot exist without distinguishing itself from itself—which simply means, without being directly aware of itself, without having and being the certainty of itself. For this reason, certainty is related to the 'I' as freedom is to the will. Just as the former constitutes the nature of the 'I', so does the latter constitute the nature of the will. To begin with, however, certainty is to be equated only with subjective freedom, with caprice; it is only objective certainty, truth, that corresponds to the genuine freedom of the will.

Accordingly, the self-certain 'I' is, to begin with, the still quite simple subjectivity, whose freedom is quite abstract, the completely indeterminate ideality or negativity of all limitation. Repelling itself from itself, the 'I' attains, therefore, at first a merely formal, not an actual, difference from itself. But as is demonstrated in Logic, the *implicit* difference must also be made *explicit*, must be developed into an *actual* difference. The manner in which this development proceeds in regard to the 'I' is that the latter—not relapsing into the anthropological sphere, into the unconscious unity of the mental or spiritual [*Geistige*] and the natural, but remaining self-certain and maintaining itself in its freedom—lets its Other unfold itself into a totality similar to the totality of the 'I', and by this very action lets a corporeal being appertaining to the soul become an independent being confronting it, an object [*Gegenstand*] in the strict sense of this word. Since the 'I' is at first only a wholly abstract subjectivity, the merely formal, empty distinguishing of itself from itself, the *actual* difference, the *determinate* content, exists outside of the 'I', belongs solely to the objects. But since the 'I' already possesses *in itself*, or in principle, difference within itself, or, in other words, since it is *in itself* the unity of itself and its Other, it is necessarily related to the difference existent in the object and immediately reflected out of this its Other into itself. The 'I' overlaps or overarches, therefore, the actual difference from itself, is at home with itself in this its Other, and in every intuition remains self-certain. Only when I come to apprehend myself as 'I', does the Other become objective to me, confronts me, and is at the same time converted into an ideal moment in me, and hence brought back to unity with me. That is why in the above Paragraph the 'I' was compared to light. Just as light is the manifestation of itself and its Other, darkness, and can manifest itself only by manifesting that Other, so too the 'I' is manifest to itself only in so far as its Other is manifest to it in the shape of something independent of it.

From this general exposition of the nature of the 'I' it is sufficiently evident that since the 'I' enters into conflict with external objects, it is superior to the impotent natural soul which is entrapped, so to speak, in a childlike unity with the world. * * *

§ 414.] The self-identity of the mind, thus first made explicit as the Ego, is only its abstract formal ideality. As *soul* it was under the phase of *substantial* universality; now, as subjective reflection in itself, it is referred to this substantiality as to its negative, something dark and beyond it. Hence consciousness, like reciprocal dependence in general, is the contradiction between the independence of the two sides and their identity in which they are merged into one. The mind as ego is *essence* [*Wesen*]; but since reality, in the sphere of essence, is represented as in immediate being and at the same time as 'ideal', it is as consciousness only the *appearance* (phenomenon) [*Erscheinung*] of mind [*Geist*].

Zusatz. The negativity which the wholly *abstract* 'I', or mere consciousness, exercises on its Other is as yet completely indeterminate, superficial, not absolute. Consequently, at this stage there arises the contradiction that the object, on the one hand is in me, and on the other hand, has an independent existence outside of me similar to that of darkness outside of light. To consciousness the object appears not as something posited by the 'I', but as something immediate, merely present, given; for consciousness does not as yet know that the object is in itself identical with mind and is released into a seemingly complete independence only by a self-diremption[4] of mind. That this is so, is known only by *us* who have pressed forward to the Idea of mind [*Geist*] and therefore have raised ourselves above the abstract, formal identity of the 'I'.

* * *

§ 417.] The grades [*Stufen*] of this elevation of certainty to truth are three in number: first (*a*) consciousness [*Bewusstsein*] in general, with an object set against it; (*b*) self-consciousness [*Selbstbewusstsein*] for which *ego* is the object; (*c*) unity of consciousness and self-consciousness, where the mind sees itself embodied in the object and sees itself as implicitly and explicitly determinate, as Reason, the *notion* of mind [*Begriff of Geist*].

Zusatz. The three stages of the rise of consciousness to Reason indicated in the above Paragraph are determined by the power of the Notion, which is active alike in the subject as in the object. These stages can therefore be considered as three *judgements* [*Urteile*]. But as we have already remarked, the

---

4. Self-separation or self-division.

abstract 'I', mere consciousness, as yet knows nothing of this. Consequently when the 'non-I' which, to begin with, is for consciousness self-subsistent, is deprived of its self-subsistent status by the power of the Notion active in it, when the object is given the form not of immediacy, externality, and individuality but of a universal, of an inwardness, and consciousness has received this inwardness into itself, the 'I's *own* internalization thereby brought about appears to it as an internalization of the object. Only when the object has been internalized into the 'I' and consciousness has in this way developed into self-consciousness, does mind know the power of its own inwardness as a power present and active in the object. Therefore, what in the sphere of consciousness is only for *us* who contemplate it, becomes in the sphere of self-consciousness for mind itself. Self-consciousness has consciousness for its object, hence sets itself over against it. But, at the same time, consciousness is also retained as a *moment* in self-consciousness itself. Self-consciousness progresses, therefore, to the stage where, by the repulsion of itself from itself, it confronts itself with another self-consciousness and in this gives itself an object with which it is identical and yet which is at the same time self-subsistent. This object is, in the first instance, an immediate, single 'I'. But when this is freed from the form of one-sided subjectivity still clinging to it and grasped as a reality pervaded by the subjectivity of the Notion, consequently as Idea, then self-consciousness leaves behind its opposition to consciousness and moves on to a mediated unity with it and thereby becomes the concrete being-for-self of the 'I', the absolutely free Reason which cognizes in the objective world its own self.

It is hardly necessary to remark that Reason, which in our exposition appears as the third and last stage, is not merely a last stage that has resulted from something extraneous to it but is, on the contrary, the foundation of consciousness and self-consciousness, therefore the *prius*,[5] and by the supersession [*Aufhebung*] of these two one-sided forms it proves itself to be their original unity and their truth.

* * *

SELF-CONSCIOUSNESS

§ 424.] *Self-consciousness* is the truth of consciousness: the latter is a consequence of the former, all consciousness of an other object being as a matter of fact also self-consciousness.[6] The object is my idea[7]: I am aware of the object as mine; and thus in it I am aware of me. The formula of self-consciousness is I = I:—abstract freedom, pure 'Ideality'; and thus it lacks 'reality': for as it is its own object, there is strictly speaking no object, because there is no distinction between it and the object.

Zusatz. In the formula, I = I, is enunciated the principle of absolute Reason and freedom. Freedom and Reason consist in this, that I raise myself to the

---

5. Precondition (literally, "something that precedes"; Latin).
6. Better translated: "The truth of consciousness [what it turns out essentially to be and developmentally to become] is *self-consciousness*, and the latter is the ground [*Grund*, 'foundation' or 'basis'] of the former, so that in existence [*in der Existenz*, 'in reality'] all consciousness of another object is self-consciousness."
7. That is, representation (*Vorstellung*).

form of I = I, that I know everything as mine, as 'I', that I grasp every object as a member in the system of what I myself am, in short, that I have in one and the same consciousness myself and the world, that in the world I find myself again, and conversely, in my consciousness have what *is*, what possesses *objectivity*.[8] This unity of the 'I' and the object which constitutes the principle of mind is, however, at first only *abstractly* present in *immediate* self-consciousness, and is known only by *us* who reflect on it, not as yet by self-consciousness itself. Immediate self-consciousness has not as yet for its object the I = I, but only the 'I'; therefore, it is free only for us, not for itself, is not as yet aware of its freedom, and contains only the foundation of it, but not as yet freedom that is truly *actual*.

§ 425.] Abstract self-consciousness is the first negation of consciousness, and for that reason it is burdened with an external object, or, nominally, with the negation of it. Thus it is at the same time the antecedent stage, consciousness: it is the contradiction of itself as self-consciousness and as consciousness. But the latter aspect and the negation in general is in I = I potentially suppressed; and hence as this certitude of self against the object it is the *impulse* to realize its implicit nature, by giving its abstract self-awareness content and objectivity, and in the other direction to free itself from its sensuousness, to set aside the given objectivity and identify it with itself. The two processes are one and the same, the identification of its consciousness and self-consciousness.

Zusatz. The defect of abstract self-consciousness lies in the fact that it and consciousness are still simply two different things, that they have not yet made themselves equal to each other. In consciousness, we see the tremendous *difference*, on the one side, of the 'I', this wholly *simple* existence, and on the other side, of the infinite variety of the world. It is this opposition of the 'I' and the world which has not yet reached a genuine mediation, that constitutes the finitude of consciousness. Self-consciousness, on the other hand, has its finitude in its still quite abstract self-identity. What is present in the I = I of immediate self-consciousness is a difference that merely *ought* to be, not yet a *posited* or *actual* difference.

This disunion between self-consciousness and consciousness forms an internal contradiction of self-consciousness with itself, because the latter is also its immediately antecedent stage—consciousness—consequently, is the opposite of itself. In other words, since abstract self-consciousness is only the *first*, hence still *conditioned*, negation of the immediacy of consciousness, and not already *absolute* negativity, that is, negation of that negation, infinite affirmation, it has itself still the form of mere being, of an immediate, of a being which in spite of, or rather just on account of, its differenceless internal being is still filled with external being. Therefore, it contains negation not merely within

---

8. For Hegel, self-identity ("I = I") is not just true in a formal-logical sense of everything: it also (and more importantly and substantively) reflects an essential identity of subjectivity and objectivity, and thus of the essential nature of the self and that of the various sorts of reality—objects, institutions, culture, and the entire world of nature and history more generally—with which we find ourselves confronted (seemingly as "alien" realities, but actually as expressions of an essential reality that is also our own). This bears importantly on his conception of the relation of the self (and self-identity) to the various sorts of objectivity we encounter in our experience.

it but also outside of it as an external object, as a 'non-I', and it is just this that makes it consciousness.

The contradiction here outlined must be resolved, and the way in which this happens is that self-consciousness which has itself as consciousness, as 'I', for object, goes on to develop the simple ideality of the 'I' into a real difference, and thus by superseding its one-sided subjectivity gives itself objectivity; this process is identical with its converse, by which the object is at the same time given a subjective determination by the 'I', is immersed in the inwardness of the self, and in this way the dependence of the 'I' on an external reality which is a feature of consciousness is destroyed. Self-consciousness thus reaches the stage where it does not have consciousness *alongside* it, is not externally connected with it, but truly pervades it and contains it dissolved within it.

To reach this goal, self-consciousness has to traverse three developmental stages.

1. The first of these stages presents us with the single self-consciousness which is immediate, simply self-identical, and at the same time and contradictorily, is related to an external object. As thus determined, self-consciousness is the certainty of itself as merely being, in face of which the object has the determination of something only seemingly independent, but is in fact a nullity. This is *appetitive*[9] *self-consciousness*.

2. On the second stage, the objective 'I' acquires the determination of another 'I', and hence there arises the relation of one self-consciousness to another self-consciousness, and between these two the *process* of *recognition*. Here, self-consciousness is no longer merely a single self-consciousness, but in it there already begins a union of *individuality*[1] and *universality* [*Allgemeinheit*].[2]

3. Furthermore, since the otherness of the selves confronting each other is overcome and these, though independent are yet identical with each other, there emerges the third stage, *universal self-consciousness*.

* * *

SELF-CONSCIOUSNESS RECOGNITIVE[3]

§ 430.] Here there is a self-consciousness for a self-consciousness, at first *immediately*, as one of two things for another. In that other as ego I behold myself, and yet also an immediately existing object, another ego absolutely independent of me and opposed to me. (The suppression of the singleness of self-consciousness was only a first step in the suppression, and it merely led to the characterization of it as *particular*.) This contradiction gives either self-consciousness the impulse to *show* itself as a free self, and to exist as such for the other:—the process of *recognition* [*Anerkennen*].

* * *

§ 431.] The process is a battle. I cannot be aware of me as myself in another individual, so long as I see in that other an other and an immediate existence:

---

9. That is, desiring (*begehrende*).
1. That is, particularity (*Einzelheit*).
2. That is, generality.
3. "Das anerkennende Selbstbewusstsein": that is, the sort of self-consciousness associated with the mutual encounter of subjects who recognize each other to be like themselves (conscious desiring agents). Mutual *recognition* of this sort is a phenomenon of great significance in Hegel's philosophy (and phenomenology) of *Geist*.

and I am consequently bent upon the suppression of this immediacy of his. But in like measure *I* cannot be recognized as immediate, except so far as I overcome the mere immediacy on my own part, and thus give existence to my freedom. But this immediacy is at the same time the corporeity of self-consciousness, in which as in its sign and tool the latter has its own *sense of self*, and its being *for others*, and the means for entering into relation with them.

* * *

§ 432.] The fight of recognition is a life and death struggle: either self-consciousness imperils the other's life, and incurs a like peril for its own— but only peril, for either is no less bent on maintaining his life, as the existence of his freedom. Thus the death of one, though *** it, from one point of view, solves the contradiction, is yet, from the essential point of view (i.e. the outward and visible recognition), a new contradiction (for that recognition is at the same time undone by the other's death), greater than the other.

Zusatz. *** To prevent any possible misunderstandings with regard to the standpoint just outlined, we must here remark that the fight for recognition pushed to the extreme here indicated can only occur in the natural state, where men exist only as single, separate individuals; but it is absent in civil society and the State because here the recognition for which the combatants fought already exists. For although the State may originate in violence, it does not rest on it; violence, in producing the State, has brought into existence only what is justified in and for itself, namely, laws and a constitution. What dominates in the State is the spirit [*Geist*] of the people [*Volk*], custom, and law. There man is recognized and treated as a *rational* being, as free, as a person; and the individual, on his side, makes himself worthy of this recognition by overcoming the natural state of his self-consciousness and obeying a universal [*Allgemeine*],[4] the will that is in essence and actuality will, the *law*; he behaves, therefore, towards others in a manner that is universally valid [*allgemeingültig*],[5] recognizing them—as he wishes others to recognize him—as free, as persons. In the State, the citizen derives his honour from the post he fills, from the trade he follows, and from any other kind of working activity. His honour thereby has a content that is substantial, universal [*allgemein*], objective, and no longer dependent on an empty subjectivity; honour of this kind is still lacking in the natural state where individuals, whatever they may be and whatever they may do, want to compel others to recognize them.

* * *

§ 433.] But because life is as requisite as liberty[6] to the solution, the fight ends in the first instance as a one-sided negation with inequality. While the one combatant prefers life, retains his single self-consciousness, but surrenders his claim for recognition, the other holds fast to his self-assertion and is recognized by the former as his superior. Thus arises the status of *master and slave*.[7]

---

4. That is, something general.
5. That is, valid for all within the community.
6. That is, freedom (*Freiheit*).

7. Better translated: "the relationship [*Verhältnis*] of *mastery* [*Herrschaft*, 'dominance'] and *servitude* [*Knechtschaft*, 'subjection']."

In the battle for recognition and the subjugation under a master, we see, on their phenomenal side, the emergence of man's social life and the commencement of political union. *Force*, which is the basis of this phenomenon, is not on that account a basis of right [*Recht*], but only the necessary and legitimate factor in the passage from the state of self-consciousness sunk in appetite and selfish isolation into the state of universal [*allgemein*] self-consciousness. Force, then, is the external or phenomenal commencement of states, not their underlying and essential principle.

Zusatz. The relationship of master and slave [*Herrschaft und Knechtschaft*] contains only a *relative* removal of the contradiction between the particularity, reflected into itself, of the distinct self-conscious subjects and their mutual identity. For in this relationship the immediacy of particular self-consciousness is, to begin with, removed only on the side of the slave,[8] but on the master's side it is preserved. As long as the natural state of life persists on both sides, the self-will of the slave surrenders itself to that of his master, receives for its content the purposes of his master who, on his part, receives into his self-consciousness, not the slave's will, but only care for the support of the slave's physical life; in such a manner that in this relationship the *realized* identity of the self-consciousness of the subjects in relation is achieved only onesidedly.

As regards the historical side of this relationship, it can be remarked that ancient peoples, the Greeks and Romans, had not yet risen to the Notion of absolute freedom, since they did not know that man as such, man as this universal [*allgemein*] 'I', as rational self-consciousness, is entitled to freedom. On the contrary, with them a man was held to be free only if he was born free. With them, therefore, freedom still had the character of a natural state. That is why slavery [*Sklaverei*] existed in their free States and bloody wars developed in which the slaves tried to free themselves, to obtain recognition of their eternal human rights.

§ 434. This status, in the first place, implies *common* [*Gemeinsamkeit*][9] wants and common concern for their satisfaction—for the means of mastery, the slave, must likewise be kept in life.[1] In place of the rude destruction of the immediate object there ensues acquisition, preservation, and formation of it, as the instrumentality in which the two extremes of independence and non-independence are welded together. The form of universality [*Allgemeinheit*] thus arising in satisfying the want, creates a *permanent* means and a provision which takes care for and secures the future.

§ 435.] But secondly, when we look to the distinction of the two, the master beholds in the slave and his servitude the supremacy of his *single* self-hood resulting from the suppression of immediate self-hood, a suppression, however, which falls on another. This other, the slave, however, in the service of the master, works off his individualist self-will,[2] overcomes the inner immediacy of appe-

---

8. That is, servant (*Knecht*).
9. That is, commonality of.
1. That is, the slave or servant, upon whose existence the master's existence and position depends,
must be kept alive.
2. That is, in the service of the master, the slave/servant works off (overcomes) his own particular will (*seinen Einzel- und Eigenwillen*).

tite, and in this divestment of self and in 'the fear of his lord' makes 'the beginning of wisdom'[3]—the passage to universal [*allgemein*] self-consciousness.

Zusatz. Since the slave works for the master and therefore not in the exclusive interest of his own individuality,[4] his desire is expanded into being not only the desire of this particular individual but also the desire of another. Accordingly, the slave rises above the selfish individuality of his natural will, and his worth to that extent exceeds that of his master who, imprisoned in his egotism, beholds in the slave only his immediate will and is only formally recognized by an unfree consciousness. This subjugation[5] of the slave's egotism forms the *beginning* of true human freedom. This quaking of the single, isolated will, the feeling of the worthlessness of egotism, the habit of obedience, is a necessary moment in the education [*Bildung*] of all men. Without having experienced the discipline which breaks self-will, no one becomes free, rational, and capable of command. To become free, to acquire the capacity for self-control, all nations [*Völker*][6] must therefore undergo the severe discipline of subjection to a master. * * *

As we have said, this servile obedience forms only the *beginning* of freedom, because that to which the natural individuality of self-consciousness subjects itself is not the truly universal [*allgemein*], rational will which is in and for itself, but the single, contingent will of another person. Here, then, only one moment of freedom is manifested, that of the negativity of the egotistic individuality; whereas the positive side of freedom attains actuality only when, on the one hand, the servile self-consciousness, freeing itself both from the individuality [*Einzelheit*] of the master and from its own individuality [*Einzelheit*], grasps the absolutely rational in its universality [*Allgemeinheit*] which is independent of the particularity of the subjects; and when, on the other hand, the master's self-consciousness is brought by the *community* [*Gemeinsamkeit*] of needs and the concern for their satisfaction existing between him and the slave, and also by beholding the suppression of the immediate individual [*einzelne*] will made objective in the slave, to realize that this suppression is the truth in regard to himself, too, and therefore to subject his own selfish will to the law of the will that is in and for itself.

UNIVERSAL [*ALLGEMEIN*] SELF-CONSCIOUSNESS

§ 436.] Universal [*Allgemein*] self-consciousness is the affirmative awareness of self in an other self: each self as a free individuality [*Einzelheit*] has his own 'absolute' independence, yet in virtue of the negation of its immediacy or appetite without distinguishing itself from that other. Each is thus universal [*allgemein*] self-consciousness and objective; each has 'real' universality in the shape of reciprocity, so far as each knows itself recognized in the other freeman, and is aware of this in so far as it recognizes the other and knows him to be free.

This universal reappearance of self-consciousness—the Notion which is aware of itself in its objectivity as a subjectivity identical with itself and for that reason universal—is the form of consciousness which lies at the root of all true mental or spiritual life [*Geistigkeit*][7]—in family, fatherland, state,

---

3. An echo of Psalm 111:10, which begins "The fear of the LORD is the beginning of wisdom" (RSV).
4. That is, "particularity," "idiosyncrasy" (*Einzelheit*).

5. That is, suppression (*Unterwerfung*).
6. That is, peoples.
7. That is, spirituality.

and of all virtues, love, friendship, valour, honour, fame. But this appearance of the underlying essence[8] may also be severed from that essence, and be maintained apart in worthless honour, idle fame, etc.

* * *

FROM C. PSYCHOLOGY: MIND [GEIST]

§ 440.] Mind [Geist] has defined itself[9] as the truth of soul and consciousness—the former a simple immediate totality, the latter now an infinite form which is not, like consciousness, restricted by that content, and does not stand in mere correlation to it as to its object, but is an awareness of this substantial totality, neither subjective nor objective. Mind, therefore, starts only from its own being and is in correlation only with its own features.

Psychology accordingly studies the faculties or general modes of mental activity qua mental[1]—mental vision, ideation, remembering, etc., desires, etc.—apart both from the content, which on the phenomenal side is found in empirical ideation, in thinking also and in desire and will, and from the two forms in which these modes exist, viz. in the soul as a physical mode, and in consciousness itself as a separately existent object of that consciousness. This, however, is not an arbitrary abstraction by the psychologist. Mind [Geist] is just this elevation above nature and physical modes, and above the complication with an external object—in one word, above the material, as its concept has just shown. All it has now to do is to realize this Notion of its freedom, and get rid of the form of immediacy with which it once more begins. The content which is elevated to intuitions[2] is its sensations: it is its intuitions also which are transmuted into representations [Vorstellungen], and its representations which are transmuted again into thoughts [Gedanken], etc.

Zusatz. Free mind or spirit [Geist],[3] or mind as such, is Reason which sunders itself, on the one hand, into pure infinite form, into a limitless Knowing, and, on the other hand, into the object that is identical with that Knowing. Here, this Knowing has as yet no other content but itself, but it is determined as embracing within itself all objectivity, so that the object is not anything externally related to mind or anything mind cannot grasp. Mind is thus the absolutely universal certainty of itself, free from any opposition whatever. Therefore, it is confident that in the world it will find its own self, that the world must be reconciled with it, that, just as Adam said of Eve that she was flesh of his flesh,[4] so mind has to seek in the world Reason that is its own Reason. We have found Reason to be the unity of subjectivity and objectivity, of the Notion that exists for itself, and of reality. Since, therefore, mind is the absolute certainty of itself, a knowing of Reason, it is knowledge of the unity

---

8. That is, substantiality (Substantiellen).
9. That is, "has determined itself" (hat sich bestimmt).
1. What Hegel actually writes is "des Geistes als solchen." His point is that his kind of philosophical psychology deals with the faculties or general modes "of Geist as such"—that is, with the things he goes on to list "as faculties or general modes of

Geist."
2. That is, perceptions (Anschauungen).
3. That is, the specific type or form of Geist Hegel is discussing here: it is the highest form or level of subjective Geist, but not the highest of all forms or levels of Geist.
4. Genesis 2:23.

of subjectivity and objectivity, knowledge that its object is the Notion [*Begriff*] and that the Notion is objective. *Free* mind or spirit [*Geist*] thereby shows itself to be the unity of the two universal [*allgemein*] stages of development considered in the first and second main parts of the doctrine of subjective mind, namely, of the soul, this simple spiritual [*geistig*] substance, or of mind [*Geist*] in its immediacy, and of consciousness or manifested mind, the self-diremption of this substance. For the determinations of *free* mind have, in common with those of the soul, the subjective element, and in common with those of consciousness, the objective element. The principle of free mind [*Geist*] is to make the merely given element [*das Seiende*] in consciousness into something mental [*Seelenhaftes*], and conversely to make what is mental [*das Seelenhafte*] into an objectivity. *Free* mind stands, like consciousness, as one side over against the object, and is at the same time both sides and there-fore, like the soul, a totality. Accordingly, whereas soul was truth only as an immediate unconscious totality, and whereas in consciousness, on the con-trary, this totality was divided into the 'I' and the object external to it, *free* mind or spirit [*Geist*], is to be cognized as *self-knowing truth*.

* * *

§ 442.] The progress of mind [*Geist*] is *development*, in so far as its existent phase, viz. knowledge [*Wissen*], involves as its intrinsic purpose and burden that utter and complete autonomy which is rationality; in which case the action of translating this purpose into reality is strictly only a nominal passage over into manifestation, and is even there a return into itself. So far as knowl-edge [*Wissen*] which has not shaken off its original quality of *mere* knowl-edge is only abstract or formal, the goal of mind [*Geist*] is to give it objective fulfilment, and thus at the same time produce its freedom.

The development here meant is not that of the individual (which has a cer-tain *anthropological* character), where faculties and forces are regarded as suc-cessively emerging and presenting themselves in external existence—a series of steps, on the ascertainment of which there was for a long time great stress laid (by the system of Condillac),[5] as if a conjectural natural emergence could exhibit the origin of these faculties and *explain* them. * * *

Similarly, if the activities of mind [*Geist*] are treated as mere manifesta-tions, forces, perhaps in terms stating their utility or suitability for some other interest of head or heart, there is no indication of the true final aim of the whole business. That can only be the intelligible unity of mind, and its activ-ity can only have itself as aim; i.e. its aim can only be to get rid of the form of immediacy or subjectivity, to reach and get hold of itself, and to liberate itself to itself. In this way the so-called faculties of mind [*Geist*] as thus distin-guished are only to be treated as steps of this liberation. And this is the only *rational* mode of studying the mind and its various activities.

Zusatz. The existence of mind, or *Knowing* [*das Wissen*], is the absolute form, that is, the form that itself contains the content, or the Notion that

---

5. Etienne Bonnot de Condillac (1715–1780), a French philosopher of the Enlightenment who rejected the doctrine of innate ideas and advo-cated a radical empiricism, known as "sensational-ism," according to which everything in and about knowledge and cognition derives from sense experience.

exists as Notion and gives itself its own reality. Consequently, the fact that the content or object is for our Knowing something *given*, something coming to it *from outside*, is only an illusory appearance and mind, by removing [*Aufhebung*] this appearance, proves itself to be what it is in itself, namely, absolutely self-determining, the infinite negativity of what is external to mind and to itself, the ideal existence that produces all reality *from itself*.[6] The progress of mind has, therefore, only this meaning, that this illusory appearance is removed, that Knowing proves itself to be the form that develops all content from itself. Consequently, the activity of mind [*Geist*], far from being restricted to a mere acceptance of a given material must, on the contrary, be called a creative activity even though the products of mind, in so far as mind is only subjective, do not as yet receive the form of immediate actuality but retain a more or less ideal existence.

§ 443.] As consciousness has for its object the stage which preceded it, viz. the natural soul (§ 413), so mind [*Geist*] has or rather makes consciousness its object: i.e. whereas consciousness is only the virtual identity of the ego with its other (§ 415), mind realizes that identity as the concrete unity which it and it only knows. Its productions are governed by the principle of all reason that the contents are at once potentially existent, and are mind's own, in freedom. Thus, if we consider the initial aspect of mind, that aspect is twofold—as *being* and as *its own*: by the one, mind finds in itself something which *is*, by the other it affirms it to be only *its own*. The way of mind [*Geist*] is therefore

(a) to be theoretical: it has to do with the rational as its immediate affection[7] which it must render its own: or it has to free knowledge from its presupposedness and therefore from its abstractness, and make the affection subjective. When the affection [*Bestimmtheit*] has been rendered its own, and the knowledge consequently characterized as free intelligence, i.e. as having its full and free characterization in itself, it is

(b) Will: *practical* mind [*Geist*], which in the first place is likewise formal— i.e. its content is at first *only* its own, and is immediately willed; and it proceeds next to liberate its volition from its subjectivity, which is the one-sided form of its contents, so that it

(c) confronts itself as *free*[8] mind [*Geist*] and thus gets rid of both its defects of one-sidedness.

Zusatz. Whereas one cannot very well say of consciousness that it possesses impulse [*Trieb*] since it possesses the object *immediately*, mind [*Geist*], on the other hand, must be grasped as impulse because it is essentially activity. This is, in the first place,

(a) the activity by which the seemingly *alien* object receives, instead of the shape of something given, isolated and contingent, the form of something inwardized, subjective, universal [*allgemein*], necessary, and rational. Mind, by undertaking this alteration of the object, reacts against the one-sidedness

---

6. In speaking of *das Ideelle* (here translated as "the ideal existence," but better rendered as "the very nature of the *Idee*") as that which "produces all reality *from itself*," and also as *Geist*, Hegel is referring not to "subjective *Geist*" or to particular instances of *Geist*, but rather to "what it is in itself"—to *Geist*'s essential nature, which is fundamentally identical with that of the *Idee*.
7. That is, determinateness (*Bestimmtheit*).
8. That is, self-determining.

of consciousness which relates itself to objects as to things immediately given and does not know them in a subjective form. As such it is theoretical mind. In this, the urge to know is dominant, the craving for knowledge [of external things].[9] Of the content of this knowledge I know that it *is*, that it has objectivity, and at the same time that it is in me and therefore subjective. Here, therefore, the object no longer has, as at the stage of consciousness, the determination of being negative towards the 'I'.

(*b*) Practical mind [*Geist*] pursues the opposite course. Unlike theoretical mind, it does not start from the seemingly alien object, but from its own aims and interests, that is, from subjective determinations, and *then* proceeds to make these into an objectivity. In doing this it reacts against the one-sided subjectivity of self-consciousness that is shut up within itself, just as theoretical mind reacts against the consciousness that is dependent on a given object.

* * *

MIND [*GEIST*] PRACTICAL [*DER PRAKTISCHE GEIST*]

§ 469.] As will, mind [*Geist*] is aware that it is the author of its own conclusions, the origin of its self-fulfilment.[1] Thus fulfilled, this independency or individuality forms the side of existence or of *reality* for the Idea of mind. As will, the mind [*Geist*] steps into actuality; whereas as cognition it is on the soil of notional generality.[2] Supplying its own content, the will is self-possessed, and in the widest sense free: this is its characteristic trait. Its finitude lies in the formalism that the spontaneity of its self-fulfilment means no more than a general and abstract ownness, not yet identified with matured reason. It is the function of the essential will to bring liberty [*Freiheit*] to exist in the formal will, and it is therefore the aim of that formal will to fill itself with its essential nature, i.e. to make liberty [*Freiheit*] its pervading character, content, and aim, as well as its sphere of existence. The essential freedom of will is, and must always be, a thought:[3] hence the way by which will can make itself objective mind [*Geist*] is to rise to be a thinking will—to give itself the content which it can only have as it thinks itself.

True liberty [*Freiheit*], in the shape of moral life[4], consists in the will finding its purpose in a universal [*allgemein*] content, not in subjective or selfish interests.[5] But such a content is only possible in thought and through thought: it is nothing short of absurd to seek to banish thought from the moral, religious, and law-abiding life.[6]

Zusatz. * * * [W]ill at the start of its self-objectification is still burdened with the form of subjectivity. But here, in the sphere of *subjective* mind, we have only to pursue this externalization to the point where volitional intelligence

9. Translator's brackets.
1. Better translated: "As will, *Geist* knows itself [*weiss sich*] as determining itself [i.e., making decisions] internally [*sich in sich beschliessend*] and fulfilling itself externally [*sich aus sich erfüllend*]."
2. This translates "the *Allgemeinheit* of the *Begriff*." The point is that, in contrast with *knowing* (*Wissen*), in which *Geist* is operating on the plane of conceptual/structural generalty, in *willing* it actively engages with the real world.

3. That is, this *Begriff*, freedom, essentially involves thought (*Denken*).
4. That is, ethicality (*Sittlichkeit*).
5. That is, *true* freedom, as ethicality (*Sittlichkeit*), involves the will taking as its objectives (*Zwecken*) content that is not subjective (i.e., "selfish," *eigensüchtig*) but rather *general* (*allgemein*).
6. Better translated: "from ethicality, religiousness, lawfulness, and so forth" (*Sittlichkeit, Religiosität, Rechtlichkeit, usf.*).

becomes objective mind [*Geist*], that is, to the point where the product of will ceases to be merely enjoyment and starts to become deed and action.

Now, in general, the course of development of practical mind [*Geist*] is as follows.

At first, will appears in the form of immediacy; it has not yet *posited* itself as intelligence freely and objectively determining itself, but only *finds* itself as such objective determining. As such, it is (1) *practical feeling*, has a *single* content and is itself an *immediately individual, subjective* will which, as we have just said, feels itself as objectively determining, but still lacks a content that is liberated from the form of subjectivity, a content that is truly objective and universal [*allgemein*] in and for itself. For this reason, will is, to begin with, only *implicitly* or notionally [*seinen Begriff nach*][7] free. But it belongs to the Idea of freedom that the will should make its Notion, which is *freedom itself*, its content or aim. When it does this it becomes *objective* mind [*Geist*], constructs for itself a world of its freedom, and thus gives to its true Content a self-subsistent existence. But will achieves this aim only by ridding itself of its [abstract][8] individuality, by developing its initially only implicit universality [*Allgemeinheit*] into a content that is universality [*allgemein*] in and for itself.

The next step on this path is made by will when (2), as impulse, it goes on to make the agreement of its inward determinateness with objectivity, which in feeling is only *given*, into an agreement that *ought* first to be *posited* by will.

The further step consists (3) in the subordination of *particular* impulses to a *universal* one [*Allgemeinen*]—happiness. But since this universal [*Allgemeine*][9] is only a universality of reflection, it remains external to the particular aspect of the impulses, and is connected with this particular aspect only by the wholly abstract individual will, that is, by *caprice*.

Both the indeterminate universal of happiness as well as the immediate particularity of impulses and the abstract individuality of caprice are, in their mutual externality, untrue, and that is why they come together in the will that wills the *concrete* universal [*Allgemeine*], the Notion of freedom which, as already remarked, forms the goal of practical mind [*Geist*].

* * *

§ 474.] Inclinations and passions embody the same constituent features as the practical feeling. Thus, while, on one hand, they are based on the rational nature of the mind [*Geist*]; they, on the other, as part and parcel of the still subjective and single will, are infected with contingency, and appear as particular to stand to the individual and to each other in an external relation and with a necessity which creates bondage.[1]

The special note in *passion* is its restriction to one special mode of volition, in which the whole subjectivity of the individual is merged, be the value of that mode what it may. In consequence of this formalism, passion is neither good nor bad; the title only states that a subject has thrown his whole soul— his interests of intellect, talent, character, enjoyment—on one aim and object. Nothing great has been and nothing great can be accomplished without

---

7. That is, essentially.
8. Translator's brackets.
9. That is, general principle.
1. That is, the inclinations and passions are related

to the individual and to each other in a merely contingent and haphazard way, owing to an unfree (i.e., imposed rather than self-determined) necessity (*hiermit nach unfreier Notwendigkeit*).

passion.[2] It is only a dead, too often, indeed, a hypocritical moralizing which inveighs against the form of passion as such.

But with regard to the inclinations, the question is directly raised, Which are good and bad?—Up to what degree the good continue good;—and (as there are many, each with its private range) In what way have they, being all in one subject and hardly all, as experience shows, admitting of gratification, to suffer at least reciprocal restriction? And, first of all, as regards the numbers of these impulses and propensities, the case is much the same as with the psychical powers, whose aggregate is to form the mind theoretical—an aggregate which is now increased by the host of impulses. The nominal rationality of impulse and propensity lies merely in their general impulse not to be subjective merely, but to get realized, overcoming the subjectivity by the subject's own agency. Their genuine rationality cannot reveal its secret to a method of outer reflection which pre-supposes a number of *independent* innate tendencies and immediate instincts, and therefore is wanting[3] in a single principle and final purpose for them. But the immanent 'reflection' of mind itself carries it beyond their particularity and their natural immediacy, and gives their contents a rationality and objectivity, in which they exist as necessary ties of social relation, as rights and duties. It is this objectification which evinces their real value, their mutual connections, and their truth. And thus it was a true perception when Plato (especially including as he did the mind's whole nature under its right)[4] showed that the full reality of justice could be exhibited only in the *objective* phase of justice, namely in the construction of the State as the ethical life [*sittliche Leben*].

The answer to the question, therefore, What are the good and rational propensities, and how they are to be co-ordinated with each other? resolves itself into an exposition of the laws and forms of common life produced by mind [*Geist*] when developing itself as *objective* mind [*Geist*]—a development in which the *content* of autonomous action loses its contingency and optionality. The discussion of the true intrinsic worth of the impulses, inclinations, and passions is thus essentially the theory of legal, moral, and social *duties*.

* * *

FREE MIND [*DER FREIE GEIST*]

§ 481.] Actual free will is the unity of theoretical and practical mind: a free will, which realizes its own freedom of will, now that the formalism, fortuitousness, and contractedness of the practical content up to this point have been superseded [*aufgehoben*]. By superseding the adjustments of means therein contained, the will is the *immediate individuality* self-instituted—an individuality, however, also purified of all that interferes with its universalism [*Allgemeinheit*],[5]

2. This famous statement is an important corrective to a simplistic, overly rationalistic understanding of Hegel's emphasis on "reason" and the fundamentally "rational" nature of *Geist* and of reality generally (social and historical as well as natural).
3. That is, lacking.
4. That is, also insofar as Plato construed the entire nature of *Geist* in terms of the "right" (rightness, normativity) of *Geist* (*unter dem Rechte des Geistes*). In the *Republic*, the Greek philosopher

Plato (ca. 427–ca. 347 B.C.E.) discusses ethical life by describing the structure of his conception of an ideal city-state.
5. That is, purified of all that interferes with its "*general* determination" (*allgemeinen Bestimmung*)—in other words, of all that interferes with its determination in accordance with *general rules* rather than particular impulses. That, Hegel immediately goes on to say, is "freedom itself [*Freiheit selbst*]."

i.e. with freedom itself. This universalism [*allgemein Bestimmung*] the will has as its object and aim, only so far as it thinks itself, knows this its concept, and is *will* as free *intelligence*.

§ 482.] The mind [*Geist*] which knows itself as free and wills itself as this its object, i.e. which has its true being for characteristic and aim, is in the first instance the rational will in general, or *implicit* Idea, and because implicit only the Notion of absolute mind. As *abstract* again, it is existent only in the *immediate* will—it is the *existential* side of reason—the *single* will as aware of this its universality [*Allgemeinheit*] constituting its contents and aim, and of which it is only the formal activity. If the will, therefore, in which the Idea thus appears is only finite, that will is also the act of developing the Idea, and of investing its self-unfolding content with an existence which, as realizing the Idea, is *actuality* [*Wirklichkeit*]. It is thus 'Objective' Mind [*Geist*].

No idea is so generally recognized as indefinite, ambiguous, and open to the greatest misconceptions (to which therefore it actually falls a victim) as the idea of Liberty [*Freiheit*]: none in common currency with so little appreciation of its meaning. Remembering that *free* mind [*Geist*] is *actual* mind [*Geist*], we can see how misconceptions about it are of tremendous consequence in practice. When individuals and nations[6] have once got in their heads the abstract concept of full-blown liberty [*Freiheit*], there is nothing like it in its uncontrollable strength, just because it is the very essence of mind [*Geist*], and that as its very actuality. Whole continents, Africa and the East, have never had this Idea, and are without it still. The Greeks and Romans, Plato and Aristotle, even the Stoics,[7] did not have it. On the contrary, they saw that it is only by birth (as, for example, an Athenian or Spartan citizen), or by strength of character, education, or philosophy (—the sage is free even as a slave and in chains) that the human being is actually free. It was through Christianity that this idea came into the world. According to Christianity, the individual *as such* has an infinite value as the object and aim of divine love, destined as mind [*Geist*] to live in absolute relationship with God himself, and have God's mind [*Geist*] dwelling in him: i.e. man is implicitly destined to supreme freedom. If, in religion as such, man is aware of this relationship to the absolute mind [*Geist*], as his true being, he has also, even when he steps into the sphere of secular existence, the divine mind [*Geist*] present with him, as the substance of the state, of the family, etc. These institutions are due to the guidance of that spirit [*Geist*], and are constituted after its measure; whilst by their existence the moral temper comes to be indwelling in the individual,[8] so that in this sphere of particular existence, of present sensation and volition, he is *actually* free.

If to be aware of the Idea [*Idee*]—to be aware, that is, that men[9] are aware of freedom as their essence, aim, and object—is matter of *speculation*, still this very Idea itself is the actuality of men—not something which they *have*, as men, but which they *are*.[1] Christianity in its adherents has realized an

---

6. That is, peoples (*Völker*).
7. Stoicism, a philosophical school founded in 3rd c. B.C.E. Greece, stressed freedom but conceived of it in a fundamentally external way, as freedom from dependence on things beyond one's control.
8. Better translated: "while the disposition of ethicality [*die Gesinnung der Sittlichkeit*] is instilled in

the individual through these institutions."
9. That is, humans (*Menschen*).
1. A sentence that illustrates Hegel's distinctive use of the term *Idee*, here referring to the "actuality" of human beings who do not merely exist but do so in a manner that fully accords with their essential nature, and so are human beings "in truth."

ever-present sense that they are not and cannot be slaves; if they are made slaves, if the decision as regards their property rests with an arbitrary will, not with laws or courts of justice, they would find the very substance of their life outraged. This will to liberty [*Freiheit*] is no longer an *impulse* which demands its satisfaction, but the permanent character—the spiritual [*geistig*] consciousness grown into a non-impulsive nature. But this freedom, which the content and aim of freedom has, is itself only a Notion [*Begriff*]—a principle of the mind [*Geist*] and heart, intended to develop into an objective phase, into legal, moral [*sittlich*], religious, and not less into scientific [*wissenschaftlich*] actuality.

SOURCE: *Hegel's Philosophy of Mind: Being Part Three of the "Encyclopaedia of the Philosophical Sciences" (1830)*, trans. William Wallace and A. V. Miller (Oxford: Clarendon Press, 1971), pp. 25–30, 51, 147, 151–55, 157–58, 165–47, 170–76, 179–80, 183–85, 228–29, 235–36, 238–40. Except where otherwise indicated, German words in brackets are the terminology used in the German original, inserted by the editor in addition to their renderings in the translation. This edition adds to Wallace's 1894 translation of the 1830 *Philosophie des Geistes*, part 3 of *Enzyklopädie der philosophischen Wissenschaften*, Miller's translation of the *Zusätze* or "additions" (marked *Zusatz*) that were incorporated into the work in 1845; they were compiled after Hegel's death from lecture notes (both his students' and his own).

On Consciousness and Self-Consciousness

From Phenomenology of *Geist*

From *Part A. Consciousness*

FROM SENSE-CERTAINTY [*DIE SINNLICHE GEWISSHEIT*] —THE "THIS," AND "MEANING."

The knowledge [*Wissen*], which is at the start or immediately our object, can be nothing else than just that which is immediate[1] knowledge, knowledge of the immediate, of what *is*. We have, in dealing with it, to proceed, too, in an immediate way, to accept what is given, not altering anything in it as it is presented before us, and keeping mere apprehension [*Auffassen*] free from conceptual comprehension [*Begreifen*].

The concrete content which sensuous certainty furnishes makes this immediately[2] appear to be the richest kind of knowledge, to be even a knowledge of endless wealth—a wealth to which we can as little find any limit when we traverse its *extent* in space and time, where that content is presented before us, as when we take a fragment out of the abundance it offers us and by dividing and dividing seek to penetrate its *intent*. Besides that, it seems to be the truest, most genuine [*wahrhafteste*] knowledge: for it has not as yet dropped anything from the object, having it before itself in its entirety and completeness. This bare fact of *certainty*, however, is in fact the abstractest and the poorest kind of *truth*. It merely says regarding what it knows: it *is*; and its truth contains solely the *being* of the matter [*Sache*][3] before it. Consciousness,

---

1. That is, unmediated (*unmittelbares*).
2. That is, initially (*unmittelbar*).

3. In the sense of "the matter at hand" (not "material substance").

on its part, in this form of certainty, takes the shape merely of pure I [*Ich*]. In other words, I here *am* merely as pure This, and the object likewise *is* merely as pure This. I—*this* particular conscious I—am certain of *this* matter before me, not because I as consciousness have developed myself in connection with it and in manifold ways set thought to work about it: and not, again, because the matter, of which I am certain, in virtue of its having a multitude of distinct qualities, was replete with possible modes of relation and a variety of connections with other things. Neither has anything to do with the truth sensuous certainty contains: neither the I nor the thing has here the meaning of a manifold relation with a variety of other things, of mediation in a variety of ways. The I does not contain or imply a manifold of representations [*Vorstellen*], the I here does not *think*: nor does the matter [*Sache*] have the meaning of a multiplicity of qualities. Rather, it simply *is*; and it *is* merely because it *is*. It *is*—that is the essential point for sense-knowledge, and that bare *being* [*reine Sein*], that simple immediacy, constitutes its truth. In the same way the certainty as *relation*, the certainty "of" something, is an immediate pure relation; consciousness is I—nothing more, a pure *this*; the *particular*[4] knows a pure *this*, something particular [*Einzelne*].

But, when we look closely, there is a good deal more implied in that bare pure being, which constitutes the kernel of this form of certainty, and is given out by it as its truth. A concrete actual certainty of sense is not merely this pure immediacy, but an *example of* such immediacy. Amongst the innumerable distinctions that here come to light, we find in all cases the fundamental difference—viz. that in sense-experience pure being at once breaks up into the two "thises," as we have called them: one this as I, and one as object. When *we*[5] reflect on this distinction, it is seen that neither the one nor the other is merely immediate, merely *is* in sense-certainty, but is at the same time *mediated*: I[6] have certainty through something "other," viz. through the matter at hand[7]; and this, again, exists in that certainty through something "other," viz. through the I.

It is not only we who make this distinction of essential truth and particular example, of essence and instance [*Wesen* and *Beispiel*], immediacy and mediation; we *find* it in sense-certainty itself, and it has to be taken up in the form in which it exists there, not as we have just determined it. One of this pair [the instance] is put forward in it as existing in simple immediacy, as the essential reality: the *object* [*Gegenstand*].[8] The other,[9] however, is put forward as the non-essential, as *mediated*, something which is not *per se* [*an sich*] in the certainty, but there through something else, I, a state of knowledge which only knows the object because the *object* is, and which can as well be as *not* be. The object, however, is the real truth, is the essential reality[1]; it *is*, quite indifferent to whether it is known or not; it remains and stands even though it is not known, while the knowledge does not exist if the object is not there.

---

4. That is, particular consciousness (*der Einzelne*).
5. That is, Hegel and we as his readers, who are contemplating this type of experience and what it involves. *He and we* (with his help) can see something about the (mediated) structure of this type of experience—as we view it analytically and from the outside—that is not evident from within the standpoint of that type of experience itself.
6. That is, the "I" having the sense-experience.
7. That is, the content of the sense-experience.
8. In Hegel's German, "*Gegenstand*": that is, liter-

ally, that which *stands* (over) *against* (me)—as the content of sense-experience stands over against the "I" experiencing it. ("Object" here is to be understood in a simple and neutral sense, as "something there," rather than as an objectively conceived "external thing" of some specific sort.)
9. That is, the essence (*Wesen*), or nature of the type, which the instance exemplifies.
1. That is, it is so for the type of consciousness under consideration. That is part of what it feels so "certain" about.

We have thus to consider as to the object, whether in point of fact it does exist in sense-certainty itself as such an essential reality as that certainty takes it to be; whether its *Begriff*, which is to be essential reality, corresponds to the way it is present in that certainty. We have for that purpose not to reflect about it and ponder what it might be in truth, but to deal with it merely as sense-certainty contains it.

Sense-certainty itself has thus to be asked: What is the This? If we take it in the two-fold form of its existence, as the *Now* and as the *Here*, the dialectic it has in it will take a form as intelligible as the This itself. To the question, What is the Now? we[2] reply, for example, the Now is night-time. To test the truth of this [instance of] sense-certainty, a simple experiment is all we need: write that truth down. A truth cannot lose anything by being written down, and just as little by our preserving and keeping it. If we look again at the truth we have written down, look at it *now, at this noon-time,* we shall have to say it has turned stale and become out of date.

The Now that is night is kept fixed, i.e. it is treated as what it is made out to be,[3] as something which *is;* but it proves to be rather a something which is *not.* The Now itself no doubt maintains itself, but as what is *not* night; similarly in its relation to the day which the Now is at present, it maintains itself as something that is also not day, or as altogether something negative. This self-maintaining Now is therefore not something immediate but something mediated; for, as something that remains and preserves itself, it is determined through and *by means of* the fact that something else, namely day and night, is *not.* Thereby it is just as much as ever it was before, Now, and in being this simple fact, it is indifferent to what is still associated with it; just as little as night or day is its being, it is just as truly *also* day and night; it is not in the least affected by this otherness through which it is what it is. A simple entity of this sort, which is by and through negation, which is neither this nor that, which is a *not-this*, and with equal indifference this as well as that—a thing of this kind we call *ein Allgemeine*.[4] The *Allgemeine* is therefore in point of fact the truth [*das Wahre*] of sense-certainty.[5]

It is as *ein Allgemeines*, too, that we give utterance to sensuous experience [*das Sinnliche*.] What we say is: "This," i.e. the general [*allgemein*] *this*; or we say: "it is," i.e. *being* in general. Of course in saying that we do not have in mind [*vorstellen*] the general *this*, or *being* in general, but we *express* something general [*das Allgemeine*]; in other words, we do not actually say what in this sense-certainty we really *mean*. Language, however, as we see, is the more truthful; in it we ourselves directly refute our own "meaning"; and since the general [*das Allgemeine*] is the real truth of sense-certainty, and language merely expresses *this* truth, it is simply not possible for us to express in words any sensuous existence which we "mean."[6]

2. That is, "we" as instances of consciousness at the level at which sense-certainty is taken to be paradigmatic of knowledge.
3. Literally, "as what it is given out to be" (*für was es ausgegeben wird*), comes across as being.
4. That is, "something general." See the Hegel glossary, p. 144.
5. That is, the true upshot of the form of knowl-

edge in which sense-certainty consists (not specific particular contents but rather the general forms of such contents).
6. That is, it is not possible for us to capture distinctively in words any particular content of sense-experience that we might intend to try to point to by means of a demonstrative pronoun such as "this."

The same will be the case when we take the *Here*, the other form of the This. The Here[7] is e.g. the tree. I turn about and this truth has disappeared and has changed round into its opposite: the Here is not a tree, but a house. The Here itself does not disappear; it *is* and remains in the disappearance of the house, tree, and so on, and is indifferently house, tree [etc.]. The This is shown thus again to be *mediated simplicity*, in other words, to be generality.

Pure being [*reines Sein*], then, remains as the essential element for this sense-certainty, since sense-certainty in its very nature proves the general [*Allgemeine*] to be the truth of its object. But that pure being is not in the form of something immediate, but of something in which the process of negation and mediation is essential. Consequently it is not what we *intend* or "mean" by being, but being with the characteristic that it is an abstraction, the purely *Allgemeine*; and our intended "meaning," which takes the truth of sense-certainty to be *not* something general [*allgemein*],[8] is alone left standing in contrast to this empty, indifferent Now and Here.

If we compare the relation in which knowledge and the object first stood with the relation they have come to assume in this result, it is found to be just the reverse of what first appeared. The object [*Gegenstand*], which professed to be the essential reality, is now the non-essential element of sense-certainty; for the *Allgemeine*, which the object has come to be, is no longer such as the object essentially was to be for sense-certainty. The certainty is now found to lie in the opposite element, namely in knowledge [*Wissen*], which formerly was the non-essential factor. Its truth lies in the object as my [*meinem*] object, or lies in the "meaning" [*Meinen*], in what I "mean"; it *is*, because *I* know it. Sense-certainty is thus indeed banished from the object, but it is not yet thereby done away with; it is merely forced back into the I. We have still to see what experience reveals regarding its reality in this sense.

The force of its truth thus lies now in the I, in the immediate fact of my being conscious of seeing, hearing, and so on; the disappearance of the particular Now and Here that we "mean" is prevented by the fact that *I* keep hold on them. The Now is daytime, because *I* see it; the Here is a tree for a similar reason. Sense-certainty, however, goes through the same dialectic process in this connection as in the former case. I, *this* I, see the tree, and assert the tree to be the Here; *another* I, however, sees the house and maintains the Here is not a tree but a house. Both truths have the same authenticity—the immediacy of seeing and the certainty and assurance both have as to their specific way of knowing; but the one certainty disappears in the other.

In all this, what does not disappear is the I, as *Allgemeine*,[9] whose seeing is neither the seeing of this tree nor of this house, but just simply seeing, which is mediated through the negation of this house, etc., and, in being so, is all the same simple and indifferent to what is associated with it—the house, the tree, and so on. I is merely *allgemein*, like Now, Here, or This in general. No doubt I "mean" a particular I, but just as little as I am able to say what I "mean" by Now, Here, so it is impossible in the case of the I too. By

---

7. That is, what is at one moment the referent of "here" for me.
8. That is, what we *take ourselves* to be *certain of* in sense-certainty is something radically particular—

namely, *this* particular sense-content—rather than something general.
9. That is, something general.

saying "this Here," "this Now," "a particular thing," I say all Thises, Heres, Nows, or Particulars [*Einzelne*]. In the same way when I say "I," "this particular I," I say quite generally "all I's," every one is what I say, every one is "I," this particular I. When philosophy is requested, by way of putting it to a crucial test—a test which it could not possibly sustain—to "deduce," to "construe," "to find a priori," or however it is put, a so-called *this thing*, or *this particular man*, it is quite fair to ask that this demand should say *what* "this thing," or *what* "this I" it means: but to say this is quite impossible.[1]

Sense-certainty discovers by experience, therefore, that its essential nature lies neither in the object nor in the I; and that the immediacy peculiar to it is neither an immediacy of the one nor of the other. For, in the case of both, what I "mean" is rather something non-essential; and the object and the I are *Allgemeine*, in which that Now and Here and I, which I "mean," do not persist or exist. We arrive in this way at the result, that we have to put the *whole* of sense-certainty as its essential reality, and no longer merely one of its moments, as happened in both cases, where first the object as against the I, and then the I, was to be its true reality. Thus it is only the whole sense-certainty itself which persists therein as immediacy, and in consequence excludes from itself all the opposition which in the foregoing had a place there.

* * *

From *Part B. On Self-Consciousness*

From The Truth of Self-Certainty [*Gewissheit Seiner Selbst*]

[INTRODUCTION]

In the kinds of certainty previously considered, the truth for consciousness is something other than consciousness itself. The *Begriff* of this truth, however, vanishes in the course of our experience of it. What the object immediately was *in itself*—whether mere *being* in sense-certainty, a concrete *thing* in perception, or *force* in the case of understanding—turns out in truth actually not to be this; rather, this inherent nature [*Ansich*] proves to be a way in which it is *for an "other"* [*fur ein Anderes*]. The abstract *Begriff* of the object gives way before the actual concrete object, or the first immediate representation [*Vorstellung*] is superseded in the course of experience. Mere certainty vanished in favour of the truth.[2] There has now arisen, however, what was not established in the case of these previous relationships, viz. a certainty which is on a par with its truth, for the certainty is to itself its own object, and consciousness is to itself the truth. Otherness, no doubt, is also found there; consciousness, that is, makes a distinction. But what is distinguished is of such a kind that consciousness, at the same time, holds there is no distinction made. If we call the movement of knowledge <u>*Begriff*</u>,[3] and

---

1. That is, it is impossible to use general words (specifically, general demonstratives) to pick out and identify any particular referent of such terms.
2. For Hegel, "truth" (philosophically speaking) is to be conceived in terms of the accordance or correspondence of something with its *Begriff*

("concept" or essential nature), or—conversely—of a *Begriff* of some sort and its objectification or instantiation in reality.
3. That is, comprehension (*Begreifen*) by way of appropriate concepts (*Begriffe*).

knowledge *qua* simple unity or Ego the *object* [*Gegenstand*], we see that not only for us [tracing the process], but likewise for knowledge itself, the object corresponds to the *Begriff*. Or, if we put it in the other form and call *Begriff* what the object is in itself, while applying the term "object" to what the object is *qua* object or *for an other*, it is clear that being "in-itself" and being "for an other" are here the same. For the inherent being [*Ansich*] is consciousness; yet it is still just as much that for which an other (viz. what is "in-itself") is. And it is *for* consciousness that the inherent nature [*Ansich*] of the object, and its "being for an other" *are* one and the same. Ego is the content of the relation, and itself the process of relating. It is Ego itself which is opposed to an other and, at the same time, reaches out beyond this other, which other is all the same taken to be only itself.

With self-consciousness, then, we have now passed into the native land of truth, into that kingdom where it is at home. We have to see how the form or attitude of self-consciousness in the first instance appears. When we consider this new form and type of knowledge—the knowledge *of self* [*das Wissen von sich selbst*]—in its relation to that which preceded, namely, the knowledge *of an "other"* [*einem Anderen*], we find, indeed, that this latter has vanished, but that its moments have, at the same time, been preserved; and the loss consists in this: that those moments are here present as they are implicitly, as they are in themselves. The being which "meaning" dealt with—particularity and the generality [*Allgemeinheit*] of perception opposed to it, as also the empty, inner region, of understanding—these are no longer present as substantial elements [*Wesen*], but as aspects [*Momente*] of self-consciousness, i.e. as abstractions or differences, which are, at the same time, of no account for consciousness itself, or are not differences at all, and are purely vanishing entities [*Wesen*].

What seems to have been lost, then, is only the principal aspect, viz. the simple fact of having independent subsistence for consciousness. But, in reality, self-consciousness is reflexion out of the bare being that belongs to the world of sense and perception, and is essentially the return out of otherness. As self-consciousness, it is movement; but since it is only its self as such which it distinguishes from itself, the difference is straightway taken to be superseded *qua* otherness. The distinction *is* not, and self-consciousness is only the lifeless tautology, "I am I": since for self-consciousness the distinction does not also have the shape of *being*, it is *not* self-consciousness. For self-consciousness, then, otherness is a fact, it does exist as a distinct aspect [*Moment*]; but the unity of itself with this difference is also a fact for self-consciousness, and is a second distinct aspect [*Moment*]. With that first aspect, self-consciousness occupies the position of consciousness, and the whole expanse of the world of sense is conserved as its object, but at the same time only as related to the second aspect, the unity of self-consciousness with itself. And, consequently, the sensible world is regarded by self-consciousness as having a subsistence which is, however, only appearance, or forms a distinction from self-consciousness that *per se* has no being.

This opposition of its appearance and its truth [*seiner Wahrheit*] finds its real essence, however, only in the truth [*die Wahrheit*]—in the unity of self-consciousness with itself. This unity must become essential to self-consciousness, i.e. self-consciousness is the state of *Desire* in general.

Consciousness has, *qua* self-consciousness, henceforth a twofold object. One is immediate—the object of sense-certainty and of perception, which, however, is here found to be marked by the character of negation. The second is itself, which is the true essence, and is found in the first instance only in the opposition of the first object to it. Self-consciousness presents itself here as the process in which this opposition is removed, and oneness or identity with itself established.

* * *

From *Part B. Self-Consciousness*

From Dependence and Independence of Self-Consciousness: Master and Servant [*Herrschaft und Knechtschaft*]

* * *

Self-consciousness is primarily simple existence for self, self-identity by exclusion of every other from itself. It takes its essential nature and absolute object to be I [*Ich*]; and in this immediacy, in this bare fact of its self-existence, it is particular. That which for it is other stands as unessential object, as object with the character of negation. But the other is also a self-consciousness;[4] an individual [*Individuum*] comes upon and encounters an individual. Appearing thus in their immediacy, they are for each other in the manner of ordinary objects. They are independent forms [*Gestalten*], consciousnesses that have not risen above the level of *life* [*Leben*]. (The existent object here has been determined as living.) They are, moreover, forms of consciousness which have not yet accomplished for one another the process of absolute abstraction, of uprooting all immediate existence, and of being merely the bare, negative fact of self-identical consciousness. In other words, they have not yet revealed themselves to each other as existing purely "for themselves," i.e. as self-consciousness. Each is indeed certain of its own self, but not of the other, and hence its own certainty of itself is still without truth.[5] For its truth would be merely that its own individual existence for itself would be shown to it to be an independent object, or, which is the same thing, that the object would be exhibited as this pure certainty of itself. By the *Begriff* of recognition,[6] however, this is not possible, except in the form that as the other is for it, so it is for the other; each in its self through its own action and again through the action of the other achieves this pure abstraction of "existence for self" [*Fürsichsein*].

The depiction of itself, however, as pure abstraction of self-consciousness, consists in showing itself as a pure negation of its objective form, or in showing that it is fettered to no determinate existence—that it is not bound at all by the particularity everywhere characteristic of existence as such, and is *not* completely bound up with [mere] life. The process of bringing all this out

4. The encounter here envisioned is between one self-conscious existence with another (rather than with a mere thing of some sort).
5. That is, its own certainty of itself has not yet come true, because the "self" it takes itself to be has not yet become something actual.
6. That is, by the very nature (*Begriff*) of recognition (*Anerkennen*), which, for Hegel, is an essential prerequisite and aspect of genuine actual selfhood.

involves a twofold action—action on the part of the other, and action on the part of itself. In so far as it is the other's action, each aims at the destruction and death of the other. But in this there is implicated also the second kind of action, self-activity; for each implies that it risks its own life. The relation of both self-consciousnesses is in this way so constituted that they prove themselves and each other through a life-and-death struggle.

They must enter into this struggle, for they must bring their certainty of themselves, the certainty of being "for themselves,"[7] to the level of objective truth, and make this a fact both in the case of the other and in their own case as well. And it is solely by risking life that freedom is obtained; only thus is it tried and proved that the essential nature of self-consciousness is not bare existence, is not the merely immediate form in which it at first makes its appearance, is not its mere absorption in the expanse of life. Rather it is thereby guaranteed that there is nothing present but what might be taken as a vanishing moment—that self-consciousness is merely pure self-existence, being-for-self. The individual [Individuum] who has not staked his life may, no doubt, be recognised as a Person; but he has not attained the truth[8] of this recognition as an independent self-consciousness. In the same way each must aim at the death of the other, as it risks its own life thereby; for that other is to it of no more worth than itself. The other's reality is presented to the former as an external other, as outside itself; it must overcome [aufheben][9] that externality. The other is a purely existent consciousness and entangled in manifold ways; it must regard its otherness as pure existence for itself or as absolute negation.

This trying and testing through death,[1] however, cancels both the truth which was to result from it, and therewith the certainty of self altogether. For just as life is the natural "position" of consciousness, independence without absolute negativity, so death is the natural "negation" of consciousness, negation without independence, which thus remains without the requisite significance of actual recognition. Through death, doubtless, there has arisen the certainty that both did stake their life, and held it lightly both in their own case and in the case of the other; but that is not for those who underwent this struggle. They cancel their consciousness which had its place in this alien element of natural existence; in other words, they cancel themselves as terms or extremes seeking to have existence on their own account. But along with this there vanishes from the play of change the essential moment, viz. that of breaking up into extremes with opposite characteristics; and the middle term collapses into a lifeless unity which is broken up into lifeless extremes, merely existent and not opposed. And the two do not mutually give and receive one another back from each other through consciousness; they let one another go quite indifferently, like things. Their act is abstract negation, not the negation characteristic of consciousness, which cancels in such a way that it preserves and maintains what is superseded [aufgehoben], and thereby survives its being aufgehoben.

In this experience self-consciousness becomes aware that life is as essential to it as pure self-consciousness. In immediate self-consciousness the

---

7. That is, of being self-conscious (Fürsichsein), and indeed of most truly being self-consciousness.
8. That is, the actually existing reality.

9. See the Hegel glossary, p. 144.
1. That is, the struggle carried all the way to the actual death of one (or both) of the parties.

simple ego is absolute object, which, however, is for us or in itself absolute mediation, and has as its essential moment substantial and solid independence. The dissolution of that simple unity is the result of the first experience; through this there is posited a pure self-consciousness, and a consciousness which is not purely for itself, but for another, i.e. as an existent consciousness, consciousness in the form and shape of thinghood. Both aspects [*Momente*] are essential; but since, in the first instance, they are unlike and opposed, and their reflexion into unity has not yet come to light, they stand as two opposed forms or modes [*Gestalten*] of consciousness. The one, whose nature is to be *for itself* [*Fürsichsein*], is independent; the other, whose nature is life or existence for another, is dependent. The former is the Master [*Herr*], the latter the servant [*Knecht*].

The master is the consciousness that exists *for itself*—but no longer merely the *Begriff* of existence for self. Rather, it is consciousness which, while existing on its own account, is *mediated* with itself through *another* consciousness, whose nature is bound up with independent reality [*Sein*] or with thinghood in general. The master brings himself into relation to both these moments— to a thing as such, the object of desire, and to the consciousness [of the servant] whose essential character is thinghood. The master, in accordance with the *Begriff* of self-consciousness, is (*a*) an immediate relation of self-existence, but is now moreover at the same time (*b*) mediation, or a being-for-self which is for itself only through an other—he [the master] stands in relation (*a*) immediately to both (*b*) mediately to each through the other. The master relates himself to the servant mediately through independent existence,[2] for that is precisely what keeps the servant in bondage; it is his chain, from which he could not in the struggle get away, and for that reason he proves himself dependent, shows that his independence consists in being a thing.[3] The master, however, is the power controlling this state of existence, for he has shown in the struggle[4] that he holds existence to be merely something negative.[5] Since he is the power dominating the negative nature of existence, while this existence again is the power controlling the other [the servant], the master holds this other in subjection.

In the same way the master relates himself to the thing mediately through the servant. The servant, being a self-consciousness in the broad sense as well, also takes up a negative attitude to things and transcends [*aufhebt*] them; but the thing is, at the same time, independent for him, and thus, despite his negative relation to it, he cannot get so far as to annihilate it outright and be done with it. That is to say, he merely works on it. To the master, on the other hand, by means of this mediating process, belongs the immediate relation, in the sense of the pure negation of it: in other words, he gets the enjoyment of it.

2. That is, through the things that are the objects of the master's desire, which the servant is in servitude to provide.
3. That is, the servant's independence amounts to no more than the independence of the things—as mere external things—that are the objects of the master's desire.

4. The suspended "struggle to the death" discussed above, in which each self-conscious subject asserted itself unconditionally in relation to the other.
5. That is, he holds mere life without independence and honor to be abhorrent, to which death would be preferable.

What mere desire did not attain, he now succeeds in attaining, viz. to have done with the thing, and find satisfaction in enjoyment. Desire alone did not accomplish this, because of the independence of the thing. The master, however, who has interposed the servant between it and himself, thereby relates himself merely to the dependence of the thing, and enjoys it without qualification and without reserve. The aspect of its independence he leaves to the servant, who labours upon it.

In these two respects [*Momente*], the master gets his *recognition* through an "other" consciousness; for in them the latter [the servant] affirms itself as unessential, both by working upon the thing, and, on the other hand, by the fact of being dependent on a determinate existence.[6] In neither case can this "other" [the servant] get the mastery over existence, and succeed in absolutely negating it. We thus have here this moment [in the dialectic] of recognition: the "other" [servant's] consciousness cancels [*aufhebt*] itself as self-existent, and thereby itself does what the first does to it. We likewise have this other moment: this action on the part of the second ["other" consciousness] is the action proper of the first ["master's" consciousness]; for what is done by the servant is properly an action on the part of the master. The latter exists only *for himself*, that is his nature [*Wesen*]; he is the negative power without qualification, a power to which the thing is nothing, and his is thus the essential action in this situation. The servant's, on the other hand, is not so; his is an unessential activity. But for recognition proper there is needed the moment that what the master does to the other he should also do to himself, and that what the servant does to himself, he should do to the other also. On that account a form of recognition has arisen that is one-sided and unequal.

In all this, the unessential consciousness is, for the master, the object which embodies the truth of his certainty of himself. But it is evident that this object does not correspond to its *Begriff*; for, just where the master has effectively achieved dominance it turns out that something has come about quite different from an independent consciousness. It is not an independent, but rather a *dependent* consciousness that he has achieved. He is thus not assured of self-existence as his truth;[7] he finds that his truth[8] is rather the unessential consciousness, and the unessential action of that consciousness.

The truth[9] of the independent consciousness is accordingly the consciousness of the servant. This doubtless appears in the first instance as external to it, and not as the truth of self-consciousness. But just as masterhood showed its essential nature to be the reverse of what it wants to be, so too servitude will, when completed, pass into the opposite of what it immediately is: beginning as a consciousness repressed within itself, it will enter into itself, and change round into real and true independence.

We have seen what servitude is only in relation to mastership. But it is a self-consciousness, and we have now to consider what it is, in this regard, in and for itself. In the first instance, the master is taken to be the essential real-

---

6. That is, the servant depends for his very existence on his ability to provide the things (the "determinate existence") that the master wants.
7. That is, as what has come about in this case; the upshot for him.

8. That is, the truth with respect to what he has become.
9. That is, the true and significant upshot or outcome.

ity for the state of servitude. Hence, for it, the truth is the independent consciousness existing for itself. This truth is not yet taken as inherent in servitude itself. Still, it does in fact contain within itself this truth of pure negativity and self-existence, because it has experienced this reality within it. For this self-consciousness was not in peril and fear for this element or that, nor for this or that moment of time, it was afraid for its entire being; it felt the fear of death, it was in mortal terror of its sovereign master. In that experience it has been melted to its inmost soul, has trembled throughout its every fibre; the stable foundations of its whole being have quaked within it. This complete perturbation of its entire substance, however, this absolute dissolution of all its stability into fluent continuity, is the simple, ultimate nature of self-consciousness—absolute negativity, pure self-referent existence, which consequently is involved in this type of consciousness. This moment of pure self-existence is moreover a fact for it; for in the master this moment is consciously his object. Further, this servant's consciousness is not only this total dissolution in a general way; in serving the servant actually carries this out. In every particular moment of service he supersedes [*aufhebt*] his dependence on and attachment to natural existence, and works this existence away.

The feeling of absolute power, however, realised both in general and in the particular form of service, is only dissolution implicitly; and while the fear of his lord is the beginning of wisdom,[1] consciousness is not therein aware of being self-existent. Through work and labour [*Arbeit*], however, this consciousness of the servant comes to itself. In the moment which corresponds to desire in the case of the master's consciousness, the aspect of the non-essential relation to the thing seemed to fall to the lot of the servant, since the thing there retained its independence. Desire has reserved to itself the pure negating of the object and thereby unalloyed feeling of self. This satisfaction, however, just for that reason is itself only a state of evanescence, for it lacks objectivity or subsistence. Labour, on the other hand, is desire restrained and checked, evanescence delayed and postponed; in other words, labour *shapes and fashions* [*bildet*]. The negative relation to the object passes into the *form* of the object, into something that is permanent and remains; because it is just for the labourer that the object has independence. This negative mediating agency, this activity giving shape and form, is at the same time the individual existence, the pure self-existence of that consciousness, which now in the work it does is externalised and passes into the condition of permanence. Working consciousness[2] accordingly comes by this means to view that independent being as its self.[3]

But again, shaping or forming [*formieren*] has not only the positive significance that the servant becomes thereby aware of himself as objectively self-existent; this type of consciousness has also a negative import, in contrast with its first moment—the element of fear. For in shaping the thing [*Bilden des Dinges*] it only becomes aware of its own proper negativity, its existence on its own account, as an object, through the fact that it supersedes [*aufhebt*] the

---

1. An echo of Psalm 111:10, which begins "The fear of the LORD is the beginning of wisdom" (RSV).
2. "Das arbeitende Bewusstsein": that is, the form or type of consciousness associated with and developed in the kind of *Arbeit* (work or labor) that

"shapes and fashions," or transforms the things on which it works.
3. That is, comes to see the products of its working activity as expressions and realizations of itself (and so of "its self" [*seiner selbst*]).

actual form confronting it. But this objective negative element is precisely the alien, external reality before which it trembled. Now, however, it destroys this extraneous alien negative, affirms and sets itself up as a negative in the element of permanence, and thereby becomes aware of being objectively for itself. In the master, this self-existence is felt to be an "other," and is only external. In fear, the self-existence is present implicitly; in fashioning the thing, self-existence comes to be felt explicitly as its own proper being, and it attains the consciousness that itself exists in its own right and on its own account [*an und für sich*]. By the fact that the form is objectified, it does not become something other than the consciousness moulding the thing through work; for just that form is his pure self-existence, which therein becomes truly realised. Thus precisely in labour, where there seemed to be merely someone else's mind [*fremder Sinn*] involved, the servant becomes aware, through this re-discovery of himself by himself, of having and being a "mind of his own" [*eigener Sinn*].

For this reflexion of self into self the two moments, fear and service in general, as also that of formative activity, are necessary: and at the same time both must exist in a general manner. Without the discipline of service and obedience, fear remains formal and does not spread over the whole known reality of existence. Without the formative activity shaping the thing, fear remains inward and mute, and consciousness does not become objective for itself. Should consciousness shape and form the thing without the initial state of absolute fear, then it has merely a vain and futile "mind of its own"; for its form or negativity is not negativity *per se*, and hence its formative activity cannot furnish the consciousness of itself as essentially real. If it does not endure absolute fear, but merely some slight anxiety, the negative reality will remain external to it, and its substance will not be through and through infected thereby. Since the entire content of its natural consciousness has not been shaken, it is still inherently a determinate mode of being; having a "mind of its own" [*eigen Sinn*] is simply obstinateness [*Eigensinn*]—a type of freedom which does not get beyond the attitude of servitude. The less the pure form [of self-consciousness] becomes its essential nature, the less that form is a general formative activity, an absolute *Begriff*, encompassing the particular; it is rather only a piece of cleverness which has mastery within a certain range, but has no more general power and control with respect to the whole of objective reality.

SOURCE: From G. W. F. Hegel, *The Phenomenology of Mind*, trans. J. B. Baillie (London: Swan Sonnenschein; New York: Macmillan, 1910), 1:90–97, 163–67, 178–88 (translation modified by the editor). Except where otherwise indicated, German words in brackets are the terminology used in the German original, inserted by the editor in addition to their renderings in the translation; and unbracketed German words are the original terminology, substituted in place of their renderings in the translation by the editor for reasons given in notes and in the Hegel glossary (p. 144). *Phänomenologie des Geistes* was first published in 1807. "Sense-certainty" (*die sinnliche Gewissheit*) is the kind of knowledge that sense-experience as such affords.

Objective *Geist*

On Objective *Geist*

From Philosophy of Mind [*Geist*]

From *Section Two. Mind* [Geist] *Objective*

[INTRODUCTION]

483.] Objective *Geist* is the absolute *Idee*, but only existing *in posse*:[1] and as it is thus on the territory of finitude, its actual rationality retains the aspect of external apparency. The free will finds itself immediately confronted by differences which arise from the circumstance that freedom [*Freiheit*] is its *inward* function and aim, and is in relation to an external and already subsisting objectivity, which splits up into different heads: viz. anthropological data (i.e. private and personal needs), external things of nature which exist for consciousness, and the ties of relation between individual wills which are conscious of their own diversity and particularity. These aspects constitute the external material for the embodiment of the will.

484.] But the purposive action of this will is to realise its *Begriff*, freedom [*Freiheit*],[2] in these externally-objective aspects, making the latter a world moulded by the former, which in it is thus at home with itself, locked together with it: the *Begriff* accordingly perfected to the *Idee*.[3] Freedom, shaped into the actuality of a world, receives the *form of Necessity* the deeper substantial nexus of which is the system or organisation of the principles of freedom, whilst its phenomenal nexus is power or authority, and the sentiment of obedience awakened in consciousness.[4]

485.] This unity of the rational will with the single will (this being the peculiar and immediate medium in which the former is actualised) constitutes the simple actuality of freedom. As it (and its content) belongs to thought, and is the virtual <u>Allgemeine</u>,[5] the content has its right and true character only in the form of *Allgemeinheit*. When invested with this character for the intelligent consciousness, or instituted as an authoritative power, it is a *Law*.[6] When, on the other hand, the content is freed from the mixedness and fortuitousness attaching to it in the practical feeling and in impulse[7] and is set and

1. Potentially (Latin).
2. That is, for Hegel, self-determination.
3. That is, the *Begriff* of freedom is "realized" (*realiziert*) or made a concretely existing reality, and so is "perfected" (*vollendet*, "fulfilled," "completed")—thereby coming to have the status of *Idee* (i.e., become fully "actual")—when *Geist* as "practical will" embodies itself adequately in the kinds of "external material" mentioned in §483.
4. Better translated: "Freedom, when shaped into the actuality of a world [i.e., a particular human society], receives the *form of necessity* [i.e., obligatory rules, laws, norms]—the substantial configuration [*Zusammenhang*] of which is the system of the determinations or conditions of freedom [*Freiheitsbestimmungen*], and the overt configuration of which is power or authority [*Macht*] and its acknowledgment [*Anerkanntsein*], that is, its acceptance as valid in consciousness."
5. That is, the inherently general; see the Hegel glossary, p. 144.
6. That is, the law.
7. This entire sentence is better translated: "When [cultural] content is freed from the dross and fortuitousness that attaches to it in practical feeling and impulse and is inculcated [*eingebildet*] into the subjective will [of the members of a society], not in the form of mere impulse, but in its *Allgemeinheit* [as general norms and rules], as habit, disposition, and character, it exists as *custom* [*Sitte*]."

grafted in the individual will, not in the form of impulse, but in its *Allgemeinheit*, so as to become its habit, temper and character, it exists as custom, or *Sitte*.[8]

486.] This 'reality', in general, where free will has *existence*, is the *Law* (Right [*Recht*]),—the term being taken in a comprehensive sense not merely as the limited juristic law, but as the actual body of all the conditions of freedom.[9] These conditions, in relation to the *subjective* will, where they, being *allgemein*, ought to have and can only have their existence, are its *Duties*; whereas as its temper and habit they are *Sitte*.[1] What is a right is also a duty, and what is a duty, is also a right. For a mode of existence is a right, only as a consequence of the free substantial will: and the same content of fact, when referred to the will distinguished as subjective and individual, is a duty. It is the same content which the subjective consciousness recognises as a duty, and brings into existence in these several wills. The finitude of the objective will thus creates the semblance of a distinction between rights and duties.

In the phenomenal range right and duty are *correlata*,[2] at least in the sense that to a right on my part corresponds a duty in some one else. But, in the light of the *Begriff*, my right to a thing is not merely possession, but as possession by a *person* it is *property*, or legal possession, and it is a *duty* to possess things as *property*, i.e. to be as a person. Translated into the phenomenal relationship, viz. relation to another person—this grows into the duty of some one *else* to respect *my* right. In the morality of the conscience, duty in general is in me—a free subject—at the same time a right of my subjective will or disposition. But in this individualist moral sphere, there arises the division between what is only inward purpose (disposition or intention), which only has its being in me and is merely subjective duty, and the actualisation of that purpose: and with this division a contingency and imperfection which makes the inadequacy of mere individualistic morality. In social ethics [*Sittlichkeit*][3] these two parts have reached their truth, their absolute unity.[4] * * *

SOURCE: From *Hegel's Philosophy of Mind: Translated from the "Encyclopaedia of the Philosophical Sciences," with Five Introductory Essays*, trans. William Wallace (Oxford: Clarendon, 1894), pp. 240–41 (translation modified by the editor). Except where otherwise indicated, German words in brackets are the terminology used in the German original, inserted by the editor in addition to their renderings in the translation; and unbracketed German words are the original terminology, substituted in place of their renderings in the translation by the editor for reasons given in notes and in the Hegel glossary (p. 144). Translated from the 1830 edition of *Philosophie des Geistes*, part 3 of *Enzyklopädie der philosophischen Wissenschaften*.

8. The root, for Hegel, of *Sittlichkeit* (ethicality).

9. That is, as the existing forms (*Dasein*) of all of the determinations or conditions (*Bestimmungen*) that make freedom concretely possible.

1. That is, customs.

2. Things that are correlated (Latin).

3. That is, ethicality.

4. Here (as in *Philosophy of Right*; see selections below) Hegel is marking what for him is the important distinction between "morality" (*Moralität*) and "moral duty" (*moralischen Pflicht*), on one hand, and "ethicality" (*Sittlichkeit*, often translated as "ethical life," and here translated as "social ethics"), on the other, as well as distinguishing both of them from "legality" (i.e., legal "right" and obliga-

tion). Legality is strictly "positive"—that is, a matter of what formally established law requires, permits, or forbids. "Morality," in contrast, is an essentially "subjective" (even though also general) requirement of conscience that one "do what is right"—a duty abstracted from all generally but definitely specified content, just as legal duty abstracts from all individual particularity and circumstances. "Ethicality" represents a form of "rightness" or normativity that is the "supersession" (*Aufhebung*), "unification," and "truth" of both of these "abstract" forms of "rightness," tying duty to specific social forms of normativity that are at once "objective" and "one's own" (if one can and does identify with one's "people" and *Volksgeist*).

On *Geist* Proper

From Phenomenology of *Geist*

From *Part BB*. Geist

[INTRODUCTION]

Reason is *Geist*,[1] when its certainty of being all reality has been raised to the level of truth, and reason is *consciously* aware of itself as its own world, and of the world as itself. The becoming [*Werden*] of *Geist* was indicated in the immediately preceding development, in which the object of consciousness, the category [*Kategorie*] pure and simple, rose to be the *Begriff* of reason. When reason "observes," this pure unity of ego and existence, the unity of subjectivity and objectivity, of for-itself-ness and in-itself-ness—this unity is immanent, has the character of implicitness or of being; and consciousness of reason *finds itself*. But the true nature of "observation" is rather the supersession [*Aufhebung*] of this instinct of *finding* its object lying directly at hand, and passing beyond this unconscious state of existence. The directly perceived [*angeschaut*] category, the thing simply "found," enters consciousness as the self-existence of the I [*Ich*]—which now knows itself in the objective reality, and knows itself there as the *self*. But this feature of the category, viz. of being "for-itself" as opposed to being immanent within itself, is equally one-sided, and a moment that supersedes itself. The category therefore gets for consciousness the character which it possesses in its general [*allgemein*] truth—it is self-contained and self-aware reality [*an und fürsichseiendes Wesen*].[2] This character, still abstract, which constitutes the matter itself [*die Sache selbst*], is to begin with "*geistig* reality": and its mode of consciousness is here a formal knowledge of that reality—a knowledge which is occupied with the varied and manifold content thereof. This consciousness is still, in point of fact, a particular individual [*ein Einzelne*] distinct from the *allgemein* substance,[3] and either prescribes arbitrary laws or pretends to possess the laws as they intrinsically are [*an und für sich*] within its own knowledge as such, and takes itself to be the power that passes judgment on them. Or again, looked at from the side of the substance, this is seen to be the self-contained and self-aware *geistig* reality, which is not yet a consciousness of its own self. The self-contained and self-aware reality, however, which is at once actual in consciousness and represents [*vorstellt*] itself to itself, is *Geist*.

Its essential *geistig* reality has been above designated as the ethical substance [*sittliche Substanz*]; *Geist*, however, is ethical actuality [*sittliche Wirklichkeit*]. *Geist* is the *self* of the actual consciousness, to which *Geist* stands opposed, or rather which appears over against itself, as an objective actual world[4] that has lost, however, all sense of alienness [*Fremden*] for the

---

1. As in previous selections (where possible), Hegel's term *Geist* is left untranslated. See the Hegel glossary on p. 144.
2. Literally, a reality that is both *an sich* (it is what it is in and of itself) and *für sich* (it involves and is mediated by some degree and form of self-representing consciousness).

3. That is, the "substance" or specific content of the life and culture of a people or community (often referred to by Hegel as its "social" or "ethical [*sittliche*] substance").
4. That is, the "objective actual world" of an existing culture and society (the *sittliche Substanz* of a people).

self, just as the self has lost all sense of having a dependent or independent existence by itself, cut off and separated from that world. Being substance and *allgemein* self-identical enduring essential reality, *Geist* is the immovable irreducible basis and the starting point for the action of all and every one; it is their purpose and their goal, as the thought-borne implicit nature [*gedachte Ansich*] of all self-consciousnesses.

This substance is likewise the *allgemein* product, wrought and created by the action of each and all, and giving them unity and likeness and identity of meaning; for it is self-existence [*Fürsichsein*], the self, action. As substance *Geist* is unbending righteous self-sameness, self-identity; but as being foritself [*Fürsichsein*], its continuity is resolved into discrete elements: it is the self-sacrificing soul of goodness, the benevolent essential nature, in which each fulfils his own special work, fragments the *allgemein* substance, and takes his own share of it. This resolution of the essential reality into individual forms is just the aspect [*Moment*] of the separate action and the separate self of all the several individuals; it is the moving soul of the ethical substance, the effectuated *allgemein* essential reality. Just because this substance is a being resolved into the self,[5] it is not a lifeless essence, but actual and alive.

Geist is thus the self-supporting absolutely real essential reality. All the previous modes of consciousness are abstractions from it: they are constituted by the fact that *Geist* analyses itself, distinguishes its moments, and halts at each individual mode in turn. The isolating of such moments presupposes *Geist* itself and requires *Geist* for its subsistence. In other words, this isolation of modes only exists within *Geist*, which is existence [*Existenz*]. Taken in isolation they appear as if they existed as they stand. But their advance and return upon their real ground and essential being showed that they are merely moments or vanishing quantities; and this essential being is precisely this movement and resolution of these moments.

Here, where *Geist*, the reflection of these moments into itself, has become established, our reflection may briefly recall them in this connexion: they were consciousness, self-consciousness, and reason. *Geist* is thus *Consciousness* in general, which contains sense-experience, perception and understanding, so far as in analysing its own self it holds fast by the moment of being a reality objective to itself, and by abstraction eliminates the fact that this reality is its own self objectified, its own self-existence. When again it holds fast by the other abstract moment produced by analysis, the fact that its object is its own self become objective to itself, is its self-existence, then it is *Self-consciousness*. But as immediate consciousness of its inherent and its explicit being, of its immanent self and its objective self, as the unity of consciousness and self-consciousness, it is that type of consciousness which *has* Reason: it is the consciousness which, as the word "has" indicates, has the object in a shape which is implicitly and inherently rational, or is categorised, but in such a way that the object is not yet taken by the consciousness in question to have the value of a category. *Geist* here is that consciousness from the immediately preceding consideration of which we have arrived at the present stage. Finally, when this reason, which *Geist* "has," is seen by *Geist* to be reason which actually *is*—to be reason which is actual in *Geist* and is its world—then *Geist* has

---

5. That is, into a multiplicity of selves.

come to its truth;[6] it *is* Geist, it is the *actual ethical* reality [*das wirkliche sitt-liche Wesen*].

Geist, so far as it is the immediate truth, is the ethical life [*sittliche Leben*] of a people [*Volk*]:—the individual, which is a world.[7] It has to advance to the consciousness of what it is immediately; it has to abandon and transcend the beautiful simplicity of ethical life, and get to a knowledge of itself by passing through a series of stages and forms. The distinction between these and those that have gone before consists in their being real spiritual individualities [*Geister*], actualities proper, and instead of being forms of consciousness, they are forms of a world.

The living ethical world is *Geist* in its truth. As it first comes to an abstract *knowledge* of its essential nature, ethical life [*Sittlichkeit*] is destroyed in the formal generality [*Allgemeinheit*] of "right" or legality [*Recht*]. *Geist*, being now sundered within itself, traces one of its worlds in the element of its objectivity as in a crass solid actuality; this is the realm of Culture [*Bildung*]. Over against this in the element of thought is traced the world of Belief or Faith [*Glaube*], the realm of essential being [*Wesen*]. Both worlds, however, when in the grip of the *Begriff*—when grasped by *Geist* which, after this loss of self through self-diremption,[8] penetrates itself—are thrown into confusion and revolutionised through individual Insight [*Einsicht*], and the general diffusion of this attitude, known as "Enlightenment" [*Aufklärung*]. And the realm which had thus been divided and expanded into the "here and now" and the "beyond" turns back into self-consciousness. This self-consciousness, again, taking now the form of Morality (the *inner* moral life) apprehends itself as the essential truth, and the real essence as its actual self, no longer puts its world and its ground and basis away outside itself, but lets everything fade into itself, and in the form of Conscience [*Gewissen*] is *Geist* sure and certain [*gewiss*] of itself.

The ethical world [*Die sittliche Welt*],[9] the world rent asunder into the "here and now" and the "beyond," and the moral worldview [*moralische Weltanschauung*], are then forms of spirituality [*Geister*] whose process and whose return into the self of *Geist*, a simple self-relating [*fürsichseiend*] self, will be developed. When these attain their goal and final result, the actual self-consciousness of Absolute *Geist* will make its appearance.[1]

FROM TRUE (*WAHRE*) GEIST: ETHICALITY (*SITTLICHKEIT*)

Geist, in its ultimate simple truth, is consciousness, and breaks asunder its moments from one another. Action divides *Geist* into substance[2] on the one

6. That is, then *Geist* has come to be in reality what it is essentially—"*Geist* in truth" or, one might appropriately say, "*Geist* come true."
7. That is, the basic unit of *Geist*—the true *geistig* "individual" (*Individuum*)—is not the particular person but rather the "ethical life" or cultural life of a *people*, conceived as a unified totality and a self-developing, self-sustaining, and self-perpetuating autonomous whole (and thus "a world").
8. Self-separation or self-division.
9. The kind of "ethical world" best exemplified by premodern societies and cultures that could actually

exist as worlds unto themselves (in contrast with modern-day "ethicality" in the institutionalized and interacting societies that Hegel calls "states").
1. This was written by Hegel in 1807. By the time of his *Philosophy of Geist* and *Philosophy of Right*, he had made room for an all-important mature modern form of *Sittlichkeit* that was the culminating form of "objective" (but still less than "absolute") *Geist* and *Geistigkeit*.
2. That is, the *sittliche* substance—the cultural content and social institutions and rules of a society.

side, and *consciousness of* the substance on the other; and divides the substance as well as consciousness. The substance appears in the shape of an *allgemein* inner nature and purpose, standing over against itself as particularised reality.[3] The middle or mediating term, infinite in character, is self-consciousness, which, being *implicitly* the unity of itself and that substance, becomes so, now, explicitly [*für sich*], unites the *allgemein* inner nature and its particular realisation, raises the latter to the former and becomes *ethical* action: and, on the other hand, brings the former down to the latter and carries out the purpose, the substance presented merely in thought. In this way it brings to light the unity of its self and the substance, and produces this unity in the form of a "work" done, and thus as actual concrete reality [*Wirklichkeit*].

When consciousness breaks up into these elements, the simple substance has in part preserved the attitude of opposition to self-consciousness; in part it thereby manifests in itself the very nature of consciousness, which consists in distinguishing its own content within itself—manifests a world articulated into separate areas. The substance is thus an ethical reality split up into distinct elemental forms: a human and a divine law.[4] In the same way, the self-consciousness appearing over against the substance assigns itself, in virtue of its inner nature, to one of these powers, and, as involving knowledge, gets broken up into ignorance of what it is doing on the one hand, and knowledge of this on the other—a knowledge which for that reason proves a deception. It learns, therefore, through its own act, both the contradictory nature of those powers into which the inner substance divided itself, and their mutual overthrow—as well as the contradiction between its knowledge of the ethical character of its act and what is truly and essentially ethical—and so finds *its own* destruction. In point of fact, however, the ethical substance has by this process become actual concrete self-consciousness: in other words *this* particular self has become self-sufficient and self-dependent [*An und Fürsichseienden*], but precisely thereby the ethical order has been overthrown and destroyed.

* * *

The *allgemein* elements of ethical reality are thus the (ethical) substance as something *Allgemein*, and that substance as particular consciousness. Their *allgemein* actuality is the people and the family; while they get their natural self, and their operative individuality, in man and woman. Here in this content of the ethical world, we see attained those purposes which the previous insubstantial modes of conscious life set before them. What Reason apprehended only as an object has become Self-consciousness, and what self-consciousness merely contained within it is here explicit true reality. What Observation knew—an object given externally and picked up, and one in the constitution of which the subject knowing had no share—is here a given ethical condition, a custom found lying ready at hand, but a reality which is at the same time the deed and the product of the subject finding it. The individual who seeks the "pleasure" of enjoying his particular individuality [*Einzelheit*] finds it in the family, and the "necessity" in which that pleasure passes

---

3. That is, a particular individual (who is at odds with it).
4. Hegel is here thinking of the paradigmatic conflict in Sophocles' *Antigone* (ca. 441 B.C.E.) between Antigone (and the religious obligation she believes she has) and Creon, the ruler who issued the edict that she disobeys.

away is his own self-consciousness as a citizen [*Bürger*] of his *Volk*. Or, again, it is knowing the "law of his own heart" as the law of all hearts, knowing the consciousness of self to be the recognised *allgemein* ordinance of society: it is "virtue," which enjoys the fruits of its own sacrifice, which brings about what it sets out to do, viz. to bring the essential nature into the light of the actual present—and its enjoyment lies in this *allgemein* life. Finally, consciousness of "the matter itself" [*der Sache selbst*] gets satisfaction in the real substance, which contains and maintains in positive form the abstract aspects of that empty category. That substance finds a genuine content in the powers of the ethical order—a content that takes the place of those insubstantial commands which the "healthy human reason" wanted to give and to know: and in consequence thus gets a concrete inherently determinate standard for "testing"—not the laws, but what is to be done.

The whole is a stable equilibrium [*Gleichgewicht*] of all the parts, and each part is a *Geist* that is very much at home, not seeking its satisfaction beyond itself, but finding its satisfaction within itself in this equilibrium within the whole. This condition of stable equilibrium can, of course, only be living by imbalance arising within it, and being brought back again to balance by justice [*Gerechtigkeit*]. Justice, however, is neither an alien principle [*Wesen*] holding somewhere remote from the present, nor the realisation (unworthy of the name of justice) of mutual malice, treachery, ingratitude, etc., which, in the unintelligent way of chance and accident, would fulfil the law by a kind of irrational connection without any controlling idea, action by commission or omission, or consciousness of what was involved. On the contrary, as justice in *human* right [*Recht*] it brings back into the *Allgemeine* the equilibrium—disrupting self-conscious elements that have broken away separately from it: the independent classes and individuals. In this way justice is the governing of the *Volk*, and is both the *allgemein* essential reality in a contemporary particular form and the own most self-conscious will of all.

That justice, however, which restores the *Allgemeine* to equilibrium by bringing a particular individual under control, is equally the simple *Geist* of those who have suffered wrong. It is not broken up into the two elements—one who has suffered wrong and a remote reality [*Wesen*].[5] The individual himself is the power of the "nether" world, and that reality is *his* "fury," wreaking vengeance upon him. For his individuality, his blood, still lives in the house, his substance has a lasting actuality.[6] The wrong, which can be brought upon the individual in the realm of the ethical world, consists merely in this, that a bare something by chance happens to him. The power which perpetrates on the conscious individual this wrong of making him into a mere thing, is "nature"; it is not the *Allgemeinheit* of the community, but the abstract *Allgemeinheit* of mere existence. And the particular individual, in wiping out the wrong suffered, turns not against the community—for he has not suffered at its hands—but against the latter. As we saw, those who consciously share the blood of the

---

5. That is, the locus or agent of this "justice" is not to be conceived as a being or entity of some sort (God or government) that exists separately and distantly from the person affected.
6. Hegel is alluding to the Greek myth of Orestes, who, after killing his mother, was pursued by the

Furies—spirits of punishment who avenge wrongs done to kindred. The locus of such justice actually lies within those who have internalized the norms and values of the "ethical substance" as their own true substance, making them their own.

individual remove this wrong in such a way that what has happened becomes rather a work of their own doing, and hence bare existence, the last state, gets also to be something willed, and thus an object of gratification.

The ethical [*sittlich*] realm persists in this way as a world without blot or stain, a world untainted by any internal dissension. So, too, its process is an untroubled transition from one of its powers to the other, in such a way that each preserves and produces the other. We see it no doubt divided into two ultimate elements and their realisation: but their opposition is rather the confirming and substantiation of one through the other; and where they directly come in contact and affect each other as actual factors, their mediating common element straightway permeates and suffuses the one with the other. The one extreme, *allgemein Geist* conscious of itself, becomes, through the individuality of *man*, linked together with its other extreme, its force and its element, with *unconscious Geist*. On the other hand, divine law is individualised, the unconscious *Geist* of the particular individual finds its existence, in *woman*, through the mediation of whom the *Geist* of the individual comes out of its unrealisedness into actuality, out of the state of unknowing and unknown, and rises into the conscious realm of *allgemein Geist*.[7] The union of man with woman constitutes the operative mediating agency for the whole, and constitutes the element which, while separated into the extremes of divine and human law, is, at the same time, their immediate union. This union, again, turns both those first mediate connections [*Schlusse*] into one and the same synthesis, and unites into one process the twofold movement in opposite directions: one from reality to unreality, the downward movement of human law, organised into independent members, to the danger and trial of death; the other, from unreality to reality, the upward movement of the law of the nether world to the daylight of conscious existence. Of these movements the former falls to man, the latter to woman.

SOURCE: From G. W. F. Hegel, *The Phenomenology of Mind*, trans. J. B. Baillie (London: Swan Sonnenschein; New York: Macmillan, 1910), 2:430–37, 454–58 (translation modified by the editor). Except where otherwise indicated, German words in brackets are the terminology used in the German original, inserted by the editor in addition to their renderings in the translation; and unbracketed German words are the original terminology, substituted in place of their renderings in the translation by the editor for reasons given in notes and in the Hegel glossary (p. 144). *Phänomenologie des Geistes* was first published in 1807.

On Right [*Recht*]

From The Philosophy of Right

From *Preface*

* * *

As to rights, ethicality [*Sittlichkeit*], and the state, the truth is as old as that in which it is openly displayed and recognized, namely, the law, morality, and

7. Another allusion to *Antigone* (the "man" here is Creon; the "woman," Antigone), to characterize the juxtaposition and conflict of two types of normativity within an "ethical world" that have the potential to disrupt and shatter the equilibrium of which Hegel has been speaking (discussed at length in the following section of the *Phenomenology*).

religion. But as the thinking *Geist* is not satisfied with possessing the truth in this simple way, it must conceive it, and thus acquire a rational form for a content which is already rational implicitly. In this way the substance is justi-fied before the bar of free thought. Free thought cannot be satisfied with what is given to it, whether by the external positive authority of the state or human agreement, or by the authority of internal feelings, the heart, and the witness of the spirit, which coincides unquestioningly with the heart. It is the nature of free thought rather to proceed out of its own self, and hence to demand that it should know itself as thoroughly one with truth.

The ingenuous[1] mind adheres with simple conviction to the truth which is publicly acknowledged. On this foundation it builds its conduct and way of life. In opposition to this naïve view of things rises the supposed difficulty of detecting amidst the endless differences of opinion anything of general appli-cation and validity. This trouble may easily be supposed to spring from a spirit of earnest inquiry. But in point of fact those who pride themselves upon the existence of this obstacle are in the plight of him who cannot see the woods for the trees. The confusion is all of their own making. Nay, more: this con-fusion is an indication that they are in fact not seeking for what is generally valid in right and the ethical order. If they were at pains to find that out, and refused to busy themselves with empty opinion and minute detail, they would adhere to and act in accordance with substantive right, namely the commands of ethicality and of the state. But a further difficulty lies in the fact that man thinks, and seeks freedom and a basis for conduct in thought. Divine as his right to act in this way is, it becomes a wrong, when it takes the place of think-ing. Thought then regards itself as free only when it is conscious of being at variance with what is generally recognized, and of setting itself up as some-thing original.

The idea that freedom of thought and mind is indicated only by deviation from, or even hostility to, what is everywhere recognized is most persistent with regard to the state. The essential task of a philosophy of the state would thus seem to be the discovery and publication of a new and original theory. When we examine this idea and the way it is applied, we are almost led to think that no state or constitution has ever existed, or now exists. We are tempted to suppose that we must now begin and keep on beginning afresh for ever. We are to fancy that the founding of the social order has depended upon present devices and discoveries. As to nature, philosophy, it is admit-ted, has to understand it as it is. The philosophers' stone[2] must be concealed somewhere, we say, in nature itself, as nature is in itself rational. Knowledge must, therefore, examine, apprehend and conceive the reason actually present in nature. It is not with the superficial shapes and accidents of nature, but with its eternal harmony—that is to say, its inherent law and essence—that knowledge has to cope. But the ethical world or the state, which is in fact reason [*Vernunft*] potently and permanently actualized in self-consciousness, is not permitted to enjoy the happiness of being reason [*Vernunft*] at all. On the contrary the *geistig* universe is looked upon as abandoned by God, and

---

1. That is, "natural" or "unsophisticated" (*unbe-fangenen*); Hegel is here referring to the ordinary decent person.

2. An unknown substance that Western alche-mists believed could transform base metals into gold; they searched for it for centuries.

given over as a prey to accident and chance. As in this way the divine is eliminated from the ethical world, truth must be sought outside of it. And since at the same time reason should and does belong to the ethical world, truth, being divorced from reason, is reduced to a mere speculation.

* * *

What is rational is actual [*wirklich*];
And what is actual [*wirklich*] is rational.[3]

Upon this conviction stands not only philosophy but even every unsophisticated consciousness, with respect to the contemplation of the spiritual universe as well as the natural. When reflection, feeling, or whatever other form the subjective consciousness may assume, regards the present as vanity, and thinks itself to be beyond it and wiser, it finds itself in emptiness, and, as it has actuality only in the present, it is vanity throughout. Against the doctrine that the *Idee*[4] is a mere idea, figment or opinion, philosophy preserves the more profound view that nothing is actual [*wirklich*] except the *Idee*. Hence arises the effort to recognize in the temporal and transient the substance, which is immanent, and the eternal, which is present. The rational is synonymous with the *Idee*, because in realizing itself it passes into external existence. It thus appears in an endless wealth of forms, figures and phenomena. It wraps its kernel round with a robe of many colours, in which consciousness finds itself at home. Through this varied husk the *Begriff*[5] first of all penetrates, in order to touch the pulse, and then feel it throbbing in its external manifestations. To bring to order the endlessly varied relations, which constitute the outer appearance of the rational essence is not the task of philosophy. Such material is not suitable for it, and it can well abstain from giving good advice about these things. Plato could well have refrained from recommending to the nurses not to stand still with children, but always to dandle them in their arms.[6]

* * *

This treatise, in so far as it contains a political *science*,[7] is nothing more than an attempt to conceive of and present the state as in itself rational. As a philosophic writing it must be on its guard against constructing a state as it ought to be. Philosophy cannot teach the state what it should be, but only how it, the ethical universe,[8] is to be known.

Ἰδοὺ Ῥόδος, ἰδοὺ καὶ τὸ πήδημα.
Hic Rhodus, hic saltus.[9]

3. *Wirklich* is often taken to be synonymous with *real* (real). For Hegel, however, it signifies not mere existence but existence as everything that a thing of that kind ought to be if it is a "genuine," "good," or "true" thing of its type—in full and complete accord with its *Begriff* ("concept" or essential nature). Since a *Begriff* for Hegel is a rational structure, this maxim expresses the conviction of the deep connection of "the rational" and "the most truly real."
4. See the Hegel glossary, p. 144.
5. See the Hegel glossary, p. 144.
6. See *The Laws* (7.790c–e), probably the last work by the Greek philosopher Plato (ca. 427–ca. 347 B.C.E.).

7. That is, insofar as it involves cognitive inquiry into the state (*Staatswissenschaft*).
8. That is, for Hegel, "the state" is the totality of the norms and associated institutions and practices of a society, not merely its political structure.
9. Literally, "*Here* is Rhodes; *here* is the leap" (the Greek is from one of Aesop's fables; its Latin translation in the second line became a proverbial phrase). That is, the "state" or "ethical universe" in its existing reality (rather than some imagined ideal) is what the political scientist and philosopher should be concerned with.

To apprehend *what is* is the task of philosophy, because *what is* is reason. As for the individual, every one is a son of his time; so philosophy also is its time apprehended in thoughts. It is just as foolish to fancy that any philosophy can transcend its present world, as that an individual could leap out of his time or jump over Rhodes. If a theory transgresses its time, and builds up a world as it ought to be, it has an existence merely in the unstable element of opinion, which gives room to every wandering fancy.

With little change the above saying would read:

Here is the rose, *here* dance.[1]

The barrier which stands between reason, as self-conscious spirit, and reason as present reality, and does not permit spirit to find satisfaction in reality, is some abstraction that is not freed for the *Begriff*.[2] To recognize reason as the rose in the cross[3] of the present, and to find delight in it, is a rational insight which implies reconciliation with reality. This reconciliation philosophy grants to those who have felt the inward demand to conceive clearly, to preserve subjective freedom while present in substantive reality, and yet though possessing this freedom to stand not upon the particular and contingent, but upon what is self-originated and self-completed.

This also is the more concrete meaning of what was a moment ago more abstractly called the unity of form and content. Form in its most concrete significance is reason, as an intellectual apprehension which conceives its object. Content, again, is reason as the substantive essence of social order and nature. The conscious identity of form and content is the philosophical *Idee*.

It is an obstinacy, and one which does honour to man, to acknowledge nothing in sentiment which is not justified by thought. This self-will is a feature of modern times, being indeed the peculiar principle of Protestantism. What was initiated by Luther[4] as faith in feeling and the witness of the spirit, the more mature mind strives to apprehend in conception. In that way it seeks to free itself in the present, and so find there itself. It is a celebrated saying that a half philosophy[5] leads away from God, while a true philosophy leads to God. (It is the same "halfness," I may say in passing, which regards knowledge as an approximation to truth.) This saying is applicable to the study of the state [*Staatswissenschaft*]. Reason cannot content itself with a mere approximation, something which is neither cold nor hot, and must be spewed out of the mouth. As little can it be contented with the cold skepticism that in this world of time things go badly, or at best only moderately well, and that we must keep the peace with reality, merely because there is nothing better to be had. Knowledge creates a much more vital peace.

Only one word more concerning the desire to teach the world what it ought to be. For such a purpose philosophy at any rate always comes too late. Philosophy, as the thought of the world, does not appear until reality has completed

1. Hegel has changed the Greek *Rhodos* to *rhodon*, and the Latin *saltus* to *salta*.
2. That is, this barrier is the result of a failure of comprehension.
3. An allusion to the Rosicrucian movement, which began in the 17th century; its members claimed to have esoteric and occult wisdom handed down from ancient times.
4. Martin Luther (1483–1546), a German theologian and religious reformer whose writings catalyzed the Protestant Reformation.
5. That is, a half-developed (and therefore inadequately developed) philosophy.

its formative process, and made itself ready. History thus corroborates the teaching of the conception that only in the maturity of reality does the ideal appear as counterpart to the real, apprehends the real world in its substance, and shapes it into an intellectual kingdom. When philosophy paints its grey in grey, a form of life has become old, and by means of grey it cannot be rejuvenated, but only known. The owl of Minerva takes its flight only when the shades of night are gathering.[6]

* * *

BERLIN, *June 25th*, 1820.

From *Introduction*

1. The philosophical science of right [*Rechtswissenschaft*] has as its object the *Idee* of right, *i.e.*, the *Begriff* of right and its realization.[7]

Note.—Philosophy has to do with *Ideen*, and hence not with what are commonly called *mere* concepts. It has indeed to exhibit the onesidedness and untruth of these mere concepts, and to show that, while that which commonly bears the name concept [*Begriff*] is only an abstract product of the understanding, the *true Begriff* alone has actuality and gives this actuality to itself. Everything other than the actuality which is established by the *Begriff* is transient surface existence, external accident, opinion, appearance void of essence, untruth, delusion, and so forth. It is through the actual shape[8] it gives itself in its realization that the *Begriff* itself is understood. This shape is the other essential element of the *Idee*, and is to be distinguished from the *form*, which exists only as *Begriff*.

2. The *Wissenschaft* of right is a part of philosophy. Hence it must develop the *Idee*, which is the reason[9] of an object, out of the *Begriff*. It is the same thing to say that it must regard the peculiar internal development of the thing itself. Since it is a part, it has a definite beginning, which is the result and truth of what goes before, and this, that goes before, constitutes its so-called proof.[1] Hence the origin of the *Begriff* of right falls outside of the *Wissenschaft* of right. The deduction[2] of the *Begriff* is presupposed in this treatise, and is to be considered as already given.

3. Right is positive[3] in general (*a*) in its form, since it has validity in a state; and this established authority is the principle for the knowledge of right. Hence we have the positive *Wissenschaft* of right. (*b*) On the side of content this right receives a positive element (α) through the particular ethnic character of a people [*Volk*], the stage of its historical development, and the interconnection of all the relations which are necessitated by nature: (β) through the necessity that a system of legalized right must contain the application of the

---

6. That is, wisdom develops only as its object is already coming to an end. Minerva is the Roman goddess of wisdom, through her identification with the Greek Athena.

7. This is an excellent example of Hegel's use of the term *Idee*: by "the *Idee* of right" he means the concept of "right" together with the sorts of conditions its realization involves and requires.

8. "Gestaltung": that is, the real-world configuration (involving practices, institutions, laws or rules, etc.).

9. "Die Vernunft": that is, the rational nature of that which is under consideration.

1. "Beweis": that is, demonstration, substantiation, derivation, and explanation.

2. "Deduktion": that is, "proof" (*Beweis*) in the broad Hegelian-"logical" sense (see previous note).

3. "Positiv": that is: specifically "posited" or formulated and established.

general *Begriff* to objects and cases whose qualities are given externally. Such an application is not the speculative thought or the development of the *Begriff*, but a subsumption made by the understanding: (γ) through the *final* determination [*Bestimmung*] that is required for *decision* in the actual world.

4. The terrain of right is in general the spiritual [*Geistige*], and its more specific place and origin is the will, which is free. Thus freedom constitutes the substance and essential character of the will, and the system of right is the realm of actualized freedom. It is the world of *Geist*, which is produced out of itself, and is a second nature.

Addition. * * * It is worth while to recall the older way of proceeding with regard to the freedom of the will. First of all, the *Vorstellung* of the will was assumed, and then an effort was made to deduce from it and establish a definition of the will. Next, the method of the older empirical psychology was adopted, and different perceptions and general phenomena of the ordinary consciousness were collected, such as remorse, guilt, and the like, on the ground that these could be explained only as proceeding out of a will that is free. Then from these phenomena was deduced the so-called proof that the will is free. But it is more convenient to take a short cut and hold that freedom is given as a fact of consciousness, and must be believed in.

The nature of the will and of freedom, and the proof that the will is free, can be shown, as has already been observed (§ 2), only in connection with the whole. The fundamental principles of the premises—that *Geist* is in the first instance intelligence, and that the phases through which it passes in its development, namely from feeling through representation or imagery [*Vorstellung*] to thought, are the way by which it produces itself as will, which, in turn, as the practical *Geist* in general, is the most direct truth of intelligence— I have presented in my *Encyclopædia of the Philosophical Wissenschaften* (Heidelberg, 1817), and hope some day to be able to give of them a more complete exposition. There is, to my mind, so much the more need for me to give my contribution to, as I hope, the more thorough knowledge of the nature of *Geist*, since, as I have there said, it would be difficult to find a philosophical discipline in a more neglected and sorry state than is that theory of *Geist* which is commonly called psychology.

Some elements of the conception of will, resulting from the premises enumerated above are mentioned in this and the following paragraphs. As to these, appeal may moreover be made to every individual to see them in his own self-consciousness. Everyone will, in the first place, find in himself the ability to abstract himself from all that he is, and in this way prove himself able of himself to set every content within himself, and thus have in his own consciousness an illustration of all the subsequent phases.

5. The will contains (α) the element of pure indeterminateness, *i.e.*, the pure doubling of the "I" back in thought upon itself. In this process every limit or content, present though it be directly by way of nature, as in needs, desires, and drives, or given in any specific way, is dissolved. Thus we have the limitless infinitude of absolute abstraction, or universality, the pure thought of itself.

Note.—Those who treat thinking and willing as two special, peculiar, and separate faculties, and, further, look upon thought as detrimental to the will, especially the good will, show from the very start that they know nothing of the nature of willing—a remark which we shall be called upon to make a number of times upon the same attitude of mind. The will on one side is the possibility of abstraction from every aspect in which the "I" finds itself or has set itself up. It reckons any content as a limit, and flees from it. This is one of the forms of the self-direction of the will, and is by imaginative thinking insisted upon as of itself freedom. It is the negative side of the will, or freedom as apprehended by the understanding. This freedom is that of the void, which has taken actual shape, and is stirred to passion. It, while remaining purely theoretical, appears in Hindu religion as the fanaticism of pure contemplation; but becoming actual it assumes both in politics and religion the form of a fanaticism which would destroy the established social order, remove all individuals suspected of desiring any kind of order, and demolish any organization which then sought to rise out of the ruins. Only in devastation does the negative will feel that it has reality. It intends, indeed, to bring to pass some positive social condition, such as universal equality or universal religious life. But in fact it does not will the positive reality of any such condition, since that would carry in its train a system, and introduce a separation by way of institutions and between individuals. But classification and objective system attain self consciousness only by destroying negative freedom. Negative freedom is actuated by a mere solitary abstract idea, whose realization is nothing but the fury of destruction.

6. (β) The "I" is also the transition from blank indefiniteness to the distinct and definite establishment of a definite content and object, whether this content be given by nature or produced out of the *Begriff* of *Geist*. Through this establishment of itself as a definite thing the "I" becomes a reality. This is the absolute aspect [*Moment*] of the finitude or specificity of the "I."

7. (γ) The will is the unity of these two elements. It is specificity [*Besonderheit*] turned back within itself and thus led back to *Allgemeinheit*; it is particularity [*Einzelheit*]; it is the self-direction[4] of the "I." Thus at one and the same time it establishes itself as its own negation, that is to say, as definite and limited, and it also abides by itself, in its self-identity and *Allgemeinheit*, and in this position remains purely self-enclosed. The "I" determines itself in so far as it is the reference of negativity to itself; and yet in this self-reference it is indifferent to its own definite character. This it knows as its own, that is, as an ideal or a mere possibility, by which it is not bound, but rather exists in it merely because it establishes itself there. This is the freedom of the will, constituting its *Begriff* or substantive reality. It is its gravity, as it were, just as gravity is the substantive reality of a body.

Note.—Every self-consciousness knows itself as at once general [*Allgemeine*], or the possibility of abstracting itself from everything definite, and also particular [*Besonderes*], with a fixed object, content or aim. These two elements, however, are only abstractions. The concrete and true—and all that is true is concrete—is the *Allgemeinheit* to which the particular is at first opposed, but, when it has been turned back into itself, is in the end made equal. This unity is individuality [*Einzelheit*], but it is not a simple unit as is the individuality of [image-using] thought [*Vorstellung*], but a unity in terms of its *Begriff* (*Encyclopædia of the Philosophical Sciences*, §§ 112–114). In other words, this individuality is properly nothing else than the *Begriff*. The first two elements of

4. That is, "self-determination" (*Selbstbestimmung*), which is the essence of Hegel's conception of freedom.

the will—that it can abstract itself from everything, and that it is definite through either its own activity or something else—are easily admitted and comprehended, because in their separation they are untrue, and characteristic of the mere understanding. But into the third, the true and speculative—and all truth, as far as it is conceived, must be thought speculatively—the understanding declines to venture, always calling the *Begriff* the inconceivable. The proof and more detailed explanation of this inmost reserve of speculation, of infinitude as the negativity which refers itself to itself, and of this ultimate source of all activity, life and consciousness, belong to logic, as the purely speculative philosophy. Here it can be noticed only in passing that, in the sentences, "The will is *allgemein*," "The will directs itself," the will is already regarded as presupposed subject or substratum; but it is not something finished and general [*Allgemeine*] and complete before it determines itself, nor yet before the superseding [*Aufheben*] and idealization [*Idealität*] of this determining [*Bestimmen*]. It is will only as this self-mediated activity and return into itself.

* * *

27. The absolute determination [*Bestimmung*] or, if you like, the absolute impulse of the free *Geist* is, as has been observed, that its freedom shall be for it an object. It is to be objective in a two-fold sense: it is the rational system of itself, and this system is to be directly real. There is thus actualized as *Idee* what the will is implicitly. Hence, the abstract conception of the *Idee* of the will is in general the free will which wills the free will.

28. The activity of the will, directed to the task of transcending the contradiction between subjectivity and objectivity, of transferring its end from subjectivity into objectivity, and yet while in objectivity of remaining with itself, is beyond the formal method of consciousness, in which objectivity is only direct actuality. This activity is the essential development of the substantive content of the *Idee*. In this development the *Begriff* shapes the *Idee*, which is in the first instance abstract, into the totality of a system. This totality as substantive is independent of the opposition between mere subjective end and its realization, and in both of these forms is the same.

29. "Right" [*das Recht*] is an existing reality through which the free will is an existing reality. Right, therefore, is, in general, freedom as *Idee*.

Note.—In the Kantian doctrine (Introduction to Kant's *Theory of Right*),[5] now generally accepted, "the highest factor is a limitation of my freedom or caprice, in order that it may be able to subsist alongside of every other individual's caprice in accordance with a universal [*allgemein*] law." This doctrine contains only a negative phase, that of limitation. And besides, the positive phase, the "universal law" or so-called law of reason, consisting in the agreement of the caprice of one with that of another, goes beyond the well-known formal identity and the proposition of contradiction. The definition of right just quoted contains the view which has especially since Rousseau[6] spread widely. According to this view neither the absolute and rational will, nor the true *Geist*, but the will and spirit of the particular individual in their

5. See KANT's *Groundwork to the Metaphysics of Morals* (1785).
6. Jean-Jacques Rousseau (1712–1778), Swiss-born French philosopher; he sets out his idea of true liberty in *The Social Contract* (1762).

idiosyncratic caprice, are the substantive and primary basis. When once this principle is accepted, the rational can announce itself only as limiting this freedom. Hence it is not an inherent rationality, but only a mere external and formal universality [*Allgemeine*].[7] This view is accordingly devoid of speculative thought, and is ruled out by the philosophical *Begriff*. In the minds of men and in the actual world it has assumed a shape whose horror is without parallel, except in the shallowness of the thoughts upon which it was founded.

30. Right in general is something holy, because it is the embodiment of the absolute *Begriff* and self-conscious freedom. But the formalism of right (and subsequently of duty) is due to distinctions arising out of the development of the *Begriff* of freedom. In contrast with the more formal, abstract and limited right, there is that sphere or stage of *Geist* in which *Geist* has brought to definite actuality the further elements contained in the *Idee*. This stage is the richer and more concrete; it is truly *allgemein* and has therefore a higher right.

Note.—Every stage in the development of the *Idee* of freedom has its distinctive right,[8] because it is the embodiment of a phase of freedom. When morality and ethicality [*Sittlichkeit*] are spoken of as being in opposition to right, only the first or formal right of the abstract personality is meant. Morality, ethicality, state-interest,[9] are every one a special right, because each of these is a definite realization of freedom. They can come into collision only in so far as they occupy the same plane. If the moral standpoint of *Geist* were not also a right and one of the forms of freedom, it could not collide with the right of personality or any other right. A right contains the *Begriff* of freedom which is the highest phase of *Geist* and in opposition to it any other kind of thing is lacking in real substance. Yet collision also implies a limit and a subordination of one phase to another. Only the right of the *Weltgeist* is the unlimited absolute.

31. The method in the *Wissenschaft* of the *Begriff*, by which the *Begriff* is developed out of itself in an immanent progression and elaboration of its features, is not first of all an assurance that certain relations are given from somewhere else, and then the application of them to the matter at hand. The true process is found in the logic, and here is presupposed.

Note.—The efficient or motive principle, which is not merely the analysis but the production of the several elements of the *Allgemeine*, I call dialectic. Dialectic is not that process in which an object or proposition, presented to feeling or the direct consciousness, is analyzed, entangled, taken hither and thither, until at last its contrary is derived. Such a merely negative method appears frequently in Plato. It may fix the opposite of any notion, or reveal the contradiction contained in it, as did the ancient skepticism, or it may in a feeble way consider an approximation to truth, or modern half-and-half attainment of it, as its goal. But the higher dialectic of the *Begriff* does not merely apprehend any phase as a limit and opposite, but produces out of this negative a positive content and result. Only by such a course is there development

---

7. That is, on the view under consideration, freedom has no rational content, and reason enters the picture only with respect to action as a formal, external constraint on freedom, which is conceived in terms of the "idiosyncratic caprice" of "the will and spirit of the particular individual."

8. That is, its particular form of rightness and normativity (this is often a helpful construal of Hegel's use of the term *Recht*).

9. "Staatsinteresse": that is, civic-mindedness, good citizenship, patriotism.

and inherent progress. Hence this dialectic is not the external agency of sub-jective thinking, but the private soul of the content, which unfolds its branches and fruit organically. Thought[1] regards this development of the *Idee* and of the peculiar activity of the reason of the *Idee* as only subjective, but is on its side unable to make any addition. To consider anything rationally is not to bring reason to it from the outside, and work it up in this way, but to count it as itself reasonable. Here it is *Geist* in its freedom, the summit of self-conscious reason, which gives itself actuality, and produces itself as the existing world. The business of philosophical *Wissenschaft* is simply to bring the specific work of reason, which is in the thing, to consciousness.

32. The phases of the development of the *Begriff* are themselves *Begriffe*. And yet, because the *Begriff* is essentially the *Idee*, they have the form of existing realities [*Dasein*]. Hence the sequence of the *Begriffe*, which arise in this way, is at the same time a sequence of configurations [*Gestaltungen*] and are to be by *Wissenschaft* so considered.

Note.—In a speculative sense the way in which a *Begriff* is manifested in reality is identical with a definite phase of the *Begriff*. But it is noteworthy that, in the *wissenschaftlich* development of the *Idee*, the elements, which result in a further definite form, although preceding this result as phases of the *Begriff*, do not in the temporal development go before it as concrete realiza-tions. Thus, as will be seen later, that stage of the *Idee* which is the *family* presupposes phases of the *Begriff* whose result it is. But that these internal presuppositions should be present in such visible realizations as right of property, contract, morality, etc., is the other side of the process, which only in a highly developed civilization[2] has attained to a specific realization of its elements.

* * *

DIVISION OF THE WORK

33. In accordance with the stages in the development of the *Idee* of the intrin-sically free will,

A. The will is direct or immediate; its *Begriff* is therefore abstract, *i.e.*, per-sonality [*Persönlichkeit*], and its embodied reality is a direct external thing. This is the sphere of abstract or formal right.

B. The will, passing out of external reality, turns back into itself. Its phase is subjective individuality [*Einzelheit*], over against the *Allgemeine*, which is on its internal side *the good*, and on its external side an *established world*, these two sides of the *Idee* only being *mediated* by each other. In this sphere the *Idee* is divided, and exists in separate elements. The right of the subjective will is in a relation of contrast to the right of the world, or the right of the *Idee*. Here, however, the *Idee* exists only implicitly. This is the sphere of *morality* [*Moralität*].

C. The unity and truth of these two abstract elements. The conceived *Idee* of the good is realized both in the will turned back into itself, and also in the

---

1. "Denken": that is, a superficial kind of thinking; mere analytical understanding, in contrast to Hegelian "speculative" (interpretive) reasoning.

2. "Nur in höher vollendeter Bildung": that is, only with the attainment of a more highly developed level of (spiritual, cultural, and social) cultivation.

external world. Thus freedom exists as real substance, which is just as much actuality and necessity as it is subjective will. The *Idee* here is in its intrinsically and explicitly general [*an und für sich allgemein*] existence, viz., ethicality [*Sittlichkeit*].

The ethical substance is again,

a. Natural *Geist*; the *family*;

b. *Geist* in its bifurcation and mere appearance; *civil society*;

c. *The state*, as freedom, which, while established in the free self-dependence of the particular will is also *allgemein* and objective. This actual and organic *Geist* (α) is the *Geist* of a people [*Volk*], (β) is found in the relation to one another of particular *Volksgeister*, and (γ) passing through and beyond this relation is actualized and revealed in world history as the *allgemein Weltgeist*, whose right is the highest.

Note.—* * * Morality and ethicality [*Sittlichkeit*], which are usually supposed to mean the same thing, are here taken in essentially different meanings. Even representational thought [*Vorstellung*] seems to make a distinction between them. In the usage of Kant the preference is given to the term morality, and the practical principles of his philosophy limit themselves wholly to this standpoint, making impossible the standpoint of ethicality, and indeed expressly destroying and abolishing it. Although morality and ethicality have the same meaning according to their etymology,[3] these different words may be used for different conceptions.

From First Part. Abstract Right

34. The intrinsically free will, when it is at the level of its abstract *Begriff*, is in a condition of *immediacy*.[4] What actuality it is when taken in this abstract way consists in a negative attitude towards reality, and a bare abstract relation of itself to itself. Such an abstract will is the particular will of a subject. In accordance with the will's aspect of specificity, it has definite ends, and, as exclusively particular, has these ends before itself as well as an external directly encountered world.

35. The *Allgemeinheit* of this consciously free will consists in a formal, self-conscious but otherwise content-less simple relation to itself in its particularity. The subject is thus so far a *person*. It is implied in personality that I, as a distinct being, am on all sides completely bounded and limited, on the side of inner caprice, impulse and appetite, as well as in my direct and visible outer life. But it is implied likewise that I stand in absolutely pure relation to myself. Hence it is that in this finitude I know myself as infinite, *allgemein*, and free.

Note.—*Personality* does not arise till the subject has not merely a general consciousness of himself in some determinate mode of concrete existence, but rather a consciousness of himself as a completely abstract "I," in which all concrete limits and values are negated and declared invalid. Hence personality involves the knowledge of one self as an object—raised, however, by thought

---

3. The roots of *Moralität* (Latin *mos*, plural *mores*) and of *Sittlichkeit* (German *Sitte*) both mean "custom" (as does the Greek *ethos*, the root of "ethics" and "ethicality").

4. That is, "unmediatedness" (*Unmittelbarkeit*); being not mediated by anything (and therefore very simple and rudimentary).

into the realm of pure infinitude: a realm, that is, in which it is purely identical with itself. Individuals and peoples have no personality, if they have not reached this pure thought and self-consciousness. In this way, too, *Geist* that is in and for itself[5] may be distinguished from its mere semblance. The semblance, though self-conscious, is aware of itself only as a merely natural will with its external objects. *Geist*, on the other hand, as an abstract and pure "I," has itself as its end and object, and is therefore a *person*.

36. (1) Personality implies, in general, a capacity to possess rights, and constitutes the *Begriff* and abstract basis of abstract right. This right, being abstract, must be formal also. Its mandate is: Be a person and respect others as persons.

* * *

From First Section. Property[6]

41. A person must give to his freedom an external sphere, in order that he may reach the completeness implied in the *Idee*. Since a person is as yet the first abstract phase of the completely existent, infinite will, the external sphere of freedom is not only distinguishable from him but directly different and separable.

42. That which is defined as different from the free *Geist* is—both *in* its own nature and also *for* this *Geist*—the external. It is a *thing* [*Sache*], something not free, impersonal and without rights.

Note.—"Thing" [*Sache*], like "objective," has two opposite meanings. When we say "That is the thing or fact [*Sache*]," "It depends on the thing [*Sache*] itself, not on the person," we mean by "thing" [*Sache*] that which is real and substantive. But it is also contrasted with person, which here includes more than a particular subject, and then it means the opposite of the real and substantive, and is something merely external.—What is external for the free *Geist*, which is different from mere consciousness, is absolutely external. Hence nature is to be conceived as that which is external in its very self.

43. The person, in immediate *Begriff* and also as a particular individual, has an existence which is purely natural. This existence is something partly in and of itself, and partly akin in its nature to the external world.—As the individual is considered in his first abstract simplicity, reference is here made only to those features of personality with which he is directly endowed, not to those which he might proceed to acquire by voluntary effort.

* * *

57. In his immediate [unmediated] existence, before it is idealized by self-consciousness, man is merely a natural being, standing outside of his true *Begriff*.[7] Only through the cultivation [*Ausbildung*] of his body and *Geist*, mainly by his becoming conscious of himself as free, does he take possession

---

5. "Der an und für sich seiende Geist": that is, *Geist* that is "for itself" (or explicitly and self-consciously) what it is "in itself" (or essentially), and thus is fully developed and fully "actual" (in Hegel's sense of the term). Such *Geist* is also what Hegel calls "the *Idee* of Geist"—that is, *Geist* whose existing form fully accords with and "realizes" its *Begriff* or structurally articulated essence.

6. Literally, "own-ness" (*das Eigentum*)—that is, that which is "one's own."

7. That is, his existence is far from being in accord with the *Begriff* of fully articulated human nature.

of himself, become his own property, and stand over against others. This active possession of himself, conversely, is the giving of actuality to what he is in *Begriff*, in his possibilities, faculties, and disposition. By this process he is for the first time securely established as his own, becomes a tangible reality as distinguished from a simple consciousness of himself, and thereby becomes capable of being given the form of a thing [*Sache*].

Note.—We are now in a position to consider slavery. We may set aside the justification of slavery based upon the argument that it originates in superior physical force, the taking of prisoners in war, the saving and preserving of life, upbringing, education, or bestowal of kindnesses. These reasons all rest ultimately on the ground that man is to be taken as a merely natural being, living (or, it may even be, choosing) a life which is not adequate to his *Begriff*. Upon the same footing stands the attempted justification of ownership as merely the status of masters, as also all views of the right to slaves founded on history. The assertion of the absolute injustice of slavery on the contrary, clinging to the *Begriff* of man as *Geist*, and as free as such, is also a one-sided idea, since it supposes man to be free *by nature*. In other words, it takes as the truth the *Begriff* in its direct and unreflective form rather than the *Idee*. This antinomy, like all others, rests upon external thinking, which keeps separate and independent each of two aspects of a single complete idea. In point of fact, neither aspect, if separated from the other, is able to measure the *Idee*, and present it in its truth. It is the mark of the free *Geist* that it does not exist merely as *Begriff* or naturally, but that it supersedes its own formalism, transcending thereby its naked natural existence, and gives to itself an existence which, being its own, is free.

Hence the side of the antinomy that insists upon the *Begriff* of freedom is to be preferred, since it contains at least the necessary point of departure for the truth. The other side, refusing to look beyond existence that is utterly at variance with the *Begriff*, has in it nothing reasonable or right at all. The standpoint of the free will, with which right and the *Wissenschaft* of right begin, is already beyond the wrong view that man is simply a natural being, who, as he cannot exist for himself, is fit only to be enslaved. This untrue phenomenon [slavery] had its origin in the circumstance that *Geist* had at that time just attained the level of consciousness. Hence through the dialectical movement of the *Begriff* arises the first inkling of the consciousness of freedom. There is thus by this movement brought to pass a struggle for recognition, and, as a necessary result, the relation of master and slave. But in order that objective *Geist*, which gives substance to right, may not again be apprehended only on its subjective side, and that it may not again appear to be a mere imperative [*Sollen*] that man in his real nature is not fit for slavery, it must come to be recognized that the *Idee* of freedom can truly exist only in the form of *the state* [*nur als der Staat*].

* * *

From *Second Part. Morality* [Moralität]

105. The moral standpoint is the standpoint of the will, not in its abstract or implicit existence, but in its existence for itself, an existence which is infi-

nite. This turning back of the will upon itself, or its actual self-identity, with its associated phases stands in contrast to its abstract implicit existence, and converts person into subject.

106. Subjectivity is the *Begriff* made determinate, differing therefore from the abstract, general will. Further, the will of the subject, though it still retains immediacy, is the will of an individual, who is an object for himself. Hence subjectivity is the *real existence* [*Dasein*] of the *Begriff.*—This gives freedom a higher ground. Now at last there appears in the *Idee* the side of its real existence, the subjectivity of the will. It is only in the will as subjective that freedom, or the potentially existing will, can be actual.

Note.—Morality, the second sphere, gives an indication of the real side of the *Begriff* of freedom. Observe the process through which morality passes. As the will has now withdrawn into itself, it appears at the outset as existing independently, having merely an intrinsic identity with the intrinsically existing or *allgemein* will. After this differentiation—in which it deepens itself within itself—is superseded, the will is able to make itself consciously identical with the intrinsically existing or *allgemein* will. Freedom is at first abstract and distinct from its *Begriff.* By means of this movement the ground of freedom, subjectivity, is sufficiently prepared to align it with its *Begriff,* and thereby to support the true realization of the *Idee.* The process ends, therefore, when the subjective will has become an objective and truly concrete will.

107. As self-determination of will is at the same time a factor of the will's conception, subjectivity is not merely the outward reality of will, but its inner being. This free and independent will, having now become the will of a subject, and assuming in the first instance the form of the *Begriff,* has itself a visible realization; otherwise it could not attain to the *Idee.* The moral standpoint is in its realized form the right of the subjective will. In accordance with this right the will *recognizes* and *is* something only in so far as it is the will's own, and the will in it is itself and subjective.

* * *

121. The *allgemein* quality of action is the manifold content reduced to the simple form of *Allgemeinheit.* But the subject turned back into himself is particular, in opposition to the particulars of the objective world. He has in his end his own particular content, which constitutes the determinate soul of his act. It is the ability of the acting subject to preserve and carry out this element of his particularity in the action that constitutes his *subjective freedom* in its concrete character. This is the subject's right to find in the act his *satisfaction.*

122. By virtue of the particular element the act has for me subjective value or interest. In contrast with this end, whose content is the intention, the direct act in its wider content is reduced to a means. This end, as far as it is finite, can again be reduced to a means for a wider intention, and so on indefinitely.

123. The content of these ends is only (α) formal activity, that is, the subject's interest or aim is to be effected by his agency. Men desire to be themselves actively interested in whatever is or ought to be their own. (β) Further definite content is found for the still abstract and formal freedom of subjectivity only in its natural subjective embodiment, as inclinations, passions, opinions, whims, etc. The satisfaction of this content is *well-being* or *happiness* in

its particularity as also in its *Allgemeinheit*. In this satisfaction consist the ends of finitude generally.

124. Since the subjective satisfaction of the individual—for example, the recognition of oneself as honoured or famous—is involved in the realization of intrinsically valid ends, the demand that only subjective satisfaction should appear as willed and attained, and also the view that in action subjective and objective ends exclude each other, are empty assertions of the abstract understanding. Nay, more, the argument becomes a positive evil when it is held that, because subjective satisfaction is always found in every finished work, it must be the essential intention of the agent, the objective end being only a means to the attainment of this satisfaction. The subject is the series of his acts. If these are a series of worthless productions, the subjectivity of the will is also worthless; if the acts are substantial and sound, so likewise is the inner will of the individual.

* * *

FROM THIRD SECTION. THE GOOD AND CONSCIENCE

129. The good is the *Idee*, or unity of the *Begriff* of the will with the [existing] particular will. Abstract right, well-being, the subjectivity of consciousness, and the contingency of external reality are in their independent and separate existences superseded [*aufgehoben*] in this unity, although in their real essence they are contained in it and preserved. This unity is *realized freedom*, the absolute ultimate aim [*Endzweck*] of the world.

* * *

133. Since the good is of the essence [*das Wesentliche*] of the will of the particular subject, it is his obligation. As the good is distinct from particularity, and particularity occurs in the subjective will, the good has at the outset only the character of abstract *allgemein* essentiality—*duty*. Hence duty, as is required by its character, must be done for duty's sake.

134. Since an act requires its own special content and definite end, and duty in the abstract contains no such end, there arises the question, "What is duty?" No answer is at once forthcoming, except "To do right and to pursue well-being—one's own well-being and well-being more generally, the well-being of others."

* * *

136. Owing to the abstract nature of the good, the other side of the *Idee*, i.e., particularity in general, falls within subjectivity. This subjectivity, attaining *Allgemeinheit* by being turned back into itself, is absolute certainty [*Gewissheit*] of itself within itself, as it establishes particularity, determines and judges. This is *conscience* [*Gewissen*].

137. True conscience is the disposition to desire what is absolutely good. It has therefore fixed rules, which are for it objective determinations and duties. Apart from this, which is its content or truth, conscience is only the formal side of the activity of the will, and the will as particular has no content peculiarly its own. The objective system of rules and duties and the union of them

with the subjective consciousness appear first in the sphere of ethicality [*Sittlichkeit*]. But at the formal standpoint of morality, conscience is devoid of objective content. It is merely an unbounded certainty of itself and is formal and abstract. It is the certainty of a particular subject.

Note.—Conscience expresses the absolute claim of the subjective self-consciousness to know in itself and from itself what right and duty are, and to recognize nothing except what it thus knows to be good. It asserts also that what it so knows and wills is right and duty in very truth. Conscience, as the unity of the subject's will with the absolute, is a holy place which it would be sacrilege to assault. But whether the conscience of a certain individual is proportionate to this *Idee* of conscience—in other words, whether what the individual conscience holds and gives out to be good is really good—can be ascertained only by an examination of the contents of the intended good. Right and duty, viewed as intrinsically rational determinations of will, are not in essence the particular property of an individual. Nor do they take the form of feeling or any other sort of mere individual consciousness, such as knowledge by way of the senses. Rather, they are essentially *allgemein* thought-out determinations, and take the form of laws and principles. Conscience is therefore subject to the judgment whether it is true or not, and its appeal merely to itself is directly opposed to what it wills to be—the rule of a rational, intrinsically valid *allgemein* way of acting. For this reason the state cannot recognize conscience in its peculiar form as subjective consciousness, just as subjective opinion, or the dogmatic appeal to a subjective opinion, can be of no avail in science.

The elements which are united in true conscience can be separated. The determining subjectivity of consciousness and will may separate itself from the true content, set itself up on its own, and reduce true content to form and illusion. Thus the term conscience is ambiguous. On the one hand it is presupposed in the identity of subjective consciousness and will with the true good, and is therefore maintained and recognized to be a holy thing. On the other hand it can be the mere subjective return of consciousness into itself, claiming the authority which conscience in its first form possesses solely because of its intrinsically valid and rational content.

* * *

TRANSITION FROM MORALITY TO ETHICALITY [*SITTLICHKEIT*]

141. In the case of conscience, as the mere abstract principle of determining [*Bestimmen*], it is demanded that its determinations shall have *Allgemeinheit* and objectivity. In the same way in the case of the good which, though it is the substantial *Allgemeine* of freedom, is still abstract, are also required definite determinations; and for them is further demanded a principle which must, however, be identical with the good. The good and conscience, when each is raised into a separate totality, are void of all definiteness, and yet need to be made definite. Still, the integration of these two relative totalities into an absolute identity is already accomplished in germ, since even the subjectivity or pure self-certainty, which vanishes by degrees in its own vacuity, is identical with the abstract *Allgemeinheit* of the good. But the concrete identity of the good and the subjective will, the truth of these two, is completed only in ethicality [*Sittlichkeit*].

From *Third Part. Ethicality* [*Sittlichkeit*][8]

142. Ethicality [*Sittlichkeit*] is the *Idee*[9] *of freedom*, as the living good, which has in self-consciousness its knowing and willing, and through corresponding action has its actuality. Self-consciousness, on the other hand, finds in ethicality its absolute basis and motive. Ethicality is thus the *Begriff* of freedom developed into a present world, and also into the nature of self-consciousness.

143. The unity of the *Begriff* of will and its realization, which is the particular will, is knowing [*Wissen*]. Hence arises the consciousness of the distinction between these two aspects of the *Idee*. But the consciousness is now present in such a way that each aspect is separately the totality of the *Idee*, and has the *Idee* as its content and foundation.

144. The objective ethical principle which takes the place of the abstract good is in its substance concrete, through the presence in it of subjectivity as its infinite form. Hence it generates differences which are within itself, and therefore are due to the *Begriff*. By means of these differences, it obtains definite content, which is independent and binding [*notwendig*], and constitutes firm ground raised above subjective opinion and preference. This content is the existing and recognized *laws and institutions*.[1]

145. The fact that the ethical [*das Sittliche*] is the *system* of these determinations of the *Idee* is constitutive of its *rationality*. Thus freedom, the absolute will, the objective, and the circle of necessity are all one principle, whose elements are the ethical forces. They govern the lives of individuals, and in individuals as their modes have their shape, manifestation, and actuality.

146. (β) This ethical substance [*Substanz*] in its actual self-consciousness knows itself, and is therefore an object of knowledge. It, with its laws and forces, has for the subject a real existence, and is in the fullest sense independent. It has an absolute and infinitely greater authority or force than anything merely natural.

Note.—The sun, moon, mountains, rivers, and all objects of nature doubtless exist. They not only have for consciousness the authority of existence in general, but have also a particular nature. This nature consciousness regards as valid, and in its varied relation and commerce with objects and their use comports itself accordingly. But the authority of social laws [*sittliche Gesetze*] is infinitely higher, because natural things represent reason only in a quite external and particular way, and hide it under the guise of contingency.

147. On the other hand, the various social forces are not something foreign to the subject. His *Geist* bears witness to them as to his own being. In them he feels that he is himself, and in them, too, he lives as in an element indistinguishable from himself. This relation is more direct and intuitive than even faith or trust.

---

8. *Sittlichkeit* is often translated as "ethical life" or with a similar phrase (e.g., Dyde used "the ethical system"). But since Hegel means it to be understood as a third type of "rightness" and normativity, comparable to but distinct from "legality" and "morality," "ethicality" is a better rendering. (See the Hegel glossary, p. 144.) Note, however, that Hegel's analysis of what "being ethical" or "living ethically" properly means and amounts to differs in important ways from both the common and the usual philosophical understanding. See §144 and the footnote to it.

9. That is (in this context), realization.
1. "Die an und für sich seienden Gesetze und Einrichtungen": that is, the established and generally recognized and accepted rules, norms, and institutions (both official and more informal) of one's society. Where there are no such established and accepted normative structures, for Hegel, there is and can be no "ethicality"—and thus no normativity other than that of mere "positive" legality and that of morality, which on his analysis is essentially contentless.

148. The individual may distinguish himself from these substantive determinations, regarding himself as subjective and essentially undetermined, or as determined otherwise in some particular way. In this case he relates to them as to a substantive reality, and they are duties binding upon his will.

Note.—The ethical theory of duties in their objective character is not comprised under the empty principle of moral subjectivity, in which, indeed, nothing is determined (§ 134), but is rightly taken up in the third part of our work, in which is found a systematic development of the sphere of ethical necessity. In this present method of treatment, as distinguished from a theory of duties, the ethical factors are deduced as necessary relations. It is, then, needless to add, with regard to each of them, the remark that it is thus for men a duty. A theory of duties, so far as it is not a philosophical discipline, simply takes its material out of the relations at hand, and shows how it is connected with personal ideas, with widely prevalent principles and thoughts, with ends, impulses, and experiences. It may also adduce as reasons the consequences which arise when each duty is referred to other ethical relations, as well as to general well-being and common opinion. But a theory of duties, which keeps to the logical settlement of its own inherent material, must be the development of the relations which are made necessary through the *Idee* of freedom, and are hence in their entire context actual. This is found only in the state.

149. A duty or obligation appears as a limitation merely of undetermined subjectivity and abstract freedom, or of the impulse of the natural will, or of the moral will which fixes upon its undetermined good capriciously. But in point of fact the individual finds in duty *liberation*. He is freed from subjection to mere natural impulse; he is freed from the dependence which he as subjective and particular felt towards moral permission and command; he is freed, also, from that indefinite subjectivity, which does not issue in the objective realization implied in action, but remains wrapped up in its own unreality. In duty the individual freely enters upon a freedom that is substantive.

150. The ethical, in so far as it is reflected simply in the naturally determined character of the individual, is virtue [*Tugend*]. When it contains nothing more than conformity to the duties of the context of relations to which the individual belongs, it is dutifulness [*Rechtschaffenheit*].

Note.—What a man ought to do, or what duties he should fulfil in order to be virtuous, is in an ethical community not difficult to determine. He has to do nothing more than what is presented, expressed and recognized in his established relations. Dutifulness is the general trait which should be found in his character, partly on legal, partly on ethical grounds. But from the moral standpoint one often looks upon dutifulness both for oneself and others as secondary and unessential. The longing to be distinctive is not satisfied with what is inherently worthy and *allgemein*, but only with something exceptional.

The name "virtue" may quite as well be applied to the different aspects of dutifulness, because they, too, although they contain nothing belonging exclusively to the individual in contrast with others, are yet his possession. But discourse about the virtues easily passes into mere declamation, since its subject matter is abstract and indefinite, and its reasons and declarations are directed to the individual's caprice and subjective inclination. In any present ethical circumstance, whose relations are fully developed and actualized, virtue in the strict sense has place and reality only when these relations come into collision. But genuine collisions are rare, although moral reflection can, on the slightest provocation, create them. It can also provide itself with the consciousness that, in order to fulfil its special mission, it must make sacrifices. Hence, in undeveloped conditions of social life virtue as such occurs more frequently, because ethical principles and the realization of them are more a matter of private liking, belonging indeed to the nature of peculiarly gifted individuals. Thus, the ancients have attributed virtue in a special way to Hercules.[2] So, too, in the ancient states, where ethical principles had not expanded into a system of free self-dependent development and objectivity, ethical defects had to be compensated for by the genius of the private individual. Thus the theory of the virtues, so far as it differs from a mere theory of duties, embraces the special features of character due to natural endowments, and thus becomes a spiritual history of the natural in man.

* * *

151. If there is a simple identity of the individual with [social] actuality, the ethical [das Sittliche] appears as a generally adopted mode of action, or custom [Sitte]. This is habit [Gewohnheit], which as a second nature has been substituted for the original and merely natural will, and has become the very soul, meaning, and reality of one's daily life. It is the living Geist actualized as a world; by this actualization does the substance of Geist exist as Geist.

152. Substantive ethical reality attains its right, and this right receives its due, when the individual in his private will and conscience drops his self-assertion and antagonism to the ethical. His character, moulded by ethical principles, takes as its motive the unmoved Allgemeine, which is open on all its sides to actual rationality. He recognizes that his worth and the stability of his private ends are grounded upon the Allgemeine and derive their reality from it. Subjectivity is the absolute form and the existing actuality of the substance. The difference between the subject and substance, as the object, end, and power of the subject, forthwith vanishes, like the difference between form and matter.

Note.—Subjectivity, which is the foundation for the real existence of the Begriff of freedom (§ 106), is at the moral standpoint still [in distinction] from the Begriff. In [the ethical] it is adequate to the Begriff, whose existence it is.

153. In that individuals belong to the ethical and social fabric they have a right to determine themselves subjectively and freely. Assurance of their freedom has its truth in the objectivity of ethicality in which they realize their own peculiar being and inner Allgemeinheit (§ 147).

Note.—To a father seeking the best way to bring up his son, a Pythagorean,[3] or some other thinker, replied, "Make him a citizen of a state [that] has good laws."

154. The right of individuals to their particularity is contained in the concrete ethical order, because particularity is the visible outward way in which the ethical [das Sittliche] exists.

2. The greatest hero of classical mythology.
3. A follower of the teachings of the Greek philosopher Pythagoras (6th c. B.C.E.).

155. Right and duty coincide in the identity of the *allgemein* and the particular wills. By virtue of the ethical fabric man has rights so far as he has duties, and duties so far as he has rights. In abstract right, on the contrary, I have the right and another person the corresponding duty; while in the case of moral right, I resolve to consider as an objective duty only the right of my own knowledge and will and of my own well-being.

156. The ethical substance [*Die sittliche Substanz*], as the union of self-consciousness with its *Begriff*, is the actual *Geist* of a family and a people [*Volk*].

157. The *Begriff* of this *Idee* exists only as *Geist*, as active self-knowledge and reality, since it objectifies itself by passing through the form of its elements. Hence it is,

A. The direct or natural ethical *Geist*, the *family*. This reality, losing its unity, passes over into dismemberment, and assumes the nature of the relational. It thus becomes—

B. civil society [*bürgerliche Gesellschaft*], an association of members or independent individuals in a formal *Allgemeinheit*. Such an association is occasioned by needs, and is preserved by the law, which secures one's person and property, and by an external system for private and common interests. This external "state"—

C. returns to, and finds its central principle in, the end and actuality of the substantive *Allgemeine*, and of the public life dedicated to its maintenance. This is the *state-constitution* [*Staatsverfassung*].

FROM FIRST SECTION. THE FAMILY

158. The family is the direct substantive reality of *Geist*. The unity of the family is one of feeling, the feeling of love. The true disposition here is that which esteems the unity as absolutely essential, and within it places the consciousness of oneself as an individuality. Hence, in the family we are not independent persons but members.

* * *

163. The ethical significance of marriage consists in the consciousness that the union is a substantive end. Marriage thus rests upon love, confidence, and the commonality [*Gemeinsamkeit*] of the whole individual existence. In this sensibility and actuality natural impulse is reduced to the mode of a merely natural element, which is extinguished in the moment of its satisfaction. On the other hand, the *geistig* bond of union, when its right as a substantive fact is recognized, is raised above the vicissitudes of passion and of temporary particular inclination, and is of itself indissoluble.

Note.—It has already been remarked that there is no contract in connection with the essential character of marriage. Marriage leaves behind and transcends the standpoint of contract, occupied by the person who is sufficient for himself. Substance is such as to be in essential relation to its accidents. The union of personalities, whereby the family becomes one person, and its members its accidents, is the ethical spirit [*sittliche Geist*].

* * *

FROM SECOND SECTION. CIVIL SOCIETY
[DIE BÜRGERLICHE GESELLSCHAFT]

182. The concrete person, who as particular is an end to himself, is a totality of wants and a mixture of necessity and caprice. As such he is one of the principles of civil society. But the particular person is essentially connected with others. Hence each establishes and satisfies himself by means of others, and so must call in the assistance of the form of *Allgemeinheit*. This *Allgemeinheit* is the other principle of the civic community.

183. The self-seeking end is conditioned in its realization by *Allgemeinheit*. Hence is formed a system of mutual dependence, a system which interweaves the subsistence, happiness, and rights of the individual with the subsistence, happiness, and right of all. The general right and well-being form the basis of the individual's right and well-being, which only by this connection receives actuality and security. This system we may in the first instance call the *external state*, the state which satisfies one's needs, and meets the requirement of comprehensibility.

184. When the *Idee* is thus at variance with itself, it imparts to the different aspects of possessive existence—to particularity, the right to develop and promote itself on all sides; and, to *Allgemeinheit*, the right to evince itself as the foundation and necessary form, predominating power and final end of the particular.[4] In this situation ethicality is lost in its own extremes. This is a system characterized by external appearance and constituted by the abstract side of the reality of the *Idee*. In it the *Idee* is found only as relative totality, and inner necessity.

185. When independent particularity gives free rein to the satisfaction of want, caprice, and subjective predilection, it destroys in its extravagance both itself and its substantive *Begriff*. On the other hand satisfaction—whether of necessary or of contingent want—is contingent, since it contains no inherent limit, and is wholly dependent on external chance, caprice, and the power of the *Allgemeine*.[5] In these conflicts and complexities civil society affords a spectacle of excess, misery, and physical and social corruption.

186. But the principle of particularity develops of its own accord into a totality, and thus goes over into *Allgemeinheit*, in which it has its truth and its right to positive realization. Owing to the independence of these principles of particularity and *Allgemeinheit*, however, their unity is not an ethical identity. It does not exist as freedom, but as a necessity. That is to say the particular has to raise itself to the form of *Allgemeinheit*, and in it it has to seek and find its subsistence.

187. Individuals as citizens in such societies are private persons, who pursue their own interests. As these interests are mediated by the *Allgemeine*, which appears as a means, they can be obtained only in so far as individuals in their desire, will, and conduct, conform to the *Allgemeine*, and become a link in the chain of the whole. The interest of the *Idee* as such does not, it is true, lie in the consciousness of the citizens; yet it is not wholly lacking. It is found in the process by means of which the individual, through necessity

---

4. That is, in "civil (bourgeois) society," the dynamics of the situation lead to extreme forms of both individualistic particularity and political authority.

5. That is, in this context, the power of political authority.

of nature and the caprice of his wants, seeks to raise his individual natural existence into formal freedom and the formal *Allgemeinheit* of knowing and willing. Thus subjectivity in its particularity is educated and transformed [*gebildet*].

Note.—The view that educated civilization [*Bildung*] is an external and degenerate form of life is allied to the idea that the natural condition of uncivilized peoples is one of unsophisticated innocence. So also the view that education [*Bildung*] is a mere means for the satisfaction of one's needs, and for the enjoyment and comfort of one's particular life, takes for granted that these selfish ends are absolute. Both theories manifest ignorance of the nature of *Geist* and the end of reason. *Geist* is real only when by its own motion it divides itself, gives itself limit and finitude in the natural needs and the region of external necessity, and then, by moulding and shaping itself in them, overcomes them, and secures for itself an objective embodiment. The rational end, therefore, is neither the simplicity of nature nor the enjoyments resulting from *Bildung* through the development of particularity. It rather works away from the condition of simple nature, in which there is either no self or a crude state of consciousness and will, and transcends the naïve individuality in which *Geist* is initially submerged. Its externality thus in the first instance receives the rationality of which it is capable—namely, the form of *Allgemeinheit* characteristic of the understanding. Only in this way is *Geist* at home and with itself in this externality as such. Hence in it the freedom of *Geist* is realized. *Geist*, becoming actualized in an element which of itself was foreign to its free character, has to do only with what is produced by itself and bears its own impress. In this way the form of *Allgemeinheit* comes into independent existence in thought—a form which is the only worthy element for the existence of the *Idee*.

Bildung is, as we may thus conclude, in its ultimate sense a liberation, and that of a high kind. Its task is to make possible the infinitely subjective substantiality of ethicality. In the process we pass upwards from the direct and natural existence to what is *geistig* and has the form of *Allgemeinheit*. In the individual agent this liberation involves a struggle against mere subjectivity, immediate desire, subjective vanity, and capricious preference. The hardness of the task is in part the cause of the disfavour under which it falls. None the less is it through the labour of *Bildung* that the subjective will itself wins possession of the objectivity in which alone it is able and worthy to be the embodiment of the *Idee*.

At the same time the form of *Allgemeinheit*, into which particularity has moulded itself and worked itself up, gives rise to that general principle of the understanding in accordance with which the particular passes upward into the true, independent existence of the individual. And since the particular gives to the *Allgemeine* its adequate content and unconditioned self-direction, it even in the ethical sphere is infinitely independent and free subjectivity. *Bildung* is thus proved to be an inherent element of the absolute, and is shown to have infinite value.

188. Civil society contains three elements:

A. The mediation [and transformation] of need, and the satisfaction of the individual through his work, through the work of all others, and through the satisfaction of their needs. This is a system of *needs*.

B. Actualization of the *Allgemeine* of freedom required for this, *i.e.*, the protection of property by the administration of justice.

C. Provision against possible contingencies, and care for the particular interest as a common one [*Gemeinsame*], by means of police and the corporation.[6]

THE SYSTEM OF NEEDS [*BEDÜRFNISSE*][7]

189. The particularity, which is in the first instance opposed to the *Allgemeine* of will, is subjective need. It gets objectivity, *i.e.*, is satisfied (α), through external objects, which are at this stage the property of others, and the product of their needs and wills, and (β) through active labour, as connecting link between subjective and objective. Labour has as its aim to satisfy subjective particularity. Yet by the introduction of the needs and free choice of others *Allgemeinheit* is realized. Hence rationality comes as an appearance into the sphere of the finite. This partial presence of rationality is the understanding, to which is assigned the function of reconciling the opposing elements of the finite sphere.

(A) NEED AND ITS SATISFACTION

190. The animal has a limited range of ways and means for satisfying its limited needs. Man in his dependence proves his *Allgemeinheit* and his ability to become independent, firstly, by multiplying his needs and means, and, secondly, by dissecting the concrete need into parts. The parts then become other needs, and through being specialized are more abstract than the first.

Note.—In abstract right [i.e., law] the object is a *person*; in the moral standpoint, a *subject*; in the family, a *member*; in civil society generally, a *citizen* [*Bürger*] (as *bourgeois*); and here, at the standpoint of need he is the concrete object of representation [*Vorstellung*] which we call *man* [*Mensch*]. Here, and properly only here, is it that we first speak of "man" in this sense.

191. The means for satisfying the specialized needs similarly divided and increased. These means become in their turn relative ends and abstract needs. Hence the multiplication expands into an infinite series of distinctions with regard to these phases, and of judgments concerning the suitability of the means to their ends. This is *refinement* [*Verfeinerung*].

192. The satisfaction of need and the attainment of means thereto become a realized possibility for others, through whose wants and labour satisfaction is in turn conditioned. The abstraction, which becomes a quality of needs and means (§ 191), helps to determine the mutual relation of individuals. This *Allgemeinheit* as *being recognized* [*Anerkanntsein*] is the dimension [*Moment*]

---

6. "Die Polizei und Korporation": that is, administrative authorities (*Polizei*) and professional associations (*Korporationen*), which control access to and standards in the professions they organize and oversee. Hegel chiefly had in mind guilds, but their diverse descendants—from trade unions to credentialing and standards-enforcing bodies such as the American Medical Association—continue to play significant roles in contemporary socioeconomic life.

7. *Bedürfnis* is sometimes translated as "want"

(which can have the sense of "lack"). One of Hegel's points about *Bedürfnisse* is that the line between what we now generally mean by "wants" and "needs" is a very fine one, if it can be drawn at all, since we can experience as needs things inessential to bare survival that were once (and perhaps for many still are) merely objects of desire, or even matters of indifference or distaste. But for the most part "need" would seem to be the more apt contemporary translation of Hegel's term.

which makes the isolated abstract needs, ways and means concrete and *social* [*gesellschaftlich*].

193. The social dimension is a special instrument both of the simple acquisition of the means, and also of the reduplication of the ways by which need is satisfied. Further, it contains directly the claim of equality with others. Both the desire for equality, including the imitation of others, and also the desire of each person to be unique, become real sources of the multiplication and extension of needs.

194. In [simplistic] representational thinking [*Vorstellung*], social need conjoins unmediated or natural need and *geistig* need;[8] but the latter, as the *Allgemeine*, outweighs the former. The social element brings a liberation, by which the stringent necessity of nature is turned aside, and man is determined by his own *allgemein intention* [*Meinung*]. He makes his own necessity, in place of that which is owing merely to external or internal contingencies or to arbitrary choice.

Note.—There is a crude idea [*Vorstellung*], with respect to need, that man is free in a so-called state of nature, in which he has only the so-called simple needs of nature, requiring for their satisfaction merely the means furnished directly and at random by nature. In this view no account is taken of the freedom which lies in *work*, of which more hereafter. Such a view is not true, because in natural need and its direct satisfaction, *Geistigkeit* is submerged in mere nature. Hence, a state of nature is a state of brutishness and unfreedom. Freedom is nowhere to be found except in the reflection of *Geist* within itself—a process by which it distinguishes itself from the natural and turns away from it.

* * *

(c) WEALTH.

199. Through the dependence and co-operation involved in labour, subjective self-seeking is converted into a contribution towards the satisfaction of the needs of all others. The *Allgemeine* so mediates the particular by its dialectic movement that the individual, while acquiring, producing, and enjoying for himself, at the same time produces and acquires for the enjoyment of others. This is a necessity, and in this necessity arising out of mutual dependence is contained the fact of an *allgemein*, enduring wealth. In it each person may share by means of his cultivation [*Bildung*] and skill. Each, too, is by it assured of subsistence, while the results of his labour preserve and increase the general wealth.

* * *

256.* * * *Note.*—* * * The development of simple ethicality [*Sittlichkeit*] through the [stage of division] marking civil society, and then [onward] into the *state*, which is shown to be the true foundation of these more abstract

---

8. That is, because representational thinking (*Vorstellung*) operates with simplistic models or mental images, it lumps all forms of need together under the same simple picture of "need," thereby obscuring significant differences.

phases, is the only *wissenschaftlich* demonstration of the *Begriff* of the state.—Although in the course of the *wissenschaftlich* exposition the state has the appearance of a result, it is in reality the true foundation. This intermediary account must now be superseded by a direct one. In actual fact the state is in general rather more *primary*. Within it the family develops into civil society, the *Idee* of the state being one that sunders itself into these two elements. In the development of civil society the ethical substance reaches its infinite form, which contains the following elements: (1) infinite differentiation, even at the point at which consciousness as it is in itself exists for itself, and (2) the form of *Allgemeinheit*, which in culture [*Bildung*] is the form of thought, that form by which *Geist* is itself in its laws and institutions. They are its reflected [*gedachten*] will,[9] and it and they together become objective and real in an organic whole.

FROM THIRD SECTION. THE STATE [*DER STATT*]

257. The state is the actuality of the ethical *Idee*—the ethical *Geist*, as the will which manifests itself, makes itself clear and visible, substantiates itself. It is the will which thinks and knows itself, and carries out what it knows, and in so far as it knows. The state finds in *custom* [*Sitte*] its direct and unreflected existence, and finds its indirect and reflected existence in the self-consciousness of the individual and in his knowledge and activity. Self-consciousness in the form of *disposition* likewise finds in the state, as the essence, purpose, and product of its activity, its *substantive freedom*.

258. The state, which is the realized substantive will, having its reality in the particular self-consciousness raised to its inherent *Allgemeinheit*, is intrinsically rational. This substantive unity is its own motive and absolute end. In this end freedom attains its highest right. This end has the highest right over the individual, whose highest duty in turn is to be a member of the state.

Note. Were the state to be considered as exchangeable with civil society, and were its decisive features to be regarded as the security and protection of property and personal freedom, the interest of the individual as such would be the ultimate purpose of the social union. It would then be one's option whether to be a member of the state. But the state has a totally different relation to the individual [*Individuum*]. It is objective *Geist*, and the individual has his truth, real existence, and ethical status only in being a member of it. Union [*Vereinigung*], as such, is itself the true content and end, since the individual is intended to lead an *allgemein* life.[1] His particular satisfactions, activities, and way of life have in this substantive and generally valid [*allgemeingültig*] principle their origin and result.

Rationality, viewed abstractly, consists in the thorough unity of *Allgemeinheit* and particularity [*Einzelheit*]. Taken concretely, and from the standpoint of the content, it is the unity of objective freedom with subjective freedom, of

9. That is, the laws and institutions of a society and people are their collective (general, *allgemein*) will as it has been articulated and developed in thought and given these sorts of objective expressions and form.
1. "Die Bestimmung der Individuen, ein allgemeines Leben zu führen": in Hegel's view, *Allgemeinheit*

(literally, having characteristics that are "common to all" in various contexts) is what is most essential to our human-*geistig* nature. *Bestimmung* here has the sense of "vocation," "calling," or "true nature"; see the source note to FICHTE's *Vocation of Man* (1800), above.

the *allgemein* substantive will with the individual consciousness and the individual will seeking particular ends. From the standpoint of the form it consists in action determined by thought-out and thus *allgemein* laws and principles. This *Idee* is the intrinsically eternal and necessary being of *Geist*.

The *Idee* of the state is not concerned with the historical origin of either the state in general or of any particular state with its special rights and characters. Hence, it is indifferent whether the state arose out of the patriarchal condition, out of fear or confidence, or out of the corporation. It does not care whether the basis of state rights is declared to be in the divine, or in positive right, or contract, or custom. When we are dealing simply with the *Wissenschaft* of the state, these things are mere appearances, and belong to history. The causes or grounds of the authority of an actual state, in so far as they are required at all, must be derived from the forms of right, which have their validity in the state.

* * *

259. The *Idee* of the state (*a*) has direct actuality in the individual state. It, as a self-relating organism, is the constitution or internal state-organization [*Staatsrecht*].

(*b*) It passes over into a relation of the individual state to other states. This is its external organization.

(*c*) This *Idee* is also the *allgemein Idee* as species or kind, and as such it has absolute power over individual states. This is the *Geist* which gives itself actuality in the process of world-history.

INTERNAL POLITY.

260. The state is the actuality of concrete freedom.[2] In this concrete freedom, personal individuality and its particular interests, as found in the family and civil society, have their complete development. In this concrete freedom, too, the rights of personal individuality receive adequate recognition. These interests and rights pass partly of their own accord into the interest of the *Allgemeine*—which the individuals also recognize by their own knowledge and will as their own substantive *Geist*, and work for as their own end. Hence, neither is the *Allgemeine* completed without the assistance of the particular interest, knowledge, and will, nor, on the other hand, do individuals, as private persons, live merely for their own special concern. They regard the *allgemein* end, and are in all their activities conscious of this end. The modern state has enormous strength and depth, in that it allows the principle of subjectivity to complete itself to an independent extreme of personal particularity, and yet at the same time brings it back into the substantive unity, and thus preserves particularity in the principle of the state.

261. In contrast with the spheres of private right and private good, of the family and of civil society, the state is on the one hand an external necessity. It is thus a higher authority, in regard to which the laws and interests of the family and community are subject and dependent. On the other hand, however,

---

2. That is, the genuine Hegelian "state" is what enables concrete freedom (*konkrete Freiheit*) to be fully actualized, by way of the various functions it performs.

the state is the immanent end of these things, and has its strength in its union of the *allgemein* end with the particular interests of individuals. Thus, in so far as people have duties to fulfil towards it, they likewise have rights (§ 155).

Note. * * * Duty is, in the first instance, a relation to something, which is for me a substantial and self-subsisting *Allgemeine*. Right, on the other hand, is in general some embodiment of this substantive reality, and hence brings to the front its particular side and my particular freedom. These two things, treated formally, appear as deputed to different phases or persons. But the state as ethical [*sittlich*], implying thorough interpenetration of the substantive and the particular, brings to light the fact that my obligation to the substantive reality is at the same time the realization of my particular freedom. In the state, duty and right are bound together in one and the same relation. * * *

* * * The *Begriff* of the union of duty and right is one of the most important features of states, and to it is due their internal strength. The abstract treatment of duty insists upon casting aside and banishing the particular interest as something unessential and even unworthy. But the concrete approach, or the *Idee*, shows particularity to be essential, and the satisfaction of the particular to be a sheer necessity. In carrying out his duty the individual must in some way or other discover his own interest, his own satisfaction and recompense. A right must accrue to him out of his relation to the state, whereby the *allgemein* concern becomes *his own particular* concern. The particular interest must in truth be neither set aside nor suppressed, but be placed in open concord with the *Allgemeine*. In this concord both particular and *Allgemeine* are included. The individual, who from the point of view of his duties is a subject, finds, in fulfilling his civic duties, protection of person and property, satisfaction of his real self, and the consciousness and self-respect implied in his being a member of this whole. Since the citizen discharges his duty as a performance and business for the state, the state is enduringly preserved. Viewed from the plane of abstraction, on the other hand, the interest of the *Allgemeine* would be satisfied if the contracts and business required of him are by him simply fulfilled as duties.

262. The actual *Idee*, *Geist*, divides itself, as we have said, into the two ideal spheres of its *Begriff*, the family and civil society. It descends into its two ideal and finite spheres, in order that it may by way of them become actually infinite and actual. Hence, *Geist* distributes to individuals generally the material of its finite realization in these spheres, in such a way that its apportionment to them has the appearance of being occasioned by circumstances, caprice, and private choice.

263. In these two spheres, in which the elements of particularity and specificity [*Einzelheit* and *Besonderheit*] have their unmediated and reflected reality (respectively), *Geist* is their objective *Allgemeinheit* in the form of appearance. It is the power of the rational in necessity (§ 184)—namely, as the above-mentioned institutions.

264. Individuals in general, because they have a *geistig* nature, have a twofold character: at one extreme, independently conscious and willing individuality, and at the other, *Allgemeinheit*, which knows and wills what is substantive. They obtain the rights of both these aspects only in so far as they themselves are actual, both as private and as substantive persons. One right

they have directly in the family, the other in civil society. In these two institutions, reflecting the intrinsic *Allgemeinheit* of their specific interests, individuals have their real self-conscious existence. And in the corporation[3] they provide for these particular interests a wider scope, and an activity directed to an *allgemein* end.

265. These institutions comprise in detail the constitution [*Verfassung*], that is, developed and actualized rationality *in specific forms* [*im Besonderen*]. They are the steadfast basis of the state, determining the disposition of individuals towards the state, and their confidence in it. They are, moreover, the foundation-stones of public freedom, because in them particular freedom becomes realized in a rational form. They thus involve an intrinsic union of freedom and necessity.

266. But *Geist* is realized and becomes its own object, not only as this necessity[4] and as a domain of appearances, but as their ideality and inner being. Substantive *Allgemeinheit* is thus an object and end for itself, and this necessity thereby assumes the form of freedom.

267. The necessity within this ideality pertains to the development of the *Idee* within itself. As subjective substantiality the *Idee* is a political disposition [*politische Gesinnung*]; and in distinction from this, as objective substantiality, it is the organism of the state, *i.e.*, the strictly political state, and its constitution.

268. Political disposition, or, in general terms, patriotism, may be defined as the certainty [*Gewissheit*] which stands in truth, and willingness [*Wollen*] that has become habitual [*Gewohnheit*]. Mere subjective certainty does not proceed out of truth, and is only opinion. Genuine patriotism is simply a result of the institutions which exist in the state as in the actuality of reason. Hence, patriotic feeling is operative in the act, which is in accord with these institutions. Political sentiment is, in general, a confidence, which may pass over into a more or less intelligent insight; it is a consciousness that my substantive and particular interest is contained and preserved in the interest and end of another—here the state—in its relation to me, the individual. Wherefore the state is for me forthwith not another, and I in this consciousness am free.[5]

Note.—By patriotism is frequently understood merely a readiness to submit to exceptional sacrifices or do exceptional acts. But in reality it is the sentiment which arises in ordinary circumstances and ways of life, and is wont to regard the commonweal as its substantive basis and end. This consciousness is kept intact in the routine of life, and upon it the readiness to submit to exceptional effort is based. But as men would rather be magnanimous than merely right, they easily persuade themselves that they possess this

---

3. That is, profession-centered organizations that both maintain professional standards and serve the well-being of their members. On *Korporation*, see n. 6, p. 322.

4. That is, the institutions discussed in the previous paragraph—whose established laws, rules, norms, and practices have the character of (practical) "necessity" or obligatoriness for all concerned (hence their *Allgemeinheit* or general applicability to their members in the relevant roles or situations).

5. That is, if I view the state (the society of which I am a part) in the manner just described, I in effect identify myself with it; if I identify with it, it is not something "other" in relation to me. By virtue of this "consciousness" (identification), I can be said to be "self-determining" (rather than being determined by something alien to or other than myself, with which I do not identify) when I am acting willingly (and thus "patriotically") in accordance with my society's institutions, laws, rules, and the like—and so, as "self-determining," am concretely *free*. This is what it turns out to mean to be actually and concretely "free" at the level of "objective *Geist*" and practical rationality.

extraordinary patriotism, in order to spare themselves the burden of the true sentiment, and to excuse the lack of it. If this feeling be regarded as something which provides its own basis, and can proceed out of [simplistic] notions [*Vorstellungen*] and thoughts, it is confounded with mere opinion [*Meinung*], and in that case is devoid of its true basis in objective reality.

* * *

270. (1) The abstract actuality or substantiality of the state consists in this, that the end pursued by the state is the general [*allgemein*] interest, which, being the substance of all particular interests, includes their preservation. (2) But the actuality of the state is also the necessity of the state, since it breaks up into the various determinations of state-activity, which are implied in the *Begriff*. Its substantiality involves these distinctions becoming real and tangible as the different public offices. (3) This substantiality is further precisely the *Geist* that, having been thoroughly permeated by education [*Bildung*], knows and wills itself. Hence, the state *knows* what it wills, and knows it in its *Allgemeinheit* and as something thought out [*Gedachtes*]. The state works and acts in accordance with conscious ends and recognized principles and laws, which are not merely implied, but are expressly before its consciousness. So, too, it works with a definite knowledge of all the actual circumstances and relations to which its acts pertain.

* * *

340. As states are particular, there is manifested in their relation to one another a shifting play [*Spiel*] of internal particularity of passions, interests, aims, talents, virtues, force, wrong, vice, and external contingency on the very largest scale. In this play the ethical whole itself, national independence, is exposed to chance. The principles of different *Volksgeister* are limited, owing to the particularities required for their actuality and self-consciousness as existing individuals. The destinies and deeds of states in their connection with one another are the visible dialectic of the finite nature of these *Volksgeister*. Out of this dialectic the *allgemein Geist*, the *Geist* of the world, produces itself subject to no such limits [*unbeschränkt*]. It has the highest right of all, and exercises its right upon them in world-history [*Weltgeschichte*], which is the world's court of judgment [*Weltgericht*].

WORLD-HISTORY.

341. The *allgemein Geist* exists concretely in art in the form of perception and image, in religion in the form of feeling and representational thinking, and in philosophy in the form of pure free thought. In world-history this concrete existence of *Geist* is the *geistig* actuality in the total range of its internality and externality. It is a court of judgment because in its intrinsic *Allgemeinheit* the particulars—namely, the Penates,[6] civil society, and the *Volksgeister* in their many-coloured reality—are all merely ideal.[7] The movement of *Geist* in this case consists in making this evident.

---

6. The guardian deities of each ancient Roman household; they were also protectors of the Roman state.
7. That is, they have meaning and significance only by virtue of their relation to the *Idee*, as objectifications or instances of the *Begriff* in question.

342. Moreover, world-history is not a court of judgment whose principle is force, nor is it the abstract and irrational necessity of blind fate. It is self-caused and self-realized reason, and its actualized existence in *Geist* is knowledge. Hence, its development issuing solely out of the *Begriff* of its freedom is a necessary development of the elements of reason. It is, therefore, an unfolding of *Geist's* self-consciousness and freedom. It is the exhibition and actualization of *allgemein Geist*.

343. The history of *Geist* is its overt deeds, for it is only what it does, and its deed is to make itself as *Geist* the object of its consciousness, to comprehend itself as self-elaborating [*sich selbst auslegend*]. To comprehend [*erfassen*] itself is its being and principle, and the completion of this act is at the same time self-relinquishment and transformation. To express the matter formally: *Geist* that comprehends anew what has already been comprehended, or, what is the same thing, passes through self-relinquishment into itself, is *Geist* of a higher stage.

Note.—Here occurs the question of the perfection and education [*Erziehung*] of humankind.[8] They who have argued in favour of this perfectability have surmised something of the nature of *Geist*. They have understood that *Geist* has Γνῶθι σεαυτὸν[9] as a law of its being, and that when it comprehends what it itself is, it assumes a higher form. To those who have rejected this thought, *Geist* has remained an empty word and history a superficial play of accidental and so-called merely human strife and passion. Though in their use of the words "providence" and "design of providence" they express their belief in a higher control, they leave these images [*Vorstellungen*] unrefined, and proclaim the design unknowable and incomprehensible.

344. States, peoples, and individuals are established upon their own particular definite principle, which has systematized reality in their constitutions and in the entire compass of their surroundings. Of this systematized reality they are aware, and in its interests are absorbed. Yet are they the unconscious tools and organs of the *Weltgeist*, through whose inner activity the lower forms pass away. Thus *Geist* by its own motion and for its own end makes ready and works out the transition into its next higher stage.

345. Justice and virtue, wrong, force, and crime, talents and their results, small and great passions, innocence and guilt, the splendor of individuals, the ways of life of peoples [*Volksleben*], independence, the fortune and misfortune of states and individuals, have in the sphere of conscious reality their definite meaning and value, and find in that sphere judgment and their due. This due is, however, as yet incomplete. In world-history, which lies beyond this range of vision, the *Idee* of the *Weltgeist*, in that necessary phase of it which constitutes at any time its actual stage, is given its absolute right. The living *Volk* then attains to happiness and renown, and its deeds attain completion.

346. Since history is the embodiment of *Geist* in the form of events, that is, of direct natural reality, the stages of development are present as unmediated

8. Or, "of the human race" (*des Menschengeschlechts*). By here using the term *Erziehung* (rather than *Bildung*, which he usually uses when discussing the "education" or cultivation and development of *Geist*), Hegel echoes the language employed by SCHILLER in *The Aesthetic Education* [*Erziehung*] *of Man* (1794; see above).
9. Know thyself (*Gnōthi seauton*, Greek); see n. 3, p. 241.

natural principles. Because they are natural, they have the character of a multiplicity, and exist alongside each other. Hence, to each *Volk* is to be ascribed a single principle, comprised under its geographical and anthropological existence.

347. To a *Volk* whose natural principle is one of these stages is assigned the accomplishment of it through the process characteristic of the self-developing self-consciousness of the *Weltgeist*. In the history of the world this *Volk* is dominant for a particular epoch, although it can make an epoch only once (§ 346). In contrast with the absolute right of this *Volk* to be the bearer of the current phase in the development of the *Weltgeist*, the *Geister* of other *Völker* are void of right, and they, like those whose epochs are gone, figure no longer in world-history.

Note.—The special history of a world-historic *Volk* contains the unfolding of its principle from its undeveloped infancy up to the time when, in the full maturity of free ethical self-consciousness, it injects itself into *allgemein* history. It contains, moreover, the period of decline and destruction, the subsequent rise of a higher principle being marked in it simply as the negative of its own. Hence, that *Geist* passes over into the higher principle, and thus points in world-history toward another *Volk*. From that time onward the first *Volk* has lost absolute interest, perhaps absorbs the higher principle positively and fashions itself in accordance with it, but is at that point only a recipient, and has no indwelling vitality and freshness. Perhaps it loses its independence, perhaps continues to drag itself on as a particular state or circle of states, and spends itself in various random civil enterprises and foreign conflicts.[1]

348. At the summit of all actions, including world-historical actions, stand individuals. Each of these individuals is a subjectivity who actualizes what is substantive. He is a living embodiment of the substantive deed of the *Weltgeist*, and is, therefore, directly identical with this deed. It is concealed even from himself, and is not his object and end (§ 344). Thus these individuals do not receive honour and thanks for their acts either from their contemporaries (§ 344), or from the public opinion of posterity. In that opinion they are viewed merely as formal subjectivities, and, as such, are simply given their part in immortal fame.

349. A *Volk* is not as yet a state. The transition from the family, horde, clan, or multitude into a state constitutes the formal realization in it of the *Idee*. If the ethical substance, which every *Volk* has implicitly, lacks this form, it is without that objectivity which comes from laws and thought-out regulations. It has—neither for itself nor for others any *allgemein* or generally acknowledged reality. It will not be recognized. Its independence, being devoid of objective law or secure realized rationality, is formal only, and is not a sovereignty.

Note.—From the ordinary point of view we do not call the patriarchal condition a constitution, or a *Volk* in this condition a state, or its independence sovereignty. Before the beginning of actual history there are found uninteresting stupid innocence and the bravery arising out of the formal struggle for recognition and out of revenge (§ 57, *Note*).

350. It is the absolute right of the *Idee* to come visibly forth, and proceeding from marriage and agriculture realize itself in laws and objective institu-

---

1. Here Hegel has in mind the fate of Greece after its world-historical "moment" had passed, when it was replaced on the world-historical stage by (and absorbed into) the Roman Empire.

tions. This is true whether its realization appears in the form of divine law and beneficence or in the form of force and wrong. This right is the right of heroes to found states.

351. In the same way civilized nations may treat as barbarians the *Völker* who are behind them in the essential elements of the state. Thus, the rights of mere herdsmen, hunters, and tillers of the soil are inferior, and their independence is merely formal.

Note.—Wars and contests arising under such circumstances are struggles for recognition in behalf of a certain definite content. It is this feature of them which is significant in world-history.

352. The concrete *Ideen*, the *Völkergeister*, have their truth in the concrete *Idee* in its absolute *Allgemeinheit*—the *Weltgeist*, around whose throne stand the *Völkergeister* as accomplishers of its actuality, and witnesses and ornaments of its splendour. Since it is, as *Geist*, only the movement of its activity in order to know itself absolutely, to free its consciousness from mere direct naturalness, and to come to itself, the principles of the different forms of its self-consciousness, as they appear in the process of liberation, are four. They are the principles of the four world-historic realms.

353. In its first and unmediated revelation the *Weltgeist* has as its principle the form of the substantive *Geist*, in whose identity individuality is in its essence submerged and without explicit justification.

The second principle is the knowledge [*Wissen*] of substantive *Geist*. Here *Geist* is the positive content and filling, and is also at the same time the living form, which is in its nature "for-itself" or self-conscious—beautiful ethical *sittlich* individuality.

The third principle is the retreat into itself of this knowing self-conscious existence. There thus arises an abstract *Allgemeinheit*, and with it an infinite opposition to objectivity, which is regarded as bereft of *Geist*.

In the fourth principle this opposition of *Geist* is overturned in order that *Geist* may receive into its inner self its truth and concrete essence. It thus becomes at home with objectivity, and the two are reconciled. Because *Geist* has come back to its formal substantive reality by returning out of this infinite opposition, it seeks to produce and know its truth as thought, and as a world of established reality.

354. In accordance with these four principles the four world-historic realms are (1) the Oriental, (2) the Greek, (3) the Roman, and (4) the Germanic.[2]

* * *

360. These realms are based upon the distinction, which has now won the form of absolute antagonism, and yet at the same time are rooted in a single unity and *Idee*. In the obdurate struggle which thus ensues, the *Geistliche* has to lower its heaven to the level of an earthly and temporal condition, to common worldliness, and to ordinary life and thought. On the other hand the abstract actuality of the worldly is exalted to thought, to the principle of rational being and knowing, and to the rationality of right and law. Consequently the contradiction has essentially become a bloodless specter. The present has stripped off its barbarism and its lawless caprice, and truth has stripped off

2. That is, northern European (*germanisch*).

its otherworldliness and its arbitrary force.[3] The true atonement and reconciliation has become objective, and reveals the state as the image and reality of reason. In the state, self-consciousness finds the organic development of its real substantive knowing and will, in religion it finds in the form of ideal essence the feeling and the vision of this its truth, and in [philosophical] *Wissenschaft* it finds the free conceptually comprehended [*begriffene*] knowledge of this truth, seeing it to be one and the same in all its mutually completing manifestations—namely, the state, nature, and the world as *Idee*.[4]

SOURCE: *Hegel's Philosophy of Right*, trans. S. W. Dyde (London: George Bell and Sons, 1896), pp. xvii–xx, xxvii–xxx, 1–2, 4, 10–11, 13–19, 34–40, 43–45, 48–49, 61–63, 104–5, 116–19, 123, 127, 129–31, 152, 155–64, 168, 185–96, 198, 239–41, 247–58, 341–46, 349–50 (translation modified by the editor). Except where otherwise indicated, German words in brackets are the terminology used in the German original, inserted by the editor in addition to their renderings in the translation; and unbracketed German words are the original terminology, substituted in place of their renderings in the translation by the editor for reasons given in notes and in the Hegel glossary (p. 144). Hegel intended this work, first published as *Grundlinien der Philosophie des Rechts* (*Outline of the Philosophy of Right*, 1821), to be used in conjunction with his course of lectures on what he considered to be the three basic forms of "rightness" or normativity—legal, moral, and ethical. This translation is of an 1833 edition, published after Hegel's death, that incorporated both his own handwritten notes to the various sections (marked "*Note.*") and additions (*Zusätze*, marked "*Addition.*"), compiled from the lecture notes of his students (omission of these notes and additions is not marked in the text); it is rather free but generally faithful to the gist of what Hegel is saying.

Absolute *Geist*

On Absolute *Geist*

From Philosophy of Mind [*Geist*]

From *Section III. Absolute Mind* [Geist]

553.] The *Begriff* of *Geist* has its *reality* in *Geist*.[1] If this reality in identity with that *Begriff* is to exist as the consciousness of the absolute *Idee*, then the necessary aspect is that the *implicitly* free intelligence be in its actuality liberated to its *Begriff*, if that actuality is to be a vehicle worthy of it. Subjective and objective *Geist* are to be looked on as the road on which this aspect of *reality* or existence rises to maturity.

* * *

FROM A. ART

556.] As this consciousness of the Absolute first takes shape, its immediacy produces the factor of finitude in Art. On one hand, that is, it breaks up into a

---

3. A reference to the time when otherworldly religious dogmatism was believed to hold a monopoly on ultimate "truth."
4. "Der ideellen Welt": that is, the world comprehended not merely as contingent material reality but as *Idee*.
1. That is, when the *Begriff* of *Geist* is realized, that reality is a matter of the form of *Geist* that has been attained. On *Begriff*, *Geist*, and *Idee*, see the Hegel glossary, p. 144.

work of external common existence, into the subject which produces that work, and the subject which contemplates and worships it. But, on the other hand, it is the concrete *contemplation* and mental picture [*Vorstellung*] of implicitly absolute *Geist* as the *Ideal*. In this ideal, or the concrete shape born of subjective spirit [*Geist*], its natural immediacy, which is only a *sign* of the *Idee*, is so transfigured by the informing *Geist* in order to express the *Idee*, that the figure shows it and it alone:—the shape or form of *Beauty*.

* * *

559.] In such single shapes 'absolute' *Geist* cannot be made explicit: in and to art, therefore, *Geist* is a limited *Volksgeist* whose implicit *Allgemeinheit*, when steps are taken to specify its fullness in detail, breaks up into an indeterminate polytheism. With the essential restrictedness of its content, Beauty in general goes no further than a pervading of the vision or image by the *Geistige*[2]—something formal, so that the content of the thought embodied or representation can, like the material which it uses to work in, be of the most diverse and unessential kind, and still the work be something beautiful and a work of art.

* * *

562.] In another way the *Idee* and the sensuous figure it appears in are incompatible; and that is where the infinite form, subjectivity, is not as in the first extreme a mere superficial personality, but its inmost depth, and God is known not as only seeking his form or satisfying himself in an external form, but as only finding himself in himself, and thus giving hmself his adequate figure in the *Geistige* alone. *Romantic art* gives up the task of showing him as such in external form and by means of beauty: it presents him as only condescending to appearance, and the divine as the heart of hearts in an externality from which it always disengages itself. Thus the external can here appear as contingent towards its significance.

* * *

As regards the close connexion of art with the various religions it may be specially noted that *beautiful* art can only belong to those religions in which the spirituality principle,[3] though concrete and intrinsically free, is not yet absolute. In religions where the *Idee* has not yet been revealed and known in its free character, though the craving for art is felt in order to bring in imaginative visibility to consciousness the idea [*Vorstellung*] of a being [*Wesen*],[4] and though art is the sole organ in which the abstract and radically indistinct content,—a mixture from natural and spiritual sources,—can try to bring itself to consciousness;—still this art is defective; its form is defective because its subject-matter and theme is so,—for the defect in subject-matter comes from the form not being immanent in it. The representations of this symbolic art keep a certain tastelessness and stolidity—for the principle it embodies is itself stolid and dull, and hence has not the power freely to transmute the external

2. That is, an imbuement (*Durchdringung*) of the vision or image with the spiritual (*das Geistige*), enabling it to come through and be discerned.
3. That is, *Geistigkeit*.
4. Hegel's emphasis. *Wesen* can also mean "essence," "reality, "existence," or the "nature" of something; but here the point is that in this sort of

spirituality, the *Idee* or highest sort of reality can only be imagined as a "being" or entity of some sort. Hegel is suggesting that in art-centered religions a "craving for art is felt" in order to give visual expression to an as-yet inarticulatable sense of the most essential sort of reality.

to significance and shape. Beautiful art, on the contrary, has for its condition the self-consciousness of the free *Geist*,—the consciousness that compared with it the natural and sensuous has no standing of its own: it makes the natural wholly into the mere expression of *Geist*, which is thus the inner form that gives utterance to itself alone.

But with a further and deeper study, we see that the advent of art, in a religion still in the bonds of sensuous externality, shows that such religion is on the decline.[5] At the very time it seems to give religion the supreme glorification, expression and brilliancy, it has lifted the religion away over its limitation. In the sublime divinity to which the work of art succeeds in giving expression the artistic genius and the spectator find themselves at home, with their personal sense and feeling, satisfied and liberated: to them the vision and the consciousness of free *Geist* has been vouchsafed and attained. Beautiful art, from its side, has thus performed the same service as philosophy: it has purified *Geist* from its thraldom.[6] The older religion, in which the need of fine art—and just for that reason—is first generated, looks up in its principle to an other-world which is sensuous and unmeaning: the images adored by its devotees are hideous idols regarded as wonder-working talismans, which point to the unspiritual objectivity of that other world,—and bones perform a similar or even a better service than such images. But even fine art is only a grade of liberation, not the supreme liberation itself.—The genuine objectivity, which is only in the medium of thought,—the medium in which alone the pure *Geist* is for *Geist*, and where the liberation is accompanied with reverence,—is still absent in the sensuous beauty of the work of art, still more in that external, unbeautiful sensuousness.

563.] Beautiful Art, like the religion peculiar to it, has its future in true religion. The restricted value of the *Idee* passes utterly and naturally into the *Allgemeinheit* identical with the infinite form;—the vision in which consciousness has to depend upon the senses passes into a self-mediating knowledge, into an existence which is itself knowledge,—into *revelation*. Thus the principle which gives the *Idee* its content is that it embody free intelligence, and as 'absolute' *Geist* it is *for Geist*.[7]

FROM B. REVEALED RELIGION

564.] It lies essentially in the *Begriff* of religion,—the religion i.e. whose content is absolute *Geist*—that it be *revealed*, and, what is more, revealed *by God*. Knowledge (the principle by which the substance is *Geist*) is a self-determining principle, as infinite self-realising form,—it therefore is manifes-

---

5. That is, the type of religion that has not yet transcended dependence on artistic images to convey its sense of the divine.
6. That is, "beautiful art"—no longer in the service of a kind of religion that itself is limited to sensuous images in its conception of spirituality and divinity—performs the same function as philosophy: it liberates the human spirit from the limitations of a conception of reality that is modeled on natural sensuous form and that takes such form to be paradigmatic of the real.

7. That is, the kind of religion that focuses on "revelation" of the divine (rather than visualization in artistic form) represents an advance: it signifies a recognition (however vague) that "the principle that gives the *Idee* its content is the (self-)determination [*Bestimmung*] of free intelligence, and as absolute, is *Geist* for *Geist* [*und als absolut Geist für Geist ist*]"—or, as Hegel elsewhere puts it, is "*Geist* knowing itself as *Geist*," even if only inadequately, in symbolic and figurative rather than properly conceptual form.

tation out and out. *Geist* is only *Geist* in so far as it is *for Geist*, and in the absolute religion it is the absolute *Geist* which manifests no longer abstract *elements* of its being but *itself*.[8]

* * *

If we recollect how intricate is the knowledge of the divine *Geist* for those who are not content with the homely pictures[9] of faith but proceed to thought,—at first only 'rationalising' reflection, but afterwards, as in duty bound, to speculative comprehension, it may almost create surprise that so many, and especially theologians whose vocation it is to deal with these Ideas, have tried to get off[1] their task by gladly accepting anything offered them for this behoof.[2] And nothing serves better to shirk it than to adopt the conclusion that man knows nothing of God. To know what God as *Geist* is—to apprehend this accurately and distinctly in thoughts—requires careful and thorough speculation. It includes, in its fore-front, the propositions: God is God only so far as he knows himself: his self-knowledge is, further, his self-consciousness in man, and man's knowledge *of* God, which proceeds to man's self-knowledge *in* God. * * *

565.] When the immediacy and sensuousness of shape and knowledge is superseded, God is, in point of content, the essential and actual *Geist* of nature and *Geist*, while in point of form he is, first of all, presented to consciousness as a mental representation [*Vorstellung*]. This quasi-pictorial representation gives to the elements of his content, on one hand, a separate being, making them presuppositions towards each other, and phenomena which succeed each other; their relationship it makes a series of events according to finite reflective categories. But, on the other hand, such a form of finite representationalism is also overcome and superseded [*aufgehoben*] in the belief in a single *Geist* and in the devotion of worship.[3]

566.] In this separating, the form parts from the content: and in the form the different functions of the *Begriff* part off into special spheres or media, in each of which absolute *Geist* exhibits itself; (α) as eternal content, abiding self-centred, even in its manifestation; (β) as distinction of the eternal essence [*Wesen*] from its manifestation, which by this difference becomes the phenomenal world into which the content enters; (γ) as infinite return, and reconciliation with the eternal being [*Wesen*], of the world it gave away—the withdrawal of the eternal from the phenomenal into the unity of its fullness.

* * *

From C. Philosophy

572.] This *Wissenschaft* is the unity of Art and Religion. Whereas the vision-method of Art, external in point of form, is but subjective production

8. That is, in "absolute religion" (which is "revealed" religion, and paradigmatically Christianity), "absolute *Geist*" is taken to manifest *itself*, rather than merely abstract elements or aspects of itself.
9. That is, the simplistic images (*schlichten Vorstellungen*) of faith (*Glauben*).
1. Evade.

2. For this purpose; to this end.
3. That is, religion makes up for the disadvantage of operating with "finite representations [*Vorstellungen*]" that distort its content, through belief in the ultimacy of *Geist* and its fundamental unity, and "the devotion of worship" (*Andacht des Kultus*).

and shivers[4] the substantial content into many separate shapes, and whereas
Religion, with its separation into parts, opens it out in mental picturing [*Vorstellung*] and mediates what is thus opened out; Philosophy not merely keeps
them together to make a total, but even unifies them into the simple *geistig*
vision, and then in that raises them to self-conscious thought. Such consciousness is thus the intelligible unity (cognised by thought) of art and religion, in
which the diverse elements in the content are cognised as necessary, and this
necessary as free.

573.] Philosophy thus characterizes itself as a cognition of the necessity in
the content of the absolute picture-idea [*Vorstellung*], as also of the necessity
in the two forms—on one hand, immediate vision and its poetry, and the objective and external revelation presupposed by representation,—on the other
hand, first the subjective retreat inwards, then the subjective movement of
faith and its final identification with the presupposed object. This cognition
is thus the *recognition* of this content and its form; it is the liberation from
the one-sidedness of the forms and their elevation into the absolute form, which
determines itself to content, remains identical with it, and is thereby the cognition of that essential and actual necessity. This movement, which philosophy is, finds itself already accomplished, when at the close it seizes its own
notion,—i.e. only *looks back* on its knowledge.

Here might seem to be the place to treat in a definite exposition of the reciprocal relations of philosophy and religion. The whole question turns entirely
on the difference of the forms of speculative thought from the forms of mental representation [*Vorstellung*] and 'reflecting' intellect.[5] But it is the whole
cycle of philosophy, and of logic in particular, which has not merely taught
and made known this difference, but also criticized it, or rather has let its
nature develop and judge itself by these very categories. It is only by an insight
into the value of these forms that the true and needful conviction can be
gained that the content of religion and philosophy is the same,—leaving out,
of course, the further details of external nature and finite *Geist* which fall
outside the range of religion. But religion is the truth *for all men*: faith rests
on the *witness* of *Geist*, which as *witnessing* is *Geist* in man. This witness—
the underlying essence in all humanity—takes, when driven to expound
itself, its first definite form under those acquired habits of thought which
secular consciousness and intellect otherwise employs. In this way the truth
becomes liable to the terms and conditions of finitude in general. This does
not prevent *Geist*, even in employing sensuous ideas and finite categories of
thought, from retaining its content (which as religion is essentially speculative) with a tenacity which does violence to them, and acts *inconsistently*
towards them. By this inconsistency it corrects their defects. Nothing easier
therefore for the 'Rationalist' than to point out contradictions in the exposition of the faith, and then to prepare triumphs for its principle of formal
identity. If *Geist* yields to this finite reflection, which has usurped the title of
reason and philosophy—('Rationalism')—it strips religious truth of its infinity and makes it in reality nothing. Religion in that case is completely in the
right in guarding herself against such reason and philosophy and treating

4. Splinters.   5. That is, "understanding" (*Verstand*).

them as enemies. But it is another thing when religion sets herself against comprehending reason, and against philosophy in general, and specially against a philosophy of which the doctrine is speculative, and so religious. Such an opposition proceeds from failure to appreciate the difference indicated and the value of *geistig* form in general, and particularly of the logical form; or, to be more precise, still from failure to note the distinction of the content—which may be in both the same—from these forms. It is on the ground of form that philosophy has been reproached and accused by the religious party; just as conversely its speculative content has brought the same charges upon it from a self-styled philosophy—and from a pithless orthodoxy.[6] It had too little of God in it for the former; too much for the latter.

* * *

574.] This *Begriff* of philosophy is the self-thinking *Idee*, the truth aware of itself (§ 236),—the logical system, but with the signification that it is *Allgemeinheit* approved and certified in concrete content as in its actuality. In this way the *Wissenschaft* has gone back to its beginning: its result is the logical system but as a *geistig* principle: out of the presupposing judgment, in which the notion was only implicit and the beginning an immediate,—and thus out of the *appearance* which it had there—it has risen into its pure principle and thus also into its proper medium.

575.] It is this appearing which originally gives the motive of the further development. The first appearance is formed by the syllogism [*Schluss*][7] which is based on the Logical system as starting-point, with Nature for the middle term which couples *Geist* with it. The Logical principle turns to Nature and Nature to *Geist*. Nature, standing between *Geist* and its essence, sunders itself, not indeed to extremes of finite abstraction, nor itself to something away from them and independent,—which, as other than they, only serves as a link between them: for the syllogism is *in the <u>Idee</u>*, and Nature is essentially defined as a transition-point and negative factor, and as implicitly *Idee*. Still the mediation of the *Begriff* has the external form of *transition*, and the *Wissenschaft* of Nature presents itself as the course of necessity, so that it is only in the one extreme that the freedom of the *Begriff* is explicit as a self-amalgamation.[8]

576.] In the second syllogism [*Schluss*] this appearance is so far superseded [*aufgehoben*], that that syllogism is the standpoint of *Geist* itself, which—as the mediating agent in the process—presupposes Nature and couples it with the Logical principle. It is the syllogism where *Geist* reflects on itself in the *Idee*: philosophy appears as a subjective cognition, of which freedom is the aim, and which is itself the way to produce it.

577.] The third syllogism [*Schluss*] is the *Idee* of philosophy, which has self-knowing reason, the absolutely *Allgemeine*, for its middle term: a middle, which divides itself into *Geist* and Nature, making the former its presupposition, as

<hr/>

6. That is, an empty piety (*inhaltslosen Frommigkeit*).
7. Hegel uses the term *Schluss* ("syllogism" in logic, but more often "end" or "conclusion") to convey the idea of a "logical" conclusion or connection within his system of "logical" *Begriffe* ("concepts" or

structures).
8. Better translated: "so that it is only in the former case [that is, in Hegel's 'Logic' rather than in the *Wissenschaft* of Nature] that the freedom of the *Begriff* is set forth as its self-integration [*Zusammenschliessen*]."

process of the *Idee*'s subjective activity, and the latter its *allgemein* extreme, as process of the objectively and implicitly existing *Idee*. The self-judging[9] of the *Idee* into its two appearances (§§ 575, 576) characterises both as its (the self-knowing reason's) manifestations: and in it there is a unification of the two aspects:—it is the nature of the *Sache*,[1] the *Begriff*, which causes the movement and development, yet this same movement is equally the action of cognition. The eternal *Idee*, in full fruition of its essence, eternally sets itself to work, engenders and enjoys itself as absolute *Geist*.[2]

* * *

SOURCE: From *Hegel's Philosophy of Mind: Translated from the "Encyclopaedia of the Philosophical Sciences," with Five Introductory Essays*, trans. William Wallace (Oxford: Clarendon Press, 1894), pp. 291, 293–99, 303–5, 315–16 (translation modified by the editor). Except where otherwise indicated, German words in brackets are the terminology used in the German original, inserted by the editor in addition to their renderings in the translation; and unbracketed German words are the original terminology, substituted in place of their renderings in the translation by the editor, for reasons given in notes and in the Hegel glossary (p. 144). Translated from the 1830 edition of *Philosophie des Geistes*, part 3 of *Enzyklopädie der philosophischen Wissenschaften*.

On Art

From Lectures on the Philosophy of Fine Art

From *Introduction*

* * *

* * * In the first place, as regards the *worthiness* of art to be philosophically[1] considered, it is no doubt the case that art can be employed as a fleeting pastime, to serve the ends of pleasure and entertainment, to decorate our surroundings, to impart pleasantness to the external conditions of our life, and to emphasize other objects by means of ornament. In this mode of employment art is indeed not independent, not free, but servile. But what *we* mean to consider, is the art which is *free* in its end as in its means.

That art is in the abstract capable of serving other aims, and of being a mere pastime, is moreover a relation which it shares with thought. For, on the one hand, cognitive inquiry [*Wissenschaft*], in the shape of the subservient understanding, may be used for finite purposes, and as an accidental means, and in that case is not self-determined, but determined by alien objects and relations; but, on the other hand, *Wissenschaft* liberates itself from this service to rise in free independence to the attainment of truth, in which medium, free from all interference, it fulfils itself in conformity with its proper aims.

9. A standard translation of "das *Sich-Urteilen*" (Hegel's emphasis). But Hegel is drawing here on the literal meaning of *Urteilen* as *ur-Teilen*, "primordial division," as well as on its connotation of "passing judgment on oneself," to bring out the necessity of the kind of bifurcation he is discussing—the two basic ways in which the *Idee* manifests itself (i.e., as Nature and as *Geist*). See n. 5, p. 201.
1. That is, "the matter" (*der Sache*) under consideration.

2. Hegel deals with the same topics relating to "absolute *Geist*" in the concluding section of his earlier *Phenomenology of Geist*, selections from which appear earlier in the volume.
1. "*Wissenschaftlich*": that is, "cognitively" in the manner of his kind of philosophy as well as the disciplines that inquire into and reflect in a rigorous and sophisticated way on both nature and *Geist*. See the Hegel glossary, p. 144.

Fine art is not real art till it is in this sense free, and only achieves its highest task when it has taken its place in the same sphere with religion and philosophy, and has become simply a mode of revealing to consciousness and bringing to expression the Divine [*das Göttliche*], the deepest interests of humanity, and the most comprehensive truths of *Geist*. It is in works of art that peoples[2] have deposited the profoundest intuitions and ideas of their hearts; and fine art is frequently the key—with many peoples there is no other—to the understanding of their wisdom and of their religion.

This is an attribute which art shares with religion and philosophy, only in this peculiar mode, that it represents even the highest ideas *in sensuous forms*, thereby bringing them nearer to the character of natural phenomena, to the senses, and to feeling. The world, into whose depths *thought* penetrates, is a supra-sensuous world,[3] which is thus, to begin with, erected as a *beyond* over against immediate consciousness and present sensation; the power which thus rescues itself from the *here*, that consists in the actuality and finiteness of sense, is the freedom of thought in cognition. But *Geist* is able to heal this schism which its advance creates; it generates out of itself the works of fine art as the first middle term of reconciliation between pure thought and what is external, sensuous, and transitory, between nature with its finite actuality and the infinite freedom of comprehending thinking.[4]

* * *

The universal need for expression in art lies in man's rational impulse to exalt the inner and outer world into a *geistig* consciousness for himself, as an object in which he recognizes his own self. He satisfies the need of this spiritual freedom when he makes all that exists explicit for himself *within*, and in a corresponding way realizes this his explicit self *without*, evoking thereby, in this reduplication of himself, what is in him into vision and into knowledge for his own mind and for that of others. This is the free rationality of man, in which, as in the case of all action and knowledge, so also art has its ground and necessary origin.

* * *

But inasmuch as the task of art is to present [*darstellen*] the *Idee* to direct perception in sensuous form [*Gestalt*], and not in the form of thought or of pure spirituality as such, and seeing that this presentation [*Darstellen*] has its value and dignity in the correspondence and the unity of the two sides, *i.e.* of the *Idee* and its sensuous embodiment [*Gestalt*], it follows that the level and excellence of art in attaining a realization adequate to its *Idee*, must depend upon the grade of inwardness and unity with which *Idee* and sensuous form [*Gestalt*] display themselves as fused into one.

---

2. "Völker": not simply political "nations" but rather societies with a historical and cultural as well as a political (and often also linguistic) identity and broad homogeneity. See the Hegel glossary, p. 144.
3. That is, "a supersensible world" (*einer übersinnlicher Welt*): for Hegel (as for KANT) a dimension of reality transcending that of merely "sensuous" phenomena of the sort to which our senses give us access, which may generally be characterized as the realm of "nature." Its relation to the "sensible world" of nature was a highly contentious question, concerning which Kant and his successors (including Hegel) differed greatly and significantly.
4. "Begreifenden Denken": that is, the freedom of the kind of thinking that attains to the level of genuine comprehension subservient to no natural or other extraneous motivations and constraints.

Thus the higher truth is *geistig* being that has attained a formation [*Gestaltung*] adequate to the *Begriff* of spirit. This is what furnishes the principle of division for the *Wissenschaft* of art.[5] For before *Geist* can attain the true *Begriff* of its absolute essence [*Wesen*], it has to traverse a course of stages whose ground is in this *Idee* itself. And to this evolution of the content with which it supplies itself, there corresponds an evolution, immediately connected therewith, of the plastic forms of art, under the shape of which *Geist* as artist presents to itself the consciousness of itself.

This evolution within the art-spirit [*Kunstgeist*] has again in its own nature two sides. In the *first* place the development itself is a *geistig* and *allgemein* one, in so far as the graduated series of definite *views of the world* [*Weltanschauungen*] as the definite but comprehensive consciousness of the natural, the human and the divine gives itself artistic expression; and, in the *second* place, this inward development of art is obliged to provide itself with external existence and sensuous form, and the definite modes of the sensuous art-existence are themselves a totality of necessary distinctions in the realm of art—which are *the several arts*. It is true, indeed, that the necessary kinds of artistic representation are on the one hand *qua* spiritual of a very general nature, and not restricted to any one material; while sensuous existence contains manifold varieties of matter. But as this latter, like *Geist*, has the *Idee* potentially for its inner soul, it follows from this that particular sensuous materials have a close affinity and secret accord with the spiritual distinctions and types of art presentation.

* * *

Only in the highest art are the *Idee* and the presentation [*Darstellung*] genuinely adequate to one another, in the sense that the outward shape given to the *Idee* is in itself essentially and actually the true *Gestalt*, because the content of the *Idee*, which that *Gestalt* expresses, is itself the true and real content. It is a corollary from this, as we indicated above, that the *Idee* must be defined in and through itself as concrete totality, and thereby possess in itself the principle and standard of its particularization and determination in external appearance. For example, the Christian imagination will be able to represent God only in human form and with man's intellectual expression, because it is herein that God himself is completely known in himself as *Geist*. Determinateness is, as it were, the bridge to phenomenal existence. Where this determinateness is not totality derived from the *Idee* itself, where the *Idee* is not conceived as self-determining and self-particularizing, the *Idee* remains abstract and has its determinateness, and therefore the principle that dictates its particular and exclusively appropriate mode of presentation, not in itself but external to it. Therefore, the *Idee* when still abstract has even its shape external, and not dictated by itself. The *Idee*, however, which is concrete in itself bears the principle of its mode of manifestation within itself, and is by that means the free process of giving shape to itself. Thus it is only the truly concrete *Idee* that can generate the true *Gestalt*, and this correspondence of the two is the Ideal [*das Ideal*].

Now because the *Idee* is in this fashion concrete unity, it follows that this unity can enter into the art-consciousness only by the expansion and re-

5. That is, for the philosophy of art.

conciliation of the particularities of the *Idee*, and it is through this evolution that artistic beauty comes to possess a *totality of particular stages and forms*. Therefore, after we have studied the beauty of art in itself and on its own merits, we must see how beauty as a whole breaks up into its particular determinations. This gives, as our *second part, the doctrine of the types of art*. These forms find their genesis in the different modes of grasping the *Idee* as artistic content, whereby is conditioned a difference of the form in which it manifests itself. Hence the types of art are nothing but the different relations of content and form [*Gestalt*], relations which emanate from the *Idee* itself, and furnish thereby the true basis of division for this sphere. For the principle of division must always be contained in that *Begriff* whose particularization and division is in question.

* * *

Now, after architecture [first] has erected the temple, and the hand of sculpture [second] has supplied it with the statue of the God, then, in the third place, this god present to sense is confronted in the spacious halls of his house by the *community* [*Gemeinde*]. The community is the spiritual reflection into itself of such sensuous existence, and is the animating subjectivity and inner life which brings about the result that the determining principle for the content of art, as well as for the medium which represents it in outward form, comes to be particularization [dispersion into various shapes, attributes, incidents, etc.], individualization, and the subjectivity which they require. The solid unity which the God has in sculpture breaks up into the multitudinous inner lives of individuals, whose unity is not sensuous, but purely ideal.[6]

It is only in this stage that God himself comes to be really and truly *Geist*— *Geist* in his (God's) community; for he here begins to be a to-and-fro, an alternation between his unity within himself and his realization in the individual's knowledge and in its separate being, as also in the common nature and union of the multitude. In the community, God is released from the abstractness of unexpanded self-identity, as well as from the simple absorption in a bodily medium, by which sculpture represents him. And he is thus exalted into *geistig* existence and into knowledge, into the reflected appearance which essentially displays itself as inward and as subjectivity. Therefore the higher content is now the *geistig* nature, and that in its absolute shape.

But the dispersion of which we have spoken reveals this at the same time as particular *geistig* being, and as individual character. Now, what manifests itself in this phase as the main thing is not the serene quiescence of the God in himself, but appearance as such, being which is *for* another, self-manifestation. And hence, in the phase we have reached, all the most manifold subjectivity in its living movement and operation—as human passion, action, and incident, and, in general, the wide realm of human feeling, will, and its negation—is for its own sake the object of artistic representation. In conformity with this content, the sensuous element of art has at once to show itself as made particular in itself and as adapted to subjective inwardness.

Media that fulfil this requirement we have in colour, in musical sound, and finally in sound as the mere indication of inward perceptions and ideas; and

6. That is, their unity is mediated and made possible by the ideas (traditions, values, beliefs, etc.) that they share.

as modes of realizing the import in question by help of these media we obtain painting, music, and poetry. In this region the sensuous medium displays itself as subdivided in its own being and universally set down as ideal. Thus it has the highest degree of conformity with the content of art, which, as such, is *geistig*, and the connection of intelligible import and sensuous medium develops into closer intimacy than was possible in the case of architecture and sculpture. The unity attained, however, is a more inward unity, the weight of which is thrown wholly on the subjective side, and which, in as far as form and content are compelled to particularize themselves and give themselves merely ideal existence, can only come to pass at the expense of the objective *Allgemeinheit* of the content and also of its amalgamation with the immediately sensuous element.

The arts, then, of which form and content exalt themselves to ideality, abandon the character of symbolic architecture and the *classical* ideal of sculpture, and therefore borrow their type from the *romantic* form of art, whose mode of formation they are most adequately adapted to express. And they constitute a *totality* of arts, because the romantic type is the most concrete in itself.

i. The articulation of this *third sphere* of the individual arts may be determined as follows. The *first* art in it, which comes next to sculpture, is *painting*. It employs as a medium for its content and for the embodiment of that content visibility as such in as far as it is specialized in its own nature, *i.e.* as developed into colour. It is true that the material employed in architecture and sculpture is also visible and coloured; but it is not, as in painting, visibility as such, not the simple light which, differentiating itself in virtue of its contrast with darkness, and in combination with the latter, gives rise to colour. This quality of visibility, made subjective in itself and treated as ideal, needs neither, like architecture, the abstractly mechanical attribute of mass as operative in the properties of heavy matter, nor, like sculpture, the complete sensuous attributes of space, even though concentrated into organic shapes. The visibility and the rendering visible which belong to painting have their differences in a more ideal form, in the several kinds of colour, and they liberate art from the sensuous completeness in space which attaches to material things, by restricting themselves to a plane surface.

On the other hand, the content also attains the most comprehensive specification. Whatever can find room in the human heart, as feeling, idea, and purpose; whatever it is capable of shaping into act—all this diversity of material is capable of entering into the varied content of painting. The whole realm of particular existence, from the highest embodiment of *Geist* down to the most isolated object of nature, finds a place here. For it is possible even for finite nature, in its particular scenes and phenomena, to make its appearance in the realm of art, if only some allusion to an element of *Geist* endows it with affinity to thought and feeling.

ii. The *second* art in which the romantic type realizes itself is contrasted with painting, and is *music*. Its medium, though still sensuous, yet develops into still more thorough subjectivity and particularization. Music, too, idealizes [*Idealsetzen*] the sensuous, and does so by superseding [*aufheben*][7]—and idealizing into the individual isolation of a single point—the indifferent externality of space, whose complete mode of appearance is accepted and imitated by painting. The

---

7. That is, at once negating, preserving, and transcending. *Aufheben* can mean any of these three things, and Hegel often uses it to mean all three at once. See the Hegel glossary, p. 144.

single point, *qua* such a negativity (excluding space), is in itself a concrete and active process of superseding [*aufheben*] within the attributes of matter, in the shape of a motion and tremor of the material body within itself and in its relation to itself. Such an initial ideality of matter,[8] which appears no longer as under the form of space, but as temporal ideality, is *sound*, the sensuous set down and yet negated, with its abstract visibility converted into audibility, inasmuch as sound, so to speak, liberates the ideal content from its immersion in matter.

This internalization and ensoulment [*Beseelung*] of matter furnishes the medium for *Geist* to attain an as yet indefinite inwardness and soul [*Seele*], and finds utterance in its tones for the heart with its whole gamut of feelings and passions. Thus music forms the centre of the romantic arts, just as sculpture represents the central point between architecture and the arts of romantic subjectivity. Thus, too, it forms the point of transition between abstract spatial sensuousness, such as painting employs, and the abstract spirituality of poetry. Music has within itself, like architecture, a relation of quantity conformable to the understanding, as the antithesis to emotion and inwardness; and has also as its basis a solid conformity to law on the part of the tones, of their conjunction, and of their succession.

iii. As regards the *third* and most *geistig* mode of presentation of the romantic art-type, we must look for it in *poetry*. Its characteristic peculiarity lies in the power with which it subjects the sensuous element—from which music and painting in their degree begin to liberate art—to *Geist* and its representations [*Vorstellungen*]. For sound, the only external matter which poetry retains, is in it no longer the feeling of the sonorous itself, but is a *sign* [*Zeichen*], which by itself is void of import. And it is a sign of representation that has become concrete in itself, and not merely of indefinite feeling and of its *nuances* and grades. This is how sound develops into the *Word*, as voice articulate in itself, whose import it is to indicate representations and thoughts. The merely negative point up to which music had developed now makes its appearance as the completely concrete point, as the point of *Geist* as the self-conscious individual, which out of itself unites the infinite space of its representations with the temporal character of sound. Yet this sensuous element, which in music was still immediately one with inward feeling, is in poetry separated from the content of consciousness. In poetry *Geist* determines this content for its own sake, and apart from all else, into representations [*Vorstellungen*], and though it employs sound to express them, yet treats it solely as a sign without value or import. Thus considered, sound may just as well be reduced to a mere letter, for the audible, like the visible, is thus depressed into a mere indication of *Geist*. For this reason the proper element of poetical presentation is poetical *representation* and *geistig* portrayal itself. And as this element is common to all types of art, it follows that poetry runs through them all and develops itself independently in each. Poetry is the *allgemein* art of *Geist* which has become free in its own nature, and which is not tied to find its realization in external sensuous matter, but unfolds itself exclusively in the inner space and inner time of representations and feelings. Yet just in this its highest phase art ends by transcending itself, inasmuch as it abandons the medium of a harmonious embodiment of *Geist* in sensuous form, and passes from the poetry of representation [*Vorstellung*] into the prose of thought [*Denken*].

8. That is, endowment of matter with meaning.

Such we may take to be the articulated totality of the particular arts, viz. the external art of architecture, the objective art of sculpture, and the subjective art of painting, music and poetry. Many other classifications have been attempted, for a work of art presents so many aspects that, as has often been the case, first one and then another is made the basis of classification. For instance, one might take the sensuous medium. Thus architecture is treated as crystallization; sculpture, as the organic modeling of the material in its sensuous and spatial totality; painting, as the coloured surface and line; while in music, space, as such, passes into the point of time possessed of content within itself, until finally the external medium is in poetry depressed into complete insignificance. Or, again, these differences have been considered with reference to their purely abstract attributes of space and time. Such abstract peculiarities of works of art may, like their material medium, be consistently explored in their characteristic traits; but they cannot be worked out as the ultimate and fundamental law, because any such aspect itself derives its origin from a higher principle, and must therefore be subordinate thereto.

This higher principle we have found in the types of art—symbolic, classical, and romantic—which are the general moments or elements [*allgemeinen Momente*] of the *Idee* of beauty itself. For *symbolic art* attains its most adequate reality and most complete application in *architecture*, in which it holds sway in the full import of its *Begriff*, and is not yet degraded to be, as it were, the inorganic nature dealt with by another art. The *classical* type of art, on the other hand, finds adequate realization in sculpture, while it treats architecture only as furnishing an enclosure in which it is to operate, and has not acquired the power of developing painting and music as absolute forms for its content. The *romantic* type of art, finally, takes possession of painting and music, and in like manner of poetic representation, as substantive and unconditionally adequate modes of utterance. Poetry, however, is conformable to all types of the beautiful, and extends over them all, because the artistic imagination is its proper medium, and imagination is essential to every product that belongs to the beautiful, whatever its type may be.

And, therefore, what the particular arts realize in individual works of art, are according to their *Begriff* simply the general types which constitute the self-unfolding *Idee* of beauty. It is as the external realization of this *Idee* that the wide Pantheon of art is being erected, whose architect and builder is the self-comprehending spirit of beauty, for the completion [*Vollendung*] of which world-history will need its millennia-long evolution.

SOURCE: From *The Introduction to Hegel's "Philosophy of Fine Art,"* trans. Bernard Bosanquet (1886; reprint, London: Kegan Paul, Trench, Trübner, 1905), pp. 47–49, 96, 174–76, 179–81, 200–211 (translation modified by the editor). Except where otherwise indicated, German words in brackets are the terminology used in the German original, inserted by the editor in addition to their renderings in the translation; and unbracketed German words are the original terminology, substituted in place of their renderings in the translation by the editor for reasons given in notes and in the Hegel glossary (p. 144). This is a partial translation of Hegel's posthumously edited and published lectures, *Vorlesungen über die Aesthetik* (1835).

On Religion

From Lectures on the Philosophy of Religion

From *Introduction*

* * *

To begin with, it is necessary to recollect generally what object we have before us in the Philosophy of Religion, and what is our ordinary idea of religion. We know that in religion we withdraw ourselves from what is temporal, and that religion is for our consciousness that region in which all the enigmas of the world are solved, all the contradictions of deeper-reaching thought have their meaning unveiled, and where the voice of the heart's pain is silenced—the region of eternal truth, of eternal rest, of eternal peace. Speaking generally, it is through thought, concrete thought, or, to put it more definitely, it is by reason of his being *Geist*, that man is man; and from man as *Geist* proceed all the many developments of the *Wissenschaften*[1] and arts, the interests of political life, and all those conditions which have reference to man's freedom and will. But all these manifold forms of human relations, activities, and pleasures, and all the ways in which these are intertwined; all that has worth and dignity for man, all wherein he seeks his happiness, his glory, and his pride, finds its ultimate centre in religion, in the thought, the consciousness, and the feeling of God.[2] Thus God is the beginning of all things, and the end of all things. As all things proceed from this point, so all return back to it again. He is the centre which gives life and quickening to all things, and which animates and preserves in existence all the various forms of being. In religion man places himself in a relation to this centre, in which all other relations concentrate themselves, and in so doing he rises up to the highest level of consciousness and to the region which is free from relation to what is other than itself, to something which is absolutely self-sufficient, the unconditioned, what is free, and is its own object and end.

* * *

FROM THE POSITION OF THE PHILOSOPHY OF RELIGION RELATIVELY TO PHILOSOPHY AND TO RELIGION

1. THE RELATION OF PHILOSOPHY TO RELIGION GENERALLY

* * *

The object of religion as well as of philosophy is eternal truth in its objectivity, God and nothing but God, and the explication of God. Philosophy is not a wisdom of the world, but is knowledge of what is not of the world; it is not knowledge which concerns external mass, or empirical existence and life, but is knowledge of that which is eternal, of what God is, and what flows out of his nature. For this his nature must reveal and develop itself. Philosophy, therefore, only unfolds itself when it unfolds religion, and in unfolding itself it

---

1. *Wissenschaft* is a key term in Hegel; see the Hegel glossary, p. 144.

2. That is, of "the Absolute," expressed in the language of religion.

unfolds religion. As thus occupied with eternal truth which exists on its own account, or is in and for itself, and, as in fact, a dealing on the part of the thinking spirit, and not of individual caprice and particular interest, with this object, it is the same kind of activity as religion is. *Geist* in so far as it thinks philosophically immerses itself with like living interest in this object, and renounces its particularity in that it permeates its object, in the same way as religious consciousness does, for the latter also does not seek to have anything of its own, but desires only to immerse itself in this content.

Thus religion and philosophy come to be one. Philosophy is itself, in fact, worship; it is religion, for in the same way it renounces subjective notions [*Einfälle*] and opinions in order to occupy itself with God. Philosophy is thus identical with religion, but the distinction is that it is so in a peculiar manner, distinct from the manner of looking at things which is commonly called religion as such. What they have in common is that they are religion; what distinguishes them from each other is merely the kind and manner of religion we find in each. It is in the distinctive way in which they both occupy themselves with God that they distinguish themselves.

* * *

2. THE RELATION OF THE PHILOSOPHY OF RELIGION
TO THE SYSTEM OF PHILOSOPHY

a. In philosophy, the Highest is called the Absolute, the *Idee*.[3] It is superfluous to go further back here, and to mention that this Highest was in the Wolffian philosophy[4] called *ens*, Thing [*Ding*]; for that at once proclaims itself an abstraction, which corresponds very inadequately to our idea of God. In the more recent philosophy, the Absolute is not so complete an abstraction, but yet it has not on that account the same signification as is implied in the term, God. In order even to make the difference apparent, we must in the first place consider what the word signify itself signifies. When we ask, "What does this or that signify?" we are asking about two kinds of things, and, in fact, about things which are opposed. In the first place, we call what we are thinking of, the meaning, the end or intention, the general thought of this or that expression, work of art, &c.; if we ask about its intrinsic character, it is essentially the *thought content* [*Gedanke*] that is in it of which we wish to have an idea [*Vorstellung*]. When we thus ask "What is God?" "What does the expression 'God' signify?" it is the thought content that we seek; the basic idea [*Vorstellung*] we possess already. Accordingly, what is signified here is that we have got to specify the *Begriff*;[5] and thus it follows that the *Begriff* is the signification [*Bedeutung*].[6] It is the Absolute, the nature of God as grasped by thought, the logical knowledge of this, to which we desire to attain. This, then, is the

---

3. A key term whose meaning in Hegel differs greatly from the everyday or philosophical understanding of the English "idea." See the Hegel glossary at the end of the introductory headnote.
4. That is, the philosophy of Christian Wolff (1679–1750), the most eminent philosopher in central Europe after Leibniz and before KANT, whom Kant had most specifically in mind in his critique of metaphysics. Wolff continued the Cartesian-

Leibnizian tradition of metaphysical philosophy (but with a strongly Protestant-Christian orientation). The word *ens* is Latin for "being" (an entity).
5. A key Hegelian term, designating the true conceptual content specifying the nature or essential structure of some kind of thing, or that structure itself. See the Hegel glossary, p. 144.
6. That is, "meaning."

one signification of signification, and so far, that which we call "the Absolute" has a meaning identical with the expression "God."

b. But we put the question again, in a second sense, according to which it is the opposite of this which is sought after. When we begin to occupy ourselves with pure thought-determinations, rather than representations [*Vorstellungen*], it may be that the mind does not feel satisfied, is not at home, in these, and asks what this pure thought-determination signifies. For example, everyone can understand for himself what is meant by the terms unity, objective, subjective, &c., and yet it may very well happen that the specific form of thought we call the unity of subjective and objective, the unity of real and ideal, is not understood. What is asked for in such a case is the meaning [*Bedeutung*] in the very opposite sense from that which was required before. Here it is a representation [*Vorstellung*] of the thought-determination which is demanded, an example of the content, which has as yet only been given in thought. If we find a thought-content difficult to understand, the difficulty lies in this, that we possess no representation of it; it is by means of an example that it becomes clear to us, and that the mind first feels at home with itself in this content. When, accordingly, we start with the ordinary conception of God, the philosophy of religion has to consider its signification—this, namely, that God is the *Idee*, the Absolute, the essential reality [*Wesen*] which is grasped in thought and in *Begriff*, and this it has in common with logical philosophy; the logical *Idee* is God as he is in himself. But it is just the nature of God that he should not be implicit or "in himself" only. He is as essentially "*for* himself,"[7] the absolute *Geist*, the *Wesen* that not only keeps itself within thought but also manifests itself, and gives itself objectivity.

c. Thus, in contemplating the *Idee* of God, in the philosophy of religion, we have at the same time to do with the manner of its representation [*Vorstellung*] to us; it simply makes itself apparent, represents itself to itself. This is the aspect of the determinate being or existence of the Absolute. In the philosophy of religion we have thus the Absolute as object; not, however, merely in the form of thought, but also in the form of its manifestation. The *allgemeine Idee* is thus to be conceived of with the purely concrete meaning of essentiality in general, regarded from the point of view of its activity in displaying itself, in appearing, in revealing itself.[8] Popularly speaking, we say God is the Lord of the natural world and of the realm of *Geist*. He *is* the absolute harmony of the two, and it is he who produces and carries on this harmony. Here neither thought and *Begriff* nor their manifestation—determinate being or existence—are lacking. This aspect, thus represented by determinate being, is itself, however, to be grasped again in thought, since we are here in the region of philosophy.

Philosophy to begin with contemplates the Absolute as logical *Idee*—the *Idee* as it is in thought, under the aspect in which its content is constituted

---

7. For Hegel, the phrase "in itself" means the intrinsic nature or potentiality of something; "for itself" refers to a self-consciousness and expression of something that is more or less (and often less) adequate to what it is "in itself."

8. That is, "the *allgemeine Idee*" refers to the structural nature of anything and everything *making* *itself manifest*, attaining embodiment in real existence, and so realizing itself. That principle is the centerpiece of Hegel's entire philosophy, and also of his philosophy of religion and explication of the real meaning of the notion of "God." On the key term *allgemein*, see the Hegel glossary, p. 144.

by the specific forms of thought. Further, philosophy exhibits the Absolute in its activity, in its creations. This is the manner in which the Absolute becomes actual or "for itself," becomes *Geist*; and God is thus the result of philosophy.[9] It becomes apparent, however, that this is not merely a result, but is something which eternally creates itself, and is that which precedes all else. The onesidedness of the result is abrogated and absorbed in the very result itself.

Nature, finite *Geist*, the world of consciousness, of intelligence, and of will, are embodiments of the divine *Idee*, but they are definite shapes, special modes of the appearance of the *Idee*, forms, in which the *Idee* has not yet penetrated to itself, so as to be absolute *Geist*.

In the philosophy of religion, however, we do not contemplate the implicitly existing logical *Idee* merely in its determinate character as pure thought, nor in those finite determinations where its mode of appearance is a finite one, but as it is in itself or implicitly in thought, and at the same time as it appears, manifests itself, and thus in infinite manifestation as *Geist*, which reflects itself in itself; for *Geist* which does not appear, *is* not.[1] In this characteristic of appearance *finite* appearance is also included—that is, the world of nature, and the world of finite *Geist*,—but *Geist* is regarded as the power or force of these worlds, as producing them out of itself, and out of them producing itself.

* * *

FROM OF JUDGMENT,[2] OR DEFINITE RELIGION

If in the first part we have considered religion in its *Begriff*, the simple conception of religion, the character of the content, the *Allgemeine*, it is now necessary to leave this sphere of generality [*Allgemeinheit*] and go on to treat of determinateness [*Bestimmtheit*] in religion.

The *Begriff* as such is not as yet unfolded; the determinate qualities, the moments are contained in it, but are not as yet openly displayed, and have not received the right distinction or difference which belongs to them. It is only by means of the judgment (*i.e.*, the act of differentiation) that they receive this. It is when God, the *Begriff*, performs the act of judgment, and the category of determinateness enters, that we first come to have existing religion, which is at the same time definitely existing religion.

The course followed in passing from the abstract to the concrete is based upon our method, upon the concept, and not on the fact that much special content is present. There is a complete distinction between this and our point of view. *Geist*, to which belongs being which is absolute and supreme, is, exists only as activity; that is to say, in so far as it posits itself, is actual or for itself, and produces itself. But in this its activity it has the power of *knowing*, and

---

9. That is, it is only with the emergence of philosophical thinking in which the world's true nature is grasped in thought that is adequate to it that God becomes fully actual.
1. That is, *Geist* is nothing real if it does not manifest itself in some way or another in this life and world; and such manifestations (in experience,

activity, and objective form) are precisely what its realization and reality consist in.
2. Hegel sometimes plays on the literal meaning of *das Urteil* (judgment) as *ur-teilen*, "primordial division," to suggest the idea of the differentiation of what is fundamentally one and the same thing into distinct and differing forms. See n. 5, p. 201.

only as it thus knows is it that which it is. It is thus essential to religion not only to exist in its *Begriff*, but also to be the consciousness of that which it is the *Begriff* of, and the material in which the *Begriff* as the plan, so to speak, realizes itself, which it makes its own, which it moulds in accordance with itself, is human consciousness. So too, Right, for example, only is when it exists in *Geist*, when it takes possession of the wills of men, and they know of it as the determination of their wills. And it is in this way that the *Idee* first realizes itself, having before only been posited as the form of the *Begriff*.

Geist, in short, is not immediate; natural things are immediate, and remain in this condition of immediate being. The being [*Sein*] of *Geist* is not thus immediate, but is, exists only as producing itself, as making itself for itself by means of negation as subject; otherwise it would be substance only. And this coming to itself on the part of *Geist* is movement, activity, and mediation of itself with itself.

A stone is immediate, it is complete. Wherever there is life, however, this activity is already to be found. Thus the first form of the existence of plants is the feeble existence of the germ, and out of this it has to develop itself and to produce itself. Finally the plant epitomizes itself when it has unfolded itself in the seed; this beginning of the plant is also its ultimate product. In like manner man is at first a child, and as belonging to Nature he goes through this cycle in order to beget another.

In plants there are two kinds of individual forms: this germ which begins is different from the one which is the completion of its life, and in which this evolution reaches maturity. But it is the very nature of *Geist*, just because it is living, to be at first only potential, to be in its *Begriff*, then to come forward into existence, to unfold, produce itself, become mature, bringing forth the notion of itself, that which it implicitly is, so that what it is in itself or implicitly may be its notion actually or for itself. The child is not as yet a reasonable person; it has capacities only, it is at first reason—*Geist*—potentially only. It is by means of education and development that it becomes *Geist*.

This, then, is what is called self-determination entering into existence, being "for other," bringing one's moments into distinction, and unfolding one's self. These distinctions are no other than the characteristics which the *Begriff* itself implicitly contains.

The development of these distinctions, and the course of the tendencies which result from them, are the way by which *Geist* comes to itself; it is itself, however, the goal. The absolute end, which is that *Geist* should know itself, comprehend itself, should become object to itself as it is in itself, arrive at perfect knowledge of itself, first appears as its true being. Now this process, followed by self-producing *Geist*, this path taken by it, includes distinct moments; but the path is not as yet the goal, and *Geist* does not reach the goal without having traversed the path. It is not originally at the goal; even what is most perfect must traverse the path to the goal in order to attain it. *Geist*, in these halting-places of its progress, is not as yet perfect; its knowledge, its consciousness regarding itself, is not what is true, and it is not as yet revealed to itself. *Geist* being essentially this activity of self-production, it follows that there are stages of its consciousness, but its consciousness of itself is always in proportion only to the stage which has been reached. Now these stages supply us with definite religion; here religion is consciousness of the *allgemeine Geist*, which is not as yet fully developed as absolute; this consciousness of *Geist* at each stage is definite consciousness of itself, it is the path of the education [*Erziehung*] of *Geist*.[3] We have therefore to consider the definite forms of religion. These, as being stages on the road followed by *Geist*, are imperfect.

The different forms or specific kinds of religion are, in one aspect, moments of religion in general, or of perfected religion. They have, however, an independent aspect too, for in them religion has developed itself in time, and historically.

Religion, in so far as it is determinate,[4] and has not as yet completed the circle of its determinateness—so far that is as it is finite religion, and exists as finite—is historical religion, or a particular form of religion. Its principal moments, and also the manner in which they exist historically, being exhibited in the progress of religion from stage to stage, and in its development, there thus arises a series of forms of religion, or a history of religion.

That which is determined by means of the *Begriff* must of necessity have existed, and the religions, as they have followed upon one another, have not arisen accidentally. It is *Geist* which rules inner life, and to see only chance here, after the fashion of the historical school, is absurd.

The essential moments of the *Begriff* of religion show themselves and make their appearance at every stage in which religion exists at all. It is only because the moments are not as yet posited in the totality of the *Begriff*, that any difference between it and its true form arises. These definite religions are not indeed *our* religion, yet they are included in ours as essential, although as subordinate moments, which cannot miss having in them absolute truth. Therefore in them we have not to do with what is foreign to us, but with what is our own, and the knowledge that such is the case is the reconciliation of the true religion with the false. Thus the moments of the *Begriff* of religion appear on lower stages of development, though as yet in the shape of anticipations or presentiments, as natural flowers and creations of fancy which have, so to speak, blossomed forth by chance. What determines the characteristics of these stages, however, through their entire history, is the determinateness of the *Begriff* itself, which can at no stage be absent.

The thought of the Incarnation,[5] for example, pervades every religion. Such general conceptions make their presence felt too in other spheres of *Geist*. What is substantial in ethical relations, as, for example, property, marriage, protection of the sovereign and of the state, and the ultimate decision which rests with subjectivity regarding that which is to be done for the whole—all this is to be found in an unsophisticated [*unausgebildet*] society as well as in a fully developed [*vollendet*] state; only the definite form of this substantial element differs according to the degree of development [*Ausbildung*] which such a society has reached. What is here of special importance, however, is that the *Begriff* should also become actually known in its totality, and in exact

---

3. A phrase that echoes SCHILLER'S in *The Aesthetic Education* [Erziehung] *of Man* [Menschen] (1794; see above).
4. That is, insofar as it is some specific religion, distinguished from other specific religions by its particular determinate features.
5. Literally, "becoming human" (*Menschwerdung*); that is, taking human form, coming to exist in the concrete and specific way in which we human beings exist.

accordance with the degree in which this knowledge is present, is the stage at which the religious spirit is, higher or lower, richer or poorer. *Geist* may have something in its possession without having a developed consciousness of it. It actually has the immediate, proper nature of *Geist*, has a physical, organic nature, but it does not know that nature in its essential character and truth, and has only an approximate, general idea of it. Men live in the state, they are themselves the life, activity, actuality of the state, but the positing, the becoming conscious of what the state is, does not on that account take place, and yet the fully developed state just means that everything which is *potentially* in it—that is to say, in its *Begriff*—should be developed, posited, and made into rights and duties, into law. In like manner the moments of the *Begriff* are actually present in the specific religions in images [*Anschauungen*], feelings, or immediate imagery; but the *consciousness* of these moments is not as yet evolved—or, in other words, they have not as yet been elevated to the point at which they are the determination of the absolute object, and God is not as yet actually represented under these determinations of the totality of the conception of religion.

It is undoubtedly true that the definite religions of the various peoples often enough exhibit the most distorted, confused, and abortive ideas of the divine nature [*göttliche Wesen*], and likewise of duties and relations as expressed in worship. But we must not treat the matter so lightly, and conceive of it in so superficial a manner, as to reject these ideas and these rites as superstition, error, and deceit, or only trace back their origin to pious feeling, and thus value them as merely representing some sort of religious feeling, without caring how they may chance to be constituted. The mere collection and elaboration of the external and visible elements cannot satisfy us either. On the contrary, something higher is necessary—namely, to recognize the meaning, the truth, and the connection with truth; in short, to get to know what is *rational* [*Vernünftige*] in them. It is *human beings* [*Menschen*] who have hit upon such religions; therefore there must be *reason* [*Vernunft*] in them, and amidst all that is accidental in them, a higher necessity. We must do them this justice, for what is human, rational in them, is *our own* too, although it exists in our higher consciousness as an aspect only.

To get a grasp of the history of religions, in this sense, means to reconcile ourselves even with what is horrible, dreadful, or absurd in them—and to justify it. We are on no account to regard it as right or true, as it presents itself in its purely immediate form—there is no question of doing this—but we are at least to recognise its beginning, the source from which it has originated as *human* [*als ein Menschliches*]. Such is the reconciliation with this entire sphere, the reconciliation which completes itself in the *Begriff*. Religions, as they follow upon one another, are determined by means of the *Begriff*. Their nature and succession are not determined from without; on the contrary, they are determined by the nature of *Geist*, which has entered into the world to bring itself to consciousness of itself. Since we look at these definite religions in accordance with the *Begriff*, this is a purely philosophical study of what actually is or exists. Philosophy indeed treats of nothing which is not, and does not concern itself with what is so powerless as not even to have the energy to force itself into existence.

Now in development [*Entwicklung*] as such, in so far as it has not as yet reached its goal, the moments of the *Begriff* are still in a state of separation or mutual exclusion, so that the reality has not as yet come to be equal to the *Begriff*. The finite religions[6] are the appearance in history of these moments. In order to grasp these in their truth, it is necessary to consider them under two aspects; on the one hand, we have to consider how God is known, how he is characterized; and on the other, how the subject at the same time knows itself. For the two aspects the objective and subjective have but one foundation for their further determination, and but one specific character pervades them both. The idea which man [*der Mensch*] has of God corresponds with that which he has of himself, of his freedom. Knowing himself in God, he at the same time knows his imperishable life in God; he knows of the truth of his being. The idea [*Vorstellung*] of the *immortality of the soul*[7] here enters as an essential moment into the history of religion. The ideas [*Vorstellungen*] of God and of immortality have a necessary relation to each other; when man knows truly about God, he knows truly about himself too: the two sides correspond with each other. At first God is something quite undetermined; but in the course of spiritual development the consciousness of that which God is gradually forms and matures itself, losing more and more of its initial indefiniteness—and with this the development of true *self*-consciousness advances also. The "proofs of the existence of God" fall within the sphere of this progressive development, it being their aim to set forth the necessary elevation of the spirit to God. For the diversity of the characteristics which in this process of elevation are attributed to God is fixed by the diversity of the points of departure, and this diversity again has its foundation in the nature of the historical stage of actual self-consciousness which has been reached. The different forms which this development takes will always indicate the metaphysical spirit of the period in question, to which the prevailing idea [*Vorstellung*] of God and form of worship [*Kultus*] correspond.

* * *

SOURCE: From Georg Wilhelm Friedrich Hegel, *Lectures on the Philosophy of Religion: Together with a Work on the Proofs of the Existence of God*, trans. E. B. Spiers and J. Burdon Sanderson (London: Kegan Paul, Trench, Trübner, 1895), 1:1–2, 19–20, 23–26, 73–80 (translation modified by the editor). Except where otherwise indicated, German words in brackets are the terminology used in the German original, inserted by the editor in addition to their renderings in the translation; and unbracketed German words are the original terminology, substituted in place of their renderings in the translation by the editor for reasons given in notes and in the Hegel glossary (p. 144). This is a translation of the second German edition (1840) of another set of Hegel's posthumously edited and published lectures, *Vorlesungen über die Philosophie der Religion*.

6. That is, the various particular religions.
7. "die Unsterblichkeit der Seele": for Hegel, this is not a philosophically viable concept but rather a *Vorstellung*—a "representation" or image of something significant about *Geist* that requires explication and more exact expression.

On Absolute Knowing

From Phenomenology of *Geist*

From *Absolute Knowing* [Wissen].

* * *

What was in the case of religion *content*, or a way of representing [*Vorstellen*] an "other," is here the action proper of the self. The *Begriff* is the connecting principle securing that the content is the action proper of the self. For this *Begriff* is, as we see, the knowledge that the action of the self within itself is all that is essential and all existence, the knowledge of this Subject as Substance and of the Substance as this knowledge of its action. What we have done here, in addition, is simply to gather together the particular aspects [*Momente*], each of which in principle exhibits the life of *Geist* in its entirety, and again to fix and secure the *Begriff* in the form of the *Begriff*, whose content was disclosed in those "moments" and had already presented itself in the form of a mode or type of consciousness.

This last form [*Gestalt*] of *Geist*—*Geist* which at once gives its complete and true content the form of self, and thereby realises its *Begriff* and in doing so remains within its own *Begriff*—this is *Absolute Knowing*. It is *Geist* knowing itself in the form of *Geist*, or conceptualizing [*begreifende*] knowing [*Wissen*].[1] Truth is here not merely *in itself* absolutely identical with certainty; it has also the typical form of certainty of self, or in its existence—i.e. for *Geist* knowing it—it is in the *form* of knowledge of itself. Truth is the content, which in the case of religion is not as yet at one with its certainty. This identification, however, is secured when the content has received the form and character of self. By this means, what constitutes the very essence, viz. the *Begriff*, comes to have the nature of existence, i.e. assumes the form of what is objective to consciousness. *Geist*, appearing before consciousness in this element of existence, or, what is here the same thing, produced by it in this element, is *Wissenschaft*.[2]

The nature, "moments" and process of this type of knowing have then come about in such a way that this knowing is pure self-existence of self-consciousness. It is the "I" [*Ich*], which is *this* "I"[3] and no other, and yet it is also immediately mediated superseded [*aufgehoben*] "I."[4] It has a content, which it distinguishes from itself; for it is pure negativity, or self-diremption;[5] it is consciousness. This content in its distinction is itself the I, for it is the process of self-superseding [*Sichselbstaufheben*], or the same pure negativity which constitutes ego. The I is in it, as distinguished, reflected into

---

1. That is, knowing in the form of genuine philosophically refined *Begriffe* (on *Begriff*, see the Hegel glossary at the end of the introductory headnote).
2. That is, systematic knowledge and cognitive inquiry. See the Hegel glossary, p. 144.
3. That is, some particular existing "I."
4. That is, the actual "I" at the level of "absolute *Geist*" (and "absolute knowing") is not only always some particular existing "I" but also an "I" that has emerged from a whole series of mediations and transformations that have raised it to the highest

level of *Allgemeinheit* (generality or universality)—which itself has been *aufgehoben* (superseded) by the attainment of particular existence. (On these terms, see the Hegel glossary on p. 144.) This is Hegel's philosophical-conceptual restatement of the "truth" of the religious image or symbol of the incarnation, in which "the Word [*Logos*] becomes flesh" (John 1:14), and "flesh" is raised to union or accord with the *Logos*.
5. Self-separation or self-division.

itself; and when the content is conceptually comprehended [*begriffen*], the I in its otherness is at home with itself. More precisely stated, this content is nothing else than the very process just spoken of; for the content is *Geist* which traverses the whole range of its own being, and does this for itself as *Geist*, by the fact that it possesses the form of the *Begriff* in its objectivity.

As to the actual existence of this *Begriff*, *Wissenschaft*[6] does not appear in time and in reality till *Geist* has arrived at this stage of being conscious regarding itself. As *Geist* which knows what it is, it did not exist before, and is not to be found at all till after the completion of the task of mastering and overcoming the imperfection of its form—thereby to produce for its consciousness the shape of its inmost essence, and in this manner to square its self-consciousness with its consciousness. *Geist* in and for itself is, when distinguished into its separate "moments" or aspects, self-conscious knowing, conceptual comprehension *in general,* which *as such* has not yet reached the substance, or is not in itself absolute knowing.

Now in actual reality the knowing substance is arrived at earlier than its form or *Begriff*-configuration [*Begriffsgestalt*]. For the substance is the undeveloped inherent nature or the ground and *Begriff* in its inert simplicity, the state of inwardness or the self of *Geist* not yet objectified. What is there, what does exist, is in the shape of unexpressed simplicity, the undeveloped immediate, or the object of representational [*vorstellenden*] consciousness in general. Because knowing [*Erkennen*] is a *geistig* consciousness, which is only aware of what implicitly and inherently is so far as this is a being for the self and a being *of* the self or a *Begriff*—knowing has on this account merely a barren object to begin with, in contrast to which the substance and the consciousness of this substance are richer in content. Revelation[7] in such a case is, in fact, concealment; for the substance is here still self-less existence, and nothing but certainty of self is manifest or revealed to it.

To begin with, therefore, it is only the abstract moments that fall to self-consciousness when dealing with the substance. But since these moments are pure activities and must move forward by their very nature, self-consciousness enriches itself till it has torn from consciousness the entire substance, and absorbed into itself the entire structure of the substance with all its constituent elements. Since this negative attitude towards objectivity is positive as well, establishes and fixes the content, it goes on till it has produced these elements out of itself and thereby reinstated them once more as objects of consciousness. In the *Begriff* knowing itself as *Begriff,* the "moments" [*Momente* in this development] thus make their appearance prior to the whole in its complete fulfillment; the movement of these "moments" is the process by which the whole comes into being. In consciousness, on the other hand, the whole—but not as comprehended conceptually [*unbegriffen*]—is prior to the moments.

Time is the *Begriff* itself as definitely existent, represented [*vorstellt*] to consciousness in the form of empty pure intuition. Hence *Geist* necessarily appears

---

6. In its ultimate form, Hegelian "absolute knowing" and "absolute knowledge" (the final form of "absolute *Geist*"); and the *Begriff* attains "actual existence" in the form appropriate to it when *Wissenschaft* in that ultimate form attains "actual existence"—that is, when there come to be actually existing thinkers in whose thought "absolute knowing" and "absolute knowledge" are existing realities.

7. That is, in a religion such as Christianity. Such "revelation," expressed representationally in religion's imagery (*Vorstellungen*) embraced in faith (*Glaube*), is inferior, at the level of "absolute *Geist*," to philosophical *Begriffe* and *Wissen*.

in time, and it appears in time so long as it does not grasp its pure *Begriff*, i.e. so long as it does not annul time. Time is the pure self in external form, apprehended in intuition [*Anschauung*], and not grasped and understood by the self; it is the *Begriff* directly apprehended through intuition. When this *Begriff* grasps itself, it supersedes [*aufhebt*] the time character, conceptually comprehends intuition, and is intuition comprehended and comprehending [*begriffenes* and *begriffendes*]. Time therefore appears as *Geist*'s destiny and necessity, where *Geist* is not yet complete within itself. It is the necessity compelling *Geist* to increase and enrich the share self-consciousness has in consciousness, to put into motion the immediacy of the inherent nature (which is the form in which the substance is present in consciousness); or, conversely, to realise and make manifest what is inherent, regarded as inward and immanent, to make manifest that which is at first within—i.e. to vindicate and secure for it the certainty of self.

For this reason it must be said that nothing is *known* [*gewusst*] which does not fall within experience, or (as it is also expressed) which is not *felt* to be true, which is not given as an inwardly revealed eternal verity, as a sacred object of belief, or whatever other expressions one might care to employ. For experience just consists in this: that the content—and the content is *Geist*—in its inherent nature is substance and so object of consciousness. But this substance in which *Geist* consists is the development of itself explicitly to what it is inherently and implicitly; and only by this process of reflecting itself into itself is it then essentially and in truth *Geist*. It is inherently the movement which constitutes the process of knowing—the transforming of that implicit inherent nature into explicitness and objectivity, of Substance into Subject, of the object of consciousness into the object of self-consciousness, i.e. into an object that is at the same time superseded and transcended—in other words, into the *Begriff*. This transforming process is a cycle that returns into itself—a cycle that presupposes its beginning, and reaches its beginning only at the end.

So far as *Geist* thus is of necessity this process of self-articulation [*Unterscheiden*], it appears as a single whole, intuitively apprehended, over against its simple self-consciousness. And since that whole is the articulation, it is articulation into the intuitively apprehended pure *Begriff*, Time, and the content, the inherent implicit nature. Substance, *qua* subject, involves the necessity—at first an *inner* necessity—to set forth in itself what it inherently is, to show itself to be *Geist*. The completed systematic expression in objective form becomes, then, at the same time the reflection of substance, the development of it into a self or subject. Consequently, until and unless *Geist* is inherently completed, completed as *Weltgeist*, it cannot reach its completion as self-conscious *Geist*. The content of religion therefore expresses earlier in time than [philosophical] *Wissenschaft* what *Geist* is; but the latter alone is the perfect form in which *Geist* truly knows itself.

The process of carrying forward this form of knowledge of itself constitutes the task which *Geist* accomplishes in the concrete actual shape of History. The religious community [*Gemeine*], in so far as it is at the outset the substance of Absolute *Geist*, is the crude form of consciousness, which has an existence all the harsher and more barbaric the deeper is its inner *Geist*; and its inarticulate stolid self has all the harder task in dealing with its essence, the [unconceptualized] content alien to its consciousness. Not till it has surrendered the hope of superseding that foreignness by an external, i.e. alien method,[8] does it turn to itself, to its own peculiar world in the actual present. It turns thither because to supersede that alien method means returning into self-consciousness.

It thus discovers this world in the living present to be its own property, and so has taken the first step to descend from the ideal intelligible world, the world of the intellect, or rather to endow the abstract element of the intellect with concrete self-hood. Through "observation," on the one hand, it finds existence in the shape of thought, and comprehends existence; and, conversely, it finds in its thought—existence. When, in the first instance, it has thus itself expressed in an abstract way the immediate unity of thought and existence, of abstract Being and Self; and when it has expressed the primal principle of "Light" in a purer form, viz. as unity of extension and existence—for "existence" is an ultimate simple term more akin to thought than "Light"—and in this way has revived again in thought the Substance of the Orient, the Absolute Substance of Eastern Religions;[9] thereupon *Geist* at once recoils in horror from this abstract unity, from this self-less substance, and maintains as against it the principle of Individuality. But after *Geist* has relinquished this principle and brought it under the ordeal of culture [*Bildung*], has thereby made it an objective existence and established it throughout the whole of existence, has arrived at the idea of "Utility" and in the sphere of absolute freedom has found the key to existence to be Individual Will—after these stages *Geist* then brings to light the thought that lies in its inmost depths, and expresses ultimate reality in the form "I = I."

This "I = I" is, however, an inward, self-reflecting process; for since this identity *qua* absolute negativity is absolute distinction, the self-identity of the I stands in contrast to this absolute distinction, which—being pure distinction and at the same time objective to the self that knows itself—has to be expressed as Time. In this way, just as formerly ultimate reality was expressed as unity of thought and *extension*, it would here be interpreted as unity of thought and *time*. But distinction left to itself—unresting and unhalting time—really collapses upon itself. It is objective rest, the stable continuity of extension; while this latter is pure identity with self—the "I."

Or: "I" is not merely self—it is identity of self with itself. This identity, however, is complete and immediate unity with self; in other words this Subject is just as much Substance. Substance by itself alone would be void and empty Intuition [*Anschauen*], or the intuition of a content which *qua* something specific would have merely a contingent character and would be devoid of necessity. Substance would only stand for the Absolute in so far as Substance was thought of or "intuited" as absolute unity; and all content would, as regards its diversity, have to fall outside the Substance and be due to reflection—a process which does not belong to Substance, because Substance would not be Subject, would not be conceived as *Geist*, as reflecting about self and reflecting itself into self. If, nevertheless, a content were to be spoken of, then on the one hand, it would only exist in order to be thrown into the empty abyss of the

---

8. That is, by a religious "mystery" or rite that is incomprehensible to it.

9. That is, the "One"—the sole true reality, all else being illusion.

Absolute, while on the other it would be picked up in external fashion from sense perception. Knowledge would appear to have come by things, by what is distinct from knowledge itself, and to have got at the distinctions between the endless variety of things, without any one understanding how or where all this came from.

Geist, however, has shown itself to be neither the mere withdrawal of self-consciousness into its pure inwardness, nor the mere absorption of self-consciousness into blank Substance devoid of all distinctions. *Geist* is the movement of the self which empties itself of self and sinks itself within its own substance, and *qua* subject, both goes out of that substance into itself, making its substance an object and a content, and also supersedes this distinction of objectivity and content. That first reflection out of immediacy is the subject's distinction of self from its substance, the *Begriff* in a state of self-diremption, the subjectification of the self, and the coming of the pure "I" into being. Since this distinction is the action pure and simple of "I = I," the *Begriff* is the necessity for and the emergence [*Aufgehen*] of existence, which has the substance for its essential nature and subsists on its own account. But this subsisting of existence for itself is the *Begriff* established and realised in determinate form, and is thereby the *Begriff*'s own inherent movement— that of descending into the bare and simple substance, which is only subject by being this negativity and going through this process.

The "I" does not have to take its stand on the form of self-consciousness in opposition to the form of substantiality and objectivity, as if it were afraid of emptying itself and becoming objective. The power of *Geist* lies rather in remaining one with itself when giving up itself, and, because it is self-contained and self-subsistent, in establishing as mere moments its explicit self-existence as well as its implicit inherent nature. Nor again is the "I" some sort of "nei-ther/nor" third thing which casts distinctions back into the abyss of the abso-lute, and declares them all to mean the same there. On the contrary, true knowing lies rather in the seeming inactivity which merely watches and con-siders how the element distinguished proceeds, how it is self-moved by its very nature and returns again into its own unity.

With absolute knowing, then, *Geist* has wound up the process of its vari-ous forms and modes, so far as in assuming these various shapes and forms it is affected with the insurmountable distinction which consciousness implies [i.e. the distinction of consciousness from its object or content]. *Geist* has attained the pure element of its existence, the *Begriff*. The content is, in view of the freedom of its own existence, the self that empties and gives up itself to objectivity; in other words, that content is the *immediate* unity of self-knowledge. The pure process of thus relinquishing itself to externality constitutes—when we consider this process in its bearing on the content— the *necessity* of this content. The diversity of content is, *qua* determinate and specific, due to relation, and is not inherent; it is its restless activity of can-celling and superseding [*aufheben*] itself, or its negativity. Thus the necessity or diversity, like its free existence, is the self too; and in this self-form, in which existence is immediately thought, the content is a *Begriff*. Seeing, then, that *Geist* has attained the *Begriff*, it unfolds its existence and develops its pro-cesses in this ether of its life and is *Wissenschaft*. The moments of its process are set forth in [philosophical] *Wissenschaft* no longer as determinate modes or forms of consciousness, but—since the distinction, which consciousness implies, has reverted to and has become a distinction within the self—as determinate *Begriffe*, and as the organic self-explaining and self-constituted process of these conceptions.

While in the *Phenomenology of Geist* each moment is the distinction of knowledge and truth, and the process in which that distinction is cancelled and transcended, on the other hand [philosophical] *Wissenschaft* does not contain this distinction and its supersession [*Aufhebung*]. Rather, since each moment has the form of the *Begriff*, it unites the objective form of truth and the knowing self in an immediate unity. In *Wissenschaft* the individual moment does not appear as the process of passing back and forward from consciousness or representation to self-consciousness and conversely: there the pure form, liberated from the condition of being an appearance in mere consciousness—the pure *Begriff* with its further development, depends solely and purely on its characteristic and specific nature. Conversely, again, there corresponds to every abstract moment of absolute *Wissenschaft* a form or mode in which *Geist* as a whole makes it appearance. As the *Geist* that actually exists and historically appears is not richer than *Wissenschaft*, so, too, *Geist* in its actual content is not poorer. To know the pure *Begriffe* of *Wissenschaft* in the form in which they are modes or types of consciousness—this constitutes the aspect of their reality, in which its essential element, the *Begriff*, appearing there in its simple mediating activity as thinking, breaks up and separates the moments of this mediation, and exhibits its content by reference to the internal and immanent opposition of its elements.

Wissenschaft contains within itself this necessity of relinquishing and divesting [*entäussern*][1] itself of the form of the pure *Begriff*, and necessarily involves the transition of the *Begriff* into consciousness. For *Geist* that knows itself is, just for the reason that it grasps its own *Begriff*, immediate identity with itself; and this, in the distinction it implies, is the certainty of what is immediate or is sense-consciousness—the beginning from which we started. This process of releasing itself from the form of its self is the highest freedom and security of its knowledge of itself.

All the same, this relinquishment of self and abandonment to externality are still incomplete. This process expresses the relation of the certainty of its self to the object, an object which, just by being in relation, has not yet attained its full freedom. Systematic knowing is aware not only of itself, but also of the negative of itself, or its limit. Knowing its limit means knowing how to sacrifice itself. This sacrifice is the emptying of self, the self-abandonment, in which *Geist* sets forth, in the form of free and unconstrained fortuitous contingency, its process of becoming *Geist*, intuitively apprehending outside it its pure self as Time, and likewise its existence as Space. This last form into which *Geist* passes, *Nature*, is its living immediate process of development.

---

1. The term *Entäusserung* and its variants, meaning something like "relinquishing and divesting oneself of something," is in Hegel a near-synonym of *Entfremdung*—"making alien" or "alienation," a concept that would take on great importance both in MARX's writings and in later philosophical and social theory and criticism.

Nature—*Geist* divested of self and given over to externality—is, in its actual existence, nothing but this eternal process of abandoning its own independent subsistence, and the movement which reinstates Subject.

The other dimension [*Seite*], however, in which *Geist* comes into being, *History*, is process in terms of *knowing* [*Wissen*], a conscious self-mediating process—*Geist* given over to and emptied into Time. But this form of abandonment is, similarly, an emptying of itself by itself; the negative is negative of itself. This way of becoming presents a slow procession and succession of *Geistern*,[2] a gallery of pictures, each of which is endowed with the entire wealth of *Geist*, and moves so slowly just for the reason that the self has to permeate and assimilate all this wealth of its substance. Since its accomplishment consists in *Geist* coming to know what it is in fully comprehending its substance, this knowledge means its subjectification—a state in which *Geist* leaves its external existence behind and gives itself over to the attitude of Recollection [*Erinnerung*]. In this subjectification, *Geist* is engulfed in the darkness and night of its own self-consciousness. Its vanished existence is, however, conserved therein; and this superseded existence—the previous state, but born anew through knowing—is the new stage of existence, a new world, and a new type and mode of *Geist*. Here it has to begin all over again at its immediacy, as freshly as before, and thence rise once more to the measure of its stature, as if, for it, all that preceded were lost, and as if it had learned nothing from the experience of the preceding forms of *Geist* that preceded. But re-collection [*Er-Innerung*] has conserved that experience, and is the inner being, and, in fact, the higher form of the substance.

While, then, this phase of *Geist* begins all over again its formative development, apparently starting solely from itself, yet at the same time it commences at a higher level. The realm of *Geister* developed in this way, and assuming definite shape in existence, constitutes a succession in which one detaches and sets loose the other, and each takes over from its predecessor the reign of this world. The goal of the process is the revelation of its depths, and this is the Absolute *Begriff*. This revelation is thereby the supersession [*Aufheben*] of its "depth," or its "extension" or *spatial* embodiment, the negation of this subjectivity of the "I"—a negativity which is its self-relinquishment, its externalization, or its substance. And this revelation is also its *temporal* embodiment, in that this externalisation in its very nature relinquishes, externalises itself, and so exists at once in its spatial "extension" as well as in its "depth" or the self. The goal, which is Absolute Knowing or *Geist* knowing itself as *Geist*, finds its pathway in the recollection of these forms of *Geist* as they are in themselves and as they accomplish the organisation of their realm. Their conservation, looked at from the side of their free phenomenal existence in the sphere of contingency, is *History*. Looked at from the side of their conceptually comprehended organization, it is the *Wissenschaft* of phenomenal knowledge—of the ways in which knowledge appears.[3] Both together, or History comprehended conceptually [*begriffene Geschichte*], form at once

---

2. That is, of social, cultural, intellectual, and spiritual forms of *Geist*.

3. That is, Hegel's kind of phenomenology: "*die Wissenschaft der erscheinenden Wissens.*"

the recollection and the Golgotha[4] of Absolute *Geist*—the actuality, truth, and certainty of its throne, without which it would be a lifeless loner [*leblose Einsame*]; only—

aus dem Kelche dieses Geisterreiches	out of the chalice of this *Geister*-realm
schäumt ihm seine Unendlichkeit.	foams forth for it its infinitude.[5]

SOURCE: From G. W. F. Hegel, *The Phenomenology of Mind*, trans. J. B. Baillie (London: Swan Sonnenschein; New York: Macmillan, 1910), 2:809–23 (translation modified by the editor). Except where otherwise indicated, German words in brackets are the terminology used in the German original, inserted by the editor in addition to their renderings in the translation; and unbracketed German words are the original terminology, substituted in place of their renderings in the translation by the editor for reasons given in notes and in the Hegel glossary (p. 144). *Phänomenologie des Geistes* was first published in 1807.

4. Place of torment, death, and burial.
5. An adaptation of the concluding lines of SCHIL-LER's poem *"Die Freundschaft"* ("Friendship," 1781). This, for Hegel, is what remains of the idea of divine reality: the "foaming forth" in nature and history of the possibility—he would say necessity—of *Geist*, in the wealth of this gallery of forms of actualized spirituality come true.

RALPH WALDO EMERSON
(1803 – 1882)

Emerson, philosophically speaking, was America's counterpart to SCHILLER. Neither was philosophically trained, neither was an academic philosopher, and neither was inclined to think and write in a philosophically rigorous manner. Both were "men of letters" first and foremost, and public intellectuals who addressed themselves primarily to wider audiences. Yet both were philosophically inclined and interesting, and both had things to say that contributed significantly to the emergence and development of the interpretive tradition. Both were even associated with German "idealism"—Schiller in its beginnings, and Emerson in its American reception and adaptation, under the banner of "Transcendentalism." Emerson first became acquainted with it indirectly, primarily through the English writer Samuel Taylor Coleridge (1772–1834); but he drew strongly on the impressions of it that he gained.

Emerson also was inspired by other currents of German and English Romanticism to champion and celebrate an unabashed individualism that found echoes and amplifications in writers as diverse as Henry David Thoreau (1817–1862), Walt Whitman (1819–1892), and FRIEDRICH NIETZSCHE. He was primarily a public lecturer and essayist, who lectured and wrote in the manner more of a preacher delivering a sermon than of a philosopher advancing an argument or making a case for an interpretation; and he never worked out any of his ideas systematically and at length. Like Schiller's *Letters*, however, his writings not only are readily accessible but are powerfully and eloquently written, giving the ideas he is seeking to develop and convey compelling expression.

Ralph Waldo Emerson was born and raised in Boston. His father, a Unitarian minister, died when he was only 7. His education got off to a strong start at Boston Public Latin School, and he was admitted to Harvard College at the tender age of 14. Upon graduation four years later he supported himself as a schoolmaster, and then began studies at the Harvard Divinity School, eventually deciding to follow in his father's footsteps and become a Unitarian minister. In addition he read extensively on his own in classical and modern religious, theological, and philosophical sources; and by the time he obtained a position as pastor at a Unitarian church in Boston in 1829, his thinking had already moved well beyond the confines of conventional Unitarian Christianity. He also married at about the same time; but his young wife died of tuberculosis less than two years later, causing him great personal distress and prompting deep religious doubts. He found the ministry increasingly confining and dissatisfying, and his unorthodox thinking proved to be a problem as well. In 1832 he resigned his position, and he never returned to the ministry.

Emerson's interests in intellectual developments in Europe led him to travel there in 1833, the first of his several lengthy European stays. He spent much of his time in England, where he became acquainted with many of the leading writers and thinkers of the day, including Coleridge (through whose writings he had already become aware of recent philosophical developments in Germany), William Wordsworth, JOHN STUART MILL, and Thomas Carlyle, with whom he developed a continuing relationship. Upon returning to America, he settled near Boston in Concord, remarried, and began a career as a public speaker and popular writer that satisfied his needs and ambitions both intellectually and practically. His home in Concord became a center of intellectual life in New England, serving as his base for the rest of his life. He traveled and lectured extensively in the United States and abroad, achieving considerable fame and acclaim on both sides of the Atlantic.

In 1836, shortly after his move to Concord, Emerson and a number of others formed the Transcendental Club to pursue their shared interest in what was coming to be called "Transcendentalism"—an American version or adaptation of what in Europe was called "idealism," centering on the thought of KANT, FICHTE, SCHELLING, and HEGEL. That same year, he anonymously published a Transcendentalist manifesto—an essay titled "Nature." The group began publishing a journal, *The Dial*, in 1840.

Transcendentalism was inspired by Kant's use of the term "transcendental" and by the impression that it refers to the sort of "supersensible" reality that he distinguishes from the empirical reality of the natural world (as in the conclusion of his *Critique of Practical Reason* [1788]; see above). It thus was opposed to a purely materialistic worldview, emphasizing not only the reality of the spiritually "transcendental"—in ourselves and beyond ourselves—but also the idea that it is a higher and truer sort of reality than mere empirical natural reality, which is subordinate to and derivative of it. In addition, it was opposed to traditional religious and theological (and in particular orthodox Christian) ways of conceiving of this spiritual reality. This made it highly controversial; and when Emerson was candid about these matters in a commencement address he was invited to deliver at the Harvard Divinity School in 1838 (included in the following selections), it caused a great scandal—as a result of which it was decades before he was again invited to lecture at Harvard. (All was eventually forgiven, however, and in fact the building in which the Harvard philosophy department today is housed bears Emerson's name.)

Emerson is included in this volume and grouped in it with the main figures associated with German idealism because he embraces Transcendentalism as the name of his own philosophical position, because the views he expresses so often clearly derive from views of theirs (or from certain ways of understanding their views), and because he himself expressly states—in his 1842 lecture "The Transcendentalist" (see below)—that "What is popularly called Transcendentalism among us, is Idealism: Idealism as it appears [i.e., as it appears to 'us'] in 1842." This lecture consists chiefly of his summary of those "Idealist" ideas that he considers most relevant to the understanding of its Transcendentalist version; but it is evident from his presentation of them that they are ideas to which he and his fellow Transcendentalists were strongly drawn.

"The Over-Soul" (1841), an essay whose very title echoes Schelling's *Weltseele* (World-Soul), is very much in the spirit of "absolute idealism" at its most Romantic—that of Schelling in particular. Among other things, it shows what becomes of the idea of God in Emerson's Transcendentalist replacement for traditional religious and philosophical ways of thinking. As the affirmation of a kind of unifying spiritual force underlying, pervading, and animating all of life and nature, it seemed to Emerson to be a very attractive alternative both to traditional religious belief and to a bleak godless materialism. (It continues to resonate in American culture, as in the familiar mantra "May the Force be with you!") But Emerson does not think of this force in a reifying way as a kind of deity, as may be seen in his "Divinity School Address." There he takes a more Kantian line, holding that the real content of religion is morality, and that what is divine is moral goodness and the spirit that accompanies and strives for it.

Yet it would also seem that Emerson thinks and is prepared to affirm other things that go well beyond these "idealist" ideas, and indeed appear to go in a very different direction—whether they are to be understood as aspects of his "transcendentalism" or as supplements to it. Some are central themes in selections below. One is his ideal of human wholeness: Emerson believes that human abilities and excellences are best cultivated not in isolation but in concert, as aspects of what it means to be fully and truly human. This not only is the sort of scholar he proclaims the newly emerging "American scholar" to be but also is the sort of human being he considers it best to be.

A related supplemental theme, sounded in "The Divinity School Address," is that of moral perfectionism, revolving around the idea that the basic moral imperative is to strive to perfect ourselves in the humanity and goodness of our lives. Another is what Emerson calls "self-reliance," by which he means something like self-assertive independence and autonomy. In the essay of that title, he fully and vividly expresses the ideal of a kind of individuality and ethos of individualism that may already have been in the air but that received a powerful impetus from him here and in subsequent writings.

Emerson could never be accused of having made a fetish of what he famously calls "foolish consistency"—which he (perhaps self-justifyingly) disdainfully dismisses as "the hobgoblin of little minds." He allowed the flow of his rhetoric and lines of thought to go as the spirit moved him, and it moved him in different ways on different occasions. He frequently revisited the same or similar topics, but he seldom stayed with any of them for long, or took any pains to think through and work out his ideas about them. This characteristic may well explain at least in part why even Nietzsche became exasperated enough with him to observe: "I fear that in Emerson we have lost a philosopher." Nonetheless Nietzsche admired him, and for good reason. Emerson may not have been a deeply original thinker, but he was an adventurous thinker with a great appetite for new ideas, giving off sparks as he encountered them. He was well aware that traditional ways of thinking were becoming problematic and that there was much in need of reconsideration and reassessment; and he was eager to get on with it. Moreover, as Nietzsche's interest in him shows, his Americanized version of both the spiritualistic and the individualistic strands of European Romanticism had appeal beyond American shores.

From The American Scholar

* * *

It is one of those fables which out of an unknown antiquity convey an unlooked-for wisdom, that the gods, in the beginning, divided Man into men, that he might be more helpful to himself;[1] just as the hand was divided into fingers, the better to answer its end.

The old fable covers a doctrine ever new and sublime; that there is One Man,—present to all particular men only partially, or through one faculty; and that you must take the whole society to find the whole man. Man is not a farmer, or a professor, or an engineer, but he is all. Man is priest, and scholar, and statesman, and producer, and soldier. In the *divided* or social state these functions are parcelled out to individuals, each of whom aims to do his stint of the joint work, whilst each other performs his. The fable implies that the individual, to possess himself, must sometimes return from his own labor to embrace all the other laborers. But, unfortunately, this original unit, this fountain of power, has been so distributed to multitudes, has been so minutely subdivided and peddled out, that it is spilled into drops, and cannot be gathered. The state of society is one in which the members have suffered amputation from the trunk, and strut about so many walking monsters,—a good finger, a neck, a stomach, an elbow, but never a man.[2]

1. A story told in one of the essays in Plutarch's *Moralia* (ca. 100 C.E.), "Of Brotherly Love."
2. This discussion of the fragmentation of humanity by the division of labor in modern society recalls SCHILLER's *Letters on the Aesthetic Education of* *Man* (1794; see above)—as does Emerson's subsequent celebration of human "wholeness" as the key to genuine humanity, which he applies to the newly emerging "American scholar" or intellectual that he here celebrates (and aspires to exemplify).

Man is thus metamorphosed into a thing, into many things. The planter, who is Man sent out into the field to gather food, is seldom cheered by any idea of the true dignity of his ministry. He sees his bushel and his cart, and nothing beyond, and sinks into the farmer, instead of Man on the farm. The tradesman scarcely ever gives an ideal worth to his work, but is ridden by the routine of his craft, and the soul is subject to dollars. The priest becomes a form; the attorney a statute-book; the mechanic a machine; the sailor a rope of the ship.

In this distribution of functions the scholar is the delegated intellect. In the right state he is *Man Thinking*. In the degenerate state, when the victim of society, he tends to become a mere thinker, or still worse, the parrot of other men's thinking.

In this view of him, as Man Thinking, the theory of his office[3] is contained. Him Nature solicits with all her placid, all her monitory pictures; him the past instructs; him the future invites. Is not indeed every man a student, and do not all things exist for the student's behoof? And, finally, is not the true scholar the only true master? But the old oracle said, "All things have two handles: beware of the wrong one."[4] In life, too often, the scholar errs with mankind and forfeits his privilege. Let us see him in his school, and consider him in reference to the main influences he receives.

———

I. The first in time and the first in importance of the influences upon the mind is that of nature. Every day, the sun; and, after sunset, Night and her stars. Ever the winds blow; ever the grass grows. Every day, men and women, conversing—beholding and beholden. The scholar is he of all men whom this spectacle most engages. He must settle its value in his mind. What is nature to him? There is never a beginning, there is never an end, to the inexplicable continuity of this web of God, but always circular power returning into itself. Therein it resembles his own spirit, whose beginning, whose ending, he never can find,—so entire, so boundless. Far too as her splendors shine, system on system shooting like rays, upward, downward, without centre, without circumference,—in the mass and in the particle, Nature hastens to render account of herself to the mind. Classification begins. To the young mind every thing is individual, stands by itself. By and by, it finds how to join two things and see in them one nature; then three, then three thousand; and so, tyrannized over by its own unifying instinct, it goes on tying things together, diminishing anomalies, discovering roots running under ground whereby contrary and remote things cohere and flower out from one stem. * * *

Thus to him, to this schoolboy under the bending dome of day, is suggested that he and it proceed from one root; one is leaf and one is flower; relation, sympathy, stirring in every vein. And what is that root? Is not that the soul of his soul? A thought too bold; a dream too wild. Yet when this spiritual light shall have revealed the law of more earthly natures,—when he has learned to worship the soul, and to see that the natural philosophy that now is, is only

3. Function.
4. An allusion to Epictetus, *Enchiridion* 43 (ca. 135 C.E.).

the first gropings of its gigantic hand, he shall look forward to an ever expanding knowledge as to a becoming creator. He shall see that nature is the opposite of the soul, answering to it part for part. One is seal and one is print. Its beauty is the beauty of his own mind. Its laws are the laws of his own mind. Nature then becomes to him the measure of his attainments. So much of nature as he is ignorant of, so much of his own mind does he not yet possess. And, in fine, the ancient precept, "Know thyself," and the modern precept, "Study nature,"[5] become at last one maxim.

II. The next great influence into the spirit of the scholar is the mind of the Past,—in whatever form, whether of literature, of art, of institutions, that mind is inscribed. Books are the best type of the influence of the past, and perhaps we shall get at the truth,—learn the amount of this influence more conveniently,—by considering their value alone.

The theory of books is noble. The scholar of the first age received into him the world around; brooded thereon; gave it the new arrangement of his own mind, and uttered it again. It came into him life; it went out from him truth. It came to him short-lived actions; it went out from him immortal thoughts. It came to him business; it went from him poetry. It was dead fact; now, it is quick[6] thought. It can stand, and it can go.[7] It now endures, it now flies, it now inspires. Precisely in proportion to the depth of mind from which it issued, so high does it soar, so long does it sing.

Or, I might say, it depends on how far the process had gone, of transmuting life into truth. In proportion to the completeness of the distillation, so will the purity and imperishableness of the product be. But none is quite perfect. As no air-pump can by any means make a perfect vacuum, so neither can any artist entirely exclude the conventional, the local, the perishable from his book, or write a book of pure thought, that shall be as efficient, in all respects, to a remote posterity, as to contemporaries, or rather to the second age. Each age, it is found, must write its own books; or rather, each generation for the next succeeding. The books of an older period will not fit this.

* * *

III. * * * Action is with the scholar subordinate, but it is essential. Without it he is not yet man. Without it thought can never ripen into truth. Whilst the world hangs before the eye as a cloud of beauty, we cannot even see its beauty. Inaction is cowardice, but there can be no scholar without the heroic mind. The preamble of thought, the transition through which it passes from the unconscious to the conscious, is action. Only so much do I know, as I have lived. Instantly we know whose words are loaded with life, and whose not.

The world,—this shadow of the soul, or *other me*,—lies wide around.[8] Its attractions are the keys which unlock my thoughts and make me acquainted with myself. I run eagerly into this resounding tumult. I grasp the hands of those next me, and take my place in the ring to suffer and to work, taught by an instinct that so shall the dumb abyss be vocal with speech. I pierce its

5. A motto of Romanticism. "Know thyself": a Greek maxim (*gnōthi seauton*) carved into the temple of Apollo at Delphi (4th c. B.C.E.), home of the god's oracle.
6. Living.

7. Walk.
8. This characterization of "the world" as the "shadow" or "other me" (alter ego) of "the soul" echoes SCHELLING's conception of the relation of "nature" to *Geist* (spirit).

order; I dissipate its fear; I dispose of it within the circuit of my expanding life. So much only of life as I know by experience, so much of the wilderness have I vanquished and planted, or so far have I extended my being, my dominion. I do not see how any man can afford, for the sake of his nerves and his nap, to spare any action in which he can partake. It is pearls and rubies to his discourse. Drudgery, calamity, exasperation, want, are instructors in eloquence and wisdom. The true scholar grudges every opportunity of action past by, as a loss of power. It is the raw material out of which the intellect moulds her splendid products. A strange process too, this by which experience is converted into thought, as a mulberry leaf is converted into satin.[9] The manufacture goes forward at all hours.

* * *

But the final value of action, like that of books, and better than books, is that it is a resource. That great principle of Undulation in nature, that shows itself in the inspiring and expiring of the breath; in desire and satiety; in the ebb and flow of the sea; in day and night; in heat and cold; and, as yet more deeply ingrained in every atom and every fluid, is known to us under the name of Polarity,—these "fits of easy transmission and reflection," as Newton called them, are the law of nature because they are the law of spirit.[1]

The mind now thinks, now acts, and each fit reproduces the other. When the artist has exhausted his materials, when the fancy no longer paints, when thoughts are no longer apprehended and books are a weariness,—he has always the resource *to live*. Character is higher than intellect. Thinking is the function. Living is the functionary. The stream retreats to its source. A great soul will be strong to live, as well as strong to think. Does he lack organ or medium to impart his truths? He can still fall back on this elemental force of living them. This is a total act. Thinking is a partial act. Let the grandeur of justice shine in his affairs. Let the beauty of affection cheer his lowly roof. Those "far from fame," who dwell and act with him, will feel the force of his constitution in the doings and passages of the day better than it can be measured by any public and designed display. Time shall teach him that the scholar loses no hour which the man lives. Herein he unfolds the sacred germ of his instinct, screened from influence. What is lost in seemliness is gained in strength. Not out of those on whom systems of education have exhausted their culture, comes the helpful giant to destroy the old or to build the new, but out of unhandselled[2] savage nature; out of terrible Druids and Berserkers come at last Alfred[3] and Shakspeare.

I hear therefore with joy whatever is beginning to be said of the dignity and necessity of labor to every citizen. There is virtue yet in the hoe and the spade, for learned as well as for unlearned hands. And labor is everywhere welcome; always we are invited to work; only be this limitation observed, that a man

---

9. Mulberry leaves are eaten by silkworms, whose cocoons yield the silk thread that is woven into satin.

1. This accordance of a kind of fundamental essential priority of "spirit" to "nature," which echoes not only Schelling but KANT, FICHTE, and HEGEL, is a basic theme and guiding idea of American Transcendentalism. The quotation is a slight paraphrase of Proposition 1 and 11 of the *Opticks* (1704), by the British mathematician and scientist Sir Isaac Newton (1642–1727).

2. Apparently Emerson's coinage, perhaps intended to mean "untried" or "unproven."

3. Saxon king of Wessex (849–899; r. 871–99), renowned for his support of learning. "Terrible Druids and Berserkers": Celts and Norse warriors.

shall not for the sake of wider activity sacrifice any opinion to the popular judgments and modes of action.

———————

I have now spoken of the education of the scholar by nature, by books, and by action. It remains to say somewhat of his duties.

They are such as become Man Thinking. They may all be comprised in self-trust. The office of the scholar is to cheer, to raise, and to guide men by showing them facts amidst appearances. He plies the slow, unhonored, and unpaid task of observation. * * * He is to find consolation in exercising the highest functions of human nature. He is one who raises himself from private considerations and breathes and lives on public and illustrious thoughts. He is the world's eye. He is the world's heart. He is to resist the vulgar prosperity that retrogrades ever to barbarism, by preserving and communicating heroic sentiments, noble biographies, melodious verse, and the conclusions of history. Whatsoever oracles the human heart, in all emergencies, in all solemn hours, has uttered as its commentary on the world of actions,—these he shall receive and impart. And whatsoever new verdict Reason from her inviolable seat pronounces on the passing men and events of to-day,—this he shall hear and promulgate.

* * *

In self-trust all the virtues are comprehended. Free should the scholar be,—free and brave. Free even to the definition of freedom, "without any hindrance that does not arise out of his own constitution." Brave; for fear is a thing which a scholar by his very function puts behind him. Fear always springs from ignorance. It is a shame to him if his tranquillity, amid dangerous times, arise from the presumption that like children and women his is a protected class; or if he seek a temporary peace by the diversion of his thoughts from politics or vexed questions, hiding his head like an ostrich in the flowering bushes, peeping into microscopes, and turning rhymes, as a boy whistles to keep his courage up. So is the danger a danger still; so is the fear worse. Manlike let him turn and face it. Let him look into its eye and search its nature, inspect its origin,—see the whelping of this lion,—which lies no great way back; he will then find in himself a perfect comprehension of its nature and extent; he will have made his hands meet on the other side, and can henceforth defy it and pass on superior. The world is his who can see through its pretension. What deafness, what stone-blind custom, what overgrown error you behold is there only by sufferance,—by your sufferance. See it to be a lie, and you have already dealt it its mortal blow.

Yes, we are the cowed,—we the trustless. It is a mischievous notion that we are come late into nature; that the world was finished a long time ago. As the world was plastic and fluid in the hands of God, so it is ever to so much of his attributes as we bring to it. To ignorance and sin, it is flint. They adapt themselves to it as they may; but in proportion as a man has any thing in him divine, the firmament flows before him and takes his signet and form. Not he is great who can alter matter, but he who can alter my state of mind. They are the kings of the world who give the color of their present thought to all

nature and all art, and persuade men by the cheerful serenity of their carrying the matter, that this thing which they do is the apple which the ages have
desired to pluck, now at last ripe, and inviting nations to the harvest. The
great man makes the great thing. Wherever Macdonald[4] sits, there is the head
of the table. Linnæus makes botany the most alluring of studies, and wins it
from the farmer and the herb-woman; Davy, chemistry; and Cuvier, fossils.[5]
The day is always his who works in it with serenity and great aims. The unstable estimates of men crowd to him whose mind is filled with a truth, as the
heaped waves of the Atlantic follow the moon.

For this self-trust, the reason is deeper than can be fathomed,—darker than
can be enlightened. I might not carry with me the feeling of my audience in
stating my own belief. But I have already shown the ground of my hope, in
adverting to the doctrine that man is one. I believe man has been wronged;
he has wronged himself. He has almost lost the light that can lead him back
to his prerogatives. Men are become of no account. Men in history, men in
the world of to-day, are bugs, are spawn, and are called "the mass" and "the
herd." In a century, in a millennium, one or two men; that is to say, one or
two approximations to the right state of every man.[6] All the rest behold in the
hero or the poet their own green and crude being,—ripened; yes, and are content to be less, so *that* may attain to its full stature. What a testimony, full of
grandeur, full of pity, is borne to the demands of his own nature, by the poor
clansman, the poor partisan, who rejoices in the glory of his chief. The poor
and the low find some amends to their immense moral capacity, for their
acquiescence in a political and social inferiority. They are content to be
brushed like flies from the path of a great person, so that justice shall be done
by him to that common nature which it is the dearest desire of all to see
enlarged and glorified. They sun themselves in the great man's light, and feel
it to be their own element. They cast the dignity of man from their downtrod
selves upon the shoulders of a hero, and will perish to add one drop of blood
to make that great heart beat, those giant sinews combat and conquer. He
lives for us, and we live in him.[7]

Men, such as they are, very naturally seek money or power; and power
because it is as good as money,—the "spoils," so called, "of office." And why
not? for they aspire to the highest, and this, in their sleep-walking, they dream
is highest. Wake them and they shall quit the false good and leap to the true,
and leave governments to clerks and desks. This revolution is to be wrought
by the gradual domestication of the idea of Culture.[8] The main enterprise of
the world for splendor, for extent, is the upbuilding of a man. Here are the
materials strewn along the ground. The private life of one man shall be a more
illustrious monarchy, more formidable to its enemy, more sweet and serene

4. That is, a Scottish lord (the saying more often
has the name "Macgregor").
5. Three eminent scientists: Carolus Linnaeus (Carl
von Linné, 1707–1778), Swedish naturalist who
devised the basic system used to classify all organisms; Sir Humphrey Davy (1778–1829), English
chemist; and Georges, Baron Cuvier (1769–1832),
French zoologist and pioneering paleontologist.
6. That is, all human beings should be fully and
truly human, but very few actually are. This idea of a
wide and common gap between genuine humanity

and the reality of human life, as it generally has been
and continues to be lived, is a central theme of the
interpretive tradition before and after Emerson.
7. This emphasis on the hero shows the influence
of the Scottish historian and essayist Thomas Carlyle (1795–1881), and anticipates NIETZSCHE, whose
early essay "Schopenhauer as Educator" (1874;
excerpted below) clearly echoes these ideas.
8. A statement that recalls the basic theme of
Schiller's *Aesthetic Education of Man*.

in its influence to its friend, than any kingdom in history. For a man, rightly viewed, comprehendeth the particular natures of all men. Each philosopher, each bard, each actor has only done for me, as by a delegate, what one day I can do for myself. The books which once we valued more than the apple of the eye, we have quite exhausted. What is that but saying that we have come up with the point of view which the universal mind took through the eyes of one scribe; we have been that man, and have passed on. First, one, then another, we drain all cisterns, and waxing greater by all these supplies, we crave a better and more abundant food. The man has never lived that can feed us ever. The human mind cannot be enshrined in a person who shall set a barrier on any one side to this unbounded, unboundable empire. It is one central fire, which, flaming now out of the lips of Etna, lightens the capes of Sicily, and now out of the throat of Vesuvius,[9] illuminates the towers and vineyards of Naples. It is one light which beams out of a thousand stars. It is one soul which animates all men.[1]

* * *

SOURCE: From Ralph Waldo Emerson, *Nature: Addresses and Lectures*, vol. 1 of *Emerson's Complete Works*, Riverside Edition (Boston: Houghton, Mifflin, 1876), pp. 82–88, 94–96, 98–102, 104–8. Originally published in 1837 as a pamphlet, "An Oration, Delivered before the Phi Beta Kappa Society at Cambridge, August 31, 1837." By changing its title to "The American Scholar" in the 1849 collection, Emerson signaled its broader application. It is sometimes referred to as a kind of second American "declaration of independence," specifically from the intellectual domination of England; in his introductory remarks, not included here, Emerson announced: "Our day of dependence, our long apprenticeship to the learning of other lands, draws to a close." (Yet his Transcendentalism is clearly indebted to philosophical developments in German-speaking central Europe. And these developments were made accessible to Americans largely via English translators and interpreters.)

From The Divinity School Address

In this refulgent summer, it has been a luxury to draw the breath of life. The grass grows, the buds burst, the meadow is spotted with fire and gold in the tint of flowers. The air is full of birds, and sweet with the breath of the pine, the balm-of-Gilead, and the new hay. Night brings no gloom to the heart with its welcome shade. Through the transparent darkness the stars pour their almost spiritual rays. Man under them seems a young child, and his huge globe a toy. The cool night bathes the world as with a river, and prepares his eyes again for the crimson dawn. The mystery of nature was never displayed more happily. The corn[1] and the wine have been freely dealt to all creatures, and the never-broken silence with which the old bounty goes forward has not yielded yet one word of explanation. One is constrained to respect the perfection of this world in which our senses converse. How wide; how rich; what invitation from every property it gives to every faculty of man! In its fruitful

---

9. Like Etna, an active volcano.
1. A concise summary of one of the main ideas that Emerson derived from his understanding of post-

Kantian German idealism.
1. That is, the staple cereal crop.

soils; in its navigable sea; in its mountains of metal and stone; in its forests of all woods; in its animals; in its chemical ingredients; in the powers and path of light, heat, attraction and life, it is well worth the pith and heart of great men to subdue and enjoy it. The planters, the mechanics, the inventors, the astronomers, the builders of cities, and the captains, history delights to honor.

But when the mind opens and reveals the laws which traverse the universe and make things what they are, then shrinks the great world at once into a mere illustration and fable of this mind. What am I? and What is? asks the human spirit with a curiosity new-kindled, but never to be quenched. Behold these outrunning laws, which our imperfect apprehension can see tend this way and that, but not come full circle. Behold these infinite relations, so like, so unlike; many, yet one. I would study, I would know, I would admire forever. These works of thought have been the entertainments of the human spirit in all ages.

A more secret, sweet, and overpowering beauty appears to man when his heart and mind open to the sentiment of virtue. Then he is instructed in what is above him. He learns that his being is without bound; that to the good, to the perfect, he is born, low as he now lies in evil and weakness. That which he venerates is still his own, though he has not realized it yet. *He ought.* He knows the sense of that grand word, though his analysis fails to render account of it. When in innocency or when by intellectual perception he attains to say,—"I love the Right; Truth is beautiful within and without for evermore. Virtue, I am thine; save me; use me; thee will I serve, day and night, in great, in small, that I may be not virtuous, but virtue;"—then is the end of the creation answered, and God is well pleased.

The sentiment of virtue is a reverence and delight in the presence of certain divine laws. It perceives that this homely game of life we play, covers, under what seem foolish details, principles that astonish. The child amidst his baubles is learning the action of light, motion, gravity, muscular force; and in the game of human life, love, fear, justice, appetite, man, and God, interact. These laws refuse to be adequately stated. They will not be written out on paper, or spoken by the tongue. They elude our persevering thought; yet we read them hourly in each other's faces, in each other's actions, in our own remorse. The moral traits which are all globed into every virtuous act and thought,—in speech we must sever, and describe or suggest by painful enumeration of many particulars. Yet, as this sentiment is the essence of all religion, let me guide your eye to the precise objects of the sentiment, by an enumeration of some of those classes of facts in which this element is conspicuous.

The intuition of the moral sentiment is an insight of the perfection of the laws of the soul. These laws execute themselves. They are out of time, out of space, and not subject to circumstance.[2] Thus in the soul of man there is a justice whose retributions are instant and entire. He who does a good deed is instantly ennobled. He who does a mean deed is by the action itself contracted. He who puts off impurity, thereby puts on purity. If a man is at heart just, then in so far is he God; the safety of God, the immortality of God,

---

2. The preceding restates the ideas sets forth by KANT in the conclusion of his *Critique of Practical Reason* (1788; see above).

the majesty of God do enter into that man with justice. If a man dissemble, deceive, he deceives himself, and goes out of acquaintance with his own being. A man in the view of absolute goodness, adores, with total humility. Every step so downward, is a step upward. The man who renounces himself, comes to himself.

See how this rapid intrinsic energy worketh everywhere, righting wrongs, correcting appearances, and bringing up facts to a harmony with thoughts. Its operation in life, though slow to the senses, is at last as sure as in the soul. By it a man is made the Providence to himself, dispensing good to his goodness, and evil to his sin. Character is always known. Thefts never enrich; alms never impoverish; murder will speak out of stone walls. The least admixture of a lie,—for example, the taint of vanity, any attempt to make a good impression, a favorable appearance,—will instantly vitiate the effect. But speak the truth, and all nature and all spirits help you with unexpected furtherance. Speak the truth, and all things alive or brute are vouchers, and the very roots of the grass underground there do seem to stir and move to bear you witness. See again the perfection of the Law as it applies itself to the affections, and becomes the law of society. As we are, so we associate. The good, by affinity, seek the good; the vile, by affinity, the vile. Thus of their own volition, souls proceed into heaven, into hell.

These facts have always suggested to man the sublime creed that the world is not the product of manifold power, but of one will, of one mind; and that one mind is everywhere active, in each ray of the star, in each wavelet of the pool; and whatever opposes that will is everywhere balked and baffled, because things are made so, and not otherwise. Good is positive. Evil is merely privative, not absolute: it is like cold, which is the privation of heat. All evil is so much death or nonentity. Benevolence is absolute and real. So much benevolence as a man hath, so much life hath he. For all things proceed out of this same spirit, which is differently named love, justice, temperance, in its different applications, just as the ocean receives different names on the several shores which it washes. All things proceed out of the same spirit, and all things conspire with it. Whilst a man seeks good ends, he is strong by the whole strength of nature. In so far as he roves from these ends, he bereaves himself of power, or auxiliaries; his being shrinks out of all remote channels, he becomes less and less, a mote, a point, until absolute badness is absolute death.[3]

The perception of this law of laws awakens in the mind a sentiment which we call the religious sentiment, and which makes our highest happiness. Wonderful is its power to charm and to command. It is a mountain air. It is the embalmer of the world. It is myrrh and storax, and chlorine[4] and rosemary. It makes the sky and the hills sublime, and the silent song of the stars is it. By it is the universe made safe and habitable, not by science or power. Thought may work cold and intransitive in things, and find no end or unity; but the dawn of the sentiment of virtue on the heart, gives and is the assurance that Law is sovereign over all natures; and the worlds, time, space, eternity, do seem to break out into joy.

3. This summary of a number of ideas derived from German idealist sources sets the stage for the non-traditional characterization of true religiousness that is Emerson's main subject here.

4. The gas, used as a disinfectant or for purification.

This sentiment is divine and deifying. It is the beatitude of man. It makes him illimitable. Through it, the soul first knows itself. It corrects the capital mistake of the infant man, who seeks to be great by following the great, and hopes to derive advantages *from another*,—by showing the fountain of all good to be in himself, and that he, equally with every man, is an inlet into the deeps of Reason. When he says, "I ought;" when love warms him; when he chooses, warned from on high, the good and great deed; then, deep melodies wander through his soul from Supreme Wisdom.—Then he can worship, and be enlarged by his worship; for he can never go behind this sentiment. In the sublimest flights of the soul, rectitude is never surmounted, love is never outgrown.

This sentiment lies at the foundation of society, and successively creates all forms of worship. The principle of veneration never dies out. Man fallen into superstition, into sensuality, is never quite without the visions of the moral sentiment. In like manner, all the expressions of this sentiment are sacred and permanent in proportion to their purity. The expressions of this sentiment affect us more than all other compositions. The sentences of the oldest time, which ejaculate this piety, are still fresh and fragrant. This thought dwelled always deepest in the minds of men in the devout and contemplative East; not alone in Palestine, where it reached its purest expression, but in Egypt, in Persia, in India, in China. Europe has always owed to oriental genius its divine impulses. What these holy bards said, all sane men found agreeable and true. And the unique impression of Jesus upon mankind, whose name is not so much written as ploughed into the history of this world, is proof of the subtle virtue of this infusion.

Meantime, whilst the doors of the temple stand open, night and day, before every man, and the oracles of this truth cease never, it is guarded by one stern condition; this, namely it is an intuition.[5] It cannot be received at second hand. Truly speaking, it is not instruction, but provocation, that I can receive from another soul. What he announces, I must find true in me, or reject; and on his word, or as his second, be he who he may, I can accept nothing. On the contrary, the absence of this primary faith is the presence of degradation. As is the flood, so is the ebb. Let this faith depart, and the very words it spake and the things it made become false and hurtful. Then falls the church, the state, art, letters, life. The doctrine of the divine nature being forgotten, a sickness infects and dwarfs the constitution. Once man was all; now he is an appendage, a nuisance. And because the indwelling Supreme Spirit cannot wholly be got rid of, the doctrine of it suffers this perversion, that the divine nature is attributed to one or two persons, and denied to all the rest, and denied with fury. The doctrine of inspiration is lost; the base doctrine of the majority of voices usurps the place of the doctrine of the soul. Miracles, prophecy, poetry, the ideal life, the holy life, exist as ancient history merely; they are not in the belief, nor in the aspiration of society; but, when suggested, seem ridiculous. Life is comic or pitiful as soon as the high ends of being fade out of sight, and man becomes near-sighted, and can only attend to what addresses the senses.

5. This statement is a gesture toward—but also a radical departure from—the Christian idea of divine revelation.

* * *

* * * In the soul then let the redemption be sought. Wherever a man comes, there comes revolution. The old is for slaves. When a man comes, all books are legible, all things transparent, all religions are forms. He is religious. Man is the wonderworker. He is seen amid miracles. * * *

Let me admonish you, first of all, to go alone; to refuse the good models, even those which are sacred in the imagination of men, and dare to love God without mediator or veil. Friends enough you shall find who will hold up to your emulation Wesleys and Oberlins,[6] Saints and Prophets. Thank God for these good men, but say, 'I also am a man.' Imitation cannot go above its model. The imitator dooms himself to hopeless mediocrity. The inventor did it because it was natural to him, and so in him it has a charm. In the imitator something else is natural, and he bereaves himself of his own beauty, to come short of another man's.

* * *

And, to this end, let us not aim at common degrees of merit. Can we not leave, to such as love it, the virtue that glitters for the commendation of society, and ourselves pierce the deep solitudes of absolute ability and worth? We easily come up to the standard of goodness in society. Society's praise can be cheaply secured, and almost all men are content with those easy merits; but the instant effect of conversing with God will be to put them away. * * *

In such high communion let us study the grand strokes of rectitude: a bold benevolence, an independence of friends, so that not the unjust wishes of those who love us shall impair our freedom, but we shall resist for truth's sake the freest flow of kindness, and appeal to sympathies far in advance; and,— what is the highest form in which we know this beautiful element,—a certain solidity of merit, that has nothing to do with opinion, and which is so essentially and manifestly virtue, that it is taken for granted that the right, the brave, the generous step will be taken by it, and nobody thinks of commending it. You would compliment a coxcomb doing a good act, but you would not praise an angel. The silence that accepts merit as the most natural thing in the world, is the highest applause. Such souls, when they appear, are the Imperial Guard of Virtue, the perpetual reserve, the dictators of fortune. One needs not praise their courage,—they are the heart and soul of nature. O my friends, there are resources in us on which we have not drawn.

* * *

* * * The Hebrew and Greek Scriptures contain immortal sentences, that have been bread of life to millions. But they have no epical integrity; are fragmentary; are not shown in their order to the intellect. I look for the new Teacher that shall follow so far those shining laws that he shall see them come full circle; shall see their rounding complete grace; shall see the world to be the mirror of the soul; shall see the identity of the law of gravitation with

---

6. That is, men of religion who do good works. The brothers John (1703–1791) and Charles Wesley (1707–1788) were clergymen who founded the Methodist movement in the Church of England; Johann Friedrich Oberlin (1740–1826) was an Alsatian Lutheran pastor and philanthropist, focusing particularly on early education.

purity of heart; and shall show that the Ought, that Duty, is one thing with Science, with Beauty, and with Joy.

SOURCE: From Ralph Waldo Emerson, "Address," in *Nature: Addresses and Lectures*, vol. 1 of *Emerson's Complete Works*, Riverside Edition (Boston: Houghton, Mifflin, 1876), pp. 119–28, 144–49, 151. Originally published in 1838 as a pamphlet, "An Address Delivered before the Senior Class in Divinity College, Cambridge, Sunday Evening 15 July, 1838."

From The Transcendentalist

The first thing we have to say respecting what are called *new views* here in New England, at the present time, is, that they are not new, but the very oldest of thoughts cast into the mould of these new times. The light is always identical in its composition, but it falls on a great variety of objects, and by so falling is first revealed to us, not in its own form, for it is formless, but in theirs; in like manner, thought only appears in the objects it classifies. What is popularly called Transcendentalism among us, is Idealism; Idealism as it appears in 1842. As thinkers, mankind have ever divided into two sects, Materialists and Idealists; the first class founding on experience, the second on consciousness; the first class beginning to think from the data of the senses, the second class perceive that the senses are not final, and say, The senses give us representations of things, but what are the things themselves, they cannot tell. The materialist insists on facts, on history, on the force of circumstances and the animal wants of man; the idealist on the power of Thought and of Will, on inspiration, on miracle, on individual culture. These two modes of thinking are both natural, but the idealist contends that his way of thinking is in higher nature. He concedes all that the other affirms, admits the impressions of sense, admits their coherency, their use and beauty, and then asks the materialist for his grounds of assurance that things are as his senses represent them. But I, he says, affirm facts not affected by the illusions of sense, facts which are of the same nature as the faculty which reports them, and not liable to doubt; facts which in their first appearance to us assume a native superiority to material facts, degrading these into a language by which the first are to be spoken; facts which it only needs a retirement from the senses to discern. Every materialist will be an idealist;[1] but an idealist can never go backward to be a materialist.

The idealist, in speaking of events, sees them as spirits. He does not deny the sensuous fact: by no means; but he will not see that alone. He does not deny the presence of this table, this chair, and the walls of this room, but he looks at these things as the reverse side of the tapestry, as the *other end*, each being a sequel or completion of a spiritual fact which nearly concerns him. This manner of looking at things transfers every object in nature from an independent and anomalous position without there, into the consciousness. Even the materialist Condillac,[2] perhaps the most logical expounder of material-

---

1. That is, idealism is more sophisticated than materialism, and so materialists will become idealists if they are not obtusely dogmatic in their materialism and give a serious hearing to the case for idealism.
2. Étienne Bonnot de Condillac (1715–1780), a French philosopher of the Enlightenment who rejected the doctrine of innate ideas and advocated a radical empiricism, known as "sensationalism," according to which everything in and about knowledge and cognition derives from sense experience. The quotation is the opening sentence of his *Essay on the Origin of Human Knowledge* (1746).

ism, was constrained to say, "Though we should soar into the heavens, though we should sink into the abyss, we never go out of ourselves; it is always our own thought that we perceive." What more could an idealist say?[3]

The materialist, secure in the certainty of sensation, mocks at fine-spun theories, at star-gazers and dreamers, and believes that his life is solid, that he at least takes nothing for granted, but knows where he stands, and what he does. Yet how easy it is to show him that he also is a phantom walking and working amid phantoms, and that he need only ask a question or two beyond his daily questions to find his solid universe growing dim and impalpable before his sense. The sturdy capitalist, no matter how deep and square on blocks of Quincy granite[4] he lays the foundations of his banking-house or Exchange, must set it, at last, not on a cube corresponding to the angles of his structure, but on a mass of unknown materials and solidity, red-hot or white-hot perhaps at the core, which rounds off to an almost perfect sphericity, and lies floating in soft air, and goes spinning away, dragging bank and banker with it at a rate of thousands of miles the hour, he knows not whither,—a bit of bullet, now glimmering, now darkling through a small cubic space on the edge of an unimaginable pit of emptiness. And this wild balloon, in which his whole venture is embarked, is a just symbol of his whole state and faculty. One thing at least, he says, is certain, and does not give me the headache, that figures do not lie; the multiplication table has been hitherto found unimpeachable truth; and, moreover, if I put a gold eagle[5] in my safe, I find it again to-morrow;—but for these thoughts, I know not whence they are. They change and pass away. But ask him why he believes that an uniform experience will continue uniform, or on what grounds he founds his faith in his figures, and he will perceive that his mental fabric is built up on just as strange and quaking foundations as his proud edifice of stone.

In the order of thought, the materialist takes his departure from the external world, and esteems a man as one product of that. The idealist takes his departure from his consciousness, and reckons the world an appearance. The materialist respects sensible masses, Society, Government, social art and luxury, every establishment, every mass, whether majority of numbers, or extent of space, or amount of objects, every social action. The idealist has another measure, which is metaphysical, namely the *rank* which things themselves take in his consciousness; not at all the size or appearance. Mind is the only reality, of which men and all other natures are better or worse reflectors. Nature, literature, history, are only subjective phenomena. Although in his action overpowered by the laws of action, and so, warmly cooperating with men, even preferring them to himself, yet when he speaks scientifically, or after the order of thought, he is constrained to degrade persons into representatives of truths. He does not respect labor, or the products of labor, namely property, otherwise than as a manifold symbol, illustrating with wonderful fidelity of details the laws of being; he does not respect government, except as far as it reiterates the law of his mind; nor the church, nor charities, nor arts, for themselves; but hears, as at a vast distance, what they say, as if his

3. The following characterization is much closer to the "subjective" idealism of George Berkeley (1685–1753), who wrote "to be is to be perceived," than to what KANT, SCHELLING, and HEGEL had in mind; however, FICHTE could have been read and understood in something like this way.
4. Quincy, Massachusetts, became famous in the 19th century for its granite quarries.
5. A $10 gold coin.

consciousness would speak to him through a pantomimic scene. His thought,— that is the Universe. His experience inclines him to behold the procession of facts you call the world, as flowing perpetually outward from an invisible, unsounded centre in himself, centre alike of him and of them, and necessitating him to regard all things as having a subjective or relative existence, relative to that aforesaid Unknown Centre of him.

From this transfer of the world into the consciousness, this beholding of all things in the mind, follow easily his whole ethics. It is simpler to be self-dependent. The height, the deity of man is to be self-sustained, to need no gift, no foreign force. Society is good when it does not violate me, but best when it is likest to solitude. Everything real is self-existent. Everything divine shares the self-existence of Deity. All that you call the world is the shadow of that substance which you are, the perpetual creation of the powers of thought, of those that are dependent and of those that are independent of your will. Do not cumber yourself with fruitless pains to mend and remedy remote effects; let the soul be erect, and all things will go well.

* * *

It is well known to most of my audience that the Idealism of the present day acquired the name of Transcendental from the use of that term by Immanuel Kant, of Königsberg, who replied to the skeptical philosophy of Locke,[6] which insisted that there was nothing in the intellect which was not previously in the experience of the senses, by showing that there was a very important class of ideas or imperative forms, which did not come by experience, but through which experience was acquired; that these were intuitions of the mind itself; and he denominated them *Transcendental* forms. The extraordinary profoundness and precision of that man's thinking have given vogue to his nomenclature, in Europe and America, to that extent that whatever belongs to the class of intuitive thought is popularly called at the present day *Transcendental*.

Although, as we have said, there is no pure Transcendentalist, yet the tendency to respect the intuitions and to give them, at least in our creed, all authority over our experience, has deeply colored the conversation and poetry of the present day; and the history of genius and of religion in these times, though impure, and as yet not incarnated in any powerful individual, will be the history of this tendency.

* * *

SOURCE: From Ralph Waldo Emerson, *Nature: Addresses and Lectures*, vol. 1 of *Emerson's Complete Works*, Riverside Edition (Boston: Houghton, Mifflin, 1876), pp. 329–34, 339–40. Delivered at Boston's Masonic Temple in December 1841, "The Transcendentalist" was first published in *The Dial* in January 1843.

From Self-Reliance

I read the other day some verses written by an eminent painter which were original and not conventional. The soul always hears an admonition in such

6. The English philosopher John Locke (1632–1704), whose theory of knowledge is set forth in *An Essay Concerning Human Understanding* (1690).

lines, let the subject be what it may. The sentiment they instil is of more value than any thought they may contain. To believe your own thought, to believe that what is true for you in your private heart is true for all men,—that is genius. Speak your latent conviction, and it shall be the universal sense: for the inmost in due time becomes the outmost, and our first thought is rendered back to us by the trumpets of the Last Judgment. Familiar as the voice of the mind is to each, the highest merit we ascribe to Moses, Plato and Milton[1] is that they set at naught books and traditions, and spoke not what men, but what *they* thought. A man should learn to detect and watch that gleam of light which flashes across his mind from within, more than the lustre of the firmament of bards and sages. Yet he dismisses without notice his thought, because it is his. In every work of genius we recognize our own rejected thoughts; they come back to us with a certain alienated majesty. Great works of art have no more affecting lesson for us than this. They teach us to abide by our spontaneous impression with good-humored inflexibility then most when the whole cry of voices is on the other side. Else to-morrow a stranger will say with masterly good sense precisely what we have thought and felt all the time, and we shall be forced to take with shame our own opinion from another.

* * *

Trust thyself: every heart vibrates to that iron string. Accept the place the divine providence has found for you, the society of your contemporaries, the connection of events. Great men have always done so, and confided themselves childlike to the genius of their age, betraying their perception that the absolutely trustworthy was seated at their heart, working through their hands, predominating in all their being. And we are now men, and must accept in the highest mind the same transcendent destiny; and not minors and invalids in a protected corner, not cowards fleeing before a revolution, but guides, redeemers and benefactors, obeying the Almighty effort and advancing on Chaos and the Dark.

* * *

Whoso would be a man, must be a nonconformist. He who would gather immortal palms must not be hindered by the name of goodness, but must explore if it be goodness. Nothing is at last sacred but the integrity of your own mind.[2] Absolve you to yourself, and you shall have the suffrage of the world. I remember an answer which when quite young I was prompted to make to a valued adviser who was wont to importune me with the dear old doctrines of the church. On my saying, "What have I to do with the sacredness of traditions, if I live wholly from within?" my friend suggested,—"But these impulses may be from below, not from above." I replied, "They do not seem to me to be such; but if I am the Devil's child, I will live then from the Devil." No law can be sacred to me but that of my nature. Good and bad are but names very readily transferable to that or this; the only right is what is after[3] my constitution;

---

1. John Milton (1608–1674), English writer of prose tracts and poetry, best known for the epic poem *Paradise Lost* (1667, 1674). Moses was traditionally credited with writing the first five books of the Bible; the Greek philosopher Plato (ca. 427–ca. 347 B.C.E.) wrote many dialogues.
2. An anticipation of the 20th-century existentialist concept of authenticity.
3. In accordance with.

the only wrong what is against it. A man is to carry himself in the presence of all opposition as if every thing were titular and ephemeral but he.

* * *

What I must do is all that concerns me, not what the people think. This rule, equally arduous in actual and in intellectual life, may serve for the whole distinction between greatness and meanness. It is the harder because you will always find those who think they know what is your duty better than you know it. It is easy in the world to live after the world's opinion; it is easy in solitude to live after our own; but the great man is he who in the midst of the crowd keeps with perfect sweetness the independence of solitude.

The objection to conforming to usages that have become dead to you is that it scatters your force. It loses your time and blurs the impression of your character. If you maintain a dead church, contribute to a dead Bible-society, vote with a great party either for the government or against it, spread your table like base housekeepers,—under all these screens I have difficulty to detect the precise man you are: and of course so much force is withdrawn from your proper life. But do your work, and I shall know you. Do your work, and you shall reinforce yourself.

* * *

A foolish consistency is the hobgoblin of little minds,[4] adored by little statesmen and philosophers and divines. With consistency a great soul has simply nothing to do. He may as well concern himself with his shadow on the wall. Speak what you think now in hard words and to-morrow speak what to-morrow thinks in hard words again, though it contradict every thing you said to-day.— 'Ah, so you shall be sure to be misunderstood.'—Is it so bad then to be misunderstood? Pythagoras was misunderstood, and Socrates, and Jesus, and Luther, and Copernicus, and Galileo, and Newton,[5] and every pure and wise spirit that ever took flesh. To be great is to be misunderstood.

I suppose no man can violate his nature. All the sallies of his will are rounded in by the law of his being, as the inequalities of Andes and Himmaleh[6] are insignificant in the curve of the sphere. Nor does it matter how you gauge and try him. A character is like an acrostic or Alexandrian stanza;[7]— read it forward, backward, or across, it still spells the same thing. In this pleasing contrite wood-life which God allows me, let me record day by day my honest thought without prospect or retrospect, and, I cannot doubt, it will be found symmetrical, though I mean it not and see it not. My book should smell of pines and resound with the hum of insects. The swallow over my window should interweave that thread or straw he carries in his bill into my web also. We pass for what we are.[8] Character teaches above our wills. Men imagine

4. That is, an obsession with consistency is a sign of small-mindedness (often misquoted with the word "foolish" omitted).
5. A mixture of philosophers, religious figures, and scientists: the Greek philosopher and mathematician Pythagoras (6th c. B.C.E.), the Greek philosopher Socrates (469–399 B.C.E.), the German theologian Martin Luther (1483–1546), the Polish astronomer Nicolaus Copernicus (1473–1543), the

Italian astronomer and mathematician Galileo Galilei (1564–1642), and the English physicist Sir Isaac Newton (1642–1727).
6. Mountain ranges in South America and Asia (the Himalayas).
7. That is, a palindrome (the reference to acrostics and "Alexandrian stanzas" is obscure).
8. That is, we will be seen for what we are (however we might try to appear otherwise).

that they communicate their virtue or vice only by overt actions, and do not see that virtue or vice emit a breath every moment.

There will be an agreement in whatever variety of actions, so they be each honest and natural in their hour. For of one will, the actions will be harmonious, however unlike they seem. These varieties are lost sight of at a little distance, at a little height of thought. One tendency unites them all. The voyage of the best ship is a zigzag line of a hundred tacks. See the line from a sufficient distance, and it straightens itself to the average tendency. Your genuine action will explain itself and will explain your other genuine actions. Your conformity explains nothing. Act singly, and what you have already done singly will justify you now. Greatness appeals to the future. If I can be firm enough to-day to do right and scorn eyes, I must have done so much right before as to defend me now. Be it how it will, do right now. Always scorn appearances and you always may. The force of character is cumulative. All the foregone days of virtue work their health into this. What makes the majesty of the heroes of the senate and the field, which so fills the imagination? The consciousness of a train of great days and victories behind. They shed a united light on the advancing actor. He is attended as by a visible escort of angels. That is it which throws thunder into Chatham's voice, and dignity into Washington's port, and America into Adams's eye.[9] Honor is venerable to us because it is no ephemera. It is always ancient virtue. We worship it to-day because it is not of to-day. We love it and pay it homage because it is not a trap for our love and homage, but is self-dependent, self-derived, and therefore of an old immaculate pedigree, even if shown in a young person.

I hope in these days we have heard the last of conformity and consistency. Let the words be gazetted and ridiculous henceforward. Instead of the gong for dinner, let us hear a whistle from the Spartan fife.[1] Let us never bow and apologize more. A great man is coming to eat at my house. I do not wish to please him; I wish that he should wish to please me. I will stand here for humanity, and though I would make it kind, I would make it true.[2] Let us affront and reprimand the smooth mediocrity and squalid contentment of the times, and hurl in the face of custom and trade and office, the fact which is the upshot of all history, that there is a great responsible Thinker and Actor working wherever a man works; that a true man belongs to no other time or place, but is the centre of things. Where he is, there is nature. He measures you and all men and all events. Ordinarily, every body in society reminds us of somewhat else, or of some other person. Character, reality, reminds you of nothing else; it takes place of the whole creation. The man must be so much that he must make all circumstances indifferent. Every true man is a cause, a country, and an age; requires infinite spaces and numbers and time fully to accomplish his design;—and posterity seem to follow his steps as a train of clients.

* * *

9. Three major political figures: William Pitt, first earl of Chatham (1708–1778), English statesman and noted orator; George Washington (1732–1799), first president of the United States; and probably John Quincy Adams (1767–1848), sixth U.S. president and, at the time this essay was written, a powerful member of the House of Representatives. "Port": bearing, demeanor.
1. A small flute used by the soldiers of the ancient Greek city-state of Sparta.
2. Genuine, authentic.

The magnetism which all original action exerts is explained when we inquire the reason of self-trust. Who is the Trustee? What is the aboriginal Self, on which a universal reliance may be grounded? What is the nature and power of that science-baffling star, without parallax,[3] without calculable elements, which shoots a ray of beauty even into trivial and impure actions, if the least mark of independence appear? The inquiry leads us to that source, at once the essence of genius, of virtue, and of life, which we call Spontaneity or Instinct. We denote this primary wisdom as Intuition, whilst all later teachings are tuitions.[4] In that deep force, the last fact behind which analysis cannot go, all things find their common origin. For the sense of being which in calm hours rises, we know not how, in the soul, is not diverse from things, from space, from light, from time, from man, but one with them and proceeds obviously from the same source whence their life and being also proceed. We first share the life by which things exist and afterwards see them as appearances in nature and forget that we have shared their cause. Here is the fountain of action and of thought. Here are the lungs of that inspiration which giveth man wisdom and which cannot be denied without impiety and atheism. We lie in the lap of immense intelligence, which makes us receivers of its truth and organs of its activity. When we discern justice, when we discern truth, we do nothing of ourselves, but allow a passage to its beams. If we ask whence this comes, if we seek to pry into the soul that causes, all philosophy is at fault. Its presence or its absence is all we can affirm. Every man discriminates between the voluntary acts of his mind and his involuntary perceptions, and knows that to his involuntary perceptions a perfect faith is due. He may err in the expression of them, but he knows that these things are so, like day and night, not to be disputed. My wilful actions and acquisitions are but roving;—the idlest reverie, the faintest native emotion, command my curiosity and respect. Thoughtless people contradict as readily the statement of perceptions as of opinions, or rather much more readily; for they do not distinguish between perception and notion. They fancy that I choose to see this or that thing. But perception is not whimsical, but fatal.[5] If I see a trait, my children will see it after me, and in course of time all mankind,—although it may chance that no one has seen it before me. For my perception of it is as much a fact as the sun.

* * *

And now at last the highest truth on this subject remains unsaid; probably, cannot be said; for all that we say is the far-off remembering of the intuition. That thought by what I can now nearest approach to say it, is this. When good is near you, when you have life in yourself, it is not by any known or accustomed way; you shall not discern the footprints of any other; you shall not see the face of man; you shall not hear any name;—the way, the thought, the good, shall be wholly strange and new. It shall exclude example and experience. You take the way from man, not to man. All persons that ever existed are its forgotten ministers. Fear and hope are alike beneath it. There is somewhat low even

3. That is, without an apparent difference of position caused by a change in the point from which it is observed.
4. The contrast here is between personal insight ("Intuition") and mere instruction by someone ("tuition").
5. That is, fateful.

in hope. In the hour of vision there is nothing that can be called gratitude, nor properly joy. The soul raised over passion beholds identity and eternal causation, perceives the self-existence of Truth and Right, and calms itself with knowing that all things go well. Vast spaces of nature, the Atlantic Ocean, the South Sea; long intervals of time, years, centuries, are of no account. This which I think and feel underlay every former state of life and circumstances, as it does underlie my present, and what is called life and what is called death.

Life only avails,[6] not the having lived. Power ceases in the instant of repose; it resides in the moment of transition from a past to a new state, in the shooting of[7] the gulf, in the darting to an aim. This one fact the world hates; that the soul *becomes*; for that forever degrades the past, turns all riches to poverty, all reputation to a shame, confounds the saint with the rogue, shoves Jesus and Judas equally aside. Why then do we prate of self-reliance? Inasmuch as the soul is present, there will be power not confident but agent.[8] To talk of reliance is a poor external way of speaking. Speak rather of that which relies because it works and is. Who has more obedience[9] than I masters me, though he should not raise his finger. Round him I must revolve by the gravitation of spirits. We fancy it rhetoric when we speak of eminent virtue. We do not yet see that virtue is Height, and that a man or a company of men, plastic and permeable to principles, by the law of nature must overpower and ride all cities, nations, kings, rich men, poets, who are not.

This is the ultimate fact which we so quickly reach on this, as on every topic, the resolution of all into the ever-blessed ONE. Self-existence is the attribute of the Supreme Cause, and it constitutes the measure of good by the degree in which it enters into all lower forms. All things real are so by so much virtue[1] as they contain. Commerce, husbandry, hunting, whaling, war, eloquence, personal weight, are somewhat, and engage my respect as examples of its presence and impure action. I see the same law working in nature for conservation and growth. Power is, in nature, the essential measure of right.[2] Nature suffers nothing to remain in her kingdoms which cannot help itself. The genesis and maturation of a planet, its poise and orbit, the bended tree recovering itself from the strong wind, the vital resources of every animal and vegetable, are demonstrations of the self-sufficing and therefore self-relying soul.

Thus all concentrates: let us not rove; let us sit at home with the cause. Let us stun and astonish the intruding rabble of men and books and institutions by a simple declaration of the divine fact. Bid the invaders take the shoes from off their feet, for God is here within.[3] Let our simplicity judge them, and our docility to our own law demonstrate the poverty of nature and fortune beside our native riches.

* * *

The populace think that your rejection of popular standards is a rejection of all standard, and mere antinomianism; and the bold sensualist will use the

---

6. That is, it is only living that matters.
7. The swift passage across.
8. That is, to the extent that the soul (your true self) is present, there will be active rather than merely presumed power.
9. That is, one who inspires more obedience (by projecting more authority).
1. Excellence; power.
2. An anticipation of (and possible inspiration for) NIETZSCHE.
3. An echo of Exodus 3:5.

name of philosophy to gild his crimes. But the law of consciousness abides. There are two confessionals, in one or the other of which we must be shriven. You may fulfil your round of duties by clearing yourself in the *direct*, or in the *reflex* way. Consider whether you have satisfied your relations to father, mother, cousin, neighbor, town, cat and dog—whether any of these can upbraid you. But I may also neglect this reflex standard and absolve me to myself. I have my own stern claims and perfect circle. It denies the name of duty to many offices[4] that are called duties. But if I can discharge its debts it enables me to dispense with the popular code. If any one imagines that this law is lax, let him keep its commandment one day.

And truly it demands something godlike in him who has cast off the common motives of humanity and has ventured to trust himself for a taskmaster. High be his heart, faithful his will, clear his sight, that he may in good earnest be doctrine, society, law, to himself, that a simple purpose may be to him as strong as iron necessity is to others!

* * *

* * * It is only as a man puts off all foreign support and stands alone that I see him to be strong and to prevail. He is weaker by every recruit to his banner. Is not a man better than a town? Ask nothing of men, and, in the endless mutation, thou only firm column must presently appear the upholder of all that surrounds thee. He who knows that power is inborn, that he is weak because he has looked for good out of him and elsewhere, and, so perceiving, throws himself unhesitatingly on his thought, instantly rights himself, stands in the erect position, commands his limbs, works miracles; just as a man who stands on his feet is stronger than a man who stands on his head.

So use all that is called Fortune. Most men gamble with her, and gain all, and lose all, as her wheel rolls. But do thou leave as unlawful these winnings, and deal with Cause and Effect, the chancellors of God. In the Will work and acquire, and thou hast chained the wheel of Chance, and shall sit hereafter out of fear from[5] her rotations. A political victory, a rise of rents, the recovery of your sick or the return of your absent friend, or some other favorable event raises your spirits, and you think good days are preparing for you. Do not believe it. Nothing can bring you peace but yourself. Nothing can bring you peace but the triumph of principles.

SOURCE: From Ralph Waldo Emerson, *Nature: Addresses and Lectures*, vol. 1 of *Emerson's Complete Works*, Riverside Edition (Boston: Houghton, Mifflin, 1876), pp. 39–40, 47, 50–51, 53–54, 57–61, 63–65, 68–71, 74–75, 89–90. First published in *Essays* (1841), this essay is drawn largely from various journal entries and lectures of 1832 to 1840.

From The Over–Soul

There is a difference between one and another hour of life in their authority and subsequent effect. Our faith comes in moments; our vice is habitual. Yet there is a depth in those brief moments which constrains us to ascribe

4. Services, functions.
5. That is, without fear of.

more reality to them than to all other experiences. For this reason the argument which is always forthcoming to silence those who conceive extraordinary hopes of man, namely the appeal to experience, is for ever invalid and vain. We give up the past to the objector, and yet we hope. He must explain this hope. We grant that human life is mean,[1] but how did we find out that it was mean? What is the ground of this uneasiness of ours; of this old discontent? What is the universal sense of want and ignorance, but the fine innuendo by which the soul makes its enormous claim? Why do men feel that the natural history of man has never been written, but he is always leaving behind what you have said of him, and it becomes old, and books of metaphysics worthless? The philosophy of six thousand years has not searched the chambers and magazines of the soul. In its experiments there has always remained, in the last analysis, a residuum it could not resolve. Man is a stream whose source is hidden. Our being is descending into us from we know not whence. The most exact calculator has no prescience that somewhat[2] incalculable may not balk the very next moment. I am constrained every moment to acknowledge a higher origin for events than the will I call mine.

As with events, so is it with thoughts. When I watch that flowing river, which, out of regions I see not, pours for a season its streams into me, I see that I am a pensioner; not a cause but a surprised spectator of this ethereal water; that I desire and look up and put myself in the attitude of reception, but from some alien energy the visions come.

The Supreme Critic on the errors of the past and the present, and the only prophet of that which must be, is that great nature in which we rest as the earth lies in the soft arms of the atmosphere; that Unity, that Over-Soul, within which every man's particular being is contained and made one with all other; that common heart of which all sincere conversation is the worship, to which all right action is submission; that overpowering reality which confutes our tricks and talents, and constrains every one to pass for what he is, and to speak from his character and not from his tongue, and which evermore tends to pass into our thought and hand and become wisdom and virtue and power and beauty. We live in succession, in division, in parts, in particles. Meantime within man is the soul of the whole; the wise silence; the universal beauty, to which every part and particle is equally related; the eternal ONE. And this deep power in which we exist and whose beatitude is all accessible to us, is not only self-sufficing and perfect in every hour, but the act of seeing and the thing seen, the seer and the spectacle, the subject and the object, are one. We see the world piece by piece, as the sun, the moon, the animal, the tree; but the whole, of which these are the shining parts, is the soul.[3] Only by the vision of that Wisdom can the horoscope of the ages be read, and by falling back on our better thoughts, by yielding to the spirit of prophecy which is innate in every man, we can know what it saith. Every man's words who speaks from that life must sound vain to those who do not dwell in the same thought on their own part. I dare not speak for it. My words do not carry its august sense; they fall short and cold. Only itself can inspire whom it will, and behold! their speech shall be lyrical, and sweet, and universal

1. Lacking; miserable.
2. Something.
3. The influence of SCHELLING—specifically, his conception of a kind of power he calls the "world-

soul" (Weltseele), of which all of nature and human-spiritual reality are manifestations—pervades this essay and is particularly evident here.

as the rising of the wind. Yet I desire, even by profane words, if I may not use sacred, to indicate the heaven of this deity and to report what hints I have collected of the transcendent simplicity and energy of the Highest Law.

If we consider what happens in conversation, in reveries, in remorse, in times of passion, in surprises, in the instructions of dreams, wherein often we see ourselves in masquerade,—the droll disguises only magnifying and enhancing a real element and forcing it on our distant notice,—we shall catch many hints that will broaden and lighten into knowledge of the secret of nature. All goes to show that the soul in man is not an organ, but animates and exercises all the organs; is not a function, like the power of memory, of calculation, of comparison, but uses these as hands and feet; is not a faculty, but a light; is not the intellect or the will, but the master of the intellect and the will; is the background of our being, in which they lie,—an immensity not possessed and that cannot be possessed. From within or from behind, a light shines through us upon things and makes us aware that we are nothing, but the light is all. A man is the façade of a temple wherein all wisdom and all good abide. What we commonly call man, the eating, drinking, planting, counting man, does not, as we know him, represent himself, but misrepresents himself. Him we do not respect, but the soul, whose organ he is, would he let it appear through his action, would make our knees bend. When it breathes through his intellect, it is genius; when it breathes through his will, it is virtue; when it flows through his affection, it is love. And the blindness of the intellect begins when it would be something of itself. The weakness of the will begins when the individual would be something of himself. All reform aims in some one particular to let the soul have its way through us; in other words, to engage us to obey.

Of this pure nature every man is at some time sensible. Language cannot paint it with his colors. It is too subtile. It is undefinable, unmeasurable; but we know that it pervades and contains us. We know that all spiritual being is in man. A wise old proverb says, "God comes to see us without bell;" that is, as there is no screen or ceiling between our heads and the infinite heavens, so is there no bar or wall in the soul, where man, the effect, ceases, and God, the cause, begins. The walls are taken away. We lie open on one side to the deeps of spiritual nature, to the attributes of God. Justice we see and know, Love, Freedom, Power. These natures no man ever got above, but they tower over us, and most in the moment when our interests tempt us to wound them.

The sovereignty of this nature whereof we speak is made known by its independency of those limitations which circumscribe us on every hand. The soul circumscribes all things. As I have said, it contradicts all experience. In like manner it abolishes time and space. The influence of the senses has in most men overpowered the mind to that degree that the walls of time and space have come to look real and insurmountable; and to speak with levity of these limits is, in the world, the sign of insanity. Yet time and space are but inverse measures of the force of the soul. The spirit sports with time,—

> "Can crowd eternity into an hour,
> Or stretch an hour to eternity."[4]

---

4. Quoted from George Gordon, Lord Byron, *Cain: A Mystery* (1821), 1.1.536–37 (lines spoken by Lucifer).

We are often made to feel that there is another youth and age than that which is measured from the year of our natural birth. Some thoughts always find us young, and keep us so. Such a thought is the love of the universal and eternal beauty. Every man parts from that contemplation with the feeling that it rather belongs to ages than to mortal life. The least activity of the intellectual powers redeems us in a degree from the conditions of time. In sickness, in languor, give us a strain of poetry or a profound sentence, and we are refreshed; or produce a volume of Plato or Shakspeare,[5] or remind us of their names, and instantly we come into a feeling of longevity. See how the deep divine thought reduces centuries and millenniums, and makes itself present through all ages. Is the teaching of Christ less effective now than it was when first his mouth was opened? The emphasis of facts and persons in my thought has nothing to do with time. And so always the soul's scale is one, the scale of the senses and the understanding is another.[6] Before the revelations of the soul, Time, Space and Nature shrink away. In common speech we refer all things to time, as we habitually refer the immensely sundered stars to one concave sphere. And so we say that the Judgment[7] is distant or near, that the Millennium approaches, that a day of certain political, moral, social reforms is at hand, and the like, when we mean that in the nature of things one of the facts we contemplate is external and fugitive, and the other is permanent and connate with the soul. The things we now esteem fixed shall, one by one, detach themselves like ripe fruit from our experience, and fall. The wind shall blow them none knows whither. The landscape, the figures, Boston, London, are facts as fugitive as any institution past, or any whiff of mist or smoke, and so is society, and so is the world. The soul looketh steadily forwards, creating a world before her, leaving worlds behind her. She has no dates, nor rites, nor persons, nor specialties nor men. The soul knows only the soul; the web of events is the flowing robe in which she is clothed.

After its own law and not by arithmetic is the rate of its progress to be computed. The soul's advances are not made by gradation, such as can be represented by motion in a straight line, but rather by ascension of state, such as can be represented by metamorphosis,—from the egg to the worm, from the worm to the fly. The growths of genius are of a certain *total* character, that does not advance the elect individual first over John, then Adam, then Richard, and give to each the pain of discovered inferiority,—but by every throe of growth the man expands there where he works, passing, at each pulsation, classes, populations, of men. With each divine impulse the mind rends the thin rinds of the visible and finite, and comes out into eternity, and inspires and expires its air. It converses with truths that have always been spoken in the world, and becomes conscious of a closer sympathy with Zeno and Arrian[8] than with persons in the house.

This is the law of moral and of mental gain. The simple rise as by specific levity not into a particular virtue, but into the region of all the virtues. They are in the spirit which contains them all. The soul requires purity, but purity

---

5. Shakespeare. Plato (ca. 427–ca. 347 B.C.E.), Greek philosopher.
6. Emerson echoes the main idea of the conclusion of KANT's *Critique of Practical Reason* (1788; see above), which was the point of departure for the worldview and line of thought he is elaborating.

7. The Last Judgment, when Christians believe God will judge all humans ("the Millennium" also has eschatological resonance; see Revelation 20).
8. That is, with long-dead and obscure Greek philosophers (335–263 B.C.E. and 92–175 C.E., respectively).

is not it; requires justice, but justice is not that; requires beneficence, but is somewhat better; so that there is a kind of descent and accommodation felt when we leave speaking of moral nature to urge a virtue which it enjoins. To the well-born child all the virtues are natural, and not painfully acquired. Speak to his heart, and the man becomes suddenly virtuous.

Within the same sentiment is the germ of intellectual growth, which obeys the same law. Those who are capable of humility, of justice, of love, of aspiration, stand already on a platform that commands the sciences and arts, speech and poetry, action and grace. For whoso dwells in this moral beatitude already anticipates those special powers which men prize so highly. The lover has no talent, no skill, which passes for quite nothing with his enamored maiden, however little she may possess of related faculty; and the heart which abandons itself to the Supreme Mind finds itself related to all its works, and will travel a royal road to particular knowledges and powers. In ascending to this primary and aboriginal sentiment we have come from our remote station on the circumference instantaneously to the centre of the world, where, as in the closet[9] of God, we see causes, and anticipate the universe, which is but a slow effect.

One mode of the divine teaching is the incarnation of the spirit in a form,— in forms, like my own. I live in society; with persons who answer to thoughts in my own mind, or express a certain obedience to the great instincts to which I live. I see its presence to them. I am certified of a common nature; and these other souls, these separated selves, draw me as nothing else can. They stir in me the new emotions we call passion; of love, hatred, fear, admiration, pity; thence come conversation, competition, persuasion, cities and war. Persons are supplementary to the primary teaching of the soul. In youth we are mad for persons. Childhood and youth see all the world in them. But the larger experience of man discovers the identical nature appearing through them all. Persons themselves acquaint us with the impersonal. In all conversation between two persons tacit reference is made, as to a third party, to a common nature. That third party or common nature is not social; it is impersonal; is God.

* * *

* * * Great is the soul, and plain. It is no flatterer, it is no follower; it never appeals from itself. It believes in itself. Before the immense possibilities of man all mere experience, all past biography, however spotless and sainted, shrinks away. Before that heaven which our presentiments foreshow us, we cannot easily praise any form of life we have seen or read of. We not only affirm that we have few great men, but, absolutely speaking, that we have none; that we have no history, no record of any character or mode of living that entirely contents us. The saints and demigods whom history worships we are constrained to accept with a grain of allowance. Though in our lonely hours we draw a new strength out of their memory, yet, pressed on our attention, as they are by the thoughtless and customary, they fatigue and invade. The soul gives itself, alone, original and pure, to the Lonely, Original and Pure, who, on that condition, gladly inhabits, leads and speaks through it. Then is it glad, young and nimble. It is not wise, but it sees through all things.

9. Inner chamber; private apartment.

It is not called religious, but it is innocent. It calls the light its own, and feels that the grass grows and the stone falls by a law inferior to, and dependent on, its nature. Behold, it saith, I am born into the great, the universal mind. I, the imperfect, adore my own Perfect. I am somehow receptive of the great soul, and thereby I do overlook the sun and the stars and feel them to be the fair accidents and effects which change and pass. More and more the surges of everlasting nature enter into me, and I become public and human in my regards and actions. So come I to live in thoughts and act with energies which are immortal. Thus revering the soul, and learning, as the ancient[1] said, that "its beauty is immense," man will come to see that the world is the perennial miracle which the soul worketh, and be less astonished at particular wonders; he will learn that there is no profane history; that all history is sacred; that the universe is represented in an atom, in a moment of time. He will weave no longer a spotted life of shreds and patches, but he will live with a divine unity. He will cease from what is base and frivolous in his life and be content with all places and with any service he can render. He will calmly front the morrow in the negligency of that trust which carries God with it and so hath already the whole future in the bottom of the heart.[2]

SOURCE: From Ralph Waldo Emerson, *Nature: Addresses and Lectures*, vol. 1 of *Emerson's Complete Works*, Riverside Edition (Boston: Houghton, Mifflin, 1876), pp. 267–77, 295–97. First published in *Essays* (1841).

1. The ancient philosopher Plotinus (205–270 C.E.), who expressed the following sentiment in *Ennead* 1.6 (often called "On Beauty").

2. That is, will calmly proceed in the carelessness (emancipation from all cares) of divinely grounded trustingness that extends to the whole future.

SØREN KIERKEGAARD
(1813 – 1855)

There is no chapter on Kierkegaard in Bertrand Russell's classic and influential *History of Western Philosophy* (1945). He does not even appear in its index. Russell despised HEGEL and NIETZSCHE, and so devoted polemical chapters to them. MARX, too, received a chapter. But as far as Russell was concerned, Kierkegaard was not a philosopher at all, and so did not deserve any attention whatsoever. This might well have pleased Kierkegaard, both because he undoubtedly would have agreed that he was nothing like Russell's idea of a philosopher, and because he would never have wanted to wind up as a paragraph or chapter in anyone's systematic "history of philosophy." He scorned the philosophical establishment of his day (along with the religious establishment of his native Denmark, and its social and cultural establishments more generally). He had no interest in contributing to the philosophical literature and philosophical debate, or in thinking or writing in ways that philosophers would find respectable. Critical as he was of Hegel, who in his time dominated the philosophical scene in Denmark as well as in Germany and elsewhere, he did not seek to reform or change philosophy. He cared infinitely more about becoming a Christian "in truth"—and about trying to get others both to understand what this really meant and to take this human possibility seriously—than he did about philosophy conceived independently of that quest.

Kierkegaard was a passionate and brilliant thinker and writer, however, and some of his many interests encompassed matters that were or became of tremendous importance to philosophers of widely differing orientations. It was his challenge to Hegel's way of dealing with human reality that was the primary impetus for the emergence in the twentieth century of existential philosophy, with its focus on Kierkegaard's question of "what it means to exist as a human being" and its insistence on giving priority to the first-person singular standpoint in attempting to elucidate human "existing." His many writings contributing to that elucidation, most of which were published in a single decade of literary-philosophical activity, are unsurpassed and inexhaustible both as sources of insight and as provocations to personal as well as philosophical self-examination. Kierkegaard also poses a profound challenge to those who suppose that it is possible and desirable to replace religion with philosophy, and that the idea of a transcendent personal God can be abandoned without grave consequences. Like KANT, he found it necessary to "deny knowledge" (Kant's expression for rejecting the pretension of rational thought to be the ultimate arbiter of all truth) in order to make legitimate "room for faith." But much more radically, he deemed it necessary to embrace the rationally paradoxical and absurd as a part of what he called the "leap of faith."

Søren Kierkegaard ("KEER-keh-gard") was born in 1813 in Copenhagen, where he spent most of his short life. He was the youngest of seven children. His father, who had risen from humble beginnings in the countryside to success and affluence as a self-made businessman, was an older man (he was 57 when Kierkegaard was born), fiercely religious, guilt-ridden, often morose, and rather distant. He also had an interest in philosophy (of a pre-Kantian sort), which no doubt influenced the development of Kierkegaard's own ambivalent interest in it. Kierkegaard's mother, who had been the maid of his father's first wife (and whom his father had impregnated not long after that wife's death), was a simple, devoutly religious woman. His father's affluence not only made it possible for Kierkegaard to receive a very good education but also provided him in his mid-20s with an inheritance that made him a man of independent means, enabling him to devote himself to whatever interests he wished to pursue. He became something of a gadfly on the cultural scene in Copenhagen. He also wrote an enormous amount—not only books but also reviews, commentaries in the newspapers and journals, discourses and essays, and much else.

Kierkegaard attended the University of Copenhagen, where he undertook a serious study of Hegel, for whom he developed both great respect and great disdain—respect for his intellect and accomplishments, and disdain for what Kierkegaard believed to be the utter failure of his grand philosophical system to even begin to do justice to religion and to "what it means to exist as a human being." Kierkegaard completed his theology examinations in 1840, but focused on literature and philosophy. In his dissertation, "On the Concept of Irony with Constant Reference to Socrates," he argued that "irony" and the kind of thinker Socrates was have no place in Hegel's kind of philosophy and system, which thus are revealed to be inadequate.

After defending his dissertation in 1841, Kierkegaard made one of his very few trips abroad—to Berlin, to attend the lectures of SCHELLING, whom he had heard was attempting to develop a new postmetaphysical alternative to Hegel (and to Schelling's own earlier idealist philosophy). He returned to Copenhagen disappointed. The following year (1843) marked the beginning of his extraordinary burst of literary output, which fell off sharply after 1851. He became ill in the fall of 1855, and died not long thereafter.

Kierkegaard never married, though in his late 30s he became engaged to a woman almost ten years his junior, Regine Olsen. Less than a year later he broke off the engagement, after much wrestling with the question of what kind of life it would be best for him to live. Since they loved each other deeply, it seems an absurd thing for him to have done; but the absurdity of making that choice may have been part of why he made it—as was also true of making what he called "the leap of faith." (This is one of the hallmarks of his thought, discussed below.) He was an enormously complex person, whose dispositions and passions, intellectual powers and religiousness, combativeness and convictions, provocations and literary ability combined to make him one of the most extraordinary figures in the history of modern philosophy—to which he stands in a very problematic but now undeniable relationship.

Most of Kierkegaard's philosophically interesting and important writings were written under pseudonyms, which he used not because he was trying to conceal his authorship but rather because he wanted to develop lines of thought from a variety of standpoints, and to force his readers to make up their own minds about the issues he was trying to get them to think about. It therefore is something of a mistake to attribute views "to Kierkegaard" simply because they are advanced in books that he wrote. He did not want to be thought to be advancing another philosophical "system" or position in rivalry with those of Kant, Hegel, and others. What will be said here about his thinking, therefore, should be read (with this caution in mind) as an attempt to characterize the apparent upshot of what emerges from the writings by Kierkegaard from which the following selections are excerpted.

As difficult as it can be to disentangle Kierkegaard from his various personae, there can be no doubt about his passionate and unconditional commitment to Christianity, even though it was one of his deepest concerns to make the point that genuine Christianity (whatever that turns out to be) is a far cry from what commonly passes for it—particularly in a country like his Denmark, in which it was the official state religion. There also can be no doubt about his vehement rejection of Hegel's subordination of religion generally and Christianity specifically to Hegel's own kind of philosophy and philosophical interpretation of the idea of God. Moreover, Kierkegaard clearly was fundamentally dissatisfied with Hegel's approach to and understanding of human existence and the self, and with Hegel's approach to the question of what it means to be genuinely, fully, and truly human.

God, for Kierkegaard, is the God of Judeo-Christianity—not as reinterpreted by Hegel but rather as celebrated by the biblical patriarch Abraham and envisioned by St. Paul. And genuine religiousness, for him, is a matter of an extraordinary sort of faith rather than of reason of any kind—except insofar as reason can help sharpen one's sense of the unreasonableness of that sort of "leap of faith," not only beyond but against the rational and reasonable. For such unreasonableness marks the paradoxicality of the faith of Abraham, for whom the humanly unthinkable can become something not only thinkable but undertaken willingly, and for whom even the seemingly impossible is deemed possible. And it marks the absurdity of the faith of the Kierekgaardian Christian, for whom even the logically impossible—the incarnation of the infinite and eternal God in finite and mortal human form—not only is possible but actually happened. Reason's chief role in relation to religion, for Kierkegaard (in great contrast to Kant as well as to Hegel), is to make clear how utterly irrational the leap of faith is—and then to get out of the way.

Kierkegaard thus takes a very radical position in defending and advocating the kind of faith that centers on the idea of an utterly transcendent personal God, the incarnation of that God in human form, the possibility of a personal relationship to that God, and the all-importance of such a relationship. His defense and advocacy concede every argument and criticism that a rationally minded critic might make, remain undaunted, and use the very irrationality of the leap to fire the passion that alone can enable one to make it. Though his way of giving this religiousness a new lease on life (notwithstanding the apparent triumph of the Enlightenment) may seem to be desperate, his is a strategy that remains available to someone unwilling to settle for the kinds of religiousness left when

the ideas traditionally at the heart of religion are abandoned, demythologized, or reinterpreted in ways that cease to have real referents.

The God of radical Christianity is all-important, for Kierkegaard; and the difference that God makes to meaning, mattering, and the significance of the individual human being could not be greater. The first selection below ("The Unchangeableness of God"), a sermon delivered in 1851 and published in the last year of his life, eloquently testifies to this conviction. In his view, to remove that God from the picture (as Hegel does, even though he retains the idea of God in reinterpreted form), has dire consequences. Neither we ourselves nor anything in or about the world in which we find ourselves can ground and sustain real meaning, or make anything truly matter, or endow our individual existence with enduring significance, or enable us to achieve anything like an unshakable and eternal happiness. It is (so to speak) God or bust. Thus for Kierkegaard a faith capable of taking paradoxicality and absurdity in stride is required to open the way to the possibility of a genuine God-relationship. Only a genuine God-relationship, in turn, can make sense of the idea that true human self-realization and selfhood have a radically individual character.

For Hegel, it is the big picture that matters—and what counts in the big picture is the emergence and development in the world of *Geist* (spirituality) in its various forms—"subjective," "objective," and "absolute." Human beings are important because it is only through embodiment in their lives that such forms of spirituality can attain reality and existence. As particular individuals, even with developed "subjective" spirituality, we have little significance. Our lives have greater "objective" significance through our participation in objective sociocultural reality. And they may even attain a form of "absolute" significance through the forms of "absolute spirituality" in which we participate, by way of artistic, religious, scientific, and philosophical experience and activity. There is nothing higher than that to which we might aspire, however, and indeed there is nothing higher in or beyond the world from which we are excluded. Our personal lives and personalities are real enough; but their significance is neither objective nor absolute. They are simply particular instantiations of subjective spirituality, which transcends mere human vitality but is of lesser significance than either of those sorts of more general (*allgemein*) attainable human identity and spirituality—"objective" and "absolute."

Kierkegaard vehemently objects to this picture. For him it is what is most *individual* about us that matters most—even though his stance makes sense only on the supposition that such individuality is what matters most about us *to the kind of God* he envisions. This most individual self and selfhood—their more and less genuine forms, and what is involved in their realization "in truth"—are the focus of his attention and concern. Everyone exists as a human being; but what it means to exist "in truth," as a *truly* human being, is something different and much more uncommon. It is a matter not just of individuality but of *genuine* individuality—and a matter not just of "subjectivity" but of *genuine* subjectivity. Kierkegaard suggests that attaining genuine subjectivity has to do with a certain sort of intensification of subjectivity that requires "passion" rather than the cultivation of our capacity for any kind of rationality.

There are different sorts of "passion" that can and do contribute in different ways to the intensification and development of human subjectivity; and for Kierkegaard, as he explores his alternative to Hegel's dialectic of human spirituality, it turns out that the kind of passion most perfectly suited to attaining the highest form of subjectivity and selfhood of which a human being is capable is the very kind that is involved in the leap of faith. Human-spiritual self-realization and human-religious God-relation therefore are a perfect match, and go hand in hand. The "truth" of human selfhood is to be conceived in terms of "subjectivity" (rather than any sort of Hegelian "objective" or "absolute" spirituality). Moreover, "subjectivity" is importantly constitutive of "truth" where some of the matters of greatest human significance—particularly faith, but perhaps love as well—are concerned. These points are developed at length in the selection from *Concluding Unscientific Postscript* (1846).

While Kierkegaard has nothing like an "ethical theory," several different sorts of ethics figure prominently in his writings. He discusses one sort of ethical orientation that is reminiscent of Hegelian "ethicality," for example, contrasting it favorably with an "aesthetic" orientation in which some type of pleasure is the locus of value (in *Either/Or* [1843])—which itself at least represents a kind of spiritual advance beyond the dull immersion in the mindless and spiritless routines and diversions of life in the modern world that he laments in *The Present Age* (1846) and elsewhere. But he by no means considers these orientations to be the only alternatives available to an existing human being.

So in *Fear and Trembling* (1843) Kierkegaard conjures up another dramatic "either/or"—of the sort faced by the biblical Abraham, who was confronted with the need to choose between his deep commitment to that kind of ethical life and his further commitment to obedience to God's will. The unconditionality of the latter commitment appears to be the basis of Abraham's readiness to act in a radically "unethical" manner (offering his son as blood sacrifice). It is paradigmatic of what Kierkegaard calls "the teleological suspension of the ethical"—that is, giving precedence over ethical considerations to something that matters more (for Abraham, God and his God-relationship). Kierkegaard uses this case study to make clear the difference between the ethicality that focuses on adherence to general norms of conduct and a religiousness that revolves around a radically particular relationship to a transcendent ultimate reality. This is the topic of the selection below from *Fear and Trembling*.

In *Concluding Unscientific Postscript*, on the other hand, we encounter another kind of ethic. It too is distinct from Kierkegaardian religiousness; but it has as its focus and locus of value the attainment of genuine subjectivity, individuality, and selfhood rather than any general norms of conduct. It might be characterized as an existential rather than Hegelian ethic—and one that Hegel is faulted for lacking. It is an ethic of radically personal self-realization and authenticity, in which the central issue and concern are one's self and relation to one's self. In Kierkegaardian religiousness, in marked contrast, one's ultimate concern is with God and one's God-relationship. And in *Sickness unto Death* (1849), Kierkegaard sets out an analysis purporting to show that nothing but that sort of religiousness—including even this existential-ethical orientation, if pursued in its absence—is sustainable, and that despair is the inevitable outcome of anything short of the leap of faith.

As mentioned above, the selections from these three works are preceded by a portion of a late essay (written two years after *Sickness*), "The Unchangeableness of God," which—unlike these and most of his other main writings—was published under his own name. That essay is a good place to start; but it is also a good place to finish, because it is closer than any of these other writings to being his last word. The reader is therefore encouraged to revisit it after having read the other selections, to be reminded of the themes it sounds and the central elements of the thinking that animates all of the rest of his work.

Kierkegaard had no interest in the contest of interpretations for its own sake, or as a quest for knowledge of ourselves, our world, or indeed the answers to philosophy's Big Questions. For him, the point of reflecting on what it means to exist as a human being, and on what genuine subjectivity and selfhood and faith are, is not to come to *know* these things: it is to *live* them. And the point of writing about them was neither more nor less than to try to move both others and

himself in that direction. His writings were intended to change how his readers live and lead their lives—though not by giving them any sort of substantive knowledge, or telling them what they ought to think, or believe, or do, or be.

Philosophers were by no means Kierkegaard's only or primary intended audience. He sought to reach and affect many others, with other sorts of writing and preaching. But among his intended audience were readers who knew of and were much taken by the prevailing (Hegelian) philosophical and intellectual fashion of the day—to which he was no stranger. He saw Hegel's philosophy as a problem for those who were seduced by it, and he attempted to provide an antidote, in language they would understand—meeting them halfway, as it were, to connect with them and help them reconsider themselves and their options. If he had been writing in a different time and place—for example, when and where the sciences rather than Hegelian philosophy have come to reign supreme—he undoubtedly would have written in another manner, to challenge other ways of thinking that he would have considered to be differently but no less unfortunately forgetful of what it means to exist as a human being, and of what it can mean and what it requires to be sustained by his kind of faith.

Kierkegaard opens his meditation on Abraham in *Fear and Trembling* with a powerfully evocative sentence that vividly shows his main concern as he considers what is at stake here: "If there was no eternal consciousness in man, if at the bottom of everything there was only a wildly seething power which, convulsed by dark passions, brought forth everything, both the great and the small, if beneath everything there lurked a bottomless void never to be filled—what else were life but despair!" Kierkegaard's nightmare here is SCHOPENHAUER's reality (setting the stage for what Nietzsche called "the advent of nihilism"). Kierkegaard and Schopenhauer could not be more profoundly different—and yet, in this respect, they are in fundamental agreement. For Kierkegaard, of course, this is not the way it is—but he is able to avoid Schopenhauer's conclusion and radical pessimism only by a leap of faith that requires an embrace of something that he himself characterizes as "absurd" and that makes no rational sense. Both of them reject Hegel's attempt to make positive sense of life and the world in a postreligious and postmetaphysical way; and both consider (or would consider) all forms of secular humanism and historical optimism (such as that of Marx) to be untenable. They thus are a philosophical odd couple, whose radical "God or bust" either/or posed a profound and unsettling challenge not only to their contemporaries but also to their successors—Nietzsche and the nonreligious existentialists among them.

From The Unchangeableness of God

* * *

God is unchangeable. In His omnipotence He created this visible world—and made Himself invisible. He clothed Himself in the visible world as in a garment; He changes it as one who shifts a garment—Himself unchanged. Thus in the world of sensible things. In the world of events He is present everywhere in every moment; in a truer sense than we can say of the most watchful human justice that it is present everywhere, God is omnipresent, though never seen by any mortal; present everywhere, in the least event as well as in the greatest, in that which can scarcely be called an event and in that which is the only event, in the death of a sparrow[1] and in the birth of the Saviour of mankind. In each moment every actuality is a possibility in His almighty hand; He holds all in readiness, in every instant prepared to change everything: the opinions of men, their judgements, human greatness and human abasement; He changes all, Himself unchanged. When everything seems stable (for it is only in appearance that the external world is for a time unchanged, in reality it is always in flux) and in the overturn of all things, He remains equally unchanged; no change touches Him, not even the shadow of a change; in unaltered clearness He, the father of lights, remains eternally unchanged. In unaltered clearness—aye, this is precisely why He is unchanged, because He is pure clearness, a clarity which betrays no trace of dimness, and which no dimness can come near. With us men it is not so. We are not in this manner clear, and precisely for this reason we are subject to change: now something becomes clearer in us, now something is dimmed, and we are changed; now changes take place about us, and the shadow of these changes glides over us to alter us; now there falls upon us from the surroundings an altering light, while under all this we are again changed within ourselves.

This thought *is terrifying, all fear and trembling.*[2] This aspect of it is in general perhaps less often emphasized; we complain of men and their mutability, and of the mutability of all temporal things, but God is unchangeable, this is

1. See Matthew 10:29; Shakespeare, *Hamlet* (ca. 1600), 5.2.157–68.
2. The phrase "fear and trembling" appears repeatedly in the New Testament (2 Corinthians 7:15; Ephesians 6:5; Philippians 2:12), and Kierkegaard had used it as the title of one of his best-known books (see the next work excerpted below).

our consolation, an entirely comforting thought: so speaks even frivolity. Aye, God is in very truth unchangeable.

But first and foremost, do you also have an understanding with God? Do you earnestly consider and sincerely strive to understand—and this is God's eternally unchangeable will for you as for every human being, that you should sincerely strive to attain this understanding—what God's will for you may be? Or do you live your life in such a fashion that this thought has never so much as entered your mind? How terrifying then that He is eternally unchangeable! For with this immutable will you must nevertheless some time, sooner or later, come into collision—this immutable will, which desired that you should consider this because it desired your welfare; this immutable will, which cannot but crush you if you come into hostile collision with it.

In the second place, you who have some degree of understanding with God, do you also have a good understanding with Him? Is your will unconditionally His will, your wishes, each one of them, His commandments, your thoughts, first and last, His thoughts? If not, how terrifying that God is unchangeable, everlastingly, eternally, unchangeable! Consider but in this connexion what it means to be at odds with merely a human being. But perhaps you are the stronger, and console yourself with the thought that the other will doubtless be compelled to change his attitude. But now if he happens to be the stronger—well, perhaps you think to have more endurance. But suppose it is an entire contemporary generation with which you are at odds; and yet, in that case you will perhaps say to yourself: seventy years[3] is no eternity. But when the will is that of one eternally unchangeable—if you are at odds with this will it means an eternity: how terrifying!

Imagine a wayfarer. He has been brought to a standstill at the foot of a mountain, tremendous, impassable. It is this mountain . . . no, it is not his destiny to cross it, but he has set his heart upon the crossing; for his wishes, his longings, his desires, his very soul, which has an easier mode of conveyance, are already on the other side; it only remains for him to follow. Imagine him coming to be seventy years old; but the mountain still stands there, unchanged, impassable. Let him become twice seventy years; but the mountain stands there unalterably blocking his way, unchanged, impassable. Under all this he undergoes changes, perhaps; he dies away from his longings, his wishes, his desires; he now scarcely recognizes himself. And so a new generation finds him, altered, sitting at the foot of the mountain, which still stands there, unchanged, impassable. Suppose it to have happened a thousand years ago: the altered wayfarer is long since dead, and only a legend keeps his memory alive; it is the only thing that remains—aye, and also the mountain, unchanged, impassable. And now think of Him who is eternally unchangeable, for whom a thousand years are but as one day—ah, even this is too much to say, they are for Him as an instant, as if they did not even exist—consider then, if you have in the most distant manner a will to walk a different path than that which He wills for you: how terrifying!

True enough, if your will, if my will, if the will of all these many thousands happens to be not so entirely in harmony with God's will: things nevertheless take their course as best they may in the hurly-burly of the so-called actual

3. The life span allotted in the Bible (Psalms 90:10).

world; it is as if God did not pay any attention. It is rather as if a just man—if there were such a man!—contemplating this world, a world which, as the Scriptures say, is dominated by evil, must needs feel disheartened because God does not seem to make Himself felt. But do you believe on that account that God has undergone any change? Or is the fact that God does not seem to make Himself felt any the less a terrifying fact, as long as it is neverthe-less certain that He is eternally unchangeable? To me it does not seem so. Consider the matter, and then tell me which is the more terrible to contem-plate: the picture of one who is infinitely the stronger, who grows tired of letting himself be mocked, and rises in his might to crush the refractory spirits—a sight terrible indeed, and so represented when we say that God is not mocked, pointing to the times when His annihilating punishments were visited upon the human race—but is this really the most terrifying sight? Is not this other sight still more terrifying: one infinitely powerful, who—eternally unchanged!—sits quite still and sees everything, without altering a feature, almost as if He did not exist; while all the time, as the just man must needs complain, lies achieve success and win to power, violence and wrong gain the victory, to such an extent as even to tempt a better man to think that if he hopes to accomplish anything for the good he must in part use the same means; so that it is as if God were being mocked, God the infi-nitely powerful, the eternally unchangeable, who none the less is neither mocked nor changed—is not this the most terrifying sight? For why, do you think, is He so quiet? Because He knows with Himself that He is eternally unchangeable. Anyone not eternally sure of Himself could not keep so still, but would rise in His strength. Only one who is eternally immutable can be in this manner so still.

He gives men time, and He can afford to give them time, since He has eter-nity and is eternally unchangeable. He gives time, and that with premedita-tion. And then there comes an accounting in eternity, where nothing is forgotten, not even a single one of the improper words that were spoken; and He is eternally unchanged. And yet, it may be also an expression for His mercy that men are thus afforded time, time for conversion and betterment. But how fearful if the time is not used for this purpose! For in that case the folly and frivolity in us would rather have Him straightway ready with His punishment, instead of thus giving men time, seeming to take no cognizance of the wrong, and yet remaining eternally unchanged. Ask one experienced in bringing up children—and in relation to God we are all more or less as children; ask one who has had to do with transgressors—and each one of us has at least once in his life gone astray, and goes astray for a longer or a shorter time, at longer or shorter intervals: you will find Him ready to confirm the observation that for the frivolous it is a great help, or rather, that it is a preventive of frivolity (and who dares wholly acquit himself of frivolity!) when the punishment fol-lows if possible instantly upon the transgression, so that the memory of the frivolous may acquire the habit of associating the punishment immediately with the guilt. Indeed, if transgression and punishment were so bound up with one another that, as in a double-barrelled shooting weapon, the pressure on a spring caused the punishment to follow instantly upon the seizure of the forbidden fruit, or immediately upon the commitment of the transgression—then I think that frivolity might take heed. But the longer the interval between guilt and punishment (which when truly understood is an expression for the gravity of the case) the greater the temptation to frivolity; as if the whole might perhaps be forgotten, or as if justice itself might alter and acquire different ideas with the passage of time, or as if at least it would be so long since the wrong was committed that it will become impossible to make an unaltered presentation of it before the bar of justice. Thus frivolity changes, and by no means for the better. It comes to feel itself secure; and when it has become secure it becomes more daring; and so the years pass, punishment is withheld, forgetfulness intervenes, and again the punishment is withheld, but new transgressions do not fail, and the old evil becomes still more malignant. And then finally all is over; death rolls down the curtain—and to all this (it was only frivolity!) there was an eternally unchangeable witness: is this also frivolity? One eternally unchangeable, and it is with this witness that you must make your reckoning. In the instant that the minute-hand of time showed seventy years, and the man died, during all that time the clock of eternity has scarcely moved perceptibly: to such a degree is everything present for the eternal, and for Him who is unchangeable.

And therefore, whoever you may be, take time to consider what I say to myself, that for God there is nothing significant and nothing insignificant, that in a certain sense the significant is for Him insignificant, and in another sense even the least significant is for Him infinitely significant. If then your will is not in harmony with His will, consider that you will never be able to evade Him. Be grateful to Him if through the use of mildness or of severity He teaches you to bring your will into agreement with His—how fearful if He makes no move to arrest your course, how fearful if in the case of any human being it comes to pass that He almost defiantly relies either upon the notion that God does not exist, or upon His having been changed, or even upon His being too great to take note of what we call trifles! For the truth is that God both exists and is eternally unchangeable; and His infinite greatness consists precisely in seeing even the least thing, and remembering even the least thing. Aye, and if you do not will as He wills, that He remembers it unchanged for an eternity!

There is thus sheer fear and trembling, for us frivolous and inconstant human beings, in this thought of God's unchangeableness. Oh, consider it well! Whether God makes Himself immediately felt or not, He is eternally unchangeable. He is eternally unchangeable, consider this, if as we say you have any matter outstanding with Him; He is unchangeable. You have perhaps promised Him something, obligated yourself in a sacred pledge . . . but in the course of time you have undergone a change, and now you rarely think of God—now that you have grown older, have you perhaps found more important things to think about? Or perhaps you now have different notions about God, and think that He does not concern Himself with the trifles of your life, regarding such beliefs as childishness. In any case you have just about forgotten what you promised Him; and thereupon you have proceeded to forget that you promised Him anything; and finally, you have forgotten, forgotten—aye, forgotten that He forgets nothing, since He is eternally unchangeable, forgotten that it is precisely the inverted childishness of mature years to imagine that anything is insignificant for God, or that God forgets anything, He who is eternally unchangeable!

In human relationships we so often complain of inconstancy, one party accuses the other of having changed. But even in the relationship between man and man, it is sometimes the case that the constancy of one party may come to seem like a tormenting affliction for the other. A man may, for example, have talked to another person about himself. What he said may have been merely a little childish, pardonably so. But perhaps, too, the matter was more serious than this: the poor foolish vain heart was tempted to speak in lofty tones of its enthusiasm, of the constancy of its feelings, and of its purposes in this world. The other man listened calmly; he did not even smile, or interrupt the speech; he let him speak on to the end, listened and kept silence; only he promised, as he was asked to do, not to forget what had been said. Then some time elapsed, and the first man had long since forgotten all this; only the other had not forgotten. Aye, let us suppose something still stranger: he had permitted himself to be moved inwardly by the thoughts that the first man had expressed under the influence of his mood, when he poured out, so to speak, his momentary feeling; he had in sincere endeavour shaped his life in accordance with these ideas. What torment in this unchanged remembrance by one who showed only too clearly that he had retained in his memory every last detail of what had been said in that moment!

And now consider Him, who is eternally unchangeable—and this human heart! O this human heart, what is not hidden in your secret recesses, unknown to others—and that is the least of it—but sometimes almost unknown to the individual himself! When a man has lived a few years it is almost as if it were a burial-plot, this human heart! There they lie buried in forgetfulness, promises, intentions, resolutions, entire plans and fragments of plans, and God knows what—aye, so say we men, for we rarely think about what we say; we say: there lies God knows what. And this we say half in a spirit of frivolity, and half weary of life—and it is so fearfully true that God does know what to the last detail, knows what you have forgotten, knows what for your recollection has suffered alteration, knows it all unchanged. He does not remember it merely as having happened some time ago, nay, He remembers it as if it were to-day. He knows whether, in connexion with any of these wishes, intentions, resolutions, something so to speak was said to Him about it—and He is eternally unchanged and eternally unchangeable. Oh, if the remembrance that another human being carries about with him may seem as it were a burden to you—well, this remembrance is after all not always so entirely trustworthy, and in any case it cannot endure for an eternity: some time I may expect to be freed from this other man and his remembrance. But an omniscient witness and an eternally unchangeable remembrance, one from which you can never free yourself, least of all in eternity: how fearful! No, in a manner eternally unchanged, everything is for God eternally present, always equally before Him. No shadow of variation, neither that of morning nor of evening, neither that of youth nor of old age, neither that of forgetfulness nor of excuse, changes Him; for Him there is no shadow. If we human beings are mere shadows, as is sometimes said, He is eternal clearness in eternal unchangeableness. If we are shadows that glide away—my soul, look well to thyself; for whether you will it or not, you go to meet eternity, to meet Him, and He is eternal clearness. Hence it is not so much that He keeps a reckoning, as that He is Himself the reckoning. It is said that we must render up an account, as if we perhaps had a long time to prepare for it, and also perhaps as if it were likely to be cluttered up with such an enormous mass of detail as to make it impossible to get the reckoning finished: O my soul, the account is every moment complete! For the unchangeable clearness of God is the reckoning, complete to the last detail, preserved by Him who is eternally unchangeable, and who has forgotten nothing of the things that I have forgotten, and who does not, as I do, remember some things otherwise than they really were.

There is thus sheer fear and trembling in this thought of the unchangeableness of God, almost as if it were far, far beyond the power of any human being to sustain a relationship to such an unchangeable power; aye, as if this thought must drive a man to such unrest and anxiety of mind as to bring him to the verge of despair.

But then it is also true that *there is rest and happiness in this thought*. It is really true that when, wearied with all this human inconstancy, this temporal and earthly mutability, and wearied also of your own inconstancy, you might wish to find a place where rest may be found for your weary head, your weary thoughts, your weary spirit, so that you might rest and find complete repose: Oh, in the unchangeableness of God there is rest! When you therefore permit this unchangeableness to serve you according to His will, for your own welfare, your eternal welfare; when you submit yourself to discipline, so that your selfish will (and it is from this that the change chiefly comes, more than from the outside) dies away, the sooner the better—and there is no help for it, you must whether willing or resisting, for think how vain it is for your will to be at odds with an eternal immutability; be therefore as the child when it profoundly feels that it has over against itself a will in relation to which nothing avails except obedience—when you submit to be disciplined by His unchangeable will, so as to renounce inconstancy and changeableness and caprice and self-will: then you will steadily rest more and more securely, and more and more blessedly, in the unchangeableness of God. For that the thought of God's unchangeableness is a blessed thought—who can doubt it? But take heed that you become of such a mind that you can rest happily in this immutability! Oh, as one is wont to speak who has a happy home, so speaks such an individual. He says: my home is eternally secure, I rest in the unchangeableness of God. This is a rest that no one can disturb for you except yourself; if you could become completely obedient in invariable obedience, you would each and every moment, with the same necessity as that by which a heavy body sinks to the earth or a light body moves upward, freely rest in God.

And as for the rest, let all things change as they do. If the scene of your activity is on a larger stage, you will experience the mutability of all things in greater measure; but even on a lesser stage, or on the smallest stage of all, you will still experience the same, perhaps quite as painfully. You will learn how men change, how you yourself change; sometimes it will even seem to you as if God Himself changed, all of which belongs to the upbringing. On this subject of the mutability of all things one older than I would be able to speak in better fashion, while perhaps what I could say might seem to someone very young as if it were new. But this we shall not further expound, leaving it rather for the manifold experiences of life to unfold for each one in particular, in a manner intended especially for him, that which all other men have experienced before him. Sometimes the changes will be such as to call to mind the saying that variety is a pleasure—an indescribable pleasure! There will also come times when you will have occasion to discover for yourself a saying which the language has suppressed, and you will say to yourself: 'Change is not pleasant—how could I ever have said that variety is a pleasure!' When this experience comes to you, you will have especial occasion (though you will surely not forget this in the first case either) to seek Him who is unchangeable.

My hearer, this hour is now soon past, and the discourse. Unless you yourself will it otherwise, this hour and its discourse will soon be forgotten. And unless you yourself will it otherwise, the thought of God's unchangeableness will also soon be forgotten in the midst of life's changes. But for this He will surely not be responsible, He who is unchangeable! But if you do not make yourself guilty of forgetfulness with respect to it, you will in this thought have found a sufficiency for your entire life, aye, for eternity.

Imagine a solitary wayfarer, a desert wanderer. Almost burned by the heat of the sun, languishing with thirst, he finds a spring. O refreshing coolness! Now God be praised, he says—and yet it was merely a spring he found; what then must not he say who found God! and yet he too must say: 'God be praised, I have found God—now I am well provided for. Your faithful coolness, O beloved well-spring, is not subject to any change. In the cold of winter, if winter visited this place, you would not become colder, but would preserve the same coolness unchanged, for the waters of the spring do not freeze! In the midday heat of the summer sun you preserve precisely the same coolness, for the waters of the spring do not become lukewarm!' There is nothing untrue in what he says, no false exaggeration in his eulogy. (And he who chooses a spring as subject for his eulogy chooses in my opinion no ungrateful theme, as anyone may better understand the more he knows what the desert signifies, and solitude.) However, the life of our wanderer took a turn otherwise than he had thought; he lost touch with the spring, and went astray in the wide world. Many years later he returned to the same place. His first thought was of the spring—but it was not, it had run dry. For a moment he stood silent in grief. Then he gathered himself together and said: 'No, I will not retract a single word of all that I said in your praise; it was all true. And if I praised your refreshing coolness while you were still in being, O beloved well-spring, let me now also praise it when you have vanished, in order that there may be some proof of unchangeableness in a human breast. Nor can I say that you deceived me; had I found you, I am convinced that your coolness would have been quite unchanged—and more you had not promised.'

But Thou O God, who art unchangeable, Thou art always and invariably to be found, and always to be found unchanged. Whether in life or in death, no one journeys so far afield that Thou art not to be found by Him, that Thou art not there, Thou who art everywhere. It is not so with the well-springs of earth, for they are to be found only in special places. And besides—overwhelming security!—Thou dost not remain, like the spring, in a single place, but Thou dost follow the traveller on his way. Ah, and no one ever wanders so far astray that he cannot find the way back to Thee, Thou who art not merely as a spring that may be found—how poor and inadequate a description of what Thou art!—but rather as a spring that itself seeks out the thirsty traveller, the errant wanderer: who has ever heard the like of any spring! Thus Thou art unchangeably always and everywhere to be found. And whenever any human being comes to Thee, of whatever age, at whatever time of the day, in whatever state: if he comes in sincerity he always finds Thy love equally warm, like the spring's unchanged coolness, O Thou who art unchangeable! Amen!

SOURCE: From Søren Kierkegaard, "For Self-Examination" and "Judge for Yourselves!" And Three Discourses, trans. Walter Lowrie (Princeton: Princeton University Press; London: Oxford University Press, 1944), pp. 230–40. In this sermon preached in 1851, which was printed in 1855 under his own name, Kierkegaard is clearly speaking for himself, and giving expression to the kind of religiousness that underlies his earlier pseudonymous writings. For that reason it is placed here, out of chronological order.

From Fear and Trembling

From In Praise of Abraham

If there was no eternal consciousness in man, if at the bottom of everything there was only a wildly seething power which, convulsed by dark passions, brought forth everything, both the great and the small, if beneath everything there lurked a bottomless void never to be filled—what else were life but despair! If it were thus, and if there were no sacred bonds which knit mankind together, if one generation followed upon another like leaves in the forest, if one generation succeeded another like the song of birds in the wood, if each generation passed through the world like a ship through the sea or like a wind through the desert, a vain and fruitless thing: if eternal oblivion like a hungry animal lay in wait for her prey and there was no power strong enough to snatch it from her, how hollow and without consolation life would be! But, therefore, life is not like this, and just as God made man and woman, so He created the hero and the poet or orator. The poet cannot perform the deeds of the hero, he can only admire and love him and rejoice in him; yet he also is happy and not less so: for the hero is, as it were, his better self, of which he is enamoured, and he rejoices that he is not himself the hero, he rejoices that his love can express itself in admiration. He is the genius of recollection and he can do nothing except recall what has been done; he can do nothing except admire what has been done; adding nothing of his own, he is still jealous of what has been entrusted to him. He follows the choice of his heart, but when he has found what he has been seeking, he visits every man's door with his song and speech, so that all may admire the hero as he does and be proud of the hero as he is. This is his work, his humble task, his loyal service in the house of the hero. If he is thus faithful to his love, and battles day and night against the guile of oblivion which wishes to steal the hero away from him, then he has accomplished his task, then he will be gathered to the hero who loves him with the same faithful love: for the poet is as it were the hero's better self, as faint as memory, but also like memory transfigured. Therefore no one shall be forgotten who was great in the world, and even if there be delay, even if the cloud of misunderstanding obscure the hero from our vision, his lover will come to him in time, and the longer time the more faithfully will he cleave to him.

No, not one shall be forgotten who was great in the world; but each was great in his own way, according to the greatness of the thing he *loved*. For he who loved himself became great through himself, and he who loved others became great through his devotion, but he who loved God became greater than any of these. All will be remembered, but each became great in proportion to his expectation. One became great by hoping for the possible, another by hoping for eternity, but the one who hoped for the *impossible* was greater than any of these. All will be remembered, but all were great according to the greatness of the things they *strove against*. For he who strove with the world became great by overcoming the world, and he who strove with himself became greater by overcoming himself; but he who strove with God became greater than any of these. So there was strife in the world, man against man, one against thousands, but he who strove with God was greater than any of these. So there was strife on earth; there was the man who overcame everything by his strength and there was the man who overcame God by his weakness. There was the man who relied upon himself and won all, there was the man who was confident in his strength and sacrificed all: but the man who believed in God was greater than all of these. There was the man who was great through his strength, and the man who was great through his wisdom, and the man who was great through his hope, and the man who was great through his love: but Abraham[1] was greater than any of these, great through the power whose strength is weakness, great through the wisdom whose secret is foolishness, great through the hope whose expression is madness, great through the love which is hatred of oneself.

* * *

From *Preliminary Expectoration*[2]
* * *

* * * It is said to be difficult to understand Hegel,[3] and only a small matter to understand Abraham! To go beyond Hegel is a miracle, but there is nothing easier than to go beyond Abraham. Personally, I have devoted a considerable amount of time to the study of Hegelian philosophy, and I believe that I understand it fairly well; I am even rash enough to think that when, in spite of all my efforts, I fail to understand him in certain passages, it is because he is not clear on the matter himself. All this I do easily and naturally, and my head never suffers from it. On the other hand, whenever I try to think about Abraham, I am as it were annihilated. At every moment I am aware of the enormous paradox[4] which forms the content of Abraham's life, at every moment I am repulsed by him, and in spite of all its passion, my thought cannot penetrate the paradox, even by a hair's-breadth. I strain every muscle to achieve my aim, and at the same moment I become as one paralysed.

---

1. First of the Hebrew patriarchs (see Genesis 11–25).
2. That is, throat-clearing.
3. HEGEL was the dominant figure in philosophy when Kierkegaard was writing.

4. A key term (and concept) for Kierkegaard. A "paradox" literally is something "beyond opinion"— that is, contrary to expectation, hard to make sense of, perhaps even self-contradictory, and therefore seemingly impossible.

I am not unacquainted with what has been admired as great and noble in the world; my soul feels kinship with it, assured in all humility, that it was also my cause which the hero espoused, and in the moment of contemplation, I cry out to myself: *jam tua res agitur.*[5] I *think* myself into the hero, but I cannot think myself into Abraham; whenever I reach these heights, I fall back again, for there I am confronted with a paradox. By this I do not mean that faith is something inferior, but on the contrary that it is the highest of all things; and I think that it is dishonest of philosophy to offer something in its place and to pour scorn on faith. Philosophy cannot and should not give faith; instead it should understand itself and know what it has to offer and take nothing, and least of all should it trick men out of something as though it were nothing. I am not unacquainted with the dangers and vicissitudes of life, but I do not fear them and cheerfully go forth to meet them. I am not unacquainted with terror, my memory is a gentle spouse and my imagination is, as I am not, a tireless little girl who spends the whole day sitting quietly over her work and who, in the evening, chatters about it so sweetly that although what she paints is not always a landscape or a flower-study or a pastoral, I still have to look at it. With my own eyes I have seen terrible things, and I have not turned back afraid; but I know that, although I have gone courageously forward to meet them, my courage is not the courage of faith and is as nothing compared with the courage of faith. I cannot perform the movement of faith,[6] I cannot close my eyes and confidently plunge into the absurd,[7] to me an impossible thing, but neither do I boast about it. I am certain that God is love, and this thought has for me a fundamental lyrical validity. When it is present, I am unspeakably happy; when it is absent, I long for it with more ardour than a lover longs for the object of his desire: but I do not believe that courage is lacking in me. For me the love of God is, both in the direct and opposite sense, incommensurable with the whole of reality. I am not so cowardly as therefore to whimper and complain, neither am I so sly and cunning as to deny that faith is something far superior. It is not difficult for me to live as I live now, I am happy and contented, but my joy is not the joy of faith, and in comparison it is almost unhappy. I do not burden God with my small sorrows and individual sorrows do not trouble me at all: I think only of my love and I guard its virginal flame so that it shines with a pure and clear light; faith itself is convinced that God looks after the smallest things. In this life I am content to be married by the left hand; while faith is sufficiently humble to demand the right hand; and that this is indeed humility is something I shall never deny.

I wonder whether all my contemporaries are really able to perform the movements of faith? Unless I am very much mistaken, they are, rather, inclined to be proud of doing what they certainly think I am incapable of doing: the imperfect movement. It is repugnant to me to do what is so often done, to speak inhumanly about great deeds, as though a few thousand years were an immense space of time; about such things I prefer to speak humanly, as though they were done but yesterday, and I prefer that the great deed itself should be the

---

5. Now it is your concern (Latin); quoted from Horace, *Epistles* 1.18.84 (ca. 20 B.C.E.).
6. In this context Kierkegaard also uses the expression "leap of faith," which similarly emphasizes the idea that faith is in an important sense a kind of *act*.
7. A key term for Kierkegaard. Something "absurd," strictly speaking, is contrary to reason or illogical.

distance which inspires or condemns. If I (*as tragic hero*; for I cannot reach higher) had been summoned to take part in such an extraordinary royal progress as the journey to Mount Moriah,[8] I know very well what I would have done. I would not have been a coward and remained at home, neither would I have dawdled on the way, nor forgotten the knife so as to cause a little delay. I am almost certain that I would have been there, with everything ready, at the proper time—I might even have arrived too early, in order to get it over sooner. But I know too all the other things I would have done. The moment I got into the saddle, I would have told myself: now everything is lost, God demands Isaac, I shall sacrifice him and with him all my joy—and yet God is love and so He will always remain; for in the temporal world God and I cannot speak together, we have no language in common. Perhaps among my contemporaries there will be one so stupid and so jealous of great deeds that he will try to convince us both that if I had done this, I would have been doing something far greater than Abraham's deed; for he will imagine that my immense resignation was more ideal, more poetical than Abraham's prosaic deed. How absolutely untrue this is! My immense resignation was simply the surrogate of faith. Nor could I perform more than the infinite movement in order to find myself and again repose in myself. Nor would I have loved Isaac as Abraham loved him. That I was sufficiently resolute to make the movement proves only that I was courageous in the human sense; and that I loved him with all my soul was no more than the pre-supposition without which my action would have been a crime; and yet I did not love him as Abraham loved him; or else I would have hesitated at the last moment, although I would still have arrived on Mount Moriah in good time. Besides, I would have spoiled the whole course of the story by my behaviour; for if Isaac had been given back to me, I would only have been embarrassed. What might have been difficult for me was the easiest thing of all for Abraham: it was easy for him to rejoice once more over Isaac! for he who, with all the infinity of his soul, *proprio motu et propriis auspiciis*,[9] has performed the infinite movement and cannot do more retains Isaac only in his pain.

What did Abraham do? He came neither *too early* nor too late. He mounted the ass and rode slowly on his way. All the while he believed, believed that God would not demand Isaac of him, and yet he was willing to sacrifice him if it was demanded of him. He believed by virtue of the absurd; for there could be no question of human calculation, and the absurdity lay precisely in the fact that God demanded it of him one moment and recalled the demand the next. He climbed the mountain and even at the moment when the knife gleamed, he believed—that God would not demand Isaac. Certainly, he was surprised by the result; but through a double movement he had returned to his first state and therefore he received Isaac more gladly than the first time. Let us go further. Imagine that Isaac had really been sacrificed. Abraham believed. He believed, not that one day he would be blessed in Heaven, but that he would be happy here on earth. God could give him a new Isaac and bring back to life the one who had been sacrificed. He believed by virtue of

---

8. That is, Abraham's journey up into the mountains, on God's instruction, to sacrifice his son Isaac—born when Abraham was 100 and his wife Sarah was 90—as a burnt offering (Genesis 22:1–19).

9. By his own impulse and under his own auspices (Latin).

the absurd; for all human calculation had long since been abandoned. We know that grief can drive a man mad, and that is hard enough to bear; we know too that the power of the will can haul so strongly to windward that it saves the reason, though this man may become a little queer, and I have no desire to disparage it; but to be capable of losing one's reason and with it the whole finite world, of which reason is the stockbroker, and then to recover the finite world by virtue of the absurd, this is something which really terrifies me; and therefore I do not say that it is a small thing, but that on the contrary it is the one and only miracle. It is generally held that the product of faith is far from being a work of art, that it is coarse and vulgar work fit only for uncultivated natures; yet this is far from the truth. The dialectic of faith is the most subtle and remarkable of all; it possesses a sublimity which it is true that I can conceive, though I can do no more than conceive it. I can make the great dive from the spring-board which takes me into infinity; my spine, like the spine of a tightrope dancer, was twisted in childhood; and so it is easy for me to make this dive; one, two, three! and I go through life standing on my head! But I cannot take the next step; I cannot perform the miracle; I am only amazed by it. If Abraham, while he was swinging his legs over the ass's back, had said to himself: Isaac is lost, whether I sacrifice him here at home or whether I undertake the long journey to Moriah—I would have had no use for him, while now I bow seven times before his name and seventy times[1] before his deed. He did not say this, and the proof is his great inward joy in receiving Isaac and in the fact that he had no need for preparation or for time to collect himself before the finite world and its joys. If it had been otherwise with Abraham, it may be that he would have loved God, but he would not have believed; for he who loves God without faith reflects upon himself, but he who loves God with faith reflects upon God.

On these heights stands Abraham. The last stage which he loses sight of is the stage of infinite resignation. But Abraham goes even further and arrives at faith; for all those caricatures of faith—the miserable tepid indolence which thinks there is no hurry and no need to sorrow before the time comes; the pitiable hopefulness which says, you can never tell what is going to happen and it may be that . . .—these caricatures belong to what is wretched in life and already they have incurred the infinite scorn of infinite resignation.

Abraham I cannot understand. In a certain sense I can learn nothing from him except it be amazement. Those who imagine that they will come to believe by thinking about the dénouement of this story only deceive themselves and desire to cheat God of the first movement of faith: infinite resignation; one could as well extract worldly-wisdom from the paradox. But perhaps one or other of them will succeed; for our times are not satisfied with faith, not even with the miracle of changing water into wine;[2] they go further, they change wine into water.

Surely it is better to stand fast by faith? Surely it is a revolting thing that every one should desire to go further? If men in our times, as may be seen in so many different ways, have no desire to stand fast by love, where will they end? In worldly cunning, in mean calculation, in wretchedness and misery, in all those things which render man's divine origin doubtful. Surely it is better

---

1. An echo of Matthew 18:21–22.   2. See John 2:1–11.

to stand fast by faith and that those who stand should see to it that they do not fall; for the movement of faith must always be performed by virtue of the absurd, and—this is important—in such a way that the things of the world are not lost but entirely regained. I can, I think, perform the movements of faith perfectly, but I can never make them. When you are learning to swim, they allow you to support yourself on traces[3] hung from the roof: you perform the movements perfectly, but you are not swimming. In the same way I can perform the movements of faith, and when I am thrown into the water, it is true that I swim (for I refuse to wade in the shallows), but I am performing altogether different movements; I am making the movements of infinity; while faith does the opposite and having made the movements of infinity, makes those of finiteness. Blessed is he who can make these movements, for he performs a miracle, and I shall never grow tired of admiring him; it is the same to me whether he is Abraham or the slave in Abraham's house, whether he is a professor of philosophy or a poor servant-girl, for I have regard only for the movements he makes. But I watch them closely: I refuse to be deceived, either by myself or by anyone else. The knights of infinite resignation can be easily distinguished by the hovering and daring of their gait, but those who bear the jewel of faith are not so easily recognizable, because in their outward appearance they bear a striking resemblance to a class of people which is bitterly despised by faith and infinite resignation alike—they bear a close resemblance to the narrow *bourgeoisie*.

Let me say frankly that I have never, in the course of my experience, seen a reliable example of the knight of faith, but I do not for a moment deny that every other man may be such a knight. Meanwhile I have spent years searching for him in vain. Men are accustomed to travelling the world, looking for rivers and mountains, new stars, birds of gay-coloured plumage, monstrous fishes, ridiculous races of men; they abandon themselves to an animal stupor and gaze open-mouthed at life, believing that they have seen something. None of these things interest me at all. But if I knew where there lived a single knight of the faith, I would make a pilgrimage on foot to greet him; for this is the miracle which occupies my thoughts exclusively. Not for a moment would I let him out of my sight; I would watch how he performed each movement and consider myself made for life; I would divide my time between watching him and practising the movements he made, and thus spend all my time in admiring him. As I have said, I have never discovered a knight of the faith, but I can easily imagine one. Here he is. I make his acquaintance, I am introduced to him. And the moment I lay eyes on him, I push him away and leap back suddenly, clap my hands together and say half aloud: 'Good God! Is this really he? Why, he looks like an Inspector of Taxes!' But it is really he. I draw closer to him, I watch every movement he makes to see whether he shows any sign of the least telegraphic communication with the infinite, a glance, a look, a gesture, an air of melancholy, a smile to betray the contrast of infinity and the finite. But no! I examine him from head to foot, hoping to discover a chink through which the infinite can peer. But no! He is completely solid. How does he walk? Firmly. He belongs wholly to the finite; and there is no townsman dressed in his Sunday best, who spends his Sunday afternoon in

---

3. Straps, harnesses.

Frederiksberg, who treads the earth more firmly than he; he belongs altogether to the earth, no *bourgeois* more so. In him you will find no trace of that exquisite exclusiveness which distinguishes the knight of the infinite. He takes pleasure in all things, takes part in everything, and everything he does, he does with the perseverance of earthly men whose souls hang fast to what they are doing. He does his job thoroughly. At first glance you would think he was a clerk who had lost his soul to double-entry book-keeping, so punctilious he is. On Sundays he takes a holiday. He goes to church. No heavenly glance, no sign of incommensurability betrays him; and without knowing him it would be impossible to distinguish him from the rest of the congregation, for his healthy bellowing of the psalms proves only that he has got a sound pair of lungs. During the afternoons he walks out to the woods. His heart rejoices over everything he sees, the crowds, the new omnibuses, the Sound.[4] If you met him on the *Strandvej*,[5] you would think he was a shopkeeper having a good time, his delight being of that kind: for he is not a poet and I have tried in vain to detect in him any sign of poetic incommensurability. When he comes home in the evening, he walks as sturdily as a postman. On his way he thinks about the special hot dish which his wife has been preparing for him, a grilled lamb's head garnished with herbs perhaps. If he meets someone similarly disposed, he is quite capable of walking as far as Østerport if only he can discuss the dish, and he will discuss it with a passion which would give credit to a *maître d'hôtel*. As it happens, he has not fourpence to spare: but he still believes that his wife has a hot meal waiting for him. If she has, it will be an enviable sight for distinguished people and an inspiring one for common folk to see him eat; for his appetite is stronger than Esau's.[6] If his wife has not prepared it he remains—oddly enough—unmoved. On his way he comes to a building site and meets another man. They begin talking and before you can say jack-knife, he has erected a new building, himself disposing of all that is necessary. The stranger will leave him, thinking he has met a capitalist, while the knight will be marvelling at the thought that if it really came to the point, nothing would be easier. He leans out of the window and looks across the square in which he lives. He is interested in everything he sees, even if it is only a rat creeping into a gutter-hole or children playing; he regards life as peacefully as a girl of sixteen. Yet he is not a genius, and I have tried in vain to detect in him the incommensurability of genius. In the evening he smokes his pipe, and to see him you would swear that he was the butcher from over the way, vegetating in the evening twilight. He is as free from cares as any ne'er-do-well, but every moment of his life he purchases his leisure at the highest price; for he makes not the least movement except by virtue of the absurd. And yet—and yet I could become furious at the thought of it, if only out of envy—this man is making and has made at every moment the movement of infinity! In infinite resignation he drains the dark waters of melancholy to the last drop; he knows the blessedness of infinity; he has known the pain of forsaking everything in the world that was most dear to him; and yet the taste of the finite is as pleasing to him as if he had never known anything higher, for

---

4. Øresund, the narrow strait that separates the Danish island on which Copenhagen is located from southern Sweden.

5. The road that runs along the Sound (literally, "Coastal Road").

6. Esau, Abraham's grandson, was so hungry that he sold his birthright to his brother in exchange for bread and lentil stew (Genesis 25:29–34).

he remains in the finite without betraying any sign of his uneasy and tortured training, and yet rejoices in it with so much assurance that for him there appears to be nothing more certain. Yet the whole earthly shape which he assumes is something newly created by virtue of the absurd. In his infinite resignation he gave up everything and then regained everything by virtue of the absurd. He is always making the movement of infinity, but he makes the movement with so much precision and assurance that he possesses himself of the finite without anyone, even for a moment, suspecting anything else. The most difficult feat which a dancer can attempt is said to be to leap and take up a definite attitude, so that at no particular moment does he appear to be trying to take up this position, but assumes the attitude as he leaps. Perhaps there are no dancers who can perform this feat—but the knight performs it. Most men's lives are lost among the joys and sorrows of the world: they 'sit out' and take no part in the dance. The knights of infinite resignation are dancers and have elevation. They make the upward movement and fall down again; and this pastime has much to commend itself and is not unpleasing to the eye. But every time they fall down, they cannot immediately take up their positions, they falter for a moment and their faltering shows that they are strangers in the world. This is more or less apparent according to the degree of their art, but even the most masterly of them cannot conceal his faltering. It is not necessary to watch them in the air, one need only watch them at the moment when they touch and have touched the earth—then you will recognize them. To be able to fall in such a way as to appear at once standing and walking, to be able to transform the leap of life into a normal gait, to be able to express perfectly the sublime in terms of the pedestrian—only the knight can do this—and this is the single miracle.

But this miracle can be easily deceptive, and therefore I shall describe these movements by means of a given example which will explain their relation to reality: for that is the important thing. A youth falls in love with a princess and the whole of his life is bound up with this love, although the relation is such that it is impossible for it to realize itself or to translate itself from ideality into reality.[7] The slaves of the finite and those frogs which inhabit the swamps of life will naturally cry out: 'What a stupid love-story! The rich brewer's widow would make just as good a match.' Let those who are in the swamps croak undisturbed! The knight of infinite resignation does not follow their advice; he refuses to surrender his love even for all the glory in the world. He is not a fool. First of all he makes certain whether his love is the whole content of his life, since his soul is too healthy and too proud to waste the least of itself on intoxication. He is not a coward; he is not afraid to let love steal into his remote and secret thoughts; he is not afraid to let it wind itself in innumerable coils round every ligament of his consciousness—if his love becomes unhappy, he will never be able to extricate himself from it. He experiences a voluptuous pleasure in allowing love to run shuddering through his nerves; and yet his soul remains as solemn as the soul of a man who has

7. It follows that any other interest in which the individual concentrates the whole of reality can, when it shows itself to be unrealizable, provoke the movement of resignation. I have, however, chosen love as a means of explaining these movements because its interest is more easy to understand, and therefore I can at once excuse myself from discussing preliminary considerations which, in a profounder sense, could only interest very few people [author's note].

drained the cup of poison and feels the liquid mingling with his blood—for this moment is both life and death. When he has wholly absorbed this love and plunged deeply into it, he does not lack the courage to attempt everything and to risk all. He surveys the circumstances of his life, he summons his swift thoughts which are like doves returning to their dove-cotes, taught to obey him at a nod: he brandishes the magic wand over them and they dart out in all directions. But when they return, each one of them a messenger of sorrow, when they explain to him that it is an impossibility: he remains calm, he dismisses them and stands alone and thereupon he undertakes the movement. But what I have said here can have no meaning unless the movement is effected normally.[8] In the first place the knight has the strength to be able to concentrate the whole content of his life and the whole significance of reality into a single desire. If a man lacks this concentration, this determination, his soul from the very beginning is scattered in the manifold: he will never be able to perform the movement and he will be as worldly-wise in the conduct of his life as the financier who invests his money in a number of different securities, hoping to gain on one what he loses on the other—in short, he is not a knight. Further, the knight will have the strength to be able to concentrate all the solutions of his thought into a single act of consciousness. If he lacks this determination, his soul from the very beginning will be scattered in the manifold and he will never have time to make the movement, he will always be running errands in life, without ever entering into eternity; for in the very moment when he approaches eternity, he will suddenly remember that he has forgotten something and have to go back for it. The next moment, he says, it will be possible; and so indeed it is; but with such reflections he will never be able to perform the movement, but instead, with their help, he will sink deeper and deeper into the mire.

The knight, then, performs the movement, but which movement? Will he forget the whole: for in this also there lies a kind of concentration? No! For the knight does not contradict himself, and it is a contradiction to forget the whole content of one's life and remain the same. The knight feels no desire to become another person, he sees no greatness in assuming another role. It is only the lower natures who forget themselves and change into something new. So the butterfly entirely forgets that it was once a caterpillar, and perhaps there will come a time when it will forget so completely that it was once a butterfly that it will be able to turn into a fish. Deeper natures never forget themselves and never become anything other than they are, and so the knight remembers everything; but this remembering is what is painful to him, and nevertheless in infinite resignation he is reconciled with existence. Love for the princess became the expression of an eternal love; it assumed a religious

8. *There is need for passion here. Every infinite movement is effected through passion, and no reflection can ever produce such a movement. This is the perpetual leap into existence which explains the movement, while mediation is a chimera which, according to Hegel, explains everything, although it is itself the one thing which he never attempted to explain.* Even to make the famous Socratic distinction between what is understood and what is not understood, passion is necessary, and it is still more necessary of course to those who want to make the real Socratic movement, which is that of ignorance. What is lacking in our times is not reflection, but passion. It follows, therefore, that our times are, in a sense, too tenacious of life to die; for death is one of the most remarkable leaps, and there is a verse by a poet which I have always liked, because after five or six lines of a quite simple beauty, in which he desires the good things of life, he ends: "*ein seliger Sprung in die Ewigkeit* / (a blessed leap into eternity)" [author's note]. On Socratic ignorance, see Plato's *Apology* (ca. 395 B.C.E.), 21–23.

character; it became transfigured into love for the eternal being which, though denying him the fulfilment, nevertheless appeased him once again with the eternal consciousness of the truth of his love as a form of eternity which no reality can take away from him. There are fools and young men who boast that everything is possible to man. This is indeed a great delusion. In the world of the spirit everything is possible, but in the finite world there is much that is not possible. Nevertheless, the knight makes the impossible possible by expressing it in terms of the spirit, but he expresses it in terms of the spirit only by renouncing it. That desire, which would have led him into reality but which was frustrated by its impossibility, is then forced inward: but it does not follow that it is either lost or forgotten. Sometimes the memory is awakened in him by the dark impulses of desire, sometimes he himself awakens it; for he is too proud to admit that what was once the whole content of his life has become nothing more than the affair of a fleeting moment. He preserves the freshness of his love and it grows with him with the years and in beauty. On the other hand, the growth of his love in no way depends upon the intervention of the finite. From the moment he has completed the movement, the princess is lost. He has no need of the nervous excitement provoked by passion at the sight of the beloved, or of anything of this kind; he has no need to bid her endless farewells in the finite sense, since he bears a memory of her which is eternal. He knows too well that lovers who are eager to see each other once more for the last time so that they can say farewell to each other are right in their eagerness and right in their belief that it is the last time; they will soon forget each other. The knight, however, has discovered the profound secret that even in love a man should be sufficient to himself. He no longer takes any finite interest in what the princess is doing, and it is precisely this which proves that he has made the movement in an infinite sense; and here we have an opportunity of discovering whether the movement of an individual is real or only apparent. Imagine someone who believed that he had performed this movement. Time passed and the princess did something else, for example, married a prince. Then his soul lost the elasticity of resignation. He shows thereby that he has not performed the movement correctly; for he who has resigned himself in an infinite sense is sufficient to himself. The knight does not abandon his resignation, he preserves his love for her as fresh as it was in the first moment, he never allows it to escape him, precisely because he has made the movement in an infinite sense. Whatever the princess does cannot disturb him, for it is only lower natures who discover in others the laws which govern their own actions, who discover the premises of their actions outside themselves. On the other hand, if the princess is similarly disposed, the beauty of her love will appear. She will then enter the order of knighthood, into which no one is received by ballot, but of which everyone becomes a member if they have the courage to present themselves: the order of knighthood which proves its immortality by the fact that it makes no distinction between man and woman. And she will keep her love young and healthy; she too will have overcome her agony, even though she will not, in the words of the ballad, 'lie every night by her lord's side'.[9] The two lovers then will remain in harmony for all eternity, in a *harmonia*

9. A line from a medieval Danish folk song.

praestabilita[1] so perfect that if ever there came a moment—a moment which will never concern them in the finite, unless they are old—if ever there came a moment when they could give to love its expression in time, they would be able to begin from where they would have begun if they had been united originally. Those who understand this, men or women, will never be deceived, for it is only the lower natures who imagine they are deceived. No girl knows how to love until she has this pride; and those who have this pride can never be deceived by the cunning wiles of the world.

In infinite resignation there is peace and rest; everyone who desires it, who has not humiliated himself by looking down upon himself, which is even more terrible than being too proud, can discipline himself to make this movement, which in its pain and suffering reconciles one with life. Infinite resignation is like the shirt in the fable.[2] The thread is spun with tears and the cloth is bleached with tears and sewn with tears, but afterwards it is a better armour than iron or steel. The one imperfection in the fable is that a third person could weave the linen. The secret of life is that everyone must sew it for himself, and the curious thing is that a man can sew it as well as a woman. In infinite resignation there is peace and rest and consolation in pain—but only if the movement is performed normally. I should not, however, find it difficult to write a whole book on the different misunderstandings, the perverse attitudes and abortive movements which I have come across in my short experience. Men have little faith in the spirit, and yet spirit is the essential thing in performing this movement, and the whole point is that it should not be the one-sided result of a *dira necessitas*;[3] and the greater the influence of the *dira necessitas*, the more questionable it becomes whether the movement is normal. And if this is said to imply that cold and sterile necessity must necessarily be present, it would follow that no one can live his death before he has died—a statement which seems to me to be no more than crass materialism. Nowadays people are less concerned than formerly to make the pure movements. If someone who wanted to learn how to dance were to say: for hundreds of years one generation after another has learned the steps, and it is high time that I profited by their experience and learned the French dances, people would laugh at him a little; but in the world of the spirit a statement like this would be entirely plausible. What then is education? I thought education was the course which the individual had to follow in order to catch himself up; and those who will not follow the course derive little profit from being born into even the most enlightened age.

Infinite resignation is the last stage which goes before faith, so that those who have not made this movement have not got faith; for it is only in infinite resignation that I become conscious of my eternal worth, and it is only then that there can be any question of grasping existence by virtue of faith.

Now let us imagine the knight of faith in the same situation. He behaves in precisely the same way as the other knight; he renounces in an infinite sense the love which is the content of his life, he is reconciled in suffering; it

---

1. Preestablished harmony (Latin): the idea of a divinely ordained harmony of the mental and material realms, proposed by the German philosopher Gottfried Wilhelm Leibniz (1646–1716) to explain their apparent causal interactions. (Actual causality between them was deemed impossible, because mind and body were assumed to be radically different kinds of substance.)
2. A Hungarian folktale.
3. Dreadful necessity (Latin); quoted from Horace, *Odes* 3.24.6 (ca. 23 B.C.E.).

is then that the miracle happens: he performs a further movement more extraordinary than any of the others, for he says: I believe, nevertheless, that I shall marry her, namely, by virtue of the absurd, by virtue of the fact that all things are possible to God. The absurd does not belong among the differences which lie within the peculiar sphere of reason. It is not identical with the improbable, the unforeseen, the unexpected. At the moment when the knight resigned himself, he was convinced that, humanly speaking, the fulfilment of his wish was impossible; this was the result of reason and he had sufficient energy to think in this way. On the other hand, in an infinite sense, it was perfectly possible, as a result of his resignation, but this possession is at the same time a renunciation—and yet this possession is not absurd in the eyes of reason; for reason still maintained rightly that in this world of the finite where it is sovereign, it must always be an impossibility. The knight of the faith is just as aware of this as the knight of resignation; and therefore the only thing that can save him is the absurd, and he lays hold of this by faith. He recognizes therefore the impossibility and in the same moment he believes in the absurd: for if he were to imagine that he had faith without recognizing with his whole heart and with all the passion of his soul that his love was impossible, he would be deceiving himself and his testimony would be valueless, since he has not even reached the stage of infinite resignation.

Faith, therefore, is not an aesthetic impulse, but something far higher, precisely because it presupposes resignation; it is not the immediate instinct of the heart, but the paradox of existence. When a young girl, in spite of all difficulties, is still convinced that her desire will be fulfilled, her assurance is not the assurance of faith, even if she has been brought up by Christian parents, even if she has attended catechism classes for a whole year. She is convinced in childish *naïveté* and innocence, and this conviction ennobles her existence and gives her preternatural greatness, so that like a thaumaturge[4] she can exorcise the finite powers of life and wring tears from stones, while, on the other hand, in her bewilderment, she can appeal to Herod as well as to Pilate,[5] and move the whole world with her prayers. Her assurance is certainly charming, and one can learn much from her, but there is one thing one cannot learn from her: how to make this movement, for her assurance dares not look impossibility in the eyes while suffering the pain of resignation.

I can therefore understand the necessity of strength and energy and freedom of the spirit, in order to make the infinite movement of resignation; I can also understand how such a movement becomes possible. But the next step utterly astounds me and my brain twists and turns in its skull; for after making the movement of resignation and obtaining everything by virtue of the absurd, to have one's desire wholly and utterly fulfilled—this is beyond the power of man and remains a miracle. At the same time I can understand that the young girl's assurance is only frivolity in comparison to the rigour of the unshakable rock of faith, even though she has recognized the impossibility. Every time I try to make this movement, my eyes grow dim, at the

4. A miracle worker.
5. See Luke 23:1–25. In classical mythology, the poet Orpheus had the power to cause nature (including stones) to weep by playing his lyre and singing.

same moment I am overwhelmed with admiration for it, and at that moment a terrible dread seizes upon my soul; for what does it mean to tempt God? And yet this is the movement of faith, and always will be, even if philosophy, in order to spread confusion among its concepts, tries to make us believe that philosophy possesses faith, and even if theology sells it outright at a profit.

Resignation does not imply faith, for what I obtain in resignation is my eternal consciousness, and this is a purely philosophical movement which I have the courage to make whenever it is demanded of me, and I can force myself to make it; for whenever finite circumstances threaten to grow above my head, I starve myself until I make the movement; for my eternal consciousness is my love for God, and to me this is the highest of all things. In resignation there is no need for faith, but faith is indeed necessary if I am to obtain the least thing over and above my eternal consciousness; and herein lies the paradox. The movements are often confused. One hears it said that it is necessary to have faith in order to renounce everything—and one hears the still more curious thing, a man complaining that he has lost his faith, but when one looks at the ladder in order to see what rung he is on, one sees, curiously enough, that he has only reached the point where he has to make the infinite movement of resignation. By resignation I renounce everything, and this is a movement which I perform by myself, and if I do not perform it, then it is because I am cowardly, effeminate, and without enthusiasm, and because I lack any sense of the high dignity which is awarded to everyone, the office of being one's own censor, a dignity which is more distinguished than the title of general censor to the whole Roman republic.[6] I perform this movement by myself, and the reward is therefore myself in my eternal consciousness, in a sacred understanding with my love for the eternal being. By faith I renounce nothing; on the contrary, by faith I receive everything, in precisely the sense in which it is said that he who has faith as a grain of mustard-seed shall remove mountains.[7] It needs a purely human courage to be able to renounce all temporality in order to gain eternity, but this I achieve, and in all eternity I cannot renounce it without self-contradiction; but it needs the paradox and the most humble courage to seize upon the whole of temporality by virtue of the absurd, and this courage is the courage of faith. It was not by faith that Abraham renounced Isaac, but by faith that Abraham obtained Isaac. By virtue of resignation the rich young man should have given everything away, but when he had done so the knight of the faith would have said to him: by virtue of the absurd every penny will be returned to you, can you believe this? And the rich young man should have been in no way indifferent to this speech; for if he gave his goods away because he was bored with them, his resignation leaves much to be desired.

Here everything turns upon the temporal and the finite. With my own strength I can renounce everything, and find peace and rest in suffering; I can bear everything, and even if that cruel demon, more terrible than the skeleton which terrifies men, even if madness holds her fool's cap before my eyes

---

6. In the Roman Republic, the censors were the two magistrates who maintained the official list of citizens (penalizing those who acted contrary to public morals).
7. See Matthew 17:20.

and by the expression on her face makes me understand that it is for me to wear it, I can still save my soul, so long as it is of more consequence to me that my love for God should conquer in me, rather than my earthly happiness. It is still possible for a man in that last moment to gather his whole soul into a single glance towards Heaven, from which all blessings come, and this glance will be understood by him and by Him whom he is seeking as a sign that he is still faithful to his love. Therefore he will wear the fool's cap contentedly. The man whose soul has not this sense of the romantic has indeed sold his soul, whether he has sold it for a kingdom or only for a miserable silver-piece.[8] But by my own strength I cannot obtain the least of the things which belong to the finite; for I continually employ my strength in renouncing everything. I can surrender the princess by my own strength, and instead of lamenting my fate, it is my duty to find joy and rest and peace in my suffering; but by my own strength I cannot obtain her again, for in fact I employ my strength in renunciation. But through faith, says that amazing knight, through faith you will obtain her by virtue of the absurd.

Alas, I cannot perform this movement. As soon as I begin, everything is reversed and I retreat into the suffering of resignation. I can swim in life, but I am too heavy for this mystical soaring. To exist in such a way that my opposition to existence at every moment expresses itself in the most serene and beautiful harmony with it—that I cannot do. And yet it must be a glorious thing to obtain the princess, as I say at every moment, and the knight of resignation who does not say this is a deceiver, he has not known a single desire, and has not retained the freshness of his desire in suffering. Perhaps there has been someone who thought it convenient that the desire should no longer be alive, that the barb of suffering should be dulled; but men such as those are not knights. Any free-born soul who caught himself thinking like this would despise himself and begin again from the beginning; above all he would never allow his soul to be deceived by himself; and yet it must be a glorious thing to obtain the princess; and yet the knight of the faith is the only happy man, heir to the whole world of the finite, while the knight of resignation is a stranger and a foreigner. Thus to obtain the princess is a marvellous thing, to live with her in gladness and in joy, day after day (for it is also conceivable that the knight of resignation might obtain the princess, although his soul had seen the impossibility of any future happiness), to live every moment in gladness and joy by virtue of the absurd, to see at every moment the sword hanging over the head of the beloved, and finding no peace in the suffering of resignation, but instead joy by virtue of the absurd—how wonderful that is. Whoever can do this is great, and he alone is great; and the thought of it rejoices my soul, which has never been niggardly in its admiration of greatness.

If each one of my contemporaries who refuse to stop at faith has understood the terror of life, if he has understood what Daub[9] means when he says that a soldier standing alone at his post near a powder-magazine with a loaded rifle in his hand during a thunderstorm will think strange thoughts; if each one of those who refuse to stop at faith was a man with the strength of soul

---

8. An echo of the 30 pieces of silver that Judas received for betraying Jesus (Matthew 26:15).

9. Karl Daub (1765–1836), a German theologian and philosopher.

to understand, and then give himself time to remain alone with the thought, that the desire was an impossibility; if each one of those who refuse to stop at faith was a man who was reconciled to suffering and reconciled through suffering: if each one of those who refuse to hold by faith had also (and if he had not done all that has gone before, he need not disturb himself at all when faith is under discussion) performed the miracle and seized upon the whole of existence by virtue of the absurd—if each one had done all this, then these words of mine would be words of the highest praise directed to my contemporaries by the least worthy of them all, who has only been able to perform the movement of resignation. Why do men refuse to hold by faith? Why is it that you will sometimes hear that there are men who are ashamed to confess that they have faith? To me it is incomprehensible. For if ever I reach a point where I can perform this movement, I shall in future always drive in a carriage drawn by four horses.

But is it really true that all the *bourgeois* narrowmindedness which I see in life, that narrowmindedness which I do not condemn with words but by my deeds, is it really not what it seems to be, but the miracle? Perhaps it is so; for the hero of faith bears a striking resemblance to it; for the hero of faith was not even an ironist or a humorist, but something still higher. A great deal is said nowadays about irony and humour, especially by those who have never been able to practise them, but who nevertheless know exactly how to explain them. I am not entirely unacquainted with these two passions, and I know a little more about them than is to be found in the Danish and German-Danish miscellanies.[1] For example, I know that these two passions are essentially different from the passion of faith. Irony and humour also reflect upon themselves and therefore belong to the sphere of infinite resignation, and their elasticity is derived from the fact that the individual is incommensurable in terms of reality.

The last movement, the paradoxical movement of faith, I cannot perform, whether it is my duty or no, although there is nothing I would sooner do. Whether a man has the right to say this is something which must be left to his own discretion; it is a matter between him and the eternal being who is the object of faith, whether in this respect he is able to come to an amicable agreement. But it is in the power of everyone to perform the movement of infinite resignation, and for my part I would not hesitate to call him a coward who imagines he cannot perform it. It is quite another matter with faith. But what no one has the right to do is to make others believe that faith is something of no importance, or that it is an easy matter, when it is the greatest and most difficult of all things.

The story of Abraham is usually interpreted in a different way. God is praised for his mercy in returning Isaac to him; it was all a trial. This is a word which may mean much or little, and yet the whole thing happens in less time than it takes to tell. You mount a winged horse and the moment you arrive on Mount Moriah, your eyes alight upon the ram. You forget that Abraham rode upon an ass which travels slowly along the road; you forget that it was a three days' journey, that it takes time to split the wood, to bind Isaac, to whet the knife.

1. Encyclopedias or reference volumes of information on various matters.

And yet we praise Abraham. The priest who is going to give the sermon can sleep comfortably until a quarter of an hour before the sermon begins, and the congregation can sleep as comfortably during the sermon: for everything is made easy for them and there is no inconvenience on either side. But if there was a man present who suffered from insomnia, he would have gone home, sat down in a corner and thought: the whole thing was only the matter of a moment, if you only wait for a minute you will see the ram, and the trial will be over. Now if the priest were to find him in this frame of mind, I think he would confront the man in all his dignity and say, 'Miserable sinner, to let thy soul sink into such folly! Miracles do not happen and all life is a trial.' As he proceeded with his peroration he would become more and more passionate, more and more pleased with himself, and while he had failed to notice any congestion of the blood during his sermon about Abraham, he can now feel the veins swelling on his forehead. But he might even lose his voice as well as his breath if the sinner answered him quietly and with dignity: I was only trying to do what you preached last Sunday.

Let us therefore either forget Abraham or learn to be terrified of the tremendous paradox which is the significance of his life, so that we may learn to understand that men can rejoice in our times, as in all other times, if they have faith. Unless the story of Abraham is a mere nothing, an illusion, a show and a pastime, it can never be a mistake for a sinner to want to do likewise, but it is necessary to find out how great was the deed which Abraham performed, in order that he should judge of himself whether he has the courage and the mission to do likewise. The comic contradiction in the behaviour of the priest lies in the fact that he reduced Abraham to the most complete insignificance, and yet wanted to forbid the other behaving in the same way.

Should we then no longer dare to speak of Abraham? I do not really think so. But if I had to speak of him, I would first describe the terrors of the trial. To that end leech-like I would suck all the agony and terror and distress from a father's suffering, in order to describe what Abraham suffered though all the while believing. I would remind my audience that the journey lasted three days and a good part of the fourth, and these three and a half days would become infinitely longer than the few thousand years which separate me from Abraham. I would remind them that in my opinion everyone is allowed to turn away before he undertakes such a thing; at any moment he may turn back penitent. If this is done I fear no danger, nor do I fear that I have awakened any desire among men to be tried like Abraham. But to hand out a cheap edition of Abraham, while forbidding everyone to do as he did, this is ridiculous!

It is now my intention to draw out of the story of Abraham the dialectic which lies concealed within it, and to do this in the form of problemata,[2] in order to discover what a tremendous paradox is faith, a paradox which can transform a murder into a holy act pleasing to God, a paradox by which Isaac is returned to Abraham, a paradox which no thought can encompass because faith begins where thought leaves off.

---

2. Problems (Greek plural); the term is specifically associated with the dialectics of Aristotle (384–322 B.C.E.).

From *Problem 1. Can There Be a Teleological Suspension of Ethics?*

Ethics is as such the universal,[3] and as the universal it is valid for all, which may be expressed in another way by saying that it is valid at every moment. It rests immanent in itself, having nothing outside itself which is its τέλος,[4] being itself the τέλος of everything outside itself, and once this has been integrated in ethics, it goes no further. Defined as a being, immediate, physical, and spiritual, the Individual is the Individual who has his τέλος in the universal and his ethical task is to express himself continually in the universal, to strip himself of his individuality in order to become the universal. As soon as the Individual desires to assert his individuality over against the universal, he sins and he can only become reconciled with the universal again by recognizing it. Each time the Individual, after entering the universal, feels compelled to assert himself as Individual, he is in a tribulation from which he cannot escape except by repentance and by renouncing himself as Individual in the universal. If this is the highest that can be said of man and his existence, then morality [ethicality] is of the same nature as man's eternal blessedness, which is his τέλος in all eternity and at every moment, for it would be a contradiction to let it be abandoned (i.e. teleologically suspended), since, as soon as it is suspended, it is lost, while that which is suspended is not lost, but remains preserved in the higher sphere which is its τέλος.

If this is so, then Hegel is right in his chapter on 'Conscience and the Good', where he defines man solely as the Individual, and he is right in considering this definition as a 'moral form of evil' (cf. especially: *The Philosophy of Law* [*Right*]) which must be suppressed in the teleology of morals, so that the Individual who remains at this stage either sins or endures tribulation. On the other hand, Hegel is wrong in speaking about faith and wrong in not protesting loudly and clearly against the respect and admiration enjoyed by Abraham as the father of faith, when he should have been brought to trial and banished as a murderer.

For faith is this paradox, that the Individual is superior to the universal, but in such a way, however, that the movement repeats itself, and therefore in such a way that the Individual, after he has once been in the universal, then as Individual isolates himself as superior to the universal. If this is not faith, then Abraham is lost, then faith has never existed in the world, precisely because it always has existed. For if ethics (i.e. morality)[5] is the highest, and nothing incommensurable remains in man except it be evil (i.e. the particular which ought to be expressed in the universal), then there is no need for any other categories besides those of Greek philosophy and those which can be logically deduced from them. Hegel ought never to have concealed this; for after all he had read the Greeks.

It is not seldom that one finds men who, although they have not buried themselves in study, have managed to lose themselves among *clichés*, and one

---

3. Kierkegaard is here invoking and making use of the Hegelian notion of the *Allgemeine* or *Allgemeinheit* (generality or universality, in the sense of something that is applicable to all, either in a specific context or regardless of context), and the concept of "ethics" he is employing here is essentially Hegelian "ethicality" (*Sittlichkeit*). See the Hegel glossary, p. 144.

4. End, purpose (Greek, *telos*).

5. Hegel's distinction between "morality" (*Moralität*) and "ethicality" (*Sittlichkeit*) is here ignored, since all such normativity is being distinguished from "faith."

hears them proclaim that a light shines over the Christian world and darkness broods over paganism. This has always seemed to me a singular statement to make when every thorough thinker and every serious artist is still rejuvenating himself in the eternal youth of the Greeks. Such a statement can be explained by the fact that people do not know what to say, but only that it is necessary to say something. It is quite right to say that the pagans did not have faith, but if, in saying this, they imagine that they have said anything, they will have to attain to a little more clarity about what is meant by faith: since otherwise one reverts into such *clichés*. It is easy to explain the whole of existence, including faith, without having any conception of what faith is; and the man who reckons on the admiration which will be accorded to an explanation of this nature is by no means the worst off; for as Boileau rightly says: *un sot trouve toujours un plus sot, qui l'admire.*[6]

Faith is in fact this paradox, that the Individual as Individual is superior to the universal, is justified over against it, not subordinate, but superior to it, but always, however, in such a way that the Individual, after having been as Individual subordinate in the universal, becomes the Individual through the universal, and as Individual superior to it; so that the Individual as Individual stands in an absolute relationship to the absolute. This standpoint cannot be mediated; for mediation is only possible by virtue of the universal; it is precisely by virtue of the universal that all mediation occurs; it is and remains for all eternity a paradox, and inaccessible to thought. And yet faith is this paradox[7] (these are the consequences which I would beg the reader to bear in mind at every point, for it would be prolix to reiterate them on each occasion) or else there never has been faith, faith precisely because it has always been, or else Abraham is lost.

It is certainly true that this paradox may easily be confused by the Individual with spiritual tribulation, but it does not follow from this that one should conceal it. It is also true that the system of many thinkers is such that they are repulsed by the paradox, but that is no reason for making faith something other than it is in order to be able to possess it; rather one should admit that one lacks faith, while those who have faith ought to have concerned themselves with erecting a few signposts so that one could distinguish between the paradox and a spiritual tribulation.

Now the story of Abraham presents a teleological suspension of ethics of this kind. There has been no lack of sharp-witted heads and thorough investigators to find analogies to it. Their wisdom is founded upon the beautiful principle that fundamentally everything is the same. If one looks a little more closely, I doubt very much whether one will find in the whole world a single analogy except a later one, which proves nothing, if it is certain that Abraham represents faith and that it is normally expressed in him whose life is not only the most paradoxical that one can think of, but so paradoxical that it cannot be thought at all. He acts by virtue of the absurd; for the absurd lies precisely in the fact that he as Individual is superior to the universal.[8] This

6. A fool always finds a greater fool who admires him (French); quoted from *The Art of Poetry* 1.232 (1674), by the poet and critic Nicolas Boileau (1636–1711).
7. Hegelian language, used to characterize the difference between Hegel's conception of "absolute spirituality" and the conception of "faith" presented here.
8. That is, the Hegelian "ethical" type of "universal" (*Allgemeine*).

paradox does not lay itself open to mediation; for as soon as he begins with it, he must confess that he was in tribulation, and if that is the case he would never be able to sacrifice Isaac, or if he has sacrificed Isaac, he must return repentant to the universal. By virtue of the absurd, he once again receives Isaac. At no moment, therefore, is Abraham a tragic hero; he is something quite different, either a murderer or a believer. He does not possess the intermediary condition which saves the tragic hero. That is why I can understand the tragic hero, but cannot understand Abraham, although, in an insane sort of way, I admire him more than any other man.

In terms of ethics, Abraham's relationship to Isaac can be expressed simply: the father ought to love his son more than himself. There are, however, different degrees within the sphere of ethics; and we shall see whether a higher expression of ethics is to be found in the story capable of explaining Abraham's behaviour ethically and of giving him the ethical justification for the suspension of his ethical duty towards his son, without, however, going beyond the teleology of ethics.

When an undertaking affecting a whole nation is thwarted, when it is brought to an end by the displeasure of Heaven, when the angry deity sends among them a calm which laughs at all their efforts, when the oracle fulfils her heavy task and proclaims that the God demands the sacrifice of a young girl—then the father has to carry out the sacrifice heroically.[9] In spite of his desire to be 'a poor man who dares to weep', and not the king who must behave in kingly fashion, he must conceal his grief nobly. And if, when he is alone, he is overcome by his grief, and if throughout the whole kingdom there are only three men who know why he is sorrowing, soon all his subjects will be companions in his sorrow, but also in his deed, knowing that he has consented to sacrifice his beautiful young daughter for the common good. 'O face, dear face, O breast, O golden hair' (*Iphigenia in Aulis*, 687). And the daughter will move him with her tears and the father will turn away his face; but the hero will raise his knife.—When the tidings are borne to the land of his fathers, the maidens of Greece will blush with enthusiasm, and if his daughter is betrothed, instead of showing his anger, her lover will be proud to share in the deed of the father, for she belonged to him more tenderly than she belonged to the father.

When the brave judge[1] who saved Israel in the hour of her distress bound God and himself in one and the same vow, he had to turn the rejoicing of the young girl, the joy of his beloved daughter, into sorrow, while the whole of Israel sorrowed with her over her maidenly youth; but every freeman will understand and every resolute woman will admire Jephthah, and all the maidens of Israel will desire to behave like his daughter; for of what use would be a victory obtained by the vow, if Jephthah did not keep the vow? Would not the victory be taken away from the people?

---

9. A reference to the story of Iphigenia, as told in Euripides' tragedy *Iphigenia in Aulis* (405 B.C.E.), quoted below (the unattributed quotation echoes line 447): her father, Agamemnon, was the leader of the Greeks gathered to wage the Trojan War, but the fleet could not set sail from Aulis for Troy before he sacrificed her to appease the anger of the goddess Artemis.

1. Jephthah, described as a "mighty warrior" (Judges 11:1, RSV). He vowed that if he was victorious in his battle with the Ammonites, he would sacrifice as a burnt offering whoever came out of his house; after his victory, he was met by his only child, a daughter (Judges 11:30–39).

When a son forgets his duty, when the state entrusts the sword of justice to the father, when the laws decree that the punishment shall be inflicted by the hand of the father, then must the father heroically forget that the guilty one is his son, and nobly conceal his sorrow; but there will be no one among the people, not even the son, who will not admire the father; and every time the laws of Rome are expounded, it will be remembered that many have commented upon them more learnedly, but none so nobly as Brutus.[2]

If, on the other hand, while a favourable wind was bearing the fleet under full sail towards the harbour, Agamemnon had sent the messenger to call Iphigenia to the sacrifice; if Jephthah, without being bound by an oath upon which depended the fate of his people, had said to his daughter: go alone two months and bewail thy short youth and then I shall sacrifice thee on the altar; if Brutus had had an upright son and yet called the lictors[3] to put him to death—who would have understood them? If they were asked why they had done this, and if all three had replied: it is a trial in which we are tempted, would anyone have understood them better?

At the decisive moment when Agamemnon, Jephthah and Brutus heroically overcome their suffering, when they have heroically lost what is dear to them and they have only to accomplish the exterior sacrifice, then surely every noble soul will shed tears of compassion for their suffering and of admiration for their deed. If, on the contrary, at the decisive moment of the heroic courage with which they bear their suffering, they were to say, simply: it will not happen all the same, who would understand them? And if they added, as explanation: we believe this by virtue of the absurd, would anyone understand them better? For if it is easy to understand how absurd the statement is, it is more difficult to understand how they can believe in it.

There is a striking difference between Abraham and the tragic hero. The tragic hero remains within the domain of morality [ethicality]. He gives to an expression of ethics a $\tau \acute{\epsilon} \lambda o \varsigma$ in a still higher expression of ethics; he reduces the ethical relationship between father and son or daughter and father to a sentiment the dialectic of which is related to the idea of morality. In this case then, there can be no question of a teleological suspension of ethics itself.

But the case of Abraham is quite different. By his action he went beyond the ethical stage and possessed a higher $\tau \acute{\epsilon} \lambda o \varsigma$ outside it, in favour of which he suspended ethics. For I would like to know how it is possible to relate Abraham's action to the universal, and whether it is possible to discover any point of contact between what Abraham did and the universal, other than that he overstepped it. There was no question of saving a nation, or of defending the idea of the state, or of appeasing the anger of the gods. If there was any question of the divinity being angry, then it could only have been with Abraham, and his entire action stands in no relation to the universal and remained a purely private undertaking. While therefore the tragic hero is great through his moral virtue, Abraham is great through his purely personal virtue. In the life of Abraham there is no higher expression of ethics than that the father should love his son. Here there can be no question of ethics in the sense of

---

2. Lucius Junius Brutus, traditional founder of the Roman Republic (509 B.C.E.); according to legend, he condemned his own two sons to death when they joined a conspiracy to restore the monarchy.
3. Attendants of Roman magistrates; in early Rome, their duties included carrying out executions.

morality. In so far as the universal was present, it was concealed in Isaac, hidden, as one might say, in his loins and was compelled to cry out through Isaac's mouth: Do not do this, you annihilate everything.

Then why did Abraham do this? For God's sake, and so, what is absolutely identical, for his own sake. For God's sake, because God demands this proof of his faith; for his own sake, because he wanted to furnish this proof. The identification of these two experiences is perfectly expressed in the word which is always used to describe this condition: it is a trial, a temptation. But what is a temptation? Ordinarily speaking, a temptation is something which tries to stop a man from doing his duty, but in this case it is ethics itself which tries to prevent him from doing God's will. But what, then is duty? Duty is quite simply the expression of the will of God.

It here becomes clear that in order to understand Abraham, we require a new category. Such a relationship to the divinity is unknown to paganism. The tragic hero never enters into a private relationship with the divinity; but ethics is to him the divine, and therefore the paradox therein can be mediated in the universal.

Abraham cannot be mediated; in other words, he cannot speak. As soon as I speak, I express the universal,[4] and when I remain silent, no one can understand me. As soon then as Abraham desires to express himself in the universal, he is obliged to say that his situation is a tribulation; for he has no higher expression for the universal which exists above the universal he has transgressed.

While therefore Abraham excites my admiration, he also terrifies me. He who denies himself and sacrifices himself for his duty surrenders the finite to grasp the infinite; he has no lack of security. The tragic hero abandons certainty for a greater certainty and one can watch him with confidence. But what of the man who abandons the universal in order to grasp something still higher, which is not the universal? Can this be anything but a tribulation? And if it were possible, but the Individual was mistaken, what salvation is there for him? He bears all the suffering of the tragic hero, he annihilates his own joy in the world, he renounces everything, and in that same moment, perhaps, he shuts himself off from the one supreme joy which is so dear to him that he would purchase it at any price. Seeing him, it is impossible to understand him, impossible to watch him confidently. Perhaps what the believer desires cannot be done at all, since it is inconceivable. Or if it could be done, and the Individual had misunderstood the divinity, what salvation would there be for him? The tragic hero has need of tears and he demands tears, and who, watching Agamemnon with envious eyes, would be so barren as not to weep with him? But where is the man with a soul so perplexed as to presume to shed tears over Abraham? The tragic hero fulfils his task in a given moment of time, but in the course of time he accomplishes something of no less value: he visits those who are weighed down by sorrow, those whose lungs cannot breathe enough for their stifled sighs, those whose thoughts hang heavily about them and who are pregnant with tears; he shows himself to them, waves away the magic spells of sorrow, unbinds their bonds, dries their tears, and in the sorrows of the tragic hero they forget their own. No one can shed tears over Abraham. You approach

4. A famous Hegelian point, made in the discussion of "sense-certainty" in "Consciousness," section A of *Phenomenology of Geist* (1807; see above).

him with a *horror religiosus*[5] as Israel approached Mount Sinai. But what if this solitary man climbing Moriah, whose summit is higher than the plains of Aulis by a whole heaven's breadth—what if he is not a sleep-walker, walking with certainty over the abyss (while below, at the foot of the mountain, those who are watching tremble with awe and veneration and terror, and dare not call out to him), what if his mind is unhinged, what if he is mistaken! Praise and thanks be to the man who offers to him who is assailed by the sorrows of life and is left naked by the roadside, the word, the verbal fig-leaf which allows him to conceal his misery! O praise great Shakespeare, who could say everything, everything without exception, exactly as it is.—But why did you never express this torment? Did you keep it perhaps to yourself? like the beloved whose name one cannot bear to let the world name;[6] for the poet purchases the power of this word, which enables him to pronounce all the dread secrets of others, at the price of a little secret which he cannot pronounce; and a poet is not an apostle, only with the power of the devil can he cast out devils.

But when ethics is teleologically suspended in this way, how does the Individual, in whom it is suspended, exist? He exists as the Individual in contradiction to the universal. Does it follow that he sins? for in the eyes of the Idea, this is the form of sin; thus the existence of a child who does not sin because it is not conscious of its existence as such, is nevertheless sin in the eyes of the Idea, and is at every moment subject to ethics. If one denies that this form can be repeated in such a way that it is not sin, then Abraham is condemned. How then did Abraham exist? He believed. This is the paradox which keeps him on the summit and which he cannot explain to anyone else; for this paradox consists in setting himself as the Individual in an absolute relationship to the absolute. Is he justified? His justification, once more, is the paradox; for if he is justified, it is not by virtue of being in any way the universal, but by virtue of being the Individual.

* * *

The story of Abraham then involves a teleological suspension of ethics. As the Individual he has become superior to the [ethical] universal. This is the paradox which cannot be mediated. It is just as impossible to explain how he enters it as to explain how he remains within it. If this is not the case, then Abraham is not a hero, but a murderer. It is senseless to desire to continue to call him the father of the faith, and to speak of him to men who have no other concern except their concern for words. A man can become a tragic hero by his own strength, but he can never, by his own strength, become a knight of the faith. When a man enters what is, in a sense, the difficult path of the tragic hero, there are many who could give him counsel; but when he enters the narrow path of faith, there is no one who can give him counsel, no one who can understand him. Faith is a miracle, yet no one is excluded from it; for passion is common to all men, and faith is a passion.

SOURCE: From *Fear and Trembling: A Dialectical Lyric*, trans. Robert Payne, rev. ed. (Oxford: Oxford University Press, 1946), pp. 10–13, 32–78, 85–86. Originally published as *Frygt og*

5. Religious horror (Latin).
6. Perhaps the unnamed dedicatee of Shakespeare's *Sonnets* (published 1609).

bæven: Dialektisk lyrik (1843), under the pseudonym "Johannes de Silentio." This is one of many pseudonyms that Kierkegaard used to allow him to assume different authorial identities and standpoints. In this instance the "author" writes as one who is trying to understand the sort of faith paradigmatically exemplified by the biblical Abraham from the outside.

From Concluding Unscientific Postscript

From *Book One. The Objective Problem Concerning the Truth of Christianity*

FROM INTRODUCTORY REMARKS CONCERNING THE OBJECTIVE PROBLEM

From an objective standpoint Christianity is a *res in facto posita*,[1] whose truth it is proposed to investigate in a purely objective manner, for the accommodating subject is much too objective not to leave himself out; or perhaps he even unhesitatingly counts himself in, as one who possesses faith as a matter of course. The truth in this objective sense may mean, first, the historical truth; second, the philosophical truth. Viewed as historical, the truth of Christianity must be determined through a critical examination of the various sources, and so forth; in short, in the same manner that historical truth generally is determined. When the question of the philosophical truth is raised, the object is to determine the relationship of the doctrine thus historically given and verified, to the eternal truth.

The inquiring, speculating, and knowing subject thus raises a question of truth. But he does not raise the question of a subjective truth, the truth of appropriation and assimilation. The inquiring subject is indeed interested; but he is not infinitely and personally and passionately interested on behalf of his own eternal happiness for his relationship to this truth. Far be it from the objective subject to display such presumption, such vanity of spirit.

* * *

FROM CHAPTER II. THE SPECULATIVE POINT OF VIEW

* * *

Now if Christianity is essentially something objective, it is necessary for the observer to be objective. But if Christianity is essentially subjectivity, it is a mistake for the observer to be objective. In every case where the object of knowledge is the very inwardness of the subjectivity of the individual, it is necessary for the knower to be in a corresponding condition. But the utmost tension of human subjectivity finds its expression in the infinite passionate interest in an eternal happiness. Even in the case of earthly love it is a necessary requirement for a would-be observer, that he should know the inwardness of love. But here the interest is not so great as it is in the case of an eternal happiness, because all love is affected by illusion, and hence has a quasi-objective aspect, which makes it possible to speak of something like an experience at second-hand. But when love is interpenetrated with a

---

1. A thing posited as a fact (Latin); that is, "a given fact."

God-relationship, this imperfection of illusion disappears, together with the remaining semblance of objectivity; and now it holds true that one not in this condition can gain nothing by all his efforts to observe. In the infinite passionate interest for his eternal happiness, the subject is in a state of the utmost tension, in the very extremity of subjectivity, not indeed where there is no object, which is the imperfect and undialectical distinction, but where God is negatively present in the subject; whose mode of subjectivity becomes, by virtue of this interest, the form for an eternal happiness.

* * *

That the speculative[2] point of view is objective I do not deny. On the contrary, and in order to give a further demonstration of this fact, I shall here again repeat the experiment of placing a subject who is in passion infinitely concerned for his eternal happiness, in relation to speculative philosophy; when it will become evident that the speculative point of view is objective, from the fact that the so interested subject becomes comical. He does not become comical because he is infinitely interested; on the other hand, everyone who is not infinitely and passionately interested, but tries nevertheless to make people believe that he has an interest in his eternal happiness, is a comic figure. No, the comical inheres precisely in the incommensurability between his interest and the speculative objectivity.

If the speculative philosopher is at the same time a believer, as is also affirmed, he must long ago have perceived that philosophy can never acquire the same significance for him as faith. It is precisely as a believer that he is infinitely interested in his eternal happiness, and it is in faith that he is assured of it. (It should be noted that this assurance is the sort of assurance that can be had in faith, i.e. not an assurance once for all, but a daily acquisition of the sure spirit of faith through the infinite personal passionate interest.) And he does not base his eternal happiness upon his philosophical speculations. Rather, he associates circumspectly with philosophy, lest it lure him away from the certainty of faith (which has in every moment the infinite dialectic of uncertainty present with it) so as to rest in an indifferent objective knowledge. This is the simple dialectical analysis of the situation. If, therefore, he says that he bases his eternal happiness on his speculation, he contradicts himself and becomes comical, because philosophy in its objectivity is wholly indifferent to his and my and your eternal happiness. An eternal happiness inheres precisely in the recessive self-feeling of the subject, acquired through his utmost exertion. And besides contradicting himself, such a philosopher lies, with respect to his pretensions to be a believer.

Or the speculative philosopher is not a believer. In this case, he is of course not comical, since he does not raise the question of his eternal happiness at all. The comical appears only when the subject with an infinite passionate interest tries to attach his eternal happiness to philosophical speculation. But the speculative philosopher does not pose the problem of which we speak; for precisely as a speculative philosopher he becomes too objective to concern himself about an eternal happiness.

* * *

2. That is, Hegelian-philosophical.

From *Book Two. The Subjective Problem: The Relation of the Subject to the Truth of Christianity; The Problem of Becoming a Christian*

From Part One. Something about Lessing

From Chapter II. Theses Possibly or Actually Attributable to Lessing[3]

* * *

Objective thinking is wholly indifferent to subjectivity, and hence also to inwardness and appropriation; its mode of communication is therefore direct. It goes without saying that it need not on that account be at all easy. But it is direct, and lacks the elusiveness and the art of a double reflection, the godly and humane solicitude in communicating itself, which belongs to subjective thinking. It can be understood directly and be recited by rote. Objective thinking is hence conscious only of itself, and is not in the strict sense of the word a form of communication at all, at least not an artistic form, in so far as artistry would always demand a reflection within the recipient, and an awareness of the form of the communication in relation to the recipient's possible misunderstanding. Objective thinking[4] is, like most human beings, so touchingly kind and communicative. It imparts itself without further ado, and, at the most, takes refuge in assurances respecting its own truth, in recommendations as to its trustworthiness, and in promises that all men will some time accept it—it is so certain. Or perhaps rather so uncertain; for the assurances and the recommendations and the promises, which are presumably for the sake of the others who are asked to accept it, may also be for the sake of the teacher, who feels the need of the security and dependability afforded by being in a majority. If his contemporaries deprive him of this consolation, he makes a draft on the future—so certain is he. This type of certainty has something in common with that independence, which in independence of the world needs the world as witness to its independence, to feel sure that it really is independent.

The form of a communication must be distinguished from its expression. When the thought has found its suitable expression in the word, which is realized by means of a first reflection, there follows a second reflection, concerned with the relation between the communication and the author of it, and reflecting the author's own existential relationship to the Idea. Let us yet again cite a few examples; for we have plenty of time, since what I write is not the expected last paragraph which will complete the System. Suppose that someone wished to communicate the following conviction: Truth is inwardness; there is no objective truth, but the truth consists in personal appropriation.[5] Suppose him to display great zeal and enthusiasm for the propagation

---

3. The author (Climacus) begins this chapter by expressing his gratitude to the German dramatist and philosopher Gotthold Ephraim Lessing (1729–1781) for "the fact that he did not permit himself to be deceived into becoming world-historical and systematic with respect to the religious."
4. It must always be remembered that I speak of the religious, in which sphere objective thinking, when it ranks as highest, is precisely irreligious. But wherever objective thinking is within its rights, its direct form of communication is also in order,

precisely because it is not supposed to have anything to do with subjectivity [author's note].
5. I say only "suppose"; and in this form I have the right to posit both what is most certain and what is most absurd. For even the certain is not posited as certain, but only as a supposition, to throw light on the relationship involved; and even the absurd is not posited essentially, but only hypothetically, in order to illustrate the consequence of the relationship [author's note].

of this truth, since if people could only be made to listen to it they would of course be saved; suppose he announced it on all possible occasions, and succeeded in moving not only those who perspire easily, but also the hard-boiled temperaments: what then? Why then, there would doubtless be found a few laborers, who had hitherto stood idle in the market-place, and only after hearing this call went to work in the vineyard—engaging themselves to proclaim this doctrine to all. And then what? Then he would have contradicted himself still further, as he had contradicted himself from the beginning; for the zeal and enthusiasm which he directed toward the end of getting it said and heard, was in itself a misunderstanding. The matter of prime importance was, of course, that he should be understood; the inwardness of the understanding would consist precisely in each individual coming to understand it by himself. Now he had even succeeded in obtaining town criers of inwardness, and a town crier of inwardness is quite a remarkable species of animal. Really to communicate such a conviction would require both art and self-control: self-control to understand inwardly that the God-relationship of the individual man is the thing of prime importance, and that the busy intermeddling of third parties constitutes lack of inwardness, and an excess of amiable stupidity; art enough to vary inexhaustibly the doubly reflected form of the communication, just as the inwardness itself is inexhaustible. The greater the artistry, the greater the inwardness. If the author of the communication had much art, he could even afford to say that he was using art, certain of being able in the next moment to insure the inwardness of his communication, because he was infinitely concerned for the preservation of his own inwardness; it is this concern which saves the individual from every form of slovenly positivity.

* * *

* * * The positiveness of historical knowledge is illusory, since it is approximation-knowledge; the speculative result is a delusion. For all this positive knowledge fails to express the situation of the knowing subject in existence. It concerns rather a fictitious objective subject, and to confuse oneself with such a subject is to be duped. Every subject is an existing subject, which should receive an essential expression in all his knowledge. Particularly, it must be expressed through the prevention of an illusory finality, whether in perceptual certainty, or in historical knowledge, or in illusory speculative results. In historical knowledge, the subject learns a great deal about the world, but nothing about himself. He moves constantly in a sphere of approximation-knowledge, in his supposed positivity deluding himself with the semblance of certainty; but certainty can be had only in the infinite, where he cannot as an existing subject remain, but only repeatedly arrive. Nothing historical can become infinitely certain for me except the fact of my own existence (which again cannot become infinitely certain for any other individual, who has infinite certainty only of his own existence), and this is not something historical. The speculative result is in so far illusory, as the existing subject proposes *qua* thinker to abstract from the fact that he is occupied in existing, in order to be *sub specie aeterni.*[6]

* * *

6. Under the aspect of eternity (Latin); that is, to think from the standpoint of the eternal.

B. An existential system is impossible.

An existential system cannot be formulated. Does this mean that no such system exists? By no means; nor is this implied in our assertion. Reality itself is a system—for God; but it cannot be a system for any existing spirit. System and finality correspond to one another, but existence is precisely the opposite of finality. It may be seen, from a purely abstract point of view, that system and existence are incapable of being thought together; because in order to think existence at all, systematic thought must think it as abrogated, and hence as not existing. Existence separates, and holds the various moments of existence discretely apart; the systematic thought consists of the finality which brings them together.

In reality we are likely to encounter a deception, an illusion. This was dealt with in the *Fragments*,[7] and to this treatment I must here refer. It will be found in the Interlude, in the discussion of the question whether the past is more necessary than the future. Whenever a particular existence has been relegated to the past, it is complete, has acquired finality, and is in so far subject to a systematic apprehension. Quite right—but for whom is it so subject? Anyone who is himself an existing individual cannot gain this finality outside existence which corresponds to the eternity into which the past has entered. If a thinker is so absent-minded as to forget that he is an existing individual, still, absent-mindedness and speculation are not precisely the same thing. On the contrary, the fact that the thinker is an existing individual signifies that existence imposes its own requirement upon him. And if he is a great individual, it may signify that his own contemporary existence may, when it comes to be past, have the validity of finality for the systematic thinker. But who is this systematic thinker? Aye, it is he who is outside of existence and yet in existence, who is in his eternity forever complete, and yet includes all existence within himself—it is God. Why the deception? Because the world has stood now for six thousand years,[8] does not existence have the same claim upon the existing individual as always? And this claim is, not that he should be a contemplative spirit in imagination, but an existing spirit in reality. All understanding comes after the fact. Now, while the existing individual undoubtedly comes after the preceding six thousand years, if we assume that he spends his life in arriving at a systematic understanding of these, the strangely ironical consequence would follow, that he could have no understanding of himself in his existence, because he had no existence, and thus had nothing which required to be understood afterwards. Such a thinker would either have to be God, or a fantastic *quodlibet*.[9] Everyone doubtless perceives the immorality of such a situation, and doubtless also perceives that it is quite in order, as another author[1] has said respecting the Hegelian system, that we owe to Hegel the completion of the System, the Absolute System—without the inclusion of an Ethics.[2] Let us smile if we will at the ethico-religious extravaganzas of the Middle Ages in asceticism and the like; but let us above all not forget, that

7. That is, Climacus's *Philosophical Fragments*.
8. The age of the earth, as calculated by genealogies and chronologies in the Bible.
9. Anything at all (Latin); that is, an abstraction.
1. Kierkegaard himself, writing as Frater Taciturnus in *Stages on Life's Way* (1845).
2. That is, an ethics as Kierkegaard/Climacus thinks

of it (for the "existing individual"), which is something quite different from Hegel's concept of "ethicality" or "ethical life"—*Sittlichkeit*, dealt with at length in both his *Philosophy of Geist* and his *Philosophy of Right* (for both, see above)—as well as from his conception of "morality" (*Moralität*).

the speculative low-comedy extravagance of assuming to be an I-am-I, and nevertheless *qua* human being often so Philistine a character that no man of enthusiasm could endure to live such a life—is equally ridiculous.

Respecting the impossibility of an existential system, let us then ask quite simply, as a Greek youth might have asked his teacher (and if the superlative wisdom can explain everything, but cannot answer a simple question, it is clear that the world is out of joint): "Who is to write or complete such a system?" Surely a human being; unless we propose again to begin using the strange mode of speech which assumes that a human being becomes speculative philosophy in the abstract, or becomes the identity of subject and object. So then, a human being—and surely a living human being, i.e. an existing individual. Or if the speculative thought which brings the systems to light is the joint effort of different thinkers: in what last concluding thought does this fellowship finally realize itself, how does it reach the light of day? Surely through some human being? And how are the individual participants related to the joint effort, what are the categories which mediate between the individual and world-process, and who is it again who strings them all together on the systematic thread? Is he a human being, or is he speculative philosophy in the abstract? But if he is a human being, then he is also an existing individual. Two ways, in general, are open for an existing individual: *Either* he can do his utmost to forget that he is an existing individual, by which he becomes a comic figure, since existence has the remarkable trait of compelling an existing individual to exist whether he wills it or not. (The comical contradiction in willing to be what one is not, as when a man wills to be a bird, is not more comical than the contradiction of not willing to be what one is, as *in casu*[3] an existing individual; just as the language finds it comical that a man forgets his name, which does not so much mean forgetting a designation, as it means forgetting the distinctive essence of one's being.) Or he can concentrate his entire energy upon the fact that he is an existing individual. It is from this side, in the first instance, that objection must be made to modern philosophy; not that it has a mistaken presupposition, but that it has a comical presupposition, occasioned by its having forgotten, in a sort of world-historical absent-mindedness, what it means to be a human being. Not indeed, what it means to be a human being in general; for this is the sort of thing that one might even induce a speculative philosopher to agree to; but what it means that you and I and he are human beings, each one for himself.[4]

The existing individual who concentrates all his attention upon the circumstance that he is an existing individual, will welcome these words of Lessing about a persistent striving, as a beautiful saying.[5] To be sure, it did not indeed win for its author an immortal fame, because it is very simple; but every thoughtful individual must needs confirm its truth. The existing individual who forgets that he is an existing individual, will become more and more absent-minded; and as people sometimes embody the fruits of their leisure moments in books, so we may venture to expect as the fruit of his absent-mindedness the expected existential system—well, perhaps not all of us, but

---

3. In this case (Latin).
4. This sentence may be seen as providing the impetus for the development of "existential philosophy."

5. Lessing's famous thesis that the striving for knowledge or wisdom is more important than its possession is the point of departure for the *Postscript*.

only those who are almost as absent-minded as he is. While the Hegelian philosophy goes on and becomes an existential system in sheer distraction of
mind, and what is more, is finished—without having an Ethics (where existence properly belongs), the more simple philosophy which is propounded by
an existing individual for existing individuals, will more especially emphasize
the ethical.

As soon as it is remembered that philosophizing does not consist in addressing fantastic beings in fantastic language,[6] but that those to whom the philosopher addresses himself are human beings; so that we have not to determine
fantastically *in abstracto*[7] whether a persistent striving is something lower than
the systematic finality, or *vice versa*, but that the question is what existing
human beings, in so far as they are existing beings, must needs be content
with: then it will be evident that the ideal of a persistent striving is the only
view of life that does not carry with it an inevitable disillusionment. Even
if a man has attained to the highest, the repetition by which life receives
content (if one is to escape retrogression or avoid becoming fantastic) will
again constitute a persistent striving; because here again finality is moved
further on, and postponed. It is with this view of life as it is with the Platonic
interpretation of love[8] as a want; and the principle that not only he is in want
who desires something he does not have, but also he who desires the continued possession of what he has. In a speculative-fantastic sense we have a
positive finality in the System, and in an aesthetic-fantastic sense we have
one in the fifth act of the drama. But this sort of finality is valid only for fantastic beings.

The ideal of a persistent striving expresses the existing subject's ethical view
of life. It must therefore not be understood in a metaphysical sense, nor indeed
is there any individual who exists metaphysically. One might thus by way of
misunderstanding set up an antithesis between finality and the persistent
striving for truth. But this is merely a misunderstanding in this sphere. In the
ethical sense, on the contrary, the persistent striving represents the consciousness of being an existing individual; the constant learning is the expression for
the incessant realization, in no moment complete as long as the subject is in
existence; the subject is aware of this fact, and hence is not deceived.

* * *

FROM PART TWO. HOW THE SUBJECTIVITY OF THE INDIVIDUAL
MUST BE QUALIFIED IN ORDER THAT THE PROBLEM[9]
MAY EXIST FOR HIM

FROM CHAPTER I. THE TASK OF BECOMING SUBJECTIVE

Objectively we consider only the matter at issue, subjectively we have regard
to the subject and his subjectivity; and behold, precisely this subjectivity is
the matter at issue. This must constantly be borne in mind, namely, that the
subjective problem is not something about an objective issue, but is the sub-

---

6. That is, addressing fantasized (Hegelian) beings
in overly imaginative (Hegelian) language.
7. In the abstract (Latin).
8. As expressed in Plato's *Symposium* 206a (ca.

384 B.C.E.): "Love is love for the eternal possession
of the good."
9. That is, the "problem" as stated in the title of
Book Two.

jectivity itself. For since the problem in question poses a decision, and since all decisiveness, as shown above, inheres in subjectivity, it is essential that every trace of an objective issue should be eliminated. If any such trace remains, it is at once a sign that the subject seeks to shirk something of the pain and crisis of the decision; that is, he seeks to make the problem to some degree objective. If the Introduction still awaits the appearance of another work before bringing the matter up for judgment, if the System still lacks a paragraph, if the speaker has still another argument up his sleeve, it follows that the decision is postponed. Hence we do not here raise the question of the truth of Christianity in the sense that when this has been determined, the subject is assumed ready and willing to accept it. No, the question is as to the mode of the subject's acceptance; and it must be regarded as an illusion rooted in the demoralization which remains ignorant of the subjective nature of the decision, or as an evasion springing from the disingenuousness which seeks to shirk the decision by an objective mode of approach, wherein there can in all eternity be no decision, to assume that the transition from something objective to the subjective acceptance is a direct transition, following upon the objective deliberation as a matter of course. On the contrary, the subjective acceptance is precisely the decisive factor; and an objective acceptance of Christianity (*sit venia verbo*)[1] is paganism or thoughtlessness.

Christianity proposes to endow the individual with an eternal happiness, a good which is not distributed wholesale, but only to one individual at a time. Though Christianity assumes that there inheres in the subjectivity of the individual, as being the potentiality of the appropriation of this good, the possibility for its acceptance, it does not assume that the subjectivity is immediately ready for such acceptance, or even has, without further ado, a real conception of the significance of such a good. The development or transformation of the individual's subjectivity, its infinite concentration in itself over against the conception of an eternal happiness, that highest good of the infinite—this constitutes the developed potentiality of the primary potentiality which subjectivity as such presents. In this way Christianity protests every form of objectivity; it desires that the subject should be infinitely concerned about himself. It is subjectivity that Christianity is concerned with, and it is only in subjectivity that its truth exists, if it exists at all; objectively, Christianity has absolutely no existence. If its truth happens to be in only a single subject, it exists in him alone; and there is greater Christian joy in heaven over this one individual than over universal history and the System, which as objective entities are incommensurable for that which is Christian.

It is commonly assumed that no art or skill is required in order to be subjective. To be sure, every human being is a bit of a subject, in a sense. But now to strive to become what one already is: who would take the pains to waste his time on such a task, involving the greatest imaginable degree of resignation? Quite so. But for this very reason alone it is a very difficult task, the most difficult of all tasks in fact, precisely because every human being has a strong natural bent and passion to become something more and different. And so it is with all such apparently insignificant tasks, precisely their seeming insignificance makes them infinitely difficult. In such cases the task itself is

1. May there be forgiveness for the word (Latin); that is, "pardon the expression."

not directly alluring, so as to support the aspiring individual; instead, it works against him, and it needs an infinite effort on his part merely to discover that his task lies here, that this is his task—an effort from which he is otherwise relieved. To think about the simple things of life, about what the plain man also knows after a fashion, is extremely forbidding; for the differential distinction attainable even through the utmost possible exertion is by no means obvious to the sensual man. No indeed, thinking about the high-falutin is very much more attractive and glorious.

When one overlooks this little distinction, humoristic from the Socratic standpoint and infinitely anxious from the Christian, between being something like a subject so called, and being a subject, or becoming one, or being what one is through having become what one is:[2] then it becomes wisdom, the admired wisdom of our own age, that it is the task of the subject increasingly to divest himself of his subjectivity in order to become more and more objective. It is easy to see what this guidance understands by being a subject of a sort. It understands by it quite rightly the accidental, the angular, the selfish, the eccentric, and so forth, all of which every human being can have enough of. Nor does Christianity deny that such things should be gotten rid of; it has never been a friend of loutishness. But the difference is, that philosophy teaches that the way is to become objective, while Christianity teaches that the way is to become subjective, i.e. to become a subject in truth. Lest this should seem a mere dispute about words, let me say that Christianity wishes to intensify passion to its highest pitch; but passion is subjectivity, and does not exist objectively.

* * *

* * * The question I would ask is this: *What conclusion would inevitably force itself upon Ethics, if the becoming a subject were not the highest task confronting a human being?* And to what conclusion would Ethics be forced? Aye, it would, of course, be driven to despair. But what does the System care about that? It is consistent enough not to include an Ethic in its systematic scheme.

The Idea of a universal history tends to a greater and greater systematic concentration of everything. A Sophist has said that he could carry the whole world in a nutshell, and this is what modern surveys of world history seem to realize: the survey becomes more and more compendious. It is not my intention to show how comical this is, but rather to try to make it clear, through the elaboration of several different thoughts all leading to the same end, what objection Ethics and the ethical have to raise against this entire order of things. For in our age it is not merely an individual scholar or thinker here and there who concerns himself with universal history; the whole age loudly demands it. Nevertheless, Ethics and the ethical, as constituting the essential anchorage for all individual existence, have an indefeasible claim upon every existing individual; so indefeasible a claim, that whatever a man may accomplish in the world, even to the most astonishing of achievements, it is none the less quite dubious in its significance, unless the individual has been ethically clear when he made his choice, has ethically clarified his choice to himself. The ethical quality is jealous for its own integrity, and is quite unimpressed by the most astounding quantity.

---

2. This striking formulation—"becoming what one is"—also figures centrally in Nietzsche's thinking.

It is for this reason that Ethics looks upon all world-historical knowledge with a degree of suspicion, because it may so easily become a snare, a demoralizing aesthetic diversion for the knowing subject, in so far as the distinction between what does or does not have historical significance obeys a quantitative dialectic. * * *

* * * Demoralized by too assiduous an absorption in world-historical considerations, people no longer have any will for anything except what is world-historically significant, no concern for anything but the accidental, the world-historical outcome, instead of concerning themselves solely with the essential, the inner spirit, the ethical, freedom.

The constant intercourse with the world-historical tends in fact to make the individual unfit for action. The true ethical enthusiasm consists in willing to the utmost limits of one's powers, but at the same time being so uplifted in divine jest as never to think about the accomplishment. As soon as the will begins to look right and left for results, the individual begins to become immoral. The energy of the will is slackened; or it is abnormally developed in the direction of an unwholesome and unethical craving, greedy for reward, and even if it accomplishes what is great, it does not do so ethically: the individual demands something else than the ethical itself. A truly great ethical personality would seek to realize his life in the following manner. He would strive to develop himself with the utmost exertion of his powers; in so doing he would perhaps produce great effects in the external world. But this would not seriously engage his attention, for he would know that the external result is not in his power, and hence that it has no significance for him, either *pro* or *contra*. He would therefore *choose* to remain in ignorance of what he had accomplished, in order that his striving might not be retarded by a preoccupation with the external, and lest he fall into the temptation which proceeds from it. For what a logician chiefly fears, namely a fallacy, a μετάβασις εἰς ἄλλο γένος,[3] that the ethicist fears quite as profoundly, namely a conclusion or transition from the ethical to something non-ethical. He would therefore keep himself in ignorance of his accomplishment by a resolution of the will; and even in the hour of death he would will not to know that his life had any other significance than that he had ethically striven to further the development of his own self. If then the power that rules the world should so shape the circumstances that he became a world-historic figure: aye, that would be a question he would first ask jestingly in eternity, for there only is there time for carefree and frivolous questions.

* * *

The task of becoming subjective, then, may be presumed to be the highest task, and one that is proposed to every human being; just as, correspondingly, the highest reward, an eternal happiness, exists only for those who are subjective; or rather, comes into being for the individual who becomes subjective. Furthermore, it is the presumption that the task of becoming subjective furnishes a human being with enough to do to suffice him for his entire life; so that it is not the zealous individual but only the restless one who

---

3. A shift to another kind or genus (Greek, *metabasis eis allo genos*); that is, an error about what category of thing something is.

manages to get through with life before life gets through with him. And such an individual is scarcely justified in speaking lightly of life, but is rather under obligations to understand that he has doubtless not rightly apprehended the task of life; for otherwise it would follow as a matter of course that this task lasts as long as life does, since it is the task of living. And when the individual apprehends it as his highest task to become subjective, under the progressive execution of this task, problems will reveal themselves which again might prove to be as sufficient for the subjective thinker as the objective problems that the objective thinker has before him—this man who goes on and on, never repeating himself, disdaining the repetition which immerses him more and more profoundly in the one thought, but astonishing the age first as systematician, then as philosopher of world-history, then as astronomer, as veterinarian, as water-inspector, as geographer, and so forth.

* * *

* * * All honor to learning! All honor to him who can handle learnedly the learned question of immortality! But the question of immortality is essentially not a learned question, rather it is a question of inwardness, which the subject by becoming subjective must put to himself. Objectively the question cannot be answered, because objectively it cannot be put, since immortality precisely is the potentiation and highest development of the developed subjectivity. Only by really willing to become subjective can the question properly emerge, therefore how could it be answered objectively? The question cannot be answered in social terms, for in social terms it cannot be expressed, inasmuch as only the subject who wills to become subjective can conceive the question and ask rightly, "Do *I* become immortal, or am *I* immortal?" Of course, people can combine for many things; thus several families can combine for a box at the theater, and three single gentlemen can combine for a riding horse, so that each of them rides every third day. But it is not so with immortality; the consciousness of my immortality belongs to me alone, precisely at the moment when I am conscious of my immortality I am absolutely subjective, and I cannot become immortal in partnership with three single gentlemen in turn. People who go about with a paper soliciting the endorsement of numerous men and women, who feel a need in general to become immortal, get no reward for their pains, for immortality is not a possession which can be extorted by a list of endorsements. Systematically, immortality cannot be proved at all. The fault does not lie in the proofs, but in the fact that people will not understand that viewed systematically the whole question is nonsense, so that instead of seeking outward proofs, one had better seek to become a little subjective. Immortality is the most passionate interest of subjectivity; precisely in the interest lies the proof. When for the sake of objectivity (quite consistently from the systematic point of view), one systematically ignores the interest, God only knows in this case what immortality is, or even what is the sense of wishing to prove it, or how one could get into one's head the fixed idea of bothering about it. If one were systematically to hang up immortality on the wall, like Gessler's hat,[4] before which we take off our hats

---

4. In SCHILLER's play *William Tell* (1804), the tyrannical Austrian governor Gessler ordered his Swiss subjects to bow to his hat, raised on a pole in the marketplace.

as we pass by, that would not be equivalent to being immortal or to being conscious of one's immortality. The incredible pains the System takes to prove immortality is labor lost and a ludicrous contradiction—to want to answer systematically a question which possesses the remarkable trait that systematically it cannot be put. This is like wanting to paint Mars[5] in the armor which rendered him invisible. The very point lies in the invisibility; and in the case of immortality, the point lies in the subjectivity and in the subjective development of the subjectivity.

Quite simply therefore the existing subject asks, not about immortality in general, for such a phantom has no existence, but about his immortality, about what it means to become immortal, whether he is able to contribute anything to the accomplishment of this end, or whether he becomes immortal as a matter of course, or whether he is that and can become it. In the first case, he asks what significance it may have, if any, that he has let time pass unutilized, whether there is perhaps a greater and a lesser immortality. In the second case, he asks what significance it may have for the whole of his human existence that the highest thing in life becomes something like a prank, so that the passion of freedom within him is relegated to lower tasks but has nothing to do with the highest, not even negatively, for a negative employment with relation to the highest thing would in a way be the most extenuating— when one wanted to do everything enthusiastically with all one's might, and then to ascertain that the utmost one can do is to maintain a receptive attitude towards that thing which one would more than gladly do everything to earn. The question is raised, how he is to comport himself in talking about his immortality, how he can at one and the same time talk from the standpoint of infinity and of finiteness and think these two together in one single instant, so that he does not say now the one and now the other; how language and all modes of communication are related thereto, when all depends upon being consistent in every word, lest the little heedless supplementary word, the chatty subordinate phrase, might intervene and mock the whole thing; where may be the place, so to speak, for talking about immortality, where such a place exists, since he well knows how many pulpits there are in Copenhagen, and that there are two chairs of philosophy, but where the place is which is the unity of infinitude and finiteness, where he, who is at one and the same time infinite and finite, can talk in one breath of his infinitude and his finiteness, whether it is possible to find a place so dialectically difficult, which nevertheless is so necessary to find. The question is raised, how he, while he exists, can hold fast his consciousness of immortality, lest the metaphysical conception of immortality proceed to confuse the ethical and reduce it to an illusion; for ethically, everything culminates in immortality, without which the ethical is merely use and wont, and metaphysically, immortality swallows up existence, yea, the seventy years[6] of existence, as a thing of naught, and yet ethically this naught must be of infinite importance. The question is raised, how immortality practically transforms his life; in what sense he must have the consciousness of it always present to him, or whether perhaps it is enough to think this thought once for all, whether it is not true that, if the answer is to this effect, the answer shows that the problem has not been

5. Roman god of war.　　　　　　　　6. The life span allotted in the Bible (Psalms 90:10).

stated, inasmuch as to such a consciousness of immortality once for all there would correspond the notion of being a subject as it were in general, whereby the question about immortality is made fantastically ludicrous, just as the converse is ludicrous, when people who have fantastically made a mess of everything and have been every possible sort of thing, one day ask the clergyman with deep concern whether in the beyond they will then really be the same—after never having been able in their lifetime to be the same for a fortnight, and hence have undergone all sorts of transformations. Thus immortality would be indeed an extraordinary metamorphosis if it could transform such an inhuman centipede into an eternal identity with itself, which this "being the same" amounts to. He asks about whether it is now definitely determined that he is immortal, about what this determinateness of immortality is; whether this determinateness, when he lets it pass for something once for all determined (employing his life to attend to his fields, to take to himself a wife, to arrange world-history) is not precisely indeterminateness, so that in spite of all determinateness he has not got any further, because the problem is not even conceived, but since he has not employed his life to become subjective, his subjectivity has become some sort of an indeterminate something in general, and that abstract determinateness has become therefore precisely indeterminateness; whether this determinateness (if he employs his life to become subjective) is not rendered so dialectically difficult, by the constant effort to adapt himself to the alternation which is characteristic of existence, that it becomes indeterminateness; whether, if this is the highest he attains to (namely, that the determinateness becomes indeterminateness), it were not better to give the whole thing up; or whether he is to fix his whole passion upon the indeterminateness, and with infinite passionateness embrace the indeterminateness of the determinate; and whether this might be the only way by which he can attain knowledge of his immortality so long as he is existing, because as exister he is marvelously compounded, so that the determinateness of immortality can only be possessed determinately by the Eternal, but by an exister can be possessed only in indeterminateness.

And the fact of asking about his immortality is at the same time for the existing subject who raises the question a deed—as it is not, to be sure, for absent-minded people who once in a while ask about the matter of being immortal quite in general, as if immortality were something one has once in a while, and the question were some sort of thing in general. So he asks how he is to behave in order to express in existence his immortality, whether he is really expressing it; and for the time being, he is satisfied with this task, which surely must be enough to last a man a lifetime since it is to last for an eternity. And then? Well, then, when he has completed this task, then comes the turn for world-history. In these days, to be sure, it is just the other way round: now people apply themselves first to world-history, and therefore there comes out of this the ludicrous result (as another author[7] has remarked), that while people are proving and proving immortality quite in general, faith in immortality is more and more diminishing.

* * *

7. Kierkegaard himself, writing as Vigilius Haufniensis in *The Concept of Anxiety* (1844).

FROM CHAPTER II. THE SUBJECTIVE TRUTH, INWARDNESS;
TRUTH IS SUBJECTIVITY

* * *

The subjective reflection turns its attention inwardly to the subject, and desires in this intensification of inwardness to realize the truth. And it proceeds in such fashion that, just as in the preceding objective reflection, when the objectivity had come into being, the subjectivity had vanished, so here the subjectivity of the subject becomes the final stage, and objectivity a vanishing factor. Not for a single moment is it forgotten that the subject is an existing individual, and that existence is a process of becoming, and that therefore the notion of the truth as identity of thought and being is a chimera of abstraction, in its truth only an expectation of the creature; not because the truth is not such an identity, but because the knower is an existing individual for whom the truth cannot be such an identity as long as he lives in time. Unless we hold fast to this, speculative philosophy will immediately trans-port us into the fantastic realism of the I-am-I, which modern speculative thought has not hesitated to use without explaining how a particular indi-vidual is related to it; and God knows, no human being is more than such a particular individual.

If an existing individual were really able to transcend himself, the truth would be for him something final and complete; but where is the point at which he is outside himself? The I-am-I is a mathematical point which does not exist, and in so far there is nothing to prevent everyone from occupying this standpoint; the one will not be in the way of the other. It is only momen-tarily that the particular individual is able to realize existentially a unity of the infinite and the finite which transcends existence. This unity is realized in the moment of passion. Modern philosophy has tried anything and everything in the effort to help the individual to transcend himself objectively, which is a wholly impossible feat; existence exercises its restraining influence, and if philosophers nowadays had not become mere scribblers in the service of a fantastic thinking and its preoccupation, they would long ago have perceived that suicide was the only tolerable practical interpretation of its striving. But the scribbling modern philosophy holds passion in contempt; and yet passion is the culmination of existence for an existing individual—and we are all of us existing individuals. In passion the existing subject is rendered infinite in the eternity of the imaginative representation, and yet he is at the same time most definitely himself. The fantastic I-am-I is not an identity of the infinite and the finite, since neither the one nor the other is real; it is a fantastic ren-dezvous in the clouds, an unfruitful embrace, and the relationship of the individual self to this mirage is never indicated.

All essential knowledge relates to existence, or only such knowledge as has an essential relationship to existence is essential knowledge. All knowledge which does not inwardly relate itself to existence, in the reflection of inward-ness, is, essentially viewed, accidental knowledge; its degree and scope is essentially indifferent. That essential knowledge is essentially related to exis-tence does not mean the above-mentioned identity which abstract thought postulates between thought and being; nor does it signify, objectively, that knowledge corresponds to something existent as its object. But it means that knowledge has a relationship to the knower, who is essentially an existing individual, and that for this reason all essential knowledge is essentially related to existence. Only ethical and ethico-religious knowledge has an essential relationship to the existence of the knower.

Mediation is a mirage, like the I-am-I. From the abstract point of view everything is and nothing comes into being. Mediation can therefore have no place in abstract thought, because it presupposes *movement*. Objective knowledge may indeed have the existent for its object; but since the knowing subject is an existing individual, and through the fact of his existence in process of becoming, philosophy must first explain how a particular existing subject is related to a knowledge of mediation. It must explain what he is in such a moment, if not pretty nearly *distrait*; where he is, if not in the moon? There is constant talk of mediation and mediation; is mediation then a man, as Peter Deacon[8] believes that *Imprimatur*[9] is a man? How does a human being manage to become something of this kind? Is this dignity, this great *philosophicum*,[1] the fruit of study, or does the magistrate give it away, like the office of deacon or grave-digger? Try merely to enter into these and other such plain questions of a plain man, who would gladly become mediation if it could be done in some lawful and honest manner, and not either by saying *ein zwei drei kokolorum*,[2] or by forgetting that he is himself an existing human being, for whom existence is therefore something essential, and an ethico-religious existence a suitable *quantum satis*.[3] A speculative philosopher may perhaps find it in bad taste to ask such questions. But it is important not to direct the polemic to the wrong point, and hence not to begin in a fantastic objective manner to discuss *pro* and *contra* whether there is a mediation or not, but to hold fast what it means to be a human being.

In an attempt to make clear the difference of way that exists between an objective and a subjective reflection, I shall now proceed to show how a subjective reflection makes its way inwardly in inwardness. Inwardness in an existing subject culminates in passion; corresponding to passion in the subject the truth becomes a paradox; and the fact that the truth becomes a paradox is rooted precisely in its having a relationship to an existing subject. Thus the one corresponds to the other. By forgetting that one is an existing subject, passion goes by the board and the truth is no longer a paradox; the knowing subject becomes a fantastic entity rather than a human being, and the truth becomes a fantastic object for the knowledge of this fantastic entity.

When the question of truth is raised in an objective manner, reflection is directed objectively to the truth, as an object to which the knower is related. Reflection is not focussed upon the relationship, however, but upon the question of whether it is the truth to which the knower is related. If only the object to which he is related is the truth, the subject is accounted to be in the truth. When the question of the truth is raised subjectively, reflection is directed subjectively to the nature of the individual's relationship; if only the mode of this relationship is in the truth, the individual is in the truth even if he should happen

8. As in Holberg's comedy *Erasmus Montanus* [1731], Act III, Scene 3 [translator's note].
9. Literally, "let it be printed" (Latin): this word, printed in a book, signified that its publication was authorized.
1. A reference to the *examen philosophicum*, an examination in philosophy and the natural sciences required of all first-year university students in Denmark.
2. One, two, three, presto! (German); that is, a magical phrase, such as abracadabra.
3. Sufficient amount (Latin).

to be thus related to what is not true.[4] Let us take as an example the knowledge of God. Objectively, reflection is directed to the problem of whether this object is the true God; subjectively, reflection is directed to the question whether the individual is related to a something *in such a manner* that his relationship is in truth a God-relationship. On which side is the truth now to be found? Ah, may we not here resort to a mediation, and say: It is on neither side, but in the mediation of both? Excellently well said, provided we might have it explained how an existing individual manages to be in a state of mediation. For to be in a state of mediation is to be finished, while to exist is to become. Nor can an existing individual be in two places at the same time— he cannot be an identity of subject and object. When he is nearest to being in two places at the same time he is in passion; but passion is momentary, and passion is also the highest expression of subjectivity.

The existing individual who chooses to pursue the objective way enters upon the entire approximation-process by which it is proposed to bring God to light objectively. But this is in all eternity impossible, because God is a subject, and therefore exists only for subjectivity in inwardness. The existing individual who chooses the subjective way apprehends instantly the entire dialectical difficulty involved in having to use some time, perhaps a long time, in finding God objectively; and he feels this dialectical difficulty in all its painfulness, because every moment is wasted in which he does not have God.[5] That very instant he has God, not by virtue of any objective deliberation, but by virtue of the infinite passion of inwardness. The objective inquirer, on the other hand, is not embarrassed by such dialectical difficulties as are involved in devoting an entire period of investigation to finding God—since it is possible that the inquirer may die tomorrow; and if he lives he can scarcely regard God as something to be taken along if convenient, since God is precisely that which one takes *à tout prix*,[6] which in the understanding of passion constitutes the true inward relationship to God.

It is at this point, so difficult dialectically, that the way swings off for everyone who knows what it means to think, and to think existentially; which is something very different from sitting at a desk and writing about what one has never done, something very different from writing *de omnibus dubitandum*[7] and at the same time being as credulous existentially as the most sensuous of men. Here is where the way swings off, and the change is marked by the fact that while objective knowledge rambles comfortably on by way of the long road of approximation without being impelled by the urge of passion, subjective knowledge counts every delay a deadly peril, and the decision so infinitely important and so instantly pressing that it is as if the opportunity had already passed.

---

4. The reader will observe that the question here is about essential truth, or about the truth which is essentially related to existence, and that it is precisely for the sake of clarifying it as inwardness or as subjectivity that this contrast is drawn [author's note].
5. In this manner God certainly becomes a postulate, but not in the otiose manner in which this word is commonly understood. It becomes clear rather that the only way in which an existing individual comes into relation with God, is when the dialectical contradiction brings his passion to the point of despair, and helps him to embrace God with the "category of despair" (faith). Then the postulate is so far from being arbitrary that it is precisely a life-necessity. It is then not so much that God is a postulate, as that the existing individual's postulation of God is a necessity [author's note].
6. At any price (French).
7. Everything must be doubted (Latin).

Now when the problem is to reckon up on which side there is most truth, whether on the side of one who seeks the true God objectively, and pursues the approximate truth of the God-idea; or on the side of one who, driven by the infinite passion of his need of God, feels an infinite concern for his own relationship to God in truth (and to be at one and the same time on both sides equally, is as we have noted not possible for an existing individual, but is merely the happy delusion of an imaginary I-am-I): the answer cannot be in doubt for anyone who has not been demoralized with the aid of science. If one who lives in the midst of Christendom goes up to the house of God, the house of the true God, with the true conception of God in his knowledge, and prays, but prays in a false spirit; and one who lives in an idolatrous community prays with the entire passion of the infinite, although his eyes rest upon the image of an idol: where is there most truth? The one prays in truth to God though he worships an idol; the other prays falsely to the true God, and hence worships in fact an idol.

When one man investigates objectively the problem of immortality, and another embraces an uncertainty with the passion of the infinite: where is there most truth, and who has the greater certainty? The one has entered upon a never-ending approximation, for the certainty of immortality lies precisely in the subjectivity of the individual; the other is immortal, and fights for his immortality by struggling with the uncertainty. Let us consider Socrates.[8] Nowadays everyone dabbles in a few proofs; some have several such proofs, others fewer. But Socrates! He puts the question objectively in a problematic manner: *if* there is an immortality. He must therefore be accounted a doubter in comparison with one of our modern thinkers with the three proofs? By no means. On this "if" he risks his entire life, he has the courage to meet death, and he has with the passion of the infinite so determined the pattern of his life that it must be found acceptable—*if* there is an immortality. Is any better proof capable of being given for the immortality of the soul? But those who have the three proofs do not at all determine their lives in conformity therewith; if there is an immortality it must feel disgust over their manner of life: can any better refutation be given of the three proofs? The bit of uncertainty that Socrates had, helped him because he himself contributed the passion of the infinite; the three proofs that the others have do not profit them at all, because they are dead to spirit and enthusiasm, and their three proofs, in lieu of proving anything else, prove just this. A young girl may enjoy all the sweetness of love on the basis of what is merely a weak hope that she is beloved, because she rests everything on this weak hope; but many a wedded matron more than once subjected to the strongest expressions of love, has in so far indeed had proofs, but strangely enough has not enjoyed *quod erat demonstrandum*.[9] The Socratic ignorance,[1] which Socrates held fast with the entire passion of his inwardness, was thus an expression for the principle that the eternal truth is related to an existing individual, and that this truth must

---

8. As recorded in the dialogues of Plato, the Greek philosopher Socrates (469–399 B.C.E.) presented himself as a profoundly ignorant inquirer, asking questions of his interlocutors and seeking answers, which he would then show to be unsatisfactory, in the service of greater wisdom and understanding. Accused of impiety and corrupting the young, he refused to renounce this activity and was sentenced to death by poison.
9. That which was to be proven (Latin).
1. That is, knowing that one does not know. On Socratic ignorance, see Plato's *Apology* (ca. 395 B.C.E.), 21–23.

therefore be a paradox for him as long as he exists; and yet it is possible that there was more truth in the Socratic ignorance as it was in him, than in the entire objective truth of the System, which flirts with what the times demand and accommodates itself to *Privatdocents*.[2]

The objective accent falls on WHAT is said, the subjective accent on HOW it is said. This distinction holds even in the aesthetic realm, and receives definite expression in the principle that what is in itself true may in the mouth of such and such a person become untrue. In these times this distinction is particularly worthy of notice, for if we wish to express in a single sentence the difference between ancient times and our own, we should doubtless have to say: "In ancient times only an individual here and there knew the truth; now all know it, except that the inwardness of its appropriation stands in an inverse relationship to the extent of its dissemination." Aesthetically the contradiction that truth becomes untruth in this or that person's mouth, is best construed comically: In the ethico-religious sphere, accent is again on the "how." But this is not to be understood as referring to demeanor, expression, or the like; rather it refers to the relationship sustained by the existing individual, in his own existence, to the content of his utterance. Objectively the interest is focussed merely on the thought-content, subjectively on the inwardness. At its maximum this inward "how" is the passion of the infinite, and the passion of the infinite is the truth. But the passion of the infinite is precisely subjectivity, and thus subjectivity becomes the truth. Objectively there is no infinite decisiveness, and hence it is objectively in order to annul the difference between good and evil, together with the principle of contradiction, and therewith also the infinite difference between the true and the false. Only in subjectivity is there decisiveness, to seek objectivity is to be in error. It is the passion of the infinite that is the decisive factor and not its content, for its content is precisely itself. In this manner subjectivity and the subjective "how" constitute the truth.

But the "how" which is thus subjectively accentuated precisely because the subject is an existing individual, is also subject to a dialectic with respect to time. In the passionate moment of decision, where the road swings away from objective knowledge, it seems as if the infinite decision were thereby realized. But in the same moment the existing individual finds himself in the temporal order, and the subjective "how" is transformed into a striving, a striving which receives indeed its impulse and a repeated renewal from the decisive passion of the infinite, but is nevertheless a striving.

When subjectivity is the truth, the conceptual determination of the truth must include an expression for the antithesis to objectivity, a memento of the fork in the road where the way swings off; this expression will at the same time serve as an indication of the tension of the subjective inwardness. Here is such a definition of truth: *An objective uncertainty held fast in an appropriation-process of the most passionate inwardness is the truth*, the highest truth attainable for an *existing* individual. At the point where the way swings off (and where this is cannot be specified objectively, since it is a matter of subjectivity), there objective knowledge is placed in abeyance. Thus the

2. Unsalaried university lecturers (the lowest rank of instructors in 19th-century central European universities).

subject merely has, objectively, the uncertainty; but it is this which precisely increases the tension of that infinite passion which constitutes his inwardness. The truth is precisely the venture which chooses an objective uncertainty with the passion of the infinite. I contemplate the order of nature in the hope of finding God, and I see omnipotence and wisdom; but I also see much else that disturbs my mind and excites anxiety. The sum of all this is an objective uncertainty. But it is for this very reason that the inwardness becomes as intense as it is, for it embraces this objective uncertainty with the entire passion of the infinite. In the case of a mathematical proposition the objectivity is given, but for this reason the truth of such a proposition is also an indifferent truth.

But the above definition of truth is an equivalent expression for faith. Without risk there is no faith. Faith is precisely the contradiction between the infinite passion of the individual's inwardness and the objective uncertainty. If I am capable of grasping God objectively, I do not believe, but precisely because I cannot do this I must believe. If I wish to preserve myself in faith I must constantly be intent upon holding fast the objective uncertainty, so as to remain out upon the deep, over seventy thousand fathoms of water, still preserving my faith.

* * *

Subjectivity is the truth. By virtue of the relationship subsisting between the eternal truth and the existing individual, the paradox came into being. Let us now go further, let us suppose that the eternal essential truth is itself a paradox. How does the paradox come into being? By putting the eternal essential truth into juxtaposition with existence. Hence when we posit such a conjunction within the truth itself, the truth becomes a paradox. The eternal truth has come into being in time: this is the paradox. If in accordance with the determinations just posited, the subject is prevented by sin from taking himself back into the eternal, now he need not trouble himself about this; for now the eternal essential truth is not behind him but in front of him, through its being in existence or having existed, so that if the individual does not existentially and in existence lay hold of the truth, he will never lay hold of it.

Existence can never be more sharply accentuated than by means of these determinations. The evasion by which speculative philosophy attempts to recollect itself out of existence has been made impossible. With reference to this, there is nothing for speculation to do except to arrive at an understanding of this impossibility; every speculative attempt which insists on being speculative shows *eo ipso*[3] that it has not understood it. The individual may thrust all this away from him, and take refuge in speculation; but it is impossible first to accept it, and then to revoke it by means of speculation, since it is definitely calculated to prevent speculation.

When the eternal truth is related to an existing individual it becomes a paradox. The paradox repels in the inwardness of the existing individual, through the objective uncertainty and the corresponding Socratic ignorance. But since the paradox is not in the first instance itself paradoxical (but only in its relationship to the existing individual), it does not repel with a sufficient intensive

---

3. By that [fact] itself (Latin).

inwardness. For without risk there is no faith, and the greater the risk the greater the faith; the more objective security the less inwardness (for inwardness is precisely subjectivity), and the less objective security the more profound the possible inwardness. When the paradox is paradoxical in itself, it repels the individual by virtue of its absurdity, and the corresponding passion of inwardness is faith. But subjectivity, inwardness, is the truth; for otherwise we have forgotten what the merit of the Socratic position is. But there can be no stronger expression for inwardness than when the retreat out of existence into the eternal by way of recollection is impossible; and when, with truth confronting the individual as a paradox, gripped in the anguish and pain of sin, facing the tremendous risk of the objective insecurity, the individual believes. But without risk no faith, not even the Socratic form of faith, much less the form of which we here speak.

When Socrates believed that there was a God, he held fast to the objective uncertainty with the whole passion of his inwardness, and it is precisely in this contradiction and in this risk, that faith is rooted. Now it is otherwise. Instead of the objective uncertainty, there is here a certainty, namely, that objectively it is absurd; and this absurdity, held fast in the passion of inwardness, is faith. The Socratic ignorance is as a witty jest in comparison with the earnestness of facing the absurd; and the Socratic existential inwardness is as Greek light-mindedness in comparison with the grave strenuosity of faith.

What now is the absurd? The absurd is—that the eternal truth has come into being in time, that God has come into being, has been born, has grown up, and so forth, precisely like any other individual human being, quite indistinguishable from other individuals. For every assumption of immediate recognizability is pre-Socratic paganism, and from the Jewish point of view, idolatry; and every determination of what really makes an advance beyond the Socratic must essentially bear the stamp of having a relationship to God's having come into being; for faith *sensu strictissimo*,[4] as was developed in the *Fragments*, refers to becoming. When Socrates believed that there was a God, he saw very well that where the way swings off there is also an objective way of approximation, for example by the contemplation of nature and human history, and so forth. His merit was precisely to shun this way, where the quantitative siren song enchants the mind and deceives the existing individual.

In relation to the absurd, the objective approximation-process is like the comedy, *Misunderstanding upon Misunderstanding*,[5] which is generally played by *Privatdocents* and speculative philosophers. The absurd is precisely by its objective repulsion the measure of the intensity of faith in inwardness. Suppose a man who wishes to acquire faith; let the comedy begin. He wishes to have faith, but he wishes also to safeguard himself by means of an objective inquiry and its approximation-process. What happens? With the help of the approximation-process the absurd becomes something different; it becomes probable, it becomes increasingly probable, it becomes extremely and emphatically probable. Now he is ready to believe it, and he ventures to claim for himself that he does not believe as shoemakers and tailors and simple folk believe, but only after long deliberation. Now he is ready to believe it; and lo,

---

4. In the strictest sense (Latin).
5. A one-act Danish comedy (1828) by Thomas Overskou.

now it has become precisely impossible to believe it. Anything that is almost probable, or probable, or extremely and emphatically probable, is something he can almost know, or as good as know, or extremely and emphatically almost *know*—but it is impossible to *believe*. For the absurd is the object of faith, and the only object that can be believed.

* * *

Let us now proceed to show by a few examples how speculative philosophy, precisely because it refuses to understand that subjectivity is truth, has maltreated Christianity, which is once for all the paradox, and paradoxical at every point. Speculative philosophy remains in the sphere of the immanent, where recollection takes itself out of existence, and at every point in the Christian thought-structure brings about an emasculation, simply by not thinking anything decisive in connection with the most decisive categories, which precisely by means of their decisiveness are calculated to prevent the individual from taking refuge in the immanent. It uses the decisive expressions merely as phraseology, and thus becomes a pagan reminiscence against which there is nothing to object to if it straightforwardly breaks with Christianity, but much to object to if it assumes to be Christianity.

That God has existed in human form, has been born, grown up, and so forth, is surely the paradox *sensu strictissimo,* the absolute paradox. As such it cannot relate itself to a relative difference between men. A relative paradox relates itself to the relative difference between more or less cleverness and brains; but the absolute paradox, just because it is absolute, can be relevant only to the absolute difference that distinguishes man from God, and has nothing to do with the relative wrangling between man and man with respect to the fact that one man has a little more brains than another. But the absolute difference between God and man consists precisely in this, that man is a particular existing being (which is just as much true of the most gifted human being as it is of the most stupid), whose essential task cannot be to think *sub specie aeterni,* since as long as he exists he is, though eternal, essentially an existing individual, whose essential task it is to concentrate upon inwardness in existing; while God is infinite and eternal. As soon as I make the understanding of the paradox commensurable for the difference between more or less of intellectual talent (a difference which cannot take us beyond being human, unless a man were to become so gifted that he was not merely a man but also God), my words show *eo ipso* that what I have understood is not the absolute paradox but a relative one, for in connection with the absolute paradox the only understanding possible is that it cannot be understood. "But if such is the case, speculative philosophy cannot get hold of it at all." "Quite right, this is precisely what the paradox says; it merely thrusts the understanding away in the interests of inwardness in existing." This may possibly have its ground in the circumstance that there is objectively no truth for existing beings, but only approximations; while subjectively the truth exists for them in inwardness, because the decisiveness of the truth is rooted in the subjectivity of the individual.

The modern mythical allegorizing tendency declares out and out that the whole of Christianity is a myth. This at least is open and above-board, and everyone can readily make up his mind about it for himself. But the friendship of speculative philosophy is of a different character. For safety's sake, speculative philosophy declares its opposition to the ungodly mythical-allegorizing tendency, and then continues: "Speculative philosophy accepts, on the contrary, the paradox, but does not stand still at this position." "Nor is there any need of standing still, for when a man persists in holding the paradox fast as a believer, more and more profoundly exploring existentially the inwardness of faith, he does not stand still." Speculative philosophy does not remain standing at the standpoint of the paradox—what does this mean? Does it mean that speculative philosophers cease to be human beings, particular existing human beings, and become *en famille*[6] I know not what? Otherwise there is no escape from remaining at the standpoint of the paradox, which is grounded in and expresses the fact that the eternal essential truth is related to existing individuals, bringing home to them the requirement of advancing further into the inwardness of faith.

* * *

There has been said much that is strange, much that is deplorable, much that is revolting about Christianity; but the most stupid thing ever said about it is, that it is to a certain degree true. There has been said much that is strange, much that is deplorable, much that is revolting about enthusiasm; but the most stupid thing ever said about it is, that it is to a certain degree. There has been said much that is strange, much that is deplorable, much that is revolting about love, but the most stupid thing ever said about it is, that it is to a certain degree. And when a man has prostituted himself by speaking in this manner about enthusiasm and love, he has betrayed his stupidity, which in this case is not in the direction of intelligence, however, since it has its ground rather in the fact that the understanding has become too large, in the same sense as when a disease of the liver is caused by an enlargement of the liver, and hence, as another author[7] has remarked, "is the flatness that salt takes on when it loses its savor": then there is still one phenomenon left, Christianity. If the sight of enthusiasm has not sufficed to help him break with the understanding, if love has not been able to emancipate him from his slavery: then let him consider Christianity. Let him be offended, he is still human; let him despair of ever himself becoming a Christian, he is yet perhaps nearer than he believes; let him fight to the last drop of blood for the extermination of Christianity, he is still human—but if he is able here to say: it is true to a certain degree, then he is stupid.

Perhaps someone will think that I tremble to say this, that I must be prepared for a terrible castigation at the hands of speculative philosophy. By no means. The speculative philosopher will here again be quite consistent with himself, and say: "There is a certain degree of truth in what the man says, only we cannot stop there, but must advance beyond it." It would also be strange if my insignificance should succeed where even Christianity had failed, namely, in bringing the speculative philosopher to the point of passion; if so, then my little fragment of philosophy would suddenly take on a significance I had least of all dreamed of.

---

6. In the family (French); that is, "among themselves," "informally."

7. Kierkegaard himself, writing as Vigilius Haufniensis in *The Concept of Anxiety*.

But whoever is neither cold nor hot is nauseating; and just as the hunter is ill-served by a weapon that misses fire at the crucial moment, so God is ill-served by misfiring individuals. Had not Pilate asked objectively what truth is,[8] he would never have condemned Christ to be crucified. Had he asked subjectively, the passion of his inwardness respecting what in the decision facing him he had *in truth to do*, would have prevented him from doing wrong. It would then not have been merely his wife who was made anxious by the dreadful dream, but Pilate himself would have become sleepless. But when a man has something so infinitely great before his eyes as the objective truth, he can afford to set at naught his little bit of subjectivity, and what he as subject has to do. And the approximation-process of the objective truth is figuratively expressed in washing the hands, for objectively there is no decision, and the subjective decision shows that one was in error nevertheless, through not understanding that the decision inheres precisely in subjectivity.

Suppose, on the other hand, that subjectivity is the truth, and that subjectivity is an existing subjectivity, then, if I may so express myself, Christianity fits perfectly into the picture. Subjectivity culminates in passion, Christianity is the paradox, paradox and passion are a mutual fit, and the paradox is altogether suited to one whose situation is, to be in the extremity of existence. Aye, never in all the world could there be found two lovers so wholly suited to one another as paradox and passion, and the strife between them is like the strife between lovers, when the dispute is about whether he first aroused her passion, or she his. And so it is here; the existing individual has by means of the paradox itself come to be placed in the extremity of existence. And what can be more splendid for lovers than that they are permitted a long time together without any alteration in the relationship between them, except that it becomes more intensive in inwardness? And this is indeed granted to the highly unspeculative understanding between passion and the paradox, since the whole of life in time is vouchsafed, and the change comes first in eternity.

* * *

Faith has in fact two tasks: to take care in every moment to discover the improbable, the paradox; and then to hold it fast with the passion of inwardness. The common conception is that the improbable, the paradoxical, is something to which faith is related only passively; it must provisionally be content with this relationship, but little by little things will become better, as indeed seems probable. O miraculous creation of confusions in speaking about faith! One is to begin believing, in reliance upon the probability that things will soon become better. In this way probability is after all smuggled in, and one is prevented from believing; so that it is easy to understand that the fruit of having been for a long time a believer is, that one no longer believes, instead of, as one might think, that the fruit is a more intensive inwardness in faith. No, faith is self-active in its relation to the improbable and the paradoxical, self-active in the discovery, and self-active in every moment holding it fast—in order to believe. Merely to lay hold of the improbable requires all the passion of the infinite and its concentration in itself; for the improbable

---

8. John 18:38. For the dream of Pilate's wife and for his hand washing, mentioned later in this paragraph, see Matthew 27:19, 24.

and the paradoxical are not to be reached by the understanding's quantitative calculation of the more and more difficult. Where the understanding despairs, faith is already present in order to make the despair properly decisive, in order that the movement of faith may not become a mere exchange within the bargaining sphere of the understanding. But to believe against the understanding is martyrdom; to begin to get the understanding a little in one's favor, is temptation and retrogression. This martyrdom is something that the speculative philosopher is free from. That he must pursue his studies, and especially that he must read many modern books, I admit is burdensome; but the martyrdom of faith is not the same thing. What I therefore fear and shrink from, more than I fear to die and to lose my sweetheart, is to say about Christianity that it is to a certain degree true. If I lived to be seventy years old, if I shortened the night's sleep and increased the day's work from year to year, inquiring into Christianity—how insignificant such a little period of study, viewed as entitling me to judge in so lofty a fashion about Christianity! For to be so embittered against Christianity after a casual acquaintance with it, that I declared it to be false: that would be far more pardonable, far more human. But this lordly superiority seems to me the true corruption, making every saving relationship impossible—and it may possibly be the case, that Christianity is the truth.

This sounds almost as if I were in earnest. If I now dared loudly to proclaim that I had come into the world for the purpose of opposing speculative philosophy, and had received a call to that effect; that this was my mission of judgment, while my prophetic mission was to divine the coming of a matchless future, for which reason men might safely rely on what I said because I had a loud voice and had received a call—then doubtless there would be many who, in lieu of considering the whole to be a fantastic reminiscence in the head of a fool, would regard it as earnest. But I can say nothing of this kind about myself. The resolve with which I began must rather be regarded as a notion that occurred to me.

* * *

My principal thought was that in our age, because of the great increase of knowledge, we had forgotten what it means to *exist*, and what *inwardness* signifies, and that the misunderstanding between speculative philosophy and Christianity was explicable on that ground. I now resolved to go back as far as possible, in order not to reach the religious mode of existence too soon, to say nothing of the specifically Christian mode of religious existence, in order not to leave difficulties unexplored behind me. If men had forgotten what it means to exist religiously, they had doubtless also forgotten what it means to exist as human beings; this must therefore be set forth. But above all it must not be done in a dogmatizing manner, for then the misunderstanding would instantly take the explanatory effort to itself in a new misunderstanding, as if existing consisted in getting to know something about this or that. If communicated in the form of knowledge, the recipient is led to adopt the misunderstanding that it is knowledge he is to receive, and then we are again in the sphere of knowledge. Only one who has some conception of the enduring capacity of a misunderstanding to assimilate even the most strenuous effort of explanation and still remain the same misunderstanding, will be able to appreciate the difficulties of an authorship where every word must be watched, and every sentence pass through the process of a double reflection.

* * *

FROM CHAPTER III. REAL OR ETHICAL SUBJECTIVITY— THE SUBJECTIVE THINKER

* * *

* * * Existing is ordinarily regarded as no very complex matter, much less an art, since we all exist; but abstract thinking takes rank as an accomplishment. But really to exist, so as to interpenetrate one's existence with consciousness, at one and the same time eternal and as if far removed from existence, and yet also present in existence and in the process of becoming: that is truly difficult. If philosophical reflection had not in our time become something queer, highly artificial, and capable of being learned by rote, thinkers would make quite a different impression upon people, as was the case in Greece, where a thinker was an existing individual stimulated by his reflection to a passionate enthusiasm; and as was also once the case in Christendom, when a thinker was a believer who strove enthusiastically to understand himself in the existence of faith.

* * *

* * * Now while pure thought either abrogates motion altogether, or meaninglessly imports it into logic, the difficulty facing an existing individual is how to give his existence the continuity without which everything simply vanishes. An abstract continuity is no continuity, and the very existence of the existing individual is sufficient to prevent his continuity from having essential stability; while passion gives him a momentary continuity, a continuity which at one and the same time is a restraining influence and a moving impulse. The goal of movement for an existing individual is to arrive at a decision, and to renew it. The eternal is the factor of continuity; but an abstract eternity is extraneous to the movement of life, and a concrete eternity within the existing individual is the maximum degree of his passion.

* * *

* * * In pure thought we are over our ears in profundity, and yet there is something rather absent-minded about it all, because the pure thinker is not clear about what it means to be a human being.

All knowledge about reality is possibility. The only reality to which an existing individual may have a relation that is more than cognitive, is his own reality, the fact that he exists; this reality constitutes his absolute interest. Abstract thought requires him to become disinterested in order to acquire knowledge; the ethical demand is that he become infinitely interested in existing.[9]

9. This is a different type of "ethical demand" and "ethics" than that discussed in *Fear and Trembling* (1843; see above), which is modeled on Hegelian "ethicality" (*Sittlichkeit*). Its focus is on "existing"— more specifically, on *genuine* (authentic) "existing"—and thus (for Kierkegaard) on "subjectivity" and its development and intensification.

The only reality that exists for an existing individual is his own ethical reality. To every other reality he stands in a cognitive relation; but true knowledge consists in translating the real into the possible.

The apparent trustworthiness of sense is an illusion. This was shown adequately as early as in Greek scepticism, and modern idealism has likewise demonstrated it. The trustworthiness claimed by a knowledge of the historical is also a deception, in so far as it assumes to be the very trustworthiness of reality; for the knower cannot know an historical reality until he has resolved it into a possibility. (On this point, more in what follows.) Abstract thought embraces the possible, either the preceding or the subsequent possibility; pure thought is a phantom.

The real subject is not the cognitive subject, since in knowing he moves in the sphere of the possible; the real subject is the ethically existing subject.

* * *

It is a misunderstanding to be concerned about reality from the aesthetic or intellectual point of view. And to be concerned ethically about another's reality is also a misunderstanding, since the only question of reality that is ethically pertinent, is the question of one's own reality. Here we may clearly note the difference that exists between faith *sensu strictissimo* on the one hand (referring as it does to the historical, and the realms of the aesthetic, the intellectual) and the ethical on the other. To ask with infinite interest about a reality which is not one's own, is faith, and this constitutes a paradoxical relationship to the paradoxical. Aesthetically it is impossible to raise such a question except in thoughtlessness, since possibility is aesthetically higher than reality. Nor is it possible to raise such a question ethically, since the sole ethical interest is the interest in one's own reality. The analogy between faith and the ethical is found in the infinite interest, which suffices to distinguish the believer absolutely from an aesthetician or a thinker. But the believer differs from the ethicist in being infinitely interested in the reality of another (in the fact, for example, that God has existed in time).

* * *

When the different spheres are not decisively distinguished from one another, confusion reigns everywhere. When people are curious about a thinker's reality and find it interesting to know something about it, and so forth, this interest is intellectually reprehensible. The maximum of attainment in the sphere of the intellectual is to become altogether indifferent to the thinker's reality. But by being thus muddle-headed in the intellectual sphere, one acquires a certain resemblance to a believer. A believer is one who is infinitely interested in another's reality. This is a decisive criterion for faith, and the interest in question is not just a little curiosity, but an absolute dependence upon faith's object.

The object of faith is the reality of another, and the relationship is one of infinite interest. The object of faith is not a doctrine, for then the relationship would be intellectual, and it would be of importance not to botch it, but to realize the maximum intellectual relationship. The object of faith is not a teacher with a doctrine; for when a teacher has a doctrine, the doctrine is *eo ipso* more important than the teacher, and the relationship is again intellectual, and it again becomes important not to botch it, but to realize the maximum intellectual relationship. The object of faith is the reality of the teacher, that the teacher really exists. The answer of faith is therefore unconditionally yes or no. For it does not concern a doctrine, as to whether the doctrine is true or not; it is the answer to a question concerning a fact: "Do you or do you not suppose that he has really existed?" And the answer, it must be noted, is with infinite passion. In the case of a human being, it is thoughtlessness to lay so great and infinite a stress on the question whether he has existed or not. If the object of faith is a human being, therefore, the whole proposal is the vagary of a stupid person, who has not even understood the spirit of the intellectual and the aesthetic. The object of faith is hence the reality of the God-man in the sense of his existence. But existence involves first and foremost particularity, and this is why thought must abstract from existence, because the particular cannot be thought, but only the universal. The object of faith is thus God's reality in existence as a particular individual, the fact that God has existed as an individual human being.

Christianity is no doctrine concerning the unity of the divine and the human, or concerning the identity of subject and object; nor is it any other of the logical transcriptions of Christianity. If Christianity were a doctrine, the relationship to it would not be one of faith, for only an intellectual type of relationship can correspond to a doctrine. Christianity is therefore not a doctrine, but the fact that God has existed.

The realm of faith is thus not a class for numskulls in the sphere of the intellectual, or an asylum for the feeble-minded. Faith constitutes a sphere all by itself, and every misunderstanding of Christianity may at once be recognized by its transforming it into a doctrine, transferring it to the sphere of the intellectual. The maximum of attainment within the sphere of the intellectual, namely, to realize an entire indifference as to the reality of the teacher, is in the sphere of faith at the opposite end of the scale. The maximum of attainment within the sphere of faith is to become infinitely interested in the reality of the teacher.

* * *

All existential problems are passionate problems, for when existence is interpenetrated with reflection it generates passion. To think about existential problems in such a way as to leave out the passion, is tantamount to not thinking about them at all, since it is to forget the point, which is that the thinker is himself an existing individual. But the subjective thinker is not a poet, though he may also be a poet; he is not an ethicist, though he may also be an ethicist; he is not a dialectician, though he may also be a dialectician. He is essentially an existing individual, while the existence of the poet is nonessential in relation to the poem, the existence of the ethicist, in relation to his doctrine, the existence of the dialectician, in relation to his thought. The subjective thinker is not a man of science, but an artist. Existing is an art. The subjective thinker is aesthetic enough to give his life aesthetic content, ethical enough to regulate it, and dialectical enough to interpenetrate it with thought.

The subjective thinker has the task of understanding himself in his existence. Abstract thought is wont to speak of contradiction, and of its immanent propulsive power, although by abstracting from existence and from existing it removes the difficulty and the contradiction. The subjective thinker is an existing individual and a thinker at one and the same time; he does not abstract from the contradiction and from existence, but lives in it while at the same time thinking. In all his thinking he therefore has to think the fact that he is an existing individual. For this reason he always has enough to think about. Humanity in the abstract is a subject soon disposed of, and likewise world-history; even such tremendous portions as China, Persia, and so forth, are as nothing to the hungry monster of the historical process. The abstract concept of faith is soon disposed of; but the subjective thinker who in all his thinking remains at home in his existence, will find an inexhaustible subject for thought in his faith, when he seeks to follow its declension in all the manifold *casibus*[1] of life. Such subjective reflection is by no means a light matter; for existence is the most difficult of all subjects to penetrate when the thinker has to remain in it, because the moment is commensurable for the highest decision, and yet again a vanishing instant in the possible seventy years of a human life.

* * *

Every human being must be assumed in essential possession of what essentially belongs to being a man. The task of the subjective thinker is to transform himself into an instrument that clearly and definitely expresses in existence whatever is essentially human.[2] To rely on a differential trait in this connection is a misunderstanding, for to have a little more brain and the like is insignificant. That our age has forsaken the individuals in order to take refuge in the collective idea, has its natural explanation in an aesthetic despair which has not yet found the ethical. Men have perceived that it avails nothing to be ever so distinguished an individual man, since no difference avails anything. A new difference has consequently been hit upon: the difference of being born in the nineteenth century. Everyone tries to determine his bit of existence in relation to the age as quickly as possible and so consoles himself. But it avails nothing, being only a higher and more glittering illusion. And just as there have lived fools in ancient times, as well as in every generation, who have confounded themselves, in the vanity of their delusion, with one or another distinguished man, pretending to be this or that individual, so the peculiarity of our age is that the fools are not even content to confuse themselves with some great man, but identify themselves with the age, with the century, with the contemporary generation, with humanity at large. To wish to live as a particular human being (which is what everyone undoubtedly is), relying upon a difference, is the weakness of cowardice; to will to live as a particular human being (which everyone undoubtedly is) in the same sense as is open to every other human being, is the ethical victory over life and all its illusions. And this victory is perhaps the hardest of all to win in the theocentric nineteenth century.

* * * The subjective thinker has only a single scene, existence, and he has nothing to do with beautiful valleys and the like. His scene is not the fairyland of the imagination, where the poet's love evokes the perfect; nor is the scene in England, and the task to make sure of local color and historical

1. (Grammatical) cases (Latin), which make up the "declension" of Latin nouns and adjectives.
2. This thought animates much of the interpretive tradition (with varying characterizations of the human subject).

450 / SØREN KIERKEGAARD

exactness. His scene is—inwardness in existing as a human being; concreteness is attained through bringing the existential categories into relationship with one another. In comparison with the existential categories, historical actuality and accuracy constitute breadth.

But existential reality is incommunicable, and the subjective thinker finds his reality in his own ethical existence. When reality is apprehended by an outsider it can be understood only as possibility. Everyone who makes a communication, in so far as he becomes conscious of this fact, will therefore be careful to give his existential communication the form of a possibility, precisely in order that it may have a relationship to existence. A communication in the form of a possibility compels the recipient to face the problem of existing in it, so far as this is possible between man and man.

* * *

FROM CHAPTER IV. THE PROBLEM OF THE FRAGMENTS: HOW CAN AN ETERNAL HAPPINESS BE BASED UPON HISTORICAL KNOWLEDGE?

* * *

* * * The existing individual who has once received the absolute direction toward the absolute telos,[3] and understands it as his task to exercise himself in this relationship, is perhaps an alderman, perhaps like any one of the other aldermen; and yet he is not like them, though when you look at him he seems wholly like them. He may possibly gain the whole world, but he is not as one who desires it. He may be a king; but every time he holds his scepter in his outstretched hand, resignation looks first to see whether he expresses existentially the absolute respect for the absolute telos—and the glory of his crown fades, although he wears it royally. It fades as it once faded in the great moment of resignation, though he now wears it in the third decade of his reign; it fades as it will some time fade in the hour of death, before the eyes of the witnesses standing by, and for his own failing sight. But thus it fades for him also in the hour of the fullness of his power. What then became of mediation? And yet there was no one who entered a cloister.

The individual does not cease to be a human being, nor does he divest himself of the manifold composite garment of the finite in order to clothe himself in the abstract garment of the cloister. But he does not mediate between the absolute telos and finite ends. In his immediacy the individual is rooted in the finite. But when resignation has convinced itself that he has acquired the absolute direction toward the absolute telos, all is changed, and the roots have been severed. He still lives in the finite, but he does not have his life in the finite. His life has, like that of other human beings, the various predicates of a human existence, but he is in them as one who is clothed in the borrowed garments of a stranger. He is a stranger in the world of the finite, but does not manifest his heterogeneity, his separation from worldliness, by a foreign mode of dress. This would be a contradiction, since he would thereby qualify himself in a worldly manner. He is incognito, but his incognito consists in having an appearance entirely like others. Just as the

---

3. Ultimate end or purpose.

dentist has loosened the soft tissues about a tooth and cut the nerve, so the roots of his life in the finite have been severed. It is not his task to give the tooth an opportunity to grow fast again, which would be mediation. In the great moment of resignation he had no thought of mediation, but committed himself by a choice, and it is now similarly his task to acquire the requisite facility in the renewal of this choice, and in giving it existential expression. The individual does indeed remain in the finite, where he confronts the difficulty of maintaining himself in the absolute choice while still living in the finite; but just as he deprived the finite of its unchecked vitality in the moment of resignation, so it remains his task to reinstate repeatedly the determination by which this was first accomplished. Let the world give him everything, it is possible that he will see fit to accept it. But he says: "Oh, well," and this "Oh, well" means the absolute respect for the absolute *telos*. If the world takes everything from him, he suffers no doubt; but he says again: "Oh, well"—and this "Oh, well" means the absolute respect for the absolute *telos*. Men do not exist in this fashion when they live immediately in the finite.

* * *

* * * It is always madness to venture, but to risk everything for the expectation of an eternal happiness is the height of madness. To ask for certainty is on the other hand prudence, for it is an excuse to evade the venture and its strenuosity, and to transfer the problem into the realm of knowledge and of prattle. No, if I am in truth resolved to venture, in truth resolved to strive for the attainment of the highest good, the uncertainty must be there, and I must have room to move, so to speak. But the largest space I can obtain, where there is room for the most vehement gesture of the passion that embraces the infinite, is uncertainty of knowledge with respect to an eternal happiness, or the certain knowledge that the choice is in the finite sense a piece of madness: now there is room, now you can venture!

And this is why an eternal happiness as the absolute good has the remarkable trait of *being definable solely in terms of the mode of acquisition*. Other goods, precisely because the mode of acquisition is accidental, or at any rate subject to a relative dialectic, must be defined in terms of the good itself. Money, for example, may be acquired both with and without effort on the part of the possessor, and both modes of acquisition are again subject to manifold variations; but money, nevertheless, remains the same good. And knowledge is also variously obtainable, in relation to talent and external circumstances, and cannot therefore be defined solely in terms of the mode of acquisition. But there is nothing to be said of an eternal happiness except that it is the good which is attained by venturing everything absolutely. Every description of the glory of this good is already as it were an attempt to make several different modes of acquisition possible, one easier for example, and one more difficult. This is enough to prove that the description does not really describe the absolute good, but only imagines itself doing so, while essentially dealing with relative goods. Hence it is so easy, in a certain sense, to talk about this good; for it is certain—when everything else is made uncertain, and because the speaker will never, as is so often the case with relative goods, be embarrassed by the revelation that what helps one to gain it will not help another.

This is why discourse concerning this good may be so brief, for there is only one thing to say: venture everything!

* * *

SOURCE: From *Kierkegaard's Concluding Unscientific Postscript*, trans. David F. Swenson and Walter Lowrie (Princeton: Princeton University Press, for American Scandinavian Foundation; [n.p.]: Oxford University Press, 1941), pp. 23, 51–54, 70–72, 75, 107–10, 115–19, 119–21, 146, 154–58, 175–82, 187–89, 194–96, 205–6, 209–10, 223, 273, 277, 280–81, 287–88, 290–91, 313–14, 318–20, 366–68, 381–82. Originally published as *Afsluttende uvidenskabelig efterskrift* (1846), nominally by "Johannes Climacus." This lengthy work (by far Kierkegaard's longest) is supposedly a mere "postscript" to *Philosophical Fragments* (1844), a much shorter work presented under the same pseudonym whose title likewise signals a standpoint differing radically from HEGEL's. It is "unscientific" in defiant opposition to Hegel's proudly *wissenschaftlich* approach to reality in general and to human reality and "spirituality" in particular—as well as contrary in spirit to the very idea of a philosophical "system" like Hegel's that purports to include and do justice to human reality.

From The Sickness unto Death

From *Part First. The Sickness unto Death is Despair*

From I. That Despair is the Sickness unto Death

A. Despair is a Sickness in the Spirit, in the Self, and so it may assume a Triple Form: In Despair at not being Conscious of having a Self (Despair Improperly so called); In Despair at not willing to be Oneself; In Despair at willing to be Oneself.

Man is spirit. But what is spirit? Spirit is the self. But what is the self? The self is a relation which relates itself to its own self, or it is that in the relation [which accounts for it] that the relation relates itself to its own self; the self is not the relation but [consists in the fact] that the relation relates itself to its own self. Man is a synthesis of the infinite and the finite, of the temporal and the eternal, of freedom and necessity, in short it is a synthesis. A synthesis is a relation between two factors. So regarded, man is not yet a self.[1]

In the relation between two, the relation is the third term as a negative unity, and the two relate themselves to the relation, and in the relation to the relation; such a relation is that between soul and body, when man is regarded as soul. If on the contrary the relation relates itself to its own self, the relation is then the positive third term, and this is the self.

Such a relation which relates itself to its own self (that is to say, a self) must either have constituted itself or have been constituted by another.

If this relation which relates itself to its own self is constituted by another, the relation doubtless is the third term, but this relation (the third term) is in turn a relation relating itself to that which constituted the whole relation.

---

1. The opening paragraphs of this section are a parody of Hegelian language, though they make important points.

Such a derived, constituted, relation is the human self, a relation which relates itself to its own self, and in relating itself to its own self relates itself to another. Hence it is that there can be two forms of despair properly so called. If the human self had constituted itself, there could be a question only of one form, that of not willing to be one's own self, of willing to get rid of oneself. This formula [i.e. that the self is constituted by another] is the expression for the total dependence of the relation (the self namely), the expression for the fact that the self cannot of itself attain and remain in equilibrium and rest by itself, but only by relating itself to that Power which constituted the whole relation. Indeed, so far is it from being true that this second form of despair (despair at not willing to be one's own self) denotes only a particular kind of despair, that on the contrary all despair can in the last analysis be reduced to this. If a man in despair is as he thinks conscious of his despair, does not talk about it meaninglessly as of something which befell him (pretty much as when a man who suffers from vertigo talks with nervous self-deception about a weight upon his head or about its being like something falling upon him, etc., this weight and this pressure being in fact not something external but an inverse reflection from an inward experience), and if by himself and by himself only he would abolish the despair, then by all the labor he expends he is only laboring himself deeper into a deeper despair. The disrelationship of despair is not a simple disrelationship but a disrelationship in a relation which relates itself to its own self and is constituted by another, so that the disrelationship in that self-relation reflects itself infinitely in the relation to the Power which constituted it.

This then is the formula which describes the condition of the self when despair is completely eradicated: by relating itself to its own self and by willing to be itself the self is grounded transparently in the Power which posited it.

* * *

FROM II. THE UNIVERSALITY OF THIS SICKNESS (SIN)

* * *

So long as one does not regard man as spirit (in which case we cannot talk about despair) but only as a synthesis of soul and body, health is an "immediate" determinant, and only the sickness of soul or body is a dialectical determinant. But despair is expressed precisely by the fact that a person is unaware of being characterized as spirit. Even that which, humanly speaking, is the most beautiful and lovable thing of all, a feminine youthfulness which is sheer peace and harmony and joy—even that is despair. For this indeed is happiness, but happiness is not a characteristic of spirit, and in the remote depths, in the most inward parts, in the hidden recesses of happiness, there dwells also the anxious dread[2] which is despair; it would be only too glad to be allowed to remain therein, for the dearest and most attractive dwelling-place of despair is in the very heart of immediate happiness. All immediacy, in spite of its illu-

---

2. In Danish, *Angest,* "anxiety," cognate with the German *Angst*—a term and concept that came to figure prominently in existentialism, especially in the existential philosophy of HEIDEGGER. Kierke-gaard wrote at length about anxiety in *Begrebet Angest* (1844), first translated into English in 1944 as *The Concept of Dread.*

sory peace and tranquillity, is dread, and hence, quite consistently, it is dread of nothing; one cannot make immediacy so anxious by the most horrifying description of the most dreadful something, as by a crafty, apparently casual half word about an unknown peril which is thrown out with the surely calculated aim of reflection; yea, one can put immediacy most in dread by slyly imputing to it knowledge of the matter referred to. For immediacy doubtless does not know; but never does reflection catch its prey so surely as when it makes its snare out of nothing, and never is reflection so thoroughly itself as when it is . . . nothing. There is need of an eminent reflection, or rather of a great faith, to support a reflection based upon nothing, i.e. an infinite reflection. So even the most beautiful and lovable thing of all, a feminine youthfulness which is sheer peace and harmony and joy, is nevertheless despair, is happiness. Hardly will one have the good hap[3] to get through life on the strength of this immediacy. And if this happiness has the hap to get through, it would be of little help for it is despair. Despair, just because it is wholly dialectical, is in fact the sickness of which it holds that it is the greatest misfortune not to have had it—the true good hap to get it, although it is the most dangerous sickness of all, if one does not wish to be healed of it. In other cases one can only speak of the good fortune of being healed of a sickness, sickness itself being misfortune.

Therefore it is as far as possible from being true that the vulgar view is right in assuming that despair is a rarity; on the contrary, it is quite universal. It is as far as possible from being true that the vulgar view is right in assuming that everyone who does not think or feel that he is in despair is not so at all, and that only he is in despair who says that he is. On the contrary, one who without affectation says that he is in despair is after all a little bit nearer, a dialectical step nearer to being cured than all those who are not regarded and do not regard themselves as being in despair. But precisely this is the common situation (as the physician of souls will doubtless concede), that the majority of men live without being thoroughly conscious that they are spiritual beings—and to this is referable all the security, contentment with life, etc., etc., which precisely is despair. Those, on the other hand, who say that they are in despair are generally such as have a nature so much more profound that they must become conscious of themselves as spirit, or such as by the hard vicissitudes of life and its dreadful decisions have been helped to become conscious of themselves as spirit—either one or the other, for rare is the man who truly is free from despair.

Ah, so much is said about human want and misery—I seek to understand it, I have also had some acquaintance with it at close range; so much is said about wasted lives—but only that man's life is wasted who lived on, so deceived by the joys of life or by its sorrows that he never became eternally and decisively conscious of himself as spirit, as self, or (what is the same thing) never became aware and in the deepest sense received an impression of the fact that there is a God, and that he, he himself, his self, exists before this God, this gain of infinity, which is never attained except through despair. And, oh, this misery, that so many live on and are defrauded of this most blessed of all thoughts; this misery, that people employ themselves about everything else,

3. Chance, fortune.

or, as for the masses of men, that people employ them about everything else, utilize them to generate the power for the theater of life, but never remind them of their blessedness; that they heap them in a mass, instead of splitting them apart so that they might gain the highest thing, the only thing worth living for, and enough to live in for an eternity—it seems to me that I could weep for an eternity over the fact that such misery exists! And, oh, to my thinking this is one expression the more of the dreadfulness of this most dreadful sickness and misery, namely, its hiddenness—not only that he who suffers from it may wish to hide it and may be able to do so, to the effect that it can so dwell in a man that no one, no one whatever discovers it; no, rather that it can be so hidden in a man that he himself does not know it! And, oh, when the hour-glass has run out, the hour-glass of time, when the noise of worldliness is silenced, and the restless or the ineffectual busyness comes to an end, when everything is still about thee as it is in eternity—whether thou wast man or woman, rich or poor, dependent or independent, fortunate or unfortunate, whether thou didst bear the splendor of the crown in a lofty station, or didst bear only the labor and heat of the day in an inconspicuous lot; whether thy name shall be remembered as long as the world stands (and so was remembered as long as the world stood), or without a name thou didst cohere as nameless with the countless multitude; whether the glory which surrounded thee surpassed all human description, or the judgment passed upon thee was the most severe and dishonoring human judgement can pass— eternity asks of thee and of every individual among these million millions only one question, whether thou hast lived in despair or not, whether thou wast in despair in such a way that thou didst not know thou wast in despair, or in such a way that thou didst hiddenly carry this sickness in thine inward parts as thy gnawing secret, carry it under thy heart as the fruit of a sinful love, or in such a way that thou, a horror to others, didst rave in despair. And if so, if thou hast lived in despair (whether for the rest thou didst win or lose), then for thee all is lost, eternity knows thee not, it never knew thee, or (even more dreadful) it knows thee as thou art known, it puts thee under arrest by thyself in despair.

FROM III. THE FORMS OF THIS SICKNESS, I.E. OF DESPAIR

The forms of despair must be discoverable abstractly by reflecting upon the factors which compose the self as a synthesis. The self is composed of infinity and finiteness. But the synthesis is a relationship, and it is a relationship which, though it is derived, relates itself to itself, which means freedom. The self is freedom. But freedom is the dialectical element in the terms possibility and necessity.

Principally, however, despair must be viewed under the category of consciousness: the question whether despair is conscious or not, determines the qualitative difference between despair and despair. In its concept[4] all despair is doubtless conscious; but from this it does not follow that he in whom it exists, he to whom it can rightly be attributed in conformity with the concept, is himself conscious of it. It is in this sense that consciousness is decisive.

4. That is, by its very nature; the phrase is another Hegelianism.

Generally speaking, consciousness, i.e. consciousness of self, is the decisive criterion of the self. The more consciousness, the more self; the more consciousness, the more will, and the more will the more self. A man who has no will at all is no self; the more will he has, the more consciousness of self he has also.

From A. Despair regarded in such a way that one does not reflect whether it is Conscious or not, so that one reflects only upon the Factors of the Synthesis.

from (a). despair viewed under the aspects of finitude/infinitude.

The self is the conscious synthesis of infinitude and finitude which relates itself to itself, whose task is to become itself, a task which can be performed only by means of a relationship to God. But to become oneself is to become concrete. But to become concrete means neither to become finite nor infinite, for that which is to become concrete is a synthesis. Accordingly, the development consists in moving away from oneself infinitely by the process of infinitizing oneself, and in returning to oneself infinitely by the process of finitizing. If on the contrary the self does not become itself, it is in despair, whether it knows it or not. However, a self, every instant it exists, is in process of becoming, for the self κατὰ δύναμιν[5] does not actually exist, it is only that which it is to become. In so far as the self does not become itself, it is not its own self; but not to be one's own self is despair.

* * *

From B. Despair viewed under the Aspect of Consciousness.

from (a). despair which is unconscious that it is despair, or the despairing unconsciousness of having a self and an eternal self.

* * *

* * * However vain and conceited men may be, they have nevertheless for the most part a very lowly conception of themselves, that is to say, they have no conception of being spirit, the absolute of all that a man can be—but vain and conceited they are . . . by of comparison. In case one were to think of a house, consisting of cellar, ground-floor and *premier étage*,[6] so tenanted, or rather so arranged, that it was planned for a distinction of rank between the dwellers on the several floors; and in case one were to make a comparison between such a house and what it is to be a man—then unfortunately this is the sorry and ludicrous condition of the majority of men, that in their own house they prefer to live in the cellar. The soulish-bodily synthesis in every man is planned with a view to being spirit, such is the building; but the man prefers to dwell in the cellar, that is, in the determinants of sensuousness. And not only does he prefer to dwell in the cellar; no, he loves that to such a degree that he

---

5. In accordance with its power (Greek, *kata duna-min*); that is, "potentially."

6. First floor (French); that is, the floor above the ground floor.

becomes furious if anyone would propose to him to occupy the *bel étage*[7] which stands empty at his disposition—for in fact he is dwelling in his own house.

* * *

* * * Every human existence which is not conscious of itself as spirit, or conscious of itself before God as spirit, every human existence which is not thus grounded transparently in God but obscurely reposes or terminates in some abstract universality (state, nation, etc.), or in obscurity about itself takes its faculties merely as active powers, without in a deeper sense being conscious whence it has them, which regards itself as an inexplicable something which is to be understood from without—every such existence, whatever it accomplishes, though it be the most amazing exploit, whatever it explains, though it were the whole of existence, however intensely it enjoys life aesthetically— every such existence is after all despair.

* * *

FROM (B). THE DESPAIR WHICH IS CONSCIOUS OF BEING DESPAIR, AS ALSO IT IS CONSCIOUS OF BEING A SELF WHEREIN THERE IS AFTER ALL SOMETHING ETERNAL, AND THEN IS IN DESPAIR AT NOT WILLING TO BE ITSELF, OR IN DESPAIR AT WILLING TO BE ITSELF.

* * *

In what follows I shall go on to examine the two forms of conscious despair, in such a way as to display at the same time a heightening of the consciousness of what despair is, and of the consciousness of the fact that one's own condition is despair—or, what is the same thing and the decisive thing, a heightening of the consciousness of the self. But the opposite of being in despair is believing; hence we may perceive the justification for what was stated above (I.A) as the formula which describes a condition in which no despair at all exists, for this same formula is also the formula for believing: by relating itself to its own self, and by willing to be itself, the self is grounded transparently in the Power which constituted it.

(1). In despair at not willing to be oneself, the despair of weakness.

* * *

(i). *Despair over the earthly or over something earthly.* This is pure immediacy, or else an immediacy which contains a quantitative reflection.—Here there is no infinite consciousness of the self, of what despair is, or of the fact that the condition is one of despair; the despair is passive, succumbing to the pressure of the outward circumstance, it by no means comes from within as action. It is, if I may say so, by an innocent misuse of language, a play upon words, as when children play at being soldiers, that in the language of immediacy such words as the self and despair occur.

The *immediate* man (in so far as immediacy is to be found without any reflection) is merely soulishly determined, his self or he himself is a something

7. Literally, "beautiful floor" (French), the principal (best) floor of a large house.

included along with "the other" in the compass of the temporal and the worldly, and it has only an illusory appearance of possessing in it something eternal. Thus the self coheres immediately with "the other," wishing, desiring, enjoying, etc., but passively; even in desiring, the self is in the dative case, like the child when it says "me" for I. Its dialectic is: the agreeable and the disagreeable; its concepts are: good fortune, misfortune, fate.

* * *

This form of despair is: in despair at not willing to be oneself; or still lower, in despair at not willing to be a self; or lowest of all, in despair at willing to be another than himself. Properly speaking, immediacy has no self, it does not recognize itself, so neither can it recognize itself again, it terminates therefore preferably in the romantic. When immediacy despairs it possesses not even enough self to wish or to dream that it had become what it did not become. The immediate man helps himself in a different way: he wishes to be another. Of this one may easily convince oneself by observing immediate men. At the moment of despair no wish is so natural to them as the wish that they had become or might become another. In any case one can never forbear to smile at such a despairer, who, humanly speaking, although he is in despair, is so very innocent. Commonly such a despairer is infinitely comic. Think of a self (and next to God there is nothing so eternal as a self), and then that this self gets the notion of asking whether it might not let itself become or be made into another . . . than itself. And yet such a despairer, whose only wish is this most crazy of all transformations, loves to think that this change might be accomplished as easily as changing a coat. For the immediate man does not recognize his self, he recognizes himself only by his dress, he recognizes (and here again appears the infinitely comic trait) he recognizes that he has a self only by externals. There is no more ludicrous confusion, for a self is just infinitely different from externals. When then the whole of existence has been altered for the immediate man and he has fallen into despair, he goes a step further, he thinks thus, this has become his wish: "What if I were to become another, were to get myself a new self?" Yes, but if he did become another, I wonder if he would recognize himself again! It is related of a peasant who came cleanly shaven to the Capital, and had made so much money that he could buy himself a pair of shoes and stockings and still had enough left over to get drunk on—it is related that as he was trying in his drunken state to find his way home he lay down in the middle of the highway and fell asleep. Then along came a wagon, and the driver shouted to him to move or he would run over his legs. Then the drunken peasant awoke, looked at his legs, and since by reason of the shoes and stockings he didn't recognize them, he said to the driver, "Drive on, they are not my legs." So in the case of the immediate man when he is in despair it is impossible to represent him truly without a touch of the comic; it is, if I may say so, a clever trick to talk in this jargon about a self and about despair.

When immediacy is assumed to have self-reflection, despair is somewhat modified; there is somewhat more consciousness of the self, and therewith in turn of what despair is, and of the fact that one's condition is despair; there is some sense in it when such a man talks of being in despair: but the despair is essentially that of weakness, a passive experience; its form is, in despair at not wanting to be oneself.

The progress in this case, compared with pure immediacy, is at once evident in the fact that the despair does not always come about by reason of a blow, by something that happens, but may be occasioned by the mere reflection within oneself, so that in this case despair is not a purely passive defeat by outward circumstances, but to a certain degree is self-activity, action. Here there is in fact a certain degree of self-reflection, and so a certain degree of observation of oneself. With this certain degree of self-reflection begins the act of discrimination whereby the self becomes aware of itself as something essentially different from the environment, from externalities and their effect upon it. But this is only to a certain degree. Now when the self with a certain degree of self-reflection wills to accept itself, it stumbles perhaps upon one difficulty or another in the composition of the self. For as no human body is perfection, so neither is any self. This difficulty, be it what it may, frightens the man away shudderingly. Or something happens to him which causes within him a breach with immediacy deeper than he has made by reflection. Or his imagination discovers a possibility which, if it were to come to pass, would likewise become a breach with immediacy.

So he despairs. His despair is that of weakness, a passive suffering of the self, in contrast to the despair of self-assertion; but, by the aid of relative self-reflection which he has, he makes an effort (which again distinguished him from the purely immediate man) to defend his self. He understands that the thing of letting the self go is a pretty serious business after all, he is not so apoplectically muddled by the blow as the immediate man is, he understands by the aid of reflection that there is much he may lose without losing the self; he makes admissions, is capable of doing so—and why? Because to a certain degree he has dissociated his self from external circumstances, because he has an obscure conception that there may even be something eternal in the self. But in vain he struggles thus; the difficulty he stumbled against demands a breach with immediacy as a whole, and for that he has not sufficient self-reflection or ethical reflection; he has no consciousness of a self which is gained by the infinite abstraction from everything outward, this naked, abstract self (in contrast to the clothed self of immediacy) which is the first form of the infinite self and the forward impulse in the whole process whereby a self infinitely accepts its actual self with all its difficulties and advantages.

So then he despairs, and his despair is: not willing to be himself. On the other hand, it strikes him as ridiculous to want to be another; he maintains the relationship to his self—to that extent reflection has identified him with the self. He then is in just such a situation with regard to the self as a man may be with regard to his dwelling-place. The comic feature is that a self certainly does not stand in such a casual relation to itself as does a man to his dwelling-place. A man finds his dwelling-place distasteful, either because the chimney smokes, or for any other reason whatsoever; so he leaves it, but he does not move out, he does not engage a new dwelling, he continues to regard the old one as his habitation; he reckons that the offense will pass away. So it is with the despairer. As long as the difficulty lasts he does not dare to come to himself (as the common phrase expresses it with singular pregnancy), he does not want to be himself—but that surely will pass by, perhaps things will change, the dark possibility will surely be forgotten. So meanwhile he comes to himself only once in a while, as it were on a visit, to see whether the change has not occurred, and so soon as it has occurred he moves home again, "is again himself," so he says. However, this only means that he begins again where he left off; he was to a certain degree a self of a sort, and he became nothing more.

But if no change occurs, he helps himself in another way. He swings away entirely from the inward direction which is the path he ought to have followed in order to become truly a self. The whole problem of the self in a deeper sense becomes a sort of blind door in the background of his soul behind which there is nothing. He accepts what in his language he calls his self, that is to say, whatever abilities, talents, etc. may have been given him; all this he accepts, yet with the outward direction toward what is called life, the real, the active life; he treats with great precaution the bit of self-reflection which he has in himself, he is afraid that this thing in the background might again emerge. So little by little he succeeds in forgetting it; in the course of years he finds it almost ludicrous, especially when he is in good company with other capable and active men who have a sense and capacity for real life. *Charmant!*[8] He has now, as they say in romances, been happily married for a number of years, is an active and enterprising man, a father and a citizen, perhaps even a great man; at home in his own house the servants speak of him as "him"; in the city he is among the *honoratiores;*[9] his bearing suggests "respect of persons," or that he is to be respected as a person, to all appearance he is to be regarded as a person. In Christendom he is a Christian (quite in the same sense in which in paganism he would have been a pagan, and in England an Englishman), one of the cultured Christians. The question of immortality has often been in his mind, more than once he has asked the parson whether there really was such an immortality, whether one would really recognize oneself again—which indeed must have for him a very singular interest, since he has no self.

It is impossible to represent truly this sort of despair without a certain admixture of satire. The comical thing is that he will talk about having been in despair; the dreadful thing is that after having, as he thinks, overcome despair, he is then precisely in despair. It is infinitely comic that at the bottom of the practical wisdom which is so much extolled in the world, at the bottom of all the devilish lot of good counsel and wise saws and "wait and see" and "put up with one's fate" and "write in the book of forgetfulness"—that at the bottom of all this, ideally understood, lies complete stupidity as to where the danger really is and what the danger really is. But again this ethical[1] stupidity is the dreadful thing.

Despair over the earthly or over something earthly is the commonest sort of despair, especially in the second form of immediacy with a quantitative reflection. The more thoroughly reflected the despair is, the more rarely it occurs in the world. But this proves that most men have not become very deep even in despair; it by no means proves, however, that they are not in despair.

8. Charming! (French).
9. More honored men (Latin).
1. "Ethical" in the sense in which the word is used in *Concluding Unscientific Postscript* (1846; see above), having to do with genuine human existing conceived in terms of "subjectivity," rather than on the Hegelian model of "ethicality."

There are very few men who live even only passably in the category of spirit; yea, there are not many even who merely make an attempt at this life, and most of those who do so, shy away. They have not learned to fear, they have not learned what "must" means, regardless, infinitely regardless of what it may be that comes to pass. Therefore they cannot endure what even to them seems a contradiction, and which as reflected from the world around them appears much more glaring, that to be concerned for one's own soul and to want to be spirit is a waste of time, yes, an inexcusable waste of time, which ought if possible to be punishable by law, at all events is punished by contempt and ridicule as a sort of treason against men, as a froward madness which crazily fills up time with nothing. Then there is a period in their lives (alas, their best period) when they begin after all to take the inward direction. They get about as far as the first difficulties, there they veer away; it seems to them as though this road were leading to a disconsolate desert—*und rings umher liegt schöne grüne Weide.*[2] So they are off, and soon they forget that best period of theirs; and, alas, they forget it as though it were a bit of childishness. At the same time they are Christians, tranquilized by the parson with regard to their salvation. This despair, as I have said, is the commonest, it is so common that only thereby can one explain the rather common opinion in common intercourse that despair is something belonging to youth, which appears only in youthful years, but is not to be found in the settled man who has come to the age of maturity and the years of wisdom. This is a desperate error, or rather a desperate mistake, which overlooks (yes, and what is worse, it overlooks the fact that what it overlooks is pretty nearly the best thing that can be said of a man, since far worse often occurs)—it overlooks the fact that the majority of men do never really manage in their whole life to be more than they were in childhood and youth, namely, immediacy with the addition of a little dose of self-reflection.

* * *

(ii). *Despair about the eternal or over oneself.* Despair over the earthly or over something earthly is really despair also about the eternal and over oneself, in so far as it is despair, for this is the formula for all despair. But the despairer, as he was depicted in the foregoing,[3] did not observe what was happening behind him, so to speak; he thinks he is in despair over something earthly and constantly talks about what he is in despair over, and yet he is in despair about the eternal; for the fact that he ascribes such great value to the earthly, or, to carry the thought further, that he ascribes to something earthly such great value, or that he first transforms something earthly into everything earthly, and then ascribes to the earthly such great value, is precisely to despair about the eternal.

This despair is now well in advance. If the former was the despair of *weakness*, this is *despair over his weakness*, although it still remains as to its nature under the category "despair of weakness," as distinguished from defiance in the next section. So there is only a relative difference. This difference

2. And all around lie beautiful green meadows (German); quoted from Goethe's *Faust*, part 1 (1808).
3. The preceding section, not included here, which focuses on despair about the loss or lack of something "earthly."

consists in the fact that the foregoing form has the consciousness of weakness as its final consciousness, whereas in this case consciousness does not come to a stop here but potentiates itself to a new consciousness, a consciousness of its weakness. The despairer understands that it is weakness to take the earthly so much to heart, that it is weakness to despair. But then, instead of veering sharply away from despair to faith, humbling himself before God for his weakness, he is more deeply absorbed in despair and despairs over his weakness. Therewith the whole point of view is inverted, he becomes now more clearly conscious of his despair, recognizing that he is in despair about the eternal, he despairs over himself that he could be weak enough to ascribe to the earthly such great importance, which now becomes his despairing expression for the fact that he has lost the eternal and himself.

Here is the scale of ascent. First, in consciousness of himself: for to despair about the eternal is impossible without having a conception about the self, that there is something eternal in it, or that it has had something eternal in it. And if a man is to despair over himself, he must indeed be conscious also of having a self; that, however, is the thing over which he despairs—not over the earthly or over something earthly, but over himself. Moreover there is in this case a greater consciousness of what despair is; for despair is precisely to have lost the eternal and oneself. As a matter of course there is greater consciousness of the fact that one's condition is that of despair. Furthermore, despair in this case is not merely passive suffering but action. For when the earthly is taken away from the self and a man despairs, it is as if despair came from without, though it comes nevertheless always from the self, indirect-directly from the self, as counter-pressure (reaction), differing in this respect from defiance, which comes directly from the self. Finally, there is here again, though in another sense, a further advance. For just because this despair is more intense, salvation is in a certain sense nearer. Such a despair will hardly forget, it is too deep; but despair is held open every instant, and there is thus possibility of salvation.

* * *

(2). The despair of willing despairingly to be oneself—defiance.

* * *

The despair described in section 1 (ii) was despair over one's weakness, the despairer does not want to be himself. But if one goes one single dialectical step further, if despair thus becomes conscious of the reason why it does not want to be itself, then the case is altered, then defiance is present, for then it is precisely because of this a man is despairingly determined to be himself.

First comes despair over the earthly or something earthly, then despair over oneself about the eternal. Then comes defiance, which really is despair by the aid of the eternal, the despairing abuse of the eternal in the self to the point of being despairingly determined to be oneself. But just because it is despair by the aid of the eternal it lies in a sense very close to the true, and just because it lies very close to the true it is infinitely remote. The despair which is the passage-way to faith is also by the aid of the eternal: by the aid of the eternal the self has courage to lose itself in order to gain itself. Here on the contrary it is not willing to begin by losing itself but wills to be itself.

In this form of despair there is now a mounting consciousness of the self, and hence greater consciousness of what despair is and of the fact that one's condition is that of despair. Here despair is conscious of itself as a deed, it does not come from without as a suffering under the pressure of circumstances, it comes directly from the self. And so after all defiance is a new qualification added to despair over one's weakness.

In order to will in despair to be oneself there must be consciousness of the infinite self. This infinite self, however, is really only the abstractest form, the abstractest possibility of the self, and it is this self the man despairingly wills to be, detaching the self from every relation to the Power which posited it, or detaching it from the conception that there is such a Power in existence. By the aid of this infinite form the self despairingly wills to dispose of itself or to create itself, to make itself the self it wills to be, distinguishing in the concrete self what it will and what it will not accept. The man's concrete self, or his concretion, has in fact necessity and limitations, it is this perfectly definite thing, with these faculties, dispositions, etc. But by the aid of the infinite form, the negative self, he wills first to undertake to refashion the whole thing, in order to get out of it in this way a self such as he wants to have, produced by the aid of the infinite form of the negative self—and it is thus he wills to be himself. That is to say, he is not willing to begin with the beginning but "in the beginning."[4] He is not willing to attire himself in himself, nor to see his task in the self given him; by the aid of being the infinite form he wills to construct it himself.[5]

If one would have a common name for this despair, one might call it Stoicism—yet without thinking only of this philosophic sect. And to illuminate this sort of despair more sharply one would do well to distinguish between the active and the passive self, showing how the self is related to itself when it is active, and how it is related to itself in suffering when it is passive, and showing that the formula constantly is: in despair to will to be oneself.

If the despairing *self* is *active*, it really is related to itself only as experimenting with whatsoever it be that it undertakes, however great it may be, however astonishing, however persistently carried out. It acknowledges no power over it, hence in the last resort it lacks seriousness and is able only to conjure up a show of seriousness when the self bestows upon its experiments its utmost attention. Like the fire which Prometheus stole from the gods,[6] so does this mean to steal from God the thought which is seriousness, that God is regarding one, instead of which the despairing self is content with regarding itself, and by that it is supposed to bestow upon its undertakings infinite interest and importance, whereas it is precisely this which makes them mere experiments. For though this self were to go so far in despair that it becomes an experimental god, no derived self can by regarding itself give itself more than it is: it nevertheless remains from first to last the self, by self-duplication it becomes neither more nor less than the self. Hence the self in its despairing

---

4. The opening of Genesis, the first book of the Bible; the contrast is between concern with the beginning and reality of one's own "concrete self" and a (grandiose but misplaced) concern with the beginning of everything.
5. This paragraph and those that follow vividly depict the stance and conception of authenticity championed by the nonreligious existential philosophers and offers a hint of Kierkegaard's own contrasting version of authenticity.
6. In classical mythology, the Titan Prometheus stole fire from the gods and gave it to humankind; as punishment, he was nailed to a mountain in the Caucasus (where every day an eagle ate his liver).

effort to will to be itself labors itself into the direct opposite, it becomes really no self. In the whole dialectic within which it acts there is nothing firm, what the self is does not for an instant stand firm, that is, eternally firm. The negative form of the self exercises quite as much the power of loosing as of binding, every instant it can quite arbitrarily begin all over again, and however far a thought may be pursued, the whole action is within a hypothesis. It is so far from being true that the self succeeds more and more in becoming itself, that in fact it merely becomes more and more manifest that it is a hypothetical self. The self is its own lord and master, so it is said, its own lord, and precisely this is despair, but so also is what it regards as its pleasure and enjoyment. However, by closer inspection one easily ascertains that this ruler is a king without a country, he rules really over nothing; his condition, his dominion, is subjected to the dialectic that every instant revolution is legitimate. For in the last resort this depends arbitrarily upon the self.

So the despairing self is constantly building nothing but castles in the air, it fights only in the air. All these experimented virtues make a brilliant showing; for an instant they are enchanting like an oriental poem: such self-control, such firmness, such ataraxia,[7] etc., border almost on the fabulous. Yes, they do to be sure; and also at the bottom of it all there is nothing. The self wants to enjoy the entire satisfaction of making itself into itself, of developing itself, of being itself; it wants to have the honor of this poetical, this masterly plan according to which it has understood itself. And yet in the last resort it is a riddle how it understands itself; just at the instant when it seems to be nearest to having the fabric finished it can arbitrarily resolve the whole thing into nothing.

If the despairing self is a *passive* sufferer, we have still the same formula: in despair at willing to be oneself. Perhaps such an experimenting self which in despair wills to be itself, at the moment when it is making a preliminary exploration of its concrete self, stumbles upon one or another hardship of the sort that the Christian would call a cross, a fundamental defect, it matters not what. The negative self, the infinite form of the self, will perhaps cast this clean away, pretend that it does not exist, want to know nothing about it. But this does not succeed, its virtuosity in experimenting does not extend so far, nor does its virtuosity in abstraction; like Prometheus the infinite, negative self feels that it is nailed to this servitude. So then it is a passively suffering self. How then does the despair which despairingly wills to be itself display itself in this case?

Note that in the foregoing the form of despair was represented which is in despair over the earthly or over something earthly, so understood that at bottom this is and also shows itself to be despair about the eternal, i.e. despair which wills not to let itself be comforted by the eternal, which rates the earthly so high that the eternal can be of no comfort. But this too is a form of despair: not to be willing to hope that an earthly distress, a temporal cross, might be removed. This is what the despair which wills desperately to be itself is not willing to hope. It has convinced itself that this thorn in the flesh gnaws so profoundly that he cannot abstract it—no matter whether this is actually so

---

7. Tranquillity, involving emotional and intellectual detachment (a state that Stoics as well as Epicureans seek to attain).

or his passion makes it true for him,[8] and so he is willing to accept it as it were eternally. So he is offended by it, or rather from it he takes occasion to be offended at the whole of existence, in spite of it he would be himself, not despitefully be himself without it (for that is to abstract from it, and that he cannot do, or that would be a movement in the direction of resignation); no, in spite of or in defiance of the whole of existence he wills to be himself with it, to take it along, almost defying his torment. For to hope in the possibility of help, not to speak of help by virtue of the absurd, that for God all things are possible—no, that he will not do. And as for seeking help from any other— no, that he will not do for all the world; rather than seek help he would prefer to be himself—with all the tortures of hell, if so it must be.

And of a truth it is not quite so true after all when people say that "it is a matter of course that a sufferer would be so glad to be helped, if only some- body would help him"—this is far from being the case, even though the oppo- site case is not always so desperate as this. The situation is this. A sufferer has one or more ways in which he would be glad to be helped. If he is helped thus, he is willing to be helped. But when in a deeper sense it becomes seri- ousness with this thing of needing help, especially from a higher or from the highest source—this humiliation of having to accept help unconditionally and in any way, the humiliation of becoming nothing in the hand of the Helper for whom all things are possible, or merely the necessity of deferring to another man, of having to give up being oneself so long as one is seeking help—ah, there are doubtless many sufferings, even protracted and agonizing sufferings, at which the self does not wince to this extent, and which therefore at bottom it prefers to retain and to be itself.

But the more consciousness there is in such a sufferer who in despair is determined to be himself, all the more does despair too potentiate itself and become demoniac. The genesis of this is commonly as follows. A self which in despair is determined to be itself winces at one pain or another which sim- ply cannot be taken away or separated from its concrete self. Precisely upon this torment the man directs his whole passion, which at last becomes a demo- niac rage. Even if at this point God in heaven and all his angels were to offer to help him out of it—no, now he doesn't want it, now it is too late, he once would have given everything to be rid of this torment but was made to wait, now that's all past, now he would rather rage against everything, he, the one man in the whole of existence who is the most unjustly treated, to whom it is especially important to have his torment at hand, important that no one should take it from him—for thus he can convince himself that he is in the right. This at last becomes so firmly fixed in his head that for a very peculiar reason

---

8. From this standpoint, it is well to note here, one will see also that much which is embellished by the name of resignation is a kind of despair, that of will- ing despairingly to be one's abstract self, of willing despairingly to be satisfied with the eternal and thereby be able to defy or ignore suffering in the earthly and temporal sphere. The dialectic of resig- nation is commonly this: to will to be one's eternal self, and then with respect to something positive wherein the self suffers, not to will to be oneself, contenting oneself with the thought that after all this will disappear in eternity, thinking itself therefore justified in not accepting it in time, so that, although suffering under it, the self will not make it to the concession that it properly belongs to the self, that is, it will not humble itself under it in faith. Resignation regarded as despair is essentially different from the form, "in despair at not willing to be oneself," for it wills desperately to be itself—with exception, how- ever, of one particular, with respect to which it wills despairingly not to be itself [author's note].

This is the kind of "resignation" that in *Fear and Trembling* (see above) is contrasted with "faith"— "the knight of infinite resignation" vs. "the knight of faith"—which is both very near to and very far from faith as Kierkegaard understands it.

he is afraid of eternity—for the reason, namely, that it might rid him of his (demoniacally understood) infinite advantage over other men, his (demoniacally understood) justification for being what he is. It is himself he wills to be; he began with the infinite abstraction of the self, and now at last he has become so concrete that it would be an impossibility to be eternal in that sense, and yet he wills in despair to be himself. Ah, demoniac madness! He rages most of all at the thought that eternity might get it into its head to take his misery from him!

This sort of despair is seldom seen in the world, such figures generally are met with only in the works of poets, that is to say, of real poets, who always lend their characters this "demoniac" ideality (taking this word in the purely Greek sense[9]). Nevertheless such a despairer is to be met with also in real life. What then is the corresponding outward mark? Well, there is no "corresponding" mark, for in fact a corresponding outward expression corresponding to close reserve is a contradiction in terms; for if it is corresponding, it is then of course revealing. But outwardness is the entirely indifferent factor in this case where introversion, or what one might call inwardness with a jammed lock, is so much the predominant factor. The lowest forms of despair, where there really was no inwardness, or at all events none worth talking about, the lowest forms of despair one might represent by describing or by saying something about the outward traits of the despairer. But the more despair becomes spiritual, and the more inwardness becomes a peculiar world for itself in introversion, all the more is the self alert with demoniac shrewdness to keep despair shut up in close reserve, and all the more intent therefore to set the outward appearance at the level of indifference, to make it as unrevealing and indifferent as possible. As according to the report of superstition the troll disappears through a crack which no one can perceive, so it is for the despairer all the more important to dwell in an exterior semblance behind which it ordinarily would never occur to anyone to look for it. This hiddenness is precisely something spiritual and is one of the safety-devices for assuring oneself of having as it were behind reality an enclosure, a world for itself locking all else out, a world where the despairing self is employed as tirelessly as Tantalus[1] in willing to be itself.

We began in section 1 (ii) with the lowest form of despair, which in despair does not will to be itself. The demoniac despair is the most potentiated form of the despair which despairingly wills to be itself. This despair does not will to be itself with Stoic doting upon itself, nor with self-deification, willing in this way, doubtless mendaciously, yet in a certain sense in terms of its perfection; no, with hatred for existence it wills to be itself, to be itself in terms of its misery; it does not even in defiance or defiantly will to be itself, but to be itself in spite; it does not even will in defiance to tear itself free from the Power which posited it, it wills to obtrude upon this Power in spite, to hold on to it out of malice. And that is natural, a malignant objection must above all take

9. That is, an "idealized" or exceptionally paradigmatic representation of a type.
1. In classical mythology, Tantalus is punished in the underworld by having food and water elude him as he continually seeks to reach them.

care to hold on to that against which it is an objection. Revolting against the whole of existence, it thinks it has hold of a proof against it, against its goodness. This proof the despairer thinks he himself is, and that is what he wills to be, therefore he wills to be himself, himself with his torment, in order with this torment to protest against the whole of existence. Whereas the weak despairer will not hear about what comfort eternity has for him, so neither will such a despairer hear about it, but for a different reason, namely, because this comfort would be the destruction of him as an objection against the whole of existence. It is (to describe it figuratively) as if an author were to make a slip of the pen, and that this clerical error became conscious of being such— perhaps it was no error but in a far higher sense was an essential constituent in the whole exposition—it is then as if this clerical error would revolt against the author, out of hatred for him were to forbid him to correct it, and were to say, "No, I will not be erased, I will stand as a witness against thee, that thou art a very poor writer."

From *Part Second. Despair Is Sin*

FROM I. DESPAIR IS SIN

Sin is this: *before God, or with the conception of God, to be in despair at not willing to be oneself, or in despair at willing to be oneself.* Thus sin is potentiated weakness or potentiated defiance: sin is the potentiation of despair. The point upon which the emphasis rests is *before God*, or the fact that the conception of God is involved; the factor which dialectically, ethically, religiously, makes "qualified" despair (to use a juridical term) synonymous with sin is the conception of God.

Although in this Second Part, and especially in this section, there is no place or occasion for psychological description, there here may be introduced, as the most dialectical borderline between despair and sin, what one might call a poet-existence in the direction of the religious, an existence which has something in common with the despair of resignation, only that the conception of God is involved. Such an existence (as is to be seen from the conjunction and position of the categories) will be the most eminent poet-existence. From a Christian standpoint such an existence (in spite of all aesthetic) is sin, it is the sin of poetizing instead of being, of standing in relation to the Good and the True through imagination instead of being that, or rather existentially striving to be it. The poet-existence here in question is distinguished from despair by the fact that it includes the conception of God or is before God; but it is prodigiously dialectical, and is in an impenetrable dialectical confusion as to how far it is conscious of being sin. Such a poet may have a very deep religious need, and the conception of God is included in his despair. He loves God above everything, God is for him the only comfort in his secret torment, and yet he loves the torment, he will not let it go. He would so gladly be himself before God, but not with respect to this fixed point where the self suffers, there despairingly he will not be himself; he hopes that eternity will remove it, and here in the temporal, however much he suffers under it, he cannot will to accept it, cannot humble himself under it in faith. And yet he continues to hold to God, and this is his only happiness, for him it would be the greatest horror to have to do without God, "it would be enough to drive one to despair"; and yet he permits himself commonly, but perhaps unconsciously, to poetize God, making him a little bit other than He is, a little bit more like a loving father who all too much indulges the child's "only wish." He who became unhappy in love, and therefore became a poet, blissfully extolls the happiness of love—so he became a poet of religiousness, he understands obscurely that it is required of him to let this torment go, that is, to humble himself under it in faith and to accept it as belonging to the self—for he would hold it aloof from him, and thereby precisely he holds it fast, although doubtless he thinks (and this, like every other word of despair, is correct in the opposite sense and therefore must be understood inversely) that this must mean separating himself from it as far as possible, letting it go as far as it is possible for a man to do so. But to accept it in faith, that he cannot do, or rather in the last resort he will not, or here is where the self ends in obscurity. But like that poet's description of love, so this poet's description of the religious possesses an enchantment, a lyrical flight, such as no married man's description has, nor that of his Reverence. What he says is not untrue, by no means, his representation reflects his happier, his better *ego*. With respect to the religious he is an unhappy lover, that is, he is not in a strict sense a believer, he has only the first prerequisite of faith, and with that an ardent longing for the religious. His collision is essentially this: is he the elect, is the thorn in the flesh the expression for the fact that he is to be employed as the extraordinary, is it before God quite as it should be with respect to the extraordinary figure he has become? or is the thorn in the flesh the experience he must humble himself under in order to attain the universal human? But enough of this. I can say with the emphasis of truth, "To whom am I talking?" Who will bother about such psychological investigations carried to the *nth* power? The Nüremburg Picture Books[2] painted by priests are easily understood, they all resemble one another—deceptively—and spiritually understood they are nothing.

CHAPTER 1. GRADATIONS IN THE CONSCIOUSNESS OF THE SELF (THE QUALIFICATION "BEFORE GOD")

In the foregoing there is steadily pointed out a gradation in the consciousness of the self: first came unconsciousness of being an eternal self (III.B a), then a knowledge of having a self in which there is after all something eternal (III.B b), and under this (1 i and ii, 2) there were again pointed out gradations. This whole situation must now be turned about and viewed in a new way. The point is this. The gradations in the consciousness of the self with which we have hitherto been employed are within the definition of the human self, or the self whose measure is man. But this self acquires a new quality or qualification in the fact that it is the self directly in the sight of God. This self is no longer the merely human self but is what I would call, hoping not to be misunderstood, the theological self, the self directly in the sight of God. And what an infinite reality this self acquires by being before God! A herdsman who (if this were possible), is a self only in the sight of cows is a very low

2. A genre of 15th-century books (the most famous example, the *Nuremberg Chronicle* of 1493, was printed). Nuremberg (in German, Nürnberg), a town of particular prominence in the Middle Ages, is located in what is now the German state of Bavaria (Bayern).

self, and so also is a ruler who is a self in the sight of slaves—for in both cases the scale or measure is lacking. The child who hitherto has had only the parents to measure himself by, becomes a self when he is a man by getting the state as a measure. But what an infinite accent falls upon the self by getting God as a measure! The measure for the self always is that in the face of which it is a self; but this does not define what "measure" is. As one can add up only magnitudes of the same order, so each thing is qualitatively that by which it is measured; and that which is qualitatively its measure (*Maalestok*) is ethically its goal (*Maal*); and the measure and goal are qualitatively that which something is—with exception of the relation which obtains in the world of freedom, where a man by not being qualitatively that which is his goal and his measure must himself have deserved this disqualification, so that the goal and the measure remain the same . . . condemningly, making manifest what it is he is not: that, namely which is his goal and his measure.

It was a very just thought to which the older dogmatic frequently recurred, whereas a later dogmatic so often censored it for lack of understanding and a proper sense of its meaning—it was a very just thought, although sometimes a wrong application was made of it: the thought that what makes sin so frightful is that it is before God. From this the theologians proved the eternity of hell-punishment. Subsequently they became shrewder and said, "Sin is sin; sin is not greater because it is against God or before God." Strange! For even the jurists talk about "qualified" crimes and extenuating circumstances, even the jurists make distinction with regard to a crime, inquiring, for example, whether it is committed against a public functionary or a private person, they prescribe a different punishment for the murder of a father and an ordinary murder.

No, the earlier dogmatic was right in asserting that the fact that the sin was before God infinitely potentiated it. Their fault lay in regarding God as something external; and in assuming that it was only now and then men sinned against God. But God is not something external in the sense that a policeman is. What we need to emphasize is that the self has the conception of God, and that then it does not will as He wills, and so is disobedient. Nor is it only now and then one sins before God; for every sin is before God, or rather it is this which properly makes human guilt to be sin.

Despair is potentiated in proportion to consciousness of self; but the self is potentiated in the ratio of the measure proposed for the self, and infinitely potentiated when God is the measure. The more conception of God, the more self; the more self, the more conception of God. Only when the self as this definite individual is conscious of existing before God, only then is it the infinite self; and then this self sins before God. The selfishness of paganism, therefore, in spite of all that can be said about it, is not nearly so "qualified" as that of Christendom, in so far as here also there is selfishness; for the pagan did not possess his self directly in the face of God. The pagan and the natural man have as their measure the merely human self. One may be right therefore from a higher standpoint in regarding paganism as lying in sin, but properly the sin of paganism was the despairing unawareness of God, unawareness of existing before God; this means to be "without God in the world."[3] On the

3. Ephesians 2:12.

other hand, it is for this reason true that the pagan did not sin in the strictest sense, for he did not sin before God. Moreover, it is also in a sense quite certain that many a time a pagan is enabled in a way to slip through the world irreproachably precisely because his light-minded Pelagian interpretation[4] saved him; but then his sin is a different one, namely, this light-minded interpretation. On the other hand and in a different aspect it is quite certain that just by being brought up strictly in Christianity a man has in a certain sense been plunged into sin, because the whole Christian view was too serious for him, especially in an earlier period of his life; but then in another sense this is again of some help to him, this deeper apprehension of what sin is.

Sin is: before God in despair not to will to be oneself, or before God in despair to will to be oneself. But is not this definition, even though in other aspects it may be conceded to have advantages (and among them this which is the weightiest of all, that it is the only Scriptural definition, for the Scripture always defines sin as disobedience), is it not after all too spiritual? To this one must first of all make answer that a definition of sin can never be too spiritual (unless it becomes so spiritual that it does away with sin); for sin is precisely a determinant of spirit. And in the next place, why should it then be too spiritual? Because it does not talk about murder, theft, unchastity, etc.? But does it not talk of them? Is it not also self-assertion against God when one is disobedient and defies His commandment? But on the other hand, when in talking about sin one talks only of such sins, it is so easily forgotten that in a way it may be all right, humanly speaking, with respect to all such things up to a certain point, and yet the whole life may be sin, the well-known kind of sin: glittering vices, wilfulness, which either spiritlessly or impudently continues to be or wills to be unaware in what an infinitely deeper sense a human self is morally under obligation to God with respect to every most secret wish and thought, with respect to quickness in comprehending and readiness to follow every hint of God as to what His will is for this self. The sins of the flesh are the self-assertion of the lower self; but how often one devil is cast out by the devil's help, and the last state becomes worse than the first. For so it is with men in this world: first a man sins from frailty and weakness; and then—yes, then perhaps he learns to flee to God and to be helped by faith which saves from all sin; but of this we are not talking here—then he despairs over his weakness and becomes, either a Pharisee[5] who in despair manages to attain a certain legal righteousness, or he despairs and plunges again into sin.

The definition therefore certainly embraces every conceivable and actual form of sin; it certainly throws into relief the decisive fact that sin is despair (for sin is not the wildness of flesh and blood, but it is the spirit's consent thereto), and it is . . . before God. As a definition it is algebraic. In this little work it would be out of place, and an effort moreover which perhaps would not succeed, were I to begin by describing the particular sins. The principal thing here is that the definition like a net must embrace all forms. And that it does, as can be seen when one tests it by setting up the opposite, namely, the definition of faith, by which I steer my course in the whole of this work,

---

4. That is, following the heresy of Pelagius (ca. 354– after 418), who held that humans could freely choose between good and evil (vs. being wholly dependent on the grace of God).

5. A member of a Jewish religious sect (repeatedly criticized by Jesus in the New Testament) that emphasized the binding force of oral tradition.

as by a sure mariners' mark. Faith is: that the self in being itself and in willing to be itself is grounded transparently in God.

But too often it has been overlooked that the opposite of sin is not *virtue*, not by any manner of means. This is in part a pagan view which is content with a merely human measure and properly does not know what *sin* is, that all sin is before God. No, *the opposite of sin is faith*, as is affirmed in Rom.14:23, "whatsoever is not of faith is sin." And for the whole of Christianity it is one of the most decisive definitions that the opposite of sin is not virtue but faith.

* * *

SOURCE: From Søren Kierkegaard, *The Sickness unto Death*, trans. Walter Lowrie (Princeton: Princeton University Press, 1941), pp. 17–19, 37–45, 67–68, 72, 77–81, 83–92, 97–99, 107–32. All bracketed additions to the text are the translator's. Originally published as *Sygdommen til døden* (1849), under the pseudonym Anti-Climacus.

Part II

Naturalisms: Humanity, Nature, and History

The competing "Idealisms" inspired by KANT provoked not only the proto-existentialist (and defiantly retro-religious) protest of KIERKEGAARD but also a variety of post-Idealist alternatives that may be loosely characterized in contrast as "naturalisms." Their point of departure was the countervailing conviction that the natural order in which we find ourselves is the only world there is—a world of which human life was originally and remains fundamentally a part, all human-spiritual reality and possibility included. Their thinking—or at any rate their interest—tended to focus on *human life* rather than on life and the world more generally. It may be considered "naturalistic" in the broad sense of cutting loose from the Kantian premises of the Idealisms of their predecessors, as well as from the idea that there is anything above and beyond this life in this world of which it is meaningful and warranted to speak, and of which account must be taken in interpreting human abilities and possibilities.

The "naturalistic turn" thus involved coming to take for granted or to presuppose certain things about ourselves—and our world—that had seemed problematic to many earlier modern philosophers. Our basic identity was simply assumed—as something no one could seriously question or deny—to be that of a certain type of living creature, whose various features, capacities, and requirements make it similar to other types of living creature in some respects and different from them in others. It thus was taken for granted that human reality is human *life*—and that human life is fundamentally a biological phenomenon that as such has no supernatural or metaphysical special status in relation to other forms of life. The thinkers making this turn, however, were far from oblivious to the many ways in which human life differs from other forms of life, and indeed differs within the species and under different sorts of circumstances. It became a significant part of their task, therefore, to develop interpretations of these very differences, and of the relation of the various forms of human spirituality to our kind of animality.

Their naturalisms thus typically emphasize the idea of *development*, but also differ in their accounts of it from mere mechanistic or biological materialisms. Our entirely natural (biological) origins notwithstanding, they generally allow for—and often make much of—the reality and possibility of developments of one sort or another that have been and continue to be quali-tatively transformative of the character of human life, with the result that it has come to be something that is more than merely physical, chemical, or even biological. They are "naturalistic" in the sense that their interpretations make no appeal to any principles or agencies that transcend the dynamics of human life; and yet those dynamics are often conceived to be such that they have made human life something that is or can be significantly different from other forms of life.

However greatly these naturalisms may differ from Hegelianism, they for the most part have something in common with it that many of them learned from it. HEGEL, following SCHILLER, conceived of human spirituality as hav-ing come to be what it is by way of a long course of historical development that was social and cultural in character. His naturalistic successors consid-ered his basic point to be important and right—but held that it is better inter-preted and expressed in terms of circumstances relating to the historical development of our humanity. With the advent of society and the invention of culture, human development ceased to be a merely biological affair. Soci-ety and culture became a kind of historically developing "second nature" in whose context human reality began to be transformed, availing itself both of resources of the natural world around it and of aspects of its own natural con-stitution to become a different sort of creature. With no supernatural assis-tance or internal metaphysical guidance, but by way of this humanly produced second nature, humankind bootstrapped its way from its original animality to a human reality that has attained a significant and rich (even if naturalis-tically engendered) dimension of a kind of spirituality.

These naturalistic thinkers thus did not reject the very idea of a human spirituality that is not reducible to human biology, but rather tried to make the case that it could and should be interpreted quite differently from the way in which Hegel had interpreted it. In doing so, they were in effect proposing to return to the idea of an interpretation along the lines suggested by Schiller in his *On the Aesthetic Education of Man* (1794) and start over again—without forgetting the lessons to be learned from Hegel's discussion of the indis-pensability of historically emerging and developing social and cultural for-mations as conditions of the possibility of any and all forms of that spirituality. With a few notable exceptions—NIETZSCHE and DILTHEY in particular—they quite understandably tended to be reluctant to retain and employ the lan-guage of *Geist* (spirit) in their discussions, since that language was too heavily freighted with Hegel's prevailing interpretation of it for most of them to feel comfortable with it. They all were very much concerned, however, to attempt to do interpretive justice (in naturalistic ways) to what they took to be the most significant instances of human possibilities to which it may be used to refer.

The thinker with whom this part begins is LUDWIG FEUERBACH (1804–1872). He was one of the leading figures in the post-Hegelian turn from Hegelian "Idealism" and "philosophy of *Geist*" to an avowedly naturalistic revision of it, in which all talk of "spirit" was replaced by and translated into the lan-guage of "man" and the "human." Like many young philosophers of his gen-eration, Feuerbach had been an avid Hegelian as a student, and he retained a great appreciation for Hegel's philosophical genius. But he came to be convinced that Hegel's philosophy needed to be "de-mystified" and brought down to earth, and that his insights needed to be—and could be—liberated from the "Idealist" language and system in which Hegel had expressed and framed them. He is often thought of as merely a transitional figure between Hegel and MARX; but he was more than that, even though he did greatly influence and inspire the young Marx's philosophical thinking. He showed the way to the possibility of a secular humanist alternative to the religions, idealisms, and materialisms of the time, and to the development of a naturalistic philosophical "anthropology" that could serve as its foundation.

Karl Marx (1818–1883) is known today primarily for the economic theory and critique of classical capitalism that he developed in *Das Kapital* (1867–94), as well as for the revolutionary political movement that he and FRIEDRICH ENGELS championed in *The Communist Manifesto* (1848). (Engels co-authored several other writings with Marx as well; but as Engels himself acknowledged, the ideas were mainly Marx's.) Marx was educated in philosophy, however, and initially aspired to a philosophical career; and his earlier writings reveal the kind of philosophical thinking to which he was inclined and the level of philosophical ability he brought to it. When these writings came to light in the second quarter of the twentieth century, they attracted considerable attention and earned him a place among the significantly original and powerful thinkers in the interpretive tradition. Like Feuerbach, he began as a Hegelian; but then, partly under Feuerbach's influence, he moved in the direction of Feuerbach's naturalistic humanism (or humanistic naturalism). He went on to develop a philosophical anthropology and conception of genuine humanity differing significantly from Feuerbach's, and a conviction that it would take a radical transformation of human society to make fully and truly human self-realization possible for each and all.

MARY WOLLSTONECRAFT (1759–1797) is best read together with JOHN STUART MILL (who follows her in this volume), because both focused significantly and importantly on an issue that had not previously been addressed (in an enlightened way) in the philosophical literature: the status of women in their society, which they felt left much to be desired. Wollstonecraft, who was Mill's senior by nearly half a century, anticipated both Mill's approach to the issue—within the context of a philosophical consideration of human flourishing—and his emphasis on the need for men and women alike to reform not just existing social, cultural, and educational practices but also existing ways of thinking about women and their lives. Mill was arguably far ahead of his time, but Wollstonecraft was even more so. Indeed, she was an exact English contemporary of the first post-Kantian figure featured in this volume, Friedrich Schiller (they were born in the same year), whose fervent Enlightenment ideas and ideals she shared. The book that has earned her a place in the history of modern philosophy, *A Vindication of the Rights of Woman* (1792), was her second "vindication" book and a kind of sequel to her first, *A Vindication of the Rights of Men* (1790), in which she championed one of the most revolutionary ideas of her time: the idea of "human rights" that are essential to human flourishing.

John Stuart Mill (1806–1873) was in important respects a kindred spirit to his contemporaries Feuerbach and Marx, to Schiller before him and to the early Nietzsche after him, and even to EMERSON (at least in Emerson's individualist rather than Transcendentalist moments). He too was a fundamentally humanistic thinker who sought to reinterpret human life in a broadly naturalistic way. There was no question in his mind that human beings were significantly different from other types of living creature. What interested him more, however, was the reality and importance of qualitative differences between merely or minimally human life and a kind of attainable but uncommon human life that is more genuinely, fully, and truly human, and so of higher worth. He further attempted to develop a naturalistic value theory and approach to ethics (to which he gave the name "utilitarianism") to go along with such a reinterpretation.

ARTHUR SCHOPENHAUER (1788–1860), like FICHTE, was a self-styled Kantian attempting to work out what he took to be the upshot of Kant's philosophical revolution. He arguably was a kind of metaphysical Idealist despite his vehement contempt for the "Idealisms" of Fichte, SCHELLING, and (in particular) Hegel, and notwithstanding his dark pessimism. He conceived of the world of experience as "representation," of the basic nature of the reality underlying it as nothing more than a kind of blind striving he called "will" (rather than anything material), and of nature and life as its expressions. Yet he also arguably was at least a kind of proto-naturalist, in his conception of human reality as a form of life among other forms of life. But for him this means that it is fundamentally an instance of the same ultimately irrational and meaningless dynamic that is manifested in everything else in the world of nature—except that it is more complex, and is able both to gain knowledge of and to say "No" to it all. He sought to carry out what Nietzsche called a radical "de-deification" of our thinking about life and the world, and about ourselves and matters of meaning, morals, and values. But for Schopenhauer this leaves us with nothing but a world of pointless striving and suffering, to which oblivion would be preferable. No one in the history of philosophy has drawn conclusions that were more profoundly pessimistic.

Friedrich Nietzsche (1844–1900) initially was impressed both by Schopenhauer's de-deified reinterpretation of the world and human reality and by his pessimistic conclusions. Persuasion gave way to dissatisfaction, and to inspiration to seek some way of avoiding his conclusions and of improving on his interpretation, even while granting that Schopenhauer was fundamentally right about the untenability of optimistic assessments of the human condition. What Nietzsche called "the death of God" might seem to lead not only to the abandonment of the morality of "good and evil" (which he advocated) but also to nihilism, whose advent concerned him greatly. He sought to find and show a way to a "philosophy of the future" that would overcome nihilism as well as religious and moralistic ways of thinking, and would be as strongly "life-affirming" as Schopenhauer's thought was "life-negating." In place of Schopenhauer's metaphysics of "will," he developed and advanced a reinterpretation of human psychology and human life—and even of life and the world more generally—whose fundamental principle is a basic disposition he called "will to power." He further supplemented his attempt to launch a naturalistic reinterpretation of human reality with a radical "revaluation of values" and reconsideration of morality that would render it conducive rather than detrimental to "the enhancement of life."

HENRI BERGSON (1859–1941) was also drawn to the concept of "life" and to the project of a "philosophy of life" that would illuminate our understanding of human reality and its relation to the phenomenon of life more generally. Like Nietzsche, he believed it important to take account of what can be learned about life from the life sciences—but also to be prepared to draw on further sources of insight and understanding in its interpretation. His concepts of "creative evolution" and of the *élan vital* (vital spirit) of life suggest the flavor of the interpretation he developed, in which the creativity and vitality of the human spirit are traced to fundamental features of life itself.

Wilhelm Dilthey (1833–1911) was also a "philosopher of life," but the form of life in which he was primarily interested was *human* life. Moreover, like Hegel (whose "philosophy of *Geist*" he saw himself as reviving and advancing), that for him meant human-*spiritual* life, and what human life has become as a historically developing reality. He thus focused on human social reality and its historicality. Dilthey further maintained that historical phenomena and historical developments, while "naturalistic" in the sense that they have to do entirely with human life in this world, are fundamentally different in character from biological and other merely natural phenomena and processes. They therefore require a different sort of comprehension ("understanding") from the sort that is appropriate to the latter ("explanation").

"Naturalism" (as this expression is to be understood here) thus is to be distinguished from the sort of mechanistically deterministic "materialism" best exemplified by the French Enlightenment thinker Julien de La Mettrie in his *Man a Machine* (1747). It likewise is not to be construed along the lines of the sort of comparably deterministic "biologism" that proclaims all of human life to be comprehensible and explainable in biological terms. Rather, it is intended to designate the general position that we fundamentally are living creatures, human beings (in German, *Menschen*) living in a world that is natural, social, cultural, and interpersonal. Its basic commitment is to the idea that while there may well be things about human life that cannot be fully comprehended and adequately explained in terms of biological (or, for that matter, mechanistic) principles, they are to be presumed to have come to be humanly possible owing to developments in the course of human events—for example, of a social or cultural nature. All such events are taken to involve nothing more than human actions, interactions, and experience of an entirely mundane nature, requiring no appeal to anything beyond this life in this world.

The rubric of "naturalisms" as employed here is intended to leave open the question of whether there are things about human life that have emerged under such circumstances but need to be differently comprehended and explained than those circumstances themselves, because they differ qualitatively from the conditions that made them possible. As has been indicated above (and will now be seen), human reality can be interpreted in strikingly different ways within these general parameters. A number of further cases in point will be encountered in Part IV of this volume.

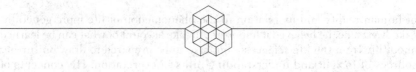

LUDWIG FEUERBACH
(1804 – 1872)

Ludwig Andreas Feuerbach (whose surname literally means "stream of fire") was more than a transitional figure between HEGEL and KARL MARX. He was an early leading light in the naturalistic turn in German philosophy after Hegel, seizing upon the idea of a philosophical anthropology that had played only a minor role in the thinking of KANT and Hegel and elevating it to a central position in his heralded "philosophy of the future." He also was a passionate early proponent of what later came to be called "secular humanism," seeking to develop a new value theory and moral philosophy upon philosophical-anthropological foundations. He was an inspiration not only to the young Marx but also to many other young philosophers, intellectuals, and artistically minded thinkers (including the young composer Richard Wagner) in the middle decades of the nineteenth century.

Feuerbach ("FOYER-bach") was born in Landshut, Bavaria. He studied first theology and then philosophy at Heidelberg and Berlin, where he encountered Hegel and came under his influence. After receiving his doctorate at Erlangen in 1828 he began teaching there; but he lost his position when his authorship of an anonymously published critique of Christianity (*Thoughts on Death and Immortality*, 1830) became known. That ended his academic career. It also made him something of a celebrity in the intellectual community in Germany. His best-known book, *The Essence of Christianity* (1841), attracted considerable attention in Britain as well, through an 1854 translation by Marian Evans (who later gained fame in her own right as a novelist, writing under the name of George Eliot). It was followed by *Principles of the Philosophy of the Future* (1843) and the essay "The Essence of Religion" (1845). Thereafter he turned his attention to the natural sciences and their philosophical implications—the subject of his intended magnum opus titled *Theogonie* (*Theogony*, 1857), which languishes in obscurity. Because he was a liberal rather than a radical, and less sophisticated than the rising generation of scientifically minded philosophers whom he had helped to inspire, his star waned well before his death in 1872.

Feuerbach first attracted attention as a critic of Hegel, seeking to recast what he took to be the most valuable aspects of Hegel's thought in a naturalistic form purged of the encumbrances of Hegelian Idealism. It was his vigorous critique of religion, however—undoubtedly inspired by Hegel's own more veiled but actually rather critical assessment of it—that made some regard him as a champion of Enlightenment and others see him as a dangerous threat, unfit for academic life. In his first anonymous book on religion he had taken a deeply critical view of the central doctrines of Christianity and of the motivation of those attracted to them. He later modified his interpretation in both respects, taking a demythologizing (rather than debunking) approach that had been anticipated by Hegel himself.

For Feuerbach religion is a sort of confusion that results from our tendency to project aspects of our own nature into an imaginary realm beyond this life and this world. He therefore called for the "reduction" or transformation of theology into anthropology, to undo the mischief resulting from this projection and to salvage its human meaning. Feuerbach saw Hegelian philosophy as an important first step in beginning this reduction; but Hegel had taken it only as far as the transformation of religious thought and imagery into his speculative philosophical Idealism, whose centerpiece is the idea of "spirit" (*Geist*). That, for Feuerbach, was still a mystification of the truth of the matter, which is properly to be conceived as human reality, or "man." Hegel's spiritualist Idealism was thus only a transitional stage in the reduction of religion to a philosophical anthropology.

Feuerbach therefore called for a "philosophy of the future" in which both theology and metaphysics would give way to a scientifically informed philosophy centering on a broadly naturalistic reinterpretation of human life, human knowledge, and human value. For him, however, the key to understanding our humanity is not merely recognizing that we are a part of living nature but also grasping that a developmental process has occurred during which humanity has come to be qualitatively different from mere animality, as our nature has been transformed under the social conditions of human existence. Our humanity is an emergent phenomenon, owing to the ways in which community has affected our emotional, sensuous, and intellectual capacities. But for Feuerbach, in contrast to Hegel before him and Marx after him, "community" is conceived primarily in interpersonal rather than social-institutional terms. The first chapter of *The Essence of Christianity*, excerpted below, is perhaps the best introduction to his thinking with respect to human reality, as well as the idea of "God," and the relation between philosophy and religion.

The excerpts that follow from Feuerbach's *Principles of the Philosophy of the Future*, his concise outline of his philosophical position, illustrate both how he attempted to position himself in relation to Hegel and how he distanced himself from Hegel and sought to chart a different course. They also sketch out the kind of account of our nature he proposes in place of Hegel's. One can easily see from them why Feuerbach had such appeal to those who were ready for something new and different after Hegel, and also why his chief legacy has been to inspire others to pursue the kind of naturalistic and humanistic reinterpretation of human reality he called for and attempted to initiate.

From The Essence of Christianity

From *Chapter I. Introduction*

§ 1. THE ESSENTIAL NATURE OF MAN

Religion has its basis in the essential difference between man and the brute[1]—the brutes have no religion. It is true that the old uncritical writers on natural history[2] attributed to the elephant, among other laudable qualities, the virtue of religiousness; but the religion of elephants belongs to the realm of

---

1. That is, the subhuman animal.
2. Notably the Roman author Pliny the Elder (23/4–

79 C.E.), who so described elephants in his encyclopedic *Natural History*.

fable. Cuvier,[3] one of the greatest authorities on the animal kingdom, assigns, on the strength of his personal observations, no higher grade of intelligence to the elephant than to the dog.

But what is this essential difference between man and the brute? The most simple, general, and also the most popular answer to this question is— consciousness:—but consciousness in the strict sense; for the consciousness implied in the feeling of self as an individual, in discrimination by the senses, in the perception and even judgment of outward things according to definite sensible signs, cannot be denied to the brutes. Consciousness in the strictest sense is present only in a being to whom his species, his essential nature, is an object of thought.[4] The brute is indeed conscious of himself as an individual—and he has accordingly the feeling of self as the common centre of successive sensations—but not as a species: hence, he is without that consciousness which in its nature, as in its name, is akin to science [*Wissenschaft*]. Where there is this higher consciousness there is a capability of *Wissenschaft*. *Wissenschaft* is the cognisance of species. In practical life we have to do with individuals; in *Wissenschaft*, with species. But only a being to whom his own species, his own nature, is an object of thought, can make the essential nature of other things or beings an object of thought.

Hence the brute has only a simple, man a twofold life: in the brute, the inner life is one with the outer; man has both an inner and an outer life. The inner life of man is the life which has relation to his species, to his general, as distinguished from his individual, nature. Man thinks—that is, he converses with himself. The brute can exercise no function which has relation to its species without another individual external to itself; but man can perform the functions of thought and speech, which strictly imply such a relation, apart from another individual. Man is himself at once I and thou;[5] he can put himself in the place of another, for this reason, that to him his species, his essential nature, and not merely his individuality, is an object of thought.[6]

Religion, being identical with the distinctive characteristic of man, is then identical with self-consciousness—with the consciousness which man has of his nature. But religion, expressed generally, is consciousness of the infinite; thus it is and can be nothing else than the consciousness which man has of his own—not finite and limited, but infinite—nature.[7] A really finite being has not even the faintest adumbration, still less consciousness, of an infinite being, for the limit of the nature is also the limit of the consciousness. The consciousness of the caterpillar, whose life is confined to a particular species of plant, does not extend itself beyond this narrow domain. It does, indeed, discriminate between this plant and other plants, but more it knows not. A

3. Georges, Baron Cuvier (1769–1832), French zoologist; he made the following observation in *The Animal Kingdom, Distributed According to Its Organization* (1817).
4. This is what Feuerbach means by "species-being" (*Gattungswesen*)—his expression coined in an attempt to recharacterize Hegelian conception of "spirit knowing itself as spirit" in a naturalistic way. A being of this sort—of our sort, Feuerbach is contending—is capable of self-cognizing self-consciousness; and, as he goes on to say, a being capable of such self-cognition is capable of cognition (*Wissen*) and therefore of its refinement, *Wis-*

senschaft (that is, scientific and other rigorous cognitive inquiry). (See the Hegel glossary, p. 144.)
5. A phrase (*Ich und Du*) made famous by MARTIN BUBER's 1923 book of that title (see below). It also figures significantly in Feuerbach's *Principles of the Philosophy of the Future* (1843, see below).
6. In this way Feuerbach attempts to derive the imperative of human sociality from our "species-being," which involves the capacity not only for self-consciousness but also for self-knowledge of our "species-nature."
7. These two sentences are paradigmatic of Feuerbach's manner of reasoning.

consciousness so limited, but on account of that very limitation so infallible, we do not call consciousness, but instinct. Consciousness, in the strict or proper sense, is identical with consciousness of the infinite; a limited consciousness is no consciousness; consciousness is essentially infinite in its nature. The consciousness of the infinite is nothing else than the consciousness of the infinity of the consciousness; or, in the consciousness of the infinite, the conscious subject has for his object the infinity of his own nature.

What, then, *is* the nature of man, of which he is conscious, or what constitutes the specific distinction, the proper humanity of man?[8] Reason, Will, Affection. To a complete man belong the power of thought, the power of will, the power of affection.[9] The power of thought is the light of the intellect, the power of will is energy of character, the power of affection is love. Reason, love, force of will, are perfections—the perfections of the human being—nay, more, they are absolute perfections of being. To will, to love, to think, are the highest powers, are the absolute nature of man as man, and the basis of his existence. Man exists to think, to love, to will. Now that which is the end, the ultimate aim, is also the true basis and principle of a being. But what is the end of reason? Reason. Of love? Love. Of will? Freedom of the will. We think for the sake of thinking; love for the sake of loving; will for the sake of willing— *i.e.*, that we may be free.[1] True existence is thinking, loving, willing existence. That alone is true, perfect, divine, which exists for its own sake. But such is love, such is reason, such is will. The divine trinity in man, above the individual man, is the unity of reason, love, will. Reason, Will, Love, are not powers which man possesses, for he is nothing without them, he is what he is only by them;[2] they are the constituent elements of his nature, which he neither has nor makes, the animating, determining, governing powers—divine, absolute powers—to which he can oppose no resistance.

How can the feeling man resist feeling, the loving one love, the rational one reason? Who has not experienced the overwhelming power of melody? And what else is the power of melody but the power of feeling? Music is the language of feeling; melody is audible feeling—feeling communicating itself. Who has not experienced the power of love, or at least heard of it? Which is the stronger—love or the individual man? Is it man that possesses love, or is it not much rather love that possesses man? When love impels a man to suffer death even joyfully for the beloved one, is this death-conquering power his own individual power, or is it not rather the power of love? And who that ever truly thought has not experienced that quiet, subtle power—the power of thought? When thou sinkest into deep reflection, forgetting thyself and what is around thee, dost thou govern reason, or is it not reason which governs and absorbs thee? *Wissenschaftlich* enthusiasm—is it not the most glorious

---

8. The obtuse Materialist says: "Man is distinguished from the brute *only* by consciousness—he is an animal with consciousness superadded"; not reflecting, that in a being which awakes to consciousness, there takes place a qualitative change, a differentiation of the entire nature. For the rest, our words are by no means intended to depreciate the nature of the lower animals. This is not the place to enter further into that question [Feuerbach's note].
9. That is, the capacity to be affected.
1. Feuerbach here links "will" or "willing" and "free-

dom" because he supposes that his readers will know from KANT and HEGEL that the essence of both is *self-determination*.
2. One of Feuerbach's central premises (derived from Hegel) is that "the nature of the subject is exhausted in the predicate"—that is, there is nothing more to the idea of the subject of a definition than is contained in the predicates of such statements. Thus to say "God is love" is simply to say that "love" is (one of the things that is meant by) "God."

triumph of intellect over thee? The desire of knowledge—is it not a simply irresistible, and all-conquering power? And when thou suppressest a passion, renouncest a habit, in short, achievest a victory over thyself, is this victorious power thy own personal power, or is it not rather the energy of will, the force of morality, which seizes the mastery of thee, and fills thee with indignation against thyself and thy individual weaknesses?

Man is nothing without an object.[3] The great models of humanity, such men as reveal to us what man is capable of, have attested the truth of this proposition by their lives. They had only one dominant passion—the realisation of the aim which was the essential object of their activity. But the object to which a subject essentially, necessarily relates, is nothing else than this subject's own, but objective, nature. If it be an object common to several individuals of the same species, but under various conditions, it is still, at least as to the form under which it presents itself to each of them according to their respective modifications, their own, but objective, nature.

Thus the Sun is the common object of the planets, but it is an object to Mercury, to Venus, to Saturn, to Uranus, under other conditions than to the Earth. Each planet has its own sun. The Sun which lights and warms Uranus has no physical (only an astronomical, scientific) existence for the Earth; and not only does the Sun appear different, but it really is *another* sun on Uranus than on the Earth. The relation of the Sun to the Earth is therefore at the same time a relation of the Earth to itself, or to its own nature, for the measure of the size and of the intensity of light which the Sun possesses as the object of the Earth is the measure of the distance which determines the peculiar nature of the Earth. Hence each planet has in its sun the mirror of its own nature.[4]

In the object which he contemplates, therefore, man becomes acquainted with himself; consciousness of the objective is the self-consciousness of man. We know the man by the object, by his conception of what is external to himself; in it his nature becomes evident; this object is his manifested nature, his true objective *ego*. And this is true not merely of spiritual, but also of sensuous objects. Even the objects which are the most remote from man, *because* they are objects to him, and to the extent to which they are so, are revelations of human nature. Even the moon, the sun, the stars, call to man Γνῶθι σεαυτόν.[5] That he sees them, and so sees them, is an evidence of his own nature. The animal is sensible only of the beam which immediately affects life; while man perceives the ray, to him physically indifferent, of the remotest star. Man alone has purely intellectual, disinterested joys and passions; the eye of man alone keeps theoretic festivals. The eye which looks into the starry heavens, which gazes at that light, alike useless and harmless, having nothing in common with the earth and its necessities—this eye sees in that light its own nature, its own origin. The eye is heavenly in its nature. Hence man elevates himself above the earth only with the eye; hence theory begins with the contemplation of the heavens. The first philosophers were astrono-

---

3. In what follows, Feuerbach develops his naturalistic version of Hegel's view that objectification is necessary to the realization or actualization of *Geist* (our human-spiritual essential nature).
4. This is Feuerbach's version of Hegel's doctrine that things are what they are only in the context of

(and by virtue of) their relations to whatever else they are related to.
5. Know thyself (Greek, *Gnōthi seauton*), a maxim carved into the temple of Apollo at Delphi (4th c. B.C.E.), home of the god's oracle.

mers. It is the heavens that admonish man of his destination, and remind him that he is destined not merely to action, but also to contemplation.

The *absolute* to man is his own nature.[6] The power of the object over him is therefore the power of his own nature. Thus the power of the object of feeling is the power of feeling itself; the power of the object of the intellect is the power of the intellect itself; the power of the object of the will is the power of the will itself. The man who is affected by musical sounds is governed by feeling; by the feeling, that is, which finds its corresponding element in musical sounds. But it is not melody as such, it is only melody pregnant with meaning and emotion, which has power over feeling. Feeling is only acted on by that which conveys feeling, *i.e.*, by itself, its own nature. Thus also the will; thus, and infinitely more, the intellect. Whatever kind of object, therefore, we are at any time conscious of, we are always at the same time conscious of our own nature; we can affirm nothing without affirming ourselves. And since to will, to feel, to think, are perfections, essences, realities, it is impossible that intellect, feeling, and will should feel or perceive themselves as limited, finite powers, *i.e.*, as worthless, as nothing. For finiteness and nothingness are identical; finiteness is only a euphemism for nothingness. Finiteness is the metaphysical, the theoretical—nothingness the pathological, practical expression. What is finite to the understanding is nothing to the heart. But it is impossible that we should be conscious of will, feeling, and intellect, as finite powers, because every perfect existence, every original power and essence, is the immediate verification and affirmation of itself. It is impossible to love, will, or think, without perceiving these activities to be perfections—impossible to feel that one is a loving, willing, thinking being, without experiencing an infinite joy therein. Consciousness consists in a being becoming objective to itself; hence it is nothing apart, nothing distinct from the being which is conscious of itself. How could it otherwise become conscious of itself? It is therefore impossible to be conscious of a perfection as an imperfection, impossible to feel feeling limited, to think thought limited.

Consciousness is self-verification, self-affirmation, self-love, joy in one's own perfection. Consciousness is the characteristic mark of a perfect nature; it exists only in a self-sufficing, complete being. Even human vanity attests this truth. A man looks in the glass; he has complacency in his appearance. This complacency is a necessary, involuntary consequence of the completeness, the beauty of his form. A beautiful form is satisfied in itself; it has necessarily joy in itself—in self-contemplation. This complacency becomes vanity only when a man piques himself on his form as being his individual form, not when he admires it as a specimen of human beauty in general. It is fitting that he should admire it thus: he can conceive no form more beautiful, more sublime than the human.[7] Assuredly every being loves itself, its existence—and fitly so. To

6. Feuerbach's signature statement, his "anthropological reduction" of Hegel's contention that (analogously expressed) the absolute to *Geist* is the very nature of *Geist*—for "the absolute," according to Hegel, is "*Geist* knowing itself as *Geist*."

7. *Homini homine nihil pulchrius* [To the human nothing (is) more beautiful than the human]. (Cic. de Nat. D. 1.1) And this is no sign of limitation, for he regards other beings as beautiful besides

himself; he delights in the beautiful forms of animals, in the beautiful forms of plants, in the beauty of nature in general. But only the absolute, the perfect form, can delight without envy in the forms of other beings [Feuerbach's note]. Slightly misquoted from *On the Nature of the Gods* 1.77 by the Roman statesman and scholar Cicero (106–42 B.C.E.).

exist is a good. *Quidquid essentia dignum est, scientia dignum est.*[8] Everything that exists has value, is a being of distinction—at least this is true of the species: hence it asserts, maintains itself. But the highest form of self-assertion, the form which is itself a superiority, a perfection, a bliss, a good, is consciousness.

Every limitation of the reason, or in general of the nature of man, rests on a delusion, an error. It is true that the human being, as an individual, can and must—herein consists his distinction from the brute—feel and recognise himself to be limited; but he can become conscious of his limits, his finiteness, only because the perfection, the infinitude of his species, is perceived by him, whether as an object of feeling, of conscience, or of the thinking consciousness. If he makes his own limitations the limitations of the species, this arises from the mistake that he identifies himself immediately with the species—a mistake which is intimately connected with the individual's love of ease, sloth, vanity, and egoism. For a limitation which I know to be merely mine humiliates, shames, and perturbs me. Hence to free myself from this feeling of shame, from this state of dissatisfaction, I convert the limits of my individuality into the limits of human nature in general. What is incomprehensible to me is incomprehensible to others; why should I trouble myself further? It is no fault of mine; my understanding is not to blame, but the understanding of the race. But it is a ludicrous and even culpable error to define as finite and limited what constitutes the essence of man, the nature of the species, which is the absolute nature of the individual. Every being is sufficient to itself. No being can deny itself, *i.e.*, its own nature; no being is a limited one to itself. Rather, every being is in and by itself infinite—has its God, its highest conceivable being, in itself. Every limit of a being is cognisable only by another being out of and above him. The life of the ephemera[9] is extraordinarily short in comparison with that of longer-lived creatures; but nevertheless, for the ephemera this short life is as long as a life of years to others. The leaf on which the caterpillar lives is for it a world, an infinite space.

That which makes a being what it is, is its talent, its power, its wealth, its adornment. How can it possibly hold its existence non-existence, its wealth poverty, its talent incapacity? If the plants had eyes, taste, and judgment, each plant would declare its own flower the most beautiful; for its comprehension, its taste, would reach no farther than its natural power of production. What the productive power of its nature has brought forth as the highest, that must also its taste, its judgment, recognise and affirm as the highest. What the nature affirms, the understanding, the taste, the judgment, cannot deny; otherwise the understanding, the judgment, would no longer be the understanding and judgment of this particular being, but of some other. The measure of the nature is also the measure of the understanding. If the nature is limited, so also is the feeling, so also is the understanding. But to a limited being its limited understanding is not felt to be a limitation; on the contrary, it is perfectly happy and contented with this understanding; it regards it, praises and values it, as a glorious, divine power; and the limited understanding,

---

8. Whatever is worthy of existing is worthy of being known (Latin). Slightly misquoted from Sir Francis Bacon's *Novum Organum* 1.120 (1620).

9. The mayfly, which in its adult form may live only a few hours.

on its part, values the limited nature whose understanding it is. Each is exactly adapted to the other; how should they be at issue with each other? A being's understanding is its sphere of vision. As far as thou seest, so far extends thy nature; and conversely. The eye of the brute reaches no farther than its needs, and its nature no farther than its needs. And so far as thy nature reaches, so far reaches thy unlimited self-consciousness, so far art thou God.[1] The discrepancy between the understanding and the nature, between the power of conception and the power of production in the human consciousness, on the one hand, is merely of individual significance and has not a universal application; and, on the other hand, it is only apparent. He who, having written a bad poem, knows it to be bad, is in his intelligence, and therefore in his nature, not so limited as he who, having written a bad poem, admires it and thinks it good.

It follows that if thou thinkest the infinite, thou perceivest and affirmest the infinitude of the power of thought; if thou feelest the infinite, thou feelest and affirmest the infinitude of the power of feeling. The object of the intellect is intellect objective to itself; the object of feeling is feeling objective to itself. If thou hast no sensibility, no feeling for music, thou perceivest in the finest music nothing more than in the wind that whistles by thy ear, or than in the brook which rushes past thy feet. What, then, is it which acts on thee when thou art affected by melody? What dost thou perceive in it? What else than the voice of thy own heart? Feeling speaks only to feeling; feeling is comprehensible only by feeling, that is, by itself—for this reason, that the object of feeling is nothing else than feeling. Music is a monologue of emotion. But the dialogue of philosophy also is in truth only a monologue of the intellect; thought speaks only to thought. The splendours of the crystal charm the sense, but the intellect is interested only in the laws of crystallisation. The intellectual only is the object of the intellect.

All therefore which, in the point of view of metaphysical, transcendental speculation and religion, has the significance only of the secondary, the subjective, the medium, the organ—has in truth the significance of the primary, of the essence, of the object itself. If, for example, feeling is the essential organ of religion, the nature of God is nothing else than an expression of the nature of feeling.[2] The true but latent sense of the phrase, "Feeling is the organ of the divine," is, feeling is the noblest, the most excellent, *i.e.*, the divine, in man. How couldst thou perceive the divine by feeling, if feeling were not itself divine in its nature? The divine assuredly is known only by means of the divine—God is known only by himself. The divine nature which is discerned by feeling is in truth nothing else than feeling enraptured, in ecstasy with itself—feeling intoxicated with joy, blissful in its own plenitude.

It is already clear from this that where feeling is held to be the organ of the infinite, the subjective essence of religion,—the external data of religion lose their objective value. And thus, since feeling has been held the cardinal principle in religion, the doctrines of Christianity, formerly so sacred, have lost their

---

1. This is the essence of Feuerbach's philosophy of religion, developed at length both in this book and in its sequel, *Lectures on the Essence of Religion* (1851).
2. Here Feuerbach takes his "subject is exhausted in the predicate" principle one step further, maintaining that exalted objects are but the objectifications of the expressions associated with them. (This too is an adaptation of a Hegelian theme.)

importance. If, from this point of view, some value is still conceded to Christian ideas, it is a value springing entirely from the relation they bear to feeling; if another object would excite the same emotions, it would be just as welcome. But the object of religious feeling is become a matter of indifference, only because when once feeling has been pronounced to be the subjective essence of religion, it in fact is also the objective essence of religion, though it may not be declared, at least directly, to be such. I say directly; for indirectly this is certainly admitted, when it is declared that feeling, as such, is religious, and thus the distinction between specifically religious and irreligious, or at least non-religious, feelings is abolished—a necessary consequence of the point of view in which feeling only is regarded as the organ of the divine. For on what other ground than that of its essence, its nature, dost thou hold feeling to be the organ of the infinite, the divine being? And is not the nature of feeling in general also the nature of every special feeling, be its object what it may? What, then, makes this feeling religious? A given object? Not at all; for this object is itself a religious one only when it is not an object of the cold understanding or memory, but of feeling. What then? The nature of feeling—a nature of which every special feeling, without distinction of objects, partakes. Thus, feeling is pronounced to be religious, simply because it is feeling; the ground of its religiousness is its own nature—lies in itself. But is not feeling thereby declared to be itself the absolute, the divine? If feeling in itself is good, religious, i.e., holy, divine, has not feeling its God in itself?[3]

But if, notwithstanding, thou wilt posit an object of feeling, but at the same time seekest to express thy feeling truly, without introducing by thy reflection any foreign element, what remains to thee but to distinguish between thy individual feeling and the general nature of feeling;—to separate the universal in feeling from the disturbing, adulterating influences with which feeling is bound up in thee, under thy individual conditions? Hence what thou canst alone contemplate, declare to be the infinite, and define as its essence, is merely the nature of feeling. Thou hast thus no other definition of God than this: God is pure, unlimited, free Feeling. Every other God, whom thou supposest, is a God thrust upon thy feeling from without. Feeling is atheistic in the sense of the orthodox belief, which attaches religion to an external object; it denies an objective God—it is itself God. In this point of view only the negation of feeling is the negation of God. Thou art simply too cowardly or too narrow to confess in words what thy feeling tacitly affirms. Fettered by outward considerations, still in bondage to vulgar empiricism, incapable of comprehending the spiritual grandeur of feeling, thou art terrified before the religious atheism of thy heart. By this fear thou destroyest the unity of thy feeling with itself, in imagining to thyself an objective being distinct from thy feeling, and thus necessarily sinking back into the old questions and doubts—is there a God or not?—questions and doubts which vanish, nay, are impossible, where feeling is defined as the essence of religion. Feeling is thy own inward power, but at the same time a power distinct from thee, and independent of thee; it is in thee, above thee; it is itself that which constitutes the objective in thee—thy own being which impresses thee as another being; in

3. A passage that encapsulates the effusively ecstatic Romanticism of Feuerbach's secular-humanistic naturalism and makes understandable his immense appeal to readers seeking a substitute for traditional Christianity.

short, thy God. How wilt thou, then, distinguish from this objective being within thee another objective being? how wilt thou get beyond thy feeling?

But feeling has here been adduced only as an example. It is the same with every other power, faculty, potentiality, reality, activity—the name is indifferent—which is defined as the essential organ of any object. Whatever is a subjective expression of a nature is simultaneously also its objective expression. Man cannot get beyond his true nature. He may indeed by means of the imagination conceive individuals of another so-called higher kind, but he can never get loose from his species, his nature; the conditions of being, the positive final predicates which he gives to these other individuals, are always determinations or qualities drawn from his own nature—qualities in which he in truth only images and projects himself. There may certainly be thinking beings besides men on the other planets of our solar system. But by the supposition of such beings we do not change our standing point—we extend our conceptions *quantitatively* not *qualitatively*. For as surely as on the other planets there are the same laws of motion, so surely are there the same laws of perception and thought as here. In fact, we people the other planets, not that we may place there different beings from ourselves, but *more* beings of our own or of a similar nature.

FROM § 2. THE ESSENCE OF RELIGION[4] CONSIDERED GENERALLY

What we have hitherto been maintaining generally, even with regard to sensational impressions, of the relation between subject and object, applies especially to the relation between the subject and the religious object.

In the perceptions of the senses consciousness of the object is distinguishable from consciousness of self; but in religion, consciousness of the object and self-consciousness coincide. The object of the senses is out of man, the religious object is within him, and therefore as little forsakes him as his self-consciousness or his conscience; it is the intimate, the closest object. "God," says Augustine, for example, "is nearer, more related to us, and therefore more easily known by us, than sensible, corporeal things."[5] The object of the senses is in itself indifferent—independent of the disposition or of the judgment; but the object of religion is a selected object; the most excellent, the first, the supreme being; it essentially presupposes a critical judgment, a discrimination between the divine and the non-divine, between that which is worthy of adoration and that which is not worthy. And here may be applied, without any limitation, the proposition: the object of any subject is nothing else than the subject's own nature taken objectively. Such as are a man's thoughts and dispositions, such is his God; so much worth as a man has, so much and no more has his God. Consciousness of God is self-consciousness, knowledge of God is self-knowledge. By his God thou knowest the man, and by the man his God; the two are identical. Whatever is God to a man, that is his heart and soul; and conversely, God is the manifested inward nature, the expressed self of a man[6]—religion the solemn unveiling of a man's hidden treasures,[7]

4. That is, the essential nature or reality (*Wesen*) of religion.
5. Quoted from *The Literal Meaning of Genesis*, by

Saint Augustine of Hippo (354–430).
6. That is, of human being, human reality, humanity.
7. That is, the hidden treasures of man's humanity.

the revelation of his intimate thoughts, the open confession of his love-secrets.

But when religion—consciousness of God—is designated as the self-consciousness of man, this is not to be understood as affirming that the religious man is directly aware of this identity; for, on the contrary, ignorance of it is fundamental to the peculiar nature of religion. To preclude this misconception, it is better to say, religion is man's earliest and also indirect form of self-knowledge. Hence, religion everywhere precedes philosophy, as in the history of the race, so also in that of the individual. Man first of all sees his nature as if *out of* himself, before he finds it in himself. His own nature is in the first instance contemplated by him as that of another being.[8] Religion is the childlike condition of humanity; but the child sees his nature—man—out of himself; in childhood a man is an object to himself, under the form of another man. Hence the historical progress of religion consists in this: that what by an earlier religion was regarded as objective, is now recognised as subjective; that is, what was formerly contemplated and worshipped as God is now perceived to be something *human*. What was at first religion becomes at a later period idolatry; man is seen to have adored his own nature. Man has given objectivity to himself, but has not recognised the object as his own nature: a later religion takes this forward step; every advance in religion is therefore a deeper self-knowledge. But every particular religion, while it pronounces its predecessors idolatrous, excepts itself—and necessarily so, otherwise it would no longer be religion—from the fate, the common nature of all religions: it imputes only to other religions what is the fault, if fault it be, of religion in general. Because it has a different object, a different tenor, because it has transcended the ideas of preceding religions, it erroneously supposes itself exalted above the necessary eternal laws which constitute the essence of religion—it fancies its object, its ideas, to be superhuman.[9] But the essence of religion, thus hidden from the religious, is evident to the thinker, by whom religion is viewed objectively, which it cannot be by its votaries. And it is our task to show that the antithesis of divine and human is altogether illusory, that it is nothing else than the antithesis between the human nature in general and the human individual; that, consequently, the object and contents of the Christian religion are altogether human.

Religion, at least the Christian, is the relation of man to himself, or more correctly to his own nature (*i.e.*, his subjective nature); but a relation to it, viewed as a nature apart from his own. The divine being is nothing else than the human being, or, rather, the human nature purified, freed from the limits of the individual man, made objective—*i.e.*, contemplated and revered as another, a distinct being. All the attributes of the divine nature are, therefore, attributes of the human nature.[1]

In relation to the attributes, the predicates, of the Divine Being, this is admitted without hesitation, but by no means in relation to the subject of these predicates. The negation of the subject is held to be irreligion, nay, atheism;

---

8. This is a clearer (and blunter) expression of what Hegel thought and said regarding religion and our human-spiritual nature.

9. In German, *übermenschlich*; this is an early anticipation of Nietzsche's concept of the *Übermensch* as a figurative representation of what human reality has it in it to become through the ongoing "enhancement of life."

1. This summarizes Feuerbach's "reduction" of theology to (a normative) philosophical anthropology.

though not so the negation of the predicates. But that which has no predicates or qualities, has no effect upon me; that which has no effect upon me has no existence for me. To deny all the qualities of a being is equivalent to denying the being himself. A being without qualities is one which cannot become an object to the mind, and such a being is virtually non-existent. Where man deprives God of all qualities, God is no longer anything more to him than a negative being. To the truly religious man, God is not a being without qualities, because to him he is a positive, real being. The theory that God cannot be defined, and consequently cannot be known by man, is therefore the offspring of recent times, a product of modern unbelief.

As reason is and can be pronounced finite only where man regards sensual enjoyment, or religious emotion, or æsthetic contemplation, or moral sentiment, as the absolute, the true; so the proposition that God is unknowable or undefinable, can only be enunciated and become fixed as a dogma, where this object has no longer any interest for the intellect; where the real, the positive, alone has any hold on man, where the real alone has for him the significance of the essential, of the absolute, divine object, but where at the same time, in contradiction with this purely worldly tendency, there yet exist some old remains of religiousness. On the ground that God is unknowable, man excuses himself to what is yet remaining of his religious conscience for his forgetfulness of God, his absorption in the world: he denies God practically by his conduct,—the world has possession of all his thoughts and inclinations,— but he does not deny him theoretically, he does not attack his existence; he lets that rest. But this existence does not affect or incommode him; it is a merely negative existence, an existence without existence, a self-contradictory existence,—a state of being which, as to its effects, is not distinguishable from non-being. The denial of determinate, positive predicates concerning the divine nature is nothing else than a denial of religion, with, however, an appearance of religion in its favour, so that it is not recognised as a denial; it is simply a subtle, disguised atheism. The alleged religious horror of limiting God by positive predicates is only the irreligious wish to know nothing more of God, to banish God from the mind. Dread of limitation is dread of existence. All real existence, i.e., all existence which is truly such, is qualitative, determinative existence. He who earnestly believes in the Divine existence is not shocked at the attributing even of gross sensuous qualities to God. He who dreads an existence that may give offence, who shrinks from the grossness of a positive predicate, may as well renounce existence altogether. A God who is injured by determinate qualities has not the courage and the strength to exist. Qualities are the fire, the vital breath, the oxygen, the salt of existence. An existence in general, an existence without qualities, is an insipidity, an absurdity. But there can be no more in God than is supplied by religion. Only where man loses his taste for religion, and thus religion itself becomes insipid, does the existence of God become an insipid existence—an existence without qualities.

There is, however, a still milder way of denying the divine predicates than the direct one just described. It is admitted that the predicates of the divine nature are finite, and, more particularly, human qualities, but their rejection is rejected; they are even taken under protection, because it is necessary to man to have a definite conception of God, and since he is man he can form no other than a human conception of him. In relation to God, it is said, these predicates are certainly without any objective validity; but to me, if he is to exist for me, he cannot appear otherwise than as he does appear to me, namely, as a being with attributes analogous to the human. But this distinction between what God is in himself, and what he is for me destroys the peace of religion, and is besides in itself an unfounded and untenable distinction. I cannot know whether God is something else in himself or for himself than he is for me; what he is to me is to me all that he is. For me, there lies in these predicates under which he exists for me, what he is in himself, his very nature; he is for me what he can alone ever be for me. The religious man finds perfect satisfaction in that which God is in relation to himself; of any other relation he knows nothing, for God is to him what he can alone be to man. In the distinction above stated, man takes a point of view above himself, *i.e.*, above his nature, the absolute measure of his being; but this transcendental-ism is only an illusion; for I can make the distinction between the object as it is in itself, and the object as it is for me, only where an object can really appear otherwise to me, not where it appears to me such as the absolute measure of my nature determines it to appear—such as it must appear to me. It is true that I may have a merely subjective conception, *i.e.*, one which does not arise out of the general constitution of my species; but if my conception is deter-mined by the constitution of my species, the distinction between what an object is in itself, and what it is for me ceases; for this conception is itself an absolute one. The measure of the species is the absolute measure, law, and criterion of man. And, indeed, religion has the conviction that its concep-tions, its predicates of God, are such as every man ought to have, and must have, if he would have the true ones—that they are the conceptions neces-sary to human nature; nay, further, that they are objectively true, represent-ing God as he is. To every religion the gods of *other* religions are only notions concerning God, but its own conception of God is to it God himself, the true God—God such as he is in himself. Religion is satisfied only with a complete Deity, a God without reservation; it will not have a mere phantasm of God; it demands God himself. Religion gives up its own existence when it gives up the nature of God; it is no longer a truth when it renounces the pos-session of the true God. Scepticism is the arch-enemy of religion; but the distinction between object and conception—between God as he is in him-self, and God as he is for me—is a sceptical distinction, and therefore an irreligious one.

That which is to man the self-existent, the highest being, to which he can conceive nothing higher—that is to him the Divine Being. How then should he inquire concerning this being, what he is in himself? If God were an object to the bird, he would be a winged being: the bird knows nothing higher, nothing more blissful, than the winged condition. How ludicrous would it be if this bird pronounced: To me God appears as a bird, but what he is in himself I know not. To the bird the highest nature is the bird-nature; take from him the conception of this, and you take from him the conception of the highest being. How, then, could he ask whether God in himself were winged? To ask whether God is in himself what he is for me, is to ask whether God is God, is to lift oneself above one's God, to rise up against him.

Wherever, therefore, this idea, that the religious predicates are only anthropomorphisms, has taken possession of a man, there has doubt, has unbelief, obtained the mastery of faith. And it is only the inconsequence of faint-heartedness and intellectual imbecility which does not proceed from this idea to the formal negation of the predicates, and from thence to the negation of the subject to which they relate. If thou doubtest the objective truth of the predicates, thou must also doubt the objective truth of the subject whose predicates they are. If thy predicates are anthropomorphisms, the subject of them is an anthropomorphism too. If love, goodness, personality, &c., are human attributes, so also is the subject which thou presupposest, the existence of God, the belief that there is a God, an anthropomorphism—a presupposition purely human. Whence knowest thou that the belief in a God at all is not a limitation of man's mode of conception? Higher beings—and thou supposest such—are perhaps so blest in themselves, so at unity with themselves, that they are not hung in suspense between themselves and a yet higher being. To know God and not oneself to be God, to know blessedness and not oneself to enjoy it, is a state of disunity, of unhappiness. Higher beings know nothing of this unhappiness; they have no conception of that which they are not.

Thou believest in love as a divine attribute because thou thyself lovest; thou believest that God is a wise, benevolent being because thou knowest nothing better in thyself than benevolence and wisdom; and thou believest that God exists, that therefore he is a subject—whatever exists is a subject, whether it be defined as substance, person, essence, or otherwise—because thou thyself existest, art thyself a subject. Thou knowest no higher human good than to love, than to be good and wise; and even so thou knowest no higher happiness than to exist, to be a subject; for the consciousness of all reality, of all bliss, is for thee bound up in the consciousness of being a subject, of existing. God is an existence, a subject to thee, for the same reason that he is to thee a wise, a blessed, a personal being. The distinction between the divine predicates and the divine subject is only this, that to thee the subject, the existence, does not appear an anthropomorphism, because the conception of it is necessarily involved in thy own existence as a subject, whereas the predicates do appear anthropomorphisms, because their necessity—the necessity that God should be conscious, wise, good, &c.,—is not an immediate necessity, identical with the being of man, but is evolved by his self-consciousness, by the activity of his thought. I am a subject, I exist, whether I be wise or unwise, good or bad. To exist is to man the first datum; it constitutes the very idea of the subject; it is presupposed by the predicates. Hence man relinquishes the predicates, but the existence of God is to him a settled, irrefragable, absolutely certain, objective truth. But, nevertheless, this distinction is merely an apparent one. The necessity of the subject lies only in the necessity of the predicate. Thou art a subject only in so far as thou art a human subject; the certainty and reality of thy existence lie only in the certainty and reality of thy human attributes. What the subject is lies only in the predicate; the predicate is the *truth* of the subject—the subject only the personified, existing predicate, the predicate conceived as existing. Subject and predicate are distinguished only as existence and essence. The negation of the predicates is therefore the negation of the subject. What remains of the human subject when abstracted from the human attributes? Even in the language of common life the divine predicates—Providence, Omniscience, Omnipotence[2]—are put for the divine subject.

The certainty of the existence of God, of which it has been said that it is as certain, nay, more certain to man than his own existence, depends only on the certainty of the qualities of God—it is in itself no immediate certainty. To the Christian the existence of the Christian God only is a certainty; to the heathen that of the heathen God only. The heathen did not doubt the existence of Jupiter,[3] because he took no offence at the nature of Jupiter, because he could conceive of God under no other qualities, because to him these qualities were a certainty, a divine reality. The reality of the predicate is the sole guarantee of existence.

Whatever man conceives to be true, he immediately conceives to be real (that is, to have an objective existence), because, originally, only the real is true to him—true in opposition to what is merely conceived, dreamed, imagined. The idea of being, of existence, is the original idea of truth; or, originally, man makes truth dependent on existence, subsequently, existence dependent on truth. Now God is the nature of man regarded as absolute truth,—the truth of man;[4] but God, or, what is the same thing, religion, is as various as are the conditions under which man conceives this his nature, regards it as the highest being. These conditions, then, under which man conceives God, are to him the truth, and for that reason they are also the highest existence, or rather they are existence itself; for only the emphatic, the highest existence, is existence, and deserves this name. Therefore, God is[5] an existent, real being, on the very same ground that he is a particular, definite being; for the qualities of God are nothing else than the essential qualities of man himself[.]

* * *

SOURCE: From Ludwig Feuerbach, *The Essence of Christianity*, translated from the second German edition by Marian Evans (1854; reprint, London: Kegan Paul, Trench, Trübner, 1893), pp. 1–20 (translation modified by the editor). Except where otherwise indicated, German words in brackets are the terminology used in the German original, inserted by the editor in addition to their renderings in the translation; and unbracketed German words are the original terminology, substituted in place of their renderings in the translation by the editor for reasons given in notes and in the Hegel glossary (p. 144). Originally published in 1841 as *Das Wesen des Christentums* (2nd ed., 1843).

From Principles of the Philosophy of the Future

I

The task of the modern era[1] was the realization and humanization of God—the transformation and dissolution of theology into anthropology.

2. That is, making provision for a benevolent future, knowing all, and being all-powerful.
3. In Roman mythology, the king of the gods.
4. This is Feuerbach's revision of what Hegel says about *Geist*.

5. That is, "is taken to be" (so too later in the sentence).
1. That is, modern philosophy from René Descartes (1596–1650) to HEGEL.

2

The *religious* or *practical* form of this humanization was Protestantism. The God who is man, that is to say the human God, Christ, this and only this is the God of Protestantism. Unlike Catholicism, Protestantism is no longer concerned with what God is in himself, but only with what he is for man; hence, it knows no speculative or contemplative tendency like Catholicism. It has ceased to be *theology*—it is essentially *Christology; that is, religious anthropology.*

3

However, Protestantism negated God-in-himself or God as God—for only God-in-himself is, strictly speaking, God—*only in practice;* theoretically, it left him intact. He *exists;* however, not for man; that is, the *religious* man. He is a transcendent being or a being that will one day become an object *for man* up there in heaven. But that which is *other-worldly* to religion, is *this-worldly* to philosophy; what does not constitute an object for the former, does so precisely for the latter.

4

The *rational* or *theoretical* assimilation and dissolution of the God who is other-worldly to religion, and hence *not given to it as an object*, is the speculative philosophy.[2]

5

The *essence* of speculative philosophy is nothing other than the *rationalized, realized, actualized essence of God.* The speculative philosophy is the *true, consistent, rational* theology.

6

Taken as an *intelligible* [*geistig*] or an *abstract* being, that is, regarded *neither* as human *nor* as sensuous, but rather as one that is an *object for and accessible only to reason or intelligence,* God qua God is *nothing but the essence of reason* itself.[3] But, *basing* themselves *rather on imagination, ordinary theology* and *Theism regard* him as *an independent being existing separately from reason.* Under these circumstances, it is an inner, a sacred *necessity* that the essence of reason as distinguished from reason itself be at last *identified with it* and the divine being thus be apprehended, realized, *as the essence* of reason. It is on this necessity that *the great historical significance of speculative philosophy* rests. The proof of the proposition that the divine essence is the essence of reason or intelligence lies in the fact that the *determinations* or

2. That is, Hegelian philosophy.
3. The term *geistig* would be better translated here as "spiritual." Feuerbach is saying that if God is conceived as (taken to be) a *spiritual* (and therefore abstract) being that is neither human nor perceivable by the senses at all, but rather one that is only an object of reason or thought, then God qua God is nothing but the essence of reason.

qualities of God, in so far as they are *rational* or *intelligible* and not *determinations* of *sensuousness* or *imagination,* are, in fact, *qualities of reason.*

"God is *the infinite being* or *the being without any limitations whatsoever.*" But what cannot be a limit or boundary on God can also not be a limit or boundary on reason. If, for example, God is elevated above all limitations of sensuousness, so, too, is reason. He who cannot conceive of any entity except as sensuous, that is, he whose reason is limited by sensuousness, can only have a God who is limited by sensuousness. Reason, which conceives God as an infinite being, conceives, in point of fact, *its own* infinity in God. What is divine to reason is also truly *rational* to it, or in other words, it is a being that perfectly corresponds to and satisfies it. That, however, in which a being finds satisfaction, is nothing but the being *in which it encounters itself as its own object.* He who finds satisfaction in a philosopher is himself of a philosophical nature. That he is of this nature is precisely what he and others encounter in this satisfaction. Reason "does not, however, pause at the finite, sensuous things; it finds satisfaction in the infinite being alone"—that is to say, the essence of reason is disclosed to us primarily in the infinite being.

"God is *the necessary being.*" But his necessity rests on the ground that he is a *rational, intelligent* being. The ground for what the world or matter is does not lie in the world or matter itself, for it is completely indifferent to whether it is or is not, or to why it is so and not otherwise.[4] Hence, it must necessarily presuppose another being as its cause, a being that is *intelligent* and *self-conscious* and acts according to reasons and goals. For if this being were to be conceived of as lacking intelligence, the question as to its own ground must arise again. The necessity of the primary and the highest being rests, therefore, on the presupposition that the *intellect* alone is the being that is *primary, highest, necessary,* and *true.* Just as the truth and reality of metaphysical or ontotheological[5] determinations depend on their reducibility to psychological or rather anthropological determinations, so the necessity of the divine being in the old metaphysics or ontotheology has meaning, truth, and reality only in the psychological or anthropological characterization of God as an intelligent being. The necessary being is one that it is necessary to think of, that must be affirmed absolutely and which it is simply impossible to deny or annul, but only to the extent to which it is a *thinking* being *itself.* Thus, it is its own necessity and reality which reason demonstrates in the necessary being.

"God is *unconditional, general*—'God is not this or that particular thing'—*immutable, eternal, or timeless being.*" But absoluteness, immutability, eternality, and generality are, according to the judgment of metaphysical theology itself, also qualities of the truths or laws of reason, and hence the qualities of reason itself; for what else are these immutable, general, absolute, and universally valid truths of reason if not expressions of the essence of reason itself?

"God is *the independent, autonomous being not requiring any other being in order to exist, hence subsisting entirely by and through itself.*" But even this abstract, metaphysical characterization has meaning and reality only as a

---

4. It is quite obvious here, as in all sections where the problem is to deal with, and present the development of, historical phenomena, I do not speak and argue from my point of view, but rather let each phenomenon speak for itself. This applies also to my treatment of theism here [Feuerbach's note].

5. Pertaining to theological ontology (the theological treatment of the natures of beings or entities such as "God" and "the soul").

definition of the essence of intelligence and, as such, it states only that God is a thinking and intelligent being or, vice versa, that the thinking being is the divine being; for only a *sensuous* being will need some other being outside itself in order to exist. I need air to breathe, water to drink, light to be able to see, plants and animals to eat, but nothing—not directly at any rate—in order to think. I cannot conceive of a breathing being without air, nor of a seeing being without light, but I can conceive of a thinking being as existing in complete isolation. A breathing being is *necessarily* referred to a being outside itself, that is to say, it has the *essential* object, through which it is what it is, *outside itself;* but the thinking being is *referred only to itself*, is its own object, carries its essence within itself and is what it is only through itself.

7

That which is *object* in *theism*[6] is subject in *speculative philosophy.* That which is only the conceived and *imagined* essence of reason in theism, is the *thinking* essence of reason itself in speculative philosophy.

The theist represents to himself God as a *personal* being *existing outside reason* and man; as a subject, he thinks God as an object. He conceives God as a being, i.e., as an *intelligible, non-sensuous* being with regard to his idea of it, but as a *sensuous* being with respect to its actual *existence* or its *truth;* for the *essential characteristic* of an objective existence; i.e., of an existence outside thought or perception, is *sensuousness.* He distinguishes God from himself in the same sense in which he distinguishes the sensuous objects and beings from himself as existing outside himself; in short, he thinks God from the *standpoint of sensuousness.* In contrast to this, the speculative theologian or philosopher thinks of God from the *standpoint of thought;* that is why the distracting idea of a sensuous being does not interpose itself between him and God; and, thus unhindered, he identifies the objective, conceived being with the *subjective,* thinking being.

The inner necessity by which God is turned from an *object* of man into his *subject, into his thinking ego,* can be demonstrated more specifically in the following way: God is an object of man and of man alone and not of the animal. However, *what* a being is can be known only through its *object;* the object to which a being is necessarily related is nothing but its own *manifest* being. Thus, the object of the herbivorous animals is the plant; it is, however, precisely through their object that these are distinguished from other animals, the carnivorous ones. Similarly, the object of the eye is light and not sound or smell, and it is through this object that the eye reveals its essence to us. It therefore comes down to the same thing whether someone cannot see or has no eyes. That is also why we name things in life with respect to their objects. The eye is the "light organ." He who cultivates land is a land cultivator (peasant); someone else, the object of whose activity is hunting, is a hunter; he who catches fish is a fisher, and so forth. Now, if God is an object of man—and he is indeed that necessarily and essentially—the essence of this object expresses nothing but man's own essence. Imagine to yourself that a thinking being on

---

6. That is, belief in the existence of God as a being that is separate from anything in or about the world (ourselves included), a being that is respon- sible for its (and our) existence, and a being with whom we can have a personal relationship.

some planet, or even on a comet, happened to glance at a few paragraphs of Christian dogmatics dealing with the being of God. What would this being infer from these paragraphs? Perhaps the existence of a God in the sense of Christian dogmatics? No. Its inference would be that the earth, too, is inhabited by thinking beings; in their definitions of God, it would discover only the definitions of their own essence. For example, in the definition "God is spirit," it would only see the proof and expression of their own spirit; in short, it would infer the essence and the qualities of the subject from those of the object. And with complete justification, because in the case of *this particular* object the distinction between what the object is in itself and what it is for man dissolves itself. This distinction is valid only in the case of an object which is given in immediate sense perception and which, precisely for that reason, is also given to other beings besides man. Light is there not only for man; it also affects animals, plants, and inorganic substances; it is a being of a general nature. In order to know what light is, we therefore observe not only the impressions and effects it makes upon ourselves, but also upon beings different from us. Hence, in this context, the distinction between the object *in itself* and the object *for us*, that is, between the object in reality and the object in our thought and imagination is necessary and objectively founded. God, however, is an object *only* for man. Animals and stars praise God *only in a human sense*. It belongs therefore to the essence of God himself that he is not an object of any other being except man, that he is a specifically human object, that he is a secret of man. But, if God is an object *only* for man, what does his essence disclose to us? Nothing but the essence of man. He whose object is the highest being is himself the highest being. The more man is the object of animals, the higher they must rank, and the closer must their approximation be to man. An animal whose object was man qua man, that is, man in his specific human nature, would itself be a man and no longer simply an animal. Only equal beings are equal objects for one another; that is, beings as they are *in themselves*. Now, it is true that theism, too, knows the identity of the divine and the human essence, but this identity forms its object only as *sensuous* identity, only as *similarity* or *affinity*, because, even if it grounds the essence of God in the spirit, it conceives God as a sensuous being existing outside man. Affinity expresses the same thing as identity; but concurrently connected with it is the sensuous idea that the related beings are two independents; that is, sensuous, beings existing apart from each other.

* * *

FROM 17

* * *

* * * Fichte embodies theistic, whereas Hegel embodies pantheistic, idealism.[7]

18

Modern philosophy has realized and superseded the Divine Being which is severed and distinguished from sensuousness, the world, and man, but

---

7. Pantheists believe the essential reality of God and that of the world to be one and the same.

only in thought, only in reason, and indeed in a reason that is *equally severed and distinguished from sensuousness, the world, and man.* That is to say, modern philosophy has proved only *the divinity of the intellect;* it recognized only the abstract *intellect* as the *divine and absolute being. Descartes' definition of himself as mind*—"*my being* consists *solely of the fact that I think*"[8]—is *modern philosophy's definition of itself.* The *will* in both the Kantian and the Fichtean idealism is itself a *pure being of the intellect,* and sense perception, which Schelling, in opposition to Fichte, connected with the intellect, is mere fantasy; it is not the truth and hence does not come into consideration.

Modern philosophy proceeded from theology; it is itself nothing else but theology dissolved and transformed into philosophy. The abstract and transcendent being of God could therefore be realized and superseded *only in an abstract and transcendent way.* In order to transform God into reason, reason itself had to assume the quality of an abstract, divine being. The senses, says Descartes, do not yield true reality, nor being, nor certainty; only the intellect separated from all sensuousness delivers the truth. Where does this dichotomy between the intellect and the senses come from? It comes only from theology. God is not a sensuous being; rather, he is the negation of all sensuous determinations and is known only through abstraction from the senses. But he is God; that is, the *truest, the most real, the most certain* being. Whence should the truth enter into the senses, the born atheists? God is the being in which existence cannot be separated from essence and concept; God is the being that cannot be thought of in any other way except as existing. Descartes transforms this objective being into a subjective one and the ontological proof into a psychological one; he transforms the proposition, "because God is thinkable, therefore he exists," into the proposition, "I think, therefore I am." Just as in God, being cannot be separated from being thought, so in me—as I am essentially mind—being cannot be separated from thought; and just as this inseparability is constitutive of the essence in the former, so also is it in the latter. A being—no matter whether in itself or for me—that *exists only to the extent that it is thought of,* and only to the extent that it forms the object of abstraction from all sensuousness, necessarily realizes and subjectifies itself in a being that *exists only to the extent that it thinks* and whose essence is abstract thought.

19

The *culmination* of modern philosophy is the *Hegelian* philosophy. The *historical necessity* and *justification* of the new philosophy must therefore be derived mainly from a *critique of Hegel's.*

20

According to its historical point of departure, the new philosophy has *the same* task and position in relation to the *hitherto existing philosophy* as *the latter* had in relation to theology. The new philosophy is the *realization* of the

---

8. A significant extension of Descartes' famous dictum "Cogito, ergo sum" (I think, therefore I am; Latin).

Hegelian philosophy or of all preceding philosophy, but a realization which is simultaneously the *negation*, and indeed the negation *without contradiction* of this philosophy.[9]

From 21

The *contradiction* of the modern philosophy, especially of pantheism, consists of the fact that it is the *negation of theology from the standpoint of theology* or *the* negation of theology which itself is *again theology*; this contradiction *especially characterizes the Hegelian philosophy.*

* * *

32

Taken in its reality or regarded as *real*, the real is the object of the senses—the *sensuous*.[1] Truth, reality, and sensuousness are one and the same thing. Only a sensuous being is a *true* and *real* being. Only through the senses is an object given *in the true sense*, not through thought *for itself.* The object given by and identical with ideation is merely thought.

An object, i.e., a real object, is given to me only if a being is given to me in a way that it affects me, only if my own activity—when I proceed from the standpoint of thought—experiences the activity of another being as a *limit* or boundary to itself. The concept of the object is originally nothing else but the concept of another *I*—everything appears to man in childhood as a freely and arbitrarily acting being—which means that in principle the concept of the *object* is mediated through the concept of You, the *objective ego.* To use the language of Fichte,[2] an object or an alter ego is given not to the ego, but to the non-ego in me; for only where I am transformed from an ego into a You—that is, where I am passive—does the idea of an activity *existing outside myself*, the idea of objectivity, really originate. But it is only through the senses that the ego is also non-ego.

A question characteristic of earlier abstract philosophy[3] is the following: How can different independent entities or substances act upon one another, for example, the body upon the soul or ego? In so far as this question was an abstraction from sensuousness, in so far as the supposedly interacting substances were abstract entities, purely intellectual creatures, philosophy was unable to resolve it. The mystery of their interaction can be solved only by sensuousness. Only sensuous beings act upon one another. I am I—for myself—and at the same time You—for others. But I am You only in so far as I am a sensuous being. But the abstract intellect isolates being-for-self as substance, ego, or God; it can, therefore, only arbitrarily connect being-for-others with being-for-self, for the necessity for this connection is sensuousness

9. Feuerbach is thus saying that his philosophy of the future is—to use a Hegelian term—the *Aufhebung* or supersession of the Hegelian philosophy: in it, the Hegelian philosophy is at once negated, preserved, and transcended (thereby "realizing" itself in the sense of becoming that which it was not yet but had it in itself to become).
1. That is, something that is capable of registering

by way of one or more of our (or other such) senses; a "sensuous being" in the fullest sense of the expression is a being (like ourselves) capable of sensing as well as of being sensed.
2. See FICHTE, First Introduction to *Science of Knowledge* (1797), § 7 (see above).
3. That is, pre-Kantian rationalism.

alone. But then it is precisely sensuousness from which the abstract intellect abstracts. What I think in isolation from sensuousness is what I think without and outside all connections. Hence the question: How can I think the unconnected to be at the same time connected?

33

The new philosophy looks upon *being*—being as given to us not only as thinking, but also as really existing being—*as the object of being*, as *its own* object. Being as the object of being—and *this* alone is truly, and deserves the name of, being—is sensuous being; that is, the being involved in sense perception, feeling, and love.[4] Or in other words, being is a *secret* underlying sense perception, feeling, and love.

Only in feeling and love has the demonstrative *this*—this person, this thing, that is, the particular—absolute value; only then is the *finite infinite*: In this and this alone does the infinite depth, divinity, and truth of love consist. In love alone resides the truth and reality of the God who counts the hairs on your head. The Christian God himself is only an abstraction from human love and an image of it. And since the demonstrative *this* owes its absolute value to love alone, it is only in love—not in abstract thought—that the secret of being is revealed. Love is passion, and passion alone is the distinctive mark of existence.[5] Only that which is an object of passion, exists—whether as reality or possibility. Abstract thought, which is devoid of feeling and passion, abolishes *the distinction between being and non-being*; non-existent for thought, this distinction is a reality for love. To love is nothing else than to become aware of this distinction. It is a matter of complete indifference to someone who loves nothing whether something exists or not, and be that what it may. But just as being as distinguished from non-being is given to me through love or feeling in general, so is everything else that is other than me given to me through love. Pain is a loud protest against identifying the subjective with the objective. The pain of love means that what is in the mind is not given in reality, or in other words, the subjective is here the objective, the concept itself the object. But this is precisely what ought not to be, what is a contradiction, an untruth, a misfortune—hence, the desire for that true state of affairs in which the subjective and the objective are not identical. Even physical pain clearly expresses this distinction. The pain of hunger means that there is nothing objective inside the stomach, that the stomach is, so to speak, its own object, that its empty walls grind against each other instead of grinding some content. Human feelings have, therefore, no empirical or anthropological significance in the sense of the old transcendental philosophy; they have, rather, an ontological and metaphysical significance: Feelings, everyday feelings, contain the deepest and highest truths. Thus, for example, love is the true *ontological* demonstration of the existence of objects apart from our head: There is no other proof of being except love or feeling in general. Only that whose *being brings you joy* and whose *not-being, pain*, has existence. The

4. For Feuerbach, sensuousness includes inner sensing ("feeling and love") as well as external sensing ("sense perception").

5. That is, human existence (a striking assertion with which KIERKEGAARD would be in emphatic agreement).

difference between subject and object, being and non-being is as *happy* a difference as it is *painful*.

34

The new philosophy bases itself on the *truth of love*, on the *truth of feeling*. In love, in feeling in general, *every human being confesses to the truth of the new philosophy*. As far as its basis is concerned, the new philosophy is nothing but *the essence of feeling raised to consciousness*—it only *affirms in the form and through the medium of reason what every man*—every real man—*admits in his heart*. It is the heart made aware of itself as reason. The *heart* demands *real* and *sensuous objects, real and sensuous beings*.

35

The *old* philosophy maintained that that which *could not be thought of also did not exist;* the *new* philosophy maintains that that which is not loved or *cannot be loved does not exist*. But that which cannot be loved can also not be adored.[6] That which is the *object of religion* can alone be the object of philosophy.

Love is not only objectively but also subjectively the criterion of being, the criterion of truth and reality. *Where there is no love there is also no truth*. And only he who *loves* something *is* also something—*to be nothing and to love nothing* is one and the same thing. The more one is, the more one loves, and vice versa.

36

The old philosophy had its point of departure in the proposition: I am an abstract, a merely thinking being to which the body does not belong. The new philosophy proceeds from the principle: I am a real and sensuous *being; indeed, the whole of my body is my ego, my being itself*. The old philosopher, therefore, thought in a *constant contradiction to and conflict with the senses* in order to avoid sensuous conceptions, or in order not to pollute abstract concepts. In contrast, the new philosopher thinks *in peace and harmony with the senses*. The old philosophy conceded the truth of sensuousness *only in a concealed way*, only in terms of the *concept*, only *unconsciously* and *unwillingly*, only because it had to. This is borne out even by its concept of God as the being who encompasses all other beings within himself, for he was held to be distinct from a merely conceived being; that is, he was held to be existing outside the mind, outside thought—a really objective, sensuous being. In contrast, the new philosophy *joyfully* and *consciously* recognizes the truth of sensuousness: It is a *sensuous* philosophy with an *open heart*.

---

6. Or "worshipped" (*angebetet*), a term that can be construed either religiously or nonreligiously. Adoration is here the common essential character of both religiousness and the spirit that animates genuinely philosophical thinking.

37

The philosophy of the modern era was in search of something *immediately certain*. Hence, it rejected the *baseless* thought of the Scholastics[7] and grounded philosophy on *self-consciousness*. That is, it posited the *thinking* being, the *ego*, the *self-conscious mind* in place of the merely conceived being or in place of God, the highest and ultimate being of all Scholastic philosophy; for a being who thinks is infinitely closer to a thinking being, infinitely more actual and certain than a being who is only conceived. Doubtful is the existence of God, doubtful is in fact anything I could think of; but indubitable is that I am, I who think and doubt. Yet this self-consciousness in modern philosophy is again something that is only conceived, only mediated through abstraction, and hence something that can be doubted. *Indubitable* and *immediately certain* is only that which is *the object of the senses, of perception and feeling.*

* * *

41

It is not only "external" things that are objects of the senses. *Man,* too, is *given to himself only through the senses;* only as a sensuous object is he an object for himself. The *identity* of *subject and object*—in self-consciousness only an abstract thought—has the character of *truth* and reality only in *man's sensuous perception of* man.

We feel not only stones and wood, not only flesh and bones, but also feelings when we press the hands or lips of a feeling being; we perceive through our ears not only the murmur of water and the rustle of leaves, but also the soulful voice of love and wisdom; we see not only mirror-like surfaces and specters of color, but we also gaze into the gaze of man. Hence, not only that which is external, but also that which is internal, not only flesh, but also spirit, not only things, but also the *ego* is an object of the senses. All is therefore capable of being perceived through the senses, even if only in a mediated and not immediate way, even if not with the help of crude and vulgar senses, but only through those that are cultivated; even if not with the eyes of the anatomist and the chemist, but only with those of the philosopher. Empiricism is therefore perfectly justified in regarding ideas as originating from the senses; but what it forgets is that the most essential sensuous object for man is *man himself;* that only in man's glimpse of man does the spark of consciousness and intellect spring. And this goes to show that idealism is right in so far as it sees the origin of ideas *in* man; but it is wrong in so far as it derives these ideas from man understood as an isolated being, as mere soul existing for himself; in one word, it is wrong when it derives the ideas from an ego that is not given in the context of its togetherness with a perceptibly given You. Ideas spring only from conversation and communication. Not alone but only within a dual relationship does one have concepts and reason in general. It takes two human beings to give birth to a man, to physical as well as spiritual man; the togetherness of man with man is the first principle and the criterion of truth

---

7. Medieval Christian thinkers ("schoolmen") whose thought depended on what Kierkegaard called a "leap of faith."

and universality. Even the certitude of those things that exist outside me is given to me through the certitude of the existence of other men besides myself. That which is seen by me alone is open to question, but that which is seen also by another person is certain.

* * *

50

The real in its reality and totality,[8] *the object of the new philosophy,* is the object also of a *real* and *total* being. The new philosophy therefore regards as its *epistemological principle,* as its *subject, not the ego, not the absolute*—i.e., abstract spirit, *in short, not reason for itself alone*—but the *real* and the *whole being of man.*[9] *Man* alone is the *reality,* the *subject* of *reason.* It is man who thinks, not the ego, not reason. The new philosophy does not depend on the divinity; i.e., the truth of reason for itself alone. Rather, it depends on the *divinity; i.e.; the truth of the whole man.*[1] Or, to put it more appropriately, the new philosophy is certainly based on reason as well, but on a reason whose *being* is the same as the *being of man;* that is, it is based not on an empty, colorless, nameless reason, but on a reason that is *of the very blood of man.* If the motto of the old philosophy was: "The rational alone is the true and real,"[2] the motto of the new philosophy is: "The *human* alone is the *true* and *real,*" for the human alone is the rational;[3] *man is the measure of reason.*

51

The *unity* of *thought* and *being* has *meaning* and *truth* only if *man* is comprehended as the *basis and subject of this unity.* Only a *real being* cognizes *real things;* only where thought is not its own subject but the *predicate* of a *real* being is it *not separated from being.* The unity of thought and being is therefore not formal, meaning that *being as a determination* does not belong to *thought in and for itself;* rather, this unity depends on the *object,* the *content* of thought.

From this arises the following categorical imperative:[4] Desire not to be a philosopher if being a philosopher means being different to man; do not be anything more than a *thinking man;* think not as a thinker, that is, not as one confined to a faculty which is *isolated* in so far as it is *torn away* from the totality of the real being of man; think as a *living, real* being, in which capacity you are exposed to the vivifying and refreshing waves of the ocean of the world; think as one who exists, as one who is *in the world* and is part of

8. In Feuerbach's German: "Das Wirkliche in seiner Wirklichkeit und Totalität," better translated as "The actual in its actuality and totality," to capture the Hegelian distinction (which Feuerbach is here following) between a simply *real* being of some sort (one that has *Realität,* reality) and an *actual* one that not only has reality but also fully manifests its essential nature (and so has *Wirklichkeit,* full actuality)—e.g., the distinction between a living human being and one that is fully and truly human. 9. That is, "das wirklich und ganze Wesen des Menschen." This echoes SCHILLER in *On the Aesthetic Education of Man* (1794; see above), and is in turn echoed by MARX (especially in the *Economic and Philosophical Manuscripts of 1844;* see below).

1. That is, the new philosophy does not depend on the abstract divinity of a theistic "God"; rather, it depends on what is *truly* divine (which is the basis of the idea of such a being)—namely, the "truth" of the "whole *Mensch* (human being)." 2. A slight variation on Hegel's phrase, from the preface to his *Philosophy of Right* (1821; see above): better translated as "the rational alone is the true and *actual,*" in Hegel's special sense of that term. 3. That is, the human alone *defines* (is definitive of) the rational. 4. What follows is almost identical to what EMERSON said on this topic six years earlier in "The American Scholar" (1837; see above).

the world, not as one in the vacuum of abstraction, not as a solitary monad,[5] not as an absolute monarch, not as an unconcerned, extra-worldly God; only then can you be sure that being and thought are united in all your thinking. How should thought as the activity of a real being not grasp real things and entities? Only when thought is cut off from man and confined to itself do embarrassing, fruitless, and, from the standpoint of an isolated thought, unresolvable questions arise: How does thought reach being, reach the object? For *confined to itself,* that is, posited *outside man,* thought is outside all ties and connections with the world. You elevate yourself to an object only in so far as you lower yourself so as to be an object for others. You think only because *your thoughts* themselves can be thought, and they are true only if they pass the test of objectivity, that is, when someone else, to whom they are given as objects, acknowledges them as such. You see because you are yourself a visible being, you feel because you are yourself a feelable being. Only to an open mind does the world stand open, and the *openings of the mind* are only the senses. But the thought that exists in isolation, that is *enclosed in itself,* is *detached from the senses, cut off from man,* is *outside* man—that thought is *absolute subject* which cannot or ought not to be an object for others. But precisely for that reason, and despite all efforts, it is *forever unable to cross over to the object, to being;* it is like a head separated from the body, which must remain unable to seize hold of an object because it lacks the means, the organs to do so.

52

The new philosophy is the *complete* and *absolute dissolution of theology into anthropology,*[6] dissolution *in which all contradictions have been overcome;* for the new philosophy is the dissolution of theology not only in reason—this was effected by the old philosophy—but also in the *heart;* in short, in the *whole* and *real* [*wirklich*] being of man. In this regard, it is only the *necessary outcome* of the old philosophy; for that which was once dissolved in reason must dissolve itself in *life,* in the *heart,* in the *blood* of man; but as a *new* and *independent* truth, the new philosophy is also the truth of the old philosophy, for only *a truth that has become flesh and blood is the truth.* The old philosophy *necessarily* relapsed into theology, for that which is sublated only *in reason,* only in the concept, still has an *antithesis* in the *heart.* The new philosophy, on the other hand, *cannot suffer such a relapse* because there is nothing to relapse into; that which is dead in both body and soul cannot return even as a ghost.

53

It is *by no means only through thinking that man is distinguished from the animal.* Rather, his *whole being* constitutes his *distinction from* the *animal.*[7] It is true that he who does not think is not a man; but this is so not because thinking is the cause, but only because it is a *necessary consequence* and *quality* of man's being.

5. A term originating in Greek philosophy but particularly associated with Gottfried Wilhelm Leibniz (1646–1716), who applied it to the basic substances that are immaterial but make up all of reality.
6. A phrase elsewhere expressed (or translated) as the complete "reduction" (boiling down and translation) of theology—and of Hegelian "speculative" philosophy—into (philosophical) anthropology.
7. This is a very important point, picked up by 20th-century "philosophical anthropologists" such as ARNOLD GEHLEN and HELMUTH PLESSNER (see below).

Hence, here too we need not go beyond the realm of sensuousness in order to recognize man as a being superior to animals. Man is not a particular being like the animal; rather, he is a *universal* being;[8] he is therefore not a limited and unfree but an unlimited and free being, for universality, being without limit, and freedom are inseparable. And this freedom is not the property of just one *special* faculty, say, the will, nor does this universality reside in a special faculty of thinking called reason; this freedom, this universality applies to the *whole* being of man. The senses of the animal are certainly keener than those of man, but they are so only in relation to certain things that are necessarily linked with the needs of the animal; and they are keener precisely because of the determination that they are limited by being exclusively directed towards some definite objects. Man does not possess the sense of smell of a hunting dog or a raven, but because his sense of smell encompasses all kinds of smell, it is free and also indifferent to particular smells. But where a sense is elevated above the limits of particularity and above being tied down to needs, it is elevated to an *independent*, to a *theoretical* significance and dignity—*universal* sense is *intellect* [*Verstand*], and *universal* sensuousness is *intellectuality* [*Geistigkeit*]. Even the lowest senses—smell and taste—are elevated in man to intellectual and scientific activities. The smell and taste of things are objects of natural science. Indeed, even the *stomach* of man, no matter how contemptuously we look down upon it, is something *human* and not animal because it is universal; that is, not limited to certain kinds of food. That is why man is free from that ferocious voracity with which the animal hurls itself on its prey. Leave a man his head, but give him the stomach of a lion or a horse, and he will certainly cease to be a man. A limited stomach is compatible only with a limited, that is, animal sense. Man's moral and rational relationship to his stomach consists therefore in his according it a human and not a beastly treatment. He who thinks that what is important to mankind is stomach, and that stomach is something animal, also authorizes man to be bestial in his eating.

54

The new philosophy makes *man, together with nature* as the basis of man, the *exclusive, universal,* and *highest object* of philosophy; it makes *anthropology, together with physiology,* the *universal science* [*Universalwissenschaft*].

55

Art, religion, philosophy, and *science*[9] are only expressions or manifestations of the *true being of man.* A man is truly and perfectly man only when he possesses an *aesthetic* or *artistic, religious* or *moral, philosophical* or *scientific* sense. And only he who *excludes from himself nothing that is essentially human* is, strictly speaking, man. *Homo sum, humani nihil a me alienum puto*[1]—this sentence, taken in its *universal* and *highest* meaning, is the *motto* of the *new philosophy.*

---

8. That is, human reality is characterized by forms of universality or generality that are not to be found among nonhuman animals (a key point for Hegel).
9. That is, *Wissenschaft.* These are the constituent elements of Hegelian "absolute spirituality" and forms of Hegelian "absolute knowing" (or knowing that transcends the limitations and contingencies of the merely sociocultural). (See glossary, p. 144.)
1. I am a human being; I consider nothing human to be alien to me (Latin); quoted from the Roman comic dramatist Terence, *Heauton Timorumenos* 77 (163 B.C.E.).

56

The *philosophy of Absolute Identity* has *completely mislocated the standpoint of truth.* The *natural standpoint* of man, the standpoint of the *distinction* between "I" and *"You,"* between *subject* and *object* is the *true,* the *absolute* standpoint and, hence, also the *standpoint of philosophy.*

57

The *true unity of head and heart*[2] does not consist in wiping out or covering up their difference, but rather in the recognition that *the essential object of the heart* is also *the essential object of the head,* or in the identity of the *object.* The new philosophy, which makes the essential and highest object of the heart—man—also the essential and highest object of the intellect, lays the foundation of a rational unity of head and heart, of thought and life.

58

Truth does not exist in thought, nor in cognition confined to itself. *Truth is only the totality of man's life and being.*

59

The single man *in isolation* possesses in himself the *essence* of man neither as a *moral* nor as a *thinking* being. The *essence* of man is contained only in the community, in the *unity of man with man*—a unity, however, that rests on the *reality* of the *distinction* between "I" and "You."[3]

60

Solitude means being *finite* and *limited, community* means being *free* and *infinite.* For *himself* alone, man is just man (in the ordinary sense); but man *with* man—*the unity of "I" and "You"*—that is God.[4]

61

The *absolute* philosopher said, or at least thought of himself—naturally as a *thinker* and not as a man—"*La vérité c'est moi,*"[5] in a way analogous to the absolute monarch claiming, *"L'Etat c'est moi,"* or the absolute God claiming, *"L'être c'est moi."*[6] The human philosopher, on the other hand, says: *Even in thought, even as a philosopher, I am a man in togetherness with men.*

---

2. That is, of reason and feeling.
3. That is, the essence of humanity requires and involves a community that is a union in which distinctness of personal identity is both respected and transcended.
4. That is, the genuine interpersonal unity of one genuine person with another—of "I" and "You" (*Ich* and *Du*)—is what is truly divine and sacred.

5. *I am the truth!* (literally, "The truth is me"; French). Feuerbach has in mind Hegel, who never said this but was, Feuerbach believed, as grandiose in his thinking as Louis XIV, king of France (reigned 1643–1715), who is popularly (though probably falsely) believed to have declared, "L'état, c'est moi" (*I* am the state).
6. *I am [true] being!* (French).

62

The *true* dialectic is *not a monologue of the solitary thinker with himself;* it is a *dialogue between "I" and "You."*[7]

63

The *Trinity* was the *highest mystery,* the *central point* of the *absolute philosophy* and *religion.* But the secret of the Trinity, as demonstrated historically and philosophically in the *Essence of Christianity,*[8] is the secret of *communal* and *social life*—the secret of the *necessity of a "You" for an "I."* It is the truth that *no being whatsoever,* be it man or God and be it called "spirit" or "I," can be a *true, perfect,* and *absolute* being *in isolation,* that the *truth* and *perfection* are only the *union* and *unity* of beings that are similar in essence. Hence, the highest and ultimate principle of philosophy is *the unity of man with man.* All essential relationships—the principles of various sciences [*Wissenschaften*]— are only *different kinds and modes of this unity.*

64

The old philosophy possesses a *double truth;* first, its *own* truth—*philosophy*— which is not concerned with man, and second, the truth *for man*—*religion.* The new philosophy as the philosophy of man, on the other hand, is also essentially the *philosophy for man;* it has, without in the least compromising the dignity and autonomy of theory—indeed it is in perfect harmony with it— essentially a *practical* tendency, and is practical in the highest sense. The new philosophy takes the place of religion; it has within itself the *essence* of religion; in truth, it is *itself religion.*[9]

65

All attempts undertaken so far to reform philosophy are not very different from the old philosophy to the extent that they are *species* belonging to the same *genus.* The most indispensable condition for a really new—i.e., independent— philosophy corresponding to the need of mankind and of the future is, however, that it distinguish itself *in essence* from the old philosophy.[1]

SOURCE: From *The Fiery Brook: Selected Writings of Ludwig Feuerbach*, trans. Zawar Hanfi (Garden City, N.Y.: Anchor Books, 1972), pp. 177–83, 202–4, 224–28, 231–32, 239–45 (the collection takes as its title the literal meaning of "Feuerbach"). Originally published in 1843 as *Grundsätze der Philosophie der Zukunft.* Except where otherwise indicated, German words in brackets are the terminology used in the German original, inserted by the editor in addition to their renderings in the translation.

7. A theme subsequently taken up by KARL JASPERS and MARTIN BUBER (see below), among others.
8. This portion of the work is not included in the previous selection from it.
9. Feuerbach's "new philosophy" is thus the full expression of what religion anticipates and

attempts—less adequately, in a confused and confusing way—to express (a claim that Hegel had made for his own "new philosophy").
1. The last of Marx's "Theses on Feuerbach" (see below) is undoubtedly a critical response to this concluding section.

KARL MARX
(1818 – 1883)

FRIEDRICH ENGELS
(1820 – 1895)

Marx published virtually nothing of a philosophical nature; yet his influence on philosophy in the interpretive tradition in the twentieth century was profound. Indeed, he continues to be of philosophical interest despite—rather than because of—the ponderous "dialectical materialism" that became the official "philosophy" of the movement that took his name after his death. The belated publication of his previously unknown early philosophical writings from the 1840s (nearly a century after they were written) made possible a new view and appreciation of the kind of philosophical thinking he had begun to do in that decade, before his interests and priorities shifted toward the economic analysis of capitalism and toward revolutionary activism. That shift effectively ended his own development as a philosopher, but those early writings attracted considerable attention (owing in no small measure to the unique place Marx had come to occupy in the political imagination). The ideas they contained and inspired initiated a significant new mode of philosophical analysis and discourse, which during the middle decades of the twentieth century rivaled existential philosophy in the interpretive tradition.

Karl Marx was born in Trier, a historic old German Rhineland town (then a part of Prussia). His parents were both ethnically Jewish, and indeed were descended from rabbis; but his intellectually and politically liberal father, a well-educated lawyer, had converted to Lutheran Protestantism several years earlier for the sake of his career. The third of nine children, Marx became the oldest son (with the attendant expectations) when his older brother died in early childhood. After receiving a humanistic education first at home (by his father) and then at a local school, he entered the university at

Bonn in 1835, intending to follow his father into the practice of law. When he transferred to the University of Berlin a year later he broadened his studies to include philosophy and history, while continuing to indulge his love of literature—and to write a good deal of poetry.

HEGEL had died just five years earlier, in 1831, and his influence at Berlin was still strong. Like many other philosophy students of his generation, at Berlin and elsewhere, Marx became interested in Hegel's thought and studied him closely. These "Young Hegelians" were already beginning to compete with each other in interpreting Hegelian philosophy and seeking to develop it further, in different directions. Marx found himself drawn to those who were nonreligious, liberal, and reformist. He chose to write his dissertation on ancient philosophy, "The Difference between the Democritean and Epicurean Philosophies of Nature," and received his doctorate in 1841. Within a few years, after unsuccessfully seeking a teaching position, he gave up any hope of an academic career and turned his attention to social reform. His father had died in 1838, which was a blow to him both personally and financially. He eked out a living, first as a contributor to and then as editor of the liberal journal *Rheinische Zeitung* (*Rhinelander Gazette*). The Prussian government suppressed it, and Marx agreed to co-edit a new review published in Paris, the *Deutsch-Französische Jahrbücher* (*German-French Yearbooks*).

Marx did not move to Paris alone; a few months earlier, in June 1843, he married a childhood friend to whom he had been engaged for many years, Jenny von Westphalen. The radical journal was short-lived, but in Paris Marx wrote what would become known as *The Economic and Philosophical Manuscripts of 1844* and became acquainted with Friedrich Engels. In Engels, born in Barmen (Prussia) and the son of a wealthy textile manufacturer, he found a kindred spirit (and source of financial support); and the two developed a close and enduring relationship. Considered a dangerous revolutionary by the French authorities, Marx was banished in 1845 and relocated to Brussels (Belgium), where his and his wife's first three children were born. He returned to Germany during the revolution of 1848–49, in which he took an active part as co-editor of the radical *Neue Rheinische Zeitung* (*New Rhinelander Gazette*) in the city of Cologne. After the counterrevolution, he was banished again.

In 1849 Marx and his wife settled in London, where he finally found lasting political refuge. There he could write as he pleased, and the British Museum became his primary workplace as he pursued his economic research. He earned some money as a correspondent for Horace Greeley's *New York Daily Tribune* on social and political affairs (initially writing on Britain, and eventually on the European Continent and even the Far East). For the most part, however, Marx and his growing family depended for support on Engels, who eventually became a partner in his family's cotton factory in Manchester. They were desperately poor much of the time, and three of Marx's four children born in England died at birth or in infancy (two of the three born in Belgium survived to adulthood). His wife, who was devoted to him, was often in poor health, and died in 1881. He lived only two years longer.

Marx died before the publication of the second and third volumes of his masterwork *Das Kapital* (*Capital*), which appeared—edited by Engels, and thanks to his efforts—in 1885 and 1894, respectively. But Marx did publish the first volume in 1867, completed drafts of the other two volumes, and wrote a good deal else as well after settling in London, including *A Contribution to the Critique of Political Economy* (1859), *Theories of Surplus Value* (1863), and *The Civil War*

in France (1871). Much of his time, however, was spent in revolutionary political activity and work for the General Council of the International Working Men's Association, which he helped found in 1864. No less a force in person than he was with a pen, he was surely one of the most remarkable personalities of Anglo-European social and intellectual history in the second half of the nineteenth century.

Marx's forceful personality and powers of intellect and expression impressed many (including JOHN STUART MILL), making him both enemies and devoted friends and admirers. Foremost among the latter was Engels. From the time they met in 1844, Engels was Marx's supporter, ally, advocate, and occasional collaborator. Without Engels there probably would have been no post-1840s Marx and no Marxism. Yet Marx was clearly the senior partner and the force behind the more theoretical parts of the most significant works that they co-authored— particularly the first part of *The German Ideology*, which they wrote in 1845–46 (published 1932), and the *Manifesto of the Communist Party* (1848; reprinted as *The Communist Manifesto*). Engels's own works are both much less rich intellectually than Marx's and much more pretentious philosophically; and while Engels made Marxism after Marx possible (by preserving, editing, publishing, and promoting his friend's work), the scientistic and yet crudely "dialectical" Marxism that he fostered impeded more than aided the understanding of Marx's thought. But worse was yet to come: its subsequent transformation into the doctrine of "dialectical materialism"—culminating in the travesty of Stalin's simplistic dogmatic version (commonly called "diamat")— which eventually blackened the very name of "Marxist philosophy" even in the former Soviet Union and Eastern Europe, while making it an object of ridicule in the West.

Hegel was Marx's point of departure, though Marx's dissatisfaction with Hegel's philosophy was as great as his admiration of it. Then, in 1843, two years after receiving his doctorate, he discovered FEUERBACH's writings, and initially was greatly impressed. Feuerbach's program of a "reduction" or transformation of Hegel's "philosophy of *Geist* (spirit)" into a naturalistic and humanistic philosophical "anthropology" seemed to Marx to be just what was needed to recast Hegel's insights into "the self-creation of man" in a more tenable form. Marx agreed with Feuerbach that it is really our *human* reality that Hegel was talking about, and our *human* self-realization in the course of our *human*-historical development that he sought to reinterpret and comprehend—and to project beyond the present, in which he believed much more remained to be desired and attained than Hegel had recognized.

Marx further was attracted to Feuerbach's emphasis on human "community" as a corrective to Hegel's institutionally oriented approach to what was most important about human social reality. The "communism" he would soon champion was meant to foster and sustain a more genuine form of interpersonal "community" than he believed to be possible either in the bourgeois and capitalistic societies of his day or in the kind of state Hegel envisioned as a corrective to them. But it did not take Marx long to conclude that Feuerbach's thinking was simplistic in both its naturalism and its conception of human social life, in ways that he outlined in his "Theses on Feuerbach" and sought to correct in the essay nominally dealing with Feuerbach in *The German Ideology* (for both, see the selections below).

What Marx took to be lacking in Feuerbach was something that his own studies of Hegel had enabled him to understand: the ways in which our human reality at all levels has been developed and transformed by the kinds of interactions and practices in our dealings with the world around us, other human beings, the products of our labor, and the social realities to which our social relations have given rise, even as they themselves have been transformed by our activities. He therefore undertook to develop a more sophisticated version of the kind of socio-naturalistic reinterpretation of human reality and possibility that Feuerbach had advocated—one that would more fully capture both its historical character and the crucial role played by "social relations" and social-institutional structures in the shaping of human life.

At the same time, Marx sought to give an account of the historical development of human reality that would dispense altogether with the apparatus of Hegel's "logic" and his "absolute-idealist" system, while also avoiding the opposite error of treating human reality as nothing more than a complex sort of causally operating matter in motion. It was to be a "materialism" in the different sense of according primacy to the kinds of material realities of economic and social-institutional life—and recognizing their difference from merely natural processes and phenomena. They have a human history, and their development reflects the supra-biological dynamics of human social relations and productive activities. Marx's materialism was thus to be a "*historical* materialism" that would do justice to the formations and transformations of human reality in the course of human-historical development, and to the distinctive character (as neither Hegelian-logical nor merely physical and biological), laws, and necessities of that development.

In the first part of *The German Ideology*, Marx (with Engels) can be seen working out the principles and general outlines of this reinterpretation of human history and human reality. This treatise is probably the best existing statement of Marx's philosophical thinking before his attention shifted in the late 1840s to the kinds of economic analysis and sociopolitical critique and activism that were to preoccupy him for the rest of his life. In his and Engels's famous *Communist Manifesto* and his "Critique of the Gotha Program," he attempts to use those principles to chart a course of political action, broadly envisioned. The last of his "Theses on Feuerbach" had been a call to such action: "Philosophers have only *interpreted* the world, in various ways; the point, however, is to *change* it." Marx seems to have decided that he had done as much as he needed to do philosophically to equip himself for this task, and for the kind of analysis and critique of the social, economic, and political world in which he found himself that he went on to undertake.

The early Marx, like Feuerbach, sought to go beyond and improve on Hegel by replacing talk of *Geist* (spirit) with the concept of "man" (*der Mensch*). Marx further proposed that man's nature be understood in terms of the features or characteristics of human *life*, conceiving of human life in terms of the general sorts of *activities* characteristic of human living, and conceiving of human "life activities" as forms of human "practice" (or "praxis"). Such human action is the outcome of successive transformations of human life in the course of human history, which now differs significantly from animal activity and has the potential to undergo further transformations as the conditions of human life are themselves transformed. It generally is mediated by forms of consciousness, is structured socially, has some sort of objective expression, and involves interaction with environmental, social, and interpersonal reality. (Thus it has both subjective and objective dimensions.)

Through forms of praxis—of which "labor" (*Arbeit*), or productive activity, is paradigmatic for Marx—human beings sustain, express, confirm, objectify, develop, and realize themselves. It also is through the prevalence of certain types of labor that they can become distorted, stunted, dehumanized, and alienated from their products, their fellow human beings, and themselves. And Marx contends that historically varying types of social and economic relations are what determine which forms of labor and of praxis more generally prevail—and so determine the character and quality of the lives of the human beings whose "life activities" they structure.

This thesis is the heart of Marx's "historical materialism"; and this is the point of his repeated insistence—against at least some forms of "Idealism"—that "consciousness is determined by life [or 'reality' or 'being'], rather than life by consciousness." However, it does not commit Marx to a "materialistic determinism" as that expression is ordinarily understood. The term he generally uses when making this claim that here (and commonly elsewhere) is translated "determined" is *bestimmt*—and the verb *bestimmen* (noun, *Bestimmung*) has a range of possible meanings. Even in this context, *bestimmt* may mean "strictly determined" in a rigidly and completely causal way; but it may also indicate some less complete influence, such as "strongly constrained" or "significantly conditioned." The same point applies to Marx's further contention that within the "ensemble of the social relations" (as Marx puts it in the sixth of his "Theses on Feuerbach") that structure and so constitute human reality, it is *economic* relations relating to the prevailing "forms and relations of production" and exchange that "determine" the rest of the "ensemble," and so also the character of the lives of those involved. Moreover, the general claim of *Bestimmung* leaves open the possibility that while this "determination" may be quite strict under some conditions in human life, it may be much looser under others. In fact, it is consistent with a seemingly very different sort of claim—which we find Marx himself making in the selection below from the third volume of *Capital*—that a significant sort of human freedom becomes humanly possible for the first time only under social conditions that do not yet obtain but that can and should become a reality.

Thus while insisting on the decisiveness of economic and social relations for the character of human life at any particular historical juncture, Marx also argues for the real possibility—indeed, the historical inevitability—of a form of human society in which human "self-activity" will at last be able to be fully and truly human, self-expressive, and self-realizing. This combination of claims is the hallmark of his thinking, and the key to its great appeal to those seeking a hopeful alternative to implausible idealisms, naïve naturalisms, and meaningless materialisms. But it requires a conception of human nature and human reality that makes this combination coherent and plausible. The 1844 manuscripts indicate how Marx sought to develop and argue for such a conception.

As we attempt to understand ourselves, Marx would have us presuppose neither too much nor too little. We must not make unwarranted assumptions about the status of our consciousness and all that Hegel called *Geist*, for example, even though we must not ignore their human reality. On the other hand, we must not ignore the human reality of our existence as living creatures in a world in which our subsistence is both possible and difficult, and requires productive activity. We are creatures whose existence is *life*, and whose life involves *action*—action that does not merely appropriate our environment but transforms it, in ways through which our lives and identities take shape. To this basic characterization Marx adds that we are *conscious and self-conscious* creatures, in ways that make a difference to our action, as well as *sensuous* creatures, whose senses mediate not only our action and interaction with everything we encounter but also our consciousness and self-consciousness. Moreover, we are *social* creatures, who both can and must interact with our fellow human creatures, in ways mediated by language and also by interests and desires that both give us much in common with and pit us against each other in competition and rivalry.

But that is not all. We are creatures of great *plasticity*, as well as of specific endowments and needs that must be met in some way or another. All the features just mentioned—our sensuousness, consciousness and self-consciousness, sociality, and productive capability—can be developed and filled out in very different ways that are not dictated with specificity by either our general or our particular natures. Their variations can be socially regulated, modified, and transmitted (making us historical creatures). The reality of our human existence is always

a function of what Marx calls the ensemble of social relations, within some specific array of which all human beings live their lives. Whatever we are or can become individually is an outcome of what these social relations—as internalized and also as encountered—make possible.

Human reality has transformed and shaped itself in the course of our collective historical development of the forms of sensuous, social, productive, conscious, and self-conscious life that have arisen in response to our basic needs, the circumstances of our existence, and previous ways of organizing and carrying on with our life activities. And it turns out that these abilities, sensibilities, and activities are capable, under the appropriate conditions, of becoming emancipated from subordination to basic biological needs, as well as from general imperatives of social life and more specific dispositions associated with the structures of various types of society—in ways that afford a glimpse of what human reality is capable of becoming.

For example: our human senses *can* be cultivated in ways that emancipate them from merely utilitarian employment and enlist them in the further service of a refined sensibility, enabling us to experience and derive satisfaction from aesthetic qualities. Our human sociality *can* be shaped in such a way that human beings learn to respect and care for each other in ways emancipated from both exploitative and competitive relationships, and to value such personal relationships for their own sake. And our human productive capabilities *can* be developed in ways that emancipate them both from the imperatives of human subsistence and from the requirements of the marketplace, enabling them to be genuinely self-expressive and intrinsically satisfying as well as socially valuable. The 1844 manuscripts are richly evocative on all these points.

In Marx's analysis, the society around him was developing the productive capacity to support the general realization of these possibilities; but it was structured in such a way that people in it were for the most part warped by it, impelled by need or disposed by greed to live lives that were barely even human. But happily for humanity (according to Marx), the very sort of society toward which history is inexorably moving, impelled by the "logic" of economics, is one that will bring the full development of our human possibilities within the reach of all—although making this dream come true will take a revolutionary restructuring of society and reeducation of its members. The validity of this assessment is obviously debatable, as is the possibility of deriving Marx's evaluative and normative views from his minimalistic philosophical anthropology. Yet his embryonic philosophical thinking remains fascinating, in part because the stakes are so high. If he really was on to something here, it is of great importance to understand what it is.

The "dialectical materialist" and "economic determinist" version of Marxism—for which (at least as elaborated) Engels was more responsible than Marx himself—was challenged by the more humanistic "neo-Marxism" inspired by the writings of the young Marx. That challenge in turn provoked a vigorous and more sophisticated "neo-orthodox" counterattack, which dismissed the humanistic tendencies of the early Marx as mere residues of Hegelian and other influences he later overcame while seeking a more rigorous and respectable reformulation of the traditional version. It is at least arguable, however, that Marx would not have been content with such a "scientific" and normatively neutral variant of his thought, and that his philosophical project required finding a way of making room for (and making sense of) significant elements of those humanistic tendencies within the de-"idealized" and economically centered reinterpretation of human reality that he went on to develop. Indeed, it is hard to imagine what might have fueled his revolutionary passion other than a conviction that this was possible.

In any event, both the reinterpretive and the normative aspirations and directions of Marx's philosophical project may be able to survive the demise of the revolutionary and economic-theoretical parts of his legacy. It is well worth finding out; for whatever one may think of them, that project is a distinctive and significant post-Hegelian development within the interpretive tradition.

Theses on Feuerbach

By Karl Marx

I

The chief defect of all hitherto existing materialism—that of Feuerbach included—is that the thing, reality, sensuousness, is conceived only in the form of the object or of *contemplation*, but not as *human sensuous activity, practice*, not subjectively. Hence it happened that the *active* side, in contradistinction to materialism, was developed by idealism—but only abstractly, since, of course, idealism does not know real, sensuous activity as such. Feuerbach wants sensuous objects, really distinct from the thought objects, but he does not conceive human activity itself as *objective* activity. Hence, in *Das Wesen des Christentums*,[1] he regards the theoretical attitude as the only genuinely human attitude, while practice is conceived and fixed only in its dirty-judaical manifestation. Hence he does not grasp the significance of "revolutionary," of practical-critical, activity.

---

1. *The Essence of Christianity* (1841); see above.

II

The question whether objective truth can be attributed to human thinking is not a question of theory but is a *practical* question. Man must prove the truth, that is, the reality and power, the this-sidedness of his thinking in practice. The dispute over the reality or non-reality of thinking which is isolated from practice is a purely *scholastic* question.

III

The materialist doctrine that men are products of circumstances and upbringing, and that, therefore, changed men are products of other circumstances and changed upbringing, forgets that it is men who change circumstances and that it is essential to educate the educator himself. Hence, this doctrine necessarily arrives at dividing society into two parts, one of which is superior to society.

The coincidence of the changing of circumstances and of human activity can be conceived and rationally understood only as revolutionising practice.

IV

Feuerbach starts out from the fact of religious self-alienation, of the duplication of the world into a religious, imaginary world and a real one. His work consists in resolving the religious world into its secular basis. He overlooks the fact that after completing this work, the chief thing still remains to be done. For the fact that the secular basis detaches itself from itself and establishes itself in the clouds as an independent realm can only be explained by the cleavage and self-contradictions within this secular basis. The latter must itself, therefore, first be understood in its contradiction and then, by the removal of the contradiction, revolutionised in practice. Thus, for instance, after the earthly family is discovered to be the secret of the holy family, the former must then itself be criticised in theory and revolutionised in practice.

V

Feuerbach, not satisfied with *abstract thinking*, appeals to *sensuous contemplation*; but he does not conceive sensuousness as practical, human-sensuous activity.

VI

Feuerbach resolves the religious essence into the human essence. But the human essence is no abstraction inherent in each single individual. In its reality it is the ensemble of the social relations.[2]

---

2. Perhaps better translated: "Feuerbach resolves the essential reality [*Wesen*] of religion into the essential nature of human reality. But human reality is no abstraction inherent in each single individual. It is actually the ensemble [or totality] of social relations." By "social relations" Marx is referring to the kinds of relations and structures that HEGEL subsumes under the rubric of "objective *Geist* [spirit]."

Feuerbach, who does not enter upon a criticism of this real essence, is consequently compelled:

(1) To abstract from the historical process and to fix the religious sentiment as something by itself and to presuppose an abstract—*isolated*—human individual.

(2) The human essence,[3] therefore, can with him be comprehended only as "genus," as an internal, dumb generality which merely *naturally* unites the many individuals.

VII

Feuerbach, consequently, does not see that the "religious sentiment" is itself a social product, and that the abstract individual whom he analyses belongs in reality to a particular form of society.

VIII

Social life is essentially *practical*. All mysteries which mislead theory into mysticism find their rational solution in human practice[4] and in the comprehension of this practice.

IX

The highest point attained by contemplative materialism, that is, materialism which does not comprehend sensuousness as practical activity, is the contemplation of single individuals in civil society.[5]

X

The standpoint of the old materialism is *"civil"* society; the standpoint of the new is *human* society, or socialised humanity.[6]

XI

The philosophers have only *interpreted* the world, in various ways; the point, however, is to *change* it.

SOURCE: From *The Marx-Engels Reader*, ed. Robert C. Tucker, 2nd ed. (New York: W. W. Norton, 1978), pp. 143–45. Marx wrote this brief outline of a critique of FEUERBACH (see above) in 1845, and it was among the unpublished manuscripts that Engels took charge of after Marx's death. Engels published it as an appendix to his own 1888 monograph, *Ludwig Feuerbach and the End of Classical German Philosophy*.

3. That is, the essential (fundamental, central) character (*Wesen*) of human reality.
4. *Praxis*, a term of crucial importance for Marx and later Marxist philosophy (especially that version inspired by the discovery and publication in the 1920s and 1930s of Marx's early manuscripts). It refers to a conception of human action as activity that is transformative of material reality, mediated by consciousness, socially structured, humanly interactive, and evaluatively significant.
5. That is, the type of society that Hegel identifies and describes in his *Philosophy of Right* (1821) as the realm of social-institutionally sanctioned, regulated, and facilitated egoistic self-assertion.
6. This is Marx's version of Hegelian "ethicality" (*Sittlichkeit*)—the most mature form of human social reality (or what Hegel called "objective spirituality"). (See Hegel glossary, p. 144.)

From Economic and Philosophical Manuscripts of 1844

BY KARL MARX

From *Estranged Labour*[1]

We have proceeded from the premises of political economy.[2] We have accepted its language and its laws. We presupposed private property, the separation of labour, capital and land, and of wages, profit of capital and rent of land—likewise division of labour, competition, the concept of exchange-value, etc. On the basis of political economy itself, in its own words, we have shown that the worker sinks to the level of a commodity and becomes indeed the most wretched of commodities; that the wretchedness of the worker is in inverse proportion to the power and magnitude of his production; that the necessary result of competition is the accumulation of capital in a few hands, and thus the restoration of monopoly in a more terrible form; that finally the distinction between capitalist and land-rentier, like that between the tiller of the soil and the factory-worker, disappears and that the whole of society must fall apart into the two classes—the property-*owners* and the propertyless *workers*.

Political economy proceeds from the fact of private property, but it does not explain it to us. It expresses in general, abstract formulae the *material* process through which private property actually passes, and these formulae it then takes for *laws*. It does not *comprehend* these laws—i.e., it does not demonstrate how they arise from the very nature of private property. Political economy does not disclose the source of the division between labour and capital, and between capital and land. When, for example, it defines the relationship of wages to profit, it takes the interest of the capitalists to be the ultimate cause; i.e., it takes for granted what it is supposed to evolve. Similarly, competition comes in everywhere. It is explained from external circumstances. As to how far these external and apparently fortuitous circumstances are but the expression of a necessary course of development, political economy teaches us nothing. We have seen how, to it, exchange itself appears to be a fortuitous fact. The only wheels which political economy sets in motion are *avarice* and the *war amongst the avaricious—competition*.

Precisely because political economy does not grasp the connections within the movement, it was possible to counterpose, for instance, the doctrine of competition to the doctrine of monopoly, the doctrine of craft-liberty to the doctrine of the corporation, the doctrine of the division of landed property to the doctrine of the big estate—for competition, craft-liberty and the division of landed property were explained and comprehended only as fortuitous, premeditated and violent consequences of monopoly, the corporation, and feudal property, not as their necessary, inevitable and natural consequences.

Now, therefore, we have to grasp the essential connection between private property, avarice, and the separation of labour,[3] capital and landed property;

---

1. That is, "alienated labor" (*die entfremdete Arbeit*)—labor that is "alienated" from the worker because it is under the control of an "alien" power (namely, an employer whose interests are at odds with those of the worker). This "alienation" (*Entfremdung*), together with the resulting "self-

alienation," is Marx's critical focus and topic in these manuscripts.
2. That is, economics.
3. That is, the division of labor (into different types of specialized labor necessary for or supplementary to the sustenance of human life).

between exchange and competition, value and the devaluation of men, monopoly and competition, etc.; the connection between this whole estrangement and the *money*-system.

Do not let us go back to a fictitious primordial condition as the political economist does, when he tries to explain. Such a primordial condition explains nothing. He merely pushes the question away into a grey nebulous distance. He assumes in the form of fact, of an event, what he is supposed to deduce— namely, the necessary relationship between two things—between, for example, division of labour and exchange. Theology in the same way explains the origin of evil by the fall of man: that is, it assumes as a fact, in historical form, what has to be explained.

We proceed from an *actual* economic fact.

The worker becomes all the poorer the more wealth he produces, the more his production increases in power and range. The worker becomes an ever cheaper commodity the more commodities he creates. With the *increasing value* of the world of things proceeds in direct proportion the *devaluation* of the world of men. Labour produces not only commodities; it produces itself and the worker as a *commodity*—and does so in the proportion in which it produces commodities generally.

This fact expresses merely that the object which labour produces—labour's product—confronts it as *something alien*, as a *power independent* of the producer. The product of labour is labour which has been congealed in an object, which has become material: it is the *objectification* of labour. Labour's realization is its objectification. In the conditions dealt with by political economy this realization of labour appears as *loss of reality* for the workers; objectification as *loss of the object* and *object-bondage*; appropriation as *estrangement*, as *alienation*.[4]

So much does labour's realization appear as loss of reality that the worker loses reality to the point of starving to death. So much does objectification appear as loss of the object that the worker is robbed of the objects most necessary not only for his life but for his work. Indeed, labour itself becomes an object which he can get hold of only with the greatest effort and with the most irregular interruptions. So much does the appropriation of the object appear as estrangement that the more objects the worker produces the fewer can he possess and the more he falls under the dominion of his product, capital.

All these consequences are contained in the definition that the worker is related to the *product of his labour* as to an *alien* object. For on this premise it is clear that the more the worker spends himself, the more powerful the alien objective world becomes which he creates over-against himself, the poorer he himself—his inner world—becomes, the less belongs to him as his own. It is the same in religion. The more man puts into God, the less he retains in himself. The worker puts his life into the object; but now his life no longer belongs to him but to the object. Hence, the greater this activity, the greater is the worker's lack of objects. Whatever the product of his labour is, he is not. Therefore the greater this product, the less is he himself. The *alienation*

---

4. "Alienation" here translates *Entäusserung*, meaning "making external to and thereby other than oneself": that is, relinquishing to others something in which one has expressed and objecti- fied something of oneself, thereby making "alien" something inherently one's own. For Marx, this is one of the key senses of the ideas of alienation and "self-alienation."

of the worker in his product means not only that his labour becomes an object, an *external* existence, but that it exists *outside him*, independently, as something alien to him, and that it becomes a power of its own confronting him; it means that the life which he has conferred on the object confronts him as something hostile and alien.

Let us now look more closely at the *objectification*, at the production of the worker; and therein at the *estrangement*, the *loss* of the object, his product.[5]

The worker can create nothing without *nature*, without the *sensuous external world*. It is the material on which his labor is manifested, in which it is active, from which and by means of which it produces.

But just as nature provides labor with the *means of life* in the sense that labour cannot *live* without objects on which to operate, on the other hand, it also provides the *means of life* in the more restricted sense—i.e., the means for the physical subsistence of the *worker* himself.

Thus the more the worker by his labour *appropriates* the external world, sensuous nature, the more he deprives himself of *means of life* in the double respect: first, that the sensuous external world more and more ceases to be an object belonging to his labour—to be his labour's *means of life*; and secondly, that it more and more ceases to be *means of life* in the immediate sense, means for the physical subsistence of the worker.

Thus in this double respect the worker becomes a slave of his object, first, in that he receives an *object of labour*, i.e., in that he receives *work*; and secondly, in that he receives *means of subsistence*. Therefore, it enables him to exist, first, as a *worker*; and, second, as a *physical subject*. The extremity of this bondage is that it is only as a *worker* that he continues to maintain himself as a *physical subject*, and that it is only as a *physical subject* that he is a *worker*.

(The laws of political economy express the estrangement of the worker in his object thus: the more the worker produces, the less he has to consume; the more values he creates, the more valueless, the more unworthy he becomes; the better formed his product, the more deformed becomes the worker; the more civilized his object, the more barbarous becomes the worker; the mightier labour becomes, the more powerless becomes the worker; the more ingenious labour becomes, the duller becomes the worker and the more he becomes nature's bondsman.)

Political economy conceals the estrangement inherent in the nature of labour by not considering the direct relationship between the worker (labour) *and production.* It is true that labour produces for the rich wonderful things—but for the worker it produces privation. It produces palaces—but for the worker, hovels. It produces beauty—but for the worker, deformity. It replaces labour by machines—but some of the workers it throws back to a barbarous type of labour, and the other workers it turns into machines. It produces intelligence—but for the worker idiocy, cretinism.

The direct relationship of labour to its produce is the relationship of the worker to the objects of his production. The relationship of the man of means to the objects of production and to production itself is only a *consequence* of this first relationship—and confirms it. We shall consider this other aspect later.

5. In what follows, Marx interprets and extends HEGEL's analysis of the situation and dehumanization of the "servant" in the "master–servant" relation found in his *Phenomenology of Geist* (1807; see above).

When we ask, then, what is the essential relationship of labour we are asking about the relationship of the *worker* to production.

Till now we have been considering the estrangement, the alienation of the worker only in one of its aspects, i.e., the worker's *relationship to the products of his labour.* But the estrangement is manifested not only in the result but in the *act of production*—within the *producing activity* itself. How would the worker come to face the product of his activity as a stranger, were it not that in the very act of production he was estranging himself from himself? The product is after all but the summary of the activity of production. If then the product of labour is alienation, production itself must be active alienation, the alienation of activity, the activity of alienation. In the estrangement of the object of labour is merely summarized the estrangement, the alienation, in the activity of labour itself.[6]

What, then, constitutes the alienation of labour?

First, the fact that labour is *external* to the worker, i.e., it does not belong to his essential being; that in his work, therefore, he does not affirm himself but denies himself, does not feel content but unhappy, does not develop freely his physical and mental energy but mortifies his body and ruins his mind. The worker therefore only feels himself outside his work, and in his work feels outside himself. He is at home when he is not working, and when he is working he is not at home. His labour is therefore not voluntary, but coerced; it is *forced labour.* It is therefore not the satisfaction of a need; it is merely a *means* to satisfy needs external to it. Its alien character emerges clearly in the fact that as soon as no physical or other compulsion exists, labour is shunned like the plague. External labour, labour in which man alienates himself, is a labour of self-sacrifice, of mortification. Lastly, the external character of labour for the worker appears in the fact that it is not his own, but someone else's, that it does not belong to him, that in it he belongs, not to himself, but to another. Just as in religion the spontaneous activity of the human imagination, of the human brain and the human heart, operates independently of the individual— that is, operates on him as an alien, divine or diabolical activity—in the same way the worker's activity is not his spontaneous activity. It belongs to another; it is the loss of his self.

As a result, therefore, man (the worker) no longer feels himself to be freely active in any but his animal functions—eating, drinking, procreating, or at most in his dwelling and in dressing-up, etc.; and in his human functions he no longer feels himself to be anything but an animal. What is animal becomes human and what is human becomes animal.

Certainly eating, drinking, procreating, etc., are also genuinely human functions. But in the abstraction which separates them from the sphere of all other human activity and turns them into sole and ultimate ends, they are animal.

We have considered the act of estranging practical human activity, labour, in two of its aspects. (1) The relation of the worker to the *product of labour* as an alien object exercising power over him. This relation is at the same time the relation to the sensuous external world, to the objects of nature as an alien world antagonistically opposed to him. (2) The relation of labour to the *act of*

6. Marx plays on the legal meaning of "alienation" as a conveyance of property to another.

production within the *labour* process. This relation is the relation of the worker to his own activity as an alien activity not belonging to him; it is activity as suffering, strength as weakness, begetting as emasculating, the worker's *own* physical and mental energy, his personal life or what is life other than activity— as an activity which is turned against him, neither depends on nor belongs to him. Here we have *self-estrangement*, as we had previously the estrangement of the *thing*.

We have yet a third aspect of *estranged labour* to deduce from the two already considered.

Man is a species being,[7] not only because in practice and in theory he adopts the species as his object (his own as well as those of other things), but—and this is only another way of expressing it—but also because he treats himself as the actual, living species; because he treats himself as a *universal* and therefore a free being.[8]

The life of the species, both in man and in animals, consists physically in the fact that man (like the animal) lives on inorganic nature; and the more universal man is compared with an animal, the more universal is the sphere of inorganic nature on which he lives. Just as plants, animals, stones, the air, light, etc., constitute a part of human consciousness in the realm of theory, partly as objects of natural science, partly as objects of art—his spiritual [*geistig*] inorganic nature, spiritual nourishment which he must first pre- pare to make it palatable and digestible—so too in the realm of practice they constitute a part of human life and human activity. Physically man lives only on these products of nature, whether they appear in the form of food, heat- ing, clothes, a dwelling, or whatever it may be. The universality of man is in practice manifested precisely in the universality which makes all nature his *inorganic* body—both inasmuch as nature is (1) his direct means of life, and (2) the material, the object, and the instrument of his life-activity. Nature is man's *inorganic body*—nature, that is, in so far as it is not itself the human body. Man *lives* on nature—means that nature is his *body*, with which he must remain in continuous intercourse if he is not to die. That man's physi- cal and spiritual [*geistig*] life is linked to nature means simply that nature is linked to itself, for man is a part of nature.

In estranging from man (1) nature, and (2) himself, his own active func- tions, his life-activity, estranged labour estranges the *species* from man. It turns for him the *life of the species* into a means of individual life. First it estranges the life of the species and individual life, and secondly it makes indi- vidual life in its abstract form the purpose of the life of the species, likewise in its abstract and estranged form.

For in the first place labour, *life-activity, productive life* itself, appears to man merely as a *means* of satisfying a need—the need to maintain the physi- cal existence. Yet the productive life is the life of the species. It is life- engendering life. The whole character of a species—its species character—is

---

7. "Species being" translates the term *Gattungs- wesen*: that is, a being that can recognize, identify, and affirm itself and its fellow creatures as being of a certain type. Here Marx is attempting to incorporate Hegel's emphasis on both the *allgemein* (general) character of *Geist* and on that *allgemein* character (or *Allgemeinheit*, "generality") being explicitly and self-consciously recognized and known.
8. That is, an autonomously self-determining being, whose *Allgemeinheit* is a liberation from every sort of identity that is merely contingent and imposed by circumstance.

contained in the character of its life-activity; and free, conscious activity is man's species character. Life itself appears only as *a means to life*.

The animal is immediately identical with its life-activity. It does not distinguish itself from it. It is *its life-activity*. Man makes his life-activity itself the object of his will and of his consciousness. He has conscious life-activity. It is not a determination with which he directly merges. Conscious life-activity directly distinguishes man from animal life-activity. It is just because of this that he is a species being. Or it is only because he is a species being that he is a Conscious Being, i.e., that his own life is an object for him. Only because of that is his activity free activity. Estranged labour reverses this relationship, so that it is just because man is a conscious being that he makes his life-activity, his *essential* being, a mere means to his *existence*.

In creating an *objective world* by his practical activity, in *working-up* inorganic nature, man proves himself a conscious species being, i.e., as a being that treats the species as its own essential being, or that treats itself as a species being. Admittedly animals also produce. They build themselves nests, dwellings, like the bees, beavers, ants, etc. But an animal only produces what it immediately needs for itself or its young. It produces one-sidedly, whilst man produces universally.[9] It produces only under the dominion of immediate physical need, whilst man produces even when he is free from physical need and only truly produces in freedom therefrom. An animal produces only itself, whilst man reproduces the whole of nature. An animal's product belongs immediately to its physical body, whilst man freely confronts his product. An animal forms things in accordance with the standard and the need of the species to which it belongs, whilst man knows how to produce in accordance with the standard of every species, and knows how to apply everywhere the inherent standard to the object. Man therefore also forms things in accordance with the laws of beauty.

It is just in the working-up of the objective world, therefore, that man first really proves himself to be a *species being*. This production is his active species life. Through and because of this production, nature appears as *his* work and his reality. The object of labour is, therefore, the *objectification of man's species life*: for he duplicates himself not only, as in consciousness, intellectually, but also actively, in reality, and therefore he contemplates himself in a world that he has created. In tearing away from man the object of his production, therefore, estranged labour tears from him his *species life*, his real species objectivity, and transforms his advantage over animals into the disadvantage that his inorganic body, nature, is taken from him.

Similarly, in degrading spontaneous activity, free activity, to a means, estranged labour makes man's species life a means to his physical existence.

The consciousness which man has of his species is thus transformed by estrangement in such a way that the species life becomes for him a means.

Estranged labour turns thus:

(3) *Man's species being*, both nature and his spiritual species property, into a being *alien* to him, into a *means* to his *individual existence*. It estranges

9. That is, man can produce not simply in a way linked directly and closely to specific biological necessities ("one-sidedly") but in indefinitely many ways ("universally," or generally).

man's own body from him, as it does external nature and his spiritual essence [*geistigen Wesen*], his *human* being.

(4) An immediate consequence of the fact that man is estranged from the product of his labour, from his life-activity, from his species being is the *estrangement of man* from *man*. If a man is confronted by himself, he is confronted by the *other* man. What applies to a man's relation to his work, to the product of his labour and to himself, also holds of a man's relation to the other man, and to the other man's labour and object of labour.

In fact, the proposition that man's species nature is estranged from him means that one man is estranged from the other, as each of them is from man's essential nature.[1]

The estrangement of man, and in fact every relationship in which man stands to himself, is first realized and expressed in the relationship in which a man stands to other men.

Hence within the relationship of estranged labour each man views the other in accordance with the standard and the position in which he finds himself as a worker.

We took our departure from a fact of political economy—the estrangement of the worker and his production. We have formulated the concept of this fact—*estranged, alienated* labour. We have analysed this concept—hence analysing merely a fact of political economy.

Let us now see, further, how in real life the concept of estranged, alienated labour must express and present itself.

If the product of labour is alien to me, if it confronts me as an alien power, to whom, then, does it belong?

If my own activity does not belong to me, if it is an alien, a coerced activity, to whom, then, does it belong?

To a being *other* than me.

Who is this being?

The *gods*? To be sure, in the earliest times the principal production (for example, the building of temples, etc., in Egypt, India and Mexico) appears to be in the service of the gods, and the product belongs to the gods. However, the gods on their own were never the lords of labour. No more was *nature*. And what a contradiction it would be if, the more man subjugated nature by his labour and the more the miracles of the gods were rendered superfluous by the miracles of industry, the more man were to renounce the joy of production and the enjoyment of the produce in favour of these powers.

The *alien* being, to whom labour and the produce of labour belongs, in whose service labour is done and for whose benefit the produce of labour is provided, can only be *man* himself.

If the product of labour does not belong to the worker, if it confronts him as an alien power, this can only be because it belongs to some *other man than the worker*. If the worker's activity is a torment to him, to another it must be

---

1. "Man's essential nature" translates *menschlichen Wesen*. *Wesen* can mean something's "essence" or "essential nature" (as often used in Hegel, whose usage Marx is echoing here); but it can also mean its "nature" or "reality." Thus the discussion's focus shifts easily between the fundamental nature and general character of something (e.g., human reality or labor) and the way it would need to be if it were to become "genuine" or true to its essential nature (its *Begriff*, in Hegel's language).

delight and his life's joy. Not the gods, not nature, but only man himself can be this alien power over man.

We must bear in mind the above-stated proposition that man's relation to himself only becomes *objective* and *real* for him through his relation to the other man. Thus, if the product of his labour, his labour *objectified*, is for him an *alien*, hostile, powerful object independent of him, then his position towards it is such that someone else is master of this object, someone who is alien, hostile, powerful, and independent of him. If his own activity is to him an unfree activity, then he is treating it as activity performed in the service, under the dominion, the coercion and the yoke of another man.

Every self-estrangement of man from himself and from nature appears in the relation in which he places himself and nature to men other than and differentiated from himself. For this reason religious self-estrangement necessarily appears in the relationship of the layman to the priest, or again to a mediator, etc., since we are here dealing with the intellectual world. In the real practical world self-estrangement can only become manifest through the real practical relationship to other men. The medium through which estrangement takes place is itself *practical*. Thus through estranged labour man not only engenders his relationship to the object and to the act of production as to powers that are alien and hostile to him; he also engenders the relationship in which other men stand to his production and to his product, and the relationship in which he stands to these other men. Just as he begets his own production as the loss of his reality, as his punishment; just as he begets his own product as a loss, as a product not belonging to him; so he begets the dominion of the one who does not produce over production and over the product. Just as he estranges from himself his own activity, so he confers to the stranger activity which is not his own.

Till now we have only considered this relationship from the standpoint of the worker and later we shall be considering it also from the standpoint of the non-worker.

Through *estranged, alienated labour*, then, the worker produces the relationship to this labour of a man alien to labour and standing outside it. The relationship of the worker to labour engenders the relation to it of the capitalist, or whatever one chooses to call the master of labour. *Private property* is thus the product, the result, the necessary consequence, of *alienated labour*, of the external relation of the worker to nature and to himself.

Private property thus results by analysis from the concept of *alienated labour*—i.e., of *alienated man*, of estranged labour, of estranged life, of *estranged* man.

True, it is as a result of the *movement of private property* that we have obtained the concept of *alienated labour* (of *alienated life*) from political economy. But on analysis of this concept it becomes clear that though private property appears to be the source, the cause of alienated labour, it is really its consequence, just as the gods *in the beginning* are not the cause but the effect of man's intellectual confusion. Later this relationship becomes reciprocal.

Only at the very culmination of the development of private property does this, its secret, re-emerge, namely, that on the one hand it is the *product* of alienated labour, and that secondly it is the *means* by which labour alienates itself, the *realization of this alienation*.[2]

* * *

From *Private Property and Communism*

* * *

(3) *Communism*[3] as the *positive* transcendence of *private property*, or *human self-estrangement*, and therefore as the real *appropriation of the human* essence by and for man; communism therefore as the complete return of man to himself as a *social* (i.e., human) being[4]—a return become conscious, and accomplished within the entire wealth of previous development. This communism, as fully-developed naturalism, equals humanism, and as fully-developed humanism equals naturalism; it is the *genuine* resolution of the conflict between man and nature and between man and man—the true resolution of the strife between existence and essence, between objectification and self-confirmation, between freedom and necessity, between the individual and the species. Communism is the riddle of history solved, and it knows itself to be this solution.

The entire movement of history is, therefore, both its *actual* act of genesis (the birth act of its empirical existence) and also for its thinking consciousness the *comprehended* and *known* process of its *coming-to-be*. That other, still immature communism, meanwhile, seeks an *historical* proof for itself—a proof in the realm of the existent—amongst disconnected historical phenomena opposed to private property, tearing single phases from the historical process and focussing attention on them as proofs of its historical pedigree[.] * * * By so doing it simply makes clear that by far the greater part of this process contradicts its claims, and that, if it has once been, precisely its being in the *past* refutes its pretension to being *essential*.

That the entire revolutionary movement necessarily finds both its empirical and its theoretical basis in the movement of *private property*—in that of the economy, to be precise—is easy to see.

This *material*, immediately *sensuous* private property is the material sensuous expression of *estranged human* life. Its movement—production and consumption—is the *sensuous* revelation of the movement of all production hitherto—i.e., the realization or the reality of man. Religion, family, state, law, morality, science, art, etc., are only *particular* modes of production, and fall under its general law. The positive transcendence of *private property* as the appropriation of *human* life is, therefore, the positive transcendence of all estrangement—that is to say, the return of man from religion, family, state, etc., to his *human*, i.e., *social* mode of existence. Religious estrangement as such

2. That is, analysis reveals that the *institution* of "private property" and the practices associated with it are what make possible and promote the systematic "alienation of labor" and of the products of the worker's labor.
3. The communal or general societal (as opposed to "private," individual) ownership and control of the means of production.
4. This is Marx's revision (and adoption as revised) of Hegel's conception of "objective *Geist*" and ethicality (*Sittlichkeit*).

occurs only in the realm of *consciousness*, of man's inner life, but economic estrangement is that of *real life*; its transcendence therefore embraces both aspects. It is evident that the *initial* stage of the movement amongst the various peoples depends on whether the true and for them *authentic* life of the people manifests itself more in consciousness or in the external world—is more ideal or real. Communism begins from the outset (*Owen*)[5] with atheism; but atheism is at first far from being *communism*; indeed, it is still mostly an abstraction.

The philanthropy of atheism is therefore at first only *philosophical*, abstract, philanthropy, and that of communism is at once *real* and directly bent on *action*.

We have seen how on the premise of positively annulled[6] private property man produces man—himself and the other man; how the object, being the direct embodiment of his individuality, is simultaneously his own existence for the other man, the existence of the other man, and that existence for him. Likewise, however, both the material of labour and man as the subject, are the point of departure as well as the result of the movement (and precisely in this fact, that they must constitute the *point of departure*, lies the historical *necessity* of private property). Thus the *social* character is the general character of the whole movement: *just as* society itself produces *man as man*, so is society *produced* by him. Activity and consumption, both in their content and in their *mode of existence*, are *social: social* activity and *social* consumption; the *human* essence of nature first exists only for *social* man; for only here does nature exist for him as a *bond* with *man*—as his existence for the other and the other's existence for him—as the life-element of the human world; only here does nature exist as the *foundation* of his own *human* existence. Only here has what is to him his *natural* existence become his *human* existence, and nature become man for him. Thus *society* is the consummated oneness in substance of man and nature—the true resurrection of nature—the naturalism of man and the humanism of nature both brought to fulfilment.

Social activity and social consumption exist by no means *only* in the form of some *directly* communal activity and directly *communal* consumption, although *communal* activity and *communal* consumption—i.e., activity and consumption which are manifested and directly confirmed in *real association* with other men—will occur wherever such a *direct* expression of sociality stems from the true character of the activity's content and is adequate to the nature of consumption.

But again when I am active *scientifically*,[7] etc.,—when I am engaged in activity which I can seldom perform in direct community with others—then I am *social*, because I am active as a *man* [*Mensch*]. Not only is the material of my activity given to me as a social product (as is even the language in which the thinker is active): my *own* existence *is* social activity, and therefore that which I make of myself, I make of myself for society and with the consciousness of myself as a social being.

<hr />

5. Robert Owen (1771–1858), Welsh social theorist and reformer, and a founding figure of British socialism.

6. That is, "positively superseded" (*positiv aufgehobenen*). *Aufhebung* was a favorite term of Hegel's, because it can mean cancellation, preservation,

transformation, or all of these things at once; Marx similarly relied on its complexity. (On *Aufhebung*, see the Hegel glossary, p. 144.)

7. That is, when I am engaged in cognitive inquiry (*wissenschaftlich* activity).

My *general* consciousness is only the *theoretical* shape of that of which the *living* shape is the *real* community, the social fabric, although at the present day *general* consciousness is an abstraction from real life and as such antagonistically confronts it. Consequently, too, the *activity* of my general consciousness, as an activity, is my *theoretical* existence as a social being.

What is to be avoided above all is the re-establishing of "Society" as an abstraction *vis-à-vis* the individual. The individual *is the social being*. His life, even if it may not appear in the direct form of a *communal* life carried out together with others—is therefore an expression and confirmation of *social life*. Man's individual and species life are not *different*, however much—and this is inevitable—the mode of existence of the individual is a more *particular,* or more *general* mode of the life of the species, or the life of the species is a more *particular* or more *general* individual life.

In his *consciousness of species* man confirms his real *social life* and simply repeats his real existence in thought, just as conversely the being of the species confirms itself in species-consciousness and is for *itself* in its generality as a thinking being.

Man, much as he may therefore be a *particular* individual (and it is precisely his particularity which makes him an individual, and a real *individual* social being), is just as much the *totality*—the ideal totality—the subjective existence of thought and experienced society present for itself; just as he exists also in the real world as the awareness and the real enjoyment of social existence, and as a totality of human life-activity.

Thinking and being are thus no doubt *distinct*, but at the same time they are in *unity* with each other.

Death seems to be a harsh victory of the species over the *definite* individual and to contradict their unity. But the determinate individual is only a *determinate species being*, and as such mortal.

(4) Just as *private property* is only the sensuous expression of the fact that man becomes *objective* for himself and at the same time becomes to himself a strange and inhuman object; just as it expresses the fact that the assertion of his life is the alienation of his life, that his realization is his loss of reality, is an *alien* reality: conversely, the positive transcendence [*Aufhebung*] of private property—i.e., the *sensuous* appropriation for and by man of the human essence[8] and of human life, of objective man, of human *achievements*—is not to be conceived merely in the sense of *direct*, one-sided *gratification*—merely in the sense of *possessing*, of *having*. Man appropriates his total essence in a total manner, that is to say, as a whole man. Each of his *human* relations to the world—seeing, hearing, smelling, tasting, feeling, thinking, being aware, sensing, wanting, acting, loving—in short, all the organs of his individual being, like those organs which are directly social in their form, are in their *objective* orientation or in their *orientation to the object*, the appropriation of that object, the appropriation of the *human* world; their orientation to the object is the *manifestation of the human world*; it is human *efficaciousness* and human *suffering*,[9] for suffering, apprehended humanly, is an enjoyment of self in man.

---

8. That is, the essential or central character of human reality (*menschlichen Wesen*).
9. That is, being affected.

Private property has made us so stupid and one-sided that an object is only *ours* when we have it—when it exists for us as capital, or when it is directly possessed, eaten, drunk, worn, inhabited, etc.,—in short, when it is *used* by us. Although private property itself again conceives all these direct realizations of possession as *means of life*, and the life which they serve as means is the *life of private property*—labour and conversion into capital.

In place of *all* these physical and mental [*geistig*] senses there has therefore come the sheer estrangement of *all* these senses—the sense of *having*. The human being had to be reduced to this absolute poverty in order that he might yield his inner wealth to the outer world. * * *

The transcendence of private property[1] is therefore the complete *emancipation* of all human senses and attributes; but it is this emancipation precisely because these senses and attributes have become, subjectively and objectively, *human*. The eye has become a *human* eye, just as its *object* has become a social, *human* object—an object emanating from man for man. The *senses* have therefore become directly in their practice *theoreticians*. They relate themselves to the *thing* for the sake of the thing, but the thing itself is an *objective human* relation to itself and to man, and vice versa. Need or enjoyment have consequently lost their *egotistical* nature, and nature has lost its mere *utility* by use becoming *human* use.

In the same way, the senses and enjoyments of other men have become my *own* appropriation. Besides these direct organs, therefore, *social* organs develop in the *form* of society; thus, for instance, activity in direct association with others, etc., has become an organ for *expressing* my own *life*, and a mode of appropriating *human life*.

It is obvious that the *human* eye gratifies itself in a way different from the crude, non-human eye; the human *ear* different from the crude ear, etc.

To recapitulate; man is not lost in his object only when the object becomes for him a *human* object or objective man. This is possible only when the object becomes for him a *social* object, he himself for himself a social being, just as society becomes a being for him in this object.

On the one hand, therefore, it is only when the objective world becomes everywhere for man in society the world of man's essential powers—human reality, and for that reason the reality of his *own* essential powers—that all *objects* become for him the *objectification of himself*, become objects which confirm and realize his individuality, become *his* objects: that is, *man himself* becomes the object. The manner in which they become *his* depends on the *nature of the objects* and on the nature of the *essential power* corresponding *to it*; for it is precisely the *determinateness* of this relationship which shapes the particular, *real* mode of affirmation. To the *eye* an object comes to be other than it is to the *ear*, and the object of the eye is another object than the object of the *ear*. The peculiarity of each essential power is precisely its *peculiar essence*, and therefore also the peculiar mode of its objectification, of its *objectively actual* living *being*. Thus man is affirmed in the objective world not only in the act of thinking, but with *all* his senses.

On the other hand, looking at this in its subjective aspect: just as music

---

1. That is, the transcendence of private property *as an institution* that permits and facilitates exploitative and abstract ownership (in contrast to *personal property*, which Marx would retain, as indispensable to the expression, development, and realization of human personality).

alone awakens in man the sense of music, and just as the most beautiful music has *no* sense for the unmusical ear—is no object for it, because my object can only be the confirmation of one of my essential powers and can therefore only be so for me as my essential power is present for itself as a subjective capacity, because the sense of an object for me goes only so far as *my* senses go (has only sense for a sense corresponding to that object)—for this reason the *senses* of the social man are *other* senses than those of the non-social man. Only through the objectively unfolded richness of man's essential being is the richness of subjective *human* sensibility (a musical ear, an eye for beauty of form—in short, *senses* capable of human gratifications, senses confirming themselves as essential powers of *man*) either cultivated or brought into being. For not only the five senses but also the so-called mental [*geistig*] senses— the practical senses (will, love, etc.)—in a word, *human* sense—the human- ness of the senses—comes to be by virtue of its object, by virtue of *humanized* nature. The *forming*[2] of the five senses is a labour of the entire history of the world down to the present.

The *sense* caught up in crude practical need has only a *restricted* sense. For the starving man, it is not the human form of food that exists, but only its abstract being as food; it could just as well be there in its crudest form, and it would be impossible to say wherein this feeding-activity differs from that of *animals*. The care-burdened man in need has no sense for the finest play; the dealer in minerals sees only the mercantile value but not the beauty and the unique nature of the mineral: he has no mineralogical sense. Thus, the objectification of the human essence both in its theoretical and practical aspects is required to make man's *sense human*, as well as to create the *human sense* corresponding to the entire wealth of human and natural substance.

Just as resulting from the movement of *private property*, of its wealth as well as its poverty—or of its material and spiritual wealth and poverty—the bud- ding society finds to hand all the material for this *development*: so *established* society produces man in this entire richness of his being—produces the *rich* man *profoundly endowed with all the senses*—as its enduring reality.

It will be seen how subjectivism and objectivism, spiritualism and materi- alism, activity and suffering, only lose their antithetical character, and thus their existence, as such antitheses in the social condition; it will be seen how the resolution of the *theoretical* antitheses is *only* possible *in a practical* way, by virtue of the practical energy of men. Their resolution is therefore by no means merely a problem of knowledge, but a *real* problem of life, which *phi- losophy*[3] could not solve precisely because it conceived this problem as *merely* a theoretical one.

It will be seen how the history of *industry* and the established *objective* exis- tence of industry are the *open* book of *man's essential powers*, the exposure to the senses of human *psychology*. Hitherto this was not conceived in its insep- arable connection with man's *essential being*, but only in an external relation of utility, because, moving in the realm of estrangement, people could only think man's general mode of being—religion or history in its abstract- general character as politics, art, literature, etc.,—to be the reality of man's essential powers and *man's species-activity*. We have before us the *objectified*

2. That is, the education, cultivation, development, refinement (*Bildung*).   3. That is, Hegel's philosophy.

essential powers of man in the form of *sensuous, alien, useful objects*, in the form of estrangement, displayed in *ordinary material industry* (which can be conceived as a part of that general movement, just as that movement can be conceived as a particular part of industry, since all human activity hitherto has been labour—that is, industry—activity estranged from itself).

A *psychology* for which this, the part of history most contemporary and accessible to sense, remains a closed book, cannot become a genuine, comprehensive and *real* science [*Wissenschaft*]. What indeed are we to think of a science which *airily* abstracts from this large part of human labour and which fails to feel its own incompleteness, while such a wealth of human endeavour unfolded before it means nothing more to it than, perhaps, what can be expressed in one word—*"need," "vulgar need"*?

The *natural sciences* have developed an enormous activity and have accumulated a constantly growing mass of material. Philosophy, however, has remained just as alien to them as they remain to philosophy. Their momentary unity was only a *chimerical illusion*. The will was there, but the means were lacking. Even historiography pays regard to natural science only occasionally, as a factor of enlightenment and utility arising from individual great discoveries. But natural science has invaded and transformed human life all the more *practically* through the medium of industry; and has prepared human emancipation, however directly and much it had to consummate dehumanization. *Industry* is the *actual*, historical relation of nature, and therefore of natural science, to man. If, therefore, industry is conceived as the *exoteric* revelation of man's *essential powers*, we also gain an understanding of the *human* essence of nature or the *natural* essence of man. In consequence, natural science will lose its abstractly material—or rather, its idealistic—tendency, and will become the basis of *human* science, as it has already become the basis of actual human life, albeit in an estranged form. *One* basis for life and another basis for *science* is *a priori* a lie. The nature which comes to be in human history—the genesis of human society—is man's *real* nature; hence nature as it comes to be through industry, even though in an *estranged* form, is true *anthropological* nature.

Sense-perception (see Feuerbach) must be the basis of all science [*Wissenschaft*]. Only when it proceeds from sense-perception in the twofold form both of *sensuous* consciousness and of *sensuous* need—that is, only when science proceeds from nature—is it *true* science. All history is the preparation for *"man"* to become the object of *sensuous* consciousness, and for the needs of "man as man" to become [natural, sensuous][4] needs. History itself is a *real* part of *natural history*—of nature's coming to be man. Natural science will in time subsume under itself the science [*Wissenschaft*] of man, just as the science of man will subsume under itself natural science: there will be *one* science.

Man is the immediate object of natural science: for immediate, *sensuous nature* for man is, immediately, human sensuousness (the expressions are identical)—presented immediately in the form of the *other* man sensuously present for him. For his own sensuousness first exists as human sensuousness for himself through the *other* man. But *nature* is the immediate object

---

4. This bracketed phrase was crossed out by Marx in his manuscript.

of the *science* [*Wissenschaft*] *of man*: the first object of man—man—is nature, sensuousness; and the particular human sensuous essential powers can only find their self-knowledge in the science of the natural world in general, since they can find their objective realization in *natural* objects only. The element of thought itself—the element of thought's living expression—*language*—is of a sensuous nature. The *social* reality of nature, and *human* natural science, or the *natural science about man*, are identical terms.

It will be seen how in place of the *wealth* and *poverty* of political economy come the *rich human being* and rich *human* need. The *rich* human being is simultaneously the human being *in need of* a totality of human life-activities— the man in whom his own realization exists as an inner necessity, as *need*. Not only *wealth*, but likewise the *poverty* of man—given socialism—receives in equal measure a *human* and therefore social significance. Poverty is the passive bond which causes the human being to experience the need of the greatest wealth—the *other* human being. The dominion of the objective being in me, the sensuous outburst of my essential activity, is *emotion*, which thus becomes here the *activity* of my being.

(5) A *being* only considers himself independent when he stands on his own feet; and he only stands on his own feet when he owes his *existence* to himself. A man who lives by the grace of another regards himself as a dependent being. But I live completely by the grace of another if I owe him not only the sustenance of my life, but if he has, moreover, *created* my *life*—if he is the *source* of my life; and if it is not of my own creation, my life has necessarily a source of this kind outside it. The *Creation* is therefore an idea very difficult to dislodge from popular consciousness. The self-mediated being of nature and of man is *incomprehensible* to it, because it contradicts everything *palpable* in practical life.

The creation of the *earth* has received a mighty blow from *geogeny*— i.e., from the science which presents the formation of the earth, the coming to be of the earth, as a process, as self-generation. *Generatio aequivoca*[5] is the only practical refutation of the theory of creation.

Now it is certainly easy to say to the single individual what Aristotle has already said. You have been begotten by your father and your mother; therefore in you the mating of two human beings—a species-act of human beings— has produced the human being.[6] You see, therefore, that even physically, man owes his existence to man. Therefore you must not only keep sight of the *one* aspect—the *infinite* progression which leads you further to enquire: "Who begot my father? Who his grandfather?", etc. You must also hold on to the *circular movement* sensuously perceptible in that progression, by which *man* repeats himself in procreation, thus always remaining the subject. You will reply, however: I grant you this circular movement; now grant me the progression which drives me even further until I ask: Who begot the first man, and nature as a whole? I can only answer you: Your question is itself a product of abstraction. Ask yourself how you arrived at that question. Ask yourself whether your question is not posed from a standpoint to which I

5. Spontaneous (literally, "ambiguous") generation (Latin).
6. The Greek philosopher Aristotle (384–322 b.c.e.)
begins his explanation of the development of the city-state with the union of the male and the female (*Politics* 1.1).

cannot reply, because it is a perverse one. Ask yourself whether that progression as such exists for a reasonable mind. When you ask about the creation of nature and man, you are abstracting, in so doing, from man and nature. You postulate them as *non-existent*, and yet you want me to prove them to you as *existing*. Now I say to you: Give up your abstraction and you will also give up your question. Or if you want to hold on to your abstraction, then be consistent, and if you think of man and nature as *non-existent*, then think of yourself as non-existent, for you too are surely nature and man. Don't think, don't ask me, for as soon as you think and ask, your *abstraction* from the existence of nature and man has no meaning. Or are you such an egoist that you postulate everything as nothing, and yet want yourself to be?

You can reply: I do not want to postulate the nothingness of nature. I ask you about *its genesis*, just as I ask the anatomist about the formation of bones, etc.

But since for the socialist man the *entire so-called history of the world* is nothing but the begetting of man through human labour, nothing but the coming-to-be of nature for man, he has the visible, irrefutable proof of his *birth* through himself, of his *process* of *coming-to-be*. Since the *real existence* of man and nature has become practical, sensuous and perceptible—since man has become for man as the being of nature, and nature for man as the being of man—the question about an *alien* being, about a being above nature and man—a question which implies the admission of the inessentiality of nature and of man—has become impossible in practice. *Atheism*, as the denial of this inessentiality, has no longer any meaning, for atheism is a *negation of God*, and postulates the *existence of man* through this negation; but socialism as socialism no longer stands in any need of such a mediation. It proceeds from the *practically and theoretically sensuous consciousness* of man and of nature as the *essence*. Socialism is man's *positive self-consciousness* no longer mediated through the annulment of religion, just as *real life* is man's positive reality, no longer mediated through the annulment of private property, through *communism*. Communism is the position as the negation of the negation, and is hence the *actual* phase necessary for the next stage of historical development in the process of human emancipation and recovery. *Communism* is the necessary pattern and the dynamic principle of the immediate future, but communism as such is not the goal of human development—the structure of human society.

From *Phenomenology*

* * *

The outstanding thing in Hegel's *Phenomenology* and its final outcome—that is, the dialectic of negativity as the moving and generating principle—is thus first that Hegel conceives the self-genesis of man as a process, conceives objectification as loss of the object, as alienation and as transcendence of this alienation; that he thus grasps the essence of *labour* and comprehends objective man—true, because real man—as the outcome of man's *own labour*. The *real*, active orientation of man to himself as a species being, or his manifestation as a real species being (i.e., as a human being), is only possible by his really bringing out of himself all the *powers* that are his as the *species* man—something which in turn is only possible through the totality of man's actions, as the result of history—is only possible by man's treating these generic powers as objects: and this, to begin with, is again only possible in the form of estrangement.

* * *

For Hegel the *essence of man—man—*equals *self-consciousness.* All estrangement of the human essence is therefore *nothing but estrangement of self-consciousness.* The estrangement of self-consciousness is not regarded as an *expression* of the *real* estrangement of the human being—its expression reflected in the realm of knowledge and thought. Instead, the *real* estrangement—that which appears real—is from its *innermost,* hidden nature (a nature only brought to light by philosophy) nothing but the *manifestation* of the estrangement of the real essence of man, of *self-consciousness.* The science which comprehends this is therefore called *Phenomenology.* All re-appropriation of the estranged objective essence appears, therefore, as a process of incorporation into self-consciousness: The man who takes hold of his essential being is *merely* the self-consciousness which takes hold of objective essences. Return of the object into the self is therefore the re-appropriation of the object.

* * *

* * * *The alienation of self-consciousness* [in Hegel] establishes *thinghood.* Because man equals self-consciousness, his alienated, objective essence, or *thinghood, equals alienated self-consciousness,* and *thinghood* is thus established through this alienation (thinghood being *that* which is an *object for man* and an object for him is really only that which is to him an essential object, therefore his *objective essence.* And since it is not *real Man,* nor therefore *Nature*—Man being *human Nature*—who as such is made the subject, but only the abstraction of man—self-consciousness—thinghood cannot be anything but alienated self-conciousness). It is only to be expected that a living, natural being equipped and endowed with objective (i.e., material) essential powers should have *real natural objects* of his essence; as is the fact that his self-alienation should lead to the establishing of a *real,* objective world— but a world in the form of *externality*—a world, therefore, not belonging to his own essential being, and an overpowering world. There is nothing incomprehensible or mysterious in this. It would be mysterious, rather, if it were otherwise. But it is equally clear that a *self-consciousness* can only establish *thinghood* through its alienation—i.e., establish something which itself is only an abstract thing, a thing of abstraction and not a *real* thing. It is clear, further, that thinghood is therefore utterly without any *independence,* any *essentiality vis-à-vis* self-consciousness; that on the contrary, it is a mere creature—something *posited* by self-consciousness. And what is posited, instead of confirming itself, is but a confirmation of the act of positing in which is concentrated for a moment the energy of the act as its product, *seeming* to give the de-posit[7]—but only for a moment—the character of an independent, real substance.[8]

7. That is, that which is "posited" (established).   8. That is, "being" (*Wesen*).

Whenever real, corporeal *man*, man with his feet firmly on the solid ground, man exhaling and inhaling all the forces of nature, *establishes* his real, objective *essential powers* as alien objects by his externalization, it is not the *act of positing* which is the subject in this process: it is the subjectivity of *objective* essential powers, whose action, therefore, must also be something *objective*. A being who is objective acts objectively, and he would not act objectively if the objective did not reside in the very nature of his being. He creates or establishes only *objects*, *because* he is established by objects—because at bottom he is *nature*. In the act of establishing, therefore, this objective being does not fall from his state of "pure activity" into a *creating of the object*; on the contrary, his *objective* product only confirms his *objective* activity, establishing his activity as the activity of an objective, natural being.

Here we see how consistent naturalism or humanism distinguishes itself both from idealism and materialism, constituting at the same time the unifying truth of both. We see also how only naturalism is capable of comprehending the act of world history.

Man is directly a *natural being*. As a natural being and as a living natural being he is on the one hand furnished with *natural powers of life*—he is an *active* natural being. These forces exist in him as tendencies and abilities— as *impulses*. On the other hand, as a natural, corporeal, sensuous, objective being he is a *suffering*,[9] conditioned and limited creature, like animals and plants. That is to say, the *objects* of his impulses exist outside him, as *objects* independent of him; yet these objects are *objects* of his *need*—essential *objects*, indispensable to the manifestation and confirmation of his essential powers. To say that man is a *corporeal*, living, real, sensuous, objective being full of natural vigour is to say that he has *real, sensuous, objects* as the objects of his being or of his life, or that he can only *express* his life in real, sensuous objects. To be objective, natural and sensuous, and at the same time to have object, nature and sense outside oneself, or oneself to be object, nature and sense for a third party, is one and the same thing. *Hunger* is a natural *need*; it therefore needs a *nature* outside itself, an *object* outside itself, in order to satisfy itself, to be stilled. Hunger is an acknowledged need of my body for an *object* existing outside it, indispensable to its integration and to the expression of its essential being. The sun is the *object* of the plant—an indispensable object to it, confirming its life—just as the plant is an object of the sun, being an *expression* of the life-awakening power of the sun, of the sun's *objective* essential power.

A being which does not have its nature outside itself is not a *natural* being, and plays no part in the system of nature. A being which has no object outside itself is not an objective being. A being which is not itself an object for some third being has no being for its *object*; i.e., it is not objectively related. Its be-ing[1] is not objective.

An unobjective being is a *nullity*—an *un-being*.

Suppose a being which is neither an object itself, nor has an object. Such a being, in the first place, would be the *unique* being: there would exist no being outside it—it would exist solitary and alone. For as soon as there are objects outside me, as soon as I am not *alone*, I am *another*—*another reality* than the

---

9. That is, passive: something to which *things happen*, owing to the action of external forces that cannot be controlled.

1. That is, mode of existing (*Sein*).

object outside me. For this third object I am thus an *other reality* than it; that is, I am *its* object. Thus, to suppose a being which is not the object of another being is to presuppose that *no* objective being exists. As soon as I have an object, this object has me for an object. But a *non-objective* being is an unreal, nonsensical thing—something merely thought of (merely imagined, that is)—a creature of abstraction. To be *sensuous*, that is, to be an object of sense, to be a *sensuous* object, and thus to have sensuous objects outside oneself—objects of one's sensuousness. To be sensuous is to *suffer*.[2]

Man as an objective, sensuous being is therefore a *suffering* being—and because he feels what he suffers, a *passionate* being. Passion is the essential force of man energetically bent on its object.

But man is not merely a natural being: he is a *human* natural being. That is to say, he is a being for himself. Therefore he is a *species being*, and has to confirm and manifest himself as such both in his being and in his knowing. Therefore, *human* objects are not natural objects as they immediately present themselves, and neither is *human sense* as it immediately *is*—as it is objectively—*human* sensibility, human objectivity. Neither nature objectively nor nature subjectively is directly given in a form adequate to the *human* being. And as everything natural has to have its *beginning, man* too has his act of coming-to-be—*history*—which, however, is for him a known history, and hence as an act of coming-to-be it is a conscious self-transcending act of coming-to-be. History is the true natural history of man[.]

* * *

SOURCE: From *The Marx-Engels Reader*, ed. Robert C. Tucker, 2nd ed. (New York: W. W. Norton, 1978), pp. 70–79, 84–93, 112–17 [translated by Martin Milligan]. Except where otherwise indicated, German words in brackets are the terminology used in the German original, inserted by the editor in addition to their renderings in the translation. These manuscripts were written in 1844, while Marx was reading extensively in economics as well as philosophy in an attempt to "demystify" some of the parts of HEGEL's "philosophy of *Geist* [spirit]" that were of greatest interest to him, expanding the scope of FEUERBACH's project of an "anthropological reduction" of Hegel's interpretation of our nature and existence into the language of "human" life and reality. These manuscripts were first published in part in a 1927 Russian edition of his collected writings; they were published in full in German in 1932.

From The German Ideology

By KARL MARX AND FRIEDRICH ENGELS

From *Part One. Ludwig Feuerbach*

The premises from which we begin are not arbitrary ones, not dogmas, but real premises from which abstraction can only be made in the imagination. They are the real individuals, their activity and the material conditions under which they live, both those which they find already existing and those produced by their activity. These premises can thus be verified in a purely empirical way.

2. That is, to be affected.

The first premise of all human history is, of course, the existence of living human individuals. Thus the first fact to be established is the physical organisation of these individuals and their consequent relation to the rest of nature. Of course, we cannot here go either into the actual physical nature of man, or into the natural conditions in which man finds himself—geological, oro-hydrographical,[1] climatic and so on. The writing of history must always set out from these natural bases and their modification in the course of history through the action of men.

Human beings[2] can be distinguished from animals by consciousness, by religion or anything else you like. They themselves begin to distinguish themselves from animals as soon as they begin to *produce* their means of subsistence, a step which is conditioned by their physical organisation. By producing their means of subsistence men are indirectly producing their actual material life.

The way in which humans [*Menschen*] produce their means of subsistence depends first of all on the nature of the actual means of subsistence they find in existence and have to reproduce. This mode of production must not be considered simply as being the reproduction of the physical existence of the individuals. Rather it is a definite form of activity of these individuals, a definite form of expressing their life, a definite *mode of life* [*Lebensweise*] on their part. As individuals express their life, so they are. What they are, therefore, coincides with their production, both with *what* they produce and with *how* they produce. The nature of individuals thus depends on the material conditions determining their production.

This production only makes its appearance with the *increase of population.* In its turn this presupposes the *interaction* [*Verkehr*][3] of individuals with one another. The form of this interaction is again determined by production.

The relations of different nations among themselves depend upon the extent to which each has developed its productive forces, the division of labour and internal interaction. This statement is generally recognised. But not only the relation of one nation to others, but also the whole internal structure of the nation itself depends on the stage of development reached by its production and its internal and external interaction. How far the productive forces of a nation are developed is shown most manifestly by the degree to which the division of labour has been carried. Each new productive force, insofar as it is not merely a quantitative extension of productive forces already known (for instance the bringing into cultivation of fresh land), causes a further development of the division of labour.

* * *

The fact is, therefore, that definite individuals who are productively active in a definite way enter into these definite social and political relations. Empirical observation must in each separate instance bring out empirically, and without any mystification and speculation, the connection of the social and political structure with production. The social structure and the State are

---

1. Relating to the watersheds or drainage of mountains.
2. *Menschen*, humans. (In the translation used, rendered exclusively as "men.")

3. That is, practical (and generally socially structured) human interaction. (In the translation used, rendered as "intercourse.")

continually evolving out of the life process of definite individuals, but of individuals, not as they may appear in their own or other people's imagination, but as they *really* are; i.e., as they operate, produce materially, and hence as they work under definite material limits, presuppositions and conditions independent of their will.

The production of ideas, of conceptions [*Vorstellungen*], of consciousness, is at first directly interwoven with the material activity and the material interaction of men [*Menschen*], the language of real life. Conceiving, thinking, the mental [*geistig*] interaction of men, appear at this stage as the direct efflux[4] of their material behaviour. The same applies to *geistig* production as expressed in the language of politics, laws, morality, religion, metaphysics, etc., of a people. Humans are the producers of their conceptions, ideas, etc.—real, active human beings, as they are conditioned by a definite development of their productive forces and of the interaction corresponding to these, up to its furthest forms. Consciousness can never be anything else than conscious existence, and the existence of humans is their actual life-process. If in all ideology humans and their circumstances appear upside-down as in a *camera obscura*,[5] this phenomenon arises just as much from their historical life-process as the inversion of objects on the retina does from their physical life-process.

In direct contrast to German philosophy[6] which descends from heaven to earth, here we ascend from earth to heaven. That is to say, we do not set out from what men say, imagine, conceive, nor from men as narrated, thought of, imagined, conceived, in order to arrive at men in the flesh. We set out from real, active human beings, and on the basis of their real life-process we demonstrate the development of the ideological reflexes and echoes of this life-process. The phantoms formed in the human brain are also, necessarily, sublimates of their material life-process, which is empirically verifiable and bound to material premises. Morality, religion, metaphysics, all the rest of ideology and their corresponding forms of consciousness, thus no longer retain the semblance of independence. They have no history, no development; but humans, developing their material production and their material interaction, alter, along with this their real existence, their thinking and the products of their thinking. Life is not determined by consciousness, but consciousness by life. In the first method of approach the starting-point is consciousness taken as the living individual; in the second method, which conforms to real life, it is the real living individuals themselves, and consciousness is considered solely as *their* consciousness.

This method of approach is not devoid of premises.[7] It starts out from the real premises and does not abandon them for a moment. Its premises are human beings, not in any fantastic isolation and rigidity, but in their actual, empirically perceptible process of development under definite conditions. As soon as this active life-process is described, history ceases to be a collection of dead facts as it is with the empiricists (themselves still abstract), or an imagined activity of imagined subjects, as with the idealists.

4. That is, the resulting correlative effects.
5. Literally, "dark chamber" (Latin), an apparatus invented in the 17th century: a darkened box with an aperture (usually a lens) through which an (inverted) image is projected on the opposite wall.
6. Here, the philosophy not only of KANT and HEGEL but also of FEUERBACH.
7. That is, it is unlike the "Idealist" Germans who (like other classical modern philosophers) aspire to begin by presupposing nothing of a substantive nature in their thinking about the world and ourselves.

Where speculation[8] ends—in real life—there real, positive science[9] begins: the representation of the practical activity, of the practical process of development of human beings. Empty talk about consciousness ceases, and real knowledge has to take its place. When reality is depicted, philosophy as an independent branch of knowledge loses its medium of existence. At the best its place can only be taken by a summing-up of the most general results, abstractions which arise from the observation of the historical development of human beings. Viewed apart from real history, these abstractions have in themselves no value whatsoever. They can only serve to facilitate the arrangement of historical material, to indicate the sequence of its separate strata. But they by no means afford a recipe or schema, as does philosophy, for neatly trimming the epochs of history. On the contrary, our difficulties begin only when we set about the observation and the arrangement—the real depiction—of our historical material, whether of a past epoch or of the present. The removal of these difficulties is governed by premises which it is quite impossible to state here, but which only the study of the actual life-process and the activity of the individuals of each epoch will make evident. We shall select here some of these abstractions, which we use in contradistinction to the ideologists,[1] and shall illustrate them by historical examples.

FROM 1. HISTORY

Since we are dealing with the Germans, who are devoid of premises, we must begin by stating the first premise of all human existence and, therefore, of all history, the premise, namely, that humans must be in a position to live in order to be able to "make history." But life involves before everything else eating and drinking, a habitation, clothing and many other things. The first historical act is thus the production of the means to satisfy these needs, the production of material life itself. And indeed this is an historical act, a fundamental condition of all history, which today, as thousands of years ago, must daily and hourly be fulfilled merely in order to sustain human life. * * * Therefore in any interpretation of history one has first of all to observe this fundamental fact in all its significance and all its implications and to accord it its due importance. * * *

The second point is that the satisfaction of the first need (the action of satisfying, and the instrument of satisfaction which has been acquired) leads to new needs; and this production of new needs is the first historical act. * * *

The third circumstance which, from the very outset, enters into historical development, is that human beings, who daily remake their own life, begin to make other human beings, to propagate their kind: the relation between man and woman, parents and children, the *family*. The family, which to begin with is the only social relationship, becomes later, when increased needs create new social relations and the increased population new needs, a

---

8. That is, Hegelian "speculative" philosophy, which "ended" with the elaboration of the section of *Philosophy of Geist* on "objective *Geist*" into his *Philosophy of Right* (for both, see above), which deals at length with economic, social, and political matters.

9. That is, empirically based (as opposed to speculative-interpretive) *Wissenschaft* (cognitive inquiry), focusing on the study of the "positive" facts about contemporary socioeconomic reality.

1. That is, those whose thinking is based on and deals with abstract "ideas."

subordinate one (except in Germany), and must then be treated and analysed according to the existing empirical data, not according to "the concept of the family," as is the custom in Germany. These three aspects of social activity are not of course to be taken as three different stages, but just as three aspects or, to make it clear to the Germans, three "moments,"[2] which have existed simultaneously since the dawn of history and the first humans, and which still assert themselves in history today.

The production of life, both of one's own in labour and of fresh life in procreation, now appears as a double relationship: on the one hand as a natural, on the other as a social relationship. By social we understand the co-operation of several individuals, no matter under what conditions, in what manner and to what end. It follows from this that a certain mode of production, or industrial stage, is always combined with a certain mode of co-operation, or social stage, and this mode of co-operation is itself a "productive force." Further, that the multitude of productive forces accessible to humans determines the nature of society, hence, that the "history of humanity" must always be studied and treated in relation to the history of industry and exchange. * * * Thus it is quite obvious from the start that there exists a materialistic connection of humans with one another, which is determined by their needs and their mode of production, and which is as old as human beings themselves. This connection is ever taking on new forms, and thus presents a "history" independently of the existence of any political or religious nonsense which would especially hold humans together.

Only now, after having considered four moments, four aspects of the primary historical relationships, do we find that man also possesses "consciousness";[3] but, even so, not inherent, not "pure" consciousness. From the start the "spirit" is afflicted with the curse of being "burdened" with matter, which here makes its appearance in the form of agitated layers of air, sounds, in short, of language. Language is as old as consciousness, language *is* practical consciousness that exists also for other humans, and for that reason alone it really exists for me personally as well; language, like consciousness, only arises from the need, the necessity, of interaction with other humans. Where there exists a relationship, it exists for me: the animal does not enter into *"relations"* with anything, it does not enter into any relation at all.[4] For the animal, its relation to others does not exist as a relation. Consciousness is, therefore, from the very beginning a social product, and remains so as long as human beings exist at all. Consciousness is at first, of course, merely consciousness concerning the *immediate* sensuous environment and consciousness of the limited connection with other persons and things outside the individual who is growing self-conscious. At the same time it is consciousness of nature, which first appears to humans as a completely alien, all-powerful and unassailable force, with which humans' relations are purely animal and by which they are overawed like beasts; it is thus a purely animal consciousness of nature (natural religion).

2. In German, *Momente* (sing. *Moment*): a term often used by Hegel in similar contexts to refer to the aspects of something.
3. Marginal note by Marx in the manuscript: "Men have history because they must *produce* their life, and because they must produce it moreover in a

specific way: this is required [*gegeben*] by their physical organization, just as is [*ebenso wie*] their consciousness" [translation revised by ed.].
4. That is, into any relation that involves consciousness (as a relation that "really exists for me personally").

We see here immediately: this natural religion or this particular relation of humans to nature is determined by the form of society and vice versa. Here, as everywhere, the identity of nature and man appears in such a way that the restricted relation of humans to nature determines their restricted relation to one another, and their restricted relation to one another determines their restricted relation to nature, just because nature is as yet hardly modified historically; and, on the other hand, man's consciousness of the necessity of associating with the individuals around him is the beginning of the consciousness that he is living in society at all. This beginning is as animal as social life itself at this stage. It is mere herd-consciousness, and at this point man is only distinguished from sheep by the fact that with him consciousness takes the place of instinct or that his instinct is a conscious one. This sheep-like or tribal consciousness receives its further development and extension through increased productivity, the increase of needs, and, what is fundamental to both of these, the increase of population. With these there develops the division of labour, which was originally nothing but the division of labour in the sexual act, then that division of labour which develops spontaneously or "naturally" by virtue of natural predisposition (e.g., physical strength), needs, accidents, etc., etc. Division of labour only becomes truly such from the moment when a division of material and mental labour appears. From this moment onwards consciousness *can* really flatter itself that it is something other than consciousness of existing practice, that it *really* represents something without representing something real; from now on consciousness is in a position to emancipate itself from the world and to proceed to the formation of "pure" theory, theology, philosophy, ethics, etc. But even if this theory, theology, philosophy, ethics, etc., comes into contradiction with the existing relations, this can only occur because existing social relations have come into contradiction with existing forces of production; this, moreover, can also occur in a particular national sphere of relations through the appearance of the contradiction, not within the national orbit, but between this national consciousness and the practice of other nations, i.e., between the national and the general consciousness of a nation (as we see it now in Germany).

Moreover, it is quite immaterial what consciousness starts to do on its own: out of all such muck we get only the one inference that these three moments, the forces of production, the state of society, and consciousness, can and must come into contradiction with one another, because the *division of labour* implies the possibility, nay the fact that intellectual [*geistig*] and material activity—enjoyment and labour, production and consumption—devolve on different individuals, and that the only possibility of their not coming into contradiction lies in the negation in its turn of the division of labour. It is self-evident, moreover, that "spectres," "bonds," "the higher being," "concept," "scruple," are merely the idealistic, *geistig* expression, the conception apparently of the isolated individual, the image of very empirical fetters and limitations, within which the mode of production of life and the form of interaction coupled with it move.

With the division of labour, in which all these contradictions are implicit, and which in its turn is based on the natural division of labour in the family and the separation of society into individual families opposed to one another, is given simultaneously the *distribution*, and indeed the *unequal* distribution, both quantitative and qualitative, of labour and its products, hence property: the nucleus, the first form, of which lies in the family, where wife and children are the slaves of the husband. This latent slavery in the family, though still very crude, is the first property, but even at this early stage it corresponds perfectly to the definition of modern economists who call it the power of disposing of the labour-power of others. Division of labour and private property are, moreover, identical expressions: in the one the same thing is affirmed with reference to activity as is affirmed in the other with reference to the product of the activity.

Further, the division of labour implies the contradiction between the interest of the separate individual or the individual family and the communal interest of all individuals who have interaction with one another. And indeed, this communal interest does not exist merely in the imagination, as the "general interest," but first of all in reality, as the mutual interdependence of the individuals among whom the labour is divided. And finally, the division of labour offers us the first example of how, as long as man remains in natural society, that is, as long as a cleavage exists between the particular and the common interest, as long, therefore, as activity is not voluntarily, but naturally, divided, man's own deed becomes an alien power opposed to him, which enslaves him instead of being controlled by him. For as soon as the distribution of labour comes into being, each person [*Mensch*] has a particular, exclusive sphere of activity, which is forced upon him and from which he cannot escape. He is a hunter, a fisherman, a shepherd, or a critical critic, and must remain so if he does not want to lose his means of livelihood; while in communist society, where nobody has one exclusive sphere of activity but each can become accomplished in any branch he wishes, society regulates the general production and thus makes it possible for me to do one thing today and another tomorrow, to hunt in the morning, fish in the afternoon, rear cattle in the evening, criticise after dinner, just as I have a mind, without ever becoming hunter, fisherman, shepherd or critic. This fixation of social activity, this consolidation of what we ourselves produce into an objective power above us, growing out of our control, thwarting our expectations, bringing to naught our calculations, is one of the chief factors in historical development up till now.

And out of this very contradiction between the interest of the individual and that of the community the latter takes an independent form as the *State*, divorced from the real interests of individual and community, and at the same time as an illusory communal life, always based, however, on the real ties existing in every family and tribal conglomeration—such as flesh and blood, language, division of labour on a larger scale, and other interests—and especially, as we shall enlarge upon later, on the classes, already determined by the division of labour, which in every such mass of men separate out, and of which one dominates all the others. It follows from this that all struggles within the State, the struggle between democracy, aristocracy, and monarchy, the struggle for the franchise, etc., etc., are merely the illusory forms in which the real struggles of the different classes are fought out among one another[.] * * * Further, it follows that every class which is struggling for mastery, even when its domination, as is the case with the proletariat, postulates the abolition of the old form of society in its entirety and of domination itself, must first conquer for itself political power in order to represent its interest in turn as the general interest, which in the first moment it is forced to do. Just because individuals seek *only* their particular interest, which for them does not coincide with their communal interest (in fact the general is the illusory form of communal life), the latter will be imposed on them as an interest "alien" to them, and "independent" of them, as in its turn a particular, peculiar "general" interest; or they themselves must remain within this discord, as in democracy. On the other hand, too, the *practical* struggle of these particular interests, which constantly *really* run counter to the communal and illusory communal interests, makes *practical* intervention and control necessary through the illusory "general" interest in the form of the State. The social power, i.e., the multiplied productive force, which arises through the co-operation of different individuals as it is determined by the division of labour, appears to these individuals, since their co-operation is not voluntary but has come about naturally, not as their own united power, but as an alien force existing outside them, of the origin and goal of which they are ignorant, which they thus cannot control, which on the contrary passes through a peculiar series of phases and stages independent of the will and the action of man, nay even being the prime governor of these.

This *"estrangement"*[5] (to use a term which will be comprehensible to the philosophers) can, of course, only be abolished given two *practical* premises. For it to become an "intolerable" power, i.e., a power against which men make a revolution, it must necessarily have rendered the great mass of humanity "propertyless," and produced, at the same time, the contradiction of an existing world of wealth and culture, both of which conditions presuppose a great increase in productive power, a high degree of its development. And, on the other hand, this development of productive forces (which itself implies the actual empirical existence of men in their *world-historical*, instead of local, being) is an absolutely necessary practical premise because without it *want* is merely made general, and with *destitution* the struggle for necessities and all the old filthy business would necessarily be reproduced; and furthermore, because only with this universal development of productive forces is a *universal*[6] human interaction [*Verkehr*] established, which produces in all nations simultaneously the phenomenon of the "propertyless" mass (universal competition), makes each nation dependent on the revolutions of the others, and finally has put *world-historical*, empirically universal individuals in place of local ones. Without this, (1) communism could only exist as a local event; (2) the *forces* of interaction themselves could not have developed as *universal*, hence intolerable powers: they would have remained home-bred conditions surrounded by superstition; and (3) each extension of interaction would abolish local communism. Empirically, communism is only possible as the act of the dominant peoples "all at once" and simultaneously, which presupposes the universal development of productive forces and the worldwide interaction [*Weltverkehr*] bound up with communism. * * *

Communism is for us not a *state of affairs* which is to be established, an *ideal* to which reality [will][7] have to adjust itself. We call communism the *real*

---

5. That is, "alienation" (*Entfremdung*)—a term that Marx (following Hegel) had used very extensively in his 1844 manuscripts (see above).
6. That is, "general" (*allgemein*); Marx often echoes Hegel's emphasis on *Allgemeinheit* (universality,

generality) as an essential feature of genuine humanity but shifts its focus, in ways that are evident here.
7. Translator's brackets.

movement which abolishes the present state of things. The conditions of this movement result from the premises now in existence. Moreover, the mass of *propertyless* workers—the utterly precarious position of labour-power on a mass scale cut off from capital or from even a limited satisfaction and, therefore, no longer merely temporarily deprived of work itself as a secure source of life—presupposes the *world market* through competition. The proletariat can thus only exist *world-historically*, just as communism, its activity, can only have a "world-historical" existence. World-historical existence of individuals, i.e., existence of individuals which is directly linked up with world history.

The form of interaction determined by the existing productive forces at all previous historical stages, and in its turn determining these, is *civil society*. The latter, as is clear from what we have said above, has as its premises and basis the simple family and the multiple, the so-called tribe, and the more precise determinants of this society are enumerated in our remarks above. Already here we see how this civil society is the true source and theatre of all history, and how absurd is the conception of history held hitherto, which neglects the real relationships and confines itself to high-sounding dramas of princes and states.

Civil society embraces the whole material interaction of individuals within a definite stage of the development of productive forces. It embraces the whole commercial and industrial life of a given stage and, insofar, transcends the State and the nation, though, on the other hand again, it must assert itself in its foreign relations as nationality, and inwardly must organise itself as State. The term "civil society" [*bürgerliche Gesellschaft*] emerged in the eighteenth century, when property relationships had already extricated themselves from the ancient and medieval communal society. Civil society as such only develops with the bourgeoisie; the social organisation evolving directly out of production and commerce, which in all ages forms the basis of the State and of the rest of the idealistic superstructure, has, however, always been designated by the same name.

From 2. Concerning the Production of Consciousness

In history up to the present it is certainly an empirical fact that separate individuals have, with the broadening of their activity into world-historical activity, become more and more enslaved under a power alien to them (a pressure which they have conceived of as a dirty trick on the part of the so-called universal spirit, etc.), a power which has become more and more enormous and, in the last instance, turns out to be the *world market*. But it is just as empirically established that, by the overthrow of the existing state of society by the communist revolution (of which more below) and the abolition of private property which is identical with it, this power, which so baffles the German theoreticians, will be dissolved; and that then the liberation of each single individual will be accomplished in the measure in which history becomes transformed into world history. From the above it is clear that the real intellectual wealth of the individual depends entirely on the wealth of his real connections. Only then will the separate individuals be liberated from the various national and local barriers, be brought into practical connection with the material and intellectual production of the whole world and be put in a position to acquire the capacity to enjoy this all-sided production of the whole earth (the creations of man). *All-round* dependence, this natural form of the *world-historical* co-operation of individuals, will be transformed by this communist revolution into the control and conscious mastery of these powers, which, born of the action of men on one another, have till now over-awed and governed men as powers completely alien to them. * * *

This conception of history depends on our ability to expound the real process of production, starting out from the material production of life itself, and to comprehend the form of interaction connected with this and created by this mode of production (i.e., civil society in its various stages), as the basis of all history; and to show it in its action as State, to explain all the different theoretical products and forms of consciousness, religion, philosophy, ethics, etc., etc., and trace their origins and growth from that basis; by which means, of course, the whole thing can be depicted in its totality (and therefore, too, the reciprocal action of these various sides on one another). It has not, like the idealistic view of history, in every period to look for a category, but remains constantly on the real *ground* of history; it does not explain practice from the idea[8] but explains the formation of ideas from material practice; and accordingly it comes to the conclusion that all forms and products of consciousness cannot be dissolved by mental criticism, by resolution into "self-consciousness" or transformation into "apparitions," "spectres," "fancies," etc., but only by the practical overthrow of the actual social relations which gave rise to this idealistic humbug; that not criticism but revolution is the driving force of history, also of religion, of philosophy and all other types of theory. It shows that history does not end by being resolved into "self-consciousness" as "spirit of the spirit," but that in it at each stage there is found a material result: a sum of productive forces, a historically created relation of individuals to nature and to one another, which is handed down to each generation from its predecessor; a mass of productive forces, capital funds and conditions, which, on the one hand, is indeed modified by the new generation, but also on the other prescribes for it its conditions of life and gives it a definite development, a special character. It shows that circumstances make men just as much as men make circumstances. This sum of productive forces, capital funds and social forms of interaction [*Verkehr*], which every individual and generation finds in existence as something given, is the real basis of what the philosophers have conceived as "substance" and "essence of man," and what they have deified and attacked: a real basis which is not in the least disturbed, in its effect and influence on the development of men, by the fact that these philosophers revolt against it as "self-consciousness" and the "Unique." These conditions of life, which different generations find in existence, decide also whether or not the periodically recurring revolutionary convulsion will be strong enough to overthrow the basis of the entire existing system. And if these material elements of a complete revolution are not present (namely, on the one hand the existing productive forces, on the other the formation of a revolutionary mass, which revolts not only against separate conditions of society up till then, but against the very "production of life" till then, the "total activity" on which it was based), then, as far as practical development is concerned, it is

8. The reference is to Hegel's *Idee* (see the Hegel glossary, p. 144).

absolutely immaterial whether the *idea* of this revolution has been expressed a hundred times already, as the history of communism proves.

In the whole conception of history up to the present this real basis of history has either been totally neglected or else considered as a minor matter quite irrelevant to the course of history. History must, therefore, always be written according to an extraneous standard; the real production of life seems to be primeval history, while the truly historical appears to be separated from ordinary life, something extra-superterrestrial. With this the relation of man to nature is excluded from history and hence the antithesis of nature and history is created. The exponents of this conception of history have consequently only been able to see in history the political actions of princes and States, religious and all sorts of theoretical struggles, and in particular in each historical epoch have had to *share the illusion of that epoch*. For instance, if an epoch imagines itself to be actuated by purely "political" or "religious" motives, although "religion" and "politics" are only forms of its true motives, the historian accepts this opinion. The "idea," the "conception" of the people in question about their real practice, is transformed into the sole determining, active force, which controls and determines their practice. When the crude form in which the division of labour appears with the Indians and Egyptians calls forth the caste-system in their State and religion, the historian believes that the caste-system is the power which has produced this crude social form. While the French and the English at least hold by the political illusion, which is moderately close to reality, the Germans move in the realm of the "pure spirit," and make religious illusion the driving force of history. The Hegelian philosophy of history is the last consequence, reduced to its "finest expression," of all this German historiography, for which it is not a question of real, nor even of political, interests, but of pure thoughts[.]

* * *

* * * As an example of Feuerbach's acceptance and at the same time misunderstanding of existing reality, which he still shares with our opponents, we recall the passage in the *Philosophie der Zukunft*[9] where he develops the view that the existence of a thing or a human being is at the same time its or his essence, that the conditions of existence, the mode of life and activity of an animal or human individual are those in which its "essence" feels itself satisfied. Here every exception is expressly conceived as an unhappy chance, as an abnormality which cannot be altered. Thus if millions of proletarians feel by no means contented with their living conditions, if their "existence" does not in the least correspond to their "essence,"[1] then, according to the passage quoted, this is an unavoidable misfortune, which must be borne quietly. The millions of proletarians and communists, however, think differently and will prove this in time, when they bring their "existence" into harmony with their "essence" in a practical way, by means of a revolution. Feuerbach, therefore, never speaks of the world of man in such cases, but always takes refuge in external nature, and moreover in *nature* which has not yet been

---

9. [*Principles of the*] *Philosophy of the Future* (1843; excerpted above).

1. This is Hegel's basic conception of self-alienation, which Marx adopts but revises regarding what its nature is, how it should be explored, and what its overcoming requires.

subdued by men. But every new invention, every advance made by industry, detaches another piece from this domain, so that the ground which produces examples illustrating such Feuerbachian propositions is steadily shrinking. The "essence" of the fish is its "existence," water—to go no further than this one proposition. The "essence" of the freshwater fish is the water of a river. But the latter ceases to be the "essence" of the fish and is no longer a suitable medium of existence as soon as the river is made to serve industry, as soon as it is polluted by dyes and other waste products and navigated by steamboats, or as soon as its water is diverted into canals where simple drainage can deprive the fish of its medium of existence. * * *

We shall, of course, not take the trouble to enlighten our wise philosophers by explaining to them that the "liberation" of "man" is not advanced a single step by reducing philosophy, theology, substance and all the trash to "self-consciousness" and by liberating man from the domination of these phrases, which have never held him in thrall. Nor will we explain to them that it is only possible to achieve real liberation in the real world and by employing real means, that slavery cannot be abolished without the steam-engine and the mule and spinning-jenny, serfdom cannot be abolished without improved agriculture, and that, in general, people cannot be liberated as long as they are unable to obtain food and drink, housing and clothing in adequate quality and quantity. "Liberation" is a historical and not a mental act, and it is brought about by historical conditions, the [development] of industry, commerce, [agri]culture[.][2]

* * *

In reality and for the *practical* materialist, i.e., the *communist*, it is a question of revolutionising the existing world, of practically attacking and changing existing things. When occasionally we find such views with Feuerbach, they are never more than isolated surmises and have much too little influence on his general outlook to be considered here as anything else than embryos capable of development. Feuerbach's "conception" of the sensuous world is confined on the one hand to mere contemplation of it, and on the other to mere feeling; he says "Man" instead of "real historical man." "Man" is really "the German." In the first case, the *contemplation* of the sensuous world, he necessarily lights on things which contradict his consciousness and feeling, which disturb the harmony he presupposes, the harmony of all parts of the sensuous world and especially of man and nature. To remove this disturbance, he must take refuge in a double perception, a profane one which only perceives the "flatly obvious" and a higher, philosophical, one which perceives the "true essence" of things. He does not see how the sensuous world around him is not a thing given direct from all eternity, remaining ever the same, but the product of industry and of the state of society; and, indeed, in the sense that it is an historical product, the result of the activity of a whole succession of generations, each standing on the shoulders of the preceding one, developing its industry and its intercourse, modifying its social system according to the changed needs. Even the objects of the simplest "sensuous certainty" are only given him through social development, industry and commercial interaction. The cherry-tree, like almost all fruit-trees, was, as is well known,

2. Translator's brackets.

only a few centuries ago transplanted by *commerce* into our zone, and therefore only *by* this action of a definite society in a definite age it has become "sensuous certainty" for Feuerbach.

Incidentally, when we conceive things thus, as they really are and happened, every profound philosophical problem is resolved, as will be seen even more clearly later, quite simply into an empirical fact. * * *

Certainly Feuerbach has a great advantage over the "pure" materialists in that he realises how man too is an "object of the senses." But apart from the fact that he only conceives him as an "object of the senses," not as "sensuous activity," because he still remains in the realm of theory and conceives of men not in their given social connection, not under their existing conditions of life, which have made them what they are, he never arrives at the really existing active human beings, but stops at the abstraction "man," and gets no further than recognising "the true, individual, corporeal man" emotionally, i.e., he knows no other "human relationships" "of man to man" than love and friendship, and even then idealised. He gives no criticism of the present conditions of life. Thus he never manages to conceive the sensuous world as the total living sensuous *activity* of the individuals composing it; and therefore when, for example, he sees instead of healthy humans a crowd of scrofulous, overworked and consumptive starvelings, he is compelled to take refuge in the "higher perception" and in the ideal "compensation in the species," and thus to relapse into idealism at the very point where the communist materialist sees the necessity, and at the same time the condition, of a transformation both of industry and of the social structure.

As far as Feuerbach is a materialist he does not deal with history, and as far as he considers history he is not a materialist. With him materialism and history diverge completely, a fact which incidentally is already obvious from what has been said.

History is nothing but the succession of the separate generations, each of which exploits the materials, the capital funds, the productive forces handed down to it by all preceding generations, and thus, on the one hand, continues the traditional activity in completely changed circumstances and, on the other, modifies the old circumstances with a completely changed activity. This can be speculatively distorted so that later history is made the goal of earlier history, e.g., the goal ascribed to the discovery of America is to further the eruption of the French Revolution. Thereby history receives its own special aims and becomes "a person ranking with other persons" (to wit: "Self-Consciousness, Criticism, the Unique," etc.), while what is designated with the words "destiny," "goal," "germ," or "ideal" of earlier history is nothing more than an abstraction formed from later history, from the active influence which earlier history exercises on later history.

The further the separate spheres, which act on one another, extend in the course of this development, the more the original isolation of the separate nationalities is destroyed by the developed mode of production and interaction and the division of labour between various nations naturally brought forth by these, the more history becomes world history. Thus, for instance, if in England a machine is invented, which deprives countless workers of bread in India and China, and overturns the whole form of existence of these empires, this invention becomes a world-historical fact. Or again, take the case of sugar and coffee which have proved their world-historical importance in the nineteenth century by the fact that the lack of these products, occasioned by the Napoleonic Continental System, caused the Germans to rise against Napoleon, and thus became the real basis of the glorious Wars of Liberation of 1813.[3] From this it follows that this transformation of history into world history is not indeed a mere abstract act on the part of the "self-consciousness," the world spirit, or of any other metaphysical spectre, but a quite material, empirically verifiable act, an act the proof of which every individual furnishes as he comes and goes, eats, drinks and clothes himself.

The ideas of the ruling class are in every epoch the ruling ideas: i.e., the class which is the ruling *material* force of society, is at the same time its ruling *intellectual* [*geistig*] force. The class which has the means of material production at its disposal, has control at the same time over the means of *geistig* production, so that thereby, generally speaking, the ideas of those who lack the means of *geistig* production are subject to it. The ruling ideas are nothing more than the ideal expression of the dominant material relationships, the dominant material relationships grasped as ideas; hence of the relationships which make the one class the ruling one, therefore, the ideas of its dominance. The individuals composing the ruling class possess among other things consciousness, and therefore think. Insofar, therefore, as they rule as a class and determine the extent and compass of an epoch, it is self-evident that they do this in its whole range, hence among other things rule also as thinkers, as producers of ideas, and regulate the production and distribution of the ideas of their age: thus their ideas are the ruling ideas of the epoch. For instance, in an age and in a country where royal power, aristocracy and bourgeoisie are contending for mastery and where, therefore, mastery is shared, the doctrine of the separation of powers proves to be the dominant idea and is expressed as an "eternal law."

The division of labour, which we have already seen above as one of the chief forces of history up till now, manifests itself also in the ruling class as the division of mental and material labour, so that inside this class one part appears as the thinkers of the class (its active, conceptive ideologists, who make the perfecting of the illusion of the class about itself their chief source of livelihood), while the others' attitude to these ideas and illusions is more passive and receptive, because they are in reality the active members of this class and have less time to make up illusions and ideas about themselves. Within this class this cleavage can even develop into a certain opposition and hostility between the two parts, which, however, in the case of a practical collision, in which the class itself is endangered, automatically comes to nothing, in which case there also vanishes the semblance that the ruling ideas were not the ideas of the ruling class and had a power distinct from the power of this class. The existence of revolutionary ideas in a particular period presupposes the existence of a revolutionary class; about the premises for the latter sufficient has already been said above.

If now in considering the course of history we detach the ideas of the ruling class from the ruling class itself and attribute to them an independent existence, if we confine ourselves to saying that these or those ideas were dom-

---

3. A series of battles, following the retreat of Napoleon (1769–1821) and his armies from Russia in 1812, in which the French were driven out of German lands by a coalition of Prussian, Russian, Swedish, and Austrian troops. "Napoleonic Continental System": Napoleon's blockade of Great Britain during the Napoleonic Wars.

inant at a given time, without bothering ourselves about the conditions of production and the producers of these ideas, if we thus ignore the individuals and world conditions which are the source of the ideas, we can say, for instance, that during the time that the aristocracy was dominant, the concepts honour, loyalty, etc., were dominant, during the dominance of the bourgeoisie the concepts freedom, equality, etc. The ruling class itself on the whole imagines this to be so. This conception of history, which is common to all historians, particularly since the eighteenth century, will necessarily come up against the phenomenon that increasingly abstract ideas hold sway, i.e., ideas which increasingly take on the form of universality. For each new class which puts itself in the place of one ruling before it, is compelled, merely in order to carry through its aim, to represent its interest as the common interest of all the members of society, that is, expressed in ideal form: it has to give its ideas the form of universality, and represent them as the only rational, universally valid ones. The class making a revolution appears from the very start, if only because it is opposed to a *class*, not as a class but as the representative of the whole of society; it appears as the whole mass of society confronting the one ruling class.[4] It can do this because, to start with, its interest really is more connected with the common interest of all other non-ruling classes, because under the pressure of hitherto existing conditions its interest has not yet been able to develop as the particular interest of a particular class. Its victory, therefore, benefits also many individuals of the other classes which are not winning a dominant position, but only insofar as it now puts these individuals in a position to raise themselves into the ruling class. When the French bourgeoisie overthrew the power of the aristocracy, it thereby made it possible for many proletarians to raise themselves above the proletariat, but only insofar as they became bourgeois. Every new class, therefore, achieves its hegemony only on a broader basis than that of the class ruling previously, whereas the opposition of the non-ruling class against the new ruling class later develops all the more sharply and profoundly. Both these things determine the fact that the struggle to be waged against this new ruling class, in its turn, aims at a more decided and radical negation of the previous conditions of society than could all previous classes which sought to rule.

This whole semblance, that the rule of a certain class is only the rule of certain ideas, comes to a natural end, of course, as soon as class rule in general ceases to be the form in which society is organised, that is to say, as soon as it is no longer necessary to represent a particular interest as general or the "general interest" as ruling.

Once the ruling ideas have been separated from the ruling individuals and, above all, from the relationships which result from a given stage of the mode of production, and in this way the conclusion has been reached that history is always under the sway of ideas, it is very easy to abstract from these various ideas "*the* idea," the notion,[5] etc., as the dominant force in history, and thus to understand all these separate ideas and concepts as "forms of self-determination" on the part of *the* concept developing in history. It follows then

4. Marginal note by Marx in the manuscript: "Universality [*Allgemeinheit*] corresponds to (1) the class versus the estate, (2) the competition, world-wide interaction, etc., (3) the great numerical strength of the ruling class, (4) the illusion of the *common* interests (in the beginning this illusion is true), (5) the delusion of the ideologists and the division of labour."
5. "'The *Idee*,' the *Begriff*": key terms in Hegel's philosophy of history and interpretation of reality (see the Hegel glossary, p. 144).

naturally, too, that all the relationships of human beings [*Menschen*] can be derived from the concept of man, man as conceived, the essence of man, *Man* [*der Mensch*]. This has been done by the speculative philosophers. Hegel himself confesses at the end of the *Geschichtsphilosophie*[6] that he "has considered the progress of the *concept* only", and has represented in history the "true *theodicy*."[7] Now one can go back again to the producers of the "concept," to the theorists, ideologists and philosophers, and one comes then to the conclusion that the philosophers, the thinkers as such, have at all times been dominant in history: a conclusion, as we see, already expressed by Hegel. The whole trick of proving the hegemony of the spirit in history * * * is thus confined to the following three efforts.

No. 1. One must separate the ideas of those ruling for empirical reasons, under empirical conditions and as empirical individuals, from these actual rulers, and thus recognise the rule of ideas or illusions in history.

No. 2. One must bring an order into this rule of ideas, prove a mystical connection among the successive ruling ideas, which is managed by understanding them as "acts of self-determination on the part of the concept" (this is possible because by virtue of their empirical basis these ideas are really connected with one another and because, conceived as *mere* ideas, they become self-distinctions, distinctions made by thought).

No. 3. To remove the mystical appearance of this "self-determining concept" it is changed into a person—"Self-Consciousness"—or, to appear thoroughly materialistic, into a series of persons, who represent the "concept" in history, into the "thinkers," the "philosophers," the ideologists, who again are understood as the manufacturers of history, as the "council of guardians," as the rulers.[8] Thus the whole body of materialistic elements has been removed from history and now full rein can be given to the speculative steed.

Whilst in ordinary life every shopkeeper is very well able to distinguish between what somebody professes to be and what he really is, our historians have not yet won even this trivial insight. They take every epoch at its word and believe that everything it says and imagines about itself is true.

This historical method which reigned in Germany and especially the reason why, must be understood from its connection with the illusion of ideologists in general, e.g., the illusions of the jurists, politicians (of the practical statesmen among them, too), from the dogmatic dreamings and distortions of these fellows; this is explained perfectly easily from their practical position in life, their job, and the division of labour.

* * *

* * * Private property, insofar as within labour itself it is opposed to labour, evolves out of the necessity of accumulation, and has still, to begin with, rather the form of the communality; but in its further development it approaches more and more the modern form of private property. The division of labour implies from the outset the division of the *conditions* of labour, of tools and materials, and thus the splitting-up of accumulated capital among different

---

6. [*Lectures on the*] *Philosophy of History* (excerpted above).
7. The justification of God's ways, reconciling his existence and assumed perfections with the existence of evil.
8. Marginal note by Marx in the manuscript: "Man = the 'rational human spirit [*Geist*].'"

owners, and thus, also, the division between capital and labour, and the different forms of property itself. The more the division of labour develops and accumulation grows, the sharper are the forms that this process of differentiation assumes. Labour itself can only exist on the premise of this fragmentation.

Thus two facts are here revealed. First the productive forces appear as a world for themselves, quite independent of and divorced from the individuals, alongside the individuals: the reason for this is that the individuals, whose forces they are, exist split up and in opposition to one another, whilst, on the other hand, these forces are only real forces in the interaction and association of these individuals. Thus, on the one hand, we have a totality of productive forces, which have, as it were, taken on a material form and are for the individuals no longer the forces of the individuals but of private property, and hence of the individuals only insofar as they are owners of private property themselves. Never, in any earlier period, have the productive forces taken on a form so indifferent to the interaction of individuals *as* individuals, because their interaction itself was formerly a restricted one. On the other hand, standing over against these productive forces, we have the majority of the individuals from whom these forces have been wrested away, and who, robbed thus of all real life-content, have become abstract individuals, but who are, however, only by this fact put into a position to enter into relation with one another *as individuals*.

The only connection which still links them with the productive forces and with their own existence—labour—has lost all semblance of self-activity[9] and only sustains their life by stunting it. While in the earlier periods self-activity and the production of material life were separated, in that they devolved on different persons, and while, on account of the narrowness of the individuals themselves, the production of material life was considered as a subordinate mode of self-activity, they now diverge to such an extent that altogether material life appears as the end, and what produces this material life, labour (which is now the only possible but, as we see, negative form of self-activity), as the means.

Thus things have now come to such a pass, that the individuals must appropriate the existing totality of productive forces, not only to achieve self-activity, but, also, merely to safeguard their very existence. This appropriation is first determined by the object to be appropriated, the productive forces, which have been developed to a totality and which only exist within a universal interaction [*Verkehr*]. From this aspect alone, therefore, this appropriation must have a universal character corresponding to the productive forces and the interaction. The appropriation of these forces is itself nothing more than the development of the individual capacities corresponding to the material instruments of production. The appropriation of a totality of instruments of production is, for this very reason, the development of a totality of capacities in the individuals themselves. This appropriation is further determined by the persons appropriating. Only the proletarians of the present day, who are completely shut off from all self-activity, are in a position to achieve a complete and no longer restricted self-activity, which consists in the appro-

---

9. That is, self-directed productive activity. For Marx, "self-activity" is a very important concept. It is said to be "universal" at this point because it is no longer "limited" or restricted in its expression.

priation of a totality of productive forces and in the thus postulated development of a totality of capacities. All earlier revolutionary appropriations were restricted; individuals, whose self-activity was restricted by a crude instrument of production and a limited interaction, appropriated this crude instrument of production, and hence merely achieved a new state of limitation. Their instrument of production became their property, but they themselves remained subordinate to the division of labour and their own instrument of production. In all expropriations up to now, a mass of individuals remained subservient to a single instrument of production; in the appropriation by the proletarians, a mass of instruments of production must be made subject to each individual, and property to all. Modern universal interaction can be controlled by individuals, therefore, only when controlled by all.

This appropriation is further determined by the manner in which it must be effected. It can only be effected through a union, which by the character of the proletariat itself can again only be a universal one, and through a revolution, in which, on the one hand, the power of the earlier mode of production and interaction and social organisation is overthrown, and, on the other hand, there develops the universal character and the energy of the proletariat, without which the revolution cannot be accomplished; and in which, further, the proletariat rids itself of everything that still clings to it from its previous position in society.

Only at this stage does self-activity coincide with material life, which corresponds to the development of individuals into complete individuals and the casting-off of all natural limitations. The transformation of labour into self-activity corresponds to the transformation of the earlier limited interaction into the interaction of individuals as such. With the appropriation of the total productive forces through united individuals, private property comes to an end. Whilst previously in history a particular condition always appeared as accidental, now the isolation of individuals and the particular private gain of each man have themselves become accidental.

The individuals, who are no longer subject to the division of labour, have been conceived by the philosophers as an ideal, under the name "Man." They have conceived the whole process which we have outlined as the evolutionary process of "Man," so that at every historical stage "Man" was substituted for the individuals and shown as the motive force of history. The whole process was thus conceived as a process of the self-estrangement[1] of "Man," and this was essentially due to the fact that the average individual of the later stage was always foisted on to the earlier stage, and the consciousness of a later age on to the individuals of an earlier. Through this inversion, which from the first is an abstract image of the actual conditions, it was possible to transform the whole of history into an evolutionary process of consciousness.

Finally, from the conception of history we have sketched we obtain these further conclusions: (1) In the development of productive forces there comes a stage when productive forces and means of interaction are brought into being,

---

1. That is, self-alienation, understood as the failure of "existence" to accord with "essence."

which, under the existing relationships, only cause mischief, and are no longer productive but destructive forces (machinery and money); and connected with this a class is called forth, which has to bear all the burdens of society without enjoying its advantages, which, ousted from society, is forced into the most decided antagonism to all other classes; a class which forms the majority of all members of society, and from which emanates the consciousness of the necessity of a fundamental revolution, the communist consciousness, which may, of course, arise among the other classes too through the contemplation of the situation of this class. (2) The conditions under which definite productive forces can be applied are the conditions of the rule of a definite class of society, whose social power, deriving from its property, has its *practical-idealistic* expression in each case in the form of the State; and, therefore, every revolutionary struggle is directed against a class, which till then has been in power. (3) In all revolutions up till now the mode of activity always remained unscathed and it was only a question of a different distribution of this activity, a new distribution of labour to other persons, whilst the communist revolution is directed against the preceding *mode* of activity, does away with *labour*, and abolishes the rule of all classes with the classes themselves, because it is carried through by the class which no longer counts as a class in society, is not recognised as a class, and is in itself the expression of the dissolution of all classes, nationalities, etc., within present society; and (4) Both for the production on a mass scale of this communist consciousness, and for the success of the cause itself, the alteration of men on a mass scale is necessary, an alteration which can only take place in a practical movement, a *revolution*; this revolution is necessary, therefore, not only because the *ruling* class cannot be overthrown in any other way, but also because the class *overthrowing* it can only in a revolution succeed in ridding itself of all the muck of ages and become fitted to found society anew.

Communism differs from all previous movements in that it overturns the basis of all earlier relations of production and interaction, and for the first time consciously treats all natural premises as the creatures of hitherto existing men, strips them of their natural character and subjugates them to the power of the united individuals. Its organisation is, therefore, essentially economic, the material production of the conditions of this unity; it turns existing conditions into conditions of unity. The reality, which communism is creating, is precisely the true basis for rendering it impossible that anything should exist independently of individuals, insofar as reality is only a product of the preceding interaction of individuals themselves. Thus the communists in practice treat the conditions created up to now by production and interaction as inorganic conditions, without, however, imagining that it was the plan or the destiny of previous generations to give them material, and without believing that these conditions were inorganic for the individuals creating them. The difference between the individual as a person and what is accidental to him is not a conceptual difference but a historical fact. This distinction has a different significance at different times—e.g., the estate as something accidental to the individual in the eighteenth century, the family more or less too. It is not a distinction that we have to make for each age, but one which each age makes itself from among the different elements which it finds in existence, and indeed not according to any theory, but compelled by material collisions in life. What appears accidental to the later age as opposed to the earlier— and this applies also to the elements handed down by an earlier age—is a form of interaction [*Verkehr*] which corresponded to a definite stage of development of the productive forces. The relation of the productive forces to the form of interaction is the relation of the form of interaction to the occupation or activity of the individuals. (The fundamental form of this activity is, of course, material, on which depend all other forms—*geistig*, political, religious, etc. The various shaping of material life is, of course, in every case dependent on the needs which are already developed, and the production, as well as the satisfaction, of these needs is an historical process, which is not found in the case of a sheep or a dog. (* * * [A]lthough sheep and dogs in their present form certainly, but *malgré eux*,[2] are products of an historical process.) The conditions under which individuals have interaction with each other, so long as the above-mentioned contradiction is absent, are conditions appertaining to their individuality, in no way external to them; conditions under which these definite individuals, living under definite relations, can alone produce their material life and what is connected with it, are thus the conditions of their self-activity and are produced by this self-activity. The definite condition under which they produce, thus corresponds, as long as the contradiction has not yet appeared, to the reality of their conditioned nature, their one-sided existence, the one-sidedness of which only becomes evident when the contradiction enters on the scene and thus exists for the later individuals. Then this condition appears as an accidental fetter, and the consciousness that it is a fetter is imputed to the earlier age as well.

These various conditions, which appear first as conditions of self-activity, later as fetters upon it, form in the whole evolution of history a coherent series of forms of interaction, the coherence of which consists in this: in the place of an earlier form of interaction, which has become a fetter, a new one is put, corresponding to the more developed productive forces and, hence, to the advanced mode of the self-activity of individuals—a form which in its turn becomes a fetter and is then replaced by another. Since these conditions correspond at every stage to the simultaneous development of the productive forces, their history is at the same time the history of the evolving productive forces taken over by each new generation, and is, therefore, the history of the development of the forces of the individuals themselves.

* * *

The transformation, through the division of labour, of personal powers (relationships) into material powers, cannot be dispelled by dismissing the general idea of it from one's mind, but can only be abolished by the individuals again subjecting these material powers to themselves and abolishing the division of labour. This is not possible without the community. Only in community [with others has each][3] individual the means of cultivating his gifts in all directions; only in the community, therefore, is personal freedom possible. In

---

2. Despite themselves (French).　　　　3. Translator's brackets.

the previous substitutes for the community, in the State, etc., personal freedom has existed only for the individuals who developed within the relationships
of the ruling class, and only insofar as they were individuals of this class. The
illusory community, in which individuals have up till now combined, always
took on an independent existence in relation to them, and was at the same time,
since it was the combination of one class over against another, not only a completely illusory community, but a new fetter as well. In the real community the
individuals obtain their freedom in and through their association.

It follows from all we have been saying up till now that the communal relationship into which the individuals of a class entered, and which was determined by their common interests over against a third party, was always a
community to which these individuals belonged only as average individuals,
only insofar as they lived within the conditions of existence of their class—a
relationship in which they participated not as individuals but as members of
a class. With the community of revolutionary proletarians, on the other hand,
who take their conditions of existence and those of all members of society
under their control, it is just the reverse; it is as individuals that the individuals participate in it. It is just this combination of individuals (assuming the
advanced stage of modern productive forces, of course) which puts the conditions of the free development and movement of individuals under their
control—conditions which were previously abandoned to chance and had won
an independent existence over against the separate individuals just because
of their separation as individuals, and because of the necessity of their combination which had been determined by the division of labour, and through
their separation had become a bond alien to them. Combination up till now
(by no means an arbitrary one, such as is expounded for example in the *Contrat
social*,[4] but a necessary one) was an agreement upon these conditions, within
which the individuals were free to enjoy the freaks of fortune (compare, e.g.,
the formation of the North American State and the South American republics). This right to the undisturbed enjoyment, within certain conditions, of
fortuity and chance has up till now been called personal freedom. These
conditions of existence are, of course, only the productive forces and forms of
interaction at any particular time.

If from a *philosophical* point of view one considers this evolution of individuals in the common conditions of existence of estates and classes, which
followed on one another, and in the accompanying general conceptions forced
upon them, it is certainly very easy to imagine that in these individuals the
species, or "Man," has evolved, or that they evolved "Man"—and in this way
one can give history some hard clouts on the ear. One can conceive these various estates and classes to be specific terms of the general expression, subordinate varieties of the species, or evolutionary phases of "Man."

This subsuming of individuals under definite classes cannot be abolished
until a class has taken shape, which has no longer any particular class interest to assert against the ruling class.

Individuals have always built on themselves, but naturally on themselves
within their given historical conditions and relationships, not on the "pure"

---

4. Social contract (French): in political philosophy, a hypothetical agreement among individuals to live
together in a society.

individual in the sense of the ideologists. But in the course of historical evolution, and precisely through the inevitable fact that within the division of labour social relationships take on an independent existence, there appears a division within the life of each individual, insofar as it is personal and insofar as it is determined by some branch of labour and the conditions pertaining to it. (We do not mean it to be understood from this that, for example, the rentier, the capitalist, etc., cease to be persons; but their personality is conditioned and determined by quite definite class relationships, and the division appears only in their opposition to another class and, for themselves, only when they go bankrupt.) In the estate (and even more in the tribe) this is as yet concealed: for instance, a nobleman always remains a nobleman, a commoner always a commoner, apart from his other relationships, a quality inseparable from his individuality. The division between the personal and the class individual, the accidental nature of the conditions of life for the individual, appears only with the emergence of the class, which is itself a product of the bourgeoisie. This accidental character is only engendered and developed by competition and the struggle of individuals among themselves. Thus, in imagination, individuals seem freer under the dominance of the bourgeoisie than before, because their conditions of life seem accidental; in reality, of course, they are less free, because they are more subjected to the violence of things. The difference from the estate comes out particularly in the antagonism between the bourgeoisie and the proletariat. When the estate of the urban burghers, the corporations, etc., emerged in opposition to the landed nobility, their condition of existence—movable property and craft labour, which had already existed latently before their separation from the feudal ties—appeared as something positive, which was asserted against feudal landed property, and, therefore, in its own way at first took on a feudal form. Certainly the refugee serfs treated their previous servitude as something accidental to their personality. But here they only were doing what every class that is freeing itself from a fetter does; and they did not free themselves as a class but separately. Moreover, they did not rise above the system of estates, but only formed a new estate, retaining their previous mode of labour even in their new situation, and developing it further by freeing it from its earlier fetters, which no longer corresponded to the development already attained.

For the proletarians, on the other hand, the condition of their existence, labour, and with it all the conditions of existence governing modern society, have become something accidental, something over which they, as separate individuals, have no control, and over which no *social* organisation can give them control. The contradiction between the individuality of each separate proletarian and labour, the condition of life forced upon him, becomes evident to him himself, for he is sacrificed from youth upwards and, within his own class, has no chance of arriving at the conditions which would place him in the other class.

Thus, while the refugee serfs only wished to be free to develop and assert those conditions of existence which were already there, and hence, in the end, only arrived at free labour, the proletarians, if they are to assert themselves as individuals, will have to abolish the very condition of their existence hitherto (which has, moreover, been that of all society up to the present), namely, labour. Thus they find themselves directly opposed to the form in which, hitherto, the individuals, of which society consists, have given themselves collective expression, that is, the State. In order, therefore, to assert themselves as individuals, they must overthrow the State.

SOURCE: From "Feuerbach: Opposition of the Materialistic and Idealistic Outlook," Part I of *The German Ideology*, in *The Marx-Engels Reader*, ed. Robert C. Tucker, 2nd ed. (New York: W. W. Norton, 1978), pp. 149–50, 154–66, 168–75, 190–95, 197–200 [translated by S. Ryazanskaya, based on an earlier translation by W. Lough; translation modified by the editor]. Except where otherwise indicated, German words in brackets are the terminology used in the German original, inserted by the editor in addition to their renderings in the translation; and unbracketed German words are the original terminology, substituted in place of their renderings in the translation by the editor for reasons given in notes and in the Hegel glossary (p. 144). *The German Ideology*, written by Marx and Engels in 1845–46, was first published in 1932, and appeared in a fuller version in 1966. This first section is thought to be mainly the work of Marx.

From Manifesto of the Communist Party

By Karl Marx and Friedrich Engels

From I. Bourgeois and Proletarians[1]

* * *

Hitherto, every form of society has been based, as we have already seen, on the antagonism of oppressing and oppressed classes. But in order to oppress a class, certain conditions must be assured to it under which it can, at least, continue its slavish existence. The serf, in the period of serfdom, raised himself to membership in the commune, just as the petty bourgeois, under the yoke of feudal absolutism, managed to develop into a bourgeois. The modern labourer, on the contrary, instead of rising with the progress of industry, sinks deeper and deeper below the conditions of existence of his own class. He becomes a pauper, and pauperism develops more rapidly than population and wealth. And here it becomes evident, that the bourgeoisie is unfit any longer to be the ruling class in society, and to impose its conditions of existence upon society as an over-riding law. It is unfit to rule because it is incompetent to assure an existence to its slave within his slavery, because it cannot help letting him sink into such a state, that it has to feed him, instead of being fed by him. Society can no longer live under this bourgeoisie, in other words, its existence is no longer compatible with society.

The essential condition for the existence, and for the sway of the bourgeois class, is the formation and augmentation of capital; the condition for capital is wage-labour. Wage-labour rests exclusively on competition between the labourers. The advance of industry, whose involuntary promoter is the bourgeoisie, replaces the isolation of the labourers, due to competition, by their revolutionary combination, due to association. The development of Modern Industry, therefore, cuts from under its feet the very foundation on which the bourgeoisie produces and appropriates products. What the bourgeoisie,

1. By bourgeoisie is meant the class of modern Capitalists, owners of the means of social production and employers of wage-labour. By proletariat, the class of modern wage-labourers who, having no means of production of their own, are reduced to selling their labour-power in order to live [Engels's note to the English edition of 1888]. These categories and concepts are related to HEGEL's discussion of the "Master–Servant" relation in his *Phenomenology of Geist* (see selection above).

therefore, produces, above all, is its own grave-diggers. Its fall and the victory of the proletariat are equally inevitable.

II. Proletarians and Communists

In what relation do the Communists stand to the proletarians as a whole?

The Communists do not form a separate party opposed to other working-class parties.

They have no interests separate and apart from those of the proletariat as a whole.

They do not set up any sectarian principles of their own, by which to shape and mould the proletarian movement.

The Communists are distinguished from the other working-class parties by this only: (1) In the national struggles of the proletarians of the different countries, they point out and bring to the front the common interests of the entire proletariat, independently of all nationality. (2) In the various stages of development which the struggle of the working class against the bourgoisie has to pass through, they always and everywhere represent the interests of the movement as a whole.

The Communists, therefore, are on the one hand, practically, the most advanced and resolute section of the working-class parties of every country, that section which pushes forward all others; on the other hand, theoretically, they have over the great mass of the proletariat the advantage of clearly understanding the line of march, the conditions, and the ultimate general results of the proletarian movement.

The immediate aim of the Communists is the same as that of all the other proletarian parties: formation of the proletariat into a class, overthrow of the bourgeois supremacy, conquest of political power by the proletariat.

The theoretical conclusions of the Communists are in no way based on ideas or principles that have been invented, or discovered, by this or that would-be universal reformer.

They merely express, in general terms, actual relations springing from an existing class struggle, from a historical movement going on under our very eyes. The abolition of existing property relations is not at all a distinctive feature of Communism.

All property relations in the past have continually been subject to historical change consequent upon the change in historical conditions.

The French Revolution, for example, abolished feudal property in favour of bourgeois property.

The distinguishing feature of Communism is not the abolition of property generally, but the abolition of bourgeois property.[2] But modern bourgeois private property is the final and most complete expression of the system of producing and appropriating products, that is based on class antagonisms, on the exploitation of the many by the few.

In this sense, the theory of the Communists may be summed up in the single sentence: Abolition of private property.

2. This important distinction is between *personal* property—that is, property that stands in some meaningful relation to the personality and related needs and self-expressive interests of the individual— and "modern bourgeois *private* property," or simply "private property": the institution that permits the private ownership of major elements of the productive capacity of modern industrial societies.

We Communists have been reproached with the desire of abolishing the right of personally acquiring property as the fruit of a man's own labour, which property is alleged to be the groundwork of all personal freedom, activity and independence.

Hard-won, self-acquired, self-earned property! Do you mean the property of the petty artisan and of the small peasant, a form of property that preceded the bourgeois form? There is no need to abolish that; the development of industry has to a great extent already destroyed it, and is still destroying it daily.

Or do you mean modern bourgeois private property?

But does wage-labour create any property for the labourer? Not a bit. It creates capital, *i.e.*, that kind of property which exploits wage-labour, and which cannot increase except upon condition of begetting a new supply of wage-labour for fresh exploitation. Property, in its present form, is based on the antagonism of capital and wage-labour. Let us examine both sides of this antagonism.

To be a capitalist, is to have not only a purely personal, but a social *status* in production. Capital is a collective product, and only by the united action of many members, nay, in the last resort, only by the united action of all members of society, can it be set in motion.

Capital is, therefore, not a personal, it is a social power.

When, therefore, capital is converted into common property, into the property of all members of society, personal property is not thereby transformed into social property. It is only the social character of the property that is changed. It loses its class-character.[3]

Let us now take wage-labour.

The average price of wage-labour is the minimum wage, *i.e.*, that quantum of the means of subsistence, which is absolutely requisite to keep the labourer in bare existence as a labourer. What, therefore, the wage-labourer appropriates by means of his labour, merely suffices to prolong and reproduce a bare existence. We by no means intend to abolish this personal appropriation of the products of labour, an appropriation that is made for the maintenance and reproduction of human life, and that leaves no surplus wherewith to command the labour of others. All that we want to do away with, is the miserable character of this appropriation, under which the labourer lives merely to increase capital, and is allowed to live only in so far as the interest of the ruling class requires it.

In bourgeois society, living labour is but a means to increase accumulated labour. In Communist society, accumulated labour is but a means to widen, to enrich, to promote the existence of the labourer.

In bourgeois society, therefore, the past dominates the present; in Communist society, the present dominates the past. In bourgeois society capital is independent and has individuality, while the living person is dependent and has no individuality.

And the abolition of this state of things is called by the bourgeois, abolition of individuality and freedom! And rightly so. The abolition of bourgeois individuality, bourgeois independence, and bourgeois freedom is undoubtedly aimed at.[4]

---

3. In a major shift away from Hegel's thought, for Marx the basic units of humanity are (transnational) socioeconomic "classes" rather than "peoples."
4. An echo of Hegel's point that things such as "individuality," "independence," and "freedom" have a different meaning and character (and conditions of attainment and forms of expression) in different types of human socioeconomic reality.

By freedom is meant, under the present bourgeois conditions of production, free trade, free selling and buying.

But if selling and buying disappears, free selling and buying disappears also. This talk about free selling and buying, and all the other "brave words" of our bourgeoisie about freedom in general, have a meaning, if any, only in contrast with restricted selling and buying, with the fettered traders of the Middle Ages, but have no meaning when opposed to the Communistic abolition of buying and selling, of the bourgeois conditions of production, and of the bourgeoisie itself.

You are horrified at our intending to do away with private property. But in your existing society, private property is already done away with for nine-tenths of the population; its existence for the few is solely due to its non-existence in the hands of those nine-tenths. You reproach us, therefore, with intending to do away with a form of property, the necessary condition for whose existence is the non-existence of any property for the immense majority of society.

In one word, you reproach us with intending to do away with your property. Precisely so; that is just what we intend.

From the moment when labour can no longer be converted into capital, money, or rent, into a social power capable of being monopolised, i.e., from the moment when individual property can no longer be transformed into bourgeois property, into capital, from that moment, you say, individuality vanishes.

You must, therefore, confess that by "individual" you mean no other person than the bourgeois, than the middle-class owner of property. This person must, indeed, be swept out of the way, and made impossible.

Communism deprives no man of the power to appropriate the products of society; all that it does is to deprive him of the power to subjugate the labour of others by means of such appropriation.[5]

It has been objected that upon the abolition of private property all work will cease, and universal laziness will overtake us.

According to this, bourgeois society ought long ago to have gone to the dogs through sheer idleness; for those of its members who work, acquire nothing, and those who acquire anything, do not work. The whole of this objection is but another expression of the tautology: that there can no longer be any wage-labour when there is no longer any capital.

All objections urged against the Communistic mode of producing and appropriating material products, have, in the same way, been urged against the Communistic modes of producing and appropriating intellectual products. Just as, to the bourgeois, the disappearance of class property is the disappearance of production itself, so the disappearance of class culture is to him identical with the disappearance of all culture.

That culture, the loss of which he laments, is, for the enormous majority, a mere training to act as a machine.

But don't wrangle with us so long as you apply, to our intended abolition of bourgeois property, the standard of your bourgeois notions of freedom, culture, law, &c. Your very ideas are but the outgrowth of the conditions of your

---

5. The fundamental concept underlying the theory and revolutionary assertion and practice of "communism" is "community" or commonality, and so in essence is the Hegelian idea of *Allgemeinheit*—but differently construed and applied than by Hegel.

bourgeois production and bourgeois property, just as your jurisprudence is but the will of your class made into a law for all—a will whose essential character and direction are determined by the economical conditions of existence of your class.

The selfish misconception that induces you to transform into eternal laws of nature and of reason, the social forms springing from your present mode of production and form of property—historical relations that rise and disappear in the progress of production—this misconception you share with every ruling class that has preceded you. What you see clearly in the case of ancient property, what you admit in the case of feudal property, you are of course forbidden to admit in the case of your own bourgeois form of property.

Abolition of the family! Even the most radical flare up at this infamous proposal of the Communists.

On what foundation is the present family, the bourgeois family, based? On capital, on private gain. In its completely developed form this family exists only among the bourgeoisie. But this state of things finds its complement in the practical absence of the family among the proletarians, and in public prostitution.

The bourgeois family will vanish as a matter of course when its complement vanishes, and both will vanish with the vanishing of capital.

Do you charge us with wanting to stop the exploitation of children by their parents? To this crime we plead guilty.

But, you will say, we destroy the most hallowed of relations, when we replace home education by social.

And your education! Is not that also social, and determined by the social conditions under which you educate, by the intervention, direct or indirect, of society, by means of schools, &c? The Communists have not invented the intervention of society in education; they do but seek to alter the character of that intervention, and to rescue education from the influence of the ruling class.

The bourgeois clap-trap about the family and education, about the hallowed co-relation of parent and child, becomes all the more disgusting, the more, by the action of Modern Industry, all family ties among the proletarians are torn asunder, and their children transformed into simple articles of commerce and instruments of labour.

But you Communists would introduce community of women, screams the whole bourgeoisie in chorus.

The bourgeois sees in his wife a mere instrument of production. He hears that the instruments of production are to be exploited in common, and, naturally, can come to no other conclusion than that the lot of being common to all will likewise fall to the women.

He has not even a suspicion that the real point aimed at is to do away with the status of women as mere instruments of production.

For the rest, nothing is more ridiculous than the virtuous indignation of our bourgeois at the community of women which, they pretend, is to be openly and officially established by the Communists. The Communists have no need to introduce community of women; it has existed almost from time immemorial.

Our bourgeois, not content with having the wives and daughters of their proletarians at their disposal, not to speak of common prostitutes, take the greatest pleasure in seducing each other's wives.

Bourgeois marriage is in reality a system of wives in common and thus, at the most, what the Communists might possibly be reproached with, is that they desire to introduce, in substitution for a hypocritically concealed, an openly legalised community of women. For the rest, it is self-evident that the abolition of the present system of production must bring with it the abolition of the community of women springing from that system, *i.e.*, of prostitution both public and private.

The Communists are further reproached with desiring to abolish countries and nationality.

The working men have no country. We cannot take from them what they have not got. Since the proletariat must first of all acquire political supremacy, must rise to be the leading class of the nation, must constitute itself *the* nation, it is, so far, itself national, though not in the bourgeois sense of the word.

National differences and antagonisms between peoples are daily more and more vanishing, owing to the development of the bourgeoisie, to freedom of commerce, to the world-market, to uniformity in the mode of production and in the conditions of life corresponding thereto.

The supremacy of the proletariat will cause them to vanish still faster. United action, of the leading civilised countries at least, is one of the first conditions for the emancipation of the proletariat.

In proportion as the exploitation of one individual by another is put an end to, the exploitation of one nation by another will also be put an end to. In proportion as the antagonism between classes within the nation vanishes, the hostility of one nation to another will come to an end.

The charges against Communism made from a religious, a philosophical, and, generally, from an ideological standpoint, are not deserving of serious examination.

Does it require deep intuition to comprehend that man's ideas, views and conceptions, in one word, man's consciousness, changes with every change in the conditions of his material existence, in his social relations and in his social life?

What else does the history of ideas prove, than that intellectual production changes its character in proportion as material production is changed? The ruling ideas of each age have ever been the ideas of its ruling class.

When people speak of ideas that revolutionise society, they do but express the fact, that within the old society, the elements of a new one have been created, and that the dissolution of the old ideas keeps even pace with the dissolution of the old conditions of existence.

When the ancient world was in its last throes, the ancient religions were overcome by Christianity. When Christian ideas succumbed in the 18th century to rationalist ideas, feudal society fought its death battle with the then revolutionary bourgeoisie. The ideas of religious liberty and freedom of conscience merely gave expression to the sway of free competition within the domain of knowledge.

"Undoubtedly," it will be said, "religious, moral, philosophical and juridical ideas have been modified in the course of historical development. But religion, morality, philosophy, political science, and law, constantly survived this change."

"There are, besides, eternal truths, such as Freedom, Justice, etc., that are common to all states of society. But Communism abolishes eternal truths, it abolishes all religion, and all morality, instead of constituting them on a new basis; it therefore acts in contradiction to all past historical experience."

What does this accusation reduce itself to? The history of all past society has consisted in the development of class antagonisms, antagonisms that assumed different forms at different epochs.

But whatever form they may have taken, one fact is common to all past ages, viz., the exploitation of one part of society by the other. No wonder, then, that the social consciousness of past ages, despite all the multiplicity and variety it displays, moves within certain common forms, or general ideas, which cannot completely vanish except with the total disappearance of class antagonisms.

The Communist revolution is the most radical rupture with traditional property relations; no wonder that its development involves the most radical rupture with traditional ideas.

But let us have done with the bourgeois objections to Communism.

We have seen above, that the first step in the revolution by the working class, is to raise the proletariat to the position of ruling class, to win the battle of democracy.

The proletariat will use its political supremacy to wrest, by degrees, all capital from the bourgeoisie, to centralise all instruments of production in the hands of the State, i.e., of the proletariat organised as the ruling class; and to increase the total of productive forces as rapidly as possible.

Of course, in the beginning, this cannot be effected except by means of despotic inroads on the rights of property, and on the conditions of bourgeois production; by means of measures, therefore, which appear economically insufficient and untenable, but which, in the course of the movement, outstrip themselves, necessitate further inroads upon the old social order, and are unavoidable as a means of entirely revolutionising the mode of production.

These measures will of course be different in different countries.

Nevertheless in the most advanced countries, the following will be pretty generally applicable.

1. Abolition of property in land and application of all rents of land to public purposes.

2. A heavy progressive or graduated income tax.

3. Abolition of all right of inheritance.

4. Confiscation of the property of all emigrants and rebels.

5. Centralisation of credit in the hands of the State, by means of a national bank with State capital and an exclusive monopoly.

6. Centralisation of the means of communication and transport in the hands of the State.

7. Extension of factories and instruments of production owned by the State; the bringing into cultivation of waste-lands, and the improvement of the soil generally in accordance with a common plan.

8. Equal liability of all to labour. Establishment of industrial armies, especially for agriculture.

9. Combination of agriculture with manufacturing industries; gradual abolition of the distinction between town and country, by a more equable distribution of the population over the country.

10. Free education for all children in public schools. Abolition of children's factory labour in its present form. Combination of education with industrial production, &c, &c.

When, in the course of development, class distinctions have disappeared, and all production has been concentrated in the hands of a vast association of the whole nation, the public power will lose its political character. Political power, properly so called, is merely the organised power of one class for oppressing another. If the proletariat during its contest with the bourgeoisie is compelled, by the force of circumstances, to organise itself as a class, if, by means of a revolution, it makes itself the ruling class, and, as such, sweeps away by force the old conditions of production, then it will, along with these conditions, have swept away the conditions for the existence of class antagonisms and of classes generally, and will thereby have abolished its own supremacy as a class.

In place of the old bourgeois society, with its classes and class antagonisms, we shall have an association, in which the free development of each is the condition for the free development of all.

SOURCE: From *The Marx-Engels Reader*, ed. Robert C. Tucker, 2nd ed. (New York: W. W. Norton, 1978), pp. 483–91 [translated by Samuel Moore, with Friedrich Engels]. Originally published in London in 1848 as *Manifest der Kommunistischen Partei*, and written primarily by Marx, in collaboration with Engels.

From Capital, Volume Three

BY KARL MARX

[ON NECESSITY AND FREEDOM]

We have seen that the capitalist process of production is a historically determined form of the social process of production in general. The latter is as much a production process of material conditions of human life as a process taking place under specific historical and economic production relations, producing and reproducing these production relations themselves, and thereby also the bearers of this process, their material conditions of existence and their mutual relations, i.e., their particular socio-economic form. For the aggregate of these relations, in which the agents of this production stand with respect to Nature and to one another, and in which they produce, is precisely society, considered from the standpoint of its economic structure. Like all its predecessors, the capitalist process of production proceeds under definite material conditions, which are, however, simultaneously the bearers of definite social relations entered into by individuals in the process of reproducing their life. Those conditions, like these relations, are on the one hand prerequisites, on the other hand results and creations of the capitalist process of production; they are produced and reproduced by it. We saw also that capital—and the capitalist is merely capital personified and functions in the process of production solely as the agent of capital—in its corresponding social process of production, pumps a definite quantity of surplus labour out of the direct producers, or labourers; capital obtains this surplus labour without an equivalent, and in essence it always remains forced labour—no matter how much it may seem to result from free contractual agreement. This surplus labour appears as surplus value, and this surplus value exists as a surplus product. Surplus labour in general, as labour performed over and above the given requirements, must always remain. In the capitalist as well as in the slave system, etc., it merely assumes an antagonistic form and is supplemented by complete idleness of a stratum of society. A definite quantity of surplus labour is required as insurance against accidents, and by the necessary and progressive expansion of the process of reproduction in keeping with the development of the needs and the growth of population, which is called accumulation from the viewpoint of the capitalist. It is one of the civilizing aspects of capital that it enforces this surplus labour in a manner and under conditions which are more advantageous to the development of the productive forces, social relations, and the creation of the elements for a new and higher form than under the preceding forms of slavery, serfdom, etc. Thus it gives rise to a stage, on the one hand, in which coercion and monopolization of social development (including its material and intellectual advantages) by one portion of society at the expense of the other are eliminated; on the other hand, it creates the material means and embryonic conditions, making it possible in a higher form of society to combine this surplus labour with a greater reduction of time devoted to material labour in general. For, depending on the development of labour productivity, surplus labour may be large in a small total working day, and relatively small in a large total working day. If the necessary labour time = 3 and the surplus labour = 3, then the total working day = 6 and the rate of surplus labour = 100%. If the necessary labour = 9 and the surplus labour = 3, then the total working day = 12 and the rate of surplus labour only 33⅓%. In that case, it depends upon the labour productivity how much use value shall be produced in a definite time, hence also in a definite surplus labour time. The actual wealth of society, and the possibility of constantly expanding its reproduction process, therefore, do not depend upon the duration of surplus labour, but upon its productivity and the more or less copious conditions of production under which it is performed. In fact, the realm of freedom actually begins only where labour which is determined by necessity and mundane considerations ceases; thus in the very nature of things it lies beyond the sphere of actual material production. Just as the savage must wrestle with Nature to satisfy his wants, to maintain and reproduce life, so must civilized man, and he must do so in all social formations and under all possible modes of production. With his development this realm of physical necessity expands as a result of his wants; but, at the same time, the forces of production which satisfy these wants also increase. Freedom in this field can only consist in socialized man, the associated producers, rationally regulating their interchange with Nature, bringing it under their common control, instead of being ruled by it as by the blind forces of Nature; and achieving this with the least expenditure of energy and under conditions most favourable to, and worthy of, their human nature.[1] But it nonetheless still remains a realm of necessity.

---

1. That is, there is a normative conception of "human nature," with which the actual condition of existing human beings is too often at variance.

Beyond it begins that development of human energy which is an end in itself, the true realm of freedom, which, however can blossom forth only with the realm of necessity as its basis.[2] The shortening of the working day is its basic prerequisite.

SOURCE: From *The Marx-Engels Reader*, ed. Robert C. Tucker, 2nd ed. (New York: W. W. Norton, 1978), pp. 439–41 [translation published by International Publishers]. Written 1863–83 and originally published in 1894 (edited by Engels after Marx's death) as *Das Kapital, Kritik der Politischen Ökonomie*, vol. 3, *Der Gesamtprozeß der kapitalistischen Produktion*.

From Critique of the Gotha Program

By Karl Marx

* * *

[On Socialism and Communism]

Let us take first of all the words "proceeds of labour" in the sense of the product of labour; then the co-operative proceeds of labour are the *total social product*.

From this must now be deducted:

First, cover for replacement of the means of production used up.

Secondly, additional portion for expansion of production.

Thirdly, reserve or insurance funds to provide against accidents, dislocations caused by natural calamities, etc.

These deductions from the "undiminished proceeds of labour" are an economic necessity and their magnitude is to be determined according to available means and forces, and partly by computation of probabilities, but they are in no way calculable by equity.

There remains the other part of the total product, intended to serve as means of consumption.

Before this is divided among the individuals, there has to be deducted again, from it:

First, the general costs of administration not belonging to production.

This part will, from the outset, be very considerably restricted in comparison with present-day society and it diminishes in proportion as the new society develops.

Secondly, that which is intended for the common satisfaction of needs, such as schools, health services, etc.

From the outset this part grows considerably in comparison with present-day society and it grows in proportion as the new society develops.

Thirdly, funds for those unable to work, etc., in short, for what is included under so-called official poor relief today.

Only now do we come to the "distribution" which the programme, under Lassallean[1] influence, alone has in view in its narrow fashion, namely, to that

---

2. That is, the conditions in which human life is lived can be fundamentally transformed, enabling the emergence of a kind of "freedom" that has not been and at present still is not humanly possible.

1. Ferdinand Lassalle (1825–1864), a German leftist- Hegelian and socialist theorist who drew Marx's scorn because he believed that state socialism would come through constitutional reform rather than revolution. The Social Democratic movement and party in Germany later grew out of his efforts.

part of the means of consumption which is divided among the individual producers of the co-operative society.

The "undiminished proceeds of labour" have already unnoticeably become converted into the "diminished" proceeds, although what the producer is deprived of in his capacity as a private individual benefits him directly or indirectly in his capacity as a member of society.

Just as the phrase of the "undiminished proceeds of labour" has disappeared, so now does the phrase of the "proceeds of labour" disappear altogether.

Within the co-operative society based on common ownership of the means of production, the producers do not exchange their products; just as little does the labour employed on the products appear here *as the value* of these products, as a material quality possessed by them, since now, in contrast to capitalist society, individual labour no longer exists in an indirect fashion but directly as a component part of the total labour. The phrase "proceeds of labour," objectionable also today on account of its ambiguity, thus loses all meaning.

What we have to deal with here is a communist society, not as it has *developed* on its own foundations, but, on the contrary, just as it *emerges* from capitalist society; which is thus in every respect, economically, morally and intellectually, still stamped with the birth marks of the old society from whose womb it emerges. Accordingly, the individual producer receives back from society—after the deductions have been made—exactly what he gives to it. What he has given to it is his individual quantum of labour. For example, the social working day consists of the sum of the individual hours of work; the individual labour time of the individual producer is the part of the social working day contributed by him, his share in it. He receives a certificate from society that he has furnished such and such an amount of labour (after deducting his labour for the common funds), and with this certificate he draws from the social stock of means of consumption as much as costs the same amount of labour. The same amount of labour which he has given to society in one form he receives back in another.

Here obviously the same principle prevails as that which regulates the exchange of commodities, as far as this is exchange of equal values. Content and form are changed, because under the altered circumstances no one can give anything except his labour, and because, on the other hand, nothing can pass to the ownership of individuals except individual means of consumption. But, as far as the distribution of the latter among the individual producers is concerned, the same principle prevails as in the exchange of commodity equivalents; a given amount of labour in one form is exchanged for an equal amount of labour in another form.

Hence, *equal right* here is still in principle—*bourgeois right*, although principle and practice are no longer at loggerheads, while the exchange of equivalents in commodity exchange only exists *on the average* and not in the individual case.

In spite of this advance, this *equal right* is still constantly stigmatised by a bourgeois limitation. The right of the producers is *proportional* to the labour they supply; the equality consists in the fact that measurement is made with an *equal standard*, labour.

But one man is superior to another physically or mentally and so supplies more labour in the same time, or can labour for a longer time; and labour, to serve as a measure, must be defined by its duration or intensity, otherwise it ceases to be a standard of measurement. This *equal* right is an unequal right for unequal labour. It recognises no class differences, because everyone is only a worker like everyone else; but it tacitly recognises unequal individual endowment and thus productive capacity as natural privileges. *It is, therefore, a right of inequality, in its content, like every right.* Right by its very nature can consist only in the application of an equal standard; but unequal individuals (and they would not be different individuals if they were not unequal) are measurable only by an equal standard in so far as they are brought under an equal point of view, are taken from one *definite* side only, for instance, in the present case, are regarded *only as workers* and nothing more is seen in them, everything else being ignored. Further, one worker is married, another not; one has more children than another, and so on and so forth. Thus, with an equal performance of labour, and hence an equal share in the social consumption fund, one will in fact receive more than another, one will be richer than another, and so on. To avoid all these defects, right instead of being equal would have to be unequal.

But these defects are inevitable in the first phase of communist society as it is when it has just emerged after prolonged birth pangs from capitalist society. Right can never be higher than the economic structure of society and its cultural development conditioned thereby.

In a higher phase of communist society, after the enslaving subordination of the individual to the division of labour, and therewith also the antithesis between mental and physical labour, has vanished; after labour has become not only a means of life but life's prime want;[2] after the productive forces have also increased with the all-round development of the individual, and all the springs of co-operative wealth flow more abundantly—only then can the narrow horizon of bourgeois right be crossed in its entirety and society inscribe on its banner: From each according to his ability, to each according to his needs![3]

* * *

SOURCE: From *The Marx-Engels Reader*, ed. Robert C. Tucker, 2nd ed. (New York: W. W. Norton, 1978), pp. 528–31 [translation published by Progress Publishers]. Originally a letter written by Marx in May 1875 to a group of fellow revolutionaries in Germany, criticizing their draft of a program of socialist goals for a congress soon to be held in the German city of Gotha; edited by Engels after Marx's death and first published in 1891. It is indicative of the difference between that program and "communism" as Marx envisioned it.

2. That is, labor as productive activity has become an essential means of self-expression and self-realization as well as of supporting life.
3. This basic principle of Marx's "higher phase of communist society" is thus to be contrasted with the principle he expects to prevail in its "first phase," following its "emergence from capitalist society," in which what a worker receives from society would still be determined by "what he gives to it." His point is that the embrace of that principle by socialists is empty unless conjoined with a much more radical transformation of the economic structure and culture of society than can be accomplished by the kinds of reforms socialists are content to advocate.

MARY WOLLSTONECRAFT
(1759 – 1797)

Wollstonecraft was a force. In the difficult and tumultuous two decades of her brief adult life, through the sheer power of her intelligence and strength of her will, and without the advantages of a formal education, she become a publishing public intellectual of a sort that was extraordinary for a woman in her time and society. She was an ardent adherent and advocate of Enlightenment ideas and values, and yet she epitomized the very different sort of passion-charged human reality that would preoccupy the dramatic Romantic challenge to them in the decades following her death. She preached reason and the rational transformation of education, society and women's place in it, and institutions such as marriage, in opposition to the oppressive weight of custom and tradition; but her personal life was seemingly as heedless of the sober rationality she prized as it was of the conventionality she despised. The work for which she is best known, *A Vindication of the Rights of Woman* (1792), has led many to think of her primarily as a forerunner of feminism and feminist theory; but she was a moral, social, and political thinker and interpreter of human reality and possibility as well, deserving of recognition and attention in the history of modern philosophy prior to its post-Kantian era—and perhaps the first woman of whom this can justifiably be said. And like her compatriot JOHN STUART MILL, who was in many respects a kindred spirit, she may appropriately be associated with both of its emerging traditions.

Mary Wollstonecraft was born in London in 1759, the second of seven children in a family whose fortunes—initially comfortable—declined markedly through her childhood. Like most of her siblings, she received no formal education, but she was an avid reader and worked hard to educate herself as best she could under the burden of onerous household duties.

She also had aptitude as a writer, which she developed under the guidance of a supportive family friend. Approaching 20, and with few options open to her, she left home in 1778 for a domestic position as companion to a widow. She returned to London three years later to help and care for her ailing mother, who died in 1782. After her mother's death she lived for a time with the family of her best friend, Fanny Blood (whose name she would give to her first daughter). In 1784 she joined her unhappily married sister Eliza, who had recently given birth. In the first of many scandals in which she was to become embroiled, Mary and her troubled sister fled (initially into hiding), leaving the baby with Eliza's husband. (The baby died within a year.)

To support themselves, the two sisters, together with a third sister and Fanny Blood, established a school for girls in Newington Green (near London). Fanny soon married, and she and her husband moved to Portugal when she became pregnant, for the sake of her health. In 1785 Wollstonecraft traveled to Lisbon to aid her friend as her due date approached, and was devastated when, shortly after the birth, both mother and baby died. Wollstonecraft returned to England, where her school was foundering. It closed the next year, in 1786. However, her brief time in Newington Green was of great importance; for she happened to hear and became acquainted with Richard Prior, a prominent Dissenting preacher, moralist, and political writer who resided there and took an interest in her. That enabled her to enter into an intellectual milieu that fueled her intellectual interest in progressive causes.

During that same time Wollstonecraft also had the good fortune to meet Joseph Johnson, a bookseller and publisher associated with London's leading religious and political radicals. Johnson became a friend, supported her, encouraged her to write, and was willing to publish her. He provided an advance for her first book, *Thoughts on the Education of Daughters* (1787), which drew on her experience in the school and as a governess. In 1788 he published two more of her books. One, intended for children, combined her pedagogical and moral interests: *Original Stories from Real Life; with Conversations, Calculated to Regulate the Affections, and Form the Mind to Truth and Goodness.* (A 1796 edition was illustrated by William Blake.) The other, *Mary: A Fiction*, was a novel inspired by her friend Fanny's life and death. She now saw herself as attempting—with some success— to become what she called (with more pride than accuracy) "the first of a new genus": a woman able to support herself as a writer.

In 1788 Johnson began publishing a journal, *Analytical Review*, to which Wollstonecraft contributed essays and reviews, thereby furthering her philosophical self-education. She also translated French and German texts. These activities gave her the opportunity to become aware of the latest works and developments in French and German philosophy—KANT's thought and his *Critique of Pure Reason* (1781; 2nd ed., 1787) and *Critique of Practical Reason* (1789) among them.

Inspired by the French Revolution (1789), Wollstonecraft's philosophical focus in her writings shifted from moral and aesthetic topics to issues that were more social and political. A major factor was her anger at Edmund Burke's *Reflections on the Revolution in France and on the Proceedings in Certain Societies in London Relative to That Event* (1790), in which Burke—an Irish-born British conservative—attacked the French Revolution and its English defenders, singling out her friend Richard Price. Burke considered it to be folly to attempt to legislate things like human rights in texts such as the recent proclamation of "rights of man" by the Enlightenment-minded revolutionary new French National Assembly.

His harsh critique prompted Wollstonecraft to counterattack, with a polemic whose very title echoed that proclamation: *A Vindication of the Rights of Men* (1790). It brought her instant celebrity, and also linked her to Thomas Paine (whom she had met), whose even better-known attack on Burke, *The Rights of Man*, appeared the following year.

The title of Wollstonecraft's *A Vindication of the Rights of Woman with Strictures on Political and Moral Subjects*, and its contents as well, should be viewed and understood in this context. The title signals her intent to situate what she has to say about "woman" and women in relation to the ongoing "rights of man" discussion—into which she had already entered (in her previous book)—and thus to place the book in the larger context of the Enlightenment project of a rational and enlightened reform of social relations and social structures in our modern societies. She begins it by affirming the idea and basic content of such "rights" of all human beings, and then proceeds to explore the special circumstances of women in her society that complicate the realization of these rights. She dedicated the book's second edition, also published in 1792, to the French statesman and politician Charles Talleyrand, whom she had met while he was in London that year, thereby emphasizing its connection to the ideals and agenda of revolutionary France.

Wollstonecraft had good reason to curry Talleyrand's favor, as she was about to travel to France—eager both to see the revolution in action and to flee the recent humiliation of her thwarted love for a married artist. In Paris, she soon met and fell in love with an American adventurer, Gilbert Imlay, by whom she became pregnant (a daughter, Fanny, was born in May 1794). They never married, but Imlay registered her as his wife at the American embassy because France was growing increasingly dangerous for English visitors. Astonishingly, given the circumstances, at the end of that year she also produced another book, of a completely different sort from anything she had written previously: *A Historical and Moral View of the Origin and Progress of the French Revolution and the Effect It Has Produced in Europe.*

In despair over the state of her relationship with Imlay, Wollstonecraft attempted suicide. Soon thereafter, she undertook a four-month trip to Scandinavia (accompanied by her infant and a nurse) in an attempt to straighten out a complex business matter for him—as memorialized in her *Letters Written during a Short Residence in Denmark, Norway, and Sweden* (1796). When she returned to London and discovered that Imlay had a new mistress, she again attempted suicide. But within months she entered into another relationship, this time with a friend she knew well, who was her intellectual equal and a better match: William Godwin, whom she had first met in 1791. After she became pregnant, they married (in March 1797), she took his name, and a daughter was born to them that August. But like Fanny Blood, Wollstonecraft did not long survive childbirth; she died, of related complications, on September 10, at the age of just 38. In this case, however, the baby survived. (Named Mary Godwin at her birth, she would become famous as Mary Shelley, the author of *Frankenstein* [1818].) At the end of her life Wollstonecraft was working on her second novel, *The Wrongs of Woman; or, Maria.* The incomplete manuscript was published in 1799 in her *Posthumous Works*, edited by Godwin.

The high drama of the second half of Wollstonecraft's life makes a strange sort of sense of the emphasis in her two *Vindication* books on the importance of fostering—in men and women alike—rationality, self-mastery, and self-control: these are precisely the virtues she must have been acutely aware that she herself greatly needed. Her primary concern, however, as she assessed what ailed the women in her world and gauged their needs even in materially comfortable circumstances, was not passion-driven irrationality but rather their socially and culturally fostered childishness, shallowness, and dependency. Her view of men

in her world was also dim but for different reasons, revealed not only in their dealings with women (and the upbringing of their daughters) but also in what they do with themselves.

For Wollstonecraft the fundamental questions requiring attention relate to how it is (or would be) best for human beings to turn out, and what kinds of social conditions and forms of education those best outcomes require. It ought, in her eyes, to go without saying that the answers should be the same for men and women alike; but since in her world the opposite was taken for granted, she undertook to make the case. Wollstonecraft argues that it would be in the best interest of all for women to receive the same advantages and opportunities as men, and for both sexes to accord each other—and themselves—the same respect, within marriage as well as in the world of society. Her point of departure, as the title of her first "vindication" book indicates, is a consideration of the "rights" of "men" (in the sense of "human beings") generally—that is, *human* rights and associated expectations. That also is the topic of the first chapter of her second "vindication" book: "The Rights and Involved Duties of Mankind Considered." And the manifesto that appears in the beginning of that chapter (excerpted below) is ringing and succinct:

> In what does man's pre-eminence over the brute creation consist? The answer is as clear as that a half is less than the whole; in Reason.
>
> What acquirement exalts one being above another? Virtue; we spontaneously reply.
>
> For what purpose were the passions implanted? That man by struggling with them might attain a degree of knowledge denied to the brutes; whispers Experience.
>
> Consequently the perfection of our nature and capability of happiness, must be estimated by the degree of reason, virtue, and knowledge, that distinguish the individual, and direct the laws which bind society[.]

Wollstonecraft's conception of what it is to be a fully and truly human being is strikingly similar to that of Kant, as set forth in his just-published *Critique of Practical Reason*. But her conception of what it takes to *become* such a human being is closer in spirit to that of David Hume (1711–1776), before her, and closer still to that of Mill a half-century later. A necessary (although not entirely sufficient) condition of a human being's turning out humanly well, for her, is that the social, cultural, and educational circumstances of that person's life, from childhood on, be conducive rather than detrimental to his or her spiritual (intellectual, moral, and emotional) development—that is, to what she here calls "the perfection of our nature and capability of happiness." Providing the opportunity for such development and for such a life, making the most of this opportunity, and endeavoring to make it available to all are what she takes the "rights and duties of man" fundamentally to be, "thus simplified." And the sort of society that is "formed in the wisest manner," she goes on to contend, and thus is to be desired and sought, is one "whose constitution is founded on the nature of man" so conceived, with all due consideration given to the conditions of its possibility and requirements of its fulfillment.

This is Wollstonecraft's Enlightenment vision and basic set of principles, which she and her kindred spirits on both sides of the Atlantic deemed so "self-evident" as to require no argument beyond their appeal to this conception of the nobler elements of our human nature, with "reason" and "virtue" as its crown jewels. To be sure, as she immediately notes, our powers of reason are too often ignobly employed, as when benighted men use them to "justify prejudices" and secure unfair and even harmful advantages over their fellow human beings. It is therefore of the utmost importance that "virtue" be cultivated and guide the critical employment of these powers to counter such rationalizing abuses of this faculty—as she herself undertakes to do in the remainder of the book. (The thought that this should suffice, and its accompanying faith in the fundamental reasonableness of human beings, when shown the errors of their ways, are among the elements of Enlightenment thinking that now seem more than a little wishful.)

One other notable aspect of this vision is the role it assigns to the "passions"— that is, to our affective nature (with its drives, feelings, emotions, and desires), whose power and unruliness Wollstonecraft knew all too well. Many philosophers from Socrates to Kant have tended to be suspicious of and even hostile to the passions. Enlightenment thinkers, though still guarded in their attitude, were more accepting. They regarded the passions as ineliminable but potentially beneficial as well as troublesome, and so concluded that they are best neither opposed nor indulged but instead mastered, tamed, and brought under rational management, to ensure that they do not overstep their bounds as harmless elements of vitality and sources of enjoyment contributing to human happiness. Wollstonecraft recognizes them as part of our human nature, but—perhaps knowing and fearing their power (as her reference to the "whisper[ed]" wisdom of "Experience" suggests)—does not affirm them, even to that limited extent. She considers the passions to be deserving of mention here only as something to be "struggled with" rather than embraced even when harnessed. She accords them value, but only for the challenges they pose, as occasions for the exercise of "virtue," and for the impetus they give to the attainment of that higher (and nobler) "degree of knowledge" transcending all mere vitality that the ability to subdue them requires.

Wollstonecraft thus overtly remained aligned philosophically with the party of those for whom nature (and the passions associated with our embodiment as living creatures) is what we were put in this world to rise above. Yet time and again her choices in her personal life showed that, for her, more mattered in life than just its "degree of reason, virtue, and knowledge." While that awareness is palpable in this second *Vindication*, she seems not to have yet figured out what to make of it and do with it. Had she lived into the coming decades of the Romantic revolution, which made it possible for the passions to be embraced with a good conscience (even if not in all forms and without reserve), we surely would have found out. SCHILLER's *Letters on the Aesthetic Education of Man* (1795; see above)—in which he worked his way beyond this Kantian way of thinking to a new conception of truly human wholeness—would soon appear; and Wollstonecraft could well have wound up doing so as well. Her thought was a work in progress that, like her life, was interrupted all too soon. Her *Vindication* makes clear its point of departure, but the book also—when illuminated by her life—tantalizingly hints at what direction it might have taken.

A Vindication of the Rights of Woman

Introduction

After considering the historic page, and viewing the living world with anxious solicitude, the most melancholy emotions of sorrowful indignation have depressed my spirits, and I have sighed when obliged to confess, that either nature has made a great difference between man and man, or that the civilization which has hitherto taken place in the world has been very partial. I have turned over various books written on the subject of education, and patiently observed the conduct of parents and the management of schools; but what has been the result?—a profound conviction that the neglected education of my fellow-creatures is the grand source of the misery I deplore; and that women, in particular, are rendered weak and wretched by a variety of concurring causes, originating from one hasty conclusion. The conduct and manners of women, in fact, evidently prove that their minds are not in a healthy state; for, like the flowers which are planted in too rich a soil, strength and usefulness are sacrificed to beauty; and the flaunting leaves, after having pleased a fastidious eye, fade, disregarded on the stalk, long before the season when they ought to have arrived at maturity.—One cause of this barren blooming I attribute to a false system of education, gathered from the books written on this subject by men who, considering females rather as women than human creatures, have been more anxious to make them alluring mistresses than affectionate wives and rational mothers; and the understanding of the sex has been so bubbled[1] by this specious homage, that the civilized women of the present century, with a few exceptions, are only anxious to inspire love, when they ought to cherish a nobler ambition, and by their abilities and virtues exact respect.

In a treatise, therefore, on female rights and manners, the works which have been particularly written for their improvement must not be overlooked; especially when it is asserted, in direct terms, that the minds of women are enfeebled by false refinement; that the books of instruction, written by men of genius, have had the same tendency as more frivolous productions; and that, in the true style of Mahometanism,[2] they are treated as a kind of subordinate

---

1. Deluded, cheated (archaic). [Unless otherwise indicated, notes are the edition editor's. See Source paragraph (editor's note).]

2. Islam (Wollstonecraft reflects popular caricatures of and prejudices about that religion) [editor's note].

beings, and not as a part of the human species, when improveable reason is allowed to be the dignified distinction which raises men above the brute creation, and puts a natural sceptre in a feeble hand.

Yet, because I am a woman, I would not lead my readers to suppose that I mean violently to agitate the contested question respecting the equality or inferiority of the sex; but as the subject lies in my way, and I cannot pass it over without subjecting the main tendency of my reasoning to misconstruction, I shall stop a moment to deliver, in a few words, my opinion.—In the government of the physical world it is observable that the female in point of strength is, in general, inferior to the male. This is the law of nature; and it does not appear to be suspended or abrogated in favour of woman. A degree of physical superiority cannot, therefore, be denied—and it is a noble prerogative! But not content with this natural pre-eminence, men endeavour to sink us still lower, merely to render us alluring objects for a moment; and women, intoxicated by the adoration which men, under the influence of their senses, pay them, do not seek to obtain a durable interest in their hearts, or to become the friends of the fellow creatures who find amusement in their society.

I am aware of an obvious inference:—from every quarter have I heard exclamations against masculine women; but where are they to be found? If by this appellation men mean to inveigh against their ardour in hunting, shooting, and gaming, I shall most cordially join in the cry; but if it be against the imitation of manly virtues, or, more properly speaking, the attainment of those talents and virtues, the exercise of which ennobles the human character, and which raise females in the scale of animal being, when they are comprehensively termed mankind;—all those who view them with a philosophic eye must, I should think, wish with me, that they may every day grow more and more masculine.

This discussion naturally divides the subject. I shall first consider women in the grand light of human creatures, who, in common with men, are placed on this earth to unfold their faculties; and afterwards I shall more particularly point out their peculiar designation.

I wish also to steer clear of an error which many respectable writers have fallen into; for the instruction which has hitherto been addressed to women, has rather been applicable to *ladies*, if the little indirect advice, that is scattered through Sandford and Merton,[3] be excepted; but, addressing my sex in a firmer tone, I pay particular attention to those in the middle class, because they appear to be in the most natural state.[4] Perhaps the seeds of false-refinement, immorality, and vanity, have ever been shed by the great. Weak, artificial beings, raised above the common wants and affections of their race, in a premature unnatural manner, undermine the very foundation of virtue, and spread corruption through the whole mass of society! As a class of mankind they have the strongest claim to pity; the education of the rich tends to render them vain and helpless, and the unfolding mind is not strengthened by the

3. *The History of Sandford and Merton* (3 vols., 1783–89), Thomas Day's best-selling work of instructive fiction for children [editor's note].
4. Wollstonecraft considers the middle classes to be more "natural" and also more educable than the aristocracy—"the great"—because they are as yet uncorrupted by the artificiality of leisure-class life.

practice of those duties which dignify the human character.—They only live to amuse themselves, and by the same law which in nature invariably produces certain effects, they soon only afford barren amusement.

But as I purpose taking a separate view of the different ranks of society, and of the moral character of women, in each, this hint is, for the present, sufficient; and I have only alluded to the subject, because it appears to me to be the very essence of an introduction to give a cursory account of the contents of the work it introduces.

My own sex, I hope, will excuse me, if I treat them like rational creatures, instead of flattering their *fascinating* graces, and viewing them as if they were in a state of perpetual childhood, unable to stand alone. I earnestly wish to point out in what true dignity and human happiness consists— I wish to persuade women to endeavour to acquire strength, both of mind and body, and to convince them that the soft phrases, susceptibility of heart, delicacy of sentiment, and refinement of taste, are almost synonymous with epithets of weakness, and that those beings who are only the objects of pity and that kind of love, which has been termed its sister, will soon become objects of contempt.

Dismissing then those pretty feminine phrases, which the men condescendingly use to soften our slavish dependence, and despising that weak elegancy of mind, exquisite sensibility, and sweet docility of manners, supposed to be the sexual characteristics of the weaker vessel,[5] I wish to shew that elegance is inferior to virtue, that the first object of laudable ambition is to obtain a character as a human being, regardless of the distinction of sex; and that secondary views should be brought to this simple touchstone.

This is a rough sketch of my plan; and should I express my conviction with the energetic emotions that I feel whenever I think of the subject, the dictates of experience and reflection will be felt by some of my readers. Animated by this important object, I shall disdain to cull my phrases or polish my style;—I aim at being useful, and sincerity will render me unaffected; for, wishing rather to persuade by the force of my arguments, than dazzle by the elegance of my language, I shall not waste my time in rounding periods,[6] or in fabricating the turgid bombast of artificial feelings, which, coming from the head, never reach the heart.—I shall be employed about things, not words!—and, anxious to render my sex more respectable members of society, I shall try to avoid that flowery diction which has slided from essays into novels, and from novels into familiar letters and conversation.

These pretty superlatives, dropping glibly from the tongue, vitiate the taste, and create a kind of sickly delicacy that turns away from simple unadorned truth; and a deluge of false sentiments and overstretched feelings, stifling the natural emotions of the heart, render the domestic pleasures insipid, that ought to sweeten the exercise of those severe duties, which educate a rational and immortal being for a nobler field of action.

5. See 1 Peter 3:7 for this characterization of wives [editor's note].   6. Formulating balanced sentences.

The education of women has, of late, been more attended to than formerly; yet they are still reckoned a frivolous sex, and ridiculed or pitied by the writers who endeavour by satire or instruction to improve them. It is acknowledged that they spend many of the first years of their lives in acquiring a smattering of accomplishments;[7] meanwhile strength of body and mind are sacrificed to libertine notions of beauty, to the desire of establishing themselves,— the only way women can rise in the world,—by marriage. And this desire making mere animals of them, when they marry they act as such children may be expected to act:—they dress; they paint, and nickname God's creatures.[8]—Surely these weak beings are only fit for a seraglio![9]—Can they be expected to govern a family with judgment, or take care of the poor babes whom they bring into the world?

If then it can be fairly deduced from the present conduct of the sex, from the prevalent fondness for pleasure which takes place of ambition and those nobler passions that open and enlarge the soul; that the instruction which women have hitherto received has only tended, with the constitution of civil society, to render them insignificant objects of desire—mere propagators of fools!—if it can be proved that in aiming to accomplish them, without cultivating their understandings, they are taken out of their sphere of duties, and made ridiculous and useless when the short-lived bloom of beauty is over,[1] I presume that *rational* men will excuse me for endeavouring to persuade them to become more masculine and respectable.

Indeed the word masculine is only a bugbear: there is little reason to fear that women will acquire too much courage or fortitude; for their apparent inferiority with respect to bodily strength, must render them, in some degree, dependent on men in the various relations of life; but why should it be increased by prejudices that give a sex to virtue, and confound simple truths with sensual reveries?

Women are, in fact, so much degraded by mistaken notions of female excellence, that I do not mean to add a paradox when I assert that this artificial weakness produces a propensity to tyrannize, and gives birth to cunning, the natural opponent of strength, which leads them to play off those contemptible infantine airs that undermine esteem even whilst they excite desire. Let men become more chaste and modest, and if women do not grow wiser in the same ratio, it will be clear that they have weaker understandings. It seems scarcely necessary to say, that I now speak of the sex in general. Many individuals have more sense than their male relatives; and, as nothing preponderates where there is a constant struggle for an equilibrium, without it has[2] naturally more gravity, some women govern their husbands without degrading themselves, because intellect will always govern.

---

7. I.e., the lessons in music, dancing, art, and needlework that were central elements in the education provided for genteel young women and that were supposed to enhance their value on the marriage market.
8. An echo of Shakespeare's *Hamlet* (ca. 1600), 3.1.143–44 [editor's note].

9. Harem, the women's quarters in a Muslim household.
1. "A lively writer, I cannot recollect his name, asks what business women turned of forty have to do in the world?" [Wollstonecraft's note].
2. We would probably say, "without its having."

Chapter I

The Rights and Involved Duties of Mankind Considered

In the present state of society it appears necessary to go back to first principles in search of the most simple truths, and to dispute with some prevailing prejudice every inch of ground. To clear my way, I must be allowed to ask some plain questions, and the answers will probably appear as unequivocal as the axioms on which reasoning is built; though, when entangled with various motives of action, they are formally contradicted, either by the words or conduct of men.

In what does man's pre-eminence over the brute creation consist? The answer is as clear as that a half is less than the whole; in Reason.

What acquirement exalts one being above another? Virtue; we spontaneously reply.

For what purpose were the passions implanted? That man by struggling with them might attain a degree of knowledge denied to the brutes; whispers Experience.

Consequently the perfection of our nature and capability of happiness, must be estimated by the degree of reason, virtue, and knowledge, that distinguish the individual, and direct the laws which bind society: and that from the exercise of reason, knowledge and virtue naturally flow, is equally undeniable, if mankind be viewed collectively.

The rights and duties of man thus simplified, it seems almost impertinent to attempt to illustrate truths that appear so incontrovertible; yet such deeply rooted prejudices have clouded reason, and such spurious qualities have assumed the name of virtues, that it is necessary to pursue the course of reason as it has been perplexed and involved in error, by various adventitious circumstances, comparing the simple axiom with casual deviations.

Men, in general, seem to employ their reason to justify prejudices, which they have imbibed, they can scarcely trace how, rather than to root them out. The mind must be strong that resolutely forms its own principles; for a kind of intellectual cowardice prevails which makes many men shrink from the task, or only do it by halves. Yet the imperfect conclusions thus drawn, are frequently very plausible, because they are built on partial experience, on just, though narrow, views.

Going back to first principles, vice skulks, with all its native deformity, from close investigation; but a set of shallow reasoners are always exclaiming that these arguments prove too much, and that a measure rotten at the core may be expedient. Thus expediency is continually contrasted with simple principles, till truth is lost in a mist of words, virtue, in forms, and knowledge rendered a sounding nothing, by the specious prejudices that assume its name.

That the society is formed in the wisest manner, whose constitution is founded on the nature of man, strikes, in the abstract, every thinking being so forcibly, that it looks like presumption to endeavour to bring forward proofs; though proof must be brought, or the strong hold of prescription will never be forced by reason; yet to urge prescription as an argument to justify the depriving men (or women) of their natural rights, is one of the absurd sophisms which daily insult common sense.

* * *

Chapter II

The Prevailing Opinion of a Sexual Character Discussed

To account for, and excuse the tyranny of man, many ingenious arguments have been brought forward to prove, that the two sexes, in the acquirement of virtue, ought to aim at attaining a very different character: or, to speak explicitly, women are not allowed to have sufficient strength of mind to acquire what really deserves the name of virtue. Yet it should seem, allowing them to have souls, that there is but one way appointed by Providence to lead *mankind* to either virtue or happiness.

If then women are not a swarm of ephemeron triflers,[3] why should they be kept in ignorance under the specious name of innocence? Men complain, and with reason, of the follies and caprices of our sex, when they do not keenly satirize our headstrong passions and groveling vices.—Behold, I should answer, the natural effect of ignorance! The mind will ever be unstable that has only prejudices to rest on, and the current will run with destructive fury when there are no barriers to break its force. Women are told from their infancy, and taught by the example of their mothers, that a little knowledge of human weakness, justly termed cunning, softness of temper, *outward* obedience, and a scrupulous attention to a puerile kind of propriety, will obtain for them the protection of man; and should they be beautiful, every thing else is needless, for, at least, twenty years of their lives.

Thus Milton describes our first frail mother; though when he tells us that women are formed for softness and sweet attractive grace,[4] I cannot comprehend his meaning, unless, in the true Mahometan strain, he meant to deprive us of souls,[5] and insinuate that we were beings only designed by sweet attractive grace, and docile blind obedience, to gratify the senses of man when he can no longer soar on the wing of contemplation.

How grossly do they insult us who thus advise us only to render ourselves gentle, domestic brutes! For instance, the winning softness so warmly, and frequently, recommended, that governs by obeying. What childish expressions, and how insignificant is the being—can it be an immortal one?—who will condescend to govern by such sinister methods! 'Certainly,' says Lord Bacon, 'man is of kin to the beasts by his body; and if he be not of kin to God by his spirit, he is a base and ignoble creature!'[6] Men, indeed, appear to me to act in a very unphilosophical manner when they try to secure the good conduct of women by attempting to keep them always in a state of childhood. Rousseau[7] was more consistent when he wished to stop the progress of reason in both sexes, for if men eat of the tree of knowledge, women will come in for a taste; but, from the imperfect cultivation which their understandings now receive, they only attain a knowledge of evil.[8]

---

3. That is, like frivolous insects who live only a day [editor's note].
4. See *Paradise Lost* (1674), 4.298, by the English poet John Milton (1608–1674) [editor's note].
5. That is, deny that we have souls [editor's note].
6. Quoted from "Of Atheism," essay 16 in *The Essays or Counsels, Civil and Moral* (1597), by the English philosopher and statesman Francis Bacon (1561–1626); Wollstonecraft's exclamation mark [editor's note].

7. Jean-Jacques Rousseau (1712–1778), Swiss-born French philosopher and political theorist who was a major influence on Wollstonecraft, though she attacked his views on women [editor's note].
8. Both Adam and Eve ate the fruit from the tree of knowledge of good and evil in the garden of Eden. In the fallen state both men and women need to work at virtue, but according to Wollstonecraft, women have been denied the education, and thus the means, to attain it.

Children, I grant, should be innocent; but when the epithet is applied to men, or women, it is but a civil term for weakness. For if it be allowed that women were destined by Providence to acquire human virtues, and by the exercise of their understandings, that stability of character which is the firmest ground to rest our future hopes upon, they must be permitted to turn to the fountain of light, and not forced to shape their course by the twinkling of a mere satellite. Milton, I grant, was of a very different opinion; for he only bends to the indefeasible right of beauty, though it would be difficult to render two passages which I now mean to contrast, consistent. But into similar inconsistencies are great men often led by their senses.

> 'To whom thus Eve with *perfect beauty* adorn'd.
> 'My Author and Disposer, what thou bidst
> '*Unargued* I obey; So God ordains;
> 'God is *thy law, thou mine:* to know no more
> 'Is Woman's *happiest* knowledge and her *praise*.[9]

These are exactly the arguments that I have used to children; but I have added, your reason is now gaining strength, and, till it arrives at some degree of maturity, you must look up to me for advice—then you ought to *think*, and only rely on God.

Yet in the following lines Milton seems to coincide with me; when he makes Adam thus expostulate with his Maker.

> 'Hast thou not made me here thy substitute,
> 'And these inferior far beneath me set?
> 'Among *unequals* what society
> 'Can sort, what harmony or true delight?
> 'Which must be mutual, in proportion due
> 'Giv'n and receiv'd; but in *disparity*
> 'The one intense, the other still remiss
> 'Cannot well suit with either, but soon prove
> 'Tedious alike: of *fellowship* I speak
> 'Such as I seek, fit to participate
> 'All rational delight[1]—

In treating, therefore, of the manners of women, let us, disregarding sensual arguments, trace what we should endeavour to make them in order to co-operate, if the expression be not too bold, with the supreme Being.

By individual education, I mean, for the sense of the word is not precisely defined, such an attention to a child as will slowly sharpen the senses, form the temper,[2] regulate the passions as they begin to ferment, and set the understanding to work before the body arrives at maturity; so that the man may only have to proceed, not to begin, the important task of learning to think and reason.

To prevent any misconstruction, I must add, that I do not believe that a private education can work the wonders which some sanguine writers have

---

9. *Paradise Lost* 4.634–38. The italics are Wollstonecraft's.
1. *Paradise Lost* 8.381–91. The italics are Wollstonecraft's.
2. Temperament, character.

attributed to it. Men and women must be educated, in a great degree, by the opinions and manners of the society they live in. In every age there has been a stream of popular opinion that has carried all before it, and given a family character, as it were, to the century. It may then fairly be inferred, that, till society be differently constituted, much cannot be expected from education. It is, however, sufficient for my present purpose to assert, that, whatever effect circumstances have on the abilities, every being may become virtuous by the exercise of its own reason; for if but one being was created with vicious inclinations, that is positively bad, what can save us from atheism? or if we worship a God, is not that God a devil?

Consequently, the most perfect education, in my opinion, is such an exercise of the understanding as is best calculated to strengthen the body and form the heart. Or, in other words, to enable the individual to attain such habits of virtue as will render it independent. In fact, it is a farce to call any being virtuous whose virtues do not result from the exercise of its own reason. This was Rousseau's opinion respecting men: I extend it to women, and confidently assert that they have been drawn out of their sphere by false refinement, and not by an endeavour to acquire masculine qualities. Still the regal homage which they receive is so intoxicating, that till the manners of the times are changed, and formed on more reasonable principles, it may be impossible to convince them that the illegitimate power, which they obtain, by degrading themselves, is a curse, and that they must return to nature and equality if they wish to secure the placid satisfaction that unsophisticated affections impart. But for this epoch we must wait—wait, perhaps, till kings and nobles, enlightened by reason, and, preferring the real dignity of man to childish state, throw off their gaudy hereditary trappings: and if then women do not resign the arbitrary power of beauty—they will prove that they have *less* mind than man.

I may be accused of arrogance; still I must declare what I firmly believe, that all the writers who have written on the subject of female education and manners from Rousseau to Dr. Gregory,[3] have contributed to render women more artificial, weak characters, than they would otherwise have been; and, consequently, more useless members of society. I might have expressed this conviction in a lower key; but I am afraid it would have been the whine of affectation, and not the faithful expression of my feelings, of the clear result, which experience and reflection have led me to draw. When I come to that division of the subject, I shall advert to the passages that I more particularly disapprove of, in the works of the authors I have just alluded to; but it is first necessary to observe, that my objection extends to the whole purport of those books, which tend, in my opinion, to degrade one half of the human species, and render women pleasing at the expense of every solid virtue.

Though, to reason on Rousseau's ground, if man did attain a degree of perfection of mind when his body arrived at maturity, it might be proper, in order to make a man and his wife *one*, that she should rely entirely on his understanding; and the graceful ivy, clasping the oak that supported it, would form a whole in which strength and beauty would be equally conspicuous. But, alas! husbands, as well as their helpmates, are often only overgrown children;

3. John Gregory (1724–1773), Scottish physician, philosopher, and professor at the University of Edinburgh; author of a widely read advice book, *A Father's Legacy to His Daughters* (1774).

nay, thanks to early debauchery, scarcely men in their outward form—and if the blind lead the blind, one need not come from heaven to tell us the consequence.[4]

Many are the causes that, in the present corrupt state of society, contribute to enslave women by cramping their understandings and sharpening their senses. One, perhaps, that silently does more mischief than all the rest, is their disregard of order.

To do every thing in an orderly manner, is a most important precept, which women, who, generally speaking, receive only a disorderly kind of education, seldom attend to with that degree of exactness that men, who from their infancy are broken into method, observe. This negligent kind of guess-work, for what other epithet can be used to point out the random exertions of a sort of instinctive common sense, never brought to the test of reason? prevents their generalizing matters of fact—so they do to-day, what they did yesterday, merely because they did it yesterday.

This contempt of the understanding in early life has more baneful consequences than is commonly supposed; for the little knowledge which women of strong minds attain, is, from various circumstances, of a more desultory kind than the knowledge of men, and it is acquired more by sheer observations on real life, than from comparing what has been individually observed with the results of experience generalized by speculation. Led by their dependent situation and domestic employments more into society, what they learn is rather by snatches; and as learning is with them, in general, only a secondary thing, they do not pursue any one branch with that persevering ardour necessary to give vigour to the faculties, and clearness to the judgment. In the present state of society, a little learning is required to support the character of a gentleman; and boys are obliged to submit to a few years of discipline. But in the education of women, the cultivation of the understanding is always subordinate to the acquirement of some corporeal accomplishment; even while enervated by confinement and false notions of modesty, the body is prevented from attaining that grace and beauty which relaxed half-formed limbs never exhibit. Besides, in youth their faculties are not brought forward by emulation; and having no serious scientific study, if they have natural sagacity it is turned too soon on life and manners. They dwell on effects, and modifications, without tracing them back to causes; and complicated rules to adjust behaviour are a weak substitute for simple principles.

As a proof that education gives this appearance of weakness to females, we may instance the example of military men, who are, like them, sent into the world before their minds have been stored with knowledge or fortified by principles. The consequences are similar; soldiers acquire a little superficial knowledge, snatched from the muddy current of conversation, and, from continually mixing with society, they gain, what is termed a knowledge of the world; and this acquaintance with manners and customs has frequently been confounded with a knowledge of the human heart. But can the crude fruit of casual observation, never brought to the test of judgment, formed by comparing speculation and experience, deserve such a distinction? Soldiers,

4. Matthew 15:14: "And if the blind lead the blind, both shall fall into the ditch." "One . . . from heaven": Jesus.

as well as women, practice the minor virtues with punctilious politeness. Where is then the sexual difference, when the education has been the same? All the difference that I can discern, arises from the superior advantage of liberty, which enables the former to see more of life.

It is wandering from my present subject, perhaps, to make a political remark; but, as it was produced naturally by the train of my reflections, I shall not pass it silently over.

Standing armies can never consist of resolute, robust men; they may be well disciplined machines, but they will seldom contain men under the influence of strong passions, or with very vigorous faculties. And as for any depth of understanding, I will venture to affirm, that it is as rarely to be found in the army as amongst women; and the cause, I maintain, is the same. It may be further observed, that officers are also particularly attentive to their persons, fond of dancing, crowded rooms, adventures, and ridicule.[5] Like the *fair* sex,[6] the business of their lives is gallantry.—They were taught to please, and they only live to please. Yet they do not lose their rank in the distinction of sexes, for they are still reckoned superior to women, though in what their superiority consists, beyond what I have just mentioned, it is difficult to discover.

The great misfortune is this, that they both acquire manners before morals, and a knowledge of life before they have, from reflection, any acquaintance with the grand ideal outline of human nature. The consequence is natural; satisfied with common nature, they become a prey to prejudices, and taking all their opinions on credit, they blindly submit to authority. So that, if they have any sense, it is a kind of instinctive glance, that catches proportions, and decides with respect to manners; but fails when arguments are to be pursued below the surface, or opinions analyzed.

May not the same remark be applied to women? Nay, the argument may be carried still further, for they are both thrown out of a useful station by the unnatural distinctions established in civilized life. Riches and hereditary honours have made cyphers of women to give consequence to the numerical figure;[7] and idleness has produced a mixture of gallantry and despotism into society, which leads the very men who are the slaves of their mistresses to tyrannize over their sisters, wives, and daughters. This is only keeping them in rank and file, it is true. Strengthen the female mind by enlarging it, and there will be an end to blind obedience; but, as blind obedience is ever sought for by power, tyrants and sensualists are in the right when they endeavour to keep women in the dark, because the former only want slaves, and the latter a play-thing. The sensualist, indeed, has been the most dangerous of tyrants, and women have been duped by their lovers, as princes by their ministers, whilst dreaming that they reigned over them.

I now principally allude to Rousseau, for his character of Sophia[8] is, undoubtedly, a captivating one, though it appears to me grossly unnatural;

---

5. "Why should women be censured with petulant acrimony, because they seem to have a passion for a scarlet coat? Has not education placed them more on a level with soldiers than any other class of men?" [Wollstonecraft's note].

6. Women.

7. As a zero added to a number multiplies its value by a factor of ten, in a hierarchical society women magnify the status of the men with whom they are allied.

8. "*Sophie on la Femme*" is the title of Book 5 of *Émile* [1762] (translatable either as "Sophie, or, The Wife" or "Sophie, or, The Woman"). Having tracked the development of Émile, his imaginary pupil, up to age twenty, Rousseau invents the character of Sophie (Sophia in the 1762 English translation) to supply his hero with a wife and to address, belatedly, the topic of female education.

however it is not the superstructure, but the foundation of her character, the principles on which her education was built, that I mean to attack; nay, warmly as I admire the genius of that able writer, whose opinions I shall often have occasion to cite, indignation always takes place of admiration, and the rigid frown of insulted virtue effaces the smile of complacency, which his eloquent periods are wont to raise, when I read his voluptuous reveries. Is this the man, who, in his ardour for virtue, would banish all the soft arts of peace, and almost carry us back to Spartan discipline? Is this the man who delights to paint the useful struggles of passion, the triumphs of good dispositions, and the heroic flights which carry the glowing soul out of itself?—How are these mighty sentiments lowered when he describes the pretty foot and enticing airs of his little favourite! But, for the present, I wave[9] the subject, and, instead of severely reprehending the transient effusions of overweening sensibility, I shall only observe, that whoever has cast a benevolent eye on society, must often have been gratified by the sight of a humble mutual love, not dignified by sentiment, or strengthened by a union in intellectual pursuits. The domestic trifles of the day have afforded matters for cheerful converse, and innocent caresses have softened toils which did not require great exercise of mind or stretch of thought: yet, has not the sight of this moderate felicity excited more tenderness than respect? An emotion similar to what we feel when children are playing, or animals sporting, whilst the contemplation of the noble struggles of suffering merit has raised admiration, and carried our thoughts to that world where sensation will give place to reason.

Women are, therefore, to be considered either as moral beings, or so weak that they must be entirely subjected to the superior faculties of men.

Let us examine this question. Rousseau declares that a woman should never, for a moment, feel herself independent, that she should be governed by fear to exercise her natural cunning, and made a coquetish slave in order to render her a more alluring object of desire, a *sweeter* companion to man, whenever he chooses to relax himself. He carries the arguments, which he pretends to draw from the indications of nature, still further, and insinuates that truth and fortitude, the corner stones of all human virtue, should be cultivated with certain restrictions, because, with respect to the female character, obedience is the grand lesson which ought to be impressed with unrelenting rigour.

What nonsense! when will a great man arise with sufficient strength of mind to puff away the fumes which pride and sensuality have thus spread over the subject! If women are by nature inferior to men, their virtues must be the same in quality, if not in degree, or virtue is a relative idea; consequently, their conduct should be founded on the same principles, and have the same aim.

Connected with man as daughters, wives, and mothers, their moral character may be estimated by their manner of fulfilling those simple duties; but the end, the grand end of their exertions should be to unfold their own faculties and acquire the dignity of conscious virtue. They may try to render their road pleasant; but ought never to forget, in common with man, that life yields

9. Waive; pass over [editor's note].

not the felicity which can satisfy an immortal soul. I do not mean to insinuate, that either sex should be so lost in abstract reflections or distant views,
as to forget the affections and duties that lie before them, and are, in truth,
the means appointed to produce the fruit of life; on the contrary, I would
warmly recommend them, even while I assert, that they afford most satisfaction when they are considered in their true, sober light.

Probably the prevailing opinion, that woman was created for man, may
have taken its rise from Moses's poetical story;[1] yet, as very few, it is presumed, who have bestowed any serious thought on the subject, ever supposed
that Eve was, literally speaking, one of Adam's ribs, the deduction must be
allowed to fall to the ground; or, only be so far admitted as it proves that man,
from the remotest antiquity, found it convenient to exert his strength to subjugate his companion, and his invention to shew that she ought to have her
neck bent under the yoke, because the whole creation was only created for his
convenience or pleasure.

Let it not be concluded that I wish to invert the order of things; I have
already granted, that, from the constitution of their bodies, men seem to be
designed by Providence to attain a greater degree of virtue. I speak collectively of the whole sex; but I see not the shadow of a reason to conclude that
their virtues should differ in respect to their nature. In fact, how can they, if
virtue has only one eternal standard? I must therefore, if I reason consequentially, as strenuously maintain that they have the same simple direction,
as that there is a God.

It follows then that cunning should not be opposed to wisdom, little cares
to great exertions, or insipid softness, varnished over with the name of
gentleness, to that fortitude which grand views alone can inspire.

I shall be told that woman would then lose many of her peculiar graces,
and the opinion of a well known poet might be quoted to refute my unqualified assertion. For Pope has said, in the name of the whole male sex,

> 'Yet ne'er so sure our passion to create,
> 'As when she touch'd the brink of all we hate.'[2]

In what light this sally[3] places men and women, I shall leave to the judi-
cious to determine; meanwhile I shall content myself with observing, that
I cannot discover why, unless they are mortal,[4] females should always be
degraded by being made subservient to love or lust.

To speak disrespectfully of love is, I know, high treason against sentiment
and fine feelings; but I wish to speak the simple language of truth, and rather
to address the head than the heart. To endeavour to reason love out of the
world, would be to out Quixote Cervantes,[5] and equally offend against common sense; but an endeavour to restrain this tumultuous passion, and to
prove that it should not be allowed to dethrone superior powers, or to usurp

---

1. See Genesis 2:21–23 for one account of the creation of woman. Moses was thought to be the
author of the first five books of the Old Testament
(the Pentateuch).
2. Quoted from Epistle 2, *To a Lady. Of the Characters of Women* (1735), lines 51–52, the second of
the *Moral Essays* by the English poet Alexander

Pope (1688–1744) [editor's note].
3. Quip [editor's note].
4. That is, unless they are thought to lack immortal
souls [editor's note].
5. I.e., to outdo the idealistic but ineffectual hero
of Miguel de Cervantes's *Don Quixote* (1605) in
trying to accomplish the impossible.

the sceptre which the understanding should ever coolly wield, appears less wild.

Youth is the season for love in both sexes; but in those days of thoughtless enjoyment provision should be made for the more important years of life, when reflection takes place of sensation. But Rousseau, and most of the male writers who have followed his steps, have warmly inculcated that the whole tendency of female education ought to be directed to one point:—to render them pleasing.

Let me reason with the supporters of this opinion who have any knowledge of human nature, do they imagine that marriage can eradicate the habitude of life? The woman who has only been taught to please will soon find that her charms are oblique sunbeams, and that they cannot have much effect on her husband's heart when they are seen every day, when the summer is passed and gone. Will she then have sufficient native[6] energy to look into herself for comfort, and cultivate her dormant faculties? or, is it not more rational to expect that she will try to please other men; and, in the emotions raised by the expectation of new conquests, endeavour to forget the mortification her love or pride has received? When the husband ceases to be a lover—and the time will inevitably come, her desire of pleasing will then grow languid, or become a spring of bitterness; and love, perhaps, the most evanescent of all passions, gives place to jealousy or vanity.

I now speak of women who are restrained by principle or prejudice; such women, though they would shrink from an intrigue[7] with real abhorrence, yet, nevertheless, wish to be convinced by the homage of gallantry that they are cruelly neglected by their husbands; or, days and weeks are spent in dreaming of the happiness enjoyed by congenial souls till their health is undermined and their spirits broken by discontent. How then can the great art of pleasing be such a necessary study? It is only useful to a mistress; the chaste wife, and serious mother, should only consider her power to please as the polish of her virtues, and the affection of her husband as one of the comforts that render her task less difficult and her life happier.—But, whether she be loved or neglected, her first wish should be to make herself respectable, and not to rely for all her happiness on a being subject to like infirmities with herself.

The worthy Dr. Gregory fell into a similar error. I respect his heart; but entirely disapprove of his celebrated Legacy to his Daughters.

He advises them to cultivate a fondness for dress, because a fondness for dress, he asserts, is natural to them.[8] I am unable to comprehend what either he or Rousseau mean, when they frequently use this indefinite term.[9] If they told us that in a pre-existent state the soul was fond of dress, and brought this inclination with it into a new body, I should listen to them with a half smile, as I often do when I hear a rant about innate elegance.—But if he only meant to say that the exercise of the faculties will produce this fondness—I deny it.—It is not natural; but arises, like false ambition in men, from a love of power.

6. Innate [editor's note].
7. Illicit affair [editor's note].
8. "The love of dress is natural to you, and therefore it is proper and reasonable." John Gregory, A

Father's Legacy to His Daughters, 2nd ed. [London, 1775], p. 55; all references are to this edition.
9. I.e., "natural."

Dr. Gregory goes much further; he actually recommends dissimulation, and advises an innocent girl to give the lie to her feelings, and not dance with spirit, when gaiety of heart would make her feel eloquent without making her gestures immodest. In the name of truth and common sense, why should not one woman acknowledge that she can take more exercise than another? or, in other words, that she has a sound constitution; and why, to damp innocent vivacity, is she darkly to be told that men will draw conclusions which she little thinks of?[1]—Let the libertine draw what inference he pleases; but, I hope, that no sensible mother will restrain the natural frankness of youth by instilling such indecent cautions. Out of the abundance of the heart the mouth speaketh;[2] and a wiser than Solomon hath said, that the heart should be made clean,[3] and not trivial ceremonies observed, which it is not very difficult to fulfill with scrupulous exactness when vice reigns in the heart.

Women ought to endeavour to purify their heart; but can they do so when their uncultivated understandings make them entirely dependent on their senses for employment and amusement, when no noble pursuit sets them above the little vanities of the day, or enables them to curb the wild emotions that agitate a reed over which every passing breeze has power? To gain the affections of a virtuous man is affectation necessary? Nature has given woman a weaker frame than man; but, to ensure her husband's affections, must a wife, who by the exercise of her mind and body whilst she was discharging the duties of a daughter, wife, and mother, has allowed her constitution to retain its natural strength, and her nerves a healthy tone, is she, I say, to condescend to use art and feign a sickly delicacy in order to secure her husband's affection? Weakness may excite tenderness, and gratify the arrogant pride of man; but the lordly caresses of a protector will not gratify a noble mind that pants for, and deserves to be respected. Fondness is a poor substitute for friendship!

In a seraglio, I grant, that all these arts are necessary; the epicure must have his palate tickled, or he will sink into apathy; but have women so little ambition as to be satisfied with such a condition? Can they supinely dream life away in the lap of pleasure, or the languor of weariness, rather than assert their claim to pursue reasonable pleasures and render themselves conspicuous by practising the virtues which dignify mankind? Surely she has not an immortal soul who can loiter life away merely employed to adorn her person, that she may amuse the languid hours, and soften the cares of a fellow-creature who is willing to be enlivened by her smiles and tricks, when the serious business of life is over.

Besides, the woman who strengthens her body and exercises her mind will, by managing her family and practising various virtues, become the friend, and not the humble dependent of her husband; and if she, by possessing such substantial qualities, merit his regard, she will not find it necessary to conceal her affection; nor to pretend to an unnatural coldness of constitution to excite her husband's passions. In fact, if we revert to history, we shall find

---

1. For this and the previous sentence see Gregory, pp. 57–58: "I would have you to dance with spirit; but never allow yourselves to be so far transported with mirth, as to forget the delicacy of your sex.— Many a girl dancing in the gaiety and innocence of her heart, is thought to discover a spirit she little dreams of."

2. Matthew 12:34.
3. "Wiser than Solomon": Jesus (who describes himself in comparable terms in Luke 11:31). In Luke 11:39–44 and Matthew 23:25–28, Jesus speaks of purifying the inner self and denounces the Pharisees' self-righteous observance of the letter of the law.

that the women who have distinguished themselves have neither been the most beautiful nor the most gentle[4] of their sex.

Nature, or, to speak with strict propriety, God, has made all things right; but man has sought him out many inventions to mar the work. I now allude to that part of Dr. Gregory's treatise, where he advises a wife never to let her husband know the extent of her sensibility or affection.[5] Voluptuous precaution, and as ineffectual as absurd.—Love, from its very nature, must be transitory. To seek for a secret that would render it constant, would be as wild a search as for the philosopher's stone, or the grand panacea:[6] and the discovery would be equally useless, or rather pernicious to mankind. The most holy band of society is friendship. It has been well said, by a shrewd satirist, "that rare as true love is, true friendship is still rarer."[7]

This is an obvious truth, and the cause not lying deep, will not elude a slight glance of inquiry.

Love, the common[8] passion, in which chance and sensation take place of choice and reason, is, in some degree, felt by the mass of mankind; for it is not necessary to speak, at present, of the emotions that rise above or sink below love. This passion, naturally increased by suspense and difficulties, draws the mind out of its accustomed state, and exalts the affections; but [in] the security of marriage, allowing the fever of love to subside, a healthy temperature is thought insipid only by those who have not sufficient intellect to substitute the calm tenderness of friendship, the confidence of respect, instead of blind admiration, and the sensual emotions of fondness.

This is, must be, the course of nature.—Friendship or indifference inevitably succeeds love.—And this constitution seems perfectly to harmonize with the system of government which prevails in the moral world. Passions are spurs to action, and open the mind; but they sink into mere appetites, become a personal and momentary gratification, when the object is gained, and the satisfied mind rests in enjoyment. The man who had some virtue whilst he was struggling for a crown, often becomes a voluptuous tyrant when it graces his brow; and, when the lover is not lost in the husband, the dotard, a prey to childish caprices, and fond jealousies, neglects the serious duties of life, and the caresses which should excite confidence in his children are lavished on the overgrown child, his wife.

In order to fulfil the duties of life, and to be able to pursue with vigour the various employments which form the moral character, a master and mistress of a family ought not to continue to love each other with passion. I mean to say, that they ought not to indulge those emotions which disturb the order of society, and engross the thoughts that should be otherwise employed. The mind that has never been engrossed by one object wants[9] vigour—if it can long be so, it is weak.

A mistaken education, a narrow, uncultivated mind, and many sexual

<hr />

4. Noble, refined [editor's note].
5. Gregory, pp. 86–87: "If you love him, let me advise you never to discover to him the full extent of your love, no, not although you marry him."
6. A medicine reputed to cure all diseases. "Philosopher's stone": sought by alchemists because it was supposed to have the power to transmute base metals into gold.

7. La Rochefoucauld (1613–1680, French noble), Les Maximes, No. 473: "Quelque rare que soit que la véritable amour, il l'est encore moins que la véritable amitié."
8. That is: love, considered as the commonplace passion it so often is [editor's note].
9. Lacks [editor's note].

prejudices, tend to make women more constant than men; but, for the present, I shall not touch on this branch of the subject. I will go still further, and advance, without dreaming of a paradox, that an unhappy marriage is often very advantageous to a family, and that the neglected wife is, in general, the best mother.[1] And this would almost always be the consequence if the female mind were more enlarged: for, it seems to be the common dispensation of Providence, that what we gain in present enjoyment should be deducted[2] from the treasure of life, experience; and that when we are gathering the flowers of the day and revelling in pleasure, the solid fruit of toil and wisdom should not be caught[3] at the same time. The way lies before us, we must turn to the right or left; and he who will pass life away in bounding from one pleasure to another, must not complain if he acquire neither wisdom nor respectability of character.

Supposing, for a moment, that the soul is not immortal, and that man was only created for the present scene,—I think we should have reason to complain that love, infantine fondness, ever grew insipid and palled upon the sense. Let us eat, drink, and love, for tomorrow we die, would be, in fact, the language of reason, the morality of life; and who but a fool would part with a reality for a fleeting shadow? But, if awed by observing the improbable[4] powers of the mind, we disdain to confine our wishes or thoughts to such a comparatively mean field of action, that only appears grand and important, as it is connected with a boundless prospect and sublime hopes, what necessity is there for falsehood in conduct, and why must the sacred majesty of truth be violated to detain a deceitful good that saps the very foundation of virtue? Why must the female mind be tainted by coquetish arts to gratify the sensualist, and prevent love from subsiding into friendship, or compassionate tenderness, when there are not qualities on which friendship can be built? Let the honest heart shew itself, and *reason* teach passion to submit to necessity; or, let the dignified pursuit of virtue and knowledge raise the mind above those emotions which rather imbitter than sweeten the cup of life, when they are not restrained within due bounds.

I do not mean to allude to the romantic passion, which is the concomitant of genius.—Who can clip its wing? But that grand passion not proportioned to the puny enjoyments of life, is only true to the sentiment, and feeds on itself. The passions which have been celebrated for their durability have always been unfortunate. They have acquired strength by absence and constitutional melancholy.—The fancy has hovered round a form of beauty dimly seen—but familiarity might have turned admiration into disgust; or, at least, into indifference, and allowed the imagination leisure to start fresh game. With perfect propriety, according to this view of things, does Rousseau make the mistress of his soul, Eloisa, love St. Preux, when life was fading before her;[5] but this is no proof of the immortality of the passion.

---

1. Wollstonecraft's point is that a woman who is not preoccupied with her husband (and his attentions to her) has more time and energy for her children.
2. That is, will be subtracted [editor's note].
3. That is, cannot be attained [editor's note].
4. The first edition reads "improvable" here, which makes more sense in context.
5. In Rousseau's *Julie; ou la Nouvelle Héloïse* (1761), the heroine, Julie, reveals her long-held passionate love for St. Preux as she is dying, even though she has been a faithful wife to Wolmar throughout the novel.

Of the same complexion is Dr. Gregory's advice respecting delicacy of sentiment, which he advises a woman not to acquire, if she have determined to marry.[6] This determination, however, perfectly consistent with his former advice, he calls *indelicate*, and earnestly persuades his daughters to conceal it, though it may govern their conduct;—as if it were indelicate to have the common appetites of human nature.

Noble morality! and consistent with the cautious prudence of a little soul that cannot extend its views beyond the present minute division of existence. If all the faculties of woman's mind are only to be cultivated as they respect her dependence on man; if, when a husband be obtained, she have arrived at her goal, and meanly proud rests satisfied with such a paltry crown, let her grovel contentedly, scarcely raised by her employments above the animal kingdom; but, if, struggling for the prize of her high calling,[7] she look beyond the present scene, let her cultivate her understanding without stopping to consider what character the husband may have whom she is destined to marry. Let her only determine, without being too anxious about present happiness, to acquire the qualities that ennoble a rational being, and a rough inelegant husband may shock her taste without destroying her peace of mind. She will not model her soul to suit the frailties of her companion, but to bear with them: his character may be a trial, but not an impediment to virtue.

If Dr. Gregory confined his remark to romantic expectations of constant love and congenial feelings, he should have recollected that experience will banish what advice can never make us cease to wish for, when the imagination is kept alive at the expence of reason.

I own it frequently happens that women who have fostered a romantic unnatural delicacy of feeling, waste their lives in *imagining* how happy they should have been with a husband who could love them with a fervid increasing affection every day, and all day. But they might as well pine married as single—and would not be a jot more unhappy with a bad husband than longing for a good one. That a proper education; or, to speak with more precision, a well stored mind, would enable a woman to support a single life with dignity, I grant; but that she should avoid cultivating her taste, lest her husband should occasionally shock it, is quitting a substance for a shadow. To say the truth, I do not know of what use is an improved taste, if the individual be not rendered more independent of the casualties[8] of life; if new sources of enjoyment, only dependent on the solitary operations of the mind, are not opened. People of taste, married or single, without distinction, will ever be disgusted by various things that touch not[9] less observing minds. On this conclusion the argument must not be allowed to hinge; but in the whole sum of enjoyment is taste to be denominated a blessing?

The question is, whether it procures most pain or pleasure? The answer will decide the propriety of Dr. Gregory's advice, and shew how absurd and tyrannic it is thus to lay down a system of slavery; or to attempt to educate

---

6. Gregory, pp. 116–18: "But if you find that marriage is absolutely essential to your happiness . . . shun . . . reading and conversation that warms the imagination, which engages and softens the heart, and raises the taste above the level of common life . . . [otherwise] you may be tired with insipidity and dullness; shocked with indelicacy, or morti-

fied by indifference."
7. An echo of Philippians 3:14, where Saint Paul writes, "I press toward the mark for the prize of the high calling of God in Christ Jesus."
8. Chance occurrences [editor's note]
9. That do not touch; that are not noticed by [editor's note].

moral beings by any other rules than those deduced from pure reason, which apply to the whole species.

Gentleness[1] of manners, forbearance and long-suffering, are such amiable Godlike qualities, that in sublime poetic strains the Deity has been invested with them; and, perhaps, no representation of his goodness so strongly fastens on the human affections as those that represent him abundant in mercy and willing to pardon. Gentleness, considered in this point of view, bears on its front all the characteristics of grandeur, combined with the winning graces of condescension;[2] but what a different aspect it assumes when it is the submissive demeanour of dependence, the support of weakness that loves, because it wants protection; and is forbearing, because it must silently endure injuries; smiling under the lash at which it dare not snarl. Abject as this picture appears, it is the portrait of an accomplished woman, according to the received opinion of female excellence, separated by specious reasoners from human excellence.[3] Or, they[4] kindly restore the rib,[5] and make one moral being of a man and woman; not forgetting to give her all the 'submissive charms.'[6]

How women are to exist in that state where there is to be neither marrying nor giving in marriage, we are not told.[7] For though moralists have agreed that the tenor of life seems to prove that *man* is prepared by various circumstances for a future state, they constantly concur in advising *woman* only to provide for the present. Gentleness, docility, and a spaniel-like affection are, on this ground, consistently recommended as the cardinal virtues of the sex; and, disregarding the arbitrary economy of nature, one writer has declared that it is masculine for a woman to be melancholy. She was created to be the toy of man, his rattle, and it must jingle in his ears whenever, dismissing reason, he chooses to be amused.

To recommend gentleness, indeed, on a broad basis is strictly philosophical. A frail being should labour to be gentle. But when forbearance confounds right and wrong, it ceases to be a virtue; and, however convenient it may be found in a companion—that companion will ever be considered as an inferior, and only inspire a vapid tenderness, which easily degenerates into contempt. Still, if advice could really make a being gentle, whose natural disposition admitted not of such a fine polish, something towards the advancement of order would be attained; but if, as might quickly be demonstrated, only affectation be produced by this indiscriminate counsel, which throws a stumbling-block in the way of gradual improvement, and true melioration of temper, the sex is not much benefited by sacrificing solid virtues to the attainment of superficial graces, though for a few years they may procure the individuals regal sway.

As a philosopher, I read with indignation the plausible[8] epithets which men use to soften their insults; and, as a moralist, I ask what is meant by such het-

---

1. Refinement [editor's note].
2. Courteous disregard of difference in rank. "Front": face.
3. Note the intended emphases: "according to the received opinion of *female* excellence, separated by specious [i.e., deceptively appealing but faulty] reasoners from *human* excellence"—for Wollstonecraft, a grievous error and serious wrong [editor's note].
4. "Vide Rousseau, and Swedenborg" [Wollstonecraft's note]. The Swedish mystic Emmanuel Swedenborg (1688–1772) believed that in the afterlife

each married couple would form a single angel, with the wife contributing her capacity for love and the husband his wisdom.
5. According to an account given in Genesis 2:21–23, God took one of the ribs of man (Adam) to create woman (Eve) [editor's note].
6. *Paradise Lost* 4.497–99: "he in delight / Both of her Beauty and submissive charms / Smil'd with superior love."
7. An echo of Jesus' account of the resurrection in Matthew 22:30.
8. Agreeable, ingratiating [editor's note].

erogeneous associations, as fair defects, amiable weaknesses, &c.?[9] If there be but one criterion of morals, but one archetype for man, women appear to be suspended by destiny, according to the vulgar tale of Mahomet's coffin;[1] they have neither the unerring instinct of brutes, nor are allowed to fix the eye of reason on a perfect model. They were made to be loved, and must not aim at respect, lest they should be hunted out of society as masculine.

But to view the subject in another point of view. Do passive indolent women make the best wives? Confining our discussion to the present moment of existence, let us see how such weak creatures perform their part? Do the women who, by the attainment of a few superficial accomplishments, have strengthened the prevailing prejudice, merely contribute to the happiness of their husbands? Do they display their charms merely to amuse them? And have women, who have early imbibed notions of passive obedience, sufficient character to manage a family or educate children? So far from it, that, after surveying the history of woman, I cannot help, agreeing with the severest satirist, considering the sex as the weakest as well as the most oppressed half of the species. What does history disclose but marks of inferiority, and how few women have emancipated themselves from the galling yoke of sovereign man?—So few, that the exceptions remind me of an ingenious conjecture respecting Newton: that he was probably a being of a superior order, accidentally caged in a human body.[2] Following the same train of thinking, I have been led to imagine that the few extraordinary women who have rushed in eccentrical directions out of the orbit prescribed to their sex, were *male* spirits, confined by mistake in female frames. But if it be not philosophical to think of sex when the soul is mentioned, the inferiority must depend on the organs; or the heavenly fire, which is to ferment the clay, is not given in equal portions.

But avoiding, as I have hitherto done, any direct comparison of the two sexes collectively, or frankly acknowledging the inferiority of woman, according to the present appearance of things, I shall only insist that men have increased that inferiority till women are almost sunk below the standard of rational creatures. Let their faculties have room to unfold, and their virtues to gain strength, and then determine where the whole sex must stand in the intellectual scale. Yet let it be remembered, that for a small number of distinguished women I do not ask a place.

It is difficult for us purblind mortals to say to what height human discoveries and improvements may arrive when the gloom of despotism subsides, which makes us stumble at every step; but, when morality shall be settled on a more solid basis, then, without being gifted with a prophetic spirit, I will venture to predict that woman will be either the friend or slave of man. We shall not, as at present, doubt whether she is a moral agent, or the link which unites man with brutes. But, should it then appear, that like the brutes they

9. *Paradise Lost* 10.891–92: "This fair defect / Of nature"; and Pope, *Of the Characters of Women*, line 44: "Fine by defect, and delicately weak."
1. Wollstonecraft refers to a discredited European legend maintaining that at Muhammad's tomb in Medina giant magnets were used to suspend his coffin in midair.
2. Possibly a reference to Pope's 1733–34 *Essay on*

Man, Epistle II, lines 31–34: "Superior beings, when of late they saw / A mortal Man unfold all Nature's law, / Admir'd such wisdom in an earthly shape, / And shew'd a NEWTON as we shew an Ape." Isaac Newton (1643–1727) was revered across Europe for his foundational work of physics, the *Principia* (1687), in which he formulated the laws of gravitation and motion.

were principally created for the use of man, he will let them patiently bite the bridle, and not mock them with empty praise; or, should their rationality be proved, he will not impede their improvement merely to gratify his sensual appetites. He will not, with all the graces of rhetoric, advise them to submit implicitly their understanding to the guidance of man. He will not, when he treats of the education of women, assert that they ought never to have the free use of reason, nor would he recommend cunning and dissimulation to beings who are acquiring, in like manner as himself, the virtues of humanity.

Surely there can be but one rule of right, if morality has an eternal foundation, and whoever sacrifices virtue, strictly so called, to present convenience, or whose *duty* it is to act in such a manner, lives only for the passing day, and cannot be an accountable creature.

The poet then should have dropped his sneer when he says,

> "If weak women go astray,
> "The stars are more in fault than they."[3]

For that they are bound by the adamantine chain of destiny is most certain, if it be proved that they are never to exercise their own reason, never to be independent, never to rise above opinion, or to feel the dignity of a rational will that only bows to God, and often forgets that the universe contains any being but itself and the model of perfection to which its ardent gaze is turned,[4] to adore attributes that, softened into virtues, may be imitated in kind, though the degree overwhelms the enraptured mind.

If, I say, for I would not impress by declamation when Reason offers her sober light, if they be really capable of acting like rational creatures, let them not be treated like slaves; or, like the brutes who are dependent on the reason of man, when they associate with him; but cultivate their minds, give them the salutary, sublime curb of principle, and let them attain conscious dignity by feeling themselves only dependent on God. Teach them, in common with man, to submit to necessity, instead of giving, to render them more pleasing, a sex to morals.[5]

Further, should experience prove that they cannot attain the same degree of strength of mind, perseverance, and fortitude, let their virtues be the same in kind, though they may vainly struggle for the same degree; and the superiority of man will be equally clear, if not clearer; and truth, as it is a simple principle, which admits of no modification, would be common to both. Nay, the order of society as it is at present regulated would not be inverted, for woman would then only have the rank that reason assigned her, and arts could not be practised to bring the balance even, much less to turn it.

These may be termed Utopian dreams.—Thanks to that Being who impressed them on my soul, and gave me sufficient strength of mind to dare to exert my own reason, till, becoming dependent only on him for the support of my virtue, I view, with indignation, the mistaken notions that enslave my sex.

3. Matthew Prior, "Hans Carvel" (1700), lines 11–12.
4. That is, the material universe (in which causal determinism prevails) contains all beings *with the exceptions of* our "rational will" and God ("the model of perfection") [editor's note].

5. That is, teach women that they as well as men are bound by the rational necessity of morality—which does not have a sex—rather than being creatures exempt from it (and so supposedly more pleasing to men) [editor's note].

I love man as my fellow; but his scepter, real, or usurped, extends not to me, unless the reason of an individual demands my homage; and even then the submission is to reason, and not to man. In fact, the conduct of an accountable being must be regulated by the operations of its own reason; or on what foundation rests the throne of God?

It appears to me necessary to dwell on these obvious truths, because females have been insulated, as it were; and, while they have been stripped of the virtues that should clothe humanity, they have been decked with artificial graces that enable them to exercise a short-lived tyranny. Love, in their bosoms, taking place of every nobler passion, their sole ambition is to be fair, to raise emotion instead of inspiring respect; and this ignoble desire, like the servility in absolute monarchies, destroys all strength of character. Liberty is the mother of virtue, and if women be, by their very constitution, slaves, and not allowed to breathe the sharp invigorating air of freedom, they must ever languish like exotics,[6] and be reckoned beautiful flaws in nature.

As to the argument respecting the subjection in which the sex has ever been held, it retorts on man. The many have always been enthralled by the few; and monsters, who scarcely have shewn any discernment of human excellence, have tyrannized over thousands of their fellow-creatures. Why have men of superior endowments submitted to such degradation? For, is it not universally acknowledged that kings, viewed collectively, have ever been inferior, in abilities and virtue, to the same number of men taken from the common mass of mankind—yet, have they not, and are they not still treated with a degree of reverence that is an insult to reason? China is not the only country where a living man has been made a God.[7] *Men* have submitted to superior strength to enjoy with impunity the pleasure of the moment—*women* have only done the same, and therefore till it is proved that the courtier, who servilely resigns the birthright of a man, is not a moral agent, it cannot be demonstrated that woman is essentially inferior to man because she has always been subjugated.

Brutal force has hitherto governed the world, and that the science of politics is in its infancy, is evident from philosophers scrupling to give the knowledge most useful to man that determinate distinction.

I shall not pursue this argument any further than to establish an obvious inference, that as sound politics diffuse liberty, mankind, including woman, will become more wise and virtuous.

---

6. Hothouse plants, which do not thrive in the English climate.

7. The emperors of China were known as the "sons of heaven."

Chapter III

The Same Subject Continued

* * *

I wish to sum up what I have said in a few words, for I here throw down my gauntlet, and deny the existence of sexual virtues, not excepting modesty. For man and woman, truth, if I understand the meaning of the word, must be the same; yet the fanciful female character, so prettily drawn by poets and novelists, demanding the sacrifice of truth and sincerity, virtue becomes a relative idea, having no other foundation than utility, and of that utility men pretend arbitrarily to judge, shaping it to their own convenience.

Women, I allow, may have different duties to fulfil; but they are *human* duties, and the principles that should regulate the discharge of them, I sturdily maintain, must be the same.

To become respectable, the exercise of their understanding is necessary, there is no other foundation for independence of character; I mean explicitly to say that they must only bow to the authority of reason, instead of being the *modest* slaves of opinion.

In the superior ranks of life how seldom do we meet with a man of superior abilities, or even common acquirements? The reason appears to me clear, the state they are born in was an unnatural one. The human character has ever been formed by the employments the individual, or class, pursues; and if the faculties are not sharpened by necessity, they must remain obtuse. The argument may fairly be extended to women; for, seldom occupied by serious business, the pursuit of pleasure gives that insignificancy to their character which renders the society of the *great* so insipid. The same want of firmness, produced by a similar cause, forces them both to fly from themselves to noisy pleasures, and artificial passions, till vanity takes place of every social affection, and the characteristics of humanity can scarcely be discerned. Such are the blessings of civil governments, as they are at present organized, that wealth and female softness equally tend to debase mankind, and are produced by the same cause; but allowing women to be rational creatures, they should be incited to acquire virtues which they may call their own, for how can a rational being be ennobled by any thing that is not obtained by its *own* exertions?

* * *

Chapter XIII

* * * Concluding Reflections on the Moral Improvement That a Revolution in Female Manners Might Naturally Be Expected to Produce

* * *

SECT. VI

It is not necessary to inform the sagacious reader, now I enter on my concluding reflections, that the discussion of this subject merely consists in opening a few simple principles, and clearing away the rubbish which obscured them. But, as all readers are not sagacious, I must be allowed to add some explanatory remarks to bring the subject home to reason—to that sluggish reason, which supinely takes opinions on trust, and obstinately supports them to spare itself the labour of thinking.

Moralists have unanimously agreed, that unless virtue be nursed by liberty, it will never attain due strength—and what they say of man I extend to mankind, insisting that in all cases morals must be fixed on immutable principles; and, that the being cannot be termed rational or virtuous, who obeys any authority, but that of reason.

To render women truly useful members of society, I argue that they should be led, by having their understandings cultivated on a large scale, to acquire a rational affection for their country, founded on knowledge, because it is obvious that we are little interested about what we do not understand. And to render this general knowledge of due importance, I have endeavoured to shew that private duties are never properly fulfilled unless the understanding enlarges the heart; and that public virtue is only an aggregate of private. But, the distinctions established in society undermine both, by beating out[8] the solid gold of virtue, till it becomes only the tinsel-covering of vice; for whilst wealth renders a man more respectable than virtue, wealth will be sought before virtue; and, whilst women's persons are caressed, when a childish simper shews an absence of mind—the mind will lie fallow. Yet, true voluptuousness[9] must proceed from the mind—for what can equal the sensations produced by mutual affection, supported by mutual respect? What are the cold, or feverish caresses of appetite, but sin embracing death,[1] compared with the modest overflowings of a pure heart and exalted imagination? Yes, let me tell the libertine of fancy when he despises understanding in woman— that the mind, which he disregards, gives life to the enthusiastic affection from which rapture, short-lived as it is, alone can flow! And, that, without virtue, a sexual attachment must expire, like a tallow candle in the socket, creating intolerable disgust. To prove this, I need only observe, that men who have wasted great part of their lives with women, and with whom they have sought for pleasure with eager thirst, entertain the meanest opinion of the sex.— Virtue, true refiner of joy!—if foolish men were to fright[2] thee from earth, in order to give loose to all their appetites without a check—some sensual wight[3] of taste would scale the heavens to invite thee back, to give a zest to pleasure!

That women at present are by ignorance rendered foolish or vicious, is, I think, not to be disputed; and, that the most salutary effects tending to improve mankind might be expected from a REVOLUTION in female manners, appears, at least, with a face of probability, to rise out of the observation. For as marriage has been termed the parent of those endearing charities which draw man from the brutal herd, the corrupting intercourse that wealth, idleness, and folly, produce between the sexes, is more universally injurious to morality than all the other vices of mankind collectively considered. To adulterous lust the most sacred duties are sacrificed, because before marriage, men, by a promiscuous intimacy with women, learned to consider love as a selfish gratification—learned to separate it not only from esteem, but from

8. That is, hammering thin [editor's note].
9. Refinement that gratifies the senses [editor's note].
1. In *Paradise Lost* (2.746–802), Sin is the mother of Death, who rapes her [editor's note].
2. Frighten off; drive away, banish [editor's note].
3. Creature; person [editor's note].

the affection merely built on habit, which mixes a little humanity with it. Justice and friendship are also set at defiance, and that purity of taste is vitiated which would naturally lead a man to relish an artless display of affection rather than affected airs. But that noble simplicity of affection, which dares to appear unadorned, has few attractions for the libertine, though it be the charm, which by cementing the matrimonial tie, secures to the pledges of a warmer passion the necessary parental attention; for children will never be properly educated till friendship subsists between parents. Virtue flies from a house divided against itself[4]—and a whole legion of devils take up their residence there.

The affection of husbands and wives cannot be pure when they have so few sentiments in common, and when so little confidence is established at home, as must be the case when their pursuits are so different. That intimacy from which tenderness should flow, will not, cannot subsist between the vicious.

Contending, therefore, that the sexual distinction which men have so warmly insisted upon, is arbitrary, I have dwelt on an observation, that several sensible men, with whom I have conversed on the subject, allowed to be well founded; and it is simply this, that the little chastity to be found amongst men, and consequent disregard of modesty, tend to degrade both sexes; and further, that the modesty of women, characterized as such, will often be only the artful veil of wantonness instead of being the natural reflection of purity, till modesty be universally respected.

From the tyranny of man, I firmly believe, the greater number of female follies proceed; and the cunning, which I allow makes at present a part of their character, I likewise have repeatedly endeavoured to prove, is produced by oppression.

Were not dissenters,[5] for instance, a class of people, with strict truth, characterized as cunning? And may I not lay some stress on this fact to prove, that when any power but reason curbs the free spirit of man, dissimulation is practised, and the various shifts of art are naturally called forth? Great attention to decorum, which was carried to a degree of scrupulosity, and all that puerile bustle about trifles and consequential solemnity, which Butler's[6] caricature of a dissenter, brings before the imagination, shaped their persons as well as their minds in the mould of prim littleness. I speak collectively, for I know how many ornaments to human nature have been enrolled amongst sectaries; yet, I assert, that the same narrow prejudice for their sect, which women have for their families, prevailed in the dissenting part of the community, however worthy in other respects; and also that the same timid prudence, or headstrong efforts, often disgraced the exertions of both. Oppression thus formed many of the features of their character perfectly to coincide with that of the oppressed half of mankind; or is it not notorious that dissenters were, like women, fond of deliberating together, and asking advice of each other, till by a complication of little contrivances, some little end was brought

---

4. Matthew 12:25: "every city or house divided against itself shall not stand."
5. Members of Protestant denominations outside the established (Anglican) church. In 1792 men who were Dissenters were still barred from political and public office in Britain.
6. Samuel Butler (1612–1860), English poet and satirist; the specific reference is not certain [editor's note].

about? A similar attention to preserve their reputation was conspicuous in the dissenting and female world, and was produced by a similar cause.

Asserting the rights which women in common with men ought to contend for, I have not attempted to extenuate their faults; but to prove them to be the natural consequence of their education and station in society. If so, it is reasonable to suppose that they will change their character, and correct their vices and follies, when they are allowed to be free in a physical, moral, and civil sense.[7]

Let woman share the rights and she will emulate the virtues of man; for she must grow more perfect when emancipated, or justify the authority that chains such a weak being to her duty.—If the latter, it will be expedient to open a fresh trade with Russia for whips; a present which a father should always make to his son-in-law on his wedding day, that a husband may keep his whole family in order by the same means;[8] and without any violation of justice reign, wielding this sceptre, sole master of his house, because he is the only being in it who has reason:—the divine, indefeasible earthly sovereignty breathed into man by the Master of the universe. Allowing this position, women have not any inherent rights to claim; and, by the same rule, their duties vanish, for rights and duties are inseparable.

Be just then, O ye men of understanding! and mark not more severely what women do amiss, than the vicious tricks of the horse or the ass for whom ye provide provender—and allow her the privileges of ignorance, to whom ye deny the rights of reason, or ye will be worse than Egyptian task-masters,[9] expecting virtue where nature has not given understanding!

SOURCE: Mary Wollstonecraft, *A Vindication of the Rights of Woman*, ed. Deidre Shauna Lynch, Norton Critical Edition, 3rd ed. (New York: W. W. Norton, 2009), pp. 9–15, 21–41, 55–56, 201–4. Except as otherwise indicated, notes are Lynch's; some of her notes have been omitted and some have been shortened. In the notes "editor" refers to the volume editor (RS).

7. "I had further enlarged on the advantages which might reasonably be expected to result from an improvement in female manners, towards the general reformation of society; but it appeared to me that such reflections would more properly close the last volume" [Wollstonecraft's note].

8. That is, secure and maintain the submission to his will of wife and children alike [editor's note].

9. Those who enslaved the Israelites; see Exodus 1:8–14 [editor's note].

JOHN STUART MILL
(1806 – 1873)

Mill is among the great contributors to the analytical tradition in Anglo-American philosophy—arguably the greatest of them in the nineteenth century. Yet he also is as deserving as FEUERBACH, MARX, SCHOPENHAUER, and NIETZSCHE of inclusion in the interpretive tradition. Mill deeply shared their concern with the quality of human life and with the conditions that affect it, with the question of how human reality is to be reconceived in the aftermath of the demise of traditional metaphysical and religious ways of understanding ourselves, and with the problem of value when it becomes detached from its long-standing dependence on those traditional understandings. The positions he takes on such matters are frequently either similar to or in competition with theirs.

John Stuart Mill was a child prodigy. Educated at home by his father, the philosopher James Mill (1773–1836), he began the study of Greek at the age of 3, and by his early teens he was well read in literature, history, logic, and mathematics— at which time he began the study of law, only to take a position as a clerk in the East India Company at 17. He never pursued an academic career, remaining in the employment of the East India Company until 1857, when its charter was not renewed.

Mill's personal life, unlike his professional life, connected significantly with his intellectual life. In 1830, he met Harriet Taylor, a true kindred spirit and intellectual partner who became the love of his life, and who also influenced his thinking not only on women's issues but on other matters throughout the rest of his career. Their relationship was for many years close but limited, because she was a married woman with children. It was only in 1851, two years after her husband's death, that she and Mill were able to marry; and then, just six years

later, she died. Mill was devastated: he had lost both the person dearest to him and the mind nearest to him, in all areas of his interests. He was elected to a term in Parliament in 1865, but he was ill-suited to political life and withdrew from it after his 1868 reelection bid failed. Though he spent his last years in relative seclusion, he remained highly and widely esteemed as one of the great minds of his age.

Mill's most substantial philosophical works, dealing with topics in the theory of knowledge and perception, philosophy of science, and philosophy of mind, were his early *System of Logic* (1843) and his much later *An Examination of Sir William Hamilton's Philosophy* (1865), selections from which are included in the analytic tradition volume. He has long been best known, however, for two quite different short works written relatively late in his life: *On Liberty* (1859) and *Utilitarianism* (1861), from which the main selections below are taken. The selection from *On Liberty* is of interest both for its discussion of the relation between individuality and freedom and for the light it sheds on Mill's thinking concerning the nature of individuality and human reality more generally. The selections from *Utilitarianism* are indicative of his value theory and conception of the human good as well as of his "utilitarian" moral philosophy, which has long been considered the leading rival to that of KANT.

Mill's polemic (against) *The Subjection of Women* (published in 1869, but written in 1861, not long after his wife's death), from which the third selection is taken, is an important extension and application of his thinking on all of these matters to the topic of the inequality of the sexes. One of the first attempts by a major modern philosopher to address this general issue, it is striking for its anticipation of a central part of SIMONE DE BEAUVOIR's analysis nearly a century later, in *The Second Sex* (1949; see the selection included below). It also vividly elaborates Mill's conception of what is conducive and detrimental to the quality of human life, and his views on the extent to which human identity and selfhood are shaped by social circumstances and influences.

Mill, like David Hume (1711–1776) before him, was very much in the post-Christian Enlightenment tradition, and was an advocate of a version of what has come to be called "secular humanism." Sharing Hume's antipathy to both metaphysical and religious thinking, he considered it imperative to align philosophy with the newly ascendant natural sciences and thereby to give the philosophy of mind, the theory of value, and even the theory of knowledge a significantly naturalistic turn. For Mill (as for Hume), mind, value, and knowledge are fundamentally psychological phenomena; human psychology is a piece of human nature; and human nature is itself fundamentally a natural phenomenon—though one whose very nature makes the way human beings turn out depend crucially on social and cultural variables. A reconsideration of human life based on a "science of man," rather than the speculative flights of fancy to which philosophers remain all too prone, was what Mill believed philosophy needed to develop. This new approach would be practical as well as theoretical, guiding social reform as well as advancing human knowledge. Mill gave classical expression to the liberal idea that social circumstances are the key to what can go both right and wrong in human life, and that social policy therefore can and should be brought to bear upon them.

Mill champions what has come to be known as a "utilitarian" value theory and moral philosophy, by which he thought such enlightened social policy should be guided, and to which his *Utilitarianism* gives classic articulation and elaboration. The key to what he calls this "theory of life" is the idea that what matters above all else is "happiness" and its maximization—with "happiness" defined as fundamentally a matter of "pleasure and freedom from pain." He insists upon construing all *desirability* in terms of what actually is or would under certain circumstances *be desired*; and these, for him, "are the only things desirable as ends." All other things, he contends, are desirable or undesirable only if and only insofar as they either are themselves inherently pleasurable or painful or are conducive to those states. Mill supposes this way of thinking to be congenial to a scientific outlook, and to be the only understanding of value and morality that begs no big questions, makes good sense, and is (or ought to be) beyond dispute. If there can be a naturalistic ethics and value theory, this would certainly seem to be one.

What makes Mill's discussion so fascinating is the moves he feels he must make to show that there is room for a much more substantial view of human "well-being" (as he himself refers to the human good) than this seemingly simplistic way of thinking might lead one to suppose. In his hands, the ideas of "pleasure" and "happiness" are extended well beyond mere sensations and feelings. Indeed, he attempts to stretch them far enough to justify the privileging of a conception of well-being that might seem to make him a kind of philosophical perfectionist—that is, one who accords evaluative priority to a certain conception of genuinely, fully, or truly human life (grounded in something objectively true about human nature) over other possible ways of living.

So, for example, in his discussion of "individuality," Mill aligns himself with the argument of Wilhelm von Humboldt (1767–1835) for its indispensability to attaining "the end of man," or highest human good, which for von Humboldt is "the highest and most harmonious development of [man's] powers to a complete and consistent whole." Mill goes on to speak of "well-developed human beings" in whom humanity "become[s] a noble and beautiful object of contemplation," thereby "making the race infinitely better worth belonging to." And he further argues that a human life of mere "contentment"—

pleasant but devoid of "self-determination," real choice-making, originality, and genuine enjoyment in one's activities—is not a life of that sort. (This is a point he makes much of in *The Subjection of Women* as well as in the third chapter of *On Liberty*.) He contends that the evaluative difference can be established and vindicated by pointing to the superiority of the kinds of "pleasure" and "happiness" associated with living as a well-developed human being, thereby providing this seemingly perfectionist picture with an entirely "utilitarian" (in Mill's sense) basis and rationale. Beyond the attractiveness of the picture, it raises two basic questions: Is Mill's strategy (or something like it) for advocating and defending his position sufficient to the task? And if it is not, in the absence of any such argument is there any other approach or strategy for legitimizing adherence to it?

Mill prized rationality, in practical as well as theoretical matters, and in all areas of human inquiry he takes a thoroughgoing empiricism for granted. Yet in matters touching on human meaning and human happiness, he also attempted to do justice to the importance of the emotions in human life. The lessons of Romanticism were not lost on him; the cultivation of our feelings was for him no less essential to human well-being than the cultivation of our rational capacities. And as the following selections show, Mill brought great passion to his concern with human flourishing, as he actively promoted it and sought to identify obstacles to it.

From On Liberty

Chapter III. Of Individuality, as One of the Elements of Well-Being

Such being the reasons[1] which make it imperative that human beings should be free to form opinions, and to express their opinions without reserve; and such the baneful consequences to the intellectual, and through that to the moral nature of man, unless this liberty is either conceded, or asserted in spite of prohibition; let us next examine whether the same reasons do not require that men should be free to act upon their opinions—to carry these out in their lives, without hindrance, either physical or moral, from their fellow-men, so long as it is at their own risk and peril. This last proviso is of course indispensable. No one pretends that actions should be as free as opinions. On the contrary, even opinions lose their immunity when the circumstances in which they are expressed are such as to constitute their expression a positive instigation to some mischievous act. An opinion that corn-dealers[2] are starvers of the poor, or that private property is robbery, ought to be unmolested when simply circulated through the press, but may justly incur punishment when delivered orally to an excited mob assembled before the house of a corn-dealer, or when handed about among the same mob in the form of a placard. Acts, of whatever kind, which, without justifiable cause, do harm to others, may be, and in the more important cases absolutely require to be, controlled by the unfavourable sentiments, and, when needful, by the active interference of mankind. The liberty of the individual must be thus far limited; he must not make himself a nuisance to other people. But if he refrains from molesting others in what concerns them, and merely acts according to his own inclination and judgment in things which concern himself, the same reasons which

1. Given in the previous chapter, "Of the Liberty of Thought and Discussion."

2. Sellers of wheat.

show that opinion should be free, prove also that he should be allowed, without molestation, to carry his opinions into practice at his own cost. That mankind are not infallible; that their truths, for the most part, are only half-truths; that unity of opinion, unless resulting from the fullest and freest comparison of opposite opinions, is not desirable, and diversity not an evil, but a good, until mankind are much more capable than at present of recognising all sides of the truth, are principles applicable to men's modes of action, not less than to their opinions. As it is useful that while mankind are imperfect there should be different opinions, so it is that there should be different experiments of living; that free scope should be given to varieties of character, short of injury to others; and that the worth of different modes of life should be proved practically, when any one thinks fit to try them. It is desirable, in short, that in things which do not primarily concern others, individuality should assert itself. Where, not the person's own character, but the traditions or customs of other people are the rule of conduct, there is wanting one of the principal ingredients of human happiness, and quite the chief ingredient of individual and social progress.

In maintaining this principle, the greatest difficulty to be encountered does not lie in the appreciation of means towards an acknowledged end, but in the indifference of persons in general to the end itself. If it were felt that the free development of individuality is one of the leading essentials of well-being; that it is not only a co-ordinate element with all that is designated by the terms civilisation, instruction, education, culture, but is itself a necessary part and condition of all those things; there would be no danger that liberty should be undervalued, and the adjustment of the boundaries between it and social control would present no extraordinary difficulty. But the evil is, that individual spontaneity is hardly recognised by the common modes of thinking as having any intrinsic worth, or deserving any regard on its own account. The majority, being satisfied with the ways of mankind as they now are (for it is they who make them what they are), cannot comprehend why those ways should not be good enough for everybody; and what is more, spontaneity forms no part of the ideal of the majority of moral and social reformers, but is rather looked on with jealousy, as a troublesome and perhaps rebellious obstruction to the general acceptance of what these reformers, in their own judgment, think would be best for mankind. Few persons, out of Germany, even comprehend the meaning of the doctrine which Wilhelm von Humboldt,[3] so eminent both as a *savant* and as a politician, made the text of a treatise—that "the end of man, or that which is prescribed by the eternal or immutable dictates of reason, and not suggested by vague and transient desires, is the highest and most harmonious development of his powers to a complete and consistent whole;" that, therefore, the object "towards which every human being must ceaselessly direct his efforts, and on which especially those who design to influence their fellow-men must ever keep their eyes, is the individuality of power and development;" that for this there are two requisites, "freedom, and variety of situations;" and that from the union of these arise

---

3. An intellectual, statesman, and social reformer who was a leading figure of the German Enlightenment (1767–1835). The treatise quoted is *The* *Sphere and Duties of Government* (written 1791; published 1851).

"individual vigour and manifold diversity," which combine themselves in "originality."

Little, however, as people are accustomed to a doctrine like that of von Humboldt, and surprising as it may be to them to find so high a value attached to individuality, the question, one must nevertheless think, can only be one of degree. No one's idea of excellence in conduct is that people should do absolutely nothing but copy one another. No one would assert that people ought not to put into their mode of life, and into the conduct of their concerns, any impress whatever of their own judgment, or of their own individual character. On the other hand, it would be absurd to pretend that people ought to live as if nothing whatever had been known in the world before they came into it; as if experience had as yet done nothing towards showing that one mode of existence, or of conduct, is preferable to another. Nobody denies that people should be so taught and trained in youth as to know and benefit by the ascertained results of human experience. But it is the privilege and proper condition of a human being, arrived at the maturity of his faculties, to use and interpret experience in his own way. It is for him to find out what part of recorded experience is properly applicable to his own circumstances and character. The traditions and customs of other people are, to a certain extent, evidence of what their experience has taught *them;* presumptive evidence, and as such, have a claim to his deference: but, in the first place, their experience may be too narrow; or they may not have interpreted it rightly. Secondly, their interpretation of experience may be correct, but unsuitable to him. Customs are made for customary circumstances and customary characters; and his circumstances or his character may be uncustomary. Thirdly, though the customs be both good as customs, and suitable to him, yet to conform to custom, merely *as* custom, does not educate or develop in him any of the qualities which are the distinctive endowment of a human being. The human faculties of perception, judgment, discriminative feeling, mental activity, and even moral preference, are exercised only in making a choice. He who does anything because it is the custom makes no choice. He gains no practice either in discerning or in desiring what is best. The mental and moral, like the muscular powers, are improved only by being used. The faculties are called into no exercise by doing a thing merely because others do it, no more than by believing a thing only because others believe it. If the grounds of an opinion are not conclusive to the person's own reason, his reason cannot be strengthened, but, is likely to be weakened, by his adopting it: and if the inducements to an act are not such as are consentaneous to[4] his own feelings and character (where affection, or the rights of others, are not concerned) it is so much done towards rendering his feelings and character inert and torpid, instead of active and energetic.

He who lets the world, or his own portion of it, choose his plan of life for him, has no need of any other faculty than the ape-like one of imitation. He who chooses his plan for himself, employs all his faculties. He must use observation to see, reasoning and judgment to foresee, activity to gather materials for decision, discrimination to decide, and when he has decided, firmness and self-control to hold to his deliberate decision. And these qualities he requires

---

4. In agreement with; suited to.

and exercises exactly in proportion as the part of his conduct which he determines according to his own judgment and feelings is a large one. It is possible that he might be guided in some good path, and kept out of harm's way, without any of these things. But what will be his comparative worth as a human being? It really is of importance, not only what men do, but also what manner of men they are that do it. Among the works of man, which human life is rightly employed in perfecting and beautifying, the first in importance surely is man himself. Supposing it were possible to get houses built, corn grown, battles fought, causes tried, and even churches erected and prayers said, by machinery—by automatons in human form—it would be a considerable loss to exchange for these automatons even the men and women who at present inhabit the more civilised parts of the world, and who assuredly are but starved specimens of what nature can and will produce. Human nature is not a machine to be built after a model, and set to do exactly the work prescribed for it, but a tree, which requires to grow and develop itself on all sides, according to the tendency of the inward forces which make it a living thing.[5]

It will probably be conceded that it is desirable people should exercise their understandings, and that an intelligent following of custom, or even occasionally an intelligent deviation from custom, is better than a blind and simply mechanical adhesion to it. To a certain extent it is admitted that our understanding should be our own: but there is not the same willingness to admit that our desires and impulses should be our own likewise; or that to possess impulses of our own, and of any strength, is anything but a peril and a snare. Yet desires and impulses are as much a part of a perfect human being as beliefs and restraints: and strong impulses are only perilous when not properly balanced; when one set of aims and inclinations is developed into strength, while others, which ought to co-exist with them, remain weak and inactive. It is not because men's desires are strong that they act ill; it is because their consciences are weak. There is no natural connection between strong impulses and a weak conscience. The natural connection is the other way. To say that one person's desires and feelings are stronger and more various than those of another, is merely to say that he has more of the raw material of human nature, and is therefore capable, perhaps of more evil, but certainly of more good. Strong impulses are but another name for energy. Energy may be turned to bad uses; but more good may always be made of an energetic nature, than of an indolent and impassive one. Those who have most natural feeling are always those whose cultivated feelings may be made the strongest. The same strong susceptibilities which make the personal impulses vivid and powerful, are also the source from whence are generated the most passionate love of virtue, and the sternest self-control. It is through the cultivation of these that society both does its duty and protects its interests: not by rejecting the stuff of which heroes are made, because it knows not how to make them. A person whose desires and impulses are his own—are the expression of his own nature, as it has been developed and modified by his own culture—is said to have a character. One whose desires and impulses are not his own, has no character, no more than a steam-engine has a character. If, in addition to being his own,

5. This metaphor invites comparison of Mill's thinking here with the thought of SCHILLER, MARX, and NIETZSCHE, among others.

his impulses are strong, and are under the government of a strong will, he has an energetic character. Whoever thinks that individuality of desires and impulses should not be encouraged to unfold itself, must maintain that society has no need of strong natures—is not the better for containing many persons who have much character—and that a high general average of energy is not desirable.[6]

In some early states of society, these forces might be, and were, too much ahead of the power which society then possessed of disciplining and controlling them. There has been a time when the element of spontaneity and individuality was in excess, and the social principle had a hard struggle with it. The difficulty then was to induce men of strong bodies or minds to pay obedience to any rules which required them to control their impulses. To overcome this difficulty, law and discipline, like the Popes struggling against the Emperors, asserted a power over the whole man, claiming to control all his life in order to control his character—which society had not found any other sufficient means of binding. But society has now fairly got the better of individuality; and the danger which threatens human nature is not the excess, but the deficiency, of personal impulses and preferences. Things are vastly changed since the passions of those who were strong by station or by personal endowment were in a state of habitual rebellion against laws and ordinances, and required to be rigorously chained up to enable the persons within their reach to enjoy any particle of security. In our times, from the highest class of society down to the lowest, every one lives as under the eye of a hostile and dreaded censorship. Not only in what concerns others, but in what concerns only themselves, the individual or the family do not ask themselves—what do I prefer? or, what would suit my character and disposition? or, what would allow the best and highest in me to have fair play, and enable it to grow and thrive? They ask themselves, what is suitable to my position? what is usually done by persons of my station and pecuniary circumstances? or (worse still) what is usually done by persons of a station and circumstances superior to mine? I do not mean that they choose what is customary in preference to what suits their own inclination. It does not occur to them to have any inclination, except for what is customary. Thus the mind itself is bowed to the yoke: even in what people do for pleasure, conformity is the first thing thought of; they like in crowds; they exercise choice only among things commonly done: peculiarity of taste, eccentricity of conduct, are shunned equally with crimes: until by dint of not following their own nature they have no nature to follow: their human capacities are withered and starved: they become incapable of any strong wishes or native pleasures, and are generally without either opinions or feelings of home growth, or properly their own. Now is this, or is it not, the desirable condition of human nature?

It is so, on the Calvinistic theory.[7] According to that, the one great offence of man is self-will. All the good of which humanity is capable is comprised in obedience. You have no choice; thus you must do, and no otherwise: "whatever is not a duty, is a sin." Human nature being radically corrupt, there is no

---

6. The ideas advanced here and through much of what follows are strikingly similar to themes subsequently found in Nietzsche.
7. The theology of the French Protestant reformer

John Calvin (1509–1564) emphasized the depravity of human beings after the fall of Adam and Eve, predestination, and salvation through grace rather than through good works.

redemption for any one until human nature is killed within him. To one holding this theory of life, crushing out any of the human faculties, capacities, and susceptibilities, is no evil: man needs no capacity, but that of surrendering himself to the will of God: and if he uses any of his faculties for any other purpose but to do that supposed will more effectually, he is better without them. This is the theory of Calvinism; and it is held, in a mitigated form, by many who do not consider themselves Calvinists; the mitigation consisting in giving a less ascetic interpretation to the alleged will of God; asserting it to be his will that mankind should gratify some of their inclinations; of course not in the manner they themselves prefer, but in the way of obedience, that is, in a way prescribed to them by authority; and, therefore, by the necessary condition of the case, the same for all.

In some such insidious form there is at present a strong tendency to this narrow theory of life, and to the pinched and hidebound type of human character which it patronises. Many persons, no doubt, sincerely think that human beings thus cramped and dwarfed are as their Maker designed them to be; just as many have thought that trees are a much finer thing when clipped into pollards, or cut out into figures of animals, than as nature made them. But if it be any part of religion to believe that man was made by a good Being, it is more consistent with that faith to believe that this Being gave all human faculties that they might be cultivated and unfolded, not rooted out and consumed, and that he takes delight in every nearer approach made by his creatures to the ideal conception embodied in them, every increase in any of their capabilities of comprehension, of action, or of enjoyment. There is a different type of human excellence from the Calvinistic: a conception of humanity as having its nature bestowed on it for other purposes than merely to be abnegated. "Pagan self-assertion" is one of the elements of human worth, as well as "Christian self-denial."[8] There is a Greek ideal of self-development, which the Platonic and Christian ideal of self-government blends with, but does not supersede. It may be better to be a John Knox than an Alcibiades, but it is better to be a Pericles than either;[9] nor would a Pericles, if we had one in these days, be without anything good which belonged to John Knox.

It is not by wearing down into uniformity all that is individual in themselves, but by cultivating it, and calling it forth, within the limits imposed by the rights and interests of others, that human beings become a noble and beautiful object of contemplation; and as the works partake the character of those who do them, by the same process human life also becomes rich, diversified, and animating, furnishing more abundant aliment to high thoughts and elevating feelings, and strengthening the tie which binds every individual to the race, by making the race infinitely better worth belonging to. In proportion to the development of his individuality, each person becomes more valuable to himself, and is therefore capable of being more valuable to others. There is a greater fulness of life about his own existence, and when there is

---

8. Sterling's *Essays* [Mill's note]. John Sterling (1806–1844), English writer and poet who was a friend of Mill's. See "On Simonides," in *Essays and Tales* (London: John W. Parker, 1848), 1:190.
9. Pericles (ca. 495–429 B.C.E.) was the Greek statesman and general who led Athens during its golden age of democracy and empire; Knox (ca. 1514–1572) was a leader of the Scottish Reformation, while Alcibiades (ca. 450–404 B.C.E.) was a gifted but unscrupulous Athenian military and political leader.

more life in the units there is more in the mass which is composed of them. As much compression as is necessary to prevent the stronger specimens of human nature from encroaching on the rights of others cannot be dispensed with; but for this there is ample compensation even in the point of view of human development. The means of development which the individual loses by being prevented from gratifying his inclinations to the injury of others, are chiefly obtained at the expense of the development of other people. And even to himself there is a full equivalent in the better development of the social part of his nature, rendered possible by the restraint put upon the selfish part. To be held to rigid rules of justice for the sake of others, develops the feelings and capacities which have the good of others for their object. But to be restrained in things not affecting their good, by their mere displeasure, develops nothing valuable, except such force of character as may unfold itself in resisting the restraint. If acquiesced in, it dulls and blunts the whole nature. To give any fair play to the nature of each, it is essential that different persons should be allowed to lead different lives. In proportion as this latitude has been exercised in any age, has that age been noteworthy to posterity. Even despotism does not produce its worst effects, so long as individuality exists under it; and whatever crushes individuality is despotism, by whatever name it may be called, and whether it professes to be enforcing the will of God or the injunctions of men.

Having said that the individuality is the same thing with development, and that it is only the cultivation of individuality which produces, or can produce, well-developed human beings, I might here close the argument: for what more or better can be said of any condition of human affairs than that it brings human beings themselves nearer to the best thing they can be? or what worse can be said of any obstruction to good than that it prevents this? Doubtless, however, these considerations will not suffice to convince those who most need convincing; and it is necessary further to show, that these developed human beings are of some use to the undeveloped—to point out to those who do not desire liberty, and would not avail themselves of it, that they may be in some intelligible manner rewarded for allowing other people to make use of it without hindrance.

In the first place, then, I would suggest that they might possibly learn something from them. It will not be denied by anybody, that originality is a valuable element in human affairs. There is always need of persons not only to discover new truths, and point out when what were once truths are true no longer, but also to commence new practices, and set the example of more enlightened conduct, and better taste and sense in human life. This cannot well be gainsaid by anybody who does not believe that the world has already attained perfection in all its ways and practices. It is true that this benefit is not capable of being rendered by everybody alike: there are but few persons, in comparison with the whole of mankind, whose experiments, if adopted by others, would be likely to be any improvement on established practice. But these few are the salt of the earth; without them, human life would become a stagnant pool. Not only is it they who introduce good things which did not before exist; it is they who keep the life in those which already exist. If there were nothing new to be done, would human intellect cease to be necessary? Would it be a reason why those who do the old things should forget why they are done, and do them like cattle, not like human beings? There is only too great a tendency in the best beliefs and practices to degenerate into the mechanical; and unless there were a succession of persons whose ever-recurring originality prevents the grounds of those beliefs and practices from becoming merely traditional, such dead matter would not resist the smallest shock from anything really alive, and there would be no reason why civilisation should not die out, as in the Byzantine Empire. Persons of genius, it is true, are, and are always likely to be, a small minority; but in order to have them, it is necessary to preserve the soil in which they grow. Genius can only breathe freely in an *atmosphere* of freedom. Persons of genius are, *ex vi termini*,[1] more individual than any other people—less capable, consequently, of fitting themselves, without hurtful compression, into any of the small number of moulds which society provides in order to save its members the trouble of forming their own character. If from timidity they consent to be forced into one of these moulds, and to let all that part of themselves which cannot expand under the pressure remain unexpanded, society will be little the better for their genius. If they are of a strong character, and break their fetters, they become a mark for the society which has not succeeded in reducing them to commonplace, to point out with solemn warning as "wild," "erratic," and the like; much as if one should complain of the Niagara river for not flowing smoothly between its banks like a Dutch canal.

I insist thus emphatically on the importance of genius, and the necessity of allowing it to unfold itself freely both in thought and in practice, being well aware that no one will deny the position in theory, but knowing also that almost every one, in reality, is totally indifferent to it. People think genius a fine thing if it enables a man to write an exciting poem, or paint a picture. But in its true sense, that of originality in thought and action, though no one says that it is not a thing to be admired, nearly all, at heart, think that they can do very well without it. Unhappily this is too natural to be wondered at. Originality is the one thing which unoriginal minds cannot feel the use of. They cannot see what it is to do for them: how should they? If they could see what it would do for them, it would not be originality. The first service which originality has to render them, is that of opening their eyes: which being once fully done, they would have a chance of being themselves original. Meanwhile, recollecting that nothing was ever yet done which some one was not the first to do, and that all good things which exist are the fruits of originality, let them be modest enough to believe that there is something still left for it to accomplish, and assure themselves that they are more in need of originality, the less they are conscious of the want.

In sober truth, whatever homage may be professed, or even paid, to real or supposed mental superiority, the general tendency of things throughout the world is to render mediocrity the ascendant power among mankind. In ancient history, in the Middle Ages, and in a diminishing degree through the long transition from feudality to the present time, the individual was a power in himself; and if he had either great talents or a high social position, he was a considerable power. At present individuals are lost in the crowd. In politics it is almost a triviality to say that public opinion now rules the world. The only

---

1. By the force of the term (Latin); that is, "by definition."

power deserving the name is that of masses, and of governments while they make themselves the organ of the tendencies and instincts of masses. This is as true in the moral and social relations of private life as in public transactions. Those whose opinions go by the name of public opinion are not always the same sort of public: in America they are the whole white population; in England, chiefly the middle class. But they are always a mass, that is to say, collective mediocrity. And what is a still greater novelty, the mass do not now take their opinions from dignitaries in Church or State, from ostensible leaders, or from books. Their thinking is done for them by men much like themselves, addressing them or speaking in their name, on the spur of the moment, through the newspapers. I am not complaining of all this. I do not assert that anything better is compatible, as a general rule, with the present low state of the human mind. But that does not hinder the government of mediocrity from being mediocre government. No government by a democracy or a numerous aristocracy, either in its political acts or in the opinions, qualities, and tone of mind which it fosters, ever did or could rise above mediocrity, except in so far as the sovereign Many have let themselves be guided (which in their best times they always have done) by the counsels and influence of a more highly gifted and instructed One or Few. The initiation of all wise or noble things comes and must come from individuals; generally at first from some one individual. The honour and glory of the average man is that he is capable of following that initiative; that he can respond internally to wise and noble things, and be led to them with his eyes open. I am not countenancing the sort of "hero-worship" which applauds the strong man of genius for forcibly seizing on the government of the world and making it do his bidding in spite of itself.[2] All he can claim is, freedom to point out the way. The power of compelling others into it is not only inconsistent with the freedom and development of all the rest, but corrupting to the strong man himself. It does seem, however, that when the opinions of masses of merely average men are everywhere become or becoming the dominant power, the counterpoise and corrective to that tendency would be the more and more pronounced individuality of those who stand on the higher eminences of thought. It is in these circumstances most especially, that exceptional individuals, instead of being deterred, should be encouraged in acting differently from the mass. In other times there was no advantage in their doing so, unless they acted not only differently but better. In this age, the mere example of non-conformity, the mere refusal to bend the knee to custom, is itself a service. Precisely because the tyranny of opinion is such as to make eccentricity a reproach, it is desirable, in order to break through that tyranny, that people should be eccentric. Eccentricity has always abounded when and where strength of character has abounded; and the amount of eccentricity in a society has generally been proportional to the amount of genius, mental vigour, and moral courage it contained. That so few now dare to be eccentric marks the chief danger of the time.

I have said that it is important to give the freest scope possible to uncustomary things, in order that it may in time appear which of these are fit to be converted into customs. But independence of action, and disregard of

---

2. An allusion to Thomas Carlyle's *On Heroes, Hero-Worship, and the Heroic in History* (1841).

custom, are not solely deserving of encouragement for the chance they afford that better modes of action, and customs more worthy of general adoption, may be struck out; nor is it only persons of decided mental superiority who have a just claim to carry on their lives in their own way. There is no reason that all human existence should be constructed on some one or some small number of patterns. If a person possesses any tolerable amount of common sense and experience, his own mode of laying out his existence is the best, not because it is the best in itself, but because it is his own mode. Human beings are not like sheep; and even sheep are not undistinguishably alike. A man cannot get a coat or a pair of boots to fit him unless they are either made to his measure, or he has a whole warehouseful to choose from: and is it easier to fit him with a life than with a coat, or are human beings more like one another in their whole physical and spiritual conformation than in the shape of their feet? If it were only that people have diversities of taste, that is reason enough for not attempting to shape them all after one model. But different persons also require different conditions for their spiritual develop-ment; and can no more exist healthily in the same moral, than all the variety of plants can in the same physical, atmosphere and climate. The same things which are helps to one person towards the cultivation of his higher nature are hindrances to another. The same mode of life is a healthy excitement to one, keeping all his faculties of action and enjoyment in their best order, while to another it is a distracting burthen, which suspends or crushes all internal life. Such are the differences among human beings in their sources of plea-sure, their susceptibilities of pain, and the operation on them of different physical and moral agencies, that unless there is a corresponding diversity in their modes of life, they neither obtain their fair share of happiness, nor grow up to the mental, moral, and aesthetic stature of which their nature is capable. Why then should tolerance, as far as the public sentiment is concerned, extend only to tastes and modes of life which extort acquiescence by the multitude of their adherents? Nowhere (except in some monastic institutions) is diversity of taste entirely unrecognised; a person may, without blame, either like or dislike rowing, or smoking, or music, or athletic exercises, or chess, or cards, or study, because both those who like each of these things, and those who dislike them, are too numerous to be put down. But the man, and still more the woman, who can be accused either of doing "what nobody does," or of not doing "what everybody does," is the subject of as much depreciatory remark as if he or she had committed some grave moral delinquency. Persons require to possess a title, or some other badge of rank, or of the consideration of people of rank, to be able to indulge somewhat in the luxury of doing as they like without detriment to their estimation. To indulge somewhat, I repeat: for whoever allow themselves much of that indulgence, incur the risk of something worse than disparaging speeches—they are in peril of a com-mission de lunatico,[3] and of having their property taken from them and given to their relations.

There is one characteristic of the present direction of public opinion pecu-liarly calculated to make it intolerant of any marked demonstration of indi-

---

3. A shortening of de lunatico inquirendo (literally, "for inquiring about the lunatic"; Latin), a legal term for a writ to establish whether an individual is insane.

viduality. The general average of mankind are not only moderate in intellect, but also moderate in inclinations: they have no tastes or wishes strong enough to incline them to do anything unusual, and they consequently do not understand those who have, and class all such with the wild and intemperate whom they are accustomed to look down upon. Now, in addition to this fact which is general, we have only to suppose that a strong movement has set in towards the improvement of morals, and it is evident what we have to expect. In these days such a movement has set in; much has actually been effected in the way of increased regularity of conduct and discouragement of excesses; and there is a philanthropic spirit abroad, for the exercise of which there is no more inviting field than the moral and prudential improvement of our fellow-creatures. These tendencies of the times cause the public to be more disposed than at most former periods to prescribe general rules of conduct, and endeavour to make every one conform to the approved standard. And that standard, express or tacit, is to desire nothing strongly. Its ideal of character is to be without any marked character; to maim by compression, like a Chinese lady's foot,[4] every part of human nature which stands out prominently, and tends to make the person markedly dissimilar in outline to commonplace humanity.

As is usually the case with ideals which exclude one-half of what is desirable, the present standard of approbation produces only an inferior imitation of the other half. Instead of great energies guided by vigorous reason, and strong feelings strongly controlled by a conscientious will, its result is weak feelings and weak energies, which therefore can be kept in outward conformity to rule without any strength either of will or of reason. Already energetic characters on any large scale are becoming merely traditional. There is now scarcely any outlet for energy in this country except business. The energy expended in this may still be regarded as considerable. What little is left from that employment is expended on some hobby; which may be a useful, even a philanthropic hobby, but is always some one thing, and generally a thing of small dimensions. The greatness of England is now all collective; individually small, we only appear capable of anything great by our habit of combining; and with this our moral and religious philanthropists are perfectly contented. But it was men of another stamp than this that made England what it has been; and men of another stamp will be needed to prevent its decline.

The despotism of custom is everywhere the standing hindrance to human advancement, being in unceasing antagonism to that disposition to aim at something better than customary, which is called, according to circumstances, the spirit of liberty, or that of progress or improvement. The spirit of improvement is not always a spirit of liberty, for it may aim at forcing improvements on an unwilling people; and the spirit of liberty, in so far as it resists such attempts, may ally itself locally and temporarily with the opponents of improvement; but the only unfailing and permanent source of improvement is liberty, since by it there are as many possible independent centres of improvement as there are individuals. The progressive principle, however, in either shape, whether as the love of liberty or of improvement, is antagonistic to the sway of Custom, involving at least emancipation from that yoke; and the contest

4. A reference to foot-binding, a common practice among Chinese women until the early 20th century.

between the two constitutes the chief interest of the history of mankind. The greater part of the world has, properly speaking, no history, because the despotism of Custom is complete. This is the case over the whole East. Custom is there, in all things, the final appeal; justice and right mean conformity to custom; the argument of custom no one, unless some tyrant intoxicated with power, thinks of resisting. And we see the result. Those nations must once have had originality; they did not start out of the ground populous, lettered, and versed in many of the arts of life; they made themselves all this, and were then the greatest and most powerful nations of the world. What are they now? The subjects or dependents of tribes whose forefathers wandered in the forests when theirs had magnificent palaces and gorgeous temples, but over whom custom exercised only a divided rule with liberty and progress. A people, it appears, may be progressive for a certain length of time, and then stop: when does it stop? When it ceases to possess individuality. If a similar change should befall the nations of Europe, it will not be in exactly the same shape: the despotism of custom with which these nations are threatened is not precisely stationariness. It proscribes singularity, but it does not preclude change, provided all change together. We have discarded the fixed costumes of our forefathers; every one must still dress like other people, but the fashion may change once or twice a year. We thus take care that when there is a change, it shall be for change's sake, and not from any idea of beauty or convenience; for the same idea of beauty or convenience would not strike all the world at the same moment, and be simultaneously thrown aside by all at another moment. But we are progressive as well as changeable: we continually make new inventions in mechanical things, and keep them until they are again superseded by better; we are eager for improvement in politics, in education, even in morals, though in this last our idea of improvement chiefly consists in persuading or forcing other people to be as good as ourselves. It is not progress that we object to; on the contrary, we flatter ourselves that we are the most progressive people who ever lived. It is individuality that we war against: we should think we had done wonders if we had made ourselves all alike; forgetting that the unlikeness of one person to another is generally the first thing which draws the attention of either to the imperfection of his own type, and the superiority of another, or the possibility, by combining the advantages of both, of producing something better than either. We have a warning example in China—a nation of much talent, and, in some respects, even wisdom, owing to the rare good fortune of having been provided at an early period with a particularly good set of customs, the work, in some measure, of men to whom even the most enlightened European must accord, under certain limitations, the title of sages and philosophers. They are remarkable, too, in the excellence of their apparatus for impressing, as far as possible, the best wisdom they possess upon every mind in the community, and securing that those who have appropriated most of it shall occupy the posts of honour and power.[5] Surely the people who did this have discovered the secret of human progressiveness, and must have kept themselves steadily at the head of the movement of the world. On the contrary, they have become stationary—have remained so for thousands

5. From the 7th to the early 20th century, men seeking jobs in China's imperial bureaucracy had to pass civil service examinations, which focused largely on the Confucian classics.

of years; and if they are ever to be farther improved, it must be by foreigners. They have succeeded beyond all hope in what English philanthropists are so industriously working at—in making a people all alike, all governing their thoughts and conduct by the same maxims and rules; and these are the fruits. The modern *régime* of public opinion is, in an unorganised form, what the Chinese educational and political systems are in an organised; and unless individuality shall be able successfully to assert itself against this yoke, Europe, notwithstanding its noble antecedents and its professed Christianity, will tend to become another China.

What is it that has hitherto preserved Europe from this lot? What has made the European family of nations an improving, instead of a stationary portion of mankind? Not any superior excellence in them, which, when it exists, exists as the effect not as the cause; but their remarkable diversity of character and culture. Individuals, classes, nations, have been extremely unlike one another: they have struck out a great variety of paths, each leading to something valuable; and although at every period those who travelled in different paths have been intolerant of one another, and each would have thought it an excellent thing if all the rest could have been compelled to travel his road, their attempts to thwart each other's development have rarely had any permanent success, and each has in time endured to receive the good which the others have offered. Europe is, in my judgment, wholly indebted to this plurality of paths for its progressive and many-sided development. But it already begins to possess this benefit in a considerably less degree. It is decidedly advancing towards the Chinese ideal of making all people alike. M. de Tocqueville,[6] in his last important work, remarks how much more the Frenchmen of the present day resemble one another than did those even of the last generation. The same remark might be made of Englishmen in a far greater degree. In a passage, already quoted from Wilhelm von Humboldt, he points out two things as necessary conditions of human development, because necessary to render people unlike one another; namely, freedom, and variety of situations. The second of these two conditions is in this country every day diminishing. The circumstances which surround different classes and individuals, and shape their characters, are daily becoming more assimilated. Formerly, different ranks, different neighbourhoods, different trades and professions, lived in what might be called different worlds; at present to a great degree in the same. Comparatively speaking, they now read the same things, listen to the same things, see the same things, go to the same places, have their hopes and fears directed to the same objects, have the same rights and liberties, and the same means of asserting them. Great as are the differences of position which remain, they are nothing to those which have ceased. And the assimilation is still proceeding. All the political changes of the age promote it, since they all tend to raise the low and to lower the high. Every extension of education promotes it, because education brings people under common influences, and gives them access to the general stock of facts and sentiments. Improvement in the means of communication promotes it, by bringing the inhabitants of distant places into personal contact, and keeping up a rapid flow of changes of residence

6. Alexis de Tocqueville (1805–1859), French political and social observer and theorist; his "last important work" is *The Old Regime and the Revolution* (1856).

between one place and another. The increase of commerce and manufactures promotes it, by diffusing more widely the advantages of easy circumstances, and opening all objects of ambition, even the highest, to general competition, whereby the desire of rising becomes no longer the character of a particular class, but of all classes. A more powerful agency than even all these, in bringing about a general similarity among mankind, is the complete establishment, in this and other free countries, of the ascendancy of public opinion in the State. As the various social eminences which enabled persons entrenched on them to disregard the opinion of the multitude gradually become levelled; as the very idea of resisting the will of the public, when it is positively known that they have a will, disappears more and more from the minds of practical politicians; there ceases to be any social support for nonconformity—any substantive power in society which, itself opposed to the ascendancy of numbers, is interested in taking under its protection opinions and tendencies at variance with those of the public.

The combination of all these causes forms so great a mass of influences hostile to Individuality, that it is not easy to see how it can stand its ground. It will do so with increasing difficulty, unless the intelligent part of the public can be made to feel its value—to see that it is good there should be differences, even though not for the better, even though, as it may appear to them, some should be for the worse. If the claims of Individuality are ever to be asserted, the time is now, while much is still wanting to complete the enforced assimilation. It is only in the earlier stages that any stand can be successfully made against the encroachment. The demand that all other people shall resemble ourselves grows by what it feeds on. If resistance waits till life is reduced *nearly* to one uniform type, all deviations from that type will come to be considered impious, immoral, even monstrous and contrary to nature. Mankind speedily become unable to conceive diversity, when they have been for some time unaccustomed to see it.

SOURCE: From John Stuart Mill, *Utilitarianism, Liberty, and Representative Government* (London: Dent; New York: Dutton, 1910), pp. 114–31. First published in 1859.

From Utilitarianism

Chapter II. What Utilitarianism Is

A passing remark is all that needs be given to the ignorant blunder of supposing that those who stand up for utility as the test of right and wrong, use the term in that restricted and merely colloquial sense in which utility is opposed to pleasure. An apology is due to the philosophical opponents of utilitarianism, for even the momentary appearance of confounding them with any one capable of so absurd a misconception; which is the more extraordinary, inasmuch as the contrary accusation, of referring everything to pleasure, and that too in its grossest form, is another of the common charges against utilitarianism: and, as has been pointedly remarked by an able writer, the same sort of persons, and often the very same persons, denounce the theory "as impracticably dry when the word utility precedes the word pleasure, and as too practicably voluptuous when the word pleasure precedes the word utility."[1] Those who know anything about the matter are aware that every writer, from Epicurus[2] to Bentham, who maintained the theory of utility, meant by it, not something to be contradistinguished from pleasure, but pleasure itself, together with exemption from pain; and instead of opposing the useful to the agreeable or the ornamental, have always declared that the useful means these, among other things. Yet the common herd, including the herd of writers, not only in newspapers and periodicals, but in books of weight and pretension, are perpetually falling into this shallow mistake. Having caught up the word utilitarian, while knowing nothing whatever about it but its sound, they habitually express by it the rejection, or the neglect, of pleasure in some of its forms; of beauty, of ornament, or of amusement. Nor is the term thus ignorantly misapplied solely in disparagement, but occasionally in compliment; as though it implied superiority to frivolity and the mere pleasures of the moment. And this perverted use is the only one in which the word is popularly known, and the one from which the new generation are acquiring their sole notion of its meaning. Those who introduced the word, but who had for many years discontinued it as a distinctive appellation, may well feel themselves called upon to resume it, if by doing so they can hope to contribute anything towards rescuing it from this utter degradation.[3]

The creed which accepts as the foundation of morals, Utility, or the Greatest Happiness Principle, holds that actions are right in proportion as they tend to promote happiness, wrong as they tend to produce the reverse of happiness. By happiness is intended pleasure, and the absence of pain; by unhappiness, pain, and the privation of pleasure. To give a clear view of the moral standard set up by the theory, much more requires to be said; in particular, what things it includes in the ideas of pain and pleasure; and to what extent this is left an open question. But these supplementary explanations do not affect the theory of life on which this theory of morality is grounded—namely, that pleasure, and freedom from pain, are the only things desirable as ends; and that all desirable things (which are as numerous in the utilitarian as in any other scheme) are desirable either for the pleasure inherent in themselves, or as means to the promotion of pleasure and the prevention of pain.

Now, such a theory of life excites in many minds, and among them in some of the most estimable in feeling and purpose, inveterate dislike. To suppose that life has (as they express it) no higher end than pleasure—no better and nobler object of desire and pursuit—they designate as utterly mean and grovelling; as a doctrine worthy only of swine, to whom the followers of Epicurus were, at a very early period, contemptuously likened; and modern holders of

1. Quoted from Thomas Love Peacock's anonymous review of *The Epicurean*, by Thomas Moore, *Westminster Review* 8 (1827): 375.
2. Greek philosopher (341–270 B.C.E.), who identified the good with pleasure (achieved by limiting desires and practicing virtues).
3. The author of this essay has reason for believing himself to be the first person who brought the word utilitarian into use. He did not invent it, but adopted it from a passing expression in Mr. Galt's *Annals of the Parish* [1839]. After using it as a designation for several years, he and others abandoned it from a growing dislike to anything resembling a badge or watchword of sectarian distinction. But as a name for one single opinion, not a set of opinions—to denote the recognition of utility as a standard, not any particular way of applying it—the term supplies a want in the language, and offers, in many cases, a convenient mode of avoiding tiresome circumlocution [Mill's note]. John Galt (1779–1839), Scottish novelist.

the doctrine are occasionally made the subject of equally polite comparisons by its German, French, and English assailants.

When thus attacked, the Epicureans have always answered, that it is not they, but their accusers, who represent human nature in a degrading light; since the accusation supposes human beings to be capable of no pleasures except those of which swine are capable. If this supposition were true, the charge could not be gainsaid, but would then be no longer an imputation; for if the sources of pleasure were precisely the same to human beings and to swine, the rule of life which is good enough for the one would be good enough for the other. The comparison of the Epicurean life to that of beasts is felt as degrading, precisely because a beast's pleasures do not satisfy a human being's conceptions of happiness. Human beings have faculties more elevated than the animal appetites, and when once made conscious of them, do not regard anything as happiness which does not include their gratification. I do not, indeed, consider the Epicureans to have been by any means faultless in drawing out their scheme of consequences from the utilitarian principle. To do this in any sufficient manner, many Stoic,[4] as well as Christian elements require to be included. But there is no known Epicurean theory of life which does not assign to the pleasures of the intellect, of the feelings and imagination, and of the moral sentiments, a much higher value as pleasures than to those of mere sensation. It must be admitted, however, that utilitarian writers in general have placed the superiority of mental over bodily pleasures chiefly in the greater permanency, safety, uncostliness, etc., of the former— that is, in their circumstantial advantages rather than in their intrinsic nature. And on all these points utilitarians have fully proved their case; but they might have taken the other, and, as it may be called, higher ground, with entire consistency. It is quite compatible with the principle of utility to recognise the fact, that some *kinds* of pleasure are more desirable and more valuable than others. It would be absurd that while, in estimating all other things, quality is considered as well as quantity, the estimation of pleasures should be supposed to depend on quantity alone.

If I am asked, what I mean by difference of quality in pleasures, or what makes one pleasure more valuable than another, merely as a pleasure, except its being greater in amount, there is but one possible answer. Of two pleasures, if there be one to which all or almost all who have experience of both give a decided preference, irrespective of any feeling of moral obligation to prefer it, that is the more desirable pleasure. If one of the two is, by those who are competently acquainted with both, placed so far above the other that they prefer it, even though knowing it to be attended with a greater amount of discontent, and would not resign it for any quantity of the other pleasure which their nature is capable of, we are justified in ascribing to the preferred enjoyment a superiority in quality, so far outweighing quantity as to render it, in comparison, of small account.

Now it is an unquestionable fact that those who are equally acquainted with, and equally capable of appreciating and enjoying, both, do give a most marked preference to the manner of existence which employs their higher

4. Stoicism, a school of classical philosophy founded by Zeno (335–263 b.c.e.), emphasized duty, justice, and acting in harmony with reason.

faculties. Few human creatures would consent to be changed into any of the lower animals, for a promise of the fullest allowance of a beast's pleasures; no intelligent human being would consent to be a fool, no instructed person would be an ignoramus, no person of feeling and conscience would be selfish and base, even though they should be persuaded that the fool, the dunce, or the rascal is better satisfied with his lot than they are with theirs. They would not resign what they possess more than he for the most complete satisfaction of all the desires which they have in common with him. If they ever fancy they would, it is only in cases of unhappiness so extreme, that to escape from it they would exchange their lot for almost any other, however undesirable in their own eyes. A being of higher faculties requires more to make him happy, is capable probably of more acute suffering, and certainly accessible to it at more points, than one of an inferior type; but in spite of these liabilities, he can never really wish to sink into what he feels to be a lower grade of existence. We may give what explanation we please of this unwillingness; we may attribute it to pride, a name which is given indiscriminately to some of the most and to some of the least estimable feelings of which mankind are capable: we may refer it to the love of liberty and personal independence, an appeal to which was with the Stoics one of the most effective means for the inculcation of it; to the love of power, or to the love of excitement, both of which do really enter into and contribute to it: but its most appropriate appellation is a sense of dignity, which all human beings possess in one form or other, and in some, though by no means in exact, proportion to their higher faculties, and which is so essential a part of the happiness of those in whom it is strong, that nothing which conflicts with it could be, otherwise than momentarily, an object of desire to them. Whoever supposes that this preference takes place at a sacrifice of happiness—that the superior being, in anything like equal circumstances, is not happier than the inferior—confounds the two very different ideas, of happiness, and content. It is indisputable that the being whose capacities of enjoyment are low, has the greatest chance of having them fully satisfied; and a highly endowed being will always feel that any happiness which he can look for, as the world is constituted, is imperfect. But he can learn to bear its imperfections, if they are at all bearable; and they will not make him envy the being who is indeed unconscious of the imperfections, but only because he feels not at all the good which those imperfections qualify. It is better to be a human being dissatisfied than a pig satisfied; better to be Socrates[5] dissatisfied than a fool satisfied. And if the fool, or the pig, are of a different opinion, it is because they only know their own side of the question. The other party to the comparison knows both sides.

It may be objected, that many who are capable of the higher pleasures, occasionally, under the influence of temptation, postpone them to the lower. But this is quite compatible with a full appreciation of the intrinsic superiority of the higher. Men often, from infirmity of character, make their election for the nearer good, though they know it to be the less valuable; and this no less when the choice is between two bodily pleasures, than when it is between bodily and mental. They pursue sensual indulgences to the injury of health,

5. Greek philosopher (469–399 B.C.E.), who was notable for his dissatisfaction with his interlocutors' quick and easy answers to his probing questions.

though perfectly aware that health is the greater good. It may be further objected, that many who begin with youthful enthusiasm for everything noble, as they advance in years sink into indolence and selfishness. But I do not believe that those who undergo this very common change, voluntarily choose the lower description of pleasures in preference to the higher. I believe that before they devote themselves exclusively to the one, they have already become incapable of the other. Capacity for the nobler feelings is in most natures a very tender plant, easily killed, not only by hostile influences, but by mere want of sustenance; and in the majority of young persons it speedily dies away if the occupations to which their position in life has devoted them, and the society into which it has thrown them, are not favourable to keeping that higher capacity in exercise. Men lose their high aspirations as they lose their intellectual tastes, because they have not time or opportunity for indulging them; and they addict themselves to inferior pleasures, not because they deliberately prefer them, but because they are either the only ones to which they have access, or the only ones which they are any longer capable of enjoying. It may be questioned whether any one who has remained equally susceptible to both classes of pleasures, ever knowingly and calmly preferred the lower; though many, in all ages, have broken down in an ineffectual attempt to combine both.

From this verdict of the only competent judges, I apprehend there can be no appeal. On a question which is the best worth having of two pleasures, of which of two modes of existence is the most grateful[6] to the feelings, apart from its moral attributes and from its consequences, the judgment of those who are qualified by knowledge of both, or, if they differ, that of the majority among them, must be admitted as final. And there needs be the less hesitation to accept this judgment respecting the quality of pleasures, since there is no other tribunal to be referred to even on the question of quantity. What means are there of determining which is the acutest of two pains, or the intensest of two pleasurable sensations, except the general suffrage of those who are familiar with both? Neither pains nor pleasures are homogeneous, and pain is always heterogeneous with pleasure. What is there to decide whether a particular pleasure is worth purchasing at the cost of a particular pain, except the feelings and judgment of the experienced? When, therefore, those feelings and judgment declare the pleasures derived from the higher faculties to be preferable *in kind*, apart from the question of intensity, to those of which the animal nature, disjoined from the higher faculties, is susceptible, they are entitled on this subject to the same regard.

I have dwelt on this point, as being a necessary part of a perfectly just conception of Utility or Happiness, considered as the directive rule of human conduct. But it is by no means an indispensable condition to the acceptance of the utilitarian standard; for that standard is not the agent's own greatest happiness, but the greatest amount of happiness altogether; and if it may possibly be doubted whether a noble character is always the happier for its nobleness, there can be no doubt that it makes other people happier, and that the world in general is immensely a gainer by it. Utilitarianism, therefore, could only attain its end by the general cultivation of nobleness of character, even if

6. Pleasing, welcome.

each individual were only benefited by the nobleness of others, and his own, so far as happiness is concerned, were a sheer deduction from the benefit. But the bare enunciation of such an absurdity as this last, renders refutation superfluous.

————————

According to the Greatest Happiness Principle, as above explained, the ultimate end, with reference to and for the sake of which all other things are desirable (whether we are considering our own good or that of other people), is an existence exempt as far as possible from pain, and as rich as possible in enjoyments, both in point of quantity and quality; the test of quality, and the rule for measuring it against quantity, being the preference felt by those who in their opportunities of experience, to which must be added their habits of self-consciousness and self-observation, are best furnished with the means of comparison. This, being, according to the utilitarian opinion, the end of human action, is necessarily also the standard of morality; which may accordingly be defined, the rules and precepts for human conduct, by the observance of which an existence such as has been described might be, to the greatest extent possible, secured to all mankind; and not to them only, but, so far as the nature of things admits, to the whole sentient creation.

Against this doctrine, however, arises another class of objectors, who say that happiness, in any form, cannot be the rational purpose of human life and action; because, in the first place, it is unattainable: and they contemptuously ask, what right hast thou to be happy? a question which Mr. Carlyle[7] clenches by the addition, What right, a short time ago, hadst thou even *to be?* Next, they say, that men can do *without* happiness; that all noble human beings have felt this, and could not have become noble but by learning the lesson of Entsagen, or renunciation; which lesson, thoroughly learnt and submitted to, they affirm to be the beginning and necessary condition of all virtue.

The first of these objections would go to the root of the matter were it well founded; for if no happiness is to be had at all by human beings, the attainment of it cannot be the end of morality, or of any rational conduct. Though, even in that case, something might still be said for the utilitarian theory; since utility includes not solely the pursuit of happiness, but the prevention or mitigation of unhappiness; and if the former aim be chimerical, there will be all the greater scope and more imperative need for the latter, so long at least as mankind think fit to live, and do not take refuge in the simultaneous act of suicide recommended under certain conditions by Novalis.[8] When, however, it is thus positively asserted to be impossible that human life should be happy, the assertion, if not something like a verbal quibble, is at least an exaggeration. If by happiness be meant a continuity of highly pleasurable excitement, it is evident enough that this is impossible. A state of exalted pleasure lasts only moments, or in some cases, and with some intermissions,

7. Thomas Carlyle (1795–1881), Scottish essayist and historian. Mill is paraphrasing a passage from his *Sartor Resartus* (1833–34); in that work, he identifies Entsagen ("renunciation" in German) with moral action.

8. The pseudonym of Friedrich von Hardenberg (1772–1801), a German poet and philosophical writer who studied with and was influenced by both SCHILLER and FICHTE.

hours or days, and is the occasional brilliant flash of enjoyment, not its permanent and steady flame. Of this the philosophers who have taught that happiness is the end of life were as fully aware as those who taunt them. The happiness which they meant was not a life of rapture; but moments of such, in an existence made up of few and transitory pains, many and various pleasures, with a decided predominance of the active over the passive, and having as the foundation of the whole, not to expect more from life than it is capable of bestowing. A life thus composed, to those who have been fortunate enough to obtain it, has always appeared worthy of the name of happiness. And such an existence is even now the lot of many, during some considerable portion of their lives. The present wretched education, and wretched social arrangements, are the only real hindrance to its being attainable by almost all.

The objectors perhaps may doubt whether human beings, if taught to consider happiness as the end of life, would be satisfied with such a moderate share of it. But great numbers of mankind have been satisfied with much less. The main constituents of a satisfied life appear to be two, either of which by itself is often found sufficient for the purpose: tranquillity, and excitement. With much tranquillity, many find that they can be content with very little pleasure: with much excitement, many can reconcile themselves to a considerable quantity of pain. There is assuredly no inherent impossibility in enabling even the mass of mankind to unite both; since the two are so far from being incompatible that they are in natural alliance, the prolongation of either being a preparation for, and exciting a wish for, the other. It is only those in whom indolence amounts to a vice, that do not desire excitement after an interval of repose: it is only those in whom the need of excitement is a disease, that feel the tranquillity which follows excitement dull and insipid, instead of pleasurable in direct proportion to the excitement which preceded it. When people who are tolerably fortunate in their outward lot do not find in life sufficient enjoyment to make it valuable to them, the cause generally is, caring for nobody but themselves. To those who have neither public nor private affections, the excitements of life are much curtailed, and in any case dwindle in value as the time approaches when all selfish interests must be terminated by death: while those who leave after them objects of personal affection, and especially those who have also cultivated a fellow-feeling with the collective interests of mankind, retain as lively an interest in life on the eve of death as in the vigour of youth and health. Next to selfishness, the principal cause which makes life unsatisfactory is want of mental cultivation. A cultivated mind—I do not mean that of a philosopher, but any mind to which the fountains of knowledge have been opened, and which has been taught, in any tolerable degree, to exercise its faculties—finds sources of inexhaustible interest in all that surrounds it; in the objects of nature, the achievements of art, the imaginations of poetry, the incidents of history, the ways of mankind, past and present, and their prospects in the future. It is possible, indeed, to become indifferent to all this, and that too without having exhausted a thousandth part of it; but only when one has had from the beginning no moral or human interest in these things, and has sought in them only the gratification of curiosity.

Now there is absolutely no reason in the nature of things why an amount of mental culture sufficient to give an intelligent interest in these objects of contemplation, should not be the inheritance of every one born in a civilised country. As little is there an inherent necessity that any human being should be a selfish egotist, devoid of every feeling or care but those which centre in his own miserable individuality. Something far superior to this is sufficiently common even now, to give ample earnest of what the human species may be made. Genuine private affections, and a sincere interest in the public good, are possible, though in unequal degrees, to every rightly brought up human being. In a world in which there is so much to interest, so much to enjoy, and so much also to correct and improve, every one who has this moderate amount of moral and intellectual requisites is capable of an existence which may be called enviable; and unless such a person, through bad laws, or subjection to the will of others, is denied the liberty to use the sources of happiness within his reach, he will not fail to find this enviable existence, if he escape the positive evils of life, the great sources of physical and mental suffering—such as indigence, disease, and the unkindness, worthlessness, or premature loss of objects of affection. The main stress of the problem lies, therefore, in the contest with these calamities, from which it is a rare good fortune entirely to escape; which, as things now are, cannot be obviated, and often cannot be in any material degree mitigated. Yet no one whose opinion deserves a moment's consideration can doubt that most of the great positive evils of the world are in themselves removable, and will, if human affairs continue to improve, be in the end reduced within narrow limits. Poverty, in any sense implying suffering, may be completely extinguished by the wisdom of society, combined with the good sense and providence of individuals. Even that most intractable of enemies, disease, may be indefinitely reduced in dimensions by good physical and moral education, and proper control of noxious influences; while the progress of science holds out a promise for the future of still more direct conquests over this detestable foe. And every advance in that direction relieves us from some, not only of the chances which cut short our own lives, but, what concerns us still more, which deprive us of those in whom our happiness is wrapt up. As for vicissitudes of fortune, and other disappointments connected with worldly circumstances, these are principally the effect either of gross imprudence, of ill-regulated desires, or of bad or imperfect social institutions. All the grand sources, in short, of human suffering are in a great degree, many of them almost entirely, conquerable by human care and effort; and though their removal is grievously slow—though a long succession of generations will perish in the breach before the conquest is completed, and this world becomes all that, if will and knowledge were not wanting, it might easily be made—yet every mind sufficiently intelligent and generous to bear a part, however small and unconspicuous, in the endeavour, will draw a noble enjoyment from the contest itself, which he would not for any bribe in the form of selfish indulgence consent to be without.[9]

And this leads to the true estimation of what is said by the objectors concerning the possibility, and the obligation, of learning to do without happiness. Unquestionably it is possible to do without happiness; it is done involuntarily by nineteen-twentieths of mankind, even in those parts of our present world which are least deep in barbarism; and it often has to be done

9. Here one can see both Mill's similarity to and his difference from MARX.

voluntarily by the hero or the martyr, for the sake of something which he prizes more than his individual happiness. But this something, what is it, unless the happiness of others, or some of the requisites of happiness? It is noble to be capable of resigning entirely one's own portion of happiness, or chances of it: but, after all, this self-sacrifice must be for some end; it is not its own end; and if we are told that its end is not happiness, but virtue, which is better than happiness, I ask, would the sacrifice be made if the hero or martyr did not believe that it would earn for others immunity from similar sacrifices? Would it be made if he thought that his renunciation of happiness for himself would produce no fruit for any of his fellow creatures, but to make their lot like his, and place them also in the condition of persons who have renounced happiness? All honour to those who can abnegate for themselves the personal enjoyment of life, when by such renunciation they contribute worthily to increase the amount of happiness in the world; but he who does it, or professes to do it, for any other purpose, is no more deserving of admiration than the ascetic mounted on his pillar.[1] He may be an inspiriting proof of what men *can* do, but assuredly not an example of what they *should*.

Though it is only in a very imperfect state of the world's arrangements that any one can best serve the happiness of others by the absolute sacrifice of his own, yet so long as the world is in that imperfect state, I fully acknowledge that the readiness to make such a sacrifice is the highest virtue which can be found in man. I will add, that in this condition of the world, paradoxical as the assertion may be, the conscious ability to do without happiness gives the best prospect of realising such happiness as is attainable. For nothing except that consciousness can raise a person above the chances of life, by making him feel that, let fate and fortune do their worst, they have not power to subdue him: which, once felt, frees him from excess of anxiety concerning the evils of life, and enables him, like many a Stoic in the worst times of the Roman Empire, to cultivate in tranquillity the sources of satisfaction accessible to him, without concerning himself about the uncertainty of their duration, any more than about their inevitable end.

Meanwhile, let utilitarians never cease to claim the morality of self-devotion as a possession which belongs by as good a right to them, as either to the Stoic or to the Transcendentalist.[2] The utilitarian morality does recognise in human beings the power of sacrificing their own greatest good for the good of others. It only refuses to admit that the sacrifice is itself a good. A sacrifice which does not increase, or tend to increase, the sum total of happiness, it considers as wasted. The only self-renunciation which it applauds, is devotion to the happiness, or to some of the means of happiness, of others; either of mankind collectively, or of individuals within the limits imposed by the collective interests of mankind.

I must again repeat, what the assailants of utilitarianism seldom have the justice to acknowledge, that the happiness which forms the utilitarian standard of what is right in conduct, is not the agent's own happiness, but that of all concerned. As between his own happiness and that of others, utilitarianism

1. A reference to the "stylites," early Christian ascetics in Greece and the Middle East who in some cases spent years living on top of pillars.

2. On Transcendentalism, see the introduction to EMERSON, above.

requires him to be as strictly impartial as a disinterested and benevolent spectator. In the golden rule of Jesus of Nazareth,[3] we read the complete spirit of the ethics of utility. To do as you would be done by, and to love your neighbour as yourself, constitute the ideal perfection of utilitarian morality. As the means of making the nearest approach to this ideal, utility would enjoin, first, that laws and social arrangements should place the happiness, or (as speaking practically it may be called) the interest, of every individual, as nearly as possible in harmony with the interest of the whole; and secondly, that education and opinion, which have so vast a power over human character, should so use that power as to establish in the mind of every individual an indissoluble association between his own happiness and the good of the whole; especially between his own happiness and the practice of such modes of conduct, negative and positive, as regard for the universal happiness prescribes; so that not only he may be unable to conceive the possibility of happiness to himself, consistently with conduct opposed to the general good, but also that a direct impulse to promote the general good may be in every individual one of the habitual motives of action, and the sentiments connected therewith may fill a large and prominent place in every human being's sentient existence. If the impugners of the utilitarian morality represented it to their own minds in this its true character, I know not what recommendation possessed by any other morality they could possibly affirm to be wanting to it; what more beautiful or more exalted developments of human nature any other ethical system can be supposed to foster, or what springs of action, not accessible to the utilitarian, such systems rely on for giving effect to their mandates.

The objectors to utilitarianism cannot always be charged with representing it in a discreditable light. On the contrary, those among them who entertain anything like a just idea of its disinterested character, sometimes find fault with its standard as being too high for humanity. They say it is exacting too much to require that people shall always act from the inducement of promoting the general interests of society. But this is to mistake the very meaning of a standard of morals, and confound the rule of action with the motive of it. It is the business of ethics to tell us what are our duties, or by what test we may know them; but no system of ethics requires that the sole motive of all we do shall be a feeling of duty; on the contrary, ninety-nine hundredths of all our actions are done from other motives, and rightly so done, if the rule of duty does not condemn them. It is the more unjust to utilitarianism that this particular misapprehension should be made a ground of objection to it, inasmuch as utilitarian moralists have gone beyond almost all others in affirming that the motive has nothing to do with the morality of the action, though much with the worth of the agent. He who saves a fellow creature from drowning does what is morally right, whether his motive be duty, or the hope of being paid for his trouble; he who betrays the friend that trusts him, is guilty of a crime, even if his object be to serve another friend to whom he is under greater obligations. But to speak only of actions done from the motive of duty, and in direct obedience to principle: it is a misapprehension of the utilitarian mode of thought, to conceive it as implying that people should fix their minds upon so wide a generality as the world, or society at large. The great majority

---

3. See Matthew 7:12, 19:19.

of good actions are intended not for the benefit of the world, but for that of individuals, of which the good of the world is made up; and the thoughts of the most virtuous man need not on these occasions travel beyond the particular persons concerned, except so far as is necessary to assure himself that in benefiting them he is not violating the rights, that is, the legitimate and authorised expectations, of any one else. The multiplication of happiness is, according to the utilitarian ethics, the object of virtue: the occasions on which any person (except one in a thousand) has it in his power to do this on an extended scale, in other words to be a public benefactor, are but exceptional; and on these occasions alone is he called on to consider public utility; in every other case, private utility, the interest or happiness of some few persons, is all he has to attend to. Those alone the influence of whose actions extends to society in general, need concern themselves habitually about so large an object. In the case of abstinences indeed—of things which people forbear to do from moral considerations, though the consequences in the particular case might be beneficial—it would be unworthy of an intelligent agent not to be consciously aware that the action is of a class which, if practised generally, would be generally injurious, and that this is the ground of the obligation to abstain from it. The amount of regard for the public interest implied in this recognition, is no greater than is demanded by every system of morals, for they all enjoin to abstain from whatever is manifestly pernicious to society.

The same considerations dispose of another reproach against the doctrine of utility, founded on a still grosser misconception of the purpose of a standard of morality, and of the very meaning of the words right and wrong. It is often affirmed that utilitarianism renders men cold and unsympathising; that it chills their moral feelings towards individuals; that it makes them regard only the dry and hard consideration of the consequences of actions, not taking into their moral estimate the qualities from which those actions emanate. If the assertion means that they do not allow their judgment respecting the rightness or wrongness of an action to be influenced by their opinion of the qualities of the person who does it, this is a complaint not against utilitarianism, but against having any standard of morality at all; for certainly no known ethical standard decides an action to be good or bad because it is done by a good or a bad man, still less because done by an amiable, a brave, or a benevolent man, or the contrary. These considerations are relevant, not to the estimation of actions, but of persons; and there is nothing in the utilitarian theory inconsistent with the fact that there are other things which interest us in persons besides the rightness and wrongness of their actions. The Stoics, indeed, with the paradoxical misuse of language which was part of their system, and by which they strove to raise themselves above all concern about anything but virtue, were fond of saying that he who has that has everything; that he, and only he, is rich, is beautiful, is a king. But no claim of this description is made for the virtuous man by the utilitarian doctrine. Utilitarians are quite aware that there are other desirable possessions and qualities besides virtue, and are perfectly willing to allow to all of them their full worth. They are also aware that a right action does not necessarily indicate a virtuous character, and that actions which are blamable, often proceed from qualities entitled to praise. When this is apparent in any particular case, it modifies their estimation, not certainly of the act, but of the agent. I grant that they are, notwithstanding, of opinion, that in the long run the best proof of a good character is good actions; and resolutely refuse to consider any mental disposition as good, of which the predominant tendency is to produce bad conduct. This makes them unpopular with many people; but it is an unpopularity which they must share with every one who regards the distinction between right and wrong in a serious light; and the reproach is not one which a conscientious utilitarian need be anxious to repel.

If no more be meant by the objection than that many utilitarians look on the morality of actions, as measured by the utilitarian standard, with too exclusive a regard, and do not lay sufficient stress upon the other beauties of character which go towards making a human being lovable or admirable, this may be admitted. Utilitarians who have cultivated their moral feelings, but not their sympathies nor their artistic perceptions, do fall into this mistake; and so do all other moralists under the same conditions. What can be said in excuse for other moralists is equally available for them, namely, that, if there is to be any error, it is better that it should be on that side. As a matter of fact, we may affirm that among utilitarians as among adherents of other systems, there is every imaginable degree of rigidity and of laxity in the application of their standard: some are even puritanically rigorous, while others are as indulgent as can possibly be desired by sinner or by sentimentalist. But on the whole, a doctrine which brings prominently forward the interest that mankind have in the repression and prevention of conduct which violates the moral law, is likely to be inferior to no other in turning the sanctions of opinion again such violations. It is true, the question, What does violate the moral law? is one on which those who recognise different standards of morality are likely now and then to differ. But difference of opinion on moral questions was not first introduced into the world by utilitarianism, while that doctrine does supply, if not always an easy, at all events a tangible and intelligible mode of deciding such differences.

———

It may not be superfluous to notice a few more of the common misapprehensions of utilitarian ethics, even those which are so obvious and gross that it might appear impossible for any person of candour and intelligence to fall into them; since persons, even of considerable mental endowments, often give themselves so little trouble to understand the bearings of any opinion against which they entertain a prejudice, and men are in general so little conscious of this voluntary ignorance as a defect, that the vulgarest misunderstandings of ethical doctrines are continually met with in the deliberate writings of persons of the greatest pretensions both to high principle and to philosophy. We not uncommonly hear the doctrine of utility inveighed against as a *godless* doctrine. If it be necessary to say anything at all against so mere an assumption, we may say that the question depends upon what idea we have formed of the moral character of the Deity. If it be a true belief that God desires, above all things, the happiness of his creatures, and that this was his purpose in their creation, utility is not only not a godless doctrine, but more profoundly religious than any other. If it be meant that utilitarianism does not recognise the revealed will of God as the supreme law of morals, I answer, that a utilitarian who believes in the perfect goodness and wisdom of God, necessarily believes that whatever God has thought fit to reveal on the subject of morals, must fulfil the requirements of utility in a supreme degree. But others besides utilitarians have been of opinion that the Christian revelation was intended, and is fitted, to inform the hearts and minds of mankind with a spirit which should enable them to find for themselves what is right, and incline them to do it when found, rather than to tell them, except in a very general way, what it is; and that we need a doctrine of ethics, carefully followed out, to *interpret* to us the will of God. Whether this opinion is correct or not, it is superfluous here to discuss; since whatever aid religion, either natural or revealed, can afford to ethical investigation, is as open to the utilitarian moralist as to any other. He can use it as the testimony of God to the usefulness or hurtfulness of any given course of action, by as good a right as others can use it for the indication of a transcendental law, having no connection with usefulness or with happiness.

Again, Utility is often summarily stigmatised as an immoral doctrine by giving it the name of Expediency, and taking advantage of the popular use of that term to contrast it with Principle. But the Expedient, in the sense in which it is opposed to the Right, generally means that which is expedient for the particular interest of the agent himself; as when a minister sacrifices the interests of his country to keep himself in place. When it means anything better than this, it means that which is expedient for some immediate object, some temporary purpose, but which violates a rule whose observance is expedient in a much higher degree. The Expedient, in this sense, instead of being the same thing with the useful, is a branch of the hurtful. Thus, it would often be expedient, for the purpose of getting over some momentary embarrassment, or attaining some object immediately useful to ourselves or others, to tell a lie. But inasmuch as the cultivation in ourselves of a sensitive feeling on the subject of veracity, is one of the most useful, and the enfeeblement of that feeling one of the most hurtful, things to which our conduct can be instrumental; and inasmuch as any, even unintentional, deviation from truth, does that much towards weakening the trustworthiness of human assertion, which is not only the principal support of all present social well-being, but the insufficiency of which does more than any one thing that can be named to keep back civilisation, virtue, everything on which human happiness on the largest scale depends; we feel that the violation, for a present advantage, of a rule of such transcendant expediency, is not expedient, and that he who, for the sake of a convenience to himself or to some other individual, does what depends on him to deprive mankind of the good, and inflict upon them the evil, involved in the greater or less reliance which they can place in each other's word, acts the part of one of their worst enemies. Yet that even this rule, sacred as it is, admits of possible exceptions, is acknowledged by all moralists; the chief of which is when the withholding of some fact (as of information from a malefactor, or of bad news from a person dangerously ill) would save an individual (especially an individual other than oneself) from great and unmerited evil, and when the withholding can only be effected by denial. But in order that the exception may not extend itself beyond the need, and may have the least possible effect in weakening reliance on veracity, it ought to be recognised, and, if possible, its limits defined; and if the principle of utility is good for anything, it must be good for weighing these conflicting utilities against one another, and marking out the region within which one or the other preponderates.

Again, defenders of utility often find themselves called upon to reply to such objections as this—that there is not time, previous to action, for calculating and weighing the effects of any line of conduct on the general happiness. This is exactly as if any one were to say that it is impossible to guide our conduct by Christianity, because there is not time, on every occasion on which anything has to be done, to read through the Old and New Testaments. The answer to the objection is, that there has been ample time, namely, the whole past duration of the human species. During all that time, mankind have been learning by experience the tendencies of actions; on which experience all the prudence, as well as all the morality of life, are dependent. People talk as if the commencement of this course of experience had hitherto been put off, and as if, at the moment when some man feels tempted to meddle with the property or life of another, he had to begin considering for the first time whether murder and theft are injurious to human happiness. Even then I do not think that he would find the question very puzzling; but, at all events, the matter is now done to his hand. It is truly a whimsical supposition that, if mankind were agreed in considering utility to be the test of morality, they would remain without any agreement as to what *is* useful, and would take no measures for having their notions on the subject taught to the young, and enforced by law and opinion. There is no difficulty in proving any ethical standard whatever to work ill, if we suppose universal idiocy to be conjoined with it; but on any hypothesis short of that, mankind must by this time have acquired positive beliefs as to the effects of some actions on their happiness; and the beliefs which have thus come down are the rules of morality for the multitude, and for the philosopher until he has succeeded in finding better. That philosophers might easily do this, even now, on many subjects; that the received code of ethics is by no means of divine right; and that mankind have still much to learn as to the effects of actions on the general happiness, I admit, or rather, earnestly maintain. The corollaries from the principle of utility, like the precepts of every practical art, admit of indefinite improvement, and, in a progressive state of the human mind, their improvement is perpetually going on. But to consider the rules of morality as improvable, is one thing; to pass over the intermediate generalisations entirely, and endeavour to test each individual action directly by the first principle, is another. It is a strange notion that the acknowledgment of a first principle is inconsistent with the admission of secondary ones. To inform a traveller respecting the place of his ultimate destination, is not to forbid the use of landmarks and direction-posts on the way. The proposition that happiness is the end and aim of morality, does not mean that no road ought to be laid down to that goal, or that persons going thither should not be advised to take one direction rather than another. Men really ought to leave off talking a kind of nonsense on this subject, which they would neither talk nor listen to on other matters of practical concernment. Nobody argues that the art of navigation is not founded on astronomy, because sailors cannot wait to calculate the Nautical Almanack. Being rational creatures, they go to sea with it ready calculated; and all rational creatures go out upon the sea of life with their minds made up on the common questions of right and wrong, as well as on many of the far more difficult questions of wise and foolish. And this, as long as foresight is a human quality, it is to be presumed they will continue to do. Whatever we adopt as the fundamental principle of morality, we require subordinate principles to apply it by; the impossibility of doing without them, being common to all systems, can afford no argument against any one in particular; but gravely to argue as if no such secondary principles could be had, and as if mankind had remained till now, and always must remain, without drawing any general conclusions from the experience of human life, is as high a pitch, I think, as absurdity has ever reached in philosophical controversy.

The remainder of the stock arguments against utilitarianism mostly consist in laying to its charge the common infirmities of human nature, and the general difficulties which embarrass conscientious persons in shaping their course through life. We are told that a utilitarian will be apt to make his own particular case an exception to moral rules, and, when under temptation, will see a utility in the breach of a rule, greater than he will see in its observance. But is utility the only creed which is able to furnish us with excuses for evil doing, and means of cheating our own conscience? They are afforded in abundance by all doctrines which recognise as a fact in morals the existence of conflicting considerations; which all doctrines do, that have been believed by sane persons. It is not the fault of any creed, but of the complicated nature of human affairs, that rules of conduct cannot be so framed as to require no exceptions, and that hardly any kind of action can safely be laid down as either always obligatory or always condemnable. There is no ethical creed which does not temper the rigidity of its laws, by giving a certain latitude, under the moral responsibility of the agent, for accommodation to peculiarities of circumstances; and under every creed, at the opening thus made, self-deception and dishonest casuistry get in. There exists no moral system under which there do not arise unequivocal cases of conflicting obligation. These are the real difficulties, the knotty points both in the theory of ethics, and in the conscientious guidance of personal conduct. They are overcome practically, with greater or with less success, according to the intellect and virtue of the individual; but it can hardly be pretended that any one will be the less qualified for dealing with them, from possessing an ultimate standard to which conflicting rights and duties can be referred. If utility is the ultimate source of moral obligations, utility may be invoked to decide between them when their demands are incompatible. Though the application of the standard may be difficult, it is better than none at all: while in other systems, the moral laws all claiming independent authority, there is no common umpire entitled to interfere between them; their claims to precedence one over another rest on little better than sophistry, and unless determined, as they generally are, by the unacknowledged influence of considerations of utility, afford a free scope for the action of personal desires and partialities. We must remember that only in these cases of conflict between secondary principles is it requisite that first principles should be appealed to. There is no case of moral obligation in which some secondary principle is not involved; and if only one, there can seldom be any real doubt which one it is, in the mind of any person by whom the principle itself is recognised.

Chapter IV. Of What Sort of Proof the Principle of Utility is Susceptible

It has already been remarked, that questions of ultimate ends do not admit of proof, in the ordinary acceptation of the term. To be incapable of proof by reasoning is common to all first principles; to the first premises of our knowledge, as well as to those of our conduct. But the former, being matters of fact, may be the subject of a direct appeal to the faculties which judge of fact—namely, our senses, and our internal consciousness. Can an appeal be made to the same faculties on questions of practical ends? Or by what other faculty is cognisance taken of them?

Questions about ends are, in other words, questions of what things are desirable. The utilitarian doctrine is, that happiness is desirable, and the only thing desirable, as an end: all other things being only desirable as means to that end. What ought to be required of this doctrine—what conditions is it requisite that the doctrine should fulfil—to make good its claim to be believed?

The only proof capable of being given that an object is visible, is that people actually see it. The only proof that a sound is audible, is that people hear it: and so of the other sources of our experience. In like manner, I apprehend, the sole evidence it is possible to produce that anything is desirable, is that people do actually desire it. If the end which the utilitarian doctrine proposes to itself were not, in theory and in practice, acknowledged to be an end, nothing could ever convince any person that it was so. No reason can be given why the general happiness is desirable, except that each person, so far as he believes it to be attainable, desires his own happiness. This, however, being a fact, we have not only all the proof which the case admits of, but all which it is possible to require, that happiness is a good: that each person's happiness is a good to that person, and the general happiness, therefore, a good to the aggregate of all persons. Happiness has made out its title as *one* of the ends of conduct, and consequently one of the criteria of morality.[4]

But it has not, by this alone, proved itself to be the sole criterion. To do that, it would seem, by the same rule, necessary to show, not only that people desire happiness, but that they never desire anything else. Now it is palpable that they do desire things which, in common language, are decidedly distinguished from happiness. They desire, for example, virtue, and the absence of vice, no less really than pleasure and the absence of pain. The desire of virtue is not as universal, but it is as authentic a fact, as the desire of happiness. And hence the opponents of the utilitarian standard deem that they have a right to infer that there are other ends of human action besides happiness, and that happiness is not the standard of approbation and disapprobation.

But does the utilitarian doctrine deny that people desire virtue, or maintain that virtue is not a thing to be desired? The very reverse. It maintains not only that virtue is to be desired, but that it is to be desired disinterestedly, for itself. Whatever may be the opinion of utilitarian moralists as to the original conditions by which virtue is made virtue; however they may believe (as they do) that actions and dispositions are only virtuous because they promote another end than virtue; yet this being granted, and it having been

---

4. Mill's reasoning here and in the following paragraphs is crucial to his position and his form of utilitarianism.

decided, from considerations of this description, what *is* virtuous, they not only place virtue at the very head of the things which are good as means to the ultimate end, but they also recognise as a psychological fact the possibility of its being, to the individual, a good in itself, without looking to any end beyond it; and hold, that the mind is not in a right state, not in a state conformable to Utility, not in the state most conducive to the general happiness, unless it does love virtue in this manner—as a thing desirable in itself, even although, in the individual instance, it should not produce those other desirable consequences which it tends to produce, and on account of which it is held to be virtue. This opinion is not, in the smallest degree, a departure from the Happiness principle. The ingredients of happiness are very various, and each of them is desirable in itself, and not merely when considered as swelling an aggregate. The principle of utility does not mean that any given pleasure, as music, for instance, or any given exemption from pain, as for example health, is to be looked upon as means to a collective something termed happiness, and to be desired on that account. They are desired and desirable in and for themselves; besides being means, they are a part of the end. Virtue, according to the utilitarian doctrine, is not naturally and originally part of the end, but it is capable of becoming so; and in those who love it disinterestedly it has become so, and is desired and cherished, not as a means to happiness, but as a part of their happiness.

To illustrate this farther, we may remember that virtue is not the only thing, originally a means, and which if it were not a means to anything else, would be and remain indifferent, but which by association with what it is a means to, comes to be desired for itself, and that too with the utmost intensity. What, for example, shall we say of the love of money? There is nothing originally more desirable about money than about any heap of glittering pebbles. Its worth is solely that of the things which it will buy; the desires for other things than itself, which it is a means of gratifying. Yet the love of money is not only one of the strongest moving forces of human life, but money is, in many cases, desired in and for itself; the desire to possess it is often stronger than the desire to use it, and goes on increasing when all the desires which point to ends beyond it, to be compassed by it, are falling off. It may, then, be said truly, that money is desired not for the sake of an end, but as part of the end. From being a means to happiness, it has come to be itself a principal ingredient of the individual's conception of happiness. The same may be said of the majority of the great objects of human life—power, for example, or fame; except that to each of these there is a certain amount of immediate pleasure annexed, which has at least the semblance of being naturally inherent in them; a thing which cannot be said of money. Still, however, the strongest natural attraction, both of power and of fame, is the immense aid they give to the attainment of our other wishes; and it is the strong association thus generated between them and all our objects of desire, which gives to the direct desire of them the intensity it often assumes, so as in some characters to surpass in strength all other desires. In these cases the means have become a part of the end, and a more important part of it than any of the things which they are means to. What was once desired as an instrument for the attainment of happiness, has come to be desired for its own sake. In being desired for its own sake it is, however, desired as *part* of happiness. The person is made, or thinks he would be made, happy by its mere possession; and is made unhappy by failure to obtain it. The desire of it is not a different thing from the desire of happiness, any more than the love of music, or the desire of health. They are included in happiness. They are some of the elements of which the desire of happiness is made up. Happiness is not an abstract idea, but a concrete whole; and these are some of its parts. And the utilitarian standard sanctions and approves their being so. Life would be a poor thing, very ill provided with sources of happiness, if there were not this provision of nature, by which things originally indifferent, but conducive to, or otherwise associated with, the satisfaction of our primitives desires, become in themselves sources of pleasure more valuable than the primitive pleasures, both in permanency, in the space of human existence that they are capable of covering, and even in intensity.

Virtue, according to the utilitarian conception, is a good of this description. There was no original desire of it, or motive to it, save its conduciveness to pleasure, and especially to protection from pain. But through the association thus formed, it may be felt a good in itself, and desired as such with as great intensity as any other good; and with this difference between it and the love of money, of power, or of fame, that all of these may, and often do, render the individual noxious to the other members of the society to which he belongs, whereas there is nothing which makes him so much a blessing to them as the cultivation of the disinterested love of virtue. And consequently, the utilitarian standard, while it tolerates and approves those other acquired desires, up to the point beyond which they would be more injurious to the general happiness than promotive of it, enjoins and requires the cultivation of the love of virtue up to the greatest strength possible, as being above all things important to the general happiness.

It results from the preceding considerations, that there is in reality nothing desired except happiness. Whatever is desired otherwise than as a means to some end beyond itself, and ultimately to happiness, is desired as itself a part of happiness, and is not desired for itself until it has become so. Those who desire virtue for its own sake, desire it either because the consciousness of it is a pleasure, or because the consciousness of being without it is a pain, or for both reasons united; as in truth the pleasure and pain seldom exist separately, but almost always together, the same person feeling pleasure in the degree of virtue attained, and pain in not having attained more. If one of these gave him no pleasure, and the other no pain, he would not love or desire virtue, or would desire it only for the other benefits which it might produce to himself or to persons whom he cared for.

We have now, then, an answer to the question, of what sort of proof the principle of utility is susceptible. If the opinion which I have now stated is psychologically true—if human nature is so constituted as to desire nothing which is not either a part of happiness or a means of happiness, we can have no other proof, and we require no other, that these are the only things desirable. If so, happiness is the sole end of human action, and the promotion of it the test by which to judge of all human conduct; from whence it necessarily follows that it must be the criterion of morality, since a part is included in the whole.

And now to decide whether this is really so; whether mankind do desire nothing for itself but that which is a pleasure to them or of which the absence is a pain; we have evidently arrived at a question of fact and experience, dependent, like all similar questions, upon evidence. It can only be determined by practised self-consciousness and self-observation, assisted by observation of others. I believe that these sources of evidence, impartially consulted, will declare that desiring a thing and finding it pleasant, aversion to it and thinking of it as painful, are phenomena entirely inseparable, or rather two parts of the same phenomenon; in strictness of language, two different modes of naming the same psychological fact: that to think of an object as desirable (unless for the sake of its consequences), and to think of it as pleasant, are one and the same thing; and that to desire anything, except in proportion as the idea of it is pleasant, is a physical and metaphysical impossibility.

So obvious does this appear to me, that I expect it will hardly be disputed:[5] and the objection made will be, not that desire can possibly be directed to anything ultimately except pleasure and exemption from pain, but that the will is a different thing from desire; that a person of confirmed virtue, or any other person whose purposes are fixed, carries out his purposes without any thought of the pleasure he has in contemplating them, or expects to derive from their fulfilment; and persists in acting on them, even though these pleasures are much diminished, by changes in his character or decay of his passive sensibilities, or are outweighed by the pains which the pursuit of the purposes may bring upon him. All this I fully admit, and have stated it elsewhere, as positively and emphatically as any one. Will, the active phenomenon, is a different thing from desire, the state of passive sensibility, and though originally an offshoot from it, may in time take root and detach itself from the parent stock; so much so, that in the case of an habitual purpose, instead of willing the thing because we desire it, we often desire it only because we will it. This, however, is but an instance of that familiar fact, the power of habit, and is nowise confined to the case of virtuous actions. Many indifferent things, which men originally did from a motive of some sort, they continue to do from habit. Sometimes this is done unconsciously, the consciousness coming only after the action: at other times with conscious volition, but volition which has become habitual, and is put in operation by the force of habit, in opposition perhaps to the deliberate preference, as often happens with those who have contracted habits of vicious or hurtful indulgence. Third and last comes the case in which the habitual act of will in the individual instance is not in contradiction to the general intention prevailing at other times, but in fulfilment of it; as in the case of the person of confirmed virtue, and of all who pursue deliberately and consistently any determinate end. The distinction between will and desire thus understood is an authentic and highly important psychological fact; but the fact consists solely in this—that will, like all other parts of our constitution, is amenable to habit, and that we may will from habit what we no longer desire for itself, or desire only because we will it. It is not the less true that will, in the beginning, is entirely produced by desire; including in that term the repelling influence of pain as well as the attractive one of pleasure. Let us take into consideration, no longer the person who has a confirmed will to do right, but him in whom that virtuous will

5. This was wishful thinking on Mill's part.

is still feeble, conquerable by temptation, and not to be fully relied on; by what means can it be strengthened? How can the will to be virtuous, where it does not exist in sufficient force, be implanted or awakened? Only by making the person *desire* virtue—by making him think of it in a pleasurable light, or of its absence in a painful one. It is by associating the doing right with pleasure, or the doing wrong with pain, or by eliciting and impressing and bringing home to the person's experience the pleasure naturally involved in the one or the pain in the other, that it is possible to call forth that will to be virtuous, which, when confirmed, acts without any thought of either pleasure or pain. Will is the child of desire, and passes out of the dominion of its parent only to come under that of habit. That which is the result of habit affords no presumption of being intrinsically good; and there would be no reason for wishing that the purpose of virtue should become independent of pleasure and pain, were it not that the influence of the pleasurable and painful associations which prompt to virtue is not sufficiently to be depended on for unerring constancy of action until it has acquired the support of habit. Both in feeling and in conduct, habit is the only thing which imparts certainty; and it is because of the importance to others of being able to rely absolutely on one's feelings and conduct, and to oneself of being able to rely on one's own, that the will to do right ought to be cultivated into this habitual independence. In other words, this state of the will is a means to good, not intrinsically a good; and does not contradict the doctrine that nothing is a good to human beings but in so far as it is either itself pleasurable, or a means of attaining pleasure or averting pain.

But if this doctrine be true, the principle of utility is proved. Whether it is so or not, must now be left to the consideration of the thoughtful reader.

SOURCE: From John Stuart Mill, *Utilitarianism, Liberty, and Representative Government* (London: Dent; New York: Dutton, 1910), pp. 5–24, 32–38. First published in 1861. The term "utility" had been used by the English philosopher and economist Jeremy Bentham (1748–1832), who argued that goodness is a function of utility, or usefulness in bringing about desirable consequences, which he conceived in terms of pleasure. Mill adopted the terminology to refer to his own (rather more sophisticated) general theory of value, associated moral theory, and general "theory of life," while continuing to characterize utility in terms of "pleasure" of one sort or another.

From The Subjection of Women

The object of this Essay is to explain as clearly as I am able, the grounds of an opinion which I have held from the very earliest period when I had formed any opinions at all on social or political matters, and which, instead of being weakened or modified, has been constantly growing stronger by the progress of reflection and the experience of life. That the principle which regulates the existing social relations between the two sexes—the legal subordination of one sex to the other—is wrong in itself, and now one of the chief hindrances to human improvement; and that it ought to be replaced by a principle of perfect equality, admitting no power or privilege on the one side, nor disability on the other.

* * *

The least that can be demanded is, that the question should not be considered as prejudged by existing fact and existing opinion, but open to discussion on its merits, as a question of justice and expediency: the decision on this, as on any of the other social arrangements of mankind, depending on what an enlightened estimate of tendencies and consequences may show to be most advantageous to humanity in general, without distinction of sex.[1] And the discussion must be a real discussion, descending to foundations, and not resting satisfied with vague and general assertions. It will not do, for instance, to assert in general terms, that the experience of mankind has pronounced in favour of the existing system. Experience cannot possibly have decided between two courses, so long as there has only been experience of one. If it be said that the doctrine of the equality of the sexes rests only on theory, it must be remembered that the contrary doctrine also has only theory to rest upon. All that is proved in its favour by direct experience, is that mankind have been able to exist under it, and to attain the degree of improvement and prosperity which we now see; but whether that prosperity has been attained sooner, or is now greater, than it would have been under the other system, experience does not say. On the other hand, experience does say, that every step in improvement has been so invariably accompanied by a step made in raising the social position of women, that historians and philosophers have been led to adopt their elevation or debasement as on the whole the surest test and most correct measure of the civilization of a people or an age. Through all the progressive period of human history, the condition of women has been approaching nearer to equality with men. This does not of itself prove that the assimilation must go on to complete equality; but it assuredly affords some presumption that such is the case.

Neither does it avail anything to say that the *nature* of the two sexes adapts them to their present functions and position, and renders these appropriate to them. Standing on the ground of common sense and the constitution of the human mind, I deny that any one knows, or can know, the nature of the two sexes, as long as they have only been seen in their present relation to one another. If men had ever been found in society without women, or women without men, or if there had been a society of men and women in which the women were not under the control of the men, something might have been positively known about the mental and moral differences which may be inherent in the nature of each. What is now called the nature of women is an eminently artificial thing—the result of forced repression in some directions, unnatural stimulation in others.[2] It may be asserted without scruple, that no other class of dependents have had their character so entirely distorted from its natural proportions by their relation with their masters; for, if conquered and slave races have been, in some respects, more forcibly repressed, whatever in them has not been crushed down by an iron heel has generally been let alone, and if left with any liberty of development, it has developed itself according to its own laws; but in the case of women, a hot-house and stove cultivation has always been carried on of some of the capabilities of

1. That is, the argument appeals not to a principle of essential equality but rather to (utilitarian) considerations of what is "most advantageous to humanity in general."

2. This was one of the main points of Mary Wollstonecraft's *A Vindication of the Rights of Woman* (1792).

their nature, for the benefit and pleasure of their masters. Then, because certain products of the general vital force sprout luxuriantly and reach a great development in this heated atmosphere and under this active nurture and watering, while other shoots from the same root, which are left outside in the wintry air, with ice purposely heaped all round them, have a stunted growth, and some are burnt off with fire and disappear; men, with that inability to recognise their own work which distinguishes the unanalytic mind, indolently believe that the tree grows of itself in the way they have made it grow, and that it would die if one half of it were not kept in a vapour bath and the other half in the snow.

Of all difficulties which impede the progress of thought, and the formation of well-grounded opinions on life and social arrangements, the greatest is now the unspeakable ignorance and inattention of mankind in respect to the influences which form human character. Whatever any portion of the human species now are, or seem to be, such, it is supposed, they have a natural tendency to be: even when the most elementary knowledge of the circumstances in which they have been placed, clearly points out the causes that made them what they are. Because a cottier[3] deeply in arrears to his landlord is not industrious, there are people who think that the Irish are naturally idle. Because constitutions can be overthrown when the authorities appointed to execute them turn their arms against them, there are people who think the French incapable of free government. Because the Greeks cheated the Turks, and the Turks only plundered the Greeks,[4] there are persons who think that the Turks are naturally more sincere: and because women, as is often said, care nothing about politics except their personalities, it is supposed that the general good is naturally less interesting to women than to men. History, which is now so much better understood than formerly, teaches another lesson: if only by showing the extraordinary susceptibility of human nature to external influences, and the extreme variableness of those of its manifestations which are supposed to be most universal and uniform. But in history, as in travelling, men usually see only what they already had in their own minds; and few learn much from history, who do not bring much with them to its study.

Hence, in regard to that most difficult question, what are the natural differences between the two sexes—a subject on which it is impossible in the present state of society to obtain complete and correct knowledge—while almost everybody dogmatizes upon it, almost all neglect and make light of the only means by which any partial insight can be obtained into it. This is, an analytic study of the most important department of psychology, the laws of the influence of circumstances on character. For, however great and apparently ineradicable the moral and intellectual differences between men and women might be, the evidence of their being natural differences could only be negative. Those only could be inferred to be natural which could not possibly be artificial—the residuum, after deducting every characteristic of either sex which can admit of being explained from education or external

3. In Ireland, a peasant renting and cultivating a small amount of land.
4. A reference to common stereotypes about the relationship between the subject Greek and ruling Turks in the Ottoman Empire, which were of much interest in England before and after Greece's War of Independence (1821–32).

circumstances. The profoundest knowledge of the laws of the formation of character is indispensable to entitle any one to affirm even that there is any difference, much more what the difference is, between the two sexes considered as moral and rational beings; and since no one, as yet, has that knowledge, (for there is hardly any subject which, in proportion to its importance, has been so little studied), no one is thus far entitled to any positive opinion on the subject. Conjectures are all that can at present be made; conjectures more or less probable, according as more or less authorized by such knowledge as we yet have of the laws of psychology, as applied to the formation of character.

* * *

Thus far, the benefits which it has appeared that the world would gain by ceasing to make sex a disqualification for privileges and a badge of subjection, are social rather than individual; consisting in an increase of the general fund of thinking and acting power, and an improvement in the general conditions of the association of men with women. But it would be a grievous understatement of the case to omit the most direct benefit of all, the unspeakable gain in private happiness to the liberated half of the species; the difference to them between a life of subjection to the will of others, and a life of rational freedom. After the primary necessities of food and raiment, freedom is the first and strongest want of human nature. While mankind are lawless, their desire is for lawless freedom. When they have learnt to understand the meaning of duty and the value of reason, they incline more and more to be guided and restrained by these in the exercise of their freedom; but they do not therefore desire freedom less; they do not become disposed to accept the will of other people as the representative and interpreter of those guiding principles. On the contrary, the communities in which the reason has been most cultivated, and in which the idea of social duty has been most powerful, are those which have most strongly asserted the freedom of action of the individual—the liberty of each to govern his conduct by his own feelings of duty, and by such laws and social restraints as his own conscience can subscribe to.

He who would rightly appreciate the worth of personal independence as an element of happiness, should consider the value he himself puts upon it as an ingredient of his own. There is no subject on which there is a greater habitual difference of judgment between a man judging for himself, and the same man judging for other people. When he hears others complaining that they are not allowed freedom of action—that their own will has not sufficient influence in the regulation of their affairs—his inclination is, to ask, what are their grievances? what positive damage they sustain? and in what respect they consider their affairs to be mismanaged? and if they fail to make out, in answer to these questions, what appears to him a sufficient case, he turns a deaf ear, and regards their complaint as the fanciful querulousness of people whom nothing reasonable will satisfy. But he has a quite different standard of judgment when he is deciding for himself. Then, the most unexceptionable administration of his interests by a tutor set over him, does not satisfy his feelings: his personal exclusion from the deciding authority appears itself the greatest grievance of all, rendering it superfluous even to enter into the question of mismanagement. It is the same with nations. What citizen of a free country would listen to any offers of good and skilful administration, in return for the abdication of freedom? Even if he could believe that good and skilful administration can exist among a people ruled by a will not their own, would not the consciousness of working out their own destiny under their own moral responsibility be a compensation to his feelings for great rudeness and imperfection in the details of public affairs? Let him rest assured that whatever he feels on this point, women feel in a fully equal degree. Whatever has been said or written, from the time of Herodotus[5] to the present, of the ennobling influence of free government—the nerve and spring which it gives to all the faculties, the larger and higher objects which it presents to the intellect and feelings, the more unselfish public spirit, and calmer and broader views of duty, that it engenders, and the generally loftier platform on which it elevates the individual as a moral, spiritual, and social being—is every particle as true of women as of men. Are these things no important part of individual happiness? Let any man call to mind what he himself felt on emerging from boyhood—from the tutelage and control of even loved and affectionate elders—and entering upon the responsibilities of manhood. Was it not like the physical effect of taking off a heavy weight, or releasing him from obstructive, even if not otherwise painful, bonds? Did he not feel twice as much alive, twice as much a human being, as before? And does he imagine that women have none of these feelings? But it is a striking fact, that the satisfactions and mortifications of personal pride, though all in all to most men when the case is their own, have less allowance made for them in the case of other people, and are less listened to as a ground or a justification of conduct, than any other natural human feelings; perhaps because men compliment them in their own case with the names of so many other qualities, that they are seldom conscious how mighty an influence these feelings exercise in their own lives. No less large and powerful is their part, we may assure ourselves, in the lives and feelings of women. Women are schooled into suppressing them in their most natural and most healthy direction, but the internal principle remains, in a different outward form. An active and energetic mind, if denied liberty, will seek for power: refused the command of itself, it will assert its personality by attempting to control others. To allow to any human beings no existence of their own but what depends on others, is giving far too high a premium on bending others to their purposes. Where liberty cannot be hoped for, and power can, power becomes the grand object of human desire; those to whom others will not leave the undisturbed management of their own affairs, will compensate themselves, if they can, by meddling for their own purposes with the affairs of others. Hence also women's passion for personal beauty, and dress and display; and all the evils that flow from it, in the way of mischievous luxury and social immorality. The love of power and the love of liberty are in eternal antagonism. Where there is least liberty, the passion for power is the most ardent and unscrupulous. The desire of power over

5. Greek historian (ca. 484–ca. 425 B.C.E.); his writings on the 5th-century Persian Wars contrasted the (free) Greeks of the Hellenic city-states with the "barbarians" of the Persian Empire.

others can only cease to be a depraving agency among mankind, when each of them individually is able to do without it: which can only be where respect for liberty in the personal concerns of each is an established principle.

But it is not only through the sentiment of personal dignity, that the free direction and disposal of their own faculties is a source of individual happiness, and to be fettered and restricted in it, a source of unhappiness, to human beings, and not least to women. There is nothing, after disease, indigence, and guilt, so fatal to the pleasurable enjoyment of life as the want of a worthy outlet for the active faculties. Women who have the cares of a family, and while they have the cares of a family, have this outlet, and it generally suffices for them: but what of the greatly increasing number of women, who have had no opportunity of exercising the vocation which they are mocked by telling them is their proper one? What of the women whose children have been lost to them by death or distance, or have grown up, married, and formed homes of their own? There are abundant examples of men who, after a life engrossed by business, retire with a competency to the enjoyment, as they hope, of rest, but to whom, as they are unable to acquire new interests and excitements that can replace the old, the change to a life of inactivity brings ennui, melancholy, and premature death. Yet no one thinks of the parallel case of so many worthy and devoted women, who, having paid what they are told is their debt to society—having brought up a family blamelessly to manhood and womanhood—having kept a house as long as they had a house needing to be kept—are deserted by the sole occupation for which they have fitted themselves; and remain with undiminished activity but with no employment for it, unless perhaps a daughter or daughter-in-law is willing to abdicate in their favour the discharge of the same functions in her younger household. Surely a hard lot for the old age of those who have worthily discharged, as long as it was given to them to discharge, what the world accounts their only social duty. Of such women, and of those others to whom this duty has not been committed at all—many of whom pine through life with the consciousness of thwarted vocations, and activities which are not suffered to expand— the only resources, speaking generally, are religion and charity. But their religion, though it may be one of feeling, and of ceremonial observance, cannot be a religion of action, unless in the form of charity. For charity many of them are by nature admirably fitted; but to practise it usefully, or even without doing mischief, requires the education, the manifold preparation, the knowledge and the thinking powers, of a skilful administrator. There are few of the administrative functions of government for which a person would not be fit, who is fit to bestow charity usefully. In this as in other cases (preeminently in that of the education of children), the duties permitted to women cannot be performed properly, without their being trained for duties which, to the great loss of society, are not permitted to them. * * * But what we are now discussing is not the need which society has of the services of women in public business, but the dull and hopeless life to which it so often condemns them, by forbidding them to exercise the practical abilities which many of them are conscious of, in any wider field than one which to some of them never was, and to others is no longer, open. If there is anything vitally important to the happiness of human beings, it is that they should relish their habitual pursuit. This requisite of an enjoyable life is very imperfectly granted, or altogether denied, to a large part of mankind; and by its absence many a life is a failure, which is provided, in appearance, with every requisite of success. But if circumstances which society is not yet skilful enough to overcome, render such failures often for the present inevitable, society need not itself inflict them. The injudiciousness of parents, a youth's own inexperience, or the absence of external opportunities for the congenial vocation, and their presence for an uncongenial, condemn numbers of men to pass their lives in doing one thing reluctantly and ill, when there are other things which they could have done well and happily. But on women this sentence is imposed by actual law, and by customs equivalent to law. What, in unenlightened societies, colour, race, religion, or in the case of a conquered country, nationality, are to some men, sex is to all women; a peremptory exclusion from almost all honourable occupations, but either such as cannot be fulfilled by others, or such as those others do not think worthy of their acceptance. Sufferings arising from causes of this nature usually meet with so little sympathy, that few persons are aware of the great amount of unhappiness even now produced by the feeling of a wasted life. The case will be even more frequent, as increased cultivation creates a greater and greater disproportion between the ideas and faculties of women, and the scope which society allows to their activity.

When we consider the positive evil caused to the disqualified half of the human race by their disqualification—first in the loss of the most inspiriting and elevating kind of personal enjoyment, and next in the weariness, disappointment, and profound dissatisfaction with life, which are so often the substitute for it; one feels that among all the lessons which men require for carrying on the struggle against the inevitable imperfections of their lot on earth, there is no lesson which they more need, than not to add to the evils which nature inflicts, by their jealous and prejudiced restrictions on one another. Their vain fears only substitute other and worse evils for those which they are idly apprehensive of: while every restraint on the freedom of conduct of any of their human fellow-creatures, (otherwise than by making them responsible for any evil actually caused by it), dries up *pro tanto*[6] the principal fountain of human happiness, and leaves the species less rich, to an inappreciable degree, in all that makes life valuable to the individual human being.

SOURCE: From John Stuart Mill, *The Subjection of Women*, 4th ed. (London: Longmans, Green, Reeder, and Dyer, 1878), pp. 1, 38–43, 184–94. First published in 1869. By "subjection," Mill means women's relationship of subordination to, dependence on, or control by men to whom they are thus "subject," either individually or generally.

6. For so much (Latin); that is, "to that extent."

ARTHUR SCHOPENHAUER
(1788 – 1860)

Schopenhauer is notorious for his profoundly pessimistic outlook—to which he gave relentless and powerful expression throughout his long life—and for his seemingly curious interpretation not only of human nature but of all of reality in terms of what he calls "will." He has few peers in the philosophical literature as a writer, making his works (even in translation) as pleasurable to read for their masterful prose as they are uncomfortable to read for their assessment of the human condition. Schopenhauer's bleak vision of humankind as existing pointlessly in a godless and meaningless world, ceaselessly striving and suffering to no purpose, brings him closer in spirit to the French existentialists of a century later than to most of his own contemporaries. Though he deserves to be viewed as more than just the antithesis of HEGEL and the precursor of NIETZSCHE, he certainly was Hegel's arch-opponent, relishing the role; and he did indeed set the stage for Nietzsche, at once serving as his great "educator" and provoking his efforts to arrive at a radical alternative to Schopenhauer's hostility to life.

Arthur Schopenhauer ("SHOW-penhow-er") was born in 1788—the year in which IMMANUEL KANT published his *Critique of Practical Reason*—in what was then the autonomous Germanic city-state of Danzig (now the Polish city of Gdansk) on the Baltic Sea, not far from Kant's Königsberg. Upon the death in 1805 of his well-to-do father (possibly by suicide), Schopenhauer came into an inheritance that made him financially independent. His mother moved to Weimar, then the capital city of German literature, and Schopenhauer joined her there shortly thereafter. A writer herself, she established a salon that made her a significant presence in the cultural life of the city; but Schopenhauer found that life repellant and devoted himself to studies at a prominent school in the nearby town of Gotha. After going on to study at the universities of Göttingen and Berlin, he received his doctorate from Jena in 1814.

During the next few years he published his first two books, *On the Fourfold Root of the Principle of Sufficient Reason* (1813) and *On Vision and Colors* (1816), while also working on what would turn out to be his most important work: *Die Welt als Wille und Vorstellung*, now generally translated as *The World as Will and Representation* (hereafter called simply *The World as Will*; the term *Vorstellung* is best left untranslated). This remarkable and very formidable book, completed in 1818 (when Schopenhauer was only 30), was published in the following year. That year also saw the birth and death of an illegitimate daughter by a servant; the asceticism he espoused in conjunction with his pessimism apparently was more consistently preached than practiced. Though Schopenhauer became increasingly misogynistic in the course of his long life, he did have a serious romantic attachment to a young woman he met in 1821, and subsequently proposed marriage to another, who declined his proposal.

The World as Will attracted little attention at the time but did enable Schopenhauer to obtain a teaching position in 1820 at Berlin, where Hegel also happened to be a professor and celebrity philosopher. Considering himself a Kantian whose task it was to complete Kant's revolution, and despising Hegel's pretension to supersede Kantianism, Schopenhauer quixotically sought to challenge Hegel's growing sway, even to the point of scheduling his lectures at the same time as Hegel's (to the detriment of his own attendance). His failure to have any effect embittered him and prompted him to retire to private life in Frankfurt in 1831. (An added impetus to leave was the cholera epidemic in Berlin that year that claimed Hegel as one of its victims.)

Schopenhauer continued to write in his long retirement, publishing several more elaborations of his metaphysical and moral views, as well as a greatly expanded edition of *The World as Will* in 1844. He also wrote numerous short essays, some of which he collected and published in 1851 under the deliberately puzzling title *Parerga and Paralipomena* (meaning roughly "Supplements and Extractions," presumably relating to *The World as Will*). He was much admired as an essayist, but it was only toward the end of his life that he began to be appreciated as a significant philosopher. During his last decades he lived in virtual isolation, resentful of his neglect, quick to take offense, abrasive, and generally misanthropic. Yet he remained a man of cultivated tastes and a lover of music and the arts, and he continued to play the flute; and in the right company he could be witty and engaging. In short: like KIERKEGAARD, his fellow (but radically different) anti-Hegelian, he was a complex and fascinating figure and thinker. He died in Hamburg in 1860, having outlived his nemesis Hegel by nearly thirty years.

Schopenhauer's *World as Will* sets forth an epistemology, a metaphysics, a philosophical anthropology, an aesthetics, the basic principles of his ethics (both interpersonal and personal), and more generally a worldview and outlook on life, all interrelated and presented systematically—at times turgidly, but at other times elegantly and powerfully. Accepting the Kantian distinction between the world as it is perceived ("the world as representation") and the world as it is in itself, Schopenhauer argues that the latter can and should be conceived along the lines of our own inner nature, which is discernible as "will." The world's fundamental nature must be akin to ours, writ large—operating similarly but without many of the complexities that have come to characterize our human reality. Schopenhauer thus greatly extends and generalizes the notion of "will" to this wider and indeed

ubiquitous employment, taking it to be a kind of nonrational dynamic principle, without form or content or purpose but driven by its very nature to manifest itself endlessly.

Yet Schopenhauer maintains that the forms taken by the will in these manifestations are not merely random but rather constitute a hierarchy of levels and types, distinguished by their complexity and associated representationally with an array of Platonic "Ideas." Moreover, while all particular existing things are thus related and share the same fundamental nature, they are also in constant competition and conflict, blindly struggling against each other in an attempt to maintain themselves in their ultimately pointless existence. This ceaseless strife results in equally pointless suffering, wherever consciousness is sufficient to register its consequences. Thus, for Schopenhauer, wherever there is will there is suffering. This theme—which, as he readily acknowledges, reflects Buddhist influences—underlies his pessimism. His abhorrence of suffering, taken together with its ubiquity and his contention that it can neither be justified nor outweighed by any attainable positive goods that life may afford, leads to his pessimistic conclusion, and with it his counsel of "denying" the will in every way possible. If the struggle for existence and the suffering it generates are worse than senseless, then oblivion is preferable to life, and the extinction of the will in any and all of its forms—and thus of the entire world as both will and representation—would be the greatest of goods.

Schopenhauer's ethics revolves around the abhorrence of suffering, not only in one's own case but wherever it may occur. The alleviation of suffering, wherever it is occurring, is thus for him the highest moral imperative; indeed, it is the very essence of morality. The only way truly to alleviate it, however, is to attack the root of the problem, which is the will itself. Beyond seeking to mitigate the sufferings of others, therefore, Schopenhauer commends a variety of strategies to liberate oneself from the grip of "willing." Some strategies, such as philosophical contemplation and aesthetic experience, provide partial (and temporary) relief. Though suicide might seem to offer an opportunity for subverting the will, Schopenhauer rejects it as paradigmatically willful, and so as not genuinely subversive of the will at all. It thus is paradoxically self-assertive. Ultimately, only a systematic and radical asceticism can lead to true deliverance from all assertiveness.

Most of the following readings are taken from *The World as Will*, selected to reflect all these themes, with more emphasis on Schopenhauer's development of his analysis and interpretation of the world's nature, our knowledge of it, and ourselves as a part of it than on the normative conclusions that he draws. The first two shorter selections, from *Parerga and Paralipomena*, provide a succinct introduction to his worldview in general and to his pessimism in particular.

The seeming strangeness and bleakness of Schopenhauer's interpretation and assessment of the world and the human condition can make it difficult for readers to take him seriously, and to see why he is no mere curmudgeonly curiosity in the history of philosophy after Kant. As Nietzsche (and Ludwig Wittgenstein in the twentieth century) came to appreciate, however, he matters more than the sum of his doctrines, and is—or at least can be—a philosophical "educator" even to those who may part company with him. One could plausibly argue that it is Schopenhauer (rather than Nietzsche, as MARTIN HEIDEGGER contends) who stands at the end of the history of Western metaphysics and of otherworldly religiousness and its consolations, and on the brink of postmetaphysical and postreligious thinking—which must begin by grappling with the implications of what Nietzsche called "the death of God." While much in Schopenhauer may seem to belong to an earlier era, there also is much in him that made him a kindred spirit to philosophers a century later, and that continues to speak strongly to a contemporary sensibility.

From Additional Remarks on the Doctrine of the Nullity of Existence

This nullity [*Nichtigkeit*][1] finds expression in the whole way in which things exist; in the infinite nature of Time and Space, as opposed to the finite nature of the individual in both; in the ever-passing present moment as the only mode of actual existence; in the interdependence and relativity of all things; in continual Becoming without ever Being; in constant wishing and never being satisfied; in the long battle which forms the history of life, where every effort is checked by difficulties, and stopped until they are overcome. Time is that in which all things pass away; it is merely the form under which the will to live[2]—the thing-in-itself and therefore imperishable—has revealed to it that its efforts are in vain; it is that agent by which at every moment all things in our hands become as nothing, and lose any real value they possess.

That which *has been* exists no more; it exists as little as that which has *never* been. But of everything that exists you must say, in the next moment, that it has been. Hence something of great importance now past is inferior to

---

1. That is, nothingness; amounting to nothing.
2. "The will to live" is Schopenhauer's elaboration of his conception of "will" as it is manifested in organic nature: what drives all life fundamentally amounts to nothing more than a blind impetus to exist and continue existing.

something of little importance now present, in that the latter is a *reality*, and related to the former as something to nothing.

A man finds himself, to his great astonishment, suddenly existing, after thousands and thousands of years of non-existence: he lives for a little while; and then, again, comes an equally long period when he must exist no more. The heart rebels against this, and feels that it cannot be true. The crudest intellect cannot speculate on such a subject without having a presentiment that Time is something ideal[3] in its nature. This ideality of Time and Space is the key to every true system of metaphysics; because it provides for quite another order of things than is to be met with in the domain of nature. This is why Kant is so great.

Of every event in our life we can say only for one moment that it *is*; for ever after, that it *was*. Every evening we are poorer by a day. It might, perhaps, make us mad[4] to see how rapidly our short span of time ebbs away; if it were not that in the furthest depths of our being we are secretly conscious of our share in the inexhaustible spring of eternity, so that we can always hope to find life in it again.

Considerations of the kind touched on above might, indeed, lead us to embrace the belief that the greatest *wisdom* is to make the enjoyment of the present the supreme object of life; because that is the only reality, all else being merely the play of thought. On the other hand, such a course might just as well be called the greatest *folly*: for that which in the next moment exists no more, and vanishes utterly, like a dream, can never be worth a serious effort.

The whole foundation on which our existence rests is the present—the ever-fleeting present. It lies, then, in the very nature of our existence to take the form of constant motion, and to offer no possibility of our ever attaining the rest for which we are always striving. We are like a man running downhill, who cannot keep on his legs unless he runs on, and will inevitably fall if he stops; or, again, like a pole balanced on the tip of one's finger; or like a planet, which would fall into its sun the moment it ceased to hurry forward on its way. Unrest is the mark of existence.

In a world where all is unstable, and nought can endure, but is swept onwards at once in the hurrying whirlpool of change; where a man, if he is to keep erect at all, must always be advancing and moving, like an acrobat on a rope—in such a world, happiness is inconceivable. How can it dwell where, as Plato[5] says, *continual Becoming and never Being* is the sole form of existence? In the first place, a man never is happy, but spends his whole life in striving after something which he thinks will make him so; he seldom attains his goal, and when he does, it is only to be disappointed; he is mostly shipwrecked in the end, and comes into harbour with masts and rigging gone. And then, it is all one whether he has been happy or miserable; for his life was never anything more than a present moment always vanishing; and now it is over.

At the same time it is a wonderful[6] thing that, in the world of human beings

3. That is, a feature or consequence of the manner in which things are represented in experience, rather than something that exists apart from it.
4. Drive us insane.
5. Greek philosopher (427–347 B.C.E.), who differ-

entiated between the timeless world of Forms or Ideas (being) and the world of life, change, and sensation (becoming); for the phrase "continual Becoming and never Being," see *Timaeus* 27d.
6. Astonishing, marvelous (but not admirable).

as in that of animals in general, this manifold restless motion is produced and kept up by the agency of two simple impulses—hunger and the sexual instinct; aided a little, perhaps by the influence of boredom, but by nothing else; and that, in the theatre of life, these suffice to form the *primum mobile*[7] of how complicated a machinery, setting in motion how strange and varied a scene!

On looking a little closer, we find that inorganic matter presents a constant conflict between chemical forces, which eventually works dissolution; and on the other hand, that organic life is impossible without continual change of matter, and cannot exist if it does not receive perpetual help from without. This is the realm of *finality*; and its opposite would be *an infinite existence*, exposed to no attack from without, and needing nothing to support it; ἀεὶ ὡσάυτως ὄν, the realm of eternal peace; οὔτε γιγνόμενον οὔτε ἀπολλύμενον, some timeless, changeless state, one and undiversified;[8] the negative knowledge of which forms the dominant note of the Platonic philosophy. It is to some such state as this that the denial of the will to live opens up the way.

The scenes of our life are like pictures done in rough mosaic. Looked at close, they produce no effect. There is nothing beautiful to be found in them, unless you stand some distance off. So, to gain anything we have longed for is only to discover how vain and empty it is; and even though we are always living in expectation of better things, at the same time we often repent and long to have the past back again. We look upon the present as something to be put up with while it lasts, and serving only as the way towards our goal. Hence most people, if they glance back when they come to the end of life, will find that all along they have been living *ad interim*;[9] they will be surprised to find that the very thing they disregarded and let slip by unenjoyed was just the life in the expectation of which they passed all their time. Of how many a man may it not be said that hope made a fool of him until he danced into the arms of death!

Then again, how insatiable a creature is man! Every satisfaction he attains lays the seeds of some new desire, so that there is no end to the wishes of each individual will. And why is this? The real reason is simply that, taken in itself, Will is the lord of all worlds: everything belongs to it, and therefore no one single thing can ever give it satisfaction, but only the whole, which is endless. For all that, it must rouse our sympathy to think how very little the Will, this lord of the world, really gets when it takes the form of an individual; usually only just enough to keep the body together. This is why man is so very miserable.

Life presents itself chiefly as a task—the task, I mean, of subsisting at all, *gagner sa vie*.[1] If this is accomplished, life is a burden, and then there comes the second task of doing something with that which has been won—of warding off boredom, which, like a bird of prey, hovers over us, ready to fall wherever it sees a life secure from need. The first task is to win something; the second, to banish the feeling that it has been won; otherwise it is a burden.

Human life must be some kind of mistake. The truth of this will be sufficiently obvious if we only remember that man is a compound of needs and

---

7. Prime mover (Latin); for Aristotle, and in medieval thought, that which provides motion to the whole system of the universe without itself being moved by anything else.

8. Schopenhauer paraphrases Plato's Greek, which literally mean "always being in just this manner"

(slightly misquoting *Phaedo* 79e) and "neither becoming nor destroyed" (*Symposium* 211a).

9. In the meanwhile (Latin).

1. To earn one's living (French); thus, "keeping on going."

necessities hard to satisfy; and that even when they are satisfied all he obtains is a state of painlessness, where nothing remains to him but abandonment to boredom. This is direct proof that existence has no real value in itself; for what is boredom but the feeling of the emptiness of life? If life—the craving for which is the very essence of our being—were possessed of any positive intrinsic value, there would be no such thing as boredom at all: mere existence would satisfy us in itself, and we should want for nothing. But as it is, we take no delight in existence except when we are struggling for something; and then distance and difficulties to be overcome make our goal look as though it would satisfy us—an illusion which vanishes when we reach it; or else when we are occupied with some purely intellectual interest—where in reality we have stepped forth from life to look upon it from the outside, much after the manner of spectators at a play. And even sensual pleasure itself means nothing but a struggle and aspiration, ceasing the moment its aim is attained. Whenever we are not occupied in one of these ways, but cast upon existence itself, its vain and worthless nature is brought home to us; and this is what we mean by boredom. The hankering after what is strange and uncommon—an innate and ineradicable tendency of human nature—shows how glad we are at any interruption of that natural course of affairs which is so very tedious.

That this most perfect manifestation of the will to live, the human organism, with the cunning and complex working of its machinery, must fall to dust and yield up itself and all its strivings to extinction—this is the naïve way in which Nature, who is always so true and sincere in what she says, proclaims the whole struggle of this will as in its very essence barren and unprofitable. Were it of any value in itself, anything unconditioned and absolute, it could not thus end in mere nothing.

If we turn from contemplating the world as a whole, and, in particular, the generations of men as they live their little hour of mock-existence and then are swept away in rapid succession; if we turn from this, and look at life in its small details, as presented, say, in a comedy, how ridiculous it all seems! It is like a drop of water seen through a microscope, a single drop teeming with infusoria;[2] or a speck of cheese full of mites invisible to the naked eye. How we laugh as they bustle about so eagerly, and struggle with one another in so tiny a space! And whether here, or in the little span of human life, this terrible activity produces a comic effect.

It is only in the microscope that our life looks so big. It is an indivisible point, drawn out and magnified by the powerful lenses of Time and Space.

SOURCE: Arthur Schopenhauer, "The Vanity of Existence," in *Studies in Pessimism: A Series of Essays*, selected and translated by Thomas Bailey Saunders, 9th ed. (London: George Allen, 1913), pp. 33–39 (translation modified by the editor). Except where otherwise indicated, German words in brackets are the terminology used in the German original, inserted by the editor in addition to their renderings in the translation. Excerpted from the essay originally published as "Nachträge zur Lehre von der Nichtigkeit des Daseyns" in Schopenhauer's collection *Parerga und Paralipomena* (1851). *Nichtigkeit* (rendered by Saunders as "vanity," which at the time had the sense of being "in vain," all for nothing) literally means "nothingness," in the sense of "insignificance." "Nullity" is a more accurate contemporary translation, better conveying that the topic of the essay is the insignficance and pointlessness of human existence.

2. Microscopic animal life.

From Additional Remarks on the Doctrine of the Suffering of the World

Unless *suffering* is the direct and immediate object of life, our existence must entirely fail of its aim. It is absurd to look upon the enormous amount of pain that abounds everywhere in the world, and originates in needs and necessities inseparable from life itself, as serving no purpose at all and the result of mere chance. Each separate misfortune, as it comes, seems, no doubt, to be something exceptional; but misfortune in general is the rule.

I know of no greater absurdity than that propounded by most systems of philosophy in declaring evil to be negative in its character. Evil is just what is positive;[1] it makes its own existence felt. Leibnitz is particularly concerned to defend this absurdity; and he seeks to strengthen his position by using a palpable and paltry sophism.[2] It is the good which is negative; in other words, happiness and satisfaction always imply some desire fulfilled, some state of pain brought to an end.

This explains the fact that we generally find pleasure to be not nearly so pleasant as we expected, and pain very much more painful.

The pleasure in this world, it has been said, outweighs the pain; or, at any rate, there is an even balance between the two. If the reader wishes to see shortly whether this statement is true, let him compare the respective feelings of two animals, one of which is engaged in eating the other.

The best consolation in misfortune or affliction of any kind will be the thought of other people who are in a still worse plight than yourself; and this is a form of consolation open to every one. But what an awful fate this means for mankind as a whole!

We are like lambs in a field, disporting themselves under the eye of the butcher, who chooses out first one and then another for his prey. So it is that in our good days we are all unconscious of the evil Fate may have presently in store for us—sickness, poverty, mutilation, loss of sight or reason.

No little part of the torment of existence lies in this, that Time is continually pressing upon us, never letting us take breath, but always coming after us like a taskmaster with a whip. If at any moment Time stays his hand, it is only when we are delivered over to the misery of boredom.

But misfortune has its uses; for, as our bodily frame would burst asunder if the pressure of the atmosphere were removed, so, if the lives of men were relieved of all need, hardship and adversity; if everything they took in hand were successful, they would be so swollen with arrogance that, though they might not burst, they would present the spectacle of unbridled folly—nay, they would go mad. And I may say, further, that a certain amount of care or pain or trouble is necessary for every man at all times. A ship without ballast is unstable and will not go straight.

---

1. That is, has definite reality; the "negative," as the absence of a quality, is not truly real.
2. Cf. [Leibniz's] *Theodicy* [1710] § 153. Leibnitz argued that evil is a negative quality—i.e., the absence of good; and that its active and seemingly positive character is an incidental and not an essential part of its nature. Cold, he said, is only the absence of the power of heat, and the active power of expansion in freezing water is an incidental and not an essential part of the nature of cold. The fact is that the power of expansion in freezing water is really an increase of repulsion amongst its molecules; and Schopenhauer is quite right in calling the whole argument a sophism [translator's note]. Gottfried Leibniz (1646–1716), German philosopher and mathematician.

Certain it is that *work, worry, labour* and *trouble,* form the lot of almost all men their whole life long. But if all wishes were fulfilled as soon as they arose, how would men occupy their lives? what would they do with their time? If the world were a paradise of luxury and ease, a land flowing with milk and honey, where every Jack obtained his Jill at once and without any difficulty, men would either die of boredom or hang themselves; or there would be wars, massacres, and murders; so that in the end mankind would inflict more suffering on itself than it has now to accept at the hands of Nature.

In early youth, as we contemplate our coming life, we are like children in a theatre before the curtain is raised, sitting there in high spirits and eagerly waiting for the play to begin. It is a blessing that we do not know what is really going to happen. Could we foresee it, there are times when children might seem like innocent prisoners, condemned, not to death, but to life, and as yet all unconscious of what their sentence means. Nevertheless every man desires to reach old age; in other words, a state of life of which it may be said: "It is bad to-day, and it will be worse to-morrow; and so on till the worst of all."

If you try to imagine, as nearly as you can, what an amount of misery, pain and suffering of every kind the sun shines upon in its course, you will admit that it would be much better if on the earth as little as on the moon the sun were able to call forth the phenomena of life; and if, here as there, the surface were still in a crystalline state.

Again, you may look upon life as an unprofitable episode, disturbing the blessed calm of non-existence. And, in any case, even though things have gone with you tolerably well, the longer you live the more clearly you will feel that, on the whole, life is *a disappointment, nay, a cheat.*

If two men who were friends in their youth meet again when they are old, after being separated for a life-time, the chief feeling they will have at the sight of each other will be one of complete disappointment at life as a whole; because their thoughts will be carried back to that earlier time when life seemed so fair as it lay spread out before them in the rosy light of dawn, promised so much—and then performed so little. This feeling will so completely predominate over every other that they will not even consider it necessary to give it words; but on either side it will be silently assumed, and form the ground-work of all they have to talk about.

He who lives to see two or three generations is like a man who sits some time in the conjurer's booth at a fair, and witnesses the performance twice or thrice in succession. The tricks were meant to be seen only once; and when they are no longer a novelty and cease to deceive their effect is gone.

While no man is much to be envied for his lot, there are countless numbers whose fate is to be deplored.

Life is a task to be done. It is a fine thing to say *defunctus est;*[3] it means that the man has done his task.

If children were brought into the world by an act of pure reason alone, would the human race continue to exist? Would not a man rather have so much sympathy with the coming generation as to spare it the burden of existence?

---

3. He has died (Latin); the verb's original meaning was to finish with or discharge an obligation, especially an unpleasant one.

or at any rate not take it upon himself to impose that burden upon it in cold blood.

I shall be told, I suppose, that my philosophy is comfortless—because I speak the truth; and people prefer to be assured that everything the Lord has made is good. Go to the priests, then, and leave philosophers in peace! At any rate, do not ask us to accommodate our doctrines to the lessons you have been taught. That is what those rascals of sham philosophers will do for you. Ask them for any doctrine you please, and you will get it. Your University professors[4] are bound to preach optimism; and it is an easy and agreeable task to upset their theories.

I have reminded the reader that every state of welfare, every feeling of satisfaction, is negative in its character; that is to say, it consists in freedom from pain, which is the positive element of existence. It follows, therefore, that the happiness of any given life is to be measured, not by its joys and pleasures, but by the extent to which it has been free from suffering—from positive evil. If this is the true standpoint, the lower animals appear to enjoy a happier destiny than man. Let us examine the matter a little more closely.

However varied the forms that human happiness and misery may take, leading a man to seek the one and shun the other, the material basis of it all is bodily pleasure or bodily pain. This basis is very restricted: it is simply health, food, protection from wet and cold, the satisfaction of the sexual instinct; or else the absence of these things. Consequently, as far as real physical pleasure is concerned, the man is not better off than the brute, except in so far as the higher possibilities of his nervous system make him more sensitive to every kind of pleasure, but also, it must be remembered, to every kind of pain. But then compared with the brute, how much stronger are the passions aroused in him! what an immeasurable difference there is in the depth and vehemence of his emotions!—and yet, in the one case, as in the other, all to produce the same result in the end: namely, health, food, clothing, and so on.

The chief source of all this passion is that thought for what is absent and future, which, with man, exercises such a powerful influence upon all he does. It is this that is the real origin of his cares, his hopes his fears—emotions which affect him much more deeply than could ever be the case with those present joys and sufferings to which the brute is confined. In his powers of reflection, memory and foresight, man possesses, as it were, a machine for condensing and storing up his pleasures and his sorrows. But the brute has nothing of the kind; whenever it is in pain, it is as though it were suffering for the first time, even though the same thing should have previously happened to it times out of number. It has no power of summing up its feelings. Hence its careless and placid temper: how much it is to be envied! But in man reflection comes in, with all the emotions to which it gives rise; and taking up the same elements of pleasure and pain which are common to him and the brute, it developes his susceptibility to happiness and misery to such a degree that, at one moment the man is brought in an instant to a state of delight that may even prove fatal, at another to the depths of despair and suicide.

---

4. Here assumed to be Hegelians.

If we carry our analysis a step farther, we shall find that, in order to increase his pleasures, man has intentionally added to the number and pressure of his needs, which in their original state were not much more difficult to satisfy than those of the brute. Hence luxury in all its forms: delicate food, the use of tobacco and opium, spirituous liquors, fine clothes and the thousand and one things that he considers necessary to his existence.

And above and beyond all this, there is a separate and peculiar source of pleasure, and consequently of pain, which man has established for himself, also as the result of using his powers of reflection; and this occupies him out of all proportion to its value, nay, almost more than all his other interests put together—I mean ambition and the feeling of honour and shame; in plain words, what he thinks about the opinion other people have of him. Taking a thousand forms, often very strange ones, this becomes the goal of almost all the efforts he makes that are not rooted in physical pleasure or pain. It is true that besides the sources of pleasure which he has in common with the brute, man has the pleasures of the mind as well. These admit of many gradations, from the most innocent trifling or the merest talk up to the highest intellectual achievements; but there is the accompanying boredom to be set against them on the side of suffering. Boredom is a form of suffering unknown to brutes, at any rate in their natural state; it is only the very cleverest of them who show faint traces of it when they are domesticated; whereas in the case of man it has become a downright scourge. The crowd of miserable wretches whose one aim in life is to fill their purses, but never to put anything into their heads, offers a singular instance of this torment of boredom. Their wealth becomes a punishment by delivering them up to the misery of having nothing to do; for, to escape it, they will rush about in all directions, travelling here, there and everywhere. No sooner do they arrive in a place than they are anxious to know what amusements it affords; just as though they were beggars asking where they could receive a dole! Of a truth, need and boredom are the two poles of human life. Finally, I may mention that as regards the sexual relation, man is committed to a peculiar arrangement which drives him obstinately to choose one person. This feeling grows, now and then, into a more or less passionate love, which is the source of little pleasure and much suffering.

It is, however, a wonderful thing that the mere addition of thought should serve to raise such a vast and lofty structure of human happiness and misery; resting, too, on the same narrow basis of joy and sorrow as man holds in common with the brute, and exposing him to such violent emotions, to so many storms of passion, so much convulsion of feeling, that what he has suffered stands written and may be read in the lines on his face. And yet, when all is told, he has been struggling ultimately for the very same things as the brute has attained, and with an incomparably smaller expenditure of passion and pain.

But all this contributes to increase the measure of suffering in human life out of all proportion to its pleasures; and the pains of life are made much worse for man by the fact that death is something very real to him. The brute flies from death instinctively without really knowing what it is, and therefore without ever contemplating it in the way natural to a man, who has this prospect always before his eyes. So that even if only a few brutes die a natural death, and most of them live only just long enough to transmit their species, and then, if not earlier, become the prey of some other animal,—whilst man, on the other hand, manages to make so-called natural death the rule, to which, however, there are a good many exceptions,—the advantage is on the side of the brute, for the reason stated above. But the fact is that man attains the natural term of years just as seldom as the brute; because the unnatural way in which he lives, and the strain of work and emotion, lead to a degeneration of the race; and so his goal is not often reached.

The brute is much more content with mere existence than man; the plant is wholly so; and man finds satisfaction in it just in proportion as he is dull and obtuse. Accordingly, the life of the brute carries less of sorrow with it, but also less of joy, when compared with the life of man; and while this may be traced, on the one side, to freedom from the torment of *care* and *anxiety*, it is also due to the fact that *hope*, in any real sense, is unknown to the brute. It is thus deprived of any share in that which gives us the most and the best of our joys and pleasures, the mental anticipation of a happy future, and the inspiriting play of phantasy, both of which we owe to our power of imagination. If the brute is free from care, it is also, in this sense, without hope; in either case because its consciousness is limited to the present moment, to what it can actually see before it. The brute is an embodiment of present impulses, and hence what elements of fear and hope exist in its nature—and they do not go very far—arise only in relation to objects that lie before it and within reach of those impulses: whereas a man's range of vision embraces the whole of his life, and extends far into the past and the future.

Following upon this, there is one respect in which brutes show real wisdom when compared with us—I mean their quiet, placid enjoyment of the present moment. The tranquillity of mind which this seems to give them often puts us to shame for the many times we allow our thoughts and our cares to make us restless and discontented. And, in fact, those pleasures of hope and anticipation which I have been mentioning are not to be had for nothing. The delight which a man has in hoping for and looking forward to some special satisfaction is a part of the real pleasure attaching to it enjoyed in advance. This is afterwards deducted; for the more we look forward to anything the less satisfaction we find in it when it comes. But the brute's enjoyment is not anticipated and therefore suffers no deduction; so that the actual pleasure of the moment comes to it whole and unimpaired. In the same way, too, evil presses upon the brute only with its own intrinsic weight; whereas with us the fear of its coming often makes its burden ten times more grievous.

It is just this characteristic way in which the brute gives itself up entirely to the present moment that contributes so much to the delight we take in our domestic pets. They are the present moment personified, and in some respects they make us feel the value of every hour that is free from trouble and annoyance, which we, with our thoughts and preoccupations, mostly disregard. But man, that selfish and heartless creature, misuses this quality of the brute to be more content than we are with mere existence, and often works it to such an extent that he allows the brute absolutely nothing more than mere, bare life. The bird which was made so that it might rove over half the world, he shuts up into the space of a cubic foot, there to die a slow death in longing and crying for freedom; for in a cage it does not sing for the pleasure of it. And when I see how man misuses the dog, his best friend; how he ties up this intelligent animal with a chain, I feel the deepest sympathy with the brute and burning indignation against its master.

We shall see later that by taking a very high standpoint it is possible to justify the sufferings of mankind. But this justification cannot apply to animals, whose sufferings, while in a great measure brought about by men, are often considerable even apart from their agency. And so we are forced to ask, Why and for what purpose does all this torment and agony exist? There is nothing here to give the will pause; it is not free to deny itself and so obtain redemption. There is only one consideration that may serve to explain the sufferings of animals. It is this: that the will to live, which underlies the whole world of phenomena, must in their case satisfy its cravings by feeding upon itself. This it does by forming a gradation of phenomena, every one of which exists at the expense of another.

* * *

Pardon's the word to all![5] Whatever folly men commit, be their shortcomings or their vices what they may, let us exercise forbearance; remembering that when these faults appear in others it is our follies and vices that we behold. They are the shortcomings or humanity, to which we belong; whose faults, one and all, we share; yes, even those very faults at which we now wax so indignant, merely because they have not yet appeared in ourselves. They are faults that do not lie on the surface. But they exist down there in the depths of our nature; and should anything call them forth they will come and show themselves, just as we now see them in others. One man, it is true, may have faults that are absent in his fellow; and it is undeniable that the sum total of bad qualities is in some cases very large; for the difference of individuality between man and man passes all measure.

In fact, the conviction that the world and man is something that had better not have been[6] is of a kind to fill us with indulgence towards one another. Nay, from this point of view, we might well consider the proper form of address to be, not *Monsieur, Sir, mein Herr*, but *my fellow-sufferer, Socî malorum, compagnon de misères!*[7] This may perhaps sound strange, but it is in keeping with the facts; it puts others in a right light; and it reminds us of that which is after all the most necessary thing in life—the tolerance, patience, regard, and love of neighbour, of which everyone stands in need, and which, therefore, every man owes to his fellow.

SOURCE: From Arthur Schopenhauer, "On the Sufferings of the World," in *Studies in Pessimism: A Series of Essays*, selected and translated by Thomas Bailey Saunders (London: George Allen, 1913), pp. 11–22, 29–30. Excerpted from the essay originally published as "Nachträge zur Lehre vom Leiden der Welt" in Schopenhauer's collection *Parerga und Paralipomena* (1851).

5. Shakespeare, *Cymbeline* (ca. 1610), 5.6.423 (Norton ed.).
6. That is, would better have never existed at all.
7. Literally, "companion of misfortunes" in Latin and French (the equivalents of "sir" were previously given in French and German).

From The World as Will and *Vorstellung*

From *First Book. The World as* Vorstellung—*First Aspect.*
Vorstellung *Subordinated to the Principle of Sufficient Reason:*
The Object of Experience and Wissenschaft[1]

§ 1. "The world is my *Vorstellung*[2]":—this is a truth which holds good for everything that lives and knows, though man alone can bring it into reflective and abstract consciousness. If he really does this, he has attained to philosophical wisdom. It then becomes clear and certain to him that what he knows is not a sun and an earth, but only an eye that sees a sun, a hand that feels an earth; that the world which surrounds him is there only as *Vorstellung, i.e.,* only in relation to something else, the *Vorstellende* [representer], which is himself. If any truth can be asserted *a priori,* it is this: for it is the expression of the most general form of all possible and thinkable experience: a form which is more general than time, or space, or causality, for they all presuppose it; and each of these, which we have seen to be just so many modes of the principle of sufficient reason, is valid only for a particular class of *Vorstellungen*; whereas the antithesis of object and subject is the common form of all these classes, is that form under which alone any *Vorstellung* of whatever kind it may be, abstract or intuitive, pure or empirical, is possible and thinkable. No truth therefore is more certain, more independent of all others, and less in need of proof than this, that all that exists for knowledge, and therefore this whole world, is only object in relation to subject, perception of a perceiver, in a word, *Vorstellung.* This is obviously true of the past and the future, as well as of the present, of what is farthest off, as of what is near; for it is true of time and space themselves, in which alone these distinctions arise. All that in any way belongs or can belong to the world is inevitably thus conditioned through the subject, and exists only for the subject. The world is *Vorstellung.*

This truth is by no means new. It was implicitly involved in the sceptical reflections from which Descartes[3] started. Berkeley,[4] however, was the first who distinctly enunciated it, and by this he has rendered a permanent service to philosophy, even though the rest of his teaching should not endure. Kant's primary mistake was the neglect of this principle, as is shown in the appendix.

* * *

§ 2. That which knows all things and is known by none is the subject. Thus it is the supporter of the world, that condition of all phenomena, of all objects which is always pre-supposed throughout experience; for all that exists, exists only for the subject. Every one finds himself to be subject, yet only in so far as he knows, not in so far as he is an object of knowledge. But his body is object, and therefore from this point of view we call it *Vorstellung.* For the body is an object among objects, and is conditioned by the laws of objects, although it is an immediate object. Like all objects of perception, it lies within

1. Some translations: "science," "cognitive inquiry." See Hegel glossary, p. 144.
2. Some translations: "representation," "image," "idea." See Source note, p. 684.

3. René Descartes (1596–1650), French mathematician and philosopher.
4. George Berkeley (1685–1753), Anglo-Irish idealist philosopher.

the universal forms of knowledge, time and space, which are the conditions of multiplicity. The subject, on the contrary, which is always the knower, never the known, does not come under these forms, but is presupposed by them; it has therefore neither multiplicity nor its opposite unity. We never know it, but it is always the knower wherever there is knowledge.

So then the world as *Vorstellung*, the only aspect in which we consider it at present, has two fundamental, necessary, and inseparable halves. The one half is the object, the forms of which are space and time, and through these multiplicity. The other half is the subject, which is not in space and time, for it is present, entire and undivided, in every percipient being. So that any one percipient being, with the object, constitutes the whole world as *Vorstellung* just as fully as the existing millions could do; but if this one were to disappear, then the whole world as *Vorstellung* would cease to be. These halves are therefore inseparable even for thought, for each of the two has meaning and existence only through and for the other, each appears with the other and vanishes with it. They limit each other immediately; where the object begins the subject ends. The universality of this limitation is shown by the fact that the essential and hence universal forms of all objects, space, time, and causality, may, without knowledge of the object, be discovered and fully known from a consideration of the subject, *i.e.*, in Kantian language, they lie *a priori* in our consciousness. That he discovered this is one of Kant's principal merits, and it is a great one. I however go beyond this, and maintain that the principle of sufficient reason[5] is the general expression for all these forms of the object of which we are *a priori* conscious; and that therefore all that we know purely *a priori*, is merely the content of that principle and what follows from it; in it all our certain *a priori* knowledge is expressed. In my essay on the principle of sufficient reason[6] I have shown in detail how every possible object comes under it; that is, stands in a necessary relation to other objects, on the one side as determined, on the other side as determining: this is of such wide application, that the whole existence of all objects, so far as they are objects, *Vorstellungen* and nothing more, may be entirely traced to this their necessary relation to each other, rests only in it, is in fact merely relative[.]

* * *

§ 5. It is needful to guard against the grave error of supposing that because perception[7] arises through the knowledge of causality, the relation of subject and object is that of cause and effect. For this relation subsists only between the immediate object and objects known indirectly, thus always between objects alone. It is this false supposition that has given rise to the foolish controversy about the reality of the outer world; a controversy in which dogmatism and scepticism oppose each other, and the former appears, now as realism, now as idealism.[8] Realism treats the object as cause, and the subject as its effect. The idealism of Fichte[9] reduces the object to the effect of the

---

5. The principle that every event must have a cause sufficient to explain it.
6. *On the Fourfold Root of the Principle of Sufficient Reason* (1813).
7. A translation of *Anschauung*, which here has the sense of the way things look.
8. A translation of *Idealismus*, a term that has no

connection with *Idee* and *Vorstellung*. Though Schopenhauer disassociates himself from both realism and Idealism, his own position is often viewed as a kind of Idealism, since it takes the world "in itself" to be something more "subject"-like than "object"-like.
9. On Fichte, see above.

subject. Since however, and this cannot be too much emphasised, there is absolutely no relation according to the principle of sufficient reason between subject and object, neither of these views could be proved, and therefore scepticism attacked them both with success. Now, just as the law of causality precedes perception and experience as their condition, and therefore cannot (as Hume[1] thought) be derived from them, so object and subject precede all knowledge, and hence the principle of sufficient reason in general, as its first condition; for this principle is merely the form of all objects, the whole nature and possibility of their existence as phenomena: but the object always presupposes the subject; and therefore between these two there can be no relation of reason and consequent. My essay on the principle of sufficient reason accomplishes just this: it explains the content of that principle as the essential form of every object—that is to say, as the universal nature of all objective existence, as something which pertains to the object as such; but the object as such always presupposes the subject as its necessary correlative; and therefore the subject remains always outside the province in which the principle of sufficient reason is valid. The controversy as to the reality of the outer world rests upon this false extension of the validity of the principle of sufficient reason to the subject also, and starting with this mistake it can never understand itself. On the one side realistic dogmatism, looking upon the *Vorstellung* as the effect of the object, desires to separate these two, *Vorstellung* and object, which are really one, and to assume a cause quite different from the *Vorstellung*, an object in itself, independent of the subject, a thing which is quite inconceivable; for even as object it presupposes subject, and so remains its *Vorstellung*. Opposed to this doctrine is scepticism, which makes the same false presupposition that in the *Vorstellung* we have only the effect, never the cause, therefore never real being; that we always know merely the action of the object. But this object, it supposes, may perhaps have no resemblance whatever to its effect, may indeed have been quite erroneously received as the cause, for the law of causality is first to be gathered from experience, and the reality of experience is then made to rest upon it. Thus both of these views are open to the correction, firstly, that object and *Vorstellung* are the same; secondly, that the true being of the object of perception[2] is its action, that the reality of the thing consists in this, and the demand for an existence of the object outside the *Vorstellung* of the subject, and also for an essence of the actual thing different from its action, has absolutely no meaning, and is a contradiction: and that the knowledge of the nature of the effect of any perceived object, exhausts such an object itself, so far as it is object, *i.e.*, *Vorstellung*, for beyond this there is nothing more to be known. So far then, the perceived world in space and time, which makes itself known as causation alone, is entirely real, and is throughout simply what it appears to be, and it appears wholly and without reserve as *Vorstellung*, bound together according to the law of causality. This is its empirical reality. On the other hand, all causality is *in* the understanding alone, and *for* the understanding. The whole actual, that is, active world is determined as such through the understanding, and apart from it is nothing. This, however, is not the only

---

1. David Hume (1711–1776), Scottish philosopher.
2. Better translated as "of the perceptual object" (*der anschaulichen Objekte*), having the sense of the way things look.

reason for altogether denying such a reality of the outer world as is taught by the dogmatist,[3] who explains its reality as its independence of the subject. We also deny it, because no object apart from a subject can be conceived without contradiction. The whole world of objects is and remains Vorstellung, and therefore wholly and for ever determined by the subject; that is to say, it has transcendental ideality.[4] But it is not therefore illusion or mere appearance; it presents itself as that which it is, Vorstellung, and indeed as a series of Vorstellungen of which the common bond is the principle of sufficient reason. It is according to its inmost meaning quite comprehensible to the healthy understanding, and speaks a language quite intelligible to it. To dispute about its reality can only occur to a mind perverted by over-subtilty, and such discussion always arises from a false application of the principle of sufficient reason, which binds all Vorstellungen together of whatever kind they may be, but by no means connects them with the subject, nor yet with a something which is neither subject nor object, but only the ground of the object; an absurdity, for only objects can be and always are the ground of objects. If we examine more closely the source of this question as to the reality of the outer world, we find that besides the false application of the principle of sufficient reason generally to what lies beyond its province, a special confusion of its forms is also involved; for that form which it has only in reference to concepts or abstract Vorstellungen, is applied to perceived Vorstellungen, real objects; and a ground of knowing is demanded of objects, whereas they can have nothing but a ground of being. Among the abstract Vorstellungen, the concepts united in the judgment, the principle of sufficient reason appears in such a way that each of these has its worth, its validity, and its whole existence, here called truth, simply and solely through the relation of the judgment to something outside of it, its ground of knowledge, to which there must consequently always be a return. Among real objects, Vorstellungen of perception, on the other hand, the principle of sufficient reason appears not as the principle of the ground of knowing, but of being, as the law of causality: every real object has paid its debt to it, inasmuch as it has come to be, i.e., has appeared as the effect of a cause. The demand for a ground of knowing has therefore here no application and no meaning, but belongs to quite another class of things. Thus the world of perception raises in the observer no question or doubt so long as he remains in contact with it: there is here neither error nor truth, for these are confined to the province of the abstract—the province of reflection. But here the world lies open for sense and understanding; presents itself with naive truth as that which it really is—Vorstellungen of perception which develop themselves according to the law of causality.

* * *

§ 6. For the present, however, in this first book we consider everything merely as Vorstellung, as object for the subject. And our own body, which is the starting-point for each of us in our perception of the world, we consider,

---

3. That is, the "realist," who takes the meaningfulness, legitimacy, and warrant of the idea that some sort of object-like world exists independent of all subjectivity and representational experience to be obvious and beyond reasonable dispute.
4. "Ideality" (Idealität) has a meaning quite different

from that of "idealism" (Idealismus): "transcendental ideality" designates the idea that "the whole world of objects" is something mind-constituted, rather than absolutely and ultimately real and independent of experience.

like all other real objects, from the side of its knowableness, and in this regard it is simply a *Vorstellung*. Now the consciousness of every one is in general opposed to the explanation of objects as mere *Vorstellungen*, and more especially to the explanation of our bodies as such; for the thing in itself is known to each of us immediately in so far as it appears as our own body; but in so far as it objectifies itself in the other objects of perception, it is known only indirectly. But this abstraction, this one-sided treatment, this forcible separation of what is essentially and necessarily united, is only adopted to meet the demands of our argument; and therefore the disinclination to it must, in the meantime, be suppressed and silenced by the expectation that the subsequent treatment will correct the one-sidedness of the present one, and complete our knowledge of the nature of the world.

At present therefore the body is for us immediate object; that is to say, that *Vorstellung* which forms the starting-point of the subject's knowledge; because the body, with its immediately known changes, precedes the application of the law of causality, and thus supplies it with its first data. The whole nature of matter consists, as we have seen, in its causal action. But cause and effect exist only for the understanding, which is nothing but their subjective correlative. The understanding, however, could never come into operation if there were not something else from which it starts. This is simple sensation—the immediate consciousness of the changes of the body, by virtue of which it is immediate object. Thus the possibility of knowing the world of perception depends upon two conditions; the first, *objectively expressed*, is the power of material things to act upon each other, to produce changes in each other, without which common quality of all bodies no perception would be possible, even by means of the sensibility of the animal body. And if we wish to express this condition *subjectively* we say: The understanding first makes perception possible; for the law of causality, the possibility of effect and cause, springs only from the understanding, and is valid only for it, and therefore the world of perception exists only through and for it. The second condition is the sensibility of animal bodies, or the quality of being immediate objects of the subject which certain bodies possess. The mere modification which the organs of sense sustain from without through their specific affections, may here be called *Vorstellungen*, so far as these affections produce neither pain nor pleasure, that is, have no immediate significance for the will, and are yet perceived, exist therefore only for *knowledge*. Thus far, then, I say that the body is immediately *known*, is *immediate object*. But the conception of object is not to be taken here in its fullest sense, for through this immediate knowledge of the body, which precedes the operation of the understanding, and is mere sensation, our own body does not exist specifically, as *object*, but first the material things which affect it: for all knowledge of an object proper, of a *Vorstellung* perceived in space, exists only through and for the understanding; therefore not before, but only subsequently to its operation. Therefore the body as object proper, that is, as a *Vorstellung* perceived in space, is first known indirectly, like all other objects, through the application of the law of causality to the action of one of its parts upon another, as, for example, when the eye sees the body or the hand touches it. Consequently the form of our body does not become known to us through mere feeling, but only through knowledge, only in *Vorstellung*; that is to say, only in the brain does our own body first come to appear as extended, articulate, organic.

* * *

§ 8. As from the direct light of the sun to the borrowed light of the moon, we pass from the immediate *Vorstellung* of perception, which stands by itself and is its own warrant, to reflection, to the abstract, discursive concepts of the reason, which obtain their whole content from knowledge of perception, and in relation to it. As long as we continue simply to perceive, all is clear, firm, and certain. There are neither questions nor doubts nor errors; we desire to go no further, can go no further; we find rest in perceiving, and satisfaction in the present. Perception suffices for itself, and therefore what springs purely from it, and remains true to it, for example, a genuine work of art, can never be false, nor can it be discredited through the lapse of time, for it does not present an opinion but the thing itself. But with abstract knowledge, with reason, doubt and error appear in the theoretical, care and sorrow in the practical. In the *Vorstellung* of perception,[5] illusion may at moments take the place of the real; but in the sphere of abstract thought, error may reign for a thousand years, impose its yoke upon whole nations, extend to the noblest impulses of humanity, and, by the help of its slaves and its dupes, may chain and fetter those whom it cannot deceive. It is the enemy against which the wisest men of all times have waged unequal war, and only what they have won from it has become the possession of mankind. Therefore it is well to draw attention to it at once, as we already tread the ground to which its province belongs. It has often been said that we ought to follow truth even although no utility can be seen in it, because it may have indirect utility which may appear when it is least expected; and I would add to this, that we ought to be just as anxious to discover and to root out all error even when no harm is anticipated from it, because its mischief may be very indirect, and may suddenly appear when we do not expect it, for all error has poison at its heart. If it is *Geist*,[6] if it is knowledge, that makes man the lord of creation,[7] there can be no such thing as harmless error, still less venerable and holy error. And for the consolation of those who in any way and at any time may have devoted strength and life to the noble and hard battle against error, I cannot refrain from adding that, so long as truth is absent, error will have free play, as owls and bats in the night; but sooner would we expect to see the owls and the bats drive back the sun in the eastern heavens, than that any truth which has once been known and distinctly and fully expressed, can ever again be so utterly vanquished and overcome that the old error shall once more reign undisturbed over its wide kingdom. This is the power of truth; its conquest is slow and laborious, but if once the victory be gained it can never be wrested back again.

5. Better translated as "In perceptual *Vorstellung*" (*In der anschaulichen Vorstellung*).
6. Neither "mind" (Haldane and Kemp's rendering) nor "spirit" is a satisfactory translation. Schopenhauer immediately glosses the meaning of *Geist* as used here in terms of "knowledge" (*Erkenntnis*), thereby showing that (like Hegel, in this case) he takes knowledge to be the paradigmatic and highest form of *Geist* and mental/spiritual activity. (See Hegel glossary, p. 144.) For Hegel, however, even the highest forms of knowledge are *wissenschaftlich* (and so conceptual and systematic), whereas for Schopenhauer the highest form of knowledge is fundamentally different from and beyond all *wissenschaftlich* knowing.
7. Better translated as "lord of the earth" (*Herrn der Erde*).

Besides the *Vorstellungen* we have as yet considered, which, according to their construction, could be referred to time, space, and matter, if we consider them with reference to the object, or to pure sensibility and understanding (*i.e.*, knowledge of causality), if we consider them with reference to the subject, another faculty of knowledge has appeared in man alone of all earthly creatures,[8] an entirely new consciousness, which, with very appropriate and significant exactness, is called *reflection*. For it is in fact derived from the knowledge of perception, and is a reflected appearance of it. But it has assumed a nature fundamentally different. The forms of perception do not affect it, and even the principle of sufficient reason which reigns over all objects has an entirely different aspect with regard to it. It is just this new, more highly endowed, consciousness, this abstract reflex of all that belongs to perception in that conception of the reason which has nothing to do with perception, that gives to man that thoughtfulness which distinguishes his consciousness so entirely from that of the lower animals, and through which his whole behaviour upon earth is so different from that of his irrational fellow-creatures. He far surpasses them in power and also in suffering. They live in the present alone, he lives also in the future and the past. They satisfy the needs of the moment, he provides by the most ingenious preparations for the future, yea for days that he shall never see. They are entirely dependent on the impression of the moment, on the effect of the perceptible motive; he is determined by abstract conceptions independent of the present. Therefore he follows predetermined plans, he acts from maxims, without reference to his surroundings or the accidental impression of the moment. Thus, for example, he can make with composure deliberate preparations for his own death, he can dissemble past finding out, and can carry his secret with him to the grave; lastly, he has an actual choice between several motives; for only in the abstract can such motives, present together in consciousness, afford the knowledge with regard to themselves, that the one excludes the other, and can thus measure themselves against each other with reference to their power over the will. The motive that overcomes, in that it decides the question at issue, is the deliberate determinant of the will, and is a sure indication of its character. The brute, on the other hand, is determined by the present impression; only the fear of present compulsion can constrain its desires, until at last this fear has become custom, and as such continues to determine it; this is called training. The brute feels and perceives; man, in addition to this, *thinks* and *knows*: both *will*. The brute expresses its feelings and dispositions by gestures and sounds; man communicates his thought to others, or, if he wishes, he conceals it, by means of speech. Speech is the first production, and also the necessary organ of his reason. Therefore in Greek and Italian, speech and reason [*Vernunft*] are expressed by the same word; ὁ λόγος, *il discorso*. *Vernunft*[9] is derived from *vernehmen*, which is not a synonym for the verb to hear, but signifies the consciousness of the meaning of thoughts communicated in words. It is by the help of language alone that reason accomplishes its most important achievements,—the united action of several individuals, the planned co-operation of many

---

8. In what follows, Schopenhauer indicates the sort of knowledge he specifically has in mind in attributing such distinctive significance to it—and also provides a vivid sketch of his conception of what distinguishes our human nature from that of all other ("lower") animals.
9. Reason; in contrast to *Verstehen* (understanding).

thousands, civilisation, the state; also *Wissenschaft*, the storing up of experience, the uniting of common properties in one concept, the communication of truth, the spread of error, thoughts and poems, dogmas and superstitions. The brute first knows death when it dies, but man draws consciously nearer to it every hour that he lives; and this makes life at times a questionable good even to him who has not recognised this character of constant annihilation in the whole of life. Principally on this account man has philosophies and religions, though it is uncertain whether the qualities we admire most in his conduct, voluntary rectitude and nobility of feeling, were ever the fruit of either of them. As results which certainly belong only to them, and as productions of reason in this sphere, we may refer to the marvellous and monstrous opinions of philosophers of various schools, and the extraordinary and sometimes cruel customs of the priests of different religions.

* * *

The understanding has only one function—immediate knowledge of the relation of cause and effect. Yet the perception of the real world, and all common sense, sagacity, and inventiveness, however multifarious their applications may be, are quite clearly seen to be nothing more than manifestations of that one function. So also the reason has one function; and from it all the manifestations of reason we have mentioned, which distinguish the life of man from that of the brutes, may easily be explained. The application or the non-application of this function is all that is meant by what men have everywhere and always called rational and irrational.

* * *

§ 10. Through all this, the question presses ever more upon us, how *certainty* is to be attained, how *judgments are to be established*, what constitutes *rational knowledge* [*Wissen*], and *Wissenschaft*, which we rank with language and deliberate action as the third great benefit conferred by reason.

Reason is feminine in nature;[1] it can only give after has received. Of itself it has nothing but the empty forms of its operation. There is no absolutely pure rational knowledge except the four principles to which I have attributed metalogical truth; the principles of identity, contradiction, excluded middle, and sufficient reason of knowledge. For even the rest of logic is not absolutely pure rational knowledge. It presupposes the relations and the combinations of the spheres of concepts. But concepts in general only exist after experience of *Vorstellungen* of perception,[2] and as their whole nature consists in their relation to these, it is clear that they presuppose them. No special content, however, is presupposed, but merely the existence of a content generally, and so logic as a whole may fairly pass for pure rational *Wissenschaft*. In all other *Wissenschaft* reason has received its content from *Vorstellungen* of perception;[3] in mathematics from the relations of space and time, presented in intuition or perception prior to all experience; in pure natural science

1. The grammatical gender of the German noun *Vernunft* happens to be feminine; Schopenhauer is taking advantage of this fact and its associations to make his point.
2. Better translated as "after previous perceptual *Vorstellungen*" (*nach vorhergegangenen anschaulichen Vorstellungen*).
3. Better translated as "from perceptual *Vorstellungen*."

[*Naturwissenschaft*], that is, in what we know of the course of nature prior to any experience, the content of the *Wissenschaft* proceeds from the pure understanding, *i.e.*, from the *a priori* knowledge of the law of causality and its connection with those pure intuitions or perceptions of space and time. In all other *Wissenschaften* everything that is not derived from the sources we have just referred to belongs to experience. Speaking generally, *to know rationally* [*wissen*] means to have in the power of the mind, and capable of being reproduced at will, such judgments as have their sufficient ground of knowledge in something outside themselves, *i.e.*, are true. Thus only abstract cognition is *rational knowledge* [*Wissen*], which is therefore the result of reason, so that we cannot accurately say of the lower animals that they *rationally know* [*wissen*] anything, although they have apprehension of what is presented in perception, and memory of this, and consequently imagination, which is further proved by the circumstance that they dream. We attribute consciousness to them, and therefore although the word *Bewusstsein* is derived from the verb to know rationally [*wissen*], the conception of consciousness corresponds generally with that of *Vorstellung* of whatever kind it may be. Thus we attribute life to plants, but not consciousness. *Rational knowledge* [*Wissen*] is therefore abstract consciousness, the permanent possession in concepts of the reason, of what has become known in another way.

* * *

§ 12. * * * The greatest value of rational or abstract knowledge is that it can be communicated and permanently retained. It is principally on this account that it is so inestimably important for practice. Any one may have a direct perceptive knowledge through the understanding alone, of the causal connection, of the changes and motions of natural bodies, and he may find entire satisfaction in it; but he cannot communicate this knowledge to others until it has been made permanent for thought in concepts. Knowledge of the first kind is even sufficient for practice, if a man puts his knowledge into practice himself, in an action which can be accomplished while the perception is still vivid; but it is not sufficient if the help of others is required, or even if the action is his own but must be carried out at different times, and therefore requires a preconceived plan. Thus, for example, a practised billiard-player may have a perfect knowledge of the laws of the impact of elastic bodies upon each other, merely in the understanding, merely for direct perception; and for him it is quite sufficient; but on the other hand it is only the man who has studied the science of mechanics, who has, properly speaking, a rational knowledge of these laws, that is, a knowledge of them in the abstract. Such knowledge of the understanding in perception is sufficient even for the construction of machines, when the inventor of the machine executes the work himself; as we often see in the case of talented workmen, who have no scientific knowledge. But whenever a number of men, and their united action taking place at different times, is required for the completion of a mechanical work, of a machine, or a building, then he who conducts it must have thought out the plan in the abstract, and such co-operative activity is only possible through the assistance of reason. It is, however, remarkable that in the first kind of activity, in which we have supposed that one man alone, in an uninterrupted course of action, accomplishes something, abstract knowledge, the application of reason or reflection, may often be a hindrance to him; for example, in the case of billiard-playing, of fighting, of tuning an instrument, or in the case of singing. Here perceptive knowledge must directly guide action; its passage through reflection makes it uncertain, for it divides the attention and confuses the man.

* * *

§ 15. * * * As regards the *content* of the *Wissenschaften* generally, it is, in fact, always the relation of the phenomena of the world to each other, according to the principle of sufficient reason, under the guidance of the *why*, which has validity and meaning only through this principle. *Explanation*[4] is the establishment of this relation. Therefore explanation can never go further than to show two ideas standing to each other in the relation peculiar to that form of the principle of sufficient reason which reigns in the class to which they belong. If this is done we cannot further be asked the question, *why*: for the relation proved is that one which absolutely cannot be imagined as other than it is, *i.e.*, it is the form of all knowledge. * * * But at the point at which natural science, and indeed every *Wissenschaft*, leaves things, because not only its explanation of them, but even the principle of this explanation, the principle of sufficient reason, does not extend beyond this point; there philosophy takes them up and treats them after its own method, which is quite distinct from the method of science. In my essay on the principle of sufficient reason, § 51, I have shown how in the different *Wissenschaften* the chief guiding clue is one or other form of that principle; and, in fact, perhaps the most appropriate classification of the *Wissenschaften* might be based upon this circumstance. Every explanation arrived at by the help of this clue is, as we have said, merely relative; it explains things in relation to each other, but something which indeed is presupposed is always left unexplained. In mathematics, for example, this is space and time; in mechanics, physics, and chemistry it is matter, qualities, original forces and laws of nature; in botany and zoology it is the difference of species, and life itself; in history it is the human race with all its properties of thought and will: in all it is that form of the principle of sufficient reason which is respectively applicable. It is peculiar to *philosophy* that it presupposes nothing as known, but treats everything as equally external and a problem; not merely the relations of phenomena, but also the phenomena themselves, and even the principle of sufficient reason to which the other *Wissenschaften* are content to refer everything. In philosophy nothing would be gained by such a reference, as one member of the series is just as external to it as another; and, moreover, that kind of connection is just as much a problem for philosophy as what is joined together by it, and the latter again is just as much a problem after its combination has been explained as before it. For, as we have said, just what the *Wissenschaften* presuppose and lay down as the basis and the limits of their explanation, is precisely and peculiarly the problem of philosophy, which may therefore be said to begin where *Wissenschaft* ends. It cannot be founded

---

4. A translation of *Erklärung*. Schopenhauer is here laying the groundwork for his important distinction between two types of knowledge: one in which the various *Wissenschaften* ("sciences," cognitive disciplines) specialize, which consists fundamentally in identifying such "explanations," and one (to which he attaches greater importance) that is the proper and distinctive pursuit of philosophy.

upon demonstrations, for they lead from known principles to unknown, but everything is equally unknown and external to philosophy. There can be no principle in consequence of which the world with all its phenomena first came into existence, and therefore it is not possible to construct, as Spinoza wished, a philosophy which demonstrates *ex firmis principiis.*[5] Philosophy is the most general rational knowledge, the first principles of which cannot therefore be derived from another principle still more general. The principle of contradiction establishes merely the agreement of concepts, but does not itself produce concepts. The principle of sufficient reason explains the connections of phenomena, but not the phenomena themselves; therefore philosophy cannot proceed upon these principles to seek a *causa efficiens* or a *causa finalis*[6] of the whole world. My philosophy, at least, does not by any means seek to know *whence* or *wherefore* the world exists, but merely *what* the world is. But the *why* is here subordinated to the *what*, for it already belongs to the world, as it arises and has meaning and validity only through the form of its phenomena, the principle of sufficient reason. We might indeed say that every one knows what the world is without help, for he is himself that subject of knowledge of which the world is the *Vorstellung*; and so far this would be true. But that knowledge is empirical, is in the concrete; the task of philosophy is to reproduce this in the abstract to raise to permanent rational knowledge the successive changing perceptions, and in general, all that is contained under the wide concept of feeling and merely negatively defined as not abstract, distinct, rational knowledge. It must therefore consist of a statement in the abstract, of the nature of the whole world, of the whole, and of all the parts. In order then that it may not lose itself in the endless multitude of particular judgments, it must make use of abstraction and think everything individual in the universal, and its differences also in the universal. It must therefore partly separate and partly unite, in order to present to rational knowledge the whole manifold of the world generally, according to its nature, comprehended in a few abstract concepts. Through these concepts, in which it fixes the nature of the world, the whole individual must be known as well as the universal, the knowledge of both therefore must be bound together to the minutest point.

* * *

§ 16. After this full consideration of reason as a special faculty of knowledge belonging to man alone, and the results and phenomena peculiar to human nature brought about by it, it still remains for me to speak of reason, so far as it is the guide of human action, and in this respect may be called *practical.* * * * At the commencement of our treatment of reason we remarked, in general terms, how much the action and behaviour of men differs from that of brutes, and that this difference is to be regarded as entirely due to the presence of abstract concepts in consciousness. The influence of these upon our whole existence is so penetrating and significant that, on account of them, we are related to the lower animals very much as those

---

5. From immovable principles (Latin). Benedict (Baruch) de Spinoza (1632–1677), Dutch philosopher.
6. An efficient cause (*how* the world could have come to be) or a final cause (an explanation of *why*

it came to be); these Latin phrases reflect the traditional Aristotelian account of the four causes that may enter into any explanation (the other two are material and formal).

animals that see are related to those that have no eyes (certain larvae, worms, and zoophytes). Animals without eyes know only by touch what is immediately present to them in space, what comes into contact with them; those which see, on the contrary, know a wide circle of near and distant objects. In the same way the absence of reason confines the lower animals to the [*Vorstellungen*] of perception, *i.e.*, the real objects which are immediately present to them in time; we, on the contrary, on account of knowledge in the abstract, comprehend not only the narrow actual present, but also the whole past and future, and the wide sphere of the possible; we view life freely on all its sides, and go far beyond the present and the actual. Thus what the eye is in space and for sensuous knowledge, reason is, to a certain extent, in time and for inner knowledge. But as the visibility of objects has its worth and meaning only in the fact that it informs us of their tangibility, so the whole worth of abstract knowledge always consists in its relation to what is perceived. * * *

The many-sided view of life as a whole which man, as distinguished from the lower animals, possesses through reason, may be compared to a geometrical, colourless, abstract, reduced plan of his actual life. He, therefore, stands to the lower animals as the navigator who, by means of chart, compass, and quadrant, knows accurately his course and his position at any time upon the sea, stands to the uneducated sailors who see only the waves and the heavens. Thus it is worth noticing, and indeed wonderful,[7] how, besides his life in the concrete, man always lives another life in the abstract. In the former he is given as a prey to all the storms of actual life, and to the influence of the present; he must struggle, suffer, and die like the brute. But his life in the abstract, as it lies before his rational consciousness, is the still reflection of the former, and of the world in which he lives; it is just that reduced chart or plan to which we have referred. Here in the sphere of quiet deliberation, what completely possessed him and moved him intensely before, appears to him cold, colourless, and for the moment external to him; he is merely the spectator, the observer. In respect of this withdrawal into reflection he may be compared to an actor who has played his part in one scene, and who takes his place among the audience till it is time for him to go upon the stage again, and quietly looks on at whatever may happen, even though it be the preparation for his own death (in the piece), but afterwards he again goes on the stage and acts and suffers as he must. From this double life proceeds that quietness peculiar to human beings, so very different from the thoughtlessness of the brutes[.]

* * *

From *Second Book. The World as Will—First Aspect.*
The Objectification of the Will

* * *

§ 18. The meaning for which we seek of that world which is present to us only as our *Vorstellung*, or the transition from the world as mere *Vorstellung* of the knowing subject to whatever it may be besides this, would never be

---

7. Astonishing, remarkable (but not necessarily admirable).

found if the investigator himself were nothing more than the pure knowing subject (a winged cherub without a body). But he is himself rooted in that world; he finds himself in it as an *individual*, that is to say, his knowledge, which is the necessary supporter of the whole world as *Vorstellung*, is yet always given through the medium of a body, whose affections are, as we have shown, the starting-point for the understanding in the perception of that world. His body is, for the pure knowing subject, a *Vorstellung* like every other *Vorstellung*, an object among objects. Its movements and actions are so far known to him in precisely the same way as the changes of all other perceived objects, and would be just as strange and incomprehensible to him if their meaning were not explained for him in an entirely different way. Otherwise he would see his actions follow upon given motives with the constancy of a law of nature, just as the changes of other objects follow upon causes, stimuli, or motives. But he would not understand the influence of the motives any more than the connection between every other effect which he sees and its cause. He would then call the inner nature of these manifestations and actions of his body which he did not understand a force, a quality, or a character, as he pleased, but he would have no further insight into it. But all this is not the case; indeed the answer to the riddle is given to the subject of knowledge who appears as an individual, and the answer is *will*. This and this alone gives him the key to his own existence, reveals to him the significance, shows him the inner mechanism of his being, of his action, of his movements.[8] The body is given in two entirely different ways to the subject of knowledge, who becomes an individual only through his identity with it. It is given as a *Vorstellung* in intelligent perception, as an object among objects and subject to the laws of objects. And it is also given in quite a different way as that which is immediately known to every one, and is signified by the word *will*. Every true act of his will is also at once and without exception a movement of his body. The act of will and the movement of the body are not two different things objectively known, which the bond of causality unites; they do not stand in the relation of cause and effect; they are one and the same, but they are given in entirely different ways,—immediately, and again in perception for the understanding. The action of the body is nothing but the act of the will objectified, *i.e.*, passed into percep-tion. It will appear later that this is true of every movement of the body, not merely those which follow upon motives, but also involuntary movements which follow upon mere stimuli, and, indeed, that the whole body is nothing but objectified will, *i.e.*, will become *Vorstellung*. All this will be proved and made quite clear in the course of this work. In one respect, therefore, I shall call the body the *objectivity of will*; as in the previous book,[9] and in the essay on the principle of sufficient reason, in accordance with the one-sided point of view intentionally adopted there (that of the *Vorstellung*), I called it *the immediate object*. Thus in a certain sense we may also say that will is the knowledge *a priori*[1] of the body, and the body is the knowledge *a posteriori*[2] of the will.

* * *

8. This passage (and what follows) is of crucial importance to the development of Schopenhauer's philosophical position.
9. The first book of this volume.
1. That is, knowledge that is possible before one has particular experiences of any sort, by reflect-ing on the very nature of the matter.
2. That is, knowledge that is made possible after (and with the benefit of) having particular experi-ences of some sort relevant to the matter.

The knowledge which I have of my will, though it is immediate, cannot be separated from that which I have of my body. I know my will, not as a whole, not as a unity, not completely, according to its nature, but I know it only in its particular acts, and therefore in time, which is the form of the phenomenal aspect of my body, as of every object. Therefore the body is a condition of the knowledge of my will. Thus, I cannot really imagine this will apart from my body. * * *

* * * My body and my will are one;—or, What as a *Vorstellung* of perception[3] I call my body, I call my will, so far as I am conscious of it in an entirely different way which cannot be compared to any other;—or, My body is the *objectivity* of my will;—or, My body considered apart from the fact that it is my *Vorstellung* is still my will[.] * * *

§ 19. In the first book we were reluctantly driven to explain the human body as merely *Vorstellung* of the subject which knows it, like all the other objects of this world of perception. But it has now become clear that what enables us consciously to distinguish our own body from all other objects which in other respects are precisely the same, is that our body appears in consciousness in quite another way *toto genere*[4] different from *Vorstellung*, and this we denote by the word *will*; and that it is just this double knowledge which we have of our own body that affords us information about it, about its action and movement following on motives, and also about what it experiences by means of external impressions; in a word, about what it is, not as *Vorstellung*, but as more than *Vorstellung*; that is to say, what it is *in itself*.[5] None of this information have we got directly with regard to the nature, action, and experience of other real objects.

It is just because of this special relation to one body that the knowing subject is an individual. For regarded apart from this relation, his body is for him only a *Vorstellung* like all other *Vorstellungen*. But the relation through which the knowing subject is an *individual*, is just on that account a relation which subsists only between him and one particular *Vorstellung* of all those which he has. Therefore he is conscious of this one *Vorstellung*, not merely as a *Vorstellung*, but in quite a different way as a will. * * *

The double knowledge which each of us has of the nature and activity of his own body, and which is given in two completely different ways, has now been clearly brought out. We shall accordingly make further use of it as a key to the nature of every phenomenon in nature, and shall judge of all objects which are not our own bodies, and are consequently not given to our consciousness in a double way but only as *Vorstellungen*, according to the analogy of our own bodies, and shall therefore assume that as in one aspect they are *Vorstellung*, just like our bodies, and in this respect are analogous to them, so in another aspect, what remains of objects when we set aside their existence as *Vorstellung* of the subject, must in its inner nature be the same as that in us which we call *will*. For what other kind of existence or reality should we attribute to the rest of the material world? Whence should we take the elements out of which we construct such a world? Besides will and *Vorstellung*

3. Better translated as "What as a perceptual *Vorstellung*."
4. In its entire character (Latin).
5. This is Schopenhauer's most distinctive and

radical claim, around which revolves his entire interpretation of ourselves—and indeed of "the world" itself—in terms of "will."

nothing is known to us or thinkable. If we wish to attribute the greatest known reality to the material world which exists immediately only in our *Vorstellung* we give it the reality which our own body has for each of us; for that is the most real thing for every one. But if we now analyse the reality of this body and its actions, beyond the fact that it is *Vorstellung*, we find nothing in it except the will; with this its reality is exhausted. Therefore we can nowhere find another kind of reality which we can attribute to the material world. Thus if we hold that the material world is something more than merely our *Vorstellung*, we must say that besides being *Vorstellung*, that is, in itself and according to its inmost nature, it is that which we find immediately in ourselves as *will*. I say according to its inmost nature; but we must first come to know more accurately this real nature of the will, in order that we may be able to distinguish from it what does not belong to itself, but to its manifestation, which has many grades.[6] Such, for example, is the circumstance of its being accompanied by knowledge, and the determination by motives which is conditioned by this knowledge. As we shall see farther on, this does not belong to the real nature of will, but merely to its distinct manifestation as an animal or a human being.

* * *

§ 21. Whoever has now gained from all these expositions a knowledge *in abstracto*, and therefore clear and certain, of what every one knows directly *in concreto*,[7] i.e., as feeling, a knowledge that his will is the real inner nature of his phenomenal being, which manifests itself to him as *Vorstellung*, both in his actions and in their permanent substratum, his body, and that his will is that which is most immediate in his consciousness, though it has not as such completely passed into the form of *Vorstellung* in which object and subject stand over against each other, but makes itself known to him in a direct manner, in which he does not quite clearly distinguish subject and object, yet is not known as a whole to the individual himself, but only in its particular acts,—whoever, I say, has with me gained this conviction will find that of itself it affords him the key to the knowledge of the inmost being of the whole of nature; for he now transfers it to all those phenomena which are not given to him, like his own phenomenal existence, both in direct and indirect knowledge, but only in the latter, thus merely one-sidedly as *Vorstellung* alone. He will recognise this will of which we are speaking not only in those phenomenal existences which exactly resemble his own, in men[8] and animals as their inmost nature, but the course of reflection will lead him to recognise the force which germinates and vegetates in the plant, and indeed the force through which the crystal is formed, that by which the magnet turns to the north pole, the force whose shock he experiences from the contact of two different kinds of metals, the force which appears in the elective affinities of matter as repulsion and attraction, decomposition and combination, and, lastly, even gravitation,

---

6. Schopenhauer here distinguishes between the "real nature of the will" (*Wesen des Willens*) and its "manifestations," or the various forms it takes (*Erscheinungen*), which are said to have many "grades" or gradations (*Grade*)—all of which are to be distinguished, as realities underlying all *Vorstel-* *lungen*, from the *Vorstellungen* we may have of them. He subsequently also refers to them as the will's "objectifications."
7. That is, "abstractly" and "concretely" (Latin).
8. That is, "human beings" (*Menschen*, a term that is generic in its application).

664 / Arthur Schopenhauer

which acts so powerfully throughout matter, draws the stone to the earth and the earth to the sun,—all these, I say, he will recognise as different only in their phenomenal existence, but in their inner nature as identical, as that which is directly known to him so intimately and so much better than anything else, and which in its most distinct manifestation is called *will*. It is this application of reflection alone that prevents us from remaining any longer at the phenomenon, and leads us to the *thing in itself.* Phenomenal existence is *Vorstellung* and nothing more. All *Vorstellung*, of whatever kind it may be, all *object*, is *phenomenal* existence, but the *will* alone is a *thing in itself.*[9] As such, it is throughout not *Vorstellung*, but *toto genere* different from it; it is that of which all *Vorstellung*, all object, is the phenomenal appearance, the visibility, the objectification. It is the inmost nature, the kernel, of every particular thing and also of the whole. It appears in every blind force of nature and also in the preconsidered action of man; and the great difference between these two is merely in the degree of the manifestation, not in the nature of what manifests itself.

§ 22. Now, if we are to think as an object this thing-in-itself (we wish to retain the Kantian expression as a standing formula), which, as such, is never object, because all object is its mere manifestation, and therefore cannot be it itself, we must borrow for it the name and concept of an object, of something in some way objectively given, consequently of one of its own manifestations. But in order to serve as a clue for the understanding, this can be no other than the most complete of all its manifestations, *i.e.*, the most distinct, the most developed, and directly enlightened by knowledge. Now this is the human will. It is, however, well to observe that here at any rate, we only make use of a *denominatio a potiori*,[1] through which, therefore, the concept of will receives a greater extension than it has hitherto had. Knowledge of the identical in different phenomena, and of difference in similar phenomena, is, as Plato so often remarks, a *sine qua non* of philosophy. But hitherto it was not recognised that every kind of active and operating force in nature is essentially identical with will, and therefore the multifarious kinds of phenomena were not seen to be merely different species of the same genus, but were treated as heterogeneous. Consequently there could be no word to denote the concept of this genus. I therefore name the genus after its most important species, the direct knowledge of which lies nearer to us and guides us to the indirect knowledge of all other species. But whoever is incapable of carrying out the required extension of the concept will remain involved in a permanent misunderstanding. For by the word *will* he understands only that species of it which has hitherto been exclusively denoted by it, the will which is guided by knowledge, and whose manifestation follows only upon motives, and indeed merely abstract motives, and thus takes place under the guidance of the reason. This, we have said, is only the most prominent example of the manifestation of will. We must now distinctly separate in thought the inmost essence of this manifestation which is known to us directly, and then transfer it to all the weaker, less distinct manifestations of the same nature, and thus

9. This radical claim sums up Schopenhauer's distinctive metaphysical position and warrants its characterization as a form of "Idealism" (in contrast to object-modeled "realism").
1. Naming by the stronger (Latin); that is, the designation of a thing in terms of its distinctive quality.

we shall accomplish the desired extension of the concept of will. From another point of view I should be equally misunderstood by any one who should think that it is all the same in the end whether we denote this inner nature of all phenomena by the word *will* or by any other. This would be the case if the thing-in-itself were something whose existence we merely *inferred*, and thus knew indirectly and only in the abstract. Then, indeed, we might call it what we pleased; the name would stand merely as the symbol of an unknown quantity. But the word *will*, which, like a magic spell, discloses to us the inmost being of everything in nature, is by no means an unknown quantity, something arrived at only by inference, but is fully and immediately comprehended, and is so familiar to us that we know and understand what will is far better than anything else whatever. The concept of will has hitherto commonly been subordinated to that of force, but I reverse the matter entirely, and desire that every force in nature should be thought as will.[2] It must not be supposed that this is mere verbal quibbling or of no consequence; rather, it is of the greatest significance and importance. For at the foundation of the concept of force, as of all other concepts, there ultimately lies the knowledge in sense-perception of the objective world, that is to say, the phenomenon, the *Vorstellung*; and the concept is constructed out of this. It is an abstraction from the province in which cause and effect reign, *i.e.*, from *Vorstellungen* of perception, and means just the causal nature of causes at the point at which this causal nature is no further etiologically explicable, but is the necessary presupposition of all etiological explanation. The concept will, on the other hand, is of all possible concepts the only one which has its source *not* in the phenomenal, *not* in the mere *Vorstellung* of perception, but comes from within, and proceeds from the most immediate consciousness of each of us, in which each of us knows his own individuality, according to its nature, immediately, apart from all form, even that of subject and object, and which at the same time is this individuality, for here the subject and the object of knowledge are one. If, therefore, we refer the concept of *force* to that of *will*, we have in fact referred the less known to what is infinitely better known; indeed, to the one thing that is really immediately and fully known to us, and have very greatly extended our knowledge. If, on the contrary, we subsume the concept of will under that of force, as has hitherto always been done, we renounce the only immediate knowledge which we have of the inner nature of the world, for we allow it to disappear in a concept which is abstracted from the phenomenal, and with which we can therefore never go beyond the phenomenal.

* * *

§ 25 * * * The subject which will be fully considered in the next book, and which has, doubtless, already presented itself to the mind of every student of Plato, is, that these different grades of the objectification of will which are manifested in innumerable individuals, and exist as their unattained types or as the eternal forms of things, not entering themselves into time and space, which are the medium of individual things, but remaining fixed, subject to no change, always being, never becoming, while the particular things arise

2. The question of whether there is any difference between Schopenhauer and NIETZSCHE here has provoked considerable debate.

and pass away, always become and never are,—that these *grades of the objectification of will* are, I say, simply *Plato's Ideas*. I make this passing reference to the matter here in order that I may be able in future to use the word *Idea*[3] in this sense. In my writings, therefore, the word is always to be understood in its true and original meaning given to it by Plato, and has absolutely no reference to those abstract productions of dogmatising scholastic reason, which Kant has inaptly and illegitimately used this word to denote, though Plato had already appropriated and used it most fitly. By Idea, then, I understand every definite and fixed grade of the objectification of will, so far as it is thing-in-itself, and therefore has no multiplicity.[4] These grades are related to individual things as their eternal forms or prototypes. * * *

§ 26. The lowest grades of the objectification of will are to be found in those most universal forces of nature which partly appear in all matter without exception, as gravity and impenetrability, and partly have shared the given matter among them, so that certain of them reign in one species of matter and others in another species, constituting its specific difference, as rigidity, fluidity, elasticity, electricity, magnetism, chemical properties and qualities of every kind. They are in themselves immediate manifestations of will, just as much as human action; and as such they are groundless, like human character. Only their particular manifestations are subordinated to the principle of sufficient reason, like the particular actions of men. They themselves, on the other hand, can never be called either effect or cause, but are the prior and presupposed conditions of all causes and effects through which their real nature unfolds and reveals itself. It is therefore senseless to demand a cause of gravity or electricity, for they are original forces. Their expressions, indeed, take place in accordance with the law of cause and effect, so that every one of their particular manifestations has a cause, which is itself again just a similar particular manifestation which determines that this force must express itself here, must appear in space and time; but the force itself is by no means the effect of a cause, nor the cause of an effect. It is therefore a mistake to say "gravity is the cause of a stone falling;" for the cause in this case is rather the nearness of the earth, because it attracts the stone. Take the earth away and the stone will not fall, although gravity remains. The force itself lies quite outside the chain of causes and effects, which presupposes time, because it only has meaning in relation to it; but the force lies outside time. The individual change always has for its cause another change just as individual as itself, and not the force of which it is the expression. For that which always gives its efficiency to a cause, however many times it may appear, is a force of nature. As such, it is groundless, *i.e.*, it lies outside the chain of causes and outside the province of the principle of sufficient reason in general, and is philosophically known as the immediate objectivity of will, which is the "in-itself" of the whole of nature; but in etiology, which in this reference is physics, it is set down as an original force, *i.e.*, a *qualitas occulta*.[5]

---

3. In German, *Idee*; Schopenhauer is emphasizing its continuity with the Greek *eidos*, which Plato uses for a somewhat similar philosophical purpose.
4. It is important to take note of this completely different use of the term *Idee*/Idea by Schopenhauer from Kant's and Hegel's uses of it (each very different from the other), and also from the ordinary uses of the term in both English and German—as well as from Schopenhauer's use of *Vorstellung* (sometimes translated as "Idea").
5. A hidden or concealed quality (Latin).

In the higher grades of the objectivity of will we see individuality occupy a prominent position, especially in the case of man, where it appears as the great difference of individual characters, *i.e.*, as complete personality, outwardly expressed in strongly marked individual physiognomy, which influences the whole bodily form. None of the brutes have this individuality in anything like so high a degree, though the higher species of them have a trace of it; but the character of the species completely predominates over it, and therefore they have little individual physiognomy. The farther down we go, the more completely is every trace of the individual character lost in the common character of the species, and the physiognomy of the species alone remains. We know the physiological character of the species, and from that we know exactly what is to be expected from the individual; while, on the contrary, in the human species every individual has to be studied and fathomed for himself, which, if we wish to forecast his action with some degree of certainty, is, on account of the possibility of concealment that first appears with reason, a matter of the greatest difficulty.

* * *

Thus every universal, original force of nature is nothing but a low grade of the objectification of will, and we call every such grade an eternal *Idea* in Plato's sense. But a *law of nature* is the relation of the [Platonic] Idea to the form of its manifestation. This form is time, space, and causality, which are necessarily and inseparably connected and related to each other. Through time and space the Idea multiplies itself in innumerable phenomena, but the order according to which it enters these forms of multiplicity is definitely determined by the law of causality; this law is as it were the norm of the limit of these phenomena of different Ideas, in accordance with which time, space, and matter are assigned to them. This norm is therefore necessarily related to the identity of the aggregate of existing matter, which is the common substratum of all those different phenomena. If all these were not directed to that common matter in the possession of which they must be divided, there would be no need for such a law to decide their claims. They might all at once and together fill a boundless space throughout an endless time. Therefore, because all these phenomena of the eternal Ideas are directed to one and the same matter, must there be a rule[6] for their appearance and disappearance; for if there were not, they would not make way for each other. Thus the law of causality is essentially bound up with that of the permanence of substance; they reciprocally derive significance from each other. Time and space, again, are related to them in the same way. For time is merely the possibility of conflicting states of the same matter, and space is merely the possibility of the permanence of the same matter under all sorts of conflicting states.

* * *

§ 27. * * * [E]ven crude matter has its existence only in the strife of conflicting forces. If we abstract from all chemical differences in matter, or go so far back in the chain of causes and effects that as yet there is no chemical difference, there remains mere matter,—the world rounded to a globe, whose

---

6. That is, "there must be a rule."

life, *i.e.*, objectification of will, is now constituted by the conflict between attractive and repulsive forces, the former as gravitation pressing from all sides towards the centre, the latter as impenetrability always opposing the former either as rigidity or elasticity; and this constant pressure and resistance may be regarded as the objectivity of will in its very lowest grade, and even there it expresses its character.

We should see the will express itself here in the lowest grade as blind striving, an obscure, inarticulate impulse, far from susceptible of being directly known. It is the simplest and the weakest mode of its objectification. But it appears as this blind and unconscious striving in the whole of unorganised nature, in all those original forces of which it is the work of physics and chemistry to discover and to study the laws, and each of which manifests itself to us in millions of phenomena which are exactly similar and regular, and show no trace of individual character, but are mere multiplicity through space and time, *i.e.*, through the *principium individuationis*,[7] as a picture is multiplied through the facets of a glass.

From grade to grade objectifying itself more distinctly, yet still completely without consciousness as an obscure striving force, the will acts in the vegetable kingdom also, in which the bond of its phenomena consists no longer properly of causes, but of stimuli; and, finally, also in the vegetative part of the animal phenomenon, in the production and maturing of the animal, and in sustaining its inner economy, in which the manifestation of will is still always necessarily determined by stimuli. The ever-ascending grades of the objectification of will bring us at last to the point at which the individual that expresses the Idea could no longer receive food for its assimilation through mere movement following upon stimuli. For such a stimulus must be waited for, but the food has now come to be of a more special and definite kind, and with the ever-increasing multiplicity of the individual phenomena, the crowd and confusion has become so great that they interfere with each other, and the chance of the individual that is moved merely by stimuli and must wait for its food would be too unfavourable. From the point, therefore, at which the animal has delivered itself from the egg or the womb in which it vegetated without consciousness, its food must be sought out and selected. For this purpose movement following upon motives, and therefore consciousness, becomes necessary, and consequently it appears as an agent, μηχανη,[8] called in at this stage of the objectification of will for the conservation of the individual and the propagation of the species. It appears represented by the brain or a large ganglion, just as every other effort or determination of the will which objectifies itself is represented by an organ, that is to say, manifests itself for the *Vorstellung* as an organ. But with this means of assistance, this μηχανη, the *world as Vorstellung* comes into existence at a stroke, with all its forms, object and subject, time, space, multiplicity, and causality. The world now shows its second side. Till now *mere will*, it becomes also *Vorstellung*, object of the knowing subject. The will, which up to this point followed its tendency in the dark with unerring certainty, has at this grade

---

7. Principle of individuation (Latin); for Schopenhauer, individuated existence is a merely superficial and apparent feature of the world, which does not apply to it in itself.

8. Machine, contrivance (Greek, *mēchanē*).

kindled for itself a light as a means which became necessary for getting rid of the disadvantage which arose from the throng and the complicated nature of its manifestations, and which would have accrued precisely to the most perfect of them. The hitherto infallible certainty and regularity with which it worked in unorganised and merely vegetative nature, rested upon the fact that it alone was active in its original nature, as blind impulse, will, without assistance, and also without interruption, from a second and entirely different world, the world as *Vorstellung*, which is indeed only the image of its own inner being, but is yet of quite another nature, and now encroaches on the connected whole of its phenomena. Hence its infallible certainty comes to an end. Animals are already exposed to illusion, to deception. They have, however, merely *Vorstellungen* of perception, no conceptions, no reflection, and they are therefore bound to the present; they cannot have regard for the future. * * *

Finally, when the will has attained to the highest grade of its objectification, that knowledge of the understanding given to brutes to which the senses supply the data, out of which there arises mere perception confined to what is immediately present, does not suffice. That complicated, many-sided, imaginative being, man, with his many needs, and exposed as he is to innumerable dangers, must, in order to exist, be lighted by a double knowledge; a higher power, as it were, of perceptive knowledge must be given him, and also reason, as the faculty of framing abstract conceptions. With this there has appeared reflection, surveying the future and the past, and, as a consequence, deliberation, care, the power of premeditated action independent of the present, and finally, the full and distinct consciousness of one's own deliberate volition as such. Now if with mere knowledge of perception there arose the possibility of illusion and deception, by which the previous infallibility of the blind striving of will was done away with, so that mechanical and other instincts, as expressions of unconscious will, had to lend their help in the midst of those that were conscious, with the entrance of reason that certainty and infallibility of the expressions of will (which at the other extreme in unorganised nature appeared as strict conformity to law) is almost entirely lost; instinct disappears altogether; deliberation, which is supposed to take the place of everything else, begets (as was shown in the First Book) irresolution and uncertainty; then error becomes possible, and in many cases obstructs the adequate objectification of the will in action. * * *

Thus knowledge generally, rational as well as merely sensuous, proceeds originally from the will itself, belongs to the inner being of the higher grades of its objectification as a mere μηχανή [mechanism], a means of supporting the individual and the species, just like any organ of the body. Originally destined for the service of the will for the accomplishment of its aims, it remains almost throughout entirely subjected to its service: it is so in all brutes and in almost all men. Yet we shall see in the Third Book how in certain individual men knowledge can deliver itself from this bondage, throw off its yoke, and, free from all the aims of will, exist purely for itself, simply as a clear mirror of the world, which is the source of art. Finally, in the Fourth Book, we shall see how, if this kind of knowledge reacts on the will, it can bring about self-surrender, *i.e.*, resignation, which is the final goal, and indeed the inmost nature of all virtue and holiness, and is deliverance from the world.

* * *

§ 29. I here conclude the second principal division of my exposition, in the hope that, so far as is possible in the case of an entirely new thought, which cannot be quite free from traces of the individuality in which it originated, I have succeeded in conveying to the reader the complete certainty that this world in which we live and have our being is in its whole nature through and through *will*, and at the same time through and through *Vorstellung*: that this *Vorstellung*, as such, already presupposes a form, object and subject, is therefore relative; and if we ask what remains if we take away this form, and all those forms which are subordinate to it, and which express the principle of sufficient reason, the answer must be that as something *toto genere* [essentially] different from *Vorstellung*, this can be nothing but *will*, which is thus properly the *thing-in-itself*. Every one finds that he himself is this will, in which the real nature of the world consists, and he also finds that he is the knowing subject, whose *Vorstellung* the whole world is, the world which exists only in relation to his consciousness, as its necessary supporter. Every one is thus himself in a double aspect the whole world, the microcosm; finds both sides whole and complete in himself. And what he thus recognises as his own real being also exhausts the being of the whole world—the macrocosm; thus the world, like man, is through and through *will*, and through and through *Vorstellung*, and nothing more than this. * * *

* * * Every will is a will towards something, has an object, an end of its willing; what then is the final end, or towards what is that will striving that is exhibited to us as the being-in-itself of the world? This question rests, like so many others, upon the confusion of the thing-in-itself with the manifestation. The principle of sufficient reason, of which the law of motivation is also a form, extends only to the latter, not to the former. It is only of phenomena, of individual things, that a ground can be given, never of the will itself, nor of the Idea in which it adequately objectifies itself. * * * Therefore every man has permanent aims and motives by which he guides his conduct, and he can always give an account of his particular actions; but if he were asked why he wills at all, or why in general he wills to exist, he would have no answer, and the question would indeed seem to him meaningless; and this would be just the expression of his consciousness that he himself is nothing but will, whose willing stands by itself and requires more particular determination by motives only in its individual acts at each point of time.

In fact, freedom from all aim, from all limits, belongs to the nature of the will, which is an endless striving. * * * It also discloses itself in its simplest form in the lowest grade of the objectification of will, in gravitation, which we see constantly exerting itself though a final goal is obviously impossible for it. For if, according to its will, all existing matter were collected in one mass, yet within this mass gravity, ever striving towards the centre, would still wage war with impenetrability as rigidity or elasticity. The tendency of matter can therefore only be confined, never completed or appeased. But this is precisely the case with all tendencies of all phenomena of will. * * *

From *Third Book. The World as* Vorstellung—*Second Aspect.*
Vorstellung *Independent of the Principle of Sufficient Reason:*
The Platonic Idea: The Object of Art

* * *

§ 34. The transition which we have referred to as possible, but yet to be regarded as only exceptional, from the common knowledge of particular things to the knowledge of the [Platonic] Idea,[9] takes place suddenly; for knowledge breaks free from the service of the will, by the subject ceasing to be merely individual, and thus becoming the pure will-less subject of knowledge, which no longer traces relations in accordance with the principle of sufficient reason, but rests in fixed contemplation of the object presented to it, out of its connection with all others, and rises into it.

* * *

If, raised by the power of the mind,[1] a man relinquishes the common way of looking at things, gives up tracing, under the guidance of the forms of the principle of sufficient reason, their relations to each other, the final goal of which is always a relation to his own will; if he thus ceases to consider the where, the when, the why, and the whither of things, and looks simply and solely at the *what*; if, further, he does not allow abstract thought, the concepts of the reason, to take possession of his consciousness, but, instead of all this, gives the whole power of his mind to perception, sinks himself entirely in this, and lets his whole consciousness be filled with the quiet contemplation of the natural object actually present, whether a landscape, a tree, a mountain, a building, or whatever it may be; inasmuch as he *loses* himself in this object (to use a pregnant German idiom), *i.e.*, forgets even his individuality, his will, and only continues to exist as the pure subject, the clear mirror of the object, so that it is as if the object alone were there, without any one to perceive it, and he can no longer separate the perceiver from the perception, but both have become one, because the whole consciousness is filled and occupied with one single sensuous picture; if thus the object has to such an extent passed out of all relation to something outside it, and the subject out of all relation to the will, then that which is so known is no longer the particular thing as such; but it is the [Platonic] *Idea*, the eternal form, the immediate objectivity of the will at this grade; and, therefore, he who is sunk in this perception is no longer individual, for in such perception the individual has lost himself; but he is *pure*, will-less, painless, timeless *subject of knowledge.* * * * In such contemplation the particular thing becomes at once the *Idea* of its species, and the perceiving individual becomes *pure subject of knowledge.* The individual, as such, knows only particular things; the pure subject of knowledge knows only Ideas. For the individual is the subject of knowledge in its relation to a definite particular manifestation of will, and in subjection to this. This particular manifestation of will is, as such, subordinated to the principle of sufficient reason in all its forms; therefore, all knowledge which relates itself to it also

9. That is, knowledge of the general types or forms of the various manifestations or objectifications of "will."

1. That is, raised by the power of intellectual and spiritual development (*durch die Kraft des Geistes gehoben*).

follows the principle of sufficient reason, and no other kind of knowledge is fitted to be of use to the will but this, which always consists merely of relations to the object. The knowing individual as such, and the particular things known by him, are always in some place, at some time, and are links in the chain of causes and effects. The pure subject of knowledge and [its] correlative, the Idea, have passed out of all these forms of the principle of sufficient reason: time, place, the individual that knows, and the individual that is known, have for them no meaning. * * * The particular things of all time and space are nothing but [Platonic] Ideas multiplied through the principle of sufficient reason (the form of the knowledge of the individual as such), and thus obscured as regards their pure objectivity. When the [Platonic] Idea appears, in it subject and object are no longer to be distinguished, for the [Platonic] Idea, the adequate objectivity of will, the true world as *Vorstellung*, arises only when the subject and object reciprocally fill and penetrate each other completely; and in the same way the knowing and the known individuals, as things in themselves, are not to be distinguished. For if we look entirely away from the true *world as* <u>*Vorstellung*</u>, there remains nothing but *the world as will*. * * *

Now the known thing, without me as the subject of knowledge, is just as little an object, and not mere will, blind effort, as without the object, without the *Vorstellung*, I am a knowing subject and not mere blind will. This will is in itself, *i.e.*, outside the *Vorstellung*, one and the same with mine: only in the world as *Vorstellung*, whose form is always at least that of subject and object, we are separated as the known and the knowing individual. As soon as knowledge, the world as *Vorstellung*, is abolished, there remains nothing but mere will, blind effort. That it should receive objectivity, become *Vorstellung*, supposes at once both subject and object; but that this should be pure, complete, and adequate objectivity of the will, supposes the object as [Platonic] Idea, free from the forms of the principle of sufficient reason, and the subject as the pure subject of knowledge, free from individuality and subjection to the will.

* * *

§ 35. In order to gain a deeper insight into the nature of the world, it is absolutely necessary that we should learn to distinguish the will as thing-in-itself from its adequate objectivity, and also the different grades in which this appears more and more distinctly and fully, *i.e.*, the [Platonic] Ideas themselves, from the merely phenomenal existence of these Ideas in the forms of the principle of sufficient reason, the restricted method of knowledge of the individual. We shall then agree with Plato when he attributes actual being only to the Ideas, and allows only an illusive, dream-like existence to things in space and time, the real world for the individual. Then we shall understand how one and the same Idea reveals itself in so many phenomena, and presents its nature only bit by bit to the individual, one side after another. Then we shall also distinguish the [Platonic] Idea itself from the way in which its manifestation appears in the observation of the individual, and recognise the former as essential and the latter as unessential. * * * The ice on the window-pane forms itself into crystals according to the laws of crystallisation, which reveal the essence of the force of nature that appears here, exhibit the

Idea; but the trees and flowers which it traces on the pane are unessential, and are only there for us. What appears in the clouds, the brook, and the crystal is the weakest echo of that will which appears more fully in the plant, more fully still in the beast, and most fully in man. But only the essential in all these grades of its objectification constitutes the [Platonic] Idea; on the other hand, its unfolding or development, because broken up in the forms of the principle of sufficient reason into a multiplicity of many-sided phenomena, is unessential to the Idea, lies merely in the kind of knowledge that belongs to the individual and has reality only for this. The same thing necessarily holds good of the unfolding of that Idea which is the completest objectivity of will. Therefore, the history of the human race, the throng of events, the change of times, the multifarious forms of human life in different lands and countries, all this is only the accidental form of the manifestation of the Idea, does not belong to the Idea itself, in which alone lies the adequate objectivity of the will, but only to the phenomenon which appears in the knowledge of the individual, and is just as foreign, unessential, and indifferent to the Idea itself as the figures which they assume are to the clouds, the form of its eddies and foam-flakes to the brook, or its trees and flowers to the ice.

To him who has thoroughly grasped this, and can distinguish between will and [Platonic] Idea, and between [Platonic] Idea and its manifestation, the events of the world will have significance only so far as they are the letters out of which we may read the Idea of man, but not in and for themselves.

* * *

§ 36. History follows the thread of events; it is pragmatic so far as it deduces them in accordance with the law of motivation, a law that determines the self-manifesting will wherever it is enlightened by knowledge. At the lowest grades of its objectivity, where it still acts without knowledge, natural science, in the form of etiology, treats of the laws of the changes of its phenomena, and, in the form of morphology, of what is permanent in them. This almost endless task is lightened by the aid of concepts, which comprehend what is general in order that we may deduce what is particular from it. Lastly, mathematics treats of the mere forms, time and space, in which the [Platonic] Ideas, broken up into multiplicity, appear for the knowledge of the subject as individual. All these, of which the common name is *Wissenschaft*, proceed according to the principle of sufficient reason in its different forms, and their theme is always the phenomenon, its laws, connections, and the relations which result from them.

But what kind of knowledge is concerned with that which is outside and independent of all relations, that which alone is really essential to the world, the true content of its phenomena, that which is subject to no change, and therefore is known with equal truth for all time, in a word, the *Ideas*, which are the direct and adequate objectivity of the thing-in-itself, the will? We answer, *Art*, the work of genius.[2] It repeats or reproduces the eternal [Platonic] Ideas grasped through pure contemplation, the essential and abiding in all the phenomena of the world; and according to what the material is in which it reproduces, it is sculpture or painting, poetry or music. Its one source is

2. Thus art, like philosophy, is the source of a knowledge (by a kind of direct acquaintance) with the Ideas—a deeper sort of knowledge than is yielded by the cognitive disciplines.

the knowledge of [Platonic] Ideas; its one aim the communication of this knowledge. While science, following the unresting and inconstant stream of the fourfold forms of reason and consequent, with each end attained sees further, and can never reach a final goal nor attain full satisfaction, any more than by running we can reach the place where the clouds touch the horizon; art, on the contrary, is everywhere at its goal. For it plucks the object of its contemplation out of the stream of the world's course, and has it isolated before it. And this particular thing, which in that stream was a small perishing part, becomes to art the representative of the whole, an equivalent of the endless multitude in space and time. It therefore pauses at this particular thing; the course of time stops; the relations vanish for it; only the essential, the [Platonic] Idea, is its object. We may, therefore, accurately define it as the *way of viewing things independent of the principle of sufficient reason*, in opposition to the way of viewing them which proceeds in accordance with that principle, and which is the method of experience and of science. * * * Only through the pure contemplation described above, which ends entirely in the object, can Ideas be comprehended; and the nature of *genius* consists in pre-eminent capacity for such contemplation. Now, as this requires that a man should entirely forget himself and the relations in which he stands, *genius* is simply the completest *objectivity*, *i.e.*, the objective tendency of the mind, as opposed to the subjective, which is directed to one's own self—in other words, to the will. Thus genius is the faculty of continuing in the state of pure perception, of losing oneself in perception, and of enlisting in this service the knowledge which originally existed only for the service of the will; that is to say, genius is the power of leaving one's own interests, wishes, and aims entirely out of sight, thus of entirely renouncing one's own personality for a time, so as to remain *pure knowing subject*, clear vision of the world; and this not merely at moments, but for a sufficient length of time, and with sufficient consciousness, to enable one to reproduce by deliberate art what has thus been apprehended[.]

* * *

§ 52. * * * The [Platonic] Ideas are the adequate objectification of will. To excite or suggest the knowledge of these by means of the representation of particular things (for works of art themselves are always representations of particular things) is the end of all the other arts, which can only be attained by a corresponding change in the knowing subject. Thus all these arts objectify the will indirectly only by means of the Ideas; and since our world is nothing but the manifestation of the Ideas in multiplicity, though their entrance into the *principium individuationis* (the form of the knowledge possible for the individual as such), music also, since it passes over the Ideas, is entirely independent of the phenomenal world, ignores it altogether, could to a certain extent exist if there was no world at all, which cannot be said of the other arts. Music is as *direct* an objectification and copy of the whole *will* as the world itself, nay, even as the Ideas, whose multiplied manifestation constitutes the world of individual things. Music is thus by no means like the other arts, the copy of the [Platonic] Ideas, but the *copy of the will itself*, whose objectivity the Ideas are. This is why the effect of music is so much more powerful and penetrating than that of the other arts, for they speak only of shadows, but it speaks of the thing itself.

* * *

From *Fourth Book. The World as Will—Second Aspect.*
The Assertion and Denial of the Will to Live,
When Self-Consciousness Has Been Attained

* * *

§ 54. The first three books will, it is hoped, have conveyed the distinct and certain knowledge that the world as *Vorstellung* is the complete mirror of the will, in which it knows itself in ascending grades of distinctness and completeness, the highest of which is man, whose nature, however, receives its complete expression only through the whole connected series of his actions. The self-conscious connection of these actions is made possible by reason, which enables a man constantly to survey the whole in the abstract.

The will, which, considered purely in itself, is without knowledge, and is merely a blind incessant impulse, as we see it appear in unorganised and vegetable nature and their laws, and also in the vegetative part of our own life, receives through the addition of the world as *Vorstellung*, which is developed in subjection to it, the knowledge of its own willing and of what it is that it wills. And this is nothing else than the world as *Vorstellung*, life, precisely as it exists. Therefore we called the phenomenal world the mirror of the will, its objectivity. And since what the will wills is always life, just because life is nothing but the *Darstellung* [display] of that willing for *Vorstellung*, it is all one and a mere pleonasm[3] if, instead of simply saying "the will," we say "the will to live."

Will is the thing-in-itself, the inner content, the essence of the world. Life, the visible world, the phenomenon, is only the mirror of the will. Therefore life accompanies the will as inseparably as the shadow accompanies the body; and if will exists, so will life, the world, exist. Life is, therefore, assured to the will to live; and so long as we are filled with the will to live we need have no fear for our existence, even in the presence of death. It is true we see the individual come into being and pass away; but the individual is only phenomenal, exists only for the knowledge which is bound to the principle of sufficient reason, to the *principio individuationis*. Certainly, for this kind of knowledge, the individual receives his life as a gift, rises out of nothing, then suffers the loss of this gift through death, and returns again to nothing. But we desire to consider life philosophically, *i.e.*, according to its Ideas, and in this sphere we shall find that neither the will, the thing-in-itself in all phenomena, nor the subject of knowing, that which perceives all phenomena, is affected at all by birth or by death. Birth and death belong merely to the phenomenon of will, thus to life; and it is essential to this to exhibit itself in individuals which come into being and pass away, as fleeting phenomena appearing in the form of time—phenomena of that which in itself knows no time, but must exhibit itself precisely in the way we have said, in order to objectify its peculiar nature. Birth and death belong in like manner to life, and hold the balance as reciprocal conditions of each other, or, if one likes the expression, as poles of the whole phenomenon of life. * * *

3. That is, redundancy.

The form of this phenomenon is time, space, and causality, and by means of these individuation, which carries with it that the individual must come into being and pass away. But this no more affects the will to live, of whose manifestation the individual is, as it were, only a particular example or specimen, than the death of an individual injures the whole of nature. For it is not the individual, but only the species that Nature cares for, and for the preservation of which she so earnestly strives, providing for it with the utmost prodigality through the vast surplus of the seed and the great strength of the fructifying impulse. The individual, on the contrary, neither has nor can have any value for Nature, for her kingdom is infinite time and infinite space, and in these infinite multiplicity of possible individuals. Therefore she is always ready to let the individual fall, and hence it is not only exposed to destruction in a thousand ways by the most insignificant accident, but originally destined for it, and conducted towards it by Nature herself from the moment it has served its end of maintaining the species. Thus Nature naïvely expresses the great truth that only the Ideas, not the individuals, have, properly speaking, reality, *i.e.*, are complete objectivity of the will. Now, since man is Nature itself, and indeed Nature at the highest grade of its self-consciousness, but Nature is only the objectified will to live, the man who has comprehended and retained this point of view may well console himself, when contemplating his own death and that of his friends, by turning his eyes to the immortal life of Nature, which he himself is.

* * *

* * * What we fear in death is the end of the individual, which it openly professes itself to be, and since the individual is a particular objectification of the will to live itself, its whole nature struggles against death. Now when feeling thus exposes us helpless, reason can yet step in and for the most part overcome its adverse influence, for it places us upon a higher standpoint, from which we no longer contemplate the particular but the whole. Therefore a philosophical knowledge of the nature of the world, which extended to the point we have now reached in this work but went no farther, could even at this point of view overcome the terror of death in the measure in which reflection had power over direct feeling in the given individual. A man who had thoroughly assimilated the truths we have already advanced, but had not come to know, either from his own experience or from a deeper insight, that constant suffering is essential to life, who found satisfaction and all that he wished in life, and could calmly and deliberately desire that his life, as he had hitherto known it, should endure for ever or repeat itself ever anew, and whose love of life was so great that he willingly and gladly accepted all the hardships and miseries to which it is exposed for the sake of its pleasures,—such a man would stand "with firm-knit bones on the well-rounded, enduring earth," and would have nothing to fear.[4] Armed with the knowledge we have given him, he would await with indifference the death that hastens towards him on the wings of time. He would regard it as a false illusion, an impotent

---

4. Nietzsche, unlike Schopenhauer, *does* believe that someone—or at any rate someone exceptional—could reasonably take such a life-affirming stance even after having "come to know . . . that constant suffering is essential to life": the type epitomized by his *Übermensch* (overman). This passage resonates strongly with that idea, and could well have prompted his further idea of the "eternal recurrence" as the ultimate test of one's attitude toward life, first set forth in *The Gay Science* (1882), § 341. The quotation is from Goethe's poem "Limits of Mankind" (1780).

spectre, which frightens the weak but has no power over him who knows that he is himself the will of which the whole world is the objectification or copy, and that therefore he is always certain of life, and also of the present, the peculiar and only form of the phenomenon of the will. * * * Finally, there are many men who would occupy this point of view if their knowledge kept pace with their will, *i.e.*, if, free from all illusion, they were in a position to become clearly and distinctly themselves. For this is, for knowledge, the point of view of the complete *assertion* [*Bejahung*][5] *of the will to live.*

That the will asserts itself means, that while in its objectivity, *i.e.*, in the world and life, its own nature is completely and distinctly given it as *Vorstellung*, this knowledge does not by any means check its volition; but this very life, so known, is willed as such by the will with knowledge, consciously and deliberately, just as up to this point it willed it as blind effort without knowledge. The opposite of this, the *denial* [*Verneinung*] *of the will to live*, shows itself if, when that knowledge is attained, volition ends, because the particular known phenomena no longer act as *motives* for willing, but the whole knowledge of the nature of the world, the mirror of the will, which has grown up through the comprehension of the *Ideas*, becomes a *quieter* of the will; and thus free, the will suppresses itself. These quite unfamiliar conceptions are difficult to understand when expressed in this general way, but it is hoped they will become clear through the exposition we shall give presently, with special reference to action, of the phenomena in which, on the one hand, the assertion in its different grades, and, on the other hand, the denial, expresses itself. For both proceed from knowledge, yet not from abstract knowledge, which is expressed in words, but from living knowledge, which is expressed in action and behaviour alone, and is independent of the dogmas which at the same time occupy the reason as abstract knowledge. To exhibit them both, and bring them to distinct knowledge of the reason, can alone be my aim, and not to prescribe or recommend the one or the other, which would be as foolish as it would be useless[.]

* * *

§ 56. * * * I wish the reader to recall the passage with which we closed the Second Book,—a passage occasioned by the question, which met us then, as to the end and aim of the will. Instead of the answer to this question, it appeared clearly before us how, in all the grades of its manifestation, from the lowest to the highest, the will dispenses altogether with a final goal and aim. It always strives, for striving is its sole nature, which no attained goal can put an end to. Therefore it is not susceptible of any final satisfaction, but can only be restrained by hindrances, while in itself it goes on for ever. * * *

We have long since recognised this striving, which constitutes the kernel and in-itself of everything, as identical with that which in us, where it manifests itself most distinctly in the light of the fullest consciousness, is called *will*. Its hindrance through an obstacle which places itself between it and its temporary aim we call *suffering*, and, on the other hand, its attainment of the end satisfaction, wellbeing, happiness. We may also transfer this terminology to the phenomena of the unconscious world, for though weaker in degree,

---

5. That is, affirmation; saying Yes (*Ja*) as opposed to denial or repudiation (*Verneinung*, saying No [*Nein*]). It is precisely in these terms that Nietzsche expresses his most fundamental difference from and opposition to Schopenhauer.

they are identical in nature. Then we see them involved in constant suffering, and without any continuing happiness. For all effort springs from defect—from discontent with one's estate—is thus suffering so long as it is not satisfied; but no satisfaction is lasting, rather it is always merely the starting-point of a new effort. The striving we see everywhere hindered in many ways, everywhere in conflict, and therefore always under the form of suffering. Thus, if there is no final end of striving, there is no measure and end of suffering.

But what we only discover in unconscious Nature by sharpened observation, and with an effort, presents itself distinctly to us in the intelligent world in the life of animals, whose constant suffering is easily proved. But without lingering over these intermediate grades, we shall turn to the life of man, in which all this appears with the greatest distinctness, illuminated by the clearest knowledge; for as the phenomenon of will becomes more complete, the suffering also becomes more and more apparent. In the plant there is as yet no sensibility, and therefore no pain. A certain very small degree of suffering is experienced by the lowest species of animal life—infusoria and radiata;[6] even in insects the capacity to feel and suffer is still limited. It first appears in a high degree with the complete nervous system of vertebrate animals, and always in a higher degree the more intelligence develops. Thus, in proportion as knowledge attains to distinctness, as consciousness ascends, pain also increases, and therefore reaches its highest degree in man. And then, again, the more distinctly a man knows, the more intelligent he is, the more pain he has; the man who is gifted with genius suffers most of all. * * *

We desire to consider in this way, in *human existence,* the inner and essential destiny of will. Every one will easily recognise that same destiny expressed in various degrees in the life of the brutes, only more weakly, and may also convince himself to his own satisfaction, from the suffering animal world, *how essential to all life is suffering.*

§ 57. * * * We saw that the inner being of unconscious nature is a constant striving without end and without rest. And this appears to us much more distinctly when we consider the nature of brutes and man. Willing and striving is its whole being, which may be very well compared to an unquenchable thirst. But the basis of all willing is need, deficiency, and thus pain. Consequently, the nature of brutes and man is subject to pain originally and through its very being.

* * *

* * * The ceaseless efforts to banish suffering accomplish no more than to make it change its form. It is essentially deficiency, want, care for the maintenance of life. If we succeed, which is very difficult, in removing pain in this form, it immediately assumes a thousand others, varying according to age and circumstances, such as lust, passionate love, jealousy, envy, hatred, anxiety, ambition, covetousness, sickness, &c., &c. If at last it can find entrance in no other form, it comes in the sad, grey garments of tediousness and ennui,[7] against which we then strive in various ways. If finally we succeed in driving this away, we shall hardly do so without letting pain enter in one of its earlier

---

6. Microscopic animal life (technically, a large class of protozoans) and a large category of invertebrates with radial structure (e.g., sea urchins).
7. That is, boredom.

forms, and the dance begin again from the beginning; for all human life is tossed backwards and forwards between pain and ennui. * * *

* * * It is true that we often see our pain arise only from some definite external relation, and are visibly oppressed and saddened by this only. Then we believe that if only this were taken away, the greatest contentment would necessarily ensue. But this is illusion. The measure of our pain and our happiness is on the whole, according to our hypothesis, subjectively determined for each point of time, and the motive for sadness is related to that, just as a blister which draws to a head all the bad humours otherwise distributed is related to the body. The pain which is at that period of time essential to our nature, and therefore cannot be shaken off, would, without the definite external cause of our suffering, be divided at a hundred points, and appear in the form of a hundred little annoyances and cares about things which we now entirely overlook, because our capacity for pain is already filled by that chief evil which has concentrated in a point all the suffering otherwise dispersed. This corresponds also to the observation that if a great and pressing care [*Besorgniss*][8] is lifted from our breast by its fortunate issue, another immediately takes its place, the whole material of which was already there before, yet could not come into consciousness as care because there was no capacity left for it, and therefore this material of care remained indistinct and unobserved in a cloudy form on the farthest horizon of consciousness. But now that there is room, this prepared material at once comes forward and occupies the throne of the reigning care of the day. And if it is very much lighter in its matter than the material of the care which has vanished, it knows how to blow itself out so as apparently to equal it in size, and thus, as the chief care of the day, completely fills the throne.

* * *

§ 58. * * * The life of every individual, if we survey it as a whole and in general, and only lay stress upon its most significant features, is really always a tragedy, but gone through in detail, it has the character of a comedy. For the deeds and vexations of the day, the restless irritation of the moment, the desires and fears of the week, the mishaps of every hour, are all through chance, which is ever bent upon some jest, scenes of a comedy. But the never-satisfied wishes, the frustrated efforts, the hopes unmercifully crushed by fate, the unfortunate errors of the whole life, with increasing suffering and death at the end, are always a tragedy. Thus, as if fate would add derision to the misery of our existence, our life must contain all the woes of tragedy, and yet we cannot even assert the dignity of tragic characters, but in the broad detail of life must inevitably be the foolish characters of a comedy.

* * *

§ 59. * * * Every one who has awakened from the first dream of youth, who has considered his own experience and that of others, who has studied himself in life, in the history of the past and of his own time, and finally in the works of the great poets, will, if his judgment is not paralysed by some indelibly imprinted prejudice, certainly arrive at the conclusion that this human world is the kingdom of chance and error, which rule without mercy in

8. That is, concern; worry.

great things and in small, and along with which folly and wickedness also wield the scourge. Hence it arises that everything better only struggles through with difficulty; what is noble and wise seldom attains to expression, becomes effective and claims attention, but the absurd and the perverse in the sphere of thought, the dull and tasteless in the sphere of art, the wicked and deceitful in the sphere of action, really assert a supremacy, only disturbed by short interruptions. On the other hand, everything that is excellent is always a mere exception, one case in millions, and therefore, if it presents itself in a lasting work, this, when it has outlived the enmity of its contemporaries, exists in isolation, is preserved like a meteoric stone, sprung from an order of things different from that which prevails here. But as far as the life of the individual is concerned, every biography is the history of suffering, for every life is, as a rule, a continual series of great and small misfortunes, which each one conceals as much as possible, because he knows that others can seldom feel sympathy or compassion, but almost always satisfaction at the sight of the woes from which they are themselves for the moment exempt. But perhaps at the end of life, if a man is sincere and in full possession of his faculties, he will never wish to have it to live over again, but rather than this, he will much prefer absolute annihilation.[9]

* * *

§ 67. * * * Now, however, I must remind the reader * * * that we found before that suffering is essential to life as a whole, and inseparable from it. And that we saw that every wish proceeds from a need, from a want, from suffering, and that therefore every satisfaction is only the removal of a pain, and brings no positive happiness; that the joys certainly lie to the wish, presenting themselves as a positive good, but in truth they have only a negative nature, and are only the end of an evil. Therefore what goodness, love, and nobleness do for others, is always merely an alleviation of their suffering, and consequently all that can influence them to good deeds and works of love, is simply the *knowledge of the suffering of others*, which is directly understood from their own suffering and placed on a level with it. But it follows from this that pure love (αγαπη, *caritas*[1]) is in its nature sympathy; whether the suffering it mitigates, to which every unsatisfied wish belongs, be great or small. Therefore we shall have no hesitation, in direct contradiction to Kant, who will only recognise all true goodness and all virtue to be such, if it has proceeded from abstract reflection, and indeed from the conception of duty and of the categorical imperative, and explains felt sympathy as weakness, and by no means virtue, we shall have no hesitation, I say, in direct contradiction to Kant, in saying: the mere concept is for genuine virtue just as unfruitful as it is for genuine art: all true and pure love is sympathy, and all love which is not sympathy is selfishness.

* * *

9. Here again, Schopenhauer's challenge was taken up by Nietzsche, who made much of the idea of an ecstatically positive response to the imagined prospect first of the unending recurrence of one's own life (*The Gay Science*, § 341) and then, in *Thus Spoke Zarathustra* (1883–85), of the eternal recurrence of all things as the ultimate test of one's ability to affirm life as it fundamentally is. In contrast, Schopenhauer's response to any such prospect is profoundly negative.
1. The Greek (*agapē*) and Latin (*caritas*), terms for love of the supposedly highest sort (terms appropriated by Christian theology), as distinguished from sexual love.

§ 68. After this digression about the identity of pure love and sympathy, the final return of which upon our own individuality has, as its symptom, the phenomenon of weeping, I now take up the thread of our discussion of the ethical significance of action, in order to show how, from the same source from which all goodness, love, virtue, and nobility of character spring, there finally arises that which I call the denial [*Verneinung*] of the will to live.

We saw before that hatred and wickedness are conditioned by egoism, and egoism rests on the entanglement of knowledge in the *principium individuationis*. Thus we found that the penetration of that *principium individuationis* is the source and the nature of justice, and when it is carried further, even to its fullest extent, it is the source and nature of love and nobility of character. For this penetration alone, by abolishing the distinction between our own individuality and that of others, renders possible and explains perfect goodness of disposition, extending to disinterested love and the most generous self-sacrifice for others.

If, however, this penetration of the *principium individuationis*, this direct knowledge of the identity of will in all its manifestations, is present in a high degree of distinctness, it will at once show an influence upon the will which extends still further. If that veil of Mâyâ,[2] the *principium individuationis*, is lifted from the eyes of a man to such an extent that he no longer makes the egotistical distinction between his person and that of others, but takes as much interest in the sufferings of other individuals as in his own, and therefore is not only benevolent in the highest degree, but even ready to sacrifice his own individuality whenever such a sacrifice will save a number of other persons, then it clearly follows that such a man, who recognises in all beings his own inmost and true self, must also regard the infinite suffering of all suffering beings as his own, and take on himself the pain of the whole world. No suffering is any longer strange to him. All the miseries of others which he sees and is so seldom able to alleviate, all the miseries he knows directly, and even those which he only knows as possible, work upon his mind like his own. It is no longer the changing joy and sorrow of his own person that he has in view, as is the case with him who is still involved in egoism; but, since he sees through the *principium individuationis*, all lies equally near him. He knows the whole, comprehends its nature, and finds that it consists in a constant passing away, vain striving, inward conflict, and continual suffering. He sees wherever he looks suffering humanity, the suffering brute creation, and a world that passes away. But all this now lies as near him as his own person lies to the egoist. Why should he now, with such knowledge of the world, assert this very life through constant acts of will, and thereby bind himself ever more closely to it, press it ever more firmly to himself? Thus he who is still involved in the *principium individuationis*, in egoism, only knows particular things and their relation to his own person, and these constantly become new *motives* of his volition. But, on the other hand, that knowledge of the whole, of the nature of the thing-in-itself which has been described, becomes a *quieter* of all and every volition. The will now turns away from life; it now shudders at the pleasures in which it recognises the assertion of life. Man now attains to the state

2. In Hindu philosophy, the cosmic illusion that the material world is real.

of voluntary renunciation, resignation, true indifference, and perfect will-lessness. * * *

* * * The phenomenon by which this change is marked, is the transition from virtue to asceticism. That is to say, it no longer suffices for such a man to love others as himself, and to do as much for them as for himself; but there arises within him a horror of the nature of which his own phenomenal existence is an expression, the will to live, the kernel and inner nature of that world which is recognised as full of misery. He therefore disowns this nature which appears in him, and is already expressed through his body, and his action gives the lie to his phenomenal existence, and appears in open contradiction to it. Essentially nothing else but a manifestation of will, he ceases to will anything, guards against attaching his will to anything, and seeks to confirm in himself the greatest indifference to everything. His body, healthy and strong, expresses through the genitals, the sexual impulse; but he denies the will and gives the lie to the body; he desires no sensual gratification under any condition. Voluntary and complete chastity is the first step in asceticism or the denial of the will to live. It thereby denies the assertion of the will which extends beyond the individual life, and gives the assurance that with the life of this body, the will, whose manifestation it is, ceases.

* * *

* * * And he mortifies not only the will itself, but also its visible form, its objectivity, the body. He nourishes it sparingly, lest its excessive vigour and prosperity should animate and excite more strongly the will, of which it is merely the expression and the mirror. So he practises fasting, and even resorts to chastisement and self-inflicted torture, in order that, by constant privation and suffering, he may more and more break down and destroy the will, which he recognises and abhors as the source of his own suffering existence and that of the world. If at last death comes, which puts an end to this manifestation of that will, whose existence here has long since perished through free denial of itself, with the exception of the weak residue of it which appears as the life of this body; it is most welcome, and is gladly received as a longed-for deliverance. Here it is not, as in the case of others, merely the manifestation which ends with death; but the inner nature itself is abolished, which here existed only in the manifestation, and that in a very weak degree; this last slight bond is now broken. For him who thus ends, the world has ended also.

* * *

§ 71. * * * We have recognised the inmost nature of the world as will, and all its phenomena as only the objectivity of will; and we have followed this objectivity from the unconscious working of obscure forces of Nature up to the completely conscious action of man. Therefore we shall by no means evade the consequence, that with the free denial, the surrender of the will, all those phenomena are also abolished; that constant strain and effort without end and without rest at all the grades of objectivity, in which and through which the world consists; the multifarious forms succeeding each other in gradation; the whole manifestation of the will; and, finally, also the universal forms of this manifestation, time and space, and also its last fundamental form, subject and object; all are abolished. No will: no *Vorstellung*: no world.

Before us there is certainly only nothingness. But that which resists this passing into nothing, our nature, is indeed just the will to live, which we ourselves are as it is our world. That we abhor annihilation so greatly, is simply another expression of the fact that we so strenuously will life, and are nothing but this will, and know nothing besides it. But if we turn our glance from our own needy and embarrassed condition to those who have overcome the world, in whom the will, having attained to perfect self-knowledge, found itself again in all, and then freely denied itself, and who then merely wait to see the last trace of it vanish with the body which it animates; then, instead of the restless striving and effort, instead of the constant transition from wish to fruition, and from joy to sorrow, instead of the never-satisfied and never-dying hope which constitutes the life of the man who wills, we shall see that peace which is above all reason, that perfect calm of the spirit, that deep rest, that inviolable confidence and serenity, the mere reflection of which in the countenance, as Raphael and Correggio[3] have represented it, is an entire and certain gospel; only knowledge remains, the will has vanished. We look with deep and painful longing upon this state, beside which the misery and wretchedness of our own is brought out clearly by the contrast. Yet this is the only consideration which can afford us lasting consolation, when, on the one hand, we have recognised incurable suffering and endless misery as essential to the manifestation of will, the world; and, on the other hand, see the world pass away with the abolition of will, and retain before us only empty nothingness. Thus, in this way, by contemplation of the life and conduct of saints, whom it is certainly rarely granted us to meet with in our own experience, but who are brought before our eyes by their written history, and, with the stamp of inner truth, by art, we must banish the dark impression of that nothingness which we discern behind all virtue and holiness as their final goal, and which we fear as children fear the dark; we must not even evade it like the Indians, through myths and meaningless words, such as reabsorption in Brahma or the Nirvana of the Buddhists.[4] Rather do we freely acknowledge that what remains after the entire abolition of will is for all those who are still full of will certainly nothing; but, conversely, to those in whom the will has turned and has denied itself, this our world, which is so real, with all its suns and milky-ways—is nothing.

SOURCE: From Arthur Schopenhauer, *The World as Will and Idea*, trans. R. B. Haldane and J. Kemp, 6th ed. (London: Kegan Paul, Trench, Trübner, 1907), 1:3–6, 16–19, 23–25, 45–48, 50, 64–66, 72–73, 105–12, 128–30, 132–34, 136–37, 141–45, 168–71, 174–75, 195–99, 211–14, 230–36, 238–40, 332–33, 353–56, 365–68, 398–402, 406, 408–9, 415–18, 485, 488–91, 493–94, 530–32 (translation modified by the editor). Except where otherwise indicated, German words in brackets are the terminology used in the German original, inserted by the editor in addition to their renderings in the translation; and unbracketed German words are the original terminology, substituted in place of their renderings in the translation by the editor for reasons given in notes and in the Hegel glossary (p. 144). Originally published as *Die Welt als Wille und Vorstellung*, first in 1818 and in a significantly expanded second edition in 1844. Haldane and Kemp's rendering of *Vorstellung* as "idea" is problematic, both

3. Two Italian Renaissance painters, Raffaello Sanzio (1483–1520) and Antonio Allegri da Correggio (1494–1534).
4. In Hinduism, Brahman is the abstract essence pervading the universe, the font of all things. Nirvana, the state of the cessation of the accumulated causes of future suffering and rebirth, is the goal of the Buddhist path.

because it does not accurately convey Schopenhauer's meaning and because "idea" is the obvious and natural English rendering of the German term *Idee*, which has its own (and very different) meanings and uses. (In this book, Schopenhauer employs it for something very like—and expressly modeled on—the *eidoi*, "ideas" or "forms," that, according to the Greek philosopher Plato [427–347 B.C.E.], are the essential archetypes of all things.) Thus recent translators have usually rendered *Vorstellung* as "representation"—but that too is less than ideal, because for Schopenhauer its meaning is highly specific: it denotes the way in which the world or things in the world come before us or are present to us as images or objects of perceptual and cognitive experience, in contrast to the world's underlying reality or character (the world as it is "in itself"), to which he attaches the term "will" and the expression "the world as will." (For him these two ways of thinking about the world together exhaust its meaning.) In the preceding excerpts, *Vorstellung* (plural, *Vorstellungen*) has therefore been left untranslated. In the "First Book" title, *Wissenschaft*—for Schopenhauer as for most other German philosophers of his time and subsequently—has the general sense of "cognitive inquiry." But he has in mind primarily those disciplines focused on objects of experience of one sort or another and on what transpires among them (i.e., the natural sciences and mathematics), seeing genuinely philosophical thinking as a different kind of knowing. (Here as so often elsewhere, Schopenhauer and HEGEL are in fundamental disagreement.) On both *Vorstellung* and *Wissenschaft*, see the Hegel glossary, p. 144.

FRIEDRICH NIETZSCHE
(1844 – 1900)

Nietzsche is unquestionably one of the most important and influential figures in the history of modern philosophy—and also one of the most unconventional and controversial. His philosophical writings were little heeded until long after his terminal collapse in 1889 (at the age of just 44). Yet his impact on European philosophy from the early twentieth century onward has been profound. In the latter part of that century he began to receive considerable attention in the English-speaking world as well, as the dark shadow cast by his misappropriation by the Nazis receded and philosophical fashions changed. His thought is a stronger living presence today in philosophy and in intellectual life more generally than that of almost any historical figure since KANT, and is likely to remain so in the foreseeable future. He may well have been right to give *Beyond Good and Evil* the subtitle "Prelude to a Philosophy of the Future."

Friedrich Wilhelm Nietzsche ("NEE-tcheh") was born in the Prussian province of Saxony, in the little village of Röcken. The death of his father—the village's Lutheran pastor—before Nietzsche was 5 left an emotional void in his young life, and he and his sister were brought up by their deeply religious mother in rather austere conditions. Fortunately, his scholastic abilities gained him a scholarship to a prestigious boarding school, Schulpforta (previously attended by JOHANN FICHTE), where he flourished. His education centered on classical languages and literatures, while he also pursued musical interests that included the piano and composition.

Nietzsche's academic training and brief academic career—as a professor at Basel University from 1869 to 1879—were in ancient languages and literatures rather than philosophy. But while he was a student at Leipzig, two encounters pro-foundly influenced him: he became acquainted intellectually with the philosophy of ARTHUR SCHOPENHAUER and personally with the composer Richard Wagner, both of whom he initially revered. Their influence is evident in his first book, *The Birth of Tragedy* (1872). It dealt with the emergence of tragedy in the literature and culture of the ancient Greeks—and also with its revival in the operas of Wagner, to whom he had become close (but of whom he eventually became severely critical).

In the course of his ten years at Basel, however, Nietzsche was drawn increasingly to philosophy; and after resigning from his professorship (because of poor health as well as his changing interests) at the age of just 34, he devoted the remainder of his productive life to it. He became serious about philosophy when he happened to come upon Schopenhauer's *The World as Will and Representation* (1818; 2nd ed., 1844) in a Leipzig bookstore. Though fascinated and persuaded by Schopenhauer's basic conception of the world as a godless and irrational affair of ceaseless striving and suffering, he was repelled by the work's starkly pessimistic verdict concerning the worth of existence in such a world, and sought some way of arriving at a different conclusion. Schopenhauer seemed to him to be fundamentally and importantly right about the world, and yet ultimately and even more importantly wrong in the pessimistic conclusions he drew and proclaimed. The challenge of that dilemma compelled him to abandon philology for philosophy.

Most of the works for which Nietzsche is known today were written in just ten years—between 1879, when he left Basel, and 1889, when he suffered a physical and mental collapse from which he never recovered. His productivity during that decade was all the more remarkable because he had no permanent residence, and was constantly plagued by a host of illnesses and other afflictions. It ceased completely with his breakdown; and although he did not die until 1900, his final decade was an empty one of increasing disability and insanity.

Nietzsche had deep concerns about the quality of life in the culture and society of his time. He was convinced that the interpretive and evaluative underpinnings of Western civilization are fundamentally flawed, and he was determined to come to grips with the profound crisis he believed would follow widespread recognition of that fact. He sought both to comprehend this situation and to help provide humanity with a new lease on life, beyond what he called "the death of God" (the demise of traditional religious and metaphysical ways of thinking) and the subsequent advent of "nihilism" (the conviction that everything is meaningless and valueless). The fundamental problem of how nihilism might be overcome and life affirmed without illusions preoccupied him throughout his life. He was convinced that traditional forms of religious and philosophical thought were inadequate to the task, and indeed were part of the problem; and so he attempted to develop a radical and more viable alternative to them that might show the way.

From his early essays to his last works, Nietzsche was an astute, severe, and provocative critic on many fronts. Cultural, social, political, artistic, religious, moral, scientific, and philosophical developments and phenomena of many kinds drew his polemical attention. As a result, many view the basic thrust and upshot of his thought as radically negative and see that negativity as a main cause of the nihilism that he proclaimed to be coming (and of worse things as well). But this impression is deeply mistaken. Nietzsche actually was a profoundly positive thinker, whose critiques and polemics were intended to prepare the way for the fundamentally constructive twin philosophical tasks of the "philosophy of the future": *interpretation* (and reinterpretation) and *evaluation* (and revaluation).

Nietzsche's thinking was avowedly interpretive and experimental, and he made free use of highly metaphorical and figurative language. He also was very critical of traditional and commonplace ways of thinking about truth and knowledge, maintaining that all thinking is "perspectival" and even writing that "there are no facts, only interpretations." Such claims have led some to label him a radical epistemological nihilist, arguing that he rejected the ideas of truth and knowledge altogether. Yet Nietzsche manifested a passionate commitment to truthfulness, as he pursued philosophical tasks whose aim he quite clearly supposed to be comprehension. Thinking can be "perspectival" without being devoid of all cognitive significance; and rejecting the idea that there can be "facts" independent of and prior to all "interpretation" does not entail the conclusion that no interpretation of any phenomenon is or can be cognitively superior to any other. Yet it is far from clear what humanly conceivable truth and humanly attainable knowledge do and can amount to if these suppositions are among one's points of departure. These are among the problems with which Nietzsche sought to come to grips.

But these were not the sorts of problems that drew Nietzsche to philosophy in the first place or that fueled his intense commitment to it. He was deeply concerned with basic problems of value and meaning that he believed were becoming increasingly acute and required new solutions. This is what motivated his concern with the supposedly forced choice between absolutism and nihilism. In his view, philosophy's basic challenge was to overcome both absolutistic ways of thinking and the unwarranted nihilism resulting from their abandonment. He therefore undertook to reinterpret ourselves and the world along lines that would be more tenable, and also more conducive to what he called the "flourishing" and "enhancement" of human life.

Nietzsche advocated replacing the metaphysical Holy Grail of an ultimate reality conceived along the lines of a transcendent deity or "'true world' of being," and the quest for it conceived as the proper aim and picture of true knowledge and our existence, with different (and related) paradigms of reality, knowledge, and value. His candidates were the sort of reality in which human life and the world of our activities and experience consist, the kind of comprehension of them of which they admit and we are capable, and the possibility of the creative transformation and enrichment of life so reinterpreted. The "de-deification of nature," the tracing of the "genealogy of morals" and their critique, and the elaboration of "naturalistic" accounts of knowledge, value, morality, and our entire "spiritual" nature thus came to be among the main tasks of the "new philosophers" Nietzsche called for and hoped would follow his lead. These philosophical projects mattered to him as they did, however, not merely because they might lead to an enhanced comprehension of human reality, but also and more importantly for their anticipated "value for life" (in one of his favorite phrases)—because they might thereby aid in the all-important task of creatively transforming and enriching human life.

Many of Nietzsche's books consist of numbered sections, paragraphs, or remarks—sometimes running to a page or more but often much briefer—in which he reflects on a variety of issues rather than systematically pursuing sustained lines of argument on single topics. This manner of pursing and presenting his thinking greatly complicates the task of understanding him; but it also is why his thinking on the many matters he discusses is less simplistic and more complex than it might at first appear to be. In one work after another (and also in his vast notebooks) he returns to problems repeatedly, approaching them from many different angles, and it is only by taking account of his many diverse reflections on them that we can come close to doing justice to his thinking about any of them. The following selections, ordered chronologically, are drawn from many of his writings both early and late, to provide a comprehensive introduction to his developing philosophical concerns and ways of pursuing them.

The first selections are from Nietzsche's first book, *The Birth of Tragedy*, written and published when he was a young professor of philology at Basel University, still in his twenties and a passionate believer in the cultural importance of the radical new operatic art of Richard Wagner (to whom he was then close). Nietzsche was convinced that Wagner was reviving the spirit of Greek tragedy, and that the revival of that spirit held great promise for humanity as an alternative to the failing religious, philosophical, and scientific faiths that had previously sustained Western culture. For the early Nietzsche, only illusions of one sort or another could counteract the unbearableness of the awful truth about the human condition that the Greeks, like Schopenhauer, had known all too well; and he looked for guidance and inspiration to the example of the Greeks. As a people and culture, he believed, they had found a kind of solution in the sustainable illusions of the various art forms he discusses, through whose lenses they were able to experience life very affirmatively, as a positively charged aesthetic phenomenon.

The second selection ("On Truth and Lie") is a draft of an essay Nietzsche wrote at about the same time, but never completed or published. Its topic is the very problematic status of our human cognitive abilities when considered as abilities of the kind of entirely biological and social creature we must now mundanely suppose ourselves initially to have been and then to have become. It thereby also shows the way in which he conceived of the human condition and of at least the basic character of human reality at this early stage of his intellectual and philosophical development. It and *The Birth of Tragedy* indicate his points of departure, providing initial (but by no means final) reflections on the important issues he raises in them. His point in the title's proclamation that "truth" and "lie" are to be considered in a "nonmoral sense" was to become one of the hallmarks of his kind of philosophical thinking: we need to learn to think about such things in a manner that is free of moralistic prejudices.

The next set of selections is from "Schopenhauer as Educator," written just two years later (1874). Though nominally about Schopenhauer, this essay is actually a kind of manifesto setting forth Nietzsche's own convictions at that early point in his intellectual development, while he was still a professor of philology at Basel and still closely associated with Wagner. Nietzsche was grateful to Schopenhauer "as educator" for providing the kind of inspiration and provocation that he needed so that he could find his own way beyond Schopenhauer *as philosopher*—just as he was soon to achieve his emancipation from Wagner, who still looms large in this essay as the epitome of the kind of creative genius of culture it celebrates. The essay's central theme is Nietzsche's emerging conviction that the key to making life meaningful and worth living is its enrichment and transformation through the enhancement of *culture*: the best thing we can do with our lives is to contribute to it in whatever ways we can (if not as creators ourselves, then in supporting roles).

The fourth group of selections is from the first (1882) edition of *The Gay Science*—the culminating work of Nietzsche's pre-*Zarathustra* philosophical development and of what he called his "free spirit" series. In this series, which began with *Human, All Too Human* (1878), Nietzsche inaugurated his kind of "free-spirited" philosophy, which he saw as a renewal and deepening of the spirit of Voltaire (to whose memory *Human, All Too Human* was dedicated) and of the Enlightenment. He had opened that first book of the series by asserting that the time for "metaphysical philosophy" was over, because "there are *no eternal facts*, just as there are no absolute truths"; philosophers must "learn that man has become, that the faculty of cognition has become," and indeed "everything has become." Therefore, he continued, "what is needed from now on is *historical philosophizing*," in an alliance with "natural science, the youngest of all philosophical methods." In that book and this series, and in *The Gay Science* most

clearly, he attempted to begin to practice what he there preached.

It is in *The Gay Science* that Nietzsche proclaims for the first time that "God is dead"; and he goes on to contend that "God's shadows" must now be banished from our thinking about ourselves and our world. In particular, he suggests that the death of God requires both the "de-deification of nature" and a "naturalizing" reconsideration of the whole of our human reality, attentive to how and what it has "become" as well as what it was in the first place and fundamentally continues to be. The German version of the title—*Die fröhliche Wissenschaft*—translates an Italian phrase ("la gaya scienza," Nietzsche's subtitle) long associated with the playful and this-worldly art and spirit of the troubadours, the pre-Renaissance lyric poets of southern France whom Nietzsche admired and in a sense sought to emulate philosophically. It also conveys how Nietzsche conceives of what he is doing: as a kind of cognitive endeavor—aspiring in particular to the comprehension of human reality—whose pursuit (in marked contrast to the spirit of Schopenhauer's thinking) is a fundamentally joyful affair.

Yet for Nietzsche that pursuit is also a serious affair, reflecting his sense that much is at stake, and his emerging conviction that a sustainable life-affirming stance without illusions is humanly possible after all but (as for the Greeks) requires the attainment of a "tragic"—rather than either merely pessimistic *or optimistic*—sensibility. So he chose to conclude the first edition of *The Gay Science* with the opening paragraph of the prologue to the first part of his next work, *Thus Spoke Zarathustra* (1883–85), captioned "Incipit tragoedia": "The tragedy begins."

It is from that remarkable work that the next selection is taken. The selection—the first part's prologue and initial speeches—merely hints at the richness of this monumental four-part literary-philosophical masterpiece. It features a Zarathustra who is only at the beginning of the development of the new sort of postreligious, postmetaphysical, and postscientistic *life-affirming* ("Yes-saying") sensibility that this work is intended to foster. But this brief selection does introduce some of the guiding ideas of the work (and of the later Nietzsche): "the death of God" as the point of departure, the *Übermensch* (overman)—symbolizing the enhancement of life—as "the meaning of the earth" and the new meaning of life, the distinction between ordinary "herd" humanity and the possibility of a "higher" humanity, different types of human spirituality, the delusion of "otherworldly" hopes, the need for a naturalistic reinterpretation of spirituality, and the importance of sublimation for spiritual development.

The selection that follows is from Nietzsche's first post-*Zarathustra* book, *Beyond Good and Evil* (1886), which he subtitled "Prelude to a Philosophy of the Future." Rather than returning to the same kinds of reflections he had been pursuing in his "free spirit" series, he here considers how the sort of "philosophy of the future" he envisions differs both from philosophy previously and from his own "free-spirited" alternative to it. The point of the title is that this philosophy of the future is not only to be "de-deified" but also "de-moralized"—that is, liberated from the sway of moral prejudices generally, and of the morality of the "good/evil" dichotomy in particular.

This book also offers sketches of the way in which Nietzsche proposes to reinterpret religions and moralities naturalistically, as human (and often all-too-human) phenomena, thereby rendering their status and authority dubious. And it looks ahead to a further task he now sees as even more important than taking the lead in such liberating critique, naturalistic reinterpretation, and life affirmation: he calls it "value creation." While Nietzsche does not make clear what he means, it is at least plausible to suppose that *Thus Spoke Zarathustra* had already provided something like an example, in the new sensibility it seeks to foster. He further envisions a key role for these "new philosophers" not only in the comprehension of what the enhancement of life involves and requires (and of what is

detrimental to it), but also in the "great politics" of strategizing to promote its real-world realization.

But rather than devoting himself to further efforts of either sort, Nietzsche then returned to the pre-*Zarathustra* enterprise of *The Gay Science*, with a second edition of it (1887) containing a substantial new fifth part or "book." The selections from it show him at the height of his philosophical powers—continuing the project of the four-book version of 1882 with the benefit of five more years of philosophical development, and giving at least some indications of how his thinking on various philosophical issues was developing. They also flesh out his assertion in *Beyond Good and Evil* that the new philosopher is to be all that the free-spirited philosopher of his pre-*Zarathustra* period was *and more*, rather than something else altogether.

These selections display Nietzsche at his philosophical best, reflecting incisively, clearly, and calmly on a range of important questions and issues in a way that should be of interest to anyone with a serious interest in philosophy. They begin with a thoughtful meditation on the "death of God" issue that he had first raised explicitly in the previous edition, and proceed through reflections on the "will to truth," the value of moral values, the problem of nihilism, the relation of consciousness to language, the contributions of such earlier figures as Kant and HEGEL, the shallowness of a purely "scientific" worldview, and other fascinating and important topics. This fifth book of *The Gay Science* should be required reading for anyone interested in Nietzsche.

On the Genealogy of Morals (also 1887), from which the next selections are taken, was written as a kind of supplement to his discussion of moralities in his chapter "The Natural History of Morals" in *Beyond Good and Evil*. As just noted, by this point Nietzsche had come to see the need for what he calls the "revaluation" or reassessment of moral values, and indeed of prevailing values and valuations more generally. He also had come to see the need for a preliminary sort of inquiry into the human *origins* of existing modes of moral and other valuation, and the social, psychological, and other conditions and circumstances (including prior modes of valuation) that were—or may plausibly be supposed to have been—involved. The book's three essays provide three such discussions, each intended to shed light on some aspect of the "genealogy" of modern-day morality in the Western world. Though only preliminary to an actual revaluation of that morality, they help set the stage for it. They also contribute to Nietzsche's consideration of a number of other significant features of human reality and their genealogy, thereby providing examples of the "naturalizing" reinterpretation of our human reality that he had called for in *The Gay Science*.

Nietzsche subtitled *Genealogy* "A Polemic." This book marked the beginning of the polemical turn that characterizes all of his last works, but it was not nearly as vehement as the diatribes of 1888 against Wagner and Christianity that followed it. Between them he wrote his last philosophical book, which he playfully titled *Götzen-Dämmerung* (*Twilight of the Idols*), punning on the name of the final opera of Wagner's *Ring of the Nibelung* cycle, *Götterdämmerung* (*Twilight of the Gods*). While more measured and temperate in its manner than the other two polemics of that final year of his productive life, it is no less incisive. After first taking aim at Socrates and some of the main tendencies of the Western philosophical tradition that he initiated, Nietzsche broadened his range of targets to include many more of the intellectual and cultural "idols" of his own time, and also advanced startling conjectures and proposals on a variety of philosophical and political issues. The selections from this late work are among his last words on many of the topics he discusses. Yet they were written by a thinker on the edge, whose time was running out; and, like his other writings from that stressed and frantic year just prior to his collapse, they may well leave their reader wondering what to make of them.

The same may be said about the mate-rial in the final set of selections, from Nietzsche's notebooks. These notebooks, which contain a vast amount of material, were his philosophical workshop, and much of what he published first took form in them. Prior to his collapse Nietzsche had made plans for further book projects. One of them, which he referred to (even in print) as his intended "masterwork," was to be titled either *The Will to Power* or *Revaluation of All Values* (or both). His plans for it were modified a number of times, and then were seemingly abandoned in 1888 (though it is of course possible that, had he had a longer productive life, he might have again revived them).

After Nietzsche's collapse these notebooks and unpublished manuscripts fell (by default rather than his intent) under the control of his sister, Elisabeth Förster-Nietzsche, who made herself his promoter and editor as well as conservator of his literary estate, from the time of his incapacitation to her own death in 1936. She decided to select, edit, and arrange a selection of the notebook material, which she published in 1901 under Nietzsche's name with the title *Der Wille zur Macht* (*The Will to Power*), as if it were something like the masterwork that he had intended to write. Its translation into English (1967) has until recently been the only substantial sampling from the notebooks available in English.

It is now generally recognized that we should not regard this volume as one of Nietzsche's works, or suppose that he wanted a book of this sort to exist—or that he would have approved of the publication of all or any of the contents of his notebooks, in any language. But these contents have been published in German, and are slowly appearing in English translation. Scholars disagree over whether the notebook material should be used at all in interpreting Nietzsche's thought. A small number of selections from it (from among those included in *The Will to Power*) have been presented here—arranged by topic, retranslated, and reorganized to restore chronological order—in order to give readers both a sense of what this material is like and the chance to see some of it.

The notebooks certainly are not authoritative. They simply open another window on Nietzsche's thinking. But it is also important to recognize that there is a sense in which the same caveat applies to his published writings. Nothing he says in print, in any book early or late, can be taken as it stands, in isolation and without qualification, as definitive and authoritative for the understanding of "what he thinks" on any matter being discussed; for from beginning to abrupt end, his thought was work in progress, his writings were places of experiments, and his affair with language was an adventure. That is what makes interpreting Nietzsche such an interesting challenge.

———————

Nietzsche characterizes not only ourselves but also life and the world more generally in terms of "power" dynamics, reflecting a fundamental assertive-transformative tendency he calls "will to power." He further bases his "Dionysian value-standard" on this interpretation, as its affirmation; and he suggests that values be "revalued" and moralities be reassessed accordingly, in a way that is both conceptually and evaluatively "beyond good and evil," and that presupposes "the death of God." The meaning and significance of these ideas continue to be matters of intense debate. It is undeniable, however, that Nietzsche celebrates the attainment of a kind of life in which this power-oriented disposition is both strengthened and transformed, and that he takes what he calls the "enhancement of life"—by way of the many sorts of creativity that are humanly possible—to be the key to what he has his Zarathustra proclaim to be "the meaning of the earth."

From The Birth of Tragedy

1

We shall have gained much for the science [discipline] of aesthetics when we have succeeded in perceiving directly, and not only through logical reasoning, that art derives its continuous development from the duality of the *Apolline* [*Apollinische*] and *Dionysiac* [*Dionysische*];[1] just as the reproduction of species depends on the duality of the sexes, with its constant conflicts and only periodically intervening reconciliations. These terms are borrowed from the Greeks, who revealed the profound mysteries of their artistic doctrines to the discerning mind, not in concepts but in the vividly clear forms of their deities. To the two gods of art, Apollo and Dionysus, we owe our recognition that in the Greek world there is a tremendous opposition, as regards both origins and aims, between the Apolline [*apollinisch*] art of the sculptor and the non-visual, Dionysiac [*dionysisch*] art of music. These two very different tendencies walk side by side, usually in violent opposition to one another, inciting one another to ever more powerful births, perpetuating the struggle of the opposition only apparently bridged by the word 'art'; until, finally, by a metaphysical miracle of the Hellenic 'will', the two seem to be coupled, and

———————

1. Also translated "Apollinian" or "Apollonian" and "Dionysian": characteristic of the Greek gods Apollo (god of music, medicine, and prophecy, associated with the higher developments of civilization) and Dionysus (god of vegetation and wine, associated with frenzied cult worship).

in this coupling they seem at last to beget the work of art that is as Dionysiac as it is Apolline—Attic tragedy.[2]

To reach a better understanding of these two tendencies, let us first conceive them as the separate art worlds of *dream* and *intoxication*, two physiological states which contrast similarly to the Apolline and the Dionysiac. * * *

The beautiful illusion of the dream worlds, in the creation of which every man is a consummate artist, is the precondition of all visual art, and indeed, as we shall see, of an important amount of poetry. We take pleasure in the immediate apprehension of form, all shapes speak to us, and nothing is indifferent or unnecessary. But even when this dream reality is presented to us with the greatest intensity, we still have a glimmering awareness that it is an *illusion*. That is my experience, at least[;] * * * and perhaps many, like myself, can remember calling out to themselves in encouragement, amid the perils and terrors of the dream, and with success: 'It is a dream! I want to dream on!' Just as I have often been told of people who have been able to continue one and the same dream over three and more successive nights: facts which clearly show that our innermost being, our common foundation, experiences dreams with profound pleasure and joyful necessity.

This same joyful necessity of dream experiences was also expressed by the Greeks in the figure of Apollo: Apollo, the deity of all plastic forces, is also the soothsaying god. Etymologically the 'shining one',[3] the deity of light, he also holds sway over the beautiful illusion of the inner fantasy world. The higher truth, the perfection of these states in contrast to imperfectly comprehensible daily reality, the deep awareness of nature healing and helping in sleep and dreams, is at the same time the symbolic analogue of soothsaying powers and of art in general, through which life is made both possible and worth living. But our image of Apollo must incorporate the delicate line that the dream image may not overstep without becoming pathological, in which case illusion would deceive us as solid reality; it needs that restraining boundary, that freedom from wilder impulses, that sagacious calm of the sculptor god. His eye must be sunlike, as befits his origin; even should it rage and show displeasure, it still bears the solemnity of the beautiful illusion. And thus we might say of Apollo what Schopenhauer said of man caught up in the veil of Maya[4] (*The World as Will and Representation* I):

> Just as the boatman sits in his little boat, trusting to his fragile craft in a stormy sea which, boundless in every direction, rises and falls in howling, mountainous waves, so in the midst of a world full of suffering the individual man calmly sits, supported by and trusting the *principium individuationis*.[5]

Indeed, it might be said of Apollo that the unshaken faith in that *principium* and the peaceful stillness of the man caught up in it have found their most sublime expression in him, and we might even describe Apollo as the glorious

---

2. The plays performed in Athens (the chief city of the region called Attica) at the festival of Dionysus during the 5th century B.C.E.
3. As Phoebus ("radiant") Apollo, god of light.
4. In Hindu philosophy, the cosmic illusion that the material world is real. For SCHOPENHAUER's

World as Will (1818; 2nd ed., 1844), see above.
5. The principle of individuation (Latin), which specifies that everything that exists is some sort of specific thing. For Schopenhauer, this is a merely superficial and apparent feature of the world, which does not apply to the world as it is in itself.

divine image of the *principium individuationis*, from whose gestures and looks all the delight, wisdom and beauty of 'illusion' speak to us.

In the same passage Schopenhauer has described the tremendous *dread* that grips man when he suddenly loses his way amidst the cognitive forms of appearance, because the principle of sufficient reason,[6] in one of its forms, seems suspended. If we add to this dread the blissful ecstasy which, prompted by the same fragmentation of the *principium individuationis*, rises up from man's innermost core, indeed from nature, we are vouchsafed a glimpse into the nature of the *Dionysiac*, most immediately understandable to us in the analogy of *intoxication*. Under the influence of the narcotic potion hymned by all primitive men and peoples, or in the powerful approach of spring, joyfully penetrating the whole of nature, those Dionysiac urges are awakened, and as they grow more intense, subjectivity becomes a complete forgetting of the self. In medieval Germany, too, the same Dionysiac power sent singing and dancing throngs, constantly increasing, wandering from place to place: in these dancers of Saint John and Saint Vitus we can recognize the Bacchic choruses of the Greeks, with their prehistory in Asia Minor, as far back as Babylon and the orgiastic Sacaea.[7] Some people, either through a lack of experience or through obtuseness, turn away with pity or contempt from phenomena such as these as from 'folk diseases', bolstered by a sense of their own sanity; these poor creatures have no idea how blighted and ghostly this 'sanity' of theirs sounds when the glowing life of Dionysiac revellers thunders past them.

Not only is the bond between man and man sealed by the Dionysiac magic: alienated, hostile or subjugated nature, too, celebrates her reconciliation with her lost son, man. The earth gladly offers up her gifts, and the ferocious creatures of the cliffs and the desert peacefully draw near. The chariot of Dionysus is piled high with flowers and garlands; under its yoke stride tigers and panthers. If we were to turn Beethoven's 'Hymn of Joy'[8] into a painting, and not to restrain the imagination even as the multitudes bowed awestruck into the dust: this would bring us close to the Dionysiac. Now the slave is a free man, now all the rigid and hostile boundaries that distress, despotism or 'impudent fashion' have erected between man and man break down. Now, with the gospel of world harmony, each man feels himself not only united, reconciled, and at one with his neighbour, but *one* with him, as if the veil of Maya had been rent and now hung in rags before the mysterious primal Oneness.

Singing and dancing, man expresses himself as a member of a higher community: he has forgotten how to walk and talk, and is about to fly dancing into the heavens. His gestures express enchantment. Just as the animals now speak, and the earth yields up milk and honey, he now gives voice to supernatural sounds: he feels like a god, he himself now walks about enraptured and elated as he saw the gods walk in dreams. Man is no longer an artist, he has become a work of art: the artistic power of the whole of nature reveals

---

6. The principle that every event must have a cause sufficient to explain it; this was the subject of Schopenhauer's first book, *On the Fourfold Root of the Principle of Sufficient Reason* (1813).
7. A Babylonian and Persian festival of the New Year. Nietzsche is listing a number of ecstatic cel-

ebrations (Bacchus is the Roman equivalent of Dionysus).
8. That is, SCHILLER's "Ode to Joy" (1786), incorporated by Ludwig van Beethoven (1770–1827) into the final movement of his Ninth Symphony.

itself to the supreme gratification of the primal Oneness amidst the paroxysms of intoxication. The noblest clay, the most precious marble, man, is kneaded and hewn here, and to the chisel-blows of the Dionysiac world-artist there echoes the cry of the Eleusinian mysteries, 'Do you bow low, multitudes? Do you sense the Creator, world?'[9]

2

We have so far considered the Apolline [*Apollinische*], and its opposite, the Dionysiac [*Dionysische*], as artistic powers which spring from nature itself, *without the mediation of the human artist*, and in which nature's artistic urges are immediately and directly satisfied; on the one hand as the world of dream images, whose perfection is not at all dependent on the intellectual accomplishments or artistic culture of the individual; on the other as an ecstatic reality, which again pays no heed to the individual, but even seeks to destroy individuality and redeem it with a mystical sense of unity. Faced with these immediate artistic states in nature, every artist is an 'imitator'—either an Apolline dream artist or a Dionysiac ecstatic artist or else—as for example in Greek tragedy—a dream artist and an ecstatic artist at one and the same time. This is how we must imagine him as he sinks down, lonely and apart from the revelling choruses in Dionysiac drunkenness and mystical self-negation, as his own condition, his unity with the innermost core of the world is revealed to him *in a symbolic dream-image*.

* * *

On the other hand, we do not need to rely on conjecture when we consider the massive chasm that separates the *Dionysiac Greeks* from the Dionysiac barbarians. From all corners of the ancient world—ignoring the modern world for the time being—from Rome to Babylon we can demonstrate the existence of Dionysiac festivals, which are at best related to the Greek festivals as the bearded satyr,[1] deriving his name and attributes from the goat, is related to Dionysus himself. Almost universally, the centre of those festivals was an extravagant lack of sexual discipline, whose waves engulfed all the venerable rules of family life. The most savage beasts of nature were here unleashed, even that repellent mixture of lust and cruelty that I have always held to be a 'witch's brew'. It would seem that for some time, however, the Greeks were thoroughly secured and protected against the febrile excitements of these festivals, knowledge of which forced its way to the Greeks along every route of land and sea: the figure of Apollo rose up in all its pride and held out the Gorgon's head[2] to the grotesque, barbaric Dionysiac, the most dangerous force it had to contend with. It was in Doric[3] art that Apollo's majestically repudiating stance was immortalized.

---

9. Quoted from a chorus of Schiller's "Ode to Joy." "Eleusinian mysteries": the most famous of the secret Greek cults, connected with Demeter (goddess of agriculture) and Dionysus; Eleusis was northwest of Athens.
1. In Greek mythology, a nature spirit with features of goats or horses; satyrs, who were attendants of Dionysus, were notoriously lustful.

2. A head that was incorporated into the shield of Athena, patron of Athens and goddess of war and practical reason; at the sight of the Gorgon, a snake-headed monster, the viewer was turned to stone.
3. Of Doria, the central part of ancient Greece (the Doric architectural order is the oldest and simplest).

This resistance became more questionable, even impossible, when similar impulses emerged from the deepest roots of Greek culture. Now all the Delphic god[4] could do was to disarm his powerful opponent of his destructive weapon by effecting a timely reconciliation—the most important moment in the history of Greek religion. Wherever we look we can observe the transformations wrought by this event. It was the reconciliation of two adversaries, clearly defining the boundaries that they were henceforward to respect, and periodically exchanging gifts of honour. Fundamentally the chasm had not been bridged. But if we consider how Dionysiac power revealed itself under the terms of that peace accord, and establish a comparison with the Babylonian Sacaea and its throwback of man to the condition of the tiger and the ape, we will be able to understand the meaning of those new festivals of world redemption and days of transfiguration. It was here that nature was first given its artistic celebration, here that the breakdown of the *principium individuationis* became an artistic phenomenon. That terrible 'witch's brew' of lust and cruelty had now lost its potency, and only the peculiar blend and duality of emotions amongst the Dionysiac revellers recalls it, as medicines recall deadly poisons—the phenomenon that pain is experienced as joy, that jubilation tears tormented cries from the breast. At the moment of supreme joy we hear the scream of horror or the yearning lamentation for something irrevocably lost. Those Greek festivals reveal a sentimental trait in nature, as though she were bemoaning her fragmentation into individuals. The chanting and gestures of these revellers, with their dual inspiration, was something new and unheard of in the Homeric[5] and Greek world; and Dionysiac music in particular induced feelings of awe and terror. Music was apparently already known as an Apolline art, but only because of its rhythm, as regular as the sound of waves crashing against the shore, the creative power of which was developed for the representation of Apolline states. The music of Apollo was Doric architecture transmuted into sounds, but only into suggestive sounds such as those of the cithara. Care was taken to ensure that the one element held to be non-Apolline [*unapollinisch*] was excluded, the very element of which Dionysiac music consisted—the overwhelming power of sound, the unified flow of melody and the utterly incomparable world of harmony. In the Dionysiac dithyramb,[6] man's symbolic faculties are roused to their supreme intensity: a feeling never before experienced is struggling for expression—the destruction of the veil of Maya, Oneness as the source of form, of nature itself. The essence of nature was now to find symbolic expression. A new world of symbols was required, the whole of the symbolism of the body, not only the symbolism of the mouth, the eye, the word, but the rhythmic motion of all the limbs of the body in the complete gesture of the dance. Then all the other symbolic forces, the forces of music—rhythm, dynamics and harmony— would suddenly find impetuous expression. In order to grasp this total liberation of all symbolic forces, man must already have reached that peak of self-negation that seeks symbolic expression in those powers: the dithyrambic votary of Dionysus is thus understood only by his fellows! With what

4. That is, Apollo, whose most important temple and oracle were in Delphi.
5. That is, the world of preclassical Greece; the poems attributed to Homer were composed ca. 8th

century B.C.E., describing events of the 13th century B.C.E.
6. A choral song to Dionysus.

astonishment the Apolline Greek must have looked upon him! And his astonishment would have been intensified by its combination with the terror, not
in the end so strange to him, that his Apolline consciousness alone, like a
veil, hid that Dionysiac world from his view.

3

In order to understand this we must level down, stone by stone, as it were,
the elaborate construction of *Apolline culture* until we can see its underlying
foundations. Only then will we be able to see the glorious *Olympian* figures
of the gods standing on the gables of this structure, their actions, depicted in
brilliant reliefs, ornamenting its friezes. If Apollo too stands among them, as
one deity amongst others, without any claim to privileged status, we should
not allow ourselves to be misled. The same impulse that is symbolized in
Apollo gave birth to that entire Olympian world, and in this sense we may
consider Apollo to be its father. What was the tremendous need that produced
such a brilliant society of Olympian beings?

Anyone who approaches these Olympians with a different religion in his
heart, seeking elevated morals, even sanctity, ethereal spirituality, charity and
mercy, will quickly be forced to turn his back upon them, discouraged and
disappointed. Nothing here suggests asceticism, spirituality or duty—
everything speaks of a rich and triumphant existence, in which everything is
deified, whether it be good or evil. And thus the onlooker may be disquieted
by this fantastic exuberance of life, wondering what magic potion these boisterous men must have drunk to enjoy life so much that, whichever way they
look, Helen,[7] 'floating in sweet sensuality', the ideal image of their own existence, smiles back at them. But we must call out to this onlooker, who has
already turned his back: go not, but first hear what Greek folk wisdom says of
this same life, spread out before you here with such inexplicable cheerfulness. According to the old story, King Midas had long hunted wise *Silenus*,[8]
Dionysus' companion, without catching him. When Silenus had finally fallen
into his clutches, the king asked him what was the best and most desirable
thing of all for mankind. The daemon stood silent, stiff and motionless, until
at last, forced by the king, he gave a shrill laugh and spoke these words: 'Miserable, ephemeral race, children of hazard and hardship, why do you force
me to say what it would be much more fruitful for you not to hear? The best
of all things is something entirely outside your grasp: not to be born, not to
be, to be *nothing*. But the second-best thing for you—is to die soon.'[9]

How does this folk wisdom relate to the Olympian world of the gods? As
does the ecstatic vision of the tortured martyr to his torments.

Now the Olympian magic mountain opens up before us, revealing all its
roots. The Greeks knew and felt the fears and horrors of existence: in order
to be able to live at all they had to interpose the radiant dream-birth of the

---

7. The mythological Helen of Troy, the most beautiful woman in Greece and wife of Menelaus, king
of Sparta; the Trojan War was launched to retrieve
her from Troy, where she had been taken by the
Trojan prince Paris. The quotation is from Johann
Wolfgang von Goethe, *Wilhelm Meister's Apprenticeship* (1795–96), book 4, chap. 14.

8. The mythic companion and teacher of Dionysus; more generally, a silenus is a creature closely
related to (and often identified with) the satyr.
9. The final two sentences paraphrase the Greek
tragedy *Oedipus at Colonus* 1225–27 (ca. 406
B.C.E.), by the Greek tragedian Sophocles.

Olympians between themselves and those horrors. The terrible mistrust of the Titanic[1] forces of nature; the Moira[2] mercilessly reigning over all man's knowledge; the vultures that tormented the great friend to man, Prometheus;[3] the terrible destiny of wise Oedipus;[4] the family curse of the Atreids,[5] forcing Orestes to matricide—in short the entire philosophy of the god of the woods, along with its mythical examples, which brought about the downfall of the gloomy Etruscans[6]—the Greeks repeatedly overcame all this, or at least veiled and concealed it, with the artistic *middle world* of the Olympians. In order to live, the Greeks were profoundly compelled to create those gods. We might imagine their origin as follows; the Apolline impulse to beauty led, in gradual stages, from the original Titanic order of the gods of fear to the Olympian order of the gods of joy, just as roses sprout on thorn-bushes. How else could life have been borne by a race so sensitive, so impetuous in its desires, so uniquely capable of *suffering*, if it had not been revealed to them, haloed in a higher glory, in their gods? The same impulse that calls art into existence, the complement and apotheosis of existence, also created the Olympian world with which the Hellenic 'will' held up a transfiguring mirror to itself. Thus the gods provide a justification for the life of man by living it themselves— the only satisfactory form of theodicy! Existence under the bright sunlight of gods such as these was felt to be the highest goal of mankind, and the true grief felt by Homeric man came from departure from it, especially when that departure was near. We might now reverse Silenus' wisdom to say of them: 'the worst thing of all for them would be to die soon, the second worst to die at all'. If this lament is voiced once, it is heard again . . . from short-lived Achilles,[7] mourning the leaf-like change and transformation of the human race, the collapse of the heroic age. It is not unworthy of the greatest of all heroes to long for a continuation of life, even as a day labourer. The 'will', at the Apolline stage, longs so impetuously for life, and Homeric man feels so at one with it that even lamentation becomes his song of praise.

Here we must point out that the harmony that men of more recent times have so yearned for, indeed the unity of man with nature, to which Schiller applied the artistic word 'naïve',[8] is by no means such a simple, obvious, inevitable state that we would *necessarily* encounter it at the gateway to every culture, as a paradise of humanity. The only era that could hold such a view would be one that saw Rousseau's Émile[9] as an artist, and deluded itself that in Homer it had found just such an artist-Émile, reared at nature's breast. Whenever we encounter the naïve in art, we should recognize that we are in the presence of the highest impact of Apolline culture, which must always

---

1. The Titans were the gods who preceded and were overthrown by the Olympians (led by Zeus).
2. The Fates.
3. In Greek mythology, a Titan who gave fire to mortals; as punishment, he was chained to a mountain where daily his liver was eaten by an eagle.
4. Oedipus, whose wisdom was displayed in solving the riddle of the Sphinx, was destined to kill his father and marry his mother.
5. Descendants of Atreus, who was cursed by his brother Thyestes; Atreus's son Agamemnon was murdered by his wife, Clytemnestra, on his return from the Trojan War, and her son, Orestes, killed

her to avenge his father.
6. The most powerful people of pre-Roman Italy.
7. The greatest warrior among the Greeks fighting at Troy, where he died. (In the underworld, he told Odysseus that he would rather live as the hireling of a poor man than be lord over all the dead; *Odyssey* 11.489–91.)
8. See Schiller, *On Naïve and Sentimental* [or *Reflective*] *Poetry* (1795–96).
9. The child who is raised and educated in *Emile, or On Education* (1762), a didactic novel by the Swiss-born philosopher and social theorist Jean-Jacques Rousseau (1712–1778).

overthrow a realm of Titans and slay monsters, and which must emerge triumphant over a terrible abyss in its contemplation of the world and its most intense capacity for suffering, by resorting to the most powerful and pleasurable illusions. But how rarely is the naïve, that complete immersion in the beauty of illusion, achieved! How inexpressibly sublime, for that reason, is *Homer*, who, as an individual, is related to that Apolline folk culture as the individual dream artist is related to the dream faculties of the people and of nature in general. Homeric *naïveté* can only be understood as the complete triumph of Apolline illusion: this is one of those illusions that nature so often uses in order to attain its goals. The true goal is veiled by a phantasm: we stretch our hands towards one thing, and nature deceives us to achieve the other. Amongst the Greeks the 'will' wished to contemplate itself, in the transfiguration of genius and the world of art; in order to glorify themselves, its creations had to feel worthy of glorification, they had to see themselves in a higher sphere, without this contemplation seeming either a command or a reproach. It was in this sphere of beauty that they saw reflections of themselves, the Olympians. With this reflection of beauty the Hellenic 'will' battled with the talent, correlative to the artistic talent, for suffering and the wisdom of suffering, and as a monument to its triumph stands Homer, the naïve artist.

* * *

7

We must now call upon all the aesthetic principles we have so far discussed in order to find our way around the labyrinth, which is how we must refer to the *origin of Greek tragedy*. I do not think I am making an extravagant claim when I say that the problem of this origin has not yet even been seriously tackled, however many times the tattered rags of the classical tradition have been sewn together in their various combinations, and ripped apart again. This tradition tell us quite categorically *that tragedy arose from the tragic chorus*, and was originally only chorus and nothing else.[1]

* * *

* * * Perhaps we shall find a point of departure for our reflections in the claim that the satyr, the invented natural being, relates to cultural humanity as Dionysiac music relates to civilization. Of the latter, Richard Wagner[2] says that it is annulled by music as lamplight is annulled by the light of day. In the same way, I believe, the Greek man of culture felt himself annulled in the face of the satyr chorus, and the immediate effect of Dionysiac tragedy is that state and society, the gulfs separating man from man, make way for an overwhelming sense of unity that goes back to the very heart of nature. The metaphysical consolation (with which, as I wish to point out, every true tragedy leaves us), that whatever superficial changes may occur, life is at bottom indestructibly powerful and joyful, is given concrete form as a satyr chorus, a chorus of natural beings, living ineradicably behind all civilization, as it were, remain-

---

1. Classical Greek tragedies had a limited number of actors (usually three) and a chorus. According to the traditional explanation, tragedy (literally, "goat song") developed from a chorus of satyrs.

2. German composer (1813–1883), to whom Nietzsche was at this time close, and to whom he dedicated this book, which celebrates his work.

ing the same for ever, regardless of the changing generations and the path of history.

This chorus was a consolation to the Hellene,[3] thoughtful and uniquely susceptible as he was to the tenderest and deepest suffering, whose piercing gaze has seen to the core of the terrible destructions of world history and nature's cruelty; and who runs the risk of longing for a Buddha-like denial of the will. He is saved by art, and through art life has saved him for itself.

The ecstasy of the Dionysiac state, abolishing the habitual barriers and boundaries of existence, actually contains, for its duration, a lethargic element into which all past personal experience is plunged. Thus, through this gulf of oblivion, the worlds of everyday and Dionysiac reality become separated. But when one once more becomes aware of this everyday reality, it becomes repellent; this leads to a mood of asceticism, of denial of the will. This is something that Dionysiac man shares with Hamlet: both have truly seen to the essence of things, they have *understood*, and action repels them; for their action can change nothing in the eternal essence of things, they consider it ludicrous or shameful that they should be expected to restore order to the chaotic world. Understanding kills action, action depends on a veil of illusion—this is what Hamlet teaches us, not the stock interpretation of Hamlet as a John-a-dreams[4] who, from too much reflection, from an excess of possibilities, so to speak, fails to act. Not reflection, not that!—True understanding, insight into the terrible truth, outweighs every motive for action, for Hamlet and Dionysiac man alike. No consolation will be of any use from now on, longing passes over the world towards death, beyond the gods themselves; existence, radiantly reflected in the gods or in an immortal 'Beyond', is denied. Aware of truth from a single glimpse of it, all man can now see is the horror and absurdity of existence; now he understands the symbolism of Ophelia's fate, now he understands the wisdom of Silenus,[5] the god of the woods: it repels him.

Here, in this supreme menace to the will, there approaches a redeeming, healing enchantress—*art*. She alone can turn these thoughts of repulsion at the horror and absurdity of existence into ideas compatible with life: these are the *sublime*—the taming of horror through art; and *comedy*—the artistic release from the repellence of the absurd. The satyr chorus of the dithyramb is the salvation of Greek art; the frenzies described above were exhausted in the middle world of these Dionysiac attendants.

* * *

18

It is an eternal phenomenon: the voracious will[6] always finds a way to keep its creations alive and perpetuate their existence, by casting an illusion over things. One man will be enthralled by Socratic delight in knowledge[7] and the delusion that it might heal the eternal wound of existence, while another will

---

3. That is, the Greek.
4. The proverbial name of an idle dreamer. So Hamlet self-accusingly labels himself: Shakespeare, *Hamlet* (ca. 1600), 2.2.545 (Norton ed.).
5. Sage companion of Dionysus, mentioned above. Shakespeare's Ophelia (*in Hamlet*) went mad and drowned herself.

6. Nietzsche here is in basic agreement with Schopenhauer's characterization of the fundamental nature of all reality as "will," and with his basic conception of it.
7. The Greek philosopher Socrates (469–399 B.C.E.) taught that the love and pursuit of knowledge was the path to the human soul's improvement.

be caught up in the seductive veil of beauty, art, that floats before his eyes, and yet another will be gripped by the metaphysical consolation that beneath the whirlpool of phenomena eternal life flows indestructibly onwards: not to mention the more common and perhaps yet more powerful illusions that the will keeps constantly in readiness. These three levels of illusion are meant only for those nobler spirits who experience the burden and weight of existence more profoundly, and who must be deluded away from their distress with special stimulants. That which we call culture is made up entirely of those stimulants. According to the proportions of the mixture, culture is predominantly Socratic or artistic or tragic.

* * *

While the blight that lies dormant in the womb of theoretical culture is gradually beginning to frighten modern man, and he casts uneasily around in the stores of his experience for remedies to ward off the danger without quite believing in their efficacy, while he begins to have an inkling of the consequences of his situation, great and universally minded spirits have, with incredible level-headedness, used the armoury of science to lay bare the limitations and determinations of knowledge, and have thus decisively negated the claims of science to universal validity and universal goals. In so doing, they have revealed the delusion, based on the principle of causality, which imagines it can explain the innermost essence of things. The tremendous courage and wisdom of *Kant* and *Schopenhauer* carried off the most difficult victory: victory over the optimism that lurked within the essence of logic, which in turn forms the basis of our culture. Where that optimism had believed that all the mysteries of the world could be known and explained, relying on apparently innocuous *aeternae veritates*,[8] and had treated space, time and causality as utterly unconditional and universally valid laws, Kant revealed how these in fact only served to transform mere phenomena, the work of Maya, into the sole true essence of things, and thus render true knowledge of that essence thoroughly impossible. Or, as Schopenhauer has it, to send the dreamer into an even deeper sleep (*World as Will and Representation* I). This insight ushered in a culture which I should like to call tragic. Its most important characteristic is that its highest goal lies no longer in science but in wisdom, undeceived by the enticing diversions of the sciences; that it turns a steady eye on the world as a whole, and seeks to grasp, with a sympathetic love, eternal suffering as its own.

* * *

24

Among the peculiar artistic effects of musical tragedy we stressed an Apolline [*apollinisch*] *delusion* which rescues us from immediate oneness with Dionysiac [*dionysisch*] music, while allowing our musical emotion to be discharged in an Apolline sphere and in an interposed, visible middle world. At the same time we thought we had observed how that discharge made the middle world

8. Eternal truths (Latin).

of the theatrical event, the drama itself, visible and intelligible from within to a degree unattainable in any other forms of Apolline art. Where Apolline art takes wing, uplifted by the spirit of music, we encounter the supreme intensification of its powers, and must thus acknowledge the summit of both Apolline and Dionysiac artistic aims in the fraternal bond between Apollo and Dionysus.

* * *

For to say that life really is so tragic does not in the least help to explain the origin of an art form, provided that art is not only an imitation of the truth of nature but a metaphysical supplement to that truth of nature, coexisting with it in order to overcome it. In as far as it belongs to art at all, the tragic myth participates fully in its metaphysical intention of transfiguration. But what does it transfigure, if it presents the world of phenomena in the image of the suffering hero? Least of all the 'reality' of this world of phenomena, because it says to us: 'Look! Take a close look! That is your life! That is the hour-hand of the clock of your existence!'

And are we to imagine that myth showed us this life in order to transfigure it for us? But if it did not, wherein lies the aesthetic pleasure with which we let those images pass before us? I am speaking of aesthetic pleasure, and know that many of these images could also produce a moral delight, taking the form of pity, for example, or moral victory. But no one seeking to deduce the effect of the tragic from moral sources alone, as has been customary in aesthetics for far too long, should believe that he has done any kind of service to art, which must insist on purity in its sphere above all else. The first challenge when it comes to explaining the tragic myth is that of seeking the pleasure peculiar to it in the purely aesthetic sphere, without intruding upon the sphere of pity, fear or moral sublimity. How can ugliness and discord, the content of the tragic myth, produce aesthetic pleasure?

At this point we must take a bold leap into a metaphysics of art, repeating our earlier assertion that existence and the world seem justified only as an aesthetic phenomenon.[9] Accordingly, the tragic myth has to convince us that even ugliness and discord are an artistic game which the will, in the eternal abundance of its pleasure, plays with itself. But this primal and difficult phenomenon of Dionysiac [dionysisch] art is only intelligible and can only be immediately grasped through the wonderful significance of *musical dissonance*: just as music alone, placed next to the world, can give us an idea of what we might understand by 'the justification of the world as an aesthetic phenomenon'. The pleasure produced by the tragic myth has the same origin as the pleasurable perception of dissonance in music. The Dionysiac, with its primal pleasure experienced even in pain, is the common womb of music and the tragic myth.

In referring to the musical relation of dissonance, perhaps we have made the difficult problem of the effect of tragedy considerably easier? For we now understand what it means to wish to look, in tragedy, and at the same time to long to go beyond that looking; we might characterize this condition with reference to artistically applied dissonance, by saying that we want to hear and

9. This is the basic thesis of *The Birth of Tragedy*; scholars debate whether the later Nietzsche   retains, rejects, or affirms a modified version of this idea.

long to go beyond hearing. The striving for infinity, the wingbeat of longing, that accompanies the supreme delight of clearly perceived reality, reminds us that both states are aspects of a Dionysiac [*dionysisch*] phenomenon: over and over again it shows us the spirit that playfully builds and destroys the world of individuals as the product of a primal pleasure: similarly, dark Heraclitus[1] compares the force that builds worlds to a child placing stones here and there, and building sandcastles and knocking them down again.

* * *

25

Music and tragic myth are to an equal extent expressions of the Dionysiac capacity of a people, and they are inseparable. Both originate in a sphere of art beyond the Apolline. Both transfigure a region in whose chords of delight dissonance as well as the terrible image of the world charmingly fade away; they both play with the sting of displeasure, trusting to their extremely powerful magical arts; both use this play to justify the existence even of the 'worst world'. Here the Dionysiac, as against the Apolline, proves to be the eternal and original artistic force, calling the whole phenomenal world into existence: in the midst of it a new transfiguring illusion is required if the animated world of individuation is to be kept alive. If we could imagine dissonance becoming man—and what else is man?—then in order to stay alive that dissonance would need a wonderful illusion, covering its own being with a veil of beauty. That is the real artistic intention of Apollo, in whose name we bring together all those innumerable illusions of the beauty of appearance, which at each moment make life worth living and urge us to experience the next moment.

From the foundation of all existence, the Dionysiac [*dionysisch*] substratum of the world, no more can enter the consciousness of the human individual than can be overcome once more by that Apolline [*apollinisch*] power of transfiguration, so that both of these artistic impulses are forced to unfold in strict proportion to one another, according to the law of eternal justice. Where the Dionysiac powers have risen as impetuously as we now experience them, Apollo, enveloped in a cloud, must also have descended to us; some future generation will behold his most luxuriant effects of beauty.

* * *

SOURCE: From Friedrich Nietzsche, *The Birth of Tragedy out of the Spirit of Music*, trans. Shaun Whiteside, ed. Michael Tanner (London: Penguin, 1993), pp. 14–24, 35–36, 38–40, 85–88, 113–17. Except where otherwise indicated, German words in brackets are the terminology used in the German original, inserted by the editor in addition to their renderings in the translation. Originally published by Nietzsche in 1872, as *Die Geburt der Tragödie aus dem Geiste der Musik* (*The Birth of Tragedy out of the Spirit of Music*), it was republished in 1886, with a new preface, as *Die Geburt der Tragödie, oder: Griechenthum und Pessimismus* (*The Birth of Tragedy, or: Hellenism and Pessimism*).

1. Nietzsche's favorite pre-Socratic philosopher (active ca. 500 B.C.E.); "dark" (*dunkel*) has the sense of "obscure" or "mysterious" as well as "gloomy." For the comparison, see Heraclitus fragment 52.

From On Truth and Lie in a Nonmoral Sense

1

Once upon a time, in some out of the way corner of that universe which is dispersed into numberless twinkling solar systems, there was a star upon which clever beasts invented knowing. That was the most arrogant and mendacious minute of "world history," but nevertheless, it was only a minute. After nature had drawn a few breaths, the star cooled and congealed, and the clever beasts had to die. —One might invent such a fable, and yet he still would not have adequately illustrated how miserable, how shadowy and transient, how aimless and arbitrary the human intellect looks within nature. There were eternities during which it did not exist. And when it is all over with the human intellect, nothing will have happened. For this intellect has no additional mission which would lead it beyond human life.[1] Rather, it is human, and only its possessor and begetter takes it so solemnly—as though the world's axis turned within it. But if we could communicate with the gnat, we would learn that he likewise flies through the air with the same solemnity, that he feels the flying center of the universe within himself. There is nothing so reprehensible and unimportant in nature that it would not immediately swell up like a balloon at the slightest puff of this power of knowing. And just as every porter wants to have an admirer, so even the proudest of men, the philosopher, supposes that he sees on all sides the eyes of the universe telescopically focused upon his action and thought.

It is remarkable that this was brought about by the intellect, which was certainly allotted to these most unfortunate, delicate, and ephemeral beings merely as a device for detaining them a minute within existence. For without this addition they would have every reason to flee this existence as quickly as Lessing's son.[2] The pride connected with knowing and sensing lies like a blinding fog over the eyes and senses of men, thus deceiving them concerning the value of existence. For this pride contains within itself the most flattering estimation of the value of knowing. Deception is the most general effect of such pride, but even its most particular effects contain within themselves something of the same deceitful character.

As a means for the preserving of the individual, the intellect unfolds its principle powers in dissimulation,[3] which is the means by which weaker, less robust individuals preserve themselves—since they have been denied the chance to wage the battle for existence with horns or with the sharp teeth of beasts of prey. This art of dissimulation reaches its peak in man. Deception, flattering, lying, deluding, talking behind the back, putting up a false front, living in borrowed splendor, wearing a mask, hiding behind convention, playing a role for others and for oneself—in short, a continuous fluttering around the *solitary* flame of vanity—is so much the rule and the law among men that there is almost nothing which is less comprehensible than how an honest and

---

1. This sentence flatly rejects the cosmic significance accorded to the human intellect in the larger scheme of things by HEGEL and other philosophers from the Greeks onward for whom true knowledge is the greatest of goods and the ultimate human calling.

2. The only son of the German dramatist and critic Gotthold Ephraim Lessing (1729–1781) died within days of being born.
3. That is, pretending (*Verstellen*).

pure drive for truth could have arisen among them. They are deeply immersed in illusions and in dream images; their eyes merely glide over the surface of things and see "forms." Their senses nowhere lead to truth; on the contrary, they are content to receive stimuli and, as it were, to engage in a groping game on the backs of things. Moreover, man permits himself to be deceived in his dreams every night of his life. His moral sentiment does not even make an attempt to prevent this, whereas there are supposed to be men who have stopped snoring through sheer will power. What does man actually know about himself? Is he, indeed, ever able to perceive himself completely, as if laid out in a lighted display case? Does nature not conceal most things from him—even concerning his own body—in order to confine and lock him within a proud, deceptive consciousness, aloof from the coils of the bowels, the rapid flow of the blood stream, and the intricate quivering of the fibers! She threw away the key. And woe to that fatal curiosity which might one day have the power to peer out and down through a crack in the chamber of consciousness and then suspect that man is sustained in the indifference of his ignorance by that which is pitiless, greedy, insatiable, and murderous—as if hanging in dreams on the back of a tiger. Given this situation, where in the world could the drive for truth have come from?

Insofar as the individual wants to maintain himself against other individuals, he will under natural circumstances employ the intellect mainly for dissimulation. But at the same time, from boredom and necessity, man wishes to exist socially and with the herd; therefore, he needs to make peace and strives accordingly to banish from his world at least the most flagrant *bellum omnium contra omnes.*[4] This peace treaty brings in its wake something which appears to be the first step toward acquiring that puzzling truth drive: to wit, *that* which shall count as "truth" from now on is established. That is to say, a uniformly valid and binding designation is invented for things, and this legislation of language likewise establishes the first laws of truth. For the contrast between truth and lie arises here for the first time. The liar is a person who uses the valid designations, the words, in order to make something which is unreal appear to be real. He says, for example, "I am rich," when the proper designation for his condition would be "poor." He misuses fixed conventions by means of arbitrary substitutions or even reversals of names. If he does this in a selfish and moreover harmful manner, society will cease to trust him and will thereby exclude him. What men avoid by excluding the liar is not so much being defrauded as it is being harmed by means of fraud. Thus, even at this stage, what they hate is basically not deception itself, but rather the unpleasant, hated consequences of certain sorts of deception. It is in a similarly restricted sense that man now wants nothing but truth: he desires the pleasant, life-preserving consequences of truth. He is indifferent toward pure knowledge which has no consequences; toward those truths which are possibly harmful and destructive he is even hostilely inclined. And besides, what about these linguistic conventions themselves? Are they perhaps products of knowledge, that is, of the sense of truth? Are designations congruent with things? Is language the adequate expression of all realities?

4. War of all against all (Latin), the phrase used by the political philosopher Thomas Hobbes (1588–1679) to describe the life of humans before they entered into the social contract and agreed to live together in society.

It is only by means of forgetfulness that man can ever reach the point of fancying himself to possess a "truth" of the grade just indicated. If he will not be satisfied with truth in the form of tautology, that is to say, if he will not be content with empty husks, then he will always exchange truths for illusions. What is a word? It is the copy in sound of a nerve stimulus. But the further inference from the nerve stimulus to a cause outside of us is already the result of a false and unjustifiable application of the principle of sufficient reason.[5] If truth alone had been the deciding factor in the genesis of language, and if the standpoint of certainty had been decisive for designations, then how could we still dare to say "the stone is hard," as if "hard" were something otherwise familiar to us, and not merely a totally subjective stimulation! We separate things according to gender, designating the tree as masculine and the plant as feminine.[6] What arbitrary assignments! How far this oversteps the canons of certainty! We speak of a "snake": this designation touches only upon its ability to twist itself and could therefore also fit a worm. What arbitrary differentiations! What one-sided preferences, first for this, then for that property of a thing! The various languages placed side by side show that with words it is never a question of truth, never a question of adequate expression; otherwise, there would not be so many languages. The "thing in itself" (which is precisely what the pure truth, apart from any of its consequences, would be) is likewise something quite incomprehensible to the creator of language and something not in the least worth striving for. This creator only designates the relations of things to men, and for expressing these relations he lays hold of the boldest metaphors. To begin with, a nerve stimulus is transferred into an image: first metaphor. The image, in turn, is imitated in a sound: second metaphor. And each time there is a complete overleaping of one sphere, right into the middle of an entirely new and different one. One can imagine a man who is totally deaf and has never had a sensation of sound and music. Perhaps such a person will gaze with astonishment at Chladni's sound figures;[7] perhaps he will discover their causes in the vibrations of the string and will now swear that he must know what men mean by "sound." It is this way with all of us concerning language: we believe that we know something about the things themselves when we speak of trees, colors, snow, and flowers; and yet we possess nothing but metaphors for things—metaphors which correspond in no way to the original entities. In the same way that the sound appears as a sand figure, so the mysterious X of the thing in itself first appears as a nerve stimulus, then as an image, and finally as a sound. Thus the genesis of language does not proceed logically in any case, and all the material within and with which the man of truth, the scientist, and the philosopher later work and build, if not derived from never-never land, is at least not derived from the essence of things.

In particular, let us further consider the formation of concepts. Every word instantly becomes a concept precisely insofar as it is not supposed to serve as a reminder of the unique and entirely individual original experience to which

5. That is, the principle that every event must have a cause sufficient to explain it.
6. That is, the grammatical gender in German of *Baum* (tree) and *Pflanze* (plant).
7. The figures that emerge when sand is sprinkled on a rigid surface that vibrates at different frequencies; this phenomenon was demonstrated by the German physicist Ernst Florens Friedrich Chladni (1756–1827).

it owes its origin; but rather, a word becomes a concept insofar as it simultaneously has to fit countless more or less similar cases—which means, purely and simply, cases which are never equal and thus altogether unequal. Every concept arises from the equation of unequal things. Just as it is certain that one leaf is never totally the same as another, so it is certain that the concept "leaf" is formed by arbitrarily discarding these individual differences and by forgetting the distinguishing aspects. This awakens the idea that, in addition to the leaves, there exists in nature the "leaf": the original model according to which all the leaves were perhaps woven, sketched, measured, colored, curled, and painted—but by incompetent hands, so that no specimen has turned out to be a correct, trustworthy, and faithful likeness of the original model. We call a person "honest," and then we ask "why has he behaved so honestly today?" Our usual answer is, "on account of his honesty." Honesty! This in turn means that the leaf is the cause of the leaves. We know nothing whatsoever about an essential quality called "honesty"; but we do know of countless individualized and consequently unequal actions which we equate by omitting the aspects in which they are unequal and which we now designate as "honest" actions. Finally we formulate from them a *qualitas occulta*[8] which has the name "honesty." We obtain the concept, as we do the form, by overlooking what is individual and actual; whereas nature is acquainted with no forms and no concepts, and likewise with no species, but only with an X which remains inaccessible and undefinable for us. For even our contrast between individual and species is something anthropomorphic and does not originate in the essence of things; although we should not presume to claim that this contrast does not correspond to the essence of things: that would of course be a dogmatic assertion and, as such, would be just as indemonstrable as its opposite.

What then is truth? A movable host of metaphors, metonymies,[9] and anthropomorphisms: in short, a sum of human relations which have been poetically and rhetorically intensified, transferred, and embellished, and which, after long usage, seem to a people to be fixed, canonical, and binding. Truths are illusions which we have forgotten are illusions; they are metaphors that have become worn out and have been drained of sensuous force, coins which have lost their embossing and are now considered as metal and no longer as coins.

We still do not yet know where the drive for truth comes from. For so far we have heard only of the duty which society imposes in order to exist: to be truthful means to employ the usual metaphors. Thus, to express it morally, this is the duty to lie according to a fixed convention, to lie with the herd and in a manner binding upon everyone. Now man of course forgets that this is the way things stand for him. Thus he lies in the manner indicated, unconsciously and in accordance with habits which are centuries old; and precisely *by means of this unconsciousness* and forgetfulness he arrives at his sense of truth. From the sense that one is obliged to designate one thing as "red," another as "cold," and a third as "mute," there arises a moral impulse in regard to truth. The venerability, reliability, and utility of truth is something which a person demonstrates for himself from the contrast with the liar, whom no

8. Hidden or secret quality (Latin).
9. Two figures of speech: metaphor relies on simi-
larity between two things, whereas metonymy relies on any other association.

one trusts and everyone excludes. As a *"rational"* being, he now places his behavior under the control of abstractions. He will no longer tolerate being carried away by sudden impressions, by intuitions. First he universalizes all these impressions into less colorful, cooler concepts, so that he can entrust the guidance of his life and conduct to them. Everything which distinguishes man from the animals depends upon this ability to volatilize perceptual metaphors in a schema, and thus to dissolve an image into a concept. For something is possible in the realm of these schemata which could never be achieved with the vivid first impressions: the construction of a pyramidal order according to castes and degrees, the creation of a new world of laws, privileges, subordinations, and clearly marked boundaries—a new world, one which now confronts that other vivid world of first impressions as more solid, more universal, better known, and more human than the immediately perceived world, and thus as the regulative and imperative world. Whereas each perceptual metaphor is individual and without equals and is therefore able to elude all classification, the great edifice of concepts displays the rigid regularity of a Roman columbarium[1] and exhales in logic that strength and coolness which is characteristic of mathematics. Anyone who has felt this cool breath [of logic][2] will hardly believe that even the concept—which is as bony, foursquare, and transposable as a die—is nevertheless merely the *residue of a metaphor,* and that the illusion which is involved in the artistic transference of a nerve stimulus into images is, if not the mother, then the grandmother of every single concept.[3] But in this conceptual crap game "truth" means using every die in the designated manner, counting its spots accurately, fashioning the right categories, and never violating the order of caste and class rank. * * * Here one may certainly admire man as a mighty genius of construction, who succeeds in piling up an infinitely complicated dome of concepts upon an unstable foundation, and, as it were, on running water. Of course, in order to be supported by such a foundation, his construction must be like one constructed of spiders' webs: delicate enough to be carried along by the waves, strong enough not to be blown apart by every wind. As a genius of construction man raises himself far above the bee in the following way: whereas the bee builds with wax that he gathers from nature, man builds with the far more delicate conceptual material which he first has to manufacture from himself. In this he is greatly to be admired, but not on account of his drive for truth or for pure knowledge of things. When someone hides something behind a bush and looks for it again in the same place and finds it there as well, there is not much to praise in such seeking and finding. Yet this is how matters stand regarding seeking and finding "truth" within the realm of reason. If I make up the definition of a mammal, and then, after inspecting a camel, declare "look, a mammal," I have indeed brought a truth to light in this way, but it is a truth of limited value. That is to say, it is a thoroughly anthropomorphic truth which contains not a single point which would be "true in itself" or really and universally valid apart from man. At bottom, what the investigator of such truths is seeking is only the metamorphosis of the world into man. He strives to understand the world as something analogous to man, and at best he

---

1. An underground tomb with small wall niches in which funeral urns were placed.
2. Translator's brackets.

3. I.e. concepts are derived from images, which are, in turn, derived from nerve stimuli [translator's note].

achieves by his struggles the feeling of assimilation. Similar to the way in which astrologers considered the stars to be in man's service and connected with his happiness and sorrow, such an investigator considers the entire universe in connection with man: the entire universe as the infinitely fractured echo of one original sound—man; the entire universe as the infinitely multiplied copy of one original picture—man. His method is to treat man as the measure of all things, but in doing so he again proceeds from the error of believing that he has these things [which he intends to measure][4] immediately before him as mere objects. He forgets that the original perceptual metaphors are metaphors and takes them to be the things themselves.

Only by forgetting this primitive world of metaphor can one live with any repose, security, and consistency: only by means of the petrification and coagulation of a mass of images which originally streamed from the primal faculty of human imagination like a fiery liquid, only in the invincible faith that *this* sun, *this* window, *this* table is a truth in itself, in short, only by forgetting that he himself is an *artistically creating* subject, does man live with any repose, security, and consistency. If but for an instant he could escape from the prison walls of this faith, his "self consciousness" would be immediately destroyed. It is even a difficult thing for him to admit to himself that the insect or the bird perceives an entirely different world from the one that man does, and that the question of which of these perceptions of the world is the more correct one is quite meaningless, for this would have to have been decided previously in accordance with the criterion of the *correct perception*, which means, in accordance with a criterion which is *not available*. But in any case it seems to me that "the correct perception"—which would mean "the adequate expression of an object in the subject"—is a contradictory impossibility. For between two absolutely different spheres, as between subject and object, there is no causality, no correctness, and no expression; there is, at most, an *aesthetic* relation: I mean, a suggestive transference, a stammering translation into a completely foreign tongue—for which there is required, in any case, a freely inventive intermediate sphere and mediating force. "Appearance" is a word that contains many temptations, which is why I avoid it as much as possible. For it is not true that the essence of things "appears" in the empirical world. A painter without hands who wished to express in song the picture before his mind would, by means of this substitution of spheres, still reveal more about the essence of things than does the empirical world. Even the relationship of a nerve stimulus to the generated image is not a necessary one. But when the same image has been generated millions of times and has been handed down for many generations and finally appears on the same occasion every time for all mankind, then it acquires at last the same meaning for men it would have if it were the sole necessary image and if the relationship of the original nerve stimulus to the generated image were a strictly causal one. In the same manner, an eternally repeated dream would certainly be felt and judged to be reality. But the hardening and congealing of a metaphor guarantees absolutely nothing concerning its necessity and exclusive justification.

Every person who is familiar with such considerations has no doubt felt a deep mistrust of all idealism of this sort: just as often as he has quite clearly

---

4. Translator's brackets and supplemental wording.

convinced himself of the eternal consistency, omnipresence, and infallibility of the laws of nature. He has concluded that so far as we can penetrate here—from the telescopic heights to the microscopic depths—everything is secure, complete, infinite, regular, and without any gaps. Science will be able to dig successfully in this shaft forever, and all the things that are discovered will harmonize with and not contradict each other. How little does this resemble a product of the imagination, for if it were such, there should be some place where the illusion and unreality can be divined. Against this, the following must be said: if each of us had a different kind of sense perception—if we could only perceive things now as a bird, now as a worm, now as a plant, or if one of us saw a stimulus as red, another as blue, while a third even heard the same stimulus as a sound—then no one would speak of such a regularity of nature, rather, nature would be grasped only as a creation which is subjective in the highest degree. After all, what is a law of nature as such for us? We are not acquainted with it in itself, but only with its effects, which means in its relation to other laws of nature—which, in turn, are known to us only as sums of relations. Therefore all these relations always refer again to others and are thoroughly incomprehensible to us in their essence. All that we actually know about these laws of nature is what we ourselves bring to them—time and space, and therefore relationships of succession and number. But everything marvelous about the laws of nature, everything that quite astonishes us therein and seems to demand our explanation, everything that might lead us to distrust idealism: all this is completely and solely contained within the mathematical strictness and inviolability of our representations of time and space. But we produce these representations in and from ourselves with the same necessity with which the spider spins. If we are forced to comprehend all things only under these forms, then it ceases to be amazing that in all things we actually comprehend nothing but these forms. For they must all bear within themselves the laws of number, and it is precisely number which is most astonishing in things. All that conformity to law, which impresses us so much in the movement of the stars[5] and in chemical processes, coincides at bottom with those properties which we bring to things. Thus it is we who impress ourselves in this way. In conjunction with this, it of course follows that the artistic process of metaphor formation with which every sensation begins in us already presupposes these forms and thus occurs within them. The only way in which the possibility of subsequently constructing a new conceptual edifice from metaphors themselves can be explained is by the firm persistence of these original forms. That is to say, this conceptual edifice is an imitation of temporal, spatial, and numerical relationships in the domain of metaphor.

2

We have seen how it is originally *language* which works on the construction of concepts, a labor taken over in later ages by *science* [*Wissenschaft*].[6] Just

5. A reference to KANT's "awe" at the lawfulness of the "starry heavens above," expressed in the conclusion to *Critique of Practical Reason* (1788; see above, p. 33).

6. In German, and for Nietzsche, the term *Wissenschaft* designates not only the natural sciences but also cognitive inquiry (in its many refined forms) more generally.

as the bee simultaneously constructs cells and fills them with honey, so science works unceasingly on this great columbarium of concepts, the graveyard of perceptions. It is always building new, higher stories and shoring up, cleaning, and renovating the old cells; above all, it takes pains to fill up this monstrously towering framework and to arrange therein the entire empirical world, which is to say, the anthropomorphic world. Whereas the man of action binds his life to reason and its concepts so that he will not be swept away and lost, the scientific investigator builds his hut right next to the tower of science so that he will be able to work on it and to find shelter for himself beneath those bulwarks which presently exist. And he requires shelter, for there are frightful powers which continuously break in upon him, powers which oppose scientific "truth" with completely different kinds of "truths" which bear on their shields the most varied sorts of emblems.

The drive toward the formation of metaphors is the fundamental human drive, which one cannot for a single instant dispense with in thought, for one would thereby dispense with man himself. This drive is not truly vanquished and scarcely subdued by the fact that a regular and rigid new world is constructed as its prison from its own ephemeral products, the concepts. It seeks a new realm and another channel for its activity, and it finds this in *myth* and in *art* generally. This drive continually confuses the conceptual categories and cells by bringing forward new transferences, metaphors, and metonymies. It continually manifests an ardent desire to refashion the world which presents itself to waking man, so that it will be as colorful, irregular, lacking in results and coherence, charming, and eternally new as the world of dreams. Indeed, it is only by means of the rigid and regular web of concepts that the waking man clearly sees that he is awake; and it is precisely because of this that he sometimes thinks that he must be dreaming when this web of concepts is torn by art. * * *

* * * That immense framework and planking of concepts to which the needy man clings his whole life long in order to preserve himself is nothing but a scaffolding and toy for the most audacious feats of the liberated intellect. And when it smashes this framework to pieces, throws it into confusion, and puts it back together in an ironic fashion, pairing the most alien things and separating the closest, it is demonstrating that it has no need of these makeshifts of indigence and that it will now be guided by intuitions rather than by concepts. There is no regular path which leads from these intuitions into the land of ghostly schemata, the land of abstractions. There exists no word for these intuitions; when man sees them he grows dumb, or else he speaks only in forbidden metaphors and in unheard-of combinations of concepts. He does this so that by shattering and mocking the old conceptual barriers he may at least correspond creatively to the impression of the powerful present intuition.

There are ages in which the rational man and the intuitive man stand side by side, the one in fear of intuition, the other with scorn for abstraction. The latter is just as irrational as the former is inartistic. They both desire to rule over life: the former, by knowing how to meet his principle needs by means of foresight, prudence, and regularity; the latter, by disregarding these needs and, as an "overjoyed hero," counting as real only that life which has been disguised as illusion and beauty. Whenever, as was perhaps the case in ancient Greece, the intuitive man handles his weapons more authoritatively and victoriously than his opponent, then, under favorable circumstances, a culture can take shape and art's mastery over life can be established. * * *

SOURCE: From "On Truth and Lies in a Nonmoral Sense," in *Philosophy and Truth: Selections from Nietzsche's Notebooks of the Early 1870s*, ed. and trans. Daniel Breazeale (Atlantic Highlands, N.J.: Humanities Press, 1979), pp. 79–90. Except where otherwise indicated, German words in brackets are the terminology used in the German original, inserted by the editor in addition to their renderings in the translation. Titled in German "Über Wahrheit und Lüge im aussermoralischen Sinne" (written 1873, published posthumously 1903). *Aussermoralischen*, here translated "nonmoral," is often translated "extra-moral." The point is that in considering the terms "truth" and "lies" as he proposes to do here, Nietzsche is not presupposing or implying any value judgments about either of them.

From Schopenhauer as Educator

1

A traveller who had seen many lands and peoples and several of the earth's continents was asked what quality in men he had discovered everywhere he had gone. He replied: 'They have a tendency to laziness.' To many it will seem that he ought rather to have said: 'They are all timid. They hide themselves behind customs and opinions.' In his heart every man knows quite well that, being unique, he will be in the world only once and that no imaginable chance will for a second time gather together into a unity so strangely variegated an assortment as he is: he knows it but he hides it like a bad conscience—why? From fear of his neighbour, who demands conventionality and cloaks himself with it. But what is it that constrains the individual to fear his neighbour, to think and act like a member of a herd,[1] and to have no joy in himself? Modesty, perhaps, in a few rare cases. With the great majority it is indolence, inertia, in short that tendency to laziness of which the traveller spoke. He is right: men are even lazier than they are timid, and fear most of all the inconveniences with which unconditional honesty and nakedness would burden them. Artists alone hate this sluggish promenading in borrowed fashions and appropriated opinions and they reveal everyone's secret bad conscience, the law that every man is a unique miracle; they dare to show us man as he is, uniquely himself to every last movement of his muscles, more, that in being thus strictly consistent in uniqueness he is beautiful, and worth regarding, and in no way tedious. When the great thinker despises mankind, he despises its laziness: for it is on account of their laziness that men seem like factory products, things of no consequence and unworthy to be associated with or instructed. The man who does not wish to belong to the mass needs only to cease taking himself easily; let him follow his conscience, which calls to him: 'Be your self! All you are now doing, thinking, desiring, is not you yourself.'[2]

Every youthful soul hears this call day and night and trembles when he

---

1. A characterization often employed subsequently by Nietzsche to refer to group mentality (as the mentality of "the herd"), and to the type of morality geared to "herd-like" human life (as "herd morality").

2. It is a central part of the purpose of this essay to suggest what Nietzsche conceives this to mean (and not to mean).

hears it; for the idea of its liberation gives it a presentiment of the measure of happiness allotted it from all eternity—a happiness to which it can by no means attain so long as it lies fettered by the chains of fear and convention. And how dismal and senseless life can be without this liberation! There exists no more repulsive and desolate creature in the world than the man who has evaded his genius[3] and who now looks furtively to left and right, behind him and all about him. In the end such a man becomes impossible to get hold of, since he is wholly exterior, without kernel, a tattered, painted bag of clothes, a decked-out ghost that cannot inspire even fear and certainly not pity. And if it is true to say of the lazy that they kill time, then it is greatly to be feared that an era which sees its salvation in public opinion, that is to say private laziness, is a time that really will be killed: I mean that it will be struck out of the history of the true liberation of life. How reluctant later generations will be to have anything to do with the relics of an era ruled, not by living men, but by pseudo-men dominated by public opinion; for which reason our age may be to some distant posterity the darkest and least known, because least human, portion of human history. I go along the new streets of our cities and think how, of all these gruesome houses which the generation of public opinion has built for itself, not one will be standing in a hundred years' time, and how the opinions of these house-builders will no doubt by then likewise have collapsed. On the other hand, how right it is for those who do not feel themselves to be citizens of this time to harbour great hopes; for if they were citizens of this time they too would be helping to kill their time and so perish with it—while their desire is rather to awaken their time to life and so live on themselves in this awakened life.

But even if the future gave us no cause for hope—the fact of our existing at all in this here-and-now must be the strongest incentive to us to live according to our own laws[4] and standards: the inexplicable fact that we live precisely today, when we had all infinite time in which to come into existence, that we possess only a shortlived today in which to demonstrate why and to what end we came into existence now and at no other time. We are responsible to ourselves for our own existence; consequently we want to be the true helmsman of this existence and refuse to allow our existence to resemble a mindless act of chance. One has to take a somewhat bold and dangerous line with this existence: especially as, whatever happens, we are bound to lose it. Why go on clinging to this clod of earth, this way of life, why pay heed to what your neighbour says? It is so parochial to bind oneself to views which are no longer binding even a couple of hundred miles away. Orient and Occident are chalk-lines drawn before us to fool our timidity. I will make an attempt to attain freedom, the youthful soul says to itself; and is it to be hindered in this by the fact that two nations happen to hate and fight one another, or that two continents are separated by an ocean, or that all around it a religion is taught which did not yet exist a couple of thousand years ago. All that is not you, it says to itself. No one can construct for you the bridge upon which precisely you must cross the stream of life, no one but you yourself alone. There are, to be sure, countless paths and bridges and demi-gods which would bear

---

3. That is, his true nature.
4. The literal meaning of "autonomy"; this is the essence of what both KANT and HEGEL—and now also Nietzsche—mean by "freedom."

you through this stream; but only at the cost of yourself: you would put yourself in pawn and lose yourself. There exists in the world a single path along which no one can go except you: whither does it lead? Do not ask, go along it. Who was it who said: 'a man never rises higher than when he does not know whither his path can still lead him'?[5]

But how can we find ourselves again? How can man know himself? He is a thing dark and veiled; and if the hare has seven skins, man can slough off seventy times seven[6] and still not be able to say: 'this is really you, this is no longer outer shell'. Moreover, it is a painful and dangerous undertaking thus to tunnel into oneself and to force one's way down into the shaft [Schacht] of one's being by the nearest path. A man who does it can easily so hurt himself that no physician can cure him. And, moreover again, what need should there be for it, since everything bears witness to what we are, our friendships and enmities, our glance and the clasp of our hand, our memory and that which we do not remember, our books and our handwriting. This, however, is the means by which an inquiry into the most important aspect can be initiated. Let the youthful soul look back on life with the question: what have you truly loved up to now, what has drawn your soul aloft, what has mastered it and at the same time blessed it? Set up these revered objects before you and perhaps their nature and their sequence will give you a law, the fundamental law of your own true self.[7] Compare these objects one with another, see how one completes, expands, surpasses, transfigures another, how they constitute a stepladder upon which you have clambered up to yourself as you are now; for your true nature lies, not concealed deep within you, but immeasurably high above you, or at least above that which you usually take yourself to be. Your true educators and formative teachers reveal to you what the true basic material of your being is, something in itself ineducable and in any case difficult of access, bound and paralysed: your educators can be only your liberators. And that is the secret of all culture:[8] it does not provide artificial limbs, wax noses or spectacles—that which can provide these things is, rather, only sham education. Culture [Bildung] is liberation, the removal of all the weeds, rubble and vermin that want to attack the tender buds of the plant, an outstreaming of light and warmth, the gentle rustling of nocturnal rain, it is imitation and worship of nature where nature is in her motherly and merciful mood, it is the perfecting of nature when it deflects her cruel and merciless assaults and turns them to good, and when it draws a veil over the expressions of nature's step-motherly mood and her sad lack of understanding.[9]

Certainly there may be other means of finding oneself, of coming to oneself out of the bewilderment in which one usually wanders as in a dark cloud,

---

5. Oliver Cromwell, as quoted by Cardinal de Retz in his Memoirs [translator's note]. Cromwell (1599–1658) led the parliamentary forces that overthrew Charles I in the English Civil Wars; he became in effect the ruler of Great Britain during the republican Commonwealth. Cardinal de Retz (1613–1679), a leader of an unsuccessful aristocratic rebellion against the French government, wrote his Memoirs from 1671 to 1679.
6. See Matthew 18:22. "The hare has seven skins": a German saying analogous to "the cat has nine lives."
7. This translates "deines eigentlichen Selbst." The term eigentlich, which became one of the key terms in HEIDEGGER's version of existential philosophy (see

selections from his Being and Time below) and in existentialism more generally, can also be translated as "genuine" or "authentic" (hence: "authenticity").
8. This translates as "Bildung," which can also mean "education."
9. This paragraph is crucial for understanding the difference between what Nietzsche subsequently means in speaking of "the enhancement of life," "higher humanity," and the image of "the Übermensch," in contrast to the merely natural creature we once were and what remains merely natural in us, as well as to what is "all too human" in and about ourselves and human beings generally in the kind of socialized creatures we now are.

but I know of none better than to think on one's true educators. And so today I shall remember one of the teachers and taskmasters of whom I can boast, *Arthur Schopenhauer*[1]—and later on I shall recall others.

* * *

5

But I have undertaken to exhibit my experience of Schopenhauer as an *educator*,[2] and it is thus not nearly sufficient for me to paint, and to paint imperfectly, that ideal man who, as his Platonic ideal as it were, holds sway in and around him. The hardest task still remains: to say how a new circle of duties may be derived from this ideal and how one can proceed towards so extravagant a goal through a practical activity—in short, to demonstrate that this ideal *educates*. One might otherwise think it nothing but an intoxicating vision granted us only for moments at a time, and then leaving us all the more painfully in the lurch and prey to an even deeper dissatisfaction. It is also indisputable that that is how we *begin* our association with this ideal—with a sudden contrast of light and darkness, intoxication and nausea—and that this is a repetition of an experience which is as old as ideals themselves. But we ought not to stand long in the doorway, we ought soon to get through the beginning. And so we have seriously to ask the definite question: is it possible to bring that incredibly lofty goal so close to us that it educates us while it draws us aloft?—that Goethe's mighty words may not be fulfilled in us: 'Man is born to a limited situation; he is able to understand simple, accessible, definite goals, and he accustoms himself to employing the means that happen to lie close at hand; but as soon as he oversteps his limits he knows neither what he wants nor what he ought to do, and it is all one whether he is distracted by the multiplicity of the things he encounters or whether his head is turned by their loftiness and dignity. It is always a misfortune when he is induced to strive after something which he cannot proceed towards through a practical activity.'[3] The Schopenhauerean man appears to be singularly open to this objection: his dignity and loftiness can only turn our heads and thereby exclude us from any participation in the world of action; coherent duties, the even flow of life are gone. One man perhaps at last accustoms himself to living discontentedly according to two different rules of conduct, that is to say in conflict with himself, uncertain of how to act and therefore daily more feeble and unfruitful: while another may even renounce all action on principle and almost cease to pay any attention to the actions of others. The dangers are always great when things are made too difficult for a man and when he is incapable of *fulfilling* any duties at all; stronger natures can be destroyed by it, the weaker, more numerous natures decline into a reflective laziness and in the end forfeit through laziness even their ability to reflect.

Now, in face of such objections I am willing to concede that in precisely this respect our work has hardly begun and that from my own experience I am

1. Nietzsche's portrait of SCHOPENHAUER has more to do with what Nietzsche imagined Schopenhauer to have been (and wanted himself to be) than with what Schopenhauer actually was and stood for.

2. Literally, one who "draws one [up]" (an *Erzieher*).
3. From *Wilhelm Meister's Apprenticeship* (1795–96), book 6, by Johann Wolfgang von Goethe (1749–1832), the preeminent German literary figure of his time.

sure of only one thing: that from that ideal image it is possible to fasten upon ourselves a chain of fulfillable duties, and that some of us already feel the weight of this chain. But before I can conscientiously reduce this new circle of duties to a formula I must offer the following preliminary observations.

More profoundly feeling people have at all times felt sympathy for the animals because they suffer from life and yet do not possess the power to turn the goad of life against themselves and understand their existence metaphysically; one is, indeed, profoundly indignant at the sight of senseless suffering. That is why there has arisen in more than one part of the earth the supposition that the bodies of animals contain the guilt-laden souls of men, so that this suffering which at first sight arouses indignation on account of its senselessness acquires meaning and significance as punishment and atonement before the seat of eternal justice. And it is, truly, a harsh punishment thus to live as an animal, beset by hunger and desire yet incapable of any kind of reflection on the nature of this life; and no harder fate can be thought of than that of the beast of prey[4] pursued through the wilderness by the most gnawing torment, rarely satisfied and even then in such a way that satisfaction is purchased only with the pain of lascerating combat with other animals or through inordinate greed and nauseating satiety. To hang on to life madly and blindly, with no higher aim than to hang on to it; not to know that or why one is being so heavily punished but, with the stupidity of a fearful desire, to thirst after precisely this punishment as though after happiness—that is what it means to be an animal; and if all nature presses towards man, it thereby intimates that man is necessary for the redemption of nature from the curse of the life of the animal, and that in him existence at last holds up before itself a mirror in which life appears no longer senseless but in its metaphysical significance.[5] Yet let us reflect: where does the animal cease, where does man begin?—man, who is nature's sole concern! As long as anyone desires life as he desires happiness he has not yet raised his eyes above the horizon of the animal, for he only desires more consciously what the animal seeks through blind impulse. But that is what we all do for the greater part of our lives: usually we fail to emerge out of animality, we ourselves are the animals whose suffering seems to be senseless.

But there are moments *when we realize this*: then the clouds are rent asunder, and we see that, in common with all nature, we are pressing towards man as towards something that stands high above us.[6] In this sudden illumination we gaze around us and behind us with a shudder: we behold the more subtle beasts of prey and there we are in the midst of them. The tremendous coming and going of men on the great wilderness of the earth, their founding of cities and states, their wars, their restless assembling and scattering again, their confused mingling, mutual imitation, mutual outwitting and downtreading, their wailing in distress, their howls of joy in victory—all this is a continuation of animality: as though man was to be deliberately retrogressed and defrauded of his metaphysical disposition, indeed as though nature, after

4. This expression translates *Raubtier*—a term Nietzsche uses again in later writings (notably *On the Genealogy of Morals*; see below) to designate a barbaric type of human being that he is often thought to admire. This passage suggests otherwise.

5. Nietzsche never abandoned the dim view of merely "natural," animal existence articulated here.
6. That is, toward a higher humanity, later emblematized by the figure of the *Übermensch*.

having desired and worked at man for so long, now drew back from him in fear and preferred to return to the unconsciousness of instinct. Nature needs knowledge and it is terrified of the knowledge it has need of; and so the flame flickers restlessly back and forth as though afraid of itself and seizes upon a thousand things before it seizes upon that on account of which nature needs knowledge at all. * * *

* * * But we feel at the same time that we are too weak to endure those moments of profoundest contemplation for very long and that we are not the mankind towards which all nature presses for its redemption: it is already much that we should raise our head above the water at all, even if only a little, and observe what stream it is in which we are so deeply immersed. And even this momentary emerging and awakening is not achieved through our own power, we have to be lifted up—and who are they who lift us?

They are those true [*wahrhaften*] *men, those who are no longer animal, the philosophers, artists and saints*; nature, which never makes a leap, has made its one leap in creating them, and a leap of joy moreover, for nature then feels that for the first time it has reached its goal—where it realizes it has to unlearn having goals and that it has played the game of life and becoming with too high stakes. This knowledge transfigures nature, and a gentle evening-weariness, that which men call 'beauty', reposes upon its face. That which it now utters with this transfigured countenance is the great *enlightenment* as to the character of existence; and the supreme wish that mortals can wish is lastingly and with open ears to participate in this enlightenment. If we think of how much Schopenhauer for instance must have *heard* during the course of his life, then we might well say to ourselves afterwards: 'Alas, your deaf ears, your dull head, your flickering understanding, your shrivelled heart, all that I call mine, how I despise you! Not to be able to fly, only to flutter! To see what is above you but not to be able to reach it! To know the way that leads to the immeasurable open prospect of the philosopher, and almost to set foot on it, but after a few steps to stagger back! And if that greatest of all wishes were fulfilled for only a day, how gladly one would exchange for it all the rest of life! To climb as high into the pure icy Alpine air as a philosopher ever climbed, up to where all the mist and obscurity cease and where the fundamental constitution of things speaks in a voice rough and rigid but ineluctably comprehensible! Merely to think of this makes the soul infinitely solitary; if its wish were fulfilled, however, if its glance once fell upon things straight and bright as a beam of light, if shame, fear and desire died away—what word could then describe the condition it would be in, that new and enigmatic animation without agitation with which it would, like the soul of Schopenhauer, lie extended over the tremendous hieroglyphics of existence, over the petrified doctrine of becoming, not as the darkness of night but as the glowing light of dawn streaming out over all the world. And what a fate, on the other hand, to sense sufficient of the certainty and happiness of the philosopher to be able to feel the whole uncertainty and unhappiness of the non-philosopher, of him who desires without hope! To know oneself a fruit on the tree which can never become ripe because one is too much in the shadow, and at the same time to see close at hand the sunshine that one lacks!'

There is enough torment here to make a man who is mis-talented in such a way malicious and envious, if he is capable of malice and envy at all; probably, however, he will at last turn his soul in another direction so that it shall not consume itself in vain longing—and now he will *discover* a new circle of duties.

Here I have arrived at an answer to the question whether it is possible to pursue the great ideal of the Schopenhauerean man by means of a practical activity. One thing above all is certain: these new duties are not the duties of a solitary; on the contrary, they set one in the midst of a mighty community held together, not by external forms and regulations, but by a fundamental idea. It is the fundamental idea of *culture* [*Kultur*], insofar as it sets for each one of us but one task: *to promote the production of the philosopher, the artist and the saint within us and without us and thereby to work at the perfecting[7] of nature.* For, as nature needs the philosopher, so does it need the artist, for the achievement of a metaphysical goal, that of its own self-enlightenment, so that it may at last behold as a clear and finished picture that which it could see only obscurely in the agitation of its evolution—for the end, that is to say, of self-knowledge. It was Goethe who declared, in an arrogant but profound assertion, that nature's experiments are of value only when the artist finally comes to comprehend its stammerings, goes out to meet it halfway, and gives expression to what all these experiments are really about. 'I have often said', he once exclaimed, 'and I shall often repeat, that the *causa finalis* of the activities of men and the world is dramatic poetry. For the stuff is of absolutely no other use.'[8] And so nature at last needs the saint, in whom the ego is completely melted away and whose life of suffering is no longer felt as his own life—or is hardly so felt—but as a profound feeling of oneness and identity with all living things: the saint in whom there appears that miracle of transformation which the game of becoming never hits upon, that final and supreme becoming-human after which all nature presses and urges for its redemption from itself.[9] It is incontestable that we are all related and allied to the saint, just as we are related to the philosopher and artist; there are moments and as it were bright sparks of the fire of love in whose light we cease to understand the word 'I', there lies something beyond our being which at these moments moves across into it, and we are thus possessed of a heartfelt longing for bridges between here and there. It is true that, as we usually are, we can contribute nothing to the production of the man of redemption: that is why we *hate* ourselves as we usually are, and it is this hatred which is the root of that pessimism which Schopenhauer had again to teach our age, though it has existed for as long as the longing for culture [*Kultur*] has existed. Its root, not its flower; its bottom floor, so to speak, not its roof; the commencement of its course, not its goal: for at some time or other we shall have to learn to hate something else, something more universal, and cease to hate our own individuality and its wretched limitations, changeableness and restlessness: it will be in that elevated[1] condition in which we shall also love something else, something we are now unable to love. Only when, in our present or in some future incarnation, we ourselves have been taken into that exalted order of philosophers,

---

7. This translates *Vollendung*, which might better be rendered in this context as "completion" or "fulfillment."

8. Quoted from a letter from Goethe to his good friend Charlotte von Stein, March 3, 1785. *Causa finalis*: ultimate aim (Latin).

9. Nietzsche here gives expression to what became one of his central themes: the transformation (*Verwandlung*) of life as the key to its enhancement (*Erhöhung*), highest human development (*höchste Menschwerdung*), and redemption (*Erlösung*) from the meaninglessness of the merely natural.

1. That is, enhanced (*erhöhten*, literally, "heightened").

artists and saints, shall we also be given a new goal for our love and hate—in the meantime we have our task and our circle of duties, our hate and our love. For we know what culture is. Applied to the Schopenhauerean man,[2] it demands that we prepare and promote his repeated production by getting to know what is inimical to it and removing it—in short, that we unwearyingly combat that which would deprive *us* of the supreme fulfilment of our existence by preventing us from becoming such Schopenhauerean men ourselves.—

6

Sometimes it is harder to accede to a thing than it is to see its truth; and that is how most people may feel when they reflect on the proposition: 'Mankind must work continually at the production of individual great men—that and nothing else is its task.' How much one would like to apply to society and its goals something that can be learned from observation of any species of the animal or plant world: that its only concern is the individual higher exemplar, the more uncommon, more powerful, more complex, more fruitful—how much one would like to do this if inculcated fancies as to the goal of society did not offer such tough resistance! We ought really to have no difficulty in seeing that, when a species has arrived at its limits and is about to go over into a higher species, the goal of its evolution lies, not in the mass of its exemplars and their wellbeing, let alone in those exemplars who happen to come last in point of time, but rather in those apparently scattered and chance existences which favourable conditions have here and there produced; and it ought to be just as easy to understand the demand that, because it can arrive at a conscious awareness of its goal, mankind ought to seek out and create the favourable conditions under which those great redemptive men can come into existence. But everything resists this conclusion: here the ultimate goal is seen to lie in the happiness of all or of the greatest number, there in the development of great communities; and though one may be ready to sacrifice one's life to a state, for instance, it is another matter if one is asked to sacrifice it on behalf of another individual. It seems to be an absurd demand that one man should exist for the sake of another man; 'for the sake of all others, rather, or at least for as many as possible!' O worthy man! as though it were less absurd to let number decide when value and significance are at issue! For the question is this: how can your life, the individual life, receive the highest value, the deepest significance? How can it be least squandered? Certainly only by your living for the good of the rarest and most valuable exemplars,[3] and not for the good of the majority, that is to say those who, taken individually, are the least valuable exemplars. And the young person should be taught to regard himself as a failed work of nature but at the same time as a witness to the grandiose and marvellous intentions of this artist: nature has done

2. In the previous section Nietzsche wrote: "*The Schopenhauerean man voluntarily takes upon himself the suffering involved in being truthful * * *;* and being truthful means: to believe in an existence that can in no way be denied and which is itself true and without falsehood." (His emphasis.)
3. That is, for the good (or flourishing and development) of those who exceed the typically human in

their abilities (contributing to a social order—and more specifically to a culture—that is conducive to the general enhancement of the character and quality of human life). Nietzsche here expresses his disdain for the classical "utilitarian" view (which JOHN STUART MILL attempted to refine) that what matters most is "the greatest happiness of the greatest number."

badly, he should say to himself; but I will honour its great intentions by serving it so that one day it may do better.

By coming to this resolve he places himself within the circle of *culture*; for culture is the child of each individual's self-knowledge and dissatisfaction with himself. Anyone who believes in culture is thereby saying: 'I see above me something higher and more human than I am; let everyone help me to attain it, as I will help everyone who knows and suffers as I do: so that at last the man may appear who feels himself perfect and boundless in knowledge and love, perception and power, and who in his completeness is at one with nature, the judge and evaluator of things.[4] It is hard to create in anyone this condition of intrepid self-knowledge because it is impossible to teach love; for it is love alone that can bestow on the soul, not only a clear, discriminating and self-contemptuous view of itself, but also the desire to look beyond itself and to seek with all its might for a higher self as yet still concealed from it. Thus only he who has attached his heart to some great man is by that act *consecrated to culture*; the sign of that consecration is that one is ashamed of oneself without any accompanying feeling of distress, that one comes to hate one's own narrowness and shrivelled nature, that one has a feeling of sympathy for the genius who again and again drags himself up out of our dryness and apathy and the same feeling in anticipation for all those who are still struggling and evolving, with the profoundest conviction that almost everywhere we encounter nature pressing towards man and again and again failing to achieve him, yet everywhere succeeding in producing the most marvellous beginnings, individual traits and forms: so that the men we live among resemble a field over which is scattered the most precious fragments of sculpture where everything calls to us: come, assist, complete, bring together what belongs together, we have an immeasurable longing to become whole.

This sum of inner states is, I said, the first sign that one is consecrated to culture; now, however, I have to describe the *further* stage of this consecration, and I realize that here my task is more difficult. For now we have to make the transition from the inward event to an assessment of the outward event; the eye has to be directed outwards so as to rediscover in the great world of action that desire for culture it recognized in the experiences of the first stage just described; the individual has to employ his own wrestling and longing as the alphabet by means of which he can now read off the aspirations of mankind as a whole. But he may not halt even here; from this stage he has to climb up to a yet higher one; culture demands of him, not only inward experience, not only an assessment of the outward world that streams all around him, but finally and above all an act, that is to say a struggle on behalf of culture and hostility towards those influences, habits, laws, institutions in which he fails to recognize his goal: which is the production of the genius.[5]

* * *

SOURCE: From Friedrich Nietzsche, *Untimely Meditations*, trans. R. J. Hollingdale (Cambridge: Cambridge University Press, 1983), pp. 127–30, 156–63. Except where otherwise

4. This passage foreshadows what Nietzsche takes to be the essence of the "higher humanity" of which he often speaks in his later writings.
5. That is, the production of the exceptional sort of human being in whom the creative abilities characteristic of humanity at its best are enhanced, cultivated, and educated as fully as is humanly possible.

indicated, German words in brackets are the terminology used in the German original, inserted by the editor in addition to their renderings in the translation. Originally published in 1874 as *Schopenhauer als Erzieher*, one of the four long essays that he collectively called *Unzeitgemässe Betrachtungen*.

From The Gay Science

From *Book One*

1

The teachers of the purpose of existence.—Whether I regard human beings with a good or with an evil eye, I always find them engaged in a single task, each and every one of them: to do what benefits the preservation of the human race. Not from a feeling of love for the race, but simply because within them nothing is older, stronger, more inexorable and invincible than this instinct— because this instinct constitutes *the essence*[1] of our species and herd. One might quickly enough, with the usual myopia from five steps away, divide one's neighbours into useful and harmful, good and evil; but on a large-scale assessment, upon further reflection on the whole, one grows suspicious of this tidying and separating and finally abandons it. Even the most harmful person may actually be the most useful when it comes to the preservation of the species; for he nurtures in himself or through his effects on others drives without which humanity would long since have become feeble or rotten. Hatred, delight in the misfortunes of others, the lust to rob and rule, and whatever else is called evil: all belong to the amazing economy of the preservation of the species, an economy which is certainly costly, wasteful, and on the whole most foolish—but still *proven* to have preserved our race so far. I no longer know whether you, my dear fellow man and neighbour, are even *capable* of living in a way which is damaging to the species, i.e. 'unreasonably' and 'badly'. What *might* have harmed the species may have become extinct many thousands of years ago and may by now belong to the things that are no longer possible even for God. Pursue your best or your worst desires, and above all, perish! In both cases you are probably still in some way a promoter and benefactor of humanity and are thus entitled to your eulogists—as well as to your mockers! But you will never find someone who could completely mock you, the individual, even in your best qualities, someone who could bring home to you as far as truth allows your boundless, fly- and frog-like wretchedness! To laugh at oneself as one would have to laugh in order to laugh *from the whole truth*—for that, not even the best have had enough sense of truth, and the most gifted have had far too little genius! Perhaps even laughter still has a future—when the proposition 'The species is everything, an individual is always nothing' has become part of humanity and this ultimate liberation and irresponsibility is accessible to everyone at all times. Perhaps laughter will then have formed an alliance with wisdom; perhaps only 'gay science' will remain. At present, things are still quite different; at present, the comedy of existence has not yet 'become conscious' of itself; at present, we still live in

---

1. That is, the very nature (*das Wesen*).

the age of tragedy, in the age of moralities and religions. What is the meaning of the ever-new appearance of these founders of moralities and religions, of these instigators of fights about moral valuations, these teachers of pangs of conscience and religious wars? What is the meaning of these heroes on this stage? For these have been the heroes thus far; and everything else, even if at times it was all that we could see and was far too near, has always served only to set the stage for these heroes, whether as machinery and backdrop or in the role of confidant and servant. (The poets, for example, were always the servants of some kind of morality.) It is obvious that these tragedies, too, work in the interest of the *species*, even if they should believe that they are working in the interest of God, as God's emissaries. They, too, promote the life of the species *by promoting the faith in life*. 'Life is worth living', each of them shouts, 'there is something to life, there is something behind life, beneath it; beware!' This drive, which rules the highest as well as the basest of human beings—the drive for the preservation of the species—erupts from time to time as reason and passion of mind;[2] it is then surrounded by a resplendent retinue of reasons and tries with all its might to make us forget that fundamentally it is drive, instinct, stupidity, lack of reasons. Life *ought to* be loved, *because*—! Man *ought to* advance himself and his neighbour, *because*—! What names all these Oughts and Becauses have been given and may yet be given in the future! The ethical teacher makes his appearance as the teacher of the purpose of existence in order that what happens necessarily and always, by itself and without a purpose, shall henceforth seem to be done for a purpose and strike man as reason and an ultimate commandment; to this end he invents a second, different existence and takes by means of his new mechanics the old, ordinary existence off its old, ordinary hinges. To be sure, in no way does he want us to *laugh* at existence, or at ourselves—or at him; for him, an individual is always an individual, something first and last and tremendous; for him there are no species, sums, or zeroes. Foolish and fanciful as his inventions and valuations may be, badly as he may misjudge the course of nature and deny its conditions—and all ethical systems hitherto have been so foolish and contrary to nature that humanity would have perished from every one had it gained power over humanity—all the same! Every time 'the hero' appeared on stage, something new was attained: the gruesome counterpart of laughter, that profound shock that many individuals feel at the thought: 'Yes, living is worth it! Yes, I am worthy of living!' Life and I and you and all of us became *interesting* to ourselves once again for a while. There is no denying that *in the long run* each of these great teachers of a purpose was vanquished by laughter, reason and nature: the brief tragedy always changed and returned into the eternal comedy of existence, and the 'waves of uncountable laughter'—to cite Aeschylus[3]—must in the end also come crashing down on the greatest of these tragedians. Despite all this corrective laughter, human nature on the whole has surely been altered by the recurring emergence of such teachers of the purpose of existence—*it has acquired one additional need*, the need for the repeated appearance of such teachers and such teachings of a 'purpose'. Man has gradually become a fantastic animal that must fulfil one condition of existence more than any other animal: man *must* from time to

---

2. That is, "spirit" (*Geist*).
3. Greek tragedian (ca. 525–456 B.C.E.); Nietzsche slightly misquotes *Prometheus Bound* 89–90, "countless laughter of sea waves."

time believe he knows *why* he exists; his race cannot thrive without a periodic trust in life—without faith in the *reason in life*! And ever again the human
race will from time to time decree: 'There is something one is absolutely forbidden henceforth to laugh at.' And the most cautious friend of man will add:
'Not only laughter and gay wisdom but also the tragic, with all its sublime unreason, belongs to the means and necessities of the preservation of the species.'
And therefore! Therefore! Therefore! Oh, do you understand me, my brothers?
Do you understand this new law of ebb and flood? We, too, have our time!

2

Intellectual conscience.—I keep having the same experience and keep resisting it anew each time; I do not want to believe it although I can grasp it as
with my hands: *the great majority lacks an intellectual conscience*—indeed, it
has often seemed to me as if someone requiring such a conscience would be
as lonely in the most densely populated cities as he would be in the desert.
Everyone looks at you with strange eyes and goes on handling their scales,
calling this good and that evil; nobody as much as blushes when you notice
that their weights are underweight—nor do they become indignant with you;
perhaps they laugh at your doubts. I mean: *to the great majority* it is not contemptible to believe this or that and to live accordingly *without* first becoming aware of the final and most certain reasons pro and con, and without even
troubling themselves about such reasons afterwards: the most gifted men and
the noblest women still belong to this 'great majority'. But what are goodheart-
edness, refinement, and genius to me when the person possessing these virtues tolerates slack feelings in his believing and judging and when he does
not consider *the desire for certainty* to be his inmost craving and deepest
need—as that which separates the higher human beings from the lower!

* * *

54

The consciousness of appearance.—How wonderful and new and yet how fearful and ironic my new insight makes me feel towards all of existence! I have
discovered for myself that the ancient humanity and animality, indeed the
whole prehistory and past of all sentient being, continues within me to fabu-
late,[4] to love, to hate, and to infer—I suddenly awoke in the middle of this
dream, but only to the consciousness that I am dreaming and that I *must* go
on dreaming lest I perish—as the sleepwalker has to go on dreaming in order
to avoid falling down. What is 'appearance' to me now! Certainly not the opposite of some essence[5]—what could I say about any essence [*Wesen*] except name
the predicates of its appearance! Certainly not a dead mask that one could put
on an unknown x and probably also take off x! To me, appearance is the active,
and living itself, which goes so far in its self-mockery that it makes me feel
that here there is appearance and a will-o'-the-wisp and a dance of spirits and
nothing else—that among all these dreamers, even I, the 'knower', am dancing

---

4. That is, "composes on [in the sense of 'onward']"
(*fortdichtet*). This whole phrase—"in mir fortdichtet, fortliebt, forthasst, fortschliesst"—is better

translated as "composes on, loves on, hates on,
infers on within me."
5. That is, (true) being or (essential) reality (*Wesen*).

my dance; that the one who comes to know is a means of prolonging the earthly dance and thus is one of the masters of ceremony of existence, and that the sublime consistency and interrelatedness of all knowledge may be and will be the highest means to *sustain* the universality of dreaming, the mutual comprehension of all dreamers, and thereby also *the duration of the dream.*

* * *

From *Book Two*

57

To the realists.—You sober people who feel armed against passion and phantastical conceptions and would like to make your emptiness a matter of pride and an ornament—you call yourself realists and insinuate that the world really is the way it appears to you: before you alone reality [*Wirklichkeit*]⁶ stands unveiled, and you yourselves are perhaps the best part of it—oh, you beloved images of Sais.⁷ But aren't you too in your unveiled condition still most passionate and dark creatures, compared to fish, and still all too similar to an artist in love? And what is 'reality' to an artist in love! You still carry around the valuations of things that originate in the passions and loves of former centuries! Your sobriety still contains a secret and inextirpable drunkenness! Your love of 'reality', for example—oh, that is an old, ancient 'love'! In every experience, in every sense impression there is a piece of this old love; and some fantasy, some prejudice, some irrationality, some ignorance, some fear, and whatever else, has worked on and contributed to it. That mountain over there! That cloud over there! What is 'real' [*wirklich*] about that? Subtract just once the phantasm and the whole human *contribution* from it, you sober ones! Yes, if you could do *that*! If you could forget your background, your past, your nursery school—all of your humanity and animality! There is no 'reality' for us—and not for you either, you sober ones—we are not nearly as strange to one another as you think, and perhaps our good will to transcend drunkenness is just as respectable as your belief that you are altogether *incapable* of drunkenness.

58

Only as creators!—This has caused me the greatest trouble and still does always cause me the greatest trouble: to realize that *what things are called* is unspeakably more important than what they are. The reputation, name, and appearance, the worth, the usual measure and weight of a thing—originally almost always something mistaken and arbitrary, thrown over things like a dress and quite foreign to their nature and even to their skin—has, through the belief in it and its growth from generation to generation, slowly grown onto and into the thing and has become its very body: what started as appearance in the end nearly always becomes essence and *effectively* acts as its essence! What kind of a fool would believe that it is enough to point to this origin and this

6. This is, actuality; true reality.
7. An allusion to FRIEDRICH SCHILLER's poem "The Veiled Image of Sais" (1795); the Greek biographer and essayist Plutarch (ca. 50–ca. 120 C.E.), in *Isis and Osiris* 9, reports that in the Egyptian city of Sais "the statue of Athena, whom they believe to be Isis, had the inscription 'I am all that has been and is and will be, and no mortal has yet raised my veil [literally, "uncovered my mantle"].'"

misty shroud of delusion in order to *destroy* the world that counts as 'real', so-called 'reality'! Only as creators can we destroy!—But let us also not forget that in the long run it is enough to create new names and valuations and appearances of truth in order to create new 'things'.

* * *

From *Book Three*

108

New battles.—After Buddha[8] was dead, they still showed his shadow in a cave for centuries—a tremendous, gruesome shadow. God is dead; but given the way people are, there may still for millennia be caves in which they show his shadow.—And we—we must still defeat his shadow as well!

109

Let us beware.—Let us beware of thinking that the world is a living being. Where would it stretch? What would it feed on? How could it grow and pro-create? After all, we know roughly what the organic is; are we then supposed to reinterpret what is inexpressibly derivative, late, rare, accidental, which we perceive only on the crust of the earth, as something essential, common, and eternal, as those people do who call the universe an organism? This nause-ates me. Let us beware even of believing that the universe is a machine; it is certainly not constructed to one end, and the word 'machine' pays it far too high an honour. Let us beware of assuming in general and everywhere any-thing as elegant as the cyclical movements of our neighbouring stars; even a glance at the Milky Way raises doubts whether there are not much coarser and more contradictory movements there, as well as stars with eternally lin-ear paths, etc. The astral order in which we live is an exception; this order and the considerable duration that is conditioned by it have again made possi-ble the exception of exceptions: the development of the organic. The total character of the world, by contrast, is for all eternity chaos, not in the sense of a lack of necessity but of a lack of order, organization, form, beauty, wis-dom, and whatever else our aesthetic anthropomorphisms are called. Judged from the vantage point of our reason, the unsuccessful attempts are by far the rule; the exceptions are not the secret aim, and the whole musical mech-anism repeats eternally its tune, which must never be called a melody—and ultimately even the phrase 'unsuccessful attempt' is already an anthropomor-phism bearing a reproach. But how could we reproach or praise the universe! Let us beware of attributing to it heartlessness or unreason or their opposites: it is neither perfect, nor beautiful, nor noble, nor does it want to become any of these things; in no way does it strive to imitate man! In no way do our aes-thetic and moral judgements apply to it! It also has no drive to self-preservation or any other drives; nor does it observe any laws. Let us beware of saying that there are laws in nature. There are only necessities: there is no one who com-

---

8. The historical Buddha (active ca. 5th century B.C.E.), born Siddhartha Gautama in northeastern India, who founded Buddhism.

mands, no one who obeys, no one who transgresses. Once you know that there are no purposes, you also know that there is no accident; for only against a world of purposes does the word 'accident' have a meaning. Let us beware of saying that death is opposed to life. The living is only a form of what is dead, and a very rare form. Let us beware of thinking that the world eternally creates new things. There are no eternally enduring substances; matter is as much of an error as the god of the Eleatics.[9] But when will we be done with our caution and care? When will all these shadows of god no longer darken us? When will we have completely de-deified nature? When may we begin to *naturalize* humanity with a pure, newly discovered, newly redeemed nature?[1]

110

Origin of knowledge.—Through immense periods of time, the intellect produced nothing but errors; some of them turned out to be useful and species-preserving; those who hit upon or inherited them fought their fight for themselves and their progeny with greater luck. Such erroneous articles of faith, which were passed on by inheritance further and further, and finally almost became part of the basic endowment of the species, are for example: that there are enduring things; that there are identical things; that there are things, kinds of material, bodies; that a thing is what it appears to be; that our will is free; that what is good for me is also good in and for itself. Only very late did the deniers and doubters of such propositions emerge; only very late did truth emerge as the weakest form of knowledge. It seemed that one was unable to live with it; that our organism was geared for its opposite: all its higher functions, the perceptions of sense and generally every kind of sensation, worked with those basic errors that had been incorporated since time immemorial. Further, even in the realm of knowledge those propositions became the norms according to which one determined 'true' and 'untrue'— down to the most remote areas of pure logic. Thus the *strength* of knowledge lies not in its degree of truth, but in its age, its embeddedness, its character as a condition of life. Where life and knowledge seem to contradict each other, there was never any serious fight to begin with; denial and doubt were simply considered madness. Those exceptional thinkers, like the Eleatics, who still posited and clung to the opposites of the natural errors, believed in the possibility of also *living* this opposite: they invented the sage as the man of unchangeability, impersonality, universality of intuition, as one and all at the same time, with a special capacity for that inverted knowledge; they had the faith that their knowledge was at the same time the principle of *life.* But in order to be able to claim all this, they had to *deceive* themselves about their own state: they had fictitiously to attribute to themselves impersonality and duration without change; they had to misconstrue the nature of the knower,

---

9. Members of a pre-Socratic school of Greek philosophy founded in the early 5th century B.C.E. by Parmenides in Elea, in southern Italy; they argued that all change in the world is illusory, because all that truly exists must be unchanging, indivisible, and eternal.
1. In Nietzsche's German, "Wann werden wir angefangen dürfen, uns Menschen mit der reinen, neu gefundenen, neu erlösten Natur zu *vernatürlichen?*" Better translated: "When may we be permitted to *naturalize* ourselves ['us human beings'] with a pure, newly discovered, newly redeemed nature?" This is one of the challenges to which Nietzsche conceives his own philosophical efforts—beginning with *The Gay Science*—to be a response. The very next sections are cases in point.

deny the force of impulses in knowledge, and generally conceive reason as a completely free, self-originated activity. They closed their eyes to the fact that they, too, had arrived at their propositions in opposition to what was considered valid or from a desire for tranquillity or sole possession or sovereignty. The subtler development of honesty and scepticism finally made also these people impossible; even their life and judgements proved dependent on the ancient drives and fundamental errors of all sentient existence. This subtler honesty and scepticism arose wherever two conflicting propositions seemed to be *applicable* to life because both were compatible with the basic errors, and thus where it was possible to argue about the greater or lesser degree of *usefulness* for life; also wherever new propositions showed themselves to be not directly useful, but at least also not harmful, as expressions of an intellectual play impulse, and innocent and happy like all play. Gradually the human brain filled itself with such judgements and convictions; and ferment, struggle, and lust for power developed in this tangle. Not only utility and delight, but also every kind of drive took part in the fight about the 'truths'; the intellectual fight became an occupation, attraction, profession, duty, dignity—knowledge and the striving for the true finally took their place as a need among the other needs. Henceforth, not only faith and conviction, but also scrutiny, denial, suspicion, and contradiction were a *power*; all 'evil' instincts were subordinated to knowledge and put in its service and took on the lustre of the permitted, honoured, useful and finally the eye and the innocence of the *good*. Thus knowledge became a part of life and, as life, a continually growing power, until finally knowledge and the ancient basic errors struck against each other, both as life, both as power, both in the same person. The thinker—that is now the being in whom the drive to truth and those life-preserving errors are fighting their first battle, after the drive to truth has *proven* itself to be a life-preserving power, too. In relation to the significance of this battle, everything else is a matter of indifference: the ultimate question about the condition of life is posed here, and the first attempt is made here to answer the question through experiment. To what extent can truth stand to be incorporated?—that is the question; that is the experiment.

* * *

113

On the doctrine of poisons.—So much has to come together in order for scientific thought[2] to originate, and all these necessary forces have had to be separately invented, practised, cultivated! In their separateness they have, however, very often had a totally different effect from that which they have today when in the realm of scientific thought [*wissenschaftlich Denken*] they mutually limit and keep each other in check: they have worked as poisons, e.g. the doubting drive, the denying drive, the waiting drive, the collecting drive, the dissolving drive. Many hecatombs of human beings had to be sacrificed before these drives learned to grasp their coexistence and feel

2. That is, "a rigorously cognitive thinking" (*ein wissenschaftlich Denken*). *Wissenschaft* comprises not just the natural sciences but also other cogni- tive disciplines, including linguistics, history, and philosophy.

like functions of one organizing force in one human being! And how far we still are from the time when artistic energies and the practical wisdom of life join with scientific thought [*wissenschaftlich Denken*] so that a higher organic system will develop in relation to which the scholar, the physician, the artist, and the lawmaker, as we now know them, would have to appear as paltry antiquities!

* * *

115

The four errors.—Man has been educated by his errors: first, he saw himself only incompletely; secondly, he endowed himself with fictitious attributes; thirdly, he placed himself in a false rank order in relation to animals and nature; fourthly, he invented ever new tables of goods and for a time took them to be eternal and unconditioned—so that now this, now that human drive and condition occupied first place and was ennobled as a result of this valuation. If one discounts the effect of these four errors, one has also discounted humanity, humaneness, and 'human dignity'.

116

Herd instinct.—Wherever we encounter a morality [*eine Moral*], we find an evaluation and ranking of human drives and actions. These evaluations and rankings are always the expression of the needs of a community and herd: that which benefits *it* the most—and second most, and third most—is also the highest standard of value for all individuals. With morality the individual is instructed to be a function of the herd and to ascribe value to himself only as a function. Since the conditions for preserving one community have been very different from those of another community, there have been very different moralities; and in view of essential changes in herds and communities, states and societies that are yet to come, one can prophesy that there will yet be very divergent moralities [*Moralen*]. Morality [*Moralität*] is herd-instinct in the individual.

* * *

120

Health of the soul.—The popular medical formulation of morality (the originator of which is Ariston of Chios), 'virtue is the health of the soul',[3] would, in order to be useful, have to be changed at least to read, 'your virtue is the health of your soul'. For there is no health as such, and all attempts to define such a thing have failed miserably. Deciding what is health even for your *body* depends on your goal, your horizon, your powers, your impulses, your mistakes and above all on the ideals and phantasms of your soul. Thus there are innumerable healths of the body; and the more one allows the particular and

3. According to Plutarch (*On Moral Virtue* 2), the Stoic philosopher Ariston (active ca. 250 B.C.E.) "made virtue one in its essential nature and called it health."

incomparable to rear its head again, the more one unlearns the dogma of the 'equality of men', the more the concept of a normal health, along with those of a normal diet and normal course of an illness, must be abandoned by our medical men. Only then would it be timely to reflect on the health and illness of the *soul* and to locate the virtue peculiar to each man in its health— which of course could look in one person like the opposite of health in another. Finally, the great question would still remain whether we can *do without* illness, even for the development of our virtue; and whether especially our thirst for knowledge and self-knowledge do not need the sick soul as much as the healthy; in brief, whether the will to health alone is not a prejudice, a cowardice and a piece of most refined barbarism and backwardness.

121

Life not an argument.—We have arranged for ourselves a world in which we are able to live—by positing bodies, lines, planes, causes and effects, motion and rest, form and content; without these articles of faith no one could endure living! But that does not prove them. Life is not an argument; the conditions of life might include error.

* * *

125

The madman.—Haven't you heard of that madman who in the bright morning lit a lantern and ran around the marketplace[4] crying incessantly, 'I'm looking for God! I'm looking for God!' Since many of those who did not believe in God were standing around together just then, he caused great laughter. Has he been lost, then? asked one. Did he lose his way like a child? asked another. Or is he hiding? Is he afraid of us? Has he gone to sea? Emigrated?—Thus they shouted and laughed, one interrupting the other. The madman jumped into their midst and pierced them with his eyes. 'Where is God?' he cried; 'I'll tell you! *We have killed him*—you and I! We are all his murderers. But how did we do this? How were we able to drink up the sea? Who gave us the sponge to wipe away the entire horizon? What were we doing when we unchained this earth from its sun? Where is it moving to now? Where are we moving to? Away from all suns? Are we not continually falling? And backwards, sidewards, forwards, in all directions? Is there still an up and a down? Aren't we straying as though through an infinite nothing? Isn't empty space breathing at us? Hasn't it got colder? Isn't night and more night coming again and again? Don't lanterns have to be lit in the morning? Do we still hear nothing of the noise of the grave-diggers who are burying God? Do we still smell nothing of the divine decomposition?—Gods, too, decompose! God is dead! God remains dead! And we have killed him! How can we console ourselves, the murderers of all murderers! The holiest and the mightiest thing the world has ever possessed has bled to death under our knives: who will wipe this blood from us? With what water could we clean ourselves? What festivals of atonement, what holy games will we have to invent for ourselves? Is the magnitude of this deed

---

4. Perhaps an echo of the Cynic Diogenes (ca. 400–ca. 325 B.C.E.), who was said to have carried a lighted lamp in broad daylight to search for an honest man.

not too great for us? Do we not ourselves have to become gods merely to appear worthy of it? There was never a greater deed—and whoever is born after us will on account of this deed belong to a higher history than all history up to now!' Here the madman fell silent and looked again at his listeners; they too were silent and looked at him disconcertedly. Finally he threw his lantern on the ground so that it broke into pieces and went out. 'I come too early', he then said; 'my time is not yet. This tremendous event is still on its way, wandering; it has not yet reached the ears of men. Lightning and thunder need time; the light of the stars needs time; deeds need time, even after they are done, in order to be seen and heard. This deed is still more remote to them than the remotest stars—*and yet they have done it themselves!*' It is still recounted how on the same day the madman forced his way into several churches and there started singing his *requiem aeternam deo.*[5] Led out and called to account, he is said always to have replied nothing but, 'What then are these churches now if not the tombs and sepulchres of God?'

126

Mystical explanations—Mystical explanations are considered deep; the truth is, they are not even shallow.

* * *

From *Book Four*

* * *

333

What knowing means.—*Non ridere, non lugere, neque detestari, sed intelligere!*[6] says Spinoza as simply and sublimely as is his wont. Yet in the final analysis, what is this *intelligere* other than the way we become sensible of the other three? A result of the different and conflicting impulses to laugh, lament, and curse? Before knowledge is possible, each of these impulses must first have presented its one-sided view of the thing or event; then comes the fight between these one-sided views, and occasionally out of it a mean, an appeasement, a concession to all three sides, a kind of justice and contract; for in virtue of justice and a contract all these impulses can assert and maintain themselves in existence and each can finally feel it is in the right vis-à-vis all the others. Since only the ultimate reconciliation scenes and final accounts of this long process rise to consciousness, we suppose that *intelligere* must be something conciliatory, just, and good, something essentially opposed to the instincts, when in fact *it is only a certain behaviour of the drives towards one another.* For the longest time, conscious thought was considered thought itself; only now does the truth dawn on us that by far the greatest part of our mind's activity proceeds unconscious and unfelt; but I think these drives which here fight each

---

5. Eternal rest [be granted] to God (Latin)—a startling inversion of the Roman Catholic prayer to God to grant eternal rest to the dead.
6. Not to laugh, not to lament, nor to despise, but to understand [know]! (Latin); quoted from chapter 1 of *Tractatus Politicus* (1677), by the Dutch philosopher Benedict (Baruch) de Spinoza (1632–1677).

other know very well how to make themselves felt by and how to hurt *each other.* This may well be the source of that great and sudden exhaustion that afflicts all thinkers (it is the exhaustion of the battlefield). Indeed, there may be many hidden instances for *heroism* in our warring depths, but certainly nothing divine, eternally resting in itself, as Spinoza supposed. *Conscious* thought, especially that of the philosopher, is the least vigorous and therefore also the relatively mildest and calmest type of thought; and thus precisely philosophers are most easily led astray about the nature of knowledge.

334

One must learn to love.—This happens to us in music: first one must *learn to hear* a figure and melody at all, to detect and distinguish it, to isolate and delimit it as a life in itself; then one needs effort and good will to *stand* it despite its strangeness; patience with its appearance and expression, and kind-heartedness about its oddity. Finally comes a moment when we are *used* to it; when we expect it; when we sense that we'd miss it if it were missing; and now it continues relentlessly to compel and enchant us until we have become its humble and enraptured lovers, who no longer want anything better from the world than it and it again. But this happens to us not only in music: it is in just this way that we have *learned to love* everything we now love. We are always rewarded in the end for our good will, our patience, our fair-mindedness and gentleness with what is strange, as it gradually casts off its veil and presents itself as a new and indescribable beauty. That is *its thanks* for our hospitality. Even he who loves himself will have learned it this way—there is no other way. Love, too, must be learned.

335

Long live physics!—So, how many people know how to observe? And of these few how many to observe themselves? 'Everyone is farthest from himself'[7]— every person who is expert at scrutinizing the inner life of others knows this to his own chagrin; and the saying, 'Know thyself',[8] addressed to human beings by a god, is near to malicious. *That* self-observation is in such a bad state, however, is most clearly confirmed by the way in which *nearly everyone* speaks of the nature of a moral act—that quick, willing, convinced, talkative manner, with its look, its smile, its obliging eagerness! People seem to be wanting to say to you, 'But my dear fellow, that is precisely *my* subject! You are directing your question to the person who is *competent* to answer it: there is, as it happens, nothing I am wiser about. So: when man judges "*that is right*" and infers "*hence it must come about!*" and then *does* what he thus has recognized to be right and described as necessary—then the nature of his act is *moral!*' But, my friend, you are speaking of three acts instead of one: even the judgement 'that is right', for example, is an act. Wouldn't it be possible for a person to make a judgement in a way that would be moral or immoral? *Why* do you take this and specifically this to be right? 'Because my conscience tells me

7. Reversal of common German expression "Everyone is closest to himself" [Williams's note].

8. A maxim carved into the temple of Apollo at Delphi (4th c. B.C.E.), home of the god's oracle.

so; conscience never speaks immorally, since it determines what is to count as moral!' But why do you *listen* to the words of your conscience? And what gives you the right to consider such a judgement true and infallible? For this belief—is there no conscience? Do you know nothing of an intellectual conscience? A conscience behind your 'conscience'? Your judgement, 'that is right' has a prehistory in your drives, inclinations, aversions, experiences, and what you have failed to experience; you have to ask, '*how* did it emerge there?' and then also, '*what* is really impelling me to listen to it?' You can listen to its commands like a good soldier who heeds the command of his officer. Or like a woman who loves the one who commands. Or like a flatterer and coward who fears the commander. Or like a fool who obeys because he can think of no objection. In short, there are a hundred ways to listen to your conscience. But *that* you hear this or that judgement as the words of conscience, i.e. *that* you feel something to be right may have its cause in your never having thought much about yourself and in your blindly having accepted what has been labelled *right* since your childhood; or in the fact that fulfilling your duties has so far brought you bread and honours—and you consider it right because it appears to you as *your own* 'condition of existence' (and that you have a *right* to existence seems irrefutable to you). For all that, the *firmness* of your moral judgement could be evidence of your personal wretchedness, of lack of a personality; your 'moral strength' might have its source in your stubbornness—or in your inability to envisage new ideals. And, briefly, had you reflected more subtly, observed better, and studied more, you would never continue to call this 'duty' of yours and this 'conscience' of yours duty and conscience. Your insight into *how such things as moral judgements could ever have come into existence* would spoil these emotional words for you, as other emotional words, for example, 'sin', 'salvation of the soul', and 'redemption' have been spoiled for you. And now don't bring up the categorical imperative, my friend! The term tickles my ear and makes me laugh despite your very serious presence. I am reminded of old Kant, who helped himself to (*erschlichen*) the 'thing in itself'—another very ridiculous thing!—and was punished for this when the 'categorical imperative' crept into (*beschlichen*) his heart and made him stray back to 'God', 'soul', 'freedom', 'immortality', like a fox who strays back into his cage. Yet it had been *his* strength and cleverness that had *broken open* the cage![9] What? You admire the categorical imperative within you? This 'firmness' of your so-called moral judgement? This absoluteness of the feeling, 'here everyone must judge as I do'? Rather admire your *selfishness* here! And the blindness, pettiness, and simplicity of your selfishness! For it is selfish to consider one's own judgement a universal law, and this selfishness is blind, petty, and simple because it shows that you haven't yet discovered yourself or created for yourself an ideal of your very own—for this could never be someone else's, let alone everyone's, everyone's! No one who judges, 'in this case everyone

9. In the *Critique of Pure Reason* (1781) KANT argued that the great concepts of traditional speculation—God, the soul, freedom—did not designate objects about which it was even in principle possible for us to know anything. This seemed to spell the end of traditional metaphysics and theology. In the *Critique of Practical Reason* (1788), however, Kant seemed to argue that the morality required us to accept as "postulates of pure practical reason" a number of principles such as the existence of God and the continuation of some form of life after death. This was thought by many to reintroduce the possibility of a version of the theology it had been the great glory of his earlier work to terminate. "The categorical imperative" is Kant's fundamental principle of morality [Williams's note].

would have to act like this' has yet taken five steps towards self-knowledge. For he would then know that there neither are nor can be actions that are all the same; that every act ever performed was done in an altogether unique and unrepeatable way, and that this will be equally true of every future act; that all prescriptions of action (even the most inward and subtle rules of all moralities so far) relate only to their rough exterior; that these prescriptions may yield an appearance of sameness, *but only just an appearance*; that as one observes or recollects *any* action, it is and remains impenetrable; that our opinions about 'good' and 'noble' and 'great' can never be *proven true* by our actions because every act is unknowable; that our opinions, valuations, and tables of what is good are certainly some of the most powerful levers in the machinery of our actions, but that in each case, the law of its mechanism is unprovable. Let us therefore *limit* ourselves to the purification of our opinions and value judgements and to the *creation of tables of what is good that are new and all our own*: let us stop brooding over the 'moral value of our actions'! Yes, my friends, it is time to feel nauseous about some people's moral chatter about others. Sitting in moral judgement should offend our taste. Let us leave such chatter and such bad taste to those who have nothing to do but drag the past a few steps further through time and who never live in the present—that is, to the many, the great majority! We, however, want to *become who we are* [*Die werden, die wir sind*]—human beings who are new, unique, incomparable, who give themselves laws, who create themselves! To that end we must become the best students and discoverers of everything lawful and necessary in the world: we must become *physicists* in order to be creators in this sense—while hitherto all valuations and ideals have been built on *ignorance* of physics or in *contradiction* to it. So, long live physics![1] And even more long live what *compels* us to it—our honesty![2]

* * *

337

The 'humanity' of the future.—When I view this age with the eyes of a distant age, I can find nothing odder in present-day man than his peculiar virtue and disease called 'the sense for history'. This is the beginning of something completely new and strange in history: if one gave this seed a few centuries and more, it might ultimately become a wonderful growth with an equally wonderful smell that could make our old earth more agreeable to inhabit. We present-day humans are just beginning to form the chain of a very powerful future feeling, link by link—we hardly know what we are doing. It seems to us almost as if we are dealing not with a new feeling but with a decrease in all old feelings: the sense for history is still something so poor and cold, and many are struck by it as by a frost and made even poorer and colder by it. To others it appears as the sign of old age creeping up, and they see our planet as a melancholy sick man who chronicles his youth in order to forget his present condition. Indeed, that is one colour of this new feeling: he who is able to feel the history of man altogether as his own history feels in a monstrous

1. That is, "Up with physics!" (*Hoch die Physik!*), or "Here's to physics!" 2. Better translated as "intellectual integrity" (*Redlichkeit*).

generalization all the grief of the invalid thinking of health, of the old man thinking of the dreams of his youth, of the lover robbed of his beloved, of the martyr whose ideal is perishing, of the hero on the eve after a battle that decided nothing but brought him wounds and the loss of a friend. But to bear and to be able to bear this monstrous sum of all kinds of grief and still be the hero who, on the second day of battle, greets dawn and his fortune as a person whose horizon stretches millennia before and behind him, as the dutiful heir to all the nobility of past spirit, as the most aristocratic of old nobles and at the same time the first of a new nobility the likes of which no age has ever seen or dreamt: to take this upon one's soul—the oldest, the newest, losses, hopes, conquests, victories of humanity. To finally take all this in one soul and compress it into one feeling—this would surely have to produce a happiness unknown to humanity so far: a divine happiness full of power and love, full of tears and laughter, a happiness which, like the sun in the evening, continually draws on its inexhaustible riches, giving them away and pouring them into the sea, a happiness which, like the evening sun, feels richest when even the poorest fisherman is rowing with a golden oar! This divine feeling would then be called—humanity!

* * *

341

The heaviest weight.—What if some day or night a demon were to steal into your loneliest loneliness and say to you: 'This life as you now live it and have lived it you will have to live once again and innumerable times again; and there will be nothing new in it, but every pain and every joy and every thought and sigh and everything unspeakably small or great in your life must return to you, all in the same succession and sequence—even this spider and this moonlight between the trees, and even this moment and I myself. The eternal hourglass of existence is turned over again and again, and you with it, speck of dust!' Would you not throw yourself down and gnash your teeth and curse the demon who spoke thus? Or have you once experienced a tremendous moment when you would have answered him: 'You are a god, and never have I heard anything more divine.' If this thought gained power over you, as you are it would transform and possibly crush you; the question in each and every thing, 'Do you want this again and innumerable times again?' would lie on your actions as the heaviest weight! Or how well disposed would you have to become to yourself and to life *to long for nothing more fervently* than for this ultimate eternal confirmation and seal?[3]

* * *

SOURCE: From Friedrich Nietzsche, *The Gay Science: With a Prelude in German Rhymes and an Appendix of Songs*, ed. Bernard Williams, trans. Josefine Nauckhoff, poems trans. Adrian Del Caro (Cambridge: Cambridge University Press, 2001), pp. 27–30, 63–64, 69–70, 109–17,

3. This is a preview of a version of the idea of "eternal recurrence" that figures significantly in Nietzsche's next work, *Thus Spoke Zarathustra*. The next (and final) section of this book is also the beginning of the prologue of *Zarathustra*'s first part (which follows this selection). The idea appears here as a kind of thought experiment or test, rather than as a cosmological hypothesis or doctrine, and is applied specifically to the case of one's own life rather than to all of reality or to all events.

119–21, 185–91, 194–95. Except where otherwise indicated, German words in brackets are the terminology used in the German original, inserted by the editor in addition to their renderings in the translation. First published as *Die fröhliche Wissenschaft* in 1882 in a version containing four books, shortly before the appearance of the first two parts of *Thus Spoke Zarathustra* (1883)—which opens with the transitional concluding section of book 4. In 1887 Nietzsche republished the work with a new preface and a very important new fifth book (selections from which appear below, in chronological order of publication).

The German title of the original edition was followed by a subtitle in Italian that it translates: *La gaya scienza*, which signals the idea of the pursuit of knowledge (*scienza*), and also invokes the spirit of the French troubadours of 14th-century Provence who were greatly admired by Nietzsche, to whose art and cheerfully this-worldly sensibility the phrase refers. His rendering of this phrase not only employs the German word for cognitive inquiry (*Wissenschaft*)—a form of which he both advocates and exemplifies in this work—but also underscores the idea that such inquiry can and should be associated with a "joyful" disposition diametrically opposed to SCHOPENHAUER's grim pessimism.

From Thus Spoke Zarathustra

From *First Part*

ZARATHUSTRA'S PROLOGUE

1

When Zarathustra[1] was thirty years old he left his home and the lake of his home and went into the mountains. Here he enjoyed his spirit and his solitude, and for ten years did not tire of it. But at last a change came over his heart, and one morning he rose with the dawn, stepped before the sun, and spoke to it thus:

"You great star, what would your happiness be had you not those for whom you shine?

"For ten years you have climbed to my cave: you would have tired of your light and of the journey had it not been for me and my eagle and my serpent.

"But we waited for you every morning, took your overflow from you, and blessed you for it.

"Behold, I am weary of my wisdom, like a bee that has gathered too much honey; I need hands outstretched to receive it.

"I would give away and distribute, until the wise among men find joy once again in their folly, and the poor in their riches.

"For that I must descend to the depths, as you do in the evening when you go behind the sea and still bring light to the underworld, you overrich star.

"Like you, I must *go under*—go down, as is said by man, to whom I want to descend.

"So bless me then, you quiet eye that can look even upon an all-too-great happiness without envy!

---

1. The original Zarathustra, also known as Zoroaster (ca. 628–551 B.C.E.), was a Persian sage and religious figure, an early monotheist who strictly opposed "good" and "evil." In creating this new figure, Nietzsche is attempting to undo what he took to be the damage done by his Zarathustra's namesake as one of the originators of these cornerstones of the religious and moral traditions of which Nietzsche was so critical.

"Bless the cup that wants to overflow, that the water may flow from it golden and carry everywhere the reflection of your delight.

"Behold, this cup wants to become empty again, and Zarathustra wants to become man again."

Thus Zarathustra began to go under.[2]

2

Zarathustra descended alone from the mountains, encountering no one. But when he came into the forest, all at once there stood before him an old man who had left his holy cottage to look for roots in the woods. And thus spoke the old man to Zarathustra:

"No stranger to me is this wanderer: many years ago he passed this way. Zarathustra he was called, but he has changed. At that time you carried your ashes to the mountain; would you now carry your fire into the valleys?[3] Do you not fear to be punished as an arsonist?

"Yes, I recognize Zarathustra. His eyes are pure, and around his mouth there hides no disgust. Does he not walk like a dancer?

"Zarathustra has changed, Zarathustra has become a child, Zarathustra is an awakened one; what do you now want among the sleepers? You lived in your solitude as in the sea, and the sea carried you. Alas, would you now climb ashore? Alas, would you again drag your own body?"

Zarathustra answered: "I love man."

"Why," asked the saint, "did I go into the forest and the desert? Was it not because I loved man all-too-much? Now I love God; man I love not. Man is for me too imperfect a thing. Love of man would kill me."

Zarathustra answered: "Did I speak of love? I bring men a gift."

"Give them nothing!" said the saint. "Rather, take part of their load and help them to bear it—that will be best for them, if only it does you good! And if you want to give them something, give no more than alms, and let them beg for that!"

"No," answered Zarathustra. "I give no alms. For that I am not poor enough."

The saint laughed at Zarathustra and spoke thus: "Then see to it that they accept your treasures. They are suspicious of hermits and do not believe that we come with gifts. Our steps sound too lonely through the streets. And what if at night, in their beds, they hear a man walk by long before the sun has risen—they probably ask themselves, Where is the thief going?

"Do not go to man. Stay in the forest! Go rather even to the animals! Why do you not want to be as I am—a bear among bears, a bird among birds?"

"And what is the saint doing in the forest?" asked Zarathustra.

The saint answered: "I make songs and sing them; and when I make songs, I laugh, cry, and hum: thus I praise God. With singing, crying, laughing, and humming, I praise the god who is my god. But what do you bring us as a gift?"

2. Literally, "Thus began Zarathustra's descent" (*Also begann Zarathustra's Untergang*). *Untergang*—a term Nietzsche uses repeatedly—can have the sense of "downfall," and here (as often in this work) he plays with a word's multiple meanings. The suggestion is that Zarathustra is not simply going down from the mountain into the world of ordinary human beings but is descending in a way that will be his downfall. The echo of Jesus's sojourn in the wilderness and return to the world of men at about the same age is undoubtedly deliberate.

3. Fire was at the center of the Zoroastrian religion.

When Zarathustra had heard these words he bade the saint farewell and said: "What could I have to give you? But let me go quickly lest I take something from you!" And thus they separated, the old one and the man, laughing as two boys laugh.

But when Zarathustra was alone he spoke thus to his heart: "Could it be possible? This old saint in the forest has not yet heard anything of this, that *God is dead!*"

3

When Zarathustra came into the next town, which lies on the edge of the forest, he found many people gathered together in the market place; for it had been promised that there would be a tightrope walker. And Zarathustra spoke thus to the people:

"*I teach you the overman.*[4] Man is something that shall be overcome. What have you done to overcome him?

"All beings so far have created something beyond themselves; and do you want to be the ebb of this great flood and even go back to the beasts rather than overcome man? What is the ape to man? A laughingstock or a painful embarrassment. And man shall be just that for the overman: a laughingstock or a painful embarrassment. You have made your way from worm to man, and much in you is still worm. Once you were apes, and even now, too, man is more ape than any ape.

"Whoever is the wisest among you is also a mere conflict and cross between plant and ghost. But do I bid you become ghosts or plants?

"Behold, I teach you the overman. The overman is the meaning of the earth. Let your will say: the overman *shall be* the meaning of the earth! I beseech you, my brothers, *remain faithful to the earth,* and do not believe those who speak to you of otherworldly hopes! Poison-mixers are they, whether they know it or not. Despisers of life are they, decaying and poisoned themselves, of whom the earth is weary: so let them go.

"Once the sin against God was the greatest sin; but God died, and these sinners died with him. To sin against the earth is now the most dreadful thing, and to esteem the entrails of the unknowable higher than the meaning of the earth.

"Once the soul looked contemptuously upon the body, and then this contempt was the highest: she wanted the body meager, ghastly, and starved. Thus she hoped to escape it and the earth. Oh, this soul herself was still meager, ghastly, and starved: and cruelty was the lust of this soul. But you, too, my brothers, tell me: what does your body proclaim of your soul? Is not your soul poverty and filth and wretched contentment?

"Verily, a polluted stream is man. One must be a sea to be able to receive a

4. In German, *Übermensch* ("OO-bear-mench"), a term difficult to translate into English: the two possibilities are the now comical "superman" (used by many from George Bernard Shaw to R. J. Hollingdale) and the artificial "overman" (Kaufmann's choice here). Moreover, neither conveys that *Mensch* (human being) is generic, because "man" in English is strongly gendered as male. It is there-fore best left untranslated, as a reminder that Nietzsche is adopting and adapting the term *Über-mensch* to convey the idea of a transformed and transfigured humanity attained through the "enhancement of life" and the continual "overcoming" of the "all too human." (The very artificiality of "overman" makes it the second-best choice.)

polluted stream without becoming unclean. Behold, I teach you the overman: he is this sea; in him your great contempt can go under.

"What is the greatest experience you can have? It is the hour of the great contempt. The hour in which your happiness, too, arouses your disgust, and even your reason and your virtue.

"The hour when you say, 'What matters my happiness? It is poverty and filth and wretched contentment. But my happiness ought to justify existence itself.'

"The hour when you say, 'What matters my reason? Does it crave knowledge as the lion his food? It is poverty and filth and wretched contentment.'

"The hour when you say, 'What matters my virtue? As yet it has not made me rage. How weary I am of my good and my evil! All that is poverty and filth and wretched contentment.'

"The hour when you say, 'What matters my justice? I do not see that I am flames and fuel. But the just are flames and fuel.'

"The hour when you say, 'What matters my pity? Is not pity the cross on which he is nailed who loves man? But my pity is no crucifixion.'

"Have you yet spoken thus? Have you yet cried thus? Oh, that I might have heard you cry thus!

"Not your sin but your thrift cries to heaven; your meanness even in your sin cries to heaven.

"Where is the lightning to lick you with its tongue? Where is the frenzy with which you should be inoculated?

"Behold, I teach you the overman: he is this lightning, he is this frenzy."

When Zarathustra had spoken thus, one of the people cried: "Now we have heard enough about the tightrope walker; now let us see him too!" And all the people laughed at Zarathustra. But the tightrope walker, believing that the word concerned him,[5] began his performance.

4

Zarathustra, however, beheld the people and was amazed. Then he spoke thus:

"Man is a rope, tied between beast and overman—a rope over an abyss. A dangerous across, a dangerous on-the-way, a dangerous looking-back, a dangerous shuddering and stopping.

"What is great in man is that he is a bridge and not an end: what can be loved in man is that he is an *overture* and a *going under*.

"I love those who do not know how to live, except by going under, for they are those who cross over.

"I love the great despisers because they are the great reverers and arrows of longing for the other shore.

"I love those who do not first seek behind the stars for a reason to go under and be a sacrifice, but who sacrifice themselves for the earth, that the earth may some day become the overman's.

"I love him who lives to know, and who wants to know so that the overman may live some day. And thus he wants to go under.

5. That is, as someone who literally walks "over" or high above the audience below. This is an early warning by Nietzsche against any overly literal and simplistic understanding of his idea of the *Übermensch*, which refers neither to a species that would surpass ours nor to someone of some superior ability but to the idea of *Übermenschlichkeit*, or transformed *Menschlichkeit* (humanity), through the ongoing "enhancement of life."

"I love him who works and invents to build a house for the overman and to prepare earth, animal, and plant for him: for thus he wants to go under.

"I love him who loves his virtue, for virtue is the will to go under and an arrow of longing.

"I love him who does not hold back one drop of spirit for himself, but wants to be entirely the spirit of his virtue: thus he strides over the bridge as spirit.

"I love him who makes his virtue his addiction and his catastrophe:[6] for his virtue's sake he wants to live on and to live no longer.

"I love him who does not want to have too many virtues. One virtue is more virtue than two because it is more of a noose on which his catastrophe[7] may hang.

"I love him whose soul squanders itself, who wants no thanks and returns none: for he always gives away and does not want to preserve himself.

"I love him who is abashed when the dice fall to make his fortune, and asks, 'Am I then a crooked gambler?' For he wants to perish.

"I love him who casts golden words before his deeds and always does even more than he promises: for he wants to go under.

"I love him who justifies future and redeems past generations: for he wants to perish of the present.

"I love him who chastens his god because he loves his god: for he must perish of the wrath of his god.

"I love him whose soul is deep, even in being wounded, and who can perish of a small experience: thus he goes gladly over the bridge.

"I love him whose soul is overfull so that he forgets himself, and all things are in him: thus all things spell his going under.

"I love him who has a free spirit and a free heart: thus his head is only the entrails of his heart, but his heart drives him to go under.

"I love all those who are as heavy drops, falling one by one out of the dark cloud that hangs over men: they herald the advent of lightning, and, as heralds, they perish.

"Behold, I am a herald of the lightning and a heavy drop from the cloud; but this lightning is called *overman*."

* * *

FROM ZARATHUSTRA'S SPEECHES

ON THE THREE METAMORPHOSES

Of three metamorphoses of the spirit[8] I tell you: how the spirit [*der Geist*] becomes a camel; and the camel, a lion; and the lion, finally, a child.

There is much that is difficult for the spirit, the strong reverent spirit that would bear much: but the difficult and the most difficult are what its strength demands.

What is difficult? asks the spirit that would bear much, and kneels down

---

6. Better translated: "I love him who makes his virtue his compulsion and his undoing [*Hang und Verhängnis*]," though that does not capture Nietzsche's wordplay.

7. That is, "undoing," depletion (*Verhängnis*).

8. In *Zarathustra* and in Nietzsche's other writings as well, "spirit" translates *Geist*, a term Nietzsche found very apt and valuable in connection with many human psychological and cultural capacities, experiences, and activities.

like a camel wanting to be well loaded. What is most difficult, O heroes, asks the spirit that would bear much, that I may take it upon myself and exult in my strength? Is it not humbling oneself to wound one's haughtiness? Letting one's folly shine to mock one's wisdom?

Or is it this: parting from our cause when it triumphs? Climbing high mountains to tempt the tempter?

Or is it this: feeding on the acorns and grass of knowledge and, for the sake of the truth, suffering hunger in one's soul?

Or is it this: being sick and sending home the comforters and making friends with the deaf, who never hear what you want?

Or is it this: stepping into filthy waters when they are the waters of truth, and not repulsing cold frogs and hot toads?

Or is it this: loving those who despise us and offering a hand to the ghost that would frighten us?

All these most difficult things the spirit that would bear much takes upon itself: like the camel that, burdened, speeds into the desert, thus the spirit speeds into its desert.

In the loneliest desert, however, the second metamorphosis occurs: here the spirit becomes a lion who would conquer his freedom and be master in his own desert. Here he seeks out his last master: he wants to fight him and his last god; for ultimate victory he wants to fight with the great dragon.

Who is the great dragon whom the spirit will no longer call lord and god? "Thou shalt" is the name of the great dragon. But the spirit of the lion says, "I will." "Thou shalt" lies in his way, sparkling like gold, an animal covered with scales; and on every scale shines a golden "thou shalt."

Values, thousands of years old, shine on these scales; and thus speaks the mightiest of all dragons: "All value of all things shines on me. All value has long been created, and I am all created value. Verily, there shall be no more 'I will.'" Thus speaks the dragon.

My brothers, why is there a need in the spirit for the lion? Why is not the beast of burden, which renounces and is reverent, enough?

To create new values[9]—that even the lion cannot do; but the creation of freedom for oneself for new creation—that is within the power of the lion. The creation of freedom for oneself and a sacred "No" even to duty—for that, my brothers, the lion is needed. To assume the right to new values—that is the most terrifying assumption for a reverent spirit that would bear much. Verily, to him it is preying, and a matter for a beast of prey. He once loved "thou shalt" as most sacred: now he must find illusion and caprice even in the most sacred, that freedom from his love may become his prey: the lion is needed for such prey.

But say, my brothers, what can the child do that even the lion could not do? Why must the preying lion still become a child? The child is innocence and forgetting, a new beginning, a game, a self-propelled wheel, a first movement, a sacred "Yes." For the game of creation, my brothers, a sacred "Yes" is

---

9. Value, values, creativity, value creation, and "creat[ing] new values" are a cluster of concepts and themes that are central both to *Zarathustra* and to Nietzsche's more general response to pessimism and nihilism, of which his conception of the *Übermensch* as "the meaning of the earth" is the culminating expression.

needed: the spirit now wills his own will, and he who had been lost to the world now conquers his own world.

Of three metamorphoses of the spirit I have told you: how the spirit became a camel; and the camel, a lion; and the lion, finally, a child.

* * *

ON THE AFTERWORLDLY

At one time Zarathustra too cast his delusion beyond man, like all the afterworldly.[1] The work of a suffering and tortured god, the world then seemed to me. A dream the world then seemed to me, and the fiction of a god: colored smoke before the eyes of a dissatisfied deity. Good and evil and joy and pain and I and you—colored smoke this seemed to me before creative eyes. The creator wanted to look away from himself; so he created the world.

Drunken joy it is for the sufferer to look away from his suffering and to lose himself. Drunken joy and loss of self the world once seemed to me. This world, eternally imperfect, the image of an eternal contradiction, an imperfect image—a drunken joy for its imperfect creator: thus the world once appeared to me.

Thus I too once cast my delusion beyond man, like all the afterworldly. Beyond man indeed?

Alas, my brothers, this god whom I created was man-made and madness, like all gods! Man he was, and only a poor specimen of man and ego: out of my own ashes and fire this ghost came to me, and, verily, it did not come to me from beyond. What happened, my brothers? I overcame myself, the sufferer; I carried my own ashes to the mountains; I invented a brighter flame for myself. And behold, then this ghost *fled* from me. Now it would be suffering for me and agony for the recovered to believe in such ghosts: now it would be suffering for me and humiliation. Thus I speak to the afterworldly.

It was suffering and incapacity that created all after-worlds—this and that brief madness of bliss which is experienced only by those who suffer most deeply.

Weariness that wants to reach the ultimate with one leap,[2] with one fatal leap, a poor ignorant weariness that does not want to want any more: this created all gods and afterworlds.

Believe me, my brothers: it was the body that despaired of the body and touched the ultimate walls with the fingers of a deluded spirit. Believe me, my brothers: it was the body that despaired of the earth and heard the belly of being speak to it. It wanted to crash through these ultimate walls with its head, and not only with its head—over there to "that world." But "that world" is well concealed from humans—that dehumanized inhuman world which is

---

1. In German, *Hinterweltlern*, a term coined by Nietzsche to refer to those who look beyond this life and this world for a higher and different sort of power and reality that would make their lives more meaningful: *hinter* (behind, beyond)+*Welt* (world)+*lern* (i.e., those who go in for that sort of thing). The translation "the afterworldly" (i.e., "those who are afterworldly-minded") evokes the idea of an "afterlife"; but Nietzsche's focus here is on the preference for the *other*worldly in contrast to the *this*-worldly, rather than on what might come *after* this life.

2. This idea of hoping to reach "the ultimate with a *single* leap" (*mit Einem Sprunge zum Letzten*) seems to echo KIERKEGAARD's "leap of faith" to enter into a "God-relationship," upon which Nietzsche appears to be commenting here; but though Nietzsche had heard of Kierkegaard, he knew little about him and never read him.

a heavenly nothing; and the belly of being does not speak to humans at all, except as a human.

Verily, all being is hard to prove and hard to induce to speak. Tell me, my brothers, is not the strangest of all things proved most nearly?

Indeed, this ego and the ego's contradiction and confusion still speak most honestly of its being—this creating, willing, valuing ego, which is the measure and value of things. And this most honest being, the ego, speaks of the body and still wants the body, even when it poetizes and raves and flutters with broken wings. It learns to speak ever more honestly, this ego: and the more it learns, the more words and honors it finds for body and earth.

A new pride my ego taught me, and this I teach men: no longer to bury one's head in the sand of heavenly things, but to bear it freely, an earthly head, which creates a meaning for the earth.

A new will I teach men: to *will* this way which man has walked blindly, and to affirm it, and no longer to sneak away from it like the sick and decaying.

It was the sick and decaying who despised body and earth and invented the heavenly realm and the redemptive drops of blood: but they took even these sweet and gloomy poisons from body and earth. They wanted to escape their own misery, and the stars were too far for them. So they sighed: "Would that there were heavenly ways to sneak into another state of being and happiness!" Thus they invented their sneaky ruses and bloody potions. Ungrateful, these people deemed themselves transported from their bodies and this earth. But to whom did they owe the convulsions and raptures of their transport? To their bodies and this earth.

Zarathustra is gentle with the sick. Verily, he is not angry with their kinds of comfort and ingratitude. May they become convalescents, men of overcoming, and create a higher body for themselves! Nor is Zarathustra angry with the convalescent who eyes his delusion tenderly and, at midnight, sneaks around the grave of his god: but even so his tears still betray sickness and a sick body to me.

Many sick people have always been among the poetizers and God-cravers; furiously they hate the lover of knowledge and that youngest among the virtues, which is called "honesty."[3] They always look backward toward dark ages; then, indeed, delusion and faith were another matter: the rage of reason was godlikeness, and doubt was sin.

I know these godlike men all too well: they want one to have faith in them, and doubt to be sin. All too well I also know what it is in which they have most faith. Verily, it is not in afterworlds and redemptive drops of blood, but in the body, that they too have most faith; and their body is to them their thing-in-itself. But a sick thing it is to them, and gladly would they shed their skins. Therefore they listen to the preachers of death and themselves preach afterworlds.

Listen rather, my brothers, to the voice of the healthy body: that is a more honest and purer voice. More honestly and purely speaks the healthy body that is perfect and perpendicular: and it speaks of the meaning of the earth.

Thus spoke Zarathustra.

---

3. That is, intellectual integrity (*Redlichkeit*).

ON THE DESPISERS OF THE BODY

I want to speak to the despisers of the body. I would not have them learn and teach differently, but merely say farewell to their own bodies—and thus become silent.

"Body am I, and soul"—thus speaks the child. And why should one not speak like children?

But the awakened and knowing say: body am I entirely, and nothing else; and soul is only a word for something about the body.

The body is a great reason, a plurality with one sense, a war and a peace, a herd and a shepherd. An instrument of your body is also your little reason, my brother, which you call "spirit" [Geist]—a little instrument and toy of your great reason.

"I," you say, and are proud of the word. But greater is that in which you do not wish to have faith—your body and its great reason: that does not say "I," but does "I."

What the sense feels, what the spirit knows, never has its end in itself. But sense and spirit would persuade you that they are the end of all things: that is how vain they are. Instruments and toys are sense and spirit: behind them still lies the self. The self also seeks with the eyes of the senses; it also listens with the ears of the spirit. Always the self listens and seeks: it compares, over-powers, conquers, destroys. It controls, and it is in control of the ego too.

Behind your thoughts and feelings, my brother, there stands a mighty ruler, an unknown sage—whose name is self. In your body he dwells; he is your body.

There is more reason in your body than in your best wisdom. And who knows why your body needs precisely your best wisdom?

Your self laughs at your ego and at its bold leaps. "What are these leaps and flights of thought to me?" it says to itself. "A detour to my end. I am the leading strings of the ego and the prompter of its concepts."

The self says to the ego, "Feel pain here!" Then the ego suffers and thinks how it might suffer no more—and that is why it is *made* to think.

The self says to the ego, "Feel pleasure here!" Then the ego is pleased and thinks how it might often be pleased again—and that is why it is *made* to think.

I want to speak to the despisers of the body. It is their respect that begets their contempt. What is it that created respect and contempt and worth and will? The creative self created respect and contempt; it created pleasure and pain. The creative body created the spirit as a hand for its will.

Even in your folly and contempt, you despisers of the body, you serve your self. I say unto you: your self itself wants to die and turns away from life. It is no longer capable of what it would do above all else: to create beyond itself. That is what it would do above all else, that is its fervent wish.

But now it is too late for it to do this: so your self wants to go under, O despisers of the body. Your self wants to go under, and that is why you have become despisers of the body! For you are no longer able to create beyond yourselves.

And that is why you are angry with life and the earth. An unconscious envy speaks out of the squint-eyed glance of your contempt.

I shall not go your way, O despisers of the body! You are no bridge to the overman!

Thus spoke Zarathustra.

ON ENJOYING AND SUFFERING THE PASSIONS

My brother, if you have a virtue and she is your virtue, then you have her in common with nobody. To be sure, you want to call her by name and pet her; you want to pull her ear and have fun with her. And behold, now you have her name in common with the people and have become one of the people and herd with your virtue.

You would do better to say, "Inexpressible and nameless is that which gives my soul agony and sweetness and is even the hunger of my entrails."

May your virtue be too exalted for the familiarity of names: and if you must speak of her, then do not be ashamed to stammer of her. Then speak and stammer, "This is *my* good; this I love; it pleases me wholly; thus alone do *I* want the good. I do not want it as divine law; I do not want it as human statute and need: it shall not be a signpost for me to overearths and paradises. It is an earthly virtue that I love: there is little prudence in it, and least of all the reason of all men. But this bird built its nest with me: therefore I love and caress it; now it dwells with me, siting on its golden eggs." Thus you shall stammer and praise your virtue.

Once you suffered passions and called them evil. But now you have only your virtues left: they grew out of your passions. You commended your highest goal to the heart of these passions: then they become your virtues and passions you enjoyed.

And whether you came from the tribe of the choleric or of the voluptuous or of the fanatic or of the vengeful, in the end all your passions became virtues and all your devils, angels. Once you had wild dogs in your cellar, but in the end they turned into birds and lovely singers.[4] Out of your poisons you brewed your balsam. You milked your cow, melancholy; now you drink the sweet milk of her udder.

And nothing evil grows out of you henceforth, unless it be the evil that grows out of the fight among your virtues. My brother, if you are fortunate you have only one virtue and no more: then you will pass over the bridge more easily. It is a distinction to have many virtues, but a hard lot; and many have gone into the desert and taken their lives because they had wearied of being the battle and battlefield of virtues.

My brother, are war and battle evil? But this evil is necessary; necessary are the envy and mistrust and calumny among your virtues. Behold how each of your virtues covets what is highest: each wants your whole spirit that it might become *her* herald; each wants your whole strength in wrath, hatred, and love. Each virtue is jealous of the others, and jealousy is a terrible thing. Virtues too can perish of jealousy. Surrounded by the flame of jealousy, one will in the end, like the scorpion, turn one's poisonous sting against oneself. Alas, my brother, have you never yet seen a virtue deny and stab herself?

---

4. A figurative expression of *sublimation*, one of Nietzsche's most important concepts, used to explain how human life has come to differ significantly from mere animality, human spirituality has become a reality, and the enhancement of life can continue.

Man is something that must be overcome; and therefore you shall love your virtues, for you will perish of them.

Thus spoke Zarathustra.

* * *

ON THE THOUSAND AND ONE GOALS

Zarathustra saw many lands and many peoples: thus he discovered the good and evil of many peoples. And Zarathustra found no greater power on earth than good and evil.

No people could live without first esteeming;[5] but if they want to preserve themselves, then they must not esteem as the neighbor esteems. Much that was good to one people was scorn and infamy to another: thus I found it. Much I found called evil here, and decked out with purple honors there. Never did one neighbor understand the other: ever was his soul amazed at the neighbor's delusion and wickedness.

A tablet[6] of the good hangs over every people. Behold, it is the tablet of their overcomings; behold, it is the voice of their will to power.

Praiseworthy is whatever seems difficult to a people; whatever seems indispensable and difficult is called good; and whatever liberates even out of the deepest need, the rarest, the most difficult—that they call holy.

Whatever makes them rule and triumph and shine, to the awe and envy of their neighbors, that is to them the high, the first, the measure, the meaning of all things.

Verily, my brother, once you have recognized the need and land and sky and neighbor of a people, you may also guess the law of their overcomings, and why they climb to their hope on this ladder.

"You shall always be the first and excel all others: your jealous soul shall love no one, unless it be the friend"—that made the soul of the Greek quiver: thus he walked the path of his greatness.

"To speak the truth and to handle bow and arrow well"—that seemed both dear and difficult to the people who gave me my name[7]—the name which is both dear and difficult to me.

"To honor father and mother and to follow their will to the root of one's soul"—this was the tablet of overcoming that another people[8] hung up over themselves and became powerful and eternal thereby.

"To practice loyalty and, for the sake of loyalty, to risk honor and blood even for evil and dangerous things"—with this teaching another people[9] conquered themselves; and through this self-conquest they became pregnant and heavy with great hopes.

Verily, men gave themselves all their good and evil. Verily, they did not take it, they did not find it, nor did it come to them as a voice from heaven. Only man placed values in things to preserve himself—he alone created a meaning for things, a human meaning. Therefore he calls himself "man," which means: the esteemer.

---

5. That is, valuing positively (*schätzen*; its root, *Schatz*, means "treasure").
6. An image that recalls the tablet (*Tafel*) of the Ten Commandments.
7. The Persians.
8. The Jews.
9. The Germans.

To esteem is to create: hear this, you creators! Esteeming itself is of all esteemed things the most estimable treasure. Through esteeming alone is there value: and without esteeming, the nut of existence would be hollow.[1] Hear this, you creators!

Change of values—that is a change of creators. Whoever must be a creator always annihilates.

First, peoples were creators; and only in later times, individuals. Verily, the individual himself is still the most recent creation.

Once peoples hung a tablet of the good over themselves. Love which would rule and love which would obey have together created such tablets.

The delight in the herd is more ancient than the delight in the ego; and as long as the good conscience is identified with the herd, only the bad conscience says: I.

Verily, the clever ego, the loveless ego that desires its own profit in the profit of the many—that is not the origin of the herd, but its going under.

Good and evil have always been created by lovers and creators. The fire of love glows in the names of all the virtues, and the fire of wrath.

Zarathustra saw many lands and many peoples. No greater power did Zarathustra find on earth than the works of the lovers: "good" and "evil" are their names.

Verily, a monster is the power of this praising and censuring. Tell me, who will conquer it, O brothers? Tell me, who will throw a yoke over the thousand necks of this beast?

A thousand goals have there been so far, for there have been a thousand peoples. Only the yoke for the thousand necks is still lacking: the one goal is lacking. Humanity still has no goal.

But tell me, my brothers, if humanity still lacks a goal—is humanity itself not still lacking too?

Thus spoke Zarathustra.

* * *

From *Second Part*

* * *

UPON THE BLESSED ISLES

The figs are falling from the trees; they are good and sweet; and, as they fall, their red skin bursts. I am a north wind to ripe figs.

Thus, like figs, these teachings fall to you, my friends; now consume their juice and their sweet meat. It is autumn about us, and pure sky and afternoon. Behold what fullness there is about us! And out of such overflow it is beautiful to look out upon distant seas. Once one said God when one looked upon distant seas; but now I have taught you to say: overman.

God is a conjecture; but I desire that your conjectures should not reach beyond your creative will. Could you *create* a god? Then do not speak to me of any gods. But you could well create the overman. Perhaps not you yourselves,

---

1. This paragraph provides an important key to Nietzsche's idea of "value creation."

my brothers. But into fathers and forefathers of the overman you could re-create yourselves: and let this be your best creation.

God is a conjecture; but I desire that your conjectures should be limited by what is thinkable. Could you *think* a god? But this is what the will to truth should mean to you: that everything be changed into what is thinkable for man, visible for man, feelable by man. You should think through your own senses to their consequences.

And what you have called world, that shall be created only by you: your reason, your image, your will, your love shall thus be realized. And verily, for your own bliss, you lovers of knowledge.

And how would you bear life without this hope, you lovers of knowledge? You could not have been born either into the incomprehensible or into the irrational.

But let me reveal my heart to you entirely, my friends: *if* there were gods, how could I endure not to be a god! *Hence* there are no gods. Though I drew this conclusion, now it draws me.

God is a conjecture; but who could drain all the agony of this conjecture without dying? Shall his faith be taken away from the creator, and from the eagle, his soaring to eagle heights?

God is a thought that makes crooked all that is straight, and makes turn whatever stands. How? Should time be gone, and all that is impermanent a mere lie? To think this is a dizzy whirl for human bones, and a vomit for the stomach; verily, I call it the turning sickness to conjecture thus. Evil I call it, and misanthropic—all this teaching of the One and the Plenum and the Unmoved and the Sated and the Permanent. All the permanent—that is only a parable. And the poets lie too much.

It is of time and becoming that the best parables should speak: let them be a praise and a justification of all impermanence.

Creation—that is the great redemption from suffering, and life's growing light.[2] But that the creator may be, suffering is needed and much change. Indeed, there must be much bitter dying in your life, you creators. Thus are you advocates and justifiers of all impermanence. To be the child who is newly born, the creator must also want to be the mother who gives birth and the pangs of the birth-giver.

Verily, through a hundred souls I have already passed on my way, and through a hundred cradles and birth pangs. Many a farewell have I taken; I know the heartrending last hours. But thus my creative will, my destiny, wills it. Or, to say it more honestly: this very destiny—my will wills.

Whatever in me has feeling, suffers and is in prison; but my will always comes to me as my liberator and joy-bringer. Willing liberates: that is the true teaching of will and liberty—thus Zarathustra teaches it. Willing no more and esteeming no more and creating no more[3]—oh, that this great weariness might always remain far from me! In knowledge too I feel only my will's joy in begetting and becoming; and if there is innocence in my knowledge, it is because

2. A succinct expression of the thought at the very heart of this work, and of Nietzsche's answer to SCHOPENHAUER and response to the threat of "nihilism" (the conviction that life lacks any and all value and meaning).

3. In effect, the counsel of Schopenhauerian pessimism (what Nietzsche came to call "nihilism" in practice).

the will to beget is in it. Away from God and gods this will has lured me; what could one create if gods existed?

But my fervent will to create impels me ever again toward man; thus is the hammer impelled toward the stone. O men, in the stone there sleeps an image, the image of my images. Alas, that it must sleep in the hardest, the ugliest stone! Now my hammer rages cruelly against its prison. Pieces of rock rain from the stone: what is that to me? I want to perfect it; for a shadow came to me—the stillest and lightest of all things once came to me. The beauty of the overman came to me as a shadow. O my brothers, what are the gods to me now?

Thus spoke Zarathustra.

* * *

ON SELF-OVERCOMING

"Will to truth," you who are wisest call that which impels you and fills you with lust?

A will to the thinkability of all beings: this *I* call your will. You want to *make* all being thinkable, for you doubt with well-founded suspicion that it is already thinkable. But it shall yield and bend for you. Thus your will wants it. It shall become smooth and serve the spirit as its mirror and reflection. That is your whole will, you who are wisest: a will to power[4]—when you speak of good and evil too, and of valuations. You still want to create the world before which you can kneel: that is your ultimate hope and intoxication.

The unwise, of course, the people—they are like a river on which a bark drifts; and in the bark sit the valuations, solemn and muffled up. Your will and your valuations you have placed on the river of becoming; and what the people believe to be good and evil, that betrays to me an ancient will to power.

It was you who are wisest who placed such guests in this bark and gave them pomp and proud names—you and your dominant will. Now the river carries your bark farther; it *has* to carry it. It avails nothing that the broken wave foams and angrily opposes the keel. Not the river is your danger and the end of your good and evil, you who are wisest, but that will itself, the will to power—the unexhausted procreative will of life.

But to make you understand my word concerning good and evil, I shall now say to you my word concerning life and the nature of all the living.

I pursued the living; I walked the widest and the narrowest paths that I might know its nature. With a hundredfold mirror I still caught its glance when its mouth was closed, so that its eyes might speak to me. And its eyes spoke to me.

But wherever I found the living, there I heard also the speech on obedience. Whatever lives, obeys.

And this is the second point: he who cannot obey himself is commanded. That is the nature of the living.

This, however, is the third point that I heard: that commanding is harder than obeying; and not only because he who commands must carry the burden

---

4. This idea appeared earlier in Nietzsche's published writings as a specific psychological phenomenon; here he first employs it in interpreting "life" and "the living" and connects it to the idea of "self-overcoming."

of all who obey, and because this burden may easily crush him. An experiment and hazard appeared to me to be in all commanding; and whenever the living commands, it hazards itself. Indeed, even when it commands *itself*, it must still pay for its commanding. It must become the judge, the avenger, and the victim of its own law. How does this happen? I asked myself. What persuades the living to obey and command, and to practice obedience even when it commands?

Hear, then, my word, you who are wisest. Test in all seriousness whether I have crawled into the very heart of life and into the very roots of its heart.

Where I found the living, there I found will to power; and even in the will of those who serve I found the will to be master.

That the weaker should serve the stronger, to that it is persuaded by its own will, which would be master over what is weaker still: this is the one pleasure it does not want to renounce. And as the smaller yields to the greater that it may have pleasure and power over the smallest, thus even the greatest still yields, and for the sake of power risks life. That is the yielding of the greatest: it is hazard and danger and casting dice for death.

And where men make sacrifices and serve and cast amorous glances, there too is the will to be master. Along stealthy paths the weaker steals into the castle and into the very heart of the more powerful—and there steals power.

And life itself confided this secret to me: "Behold," it said, "I am *that which must always overcome itself*. Indeed, you call it a will to procreate or a drive to an end, to something higher, farther, more manifold: but all this is one, and one secret.

"Rather would I perish than forswear this; and verily, where there is perishing and a falling of leaves, behold, there life sacrifices itself—for power. That I must be struggle and a becoming and an end and an opposition to ends—alas, whoever guesses what is my will should also guess on what *crooked* paths it must proceed.

"Whatever I create and however much I love it—soon I must oppose it and my love; thus my will wills it. And you too, lover of knowledge, are only a path and footprint of my will; verily, my will to power walks also on the heels of your will to truth.

"Indeed, the truth was not hit by him[5] who shot at it with the word of the 'will to existence': that will does not exist. For, what does not exist cannot will; but what is in existence, how could that still want existence? Only where there is life is there also will: not will to life but—thus I teach you—will to power.

"There is much that life esteems more highly than life itself; but out of the esteeming itself speaks the will to power."

Thus life once taught me; and with this I shall yet solve the riddle of your heart, you who are wisest.

Verily, I say unto you: good and evil that are not transitory, do not exist. Driven on by themselves, they must overcome themselves again and again. With your values and words of good and evil you do violence when you value; and this is your hidden love and the splendor and trembling and overflowing of your soul. But a more violent force and a new overcoming grow out of your values and break egg and eggshell.

5. That is, Schopenhauer.

And whoever must be a creator in good and evil, verily, he must first be an annihilator and break values. Thus the highest evil belongs to the highest goodness: but this is creative.

Let us speak of this, you who are wisest, even if it be bad. Silence is worse; all truths that are kept silent become poisonous.

And may everything be broken that cannot brook our truths! There are yet many houses to be built!

Thus spoke Zarathustra.

* * *

From *Third Part*

* * *

FROM ON OLD AND NEW TABLETS

1

Here I sit and wait, surrounded by broken old tablets and new tablets half covered with writing. When will my hour come? The hour of my going down and going under; for I want to go among men once more. For that I am waiting now, for first the signs must come to me that *my* hour has come: the laughing lion with the flock of doves. Meanwhile I talk to myself as one who has time. Nobody tells me anything new: so I tell myself—myself.[6]

2

When I came to men I found them sitting on an old conceit:[7] the conceit that they have long known what is good and evil for man. All talk of virtue seemed an old and weary matter to man; and whoever wanted to sleep well still talked of good and evil before going to sleep.

I disturbed this sleepiness when I taught: what is good and evil *no one knows yet*, unless it be he who creates. He, however, creates man's goal and gives the earth its meaning and its future. That anything at all is good and evil—that is his creation.

And I bade them overthrow their old academic chairs and wherever that old conceit had sat; I bade them laugh at their great masters of virtue and saints and poets and world-redeemers. I bade them laugh at their gloomy sages and at whoever had at any time sat on the tree of life like a black scarecrow. I sat down by their great tomb road among cadavers and vultures, and I laughed at all their past and its rotting, decaying glory.

Verily, like preachers of repentance and fools, I raised a hue and cry of wrath over what among them is great and small, and that their best is still so small. And that their greatest evil too is still so small—at that I laughed.

My wise longing cried and laughed thus out of me—born in the mountains, verily, a wild wisdom—my great broad-winged longing! And often it swept me

---

6. Written a year after parts 1 and 2, part 3 has Zarathustra speaking in a very different voice; he is reflecting rather than making sermon-like speeches.

7. In German, *einem alten Dünkel*, an old supposition or belief widely shared and taken for granted.

away and up and far, in the middle of my laughter; and I flew, quivering, an arrow, through sun-drunken delight, away into distant futures which no dream had yet seen, into hotter souths than artists ever dreamed of, where gods in their dances are ashamed of all clothes—to speak in parables and to limp and stammer like poets; and verily, I am ashamed that I must still be a poet.

Where all becoming seemed to me the dance of gods and the prankishness of gods, and the world seemed free and frolicsome and as if fleeing back to itself—as an eternal fleeing and seeking each other again of many gods, as the happy controverting of each other, conversing again with each other, and converging again of many gods.

Where all time seemed to me a happy mockery of moments, where necessity was freedom itself playing happily with the sting of freedom.

Where I also found again my old devil and archenemy, the spirit of gravity,[8] and all that he created: constraint, statute, necessity and consequence and purpose and will and good and evil.

For must there not be that *over* which one dances and dances away? For the sake of the light and the lightest, must there not be moles and grave dwarfs?

3

There it was too that I picked up the word "overman" by the way, and that man is something that must be overcome—that man is a bridge and no end: proclaiming himself blessed in view of his noon and evening, as the way to new dawns—Zarathustra's word of the great noon, and whatever else I hung up over man like the last crimson light of evening.

Verily, I also let them see new stars along with new nights; and over clouds and day and night I still spread out laughter as a colorful tent.

I taught them all *my* creating and striving, to create and carry together into One what in man is fragment and riddle and dreadful accident; as creator, guesser of riddles, and redeemer of accidents, I taught them to work on the future and to redeem with their creation all that *has been*. To redeem what is past in man and to re-create all "it was" until the will says, "Thus I willed it! Thus I shall will it"—this I called redemption and this alone I taught them to call redemption.

Now I wait for my own redemption—that I may go to them for the last time. For I want to go to men once more; under their eyes I want to go under; dying, I want to give them my richest gift. From the sun I learned this: when he goes down, overrich; he pours gold into the sea out of inexhaustible riches, so that even the poorest fisherman still rows with golden oars. For this I once saw and I did not tire of my tears as I watched it.

Like the sun, Zarathustra too wants to go under; now he sits here and waits, surrounded by broken old tablets and new tablets half covered with writing.

4

Behold, here is a new tablet; but where are my brothers to carry it down with me to the valley and into hearts of flesh?

8. That is, "spirit of heavy seriousness" (*Geist der Schwere*).

Thus my great love of the farthest demands it: *do not spare your neighbor!* Man is something that must be overcome.

There are many ways of overcoming: see to that *yourself!* But only a jester thinks: "Man can also be *skipped over.*"

Overcome yourself even in your neighbor: and a right that you can rob you should not accept as a gift.

What you do, nobody can do to you in turn. Behold, there is no retribution.

He who cannot command himself should obey. And many *can* command themselves, but much is still lacking before they also obey themselves.

5

This is the manner of noble souls: they do not want to have anything for nothing; least of all, life. Whoever is of the mob wants to live for nothing; we others, however, to whom life gave itself, we always think about what we might best give in return. And verily, that is a noble speech which says, "What life promises us, we ourselves want to keep to life."

One shall not wish to enjoy where one does not give joy. And one shall not *wish* to enjoy! For enjoyment and innocence are the most bashful things: both do not want to be sought. One shall *possess* them—but rather *seek* even guilt and suffering.

6

My brothers, the firstling is always sacrificed. We, however, are firstlings. All of us bleed at secret sacrificial altars; all of us burn and roast in honor of old idols. What is best in us is still young: that attracts old palates. Our flesh is tender, our hide is a mere lambskin: how could we fail to attract old idol-priests? *Even in ourselves* the old idol-priest still lives who roasts what is best in us for his feast. Alas, my brothers, how could firstlings fail to be sacrifices?

But thus our kind wants it; and I love those who do not want to preserve themselves. Those who are going under I love with my whole love: for they cross over.

7

To be true—only a few are *able!* And those who are still lack the will. But the good[9] have this ability least of all. Oh, these good men! *Good men never speak the truth;* for the spirit, to be good in this way is a disease. They give in, these good men; they give themselves up; their heart repeats and their ground obeys: but whoever heeds commands does not heed *himself.*

Everything that the good call evil must come together so that one truth may be born. O my brothers, are you evil enough for this truth? The audacious daring, the long mistrust, the cruel No, the disgust, the cutting into the living—how rarely does all this come together. But from such seed is truth begotten.

Alongside the bad conscience, all science has grown so far. Break, break, you lovers of knowledge, the old tablets!

---

9. That is, those who are very "moral" by conventional standards of "good" and "evil."

8

When the water is spanned by planks, when bridges and railings leap over the river, verily, those are not believed who say, "Everything is in flux."[1] Even the blockheads contradict them. "How now?" say the blockheads. "Everything should be in flux? After all, planks and railings are *over* the river. Whatever is *over* the river is firm; all the values of things, the bridges, the concepts, all 'good' and 'evil'—all that is *firm*."

But when the hard winter comes, the river-animal tamer, then even the most quick-witted learn mistrust; and verily, not only the blockheads then say, "Does not everything *stand still*?"

"At bottom everything stands still"—that is truly a winter doctrine, a good thing for sterile times, a fine comfort for hibernators and hearth-squatters.

"At bottom everything stands still"—*against* this the thawing wind preaches. The thawing wind, a bull that is no plowing bull, a raging bull, a destroyer who breaks the ice with wrathful horns. Ice, however, *breaks bridges!*

O my brothers, is not everything in flux *now?* Have not all railings and bridges fallen into the water? Who could still cling to "good" and "evil"?

"Woe to us! Hail to us! The thawing wind blows!"—thus preach in every street, my brothers.

9

There is an old illusion, which is called good and evil. So far the wheel of this illusion has revolved around soothsayers and stargazers. Once man believed in soothsayers and stargazers, and therefore believed: "All is destiny: you ought to, for you must."

Then man again mistrusted all soothsayers and stargazers, and therefore believed: "All is freedom: you can, for you will."

O my brothers, so far there have been only illusions about stars and the future, not knowledge; and therefore there have been only illusions so far, not knowledge, about good and evil.

10

"Thou shalt not rob! Thou shalt not kill!" Such words were once called holy; one bent the knee and head and took off one's shoes before them. But I ask you: where have there ever been better robbers and killers in this world than such holy words?

Is there not in all life itself robbing and killing? And that such words were called holy—was not truth itself killed thereby? Or was it the preaching of death that was called holy, which contradicted and contravened all life? O my brothers, break, break the old tablets!

---

1. A famous saying attributed to Heraclitus (active ca. 500 B.C.E.), Nietzsche's favorite pre-Socratic philosopher.

11

This is my pity for all that is past: I see how all of it is abandoned—abandoned to the pleasure, the spirit, the madness of every generation, which comes along and reinterprets all that has been as a bridge to itself.

A great despot might come along, a shrewd monster who, according to his pleasure and displeasure, might constrain and strain all that is past till it becomes a bridge to him, a harbinger and herald and cockcrow.

This, however, is the other danger and what prompts my further pity: whoever is of the rabble, thinks back as far as the grandfather; with the grandfather, however, time ends.

Thus all that is past is abandoned: for one day the rabble might become master and drown all time in shallow waters.

Therefore, my brothers, a *new nobility* is needed to be the adversary of all rabble and of all that is despotic and to write anew upon new tablets the word "noble."[2]

For many who are noble are needed, and noble men of many kinds, that there may be a nobility. Or as I once said in a parable: "Precisely this is godlike that there are gods, but no God."

12

O my brothers, I dedicate and direct you to a new nobility: you shall become procreators and cultivators and sowers of the future—verily, not to a nobility that you might buy like shopkeepers and with shopkeepers' gold: for whatever has its price has little value.

Not whence you come shall henceforth constitute your honor, but whither you are going! Your will and your foot which has a will to go over and beyond yourselves—that shall constitute your new honor.

Verily, not that you have served a prince—what do princes matter now?—or that you became a bulwark for what stands that it might stand more firmly.

Not that your tribe has become courtly at court and that you have learned, like a flamingo, to stand for long hours in a colorful costume in shallow ponds—for the ability to stand is meritorious among courtiers; and all courtiers believe that blessedness after death must comprise permission to sit.

Nor that a spirit which they call holy led your ancestors into promised lands, which I do not praise—for where the worst of all trees grew, the cross, that land deserves no praise. And verily, wherever this "Holy Spirit" led his knights, on all such crusades goose aids goat in leading the way, and the contrary and crude sailed foremost.

O my brothers, your nobility should not look backward but ahead! Exiles shall you be from all father- and forefather-lands! Your *children's land* shall you love: this love shall be your new nobility—the undiscovered land in the most distant sea. For that I bid your sails search and search.

---

2. This "new nobility" of quality, a "higher humanity" in which the best and most creative of human possibilities would be realized, is the alternative envisioned by Nietzsche to the two dangerous possibilities mentioned earlier: that either our "all too human" baser tendencies or the disposition to brutal manifestations of our elemental "will to power" in the rule of mere "force" (*Gewalt-Herrschen*) would prevail.

In your children you shall make up for being the children of your fathers: thus shall you redeem all that is past. This new tablet I place over you.

13

"Why live? All is vanity! Living—that is threshing straw; living—that is consuming oneself in flames without becoming warm."[3] Such antiquarian babbling is still considered "wisdom"; it is honored all the more for being old and musty. Mustiness too ennobles.

Children might speak thus: they fear the fire because it burned them. There is much childishness in the old books of wisdom. And why should those who always "thresh *straw*" be allowed to blaspheme threshing? Such oxen should be muzzled after all.

Such men sit down to the table and bring nothing along, not even a good appetite; and then they blaspheme: "All is vanity." But eating and drinking well, O my brothers, is verily no vain art. Break, break the old tablets of the never gay!

14

"To the clean all is clean," the people say. But I say unto you, "To the mean[4] all becomes mean."

Therefore the swooners and head-hangers, whose hearts also hang limply, preach, "The world itself is a filthy monster." For all these have an unclean spirit—but especially those who have neither rest nor repose except when they see the world from *abaft*,[5] the afterworldly. To these I say to their faces, even though it may not sound nice: the world is like man in having a backside abaft; that much is true. There is much filth in the world; that much is true. But that does not make the world itself a filthy monster.

There is wisdom in this, that there is much in the world that smells foul: nausea itself creates wings and water-divining powers. Even in the best there is still something that nauseates; and even the best is something that must be overcome. O my brothers, there is much wisdom in this, that there is much filth in the world.

15

Such maxims I heard pious afterworldly people speak to their conscience—verily, without treachery or falseness, although there is nothing falser in the whole world, nothing more treacherous:

"Let the world go its way! Do not raise one finger against it!"

"Let him who wants to, strangle and stab and fleece and flay the people. Do not raise one finger against it! Thus will they learn to renounce the world."

"And your own reason—you yourself should stifle and strangle it; for it is a reason of this world; thus will you yourself learn to renounce the world."

Break, break, O my brothers, these old tablets of the pious. Break the maxims of those who slander the world.

---

3. The appeal made by Schopenhauerian pessimism, whose attraction Nietzsche clearly continued to feel and therefore to fear.

4. Literally, "swine" (*Schwein*).
5. That is, "from behind" (*von hinten*).

16

"Whoever learns much will unlearn all violent desire"—that is whispered today in all the dark lanes.

"Wisdom makes weary; worth while is—nothing; thou shalt not desire!"—this new tablet I found hanging even in the open market places.

Break, O my brothers, break this *new* tablet too. The world-weary hung it up, and the preachers of death, and also the jailers; for behold, it is also an exhortation to bondage. Because they learned badly, and the best things not at all, and everything too early and everything too hastily; because they *ate* badly, therefore they got upset stomachs; for their spirit is an upset stomach which counsels death. For verily, my brothers, the spirit *is* a stomach. Life is a well of joy; but for those out of whom an upset stomach speaks, which is the father of melancholy, all wells are poisoned.

To gain knowledge is a *joy* for the lion-willed! But those who have become weary are themselves merely being "willed," and all the billows play with them. And this is always the manner of the weak: they get lost on the way. And in the end their weariness still asks, "Why did we ever pursue any way at all? It is all the same." *Their* ears appreciate the preaching, "Nothing is worth while! You shall not will!" Yet this is an exhortation to bondage.

O my brothers, like a fresh roaring wind Zarathustra comes to all who are weary of the way; many noses he will yet make sneeze. Through walls too, my free breath blows, and into prisons and imprisoned spirits. To will liberates, for to will is to create: thus I teach. And you shall learn solely in order to create.

And you shall first *learn* from me how to learn—how to learn well. He that has ears to hear, let him hear!

* * *

SOURCE: From *The Portable Nietzsche*, selected and translated by Walter Kaufmann (New York: Viking, 1954), pp. 121–28, 137–39, 142–49, 170–73, 197–200, 225–28, 308–18. Originally published as *Also Sprach Zarathustra* in four parts (1883–85).

From Beyond Good and Evil

Preface

Supposing truth is a woman[1]—what then? Are there not grounds for the suspicion that all philosophers, insofar as they were dogmatists, have been very inexpert about women? That the gruesome seriousness, the clumsy obtrusiveness with which they have usually approached truth so far have been awkward and very improper methods for winning a woman's heart? What is certain is that she has not allowed herself to be won—and today every kind of dogmatism is left standing dispirited and discouraged. *If* it is left standing at all!

1. Nietzsche is here playing on the grammatical gender of German nouns—"the truth" (*die Wahrheit*), like all nouns ending in -*heit*, is feminine— and on stereotypes about women and men. His scorn is directed not at women or the feminine but at philosophers and their general ineptness.

For there are scoffers who claim that it has fallen, that all dogmatism lies on the ground—even more, that all dogmatism is dying.

Speaking seriously, there are good reasons why all philosophical dogmatizing, however solemn and definitive its airs used to be, may nevertheless have been no more than a noble childishness and tyronism.[2] And perhaps the time is at hand when it will be comprehended again and again *how little* used to be sufficient to furnish the cornerstone for such sublime and unconditional philosophers' edifices as the dogmatists have built so far: any old popular superstition from time immemorial (like the soul superstition which, in the form of the subject and ego superstition, has not even yet ceased to do mischief); some play on words perhaps, a seduction by grammar, or an audacious generalization of very narrow, very personal, very human, all too human facts.

The dogmatists' philosophy was, let us hope, only a promise across millennia—as astrology was in still earlier times when perhaps more work, money, acuteness, and patience were lavished in its service than for any real science so far: to astrology and its "supra-terrestrial" claims we owe the grand style of architecture in Asia and Egypt. It seems that all great things first have to bestride the earth in monstrous and frightening masks in order to inscribe themselves in the hearts of humanity with eternal demands: dogmatic philosophy was such a mask; for example, the Vedanta doctrine in Asia and Platonism[3] in Europe.

Let us not be ungrateful to it, although it must certainly be conceded that the worst, most durable, and most dangerous of all errors so far was a dogmatist's error—namely, Plato's invention of the pure spirit and the good as such.[4] But now that it is overcome, now that Europe is breathing freely again after this nightmare and at least can enjoy a healthier—sleep, we, *whose task is wakefulness itself*, are the heirs of all that strength which has been fostered by the fight against this error. To be sure, it meant standing truth on her head and denying *perspective*, the basic condition of all life,[5] when one spoke of spirit and the good as Plato did. Indeed, as a physician one might ask: "How could the most beautiful growth of antiquity, Plato, contract such a disease? Did the wicked Socrates corrupt him after all? Could Socrates have been the corrupter of youth after all? And did he deserve his hemlock?"[6]

But the fight against Plato or, to speak more clearly and for "the people," the fight against the Christian-ecclesiastical pressure of millennia—for Christianity is Platonism for "the people"—has created in Europe a magnificent tension of the spirit the like of which had never yet existed on earth: with so tense a bow we can now shoot for the most distant goals. To be sure, European man experiences this tension as need and distress; twice already attempts

---

2. That is, the ineptness of a novice or beginner (*Anfängerei*).

3. Philosophy based on the thinking of the Greek philosopher Plato (ca. 427–ca. 347 B.C.E.), which accords true reality to an intelligible but imperceptible realm of eternal immutable Forms that transcend and ground the derivative world of life and experience. "The Vedanta doctrine": a system of philosophy developed from the 9th to 13th centuries C.E. that emphasizes the identity of the individual soul and the world-soul; it forms the basis of most modern schools of Hinduism.

4. That is, the Ideas or Forms of "pure spirit" (*reinen Geiste*) and "the good" ([*dem*] *Guten*), which Plato argued existed independently of and were more real than their instantiations in the sensible world.

5. This is Nietzsche's primary application of the idea of "perspective" in this book—the only book in which he makes significant use of it.

6. Socrates (469–399 B.C.E.), Plato's teacher, was prosecuted for impiety and corrupting the youth of Athens; he was found guilty and sentenced to death (by drinking hemlock, a poison).

have been made in the grand style to unbend the bow—once by means of Jesuitism,[7] the second time by means of the democratic enlightenment which, with the aid of freedom of the press and newspaper-reading, might indeed bring it about that the spirit would no longer experience itself so easily as a "need." (The Germans have invented gunpowder—all due respect for that!— but then they made up for that: they invented the press.[8]) But we who are neither Jesuits nor democrats, nor even German enough, we *good Europeans* and free, *very* free spirits—we still feel it, the whole need of the spirit and the whole tension of its bow. And perhaps also the arrow, the task, and—who knows?—the *goal*——

Sils Maria, Upper Engadine,
June 1885[9]

From *PART ONE*
On the Prejudices of Philosophers[1]

1

The will to truth which will still tempt us to many a venture, that famous truthfulness of which all philosophers so far have spoken with respect—what questions has this will to truth not laid before us! What strange, wicked, questionable questions! That is a long story even now—and yet it seems as if it had scarcely begun. Is it any wonder that we should finally become suspicious, lose patience, and turn away impatiently? that we should finally learn from this Sphinx[2] to ask questions, too? *Who* is it really that puts questions to us here? *What* in us really wants "truth"?

Indeed we came to a long halt at the question about the cause of this will— until we finally came to a complete stop before a still more basic question. We asked about the *value* of this will. Suppose we want truth: *why not rather* untruth? and uncertainty? even ignorance?

The problem of the value of truth came before us—or was it we who came before the problem? Who of us is Oedipus here? Who the Sphinx? It is a rendezvous, it seems, of questions and question marks.

And though it scarcely seems credible, it finally almost seems to us as if the problem had never even been put so far—as if we were the first to see it, fix it with our eyes, and *risk* it. For it does involve a risk, and perhaps there is none that is greater.

---

7. Nietzsche saw the Jesuits, a Catholic religious order founded in 1540 that played a prominent role in evangelism and religious education, as leading the Christian campaign to "unbend the bow" by teaching and cultivating the resolute subordination of thought to faith.
8. The printing press, invented by the German printer Johannes Gutenberg (d. 1468).
9. The date of the preface; however, much of the book was drawn from or anticipated by material from Nietzsche's notebooks of the previous several years, during which his primary focus and only

publication was *Thus Spoke Zarathustra* (1883–85; see above).
1. Literally, "prejudgments" (*Vorurtheilen* or *Vorurteilen*); that is, things assumed and taken for granted.
2. In Greek mythology, a winged female monster with a lion's body and human head that killed all who failed to answer her riddle; after it was correctly answered by Oedipus (who was rewarded by becoming king of Thebes and unwittingly marrying his mother), she killed herself.

2

"How *could* anything originate out of its opposite? for example, truth out of error? or the will to truth out of the will to deception? or selfless deeds out of selfishness? or the pure and sunlike gaze of the sage out of lust? Such origins are impossible; whoever dreams of them is a fool, indeed worse; the things of the highest value must have another, *peculiar* origin—they cannot be derived from this transitory, seductive, deceptive, paltry world, from this turmoil of delusion and lust. Rather from the lap[3] of Being, the intransitory, the hidden god, the 'thing-in-itself'—there must be their basis, and nowhere else."

This way of judging constitutes the typical prejudgment and prejudice which give away the metaphysicians of all ages; this kind of valuation looms in the background of all their logical procedures; it is on account of this "faith" that they trouble themselves about "knowledge," about something that is finally baptized solemnly as "the truth." The fundamental faith of the metaphysicians is *the faith in opposite values*. It has not even occurred to the most cautious among them that one might have a doubt right here at the threshold where it was surely most necessary—even if they vowed to themselves, *"de omnibus dubitandum."*[4]

For one may doubt, first, whether there are any opposites at all, and secondly whether these popular valuations and opposite values on which the metaphysicians put their seal, are not perhaps merely foreground estimates, only provisional perspectives, perhaps even from some nook, perhaps from below, frog perspectives, as it were, to borrow an expression painters use. For all the value that the true, the truthful, the selfless may deserve, it would still be possible that a higher and more fundamental value for life might have to be ascribed to deception, selfishness, and lust. It might even be possible that what constitutes the value of these good and revered things is precisely that they are insidiously related, tied to, and involved with these wicked, seemingly opposite things—maybe even one with them in essence. Maybe!

But who has the will to concern himself with such dangerous maybes? For that, one really has to wait for the advent of a new species of philosophers, such as have somehow another and converse taste and propensity from those we have known so far—philosophers of the dangerous "maybe" in every sense.

And in all seriousness: I see such new philosophers coming up.

3

After having looked long enough between the philosopher's lines and fingers, I say to myself: by far the greater part of conscious thinking must still be included among instinctive activities, and that goes even for philosophical thinking. We have to relearn here, as one has had to relearn about heredity and what is "innate." As the act of birth deserves no consideration in the whole process and procedure of heredity, so "being conscious" is not in any decisive sense the *opposite* of what is instinctive: most of the conscious thinking of a philosopher is secretly guided and forced into certain channels by his instincts.

Behind all logic and its seeming sovereignty of movement, too, there stand

---

3. Literally, "womb" (*Schoss*).
4. "Everything must be doubted" (Latin), a maxim attributed to the French philosopher and mathematician René Descartes (1596–1650).

valuations or, more clearly, physiological demands for the preservation of a certain type of life. For example, that the definite should be worth more than the indefinite, and mere appearance worth less than "truth"—such estimates might be, in spite of their regulative importance for *us*, nevertheless mere foreground estimates, a certain kind of *niaiserie*[5] which may be necessary for the preservation of just such beings as we are. Supposing, that is, that not just man is the "measure of things."

4

The falseness of a judgment is for us not necessarily an objection to a judgment; in this respect our new language may sound strangest. The question is to what extent it is life-promoting, life-preserving, species-preserving, perhaps even species-cultivating. And we are fundamentally inclined to claim that the falsest judgments (which include the synthetic judgments *a priori*)[6] are the most indispensable for us; that without accepting the fictions of logic, without measuring reality against the purely invented world of the unconditional and self-identical, without a constant falsification of the world by means of numbers, man could not live—that renouncing false judgments would mean renouncing life and a denial of life. To recognize untruth as a condition of life—that certainly means resisting accustomed value feelings in a dangerous way; and a philosophy that risks this would by that token alone place itself beyond good and evil.

5

What provokes one to look at all philosophers half suspiciously, half mockingly, is not that one discovers again and again how innocent they are—how often and how easily they make mistakes and go astray; in short, their childishness and childlikeness—but that they are not honest enough in their work, although they all make a lot of virtuous noise when the problem of truthfulness is touched even remotely. They all pose as if they had discovered and reached their real opinions through the self-development of a cold, pure, divinely unconcerned dialectic (as opposed to the mystics of every rank, who are more honest and doltish—and talk of "inspiration"); while at bottom it is an assumption, a hunch, indeed a kind of "inspiration"—most often a desire of the heart that has been filtered and made abstract—that they defend with reasons they have sought after the fact. They are all advocates who resent that name, and for the most part even wily spokesmen for their prejudices which they baptize "truths"—and *very* far from having the courage of the conscience that admits this, precisely this, to itself; very far from having the good taste of the courage which also lets this be known, whether to warn an enemy or friend, or, from exuberance, to mock itself.

The equally stiff and decorous Tartuffery of the old Kant as he lures us on the dialectical bypaths that lead to his "categorical imperative"[7]—really lead astray and seduce—this spectacle makes us smile, as we are fastidious and find

---

5. Folly, stupidity, silliness: one of Nietzsche's favorite French words [translator's note].
6. That is, judgments that, according to KANT, can be known before experience confirms them and yet say something that is true and significant (beyond a matter of definition) about experience or

what is experienced (e.g., "every event has a cause").
7. A moral law that is absolute for all agents (Kant's fundamental principle of morality). "Tartuffery": hypocrisy, like that shown by the title character in Molière's play *Tartuffe* (1664).

it quite amusing to watch closely the subtle tricks of old moralists and preachers of morals. Or consider the hocus-pocus of mathematical form with which Spinoza[8] clad his philosophy[.]

* * *

12

As for materialistic atomism, it is one of the best refuted theories there are, and in Europe perhaps no one in the learned world is now so unscholarly as to attach serious significance to it, except for convenient household use (as an abbreviation of the means of expression)—thanks chiefly to the Dalmatian Boscovich: he and the Pole Copernicus[9] have been the greatest and most successful opponents of visual evidence so far. For while Copernicus has persuaded us to believe, contrary to all the senses, that the earth does *not* stand fast, Boscovich has taught us to abjure the belief in the last part of the earth that "stood fast"— the belief in "substance," in "matter," in the earth-residuum and particle-atom: it is the greatest triumph over the senses that has been gained on earth so far.

One must, however, go still further, and also declare war, relentless war unto death, against the "atomistic need" which still leads a dangerous afterlife in places where no one suspects it, just like the more celebrated "metaphysical need": one must also, first of all, give the finishing stroke to that other and more calamitous atomism which Christianity has taught best and longest, the *soul atomism.* Let it be permitted to designate by this expression the belief which regards the soul as something indestructible, eternal, indivisible, as a monad, as an *atomon:* this belief ought to be expelled from science! Between ourselves, it is not at all necessary to get rid of "the soul" at the same time, and thus to renounce one of the most ancient and venerable hypotheses—as happens frequently to clumsy naturalists who can hardly touch on "the soul" without immediately losing it.[1] But the way is open for new versions and refinements of the soul-hypothesis; and such conceptions as "mortal soul," and "soul as subjective multiplicity," and "soul as social structure of the drives and affects,"[2] want henceforth to have citizens' rights in science. When the *new* psychologist puts an end to the superstitions which have so far flourished with almost tropical luxuriance around the idea of the soul, he practically exiles himself into a new desert and a new suspicion—it is possible that the older psychologists had a merrier and more comfortable time of it; eventually, however, he finds that precisely thereby he also condemns himself to *invention*—and—who knows?—perhaps to discovery.

8. Benedict (Baruch) de Spinoza (1632–1677), Dutch philosopher.
9. Nicolaus Copernicus (1473–1543), Polish astronomer in whose theory of the solar system the earth orbits the sun; in the traditional view, the earth is assumed to be stationary and at the center of the universe. Ruggero Giuseppe Boscovich (1711–1787), astronomer and mathematician from Ragusa in Dalmatia (now Dubrovnik, Croatia); in his *Theory of Natural Philosophy* (1763), he proposed an early description of atomic theory.
1. It is important to distinguish between the kind of "naturalizing" thinking and reinterpreting that Nietzsche calls for in *Gay Science* §109 (above)— the kind of naturalism he himself pursues—and the simplistic scientist kind of naturalism he disparages here and elsewhere (e.g., in *Gay Science* §373, below).
2. That is, dispositions, inclinations, passions (*Affekte*).

13

Physiologists should think before putting down the instinct of self-preservation as the cardinal instinct of an organic being. A living thing seeks above all to *discharge* its strength—life itself is *will to power*;[3] self-preservation is only one of the indirect and most frequent *results*.

In short, here as everywhere else, let us beware of *superfluous* teleological principles[4]—one of which is the instinct of self-preservation (we owe it to Spinoza's inconsistency).[5] Thus method, which must be essentially economy of principles, demands it.

14

It is perhaps just dawning on five or six minds that physics, too, is only an interpretation and exegesis of the world (to suit us, if I may say so!) and *not* a world-explanation; but insofar as it is based on belief in the senses, it is regarded as more, and for a long time to come must be regarded as more— namely, as an explanation. Eyes and fingers speak in its favor, visual evidence and palpableness do, too: this strikes an age with fundamentally plebeian tastes as fascinating, persuasive, and *convincing*—after all, it follows instinctively the canon of truth of eternally popular sensualism. What is clear, what is "explained"? Only what can be seen and felt—every problem has to be pursued to that point. Conversely, the charm of the Platonic way of thinking, which was a *noble* way of thinking, consisted precisely in *resistance* to obvious sense-evidence—perhaps among men who enjoyed even stronger and more demanding senses than our contemporaries, but who knew how to find a higher triumph in remaining masters of their senses—and this by means of pale, cold, gray concept nets which they threw over the motley whirl of the senses—the mob of the senses, as Plato said. In this overcoming of the world, and interpreting of the world in the manner of Plato, there was an *enjoyment* different from that which the physicists of today offer us—and also the Darwinists[6] and anti-teleologists among the workers in physiology, with their principle of the "smallest possible force" and the greatest possible stupidity. "Where man cannot find anything to see or to grasp, he has no further business"—that is certainly an imperative different from the Platonic one, but it may be the right imperative for a tough, industrious race of machinists and bridge-builders of the future, who have nothing but *rough* work to do.

15

To study physiology with a clear conscience, one must insist that the sense organs are *not* phenomena in the sense of idealistic philosophy; as such they

3. Here Nietzsche restates in his own voice what he said through Zarathustra in "On Self-Overcoming" in *Thus Spoke Zarathustra*, part 2 (see above).
4. That is, principles that explain natural phenomena in terms of ends, goals, or purposes.
5. While generally critical of teleological principles and explanations, Spinoza viewed the "principle of self-preservation" as a fundamental principle of reality. In Nietzsche's view, his "will to power" hypothesis makes the principle of self-preservation superfluous.
6. Those who follow the English naturalist Charles Darwin (1809–1882) in embracing the theory of natural selection to explain development.

could not be causes! Sensualism,[7] therefore, at least as a regulative hypothesis, if not as a heuristic principle.

What? And others even say that the external world is the work of our organs? But then our body, as a part of this external world, would be the work of our organs! But then our organs themselves would be—the work of our organs! It seems to me that this is a complete *reductio ad absurdum*, assuming that the concept of a *causa sui*[8] is something fundamentally absurd. Consequently, the external world is *not* the work of our organs—?

16

There are still harmless self-observers who believe that there are "immediate certainties"; for example, "I think," or as the superstition of Schopenhauer put it, "I will"; as though knowledge here got hold of its object purely and nakedly as "the thing in itself," without any falsification on the part of either the subject or the object. But that "immediate certainty," as well as "absolute knowledge" and the "thing in itself," involve a *contradictio in adjecto*,[9] I shall repeat a hundred times; we really ought to free ourselves from the seduction of words!

Let the people suppose that knowledge means knowing things entirely; the philosopher must say to himself: When I analyze the process that is expressed in the sentence, "I think,"[1] I find a whole series of daring assertions that would be difficult, perhaps impossible, to prove; for example, that it is *I* who think, that there must necessarily be something that thinks, that thinking is an activity and operation on the part of a being who is thought of as a cause, that there is an "ego," and, finally, that it is already determined what is to be designated by thinking—that I *know* what thinking is. For if I had not already decided within myself what it is, by what standard could I determine whether that which is just happening is not perhaps "willing" or "feeling"? In short, the assertion "I think" assumes that I *compare* my state at the present moment with other states of myself which I know, in order to determine what it is; on account of this retrospective connection with further "knowledge," it has, at any rate, no immediate certainty for me.

In place of the "immediate certainty" in which the people may believe in the case at hand, the philosopher thus finds a series of metaphysical questions presented to him, truly searching questions of the intellect; to wit: "From where do I get the concept of thinking? Why do I believe in cause and effect? What gives me the right to speak of an ego, and even of an ego as cause, and finally of an ego as the cause of thought?" Whoever ventures to answer these metaphysical questions at once by an appeal to a sort of *intuitive* perception, like the person who says, "I think, and know that this, at least, is true, actual, and certain"—will encounter a smile and two question marks from a philosopher nowadays. "Sir," the philosopher will perhaps give him to understand, "it is improbable that you are not mistaken; but why insist on the truth?"—

---

7. The view that what the senses (our sense organs) deliver is the basis of all knowledge; it is here proposed as a guide for interpretive thought, whether or not it is useful for problem solving.
8. Cause of itself (Latin).

9. A contradiction in what is added (Latin); that is, a contradiction in terms.
1. The famous starting point of Descartes (*cogito*), which he took to be an absolutely simple and clear noninferential certainty.

17

With regard to the superstitions of logicians, I shall never tire of emphasizing a small terse fact, which these superstitious minds hate to concede—namely, that a thought comes when "it" wishes, and not when "I" wish, so that it is a falsification of the facts of the case to say that the subject "I" is the condition of the predicate "think." It thinks; but that this "it" is precisely the famous old "ego" is, to put it mildly, only a supposition, an assertion, and assuredly not an "immediate certainty." After all, one has even gone too far with this "it thinks"—even the "it" contains an *interpretation* of the process, and does not belong to the process itself. One infers here according to the grammatical habit: "Thinking is an activity; every activity requires an agent; consequently—"

It was pretty much according to the same schema that the older atomism sought, besides the operating "power," that lump of matter in which it resides and out of which it operates—the atom. More rigorous minds, however, learned at last to get along without this "earth-residuum," and perhaps some day we shall accustom ourselves, including the logicians, to get along without the little "it" (which is all that is left of the honest little old ego).

18

It is certainly not the least charm of a theory that it is refutable; it is precisely thereby that it attracts subtler minds. It seems that the hundred-times-refuted theory of a "free will" owes its persistence to this charm alone; again and again someone comes along who feels he is strong enough to refute it.

19

Philosophers are accustomed to speak of the will as if it were the best-known thing in the world; indeed, Schopenhauer has given us to understand that the will alone is really known to us, absolutely and completely known, without subtraction or addition.[2] But again and again it seems to me that in this case, too, Schopenhauer only did what philosophers are in the habit of doing—he adopted a *popular prejudice* and exaggerated it. Willing seems to me to be above all something *complicated*, something that is a unit only as a word—and it is precisely in this one word that the popular prejudice lurks, which has defeated the always inadequate caution of philosophers. So let us for once be more cautious, let us be "unphilosophical": let us say that in all willing there is, first, a plurality of sensations, namely, the sensation of the state *"away from which,"* the sensation of the state *"towards which,"* the sensations of this *"from"* and *"towards"* themselves, and then also an accompanying muscular sensation, which, even without our putting into motion "arms and legs," begins its action by force of habit as soon as we "will" anything.

Therefore, just as sensations (and indeed many kinds of sensations) are to be recognized as ingredients of the will, so, secondly, should thinking also: in every act of the will there is a ruling thought—let us not imagine it

2. In *The World as Will and Representation* (1818; 2nd ed., 1844); see above.

possible to sever this thought from the "willing," as if any will would then remain over!

Third, the will is not only a complex of sensation and thinking, but it is above all an *affect*, and specifically the affect of the command. That which is termed "freedom of the will" is essentially the affect of superiority in relation to him who must obey: "I am free, 'he' must obey"—this consciousness is inherent in every will; and equally so the straining of the attention, the straight look that fixes itself exclusively on one aim, the unconditional evaluation that "this and nothing else is necessary now," the inward certainty that obedience will be rendered—and whatever else belongs to the position of the commander. A man who *wills* commands something within himself that renders obedience, or that he believes renders obedience.

But now let us notice what is strangest about the will—this manifold thing for which the people have only one word: inasmuch as in the given circumstances we are at the same time the commanding *and* the obeying parties, and as the obeying party we know the sensations of constraint, impulsion, pressure, resistance, and motion, which usually begin immediately after the act of will; inasmuch as, on the other hand, we are accustomed to disregard this duality, and to deceive ourselves about it by means of the synthetic concept "I," a whole series of erroneous conclusions, and consequently of false evaluations of the will itself, has become attached to the act of willing—to such a degree that he who wills believes sincerely that willing *suffices* for action. Since in the great majority of cases there has been exercise of will only when the effect of the command—that is, obedience; that is, the action—was to be *expected*, the *appearance* has translated itself into the feeling, as if there were *a necessity of effect*. In short, he who wills believes with a fair amount of certainty that will and action are somehow one; he ascribes the success, the carrying out of the willing, to the will itself, and thereby enjoys an increase of the sensation of power which accompanies all success.

"Freedom of the will"—that is the expression for the complex state of delight of the person exercising volition, who commands and at the same time identifies himself with the executor of the order—who, as such, enjoys also the triumph over obstacles, but thinks within himself that it was really his will itself that overcame them. In this way the person exercising volition adds the feelings of delight of his successful executive instruments, the useful "under-wills" or under-souls—indeed, our body is but a social structure composed of many souls—to his feelings of delight as commander. *L'effet c'est moi*:[3] what happens here is what happens in every well-constructed and happy commonwealth; namely, the governing class identifies itself with the successes of the commonwealth. In all willing it is absolutely a question of commanding and obeying, on the basis, as already said, of a social structure composed of many "souls." Hence a philosopher should claim the right to include willing as such within the sphere of morals [*Moral*]—morals being understood as the doctrine of the relations of supremacy under which the phenomenon of "life" comes to be.

---

3. *I* am the effect! (French; literally, "The effect is me"); similar playing on the statement famously (though probably falsely) ascribed to Louis XIV, king of France (r. 1643–1715): "L'état, c'est moi" (*I* am the state).

20

That individual philosophical concepts are not anything capricious or auton-omously evolving, but grow up in connection and relationship with each other; that, however suddenly and arbitrarily they seem to appear in the history of thought, they nevertheless belong just as much to a system as all the mem-bers of the fauna of a continent—is betrayed in the end also by the fact that the most diverse philosophers keep filling in a definite fundamental scheme of *possible* philosophies. Under an invisible spell, they always revolve once more in the same orbit; however independent of each other they may feel themselves with their critical or systematic wills, something within them leads them, something impels them in a definite order, one after the other— to wit, the innate systematic structure and relationship of their concepts. Their thinking is, in fact, far less a discovery than a recognition, a remem-bering, a return and a homecoming to a remote, primordial, and inclusive household of the soul, out of which those concepts grew originally: philoso-phizing is to this extent a kind of atavism[4] of the highest order.

The strange family resemblance of all Indian, Greek, and German philoso-phizing is explained easily enough. Where there is affinity of languages,[5] it cannot fail, owing to the common philosophy of grammar—I mean, owing to the unconscious domination and guidance by similar grammatical functions— that everything is prepared at the outset for a similar development and sequence of philosophical systems; just as the way seems barred against cer-tain other possibilities of world-interpretation. It is highly probable that phi-losophers within the domain of the Ural-Altaic languages (where the concept of the subject is least developed) look otherwise "into the world," and will be found on paths of thought different from those of the Indo-Germanic peo-ples and the Muslims: the spell of certain grammatical functions is ultimately also the spell of *physiological* valuations and racial conditions.

So much by way of rejecting Locke's[6] superficiality regarding the origin of ideas.

21

The *causa sui* is the best self-contradiction that has been conceived so far, it is a sort of rape and perversion of logic; but the extravagant pride of man has managed to entangle itself profoundly and frightfully with just this nonsense. The desire for "freedom of the will" in the superlative metaphysical sense, which still holds sway, unfortunately, in the minds of the half-educated; the desire to bear the entire and ultimate responsibility for one's actions oneself, and to absolve God, the world, ancestors, chance, and society involves nothing less than to be precisely this *causa sui* and, with more than

4. That is, the reappearance or survival of (or regression to) something ancient.
5. Sanskrit, Greek, and German all belong to the Indo-European language family; Ural and Altaic languages (formerly believed to be related) and Arabic (the language of Islam) belong to different families.
6. John Locke (1632–1704), English philosopher; in *An Essay Concerning Human Understanding* (1690), he argued that all ideas derive from sense perception.

Münchhausen's[7] audacity, to pull oneself up into existence by the hair, out of the swamps of nothingness. Suppose someone were thus to see through the boorish simplicity of this celebrated concept of "free will" and put it out of his head altogether, I beg of him to carry his "enlightenment" a step further, and also put out of his head the contrary of this monstrous conception of "free will": I mean "unfree will," which amounts to a misuse of cause and effect. One should not wrongly reify "cause" and "effect," as the natural scientists do (and whoever, like them, now "naturalizes" in his thinking), according to the prevailing mechanical doltishness which makes the cause press and push until it "effects" its end; one should use "cause" and "effect" only as pure concepts, that is to say, as conventional fictions for the purpose of designation and communication—*not* for explanation. In the "in-itself" there is nothing of "causal connections," of "necessity," or of "psychological non-freedom"; there the effect does *not* follow the cause, there is no rule of "law." It is *we* alone who have devised cause, sequence, for-each-other, relativity, constraint, number, law, freedom, motive, and purpose; and when we project and mix this symbol world into things as if it existed "in itself," we act once more as we have always acted—*mythologically.* The "unfree will" is mythology; in real life it is only a matter of *strong* and *weak* wills.

It is almost always a symptom of what is lacking in himself when a thinker senses in every "causal connection" and "psychological necessity" something of constraint, need, compulsion to obey, pressure, and unfreedom; it is suspicious to have such feelings—the person betrays himself. And in general, if I have observed correctly, the "unfreedom of the will" is regarded as a problem from two entirely opposite standpoints, but always in a profoundly *personal* manner: some will not give up their "responsibility," their belief in *themselves,* the personal right to *their* merits at any price (the vain races belong to this class). Others, on the contrary, do not wish to be answerable for anything, or blamed for anything, and owing to an inward self-contempt, seek to *lay the blame for themselves somewhere else.* The latter, when they write books, are in the habit today of taking the side of criminals; a sort of socialist pity is their most attractive disguise. And as a matter of fact, the fatalism of the weak-willed embellishes itself surprisingly when it can pose as "*la religion de la souffrance humaine,*"[8] that is *its* "good taste."

22

Forgive me as an old philologist who cannot desist from the malice of putting his finger on bad modes of interpretation: but "nature's conformity to law," of which you physicists talk so proudly, as though—why, it exists only owing to your interpretation and bad "philology." It is no matter of fact, no "text," but rather only a naïvely humanitarian emendation and perversion of meaning, with which you make abundant concessions to the democratic instincts of the modern soul! "Everywhere equality before the law; nature is no different in

7. Karl Friedrich Hieronymus, Freiherr (Baron) von Münchhausen (1720–1797), a famous story-teller of Hanover, Germany, who became associated with a number of tall tales; in one, he extricated himself and his horse from a swamp by pulling up on his own hair.
8. The religion of human suffering (French).

that respect, no better off than we are"—a fine instance of ulterior motivation, in which the plebeian antagonism to everything privileged and autocratic
as well as a second and more refined atheism are disguised once more. "Ni
Dieu, ni maître"[9]—that is what you, too, want; and therefore "cheers for the
law of nature!"—is it not so? But as said above, that is interpretation, not text;
and somebody might come along who, with opposite intentions and modes of
interpretation, could read out of the same "nature," and with regard to the
same phenomena, rather the tyrannically inconsiderate and relentless
enforcement of claims of power—an interpreter who would picture the
unexceptional and unconditional aspects of all "will to power" so vividly
that almost every word, even the word "tyranny" itself, would eventually
seem unsuitable, or a weakening and attenuating metaphor—being too
human—but he might, nevertheless, end by asserting the same about this world
as you do, namely, that it has a "necessary" and "calculable" course, *not* because
laws obtain in it, but because they are absolutely *lacking,* and every power
draws its ultimate consequences at every moment. Supposing that this also is
only interpretation—and you will be eager enough to make this objection?—
well, so much the better.

23

All psychology so far has got stuck in moral prejudices and fears; it has not
dared to descend into the depths. To understand it as morphology and *the doctrine of the development*[1] *of the will to power,* as I do—nobody has yet come
close to doing this even in thought—insofar as it is permissible to recognize
in what has been written so far a symptom of what has so far been kept silent.
The power of moral prejudices has penetrated deeply into the most spiritual
world, which would seem to be the coldest and most devoid of presuppositions, and has obviously operated in an injurious, inhibiting, blinding, and
distorting manner. A proper physio-psychology has to contend with unconscious resistance in the heart of the investigator, it has "the heart" against it:
even a doctrine of the reciprocal dependence of the "good" and the "wicked"
drives, causes (as refined immorality) distress and aversion in a still hale and
hearty conscience—still more so, a doctrine of the derivation of all good
impulses from wicked ones. If, however, a person should regard even the
affects of hatred, envy, covetousness, and the lust to rule as conditions of life,
as factors which, fundamentally and essentially, must be present in the general economy of life (and must, therefore, be further enhanced if life is to be
further enhanced)—he will suffer from such a view of things as from sea-
sickness. And yet even this hypothesis is far from being the strangest and most
painful in this immense and almost new domain of dangerous insights; and
there are in fact a hundred good reasons why everyone should keep away from
it who—*can.*

On the other hand, if one has once drifted there with one's bark, well! all
right! let us clench our teeth! let us open our eyes and keep our hand firm on

---

9. Neither God nor master (French); a slogan, and
the title of a journal founded in 1880 by the
French revolutionary socialist Auguste Blanqui.

1. That is, the "theory of the development (or
developmental theory) [*Entwicklungslehre*] of the
will to power."

the helm! We sail right *over* morality, we crush, we destroy perhaps the remains of our own morality by daring to make our voyage there—but what matter are *we*! Never yet did a *profounder* world of insight reveal itself to daring travelers and adventurers, and the psychologist who thus "makes a sacrifice"—it is *not* the *sacrifizio dell' intelletto*,[2] on the contrary!—will at least be entitled to demand in return that psychology shall be recognized again as the queen of the sciences, for whose service and preparation the other sciences [*Wissenschaften*] exist. For psychology is now again[3] the path to the fundamental problems.

From *PART TWO*
The Free Spirit

24

O *sancta simplicitas!*[4] In what strange simplification and falsification man lives! One can never cease wondering once one has acquired eyes for this marvel! How we have made everything around us clear and free and easy and simple! how we have been able to give our senses a passport to everything superficial, our thoughts a divine desire for wanton leaps and wrong inferences! how from the beginning we have contrived to retain our ignorance in order to enjoy an almost inconceivable freedom, lack of scruple and caution, heartiness, and gaiety of life—in order to enjoy life! And only on this now solid, granite foundation of ignorance could knowledge rise so far—the will to knowledge on the foundation of a far more powerful will: the will to ignorance, to the uncertain, to the untrue! Not as its opposite, but—as its refinement!

Even if *language*, here as elsewhere, will not get over its awkwardness, and will continue to talk of opposites where there are only degrees and many subtleties of gradation; even if the inveterate Tartuffery of morals, which now belongs to our unconquerable "flesh and blood," infects the words even of those of us who know better—here and there we understand it and laugh at the way in which precisely science at its best seeks most to keep us in this *simplified*, thoroughly artificial, suitably constructed and suitably falsified world—at the way in which, willy-nilly, it loves error, because, being alive, it loves life.

* * *

32

During the longest part of human history—so-called prehistorical times—the value or disvalue of an action was derived from its consequences. The action itself was considered as little as its origin. It was rather the way a distinction or disgrace still reaches back today from a child to its parents, in China: it was the retroactive force of success or failure that led men to think well or ill

---

2. Sacrifice of the intellect (Italian).
3. Perhaps a reference to the Greek philosopher Aristotle (385–322 B.C.E.), whose psychology in

On the Soul was very broad in scope, and for whom this may also be said to have been the case.
4. Oh holy simplicity! (Latin).

of an action. Let us call this period the *pre-moral* period of mankind: the imperative "know thyself!"[5] was as yet unknown.

In the last ten thousand years, however, one has reached the point, step by step, in a few large regions on the earth, where it is no longer the consequences but the origin of an action that one allows to decide its value. On the whole this is a great event which involves a considerable refinement of vision and standards; it is the unconscious aftereffect of the rule of aristocratic values and the faith in "descent"—the sign of a period that one may call *moral* in the narrower sense. It involves the first attempt at self-knowledge. Instead of the consequences, the origin: indeed a reversal of perspective! Surely, a reversal achieved only after long struggles and vacillations. To be sure, a calamitous new superstition, an odd narrowness of interpretation, thus become dominant: the origin of an action was interpreted in the most definite sense as origin in an *intention;* one came to agree that the value of an action lay in the value of the intention. The intention as the whole origin and prehistory of an action—almost to the present day this prejudice dominated moral praise, blame, judgment, and philosophy on earth.

But today—shouldn't we have reached the necessity of once more resolving on a reversal and fundamental shift in values, owing to another self-examination of man, another growth in profundity? Don't we stand at the threshold of a period which should be designated negatively, to begin with, as *extra-moral?*[6] After all, today at least we immoralists[7] have the suspicion that the decisive value of an action lies precisely in what is *unintentional* in it, while everything about it that is intentional, everything about it that can be seen, known, "conscious," still belongs to its surface and skin—which, like every skin, betrays something but *conceals* even more. In short, we believe that the intention is merely a sign and symptom that still requires interpretation—moreover, a sign that means too much and therefore, taken by itself alone, almost nothing. We believe that morality in the traditional sense, the morality of intentions, was a prejudice, precipitate and perhaps provisional—something on the order of astrology and alchemy—but in any case something that must be overcome. The overcoming of morality, in a certain sense even the self-overcoming of morality—let this be the name for that long secret work which has been saved up for the finest and most honest, also the most malicious, consciences of today, as living touchstones of the soul.

33

There is no other way: the feelings of devotion, self-sacrifice for one's neighbor, the whole morality of self-denial must be questioned mercilessly and taken to court—no less than the aesthetics of "contemplation devoid of all interest"[8] which is used today as a seductive guise for the emasculation of art, to give it a good conscience. There is too much charm and sugar in these feelings of

---

5. A maxim carved into the temple of Apollo at Delphi (4th c. B.C.E.), home of the god's oracle.
6. That is, outside of and beyond moralistic ways of thinking, leaving them behind (*aussermoralische*).
7. That is, we who are no longer moralistic in our thinking (and thus are "beyond good and evil").
8. The aesthetic position of Kant, expressed in his *Critique of Judgment* (1790).

"for others," "*not* for myself," for us not to need to become doubly suspicious at this point and to ask: "are these not perhaps—*seductions?*"

That they *please*—those who have them and those who enjoy their fruits, and also the mere spectator—this does not yet constitute an argument in their *favor* but rather invites caution. So let us be cautious.

34

Whatever philosophical standpoint one may adopt today, from every point of view the *erroneousness* of the world in which we think we live is the surest and firmest fact that we can lay eyes on: we find reasons upon reasons for it which would like to lure us to hypotheses concerning a deceptive principle in "the essence of things." But whoever holds our thinking itself, "the spirit," in other words, responsible for the falseness of the world—an honorable way out which is chosen by every conscious or unconscious *advocatus dei*[9]— whoever takes this world, along with space, time, form, movement, to be falsely *inferred*—anyone like that would at least have ample reason to learn to be suspicious at long last of all thinking. Wouldn't thinking have put over on us the biggest hoax yet? And what warrant would there be that it would not continue to do what it has always done?

In all seriousness: the innocence of our thinkers is somehow touching and evokes reverence, when today they still step before consciousness with the request that it should please give them *honest* answers; for example, whether it is "real," and why it so resolutely keeps the external world at a distance, and other questions of that kind. The faith in "immediate certainties" is a *moral* naïveté that reflects honor on us philosophers; but—after all we should not be "*merely* moral" men. Apart from morality, this faith is a stupidity that reflects little honor on us. In bourgeois life ever-present suspicion may be considered a sign of "bad character" and hence belong among things imprudent; here, among us, beyond the bourgeois world and its Yes and No—what should prevent us from being imprudent and saying: a philosopher has nothing less than a *right* to "bad character," as the being who has so far always been fooled best on earth; he has a *duty* to suspicion today, to squint maliciously out of every abyss of suspicion.

Forgive me the joke of this gloomy grimace and trope; for I myself have learned long ago to think differently, to estimate differently with regard to deceiving and being deceived, and I keep in reserve at least a couple of jostles for the blind rage with which the philosophers resist being deceived. Why *not?* It is no more than a moral prejudice that truth is worth more than mere appearance; it is even the worst proved assumption there is in the world. Let at least this much be admitted: there would be no life at all if not on the basis of perspective[1] estimates and appearances; and if, with the virtuous enthusiasm and clumsiness of some philosophers, one wanted to abolish the "apparent world" altogether—well, supposing *you* could do that, at least nothing would be left of your "truth" either. Indeed, what forces us at all to suppose that there is an essential opposition of "true" and "false"? Is it not sufficient

---

9. Advocate of God (Latin), an ironic inversion of the idea and role of a devil's advocate (*advocatus diaboli*), the title held by a Roman Catholic official responsible for preparing all possible arguments against an individual's beatification or canonization.

1. That is, perspectival (*perspektivisch*).

to assume degrees of apparentness and, as it were, lighter and darker shadows and shades of appearance—different "values," to use the language of painters? Why couldn't the world *that concerns us*—be a fiction? And if somebody asked, "but to a fiction there surely belongs an author?"—couldn't one answer simply: *why*? Doesn't this "belongs" perhaps belong to the fiction, too? Is it not permitted to be a bit ironical about the subject no less than the predicate and object? Shouldn't philosophers be permitted to rise above faith in grammar? All due respect for governesses—but hasn't the time come for philosophy to renounce the faith of governesses?

35

O Voltaire! O humaneness! O nonsense! There is something about "truth," about the *search* for truth; and when a human being is too human about it— *"il ne cherche le vrai que pour faire le bien"*[2]—I bet he finds nothing.

36

Suppose nothing else were "given" as real except our world of desires and passions, and we could not get down, or up, to any other "reality" besides the reality of our drives—for thinking is merely a relation of these drives to each other: is it not permitted to make the experiment and to ask the question whether this "given" would not be *sufficient* for also understanding on the basis of this kind of thing the so-called mechanistic (or "material") word? I mean, not as a deception, as "mere appearance," an "idea"[3] (in the sense of Berkeley[4] and Schopenhauer) but as holding the same rank of reality as our affect— as a more primitive form of the world of affects in which everything still lies contained in a powerful unity before it undergoes ramifications and developments in the organic process (and, as is only fair, also becomes tenderer and weaker)—as a kind of instinctive life in which all organic functions are still synthetically intertwined along with self-regulation, assimilation, nourishment, excretion, and metabolism—as a *pre-form* of life.

In the end not only is it permitted to make this experiment; the conscience of *method* demands it. Not to assume several kinds of causality until the experiment of making do with a single one has been pushed to its utmost limit (to the point of nonsense, if I may say so)—that is a moral of method which one may not shirk today—it follows "from its definition," as a mathematician would say. The question is in the end whether we really recognize the will as *efficient*, whether we believe in the causality of the will: if we do—and at bottom our faith in this is nothing less than our faith in causality itself—then we have to make the experiment of positing the causality of the will hypothetically as the only one. "Will," of course, can affect only "will"—and not "matter" (not "nerves," for example). In short, one has to risk the hypothesis whether will does not affect will wherever "effects" are recognized—and

2. He seeks the true only to do the good (French), a near-exact quotation from the poem "Epistle 118: To a Man" (1776) by the French poet, essayist, and dramatist Voltaire (pseudonym of François-Marie Arouet, 1694–1778).

3. That is, a "representation" (*Vorstellung*), or a mental image.
4. George Berkeley (1685–1753), Anglo-Irish bishop and Idealist philosopher.

whether all mechanical occurrences are not, insofar as a force is active in them, will force, effects of will.

Suppose, finally, we succeeded in explaining our entire instinctive life as the development and ramification of *one* basic form of the will—namely, of the will to power, as *my* proposition has it; suppose all organic functions could be traced back to this will to power and one could also find in it the solution of the problem of procreation and nourishment—it is *one* problem—then one would have gained the right to determine *all* efficient force univocally as— *will to power.* The world viewed from inside, the world defined and determined according to its "intelligible character"[5]—it would be "will to power" and nothing else.—

* * *

39

Nobody is very likely to consider a doctrine true merely because it makes people happy or virtuous—except perhaps the lovely "idealists" who become effusive about the good, the true, and the beautiful and allow all kinds of motley, clumsy, and benevolent desiderata to swim around in utter confusion in their pond. Happiness and virtue are no arguments. But people like to forget— even sober spirits—that making unhappy and evil are no counterarguments. Something might be true while being harmful and dangerous in the highest degree. Indeed, it might be a basic characteristic of existence that those who would know it completely would perish, in which case the strength of a spirit should be measured according to how much of the "truth" one could still barely endure—or to put it more clearly, to what degree one would *require* it to be thinned down, shrouded, sweetened, blunted, falsified.

But there is no doubt at all that the evil and unhappy are more favored when it comes to the discovery of certain *parts* of truth, and that the probability of their success here is greater—not to speak of the evil who are happy, a species the moralists bury in silence. Perhaps hardness and cunning furnish more favorable conditions for the origin of the strong, independent spirit and philosopher than that gentle, fine, conciliatory good-naturedness and art of taking things lightly which people prize, and prize rightly, in a scholar. Assuming first of all that the concept "philosopher" is not restricted to the philosopher who writes books—or makes books of *his* philosophy.

A final trait for the image of the free-spirited philosopher is contributed by Stendhal[6] whom, considering German taste, I do not want to fail to stress— for he goes against the German taste. "*Pour être bon philosophe,*" says this last great psychologist, "*il faut être sec, clair, sans illusion. Un banquier, qui a fait fortune, a une partie du caractère requis pour faire des découvertes en philosophie, c'est-à-dire pour voir clair dans ce qui est.*"[7]

* * *

5. That is, its essential, aptly conceivable, and knowable character.
6. French writer (pseudonym of Marie-henri Beyle, 1783–1843), known for his psychologically acute novels; the following quotation is from a letter of 1829.

7. To be a good philosopher, one must be dry, clear, without illusion. A banker who has made a fortune has one character trait that is needed for making discoveries in philosophy, that is to say, for seeing clearly into what it is [translator's note].

From *PART THREE*
The Religious Nature[8]

* * *

53

Why atheism today?—'The father' in God is thoroughly refuted; likewise 'the judge', 'the rewarder'. Likewise his 'free will': he does not hear—and if he heard he would still not know how to help. The worst thing is: he seems incapable of making himself clearly understood: is he himself vague about what he means?—These are what, in the course of many conversations, asking and listening, I found to be the causes of the decline of European theism;[9] it seems to me that the religious instinct is indeed in vigorous growth—but that it rejects the theistic answer with profound mistrust.

54

What, at bottom, is the whole of modern philosophy doing? Since Descartes— and indeed rather in spite of him than on the basis of his precedent—all philosophers have been making an *attentat*[1] on the ancient soul concept under the cloak of a critique of the subject-and-predicate concept—that is to say, an *attentat* on the fundamental presupposition of Christian doctrine. Modern philosophy, as an epistemological scepticism, is, covertly or openly, *anti-Christian*: although, to speak to more refined ears, by no means anti-religious. For in the past one believed in 'the soul' as one believed in grammar and the grammatical subject: one said 'I' is the condition, 'think' is the predicate and conditioned—thinking is an activity to which a subject *must* be thought of as cause. Then one tried with admirable artfulness and tenacity to fathom whether one could not get out of this net—whether the reverse was not perhaps true: 'think' the condition, 'I' conditioned; 'I' thus being only a synthesis *produced* by thinking. *Kant* wanted fundamentally to prove that, starting from the subject, the subject could not be proved—nor could the object: the possibility of an *apparent existence* of the subject, that is to say of 'the soul', may not always have been remote from him, that idea which, as the philosophy of the Vedanta,[2] has exerted immense influence on earth before.

* * *

From *PART FIVE*
On the Natural History of Morals

186

Moral sensibility is as subtle, late, manifold, sensitive and refined in Europe today as the 'science of morals' [*Wissenschaft der Moral*'] pertaining to it is still young, inept, clumsy and coarse-fingered—an interesting contrast which

---

8. That is, "religiousness" (*Das religiöse Wesen*), or the nature/essence/being/reality of being religious.
9. That is, belief in God.

1. Attempt (French); specifically, an assassination attempt.
2. See p. 727, n. 3.

sometimes even becomes visible and incarnate in the person of a moralist. Even the expression 'science [*Wissenschaft*] of morals' is, considering what is designated by it, far too proud, and contrary to *good* taste: which is always accustomed to choose the more modest expressions. One should, in all strictness, admit *what* will be needful here for a long time to come, *what* alone is provisionally justified here: assembly of material, conceptual comprehension and arrangement of a vast domain of delicate value-feelings and value-distinctions which live, grow, beget and perish—and perhaps attempts to display the more frequent and recurring forms of these living crystallizations—as preparation of a *typology* of morals. To be sure: one has not been so modest hitherto. Philosophers one and all have, with a strait-laced seriousness that provokes laughter, demanded something much higher, more pretentious, more solemn of themselves as soon as they have concerned themselves with morality as a science[3]: they wanted to furnish the *rational ground* of morality—and every philosopher hitherto has believed he has furnished this rational ground; morality itself, however, was taken as 'given'. How far from their clumsy pride was that apparently insignificant task left in dust and mildew, the task of description, although the most delicate hands and senses could hardly be delicate enough for it! It was precisely because moral philosophers knew the facts of morality only somewhat vaguely in an arbitrary extract or as a chance abridgement, as morality of their environment, their class, their church, the spirit of their times, their climate and zone of the earth, for instance—it was precisely because they were ill informed and not even very inquisitive about other peoples, ages and former times, that they did not so much as catch sight of the real problems of morality [*Moral*]—for these come into view only if we compare *many* moralities [*Moralen*]. Strange though it may sound, in all 'science of morals' hitherto the problem of morality itself has been *lacking*: the suspicion was lacking that there was anything problematic here. What philosophers called 'the rational ground of morality' and sought to furnish was, viewed in the proper light, only a scholarly form of *faith* in the prevailing morality, a new way of *expressing* it, and thus itself a fact within a certain morality, indeed even in the last resort a kind of denial that this morality *ought* to be conceived of as a problem—and in any event the opposite of a testing, analysis, doubting and vivisection of this faith. Hear, for example, with what almost venerable innocence Schopenhauer still presented his task, and draw your own conclusions as to how scientific a 'science' is whose greatest masters still talk like children and old women:—'The principle', he says (*Fundamental Problems of Ethics*),

> the fundamental proposition on whose content all philosophers of ethics are *actually* at one: *neminem laede, immo omnes, quantum potes, juva*[4] is *actually* the proposition of which all the teachers of morals endeavour to furnish the rational ground . . . the *actual* foundation of ethics which has been sought for centuries like the philosopher's stone.

—The difficulty of furnishing the rational ground for the above-quoted proposition may indeed be great—as is well known, Schopenhauer too failed

---

3. That is, as a cognitive discipline (*Wissenschaft*).
4. Harm no one, but on the contrary help all as much as you can (Latin). This extract is quoted from SCHOPENHAUER's essay "On the Basis of Morality" (1840), republished in the book *The Two Fundamental Problems of Ethics* (1840).

to do it—; and he who has ever been certain how insipidly false and sentimental this proposition is in a world whose essence is will to power—may like to recall that Schopenhauer, although a pessimist, *actually*—played the flute . . . Every day, after dinner: read his biographers on this subject. And by the way: a pessimist, a world-denier and God-denier, who *comes to a halt* before morality—who affirms morality and plays the flute, affirms *laede neminem* morality: what? is that actually—a pessimist?

187

Quite apart from the value of such assertions as 'there exists in us a categorical imperative' one can still ask: what does such an assertion say of the man who asserts it? There are moralities which are intended to justify their authors before others; other moralities are intended to calm him and make him content with himself; with others he wants to crucify and humiliate himself; with others he wants to wreak vengeance, with others hide himself, with others transfigure himself and set himself on high; this morality serves to make its author forget, that to make him or something about him forgotten; many moralists would like to exercise power and their creative moods on mankind; others, Kant perhaps among them, give to understand with their morality: 'what is worthy of respect in me is that I know how to obey—and things *ought* to be no different with you!'—in short, moralities too are only a *sign-language of the emotions*.[5]

188

Every morality is, as opposed to *laisser aller*,[6] a piece of tyranny against 'nature', likewise against 'reason': but that can be no objection to it unless one is in possession of some other morality which decrees that any kind of tyranny and unreason is impermissible. The essential and invaluable element in every morality is that it is a protracted constraint[.]

* * *

201

So long as the utility which dominates moral value-judgements is solely that which is useful to the herd, so long as the object is solely the preservation of the community and the immoral is sought precisely and exclusively in that which seems to imperil the existence of the community: so long as that is the case there can be no 'morality of love of one's neighbour'. Supposing that even there a constant little exercise of consideration, pity, fairness, mildness, mutual aid was practised, supposing that even at that stage of society all those drives are active which are later honourably designated 'virtues' and are finally practically equated with the concept 'morality': in that era they do not yet by any means belong to the domain of moral valuations—they are still *extra-moral*. An act of pity, for example, was during the finest age of Rome considered neither good nor bad, neither moral nor immoral; and even if it was commended,

5. Better translated as "of the affects" (*der Affekte*), since Nietzsche is referring to basic psychological forces (drives, instincts, dispositions, inclinations) as well as to impulses such as emotions and feelings.
6. Letting go (French); that is, "permitting all."

this commendation was entirely compatible with a kind of involuntary disdain, as soon, that is, as it was set beside any action which served the welfare of the whole, of the *res publica*.[7] Ultimately 'love of one's neighbour' is always something secondary, in part conventional and arbitrarily illusory, when compared with *fear of one's neighbour*. Once the structure of society seems to have been in general fixed and made safe from external dangers, it is this fear of one's neighbour which again creates new perspectives of moral valuation. There are certain strong and dangerous drives, such as enterprisingness, foolhardiness, revengefulness, craft, rapacity, ambition, which hitherto had not only to be honoured from the point of view of their social utility—under different names, naturally, from those chosen here—but also mightily developed and cultivated (because they were constantly needed to protect the community as a whole against the enemies of the community as a whole); these drives are now felt to be doubly dangerous—now that the diversionary outlets for them are lacking—and are gradually branded as immoral and given over to calumny. The antithetical drives and inclinations now come into moral honour; step by step the herd instinct draws its conclusions. How much or how little that is dangerous to the community, dangerous to equality, resides in an opinion, in a condition or emotion, in a will, in a talent, that is now the moral perspective: here again fear is the mother of morality. When the highest and strongest drives, breaking passionately out, carry the individual far above and beyond the average and lowlands of the herd conscience, the self-confidence of the community goes to pieces, its faith in itself, its spine as it were, is broken: consequently it is precisely these drives which are most branded and calumniated. Lofty spiritual independence, the will to stand alone, great intelligence even, are felt to be dangerous; everything that raises the individual above the herd and makes his neighbour quail is henceforth called *evil*; the fair, modest, obedient, self-effacing disposition, the *mean and average* in desires, acquires moral names and honours. Eventually, under very peaceful conditions, there is less and less occasion or need to educate one's feelings in severity and sternness; and now every kind of severity, even severity in justice, begins to trouble the conscience; a stern and lofty nobility and self-responsibility is received almost as an offence and awakens mistrust, 'the lamb', even more 'the sheep', is held in higher and higher respect. There comes a point of morbid mellowing and over-tenderness in the history of society at which it takes the side even of him who harms it, the *criminal*, and does so honestly and wholeheartedly. Punishment: that seems to it somehow unfair—certainly the idea of 'being punished' and 'having to punish' is unpleasant to it, makes it afraid. 'Is it not enough to render him *harmless*? why punish him as well? To administer punishment is itself dreadful!'—with this question herd morality, the morality of timidity, draws its ultimate conclusion. Supposing all danger, the cause of fear, could be abolished, this morality would therewith also be abolished: it would no longer be necessary, it would no longer *regard itself* as necessary!—He who examines the conscience of the present-day European will have to extract from a thousand moral recesses and hiding-places always the same imperative, the imperative of herd timidity: 'we wish that

---

7. The common good, the state (Latin).

there will one day *no longer be anything to fear!*' One day—everywhere in Europe the will and way to *that* day is now called 'progress'.

202

Let us straight away say once more what we have already said a hundred times: for ears today offer such truths—*our* truths—no ready welcome. We know well enough how offensive it sounds when someone says plainly and without metaphor that man is an animal; but it will be reckoned almost a *crime* in us that precisely in regard to men of 'modern ideas' we constantly employ the terms 'herd', 'herd instinct', and the like. But what of that! we can do no other: for it is precisely here that our new insight lies. We have found that in all principal moral judgements Europe has become unanimous, including the lands where Europe's influence predominates: one manifestly *knows* in Europe what Socrates thought he did not know,[8] and what that celebrated old serpent once promised to teach—one 'knows' today what is good and evil. Now it is bound to make a harsh sound and one not easy for ears to hear when we insist again and again: that which here believes it knows, that which here glorifies itself with its praising and blaming and calls itself good, is the instinct of the herd-animal man: the instinct which has broken through and come to predominate and prevail over the other instincts and is coming to do so more and more in proportion to the increasing physiological approximation and assimilation of which it is the symptom. *Morality is in Europe today herd-animal morality*— that is to say, as we understand the thing, only *one* kind of human morality beside which, before which, after which many other, above all *higher*, moralities are possible or ought to be possible. But against such a 'possibility', against such an 'ought', this morality defends itself with all its might: it says, obstinately and stubbornly, 'I am morality itself, and nothing is morality besides me!'—indeed, with the aid of a religion which has gratified and flattered the sublimest herd-animal desires, it has got to the point where we discover even in political and social institutions an increasingly evident expression of this morality: the *democratic* movement inherits the Christian. * * *

203

We, who have a different faith—we, to whom the democratic movement is not merely a form assumed by political organization in decay but also a form assumed by man in decay, that is to say in diminishment, in process of becoming mediocre and losing his value: whither must *we* direct our hopes?— Towards *new philosophers*, we have no other choice; towards spirits strong and original enough to make a start on antithetical evaluations and to revalue and reverse 'eternal values'; towards heralds and forerunners, towards men of the future who in the present knot together the constraint which compels the will of millennia on to *new* paths. To teach man the future of man as his *will*, as dependent on a human will, and to prepare for great enterprises and collective experiments in discipline and breeding so as to make an end of that grue-

8. Socrates famously declared that his wisdom lay in recognizing that he had no knowledge (Plato, *Apology* 21d, 23b).

some dominion of chance and nonsense that has hitherto been called 'history'—the nonsense of the 'greatest number' is only its latest form—: for that a new kind of philosopher and commander will some time be needed, in face of whom whatever has existed on earth of hidden, dreadful and benevolent spirits may well look pale and dwarfed. It is the image of such leaders which hovers before *our* eyes—may I say that aloud, you free spirits?

* * *

From PART SIX
We Scholars[9]

* * *

210

Supposing, then, that in the image of the philosophers of the future some trait provokes the question whether they will not have to be sceptics in the sense last suggested,[1] this would still designate only something about them—and *not* them themselves. They might with equal justification let themselves be called critics; and they will certainly be experimenters. Through the name with which I have ventured to baptize them I have already expressly emphasized experiment and the delight in experiment: was this because, as critics body and soul, they like to employ experiment in a new, perhaps wider, perhaps more dangerous sense? Will they, in their passion for knowledge, have to go further with audacious and painful experiments than the tender and pampered taste of a democratic century can approve of?—There can be no doubt that these coming men will want to dispense least with those serious and not indubious qualities which distinguish the critic from the sceptic: I mean certainty in standards of value, conscious employment of a unity of method, instructed courage, independence and ability to justify oneself; indeed, they confess to taking a *pleasure* in negating and dissecting and to a certain self-possessed cruelty which knows how to wield the knife with certainty and deftness even when the heart bleeds. They will be *harder* (and perhaps not always only against themselves) than humane men might wish, they will not consort with 'truth' so as to be 'pleased' by it or 'elevated' and 'inspired'—they will rather be little disposed to believe that *truth* of all things should be attended by such pleasures. They will smile, these stern spirits, if someone should say in their presence: 'This thought elevates me: how should it not be true?' Or: 'This work delights me: how should it not be beautiful?' Or: 'This artist enlarges me: how should he not be great?'—perhaps they will have not only a smile but a feeling of genuine disgust for all such fawning enthusiasm, idealism, feminism, hermaphroditism, and he who could penetrate into the secret chambers of their hearts would hardly discover there the intention of reconciling 'Christian feelings' with 'classical taste' and perhaps even with 'modern parliamentarianism' (as such a conciliatory spirit is

9. That is, "We Learned (or Sophisticated) Ones" (*Wir Gelehrten*).
1. A "masculinized" German form of skepticism,

discussed and praised in the previous section (not included here).

said to exist even among philosophers in our very uncertain and consequently conciliatory century). Critical discipline and every habit conducive to cleanliness and severity in things of the spirit will be demanded by these philosophers not only of themselves: they could even display them as their kind of decoration—none the less they still do not want to be called critics on that account. It seems to them no small insult to philosophy when it is decreed, as is so happily done today: 'Philosophy itself is criticism and critical science—and nothing whatever besides!' This evaluation of philosophy may enjoy the applause of every positivist in France and Germany (—and it might possibly have flattered the heart and taste of *Kant*: one should recall the titles of his principal works): our new philosophers will still say: critics are the philosophers' instruments and for that reason very far from being philosophers themselves! Even the great Chinaman of Königsberg[2] was only a great critic.—

211

I insist that philosophical labourers and men of science[3] in general should once and for all cease to be confused with philosophers—that on precisely this point 'to each his own' should be strictly applied, and not much too much given to the former, much too little to the latter. It may be required for the education of a philosopher that he himself has also once stood on all those steps on which his servants, the scientific labourers of philosophy,[4] remain standing—*have* to remain standing; he himself must perhaps have been critic and sceptic and dogmatist and historian and, in addition, poet and collector and traveller and reader of riddles and moralist and seer and 'free spirit' and practically everything, so as to traverse the whole range of human values and value-feelings and be *able* to gaze from the heights into every distance, from the depths into every height, from the nook-and-corner into every broad expanse with manifold eyes and a manifold conscience. But all these are only preconditions of his task: this task itself demands something different—it demands that he *create values*. Those philosophical labourers after the noble exemplar of Kant and Hegel have to take some great fact of evaluation—that is to say, former *assessments* of value, creations of value which have become dominant and are for a while called 'truths'—and identify them and reduce them to formulas, whether in the realm of *logic* or of *politics* (morals) or of *art*. It is the duty of these scholars to take everything that has hitherto happened and been valued, and make it clear, distinct, intelligible and manageable, to abbreviate everything long, even 'time' itself, and to *subdue* the entire past: a tremendous and wonderful task in the service of which every subtle pride, every tenacious will can certainly find satisfaction. *Actual philosophers, however, are commanders and law-givers*: they say 'thus it *shall* be!', it is they who determine the Wherefore and Whither of mankind, and they possess for this task the preliminary work of all the philosophical labourers, of all those

---

2. That is, Kant, who was born and lived his entire life in Königsberg, in what was then East Prussia (now Kaliningrad, part of Russia). Because the Chinese were stereotyped as strict followers of rules who fetishized duty, Nietzsche calls him "der grosse Chinese."
3. In German, *wissenschaftlich Menschen*: that is,

people who devote themselves to some variety of specialized cognitive inquiry.
4. In German, *wissenschaftlich Arbeiter der Philosophie*: that is, those in philosophy who devote themselves to working industriously and rigorously within some established paradigm of philosophical inquiry and debate.

who have subdued the past—they reach for the future with creative hand, and everything that is or has been becomes for them a means, an instrument, a hammer. Their 'knowing' is *creating*, their creating is a law-giving, their will to truth is—*will to power*.—Are there such philosophers today? Have there been such philosophers? *Must* there not be such philosophers? . . .

212

It seems to me more and more that the philosopher, being *necessarily* a man of tomorrow and the day after tomorrow, has always found himself and *had* to find himself in contradiction to his today: his enemy has always been the ideal of today. Hitherto these extraordinary promoters of mankind who have been called philosophers and have seldom felt themselves to be friends of knowledge but, rather, disagreeable fools and dangerous question-marks— have found their task, their hard, unwanted, unavoidable task, but finally the greatness of their task, in being the bad conscience of their age. By laying the knife vivisectionally to the bosom of the very *virtues of the age*[5] they betrayed what was their own secret: to know a *new* greatness of man, a new untrodden path to his enlargement.[6] Each time they revealed how much hypocrisy, indolence, letting oneself go and letting oneself fall, how much falsehood was concealed under the most honoured type of their contemporary morality, how much virtue was *outlived*; each time they said: 'We have to go thither, out yonder, where *you* today are least at home.' In face of a world of 'modern ideas' which would like to banish everyone into a corner and 'speciality', a philosopher, assuming there could be philosophers today, would be compelled to see the greatness of man, the concept 'greatness', precisely in his spaciousness and multiplicity, in his wholeness in diversity: he would even determine value and rank according to how much and how many things one could endure and take upon oneself, how *far* one could extend one's responsibility. Today the taste of the age and the virtue of the age weakens and attenuates the will, nothing is so completely timely as weakness of will: consequently, in the philosopher's ideal precisely strength of will, the hardness and capacity for protracted decisions, must constitute part of the concept 'greatness'; with just as much justification as the opposite doctrine and the ideal of a shy, renunciatory, humble, selfless humanity was appropriate to an opposite age, to one such as, like the sixteenth century, suffered from its accumulation of will and the stormiest waters and flood-tides of selfishness.[7] In the age of Socrates, among men of nothing but wearied instincts, among conservative ancient Athenians who let themselves go—'towards happiness', as they said, towards pleasure, as they behaved—and who at the same time had in their mouth the old pretentious words to which their lives had long ceased to give them any right, *irony* was perhaps required for greatness of soul, that Socratic malicious certitude of the old physician and plebeian who cut remorselessly into his own flesh as he did into the flesh and heart of the 'noble', with a look which said distinctly enough: 'do not dissemble before me! Here—we are equal!' Today, conversely, when the herd animal alone obtains and bestows honours in

---

5. That is, of their own times.
6. That is, becoming greater (*Vergrösserung*).

7. Nietzsche is presumably thinking here of the turbulent last century of the Italian Renaissance.

Europe, when 'equality of rights' could all too easily change into equality in wrongdoing: I mean into a general war on everything rare, strange, privileged, the higher man, the higher soul, the higher duty, the higher responsibility, creative fullness of power and mastery—today, being noble, wanting to be by oneself, the ability to be different, independence and the need for self-responsibility pertains to the concept 'greatness'; and the philosopher will betray something of his ideal when he asserts: 'He shall be the greatest who can be the most solitary, the most concealed, the most divergent, the man beyond good and evil, the master of his virtues, the superabundant of will; this shall be called greatness: the ability to be as manifold as whole, as vast as full.' And, to ask it again: is greatness—*possible* today?

* * *

225

Whether it be hedonism or pessimism or utilitarianism or eudaemonism: all these modes of thought which assess the value of things according to *pleasure* and *pain*, that is to say according to attendant and secondary phenomena, are foreground modes of thought and naïvetics which anyone conscious of *creative* powers and an artist's conscience will look down on with derision, though not without pity. Pity for *you*! That, to be sure, is not pity for social 'distress', for 'society' and its sick and unfortunate, for the vicious and broken from the start who lie all around us; even less is it pity for the grumbling, oppressed, rebellious slave classes who aspire after domination—they call it 'freedom'. *Our* pity is a more elevated, more farsighted pity—we see how *man* is diminishing himself, how *you* are diminishing him!—and there are times when we behold *your* pity with an indescribable anxiety, when we defend ourselves against this pity—when we find your seriousness more dangerous than any kind of frivolity. You want if possible—and there is no madder 'if possible'— *to abolish suffering*; and we?—it really does seem that *we* would rather increase it and make it worse than it has ever been! Wellbeing as you understand it— that is no goal, that seems to us an *end*! A state which soon renders man ludicrous and contemptible—which makes it *desirable* that he should perish! The discipline of suffering, of *great* suffering—do you not know that it is *this* discipline alone which has created every elevation of mankind hitherto? That tension of the soul in misfortune which cultivates its strength, its terror at the sight of great destruction, its inventiveness and bravery in undergoing, enduring, interpreting, exploiting misfortune, and whatever of depth, mystery, mask, spirit, cunning and greatness has been bestowed upon it—has it not been bestowed through suffering, through the discipline of great suffering? In man, *creature* and *creator* are united: in man there is matter, fragment, excess, clay, mud, madness, chaos; but in man there is also creator, sculptor, the hardness of the hammer, the divine spectator and the seventh day—do you understand this antithesis?[8] And that *your* pity is for the 'creature in man', for that which has to be formed, broken, forged, torn, burned, annealed,

---

8. This sentence is one of the most powerful and revealing in the entire book, expressing both Nietzsche's concerns and his hopes for humanity.

"The seventh day": that is, the day of rest after divine creation.

refined—that which has to *suffer* and *should* suffer? And *our* pity—do you not grasp whom our *opposite* pity is for when it defends itself against your pity as the worst of all pampering and weakening?—Pity *against* pity, then!—But, to repeat, there are higher problems than the problems of pleasure and pain and pity; and every philosophy that treats only of them is a piece of naïvety.

* * *

227

Honesty[9]—granted that this is our virtue, from which we cannot get free, we free spirits—well, let us labour at it with all love and malice and not weary of 'perfecting' ourselves in *our* virtue, the only one we have: may its brightness one day overspread this ageing culture and its dull, gloomy seriousness like a gilded azure mocking evening glow! And if our honesty should one day none the less grow weary, and sigh, and stretch its limbs, and find us too hard, and like to have things better, easier, gentler, like an agreeable vice: let us remain *hard*, we last of the Stoics! And let us send to the aid of our honesty whatever we have of devilry in us—our disgust at the clumsy and casual, our '*nitimur in vetitum*',[1] our adventurer's courage, our sharp and fastidious curiosity, our subtlest, most disguised, most spiritual will to power and world-overcoming which wanders avidly through all the realms of the future—let us go to the aid of our 'god' with all our 'devils'!

* * *

From *PART SEVEN*
Our Virtues

* * *

230

Perhaps what I have said here of a 'fundamental will of the spirit' may not be immediately comprehensible: allow me to explain.—That commanding something which the people calls 'spirit [*Geist*]' wants to be master within itself and around itself and to feel itself master: out of multiplicity it has the will to simplicity, a will which binds together and tames, which is imperious and domineering. In this its needs and capacities are the same as those which physiologists posit for everything that lives, grows and multiplies. The power of the spirit [*Geist*] to appropriate what is foreign to it is revealed in a strong inclination to assimilate the new to the old, to simplify the complex, to overlook or repel what is wholly contradictory: just as it arbitrarily emphasizes, extracts and falsifies to suit itself certain traits and lines in what is foreign to it, in every piece of 'external world'. Its intention in all this is the incorporation of new 'experiences', the arrangement of new things within old divisions—growth, that is to say; more precisely, the *feeling* of growth, the feeling of increased power. This same will is served by an apparently antithetical drive of the spirit,

---

9. That is, intellectual integrity (*Redlichkeit*).
1. We strive for the forbidden (Latin); quoted from Ovid, *Amores* 3.4.17 (ca. 20 B.C.E.).

a sudden decision for ignorance, for arbitrary shutting-out, a closing of the windows, an inner denial of this or that thing, a refusal to let it approach, a kind of defensive posture against much that can be known, a contentment with the dark, with the closed horizon, an acceptance and approval of ignorance: all this being necessary according to the degree of its power to appropriate, its 'digestive power', to speak in a metaphor—and indeed 'the spirit' is more like a stomach than anything else. It is here that there also belongs the occasional will of the spirit to let itself be deceived, perhaps with a mischievous notion that such and such is *not* the case, that it is only being allowed to pass for the case, a joy in uncertainty and ambiguity, an exultant enjoyment of the capricious narrowness and secrecy of a nook-and-corner, of the all too close, of the foreground, of the exaggerated, diminished, displaced, beautified, an enjoyment of the capriciousness of all these expressions of power. Finally there also belongs here that not altogether innocent readiness of the spirit to deceive other spirits and to dissemble before them, that continual pressing and pushing of a creative, formative, changeable force: in this spirit enjoys the multiplicity and cunning of its masks, it enjoys too the sense of being safe that this brings—for it is precisely through its protean arts that it is best concealed and protected! *This* will to appearance, to simplification, to the mask, to the cloak, in short to the superficial—for every surface is a cloak—is *counteracted* by that sublime inclination in the man of knowledge which takes a profound, many-sided and thorough view of things and *will*[2] take such a view: as a kind of cruelty of the intellectual conscience and taste which every brave thinker will recognize in himself, provided he has hardened and sharpened for long enough his own view of himself, as he should have, and is accustomed to stern discipline and stern language. He will say 'there is something cruel in the inclination of my spirit'—let the amiable and virtuous try to talk him out of that! In fact, it would be nicer if, instead of with cruelty, we were perhaps credited with an 'extravagant honesty'—we free, *very* free spirits—and perhaps *that* will actually one day be our posthumous fame? In the meantime—for it will be a long time before that happens—we ourselves are likely to be least inclined to dress up in moralistic verbal tinsel and valences of this sort: all our labour hitherto has spoiled us for this taste and its buoyant luxuriousness. They are beautiful, glittering, jingling, festive words: honesty, love of truth, love of wisdom, sacrifice for the sake of knowledge, heroism of the truthful—there is something about them that makes one's pride swell. But we hermits and marmots long ago became convinced that this worthy verbal pomp too belongs among the ancient false finery, lumber and gold-dust of unconscious human vanity, and that under such flattering colours and varnish too the terrible basic text *homo natura*[3] must again be discerned. For to translate man back into nature; to master the many vain and fanciful interpretations and secondary meanings which have been hitherto scribbled and daubed over that eternal basic text *homo natura*; to confront man henceforth with man in the way in which, hardened by the discipline of science [*Wissenchaft*], man today confronts the *rest* of nature with dauntless Oedipus eyes and stopped-up Odysseus ears,[4] deaf

2. That is, "*wants to*" (*will*; Nietzsche's emphasis).
3. Natural man (Latin), or humans viewed at the level of their "natural" constitution and elemental nature.
4. Two allusions to Greek mythology: Oedipus fearlessly used his sight to discover the truth (though it

so appalled him that he gouged out his own eyes); Odysseus, returning home from the Trojan War, ordered his men to shut their ears with wax and tie him to his ship's mast so that he might hear the Sirens, female half-bird creatures whose irresistible songs lured sailors to their death.

to the siren songs of old metaphysical bird-catchers who have all too long been piping to him 'you are more! you are higher! you are of a different origin!'— that may be a strange and extravagant task but it is a *task*—who would deny that? Why did we choose it, this extravagant task? Or, to ask the question differently: 'why knowledge at all?'—Everyone will ask us about that. And we, thus pressed, we who have asked ourselves the same question a hundred times, we have found and can find no better answer . . .

* * *

From *PART NINE*
What is Noble?[5]

257

Every elevation[6] of the type 'man' has hitherto been the work of an aristocratic society—and so it will always be: a society which believes in a long scale of orders of rank and differences of worth between man and man and needs slavery in some sense or other. Without the *pathos of distance* such as develops from the incarnate differences of classes, from the ruling caste's constant looking out and looking down on subjects and instruments and from its equally constant exercise of obedience and command, its holding down and holding at a distance, that other, more mysterious pathos could not have developed either, that longing for an ever-increasing widening of distance within the soul itself, the formation of ever higher, rarer, more remote, tenser, more comprehensive states, in short precisely the elevation of the type 'man', the continual 'self-overcoming of man', to take a moral formula in a supra-moral sense.[7] As to how an aristocratic society (that is to say, the precondition for this elevation of the type 'man') originates, one ought not to yield to any humanitarian illusions: truth is hard. Let us admit to ourselves unflinchingly how every higher culture on earth has hitherto *begun*! Men of a still natural nature, barbarians in every fearful sense of the word, men of prey still in possession of an unbroken strength of will and lust for power, threw themselves upon weaker, more civilized, more peaceful, perhaps trading or cattle-raising races, or upon old mellow cultures, the last vital forces in which were even then flickering out in a glittering firework display of spirit and corruption. The noble caste was in the beginning always the barbarian caste: their superiority lay, not in their physical strength, but primarily in their psychical—they were *more complete* human beings (which, on every level, also means as much as 'more complete beasts'—).

* * *

5. "Noble" translates *vornehm*: literally as well as figuratively outstanding, exceptional, distinguished. In short, for Nietzsche, "higher."
6. That is, enhancement (*Erhöhung*).
7. This is a *developmental* claim or hypothesis, about the real-world conditions in which a certain kind of "elevation" or transformation and enhancement of human reality and possibility can emerge and develop. Nietzsche's topic here, in short, is the "genealogy" of the kind of "higher humanity" that is now humanly possible; in *Thus Spoke Zarathustra* (1883–85; see above), its ultimate symbol and image is the *Übermensch*.

259

To refrain from mutual injury, mutual violence, mutual exploitation, to equate one's own will with that of another: this may in a certain rough sense become good manners between individuals if the conditions for it are present (namely if their strength and value standards are in fact similar and they both belong to *one* body). As soon as there is a desire to take this principle further, however, and if possible even as the *fundamental principle of society*, it at once reveals itself for what it is: as the will to the *denial* of life, as the principle of dissolution and decay. One has to think this matter thoroughly through to the bottom and resist all sentimental weakness: life itself is *essentially* appropriation, injury, overpowering of the strange and weaker, suppression, severity, imposition of one's own forms, incorporation and, at the least and mildest, exploitation—but why should one always have to employ precisely those words which have from of old been stamped with a slanderous intention? Even that body within which, as was previously assumed, individuals treat one another as equals—this happens in every healthy aristocracy—must, if it is a living and not a decaying body, itself do all that to other bodies which the individuals within it refrain from doing to one another: it will have to be the will to power incarnate, it will want to grow, expand, draw to itself, gain ascendancy—not out of any morality or immorality, but because it *lives*, and because life *is* will to power. On no point, however, is the common European consciousness more reluctant to learn than it is here; everywhere one enthuses, even under scientific disguises, about coming states of society in which there will be 'no more exploitation'—that sounds to my ears like promising a life in which there will be no organic functions. 'Exploitation' does not pertain to a corrupt or imperfect or primitive society: it pertains to the *essence* of the living thing as a fundamental organic function, it is a consequence of the intrinsic will to power which is precisely the will of life.—Granted this is a novelty as a theory—as a reality it is the *primordial fact* of all history: let us be at least that honest with ourselves!—

260

In a tour of the many finer and coarser moralities [*Moralen*] which have ruled or still rule on earth I found certain traits regularly recurring together and bound up with one another: until at length two basic types were revealed and a basic distinction emerged. There is *master morality* and *slave morality*—I add at once that in all higher and mixed cultures attempts at mediation between the two are apparent and more frequently confusion and mutual misunderstanding between them, indeed sometimes their harsh juxtaposition—even within the same man, within *one* soul. The moral value-distinctions have arisen either among a ruling order which was pleasurably conscious of its distinction from the ruled—or among the ruled, the slaves and dependants of every degree. In the former case, when it is the rulers who determine the concept 'good', it is the exalted, proud states of soul which are considered distinguishing and determine the order of rank. The noble [*vornehm*] human being separates from himself those natures in which the opposite of such exalted proud states find expression: he despises them. It should be noted at once that in this first type of morality the antithesis 'good' and 'bad' means the same thing as 'noble' and 'despicable'—the antithesis 'good' and *'evil'* originates elsewhere.[8] The cowardly, the timid, the petty, and those who think only of narrow utility are despised; as are the mistrustful with their constricted glance, those who abase themselves, the dog-like type of man who lets himself be mistreated, the fawning flatterer, above all the liar—it is a fundamental belief of all aristocrats that the common people are liars. 'We who are truthful'—thus did the nobility of ancient Greece designate themselves. It is immediately obvious that designations of moral value were everywhere first applied to *human beings*, and only later and derivatively to *actions*: which is why it is a grave error when moral historians start from such questions as 'why has the compassionate action been praised?' The noble type of man feels *himself* to be the determiner of values, he does not need to be approved of, he judges 'what harms me is harmful in itself', he knows himself to be that which in general first accords honour to things, he *creates values*. Everything he knows to be part of himself, he honours: such a morality is self-glorification. In the foreground stands the feeling of plenitude, of power which seeks to overflow, the happiness of high tension, the consciousness of a wealth which would like to give away and bestow—the noble human being too aids the unfortunate but not, or almost not, from pity, but more from an urge begotten by superfluity of power. The noble human being honours in himself the man of power, also the man who has power over himself, who understands how to speak and how to keep silent, who enjoys practising severity and harshness upon himself and feels reverence for all that is severe and harsh. 'A hard heart has Wotan[9] set in my breast', it says in an old Scandinavian saga: a just expression coming from the soul of a proud Viking. A man of this type is actually proud that he is *not* made for pity: which is why the hero of the saga adds as a warning: 'he whose heart is not hard in youth will never have a hard heart'. Brave and noble men who think that are at the farthest remove from that morality which sees the mark of the moral precisely in pity or in acting for others or in *désintéressement*;[1] belief in oneself, pride in oneself, a fundamental hostility and irony for 'selflessness' belong just as definitely to noble morality as does a mild contempt for and caution against sympathy and the 'warm heart'.—It is the powerful who *understand* how to honour, that is their art, their realm of invention. Deep reverence for age and the traditional—all law rests on this twofold reverence—belief in and prejudice in favour of ancestors and against descendants, is typical of the morality of the powerful; and when, conversely, men of 'modern ideas' believe almost instinctively in 'progress' and 'the future' and show an increasing lack of respect for age, this reveals clearly enough the ignoble origin of these 'ideas'. A morality of the rulers is, however, most alien and painful to contemporary taste in the severity of its principle that one has duties only towards one's equals; that towards beings of a lower rank, towards everything alien, one may act as one wishes or 'as the heart dictates' and in any case 'beyond good and evil'—: it is here that pity and the like can have a place. The capacity for and the duty of protracted gratitude and protracted

---

8. This is one of the topics of the first essay of Nietzsche's next book, *On the Genealogy of Morals* (1887; see below).

9. One of the main deities of Norse mythology (also called Odin), a war god.

1. Disinterestedness; unselfishness (French).

revenge—both only among one's equals—subtlety in requittal, a refined conception of friendship, a certain need to have enemies (as conduit systems, as it were, for the emotions of envy, quarrelsomeness, arrogance—fundamentally so as to be able to be a good *friend*): all these are typical marks of noble morality which, as previously indicated, is not the morality of 'modern ideas' and is therefore hard to enter into today, also hard to unearth and uncover. It is otherwise with the second type of morality, *slave morality*. Suppose the abused, oppressed, suffering, unfree, those uncertain of themselves and weary should moralize: what would their moral evaluations have in common? Probably a pessimistic mistrust of the entire situation of man will find expression, perhaps a condemnation of man together with his situation. The slave is suspicious of the virtues of the powerful: he is sceptical and mistrustful, *keenly* mistrustful, of everything 'good' that is honoured among them—he would like to convince himself that happiness itself is not genuine among them. On the other hand, those qualities which serve to make easier the existence of the suffering will be brought into prominence and flooded with light: here it is that pity, the kind and helping hand, the warm heart, patience, industriousness, humility, friendliness come into honour—for here these are the most useful qualities and virtually the only means of enduring the burden of existence. Slave morality is essentially the morality of utility. Here is the source of the famous antithesis 'good' and *'evil'*—power and danger were felt to exist in evil, a certain dreadfulness, subtlety and strength which could not admit of contempt. Thus, according to slave morality the 'evil' inspire fear; according to master morality it is precisely the 'good' who inspire fear and want to inspire it, while the 'bad' man is judged contemptible. The antithesis reaches its height when, consistently with slave morality, a breath of disdain finally also comes to be attached to the 'good' of this morality—it may be a slight and benevolent disdain—because within the slaves' way of thinking the good man has in any event to be a *harmless* man: he is good-natured, easy to deceive, perhaps a bit stupid, *un bonhomme*.[2] Wherever slave morality comes to predominate, language exhibits a tendency to bring the words 'good' and 'stupid' closer to each other.—A final fundamental distinction: the longing for *freedom*, the instinct for the happiness and the refinements of the feeling of freedom, belong just as necessarily to slave morality and morals as the art of reverence and devotion and the enthusiasm for them are the regular symptom of an aristocratic mode of thinking and valuating.—This makes it clear without further ado why love *as passion*—it is our European speciality—absolutely must be of aristocratic origin: it was, as is well known, invented by the poet-knights of Provence, those splendid, inventive men of the *'gai saber'*[3] to whom Europe owes so much and, indeed, almost itself.—

* * *

SOURCES: From Friedrich Nietzsche, *Beyond Good and Evil: Prelude to a Philosophy of the Future*, trans. Walter Kaufmann (New York: Vintage Books, 1966), pp. 2–13, 19–35, 43–50

2. A simple-minded man (French).
3. Gay science (Provençal), in the language of the French troubadours of 14th-century Provence. Nietzsche saw the "knowing" or "wisdom" of "those splendid, inventive men" as at least as much an artful and enlightened way of living a human life as it was any sort of cognitive endeavor. Immediately after publishing this work, and before *On the Genealogy of Morals* appeared, he issued an expanded edition of *The Gay Science* (1887, see below; for the 1st ed. of 1882, see above).

[through part 2], and trans. R. J. Hollingdale (Harmondsworth: Penguin, 1974), pp. 80–81, 108–10, 122–26, 140–44, 154–56, 160–62, 192–98 [parts 3–9]. Except where otherwise indicated, German words in brackets are the terminology used in the German original, inserted by the editor in addition to their renderings in the translation. Originally published in 1886 as *Jenseits von Gut und Böse*.

From The Gay Science

From *BOOK FIVE*
We Fearless Ones

343

The meaning of our cheerfulness.[1]—The greatest recent event—that "God is dead," that the belief in the Christian god has become unbelievable[2]—is already beginning to cast its first shadows over Europe. For the few at least, whose eyes—the *suspicion* in whose eyes is strong and subtle enough for this spectacle, some sun seems to have set and some ancient and profound trust has been turned into doubt; to them our old world must appear daily more like evening, more mistrustful, stranger, "older." But in the main one may say: The event itself is far too great, too distant, too remote from the multitude's capacity for comprehension even for the tidings of it to be thought of as having *arrived* as yet. Much less may one suppose that many people know as yet *what* this event really means—and how much must collapse now that this faith has been undermined because it was built upon this faith, propped up by it, grown into it; for example, the whole of our European morality. This long plenitude and sequence of breakdown, destruction, ruin, and cataclysm that is now impending—who could guess enough of it today to be compelled to play the teacher and advance proclaimer of this monstrous logic of terror, the prophet of a gloom and an eclipse of the sun whose like has probably never yet occurred on earth?

Even we born guessers of riddles who are, as it were, waiting on the mountains, posted between today and tomorrow, stretched in the contradiction between today and tomorrow, we firstlings and premature births of the coming century, to whom the shadows that must soon envelop Europe really *should* have appeared by now—why is it that even we look forward to the approaching gloom without any real sense of involvement and above all without any worry and fear for *ourselves*? Are we perhaps still too much under the impression of the *initial consequences* of this event—and these initial consequences, the consequences for *ourselves*, are quite the opposite of what one might perhaps expect: They are not at all sad and gloomy but rather like a new and scarcely describable kind of light, happiness, relief, exhilaration, encouragement, dawn.

Indeed, we philosophers and "free spirits" feel, when we hear the news that "the old god is dead," as if a new dawn shone on us; our heart overflows with gratitude, amazement, premonitions, expectation. At long last the horizon

---

1. Here Nietzsche uses the word *Heiterkeit*, but this opening section provides an indication of the sort of spirit in which he would now have the *Fröhlichkeit* of his *fröhlichen Wissenschaft* be conceived.
2. This elaboration indicates what Nietzsche fundamentally means by "God is dead."

appears free to us again, even if it should not be bright; at long last our ships may venture out again, venture out to face any danger; all the daring of the lover of knowledge[3] is permitted again; the sea, *our* sea, lies open again; perhaps there has never yet been such an "open sea."—

344

How we, too, are still pious.—In science[4] convictions have no rights of citizenship, as one says with good reason. Only when they decide to descend to the modesty of hypotheses, of a provisional experimental point of view, of a regulative fiction, they may be granted admission and even a certain value in the realm of knowledge—though always with the restriction that they remain under police supervision, under the police of mistrust.—But does this not mean, if you consider it more precisely, that a conviction may obtain admission to science only when it *ceases* to be a conviction? Would it not be the first step in the discipline of the scientific [*wissenschaftlich*] spirit that one would not permit oneself any more convictions?

Probably this is so; only we still have to ask: *To make it possible for this discipline to begin,* must there not be some prior conviction—even one that is so commanding and unconditional that it sacrifices all other convictions to itself? We see that science [*Wissenschaft*] also rests on a faith; there simply is no science "without presuppositions." The question whether *truth* is needed must not only have been affirmed in advance, but affirmed to such a degree that the principle, the faith, the conviction finds expression: "*Nothing* is needed *more* than truth, and in relation to it everything else has only second-rate value."

This unconditional will to truth—what is it? Is it the will *not to allow oneself to be deceived*? Or is it the will *not to deceive*? For the will to truth could be interpreted in the second way, too—if only the special case "I do not want to deceive myself" is subsumed under the generalization "I do not want to deceive." But why not deceive? But why not allow oneself to be deceived?

Note that the reasons for the former principle belong to an altogether different realm from those for the second. One does not want to allow oneself to be deceived because one assumes that it is harmful, dangerous, calamitous to be deceived. In this sense, science [*Wissenschaft*] would be a long-range prudence, a caution, a utility; but one could object in all fairness: How is that? Is wanting not to allow oneself to be deceived really less harmful, less dangerous, less calamitous? What do you know in advance of the character of existence to be able to decide whether the greater advantage is on the side of the unconditionally mistrustful or of the unconditionally trusting? But if both should be required, much trust *as well as* much mistrust, from where would science then be permitted to take its unconditional faith or conviction on which it rests, that truth is more important than any other thing, including every other conviction? Precisely this conviction could never have come into being if both truth and untruth constantly proved to be useful, which is the case. Thus—the faith in science which after all exists undeniably, cannot owe its origin to such a calculus of utility; it must have originated *in spite of*

---

3. That is, knower, pursuer of knowledge (*Erkennenden*).
4. That is, intellectually conscientious and sophisticated cognitive inquiry (*Wissenschaft*).

the fact that the disutility and dangerousness of "the will to truth," of "truth at any price" is proved to it constantly. "At any price": how well we understand these words once we have offered and slaughtered one faith after another on this altar!

Consequently, "will to truth" does *not* mean "I will not allow myself to be deceived" but—there is no alternative—"I will not deceive, not even myself"; *and with that we stand on moral ground.* For you only have to ask yourself carefully, "Why do you not want to deceive?" especially if it should seem— and it does seem!—as if life aimed at semblance, meaning error, deception, simulation, delusion, self-delusion, and when the great sweep of life has actually always shown itself to be on the side of the most unscrupulous *polytropoi.*[5] Charitably interpreted, such a resolve might perhaps be a quixotism, a minor slightly mad enthusiasm; but it might also be something more serious, namely, a principle that is hostile to life and destructive.—"Will to truth"— that might be a concealed will to death.

Thus the question "Why science?" leads back to the moral problem: *Why have morality at all* when life, nature, and history are "not moral"? No doubt, those who are truthful in that audacious and ultimate sense that is presupposed by the faith in science *thus affirm another world* than the world of life, nature, and history; and insofar as they affirm this "other world"—look, must they not by the same token negate its counterpart, this world, *our* world?— But you will have gathered what I am driving at, namely, that it is still a *metaphysical faith* upon which our faith in science [*Wissenschaft*] rests—that even we seekers after knowledge [*Erkennenden*] today, we godless anti-metaphysicians still take our fire, too, from the flame lit by a faith that is thousands of years old, that Christian faith which was also the faith of Plato,[6] that God is the truth, that truth is divine.—But what if this should become more and more incredible, if nothing should prove to be divine any more unless it were error, blindness, the lie—if God himself should prove to be our most enduring lie?—

345

Morality as a problem.—The lack of personality always takes its revenge: A weakened, thin, extinguished personality that denies itself is no longer fit for anything good—least of all for philosophy. "Selflessness" has no value either in heaven or on earth. All great problems demand *great love*, and of that only strong, round, secure spirits who have a firm grip on themselves are capable. It makes the most telling difference whether a thinker has a personal relationship to his problems and finds in them his destiny, his distress, and his greatest happiness, or an "impersonal" one, meaning that he can do no better than to touch them and grasp them with the antennae of cold, curious thought. In the latter case nothing will come of it; that much one can promise in advance, for even if great problems should allow themselves to be *grasped* by them they would not permit frogs and weaklings to *hold on* to them; such has been their taste from time immemorial—a taste, incidentally, that they share with all redoubtable females.

---

5. Literally, "men of many turns" (Greek); that is, those who have been around, have had much experience, and are wise to the ways of the world.
6. Greek philosopher (ca. 427–ca. 347 B.C.E.).

Why is it then that I have never yet encountered anybody, not even in books, who approached morality in this personal way and who knew morality as a problem, and this problem as his own personal distress, torment, voluptuousness, and passion? It is evident that up to now morality was no problem at all but, on the contrary, precisely that on which after all mistrust, discord, and contradiction one could agree—the hallowed place of peace where our thinkers took a rest even from themselves, took a deep breath, and felt revived. I see nobody who ventured a *critique* of moral valuations;[7] I miss even the slightest attempts of scientific [*wissenschaftlich*] curiosity, of the refined, experimental imagination of psychologists and historians that readily anticipates a problem and catches it in flight without quite knowing what it has caught. I have scarcely detected a few meager preliminary efforts to explore the *history of the origins* of these feelings and valuations (which is something quite different from a critique and again different from a history of ethical systems).[8] In one particular case[9] I have done everything to encourage a sympathy and talent for this kind of history—in vain, as it seems to me today.

These historians of morality (mostly Englishmen) do not amount to much. Usually they themselves are still quite unsuspectingly obedient to one particular morality and, without knowing it, serve that as shield-bearers and followers—for example, by sharing that popular superstition of Christian Europe which people keep mouthing so guilelessly to this day, that what is characteristic of moral actions is selflessness, self-sacrifice, or sympathy and pity. Their usual mistaken premise is that they affirm some consensus of the nations, at least of tame nations, concerning certain principles of morals, and then they infer from this that these principles must be unconditionally binding also for you and me; or, conversely, they see the truth that among different nations[1] moral valuations are *necessarily* different and then infer from this that *no* morality is at all binding. Both procedures are equally childish.

The mistake made by the more refined among them is that they uncover and criticize the perhaps foolish opinions of a people about their morality, or of humanity about all human morality—opinions about its origin, religious sanction, the superstition of free will, and things of that sort—and then suppose that they have criticized the morality itself. But the value of a command "thou shalt" is still fundamentally different from and independent of such opinions about it and the weeds of error that may have overgrown it—just as certainly as the value of a medication for a sick person is completely independent of whether he thinks about medicine scientifically or the way old women do. Even if a morality has grown out of an error, the realization of this fact would not as much as touch the problem of its value.

Thus nobody up to now has examined the *value* [*Wert*] of that most famous of all medicines which is called morality [*Moral*]; and the first step would be—for once to *question* it. Well then, precisely this is our task.—

---

7. That is, moral value judgments (*moralischen Werturteilen*).
8. A history of origins, and not a critique or history of systems, is exactly what Nietzsche saw himself as providing in the not-yet-published *On the Genealogy of Morals*, on which he was working.
9. A reference to the German moral philosopher Paul Rée (1849–1901), a former friend whose work Nietzsche had earlier admired; their relationship

had become strained, and Nietzsche at this point wanted to deny his indebtedness to Rée. Rée had earlier written *Der Ursprung der moralischen Empfindungen* (1877, *The Origin of Moral Feeling*), and more recently *Die Entstehung des Gewissens* (1885, *The Emergence of Conscience*)—books that were both at least apparently similar to Nietzsche's "genealogy of morals" project.
1. That is, peoples (*Völker*).

346

Our question mark.—But you do not understand this? Indeed, people will have trouble understanding us. We are looking for words; perhaps we are also looking for ears. Who are we anyway? If we simply called ourselves, using an old expression, godless, or unbelievers, or perhaps immoralists, we do not believe that this would even come close to designating us: We are all three in such an advanced stage that one—that *you*, my curious friends—could never comprehend how we feel at this point. Ours is no longer the bitterness and passion of the person who has torn himself away and still feels compelled to turn his unbelief into a new belief, a purpose, a martyrdom. We have become cold, hard, and tough in the realization that the way of this world is anything but divine; even by human standards it is not rational, merciful, or just. We know it well, the world in which we live is ungodly, immoral, "inhuman"; we have interpreted it far too long in a false and mendacious way, in accordance with the wishes of our reverence, which is to say, according to our *needs*. For man is a reverent animal. But he is also mistrustful; and that the world is *not* worth what we thought it was, that is about as certain as anything of which our mistrust has finally got hold. The more mistrust, the more philosophy.

We are far from claiming that the world is worth *less*; indeed it would seem laughable to us today if man were to insist on inventing values that were supposed to *excel*[2] the value of the actual world. This is precisely what we have turned our backs on as an extravagant aberration of human vanity and unreason that for a long time was not recognized as such. It found its final expression in modern pessimism,[3] and a more ancient and stronger expression in the teaching of Buddha;[4] but it is part of Christianity also, if more doubtfully and ambiguously so but not for that reason any less seductive.

The whole pose of "man *against* the world," of man as a "world-negating" principle, of man as the measure of the value of things, as judge of the world who in the end places existence itself upon his scales and finds it wanting— the monstrous insipidity of this pose has finally come home to us and we are sick of it. We laugh as soon as we encounter the juxtaposition of "man *and* world," separated by the sublime presumption of the little word "and." But look, when we laugh like that, have we not simply carried the contempt for man one step further? And thus also pessimism, the contempt for that existence which is knowable by *us*? Have we not exposed ourselves to the suspicion of an opposition—an opposition between the world in which we were at home up to now with our reverences that perhaps made it possible for us to *endure* life, and another world *that consists of us*—an inexorable, fundamental, and deepest suspicion about ourselves that is more and more gaining worse and worse control of us Europeans and that could easily confront coming generations with the terrifying Either/Or: "Either abolish your reverences or— *yourselves!*" The latter would be nihilism; but would not the former also be—nihilism?—This is *our* question mark.[5]

2. That is, exceed or surpass (*überragen*).
3. That is, in SCHOPENHAUER.
4. The historical Buddha (active ca. 5th century B.C.E.), born Siddhartha Gautama in northeastern India, who founded Buddhism.
5. Nietzsche wishes to suggest that this Either/Or is a false dichotomy, and that a third and more promising option exists.

347

Believers and their need to believe.—How much one needs a *faith* in order to flourish, how much that is "firm" and that one does not wish to be shaken because one *clings* to it, that is a measure of the degree of one's strength (or, to put the point more clearly, of one's weakness). Christianity, it seems to me, is still needed by most people in old Europe even today; therefore it still finds believers. For this is how man is: An article of faith could be refuted before him a thousand times—if he needed it, he would consider it "true" again and again, in accordance with that famous "proof of strength" of which the Bible speaks.[6]

* * *

349

Once more the origin of scholars.—The wish to preserve oneself is the symptom of a condition of distress, of a limitation of the really fundamental instinct of life which aims at *the expansion of power* and, wishing for that, frequently risks and even sacrifices self-preservation. It should be considered symptomatic when some philosophers—for example, Spinoza[7] who was consumptive—considered the instinct of self-preservation decisive and *had* to see it that way; for they were individuals in conditions of distress.

That our modern natural sciences have become so thoroughly entangled in this Spinozistic dogma (most recently and worst of all, Darwinism with its incomprehensibly onesided doctrine of the "struggle for existence")[8] is probably due to the origins of most natural scientists: In this respect they belong to the "common people"; their ancestors were poor and undistinguished people who knew the difficulties of survival only too well at firsthand. The whole of English Darwinism breathes something like the musty air of English overpopulation, like the smell of the distress and overcrowding of small people. But a natural scientist should come out of his human nook; and in nature it is not conditions of distress that are *dominant* but overflow and squandering, even to the point of absurdity. The struggle for existence is only an *exception*, a temporary restriction of the will to life. The great and small struggle always revolves around superiority,[9] around growth and expansion, around power—in accordance with the will to power which is the will of life.

* * *

354

On the "genius of the species."—The problem of consciousness (more precisely, of becoming conscious of something) confronts us only when we begin

6. See 1 Corinthians 2:4. Nietzsche thus scoffs at the idea that something *is* "true" if believing it makes one feel stronger (though he recognizes that that may be an important point in the psychology of belief, and even—in some circumstances—a practical reason for someone to believe something that happens to be false, erroneous, or fictitious).
7. Benedict (Baruch) de Spinoza (1632–1677), Dutch philosopher.
8. That is, the version of Darwinism popularized by the English sociologist Herbert Spencer (1820–1903; see §373, below), rather than the theory of evolution by natural selection set forth by the English naturalist Charles Darwin (1809–1882).
9. Better translated as "domination" (*Übergewicht*).

to comprehend how we could dispense with it; and now physiology and the history of animals place us at the beginning of such comprehension (it took them two centuries to catch up with *Leibniz's*[1] suspicion which soared ahead). For we could think, feel, will, and remember, and we could also "act" in every sense of that word, and yet none of all this would have to "enter our consciousness" (as one says metaphorically). The whole of life would be possible without, as it were, seeing itself in a mirror. Even now, for that matter, by far the greatest portion of our life actually takes place without this mirror effect; and this is true even of our thinking, feeling, and willing life, however offensive this may sound to older philosophers. *For what purpose,* then, any consciousness at all when it is in the main *superfluous*?

Now, if you are willing to listen to my answer and the perhaps extravagant surmise that it involves, it seems to me as if the subtlety and strength of consciousness always were proportionate to a man's (or animal's) *capacity for communication*, and as if this capacity in turn were proportionate to the *need for communication*. But this last point is not to be understood as if the individual human being who happens to be a master in communicating and making understandable his needs must also be most dependent on others in his needs. But it does seem to me as if it were that way when we consider whole races and chains of generations: Where need and distress have forced men for a long time to communicate and to understand each other quickly and subtly, the ultimate result is an excess of this strength and art of communication— as it were, a capacity that has gradually been accumulated and now waits for an heir who might squander it. (Those who are called artists are these heirs; so are orators, preachers, writers—all of them people who always come at the end of a long chain, "late born" every one of them in the best sense of that word and, as I have said, by their nature squanderers.)

Supposing that this observation is correct, I may now proceed to the surmise that *consciousness has developed only under the pressure of the need for communication*; that from the start it was needed and useful only between human beings (particularly between those who commanded and those who obeyed); and that it also developed only in proportion to the degree of this utility. Consciousness is really only a net of communication between human beings; it is only as such that it had to develop; a solitary human being who lived like a beast of prey would not have needed it. That our actions, thoughts, feelings, and movements enter our own consciousness—at least a part of them—that is the result of a "must" that for a terribly long time lorded it over man. As the most endangered animal, he *needed* help and protection, he needed his peers, he had to learn to express his distress and to make himself understood; and for all of this he needed "consciousness" first of all, he needed to "know" himself what distressed him, he needed to "know" how he felt, he needed to "know" what he thought. For, to say it once more: Man, like every living being, thinks continually without knowing it; the thinking that rises to *consciousness* is only the smallest part of all this—the most superficial and worst part—for only this conscious thinking *takes the form of*

---

1. Gottfried Wilhelm Leibniz (1646–1715), German philosopher and mathematician; his "suspicion" is explained in §357, below.

words, *which is to say signs of communication*, and this fact uncovers the origin of consciousness.

In brief, the development of language and the development of consciousness (*not* of reason but merely of the way reason enters consciousness) go hand in hand. Add to this that not only language serves as a bridge between human beings but also a mien, a pressure, a gesture. The emergence of our sense impressions into our own consciousness, the ability to fix them and, as it were, exhibit them externally, increased proportionately with the need to communicate them to *others* by means of signs. The human being inventing signs is at the same time the human being who becomes ever more keenly conscious of himself. It was only as a social animal that man acquired self-consciousness—which he is still in the process of doing, more and more.

My idea is, as you see, that consciousness does not really belong to man's individual existence but rather to his social or herd nature; that, as follows from this, it has developed subtlety only insofar as this is required by social or herd utility. Consequently, given the best will in the world to understand ourselves as individually as possible, "to know ourselves," each of us will always succeed in becoming conscious only of what is not individual but "average." Our thoughts themselves are continually governed by the character of consciousness—by the "genius of the species" that commands it—and translated back into the perspective of the herd. Fundamentally, all our actions are altogether incomparably personal, unique, and infinitely individual; there is no doubt of that. But as soon as we translate them into consciousness *they no longer seem to be*.

This is the essence of phenomenalism and perspectivism as *I* understand them:[2] Owing to the nature of *animal consciousness*, the world of which we can become conscious is only a surface- and sign-world, a world that is made common and meaner; whatever becomes conscious *becomes* by the same token shallow, thin, relatively stupid, general, sign, herd signal; all becoming conscious involves a great and thorough corruption, falsification, reduction to superficialities, and generalization. Ultimately, the growth of consciousness becomes a danger; and anyone who lives among the most conscious Europeans even knows that it is a disease.

You will guess that it is not the opposition of subject and object that concerns me here: This distinction I leave to the epistemologists who have become entangled in the snares of grammar (the metaphysics of the people). It is even less the opposition of "thing-in-itself" and appearance; for we do not "know" nearly enough to be entitled to any such distinction. We simply lack any organ for knowledge [*Erkenntnis*], for "truth": we "know" [*wissen*] (or believe or imagine) just as much as may be *useful* in the interests of the human herd, the species; and even what is here called "utility" is ultimately also a mere belief, something imaginary, and perhaps precisely that most calamitous stupidity of which we shall perish some day.

* * *

2. The "perspectivism" (*Perspektivismus*) that Nietzsche articulates and affirms here is far from the radically relativistic perspectivism with respect to truth, knowledge, and value that is commonly attributed to him.

357

On the old problem: "What is German?"—Recapitulate in your mind the real achievements of philosophical thinking that one owes to Germans. Is there any legitimate sense in which one might give the credit for these achievements to the whole race? May we say that they are at the same time the product of "the German soul," or at least symptoms of that in the sense in which, say, Plato's ideomania, his almost religious madness about Forms,[3] is usually taken also for an event and testimony of "the Greek soul"? Or should the opposite be the truth? Might they be just as individual, just as much *exceptions* from the spirit of the race as was, for example, Goethe's[4] paganism with a good conscience? Or as is Bismarck's Machiavellism with a good conscience, his so-called *"Realpolitik,"*[5] among Germans? Might our philosophers actually contradict the *need* of "the German soul"? In short, were the German philosophers really—philosophical *Germans*?

I recall three cases. First, *Leibniz's* incomparable insight that has been vindicated not only against Descartes[6] but against everybody who had philosophized before him—that consciousness is merely an *accidens* of experience[7] and *not* its necessary and essential attribute; that, in other words, what we call consciousness constitutes only one state of our spiritual and psychic world (perhaps a pathological state) and *not by any means the whole of it*. The profundity of this idea has not been exhausted to this day. Is there anything German in this idea? Is there any reason for surmising that no Latin could easily have thought of this reversal of appearances? For it is a reversal.

Let us recall, secondly, *Kant's* tremendous question mark that he placed after the concept of "causality"—without, like Hume,[8] doubting its legitimacy altogether. Rather, Kant began cautiously to delimit the realm within which this concept makes sense (and to this day we are not done with this fixing of limits).

Let us take, thirdly, the astonishing stroke of *Hegel*, who struck right through all our logical habits and bad habits when he dared to teach that species concepts[9] develop *out of each other*. With this proposition the minds of Europe were preformed for the last great scientific movement, Darwinism—for without Hegel there could have been no Darwin. Is there anything German in this Hegelian innovation which first introduced the decisive concept of "development" into science [*Wissenschaft*]?

Yes, without any doubt. In all three cases we feel that something in ourselves has been "uncovered" and guessed, and we are grateful for it and at

---

3. The abstract essences (also called Ideas) that, according to the Greek philosopher Plato (ca. 427–ca. 347 B.C.E.), exist independently of and are more real than their instantiations in the sensible world.

4. Johann Wolfgang von Goethe (1749–1832), the preeminent German literary figure of his time; the German poet and critic Heinrich Heine labeled him "the great pagan" (*der grosse Heide*).

5. Practical or realistic politics (in contrast to diplomacy based on ideology or morality); its most famous proponent was Otto von Bismarck (1815–1898), prime minister of Prussia and first chancellor of the German Empire.

6. René Descartes (1596–1650), French philosopher and mathematician.

7. Better translated as "representation" (*Vorstellung*). *Accidens*: that is, an "accidental" or secondary (rather than essential) property of something.

8. David Hume (1711–1776), Scottish philosopher; his conclusion that it is impossible to give meaningful empirical content (beyond that of constant conjunction) to the idea of causality helped spur KANT to write his *Critique of Pure Reason* (1781).

9. In German, *Artbegriffe*: that is, *Begriffe* ("concepts," in HEGEL's special sense of the term: see the glossary in the introduction to Hegel, above) of a particular species or type (*Art*) of creature.

the same time surprised. Each of these three propositions is a thoughtful piece of German self-knowledge, self-experience, self-understanding. "Our inner world is much richer, more comprehensive, more concealed," we feel with Leibniz. As Germans, we doubt with Kant the ultimate validity of the knowledge attained by the natural sciences and altogether everything that *can* be known *causaliter*;[1] whatever is know*able* immediately seems to us less valuable on that account. We Germans are Hegelians even if there never had been any Hegel, insofar as we (unlike all Latins) instinctively attribute a deeper meaning and greater value to becoming and development than to what "is"; we hardly believe in the justification of the concept of "being"—and also insofar as we are not inclined to concede that our human logic is logic as such or the only kind of logic (we would rather persuade ourselves that it is merely a special case and perhaps one of the oddest and most stupid cases).

It would be a fourth question whether *Schopenhauer*, too, with his pessimism—that is, the problem of the *value of existence*—had to be precisely a German. I believe not. The event after which this problem was to be expected for certain—an astronomer of the soul could have calculated the very day and hour for it—the decline of the faith in the Christian god, the triumph of scientific atheism, is a generally European event in which all races had their share and for which all deserve credit and honor. Conversely, one might charge precisely the Germans—those Germans who were Schopenhauer's contemporaries—that they *delayed* this triumph of atheism most dangerously for the longest time. Hegel in particular was its delayer par excellence, with his grandiose attempt to persuade us of the divinity of existence, appealing as a last resort to our sixth sense, "the historical sense." As a philosopher, Schopenhauer was the *first* admitted and inexorable atheist among us Germans: This was the background of his enmity against Hegel. The ungodliness of existence was for him something given, palpable, indisputable; he always lost his philosopher's composure and became indignant when he saw anyone hesitate or mince matters at this point. This is the locus of his whole integrity; unconditional and honest atheism is simply the *presupposition* of the way he poses his problem, being a triumph achieved finally and with great difficulty by the European conscience, being the most fateful act of two thousand years of discipline for truth that in the end forbids itself the *lie* in faith in God.

You see what it was that really triumphed over the Christian god: Christian morality itself, the concept of truthfulness that was understood ever more rigorously, the father confessor's refinement of the Christian conscience, translated and sublimated into a scientific [*wissenschaftlich*] conscience, into intellectual cleanliness at any price. Looking at nature as if it were proof of the goodness and governance of a god; interpreting history in honor of some divine reason, as a continual testimony of a moral world order and ultimate moral purposes; interpreting one's own experiences as pious people have long enough interpreted theirs, as if everything were providential, a hint, designed and ordained for the sake of the salvation of the soul—that is *all over* now, that has man's conscience *against* it, that is considered indecent and dishonest by every more refined conscience—mendaciousness, feminism, weakness,

---

1. Causally (Latin); that is, comprehended in terms of the principle of causality.

and cowardice. In this severity, if anywhere, we are *good* Europeans and heirs of Europe's longest and most courageous self-overcoming.

As we thus reject the Christian interpretation and condemn its "meaning" like counterfeit, *Schopenhauer's* question immediately comes to us in a terrifying way: *Has existence any meaning at all?* It will require a few centuries before this question can even be heard completely and in its full depth. What Schopenhauer himself said in answer to this question was—forgive me—hasty, youthful, only a compromise, a way of remaining—remaining stuck—in precisely those Christian-ascetic moral perspectives in which one had *renounced faith* along with the faith in God. But he *posed* the question—as a good European, as I have said, and *not* as a German.

* * *

360

Two kinds of causes that are often confounded.—This seems to me to be one of my most essential steps and advances: I have learned to distinguish the cause of acting from the cause of acting in a particular way, in a particular direction, with a particular goal. The first kind of cause is a quantum of dammed-up energy that is waiting to be used up somehow, for something, while the second kind is, compared to this energy, something quite insignificant, for the most part a little accident in accordance with which this quantum "discharges" itself in one particular way—a match versus a ton of powder. Among these little accidents and "matches" I include so-called "purposes" as well as the even much more so-called "vocations": They are relatively random, arbitrary, almost indifferent in relation to the tremendous quantum of energy that presses, as I have said, to be used up somehow. The usual view is different: People are accustomed to consider the goal (purposes, vocations, etc.) as the *driving force*, in keeping with a very ancient error; but it is merely the *directing* force—one has mistaken the helmsman for the steam. And not even always the helmsman, the directing force.

Is the "goal," the "purpose" not often enough a beautifying pretext, a self-deception of vanity after the event that does not want to acknowledge that the ship is *following* the current into which it has entered accidentally? that it "wills" to go that way *because it—must?* that is has a direction, to be sure, but—no helmsman at all?

We still need a critique of the concept of "purpose."

* * *

370

What is romanticism?—It may perhaps be recalled, at least among my friends, that initially[2] I approached the modern world with a few crude errors and overestimations and, in any case, hopefully. Who knows on the basis of what personal experiences,[3] I understood the philosophical pessimism of the

---

2. That is, in *The Birth of Tragedy* (1872; see above), in which Nietzsche distinguished between "Apollonian," "Dionysian," and "tragic" types of art, culture, and sensibility.
3. Better worded: "On the basis of who knows what personal experiences, . . ."

nineteenth century as if it were a symptom of a superior force of thought, of more audacious courage, and of more triumphant *fullness* of life than had characterized the eighteenth century, the age of Hume, Kant, Condillac,[4] and the sensualists. Thus tragic insight appeared to me as the distinctive *luxury* of our culture, as its most precious, noblest, and most dangerous squandering, but, in view of its over-richness, as a *permissible* luxury. In the same way, I reinterpreted German music for myself as if it signified a Dionysian power of the German soul: I believed that I heard in it the earthquake through which some primeval force that had been dammed up for ages finally liberated itself—indifferent whether everything else that one calls culture might begin to tremble. You see, what I failed to recognize at that time both in philosophical pessimism and in German music was what is really their distinctive character—their *romanticism*.

What is romanticism?—Every art, every philosophy may be viewed as a remedy and an aid in the service of growing and struggling life; they always presuppose suffering and sufferers. But there are two kinds of sufferers: first, those who suffer from the *over-fullness of life*—they want a Dionysian art and likewise a tragic view of life, a tragic insight—and then those who suffer from the *impoverishment of life* and seek rest, stillness, calm seas, redemption from themselves through art and knowledge, or intoxication, convulsions, anaesthesia, and madness. All romanticism in art and insight corresponds to the dual needs of the latter type, and that included (and includes) Schopenhauer as well as Richard Wagner,[5] to name the two most famous and pronounced romantics whom I *misunderstood* at that time—*not*, incidentally, to their disadvantage, as one need not hesitate in all fairness to admit. He that is richest in the fullness of life, the Dionysian god and man, cannot only afford the sight of the terrible and questionable but even the terrible deed and any luxury of destruction, decomposition, and negation. In his case, what is evil, absurd, and ugly seems, as it were, permissible, owing to an excess of procreating, fertilizing energies that can still turn any desert into lush farmland. Conversely, those who suffer most and are poorest in life would need above all mildness, peacefulness, and goodness in thought as well as deed—if possible, also a god who would be truly a god for the sick, a healer and savior; also logic, the conceptual understandability of existence—for logic calms and gives confidence—in short, a certain warm narrowness that keeps away fear and encloses one in optimistic horizons.

Thus I gradually learned to understand Epicurus,[6] the opposite of a Dionysian pessimist; also the "Christian" who is actually only a kind of Epicurean—both are essentially romantics—and my eye grew ever sharper for that most difficult and captious form of *backward inference* in which the most mistakes are made: the backward inference from the work to the maker, from the deed to the doer, from the ideal to those who *need it*, from every way of thinking and valuing to the commanding need behind it.

---

4. Étienne Bonnot de Condillac (1715–1780), French philosopher, psychologist, and economist.
5. German composer (1813–1883), to whom Nietzsche had been very close while writing *The Birth of Tragedy* but from whom he became estranged in the late 1870s, and against whom he later reacted strongly.
6. Greek philosopher (341–270 B.C.E.), who identified the good with pleasure (achieved more by limiting desires and practicing virtues than by indulging appetites).

Regarding all aesthetic values I now avail myself of this main distinction: I ask in every instance, "is it hunger or superabundance that has here become creative?" At first glance, another distinction may seem preferable—it is far more obvious—namely the question whether the desire to fix, to immortalize, the desire for *being* prompted creation, or the desire for destruction, for change, for future, for *becoming*. But both of these kinds of desire are seen to be ambiguous when one considers them more closely; they can be interpreted in accordance with the first scheme that is, as it seems to me, preferable. The desire for *destruction*, change, and becoming can be an expression of an overflowing energy that is pregnant with future (my term for this is, as is known, "Dionysian"); but it can also be the hatred of the ill-constituted, disinherited, and underprivileged, who destroy, *must* destroy, because what exists, indeed all existence, all being, outrages and provokes them. To understand this feeling, consider our anarchists closely.

The will to *immortalize*[7] also requires a dual interpretation. It can be prompted, first, by gratitude and love; art with this origin will always be an art of apotheoses,[8] perhaps dithyrambic like Rubens, or blissfully mocking like Hafiz,[9] or bright and gracious like Goethe, spreading a Homeric light and glory over all things. But it can also be the tyrannic will of one who suffers deeply, who struggles, is tormented, and would like to turn what is most personal, singular, and narrow, the real idiosyncrasy of his suffering, into a binding law and compulsion—one who, as it were, revenges himself on all things by forcing his own image, the image of his torture, on them, branding them with it. This last version is *romantic pessimism* in its most expressive form, whether it be Schopenhauer's philosophy of will or Wagner's music—romantic pessimism, the last *great* event in the fate of our culture.

(That there still *could* be an altogether different kind of pessimism, a classical type—this premonition and vision belongs to me as inseparable from me, as my *proprium* and *ipsissimum*;[1] only the word "classical" offends my ears, it is far too trite and has become round and indistinct. I call this pessimism of the future—for it comes! I see it coming!—*Dionysian* pessimism.[2])

* * *

373

"*Science [Wissenschaft]*" *as a prejudice.*—It follows from the laws of the order of rank that scholars, insofar as they belong to the spiritual middle class, can never catch sight of the really great problems and question marks; moreover, their courage and their eyes simply do not reach that far—and above all, their needs which led them to become scholars in the first place, their inmost assumptions and desires that things might be such and such, their fears and hopes all come to rest and are satisfied too soon. Take, for example, that

---

7. That is, "eternalize," "make eternal" (*verewigen*).
8. Deifications; exaltations.
9. Mohammad Shams al-Din Hafez (ca. 1325–ca. 1390), great Persian lyric poet. Peter Paul Rubens (1577–1640), Flemish Baroque painter whose works display sensuous exuberance. A dithyramb is a

choral song to Dionysus.
1. That is, "my very own and my veriest essence" (Latin terms).
2. That is, a "pessimism" (in that it repudiated all "optimism") that—paradoxically—would be ecstatically affirmative.

pedantic Englishman, Herbert Spencer. What makes him "enthuse" in his way and then leads him to draw a line of hope, a horizon of desirability—that eventual reconciliation of "egoism and altruism" about which he raves[3]—almost nauseates the likes of us; a human race that adopted such Spencerian perspectives as its ultimate perspectives would seem to us worthy of contempt, of annihilation! But the mere fact that he had to experience as his highest hope something that to others appears and may appear only as a disgusting possibility poses a question mark that Spencer would have been incapable of foreseeing.

It is no different with the faith with which so many materialistic natural scientists rest content nowadays, the faith in a world that is supposed to have its equivalent and its measure in human thought and human valuations—a "world of truth" that can be mastered completely and forever with the aid of our square little reason. What? Do we really want to permit existence to be degraded for us like this—reduced to a mere exercise for a calculator and an indoor diversion for mathematicians? Above all, one should not wish to divest existence of its *rich ambiguity*: that is a dictate of good taste, gentlemen, the taste of reverence for everything that lies beyond your horizon. That the only justifiable interpretation of the world should be one in which *you* are justified because one can continue to work and do research scientifically in *your* sense (you really mean, mechanistically?)—an interpretation that permits counting, calculating, weighing, seeing, and touching, and nothing more—that is a crudity and naiveté, assuming that it is not a mental illness, an idiocy.

Would it not be rather probable that, conversely, precisely the most superficial and external aspect of existence—what is most apparent, its skin and sensualization—would be grasped first—and might even be the only thing that allowed itself to be grasped? A "scientific" interpretation of the world, as you understand it, might therefore still be one of the *most stupid* of all possible interpretations of the world, meaning that it would be one of the poorest in meaning. This thought is intended for the ears and consciences of our mechanists who nowadays like to pass as philosophers and insist that mechanics is the doctrine of the first and last laws on which all existence must be based as on a ground floor. But an essentially mechanical world would be an essentially *meaningless* world. Assuming that one estimated the *value* of a piece of music according to how much of it could be counted, calculated, and expressed in formulas: how absurd would such a "scientific" estimation of music be![4] What would one have comprehended, understood, grasped of it? Nothing, really nothing of what is "music" in it!

374

Our new "infinite."[5]—How far the perspective[6] character of existence extends or indeed whether existence has any other character than this; whether existence without interpretation, without "sense," does not become "nonsense";

---

3. In *The Data of Ethics* (1879).
4. That is: Suppose that one were to appraise (*Gesetzt, dass man schätzte*) the *worth* of a music (*Wert einer Musik*) according to [. . .]. And: How absurd such a "scientific" appraisal of the music

("*wissenschaftliche*" *Abschätzung der Musik*) would be!
5. More literally, "endless" or "limitless" (*Unendliches*).
6. That is, perspectival (*perspektivisch*).

whether, on the other hand, all existence is not essentially actively engaged in *interpretation*[7]—that cannot be decided even by the most industrious and most scrupulously conscientious analysis and self-examination of the intellect; for in the course of this analysis the human intellect cannot avoid seeing itself in its own perspectives, and *only* in these. We cannot look around our own corner: it is a hopeless curiosity that wants to know what other kinds of intellects and perspectives there *might* be; for example, whether some beings might be able to experience time backward, or alternately forward and backward (which would involve another direction of life and another concept of cause and effect). But I should think that today we are at least far from the ridiculous immodesty that would be involved in decreeing from our corner that perspectives are permitted only from this corner. Rather has the world become "infinite" for us all over again, inasmuch as we cannot reject the possibility that *it may include infinite interpretations.*[8] Once more we are seized by a great shudder; but who would feel inclined immediately to deify again after the old manner this monster of an unknown world? And to worship the unknown henceforth as "the Unknown One"? Alas, too many *ungodly* possibilities of interpretation are included in the unknown, too much devilry, stupidity, and foolishness of interpretation—even our own human, all too human folly, which we know.

* * *

380

"The wanderer" speaks.— If one would like to see our European morality [*Moralität*] for once as it looks from a distance, and if one would like to measure it against other moralities, past and future, then one has to proceed like a wanderer who wants to know how high the towers in a town are: he *leaves* the town. "Thoughts about moral prejudices,"[9] if they are not meant to be prejudices about prejudices, presuppose a position *outside* morality [*Moral*], some point beyond good and evil to which one has to rise, climb, or fly—and in the present case at least a point beyond *our* good and evil, a freedom from everything "European," by which I mean the sum of the imperious value judgments that have become part of our flesh and blood. That one *wants* to go precisely out there, up there, may be a minor madness, a peculiar and unreasonable "you must"—for we seekers for knowledge [*Erkennenden*] also have our idiosyncrasies of "unfree will"—the question is whether one really *can* get up there.

This may depend on manifold conditions. In the main the question is how light or heavy we are—the problem of our "specific gravity." One has to be *very light* to drive one's will to knowledge into such a distance and, as it were, beyond one's time, to create for oneself eyes to survey millennia and, moreover,

---

7. Better translated: "every reality is essentially an *auslegendes* reality" (*alles Dasein essentiell ein auslegendes Dasein ist*). Although *auslegen* often has the sense "to interpret," it literally means "to lay out" (i.e., organize, arrange). Here, in discussing everything that exists (not just language-using creatures like ourselves), Nietzsche is suggesting that "every reality is essentially an *organizing* reality," which does its best to impose an order or arrangement upon its environing world that both expresses and enhances its ability to master and control its environment.

8. In German, *Interpretationen*; in using a synonym of *Auslegungen*, Nietzsche may be evoking the literal meaning of *auslegen* (discussed in the previous note).

9. The literally translated subtitle of Nietzsche's 1881 book, *Morgenröthe* (*Daybreak* [or *Dawn*]): *Gedanken über die moralischen Vorurteile*.

clear skies in these eyes. One must have liberated oneself from many things that oppress, inhibit, hold down, and make heavy precisely us Europeans today. The human being of such a beyond who wants to behold the supreme measures of value of his time must first of all "overcome" this time in himself—this is the test of his strength—and consequently not only his time but also his prior aversion and contradiction *against* this time, his suffering from this time, his un-timeliness, his *romanticism*.

* * *

382

The great health.[1]— Being new, nameless, hard to understand, we premature births of an as yet unproven future need for a new goal also a new means— namely, a new health, stronger, more seasoned, tougher, more audacious, and gayer than any previous health. Whoever has a soul that craves to have experienced the whole range of values and desiderata to date, and to have sailed around all the coasts of this ideal "mediterranean"; whoever wants to know from the adventures of his own most authentic[2] experience how a discoverer and conqueror of the ideal feels, and also an artist, a saint a legislator, a sage, a scholar, a pious man, a soothsayer,[3] and one who stands divinely apart in the old style—needs one thing above everything else: the *great health*—that one does not merely have but also acquires continually, and must acquire because one gives it up again and again, and must give it up.

And now, after we have long been on our way in this manner, we argonauts of the ideal, with more daring perhaps than is prudent, and have suffered shipwreck and damage often enough, but are, to repeat it, healthier than one likes to permit us, dangerously healthy, ever again healthy—it will seem to us as if, as a reward, we now confronted an as yet undiscovered country whose boundaries nobody has surveyed yet, something beyond all the lands and nooks of the ideal so far, a world so overrich in what is beautiful, strange, questionable, terrible, and divine that our curiosity as well as our craving to possess it has got beside itself—alas, now nothing will sate us any more!

After such vistas and with such a burning hunger in our conscience and science,[4] how could we still be satisfied with *present-day man*? It may be too bad but it is inevitable that we find it difficult to remain serious when we look at his worthiest goals and hopes, and perhaps we do not even bother to look any more.

Another ideal runs ahead of us, a strange, tempting, dangerous ideal to which we should not wish to persuade anybody because we do not readily concede *the right to it* to anyone: the ideal of a spirit [*Geist*] who plays naively— that is, not deliberately but from overflowing power and abundance—with all that was hitherto called holy, good, untouchable, divine; for whom those supreme things that the people naturally accept as their value standards, signify danger, decay, debasement, or at least recreation, blindness, and

---

1. Literally, "soundness" (*Gesundheit*); that is, being in sound condition.
2. That is, own most (*eigensten*), i.e., most extremely and entirely one's own.
3. That is, a truth teller (*Wahrsager*), the literal (original) meaning of "soothsayer."

4. Better translated: "with such a burning hunger in [intellectual] conscience and knowing" (*mit einem solchen Heisshunger in Gewissen und Wissen*); that is, with such a burning desire for knowledge and intellectual integrity.

temporary self-oblivion; the ideal of a human, superhuman well-being and benevolence[5] that will often appear *inhuman*—for example, when it confronts all earthly seriousness so far, all solemnity in gesture, word, tone, eye, morality, and task so far, as if it were their most incarnate and involuntary parody— and in spite of all of this, it is perhaps only with him that *great seriousness* really begins, that the real question mark is posed for the first time, that the destiny of the soul changes, the hand moves forward, the tragedy *begins*.

* * *

SOURCE: From Friedrich Nietzsche, *The Gay Science: With a Prelude in Rhymes and an Appendix of Songs*, trans. Walter Kaufmann (New York: Vintage, 1974), pp. 279–87, 291–92, 297–300, 304–8, 315–16, 327–31, 334–37, 342–43, 346–47. Except where otherwise indicated, German words in brackets are the terminology used in the German original, inserted by the editor in addition to their renderings in the translation. Nietzsche added a preface and this fifth book to a second edition of *Die fröhlichen Wissenschaft* (1887), originally published in four books in 1882 (see above).

From On the Genealogy of Morals
From *Preface*
1

We remain unknown to ourselves, we seekers after knowledge, even to ourselves: and with good reason. We have never sought after ourselves—so how should we one day find ourselves? It has rightly been said that: 'Where your treasure is, there will your heart be also';[1] *our* treasure is to be found in the beehives of knowledge. As spiritual bees from birth, this is our eternal destination, our hearts are set on one thing only—'bringing something home'. Whatever else life has to offer, so-called 'experiences'—who among us is serious enough for them? Or has enough time for them? In such matters, we were, I fear, never properly 'abreast of things': our heart is just not in it—nor, if it comes to it, are our ears! Imagine someone who, when woken suddenly from divine distraction and self-absorption by the twelve loud strokes of the noon bell, asks himself: 'What time is it?' In much the same way, we rub our ears *after the fact* and ask in complete surprise and embarrassment: '*What* was that we just experienced?', or even 'Who *are* we really?' Then we count back over in retrospect, as I said, every one of the twelve trembling strokes of our experience, our life, our *being*—and alas! lose our count in the process . . . And so we necessarily remain a mystery to ourselves, we fail to understand ourselves, we are *bound* to mistake ourselves. Our eternal sentence reads: 'Everyone is furthest from himself'—of ourselves, we have no knowledge . . .

---

5. This translates *das Ideal eines menschlich-übermenschlich Wohlseins und Wohlwollens*. The translation does not show Nietzsche's important hyphenation that links *menschlich* ("human") and *übermenschlich* ("over-human" or "more than human") in his characterization of this ideal, thereby linking his conception of the "overman" (*der Übermensch*) with that of "man" (*der Mensch*) as a transformation of the human. *Wohlsein und Wohlwollen* also might be better translated as "well-being and well-wanting" (that is, well-willing, well-intending).

1. Matthew 6:21.

2

—My thoughts on the *origin* of our moral prejudices—for such is the subject of this polemic—found their first, spare, provisional expression in the collection of aphorisms entitled *Human, All Too Human: A Book for Free Spirits*.[2] I began writing that book in Sorrento, during a winter which allowed me to make a halt, as a walker makes a halt, and to survey the distant and dangerous expanse through which my mind had been making its way up until then. This was in the winter of 1876–7; the thoughts themselves are older. For the most part, I take up the same thoughts in these present essays—let us hope that they have thrived since then, that they have matured, grown brighter, stronger, more complete! But *that* I still hold to these ideas today, and that they themselves have since become increasingly inseparable, indeed have even grown into one another and become intertwined—all this strengthens my happy assurance that, far from emerging as isolated, random, or sporadic phenomena, these ideas grew from a common root, from a *fundamental will* of knowledge,[3] a will which issued its imperatives from the depths, speaking in increasingly definite terms and demanding increasingly definite answers. For nothing else befits a philosopher. We have no right to any *isolated* act whatsoever: to make isolated errors and to discover isolated truths are equally forbidden us. Rather, our thoughts, our values, our yeses and noes and ifs and whethers grow out of us with the same necessity with which a tree bears its fruits—all related and connected to one another and evidence of a *single* will, a *single* health, a *single* earth, a *single* sun.—And as to whether these fruits of ours are to *your* taste?—But what is that to the trees! What is that to *us*, the philosophers! . . .

3

I harbour a particular reservation which I am reluctant to confess—for it concerns *morality* [*die Moral*], everything which has up to now been celebrated as morality—a reservation which emerged so unsolicited, so early and inexorably, so in contradiction with my environment, age, models, and origins, that I might almost be entitled to call it my 'A priori'.[4] As to the nature of this reservation—I found that my curiosity and suspicion were soon drawn up short at the question of the real *origin* of our notions of good and evil. In fact, as a 13-year-old boy I was already preoccupied with the problem of the origin of evil. At an age when one has 'half children's games and half God at heart',[5] I devoted my first literary piece of child's play, my first exercise in philosophical writing to this subject—and as for my 'solution' to the problem at that time, I gave God the honour, as is fitting, and made him the father of *evil*. Was *this* the very thing which my 'A priori' required of me? That new immoral, or at least amoral, 'A priori' and the alas! so anti-Kantian, so

---

2. Nietzsche's second book, published in 1878.
3. This translates "aus einem in der Tiefe gebietenden, immer bestimmter redenden, immer verlangenden *Grundwillen der Erkenntniss*"; that is, "out of an ever more precisely speaking, ever more demanding *fundamental will* of knowledge that

commands from the depths."
4. That is, something known or knowable prior to the experience of cases that might count as relevant evidence.
5. Quoted from Johann Wolfgang von Goethe, *Faust*, part 1 (1808).

enigmatic 'categorical imperative'[6] which spoke through it and to which I have since been increasingly attentive and more than just attentive? . . . Fortunately, I have since learnt to separate theology from morality[7] and ceased looking for the origin of evil *behind* the world. Some schooling in history and philology, together with an innate sense of discrimination with respect to questions of psychology, quickly transformed my problem into another one: under what conditions did man invent the value-judgements good and evil? *And what value do they themselves possess?* Have they helped or hindered the progress of mankind? Are they a sign of indigence, of impoverishment, of the degeneration of life? Or do they rather reveal the plenitude, the strength, the will of life, its courage, confidence, and future?—To these questions, I found several audacious answers. I distinguished between periods, peoples, degrees of rank among individuals, I narrowed down my problem. Out of the answers grew new questions, investigations, hypotheses, probabilities: until finally I had a land of my own, a soil of my own, a completely unknown, burgeoning, flourishing world, like a secret garden, whose existence no one had been allowed to suspect . . . Oh how *fortunate* we are, we seekers after knowledge, provided only that we do not break our silence prematurely! . . .

4

The first impetus to give expression to some of my hypotheses on the origin of morality came from a neat and tidy little book, clever even to the point of precociousness. There for the first time I clearly encountered an inverted and perverted kind of genealogical hypothesis, the genuinely *English* kind, and found myself drawn to it—as opposites attract one another. The title of this little book was *The Origin of Moral Sensations*; its author Dr Paul Rée,[8] the year of its appearance 1877. * * *

5

At that particular moment, my real concern was with something much more important than my own or anyone else's hypotheses about the origin of morality (or, to be more precise: the latter interest was completely subordinate to a single goal, to which it is merely one among many means). For me, what was at stake was the *value* of morality—and on that question I had no choice but to engage almost single-handedly with my great teacher Schopenhauer. That book of mine, its passion and its secret refutation, was addressed to him, as to a contemporary (—for that book too was a 'polemic'). At issue was the value of the 'unegoistic', the instincts of compassion [*Mitleid*],[9] self-abnegation, self-sacrifice, those very instincts which Schopenhauer had for so long made golden, godly, and transcendent, until finally they became for him 'values in themselves', on the basis of which he *said no* to life and also to himself. But it was against *these* very instincts that an increasingly fundamental suspi-

---

6. A moral law that is absolute for all agents (KANT's fundamental principle of morality).
7. The original, "das theologische Vorurteil von dem moralischen abschneiden," is better translated as "to separate theological from moral prejudice."
8. A minor German moral philosopher (1849–

1901), a former friend whose work Nietzsche had earlier admired. Their relationship had become strained, and Nietzsche at this point wanted to deny his indebtedness to Rée.
9. Literally, "suffering with," sharing (others') suffering.

cion, a scepticism which dug ever deeper, spoke out within me! It was here that I saw the *great* danger for mankind, its most sublime temptation and seduction—leading in what direction? towards nothingness?—It was here that I saw the beginning of the end, the stagnation, the tired nostalgia, the will turning *against* life, the melancholy and tender signs of the approach of the last illness. I regarded the inexorable progress of the morality of compassion, which afflicted even the philosophers with its illness, as the most sinister symptom of the sinister development of our European culture, as its detour leading in what direction? Towards a new Buddhism? towards a European Buddhism? towards—*nihilism?* . . . For the modern predilection for compassion, its overestimation in philosophy, is a recent development: the very *worthlessness* of compassion was formerly a point of agreement among philosophers. To mention only Plato, Spinoza, La Rochefoucauld,[1] and Kant, four minds as different from one another as possible, but united in one respect: in their contempt for compassion.—

6

This problem of the *value* of compassion and of the morality of compassion (—I am an opponent of the shameful modern weakening of sensibility—) seems at first merely an isolated issue, a free-standing question-mark. But whoever pauses here, whoever *learns* to ask questions here, will undergo the same experience as I—that of a huge new prospect opening up, a vertiginous possibility, as every kind of mistrust, suspicion, and fear leaps forward, and the belief in morality, all morality, falters. Finally, a new demand finds expression. Let us articulate this *new demand*: we stand in need of a *critique* of moral values, *the value of these values itself should first of all*[2] *be called into question.* This requires a knowledge [*eine Kenntniss*] of the conditions and circumstances of their growth, development, and displacement (morality as consequence, symptom, mask, Tartufferie,[3] illness, misunderstanding: but also morality as cause, cure, stimulant, inhibition, poison); knowledge the like of which has never before existed nor even been desired. The *value* of these 'values' was accepted as given, as fact, as beyond all question. Previously, no one had expressed even the remotest doubt or shown the slightest hesitation in assuming the 'good man' to be of greater worth than the 'evil man', of greater worth in the sense of his usefulness in promoting the progress of human *existence* (including the future of man). What? And if the opposite were the case? What? What if there existed a symptom of regression in the 'good man', likewise a danger, a temptation, a poison, a narcotic, by means of which the present were living *at the expense of the future*? Perhaps more comfortably and less dangerously, but also in less grand style, in a humbler manner? . . . So that none other than morality itself would be the culprit, if the *highest power and splendour* of the human type, in itself a possibility, were never to be reached? So that [*gerade*, precisely][4] morality would constitute the danger of dangers? . . .

1. The Greek philosopher Plato (ca. 427–ca. 347 B.C.E.), the Dutch philosopher Benedict (Baruch) de Spinoza (1632–1677), and the French epigrammatist François VI, duke de La Rochefoucauld (1613–1680).

2. That is, for once (*erst einmal*).
3. Hypocrisy, like that shown by the title character in Molière's play *Tartuffe* (1664).
4. Word omitted by translator.

7

Suffice it to say that, since this prospect opened up before me, I myself had reason to look around for learned, daring, and hardworking colleagues (I continue to do so). What is involved is a journey across the wide expanse of morality, so distant and so inaccessible—morality which has actually existed, which has actually been lived—a journey with nothing but new questions and with fresh eyes, as it were: does this not amount practically to *discovering* this expanse of territory for the first time?

* * *

From *FIRST ESSAY*
'Good and Evil,' 'Good and Bad'

1

—These English psychologists, to whom we owe the only attempts so far to develop a history of the genesis of morality, themselves present us with an enigma. As living and breathing enigmas, this gives them, I confess, an essential advantage over their books—*they themselves are interesting*! These English psychologists—what are they really after? Whether by accident or design, they are always to be found at the same task—pushing to the forefront the *partie honteuse*[5] of our inner world, seeking the real directing force of human development, the real decisive influence upon it, in the very place where the intellectual pride of man would least *wish* to find it (for example, in the *vis inertiae*[6] of habit or in forgetfulness or in the blind arbitrariness of a mechanistic chain of ideas, or in something purely passive, automatic, reflexlike, molecular, and fundamentally stupid). What drives these psychologists always in *this* particular direction? Is it a secret, spiteful, vulgar, and perhaps unacknowledged instinct to belittle man? Or perhaps a pessimistic suspicion, the mistrust of disappointed, gloomy idealists who have turned green and poisonous? Or a petty, subterranean, rancorous hostility towards Christianity (and Plato), which may not even have crossed the threshold of consciousness? Or even a lascivious taste for an irritant, the painful paradox, for the questionable and absurd aspects of life? Or finally, a little of all these: a little vulgarity, a little gloom, a little anti-Christianity, a little itch and need for spice? . . . But I am told that they are simply cold, boring old frogs who crawl around and hop into people, as though they were completely in their element, that is, in a *quagmire*. I hear this with reluctance—indeed, I do not believe it, and if one may wish where one cannot know, then I wish heartily that the opposite were the case—that these microscopic researchers of the soul were basically brave, generous, and proud animals, who know how to restrain their emotions as well as their pain, and have taught themselves to sacrifice all wishfulness to truth, to *every* truth, even the simple, bitter, ugly, repulsive, unChristian, immoral truth . . . For such truths do exist.—

---

5. Shameful part (French).   6. Force of inertia (Latin).

2

So the greatest respect to the good spirits who preside over these historians of morality! Unfortunately, there is no doubt that they lack the *historical spirit*, that they have been abandoned by all the good spirits of history! As is the wont of philosophers, they all think in an *essentially* unhistorical manner; there is no doubt about that. The amateurishness of their genealogy of morals comes to light as soon as they have to account for the origin of 'good' as concept and judgement. 'Originally'—so they decree— 'unegoistic actions were acclaimed and described as good by those towards whom they were directed, thus those to whom they were *useful*. The origin of this acclaim was later forgotten and unegoistic actions were simply felt to be good, because they were *habitually* always praised as such—as if they were in themselves something good.' It is clear from the outset that all the typical characteristics of the English psychologists' prejudice are already present in this first deduction— here we have 'utility', 'forgetting', 'habit', and finally 'error', all as the basis of a value-judgement which has up to now been the pride of civilized man and been accepted as a kind of essential human prerogative. The *goal* here is to humble this pride, devalue this value-judgement: is this goal attained? . . . It seems clear to me that this theory looks in the wrong place for the real origin of the concept 'good'. The judgement 'good' does *not* derive from those to whom 'goodness' is shown! Rather, the 'good' themselves—that is, the noble [*Vornehmen*],[7] the powerful, the superior, and the high-minded—were the ones who felt themselves and their actions to be good—that is, as of the first rank— and posited them as such, in contrast to everything low, low-minded, common, and plebeian. On the basis of this *pathos of distance*, they first arrogated the right to create values, to coin the names of values. What did utility matter to them? The point of view of utility could not be more alien and inappropriate to such a high-temperature outpouring of the highest value-judgements when engaged in the making and breaking of hierarchies: for here feeling is at the opposite end of the scale from the low temperature presupposed by every prudent calculation and utilitarian estimation—and not only on one occasion, not for an exceptional hour, but over the long term. As I said, the pathos of nobility [*Vornehmheit*] and distance, the enduring, dominating, and fundamental overall feeling of a higher ruling kind in relation to a lower kind, to a 'below'—*that* is the origin of the opposition between 'good' and 'bad'. (The right of the masters to confer names extends so far that one should allow oneself to grasp the origin of language itself as the expression of the power of the rulers: they say 'this *is* such and such', they put their seal on each thing and event with a sound and in the process take possession of it.) It follows from this origin that there is from the outset absolutely *no* necessary connection between the word 'good' and 'unegoistic' actions, as the superstition of the genealogists of morals would have it. Rather, it is only with the decline of aristocratic value-judgements that this whole opposition between 'egoistic' and 'unegoistic' comes to impose itself increasingly on the human conscience. To adopt my own terminology, it is the *herd-instinct*, which here finally has its

---

7. This word, as used by Nietzsche, connotes superiority and dominance rather than hereditary aristocracy. See the excerpts (above) from Part Nine of *Beyond Good and Evil*, entitled "What is *vornehm?*"

chance to put in a word (and to put itself into *words*). Even then, it is a long time before this instinct dominates to such an extent that the moral value-judgement catches and sticks fast on this opposition (as is, for example, the case in contemporary Europe: today the prejudice which takes 'moral', 'unego-istic', '*désintéressé*' as synonyms already rules with the power of an '*idée fixe*'[8] and mental illness.)

* * *

10

—The slave revolt in morals begins when *ressentiment*[9] itself becomes creative and ordains values: the *ressentiment* of creatures to whom the real reaction, that of the deed, is denied and who find compensation in an imaginary revenge. While all noble morality grows from a triumphant affirmation of itself, slave morality from the outset says no to an 'outside', to an 'other', to a 'non-self': and *this* no is its creative act. The reversal of the evaluating gaze—this *neces-sary* orientation outwards rather than inwards to the self—belongs character-istically to *ressentiment*. In order to exist at all, slave morality from the outset always needs an opposing, outer world; in physiological terms, it needs exter-nal stimuli in order to act—its action is fundamentally reaction. The oppo-site is the case with the aristocratic mode of evaluation: this acts and grows spontaneously, it only seeks out its antithesis in order to affirm itself more thankfully and more joyfully. Its negative concept, 'low', 'common', 'bad', is only a derived, pale contrast to its positive basic concept which is thoroughly steeped in life and passion—'we the noble, we the good, we the beautiful, we the happy ones!' If the aristocratic mode of evaluation errs and sins against reality, this happens in relation to the sphere with which it is *not* sufficiently familiar, and against real knowledge of which it stubbornly defends itself: it misjudges on occasion the sphere it despises—that of the common man, of the lower people. On the other hand, one may consider that this feeling of contempt, condescension, and superiority, granted that it *falsifies* the image of those despised, will trail far behind the falsification by means of which the downtrodden hatred, the revenge of the powerless will attack its opponent—*in effigie*,[1] of course. * * * The 'well-bred' *felt* themselves to be 'the fortunate'; they did not have to construe their good fortune artificially through a glance at their enemies, to persuade themselves of it, to *convince themselves through lying* (as all men of *ressentiment* usually do). Likewise, as fully developed people overladen with strength, and consequently as *necessarily* active people, they knew better than to separate action from happiness—with them, activ-ity is necessarily calculated into happiness (from where *eu prattein*[2] takes its origin). All this is diametrically opposed to 'happiness' as understood on the level of the powerless, the oppressed, of those who suppurate with poisonous and hostile feelings, those for whom happiness appears essentially as narcotic,

---

8. Fixed idea (French); that is, an idea that has taken hold to the point of obsession. *Désintéressé:* disinterestedness (French).
9. Resentment (French); Nietzsche uses this word to refer specifically to the particularly pathological emotion that arises under the circumstances dis-cussed here. It plays a major role in the origin and development of what he calls "slave morality," and in his genealogical account of the morality that has come to be taken for granted in the modern Western world.
1. In effigy (French).
2. To do well (Greek).

anaesthetic, calm, peace, 'sabbath', the expansion of feeling and the stretching of limbs, in a word, as *passivity*. While the noble [*vornehm*] man lives for himself in trust and openness (*gennaios*[3] 'of noble birth' underlines the nuance of 'honest' and also 'naïve'), the man of *ressentiment* is neither upright nor naïve in his dealings with others, nor is he honest and open with himself. His soul *squints*; his mind loves bolt-holes, secret paths, back doors, he regards all hidden things as *his* world, *his* security, *his* refreshment; he has a perfect understanding of how to keep silent, how not to forget, how to wait, how to make himself provisionally small and submissive. A race of such men of *ressentiment* is bound in the end to become *cleverer* than any noble race, and it will respect cleverness to a completely different degree: that is, as a first condition of existence. In contrast, for aristocratic people cleverness easily acquires a delicate taste of luxury and refinement. They long considered cleverness less essential than the smooth functioning of their unconscious regulating instincts, than a certain recklessness, even. This latter took the form of a bold impetuosity, whether with respect to danger, the enemy, or the instantaneous outbursts of wrath, love, respect, gratitude, and revenge, by means of which noble souls have at all times recognized one another. For the *ressentiment* of the noble man himself, if it appears at all, completes and exhausts itself in an immediate reaction. For that reason, it does not *poison*. * * * Such a man with a *single* shrug shakes off much of that which worms and digs its way into others. Here alone is actual '*love* of one's enemy'[4] possible, assuming that such a thing is at all possible on earth. How much respect a noble man has already for his enemy!—and such respect is already a bridge to love . . . The noble man claims his enemy for himself, as a mark of distinction. He tolerates no other enemy than one in whom nothing is to be despised and a *great deal* is worthy of respect! In contrast, imagine the 'enemy' as conceived by the man of *ressentiment*. This is the very place where his deed, his creation is to be found—he has conceived the 'evil enemy', the '*evil man*'. Moreover, he has conceived him as a fundamental concept, from which he now derives another as an after-image and counterpart, the 'good man'—himself! . . .

11

This, then, is the very opposite of what the noble man does[5]—for the latter conceives the fundamental concept 'good' spontaneously and in advance—that is, from his own point of view—and only then does he proceed to create for himself an idea of the 'bad'! This 'bad' of noble origin and that 'evil' which issues from the cauldron of insatiable hatred—the former being a retrospective creation, an incidental, a complementary colour, while the latter is the original, the beginning, the real *deed* in the conception of a slave morality—what a difference there is between these two words 'bad' and 'evil', in spite of the fact that they both appear to stand in opposition to one and the same concept of 'good'! But it is not the *same* concept of 'good' which is involved in

3. High-born, noble (Greek), translated by Nietzsche as "of noble birth."
4. See Matthew 5:44.
5. That is, of "how it is with the noble [type of human being]" (*wie bei dem Vornehmen*). Nietzsche uses the term *Vornehm* and its variants to refer neither to social status nor to wealth and power nor to exceptional physical attributes (although it may initially have had—and sometimes may still have—such associations), but rather to something more like a distinctive (and uncommon) cultural-psychological personality type.

each case: the question which should be asked is rather: *who* is actually 'evil' according to the morality of *ressentiment*? In all strictness, the answer is: *none other* than the 'good man' of the other morality, none other than the noble, powerful, dominating man, but only once he has been given a new colour, interpretation, and aspect by the poisonous eye of *ressentiment*. We would be the last to deny that anyone who met these 'good men' only as enemies would know them only as *evil enemies*, and that these same men, who are *inter pares*[6] so strictly restrained by custom, respect, usage, gratitude, even more by circumspection and jealousy, and who in their relations with one another prove so inventive in matters of consideration, self-control, tenderness, fidelity, pride, and friendship—these same men behave towards the outside world—where the foreign, the *foreigners*, are to be found—in a manner not much better than predators on the rampage. There they enjoy freedom from all social constraint, in the wilderness they make up for the tension built up over a long period of confinement and enclosure within a peaceful community, they *regress* to the innocence of the predator's conscience, as rejoicing monsters, capable of high spirits as they walk away without qualms from a horrific succession of murder, arson, violence, and torture, as if it were nothing more than a student prank, something new for the poets to sing and celebrate for some time to come. There is no mistaking the predator beneath the surface of all these noble races, the magnificent *blond beast* roaming lecherously in search of booty and victory; the energy of this hidden core needs to be discharged from time to time, the animal must emerge again, must return to the wilderness— Roman, Arab, German, Japanese nobility, Homeric heroes, Scandinavian Vikings,—they all share this same need. The noble races are the ones who, wherever they have gone, have left the concept 'barbarian' in their wake; an awareness of this is betrayed even by their highest culture, which actually takes pride in it (for example, when Pericles[7] says to his Athenians in that famous funeral address, 'wherever our boldness has given us access to land and sea, we have established everlasting monuments of good *and wickedness*'). * * * Assuming that what is now in any case believed to be the 'truth' were true—that it is the *meaning of all culture* [*Cultur*] to breed a tame and civilized animal, a *domestic animal*, from the predatory animal 'man'—then there is no doubt that one would have to consider all the instincts of reaction and *ressentiment*, with whose help the noble races and their ideals were finally ruined and overcome, as the real *instruments of culture*. Which is not to say that those who possess these instincts are at the same time representatives of culture itself. Rather, the opposite is not only probable—no! today it is *patently obvious*! Those who possess the oppressive and vindictive instincts, the descendants of all European and non-European slavery, of all pre-Aryan population in particular—they represent the *regression* of humanity! These supposed 'instruments of culture' are a disgrace to mankind, they arouse suspicion and actually constitute an argument against 'culture' as a whole! One may have every right to remain fearful and suspicious of the blond beast beneath all noble races: but who would not a hundred times prefer fear accom-

---

6. Among equals (Latin).
7. Greek statesman and general (ca. 495–429 B.C.E.), who led Athens during its golden age of democracy and empire; he delivered his famous funeral oration, recorded by the Greek historian

Thucydides (here quoted from *History of the Peloponnesian War* 2.41), after the first series of campaigns of the Peloponnesian War (431–404 B.C.E.)—which ultimately ended in Athens's crushing defeat.

panied by the possibility of admiration to *freedom* from fear accompanied by the disgusting sight of the failed, atrophied, and poisoned? And is this not *our* fate? What causes *our* revulsion from 'man' today?—for we *suffer* from man, there is no doubt.—*Not* fear; but rather the fact that we no longer have anything to fear from man; that 'man' squirms like a worm before us; that the 'tame man', the irremediably mediocre and unedifying man has already learnt to regard himself as goal and destination, as the meaning of history, as the 'higher man'—and even that he has a certain right to regard himself as such, in so far as he senses his superiority over the surplus of failed, sickly, tired, worn-out people who are beginning to make Europe smell, in so far as he represents something which remains at least relatively successful, something which is still capable of life, something which affirms life . . .

* * *

13

—But let us return to our problem: for our discussion of the problem of the *other* origin of 'good', of good as conceived by the man of *ressentiment*, requires its conclusion.—That lambs bear ill-will towards large birds of prey is hardly strange: but is in itself no reason to blame large birds of prey for making off with little lambs. And if the lambs say among themselves: 'These birds of prey are evil; and whoever is as little of a bird of prey as possible, indeed, rather the opposite, a lamb—should he not be said to be good?', then there can be no objection to setting up an ideal like this, even if the birds of prey might look down on it a little contemptuously and perhaps say to themselves: 'We bear them no ill-will at all, these good lambs—indeed, we love them: there is nothing tastier than a tender lamb.' To demand of strength that it should *not* express itself as strength, that it should *not* be a will to overcome, overthrow, dominate, a thirst for enemies and resistance and triumph, makes as little sense as to demand of weakness that it should express itself as strength. A quantum of force is also a quantum of drive, will, action—in fact, it is nothing more than this driving, willing, acting, and it is only through the seduction of language (and through the fundamental errors of reason petrified in it)—language which understands and misunderstands all action as conditioned by an actor, by a 'subject'—that it can appear otherwise. Just as the common people distinguish lightning from the flash of light and takes the latter as *doing*, as the effect of a subject which is called lightning, just so popular morality distinguishes strength from expressions of strength, as if behind the strong individual there were an indifferent substratum which was at *liberty* to express or not to express strength. But no such substratum exists; there is no 'being' behind doing, acting, becoming; 'the doer' is merely a fiction imposed on the doing—the doing itself is everything. Basically, the common people represent the doing twice over, when they make lightning flash—that is a doing doubled by another doing: it posits the same event once as cause and then once again as effect. The natural scientists do not fare any better when they say: 'Force moves, force causes', and the like—in spite of all its coldness, its freedom from emotion, our entire science is still subject to the seduction of language and has not shaken itself free of the monstrous changelings, the 'subjects', foisted upon it (the atom is an example of such a changeling,[8] as is the Kantian 'thing in itself'). No wonder that the downtrodden and surreptitiously smouldering emotions of revenge and hatred exploit this belief in their own interests and maintain no belief with greater intensity than that *the strong may freely choose* to be weak, and the bird of prey to be lamb—and so they win the right to blame the bird of prey for simply being a bird of prey . . . If, out of the vindictive cunning of impotence, the oppressed, downtrodden, and violated tell themselves: 'Let us be different from the evil, that is, good! And the good man is the one who refrains from violation, who harms no one, who attacks no one, who fails to retaliate, who leaves revenge to God, who lives as we do in seclusion, who avoids all evil and above all asks little of life, as we do, the patient, the humble, the just.' When listened to coldly and without prejudice, this actually means nothing more than: 'We weak men are, after all, weak; it would be good if we refrained from doing anything *for which we lack sufficient strength*.' But this dry matter-of-factness, this cleverness of the lowest rank, which even insects possess (insects which, in situations of great danger, probably play dead in order not to do 'too much'), has, thanks to the forgery and self-deception of impotence, clothed itself in the magnificence of self-abnegating, calm, and patient virtue, exactly as if the weakness of the weak man itself—that is, his *essence*, his action, his whole single, unavoidable, irredeemable reality—were a free achievement, something willed, chosen, a *deed*, a *merit*. *Bound* to do so by his instinct of self-preservation and self-affirmation, an instinct which habitually sanctifies every lie, this kind of man discovered his faith in the indifferent, freely choosing 'subject'. The subject (or, to adopt a more popular idiom, the *soul*) has, therefore, been perhaps the best article of faith on earth so far, since it enables the majority of mortals, the weak and downtrodden of all sorts, to practise that sublime self-deception—the interpretation of weakness itself as freedom, of the way they simply are, as *merit*.

* * *

16

Let us conclude. For thousands of years, a fearful struggle has raged on earth between the two opposed value-judgements, 'good and bad' and 'good and evil'; and as certain as it is that the second value-judgement has long been in the ascendant, there is even now no shortage of places where the outcome of the conflict remains undecided. It might even be said that the conflict has escalated in the interim and so become increasingly profound, more spiritual: so that today there is perhaps no more decisive mark of the '*higher nature*', of the more spiritual nature, than to be divided against oneself in this sense and to remain a battleground for these oppositions.[9] The symbol for this struggle, written in a script which has remained legible throughout the whole of human history up until now, is called 'Rome against Judaea, Judaea against Rome'— so far, there has been no greater event than *this* struggle, *this* questioning, *this* mortal enmity and contradiction. * * *

8. According to the German physicist and philosopher Ernst Mach (1838–1916), atoms are theoretical constructs and not real entities.
9. As this sentence shows, Nietzsche by no means equates the "higher nature" of the "higher humanity" he champions with the nature of the "noble" type of premodern humanity he has been discussing.

17

—Was that the end of it? Was that greatest of all ideal oppositions then placed *ad acta*[1] for all time? Or only postponed, indefinitely postponed? . . . Will the old flame not inevitably flare up again at some time in an even more fearful way, after much lengthier preparation? Moreover, is this not the very thing which we should desire with all our strength? should even will? should even promote? . . . Anyone who, like my reader, starts to reflect at this point and to pursue his thoughts will find no early end to them—reason enough for me to come to an end, assuming that my *aim* has long since become sufficiently clear, the aim of that dangerous slogan written on the body of my last book: 'Beyond Good and Evil' . . . This at the very least does *not* mean 'Beyond Good and Bad'.——

———

Note: I take the opportunity afforded by this essay to give public and formal expression to a wish which I have previously mooted only in occasional conversations with academics: that some philosophy faculty or another might render outstanding service to the promotion of the *historical* study of *morality* through offering a series of academic prizes—perhaps this book might serve to give a powerful impetus in this very direction. Should this possibility be pursued, the following question might be suggested: it merits the attention of philologists and historians as much as that of philosophers by profession—

> *'What indications for the direction of further research does linguistics, and in particular the study of etymology, provide for the history of the development of moral concepts?'*

—On the other hand, it is admittedly just as necessary to secure the interest of physiologists and physicians in the exploration of this problem (of the *value* of previous evaluations): here too it might be left to the specialist philosophers to act as spokesmen and mediators in this matter, once they have largely succeeded in reshaping the original relationship of mutual aloofness and suspicion which obtains between the disciplines of philosophy, physiology, and medicine into the most amicable and fruitful exchange. In fact, all tables of commandments, all 'Thou shalts' known to history or ethnological research, certainly require *physiological* investigation and interpretation prior to psychological examination. Equally, all await a critique from the medical sciences. The question: what is the *value* of this or that table of commandments and 'morality'? should be examined from the most varied perspectives; in particular, the question of its value *to what end?* cannot be examined too closely. For example, something possessing clear value for the greatest possible survival capacity of a race (or for increasing its powers of adaptation to a certain climate or for the preservation of the greatest number) would not have anything like the same value if what was at issue were the development of a stronger type. The welfare of the greatest number and the welfare of the few

---

1. To the records (Latin); that is, relegated to the archives as done with.

represent opposed points of view on value: to hold the former as of intrinsically higher value may be left to the naïveté of English biologists . . . From now on, *all* disciplines have to prepare the future task of the philosopher: this task being understood as the solution of the *problem of value*, the determination of the *hierarchy*[2] of values.—

From SECOND ESSAY
'Guilt,' 'Bad Conscience,' and Related Matters

1

The breeding of an animal which is *entitled to make promises*[3]—is this not the paradoxical task which nature has set itself with respect to man? Is this not the real problem which man not only poses but faces also? . . . The extent to which this problem has been solved must seem all the more surprising to someone who fully appreciates the countervailing force of *forgetfulness*. Forgetfulness is no mere *vis inertiae*, as the superficial believe; it is rather an active—in the strictest sense, positive—inhibiting capacity, responsible for the fact that what we absorb through experience impinges as little on our consciousness during its digestion (what might be called its 'psychic assimilation') as does the whole manifold process of our physical nourishment, that of so-called 'physical assimilation'. The temporary shutting of the doors and windows of consciousness; guaranteed freedom from disturbance by the noise and struggle caused by our underworld of obedient organs as they co-operate with and compete against one another; a little silence, a little *tabula rasa*[4] of consciousness, making room for the new, making room above all for the superior functions and functionaries—those of governing, anticipating, planning ahead (since our organism is structured as an oligarchy)—such is the use of what I have called active forgetfulness, an active forgetfulness whose function resembles that of a concierge preserving mental order, calm, and decorum. On this basis, one may appreciate immediately to what extent there could be no happiness, no serenity, no hope, no pride, no *present* without forgetfulness. The man in whom this inhibiting apparatus is damaged and out of order may be compared to a dyspeptic (and not only compared)—he is never 'through' with anything . . . Even this necessarily forgetful animal—in whom forgetting is a strength, a form of *robust* health—has now bred for himself a counter-faculty, a memory, by means of which forgetfulness is in certain cases suspended— that is, those which involve promising. This development is not merely the result of a passive inability to rid oneself of an impression once etched on the mind, nor of the incapacity to digest a once-given word with which one is never through, but represents rather an active *will* not to let go, an ongoing willing of what was once willed, a real *memory of the will*: so that between the original 'I will', 'I shall do', and the actual realization of the will, its *enactment*, a world of new and strange things, circumstances, even other acts of will may safely intervene, without causing this long chain of the will to break. But how much all this presupposes! In order to dispose of the future in advance in this

2. That is, rank-order (*Rangordnung*).

3. This translates "das *versprechen darf*"—that is, an animal that *may promise* because it is *capable of keeping* a promise. So the question posed thus becomes: how was *that* capacity developed?

4. Scraped tablet (Latin)—that is, a blank slate ready to be written on. This metaphor is associated particularly with the English empiricist John Locke (1632–1704).

way, how much man must first have learnt to distinguish necessity from accident! To think in terms of causality, to see and anticipate from afar, to posit ends and means with certainty, to be able above all to reckon and calculate! For that to be the case, how much man himself must have become *calculable, regular, necessary*, even to his own mind, so that finally he would be able to vouch for himself *as future*, in the way that someone making a promise does!

2

Such is the long history of the origin of *responsibility*. As we have already grasped, the task of breeding an animal which is entitled to make promises presupposes as its condition a more immediate task, that of first *making* man to a certain extent necessary, uniform, an equal among equals, regular and consequently calculable. The enormous labour of what I have called the 'morality of customs'[5]—the special work of man on himself throughout the longest era of the human race, his whole endeavour *prior to the onset of history*, all this finds its meaning, its great justification—regardless of the degree to which harshness, tyranny, apathy, and idiocy are intrinsic to it—in the following fact: it was by means of the morality of custom and the social straitjacket that man was really *made* calculable. By way of contrast, let us place ourselves at the other end of this enormous process, at the point where the tree finally bears its fruit, where society and its morality of custom finally reveal the *end* to which they were merely a means: there we find as the ripest fruit on their tree the *sovereign individual*, the individual who resembles no one but himself, who has once again broken away from the morality of custom, the autonomous supra-moral individual (since 'autonomous' and 'moral' are mutually exclusive)—in short, the man with his own independent, enduring will, the man who is *entitled to make promises*. And in him we find a proud consciousness, tense in every muscle, of *what* has finally been achieved here, of what has become incarnate in him—a special consciousness of power and freedom, a feeling of the ultimate completion of man. This liberated man, who is really *entitled* to make promises, this master of *free* will, this sovereign—how should he not be aware of his superiority over everything which cannot promise and vouch for itself? How should he not be aware of how much trust, how much fear, how much respect he arouses—he *'deserves'* all three—and how much mastery over circumstances, over nature, and over all less reliable creatures with less enduring wills is necessarily given into his hands along with this self-mastery? The 'free' man—the owner of an enduring, indestructible will—possesses also in this property his *measure of value*: looking out at others from his own vantage-point, he bestows respect or contempt. Necessarily, he respects those who are like him—the strong and reliable (those who are *entitled* to make promises), that is, anyone who promises like a sovereign—seriously, seldom, slowly—who is sparing with his trust, who *confers distinction* when he trusts, who gives his word as something which can be relied on, because he knows himself strong enough to uphold it even against accidents, even 'against fate'. Even so, he will have to keep the toe of his boot poised for the cowering dogs who make promises without entitlement, and hold his stick at the ready for the liar who breaks his word the moment he utters it. The proud

5. That is, the "ethicality of custom" (*Sittlichkeit der Sitte*), the kind of ethics or normativity centering on the authoritativeness of customs.

knowledge of this extraordinary privilege of *responsibility*, the consciousness of this rare freedom, this power over oneself and over fate has sunk down into his innermost depths and has become an instinct, a dominant instinct—what will he call it, this dominant instinct, assuming that he needs a name for it? About that there can be no doubt: this sovereign man calls it his *conscience* . . .[6]

3

His conscience? . . . It may be surmised in advance that the concept of 'conscience'—which we meet here in its highest, almost disconcerting form— is the product of a long history and series of transformations. To be able to vouch for oneself, and to do so with pride, and so to have the *right to affirm oneself*—that is, as I have said, a ripe fruit, but also a *late* fruit. How long this fruit had to hang sharp and bitter on the tree! And for an even longer time there was no sign of such a fruit—no one would have had the right to promise it, in spite of the fact that this alone was the end towards which the entire preparation and growth of the tree was directed!—'How does one give the man-animal a memory? How does one impress something on this partly insensate, partly idiotic ephemeral understanding, this incarnated forgetfulness, so that it remains present to mind?' . . . As we might imagine, the means employed to find a solution or answer to this ancient problem have been far from tender; there is, perhaps, nothing more frightening and more sinister in the whole prehistory of man than his *technique for remembering things.* 'Something is branded in, so that it stays in the memory: only that which *hurts* incessantly is remembered'—this is a central proposition of the oldest (and unfortunately also the most enduring) psychology on earth. One may even be tempted to say that something of this horror—by means of which promises were once made all over the earth, and guarantees and undertakings given— something of this *survives* still wherever solemnity, seriousness, secrecy, and sombre colours are found in the life of men and nations: the past, the longest, deepest, harshest past, breathes on us and wells up in us, whenever we become 'serious'. Things never proceeded without blood, torture, and victims, when man thought it necessary to forge a memory for himself. The most horrifying sacrifices and offerings (including sacrifice of the first-born), the most repulsive mutilations (castrations, for example), the cruellest rituals of all religious cults (and all religions are at their deepest foundations systems of cruelty)—all these things originate from that instinct which guessed that the most powerful aid to memory was pain. In a certain sense, the whole of asceticism belongs here: a few ideas are to be made inextinguishable, omnipresent, unforgettable, 'fixed'—with the aim of hypnotizing the whole nervous system and intellect by means of these 'fixed ideas'—and the ascetic procedures and forms of life are the means of freeing these ideas from competition with all other ideas, in order to make them 'unforgettable'. The worse mankind's memory was, the more frightening its customs appear; the harshness of punishment codes, in particular, gives a measure of how much effort it

---

6. This type of "conscience" is very different from the type of "bad conscience" to which Nietzsche turns in §4. And the defining characteristic of "the sovereign individual" (das *souveräne Individuum*) is not domination or mastery of *others*, but rather *self-mastery* and self-control. This "sovereign" type, while admirable in this respect, also is not yet (fully) the type of "redeeming" human being that Nietzsche glowingly envisions at the end of this essay (§24).

required to triumph over forgetfulness and to make these ephemeral slaves of emotion and desire mindful of a few primitive requirements of social cohabitation. * * * With the help of such images and procedures[7] one eventually memorizes five or six 'I will not's, thus giving one's *promise* in return for the advantages offered by society. And indeed! with the help of this sort of memory, one eventually did come to 'see reason'!—Ah, reason, seriousness, mastery over the emotions, the whole murky affair which goes by the name of thought, all these privileges and showpieces of man: what a high price has been paid for them! how much blood and horror is at the bottom of all 'good things'!

4

But how then did that other 'murky affair',[8] the sense of guilt, the whole matter of 'bad conscience', originate?—And here we return to our genealogists of morals. To repeat myself—or perhaps I have not yet said it at all?—they are of no use.

* * *

16

At this point, I can no longer avoid giving my own hypothesis as to the origin of 'bad conscience' its first, provisional expression: it does not make for easy listening and requires a long period of continuous reflection and consideration, filling waking and sleeping hours. I take bad conscience to be the deep sickness to which man was obliged to succumb under the pressure of that most fundamental of all changes—when he found himself definitively locked in the spell of society and peace. These half-animals who were happily adapted to a life of wilderness, war, nomadism, and adventure were affected in a similar way to the creatures of the sea when they were forced either to adapt to life on land or to perish—in a single stroke, all their instincts were devalued and 'suspended'. From that moment on they had to walk on their feet and 'support themselves', where previously they had been supported by water: a horrific weight bore down on them. The simplest tasks made them feel clumsy, they were without their old guides in this new, unknown world, the regulating drives with their instinctive certainty—they were reduced, these unfortunate creatures, to thinking, drawing conclusions, calculating, combining causes and effects, to their 'consciousness', their most meagre and unreliable organ! I believe that never on earth had there been such a feeling of misery, such leaden discomfort. Nor did the old instincts all of a sudden cease making their demands! Only it was difficult and seldom possible to obey them: for the most part, they had to seek new and, at the same time, subterranean satisfactions for themselves. Every instinct which does not vent itself externally *turns inwards*—this is what I call the *internalization* of man: it is at this point that what is later called the 'soul' first develops in man. The whole inner world, originally stretched thinly as between two membranes, has been extended and expanded, has acquired depth, breadth, and height in proportion as the external

---

7. Stoning, impalement, flaying alive, and other punishments mentioned in the omitted passage.

8. That is, somber thing, serious business (*düstre Sache*).

venting of human instinct has been *inhibited*. Those fearful bulwarks by means of which the state organization protected itself against the old instincts of freedom—punishment belongs above all to these bulwarks—, caused all the instincts of the wild, free, nomadic man to turn backwards *against man himself*. Hostility, cruelty, pleasure in persecution, in assault, in change, in destruction,—all that turning against the man who possesses such instincts: *such* is the origin of 'bad conscience'. The man who is forced into an oppressively narrow and regular morality, who for want of external enemies and resistance impatiently tears, persecutes, gnaws, disturbs, mistreats himself, this animal which is to be 'tamed', which rubs himself raw on the bars of his cage, this deprived man consumed with homesickness for the desert, who had no choice but to transform himself into an adventure, a place of torture, an uncertain and dangerous wilderness—this fool, this yearning and desperate prisoner became the inventor of 'bad conscience'. But with him was introduced the greatest and most sinister sickness which still afflicts man even today, man's suffering *from man, from himself*: this as a result of a violent separation from his animal past, of a leap which is also a fall into new situations and conditions of existence, of a declaration of war against the old instincts, which previously constituted the basis of his strength, pleasure, and fearfulness. On the other hand, let us add immediately that with the emergence of an animal soul turned against itself and taking sides against itself, something so new, so deep, so unprecedented, so enigmatic *and pregnant with the future*[9] came into existence that the earth's aspect was essentially altered. In fact, it took divine spectators to appreciate fully the drama which began at that time and whose end is not yet in sight, not by a long way—a drama too fine, too marvellous, too paradoxical to be allowed to run senselessly unnoticed on just any ridiculous star! Since that time, man *counts* among the most unexpected and exciting lucky throws of the dice played by Heraclitus'[1] 'great child'—whether that be Zeus[2] or chance—he arouses interest, suspense, hope, almost certainty, as if in him something were being announced, were being prepared, as if man were not an end in himself, but rather only a pathway, an incident, a bridge, a great promise . . .

17

This hypothesis as to the origin of bad conscience presupposes first that this change was not gradual and voluntary, an organic growth into new conditions, but rather a break, a leap, a compulsion, an irrefutable fate, against which there was no struggle nor even any *ressentiment*. And secondly, that the insertion of a previously unrestrained and unshaped population into a fixed form, just as it began with an act of violence, was only brought to completion through simple acts of violence—that the oldest 'state' accordingly emerged and endured as a fearful tyranny, as a crushing and thoughtless machinery, until such a raw material of common people and half-animals was finally not only thoroughly kneaded and malleable but also *formed*. I used the word 'state':

---

9. That is, opening up new possibilities, and so something *Zukunftsvolles* (literally "future-full"; figuratively, potentially game-changing).
1. Nietzsche's favorite pre-Socratic Greek philosopher (active ca. 500 B.C.E.), who held that all is in flux; the quotation refers to Heraclitus fragment 52, "Time is a child playing checkers; the kingdom of a child."
2. Ruler of the Greek gods.

it goes without saying what I mean by that—some horde or other of blond predatory animals, a race of conquerors and masters which, itself organized for war and with the strength to organize others, unhesitatingly lays its fearful paws on a population which may be hugely superior in numerical terms but remains shapeless and nomadic. Such is the beginning of the 'state' on earth: I think that the sentimental effusion which suggested that it originates in a 'contract'[3] has been done away with. He who is capable of giving commands, who is a 'master' by nature, who behaves violently in deed and gesture—what are contracts to him! One does not reckon with such beings, they arrive like fate, without motive, reason, consideration, pretext, they arrive like lightning, too fearful, too sudden, too convincing, too 'different', even to be hated. Their work is an instinctive creation and impression of form, they are the most involuntary, most unconscious artists there are—wherever they appear, something new quickly grows up, a *living* structure of domination, in which parts and functions are demarcated and articulated, where only that which has first been given a 'meaning' with respect to the whole finds a place. The meaning of guilt, responsibility, and consideration is unknown to these born organizers; the fearful egoism of the artist presides in them, with its gaze of bronze and sense of being justified in advance to all eternity in its 'work', like the mother in her child. *They* were not the ones among whom 'bad conscience' grew up, as goes without saying from the outset—but it would not have grown up *without them*, this ugly weed, it would not exist if, under the force of their hammer-blows, of their artists' violence, a vast quantity of freedom had not been expelled from the world, or at least removed from visibility and, as it were, forcibly made *latent*. This *instinct of freedom* made latent through force—as we have already understood—this instinct of freedom, forced back, trodden down, incarcerated within and ultimately still venting and discharging itself only upon itself: such is *bad conscience* at its origin, that and nothing more.

* * *

24

—I conclude with three question-marks, that much seems clear. 'Is an ideal actually being set up or broken down here?' I may be asked . . . But have you ever asked yourselves often enough how much the setting up of *every* single ideal on earth has cost? How much reality had to be defamed and denied, how many lies sanctified, how much conscience disturbed, how much 'god' sacrificed each time to that end? In order for a shrine to be set up, *another shrine must be broken into pieces*: that is the law—show me the case where it is not so! . . . We modern men, we are the heirs to centuries of the vivisection of conscience and animal self-torture: it is in this that we have our greatest experience, our artistry perhaps, in any case, our refinement, the luxury which vitiates our taste. For all too long man has looked askance at his natural inclinations, with the result that they have ultimately become interwoven with 'bad conscience'. An attempt at reversal would *in itself* be possible—but who is

---

3. That is, the social contract: in political philosophy, a hypothetical agreement among individuals to live together in a society.

strong enough to undertake it?—that is, an attempt instead to interweave bad conscience with the *unnatural* inclinations, all those aspirations to the beyond, the absurd, the anti-instinctual, the anti-animal, in short, to what have up to now been regarded as ideals, ideals which are all hostile to life, ideals which defame the world. To whom can one turn today with *such* hopes and demands? . . . The good men are the very people who would oppose it; as would, of course, the comfortable, the reconciled, the vain, the sentimentally effusive, the exhausted men . . . What is more deeply insulting to them, what isolates us more completely from them than to reveal a glimpse of our self-discipline and self-respect? And again—how accommodating, how kind the whole world shows itself to us, as soon as we behave like everyone else and 'let ourselves go' like everyone else! . . . Such a goal would require *different* kinds of spirit than are likely in this period, of all periods: spirits, who, strengthened through wars and victories, have developed a need for conquest, adventure, danger, pain; it would require acclimatization to sharp, high-altitude air, to winter expeditions, to ice and mountains in every sense, it would even require a kind of sublime wickedness, a last, self-assured intellectual malice which belongs to great health, it would require, in short—and which is bad enough—nothing less than this *great health* itself! . . . Is this still possible even today? . . . But at some time, in a period stronger than this brittle, self-doubting present, he must yet come to us, the *redeemer* of great love and contempt, the creative spirit whose compelling strength allows him no rest in any remote retreat and beyond, a spirit whose seclusion is misunderstood by the common people, as if it were a flight *from* reality—while it is only a further steeping, burrowing, plunging *into* reality, from which he may at some time return to the light, bearing the *redemption* of this reality: its redemption from the curse which the previous ideal has laid upon it. This man of the future, who will redeem us as much from the previous ideal as from *what was bound to grow out of it*, from the great disgust, from the will to nothingness, from nihilism, this midday stroke of the bell, this toll of great decision, which once again liberates the will, which once again gives the earth its goal and man his hope, this Antichristian and Antinihilist, this conqueror of God and of nothingness—*he must come one day* . . .

*   *   *

SOURCE: Friedrich Nietzsche, *On the Genealogy of Morals: A Polemic: By Way of Clarification and Supplement to My Last Book, "Beyond Good and Evil,"* trans. Douglas Smith (Oxford: Oxford University Press, 1996), pp. 3–8, 11–13, 22–30, 34–35, 37–44, 64–67, 75–76. Except where otherwise indicated, German words in brackets are the terminology used in the German original, inserted by the editor in addition to their renderings in the translation. Originally published in 1887 as *Zur Genealogie der Moral*.

From Twilight of the Idols

From *The Problem of Socrates*

1

Throughout the ages the wisest of men have passed the same judgement on life: *it is no good* . . . Always and everywhere their mouths have been heard to produce the same sound—a sound full of doubt, full of melancholy, full of weariness of life, full of resistance to life. Even Socrates said as he was dying: 'Life is one long illness: I owe the saviour Asclepius a cock.'[1] Even Socrates had had enough of it.—What does this *prove*? What does this *point to*?—In former times people would have said (—oh they did say it, and loudly enough, with our pessimists in the vanguard!): 'There must be at least something true here! The *consensus sapientium*[2] proves the truth.'—Shall we still speak in such terms today? *can* we do so? 'There must be at least something *sick* here' is the answer *we* give: these wisest of every age, we should look at them from close to! Were they all perhaps no longer steady on their feet? belated? doddery? *décadents*?[3] Would wisdom perhaps appear on earth as a raven excited by a faint whiff of carrion? . . .

2

I myself was first struck by this impertinent thought, that the great wise men are *declining types*, in the very case where it meets with its strongest opposition from scholarly and unscholarly prejudice: I recognized Socrates and Plato as symptoms of decay, as tools of the Greek dissolution, as pseudo-Greek, as anti-Greek (*Birth of Tragedy*, 1872).[4] That *consensus sapientium*—I have realized it more and more—proves least of all that they were right in what they agreed on: it proves rather that they themselves, these wisest of men, were somehow in *physiological* agreement in order to have—to *have* to have—the same negative attitude towards life. Judgements, value judgements on life, whether for or against, can ultimately never be true: they have value only as symptoms, they can be considered only as symptoms—in themselves such judgements are foolish. We must really stretch out our fingers and make the effort to grasp this astonishing *finesse*, *that the value of life cannot be assessed.*[5] Not by a living person because he is an interested party, indeed even the object of dispute, and not the judge; nor by a dead person, for a different reason. For a philosopher to see a problem in the *value* of life is thus even an objection against him, a question mark against his wisdom, a piece of unwisdom.—What? so all these great wise men were not only *decadents*, they were not even wise?

* * *

'Reason' in Philosophy

1

You ask me what are all the idiosyncrasies of the philosophers? . . . For one thing their lack of historical sense, their hatred of the very idea of becoming, their Egypticism.[6] They think they are doing a thing an *honour* when they

---

1. The Greek philosopher Socrates (469–399 B.C.E.) was sentenced to death for impiety and corrupting the youth of Athens; according to *Phaedo* (118a), written by his pupil Plato (ca. 427–ca. 347 B.C.E.), his last words were "Crito, we owe a rooster to Asclepius; pay it and do not neglect it" (accurately quoted by Nietzsche in *The Gay Science*, §340, though with the same interpretation as provided here). In the account written about the same time by the historian Xenophon (*Apology of Socrates* 1), Socrates appears to welcome avoiding

the frailties of old age. "Saviour" was a common epithet of Asclepius, the object of cult worship and recipient of sacrifices as god of healing.
2. Consensus of the wise (Latin).
3. Decadent (French).
4. Nietzsche's first book (see above).
5. That is, cannot be measured by any appropriate standard or method of evaluation (*abgeschätzt*)—for there is none.
6. That is, their preference for what is fixed and eternally unchanging.

dehistoricize it, *sub specie aeterni*[7]—when they make a mummy out of it. All that philosophers have been handling for thousands of years is conceptual mummies; nothing real has ever left their hands alive. They kill things and stuff them, these servants of conceptual idols, when they worship—they become a mortal danger to everything when they worship. Death, change, age, as well as procreation and growth, are objections—even refutations—for them. Whatever is, does not *become*; whatever becomes, *is* not . . . Now they all believe, even to the point of desperation, in [B]eing. But because they cannot gain possession of it they look for reasons as to why it is being withheld from them. 'There must be some pretence, some deception going on, preventing us from perceiving being: where's the deceiver hiding?'—'We've got him', they cry in rapturous delight, 'it's our sensuousness! These senses, *which are otherwise so immoral, too*, they are deceiving us about the *real* world. Moral: free yourself from sense-deception, from becoming, history, lies—history is nothing but belief in the senses, belief in lies. Moral: say no to anything which believes in the senses, to the whole of the rest of humanity: they are all just "the populace". Be a philosopher, be a mummy, represent monotono-theism by miming a gravedigger!—And above all away with the *body*, this pitiful *idée fixe*[8] of the senses! afflicted with every logical error there is, refuted, even impossible, though it is cheeky enough to act as if it were real!' . . .

2

I shall set apart, with great respect, the name of *Heraclitus*.[9] If the rest of the philosophical populace rejected the evidence of the senses because they showed multiplicity and change, he rejected their evidence because they showed things as if they had duration and unity. Heraclitus, too, did the senses an injustice. They do not lie either in the way that the Eleatics[1] believe, or as he believed—they do not lie at all. What we *make* of their evidence is what gives rise to the lie, for example the lie of unity, the lie of materiality, of substance, of duration . . . 'Reason' is what causes us to falsify the evidence of the senses. If the senses show becoming, passing away, change, they do not lie . . . But Heraclitus will always be right that Being is an empty fiction. The 'apparent' world is the only one: the 'real world' has just been *lied on*[2] . . .

3

—And what fine instruments of observation we have in our senses! This nose, for example, of which not one philosopher has yet spoken in reverence and gratitude, is nevertheless actually the most delicate instrument we have at our command: it can register minimal differences in movement which even the spectroscope fails to register. We possess science [*Wissenschaft*] nowadays precisely to the extent that we decided to *accept* the evidence of the senses—when we were still learning to sharpen them, arm them, think them through

---

7. Under the aspect of eternity (Latin); that is, from the perspective of the eternal.
8. Fixed idea (French); that is, an idea that has taken hold to the point of obsession.
9. Nietzsche's favorite pre-Socratic Greek philosopher (active ca. 500 B.C.E.), who held that all is in flux.

1. Members of a pre-Socratic school of Greek philosophy founded in the early 5th century B.C.E. by Parmenides in Elea, in southern Italy; they argued that all change in the world is illusory, because all that really exists is unchanging, indivisible, and eternal.
2. That is, "lied about."

to the end. The rest is abortion and not-yet-science: to wit, metaphysics, theology, psychology, theory of knowledge. *Or* the science [*Wissenschaft*] of forms, the theory of signs: like logic and that applied logic, mathematics. Reality is nowhere to be found in them, not even as a problem; nor does the question arise as to what actual value a sign-convention like logic has.—

4

The *other* idiosyncrasy of the philosophers is no less dangerous: it consists in mistaking the last for the first. They put what comes at the end—unfortunately! for it should not come anywhere!—the 'highest concepts', i.e. the most general, emptiest concepts, the last wisp of evaporating reality, at the beginning *as* the beginning. This is once again simply the expression of their kind of reverence: the higher *is not allowed* to grow out of the lower, *is not allowed* to have grown at all . . . Moral: everything first-rate must be *causa sui*.[3] If it is descended from something else, this is seen as an objection and brings its value into question. All the supreme values are first-rate; all the highest concepts—being, the absolute, the good, the true, the perfect—none of them can have become, so they *must* be *causa sui*. Equally, though, none of them can differ from the others or conflict with them . . . Hence their astounding notion of 'God' . . . The last, thinnest, emptiest, is put first, as cause in itself, as *ens realissimum*[4] . . . Oh that humanity had to take seriously the brain-feverish fantasies spun out by the sick!—And it has paid dearly for it! . . .

5

—Let us finally set against this the different way in which *we* (—I say we out of politeness . . .) contemplate the problem of error and appearance. In former times people took alteration, change, becoming in general as proof of appearance, as a sign that there must be something there leading us astray. Nowadays, conversely—and precisely in so far as the prejudice called 'reason' compels us to establish unity, identity, duration, substance, cause, materiality, Being—we see ourselves to a certain extent tangled up in error, *forced* into error; as sure as we are, on the basis of stringent checking, *that* the error is here. It is no different from the movements of the great stars: in their case error has our eye as its constant advocate, here it has our *language*. Language is assigned by its emergence to the time of the most rudimentary form of psychology: we become involved in a crude fetishism when we make ourselves conscious of the basic premises of the metaphysics of language, in plain words: of *reason*. *This* is what sees doer and deed everywhere: it believes in the will as cause in general; it believes in the 'I', in the I as Being, in the I as substance, and *projects* the belief in the I-substance onto all things—only then does it *create* the concept 'thing' . . . Being is thought in, *foisted in* everywhere as cause; only following on from the conception 'I' is the concept 'Being' derived . . . At the beginning stands the great disaster of an error that the will is something *at work*—that will is a *capacity* . . . Nowadays we know that it is just a word . . . Very much later, in a world a thousand times more enlightened, philosophers were surprised to realize how *assured*, how subjectively *cer-*

---

3. The cause of itself (Latin).   4. The most real being (Latin).

tain they were in handling the categories of reason—which, they concluded, could not come from the empirical world, since the empirical world stands in contradiction to them. *So where do they come from?*—And in India as in Greece they made the same mistake: 'we must once have been at home in a higher world (—instead of *in a very much lower one*: which would have been the truth!), we must have been divine *because* we have reason!' . . . In fact nothing has had a more naïve power of persuasion so far than the error of Being, as formulated, for example, by the Eleatics: for it has on its side every word, every sentence we speak!—Even the opponents of the Eleatics still succumbed to the seduction of their concept of Being: among others Democritus,[5] when he invented his *atom* . . . 'Reason' in language: oh what a deceitful old woman![6] I am afraid we are not getting rid of God because we still believe in grammar . . .

6

People will be grateful to me for condensing such an essential new insight into four theses: this way I am easing comprehension; this way I am inviting contradiction.

First Proposition. The reasons which have been given for designating 'this' world as apparent actually account for its reality—any *other* kind of reality is absolutely unprovable.

Second Proposition. The characteristics which have been given to the 'true Being' of things are the characteristics of non-Being, of *nothingness*—the 'real world' has been constructed from the contradiction of the actual world: an apparent world, indeed, to the extent that it is merely a *moral-optical* illusion.

Third Proposition. Concocting stories about a world 'other' than this one is utterly senseless, unless we have within us a powerful instinct to slander, belittle, cast suspicion on life: in which case we are *avenging* ourselves on life with the phantasmagoria of 'another', 'better' life.

Fourth Proposition. Dividing the world into a 'real' one and an 'apparent' one, whether in the manner of Christianity, or of Kant (a *crafty* Christian, when all's said and done), is but a suggestion of *décadence*—a symptom of *declining* life . . . The fact that the artist values appearance more highly than reality is no objection to this proposition. For 'appearance' here means reality *once more*, only selected, strengthened, corrected . . . The tragic artist is *no* pessimist—on the contrary, he says *yes* to all that is questionable and even terrible; he is *Dionysian*[7] . . .

How the 'Real World'[8] Finally Became a Fable

HISTORY OF AN ERROR

1. The real [*wahre*] world attainable for the wise man, the pious man, the virtuous man—he lives in it, *he is it.*

---

5. Greek philosopher (ca. 460–ca. 370 B.C.E.), an important figure in the development of the early atomic theory of matter.

6. A "woman," because the German noun *Vernunft* (reason) is grammatically gendered feminine.

7. In his later writings, Nietzsche's label "Dionysian" (which he embraced) has a different meaning than it had for him when he introduced it in *The*

Birth of Tragedy. There, it signified the ecstatic and emotional, in contrast to the rational and analytic ("Apollonian"); now, it conveys the idea of a kind of synthesis of the two tendencies or mentalities.

8. That is, "true world" (*wahre Welt*); the idea of a "world" or reality different from the world of ordinary life and experience that is what is *truly* real.

(Most ancient form of the idea, relatively clever, simple, convincing. Paraphrase of the proposition: 'I, Plato, *am* the truth.')

2. The real world unattainable for now, but promised to the wise man, the pious man, the virtuous man ('to the sinner who repents').

(Progress of the idea: it becomes more cunning, more insidious, more incomprehensible—*it becomes a woman,*[9] becomes Christian . . .)

3. The real world unattainable, unprovable, unpromisable, but the mere thought of it a consolation, an obligation, an imperative.

(The old sun in the background, but seen through mist and scepticism; the idea become sublime, pale, Nordic, Königsbergian.[1])

4. The real world—unattainable? At any rate unattained. And since unattained also *unknown*. Hence no consolation, redemption, obligation either: what could something unknown oblige us to do? . . .

(Break of day. First yawn of reason. Cock-crow[2] of positivism.)

5. The 'real world'—an idea with no further use, no longer even an obligation—an idea become useless, superfluous, *therefore* a refuted idea: let us do away with it!

(Broad daylight; breakfast; return of *bon sens* and cheerfulness; Plato's shameful blush; din from all free spirits.[3])

6. The real world—we have done away with it: what world was left? the apparent one, perhaps? . . . But no! *with the real [wahre] world we have also done away with the apparent [scheinbare] one!*[4]

(Noon; moment of the shortest shadow; end of the longest error; pinnacle of humanity; INCIPIT ZARATHUSTRA.[5])

From *Morality as Anti-Nature*

1

All passions have a period in which they are merely fateful, in which they draw their victims down by weight of stupidity—and a later, very much later one, in which they marry the spirit, 'spiritualize' themselves. In former times, because of the stupidity of passion, people waged war on passion itself: they plotted to destroy it—all the old moral monsters are in complete agreement that *'il faut tuer les passions'.*[6]

* * *

9. Another play on German grammar: *die Welt* (the world) is grammatically feminine.
1. That is, Kantian; KANT was born and lived his whole life in the Prussian city of Königsberg (now the Russian city of Kaliningrad).
2. That is, the dawning.
3. That is, all "enlightened" types with a humanistic focus on what can be known of and done with this life in this world. *Bon sens*: good sense, common sense (French). "Din" is translated from "Teufelsalärm"; pandemonium, uproar.
4. That is: by doing away with the "true world" idea, we also do away with the idea that what we are left with after we have done so has the status of mere "appearance."
5. Zarathustra begins (Latin); that is, the era of Nietzsche's new Zarathustra, the central figure of *Thus Spoke Zarathustra* (1883–85).
6. You must kill the passions (French).

4

—I shall make a principle into a formula. All naturalism in morality, i.e. every *healthy* morality, is governed by a vital instinct[7]—one or other of life's decrees is fulfilled through a specific canon of 'shalls' and 'shall nots', one or other of the obstructions and hostilities on life's way is thus removed. *Anti-natural* morality, i.e. almost every morality which has hitherto been taught, revered, and preached, turns on the contrary precisely *against* the vital instincts—it is at times secret, at times loud and brazen in *condemning* these instincts. In saying 'God looks at the heart'[8] it says no to the lowest and highest of life's desires, and takes God to be an *enemy of life* . . . The saint, in whom God is well pleased, is the ideal castrato . . . Life ends where the 'kingdom of God' *begins* . . .

5

Once you have grasped the heinousness of such a revolt against life, which has become almost sacrosanct in Christian morality, then fortunately you have also grasped something else: the futile, feigned, absurd, *lying* nature of such a revolt. A condemnation of life on the part of the living remains in the last resort merely the symptom of a specific kind of life: the question as to whether it is justifiable or not simply does not arise. You would need to be situated *outside* life, and at the same time to know life as well as someone—many people, everyone—who has lived it, to be allowed even to touch on the problem of the *value* of life: reason enough for realizing that the problem is an inaccessible problem to us. Whenever we speak of values, we speak under the inspiration—from the perspective—of life: life itself forces us to establish values; life itself evaluates through us *when* we posit values . . . It follows from this that even that *anti-nature of a morality* which conceives of God as the antithesis and condemnation of life is merely a value judgement on the part of life—*which* life? *what* kind of life?—But I have already given the answer: declining, weakened, tired, condemned life. Morality as it has hitherto been understood—and formulated by Schopenhauer, lastly, as 'denial of the will to life'[9]—is the *décadence instinct* itself making an imperative out of itself: it says: *'perish!'*—it is the judgement of the condemned . . .

6

Let us finally consider what naïvety it is in general to say 'man *should* be such and such!' Reality shows us a delightful abundance of types, the richness that comes from an extravagant play and alternation of forms: to which some wretched loafer of a moralist says: 'no! man should be *different*'? . . . He even knows how man should be, this maundering miseryguts:[1] he paints himself on the wall and says *'ecce homo!'*[2] . . . But even when the moralist turns just to the individual and says to him: *'you* should be such and such!' he does not stop making a fool of himself. The individual is a piece of fate from top to

7. That is, instinct of life (*Instinkte des Lebens*).
8. See 1 Samuel 16:7.
9. In SCHOPENHAUER's *The World as Will and Representation* (1818; 2nd ed., 1844); see above.
1. That is, pathetic grumbler (*Schlucker und Mucker*).

2. Behold the man! (Latin): the words of Pilate (in the Vulgate Bible) on presenting Jesus to the crowd before his crucifixion (John 19:5). Nietzsche himself used the phrase as the title of the autobiographical book he wrote in 1888 (published 1908).

bottom, one more law, one more necessity for all that is to come and will be. Telling him to change means demanding that everything should change, even backwards . . . And indeed there have been consistent moralists who wanted man to be different, namely virtuous; they wanted him to be in their image, namely a miseryguts: to which end they *denied* the world! No minor madness! No modest kind of immodesty! . . . Morality, in so far as it *condemns*—in itself, and *not* in view of life's concerns, considerations, intentions—is a specific error on which we should not take pity, a *degenerate's idiosyncrasy* which has wrought untold damage! . . . We who are different, we immoralists, on the contrary, have opened our hearts to all kinds of understanding, comprehending, *approving*. We do not readily deny; we seek our honour in being *affirmative*.[3] More and more our eyes have been opened to that economy which still needs and can exploit all that is rejected by the holy madness of the priest, of the priest's *sick* reason; to that economy in the law of life which can gain advantage even from the repulsive species of the miseryguts, the priest, the virtuous man—*what* advantage?—But we ourselves, we immoralists are the answer here . . .

From *The Four Great Errors*

1

Error of Confusing Cause and Consequence.—There is no error more dangerous than that of confusing the *consequence with the cause*: I call it the real ruination of reason. Nevertheless this error is among the most long-standing and recent of humanity's habits: it is even sanctified by us, and bears the name 'religion', 'morality'. *Every* proposition which religion and morality formulate contains it; priests and moral legislators are the originators of this ruination of reason.

* * *

3

Error of a False Causality.—People throughout the ages have believed they knew what a cause is: but where did we get our knowledge, more precisely our belief that we know? From the realm of the celebrated 'inner facts', not one of which has so far turned out to be real. We believed that we ourselves, in the act of willing, were causes; we thought that we were at least catching causality there *in the act*. Likewise people were in no doubt that all the *antecedentia*[4] of an action, its causes, were to be sought in consciousness and would be rediscovered there if sought—as 'motives': otherwise they would not have been free *to do* it, responsible *for* it. Finally, who would have denied that a thought is caused? that the 'I' causes the thought? . . . Of these three 'inner facts', by which causality seemed to be authenticated, the first and most convincing one is that of the *will as cause*; the conception of a consciousness ('mind') as cause and, later still, of the 'I' (the 'subject') as cause came only afterwards, once the causality of the will had been established as given, as *empirical* . . . Since then we have thought better of all this. Nowadays we no longer believe a word of it. The 'inner world' is full of illusions

3. "Approving": *Gutheissen*, calling things "good." "Affirmative": *Bejahende*, "yes-sayers."
4. Antecedents (Latin), a technical term in classical philosophy.

830 / Friedrich Nietzsche

and jack-o'-lanterns:[5] the will is one of them. The will no longer moves anything, and therefore no longer explains anything either—it simply accompanies events, and can even be absent. The so-called 'motive': another error. Merely a surface phenomenon of consciousness, an accessory to the act, which does more to conceal the *antecedentia* of an act than to represent them. And as for the I! It has become a fable, a fiction, a play on words: it has completely given up thinking, feeling, and willing! . . . What is the result? There are no mental causes at all! All the apparently empirical evidence for them has gone to the devil! *That* is the result!—And we had subjected this 'empirical evidence' to a pretty piece of abuse; we had *created* the world on the basis of it as a world of causes, a world of will, a spirit world . . . The most ancient and long-established psychology was at work here, and it did absolutely nothing else: in its eyes every event was an action, every action the result of a will; in its eyes the world became a multiplicity of agents, an agent (a 'subject') foisting itself onto every event. Man's three 'inner facts', the things he believed in most firmly—the will, the mind [*Geist*], the I—were projected out of himself: he derived the concept of Being from the concept of the I, and posited the existence of 'things' after his own image, after his concept of the I as cause. No wonder if, later on, he only ever rediscovered in things *what he had put in them.*—The thing itself, to say it again, the concept of thing: just a reflection of the belief in the I as cause . . . And even your atom, my dear mechanicians and physicists, how much error, how much rudimentary psychology still remains in your atom! Not to speak of the 'thing in itself', the *horrendum pudendum*[6] of the metaphysicians! The error of confusing the mind as cause with reality! And made the measure of reality! And called *God!*—

4

Error of Imaginary Causes.—To take dreams as my starting point: a specific sensation, for example one which results from a distant cannon-shot, has a cause foisted onto it after the event (often a complete little novel, in which the dreamer himself is the main character). Meanwhile the sensation persists, in a kind of resonance: it is as if it waits for the causal drive to allow it to step into the foreground—now no longer as chance, but as 'meaning'. The cannon-shot makes its appearance in a *causal* way, in an apparent reversal of time. The later thing, the motivation, is experienced first, often together with a hundred details which pass by like lightning, and the shot follows . . . What has happened? The ideas which a certain state *generated* have been mistakenly understood as its cause.

* * *

7

Error of Free Will.—We no longer have any sympathy nowadays for the concept 'free will': we know only too well what it is—the most disreputable piece of trickery the theologians have produced, aimed at making humanity 'respon-

---

5. That is, phantoms, will-o'-the-wisps (*Irrlichter*); literally, "false lights."
6. Dreadful shameful thing (Latin).

sible' in their sense, i.e. at *making it dependent on them* . . . I shall give here simply the psychology behind every kind of making people responsible.— Wherever responsibilities are sought, it is usually the instinct for *wanting to punish and judge* that is doing the searching. Becoming is stripped of its innocence once any state of affairs is traced back to a will, to intentions, to responsible acts: the doctrine of the will was fabricated essentially for the purpose of punishment, i.e. of *wanting to find guilty*. The old psychology as a whole, the psychology of the will, presupposes the fact that its originators, the priests at the head of ancient communities, wanted to give themselves the *right* to impose punishments—or give God the right to do so . . . People were thought of as 'free' so that they could be judged and punished—so that they could become *guilty*: consequently every action *had* to be thought of as willed, the origin of every action as located in consciousness (—thus the *most fundamental* piece of counterfeiting *in psychologicis*[7] became the principle of psychology itself). Nowadays, since we are engaged in a movement in the *opposite* direction, since we immoralists especially are seeking with all our strength to eliminate the concepts of guilt and punishment again and to cleanse psychology, history, nature, social institutions and sanctions of them, there is in our view no more radical opposition than that which comes from the theologians who, with their concept of the 'moral world order', persist in plaguing the innocence of becoming with 'punishment' and 'guilt'. Christianity is a metaphysics of the hangman . . .

8

What can *our* doctrine[8] be, though?—That no one *gives* man his qualities, neither God, nor society, nor his parents and ancestors, nor *man himself* (—the nonsense of the last idea rejected here was taught as 'intelligible freedom' by Kant, perhaps already by Plato, too). *No one* is responsible for simply being there, for being made in such and such a way, for existing under such conditions, in such surroundings. The fatality of one's being cannot be derived from the fatality of all that was and will be. *No one* is the result of his own intention, his own will, his own purpose; *no one* is part of an experiment to achieve an 'ideal person' or an 'ideal of happiness' or an 'ideal of morality'—it is absurd to want to *discharge* one's being onto some purpose or other. *We* invented the concept 'purpose': in reality, 'purpose' is *absent* . . . One is necessary, one is a piece of fate, one belongs to the whole, one *is* in the whole—there is nothing which could judge, measure, compare, condemn our Being, for that would mean judging, measuring, comparing, condemning the whole . . . *But there is nothing apart from the whole!* That no one is made responsible any more, that a kind of Being cannot be traced back to a *causa prima*,[9] that the world is no unity, either as sensorium or as 'mind [*Geist*]', *this alone is the great liberation*—this alone re-establishes the *innocence* of becoming . . . The concept 'God' has been the greatest *objection* to existence so far . . . We deny God, we deny responsibility in God: *this* alone is how we redeem the world.—

7. In psychological matters (Latin).
8. That is, teaching or theory (*Lehre*).

9. First cause (Latin).

From *The 'Improvers' of Humanity*

1

People are familiar with my call for the philosopher to place himself *beyond good and evil*[1]—to have the illusion of moral judgement *beneath* him. This call results from an insight which I was the first to formulate: *that there are no moral facts at all*. Moral judgement has this in common with religious judgement, that it believes in realities which do not exist. Morality is merely an interpretation of certain phenomena, more precisely a *mis*interpretation. Moral judgement pertains, like religious judgement, to a level of ignorance on which the very concept of the real, the distinction between the real and the imaginary, is still lacking: so that 'truth', on such a level, designates nothing but what we nowadays call 'illusions'. In this respect moral judgement should never be taken literally: as such it is only ever an absurdity. But as a *semiotics*[2] it remains inestimable: it reveals, at least to anyone who knows, the most valuable realities of cultures and interiorities which did not *know* enough to 'understand' themselves. Morality is merely sign language, merely symptomatology: you must already know *what* is going on in order to profit by it.

* * *

SOURCE: From Friedrich Nietzsche, *Twilight of the Idols: or, How to Philosophize with a Hammer*, trans. Duncan Large (Oxford: Oxford University Press, 1998), pp. 11–12, 16–21, 23–29, 31–33. Except where otherwise indicated, German words in brackets are the terminology used in the German original, inserted by the editor in addition to their renderings in the translation. Originally published in 1889 as *Götzen-Dämmerung; oder, Wie man mit dem Hammer philosophiert*, a title that parodies that of the final opera in Richard Wagner's 4-part *Ring of the Nibelung* cycle, *Götterdämmerung* (*Twilight of the Gods*). Nietzsche thus signals his intention to rival Wagner and his radical critique of contemporary European culture, society, and civilization—and indeed to surpass him, showing the hollowness of many more models, ideals, and values than Wagner had taken on.

From Notebooks of 1884–1888[1]

Themes of 1884–1886

1884

Our presuppositions: no God; no purpose; finite force. We want to *guard* ourselves against following and endorsing the mode of thought of the lowly. [KGW VII 25:299/WM 595]

*

(1) We want to hold fast to our senses and to belief in them—and think them through to the end! The non-sensuousness of previous philosophy as man's greatest nonsense.

---

1. In *Beyond Good and Evil* (1886; see above).
2. A theory of signs (Nietzsche's "symptomatology").
1. Material from Nietzsche's notebooks selected, edited and published after his death, in a volume given the title *Der Wille zur Macht* ("WM" below) by its compilers; translated as *The Will to Power* ("WP"). For further information, see "Source" below and discussion above (pp. 690–91).

(2) the world at hand, which everything earthly and living has been building, so that it appears as it does (durable and *slowly* changing), we want to
build *further*—but not criticize it away as false!

(3) our valuations build at it, they emphasize and underscore. What does
it matter if whole religions say: "It is all bad and false and evil!" This condemnation of the whole process can only be a judgment of misfits!

(4) to be sure, the misfits could be those who suffer most and are the most
sensitive? The contented could be of little value?

(5) one must understand the artistic fundamental phenomenon that is
called life—the *building* spirit [*Geist*], that builds under the most unfavorable
circumstances: in the slowest manner—the *proof* for all of its combinations
must first be given anew: *it preserves itself.* [KGW VII 25:438/WM 1046]

*

The best-believed *a priori* "truths"[2] are for me—*assumptions for the time
being*, e.g., the law of causality is a very well acquired habit of belief, so
ingrained that *not* to believe in it would destroy the race. But are they therefore truths? What an inference! As though it were a proof of truth that man
remains in existence. [KGW VII 26:12/WM 497]

*

The entire knowledge-apparatus is an apparatus for abstraction and simplification, directed not toward knowledge, but rather toward *getting control
of things*: "end" and "means" are as remote from its nature as are "concepts."
With "end" and "means" one gets control of a process (—one *invents* a process that is grasped!); with concepts, of the "things" that constitute the
process. [KGW VII 26:61/WM 503]

*

What the philosophers *lack*: (a) historical sense, (b) knowledge of physiology, (c) a goal in the future. To undertake a critique, without any irony and
moral condemnation. [KGW VII 26:100/WM 408]

*

If only we *could foresee* the most favorable conditions, under which beings
of the highest value arise! It is a thousand times too complicated, and the
probability of failure is *very great*: thus it is not encouraging to strive for
them!—Skepticism.

On the other hand: we can increase courage, insight, hardness, independence, the feeling of responsibility, refine the sensitivity of the scales, and anticipate that fortunate accidents will come to our aid. [KGW VII 26:117/WM 907]

*

Insight: all value-determination has to do with a particular perspective: the
preservation of the individual, of a community, a race, a state, a church, a faith,
a culture. Owing to the *forgetting* that there is only perspectival valuation, contradictory valuations and *consequently contradictory drives* of all sorts swarm in

2. That is, truths that, according to KANT, can be known independently of confirmation by experience.

a single person. This is the *expression of the sickness of man*, as opposed to the animal, in which all instincts to be found satisfy quite definite tasks.

This contradictory creature, however, has in its nature great method of *knowledge*: one feels many pros and cons—one raises oneself *to justice*—to comprehension *beyond valuations of good and evil.*

The wisest human being would be the richest in *contradictions*, who has a similar taste for all kinds of human beings: and with it all, great moments of *grand-scale harmony*—a rare happenstance even in us!—a kind of planetary movement—[KGW VII 26:119/WM 259]

*

To what extent our intellect also is a consequence of conditions of existence—we would not have it if we did not need it, and would not have it *as it is* if we did not need it as it is, if we could also live otherwise. [KGW VII 26:137/WM 498]

*

Science—the transformation of nature into concepts for the purpose of the mastery of nature—that belongs under the rubric of "means."

But the purpose and will of man must likewise *grow*, the intention with regard to the whole. [KGW VII 26:170/WM 610]

*

The philosophers are prejudiced *against* appearance, change, pain, death, the bodily, the senses, fate and unfreedom, the purposeless, everything human, even more the animal, more still the material; guided by instinctive value-determinations, in which earlier (more dangerous) cultural conditions are reflected.

They believe in absolute knowledge; knowledge for its own sake; the connection of virtue and happiness, desire and pain; the comprehensibility of human actions; good and evil. False opposites. The seductions of language. [KGW VII 26:300/WM 407]

*

I want to talk no one into philosophy; it is necessary, it is perhaps also desirable, that the philosopher is a *rare* plant. Nothing is more contrary to me than the teacherly praise of philosophy, as in Seneca or especially Cicero.[3] Philosophy has little to do with virtue. If I may say so, the scientific type also is something fundamentally different from the philosopher.—What I desire is that the genuine concept of the philosopher not be entirely extinguished in Germany. There are so many half-creatures of all kinds in Germany who would gladly conceal their wretchedness under so noble a name. [KGW VII 26:452/WM 420]

*

I teach: that there are higher and lower human beings, and that under certain conditions a single one can justify whole millennia—i.e., a full rich

---

3. Roman orator and statesman (106–43 B.C.E.), who also wrote philosophical treatises. Seneca the Younger (ca. 4 B.C.E.–65 C.E.), Roman tragedian and Stoic philosopher.

great whole human being in relation to countless incomplete human fragments. [KGW VII 27:16/WM 997]

*

Man, in contrast to the animal, has extensively cultivated an abundance of *contrary* drives and impulses: owing to this syntheses he is master of the earth. —Morals are the expression of locally limited *rank-orders* in this multifarious world of drives: in order that man should not perish from their *contradictions*. Thus: one drive as master, its opposite drive weakened, refined, as an impulse that provides the stimulus for the activity of the dominant drive.

The highest human being would have the greatest multiplicity of drives, and also in the relatively greatest strength, that can still be endured. In point of fact: where the human plant shows itself strong, one finds instincts striving powerfully *against* each other (e.g., Shakespeare), but restrained. [KGW VII 27:59/WM 986]

EARLY TO MID-1885

Philosophers (1) have always had a wonderful capacity for contradictions in terms. (2) They have trusted concepts as unconditionally as they have mistrusted the senses: they have not considered that concepts and words are our inheritance from times when what went on in the head was very murky and crude.

What dawns on philosophers last of all: they must no longer allow concepts simply to be given to them, nor simply purify and polish them, but rather above all must *make* them, *create* them, present them and make them convincing. Previously one has on the whole trusted one's concepts, as though they were a wonderful dowry from some sort of wonderland: but they are ultimately the legacy of our furthest, stupidest as well as cleverest ancestors. This *piety* toward that which is found in ourselves perhaps is part of the *moral* element in knowledge. What is needed first and foremost is absolute skepticism toward all inherited concepts (such as one philosopher *perhaps* once had—Plato:[4] naturally, he *taught* the *opposite*—). [KGW VII 34:195/WM 409]

*

The (At)tempter

There are many kinds of eyes. Even the Sphinx[5] has eyes: and consequently there are many kinds of "truths," and consequently there is no truth. [KGW VII 34:230/WM 540]

*

The victorious concept "force," with which our physicists have created God and the world, still requires an elaboration: an inner nature must be ascribed to it, which I designate as "will to power," i.e., as an insatiable craving for the manifestation of power; or for the use and exercise of power, as creative drive, etc. Physicists cannot eliminate "action at a distance" from their principles; likewise a repelling (or attracting) force. There is no alternative: one must

4. Greek philosopher (ca. 427–ca. 347 B.C.E.).
5. In Greek mythology, a winged female monster

with a lion's body and human head that killed all who failed to answer her riddle.

conceive all movements, all "appearances," all "laws" only as symptoms of an inner event and make use of the analogy of man for that purpose. In the animal it is possible to derive all of its drives from the will to power; likewise, all functions of organic life from this one source. [KGW VII 36:31/WM 619]

*

For a Plan. Introduction

1. The organic functions translated back into the fundamental will, the will to power—as having branched off from it.

2. Thinking, feeling, wanting in everything living—what is a pleasure other than: a stimulation of the feeling of power by an impediment (even stronger by rhythmic obstacles and resistances)—so that it thereby increases. Thus pain is involved in all pleasure.—If the pleasure is to become very great, the pains must last very long and the tension of the bow must be tremendous.

3. The will to power specializing itself as will to nourishment, property, tools, servants—obeying and ruling: the body.—The stronger will directs the weaker. There is no other kind of causality whatsoever than that of will upon will. It is certainly nothing mechanistic.

4. The spiritual [*geistig*] functions. Will to formation, assimilation, etc. Appendix. The great misunderstandings of the philosophers. [KGW VII 35:15/WM 658]

*

On the whole I side more with the artists than with any philosophers previously: they have not lost the scent of the great trail that life leaves, they love the things of "this world"—they have loved their senses. To strive for desensualization: that seems to me to be a misunderstanding or a sickness or a cure, where it is not mere hypocrisy or self-deception. I wish for myself, and for all those who live—who are *permitted* to live—without the anxieties of a puritanical conscience, an ever greater spiritualization and multiplication of the senses; yes, we would be thankful to the senses for their subtlety, abundance and power, and in return offer them the best we have of spirit. What do the priestly and metaphysical slanders of the senses matter to us? We have nothing more to do with these slanders; it is a sign of having turned out well when, like Goethe,[6] one clings with ever greater pleasure and affection to "the things of the world":—for in this manner one holds fast to the great conception of man, that man becomes the *transfigurer of existence* when he learns to transfigure himself.—But what are you saying? one may object to me. Are there not the most vexing pessimists among artists precisely today? For example, what do you think of Richard Wagner?[7] Is he no pessimist?—I scratch my ear: (you are right, I forgot something for a moment.) [KGW VII 37:12/WM 820]

*

"Truth": in my way of thinking this does not necessarily designate an opposite of error, but rather in the most fundamental cases only a placement of various errors in relation to each other: thus one might be older, deeper than

---

6. Johann Wolfgang von Goethe (1749–1832), the preeminent German literary figure of his time.
7. German composer (1813–1883), to whom Nie-

tzsche had been very close while writing *The Birth of Tragedy* (1872) but against whom he reacted strongly in the late 1870s.

another, perhaps even ineradicable in so far as an organic creature of our kind could not live without it; while other errors do not tyrannize over us as conditions of life in this way, and compared with such "tyrants" can be eliminated and "refuted." An assumption that is "irrefutable"—why should it thereby already be *true?* This proposition will perhaps shock the logicians, who suppose *their* limits to be the limits of things—but I have long ago declared war on this logicians' optimism. [KGW VII 38:4/WM 535]

*

And do you know what "the world" is to me? Shall I show it to you in my mirror? This world: a monster of energy, without beginning, without end; a fixed and firm quantity of energy that becomes neither larger nor smaller, that is not consumed but rather only transformed; as a whole of unchanging size, a household without expenditures and losses, but likewise without increase, without income, enclosed by "nothingness" as by a boundary; not something dissipating or squandering or infinitely extending but rather as a definite force set in a definite space—and not a space that might be "empty" anywhere, but rather as force throughout; as a play of forces and waves of force, at once one and "many," at once increasing here and diminishing there; a sea of forces raging and surging within itself, eternally changing, eternally running back again, with tremendous years of recurrence, with an ebb and flow of its forms; out of the simplest surging into the most complex, out of the stillest, stiffest, coldest into the hottest, wildest, most self-contradictory, and then homewardly returning to the simple again out of this fullness; out of the play of contradictions back to the pleasure of concord, affirming itself as that which must eternally return, as a becoming that knows no satiety, no disgust, no weariness—: This my *Dionysian* world[8] of the eternally self-creating and eternally self-destroying, this mystery-world of the twofold ecstacy; this my beyond good and evil, without goal, unless the happiness of the circle is a goal; without will, unless a ring has goodwill toward itself—do you want a *name* for this world? A *solution* for all its mysteries? A *light* too for you, you best hidden, strongest, most dauntless, most midnightly ones?—*This world is the will to power—and nothing besides!* And you yourselves are also this will to power—and nothing besides! [KGW VII 38:12/WM 1067][9]

*

FALL 1885 TO FALL 1886

Physiologists should think twice before positing the drive for preservation as the cardinal drive of an organic creature: something living wants above all to *give vent* to its force: "preservation" is only one of the consequences thereof.— Beware of *superficial* teleological principles! And the entire concept of a "drive for preservation" is among them. [KGW VIII 2:63/WM 650]

*

8. In his later writings, Nietzsche's label "Dionysian" (which he embraced) had a different meaning than when he introduced it in *The Birth of Tragedy*. There, it signified the ecstatic and emotional, as opposed to the rational and analytic "Apollonian"; now, it conveys the idea of a kind of synthesis of the two tendencies or mentalities.

9. The compilers of WM chose to end the collection with this note, though it dates from 1885 (far from the end of the period, 1883–88, during which the notes collected in WM were written). It predates what Nietzsche has to say about "will to power" in *Beyond Good and Evil* (1886; see above).

The question of the origin of our evaluations and lists of what is good by no means coincides with their critique, as is so often believed; although, to be sure, the insight into some shameful origin brings with it a felt lessening of value of that which has arisen in that manner and sets the stage for a critical attitude and stance toward it. [KGW VIII 2:189/WM 254]

What are our evaluations and moral goods-lists themselves worth? *What is the outcome of their dominance? For whom? In relation to what?*—Answer: for life. But *what is life?* Here a new, more definite conception of the concept "life" is needed. My formula for it is: life is will to power.

What is the meaning of evaluation itself? Does it refer back or down to another metaphysical world? As Kant still believed (coming as he did before the great historical movement). In short: Where did it "originate"? Or has it not "originated" at all? Answer: moral evaluation is a *construal*,[1] a kind of interpreting. The construal itself is a *symptom* of particular physiological conditions, likewise of a particular spiritual level of dominant judgments. Who *construes?*—our affects. [KGW VIII 2:190/WM 254]

*

Toward a Preface to Daybreak

An attempt to try to think about morality without coming under its spell, mistrustful against being outwitted by its beautiful gestures and glances. A world that we are able to revere, that is fitting for our worshipful drives—that is constantly *proved*—through the guidance of one and all—: this the Christian idea, from which we all descend.

Through a growth of astuteness, mistrustfulness, scientificness (also through a more elevated instinct of truthfulness, therefore again under Christian influences), *this* interpretation has become *impermissible* to us any longer. . . .

My attempt to understand moral judgments as symptoms and signlanguages, which betray processes of physiological flourishing or failure, likewise the consciousness of conditions of preservation and growth: a mode of interpretation of the same worth as astrology. Prejudices prompted by instincts (of races, communities, of various stages like growth or withering, etc.).

Applied to the specific Christian-European morality: our moral judgments are signs of decline, of no belief in life, a preparation for pessimism.

What does it mean that we have interpreted a *contradiction* into existence?— Decisive importance: behind all other evaluations these moral evaluations stand in command. Supposing they collapse—by what do we measure then? And what value then do knowledge, etc., etc. have?

My main proposition: There are no moral phenomena but rather only a moral(-istic) interpretation of these phenomena. This interpretation itself is of extramoral origin. [KGW VIII 2:165/WM 258]

*

That the value of the world lies in our interpretation (—that perhaps somewhere interpretations other than merely human ones are possible—); that previous interpretations are perspectival valuations, which have enabled us to

---

1. Or "interpretation" (*Auslegung*); similarly, in the next sentence "construes" (*auslegt*) could be "interprets." The translation differentiates the terms from *Interpretation*, which Nietzsche uses elsewhere in the passage.

preserve ourselves in life, that is, in will to power, for the growth of power; that every *elevation of man* involves the overcoming of narrower interpretations; that every attained strengthening and extension of power brings about new perspectives and means believing in new horizons—this runs through my writings. The world that *is of any concern to us* is false, i.e., is no matter of fact, but rather is a fabrication and approximation on the basis of a meager sum of observations; it is "in flux," as something becoming, as an ever newly shifting falsehood, which never approaches the truth: for—there is no "truth." [KGW VIII 2:108/WM 616]

*

The "meaninglessness of what happens":[2] the belief in this is the consequence of an insight into the falsity of previous interpretations, a generalization of discouragement and weakness—not a *necessary* belief.

The presumptuousness of man: when one does not see meaning, to *deny* it! [KGW VIII 2:109/WM 599]

*

Nihilism stands at the door: from whence comes this strangest and most sinister of all guests?

1. Starting point: it is an *error* to point to "social distress" or "psychological degeneration" or indeed to corruption as the *cause* of nihilism. These permit of a great many different construals. Nihilism lurks in an entirely specific interpretation, the Christian-moral. It is the most decent and compassionate of times. Need—need of the soul, of the body, of the intellect—is in itself incapable of giving rise to nihilism, i.e., the radical denial of value, meaning, desirability.

2. The demise of Christianity—from its morality (which is irreplaceable)—which turns against the Christian God (the sense of truthfulness, highly developed through Christianity, is nauseated by the falsehood and mendacity of all Christian interpretations of the world and history. Reaction from "God is the truth" to the fanatical belief "All is false." Buddhism of the *deed* . . .)

3. Skepticism in morals is what is decisive. The downfall of the moral world-interpretation which no longer has any sanction after it has attempted to flee into a beyond: ends in nihilism, "everything has no meaning" (the untenability of one world-interpretation—to which incredible energy has been devoted—awakens the suspicion that *all* world-interpretations are false). Buddhistic tendency, longing for nothingness. (Indian Buddhism does *not* have a fundamentally moral development behind it, therefore its nihilism contains morality that has not been overcome; existence as punishment, combined with existence as error, error thus as punishment—a moral evaluation.) The philosophical attempt to overcome the "moral God" (Hegel, pantheism). Overcoming of popular ideals: The sage. The saint. The poet. Antagonism of "true" and "beautiful" and "good."—

4. Against "meaninglessness" on the one hand, against moral value judgments on the other: to what extent all previous science and philosophy stand under moral judgments? and whether this won't earn one the hostil-

---

2. In German, *Sinnlosigkeit des Geschehens*: "what happens" appropriately translates *Geschehen*, here and elsewhere, because Nietzsche emphatically rejects the view that what goes on in the world— what happens—does so in the form of discrete and definite "events" (the translation used by Kaufmann).

ity of science in the bargain? or the anti-scientific attitude? Critique of Spinoza.[3] Christian value judgments linger on everywhere in the socialistic and positivistic systems. A *critique of Christian morality* is lacking.

5. The nihilistic consequences of contemporary natural science (together with its attempt to slip away into some beyond). From its pursuit eventually *follows* a self-disintegration, a turning against *itself*, an anti-scientificality.— Since Copernicus[4] man has been rolling from the center into X.

6. The nihilistic consequences of political and economic ways of thinking, in which all "principles" are close to belonging to play-acting: the breath of mediocrity, wretchedness, dishonesty, etc. Nationalism, anarchism, etc. Punishment. The *redeeming* class and man are lacking, the justifiers—

7. The nihilistic consequences of history and the *"practical* historians," i.e., the romantics. The position of art: absolute *un*-originality of its position in the modern world. Its darkening. Goethe's purported Olympianness.

8. Art and the preparation of nihilism. Romantic (Wagner's *Nibelungen* ending).[5] [KGW VIII 2:127/WM 1]

*

Conclusion

To what extent this self-destruction of morality is still a part of its own force. We Europeans have the blood in us of those who have died for their faith; we have looked upon morality seriously and fearfully, and there is nothing that we have not in one way or another sacrificed for it. On the other hand: our spiritual refinement has essentially been achieved through conscience-vivisection. We do not yet know the "whither" to which we are driven, now that we have in this way uprooted ourselves from our old ground. But this ground itself has provided us with the force that now drives us with the distance, into adventure, thrusting us out into the boundless, unexplored, undiscovered—we have no choice, we must be conquerors, since we have no country any longer where we are at home, where we would like to "conserve." No, you know better, my friends! The hidden Yes in you is stronger than all No's and Maybe's, by which you along with your time are sickened and addicted; and if you must go to sea, you emigrants, a *faith* thus compels you to do so. . . . [KGW VIII 2:207/WM 405]

Nihilism[6]

FALL 1886–FALL 1887

Critique of previous *pessimism*

Resistance to the eudaimonistic point of view as the final reduction of the question: what *meaning* does it have? Reduction of gloom. —*Our* pessimism: the world does not have the value that we believed—our faith itself has so

---

3. Benedict (Baruch) de Spinoza (1632–1677), Dutch philosopher.
4. Nicolaus Copernicus (1473–1543), Polish astronomer in whose theory of the solar system the earth orbits the sun; in the traditional view, the earth is assumed to be stationary and at the center of the universe.

5. *The Ring of the Nibelung (Der Ring des Nibelungen*, 1869–76), Wagner's four-opera cycle, concludes with the destruction of the gods.
6. In the following sections, entries are grouped under broad topics to aid readers in following the development of Nietzsche's thinking on them during the last three years of his productive life.

intensified our drive for knowledge that today we *must* say this. At first it thereby is taken as worth less: it is so *experienced at first*—only in this sense are we pessimists, namely, with a will to face up to this revaluation unreservedly, and no longer to tell ourselves stories, lies, in the old way. . . . Precisely thereby we find the passion that perhaps will impel us to seek *new values*. In sum: the world could be worth much more than we believed.—We must get beyond the *naivete of our ideals*, and see that while we perhaps had in mind to give it the loftiest interpretation, we may not once have given our human existence even a moderately fair value.

> what has been *deified?* The value instincts within the *community* (that which conduces to its continuation);
> what has been *slandered?* That which sets the higher human beings apart from the lower, the gap-producing drives. [KGW VIII 6:25/WM 32]

*

To *impress* the character of being upon becoming—that is the highest *will to power.*

Twofold falsification, arising from the senses and from the spirit, in order to preserve a world of beings, of what persists, of equivalences, etc.

That *everything recurs is the closest approximation of a world of becoming to being:* culmination of the reflection.

From the values accorded to that which has "being" derive the condemnations of and dissatisfactions with that which becomes: after such a world of being was first invented.

The metamorphosis of beings (body, God, ideas, laws of nature, formulas, etc.)

"Beings" as appearance; reversal of values; appearance was the *value-conferring—*

Knowledge in itself in becoming [is][7] impossible; so how is knowledge possible? As error about oneself, as will to power, as will to deception.

Becoming as inventing, wanting, self-denial, self-overcoming: no subject, but rather a deed, a positing, creative, no "cause and effect."

Art as will to the overcoming of becoming, as "eternalization," but shortsighted, depending on the perspective: as it were, repeating the tendency of the whole on a small scale.

What *all life* shows, as scaled-down formula for the overall tendency to be observed: therefore, a new specification of the concept "life," as will to power.

Instead of "cause and effect" the struggle of becomers with each other, often with absorption of the opponent; no constant number of becomers.

Uselessness of old ideals for the interpretation of all that happens, once one recognizes their animal origin and utility; all moreover contrary to life.

Uselessness of mechanistic theory—it gives the impression of *meaninglessness.*

The entire *idealism* of previous humanity is on the verge of turning into *nihilism*—into the belief in absolute *value*-lessness, that is, *meaning*-lessness. . . .

---

7. Translator's brackets.

The destruction of ideals, the new desert, the new arts needed to
endure it, we *amphibians*.
Presupposition: bravery, patience, no "going back," no hurry to go forward
NB. Zarathustra,[8] constantly adopting a parodic stance toward all
previous values, out of abundance. [KGW VIII 7:54/WM 617]

*

European Nihilism[9]

(1) What *advantage* did the Christian moral-hypothesis offer?
   (a) It ascribed an absolute *value* to man, in contrast to his smallness and
       fortuitousness in the flow of becoming and passing away.
   (b) It served the advocates of God, insofar as it granted the character of
       perfection to the world despite suffering and evil—"freedom"
       included—evil seemed full of *meaning*.
   (c) It posited a *knowledge* with respect to absolute values on the part of
       man and gave him therewith *adequate cognition* precisely for what
       is most important.
   It prevented man from despising himself as man, from taking sides against
life, from despairing about knowing: it was a *means of preservation*;—in sum,
morality was the great *antidote* against practical and theoretical nihilism.
[KGW VIII 5:71/WM 4]

(2) But among the forces that morality cultivated was *truthfulness*: this
finally turned itself against morality, discovered its *teleology*, its *interested*
point of view—and the *insight* into this long-ingrained mendacity that one
despairs of getting rid of now serves precisely as a stimulant. To nihilism. We
now find needs in ourselves, planted during the long moral-interpretation,
which appear to us as needs for untruth; on the other hand, it seems that they
are those on which the value depends by means of which we can endure to
live. This antagonism—that which we know, we do *not* esteem, and that which
we would like to lie to ourselves about, we are no longer *permitted* to esteem—
results in a process of dissolution. [KGW VIII 5:71/WM 5]

(3) Actually we no longer are so much in need of an antidote against the
first nihilism: life in our Europe is no longer so very uncertain, chancy, absurd.
Such a tremendous *heightening* of the *value* of man, of the value of evils, etc.,
is now not so needful, we can bear a significant *reduction* of this value, we
can allow much absurdity and chance to be removed: the attained *power* of
man now permits a curtailment of the means of cultivation, of which the moral
interpretation was the strongest. "God" is much too extreme a hypothesis.
[KGW VIII 5:71/WM 114]

(4) But extreme positions are not replaced by moderate ones, but rather
again by extremes—of the opposite kind. And so the belief in the absolute
immorality of nature, in aim- and meaninglessness, is the psychologically necessary *effect*, if the belief in God and an essential moral order is not held any

---

8. The central figure of *Thus Spoke Zarathustra*
(1883–85).

9. This long entry was divided into four by the
compilers of WM.

longer. Nihilism now appears, *not* because the aversion to existence is greater than previously, but rather because one has become generally mistrustful of a "meaning" in evil and, indeed, in existence. *One* interpretation has collapsed, but because it was taken to be *the* interpretation, it seems as if there were no meaning at all in existence, as if all were *pointless*.

(5) That this "Pointless!" is the character of our present-day nihilism remains to be shown. Mistrust toward our earlier valuations grows into the question: "Aren't all 'values' lures with which the comedy continues, but without coming any closer to a solution?" *Duration*, regarded as "pointless," without goal or purpose, is the most *paralyzing* thought, especially if one grasps that one is being fooled and yet is powerless to keep oneself from being fooled.

(6) Let us think this thought in its most awful form: existence, just as it is, without meaning and goal, but unavoidably recurring, without a finale in nothingness: "the eternal return."

That is the extremest form of nihilism: nothingness (the "meaningless") eternally!

European form of Buddhism: the energy of knowledge and strength *forces* one to such a belief. It is the *most scientific* of all possible hypotheses. We deny final goals: if existence had one, it would have had to have been reached. [. . .][1]

(10) [. . .] There is nothing in life that has value, other than the degree of power—given precisely that life itself is will to power. Morality protected those who have turned out badly from nihilism, in that it assigned to *each* an infinite value, a metaphysical value, and placed them in an order that did not accord with worldly power and ranking: it taught resignation, meekness, etc. Supposing that the belief in this morality perishes, then the badly turned out would no longer have their comfort—and would perish.

(11) This perishing manifests itself as *doing oneself in*, or as an instinctive selecting of that which *must destroy*. *Symptoms* of this self-destruction of the badly-turned-out: self-vivisection, intoxication, romanticism, above all the instinctive compulsion to actions by which one makes *mortal enemies* of the powerful (—like raising one's own hangman oneself), the *will to destruction* as the will of a still deeper instinct, the instinct of self-destruction, the *will to nothingness*.

(12) Nihilism, as a symptom of the badly turned out no longer having any comfort left: of their destroying in order to be destroyed, of their no longer having any reason to "resign themselves" now that they are cut loose from morality—of their having placed themselves on the ground of the opposing principle, and also *wanting power* themselves, by which they *compel* the powerful to become their hangmen. This is the European form of Buddhism, a *doing-no*, after all existence has lost its "meaning."

(13) "Distress" has not grown especially greater: on the contrary! "God, morality, resignation" were remedies on frightfully deep levels of misery: *active nihilism* makes its appearance under relatively much more favorable conditions.

1. All bracketed ellipses are the translator's.

For morality to be experienced as overcome already presupposes a considerable degree of spiritual culture—and this in turn presupposes a relatively comfortable life. A certain spiritual weariness, brought through the long conflict of philosophical opinions to a hopeless scepticism *toward* philosophy, likewise characterizes the by no means miserable situation of these nihilists. One might think of the situation in which the Buddha[2] appeared. The teaching of the eternal recurrence would have *scholarly* presuppositions (as Buddha's teaching did, e.g., the concept of causality, etc.). [. . .]

(15) Who will show themselves to be the *strongest* in this situation? The most moderate, those who have no *need* of extreme articles of faith, those who not only can tolerate but enjoy a good bit of chance and nonsense, those who are able to think of man with a significant reduction of his value without thereby becoming small and weak: the richer in health, who can take most misfortunes in stride and therefore are not so fearful of them—human beings who are *confident of their power*, and who represent the *attained* strength of humanity with conscious pride.

(16) How would such a person think of the eternal return? [KGW VIII 5:71/WM 55]

*

1. Nihilism a *normal* condition.[3]
   Nihilism: the goal is lacking; there is no answer to the question "Why?"
   What does nihilism mean?—*that the highest values devalue themselves.*
   It is *ambiguous:*
   A. Nihilism as sign of *increased power of the spirit: as active nihilism.*
      It can be a sign of *strength:* the energy of the spirit can have grown so great that *previous* goals ("convictions," articles of faith) are insufficient.
      —a belief in general expresses the pressure of *conditions of existence*, a subjugation under the authority of relations under which a creature *flourishes, grows, attains power.* . . .
      On the other hand, a sign of *insufficient* strength now to go on productively to *posit* a goal, a why, a faith.
      Its *maximum* of relative strength is attained as the violent strength of *destruction:* as *active nihilism.* Its opposite would be the tired nihilism that no longer *asserts itself:* Buddhism, its most famous form: as *passive* nihilism.
      Nihilism represents a pathological transitional condition (what is pathological is the tremendous generalization, the inference *to no meaning at all*): whether because the productive forces are not yet strong enough, or because decadence still lingers on and has not yet discovered this remedy.
   B. Nihilism as *decline and decrease of the power of the spirit: passive nihilism:*
      as a sign of weakness: the strength of the spirit can be tired, exhausted, so that the previous goals and values are insufficient and no longer inspire belief—

---

2. Siddhartha Gautama (active ca. 5th century B.C.E.), born in northeastern India, who founded Buddhism.

3. This entry was divided into four by the compilers of WM.

That the synthesis of values and goals (on which every strong culture depends) dissolves, so that the various values war with each other: disintegration.

That everything that delights, heals, soothes, anesthetizes comes to the foreground, in various *disguises*, religious, or moral or political or aesthetic etc.

2. Presupposition of this hypothesis.

That there is no truth; that there is no absolute constitution of things, no "thing in itself."

—*This is itself a nihilism*, and *indeed the most extreme*. It takes the value of things to consist precisely in that this value corresponds and has corresponded to *no* reality, but rather is only a symptom of strength on the part of the *value-determiner*, a simplification for the purpose of life. [KGW VIII 9:35/WM 2, 13, 22, 23]

*

What is a *belief*? How does it arise? Every belief is a *taking-to-be-true*. The most extreme form of nihilism would be: that *every* belief, every taking-to-be-true, is necessarily false: *because there is absolutely no true world*. Thus: a *perspectival appearance*, whose origin lies in us (insofar as we continually have *need* of a narrower, abbreviated, simplified world).

—that it is the *measure of strength* how far we are able to acknowledge *appearance* and the necessity of lies—without perishing.

To that extent *nihilism*, as the *denial of a truthful world*, of being, *could be a divine way of thinking;*—[KGW VIII 9:41/WM 15]

*

On the Genesis of the Nihilist

It is only late that one comes to have the courage for what one really *knows*. That I have previously been fundamentally a nihilist is something I have recognized only recently: the energy, the nonchalance with which I have gone ahead as a nihilist deceived me about this basic fact. If one is moving toward a goal, it seems impossible that our most basic assumption is "goal-lessness as such." [KGW VIII 9:123/WM 25]

*

Toward a Plan[4]

Radical nihilism is the conviction of the absolute untenability of existence as far as the highest values one acknowledges are concerned, together with the *insight* that we do not have the slightest right to posit a beyond or an in-itself of things that is "divine" or the embodiment of morality.

This insight is a consequence of highly developed "truthfulness": thereby itself a consequence of the belief in morality. [WM 3]

This is the antinomy: to the extent that we believe in morality, we *condemn* existence.

---

4. This entry was divided into two sections by the compilers of WM.

The logic of pessimism carried all the way to *nihilism: what is at work there?*—Concept of *valuelessness, meaninglessness:* to what extent moral valuations lurk behind all other high values.

—Result: *moral valuations are condemnations, negations, morality is the denial of the will to existence . . .*

Problem: *but what is morality?* [KGW VIII 10:192/WM 11]

LATE 1887–1888

Critique of Nihilism

(1) Nihilism as a psychological condition will have to arrive *first* when we have sought a "meaning" in all that happens that is not there: so that the seeker finally becomes dismayed. Nihilism in this instance is the realization of the long *waste* of strength, the torment of the "pointless," the insecurity, the lack of opportunity somehow to recover and in some way to regain one's composure—being ashamed of oneself, as if one had *deceived* oneself for all too long. . . . This sought-for *meaning* might have been: the "fulfillment" of an ethically supreme principle in all that happens, the ethical world-order; or the increase of love and harmony in the interactions of creatures; or the approach of a general condition of happiness; or even the movement toward a general condition of nothingness—a goal is still a meaning. The common denominator of all of these notions is that something or other is to be attained through the process: and now one comprehends that in all this becoming *nothing* is achieved, *nothing* is attained. . . . Thus: disappointment concerning a supposed *goal* of *becoming* as cause of nihilism: whether it is with reference to a quite specific goal or is generalized, the insight into the untenability of all previous goal-hypotheses that apply to the entire "development" (—man *no longer* collaborator of becoming, let alone its centerpoint).

Nihilism as a psychological condition arrives *second* when one has postulated a *totality,* a *systematization,* even an *organization* in all that happens and beneath all that happens: so that the soul that craves to admire and revere can revel in the totalizing conception of a supreme form of domination and control (—if it is the soul of a logician, mere complete consistency and derivability suffice for reconciliation with everything . . .); a kind of unity, some form of "monism": such a belief is enough to give one a deep feeling of belonging and dependence in relation to a whole that infinitely transcends him, a mode of the divinity. . . . "The general well-being requires the devotion of the individual." . . . But now one sees that there *is* no such thing! At bottom man has lost the belief in his own value if no infinitely valuable whole is working through him: i.e., he has conceived of such a whole *in order to be able to believe in his own value.*

Nihilism as a psychological condition has a *third* and *last* form. Assuming these two *insights,*—that in becoming nothing is to be attained, and that there is no great unity at work beneath all becoming in which the individual may completely immerse himself as in a substance of the highest value—the *subterfuge* remains to condemn this entire world of becoming as deception and to discover a world lying beyond it as the *true* world. But as soon as one finds out that this world is constructed merely out of psychological needs, and that one has no right whatsoever to it, the last form of nihilism arises, which involves *disbelief in a metaphysical world*—which rules out belief in a *true* world. From this standpoint one affirms the reality of becoming as the *only* reality, rules out every sort of sneak-path to afterworlds and false divinities— but *finds unendurable this world that one refuses to deny.* . . .

What at bottom has happened? The feeling of *valuelessness* was reached when one comprehended that it is not permitted to interpret the general character of existence either with the concept "purpose" or with the concept "unity" or with the concept "truth." Existence achieves and attains nothing, any overarching unity in the multiplicity of happening is lacking; the character of existence is not "true," it is *false,* . . . one simply no longer has any way to persuade oneself of a true world. . . .

In short: the categories "purpose," "unity," "being," with which we have attributed value to the world, are *withdrawn* by us again—and now the world *looks valueless.* . . .

(2) Suppose we have recognized to what extent the world may no longer be *interpreted* with these three categories, and that after having this insight the world begins to seem valueless for us: we then must ask, Where did our faith in these three categories come from?—let us see whether it might not be possible to terminate our faith in *them.* If we *devalue* these three categories, then the demonstration of their inapplicability to the universe is no longer any reason *to devalue the universe.*

Upshot: the faith in the categories of reason is the cause of nihilism—we have measured the value of the world by categories *that have to do with a purely fictitious world.*

Final upshot: all values with which we up to now have sought to make the world estimable for ourselves, and which finally have *devalued* it as they have turned out not to apply—all these values are, psychologically considered, results of specific perspectives of utility for the maintenance and extension of human forms of domination: and only falsely *projected* into the nature of things. It is always the *hyperbolic naivete* of man to take himself as the meaning and value-standard of things. . . . [KGW VIII 11:99/WM 12]

*

The highest values, in whose service human beings are supposed to live, especially if they are very burdensome and impose a high cost: for the purpose of amplification, as if they were commandments of God, these *social values* were erected over humanity, as "reality," as "true" world, as hope and *future* world. Now, when the unsavory origins of these values have become clear, it seems to us that everything has therewith been devalued and has become "meaningless" . . . but that is only a *transitional condition.* [KGW VIII 11:100/WM 7]

*

The time is coming when we will have to *pay* for having been *Christians* for two thousand years: we are losing the *importance* that has enabled us to live— we don't know for a while what to do. We plunge abruptly into the *opposed* valuations, with the same degree of energy with which we have been Christians— with which we have gone in for Christian nonsensical exaggeration—

(1) The "immortal soul"; the eternal value of the "person"
(2) Salvation, judgment, evaluation in the "beyond"

(3) Moral value as the highest value, the "salvation of the soul" as cardinal interest

(4) "sin," "earthly," "flesh," "pleasures"—stigmatized as "world"

Now everything is false through and through, mere "words," jumbled, weak or overheated. [. . .] [KGW VIII 11:148/WM 30]

*

Preface

(1) Great things require that one either remain silent or speak with greatness about them: with greatness, that means cynically and with innocence.

(2) What I relate is the history of the next two centuries. I describe what is coming, what no longer can come otherwise: *the advent of nihilism*. This history can now already be told; for necessity itself is here at work. This future already speaks in a hundred signs, this destiny everywhere announces itself; for this music of the future all ears are already perked. Our entire European culture has long been moving, with a tortured tension that has grown from decade to decade, as if toward a catastrophe: restlessly, violently, plunging: like a river that wants to reach its end, that reflects no longer, that is afraid to reflect about it.

(3) He who speaks here, in contrast, has previously done nothing but *reflect*: as a philosopher and hermit by instinct, who has found his advantage in being apart and outside, in patience, in delay, in hanging back; as a daring and experimenting spirit that has already gotten lost in every labyrinth of the future; as a prophetic bird of a spirit that *looks back* when it relates what is to come; as the first consummate nihilist of Europe, who however has already lived nihilism itself through to the end in himself—who has left it behind himself, beneath himself, outside himself. . . .

(4) For one should not misconstrue the meaning of the title with which this gospel of the future wants to be named. *"The Will to Power: Attempt at a Revaluation of All Values"*—with this formula a *countermovement* is brought to expression, with respect to principle and task: a movement that in some future time will replace this consummate nihilism, but that *presupposes* it, logically and psychologically, and that in any event can only come *after it* and *out of it*. For why is the advent of nihilism *necessary*? Because it is our previous values themselves that draw out their final consequence in it; because nihilism is the logical outcome of our great values and ideas thought through to the end—because we must first experience nihilism, in order to get to the bottom of what the *value* of these "values" really is. . . . We have need, sometime, of *new values*. . . . [KGW VIII 11:411/WM Preface]

Reason and Knowledge

1886–1888

Fundamental solution:

We have faith in reason: but this is the philosophy of gray *concepts*; language is built on the most naive prejudices.

Now we read disharmonies and problems into things, because we *think only in linguistic form*—and along with it believe in the "eternal truth" of reason (e.g. subject, predicate, etc.).

We cease to think if we are unwilling to do so under linguistic constraint, we hardly even reach the doubt that sees a boundary as a boundary here.

Rational thought is an interpretation in accordance with a scheme that we are unable to let go of. [KGW VIII 5:22/WM 552]

*

Against positivism, which stops at phenomena—"there are only facts"—I would say: No, there precisely are no facts, only interpretations. We are unable to ascertain any fact "in itself": perhaps it is nonsense to want to do any such thing. "It is all subjective," you say; but that is already *interpretation*, the "subject" is nothing given, but rather something fictitiously added, stuck in underneath.—Is it even necessary to posit an interpreter behind the interpretation? That is already invention, hypothesis.

To the extent that the word "knowledge" has meaning, the world is knowable: but it can be *construed* otherwise; it has no meaning behind it, but rather countless meanings. "Perspectivism."

It is our needs *that interpret the world*: our drives and their for and against. Every drive is a kind of lust to dominate; each has its perspective, which it would like to impose as a norm on all other drives. [KGW VIII 7:60/WM 481]

*

Psychological Derivation of Our Faith in Reason

The concept "reality/being" is borrowed from our "subject"-feeling.

"Subject": interpreted out of ourselves, so that the ego is taken as subject, as cause of all doings, as *doer*.

The logical-metaphysical postulates, the belief in substance, accident, attribute etc. gets its convincing force from the habit of regarding all our doings as consequences of our will:—so that the ego, as substance, does not dissolve in the multiplicity of change.—*But there is no will.*

We have no categories at all that allow us to distinguish a "world in itself" from a world as appearance. All our *categories of reason* are of sensual origin: read off of the empirical world. "The soul," "the ego"—here too the history of these concepts shows the oldest distinction ("breath," "life")—

If there is nothing material, there is nothing immaterial either. The concept no longer *contains* anything . . .

No subject-"atoms." The sphere of a subject continually *growing* or *diminishing*—the center of the system continually *shifting*—; in cases in which it is unable to organize the appropriated mass, it breaks in two. On the other hand it can turn a weaker subject into its functionary without destroying it, and to a certain extent constitute a new unity together with it. No "substance"; rather, something that intrinsically strives for strengthening, and that only indirectly wants to "preserve" itself (it wants to *surpass* itself—) [KGW VIII 9:98/WM 488]

*

On "Logical Apparentness"

The concepts "individual" and "species" [are][5] equally false and merely apparent. "Species" only expresses the fact that a multitude of similar creatures come along at the same time and that the tempo of further growth and self-alteration has slowed down for a long time: so that the actual small continuations and increases are not very noticeable (—a developmental phase in which the self-developing is not visible, so that an equilibrium *seems* to have been reached, and the false idea is made possible that *here a goal has been attained*—and that the development has a given goal . . .)

The *form* is taken to be something enduring and therefore valuable; but the form is merely invented by us; and however often "the same form is attained," that does not mean that it is *the same* form—*rather it is always something new that appears*—and it is only we who compare them, who reckon the new, insofar as it is similar to the old, together in the unity of "form." As if a *type* is supposedly attained, and so to speak is intended by and inherent in the formative process.

Form, species, law, idea, purpose—the same error is made here in all of them, of wrongly attributing a false reality to a fiction: as if what happens has something obedient about it—an artificial distinction in what happens is then drawn between *what* does the doing and *that toward which* this doing is directed (but the *what* and the *toward which* are only laid down by us in obedience to our metaphysical-logical dogmatism; no "matter of fact")

One should not understand this *compulsion* to fashion concepts, species, forms, purposes, laws—"a world of identical cases"—as if we were in a position to ascertain the *true* world by means of them; but rather, as the compulsion to arrange for ourselves a world in which *our existence* is facilitated—with them we create a world that is calculable, simplified, comprehensible, etc. for us.

This same compulsion is to be found in the *sense-activities* that support the understanding—the simplifying, coarsening, emphasizing, and elaborating, on which all "re-cognition," all being-able-to-make-oneself-understandable depends. Our *needs* have made our senses so precise that the "same world of appearance" always recurs and thereby has acquired the semblance of *reality*.

Our subjective compulsion to have faith in logic only shows that, long before logic itself came to consciousness, we did nothing less than *insert its postulates into what happens:* now we discover them in what happens—we no longer can do otherwise—and suppose that this compulsion establishes something about "truth." It is we who have created "the thing," "the identical thing," subject, attribute, doing, object, substance, form, after we have long pursued *making* the identical, *making* the coarse and simple.

The world *appears* logical to us, because *we* first logicized it. [KGW VIII 9:144/WM 521]

*

On Theory of Knowledge: entirely empirical

There is neither "spirit" nor reason nor thought nor consciousness nor soul nor will nor truth: all fictions that are useless. We have to do not with

5. Translator's insertion.

"subject and object" but rather a particular animal species that can flourish only through a certain relative *accuracy*, above all *regularity* of its perceptions (so that it can capitalize on its experience). . . .

Knowledge works as a *tool* of power. Thus it is obvious that it grows with every increase of power. . . .

Meaning of "knowledge": here, as in the cases of "good" or "beautiful," the concept is to be taken in a strict and narrow anthropocentric and biological sense. In order for a particular species to preserve itself—and grow in its power—it must register enough of the calculable and constant in its conception of reality to be able to construct a scheme of behavior on it. *The utility of preservation*, not some abstract-theoretical need not to be deceived, stands as the motive behind the development of the organs of knowledge. . . . They develop in such a way that their observations suffice to preserve us. In other words: the *extent* of the desire for knowledge depends upon the extent of the growth of the *will to power* of a species: a species grasps a certain amount of reality *in order to become master over it, in order to make use of it.* [KGW VIII 14:122/WM 480]

*

Will to Power as Knowledge

Not "to know," but rather to schematize, to impose as much regularity and form on chaos as will be sufficient for our practical needs.

In the formation of reason, logic, the categories, it was need that was decisive: the need not to "know" but rather to subsume, to schematize, for the purpose of comprehensibility, of calculation. . . .

Adjustment, filling out to make similar, equal—the development of reason is the same process that every sense-impression undergoes!

There was no pre-existing "Idea" at work here: but rather usefulness, that it is only when we see things as made coarse and equal that they become calculable and manageable for us. . . .

Finality in reason is an effect, not a cause: with any other kind of reason, to which there are constant impulses, life goes badly—it is poorly arranged—too unequal—

The categories are "truths" only in the sense that they are conditions of life for us: as Euclidean space[6] is such a conditioned "truth." (Candidly speaking: since no one will seriously maintain the necessity of the existence of human beings exactly as they are, reason as well as Euclidean space is a mere idiosyncrasy of a particular animal species and one among many others. . . .)

The subjective compulsion to be unable to contradict here is a biological compulsion: the instinct for the utility of inferring as we infer is implanted in our bodies, we almost *are* this instinct. . . . But what naivete to draw from that a proof that we therewith possess a "truth as such."

Not being able to contradict is proof of an inability, not a "truth." [KGW VIII 14:152/WM 515]

---

6. That is, three-dimensional space to which plane and solid geometry applies (Euclid was a Greek mathematician, active ca. 300 B.C.E.).

The World and Life

1888

Will to Power   Philosophy

Power quanta. *Critique of Mechanism*[7]

Let us here put aside the two popular concepts "necessity" and "law": the first inserts a false compulsion into the world, the second a false freedom. "Things" do not conduct themselves regulatedly, in accordance with a *rule*; there are no things (—that is a fiction of ours); they conduct themselves just as little under a compulsion of necessity. Here there is no obeying; for *that something is as it is*, as strong or as weak, is not the consequence of obedience or of a rule or of a compelling. . . .

The degree of resistance and the degree of superior power—in all that happens that is what is decisive: if, for our ordinary purposes of calculation, we know how to express that in formulas of "laws," all the better for us! But we have not inserted any "morality" into the world by imagining it to be obedient.

There are no laws: every power draws its ultimate consequence in every moment. Calculability depends precisely on the fact that there is no middle term.

A power-quantum is characterized by the effect that it produces and that it resists. The adiaphorous[8] state is lacking, conceivable in principle though it may be. It is essentially a will to violate and to defend itself against violation. Not self-preservation: every atom affects the whole of reality—it is thought away if one thinks away this radiation of power-will. That is why I call it a quantum of "will to power": the characteristic is thereby expressed that cannot *be* thought away from the mechanistic order without thinking it itself away.

A translation of this world of effect into a *visible* world—a world for the eye—is the concept "movement." Here it is always taken for granted that *something* is moved—thereby a thing that does the effecting is always supposed, whether it be now in the fiction of a clump-atom or even as its abstraction, the dynamic atom—i.e., we have not gotten rid of the habits to which the senses and language seduce us. Subject, object, a doer added to a doing, the doing and that which does it sundered: let us not forget that what is thereby indicated is mere semiotics and nothing real. Mechanics as a doctrine of *motion* is already a translation into the sense-language of man. [KGW VIII 14:79/WM 634]

We have need of unities in order to be able to calculate: it does not follow that there are such unities. We have derived the concept of unity from our "ego"-concept—our oldest article of faith. If we did not take ourselves to be unities, we never would have formed the concept "thing." Now, much later, we are honestly convinced that our conception of the ego-concept does not attest to any real unity. Thus in order to uphold the mechanistic theory of the world, we must always enter a caveat concerning the extent to which we rely on fictions in doing so: the concept of movement (taken from our sense language) and the concept of the atom=unity (deriving from our psychical "experience"): it has a *sense prejudice* and a *psychological prejudice* among its presuppositions.

The *mechanistic* world is imagined in the only way the eye and touch can picture such a world (as "moved").

---

7. This long entry was divided into two sections by the compilers of WM.

8. Indifferent, neutral; incapable of doing either harm or good.

to enable it to be calculated—unities are invented
in order to invent causal unities, "things" (atoms), whose effect remains
  constant (—transference of the false subject-concept to the
  atom-concept)
concept of number
concept of thing (concept of the subject)
concept of activity (separation of being-a-cause and effect)
movement (eye and touch)
that all effect is *movement*
that where there is movement, *something* is moved

Phenomenal therefore are: the mixing in of the concept of number, the concept of the subject, the concept of movement; our *eye*, our *psychology* are still involved.

If we eliminate these additions, then no things remain, but rather dynamic quanta, in a relation of tension to all other dynamic quanta: whose nature consists in their relation to all other quanta, in their "effect" on them—The will to power, not a being, not a becoming, but rather a *pathos*, is the most elemental fact, from which becoming and effecting first emerge. . . .

Mechanics formulates succession-phenomena semiotically, going beyond that, using sensuous and psychological means of expression; it does not touch upon the causal force. . . . [KGW VIII 14:79/WM 635]

*

Critique of the Concept "Cause"

Psychologically regarded: the concept "cause" is our feeling of power from so-called willing—our concept "effect," the superstition that the feeling of power is itself the power that impels. . . .

  a condition that accompanies an event, and already is an effect of the
    event, is projected as its "sufficient basis"
  the relation of tension in our feeling of power: pleasure as the feeling of
    power: of resistance overcome—are these illusions?
  if we translate the concept "cause" back again into the only sphere
    known to us, from which we have taken it: we cannot conceive of
    any *change* in which there is not a will to power. We do not know
    how to explain a change except as the encroachment of power upon
    other power.
  mechanics shows us only results, and then only in images (motion is a
    speech-image)
  gravitation itself has no mechanistic cause, since it is the initial basis
    for mechanistic results
  the will to accumulation of force as specific for the phenomena of life,
    for nourishment, reproduction, heredity
  for society, state, custom, authority
  should we not be permitted to assume this will as the moving cause in
    chemistry as well?
  and in the cosmic order?
  not merely conservation of energy, but rather maximal economy of use:
    so that the *will-to-become-stronger of every force-center* is the only

reality—not self-preservation, but rather appropriation, willing to become master, more, stronger.

that science is possible—that is supposed to *prove* to us a principle of causality?

"from like causes, like effects"

"a permanent law of things"

"an immutable order"

just because something is calculable, is it therefore necessary?

if something happens thus and not otherwise, that involves no "principle," no "law," no "order"

Power-quanta, whose nature consists in the exercise of power on all other power-quanta

In the belief in cause and effect the main thing is always forgotten: the *happening* itself.

one has inserted a doer, one has again hypothesized the done [KGW VIII 14:81/WM 689]

*

Can we assume a *striving for power* without a sensation of pleasure and displeasure, i.e., without a feeling of the increase and decrease of power?

is mechanism only a sign language for the *internal* factual world of struggling and conquering will-quanta?

all presuppositions of mechanism, matter, atom, pressure and impact, gravity are not "facts in themselves," but rather interpretations with the aid of *psychical* fictions.

life as the form of being best known to us is specifically a will to the accumulation of force

all processes of life have their impetus here

nothing wants to preserve itself, all is to be added and accumulated

Life as a special case: hypothesis from it to the total character of existence.

strives for a *maximal feeling of power*

is essentially a striving for an increase of power

striving is nothing other than striving for power

that which is most basic and innermost remains this will: mechanics is a mere semiotics of the results. [KGW VIII 14:82/WM 689][9]

*

Will to power psychologically

Unitary Conception of Psychology

We are used to considering the development of an incredible abundance of forms to be consistent with an origin from a unity.

So that the will to power is the primitive affect-form, and that all other affects are only its developments;

So that it is importantly enlightening to replace individual "happiness," as that for which everything living supposedly strives, with power: "it strives for

---

9. Some of the entries in Nietzsche's notebooks were polished, as if being readied for publication, while others (like this one) are jotted-down thoughts. The compilers of WM tried to turn such jottings into complete sentences and paragraphs.

power, for an increase in power"—pleasure is only a symptom of the feeling of attained power, a consciousness of a difference—

—it does not strive for pleasure; rather, pleasure occurs when that for which it strives is attained: pleasure accompanies, pleasure does not impel. . . .

So that all driving force is will to power, and that there is no other physical, dynamic or psychical force. [. . .] [KGW VIII 14:121/WM 688]

*

Physicists believe in a "true world" in their way: a firm atom-systematization in necessary motion, the same for all creatures—so that for them the "apparent world" is reduced to the aspect of universal and universally necessary being accessible to each creature after its own fashion (accessible and at the same time adjusted—made "subjective"). But they are thereby mistaken: the atom that they posit is derived in accordance with the logic of the perspectivism of consciousness—and is thereby also itself a subjective fiction. This world-picture that they devise is throughout not essentially different from the subjective world-picture: it is merely constructed with more widely extended senses, but throughout with *our* senses. . . . And in the end they have left something out of the constellation without knowing it: precisely the necessary perspectivism, owing to which every power-center—and not only man—construes the entire rest of the world out of itself, i.e., measures, feels, forms in accordance with its power. . . . They have forgotten to include this perspective-*establishing* force in "true being." . . . Put in academic language: subjectivity. They think this was "developed," added subsequently—

But even the chemists require it: it is *specificity*, acting and reacting thus and so in particular ways, accordingly.

Perspectivism is only a complex form of specificity.

My idea is that every particular body thus strives to become master of all space and to extend its force (—its will to power:) and to push back whatever resists its extension. But it continually runs up against similar efforts of other bodies and ends up coming to an arrangement ("unification") with those that are sufficiently related: *they then conspire together for power.* And the process goes on. . . . [KGW VIII 14:186/WM 636]

*

(1) The world exists; it is nothing that comes to be, nothing that passes away. Or rather: it comes to be, it passes away, but it has never begun to come to be and never ceases to pass away—it *maintains* itself in both. . . . It lives on itself: its excrements are its nourishment. . . .

(2) The hypothesis of a *created* world should not for a moment concern us. The concept "create" is today completely indefinable, inoperable; merely a word, rudimentary from superstitious times; with a word one explains nothing. The latest attempt to conceive of a world that *began* has recently been made with the aid of a logical procedure—for the most part, as is to be suspected, with an ulterior theological aim. [. . .]

(4) I have run into this thought in earlier thinkers; every time it was conditioned by other, ulterior considerations (—mostly theological, to the advantage of the *creator spiritus*[1]). If the world as a whole could become rigid, dry,

---

1. Creator spirit (Latin); that is, God.

dead, *nothing*, or if it could reach a condition of equilibrium, or if it as a whole had some sort of goal that involved duration, immutability, some once-and-for-all-time (in short, metaphysically expressed: if becoming *could* wind up in being or in nothingness), this condition would have had to have been reached. But it has not been reached: from which it follows. . . . That is the only certainty that we can get our hands on, to serve as a corrective to a great many intrinsically possible world-hypotheses. If, e.g., mechanistic theory cannot avoid the consequence of a final condition, which Thompson[2] has derived from it, mechanistic theory is thereby *refuted*.

(5) If the world *permits* of being thought of as a determinate quantity of force and as a determinate number of force-centers—and every other representation remains indeterminate and consequently *unusable*—then it follows from this that it has to pass through a calculable number of combinations, in the great dice-game of its existence. In an infinite time, every possible combination would have to be reached at some time or other; moreover, it would have to be reached infinitely many times. And since between every "combination" and its next "recurrence" all combinations that are in any way possible would have to come about, and each of these combinations conditions the entire sequence of combinations in the same series, then a circular course of absolutely identical series would thereby be demonstrated: the world as a circular course that has already repeated itself infinitely often and that plays its game *in infinitum*.[3]

This conception is not simply a mechanistic one; for if it were, it would not necessitate an infinite recurrence of identical cases, but rather a final state. *Because* the world has not reached such a state, mechanistic theory must be considered an imperfect and only provisional hypothesis. [KGW VIII 14:188/ WM 1066][4]

Values, Moralities, Religions

1887

Toward a Plan[5]

In place of *moral values*, purely *naturalistic* values. Naturalization of morality.

In place of "sociology," a doctrine of the *forms of domination*.

In place of "theory of knowledge," a *perspective-doctrine of the affects* (to which a hierarchy of the affects belongs).

the *transfigured* affects: their *higher ordering*, their "spirituality."

In place of metaphysics and religion, *the doctrine of the eternal recurrence* (this as a means of breeding and selection). [KGW VIII 9:8/WM 462]

*

In place of "society," the *culture-complex* as *my* chief interest (both as a whole and with regard to its parts). [KGW VIII 10:28/WM 462]

2. That is, William Thomson, Lord Kelvin (1824–1907), Scottish engineer and physicist; the "final condition" is of maximum entropy (with no energy available to do any work).
3. To infinity (Latin).
4. This [entry] is the main place in Nietzsche's writings where he attempts to construct and spell out an argument for the idea and teaching of "eternal recurrence" construed as a cosmological hypothesis applying to all events and sequences of events [translator's note].
5. The compilers of WM combined the following note with this one, and also substituted "Fundamental Innovations" as the heading of the first note.

*

To take into service everything terrible, singly, gradually, experimentally: this is what the task of culture requires; but until it is *strong* enough for this, it must oppose, moderate, conceal, even curse. . . .

—everywhere, where a culture *posits* something as *evil*, it gives expression to a relation of *fear*, thus a *weakness* . . .

Thesis: everything good is a former evil made serviceable.

Standard: the more terrible and the greater the passions are that an age, a people, an individual can permit themselves, because they are able to employ them *as means, the higher stands their culture* (—the realm of the evil grows ever *smaller* . . .)

—the more mediocre, weak, submissive and cowardly a person is, the more he will take to *be evil:* for him the realm of the evil is the most encompassing; the lowest person will see the realm of the evil (i.e., of that which is forbidden and dangerous to him) everywhere. [KGW VIII 9:138/WM 1025]

*

In summa:[6] mastery over the passions, *not* their weakening or eradication!

The greater the mastering strength of a will is, the more freedom may be allowed to the passions.

The "great man" is great owing to the freedom of scope of his desires and through the even greater power that knows how to take these magnificent monsters into service.

—the "good man" at every stage of civilization is at once the *undangerous and the useful* one: a kind of *mean;* the expression in the common mind of one *of whom one has nothing to fear and whom one nonetheless is not permitted to despise* . . .

Schooling: essentially the means of *ruining* the exception, by distraction, seduction, sickening, for the benefit of the rule.

That is harsh; but economically considered, perfectly reasonable. At least for a long time.—

Acculturating: essentially, the means of setting taste against the exception for the benefit of the mediocre.

A culture of the exception, of attempts, of danger, of nuance as the consequence of a great *wealth of energies: every* aristocratic culture tends that way.

It is only when a culture has an overflow of energies at its disposal that a hothouse of cultural surplus can arise on its foundation—[KGW VIII 9:139/WM 933]

*

Whose Will to Power Is Morality?

The *common* theme in the history of Europe since Socrates[7] is the attempt to bring about the dominance of *moral values* over all other values: so that they are to be the leader and judge not only of life but also of (1) knowledge, (2) art, (3) political and social affairs.

---

6. In summary (Latin). 7. Greek philosopher (469–399 B.C.E.).

"becoming better" as the sole task, everything else the *means* to it (or disturbance, restriction, danger: consequently to be combated unto annihilation . . .)
A similar movement in *China*. A similar movement in *India*.

What is signified by this *will to power on the part of moral powers*, which
has been manifested on earth in such tremendous developments?

Answer: *three powers are at work within it*: (1) the instinct of the *herd* against
the strong and independent; (2) the instinct of the *suffering* and of those who
have turned out badly against the fortunate; (3) the instinct of the *mediocre*
against the exceptions.—*Tremendous advantage of this movement*, how much
cruelty, falseness and narrow-mindedness have also assisted in it (for the history
of the *struggle of morality with the fundamental instincts of life* is itself the greatest immorality that there has ever been on earth . . .) [KGW VIII 9:159/WM 274]

*

The affects are one and all *useful*, some directly, others indirectly; with respect to utility it is utterly impossible to specify a gradation of values—thus
certainly, economically considered, the forces of nature are one and all
good, i.e., useful, just as terrible and irrevocable consequences also follow
from them. The most one can say is that the most powerful affects are the
most valuable: insofar as there are no greater sources of energy. [KGW VIII
10:133/WM 931]

*

Points of view for *my* values: whether out of abundance or out of longing . . . ;
whether one looks on or gets involved . . . or looks away, passes by . . . ; whether
"spontaneously" out of pent up force or merely *reactively* stimulated, incited . . . ;
whether *simply* out of paucity of elements *or* out of overwhelming mastery over
many, so that they are pressed into service when they are needed . . . ; whether
one is *problem* or *solution* [. . .] [KGW VIII 10:145/WM 1009]

*

Consider the *damage* that is done to all human institutions, whenever a
divine and otherworldly *higher sphere* is posited that must first *sanction* these
institutions. By then becoming accustomed to seeing their value in this sanction (e.g., in the case of marriage), one has *diminished their natural worth*, in
some situations *denied* it. . . . To the extent that one has bestowed honor upon
the anti-nature of a God, nature is unfavorably assessed. "Nature" becomes
akin to "despicable," "bad" . . .

The fatefulness of a belief in the *reality of the highest moral qualities as God*:
with it all actual values were denied and fundamentally construed as *un-values*.
Thus *antinaturalness* ascended to the throne. With an inexorable logic one
arrived at the absolute call for the *denial of nature*. [KGW VIII 10:152/WM 245]

*

"*Morality for morality's sake*"—an important stage in its denaturalization: it
itself appears as the ultimate value. In this phase it permeates religion: e.g.,
in Judaism. And there likewise is a phase in which it *separates itself* again from
religion, and in which no God is "moral" enough for it: then it gives preference to the impersonal ideal. . . . That is now the case.

"Art for art's sake"—that is the most dangerous principle: one thereby introduces a false opposition into things,—it leads to a slandering of reality ("idealization" into *ugliness*). When one separates an ideal from reality, one denigrates reality, one impoverishes it, one slanders it. "The beautiful for its own sake," "the true for its own sake," "the good for its own sake"—these are three forms of the *evil eye* for reality.

—*Art, knowledge, morality* are *means:* instead of recognizing in them the aim of enhancing life, one has related them to the *opposite of life*, to "God"—so to speak, as revelations of a higher world, which in them peeks through here and there. . . .

—"beautiful and ugly," "true and false," "good and evil"—these *distinctions* and *antagonisms* betray conditions of existence and advancement not of humanity in general, but rather of certain fixed and enduring complexes which separate themselves from their adversaries. The *war* that is thereby created is the essential thing about them: as a means of *separation* that *strengthens* the isolation. . . . [KGW VIII 10:194/WM 298]

*

We Hyperboreans[8]

My conclusion is: that the *actual* human being represents a much higher value than the "wished-for" human being of any previous ideal; that all "wishful-nesses" with respect to man have been absurd and dangerous extravagances, with which a particular sort of human being sought to hang *its* conditions of preservation and growth over humanity as a law; that every "wishfulness" of such an origin that has been brought to dominance up to now has *diminished* the value of man, his strength, his certainty of a future; that the poverty and small-mindedness of man reveals itself most, even today, when he *wishes;* that the capacity of human beings to establish values has up to now been too little developed to do justice to the actual and not merely "wishful" *value of man;* that "the ideal" up to now has been the truly world- and humanity-slandering force, the poison cloud over reality, the great *seduction to nothingness.* . . . [KGW VIII 11:118/WM 390]

*

1888[9]

Which values have prevailed so far

1. Morality as the highest value, in all phases of philosophy (even among the skeptics).

Result: this world is worthless, there must be a "true world."

2. *What* really determined the highest value here? What really is morality? The instinct of decadence; it is the exhausted and disinherited that take their *revenge* in this way and play the *masters.* . . .

---

8. In Greek mythology, a legendary people who lived in a paradisial region in the far north (their name is usually understood to mean "beyond the north wind").

9. The final productive year of Nietzsche's life; in January 1889 he collapsed, never to recover.

Historical proof: the philosophers [are][1] always decadents, always in the service of nihilistic religions.

3. The instinct of decadence, which steps forth as will to power. Introduction of its system of means: absolute unmorality of the means.

General view: the highest values so far are a special case of the will to power: morality itself is a special case of *unmorality*. [KGW VIII 14:137/WM 401]

Purification of formerly depreciated values.

We have grasped *what* so far has determined the highest value and *why* it has become master over the opposing valuation: it was *stronger.* . . .

Let us now purify the *opposing valuation* of the infection and half-heartedness, of the *degeneration*, in which it is familiar to us all.

Theory of their *denaturing* and *restoration of nature: moraline-free.*[2] [. . .] [KGW VIII 14:138/WM 401]

*

A Preface

I have the fortune, and the honor that goes along with it, after whole millennia of error and confusion, to have rediscovered the path that leads to a Yes and a No.

I teach No to all that makes weak—that exhausts.

I teach Yes to all that strengthens, that accumulates energy, that conduces to pride—

Previously one has taught neither the one nor the other: one has taught virtue, becoming selfless, pity, even the negation of life. . . . These are all values of the exhausted. [. . .] [KGW VIII 15:13/WM 54]

*

Christianity

One has previously always attacked Christianity in a false and not merely timid way.[3] As long as one has not seen the morality of Christianity as a *capital crime against life*, its defenders have had the advantage. The question of the mere "truth" of Christianity, whether with respect to the existence of its God or to the historicity of the legend of its origin, not even to speak of Christian astronomy and natural science—is an entirely incidental matter, as long as the question of the value of Christian morality is not addressed. Is the morality of Christianity *worth* anything, or is it a shame and disgrace despite all the holiness of its arts of seduction? There are hiding places of all sorts for the problem of truth; and the most faithful are ultimately able to make use of the logic of the unbelievers in order to devise for themselves a right to affirm certain things as—irrefutable that is, as *beyond* the means of refutation (—this ploy today is called "Kantian criticism"—). [KGW VIII 15:19/WM 251]

*

1. Translator's insertion.
2. "Moraline": a term coined by Nietzsche to indicate that morality has an effect (as stimulant or narcotic) similar to that of caffeine or codeine.

3. One of the polemics that Nietzsche wrote in 1888 was against Christianity—*Der Antichrist* (*The Antichrist* or, better, *The Anti-Christian*); its basic themes are anticipated in a number of these entries.

One should never forgive Christianity for having destroyed such men as Pascal.[4] One should never cease combating exactly this in Christianity, that it has the will to break precisely the strongest and noblest souls. One should never rest as long as this one thing is not completely destroyed: the ideal of man that was invented by Christianity. The entire absurd remainder of Christian fable, concept-cobwebs and theology do not matter to us; it could be a thousand times more absurd, and we would not lift a finger against it. But we do combat this ideal, which with its sickly beauty and feminine seductiveness, with its stealthy eloquence of slander, appeals to all the cowardices and vanities of wearied souls (for even the strongest have weary hours), as if all of that which might in such circumstances seem most useful and desirable—trust, guilelessness, modesty, patience, love of one's fellows, resignation, submission to God, a sort of unharnessing and dismissing of one's entire ego—were also intrinsically the most useful and desirable things; as if the paltry modest abortion of a soul—the virtuous average-animal and herd-sheep human being— not only were superior to the stronger, more evil, more covetous, more defiant, more extravagant and therefore a hundred times more endangered kind of human being, but moreover provided the ideal, the goal, the standard, the highest desirability for humanity in general. The erection of *this* ideal was the most sinister temptation ever placed before man; for with it the more strongly constituted exceptions and fortunate cases among human beings, in whom the will to power and to growth of the entire type man takes a step forward, were threatened with going under. With its values, it cuts at the roots of the growth of these higher human beings—who for the sake of their higher demands and tasks willingly endure a more dangerous life (economically expressed: an increase in the cost to the entrepreneurs as well as in the improbability of success). What is it that we combat in Christianity? That it wants to break the strong, that it wants to discourage their courage, exploit their bad hours and weariness, invert their proud assurance into distress and bad conscience, that it knows how to poison and sicken the noble instincts to the point that their strength, their will to power turns backward, turns against itself— until the strong perish through orgies of self-contempt and self-torment: that horrible sort of perishing the most famous example of which is provided by Pascal. [KGW VIII 11:55/WM 252]

*

Countermovement: Religion

The two types: *Dionysus* and the *Crucified*[5]

To bear in mind: the typical *religious* person—a decadence-type?

The great innovators are one and all pathological and epileptic . . . but aren't we then leaving out one type of religious person, the *pagan*? Isn't the pagan

---

4. Blaise Pascal (1623–1662), a brilliant French mathematician and scientist, whose intellect Nietzsche greatly admired; following a religious experience at age 32, he abandoned those studies and moved to a convent. His famous *Pensées* (*Thoughts*, published 1670) reflects his later inter-

ests in religion and religiously inspired philosophy. 5. Jesus, as interpreted by Christianity. Dionysus: Greek god of wine, a figure of ecstatic cult worship; in one version of his myth, he was torn apart as an infant and then reborn.

cult a form of thanksgiving and affirmation of life? Mustn't its highest representation be a justification and deification of life?

Type of a well-turned-out and ecstatic-overflowing spirit. . . . A type that takes into itself and *redeems* the contradictions and questionable aspects of existence?

It is here that I locate the *Dionysus* of the Greeks: the religious affirmation of life, life as a whole, not denied or divided; typical that the sex-act awakens profundity, mystery, reverence.

Dionysus versus the "Crucified": there you have the antithesis. It is *not* a difference with respect to martyrdom—the same thing has a different meaning. Life itself, its eternal fruitfulness and recurrence gave rise to torment, destruction, the will to annihilation. . . . In the other case suffering, the "Crucified as the innocent," was taken to be objection against life, as a formula for its condemnation.

One discerns: the problem is that of the meaning of life: whether a Christian meaning or a tragic meaning. . . . In the first case, it is supposed to be the way to a blessed state of being; ultimately, being is taken to be *blessed enough* to be able to justify a monstrous amount of suffering.

The tragic human being affirms even the harshest suffering: he is strong, full, deifying enough to do so.

The Christian denies even the happiest lot on earth; he is weak, poor, discontented enough to suffer of life in every form. . . .

"The God on the cross" is a curse on life, a sign to free oneself from it. Dionysus cut in pieces is a *promise* of life: it will ever again be born and come back from destruction. [KGW VIII 14:89/WM 1052]

*

That nothing of that which formerly was taken to be true is true; that what was formerly rejected by us as unholy, forbidden, despicable, disastrous—all these flowers grow today along the lovely paths of truth.

This entire old morality no longer matters to us: there is not a concept in it that still deserves respect. We have outlived it—we are no longer crude and naive enough to have to allow ourselves to tell ourselves lies in this way. . . . More politely expressed: we are too virtuous for that. . . .

And if truth in the old sense was only "truth" because the old morality affirmed it, was allowed to affirm it: then it also follows that we have no more such truth left. . . . Our *criterion* of truth is by no means morality: we *refute* a supposition by showing that it is dependent on morality, that it is inspired by lofty feelings. [KGW VIII 15:77/WM 459]

*

How I recognize my kindred spirits: Philosophy, as I have so far understood and lived it, is the voluntary search even for the accursed and heinous sides of existence. From long experience, gained from such wanderings through ice and desert, I learned to see differently all that has previously philosophized:— the *hidden* history of philosophy, the psychology of its great names came to light for me. "How much truth does a spirit *endure*, how much truth does it *dare*?"—This became the real measure of value for me. Error is *cowardice*, . . . every achievement of knowledge *derives* from courage, from hardness against oneself, from cleanliness toward oneself. . . . Such an experimental philosophy as I live anticipates even the possibility of the most fundamental nihilism: but this is not to say that it must stop with a No, with a negation, with a will to say No. It wants far more to come through to the opposite—to a *Dionysian affirmation* of the world, as it is, without subtraction, exception or selection—it wants the eternal circulation—the same things, the same logic and unlogic of things knotted together. Highest condition that a philosopher can attain: to stand in a Dionysian manner to existence—; my formula for this is *amor fati.*[6] . . .

It is a part of this to comprehend the previously repudiated sides of existence not only as *necessary* but also as desirable: and not only as desirable in relation to the previously affirmed sides (as something like their complements or preconditions) but rather for their own sake, as the more powerful, more fruitful, *truer* sides of existence, in which its will more clearly expresses itself. Along with this belongs the depreciation of the previously exclusively *affirmed* sides of existence; to comprehend where these valuations came from and how little they are binding upon a Dionysian value standard for existence: I extracted and comprehended *what* it is that really says Yes here (in one kind of case the instinct of the suffering, in another the instinct of the herd, and in a third the *instinct of the majority* in opposition to the exceptions—). I therewith surmised to what extent another stronger sort of human being necessarily would have to think of the enhancement and elevation of mean along different lines: *higher creatures,* beyond good and evil, beyond those values that cannot deny their origin in the sphere of suffering, of the herd and of the majority—I sought for the beginnings of this inverted formation of ideals in history (the concepts "pagan," "classical," "noble" newly discovered and presented—). [KGW VIII 16:32/WM 1041]

SOURCE: From *Nietzsche: Selections,* ed. Richard Schacht (New York: Macmillan; Toronto: Maxwell Macmillan Canada, 1993), pp. 145–55, 265–93. Entries from the notebooks kept by Nietzsche from the years 1883 to 1888 were drawn on by his sister, Elisabeth Förster-Nietzsche, with the assistance of his devoted friend Heinrich Köselitz (whom Nietzsche called Peter Gast), to construct a volume to serve as the "masterwork" he had contemplated. Arranging the selected entries thematically rather than chronologically, they published the result with great fanfare in 1901, after his death, as *Der Wille zur Macht: Versuch einer Umwertung aller Werte* (*The Will to Power: Attempt at a Revaluation of All Values*). An expanded second edition was published in 1906, which was reprinted with an index in 1911 (this edition is referred to as "WM"). It was translated into English in 1967 by Walter Kaufmann and R. J. Hollingdale as *The Will to Power* ("WP"); selections here edited and translated by Richard Schacht. For the convenience of readers, each entry is identified by its number in WM (and WP) as well as by its location in *Nietzsche Werke: Kritische Gesamtausgabe* (*Nietzsche Works: Critical Edition*), edited by Georgio Colli and Mazzino Montinare (*Kritische Gesamtausgabe,* or KGW), specified by multivolume part (*Abteilung*) number, notebook number within that part (ordered chronologically), and entry number. This translation follows the KGW text; thus, it does not always correspond exactly to the presentation of the material in WM (and WP). (Indications of the locations of the notebook material provided in the original publication in *Nietzsche: Selections* have been reformatted by the editor.)

6. Love of fate (Latin).

HENRI BERGSON
(1859 – 1941)

Bergson was a philosophical phenomenon. It is difficult to imagine any philosopher today, or even during the last third of the twentieth century, attaining the celebrity status he enjoyed during the decades before and after the First World War. His interests were wide-ranging, his writing style was engaging and accessible, and his ideas on the many topics on which he wrote were unconventional, intriguing and inspiring to many, often mystifying, but seemingly profound. He challenged many philosophical orthodoxies, as he sought to come to terms both with recent scientific developments (particularly those relating to evolutionary theory) and with artistic and religious experience. (He was born, fittingly enough, in the year that Darwin's *On the Origin of Species* was published.) Because one of his central interests was in the phenomenon of "life" in general and of human life in particular, he is often linked with others such as NIETZSCHE and DILTHEY who contributed to the emergence of the "philosophy of life" as a major philosophical theme in the late nineteenth and early twentieth century. But his thinking on these questions differs markedly from theirs, as well as from the materialistic and scientistic treatments to which he was so strongly and vigorously opposed.

The life of Henri Louis Bergson ("BARE-KSAWN") was remarkable, in a number of respects. Though he was French by birth (in Paris), education, and eventual citizenship, his father was Polish and his mother was English. Both were Jewish. During his early years the family lived in London, but they relocated to Paris while he was still a child. A precocious student, he was initially attracted to mathematics, at which he excelled, publishing a solution to a long-standing problem while still in his teens. By the time he was admitted to the elite École Normale

Supérieure, however, he had decided to pursue studies in the humanities rather than in mathematics or the sciences, though he developed an interest in evolutionary theory. He graduated in 1881 with a specialization in philosophy. In the following years he taught at the secondary level, published his first philosophy paper in 1886, and prepared the two dissertations (one in Latin and one in French) required by the University of Paris for his doctorate, which he received in 1889. The Latin dissertation, on Aristotle, remained unpublished; the French one, on consciousness, appeared under the title *Time and Free Will* (1889).

In 1891 Bergson married Louise Neuberger, who was a cousin of Marcel Proust. (The future novelist, then still a student, would count Bergson among his influences.) During the next ten years he held a number of teaching appointments and continued to write. His reputation grew, and he was appointed in 1910 to the chair in Greek and Latin philosophy at the distinguished Collége de France and then, four years later, to the chair in modern philosophy. In 1907 he published *Creative Evolution*, which was a sensation not only in France but also internationally, gaining him the 1927 Nobel Prize in Literature. As he became a celebrity, his lectures at the Collége came to be major events.

Until the First World War broke out in 1914, Bergson lectured widely—in Britain and America as well as Europe—drawing large audiences and receiving much attention. In 1908 he met the American philosopher and psychologist William James, who did much to draw attention to him in the English-speaking world. Each admired the other's work. In 1914 Bergson became the first Jew elected to the forty-member Académie Française (in which he officially took his place four years later). In the same year, his writings were condemned by the Roman Catholic Church on the grounds of his purported pantheism and his embrace of evolution.

During and following the First World War, while continuing to pursue his philosophical interests, Bergson was drawn into international politics. He was a member of the French mission to Washington in 1917 that sought America's involvement in the war, worked toward the formation of the League of Nations, and was appointed the first president of its International Commission for Intellectual Cooperation in 1922. Later in the decade worsening arthritis forced him to curtail and finally give up these activities. Bergson published his final two books in the early 1930s. He died in 1941, soon after complying with the new regulation of the German-controlled Vichy government that Jews register with the state (refusing the exemption from this requirement he had been offered).

Bergson wrote on many topics: body and mind, space and time, action and freedom, perception and memory, matter and life, religion and morality, and much else. Throughout his career he resisted mechanistic reductionism and the dominance of the kind of rationality that tends to go along with it, insisting that human experience, action, and life—and indeed life and reality more generally—cannot be reduced to the causally deterministic materialist paradigm. So, for example, he argues that the temporality of experience (or "lived time") is fundamentally different from "clock time" and its scientific refinement, and that the latter is an artificial abstraction from time's fundamental reality. He characterizes that reality as "duration" (la durée), which he associates with "mobility," and distinguishes its heterogeneous "qualitative multiplicity" from the homogeneous "quantitative multiplicity" of clock time. He takes a similar position regarding life and the world—our own bodily and mental reality most definitely included—which he thus fundamentally conceives in terms of duration-like processes.

As might be expected, therefore, Bergson rejects the idea that consciousness can be reduced to brain states. He even contends that it is a mistake to conceive of the brain and the body in a materialistically deterministic way. Life, for him, is irreducibly "vital"; and the vitality of life is only abstractly represented, but not truly comprehended, when conceived and described in terms of material causality. He famously invoked the idea of an élan vital, or "vital spirit," that is essential to all life, and argued that it must be grasped intuitively on its own terms rather than conceived in an abstractly "intellectual" way (in accordance with the requirements of theoretical rationality).

Bergson makes much of this distinction between "intuition" and "intellect." Intellect, he argues, is a way of thinking that has evolved and been developed because in certain contexts it is not only possible but helpful to operate with a simplified model of discrete interacting units and structural relations. Those contexts are limited, however, and thus this way of thinking fails to capture the underlying reality of actions, experiences, life processes, and the world more generally—which can only be apprehended intuitively. Because our language and rationality are geared to the artificial simplification required by intellect, we find it difficult to express and discuss the character of this underlying reality, and therefore are strongly disposed to misunderstand it. The crucial but commonly neglected task of philosophy, for Bergson, is to criticize and counter the tendencies associated with that sort of rationalistic intellectuality by strengthening our relatively weak intuitive abilities and powers.

Bergson's concept of "creative evolution," while inspired by his reading of Charles Darwin's theory of natural selection, was provoked and shaped by his dissatisfaction with Herbert Spencer's naturalistic philosophical elaboration of it, and by his antipathy to the increasing tendency to suppose that life must be a mechanistic-materialistic, causally deterministic phenomenon. He embraces the idea of human life as a form of life, which along with all other forms of life is the outcome of evolutionary processes; but he holds that those processes can and should be comprehended in a different manner. Many fear that evolution dispenses with or even rules out spirituality and creativity; but for him evolution—not only of human life but of life more generally—is itself to be understood in terms of spirituality and creativity. (Indeed, he takes the same position with respect to divinity—giving some legitimacy to the charge of pantheism leveled at him by the Roman Catholic Church.) Bergson does accord a very special place to human life in the larger scheme of things, however, and even envisions the possibility that the very spirituality manifest in human life may be emancipated from the bounds of natural existence and mortality.

The following selections from *Creative Evolution* show Bergson addressing these topics at his rhetorical best. One can easily see why so many people were excited and inspired when they encountered this work and the lectures and other writings in which he set forth his thinking on related matters. Bergson offered the hope of a way to avoid having to choose between science and spirituality, and indeed to find a way of combining them that made both more attractive and meaningful. Whether it is possible to do so, either by his approach or by some other, doing justice to science while supporting a robust conception of spirituality in a manner that makes sense philosophically, is a question that he does not clearly answer. Yet it is a challenge to which he rose with courage and originality—and with an undeniable and unsurpassable *élan vital*. And his thinking on consciousness and "lived experience" had a significant impact on the subsequent development of phenomenology, particularly in France.

From Creative Evolution

From *Introduction*

The history of the evolution of life, incomplete as it yet is, already reveals to us how the intellect has been formed, by an uninterrupted progress, along a line which ascends through the vertebrate series up to man. It shows us in the faculty of understanding an appendage of the faculty of acting, a more and more precise, more and more complex and supple adaptation of the consciousness of living beings to the conditions of existence that are made for them. Hence should result this consequence that our intellect, in the narrow sense of the word, is intended to secure the perfect fitting of our body to its environment, to represent the relations of external things among themselves—in short, to think matter.[1] Such will indeed be one of the conclusions of the present essay. We shall see that the human intellect feels at home among inanimate objects, more especially among solids, where our action finds its fulcrum and our industry its tools; that our concepts have been formed on the model of solids; that our logic is, pre-eminently, the logic of solids; that, consequently, our intellect triumphs in geometry, wherein is revealed the kinship of logical thought with unorganized matter, and where the intellect has only to follow its natural movement, after the lightest possible contact with experience, in order to go from discovery to discovery, sure that experience is following behind it and will justify it invariably.

1. That is, to think in ways that are suited to dealing with the sorts of "matter" or material objects with which we find ourselves confronted in our ordinary practical dealings with the world around us.

But from this it must also follow that our thought, in its purely logical form, is incapable of presenting the true nature of life, the full meaning of the evolutionary movement. Created by life, in definite circumstances, to act on definite things, how can it embrace life, of which it is only an emanation or an aspect? Deposited by the evolutionary movement in the course of its way, how can it be applied to the evolutionary movement itself? As well contend that the part is equal to the whole, that the effect can reabsorb its cause, or that the pebble left on the beach displays the form of the wave that brought it there. In fact, we do indeed feel that not one of the categories of our thought—unity, multiplicity, mechanical causality, intelligent finality, etc.—applies exactly to the things of life: who can say where individuality begins and ends, whether the living being is one or many, whether it is the cells which associate themselves into the organism or the organism which dissociates itself into cells? In vain we force the living into this or that one of our molds. All the molds crack. They are too narrow, above all too rigid, for what we try to put into them. Our reasoning, so sure of itself among things inert, feels ill at ease on this new ground. It would be difficult to cite a biological discovery due to pure reasoning. And most often, when experience has finally shown us how life goes to work to obtain a certain result, we find its way of working is just that of which we should never have thought.

Yet evolutionist philosophy[2] does not hesitate to extend to the things of life the same methods of explanation which have succeeded in the case of unorganized matter. It begins by showing us in the intellect a local effect of evolution, a flame, perhaps accidental, which lights up the coming and going of living beings in the narrow passage open to their action; and lo! forgetting what it has just told us, it makes of this lantern glimmering in a tunnel a Sun which can illuminate the world. Boldly it proceeds, with the powers of conceptual thought alone, to the ideal reconstruction of all things, even of life. True, it hurtles in its course against such formidable difficulties, it sees its logic end in such strange contradictions, that it very speedily renounces its first ambition. "It is no longer reality itself," it says, "that it will reconstruct, but only an imitation of the real, or rather a symbolical image; the essence of things escapes us, and will escape us always; we move among relations; the absolute is not in our province; we are brought to a stand before the Unknowable."—But for the human intellect, after too much pride, this is really an excess of humility. If the intellectual form of the living being has been gradually modeled on the reciprocal actions and reactions of certain bodies and their material environment, how should it not reveal to us something of the very essence of which these bodies are made? Action cannot move in the unreal. A mind born to speculate or to dream, I admit, might remain outside reality, might deform or transform the real, perhaps even create it—as we create the figures of men and animals that our imagination cuts out of the passing cloud. But an intellect bent upon the act to be performed and the reaction to follow, feeling its object so as to get its mobile impression at every instant, is an intellect that touches something of the absolute. Would the idea ever

2. That is, philosophy that embraces the basic premises of the idea of evolution in interpreting human reality and analyzing human abilities (including action and cognition). Bergson embraces this label for his own philosophy, but attempts to counter its tendency to scientism.

have occurred to us to doubt this absolute value of our knowledge if philosophy had not shown us what contradictions our speculation meets, what dead-locks it ends in? But these difficulties and contradictions all arise from try-ing to apply the usual forms of our thought to objects with which our industry has nothing to do, and for which, therefore, our molds are not made. Intel-lectual knowledge, in so far as it relates to a certain aspect of inert matter, ought, on the contrary, to give us a faithful imprint of it, having been stereo-typed[3] on this particular object. It becomes relative only if it claims, such as it is, to present to us life—that is to say, the maker of the stereotype-plate.

Must we then give up fathoming the depths of life? Must we keep to that mechanistic idea of it which the understanding will always give us—an idea necessarily artificial and symbolical, since it makes the total activity of life shrink to the form of a certain human activity which is only a partial and local manifestation of life, a result or by-product of the vital process? We should have to do so, indeed, if life had employed all the psychical potentialities it possesses in producing pure understandings—that is to say, in making geo-metricians. But the line of evolution that ends in man is not the only one. On other paths, divergent from it, other forms of consciousness have been devel-oped, which have not been able to free themselves from external constraints or to regain control over themselves, as the human intellect has done, but which, none the less, also express something that is immanent and essential in the evolutionary movement. Suppose these other forms of consciousness brought together and amalgamated with intellect: would not the result be a consciousness as wide as life? And such a consciousness, turning around sud-denly against the push of life which it feels behind, would have a vision of life complete—would it not?—even though the vision were fleeting.

It will be said that, even so, we do not transcend our intellect, for it is still with our intellect, and through our intellect, that we see the other forms of consciousness. And this would be right if we were pure intellects, if there did not remain, around our conceptual and logical thought, a vague nebulosity, made of the very substance out of which has been formed the luminous nucleus that we call the intellect. Therein reside certain powers that are com-plementary to the understanding, powers of which we have only an indistinct feeling when we remain shut up in ourselves, but which will become clear and distinct when they perceive themselves at work, so to speak, in the evolu-tion of nature. They will thus learn what sort of effort they must make to be intensified and expanded in the very direction of life.

This amounts to saying that *theory of knowledge* and *theory of life*[4] seem to us inseparable. A theory of life that is not accompanied by a criticism of knowl-edge is obliged to accept, as they stand, the concepts which the understand-ing puts at its disposal: it can but enclose the facts, willing or not, in pre-existing frames which it regards as ultimate. It thus obtains a symbolism which is con-

---

3. Literally, printed from a solid metal plate cast from a plaster mold.　　4. That is, philosophical biology and anthropology.

venient, perhaps even necessary to positive science, but not a direct vision of its object. On the other hand, a theory of knowledge which does not replace the intellect in the general evolution of life will teach us neither how the frames of knowledge have been constructed nor how we can enlarge or go beyond them. It is necessary that these two inquiries, theory of knowledge and theory of life, should join each other, and, by a circular process, push each other on unceasingly.

* * *

From CHAPTER I
The Evolution of Life—Mechanism and Teleology

* * *

A manufactured thing delineates exactly the form of the work of manufacturing it. I mean that the manufacturer finds in his product exactly what he has put into it. If he is going to make a machine, he cuts out its pieces one by one and then puts them together: the machine, when made, will show both the pieces and their assemblage. The whole of the result represents the whole of the work; and to each part of the work corresponds a part of the result.

Now I recognize that positive science can and should proceed as if organization was like making a machine. Only so will it have any hold on organized bodies. For its object is not to show us the essence of things, but to furnish us with the best means of acting on them. Physics and chemistry are well advanced sciences, and living matter lends itself to our action only so far as we can treat it by the processes of our physics and chemistry. Organization can therefore only be studied scientifically if the organized body has first been likened to a machine. The cells will be the pieces of the machine, the organism their assemblage, and the elementary labors which have organized the parts will be regarded as the real elements of the labor which has organized the whole. This is the standpoint of science. Quite different, in our opinion, is that of philosophy.

For us, the whole of an organized machine may, strictly speaking, represent the whole of the organizing work (this is, however, only approximately true), yet the parts of the machine do not correspond to parts of the work, because *the materiality of this machine does not represent a sum of means employed, but a sum of obstacles avoided*: it is a negation rather than a positive reality. So, as we have shown in a former study, vision is a power which should attain *by right* an infinity of things inaccessible to our eyes. But such a vision would not be continued into action; it might suit a phantom, but not a living being. The vision of a living being is an *effective* vision, limited to objects on which the being can act: it is a vision that is *canalized*,[5] and the visual apparatus simply symbolizes the work of canalizing. Therefore the creation of the visual apparatus is no more explained by the assembling of its anatomic elements than the digging of a canal could be explained by the heaping-up of the earth which might have formed its banks. A mechanistic theory would maintain that the earth had been brought cart-load by cart-load;

---

5. Channeled.

finalism would add that it had not been dumped down at random, that the carters had followed a plan. But both theories would be mistaken, for the canal has been made in another way.

With greater precision, we may compare the process by which nature constructs an eye to the simple act by which we raise the hand. But we supposed at first that the hand met with no resistance. Let us now imagine that, instead of moving in air, the hand has to pass through iron filings which are compressed and offer resistance to it in proportion as it goes forward. At a certain moment the hand will have exhausted its effort, and, at this very moment, the filings will be massed and coördinated in a certain definite form, to wit, that of the hand that is stopped and of a part of the arm. Now, suppose that the hand and arm are invisible. Lookers-on will seek the reason of the arrangement in the filings themselves and in forces within the mass. Some will account for the position of each filing by the action exerted upon it by the neighboring filings: these are the mechanists. Others will prefer to think that a plan of the whole has presided over the detail of these elementary actions: they are the finalists. But the truth is that there has been merely one indivisible act, that of the hand passing through the filings: the inexhaustible detail of the movement of the grains, as well as the order of their final arrangement, expresses negatively, in a way, this undivided movement, being the unitary form of a resistance, and not a synthesis of positive elementary actions. For this reason, if the arrangement of the grains is termed an "effect" and the movement of the hand a "cause," it may indeed be said that the whole of the effect is explained by the whole of the cause, but to parts of the cause parts of the effect will in no wise correspond. In other words, neither mechanism nor finalism will here be in place, and we must resort to an explanation of a different kind. Now, in the hypothesis we propose, the relation of vision to the visual apparatus would be very nearly that of the hand to the iron filings that follow, canalize and limit its motion.

The greater the effort of the hand, the farther it will go into the filings. But at whatever point it stops, instantaneously and automatically the filings coördinate and find their equilibrium. So with vision and its organ. According as the undivided act constituting vision advances more or less, the materiality of the organ is made of a more or less considerable number of mutually coördinated elements, but the order is necessarily complete and perfect. It could not be partial, because, once again, the real process which gives rise to it has no parts. That is what neither mechanism nor finalism takes into account, and it is what we also fail to consider when we wonder at the marvelous structure of an instrument such as the eye. At the bottom of our wondering is always this idea, that it would have been possible for *a part only* of this coördination to have been realized, that the complete realization is a kind of special favor. This favor the finalists consider as dispensed to them all at once, by the final cause; the mechanists claim to obtain it little by little, by the effect of natural selection; but both see something positive in this coördination, and consequently something fractionable in its cause,—something which admits of every possible degree of achievement. In reality, the cause, though more or less intense, cannot produce its effect except in one piece, and completely finished. According as it goes further and further in the direction of vision, it gives the simple pigmentary masses of a lower organism, or the rudimentary eye of a Serpula, or the slightly differentiated eye of the Alciope,[6] or the marvelously perfected eye of the bird; but all these organs, unequal as is their complexity, necessarily present an equal coördination. For this reason, no matter how distant two animal species may be from each other, if the progress toward vision has gone equally far in both, there is the same visual organ in each case, for the form of the organ only expresses the degree in which the exercise of the function has been obtained.

But, in speaking of a progress toward vision, are we not coming back to the old notion of finality? It would be so, undoubtedly, if this progress required the conscious or unconscious idea of an end to be attained. But it is really effected in virtue of the original impetus of life; it is implied in this movement itself, and that is just why it is found in independent lines of evolution. If now we are asked why and how it is implied therein, we reply that life is, more than anything else, a tendency to act on inert matter.[7] The direction of this action is not predetermined; hence the unforeseeable variety of forms which life, in evolving, sows along its path. But this action always presents, to some extent, the character of contingency; it implies at least a rudiment of choice. Now a choice involves the anticipatory idea of several possible actions. Possibilities of action must therefore be marked out for the living being before the action itself. Visual perception is nothing else: the visible outlines of bodies are the design of our eventual action on them. Vision will be found, therefore, in different degrees in the most diverse animals, and it will appear in the same complexity of structure wherever it has reached the same degree of intensity.

We have dwelt on these resemblances of structure in general, and on the example of the eye in particular, because we had to define our attitude toward mechanism on the one hand and finalism on the other. It remains for us to describe it more precisely in itself. This we shall now do by showing the divergent results of evolution not as presenting analogies, but as themselves mutually complementary.

From CHAPTER II
The Divergent Directions of the Evolution of Life:
Torpor, Intelligence, Instinct

* * *

Instinct is sympathy. If this sympathy could extend its object and also reflect upon itself, it would give us the key to vital operations—just as intelligence, developed and disciplined, guides us into matter. For—we cannot too often repeat it—intelligence and instinct are turned in opposite directions, the former towards inert matter, the latter towards life. Intelligence, by means of science, which is its work, will deliver up to us more and more completely the secret of physical operations; of life it brings us, and moreover only claims to bring us, a translation in terms of inertia. It goes all round life, taking from outside the greatest possible number of views of it, drawing it into itself instead of entering into it. But it is to the very inwardness of life that *intuition* leads

---

6. An African butterfly. "Serpula": a genus of sea tube worm.

7. This is Bergson's initial characterization of his alternative to NIETZSCHE's "will to power."

us—by intuition I mean instinct that has become disinterested, self-conscious, capable of reflecting upon its object and of enlarging it indefinitely.[8]

That an effort of this kind is not impossible, is proved by the existence in man of an aesthetic faculty along with normal perception. Our eye perceives the features of the living being, merely as assembled, not as mutually organized. The intention of life, the simple movement that runs through the lines, that binds them together and gives them significance, escapes it. This intention is just what the artist tries to regain, in placing himself back within the object by a kind of sympathy, in breaking down, by an effort of intuition, the barrier that space puts up between him and his model. It is true that this aesthetic intuition, like external perception, only attains the individual. But we can conceive an inquiry turned in the same direction as art, which would take life *in general* for its object, just as physical science, in following to the end the direction pointed out by external perception, prolongs the individual facts into general laws. No doubt this philosophy will never obtain a knowledge of its object comparable to that which science has of its own. Intelligence remains the luminous nucleus around which instinct, even enlarged and purified into intuition, forms only a vague nebulosity. But, in default of knowledge properly so called, reserved to pure intelligence, intuition may enable us to grasp what it is that intelligence fails to give us, and indicate the means of supplementing it. On the one hand, it will utilize the mechanism of intelligence itself to show how intellectual molds cease to be strictly applicable; and on the other hand, by its own work, it will suggest to us the vague feeling, if nothing more, of what must take the place of intellectual molds. Thus, intuition may bring the intellect to recognize that life does not quite go into the category of the many nor yet into that of the one; that neither mechanical causality nor finality can give a sufficient interpretation of the vital process. Then, by the sympathetic communication which it establishes between us and the rest of the living, by the expansion of our consciousness which it brings about, it introduces us into life's own domain, which is reciprocal interpenetration, endlessly continued creation. But, though it thereby transcends intelligence, it is from intelligence that has come the push that has made it rise to the point it has reached. Without intelligence, it would have remained in the form of instinct, riveted to the special object of its practical interest, and turned outward by it into movements of locomotion.

How theory of knowledge must take account of these two faculties, intellect and intuition, and how also, for want of establishing a sufficiently clear distinction between them, it becomes involved in inextricable difficulties, creating phantoms of ideas to which there cling phantoms of problems, we shall endeavor to show a little further on. We shall see that the problem of knowledge, from this point of view, is one with the metaphysical problem, and that both one and the other depend upon experience. On the one hand, indeed, if intelligence is charged with matter and instinct with life, we must squeeze them both in order to get the double essence from them; metaphysics is therefore dependent upon theory of knowledge. But, on the other hand, if consciousness has thus split up into intuition and intelligence, it is because

---

8. This definition recalls SCHOPENHAUER on our intuitive knowledge of what he calls "will"; see the selection above from *The World as Will and Representation* (1818; 2nd ed., 1844).

of the need it had to apply itself to matter at the same time as it had to follow the stream of life. The double form of consciousness is then due to the double form of the real, and theory of knowledge must be dependent upon metaphysics. In fact, each of these two lines of thought leads to the other; they form a circle, and there can be no other centre to the circle but the empirical study of evolution. It is only in seeing consciousness run through matter, lose itself there and find itself there again, divide and reconstitute itself, that we shall form an idea of the mutual opposition of the two terms, as also, perhaps, of their common origin. But, on the other hand, by dwelling on this opposition of the two elements and on this identity of origin, perhaps we shall bring out more clearly the meaning of evolution itself.

Such will be the aim of our next chapter. But the facts that we have just noticed must have already suggested to us the idea that life is connected either with consciousness or with something that resembles it.

Throughout the whole extent of the animal kingdom, we have said, consciousness seems proportionate to the living being's power of choice. It lights up the zone of potentialities that surrounds the act. It fills the interval between what is done and what might be done. Looked at from without, we may regard it as a simple aid to action, a light that action kindles, a momentary spark flying up from the friction of real action against possible actions. But we must also point out that things would go on in just the same way if consciousness, instead of being the effect, were the cause. We might suppose that consciousness, even in the most rudimentary animal, covers by right an enormous field, but is compressed in fact in a kind of vise: each advance of the nervous centres, by giving the organism a choice between a larger number of actions, calls forth the potentialities that are capable of surrounding the real, thus opening the vise wider and allowing consciousness to pass more freely. In this second hypothesis, as in the first, consciousness is still the instrument of action; but it is even more true to say that action is the instrument of consciousness; for the complicating of action with action, and the opposing of action to action, are for the imprisoned consciousness the only possible means to set itself free. How, then, shall we choose between the two hypotheses? If the first is true, consciousness must express exactly, at each instant, the state of the brain; there is strict parallelism (so far as intelligible) between the psychical and the cerebral state. On the second hypothesis, on the contrary, there is indeed solidarity and interdependence between the brain and consciousness, but not parallelism: the more complicated the brain becomes, thus giving the organism greater choice of possible actions, the more does consciousness outrun its physical concomitant. Thus, the recollection of the same spectacle probably modifies in the same way a dog's brain and a man's brain, if the perception has been the same; yet the recollection must be very different in the man's consciousness from what it is in the dog's. In the dog, the recollection remains the captive of perception; it is brought back to consciousness only when an analogous perception recalls it by reproducing the same spectacle, and then it is manifested by the recognition, *acted* rather than *thought*, of the present perception much more than by an actual reappearance of the recollection itself. Man, on the contrary, is capable of calling up the recollection at will, at any moment, independently of the present perception. He is not limited to *playing* his past life again; he *represents* and *dreams* it. The local modification of the brain to which the recollection is attached being the same in each case, the psychological difference between the two recollections cannot have its ground in a particular difference of detail between the two cerebral mechanisms, but in the difference between the two brains taken each as a whole. The more complex of the two, in putting a greater number of mechanisms in opposition to one another, has enabled consciousness to disengage itself from the restraint of one and all and to reach independence. That things do happen in this way, that the second of the two hypotheses is that which must be chosen, is what we have tried to prove, in a former work, by the study of facts that best bring into relief the relation of the conscious state to the cerebral state, the facts of normal and pathological recognition, in particular the forms of aphasia.[9] But it could have been proved by pure reasoning, before even it was evidenced by facts. We have shown on what self-contradictory postulate, on what confusion of two mutually incompatible symbolisms, the hypothesis of equivalence between the cerebral state and the psychic state rests.[1]

The evolution of life, looked at from this point, receives a clearer meaning, although it cannot be subsumed under any actual *idea*. It is as if a broad current of consciousness had penetrated matter, loaded, as all consciousness is, with an enormous multiplicity of interwoven potentialities. It has carried matter along to organization, but its movement has been at once infinitely retarded and infinitely divided. On the one hand, indeed, consciousness has had to fall asleep, like the chrysalis in the envelope in which it is preparing for itself wings; and, on the other hand, the manifold tendencies it contained have been distributed among divergent series of organisms which, moreover, express these tendencies outwardly in movements rather than internally in representations. In the course of this evolution, while some beings have fallen more and more asleep, others have more and more completely awakened, and the torpor of some has served the activity of others. But the waking could be effected in two different ways. Life, that is to say consciousness launched into matter, fixed its attention either on its own movement or on the matter it was passing through; and it has thus been turned either in the direction of intuition or in that of intellect. Intuition, at first sight, seems far preferable to intellect, since in it life and consciousness remain within themselves. But a glance at the evolution of living beings shows us that intuition could not go very far. On the side of intuition, consciousness found itself so restricted by its envelope that intuition had to shrink into instinct, that is, to embrace only the very small portion of life that interested it; and this it embraces only in the dark, touching it while hardly seeing it. On this side, the horizon was soon shut out. On the contrary, consciousness, in shaping itself into intelligence, that is to say in concentrating itself at first on matter, seems to externalize itself in relation to itself; but, just because it adapts itself thereby to objects from without, it succeeds in moving among them and in evading the barriers they oppose to it, thus opening to itself an unlimited field. Once freed,

---

9. *Matière et mémoire* [*Matter and Memory*, 1896], chaps. ii and iii [Bergson's note].
1. [Bergson,] "Le Paralogisme psycho-physiologique," (*Revue de metaphysique*, Nov. 1904) [Bergson's note]. "The Psychophysiological Paralogism [i.e., Fallacy]," a famous 1904 lecture, published in the *Review of Metaphysics and Morals*.

moreover, it can turn inwards on itself, and awaken the potentialities of intuition which still slumber within it.

From this point of view, not only does consciousness appear as the motive principle of evolution, but also, among conscious beings themselves, man comes to occupy a privileged place. Between him and the animals the difference is no longer one of degree, but of kind. We shall show how this conclusion is arrived at in our next chapter. Let us now show how the preceding analyses suggest it.

A noteworthy fact is the extraordinary disproportion between the consequences of an invention and the invention itself. We have said that intelligence is modeled on matter and that it aims in the first place at fabrication. But does it fabricate in order to fabricate or does it not pursue involuntarily, and even unconsciously, something entirely different? Fabricating consists in shaping matter, in making it supple and in bending it, in converting it into an instrument in order to become master of it. It is this *mastery* that profits humanity, much more even than the material result of the invention itself. Though we derive an immediate advantage from the thing made, as an intelligent animal might do, and though this advantage be all the inventor sought, it is a slight matter compared with the new ideas and new feelings that the invention may give rise to in every direction, as if the essential part of the effect were to raise us above ourselves and enlarge our horizon. Between the effect and the cause the disproportion is so great that it is difficult to regard the cause as *producer* of its effect. It releases it, whilst settling, indeed, its direction. Everything happens as though the grip of intelligence on matter were, in its main intention, to *let something pass* that matter is holding back.

The same impression arises when we compare the brain of man with that of the animals. The difference at first appears to be only a difference of size and complexity. But, judging by function, there must be something else besides. In the animal, the motor mechanisms that the brain succeeds in setting up, or, in other words, the habits contracted voluntarily, have no other object nor effect than the accomplishment of the movements marked out in these habits, stored in these mechanisms. But, in man, the motor habit may have a second result, out of proportion to the first: it can hold other motor habits in check, and thereby, in overcoming automatism, set consciousness free. We know what vast regions in the human brain language occupies. The cerebral mechanisms that correspond to the words have this in particular, that they can be made to grapple with other mechanisms, those, for instance, that correspond to the things themselves, or even be made to grapple with one another. Meanwhile consciousness, which would have been dragged down and drowned in the accomplishment of the act, is restored and set free.[2]

The difference must therefore be more radical than a superficial examination would lead us to suppose. It is the difference between a mechanism which engages the attention and a mechanism from which it can be diverted. The primitive steam-engine, as Newcomen[3] conceived it, required the presence

2. A geologist whom we have already had occasion to cite, N. S. Shaler, well says that "when we come to man, it seems as if we find the ancient subjection of mind to body abolished, and the intellectual parts develop with an extraordinary rapidity, the structure of the body remaining identical in essentials" (Shaler, *The Interpretation of Nature*, Boston, 1899, p. 187) [Bergson's note]. Nathaniel Shaler (1841–1906), American geologist and paleontologist.
3. Thomas Newcomen (1664–1729), English engineer and inventor of the earliest practical steam engine.

of a person exclusively employed to turn on and off the taps, either to let the steam into the cylinder or to throw the cold spray into it in order to condense the steam. It is said that a boy employed on this work, and very tired of having to do it, got the idea of tying the handles of the taps, with cords, to the beam of the engine. Then the machine opened and closed the taps itself; it worked all alone. Now, if an observer had compared the structure of this second machine with that of the first without taking into account the two boys left to watch over them, he would have found only a slight difference of complexity. That is, indeed, all we can perceive when we look only at the machines. But if we cast a glance at the two boys, we shall see that whilst one is wholly taken up by the watching, the other is free to go and play as he chooses, and that, from this point of view, the difference between the two machines is radical, the first holding the attention captive, the second setting it at liberty. A difference of the same kind, we think, would be found between the brain of an animal and the human brain.

If, now, we should wish to express this in terms of finality, we should have to say that consciousness, after having been obliged, in order to set itself free, to divide organization into two complementary parts, vegetables on one hand and animals on the other, has sought an issue in the double direction of instinct and of intelligence. It has not found it with instinct, and it has not obtained it on the side of intelligence except by a sudden leap from the animal to man. So that, in the last analysis, man might be considered the reason for the existence of the entire organization of life on our planet. But this would be only a manner of speaking. There is, in reality, only a current of existence and the opposing current; thence proceeds the whole evolution of life. We must now grasp more closely the opposition of these two currents. Perhaps we shall thus discover for them a common source. By this we shall also, no doubt, penetrate the most obscure regions of metaphysics. However, as the two directions we have to follow are clearly marked, in intelligence on the one hand, in instinct and intuition on the other, we are not afraid of straying. A survey of the evolution of life suggests to us a certain conception of knowledge, and also a certain metaphysics, which imply each other. Once made clear, this metaphysics and this critique may throw some light, in their turn, on evolution as a whole.

From *CHAPTER III*
On the Meaning of Life:
The Order of Nature and the Form of Intelligence

* * *

When we put back our being into our will, and our will itself into the impulsion it prolongs, we understand, we feel, that reality is a perpetual growth, a creation pursued without end. Our will already performs this miracle. Every human work in which there is invention, every voluntary act in which there is freedom, every movement of an organism that manifests spontaneity, brings something new into the world. True, these are only creations of form. How could they be anything else? We are not the vital current itself; we are this current already loaded with matter, that is, with congealed parts of its own substance which it carries along its course. In the composition of a work of genius, as in a simple free decision, we do, indeed, stretch the spring of our activity to the utmost and thus create what no mere assemblage of materials could have given (what assemblage of curves already known can ever be equivalent to the pencil-stroke of a great artist?) but there are, none the less, elements here that pre-exist and survive their organization. But if a simple arrest of the action that generates form could constitute matter (are not the original lines drawn by the artist themselves already the fixation and, as it were, congealment of a movement?), a creation of matter would be neither incomprehensible nor inadmissible. For we seize from within, we live at every instant, a creation of form, and it is just in those cases in which the form is pure, and in which the creative current is momentarily interrupted, that there is a creation of matter. Consider the letters of the alphabet that enter into the composition of everything that has ever been written: we do not conceive that new letters spring up and come to join themselves to the others in order to make a new poem. But that the poet creates the poem and that human thought is thereby made richer, we understand very well: this creation is a simple act of the mind, and action has only to make a pause, instead of continuing into a new creation, in order that, of itself, it may break up into words which dissociate themselves into letters which are added to all the letters there are already in the world. Thus, that the number of atoms composing the material universe at a given moment should increase runs counter to our habits of mind, contradicts the whole of our experience; but that a reality of quite another order, which contrasts with the atom as the thought of the poet with the letters of the alphabet, should increase by sudden additions, is not inadmissible; and the reverse of each addition might indeed be a world, which we then represent to ourselves, symbolically, as an assemblage of atoms.

The mystery that spreads over the existence of the universe comes in great part from this, that we want the genesis of it to have been accomplished at one stroke or the whole of matter to be eternal. Whether we speak of creation or posit an uncreated matter, it is the totality of the universe that we are considering at once. At the root of this habit of mind lies the prejudice which we will analyze in our next chapter, the idea, common to materialists and to their opponents, that there is no really acting duration, and that the absolute—matter or mind—can have no place in concrete time, in the time which we feel to be the very stuff of our life. From which it follows that everything is given once for all, and that it is necessary to posit from all eternity either material multiplicity itself, or the act creating this multiplicity, given in block in the divine essence. Once this prejudice is eradicated, the idea of creation becomes more clear, for it is merged in that of growth. But it is no longer then of the universe in its totality that we must speak.

* * *

The impetus of life, of which we are speaking, consists in a need of creation. It cannot create absolutely, because it is confronted with matter, that is to say with the movement that is the inverse of its own. But it seizes upon this matter, which is necessity itself, and strives to introduce into it the largest possible amount of indetermination and liberty. How does it go to work?

An animal high in the scale may be represented in a general way, we said, as a sensori-motor nervous system imposed on digestive, respiratory, circulatory systems, etc. The function of these latter is to cleanse, repair and protect the nervous system, to make it as independent as possible of external circumstances, but, above all, to furnish it with energy to be expended in movements. The increasing complexity of the organism is therefore due theoretically (in spite of innumerable exceptions due to accidents of evolution) to the necessity of complexity in the nervous system. No doubt, each complication of any part of the organism involves many others in addition, because this part itself must live, and every change in one point of the body reverberates, as it were, throughout. The complication may therefore go on to infinity in all directions; but it is the complication of the nervous system which conditions the others in right, if not always in fact. Now, in what does the progress of the nervous system itself consist? In a simultaneous development of automatic activity and of voluntary activity, the first furnishing the second with an appropriate instrument. Thus, in an organism such as ours, a considerable number of motor mechanisms are set up in the medulla and in the spinal cord, awaiting only a signal to release the corresponding act: the will is employed, in some cases, in setting up the mechanism itself, and in the others in choosing the mechanisms to be released, the manner of combining them and the moment of releasing them. The will of an animal is the more effective and the more intense, the greater the number of the mechanisms it can choose from, the more complicated the switchboard on which all the motor paths cross, or, in other words, the more developed its brain. Thus, the progress of the nervous system assures to the act increasing precision, increasing variety, increasing efficiency and independence. The organism behaves more and more like a machine for action, which reconstructs itself entirely for every new act, as if it were made of india-rubber[4] and could, at any moment, change the shape of all its parts. But, prior to the nervous system, prior even to the organism properly so called, already in the undifferentiated mass of the amoeba, this essential property of animal life is found. The amoeba deforms itself in varying directions; its entire mass does what the differentiation of parts will localize in a sensori-motor system in the developed animal. Doing it only in a rudimentary manner, it is dispensed from the complexity of the higher organisms; there is no need here of the auxiliary elements that pass on to motor elements the energy to expend; the animal moves as a whole, and, as a whole also, procures energy by means of the organic substances it assimilates. Thus, whether low or high in the animal scale, we always find that animal life consists (1) in procuring a provision of energy; (2) in expending it, by means of a matter as supple as possible, in directions variable and unforeseen.

Now, whence comes the energy? From the ingested food, for food is a kind of explosive, which needs only the spark to discharge the energy it stores. Who has made this explosive? The food may be the flesh of an animal nourished on animals and so on; but, in the end it is to the vegetable we always come back. Vegetables alone gather in the solar energy, and the animals do but borrow it from them, either directly or by some passing it on to others. How then has the plant stored up this energy? Chiefly by the chlorophyllian function, a

4. Natural rubber, a highly elastic substance.

chemicism *sui generis*[5] of which we do not possess the key, and which is probably unlike that of our laboratories. The process consists in using solar energy to fix the carbon of carbonic acid, and thereby to store this energy as we should store that of a water-carrier by employing him to fill an elevated reservoir: the water, once brought up, can set in motion a mill or a turbine, as we will and when we will. Each atom of carbon fixed represents something like the elevation of the weight of water, or like the stretching of an elastic thread uniting the carbon to the oxygen in the carbonic acid. The elastic is relaxed, the weight falls back again, in short the energy held in reserve is restored, when, by a simple release, the carbon is permitted to rejoin its oxygen.

So that all life, animal and vegetable, seems in its essence like an effort to accumulate energy and then to let it flow into flexible channels, changeable in shape, at the end of which it will accomplish infinitely varied kinds of work. That is what the *vital impetus*,[6] passing through matter, would fain do all at once. It would succeed, no doubt, if its power were unlimited, or if some reinforcement could come to it from without. But the impetus is finite, and it has been given once for all. It cannot overcome all obstacles. The movement it starts is sometimes turned aside, sometimes divided, always opposed; and the evolution of the organized world is the unrolling of this conflict. The first great scission[7] that had to be effected was that of the two kingdoms, vegetable and animal, which thus happen to be mutually complementary, without, however, any agreement having been made between them. It is not for the animal that the plant accumulates energy, it is for its own consumption; but its expenditure on itself is less discontinuous, and less concentrated, and therefore less efficacious, than was required by the initial impetus of life, essentially directed toward free actions: the same organism could not with equal force sustain the two functions at once, of gradual storage and sudden use. Of themselves, therefore, and without any external intervention, simply by the effect of the duality of the tendency involved in the original impetus and of the resistance opposed by matter to this impetus, the organisms leaned some in the first direction, others in the second. To this scission there succeeded many others. Hence the diverging lines of evolution, at least what is essential in them. But we must take into account retrogressions, arrests, accidents of every kind. And we must remember, above all, that each species behaves as if the general movement of life stopped at it instead of passing through it. It thinks only of itself, it lives only for itself. Hence the numberless struggles that we behold in nature. Hence a discord, striking and terrible, but for which the original principle of life must not be held responsible.

The part played by contingency in evolution is therefore great. Contingent, generally, are the forms adopted, or rather invented. Contingent, relative to the obstacles encountered in a given place and at a given moment, is the dissociation of the primordial tendency into such and such complementary tendencies which create divergent lines of evolution. Contingent the arrests and

5. A unique chemical action.
6. In French, *élan vital* (vital spirit)—that is, the vital impulse or disposition that Bergson believes must be supposed to be at work in all life. This is Bergson's definitive characterization of his alterna-

tive to Nietzsche's "will to power," and is the fundamental principle of his distinctive cosmology or world interpretation.
7. Splitting.

set-backs; contingent, in large measure, the adaptations. Two things only are necessary: (1) a gradual accumulation of energy; (2) an elastic canalization of this energy in variable and indeterminable directions, at the end of which are free acts.

* * *

It is precisely because a cerebral state expresses simply what there is of nascent action in the corresponding psychical state, that the psychical state tells us more than the cerebral state. The consciousness of a living being, as we have tried to prove elsewhere, is inseparable from its brain in the sense in which a sharp knife is inseparable from its edge: the brain is the sharp edge by which consciousness cuts into the compact tissue of events, but the brain is no more coextensive with consciousness than the edge is with the knife.[8] Thus, from the fact that two brains, like that of the ape and that of the man, are very much alike, we cannot conclude that the corresponding consciousnesses are comparable or commensurable.

But the two brains may perhaps be less alike than we suppose. How can we help being struck by the fact that, while man is capable of learning any sort of exercise, of constructing any sort of object, in short of acquiring any kind of motor habit whatsoever, the faculty of combining new movements is strictly limited in the best-endowed animal, even in the ape? The cerebral characteristic of man is there. The human brain is made, like every brain, to set up motor mechanisms and to enable us to choose among them, at any instant, the one we shall put in motion by the pull of a trigger. But it differs from other brains in this, that the number of mechanisms it can set up, and consequently the choice that it gives as to which among them shall be released, is unlimited. Now, from the limited to the unlimited there is all the distance between the closed and the open. It is not a difference of degree, but of kind.

Radical therefore, also, is the difference between animal consciousness, even the most intelligent, and human consciousness. For consciousness corresponds exactly to the living being's power of choice; it is co-extensive with the fringe of possible action that surrounds the real action: consciousness is synonymous with invention and with freedom. Now, in the animal, invention is never anything but a variation on the theme of routine. Shut up in the habits of the species, it succeeds, no doubt, in enlarging them by its individual initiative; but it escapes automatism only for an instant, for just the time to create a new automatism. The gates of its prison close as soon as they are opened; by pulling at its chain it succeeds only in stretching it. With man, consciousness breaks the chain.[9] In man, and in man alone, it sets itself free. The whole history of life until man has been that of the effort of consciousness to raise matter, and of the more or less complete overwhelming of consciousness by the matter which has fallen back on it. The enterprise was paradoxical, if, indeed, we may speak here otherwise than by metaphor of enterprise and of effort. It was to create with matter, which is necessity itself, an instrument of freedom, to make a machine which should triumph over

---

8. An important point, which depends largely on the soundness (as well as the comprehensibility) of Bergson's analogy (typical of his reasoning).
9. The points made here and in the remainder of the paragraph are of the greatest importance for understanding Bergson's general philosophical-interpretive way of thinking.

mechanism, and to use the determinism of nature to pass through the meshes of the net which this very determinism had spread. But, everywhere except in man, consciousness has let itself be caught in the net whose meshes it tried to pass through: it has remained the captive of the mechanisms it has set up. Automatism, which it tries to draw in the direction of freedom, winds about it and drags it down. It has not the power to escape, because the energy it has provided for acts is almost all employed in maintaining the infinitely subtle and essentially unstable equilibrium into which it has brought matter. But man not only maintains his machine, he succeeds in using it as he pleases. Doubtless he owes this to the superiority of his brain, which enables him to build an unlimited number of motor mechanisms, to oppose new habits to the old ones unceasingly, and, by dividing automatism against itself, to rule it. He owes it to his language, which furnishes consciousness with an imma-terial body in which to incarnate itself and thus exempts it from dwelling exclusively on material bodies, whose flux would soon drag it along and finally swallow it up. He owes it to social life, which stores and preserves efforts as language stores thought, fixes thereby a mean level to which individuals must raise themselves at the outset, and by this initial stimulation prevents the aver-age man from slumbering and drives the superior man to mount still higher. But our brain, our society, and our language are only the external and vari-ous signs of one and the same internal superiority. They tell, each after its manner, the unique, exceptional success which life has won at a given moment of its evolution. They express the difference of kind, and not only of degree, which separates man from the rest of the animal world. They let us guess that, while at the end of the vast spring-board from which life has taken its leap, all the others have stepped down, finding the cord stretched too high, man alone has cleared the obstacle.

It is in this quite special sense that man is the "term"[1] and the "end" of evolution. Life, we have said, transcends finality as it transcends the other categories. It is essentially a current sent through matter, drawing from it what it can. There has not, therefore, properly speaking, been any project or plan. On the other hand, it is abundantly evident that the rest of nature is not for the sake of man: we struggle like the other species, we have struggled against other species. Moreover, if the evolution of life had encountered other acci-dents in its course, if, thereby, the current of life had been otherwise divided, we should have been, physically and morally, far different from what we are. For these various reasons it would be wrong to regard humanity, such as we have it before our eyes, as pre-figured in the evolutionary movement. It can-not even be said to be the outcome of the whole of evolution, for evolution has been accomplished on several divergent lines, and while the human spe-cies is at the end of one of them, other lines have been followed with other species at their end. It is in a quite different sense that we hold humanity to be the ground of evolution.

From our point of view, life appears in its entirety as an immense wave which, starting from a centre, spreads outwards, and which on almost the whole of its circumference is stopped and converted into oscillation: at one single point the obstacle has been forced, the impulsion has passed freely. It

1. Terminus, end point.

is this freedom that the human form registers. Everywhere but in man, consciousness has had to come to a stand;[2] in man alone it has kept on its way. Man, then, continues the vital movement indefinitely, although he does not draw along with him all that life carries in itself. On other lines of evolution there have traveled other tendencies which life implied, and of which, since everything interpenetrates, man has, doubtless, kept something, but of which he has kept only very little. *It is as if a vague and formless being, whom we may call, as we will, man or superman,[3] had sought to realize himself, and had succeeded only by abandoning a part of himself on the way.* The losses are represented by the rest of the animal world, and even by the vegetable world, at least in what these have that is positive and above the accidents of evolution.

From this point of view, the discordances of which nature offers us the spectacle are singularly weakened. The organized world as a whole becomes as the soil on which was to grow either man himself or a being who morally must resemble him. The animals, however distant they may be from our species, however hostile to it, have none the less been useful traveling companions, on whom consciousness has unloaded whatever encumbrances it was dragging along, and who have enabled it to rise, in man, to heights from which it sees an unlimited horizon open again before it.

It is true that it has not only abandoned cumbersome baggage on the way; it has also had to give up valuable goods. Consciousness, in man, is preeminently intellect. It might have been, it ought, so it seems, to have been also intuition.[4] Intuition and intellect represent two opposite directions of the work of consciousness: intuition goes in the very direction of life, intellect goes in the inverse direction, and thus finds itself naturally in accordance with the movement of matter. A complete and perfect humanity would be that in which these two forms of conscious activity should attain their full development. And, between this humanity and ours, we may conceive any number of possible stages, corresponding to all the degrees imaginable of intelligence and of intuition. In this lies the part of contingency in the mental structure of our species. A different evolution might have led to a humanity either more intellectual still or more intuitive. In the humanity of which we are a part, intuition is, in fact, almost completely sacrificed to intellect. It seems that to conquer matter, and to reconquer its own self, consciousness has had to exhaust the best part of its power. This conquest, in the particular conditions in which it has been accomplished, has required that consciousness should adapt itself to the habits of matter and concentrate all its attention on them, in fact determine itself more especially as intellect. Intuition is there, however, but vague and above all discontinuous. It is a lamp almost extinguished, which only glimmers now and then, for a few moments at most. But it glimmers wherever a vital interest is at stake. On our personality, on our liberty, on the place we occupy in the whole of nature, on our origin and perhaps also on

2. Standstill.
3. In French *sur-homme*, undoubtedly a reference to Nietzsche and his idea of the *Übermensch* (who is human but more than merely and ordinarily human).
4. Bergson's contrast between "intellect" (*intelligence*) and "intuition" (*intuition*) is his counterpart

to the Romantics' contrast between "rationality" and "feeling," to HEGEL's contrast between "reason" (*Vernunft*) and mere "understanding" (*Verstand*), and to DILTHEY's contrast between "understanding" (*Verstehen*) and "explanation" (*Erklären*). It is also a contrast drawn in other terms by both Schopenhauer and Nietzsche.

our destiny, it throws a light feeble and vacillating, but which none the less pierces the darkness of the night in which the intellect leaves us.

These fleeting intuitions, which light up their object only at distant intervals, philosophy ought to seize, first to sustain them, then to expand them and so unite them together. The more it advances in this work, the more will it perceive that intuition is mind itself, and, in a certain sense, life itself: the intellect has been cut out of it by a process resembling that which has generated matter. Thus is revealed the unity of the spiritual life. We recognize it only when we place ourselves in intuition in order to go from intuition to the intellect, for from the intellect we shall never pass to intuition.

Philosophy introduces us thus into the spiritual life. And it shows us at the same time the relation of the life of the spirit to that of the body. The great error of the doctrines on the spirit has been the idea that by isolating the spiritual life from all the rest, by suspending it in space as high as possible above the earth, they were placing it beyond attack, as if they were not thereby simply exposing it to be taken as an effect of mirage! Certainly they are right to listen to conscience when conscience affirms human freedom; but the intellect is there, which says that the cause determines its effect, that like conditions like, that all is repeated and that all is given. They are right to believe in the absolute reality of the person and in his independence toward matter; but science is there, which shows the interdependence of conscious life and cerebral activity. They are right to attribute to man a privileged place in nature, to hold that the distance is infinite between the animal and man; but the history of life is there, which makes us witness the genesis of species by gradual transformation, and seems thus to reintegrate man in animality. When a strong instinct assures the probability of personal survival, they are right not to close their ears to its voice; but if there exist "souls" capable of an independent life, whence do they come? When, how and why do they enter into this body which we see arise, quite naturally, from a mixed cell derived from the bodies of its two parents? All these questions will remain unanswered, a philosophy of intuition will be a negation of science, will be sooner or later swept away by science, if it does not resolve to see the life of the body just where it really is, on the road that leads to the life of the spirit. But it will then no longer have to do with definite living beings. Life as a whole, from the initial impulsion that thrust it into the world, will appear as a wave which rises, and which is opposed by the descending movement of matter. On the greater part of its surface, at different heights, the current is converted by matter into a vortex. At one point alone it passes freely, dragging with it the obstacle which will weigh on its progress but will not stop it. At this point is humanity; it is our privileged situation. On the other hand, this rising wave is consciousness, and, like all consciousness, it includes potentialities without number which interpenetrate and to which consequently neither the category of unity nor that of multiplicity is appropriate, made as they both are for inert matter. The matter that it bears along with it, and in the interstices of which it inserts itself, alone can divide it into distinct individualities. On flows the current, running through human generations, subdividing itself into individuals. This subdivision was vaguely indicated in it, but could not have been made clear without matter. Thus souls are continually being created, which, nevertheless, in a certain sense pre-existed. They are nothing else than the little rills into which the great river of life divides itself, flowing through the body of humanity. The movement of the stream is distinct from the river bed, although it must adopt its winding course. Consciousness is distinct from the organism it animates, although it must undergo its vicissitudes. As the possible actions which a state of consciousness indicates are at every instant beginning to be carried out in the nervous centres, the brain underlines at every instant the motor indications of the state of consciousness; but the interdependency of consciousness and brain is limited to this; the destiny of consciousness is not bound up on that account with the destiny of cerebral matter. Finally, consciousness is essentially free; it is freedom itself; but it cannot pass through matter without settling on it, without adapting itself to it: this adaptation is what we call intellectuality; and the intellect, turning itself back toward active, that is to say free, consciousness, naturally makes it enter into the conceptual forms into which it is accustomed to see matter fit. It will therefore always perceive freedom in the form of necessity; it will always neglect the part of novelty or of creation inherent in the free act; it will always substitute for action itself an imitation artificial, approximative, obtained by compounding the old with the old and the same with the same. Thus, to the eyes of a philosophy that attempts to reabsorb intellect in intuition, many difficulties vanish or become light. But such a doctrine does not only facilitate speculation; it gives us also more power to act and to live. For, with it, we feel ourselves no longer isolated in humanity, humanity no longer seems isolated in the nature that it dominates. As the smallest grain of dust is bound up with our entire solar system, drawn along with it in that undivided movement of descent which is materiality itself, so all organized beings, from the humblest to the highest, from the first origins of life to the time in which we are, and in all places as in all times, do but evidence a single impulsion, the inverse of the movement of matter, and in itself indivisible. All the living hold together, and all yield to the same tremendous push. The animal takes its stand on the plant, man bestrides animality, and the whole of humanity, in space and in time, is one immense army galloping beside and before and behind each of us in an overwhelming charge able to beat down every resistance and clear the most formidable obstacles, perhaps even death.

SOURCE: From Henri Bergson, *Creative Evolution*, trans. Arthur Mitchell (New York: Henry Holt, 1911), pp. ix–xiii, 92–97, 176–85, 239–41, 251–55, 262–71. Originally published in 1907 as *L'Evolution créatrice*.

WILHELM DILTHEY
(1833 – 1911)

Although Wilhelm Dilthey is almost unknown to most English-speaking philosophers, he is an important figure in the interpretive tradition. Along with NIE-TZSCHE and BERGSON, he played a major role in the emergence of *Lebensphiloso-phie*, or "the philosophy of (human) life," in the late nineteenth and early twentieth centuries. His distinctive contribution was his emphasis on the historical, social, and cultural dimensions of human existence, and on the need for an appropriately interpretive approach to do justice to them. MARTIN HEIDEGGER acknowledged a debt to him in *Being and Time* (1927), but the subsequent movements with which he had the greatest affinity were philosophical anthropology and hermeneutics rather than Heideggerian existential philosophy. Dilthey also showed how some of the basic ideas in HEGEL's "philosophy of *Geist* [spirit]," and of "objective *Geist*" in particular, could be developed independently of Hegel's system and kind of "idealism" into a vital philosophy of human social and cultural (and therefore historical) reality—one that needs to be pursued in ways very different from those characteristic of perspectives on human life that focus on its biological character.

Dilthey ("DILL-tye") emphasized the inadequacy of methods and concepts drawn from or modeled on those of the natural sciences for comprehending those aspects of human reality that have developed historically, by way of the kinds of social and cultural phenomena embraced by Hegel's rubric of "objective spirit [*Geist*]." He argued that the proper and distinctive task of disciplines that study such phenomena—which he called the *Geisteswissenschaften* (human disciplines; literally, "*Geist* disciplines"), and which include the whole range of the humanities and the interpretive parts of the social sciences—is *understanding*

(*Verstehen*) through attending to meanings, rather than *explanation* (*Erklären*) in terms of causal laws. Dilthey was no Hegelian, but he gave new and important philosophical life to some of Hegel's most important contributions to the development of the interpretive tradition—including the fundamental conception of philosophy as an interpretive endeavor. He seized on the central themes and focal points around which Hegel had developed his all-encompassing system and big picture story, freed them of that system and story, and made the most of them.

Dilthey was born in 1833, two years after Hegel's death. Like Hegel, he was from the southwestern part of Germany—in his case, the Rhineland town of Biebrich, where he spent his childhood years. An even more important biographical connection between the two men was that Dilthey held Hegel's chair in philosophy at the University of Berlin for longer than Hegel himself had, from 1882 until his death in 1911. His father was a Protestant theologian, and for a time he considered following in his father's footsteps. He studied theology first at Heidelberg and then at Berlin, where Hegel's influence was still strong, but where KANT's thought and philosophical program were also attracting renewed interest. Dilthey was drawn to literature and history, and even more to philosophy, in which he received his doctorate. He had the good fortune to obtain a teaching appointment in philosophy at Basel University (in the German part of Switzerland) in 1866, and might have become Nietzsche's colleague there; but he left to take another position at Kiel (in Germany) in 1868, just a year before Nietzsche arrived at Basel to take a position in classical philology. He made one more move—to Breslau, in 1871—before being offered the chair at Berlin.

Dilthey's philosophical education gave him a strong appreciation of Hegel's philosophy of *Geist* in its many manifestations, and of Hegel's emphasis on the historical, social, cultural, and institutional character of human-spiritual life. He was also shaped by the growing Neo-Kantian movement's sensitivity to the need for greater rigor and caution in "speculative" interpretation than had been characteristic of the post-Kantian idealist thinkers. But at Berlin he had come under the influence of several students of Friedrich Schleiermacher (1768–1864), who was one of the greatest post-Hegelian apostles of the idea of "interpretation"—specifically in theology and philology, but by implication also in philosophy and the *Geisteswissenschaften* more generally. Schleiermacher had himself taught at Berlin; and it was the explicitness with which he raised and pursued issues relating to the need for interpretation to deal with literary, linguistic, religious, and other such expressions of human cultural and spiritual life that prompted Dilthey to develop his distinctive philosophical program and position, partly Neo-Kantian and partly Neo-Hegelian.

Dilthey was convinced that Hegel was right to focus on the broad range of historically developed forms of human-spiritual experience and activity that constitute human social and cultural life in his attempt to comprehend human life and human reality. He also was convinced both that philosophy had a significant role to play in the methodological and conceptual development of the emerging special disciplines focusing on various aspects of social and cultural life, and that the philosophical investigation of such phenomena required something closer to Kantian rigor. He therefore sought to perform for these *Geisteswissenschaften* something like the function that he took Kant to have performed for the natural sciences and for the study of ethics, while at the same time carrying out the Hegelian program of identifying and analyzing the basic structures of human-spiritual reality as they come to light in social and cultural life.

Like Hegel, Dilthey thought that it made sense to regard social and cultural phenomena as expressions of the human spirit. It was also essential, in his view, to base our conception and understanding of the human spirit on the investigation of such phenomena by the various *Geisteswissenschaften* and philosophy. He insisted that such investigation needs to be "empirical," in the sense of focusing on the kinds of observable objects, products, expressions, institutions, and practices associated with the various domains of social and cultural life. Yet he also stressed that its central concern must be not merely the outward forms of such things but rather the *meanings* they elaborate, communicate, and sustain. Thus such investigation must be "interpretive," as well. Its aim goes beyond accurate description, prediction, and explanation to an understanding of the human reality of which social and cultural phenomena are the central, historically developing fabric.

Dilthey called what he is doing *Lebensphilosophie* rather than *Geistesphilosophie*, despite his constant references to *Geist* and the *geistig*, because he wanted to make clear that there is nothing religious, metaphysical, or even Hegelian-"idealistic" about his basic conception of human reality—which is that it is fundamentally a form of *life* (*Leben*), and a part of nature, with no special connection with anything transcendent or "absolute." Yet he does repeatedly refer to *Geist* because he wanted to emphasize just as strongly that human life is no longer *merely* life in the biological sense: somewhere and somehow along the way, through the emergence and development of the social and cultural dimension of human reality, and the associated transformations of the character of experience and activity, it has become something qualitatively different from biological reality.

Dilthey felt no need to give an account of precisely how this has come about. For his purposes, it sufficed to recognize that this special character of our form of life is a reality. His task was to attempt to develop a *Lebensphilosophie*—or, more accurately but cumbersomely, a *Menschlichenlebensphilosophie* (philosophy of *human* life)—that does justice to it. And for him, this meant not only acknowledging the fact that human life is socioculturally structured to a very significant degree but also recognizing that this sociocultural structuring has been and continues to be a *historical* affair involving something invisible to the natural sciences: namely, *meaning*, developing in great profusion. Dilthey saw nothing "absolute" about such meaning (or meanings); rather, it is something that itself is to be understood as a historical phenomenon, within the contexts of sociocultural human life.

For Dilthey as for Hegel, *Geist* or human spirituality is fundamentally "objective"—that is, historically determinate and socioculturally objectified—and "general" rather than subjective and individual, as the example of language illustrates. Individuals for him are bearers and representatives of socially and culturally structured forms of life, which they encounter and internalize, and which guide how they experience, think, feel, and do whatever they do—even though they also are involved in the processes and dynamics whereby such structures develop, change, and fade. Individuals are crossing points of systems of relations, not monadic units with fixed identities apart from all such relations; and it is by virtue of these sociocultural systems of relations that they are enabled to override and transcend the systems of internal and external biological and natural relations that determine the lives of creatures of other sorts. Individuality, subjectivity, creativity, and freedom are real, for Dilthey; but they depend and draw on these internalized systems of relations and their historically developed contents.

Human experience, for Dilthey, differs from mere animal sentience, in that it is structured by general categories of value, purpose and meaning, and involves the relation of the present to the past and the future. It is a distinctive feature of human life (at least in relation to other types of living creature) that it is permeated by *meaning* relationships. The meanings in question are structured by social and cultural values, norms, practices, traditions, and institutions, and they are inseparable from the human languages that are the medium of their existence. But they are a living reality only to the extent that their objective content is internalized by specific human beings, informing their experience and activity in a dynamic way mediated by consciousness. Thus for Dilthey it also is a crucial feature of human-spiritual reality that it is subjective as well as objective.

In all of this one can easily see the influence of Hegel; but Dilthey departs from Hegel precisely in his rejection of anything like the "logic" and rationality that Hegel takes to underlie the whole unfolding process of nature, *Geist*, and "world-historical" development. There is no grand narrative of world history, for Dilthey, and no all-encompassing structure that undergirds it, guides it, and endows it with "absolute" meaning. Human life is full of norms, values, and purposes; but they are all *human* and historical rather than unconditional and absolute. What is universal (or at any rate pervasive), constant, and enduring is only the continuousness of the creative forces in human life that give rise to the changing richness of cultural meaning. This "historicism" is a kind of radical relativism—but for Dilthey that is no cause for anguish. On the contrary: he considers it liberating and exhilarating.

Dilthey is thus appropriately linked with Nietzsche as well as with Hegel—and with subsequent figures associated with seemingly quite different developments in the interpretive tradition. He can be seen, for example, as a kind of halfway house between Hegel and FOU-CAULT. But as was observed above, he was also an acknowledged important influence on Heidegger, whose own "existential-philosophical" account of human reality is closer to Dilthey's than is often recognized. Moreover, he has a close kinship with such representatives of philosophical anthropology as HELMUTH PLESSNER and ERNST CASSIRER. He therefore stands at the center of the two-century interpretive tradition to date, where different strands converged and from which new paths went forward in a number of different directions. But he was not merely a transitional figure. The position he attempted to stake out deserves to be taken seriously in its own right, and there is much to be gained philosophically from engaging with it. The following selection was published just a year before his death, and so reflects the final version of his evolving thinking.

From The Construction of the Historical World in the Human Studies

The Delimitation of the Human Studies

I

I shall start from the whole range of facts which forms the firm basis for any reasoning about the human studies.[1] Side by side with the sciences a group of studies, linked by their common subject-matter, has grown naturally from the problems of life itself. These include history, economics, jurisprudence, politics, the study of religion, literature, poetry, architecture, music, and of philosophic world views and systems, and, finally, psychology. All these studies refer to the same great fact: mankind—which they describe, recount and judge and about which they form concepts and theories.

What is usually separated into physical and mental [*Psychisches*][2] is vitally linked in mankind. For we, ourselves, are part of nature and nature is active in our obscure and unconscious instincts; states of mind are constantly expressed in gestures, facial changes and words and have an objective existence in institutions, states, churches and seats of learning; these provide the contexts of history.

This does not preclude the human studies from distinguishing, where required, the physical from the mental [*Psychischen*]. But we must remember that they work with abstractions, not with entities, and that these abstractions are only valid within the limits imposed by the point of view from which they arose. I shall now describe the point of view according to which I distinguish the mental [*Psychisches*] from the physical and determine the meaning I give these expressions in what follows. What comes first are experiences. As I have tried to prove earlier, these occur in a context which, in the midst of change remains the same throughout life. On the basis of this context, what I have earlier called the acquired structure of mental life [*Seelenleben*] develops. It includes our ideas, valuations and purposes and exists as a link

1. "Human studies" translates *Geisteswissenschaften*: that is, the disciplines that deal with "*Geist*," the human spirit in its various dimensions and manifestations.
2. The translator uses the terms "mind" and "mental" to translate three different terms: here, and again occasionally, (the) *Psychische* (the "psychic" or psychological); in the next paragraph, *Seelenleben* (life of the soul); and, most often sub-

sequently, *Geist* and *geistig*. His aim is to replace the first two (commonly used) expressions with the third, which he considers more appropriate. Whenever "mind" and "mental" appear in these texts, readers should remember that Dilthey is talking about the human spirit (*Geist*) and its *geistig* (spiritual—that is, cultural, historical, artistic, literary, linguistic, social-institutional, etc.) expressions.

between them. In each of them the acquired structure exists in particular combinations, in relationships between ideas, evaluations and goal preferences. This structure constantly affects our actions, colouring our ideas and states, organizing our impressions and regulating our emotions; it is constantly present and constantly active, without our being aware of it. I see no objection to our abstracting this structure of experiences from the pattern of a man's life, calling it the mental [*das Psychische*] and making it the subject of judgments and theoretical discussions. We are justified in forming this concept because what we have thus singled out as the logical subject makes possible the judgments and theories required in the human studies. The concept of the physical is equally legitimate. Impressions and images are part of experience. To make them comprehensible we must in practice treat them as emanating from physical objects. Both concepts can only be used when we remember that they are abstracted from the fact—man; they do not denote full realities but only legitimately formed abstractions.

In the studies listed the subjects of assertions vary in comprehensiveness from individuals, families, more complex associations, nations, Ages, historical movements or evolutionary series, social organizations, systems of culture and other sections of the whole of humanity, to humanity itself. These can be talked about and described and theories can be developed about them, but they always refer to the same fact, humanity or human—social—historical reality.[3] So it is possible to define this group of disciplines in terms of its common reference to the same face—humanity—and thus to distinguish them from the sciences. In addition, because of this common reference, assertions about the logical subjects comprised in the fact, humanity, support each other. The two great classes of the disciplines listed, the study of history (including the description of the contemporary state of society) and the systematic human studies are, throughout, dependent on each other and form a solid whole.

II

This definition of the human studies, though true as far as it goes, is not exhaustive. We must discover *how* the human studies are related to the fact of humanity.[4] Only then can we define their subject-matter precisely. For clearly it cannot be logically correct to distinguish the human studies from sciences on the grounds that they cover different ranges of facts. After all, physiology deals with an aspect of man and is a science. The basis for distinguishing the two classes of disciplines cannot lie in the facts *per se*. The human studies must be related differently to the mental and the physical aspects of man. And this, indeed, is the case.

In these studies a tendency inherent in the subject-matter itself is at work. The study of language embraces the physiology of the speech-organs as well as the semantics of words and sentences. The chemical effects of gunpowder are as much part of the course of modern war as the moral qualities of the soldiers who stand in its smoke. But, in the nature of the group of disciplines

3. Here Dilthey makes it clear that like HEGEL, MARX, and many others, he considers "human reality" to be social, cultural, and historical as well as biological, and considers human social, cultural, and historical reality to be significantly different from human biological reality (in which it is grounded, out of and beyond which it has developed, and on which it depends).

4. That is, to human reality as it actually exists.

with which we are dealing there is a tendency, which grows stronger and stronger as they develop, to relegate the physical side of events to the role of conditions and means of comprehension. This is the turn towards reflection, the movement of understanding from the external to the internal. This tendency makes use of every expression of life in order to understand the mental content from which it arises. In history we read of economic activities, settlements, wars and the creating of states. They fill our souls with great images and tell us about the historical world which surrounds us: but what moves us, above all, in these accounts is what is inaccessible to the senses and can only be experienced inwardly; this is inherent in the outer events which originate from it and, in its turn, is affected by them. The tendency I am speaking of does not depend on looking at life from the outside but is based on life itself.[5] For all that is valuable in life is contained in what can be experienced and the whole outer clamour of history revolves round it: goals unknown to nature arise within it. The will strives to achieve development and organization. Only in the world of the mind which creatively, responsibly and autonomously, stirs within us, has life its value, its goal and its meaning.

One can say that in all scholarly work two tendencies assert themselves.

Man finds himself determined[6] by nature, which embraces the sparse, sporadic mental [psychisch] processes. Seen in this way they appear to be interpolations in the great text of the physical world. At the same time our conception of a spatial world is the original basis for our knowledge of uniformities on which we must rely from the outset. We are able to control the physical world by studying its laws. These can only be discovered if the way we experience nature, our involvement in it, and the living feeling with which we enjoy it, recedes behind the abstract apprehension of the world in terms of space, time, mass and motion. All these factors combine to make man efface himself so that, from his impressions, he can map out this great object, nature, as a structure governed by laws. Thus it becomes the centre of reality for man.

But that same man then turns back to life, to himself. To return to experience, through which alone we have access to nature and to life, the only source of meaning, value and purpose is the other great tendency which determines scholarly work. From this a second centre comes into being. It gives unity to all that happens to man, what he creates and does, the systems of purposes through which he lives and the outer organization of society in which individuals congregate. Here understanding [Verstehen] penetrates the observable facts of human history to reach what is not accessible to the senses and yet affects external facts and expresses itself through them.[7]

---

5. That is, on *human* life itself. This tendency to use the word "life" (*Leben*) to refer specifically to life in its full human reality—and not to life of any sort, or even to human life considered as a simply biological phenomenon—is reflected in the emergence of the term *Lebensphilosophie* (philosophy of life), used by German-speaking European philosophers in the late 19th and early 20th centuries to refer to philosophical inquiry into and reflection on the character of *human life* as the key to comprehending ourselves and whatever content the ideas of "human nature" and "human reality" may have.
6. That is, "constrained and conditioned" (*bestimmt*). For Dilthey, as for many of the earlier German-speaking philosophers encountered in this volume, the term *bestimmen* and its variants

do not have the sense of being specifically and completely causally determined.
7. Dilthey uses "understanding" (*Verstehen*) to designate the type of comprehension he considers essential in dealing with human *geschichtlich* (historically developed and ongoing) reality in its diverse manifestations and expressions, in contrast to the kind of "explanation" (*Erklären*) that is the specialty and aim of the sciences of nature. (Note that what Hegel and many others call *Verstand*—also usually translated "understanding"—is a more analytical and less interpretive kind of thinking and reasoning than Dilthey has in mind in speaking of *Verstehen*, which is fundamentally aligned with Hegel's conception of reason as "speculative" *Vernunft*.)

The first tendency aims at grasping mental [*psychischen*] contexts in the language, concepts and methods of science and so it alienates itself. The other tendency is to seek out, and reflect upon, the unobservable content which manifests itself in the observable outer course of human events. History shows that, through the human studies, man is getting nearer and nearer to his distant goal—self-knowledge.

This second tendency is also directed towards interpreting not only the human world but also nature (which can only be explained but never understood) in mental terms. Men like Fichte, Schelling, Hegel, Schopenhauer, Fechner, Lotze[8] and their successors tried to do this and to eavesdrop on the hidden meaning of nature.

At this point the meaning of the concepts inner and outer and the justification for using them become clear. They designate the relationship which exists in the understanding between the outer phenomena of life and what produces them and is expressed in them. The relationship between inner and outer exists only for understanding, just as the relationship between phenomena and that by which they are explained exists only for scientific [*wissenschaftlich*] cognition.

III

At this point the nature and relationship of the group of disciplines we started with can be determined more precisely.

We have already distinguished humanity from organic nature, which is most closely related to it, as well as from inorganic nature. This meant making a distinction between parts of the world. These parts form stages and mankind can be distinguished from the animal world because it has reached the stage in which concepts, valuations, realization of purposes, responsibility and consciousness of the meaning of life occur. We have already described the most general, common characteristic of our group of disciplines as its reference to man and mankind. This forms the bond between the disciplines. When we examine the special nature of this relationship between man and the human studies we find that it is not enough to describe man as their common subject-matter. Indeed, that subject-matter only comes into being through a particular attitude to humanity which is not imported from outside but based on man's nature. When we have to deal with states, churches, institutions, customs, books and works of art we find that, like man himself, they always contain a relationship between what is outside and perceived by the senses and something they cannot reach which is inside.

We must now determine what this inner side is. It is a common error to identify our knowledge of it with psychology. I shall try to eliminate this error by making the following points.

The apparatus of law-books, judges, litigants, defendants, at a particular time and place is, first of all, the expression of a purposive system of laws which makes this apparatus effective. This purposive system is directed towards an unambiguous, external regulation of individual wills; it creates the

8. Hermann Lotze (1817–1881), German philosopher who was an important transitional figure away from post-Kantian idealism. Gustav Fechner (1801–1887), German physicist, psychologist, and philosopher.

conditions for the perfect life, as far as they can be realized by compulsion, and delimits the power spheres of individuals in relation to each other, to things and to the general will. The law must, therefore, take the form of imperatives backed by the power of a community to enforce them. Thus historical understanding of the law in force in a certain community at a given time can be achieved by going back from the outer apparatus to what it manifests, the intellectual system of legal imperatives produced by the collective will and enforced by it. Ihering[9] discusses the spirit of Roman law in this way. His understanding of this spirit [*Geist*] is not psychological insight. It is achieved by going back to a mind-created structure [*geistig Gebilde*] with a pattern and law of its own. Jurisprudence, from the interpretation of a passage in the Corpus Juris[1] to the understanding of the whole Roman law and thence to the comparison of legal systems, is based on this. Hence its subject-matter is not identical with the outer facts and occurrences through, and in, which the law takes its course. These facts are the concern of jurisprudence only in so far as they embody the law. The actual capture of the criminal, the illness of witnesses, or the apparatus of execution belong to pathology and technology.

It is the same with aesthetics. The work of a poet lies in front of me. It consists of letters, is put together by compositors and printed by machines. But literary history and criticism are only concerned with what the pattern of words refers to, not—and this is decisive—with the processes in the poet's mind but with a structure created by these processes yet separable from them. The structure of a drama lies in its particular combination of subject, poetic mood, plot and means of presentation. Each contributes to the structure of the work according to a law intrinsic to poetry. Thus the primary subject-matter of literary history or criticism is wholly distinct from the mental processes of the poet or his reader. A mind-created [*geistig*] structure comes into being and enters the world of the senses; we can understand it only by penetrating that world.

These illustrations throw light on the subject-matter of the disciplines under consideration, their nature and their difference from the sciences. Their subject-matter, too, is not impressions as they are experienced, but objects created by cognition in order to organize them. In both cases the object is created according to the law imposed by the facts. In this both groups of disciplines agree. But they differ in the way in which their subject-matter is formed, that is, in the procedure which constitutes these disciplines. In the one a mental object emerges in the understanding; in the other a physical object in knowledge.

Now we may pronounce the word 'Geisteswissenschaften',[2] for its meaning is clear. In the eighteenth century, when the need to find a common name for this group of disciplines arose, they were called the moral sciences, Geisteswissenschaften, or even the cultural sciences. The change of name alone shows that none of them is quite appropriate for what is to be referred to. So I want to indicate here the sense in which I use the word. It is the sense in which

9. Rodolf von Jihering or Ihering (1818–1892), German legal scholar who specialized in Roman law.
1. Body of Law (Latin); specifically, the *Corpus Juris Civilis* (*Body of Civil Law*) or Code of Justinian (529–565 C.E.), the collection of Roman laws and legal interpretations sponsored by the Byzantine emperor Justinian.

2. That is, the disciplines that study the various forms and expressions of the human spirit (*Geist*), which typically require and employ concepts, methods, and ways of thinking differing from those required and employed in the *Naturwissenschaften*, or natural sciences (literally, "nature sciences" or "nature disciplines").

Montesquieu[3] spoke of the spirit of the laws[,] Hegel of the objective mind [*Geist*], or Ihering of the spirit of the Roman law. To compare the usefulness of this expression with that of others used now will be possible later.

IV

Now we can meet the final requirement for a definition of the human studies. We can distinguish the human studies from the sciences by certain, clear, characteristics. These are to be found in the attitude of mind, already described, which moulds the subject-matter of the human studies quite differently from that of scientific knowledge. Humanity seen through the senses is just a physical fact which can only be explained scientifically. It only becomes the subject-matter of the human studies when we experience human states, give expressions to them and understand these expressions. The interrelation of life, expression and understanding, embraces gestures, facial expressions and words, all of which men use to communicate with each other; it also includes permanent mental [*geistig*] creations which reveal their author's deeper meaning, and lasting objectifications of the mind in social structures where common human nature is surely, and for ever, manifest. The psycho-physical unit, man, knows even himself through the same mutual relationship of expression and understanding; he becomes aware of himself in the present; he recognizes himself in memory as something that once was; but, when he tries to hold fast and grasp his states of mind by turning his attention upon himself, the narrow limits of such an introspective method of self-knowledge show themselves; only his actions and creations and the effect they have on others teach man about himself. So he only gains self-knowledge by the circuitous route of understanding. We learn what we once were and how we became what we are by looking at the way we acted in the past, the plans we once made for our lives, and the professional career we pursued. We have to consult old, forgotten letters and the judgments made about us long ago. In short, we can only know ourselves thoroughly through understanding; but we cannot understand ourselves and others except by projecting what we have actually experienced into every expression of our own and others' lives. So man becomes the subject-matter of the human studies only when we relate experience, expression and understanding to each other. They are based on this connection, which is their distinguishing characteristic. A discipline only belongs to the human studies when we can approach its subject-matter through the connection between life, expression and understanding.

All the properties which have been singled out as constituting the character of the human studies, the cultural sciences and history, follow from this common characteristic. The special relationship in which the unique and individual stands to general uniformities is one example. The connection between factual assertions, valuations and concepts of ends is another. It also follows that 'the apprehension of the unique and individual is as much a final goal in these disciplines as the development of abstract uniformities'.[4] There

---

3. Charles-Louis de Secondat, Baron de La Brède et de Montesquieu (1689–1755), French political philosopher.

4. Dilthey, *Einleitung in die Geisteswissenschaften* (*Introduction to the Spiritual/Human Disciplines*, 1883), vol. 1 of *Gesammelte Schriften* (1922), p. 33.

are further consequences; all the basic concepts with which this group of disciplines operates are different from the corresponding ones in the sphere of science.

We are justified in describing disciplines as human studies when they endeavour to trace what is creative, valuable and active in man and the objective mind [*Geist*] he has produced.

From *General Theses about the System of the Human Sciences*

* * *

From The Structure of the Human Studies

The special structure of the human studies is the product of the conditions under which they apprehend objects; particular problems arise from the forms and general processes of thought and are solved by a particular combination of methods.

In the development of these procedures the human studies have always been influenced by the physical sciences. Their methods, having developed earlier, were extensively adapted to the problems of the human studies. This is especially clear in two cases. The comparative methods increasingly applied in the systematic human studies were first evolved in biology, and experimental methods developed in astronomy and physiology were transferred to psychology, aesthetics and educational theory. Even today a psychologist, educationalist, philologist or art-critic will often ask himself when tackling individual problems if the techniques and methods for the solution of analogous problems in the physical sciences could be fruitfully applied in his own field.

But in spite of such individual points of contact, the methodology of the human studies is, from its starting-point onwards, different from that of the physical sciences.

FROM LIFE AND THE HUMAN STUDIES

Here I am only concerned with the general principles which are decisive for insight into the human studies as a whole: the description of methods belongs to the exposition of the construction of the human studies. I shall prefix two explanations of terms. By 'persons' I understand the constituents of the social-historical world. By 'mental [*geistig*] structure' I refer to the inter-relationship between various processes within the person.

1. LIFE

The human studies rest on the relationship between experience, expression and understanding. So their development depends as much on the depth of experience as on the increasing revelation of its content; it is also conditioned by the spread of understanding over all objective manifestations of mind [*Geist*] and by the increasingly complete and methodical extraction of the mental [*geistig*] content from different expressions.

What we grasp through experience and understanding is life as the inter-weaving of all mankind. When we first confront this vast fact, which is our starting-point not only for the human studies but also for philosophy, we must try to get behind its scientific elaboration and grasp life in its raw state.

The distinctive facts of the life of mankind present themselves to us as the special characteristics of individual persons, as their relations, attitudes, conduct, their effect on things and people, and what they suffer from them. This permanent basis, from which differentiated processes arise, contains nothing which is not vitally related to an I. As everything is related to it the state of the I changes constantly according to how things and people respond to it. There is not a person or a thing which is merely an object to me, which does not represent pressure or furtherance, the goal of some striving or a restriction on my will; every object is important, worthy of consideration, close or distant, resistant or strange. Through this vital relationship, either transitory or permanent, these people and things bring me happiness, expend my existence and heighten my powers; or they confine the scope of my life, bring pressure to bear on me and drain my strength. Changes in me correspond to the characteristics which things acquire through this vital relationship. From this basis of life, objective cognition, valuation and the setting of purposes emerge as types of conduct with countless nuances in a state of flux. In the course of a life they are internally interwoven and themselves embrace and determine all activity and development.

We can illustrate this by the way in which the lyrical poet expresses an experience; he starts from a situation and shows men and things in a vital relationship to an ideal I in which his own existence and, within it, his experiences, are imaginatively heightened; this vital relationship determines what the genuine lyrical poet sees and expresses about men, things and himself. Similarly the epic poet must only say what stands out in the vital relationship he has described. The historian, describing historical situations and characters, will give a stronger impression of real life the more he reveals of these vital relationships—he must accentuate those characteristics of men and things which are prominent and active in these relationships—he must, I would say, give the characters, things and events the form and colour of the perceptions and memories to which they gave rise in these vital relationships.

2. KNOWLEDGE OF LIFE

The cognition of objects is a temporal process and, therefore, contains memory pictures. As, with the progress of time, experience accumulates and constantly recedes, we come to remember our passage through life. In the same way understanding of other people produces memories of their circumstances and images of different situations. All these memories of external facts, events and persons are invariably combined with a sense of the context to which they belong. The individual's knowledge of life springs from the generalization of what has thus accumulated. It arises through procedures which are equivalent to induction. The number of cases on which the induction is based constantly increases in the course of a lifetime and the generalizations formed are constantly corrected. The certainty attributable to personal knowledge of life is different from scientific validity, for these generalizations are not methodically made and cannot be formalized.

The individual slant which colours the personal knowledge of life is corrected and enlarged by the common experience. By this I mean the shared beliefs emerging in any coherent circle of people. These are assertions about the passage of life, judgments of value, rules of conduct, definitions of goals and of what is good. It is characteristic of them that they are the products of the common life. They apply as much to the life of individuals as to that of communities. As custom, tradition and public opinion they influence individuals and their experience; because the community has the weight of numbers behind it and outlasts the individual, this power usually proves superior to his will. The certainty of this common knowledge of life is greater than that of individuals because, in common knowledge, individual points of view cancel each other out and the number of cases on which the induction rests is much greater. On the other hand, in the case of common knowledge, we know less where it comes from than in the case of individuals.

3. DIFFERENCES OF CONDUCT AND CLASSES OF STATEMENTS IN THE KNOWLEDGE OF LIFE

The knowledge of life contains classes of statements based on differences of conduct. For life is not only the source of the empirical content of knowledge; the typical classes of assertions are also conditioned by typical forms of human conduct. Now I merely want to affirm the existence of this relationship between the differences of conduct and the assertions of the knowledge of life.

From individual factual relations between the I and things and men, individual situations of life arise: differentiated states of the self, feelings of pressure or exhilaration, desire for an object, fear or hope. In so far as things or people which make a demand on the self come to occupy a place in its existence, become sources of help or hindrance, objects of desire, striving or recoil, they acquire, through these vital relationships, a meaning over and above our factual comprehension of them. All these characterizations of self, things or people, because they arise from these vital relationships, become conscious and are expressed in language. Therefore it contains distinctions between factual assertion, wish, exclamation and command. A survey of the expressions used for the behaviour and the attitudes of the self towards men and things shows that they fall into certain main classes. They assert a fact or a value, affirm a purpose, formulate a rule, or express the significance of a fact in the wider context into which it is interwoven. There are also relationships between the various kinds of assertions contained in the knowledge of life. Factual assertions form a layer on which valuations rest; the layer of valuations, in turn, serves as a basis for the setting of purposes.

The various forms of conduct and their products are objectified in statements which assert that they are facts. The resulting observations of people and things then become independent of the vital relationships from which they emerge. The facts are raised to a general knowledge of life by a procedure equivalent to induction. This is the origin of the many kinds of statements which emerged in generalized folk-wisdom and literature as proverbs, maxims and reflections about passions, characters and values of life. In them the differences which we noticed in the expressions of attitudes or forms of conduct recur.

There are further differences in the way our knowledge of life is formulated. In life itself cognition, valuation, the giving of rules and setting of purposes occurs at different levels which mutually presuppose each other. We have already pointed to such levels in the cognition of objects: they exist in the other forms of conduct. Thus, estimating the practical value of things or people presupposes that we have ascertained their capacity to help or harm; a decision only becomes possible when we have considered the relation between goals and reality and how the latter contains the means for achieving the former.

4. IDEAL UNITS AS THE BASIS OF LIFE AND OUR KNOWLEDGE OF IT

The lives of individuals are infinitely enriched through their relationships to their environment, to other people and to things. But every individual is also a point where webs of relationships intersect; these relationships go through individuals, exist within them, but also reach beyond their life and possess an independent existence and development of their own through the content, value and purpose which they realize. Thus they are subjects of an ideal kind. Some kind of knowledge of reality is inherent in them; standpoints for valuation develop within them; purposes are realized in them; they have a meaning which they sustain in the context of the mind [*Geist*]-constructed world.

This is already the case in some of the systems of culture, for instance, art and philosophy, where there is no organization to link their parts. But organized associations also develop. Economic life produces its own associations, science its own research centres, religions develop the strongest of all cultural organizations. The highest development of common goals within a community is found in the family and the state and in the different intermediate forms between them.

Every organized unit in a state acquires a knowledge of itself, of the rules on which its existence is founded and of its place in the whole. It enjoys what has become valuable within it and realizes the intrinsic purposes which maintain and further its existence. Being itself a value of mankind it realizes values. It has a meaning of its own in the context of mankind.

At this point society and history unfold before us. But it would be wrong to confine history to the co-operation of human beings for common purposes. The individual person in his independent existence is a historical being. He is determined by his position in time and space and in the interaction of cultural systems and communities. The historian has, therefore, to understand the whole life of an individual as it reveals itself at a certain time and place. It is the whole web of relationships which stretches from individuals furthering their own existence to the cultural systems and communities and, finally, to the whole of mankind, which makes up the character of society and history. Individuals, as much as communities and contexts, are the logical subjects of history.

* * *

FROM THE OBJECTIFICATIONS OF LIFE

I

The totality of understanding reveals—in contrast with the subjectivity of experience—the objectifications of life. A realization of the objectivity of life, i.e. of its externalizations in many kinds of structural systems, becomes an additional basis for the human studies [*Geisteswissenschaften*]. The individual, the communities and the works into which life and mind [*Geist*] have entered, form the outer realm of the mind [*Geist*]. These manifestations of life, as they present themselves to understanding in the external world, are, as it were, embedded in the context of nature. The great outer reality of mind [*Geist*] always surrounds us. It is a manifestation of the mind [*Geist*] in the world of the senses—from a fleeting expression to the century-long rule of a constitution or code of law. *Every single expression represents a common [allgemein] feature* in the realm of this objective mind [*Geist*]. Every word, every sentence, every gesture or polite formula, every work of art and every political deed is intelligible because the people who expressed themselves through them and those who understood them have something in common; the individual always experiences, thinks and acts in a common sphere and only there does he understand.[5] Everything that is understood carries, as it were, the hallmark of familiarity derived from such common features. We live in this atmosphere, it surrounds us constantly. We are immersed in it. We are at home everywhere in this historical and understood world; we understand the sense and meaning of it all; we ourselves are woven into this common sphere.[6]

The change of expressions which affect us challenges us constantly to new understanding, but, because every expression and the understanding of it is, at the same time, connected with others, our understanding carries us along naturally from the given particular to the whole. As the relations between what is alike increase, the possibilities of generalization, already contained in the common features of what is understood, grow.

Understanding highlights a further characteristic of the objectification of life which determines both classification and generalization. The objectification of life contains in itself many differentiated systems. From the distinctions of race down to the difference of expressions and customs of a people [*Volk*] or, indeed, a country town, there exist natural divisions based on mental [*geistig*] differences. Differentiations of another kind arise in the cultural systems; yet others distinguish Ages from each other. In short, many lines, which mark out areas of related life from some point of view or other, traverse the world of objective mind [*Geist*] and cross in it. The fullness of life expresses itself in innumerable nuances and can only be understood through the recurrence of these differences.

Only through the idea of the objectification of life do we gain insight into the nature of the historical. Here everything arose from mental [*geistig*] activity and therefore bears the hallmark of historicity. It is interwoven into the world of the senses as a product of history. From the distribution of trees in a park, the arrangement of houses in a street, the functional tool of an artisan, to the sentence pronounced in the courtroom, we are hourly surrounded by the products of history. Whatever characteristics of its own the mind [*Geist*] puts into expressions today, are, tomorrow, if they persist, history. With the passage of time we are surrounded by Roman ruins, cathedrals and the

5. The word "understanding" (*Verstehen*) should be emphasized here. Genuine *understanding* or comprehension, for Dilthey, is possible only in this kind of meaning-structured context.

6. Dilthey makes significant use of Hegel's concept of *Allgemeinheit* (generality); *allgemein* (here translated as "common," elsewhere often as "universality") literally means "common to all."

summer castles of autocrats. History is not something separated from life or remote in time from the present.

To summarize. The human studies [*Geisteswissenschaften*] have as their comprehensive subject-matter the objectification of life. But, in so far as this becomes something we understand [*verstehen*], it contains the relation of inner to outer throughout. Accordingly this objectification is always related, in understanding, to experience in which the person becomes aware of his own inner life and capable of interpreting that of others. If the facts of the human studies are contained in this then everything inflexible and everything alien, because it belongs to the images of the physical world, must be removed from the idea of these facts. Every fact is man-made and, therefore, historical; it is understood and, therefore, contains common features; it is known because understood, and it contains a classification of the manifold because every interpretation of an expression by the higher understanding rests on such a classification. The classifying of expressions is already rooted in the facts of the human studies.

Here the concept of the human studies [*Geisteswissenschaften*] is completed. Their range is identical with that of understanding and understanding consistently has the objectification of life as its subject-matter. Thus the range of the human studies is determined by the objectification of life in the external world. Mind [*Geist*] can only understand what it has created.[7] Nature, the subject-matter of the physical sciences, embraces the reality which has arisen independently of the activity of mind [*Geist*]. Everything on which man has actively impressed his stamp forms the subject-matter of the human studies. Up till now I have also called the objectification of life 'objective mind [*Geist*]'. The term is a profound and fortunate creation of Hegel's. However, I must distinguish precisely and clearly the sense in which I use it from that which Hegel gave it. This difference applies as much to the place of the concept in the system as to its function and denotation.

II

* * *

Today we can no longer retain the presuppositions on which Hegel based this concept. He constructed communities from the universal [*allgemein*], rational will. Today we must start from the reality of life; life contains the sum of all mental [*geistig*] activities. Hegel constructed metaphysically; we analyse the given. The contemporary analysis of human existence fills us all with a sense of fragility, of the power of dark instincts, of the suffering from ignorance and illusion and of how ephemeral life is, even where the highest creations of communal life arise from it. Thus we cannot understand the objective mind [*Geist*][8] through reason but must go back to the structural connections of persons, and by extension, of communities. We cannot assign the objective

7. This proposition summarizes Dilthey's central thesis—which echoes Hegel and Giambattista Vico (1668–1744), an Italian philosopher who had advanced the radical thesis that we can truly comprehend only that which we have created.
8. Here and in what follows, it is best to ignore the article "the" retained by the translator; Dilthey (like Hegel) is talking about not "*the* objective *Geist*," as some particular sort of immaterial being or agency, but rather the phenomenon and reality of "objective *Geist*" in contrast to merely "subjective *Geist*." By "objective *Geist*" they mean objectively expressed and embodied "spiritual" or social and cultural content (meanings, customs, rules, laws, norms, practices, institutions), as exemplified by human languages, cultures, and societies and their various constituent elements.

mind [*Geist*] a place in an ideal construction, but must start with its historical reality. This we try to understand and describe in adequate concepts.
Once the objective mind [*Geist*] is divorced from its one-sided foundation on
a universal reason (which expresses the nature of the world-spirit [*Weltgeist*])
and from any ideal construction, a new conception of it becomes possible;
the objective mind [*Geist*] embraces language, custom and every form or
style of life as well as the family, society, the state and the law. Consequently,
what Hegel distinguished from objective mind [*Geist*] as absolute mind
[*Geist*]—namely art, religion and philosophy—also falls under this same
concept. These, because they reflect the common factors expressed by creative individuals, are powerful objectifications of mind [*Geist*] which thus
becomes accessible to knowledge.

This objective mind [*Geist*] is differentiated into structures from mankind
down to the most narrowly defined types. This differentiation gives rise to
individuality. If we can understand individual human expressions on the basis,
and by means of, the universally [*allgemein*] human, we re-experience the
inner connections which lead from the latter to the former. Once this process is comprehended individual psychology can explain theoretically how
individuality arises.

The same combination of fundamental regularities and the resultant differentiation into individuals (and, therefore, the combination of general theory
and comparative procedure) forms the basis of the systematic human studies.
Their generalizations about moral life or poetry thus become the foundation for
insight into the differences between various moral ideals or poetic activities.

In the objective mind [*Geist*], past ages, in which the great, total forces of
history have taken shape, are contemporary reality. The individual, as bearer
and representative of the general feature interwoven in him, enjoys and grasps
the history in which they arose. He understands history because he himself
is a historical being.

In one final point the concept of objective mind [*Geist*] here developed
diverges from that of Hegel. Once we replace Hegel's reason by life in its totality (experience, understanding, historical context and power of the irrational), the problem of how scientific history is possible arises. For Hegel this
problem did not exist. His metaphysic (in which the world-spirit [*Weltgeist*]
with nature as its manifestation, the objective mind [*Geist*] as its actualization
and the absolute mind [*Geist*], culminating in philosophy, as the realization
of the knowledge of it, are in themselves identical) has left this problem
behind. But, today, the task is the reverse—to recognize the actual historical
expressions as the true foundation of historical knowledge and to find a method
of answering the question how universally valid knowledge of the historical
world can be based on what is thus given.

FROM THE MIND [*GEIST*]-CONSTRUCTED WORLD AS A SYSTEM OF INTERACTIONS

Experience and understanding of the objectifications of life disclose the mind
[*Geist*]-constructed world. We must now define more closely the nature of this
world (the historical and social world) as the object of the human studies.

Let us first summarize the results of the preceding investigations about the interrelatedness of the human studies. This rests on the relationship between experience and understanding from which three main principles have emerged. Our knowledge of what is given in experience is extended through the interpretation of the objectifications of life and this interpretation, in turn, is only made possible by plumbing the depths of subjective experience. Similarly, understanding of the particular depends on knowledge of the general which, in turn, presupposes understanding. Finally, a part of the historical course of events can only be understood completely in terms of its relation to the whole and a universal-historical survey of the whole presupposes the understanding of the parts united in it.

As a result, the comprehension of every particular state of affairs of the human studies within its common historical whole and the comprehension of the conceptual representation of this whole in the systematic human studies are mutually interdependent. In the progress of the human studies the interaction of experience and understanding in the comprehension of the mind-constructed [*Geist*-constructed] world, the mutual dependence of general and particular knowledge and, finally, the gradual illumination of the mind-constructed [*Geist*-constructed] world, are everywhere present. Therefore, we find them again in all the operations of the human studies whose structure is universally based on them. So we shall have to recognize the interdependence of interpretation, criticism, linking of sources, and synthesis in a historical whole. The concepts of such subjects as economics, law, philosophy, art and religion which refer to the interactions of different persons in a common task, originate in a similar way. In scientific thought a concept can only be formed when we have ascertained the facts which are to be subsumed under it; but to ascertain and select these facts we must be able to recognize them as coming under this concept. To define the concept of poetry I must abstract it from all the facts which constitute its denotation and to ascertain which works belong to poetry. I must already know how to recognize a work as poetical.

This relation is, therefore, the most general feature of the structure of the human studies.

1. THE GENERAL CHARACTER OF THE SYSTEM OF INTERACTION OF THE MIND [*GEIST*]-CONSTRUCTED WORLD

Thus we learn to comprehend the mind-constructed [*Geist*-constructed] world as a system of interactions or as an inter-relationship contained in its enduring creations. This system of interactions and its creations is the subject-matter of the human studies. They analyse either that system of interactions or the logical, aesthetic or religious structure characteristic of a sub-system, or that of a constitution or code (which points back to the system of interactions from which it originated).

This system of interactions is distinguished from the causal order of nature by the fact that, in accordance with the structure of mental [*geistig*] life, it creates objects of value and realizes *purposes*: and this, not occasionally, not here and there, but as a result of the mind's dynamic structure to do this once it understands. I call this the immanent ideological character[9] of the mind's system of interaction. By this I mean a combination of creative acts based on

9. That is, the purpose-filled character of sociocultural life.

the structure of a system of interactions. Historical life is productive. It constantly creates goods and things of value and all concepts about them are reflections of this activity.

Objects of value and goods in the mind-constructed [*Geist*-constructed] world are created by individuals, communities and cultural systems in which the individuals co-operate. This co-operation is determined by the fact that, in order to realize objects of value, individuals subject themselves to rules and set themselves purposes. Every kind of co-operation contains a vital relationship—basic to human nature and linking individuals—a core, as it were, which cannot be grasped psychologically but is revealed in every such system of relations. Any achievement is determined by the structural connections between comprehension and the mental [*geistig*] states expressed in valuation and the positing of purposes, goods and norms. Such a system of interactions operates primarily in individuals. They are thus the crossing points of systems of relations, each of which is a continual source of activity. Consequently, in each system, common values and orderly procedures for realizing them are established and accepted as unconditionally valid. So in every permanent relationship between individuals values, rules and purposes are developed, made conscious and consolidated by reflection. This creative activity, under the natural conditions which constantly provide material and stimulation for it, occurs in individuals, communities, cultural systems and nations and becomes conscious of itself in the human studies.

In accordance with the structural system, every mental [*geistig*] unit has its centre within itself. Like the individual every cultural system, every community has its own focal point. In it, a conception of reality, valuation and the attainment of goals are linked into a whole.

A fundamental relation in the system of interactions, the subject-matter of the human studies, now stands revealed. The different units from which creative activity proceeds are woven into wider social-historical contexts; these are nations, Ages, historical periods. In this way complex forms of historical connections develop. The historian must bring together the values, purposes and commitments sustained by individuals, communities and systems of relations which occur in them. He compares them, emphasizes what is common to them and synthesizes the various systems of interactions; a different form of unity arises from the fact that every historical unit has its own centre. Individuals, cultural systems or communities which are contemporaneous and constantly interacting, communicate with each other and thus supplement their own lives with that of others; nations are often relatively self-contained and, because of this, have their own horizons; but, if I now consider the period of the Middle Ages, I find its horizon to be different from that of previous periods. Even where the results of these periods persist they are assimilated into the system of the medieval world which has a *closed horizon*. Thus an *epoch is centred on itself in a new sense*. The common practices of an epoch become the norm for the activities of individuals who live in it. The society of an epoch has a pattern of interactions which has uniform features. There is an inner affinity in the comprehension of objects. The ways of feeling, the emotions and the impulses which arise from them, are similar to each other. The will, too, choses uniform goals, strives for related goods, and finds itself committed in a similar way. It is the task of historical analysis to discover the consensus which governs the concrete purposes, values and ways of thought of a period. Even the prevailing contrasts are determined by this common background. Thus, every action, every thought, every common activity, in short, every part of this historical whole, has its significance through its relationship to the whole of the epoch or Age. The historian's judgment ascertains what the individual has achieved within this context and how far his vision and activity may have extended beyond it.

The system of the human studies to which we aspire must, therefore, be thought of in terms of the following points of view. We must see the historical world as a whole, this whole as a system of interactions, and this system of interactions as a source of objects of value and purposes (that is as creative). We must understand this whole from within itself and its values and purposes as centred in Ages or epochs of universal history. So the direct relationship between life with its values and purposes and history is replaced by scholarly concern with general validity. We must seek the inherent relationship between productive power, values, purpose, meaning and significance within the historical system of interactions. Only on the basis of such objective history do these questions arise: is prediction of the future possible and, if so, how far? and can our lives be subordinated to the common goals of mankind?

The system of interactions is primarily comprehended by the experiencing subject for whom the sequence of inner events unfolds in structural relations. These connections are then rediscovered in other individuals through understanding. Thus the fundamental form of the connections arises in the individual who combines present, past and possibilities of the future in the course of his life. This also has its place in the historical process in which the person belongs. When the wider context of an event is observed by a spectator or reported in an account, the conception of historical events arises; and, as the individual events occupy a position in time—presupposing causes in the past and consequences in the future—every event requires a sequel and the present leads into the future.

Another kind of connection prevails in works which, separated from their authors, have their own life and are a law unto themselves. Before we arrive at the system of interactions in which they originated we must grasp the connections which are there in the completed work. The logical connections which link legal principles into a code of law emerge in understanding. If we read one of Shakespeare's comedies we find the component parts of an event not only temporally and causally linked but elevated into unity according to the laws of poetical composition; this unity lifts the beginning and the end out of the causal chain and links its parts into a whole.

* * *

From *Drafts for a Critique of Historical Reason*

* * *

THE CATEGORIES OF LIFE

LIFE

The human world is the poet's proper subject-matter. It is the scene of the events which he describes and of the features through which he gives them significance. The great enigma of the poet who conjures up a new reality above life which moves us as much as life and extends and elevates the soul, can only be solved if we can explain the relations between this human world and its basic features and poetry. Then we can find a theory which transforms the history of poetry into historical scholarship.

Life is the context of actual externally-conditioned interactions between people, considered independent of particular changes in time and locations. In the human studies I shall confine the term 'life' to the human world;[1] its meaning is thus determined by the sphere in which it is used and thus not open to misunderstanding. Life consists of interactions between people; the finite course of a particular life is regarded by a spectator as belonging to one person because the body in which it occurs seems to remain the same; yet, this lifetime has the strange characteristic that every part of it is consciously linked to the others by some kind of experience of continuity, coherence and identity. In the human studies the expression interaction does not signify the relation which, in nature, is an aspect of causality (for causality presupposes that cause and effect are equal); it describes an experience and can be put into experiental terms by the relation between impulse and resistance, pressure, awareness of being helped, joy in other people etc. Impulse here does not, of course, refer to a power of spontaneity or causality assumed in some explanatory psychological theories, but only a fact which is somehow rooted in the person and which he experiences; so we experience the intention to execute movements in order to achieve a certain effect. This is the experience which is usually described as an interaction between different people.

Life is the context in which these interactions, conditioned [*bestimmt*] by the causal order of physical objects including the psychological events in bodies, take place. This life is always and everywhere spatially and temporally determined—localized, as it were, in the spatio-temporal order of people's lives. But if we emphasize what is constant in the human world and makes spatially and temporally determined events possible—not by an abstraction from the latter but an intuition which leads from the whole with its unvarying characteristics to its spatially and temporally differentiated instances—then the concept of life arises which forms the basis for all its individual forms and systems, for our experience, understanding, expressions and comparative study of them.

Then, and only then, do we discover with surprise a general property of life, not experienced in nature or even the natural objects which we call living organisms.

---

1. An important point for understanding Dilthey in general and the idea of *Lebensphilosophie* in particular; see p. 861, n. 5.

EXPERIENCE

I

Life is very closely related to the filling of time. Its whole character, its ephemeral nature and its continuity through the unity of the self is determined by time.

In time life exists in the relation of parts to a whole, that is, as a context.

Thus, too, understanding through re-living occurs.

Living and re-living contain a special relation of parts to the whole. It is that of the significance of the parts for the whole. This is clearest in the case of memory. Any reference to oneself, or relation to others contains the significance of parts for the whole. I look at, and take in, a landscape. As we must assume that this is a relationship in life and not a mere apprehension, we should not call this experience of a landscape a picture but rather an 'impression'. Basically I only have such impressions and not a self separated from them, nor something of which it is the impression. The latter I only add by a construction.

NOTE

I should like to emphasize that meaning is related to the totality of the knowing subject. We can generalize the expression so that it becomes identical with every relation which the subject discovers between parts and the whole, so that even the objects of thought, or, put more precisely, the relation of parts in thinking of an object or the setting of a purpose, is included. This would include even the general ideas under which individual images are subsumed. Then, meaning means nothing except belonging to a whole; this eliminates the enigma of life, how can an organic or psychic whole be real?

II

From the psychological point of view, the present is a temporal sequence integrated into a unity. What cannot be distinguished because of its continuity we call the present. What we can experience is a moment of life. Even when we can distinguish temporal parts in our experiencing we describe what is structurally connected by memory as one experience.

The principle of experience: everything which exists for us does so only as given in the present. Even when an experience is past, it only exists for us as given in a present experience. This principle is more general (more complete) than that of consciousness for it also embraces what is not real.

The next characteristic is this: experience is qualitative being (i.e. reality) which cannot be defined by awareness but reaches into what can be possessed without making distinctions (note: can one say possessed?). The experience of an external world exists for me in a similar way: what is not apprehended can be inferred. (I can say: my experience contains even what cannot be seen and I can elucidate it.)

The fact is that part of what my intuition (in the widest sense of the word) embraces, is focused upon and apperceived through its meaning and is distinguished from mental processes which are not apperceived. This is what we call 'I', and there is a double relation: I am and I have.

The next proof is that experience also contains the structure of life (i.e. a temporal-spatial localization stretching from the present) in which an inherent purpose is dynamically active.

When we remember experiences we can distinguish those which have a continued, dynamic, effect on the present from those which are wholly past. In the first case the feeling as such recurs; in the second an idea of feelings which in the present produces only a feeling about the idea of feelings.

Experiencing and experience are not separate; they are merely different terms for the same thing.

The presence of judgments distinguishes apperception from experience; I am sad, I observe or know about a death. This contains the double direction of statements expressing the given reality.

DURATION APPREHENDED IN UNDERSTANDING

If we give our attention to the process of experiencing we cannot apprehend the forward movement of mental [geistig] life: for every act of focusing halts the process and gives some duration to what is focused on. But here, too, the relation between experience, expression and understanding makes a solution possible. We apprehend the expression of activity and re-live it.

The advance of time leaves more and more of the past behind and moves into the future. The great problem about whether mental [geistig] events are merely a happening or an activity is solved if we seek the expression which articulates the tendency of what is happening. Movement forward in time and the mental adding up of the past are not sufficient. I must seek an expression which can occur in time and is not disturbed from outside. Instrumental music is a case in point. However it may have originated it is an occurrence which the creator sees continuing from one phrase to the next. Here we have a direction, an activity, stretching towards a realization, a movement forwards of mental [geistig] activity itself, conditioned by the past and yet containing different possibilities, a presentation which is at the same time creation.

MEANING

There is a further aspect of life which is conditioned by time but adds something new. Understanding the *nature of life* involves categories which have nothing to do with *nature*.[2] The decisive point is that these categories are not applied to life *a priori* as something strange but lie in its nature. The approach which they express abstractly is the exclusive starting-point for understanding life, for it only exists in this particular kind of relationship of a whole to its parts. The fact that we abstract these relationships as categories implies that we cannot delimit the number of these categories or formalize their relationship logically. Meaning, value, purpose, development and ideal are such categories. But the totality of a life, or any section of the life of mankind, can only be grasped in terms of the category of the meaning which the individual parts have for the understanding of the whole. All the other categories depend on this. Meaning is the comprehensive category through which life can be understood.

---

2. Emphasis added, to clarify where emphasis is intended.

The objects of scientific knowledge are as changeable as conscious life, but only in life does the present include memory pictures of the past and pictures of the future in which possibilities are imagined and selected as purposes. So the present is filled with past events and contains the future. This is the meaning of the word 'development' in the human studies. It does not mean that we can apply the concept of an unfolding purpose to the life of an individual, a nation or mankind; this would be a way of looking beyond the subject-matter and could be rejected. The concept only describes a relationship inherent in life and includes the principle of organization which is a general characteristic of life. A deeper look reveals organization even in the poorest soul. We see it most clearly where great men have a historical destiny; but no life is so poor that its course does not contain some organization. Wherever an innate and, based on it, an acquired mental [*geistig*] structure form the constant feature of a life within which change and decay occur, temporal life becomes organization. But this concept can only occur because we consider life under the category of meaning.

The category of meaning designates the relationship, inherent in life, of parts of a life to the whole. The connections are only established by memory, through which we can survey our past. Here meaning takes the form of comprehending life. We grasp the meaning of a past moment. It is significant for the individual because in it an action or an external event committed him for the future. Or, perhaps, the plan for the future conduct of life was conceived then. It is significant for communal life because the individual intervened in the shaping of mankind and contributed to it with his essential being. In all these and other cases the particular moment gains meaning from its relationship with the whole, from the connection between past and future, between individual and mankind. But in what does the particular kind of relationship of parts to a whole in a life consist of?

It is a relationship which is never quite complete. One would have to wait for the end of a life, for only at the hour of death could one survey the whole from which the relationship between the parts could be ascertained. One would have to wait for the end of history to have all the material necessary to determine its meaning. On the other hand, the whole is only there for us when it becomes comprehensible through its parts. Understanding always hovers between these two points of view. Our view of the meaning of life changes constantly. Every plan for your life expresses a view of the meaning of life. The purposes we set for the future are determined by the meaning we give to the past. The actual formation of life is judged in terms of the meaning we give to what we remember.

Just as words have meaning through which they designate something, or sentences a significance which we can construe, so can the pattern of a life be construed from the determined-undetermined meaning of its parts.

Meaning is the special relationship which the parts have to the whole in a life. We recognize this meaning as we do that of words in a sentence, through memory and future potentialities. The nature of the meaning-relationships lies in the pattern of life formed in time by the interaction between a living structure and its environment.

What is it, then, which, in the contemplation of one's life, constitutes the pattern which links the parts into a whole and makes the life comprehensible? An experience is a unit made up of parts linked by a common meaning.

The narrator achieves his effect by emphasizing the significant elements of a course of events. The historian describes certain human beings as significant and certain turning-points in life as meaningful; he recognizes the meaning of a work or a man by its special effect on the common destiny. The parts of a life have a certain meaning for the whole; put briefly, the category of meaning has obviously a particularly close *connection with understanding*; this we must now try to comprehend.

Every expression has a meaning in so far as it is a sign which signifies or points to something that is part of life. Life does not mean anything other than itself. There is nothing in it which points to a meaning outside it.

If we single out something in life by means of concepts[,] this serves above all to describe its unique quality. These general concepts serve, therefore, to express an understanding of life. Here there is only a loose progression from the presupposition to what follows from it; what is new does not follow formally from the presupposition; it is rather that understanding passes from something already grasped to something new which can be understood through it. The inner relationship between them lies in the possibility of re-creating and re-living. This is the general method that must be used as soon as understanding leaves the sphere of words and their meaning and seeks, not the meaning of signs, but the much deeper meaning of expressions. Fichte had the first inkling of this method. Life is like a melody the notes of which are not the expressions of hidden realities within. Like notes in a melody, life expresses nothing but itself.[3]

1. The simplest case in which meaning occurs is the understanding of a sentence. Each word has a meaning and, by joining them, we arrive at the meaning of a sentence. Here understanding of the sentence results from the meaning of the individual words. But there is an interaction between the whole and the parts through which ambiguities of meaning are eliminated and the meaning of individual words determined.

2. The same relation holds between the parts and the whole of a life and here, too, the understanding of the whole, the significance of life, is derived from the meaning of the parts.

3. This relationship of meaning and significance holds, therefore, for the course of a life; individual events in the external world which form it have, like the words in a sentence, a relation to something which they signify. Through this every experience is significantly connected up into a whole. Just as the words of a sentence are joined to give it meaning[,] so experiences are connected to give us the meaning of a life. It is the same with history.

4. Thus the concept of meaning arises, first of all, in relation to the process of understanding. It contains the relationship of something outward, something given to the senses, to something inward of which it is the expression. But this relationship is essentially different from the grammatical one. The expression of mental [*geistig*] content in the parts of a life is different from the expression of meaning by a word.

5. Hence such words as meaning, comprehension, significance (of a life or of history) are only points to the relationship between events and an inner pattern, contained in understanding and required by it.

3. An important sentence and proposition for the understanding of Dilthey.

6. We are looking for the kind of connection which is inherent in life itself, and we are looking for it in the individual events. In each of these which contributes to the pattern something of the meaning of life must be contained; otherwise it could not arise from their inter-connection. The paradigm of science is the concept of a causal order in the physical world[,] and its particular methodology consists of the procedures for discovering it; in an analogous way we can approach the categories of life, their relations to each other, the paradigm they constitute and the methods for apprehending them. In the one case we are dealing with abstract connections which, in their essence, are logically transparent. In the other we aim at understanding the connectedness of life itself[,] which can never be known entirely.

We can only reach an approximate understanding of life; it lies in the nature of both understanding and life that the latter reveals quite different sides to us according to the point of view from which we consider its course in time. In the act of recollection the category of meaning is first disclosed. Every present is filled with reality and we attribute a positive or negative value to it. As we turn to the future the categories of purpose, ideal and giving shape to a life originate. It is the secret of life that a supreme purpose, to which all individual purposes are subordinated, is realized in it. It realizes a supreme value, and must be determined by ideals. It achieves a shape. Each of these concepts, from its own point of view, embraces the whole of life; so it has the character of a category through which life is understood. None of these categories can be subordinated to the others because each of them makes the whole of life comprehensible from a different point of view. They are thus incommensurable. Yet there is a difference in their roles. The intrinsic values of the experienced present stand separately side by side. One can only compare them. From the point of view of value life appears as an infinite wealth of existential, negative or positive intrinsic values. It is a chaos of harmonies and dissonances—where the dissonances do not dissolve into harmonies. No arrangement of sounds which fills a present has a musical relationship to an earlier or later one. Even the relationship between intrinsic and instrumental values only presupposes causal relations which because they are mechanical in character do not reach into the depth of life.

The categories which consider life while taking account of the future presuppose the category of value; they dissolve into the different possibilities for penetrating the future.

The connectedness of life is only adequately represented in the relation which the meaning of the events of life has to the understanding and significance of the whole. Only in this category is mere co-existence or subordination overcome. Thus the categories of value and purpose, which are individual aspects of the understanding of life, become part of the comprehensive context of this understanding.

MEANING AND STRUCTURE

1. Experience in its concrete reality is made coherent by the category of meaning. This is the unity which, through memory, joins together what has been experienced directly or through empathy. Its meaning does not lie in some focal point outside our experience but is contained in them and constitutes the connections between them.

This system of connections is, thus, the peculiar form of relatedness, or category, found in all that can be experienced.

Where the meaning of the life of an individual, of myself, of another, or of a nation, lies, is not clearly determined by the fact that there is such a meaning. That it is there is always certain to the person remembering it as a series of related experiences. But only in the last moment of a life can the balance of its meaning be struck, so it can be done only for a moment, or by another who retraces that life.

Thus Luther's[4] life receives its meaning from the pattern presented by all the concrete events in which he embraced and established the new attitude to religion. This, in its turn, forms part of a more comprehensive context of actual events which precede and follow it. Here meaning is seen historically. But one can also seek this meaning in the positive values of life. There it stands in relation to subjective feelings.

2. Meaning, evidently, does not coincide with values nor with their connections in a life.

3. Meaning is the category for the whole context of life; the category of structure originates from the analysis of life's recurring features. Analysis, in this sense, seeks only what is contained in these recurrences and finds nothing except this content. This is an abstraction and its concept is only valid when it is linked to the consciousness of the context of life in which it is contained.

How far can this analysis go? Scientific, atomistic psychology was followed by the psychological scholasticism of Brentano's[5] school[,] which creates abstract entities like conduct, object, content, in order to reconstruct life from them. Husserl[6] represents this tendency at its most extreme.

In contrast we must treat life as a whole, integrated structure, conditioned by its real relationships to the external world, and consider conduct as one of these relationships. Feeling and will are only concepts which indicate how we are to reconstruct the corresponding parts of life.

MEANING, SIGNIFICANCE, VALUE

1. The whole objectification of life consists of expressions, i.e. pieces of the objective world relevant for an interpretation of life. Each of them is a whole with parts and a part of a whole because it belongs to a system of reality which is sub-divided into parts and, at the same time, belongs to a larger system of reality. It is significant, through this double relationship, as a link in the greater whole. This is the hallmark which life impresses on all experience whether directly or through empathy. For experience contains an active attitude towards all the particular, economic, personal or religious circumstances occurring within it. It is a system of interactions conditioned by this attitude. Life is related to anything to which it has taken up an attitude; [examples of] such attitudes are: strangeness, withdrawal, selection, love, isolation, longing, opposition, need, requirement, esteem, form, formlessness, conflict of

4. Martin Luther (1483–1546), German theologian whose criticism of Roman Catholicism helped drive the foundation of new Protestant traditions.
5. Franz Brentano (1838–1917), German philosopher who focused on the acts rather than the contents of the mind.
6. On EDMUND HUSSERL, see below.

life with objective facts and impotence in the face of them, the will to remove what is intolerable and restore enjoyment, ideal, remembrance, separation and unification.

Life itself contains the grief over its finitude and the desire to overcome it, striving for realization and objectification, denial or removal of existing limits, separation and combination.

Unholiness, grace, beauty, freedom, style, connectedness, development, inner logic and inner dialectic are all attributes of life[;] so are the opposites here and beyond, transcendence and immanence and reconciliation.

2. The relationships which originate in this way determine the significance of the individual parts of life. Significance is the meaning, defined by the system of interactions, which a part has for a whole. In the conduct of life it adds a relationship between the links in the system of interactions which goes beyond the experience of effective activity and so arranges them in an independent order. Effective activity constitutes everything which comes to the fore in life. Only the effects of this activity can be observed, for the activity of the self remains unknown. But conduct, or attitude, is something more profound and determines the way life produces its effects; all the concepts developed above are *concepts of life* contained in life. In every person, or period, they receive a new context. They give its colour to whatever presents itself to life. Even spatial relationships like broad, wide, high, low, receive additional meaning from conduct; it is the same with time.

3. According to this relationship anthropological reflection produces a context in art, history and philosophy in which only what is contained in life is made conscious.

Anthropological reflection comes first. It rests on such systems of interaction as passion etc: it sketches their various types and expresses their significance in the whole of life.

Contemplating, experiencing and understanding oneself as well as others and thus gaining knowledge of human nature, produces generalizations which give new expression to value, meaning and the purpose of life. They form a separate layer between life and art or historical representation. Autobiography is a literature of almost infinite extent. The question is how the historical categories facilitate understanding in it.

The historical development of the study of man is misrepresented if we confine the study to psychology as it has developed today. It has been approached from different directions. The greatest contrast, however, lies between what I once described as content psychology and what could also be called concrete psychology or anthropology and the proper science of psychology. This anthropology is still close to questions about the meaning and value of life because it is so close to concrete life. That is why it tries to distinguish types of life and stages of realizing types of significance of life.

One may think of the Neo-Platonic type, the Mysticism of the Middle Ages or the stages in Spinoza.[7] A realization of the meaning of life takes place in these schemata.

The basis of poetry is the system of interactions, i.e. events. Every poem is somehow related to an event which has either been experienced or requires

7. Benedict (Baruch) de Spinoza (1632–1677), Dutch philosopher.

understanding. It shapes the event by making its parts significant through the free play of imagination. Poetry is made up of assertions about life which it expresses vigorously. Everything is coloured by this relationship and is seen as wide, high or remote. Past and present are not mere facts; through his empathy the poet restores the relationship to life which receded in the course of intellectual development and practical interests.

4. The significance which a fact receives as a determinate link in the meaning of a whole is based on a vital relationship and not an intellectual one; it is not a question of imposing reason and thought on part of an event. We draw significance from life itself. If we call the connections which arise from the meaning of its parts the meaning of life, then a poem expresses that meaning by a free creation of meaningful connections. The event depicted in the poem becomes a symbol of life.

Starting with anthropological reflection everything, including poetry, is explanation and explication of life itself. What is contained, inaccessible to observation and reasoning, in the depth of life, is drawn forth. Thus the poet feels himself to be inspired.

The limitation of poetry is that it has no method for understanding life. Its manifestations are not systematically ordered. Its strength is the direct relationship of the event depicted to life, through which the event and the free creation which expresses its significance become an unmediated expression of life.

The realm of life, treated as a temporal and causal construction objectified in time, is history. It is a whole which can never be completed. The historian shapes the course of the system of interactions from the events contained in his sources. He is committed to making us aware of its reality.

The meaning of the part is here determined by its relation to the whole, but this whole is treated as an objectification of life and understood through this relationship.

VALUES

The life of the mind [Geist] contains an extensive realm of values. The value we attribute to objects reflects our personal relationship to them. So value is not, primarily, a product of conceptualization in the service of thought about objects. (It can become this when the result, on the one hand, represents an attitude and, on the other, enters into objective relationships.) It is the same with assessing values. This, too, is independent of the apprehension of objects. In this sense we must re-interpret the expression 'the sense of values'. Value is the abstract expression for the attitude described. It is common to explain values psychologically. This corresponds to the general procedure of psychological explanation. But this method is questionable because it makes what counts as a value and how values are related to each other, dependent on the psychological starting-point. A transcendental explanation, which contrasts unconditional and conditional values, is equally mistaken. We must use the reverse procedure. We must start from a complete survey of the expressions, in which all valuations are contained. Only then can we enquire into the attitude itself.

We colour the panorama of life with positive and negative attitudes—

pleasure, liking, approval or satisfaction; objects conceived as permanent come to sustain memories of feelings which they evoke and these make varied states of mind possible. Thought distinguishes these states of mind from the object and then applies them to it; this is the origin of the idea and concept of value. As value has this special relationship to a person whom it can affect, it is clearly distinguished from the qualities which make up the reality of an object. The ways in which an object can affect the mind multiply with life itself. What affects us in the present is increasingly overlaid by memory. Thus value becomes less affected by when an object begins and ceases to attract us. Even when objects continue to exist the concept of their value can contain nothing but the idea of past possibilities. Because, in practice, evaluations are necessary when we determine the goals for our will, we compare values and so value comes to be related to the future as a good or goal. Thus value gains a new independence as a concept; elementary acts of valuing are combined into a total, organized evaluation. Values, then, continue to exist independently even when divorced from the will. This is how experience gradually develops the concept of value. Let me repeat that we are dealing with an analytical distinction, not a temporal stage.

When we reflect, turning the 'I' upon itself, the 'I' can become an object to itself; it becomes capable of enjoying itself and being an object of enjoyment to others. In the last resort it is not different from other objects which can be enjoyed though we cannot say that they can enjoy what they are or can achieve. But when we, as sensitive beings, become objects to ourselves and thus aware of ourselves, our actions and the enjoyment we derive from them, the unique concept of the intrinsic value of the person arises—distinguishing him from everything which, as far as we know, does not enjoy itself. In this sense the Renaissance formed the idea of the monad in which 'thinghood', enjoyment, value and perfection were united. Leibniz[8] enriched German philosophy and literature with this concept and the strong emotion contained in it.

Understanding makes a different kind of contribution to the development of the concept of value. Here the primary experience in one's own life is the power with which another individual affects us. When understanding reconstructs the individuality of another, the idea and conception of value are further divorced from the experience of being affected. For they are not only reconstructed, they are also referred to another person. As a consequence the relation between the power to affect others and the self-awareness of the subject, who has this power, can be grasped much more clearly. The intrinsic value of the person becomes entirely objective and is objectively revealed in all his relations to his environment. One limitation remains which only historical distance can remove. Understanding is confused by comparing others with ourselves, conceit, envy, jealousy and suffering from an other's power; the yardstick for evaluation which we get when surveying the past, is missing.

Value is objective description by means of a concept. It has no life but it has not lost its relation to life.

Once the concept of value is formed it becomes, through its relation to life, a *power*, because it pulls together what is separated, dark and transitory in

8. Gottfried Wilhelm Leibniz (1646–1716), German philosopher and mathematician.

life. When we find in history values, and valuations expressed in documents, we can, by empathy, put back into them the relationship to life they once contained.

THE WHOLE AND ITS PARTS

Temporal and spatial life is differentiated according to the category of the whole and its parts. History as the successive or simultaneous unfolding of life is categorially a further spelling out of this relationship of the parts to the whole. Here things belong together only because they refer to a person, to a life of which they are part. The course of history is not arranged like pieces of furniture in a room which can be observed by any one who enters, or removed because they are unrelated to each other. Viewed scientifically every configuration is the meaningless result of moving masses, but movement and mass and the laws of their relationships are not subject to time. Life, in any one of its forms, has an inner relationship of part to whole so the configuration is never meaningless.

This belonging-together appears in quite different, vital relationships and is different in each of them.

DEVELOPMENT, ESSENCE AND OTHER CATEGORIES

Here two further categories emerge. Life and its course form a pattern which develops through the constant absorption of new experiences on the basis of the older ones: I call this the acquired mental [geistig] structure. The way this process takes place allows for the structure continuing even while change is going on. This fact, which can be demonstrated in all mental [geistig] life, I refer to in terms of the category of essence. But essence has for its other side constant change. This means that the change which absorbs external influences is, at the same time, determined by the uniform pattern of life itself. This makes up the character of every life, and we must try to grasp it without prejudices. All theories about stages of progressive development must be abandoned.

What, then, is the universal course of events? The definiteness of every individual existence and every one of its states includes its limitations. This concept has a distinct meaning in the mental sphere and is unlike a spatial frontier. The existence of a person constitutes his individuality. Its limitations cause suffering and a desire to overcome them. Finitude is tragic and we feel impelled to transcend it. Limitation expresses itself externally as the pressure of the world on the subject. Through the power of circumstances and the character of the mind [Geist] this can become so strong that it impedes progress. But in most cases finitude makes man try to overcome the pressure of new circumstances and new human relationships. As every state is equally finite it produces the same will to power[9] which springs from being conditioned, the same will to inner freedom which results from inner limitations. But all is held together by the inner power and inner limitation resulting from the definiteness of the individual existence and the persistence of the acquired structure deriving from it. So, the same essence affects the whole course of events.

9. This usage is clearly a reference to Nietzsche.

In everything there is the same limitation of possibilities and yet freedom to chose between them, and the beautiful feeling of being able to move forward and to realize new potentialities in one's own existence. This inwardly-determined pattern of life, which promotes the restless progress of change, I call development.

This concept is quite different from the speculative fantasies about progress to ever higher stages. It means that the subject becomes clearer and more differentiated. But the life of an individual, like the lower forms of life, can lack the realization of a higher meaning and remain tied to the natural basis of plant-like growth, of rise and decline between birth and death. It can decline early or move upwards until the end.

SOURCE: From Wilhelm Dilthey, *Selected Writings*, ed. and trans. H. P. Rickman (Cambridge: Cambridge University Press, 1976), pp. 170–81, 191–99, 231–45. Except where otherwise indicated, German words in brackets are the terminology used in the German original, inserted by the editor in addition to their renderings in the translation. Originally published in 1910 as *Der Aufbau der geschichtlichen Welt in den Geisteswissenschaften*, it was republished in 1927 as volume 7 of Dilthey's *Gesammelte Schriften* (*Collected Writings*).

Part III

Phenomenologies: Consciousness and Human Existence

The phenomenological movement changed the complexion and direction of the interpretive tradition very significantly in the first half of the twentieth century, challenging and then—for a considerable time—eclipsing the naturalisms to which it opposed itself. The existential movement to which it in part gave rise in the second quarter of the century so thoroughly co-opted the brand name "phenomenology" that the two rubrics are often taken as alternative names of the same philosophical development. But the phenomenology of EDMUND HUSSERL, who is generally regarded as that movement's founder, had little in common—either in content or in spirit—with the "existential phenomenologies" of existential philosophy's most important and influential subsequent proponents (MARTIN HEIDEGGER, KARL JASPERS, and JEAN-PAUL SARTRE). Husserl's phenomenology was even more alien in both respects to the philosophical concerns and orientation of existential philosophy's own inspiration and origin, SØREN KIERKEGAARD. These "existential" thinkers shared Husserl's hostility to naturalistic thinking in philosophy; but they were no less hostile to the interpretations of human reality advanced by those inspired by KANT's "transcendental idealism"—with which Husserl had a strong affinity.

Kierkegaard's central concern—and that of the existential philosophy he inspired—was with (in his phrase) "what it means to exist as a human being," considered as a particular concrete existing, choosing, and deciding human subject. Husserl's was with getting philosophy on the road to becoming the kind of "rigorous discipline" he believed it ought to be, capable of attaining absolute and certain knowledge of the essential natures of the possible types of objects and modes of experience. The two could hardly have been more different. Yet existential philosophy could be characterized as a hybrid of Kierkegaardian and Husserlian concerns and ways of thinking, dominated at some times by the one and at some times by the other. In any event, it certainly is one of the most important versions of phenomenology—even though it is by no means the only one.

Kierkegaard himself could be considered a "phenomenological" (as well as existential) thinker, even if of a very different kind than either Husserl or Heidegger and Sartre. His inclusion in this part of this volume therefore would have been just as appropriate as was his placement in the first part (as a contestant in the nineteenth-century competition of interpretations of human spirituality). The selections from his writings to be found there have an important relation to the texts that follow here (after Husserl's), and so can be productively read (or reread) in conjunction with them.

Of course, another philosopher in the interpretive tradition (unlike Kierkegaard) made actual and prominent use of the term "phenomenology": namely, HEGEL. Hegel's conception of phenomenology and his book *The Phenomenology of* Geist (1807) figure very importantly in his thought and work. The selections from that work included above might well be considered in the present context as well. Indeed, it could be argued that Kierkegaard's various writings add up to something like his own (unsystematic) "phenomenology of spiritual development," telling a story of a kind of dialectical progression of human-spiritual possibilities very different from—and in deep rivalry with— Hegel's story in his *Phenomenology.*

Hegel's purposes and conception of phenomenology are far removed from those of Husserl, however, and from those of the others who appear below as well; and Husserl held Hegel and his kind of philosophy in low esteem. Yet the two philosophers do share something in common that sets Husserl apart from many of the rest: the conviction that genuinely philosophical thinking does *not* have as its most important order of business anything like the elucidation of "what it means to exist" as a particular individual human being. In fact, for both of them philosophers must rise above and leave behind any such self-preoccupation, in the interest of attaining knowledge of the highest order.

At the same time, something important unites these otherwise very diverse thinkers—including Hegel, at least in his *Phenomenology*, as well as Kierkegaard—and distinguishes them from other philosophical orientations with which they have overlapping interests: they all concentrate on matters they believe to be most appropriately analyzed by focusing on *the ways in which they are experienced* (first-person singular). They also characteristically take this to include a great deal more of human reality and our world than one might expect.

Phenomenological analysis attempts to explore—and either articulate or more indirectly elucidate—the character and content of different types of experience "from the inside," as it were, in a way that illuminates their internal structural and relational features. Some phenomenologies remain at the level of such description. Others (sometimes called "transcendental phenomenologies") take the further step of considering what the implications of the results of such analysis might be—with respect, for example, to the basic character and structure of the mind or *Geist* or the "transcendental ego" or human reality, or even to the constitution of the world of experience.

It was the ambition of Hegel to do all of these things, by way of the kind of phenomenology he pursued and set forth in his *Phenomenology of* Geist, which he also conceived and presented as a *developmental* phenomenology. For him the "phenomenology of *Geist*" was the analysis, interpretation, and ultimately comprehension of the experiential character of the whole of not only human reality but also the reality of which we are a part—both natural and (socially and culturally) historical. Husserl intended his phenomenological program to be no less comprehensive; but his conception of the world of experience and of ourselves as the subjects of that experience was recalibrated in the direction of Descartes and Kant. Heidegger's ultimate ambition—to recover "the meaning [*Sinn*] of being [*Sein*]"—was all-encompassing; but his focus in his existential phenomenology, like that of Kierkegaard before him and most of those after him who are featured in this part, was on human reality.

This refocusing of phenomenologies after Husserl is not surprising. When it comes to what matters most about human reality, interpersonally as well as personally, the manner in which one's "existing" is experienced—or rather, an exploration of the ways in which it is and can be experienced—is arguably the best guide to the comprehension of what it means (and can mean) to exist as a human being. That is the fundamental project of "existential philosophy," or the phenomenological exploration of (human) "existence" or "existing." (It should not be equated with "existentialism," a label for a particular set of views on the matter held by Sartre and kindred spirits, which are by no means shared by all who pursue this project.)

Some existential philosophers, at least at times, attempt to emulate Husserl's austerely analytical style. Others prefer to proceed more in the evocative style and "unscientific" (that is, not rigorously systematic) manner of Kierkegaard. The latter style is also characteristic of a number of figures included here whose interest in "existing as a human being" has a deeply ethical character and revolves around the human possibility of genuinely personal "existing together," which is the focus of the selections from their writings.

That human possibility is not precluded or ignored in existential philosophy, but it tends to be somewhat marginalized in the thinking of its most prominent proponents (such as Heidegger and Sartre), as it had been for Kierkegaard. Kierkegaard's conception of genuinely human existing had centered on one's relation to oneself and to God; in that context, interpersonal relationships might well seem more distracting and detrimental than spiritually beneficial.

In any event, existential philosophy took over not only Kierkegaard's problem of what it means to exist as a human being but also his problem of what it means to exist as a human being "in truth" (as he put it)—or to exist "authentically" (as this idea came to be variously expressed in the existential-philosophical literature). The authors featured differ over what such authenticity involves, and how it relates not only to one's relations with others but to many other features and circumstances of one's existence as well. For Kierkegaard, it had been closely bound up with what he had called "the leap of faith" and the "God-relationship" that that leap made possible.

That is not so for most existential philosophers, who typically endorse Nietzsche's proclamation of "the death of God"—or, at any rate, of Kierkegaard's

Lutheran-Christian God—even if some write suggestively of what appear to be alternative conceptions of some sort of "transcendence." But they disagree over the consequences of this radical divergence from Kierkegaard with respect to the understanding of human "existing" and of existing "in truth." For existential philosophy, Nietzsche is significant because he insists on coming to terms with how the death of God affects the reinterpretation of human reality; but few existential philosophers follow him in his own reinterpretation, which proceeds very differently from theirs, placing him at quite a distance from any of the phenomenologies to be encountered below.

The first of them is that of Edmund Husserl (1859–1938). He was the founding father of the phenomenological movement, and a seminal figure for a number of other important thinkers and developments in the interpretive tradition in the twentieth century—most notably Heidegger and existential philosophy. Yet he was perhaps the most analytically minded figure in this entire volume: he aspired to turn philosophy into a discipline that would surpass even the philosophical enterprises of Descartes and Kant in its rigor. Indeed, he was highly critical of many of the tendencies reflected in the two previous parts of this volume precisely because he believed them to have abandoned that aspiration to rigor, which was to be realized at last by phenomenology as he conceived of it. A careful analysis of the contents and the forms of consciousness precisely as they present themselves in experience, he believed, could and would yield certain knowledge of the essential natures and structures of both the mind and its various possible objects.

Martin Heidegger (1889–1976) adapted Husserl's idea and method of phenomenological analysis to Kierkegaard's concern with what it means to exist as a human being. The result was what is often called "existentialism" but is more accurately called "existential philosophy," or "the philosophy of existence": that is, of individual human existing, approached and analyzed from a first-person-singular standpoint. Heidegger called this kind or way of being "Dasein," an ordinary German word for "existence" that he appropriated and made much of. It literally means "being-there," which he construes as "being-in-the-world." In his analysis of it, he attaches great importance to the distinction between "authentic" and "inauthentic" existing. Emphasis on this distinction, variously understood, became one of the hallmarks of existential philosophy.

Heidegger's larger concern, however, was with what he called "the meaning of being [Sein]," and with the "meaning" of our "being" and "existing" in relation to it. That concern led him, in his later writings, to abandon phenomenology and the existential emphasis on analyzing Dasein, instead approaching these questions with evocative reflections in language that became increasingly delphic and poetic. He preferred to call these late efforts "essential thinking" rather than any kind of philosophy at all.

Karl Jaspers (1883–1969) was the other primary originator of German existential philosophy. He used the term Existenz to refer to human existing, and more specifically to what he considered to be existing that is genuinely human (or rather that is simply "genuine"). For Jaspers, human existing is inescapably "with others," and thus genuine existing very fundamentally and importantly involves existing with others in a way that is itself significantly genuine. His version of existential philosophy ("Existenz-philosophy," or "philosophy of

Existenz") is not presented as an "analysis" of the basic structures of human existing; rather, it is an "elucidation" of the character of genuine existing and existing with others that also illuminates human existing more generally. His counterpoint to Heidegger's larger interest in "the meaning of being" is his emphasis on what he calls "Transcendence." That idea might seem to echo Kierkegaard's emphasis on "God," but what Jaspers has in mind here is no more to be conceived as an entity of some sort than is what he calls *Existenz*.

MARTIN BUBER (1878–1965), like Kierkegaard, was a religious thinker who also was a kind of existential philosopher before existential philosophy came to have a discernible philosophical identity. Like Jaspers, he focused his thinking regarding the understanding of human existence on the possibility and character of the way of existing that is or would be the most genuinely human, and of the way of relating to others that not only is associated with it but is essential to it. Drawing on the German *du* that is the form of "you" employed in close personal relationships, he called this way of relating an *Ich-Du* ("I-thou," or "I-personally to you-personally") relation—an expression that came to be identified with his thought.

Though SIMONE WEIL (1909–1943) wrote little during her brief lifetime, she made a powerful impression on those whom she encountered in the French and British philosophical communities, which was reinforced and broadened by her posthumous publications. She wrote with passionate intensity on the importance of attaining a kind of spirituality that transcends all self-preoccupation and is uncompromising in its reverence for the humanity of others. Her vision of the truly human differed from that of many of those associated with existential philosophy; but she was as committed as any of them to the task of illuminating what it means to exist as a human being, and what it can mean to exist as a truly human being.

EMMANUEL LEVINAS (1905–1995) was similar to Weil in his concerns and the centrality he accorded to "the other." Through his influential writings, he has ensured that this alternative to the better-known, more "self-centered" version of existential philosophy and human authenticity advanced by Heidegger, Sartre, and others cannot be regarded as a peculiarity of Jaspers and a few relatively marginal figures (such as Buber and Weil). Though well acquainted with that version, Levinas was neither daunted nor persuaded by it.

Jean-Paul Sartre (1905–1980) was the most prominent advocate of the self-centered version; indeed, his literary as well as philosophical promotion of it was so effective that his "existentialism" is commonly taken to be what "existential philosophy" is all about (much to the dismay of Heidegger, Jaspers, and many others). But it was Sartre who made "existentialism" a household word, and he did existential philosophy the great service of ensuring that it could not be dismissed as something that was merely German—or even something that was inherently and fatally tainted by Heidegger's politics.

Heidegger was a member of the Nazi Party and for a time supported Hitler enthusiastically; but Sartre was anti-Nazi and anti-fascist to the core, a participant in the French Resistance to the German Occupation, and as far left politically as Heidegger was far right. Yet he admired Heidegger's existential-philosophical project, and undertook to get involved in it himself. The result was *Being and Nothingness* (1943), a book as massive and influential as

Heidegger's own *Being and Time* (1927), and a promotional campaign that made existential philosophy the popularly dominant movement in the interpretive tradition in postwar Europe—and in its North American extension—for a generation. Kierkegaard's passion to focus on what it means to exist as a human being was mirrored in Sartre in a way that would have surprised him, and might not have pleased him. Yet Sartre eclipsed even Heidegger, making phenomenological analysis of first-person-singular human reality not only a philosophical phenomenon but a cultural one, accompanied by fascination with the idea of authenticity as a replacement for traditional morality.

MAURICE MERLEAU-PONTY (1908–1961) was perhaps Sartre's most formidable contemporary French philosophical peer—at first a comrade-in-arms politically, philosophically, and personally, and subsequently a rival and even antagonist in all three arenas. He too was committed to a phenomenological analysis of human reality, but his version of it revolved around his interest in "the body" and "perception"—as "lived" or experiential phenomena, not merely as physiological and psychological matters. Yet unlike Heidegger and Sartre, Merleau-Ponty paid serious attention to scientific perspectives on these questions, in a way that has an affinity to phenomenology's rival in dealing with human reality (represented in Part IV below) that is known in Europe as "philosophical anthropology."

EDMUND HUSSERL
(1859 – 1938)

As the father of twentieth-century phenomenology, Edmund Husserl was one of the grandfathers of several of the most significant subsequent developments in the interpretive tradition. This would seem to make him a revolutionary figure in the recent history of modern Western philosophy. Yet he had a closer kinship with many figures in the early modern part of that history and in the analytic tradition than he did with most of the figures in the interpretive tradition itself, both before him and after him—including most of those he influenced.

If Husserl was a philosophical revolutionary, he was in many respects a very conservative one. He might with equal appropriateness be called a revolutionary conservative. Indeed, he was a kindred spirit to René Descartes (1596–1650), whose mathematician's mentality and ambition to elevate philosophy to the status of a comparably rigorous discipline he shared. He had no patience or sympathy whatsoever with either the speculative interpretive adventures of the idealists or the scientifically and historically oriented reinterpretations of their naturalistically minded rivals. Yet he too was a reinterpreter, not only in relation to both of these main currents of the post-Kantian interpretive tradition (and to positivism as well) but also in relation to the ways in which classical modern philosophers from Descartes to KANT had conceived of the human mind

and knowledge, and of philosophical method itself.

Edmund Gustav Albrecht Husserl ("HOOS-earl") was born to Jewish parents in what was then the Austro-Hungarian Empire, in the Moravian town of Prossnitz (now Prostejov, in the Czech Republic), in 1859—the same year as both the French philosopher-sociologist Émile Durkheim and the American pragmatist philosopher John Dewey. He was the second of four children. After finishing elementary school locally, he was sent to Vienna and then to Olmütz for his secondary education. In 1876 he enrolled at the University of Leipzig, focusing his studies on astronomy, mathematics, and physics. There he attended lectures on philosophy by Wilhelm Wundt (one of the leading philosophers and psychologists of the day). He also became acquainted with the philosopher Thomas Masaryk (later Czechoslovakia's first president), who introduced Husserl to the thinking of Franz Brentano, his own teacher.

Initially, however, Husserl remained primarily interested in science and mathematics. In 1878 he moved on to the University of Berlin, where he studied mathematics with Karl Weierstrass and Leopold Kronecker, leading figures in the field. In 1881 he transferred again, to the University of Vienna—still concentrating on mathematics, though by that time he was becoming increasingly interested in philosophy. After completing his doctorate (in mathematics) in 1883 under Leo Kön-ingsberger, he briefly returned to Berlin to work as Weierstrass's assistant.

At that point Husserl made the decision to change direction, and to pursue his developing philosophical interests. In 1884 he returned to Vienna for two years of intensive studies. He attended the lectures of Brentano, who maintained that philosophy should be a rigorous cognitive discipline, and that a careful analysis of the contents of experience should be central to it. These came to be among Husserl's basic convictions. It is thus for good reason that Brentano is often regarded as one of phenomenology's grandfathers.

In 1886 Husserl became a Protestant Christian, was baptized, and was married to Malvina Steinschneider, who likewise had converted to Christianity from Judaism. In that same year he transferred to the University of Halle to study with Carl Stumpf, a student of Brentano's and important philosopher in his own right. Stumpf made much of the concept of a "state of affairs" (*Sachverhalt*), which became important in Husserl's phenomenology. Just a year later, Husserl defended his habilitation thesis (a higher qualification than the doctorate) on the concept of number. He then obtained a position in philosophy at the University of Halle in 1887. In 1891 he published his first work, a psychological analysis of the notion of number. It was harshly criticized by Gottlob Frege, who accused him of treating number as something merely psychological. Husserl disavowed all such "psychologism," which he vehemently and repeatedly attacked in his subsequent publications; indeed, opposition to it became one of the cornerstones of his emphatically non-naturalistic (and even antinaturalistic) phenomenology.

Husserl moved on to Göttingen in 1901, where he continued to teach until 1916, and launched his phenomenological program with the publication of a two-part work, *Logische Untersuchungen* (1900–01, *Logical Investigations*). Its very title reveals much about the character of Husserlian "phenomenology," which was to be a kind of "logic" or structural analysis of the "phenomena" of experience, exactly as they present themselves in experience. This book had considerable influence in German-speaking Europe, giving rise to a nascent explicitly "phenomenological" movement in Munich, and contributing to the growing reaction against all forms of naturalism and psychologism that the Marburg Neo-Kantians had been fomenting since the 1870s.

During the first decade of the new century, Husserl came under the influence of Kant and the Neo-Kantians; and the resultant shifts in his thinking aligned him more closely with that part of the German philosophical tradition. In 1913 he founded what was to become an important periodical called *Jahrbuch für Philosophie und phänomenologische Forschung* (*Yearbook for Philosophy and Phenomenological Research*). In 1916 he began to teach at the University of Freiburg, where he succeeded Heinrich Rickert, the leading thinker of the so-called Southwest school of Neo-Kantianism. In 1921 MARTIN HEIDEGGER came to Freiburg, and for two years was his student and assistant.

Husserl continued to teach at Freiburg until his retirement in 1929, attracting increasing attention throughout Europe. In 1928 he lectured on phenomenology in London, and the following year in Paris. At the time of his retirement he was generally regarded as the leading philosopher in Europe. Heidegger and MAX SCHELER were among those who vied to be considered his successor. He continued to work and lecture in retirement; but when the Nazis came to power in 1933, his life became increasingly difficult owing to his Jewish ancestry. Though he had offers of positions elsewhere (including in the United States), he chose to remain in Freiburg, where he died on April 27, 1938. The last of the selections below, written in the mid-1930s, conveys the deep dismay with which he regarded what was happening and looming in the Germany and Western civilization that he loved—horrors that ultimately were far worse than he or anyone else could possibly have imagined.

Like Descartes, Husserl not only aspired to return (or raise) philosophy to the status of a cognitive discipline (*Wissenschaft*), as rigorous in its own way as any other, but also sought to do so by taking mathematics—rather than the natural sciences (*Naturwissenschaften*) or socially and culturally oriented disciplines (*Geisteswissenschaften*)—as its model. (That is the topic of the first selection below.) Indeed, he sought to elevate philosophy above both the natural sciences and the historical and cultural disciplines, in opposition to tendencies—even within philosophy itself—to subordinate it to one or the other of these sorts of inquiry. Like Kant, moreover, he aspired to make philosophy the *Wissenschaft* (often but misleadingly translated as "science") of the forms and structures of all possible experience. And like Plato, he conceived of their comprehension as a kind of extralinguistic intuition or insightful grasp of the forms or essences of the various possible types of objects of experience—and modes of experience as well. (This understanding comes through quite clearly in the second selection below.)

Husserl called one of his most important works *Cartesian Meditations* (excerpted in the third selection below), because he believed that the key to getting philosophy back on the right track (as the *Wissenschaft* of experience) was to be even more rigorous than Descartes in adhering to an analysis of the contents, structures, and modes of experience, setting aside (or "bracketing") all interpretive hypotheses about what the causes or sources of experience external to it might be. In the end, Husserl concluded, it is meaningless even to postulate the existence of some sort of reality or "things in themselves" independent of these dimensions and contents of experience. For him even the natural sciences, impressive as they are, operate only within the domain to be analyzed phenomenologically, and do not penetrate beyond it.

Husserl's motto *"An den Sachen selbst!"* is commonly translated "To the things themselves!"—a rendering that invites serious confusion on this point. Far from proclaiming his intent to get beneath experience to whatever "things" underlie it, this is a call to focus on the *contents of experience* themselves, precisely as they are experienced, setting aside all questions regarding the possibility and nature of anything external to them. The term *Sachen* here does not mean "things" in any philosophically significant sense; Husserl's use of it derives from his teacher Carl Stumpf's concept of *Sachverhalt* (as noted above) to refer to something like "state of affairs." Thus his motto might perhaps best be understood as "To the matters [experienced] themselves!" Those are the "phenomena" of his "phenomenology": and his "phenomenology" is the study of them and of their "logic."

Far from reducing all objectivity to subjectivity, Husserl conceived of phenomenological analysis as enabling us to arrive at a kind of (directly intuited rather than empirical-theoretical) comprehension of the very essentials of experience—essentials that surpass all merely commonsense, cultural, historical, linguistic, and natural-scientific ways of thinking, and that cannot possibly be regarded as merely natural (physical, biological, or social) phenomena. Phenomenology was to be a discipline that stands in relation to experiential or phenomenal reality (including the experiences and sciences of "nature") as the discipline of mathematics stands in relation to mathematical reality. It was to be the rigorous, analytically pursued, and intuitively guided *Wissenschaft* of the basic features of all possible experience—and therefore of all meaningfully conceivable worldly reality.

Husserlian phenomenology thus is an attempted end run around the pretensions of the natural and historical disciplines to have the last word (or words) with respect to human reality, and indeed to reality more generally. Its centerpiece is a move intended to stop the encroachments of those disciplines in their tracks: it claims supremacy with respect to the analysis of *experience as such*—experience as experienced—that no natural-scientific or sociohistorical discipline can touch, owing to their commitment to perspectives and conceptualizations that are coherent only within the bounds of their specific domains. Husserl intends this strategy to enable philosophy not only to escape from the imperialistic pretentions of these disciplines but to turn the tables on them, by insisting that they are actually merely players in a spectacle to which phenomenology alone holds the interpretive key. They map portions or aspects of its surface and near-surface features, while it alone is able to discern its deep structures. These (as was noted above) are not features of "things" as entities apart from ourselves and our own reality, but rather are features of an underlying reality that is neither naturalistically objective nor psychologically subjective.

The seemingly strange consequences to which this line of thought may lead (and does lead Husserl) do not themselves constitute or explain the enormous appeal of Husserl's phenomenological philosophy for so many philosophers, particularly in the first half of the twentieth century. Its appeal springs instead from its insistence on *the primacy of experience*—and particularly of first-person perceptual experience, rather than the "experiences" of *observers* of human life, whether natural-scientific, psychological, social, or cultural—conjoined with its profession or promise of a *wissenschaftlich* rigor that seemed to make the yielding of any pride of place or of intellectual conscience to the "sciences" neither necessary nor warranted.

Viewed from the standpoint of what followed Husserl in European philosophy, much of which proclaimed itself to be indebted to him, as well as from the standpoint of the half century of reactions against Hegelianism and Idealism that preceded him, Husserl is something of an enigma. He is so intimately associated with such philosophers as Martin Heidegger, JEAN-PAUL SARTRE, and MAURICE MERLEAU-PONTY (not to mention others as diverse as MAX SCHELER, EMMANUEL LEVINAS, and JACQUES DERRIDA) that it is difficult to avoid seeing him through the lenses of those later associations. Yet were it not for the strength of those linkages, which represent appropriations of him more than deep affinities with the spirit of his thought and philosophical program, it would almost make more sense to consider his thought a latter-day version of the kind of philosophical "Idealism" with which this volume and the interpretive tradition began—or as a cousin of certain thinkers in the early analytic tradition. The closest philosophical kindred spirit Husserl has in this volume is its initiating figure: Immanuel Kant—and the Kant of the first "critique" (his *Critique of Pure Reason*) at that. And in the history of Western philosophy after Kant, his closest kindred spirit may well be Gottlob Frege, one of the giants of the analytic tradition.

But the banner of "phenomenology" was appropriated by Heidegger; moreover, Husserl's own late philosophical interests seem to have taken a turn away from the kind of philosophical "Idealism" that he had boldly championed in his phenomenological writings, against the philosophical tides of the times. Husserl stands as a reminder, however, that the interpretive and analytic traditions have not always been worlds apart, and that there are compelling reasons to interpret experience very differently than has been done by many of the interpretive tradition's most familiar figures, from KIERKEGAARD, MARX, and NIETZSCHE to Heidegger, Sartre, and FOUCAULT.

From Philosophy as Rigorous Science [*Wissenschaft*][1]

From its earliest beginnings philosophy has claimed to be rigorous science [*Wissenschaft*]. What is more, it has claimed to be the science [*Wissenschaft*] that satisfies the loftiest theoretical needs and renders possible from an ethico-religious point of view a life regulated by pure rational norms. This claim has been pressed with sometimes more, sometimes less energy, but it has never been completely abandoned, not even during those times when interest in and capacity for pure theory were in danger of atrophying, or when religious forces restricted freedom of theoretical investigation.

During no period of its development has philosophy been capable of living up to this claim of being rigorous science [*Wissenschaft*]; not even in its most recent period, when—despite the multiplicity and contradictory character of its philosophical orientations—it has followed from the Renaissance up to the present an essentially unitary line of development. It is, in fact, the dominant characteristic of modern philosophy that, rather than surrender itself naïvely to the philosophical impulse, it will by means of critical reflection and by ever more profound methodological investigation constitute itself as rigorous science. But the only mature fruit of these efforts has been to secure first the foundation and then the independence of rigorous natural and humanistic sciences[2] along with new purely mathematical disciplines. Philosophy itself, in the particular sense that only now has become distinguished, lacked as much as ever the character of rigorous science. The very meaning of the distinction remained without scientifically [*wissenschaftlich*] secure determination. The question of philosophy's relation to the natural and humanistic sciences—whether the specifically philosophical element of its work, essentially related as it is to nature and the human spirit [*Geist*], demands fundamentally new attitudes, that in turn involve fundamentally peculiar goals and methods; whether as a result the philosophical takes us, as it were, into a new dimension, or whether it performs its function on the same level as the empirical sciences of nature and of the human spirit—all this is to this day disputed. It shows that even the proper sense of philosophical problems has not been made scientifically [*wissenschaftlich*] clear.

Thus philosophy, according to its historical purpose the loftiest and most rigorous of all sciences [*Wissenschaften*], representing as it does humanity's imperishable demand for pure and absolute knowledge (and what is inseparably one with that, its demand for pure and absolute valuing and willing), is incapable of assuming the form of rigorous science.[3] Philosophy, whose vocation is to teach us how to carry on the eternal work of humanity, is

---

1. That is, cognitive discipline. *Wissenschaft* and *wissenschaftlich* are commonly translated as "science" and "scientific" (as they are in the translation used); but this is seriously misleading, particularly in Husserl's case (as in Hegel's). These English terms are generally understood to refer to the kind of inquiry and thinking paradigmatically exemplified by the natural sciences, whereas philosophy for him (like mathematics) is a radically different sort of cognitive endeavor and discipline. Husserl's German terms therefore should be kept in mind, and understood in the sense of "cognitive

discipline."
2. "Natur- und Geisteswissenschaften": that is, the cognitive disciplines that inquire into nature or natural phenomena and those that inquire into *Geist* (i.e., the human spirit and its expressions)—the social, cultural, linguistic, historical, and other such disciplines, including philosophy itself.
3. That is, to assume the form of rigorous science, philosophy must be changed in the ways that Husserl will be advocating, thereby transforming it into "phenomenology."

utterly incapable of teaching in an objectively valid manner. Kant was fond of saying that one could not learn philosophy, but only to philosophize.[4] What is that but an admission of philosophy's unscientific [*unwissenschaftlich*] character? As far as science, real science [*Wissenschaft*], extends, so far can one teach and learn, and this everywhere in the same sense. Certainly scientific learning is nowhere a passive acceptance of matter alien to the mind. In all cases it is based on self-activity, on an inner reproduction, in their relationships as grounds and consequences, of the rational insights gained by creative spirits. One cannot learn philosophy, because here there are no such insights objectively grasped and grounded, or to put it in another way, because here the problems, methods, and theories have not been clearly defined conceptually, their sense has not been fully clarified.

I do not say that philosophy is an imperfect science; I say simply that it is not yet a science [*Wissenschaft*] at all,[5] that as science it has not yet begun. As a criterion for this, take any portion—however small—of theoretical content that has been objectively grounded. All sciences [*Wissenschaften*] are imperfect, even the much-admired exact sciences. On the one hand they are incomplete, because the limitless horizon of open problems, which will never let the drive toward knowledge rest, lies before them; and on the other hand they have a variety of defects in their already developed doctrinal content, there remain evidences here and there of a lack of clarity or perfection in the systematic ordering of proofs and theories. Nevertheless they do have a doctrinal content that is constantly growing and branching out in new directions. No reasonable person will doubt the objective truth or the objectively grounded probability of the wonderful theories of mathematics and the natural sciences. Here there is, by and large, no room for private "opinions," "notions," or "points of view." To the extent that there are such in particular instances, the science in question is not established as such but is in the process of becoming a science [*Wissenschaft*] and is in general so judged.

The imperfection of philosophy is of an entirely different sort from that of the other sciences [*Wissenschaften*] as just described. It does not have at its disposal a merely incomplete and, in particular instances, imperfect doctrinal system; it simply has none whatever. Each and every question is herein controverted, every position is a matter of individual conviction, of the interpretation given by a school, of a "point of view."[6]

It may well be that the proposals presented in the world-renowned scientific works of philosophy in ancient and modern times are based on serious, even colossal intellectual activity. More than that, it may in large measure be work done in advance for the future establishment of scientifically strict doctrinal systems; but for the moment, nothing in them is recognizable as a basis for philosophical science, nor is there any prospect of cutting out, as

---

4. See, e.g., KANT's *Critique of Pure Reason* (1781; 2nd ed., 1787), A 837 / B 865.
5. That is, it is *not yet* a genuine rigorous *Wissenschaft*.
6. Husserl here is expressing his contempt for philosophy that amounts to nothing more than the expression of personal convictions, the development of interpretations that are merely ways of thinking favored by and identified with various schools of thought, or the elaboration of "worldviews" (*Weltanschauungen*, ways of looking at the world).

it were, with the critical scissors here and there a fragment of philosophical doctrine.

* * *

The revolutions decisive for the progress of philosophy are those in which the claim of former philosophies to be scientific are discredited by a critique of their pretended scientific [*wissenschaftlich*] procedure. Then at the helm is the fully conscious will to establish philosophy in a radically new fashion in the sense of rigorous science [*Wissenschaft*],[7] determining the order in which tasks are undertaken. First of all, thought concentrates all its energy on decisively clarifying, by means of systematic examination, the conditions of strict science that in former philosophies were naively overlooked or misunderstood, in order thereafter to attempt to construct anew a structure of philosophical docrine. Such a fully conscious will for rigorous science dominated the Socratic-Platonic revolution of philosophy[8] and also, at the beginning of the modern era, the scientific [*wissenschaftlich*] reactions against Scholasticism, especially the Cartesian revolution.[9] Its impulse carries over to the great philosophies of the seventeenth and eighteenth centuries; it renews itself with most radical vigor in Kant's critique of reason and still dominates Fichte's philosophizing. Again and again research is directed toward true beginnings, decisive formulation of problems, and correct methods.

Only with romantic philosophy does a change occur. However much Hegel insists on the absolute validity of his method and his doctrine, still his system lacks a critique of reason, which is the foremost prerequisite for being scientific [*wissenschaftlich*] in philosophy. In this connection it is clear that this philosophy, like romantic philosophy in general, acted in the years that followed either to weaken or to adulterate the impulse toward the constitution of rigorous philosophical science.

Concerning the latter tendency to adulterate, it is well known that with the progress of the exact sciences Hegelianism gave rise to reactions, as a result of which the naturalism of the eighteenth century gained an overwhelming impetus; and with its scepticism, which invalidated all absolute ideality and objectivity, it has largely determined the *Weltanschauung*[1] and philosophy of the last decades.

On the other hand, as a tendency to weaken the impulse toward philosophic science Hegelian philosophy produced aftereffects by its doctrine on the relative justification of every philosophy for its own time—a doctrine, it is true, that in Hegel's system, pretending to absolute validity, had an entirely different sense from the historistic one attributed to it by those generations that had lost along with their belief in Hegelian philosophy any belief whatever in an

7. Husserl regards the phenomenological revolution he advocates as a radical break with the philosophical tradition that began with Hegel—but as akin to the previous philosophical "revolutions" he mentions (even making favorable mention of FICHTE!).

8. Socrates (469–399 B.C.E.) was not only the teacher of Plato (ca. 427–ca. 347 B.C.E.) but also the main figure in most of his dialogues.

9. The French philosopher René Descartes (1596–1650), commonly considered to be the father of modern philosophy, aspired to make philosophy as methodologically rigorous as mathematics. "Scholastics": medieval Christian thinkers who relied on dialectical and syllogistic reasoning and sought to reconcile Christian theology with classical philosophy.

1. Worldview, general outlook.

absolute philosophy. As a result of the transformation of Hegel's metaphysical philosophy of history into a sceptical historicism, the establishment of the new *Weltanschauung* philosophy has now been essentially determined.[2] This latter seems in our day to be spreading rapidly, and what is more, warring as it does for the most part against naturalism and, when the occasion offers, even against historicism, it has not the least desire to be sceptical. To the extent, however, that it does not show itself, at least in its whole intention and procedure, any longer dominated by that radical will to scientific doctrine that constituted the great progress of modern philosophy up to Kant's time, what I said regarding a weakening of philosophy's scientific impulse referred particularly to it.

The following arguments are based on the conviction that the highest interests of human culture demand the development of a rigorously scientific [*wissenschaftlich*] philosophy; consequently, if a philosophical revolution in our times is to be justified, it must without fail be animated by the purpose of laying a new foundation for philosophy in the sense of strict science [*Wissenschaft*]. This purpose is by no means foreign to the present age. It is fully alive precisely in the naturalism that dominates the age. From the start, naturalism sets out with a firm determination to realize the ideal of a rigorously scientific reform of philosophy. It even believes at all times, both in its earlier and in its modern forms, that it has already realized this idea. But all this takes place, when we look at it from the standpoint of principle, in a form that from the ground up is replete with erroneous theory; and from a practical point of view this means a growing danger for our culture.[3] It is important today to engage in a radical criticism of naturalistic philosophy. In particular, there is need of a positive criticism of principles and methods as opposed to a purely negative criticism based on consequences. Only such a criticism is calculated to preserve intact confidence in the possibility of a scientific [*wissenschaftlich*] philosophy, a confidence threatened by the absurd consequences of a naturalism built on strict empirical science.

* * *

* * * It is in the methodical disposition and connection of experiences, in the interplay of experience and thought, which has its rigid logical laws, that valid experience is distinguished from invalid, that each experience is accorded its level of validity, and that objectively valid knowledge as such, knowledge of nature, is worked out. Still, no matter how satisfactory this kind of critique of experience may be, as long as we remain within natural science and think according to its point of view, a completely different critique of experience is still possible and indispensable, a critique that places in question all experience as such and the sort of thinking proper to empirical science.[4]

2. Husserl thus associates Hegel's philosophy and heritage with the mistake of abandoning philosophy's aspiration and determination to be a rigorous *Wissenschaft*, Hegel's pretension to "absolute knowledge" notwithstanding, because he sees Hegel as having prepared the way for the subsequent triumph of historical relativism.
3. That is, the danger of depriving our culture of the firm cognitive foundation it needs by mistakenly supposing that the way to transform philosophy into a rigorous *Wissenschaft* is to model and base it "naturalistically" on "strict *empirical* sciences" paradigmatically exemplified by the natural sciences. The idea of such a "naturalistic philosophy," for Husserl, is not only nonsense but *dangerous* nonsense, because what then passes for philosophy as a "rigorous *Wissenschaft*" can provide no such foundation and defense.
4. In what follows, Husserl sketches out the basic motivation for and ideas of what he calls "phenomenology."

How can experience as consciousness give or contact an object? How can experiences be mutually legitimated or corrected by means of each other, and not merely replace each other or confirm each other subjectively? How can the play of a consciousness whose logic is empirical make objectively valid statements, valid for things that are in and for themselves? Why are the playing rules, so to speak, of consciousness not irrelevant for things? How is natural science to be comprehensible in absolutely every case, to the extent that it pretends at every step to posit and to know a nature that is in itself—in itself in opposition to the subjective flow of consciousness? All these questions become riddles as soon as reflection on them becomes serious. It is well known that theory of knowledge is the discipline that wants to answer such questions, and also that up to the present, despite all the thoughtfulness employed by the greatest scholars in regard to those questions, this discipline has not answered in a manner scientifically [*wissenschaftlich*] clear, unanimous, and decisive.

It requires only a rigorous consistency in maintaining the level of this problematic (a consistency missing, it is true, in all theories of knowledge up to the present) to see clearly the absurdity of a theory of knowledge based on natural science, and thus, too, of any psychological theory of knowledge. If certain riddles are, generally speaking, inherent in principle to natural science, then it is self-evident that the solution of these riddles according to premises and conclusions in principle transcends natural science. To expect from natural science itself the solution of any one of the problems inherent in it as such—thus inhering through and through, from beginning to end—or even merely to suppose that it could contribute to the solution of such a problem any premises whatsoever, is to be involved in a vicious circle.

It also becomes clear that just as every scientific, so every prescientific application of nature must in principle remain excluded in a theory of knowledge that is to retain its univocal sense. So, too, must all expressions that imply thetic existential positings[5] of things in the framework of space, time, causality, etc. This obviously applies also to all existential positings with regard to the empirical being of the investigator, of his psychical faculties, and the like.

Further: if knowledge theory will nevertheless investigate the problems of the relationship between consciousness and being, it can have before its eyes only being as the correlate of consciousness, as something "intended" after the manner of consciousness:[6] as perceived, remembered, expected, represented pictorially, imagined, identified, distinguished, believed, opined, evaluated, etc. It is clear, then, that the investigation must be directed toward a scientific [*wissenschaftlich*] essential knowledge of consciousness, toward that which consciousness itself "is" according to its essence in all its distinguishable forms. At the same time, however, the investigation must be directed toward what consciousness "means," as well as toward the different ways in which—in accord with the essence of the aforementioned forms—it intends

---

5. Assertions of states of affairs.
6. The terms "intend" and "intention" ordinarily are used when we speak of something we may have it in mind to *do*. In this technical usage, which has become very important and common in philosophy, the "something" can be the "intentional" or "intended" *object of* any sort of mental act or operation, such as those Husserl goes on to list. (Consciousness is always "consciousness *of* something":

that is the principle of the "intentionality" of consciousness.) It is these kinds of "intended objects" *as they are "intended"* (that is, as they are experienced), along with the various kinds of "intending" or mental acts and operations, that Husserl proposes to make the focus of phenomenological inquiry, with the goal of attaining knowledge of their "essences."

the objective, now clearly, now obscurely, now by presenting or by presentifying,[7] now symbolically or pictorially, now simply, now mediated in thought, now in this or that mode of attention, and so in countless other forms, and how ultimately it "demonstrates" the objective as that which is "validly," "really."

Every type of object that is to be the object of a rational proposition, of a prescientific and then of a scientific [wissenschaftlich] cognition, must manifest itself in knowledge, thus in consciousness itself, and it must permit being brought to givenness, in accord with the sense of all knowledge. All types of consciousness, in the way they are, so to speak, teleologically ordered under the title of knowledge and, even more, in the way they are grouped according to the various object categories—considered as the groups of cognitive functions that especially correspond to these categories—must permit being studied in their essential connection and in their relation back to the forms of the consciousness of givenness belonging to them. The sense of the question concerning legitimacy, which is to be put to all cognitive acts, must admit of being understood, the essence of grounded legitimation and that of ideal groundableness or validity must admit of being fully clarified, in this manner—and with respect to all levels of cognition, including the highest, that of scientific cognition.

What it means, that objectivity is, and manifests itself cognitively as so being, must precisely become evident purely from consciousness itself, and thereby it must become completely understandable. And for that is required a study of consciousness in its entirety, since according to all its forms it enters into possible cognitive functions. To the extent, however, that every consciousness is "consciousness-of," the essential study of conciousness includes also that of consciousness-meaning and consciousness-objectivity as such.[8] To study any kind of objectivity whatever according to its general essence (a study that can pursue interests far removed from those of knowledge theory and the investigation of consciousness) means to concern oneself with objectivity's modes of givenness and to exhaust its essential content in the processes of "clarification" proper to it. Even if the orientation is not that which is directed toward the kinds of consciousness and an essential investigation of them, still the method of clarification is such that even here reflection on the modes of being intended and of being given cannot be avoided. In any case, however, the clarification of all fundamental kinds of objectivities is for its part indispensable for the essential analysis of consciousness, and as a result is included in it, but primarily in an epistemological analysis, that finds its task precisely in the investigation of correlations. Consequently we include all such studies, even though relatively they are to be distinguished, under the title "phenomenological."

With this we meet a science [Wissenschaft] of whose extraordinary extent our contemporaries have as yet no concept; a science, it is true, of consciousness that is still not psychology; a phenomenology of consciousness as opposed

---

7. That is, by being immediately present to one in an instance of perceiving or by being *made* present to one by some act that calls it to mind although it is not immediately present (by remembering, anticipating, wanting, imagining, etc.).
8. That is, the study of consciousness will include the study of the kinds of objectivity or object that consciousness can be "consciousness of," and also the study of the kinds of "meaning" or "sense" that such kinds of objectivity or object can *have* in and for consciousness.

to a natural science about consciousness.[9] But since there will be no question here of an accidental equivocation, it is to be expected beforehand that phenomenology and psychology must stand in close relationship to each other, since both are concerned with consciousness, even though in a different way, according to a different "orientation." This we may express by saying that psychology is concerned with "empirical consciousness," with consciousness from the empirical point of view, as an empirical being in the ensemble of nature, whereas phenomenology is concerned with "pure" consciousness, i.e., consciousness from the phenomenological point of view.

* * *

Let us now turn to the "world" of the "psychical,"[1] and let us confine ourselves to "psychical phenomena," which the new psychology looks upon as its field of objects—i.e., in beginning we leave out of consideration problems relative to the soul and to the ego. We ask, then, whether in every perception of the psychical, just as in the sense of every physical experience and of every perception of the real, there is included "nature"-objectivity? We soon see that the relationships in the sphere of the psychical are totally different from those in the physical sphere. The psychical is divided (to speak metaphorically and not metaphysically) into monads that have no windows and are in communication only through empathy. Psychical being, being as "phenomenon," is in principle not a unity that could be experienced in several separate perceptions as individually identical, not even in perceptions of the same subject. In the psychical sphere there is, in other words, no distinction between appearance and being, and if nature is a being that appears in appearances, still appearances themselves (which the psychologist certainly looks upon as psychical) do not constitute a being which itself appears by means of appearances lying behind it—as every reflection on the perception of any appearance whatever makes evident. It is then clear: there is, properly speaking, only one nature, the one that appears in the appearances of things. Everything that in the broadest sense of psychology we call a psychical phenomenon, when looked at in and for itself, is precisely phenomenon and not nature.

A phenomenon, then, is no "substantial" unity; it has no "real properties," it knows no real parts, no real changes, and no causality; all these words are here understood in the sense proper to natural science. To attribute a nature to phenomena, to investigate their real component parts, their causal connections—that is pure absurdity, no better than if one wanted to ask about the causal properties, connections, etc. of numbers. It is the absurdity of naturalizing something whose essence excludes the kind of being that nature has. A thing is what it is, and it remains in its identity forever: nature is eternal. Whatever in the way of real properties or modifications of properties belongs in truth to a thing (to the thing of nature, not to the sensible thing of practical life, the thing "as it appears sensibly") can be determined with objective validity and confirmed or corrected in constantly new experiences. On

---

9. Husserl emphasizes that what he is calling "phenomenology" is neither psychology nor cognitive science (both of which, in his view, are fundamentally naturalistic in a way that the phenomenological study of consciousness is not).

1. That is, the experiential—considered independently of anything that might be supposed to "underlie" or "cause" it, or "explain" it by way of natural-scientific laws and principles.

the other hand, something psychical, a "phenomenon," comes and goes; it retains no enduring, identical being that would be objectively determinable as such in the sense of natural science, e.g., as objectively divisible into components, "analysable" in the proper sense.

* * *

Now, to what extent is something like rational investigation and valid statement possible in this sphere? To what extent, too, are only such statements possible which we have just now given as most crude descriptions (passing over in silence entire dimensions)? It goes without saying that research will be meaningful here precisely when it directs itself purely to the sense of the experiences, which are given as experiences of the "psychical," and when thereby it accepts and tries to determine the "psychical" exactly as it demands, as it were, to be accepted and determined, when it is seen—above all where one admits no absurd naturalizings.[2] One must, it was said, take phenomena as they give themselves, i.e., as this flowing "having consciousness," intending, appearing, as this foreground and background "having consciousness," a "having consciousness" as present or pre-present, as imagined or symbolic or copied, as intuitive or represented emptily, etc. Thus, too, we must take phenomena as they turn this way or that, transforming themselves, according as the point of view or mode of attention changes in one way or another. All that bears the title "consciousness-of" and that "has" a "meaning," "intends" something "objective," which latter—whether from one standpoint or other it is to be called "fiction" or "reality"—permits being described as something "immanently objective," "intended as such," and intended in one or another mode of intending.

That one can here investigate and make statements, and do so on the basis of evidence, adapting oneself to the sense of this sphere of "experience," is absolutely evident. Admittedly, it is fidelity to the demands indicated above that constitutes the difficulty. On the single-mindedness and purity of the "phenomenological" attitude depends entirely the consistency or absurdity of the investigations that are here to be carried out. We do not easily overcome the inborn habit of living and thinking according to the naturalistic attitude, and thus of naturalistically adulterating the psychical. Furthermore, overcoming this habit depends to a great extent on the insight that in fact a "purely immanent" investigation of the psychical (using the term in its widest sense, which means the phenomenal as such) is possible, the kind of research that has just been generally characterized and that stands in contrast to any psychophysical investigation of the same, the latter being a kind of investigation we have not yet taken into consideration and which, of course, has its justification.

If the immanently psychical is not nature in itself but the respondent of nature, what are we seeking for in it as its "being"? If it is not determinable in "objective" identity as the substantial unity of real properties that must be grasped over and over again and be determined and confirmed in accordance with science and experience, if it is not to be withdrawn from the eternal flux, if it is incapable of becoming the object of an intersubjective evaluation—then what is there in it that we can seize upon, determine, and fix as an objective unity? This, however, is understood as meaning that we remain in the pure

---

2. That is, "naturalistic" accounts that purport to "explain" the contents of our experience as they are experienced in terms of natural entities, processes, causes, and the like.

phenomenological sphere and leave out of account relationships to nature and to the body experienced as a thing. The answer, then, is that if phenomena have no nature, they still have an essence, which can be grasped and adequately determined in an immediate seeing.[3] All the statements that describe the phenomena in direct concepts do so, to the degree that they are valid, by means of concepts of essence, that is, by conceptual significations of words that must permit of being redeemed in an essential intuition.[4]

* * * That the "essences" grasped in essential intuition permit, at least to a very great extent, of being fixed in definitive concepts and thereby afford possibilities of definitive and in their own way absolutely valid objective statements, is evident to anyone free of prejudice. The ultimate differences of color, its finest nuances, may defy fixation, but "color" as distinguished from "sound" provides a sure difference, than which there is in the world no surer. And such absolutely distinguishable—better, fixable—essences are not only those whose very "content" is of the senses, appearances ("apparitions," phantoms, and the like), but also the essences of whatever is psychical in the pregnant sense, of all ego "acts" or ego states, which correspond to well-known headings such as perception, imagination, recollection, judgment, emotion, will—with all their countless particular forms.

* * *

The whole thing, however, depends on one's seeing and making entirely one's own the truth that just as immediately as one can hear a sound, so one can intuit an "essence"—the essence "sound," the essence "appearance of thing," the essence "apparition," the essence "pictorial representation," the essence "judgment" or "will," etc.—and in the intuition one can make an essential judgment. On the other hand, however, it depends on one's protecting himself from the Humean confusion[5] and accordingly not confounding phenomenological intuition with "introspection," with interior experience—in short, with acts that posit not essences but individual details corresponding to them.

Pure phenomenology as science [*Wissenschaft*], so long as it is pure and makes no use of the existential positing of nature, can only be essence investigation, and not at all an investigation of being-there;[6] all "introspection" and every judgment based on such "experience" falls outside its framework. The particular can in its immanence be posited only as this—this disappearing perception, recollection, etc.—and if need be, can be brought under the strict essential concepts resulting from essential analysis. For the individual is not essence, it is true, but it "has" an essence, which can be said of it with evident validity. To fix this essence as an individual, however, to give it a position in a "world" of individual being-there, is something that such a mere subsumption under essential concepts cannot accomplish. For phenomenology, the singular is eternally the *apeiron*.[7] Phenomenology can recognize with objective validity only essences and essential relations, and thereby it can accomplish—and decisively accomplish—whatever is necessary for a correct understanding of all empirical cognition and of all cognition whatsoever: the clarification of the "origin" of all formal-logical and natural-logical principles (and whatever other guiding "principles" there may be) and of all the problems involved in correlating "being" (being of nature, being of value, etc.) and consciousness, problems intimately connected with the aforementioned principles.

* * *

Every spiritual [*geistig*] formation—taking the term in its widest possible sense, which can include every kind of social unity, ultimately the unity of the individual itself and also every kind of cultural formation—has its intimate structure, its typology, its marvelous wealth of external and internal forms which in the stream of spirit [*Geist*]-life itself grow and transform themselves, and in the very manner of the transformation again cause to come forward differences in structure and type. In the visible outer world the structure and typology of organic development afford us exact analogies. Therein there are no enduring species and no construction of the same out of enduring organic elements. Whatever seems to be enduring is but a stream of development. If by interior intuition we enter vitally into the unity of spirit [*Geist*]-life, we can get a feeling for the motivations at play therein and consequently "understand" the essence and development of the spiritual [*geistig*] structure in question, in its dependence on a spiritually [*geistig*] motivated unity and development. In this manner everything historical becomes for us "understandable," "explicable," in the "being" peculiar to it, which is precisely "spiritual [*geistig*] being," a unity of interiorly self-questioning moments of a sense and at the same time a unity of intelligible structuration and development according to inner motivation. Thus in this manner also art, religion, morals, etc. can be intuitively investigated, and likewise the *Weltanschauung* that stands so close to them and at the same time is expressed in them.

* * *

Of course, we need history too. Not, it is true, as the historian does, in order to lose ourselves in the developmental relations in which the great philosophies have grown up, but in order to let the philosophies themselves, in accord with their spiritual [*geistig*] content, work on us as an inspiration. In fact, out of these historical philosophies there flows to us philosophical life—if we understand how to peer into them, to penetrate to the soul of their words and theories—philosophical life with all the wealth and strength of living motivations. But it is not through philosophies that we become philosophers. Remaining immersed in the historical, forcing oneself to work therein in historico-critical activity, and wanting to attain philosophical science by means of eclectic elaboration or anachronistic renaissance—all that leads to nothing but hopeless efforts. The impulse to research must proceed not from philosophies but from things and from the problems connected with them. Philosophy, however, is essentially a science [*Wissenschaft*] of true

---

7. Unlimited, boundless (Greek); that is, the indefinite.

beginnings, or origins, of *rizōmata pantōn*.[8] The science concerned with what is radical must from every point of view be radical itself in its procedure. Above all it must not rest until it has attained its own absolutely clear beginnings, i.e., its absolutely clear problems, the methods preindicated in the proper sense of these problems, and the most basic field of work wherein things are given with absolute clarity. But one must in no instance abandon one's radical lack of prejudice, prematurely identifying, so to speak, such "things" with empirical "facts." To do this is to stand like a blind man before ideas, which are, after all, to such a great extent absolutely given in immediate intuition. We are too subject to the prejudices that still come from the Renaissance. To one truly without prejudice it is immaterial whether a certainty comes to us from Kant or Thomas Aquinas, from Darwin or Aristotle, from Helmholtz or Paracelsus.[9] What is needed is not the insistence that one see with his own eyes; rather it is that he not explain away under the pressure of prejudice what has been seen. Because in the most impressive of the modern sciences, the mathematico-physical, that which is exteriorly the largest part of their work, results from indirect methods, we are only too inclined to overestimate indirect methods and to misunderstand the value of direct comprehensions. However, to the extent that philosophy goes back to ultimate origins, it belongs precisely to its very essence that its scientific [*wissenschaftlich*] work move in spheres of direct intuition. Thus the greatest step our age has to make is to recognize that with the philosophical intuition in the correct sense, the phenomenological grasp of essences, a limitless field of work opens out, a science [*Wissenschaft*] that without all indirectly symbolical and mathematical methods, without the apparatus of premises and conclusions, still attains a plenitude of the most rigorous and, for all further philosophy, decisive cognitions.

SOURCE: From Edmund Husserl, "Philosophy as Rigorous Science," in *Phenomenology and the Crisis of Philosophy*, trans. Quentin Lauer (New York: Harper and Row, 1965), pp. 71–78, 87–91, 105–11, 115–16, 122–23, 146–47. Except where otherwise indicated, German words in brackets are the terminology used in the German original, inserted by the editor in addition to their renderings in the translation. Originally published in 1911 as "*Philosophie als strenge Wissenschaft*." The term *Wissenschaft* has a long tradition of use to mean "cognitive inquiry" or "cognitive discipline" (where "discipline" is understood as methodologically self-conscious systematic inquiry of some sort). So understood, it encompasses not only the natural sciences and (more recently) the social and behavioral sciences but also cognitive disciplines of other sorts, with other methodologies and their own forms of "rigor" in inquiry, such as mathematics, linguistics, history, and the various branches of philosophy (which HEGEL referred to as the philosophical *Wissenschaften*). For some, philosophy is and should be something other than a cognitive discipline that is as rigorous and systematic in its own way (or ways) as any other in the pursuit of knowledge of its proper objects of inquiry; but for Husserl that is precisely what philosophy can and should be—more truly than it ever has been before. The most apt translation of this essay's title might therefore be "Philosophy as Rigorous Cognitive Inquiry." The term *Wissenschaft* throughout this essay (and in Husserl's other writings) should always be so understood, in no way implying that philosophy for Husserl ought to model itself on the natural

8. Roots of all things (Greek). "Radical" is derived from the Latin *radix*, "root."
9. A mix of scientists and philosophers: Aquinas (1224/25–1274), Italian theologian and Scholastic philosopher; Charles Darwin (1809–1882), English naturalist; Aristotle (385–322 B.C.E.), Greek

philosopher; Hermann von Helmholtz (1821–1894), German scientist and philosopher; and Paracelsus (Philippus Aureolus Theophrastus Bombastus von Hohenheim, 1493–1541), German-Swiss physician and alchemist.

sciences. That is an idea he emphatically rejects and seeks to counter, as one of the great mistakes endangering the very essence and mission of philosophy—the other being philosophy's abandonment of the aspiration and determination to be a "rigorous *Wissenschaft*" at all.

From Ideas: General Introduction to Pure Phenomenology

From *Introduction*

Pure Phenomenology, to which we are here seeking the way, whose unique position in regard to all other sciences [*Wissenschaften*][1] we wish to make clear, and to set forth as the most fundamental region of philosophy, is an essentially new science [*Wissenschaft*], which in virtue of its own governing peculiarity lies far removed from our ordinary thinking, and has not until our own day therefore shown an impulse to develop. It calls itself a science of "phenomena." Other sciences, long known to us, also treat of phenomena. Thus one hears psychology referred to as a science of psychical, and natural science as a science of physical "appearances" or phenomena. So in history we hear speak occasionally of historical, and in the cultural sciences [*Wissenschaften*] of cultural phenomena, and similarly for all sciences that deal with realities. Now differently as the word "phenomenon" may be used in such contexts, and diverse as may be the meanings which it bears, it is certain that phenomenology also deals with all these "phenomena" and in all their meanings, but from a quite different point of view, the effect of which is to modify in a determinate way all the meanings which the term bears in the old-established sciences. Only as thus modified do these meanings enter the phenomenological sphere. To understand these modifications, or, to speak more accurately, to reach the phenomenological standpoint, and through reflexion[2] to fix its distinctive character, and that also of the natural viewpoints, in a scientific [*wissenschaftlich*] way, this is the first and by no means easy task which we must carry out in full, if we would gain the ground of phenomenology and grasp its distinctive nature scientifically.

In the last decade there has been much talk of phenomenology in German philosophy and psychology. In presumed agreement with the *Logical Studies*,[3] phenomenology is conceived as a sub-domain of empirical psychology,[4] as a region containing "immanent" descriptions of psychical events (*Erlebnisse*), which—such is their understanding of this immanence—remains strictly within the framework in inner *experience* (*Erfahrung*). My protest against this interpretation[5] has apparently been of small use, and the accompanying elucidations, which sharply delineate some at least of the main points of the difference, have not been understood or have been heedlessly set aside. Thence also the completely empty replies—empty because the plain *meaning* of my

1. On the term *Wissenschaft*, often translated "science," see the source note to "Philosophy as Rigorous Science [*Wissenschaft*]," above.
2. That is, "reflection." For Husserl this is a technical term, used to refer specifically to the kind of philosophical thinking in which he engages in what follows.
3. E. Husserl, *Logische Untersuchungen*, 2 vols.,

1900 and 1901. Republished (3rd ed.) in three vols. 1922. The references in this translation are to the three vols. of this third edition [translator's note].
4. Husserl's point here is that phenomenology is *wrongly* so conceived, and that the presumption of agreement is false or mistaken.
5. In "Philosophy as Rigorous Science [*Wissenschaft*]" (see above), a reference supplied by Husserl.

statement was missed—to my criticism of the psychological method, a criticism which in no way denied the value of modern psychology, and in no sense depreciated the experimental work carried out by men of distinction, but exposed certain, in the literal sense of the term, radical defects of method on the removal of which, in my opinion, the raising of psychology to a higher scientific [*wissenschaftlich*] level and an extraordinary extension of its field of work must depend. There will still be occasion to deal briefly with the superfluous defences of psychology against my presumed "attacks." I mention this dispute here that I may state from the outset most emphatically, in face of prevailing and far-spreading misinterpretations, *that the pure phenomenology*, to which in what follows we would prepare a way of approach, the same which emerged for the first time in the *Logical Studies*, and has revealed an ever richer and deeper meaning to me as my thought has dwelt on it through the last ten years, *is not psychology*, and that it is not accidental delimitations and considerations of terminology, but grounds *of principle*, which forbid its being counted as psychology. Great as is the importance which phenomenology must claim to possess for psychology in the matter of method, whatever the essential "bases" it provides for it, it is itself (if only as Science [*Wissenschaft*] of ideas) as little identifiable with psychology as is geometry with natural science. Indeed, the difference is more marked, and reaches deeper than this comparison would itself suggest. It makes no difference that phenomenology has to do with "consciousness," with all types of experience, with acts and their correlates; though in view of the prevailing habits of thought, it demands no small effort to see this. That we should set aside all previous habits of thought, see through and break down the mental barriers which these habits have set along the horizons of our thinking, and in full intellectual freedom proceed to lay hold on those genuine philosophical problems still awaiting completely fresh formulation which the liberated horizons on all sides disclose to us—these are hard demands. Yet nothing less is required. What makes the appropriation of the essential nature of phenomenology, the understanding of the peculiar meaning of its form of inquiry, and its relation to all other sciences (to psychology in particular) so extraordinarily difficult, is that in addition to all other adjustments *a new way of looking at things* is necessary, one that contrasts *at every point* with the natural attitude of experience and thought. To move freely along this new way without ever reverting to the old viewpoints, to learn to see what stands before our eyes, to distinguish, to describe, calls, moreover, for exacting and laborious studies.

It will be the chief task of this *First* Book to search out ways in which the excessive difficulties of penetrating into this new world can be overcome as it were bit by bit. We shall start from the standpoint of everyday life, from the world as it confronts us, from consciousness as it presents itself in psychological experience, and shall lay bare the presuppositions essential to this viewpoint. We shall then develop a method of "phenomenological Reductions,"[6] according to which we may set aside the limitations to knowledge essentially involved in every nature-directed form of investigation, deflecting the restricted line of vision proper to it, until we have eventually before us the

6. A very important concept for Husserl: it refers to a way of redescribing the content and character of an experience that restricts attention exclusively to what is immanent in the experience, purified of all interpretive or theoretical ideas and assumptions about the extra-experiential status of its contents and character.

free outlook upon "transcendentally" purified phenomena, and therewith the field of phenomenology in our own special sense of that term.

Let us trace the lines of this anticipatory sketch somewhat more firmly, and in conformity with the bias of the times, as also with inner affinities of the subject-matter, connect them with psychology.

Psychology is a science [*Wissenschaft*] of experience. Keeping to the customary sense of the word experience (*Erfahrung*), this has a twofold meaning:

1. Psychology is a science of *facts* (*Tatsachen*), of "matters of fact"—in Hume's sense of the word.[7]

2. Psychology is a science of *realities* (*Realitäten*). The "phenomena" which it handles as psychological "phenomenology" are real events which as such, in so far as they have real existence (*Dasein*), take their place with the real Subjects to which they belong in the one spatio-temporal world, the *omnitudo realitatis*.[8]

As over against this psychological "phenomenology," *pure or transcendental phenomenology will be established not as a science of facts, but as a science* [*Wissenschaft*] *of essential Being* (as "*eidetic*"[9] science); a science [*Wissenschaft*] which aims exclusively at establishing "knowledge of essences" (*Wesenserkenntnisse*) and *absolutely no "facts."* The corresponding Reduction which leads from the psychological phenomenon to the pure "essence," or, in respect of the judging thought, from factual ("empirical") to "essential" universality, is the *eidetic Reduction.*

In the second place, the phenomena of transcendental phenomenology will be characterized as non-real (*irreal*). Other reductions, the specifically transcendental, "purify" the psychological phenomena from that which lends them reality, and therewith a setting in the real "world." Our phenomenology should be a theory of essential Being, dealing not with real, but with transcendentally reduced phenomena.

What this all affirms when more closely considered will first become plain in the developments that follow. In an anticipatory way it gives an outline sketch of the preliminary series of studies. I consider it necessary at this point to add only one remark: It will surprise the reader that in the two foregoing passages in italics, in place of the single division of sciences [*Wissenschaften*] into realistic and idealistic (or into empirical and *a priori*) which is universally adopted, two divisions are preferred, corresponding to the two pairs of opposites: Fact and Essence, Real and not-Real. The distinction conveyed by this twofold opposition replacing that between real and ideal will find a thoroughgoing justification in the later course of our inquiries (as a matter of fact, in the Second Book). It will be shown that the concept of reality requires a fundamental limitation in virtue of which a difference must be set up between real Being and individual (purely temporal) Being. The transition to the pure Essence provides on the one side a knowledge of the essential nature of the Real, on the other, in respect of the domain left over, knowledge of the essential nature of the non-real (*irreal*). It will transpire further that all tran-

---

7. The Scottish philosopher David Hume (1711–1776) divided all objects of human reason into "relations of ideas" and "matters of fact."
8. The allness of reality (Latin); that is, reality in the most comprehensive sense.
9. A technical term for Husserl, meaning "essential" or "pertaining to essences as such." "Eidetic" comes from the Greek word *eidos* (plural, *eidoi*), which Plato (ca. 427–ca. 347 B.C.E.) used to designate the "Forms" or "Ideas" that are fundamental, timeless universals, in whose reality objects in the natural world (their less than perfect copies) participate or share.

scendentally purified "experiences" are non-realities, and excluded from every connexion within the "real world." These same non-realities are studied by phenomenology, but not as singular particularities (*Einzelheiten*), rather in their "essential being." The extent, however, to which transcendental phenomena as singular *facta*[1] are at all available for study, and the question of the relation which a factual study of such a kind may bear to the idea of a Metaphysic, can be considered only in the concluding series of investigations.

In the *first* Book we shall treat not only of the general theory of the phenomenological Reductions which make the transcendentally purified consciousness with its essential correlates perceptible (*sichtlich*) and accessible; we shall also seek to win definite ideas of the most general structures of this pure consciousness, and through their agency of the most general groups of problems, directions of study and methods which pertain to the new science [*Wissenschaft*].

In the *second* Book we make a thorough inquiry into certain specially important sets of problems the systematic formulation of which and solution under types is the precondition for bringing into real clearness the difficult relations of phenomenology to the physical sciences of nature, to psychology, and to the sciences of the mind [*Geisteswissenschaften*], and on another side also to the *a priori* sciences as a collective whole. The phenomenological sketches here traced in outline offer also the welcome means of considerably deepening the understanding of phenomenology reached in the *first* Book, and of winning from its immense circle of problems a far richer content of knowledge.

A *third* and concluding Book is dedicated to the Idea of Philosophy. The insight will be awakened that genuine philosophy, the idea of which is to realize the idea of Absolute Knowledge, has its roots in pure phenomenology, and this in so earnest a sense that the systematically rigorous grounding and development of this first of all philosophies remains the perpetual precondition of all metaphysics and other philosophy "which would aspire to be a *science* [*Wissenschaft*]."[2]

* * *

From *CHAPTER* 3

The Thesis[3] *of the Natural Standpoint and Its Suspension*

FROM 27. THE WORLD [*WELT*] OF THE NATURAL STANDPOINT: I AND MY WORLD ABOUT ME [*UMWELT*][4]

Our first outlook upon life is that of natural human beings, imaging, judging, feeling, willing, "*from the natural standpoint.*" Let us make clear to ourselves what this means in the form of simple meditations which we can best carry on in the first person.

I am aware of a world, spread out in space endlessly, and in time becoming and become, without end. I am aware of it, that means, first of all, I discover

1. Facts (Latin).
2. The hostility Husserl expresses toward HEGEL in "Philosophy as Rigorous Science [*Wissenschaft*]" thus is directed not at Hegel's "Idea of Philosophy," which Husserl here clearly and explicitly embraces,

but rather at Hegel's way of attempting to realize it.
3. The German word Husserl uses; here meaning "basic posit," underlying idea.
4. *Welt*: world. *Umwelt*: surrounding world, environment.

it immediately, intuitively, I experience it. Through sight, touch, hearing, etc., in the different ways of sensory perception, corporeal things somehow spatially distributed are *for me simply there*, in verbal or figurative sense "present," whether or not I pay them special attention by busying myself with them, considering, thinking, feeling, willing. Animal beings also, perhaps men, are immediately there for me; I look up, I see them, I hear them coming towards me, I grasp them by the hand; speaking with them, I understand immediately what they are sensing and thinking, the feelings that stir them, what they wish or will. They too are present as realities in my field of intuition, even when I pay them no attention. But it is not necessary that they and other objects likewise should be present precisely in my *field of perception*. For me real objects are there, definite, more or less familiar, agreeing with what is actually perceived without being themselves perceived or even intuitively present. I can let my attention wander from the writing-table I have just seen and observed, through the unseen portions of the room behind my back to the verandah, into the garden, to the children in the summer-house, and so forth, to all the objects concerning which I precisely "know" that they are there and yonder in my immediate co-perceived surroundings—a knowledge which has nothing of conceptual thinking in it, and first changes into clear intuiting with the bestowing of attention, and even then only partially and for the most part very imperfectly.

* * *

In this way, when consciously awake, I find myself at all times, and without my ever being able to change this, set in relation to a world which, through its constant changes, remains one and ever the same. It is continually "present" for me, and I myself am a member of it. Therefore this world is not there for me as a mere *world of facts and affairs*, but, with the same immediacy, as a *world of values*, a *world of goods*, a *practical world*. Without further effort on my part I find the things before me furnished not only with the qualities that befit their positive nature, but with value-characters such as beautiful or ugly, agreeable or disagreeable, pleasant or unpleasant, and so forth. Things in their immediacy stand there as objects to be used, the "table" with its "books," the "glass to drink from," the "vase," the "piano," and so forth. These values and practicalities, they too belong to *the constitution of the "actually present" objects as such*, irrespective of my turning or not turning to consider them or indeed any other objects. The same considerations apply of course just as well to the men and beasts in my surroundings as to "mere things." They are my "friends" or my "foes," my "servants" or "superiors," "strangers" or "relatives," and so forth.

* * *

FROM 31. RADICAL ALTERATION OF THE NATURAL THESIS. "DISCONNEXION," "BRACKETING"

Instead now of remaining at this standpoint, we propose to alter it radically. Our aim must be to convince ourselves of the possibility of this alteration on grounds of principle.

The General Thesis according to which the real world about me is at all times known not merely in a general way as something apprehended, but as a fact-world *that has its being out there*, does *not* consist of course *in an act proper*, in an articulated judgment *about existence*. It is and remains something all the time the standpoint is adopted, that is, it endures persistently during the whole course of our life of natural endeavour. What has been at any time perceived clearly, or obscurely made present, in short everything out of the world of nature through experience and prior to any thinking, bears in its totality and in all its articulated sections the character "present" "out there," a character which can function essentially as the ground of support for an explicit (predicative) existential judgment which is in agreement with the character it is grounded upon. If we express that same judgment, we know quite well that in so doing we have simply put into the form of a statement and grasped as a predication what already lay somehow in the original experience, or lay there as the character of something "present to one's hand [*Vorhanden*][5]."

We can treat the potential and unexpressed thesis exactly as we do the thesis of the explicit judgment. A procedure of this sort, *possible at any time*, is, for instance, *the attempt to doubt everything* which Descartes,[6] with an entirely different end in view, with the purpose of setting up an absolutely indubitable sphere of Being, undertook to carry through. We link on here, but add directly and emphatically that this attempt to doubt everything should serve us *only as a device of method*, helping us to stress certain points which by its means, as though secluded in its essence, must be brought clearly to light.

The attempt to doubt everything has its place in the realm of our *perfect freedom*. We can *attempt to doubt* anything and everything, however convinced we may be concerning what we doubt, even though the evidence which seals our assurance is completely adequate.

Let us consider what is essentially involved in an act of this kind. He who attempts to doubt is attempting to doubt "Being" of some form or other, or it may be Being expanded into such predicative forms as "It is," "It is this or thus," and the like. The attempt does not affect the form of Being itself. He who doubts, for instance, whether an object, whose Being he does not doubt, is constituted in such and such a way doubts *the way it is constituted*. We can obviously transfer this way of speaking from the doubting to the *attempt* at doubting. It is clear that we cannot doubt the Being of anything, and in the same act of consciousness (under the unifying form of simultaneity) bring what is substantive to this Being under the terms of the Natural Thesis, and so confer upon it the character of "being actually there" (*vorhanden*). Or to put the same in another way: we cannot at once doubt and hold for certain one and the same quality of Being. It is likewise clear that the *attempt* to doubt any object of awareness in respect of it *being actually there necessarily conditions a certain suspension* (*Aufhebung*) *of the thesis*; and it is precisely this that interests us. It is not a transformation of the thesis into its antithesis, of positive into negative; it is also not a transformation into presumption, suggestion, indecision, doubt (in one or another sense of the word); such shifting indeed is not at our free pleasure. *Rather is it something quite unique. We do not abandon the thesis we have adopted, we make no change in our conviction*, which remains in itself what it is so long as we do not introduce new motives of judgment, which we precisely refrain from doing. And yet the thesis undergoes a modification—whilst remaining in itself what it is, *we set it as it*

---

5. That is: simply there, at hand.
6. René Descartes (1596–1650), French mathematician and philosopher who used a strategy of systematic doubt in an attempt to attain certain knowledge.

were "*out of action,*" we "*disconnect it,*" "*bracket it.*" It still remains there like the bracketed in the bracket, like the disconnected outside the connexional system. We can also say: The thesis is experience as lived (*Erlebnis*), *but we make "no use" of it,* and by that, of course, we do not indicate privation (as when we say of the ignorant that he makes no use of a certain thesis); in this case rather, as with all parallel expressions, we are dealing with indicators that point to a definite but *unique form of consciousness,* which clamps on to the original simple thesis (whether it actually or even predicatively *posits* existence or not), and transvalues it in a quite peculiar way. *This transvaluing is a concern of our full freedom, and is opposed to all cognitive attitudes* that would set themselves up as co-ordinate with the *thesis,* and yet within the unity of "simultaneity" remain incompatible with it, as indeed it is in general with all attitudes whatsoever in the strict sense of the word.

In *the attempt to doubt* applied to a thesis which, as we presuppose, is certain and tenaciously held, the "disconnexion" takes place in and with a modification of the antithesis, namely with the "*supposition*" (*Ansetzung*) of *Non-Being,* which is thus the partial basis of the attempt to doubt. With Descartes this is so markedly the case that one can say that his universal attempt at doubt is just an attempt at universal denial. We disregard this possibility here, we are not interested in every analytical component of the attempt to doubt, nor therefore in its exact and completely sufficing analysis. *We extract only the phenomenon of "bracketing" or "disconnection,"* which is obviously not limited to that of the attempt to doubt, although it can be detached from it with special ease, but can appear *in other contexts also,* and with no less ease *independently.* In relation to every thesis and wholly uncoerced we can use this *peculiar ἐποχή*[7] (*epokhe*—abstention), *a certain refraining from judgment which is compatible with the unshaken and unshakable because self-evidencing conviction of Truth.* The thesis is "put out of action," bracketed, it passes off into the modified status of a "bracketed thesis," and the judgment *simpliciter*[8] into "*bracketed judgment.*"

* * *

32. The Phenomenological ἐποχή

We can now let the universal ἐποχή, (*epokhe*—abstention) in the sharply defined and novel sense we have given to it step into the place of the Cartesian attempt at universal doubt. But on good grounds we *limit* the universality of this ἐποχή. For were it as inclusive as it is in general capable of being, then since every thesis and every judgment can be modified freely to any extent, and every objectivity that we can judge or criticize can be bracketed, no field would be left over for unmodified judgments, to say nothing of a science. But our design is just to discover a new scientific [*wissenschaftlich*] domain, such as might be won precisely *through the method of bracketing,* though only through a definitely limited form of it.

The limiting consideration can be indicated in a word.

We put out of action the general thesis which belongs to the essence of the natural standpoint, we place in brackets whatever it includes respecting

---

7. Suspension of judgment (a technical term in Greek philosophy).

8. Simply (Latin); that is, a judgment without qualification.

the nature of Being: *this entire natural world therefore* which is continually "there for us," "present to our hand [*vorhanden*]," and will ever remain there, is a "fact-world [*Wirklichkeit*]"[9] of which we continue to be conscious, even though it pleases us to put it in brackets.

If I do this, as I am fully free to do, I do *not* then *deny* this "world," as though I were a sophist, *I do not doubt that it is there* as though I were a sceptic; but I use the "phenomenological" ἐποχή, which *completely bars me from using any judgment that concerns spatio-temporal existence (Dasein)*.

Thus *all sciences which relate to this natural world*, though they stand [ever] so firm[1] to me, though they fill me with wondering admiration, though I am far from any thought of objecting to them in the least degree, *I disconnect them all, I make absolutely no use of their standards, I do not appropriate a single one of the propositions that enter into their systems, even though their evidential value is perfect, I take none of them, no one of them serves me for a foundation*—so long, that is, as it is understood, in the way these sciences themselves understand it, as a truth *concerning the realities* of this world. *I may accept it only after I have placed it in the bracket.* That means: only in the modified consciousness of the judgment as it appears in disconnexion, and *not as it figures within the science as its proposition, a proposition which claims to be valid and whose validity I recognize and make use of.*

The ἐποχή here in question [is not to be confused][2] with that which positivism demands, and against which, as we were compelled to admit, it is itself an offender. We are not concerned at present with removing the preconceptions which trouble the pure positivity (*Sachlichkeit*) of research, with the constituting of a science "free from theory" and "free from metaphysics" by bringing all the grounding back to the immediate data, nor with the means of reaching such ends, concerning whose value there is indeed no question. What *we* demand lies along another line. The whole world as placed within the nature-setting and presented in experience as real, taken completely "free from all theory," just as it is in reality experienced, and made clearly manifest in and through the linkings of our experiences, has now no validity for us, it must be set in brackets, untested indeed but also uncontested. Similarly all theories and sciences, positivistic or otherwise, which relate to this world, however good they may be, succumb to the same fate.

From *Chapter 4. Consciousness and Natural Reality*

33. INTIMATION CONCERNING "PURE" OR "TRANSCENDENTIAL CONSCIOUSNESS" AS PHENOMENOLOGICAL RESIDUUM

We have learnt to understand the meaning of the phenomenological ἐποχή (*epokhe*—abstention), but we are still quite in the dark as to its serviceability.[3] In the first place it is not clear to what extent the limitation of the total field of the ἐποχή, as discussed in the previous pages, involves a real narrowing of its general scope. *For what can remain over when the whole world is bracketed, including ourselves and all our thinking (cogitare[4])?*

---

9. That is, actuality.
1. A correction to Gibson's translation, which reads "never so firm."
2. That is, "should not be confused" (a correction

to Gibson's translation, which reads "will not be confined").
3. That is, as to the point of it.
4. To think (Latin).

Since the reader already knows that the interest which governs these "Meditations" concerns a new eidetic science [*Wissenschaft*], he will indeed at first expect the world as fact to succumb to the disconnexion, but not *the world as Eidos*, nor any other sphere of Essential Being. The disconnecting of the world does not as a matter of fact mean the disconnecting of the number series, for instance, and the arithmetic relative to it.

However, we do not take this path, nor does our goal lie in its direction. That goal we could also refer to as *the winning of a new region of Being, the distinctive character of which has not yet been defined*, a region of *individual* Being, like every genuine region. We must leave the sequel to teach us what that more precisely means.

We proceed in the first instance by showing up simply and directly what we see; and since the Being to be thus shown up is neither more nor less than that which we refer to on essential grounds as "pure experiences (*Erlebnisse*)" "pure consciousness" with its pure "correlates of consciousness," and on the other side its "pure Ego," we observe that it is from *the Ego, the* consciousness, *the* experience as given to us from the natural standpoint, that we take our start.

I, the real human being, am a real object like others in the natural world. I carry out *cogitationes*,[5] "acts of consciousness" in both a narrower and a wider sense, and these acts, as belonging to this human subject, are events of the same natural world. And all my remaining experiences (*Erlebnisse*) likewise, out of whose changing stream the specific acts of the Ego shine forth in so distinctive a way, glide into one another, enter into combinations, and are being incessantly modified. Now in its *widest connotation* the expression "*consciousness*" (then indeed less suited for its purpose) includes *all* experiences (*Erlebnisse*), and entrenched in the natural standpoint as we are even in our scientific thinking, grounded there in habits that are most firmly established since they have never misled us, we take all these data of psychological reflexion as real world-events, as the experiences (*Erlebnisse*) of animal beings. So natural is it to us to see them only in this light that, though acquainted already with the possibility of a change of standpoint, and on the search for the new domain of objects, we fail to notice that it is from out these centres of experience (*Erlebnisse*) themselves that through the adoption of the new standpoint the new domain emerges.[6] Connected with this is the fact that instead of keeping our eyes turned towards these centres of experience, we turned them away and sought the new objects in the ontological realms of arithmetic, geometry, and the like, whereby indeed nothing truly new has [is] to be won.

Thus we fix our eyes steadily upon the sphere of Consciousness and study what it is that we find immanent in *it*. At first, without having yet carried out the phenomenological suspensions of the element of judgment, we subject this sphere of Consciousness in its essential nature to a systematic though in no sense exhaustive analysis. What we lack above all is a certain general insight into the essence of *consciousness in general*, and quite specially also of con-

---

5. Latin (singular, *cogitatio*): acts of the *cogito*—Descartes' "I think" (which Husserl uses very broadly, along the lines of "I experience," to mean and refer to something like "that which experiences" or, loosely speaking, "the experiencing mind").

6. Better translated as: "It is so natural for us to see them only in this way that, although we are already aware of the possibility of a change of standpoint, and even though we are seeking a new domain of objects, we fail to notice that it is from out of these centers of experience themselves that the new domain emerges, through the adoption of the new standpoint."

sciousness, so far as in and through its essential Being, the "natural" fact-world comes to be known. In these studies we go so far as is needed to furnish the full insight at which we have been aiming, to wit, *that Consciousness in itself has a being of its own which in its absolute uniqueness of nature*[7] *remains unaffected by the phenomenological disconnexion.* It therefore remains over as a *"phenomenological residuum,"* as a region of Being which is in principle unique, and can become in fact the field of a new science—the science [*Wissenschaft*] of Phenomenology.

Through this insight the "phenomenological" ἐποχή will for the first time deserve its name; to exercise it in full consciousness of its import will turn out to be the necessary operation which *renders "pure" consciousness accessible to us, and subsequently the whole phenomenological region.* And thus we shall be able to understand why this region and the new science [*Wissenschaft*] attached to it was fated to remain unknown. From the natural standpoint nothing can be seen except the natural world. So long as the possibility of the phenomenological standpoint was not grasped, and the method of relating the objectivities which emerge therewith to a primordial form of apprehension had not been devised, the phenomenological world must needs have remained unknown, and indeed barely divined at all.[8]

We would add yet the following to our terminology: Important motives which have their ground in epistemological requirements justify us in referring to "pure" consciousness, of which much is yet to be said, also as *transcendental consciousness,* and the operation through which it is acquired as *transcendental ἐποχή.*[9] On grounds of method this operation will split up into different steps of "disconnexion" or "bracketing," and thus our method will assume the character of a graded reduction. For this reason we propose to speak, and even preponderatingly,[1] of *phenomenological reductions* (though, in respect of their unity as a whole, we would speak in unitary form of *the* phenomenological reduction). From the epistemological viewpoint we would also speak of transcendental reductions. Moreover, these and *all* our terms must be understood exclusively in accordance with the sense which *our* presentations indicate for them, but not in any other one which history or the terminological habits of the reader may favour.

34. THE ESSENCE OF CONSCIOUSNESS AS THEME OF INQUIRY

We start with a series of observations within which we are not troubled with any phenomenological ἐποχή. We are directed to an "outer world," and, without forsaking the natural standpoint, reflect psychologically on our Ego and its experience (*Erleben*). We busy ourselves, precisely as we have done if we had never heard of the new viewpoint, with *the essential nature of "the consciousness of something,"* following, for instance, our consciousness of the existence of material things, living bodies and men, or that of technical and literary

7. That is, in the absolute uniqueness of its nature (in contrast with the natures of other sorts of being or reality).
8. That is, had to remain unknown, and indeed hardly even imagined.
9. The term "transcendental" here merely signifies that neither this consciousness nor the *epochē* in question is an object or content of consciousness—

that is, something that goes on or is encountered within experience. Husserl's use of the term draws on that of KANT, for whom it referred to the conditions of the possibility of experience and the ways in which the mind structures the contents of experience, rather than the contents of experience as such.
1. Preponderantly, predominantly.

works, and so forth. We adhere to our general principle that each individual event has its essence that can be grasped in its eiditic purity, and in this purity must belong to a field available to eidetic inquiry. In accordance herewith the universal fact of nature [*allgemeine naturliche Faktum*][2] conveyed by the words "I am," "I think," "I have a world over against me," and the like, has also its essential content, and it is on this exclusively that we now intend to concentrate. Thus we rehearse to ourselves by way of illustration certain conscious experiences chosen at random, and in their individuality just as they are in their natural setting as real facts of human life, and we make these present to ourselves through memory or in the free play of fancy. On the ground of illustrations such as these, which we assume to be presented with perfect clearness, we grasp and fix in adequate ideation the pure essences that interest us. The individual facts, the fact-character of the natural world in general, thereby escapes our theoretical scrutiny—as in all cases where our inquiry is purely eidetic.

We limit still further the theme of our inquiry. Its title ran: Consciousness, or more distinctly *Conscious experience (Erlebnis) in general*, to be taken in an extremely wide sense about whose exact definition we are fortunately not concerned. Exact definitions do not lie at the threshold of analysis of the kind we are here making, but are a later result involving great labour. As starting-point we take consciousness in a pregnant sense which suggests itself at once, most simply indicated through the Cartesian *cogito*, "I think." As is known Descartes understood this in a sense so wide as to include every case of "I perceive, I remember, I fancy, I judge, feel, desire, will," and all experiences of the Ego that in any way resemble the foregoing, in all the countless fluctuations of their special patterns. The Ego itself to which they are all related, spontaneous, in receptive or any other "attitude," and indeed the Ego in any and every sense, we leave at first out of consideration. We shall be concerned with it later, and fundamentally. For the present there is sufficient other material to serve as support for our analysis and grasp of the essential. And we shall find ourselves forthwith referred thereby to enveloping connexions of experience which compel us to widen our conception of a conscious experience beyond this circle of specific *cogitationes*.[3]

We shall consider conscious experiences *in the concrete fullness and entirety* with which they figure in their concrete context—the *stream of experience*—and to which they are closely attached through their own proper essence. It then becomes evident that every experience in the stream which our reflexion can lay hold on has *its own essence open to intuition*, a "content" which can be considered in its *singularity in and for itself*. We shall be concerned to grasp this individual content of the *cogitatio* in its *pure* singularity, and to describe it in its general features, excluding everything which is not to be found in the *cogitatio* as it is in itself. We must likewise describe the *unity of consciousness* which is demanded *by the intrinsic nature of the cogitationes*, and so necessarily demanded that they could not be without this unity.

---

2. Literally "general natural fact"—that is, the general (from the natural standpoint) "fact of the matter" we are talking about when we say such

things as "I am."
3. That is, "cogitations," instances of the various kinds of conscious events mentioned.

35. THE COGITO AS "ACT." THE MODAL FORM OF MARGINAL ACTUALITY

Let us start with an example. In front of me, in the dim light, lies this white paper. I see it, touch it. This perceptual seeing and touching of the paper as the full concrete experience *of* the paper that lies here as given in truth precisely with this relative lack of clearness, with this imperfect definition, appearing to me from this particular angle—is a *cogitatio*, a conscious experience. The paper itself with its objective qualities, its extension in space, its objective position in regard to that spatial thing I call my body, is not *cogitatio*, but *cogitatum*,[4] not perceptual experience, but something perceived. Now that which is perceived can itself very well be a conscious experience; but it is evident that an object such as a material thing, this paper, for instance, as given in perceptual experience, is in principle other than an experience, a being of a completely different kind.

Before pursuing this point farther, let us amplify the illustration. In perception properly so-called, as an explicit awareness (*Gewahren*), I am turned towards the object, to the paper, for instance, I apprehend it as being this here and now. The apprehension is a singling out, every perceived object having a background in experience. Around and about the paper lie books, pencils, inkwell, and so forth, and these in a certain sense are also "perceived," perceptually there, in the "field of intuition";[5] but whilst I was turned towards the paper there was no turning in their direction, nor any apprehending of them, not even in a secondary sense. They appeared and yet were not singled out, were not posited on their own account. Every perception of a thing has such a zone of *background intuitions* (or background awarenesses, if "intuiting" already includes the state of being turned towards), and this also is a *"conscious experience,"* or more briefly a "consciousness of" all indeed that in point of fact lies in the co-perceived objective "background." We are not talking here of course of that which is to be found as an "objective" element in the objective space to which the background in question may belong, of all the things and thing-like events which a valid and progressive experience may establish there. What we say applies exclusively to that zone of consciousness which belongs to the model essence of a perception as "being turned towards an object," and further to that which belongs to the proper essence of this zone itself. But it is here implied that certain modifications of the original experience are possible, which we refer to as a free turning of the "look"—not precisely nor merely of the physical but of the *"mental [geistig] look"*—from the paper at first *descried*[6] to objects which had already appeared before of which we had been "implicitly" aware, and whereof *subsequent* to the directing of one's look thither we are explicitly aware, perceiving them "attentively," or "noticing them near by."

We are aware of things not only in perception, but also consciously in recollections, in representations similar to recollections, and also in the free play of fancy; and this in "clear intuition" it may be, or without noticeable perceptibility after the manner of "dim" presentations; they float past us in different "characterizations" as real, possible, fancied, and so forth. All that we have stated concerning perceptual experiences holds good, obviously, of these other experiences, essentially different as they are. We shall not think of confusing

---

4. Something thought (Latin); that is, something experienced.

5. That is, field of awareness (*Anschauungsfeld*).
6. Caught sight of.

the *objects of which we are aware* under these forms of consciousness (the fancy-shaped nymphs, for instance) with the conscious experiences themselves which are a consciousness *of* them.[7] Then, again, we know that it is the essence of all such experiences—taking the same, as always, in their concrete fullness—to show that remarkable modification which transfers consciousness in the *mode of actual orientation* to consciousness in the *mode of non-actuality* and conversely. At the one time the experience is, so to speak *"explicitly"* aware of its objective content, at the other implicitly and merely *potentially*. The objective factor, whether in perception, memory, or fancy, may already be appearing to us, but *our mental gaze is not yet "directed" towards it*, not even in a secondary sense, to say nothing of being "busied" with it in some special way.

Similar remarks apply to all and any of the *cogitationes* in the sense illustrated by Descartes' use of the term, to all experiences of thought, feeling and will, except that, as will be emphasized (in the next paragraph), the "directedness towards," the "being turned towards," which is the distinctive mark of focal actuality, does not coincide, as in the favourite because simplest examples of sensory presentations, with singling out and noting the objects we are aware of. It is also obviously true of all such experiences that the focal is girt about with a "zone" of the marginal; *the stream of experience can never consist wholly of focal actualities*. These indeed determine, in a very general sense which must be extended beyond the circle of our illustrations, and through the contrast with marginal actualities already drawn, the *pregnant* meaning of the expression "cogito," "I have *consciousness* of something," "I perform an *act* of consciousness." In order to keep this well-established concept purely separate, we propose to reserve for it exclusively the Cartesian expressions *cogito* and *cogitationes*, unless through some addition, such as "marginal" or the like, we expressly indicate the modified use we are making of the term.

We can define a *"wakeful" Ego* as one that within its stream of experience is continually conscious in the specific form of the *cogito;* which, of course, does not mean that it can and does bring these experiences persistently or in general to predicative expression. Ego-subjects include animals.[8] But, according to what we have said above, it belongs to the essence of the stream of experience of a wakeful Self that the continuously prolonged chain of *cogitationes* is constantly enveloped in a medium of dormant actuality (*Inaktualität*), which is ever prepared to pass off into the wakeful mode (*Aktualität*), as conversely the wakeful into the dormant.

36. INTENTIONAL EXPERIENCE. EXPERIENCE IN GENERAL

However drastic the change which the experiences of a wakeful Consciousness undergo in their transition into the dormant state, the experiences as modified share the essential nature of the original experiences in an important respect. It belongs as a general feature to the essence of every actual *cogito* to be a consciousness *of* something. But according to what we have already said, the *modified cogitatio is likewise and in its own way Consciousness,*

---

7. That is, one must not confuse something that can be the *object of* a conscious experience or awareness with the experiencing or *awareness* of such an object.
8. For Husserl, the possibility of being "ego-subjects" (i.e., the subjects of conscious experiences) is not restricted to human beings, because he does not think that conscious experiences necessarily involve language. It does not follow, however, that animals (lacking language) are capable of thought, or reasoning, or doing phenomenology.

and *of the same* something as with the corresponding unmodified consciousness. Thus the essential property of Consciousness in its general form is preserved in the modification. All experiences which have these essential properties in common are also called *"internal experiences"* (acts in the *very wide sense* of the *Logical Studies*[9]); in so far as they are a consciousness of something they are said to be *"intentionally related"* to this something.

We must, however, be quite clear on this point that *there is no question here of a relation between a psychological event—called experience (Erlebnis)—and some other real existent (Dasein)—called Object*—or of a *psychological connexion* obtaining between the one and the other *in objective reality*. On the contrary, we are concerned with experiences in their essential purity, with *pure essences*, and with that which is *involved in* the essence *"a priori,"* in *unconditioned necessity.*

That an experience is the consciousness of something: a fiction, for instance, the fiction of this or that centaur; a perception, the perception of its "real" object; a judgment, the judgment concerning it subject-matter, and so forth, this does not relate to the experimental fact as lived within the world, more specifically within some given psychological context, but to the pure essence grasped ideationally as pure idea. In the very essence of an experience lies determined not only *that*, but also *whereof* it is a consciousness, and in what determinate or indeterminate sense it is this. So too in the essence of consciousness as dormant lies included the variety of wakeful *cogitationes*, into which it can be differentiated through the modification we have already referred to as "the noticing of what was previously unnoticed."

Under *experiences* in the *widest sense* we understand whatever is to be found in the stream of experience, not only therefore intentional experiences, *cogitationes* actual and potential taken in their full concreteness, but all the real (*reellen*) phases to be found in this stream and in its concrete sections.

For it is easily seen that *not every real phase* of the concrete unity of an intentional experience has itself the *basic character of intentionality*, the property of being a "consciousness of something." This is the case, for instance, with all sensory data, which play so great a part in the perceptive intuitions of things. In the experience of the perception of this white paper, more closely in those components of it related to the paper's quality of whiteness, we discover through properly directed noticing the sensory datum "white." This "whiteness" is something that belongs inseparably to the essence of the concrete perception, as a *real (reelles)* concrete constitutive portion of it. As the content which presents the whiteness of the paper as it appears to us it is the *bearer of* an intentionality, but not itself a consciousness of something. The same holds good of other data of experience, of the so-called *sensory feelings*, for instance. We shall be speaking of these at greater length in a later context.

* * *

39. CONSCIOUSNESS AND NATURAL REALITY.
THE VIEW OF THE "MAN IN THE STREET ['*NAIVEN' MENSCHEN*]"[1]

All the essential characteristics of experience and consciousness which we have reached are for us necessary steps towards the attainment of the end

---

9. Husserl's earlier work *Logische Untersuchungen.*
1. The "naïve" man—that is, the ordinary person in ordinary life thinking in ordinary ways. (Sometimes referred to in philosophy as "the man in the street.")

which is unceasingly drawing us on, the discovery, namely, of the essence of that *"pure" consciousness* which is to fix the limits of the phenomenological field. Our inquiries were eidetic;[2] but the individual instances of the essences we have referred to as experience, stream of experience, "consciousness" in all its senses, belonged as real events to the natural world. To that extent we have not abandoned the ground of the natural standpoint. Individual consciousness is interwoven with the *natural world* in a *twofold* way; it is some *man's* consciousness, or that of some *man* or *beast*,[3] and in a large number at least of its particularizations it is a consciousness of this world. *In respect now of this intimate attachment with the real world, what is meant by saying that consciousness has an essence "of its own,"* that with other consciousness it constitutes a self-contained *connexion determined purely through this, its own essence*, the connexion, namely, of the stream of consciousness? Moreover, since we can interpret consciousness in the widest sense to cover eventually whatever the concept of experience includes, the question concerns the experience-stream's own essential nature and that of all its components. To what extent, in the first place, must the *material world* be fundamentally different in kind, *excluded from the experience's own essential nature [Eigenwesenheit]*? And if it is this, if over against all consciousness and the essential being proper to it, it is that which is *"foreign"* and *"other,"* how can consciousness be *interwoven* with it, and consequently with the whole world that is alien to consciousness? For it is easy to convince oneself that the material world is not just any portion of the natural world, but its fundamental stratum to which all other real being is *essentially* related. It still fails to include the souls of men and animals;[4] and the new factor which these introduce is first and foremost their "experiencing" together with their conscious relationship to the world surrounding them. *But here consciousness and thinghood form a connected whole*, connected within the particular psychological unities which we call *animalia*,[5] and in the last resort within the *real unity of the world as a whole*. Can the unity of a whole be other than made one through the essential proper nature of its parts, which must therefore have some *community of essence* instead of a fundamental heterogeneity?

To be clear, let us seek out the ultimate sources whence the general thesis of the world which I adopt when taking up the natural standpoint draws its nourishment, thereby enabling me as a conscious being to discover over against me an existing world of things, to ascribe to myself in this world a body, and to find for myself within this world a proper place. This ultimate source is obviously *sensory experience*. For our purpose, however, it is sufficient to consider *sensory perception*, which in a certain proper sense plays among experiencing acts the part of an original experience, whence all other experiencing acts draw a chief part of their power to serve as a ground. Every perceiving consciousness has this peculiarity, that it is the consciousness of *the embodied (leibhaftigen) self-presence of an individual object*, which on its own side and in a pure logical sense of the term is an individual or some logico-categorical modification of the same. In our own instance, that of sensory perception, or, in

2. That is, having to do with essences.
3. That is, all actually occurring particular instances of consciousness are those of some particular human being or other such sentient being.

4. That is, the consciousnesses of human and other such sentient beings.
5. Animals (Latin).

distincter terms, perception of a world of things, the logical individual is the Thing; and it is sufficient for us to treat the perception of things as representing all other perceptions (of properties, processes, and the like).

The natural wakeful life of our Ego is a continuous perceiving, actual or potential. The world of things and our body within it are continuously present to our perception. How then does and can *Consciousness itself* separate out as a *concrete thing in itself*, from that within it, of which we are conscious, namely, the *perceived being*, "*standing over against*" consciousness "*in and for itself*"?

I meditate first as would the man "in the street" ['*naïv' Mensch*]. I see and grasp the thing itself in its bodily reality. It is true that I sometimes deceive myself, and not only in respect of the perceived constitution of the thing, but also in respect of its being there at all. I am subject to an illusion or hallucination. The perception is not then "genuine." But if it is, if, that is, we can "confirm" its presence in the actual context of experience, eventually with the help of correct empirical thinking, then the perceived thing *is real* and itself really given, and that bodily in perception. Here perceiving considered simply as consciousness, and apart from the body and the bodily organs, appears as something in itself essenceless, an empty looking of an empty "Ego" towards the object itself which comes into contact with it in some astonishing way.

40. "PRIMARY" AND "SECONDARY" QUALITIES. THE BODILY GIVEN THING [AS] "MERE APPEARANCE" OF THE "PHYSICALLY TRUE"

If as a "man in the street ['*naïv' Mensch*]" misled by sensibility I have indulged the inclination to spin out such thoughts as these, now, as a "man of science [*wissenschaftlich Mensch*],"[6] I call to mind the familiar distinction between *secondary* and *primary* qualities, according to which the specific qualities of sense should be "merely subjective" and only the geometrico-physical qualities "objective." The colour and sound of a thing, its smell, its taste, and so forth, though they appear to cleave to the thing "bodily" as though belonging to its essence, are not themselves and as they appear to be, real, but mere "signs" of certain primary qualities. But if I recall familiar theories of Physics, I see at once that the meaning of such much-beloved propositions can hardly be the one which the words warrant: as though really only the "specific" sensory qualities of the perceived thing were mere appearance; which would come to saying that the "primary" qualities which remain after the *subtraction* of these same sensory qualities belonged to the same thing as it objectively and truly is, together with other such qualities which did not show forth as appearance. So understood, the old Berkeleian objection would hold good, namely, that extension, this essential nucleus of corporeality and all primary qualities, is unthinkable apart from the secondary qualities.[7] Rather *the whole essential content of the perceived thing*, all that is present in the body, with all its qualities and all that can ever be perceived, is "*mere*

6. That is, a man of natural-scientific sophistication, who, while not being "misled by sensibility" (as the "naïve" person is), makes the different mistake of supposing "physical scientific" theory to be the last word and whole truth about reality.
7. The Anglo-Irish empiricist and subjective

Idealist philosopher George Berkeley (1685–1753) argued that the so-called primary qualities relating to spatial extension are inseparable from the so-called secondary qualities (e.g., color) held to be dependent on the character of our senses.

appearance," and the *"true thing"* is that of physical science. When the latter defines the given thing exclusively through concepts such as atoms, ions, energies, and so forth, and in every case as space-filling processes whose sole *characteristica*[8] are mathematical expressions, its reference is to *something that transcends the whole content of the thing as present to us in bodily form.* It cannot therefore mean even the thing as lying in natural sensible space; in other words, its physical space cannot be the space of the world of bodily perception: otherwise it would also fall under the Berkeleian objection.

The *"true Being"* would therefore be entirely and *fundamentally something that is defined otherwise than as that which is given in perception as corporeal reality*, which is given exclusively through its sensory determinations, among which must also be reckoned the sensori-spatial. *The thing as strictly experienced gives the mere "this," an empty X which becomes the bearer of mathematical determinations, and of the corresponding mathematical formula* and exists not in perceptual space, but in an *"objective space,"* of which the former is the mere "symbol," *a Euclidean manifold of three dimensions that can be only symbolically represented.*

Let us then accept this. Let that which is given bodily in any perception be, as is taught there, "mere appearance," in principle "merely subjective," and yet no empty illusion. Yet that which is given in perception serves in the rigorous method of natural science for the valid determination, open to anyone to carry out and to verify through his own insight of that transcendent being whose "symbol" it is. The sensory content of that which is given in perception itself continues indeed to be reckoned as other than the true thing as it is in itself, but the *substratum*, the bearer (the empty X) of the perceived determinations still continues to count as that which is determined through exact method in the form of physical predicates. *All physical knowledge serves accordingly, and in the reverse sense, as an indicator of the course of possible experiences with the sensory things found in them and the occurrences in which they figure.* Thus it helps us to find our way about in the world of actual experience in which we all live and act.[9]

From 41. The Real Nature of Perception and Its Transcendent Object

All this being presupposed, *what is it, we ask, that belongs to the concrete real nature (reellen Bestande) of the perception itself, as cogitation?* Not the physical thing, as is obvious: radically transcendent as it is, transcendent over against the whole "world of appearance." But *even the latter*, though we refer to it habitually as "merely subjective," does not belong in all its detail of things and events to the real nature of perception, but is opposed to it as "transcendent." Let us consider this more closely. We have indeed already spoken of the transcendence of the thing, but only in passing. It concerns us now to win a deeper insight into *the relation of the transcendent to the Consciousness* that knows it, and to see how this mutual connexion, which has its own riddles, is to be understood.

---

8. Characteristics (Greek).
9. That is, we can accept this (scientific) way of thinking on its own terms—but that is by no means the whole story concerning "the world of actual experience in which we all live and act," with which it merely "helps us."

We shut off the whole of physics and the whole domain of theoretical thought. We remain within the framework of plain intuition and the syntheses that belong to it, including perception. It is then evident that intuition and the intuited, perception and the thing perceived, though essentially related to each other, are in principle and of necessity *not really (reell) and essentially one and united.*

We start by taking an example. Keeping this table steadily in view as I go round it, changing my position in space all the time, I have continually the consciousness of the bodily presence out there of this one and self-same table, which in itself remains unchanged throughout. But the perception of the table is one that changes continuously, it is a continuum of changing perceptions. I close my eyes. My other senses are inactive in relation to the table. I have now no perception of it. I open my eyes, and the perception returns. The perception? Let us be more accurate. Under no circumstances does it return to me individually the same. Only the table is the same, known as identical through the synthetic consciousness which connects the new perception with the recollection. The perceived thing can be, without being perceived, without my being aware of it even as potential only (in the way of inactuality, as previously described[1]), and perhaps without itself changing at all. But the perception itself is what it is within the steady flow of consciousness, and is itself constantly in flux; the perceptual now is ever passing over into the adjacent consciousness of the just-past, a new now simultaneously gleams forth, and so on. The perceived thing in general, and all its parts, aspects, and phases, whether the quality be primary or secondary, are necessarily transcendent to the perception, and on the same grounds everywhere. The colour of the thing seen is not in principle a real phase of the consciousness of colour; it appears, but even while it is appearing the appearance can and *must* be continually changing, as experience shows. The *same* colour appears "in" continuously varying patterns of *perspective colour-variations*. Similarly for every sensory quality and likewise for every spatial shape! One and the same shape (given *as* bodily the same) appears continuously ever again "in another way," in ever-differing perspective variations of shape. That is a necessary state of things, and it has obviously a more general bearing. For it is only in the interests of simplicity that we have illustrated our point by reference to a thing that appears unchanged in perception. The transfer to changes of any other sort is a perfectly simple proceeding.

An empirical consciousness of a self-same thing that looks "all-round" its object, and in so doing is continually confirming the unity of its own nature, essentially and necessarily possesses a manifold system of continuous patterns of appearance and perspective variations, in and through which all objective phases of the bodily self-given which appear in perception manifest themselves perspectively in definite continua. Every determinate feature has *its own* system of perspective variations; and for each of these features, as for the thing as a whole, the following holds good, namely, that it remains one and the same for the consciousness that in grasping it unites recollection and fresh perception synthetically together, despite interruption in the continuity of the course of actual perception.

We now see also what it is that really and indubitably belongs to the real nature of the concrete intentional experiences which we refer to here as

---

1. Cf. supra, §35 [Husserl's note].

perceptions of things. Whilst the thing is the intentional unity, that which we are conscious of as one and self-identical within the continuously ordered flow of perceptual patterns as they pass off the one into the other, these patterns themselves have always their *definite descriptive nature* (*Bestand*), which is *essentially* correlated with that unity. To every phase of perception there necessarily belongs, for instance, a definite content in the way of perspective variations of colour, shape, and so forth. They are counted among the "*sensory data*," data of a particular region with determinate divisions, which within every such division gather together into concrete unities of experience *sui generis* (*sensory "fields"*) which, further, in ways we cannot here describe more closely, are ensouled within the concrete unity of perception through "*apprehensions*," and, in this ensouling, exercise the "*exhibitive* (*darstellende*) *function*," or in unison with it constitute that which we call the "appearing of" colour, shape, and so forth. This, after interweaving itself with still further features, constitutes the real nature (*Bestand*) of perception, which is the consciousness of one identical thing derived through the confluence into one *unity of apprehension*, a confluence grounded in the *essential Being* of the apprehensions unified, and again through the possibility, grounded in the very *essence* of different unities of this kind, of *syntheses of identification*.

* * *

46. Indubitability of Immanent, Dubitability of Transcendent Perception

From all this important consequences follow. Every immanent perception necessarily guarantees the existence (*Existenz*) of its object. If reflective apprehension is directed to my experience, I apprehend an absolute Self whose existence (*Dasein*) is, in principle, undeniable, that is, the insight that it does not exist is, in principle, impossible; it would be nonsense to maintain the possibility of an experience *given in such a way not* truly existing. The stream of experience which is mine, namely, of the one who is thinking, may be to ever so great an extent uncomprehended, unknown in its past and future reaches, yet so soon as I glance towards the flowing life and into the real present it flows through, and in so doing grasp myself as the pure subject of this life (what that means will expressly concern us at a later stage), I say forthwith and because I must: *I am*, this life is, I live: *cogito*.

To every stream of experience, and to every Ego as such, there belongs, in principle, the possibility of securing this self-evidence: each of us bears in himself the warrant of his absolute existence (*Daseins*) as a fundamental possibility. But is it not conceivable, one might ask, that an Ego might have only fancies in its stream of experience, that the latter might consist of nothing beyond fictive intuitions? Such an Ego would thus discover only fictive *cogitationes*; its reflexions, by the very nature of this experiential medium, would be exclusively reflexions within the imagination. But that is obvious nonsense. That which floats before the mind may be a mere fiction; the floating itself, the fiction-producing consciousness, is not itself imagined, and the possibility of a perceiving reflexion which lays hold on absolute existence belongs to its essence as it does to every experience. No nonsense lies in the possibility that all alien consciousness which I posit in the experience of empathy does not exist. But *my* empathy and my consciousness in general is given in a primordial and absolute sense, not only essentially but existentially. This privileged position holds only for oneself and for the stream of experience to which the self is related; here only is there, and must there be, anything of the nature of immanent perception.

In contrast to this, it is, as we know, an essential feature of the thing-world that no perception, however perfect it may be, gives us anything absolute within its domain; and with this the following is essentially connected, namely, that every experience (*Erfahrung*), however far it extends, leaves open the possibility that what is given, despite the persistent consciousness of its bodily self-presence, does *not* exist. It is an essentially valid law that *existence in the form of a thing* [_Dingliche Existenz_][2] *is never demanded as necessary by virtue of its givenness*, but in a certain way is always *contingent*. That means: It can always happen that the further course of experience will compel us to abandon what has already been set down and justified *in the light of empirical canons of rightness*. It was, so we afterwards say, mere illusion, hallucination, merely a coherent dream, and the like. Moreover, in this sphere of given data the open possibility remains of changes in apprehension, the turning of an appearance over into one which cannot unite with it harmoniously, and therewith an influence of later empirical positions on early ones whereby the intentional objects of these earlier positings suffer, so to speak, a posthumous reconstruction— eventualities which in the sphere of subject-experience (*Erlebnis*) are essentially excluded. In the absolute sphere, opposition, illusion, and being-otherwise have no place. It is a sphere of the absolutely established (*absoluter Position*).

In every way, then, it is clear that everything which is there for me in the world of things is on grounds of principle *only a presumptive reality*; that *I myself*, on the contrary, for whom it is there (excluding that which is imputed to the thing-world "by me"), I myself or my experience in its actuality am *absolute* Reality (*Wirklichkeit*),[3] given through a positing that is unconditioned and simply indissoluble.

The thesis of my pure Ego and its personal life, which is "necessary" and plainly indubitable, thus stands opposed to the thesis of the world which is "contingent." All corporeally given thing-like entities can also not be, no corporeally given experiencing can also not be:[4] that is the essential law, which defines this necessity and that contingency.

Obviously then the ontic necessity of the actual present experiencing is no pure essential necessity, that is, no pure eidetic specification of an essential law; it is the necessity of a fact (*Faktum*), and called "necessity" because an essential law is involved in the fact, and here indeed in its existence as such.

---

2. That is, "thingly" existence ("bodily" existence), thing-style existence.

3. Husserl is reiterating Descartes' basic point that the *cogito*—and therefore my own existence as *cogito*-subject—is grounded in my experience with an absoluteness or certainty that is of a completely different order from any conviction I can possibly have regarding existence that transcends my *cogito* and conscious experience.

4. This very important passage is better translated: The thesis of the world [i.e., positing the existence of a world of *Dingliche Existenz*], that is a "contingent" ["*zufällige*"] one, is to be contrasted with the thesis of my pure I and I-life [*Ich und Ichleben*], that is a "necessary" ["*notwendige*"] one [i.e., one that is necessarily valid], simply indubitable [*schlechthin zweifellose*]. Everything thingly [*Dingliche*] that is bodily given [*leibhaft gegebene*] can also not be [*nicht sein*; i.e., conceivably also might not actually be the case]; whereas no bodily given *experience* [_Erlebnis_] can also not be [i.e., conceivably also might not actually be occurring].

The ideal possibility of a reflexion which has the essential character of a self-evident unshakeable *existential* thesis has its ground in the essential nature of a pure Ego *in general* and of an experiencing *in general*.

The reflexions in which we have been indulging also make it clear that no proofs drawn from the empirical consideration of the world can be conceived which could assure us with absolute certainty of the world's existence. The world is not doubtful in the sense that there are rational grounds which might be pitted against the tremendous force of unanimous experiences, but in the sense that a doubt is *thinkable*, and this is so because the possibility of non-Being is in principle never excluded. Every empirical power, be it ever so great, can be gradually outweighed and overcome. Nothing is thereby altered in the absolute Being of experiences, indeed these remain presupposed in all this all the time.

With this conclusion our study has reached its climax. We have won the knowledge we needed. In the essential connexions it has revealed to us already involved the most important of the premises on which depend those inferences we would draw concerning the detachability in principle of the whole natural world from the domain of consciousness, the sphere in which experiences have their being; inferences in which, as we can readily convince ourselves, a central, though not fully developed, thought of the quite otherwise oriented meditations of Descartes comes at last to its own. To reach our final goal we shall need indeed to add in the sequel a few supplementary discussions, which for the rest will not trouble us too much. Meanwhile let us draw our conclusions provisionally within a compass of limited bearing.

SOURCE: From Edmund Husserl, *Ideas: General Introduction to Pure Phenomenology*, trans. W. R. Boyce Gibson (1931; reprint, New York: Collier Books, 1962), pp. 37–41, 91–93, 96–109, 113–19, 130–32. Except where otherwise indicated, German words in brackets are the terminology used in the German original, inserted by the editor after their renderings in the translation. Except where otherwise indicated, German words in brackets are the terminology used in the German original, inserted by the editor in addition to their renderings in the translation. Those in parentheses were inserted by the translator. Originally published in 1913 as *Ideen zu einer reinen Phänomenologie und phänomenologische Philosophie. Erstes Buch: Allgemeine Einführung in die reine Phänomenologie (Ideas Pertaining to a Pure Phenomenology and to a Phenomenological Philosophy. First Book: General Introduction to Pure Phenomenology)*.

From Cartesian Meditations: An Introduction to Phenomenology

From *Introduction*

FROM §1. DESCARTES' *MEDITATIONS* AS THE PROTOTYPE OF PHILOSOPHICAL REFLECTION

* * *

Every beginner in philosophy knows the remarkable train of thoughts contained in the *Meditations*.[1] Let us recall its guiding idea. The aim of the *Meditations* is a complete reforming of philosophy into a science [*Wissenschaft*][2]

---

1. *Meditations on First Philosophy* (i.e., metaphysics) by the French philosopher and mathematician René Descartes (1596–1650), commonly considered to be the father of modern (post-Scholastic) philosophy.

2. That is, "cognitive discipline." On the term *Wissenschaft*, see the source note to "Philosophy as Rigorous Science [*Wissenschaft*]," above.

grounded on an absolute foundation. That implies for Descartes a corresponding reformation of all the sciences, because in his opinion they are only non-selfsufficient members of the one all-inclusive science [*Wissenschaft*], and this is philosophy. Only within the systematic unity of philosophy can they develop into genuine sciences. As they have developed historically, on the other hand, they lack that scientific [*wissenschaftlich*] genuineness which would consist in their complete and ultimate grounding on the basis of absolute insights, insights behind which one cannot go back any further. Hence the need for a radical rebuilding that satisfies the idea of philosophy as the all-inclusive unity of the sciences [*Wissenschaften*], within the unity of such an absolutely rational grounding. With Descartes this demand gives rise to a philosophy turned toward the subject himself.

* * *

§2. THE NECESSITY OF A RADICAL NEW BEGINNING OF PHILOSOPHY

Thus far, Descartes. We ask now: It is really worth while to hunt for an eternal significance belonging to these thoughts or to some clarifiable core that may be contained in them? Are they still such thoughts as might infuse our times with living forces?

Doubt is raised at least by the fact that the positive sciences, which were to experience an absolutely rational grounding by these meditations, have paid so little attention to them. To be sure, the positive sciences, after three centuries of brilliant development, are now feeling themselves greatly hampered by obscurities in their foundations, in their fundamental concepts and methods. But, when they attempt to give those foundations a new form, they do not think of turning back to resume Cartesian meditations. On the other hand, great weight must be given to the consideration that, in philosophy, the *Meditations* were epoch-making in a quite unique sense, and precisely because of their going back to the pure *ego cogito*.[3] Descartes, in fact, inaugurates an entirely new kind of philosophy. Changing its total style, philosophy takes a radical turn: from naïve Objectivism to transcendental subjectivism[4]—which, with its ever new but always inadequate attempts, seems to be striving toward some necessary final form, wherein its true sense and that of the radical transmutation itself might become disclosed. Should not this continuing tendency imply an eternal significance and, for us, a task imposed by history itself, a great task in which we are all summoned to collaborate?

The splintering of present-day philosophy, with its perplexed activity, sets us thinking. When we attempt to view western philosophy as a unitary science [*Wissenschaft*], its decline since the middle of the nineteenth century is

---

3. I think (Latin); Husserl uses Descartes' *cogito* to mean something like "that which experiences" or, loosely speaking, "the experiencing mind."
4. That is, turning from the view that things truly are as they are perceived to be ("naïve Objectivism") to the view that things are perceived or experienced as they are owing to the way in which the mind—a kind of "subject" that "transcends" its experiences—has structured and conditioned the manner and content of their perceived or experienced characteristics ("transcendental subjectivism"— or, less misleadingly, "transcendent subject-ism"). Husserl's use of the term "transcendental" draws on that of KANT, for whom it referred to the conditions of the possibility of experience and the ways in which the mind structures the contents of experience, rather than to the contents of experience as such.

unmistakable. The comparative unity that it had in previous ages, in its aims, its problems and methods, has been lost. When, with the beginning of modern times, religious belief was becoming more and more externalized as a lifeless convention, men of intellect were lifted by a new belief, their great belief in an autonomous philosophy and science [*Wissenschaft*]. The whole of human culture was to be guided and illuminated by scientific [*wissenschaftlich*] insights and thus reformed, as new and autonomous.

But meanwhile this belief too has begun to languish. Not without reason. Instead of a unitary living philosophy, we have a philosophical literature growing beyond all bounds and almost without coherence. Instead of a serious discussion among conflicting theories that, in their very conflict, demonstrate the intimacy with which they belong together, the commonness of their underlying convictions, and an unswerving belief in a true philosophy, we have a pseudo-reporting and a pseudo-criticizing, a mere semblance of philosophizing seriously with and for one another. This hardly attests a mutual study carried on with a consciousness of responsibility, in the spirit that characterizes serious collaboration and an intention to produce Objectively valid results. "Objectively valid results"—the phrase, after all, signifies nothing but results that have been refined by mutual criticism and that now withstand every criticism. But how could actual study and actual collaboration be possible, where there are so many philosophers and almost equally many philosophies? To be sure, we still have philosophical congresses. The philosophers meet but, unfortunately, not the philosophies. The philosophies lack the unity of a mental [*geistig*] space in which they might exist for and act on one another. It may be that, within each of the many different "schools" or "lines of thought", the situation is somewhat better. Still, with the existence of these in isolation, the total philosophical present is essentially as we have described it.

In this unhappy present, is not our situation similar to the one encountered by Descartes in his youth? If so, then is not this a fitting time to renew his radicalness, the radicalness of the beginning philosopher: to subject to a Cartesian overthrow the immense philosophical literature with its medley of great traditions, of comparatively serious new beginnings, of stylish literary activity (which counts on "making an effect" but not on being studied), and to begin with new *meditationes de prima philosophia*?[5] Cannot the disconsolateness of our philosophical position be traced back ultimately to the fact that the driving forces emanating from the *Meditations* of Descartes have lost their original vitality—lost it because the spirit that characterizes radicalness of philosophical self-responsibility has been lost? Must not the demand for a philosophy aiming at the ultimate conceivable freedom from prejudice, shaping itself with actual autonomy according to ultimate evidences it has itself produced, and therefore absolutely self-responsible—must not this demand, instead of being excessive, be part of the fundamental sense of genuine philosophy? In recent times the longing for a fully alive philosophy has led to many a renaissance. Must not the only fruitful renaissance be the one that reawakens the impulse of the Cartesian *Meditations*: not to adopt their content but, in *not* doing so, to renew with greater intensity the radicalness of their spirit, the radicalness of self-responsibility, to make that radicalness true for the first time by enhancing it to the last degree, to uncover thereby for

5. Meditations on first philosophy (Latin)—the full title of Descartes' *Meditations*.

the first time the genuine sense of the necessary regress to the ego, and consequently to overcome the hidden but already felt naïveté of earlier philosophizing?

In any case, the question indicates one of the ways that has led to transcendental phenomenology.

Along that way we now intend to walk together. In a quasi-Cartesian fashion we intend, as radically beginning philosophers, to carry out meditations with the utmost critical precaution and a readiness for any—even the most far-reaching—transformation of the old-Cartesian meditations. Seductive aberrations, into which Descartes and later thinkers strayed, will have to be clarified and avoided as we pursue our course.

From FIRST MEDITATION

The Way to the Transcendental Ego

§3. THE CARTESIAN OVERTHROW AND THE GUIDING FINAL IDEA OF AN ABSOLUTE GROUNDING OF SCIENCE

And so we make a new beginning, each for himself and in himself, with the decision of philosophers who begin radically: that at first we shall put out of action all the convictions we have been accepting up to now, including all our sciences. Let the idea guiding our meditations be at first the Cartesian idea of a science [*Wissenschaft*] that shall be established as radically genuine, ultimately an all-embracing science [*Wissenschaft*].

But, now that we no longer have at our disposal any already-given science as an example of radically genuine science (after all, we are not accepting any given science), what about the indubitability of that idea itself, the idea namely of a science [*Wissenschaft*] that shall be grounded absolutely? Is it a legitimate final idea, the possible aim of some possible practice? Obviously that too is something we must not presuppose, to say nothing of taking any norms as already established for testing such possibilities—or perchance a whole system of norms in which the style proper to genuine science is allegedly prescribed. That would mean presupposing a whole logic as a theory of science [*Wissenschaft*]; whereas logic must be included among the sciences [*Wissenschaften*] overthrown in overthrowing all science. Descartes himself presupposed an ideal of science, the ideal approximated by geometry and mathematical natural science. As a fateful prejudice this ideal determines philosophies for centuries and hiddenly determines the *Meditations* themselves. Obviously it was, for Descartes, a truism from the start that the all-embracing science [*Wissenschaft*] must have the form of a deductive system, in which the whole structure rests, *ordine geometrico*,[6] on an axiomatic foundation that grounds the deduction absolutely. For him a role similar to that of geometrical axioms in geometry is played in the all-embracing science by the axiom of the ego's absolute certainty of himself, along with the axiomatic principles innate in the ego—only this axiomatic foundation lies even deeper than that of geometry and is called on to participate in the ultimate grounding even of geometrical knowledge.

---

6. In geometric order (Latin); that is, in the manner of a proof in geometry.

None of that shall determine our thinking. As beginning philosophers we do not as yet accept any normative ideal of science [*Wissenschaft*]; and only so far as we produce one newly for ourselves can we ever have such an ideal.

But this does not imply that we renounce the general aim of grounding science [*Wissenschaft*] absolutely.[7] That aim shall indeed continually motivate the course of our meditations, as it motivated the course of the Cartesian meditations; and gradually, in our meditations, it shall become determined concretely. Only we must be careful about how we make an absolute grounding of science our aim. At first we must not presuppose even its possibility. How then are we to find the legitimate manner in which to make it our aim? How are we to make our aim perfectly assured, and thus assured as a practical possibility? How are we then to differentiate the possibility, into which at first we have a general insight, and thereby mark out the determinate methodical course of a genuine philosophy, a radical philosophy that begins with what is intrinsically first?

Naturally we get the general idea of science [*Wissenschaft*] from the sciences that are factually given.[8] If they have become for us, in our radical critical attitude, merely alleged sciences, then, according to what has already been said, their general final idea has become, in a like sense, a mere supposition. Thus we do not yet know whether that idea is at all capable of becoming actualized. Nevertheless we do have it in this form, and in a state of indeterminate fluid generality; accordingly we have also the idea of philosophy:[9] as an idea about which we do not know whether or how it can be actualized. We take the general idea of science [*Wissenschaft*], therefore, as a precursory presumption, which we allow ourselves tentatively, by which we tentatively allow ourselves to be guided in our meditations. We consider how it might be thought out as a possibility and then consider whether and how it might be given determinate actualization. To be sure, we get into what are, at first, rather strange circumstantialities—but how can they be avoided, if our radicalness is not to remain an empty gesture but is to become an actual deed? Let us go on then with patience.

* * *

§5. Evidence and the Idea of Genuine Science [*Wissenschaft*]

As we go on meditating in this manner and along this line, we beginning philosophers recognize that the Cartesian idea of a science (ultimately an all-embracing science [*Wissenschaft*]) grounded on an absolute foundation, and absolutely justified, is none other than the idea that constantly furnishes

---

7. This aim—to "ground" (or provide a firm foundation for) all cognitive endeavor on something that would be as unquestionably valid and certain as "divine revelation" (whether personal or scriptural) is problematic—is one of the fundamental matters at issue in the interpretive tradition. The question is whether any such grounding or foundation can be found for any of the disciplines, rendering them fundamentally sound in a way that warrants any cognitive claims they might (on methodologically sound grounds and appropriate

evidence) be disposed to make.
8. That is, "Naturally, we get the general idea of *Wissenschaft* [cognitive inquiry] from the *Wissenschaften* [cognitive disciplines] that actually exist"—for example, physics, mathematics, biology, psychology, history, and linguistics.
9. That is, the idea of philosophy as *Wissenschaft* (cognitive inquiry)—and indeed as *strenge Wissenschaft* (rigorous cognitive inquiry), as in the title of our first selection—whose relation to other *Wissenschaften* remains to be determined.

guidance in all sciences and in their striving toward universality[1]—whatever may be the situation with respect to a de facto actualization of that idea.

Evidence is, in an *extremely broad sense*, an *"experiencing"* of something that is, and is thus; it is precisely a mental seeing of something itself. Conflict with what evidence shows, with what "experience" shows, yields the negative of evidence (or negative evidence)—put in the form of a judgment: positive evidence of the affair's non-being. In other words, negative evidence has as its content evident falsity. Evidence, which in fact includes all experiencing in the usual and narrower sense, can be more or less perfect. *Perfect evidence* and its correlate, *pure and genuine truth*, are given as ideas lodged in the striving for knowledge, for fulfilment of one's meaning intention. By immersing ourselves in such a striving, we can extract those ideas from it. Truth and falsity, criticism and critical comparison with evident data, are an everyday theme, playing their incessant part even in pre-scientific life. For this everyday life, with its changing and relative purposes, relative evidences and truths suffice. But science [*Wissenschaft*] looks for truths that are valid, and remain so, *once for all and for everyone*; accordingly it seeks verifications of a new kind, verifications carried through to the end. Though de facto, as science itself must ultimately see, it does not attain actualization of a system of absolute truths, but rather is obliged to modify its "truths" again and again, it nevertheless follows the idea of absolute or scientifically [*wissenschaftlich*] genuine truth; and accordingly it reconciles itself to an infinite horizon of approximations, tending toward that idea. By them, science believes, it can surpass *in infinitum*[2] not only everyday knowing but also itself; likewise however by its aim at systematic universality of knowledge, whether that aim concern a particular closed scientific province or a presupposed all-embracing unity of whatever exists—as it does if a "philosophy" is possible and in question. According to intention, therefore, the idea of science [*Wissenschaft*] and philosophy involves an *order of cognition, proceeding from intrinsically earlier to intrinsically later cognitions*; ultimately, then, *a beginning and a line of advance* that are not to be chosen arbitrarily but have their basis "in the nature of things themselves".

Thus, by immersing ourselves meditatively in the general intentions of scientific endeavor, we discover fundamental parts of the final idea, genuine science [*Wissenschaft*], which, though vague at first, governs that striving. Meanwhile we have made no advance judgment in favor of the possibility of those components or in favor of a supposedly unquestionable scientific ideal.

We must not say at this point: "Why bother with such investigations and ascertainments? They obviously belong to the general theory of science, to logic, which must of course be applied both now and later." On the contrary, we must guard ourselves against just this matter-of-course opinion. Let us emphasize what we said against Descartes: Like every other already-given science, logic is deprived of acceptance by the universal overthrow. Everything that makes a philosophical beginning possible we must first acquire by ourselves. Whether, later on, a genuine science [*Wissenschaft*] similar to traditional

---

1. That is, in their striving toward general or universal validity (*Allgemeinheit*).

2. Without limit, endlessly (Latin).

logic will accrue to us is an eventuality about which we can at present know nothing.

By this preliminary work, here roughly indicated rather than done explicitly, we have gained a measure of clarity sufficient to let us fix, for our whole further procedure, a *first methodological principle*. It is plain that I, as someone beginning philosophically, since I am striving toward the presumptive end, genuine science, must neither make nor go on accepting any judgment as scientific [*wissenschaftlich*] *that I have not derived from evidence*, from "experiences" in which the affairs and affair-complexes in question are present to me as "*they themselves*". Indeed, even then I must at all times reflect on the pertinent evidence; I must examine its "range" and make evident to myself *how far* that evidence, how far its "perfection", *the actual giving of the affairs themselves*, extends. Where this is still wanting, I must not claim any final validity, but must account my judgment as, at best, a possible intermediate stage on the way to final validity.

Because the sciences aim at predications that express completely and with evident fitness what is beheld pre-predicatively,[3] it is obvious that I must be careful also about this aspect of scientific [*wissenschaftlich*] evidence. Owing to the instability and ambiguity of common language and its much too great complacency about completeness of expression, we require, even where we use its means of expression, a new legitimation of significations by orienting them according to accrued insights, and a fixing of words as expressing the significations thus legitimated. That too we account as part of our normative principle of evidence, which we shall apply consistently from now on.

But how would this principle, or all our meditation up to now, help us, if it gave us no hold for making an actual beginning, that is, for starting to actualize the idea of genuine science? Since the form belonging to a systematic order of cognitions—genuine cognitions—is part of this idea, there emerges, as the *question of the beginning*, the inquiry for those cognitions that are first in themselves and can support the whole storied edifice of universal knowledge. Consequently, if our presumptive aim is to be capable of becoming a practically possible one, we meditators, while completely destitute of all scientific knowledge, must have access to evidences that already bear the stamp of fitness for such a function, in that they are recognizable as preceding all other imaginable evidences. Moreover, in respect of this evidence of preceding, they must have a certain perfection, they must carry with them an absolute certainty, if advancing from them and constructing on their basis a science [*Wissenschaft*] governed by the idea of a definitive system of knowledge—considering the infinity presumed to be part of this idea—is to be capable of having any sense.

---

3. Husserl takes it to be the case that cognitive inquiry involves aiming at descriptions that completely express (in language) with full "evident fitness" what is beheld pre-descriptively and extralinguistically. The thesis that such descriptions are possible is central to his position and program of phenomenology, for it renders at least comprehensible his conviction that the task of phenomenological philosophy is to seek knowledge of real "essences" that are not themselves intrinsically linguistic (and thus cultural, historical, and therefore contingent) phenomena with mundanely human genealogies.

§6. DIFFERENTIATIONS OF EVIDENCE.[4] THE PHILOSOPHICAL DEMAND FOR AN EVIDENCE THAT IS APODICTIC AND FIRST IN ITSELF

But here, at this decisive point in the process of beginning, we must penetrate deeper with our meditations. The phrase *absolute certainty* and the equivalent phrase *absolute indubitability* need clarifying. They call our attention to the fact that, on more precise explication, the ideally demanded *perfection of evidence becomes differentiated*. At the present introductory stage of philosophical meditation we have the boundless infinity of prescientific experiences, evidences: more or less perfect. With reference to them *imperfection*, as a rule, signifies *incompleteness*, a one-sidedness and at the same time a relative obscurity and indistinctness that qualify the givenness of the affairs themselves or the affair-complexes themselves: i.e., an infectedness of the "experience" with *unfulfilled components*, with *expectant* and *attendant meanings*. Perfecting then takes place as a synthetic course of further harmonious experiences in which these attendant meanings become fulfilled in actual experience. The corresponding idea of perfection would be that of "*adequate evidence*"—and the question whether adequate evidence does not necessarily lie at infinity may be left open.

Though this idea continuously guides the scientist's[5] intent, *a different perfection* of evidence has for him (as we see by the aforesaid process of "immersing ourselves" in his intent) a higher dignity. This perfection is "*apodicticity*"; and it can occur even in evidences that are inadequate. It is *absolute indubitability* in a quite definite and peculiar sense, the absolute indubiability that the scientist [*Wissenschaftler*] demands of all "*principles*"; and its superior value is evinced in his endeavor, where groundings already evident in and by themselves are concerned, to ground them further and at a higher level by going back to principles, and thereby to obtain for them the highest dignity, that of apodicticity. The fundamental nature of apodicticity can be characterized in the following manner:

Any evidence is a grasping of something itself that is, or is thus, a grasping in the mode "it itself", with full certainty of its being, a certainty that accordingly excludes every doubt. But it does not follow that full certainty excludes the conceivability that what is evident could subsequently become doubtful, or the conceivability that being could prove to be illusion—indeed, sensuous experience furnishes us with cases where that happens. Moreover, this open possibility of becoming doubtful, or of non-being, *in spite of evidence*, can always be recognized in advance by critical reflection on what the evidence in question does. An *apodictic* evidence, however, is not merely certainty of the affairs or affair-complexes (states-of-affairs) evident in it; rather it discloses itself, to a critical reflection, as having the signal peculiarity of being *at the same time the absolute unimaginableness* (inconceivability) of their *non-being*, and thus excluding in advance every doubt as "objectless", empty. Furthermore the evidence of that critical reflection likewise has the dignity of being apodictic, as does therefore the evidence of the unimaginableness of what is

---

4. Husserl's crucial term *Evidenz* might be translated better—that is, in a way more aptly expressive of his meaning—as "evidentness."

5. That is, the person engaged in the kind of *Wissenschaft* under consideration (Husserlian cognitive inquiry).

presented with <apodictically>[6] evident certainty. And the same is true of every critical reflection at a higher level.

We remember now the Cartesian principle for building genuine science [*Wissenschaft*]: the principle of absolute indubitability, by which every imaginable doubt (even though it were in fact groundless) was to be excluded. If, by our meditations, we have acquired that principle in a clarified form, there arises the question whether and how it might help us make an actual beginning. In accordance with what has already been said, we now formulate, as an initial definite question of beginning philosophy, the question whether it is possible for us to bring out evidences that, on the one hand, carry with them—as we now must say: apodictically—the insight that, as "first in themselves", they precede all other imaginable evidences and, on the other hand, can be seen to be themselves apodictic. If they should turn out to be inadequate, they would have to possess at least a recognizable apodictic content, they would have to give us some being that is firmly secured "once for all", or absolutely, by virtue of their apodicticity. *How*, and even *whether*, it would be possible to go on from there and build an apodictically secured philosophy must, of course, remain for later consideration.

§7. The Evidence for the Factual Existence of the World not Apodictic; Its Inclusion in the Cartesian Overthrow

The question of evidences that are first in themselves can apparently be answered without any trouble. Does not the *existence of the world* present itself forthwith as such an evidence? The life of everyday action relates to the world. All the sciences relate to it: the sciences of matters of fact relate to it immediately; the apriori sciences [*Wissenschaften*], mediately, as instruments of scientific method.[7] More than anything else the being of the world is obvious. It is so very obvious that no one would think of asserting it expressly in a proposition. After all, we have our continuous experience in which this world incessantly stands before our eyes, as existing without question. But, however much this evidence is prior in itself to all the <other> evidences of life (as turned toward the world) and to all the evidences of all the world sciences (since it is the basis that continually supports them), we soon become doubtful about the extent to which, in this capacity, it can lay claim to being apodictic. And, if we follow up this doubt, it becomes manifest that our experiential evidence of the world lacks also the superiority of being the absolutely primary evidence. Concerning the first point, we note that the universal sensuous experience in whose evidence the world is continuously given to us beforehand is obviously not to be taken forthwith as an apodictic evidence, which, as such, would absolutely exclude both the possibility of eventual doubt whether the world is actual and the possibility of its non-being. Not only can a particular experienced thing suffer devaluation as an illusion of the senses; the whole unitarily surveyable nexus, experienced throughout a period of time, can prove to be an illusion, a coherent dream. We need not take the indicating of these possible and sometimes actual reversals of evi-

---

6. Words marked with angled brackets reflect different versions of the manuscript of these lectures.
7. That is, of sound cognitive method. "The apriori sciences": disciplines in which knowledge is not a matter of what is discovered or can be confirmed by experience (i.e., empirical evidence).

dence as a sufficient criticism of the evidence in question and see in it a full proof that, in spite of the continual experiencedness of the world, a non-being of the world is conceivable. We shall retain only this much: that the evidence of world-experience would, at all events, need to be criticized with regard to its validity and range, before it could be used for the purposes of a radical grounding of science [*Wissenschaft*], and that therefore we must not take that evidence to be, without question, immediately apodictic. It follows that denying acceptance to all the sciences given us beforehand, treating them as, for us, inadmissible prejudices, is not enough. Their universal basis, the experienced world, must also be deprived of its naïve acceptance. The being of the world, by reason of the evidence of natural experience, must no longer be for us an obvious matter of fact; it too must be for us, henceforth, only an acceptance-phenomenon.

If we maintain this attitude, is any being whatever left us as a basis for judgments, let alone for evidences on which we could establish an all-embracing philosophy and, furthermore, do so apodictically? Is not "the world" the name for the universe of whatever exists? If so, how can we avoid starting *in extenso*, and as our first task, that criticism of world-experience which, a moment ago, we merely indicated? Then, if criticism were to yield the result considered likely in advance, would not our whole philosophical aim be frustrated? But what if the world were, in the end, not at all the absolutely first basis for judgments and a being that is intrinsically prior to the world were the already presupposed basis for the existence of the world?

§8. THE *EGO COGITO* AS TRANSCENDENTAL SUBJECTIVITY

At this point, following Descartes, we make the great reversal that, if made in the right manner, leads to transcendental subjectivity: the turn to the *ego cogito* as the ultimate and apodictically certain basis for judgments, the basis on which any radical philosophy must be grounded.[8]

Let us consider. As radically meditating philosophers, we now have neither a science [*Wissenschaft*] that we accept nor a world that exists for us. Instead of simply existing for us—that is, being accepted naturally by us in our experiential believing in its existence—the world is for us only something that claims being.[9] Moreover, that affects the intramundane existence of all other Egos, so that rightly we should no longer speak communicatively, in the plural. Other men than I, and brute animals, are data of experience for me only by virtue of my sensuous experience of their bodily organisms; and, since the validity of this experience too is called in question, I must not use it. Along with other Egos, naturally, I lose all the formations pertaining to sociality and culture. In short, not just corporeal Nature but the whole concrete surrounding

8. It is necessary to say that the reduction has apodictic significance, since it shows apodictically that the being of the transcendental Ego is antecedent to the being of the world [Husserl's marginal note]. This is very significant evidence that Husserl sees his form of "transcendental phenomenology" as resulting in a "transcendental idealism" that is not only epistemological but also metaphysical.
9. This translation does not capture the full strength of Husserl's language here. For "radically meditating philosophers," he states, the world is "nur ein blosser Seinsanspruch"—"only a mere being-claim": that is, the world conceived as something that transcends our experience is for the phenomenologist only a *purported* reality. This statement takes on even greater significance in view of his marginal note to the next sentence's assertion that this applies to the existence in the world of all others like myself (*aller anderen Ich*)— and, he continues: "Likewise the intramundane existence of my own *Ich* [Ego, self] as human!" (Husserl's exclamation mark).

life-world is for me, from now on, only a phenomenon of being, instead of something that is.

But, no matter what the status of this phenomenon's claim to actuality and no matter whether, at some future time, I decide critically that the world exists or that it is an illusion, still this phenomenon itself, as mine, is not nothing but is precisely what makes such critical decisions at all possible and accordingly makes possible whatever has for me sense and validity as "true" being—definitively decided or definitively decideable being. And besides: If I abstained—as I was free to do and as I did—and still abstain from every believing involved in or founded on sensuous experiencing, so that the being of the experienced world remains unaccepted by me, still this abstaining is what it is; and it exists, together with the whole stream of my experiencing life. Moreover, this life is continually there *for me*. Continually, in respect of a field of the present, it is given to consciousness perceptually, with the most originary originality, as it itself; memorially, now these and now those pasts thereof are "again" given to consciousness, and that implies: as the "pasts themselves". Reflecting, I can at any time look at this original living and note particulars; I can grasp what is present as present, what is past as past, each as itself. I do so now, as the Ego who philosophizes and exercises the aforesaid abstention.

Meanwhile the world experienced in this reflectively grasped life goes on being for me (in a certain manner) "experienced" as before, and with just the content it has at any particular time. It goes on appearing, as it appeared before; the only difference is that I, as reflecting philosophically, no longer keep in effect (no longer accept) the natural believing in existence involved in experiencing the world—though that believing too is still there and grasped by my noticing regard. The same is true of all the processes of meaning that, in addition to the world-experiencing ones, belong to my lifestream: the non-intuitive processes of meaning objects, the judgings, valuings, and decidings, the processess of setting ends and willing means, and all the rest, in particular the position-takings necessarily involved in them all when I am in the natural and non-reflective attitude—since precisely these position-takings always presuppose the world, i.e., involve believing in its existence. Here too the philosophically reflective Ego's abstention from position-takings, his depriving them of acceptance, does not signify their disappearance from his field of experience. The concrete subjective processes, let us repeat, are indeed the things to which his attentive regard is directed: but the attentive Ego, qua philosophizing Ego, practices abstention with respect to what he intuits. Likewise everything *meant* in such accepting or positing processes of consciousness (the meant judgment, theory, value, end, or whatever it is) is still retained completely—but with the acceptance-modification, "mere phenomenon".

This universal depriving of acceptance, this "inhibiting" or "putting out of play" of all positions taken toward the already-given Objective world and, in the first place, all existential positions (those concerning being, illusion, possible being, being likely, probable, etc.),—or, as it is also called, this "phenomenological epoché" and "parenthesizing"[1] of the Objective world—therefore does not leave us confronting nothing. On the contrary we gain possession of something by it; and what we (or, to speak more precisely, what I, the one

---

1. Bracketing. "Epoché": suspension of judgment; see §§31–32 of Husserl's *Ideas* (1913), above.

who is meditating) acquire by it is my pure living,[2] with all the pure subjective processes making this up, and everything meant in them, *purely as* meant in them: the universe of "phenomena" in the (particular and also the wider) phenomenological sense. The epoché can also be said to be the radical and universal method by which I apprehend myself purely: as Ego, and with my own pure conscious life, in and by which the entire Objective world exists for me and is precisely as it is for me. Anything belonging to the world, any spatiotemporal being, exists for me—that is to say, is accepted by me—in that I experience it, perceive it, remember it, think of it somehow, judge about it, value it, desire it, or the like. Descartes, as we know, indicated all that by the name *cogito*. The world is for me absolutely nothing else but the world existing for and accepted by me in such a conscious *cogito*. It gets its whole sense, universal and specific, and its acceptance as existing, exclusively from such *cogitationes*.[3] In these my whole world-life goes on, including my scientifically inquiring and grounding life. By my living, by my experiencing, thinking, valuing, and acting, I can enter no world other than the one that gets its sense and acceptance or status [*Sinn und Geltung*][4] in and from me, myself. If I put myself above all this life and refrain from doing any believing that takes "the" world straightforwardly as existing—if I direct my regard exclusively to this life itself, as consciousness *of* "the" world—I thereby acquire myself as the pure ego, with the pure stream of my *cogitationes*.

Thus the being of the pure ego and his *cogitationes*, as a being that is prior in itself, is antecedent to the natural being of the world—the world of which I always speak, the one of which I *can* speak. Natural being is a realm whose existential status [*Seinsgeltung*] is secondary; it continually presupposes the realm of transcendental being. The fundamental phenomenological method of transcendental epoché, because it leads back to this realm, is called transcendental-phenomenological reduction.

From *SECOND MEDITATION*

The Field of Transcendental Experience Laid Open in Respect of Its Universal Structures

* * *

FROM §15. NATURAL AND TRANSCENDENTAL REFLECTION

* * *

* * * If the Ego, as naturally immersed in the world, experiencingly and otherwise, is called "*interested*" *in the world*, then the phenomenologically altered—and, as so altered, continually maintained—attitude consists in a *splitting of the Ego*: in that the phenomenological Ego establishes himself[5] as

---

2. Though Husserl uses the word *Leben* here, he clearly means it to be understood in the sense of "existing" as a subject of experience (rather than "living" construed biologically).
3. Acts of the *cogito* (Latin; singular, *cogitatio*).
4. Translator's brackets, here and in the following paragraph.

5. Here and elsewhere, the translator should have used the neuter pronoun ("it," "its," "itself") in referring to the phenomenologically reduced Ego or self, both because it has no gender and because grammatically *Ich* and *Ego* (the German words Husserl uses) are both neuter, not masculine.

"*disinterested onlooker*", above the naïvely interested Ego. That this takes place is then itself accessible by means of a new reflection, which, as transcendental, likewise demands the very same attitude of looking on "*disinterestedly*"—the Ego's sole remaining interest being to see and to describe adequately what he sees, purely as seen, as what is seen and seen in such and such a manner.

Thus all occurences of the life turned toward the world, with all their simple and founded positings of being and with the correlative modes of being (such as certainly existing, being possible, being probable, also being beautiful and being good, being useful, etc.), pure of all accompanying and expectant meanings on the observer's part, become accessible to description. Only in this purity, indeed, can they become themes of a universal *criticism of consciousness*, such as our aiming at a philosophy necessarily demands. We recall the radicalness of the Cartesian idea of philosophy, as the idea of the all-embracing science [*Wissenschaft*], grounded to the utmost and apodictically. This idea demands an absolute universal criticism, which, for its part, by abstention from all positions that already give anything existent, must first create for itself a *universe of absolute freedom from prejudice*.[6] The universality of transcendental experience and description does this by inhibiting the universal "prejudice" of world-experience, which hiddenly pervades all naturalness (the belief in the world, which pervades naturalness thoroughly and continuously), and then—within the sphere that remains unaffected, the absolute sphere of egological being, as the sphere of meanings reduced to an unalloyed freedom from prejudice—striving for a universal description. This description is then called on to be the foundation for a radical and universal criticism. Naturally everything depends on strictly preserving the absolute "unprejudicedness" of the description and thereby satisfying the principle of pure evidence, which we laid down in advance. That signifies restriction to the pure data of transcendental reflection, which therefore must be taken precisely as they are given in simple evidence, purely "intuitively", and always kept free from all interpretations that read into them more than is genuinely seen.

If we follow this methodological principle in the case of the dual topic, *cogito—cogitatum*[7] (*qua cogitatum*), there become opened to us, first of all, the general descriptions to be made, always on the basis of particular *cogitationes*, with regard to each of the two correlative sides. Accordingly, on the one hand, descriptions of the intentional object as such, with regard to the determinations attributed to it in the modes of consciousness concerned, attributed furthermore with corresponding modalities, which stand out when attention is directed to them. (For example: the "modalities of being", like certainly being, possibly or presumably being, etc.; or the "subjective"-temporal modes, being present, past, or future.) This line of description is called *noematic*. Its counterpart is *noetic* description,[8] which concerns the modes of the *cogito* itself, the modes of consciousness (for example: perception, recollection, retention), with the modal differences inherent in them (for example: differences in clarity and distinctness).

6. That is, from all preconceptions, which Husserl finds inherently problematic because they are by definition lacking in "evidence" (i.e., apodictic evidentness).
7. Something thought (Latin).
8. The nouns *noema* (plural, *noemata*; adjective, *noematic*) and *noesis* (plural, *noeses*; adjective, *noetic*) are borrowed from the Greek words for "mind" (*nous*), "to think" (*noein*), and "perception" (*noēsis*) to refer to the objects (*noemata*) and modes (*noeses*) of phenomenologically reduced consciousness.

We now understand that, by our universal epoché with respect to the being or non-being of the world, we have not simply lost the world for phenomenology; we retain it, after all, *qua cogitatum*. And not only with respect to the *particular* realities that are meant (and *as* they are meant) in some set or other of separate acts of consciousness—or, stated more distinctly: that are meant selectively. For indeed their particularity is particularity within a unitary *universe*, which, even when we are directed to and grasping the particular, goes on "appearing" unitarily. In other words, there is always co-awareness of it, in the unity of a consciousness that can itself become a grasping consciousness, and often enough does. This consciousness is awareness of the world-whole in its own peculiar form, that of spatiotemporal endlessness. Throughout every change in consciousness the universe—changeable in its experienced (and otherwise selectively meant) particulars, but still the one and only universe—remains as the existing background of our whole natural life. Thus, when phenomenological reduction is consistently executed, there is left us, on the noetic side, the openly endless life of pure consciousness and, as its correlate on the noematic side, the meant world, purely as meant. Accordingly, not only in respect of particulars but also *universally*, the phenomenologically meditating Ego can become the "non-participant onlooker" at himself—including furthermore every Objectivity that "is" for him, and *as* it is for him. Obviously it can be said that, as an Ego in the natural attitude, I am likewise and at all times a transcendental Ego, but that I know about this only by executing phenomenological reduction. Only by virtue of this new attitude do I see that all the world, and therefore whatever exists naturally, exists for me only as accepted by me, with the sense it has for me at the time—that it exists for me only as *cogitatum* of my changing and, while changing, interconnected *cogitationes*; and I now accept it solely as that. Consequently I, the transcendental phenomenologist, have *objects* (singly or in universal complexes) as a theme for my universal descriptions: *solely as the intentional correlates of modes of consciousness of them.*

* * *

§21. THE INTENTIONAL OBJECT AS "TRANSCENDENTAL CLUE"

The most universal type—within which, as a form, everything particular is included—is indicated by our first universal scheme: *ego—cogito—cogitatum*. The most universal descriptions (made with the most extreme, with—so to speak—formal, universality), which we have attempted in a rough fashion concerning intentionality, concerning its peculiar synthesis, and so forth, relate to that type. In the particularization of that type, and of its description, the *intentional object*[9] (on the side belonging to the *cogitatum*) plays, for easily understood reasons, the role of "transcendental clue" to the typical infinite multiplicities of possible *cogitationes* that, in a possible synthesis, bear the intentional object within them (in the manner peculiar to consciousness) as the same meant object. Necessarily the point of departure is the object given "straightforwardly" at the particular time. From it reflection goes back to the

9. On this use of "intentional," see p. 901, n. 6.

mode of consciousness at that time and to the potential modes of consciousness included horizonally in that mode, then to those in which the object
might be otherwise intended as the same, within the unity (ultimately) of a
possible conscious life, all the possibilities of which are included in the "ego".
If we continue to limit ourselves to the most extreme universality, to *formal
universality*, if we think of just any object (with an unrestrictedly optional content) as *cogitatum*, and take it in this universality as our clue, we find that the
multiplicity of possible modes of consciousness of the Same—the formal type
that all these exemplify—is subdivided into a number of sharply differentiated *particular types*. For example, possible perception, retention, recollection,
expectation, intending as something symbolized, intuitive representation by
analogy, are such types of intentionality, which pertain to *any conceivable
object*, as do their types of synthetic combination. All these types become further particularized in their whole noetic-noematic composition as soon as we
particularize the empty universality of the intentional object. The particularization may at first be formal-logical (formal-ontological)—that is to say:
modes of the Anything Whatever, such as single object, and ultimately individual object, universal, plurality, whole, predicatively formed state (or complex) of affairs, relational complex, and so forth. Here the radical difference
between *objectivities that are real* (in a broad sense) and *categorial objectivities* also presents itself. The latter point back to an origin from "operations",
from a step-by-step generative-constructive activity of the ego: the former, to
an origin as effects of a merely passive (in any case, not an <actively> generative) synthesis. On the other hand, we have the *material-ontological* particularizations, starting from the concept of the real concrete individual, which
is differentiated into its real regions—for example: (mere) spatial thing, animate being, and so forth—and entails corresponding particularizations of the
relevant formal-logical modifications (real property, real plurality, real relational complex, and the rest).

Each type brought out by these clues is to be asked about its noetic-
noematic structure, is to be systematically explicated and established in respect of those modes of intentional flux that pertain to it, and in respect of
their horizons and the intentional processes implicit in their horizons, and so
forth. If one keeps no matter what object fixed in its form or category and
maintains continuous evidence of its identity throughout the change in
modes of consciousness of it, one sees that, no matter how fluid these may
be, and no matter how inapprehensible as having ultimate elements, still
they are by no means variable without restriction. They are always restricted
to a set of *structural types*, which is "invariable", inviolably the same: as long
as the objectivity remains intended as *this* one and as of this kind, and as
long as, throughout the change in modes of consciousness, evidence of objective identity can persist.

To explicate systematically just this set of structural types is the *task of
transcendental theory*, which, if it restricts itself to an objective universality
as its clue, is called theory of the transcendental constitution of any object
whatever, as an object of the form or category (highest of all, the region) in
question. Thus arise—first of all, as separate—many different transcendental theories: a theory of perception and the other types of intuition, a theory
of intending objects as symbolized, a theory of judgment, a theory of

volition, and so forth. They become united, however, in view of the more comprehensive synthetic complexes; they belong together functionally, and thus make up the *formally universal* constitutional theory of *any object whatever* or of an open horizon of possible *objects of any sort*, as objects of possible consciousness.

Furthermore, transcendental theories of constitution arise that, as nonformal, relate to any spatial things whatever (singly and in the all-embracing nexus of a Nature), to any psycho-physical beings, to human beings as such, to their self-comportment toward their natural and otherwise determined surrounding world, to any social communities, any cultural objects, and ultimately to any Objective world whatever—purely as a world intended in possible consciousness and, transcendentally, as a world constituted (in the manner peculiar to consciousness) purely within the transcendental ego. All of that, naturally, with consistently exercised transcendental epoché, from which all these theories derive a transcendental sense.*

Yet it must not be overlooked that types of real and ideal objects intended as "*Objective*" are not the only clues for constitutional investigations—that is, when we inquire into the universal types of possible modes of consciousness of objects. The types of *merely subjective objects*, such as all immanent subjective processes themselves, are likewise clues, since, as objects of the consciousness of internal time, they have (singly and universally) their "constitution".

Everywhere problems of *particular, separately considered* kinds of objects and *problems of universality* become distinguishable. The latter concern the ego in the universality of his being and living and in his relation to the corresponding universality of his objective correlates. If we take the unitary Objective world as a transcendental clue, it leads back to the synthesis of Objective perceptions and other Objective intuitions, which extends throughout the unity of life as a whole, and is such that the world is at all times intended—and can become thematic—as a unit. Consequently the world is a universal problem of egology, as is likewise the whole of conscious life, in its immanent temporality, when we direct our regard to the purely immanent.

---

*At about this point Husserl inserted a page of text, which may be translated as follows.

Yet I had to begin with myself, the Ego given in experience of myself as a man. After all, I could exercise reduction only by starting out from myself; and therefore I arrived only at the ego who has, as his worldly counterpart, his own psyche. My own human psyche, therefore, I can make evident as a manifestation of the absolute: What are others, what is the world, for me?—Constituted phenomena, merely something produced within me. Never can I reach the point of ascribing being in the absolute sense to others, any more than to the physical things of Nature, which exist only as transcendentally produced affairs. Meditations I–IV concern a first path, along which it becomes visible in a very general manner that, for the ego of the transcendental reduction, all that exists is and must be a constituted product. But must it not be said likewise that all that exists for me as a man must be constituted within me, in the manner peculiar to consciousness—including my own humanness? How is the latter proposition related to the former? Conscious life is likewise constituted necessarily as human in the constituted world, and as a human conscious life in which the world is intended, psychically constituted, and so forth.

The all-embracing constitution of the world within the ego is outlined as a problem only as far as the theory of clues—as far as the consideration of the world (that is to say: the ontological consideration thereof, as transformed into a constitutional-ontological consideration). Somewhere in that context, naturally, the problem *man* must present itself? But what is the proper order?

The first procedure in Meditations I–IV is to awaken the guiding thought: The world is a meaning, an accepted sense. When we go back to the ego, we can explicate the founding and founded strata with which that sense is built up [*den Fundierungsaufbau*], we can reach the absolute being and process in which the being of the world shows its ultimate truth and in which the ultimate problems of being reveal themselves—bringing into the thematic field all the disguises that unphilosophical naiveté cannot penetrate [*alle Verhüllungen der unphilosophischen Naivität*] [translator's note, including the brackets].

§22. The Idea of the Universal Unity Comprising All Objects, and the Task of Clarifying It Constitutionally.

Types of objects—viewed with the attitude established by phenomenological reduction, purely as cogitata, and not construed with the "prejudices" involved in a set of scientific concepts accepted in advance—were found to be clues for transcendental investigations, which belong together on account of their themes. The fact is that the constituting multiplicities of consciousness—those actually or possibly combined to make the unity of an identifying synthesis—are not accidental but, as regards the possibility of such a synthesis, *belong together for essential reasons.* Accordingly they are governed by *principles,* thanks to which our phenomenological investigations do not get lost in disconnected descriptions but are essentially organized. Any "Objective" object, *any object whatever* (even an immanent one), points to *a structure, within the transcendental ego, that is governed by a rule.* As something the ego objectivates,[1] something of which he is conscious in any manner, the object indicates forthwith a universal rule governing *possible* other consciousnesses of it as identical—possible, as exemplifying essentially predelineated types. And naturally the same is true of any "imaginable" object, anything conceivable as something intended. Transcendental subjectivity is not a chaos of intentional processes. Moreover, it is not a chaos of types of constitution, each organized in itself by its relation to a kind or a form of intentional objects. In other words: The *allness* of objects and types of objects conceivable for me—transcendentally speaking: for me as transcendental ego—is no chaos; and correlatively the allness of the types of the infinite multiplicities, the types corresponding to types of objects, is not a chaos either: noetically and noematically those multiplicities always belong together, in respect of their possible synthesis.

That indicates in advance a *universal constitutive synthesis,* in which all syntheses function together in a definitely ordered manner and in which therefore all actual and possible objectivities (as actual and possible for the transcendental ego), and correlatively all actual and possible modes of consciousness of them, are embraced. Furthermore we can say that an enormous task is foreshadowed, which is that of transcendental phenomenology as a whole: the task of *carrying out all phenomenological investigations* within the unity of a systematic and all-embracing order by following, as our mobile clue, a system to be found out level by level, the system namely of all objects of possible consciousness, including the system of their formal and material categories—the task, I say, of carrying out such investigations as *corresponding constitutional investigations,* one based upon another, and all of them interconnected, in a strictly systematic fashion.

But we speak more correctly if we say that here it is a matter of an infinite *regulative idea,*[2] that the evidently presupposable system of possible objects of possible consciousness is itself an anticipative idea (not however an invention, an "as if"), and that, as regards practice, it equips us with the principle for combining any relatively closed constitutional theory with any other: by an incessant uncovering of horizons—not only those belonging to objects of consciousness internally, but also those having an external reference, namely to essential forms of inter-connexions. To be sure, even the tasks that present themselves when we take single types of objects as restricted clues prove to

---

1. Objectifies, makes into an object.
2. That is, a guiding idea—an idea that functions to guide inquiry, rather than to designate or refer to an existing reality of some sort (the latter being the function of a "constitutive" idea). This terminology is Kantian.

be extremely complicated and always lead to extensive disciplines when we penetrate more deeply. That is the case, for example, with a transcendental theory of the constitution of a spatial object (to say nothing of a Nature) as such, of psycho-physical being and humanity as such, culture as such.

From FOURTH MEDITATION

Development of the Constitutional Problems Pertaining to the Transcendental Ego Himself[3]

§30. THE TRANSCENDENTAL EGO INSEPARABLE FROM THE PROCESSES MAKING UP HIS LIFE

Objects exist for me, and are for me what they are, only as objects of actual and possible consciousness. If this is not to be an empty statement and a theme for empty speculations, it must be shown what makes up concretely this existence and being-thus for me, or what sort of actual and possible consciousness is concerned, what the structure of this consciousness is, what "possibility" signifies here, and so forth. This can be done solely by constitutional investigation—first, in the broader sense introduced initially, and then in the narrower sense just now described. Moreover there is but one possible method, the one demanded by the essence of intentionality and of its horizons. Even from the preparatory analyses leading us upward to the sense of the problem, it becomes clear that the transcendental ego (in the psychological parallel, the psyche) is what it is solely in relation to intentional objectivities. Among these, however, are necessarily included for the ego existing objects and, for him as related to a world, not only objects within his (adequately verifiable) sphere of immanent time but also world Objects, which are shown to be existent only in his inadequate, merely presumptive, external experience—in the harmoniousness of its course. It is thus an essential property of the ego, constantly to have systems of intentionality— among them, harmonious ones—partly as going on within him <actually>, partly as fixed potentialities, which, thanks to predelineating horizons, are available for uncovering. Each object that the ego ever means, thinks of, values, deals with, likewise each that he ever phantasies or can phantasy, indicates its correlative system and exists only as itself the correlate of its system.

§31. THE EGO AS IDENTICAL POLE OF THE SUBJECTIVE PROCESSES

Now, however, we must call attention to a great gap in our exposition. The ego is himself *existent for himself* in continuous evidence; thus, in himself, he is *continuously constituting himself as existing*. Heretofore we have touched on only one side of this self-constitution, we have looked at only the *flowing cogito*. The ego grasps himself not only as a flowing life but also as I, who live this and that subjective process, who live through this and that cogito, *as the same I*. Since we were busied up to now with the intentional relation of consciousness to object, cogito to cogitatum, only that synthesis stood out for us which "polarizes" the multiplicities of actual and possible consciousness toward identical objects, accordingly in relation to *objects as poles*, synthetic unities. Now we encounter a second polarization, a *second kind of synthesis*,

3. That is, itself. (As previously noted, the gender of the "ego" or "I [*Ich*]," transcendental or otherwise, is supplied by the translator.)

which embraces all the particular multiplicities of *cogitationes* collectively and in its own manner, namely as belonging to the identical Ego, who, *as the active and affected subject of consciousness*, lives in all processes of consciousness and is related, *through* them, to all object-poles.

§32. THE EGO AS SUBSTRATE OF HABITUALITIES

But it is to be noted that *this centering Ego is not an empty pole of identity*, any more than any *object* is such. Rather, according to a law of "transcendental generation", with every *act* emanating from him and having a *new* objective sense, he acquires *a new abiding property*. For example: If, in an act of judgment, I decide for the first time in favor of a being and a being-thus, the fleeting act passes; but from now on I *am abidingly the Ego who is thus and so decided*, "I am of this conviction". That, however, does not signify merely that I remember the act or can remember it later. This I can do, even if meanwhile I have "given up" my conviction. After cancellation it is no longer my conviction; but it has remained abidingly my conviction up to then. As long as it is accepted by me, I can "return" to it repeatedly, and repeatedly find it as mine, habitually my own opinion or, correlatively, find myself as the Ego who *is* convinced, who, as the persisting Ego, is determined by this abiding *habitus* or state. Likewise in the case of decisions of every other kind, value-decisions, volitional decisions. I decide; the act-process vanishes but the decision persists; whether I become passive and sink into heavy sleep or live in other acts, the decision continues to be accepted and, correlatively, I am so decided from then on, as long as I do not give the decision up. If it aims at a terminating deed, it is not "revoked" by the deed that fulfils it; in the mode characteristic of fulfilled decision it continues to be accepted: "I continue to stand by my deed". *I myself,* who am persisting in my abiding volition, *become changed* if I "cancel" my decisions or repudiate my deeds. The persisting, the temporal enduring, of such determining properties of the Ego, or the peculiar change that the Ego undergoes in respect of them, manifestly is not a continuous filling of immanent time with subjective processes—just as the abiding Ego himself, as the pole of abiding Ego-properties, is not a process or a continuity of processes, even though, with such habitual determining properties, he is indeed related back to the stream of subjective processes. Since, by his *own active generating*, the Ego constitues himself as *identical substrate of Ego-properties*, he constitutes himself also as a "fixed and abiding" *personal Ego*—in a maximally broad sense, which permits us to speak of sub-human "persons".[4] Though convictions are, in general, only relatively abiding and have their modes of alteration (through modalization of the active positings—for example, "cancellation" or negation, undoing of their acceptance), the Ego shows, in such alterations, an abiding style with a unity of identity throughout all of them: a "personal character".

§33. THE FULL CONCRETION OF THE EGO AS MONAD AND THE PROBLEM OF HIS SELF-CONSTITUTION

From the Ego as identical pole, and as substrate of habitualities, we distinguish *the ego taken in full concreteness*—in that we take, in addition, that

---

4. An allusion to animals. For Husserl's inclusion of animals among possible ego-subjects, see §35 of *Ideas*, with note 8, and §39, with note 4 (pp. 950–52 above).

without which the Ego cannot after all be concrete. (The ego, taken in full concreteness, we propose to call by the Leibnizian name: monad.[5]) The Ego can be concrete only in the flowing multiformity of his intentional life, along with the objects meant—and in some cases constituted as existent for him—in that life. Manifestly, in the case of an object so constituted, its abiding existence and being-thus are a correlate of the habituality constituted in the Ego-pole himself by virtue of his position-taking.

That is to be understood in the following manner. As ego, I have a surrounding world [Umwelt], which is continually "existing for me"; and, in it, objects as "existing for me"—already with the abiding distinction between those with which I am acquainted and those only anticipated as objects with which I may become acquainted. The former, the ones that are, in the first sense, existent for me, are such by original acquisition—that is: by my original taking cognizance of what I had never beheld previously, and my explication of it in particular intuitions of its features. Thereby, in my synthetic activity, the object becomes constituted originally, perceptively, in the explicit sense-form: "something identical having its manifold properties", or "object as identical with itself and undergoing determination in respect of its manifold properties". This, my activity of positing and explicating being, sets up a habituality of my Ego, by virtue of which the object, as having its manifold determinations, is mine abidingly. Such abiding acquisitions make up my surrounding world, so far as I am acquainted with it at the time, with its horizons of objects with which I am unacquainted—that is: objects yet to be acquired but already anticipated with this formal object-structure.

I exist for myself and am continually given to myself, by experiential evidence, as "I myself". This is true of the transcendental ego and, correspondingly, of the psychologically pure ego; it is true, moreover, with respect to any sense of the word ego. Since the monadically concrete ego includes also the whole of actual and potential conscious life, it is clear that the problem of explicating this monadic ego phenomenologically (the problem of his constitution for himself[6]) must include all constitutional problems without exception. Consequently the phenomenology of this self-constitution coincides with phenomenology as a whole.

* * *

FROM §40. TRANSITION TO THE QUESTION OF TRANSCENDENTAL IDEALISM

* * *

* * * That I attain certainties, even compelling evidences, in my own domain of consciousness, in the nexus of motivation determining me, is understandable. But how can this business, going on wholly within the immanency of conscious life, acquire Objective significance? How can evidence (clara et distincta perceptio)[7] claim to be more than a characteristic of consciousness

---

5. A term originating in Greek philosophy (literally, "unit"); for the German rationalist philosopher Gottfried Wilhelm Leibniz (1646–1716), it designated the logically or conceptually ultimate fundamental units of reality that are purported to (necessarily) be the basis of all phenomenal reality, spatiotemporal as well as psychological. Husserl apparently considers his thinking to be rightly associated not only with Descartes' epistemological program and aspirations but also with Leibniz's Idealist metaphysics.

6. That is, of its constitution for itself.

7. Clear and distinct perception (Latin). Here Husserl goes so far as to use Descartes' own language as a gloss on what he means by "evidence" or evidentness.

within me? Aside from the (perhaps not so unimportant) exclusion of acceptance of the world as being, it is the Cartesian problem, which was supposed
to be solved by divine *veracitas*.[8]

From §41. Genuine Phenomenological Explication of One's Own "Ego Cogito" as Transcendental Idealism

What does phenomenology's transcendental self-investigation have to say
about this? Nothing less than that the whole problem is inconsistent. It involves
an inconsistency into which Descartes necessarily fell, because he missed the
genuine sense of his reduction to the indubitable—we were about to say: his
transcendental epoché and reduction to the pure ego. But, precisely because
of its complete disregard of the Cartesian epoché, the usual post-Cartesian
way of thinking is much cruder. We ask: Who then is the Ego who can rightly
ask such "transcendental" questions? As a natural man, can I rightly ask them?
As a natural man, can I ask seriously and transcendentally how I get outside
my island of consciousness and how what presents itself in my consciousness
as a subjective evidence-process can acquire Objective significance? When I
apperceive myself as a natural man, I have already apperceived the spatial
world and construed myself as in space, where I already have an Outside Me.
Therefore the validity of world-apperception has already been presupposed,
has already entered into the sense assumed in asking the question—whereas
the answer alone ought to show the rightness of accepting anything as
Objectively valid. Manifestly the conscious execution of phenomenological
reduction is needed, in order to attain that Ego and conscious life by which
transcendental questions, as questions about the possibility of transcendent
knowledge, can be asked. But as soon as—instead of transiently exercising a
phenomenological epoché—one sets to work, attempting in a systematic self-
investigation and as the pure ego to uncover this ego's whole field of consciousness, one recognizes that all that exists for the pure ego becomes constituted
in him himself; furthermore, that every kind of being—including every kind
characterized as, in any sense, "transcendent"—has its own particular constitution. Transcendency in every form is an immanent existential characteristic, constituted within the ego. Every imaginable sense, every imaginable
being, whether the latter is called immanent or transcendent, falls within the
domain of transcendental subjectivity, as the subjectivity that constitutes
sense and being. The attempt to conceive the universe of true being as something lying outside the universe of possible consciousness, possible knowledge,
possible evidence, the two being related to one another merely externally by
a rigid law, is nonsensical. They belong together essentially; and, as belonging together essentially, they are also concretely one, one in the only absolute
concretion: transcendental subjectivity. If transcendental subjectivity is the
universe of possible sense, then an outside is precisely—nonsense. But even
nonsense is always a mode of sense and has its non-sensicalness within the
sphere of possible insight. That is true, however, not alone in the case of the
merely de facto ego and what is in fact (thanks to his own constituting) accessible to him as existing for him—including an open plurality of other egos
who, along with their constitutive performances, exist for him. Stated more

8. Veracity, truthfulness (Latin).

precisely: If (as is in fact the case) there are transcendentally constituted in me, the transcendental ego, not only other egos but also (*as* constituted in turn by the transcendental intersubjectivity accruing to me thanks to the constitution in me of others) an Objective world common to us all, then everything said up to now is true, not alone in the case of my de facto ego and in the case of this de facto intersubjectivity and world, which receive sense and existence-status in my subjectivity. The "phenomenological self-explication" that went on in my ego, this explication of all my ego's constitut-ings and all the objectivities existing for him, necessarily assumed the methodic form of an apriori self-explication, one that gives the facts their place in the corresponding universe of pure (or eidetic) possibilities. This explication there-fore concerns my de facto ego, only so far as the latter is one of the pure pos-sibilities to be acquired by his free phantasy-variation (fictive changing) of himself. Therefore, as eidetic, the explication is valid for the universe of these, my possibilities as essentially an ego, my possibilities namely of being other-wise; accordingly then it is valid also for every possible intersubjectivity related (with a corresponding modification) to these possibilities, and valid like-wise for every world imaginable as constituted in such an intersubjectivity. Genuine theory of knowledge is accordingly possible [*sinnvoll*][9] only as a transcendental-phenomenological theory, which, instead of operating with inconsistent inferences leading from a supposed immanency to a supposed transcendency (that of no matter what "thing in itself", which is alleged to be essentially unknowable), has to do exclusively with systematic clarification of the knowledge performance, a clarification in which this must become thor-oughly understandable as an intentional performance. Precisely thereby every sort of existent itself, real or ideal, becomes understandable as a "product" of transcendental subjectivity, a product constituted in just that performance.[1] This kind of understandableness is the highest imaginable form of rational-ity. All wrong interpretations of being come from naïve blindness to the hori-zons that join in determining the sense of being, and to the corresponding tasks of uncovering implicit intentionality. If these are seen and undertaken, there results a universal phenomenology, as a self-explication of the ego, car-ried out with continuous evidence and at the same time with concreteness. Stated more precisely: First, a self-explication in the pregnant sense, showing systematically how the ego constitutes himself, in respect of his own proper essence, as existent in himself and for himself; then, secondly, a self-explication in the broadened sense, which goes on from there to show how, by virtue of this proper essence, the ego likewise constitutes in himself something "other", something "Objective", and thus constitutes everything without exception that ever has for him, in the Ego, existential status as non-Ego.

Carried out with this systematic concreteness, phenomenology is *eo ipso*[2] "*transcendental idealism*", though in a fundamentally and essentially new sense. It is not a psychological idealism, and most certainly not such an ide-alism as sensualistic psychologism proposes, an idealism that would derive a senseful world from senseless sensuous data. Nor is it a Kantian idealism,

---

9. Better translated as "meaningful."
1. This claim reflects the radical "idealism" that Husserl explicitly embraces in the next paragraph, linking him not only with Descartes and Leibniz but also with post-Kantian Idealism, which dis-

pensed with Kant's "thing-in-itself" as meaning-less and transformed Kant's "transcendental ego" into the locus and basis of all reality.
2. By that itself (Latin); that is, thereby, as such.

which believes it can keep open, at least as a limiting concept, the possibility of a world of things in themselves.[3] On the contrary, we have here a transcendental idealism that *is* nothing more than a consequentially executed self-explication in the form of a systematic egological science [*Wissenschaft*], an explication of my ego as subject of every possible cognition, and indeed with respect to every sense of what exists, wherewith the latter might be able to *have* a sense for me, the ego. This idealism is not a product of sportive argumentations, a prize to be won in the dialectical contest with "realisms". It is *sense-explication* achieved *by actual work*, an explication carried out as regards every type of existent ever conceivable by me, the ego, and specifically as regards the transcendency actually given to me beforehand through experience: Nature, culture, the world as a whole. But that signifies: systematic uncovering of the constituting intentionality itself. *The proof of this idealism is therefore phenomenology itself.*[4] Only someone who misunderstands either the deepest sense of intentional method, or that of transcendental reduction, or perhaps both, can attempt to separate phenomenology from transcendental idealism. Whoever labors under the first misunderstanding has not advanced even so far as to grasp the peculiar essence of a genuine intentional psychology (including that of an intentional-psychological theory of knowledge) or the requirement that intentional psychology become the fundamental and central part of a truly scientific [*wissenschaftlich*] psychology. On the other hand, anyone who misconstrues the sense and performance of transcendental-phenomenological reduction is still entangled in psychologism; he confounds intentional psychology and transcendental phenomenology, a parallel that arises by virtue of the essential possibility of a change in attitude; he falls a victim to the inconsistency of a transcendental philosophy that stays within the natural realm.

Our meditations have prospered to the extent that already they have made evident the necessary style of a philosophy, namely its style as transcendental-phenomenological philosophy, and correlatively, for the universe of what exists for us actually or possibly, the style of its only possible sense-interpretation:[5] the style of the latter as transcendental-phenomenological idealism. Included in this evidence is the insight that the infinity of tasks disclosed by our extremely general preliminary sketch—the self-explications of my (the meditator's) ego in respect of constituting and constituted—are a chain of particular meditations fitting into the universal frame of one unitary meditation, which can always be carried further synthetically.

* * *

SOURCE: From Edmund Husserl, *Cartesian Meditations: An Introduction to Phenomenology*, trans. Dorian Cairns (1960; reprint, The Hague: M. Nijhoff, 1970), pp. 1–2, 4–9, 11–21, 35–37,

3. It would seem significant that Husserl does not take this opportunity to disassociate his "transcendental idealism" from the Idealisms of FICHTE and SCHELLING.

4. That is, for Husserl phenomenology itself *is* the "proof" of this Idealism, in the sense that the meaning and experiential constitution (and therefore the essence) of every possible type of object of experience and mode of experience leave nothing meaningful to be said about anything else—and so render incoherent the idea that there could *be* anything else, other than the "transcendental ego" that must be supposed to be the condition of the possibility of all such experience and constitution. (The various other *Wissenschaften* are thus seen as dealing with various types of phenomena at a less fundamental level of consideration.)

5. That is, of the only possible interpretation of its meaning.

50–55, 65–68, 81–87. Except where otherwise indicated, German words in brackets are the terminology used in the German original, inserted by the editor in addition to their renderings in the translation. "The *Meditations* are an elaboration of two lectures, entitled '*Einleitung in die transzendentale Phänomenologie*' (Introduction to Transcendental Phenomenology), that Husserl delivered at the Sorbonne on the twenty-third and twenty-fifth of February, 1929" [translator's note]. *Meditations* was first published in a French version in 1931, and appeared in Husserl's German in 1950.

From Philosophy and the Crisis of European Man

I

In this lecture I will venture an attempt to awaken new interest in the oft-treated theme of the European crisis by developing the philosophico-historical idea (or the teleological sense) of European man.[1]

* * *

* * * I am referring, of course, to the spiritual form of Europe. It is now no longer a number of different nations bordering on each other, influencing each other only by commercial competition and war. Rather a new spirit [*Geist*] stemming from philosophy and the sciences [*Wissenschaften*][2] based on it, a spirit of free criticism providing norms for infinite tasks, dominates man, creating new, infinite ideals. These are ideals for individual men of each nation and for the nations themselves. Ultimately, however, the expanding synthesis of nations too has its infinite ideals, wherein each of these nations, by the very fact that it strives to accomplish its own ideal task in the spirit of infinity,[3] contributes its best to the community of nations. In this give and take the supernational totality with its graded structure of societies grows apace, filled with the spirit of one all-inclusive task, infinite in the variety of its branches yet unique in its infinity. In this total society with its ideal orientation, philosophy itself retains the role of guide, which is its special infinite task. Philosophy has the role of a free and universal theoretical disposition that embraces at once all ideals and the one overall ideal—in short, the universe of all norms. Philosophy has constantly to exercise through European man its role of leadership for the whole of mankind.

II

* * *

Is not what is here being advocated something rather out of place in our times—saving the honor of rationalism, of enlightenment, of an intellectualism that, lost in theory, is isolated from the world, with the necessarily bad

1. That is, "European humanity" (*europäischen Menschentum*). Husserl is actually speaking and thinking here of Western civilization more generally, in this time of its greatest crisis.
2. On the term *Wissenschaft*, often translated "science," see the source note to "Philosophy as Rigorous Science [*Wissenschaft*]," above.

3. "im Geiste der Unendlichkeit": that is, in the spirit of humanity's transcendence of all finite limitations (presumably in the quest for genuine knowledge above all). As critical of HEGEL as Husserl may have been, he shared Hegel's audacious aspiration for a kind of knowledge that might truly and appropriately be characterized as "absolute."

result that the quest for learning becomes empty, becomes intellectual snobbishness? Does it not mean falling back into the fatal error of thinking that science [*Wissenschaft*] makes men wise, that science [*Wissenschaft*] is called upon to create a genuine humanity, superior to destiny and finding satisfaction in itself? Who is going to take such thoughts seriously today?

This objection certainly is relatively justified in regard to the state of development in Europe from the seventeenth up to the end of the nineteenth century. But it does not touch the precise sense of what I am saying. I should like to think that I, seemingly a reactionary, am far more revolutionary than those who today in word strike so radical a pose.

I, too, am quite sure, that the European crisis has its roots in a mistaken rationalism.[4] That, however, must not be interpreted as meaning that rationality as such is an evil or that in the totality of human existence it is of minor importance. The rationality of which alone we are speaking is rationality in that noble and genuine sense, the original Greek sense, that became an ideal in the classical period of Greek philosophy—though of course it still needed considerable clarification through self-examination. It is its vocation, however, to serve as a guide to mature development. On the other hand, we readily grant (and in this regard German idealism has spoken long before us) that the form of development given to *ratio*[5] in the rationalism of the Enlightenment was an aberration, but nevertheless an understandable aberration.

Reason is a broad title. According to the good old definition, man is the rational living being, a sense in which even the Papuan is man and not beast. He has his aims, and he acts with reflection, considering practical possibilities. As products and methods grow, they enter into a tradition that is ever intelligible in its rationality. Still, just as man (and even the Papuan) represents a new level of animality—in comparison with the beast—so with regard to humanity and its reason does philosophical reason represent a new level. The level of human existence with its ideal norms for infinite tasks, the level of existence *sub specie aeternitatis*,[6] is, however, possible only in the form of absolute universality, precisely that which is a priori included in the idea of philosophy. It is true that universal philosophy, along with all the particular sciences, constitutes only a partial manifestation of European culture. Contained, however, in the sense of my entire presentation is the claim that this part is, so to speak, the functioning brain upon whose normal functioning the genuine, healthy spirit of Europe depends. The humanity of higher man, of reason, demands, therefore, a genuine philosophy.

But at this very point there lurks a danger. "Philosophy"—in that we must certainly distinguish philosophy as a historical fact belonging to this or that time from philosophy as idea, idea of an infinite task. The philosophy that at any particular time is historically actual is the more or less successful attempt to realize the guiding idea of the infinity, and thereby the totality, of truths. Practical ideals, viewed as external poles from the line of which one cannot stray during the whole of life without regret, without being untrue to oneself and thus unhappy, are in this view by no means yet clear and determined; they are anticipated in an equivocal generality. Determination comes only with concrete pursuit and with

4. That is, the (shallow) rationalism of the Enlightenment, which had faith in the ability of natural-scientific theoretical rationality and social-bureaucratic practical rationality to lead humanity to truth and solve all of its practical problems.
5. Reason (Latin).
6. Under the aspect of eternity (Latin); that is, from the perspective of the eternal.

at least relatively successful action. Here the constant danger is that of falling into one-sidedness and premature satisfaction, which are punished in subsequent contradictions. Thence the contrast between the grand claims of philosophical systems, that are all the while incompatible with each other. Added to this are the necessity and yet the danger of specialization.

In this way, of course, one-sided rationality can become an evil. It can also be said that it belongs to the very essence of reason that philosophers can at first understand and accomplish their infinite task only on the basis of an absolutely necessary one-sidedness. In itself there is no absurdity here, no error. Rather, as has been remarked, the direct and necessary path for reason allows it initially to grasp only one aspect of the task, at first without recognizing that a thorough knowledge of the entire infinite task, the totality of being, involves still other aspects. When inadequacy reveals itself in obscurities and contradiction, then this becomes a motive to engage in a universal reflection. Thus the philosopher must always have as his purpose to master the true and full sense of philosophy, the totality of its infinite horizons. No one line of knowledge, no individual truth must be absolutized. Only in such a supreme consciousness of self, which itself becomes a branch of the infinite task, can philosophy fulfill its function of putting itself, and therewith a genuine humanity,[7] on the right track. To know that this is the case, however, also involves once more entering the field of knowledge proper to philosophy on the highest level of reflection upon itself. Only on the basis of this constant reflectiveness is a philosophy a universal knowledge.

I have said that the course of philosophy goes through a period of naïveté. This, then, is the place for a critique of the so renowned irrationalism, or it is the place to uncover the naïveté of that rationalism that passes as genuine philosophical rationality, and that admittedly is characteristic of philosophy in the whole modern period since the Renaissance, looking upon itself as the real and hence universal rationalism. Now, as they begin, all the sciences, even those whose beginnings go back to ancient times, are unavoidably caught up in this naïveté. To put it more exactly, the most general title for this naïveté is objectivism, which is given a structure in the various types of naturalism, wherein the spirit [Geist] is naturalized.[8] Old and new philosophies were and remain naïvely objectivistic. It is only right, however, to add that German idealism, beginning with Kant, was passionately concerned with overcoming the naïveté that had already become very sensitive. Still, it was incapable of really attaining to the level of superior reflectiveness that is decisive for the new image of philosophy and of European man.

* * *

There are all sorts of problems that stem from naïveté, according to which objectivistic science holds what it calls the objective world to be the totality of what is, without paying any attention to the fact that no objective science can do justice to the subjectivity that achieves science. One who has been trained in the natural sciences finds it self-evident that whatever is merely

7. Husserl's conception of "genuine humanity," or humanity at its best and most fully self-realized, is comparable at least in principle to Hegel's conception of the culmination of "absolute spirituality" in "absolute knowing."

8. Here Husserl renews his campaign against naturalistic accounts (and reductions) of all human spirituality to phenomena with an entirely biological and sociohistorical basis, genealogy, and status.

subjective must be eliminated and that the method of natural science, formulated according to a subjective mode of representation, is objectively determined. In the same manner he seeks what is objectively true for the psychic too. By the same token, it is taken for granted that the subjective, eliminated by the physical scientist, is, precisely as psychic, to be investigated in psychology and of course in psychophysical psychology. The investigator of nature, however, does not make it clear to himself that the constant foundation of his admittedly subjective thinking activity is the environing world of life.[9] This latter is constantly presupposed as the basic working area, in which alone his questions and his methodology make sense. Where, at the present time, is that powerful bit of method that leads from the intuitive environing world to the idealizing of mathematics and its interpretation as objective being, subjected to criticism and clarification? Einstein's revolutionary changes[1] concern the formulas wherein idealized and naïvely objectivized nature (*physis*)[2] is treated. But regarding the question of how formulas or mathematical objectification in general are given a sense based on life and the intuitive environing world, of this we hear nothing. Thus Einstein does nothing to reformulate the space and time in which our actual life takes place.

Mathematical science of nature is a technical marvel for the purpose of accomplishing inductions whose fruitfulness, probability, exactitude, and calculability could previously not even be suspected. As an accomplishment it is a triumph of the human spirit. With regard to the rationality of its methods and theories, however, it is a thoroughly relative science. It presupposes as data principles that are themselves thoroughly lacking in actual rationality. In so far as the intuitive environing world, purely subjective as it is, is forgotten in the scientific thematic, the working subject is also forgotten, and the scientist is not studied. (Thus from this point of view the rationality of the exact sciences is on a level with the rationality of the Egyptian pyramids.)

It is true, of course, that since Kant we have a special theory of knowledge, and on the other hand there is psychology, which with its claims to scientific exactitude wants to be the universal fundamental science [*Wissenschaft*] of the spirit.[3] Still, our hope for real rationality, i.e., for real insight, is disappointed here as elsewhere. The psychologists simply fail to see that they too study neither themselves nor the scientists who are doing the investigating nor their own vital environing world. They do not see that from the very beginning they necessarily presuppose themselves as a group of men belonging to their own environing world and historical period. By the same token, they do not see that in pursuing their aims they are seeking a truth in itself, universally valid for everyone. By its objectivism psychology simply cannot make a study of the soul in its properly essential sense, which is to say, the ego that acts and is acted upon.[4]

9. The conception of a "life-world" (*Lebenswelt*) was central to Husserl's late philosophy. It provides a kind of conceptual bridge between his earlier "pure phenomenology" and the kind of "applied" or "existential" phenomenology that subsequently became quite popular—phenomenology applied to the analysis of the sorts of phenomena with which existing human subjects have common experience and must often deal.
1. That is, the theories of relativity set forth by the German-born physicist Albert Einstein (1879–1955), which fundamentally changed the scientific understanding of space, time, matter, and energy.
2. Greek.
3. That is, the fundamental "*Wissenschaft* of *Geist*."
4. This is an important shift in Husserl's thinking—from the conception of "the ego" (*das Ich*, the conscious subject or self) as something that has conscious experiences and performs conscious acts of various sorts to its conception as something that can and does act and interact in significant ways within the *Lebenswelt* both with things and with other subjects.

Though by determining the bodily function involved in an experience of evaluating or willing, it may objectify the experience and handle it inductively, can it do the same for purposes, values, norms? Can it study reason as some sort of "disposition"? Completely ignored is the fact that objectivism, as the genuine work of the investigator intent upon finding true norms, presupposes just such norms; that objectivism refuses to be inferred from facts, since in the process facts are already intended as truths and not as illusions. It is true, of course, that there exists a feeling for the difficulties present here, with the result that the dispute over psychologism is fanned into a flame. Nothing is accomplished, however, by rejecting a psychological grounding of norms, above all of norms for truth in itself. More and more perceptible becomes the overall need for a reform of modern psychology in its entirety. As yet, however, it is not understood that psychology through its objectivism has been found wanting; that it simply fails to get at the proper essence of spirit [*Geist*]; that in isolating the soul and making it an object of thought, that in reinterpreting psychophysically being-in-community, it is being absurd. True, it has not labored in vain, and it has established many empirical rules, even practically worthwhile ones. Yet it is no more a real psychology than moral statistics with its no less worthwhile knowledge is a moral science [*Wissenschaft*].

In our time we everywhere meet the burning need for an understanding of spirit [*Geist*], while the unclarity of the methodological and factual connection between the natural sciences and the sciences of the spirit [*Geisteswissenschaften*] has become almost unbearable. Dilthey, one of the greatest scientists of the spirit [*Geisteswissenschaftler*], has directed his whole vital energy to clarifying the connection between nature and spirit [*Geist*], to clarifying the role of psychophysical psychology, which he thinks is to be complemented by a new, descriptive and analytic psychology.[5] * * *

The spirit [*Der Geist*] and in fact only the spirit [*der Geist*] is a being in itself and for itself; it is autonomous and is capable of being handled in a genuinely rational, genuinely and thoroughly scientific [*wissenschaftlich*] way only in this autonomy.[6] In regard to nature and scientific truth concerning it, however, the natural sciences give merely the appearance of having brought nature to a point where for itself it is rationally known. For true nature in its proper scientific [*wissenschaftlich*] sense is a product of the spirit that investigates nature, and thus the science of nature presupposes the science [*Wissenschaft*] of the spirit. The spirit [*Der Geist*] is essentially qualified to exercise self-knowledge, and as scientific spirit [*wissenschaftlich Geist*] to exercise scientific self-knowledge, and that over and over again. Only in the kind of pure knowledge proper to science of the spirit [*Geisteswissenschaft*] is the scientist unaffected by the objection that his accomplishment is self-concealing. As a consequence, it is absurd for the sciences of the spirit to dispute with the sciences of nature for equal rights. To the extent that the former concede to the latter that their objectivity is an autonomy, they are themselves victims of objectivism. Moreover, in the way the sciences of the spirit are at present developed, with their manifold disciplines, they forfeit the ultimate, actual rationality which the spiritual *Weltanschauung* makes possible. Precisely this lack of genuine rationality on all sides is the source of what has become for man an unbearable

5. On DILTHEY, see above.
6. This entire sentence is emphasized in the German text. (It makes a point with which both KANT and Hegel would agree.)

unclarity regarding his own existence and his infinite tasks. These last are inseparably united in one task: only if the spirit returns to itself from its naïve exteriorization, clinging to itself and purely to itself, can it be adequate to itself.[7]

Now, how did the beginning of such a self-examination come about? A beginning was impossible so long as sensualism, or better, a psychology of data, a *tabula rasa*[8] psychology, held the field. Only when Brentano[9] promoted psychology to being a science of vital intentional experiences was an impulse given that could lead further—though Brentano himself had not yet overcome objectivism and psychological naturalism. The development of a real method of grasping the fundamental essence of spirit [*Geist*] in its intentionalities and consequently of instituting an analysis of spirit with a consistency reaching to the infinite, led to transcendental phenomenology. It was this that overcame naturalistic objectivism, and for that matter any form of objectivism, in the only possible way, by beginning one's philosophizing from one's own ego; and that purely as the author of all one accepts, becoming in this regard a purely theoretical spectator. This attitude brings about the successful institution of an absolutely autonomous science of spirit in the form of a consistent understanding of self and of the world as a spiritual accomplishment. Spirit [*Geist*] is not looked upon here as part of nature or parallel to it; rather nature belongs to the sphere of spirit [*Geist*]. Then, too, the ego is no longer an isolated thing alongside other such things in a pre-given world. The serious problem of personal egos external to or alongside of each other comes to an end in favor of an intimate relation of beings in each other and for each other.[1]

Regarding this question of interpersonal relations, nothing can be said here; no one lecture could exhaust the topic. I do hope, however, to have shown that we are not renewing here the old rationalism, which was an absurd naturalism, utterly incapable of grasping the problems of spirit that concern us most. The *ratio* now in question is none other than spirit [*Geist*] understanding itself in a really universal, really radical manner, in the form of a science [*Wissenschaft*] whose scope is universal, wherein an entirely new scientific thinking is established in which every conceivable question, whether of being, of norm, or of so-called "existence," finds its place.[2] It is my conviction that intentional phenomenology has for the first time made spirit as spirit [*Geist*] the field of systematic, scientific [*wissenschaftlich*] experience, thus effecting a total transformation of the task of knowledge. The universality of the absolute spirit [*Geist*] embraces all being in an absolute historicity, into which nature fits as a product of spirit [*Geistesgebilde*]. It is intentional, which is to say transcendental, phenomenology that sheds light on the subject by virtue of its point of departure and its

7. This entire sentence is emphasized in the German text.

8. Scraped tablet (Latin)—that is, a "blank slate," ready to be written on; as a metaphor of the mind, it is associated particularly with the English empiricist John Locke (1632–1704).

9. Franz Brentano (1838–1917), German philosopher and founder of act psychology, which emphasizes intentionality; see in this anthology's companion volume, *The Analytic Tradition*.

1. This almost certainly is a (necessarily oblique) reference to Martin Buber's insistence on the importance of this sort of interpersonal relationship and experience in *I and Thou* (1924; see below), which Husserl here appears to be acknowledging, as a point of phenomenological as well as human significance. If he had pursued the idea of the possibility and irreducibility of that sort of experience, he might have provided another conceptual bridge between his transcendental phenomenology and existential phenomenology.

2. Here Husserl expresses his discomfort with and dubiousness about Heidegger's philosophy of human "existence (*Existenz*)," whose popularity was already growing rapidly.

methods. Only when seen from the phenomenological point of view is naturalistic objectivism, along with the profoundest reasons for it, to be understood. Above all, phenomenology makes clear that, because of its naturalism, psychology simply could not come to terms with the activity and the properly radical problem of spirit's life [*geistig Leben*].

III

Let us summarize the fundamental notions of what we have sketched here. The "crisis of European existence," which manifests itself in countless symptoms of a corrupted life, is no obscure fate, no impenetrable destiny. Instead, it becomes manifestly understandable against the background of the philosophically discoverable "teleology of European history." As a presupposition of this understanding, however, the phenomenon "Europe" is to be grasped in its essential core. To get the concept of what is contra-essential in the present "crisis," the concept "Europe" would have to be developed as the historical teleology of infinite goals of reason; it would have to be shown how the European "world" was born from ideas of reason, i.e., from the spirit of philosophy. The "crisis" could then become clear as the "seeming collapse of rationalism." Still, as we said, the reason for the downfall of a rational culture does not lie in the essence of rationalism itself but only in its exteriorization, its absorption in "naturalism" and "objectivism."

The crisis of European existence can end in only one of two ways: in the ruin of a Europe alienated from its rational sense of life, fallen into a barbarian hatred of spirit; or in the rebirth of Europe from the spirit of philosophy, through a heroism of reason that will definitively overcome naturalism. Europe's greatest danger is weariness. Let us as "good Europeans" do battle with this danger of dangers with the sort of courage that does not shirk even the endless battle. If we do, then from the annihilating conflagration of disbelief, from the fiery torrent of despair regarding the West's mission to humanity, from the ashes of the great weariness, the phoenix of a new inner life of the spirit will arise[3] as the underpinning of a great and distant human future, for the spirit alone is immortal.[4]

SOURCE: From Edmund Husserl, *Phenomenology and the Crisis of Philosophy*, trans. Quentin Lauer (New York: Harper & Row, 1965), pp. 149, 177–81, 185–92. Except where otherwise indicated, German words in brackets are the terminology used in the German original, inserted by the editor in addition to their renderings in the translation. This essay originated as a lecture, "Die Philosophie in der Krisis der europäischen Menschheit" ("Philosophy in the Crisis of European Humanity"); it was delivered in Vienna in 1935, three years before Husserl's death, at a time when the power of Hitler and Nazi Germany was rising but Austria had not yet been incorporated into Germany. It is related to Husserl's last completed work, *Der Krisis der europäischen Wissenschaften und das transzendentale Phänomenologie* (1936, *The Crisis of European Cognitive Inquiry and Transcendental Phenomenology*).

3. That is, "a new inwardness of life and spiritualization arises [or will arise]" (*einer neuen Lebensinnerlichkiet und Vergeisterung aufersteht*).

4. "Denn der Geist allein ist unsterblich." This final clause, preceded in the original by a colon rather than simply a comma, is clearly intended to end the essay with a dramatic flourish—made all the more poignant by the ominousness of the times. This is essentially Husserl's last word, even though he proceeded to elaborate the ideas of this essay in the *Crisis* book that followed. And it shows that, in the end, he conceived of his kind of phenomenology not as a radical alternative to the philosophy of *Geist* but as its reformation.

MARTIN HEIDEGGER
(1889 – 1976)

Heidegger loomed as large in twentieth-century philosophy in the interpretive tradition as HEGEL had in the nineteenth (and as Ludwig Wittgenstein did in the twentieth-century analytic tradition). The impact of his *Being and Time* was enormous. Published in 1927, it transformed the philosophical scene in German-speaking Europe within just a few years, launching the existential-philosophical movement that many came to see as almost synonymous with Continental (i.e., European) philosophy in the middle third of the twentieth century. Heideggerian existential philosophy—the philosophical analysis of human existence (*Existenz*) and human reality (*Dasein*), or of what KIERKEGAARD had called "what it means to exist as a human being"—rapidly eclipsed the remnants of Hegelianism, the revival of Kantianism, and the fledgling "philosophical anthropology" movement emerging out of central European "life philosophy" (*Lebensphilosophie*). And it soon supplanted the kind of phenomenology that Heidegger's mentor EDMUND HUSSERL had inaugurated as the dominant philosophical development of the day. It spread to France as "existentialism" after the Second World War, and then throughout the Western world—even as Heidegger himself was moving on, to a still more radical departure from the Western philosophical tradition. By the time of his death in 1976 Heidegger had attained virtual cult status in the eyes of many, while others regarded him as the very embodiment of the most problematic tendencies of German philosophy and society in the first half of the twentieth century. Few figures in the history of philosophy have been as controversial.

Martin Heidegger ("HIGH-degger") was born in the small Black Forest town of Messkirch, and it was in that part of southwestern Germany that he lived most of his life. His feelings for it were very powerful, and significantly influenced his thinking. His family was devoutly and simply Catholic, as was most of the population in that region, and it was initially both his family's hope and his own expectation that he would enter the priesthood. He even became a Jesuit novice for a short while after concluding his early schooling, before withdrawing for reasons of health. In his early teens Heidegger attended school first in Konstanz and then in Freiburg, where the main university in that part of the country was located. He had already become interested in philosophy during his high school years, when he happened to read Franz Brentano's *On the Several Senses of Being in Aristotle* (1862). That experience inspired his lifelong interest in "the meaning of being"—the all-important question for which he considered *Being and Time* to be merely preparing the way.

Heidegger's philosophical interests initially had a strongly religious character; and when he initially entered the university at Freiburg, in 1909, it was as a theology student. Two years later, however, he shifted his studies to philosophy, becoming very interested in Husserl and his program of phenomenology. Heidegger completed his doctoral dissertation on the problem of psychologism in philosophy in 1914, under the supervision of the prominent Neo-Kantian philosopher Heinrich Rickert. At the outbreak of the First World War he enlisted in the army, but because of ill health he was released from service shortly thereafter and returned to his academic pursuits.

Heidegger aspired to the professorship of Catholic philosophy at Freiburg; and so, two years later, he completed his habilitation (the postdoctoral research credential then required for a university teaching position) with a second dissertation on the treatment of categories and meaning in the Scholastic text *On the Modes of Signifying*, at that time attributed to the medieval theologian and philosopher Duns Scotus. This research contributed further to the development of his thinking with respect to "meaning" and "being." After a year of unsalaried teaching at Freiburg (1916–1917), during which he became acquainted with Husserl (then a new member of Freiburg's philosophy faculty) and married Elfriede Petri, he was called into army service in a noncombatant role. Upon returning to Freiburg after the war's end he publicly terminated his association with Catholic philosophy and obtained an appointment as Husserl's assistant, while continuing as a lecturer on topics in phenomenology as well as in Aristotle's philosophy. But his thinking began to diverge from Husserl's almost immediately; for Husserl turned in a Cartesian and Kantian direction, while Heidegger was feeling the pull of Kierkegaard and NIETZSCHE.

In 1923 Heidegger left Freiburg to take a midlevel position at Marburg University. He was highly successful as a teacher, but published little in his first three years. Under great pressure to publish something substantial in order to secure his position and advance academically, he readied an incomplete version of a book on which he had been working for publication. He was fortunate to have it appear in 1927 in Husserl's phenomenological research "Yearbook" series, thereby gaining what amounted to Husserl's seal of approval. That book was *Being and Time*. It earned him an appointment at the rank of professor at Marburg that very year, and attracted immediate widespread attention and interest. When Husserl retired in the following year, Heidegger was appointed to his chair (professorship) at Freiburg, where he remained for the remainder of his academic career.

Heidegger dedicated *Being and Time* to Husserl, "In friendship and admiration"; but in the years that followed, as his star rose, Heidegger in effect abandoned his mentor. His writings after *Being and Time* made his departure from Husserl's kind of phenomenology and philosophical orientation increasingly clear and dramatic. That is something for which he can hardly be faulted. But he also ceased to have personal contact with Husserl during the last years of Husserl's life, as Hitler's new government began to take steps to exclude ethnic Jews (including those who, like Husserl, had converted to Christianity) from academic and public life—and he even removed the dedication to Husserl from printings of *Being and Time* after 1933. (After the war it was restored.)

Like many other German academics at that time, Heidegger was initially enthusiastic about Hitler, and even joined the Nazi Party. Indeed, when he was selected to serve as rector (or provost) of Freiburg University in 1933, he expressed his enthusiasm for the new regime in his inaugural address. (He proved to be unsuccessful as a university administrator, and resigned after only a year as rector.) Though he soon ceased to be outspokenly supportive of Hitler and his actions, and kept a low profile during the Second World War, he retained his party membership until the war ended in 1945.

Freiburg was in the French zone of occupation after the war; and, owing to his association with the Nazis, Heidegger was forbidden to teach, at Freiburg or anywhere else in Germany. That ban was lifted—to much acclaim by his admirers and the media—in 1951, when he was allowed to return to academic life as professor emeritus at Freiburg. He taught regularly until 1958, and occasionally after that. He also was much in demand as a lecturer (although he disliked travel, and preferred to remain in Freiburg and his nearby mountain hut). Before Hitler's rise, Heidegger had had many devoted students who did not at all share his political orientation. A number of them were Jewish—including HANNAH ARENDT, with whom he had a brief but intense affair. (He apparently had a number of other affairs as well, as did his wife in the early years of their marriage.) After the war many of his former students, and many of his earlier philosophical and academic colleagues as well (including KARL JASPERS), wrestled with the question of whether he could be forgiven for what he had done and said during the Hitler years—or, if not, whether resuming a relationship of some sort with him was possible and desirable. (Arendt was among those who chose to do so; Jaspers was among those who did not.)

Heidegger's thinking had undergone what has come to be known as a major "turn" (*Kehre*) in the later 1930s, moving away from the kind of phenomenological project he had pursued in *Being and Time* in a direction that led him ultimately not only to denounce metaphysics but to renounce the label of "philosophy" for the kind of thinking to which he had "turned." His thinking focused increasingly on the questions of "meaning" and "being" with which he had begun, but it became a different kind of thinking, expressed in a style that had an increasingly poetic quality. During the last decades of his life his writings—many of which began as lectures—tended to be brief and ever more obscure. The selections below that follow substantial excerpts from *Being and Time* give some indication of the trajectory of his thought from the late 1940s onward. Heidegger died in Freiburg in 1976.

When Heidegger succeeded to Husserl's chair in philosophy at Freiburg, shortly after the appearance of *Being and Time*, he still professed to be following in Husserl's footsteps, at least to the extent of doing "phenomenological" philosophy. Nevertheless, his avowedly phenomenological analysis and interpretation of human experience had a radically different focus and character than Husserl's. *Being and Time*'s focus was on what Kierkegaard had in mind in speaking of "what it means to exist as a human being" (which Heidegger calls *Dasein*); and its character reflected the urgency associated with the collapse of traditional ways of thinking about ourselves and the human condition that Nietzsche had in mind in speaking of "the death of God."

But Nietzsche and Kierkegaard were not yet being taken seriously by the academic philosophical community in Europe (or elsewhere); indeed, they drew attention only gradually, owing in no small measure to the interest taken in them by Heidegger and his fellow existential-philosophical founding father Karl Jaspers. Their relative unfamiliarity made *Being and Time* seem even more revolutionary than it was. Yet it is that book—rather than his later writings—for which Heidegger is most likely to be best remembered; and because of its importance, it provides the bulk of his work included in this volume and is the focus of most of the following commentary. The three other selections indicate the direction and character of his later thought and publications after he ceased to call what he was doing "phenomenology," or even (eventually) "philosophy," preferring to speak instead of "thought" and "essential thinking" with respect to human life and its meaning.

Heidegger's fundamental concern, from first to last, was not with human reality as a topic unto itself, but rather with the much larger and more fundamental question of how to think about "being" conceived as something like that in relation to which the nature, existence and occurrence of anything and everything in and about human reality and the world in which we find ourselves are to be understood. He calls this the question of "the meaning [*Sinn*] of being [*Sein*]." And he was convinced that while the pre-Socratic Greek philosophers may have been trying to ask and answer this question in at least the right sort of way, the entire subsequent history of Western philosophy has been the story of misunderstanding it and giving answers that contribute to its further misunderstanding, by inducing us to think about "being" (*Sein*) in ways that are deeply misguided.

Though Heidegger raises this issue at the outset of *Being and Time*, the book itself is devoted to what he sees as an unavoidable preliminary question regarding the meaning or character of the being (*Seinde*) that is attempting to ask and answer that larger question—that is, the question of *our own* being. His attempt to address that question in this book might be called a form of ontological inquiry, for it is inquiry relating to a kind or form of being; he calls it "fundamental ontology," because it is fundamental or preliminary to the project of a more general or comprehensive ontology that would proceed to the question of the meaning of being itself.

Heidegger calls our own kind of being *Dasein*—a very ordinary word in German, meaning "existence" of one sort or another—because he considers this term to be a particularly apt designation of our own very special sort of being. So he draws on its literal meaning as "there-being" (*da-sein*), or "being-there," to make and constantly reiterate the fundamental point that our being has the basic and quite essential character of "being-in-the-world." His ontological analysis of Dasein is thus to be an analysis of the general features or "structures" of our being-in-the-world. But Dasein is not the name of some kind of thing or object. It is the *character of* an entity that "exists." "Existing" is something that a human being *does*, not a property (among others) that a human being *has*. Heidegger is concerned with what it is to "exist" in the way that human beings exist; the fundamental nature of Dasein, he says, "lies in its *Existenz*." Our reality is our *manner of* existing; our being is our manner of "be-ing," not our type of thinghood.

Heidegger calls his method "phenomenological," and considers this kind of method to be appropriate and essential if this sort of reality is to be comprehended, because only phenomenological analysis that focuses on the character and content of forms of experience that we as existing Dasein have, as we have them, is capable of revealing the character of our existing. It is not something to be explained from without, as though it were a kind of object we might use or

examine. Rather, it is something that must be brought into focus from within—from the standpoint of "I myself," caught in the act of existing. "Phenomenology" and "existential analysis" are thus made for each other. No perspective other than that guided by what comes to light in properly conducted "first-person-singular" analysis is required or even relevant to this enterprise. Hence Heidegger's emphatic rejection of all "naturalism," and his insistence that there is a radical distinction between his kind of phenomenology and any "philosophical anthropology" that approaches human reality as a form of life that is fundamentally a part of living nature.

Heidegger's kind of phenomenology is by no means merely or entirely descriptive. It is a kind of "transcendentally interpretive" phenomenology, because it seeks to arrive at a comprehension of the underlying or informing structures that are presupposed by the possibility of the kinds of experiences analyzed, and thus to arrive at an ontological account of the fundamental features of Dasein's kind or way of be-ing. As he observes, in his very important methodological discussion in §63 of *Being and Time*, his analysis is and must be "guided by" preanalytic experiences and understandings (since there is nothing else by which such inquiry could properly *be* guided, and since such guidance is entirely appropriate to the matter under consideration). But these experiences and understandings must themselves be reinterpreted, as the underlying structures that they are found to presuppose come to light in the course of reflection on the conditions of their possibility.

In thinking about our kind of reality, Heidegger considers it to be no less serious a philosophical mistake to *presuppose too little* than to presuppose too much. So, for example, as has already been observed, he takes it to be evident and beyond serious question that our kind of being is not a static state but something that *goes on* (be-ing), and that goes on "in the world"—or, more accurately, "in a world": a world in which we encounter and must deal with both things that do and things that do not have the same sort of reality as we do. Our "being in the world" is a being that has the basic character of *involvements*, owing to which things and others *matter* to us in different sorts of ways. The world we are "be-ing *in*" as we go on existing is for us no mere neutral context, but rather a complex totality of relations with meanings that reflect these ways of mattering. Our being in the world further is both ontological and open-ended. It is ontological in the sense that we are capable of and disposed to ask about the being of entities other than ourselves as well as about our own reality. And it is open-ended in the sense that our being *is an issue* for us—not only because it is a *question* for us in the sense just mentioned but also because the way in which we go on existing *remains to be determined*. We find ourselves having to decide what to do with ourselves.

As Heidegger proceeds to explore the experiential character of our "being in the world," he draws attention to the ways in which our involvements are characterized by several fundamental mediating structures: specifically, *interpretation* (modes of understanding) and *state of mind* (modes of disposition) that both can and do vary greatly, and greatly affect the ways in which things are experienced. They also are experienced through the medium of language, which is a further fundamental structure of Dasein's (and thus our) kind of being. Dasein moreover has the basic structure of "being with others" as well as with things. Others matter to us in different ways—and in ways different from the ways things do; but Heidegger contends that these differing ways of mattering are all modalities of the phenomenon of "care" (*Sorge*), which he concludes is the very essence or sense (*Sinn*) of Dasein's being— not only with respect to things and others, but also with respect to our own being, identity, and possibilities.

Nor is that all. As his phenomenological analysis of Dasein develops, Hei-degger contends that "being toward death" is no less fundamental a feature or structure of Dasein's "being" than is being involved with things and (differently) with others; and later in the book he makes the same point with respect to "being from birth" and "stretching along" between birth and death. He further argues that another fundamental structural feature of Dasein is a tendency to "fall" into preoccupation with things, and to fall under the spell of the anonymous control of impersonal social norms and expectations. This tendency largely prevails, he contends; and that would be the end of the matter were it not for Dasein's disposition to experience the counteracting object-less state of mind of "anxiety" regarding the contingency of these commonplace preoccupations and determinations, and regarding one's own "being toward death," that most vividly reveals their insubstantiality.

These points are used by Heidegger to set the stage for what is perhaps the most powerful central idea of the book: the contrast between "inauthentic" and "authentic" existing. A preoccupation with that distinction, in one form or another, is one of the hallmarks of existential philosophy. Heidegger claims that his version of this distinction is purely descriptive rather than evaluative: it is the difference between living one's life in a manner that is scripted and determined by the way things are in the impersonally ordered world in which one finds oneself (and by the dispositions it has instilled in one), and living one's life in a manner that can truly be said to be "one's own." But it is difficult to read his discussion of the distinction and its various associations (featuring the language of "falling" and "losing oneself" on the one hand, and of "resolute anticipation" and "finding oneself" on the other), as anything other than a powerful appeal for existing authentically rather than inauthentically—even though Heidegger asserts that authentic existing is only a kind of modification of inauthentic existing. For him, that modification makes all the difference in the world of human reality.

While *Being and Time* is often read as offering a profoundly individuating conception of authenticity, and does indeed do so, that conception turns out to be provisional, or at any rate incomplete. It is given a significantly different twist toward the end of the book, as Heidegger proceeds to rework the analysis of Dasein he seemed to have concluded (with his revelation that "care" is the key to the "meaning" of Dasein's being). That reworking, in terms of "temporality," sets the stage for a discussion of Dasein's "historicality," with which the book (incompletely) concludes. Heidegger makes it clear that he sees Dasein's possible authenticity as pertaining not only to the radical individuation associated with authentic "being toward death" but also to the positive appropriation of one's social as well as individual historical identity associated with authentic "being from birth" and "stretching along between birth and death."

Surprising though this step may be, in view of the tone of much of the preceding discussion in the book, there is no contradiction between these two forms or dimensions of authenticity. For Heidegger is careful to characterize the former in a way that leaves entirely open what the content of one's authentic choosing is to be, and does not require rejection of one's determinate historically conditioned identity or the values and norms of one's culture and society. It even suggests the possibility of a connection between such authenticity and a positive relation to such content that is inauthentic when it is merely unreflectively accepted and followed, rather than chosen in full recognition of one's individual responsibility for one's choice and inescapable mortality.

This conception of Dasein's essential "historicality" thus brings Heidegger and his conception of "authentic" existing surprisingly close to Hegel and his conception of the kind of "objective" (historically developed social and cultural) "spirituality" that is essential to

human-spiritual self-realization. In retrospect, Heidegger's analysis of Dasein in the previous parts of *Being and Time* can be seen as his alternative version of Hegel's conception of "subjective" spirituality, which preceded (and was superseded—even if not completely supplanted—by) Hegel's discussion of "objective" spirituality in his philosophy and phenomenology of *Geist*.

With that comparison in mind, one might (helpfully but cautiously) extend it to see Heidegger's *Kehre*—and further reconsideration of human reality and authentic humanity in his later writings—as his alternative version of Hegel's conception of "absolute" spirituality. In these writings, exemplified by the final three selections below, "the later Heidegger" (as he is commonly called) turned his attention to what is humanly possible and of even greater significance beyond the levels of both individual and historically specific existence. The kind of "essential thinking" he envisions, attempting at least to position ourselves to become capable of coming to comprehend "being" and "the meaning of being" more generally, is by no means comparable either in character or in aspiration to Hegelian "absolute knowing." Yet it is purported to transcend all lesser forms of knowing and thinking (natural-scientific knowledge and thought included) in somewhat the same way, and to set humanity above and beyond the rest of reality in a somewhat similar way as well.

For Heidegger, it is only in and through language, employed in the manner of an "essential thinking" that is more poetic than scientific, that "being" attains completion; and it is only in us (as far as we know) that this can happen. Heidegger therefore goes so far as to conceive of this as (in FICHTE's language) the very "vocation of man." It is our highest calling, transcending all mere individuality and historical particularity— even though (as for Hegel) it presupposes both, and also significantly involves both. For the truth and meaning of "being," Heidegger intimates, in the words of the title of one of his late essays (included below), seems to be nothing transcendent, but rather a matter of human existing in a manner that unites genuine "building, dwelling, and thinking." That, in the end, would appear to be the essence of the later Heidegger's version of authenticity.

With Heidegger the course of the interpretive tradition in philosophy changed. It is impossible to imagine what that course would have been without him—or, for that matter, if the world and humanity had been spared Hitler's Third Reich, in which he became entangled in ways that undoubtedly affected the trajectory, character, and influence of his own thought. He was an extraordinary figure in many respects. There has never been his like in academic philosophy, nor (almost certainly) will there ever be again. Many would say: Fortunately—for there is much about Heidegger the man that is far from admirable, and even appalling. In the long run, however, what will remain and matter most is whatever the enduring interest and significance of his thought turns out to be.

From Being and Time

From INTRODUCTION
The Exposition of the Question of the Meaning of Being

From Chapter I
The Necessity, Structure, and Priority of the Question of Being

* * *

From 4. The Ontic Priority of the Question of Being

Science [*Wissenschaft*][1] in general can be defined as the totality of fundamentally coherent true propositions. This definition is not complete, nor does it get at the meaning of science [*Wissenschaft*]. As ways in which human beings [*Menschen*] behave, sciences have this being's (the human being's) kind of being. We are defining this being terminologically as Da-sein.[2] Scientific [*Wissenschaftlich*] research is neither the sole nor the most immediate kind of being of this being that is possible. Moreover, Da-sein itself is distinctly different from other beings. We must make this distinct difference visible in a preliminary way. Here the discussion must anticipate subsequent analyses which only later will become truly demonstrative.[3]

Da-sein is a being that does not simply occur among other beings. Rather it is ontically[4] distinguished by the fact that in its being this being is concerned

---

1. That is, cognitive inquiry and disciplines.
2. Heidegger's term for our kind of "being" is *Da-sein*, which until he appropriated it for this special purpose was simply a word for the ordinary "existence" of anything whatsoever. The translator chose to hyphenate it (as "Da-sein") throughout, thereby departing from (even while seemingly retaining) Heidegger's usage—presumably in order to bring out its literal meaning ("there [*da*]–being [*Sein*]," or "being-there") and perhaps also to highlight that for Heidegger our human way of existing as "being-there" has very special significance and a distinctive relation to the ways in which everything else

merely "is." Indeed, for proper emphasis in English in translating this work, our "being" (*Sein*) should be hyphenated as well—making it "be-ing"—because Heidegger understands our *Sein* in the sense of the participle (to be), akin to "doing." Human reality, for Heidegger, is not a matter of being a certain sort of "thing." Rather, it is fundamentally a matter of *da-sein*, or "be-ing there"—that is, living or existing in some particular "there" or "world" of environing and social circumstances.
3. That is, supported, justified.
4. That is, on its face, as readily apparent.

about its very being. Thus it is constitutive of the being of Da-sein to have, in its very being, a relation of being to this being. And this in turn means that Da-sein understands itself in its being in some way and with some explicitness. It is proper to this being that it be disclosed to itself with and through its being. *Understanding of being is itself a determination of being of Da-sein.*[5] The ontic distinction of Da-sein lies in the fact that it *is* ontological.[6]

To be ontological does not yet mean to develop ontology. Thus if we reserve the term ontology for the explicit, theoretical question of the meaning of beings, the intended ontological character of Da-sein is to be designated as pre-ontological. That does not signify being simply ontical, but rather being in the manner of an understanding of being.

We shall call the very being[7] to which Da-sein can relate in one way or another, and somehow always does relate, existence [*Existenz*]. And because the essential definition of this being cannot be accomplished by ascribing to it a "what" that specifies its material content, because its essence[8] lies rather in the fact that it in each instance has to be its being as its own, the term Da-sein, as a pure expression of being,[9] has been chosen to designate this being.

Da-sein always understands itself in terms of its existence [*aus seiner Existenz*], in terms of its possibility to be itself or not to be itself. Da-sein has either chosen these possibilities itself, stumbled upon them, or in each instance already grown up in them. Existence is decided only by each Da-sein itself in the manner of seizing upon or neglecting such possibilities. We come to terms with the question of existence always only through existence itself. We shall call *this* kind of understanding of itself *existentiell* understanding.[1] The question of existence is an ontic "affair" of Da-sein. For this the theoretical transparency of the ontological structure of existence is not necessary. The question of structure aims at the analysis of what constitutes existence. We shall call the coherence of these structures *existentiality.* Its analysis does not have the character of an existentiell understanding but rather an *existential* one.[2] The task of an existential analysis of Da-sein is prescribed with regard to its possibility and necessity in the ontic constitution of Da-sein.

But since existence [*Existenz*] defines Da-sein,[3] the ontological analysis of this being always requires a previous glimpse of existentiality.[4] However, we understand existentiality as the constitution of being of the being that exists. But the idea of being already lies in the idea of such a constitution of being. And thus the possibility of carrying out the analysis of Da-sein depends upon the prior elaboration of the question of the meaning of being in general.

Sciences and disciplines [*Wissenschaften*] are ways of being of Da-sein in which Da-sein also relates to beings that it need not itself be. But *being in a*

---

5. "Seinsbestimmtheit": that is, a fundamental characteristic (of the "being" or reality of Da-sein).
6. That is, it is a readily apparent surface feature of Da-sein that it is self-"understanding" or self-interpreting, in the sense that it is able and tends to have ideas about itself.
7. That is, "the be-ing itself" (*das Sein selbst*).
8. Its *Wesen*—that is, its fundamental nature or reality.
9. That is, "a term simply meaning 'being' or 'to be'" (*Seinsausdruck*).
1. That is, the kind of understanding that may

simply be based on familiarity with the way in which the matter under consideration is experienced.
2. That is, the kind of understanding that grasps something about the basic structure(s) of human reality (whether those of "Da-sein" generally or those associated with its possible alternative modes).
3. Better translated: "But now insofar as Existenz is determinative of Dasein" (*Sofern nun aber Existenz das Dasein bestimmt*).
4. "Existenzialität": that is, the basic character of Da-sein's Existenz.

world belongs essentially to Da-sein. Thus the understanding of being that belongs to Da-sein just as originally implies the understanding of something like "world" and the understanding of the being of beings accessible within the world. Ontologies which have beings unlike Da-sein as their theme are accordingly founded and motivated in the ontic structure of Da-sein itself. This structure includes in itself the determination of a pre-ontological understanding of being.

Thus *fundamental ontology*, from which alone all other ontologies can originate, must be sought in the *existential analysis of Da-sein*.[5]

Da-sein accordingly takes priority in several ways over all other beings. The first priority is an *ontic* one: this being is defined in its being by existence [*Existenz*]. The second priority is an *ontological* one: on the basis of its determination as existence Da-sein is in itself "ontological." But just as originally Da-sein possesses—in a manner constitutive of its understanding of existence—an understanding of the being of all beings unlike itself. Da-sein therefore has its third priority as the ontic-ontological condition of the possibility of all ontologies. Da-sein has proven to be what, before all other beings, is ontologically the primary being to be interrogated.

However, the roots of the existential analysis, for their part, are ultimately *existentiell*—they are *ontic*. Only when philosophical research and inquiry themselves are grasped in an existentiell way—as a possibility of being of each existing Da-sein—does it become possible at all to disclose the existentiality of existence and therewith to get hold of a sufficiently grounded set of ontological problems. But with this the ontic priority of the question of being has also become clear.

From CHAPTER II

THE DOUBLE TASK IN WORKING OUT THE QUESTION OF BEING: THE METHOD OF THE INVESTIGATION AND ITS OUTLINE

FROM 5. THE ONTOLOGICAL ANALYSIS OF DA-SEIN AS THE EXPOSURE OF THE HORIZON FOR AN INTERPRETATION OF THE MEANING OF BEING IN GENERAL

In designating the tasks involved in "formulating" the question of being, we showed that not only must we pinpoint the particular being that is to function as the primary being to be interrogated but also that an explicit appropriation and securing of correct access to this being is required. We discussed which being it is that takes over the major role within the question of being. But how should this being, Da-sein, become accessible and, so to speak, be envisaged in a perceptive interpretation?

The ontic-ontological priority that has been demonstrated for Da-sein could lead to the mistaken opinion that this being would have to be what is primar-

---

5. Beings like ourselves and having the character of "Da-sein," according to Heidegger, are beings that develop and operate with understandings of the "being" of beings generally, their own included. Their (that is, our) own "be-ing" thus underlies their own consideration of the being of beings more generally. To understand what Da-sein is doing when it does this, one has to understand its own "be-ing." Thus the "ontology of Da-sein" is "fundamental"—procedurally, at any rate—to efforts to come up with an "ontology of beings." It therefore may be called "fundamental ontology" in relation to the ontologies of other types of beings.

ily given also ontically-ontologically, not only in the sense that such a being could be grasped "immediately" but also that the prior givenness of its manner of being would be just as "immediate." True, Da-sein is ontically not only what is near or even nearest—we ourselves *are* it, each of us. Nevertheless, or precisely for this reason, it is ontologically what is farthest removed. True, it belongs to its most proper being to have an understanding of this being and to sustain a certain interpretation of it. But this does not at all mean that the most readily available pre-ontological interpretation of its own being could be adopted as an adequate guideline, as though this understanding of being had to arise from a thematically ontological reflection on the most proper constitution of its being. Rather, in accordance with the kind of being belonging to it, Da-sein tends to understand its own being in terms of that being to which it is essentially, continually, and most closely related—the "world." In Da-sein itself and therewith in its own understanding of being, as we shall show, the way the world is understood is ontologically reflected back upon the interpretation of Da-sein.

The ontic-ontological priority of Da-sein is therefore the reason why the specific constitution of the being of Da-sein—understood in the sense of the "categorial" structure that belongs to it—remains hidden from it. Da-sein is ontically "nearest" to itself, ontologically farthest away; but pre-ontologically certainly not foreign to itself.

We have merely precursorily indicated that an interpretation of this being is confronted with peculiar difficulties rooted in the mode of being of the thematic object and the way it is thematized. They do not result from some shortcoming of our powers of knowledge or lack of a suitable way of conceiving—a lack seemingly easy to remedy.

Not only does an understanding of being belong to Da-sein, but this understanding also develops or decays according to the actual manner of being of Da-sein at any given time; for this reason it has a wealth of interpretations at its disposal. Philosophical psychology, anthropology, ethics, "politics," poetry, biography, and historiography pursue in different ways and to varying extents the behavior, faculties, powers, possibilities, and destinies of Da-sein. But the question remains whether these interpretations were carried out in as original an existential manner as their existentiell originality perhaps merited. The two do not necessarily go together, but they also do not exclude one another. Existentiell interpretation can require existential analysis, provided philosophical knowledge is understood in its possibility and necessity. Only when the fundamental structures of Da-sein are adequately worked out with explicit orientation toward the problem of being will the previous results of the interpretation of Da-sein receive their existential justification.

Hence the first concern in the question of being must be an analysis of Da-sein. But then the problem of gaining and securing the kind of access that leads to Da-sein truly becomes crucial. Expressed negatively, no arbitrary idea of being and reality, no matter how "self-evident" it is, may be brought to bear on this being in a dogmatically constructed way; no "categories" prescribed by such ideas may be forced upon Da-sein without ontological deliberation. The manner of access and interpretation must instead be chosen in such a way that this being can show itself to itself on its own terms. And furthermore, this manner should show that being as it is *initially and for the most part—in its average everydayness*. Not arbitrary and accidental structures but essential ones are to be demonstrated in this everydayness, structures that remain determinative in every mode of being of factual Da-sein. By looking at the fundamental constitution of the everydayness of Da-sein we shall bring out in a preparatory way the being of this being.

The analytic of Da-sein thus understood is wholly oriented toward the guiding task of working out the question of being. Its limits are thereby determined. It cannot hope to provide a complete ontology of Da-sein, which of course must be supplied if something like a "philosophical" anthropology is to rest on a philosophically adequate basis. With a view to a possible anthropology or its ontological foundation, the following interpretation will provide only a few "parts," although not inessential ones. However, the analysis of Da-sein is not only incomplete but at first also *preliminary*. It only brings out the being of this being without interpreting its meaning. Its aim is rather to expose the horizon for the most primordial interpretation of being. Once we have reached that horizon the preparatory analytic of Da-sein requires repetition on a higher, genuinely ontological basis.

The meaning of the being of that being we call Da-sein proves to be *temporality* [*Zeitlichkeit*]. In order to demonstrate this we must repeat our interpretation of those structures of Da-sein that shall have been indicated in a preliminary way—this time as modes of temporality. While it is true that with this interpretation of Da-sein as temporality the answer to the guiding question about the meaning of being in general is not already given, the soil from which we may reap it will nevertheless be prepared.

* * *

From PART ONE, DIVISION ONE

The Preparatory Fundamental Analysis of Da-sein

FROM CHAPTER I

THE EXPOSITION OF THE TASK OF A PREPARATORY ANALYSIS OF DA-SEIN

FROM 9. THE THEME OF THE ANALYTIC OF DA-SEIN

The being [*Seiende*] whose analysis our task is, is always we ourselves. The being [*Sein*] of this being [*Seiende*] is always *mine*. In the being of this being [*Seiende*] it is related to its being. As the being of this being, it is entrusted to its own being. It is being [*Sein*] about which this being is concerned.[6] From this characteristic of Da-sein two things follow:

6. This important passage would be easier to understand if the words *Sein* and *Seiende* were translated differently. *Sein* must be translated as "being" (as a participle; see p. 964, n. 2, above), understood as the true nature of that which is under consideration, rather than its mere occurrence. *Seiende*, on the other hand, can also be translated by the neutral word "entity." (So: I as a human being am "a being" or "an entity" of a different sort than "entities" such as hammers, chairs, or trees.) A better rendering: "We ourselves are precisely the entity [*Seiende*] whose analysis is the task here. The be-ing [*Sein*] of this entity is always *mine* [*je meines*]—that is, its be-ing always has the character of 'mine-ness' or 'I-myself-ness' to an entity of our sort]. It is a feature of the be-ing of this entity that this entity actively relates itself [*verhält sich*] to its be-ing [that is, has some awareness of it and attempts to do something about it]. As the entity whose be-ing that be-ing is, it is answerable [responsible] for its own be-ing [that is, for what it does with or about it]. It is *be-ing* (and its own be-ing in particular) about which and with which this entity concerns itself."

1. The "essence" of this being lies in its to be.[7] The whatness (*essentia*) of this being must be understood in terms of its being (*existentia*)[8] insofar as one can speak of it at all. Here the ontological task is precisely to show that when we choose the word existence for the being of this being, this term does not and cannot have the ontological meaning of the traditional expression of *existentia*. Ontologically, *existentia* means *objective presence* [*Vorhandenheit*], a kind of being which is essentially inappropriate to characterize the being which has the character of Da-sein. We can avoid confusion by always using the interpretive expression *objective presence* [*Vorhandenheit*] for the term *existentia*, and by attributing existence [*Existenz*] as a determination of being only to Da-sein.

The "essence" of Da-sein lies in its existence [*Existenz*]. The characteristics to be found in this being [*Seienden*] are thus not objectively present "attributes" of an objectively present being [*Seienden*] which has such and such an "outward appearance," but rather possible ways for it to be, and only this. The thatness of this being is primarily being [*Sein*]. Thus the term "Da-sein" which we use to designate this being does not express its what, as in the case of table, house, tree, but being [*Sein*].[9]

2. The being[1] which this being is concerned about in its being is always my own. Thus, Da-sein is never to be understood ontologically as a case and instance of a genus of beings as objectively present. To something objectively present its being is a matter of "indifference," more precisely, it "is" in such a way that its being can neither be indifferent nor non-indifferent to it. In accordance with the character of *always-being-my-own-being* [*Jemeinigkeit*], when we speak of Da-sein, we must always use the *personal* pronoun along with whatever we say: "I am," "You are."[2]

Da-sein is my own [*meines*], to be always in this or that way. It has somehow always already decided in which way Da-sein is always my own. The being [*Seiende*] which is concerned in its being about its being [*Sein*] is related to its being as its truest possibility. Da-sein *is* always its possibility. It does not "have" that possibility only as a mere attribute of something objectively present. And because Da-sein is always essentially its possibility, it *can* "choose" itself in its being [*Sein*], it can win itself, it can lose itself, or it can never and only "apparently" win itself. It can only have lost itself and it can only have not yet gained itself because it is essentially possible as authentic, that is, it belongs to itself. The two kinds of being of *authenticity* and *inauthenticity*—these expressions are terminologically chosen in the strictest sense of the word[3]—are based on

---

7. That is, "The 'essential reality' of Da-sein lies [not in what it has been or now is, but rather] in its *to-be*" (*Das "Wesen" dieses Seienden* [i.e., *Dasein*] *liegt in seinem Zu-sein*). Thus Da-sein has to do with *what becomes of it* or (better) *what it does with itself and its possibilities*—or, as Heidegger says in the next paragraph, with "possible ways for it to be, and only this." He begins the next paragraph by restating this point, replacing *seinem Zu-sein* (its to-be) with *seiner Existenz* (its Existenz or distinctive kind of existence), thereby showing that he means *Existenz*—as applied to Da-sein—to take on the meaning of *Zu-sein* (to-be).

8. Heidegger borrows the Latin terms in parentheses (essence, existence) from Scholastic philosophy.

9. The *Sein* of Da-sein has thus come to mean not simply its kind of "being" but *its way of be-ing*—that is, its way of carrying on with its life and the "possible ways for it to be" (previously character-

ized as its *Zu-sein* [to-be]).

1. That is, be-ing.

2. In German, "'ich bin,' 'du bist,'" using the intimate "you" (*du* rather than the formal *Sie*)—a distinction that no longer exists in English.

3. "*Eigentlich* and *uneigentlich*"—in the strictest or most literal sense meaning "(of) one's own" and "*not* (of) one's own." This distinction is of the greatest importance, not only in this book but in later existential philosophy, as these terms became catchwords and gained wide popularity. The distinction easily lends itself to a variety of interpretations, and it therefore is crucial to attend carefully to how Heidegger actually defines and uses these expressions, and to what he does and does not mean by them and take them to imply (evaluatively as well as descriptively and analytically), rather than reading into him one's own preconceptions or the interpretations of other philosophers.

the fact that Da-sein is in general determined by always being-mine. But the inauthenticity of Da-sein does not signify a "lesser" being or a "lower" degree of being. Rather, inauthenticity can determine Da-sein even in its fullest concretion, when it is busy, excited, interested, and capable of pleasure.

The two characteristics of Da-sein sketched out—on the one hand, the priority of "*existentia*" over *essentia*, and then, always-being-mine—already show that an analytic of this being is confronted with a unique phenomenal region. This being does not and never has the kind of being of what is merely objectively present [*Vorhanden*][4] within the world. Thus, it is also not to be thematically found in the manner of coming across something objectively present. The correct presentation of it is so little a matter of course[5] that its determination itself constitutes an essential part of the ontological analytic of this being. The possibility of understanding the being of this being stands and falls with the secure accomplishment of the correct presentation of this being. No matter how provisional the analysis may be, it always demands the securing of the correct beginning.

As a being [*Seiende*], Da-sein always defines itself in terms of a possibility which it *is* and somehow understands in its being [*Sein*].[6] That is the formal meaning of the constitution of the existence of Da-sein. But for the *ontological* interpretation of this being, this means that the problematic of its being is to be developed out of the existentiality of its existence [*Existenz*].[7] However, this cannot mean that Da-sein is to be construed in terms of a concrete possible idea of existence. At the beginning of the analysis, Da-sein is precisely not to be interpreted in the differentiation of a particular existence; rather, to be uncovered in the indifferent way in which it is initially and for the most part. This indifference of the everydayness of Da-sein is *not nothing*; but rather, a positive phenomenal characteristic. All existing[8] is how it is out of this kind of being, and back into it. We call this everyday indifference of Da-sein *averageness*.

And because average everydayness constitutes the ontic immediacy of this being, it was and will be *passed over* again and again in the explication of Da-sein. What is ontically nearest and familiar is ontologically the farthest, unrecognized and constantly overlooked in its ontological significance. Augustine[9] asks: "*Quid autem propinquius meipso mihi?*" ("But what is closer to me than myself?") And must answer: "*Ego certe laboro hic et laboro in meipso: factus sum mihi terra difficultatis et sudoris nimii.*" ("Assuredly I labor here and I labor within myself: I have become to myself a land of trouble and inordinate sweat"). This holds true not only for the ontic and preontological opacity of Da-sein, but to a still higher degree for the ontological task of not only not

---

4. That is, "Da-sein does not have—and indeed never has—the kind of being of what is merely observably there."
5. That is, "is so far from being simple and straightforward."
6. That is, takes to be a part of its being.
7. That is, out of the distinctive structure of its Existenz. Heidegger uses the term *Existenzialität* to refer to the special kind of structure that Existenz has, which (as he has already stated) is

completely different from the structures of other sorts of entities. He also refers to specific structures of Existenz as *Existenzialien* (here translated as "existentials").
8. That is, all existing in Da-sein's manner of existing (*Existieren*).
9. Saint Augustine (354–430), theologian, philosopher, and one of the church fathers. The quoted Latin is from his *Confessions* 10.16.

failing to see this being in its phenomenally nearest kind of being, but of making it accessible in its positive characteristics.

But the average everydayness of Da-sein must not be understood as a mere "aspect." In it, too, and even in the mode of inauthenticity, the structure of existentiality lies *a priori*. In it, too, Da-sein is concerned with a particular mode of its being to which it is related in the way of average everydayness, if only in the way of fleeing *from* it and of forgetting *it*.

The explication of Da-sein in its average everydayness, however, does not just give average structures in the sense of a vague indeterminacy. What *is* ontically in the way of being average can very well be understood ontologically in terms of pregnant structures which are not structurally different from the ontological determinations of an *authentic* being of Da-sein.

All explications arising from an analytic of Da-sein are gained with a view toward its structure of existence [*Existenz*]. Because these explications are defined in terms of existentiality, we shall call the characteristics of being of Da-sein *existentials*. They are to be sharply delimited from the determinations of being of those beings unlike Da-sein which we call *categories*. * * *

We intimated in the introduction that a task is furthered in the existential analytic of Da-sein, a task whose urgency is hardly less than that of the question of being itself: the exposition of *the a priori* which must be visible if the question "What is human being?" is to be discussed philosophically. The existential analytic of Da-sein is *prior* to any psychology, anthropology, and especially biology.[1] By being delimited from these possible investigations of Da-sein, the theme of the analytic can become still more sharply defined. Its necessity can thus at the same time be demonstrated more incisively.

* * *

From CHAPTER II

Being-in-the-World in General as the Fundamental Constitution of Da-sein

from 12. a preliminary sketch of being-in-the-world in terms of the orientation toward being-in as such

In the preparatory discussions (section 9) we already profiled characteristics of being which are to provide us with a steady light for our further investigation, but which at the same time receive their structural concretion in this investigation. Da-sein is a being [*Seiende*] which is related understandingly in its being [*Sein*] toward that being [*Sein*]. In saying this we are calling attention to the formal concept of existence [*Existenz*]. Da-sein exists [*existiert*]. Furthermore, Da-sein is the being which I myself always am. Mineness belongs

---

1. As Heidegger here insists, "Da-sein" is not to be understood simply as a synonym for *Mensch* ("man" or "human being"). It is intended to designate the basic and essential character *of* our reality, as the kind of entity (*Seiende*) we essentially are. As human beings, we are entities of the type *Mensch*; but "Da-sein" is the type of *Sein* (being) that human reality happens to instantiate (along with a good deal else that is peculiar to human reality, but that is not at all intrinsic to or even relevant to the "existenzial" structure of Da-sein). Thus for Heidegger there is a significant difference between his analytic of Da-sein (and Existenz) and a philosophical anthropology, biology, or psychology, all of which he takes to be broader and less fundamental than his phenomenological ontology of Da-sein.

to existing Da-sein as the condition of the possibility of authenticity and inauthenticity. Da-sein exists always in one of these modes, or else in the modal indifference to them.

These determinations of being of Da-sein, however, must now be seen and understood *a priori* as grounded upon that constitution of being which we call *being-in-the-world*.[2] The correct point of departure of the analytic of Da-sein consists in the interpretation of this constitution.

The compound expression "being-in-the-world" indicates, in the very way we have coined it, that it stands for a *unified* phenomenon. This primary datum must be seen as a whole. But while being-in-the-world cannot be broken up into components that may be pieced together, this does not prevent it from having several constitutive structural factors. The phenomenal fact indicated by this expression actually gives us a threefold perspective. If we pursue it while keeping the whole phenomenon in mind from the outset we have the following:

1. "*In-the-world*": In relation to this factor, we have the task of questioning the ontological structure of "world" and of defining the idea of *worldliness* as such (cf. chapter 3 of this division).

2. The *being* [*Seiende*] which always is in the way of being-in-the-world. In it we are looking for what we are questioning when we ask about the "who?". In our phenomenological demonstration we should be able to determine who is in the mode of average everydayness of Da-sein (cf. chapter 4 of this division).

3. *Being in* [*In-Sein*] as such: The ontological constitution of in-ness itself is to be analyzed (cf. chapter 5 of this division). Any analysis of one of these constitutive factors involves the analysis of the others; that is, each time seeing the whole phenomenon. It is true that being-in-the-world is an *a priori* necessary constitution of Da-sein, but it is not at all sufficient to fully determine Da-sein's being. Before we thematically analyze the three phenomena indicated individually, we shall attempt to orient ourselves toward a characteristic of the third of these constitutive factors.

What does *being-in* mean? Initially, we supplement the expression being-in with the phrase "in the world," and are inclined to understand this being-in as "being-in [*Sein in*] something." With this term, the kind of being of a being is named which is "in" something else, as water is "in" the glass, the dress is "in" the closet. By this "in" we mean the relation of being that two beings extended "in" space have to each other with regard to their location in that space. Water and glass, dress and closet, are both "in" space "at" a location in the same way. This relation of being can be expanded; that is, the bench in the lecture hall, the lecture hall in the university, the university in the city, and so on until: the bench in "world space." These beings whose being "in" one another can be determined in this way all have the same kind of being—

2. In the German, "In-der-Welt-sein." A better phrase might have been "In-*einer*-Welt-sein"—"being-in-*a*-world"—to guard against the mistaken impression that "*der* Welt" (*the* world) here refers to the totality of the spatiotemporal universe. In Heidegger's usage, *Welt* instead has a meaning closer to that of "world" in such phrases as "the world of the Greeks," "a world unto itself," and "a world that is no longer." (This last example is Heidegger's own; see §73, below.)

that of being objectively present—as things occurring "within" the world. The objective presence "in" something objectively present, the being objectively present together with something having the same kind of being in the sense of a definite location relationship are ontological characteristics which we call *categorial*. They belong to beings whose kind of being is unlike Da-sein.

In contrast, being-in [*In-Sein*] designates a constitution of being of Da-sein, and is an *existential*. But we cannot understand by this the objective presence of a material thing (the human body) "in" a being objectively present. Nor does the term being-in designate a spatial "in one another" of two things objectively present, any more than the word "in" primordially means a spatial relation of this kind. "In" stems from *innan-*, to live, *habitare*,[3] to dwell. "*An*" means I am used to, familiar with, I take care of something. It has the meaning of *colo* in the sense of *habito* and *diligo*. We characterized this being to whom being-in belongs in this meaning as the being which I myself always am. The expression "*bin*" is connected with "*bei*." "*Ich bin*" (I am) means I dwell, I stay near . . . the world as something familiar in such and such a way. Being [*Sein*][4] as the infinitive of "I am": that is, understood as an existential, means to dwell near . . . , to be familiar with. . . . *Being-in is thus the formal existential expression of the being of Da-sein* which has the essential constitution of being-in-the-world.

"Being together with"[5] the world, in the sense of being absorbed in the world, which must be further interpreted, is an existential which is grounded in being-in. Because we are concerned in these analyses with *seeing* a primordial structure of being of Da-sein in accordance with whose phenomenal content the concepts of being must be articulated, and because this structure is fundamentally incomprehensible in terms of the traditional ontological categories, this "being together with" must also be examined more closely.

* * *

Initially it is only a matter of seeing the ontological distinction between being-in as an existential and the category of the "insideness" that things objectively present can have with regard to one another. If we define being-in in this way, we are not denying to Da-sein every kind of "spatiality." On the contrary. Da-sein itself has its own "being-in-space," which in its turn is possible only *on the basis of being-in-the-world in general*. Thus, being-in cannot be clarified ontologically by an ontic characteristic, by saying for example: being-in in a world is a spiritual [*geistig*] quality and the "spatiality" of human being is an attribute of its bodiliness which is always at the same time "based on" corporeality. Then we again have to do with a being-objectively-present-together of a spiritual thing [*Geist*] thus constituted with a corporeal thing, and the being of the beings thus compounded is more obscure than ever. The understanding of being-in-the-world as an essential structure of Da-sein first makes possible the insight into its *existential spatiality*. This insight will keep us from failing to see this structure or from previously cancelling it out, a

---

3. Latin, as are *colo* (I cultivate; I dwell), *habito* (I inhabit), and *diligo* (I value highly).
4. That is, "to be," be-ing.
5. "Sein-bei." This expression, as used by Heidegger, is difficult to translate aptly and compactly. His meaning is partly explained in the next clause. He uses it to characterize the typical sort of way in which Da-sein relates to things around it: not just as finding itself indifferently located "beside them" or "among them" but as interested in them, involved with them, occupied with them, relating to them (either positively or aversely). The basic idea is that of involvement or connectedness, as in the expression "by my side."

procedure motivated not ontologically, but "metaphysically" in the naïve opinion that human being is initially a spiritual thing[6] which is then subsequently placed "in" a space.

With its facticity, the being-in-the-world of Da-sein is already dispersed in definite ways of being-in, perhaps even split up. The multiplicity of these kinds of being-in can be indicated by the following examples: to have to do with something, to produce, order and take care of something, to use something, to give something up and let it get lost, to undertake, to accomplish, to find out, to ask about, to observe, to speak about, to determine. . . . These ways of being-in have the kind of being of *taking care of*[7] which we shall characterize in greater detail. The *deficient* modes of omitting, neglecting, renouncing, resting, are also ways of taking care of something, in which the possibilities of taking care are kept to a "bare minimum." The term "taking care" has initially its prescientific meaning and can imply: carrying something out, settling something, "to straighten it out." The expression could also mean to take care of something in the sense of "getting it for oneself." Furthermore, we use the expression also in a characteristic turn of phrase: I will see to it or take care that the enterprise fails. Here "to take care" amounts to apprehensiveness. In contrast to these prescientific ontic meanings, the expression "taking care" is used in this inquiry as an ontological term (an existential) to designate the being of a possible being-in-the-world. We do not choose this term because Da-sein is initially economical and "practical" to a large extent, but because the being of Da-sein itself is to be made visible as *care*.[8] Again, this expression is to be understood as an ontological structure concept (compare chapter 6 of this division). The expression has nothing to do with "distress," "melancholy," or "the cares of life" which can be found ontically in every Da-sein. These—like their opposites, "carefreeness" and "gaiety"—are ontically possible only because Dasein, *ontologically* understood, is care. Because being-in-the-world belongs essentially to Da-sein, its being toward the world is essentially taking care [*Besorgen*].[9]

According to what we have said, being-in is not a "quality" which Da-sein sometimes has and sometimes does not have, *without* which it could *be* just as well as it could with it. It is not the case that human being "is," and then on top of that has a relation of being to the "world" which it sometimes takes

---

6. "Ein geistiges Ding." Heidegger is ridiculing the idea that Da-sein is some kind of "spiritual thing" that is located spatially "in" (or "inside of") a physical, biological body, wherever "in the world" that body happens to be.

7. "Besorgen": that is, being interested in, concerned with, caring about. Heidegger often uses this term and its variants. The translator decided to render it "taking care of," which may on occasion be appropriate but often is not. Heidegger employs the term to characterize all of our many and diverse ways of engaging with things in our environing world as we go about our lives because of their relevance in some way to our practical purposes—relevance that leads us to "care about" or be "concerned with" them. That is what his use of the term *Besorgen* is meant to sum up and convey (rather than any general benevolent disposition to "take care of" everything in one's environing world).

8. "Sorge," a very important concept in Heidegger's analysis of Da-sein. It is the root of words like *Besorgen* (see previous note), which characterize the experiential quality of Da-sein's relations of various sorts that flesh out its "being-in-the-world" and its Existenz. It is commonly rendered as "care"—its usual sense in German—but Heidegger broadens its meaning in the direction of the general idea of *involvement* or of different kinds of connectedness (with things and with others in particular, but in quite different ways). Translators cannot always find words or phrases in relatively idiomatic English that preserve the evident connection with the basic ideas of his various key root words—like "care" (as "caring about" in one way or another)—and that also are appropriate in these different sorts of relational contexts to what Heidegger wants to bring out about them.

9. That is, "Da-sein's being toward the world [*Sein zur Welt*] is essentially interested involvement [*wesenhaft Besorgen*]."

upon itself. Da-sein is never "initially" a sort of a being which is free from being-in, but which at times is in the mood to take up a "relation" to the world. This taking up of relations to the world is possible only *because*, as being-in-the-world, Da-sein is as it is. This constitution of being is not first derived from the fact that besides the being which has the character of Da-sein there are other beings which are objectively present and meet up with it. These other beings can only "meet up" "with" Da-sein because they are able to show themselves of their own accord within a *world*.

* * *

Both in Da-sein and for it, this constitution of being is always already somehow familiar. If it is now to be recognized, the explicit *cognition* [_Erkennen_] that this task implies takes *itself* (as a knowing of the world) as the exemplary relation of the "soul" to the world. The cognition of world (*noein*)—or addressing oneself to the "world" and discussing it (*logos*[1])—thus functions as the primary mode of being-in-the-world even though being-in-the-world is not understood as such. But because this structure of being remains ontologically inaccessible, yet is ontically experienced as the "relation" between one being (world) and another (soul), and because being is initially understood by taking being as innerworldly beings for one's ontological support, one tries to conceive the relation between world and soul as grounded in these two beings and in the sense of their being; that is, as objective presence. Although it is experienced and known prephenomenologically, being-in-the-world is *invisible* if one interprets it in a way that is ontologically inadequate. One is just barely acquainted with this constitution of Da-sein only in the form given by an inadequate interpretation—and indeed, as something obvious. In this way it then becomes the "evident" point of departure for the problems of epistemology or a "metaphysics of knowledge." For what is more obvious than the fact that a "subject" is related to an "object" and the other way around? This "subject-object-relation" must be presupposed. But that is a presupposition which, although it is inviolate in its own facticity, is truly fatal, perhaps for that very reason, if its ontological necessity and especially its ontological meaning are left in obscurity.

Thus the phenomenon of being-in has for the most part been represented exclusively by a single exemplar—knowing the world. This has not only been the case in epistemology; for even practical behavior has been understood as behavior which is *not* theoretical and "atheoretical." Because knowing has been given this priority, our understanding of its ownmost kind of being is led astray, and thus being-in-the-world must be delineated more precisely with reference to knowing the world, and must itself be made visible as an existential "modality" of being-in.

FROM 13. THE EXEMPLIFICATION OF BEING-IN IN A FOUNDED MODE: KNOWING THE WORLD

If being-in-the-world is a fundamental constitution of Da-sein, and one in which it moves not only in general but especially in the mode of everydayness,

1. Speaking; word; reason (Greek). *Noein*: perceiving, thinking (literally, "to perceive," "to think"; Greek).

it must always already have been experienced ontically. It would be incomprehensible if it were totally veiled, especially since Da-sein has an understanding of its own being at its disposal, no matter how indeterminately that understanding functions. However, no sooner was the "phenomenon of knowing the world" understood than it was interpreted in an "external" formal way. The evidence for this is the interpretation of knowledge, still prevalent today, as a "relation between subject and object" which contains about as much "truth" as it does vacuity. But subject and object are not the same as Da-sein and world.

* * *

If we now ask what shows itself in the phenomenal findings of knowing, we must remember that knowing itself is grounded before-hand in already-being-in-the-world which essentially constitutes the being of Da-sein. Initially, this already-being-with is not solely a rigid staring at something merely objectively present. Being-in-the-world, as taking care of things, is *taken in by* the world which it takes care of.[2] In order for knowing to be possible as determining by observation what is objectively present, there must first be a *deficiency* of having to do with the world and taking care of it.[3] In refraining from all production, manipulation, and so on, taking care of things[4] places itself in the only mode of being-in which is left over, in the mode of simply lingering with. . . . *On the basis* of this kind of being toward the world which lets us encounter beings within the world solely in their mere *outward appearance* (*eidos*[5]), and *as* a mode of this kind of being, looking explicitly at something thus encountered is possible. This looking *at* is always a way of assuming a definite direction toward something, a glimpse of what is objectively present. It takes over a "perspective" from the beings thus encountered from the very beginning. This looking itself becomes a mode of independent dwelling together with beings in the world. In this "*dwelling*"—as the refusal of every manipulation and use—the *perception* of what is objectively present takes place. Perception takes place as *addressing* and *discussing* something as something. On the foundation of this *interpretation* in the broadest sense, perception becomes *definition*. What is perceived and defined can be expressed in propositions and as thus *expressed* can be maintained and preserved. This perceptive retention of a proposition about . . . is itself a way of being-in-the-world, and must not be interpreted as a "procedure" by which a subject gathers representations about something for itself which then remain stored up "inside" as thus appropriated, and in reference to which the question can arise at times of how they "correspond" with reality.

In directing itself toward . . . and in grasping something, Da-sein does not first go outside of the inner sphere in which it is initially encapsulated, but, rather, in its primary kind of being, it is always already "outside" together with[6] some being encountered in the world already discovered. Nor is any inner

2. "Das In-der-Welt-sein ist das Besorgen von der besorgten Welt *benommen*." *Benommen* normally means "taken in" or "dazed"; here it has the sense that Da-sein as being-in-the-world tends to be "bedazzled by" or "under the spell of" its interested involvements in the world it cares about.
3. "Einer Defizienz des besorgten Zu-tun-habens mit der Welt": that is, a deficiency in Da-sein's interested dealings ("havings-to-do," that is, involvements) with the world.
4. That is, being interested in (caring about) things.
5. Form (Greek).
6. That is, involved with, occupied with (*bei*).

sphere abandoned when Da-sein dwells together with a being to be known and determines its character. Rather, even in this "being outside" together with its object, Da-sein is "inside," correctly understood; that is, it itself exists as the being-in-the-world which knows. Again, the perception of what is known does not take place as a return with one's booty to the "cabinet" of consciousness after one has gone out and grasped it. Rather, in perceiving, preserving, and retaining, the Da-sein that knows *remains outside as Da-sein*. In "mere" knowledge about a context of the being of beings, in "only" representing it, in "solely" "thinking" about it, I am no less outside in the world together with beings than I am when I *originally* grasp them. Even forgetting something, when every relation of being to what was previously known seems to be extinguished, must be understood *as a modification of primordial being-in*, and this holds true for every deception and every error.

The foundational context shown for the mode of being-in-the-world constitutive for the knowledge of the world makes the following clear: in knowing, Da-sein gains a new *perspective of being* toward the world always already discovered in Da-sein. This new possibility of being can be independently developed. It can become a task, and as scientific [*wissenschaftlich*] knowledge can take over the guidance for being-in-the-world. But knowing neither first *creates* a "commercium"[7] of the subject with the world, nor does this commercium *originate* from an effect of the world on a subject. Knowing is a mode of Da-sein which is founded in being-in-the-world. Thus, being-in-the-world, as a fundamental constitution, requires a *prior* interpretation.

* * *

FROM CHAPTER IV

BEING-IN-THE-WORLD AS BEING-WITH AND BEING A SELF: THE "THEY"[8]

The analysis of the worldliness of the world continually brought the whole phenomenon of being-in-the-world into view without thereby delimiting all of its constitutive factors with the same phenomenal clarity as the phenomenon of world itself. The ontological interpretation of the world which discussed innerworldly things at hand[9] came first not only because Da-sein in its everydayness is in a world in general and remains a constant theme with regard to that world, but because it relates itself to the world in a predominant mode of being. Initially and for the most part, Da-sein is taken in by[1] its

---

7. That is, a practical interaction (literally, "commercial transaction"; Latin).

8. "Das 'Man.'" Often translated as "the 'one.'" In German, the word *man* does not correspond to "man" in English. The word for adult male (also for husband) is "Mann." The German *man* functions impersonally, like the English "one"; its application is not restricted to males. It is typically used in instructing or reprimanding those who don't know or aren't following accepted rules or received wisdom: e.g., "They say there's a reason for everything," or "One ought to know better," or "People won't like that." For Heidegger this is not only a very familiar sociolinguistic phenomenon

but also an important human (and, as NIETZSCHE would say, "all too human") one—and one that helps to account for the prevalence of certain common tendencies that he associates with "inauthenticity."

9. "Das innerweltliche Zuhandene": that is, things encountered within the world in which we find ourselves that are not merely objectively present (Heidegger's expression for things experienced in that way is *das Vorhandene*) but rather are of interest to us (and are available to us or affect us) as having practical significance.

1. That is, is under the spell of; is entranced, fascinated, or preoccupied by (*benommen*).

world. This mode of being, being absorbed in the world, and thus being-in which underlies it, essentially determine the phenomenon which we shall now pursue with the question: *Who* is it who is in the everydayness of Da-sein? All of the structures of being of Da-sein, thus also the phenomenon that answers to this question of who, are modes of its being. Their ontological characteristic is an existential one. Thus, we need to pose the question correctly and outline the procedure for bringing to view a broader phenomenal domain of the everydayness of Da-sein. By investigating in the direction of the phenomenon which allows us to answer the question of the who, we are led to structures of Da-sein which are equiprimordial with being-in-the-world: being-with and *Mitda-sein*.[2] In this kind of being, the mode of everyday being a self is grounded whose explication makes visible what we might call the "subject" of everydayness, the *they*. This chapter on the "who" of average Da-sein thus has the following structure: (1) The approach to the existential question of the who of Da-sein (section 25). (2) The *Mitda-sein* of the others and everyday being-with (section 26). (3) Everyday being a self and the they (section 27).

FROM 25. THE APPROACH TO THE EXISTENTIAL QUESTION OF THE WHO OF DA-SEIN

The answer to the question of who this being actually is (Da-sein) seems to have already been given with the formal indication of the basic characteristics of Da-sein (cf. section 9). Da-sein is a being which I myself am, its being is in each case mine. This determination *indicates* an *ontological* constitution, but no more than that. At the same time, it contains an *ontic* indication, albeit an undifferentiated one, that an I is always this being, and not others. The who is answered in terms of the I itself, the "subject," the "self." The who is what maintains itself in the changes throughout its modes of behavior and experiences as something identical and is, thus, related to this multiplicity. Ontologically, we understand it as what is always already and constantly objectively present in a closed region and for that region, as that which lies at its basis in an eminent sense, as the *subjectum*.[3] As something self-same in manifold otherness, this subject has the character of the *self*. Even if one rejects a substantial soul, the thingliness of consciousness and the objectivity of the person, ontologically one still posits something whose being retains the meaning of objective presence, whether explicitly or not. Substantiality is the ontological clue for the determination of beings in terms of whom the question of the who is answered. Da-sein is tacitly[4] conceived in advance as objective presence. In any case, the indeterminacy of its being always implies this meaning of being. However, objective presence is the mode of being of beings unlike Da-sein.

The ontic obviousness of the statement that it is I who is in each case Da-sein must not mislead us into supposing that the way for an ontological interpretation of what is thus "given" has been unmistakably prescribed. It is even questionable whether the ontic content of the above statement reaches the

---

2. That is, "being with and Da-sein-with" (*Mitsein und Mitdasein*). The latter term refers not just to "being with others" but to something that is added to that concept when it is specified that one is talk-

ing about "Da-sein together" (and "Existenz together").
3. The subject (Latin).
4. That is, implicitly (*unausgesprochen*).

phenomenal content of everyday Da-sein. It could be the case that the who of everyday Da-sein is precisely *not* I myself [*ich selbst*].

* * *

Just as the ontic, self-evident character of being-in-itself of innerworldly beings misleads us to the conviction of the ontological self-evident character of the meaning of this being and makes us overlook the phenomenon of world, the ontic, self-evident character that Da-sein is always my own also harbors the possibility that the ontological problematic indigenous to it might be led astray. *Initially* the who of Da-sein is not only a problem *ontologically*, it also remains concealed *ontically*.

But, then, is the existential analytical answer to the question of the who without any clues at all? By no means. To be sure, of the formal indications of the constitution of being of Da-sein given above (sections 9 and 12), it is not so much the one which we discussed which is functional, but rather, the one according to which the "essence" of Da-sein is grounded in its existence. *If the "I" is an essential determination of Da-sein, it must be interpreted existentially.* The question of the who can then be answered only by a phenomenal demonstration of a definite kind of being of Da-sein. If Da-sein is always only its self *in existing*, the constancy of the self as well as its possible "inconstancy" require an existential-ontological kind of questioning as the only adequate access to the problematic.

But if the self is conceived "only" as a way of the being of this being, then that seems tantamount to volatizing the true "core" of Da-sein. But such fears are nourished by the incorrect preconception that the being in question really has, after all, the kind of being of something objectively present, even if one avoids attributing to it the massive element of a corporeal thing. However, the "*substance*" of human being is not the spirit [*der Geist*] as the synthesis of body and soul, but *existence.*[5]

FROM 26. THE *MITDA-SEIN* OF THE OTHERS AND EVERYDAY BEING-WITH

The answer to the question of the who of everyday Da-sein is to be won through the analysis of *the* kind of being [*Seinsart*] in which Da-sein, initially and for the most part, lives. Our investigation takes its orientation from being-in-the-world. This fundamental constitution of Da-sein determines every mode of its being. If we justifiably stated that all other structural factors of being-in-the-world already came into view by means of the previous explication of the world, the answer to the question of the who must also be prepared by that explication.

The "description" of the surrounding world [*Umwelt*] nearest to us, for example, the work-world [*Werkwelt*] of the handworker, showed that together with the useful things found in work, others are "also encountered" for whom the "work" is to be done. In the kind of being of these things at hand, that is,

---

5. "Allein die 'Substanz' des Menschen ist nicht der Geist als die Synthese von Seele und Leib, sondern die *Existenz*." This is a very important sentence, making it quite clear that "Existenz" or "existing" in the way or ways in which Da-sein is capable of existing is the *only* sort of "substance" of a spiritual nature that Heidegger is prepared to acknowledge in human reality—that is, a "substance" completely devoid of any essential content other than its general *existenzial* structure.

in their relevance, there lies an essential reference to possible wearers for whom they should be "cut to the figure." Similarly, the producer or "supplier" is encountered in the material used as one who "serves" well or badly. The field, for example, along which we walk "outside" shows itself as belonging to such and such a person who keeps it in good order, the book which we use is bought at such and such a place, given by such and such a person, and so on. The boat anchored at the shore refers in its being-in-itself to an acquaintance who undertakes his voyages with it, but as a "boat strange to us," it also points to others. The others who are "encountered" in the context of useful things in the surrounding world at hand are not somehow added on in thought to an initially merely objectively present thing, but these "things" are encountered from the world in which they are at hand for the others. This world is always already from the outset my own.[6] In our previous analysis, the scope of what is encountered in the world was initially narrowed down to useful things at hand, or nature objectively present, thus to beings of a character unlike Da-sein. This restriction was not only necessary for the purpose of simplifying the explication; but, above all, because the kind of being of the existence of the others encountered within the surrounding world is distinct from handiness and objective presence. The world of Da-sein thus frees beings which are not only completely different from tools and things, but which themselves in accordance with their kind of being as *Da-sein* are themselves "in" the world as being-in-the-world in which they are at the same time encountered. These beings are neither objectively present nor at hand, but they *are like* the very Da-sein which frees them—*they are there, too, and there with it*. So, if one wanted to identify the world in general with innerworldly beings, one would have to say the "world" is also Da-sein.

But the characteristic of encountering the *others* is, after all, oriented toward one's *own* Da-sein. Does not it, too, start with the distinction and isolation of the "I," so that a transition from this isolated subject to the others must then be sought? In order to avoid this misunderstanding, we must observe in what sense we are talking about "the others." "The others" does not mean everybody else but me—those from whom the I distinguishes itself. They are, rather, those from whom one mostly does *not* distinguish oneself, those among whom one is, too.[7] This being-there-too with them does not have the ontological character of being objectively present "with" them within a world. The "with" is of the character of Da-sein, the "also" means the sameness of being as circumspect, heedful being-in-the-world. "With" and "also" are to be understood *existentially*, not categorially. On the basis of this *like-with*[8] being-in-the-world, the world is always already the one that I share with the others. The world of Da-sein is a *with-world*. Being-in is *being-with* others. The innerworldly being-in-itself of others is *Mitda-sein*.[9]

The others are not encountered by grasping and previously discriminating one's own subject, initially objectively present, from other subjects also present. They are not encountered by first looking at oneself and then ascertaining the opposite pole of a distinction. They are encountered from the *world*

---

6. By "my own," Heidegger obviously does not mean "my own *exclusively*," but rather "my own" as the town in which I live is "my own" town.
7. Thus, by "the others" Heidegger actually means something like "people generally" (implicitly understood as limited to one's community and society), oneself included—or at any rate, one's everyday social self included.
8. That is, *joint* (<u>mithaften</u>).
9. That is, being-jointly-there.

in which Da-sein, heedful and circumspect, essentially dwells. As opposed to the theoretically concocted "explanations" of the objective presence of others which easily urge themselves upon us, we must hold fast to the phenomenal fact which we have indicated of their being encountered in the *surrounding world*. This nearest and elemental way of Da-sein of being encountered in the world goes so far that even one's *own* Da-sein *initially* becomes "discoverable" by *looking away* from its "experiences" and the "center of its actions" or by not yet "seeing" them all. Da-sein initially finds "itself" in *what* it does, needs, expects, has charge of, in the things at hand which it initially *takes care of* in the surrounding world.[1]

* * *

Da-sein understands itself, initially and for the most part, in terms of its world, and the *Mitda-sein* of others is frequently encountered from inner-worldly things at hand. But when the others become, so to speak, thematic in their Da-sein, they are not encountered as objectively present thing-persons, but we meet them "at work," that is, primarily in their being-in-the-world. Even when we see the other "just standing around," he is never understood as a human-thing objectively present. "Standing around" is an existential mode of being, the lingering with everything and nothing which lacks heedfulness and circumspection. The other is encountered in his *Mitda-sein* in the world.

But, after all, the expression "Da-sein" clearly shows that this being is "initially" unrelated to others, that it can, of course, also be "with" others subsequently. But we must not overlook the fact that we are also using the term *Mitda-sein* as a designation *of* the being to which the existing others are freed within the world. The *Mitda-sein* of others is disclosed only within the world for a Da-sein and thus also for those who are *Mitda-sein*, because Da-sein in itself is essentially being-with. The phenomenological statement that Da-sein is essentially being-with has an existential-ontological meaning. It does not intend to ascertain ontically that I am factically not objectively present alone, rather that others of my kind also are.[2] If the statement that the being-in-the-world of Da-sein is essentially constituted by being-with meant something like this, being-with would not be an existential attribute that belongs to Da-sein of itself on the basis of its kind of being, but something which occurs at times on the basis of the existence of others. Being-with existentially determines Da-sein even when an other is not factically present and perceived. The being-alone of Da-sein, too, is being-with in the world. The other can be *lacking* only *in* and *for* a being-with. Being-alone is a deficient mode of being-with, its possibility is a proof for the latter. On the other hand, factical being alone is not changed by the fact that a second copy of a human being is "next to" me, or perhaps ten human beings. Even when these and still more are objectively present, Da-sein can be alone. Thus, being-with and the facticity of being-with-one-another are not based on the fact that several "subjects" are physically there together. Being alone "among" many, however, does not mean with respect to the being of others that they are simply objectively present.

---

1. That is, "in the initially *cared-about* [interested-in] things at hand in Da-sein's surrounding world" (*in dem zunächst* besorgten *umweltlich Zuhandenen*), as things that *matter to it*.
2. That is, the existential-ontological statement

"Da-sein is essentially being-with" does not mean that, in ordinary terms, I am never in fact alone; nor does it merely mean that others of my kind could appear at any time, but rather that others of my kind are always appearing (*vorkommen*).

Even in being "among them," they are *there with*. Their *Mitda-sein* is encountered in the mode of indifference and being alien. Lacking and "being away"
are modes of *Mitda-sein* and are possible only because Da-sein as being-with
lets the Da-sein of others be encountered in its world. Being-with is an attribute of one's own Da-sein. *Mitda-sein* characterizes the Da-sein of others in
that it is freed for a being-with by the world of that being-with. Only because
it has the essential structure of being-with, is one's own Da-sein *Mitda-sein*
as encounterable by others.

If *Mitda-sein* remains existentially constitutive for being-in-the-world, it
must be interpreted, as must also circumspect association with the innerworldly things at hand which we characterized by way of anticipation as taking care of things, in terms of the phenomenon of *care* which we used to
designate the being of Da-sein in general. (Cf. chapter 6 of this division.)
Taking care of things[3] is a character of being which being-with cannot have
as its own, although this kind of being is a *being toward* beings encountered
in the world, as is taking care of things. The being to which Da-sein is related
as being-with does not, however, have the kind of being of useful things at
hand; it is itself Da-sein. This being is not taken care of, but is a matter of
concern.[4]

* * *

With regard to its positive modes, concern has two extreme possibilities. It
can, so to speak, take the other's "care" away from him and put itself in his
place in taking care, it can *leap in* for him. Concern takes over what is to be
taken care of for the other. The other is thus displaced, he steps back so that
afterwards, when the matter has been attended to, he can take it over as something finished and available or disburden himself of it completely. In this
concern, the other can become one who is dependent and dominated even if
this domination is a tacit one and remains hidden from him. This kind of concern which does the job and takes away "care" is, to a large extent, determinative for being with one another and pertains, for the most part, to our taking
care of things at hand.[5]

In contrast to this, there is the possibility of a concern which does not so
much leap in for the other as *leap ahead* of him, not in order to take "care"
away from him, but to first to give it back to him as such. This concern which
essentially pertains to authentic care; that is, the existence of the other, and
not to a *what* which it takes care of, helps the other to become transparent to
himself *in* his care and *free for* it.

3. That is, being interested in things (*besorgen*).
4. That is, "This entity [i.e., 'the entity to which
Da-sein is related as being-with'] is not *cared about*
[*besorgt*, in the way that one 'cares about,' 'is interested in' or 'concerned with' *things* of various sorts,
for various reasons], but rather is one to whom Da-
sein stands in [a relation of] *concern for* [*Fürsorge*]" (*Dieses Seiende wird nicht* besorgt, *sondern
steht in der* Fürsorge). Here Heidegger chooses to
use the word *Fürsorge*—which literally means
"care for"—to designate the cluster of kinds of
"care" (or lack of "care") relations that one Da-sein
may have for other Da-sein, which are different
from the ways one may feel about (or the forms of

involvement one may have with) mere things.
5. This kind of "concern for" the other is akin to
the way in which one might be "interested in" or
"care about" things, since it treats the other as
something less than a full equal, who needs to be
"cared for." The kind discussed in the following
paragraph, in contrast, respects the other as an
autonomous equal deserving of respect, eliciting
concern or care *as* someone capable of self-caring
but as standing to benefit—precisely as regards
authenticity—from an autonomy-respecting companion. (Thus Heidegger does not regard all such
relationships as detrimental to authenticity.)

Concern proves to be constitutive of the being of Da-sein which, in accordance with its different possibilities, is bound up with its being toward the world taken care of and also with its authentic being toward itself. Being-with-one-another is based initially and often exclusively on what is taken care of together in such being. A being-with-one-another which arises from one's doing the same thing as someone else not only keeps for the most part within outer limits but enters the mode of distance and reserve. The being-with-one-another of those who are employed for the same thing often thrives only on mistrust. On the other hand, when they devote themselves to the same thing in common, their doing so is determined by their Da-sein, which has been stirred. This *authentic* alliance first makes possible the proper kind of objectivity which frees the other for himself in his freedom.

Between the two extremes of positive concern—the one which does someone's job for him and dominates him, and the one which is in advance of him and frees him—everyday being-with-one-another maintains itself and shows many mixed forms whose description and classification lie outside of the limits of this investigation.

Just as *circumspection* belongs to taking care of things as a way of discovering things at hand, concern is guided by *considerateness* and *tolerance*. With concern, both can go through the deficient and indifferent modes up to the point of *inconsiderateness* and the tolerance which is guided by indifference.

The world not only frees things at hand as beings encountered within the world, but also Da-sein, the others in their *Mitda-sein*. But in accordance with its own meaning of being, this being which is freed in the surrounding world is being-in in the same world in which, as encounterable for others, it is there with them. Worldliness was interpreted (section 18) as the referential totality of significance. In being familiar with this significance and previously understanding it, Da-sein lets things at hand be encountered as things discovered in their relevance. The referential context of significance is anchored in the being of Da-sein toward its ownmost being—a being which cannot be in a relation of relevance, but which is rather the being *for the sake of which* Da-sein itself is as it is.

But, according to the analysis which we have now completed, being-with-others belongs to the being of Da-sein, with which it is concerned in its very being. As being-with, Da-sein "is" essentially for the sake of others.[6] This must be understood as an existential statement as to its essence. But when actual, factical Da-sein does *not* turn to others and thinks that it does not need them, or misses them, it *is* in the mode of being-with. In being-with as the existential for-the-sake-of-others, these others are already disclosed in their Da-sein. This previously constituted disclosedness of others together with being-with thus helps to constitute significance, that is, worldliness. As this worldliness, disclosedness is anchored in the existential for-the-sake-of-which. Hence the worldliness of the world thus constituted in which Da-sein always already essentially is, lets things at hand be encountered in the surrounding world in such a way that the *Mitda-sein* of others is encountered at the same time with them as circumspectly taken care of.[7] The structure of the worldliness of the world is such that others are not initially objectively

6. "Als Mitsein 'ist' daher das Dasein wesentlich umwillen Anderer." *Umwillen* usually means "for the sake of," but in this context it is best understood as meaning something like "other-directed" (other-oriented, other-guided).
7. That is, as things one is interested in.

present as unattached subjects along with other things, but show themselves in their heedful being in the surrounding world in terms of the things at hand in that world.

The disclosedness of the *Mitda-sein* of others which belongs to being-with means that the understanding of others already lies in the understanding of being of Da-sein because its being is being-with. This understanding, like all understanding, is not a knowledge derived from cognition, but a primordially existential kind of being which first makes knowledge and cognition possible. Knowing oneself is grounded in primordially understanding being-with. It operates initially in accordance with the nearest kind of being of being-together-in-the-world in the understanding knowledge of what Da-sein circumspectly finds and takes care of with the others. Concernful taking care of things is understood in terms of what is taken care of and with an understanding of them. Thus the other is initially disclosed in the taking care of concern.

* * *

Being toward others is not only an autonomous irreducible relation of being, as being-with it already exists with the being of Da-sein. Of course, it is indisputable that a lively mutual acquaintanceship on the basis of being-with often depends on how far one's own Da-sein has actually understood itself, but this means that it depends only upon how far one's essential being with others has made it transparent and not disguised itself. This is possible only if Da-sein as being-in-the-world is always already with others. "Empathy [*Einfühlung*]"[8] does not first constitute being-with, but is first possible on its basis, and is motivated by the prevailing modes of being-with in their inevitability.

But the fact that "empathy" is not an original existential phenomenon, any more than is knowing in general, does not mean that there is no problem here. Its special hermeneutic will have to show how the various possibilities of being of Da-sein themselves mislead and obstruct being-with-one-another and its self-knowledge, so that a genuine "understanding" is suppressed and Da-sein takes refuge in surrogates; this positive existential condition presupposes a correct understanding of the stranger for its possibility. Our analysis has shown that being-with is an existential constituent of being-in-the-world. *Mitda-sein* has proved to be a manner of being which beings encountered within the world have as their own. In that Da-sein *is* at all, it has the kind of being of being-with-one-another. Being-with-one-another cannot be understood as a summative result of the occurrence of several "subjects." Encountering a number of "subjects" itself is possible only by treating the others encountered in their *Mitda-sein* merely as "numerals."[9] This number is discovered only by a definite being with and toward one another. "Inconsiderate" being-with "reckons" with others without seriously "counting on them" or even wishing "to have anything to do" with them.

One's own Da-sein, like the *Mitda-sein* of others, is encountered, initially and for the most part, in terms of the world-together in the surrounding world taken care of. In being absorbed in the world of taking care of things,[1] that is, at the same time in being-with toward others, Da-sein is not itself. *Who* is it, then, who has taken over being as everyday being-with-one-another?

8. Literally, "feeling at one" (with others).
9. That is, "numbers" (*Nummern*), units that are only numerically distinct.
1. That is, of things one is interested in.

27. EVERYDAY BEING ONE'S SELF AND THE THEY [DAS MAN]

The *ontologically* relevant result of the foregoing analysis of being-with is the insight that the "subject character" of one's own Da-sein and of the others is to be defined existentially, that is, in terms of certain ways to be. In what is taken care of in the surrounding world, the others are encountered as what they are; they *are* what they do.

In taking care of the things which one has taken hold of, for, and against others, there is constant care as to the way one differs from them, whether this difference is to be equalized, whether one's own Da-sein has lagged behind others and wants to catch up in relation to them, whether Da-sein in its priority over others is intent on suppressing them. Being-with-one-another is, unknown to itself, disquieted by the care about this distance. Existentially expressed, being-with-one-another has the character of *distantiality*.[2] The more inconspicuous this kind of being is to everyday Da-sein itself, all the more stubbornly and primordially does it work itself out.

But this distantiality which belongs to being-with is such that, as everyday being-with-one-another, Da-sein stands in *subservience*[3] to the others. It itself *is* not; the others have taken its being away from it. The everyday possibilities of being of Da-sein are at the disposal of the whims of the others. These others are not *definite* others. On the contrary, any other can represent them. What is decisive is only the inconspicuous domination by others that Da-sein as being-with has already taken over unawares. One belongs to the others oneself, and entrenches their power. "The others," whom one designates as such in order to cover over one's own essential belonging to them, are those who *are there* initially and for the most part in everyday being-with-one-another. The who is not this one and not that one, not oneself and not some and not the sum of them all. The "who" is the neuter, *the they* [*das Man*].[4]

We have shown earlier how the public "surrounding world" is always already at hand and taken care of in the surrounding world nearest to us. In utilizing public transportation, in the use of information services such as the newspaper, every other is like the next. This being-with-one-another dissolves one's own Da-sein completely into the kind of being of "the others" in such a way that the others, as distinguishable and explicit, disappear more and more. In this inconspicuousness and unascertainability, the they unfolds its true dictatorship. We enjoy ourselves and have fun the way *they* enjoy themselves.[5] We read, see, and judge literature and art the way *they* see and judge. But we also withdraw from the "great mass" the way *they* withdraw, we find "shocking" what *they* find shocking. The they, which is nothing definite and which all are, though not as a sum, prescribes the kind of being of everydayness.

The they [*Das Man*] has its own ways to be. The tendency of being-with which we called distantiality is based on the fact that being-with-one-another as such creates *averageness*. It is an existential character of the they. In its being, the they is essentially concerned with averageness. Thus, the they [*das Man*] maintains itself factically in the averageness of what is proper,

2. That is, interest in things in ways that may conflict with the ways in which others are interested in them *distances* one from others.
3. That is, subordination, submission (*Botmässigkeit*).
4. Pronounced "dahs Mahn." It means not the English "man" (male or humankind) but rather the (English) impersonal "one," as in "one can't be too careful," "one should keep one's promises," etc.; here translated as "the they," as in "they say crime doesn't pay."
5. That is, "the way one enjoys oneself," "the way people enjoy themselves."

what is allowed, and what is not. Of what is granted success and what is not. This averageness, which prescribes what can and may be ventured, watches over every exception which thrusts itself to the fore. Every priority is noiselessly squashed. Overnight, everything primordial is flattened down as something long since known. Everything gained by a struggle becomes something to be manipulated. Every mystery loses its power. The care of averageness reveals, in turn, an essential tendency of Da-sein, which we call the *levelling down* of all possibilities of being.

Distantiality, averageness, and levelling down, as ways of being of the they [*das Man*], constitute what we know as "publicness." Publicness initially controls every way in which the world and Da-sein are interpreted, and it is always right, not because of an eminent and primary relation of being to "things," not because it has an explicitly appropriate transparency of Da-sein at its disposal, but because it does not get to "the heart of the matter," because it is insensitive to every difference of level and genuineness. Publicness obscures everything, and then claims that what has been thus covered over is what is familiar and accessible to everybody.

The they [*Das Man*] is everywhere, but in such a way that it has always already stolen away when Da-sein presses for a decision. However, because the they presents every judgment and decision as its own, it takes the responsibility of Da-sein away from it. The they [*Das Man*] can, as it were, manage to have "them" constantly invoking it. It can most easily be responsible for everything because no one has to vouch for anything. The they [*Das Man*] always "did it," and yet it can be said that "no one" did it. In the everydayness of Da-sein, most things happen in such a way that we must say "no one did it."

Thus, the they [*das Man*] *disburdens* Da-sein in its everydayness. Not only that; by disburdening it of its being, the they accommodates Da-sein in its tendency to take things easily and make them easy. And since the they constantly accommodates Da-sein, it retains and entrenches its stubborn dominance.

Everyone is the other, and no one is himself. The *they* [*Das Man*], which supplies the answer to the *who* of everyday Da-sein, is the *nobody* to whom every Da-sein has always already surrendered itself, in its being-among-one-another.

In these characteristics of being which we have discussed—everyday being-among-one-another, distantiality, averageness, levelling down, publicness, disburdening of one's being, and accommodation—lies the initial "constancy"[6] of Da-sein. This constancy pertains not to the enduring objective presence of something, but to the kind of being of Da-sein as being-with. Existing in the modes we have mentioned, the self of one's own Da-sein and the self of the other have neither found nor lost themselves. One is in the manner of dependency and inauthenticity. This way of being does not signify a lessening of the facticity of Da-sein, just as the they [*das Man*] as the nobody is not nothing. On the contrary, in this kind of being Da-sein is an *ens realissimum*,[7] by "reality" we understand a being that is like Da-sein.

Of course, the they [*das Man*] is as little objectively present as Da-sein itself. The more openly the they [*das Man*] behaves, the more slippery and hidden it is, but the less is it nothing at all. To the unprejudiced ontic-ontological "eye," it reveals itself as the "most real subject" of everydayness. And if it is not accessible like an objectively present stone, that is not in the least decisive

6. That is, steadiness, stability, predictability (*Ständigkeit*).
7. Most real being (Latin).

about its kind of being. One may neither decree prematurely that this they [*Man*] is "really" nothing, nor profess the opinion that the phenomenon has been interpreted ontologically if one "explains" it as the result of the objective presence of several subjects which one has put together in hindsight. On the contrary, the elaboration of the concepts of being must be guided by these indubitable phenomena.

Nor is the they [*das Man*] something like a "universal subject" which hovers over a plurality of subjects. One could understand it this way only if the being of "subjects" is understood as something unlike Da-sein, and if these are regarded as factually objectively present cases of an existing genus. With this approach, the only possibility ontologically is to understand everything which is not a case of this sort in the sense of genus and species. The they [*Das Man*] is not the genus of an individual Da-sein, nor can it be found in this being as an abiding characteristic. That traditional logic also fails in the face of these phenomena, cannot surprise us if we consider that it has its foundation in an ontology of objective presence—an ontology which is still rough at that. Thus, it fundamentally cannot be made more flexible no matter how many improvements and expansions might be made. These reforms of logic, oriented toward the "humanistic sciences [*Geisteswissenschaften*]," only increase the ontological confusion.

The they [Das Man] is an existential and belongs as a primordial phenomenon to the positive constitution[8] *of Da-sein.* It itself has, in turn, various possibilities of concretion in accordance with Da-sein. The extent to which its dominance becomes penetrating and explicit may change historically.

The self of everyday Da-sein is the *they-self* [*Man-selbst*] which we distinguish from the *authentic self*, the self which has explicitly grasped itself. As the they-self, Da-sein is *dispersed* in the they and must first find itself. This dispersion characterizes the "subject" of the kind of being which we know as heedful absorption in the world nearest encountered. If *Da-sein* is familiar with itself as the they-self [*Man-selbst*], this also means that the they [*das Man*] prescribes the nearest interpretation of the world and of being-in-the-world. The they [*Das Man*] itself, for the sake of which Da-sein is every day,[9] articulates the referential context of significance. The world of Da-sein frees the beings encountered for a totality of relevance which is familiar to the they [*das Man*] in the limits which are established with the averageness of the they. *Initially*, factical Da-sein is in the with-world, discovered in an average way. *Initially*, "I" "am" not in the sense of my own self, but I am the others in the mode of the they [*das Man*]. In terms of the they [*das Man*], and as the they, I am initially "given" to "myself."[1] Initially, Da-sein is the they [*das Man*] and for the most part it remains so. If Da-sein explicitly discovers the world and brings it near, if it discloses its authentic being to itself, this discovering of "world" and disclosing of Da-sein always comes about by clearing away coverings and obscurities, by breaking up the disguises with which Da-sein cuts itself off from itself.

With this interpretation of being-with and being one's self in the they, the question of the who in the everydayness of being-with-one-another is answered.

---

8. That is, the specific constitution of Da-sein (it is not a mere lack or absence). "Positive" here has the sense of "actual, structural" (not implying favorability or approval).
9. That is, around which everyday Da-sein revolves (*worum-willen das Dasein alltäglich ist*); by which

it is guided. The expression *worum-willen* is a somewhat artificial version of *umwillen* (see p. 983, n. 6, above).
1. Better translated: "It is in terms of *das Man* [the they], and as *das Man*, that I am initially 'given' to myself."

These considerations have at the same time given us a concrete understanding of the basic constitution of Da-sein. Being-in-the-world became visible in its everydayness and averageness.

Everyday Da-sein derives the pre-ontological interpretation of its being from the nearest kind of being of the they [*Man*]. The ontological interpretation initially follows this tendency of interpretation, it understands Da-sein in terms of the world and finds it there as an innerworldly being. Not only this; the "nearest" ontology of Da-sein[2] takes the meaning of being on the basis of which these existing "subjects" are understood also in terms of the "world." But since the phenomenon of world itself is passed over in this absorption in the world, it is replaced by objective presence in the world, by things. The being of beings, which *is there, too*, is understood as objective presence. Thus, by showing the positive phenomenon of nearest, everyday being-in-the-world, we have made possible an insight into the root of missing the ontological interpretation of this constitution of being. It itself, in its everyday kind of being, is what initially misses itself and covers itself over.

If the being of everyday being-with-one-another, which seems ontologically to approach pure objective presence, is really fundamentally different from that kind of presence, still less can the being of the authentic self be understood as objective presence. *Authentic being one's self* is not based on an exceptional state of the subject, a state detached from the they [*Man*], *but is an existentiell modification of the they* [*Man*] *as an essential existential.*[3]

But, then, the sameness of the authentically existing self is separated ontologically by a gap from the identity of the I maintaining itself in the multiplicity of its "experiences."

FROM CHAPTER V

BEING-IN AS SUCH

* * *

FROM 38. FALLING PREY [*VERFALLEN*][4] AND THROWNNESS [*GEWORFENHEIT*]

Idle talk, curiosity, and ambiguity characterize the way in which Da-sein is its "there," the disclosedness of being-in-the-world, in an everyday way. As existential determinations, these characteristics are not objectively present in Da-sein; they constitute its being. In them and in the connectedness of their

---

2. That is, "the 'most natural' ontology of Da-sein," or that which most naturally suggests itself—modeled as it is on the kinds of entities with which we find ourselves surrounded in our environing world (namely, things).

3. This sentence makes a crucial point about Heidegger's conception of the status of "authenticity," or authentic selfhood, in relation to the "inauthenticity" of "they-selfhood." First, "authenticity" means "authentically being one's self" (*eigentlich Selbstsein*); and second, "authentic *Selbstsein*" is not completely separate and distinct from the kind of "self" one has at the level of "the they" (*das Man*), but rather is a real-life (*existenzielle*) *modification* of that self—i.e., of the way in which one relates oneself to that identity, whose elements are supplied out of one's everyday "they-self."

4. *Verfallen* usually means "collapsing" or "relapsing" (backsliding). Here it is (purported to be) evaluatively neutral and is used to mean *falling into absorption* in the everyday world of ordinary concerns and *das Man*–style ways of thinking. "Falling prey" is a particularly misleading translation, because it suggests that the impetus to such absorption is *external* to Da-sein; but Heidegger sees the tendency to such "falling into absorption" as a part of the very *existenzial* structure of Da-sein itself, of which the gravitational attraction of the everyday world and of *das Man* merely takes advantage. *Verfallen* (here "falling prey") designates Da-sein's inherent tendency to be *attracted to* that world of everyday life and anonymous social normativity, into which it tends to fall and in which it tends to become absorbed.

being, a basic kind of the being of everydayness reveals itself, which we call the *entanglement* [*Verfallen*][5] of Da-sein.

This term, which does not express any negative value judgment, means that Da-sein is initially and for the most part *together with* the "world" that it takes care of.[6] This absorption in . . . mostly has the character of being lost in the publicness of the they [*das Man*]. As an authentic potentiality for being a self, Da-sein has initially always already fallen away from itself and fallen prey [*verfallen*] to the "world." Falling prey [*Verfallenheit*] to the "world" means being absorbed in being-with-one-another as it is guided by idle talk, curiosity, and ambiguity. What we called the inauthenticity of Da-sein may now be defined more precisely through the interpretation of falling prey [*Verfallen*].[7] But inauthentic and unauthentic by no means signify "not really," as if Da-sein utterly lost its being in this kind of being. Inauthenticity does not mean anything like no-longer-being-in-the-world, but rather it constitutes precisely a distinctive kind of being-in-the-world which is completely taken in by the world and the *Mitda-sein* of the others in the they. Not-being-its-self functions as a *positive* possibility of beings which are absorbed in a world, essentially taking care of that world. This *nonbeing* must be conceived as the kind of being of Da-sein nearest to it and in which it mostly maintains itself.

Thus neither must the entanglement [*Verfallenheit*] of Da-sein be interpreted as a "fall" from a purer and higher "primordial condition." Not only do we not have any experience of this ontically, but also no possibilities and guidelines of interpretation ontologically.

As factical being-in-the-world, Da-sein, falling prey [*als verfallendes*], has already fallen *away from itself*; and it has not fallen prey to some being which it first runs into in the course of its being, or perhaps does not, but it has fallen prey [*verfallen*] to the *world* which itself belongs to its being. Falling prey [*Das Verfallen*] is an existential determination of Da-sein itself, and says nothing about Da-sein as something objectively present, or about objectively present relations to beings from which it is "derived" or to beings with which it has subsequently gotten into a *commercium*.

The ontological-existential structure of falling prey [*Verfallen*] would also be misunderstood if we wanted to attribute to it the meaning of a bad and deplorable ontic quality which could perhaps be removed in the advanced stages of human culture.

Neither in our first reference to being-in-the-world as the fundamental constitution of Da-sein nor in our characterization of its constitutive structural factors, did we go beyond an analysis of the *constitution* of this kind of being, and note its character as a phenomenon. It is true that the possible basic kinds of being-in, taking care and concern, were described. But we did not discuss

---

5. "Entanglement" (not the translator's usual rendering of *Verfallen*) may be an appropriate word with which to describe the usual *consequence* or result of *Verfallen*; but *Verfallen* itself designates the *tendency to "fall into"* the kind of absorption he is talking about, and so would be better translated as "fall-proneness."
6. That is, "is interested in." "*Together with*": that is, "immersed in" (*bei*); see p. 973, n. 5, above.
7. Here and in what follows in this section, Heidegger clarifies what he does and does not mean by "authenticity" and "inauthenticity." It is important to bear in mind that he views *Verfallen* not as a permanent state of "being fallen" into absorption in the everyday world and under the sway of *das Man* but rather as a *persisting tendency* or disposition to be so absorbed, which is only temporarily overcome. Authenticity thus always involves a kind of "self-overcoming" (in Nietzsche's language) of this tendency, which remains a part of the "positive" structure of Da-sein's "being." At the same time, authenticity is not a tendency but rather has the structural character of a *persisting possibility* of Da-sein's "being"—and one that can only be (temporarily) realized by way of what might be called certain galvanizing types of experience, discussed below.

the question of the everyday kind of being of these ways of being. It also became evident that being-in is quite different from a confrontation which merely observes and acts, that is, the concurrent objective presence of a subject and an object. Still, it must have seemed that being-in-the-world functions as a rigid framework within which the possible relations of Da-sein to its world occur, without the "framework" itself being touched upon in its kind of being. But this supposed "framework" itself belong to the kind of being of Da-sein. An *existential mode* of being-in-the-world is documented in the phenomenon of falling prey [*Verfallen*].

* * *

* * * We call this kind of "movement" of Da-sein in its own being the *plunge*.[8] Da-sein plunges out of itself into itself, into the groundlessness and nothingness of inauthentic everydayness. But this plunge remains concealed from it by the way things have been publicly interpreted so that it is interpreted as "getting ahead" and "living concretely."

The kind of movement of plunging into and within the groundlessness of inauthentic being in the they [*Man*] constantly tears understanding away from projecting authentic possibilities, and into the tranquillized supposition of possessing or attaining everything. Since the understanding is thus constantly torn away from authenticity and into the they (although always with a sham of authenticity), the movement of falling prey [*Verfallen*] is characterized by *eddying*.[9]

Not only does falling prey [*Verfallen*] determine being-in-the-world existentially; at the same time the eddy reveals the character of throwing and movement of thrownness [*Geworfenheit*][1] which can force itself upon Da-sein in its attunement. Not only is thrownness not a "finished fact," it is also not a self-contained fact. The facticity of Da-sein is such that Da-sein, *as long as* it is what it is, remains in the throw [*Wurf*] and is sucked into the eddy of the they's inauthenticity. Thrownness, in which facticity can be seen phenomenally, belongs to Da-sein, which is concerned in its being about that being. Da-sein exists factically.

But now that falling prey [*Verfallen*] has been exhibited, have we not set forth a phenomenon which directly speaks *against* the definition in which the formal idea of existence was indicated? Can Da-sein be conceived as a being whose being is concerned *with* potentiality for being if this being *has lost itself* precisely in its everydayness and "lives" *away from itself* in falling prey [*Verfallen*]? Falling prey [*Verfallen*] to the world is, however, phenomenal "evidence" *against* the existentiality of Da-sein only if Da-sein is posited as an isolated I-subject, as a self-point from which it moves away. Then the world is an object. Falling prey [*Verfallen*] to the world is then reinterpreted ontologically as objective presence in the manner of innerworldly beings. However, if we hold on to the being of Da-sein in the constitution indicated of *being-in-the-world*, it becomes evident

8. That is, a precipitous, rapid, and dramatic fall (*Absturz*), like that of a waterfall.
9. That is, a swirl or whirl (*Wirbel*), like the turbulence produced at the foot of a waterfall by the "plunging" water.
1. "Thrownness" (*Geworfenheit*) and "throw" (*Wurf*) are important terms here, providing a counterimage to the comforting idea of Divine Providence (an inscrutable divine plan); they suggest instead the radical contingency of Da-sein's existence, akin to the throw of dice, and set the stage for Heidegger's later discussion of all-pervading *Angst* (anxiety).

that falling prey [*Verfallen*] *as the kind of being of this being-in* rather represents the most elemental proof *for* the existentiality of Da-sein. In falling prey [*Verfallen*], nothing other than our potentiality for being-in-the-world is the issue, even if in the mode of inauthenticity. Da-sein *can* fall prey *only* because it is concerned with understanding, attuned being-in-the-world.[2] On the other hand, *authentic* existence is nothing which hovers over entangled everydayness, but is existentially only a modified grasp of everydayness.

Nor does the phenomenon of falling prey [*Verfallen*] give something like a "night view" of Da-sein, a property occurring ontically which might serve to round out the harmless aspect of this being. Falling prey [*Verfallen*] reveals an *essential*, ontological structure of Da-sein itself. Far from determining its nocturnal side, it constitutes all of its days in their everydayness.

Our existential, ontological interpretation thus does not make any ontic statement about the "corruption of human nature," not because the necessary evidence is lacking but because its problematic is *prior to* any statement about corruption or incorruption. Falling prey [*Verfallen*] is an ontological concept of motion. Ontically, we have not decided whether [the] human being is "drowned in sin," in the *status corruptionis,* or whether he walks in the *status integritatis* or finds himself in an interim stage, the *status gratiae.*[3] But faith and "worldview," when they state such and such a thing and when they speak about Da-sein as being-in-the-world, must come back to the existential structures set forth, provided that their statements at the same time claim to be *conceptually* comprehensible.

The leading question of this chapter pursued the being of the there. Its theme was the ontological constitution of the disclosedness essentially belonging to Da-sein. The being of disclosedness is constituted in attunement, understanding, and discourse. Its everyday mode of being is characterized by idle talk, curiosity, and ambiguity. These show the kind of movement of falling prey with the essential characteristics of temptation, tranquillization, alienation, and entanglement.

But with this analysis the totality of the existential constitution of Da-sein has been laid bare in its main features and the phenomenal basis has been obtained for a "comprehensive" interpretation of the being of Da-sein as care [*Sorge*].

FROM CHAPTER VI
CARE AS THE BEING OF DA-SEIN

FROM 39. THE QUESTION OF THE PRIMORDIAL TOTALITY OF THE STRUCTURAL WHOLE OF DA-SEIN

Being-in-the-world is a structure that is primordial and constantly *whole.* In the previous chapters (division I, chapters II–V) this structure was clarified

2. An echo of earlier passages not included here (§§29, 31), in which Heidegger contends that as part of Da-sein's "being-in-the-world," its experience is always characterized, mediated, and colored by two basic structures: *Verstehen* (understanding) and *Befindlichkeit* (translated in this text as "attunement" and often elsewhere as "state of mind," but perhaps best rendered as "disposition"). The latter's root is the word for "find," and the point of calling this a basic structure of Da-sein is to say that Da-sein always "finds itself" feeling disposed or "minded" in some general way or other, as well as always understands or interprets itself and what is going on in its world in some fashion.

3. Three Latin phrases: "state of corruption," "state of integrity," and "state of grace." The first and third are borrowed from Roman Catholic theology, and Heidegger uses them as models for the second (which relates to his conception of authenticity).

phenomenally as a whole and, always on this basis, in its constitutive moments. The preview given at the beginning of the whole of the phenomenon has now lost the emptiness of its first general prefiguration. However, the phenomenal *manifoldness* of the constitution of the structural whole and its everyday kind of being can now easily distort the *unified* phenomenological view of the whole as such. But this view must be held in readiness more freely and more securely when we now ask the question toward which the preparatory fundamental analysis of Da-sein was striving in general: *How is the totality of the structural whole that we pointed out to be determined existentially and ontologically?*

Da-sein exists factically.[4] We are asking about the ontological unity of existentiality and facticity, namely, whether facticity belongs essentially to existentiality. On the basis of the attunement essentially belonging to it, Da-sein has a mode of being in which it is brought before itself and it is disclosed to itself in its throwness [*Geworfenheit*]. But throwness is the mode of being of a being which always *is* itself its possibilities in such a way that it understands itself in them and from them (projects itself upon them).[5] Being-in-the-world, to which being together with [*bei*] things at hand belongs just as primordially as being-with-others, is always for the sake of itself.[6] But the self is initially and for the most part inauthentic, the they-self.[7] Being-in-the-world is always already entangled [*Verfallen*]. *The average everydayness of Da-sein can thus be determined as entangled* [*Verfallen*]-*disclosed, thrown-projecting being-in-the-world which is concerned with its ownmost potentiality in its being together with* [*bei*] *the "world" and in being-with with the others.*[8]

Can we succeed in grasping this structural whole of the everydayness of Da-sein in its totality? Can the being of Da-sein be delineated in a unified way so that in terms of it the essential equiprimordiality of the structures pointed out becomes intelligible, together with the existential possibilities of modification which belong to it? Is there a way to attain this being phenomenally on the basis of the present point of departure of the existential analytic?

To put it negatively, it is beyond question that the totality of the structural whole is not to be reached phenomenally by means of cobbling together elements. This would require a blueprint. The being of Da-sein, which ontologically supports the structural whole as such, becomes accessible by completely looking *through* this whole *at a* primordially unified phenomenon which already lies in the whole in such a way that it is the ontological basis for every structural moment in its structural possibility. Thus a "comprehensive" interpretation cannot consist of a process of piecing together what we have

---

4. That is, Da-sein always exists in some particular determinate circumstances and with particular determinate characteristics.

5. *Entwerfen* (projection) entails seizing on envisioned possibilities to develop a project (*Entwurf*), thereby orienting oneself to and into the future. Heidegger sees a close connection between such *Entwerfen*, the *Zu-sein* (to-be) of Da-sein, and the *Zukunft* (future) as the primary temporal modality of Da-sein's Existenz.

6. That is, is always self-centered (*umwillen seiner selbst*), in a way that always includes involvements with things and being with others.

7. "Das Selbst aber is zunächst und zumeist uneigentlich, das Man-selbst." This claim—that "the

self" is inauthentic not only *zunächst* (initially or in the first place) but also *zumeist* (for the most part, most of the time)—applies to Da-sein generally, even to those who do attain a measure of authentic selfhood. This is not a criticism but simply an observation that much of the daily life of even the most authentic Da-sein imaginable will have the character of absorption and impersonal, anonymous *das Man*–style normativity.

8. This long and awkward sentence summarizes the various structural features of Da-sein in its "everyday" mode of being that Heidegger has identified up to this point; he is now seeking some central thread that unites them.

hitherto gained. The question of Da-sein's existential character is essentially different from the question of the being of something objectively present [*Vorhanden*]. Everyday experience of the surrounding world, which is directed ontically and ontologically to innerworldly beings, cannot present Da-sein ontically and primordially for the ontological analysis. Similarly, our immanent perception of experiences is lacking an ontologically sufficient guideline. On the other hand, the being of Da-sein is not to be deduced from an idea of human being [*Idee des Menschen*].⁹ Can we gather from our previous interpretation of Da-sein what ontic-ontological access to itself it requires, *from itself*, as the sole appropriate one?

An understanding of being belongs to the ontological structure of Da-sein. In existing, it is disclosed to itself in its being. Attunement and understanding constitute the kind of being of this disclosedness. Is there an understanding attunement in Da-sein in which it is disclosed to itself in a distinctive way?

If the existential analytic of Da-sein is to keep a fundamental clarity as to its basic ontological function, it must search for one of the *most far-reaching* and *most primordial* possibilities of disclosure which lie in Da-sein itself for mastering its preliminary task, that of setting forth the being of Da-sein. The kind of disclosure in which Da-sein brings itself before itself must be such that in it Da-sein becomes accessible to itself, so to speak, in a *simplified* way. Together with what has been disclosed to it, the structural whole of the being we seek must then come to light in an elemental way.

As a kind of attunement¹ adequate for such methodical requirements, we shall take the phenomenon of *Angst*² as the basis of analysis. The elaboration of this fundamental kind of attunement and the ontological characteristics of what is disclosed in it as such take their point of departure from the phenomenon of entanglement, and distinguish *Angst* from the related phenomenon of fear analyzed earlier. As a possibility of being of Da-sein, together with the Da-sein itself disclosed in it, *Angst* provides the phenomenal basis for explicitly grasping the primordial totality of being of Da-sein. Its being reveals itself as *care* [*Sorge*]. The ontological development of this fundamental existential phenomenon demands that we differentiate it from phenomena which at first might seem to be identified with care. Such phenomena are will, wish, predilection, and urge. Care cannot be derived from them because they are themselves founded upon it.

* * *

40. THE FUNDAMENTAL ATTUNEMENT OF *ANGST* AS AN EMINENT DISCLOSEDNESS OF DA-SEIN

One possibility of being of Da-sein is to give ontic "information" about itself as a being. Such information is possible only in the disclosedness belonging to Da-sein which is based on attunement and understanding. To what extent is *Angst* a distinctive attunement? How is Da-sein brought before itself in it

9. That is, from philosophical anthropology; instead, Da-sein has a kind of ontological structural logic of its own (which human reality instantiates).
1. That is, general disposition, the way one is

basically "minded" or feeling (*Befindlichkeit*). See p. 991, n. 2, above.
2. "Anxiety," of the specific kind that Heidegger will be going on to discuss.

through its own being so that phenomenologically the being disclosed in *Angst* is defined as such in its being, or adequate preparations can be made for doing so?

With the intention of penetrating to the being of the totality of the structural whole, we shall take our point of departure from the concrete analysis of entanglement [*Verfallen*] carried out in the last chapter. The absorption of Da-sein in the they [*Man*] and in the "world" taken care of reveals something like a *flight* of Da-sein from itself as an authentic potentiality for being itself. This phenomenon of the flight of Da-sein *from itself* and its authenticity seems, however, to be least appropriate to serve as a phenomenal foundation for the following inquiry. In this flight, Da-sein precisely does not bring itself before itself. In accordance with its own-most trait of entanglement, this turning away leads *away from* Da-sein. But in investigating such phenomena, our inquiry must guard against conflating ontic-existentiell[3] characteristics with ontological-existential interpretation, and must not overlook the positive, phenomenal foundations provided for this interpretation by such a characterization.

It is true that existentielly[4] the authenticity of being a self is closed off and repressed in entanglement, but this closing off is only the *privation* of a disclosedness which reveals itself phenomenally in the fact that the flight of Da-sein is a flight *from* itself. That from which Da-sein flees is precisely what Da-sein comes up "behind." Only because Da-sein is ontologically and essentially brought before itself by the disclosedness belonging to it, *can* it flee *from* that from which it flees. Of course, in this entangled [*verfallend*] turning away, that from which it flees is *not grasped*, nor is it experienced in a turning toward it. But in turning away *from* it, it is "there," disclosed. On account of its character of being disclosed, this existentielly-ontic turning away makes it phenomenally possible to grasp existentially and ontologically what the flight is from. Within the ontic "away from" which lies in turning away, that from which Da-sein flees can be understood and conceptualized by "turning toward" in a way which is phenomenologically interpretive.

Thus the orientation of our analysis toward the phenomenon of entanglement [*Verfallen*] is not condemned in principle to be without any prospect of ontologically experiencing something about the Da-sein disclosed in that phenomenon. On the contrary, it is just here that our interpretation is the least likely to be surrendered to an artificial self-conception of Da-sein. It only carries the explication of what Da-sein itself discloses ontically. The possibility of penetrating to the being of Da-sein by going along with it and pursuing it interpretatively in an attuned understanding increases, the more primordially that phenomenon is which functions methodologically as disclosive attunement. To say that *Angst* accomplishes something like this is only an assertion for now.

We are not completely unprepared for the analysis of *Angst*. It is true that we are still in the dark as to how it is ontologically connected with fear. Obviously they are kindred phenomena. What tells us this is the fact that both phenomena remain mostly undifferentiated, and we designate as *Angst* what

---

3. That is, ordinary-experiential phenomena (in contrast to the ontological-*existenzial* philosophical account of the structures of Da-sein that underlie them).

4. That is, experientially, in real life.

is really fear and call fear what has the character of *Angst*. We shall attempt to penetrate to the phenomenon of *Angst* step by step.

The falling prey [*Verfallen*] of Da-sein to the they [*das Man*] and the "world" taken care of, we called a "flight" from itself. But not every shrinking back from . . . , not every turning away from . . . is necessarily flight. Shrinking back from what fear discloses, from what is threatening, is founded upon fear and has the character of flight. Our interpretation of fear as attunement showed that what we fear is always a detrimental innerworldy being, approaching nearby from a definite region, which may remain absent. In falling prey [*Verfallen*], Da-sein turns away from itself. What it shrinks back from must have a threatening character; yet this being has the same kind of being as the one which shrinks back from it—it is Da-sein itself. What it shrinks back from cannot be grasped as something "fearsome"; because anything fearsome is always encountered as an innerworldly being. The only threat which can be "fearsome" and which is discovered in fear always comes from innerworldly beings.

The turning away of falling prey [*Verfallen*] is thus not a flight which is based on a fear of innerworldly beings. Any flight based on that kind of fear belongs still less to turning away, as turning away precisely *turns toward* innerworldly beings while absorbing itself in them. *The turning away of falling prey* [*Verfallen*] *is rather based on* Angst *which in turn first makes fear possible.*

In order to understand this talk about the entangled [*verfallend*] flight of Da-sein from itself, we must recall that being-in-the-world is the basic constitution of Da-sein. *That about which one has* Angst *is being-in-the-world as such.* How is what *Angst* is anxious about phenomenally differentiated from what fear is afraid of? What *Angst* is about is not an innerworldly being. Thus it essentially cannot be relevant. The threat does not have the character of a definite detrimentality which concerns what is threatened with a definite regard to a particular factical potentiality for being. What *Angst* is about is completely indefinite. This indefiniteness not only leaves factically undecided which innerworldly being is threatening us, but also means that innerworldly beings in general are not "relevant." Nothing of that which is at hand and objectively present within the world, functions as what *Angst* is anxious about. The totality of relevance discovered within the world of things at hand and objectively present is completely without importance. It collapses. The world has the character of complete insignificance. In *Angst* we do not encounter this or that thing which, as threatening, could be relevant.

Thus neither does *Angst* "see" a definite "there" and "over here" from which what is threatening approaches. The fact that what is threatening is *nowhere* characterizes what *Angst* is about. *Angst* "does not know" what it is about which it is anxious. But "nowhere" does not mean nothing; rather, region in general lies therein, and disclosedness of the world in general for essentially spatial being-in. Therefore, what is threatening cannot approach from a definite direction within nearness, it is already "there"—and yet nowhere. It is so near that it is oppressive and stifles one's breath—and yet it is nowhere.

In what *Angst* is about, the "it is nothing and nowhere" becomes manifest. The recalcitrance of the innerworldly nothing and nowhere means phenomenally that *what* Angst *is about is the world as such*. The utter insignificance which makes itself known in the nothing and nowhere does not signify the absence of world, but means that innerworldly beings in themselves are so completely unimportant that, on the basis of this *insignificance* of what is innerworldly, the world is all that obtrudes itself in its worldliness.

What oppresses us is not this or that, nor is it everything objectively present together as a sum, but the *possibility* of things at hand in general, that is, the world itself. When *Angst* has quieted down, in our everyday way of talking we are accustomed to say "it was really nothing." This way of talking, indeed, gets at *what* it was ontically. Everyday discourse aims at taking care of things at hand and talking about them. That about which *Angst* is anxious is none of the innerworldly things at hand. But this "none of the things at hand," which is all that everyday, circumspect discourse understands, is not a total nothing. The nothing of handiness is based on the primordial "something," on the *world*. The world, however, ontologically belongs essentially to the being of Da-sein as being-in-the-world. So if what *Angst* is about exposes nothing, that is, the world as such, this means that *that about which* Angst *is anxious is being-in-the-world itself.*

Being anxious discloses, primordially and directly, the world as world. It is not the case that initially we deliberately look away from innerworldly beings and think only of the world about which *Angst* arises, but *Angst* as a mode of attunement first discloses the *world as world*. However, that does not mean that the worldliness of the world is conceptualized in *Angst*.

Angst is not only *Angst* about . . . , but is at the same time, as attunement, *Angst* for. . . . That for which *Angst* is anxious is not a *definite* kind of being and possibility of Da-sein. The threat itself is, after all, indefinite and thus cannot penetrate threateningly to this or that factically concrete potentiality of being. What *Angst* is anxious for is being-in-the-world itself. In *Angst*, the things at hand in the surrounding world sink away, and so do innerworldly beings in general. The "world" can offer nothing more, nor can the *Mitda-sein* of others. Thus *Angst* takes away from Da-sein the possibility of understanding itself, falling prey [*verfallend*], in terms of the "world" and the public way of being interpreted. It throws Da-sein back upon that for which it is anxious, its authentic potentiality-for-being-in-the-world. *Angst* individuates Da-sein to its ownmost being-in-the-world which, as understanding, projects itself essentially upon possibilities. Thus along with that for which it is anxious, *Angst* discloses Da-sein as *being-possible*, and indeed as what can be individualized in individuation of its own accord.[5]

Angst reveals in Da-sein its *being toward* its ownmost potentiality of being, that is, *being free for* the freedom of choosing and grasping itself. *Angst* brings Da-sein *before its being free for . . . (propensio in*[6]), the authenticity of its being as possibility which it always already is. But at the same time, it is this being to which Da-sein as being-in-the-world is entrusted.

That *about which Angst* is anxious reveals itself as that *for which* it is anxious: being-in-the-world. The identity of that about which and that for which one has *Angst* extends even to anxiousness itself. For as attunement, anxiousness is a fundamental mode of being-in-the-world. *The existential identity of disclosing and what is disclosed so that in what is disclosed the world is disclosed*

---

5. The role of *Angst* in the possible individuation of Da-sein is an important part of Heidegger's answer to the question of what is capable of countering *Verfallen* and making authentic selfhood possible.
6. Inclination in or to (Latin).

as world, as being-in, individualized, pure, thrown potentiality for being, makes it clear that with the phenomenon of Angst a distinctive kind of attunement has become the theme of our interpretation. Angst individualizes and thus discloses Da-sein as "*solus ipse.*"[7] This existential "solipsism," however, is so far from transposing an isolated subject-thing into the harmless vacuum of a worldless occurrence that it brings Da-sein in an extreme sense precisely before its world as world, and thus itself before itself as being-in-the-world.

Again, everyday discourse and the everyday interpretation of Da-sein furnish the most unbiased evidence that *Angst* as a basic attunement is disclosive in this way. We said earlier that attunement reveals "how one is." In *Angst* one has an "*uncanny*" feeling. Here the peculiar indefiniteness of that which Da-sein finds itself involved in with *Angst* initially finds expression: the nothing and nowhere. But uncanniness means at the same time not-being-at-home.[8] In our first phenomenal indication of the fundamental constitution of Da-sein and the clarification of the existential meaning of being-in in contradistinction to the categorial signification of "insideness," being-in was defined as dwelling with . . . , being familiar with. . . . This characteristic of being-in was then made more concretely visible through the everyday publicness of the they which brings tranquillized self-assurance, "being-at-home" with all its obviousness, into the average everydayness of Da-sein. *Angst,* on the other hand, fetches Da-sein back out of its entangled [*verfallend*] absorption in the "world." Everyday familiarity collapses. Da-sein is individuated, but *as* being-in-the-world. Being-in enters the existential "mode" of *not-being-at-home.* The talk about "uncanniness" means nothing other than this.

Now, however, what falling prey [*Verfallen*], as flight, is fleeing from becomes phenomenally visible. It is not a flight *from* innerworldly beings, but precisely *toward* them as the beings among which taking care of things, lost in the they [*das Man*], can linger in tranquillized familiarity. Entangled [*Verfallend*] flight *into* the being-at-home of publicness is flight *from* not-being-at-home, that is, from the uncanniness which lies in Da-sein as thrown, as being-in-the-world entrusted to itself in its being. This uncanniness constantly pursues Da-sein and threatens its everyday lostness in the they [*das Man*], although not explicitly. This threat can factically go along with complete security and self-sufficiency of the everyday way of taking care of things. *Angst* can arise in the most harmless situations. Nor does it have any need for darkness, in which things usually become uncanny to us more easily. In the dark there is emphatically "nothing" to see, although the world is *still* "there" *more obtrusively.*

If we interpret the uncanniness of Da-sein existentially and ontologically as a threat which concerns Da-sein itself and which comes from Da-sein itself, we are not asserting that uncanniness has always already been understood in factical *Angst* in this sense. The everyday way in which Da-sein understands uncanniness is the entangled turning away which "phases out" not-being-at-home. The everydayness of this fleeing, however, shows phenomenally that *Angst* as a fundamental kind of attunement belongs to the essential constitution of Da-sein of being-in-the-world which, as an existential one, is never objectively present, but *is* itself always in the mode of factical Da-sein, that

---

7. Itself alone (Latin); by itself, on its own.
8. The root of the German word for "uncanniness" (*Unheimlichkeit*) is *Heim,* "home."

is, in the mode of an attunement. Tranquillized, familiar being-in-the-world is a mode of the uncanniness of Da-sein, not the other way around. *Not-being-at-home must be conceived existentially and ontologically as the more primordial phenomenon.*

And only because *Angst* always already latently determines being-in-the-world, can being-in-the-world, as being together with [*bei*] the "world" taking care of things and attuned,[9] be afraid. Fear is *Angst* which has fallen prey [*verfallen*] to the "world." It is inauthentic and concealed from itself as such.[1]

Factically, the mood of uncanniness remains for the most part existentielly uncomprehended. Moreover, with the dominance of falling prey [*Verfallen*] and publicness, "real" *Angst* is rare. Often, *Angst* is "physiologically" conditioned. This fact is an *ontological* problem in its facticity, not only with regard to its ontic causes and course of development. The physiological triggering of *Angst* is possible only because Da-sein is anxious in the very ground of its being.

Still more rare than the existentiell fact[2] of real *Angst* are the attempts to interpret this phenomenon in its fundamental, existential-ontological constitution and function. The reasons for this lie partly in the general neglect of the existential analytic of Da-sein, particularly in the failure to recognize the phenomenon of attunement. The factical rarity of the phenomenon of *Angst*, however, cannot deprive it of its suitability for taking over a methodical function *in principle* for the existential analytic. On the contrary, the rarity of the phenomenon is an indication of the fact that Da-sein, which mostly remains concealed from itself in its authenticity on account of the public way of being interpreted of the they [*das Man*], can be disclosed in a primordial sense in its fundamental attunement.

It is true that it is the nature of every kind of attunement[3] to disclose complete being-in-the-world in all its constitutive factors (world, being-in, self). However, in *Angst* there lies the possibility of a distinctive disclosure, since *Angst* individualizes. This individualizing fetches Da-sein back from its falling prey [*Verfallen*][4] and reveals to it authenticity and inauthenticity as possibilities of its being.[5] The fundamental possibilities of Da-sein, which is always my own, show themselves in *Angst* as they are, undistorted by innerworldly beings to which Da-sein, initially and for the most part, clings.

To what extent has this existential interpretation of *Angst*, gained a phenomenal basis for the answering the leading question of the being of the totality of the structural whole of Da-sein?

FROM 41. THE BEING OF DA-SEIN AS CARE [*SORGE*]

With the intention of grasping the totality of the structural whole ontologically, we must first ask whether the phenomenon of *Angst* and what is

9. That is, "as interested-and-state-of-mind-colored being-absorbed in the world" (*als besorgend-befindliches Sein bei der Welt*).
1. That is, "Fear is *Angst* that has fallen into [absorption in] the 'world,' inauthentic and concealed from itself" (*Furcht ist an die "Welt" verfallene, uneigentliche und ihr selbst als solche verborgene Angst*).
2. That is, real-life experiential occurrence (*existenzielle Faktum*).
3. "*Befindlichkeit*": that is, "mindedness" or general disposition (how one "finds oneself" disposed)

with respect to oneself and the world.
4. That is, tendency to fall into absorption.
5. Heidegger here understatedly makes a series of very important points. The kind of *Angst* he is talking about has the profound *existenzielle* (real-life experiential) significance of (1) pulling Da-sein back out of its "fallen" (into absorption) state, (2) "individualizing" it, and (3) revealing to it that "authenticity" and "inauthenticity" are both possible ways of be-ing (and of being a self) for Da-sein.

disclosed in it are able to give the whole of Da-sein in a way that is phenomenally equiprimordial, so that our search for totality can be fulfilled in this givenness. The total content of what lies in it can be enumerated: As attunement,
being anxious is a way of being-in-the-world;[6] that about which we have *Angst*
is thrown being-in-the-world; that for which we have *Angst* is our potentiality-
for-being-in-the-world. The complete phenomenon of *Angst* thus shows Da-
sein as factical, existing being-in-the-world. The fundamental, ontological
characteristics of this being are existentiality, facticity, and falling prey [*Verfallen*]. These existential determinations are not pieces belonging to something composite, one of which might sometimes be missing, but a primordial
content is woven in them which constitutes the totality of the structural whole
that we are seeking. In the unity of the determinations of being of Da-sein
that we have mentioned, this being becomes ontologically comprehensible as
such. How is this unity itself to be characterized?

Da-sein is a being which is concerned in its being about that being.[7] The "is
concerned about . . ." has become clearer in the constitution of being of understanding as self-projective being toward its ownmost potentiality-for-being.
This potentiality is that for the sake of which any Da-sein is as it is. Da-sein
has always already compared itself, in its being, with a possibility of itself.
Being free *for* its ownmost potentiality-for-being, and thus for the possibility
of authenticity and inauthenticity, shows itself in a primordial, elemental concretion in *Angst*. But ontologically, being toward one's ownmost potentiality-
for-being means that Da-sein is always already *ahead* of itself in its being.
Da-sein is always already "beyond itself," not as a way of behaving toward
beings which it is *not*, but as being toward the potentiality-for-being which it
itself is. This structure of being of the essential "being concerned about" we
formulate as the *being-ahead-of-itself* of Da-sein.

But this structure concerns the whole of the constitution of Da-sein. Being-
ahead-of-itself does not mean anything like an isolated tendency in a worldless "subject," but characterizes being-in-the-world. But to being-in-the-world
belongs the fact that it is entrusted to itself,[8] that it is always already thrown
into a world. The fact that Da-sein is entrusted to itself shows itself primordially and concretely in *Angst*. More completely formulated, being-ahead-of-itself
means *being-ahead-of itself-in-already-being-in-a-world*. As soon as this essentially unitary structure is seen phenomenally, what we worked out earlier in
the analysis of worldliness also becomes clearer. There we found that the referential totality of significance (which is constitutive for worldliness) is
"anchored" in a for-the-sake-of-which. The fact that this referential totality,
of the manifold relations of the in-order-to, is bound up with that which Da-
sein is concerned about, does not signify that an objectively present "world"
of objects is welded together with a subject. Rather, it is the phenomenal
expression of the fact that the constitution of Da-sein, whose wholeness is
now delineated explicitly as being-ahead-of-itself-in-already-being-in . . . , is primordially a whole. Expressed differently: existing is always factical. Existentiality is essentially determined by facticity.[9]

---

6. That is, "Self-anxiousness, as [a special kind of]
mindedness [attunement, state of mind], is a way
of being-in-the-world" (*Das Sichängsten ist als
Befindlichkeit eine Weise des In-der-Welt-sein*).
7. This is, in its be-ing about that be-ing.
8. That is, "that it is handed over to itself" (*dass es*

ihn selbst überantwortet), i.e., is responsible for itself.
9. Better translated: "Existenziality is essentially
determined [*bestimmt*, conditioned] *through* facticity [*durch Faktizität*]"—that is, decisively conditioned through the circumstances of one's factical
(real-life) existence.

Furthermore, the factical existing of Da-sein is not only in general and indifferently a thrown potentiality-for-being-in-the-world, but is always already also absorbed in the world taken care of.[1] In this entangled [*verfallend*] being-together-with, fleeing from uncanniness (which mostly remains covered over by latent *Angst* because the publicness of the they suppresses everything unfamiliar) announces itself, whether it does so explicitly or not, and whether it is understood or not. In being-ahead-of-oneself-already-being-in-the-world, entangled *being-together* with innerworldly things at hand taken care of lies essentially included.[2]

The formal existential totality of the ontological structural whole of Da-sein must thus be formulated in the following structure: The being of Da-sein means being-ahead-of-oneself-already-in (the world) as being-together-with (innerworldly beings encountered).[3] This being fills in the significance of the term *care* [*Sorge*], which is used in a purely ontological and existential way. Any ontically intended tendency of being, such as worry or carefreeness, is ruled out.

Since being-in-the-world is essentially care, being-together-with things at hand could be taken in our previous analyses as *taking care* of them, being with the *Mitda-sein* of others encountered within the world as *concern*.[4] Being-together-with is taking care of things, because as a mode of being-in it is determined by its fundamental structure, care. Care not only characterizes existentiality, abstracted from facticity and falling prey [*Verfallen*], but encompasses the unity of these determinations of being. Nor does care mean primarily and exclusively an isolated attitude of the ego toward itself. The expression "care for oneself," following the analogy of taking care and concern, would be a tautology. Care cannot mean a special attitude toward the self, because the self is already characterized ontologically as being-ahead-of-itself; but in this determination the other two structural moments of care, already-being-in . . . and being-together-with, are *also posited*.

In being-ahead-of-oneself as the being toward one's ownmost potentiality-of-being lies the existential and ontological condition of the possibility of *being free for* authentic existentiell possibilities. It is the potentiality-for-being for the sake of which Da-sein always is as it factically is. But since this being toward the potentiality-for-being is itself determined by freedom, Da-sein *can* also be related to its possibilities *unwillingly*,[5] it *can* be inauthentic, and it is so factically initially and for the most part. The authentic for-the-sake-of-which remains ungrasped, the project of one's potentiality-of-being is left to the disposal of the they [*das Man*]. Thus in being-ahead-of-itself, the "self" actually means the self in the sense of the they-self [*Man-selbst*]. Even in inauthenticity, Da-sein remains essentially ahead-of-itself, just as the

---

1. That is, the world one is interested in.
2. That is, "falling *being-absorbed in* cared-about innerworldly things-at-hand" (*das verfallende* Sein beim *besorgten innerweltlichen Zuhandenen*) is essentially included in the characterization of Da-sein at the beginning of the sentence.
3. This crucial sentence, no less awkward in German, sums up the entire analysis of Da-sein developed so far and provides the full meaning of the one-word encapsulation of what Heidegger asserts to be the "meaning" of Da-sein's "being": "care" (*Sorge*). In the original: "Das Sein des Daseins besagt: 'Sich-Vorweg-schon-sein-in-(der-Welt-) als

Sein-bei (innerweltlich begegnenden Seienden)'"; here *begegnenden Seienden* (encountered entities) include both at-hand things and other Da-sein.
4. That is, the fact that "care" (*Sorge*) is the "being" or very nature of "being-in-the-world" (Da-sein's "being") is reflected in two findings: "caring about" (*Besorgen*, "being interested in") is the basic character of Da-sein's relations to things in its environing world, and "caring for" (*Fürsorge*, "concern") is the basic character of Da-sein's relations to other Da-sein.
5. That is, haphazardly, without willing them (*unwillentlich*).

entangled fleeing of Da-sein from itself still shows *the* constitution of being of a being that *is concerned about its being.*[6]

As a primordial structural totality, care lies "before" every factical "attitude" and "position" of Da-sein, that is, it is always already *in* them as an existential *a priori.* Thus this phenomenon by no means expresses a priority of "practical" over theoretical behavior. When we determine something objectively present by merely looking at it, this has the character of care just as much as a "political action," or resting and having a good time. "Theory" and "praxis" are possibilities of being for a being whose being must be defined as care.

The phenomenon of care in its totality is essentially something that cannot be split up; thus any attempts to derive it from special acts or drives such as willing and wishing or urge and predilection, or of constructing it out of them, will be unsuccessful.

Willing and wishing are necessarily rooted ontologically in Da-sein as care, and are not simply ontologically undifferentiated experiences which occur in a "stream" that is completely indeterminate as to the meaning of its being. This is no less true for predilection and urge. They, too, are based upon care insofar as they are purely demonstrable in Da-sein in general. This does not exclude the fact that urge and predilection are ontologically constitutive even for beings which are only "alive." The basic ontological constitution of "living," however, is a problem in its own right and can be developed only reductively and privatively in terms of the ontology of Da-sein.

Care is ontologically "prior" to the phenomena we mentioned, which can, of course, always be adequately "described" within certain limits without the complete ontological horizon needing to be visible or even known as such. For the present fundamental ontological study, which neither aspires to a thematically complete ontology of Da-sein nor even to a concrete anthropology, it must suffice to suggest how these phenomena are existentially based in care.

* * *

From PART ONE, DIVISION TWO
Da-sein and Temporality

45. THE RESULT OF THE PREPARATORY FUNDAMENTAL ANALYSIS OF DA-SEIN AND THE TASK OF A PRIMORDIAL, EXISTENTIAL INTERPRETATION OF THIS BEING

What was gained by our preparatory analysis of Da-sein, and what are we looking for? We have *found* the fundamental constitution of the being in question, being-in-the-world, whose essential structures are centered in disclosedness. The totality of this structural whole revealed itself as care. The being of Da-sein is contained in care. The analysis of this being took as its guideline existence [*Existenz*], which was defined by way of anticipation as the essence of Da-sein. The term existence [*Existenz*] formally indicates that Da-sein *is* as an understanding potentiality-of-being which is concerned in its being about its being. Thus existing, I myself am that being. The development of the phenomenon of care provided an insight into the concrete constitution of existence [*Existenz*],

6. That is, a being that thinks about its be-ing (*um sein Sein geht*); literally, revolves around its be-ing.

that is, into its equiprimordial connection with facticity and with the falling prey [Verfallen] of Da-sein.

We are *looking* for the answer to the question of the meaning of being in general, and above all the possibility of radically developing this basic question of all ontology. But freeing the horizon in which something like being in general becomes intelligible amounts to clarifying the possibility of the understanding of being in general, an understanding which itself belongs to the constitution of that being which we call Da-sein. The understanding of being, however, cannot be *radically* clarified as an essential factor in the being of Da-sein, unless the being to whose being it belongs has been *primordially* interpreted in itself with regard to its being.

Are we entitled to the claim that in characterizing Da-sein ontologically as care we have given a *primordial* interpretation of this being? By what standard is the existential analytic of Da-sein to be measured with regard to its primordiality or nonprimordiality? What then do we mean by the *primordiality* of an ontological interpretation?

Ontological inquiry is a possible way of interpretation which we characterized as a development and appropriation of an understanding. Every interpretation has its fore-having, its fore-sight, and its fore-conception. If such an interpretation becomes an explicit task of an inquiry, the totality of these "presuppositions" (which we call the *hermeneutical situation*[7]) needs to be clarified and made secure beforehand both in a fundamental experience of the "object" to be disclosed, and in terms of that experience. In ontological interpretation beings are freed with regard to their own constitution of being. Such an interpretation obliges us first to give a phenomenal characterization of the being we have taken as our theme and thus bring it into the scope of our fore-having with which all the subsequent steps of our analysis are to conform. But at the same time these steps need to be guided by the possible fore-sight[8] of the kind of being of the being in question. Fore-having and fore-sight then prefigure at the same time the conceptuality (fore-conception) to which all the structures of being are to be brought.

But a *primordial*, ontological interpretation requires not only in general that the hermeneutical situation be secured in conformity with the phenomena, but also the explicit assurance that *the totality* of the beings taken as its theme have been brought to a fore-having. Similarly, it is not sufficient just to make a first sketch of the being of these beings, even if it is phenomenally based. If we are to have a fore-sight of being, we must see it with respect to the *unity* of the possible structural factors belonging to it. Only then can the question of the meaning of the unity that belongs to the totality of being of all beings be asked and answered with phenomenal certainty.

Did the existential analysis of Da-sein which we made, arise from such a hermeneutical situation as will guarantee the primordiality that fundamental ontology requires? Can we proceed from the results attained—that the being of Da-sein is care—to the question of the primordial unity of this structural totality?

What is the status of the fore-sight which has been guiding our ontological

---

7. That is, the situation in which interpretive inquiry is obliged to proceed. "Hermeneutics" is basically the theory of interpretation, where "interpretation" is understood as the kind of analysis and thinking required to develop an understanding of the meanings of things that involve more than what is empirically ascertainable.

8. That is, preliminary image (*Vor-sicht*).

procedure up to now? We defined the idea of existence [*Existenz*] as a potentiality of being, a potentiality that understands and is concerned about its own being. But this *potentiality-of-being* that is always *mine* is free for authenticity or inauthenticity, or for a mode in which neither of these has been differentiated. Our previous interpretation was limited to an analysis of indifferent or inauthentic existence [*Existenz*], starting out with average everydayness. Of course, it was possible and necessary to reach a concrete definition of the existentiality of existence [*Existenz*] in this way. Still, our ontological characterization of the constitution of existence [*Existenz*] was flawed by an essential lack. Existence [*Existenz*] means potentiality-of-being, but also authentic potentiality-of-being. As long as the existential structure of authentic potentiality-of-being is not incorporated in the idea of existence [*Existenz*], the fore-sight guiding an *existential* interpretation lacks primordiality.

And what is the situation with the fore-having of the hermeneutical situation up to now? When and how did our existential analytic make sure that by starting with everydayness it forced *all of* Da-sein—this being from its "beginning" to its "end"—into the phenomenological view giving us our theme? We did assert that care is the totality of the structural whole of the constitution of being of Da-sein. But have we not at the very beginning of our interpretation renounced the possibility of bringing Da-sein as a whole to view? Everydayness is, after all, precisely the being "between" birth and death. And if existence [*Existenz*] determines the being of Da-sein and if its essence is also constituted by potentiality-of-being, then, as long as Da-sein exists [*existiert*], it must always, as such a potentiality, *not yet be* something? A being whose essence is made up of existence [*Existenz*] essentially resists the possibility of being comprehended as a total being. Not only has the hermeneutical situation given us no assurance of "having" the whole being up to now; it is even questionable whether the whole being is attainable at all, and whether a primordial, ontological interpretation of Da-sein must not get stranded—on the kind of being of the thematic being itself.

One thing has become unmistakable. *Our existential analytic of Da-sein up to now cannot lay claim to primordiality.* Its fore-having never included more than the *inauthentic* being of Da-sein, of Da-sein as *fragmentary*. If the interpretation of the being of Da-sein is to become primordial as a foundation for the development of the fundamental question of ontology, it will have to bring the being of Da-sein in its possible *authenticity* and *totality* existentially to light beforehand.[9]

Thus the task arises of placing Da-sein as a whole in our fore-having. However, that means that we must first unpack the question of this being's potentiality-for-being-a-whole. As long as Da-sein is, something is always still outstanding,[1] what it can and will be. But the "end" itself belongs to what is outstanding. The "end" of being-in-the-world is death. This end, belonging to the potentiality-of-being, that is, to existence [*Existenz*], limits and defines the possible totality of Da-sein. The being-at-an-end of Da-sein in death, and thus its being a whole, can, however, be included in our discussion of the possible *being* whole in a phenomenally appropriate way only if an ontologically adequate, that is, an *existential* concept of death has been attained. But

9. This is the task that Heidegger is setting for himself in Division II.
1. That is, left out of the picture.

as far as Da-sein goes, death *is* only in an existentiell *being toward death*. The existential structure of this being turns out to be the ontological constitution of the potentiality-for-being-a-whole of Da-sein. Thus, the whole existing Da-sein can be brought into our existential fore-having. But can Da-sein also exist [*existieren*] as a whole *authentically*? How is the authenticity of existence [*Existenz*] to be defined at all if not with reference to authentic existing? Where do we get our criterion for this? Obviously Da-sein itself in its being must present the possibility and way of its authentic existence [*Existenz*], if such existence is neither imposed upon it ontically, nor ontologically fabricated. But an authentic potentiality-of-being is attested by conscience. Like death, this phenomenon of Da-sein requires a genuinely existential interpretation. It leads to the insight that an authentic potentiality-of-being of Da-sein lies in wanting-to-have-a-conscience. This existentiell possibility, however, tends, from the meaning of its being, to be made definite in an existentiell way by being toward death.[2]

With the demonstration of an *authentic potentiality-for-being-a-whole* of Da-sein our existential analytic has secured the constitution of the *primordial* being of Da-sein. But the authentic *potentiality-for-being-a-whole* becomes visible as a mode of care. With this the phenomenally adequate basis for a primordial interpretation of the meaning of being of Da-sein is also secured.

The primordial ontological ground of the existentiality of Da-sein, however, is *temporality*. The articulated structural totality of the being of Da-sein as care first becomes existentially intelligible in terms of temporality. The interpretation of the meaning of being of Da-sein cannot stop with this fact. The existential-temporal analysis of this being needs concrete confirmation. We must go back and free the ontological structures of Da-sein already gained with regard to their temporal meaning. Everydayness reveals itself as a mode of temporality. But by thus repeating our preparatory fundamental analysis of Da-sein, the phenomenon of temporality itself will at the same time become more transparent. In terms of temporality, it becomes intelligible why Da-sein is and can be historical in the ground of its being and, being *historical*,[3] it can develop historiography.

If temporality constitutes the primordial meaning of being of Da-sein, and if this being is concerned *about its being* in its very being, then care must need "time" and thus reckon with "time." The temporality of Da-sein develops a "time calculation." The "time" experienced in such calculation is the nearest phenomenal aspect of temporality. From it originates the everyday, vulgar understanding of time. And that develops into the traditional concept of time.

The clarification of the origin of the "time" "in which" innerworldly beings are encountered, of time as within-timeness, reveals an essential possibility of the temporalization of temporality. Now the understanding is being prepared for a still more primordial temporalization of temporality. In it is based the understanding of being that is constitutive for the being of Da-sein. The project of a meaning of being in general can be accomplished in the horizon of time.

Thus the inquiry comprised in this division will traverse the following stages: The possible being whole of Da-sein and being toward death (chapter I); the

2. This paragraph provides two of the keys to the following discussion: "death" (or "being toward death") and "conscience" (*Gewissen*), or what Heidegger is going to call "guilt" (*Schuld*).

3. That is, *geschichtlich*, a third key concept in the development of Heidegger's further analysis of Da-sein.

attestation of Da-sein of an authentic potentiality-of-being and resolution (chapter II); the authentic potentiality-for-being-a-whole of Da-sein and temporality as the ontological meaning of care (chapter III); temporality and everydayness (chapter IV); temporality and historicity (chapter V); temporality and within-timeness as the origin of the vulgar concept of time (chapter VI).

From CHAPTER I
THE POSSIBLE BEING-A-WHOLE OF DA-SEIN AND BEING-TOWARD-DEATH

46. THE SEEMING IMPOSSIBILITY OF ONTOLOGICALLY GRASPING AND DETERMINING DA-SEIN AS A WHOLE

The inadequacy of the hermeneutical situation from which the foregoing analysis originated must be overcome. With regard to the fore-having, which must necessarily be obtained, of the whole of Da-sein, we must ask whether this being, as something existing, can become accessible at all in its being. There seem to be important reasons that speak against the possibility of our required task, reasons that lie in the constitution of Da-sein itself.

Care, which forms the totality of the structural whole of Da-sein, obviously contradicts a possible being whole of this being according to its ontological sense. The primary factor of care, "being ahead of itself," however, means that Da-sein always exists for the sake of itself. "As long as it is," up until its end, it is related to its potentiality-of-being. Even when it, still existing, has nothing further "ahead of it," and has "settled its accounts," its being is still influenced by "being ahead of itself." Hopelessness, for example, does not tear Da-sein away from its possibilities, but is only an independent mode of *being toward* these possibilities. Even when one is without illusions and "is ready *for* anything," the "ahead of itself" is there. This structural factor of care tells us unambiguously that something is always still *outstanding* in Da-sein which has not yet become "real" as a potentiality-of-its-being. A *constant unfinished quality* thus lies in the essence of the constitution of Da-sein. This lack of totality means that there is still something outstanding in one's potentiality-for-being.

However, if Da-sein "exists [*existiert*]" in such a way that there is absolutely nothing more outstanding[4] for it, it has also already thus become no-longer-being-there. Eliminating what is outstanding in its being is equivalent to annihilating its being. As long as Da-sein *is* as a being,[5] it has never attained its "wholeness." But if it does, this gain becomes the absolute loss of being-in-the-world. It is then never again to be experienced *as a being*.

The reason for the impossibility of experiencing Da-sein ontically as an existing whole and thus of defining it ontologically in its wholeness does not lie in any imperfection of our *cognitive faculties*. The hindrance lies on the side of the *being* of this being. What cannot even *be* in *such a way* that an experience of Da-sein could pretend to grasp it, fundamentally eludes being experienced. But is it not then a hopeless undertaking to try to discern the ontological wholeness of being of Da-sein?

---

4. That is, not (yet) included.
5. That is, as a *Seiende* (entity)—more specifically, as the kind of *Seiende* it is, whose *Existenz* (and

thus whose projection toward its possibilities) is its "essence" (*Wesen*).

As an essential structural factor of care, "being ahead of itself" cannot be eliminated. But is what we concluded from this tenable? Did we not conclude in a merely formal argumentation that it is impossible to grasp the whole of Da-sein? Or did we not at bottom inadvertently posit Da-sein as something objectively present ahead of which something not yet objectively present constantly moves along? Did our argumentation grasp not-yet-being and the "ahead-of-itself" in a genuinely *existential* sense? Did we speak about "end" and "totality" in a way phenomenally appropriate to Da-sein? Did the expression "death" have a biological significance or one that is existential and ontological, or indeed was it sufficiently and securely defined at all? And have we actually exhausted all the possibilities of making Da-sein accessible in its totality?

We have to answer these questions before the problem of the wholeness of Da-sein can be dismissed as nothing. The question of the wholeness of Da-sein, both the existentiell question about a possible potentiality-for-being-a-whole, as well as the existential question about the constitution of being of "end" and "wholeness," contain the task of a positive analysis of the phenomena of existence set aside up to now. In the center of these considerations we have the task of characterizing ontologically the being-toward-the-end of Da-sein and of achieving an existential concept of death. Our inquiry related to these topics is structured in the following way: The possibility of experiencing the death of others, and the possibility of grasping the whole of Da-sein (section 47); what is outstanding, end and wholeness (section 48); how the existential analysis of death is distinguished from other possible interpretations of this phenomenon (section 49); preliminary sketch of the existential and ontological structure of death (section 50); being toward death and the everydayness of Da-sein (section 51); everyday being toward death and the complete existential concept of death (section 52); the existential project of an authentic being toward death (section 53).

* * *

50. A PRELIMINARY SKETCH OF THE EXISTENTIAL AND ONTOLOGICAL STRUCTURE OF DEATH

From our considerations of something outstanding, end, and totality there has resulted the necessity of interpreting the phenomenon of death as being-toward-the-end in terms of the fundamental constitution of Da-sein. Only in this way can it become clear how a wholeness constituted by being-toward-the-end is possible in Da-sein itself, in accordance with its structure of being. We have seen that care is the fundamental constitution of Da-sein. The ontological significance of this expression was expressed in the "definition": being-ahead-of-itself-already-being-in (the world) as being-together-with beings encountered (within the world). Thus the fundamental characteristics of the being of Da-sein are expressed: in being-ahead-of-itself, existence [*Existenz*], in already-being-in . . . , facticity, in being-together-with [*sein bei*] . . . , falling prey [*Verfallen*]. Provided that death belongs to the being of Da-sein in an eminent sense, it (or being-toward-the-end) must be able to be defined in terms of these characteristics.

We must, in the first instance, make it clear in a preliminary sketch how the existence, facticity, and falling prey [*Verfallen*] of Da-sein are revealed in the phenomenon of death.

The interpretation of the not-yet, and thus also of the most extreme not-yet, of the end of Da-sein in the sense of something outstanding was rejected as inappropriate. For it included the ontological distortion of Da-sein as something objectively present. Being-at-an-end means existentially being-toward-the-end. The most extreme not-yet has the character of something *to which Da-sein relates*. The end is imminent for Da-sein. Death is not something not yet objectively present, nor the last outstanding element reduced to a minimum, but rather an *imminence*.[6]

However, many things can be imminent for Da-sein as being-in-the-world. The character of imminence is not in itself distinctive for death. On the contrary, this interpretation could even make us suspect that death would have to be understood in the sense of an imminent event to be encountered in the surrounding world. For example, a thunderstorm can be imminent, remodeling a house, the arrival of a friend, accordingly, being which are objectively present, at hand or Da-sein-with. Imminent death does not have this kind of being.

But a journey, for example, can also be imminent for Da-sein, or a discussion with others, or a renouncing something which Da-sein itself can be—its own possibilities-of-being which are founded in being-with others.

Death is a possibility of being that Da-sein always has to take upon itself. With death, Da-sein stands before itself in its ownmost potentiality-of-being.[7] In this possibility, Da-sein is concerned about its being-in-the-world absolutely. Its death is the possibility of no-longer-being-able-to-be-there. When Da-sein is imminent to itself as this possibility, it is *completely* thrown back upon its ownmost potentiality-of-being. Thus imminent to itself, all relations to other Da-sein are dissolved in it. This nonrelational ownmost possibility is at the same time the most extreme one. As a potentiality of being, Da-sein is unable to bypass the possibility of death. Death is the possibility of the absolute impossibility of Da-sein. Thus *death* reveals itself as the *ownmost nonrelational possibility not to be bypassed*. As such, it is *an eminent* imminence. Its existential possibility is grounded in the fact that Da-sein is essentially disclosed to itself, in the way of being-ahead-of-itself. This structural factor of care has its most primordial concretion in being-toward-death. Being-toward-the-end becomes phenomenally clearer as being toward the eminent possibility of Da-sein which we have characterized.

The ownmost nonrelational possibility not to be bypassed is not created by Da-sein subsequently and occasionally in the course of its being. Rather, when Da-sein exists, it is already *thrown* into this possibility. Initially and for the most part, Da-sein does not have any explicit or even theoretical knowledge of the fact that it is delivered over to its death, and that death thus belongs to being-in-the-world. Throwness into death reveals itself to it more primordially and penetratingly in the attunement of *Angst*. *Angst* in the face of death is *Angst* "in the face of" the ownmost nonrelational potentiality-of-being not to be bypassed. What *Angst* is about is being-in-the-world itself. What *Angst* is about is the potentiality-of-being of Da-sein absolutely. *Angst* about death must not be confused with a fear of one's demise. It is not an arbitrary and

6. Literally, something that stands (looms) before us (*Bevorstand*).

7. Heidegger frequently refers to Da-sein's death as "its ownmost potentiality-of-being [*Seinkönnen*, the way it has the potentiality to be]." This paragraph explains why, and what he means.

chance "weak" mood of the individual, but, as a fundamental attunement of Da-sein, the disclosedness of the fact that Da-sein exists as thrown being-*toward*-its-end. Thus the existential concept of dying is clarified as thrown being toward the ownmost nonrelational potentiality-of-being not to be bypassed. Precision is gained by distinguishing this from pure disappearance, and also from merely perishing, and finally from the "experience" of a demise.

Being-toward-the-end does not first arise through some attitude which occasionally turns up, rather it belongs essentially to the thrownness of Da-sein which reveals itself in attunement (mood) in various ways. The factical "knowledge" or "lack of knowledge" prevalent in Da-sein as to its ownmost being-toward-the-end is only the expression of the existentiell possibility of maintaining itself in this being in different ways. The fact that factically many people initially and for the most part do not know about death must not be used to prove that being-toward-death does not "generally" belong to Da-sein, but only proves that Da-sein, fleeing *from* it, initially and for the most part covers over its ownmost being-toward-death. Da-sein dies factically as long as it exists, but initially and for the most part in the mode of *falling prey* [*Verfallen*]. For factical existing is not only generally and without further differentiation a thrown potentiality-for-being-in-the-world, but it is always already absorbed in the "world" taken care of.[8] In this entangled [*verfallend*] being together with . . . , the flight from uncanniness makes itself known, that is, the flight *from* its ownmost being-toward-death. Existence, facticity, falling prey [*Verfallen*] characterize being-toward-the-end, and are accordingly constitutive for the existential concept of death. *With regard to its ontological possibility, dying* [*Sterben*] *is grounded in care.*

But if being toward death [*Sein zum Tode*] belongs primordially and essentially to the being of Da-sein, it must also be demonstrated in everydayness, although initially in an inauthentic way. And if being-toward-the-end [*Sein zum Ende*] is even supposed to offer the existential possibility for an existentiell wholeness of Da-sein, this would give the phenomenal confirmation for the thesis that care is the ontological term for the wholeness of the structural totality of Da-sein. However, for the complete phenomenal justification of this statement, a *preliminary sketch* of the connection between being-toward-death and care is not sufficient. Above all, we must be able to see this connection in the *concretion* nearest to Da-sein, its everydayness.

51. BEING-TOWARD-DEATH AND THE EVERYDAYNESS OF DA-SEIN

The exposition of everyday, average being-toward-death was oriented toward the structures of everydayness developed earlier. In being-toward-death, Da-sein is related *to itself* as an eminent potentiality-of-being. But the self of everydayness is the they which is constituted in public interpretedness which expresses itself in idle talk. Thus, idle talk must make manifest in what way everyday Da-sein interprets its being-toward-death. Understanding, which is also always attuned, that is, mooded, always forms the basis of this interpretation. Thus we must ask how the attuned understanding lying in the idle talk of the they has disclosed being-toward-death. How is the they [*das Man*]

---

8. That is, "interested in" or cared about (*besorgten*).

related in an understanding way to its ownmost nonrelational possibility not-to-be-bypassed of Da-sein?[9] What attunement discloses to the they [*das Man*] that it has been delivered over to death, and in what way?

The publicness of everyday being-with-one-another "knows" death as a constantly occurring event, as a "case of death." Someone or another "dies," be it a neighbor or a stranger. People unknown to us "die" daily and hourly. "Death" is encountered as a familiar event occurring within the world. As such, it remains in the inconspicuousness characteristic of everyday encounters. The they [*Das Man*] has also already secured an interpretation for this event. The "fleeting" talk about this which is either expressed or else mostly kept back says: One also dies at the end, but for now one is not involved.

The analysis of "one dies"[1] reveals unambiguously the kind of being of everyday being toward death. In such talk, death is understood as an indeterminate something which first has to show up from somewhere, but which right now is *not yet objectively present* for oneself, and is thus no threat. "One dies [*Man stirbt*]"[2] spreads the opinion that death, so to speak, strikes the they [*das Man*]. The public interpretation of Da-sein says that "one dies [*man stirbt*]" because in this way everybody can convince him/herself that in no case is it I myself, for this one [*Man*] is *no one*. "Dying" is levelled down to an event which does concern Da-sein, but which belongs to no one in particular. If idle talk is always ambiguous, so is this way of talking about death. Dying, which is essentially and irreplaceably mine, is distorted into a publicly occurring event which the they encounters. Characteristic talk speaks about death as a constantly occurring "case." It treats it as something always already "real," and veils its character of possibility and concomitantly the two factors belonging to it, that it is nonrelational and cannot-be-bypassed. With such ambiguity, Da-sein puts itself in the position of losing itself in the they [*das Man*] with regard to an eminent potentiality-of-being that belongs to its own self. The they justifies and aggravates the *temptation* of covering over for itself its ownmost being-toward-death.

The evasion of death which covers over, dominates everydayness so stubbornly that, in being-with-one-another, the "neighbors" often try to convince the "dying person" that he will escape death and soon return again to the tranquillized everydayness of his world taken care of. This "concern" has the intention of thus "comforting" the "dying person." It wants to bring him back to Da-sein by helping him to veil completely his ownmost nonrelational possibility. Thus, the they makes sure of a *constant tranquillization about death*. But, basically, this tranquillization is not only for the "dying person," but just as much for "those who are comforting him." And even in the case of a demise, publicness is still not to be disturbed and made uneasy by the event in the carefreeness it has made sure of. Indeed, the dying of others is seen often as a social inconvenience, if not a downright tactlessness, from which publicness should be spared.

9. "Wie verhält sich das Man verstehend zu seiner eigensten, unbezüglichen und unüberholbaren Möglichkeit des Daseins?" In other words: What is the typical *das Man* way of thinking about one's own death—which is a very special "possibility" that each of us has, because my death is something that pertains more radically *to me* than any other possibility of mine (hence "ownmost"), that pertains *directly* to me with no intermediaries involved (hence "nonrelational"), and that (in the long run, at any rate) is unavoidable (hence "inescapable")? Heidegger often uses this litany of characteristics to refer indirectly to the death that is part of the very structure of Da-sein.

1. This impersonal way of talking about death (*man stirbt*) distances it even while acknowledging it.

2. That is, the commonplace expression "man stirbt."

But along with this tranquillization, which keeps Da-sein away from its death, the they at the same time justifies itself and makes itself respectable by silently ordering the way in which *one* [*man*] is supposed to behave toward death in general. Even "thinking about death" is regarded publicly as cowardly fear, a sign of insecurity on the part of Da-sein and a dark flight from the world. *The they [Das Man] does not permit the courage to have* Angst *about death.* The dominance of the public interpretedness of the they [*das Man*] has already decided what attunement is to determine our stance toward death. In *Angst* about death, Da-sein is brought before itself as delivered over to its possibility not-to-be-bypassed. The they [*Das Man*] is careful to distort this *Angst* into the fear of a future event. Angst, made ambiguous as fear, is, moreover, taken as a weakness which no self-assured Da-sein is permitted to know. What is "proper" according to the silent decree of the they [*das Man*] is the indifferent calm as to the "fact" that one dies. The cultivation of such a "superior" indifference *estranges*[3] Da-sein from its own-most nonrelational potentiality-of-being.

Temptation, tranquillization, and estrangement, however, characterize the kind of being of *falling prey* [*Verfallen*]. Entangled [*Verfallend*], everyday being-toward-death is a constant *flight from death*. Being *toward* the end has the mode of *evading that end*—reinterpreting it, understanding it inauthentically, and veiling it. Factically one's own Da-sein is always already dying, that is, it is in a being-toward-its-end. And it conceals this fact from itself by reinterpreting death as a case of death occurring every day with others, a case which always assures us still more clearly that "one oneself [*man selbst*]" is still "alive." But in the entangled [*verfallend*] flight *from* death, the everydayness of Da-sein bears witness to the fact that the they [*das Man*] itself is always already determined *as being toward death*, even when it is not explicitly engaged in "thinking about death." *Even in average everydayness, Da-sein is constantly concerned with its ownmost nonrelational potentiality-of-being not-to-be-bypassed, if only in the mode of taking care of things in a mode of untroubled indifference* toward *the most extreme possibility of its existence.*

The exposition of everyday being-toward-death, however, gives us at the same time a directive to attempt to secure a complete existential concept of being-toward-the-end, by a more penetrating interpretation in which entangled [*verfallend*] being-toward-death is taken as an evasion *of death. That from which* one flees has been made visible in a phenomenally adequate way. We should now be able to project phenomenologically how evasive Da-sein itself understands its death.

FROM 52. EVERYDAY BEING-TOWARD-DEATH AND THE COMPLETE EXISTENTIAL CONCEPT OF DEATH

Being-toward-the-end was determined in a preliminary existential sketch as being toward one's ownmost nonrelational potentiality-of-being[4] not-to-be-bypassed. Existing being toward this possibility, brings itself before the absolute impossibility of existence. Beyond this seemingly empty characteristic of being-toward-death, the concretion of this being revealed itself in the mode

---

3. That is, alienates (*entfremdet*). Heidegger follows Hegel in employing this term in the sense of a kind of self-alienation.
4. Here, and sometimes elsewhere, Heidegger speaks of death as a special *Seinkönnen* (potenti-

ality of being) of Da-sein; at other times, as in the previous section (see n. 9), as a special *Möglichkeit des Daseins* (possibility of Da-sein). He apparently considers these expressions simply to be two different ways of saying the same thing.

of everydayness. In accordance with the tendency toward falling prey [*verfallen*] essential to everydayness, being-toward-death proved to be an evasion of it, an evasion that covers over. Whereas previously our inquiry made the transition from the formal preliminary sketch of the ontological structure of death to the concrete analysis of everyday being-toward-the-end, we now wish to reverse the direction and attain the complete existential concept of death with a supplementary interpretation of everyday being-toward-the-end.

* * *

* * * The full existential and ontological concept of death can now be defined as follows: As the end of Da-sein, death is the ownmost nonrelational, certain, and, as such, indefinite and not to be bypassed possibility of Da-sein. As the end of Da-sein, *death is* in the being[5] of this being-*toward*-its-end.

The delineation of the existential structure of being-toward-the-end helps us to develop a kind of being of Da-sein in which it can be *wholly as Da-sein*. The fact that even everyday Da-sein *is* always already *toward* its end, that is, is constantly coming to grips with its own death, even though "fleetingly," shows that this end, which concludes and defines being-whole, is not something which Da-sein ultimately arrives at only in its demise. In Da-sein, existing [*existieren*] toward its death, its most extreme not-yet which everything else precedes is always already included. So if one has given an ontologically inappropriate interpretation of the not-yet of Da-sein as something outstanding, any formal inference from this to the lack of totality of Da-sein will be incorrect. *The phenomenon of the not-yet has been taken from the ahead-of-itself; no more than the structure of care in general, can it serve as a higher court that would rule against a possible, existent wholeness; indeed, this ahead-of-itself first makes possible such a being-toward-the-end.*[6] The problem of the possible wholeness of the being which we ourselves actually are exists justifiably if care, as the fundamental constitution of Da-sein, "is connected" with death as the most extreme possibility of this being.

Yet it remains questionable whether this problem has been as yet adequately developed. Being-toward-death is grounded in care. As thrown being-in-the-world, Da-sein is always already delivered over to its death. Being toward its death, it dies factically and constantly as long as it has not reached its demise. That Da-sein dies factically means at the same time that it has always already decided in this or that way in its being-toward-death. Everyday, entangled evasion *of* death is an *inauthentic* being *toward* it. Inauthenticity has possible authenticity as its basis. Inauthenticity characterizes the kind of being in which Da-sein diverts itself and for the most part has always diverted itself, too, but it does not have to do this necessarily and constantly. Because Da-sein exists,[7] it determines itself as the kind of being it is, and it does so always in terms of a possibility which it itself *is* and understands.

Can Da-sein *authentically understand* its ownmost, nonrelational, certain possibility not-to-be-bypassed that is, as such, indefinite? That is, can it

---

5. That is, in the be-ing (*Sein*).
6. This important sentence (emphasized by Heidegger) is better translated: "The phenomenon of the 'not yet' derived from the ahead-of-itself structure (like the care structure generally) is so far from counting against a possible existent being-as-a-whole or wholeness [*ein mögliches existentes*

Ganzsein] [for Da-sein] that that ahead-of-itself structure is actually what makes such a being-toward-the-end possible."
7. That is, because Da-sein "exists" (*existiert*) in the special sense of this term that Heidegger elaborated at the outset, and reserves to Da-sein alone.

maintain itself in an authentic being-toward-its-end? As long as this authentic being-toward-death has not been set forth and ontologically determined, there is something essentially lacking in our existential interpretation of being-toward-the-end.

Authentic being-toward-death signifies an existentiell possibility[8] of Da-sein. This ontic potentiality-of-being must in its turn be ontologically possible. What are the existential conditions of this possibility? How are they themselves to become accessible?

53. EXISTENTIAL PROJECT OF AN AUTHENTIC BEING-TOWARD-DEATH

Factically, Da-sein maintains itself initially and for the most part in an inauthentic being-toward-death. How is the ontological possibility of an *authentic* being-toward-death to be characterized "objectively," if, in the end, Da-sein is never authentically related to its end, or if this authentic being must remain concealed from others in accordance with its meaning? Is not the project of the existential possibility of such a questionable existentiell potentiality-of-being a fantastical undertaking? What is needed for such a project to get beyond a merely poetizing, arbitrary construction? Does Da-sein itself provide directives for this project? Can the grounds for its phenomenal justification be taken from Da-sein itself? Can our analysis of Da-sein up to now give us any prescriptions for the ontological task we have now formulated, so that what we have before us can be kept on a secure path?

The existential concept of death has been established, and thus we have also established that to which an authentic being-toward-the-end should be able to relate itself. Furthermore, we have also characterized inauthentic being-toward-death and thus we have prescribed how authentic being-toward-death cannot be in a negative way. The existential structure of an authentic being-toward-death must let itself be projected with these positive and prohibitive instructions.

Da-sein is constituted by disclosedness, that is, by attuned understanding. *Authentic* being-toward-death can*not evade* its ownmost nonrelational possibility or *cover* it *over* in this flight and *reinterpret* it for the common sense of the they. The existential project of an authentic being-toward-death must thus set forth the factors of such a being which are constitutive for it as an understanding of death—in the sense of being toward this possibility without fleeing it or covering it over.

First of all, we must characterize being-toward-death as a being *toward a possibility*, toward an eminent possibility of Da-sein itself. Being toward a possibility, that is, toward something possible, can mean to be out for something possible, as in taking care of its actualization. In the field of things at hand and objectively present, we constantly encounter such possibilities: what is attainable, manageable, viable, and so forth. Being out for something possible and taking care of it has the tendency of *annihilating* the *possibility* of the possible by making it available. The actualization of useful things at hand in taking care of them (producing them, getting them ready, readjusting them, etc.), is, however, always merely relative, in that what has been actualized still

8. That is, a real-life experiential possibility.

has the character of being relevant. Even when actualized, as something actual it remains possible for . . . , it is characterized by an in-order-to. Our present analysis should simply make clear how being out for something and taking care of it, is related to the possible. It does so not in a thematic and theoretical reflection on the possible as possible, or even with regard to its possibility as such, but rather in such a way that it *circumspectly* looks *away* from the possible to what it is possible for.

Evidently being-toward-death, which is now in question, cannot have the character of being out for something and taking care of it with a view toward its actualization. For one thing, death as something possible is not a possible thing at hand or objectively present, but a possibility-of-being of <u>Da-sein</u>. Then, however, taking care of the actualization of what is thus possible would have to mean bringing about one's own demise. Thus Da-sein would precisely deprive itself of the very ground for an existing being-toward-death.

Thus if being-toward-death is not meant as an "actualization" of death, neither can it mean to dwell near the end in its possibility. This kind of behavior would amount to "thinking about death," thinking about this possibility, how and when it might be actualized. Brooding over death does not completely take away from it its character of possibility. It is always brooded over as something coming, but we weaken it by calculating how to have it at our disposal. As something possible, death is supposed to show as little as possible of its possibility. On the contrary, if being-toward-death has to disclose understandingly the possibility which we have characterized as *such*, then in such being-toward-death this possibility must not be weakened, it must be understood *as possibility*, cultivated *as possibility*, and *endured as possibility* in our relation to it.

However, Da-sein relates to something possible in its possibility, by *expecting* it. Anyone who is intent on something possible, may encounter it unimpeded and undiminished in its "whether it comes or not, or whether it comes after all." But with this phenomenon of expecting has our analysis not reached the same kind of being toward the possible which we already characterized as being out for something and taking care of it? To expect something possible is always to understand and "have" it with regard to whether and when and how it will really be objectively present. Expecting is not only an occasional looking away from the possible to its possible actualization, but essentially a *waiting for that actualization*. Even in expecting, one leaps away from the possible and gets a footing in the real. It is for its reality that what is expected is expected. By the very nature of expecting, the possible is drawn into the real, arising from it and returning to it.

But being toward this possibility, as being-toward-death, should relate itself to that *death* so that it reveals itself, in this being and for it, *as possibility*. Terminologically, we shall formulate this being toward possibility as *anticipation of this possibility*.[9] But does not this mode of behavior contain an approach to the possible, and does not its actualization emerge with its nearness? In this kind of coming near, however, one does not tend toward making something real available and taking care of it, but as one comes nearer understandingly,

9. "Vorlaufen in die Möglichkeit." *Vorlaufen* literally means "to run ahead," though it can also mean "to go before." "Anticipation" is perhaps the best available English term for what Heidegger has in mind here, but in the sense of "expecting" or "keeping in mind" rather than "looking forward to."

the possibility of the possible only becomes "greater." *The nearest nearness of being-toward-death as possibility is as far removed as possible from anything real*. The more clearly this possibility is understood, the more purely does understanding penetrate to it *as the possibility of the impossibility of existence* [*Existenz*] *in general*. As possibility, death gives Da-sein nothing to "be actualized" and nothing which it itself could *be* as something real. It is the possibility of the impossibility of every mode of behavior toward . . . , of every way of existing. In running ahead to this possibility, it becomes "greater and greater," that is, it reveals itself as something which knows no measure at all, no more or less, but means the possibility of the measureless impossibility of existence [*Existenz*]. Essentially, this possibility offers no support for becoming intent on something, for "spelling out" the real thing that is possible and so forgetting its possibility. As anticipation of possibility, being-toward-death first *makes* this possibility *possible* and sets it free as possibility.

Being-toward-death is the anticipation of a potentiality-of-being of *that* being whose kind of being is anticipation itself.[1] In the anticipatory revealing of this potentiality-of-being, Da-sein discloses itself to itself with regard to its most extreme possibility. But to project oneself upon one's ownmost potentiality of being means to be able to understand oneself in the being of the being thus revealed: to exist [*existieren*]. Anticipation shows itself as the possibility of understanding one's *ownmost* and extreme potentiality-of-being, that is, as the possibility of *authentic existence* [*Existenz*].[2] Its ontological constitution must be made visible by setting forth the concrete structure of anticipation of death. How is the phenomenal definition of this structure to be accomplished? Evidently by defining the characteristics of anticipatory disclosure which must belong to it so that it can become the pure understanding of the ownmost nonrelational possibility not-to-be-bypassed which is certain and, as such, indefinite. We must remember that understanding does not primarily mean staring at a meaning, but understanding oneself in the potentiality-of-being that reveals itself in the project.

Death is the *ownmost* possibility of Da-sein. Being toward it discloses to Da-sein its *ownmost* potentiality-of-being in which it is concerned about the being of Da-sein absolutely. Here the fact can become evident to Da-sein that in the eminent possibility of itself it is torn away from the they [*das Man*]; that is, anticipation can always already have torn itself away from the they. The understanding of this "ability," however, first reveals its factical lostness in the everydayness of the they-self [*Man-selbst*].

The ownmost possibility is *nonrelational*. Anticipation lets Da-sein understand that it has to take over solely from itself the potentiality-of-being in which it is concerned absolutely about its ownmost being. Death does not just "belong" in an undifferentiated way to one's own Da-sein, but it *lays claim* on it as something *individual*. The nonrelational character of death understood in anticipation individualizes Da-sein down to itself.[3] This individualizing is

---

1. That is, Da-sein's "kind of being is anticipation itself" in the sense that "being ahead of itself"— i.e., living toward possibilities of which one has an awareness—is the basic structure of what Heidegger means by "Existenz," which he has termed Da-sein's "essence." Keeping one's own inescapable death in mind (taking it seriously into account in the living of one's life) is a salient example of such

"anticipation."
2. Here Heidegger makes the crucial link between "anticipation" (in his sense) of one's death and "the possibility of authentic Existenz."
3. This "individualization" effect explains the link that Heidegger sees between "anticipation" (of one's own death) and the possibility of authenticity.

a way in which the "there" is disclosed for existence. It reveals the fact that any being-together-with what is taken care of and any being-with the others fails when one's ownmost potentiality-of-being is at stake. Da-sein can *authentically* be *itself* only when it makes that possible of its own accord. But if taking care of things and being concerned fail us, this does not, however, mean at all that these modes of Da-sein have been cut off from its authentic being a self. As essential structures of the constitution of Da-sein they also belong to the condition of the possibility of existence [*Existenz*] in general. Da-sein is authentically itself only if it projects itself, *as* being-together with things taken care of and concernful being-with . . . , primarily upon its ownmost potentiality-of-being, rather than upon the possibility of the they-self [*Man-selbst*]. Anticipation of its nonrelational possibility forces the being that anticipates into the possibility of taking over its ownmost being of its own accord.

The ownmost nonrelational possibility is *not to be bypassed*. Being toward this possibility lets Da-sein understand that the most extreme possibility of existence is imminent, that of giving itself up. But anticipation does not evade the impossibility of bypassing death, as does inauthentic being-toward-death, but *frees* itself *for* it. Becoming free *for* one's own death in anticipation frees one from one's lostness in chance possibilities urging themselves upon us, so that the factical possibilities lying before the possibility not-to-be-bypassed can first be authentically understood and chosen. Anticipation discloses to existence [*Existenz*] that its extreme inmost possibility lies in giving itself up and thus shatters all one's clinging to whatever existence [*Existenz*] one has reached. In anticipation, Da-sein guards itself against falling back behind itself, or behind the potentiality-for-being that it has understood. It guards against "becoming too old for its victories" (Nietzsche).[4] Free for its ownmost possibilities, that are determined by the *end*, and so understood as *finite*, Da-sein prevents the danger that it may, by its own finite understanding of existence [*Existenz*], fail to recognize that it is getting overtaken by the existence-possibilities [*Existenz*-possibilities] of others, or that it may misinterpret these possibilities, thus divesting itself of its ownmost factical existence. As the nonrelational possibility, death individualizes, but only, as the possibility not-to-be-bypassed, in order to make Da-sein as being-with understand the potentialities-of-being of the others. Because anticipation of the possibility not-to-be-bypassed also disclosed all the possibilities lying before it, this anticipation includes the possibility of taking the *whole* of Da-sein in advance in an existentiell way, that is, the possibility of existing as a *whole potentiality-of-being.*[5]

The ownmost nonrelational possibility not-to-be-bypassed is *certain*. The mode *of being* certain of it is determined by the truth (disclosedness) corresponding to it. But Da-sein discloses the certain possibility of death as possibility only by making this possibility as its ownmost potentiality-of-being *possible* in anticipating it. The disclosedness of this possibility is grounded in a making possible that anticipates. Holding oneself in this truth, that is, being certain of what has been disclosed, lays claim all the more upon anticipation. The certainty of death cannot be calculated in terms of ascertaining cases of

4. A paraphrase from "On Free Death" in part 1 of Nietzsche's *Thus Spoke Zarathustra* (1883): "Some become too old even for their truths and victories." 5. Here again Heidegger links "anticipation" (of one's own death) and the possibility of what he sees as the only authentic kind of "wholeness" of self that is possible for Da-sein as an entity whose essence "lies in its Existenz."

death encountered. This certainty by no means holds itself in the truth of something objectively present. When something objectively present has been discovered, it is encountered most purely by just looking at it and letting it be encountered in itself. Da-sein must first have lost itself in the factual circumstances (this can be one of care's own tasks and possibilities) if it is to gain the pure objectivity, that is, the indifference of apodictic evidence. If being-certain in relation to death does not have this character, that does not mean it is of a lower grade, but that *it does not belong at all to the order of degrees of evidence about things objectively present.*

Holding death for true (death *is* always just one's own) shows a different kind of certainty, and is more primordial than any certainty related to beings encountered in the world or to formal objects, for it is certain of being-in-the-world. As such, it claims not only *one* definite kind of behavior of Da-sein, but claims Da-sein in the complete authenticity of its existence [*Existenz*].[6] In anticipation, Da-sein can first make certain of its ownmost being in its totality not-to-be-bypassed. Thus, the evidence of the immediate givenness of experiences, of the ego or of consciousness, necessarily has to lag behind the certainty contained in anticipation. And yet this is not because the kind of apprehension belonging to it is not strict enough, but because at bottom it cannot hold *for true* (disclosed) something that it basically insists upon "having there" as true: namely, the Da-sein which I myself *am* and can be as potentiality-of-being authentically only in anticipation.[7]

The ownmost nonrelational possibility not-to-be-bypassed is *indefinite* with regard to its certainty. How does anticipation disclose this character of the eminent possibility of Da-sein? How does understanding, anticipating, project itself upon a definite potentiality-of-being which is constantly possible in such a way that the when in which the absolute impossibility of existence becomes possible remains constantly indefinite? In anticipating the indefinite certainty of death, Da-sein opens itself to a constant *threat* arising from its own there. Being-toward-the-end must hold itself in this very threat, and can so little phase it out that it rather has to cultivate the indefiniteness of the certainty. How is the genuine disclosing of this constant threat existentially possible? All understanding is attuned. Mood brings Da-sein before the thrownness of its "that-it-is-there." *But the attunement [Befindlichkeit] which is able to hold open the constant and absolute threat to itself arising from the ownmost individualized being of Da-sein is* Angst.[8] In Angst, Da-sein finds itself *faced* with the nothingness of the possible impossibility of its existence. *Angst is* anxious *about* the potentiality-of-being of the being thus determined, and

---

6. "Als solches beansprucht ist nicht nur *eine* bestimmte Verhaltung des Daseins, sondern dieses in der vollen Eigentlichkeit seiner Existenz." Heidegger is talking about authentic being-toward-death, which he calls *Vorlaufen* (anticipation) and has just characterized as "Das Für-wahr-halten des Todes" (holding death for true, taking death to be true). And what he is saying here pertains to authenticity: what is demanded of one by such "anticipation"—as recognition of the truth of death and its inescapability, which is bound up with being "certain of being-in-the world" as well—is not "only *one* specific behavior of Da-sein, but rather the full authenticity of its Existenz." See

also p. 1021, n. 5, below.
7. That is, "namely, the Da-sein which I myself *am*, and which as potentiality-for-being I can be authentically only anticipatorily [*vorlaufend*]"— i.e., only by way of the "anticipation" or "holding for true" of my own death.
8. Here Heideggerian *Angst* turns out to be a positively significant phenomenon, as a form of mindedness (*Befindlichkeit*) that is well attuned to "holding death for true" as well as to the radical contingency and non-authoritativeness of everything the world of everyday life and normativity that is ordinarily taken for granted. It thus is a perfect match for authenticity.

thus discloses the most extreme possibility. Because the anticipation of Da-sein absolutely individualizes and lets it, in this individualizing of itself, become certain of the wholeness of its potentiality-of-being, the fundamental attunement of *Angst* belongs to this self-understanding of Da-sein in terms of its ground. Being-toward-death is essentially *Angst*. This is attested unmistakably, although "only" indirectly, by being-toward-death as we characterized it, when it distorts *Angst* into cowardly fear and, in overcoming that fear, only makes known its own cowardliness in the face of *Angst*.

What is characteristic about authentic, existentially projected being-toward-death can be summarized as follows: *Anticipation reveals to Da-sein its lostness in the they-self [Man-selbst], and brings it face to face with the possibility to be itself, primarily unsupported by concern taking care of things, but to be itself in passionate anxious **freedom toward death** which is free of the illusions of the they [das Man], factical, and certain of itself.*[9]

All relations, belonging to being-toward-death, to the complete content of the most extreme possibility of Da-sein, constitute an anticipation that they combine in revealing, unfolding, and holding fast, as that which makes this possibility possible. The existential project in which anticipation has been delimited, has made visible the *ontological* possibility of an existentiell, authentic being-toward-death. But with this, the possibility then appears of an authentic potentiality-for-being-a-whole—*but only as an ontological possibility*. Of course, our existential project of anticipation stayed with those structures of Da-sein gained earlier and let Da-sein itself, so to speak, project itself upon this possibility, without proffering to Da-sein the "content" of an ideal of existence [*Existenz*] forced upon it "from the outside." And yet this existentially "possible" being-toward-death remains, after all, existentielly a fantastical demand. The ontological possibility of an authentic potentiality-for-being-a-whole of Da-sein means nothing as long as the corresponding ontic potentiality-of-being has not been shown in terms of Da-sein itself. Does Da-sein ever project itself factically into such a being-toward-death? Does it even *demand*, on the basis of its ownmost being, an authentic potentiality of being which is determined by anticipation?

Before answering these questions, we must investigate to what extent *at all* and in what way Da-sein *bears witness* to a possible *authenticity* of its existence from its ownmost potentiality-of-being, in such a way that it not only makes this known as *existentielly* possible, but *demands* it of itself.

The question hovering over us of an authentic wholeness of Da-sein and its existential constitution can be placed on a viable, phenomenal basis only if that question can hold fast to a possible authenticity of its being attested by Da-sein itself. If we succeed in discovering phenomenologically such an attestation and what is attested to in it, the problem arises again of *whether the anticipation of death projected up to now only in its **ontological** possibility has an essential connection with that authentic potentiality-of-being **attested to**.*

---

9. Heidegger stops short of claiming moral status, normative force, or even evaluative legitimacy for the idea that authenticity in one's being-toward-death and existence is to be preferred to inauthenticity; but this passage leaves no doubt about his view of the matter. Indeed, in the discussion of "conscience" that follows he purports to have identified something *within Da-sein's being* that itself "calls" for authenticity.

From CHAPTER II
The Attestation of Da-sein of an Authentic Potentiality-of-Being and Resoluteness

FROM 55. THE EXISTENTIAL AND ONTOLOGICAL FOUNDATIONS OF CONSCIENCE

The analysis of conscience [*Gewissen*] will start out with an undifferentiated fact about this phenomenon, the fact that it somehow gives one to understand something. Conscience discloses, and thus belongs to the scope of the existential phenomena which constitute the *being of the there* as disclosedness. We have analyzed the most general structures of attunement, understanding, discourse, and falling prey [*Verfallen*]. If we put conscience in this phenomenal context, this is not a matter of a schematic application of the structures gained there to a particular "case" of the disclosure of Da-sein. Rather, our interpretation of conscience will not only continue the earlier analysis of the disclosedness of the there, but will grasp it more primordially with regard to the authentic being of Da-sein.

* * *

FROM 56. THE CHARACTER OF CONSCIENCE AS A CALL

* * *

What is what is talked about[1] in the call [*Ruf*] of conscience, what is summoned?[2] Evidently Da-sein itself. This answer is just as incontestable as it is indefinite. If the call had such a vague goal, it would still be an occasion for Da-sein to pay heed to itself. But to Da-sein essentially belongs the fact that it is disclosed to itself with the disclosedness of its world, so that it always already *understands itself*. The call reaches Da-sein in this always-already-understanding-itself in everyday, average taking care of things. The call reaches the they-self [*Man-selbst*] of heedful being-with with others.

And to what is one summoned? To one's *own self*.[3] Not to what Da-sein is, can do, and takes care of in everyday being-with-one-another, not even to what has moved it, what it has pledged itself to, what it has let itself be involved with. * * *

The they-self [*Man-selbst*] is summoned to the self [*das Selbst*]. However, this is not the self that can become an "object" for itself on which to pass judgment, not the self that unrestrainedly dissects its "inner life" with excited curiosity, and not the self that stares "analytically" at states of the soul and their backgrounds. The summons of the self in the they-self [*Man-selbst*] does not force it inwards upon itself so that it can close itself off from the "external world." The call passes over all this and disperses it, so as to summon solely the self which is in no other way than being-in-the-world.

But how are we to define *what is spoken* in this discourse? *What* does conscience call to the one summoned?[4] Strictly speaking—nothing. The call does not say anything, does not give any information about events of the world,

---

1. That is: What is talked about (literally, "the talked-about," *das Beredete*)?
2. Literally, the called to (*Angerufene*).
3. That is, a call to authentic "being-a-self,"

self-being, selfhood. (Just as Heidegger's "anxiety" is a special sort of anxiety, this "conscience" clearly is not conscience in general.)
4. That is, the one called to (*Angerufene*).

has nothing to tell. Least of all does it strive to open a "conversation with itself" in the self which has been summoned. "Nothing" is called *to* the self which is summoned [*angerufen*], but it is *summoned* [*aufgerufen*]to itself,[5] that is, to its ownmost potentiality-of-being. In accordance with its tendency as call, the call does not mandate a "trial" for the self which has been summoned, but as a summons to the ownmost *potentiality*-of-being-a-self, it calls Da-sein forth (ahead-of-itself) to its most unique possibilities.

* * *

FROM 57. CONSCIENCE AS THE CALL OF CARE

Conscience calls the self of Da-sein forth from its lostness in the they [*das Man*]. The self summoned remains indifferent and empty in its what. The call passes over *what* Da-sein understands itself *as* initially and for the most part in its interpretation in terms of taking care of things. And yet the self is unequivocally and unmistakably reached.

* * *

Thus only an analysis of understanding the summons can lead to an explicit discussion of *what the call gives to understand*. But only with our foregoing, general ontological characterization of conscience is the possibility given to comprehend existentially conscience's call of "guilty [*schuldig*]." All interpretations and experiences of conscience agree that the "voice" of conscience somehow speaks of "guilt [*Schuld*]."[6]

FROM 58. UNDERSTANDING THE SUMMONS, AND GUILT

In order to grasp phenomenally what is heard in understanding the summons, we shall take up this summons anew. Summoning the they-self [*Man-selbst*] means calling forth the authentic self to its potentiality-of-being, as Da-sein, that is, being-in-the-world taking care of things and being-with others. The existential interpretation of that to which the call calls forth, thus cannot define any concrete individual possibility of existence if it understands itself correctly in its methodical possibilities and tasks. What can be established, and what seeks to get established, is not what is called in and to each particular Da-sein from an existentiell standpoint, but what *belongs to the existential condition of the possibility* of the actual, factical and existentiell potentiality-of-being.

* * *

The call is the call of care. Being guilty [*Schuldigsein*] constitutes the being that we call care. Da-sein stands primordially together with itself in uncanniness. Uncanniness brings this being face to face with its undisguised nullity [*Nichtigkeit*], which belongs to the possibility of its ownmost potentiality-of-being. In that Da-sein as care is concerned about its being, it calls itself as a they [*Man*] that has factically fallen prey [*Verfallen*], and calls itself from its uncanniness to its potentiality-of-being. The summons calls back by calling

---

5. It is only at this point that Heidegger shifts from speaking of being "called to" (*angerufen*) to being "summoned" (*aufgerufen*).
6. Heidegger's following elaboration of the idea of "guilty!" (*schuldig!*) and its association with "con-

science as the call of care" implies that "guilty" here basically means "responsible," and that "guilt" has the sense of "responsibility" (for the manner in which it responds).

forth: *forth* to the possibility of taking over in existence the thrown being that it is, *back* to thrownness in order to understand it as the null ground that it has to take up into existence. The calling back in which conscience calls forth gives Da-sein to understand that Da-sein itself—as the null ground of its null project,[7] standing in the possibility of its being—must bring itself back to itself from its lostness in the they [*das Man*], and this means that it is *guilty*.

* * *

Then the correct hearing of the summons is tantamount to understanding oneself in one's ownmost potentiality-of-being, that is, in projecting oneself upon one's *ownmost* authentic potentiality for becoming guilty.[8] When Da-sein understandingly lets itself be called forth to this possibility, this includes its *becoming free* for the call: its readiness for the potentiality-of-being summoned. Understanding the call, *Da-sein listens to its ownmost possibility of existence [Existenz]*. It has chosen itself.

* * *

FROM 60. THE EXISTENTIAL STRUCTURE OF THE AUTHENTIC POTENTIALITY-OF-BEING ATTESTED IN CONSCIENCE

The existential interpretation of conscience is to set for an *existent* attestation in Da-sein itself of its ownmost potentiality-of-being. Conscience attests not by making something known in an undifferentiated way, but by a summons that calls forth to being-guilty.

* * *

The disclosedness of Da-sein in wanting-to-have-a-conscience is thus constituted by the attunement of *Angst*, by understanding as projecting oneself upon one's ownmost being-guilty, and by discourse as reticence. We shall call the eminent, authentic disclosedness attested in Da-sein itself by its conscience—the *reticent projecting oneself upon one's ownmost being-guilty which is ready for* Angst—*resoluteness.*[9]

* * *

Now, in resoluteness the most primordial truth of Da-sein has been reached, because it is *authentic*. The disclosedness of the there [*Da*] discloses equiprimordially the whole of being-in-the-world—the world, being-in, and the self that is this being as "I am." With the disclosedness of world, innerworldly beings have always already been discovered. * * * The "world" at hand does not become different as far as "content,"[1] the circle of the others is not exchanged for a new one, and yet the being toward things at hand which understands

---

7. "Nichtiger Grund seines nichtigen Entwurfs": the reference is to the characterization of "thrownness" as the *nichtigen Grund* that Da-sein has to "take up into Existenz." The point is that Da-sein has no "ground" for the facticity of its existence other than "thrownness," which has the character of radical contingency (and thus no solid foundation). A "ground" that is no substantial "ground" is a "null ground" or "nothing-like ground"; and since "thrownness" is a structure of Da-sein, that

"nullity" or "nothing-like-ness" carries over into Da-sein's very being.
8. That is, responsible for itself.
9. "Entschlossenheit." It might be thought of as resoluteness in facing up to the consequences both of the "thrownness" of one's existence and of the radicalness of one's responsibility for the manner of one's existence in that light.
1. That is, with respect to content.

and takes care of things, and the concerned being-with with the others is now defined in terms of their ownmost potentiality-of-being-a-self.[2]

As *authentic being a self*, resoluteness does not detach Da-sein from its world, nor does it isolate it as free floating ego. How could it, if resoluteness as authentic disclosedness is, after all, nothing other than *authentically being-in-the-world*? Resoluteness brings the self right into its being together with things at hand, actually taking care of them, and pushes it toward concerned being-with with the others.[3]

In the light of the for-the-sake-of-which of the potentiality-of-being which it has chosen, resolute Da-sein frees itself for its world. The resoluteness toward itself first brings Da-sein to the possibility of letting the others who are with it "be" in their ownmost potentiality-of-being, and also discloses that potentiality in concern which leaps ahead and frees. Resolute Da-sein can become the "conscience" of others. It is from the authentic being a self of resoluteness that authentic being-with-one-another first arises,[4] not from ambiguous and jealous stipulations and talkative fraternizing in the they [*das Man*] and in what they [*man*] wants to undertake.

In accordance with its ontological essence, resoluteness always belongs to a factical Da-sein. The essence of this being is its existence [*Existenz*]. Resoluteness "exists" only as a resolution that projects itself understandingly. But to what does Da-sein resolve itself in resoluteness? On what is it to resolve? *Only* the resolution itself can answer this. It would be a complete misunderstanding of the phenomenon of resoluteness if one were to believe that it is simply a matter of receptively taking up possibilities presented and suggested. *Resolution is precisely the disclosive projection and determination of the actual factical possibility.* The *indefiniteness* that characterizes every factically projected potentiality-of-being of Da-sein *belongs* necessarily to resoluteness. Resoluteness is certain of itself only in a resolution. But the *existentiell indefiniteness* of resoluteness never makes itself definite except in a resolution; it nevertheless has its *existential definiteness*.[5]

What one resolves upon in resoluteness is prefigured ontologically in the existentiality of Da-sein in general as a potentiality-of-being in the mode of heedful concern. But, as care, Da-sein is determined by facticity and falling prey [*Verfallen*]. * * * Even resolutions are dependent upon the they [*das Man*] and its world. Understanding this is one of the things that resolution discloses, in that resoluteness first gives to Da-sein its authentic transparency. In resoluteness, Da-sein is concerned with its ownmost potentiality-of-being that, as thrown, can project itself only upon definite, factical possibilities. Resolution does not escape from "reality," but first discovers what is factically

2. Better translated: "and yet the understanding and interested [*verstehende besorgende*] being toward what is at hand [*Zuhandenen*] and the concernful [*fürsorgende*] being-with with others are now determined out of Da-sein's ownmost potentiality-of-being-a-self [*Selbstseinkönnen*]."

3. Better translated: "Resoluteness brings the self directly into ongoing interested involvement with what is at hand [*gerade in das jeweilige besorgende Sein bei Zuhandenen*] and pushes it toward concernful being-with with others."

4. Here Heidegger makes provision for the possibility of "authentic being-with-one-another" as well as for "authentic being a self" (thus making clear that "authenticity" is not inherently isolated

and isolating).

5. In this important paragraph, Heidegger makes clear that "resoluteness"—and therefore "authenticity"—does not entail or require anything in particular with respect to conduct, and has no substantive specific prescriptive normative content whatsoever. ("On what is [Da-sein] to resolve? *Only* the resolution itself can answer this.") A common criticism of existentialism is that apparently anything whatsoever can be done "authentically" as long as one does it with "anticipatory resoluteness" (or meets a similar criterion), and the value of "authenticity" trumps all other values (if there are any). For Heidegger, however, that issue falls outside his present scope. See also p. 1016, n. 6, above.

possible in such a way that it grasps it as it is possible as one's ownmost potentiality-of-being in the they [*das Man*]. The existential definiteness of possible resolute Da-sein includes the constitutive moments of the existential phenomenon that we call *situation* and which we have not yet discussed.

In the term *situation* (position—"to be in the position of"),[6] there is an overtone of a spatial significance. We shall not attempt to eliminate it from the existential concept. For such an overtone is also implied in the "there" of Da-sein. Being-in-the-world has a spatiality of its own that is characterized by the phenomena of de-distancing and directionality. Da-sein "makes room" in factically existing. But the spatiality of Da-sein, on the basis of which existence actually determines its "place," is grounded in the constitution of being-in-the-world, for which disclosedness is primarily constitutive. Just as the spatiality of the there [*Da*] is grounded in disclosedness, situation has its basis in resoluteness. Situation is the there [*Da*] disclosed in resoluteness—as which the existing [*existierend*] being is there [*da*]. It is not an objectively present framework in which Da-sein occurs or into which it could even bring itself. Far removed from any objectively present mixture of the circumstances and accidents encountered, situation *is* only through and in resoluteness. The actual factical relevant character of the circumstances is disclosed to the self only when that relevant character is such that one is resolute for the there [*Da*] which that self, in existing [*existierend*], has to be.

* * *

Resoluteness brings the being of the there to the existence of its situation. But resoluteness delineates the existential structure of the authentic potentiality-of-being attested in conscience—wanting to have a conscience. In this potentiality we recognized the appropriate understanding of the summons. This makes it quite clear that the call of conscience does not dangle an empty ideal of existence before us when it summons us to our potentiality-of-being, but *calls forth to the situation*.[7]

* * *

FROM CHAPTER III
THE AUTHENTIC POTENTIALITY-FOR-BEING-A-WHOLE OF DA-SEIN, AND TEMPORALITY AS THE ONTOLOGICAL MEANING OF CARE

FROM 61. PRELIMINARY SKETCH OF THE METHODICAL STEP FROM OUTLINING THE AUTHENTIC BEING-A-WHOLE OF DA-SEIN TO THE PHENOMENAL EXPOSITION OF TEMPORALITY

We projected existentially an authentic potentiality-for-being-a-whole of Da-sein. Analyzing this phenomenon revealed authentic being-toward-death as

6. Heidegger glosses *Situation*, the German term here translated "situation," as *Lage*, which itself is usually translated "situation." "Position" is a poor rendering of *Lage*, because it means something quite different. "Circumstances" would be more apt. Heidegger intends *Situation* to function as the Existenz-structural counterpart to the ordinary concept of one's circumstances (*Lage*), differing from the latter in the manner in which the application of "resoluteness" transforms their significance.

7. That is, "the call of conscience" is not empty, because it takes on concrete significance for existing Da-sein, which always exists as some particular Da-sein in some particular circumstances, at some particular historical juncture, etc. (specifics that constitute its "facticity"); and it is *that* with which one is called to come to terms and make one's choices regarding one's possibilities, and through which resoluteness and authenticity take on concrete meaningfulness.

anticipation. In its existentiell attestation, the authentic potentiality-of-being of Da-sein was shown to be *resoluteness*, and at the same time was interpreted existentially. How are we to bring these phenomena of anticipation and resoluteness together? Did our ontological project of the authentic potentiality-for-being-a-whole not lead us to a dimension of Da-sein that is far removed from the phenomenon of regular type[8] resoluteness? What is death supposed to have in common with the "concrete situation" of acting? Does not the attempt to bring resoluteness and anticipation forcibly together lead us astray into an intolerable, completely unphenomenological construction which may no longer even claim to have the character of an ontological project that is phenomenally grounded?

* * *

Ontologically, Da-sein is in principle different from everything objectively present and real. Its "content" is not founded in the substantiality of a substance, but in the *"self-constancy"* [*Selbständigkeit*] of the existing [*existierend*] self whose being was conceived as care. The phenomenon of the *self* included in care needs a primordial and authentic existential definition, in contrast to our preparatory demonstration of the inauthentic they-self [*Man-selbst*]. Along with this, we must establish what possible ontological questions are to be directed toward the "self," if it is neither substance nor subject.[9]

The phenomenon of care thus sufficiently clarified, can then be interrogated as to its ontological meaning. Defining this meaning will lead to the exposition of temporality. In exhibiting this, we are not led into remote, separate areas of Da-sein; we merely get a conception of the total phenomenal content of the existential fundamental constitution of Da-sein in the ultimate foundations of its own ontological intelligibility. *Temporality is experienced as a primordial phenomenon in the authentic being-a-whole of Da-sein, in the phenomenon of anticipatory resoluteness.* If temporality makes itself known primordially here, the temporality of anticipatory resoluteness is presumably a distinctive mode of that temporality. Temporality can *temporalize* itself in various possibilities and various ways. The fundamental possibilities of existence [*Existenz*], the authenticity and inauthenticity of Da-sein, are ontologically grounded in possible temporalizations of temporality.

* * *

FROM 62. THE EXISTENTIELLY AUTHENTIC POTENTIALITY-FOR-BEING-A-WHOLE OF DA-SEIN AS ANTICIPATORY RESOLUTENESS

How does resoluteness, "thought out" in accordance with its ownmost tendency of being, lead us to authentic being-toward-death? How is the connection between wanting to have a conscience and the existentially projected, authentic potentiality-of-being-a-whole of Da-sein to be conceived?

* * *

8. That is, from resoluteness as (familiar) "phenomenon."
9. That is, "the self" is not an entity of any sort for Heidegger—"neither substance nor subject"—but rather is simply the "constancy" of the ways in which Da-sein's "being" as "care" is realized and expressed in its relations to things, others, its facticity, and its possibilities (as well as its "thrownness" and its "being-toward-death").

Resolutely, Da-sein takes over authentically in its existence the fact that it *is* the null ground of its nullity.[1] We conceived of death existentially as what we characterized as the possibility of the *im*possibility of existence, that is, as the absolute nothingness of Da-sein. Death is not pieced on to Da-sein as its "end," but, as care, Da-sein is the thrown (that is, null) ground of its death. The nothingness primordially dominant in the being of Da-sein is revealed to it in authentic being-toward-death. Anticipation makes being-guilty evident only on the basis of the *whole* being of Da-sein. Care contains death and guilt equiprimordially. Only anticipatory resoluteness understands the potentiality-for-being-guilty *authentically and wholly*, that is, *primordially*.

Understanding the call of conscience reveals the lostness in the they [*das Man*]. Resoluteness brings Da-sein back to its ownmost potentiality-of-being-a-self. One's own potentiality-of-being becomes authentic and transparent in the understanding being-toward-death as the *ownmost* possibility.

* * *

Anticipatory resoluteness is not a way out fabricated for the purpose of "overcoming" death, but it is rather the understanding that follows the call of conscience and that frees for death the possibility of *gaining power over* the *existence* of Da-sein and of basically dispersing every fugitive self-covering-over. Nor does wanting to have a conscience, which we defined as being-toward-death, mean a detachment in which one flees from the world, but brings one without illusions to the resoluteness of "acting."[2] Nor does anticipatory resoluteness stem from "idealistic" expectations soaring above existence and its possibilities; but arises from the sober understanding of the basic factical possibilities of Da-sein. Together with the sober *Angst* that brings us before our individualized potentiality-of-being, goes the unshakable joy in this possibility.

* * *

63. THE HERMENEUTICAL SITUATION AT WHICH WE HAVE ARRIVED FOR INTERPRETING THE MEANING OF BEING OF CARE, AND THE METHODICAL CHARACTER OF THE EXISTENTIAL ANALYTIC IN GENERAL[3]

In its anticipatory resoluteness, Da-sein has been made phenomenally visible with regard to its possible authenticity and totality. The hermeneutical situation which was previously insufficient for the interpretation of the meaning of being of care, now has the required primordiality. Da-sein has been placed in our fore-having primordially, that is, with regard to its authentic potentiality-of-being-a-whole; the guiding fore-sight, the idea of existence [*Existenz*], has attained its definiteness through the clarification of the ownmost potentiality-of-being; with the concretely developed structure of being of Da-sein, its ontological peculiarity, as opposed to everything objectively present, has become

1. "Der nichtige Grund seiner Nichtigkeit": that is, in resoluteness Da-sein comes to terms affirmatively with its "thrownness"—with the insubstantiality, contingency, and uncanniness of its existence, and indeed of its very being, whose structure is its *nichtige Grund*, its insubstantial ground. (See

p. 1020, n. 7, above.)
2. That is, of genuine *action* (*Handeln*).
3. This section provides methodological commentary that illuminates Heidegger's procedure earlier in the book.

so clear that our fore-grasp on the existentiality of Da-sein possesses sufficient articulation to guide securely the conceptual development of the existentials.

The path of the analytic of Da-sein which we have traversed so far has led us to a concrete demonstration of the thesis only suggested at the beginning: *The being that we ourselves always are is ontologically farthest from us.* The reason for this lies in care itself. Entangled [*Verfallend*] being-together-with-the-"world" initially taken care of, guided the everyday interpretation of Da-sein, and covered over ontically the authentic being of Da-sein, thus denying the appropriate basis for an ontology oriented toward this being. Thus the primordial phenomenal fore-giving of this being is not at all self-evident, even if the ontology initially follows the course of the everyday interpretation of Da-sein. Rather, freeing the primordial being of Da-sein must be *wrested* from Da-sein *in opposition* to the entangled [*verfallend*], ontic, and ontological tendency of interpretation.

Not only the demonstration of the most elemental structures of being-in-the-world, the definition of the concept of world, the clarification of the nearest and most average who of this being, of the they-self [*Man-selbst*], the interpretation of the "there," but above all the analyses of care, death, conscience, and guilt show *how* the commonsense way of taking care of things has taken over the potentiality-of-being of Da-sein and the disclosure of that potentiality, or rather its closing off.

Thus the *kind* of being of Da-sein *requires* of an ontological interpretation that has set as its goal the primordiality of the phenomenal demonstration *that it be in charge of the being of this being*[4] *in spite of this being's own tendency to cover things over.* Thus the existential analytic constantly has the character of *doing violence*, whether for the claims of the everyday interpretation or for its complacency and its tranquillized obviousness. Of course, this character is especially distinctive of the ontology of Da-sein, but it belongs to any interpretation because the understanding that unfolds in interpretation has the structure of a project. But is not anything of this sort *guided* and *regulated* in a way of its own? Where are ontological projects to get the evidence that their "findings" are phenomenally appropriate? Ontological interpretation projects the beings given to it upon the being appropriate to them, so as to bring them to a concept with regard to their structure. Where are the guideposts to direct the projection so that being will be reached at all? And what if the being that is thematic for the existential analytic conceals the being which belongs to it and does so *in* its very way of being? To answer these questions we must initially restrict ourselves to clarifying the analytic of Da-sein, as the questions themselves demand.

Self-interpretation belongs to the being of Da-sein. In the circumspect discovery of the "world" taking care of things, taking care of things is sighted, too.[5] Da-sein always already understands itself factically in definite existentiell possibilities, even if its projects arise only from the common sense of the they [*das Man*]. Whether explicitly or not, whether appropriately or not, existence is somehow understood too. Every ontic understanding "includes" certain things, even if only *pre*-ontologically, that is, even if they are not

4. That is, in control of the be-ing of this being.
5. That is, "In the circumspect-interested discovery [*umsicht-besorgenden Entdeckung*, literally 'uncovering'] of the 'world,' interestedness [*Besorgen*] is caught sight of along with it."

grasped theoretically and thematically. Every ontologically explicit question about the being [*Sein*] of Da-sein has already had the way prepared for it by the kind of being [*Seinsart*] of Da-sein.

Nevertheless, how are we to find out what constitutes the "authentic" existence of Da-sein? Without an existentiell understanding, all analysis of existentiality remains without foundation. Does not an ontic conception of existence [*Existenz*] underlie our interpretation of the authenticity and totality of Da-sein, an ontic interpretation that might be possible, but need not be binding for every one? Existential interpretation will never seek to take over a *fiat* as to those things that, from an existentiell point of view, are possible or binding. But must it not justify itself with regard to *those* existentiell possibilities that it uses to give the ontic base for the ontological interpretation? If the being of Da-sein is essentially potentiality-of-being and being free for its ownmost possibilities, and if it always exists only in freedom or unfreedom for them, can the ontological interpretation take as its basis anything other than *ontic possibilities* (modes of potentiality-of-being) and project *these* upon *their ontological possibility*? And if Da-sein mostly interprets itself in terms of its lostness in taking care of the "world," isn't the determination of the ontic and existentiell possibilities and the existential analysis based upon them (in opposition to that lostness) the mode of its disclosure appropriate to this being? *Does not then the violence of this project amount to freeing the undisguised*[6] *phenomenal content of Da-sein?*

The "violent" presentation of possibilities of existence may be required for our method, but can it escape being merely arbitrary? If our analytic takes anticipatory resoluteness as its basis, as an existentielly authentic potentiality-of-being, and if Da-sein itself summons to this possibility right out of the ground of its existence, is this possibility then an *arbitrary* one? Is the mode of being in accordance with which the potentiality-of-being of Da-sein relates to its eminent possibility, death, picked up by chance? *Has being-in-the-world a higher instance*[7] *of its potentiality-of-being than its own death?*

The ontic and ontological project of Da-sein upon an authentic potentiality-of-being-a-whole may not be arbitrary, but is the existential interpretation of these phenomena then already justified? Where does this interpretation get its guidelines, if not from a "presupposed" idea of existence in general? How are the steps of the analysis of inauthentic everydayness regulated, if not by the concept of existence [*Existenz*] that we have posited? And if we say that Da-sein "falls prey [*verfalle*]," and that thus the authenticity of its potentiality-of-being is to be wrested from this tendency of being—from what perspective are we speaking here? Isn't everything illuminated by the light of the "presupposed" idea of existence, even if rather dimly? Where does this idea get its justification? Has our initial project, in which we called attention to it, led us nowhere? By no means.

Our formal indication of the idea of existence [*Existenz*] was guided by the understanding of being in Da-sein itself. Without any ontological transparency, it was, after all, revealed that I myself am always the being which we call Da-sein, as the potentiality-of-being that is concerned to be this being. Da-sein understands itself as being-in-the-world, although without sufficient ontological

---

6. That is, no longer disguised, unvarnished; genuine (*unverstellten*).
7. That is, a "more salient instance" (*höhere Instanz*), to which greater significance might appropriately be accorded.

definiteness. Thus existing [*seiend*],[8] it encounters beings of the kind of being of things at hand and objectively present. No matter how far removed from an ontological concept the distinction between existence [*Existenz*] and reality may be, even if Da-sein initially understands existence as reality, Da-sein is not just objectively present, but has always already *understood itself*, however mythical or magical its interpretations may be. For otherwise, Da-sein would not "live" in a myth and would not take heed of its magic in rites and cults. The idea of existence [*Existenz*] which we have posited gives us an outline of the formal structure of the understanding of Da-sein in general, and does so in a way that is not binding from an existentiell point of view.

Under the guidance of this idea the preparatory analysis of the everydayness nearest to us has been carried out as far as a first conceptual definition of care. This phenomenon enabled us to get a more precise grasp of existence [*Existenz*] and its relations to facticity and falling prey [*Verfallen*]. The definition of the structure of care has given us a basis on which to distinguish ontologically between existence [*Existenz*] and reality for the first time. This led to the thesis that the substance of human being is existence [*Existenz*].[9]

But even this formal idea of existence [*Existenz*], which is not binding in an existentiell way, already contains a definite though unprofiled ontological "content" that "presupposes" an idea of being [*Sein*] in general—just like the idea of reality contrasted with it. Only in the horizon of *that* idea of being can the distinction between existence [*Existenz*] and reality [*Realität*] be made. After all, both mean *being* [*Sein*].

But is not the ontologically clarified idea of being in general first to be attained by developing the understanding of being that belongs to Da-sein? However, that understanding can be grasped primordially only on the basis of a primordial interpretation of Da-sein guided by the idea of existence [*Existenz*]. Does it not thus finally become evident that this problem of fundamental ontology that we have set forth is moving in a "circle"?

We already showed, in the structure of understanding in general, that what is faulted with the inappropriate expression "circle" belongs to the essence and the distinctiveness of understanding itself. Still, our inquiry must now return explicitly to this "circular" argument if the problematic of fundamental ontology is to have its hermeneutical situation clarified. When it is objected that the existential interpretation is "circular," it is said that the idea of existence [*Existenz*] and of being [*Sein*] in general is "presupposed," and that Da-sein gets interpreted "accordingly" so that the idea of being may be obtained from it. But what does "presupposing" mean? In positing the idea of existence [*Existenz*], do we also posit some proposition from which we can deduce further propositions about the being of Da-sein, according to the formal rules of consistency? Or does this pre-supposing have the character of an understanding project in such a way that the interpretation developing this understanding *lets* what is to be interpreted be *put in words for the very first time, so that it may decide of its own accord whether, as this being [Seiende], it will provide the constitution of being [Sein] for which it has been disclosed in the*

8. That is, so be-ing; going along in its way of be-ing.
9. That is, "der These: Die Substanz des Menschen ist die Existenz." It is notable that as Heidegger retrospectively considers the whole book to this point, he here presents this proposition as a (or perhaps even the) "thesis" to which it has "led"

(*führte*). It is also striking that he here drops terminological pretense and speaks directly and simply of "man" (*der Mensch*) rather than of *Dasein*—his insistence at the outset that he is doing "ontology" rather than (philosophical) "anthropology" notwithstanding.

projection with regard to its formal aspect? Is there any other way that beings can put themselves into words with regard to their being at all? In the existential analytic, a "circle" in the proof cannot be "avoided," because that analytic is *not* proving anything according to the rules of logic of consistency *at all*. What common sense wishes to get rid of by avoiding the "circle," thinking that it does justice to the loftiest rigor of scientific [*wissenschaftlich*] investigation, is nothing less than the basic structure of care. Primordially constituted by care, Da-sein is always already ahead of itself. Existing [*Sei-end*],[1] it has always already projected itself upon definite possibilities of its existence [*Existenz*]; and in these existentiell projects it has also projected pre-ontologically something like existence [*Existenz*] and being. But can one deny this projecting of *that* research essential to Da-sein, which, *like all research itself is a kind of being of disclosive Da-sein*, that wants to develop and conceptualize the understanding of being belonging to Da-sein?

But the "charge of circularity" itself comes from a kind of being [*Seinsart*] of Da-sein. Something like projecting, especially ontological projecting, necessarily remains foreign for the common sense of our heedful absorption in the they [*das Man*] because common sense barricades itself against it "in principle." Whether "theoretically" or "practically," common sense only takes care of beings that are in view of its circumspection. What is distinctive about common sense is that it thinks it experiences only "factual" beings in order to be able to rid itself of its understanding of being. It fails to recognize that beings [*Seiende*] can be "factually" experienced only when being [*Sein*] has already been understood, although not conceptualized. Common sense misunderstands understanding. And *for this reason* it must also necessarily proclaim as "violent" anything lying beyond the scope of its understanding as well as any move in that direction.

The talk about the "circle" in understanding expresses the failure to recognize two things: (1) That understanding itself constitutes a basic kind of the being of Da-sein. (2) That this being is constituted as care. To deny the circle, to make a secret of it or even to wish to overcome it means to anchor this misunderstanding once and for all. Rather, our attempt must aim at leaping into this "circle" primordially and completely, so that even at the beginning of our analysis of Da-sein we make sure that we have a complete view of the circular being of Da-sein. Not too much, but *too little* is "presupposed" for the ontology of Da-sein, if one "starts out with" a worldless I in order then to provide that I with an object and an ontologically baseless relation to that object. *Our view is too short-sighted* if we make "life" a problem, *and then occasionally also* take death into account. The thematic objection is *artificially* and *dogmatically* cut out if one limits oneself "initially" to a "theoretical subject," and then complements it "on the practical side" with an additional "ethic."[2]

This will suffice to clarify the existential meaning of the hermeneutical situation of a primordial analytic of Da-sein. With the exposition of anticipatory resoluteness Da-sein has been brought before us with regard to its authentic totality. The authenticity of the potentiality-of-being-a-self guarantees the fore-sight of primordial existentiality, and this assures us of coining the appropriate existential concepts.

---

1. That is, going along in its way of be-ing.
2. This is a very important paragraph, particularly

with respect to the question of where and how (and how radically) Heidegger departs from Husserl.

At the same time, the analysis of anticipatory resoluteness led us to the phenomenon of primordial and authentic truth. Earlier we showed how the understanding of being that prevails initially and for the most part conceives being in the sense of objective presence and thus covers over the primordial phenomenon of truth. But if "there is" [es "gibt"] being only when truth "is [ist]," and if the understanding of being always varies according to the kind of truth, then primordial and authentic truth must guarantee the understanding of the being of Da-sein and of being in general. The ontological "truth" of the existential analysis is developed on the basis of primordial, existentiell truth. Yet the latter does not necessarily need the former. The most primordial and basic existential truth, for which the problematic of fundamental ontology strives in preparing the question of being in general, is the *disclosure of the meaning of being of care*.[3] In order to reveal this meaning, we need to hold in readiness, undiminished, the full structural content of care.

FROM 64. CARE AND SELFHOOD

The unity of the constitutive moments of care, existentiality, facticity, and falling prey [*Verfallen*] made possible a first ontological definition of the totality of the structural whole of Da-sein. The structure of care was given an existential formula: being-ahead-of-oneself-already-being-in (a world) as being-together-with (innerworldly beings encountered). The totality of the structure of care does not first arise from a coupling together, yet it is *articulated*. In assessing this ontological result, we have had to estimate how well it satisfies the requirements of a *primordial* interpretation of Da-sein. We found that neither the *whole* of Da-sein nor its *authentic* potentiality-of-being had been made thematic. However, the attempt to grasp phenomenally the whole of Da-sein seemed to get stranded precisely on the structure of care. The ahead-of-itself presented itself as a not-yet. But the ahead-of-itself, characterized in the sense of something outstanding, revealed itself to our genuine existential reflection as *being toward the end*, something that in the depths of its being every Da-sein is. We also made it clear that care summons Da-sein to its ownmost potentiality-of-being in the call of conscience. Understanding the summons revealed itself—primordially understood—as anticipatory resoluteness, which includes an authentic potentiality-of-being-whole of Da-sein. The structure of care does not speak *against* the possibility of being-a-whole, but is the *condition of the possibility* of such an existentiell potentiality-of-being. In the course of these analyses it became clear that the existential phenomena[4] of death, conscience, and guilt are anchored in the phenomenon of care. *The articulation of the totality of the structural whole has become still richer, and thus the existential question of the unity of this totality has become more urgent.*

How are we to grasp this unity? How can Da-sein exist as a unity in the ways and possibilities of its being that we mentioned? Evidently only in such a way that it *itself is* this being in its essential possibilities, that *I* am always this being. The "I" seems to "hold together" the totality of the structural whole. The "I" and the "self" have been conceived for a long time in the "ontology" of this being as the supporting ground (substance or subject). Even in its preparatory characterization of everydayness, our analytic also already encountered

3. That is, opening up and revealing the *Seinssinne der Sorge*.
4. That is, phenomena characterizing *Existenz*.

the question of the who of Da-sein. We found that Da-sein is initially and for the most part *not* itself, but lost in the they-self [*Man-selbst*]. The they-self is an existentiell modification of the authentic self.[5] The question of the onto-logical constitution of selfhood remained unanswered. It is true that we already established the guidelines for the problem: If the self belongs to the essential qualities of Da-sein whose "essence," however, lies in *existence* [*Existenz*], then I-hood and selfhood must be conceived *existentially*.[6] Nega-tively, we also saw that our ontological characterization of the they ruled out any application of the categories of objective presence (substance). In princi-ple it became clear that care cannot be derived ontologically from reality or be constructed with the categories of reality. Care already contains the phe-nomenon of self, if indeed the thesis is correct that the expression "care for self" would be *tautological* if it were proposed in conformity with concern as care for others. But then the problem of the ontological definition of the self-hood of Da-sein gets sharpened to the question of the existential "connec-tion" between care and selfhood.

To clarify the existentiality[7] of the self, we take as our "natural" point of departure the everyday self-interpretation of Da-sein that expresses "itself" in *saying-I*. Utterance is not necessary. With the "I," this being means itself. The content of this expression is taken to be absolutely simple. It always means only me, and nothing further. As this simple thing, the "I" is not a definition of other things: it is *itself* not a predicate, but the absolute "subject." What is expressed and addressed in saying-I is always met with as the same persisting thing. The characteristics of "simplicity," "substantiality," and "personality," which Kant, for example, takes as the foundation for his doctrine "On the paralogisms of pure reason"[8] arise from a genuine "pre-phenomenological" experience. The question remains whether what was experienced in such a way ontically may be interpreted ontologically with the aid of the "categories" mentioned.

* * *

Kant's analysis has two positive aspects: on the one hand, he sees the impos-sibility of ontically reducing the I to a "substance." On the other hand, he holds fast to the I as "I think." Nevertheless, he conceives this I again as subject, thus in an ontologically inappropriate sense. For the ontological concept of the sub-ject does *not* characterize *the selfhood of the I qua self, but the sameness and constancy of something always already objectively present*. To define the I onto-logically as a *subject* means to posit it as something always already objectively present. The being of the I is understood as the reality of the *res cogitans*.[9]

But what is the reason that while the "I think" gives Kant a genuine phe-nomenal point of departure, he cannot exploit it ontologically, but is forced to fall back upon the "subject," that is, something substantial? The I is not only an "I think," but an "I think something." However, does not Kant him-self emphasize again and again that the I remains related to its representa-tions, and would be nothing without them?

5. Heidegger says exactly the opposite near the end of §27, above (see p. 988, 3).
6. That is, in terms of the structure of *Existenz*.
7. That is, *Existenz*-structure.
8. A chapter in *Critique of Pure Reason* (1781; 2nd ed., 1787) in which KANT explains how rationalist philosophers arrived at what he sees as erroneous conclusions about the nature of the self.
9. Thinking thing (Latin); that is, the mind as con-ceived and characterized by Descartes.

But for Kant these representations are the "empirical," which is "accompanied" by the I—the appearances to which the I is "connected." But nowhere does Kant show the kind of being of this "connection" and "accompanying." At bottom, however, their kind of being is understood as the constant objective presence of the I together with its representations. Kant did avoid cutting off the I from thinking, but without positing the "I think" itself in its full essential content as "I think something," and above all without seeing the ontological "presupposition" for the "I think something" as the fundamental determination of the self. For even the point of departure of the "I think something" is not definite enough ontologically, because the "something" remains indefinite. If by this something we understand an *innerworldly* being, it tacitly implies that *world* has been presupposed; this very phenomenon of the world also determines the constitution of being of the I, if indeed it is to be possible for the I to be something like an "I think something." Saying-I means the being that I always am as "I-am-in-a-world." Kant did not see the phenomenon of world and was consistent enough to keep the "representations" at a distance from the *a priori* content of the "I think." But thus the I again was forced back to an *isolated* subject that accompanies representations in a way that is ontologically quite indefinite.

In saying-I, Da-sein expresses itself as being-in-the-world. But does everyday saying-I take *itself as* being-in-the-world [*in-der-Welt-seiend*]? Here we must make a distinction. Surely in saying-I Da-sein means the being that it itself always is. But the everyday interpretation of the self has the tendency to understand itself in terms of the "world" taken care of. When Da-sein has itself in view ontically, it *fails to see* itself in relation to the kind of being of the being that it itself is. And that is particularly true of the fundamental constitution of Da-sein, being-in-the-world.

How is this "fleeting" saying-I motivated? By the entanglement [*Verfallen*] of Da-sein, for as falling prey [*verfallend*] it *flees* from itself to the they [*das Man*]. The "natural" talk about the I takes place in the they-self [*Man-selbst*]. What expresses itself in the "I" is that self that, initially and for the most part, I am *not* authentically. When one is absorbed in the everyday multiplicity and rapid succession of what is taken care of,[1] the self of the self-forgetful "I take care of"[2] shows itself as what is constantly and identically simple, but indefinite and empty. One *is*, after all, *what* one takes care of.[3] The fact that the "natural" ontic way of saying-I overlooks the phenomenal content of Da-sein that one has in view in the I does *not* give the ontological interpretation of the I the *right* to *go along with this oversight* and to force an inappropriate "categorial" horizon upon the problematic of the self.

Of course, by refusing to go along with the everyday way in which the I talks, our ontological interpretation of the "I" has by no means *solved* the problem; but it has indeed *prescribed the direction* for further questioning. The I is the being that one is in "being-in-the-world." Already-being in-a-world as being-together-with-innerworldly-things-at-hand means, however, equiprimordially being-ahead-of-oneself. "I" means the being that is concerned *about* the being of the being[4] which it is. Care expresses itself with the "I" initially

---

1. That is, of what is cared about or of interest to one (*des Besorgten*).

2. That is, the self-forgetful "I care about" or "am interested in" (*Ich-besorge*).

3. That is, what one cares about, is interested in.

4. That is, the be-ing (*Sein*) of the being (*Seiende*).

and for the most part in the "fleeting" talk about the I in taking care of things. The they-self [*Man-selbst*] keeps on saying I most loudly and frequently because at bottom it *is not authentically* itself and evades its authentic potentiality-of-being. If the ontological constitution of the self can neither be reduced to a substantial I nor to a "subject," but if, on the contrary, the everyday, fleeting saying-I must be understood in terms of our *authentic* potentiality-of-being, the statement still does not follow that the self is the constantly objectively present ground of care. Existentially, selfhood is only to be found in the authentic potentiality-of-being-a-self, that is, in the authenticity of the being of Da-sein *as care*. In terms of care the constancy [*Ständigkeit*] *of the self*, as the supposed persistence of the subject, gets its clarification.[5] The phenomenon of this authentic potentiality-of-being, however, also opens our eyes to the *constancy of the self* in the sense of its having gained a stand. The *constancy of the self* in the double sense of constancy and steadfastness is the *authentic* counter-possibility to the lack of constancy [*Unselbst-ständigkeit*] of irresolute falling prey [*Verfallen*]. Existentially, the *constancy of the self* [*Selbst-ständigkeit*] means nothing other than anticipatory resoluteness. Its ontological structure reveals the existentiality[6] of the selfhood of the self.

Da-sein *is authentically itself* in the mode of primordial individuation of reticent resoluteness that expects *Angst* of itself. *In keeping silent*, authentic *being-one's-self* does not keep on saying "I," but rather "*is*" in reticence the thrown being that it can authentically be. The self that is revealed by the reticence of resolute existence is the primordial phenomenal basis for the question of the being of the "I." Only if we are phenomenally oriented toward the meaning of being of the authentic-potentiality-of-being-a-self are we put in a position to discuss what ontological justification there is for treating substantiality, simplicity, and personality as characteristics of selfhood. The ontological question of the being of the self must be extricated from the forehaving, constantly suggested by the predominant way of saying-I, of a persistently objectively present self-thing.

Care does not need a foundation in a self. But existentiality as a constituent of care gives the ontological constitution of the self-constancy of Da-sein to which there belongs, corresponding to the complete structural content of care, the factical falling prey [*Verfallensein*] *to unself-constancy.* The structure of care, conceived in full, includes the phenomenon of selfhood.[7] This phenomenon is clarified by interpreting the meaning of care which we defined as the totality of being of Da-sein.

FROM 65. TEMPORALITY AS THE ONTOLOGICAL MEANING OF CARE

In characterizing the "connection" between care and selfhood, our aim was not only to clarify the special problem of I-hood but also to help in the final preparation for phenomenally grasping the totality of the structural whole of Da-sein. We need the *unwavering discipline* of the existential line of

---

5. That is: The *constancy of the self*, as the purported persistence of the subject, is clarified (and should be understood) in terms of *care* (rather than any sort of substance).
6. That is, *Existenz*-structure.
7. That is, *Sorge* (care) does not presuppose the existence of a (substantial) self. On the contrary: the structure of care (*Sorge*) "includes the phenomenon of selfhood," and thus makes that

phenomenon possible. The self, for Heidegger, is a care-phenomenon—a function of the possible constancy of complexes of care-relations. If these care relations are largely internalizations of patterns of care-relations that one has simply picked up from "the they" in one's world, then the resulting self will be a "they-self" rather than an "own-self." (See p. 1023, n. 9, above.)

questioning if, for our ontological viewpoint, the kind of being of Da-sein is not finally to be distorted into a mode of objective presence, even if it is quite undifferentiated. Da-sein becomes "essential" in authentic existence that is constituted as anticipatory resoluteness. This mode of the authenticity of care contains the primordial self-constancy and totality of Da-sein. We must take an undistracted look at these and understand them existentially[8] if we are to expose the ontological meaning of the being of Da-sein.

* * *

Da-sein is disclosed to itself authentically or inauthentically with regard to its existence. Existing, it understands itself in such a way that this understanding does not just grasp something, but constitutes the existentiell being of its factical potentiality-of-being. The being that is disclosed is that of a being that is concerned about its being. The meaning [*Sinn*] of this being—that is, care—is what makes care possible in its constitution, and it is what primordially makes up the being of this potentiality-of-being. The meaning of being [*Seinssinn*] of Da-sein is not something different from it, unattached and "outside" of it, but is self-understanding Da-sein itself. What makes possible the being of Da-sein, and thus its factical existence?

What is projected in the primordial existential project of existence revealed itself as anticipatory resoluteness. What makes possible this authentic being-a-whole of Da-sein with regard to the unity of its articulated structural whole? Expressed formally and existentially, without constantly naming the complete structural content, anticipatory resoluteness is the *being toward* one's ownmost, eminent potentiality-of-being. Something like this is possible only in such way that Da-sein *can* come toward itself *at all* in its ownmost possibility and perdure[9] the possibility as possibility in this letting-itself-come-toward-itself, that is, that it exists. Letting-*come-toward-itself* that perdures the eminent possibility is the primordial phenomenon of the *future*.[1] If authentic or inauthentic *being-toward-death* belongs to the being of Da-sein, this is possible only as *futural* in the sense indicated now and to be more closely defined later. Here "future" does not mean a now that has *not yet* become "actual" and that sometime *will be* for the first time, but the coming in which Da-sein comes toward itself in its ownmost potentiality-of-being. Anticipation makes Da-sein *authentically* futural in such a way that anticipation itself is possible only in that Da-sein, *as existing*, always already comes toward itself, that is, is futural in its being in general.

Anticipatory resoluteness understands Da-sein in its essential being-guilty. This understanding means to take over being-guilty while existing, to *be* the thrown ground of nullity. But to take over thrownness means to authentically *be* Da-sein in the *way that it always already was*. Taking over thrownness, however, is possible only in such a way that futural Da-sein *can be* its ownmost "how it always already was," that is, its "having-been." Only because Da-sein in general *is* as I *am*-having-been, can it come futurally toward itself in such

8. That is, in terms of the structure of *Existenz*.
9. That is, endure (*aushalten*).
1. That is, "Letting-itself *come toward* itself [*sich auf sich Zukommen-lassen*], which underlies the exceptional possibility [of being-toward-death], is the primordial phenomenon of the *future* [*Zukunft*]." Heidegger's emphases here simply draw

attention to the linguistic kinship of *Zukommon* (come toward) and *Zukunft* (future). The middle clause is a reminder that Da-sein's "being-toward-death" (which Heidegger often refers to as the most *ausgezeichnete* [exceptional or eminent] of Da-sein's "possibilities of being") is made possible by this "future" feature of its structure.

a way that it comes-*back*. Authentically futural, Da-sein is authentically *having-been*.[2] Anticipation of the most extreme and ownmost possibility comes back understandingly to one's ownmost *having-been*. Da-sein can *be* authentically having-been only because it is futural. In a way, having-been arises from the future.

Anticipatory resoluteness discloses the actual situation of the there in such a way that existence circumspectly takes care of the factical things at hand in the surrounding world in action. Resolute being together with what is at hand in the situation, that is, letting *what presences* in the surrounding world be encountered in action, is possible only in a *making* that being *present*. Only as the *present*, in the sense of making present, can resoluteness be what it is, namely, the undistorted letting what it grasps in action be encountered.

Futurally coming back to itself, resoluteness brings itself to the situation in making it present. Having-been arises from the future in such a way that the future that has-been (or better, is in the process of having-been) releases the present from itself. We call the unified phenomenon of the future that makes present in the process of having-been *temporality*.[3] Only because Da-sein is determined as temporality does it make possible for itself the authentic potentiality-of-being-a-whole of anticipatory resoluteness which we characterized. *Temporality reveals itself as the meaning of authentic care.*

The phenomenal content of this meaning, drawn from the constitution of being of anticipatory resoluteness, fulfills the significance of the term temporality. We must now keep the terminological use of this expression at a distance from all of the meanings of "future," "past," and "present" initially urging themselves upon us from the vulgar concept of time. That is also true of the concepts of a "subjective" and an "objective," or an "immanent" and "transcendent" "time." Since Da-sein understands itself initially and for the most part inauthentically, we may suppose that the "time" of the vulgar understanding of time indeed presents a genuine phenomenon, but a derivative one. It arises from inauthentic temporality that has an origin of its own. The concepts of "future," "past," and "present" initially grew out of the inauthentic understanding of time. The terminological definition of the corresponding primordial and authentic phenomena battles with the same difficulty in which all ontological terminology is stuck. In this field of inquiry, forcing things is not an arbitrary matter, but a necessity rooted in facts. However, in order to demonstrate the origin of inauthentic temporality from primordial and authentic temporality without any gap, we first need to work out correctly the primordial phenomenon concretely, which we have thus far only sketched out roughly.

If resoluteness constitutes the mode of authentic care, and if it is itself possible only through temporality, the phenomenon at which we arrived by considering resoluteness must itself only present a modality of temporality, which makes care possible in general. The totality of being of Da-sein as care means: Ahead-of-itself-already-being-in (a world) as being-together-with (beings

---

2. That is, "having-been" (*Gewesenheit*) is no less a part of the being-structure of Da-sein than is the "phenomenon of the future," and it underlies the structure to which he is about to turn: Da-sein's "historicality" (*Geschichtlichkeit*)—which turns out to be very nearly as significant, for Heidegger, as its "being-toward-death."

3. This sentence is the heart of this key paragraph, which reveals the connection that the title of the book itself foreshadows. The "essence" of Da-sein turns out to lie not simply in its future orientation toward its possibilities but in its "temporality" more generally, which has the threefold structure that this sentence indicates.

encountered within the world). In first establishing this articulated structure, we referred to the fact that with regard to this articulation the ontological question had to be taken back further to the exposition of the unity of the totality of the structural manifold. *The primordial unity of the structure of care lies in temporality.*

Being-ahead-of-oneself is grounded in the future. Already-being-in . . . makes known having-been. Being-together-with . . . is made possible in making present. After what we have said, it is automatically ruled out to conceive the "ahead" in the "ahead-of-itself" and the "already" in terms of the vulgar understanding of time. The "ahead" does not mean the "before" in the sense of a "not-yet-now, but later." Nor does the "already" mean a "no-longer-now, but earlier." If the expressions "ahead of" and "already" had *this* temporal meaning, which they can also have, then we would be saying about the temporality of care that it is something that is "earlier" and "later," "not yet" and "no longer" at the same time. Then care would be conceived as a being that occurs and elapses "in time." The *being* of a being of the nature of Da-sein would then turn into *something objectively present.* If this is impossible, the temporal significance of these expressions must be a different one. The "before" and the "ahead of" indicate the future that first makes possible in general the fact that Da-sein can be in such a way that it is concerned *about* its potentiality-of-being. The self-project grounded in the "for the sake of itself" in the future is an essential quality of *existentiality. Its primary meaning is the future.*

Similarly, the "already" means the existential, temporal meaning of being of the being that, in that it *is,* is always already something thrown. Only because care is grounded in having-been, can Da-sein exist as the thrown being that it is. "As long as" Da-sein factically exists, it is never past, but is always already *having-been* in the sense of "I-*am*-as-having-been." And only as long as Da-sein is, *can* it *be* as having-been. On the other hand, we call beings past that are no longer objectively present. Thus existing Da-sein can never ascertain itself as an objectively present fact that comes into being and passes away "with time," and is already partially past. It always "finds itself" only as a thrown fact. In *attunement* Da-sein is invaded by itself as the being that it still is and already was, that is, that it constantly *is* as having been. The primary existential meaning of facticity lies in having-been. The formulation of the structure of care indicates the temporal meaning of existentiality of facticity with the expressions "before" and "already."

On the other hand, such an indication is lacking for the third constitutive factor of care: entangled [*verfallend*] being-together-with. . . .[4] That is not supposed to mean that falling prey [*Verfallen*] is not also grounded in temporality; it should instead intimate that *making present,* as the *primary* basis for the *falling prey* to things at hand and objectively present that we take care of, remains *included* in the future and in having-been in the mode of primordial temporality. Resolute, Da-sein has brought itself back out of falling prey in order to be all the more authentically "there" for the disclosed situation in the "Moment" [*Augenblick*].

Temporality makes possible the unity of existence, facticity, and falling prey [*Verfallen*] and thus constitutes primordially the totality of the structure of

4. That is, "fallen [and so absorbed] involvement with" (*das verfallende Sein-bei*)."

care. The factors of care are not pieced together cumulatively, any more than temporality itself has first been put together out of future, past, and present "in the course of time." Temporality "is" not a *being* at all. It is not, but rather *temporalizes* itself. Nevertheless, we still cannot avoid saying that "temporality 'is' the meaning of care," "temporality 'is' determined thus and so." The reason for this can be made intelligible only when we have clarified the idea of being and the "is" as such. Temporality temporalizes, and it temporalizes possible ways of itself. These make possible the multiplicity of the modes of being of Da-sein, in particular the fundamental possibility of authentic and inauthentic existence.

Future, having-been, and present show the phenomenal characteristics of "toward itself," "back to," "letting something be encountered." The phenomena of toward . . . , to . . . , together with . . . reveal temporality as the *ekstatikon*[5] *par excellence. Temporality is the primordial "outside of itself" in and for itself.* Thus we call the phenomena of future, having-been, and present, the *ecstasies* of temporality. Temporality is not, prior to this, a being that first emerges from *itself*; its essence is temporalizing in the unity of the *ecstasies*. What is characteristic of the "time" accessible to the vulgar understanding consists, among other things, precisely in the fact that it is a pure succession of nows, without beginning and without end, in which the ecstatic character of primordial temporality is levelled down. But this very levelling down, in accordance with its existential meaning, is grounded in the possibility of a definite kind of temporalizing, in conformity with which temporality temporalizes as inauthentic the kind of "time" we have just mentioned. Thus if we demonstrate that the "time" accessible to the common sense of Da-sein is *not* primordial, but arises rather from authentic temporality, then, according to the principle *a potiori fit denominatio*,[6] we are justified in calling the *temporality* now set forth *primordial time*.

In enumerating the ecstasies, we have always mentioned the future first. That should indicate that the future has priority in the ecstatic unity of primordial and authentic temporality, although temporality does not first originate through a cumulative sequence of the ecstasies, but always temporalizes itself in their equiprimordiality. But within this equiprimordiality, the modes of temporalizing are different. And the difference lies in the fact that temporalizing can be primarily determined out of the different ecstasies. Primordial and authentic temporality temporalizes itself out of the authentic future, and indeed in such a way that, futurally having-been, it first arouses the present. *The primary phenomenon of primordial and authentic temporality is the future.* The priority of the future will itself vary according to the modified temporalizing of inauthentic temporality, but it will still make its appearance in derivative "time."

Care is being-toward-death. We defined anticipatory resoluteness as authentic being toward the possibility that we characterized as the absolute impossibility of Da-sein. In this being-toward-the-end, Da-sein exists authentically and totally as the being that it can be when "thrown into death." It does

---

5. Displaced thing (Greek), something "out of (its) place," "outside of itself." The word has the same root as "ecstasies" (in German, *Ekstasen*). The three "ecstasies of temporality" involve three different but related ways of being displaced from (outside of, at a distance from) the immediate here-and-now.

6. The name arises from the more important (Latin).

not have an end where it just stops, but it *exists finitely*. The authentic future, which is temporalized primarily by *that* temporality which constitutes the meaning of anticipatory resoluteness, thus reveals itself *as finite*. But, in spite of my no longer being there, "does time not go on?" And can there not be an unlimited number of things that still lie "in the future" and arrive from it?

These questions are to be answered in the affirmative. Nevertheless, they do not contain any objection to the finitude of primordial temporality because they no longer deal with that at all. The question is not how many things can still occur "in an ongoing time," or about what kind of a "letting-come-toward-oneself" we can encounter "out of this time," but about how the coming-toward-oneself is itself to be primordially determined *as such*. Its finitude does not primarily mean a stopping, but is a characteristic of temporalizing itself. The primordial and authentic future is the toward-oneself, toward *oneself*, existing as the possibility of a nullity not-to-be-bypassed. The ecstatic quality of the primordial future lies precisely in the fact that it closes the potentiality-of-being, that is, the future is itself closed and as such makes possible the resolute existentiell understanding of nullity. Primordial and authentic coming-toward-oneself is the meaning of existing in one's ownmost nullity. With the thesis of the primordial finitude of temporality, we are not contesting the fact that "time goes on." We are simply holding fast to the phenomenal quality of primordial temporality that shows itself in what is projected in the primordial existential project of Da-sein.

* * *

Let us summarize the analysis of primordial temporality in the following theses: Time is primordial as the temporalizing of temporality, and makes possible the constitution of the structure of care. Temporality is essentially ecstatic. Temporality temporalizes itself primordially out of the future. Primordial time is finite.

Yet the interpretation of care as temporality cannot remain restricted to the narrow basis we have so far attained, although it did take the first steps toward the primordial, authentic being-a-whole of Da-sein. The thesis that the meaning of Da-sein is temporality must be confirmed by the concrete content of the fundamental constitution of this being which we have set forth.

66. THE TEMPORALITY OF DA-SEIN AND THE TASKS ARISING FROM IT OF A MORE PRIMORDIAL RETRIEVE[7] OF THE EXISTENTIAL ANALYSIS

The phenomenon of temporality which we have set forth requires not only a more wide-ranging confirmation of its constitutive power, it itself thus comes to view with regard to the fundamental possibilities of temporalization. We shall briefly call the demonstration of the possibility of the constitution of being of Da-sein on the basis of temporality, the "temporal" interpretation, although this is only a provisional term.

Our next task is to go beyond the temporal analysis of the authentic potentiality-of-being-a-whole of Da-sein and a general characterization of the temporality of care, so that the *inauthenticity* of Da-sein may be made visible

---

7. That is, reworking (*Wiederholung*); literally, going for (or going through) again.

in its specific temporality. Temporality first showed itself in anticipatory resoluteness. That is the authentic mode of disclosedness that for the most part stays within the inauthenticity of the entangled [*verfallen*] self-interpretation of the they [*das Man*]. The nature of the temporality of disclosedness in general leads to the temporal understanding of that heedful being-in-the-world nearest to us, and thus of the average indifference of Da-sein from which the existential analytic first started. We called the average kind of being of Da-sein, in which it initially and for the most part stays, everydayness. By retrieving[8] our earlier analysis, *everydayness* must be revealed in its *temporal* meaning so that the problematic included in temporality may come to light and the seeming "obviousness" of our preparatory analyses may disappear completely. Indeed, confirmation is to be found for temporality in all the essential structures of the fundamental constitution of Da-sein. Yet that does not lead us to repeat our analyses in the same external schema in the order of their presentation. The course of our temporal analysis has a different direction. It is to make the connection of our earlier reflections clearer and to remove their chance character and seeming arbitrariness. However, beyond these necessities of method, there are valid motives in the phenomenon itself that compel us to articulate our analysis in a different way when we retrieve it.

The ontological structure of the being that I *myself* always am is centered in the self-constancy of existence. Because the self cannot be conceived either as substance or as subject, but is rather grounded in existence, our analysis of the inauthentic self, the they [*das Man*], was left completely in the train of the preparatory interpretation of Da-sein. Now that selfhood has been *explicitly* taken back into the structure of care, and thus of temporality, the temporal interpretation of self-constancy and the lack of self-constancy acquires an importance of its own. It requires a special thematic development. But it not only gives us the right protections against the paralogisms[9] and the ontologically inappropriate question about the being of the I in general; at the same time it provides us, in accordance with its central function, with a more primordial insight into the *structure of the temporalizing of temporality*. Temporality reveals itself as the *historicity*[1] of Da-sein. The statement that Da-sein is historical is confirmed as an existential and ontological fundamental proposition. It is far removed from merely ontically ascertaining the fact that Da-sein occurs in a "world history." The historicity [*Geschichtlichkeit*] of Da-sein, however, is the ground of a possible historiographical [*historisch*] understanding that in its turn harbors the possibility of getting a special grasp of the development of historiography [*Historie*] as a science [*Wissenschaft*].

The temporal interpretation of everydayness and historicity secures the view of primordial time sufficiently to uncover it as the condition of the possibility and necessity of the everyday experience of time. *Da-sein expends itself primarily for itself* as a being that is concerned about its being, whether explicitly or not. Initially and for the most part, care is circumspect taking care of things. Expending itself for the sake of itself, Da-sein "uses itself up." Using itself up, Da-sein uses itself, that is, its time. Using its time, it reckons with it.[2] Taking care of things which is circumspect and reckoning, initially

---

8. That is, reworking.
9. That is, flawed reasonings.
1. "Geschichtlichkeit." German has two words for "history": *Geschichte*, which refers to what has happened in the course of human events, and *Historie*,

which designates the discipline devoted to its study.
2. Better translated: "Using time, Da-sein reckons with it" (*Zeit brauchend, rechnet es* [*Dasein*] *mit ihr*); that is, making use of time, Da-sein comes to terms with it.

discovers time and develops a measurement of time.[3] Measurement of time is constitutive for being-in-the-world. Measuring its time, the discovering of circumspection which takes care of things lets what it discovers at hand and objectively present be encountered in time. Innerworldly beings thus become accessible as "existing in time." We shall call the temporal quality of inner-worldly beings "*within-time-ness.*" The "time" initially found therein ontically becomes the basis for the development of the vulgar and traditional concept of time. But time as within-time-ness arises from an essential kind of tempo-ralization of primordial temporality. This origin means that the time "in which" objectively present things come into being and pass away is a genuine phenomenon of time; it is not an externalization of a "qualitative time" into space, as Bergson's interpretation of time—which is ontologically completely indeterminate and insufficient—would have it.

The elaboration of the temporality of Da-sein as everydayness, historicity, and within-time-ness first gives uncluttered insight into the *complexities* of a primordial ontology of Da-sein. As being-in-the-world Da-sein exists factically together with beings encountered within the world. Thus the being of Da-sein gets its comprehensive ontological transparency only in the horizon of the clarified being of beings unlike Da-sein, that is, even of what is not at hand and not objectively present, but only "subsists." But if the variations of being are to be interpreted for everything of which we say that it *is,* we need before-hand a sufficiently clarified idea of being in general. As long as we have not reached this, the retrieve[4] of the temporal analysis of Da-sein will remain incomplete and marred by lack of clarity,[5] not to speak extensively of the factual difficulties. The existential-temporal analysis of Da-sein requires in its turn a new retrieve in the context of a fundamental discussion of the concept of being.

* * *

FROM CHAPTER V
TEMPORALITY AND HISTORICITY [*GESCHICHTLICHKEIT*]

72. EXISTENTIAL AND ONTOLOGICAL EXPOSITION OF THE PROBLEM OF HISTORY [*GESCHICHTE*]

All our efforts in the existential analytic are geared to the one goal of finding a possibility of answering the question of the *meaning of being* [*Sinn von Sein*] in general. The development of this *question* requires that we delineate the phenomenon in which something like being itself becomes accessible—the phenomenon of the *understanding of being.* But this phenomenon belongs to the constitution of being of Da-sein. Only when this being has been inter-preted beforehand in a sufficiently primordial way, can the understanding of being contained in its constitution of being itself be grasped, and only on that basis can we formulate the question of being understood in this under-standing and the question of what such understanding "presupposes."

3. That is, "Circumspect-reckoning interest ini-tially discovers time and leads to the development of a time reckoning" (*Das umsicht-rechnende Be-sorgen endeckt zunächst die Zeit und führt zur Ausbildung einer Zeitrechnung*).
4. That is, reworking.
5. That is, "the recapitulating temporal analysis of Da-sein [up to this point in the book] remains incom-plete and burdened with unclarity" (*bleibt auch die wiederholende zeitliche Analyse des Daseins unvoll-ständig und mit Unklarheit behaftet*). Heidegger had begun this second part of the book by saying that the analysis of Da-sein given in the first part would have to be recapitulated and reworked to explicitly take account of Da-sein's temporality. Now he is declaring that a further reworking is necessary.

Although many structures of Da-sein still remain in the dark with regard to particulars, yet it seems that we have reached the requisite, primordial interpretation of Da-sein with the clarification of temporality as the primordial condition of the possibility of *care*. Temporality was set forth with regard to the authentic potentiality-of-being-a-whole of Da-sein. The temporal interpretation of care [*Sorge*] was then confirmed by demonstrating the temporality of heedful [*besorgend*][6] being-in-the-world. Our analysis of the authentic potentiality-of-being-a-whole revealed that an equiprimordial connection of death, guilt, and conscience is rooted in care. Can Da-sein be understood still more primordially than in the project of its authentic existence?

Although up to now we have not seen any possibility of a more radical starting point for our existential analytic, yet with regard to the above discussion of the ontological meaning of everydayness, a serious reservation comes to light: Has indeed the whole of Da-sein with respect to its authentic *being*-a-whole been captured in the fore-having of our existential analysis? It may be that the line of questioning related to the wholeness of Da-sein possesses a genuinely unequivocal character ontologically. The question itself may even have been answered with regard to *being-toward-the-end*. However, death is, after all, only the "end" of Da-sein, and formally speaking, it is just *one* of the ends that embraces the totality of Da-sein. But the other "end" is the "beginning," "birth." Only the being "between" birth and death presents the whole we are looking for. Then the previous orientation of our analytic would remain "one-sided," in spite of all its tendencies toward a consideration of *existing* being-a-whole and in spite of the genuineness with which authentic and inauthentic being-toward-death have been explicated. Da-sein has been our theme only as to how it exists [*existiert*], so to speak, "forward" and leaves everything that has been "behind." Not only did being-toward-the-beginning remain unnoticed, but, above all, the way Da-sein *stretches along between* birth and death.[7] Precisely the "connection of life," in which, after all, Da-sein constantly somehow holds itself, was overlooked in our analysis of being-a-whole.

Must we not then take back our point of departure of temporality as the meaning of being of the totality of Da-sein, even though what we addressed as the "connection" between birth and death is ontologically completely obscure? Or does *temporality*, as we set it forth, first give the *foundation* on which to provide an unequivocal direction for the existential and ontological question of that "connection"? Perhaps it is already a gain in the field of this inquiry if we learn not to take the problems too lightly.

What seems "more simple" than the nature of the "connection of life" between birth and death? It *consists* of a succession of experiences "in time." If we pursue this characterization of the connection in question and above all of the ontological assumption behind it in a more penetrating way, something remarkable happens. In this succession of experiences only the experience that is objectively present "in the actual now" is "really" "real." The experiences past and just coming, on the other hand, are no longer or not yet "real." Da-sein traverses the time-span allotted to it between the two boundaries in such a way that it is "real" only in the now and hops, so to speak,

---

6. That is, concernful, caring.
7. That is, "the *stretching along* of Da-sein *between* birth and death" (*die* Erstreckung *des Daseins* zwischen *Geburt und Tod*). This is a significant modification of the idea of Da-sein's "being-toward-death."

through the succession of nows of its "time." For this reason one says that Da-sein is "temporal." The self maintains itself in a certain sameness throughout this constant change of experiences. Opinions diverge as to how this persistent self is to be defined and how one is to determine what relation it may possibly have to the changing experiences. The being of this persistingly changing connection of experiences remains undetermined. But basically something objectively present [*Vorhandenes*] "in time," but of course "unthinglike," has been posited in this characterization of the connection of life, whether one admits it or not.[8]

With regard to what was developed as the meaning of being of care under the rubric of temporality, we found that while following the guideline of the vulgar interpretation of Da-sein, within its own limits, is justified and adequate, we could not carry through a genuine ontological analysis of the way Da-sein *stretches along* between birth and death if we take this interpretation as our guideline, nor could we even establish such an analysis as a problem.

Da-sein does not exist as the sum of the momentary realities of experiences that succeed each other and disappear. Nor does this succession gradually fill up a framework. For how should that framework be objectively present, when it is always only the experience that one is having "right now" that is "real," and when the boundaries of the framework—birth that is past and death that is yet to come—are lacking reality. At bottom, even the vulgar interpretation of the "connectedness of life" does not think of a framework spanned "outside" of Da-sein and embracing it, but correctly looks for it in Da-sein itself. When, however, one tacitly regards this being ontologically as something objectively present "in time," an attempt at any ontological characterization of the being "between" birth and death gets stranded.

Da-sein does not first fill up an objectively present path or stretch "of life" through the phases of its momentary realities, but stretches *itself* along in such a way that its own being is constituted beforehand as this stretching along. The "between" of birth and death already lies *in the being*[9] of Da-sein. On the other hand, it is by no means the case that Da-sein is real in a point of time, and that, in addition, it is then "surrounded" by the nonreality of its birth and its death. Understood existentially, birth is never something past in the sense of what is no longer objectively present, and death is just as far from having the kind of being of something outstanding that is not yet objectively present but will come. Factical Da-sein exists as born, and, born, it is already dying in the sense of being-toward-death. Both "ends" and their "between" *are* as long as Da-sein factically exists, and they *are* in the sole way possible on the basis of the being of Da-sein as *care*. In the unity of throwness and the fleeting[1] or else anticipatory being-toward-death, birth and death "are connected" in the way appropriate to Da-sein. As care, Da-sein *is* the "Between."[2]

8. This is a picture that Heidegger intends to challenge and replace.
9. That is, in the be-ing (*Sein*).
1. In this context, the word translated as "fleeting"—*flüchtig*—is better rendered as "fleeing"; the point is to recall the two different ways of "being-toward-death" that Heidegger has distinguished, "anticipating" contrasting with "fleeing" (*flüchten*).
2. "Als Sorge *ist* das Dasein das 'Zwischen.'" A

significant modification or elaboration of the idea of Da-sein's "being-in-the-world": Da-sein now is to be conceived as "being-in-the-world-between-birth-and-death," and understood as incorporating the essential structures of both "temporality" and "care" in relation to things, others, and possibilities, and as being able to be either "authentic" or "inauthentic."

But the constitutional totality of care has the possible *ground* of its unity in temporality. The ontological clarification of the "connectedness of life," that is, of the specific way of stretching along, movement, and persistence of Da-sein, must accordingly be approached in the horizon of the temporal constitution of this being. The movement of existence [*Existenz*] is not the motion of something objectively present. It is determined from the stretching along of Da-sein. The specific movement of the *stretched out stretching itself along*, we call the *occurrence* [*Geschehen*][3] of Da-sein. The question of the "connectedness" of Da-sein is the ontological problem of its occurrence. To expose the *structure of occurrence* and the existential and temporal conditions of its possibility means to gain an *ontological* understanding of *historicity* [*Geschichtlichkeit*].

With the analysis of the specific movement and persistence appropriate to the occurrence of Da-sein, our inquiry returns to the problem that was touched upon right before the exposition of temporality: to the question of the constancy of the self that we determined as the who of Da-sein. Self-constancy is a mode of being of Da-sein and is thus grounded in a specific temporalizing of temporality. The analysis of occurrence introduces the problems found in a thematic investigation into temporalization as such.

If the question of historicity leads back to those "origins," the *place* of the problem of history [*Geschichte*] has thus already been decided upon. We must not search in historiography [*Historie*] as the science [*Wissenschaft*] of history. Even if the scientific [*wissenschaftlich*] and theoretical kind of treatment of the problem of "history [*Historie*]" does not just aim at an "epistemological" (Simmel)[4] clarification of historiographical [*historisch*] comprehension, or at the logic of the concept formation of historiographical presentation (Rickert),[5] but is rather oriented toward the "objective side," history is accessible in this line of questioning only as the *object* of a science [*Wissenschaft*]. The basic phenomenon of history [*Geschichte*], which is prior to the possibility of making something thematic by historiography and underlies it, is thus irrevocably set aside. How history can become a possible *object* for historiography, can be gathered only from the kind of being of what is historical [*das Geschichtlich*], from historicity [*Geschichtlichkeit*] and its rootedness in temporality.[6]

If historicity itself is to be illuminated in terms of temporality, and primordially in terms of *authentic* temporality, then it is essential to this task that it can only be carried out by way of a phenomenological construction. The existential and ontological constitution of historicity must be mastered in *opposition to* the vulgar interpretation of the history of Da-sein that covers over. The existential construction of historicity has its definite support in the vulgar

---

3. That is, "happening" or "going on." Heidegger sees a deep connection between Da-sein's *Geschehen* and its *Geschichtlichkeit*.

4. Georg Simmel (1858–1918), an eminent German philosopher and sociologist, who played a major role in the emergence of sociology as a discipline.

5. Heinrich Rickert (1863–1936), an important German philosopher in the Neo-Kantian tradition. Concerned with the relation between natural-scientific and historical (or *geisteswissenschaftlich*) forms of inquiry and knowledge, he sought a way of unifying them while maintaining their distinctiveness (in effect incorporating the former into the latter).

6. Heidegger is here distinguishing between history conceived as the succession of objectively identifiable events studied by the *Wissenschaft* of "history" (*Historie*) and "the basic phenomenon of history (*Geschichte*)," conceived as the "happening" (*Geschehen*) of the sort of be-ing that has the character of *Geschichtlichkeit*—translated here as "historicity" but usually rendered as "historicality"— that calls for a different kind of analysis.

understanding of Da-sein[7] and is guided by those existential structures attained so far.

We shall first describe the vulgar concept of history, so that we may give our investigation an orientation as to the factors which are generally held to be essential for history. Here it must become clear what is primordially considered as historical. Thus the point of departure for the exposition of the ontological problem of historicity has been designated.

Our interpretation of the authentic potentiality-of-being-a-whole of Da-sein and our analysis of care as temporality arising from that interpretation, offer the guideline for the existential construction of historicity. The existential project for the historicity of Da-sein only reveals what already lies enveloped in the temporalizing of temporality. Corresponding to the rootedness of historicity in care, Da-sein always exists as authentically or inauthentically historical.[8] What we had in view under the rubric of everydayness for the existential analytic of Da-sein as the nearest horizon gets clarified as the inauthentic historicity of Da-sein.

Disclosure and interpretation belong essentially to the occurrence of Dasein. From the kind of being of this being that exists historically, there arises the existentiell possibility of an explicit disclosure and grasp of history. Making it thematic, that is, the *historiographical* disclosure of history, is the presupposition for the possibility of "building up the historical world in the sciences of the humanities [*Geisteswissenschaften*]."[9] The existential interpretation of historiography as a science [*Wissenschaft*] aims solely at a demonstration of its ontological provenance from the historicity of Da-sein. Only from here are the boundaries to be staked out within which a theory of science [*Wissenschaft*] oriented toward the factical business of science [*Wissenschaft*] may expose itself to the chance elements of its line of questioning.

The analysis of the historicity of Da-sein attempted to show that this being is not "temporal," because it "is in history," but because, on the contrary, it exists and can exist historically only because it is temporal in the ground of its being.

Nevertheless, Da-sein must also be called "temporal" in the sense of its being "in time." Factical Da-sein needs and uses the calendar and the clock even without a developed historiography. What occurs "with it," it experiences as occurring "in time." In the same way, the processes of nature, whether living or lifeless, are encountered "in time." They are within-time. So while our analysis of how the "time" of within-time-ness has its source in temporality will be deferred until the next chapter, it would be easy to put this before the discussion of the connection between historicity and temporality. What is historical is ordinarily characterized with the aid of the time of within-timeness. But if this vulgar[1] characterization is to be stripped of its seeming self-evidence and exclusiveness, historicity is to be "deduced" beforehand purely from the primordial temporality of Da-sein. This is required by the

7. That is, it is in *opposition to* the obscuring (commonplace) *interpretation* of the history of Da-sein but it is *supported by* the (commonsense and wiser) *comprehension* of Da-sein Heidegger frequently appeals to (e.g., in §63 above).

8. "Als eigentlich oder uneigentlich geschichtliches." This marks a significant change in Heidegger's use of these contrasting terms. Their meanings here are more figurative than literal (and

more akin to their meanings in ordinary usage), with the distinction coming to revolve around the idea of "genuineness" more than "own-ness."

9. A reference to DILTHEY's *The Construction of the Historical World in the Human Sciences* (1910; see above). This work was well known to and admired by Heidegger, who acknowledges his indebtedness to Dilthey below.

1. That is, commonplace (*vulgären*).

way these are "objectively" connected. But since time as within-time-ness also "stems" from the temporality of Da-sein, historicity and within-time-ness turn out to be equiprimordial. The vulgar interpretation of the temporal character of history is thus justified within its limits.

After this first characterization of the course of the ontological exposition of historicity in terms of temporality, do we still need explicit assurance that the following inquiry does not believe that the problem of history can be solved by a sleight of hand? The paucity of the available "categorial" means and the uncertainty of the primary ontological horizons become all the more obtrusive, the more the problem of history is traced to its *primordial rootedness*. In the following reflections, we shall content ourselves with indicating the ontological place of the problem of historicity. Basically, the following analysis is solely concerned with furthering the investigations of Dilthey in a preparatory way. Today's present generation has not as yet made them its own.

Our exposition of the existential problem of historicity—an exposition, moreover, that is of necessity limited by our fundamental and ontological aim—is divided up as follows: the vulgar understanding of history and the occurrence of Da-sein (section 73); the fundamental constitution of historicity (section 74); the historicity of Da-sein and world history (section 75); the existential origin of historiography from the historicity of Da-sein (section 76); the connection of the previous exposition of the problem of historicity with the investigations of Dilthey and the ideas of Count Yorck[2] (section 77).

73. THE VULGAR UNDERSTANDING OF HISTORY [*GESCHICHTE*] AND THE OCCURRENCE [*GESCHEHEN*] OF DA-SEIN

Our next goal is to find the point of departure for the primordial question of the essence of history, that is, for the existential construction of historicity. This point is designated by what is primarily historical. Thus our reflections begin with a characterization of what is meant by the expressions "history" and "historical" in the vulgar interpretation of Da-sein. They are ambiguous.

The most obvious ambiguity of the term "history" has often been noted, and it is by no means "approximate." It makes itself known in the fact that it means "historical reality" as well as the possibility of a science [*Wissenschaft*] of it. For the time being, we shall leave out the signification of "history" in the sense of a science of history (historiography).[3]

Among the meanings of the expression "history" that signify neither the science of history nor the latter as an object, but rather this being itself which has not necessarily been objectified, the one in which this being is understood as something *past* claims a preferred use. This significance makes itself known in talk such as "this or that already belongs to history." Here "past" means on the one hand "no longer objectively present," or else "indeed still objectively present, but without 'effect' on the 'present'." However, what is historical as what is past also has the opposite significance when we say that one cannot evade history. Here history means what is past, but is nevertheless still having an effect. However, what is historical as what is past is understood

2. Count (Graf) Paul Yorck von Wartenburg (1835–1897), a friend of Dilthey's. His ideas on historicity, made known through his posthumously published correspondence with Dilthey, influenced Heidegger. (Sections 76 and 77 are not included here.)

3. That is, "in the sense of the discipline that studies *Geschichte* (namely, History)" (*im Sinne von Geschichtswissenschaft* [*Historie*]).

in a positive or privative effective relation to the "present" in the sense of what is real "now" and "today." "The past" has a remarkable ambiguity here. Here "the past" belongs irrevocably to an earlier time; it belonged to former events and can yet still be objectively present "now"—for example, the remains of a Greek temple. A "bit of the past" is still "present" in it.

Thus history does not so much mean the "past" in the sense of what is past, but the *derivation* from it. Whatever "has a history" is in the context of a becoming. Here the "development" is sometimes a rise, sometimes a fall. Whatever "has a history" in this way can at the same time "make" history. "Epoch making," it "presently" determines a "future." Here history means a "connection" of events and "effects" that moves through the "past," the "present" and the "future." Here the past has no particular priority.

Furthermore, history signifies the whole of beings that change "in time," the transformations and destinies of humankind, human institutions and their "cultures," in contradistinction to nature that similarly moves "in time." History means here not so much the kind of being, the occurrence, as the region of beings that one distinguishes from nature with regard to the essential determination of the existence [*Existenz*] of human being as "spirit [*Geist*]" and "culture," although nature, too, belongs in a way to history thus understood.

And finally, what has been handed down as such is taken to be "historical," whether it be known historiographically or taken over as being self-evident and concealed in its derivation.

If we consider the four meanings together, we find that history is the specific occurrence of existing Da-sein happening in time,[4] in such a way that the occurrence in being-with-one-another that is "past" and at the same time "handed down" and still having its effect is taken to be history in the sense emphasized.

The four meanings have a connection in that they are related to human being as the "subject" of events. How is the kind of occurrence of these events to be determined? Is the occurrence a succession of processes, a changing appearance and disappearance of events? In what way does this occurrence of history belong to Da-sein? Is Da-sein factically already "objectively present" beforehand, and then at times gets into "a history"? Does Da-sein first *become* historical through a concatenation of circumstances and events? Or is the being of Da-sein first constituted by occurrence [*Geschehen*], so that *only because Dasein is historical in its being* are anything like circumstances, events, and destinies ontologically possible? Why does precisely the past have an important function in the "temporal" characterization of Da-sein occurring "in time"?

If history belongs to the being of Da-sein, and if this being is grounded in temporality, it seems logical to begin the existential analysis of historicity with *the* characteristics of what is historical that evidently have a temporal meaning. Thus a more precise characterization of the remarkable priority of the "past" in the concept of history should prepare the exposition of the fundamental constitution of historicity.

The "antiquities" preserved in museums (for example, household things) belong to a "time past," and are yet still objectively present in the "present." How are these useful things historical when they are, after all, *not yet past*? Only because they became an *object* of historiographical interest, of the cultivation of antiquity and national lore? But such useful things can only, after

---

4. That is, "history is the specific happening [*Geschehen*] of existing Da-sein occurring in time" (*Geschichte ist das in der Zeit sich begebende spezifische Geschehen des existierendes Daseins*).

all, be *historiographical objects* because they are somehow in themselves *historical*. We repeat the question: With what justification do we call these beings historical when they are not yet past? Or do these "things" "in themselves" yet have "something past" about them although they are still objectively present today? Are these objectively present things then still what they were? Evidently these "things" have changed. The tools have become fragile and worm-eaten "in the course of time." But yet *the* specific character of the past that makes them something historical does not lie in this transience that continues even during their objective presence in the museum. But then what is past about the useful thing? What *were* the "things" that they no longer are today? They are still definite useful things, but out of use. However, if they were still in use, like many heirlooms in the household, would they then not be historical? Whether in use or out of use, they are no longer what they were. What is "past"? Nothing other than the *world* within which they were encountered as things at hand belonging to a context of useful things and used by heedful Da-sein existing-in-the-world. That *world* is no longer.[5] But what was previously *innerworldly* in that world is still objectively present. As useful things belonging to that world, what is *now* still objectively present can nevertheless belong to the *"past."* But what does it mean that the world no-longer-is? World *is* only in the mode of *existing* Da-sein, that is, *factically as being-in-the-world*.

The historical character of extant antiquities is thus grounded in the "past" of Da-sein to whose world that past belongs. According to this, only "past" Da-sein would be historical, but not "present" Da-sein. However, can Da-sein be *past* at all, if we define "past" as "now *no longer objectively present or at hand"?* Evidently Da-sein can never be past, not because it is imperishable, but because it can essentially *never* be *objectively present* [*vorhand*].[6] Rather, if it is, it *exists* [*existiert*]. But a Da-sein that no longer exists is not past in the ontologically strict sense; it is rather *having-been-there*. The antiquities still objectively present have a "past" and a character of history because they belong to useful things and originate from a world that has-been—the world of a Da-sein that has-been-there. Da-sein is what is primarily historical. But does Da-sein first *become* historical by no longer being there? Or *is* it historical precisely as factically existing? *Is Da-sein something that has-been only in the sense of having-been-there, or has it been as something making present and futural, that is, in the temporalizing of its temporality?*

From this preliminary analysis of the useful things belonging to history that are still objectively present and yet somehow "past," it becomes clear that this kind of being is historical only on the basis of its belonging to the world. But the world has a historical kind of being because it constitutes an ontological determination of Da-sein. Furthermore, we can see that when one designates a time as "the past," the meaning of this is not unequivocal, but "the past" is manifestly distinct from the *having-been*, which we got to know as a constituent of the ecstatic unity of the temporality of Da-sein. But thus the enigma ultimately only becomes more acute; why is that precisely the "past" or, more appropriately, the having-been *predominately* determines what is historical when, after all, having-been temporalizes itself equiprimordially with present and future.

---

5. This sentence helps clarify what Heidegger means by *Welt* (world). So, for example, one might say that "the world of medieval Europe, like the world of the Roman Empire that preceded it, is long gone."

6. That is, its kind of reality is not that of a *vorhand* (at-hand) thing.

We asserted that Da-sein is what is *primarily* historical. But *secondarily* historical is what is encountered within the world, not only useful things at hand in the broadest sense, but also *nature* in the surrounding world as the "historical ground." We call beings unlike Da-sein that are historical by reason of their belonging to the world that which is world-historical. We can show that the vulgar concept of "world history" arises precisely from our orientation toward what is secondarily historical. What is world-historical is not first historical on the basis of a historiographical objectivation, but rather *as the being* that it is in itself encountered in the world.

The analysis of the historical character of a useful thing still objectively present not only led us back to Da-sein as what is primarily historical, but at the same time made it dubious whether the temporal characteristics of what is historical should be primarily oriented toward the being-in-time of something objectively present at all. Beings do not become "more historical" as we go on to a past ever farther away, so that what is most ancient would be the most authentically historical. But the "temporal" distance from now and today again has no primarily constitutive significance for the historicity of authentically historical beings, not because they are not "in time" or are timeless, but rather because they *primordially* exist *temporally in a way that* nothing objectively present [*vorhand*] "in time," whether passing away or coming into being, could ever, by its ontological essence, be temporal in such a way.

It will be said that these are overly complicated remarks. No one denies that human existence is basically the primary "subject" of history, and the vulgar concept of history cited says this clearly enough. But the thesis that "Da-sein is historical" not only means the ontic fact that human being presents a more or less important "atom" in the business of world history, and remains the plaything of circumstances and events, but poses the problem *why and on the basis of what ontological conditions, does historicity belong to the subjectivity of the "historical" subject as its essential constitution?*

74. THE ESSENTIAL CONSTITUTION OF HISTORICITY

Factically, Da-sein always has its "history," and it can have something of the sort because the being of this being is constituted by historicity. We want to justify this thesis with the intention of setting forth the *ontological* problem of history as an existential one. The being of Da-sein was defined as care. Care is grounded in temporality. Within the scope of temporality we must accordingly search for an occurrence that determines existence [*Existenz*] as historical. Thus the interpretation of the historicity of Da-sein turns out to be basically just a more concrete development of temporality. We revealed temporality initially with regard to the mode of authentic existing that we characterized as anticipatory resolution. Why does this involve an authentic occurrence of Da-sein?

We determined resoluteness as self-projection upon one's own being guilty that is reticent and ready for *Angst*. It attains its authenticity as *anticipatory* resoluteness. In it, Da-sein understands itself with regard to its potentiality-of-being in a way that confronts death in order to take over completely the being that it itself is in its thrownness. Resolutely taking over one's own factical "There" means at the same time the resolve for the situation. In the existential analytic we cannot, on principle, discuss what Da-sein *factically* resolves upon. Our present inquiry excludes even the existential project of factical possibilities of existence. Nevertheless, we must ask whence *in general* can the possibilities be drawn upon which Da-sein factically projects itself? Anticipatory self-projection upon the possibility of existence not to-be-bypassed—on death—guarantees only the totality and authenticity of resoluteness. But the factically disclosed possibilities of existence [*Existenz*] are not to be taken from death.[7] All the less so since anticipation of that possibility is not a speculation about it, but rather precisely signifies coming back to the factical There. Is taking over the thrownness of the self into its world supposed to disclose a horizon from which existence [*Existenz*] seizes its factical possibilities? Did we not moreover say that Da-sein never gets behind its thrownness? Before we rashly decide whether Da-sein draws its authentic possibilities of existence [*Existenz*] from thrownness or not, we must assure ourselves of the complete concept of this fundamental determination of care.

It is true that Da-sein is delivered over to itself and its potentiality-of-being, *but as being-in-the-world*. As thrown, it is dependent upon a "world," and exists factically with others. Initially and for the most part, the self is lost in the they [*das Man*]. It understands itself in terms of the possibilities of existence that "circulate" in the actual "average" public interpretedness of Da-sein today. Mostly they are made unrecognizable by ambiguity, but they are still familiar. Authentic existentiell understanding is so far from extricating itself from traditional interpretedness that it always grasps its chosen possibility in resolution from that interpretation and in opposition to it, and yet again for it.

The resoluteness in which Da-sein comes back to itself discloses the actual factical possibilities of authentic existing *in terms of the heritage* [*Erbe*] which that resoluteness *takes over* as thrown.[8] Resolute coming back to thrownness involves *handing oneself over* to traditional[9] possibilities, although not necessarily *as* traditional ones. If everything "good" is a matter of heritage [*Erbschaft*] and if the character of "goodness" lies in making authentic existence [*Existenz*] possible, then handing down a heritage is always constituted in resoluteness. The more authentically Da-sein resolves itself, that is, understands itself unambiguously in terms of its ownmost eminent possibility in anticipating death, the more unequivocal and inevitable is the choice in finding the possibility of its existence [*Existenz*]. Only the anticipation of death drives every chance and "preliminary" possibility out. Only being free *for* death gives Da-sein its absolute goal[1] and knocks[2] existence [*Existenz*] into its finitude. The finitude of existence [*Existenz*] thus seized upon tears one back out of endless multiplicity of possibilities offering themselves nearest by— those of comfort, shirking and taking things easy—and brings Da-sein to the simplicity of its *fate*. This is how we designate the primordial occurrence of Da-sein that lies in authentic resoluteness in which it *hands itself down* to itself, free for death, in a possibility that it inherited and yet has chosen.

Da-sein can only be reached[3] by the blows of fate because in the basis of its

---

7. Without the point made by these two sentences, Heidegger's earlier analyses of "being-toward-death," "resoluteness," and "authenticity" are incomplete.
8. This statement is of the greatest importance for Heidegger's reworked conception of the "facticity" of Da-sein: it now is by no means a purely individual affair, for it includes one's specific "heritage" (*Erbe*).

9. That is, handed-down, having-come-down (*überkommener*).
1. That is, "the goal (aim, end) pure and simple" (*das Ziel schlechthin*). This is no *particular* objective whatsoever, but rather *authenticity* (not a "what" or "why" of being, but a "way" of being).
2. That is, jolts.
3. That is, struck (*getroffen*), affected.

being it *is* fate in the sense described. Existing fatefully in resoluteness hand-ing itself down, Da-sein is disclosed as being-in-the-world for the "coming" of "fortunate" circumstances and for the cruelty of chance. Fate does not first originate with the collision of circumstances and events. Even an irresolute person is driven by them, more so than someone who has chosen, and yet he can "have" no fate.

When Da-sein, anticipating, lets death become powerful in itself, as free for death it understands itself in its own *higher power*, the power of its finite freedom, and takes over the *powerlessness* of being abandoned to itself in that freedom, which always only *is* in having chosen the choice, and becomes clear about the chance elements in the situation disclosed. But if fateful Da-sein essentially exists as being-in-the-world in being-with others, its occurrence is an occurrence-with and is determined as *destiny*.[4] With this term, we desig-nate the occurrence of the community, of a people. Destiny is not composed of individual fates, nor can being-with-one-another be conceived of as the mutual occurrence of several subjects. These fates are already guided before-hand in being-with-one-another in the same world and in the resoluteness for definite possibilities. In communication and in battle the power of destiny first becomes free. The fateful destiny of Da-sein in and with its "generation" con-stitutes the complete, authentic occurrence [*Geschehen*] of Da-sein.[5]

As the powerless higher power preparing itself for adversities, the power of reticent self-projection, ready for *Angst*, upon one's own being-guilty, fate requires the constitution of being of care as the ontological condition of its possibility, that is, temporality. Only if death, guilt, conscience, freedom, and finitude live together equiprimordially in the being of a being as they do in care, can that being exist in the mode of fate, that is, be historical in the ground of its existence.

Only a being that is essentially futural *in its being so that it can let itself be thrown back upon its factical There, free for its death and shattering itself on it, that is, only a being that, as futural, is equiprimordially* having-been, *can hand down to itself its inherited possibility, take over its own thrownness and be in the Moment* for *"its time." Only authentic temporality that is at the same time finite makes something like fate, that is, authentic historicity, possible.*

It is not necessary that resoluteness *explicitly* know of the provenance of its possibilities upon which it projects itself. However, in the temporality of Da-sein, and only in it, lies the possibility of fetching the existentiell potentiality-of-being upon which it projects itself *explicitly* from the traditional understanding of Da-sein. Resoluteness that comes back to itself and hands itself down then becomes the retrieve [*Wiederholung*][6] of a possibility of existence

---

4. "Geschick": the "destiny" of a community, soci-ety, or "people," in contrast to the *Schicksal* or "fate" of an individual. In the last sentence of this paragraph, they are merged.
5. This clear and powerful statement would appear to supersede Heidegger's far more individualistic statements earlier in the book regarding "authen-ticity." The *Geschehen* (occurrence, happening) of Da-sein is a more comprehensive characterization of its reality than its "Existenz"; and thus this kind of "authenticity"—in which the fate of the indi-vidual as such is transcended—is a higher, more significant kind than that which focuses on the

manner in which the individual chooses ("antici-patory resoluteness").
6. *Wiederholung* is normally translated as "repeti-tion." Heidegger here gives it a somewhat different meaning (and a very important role), drawing upon its literal meaning, that the translator uses the artificial term "retrieve" (as a noun) to attempt to convey. It literally means something like "holding" (*holen*, getting, going for) "again" (*wieder*); that is, embracing something previously embraced (embracing again, re-embracing). It would be bet-ter translated as "retrieval," and should be so understood.

[Existenz] that has been handed down. *Retrieve is explicit handing down*, that is, going back to the possibilities of the Da-sein that has been there. The authentic retrieve of a possibility of existence [Existenz] that has been—the possibility that Da-sein may choose its heroes—is existentially grounded in anticipatory resoluteness; for in resoluteness the choice is first chosen that makes one free for the struggle to come, and the loyalty to what can be retrieved.[7] The handing down of a possibility that has been in retrieving [wiederholend] it, however, does not disclose the Da-sein that has been there in order to actualize it again. The retrieve of what is possible neither brings back "what is past," nor does it bind the "present" back to what is "outdated." Arising from a resolute self-projection, retrieve is not convinced by "something past," in just letting it come back as what was once real. Rather, retrieve *responds* to the possibility of existence [Existenz] that has-been-there. But responding to the possibility in a resolution is at the same time, *as in the Moment, the disavowal* of what is working itself out today as the "past." Retrieve [Wiederholung] neither abandons itself to the past, nor does it aim at progress. In the Moment, authentic existence is indifferent to both of these alternatives.

We characterize retrieve as the mode of resolution handing itself down, by which Da-sein exists explicitly as fate. But if fate constitutes the primordial historicity of Da-sein, history has its essential weight neither in what is past nor in the today and its "connection" with what is past, but in the authentic occurrence [Geschehen] of existence [Existenz] that arises from the *future* of Da-sein. As a mode of being of Da-sein, history has its roots so essentially in the future that death, as the possibility of Da-sein we characterized, throws anticipatory existence back upon its *factical* thrownness and thus first gives to the *having-been* its unique priority in what is historical. *Authentic being-toward-death, that is, the finitude of temporality, is the concealed ground of the historicity of Da-sein.* Da-sein does not first become historical in retrieve [Wiederholung], but rather because as temporal it is historical, it can take itself over in its history, retrieving itself. Here no historiography is needed as yet.

We call the anticipatory handing oneself down to the There of the Moment that lies in resoluteness fate.[8] In it destiny is also grounded, by which we understand the occurrence of Da-sein in being-with-others. Fateful destiny can be explicitly disclosed in retrieve with regard to its being bound up with the heritage handed down to it. Repetition [Wiederholung] first makes manifest to Da-sein its own history. Retrieve first reveals to Da-sein its own history. The occurrence itself and the disclosedness belonging to it, or the appropriation of it, is existentially grounded in the fact that Da-sein is ecstatically open as a temporal being.

What we characterized as historicity in conformity with the occurrence lying in anticipatory resoluteness, we shall call the *authentic* historicity of Da-sein. It became clear in terms of the phenomena of handing down and retrieve, rooted in the future, why the occurrence of authentic history has its weight in having-been. However, it remains all the more enigmatic how this occurrence, as fate, is to constitute the whole "connection" of Da-sein from its birth to its death. What can going back to resoluteness add to this by way

---

7. That is: and for loyalty to that which is re-embraceable (*Wiederholbaren*).
8. That is, "The resoluteness-implicated anticipa-tory handing-down of oneself to the There of the Moment is what we call 'fate.'"

of clarification? Is not each resolution just *one* more single "experience" in the succession of the whole connection of experiences? Is the "connection" of authentic occurrence supposed to consist of an uninterrupted succession of resolutions? Why does the question of the constitution of the "connection of life" not find an adequate and satisfactory answer? Is not our inquiry over-hasty? Does it not, in the end, cling too much to the answer, without having tested the *question* beforehand as to its legitimacy? Nothing became more clear from the course of the existential analytic so far than the fact that the ontology of Da-sein falls prey to the temptations of the vulgar understanding of being [*Sein*] again and again. We can cope with this methodically only by pursuing the *origin* of the question of the constitution of the connection of Da-sein, no matter how "self-evident" this question may be, and by determining in what ontological horizon it moves.

If historicity belongs to the being of Da-sein, then even inauthentic existence must be historical. Did the *inauthentic* historicity of Da-sein determine our line of questioning about a "connection of life" and block the access to authentic historicity and the "connection" peculiar to it? However that may be, if the exposition of the ontological problem of history is supposed to be adequate and complete, we cannot escape considering the inauthentic historicity of Da-sein.

FROM 75. THE HISTORICITY OF DA-SEIN AND WORLD HISTORY

Initially and for the most part, Da-sein understands itself in terms of what it encounters in the surrounding world and what it circumspectly takes care of.[9] Understanding is not just a bare taking cognizance of itself which simply accompanies all the modes of behavior of Da-sein. Understanding signifies self-projection upon the actual possibility of being-in-the-world, that is, exist-ing as this possibility. Thus understanding, as common sense, also constitutes the inauthentic existence of the they [*das Man*]. What everyday taking care of things[1] encounters in public being-with-one-another is not just useful things and works, but at the same time what "is going on" with them: "affairs," undertakings, incidents, mishaps. The "world" belongs to everyday trade and traffic as the soil from which they grow and the stage where they are displayed. In public being-with-one-another the others are encountered in the activities in which "one" "swims along" with it "oneself." One always knows about it, talks about it, furthers it, fights it, retains it, and forgets it primarily with regard to *what* is being done and *what* will "come out of it." We initially cal-culate the progress, arrest, adjustment, and "output" of individual Da-sein in terms of the course, status, change, and availability of what is taken care of. As trivial as the reference to the understanding of Da-sein of everyday com-mon sense may be, ontologically this understanding is by no means transpar-ent. But then why should the "connectedness" of Da-sein not be determined in terms of what is taken care of and "experienced"? Do not useful things and works and everything that Da-sein spends time with also belong to "history"? Is the occurrence of history then only the isolated course of "streams of expe-rience" in individual subjects?

Indeed, history is neither the connectedness of movements in the altera-tion of objects, nor the free-floating succession of experiences of "subjects."

---

9. That is, is concerned with (and deals with).
1. That is, "everyday concern" (*alltäglichen Besorgen*), in the sense of "interest."

Does the occurrence of history then pertain to the "linking" of subject and object? Even if one assigns occurrence to the subject-object relationship, then we must ask about the kind of being of this linking as such, if it is that which basically "occurs." The thesis of the historicity of Da-sein does not say that the worldless subject is historical, but that what is historical is the being that exists as being-in-the-world. *The occurrence [Geschehen] of history [Geschichte] is the occurrence of being-in-the-world.*[2] The historicity of Da-sein is essentially the historicity of the world which, on the basis of its ecstatic and horizonal temporality, belongs to the temporalizing of that temporality. When Da-sein factically exists, it already encounters beings discovered within the world. *With the existence of historical being-in-the-world, things at hand and objectively present have always already been included in the history of the world.* Tools and works, for example books, have their "fates"; buildings and institutions have their history. And even nature is historical. It is *not* historical when we speak about "natural history," but nature is historical as a countryside, as areas that have been inhabited or exploited, as battlefields and cultic sites. These innerworldly beings as such *are* historical, and their history does not signify something "external" that simply accompanies the "inner" history of the "soul." We shall call these beings *world-historical*. Here we must observe that the expression "world history" that we have chosen and that is here understood ontologically, has a double meaning. On the one hand, it signifies the occurrence of world[3] in its essential existent unity with Da-sein. But at the same time it means the innerworldly "occurrence" of what is at hand and objectively present, since innerworldly beings are always discovered with the factically existent world. The historical world is factically only as the world of innerworldly beings. What "occurs" with tools and works as such has its own character of motion, and this character has been completely obscure up to now. For example, a ring that is "presented" and "worn" does not simply undergo a change of location in its being. The movement of occurrence in which "something happens to it" cannot be grasped at all in terms of motion as change of location. That is true of all world-historical "processes" and events, and in a way even of "catastrophes of nature." Quite apart from the fact that we would necessarily go beyond the limits of our theme if we were to pursue the problem of the ontological structure of world-historical occurrence, we cannot do this because the intention of this exposition is to lead us to the ontological enigma of the movement of occurrence in general.

We only want to delimit *that* range of phenomena that we also necessarily have in mind ontologically when we speak about the historicity of Da-sein. On the basis of the temporally founded transcendence of the world, what is world-historical is always already "objectively" there in the occurrence of existing being-in-the-world, *without being grasped historiographically.* And since factical Da-sein is absorbed and entangled in what it takes care of,[4] it initially understands its history as world history. And since, furthermore, the vulgar understanding of being understands "being" as objective presence without further differentiation, the being of what is world-historical is experienced and

---

2. That is, "The *Geschehen* [happening] of history is the *Geschehen* of being-in-the-world," i.e., of Da-sein.
3. That is, the happening of (the kind of structural totality Heidegger calls) "world (*Welt*)."
4. That is, what it is concerned with (*dem Besorgten*).

interpreted in the sense of objective presence that comes along, is present, and disappears. And finally since the meaning of being in general is taken to be what is absolutely self-evident, the question of the kind of being of what is world-historical and of the movement of occurrence in general is "after all really" only unfruitful and unnecessarily complicated verbal sophistry.

Everyday Da-sein is dispersed in the multiplicity of what "happens" daily. The opportunities and circumstances that taking care keeps "tactically" awaiting in advance, result in "fate." Inauthentically existing Da-sein first calculates its history in terms of what it takes care of. In so doing, it is driven about by its "affairs." So if it wants to come to itself, it must first *pull itself together* from the *dispersion* and the *disconnectedness* of what has just "happened," and because of this, it is only then that there at last arises from the horizon of the understanding of inauthentic historicity the *question* of how one is to establish Da-sein's "connectedness" if one does so in the sense of the experiences of the subject "also" objectively present. The possibility that this horizon for the question should be the dominant one, is grounded in irresoluteness that constitutes the essence of the in-constancy[5] of the self.

We have thus pointed out the *origin* of the question of Da-sein's "connectedness" in the sense of the unity with which experiences are linked together between birth and death.[6] At the same time, the provenance of this question betrays its inappropriateness with regard to a primordial existential interpretation of the totality of occurrence of Da-sein. But, on the other hand, with the predominance of this "natural" horizon of questioning, it becomes explicable why precisely the authentic historicity of Da-sein—fate and retrieve [*Wiederholung*]—looks as if it, least of all, could provide the phenomenal basis for bringing into the form of an ontologically founded problem what is fundamentally intended with the question of the "connectedness of life."

This question can not ask: how does Da-sein acquire such a unity of connection that it can subsequently link together the succession of "experiences" that has ensued and is still ensuing; rather, it asks in which of its own kinds of being *does it lose itself in such a way that it must, as it were, pull itself together only subsequently out of its dispersion, and think up for itself[7] a unity in which this together is embraced?* Lostness in the they and in world history, revealed itself earlier as a flight from death. This flight from . . . reveals being-*toward*-death as a fundamental determination of care. Anticipatory resoluteness brings this being-toward-death to authentic existence [*Existenz*]. But we interpreted the occurrence of this resoluteness that anticipates and hands down and retrieves the heritage of possibilities, as authentic historicity. Does perhaps the primordial stretching along of the whole of existence [*Existenz*], which is not lost and does not need a connection, lie in historicity? The resoluteness of the self against the inconstancy of dispersion is in itself a *steadiness that has been stretched along*[8]—the steadiness in which Da-sein as fate "incorporates" into its existence [*Existenz*] birth and death and their

5. "Un-ständigkeit"—in contrast to the "constancy" (*Ständigkeit*) of the self that Heidegger associates with "resoluteness" (and therefore "authenticity"), and with the kind of self that it makes possible.

6. The "connectedness" and "wholeness" (or "being-as-a-whole") of the kind of self that such "constancy" makes possible (and indeed constitutes) are the only such "connectedness" and "wholeness" that are humanly attainable and can be humanly real.

7. That is, envision, conceive for itself (*sich erdenken*).

8. That is, more simply, a "stretched steadiness" (*erstreckte Stätigkeit*).

"between" in such a way that in such constancy it is in the Moment for what is world-historical in its actual situation. In the fateful retrieve [*Wiederholung*] of possibilities that have-been, Da-sein brings itself back "immediately," that is, temporally and ecstatically, to what has already been before it. But when its heritage is thus handed down to itself, "birth" is *taken into existence* [*Existenz*] in coming back from the possibility of death (the possibility not-to-be-bypassed) so that existence [*Existenz*] may accept the thrownness of its own There more free from illusion.[9]

Resoluteness constitutes the *loyalty* of existence [*Existenz*] to its own self.[1] As resoluteness ready for *Angst*, loyalty is at the same time a possible reverence for the sole authority that a free existence [*Existenz*] can have, for the possibilities of existence [*Existieren*] that can be retrieved. Resoluteness would be misunderstood ontologically if one thought that it *is* real as "experience" only as long as the "act" of resolution "lasts." In resoluteness lies the existentiell constancy which, in keeping with its essence, has already anticipated every possible Moment arising from it. As fate, resoluteness is freedom to *give up* a definite resolution, as may be required in the situation. Thus the steadiness of existence [*Existenz*] is not interrupted, but precisely confirmed in the Moment. Constancy is not first formed either through or by "Moments" adjoining each other, but rather the Moments arise from the temporality, *already stretched along*, of that retrieve which is futurally in the process of having-been.

On the other hand, in inauthentic historicity the primordial stretching along of fate is concealed. With the inconstancy of the they-self [*Man-selbst*], Da-sein makes present its "today." Awaiting the next new thing, it has already forgotten what is old. The they [*Das Man*] evades choice. Blind toward possibilities, it is incapable of retrieving what has been, but only retains what is and receives "real," what has been left over, of the world-historical that has been, the remnants, and the information about them that is objectively present. Lost in the making present of the today, it understands the "past" in terms of the "present." In contrast, the temporality of authentic historicity, as the Moment that anticipates and retrieves, *undoes* the making present of the today and the habituation to the conventionalities of the they [*das Man*]. Inauthentic historical existence, on the other hand, is burdened with the legacy of a "past" that has become unrecognizable to it, looks for what is modern. Authentic historicity understands history as the "recurrence"[2] of what is possible and knows that a possibility recurs only when existence [*Existenz*] is open for it fatefully, in the Moment, in resolute retrieve [*Wiederholung*].[3]

* * *

SOURCE: From Martin Heidegger, *Being and Time: A Translation of "Sein und Zeit,"* trans. Joan Stambaugh (Albany: State University of New York Press, 1996), pp. 9–11, 13–15, 39–42, 49–58, 107–8, 110–22, 164–65, 167–81, 213–21, 231–36, 239–46, 250–53, 258, 264–65, 272–76, 279, 281–83, 286–306, 341–58. Except where otherwise indicated, German words

9. That is, in a more illusion-free (*illusionsfreier*) way.

1. In other words, "In being 'resolute,' Da-sein as Existenz is being true to its own self." "Loyalty" here translates *Treue*, or "trueness."

2. An echo of Nietzsche's formulation of his idea of "eternal recurrence" (*ewige Wiederkehr*).

3. Better rendered: Authentic *Geschichtlichkeit* understands *Geschichte* as the "recurring" of something [humanly] possible, and knows that possibility only recurs when *Existenz* is [at once] fate- and moment-sensitively (*schicksalhaft-augenblicklich*) open for it in resolute *Wiederholung* [re-embrace].

in brackets are the terminology used in the German original, inserted by the editor in addition to their renderings in the translation. The text was first published as a special issue of a journal edited by EDMUND HUSSERL, *Jahrbuch für Philosophie und phänomenologische Forschung (Yearbook for Philosophy and Phenomenological Research)*, 8 (1927). Though presented there as the work's "Erste Hälfte" (first half), no subsequent portion was ever published.

From Letter on Humanism

Our thinking about the essence of action is still far from resolute enough. Action is known only as the bringing about of an effect; it is assessed by its utility. But the essence of action is fulfillment. To fulfill is to unfold something in the fullness of its essence, to usher it forward into that fullness: *producere*.[1] Hence only that can be truly fulfilled which is already in existence. Yet that which, above all, "is," is Being [*Sein*]. Thought brings to fulfillment the relation of Being to the essence of man, it does not make or produce this relation. Thought merely offers it to Being as that which has been delivered to itself by Being. This offering consists in this: that in thought Being is taken up in language. Language is the house of Being. In its home man dwells. Whoever thinks or creates in words is a guardian of this dwelling. As guardian, he brings to fulfillment the unhiddenness of Being insofar as he, by his speaking, takes up this unhiddenness in language and preserves it in language. Thought does not become action because an effect issues from it, or because it is applied. Thought acts in that it thinks. This is presumably the simplest and, at the same time, the highest form of action: it concerns man's relation to what is. All effecting, in the end, rests upon Being, is bent upon what is. Thought, on the other hand, lets itself be called into service by Being in order to speak the truth of Being. It is thought which accomplishes this letting be (*Lassen*). Thought is *l'engagement par l'Etre pour l'Etre*.[2] I do not know if it is linguistically possible to express both ("*par*" et "*pour*") as one, i.e. by *penser, c'est l'engagement de l'Etre*.[3] Here the possessive form "*de l'* . . ." is meant simultaneously to express the genitive as *genitivus subiectivus* and *obiectivus*.[4] In this, "subject" and "object" are inadequate terms of the metaphysics which, in the form of Western "logic" and "grammar," early took possession of the interpretation of language. Today we can but begin to surmise what lies hidden in this process. The freeing of language from grammar, and placing it in a more original and essential framework, is reserved for thought and poetry. Thought is not merely *l'engagement dans l'action*[5] for and by "what is" in the sense of the actual and present situation. Thought is *l'engagement* by and for the truth of Being. Its history is never past, it is always imminent. The history of Being sustains and determines every *condition et situation humaine*.[6] In order that we may first learn how to perceive the aforesaid essence of thinking in its pure form—and that means to fulfill it as well—we must free ourselves

1. To produce, to lead forth (Latin).
2. The engagement by Being for Being (French).
3. Thought, that is the engagement of Being (French); that is, engaging with Being.
4. Subjective and objective genitive (Latin), distinguished by whether the noun in an "of" phrase

(here, the French "de l' . . .") is the subject or the object of the action implied by the preceding noun: e.g., "the love of children" can mean either love felt by children or love felt for children.
5. The engagement in action (French).
6. Human condition and situation (French).

from the technical interpretation of thought. Its beginnings reach back to Plato and Aristotle.[7] With them thought is valued as τέχνη,[8] the procedure of reflection in the service of doing and making. The reflection here is already seen from the viewpoint of πρᾶξις and ποίησις.[9] Hence thought, when taken by itself, is not "practical." The characterization of thought as θεωρία[1] and the determination of cognition as "theoretical" behavior occur already within the "technical" interpretation of thought. They constitute a reactive attempt of saving for thought an independence in the face of doing and acting. Ever since, "philosophy" has faced the constant distress of justifying its existence against "science." It believes it accomplishes this most securely by elevating itself to the rank of science [Wissenschaft]. Yet this effort is the surrender of the essence of thought. Philosophy is haunted by the fear of losing prestige and validity, unless it becomes science [Wissenschaft].[2] It is considered a failure equated with unscientific [unwissenschaftlich] rigor. Being as the element of thought has been abandoned in the technical interpretation of thought. "Logic," since sophistry and Plato, is the initial sanction of this interpretation. Thought is judged by a measure inadequate to it. This judgment is like the procedure of trying to evaluate the nature and the capability of a fish by how long it is able to live on dry land. Too long, all too long, thought has been lying on dry land. Can the effort to bring thought back to its element be called "irrationalism" now?

The questions your letter[3] raises would undoubtedly be more easily clarified in personal conversation. In writing thought tends to lose its flexibility. Above all, however, it can hardly preserve the multidimensional quality peculiar to its realm. Strictness of thought consists, in contradistinction to science [Wissenschaft], not merely in the artificial, i.e. the technico-theoretical exactitude of terms. It rests on the fact that speaking remains purely in the element of Being and lets the simplicity of the manifold dimensions of Being rule. But the written, on the other hand, offers the salutary compulsion toward thought-out composition of the spoken word. Today I should like to select only one of your questions, the discussion of which may cast light on the others too.

You ask: Comment dedonner un sens au mot "Humanisme"?[4] This question is asked with the intention of retaining the word "humanism." I wonder if it is necessary. Or is the harm wrought by all such terms not obvious enough yet? Of course, for some time now, "isms" have been suspect. But the market of public opinion always demands new ones. Again and again this demand is readily answered. And terms like "logic," "ethics," "physics" occur only when original thinking has stopped. The Greeks, in their great age, did their thinking without such terms. They did not even call it "philosophy." Thinking ceases when it withdraws from its element. The element is that by means of which thinking can be thinking. It is the element which is potent, which is potency.[5]

---

7. Two Greek philosophers (ca. 427–ca. 347 B.C.E. and 385–322 B.C.E., respectively) who are seminal figures in Western thought.
8. Skill, craft (Greek, technē); but also "art."
9. Action and creating (Greek, praxis and poiēsis). Poiēsis also means "poetry."
1. Contemplation, theory (Greek, theōria).
2. That is, "cognitive discipline" (Wissenschaft), not simply the kind of inquiry pursued in the natural sciences.
3. The letter to which Heidegger was responding in the first version of this essay (see source note, below).
4. How may one give a meaning to the word

"humanism"? (French).
5. This and the following passage depend essentially on a play on words though it is not just that. The verb "vermögen" means "to be able to," "to have the power to do . . ." The noun "Vermögen" means "potency," also "wealth," "resources," "means." "Vermögend" means accordingly "potent" and also "propertied." The play on words is that, without the prefix "ver" the word becomes "mögen" meaning "to like." "Mögen" is then used here in a fusion of the two strains of meaning, potency and liking [translator's note].

It concerns itself with thought and so brings thought into its essence. Thought is, more simply, thought of Being. The genitive has two meanings. Thought is of Being, insofar as thought, eventuated by Being, belongs to Being. Thought is at the same time thought of Being insofar as thought listens to, heeds, Being. Listening to and belonging to Being, thought constitutes what it is in its essential origin. Thought is—this means, Being has always, in the manner of destiny, concerned itself about its essence, embraced it. To concern oneself about a "thing" or a "person" means, to love, to like him or it. Such "liking," understood in a more original way, means: to confer essence. Such "liking origin" is the proper nature of potency (*Vermögen*), which not only can perform this or that, but which can let something be what it is as it stems from its true origin. It is the potency of this loving on the "strength of which something is in fact capable of being." This potency is the truly "possible," that whose essence rests on "Mögen." Being is capable of thought. The one makes the other possible. Being as the element is the "quiet power" of the loving potency, i.e. of the possible. Our words "possible" and "possibility," however, are, under the domination of "logic" and "metaphysics," taken only in contrast to "actuality," i.e. they are conceived with reference to a determined—viz. the metaphysical—interpretation of Being as *actus* and *potentia*[6] the distinction of which is identified with that of *existentia* and *essentia*.[7] When I speak of the "quiet power of the possible," I do not mean the possible of a merely represented *possibilitas*,[8] nor the *potentia* as *essentia* of an *actus* of the *existentia*, but Being itself, which in its loving potency commands thought and thus also the essence of man, which means in turn his relationship to Being. To command something is to sustain it in its essence, to retain it in its element.

When thought comes to an end of withdrawing from its element, it replaces the loss by making its validity felt as τέχνη, as an educational instrument and therefore as a scholarly matter and later as a cultural matter. Philosophy gradually becomes a technique of explanation drawn from ultimate causes. One no longer thinks, but one occupies oneself with "philosophy." In competition such occupations publicly present themselves as "isms" and try to outdo each other. The domination achieved through such terminology does not just happen. It rests, especially in modern times, on the peculiar dictatorship of the public. So-called private existence does not mean yet, however, essentially and freely being human. It merely adheres obstinately to a negation of the public. It remains an offshoot dependent on the public and nourishes itself on its mere retreat from the public. So it is witness, against its own will, of its subjection to the public. The public itself, however, is the metaphysically conditioned—as it is derived from the domination of subjectivity—establishment and authorization of the overtness of the existent in the absolute objectivization of everything. Therefore, language falls into the service of arranging the lines of communication, on which objectification as the uniform accessibility of everything for everybody expands, disregarding all limits. So language comes under the dictatorship of the public. This public predetermines what is intelligible and what must be rejected as unintelligible. What has been said in *Sein und Zeit* (1927), §§ 27 and 35, about the word "*man*"[9] (the impersonal one) is

---

6. Act and power or capacity (Latin).
7. Existence and essence (Latin).
8. Possibility (Latin).
9. On the impersonal use of *man* in German, see p.

977, n. 8, above, to *Being and Time.* (The selections from that work do not include §35.) This word in German does not mean what "man" means in English.

not simply meant to furnish, in passing, a contribution to sociology. In the same way the word *man* does not simply mean the counterpart—in an ethical existential way—to a person's self-Being. What has been said contains rather an indication—thought of from the question of the truth of Being—of the original pertinence of the word Being. This relationship remains concealed under the domination of subjectivity, which is represented as the public. When, however, the truth of Being has become memorable to thought, then reflection on the essence of language must obtain a new rank. It can no longer be mere philosophy of language. And for just this reason *Sein und Zeit* (§34) contains an indication of the essential dimension of language and broaches the simple question of what mode of Being the language as language from time to time is in. The ubiquitous and fast-spreading impoverishment of language does not gnaw only at[1] aesthetic and moral responsibility in all use of language. It rises from an endangering of man's essence. A merely cultured use of language still does not demonstrate that we have as yet escaped this essential danger. Today it may rather signify that we have not yet seen the danger and cannot see it, because we have never exposed ourselves to its gaze. The decadence of language, quite recently considered though very late, is, however, not the cause but rather a consequence of the process that language under the domination of the modern metaphysics of subjectivity almost always falls out of its element. Language still denies us its essence: that it is the house of the truth of Being. Language, moreover, leaves itself to our mere willing and cultivating as an instrument of domination over beings. This itself appears as the actual in the concatenation of cause and effect. Calculating and acting we encounter beings as the actual, but also scientifically [*wissenschaftlich*] and in philosophizing with explanations and arguments. To these also belongs the assurance that something is inexplicable. Through such assertions we believe we confront the mystery. As if it were taken for granted that the truth of Being could be set up over causes and basic explanations or, what is the same, over their incomprehensibility.

If man, however, is once again to find himself in the nearness of Being, he must first learn to exist in the nameless. He must recognize the seduction of the public, as well as the impotence of the private. Man must, before he speaks, let himself first be claimed again by Being at the risk of having under this claim little or almost nothing to say. Only in this way will the preciousness of its essence be returned to the word, and to man the dwelling where he can live in the truth of Being.

But is there not now in this claim upon man, is there not in the attempt to make man ready for this claim, an effort in behalf of man? Where else does "Care" (*Sorge*)[2] go, if not in the direction of bringing man back to his essence again? What else does this mean, but that man (*homo*) should become human (*humanus*[3])? Thus *humanitas* remains the concern of such thought; for this is humanism: to reflect and to care that man be human and not un-human, "inhuman", i.e. outside of his essence. Yet, of what does the humanity of man consist? It rests in his essence.

---

1. That is, "does not merely gnaw at" (it also does much more than that).
2. A central thesis of *Being and Time* is that *Sorge* (care) is the essence of the very being of what Heidegger calls *Dasein*, which is human reality's kind of being.
3. The Latin adjective meaning "human"; *homo* is the noun (and a primary meaning of *humanitas* is "humanity").

But whence and how is the essence of man determined? Marx demands that the "human man" be known and acknowledged. He finds this man in society. The "social" man is for him the "natural" man. In "society" the "nature" of man, which means all of his "natural needs" (food, clothing, reproduction, economic sufficiency), is equally secured. The Christian sees the humanity of man, the *humanitas* of the *homo*, as the delimitation of *deitas*.[4] He is, in the history of Grace, man as the "child of God," who hears in Christ the claim of the Father and accepts it. Man is not of this world, insofar as the "world," theoretically and Platonically understood, is nothing but a transitory passage into the other world.

* * *

But when one understands by humanism, in general, the effort of man to become free for his humanity and to find therein his dignity rather than some conceptual understanding of the "freedom" and the "nature" of man, the humanism is in each instance different. Likewise its modes of realization differ. Marx's humanism requires no return to antiquity, nor does the humanism which Sartre conceives existentialism to be. In this broad sense Christianity is also a humanism, insofar as, according to its doctrine, everything comes down to the salvation of the soul (*salus aeterna*[5]) of man and the history of mankind appears in the frame of the history of salvation. However different these kinds of humanism may be, in regard to their aims and basis, in regard to the ways and means of their respective realizations, in regard to the form of their doctrine, all of them coincide in that the *humanitas* of the homo humanus is determined from the view of an already-established interpretation of nature, of history, of world, of the basis of the world (*Weltgrund*), i.e. of beings in their totality.

Every humanism is either founded in a metaphysics or is converted into the basis for a metaphysics. Every determination of the essence of man that presupposes the interpretation of beings without asking the question of the truth of Being, be it wittingly or not, is metaphysical.[6] Therefore, and precisely in view of the way in which the essence of man is determined, the characteristic of all metaphysics shows itself in the fact that it is "humanistic." For this reason every humanism remains metaphysical. Humanism not only does not ask, in determining the humanity of man, for the relation of Being to the essence of man, but humanism even impedes this question, since, by virtue of its derivation from metaphysics it neither knows nor understands it. Inversely, the necessary and the proper way of asking the question of the truth of Being, in metaphysics but forgotten by it, can only come to light, if amidst the domination of metaphysics the question is asked: "What is metaphysics?" First of all each question of "Being," even that of the truth of Being, must be presented as a "metaphysical" question.

The first humanism, the Roman, and all the humanisms that have since appeared, presupposes as self-evident the most general "essence" of man. Man

---

4. Divine nature (Latin). For Heidegger's European audience, Christian thought regarding human nature was dominant; its chief secular rival was the thought of KARL MARX.
5. Eternal health (Latin).
6. Heidegger at this point had come to view "metaphysics" as a deeply misguided way of thinking

(about reality in general and human reality in particular), based on a fundamental misunderstanding of "the meaning of being." Recognizing and overcoming that misunderstanding, for him, is difficult but necessary if "the meaning of being" is ever to be truly comprehended (which, for the later Heidegger, is humanity's essential and most important task).

is considered as the *animal rationale*.[7] This determination is not only the Latin translation of the Greek ζῷον λόγον ἔχον[8] but a metaphysical interpretation. This essential determination of man is not wrong, but it is conditioned by metaphysics. Its essential extraction and not merely its limit has, however, become questionable in *Sein und Zeit*. This questionableness is first of all given to thought as what has to be thought, but not in such a way as to be devoured by an empty skepticism.

Certainly metaphysics posits beings in their Being and so thinks of the Being of beings. But it does not discriminate between the two (cf. "Vom Wesen des Grundes" 1929, p. 8; *Kant und das Problem der Metaphysik* 1929, p. 225;[9] *Sein und Zeit*, p. 230). Metaphysics does not ask for the truth of Being itself. Nor does it ever ask, therefore, in what way the essence of man belongs to the truth of Being. This question metaphysics has not only not asked up to now, but this question cannot be treated by metaphysics as metaphysics. Being still waits for Itself to become memorable to man. However one may—in regard to the determination of the essence of man—determine the *ratio*[1] of the animal and the reason of the living being, whether as "capacity for principles," or as "capacity for categories," or otherwise, everywhere and always the essence of reason is based upon the fact that for each perceiving of beings in their Being, Being itself is discovered and realized in its truth. In the same way, an interpretation of "life" is given in the term "animal," ζῷον, which necessarily rests on an interpretation of beings as ζωή and φύσις[2] within which what is living appears. Besides this, however, the question finally remains whether, originating and predetermining everything, the essence of man lies in the dimension of the *animalitas*.[3] Are we on the right track at all to reach the essence of man, if and as long as we delimit man as a living-being amongst others, against plant, animal and God? One can so proceed, one can in such a way put man within beings as a being amongst others. Thereby one will always be able to assert what is correct about man. But one must also be clear in this regard that by this man remains cast off in the essential realm of *animalitas*, even when one does not put him on the same level as the animal, but attributes a specific difference to him. In principle one always thinks of the *homo animalis*, even when one puts *anima* as *animus sive mens*[4] and later as subject, as person, as spirit [*Geist*]. To put it so is the way of metaphysics. But by this the essence of man is too lightly considered and is not thought of in the light of its source, that essential source which always remains for historical humanity the essential future. Metaphysics thinks of man as arising from *animalitas* and does not think of him as pointing toward *humanitas*.

Metaphysics shuts itself off from the simple essential certitude that man is essentially only in his essence, in which he is claimed by Being. Only from this claim "has" he found wherein his essence dwells. Only from this dwelling "has" he "language" as the home which preserves the ecstatic for his essence. The standing in the clearing of Being I call the ex-sistence[5] of man.

---

7. Rational animal (Latin).
8. Animal having reason (Greek, *zōon logon echon*). See Aristotle, *Nicomachean Ethics* 1.7, 1098a.
9. Heidegger's two works published immediately after *Being and Time*: "The Essence of Reasons" and *Kant and the Problem of Metaphysics*.
1. Reason (Latin); here, reasoning ability.
2. Life and natural form (Greek, *zōe* and *physis*).

3. Animal nature (Latin).
4. Living being as rational soul or mind (Latin).
5. A spelling that emphasizes the root of the Latin verb *exsistere*, which literally means "to step forth." "Ecstasy" is literally the state of being outside of oneself. Heidegger is drawing on both words and their roots to elucidate the way of thinking about human existing (*Existenz*) he is advancing.

Only man has this way to be. Ex-sistence, so understood, is not only the basis of the possibility of reason, *ratio*, but ex-sistence is that, wherein the essence of man preserves the source that determines him.

Ex-sistence can only be said of the essence of man, i.e. only of the human way "to be"; for only man, as far as we know, is admitted into the destiny of ex-sistence. Thus ex-sistence can never be thought of as a specific way, amongst other ways, of a living being, so long as man is destined to think of the essence of his Being and not merely to report theories of nature and history about his composition and activity. Thus all that we attribute to man as *animalitas* in comparing him to the "animal" is grounded in the essence of ex-sistence. The body of man is something essentially different from the animal organism. The error of biologism has not yet been overcome by the fact that one affixes the soul to corporeal man and the mind to the soul and the existential to the mind, and more strongly than ever before preaches the appreciation of the mind, in order that everything may then fall back into the experience of life, with the admonitory assurance that thought will destroy by its rigid concepts the stream of life and the thought of Being will deform existence. That physiology and physiological chemistry can scientifically examine man as an organism, does not prove that in this "organic" disposition, i.e. in the body scientifically explained, the essence of man rests. This has as little value as the opinion that the essence of nature is contained in atomic energy. It may very well be that nature hides its essence in that aspect of which human technology has taken possession. As little as the essence of man consists of being an animal organism, so little can this insufficient determination of the essence of man be eliminated and compensated for by the fact that man is equipped with an immortal soul or with the capability of reason or with the character of a person. Each time the essence is overlooked and, no doubt, on the basis of the same metaphysical design.

All that man is, i.e. in the traditional language of metaphysics the "essence" of man, rests in his ex-sistence. But ex-sistence, so thought of, is not identical with the traditional concept of *existentia*, which signifies actuality in contrast to essentia as possibility. In *Sein und Zeit* (p. 42) is the sentence, italicized: "The 'essence' of being-there (*Dasein*) lies in its existence."[6] Here, however, this is not a matter of opposing *existentia* and *essentia*, because these two metaphysical determinations of Being have not yet been placed in question, let alone their relationship. The sentence contains even less a general statement about "being-there," insofar as this term (brought into usage in the eighteenth century for the word "object") is to express the metaphysical concept of the actuality of the actual. The sentence says rather:[7] man is essentially such that he is "Here" (*Da*), i.e. within the clearing of Being. This "Being" of the Here, and only this, has the basic trait of ex-sistence: i.e. it stands outside itself within the truth of Being. The ecstatic essence of man rests in the ex-sistence that remains different from the metaphysically conceived *existentia*. Medieval philosophy conceived this *existentia* as *actualitas*.[8] Kant presents *existentia* as actuality in the sense of the objectivity of experience. Hegel determines *existentia* as the self-knowing idea of the absolute subjectivity. Nietzsche understands *existentia* as the eternal return of the same.[9] Whether,

6. See p. 969, above.
7. That is, what follows expresses how the Heidegger of 1947 wanted the words written by the

Heidegger of 1927 to be understood.
8. Actuality (Latin).
9. For KANT, HEGEL, and NIETZSCHE, see above.

however, through *existentia*, in its various interpretations as actuality, different only at first glance, the Being of the stone, or even life as the Being of plants and animals, has been sufficiently thought about, remains an open question here. In each case animals are as they are, without their standing—from their Being as such—in the truth of Being and preserving in such standing what is essentially their Being. Presumably, animals are the most difficult of all entities for us to think of, because we are, on the one hand, most akin to them and, on the other hand, they are, at the same time separated from our existential essence by an abyss. And against this it might seem that the essence of the divine is much nearer us than the strangeness of animals, nearer in an essential distance, which as distance is much more familiar to our existential essence than the barely conceivable abysmal corporeal kinship to the animal. Such reflections cast a strange light on the current and therefore still premature designation of man as an *animal rationale*. Because plants and animals, although bound to their environment, are never freely placed in the clearing of Being—and only this clearing is "world"—they have no language. But it is not because they are without language that they find themselves hanging worldless in their environment. Yet in the word "environment [*Umwelt*]" is concentrated all the enigma of the animal. Language is in its essence not utterance of an organism nor is it expression of an animal. Thus it is never thought of with exactness in its symbolical or semantic character. Language is the clearing-and-concealing advent of Being itself.

Ex-sistence, ecstatically thought of, does not coincide with *existentia* either in regard to content or form. Ex-sistence means substantially the emerging into the truth of Being. *Existentia* (existence) means, however, *actualitas*, actuality in contrast to mere possibility as idea. Ex-sistence states the characteristic of man as he is in the destiny of truth. *Existentia* remains the name for the actualization of something-that-is, as an instance of its idea. The phrase, "man exists," does not answer the question of whether there are actually men or not; it answers the question of the "essence" of man. We usually put this question in an equally unsuitable way, whether we ask what man is or who he is. For, in the Who or What we are already on the lookout for something like a person or an object. Yet the personal, no less than the objective, misses and obstructs at the same time all that is essentially ex-sistence in its historical Being. Therefore, the quoted phrase in *Sein und Zeit* (p. 42) deliberately puts the word "essence" in quotation marks. This indicates that the "essence" is not now determined either from the *esse essentiae* or from the *esse existentiae*,[1] but from the ec-static nature of "being-there." Insofar as he ex-sists, man endures the "being-there" by taking the There as the clearing of Being within his "care." The *Dasein* itself, however, is essentially the "thrown" (*geworfene*). It is essentially in the cast (*Wurf*) of Being, a destiny that destines, projects a destiny.[2]

* * *

Sartre formulates, on the other hand, the basic principle of existentialism as this: existence precedes essence, whereby he understands *existentia* and *essentia* in the sense of metaphysics, which since Plato has said *essentia* precedes

---

1. The being of essence or the being of existence (Latin).

2. *Being and Time* contains no hint of this construal of *Geworfenheit* (thrownness).

existentia. Sartre reverses this phrasing. But the reversal of a metaphysical phrase remains a metaphysical phrase. As such it remains with metaphysics in the oblivion of the truth of Being. * * *

Sartre's key phrase on the superiority of *existentia* over *essentia* undoubtedly justifies the name "existentialism" as a suitable title for this philosophy. But the key phrase of "existentialism" has not the least thing in common with the same phrase in *Sein und Zeit;* apart from the fact that in *Sein und Zeit* a phrase about the relationship between *essentia* and *existentia* cannot yet be expressed, for there we are concerned with settling something preliminary. This, as can be seen from what has been said, is done there rather clumsily. What is yet to be said today might, perhaps, become an impulse to guide the essence of man to attend in thought to the dimension of the truth of Being, which pervades it. Yet even this can only happen for the dignity of Being and for the benefit of *Dasein* which man endures in existing; not for the sake of man, but that through his works civilization and culture may be vindicated.

* * *

Man is rather "cast" by Being itself into the truth of Being,[3] in order that he, ex-sisting thus, may guard the truth of Being; in order that in the light of Being, beings as beings may appear as what it is. Whether and how it appears, whether and how God and the gods, history and nature, enter, presenting and absenting themselves in the clearing of Being, is not determined by man. The advent of beings rests in the destiny of Being. For man, however, the question remains whether he finds what is appropriate to his essence to correspond to his destiny; according to this, as an ex-sisting person, he has to guard the truth of Being. Man is the guardian of Being. The thinking in *Sein und Zeit* proceeds towards this, when ecstatic existence only is experienced as "care" (cf. §44a, p. 226 ff.).

Yet Being—what is Being? It is Itself. Future thought must learn to experience and to express this. "Being" is neither God nor the basis of the world. Being is further from all that is being and yet closer to man than every being, be it a rock, an animal, a work of art, a machine, be it an angel or God. Being is the closest. Yet its closeness remains farthest from man. Man first clings always and only to beings. But when thought represents beings as beings it no doubt refers to Being. Yet, in fact, it always thinks only of beings as such and never of Being as such. The "question of Being" always remains the question of beings.

* * *

Or to proceed in more straightforward fashion perhaps: What relation has Being to ex-sistence? Being itself is the relationship, insofar as It retains and reunites ex-sistence in its existential (i.e. ecstatic) essence—as the place of the truth of Being amidst the beings. Since man as an existing one comes to stand in this relationship which Being itself professes to be, insofar as he, man, ecstatically stands (*aussteht*) it, i.e. insofar as he, caring, takes over, he fails to recognize at first the closest and clings to the next closest. He even believes that this is the closest. Yet closer than the closest and at the same

---

3. An elaboration of the (re-)interpretation of the "thrownness" of Dasein (human reality) that Heidegger announced several paragraphs above.

time, for ordinary thought, farther than his farthest is closeness itself: the truth of Being.

The oblivion of the truth of Being under the impact of beings, which is not considered in its essence, is the sense of "decadence"[4] in *Sein und Zeit*. This word does not signify the fall of man, understood as in a "moral philosophy" that has been secularized; this word states an essential relationship between man and Being within the relation of Being to man's essence. In view of this, the terms "authenticity" and "un-authenticity" (*Eigentlichkeit und Uneigentlichkeit*) do not signify a moral-existential or an "anthropological" distinction, but the "ecstatic" relation of man's essence to the truth of Being, which is still to be realized and up to now has remained concealed from philosophy. But this relation, such as it is, does not derive from ex-sistence, but the essence of ex-sistence derives existential-ecstatically from the essence of the truth of Being.

The unique thought that *Sein und Zeit* attempts to express, wants to achieve, is something simple. As such, Being remains mysterious, the plain closeness of an unobtrusive rule. This closeness is essentially language itself. Yet the language is not merely language, insofar as we imagine it at the most as the unity of sound-form (script), melody and rhythm and meaning. We think of sound-form and script as the body of the word; of melody and rhythm as the soul and of meaning as the mind of language. We generally think of language as corresponding to the essence of man, insofar as this essence is represented as *animal rationale*, i.e. as the unity of body-soul-mind. But as in the *humanitas* of the *homo animalis* ex-sistence remains concealed and through this the relation of the truth of Being to man, so does the metaphysical-animal interpretation of language conceal its essence from the point of view of the history of Being. According to this, language is the house of Being, owned and pervaded by Being. Therefore, the point is to think of the essence of language in its correspondence to Being and, what is more, as this very correspondence, i.e., the dwelling of man's essence.

Man, however, is not only a living being, who besides other faculties possesses language. Language is rather the house of Being, wherein living, man ex-sists, while he, guarding it, belongs to the truth of Being.

Thus, what matters in the determination of the humanity of man as ex-sistence is not that man is the essential, but that Being is the essential as the dimension of the ecstatic of ex-sistence. This, however, is not the spatial dimension. All that is spatial and all time-space is essentially dimensional, which is what Being itself is.

* * *

In view of the essential homelessness[5] of man the thought of the history of Being demonstrates the future destiny of man in that he investigates the truth of Being and sets out toward its discovery. Each nationalism is metaphysically an anthropologism and as such subjectivism. Nationalism is not overcome by mere internationalism, but only expanded and elevated to a system. Nationalism is far from being annulled by it or brought to *humanitas*, as

---

4. A complete mistranslation of *Verfallen*, which in *Being and Time* is best rendered as "falling-proneness" and understood as the tendency to "fall" into absorption in and preoccupation with the things and events and common expectations of everyday human life.

5. That is, "uncanniness" (*unheimlichkeit*). In *Being and Time* this term is used to convey the idea of a kind of "not-at-home-ness" or "out-of-place-ness" ("weirdness") in relation to the settled character of the world of everyday life. Here that idea is given a more radical turn.

individualism is by historical collectivism. This is the subjectivity of man in totality. He realizes its absolute self-assertion. This cannot be canceled. It cannot even be sufficiently experienced by one-sided thinking that tries to mediate. Everywhere man, thrust out from the truth of Being, runs around in a circle as the *animal rationale.*

The essence of man, however, consists of being more than mere man, insofar as this mere man is represented as a rational animal. "More" must not be understood here in an additive sense, as if the traditional definition of man were to remain as the basic definition, in order to undergo an expansion through an addition of the existential. The "more" means: more original and, therefore, in essence more essential. But here the mysterious is manifest: man is in his throwness (*Geworfenheit*). This means that man is as the ex-sisting counter-throw (*Gegenwurf*) of Being even more than the *animal rationale,* insofar as he is less related to the man who is conceived from subjectivity. Man is not the master of beings. Man is the shepherd of Being.[6] In this "less" man does not suffer any loss, but gains, because he comes into the truth of Being. He gains the essential poverty of the shepherd whose dignity rests in the fact that he was called by Being itself into the trueness of his truth. This call comes as the throw, from which stems the throwness of the *Da-sein.* Man is in his essence (from the point of view of the history of Being) that being whose Being as ex-sistence consists of dwelling in the nearness of Being. Man is the neighbor of Being.

But no doubt, you have wanted to reply for some time now, does not such thinking think precisely of the *humanitas* of the *homo humanus*? Does it not think of this *humanitas* in such a decisive meaning as no metaphysics has thought or even can think of it? Is not this "humanism" in an extreme sense? Certainly. It is the humanism that thinks of the humanity of man from the nearness to Being. But it is at the same time the humanism for which not man, but the historical essence of man in his derivation from the truth of Being, is playing. But does not the ex-sistence of man then stand and fall in this game at the same time? Indeed, it does.

* * *

* * * The essence of man rests in ex-sistence. This essence desires from Being itself, insofar as Being raises man as the ex-sisting one for the guardianship of the truth of Being. "Humanism" means now, should we decide to retain the word: the essence of man is essential for the truth of Being, and apart from this truth of Being man himself does not matter. So we think of a "humanism" of a strange sort. The word offers a term which is a *lucus a non lucendo.*[7]

Should one still call "humanism" this view which speaks out against all earlier humanism, but which does not at all advocate the in-human? And this

6. This thought is of great significance to the Heidegger of 1947 (and thereafter), and goes to the heart of what was either a major modification or a major extension of the analysis of human reality's kind of being—*Dasein*—in *Being and Time*.
7. Literally, "a dark grove from not shining" (Latin): that is, a term whose meaning contradicts that of the root from which it appears to derive. Heidegger is here suggesting a conception of "humanism"—if it is not to be abandoned

altogether—that is radically different from its usual understanding (i.e., as the idea that humanity matters intrinsically and is what matters most). Humanity "matters," for the Heidegger of 1947, *only* in connection with "the truth of Being" and its coming to light, and *only* insofar as and to the extent that humanity does what it is capable of doing in that connection. And the same would appear to apply with respect to any idea of authenticity.

only in order to swim perhaps in the dominant currents, which are stifled in a metaphysical subjectivism and find themselves drowned in the oblivion of Being? Or should thought, resisting the word "humanism," make an effort to become more attentive to the *humanitas* of the *homo humanus* and what grounds this *humanitas*? So, if the world-historical moment has not already gone that far itself, a reflection might be awakened that would not only think of man, but of the "nature" of man, and even more than this of his nature, the original dimension in which the essence of man, determined as coming from Being itself, is at home.

* * *

* * * If thought, considering the truth of Being, determines the essence of the *humanitas* as ex-sistence from its pertinence to Being, does this thought only remain a theoretical imagining of Being and of man, or is it possible to extract from knowledge directives for action and put them to use for life?

The answer is that such thinking is neither theoretical nor practical. It occurs before such a differentiation. This thinking is, insofar as it is, the recollection of Being and nothing else.[8] Belonging to Being, because it is thrown by being into the trueness of its truth and claims for it, it thinks Being. Such thinking results in nothing. It has no effect. It suffices its own essence, in that it is. But it is, in that it expresses its matter. At each epoch of history one thing only is important to it: that it be in accord with its matter. Its material relevance is essentially superior to the validity of science [*Wissenschaft*], because it is freer. For it lets Being—be.

Thinking works at building the house of Being; in which house Being joins and as such the joining of Being enjoins that man, according to destiny, dwell in the truth of Being. This dwelling is the essence of "Being-in-the-world" (cf. *Sein und Zeit*). The reference there to the "in-Being" (*In-Sein*) as "dwelling" is no etymological game. The reference in the essay of 1936 to Hölderlin's phrase, "Laboring, yet poetically man dwells on this earth"[9] is no mere gilding of a thought that abandoning science [*Wissenschaft*], takes refuge in poetry. To talk of the house of Being is not to transfer the image of "house" to Being, but from the materially understood essence of Being we shall some day be more easily able to think what "house" and "dwelling" are.

Nonetheless, thought never creates the house of Being. Thought accompanies historical existence, i.e., the *humanitas* of the *homo humanus*, to the domain where grace arises.

With grace, evil appears in the clearing of Being. The essence of evil does not consist in pure wickedness of human action, but in the malice of anger. Both grace and anger can, however, essentially only be in Being, insofar as Being itself is what is disputed.

* * *

8. This remarkable sentence would appear to signal the replacement of anything like the analysis and comprehension of human reality, which was the focus of *Being and Time*, by "the recollection of Being" as the focus of Heidegger's thought at this point.
9. Better translated as "Fully worthy, yet

poetically . . ."; quoted from "In lovely blueness . . . ," a late poem by Friedrich Hölderlin (1770–1843), a brilliant German lyric poet who by his mid-30s was completely insane and in whom Heidegger developed a great interest. Heidegger's essay of 1936 is "Hölderlin and the Essence of Poetry."

Only Being lends to grace the ascent to graciousness and to anger the push toward disgrace.

Only so far as man, ex-sisting in the truth of Being, belongs to it, can the assigning of all the directions which must become for man law and rule, come from Being itself. The verb "assign" in Greek is νέμειν.[1] The νόμος is not only law, but more originally the assigning concealed in the destiny of Being. Only this is capable of ordering man in Being. Only such ordering is capable of bearing up and binding. Otherwise, all law remains but the handiwork of human reason. More essential than any establishment of rule is the abode in the truth of Being. Only this abode yields the experience of the tenable (*das Haltbare*). The hold (*Halt*) for all behavior (*Verhalten*) is given by the truth of Being. "Hold" in our language means "shelter." Being is the shelter that in view of its own truth shelters man in his ex-sisting essence in such a way that it lodges ex-sistence in language. Thus language is at once the house of Being and the dwelling of human beings. Only because language is the dwelling of the essence of man, can the historical ways of mankind and men not be at home in their language, so that for them it becomes the shell of their machinations.

In what relationship now does the thought of Being stand to theoretical and practical behavior? It is superior to all contemplation, because it cares for the light in which only a seeing as theory can abide and move. Thought attends to the clearing of Being by putting its speaking of Being into language as the dwelling of existence. Thus thought is an action. But an action that is superior at the same time to all practice. Thinking surpasses doing and producing, not through the magnitude of its performance, nor through the consequences of its activity, but through the humbleness of the achievement that it accomplishes without result.

Thinking, as you know, brings into language in its saying only the unspoken word of Being.

The expression used here, "to bring into language," is now to be taken quite literally. Being, clearing itself, comes into language. It is always on its way towards it. As it arrives, it in its turn brings ex-sisting thought to language in its telling, which is thus elevated into the clearing of Being. Only thus, language *is* in its mysterious and yet humanly pervasive way. Insofar as language, thus brought fully into its essence, is historical, Being is preserved in remembering. Ex-sistence inhabits as it thinks the house of Being. In all this, it is as if nothing had happened at all through the utterance of thought.

But we have just seen an example of this insignificant act of thinking. For while we specifically think the expression "to bring to language," which was given to language, only this and nothing else, and while we retain in the observance of speaking what we have thought as something that always has-to-be-thought in the future, we have ourselves brought something essential of Being into language.

* * *

* * * Thought, in its essence as thought of Being, is claimed by it. Thought is related to Being as the arriving (*l'avenant*[2]). Thought is as thought in the

---

1. Also "to divide," "to distribute," "to manage" (*nemein*); the verb shares its root with *nomos* (custom; law).

2. French (the usual meaning of *avenant* is "gracious, pleasant").

advent of Being, is bound to Being as arrival. Being has already destined itself to thought. Being *is* as the destiny of thought. The destiny, however, is in itself historical. Its history has already arrived at language in the speaking of thinkers.

To express over and over again the advent of Being, permanent and in its permanence waiting for man, is the only matter for thought. That is why the essential thinkers always say the same thing. But that does not mean: the like.[3] Yet they say this only to the one who undertakes to follow their thought. While thought, remembering historically, attends to the destiny of Being, it has already bound itself to what is according to destiny. To escape into the like is not dangerous. To venture into discord in order to say the same thing, that is the danger. Ambiguity and mere quibbling threaten.

That the speaking of Being can become the destiny of truth is the first law of thought and not the rules of logic, which can become rules only through the law of Being. To attend to the destiny of the thinking-speaking does not only include our recollecting each time *what* is to be said about Being and *how* it is to be said. It remains equally essential to consider *whether* that which has-to-be-thought may be said, to what extent, at what moment in the history of Being, in what dialogue with it, and with what claim. That threefold thing, mentioned in a previous letter, is determined in the interdependence of its parts by the law of the destiny or historical thought of Being: the rigor of reflection, the carefulness of speaking, the economy of the word.

It is about time to get rid of the habit of overestimating philosophy and thereby asking too much of it. It is necessary in the present plight of the world that there be less philosophy, but more attention to thought; less literature, but more cultivation of the letter.

Future thought[4] is no longer philosophy, because it thinks more originally than metaphysics. But neither can future thought, as Hegel demanded, lay aside the name "love of wisdom" and become wisdom itself in the form of absolute knowledge.[5] Thought is on its descent to the poverty of its provisional essence. Thought gathers language in simple speech. Language is thus the language of Being, as the clouds are the clouds of the sky. Thought by its speaking traces insignificant furrows in language. They seem even more insignificant than the furrows the peasant with deliberate steps traces in the field.

SOURCE: From Martin Heidegger, "Letter on Humanism," trans. Edgar Lohner, in *Philosophy in the Twentieth Century: An Anthology*, edited by William Barrett and Henry D. Aiken (New York: Random House, 1962), 3:270–83, 288–91, 298, 300–302. Except where otherwise indicated, German words in brackets are the terminology used in the German original, inserted by the editor in addition to their renderings in the translation. This essay began as a long letter (*Brief*) written by Heidegger in 1946, after Jean Beaufret, a French philosopher-colleague in Paris, asked Heidegger to respond to some questions relating to "humanism" and "existentialism" prompted by a public lecture given earlier that year by JEAN-PAUL SARTRE. Attempting to explain what "existentialism" was all about, Sartre had argued that it was a kind of "humanism" (see the first of the Sartre selections below). Heidegger published an expanded version of his letter under the title "Brief über den 'Humanismus'" (1947, "Letter on 'Humanism'"); it is commonly referred to as his "Humanismusbrief."

3. That is, the similar.
4. That is, the "thought" that Heidegger takes himself to be inaugurating.

5. Hegel makes this demand in the preface to and conclusion of his *Phenomenology of Geist* (1807; see above).

Building Dwelling Thinking

In what follows we shall try to think about dwelling [*Wohnen*] and building [*Bauen*]. This thinking [*Denken*] about building does not presume to discover architectural ideas, let alone to give rules for building. This venture in thought does not view building as an art or as a technique of construction; rather it traces building back into that domain to which everything that *is* belongs. We ask:

1. What is it to dwell?
2. How does building belong to dwelling?

I

We attain to dwelling, so it seems, only by means of building. The latter, building, has the former, dwelling, as its goal. Still, not every building is a dwelling. Bridges and hangars, stadiums and power stations are buildings but not dwellings; railway stations and highways, dams and market halls are built, but they are not dwelling places. Even so, these buildings are in the domain of our dwelling. That domain extends over these buildings and yet is not limited to the dwelling place. The truck driver is at home on the highway, but he does not have his shelter there; the working woman is at home in the spinning mill, but does not have her dwelling place there; the chief engineer is at home in the power station, but he does not dwell there. These buildings house man. He inhabits them and yet does not dwell in them, when to dwell means merely that we take shelter in them. In today's housing shortage[1] even this much is reassuring and to the good; residential buildings do indeed provide shelter; today's houses may even be well planned, easy to keep, attractively cheap, open to air, light, and sun, but—do the houses in themselves hold any guarantee that *dwelling* occurs in them? Yet those buildings that are not dwelling places remain in turn determined by dwelling insofar as they serve man's dwelling. Thus dwelling would in any case be the end that presides over all building. Dwelling and building are related as end and means. However, as long as this is all we have in mind, we take dwelling and building as two separate activities, an idea that has something correct in it. Yet at the same time by the means-end schema we block our view of the essential relations. For building is not merely a means and a way toward dwelling—to build is in itself already to dwell. Who tells us this? Who gives us a standard at all by which we can take the measure of the nature of dwelling and building?

It is language that tells us about the nature of a thing,[2] provided that we respect language's own nature. In the meantime, to be sure, there rages round the earth an unbridled yet clever talking, writing, and broadcasting of spoken words. Man acts as though *he* were the shaper and master of language, while in fact *language* remains the master of man. Perhaps it is before all else man's subversion of *this* relation of dominance that drives his nature into alienation. That we retain a concern for care in speaking is all to the good,

---

1. The destruction inflicted during the Second World War left Germany with an acute housing shortage, which the symposium was held to address.

2. This statement, along with his reliance on language, etymology, and even mythology in the following discussion, shows how far the later Heidegger departed from HUSSERL.

but it is of no help to us as long as language still serves us even then only as a means of expression. Among all the appeals that we human beings, on our part, can help to be voiced, language is the highest and everywhere the first.

What, then, does *Bauen*, building, *mean*? The Old English and High German word for building, *buan*, means to dwell. This signifies: to remain, to stay in a place. The real meaning of the verb *bauen*, namely, to dwell, has been lost to us. But a covert trace of it has been preserved in the German word *Nachbar*, neighbor. The neighbor is in Old English the *neahgebur*; *neah*, near, and *gebur*, dweller. The Nachbar is the *Nachgebur*, the *Nachgebauer*, the near-dweller, he who dwells nearby. The verbs *buri, büren, beuren, beuron*, all signify dwelling, the abode, the place of dwelling. Now to be sure the old word *buan* not only tells us that *bauen*, to build, is really to dwell; it also gives us a clue as to how we have to think about the dwelling it signifies. When we speak of dwelling we usually think of an activity that man performs alongside many other activities. We work here and dwell there. We do not merely dwell—that would be virtual inactivity—we practice a profession, we do business, we travel and lodge on the way, now here, now there. *Bauen* originally means to dwell. Where the word *bauen* still speaks in its original sense it also says *how far* the nature of dwelling reaches. That is, *bauen, buan, bhu, beo* are our word *bin* in the versions: *ich bin*, I am, *du bist*, you are, the imperative form *bis*, be. What then does *ich bin* mean? The old word *bauen*, to which the *bin* belongs, answers: *ich bin, du bist* mean: I dwell, you dwell. The way in which you are and I am, the manner in which we humans *are* on the earth, is *Buan*, dwelling. To be a human being means to be on the earth as a mortal. It means to dwell. The old word *bauen*, which says that man *is* insofar as he *dwells*, this word *bauen* however *also* means at the same time to cherish and protect, to preserve and care for, specifically to till the soil, to cultivate the vine. Such building only takes care—it tends the growth that ripens into its fruit of its own accord. Building in the sense of preserving and nurturing is not making anything. Shipbuilding and temple-building, on the other hand, do in a certain way make their own works. Here building, in contrast with cultivating, is a constructing. Both modes of building—building as cultivating, Latin *colere, cultura*,[3] and building as the raising up of edifices, *aedificare*—are comprised within genuine building, that is, dwelling. Building as dwelling, that is, as being on the earth, however, remains for man's everyday experience that which is from the outset "habitual"—we inhabit it, as our language says so beautifully: it is the *Gewohnte*. For this reason it recedes behind the manifold ways in which dwelling is accomplished, the activities of cultivation and construction. These activities later claim the name of *bauen*, building, and with it the fact of building, exclusively for themselves. The real sense of *bauen*, namely dwelling, falls into oblivion.

At first sight this event looks as though it were no more than a change of meaning of mere terms. In truth, however, something decisive is concealed in it, namely, dwelling is not experienced as man's being; dwelling is never thought of as the basic character of human being.

That language in a way retracts the real meaning of the word *bauen*, which is dwelling, is evidence of the primal nature of these meanings; for with the

---

3. To cultivate or dwell, cultivation.

essential words of language, their true meaning easily falls into oblivion in favor of foreground meanings. Man has hardly yet pondered the mystery of this process. Language withdraws from man its simple and high speech. But its primal call does not thereby become incapable of speech; it merely falls silent. Man, though, fails to heed this silence.

But if we listen to what language says in the word *bauen* we hear three things:

1. Building is really dwelling.
2. Dwelling is the manner in which mortals are on the earth.
3. Building as dwelling unfolds into the building that cultivates growing things and the building that erects buildings.

If we give thought to this threefold fact, we obtain a clue and note the following: as long as we do not bear in mind that all building is in itself a dwelling, we cannot even adequately *ask*, let alone properly decide, what the building of buildings might be in its nature. We do not dwell because we have built, but we build and have built because we dwell, that is, because we are *dwellers*. But in what does the nature of dwelling consist? Let us listen once more to what language says to us. The Old Saxon *wuon*, the Gothic *wunian*, like the old word *bauen*, mean to remain, to stay in a place. But the Gothic *wunian* says more distinctly how this remaining is experienced. *Wunian* means: to be at peace, to be brought to peace, to remain in peace. The word for peace, *Friede*, means the free, *das Frye*, and *fry* means: preserved from harm and danger, preserved from something, safeguarded. To free really means to spare. The sparing itself consists not only in the fact that we do not harm the one whom we spare. Real sparing is something *positive* and takes place when we leave something beforehand in its own nature, when we return it specifically to its being, when we "free" it in the real sense of the word into a preserve of peace. To dwell, to be set at peace, means to remain at peace within the free, the preserve, the free sphere that safeguards each thing in its nature. *The fundamental character of dwelling is this sparing and preserving.* It pervades dwelling in its whole range. That range reveals itself to us as soon as we reflect that human being consists in dwelling and, indeed, dwelling in the sense of the stay of mortals on the earth.

But "on the earth" already means "under the sky." Both of these *also* mean "remaining before the divinities" and include a "belonging to men's being with one another." By a *primal* oneness the four—earth and sky, divinities and mortals—belong together in one.

Earth is the serving bearer, blossoming and fruiting, spreading out in rock and water, rising up into plant and animal. When we say earth, we are already thinking of the other three along with it, but we give no thought to the simple oneness of the four.

The sky is the vaulting path of the sun, the course of the changing moon, the wandering glitter of the stars, the year's seasons and their changes, the light and dusk of day, the gloom and glow of night, the clemency and inclemency of the weather, the drifting clouds and blue depth of the ether. When we say sky, we are already thinking of the other three along with it, but we give no thought to the simple oneness of the four.

The divinities are the beckoning messengers of the godhead. Out of the holy sway of the godhead, the god appears in his presence or withdraws into his concealment. When we speak of the divinities, we are already thinking of the other three along with them, but we give no thought to the simple oneness of the four.

The mortals are the human beings. They are called mortals because they can die. To die means to be capable of death *as* death. Only man dies,[4] and indeed continually, as long as he remains on earth, under the sky, before the divinities. When we speak of mortals, we are already thinking of the other three along with them, but we give no thought to the simple oneness of the four.

This simple oneness of the four we call *the fourfold*.[5] Mortals *are* in the fourfold by *dwelling*. But the basic character of dwelling is to spare, to preserve. Mortals dwell in the way they preserve the fourfold in its essential being, its presencing. Accordingly, the preserving that dwells is fourfold.

Mortals dwell in that they save the earth—taking the word in the old sense still known to Lessing.[6] Saving does not only snatch something from a danger. To save really means to set something free into its own presencing. To save the earth is more than to exploit it or even wear it out. Saving the earth does not master the earth and does not subjugate it, which is merely one step from spoliation.[7]

Mortals dwell in that they receive the sky as sky. They leave to the sun and the moon their journey, to the stars their courses, to the seasons their blessing and their inclemency; they do not turn night into day nor day into a harassed unrest.

Mortals dwell in that they await the divinities as divinities. In hope they hold up to the divinities what is unhoped for. They wait for intimations of their coming and do not mistake the signs of their absence. They do not make their gods for themselves and do not worship idols. In the very depth of misfortune they wait for the weal that has been withdrawn.[8]

Mortals dwell in that they initiate their own nature—their being capable of death as death—into the use and practice of this capacity, so that there may be a good death. To initiate mortals into the nature of death in no way means to make death, as empty Nothing, the goal. Nor does it mean to darken dwelling by blindly staring toward the end.

In saving the earth, in receiving the sky, in awaiting the divinities, in initiating mortals, dwelling occurs as the fourfold preservation of the fourfold. To spare and preserve means: to take under our care, to look after the fourfold in its presencing. What we take under our care must be kept safe. But if dwelling preserves the fourfold, where does it keep the fourfold's nature? How do mortals make their dwelling such a preserving? Mortals would never be capable of it if dwelling were merely a staying on earth under the sky, before the

---

4. That is, lives in being-toward-death.
5. This concept of "the fourfold" takes on increasing importance in the thinking of the later Heidegger.
6. Gotthold Ephraim Lessing (1729–1781), German dramatist, critic, and philosopher.
7. Better translated as "merely one step from unlimited exploitation" (*nur ein Schritt ist zur schrankenlosen Ausbeutung*).
8. More accurately translated: "In misery they await the withdrawn *Heil*" (*Im Unheil noch warten sie des entzogenen Heils*). Though today (as it surely did in Germany in 1951) *Heil* evokes the Nazi salute, the word has a long and rich history, to which Heidegger was undoubtedly seeking to return it. It is related to the words for "holy" and "healing," and has a meaning that combines "well-being" and "salvation." *Unheil* is its opposite; its meaning combines "misfortune," "misery" and "distress," with overtones of damnation.

divinities, among mortals. Rather, dwelling itself is always a staying with things. Dwelling, as preserving, keeps the fourfold in that with which mortals stay: in things.

Staying with things, however, is not merely something attached to this fourfold preserving as a fifth something. On the contrary: staying with things is the only way in which the fourfold stay within the fourfold is accomplished at any time in simple unity. Dwelling preserves the fourfold by bringing the presencing of the fourfold into things. But things themselves secure the fourfold *only when* they themselves *as* things are let be in their presencing. How is this done? In this way, that mortals nurse and nurture the things that grow, and specially construct things that do not grow. Cultivating and construction are building in the narrower sense. *Dwelling*, insofar as it keeps or secures the fourfold in things, is, as this keeping, *a building*. With this, we are on our way to the second question.

II

In what way does building belong to dwelling?

The answer to this question will clarify for us what building, understood by way of the nature of dwelling, really is. We limit ourselves to building in the sense of constructing things and inquire: what is a built thing? A bridge may serve as an example for our reflections.[9]

The bridge swings over the stream "with ease and power." It does not just connect banks that are already there. The banks emerge as banks only as the bridge crosses the stream. The bridge designedly causes them to lie across from each other. One side is set off against the other by the bridge. Nor do the banks stretch along the stream as indifferent border strips of the dry land. With the banks, the bridge brings to the stream the one and the other expanse of the landscape lying behind them. It brings stream and bank and land into each other's neighborhood. The bridge *gathers* the earth as landscape around the stream. Thus it guides and attends the stream through the meadows. Resting upright in the stream's bed, the bridge-piers bear the swing of the arches that leave the stream's waters to run their course. The waters may wander on quiet and gay, the sky's floods from storm or thaw may shoot past the piers in torrential waves—the bridge is ready for the sky's weather and its fickle nature. Even where the bridge covers the stream, it holds its flow up to the sky by taking it for a moment under the vaulted gateway and then setting it free once more.

The bridge lets the stream run its course and at the same time grants their way to mortals so that they may come and go from shore to shore. Bridges lead in many ways. The city bridge leads from the precincts of the castle to the cathedral square; the river bridge near the country town brings wagons and horse teams to the surrounding villages. The old stone bridge's humble brook crossing gives to the harvest wagon its passage from the fields into the

9. What follows is a classic example of the late Heidegger's version of something like phenomenology. It shares with Husserlian and early Heideggerian versions its implicit but emphatic rejection of the idea that what is being described has—or even could have—any more objective (e.g., natural-scientific or metaphysical) redescription that would get any closer to the real truth or "meaning" of the matter, with respect both to the entities mentioned and to ourselves.

village and carries the lumber cart from the field path to the road. The high-way bridge is tied into the network of long-distance traffic, paced as calculated for maximum yield. Always and ever differently the bridge escorts the lingering and hastening ways of men to and fro, so that they may get to other banks and in the end, as mortals, to the other side. Now in a high arch, now in a low, the bridge vaults over glen and stream—whether mortals keep in mind this vaulting of the bridge's course or forget that they, always themselves on their way to the last bridge, are actually striving to surmount all that is common and unsound in them in order to bring themselves before the haleness of the divinities. The bridge *gathers*, as a passage that crosses, before the divinities—whether we explicitly think of, and visibly *give thanks for*, their presence, as in the figure of the saint of the bridge, or whether that divine presence is obstructed or even pushed wholly aside.

The bridge *gathers* to itself in *its own* way earth and sky, divinities and mortals.

Gathering or assembly, by an ancient word of our language, is called "thing [*Ding*]." The bridge is a thing—and, indeed, it is such *as* the gathering of the fourfold which we have described. To be sure, people think of the bridge as primarily and really *merely* a bridge; after that, and occasionally, it might possibly express much else besides; and as such an expression it would then become a symbol, for instance a symbol of those things we mentioned before. But the bridge, if it is a true bridge, is never first of all a mere bridge and then afterward a symbol. And just as little is the bridge in the first place exclusively a symbol, in the sense that it expresses something that strictly speaking does not belong to it. If we take the bridge strictly as such, it never appears as an expression. The bridge is a thing and *only that*. Only? As this thing it gathers the fourfold.

Our thinking has of course long been accustomed to *understate* the nature of the thing. The consequence, in the course of Western thought, has been that the thing is represented as an unknown X to which perceptible properties are attached. From this point of view, everything *that already belongs to the gathering nature of this thing* does, of course, appear as something that is afterward read into it. Yet the bridge would never be a mere bridge if it were not a thing.

To be sure, the bridge is a thing of its *own* kind; for it gathers the fourfold in *such* a way that it allows a *site* for it. But only something *that is itself a location* can make space for a site. The location is not already there before the bridge is. Before the bridge stands, there are of course many spots along the stream that can be occupied by something. One of them proves to be a location, and does so *because of the bridge*. Thus the bridge does not first come to a location to stand in it; rather, a location comes into existence only by virtue of the bridge. The bridge is a thing; it gathers the fourfold, but in such a way that it allows a site for the fourfold. By this site are determined the localities and ways by which a space is provided for.

Only things that are locations in this manner allow for spaces. What the word for space, *Raum*, *Rum*, designates is said by its ancient meaning. *Raum* means a place cleared or freed for settlement and lodging. A space is something that has been made room for, something that is cleared and free, namely within a boundary, Greek *peras*. A boundary is not that at which something stops but, as the Greeks recognized, the boundary is that from which something *begins its presencing*. That is why the concept is that of *horismos*, that is, the horizon,[1] the boundary. Space is in essence that for which room has been made, that which is let into its bounds. That for which room is made is always granted and hence is joined, that is, gathered, by virtue of a location, that is, by such a thing as the bridge. *Accordingly, spaces receive their being from locations and not from "space."*

Things which, as locations, allow a site we now in anticipation call buildings. They are so called because they are made by a process of building construction. Of what sort this making—building—must be, however, we find out only after we have first given thought to the nature of those things which of themselves require building as the process by which they are made. These things are locations that allow a site for the fourfold, a site that in each case provides for a space. The relation between location and space lies in the nature of these things *qua* locations, but so does the relation of the location to the man who lives at that location. Therefore we shall now try to clarify the nature of these things that we call buildings by the following brief consideration.

For one thing, what is the relation between location and space? For another, what is the relation between man and space?

The bridge is a location. As such a thing, it allows a space into which earth and heaven, divinities and mortals are admitted. The space allowed by the bridge contains many places variously near or far from the bridge. These places, however, may be treated as mere positions between which there lies a measurable distance; a distance, in Greek *stadion*, always has room made for it, and indeed by bare positions. The space that is thus made by positions is space of a peculiar sort. As distance or "stadion" it is what the same word, *stadion*, means in Latin, a *spatium*, an intervening space or interval. Thus nearness and remoteness between men and things can become mere distance, mere intervals of intervening space. In a space that is represented purely as *spatium*, the bridge now appears as a mere something at some position, which can be occupied at any time by something else or replaced by a mere marker. What is more, the mere dimensions of height, breadth, and depth can be abstracted from space as intervals. What is so abstracted we represent as the pure manifold of the three dimensions. Yet the room made by this manifold is also no longer determined by distances; it is no longer a *spatium*, but now no more than *extensio*—extension. But from space as *extensio* a further abstraction can be made, to analytic-algebraic relations. What these relations make room for is the possibility of the purely mathematical construction of manifolds with an arbitrary number of dimensions. The space provided for in this mathematical manner may be called "space," the "one" space as such. But in this sense "the" space, "space," contains no spaces and no places. We never find in it any locations, that is, things of the kind the bridge is. As against that, however, in the spaces provided for by locations there is always space as interval, and in this interval in turn there is space as pure extension. *Spatium* and *extensio* afford at any time the possibility of measuring things and what they make room for, according to distances, spans, and directions, and

---

1. *Horismos* (limitation, boundary) does not mean "horizon," though the words share the same root. (For the late Heidegger, this is sufficient to suggest a deep connection.)

of computing these magnitudes. But the fact that they are *universally* applicable to everything that has extension can in no case make numerical magnitudes the *ground* of the nature of spaces and locations that are measurable with the aid of mathematics. How even modern physics was compelled by the facts themselves to represent the spatial medium of cosmic space as a field-unity determined by body as dynamic center, cannot be discussed here.

The spaces through which we go daily are provided for by locations; their nature is grounded in things of the type of buildings. If we pay heed to these relations between locations and spaces, between spaces and space, we get a clue to help us in thinking of the relation of man and space.

When we speak of man and space, it sounds as though man stood on one side, space on the other. Yet space is not something that faces man. It is neither an external object nor an inner experience. It is not that there are men, and over and above them *space*; for when I say "a man," and in saying this word think of a being who exists in a human manner—that is, who dwells—then by the name "man" I already name the stay within the fourfold among things. Even when we relate ourselves to those things that are not in our immediate reach, we are staying with the things themselves. We do not represent distant things merely in our mind—as the textbooks have it—so that only mental representations of distant things run through our minds and heads as substitutes for the things. If all of us now think, from where we are right here, of the old bridge in Heidelberg, this thinking toward that location is not a mere experience inside the persons present here; rather, it belongs to the nature of our thinking *of* that bridge that *in itself* thinking gets through, persists through, the distance to that location. From this spot right here, we are there at the bridge—we are by no means at some representational content in our consciousness. From right here we may even be much nearer to that bridge and to what it makes room for than someone who uses it daily as an indifferent river crossing. Spaces, and with them space as such—"space"—are always provided for already within the stay of mortals. Spaces open up by the fact that they are let into the dwelling of man. To say that mortals *are* is to say that *in dwelling* they persist through spaces by virtue of their stay among things and locations. And only because mortals pervade, persist through, spaces by their very nature are they able to go through spaces. But in going through spaces we do not give up our standing in them. Rather, we always go through spaces in such a way that we already experience them by staying constantly with near and remote locations and things. When I go toward the door of the lecture hall, I am already there, and I could not go to it at all if I were not such that I am there. I am never here only, as this encapsulated body; rather, I am there, that is, I already pervade the room, and only thus can I go through it.

Even when mortals turn "inward," taking stock of themselves, they do not leave behind their belonging to the fourfold. When, as we say, we come to our senses and reflect on ourselves, we come back to ourselves from things *without ever abandoning* our stay among things. Indeed, the loss of rapport with things that occurs in states of depression would be wholly impossible if even such a state were not still what it is as a human state: that is, a staying *with* things. Only if this stay already characterizes human being can the things among which we are also *fail* to speak to us, *fail* to concern us any longer.

Man's relation to locations, and through locations to spaces, inheres in his dwelling. The relationship between man and space is none other than dwelling, strictly thought and spoken.

When we think, in the manner just attempted, about the relation between location and space, but also about the relation of man and space, a light falls on the nature of the things that are locations and that we call buildings.

The bridge is a thing of this sort. The location allows the simple onefold of earth and sky, of divinities and mortals, to enter into a site by arranging the site into spaces. The location makes room for the fourfold in a double sense. The location *admits* the fourfold and it *installs* the fourfold. The two—making room in the sense of admitting and in the sense of installing—belong together. As a double space-making, the location is a shelter for the fourfold or, by the same token, a house. Things like such locations shelter or house men's lives. Things of this sort are housings, though not necessarily dwelling-houses in the narrower sense.

The making of such things is building. Its nature consists in this, that it corresponds to the character of these things. They are locations that allow spaces. This is why building, by virtue of constructing locations, is a founding and joining of spaces. Because building produces locations, the joining of the spaces of these locations necessarily brings with it space, as *spatium* and as *extensio*, into the thingly structure of buildings. But building never shapes pure "space" as a single entity. Neither directly nor indirectly. Nevertheless, because it produces things as locations, building is closer to the nature of spaces and to the origin of the nature of "space" than any geometry and mathematics. Building puts up locations that make space and a site for the fourfold. From the simple oneness in which earth and sky, divinities and mortals belong together, building *receives the directive* for its erecting of locations. Building *takes over* from the fourfold the standard for all the traversing and measuring of the spaces that in each case are provided for by the locations that have been founded. The edifices guard the fourfold. They are things that in their own way preserve the fourfold. To preserve the fourfold, to save the earth, to receive the sky, to await the divinities, to escort mortals—this fourfold preserving is the simple nature, the presencing, of dwelling.[2] In this way, then, do genuine buildings give form to dwelling in its presencing and house this presence.

Building thus characterized is a distinctive letting-dwell. Whenever it *is* such in fact, building already *has* responded to the summons of the fourfold. All planning remains grounded on this responding, and planning in turn opens up to the designer the precincts suitable for his designs.

As soon as we try to think of the nature of constructive building in terms of a letting-dwell, we come to know more clearly what that process of making consists in by which building is accomplished. Usually we take production to be an activity whose performance has a result, the finished structure, as its consequence. It is possible to conceive of making in that way; we thereby grasp something that is correct, and yet never touch its nature, which is a producing

---

2. This sentence can be taken as summarizing the "meaning" of human reality's kind of "being," and of its possible "authenticity"—which now would have the simple sense of "genuineness"—in the late Heidegger.

that brings something forth. For building brings the fourfold *hither* into a thing, the bridge, and brings *forth* the thing as a location, out into what is already there, room for which is only now made *by* this location.

The Greek for "to bring forth or to produce" is *tikto*. The word *techne*, technique, belongs to the verb's root *tec*. To the Greeks *techne* means neither art nor handicraft but rather: to make something appear, within what is present, as this or that, in this way or that way. The Greeks conceive of *techne*, producing, in terms of letting appear. *Techne* thus conceived has been concealed in the tectonics of architecture since ancient times. Of late it still remains concealed, and more resolutely, in the technology of power machinery. But the nature of the erecting of buildings cannot be understood adequately in terms either of architecture or of engineering construction, nor in terms of a mere combination of the two. The erecting of buildings would not be suitably defined *even if* we were to think of it in the sense of the original Greek *techne* as *solely* a letting-appear, which brings something made, as something present, among the things that are already present.

The nature of building is letting dwell. Building accomplishes its nature in the raising of locations by the joining of their spaces. *Only if we are capable of dwelling, only then can we build.* Let us think for a while of a farmhouse in the Black Forest, which was built some two hundred years ago by the dwelling of peasants. Here the self-sufficiency of the power to let earth and heaven, divinities and mortals enter *in simple oneness* into things, ordered the house. It placed the farm on the wind-sheltered mountain slope looking south, among the meadows close to the spring. It gave it the wide overhanging shingle roof whose proper slope bears up under the burden of snow, and which, reaching deep down, shields the chambers against the storms of the long winter nights. It did not forget the altar corner behind the community table; it made room in its chamber for the hallowed places of childbed and the "tree of the dead"— for that is what they call a coffin there: the *Totenbaum*—and in this way it designed for the different generations under one roof the character of their journey through time. A craft which, itself sprung from dwelling, still uses its tools and frames as things, built the farmhouse.

Only if we are capable of dwelling, only then can we build. Our reference to the Black Forest farm in no way means that we should or could go back to building such houses; rather, it illustrates by a dwelling that *has been* how *it* was able to build.

Dwelling, however, is *the basic character* of Being in keeping with which mortals exist. Perhaps this attempt to think about dwelling and building will bring out somewhat more clearly that building belongs to dwelling and how it receives its nature from dwelling. Enough will have been gained if dwelling and building have become *worthy of questioning* and thus have remained *worthy of thought*.

But that thinking itself belongs to dwelling in the same sense as building, although in a different way, may perhaps be attested to by the course of thought here attempted.

Building and thinking are, each in its own way, inescapable for dwelling. The two, however, are also insufficient for dwelling so long as each busies itself with its own affairs in separation instead of listening to one another. They are able to listen if both—building and thinking—belong to dwelling, if they remain within their limits and realize that the one as much as the other comes from the workshop of long experience and incessant practice.

We are attempting to trace in thought the nature of dwelling. The next step on this path would be the question: what is the state of dwelling in our precarious age? On all sides we hear talk about the housing shortage, and with good reason. Nor is there just talk; there is action too. We try to fill the need by providing houses, by promoting the building of houses, planning the whole architectural enterprise. However hard and bitter, however hampering and threatening the lack of houses remains, the *real plight of dwelling* does not lie merely in a lack of houses. The real plight of dwelling is indeed older than the world wars with their destruction, older also than the increase of the earth's population and the condition of the industrial workers. The real dwelling plight lies in this, that mortals ever search anew for the nature of dwelling, that they *must ever learn to dwell*. What if man's homelessness consisted in this, that man still does not even think of the *real* plight of dwelling as *the* plight? Yet as soon as man *gives thought* to his homelessness, it is a misery no longer. Rightly considered and kept well in mind, it is the sole summons that *calls* mortals into their dwelling.

But how else can mortals answer this summons than by trying on *their* part, on their own, to bring dwelling to the fullness of its nature? This they accomplish when they build out of dwelling, and think for the sake of dwelling.[3]

SOURCE: Martin Heidegger, *Poetry, Language, Thought*, trans. Albert Hofstadter (New York: Harper and Row, 1971), pp. 145–61. Except where otherwise indicated, German words in brackets are the terminology used in the German original, inserted by the editor in addition to their renderings in the translation. First a lecture presented at an architectural symposium (1951), "Bauen Wohnen Denken" was published in Heidegger's collection *Vorträge und Aufsätze* (1954, *Lectures and Articles*).

The End of Philosophy and the Task of Thinking

The title designates the attempt at a reflection which persists in questioning. The questions are paths to an answer. If the answer could be given, the answer would consist in a transformation of thinking, not in a propositional statement about a matter at stake.

The following text belongs to a larger context. It is the attempt undertaken again and again ever since 1930 to shape the question of Being and Time in a more primal way. This means: to subject the point of departure of the question in *Being and Time*[1] to an immanent criticism. Thus it must become clear to what extent the *critical* question of what the matter of thinking is, necessarily and continually belongs to thinking.[2] Accordingly, the name of the task of *Being and Time* will change.

3. This closing paragraph reiterates (in different but related imagery) Heidegger's characterization in the previous two selections of man as "the shepherd of Being" and of language as "the house of Being."
1. Published in 1927 (see above).
2. At this point, for Heidegger "thinking" (*Denken*) names the kind of activity that is to supersede "philosophy" as we have known it. His point is that although philosophy is approaching its end because it is increasingly and irreversibly dissolving into the modern array of forms of sophisticated, specialized, technologically minded scientific disciplines, there is still a need and a place for the different kind of thinking it initially tried to be (before it turned into "metaphysics")—a need that is now greater than ever.

We are asking:

1. What does it mean that philosophy in the present age has entered its final stage?
2. What task is reserved for thinking at the end of philosophy?

1. *What does it mean that philosophy in the present age has entered its final stage?*

Philosophy is metaphysics. Metaphysics thinks being as a whole—the world, man, God—with respect to Being, with respect to the belonging together of beings in Being. Metaphysics thinks beings as being in the manner of representational thinking which gives reasons. For since the beginning of philosophy and with that beginning, the Being of beings has showed itself as the ground (*arche, aition*[3]). The ground is from where beings as such are what they are in their becoming, perishing and persisting as something that can be known, handled and worked upon. As the ground, Being brings beings to their actual presencing. The ground shows itself as presence. The present of presence consists in the fact that it brings what is present each in its own way to presence. In accordance with the actual kind of presence, the ground has the character of grounding as the ontic causation of the real, as the transcendental making possible of the objectivity of objects, as the dialectical mediation of the movement of the absolute Spirit [*Geist*], of the historical process of production, as the will to power positing values.[4]

What characterizes metaphysical thinking which grounds the ground for beings is the fact that metaphysical thinking departs from what is present in its presence, and thus represents it in terms of its ground as something grounded.

What is meant by the talk about the end of philosophy? We understand the end of something all too easily in the negative sense as a mere stopping, as the lack of continuation, perhaps even as decline and impotence. In contrast, what we say about the end of philosophy means the completion of metaphysics. However, completion does not mean perfection as a consequence of which philosophy would have to have attained the highest perfection at its end. Not only do we lack any criterion which would permit us to evaluate the perfection of an epoch of metaphysics as compared with any other epoch. The right to this kind of evaluation does not exist. Plato's thinking is no more perfect than Parmenides.[5] Hegel's philosophy is no more perfect than Kant's.[6] Each epoch of philosophy has its own necessity. We simply have to acknowledge the fact that a philosophy is the way it is. It is not our business to prefer one to the other, as can be the case with regard to various *Weltanschauungen*.[7]

The old meaning of the word "end" means the same as place: "from one end to the other" means: from one place to the other. The end of philosophy is the place, that place in which the whole of philosophy's history is gathered in its most extreme possibility. End as completion means this gathering.

Throughout the whole history of philosophy, Plato's thinking remains decisive in changing forms. Metaphysics is Platonism. Nietszche characterizes

---

3. Beginning, cause (Greek).
4. Heidegger here is referring to Descartes, Kant, Hegel, Marx, and Nietzsche, respectively.
5. A leading pre-Socratic Greek philosopher (b. ca.

515 B.C.E.). Plato (ca. 427–ca. 347 B.C.E.): one of the most influential of all Greek philosophers.
6. For HEGEL and KANT, see above.
7. Worldviews (German).

his philosophy as reversed Platonism. With the reversal of metaphysics which was already accomplished by Karl Marx,[8] the most extreme possibility of philosophy is attained. It has entered its final stage. To the extent that philosophical thinking is still attempted, it manages only to attain an epigonal renaissance[9] and variations of that renaissance. Is not then the end of philosophy after all a cessation of its way of thinking? To conclude this would be premature.

As a completion, an end is the gathering into the most extreme possibilities. We think in too limited a fashion as long as we expect only a development of recent philosophies of the previous style. We forget that already in the age of Greek philosophy a decisive characteristic of philosophy appears: the development of sciences [Wissenschaften] within the field which philosophy opened up. The development of the sciences [Wissenschaften] is at the same time their separation from philosophy and the establishment of their independence. This process belongs to the completion of philosophy. Its development is in full swing today in all regions of beings. This development looks like the mere dissolution of philosophy, and is in truth its completion.

It suffices to refer to the independence of psychology, sociology, anthropology as cultural anthropology, to the role of logic as logistics and semantics. Philosophy turns into the empirical science of man, of all of what can become the experiential object of his technology for man, the technology by which he establishes himself in the world by working on it in the manifold modes of making and shaping. All of this happens everywhere on the basis and according to the criterion of the scientific [wissenschaftlich] discovery of the individual areas of beings.

No prophecy is necessary to recognize that the sciences now establishing themselves will soon be determined and guided by the new fundamental science [Wissenschaft] which is called cybernetics.

This science corresponds to the determination of man as an acting social being. For it is the theory of the steering of the possible planning and arrangement of human labor.[1] Cybernetics transforms language into an exchange of news. The arts become regulated-regulating instruments of information.

The development of philosophy into the independent sciences which, however, interdependently communicate among themselves ever more markedly, is the legitimate completion of philosophy. Philosophy is ending in the present age. It has found its place in the scientific [wissenschaftlich] attitude of socially active humanity. But the fundamental characteristic of this scientific attitude is its cybernetic, that is, technological character. The need to ask about modern technology is presumably dying out to the same extent that technology more definitely characterizes and regulates the appearance of the totality of the world and the position of man in it.

The sciences [Wissenschaften] will interpret everything in their structure that is still reminiscent of the origin from philosophy in accordance with the rules of science, that is, technologically. Every science understands the categories upon which it remains dependent for the articulation and delineation of its area of investigation as working hypotheses. Their truth is measured

8. For NIETZSCHE and MARX, see above.
9. That is, an inferior imitative revival of a superior original.

1. The root of the prefix cyber- is the Greek word meaning "to steer."

not only by the effect which their application brings about within the progress of research.

Scientific truth is equated with the efficiency of these effects.

The sciences are now taking over as their own task what philosophy in the course of its history tried to present in part, and even there only inadequately, that is, the ontologies of the various regions of beings (nature, history, law, art). The interest of the sciences is directed toward the theory of the necessary structural concepts of the coordinated areas of investigation. "Theory" means now: supposition of the categories which are allowed only a cybernetical function, but denied any ontological meaning. The operational and model character of representational-calculative thinking becomes dominant.

However, the sciences still speak about the Being of beings in the unavoidable supposition of their regional categories. They just don't say so. They can deny their origin from philosophy, but never dispense with it. For in the scientific attitude of the sciences, the document of their birth from philosophy still speaks.

The end of philosophy proves to be the triumph of the manipulable arrangement of a scientific-techological [*wissenschaftlich*-technological] world and of the social order proper to this world. The end of philosophy means: the beginning of the world civilization based upon Western European thinking.

But is the end of philosophy in the sense of its development to the sciences also already the complete realization of all the possibilities in which the thinking of philosophy was posited? Or is there a *first* possibility for thinking apart from the *last* possibility which we characterized (the dissolution of philosophy in the technologized sciences), a possibility from which the thinking of philosophy would have to start out, but which as philosophy it could nevertheless not experience and adopt?

If this were the case, then a task would still have to be reserved for thinking in a concealed way in the history of philosophy from its beginning to its end, a task accessible neither to philosophy as metaphysics nor, and even less so, to the sciences stemming from philosophy. Therefore we ask:

---

2. *What task is reserved for thinking at the end of philosophy?*

The mere thought of such a task of thinking must sound strange to us. A thinking which can be neither metaphysics nor science?

A task which has concealed itself from philosophy since its very beginning, even in virtue of that beginning, and thus has withdrawn itself continually and increasingly in the time to come?

A task of thinking which—so it seems—includes the assertion that philosophy has not been up to the matter of thinking and has thus become a history of mere decline?

Is there not an arrogance in these assertions which desires to put itself above the greatness of the thinkers of philosophy?

This suspicion easily suggests itself. But it can as easily be removed. For every attempt to gain insight into the supposed task of thinking finds itself moved to review the whole of the history of philosophy. Not only this, but it is even forced to think the historicity of that which grants a possible history to philosophy.

Because of this, that supposed thinking necessarily falls short of the greatness of the philosophers. It is less than philosophy. Less also because the direct or indirect effect of this thinking on the public in the industrial age, formed by technology and science, is decisively less possible to this thinking than it was in the case of philosophy.

But above all, the thinking in question remains slight because its task is only of a preparatory, not of a founding character. It is content with awakening a readiness in man for a possibility whose contour remains obscure, whose coming remains uncertain.

Thinking must first learn what remains reserved and in store for thinking to get involved in. It prepares its own transformation in this learning.

We are thinking of the possibility that the world civilization which is just now beginning might one day overcome the technological-scientific-industrial character as the sole criterion of man's world sojourn. This may happen not of and through itself, but in virtue of the readiness of man for a determination which, whether listened to or not, always speaks in the destiny of man which has yet been decided. It is just as uncertain whether world civilization will soon be abruptly destroyed or whether it will be stabilized for a long time, in a stabilization, however, which will not rest in something enduring, but rather establish itself in a sequence of changes, each of which presenting the latest fashion.

The preparatory thinking in question does not wish and is not able to predict the future. It only attempts to say something to the present which was already said a long time ago precisely at the beginning of philosophy and for that beginning, but has not been explicitly thought. For the time being, it must be sufficient to refer to this with the brevity required. We shall take a directive which philosophy offers as an aid in our undertaking.

When we ask about the task of thinking, this means in the scope of philosophy: to determine that which concerns thinking, which is still controversial for thinking, which is the controversy. This is what the word "matter" ["*Sache*"] means in the German language. It designates that with which thinking has to do in the case at hand, in Plato's language *to pragma auto*[2] (cf. "The Seventh Letter" 341 C7).

In recent times, philosophy has of its own accord expressly called thinking "to the things themselves." Let us mention two cases which receive particular attention today. We hear this call "to the things themselves" in the "Preface" which Hegel has placed before his work which was published in 1807, *System of Science*,[3] first part: "The Phenomenology of Spirit [*Geist*]." This preface is not the preface to the *Phenomenology*, but to the *System of Science* [*Wissenschaft*], to the whole of philosophy. The call "to the things themselves" refers ultimately—and that means: according to the matter, primarily—to the *Science* [*Wissenschaft*] *of Logic*.

In the call "to the things themselves," the emphasis lies on the "themselves." Heard superficially, the call has the sense of a rejection. The inadequate relations to the matter of philosophy are rejected. Mere talk about the purpose of philosophy belongs to these relations, but so does mere reporting about the results of philosophical thinking. Both are never the real totality of philosophy.

---

2. The subject itself (Greek), quoted from a letter traditionally attributed to Plato (ca. 353 B.C.E.).
3. "Wissenschaft": that is, cognitive inquiry (for HEGEL, more specifically philosophically cognitive inquiry). For this preface, see above.

The totality shows itself only in its becoming. This occurs in the developmental presentation of the matter. In the presentation, theme and method coincide. For Hegel, this identity is called: the idea [*Idee*].[4] With the idea [*Idee*], the matter of philosophy "itself comes to appear. However, this matter is historically determined: subjectivity. With Descartes' *ego cogito*,[5] says Hegel, philosophy steps on firm ground for the first time where it can be at home. If the *fundamentum absolutum* is attained with the *ego cogito* as the distinctive *subiectum*,[6] this means: The subject is the *hypokeimenon*[7] which is transferred to consciousness, what is truly present, what is unclearly enough called "substance" in traditional language.

When Hegel explains in the Preface (ed. Hoffmeister, p. 19), "The true (in philosophy) is to be understood and expressed not as substance, but just as much as subject," then this means: The Being of beings, the presence of what is present, is only manifest and thus complete presence when it becomes present as such for itself in the absolute Idea. But since Descartes, *idea* means: *perceptio*.[8] Being's coming to itself occurs in speculative dialectic. Only the movement of the idea [*Idee*], the method, is the matter itself. The call "to the thing itself" requires a philosophical method appropriate in it.

However, what the matter of philosophy should be is presumed to be decided from the outset. The matter of philosophy as metaphysics is the Being of beings, their presence in the form of substantiality and subjectivity.

A hundred years later, the call "to the thing itself" again is uttered in Husserl's treatise *Philosophy as Exact Science* [Wissenschaft].[9] It was published in the first volume of the journal *Logos* in 1910–11 (pp. 289 ff.). Again, the call has at first the sense of a rejection. But here it aims in another direction than Hegel's. It concerns naturalistic psychology which claims to be the genuine scientific [*wissenschaftlich*] method of investigating consciousness. For this method blocks access to the phenomena of intentional consciousness from the very beginning. But the call "to the thing itself" is at the same time directed against historicism which gets lost in treatises about the standpoints of philosophy and in the ordering of types of philosophical *Weltanschauungen*. About this Husserl says in italics (*ibid.*, p. 340): "*The stimulus for investigation must start not with philosophies, but with issues and problems.*"

And what is at stake in philosophical investigation? In accordance with the same tradition, it is for Husserl as for Hegel the subjectivity of consciousness. For Husserl, the *Cartesian Meditations* were not only the topic of the Parisian lectures in February, 1920. Rather, since the time following the *Logical Investigations*,[1] their spirit accompanied the impassioned course of his philosophical investigations to the end. In its negative and also in its positive sense, the call "to the thing itself" determines the securing and development of method. It also determines the procedure of philosophy by means of which the matter itself can be demonstrated as a datum. For Husserl, "the principle of all principles" is first of all not a principle of content, but one of method.

4. See *Idee* in the Hegel glossary, p. 144.
5. I think (Latin). René Descartes (1596–1650), French mathematician and philosopher.
6. Subject, foundation (Latin). *Fundamentum absolutum*: completed foundation (Latin).
7. The underlying or fundamental matter (Greek).

8. Perception (Latin).
9. That is, "Philosophy as Rigorous Science [*Wissenschaft*]" (see excerpts above).
1. Published 1900–01. For HUSSERL'S *Cartesian Meditations*, see excerpts above.

In his work published in 1913,[2] Husserl devoted a special section (section 24) to the determination of "the principle of all principles." "No conceivable theory can upset this principle," says Husserl (*ibid.*, p. 44).

"The principle of all principles" reads:

> that very primordial dator[3] Intuition is a source of authority (Rechtsquelle) for knowledge, that whatever presents itself in "Intuition" in primordial form (as it were in its bodily reality), is simply to be accepted as it gives itself out to be, though only within the limits in which it then presents itself.

"The principle of all principles" contains the thesis of the precedence of method. This principle decides what matter alone can suffice for the method. "The principle of principles" requires reduction to absolute subjectivity as the matter of philosophy. The transcendental reduction to absolute subjectivity gives and secures the possibility of grounding the objectivity of all objects (the Being of this being) in its valid structure and consistency, that is, in its constitution, in and through subjectivity. Thus transcendental subjectivity proves to be "the sole absolute being" (*Formal and Transcendental Logic*, 1929, p. 240). At the same time, transcendental reduction as the method of "universal science [*Wissenschaft*]" of the constitution of the Being of beings has the same mode of being as this absolute being, that is, the manner of the matter most native to philosophy. The method is not only directed toward the matter of philosophy. It does not just belong to the matter as a key belongs to a lock. Rather, it belongs to the matter because it is "the matter itself." If one wanted to ask: Where does "the principle of all principles" get its unshakable right, the answer would have to be: from transcendental subjectivity which is already presupposed as the matter of philosophy.

We have chosen a discussion of the call "to the thing itself" as our guideline. It was to bring us to the path which leads us to a determination of the task of thinking at the end of philosophy. Where are we now? We have arrived at the insight that for the call "to the thing itself," what concerns philosophy as its matter is established from the outset. From the perspective of Hegel and Husserl—and not only from their perspective—the matter of philosophy is subjectivity. It is not the matter as such that is controversial for the call, but rather its presentation by which the matter itself becomes present. Hegel's speculative dialectic is the movement in which the matter as such comes to itself, comes to its own presence. Husserl's method is supposed to bring the matter of philosophy to its ultimately originary givenness, that means: to its own presence.

The two methods are as different as they could possibly be. But the matter as such which they are to present is the same, although it is experienced in different ways.

But of what help are these discoveries to us in our attempt to bring the task of thinking to view? They don't help us at all as long as we do not go beyond a mere discussion of the call and ask what remains unthought in the call "to the thing itself." Questioning in this way, we can become aware how something which it is no longer the matter of philosophy to think conceals itself

2. *Ideas* (see excerpts above).
3. Given.

precisely where philosophy has brought its matter to absolute knowledge and to ultimate evidence.

But what remains unthought in the matter of philosophy as well as in its method? Speculative dialectic is a mode in which the matter of philosophy comes to appeal of itself and for itself, and thus becomes presence. Such appearance necessarily occurs in some light. Only by virtue of light, i.e., through brightness, can what shines show itself, that is, radiate. But brightness in its turn rests upon something open, something free which might illuminate it here and there, now and then. Brightness plays in the open and wars there with darkness. Wherever a present being encounters another present being or even only lingers near it—but also where, as with Hegel, one being mirrors itself in another speculatively—there openness already rules, open region is in play. Only this openness grants to the movement of speculative thinking the passage through that which it thinks.

We call this openness which grants a possible letting-appear and show "opening [*Lichtung*]." In the history of language, the German word "opening" is a borrowed translation of the French *clairière*. It is formed in accordance with the older words *Waldung* (foresting) and *Feldung* (fielding).

The forest clearing (opening) is experienced in contrast to dense forest, called "density" (*Dickung*) in older language. The substantive "opening" goes back to the verb "to open." The adjective *licht* ("open") is the same word as "light." To open something means: To make something light, free and open, e.g., to make the forest free of trees at one place. The openness thus originating is the clearing [*Lichtung*]. What is light in the sense of being free and open has nothing in common with the adjective "light," meaning "bright"—neither linguistically nor factually. This is to be observed for the difference between openness [*Lichtung*] and light. Still, it is possible that a factual relation between the two exists. Light can stream into the clearing, into its openness, and let brightness play with darkness in it. But light never first creates openness. Rather, light [*Licht*] presupposes openness [*Lichtung*]. However, the clearing, the opening, is not only free for brightness and darkness, but also for resonance and echo, for sounding and diminishing of sound. The clearing is the open for everything that is present and absent.

It is necessary for thinking to become explicitly aware of the matter called opening [*Lichtung*] here. We are not extracting mere notions from mere words, e.g., "opening," as it might easily appear on the surface. Rather, we must observe the unique matter which is adequately named with the name "opening." What the word designates in the connection we are now thinking, free openness, is a "primal phenomenon," to use a word of Goethe's.[4] We would have to say a primal matter. Goethe notes (*Maxims and Reflections*, n. 993): "Look for nothing behind phenomena: they themselves are what is to be learned." This means: The phenomenon itself, in the present case the opening, sets us the task of learning from it while questioning it, that is, of letting it say something to us.

---

4. Johann Wolfgang von Goethe (1749–1832), the preeminent German literary figure of his time. He introduced the idea of *Urphänomen* in the context of the morphology of living things.

Accordingly, we may suggest that the day will come when we will not shun the question whether the opening [*Lichtung*], the free open, may not be that within which alone pure space and ecstatic time and everything present and absent in them have the place which gathers and protects everything.

In the same way as speculative dialectical thinking, originary intuition and its evidence remain dependent upon openness which already dominates, upon the opening. What is evident is what can be immediately intuited. *Evidentia* is the word which Cicero[5] uses to translate the Greek *enargeia*, that is, to transform it into the Roman. *Enargeia*, which has the same root as *argentum* (silver), means that which in itself and of itself radiates and brings itself to light. In the Greek language, one is not speaking about the action of seeing, about *videre*,[6] but about that which gleams and radiates. But it can only radiate if openness has already been granted. The beam of light does not first create the opening, openness, it only traverses it. It is only such openness that grants to giving and receiving at all what is free, that in which they can remain and must move.

All philosophical thinking which explicitly or inexplicitly follows the call "to the thing itself" is already admitted to the free space of the opening in its movement and with its method. But philosophy knows nothing of the opening. Philosophy does speak about the light of reason, but does not heed the opening of Being. The *lumen naturale*,[7] the light of reason, throws light only on openness. It does concern the opening, but so little does it form it that it needs it in order to be able to illuminate what is present in the opening. This is true not only of philosophy's *method*, but also and primarily of its *matter*, that is, of the presence of what is present. To what extent the *subiectum*, the *hypokeimenon*, that which already lies present, thus what is present in its presence is constantly thought also in subjectivity cannot be shown here in detail. (Refer to Heidegger, *Nietzsche*, vol. 2 (1961), pages 429 ff.)

We are concerned now with something else. Whether or not what is present is experienced, comprehended or presented, presence as lingering in openness always remains dependent upon the prevalent opening. What is absent, too, cannot be as such unless it presences in the *free space of the opening*.

All metaphysics including its opponent positivism[8] speaks the language of Plato. The basic word of its thinking, that is, of his presentation of the Being of beings, is *eidos*,[9] *idea*: the outward appearance in which beings as such show themselves. Outward appearance, however, is a manner of presence. No outward appearance without light—Plato already knew this. But there is no light and no brightness without the opening. Even darkness needs it. How else could we happen into darkness and wander through it? Still, the opening as such as it prevails through Being, through presence, remains unthought in philosophy, although the opening is spoken about in philosophy's beginning. How does this occur and with which names? Answer:

---

5. Roman statesman and scholar (106–42 B.C.E.).
6. To see (Latin).
7. Light belonging to the nature of things (Latin).
8. For Heidegger, the existence of "positivist" philosophy does not count against his contention that "philosophy is metaphysics," both because he views positivism as a reaction to metaphysics that thus bears its stamp and is essentially bound up with and a part of it, and because it incorporates the same sorts of metaphysical commitments as does the scientific thinking to which it is related.
9. Form (Greek; its base meaning is "that which is seen"); in the writings of Plato, the Forms or Ideas are fundamental, timeless universals, in whose reality objects in the natural world (their less than perfect copies) participate or share.

In Parmenides' reflective poem which, as far as we know, was the first to reflect explicitly upon the Being of beings, which still today, although unheard, speaks in the sciences [*Wissenschaften*] into which philosophy dissolves. Parmenides listens to the claim:

> . . . *kreo de se panta puthestha*
> *emen aletheies eukukleos atremes etor*
> *ede broton doxas, tais ouk emi pistis alethes.*
>> Fragment I, 28 ff.
> . . . but you should learn all:
> the untrembling heart of unconcealment, well-rounded
> and also the opinions of mortals,
> lacking the ability to trust what is unconcealed.[1]

Aletheia,[2] unconcealment, is named here. It is called well-rounded because it is turned in the pure sphere of the circle in which beginning and end are everywhere the same. In this turning, there is no possibility of twisting, deceit and closure. The meditative man is to experience the untrembling heart of unconcealment. What does the word about the untrembling heart of unconcealment mean? It means unconcealment itself in what is most its own, means the place of stillness which gathers in itself what grants unconcealment to begin with. That is the opening of what is open. We ask: openness for what? We have already reflected upon the fact that the path of thinking, speculative and intuitive, needs the traversable opening. But in that opening rests possible radiance, that is, the possible presencing of presence itself.

What prior to everything else first grants unconcealment in the path on which thinking pursues one thing and perceives it: *horos estin . . . einai*:[3] that presence presences. The opening grants first of all the possibility of the path to presence, and grants the possible presencing of that presence itself. We must think *aletheia*, unconcealment, as the opening which first grants Being and thinking and their presencing to and for each other. The quiet heart of the opening is the place of stillness from which alone the possibility of the belonging together of Being and thinking, that is, presence and perceiving, can arise at all.

The possible claim to a binding character or commitment of thinking is grounded in this bond. Without the preceding experience of *aletheia* as the opening, all talk about committed and non-committed thinking remains without foundation. Where does Plato's determination of presence as *idea* have its binding character from? With regard to what is Aristotle's interpretation of presencing as *energeia*[4] binding?

Strangely enough, we cannot even ask these questions always neglected in philosophy as long as we have not experienced what Parmenides had to experience: *aletheia*, unconcealment. The path to it is distinguished from the street

---

1. Standard translation: "It is needful that you should learn of all matters—both the unshaken heart of well-rounded truth and the opinions of mortals, which lack true belief" [translator's note].
2. Usually translated "truth."
3. That it is . . . to be (Greek); excerpted from fragment 2 of Parmenides, who is describing the only possible way of inquiry—"That it is [exists] and cannot not be [exist]." Thanks to Emily Wilson of the University of Pennsylvania for identifying and translating the pre-Socratic text.
4. Actuality (Greek), a key concept in the *Metaphysics* of the Greek philosopher Aristotle (385–322 B.C.E.).

on which the opinion of mortals must wander around. *Aletheia* is nothing mortal, just as little as death itself.

It is not for the sake of etymology that I stubbornly translate the name *aletheia* as unconcealment, but for the matter which must be considered when we think that which is called Being and thinking adequately. Unconcealment is, so to speak, the element in which Being and thinking and their belonging together exist. *Aletheia* is named at the beginning of philosophy, but afterward it is not explicitly thought as such by philosophy. For since Aristotle it became the task of philosophy as metaphysics to think beings as such onto-theologically.

If this is so, we have no right to sit in judgment over philosophy, as though it left something unheeded, neglected it and was thus marred by some essential deficiency. The reference to what is unthought in philosophy is not a criticism of philosophy. If a criticism is necessary now, then it rather concerns the attempt which is becoming more and more urgent ever since *Being and Time* to ask about a possible task of thinking at the end of philosophy. For the question now arises, late enough: Why is *aletheia* not translated with the usual name, with the word "truth"? The answer must be:

Insofar as truth is understood in the traditional "natural" sense as the correspondence of knowledge with beings demonstrated in beings, but also insofar as truth is interpreted as the certainty of the knowledge of Being, *aletheia*, unconcealment in the sense of the opening may not be equated with truth. Rather, *aletheia*, unconcealment thought as opening, first grants the possibility of truth. For truth itself, just as Being and thinking, can only be what it is in the element of the opening. Evidence, certainty in every degree, every kind of verification of *veritas*[5] already move *with* that *veritas* in the realm of the prevalent opening.

Aletheia, unconcealment thought as the opening of presence, is not yet truth. Is *aletheia* then less than truth? Or is it more because it first grants truth as *adaequatio* and *certitudo*,[6] because there can be no presence and presenting outside of the realm of the opening?

This question we leave to thinking as a task. Thinking must consider whether it can even raise this question at all as long as it thinks philosophically, that is, in the strict sense of metaphysics which questions what is present only with regard to its presence.

In any case, one thing becomes clear: To raise the question of *aletheia*, of unconcealment as such, is not the same as raising the question of truth. For this reason, it was inadequate and misleading to call *aletheia* in the sense of opening, truth. The talk about the "truth of Being" has a justified meaning in Hegel's *Science* [Wissenschaft] *of Logic*, because here truth means the certainty of absolute knowledge. But Hegel also, as little as Husserl, as little as all metaphysics, does not ask about Being as Being, that is, does not raise the question how there can be presence as such. There is presence only when opening is dominant. Opening is named with *aletheia*, unconcealment, but not thought as such.

The natural concept of truth does not mean unconcealment, not in the philosophy of the Greeks either. It is often and justifiably pointed out that the word *alethes* is already used by Homer only in the *verba dicendi*,[7] in statement

---

5. Truth (Latin).
6. Commensuration and certainty (Latin).
7. Words of speaking (Latin); that is, words used to

refer to things that are said. The works of Homer (ca. 8th century B.C.E.) are the earliest in Greek literature.

and thus in the sense of correctness and reliability, not in the sense of unconcealment. But this reference means only that neither the poets nor everyday
language usage, not even philosophy see themselves confronted with the task
of asking how truth, that is, the correctness of statements, is granted only in
the element of the opening of presence.

In the scope of this question, we must acknowledge the fact that *aletheia*,
unconcealment in the sense of the opening of presence, was originally only
experienced as *orthotes*,[8] as the correctness of representations and statements.
But then the assertion about the essential transformation of truth, that is,
from unconcealment to correctness, is also untenable.

Instead we must say: *Aletheia,* as opening of presence and presenting in
thinking and saying, originally comes under the perspective of *homoiosis*[9]
and adaequatio, that is, the perspective of adequation in the sense of the correspondence of representing with what is present.

But this process inevitably provokes another question: How is it that *aletheia,* unconcealment, appears to man's natural experience and speaking *only*
as correctness and dependability? Is it because man's ecstatic sojourn in the
openness of presencing is turned only toward what is present and the existent presenting of what is present? But what else does this mean than that
presence as such, and together with it the opening granting it, remain
unheeded? Only what *aletheia* as opening grants is experienced and thought,
not what it is as such.

This remains concealed. Does this happen by chance? Does it happen only
as a consequence of the carelessness of human thinking? Or does it happen
because self-concealing, concealment, *lethe*[1] belongs to *a-letheia,* not just as
an addition, not as shadow to light, but rather as the heart of *aletheia?* And
does not even a keeping and preserving rule in this self-concealing of the opening of presence from which unconcealment can be granted to begin with,
and thus what is present can appear in its presence?

If this were so, then the opening would not be the mere opening of presence, but the opening of presence concealing itself, the opening of a self-
concealing sheltering.

If this were so, then with these questions we would reach the path to the
task of thinking at the end of philosophy.

But isn't this all unfounded mysticism or even bad mythology, in any case
a ruinous irrationalism, the denial of *ratio?*[2]

I return to the question: What does *ratio, nous, noein,*[3] perceiving
(*Vernunft—Vernehmen*) mean?[4] What does ground and principle and especially principle of all principles mean? Can this ever be sufficiently determined
unless we experience *aletheia* in a Greek manner as unconcealment and then,
above and beyond the Greek, think it as the opening of self-concealing? As
long as *ratio* and the rational still remain questionable in what is their own,
talk about irrationalism is unfounded. The technological scientific rational-

---

8. Literally, "straightness" (Greek).
9. Resemblance, likeness (Greek).
1. Forgetfulness (Greek), though here Heidegger
treats it as a synonym of "self-concealing,
concealment."
2. Reason (Latin).

3. Mind, thinking (Greek).
4. An odd translation of Heidegger's question:
"Was heisst *ratio, nous, noein,* Vernehmen?" Best
rendered: "What is meant by reason, mind, thinking, inquiring?"

ization ruling the present age justifies itself every day more surprisingly by its immense results. But these results say nothing about what the possibility of the rational and the irrational first grants. The effect proves the correctness of technological scientific rationalization. But is the manifest character of what-is exhausted by what is demonstrable? Doesn't the insistence on what is demonstrable block the way to what-is?

Perhaps there is a thinking which is more sober than the irresistible race of rationalization and the sweeping character of cybernetics. Presumably it is precisely this sweeping quality which is extremely irrational.

Perhaps there is a thinking outside of the distinction of rational and irrational still more sober than scientific technology, more sober and thus removed, without effect and yet having its own necessity. When we ask about the task of this thinking, then not only this thinking, but also the question about it is first made questionable. In view of the whole philosophical tradition, this means:

We all still need an education in thinking, and before that first a knowledge of what being educated and uneducated in thinking means. In this respect, Aristotle gives us a hint in Book IV of his *Metaphysics* (1006a ff.). It reads: *esti gar apaideusia to me gignoskein tinon dei zetein apodeixin kai tinon ou dei.* "For it is uneducated not to have an eye for when it is necessary to look for a proof, and when this is not necessary."

This sentence demands careful reflection. For it is not yet decided in what way that which needs no proof in order to become accessible to thinking is to be experienced. Is it dialectical mediation or originary intuition or neither of the two? Only the peculiar quality of that which demands of us above all else to be admitted can decide about that. But how is this to make the decision possible for us before we have not admitted it? In what circle are we moving here, inevitably?

Is it the *eukukleos alethein,* well-rounded unconcealment itself, thought as the opening?

Does the name for the task of thinking then read instead of *Being and Time*: Opening and Presence?

But where does the opening come from and how is it given? What speaks in the "It gives"?[5]

The task of thinking would then be the surrender of previous thinking to the determination of the matter of thinking.

SOURCE: Martin Heidegger, *On Time and Being*, trans. Joan Stambaugh (New York: Harper and Row, 1972), pp. 55–73. Except where otherwise indicated, German words in brackets are the terminology used in the German original, inserted by the editor in addition to their renderings in the translation. This essay was first presented on Heidegger's behalf as a 1964 lecture in Paris in a French translation, which was published in *Kierkegaard vivant* (1966). It first appeared in the original German (in which it was written) as "Das Ende der Philosophie und die Aufgabe des Denkens," in Heidegger's collection *Zur Sache des Denkens* (1969, *On the Matter of Thinking*).

5. The literal translation of the German "Es gibt," which is (commonly and very extensively) used in impersonal constructions where English would have "there is" (e.g., "There is a book on the table"). Heidegger is suggesting that something like the literal German meaning applies and is occurring in the kinds of situations in which these forms of words (in German and in English) are appropriate.

KARL JASPERS
(1883 – 1969)

Karl Jaspers is as deserving as HEI-DEGGER of being considered an origina-tor of existential philosophy, or what he called "*Existenz*-philosophy." His major treatise relating to it—a three-volume work titled simply *Philosophie* (1932, *Philosophy*)—appeared shortly after Hei-degger's *Being and Time* (1927); and his version of the philosophy of human *Existenz* was entirely independent of Heidegger's. Indeed, the two versions were rivals, differing quite significantly. That rivalry soon became deeply personal and political as well as philosophical: in 1933 Heidegger aligned himself with the Nazi movement, which to Jaspers was an abomination. Heidegger overshadowed Jaspers, both during the Hitler era and again after he emerged from postwar dis-grace; but Jaspers kept his reputation and his humanity unblemished, and he became one of the most admired and respected public intellectuals and moral leaders in postwar Germany. He thereby demonstrated—as vividly in his own way and context as SARTRE did in France—that the case of Heidegger warrants no inferences or generalizations about the relation between existential philosophy as such and either politics or humaneness.

Karl Theodor Jaspers ("YAH-sperz") was born in Oldenburg, Germany, near the North Sea. There he and his younger brother and sister were raised with an appreciation of nature, as well as with a socially and religiously liberal and human-istic sensibility. While still in his teens, he was diagnosed with a serious disease that permanently damaged his lungs and heart, affecting him throughout his adult life.

His father was a jurist, and initially Jaspers intended to pursue a legal career. After finishing his preliminary schooling locally, from 1901 to 1902 he studied law in Heidelberg and Munich. Finding that he had no passion for the law, Jaspers began to study medicine, pursuing his studies in Berlin, Göttingen, and Heidel-berg. After passing the state medical examination in 1908, he received his medical degree in 1909. From 1908 until 1915 he worked as a research assistant in a psychiatric hospital that was associated with the University of Heidelberg. In 1910, he married Gertrud Mayer, who became his intellectual and philosophical com-panion as well as the love of his life. She was Jewish, and his commitment to her would have much to do with his decision to remain with her in Germany through the Hitler years after her departure became impossible.

In 1913 Jaspers began to teach psycho-logy in Heidelberg as a part of the phi-losophy faculty (the traditional placement of psychology, which was preserved in institutional structure long after it had become a distinct discipline). He was recommended for the position by the philosopher-sociologist Max Weber, whom he had met in 1909. When he arrived, the philosophy faculty was led by Wilhelm Windelband, who was fol-lowed by Heinrich Rickert; both were important Neo-Kantians and had very definite ideas about what was philosophi-cally respectable. Consequently, Jaspers was required to confine his teaching to psychology and was largely viewed as an outsider in the philosophy faculty, although initially no hostility was shown toward him. At first he was protected by Weber; but after Weber's death in 1920, Rickert and Jaspers had some conflicts that made them enemies. Nevertheless, Jaspers attained the rank of full profes-sor in 1922.

In that position, Jaspers was free to do as he chose—and he chose to devote himself to developing a kind of philoso-phy that would be better attuned to his concerns with human reality and possibility than either Hegelianism or the Neo-Kantianism then dominant in German universities. During the following decade he worked in isolation from his colleagues; but the fruit of those years was the three-volume *Philosophy*, his first and greatest philosophical work. Though he was previously little known in philosophical circles, it made him one of the leading philosophers in Europe. (He later characterized it as the outcome of a kind of intellectual collaboration with his wife and her brother, Ernst Mayer.)

Jaspers had become acquainted with HUSSERL and Heidegger around 1920. During the next dozen years, he and Heidegger often met and talked. However, their relationship became strained, and it ended completely in 1933 when the Nazis came to power in Germany and Heidegger chose to embrace them. Their paths diverged in other respects as well. Jaspers had never been particularly religious, but in the late 1920s and early 1930s he began to see a juncture between his conception of "transcendence" and "philosophical faith" and some forms of religious and theological thought, to which he was more receptive than Heidegger was. Ironically, it was to Heidegger rather than Jaspers that many theologians were later attracted.

During Hitler's years in power, Jaspers remained in Heidelberg, both for personal reasons (his wife, born a Jew, could not leave) and on principle. His activities were increasingly circumscribed. First he was forced to resign from administrative duties; then, in 1937, he was removed from his teaching position. He subsequently was barred from publishing as well. His prominence gave him some protection, however, which for a time also extended to his wife; eventually she hid with friends. Allied forces entered and occupied Heidelberg only a few weeks before Jaspers himself was to be sent to a concentration camp.

As a prominent academic who had never compromised with the Nazi regime, after the war Jaspers was asked to assume leadership positions both at the University of Heidelberg and in the new Ministry of Education; but his chronically poor health, worsened by hardships during and following the war, led him to decline. Moreover, the political climate during that period in what became West Germany and the direction of its social and political development distressed him, to the point that in 1948 he left the country to take a position at the University of Basel in Switzerland. He nonetheless remained very much concerned with West German affairs (though he renounced his German citizenship and became a Swiss citizen in 1967), writing extensively on matters social and political as well as philosophical during the next two decades. He also resumed his relationship with Hannah Arendt, who in the early 1930s had been his student as well as Heidegger's, and whose friendship mattered greatly to both of them. He continued to teach for a time, as his health permitted; but he became increasingly frail, and died of a stroke in Basel in 1969.

Like Heidegger, and in contrast to most of their academic-philosophical predecessors and contemporaries, Jaspers had a great appreciation of both KIERKEGAARD and NIETZSCHE—though a very different appreciation than Heidegger's, particularly of Nietzsche. For Heidegger, Nietzsche was the culmination of the Western metaphysical tradition; for Jaspers, Nietzsche was already well beyond that tradition, attempting—like Kierkegaard but in a different vein—to philosophize in a way that would help illuminate human existence and its possibilities. Jaspers came to philosophy and to his concern with that task by a very different route than Heidegger's—via medicine, psychology, and psychopathology, rather than by way of the Scholastics and Husserlian phenomenology. He also came to it with a background of northern German liberal Protestantism rather than southern German Catholicism. His kind of phenomenology owed more to the tradition of introspective and therapeutically oriented psychological analysis than to Husserl's program and methodology.

But there is still more to their difference. Another aspect of it is Jaspers's emphasis, in his account of genuinely human existing (for which he—unlike Heidegger—reserves the term *Existenz*), on several kinds of experience that figure very marginally in Heidegger's analysis of "Dasein" (human reality's kind of "being") and of authentic existence in *Being and Time*. These relate to what Jaspers calls "Existenz with other Existenz" and "Existenz and Transcendence." One of Jaspers's most significant contributions was to have made clear that existential philosophy is by no means incapable of taking seriously and even foregrounding these forms of experience—though that may be said with some justice of Heidegger's version of it in *Being and Time*, and with even greater justice of Sartre's in his *Being and Nothingness* (1943).

The human possibility that Jaspers calls "Existenz" is his underlying concern throughout all three volumes of his *Philosophy*, and it is the explicit focus of the middle volume, titled *Existenzerhellung* (*Existenz Elucidation*). That placement of his discussion of it within the structure of the entire work reflects his conviction that elucidating Existenz not only is one of the main tasks but should be the heart of philosophy as an endeavor, guiding and centering thoughtful concern with the character of human reality, the living of human life, and indeed all else that pertains to them. The first volume is devoted to what Jaspers calls *Weltorientierung* (world orientation), by which he means various ways of conceiving of and attempting to comprehend the world in which we find ourselves. He by no means neglects the forms of reality and ways of knowing that pertain to the character of this world and are appropriate to it, but he considers it important to recognize how much they differ from Existenz and its elucidation. The third volume is a philosophical reflection on what Jaspers calls *Transcendenz* (transcendence), and thus on forms of thought and experience pertaining to the idea that there is more to reality than mundane and human existence—an idea that has found expression in various forms of myth, in religion, and in some types of philosophy.

Jaspers consistently attempts to shift our thinking away from the paradigm that insists on reifying reality and conceiving of it as consisting of one or more types of "thing," substance, or entity, and to emphasize instead the forms of experience, activity, and relation that underlie all such artificial objectifications. So, for example, although Jaspers's conceptions of "Existenz" and "transcendence" occupy the places that the ideas of "soul" or "spirit" and "God" occupy in the thought of many others, he refuses to reduce them to the status of a word designating some sort of immaterial entity that either does or does not objectively exist. His thought thus bears some resemblance to that of HEGEL and of certain "demythologizing" theologians in the Hegelian tradition, who think it is not only possible but desirable to retain the language and meaningfulness of the idea of spirituality while leaving behind its reifying interpretations, in order to call attention to things about ourselves and the larger reality of which we are a part that are of the utmost importance.

Jaspers was not fond of "-isms" of any sort ("existentialism" included). Yet he made an exception in the case of "humanism"; and there is a sense in which his Existenz-philosophy can quite appropriately be seen as an admirable example of humanism at its undogmatic and nondoctrinal best. Human reality is the locus of meaning and significance for him: it is there that his conception of Existenz is centered and the meaningfulness of his conception of Transcendenz is anchored. And it is precisely the possibility and realization of Existenz—rather than human life simply as a biological reality—that he views as the key to that meaning and significance.

Existenz for Jaspers is not *something that exists*; it is *existing*, just as life is *living*. There is no Existenz apart from living; but Existenz is not simply human living, conceived in terms of biological and physiological processes. It is the first-person-singular existing of a living human being leading his or her life as a self-determining individual subject and agent—and, Jaspers adds, interacting as such with other existences of the same kind, because such interactions are indispensable to this kind of existing. One can be a living human being and yet fail to realize the human possibilities of existing in this interactively individuating and individuated manner; and one can exist in this manner in some contexts while living in a different manner in other contexts (as human beings generally do). For Jaspers Existenz may be thought of as the exception rather than the rule in human life, even though in principle it is a general possibility within the reach of all.

Existenz thus is Jaspers's version of authenticity. "Existing" in the sense of "Existenz," as he uses that term, is inherently authentic; and "Existenz elucidation" is the elucidation of the character and conditions of the possibility of such existing. Unsurprisingly, Jaspers offers no separate account of authenticity: it would be redundant, because it would simply echo his conception and characterization of Existenz. This possibility already differentiates human reality from that of other forms of life; but its realization is what distinguishes the genuinely human from the merely generally human.

What it is to exist as a human being must therefore be explored on two levels, for Jaspers—as for Kierkegaard, for whom "subjectivity" mundanely characterizes all human existing and also, much more importantly, characterizes truly human existing (subjectivity "in truth") in an intensified and transfigured form. There is garden-variety, commonplace human existing, for Jaspers—and then there is what one might call "really *existing*." Because nothing "objectively" distinguishes the one from the other, the kind of approach to it that Jaspers calls *Erhellung*—"elucidation" or "illumination"—is needed. For while this invisible difference might seem to the objectively minded to be no real difference at all, to Jaspers and Kierkegaard it means everything.

Jaspers made one other contribution to existential philosophy, of a very different sort. He was as different from both Heidegger and Sartre—both as a philosopher and as a person—as anyone could be. He was a gentle, humane man, who shared many of their philosophical concerns and some of their views, but not their harshness and posturing. His integrity was as deep as his lack of arrogance was complete. His philosophy is one of mediation, between what are often thought to be the forced alternatives of Hegel and Kierkegaard, of Nietzsche and Christianity, of empirical psychology and personal experience, of authenticity and community, and of despair and hope. The profundity of his thought lies not in its obscurity but in its simplicity, honesty, directness, and humanity. He also acquitted himself well in the trying and testing circumstances with which he was confronted in the Germany of the Nazis. In the two decades that remained to him following the war, he spoke out frequently, eloquently, and wisely on behalf of peace and justice in Germany, Europe, and the world. It is well worth making his acquaintance, and thinking of him when one thinks of existential philosophy.

From The Elucidation of Existenz [*Existenzerhellung*]

From *Chapter 1*
Existenz

MUNDANE EXISTENCE [*WELTDASEIN*] AND EXISTENZ

If by "world" I mean the sum of all that cognitive orientation can reveal to me as cogently knowable for everyone, the question arises whether the being of the world is all there is. Does cognitive thinking stop with world orientation?

What we refer to in mythical terms as the soul and God, and in philosophical language as Existenz and transcendence, is not of this world. Neither one is knowable, in the sense of things in the world. Yet both might have another kind of being. They need not be nothing, even though they are not known. They could be objects of thought, if not of cognition.

What is there, as against all mundane being [Weltsein]?[1] In the answer to this question lies the basic decision of philosophy.

We answer: there is the being [*das Sein*] which in the phenomenality of existence [*in der Erscheinung des Daseins*][2] is *not* but *can be*, *ought to be*, and therefore decides in time whether it is in eternity.

This being is myself as *Existenz*. I am Existenz if I do not become an object for myself. In Existenz I know, without being able to see it, that what I call my "self" is independent. The possibility of Existenz is what I live by; it is only in its realization that I am myself. Attempts to comprehend it make it vanish, for it is not a psychological subject. I feel more deeply rooted in its possibility than in my self-objectifying grasp of my nature and my character. Existenz appears to itself as existence [*Dasein*],[3] in the polarity of subjectivity and objectivity; but it is not the appearance of an object given anywhere, or uncoverable as underlying any reflection. It is phenomenal only for itself and for other Existenz.

It is thus not my existence [*Dasein*] that is Existenz; but, *being human*, I am possible Existenz *in existence* [*Dasein*].[4] I exist or I do not exist, but my Existenz, as a possibility, takes a step toward being or away from being, toward nothingness, in every choice or decision I make.[5] My existence [*Dasein*] differs from other existence in scope; my world can be broad or narrow. But Existenz differs from other Existenz in essence, because of its freedom. As existence [*Dasein*] I live and die; my Existenz is unaware of death but soars or declines in relation to its being.[6] Existence [*Dasein*] exists empirically, Existenz as freedom only. Existence [*Dasein*] is wholly temporal, while Existenz, in time, is more than time. My existence is finite, since it is not all existence, and yet, for me, it is concluded within itself. Existenz is not everything and not for itself alone either, for its being depends on its relation to other Existenz and to transcendence[7]—the wholly Other that makes it aware of being not by itself alone—but while existence may be termed infinite as a relatively rounded endlessness, the infinity of Existenz is unrounded, an open possibility. Action on the ground of possible Existenz disconcerts me in existence;

1. That is, the sort of being possessed by the kinds of things encountered in the world in which we find ourselves. (The word translated as "as against" [*gegenüber*] would be better translated here as "in contrast to.")
2. That is, in the phenomenon (appearance, form) of human being.
3. That is, human being as a mundane creature.
4. This sentence makes it clear that Jaspers wants to distinguish genuinely human (first-person singular) *existing* (Existenz)—which for him is a human possibility that may or may not be realized—from merely being a human being (*Dasein*, for Jaspers as for HEIDEGGER). Such "existing" might be thought of as Jaspers's version of "genuinely human" or "authentic" existing. *Dasein* is the *general reality* of being a human being; Existenz (for

Jaspers) is the *possibility* of existing in a genuinely human way.
5. This is more accurately translated: "Everyone is there (*da*) or not there (*nicht da*), but Existenz, because it is something *possible*, moves toward its being (*Sein*, realization) or disappearance (*ins Nichts*) through choice and decision (*Wahl und Entscheidung*)."
6. That is, in its realization.
7. By "other Existenz" Jaspers means other genuinely human persons or selves. By "transcendence" he means the counterpart to human Existenz that transcends any and all merely and particularly human Existenz, as well as the whole world of mundane reality, but is not itself a "being" or "thing." "Transcendence" is his concept that replaces "God," just as "Existenz" replaces "soul."

as existence, concerned with enduring in time, I cannot but turn against the doubtful path of unconditionality that may be costly, even ruinous, in existence. My concern with existence tends to make existential [*existentielle*] actions conditional upon the preservation of my existence; but to possible Existenz, the unqualified enjoyment of existence [*Dasein*] is already apostasy;[8] to Existenz, the condition of its reality in existence [*Dasein*] is that it comprehends itself as unconditional. If I merely want to exist, without qualifications, I am bound to despair when I see that the reality of my existence lies in total foundering.

Existence [*Dasein*] is fulfilled in *mundane being* [Weltsein];[9] to possible Existenz, the world is the field of its phenomenality.

The *known* world is the alien world. I am *detached* from it. What my intellect can know and what I can experience empirically repulses me as such, and I am irrelevant to it. Subject to overpowering causality in the realm of reality and to logical compulsion in the realm of validity, I am not sheltered in either. I hear no kindred language, and the more determined I am to comprehend the world, the more homeless will it make me feel; as the Other, as nothing but the world, it holds no comfort. Unfeeling, neither merciful nor unmerciful, subject to laws or floundering in coincidence, it is unaware of itself. I cannot grasp it, for it faces me impersonally, explicable in particulars but never intelligible as a whole.

And yet *there is another way in which I know the world*. It is akin to me then; I am at home in it and even sheltered in it. Its laws are the laws of my own reason. I find peace as I adjust to it, as I make my tools and expand my cognition of the world. It will speak to me now; it breathes a life that I share. I give myself up to it, and when I am in it I am with myself. It is familiar in small, present things, and thrilling in its grandeur; it will make me unwary in proximity or tend to sweep me along to its far reaches. Its ways are not the ways I expect, but though it may startle me with undreamed of fulfillments and incomprehensible failures, I shall trust it even as I perish.[1]

This is no longer the world I know about in purely cognitive orientation. But my contentment in dealing with it is ambiguous. I may *crave* the world as the font of my joy of living, may be drawn to it and deceived about it by my blind will to live. I can indeed not exist without this craving, but as an absolute impulse it becomes self-destructive; it is against this impulse that my possible Existenz warns me to detach myself from the world lest I become its prey. Or, *in the world* that is so close to me, so much my kin, I may set out to *transcend* the world. Whether seeing it, thinking about it, acting and loving, producing and developing in it—in all that, then, I deal with something else at the same time, with a phenomenon of the transcendence that speaks to me. This is not a world I know but one that seems to have lost its continuity. It will change according to times and persons, and depending on my inner attitudes; it does not say the same things to all men, and not the same things at all times. I must be ready for it if I want to hear it. If I withhold myself, the very thing I might transcend to will withdraw. For it is only for freedom and by freedom, and there is nothing cogent about it at all.

8. That is, waste (*ein Abfall*); gone to waste.
9. That is, in worldly reality.
1. In this and the preceding paragraph Jaspers sketches his version of the distinction drawn by

KANT (in the conclusion of his *Critique of Practical Reason* [1788]; see above) between the two distinct dimensions of our human reality and possibility.

Possible Existenz thus *sets itself off* from the world in order to find the right way into the world. It cuts loose from the world so that its grasp of the world will give it more than the world can be. The world attracts Existenz as the medium of its realization, and repels it as its possible decay to mere existence [*Dasein*]. There is a tension between the world and Existenz. They cannot become one, and they cannot separate either.

In philosophizing on the ground of possible Existenz we presuppose this tension. The world, as *what can be known*, and Existenz, as *what must be elucidated*,[2] are dialectically distinguished and then reconsidered as one.

Mundane being [*Weltsein*], the being we know, is *general* [*allgemein*] because it is generally valid for everyone. It is the common property of all rational creatures who can agree on its being the same thing they mean. Its validity applies, in the endlessness of real things, to the definable particular.

Existenz is *never general* [*nie allgemein*], and thus not a case that might be subsumed as particular under a universal [*ein Allgemeine*].[3] Objectified as a phenomenon, however, Existenz is also the individuality of the historic particular. We still comprehend this under general categories, limited only by the endlessness of individual factuality, which makes the individual inexhaustible and thus ineffable. But individuality as such is not Existenz.[4] All that it is, to begin with, is the visible profusion of mundane existence [*Weltdasein*]—a profusion whose existential originality can be examined by the questioner's self-being, but not by any knowledge.

The union of Existenz and the world is the incalculable process of which no one who is a part of it can be sure.

POSSIBLE EXISTENZ UNSATISFIED IN EXISTENCE [*WELTDASEIN*][5]

1. DOUBTS OF THE BEING OF EXISTENZ

Once we divorce Existenz from existence [*Dasein*], from the world, and from [everything of] a general character, there seems to be nothing left. Unless Existenz becomes an object, it seems a vain hope to think of it; such thinking cannot last or produce results, so the attempted conception of Existenz seems bound to destroy itself. We can doubt the being of Existenz in every respect and let common sense tell us to stick to objectivity as both real and true. Was the attempt the outgrowth of a chimera?

There is no way to remove our doubts about Existenz. It is neither knowable as existence [*Dasein*] nor extant as validity. We can deny Existenz as we can deny the content of any philosophical thought—as opposed to particular objective cognition, whose object is demonstrable. I can never say of myself what I am, as if I were demonstrably extant. Whatever can be said of me by way of objectification applies to my empirical individuality, and as this can be the phenomenon of my Existenz, it is not a subject to any definitive psy-

---

2. Jaspers's version of DILTHEY's distinction between that which admits of knowledge in the form of *Erklären* (explanation from without) and that which requires *Verstehen* (understanding from within) to be comprehended.

3. An echo of KIERKEGAARD on "what it means to exist as a human being." For HEGEL, on the other hand, the particular embodiment of *Allgemein-*

heit (generality, universality) is the key to human-spiritual self-realization.

4. An important point for Jaspers (as well as for Kierkegaard). Individuality as mere idiosyncrasy or outward distinctiveness is not what he means by "Existenz."

5. That is, ordinary worldly human reality.

chological analysis either—a limit of my self-knowledge which indirectly points to something else, without ever being able to compel that something to become apparent. Hence the elucidation of Existenz is a deliverance but not a fulfillment, as knowledge would be; it widens my scope, but it does not create substance by demonstrating any being that I might objectively comprehend.

Since Existenz is thus inaccessible to one who asks about it in terms of the purely objective intellect, it remains subject to lasting doubt. Yet though no proof can force me to admit its being, my thinking is still not an end: it gets beyond the bounds of objective knowability in a *leap*[6] that exceeds the capacity of rational insight. Philosophizing begins and ends at a point to which that leap takes me. Existenz is the *origin* of existential philosophizing, not its goal. Nor is its origin the same as its beginning, beyond which I would go on asking for an earlier beginning; it is not my license either, which would drive me to despair, and it is not a will resulting from the endlessness of questionable motivations. The origin is free being. This is what I transcend to as *philosophizing, not knowing, brings me to myself.* The helplessness to which philosophizing reduces me when I doubt its origin is an expression of the helplessness of my self-being, and the reality of philosophizing is the incipient upsurge of that self-being. The premise of philosophizing, therefore, is to *take hold* of Existenz—which begins as no more than a dark striving for sense and support, turns into doubt and despair as reminders of its derivation from the realm of possibility, and then appear as the incomprehensible certainty that is elucidated in philosophizing.[7]

2. BEING UNSATISFIED AS AN EXPRESSION OF POSSIBLE EXISTENZ

If I reduce all things to mundane existence [*Weltdasein*], either in theory or in practice, I feel unsatisfied. This feeling is a negative origin; in separating Existenz from mundane existence it makes me sense the truth of that separation. As there is no knowledge for which the world is conclusive, no "right" order of existence that could possibly be definitive, and no absolute final goal that all might see as one, I cannot help getting more unsatisfied the clearer I am in my mind about what I know, and the more honest I am about the sense of what I am doing.

No reasons will sufficiently explain this feeling. It expresses the being of possible Existenz, which understands itself, not something else, when it declares itself unsatisfied. What I feel then is not the impotence of knowledge. It is not the emptiness at the end of all my achievements in a world in which I face the brink of nothingness. Instead, I feel a discontent that eggs me on.

An inexplicable discontent is a step out of mere existence, the step into the *solitude of possibility* where all mundane existence disappears. This solitude is not the resignation of the scientist who buries his hopes for a cognition of intrinsic being. It is not the irritation of the man of action who has come to doubt the point of all action. Nor is it the grief of a man in flight from himself and loath to be alone. Instead, after all these disillusionments, it is my

6. An echo of Kierkegaard's emphasis on the importance of a "leap of faith" but with a shift in its focus: the leap is no longer directed toward a radically transcendent Kierkegaardian God.

7. This sentence summarizes Jaspers's version of Kierkegaard's (explicitly *unwissenschaftlich*) sense of what philosophy at its best and most important can and should be and do, in and for human life.

dissatisfaction with existence [*Daseienden*] at large,[8] *my need to have my own origin*. To be unsatisfied is a condition inadequate to existence, and when this condition has opposed me to the world, it is my freedom that conquers all disenchantment and returns me to the world, to my fellow man with whom I ascertain the origin. I do not, however, comprehend all this in thoughtful reflection—which is indeed what fails me—but in the reality of my actions and in total foundering.[9]

This possible conquest alone lends substance and significance to the otherwise irremovable relativity of theoretical *knowledge* and practical *action*.

I may well derive a peculiar and profound satisfaction from a theoretical knowledge of things in general [*das Allgemeine*], from surveying world images, from contemplating forms and existence, and from expanding all of this farther and farther, under ideas. But it is my dissatisfaction that makes me feel that this whole world, for all its universality and validity, is not all of being. My attitude in it is not one of curiosity about every particular, shared with a fellow scientist [*Wissenschaftler*][1] who might be interchangeable according to his function; it is an attitude of original curiosity about being itself, shared with a friend. What grips me is a communion in asking and answering questions, and a communication which within objective validity goes indirectly beyond it.

When I face objective tasks in *practical* life, when I deal with them and ask about their meaning, no meaning that I can grasp in the world will satisfy me. My sense of possible Existenz will not rest even if my conscious comprehension feeds on the idea of a whole in which I have my place and do my job. The thought of fulfillment in an entirety will come to be merely relative, like a temptation to conceal the boundary situations which break up any entirety. Though each idea of the whole is also a step beyond the fission into sheer coincidence, I am never able to survey the whole; eventually it will be back at the mercy of the accidents of mundane existence. A place within the whole, a place that would lend importance to the individual as a member of the body of this kind of being, is always questionable. But what remains to me as an individual is what never fits into a whole: the choice of my tasks and my striving for accomplishment are simultaneous manifestations of *another* origin, unless the annihilating thought that all I do might be senseless makes me shut my eyes. While I devote my empirical individuality to my finite tasks, my possible Existenz is more than that empirical individuality, and more than the objective, realistic impersonality of my political, scientific,[2] or economic achievements. Although its essence is realized solely by this participation in the historic process of mundane existence [*Weltdasein*], Existenz is at war with the lower depths of the encompassing world in which it finds itself. It is against those depths that, failing in the world, it seeks to hold its own in the eternity of intrinsic being.

Not unless it is indeed unsatisfied—both theoretically, with the mere knowledge and contemplation of all things in the world, and practically, with the mere performance of a task in an ideal entirety—can possible Existenz *utter*

---

8. That is, with worldly reality in general.
9. That is, collapse, crashing, shipwreck (*Scheitern*), a concept often employed by Jaspers.
1. That is, scholar.

2. That is, intellectual or cognitive (*wissenschaftlich*, which is often translated too narrowly as "scientific").

and understand this dissatisfaction. It is never *motivated* by generally valid reasons; those rather tend to induce contentment and tranquillity in the totality of a mundane existence permeated by the idea and thus spiritualized. The discontent of possible self-being has broken through mundane existence and cast the individual back upon himself, back to the origin that lets him deal with his world and, with his fellow, realize his Existenz.

3. THE BREAKTHROUGH ASCERTAINED IN EXISTENTIAL ELUCIDATION

If I am unsatisfied and want to clarify this not just by setting myself apart but by positive thoughts on what this is all about, I come to existential elucidation.

As Existenz results from the real act of breaking through mundane existence [*Weltdasein*], existential elucidation is the *thinking ascertainment* of that act.[3] The breakthrough goes from possible Existenz to its realization, without being able to leave the borderline of possibility. To have its reality—although it is not objectively demonstrable—in action itself is the peculiar quality of Existenz. In its philosophical elucidation we pursue each thought that leads to the breakthrough, no matter from what side.

a. The breakthrough occurs at the *limits* of mundane existence. Philosophical thinking leads up to such limits and puts us in mind of the experiences they involve and of the appeal they issue. From the situations in the world, it leads to "boundary situations"; from empirical consciousness, to "absolute consciousness"; from actions qualified by their purposes, to "unconditional actions."

b. But the breakthrough still does not lead us out of the world. It occurs in the world, and so philosophical thought follows the appearance of Existenz in the world, in "historic consciousness" and in the "tension of subjectivity and objectivity" in its existence.

c. The breakthrough is *original*. Events happen in the world, but in the breakthrough something is settled by me. Existenz is certain that no part of intrinsic being can stay unsettled for it as a phenomenon in temporal existence. For either I allow the course of things to decide *about* me—vanishing as myself, since there is no real decision when everything just *happens*—or I deal with being originally, as myself, with the feeling that there must be a decision. My thought, aimed at the origin, seeks to elucidate "freedom."

d. Nothing I know in the world can give me any reasons for my decision; but what I am to decide can be grasped in the medium of that knowledge. Existential elucidation pervades my existence in the world, not in the sense that what matters were now known, but so I can sense possibilities that may give me a grasp on truth—on what is true as I *become* true. "I myself" and "communication" as the premise of self-being are the things we try to cover in the fundamental thoughts of all existential elucidation.

---

3. This sentence is an important statement of Jaspers's conception of the relation between actual Existenz and its philosophical *Erhellung* (elucidation). Both the German and English words literally mean "to shed light on." The primary task of Jaspers's kind of *Existenzphilosophie* (philosophy of Existenz) is to illuminate what it means (and what it more exceptionally *can* mean) to "exist as a human being," with particular attention to the question of what genuinely human "being" or Existenz as a human possibility involves.

FROM METHODS OF ELUCIDATING EXISTENZ

The distinction of possible Existenz from mere mundane existence [*Weltdasein*], its dissatisfaction with the world as such, the sense of breaking through to its reality as we come to a decision—all these serve only to make us aware of a limit of knowledge. At first our thoughts face an area where nothing is visible. If Existenz is neither a mundane object nor a valid ideal one, the means of thought employed for its elucidation must have a peculiar character.

The thinking that elucidates Existenz aims at the reality of existential action, which in its historic situation is the same as transcending to oneself. Yet the elucidating thought requires an objective thinking as a means whereby the thinker, still as possible Existenz, can transcend to that original transcending of Existenz itself. In existential elucidation, when the philosophical thought as such is pure thought in pure objectives, it is deprived of its transcending quality and consequently misunderstood; but when the thought is part of transcending, it is a performance, not indeed of the existential reality, but of the existential possibility. Having become such a possibility, it has been adopted in its first translation. But existential action is real only as factual action; though the second translation may begin as my inner action of adopting the possibility, there still remains a difference between mere inspiration and the reality of my becoming. In philosophizing we merely turn toward Existenz. Our being is still what we think, not yet what we are. It is true that when I understand myself in these thoughts as one who conceives his own possibility, I am making the thoughts my own and mine alone; and it is also true that without such adoption, as mere general concepts, existentially elucidating thoughts would make no sense at all, would indeed be unintelligible. But this first adoption is not yet the intrinsic one, of which it gives us a touch, but not yet the reality.

When we philosophize in the field of existential elucidation, any statements we make about being refer to freedom. What they say, in the transcending thought, is what can freely be. Their truth criterion is not an objective standard by which the statement is either true or false, nor is it a given phenomenon which the statement does or does not fit. Instead, it is the affirmative or negative will itself. I am the touchstone by which I test in freedom, test not only what I am but what I can be—and what I want to be, but can want only if I am lucidly conscious. At crucial points the lucidity of philosophizing already indicates the will of freedom.

The form of any statement is tied to objective contents, and thus to a general [*allgemein*] meaning. But when the statement seeks to elucidate Existenz, it also has a meaning that goes beyond this general one [*das Allgemeine*] and is no longer generally intelligible. Existentially elucidating thought and speech is generally valid and quite personally, individually fulfilling at the same time. The universal[4] as a mere universal remains here hollow, so to speak, and its sense is misleading. Yet without a language—that is to say, without any

---

4. This translates *das Allgemeine*, the same word as is also (and more appropriately) translated as "general" above and often elsewhere. Nouns like "dog," "tree," "human being," and even "Existenz" all have meanings that are *allgemein* (general or universal) even though their specific meanings and references are different, even if their instances are distinct, unique, or even radically particular (as in the case of "Existenz").

expression of the universal—Existenz would be unreal because it could not be sure of itself.

In the elucidation of Existenz I look at its relation to its universal in which it appears to itself. I derive my thinking from what elucidates Existenz, and at the same time I help to create this source of light by the possibility of self-understanding. I look for general thoughts to cover what is incapable of outright generalization. What I mean by such thoughts is precisely not their general [*allgemein*] meaning; but the general meaning is my way of transcending to Existenz—in other words, to myself and to my communicating fellow man who, like myself, is to me not an object but a free being. For Existenz must be present as a possibility if general thoughts are to have the transcending significance of existential elucidation. They move in the realm of generality, but on the boundary of generality. They are manifestations of a philosophical energy that not only makes me seek logical clarity—which is a requisite, though deceptive by itself alone; this energy makes me strive to arrange all questions, thoughts, and views so that through them the spark of self-being will be kindled in one who thinks along with me. A direct communication of that spark is impossible. Every person is himself on his own or not at all.

The man who thus conceives himself as possible Existenz will regard his general concept as valid[5] because he lives it already; but he will know at the same time that what is purely general [*allgemein*] about it, what everyone can know identically, has a different kind of intelligibility. By using general terms as the form of existentially elucidating thought, he addresses himself and others, both in order to come to himself. He addresses other men—not all men, as he would in scientific[6] cognition. He cannot convince everyone whom anyone else might replace; he can win agreement only from the individual who sees, as possible, what cannot be generalized in so many words and yet complements this generality in himself. There are two sides to existentially elucidating thought: one is the mere generality, which by itself is untrue; the other is the mute Existenz, which by itself is impossible. Only as a whole do they coincide in a fortuitous expression that can no longer be methodically produced. This sort of thinking is methodical, to be sure, since it can be tested for truth and coherently presented; but the phrasings that carry it are interlocking grips of possible Existenz striving for communication. There are, so to speak, two wings that beat in this thinking, and it will succeed only if both really beat, possible Existenz as well as generalized thinking. If one wing fails, the soaring elucidation will plummet to the ground. It is in this elucidation that the universal [*Allgemeine*] and I myself coincide as the wings of philosophizing.

* * *

3. DEVISING A SPECIFIC GENERALITY FOR EXISTENTIAL ELUCIDATION

Whenever we speak in psychological, logical, or metaphysical terms it means that philosophically we may be slipping. The generality we use in such terms may continue in a detachment that means no Existenz has been elucidated. Or Existenz may vibrate in the generality as in something else—in something

---

5. That is, as sound (*gültig*); having actual and meaningful application.

6. That is, *wissenschaftlich*, scholarly.

that makes Existenz appear to itself but will weaken it at the same time—and then the generality as such will keep existing beside the philosophical thought.

But there is a last, different, and intrinsic manner of speaking generally in the elucidation of Existenz, and that is to speak in terms which cannot be generalized in the knowledge of world orientation. The categories we use in this type of general speech lack the power to define new objects. They are pure signs. Their generality does not exist in detachment. There "exists" no Existenz, for instance, nor does a self-being, a freedom, an existential communication, a historicity, an unconditional action, or an absolute consciousness. None of those "exist," and what the words convey if we denature them into objects of our knowledge of human existence is an out and out otherness, of which the existential signs can give only confusing indications. By the signs of existential elucidation we express what for possible Existenz is true being—not as an established objectivity, but as the being I cannot grasp without willing it because it is potentially my own. Existential signs are the general terms for freedom as the activity of a being which depends upon itself.

On the surface, as words, the specific signs we use to elucidate Existenz are derived from objects of world orientation, often explicitly characterized by the adjective "existential." In the end, however, they turn out to be not object-forming categories but indices for thoughts that appeal to existential possibilities. As signs they have a general side whose generality, however, is not mundane any more but already existential. Their proper conception requires the general statement to find an echo in Existenz. Without Existenz the signs are not just empty; they are nothing.

In elucidating Existenz I speak of the self as if it were a universal whose structures I demonstrate, but I can mean only my own self for which nothing can substitute. I am not "the I"—I am myself. I do look for the self, but only so as to find my own self, and I seek my own self for the sake of the self. When I ask about myself, my original experience is that I am utterly unable to speak of myself as incomparable. Self becomes my sign for referring to my unified conception of myself and the self. In existential elucidation I speak also of the many selves and of their Existenz; but I cannot mean it that way, because the many do not exist as cases of a universal. I speak of communication and mean my communication. And so I mean my freedom, my historic consciousness, my limit situations—and yet I can speak of them only in general [allgemein] terms.

The general side [Allgemeine] is always existentially present as well. It becomes a language vibrant with undertones of existential possibility when we use it to transcend in the philosophizing of existential elucidation. Existenz is what I can only be, not see or know; it does require the general medium of lucid knowledge, but whenever the general side tends to become all there is, the individual Existenz will set itself off again. Thus its philosophical elucidation can always generalize,[7] but cannot become generally valid.[8] It can be generally understandable, but only for possible Existenz.

When we use signs to conceive it, we are construing a formal schema of Existenz. The relation of this schema to Existenz—unlike that of the schema of a group of objects [to] those objects—is wholly incongruous. Since an Existenz

---

7. That is, translate into general terms (*in Allgemeines übersetzen*).

8. That is, cannot be objectively proven or confirmed.

is not subsumable, the schema can serve only as a guide for addressing an individual one; this alone will make it meaningful. What we contemplate is not only no single real Existenz, it is not even the generic concept of anything that exists and might be called Existenz; so the contemplation must aim at the formal schema. It may attempt only ways of elucidation that can make a real Existenz more aware of itself each time it will go along. It is only on the ground of possible Existenz, and then in singular, incomparable fashion, that the thought of existential elucidation can be truly performed. And yet, if we speak at all, we cannot help using that schema and its elements as analogs of objective concepts. Language has many words that do not denote objects and are not definable either, or whose definition, if there is one, will not preserve the essence of what lies in them: words like freedom, choice, decision, resolve, probation, loyalty, or fate. The very language empowers our philosophizing to get into the existential elucidation which *qua* language it has already performed.

We can illustrate the specific generality of existentially elucidating signs by contrasting the temporal *phenomenality* of possible Existenz with temporal existence as a generally valid *objectivity*—or, differently put, *concepts of Existenz* with the Kantian *categories*.

Both existential reality and the objective reality of the world appear in time. To make his categories for the establishment of objective reality applicable to the material of sensory perception, Kant resorted to the intermediate link of time in what he called his schemata. It is possible to confront these Kantian schemata of objective reality with altogether heterogeneous schemata of existential reality, since both of them require the medium of time. The parallel, contrasting in principle and strangely significant in kind, can be expressed in brief formulas:

Objective reality is subject to *rules* and cognoscible[9] under those rules; existential reality has no rules and is absolutely *historic* [*geschichtlich*].

The rules of reality are *causal laws*; whatever happens has its cause and its effect in the course of time. Existential reality, on the other hand, is self-originating as it appears to itself in time—in other words, it is *free*.

Substantiality is *temporal inertia*, the quality of enduring, of being neither increased nor diminished, while Existenz begins and vanishes in the phenomenality of time. The equivalent of objective duration in the contrasting parallel is to stand the *test* of time.

The *mutual causality* of substances, the Kantian reciprocity or community, confronts *communication* between self-beings.[1]

Objective reality is what corresponds to *sense perception* at large; existential reality is *unconditionality at the decisive moment*. *Empirical reality* confronts the *content* of decision.

The objectively determined, quantitatively related *magnitude* confronts something objectively undeterminable which we call the level or *rank* of Existenz.

Objective possibility, the concordance of conceptions with the conditions imposed by time, contrasts with the *unsettled future that creates the possibility of choice—which is my Existenz*.

9. That is, objectively knowable.
1. That is, beings that are "selves," self-conscious subjects.

Confronting necessity, the existence of an object *at all times*, we have, instead of endless time, the *fulfilled time of the moment*. As present eternity, this fulfilled time confronts Kant's time at large—the form of inertia whose correlative is substance. The latter is objective, measurable, and can be experienced as reality; the former is the depth of original, free Existenz. The latter is validly extant for everyone; the former turns a time that is tied to choice and decision into a phenomenon, as current time. Existenz has *its* time, not *time pure and simple*. Objective time exists for consciousness at large;[2] existential time exists for the historic consciousness of Existenz alone.

Objectively *nothing new* can come to be, as substance; for if it did it would void the unity of experience and make experience itself impossible. Existentially, on the other hand, there is no lasting and definitive objectivity; there are *leaps*, rather, and there is the phenomenal *genesis* of Existenz.

Kant himself, testing the existential signs against his objective categories, expressly rejected several. He showed, for instance, why there are no leaps in the world (in time) and no gaps (in space), why there is no coincidence (i.e., no blind, haphazard occurrence of things) and no fate (i.e., no necessity without rules that allow it to be understood as necessary). And indeed there is none of that in the objective world, as an object of cognition. We no sooner try an explication of Existenz, however, than all of these words recur. There are not two worlds lying side by side; there is but one world—it is in an altogether different dimension that Existenz comes to be lucid for us without being known. It only seems to do this in a parallel, because we cannot avoid using objective concepts and categories as means of expression. It is explicable in another sense, and in other forms, than the cognition of objects requires.

* * *

From *Chapter 12*
Existenz with Other Existenz

Existenz is not in the sense in which objects are.[3] Nor is it in the sense of the being of subjects accessible to psychology. Since it appears to itself, rather, in the protean split of existence into subjectivity and objectivity, it can neither come to be definitively objective nor be adequately understood as subjective.

By the research and the knowledge of world orientation, by purposive action and purposeless experience, by providing and serving as I do my job, I obtain a footing in existence in all directions. Having done so, I have simultaneously obtained the possibility of a sense of self-being[4]—the consciousness upon which I am cast back from all existence. Yet my self-being can neither be taken for the sole being nor permit any other universal being to be acclaimed as being pure and simple. The world and transcendence may congeal in their objectivity, but possible Existenz retrieves itself from objectivity. It comes back

2. That is, consciousness as something general and impersonal, of the sort that characterizes objective thinking and knowing (*Bewusstsein überhaupt*).
3. That is, when Existenz *is* (i.e., occurs or happens), its kind of reality or manner of occurrence is not like that of objects or things. Existenz is more

like the sort of human possibility that is realized in being a lover or friend.
4. That is, "a self-consciousness of being-a-self," of selfhood, self-identity (*eines Selbstbewusstsein des Selbstseins*).

to be that which alone can make transcendence felt, but which is present and sure of itself as freedom only.

The sense of being of possible Existenz is not an observable phenomenon. It does not exist except for *this* Existenz and the one linked with it in communication.[5] When we speak of it, we are inevitably and deceptively objectifying it as if it existed in so many specimens as it seems to our observation, while in fact the words mean no more than an appeal to self-being: to become aware of something which, if it is, is this alone and admits of no substitution. In the world, of course, the subjects are the many concrete phenomenal forms of possible Existenz; but Existenz is nothing but itself and the communicative links that are as one with its self-being.[6] Existenz in the plural is not to be contemplated as an objectivity, nor as a subjectivity; we cannot establish it as extant, nor can we count how many of it there may be. Instead, as distinct from the mundane existence of multiplicity,[7] multiple Existenz is the *being of Existenz with other Existenz*. As such it is beyond cognition but can be elucidated as a possibility. It is the *tie of being to being* which we are when we believe *really to be*, the tie that comes to bind us insofar as we enter the existential circle.

Thus, instead of a being discoverable as an objectivity and as the one generally valid truth for all, what we find in the original, mundanely possible sense of being, across the subject-object dichotomy, is Existenz with other Existenz. Its source is the *encompassing* possibility of being from which being proper arises without coming to the isolation of one object in temporal existence, or to the leveling of subjects as one of a kind. In visualizing existential truth, therefore, we must understand that an ontology, a knowledge of being, is incompatible with it. Its being has to be elucidated in mundane existence as a matter of *faith against faith* rather than as the way of the one true faith.

TRUTH IN BEING WITH EACH OTHER

1. TRUTH AS ONE AND AS MANY

The differentiation of truth—of the truth I know as *cogent*[8] from the truth I *share* (as an idea) and the truth *I am myself*—is what enables Existenz to become reality. Only the truth which rationality and empirical findings make compelling is generally valid for everyone, because it applies to consciousness at large. When, on the other hand, I look at the objectively and directly stated truth of an idea or of the self-being of Existenz, I see that men have taken varied and contrasting things for their own truths. Yet in this way I acquire no original understanding of any of these truths, because in the objective form, in the picture of a multiplicity of believed truths, only their appearance exists for me as a consciousness at large engaged in world orientation. Truths conflict, but they are not shared by one who knows them all; they are shared

---

5. That is, the "sense of being of possible Existenz" is different from the "sense of self-being" that Jaspers has just been discussing, associated with thought, action, etc., as well as embodiment. It is a radically individuated possibility that exists only in relation to and within the inwardness of the existing individual—and can only be realized in relation to *another* possible Existenz (in the form of another person) with whom one is in the kind of genuine Existenz-

level relation that he calls "communication."
6. Jaspers is here going so far as to say that the realization and "self-being" of Existenz are inseparable from and essentially involve "the communicative links" of genuine communication with other Existenz.
7. That is, in contrast to the (kinds of) multiplicity that occur in mundane existence (*Weltdasein*).
8. That is, compelling (*zwingend*).

by him who is identical with one of them. *My* truth—which as Existenz I am simply in my freedom—comes up against *other* existential truth. By and with this, it comes to be itself. It is not unique and alone, but unique and uninterchangeable in its relation to others.

I cannot step out of this truth. I cannot watch it, and I cannot know it. A departure from it would drop me into the void. I can, of course, commit the objectifying self-comprehension of its current phenomenality to infinite reflection. As a phenomenon I can take it to be absolute at the historic moment, only to relativize it again in the next moment; but I can do this only by the truth of my Existenz, which is temporal and thus always in the process of becoming; I cannot do it intellectually and unoriginally. Not until it serves an Existenz can the relativizing intellect have substance by destroying every objectivity, because the success of existential thinking will bring forth new objectivities at the same time. As Existenz I am not at home elsewhere (unless it were in the transcendence that reveals itself to this Existenz); I am in existential identity with myself. This identity lies behind all seeming dissolution, but it does not yield to the dissolution because only its current phenomena are accessible to questioning, not the identity itself. It is only in communication that I see the truth of other Existenz. Turning my back on the deceptive mirrors of those who merely recognize or reject me, I come to be sure of myself in living solely in this contact of truth with truth.

Objective truth is one for all men; and regarding the reasons for it, from a standpoint, it is always particular. Existential truth is different. Because I cannot step out of the truth that is the possibility of my Existenz, because I cannot contemplate it from outside, I cannot say, "There are several truths"; for multiplicity applies only to the outward appearance of visible forms, of thoughts and dogmas that can be stated. The truth of Existenz is not manifold, because it cannot be seen as manifold from outside, and not established as extant. Nor can I say, "I myself am the sole truth," for I am not without the others to whom I relate. The unconditionality in my Existenz is not universally valid; it is an unconditionality that can never be identically transferred.

2. THE CHOICE OF TRUTH

Truth is either cogent and thus not chosen, or it is made unconditional by a choice.

If there were many unconditional truths in existence, so that I might confront them and choose one for myself, truth would be meaningless. Truths which in their unconditionality exclude each other could then be known to me as many truths, which is impossible. Whether I know truth, share truth, or am truth—in each case there can be only one truth that *excludes* untruth as something other.

A man's choice of a world view is said to show the kind of man he is.[9] But the question there is: what are his choices? All objective alternatives are specific and particular, and that in a situation; they do not apply to a number of world views that we might choose from, because no specific particularity can be decisive when it is a matter of the whole. To assign to all possible thoughts

---

9. That is, the kind of human being (*Mensch*) one is.

their place in the idea of a totality makes sense in world orientation about thoughts that are communicated in language. But a survey of world views as cogitative structures voids them as world views; rather, it enables the man[1] who surveys their cogitativeness to choose in a radically different sense: the choice I start from, as the source of existential truth, is the choice in which *Existenz chooses itself.*[2] Instead of choosing a truth from the many types I am offered, I come to it by choosing the freedom of Existenz to elucidate itself in the world view that is true for it *alone*.

Self-understanding begins with the individual concrete acts of choice whose indeterminable sequence builds our life. I can ask, then: Why did I make this choice? What did it mean? What were its consequences? What unknown premises or principles did it rest upon? The rationally consistent contexts that unfold in the answer to such questions seem to lead to possibilities, final in principle, from which I might choose as from the premises of rationally formed world views. Yet this method, this search for consequences and ultimate premises that are no longer justifiable and yet not meant to be without an object, will always lead me only to a relative end: I am not satisfied and remain skeptical when final alternatives of the world view are set forth as necessary. What the way of rational self-understanding by final principles—starting from the concrete acts of choice—retains as its foundation and indissoluble end is the Existenz whose possibility encompasses all cognition of mutually exclusive and supposedly final principles. A purely theoretical interpretation, one not aimed at its own existential choice, helps an Existenz to understand itself only relatively, in its temporary objectifications, not in the unconditionality of its source.

An Existenz, after infinite phenomenal reflection, will understand its choice of truth as the leap to the true originality that goes with a knowledge of confronting other origins.

This original choice is what lends the most decided assurance to philosophizing in the reality of individual Existenz. Because I hold my philosophizing to be true, and to be one, I cannot *comprehend* all other truth as true in the same sense, but I can join its proponents in questioning and embattled communication. Even though I take it for the one truth, my philosophizing is to me not everything; it is a form of *Existenz reaching out for others*. It can never survey a juxtaposition of truths; only their phenomena can become surveyable in stated doctrines, in the *capita mortua*[3] that must be penetrated so as to make contact with the origin of other truth.

Such a posture of the sense of truth in a philosophizing known to me as existentially elucidative does not mean an invalidation of general validities. On the contrary, this relentlessly critical posture clings to cogency and will not let me confuse it with any other truth. Nor can it mean an abdication of Existenz in the sense that it would rather not have its truth, would rather turn itself into the case of a universal. Least of all does it mean that Existenz will set itself absolute.

What remains for the intellect is the primordial paradox of existential truth: that truth is singular and yet reaching for other truths; that there seem to be

---

1. That is, the person.
2. This statement makes clear that for Jaspers, "existential truth" is truth that has to do with individual Existenz, which is different for and fully determined by each Existenz.
3. That is, worthless residue (literally, "dead heads"; Latin).

many truths, and yet there is only one; and furthermore, that absolute validity and relativity are not to exclude each other, because validity is always absolute in Existenz alone and relativity always applies only to the objective appearance of what has been thought and said.

3. WHY THERE IS NO COUNTING EXISTENZ

In the world everything objective is one at a time; and then there are the many, which can be counted. I think of the one subjective soul and count how many such subjects there are within a certain radius, or I think of the world of human order in which everybody is not just a random part but a link in the whole. Of Existenz with other Existenz I cannot think in this fashion. Existenz does not exist as such. I can move it as a phenomenon into my field of contemplative vision, but I do not have any kind of objective criterion for what is an existential phenomenon and what is not.

That is why categories other than the nonobjective signs of freedom are only inadequately applicable to Existenz. If we could watch "cases of Existenz," they would be one at a time and then many, and as such countable in the category of quantity. But unity and multiplicity are objective forms of existence in the world; they are not forms of the being of Existenz, although Existenz will inevitably but inadequately—and hence in the mode of revocation—be spoken of in those forms. Existenz is accordingly *multiple*, but *not countable*. To myself alone, each Existenz is an Existenz in singular, uninterchangeable communication, in a mutual, noncompetitive approach. Enveloped by an indistinct darkness, I am nothing but this possible Existenz with that other multiple Existenz.[4] Not even this cycle of existential experience will make a whole; but the thought of an existential realm as a totality of which I am a member is unfathomable as a distinct thought.

We do inescapably tend to conceive Existenz in this fashion anyway, to think of it as one, as many, as an existential realm. This tendency rests on the urge to objectify Existenz like everything else. In contemplation I can potentially *step out of the world* of objective existence, and thus out of the world in which subjects exist; to me as consciousness at large this exit gives a "point outside," albeit an imaginary one; I am in the world and yet, in a sense, outside it. But I *cannot step out of Existenz.* I cannot watch it, cannot compare it with other Existenz, cannot objectively put several of it side by side. At first, of course, the fact that I myself am this one, that I am always "I" again no matter how I try not to be, bespeaks nothing but the identity of an empirical and a logical subject. But that within this identity I, as the real "I myself," cannot confront this self anymore (except in the semblance of formal speech, in which I cannot really do it after all)—this shows that Existenz is *rooted in itself.*[5] Yet to state this fact as such opens the door to misconceptions, for those roots are not fetters, not ties to a ground from which I would like to be free but cannot; in this very impossibility of escaping lies my will to be myself, because I can have no other will. Here alone lies the truth of the "I am" that makes it

---

4. That is, for Jaspers Existenz refers to a *way of existing* that is always a *possibility* for each of us, but is not something that we *are* or *have*, or that can be realized or acquired once and for all, or that can exist on its own apart from our living reality.

Moreover, it necessarily involves the relatedness of genuine interpersonal communication.
5. That is, is "rooted in itself" *as a way of existing* (not as an entity).

impossible to be myself once again, as it were, to be myself in some other way, or in many ways. It is as and in this being alone that I am;[6] beside it, or behind it, I am not. It is my being as the singular, uninterchangeable freedom that is not a case of any general, formal freedom. I know it as what is nearest and yet strange to me, what is never objective as such and yet the only certainty that matters to me. That there is something which says to itself "I am" and simply will not become an object to contemplate—this is the fixed point in the universal relativization of all objectivities and validities.

BEING AS EXISTENZ AND BEING FOR ALL

At first glance we think of the world as existence in absolute space and in absolute time. We then dissolve it into relativities and view it in its perspective character; we make it observable and explorable, depriving it of all absoluteness and bringing it into suspension. As what it is, however, the world is being for all, an identically lasting objectivity.

Existenz, on its part, stands within the world; its being lies in the interrelation of origins in which unconditionality is experienced amidst the qualifications that mark all mundane existence. This basic being is never a being for all.[7]

The one universal being for all is the mundane being [Weltdasein] whose generally valid knowability remains qualified by its relativity. The being of Existenz, on the other hand, is one at a time, a mundane phenomenon whose absoluteness not everyone can come to know, and whose unconditionality is valid only for itself in its communicative circle. Being as universality [Universalität] and being as Existenz are both interdependent and conflicting.[8] Their conjunction and the doubts they cast upon each other do not permit any durable synthesis, nor do they eliminate one of the two modes of being. What takes precedence existentially is nothing for cognitive world orientation. What is generally valid for cognition has for Existenz no being-in-itself; it is not intrinsic being.

1. TOTALITY AND ORIGINALITY

The self-isolating mundane realities of objectivity and subjectivity make me vanish; yielding to them, I exist by merely being there or merely obeying, governed from without, unless I retrieve myself to my own Existenz. Yet at the same time, objectivity and subjectivity serve as the medium of illumination for whichever Existenz may turn to mine. I am addressed and I do my own addressing in that language, for which the objective language is just a passageway. But I do not come to be a whole, and I achieve none.

Existential multiplicity does not lie in objectified truths as such. In the objective realm things are either true or false, good or evil, shared or spurned, and there are synthetic combinations as dialectical possibilities; there is the

---

6. That is: It is only *as* and *in* this way of being (*Existenz*) that *I* (truly) *am*.

7. That is: Existenz's basic way of be-ing is never the kind of being that a thing is—an enduring selfsame objectivity.

8. Jaspers here is attempting to give both Hegel (with his emphasis on *Allgemeinheit* as the basic characteristic of the larger reality of which we are a part) and Kierkegaard (with his emphasis on "subjectivity" and individuality in considering what it means to exist as a human being) their due.

one truth. Existential multiplicity is originality. It means that there will be no totality because I am myself and the other is himself. It also means that, as I am only one, I do not know the many *qua* many, nor in a totality in which all multiplicity were sublimated; I know the many only as I communicate with them. They are with me, and I am with them, en route to the One.

The phenomena of Existenz are thus *not subsumable* in the total whole of a knowledge. They are *not transferable* as the knowable being that would always be the same for all men. For while all the differences and contrasts of existence can be thought of in general terms, we cannot really think of the differences between Existenz and Existenz, because no thinker can step outside them. I could no sooner conceive such differences than I would have to regard them as existentially interdependent possibilities peculiar to this thinking Existenz itself. Running through all divisions is the stream of truth, of my truth which I actively ascertain.

There must be an Existenz to apperceive reality proper. *What reality is*, however, is thus neither defined nor identical for all men. Reality does not appear alike to each original Existenz. The question is *who* sees it and *as what*, and from any knowledge there is always a leap to the answer. What I am in conjunction with transcendence is correlative to what I apperceive as reality. As an object of cogent cognition in world orientation, of course, reality is universal, but as such it never comes to be the full reality of my experience and my actions. The first is limited, particular, and relative; the second is to me the whole reality. As I know the first, I am a consciousness at large;[9] in the second, as I experience it, I am possible Existenz related to transcendence.

2. EXISTENZ AND THE CONTEMPLATION OF PHENOMENAL EXISTENZ

Man is not the peak of creation, for there is total otherness unrelated to him. But for himself he is necessarily the center. He can step out of this, observing and exploring as consciousness at large; he can change standpoints; potentially, at least, he can reach a "standpoint outside the world." Yet no matter how thoroughly he may observe and understand himself as a phenomenon and analyze his conditions, he cannot step out of his Existenz; and so he finds out that none of his psychological and sociological knowledge enables him to grasp his real self, that he no sooner steps out of his Existenz even as a mere thought possibility than it threatens to elude him. Man does not willingly come to a halt, however. He sets no limit on his observations and analyses. In his intrinsic being he always knows himself beyond or beforehand, with a leap between himself and everything he can observe.

Looking about it in the phenomenal world, Existenz searches for Existenz by way of contemplating the phenomena. Inclined to speak of them, then, in a way that would never occur to pure contemplation, it tends to see *everything* as Existenz. But the observable world of nature will not really turn into Existenz; there is nothing which man and the Other in the world will ever have really in common. Being human, I want to ask questions and get answers, but

---

9. That is, *Bewusstsein überhaupt*, Jaspers's expression for the kind of consciousness that deals in generalities (*Allgemeinheiten*) and engages in objective knowing, rule following, and the like; a better translation of this phrase than "a consciousness at large" might be "consciousness generally" or "general consciousness."

man alone replies to man. And even among men there is no equality. In the world they differ characterologically and sociologically; only for particular rights and purposes do they make themselves equal. They are equal, and thus dealing with each other on the same plane, in their indefinitely possible relation to transcendence; but at the same time their eternal being remains, as it were, in a transcendent order of rank. To whom I relate so as to stand with him before transcendence, and who will desert me there—these are abysmal, existentially manifested inevitabilities which no intellect can remove, just as they themselves are mere parables for an inequality which no categories cover.

Although in contemplating the phenomenal inequality of men—their different goals and ways of life, their different sense of existence [*Dasein*], their different factual world—we can never grasp Existenz,[1] our contemplation is subject to the existential concern of self-searching. My explication of what man at large may be comes necessarily from *my* historic situation. I do not start out objectively from the primitiveness of aboriginal tribes, nor subjectively from my own beginnings, known or possible, or from the everyday aspects of my existence. I start out from exalted moments, from the intrinsic present. It takes an existential concern to open my eyes to what seems like primitiveness, to the existence and the thinking of the aborigines, to the stages of mankind. It takes this kind of concern to make me see a historical spirit[2] as something I have adopted and overcome or as something alien, to give me a feeling for characterological or sociological types, and to show me the way that I myself have gone, and my everyday life.

I lose my way in contemplation, however, when I cease to be addressed by Existenz. A contemplation that explores the world can only be a path; it cannot be contemplating Existenz anywhere. It would be a misconception and an abandonment of the roots of philosophizing if Existenz were studied in its historic appearance, if forms of it were posited as types and their diversity surveyed in historical sequence. The things which an objective observer sees changing and following one another are psychological characters, world images, modes of conduct, social and economic conditions, world historical situations, and so forth; Existenz is always the same thing in another form. Not until I transcend and extinguish the historical side will a contemplation of history lead to the sense of historicity that assures me of being.

I am always both: a possible Existenz and an observer. Unfolding for my observation is the stage of world history on which I see the diversity of human possibilities to date; I see that the world of my traditions is one of many, and that as a historical individual I am one figure among billions on that stage. As possible Existenz, however, I am capable of this entire contemplation without entering into it as an object, and through it I am able to make contact with alien Existenz.

But if my contemplation, instead of keeping me universally ready for existential searching, makes me pile up images of man in his history and in his possibilities, it is not my self that is in touch with what I have seen. As a

---

1. Better translated: "Although Existenz can never be encountered by contemplating (and in terms of) the kinds of observable traits that vary from person to person, rendering them different and unequal, our contemplation [. . .]." "Grasp" is a poor translation of *treffen* (meet, directly encounter).

2. That is, a particular historical spirituality (*Geistigkeit*).

feeling for diversity, this erudite contact may carry universal contemplation to the very borderline of existential concern and yet be abysmally apart from it. Ranke[3] is an example. World history, he tells us, is not an accidental mêlée of states and nations; nor is cultural advancement its sole point. We see creative, living forces at work, moral energies. There is no defining them; but they can be viewed, perceived, used to engender a sense of sharing their existence. In their life, their passing, their revival—always accompanied by increased abundance, heightened significance, a broadened scope—lies the secret of world history. The diversity of nations and their literatures is the premise of history's attraction for us. It is not the society where one man holds the floor that affords us pleasure and moves us ahead, nor is it one in which all keep saying the same things on the same level or in the same mediocrity; we feel at home only where a variety of peculiarities, purely evolved in themselves, meet on a higher common plane, where indeed they produce this plane by touching and complementing each other at the living moment. There would be nothing but odious boredom if the different literatures were to blend their peculiarities. The combination of all rests on the independence of each. The same is true of states and nations; it is from segregation and pure development that harmony will emerge.

In these phrasings Ranke would seem to have Existenz in view, or at least not to surrender it to a universal. Yet for all their seeming closeness to it, the lines call for a radical distinction from the entirety of meaning they express, and what this meaning aims at in panoramic imagery is the wealth of phenomena. Diversity, abundance, scope seem ultimate standards of worth; boredom turns into a negative criterion, and overall harmony into the premise of satisfying universal contemplation. Peculiarities which are still alien will touch, only to round each other into a whole in short order. Ranke does take independence for a premise of union; but this union, this single encompassing whole, seems to him unquestionably possible. He almost takes the position of noncommittally acknowledging whatever is not mediocre. If this position were assumed in fact—especially by someone other than Ranke, that enigmatic, uniquely important mind [Geist]—the decisive factor would be predilections that cannot fail to be narrow, however vast the visual canvas, because they do not express the peculiar existential sense of fate. For Existenz does not stand on the brink of the abyss of being, where harmony ceases. It is in accord with being—a being which, put in existentially elucidative terms, would by this accord void the sense of our predilections and would void the possibility of our Existenz if we were content with the predilections. The grandeur of contemplation shows, by contrast, that as pure contemplation it buries the originality of Existenz with other Existenz.

3. UNIVERSAL [GEMEINSAME][4] AND EXISTENTIAL COMMUNITY

In diversity we seek the unity which, if it could last, would be the end of diversity. But Existenz, at once subjective and objective, can see only a signpost pointing to realization in the one being for all. Anticipated, the one being is

---

3. Leopold von Ranke (1795–1886), German historian who advocated making the discipline of history as objective, factual, and scientific as possible.

4. That is, impersonal forms of community [Gemeinschaft] (in social and cultural life).

the ruin of Existenz; rejected, it leaves Existenz an empty possibility. And if it were the community of every Existenz, it could be realized only as their perfection in the one realm of the spirits [*Geisterreich*].[5] Whatever precedes this would only be pointing the way.

What all men have in common as intelligible and universally valid can be visualized as the task of Existenz in existence [*Dasein*], in order then to contrast it with that which can constitute original existential community [*Gemeinschaft*].

Common, first, is our existence as the object of empirical research and cogent knowledge. This is the community of consciousness at large, the ability to *know* identically what is generally valid. Realistic, critical devotion to this knowledge may, as it is jointly put into practice, initiate existential links.

The second thing we have in common is what all men[6] identically *are*. Conceiving this leads to an objectivity of man at large; but this is not the same as self-being.

We can describe the *situation* a man has identically in common with any other man. All have the same vital needs; to meet those, they depend on each other's activity (the common concern with existence and possible pleasure); they all must die; they are all at the mercy of chance, and so forth. But the common situation is just the common frame for an otherwise historically differing factuality, for the supposedly general situations become situations of a self-being only as that self-being deals with them and fulfills them. Death is never alike; from all but total indifference to an ever-present and thus life-controlling end, the meaning and the weight of death change with man's way to experience and to express it. When I seek clarity about this or another basic human situation, in awareness of its relevance, I am precisely not aiming at its timeless, general side, which all men share. Instead, I am elucidating my self-being in communication with others, asking what the situation means to them.

Finally, when we ask what common trait enables men to *understand* each other across time and space, we first have to limit our premise. This understanding is by no means given; its perfection is doubtful in principle, its course a permanent task. Within these limits, the *logical* answer to our question is consciousness at large, the structure that unites whatever exists as an objectively aimed consciousness, potentially even beyond the bounds of being human. The *psychological* answer is unvarying human nature, the character of this existing species. The *idealistic* answer is God, the One we live by and live for.

None of these common unities is perfect in temporal existence. Wherever one is claimed to be presently extant or attainable, it is an anticipation. Perfect knowledge; the complete, unbroken, lastingly existent human being; the closed world totality of the spirit [*Geist*][7] in which all things have their being as links in the whole; the dogmatic deity—none of that has a definitive existence. Instead, there is no general being for all, nor—except in objective

---

5. This echoes Kant's idea of an ideal form of spiritual community that would be a kind of "*Reich*" (realm, commonly rendered as 'kingdom') of ends" in which all regard and treat each other as "ends in themselves" (rather than as "means only").
6. This translates *Menschen*, which (here and

elsewhere) would be better rendered as "human being(s)."
7. Here Jaspers alludes to Hegel's interpretation of all of reality—and of all of human reality in particular—in terms of what he calls *Geist*. (See above.)

relativities—is there a unity, a perfect community, in which Existenz would cease to be. The being of Existenz, however, the being by which other being must be sustained to have weight for us in existence, is the self-realizing unconditionality of a community that is *established*, that remains historic, and that never becomes extant. And being established, it is not universal either.

As *friendship*, it is the community of those who really are themselves for one another—rather than the community of all, who neither are nor can be Existenz for themselves.

As *following*,[8] it is the tie of self-being to a leading self-being, subject to conditions, but in fidelity and trust. Following is distinct from mere obedience, because it is a noninterchangeable community in which one who obeys will understand at the same time. The follower keeps coming to himself in communication, in a communication that is an additional and thus a receiving one, but at each moment potentially a giving one as well. Following is accordingly not confined to concerns of existence, as something objective and general, but occurs in the roots of the being of every Existenz which so commits itself.

As a *substantial common life* evolved in unconscious continuity, existential community is due to the substance of an idea. Inwardly the existential interrelation of individuals is more original; outwardly the idea comes first, although it has its roots in Existenz. The idea is the unknown Existenz of a community; it is what makes the individual himself without delivering him to the restlessness of self-being. The historic ideas are powers in which Existenz finds itself by participating in them as objectivities of the tradition that encompasses the individual, and by participating in the idea-oriented tasks of organizing existence [*Dasein*].

As a *community of action*, existential community is the realization that decides about existence [*Dasein*], most visibly in the actions of the state.

As a *community of activity* it is the realization of the tasks whereby knowledge, inventions, technical structures, works, and the products of labor we need day by day are obtained in existence.

As its medium, each of these communities needs the transparency of a purposive conception. When this is detached from the root of existential community, however, it will be diluted into a mere common bustle. There is no community of Existenz unless self-being remains the historic mode of *understanding each other in the incomprehensible*. The bounds of general, transparent understanding are not the limit of existential community; they are where it begins. But its reality is more vigorous the more comprehensively and boundlessly the intelligible realm is crossed and constantly held on to as a medium of expression.

Throughout all standpoints, Existenz will recognize Existenz as a reality it touches in another world of being. Intrinsic truth remains unconditional, not a standpoint; existential, not general [*allgemein*]; joint, not isolated; historic, not timelessly valid; en route, not perfected.

It is thus impossible and absurd to want to survey and adopt the truth of every Existenz as one, in an entirety of its objectifications. There is one general world of philosophy and of philosophical possibilities; but knowing this

---

8. That is, "followership" (*Gefolgschaft*), in the sense of being willing and able to be guided and led (in appropriate circumstances) by another person, whom one allows to "take the lead" and "lead the way."

is still *world orientation* about the philosophy that occurs in history as a sum of thought structures. It remains possible to unite and to know all objective world views and formulas in one brain. But all this is always only a means, not truth itself. I remain this historic creature which *cannot skip its own origin* by way of knowledge. As I enter into the objectivities of a general being,[9] into its intelligibilities and techniques of thought, what I rediscover in the contents of these media is the possibility of my self-being. I can transcend myself only to my own ground, and I can do this only by coming more and more decidedly to myself.

EXISTENTIAL ELUCIDATION IS NOT ONTOLOGY

An ontology was either conceiving "the All," the thought of universality as the ground from which subjective and objective multiplicity springs, or else its original concept was "the Many," the multiplicity of individuals in the "this-ness" and singleness in which they subjectively and objectively exist.

The ontologies that began with the All never did get to the truly individual; the ones that began with the individual never got to the One, which is all.

As a doctrine of the All, an object-oriented ontology became a metaphysical realism; a subject-oriented one became an idealism that dissolved all being in self-consciousness. As a doctrine of the individual, an object-oriented ontology turned into pluralism, and a subject-oriented one into monadology—both approaches to an inquiry into Existenz.

Even now, pluralism and the doctrine of monads would be existentially expressive thought forms if Existenz could be an objectified subjectivity. But Existenz can be neither an object nor an objectified subject; it remains an origin that we can subjectively and objectively elucidate only in the form of an appeal.[1] Existential elucidation would be thwarted if we developed it as an ontological doctrine.

1. PLURALISM AND MONADOLOGY

Pluralists maintain that there is no such thing as one absolute that makes the existence and the character of all things comprehensible for objective cognition. Instead, they say, there are many *beings* which partly touch and which may tend toward unity; if there is unity, it is only as a goal, not as existence [*Dasein*]. To a pluralist, the being of the many is the font of active life and meaning, with genuine experience springing from an awareness of that being, from an open mind for its abundance.

It is correct that there can be no objective doctrine of the world in which diversity does not occur. Relative to the knowledge of each time and to the viewpoint of its world orientation is the diversity of *things*, of *categories*, of the *spheres of the mind* [*Geist*].[2] But for this objective doctrine of manifold mundane being there is unity as well.

9. That is, of common (*allgemein*) life.
1. This is important to Jaspers's conception of Existenz, and of the philosophical task of its elucidation. Hence the title of this section: "*Existenzerhellung* Is Not Ontology."
2. By "the spheres of *Geist* (spirit)," Jaspers means the various domains of cultural, intellectual, and spiritual life stressed by Hegel in his conceptions of "objective" and "absolute" *Geist*. In the following paragraphs, Jaspers acknowledges their reality and significance while also insisting that Existenz is inherently and irreducibly plural. It thus is fundamentally at odds with the very idea and ideal of assimilation into anything like a complete and final totality of "spheres of *Geist*," even while allowing for participation in them.

Not only are there scattered things that do not become one; real cognition invariably confirms the premise of universal interaction, as laid down in the principle "What does not interact does not exist." This is not the same as unity, of course, but it does mean that nowhere is a thing so separate from others as to be absolutely untouched and untouchable. Nothing is absolutely for itself; everything is really or potentially related to everything else.

Categories are conceived in a system. They do not make a definitive system for our knowledge; nevertheless, there is the idea of a unity in which they generate each other in the sense of mutual logical interdependency.

The spheres of the mind [*Geist*], initially juxtaposed, will touch in struggle. They are made over into unities by a recurrently originating substance of theirs that will not let them remain embattled powers, a substance that will round them into a whole as the concordance of the many within it.

All this is reunited, however, in the microcosm of man: things as his world, the categories as the structures of his world orientation, the mental spheres [spheres of *Geist*] as the union of the present in his existence. Yet even then there is not the one whole; once again everything is up to the Existenz that will use the whole to bring about its own appearance.

True, original plurality alone is existential. Though incapable of envisioning a total existential world in contemplation, Existenz in communication with Existenz becomes aware of a dark possibility,[3] a possibility expressed—as if it were a matter of objective diversity—in such misleading statements as that there must be many an Existenz that never meets another, and that some must be touching in appearance without entering into communication, that is to say, without mutually grasping each other's Existenz.

Monism exists as the true *idea of unity* in scientific [*wissenschaftlich*] world orientation—although the final unity is not achieved but keeps shattering on the world's inner impermanence—and it exists as the One in transcendence, in whose metaphysical conception it holds its original place. But Existenz, for us flatly inaccessible to the idea of a conclusive realm of spirits, remains pluralistic.[4] The construction of a spirit realm [*Geisterreich*] for our knowledge would be blocking the one road that may lead Existenz to such a realm: to realize, by free communicative action in the vast, unobjectifiable darkness of possibility, what links self-being with self-being.

Stated as such, the pluralism of Existenz is not objective and thus does not show the universal unity that would sublimate it. The phenomenon of Existenz, of course, can be seen in world orientation, in characters, ideas, forms of the world, without letting us draw an objective line between Existenz and unexistentiality; viewed from without, it turns into a diversity and back into a mental unity. First of all, however, this unity and diversity—as in stated tenets of faith, in state structures and forms of religious life—are never the original truth itself. And second, there is in world orientation a tendency needed and meaningful for this orientation alone: to organize that externally viewed diversity in a mental cosmos, at the cost of its existential roots. Between real

---

3. That is, becomes aware in the darkness of a possibility.
4. Better translated: "But there is an *enduring* pluralism of Existenz, because it is simply incompatible with the very idea of a final realm of *Geist* (Geister-

reich)." Jaspers here echoes Kierkegaard's protest against the absorption of the individual self in the *Allgemeinheit* (generality, universality) of Hegelian "objective" and "absolute" spirituality.

Existenz and an objectively known unification of the existential world there is a radical conflict.

Leibniz,[5] in his closely reasoned pluralism of *monads*, assigns to them an original place in a preestablished harmony, without impairing their absolute independence. His world consists of innumerable individual specimens of Existenz which do not affect each other, do not react to each other, but unfold and wither as individual worlds, each one of which is the whole. In the monads, being has become a diversity of subjects conceived as objects.

A monadology that *captured* the philosophy of Existenz, one that made it a knowledge of multiple existential being, would be confusing consciousness at large—the thinking which can attain a standpoint outside its thoughts—with Existenz, which in principle is always with itself alone. In consciousness at large I can only understand others;[6] as Existenz I enter into true communication.

But if we regarded the doctrine of monads as a pictorial *representation* of existential philosophy, something we can understand in metaphysical monadology would appear as a contradiction—namely, that monads have "no windows." Even if they had windows, this would not suffice for Existenz to view them as a parable for the being of plural Existenz, for windows would lead only to understanding. Existenz needs the possibility of closer links, of a kind that will not only let one see each other but will awaken and bring to life each other's being and substance.

The single monad is consciousness and unconsciousness at large; it is the *whole world in a particularity defined by the measure of clarity* that has been reached by this monad. Monads are the multiplication of the world entirety. Each one is all, although in the most varied degrees of awareness. Existenz, on the other hand, is not a being-for-itself. In its own eyes it is not all. Rather, it is for itself in its being with other Existenz and in its relation to transcendence.[7]

A monad is not Existenz; it has no historic definition; it is not a vanishing phenomenon of Existenz in time but the metaphysical *unit enduring throughout* time. It is thus a structure of *hypothetical* metaphysics, not of existential elucidation. Conceiving it does not involve an appeal to Existenz.

2. THE TEMPTATION IN THE WILL TO KNOW

Existential elucidation does make use of objectivities and subjectivities, but it provides no orientation about their being. In it, objectivities and subjectivities are not intended to establish facts; they are monitored, so to speak, as data from world orientation. Instead of doing once again what science [*Wissenschaft*] has done, we evoke possible Existenz on the premises of scientific

5. Gottfried Wilhelm Leibniz (1646–1716), German rationalist philosopher; he used the term "monad" (literally, "unit"; Greek) to designate the logically or conceptually ultimate fundamental units of reality that are purported to (necessarily) be the basis of all phenomenal reality, spatiotemporal as well as psychological.
6. That is: If I think about others in an objectively rational and impersonal manner, I can only *understand* (comprehend) various things *about* them (as opposed to really connecting with them).
7. That is: Existenz is nothing in and by itself. It is a reality, even for itself, only in relating in an Existenz-appropriate way with other Existenz and transcendence.

knowledge. We do not improve our cognition of the facts by steeping ourselves in the way they are, but we do make them speak in their relevance to
self-being.

If the elucidation of Existenz were to lead us to ontological statements about
it and thus to a *new objectivity* of the subjective realm, such congealment
would make our evocative thinking cognitively meaningless and a tool for
abuse.

If, for example, I lay down a passing existentially elucidative thought in the
statement "There are as many truths as there are individuals," this will in time
falsely serve to justify the arbitrary actions of each random self-existence.[8]
Citing the validity of such a statement, whatever exists can claim to find itself
of value by the mere fact that it exists. A brutal, vital atomism of the many
will then rise up against the possibility of a self-being that can come about
in communication only. The point of existential elucidation turns out to be
twisted into its opposite.

And if, objectifying in the other direction, I lay down the proposition that
"Existenz exists in communication and is true insofar as community turns into
unity," I may think I have in outward fashion what is impossible except existentially. What I am thus dogmatically claiming is the necessity of association and fraternization with everyone, of organization at all costs. I am for an
ever larger body politic, for global unity, for everything imperial. But outward
unity and entirety can be only a medium for possible Existenz; they spell its
ruin when they are absolutized with a resulting loss of their true unity in
transcendence.

The same abuse shows in the extent of the sort of talk wherein men vindicate and justify and seek support and security for themselves. Continued day
by day, an objectifying pronouncement of things existential will degrade
unconditionality into an object. We "demand" and "miss," "assure" and "confirm." We talk of love, lament about the boundary situations, and let an asserted
but unrealized unconditionality nullify all possibility and all reality. This is
where the untruth lies: what has meaning and weight at high points, as a
moment of articulating an expression and an appeal, becomes empty as a
topic of daily conversation. Against such misuse, silence is the regular expression of factual unconditionality. Tough, realistic expression, coolness, and
indirectness will more easily tie the knot of genuine communication than will
the anticipating and vulgarizing affectiveness of mouthing phrases of existential philosophy. Our daily life is sustained by the certainty of what is possible at crucial moments—by silent fidelity, not by one we know because we
say so.

Every word of existential elucidation that is not taken for an appeal but for
a statement of being—which it is only in its most literal sense—constitutes a
temptation to such abuse. Stripped of the element of appealing, of calling for
their translation into real Existenz, the signs of existential elucidation can be
talked about in terms of *applying* it, as if something were or were not so. A
consummate doctrine, indeed the very rudiment, of an ontology of Existenz
would have the same meaning. The result is the specific sophistry that accom-

---

8. That is, willful individual (*Eigendasein*).

panies all existential philosophizing. We take our worst falls when we seem nearest to the core.[9]

Faith Against Faith

In faith I collide as truth, as the truth I am as myself, with the faith in other truth. It takes this collision for my faith to come into being, and for me to come to myself.

The objection that in this case there would be no truth any longer, that it is a clear case of bottomless relativism, since a self-contradictory truth must necessarily be untrue and controversy cannot but prove the truth of one only— this objection presupposes, first, that there is no truth except the cogent, objectively extant one; the objectors are talking about something other than what is here the issue. Second, they would void Existenz in favor of an allegedly existing absolute objectivity, one we need only grasp and obey. And third, the objection reduces all communication to the joint understanding of objective validities, and the rest, perhaps, to random sympathies and antipathies, vital or erotic. In other words, it voids the genuine communication of struggling love.[1]

Only the man who becomes aware of the *faith* that is inherent in his Existenz, who can distinguish it from cogent and objective knowledge (which he seeks and has, but is not) as well as from the other faith—only such a man is originally unconditional and in true peril. He alone comes to respect Existenz as such in the other, distinguishing it from mere existence [*Dasein*] and from himself. It takes faith to understand faith. And to understand it does not here mean to make it my own, or to understand just the contents; it means that at the bounds of intelligibility the unintelligible is experienced as akin to myself but alien to me in the originality of the other faith.

In our inconclusive world, truth as self-being stands *against* other truth. Before transcendence it means extinction in time. Truths are *modes of extinction* as mundane existence in temporal phenomenality.

The struggle for existence, of whichever kind, occurs in the world as passive happening and active doing. It does not become a medium of existential struggle until the objectively incomprehensible dichotomy sets in: that all Existenz *depends upon the empirical phenomenon* in which it is realized and for whose existence it must fight like all existence, and that at the same time it is *more* than an empirical phenomenon and therefore able, not only to risk its phenomenality, but to give it up. Existenz will fight for its existence [*Dasein*], but not at any price.

1. THE STRUGGLE TO SOAR IN FAITH

As existence [*Dasein*], possible Existenz is fighting itself. It fights against *evil*, the unconquerable and yet unexistential resistance of self-will in blindly

---

9. Jaspers dismisses Heidegger's enthusiastic followers in the previous paragraph's scathing penultimate sentence, and here disassociates himself from Heidegger (and repudiates his ontological project in *Being and Time*).

1. That is, "fighting love," or "loving struggle" (*Kämpfender Liebe*): a relationship of Existenz-level communication that is loving but also challenging—as when the other does things that are unworthy.

defiant existence, the reversal of the final condition of my actions: from probation before transcendence into mere qualification of my actions by advantages to my existence [*Dasein*]. Possible Existenz fights against all ways of
deteriorating into a nonentity, by evasion and drift. It fights its own *unbelief*,
demonstrated in enjoying existence [*Dasein*] without transcendence, or in
despairing at existence. Only in this struggle, which erupts anew after each
victory and is resumed on aggravated terms after each defeat, can a possible
Existenz come to be real. Tranquil security may turn victory into perdition; a
defeat on the brink of the abyss may be most clearly uplifting.

Unchanged in substance, although different in form, the fight against oneself becomes an *outward struggle*. As such it is the fight of possible Existenz
against the superior force of what is not self-being, against the worthlessness
of an existence that makes claims simply because it exists, one which in time,
like a rising tide of mud, will manifest its worthlessness by a permanence that
is no triumph. This foe is waging the battle of hate-filled nonentity against
all being. He seeks self-confirmation and finds it, deluding himself and yet
unsatisfied, in the destruction of phenomenal Existenz in existence [*Dasein*].[2]
His will to the void [*zum Nichts*], to the nonentity he is, remains hidden from
him. He cheats all true being and is cheated himself as the achievement of
his continued existence [*Dasein*] in time strikes him as being.[3]

2. THE QUESTION OF THE ONE FAITH

In unexistential mundane existence,[4] the decisive factor is the leveling will of
nonentities who are not themselves, of existing individuals with their vitally,
characterologically given traits. Everyone wants the other to be like himself.
An Existenz alone feels the need to answer this question: if I believe in my
own truth, can I want everyone else to be as I am? May I take *my* faith, which
is to me the only true one, for the *one* faith pure and simple and want to bring
all others to it?

The negative answer follows from the situation of Existenz in existence
[*Dasein*]. To be real, Existenz must be historic [*geschichtlich*].[5] Only in case of
an existential vacuum will there be no resistance to the influx of any odd
content, but the result, then, will be only an imaginary total knowledge and
understanding, not a being. That I am myself is the very reason why I cannot
absorb any other true being. Its realization in myself would ruin me. I should
like to absorb it—for I should like to be truthful also in the sense of sharing
in all being—but it must satisfy me that the other is it. I love what is; I love it
precisely when I myself cannot be it. I dispense with an equality of levels; I
see what is flatly superior, and also what is inferior; I do without evaluation
and struggle, and yet I am in loving communication. I am at peace with the
other's being, one which, even though necessarily rejecting me, brings me so
much more resolutely to myself.

The psychological-sociological rule,[6] however, is that most world views and
tenets of religious faith tend to be regarded as solely and generally valid. Pro-

2. That is, of the realization in *Dasein* of Existenz.
3. That is (better translated): "He betrays (*betrügt*)
all genuine (*echte*) being, and is himself betrayed/
deceived (*betrogen*) precisely in that achieving his
own continued survival in time seems to him to be

being," i.e., to be what life is all about.
4. That is, Existenz-less (*existenzlosen*) *Weltdasein*.
5. That is, rooted in one's specific historical reality.
6. That is, as a psychological-sociological
generalization.

paganda is made for them, so as to bring salvation in their sense to all men. They carry the germ of an intolerance that makes believers use the means of violence available at each stage of their factual rise to power, trying to force these beliefs upon others. They imply a will to be for all men, to be catholic.[7] Only for a philosophy of freedom, and for the forms of religious faith that spring from such a philosophy, does the question arise what can and may be meaningfully willed as enforceable, and what may not and cannot be so willed.

Hence the answer to our previous question: I want everyone else to be the way I *strive to become*—to be himself in *his* truth. "Do not follow me; follow yourself!" is the existential challenge. Self-being awakens self-being but does not force itself on it.

It becomes questionable, however, whether another may be asked to be himself if he is not up to it—whether in that case an imposed faith will not be the truth, rather, because men who are not themselves can live only in such a faith. And there is the further question whether the challenge to be myself is not the most inhuman violence to be insinuated into my soul without external violence—whether self-being and the appeal to Existenz are indeed not fantastic illusions.

But in such questions we move on the level of contemplating the reality of existence psychologically—in other words, on a level on which self-being and freedom are absent from the start. This positivistic approach is not convincing; for self-being can be claimed against it as long as the other wants to continue in serious communication. What one is who does not want to be himself any more is another question. On that level philosophy has an end, but so has religion. What remains there is the purely positivistic political and sociological question how society can be organized, and whether a superstition may not perhaps suit the purpose.

Instead of belonging to one universal faith whose objective form bespeaks the will to power of a One, man will at crucial moments be cast back wholly upon himself, out of all forms. Struggle—no longer for existence, but for manifestation—*remains* thus even in the solidarity of communicative faith. I myself lovingly join the other as himself. But in all the identity which we owe to our relation to intrinsic being we remain permanently separated at the same time: every man lives on his own responsibility, without dependence, but in assurance of the other and in his echo. The *possibility* of faith against faith remains even in the closest conjunction.

3. THE STRUGGLE OF FAITH AGAINST FAITH

If there were only the fight of being against nonbeing, of truth against untruth, of good against evil, there would be one all-encompassing movement throughout existence. But the diversity of Existenz results in another pathos: that Existenz will not fight with unexistentiality, but will fight with other Existenz. The unexistential is just a repulsive nonentity, but alien Existenz has a depth of its own; the struggle between Existenz and Existenz, between faith and faith, is not covered by any of the alternatives of true or false, good or evil, faith or faithlessness. It is originally different in character from the ultimately

---

7. That is: Most worldviews and religious faiths have an inherent tendency to want to be "catholic" in the sense of being all-inclusive—"for all" (*für alle*) and embraced by all.

incomprehensible struggle against the other with whom I can communicate and whose equal worth I inwardly acknowledge. Here, though the situation in existence makes combat necessary, the combatants know they belong together in transcendence.[8]

In this struggle lies a hatred paired with love: the hatred a self-being feels for the way a strange self-being is, and its love of the being which is self-being after all. The final goal, which need not be rationally conscious and cannot be purposively willed, remains to get through this rupture of communication and establish true communication. The struggle is like an articulation in the process of manifesting myself. It thus means an uplift I lack in the pure struggle for existence, in which I know nothing but the reality of my will to live. In the struggle of faiths lies a solidarity that may suddenly break through and end the struggle.

Since Existenz is diverse and struggle cannot end in its existence,[9] it does seek communication with other Existenz; but as a community of all men this communication will not work. It will work as the real, historic [geschichtlich] community of men who belong together, men who commit themselves to that existential solidarity and whose mutual selection will, in fact, instantly pit them against other men who were excluded from that selection. All true communication is private to a few. The larger a community, the more uncommunicative it is. From a community of faith it turns into the impersonal protection of a total existence.[1] In the world the last alternative seems to lie between individualistic isolation and collective entirety, but this is an alternative for existence as such; the existential choice would lie between the possibility of Existenz in relation to transcendence and an unexistential[2] perfection in the world. The possibility of Existenz in existence [Dasein] includes the struggle of faiths; what mundane perfection accomplishes, though in utopian form, is a compromise of all unconditionalities into the order of one whole for all, without transcendence.

In the struggle of faith against faith[3] there are postures which not only show how possible Existenz deals with other possible Existenz but reveal the very essence of the faith that makes it do so. They are *intolerance, tolerance*, and *indifference*. Intolerance springs from untrue objectification and involves a loss of Existenz. People who are not themselves want to force their objectivity on others, if only a nonentity such as the color of their flag. Tolerance springs from a willingness to acknowledge others in communicative struggle. It makes me admit that what I am fighting against has a right to exist; the point of it is finally to end the struggle. Indifference indicates a lack of contact. The other, not even recognized as possible Existenz, is outside the area of my existential concern, whether because my interest in him is only vital, not a matter of faith any more, or because the narrowness of my own Existenz makes me inaccessible.

---

8. That is, in transcendence of relations that are merely objective (as happens in the case of genuine communication).
9. That is: Because Existenz (among human beings) is diverse, struggle (among them) in existence cannot cease.
1. That is, of a collective existence (*Gesamtdasein*).

2. That is, Existenz-less; without Existenz.
3. That is, the struggle between differing basic outlooks and values to which people may be committed in very genuine ways—a struggle that is by no means precluded by Existenz, genuine communication, and love.

Intolerance accompanies, above all, the abuse of objectivity I am lured into by the will to know. To maintain myself in this, I become an *intolerant rationalist*. Rational argument, thoughtful and clear in essence, comes then to be full of animosity and agitation; I am moved by psychologically intelligible needs for power and prestige, those irrational motives of escaping into self-deceptive ersatz forms of Existenz.

It is the weakness of my own faith that I want to overcome by force: unless the other believes in the same objectivity, I suspect that I might seem to him inferior, a believer in untruth; for my confusion of existential and objective, generally valid truth will let me see no truth except one that must forcibly exclude all others.

Something altogether different is true outrage, anger at the baseness, at the unexistentiality and sham which are not only existent but predominant, prestigious, presumptuous, and oppressive. Here faith stands against faithlessness.

While intolerance makes me subordinate my Existenz to generality and objectivity, true tolerance requires me to recognize the other inwardly without forcing anything on him. A strong faith begets candor in communication; it makes me ready and willing to be doubted, to test myself in my own faith, to come to myself in the free, open air where the validity of any positive faith is granted even as I fight it. No synthesis of all faiths into one is here pursued as a possible goal (the idealistic dead-end road of a total spirit as an idea without transcendence[4]). Nor is one faith made a faith for all Existenz and all time. The ultimate in this temporal-historic world is the self-realization of Existenz in the perilous process whose goal and end no knowledge tells us about. From this process the leap goes to transcendence, in a way that cannot be laid down and cannot be copied as if it were a matter of technique.[5] It is the lasting mystery for every Existenz. Tolerance knows standards, but not definitive standards. As the positive performance of recognition it is something that moves, something that will stray and find its way again, and always something yet to be acquired. Its stance is to be ready for such positivity, and never to be indifferent.

Indifference is to leave things as they are, without caring. If each act of tolerance is a personal acknowledgment, indifference is, in our social order—in which none are to be persecuted or discriminated against on account of their faith—the inevitable dilution and eventual perversion of tolerance. It is indifference to live and let live, not to disturb others as long as they do nothing vitally harmful or offensive. In the case of rulers whose rule is not threatened, an indifference that will be labeled tolerance produces the originally inhumane attitude that everyone should make a fool of himself in his own way—or, more kindly put, that everyone should seek his own salvation. In indifference there is no faith, no communication, no readiness for communication. The limitations on the forces and effective spheres of each Existenz

4. That is: the mistaken path (*Irrweg*) of idealism, which embraced the idea of a totality of spirit (*Totalität des Geistes*) without transcendence.
5. In these two sentences Jaspers contrasts a purely immanent, "temporal-historical (*zeitlich-geschichtlichen*) world" form of genuine Existenz or authenticity with one that involves a "leap" beyond that world to what he calls "transcendence" (*Transcendenz*). Its nature or meaning is difficult to discern, but Jaspers clearly conceives it as a kind of encompassing counterpart to his conception of Existenz. It might be thought of as his philosophical replacement for the religious idea of "God."

make indifference unavoidable as a social posture; but the crucial way in which it differs from true tolerance is that tolerance, even when it borders on indifference, will as a matter of principle keep me ready to listen, if possible, and to be impinged upon.

4. EXISTENZ WITH OTHER EXISTENZ AS A BOUNDARY

The diversity of truth remains a basic fact for Existenz; but attempts to find objective words for this fact will fail. To say that the one transcendence shows in many aspects is an oversimplification. As Existenz, starting out from transcendence, we can never make it comprehensible in principle by turning all of being into a whole, as the outflow of transcendence. The One would not be explicable by an explication of its diverse aspects. And neither is the diversity of Existenz the diversity of the aspects of the one being, for each Existenz is always only itself, not a picture for others. It does not become an aspect; there are aspects for it. The only solution is that of transcendence for Existenz: the unfathomable, downright otherness, is revealed only here, only for Existenz, and only if Existenz will not forget what exists in the world. The boundary situations as such are not yet the dizzying abyss that tears us from whatever ground we stand on; nothing short of this diversity of truth in the being of Existenz with Existenz will fully evoke that vertigo. Either we are freed from it by transcendence or we escape as existence [*Dasein*] into confining delusions to which we stubbornly and fearfully cling.

SOURCE: From Karl Jaspers, *Existential Elucidation*, vol. 2 of *Philosophy*, trans. E. B. Ashton (Chicago: University of Chicago Press, 1970), pp. 3–12, 15–18, 360–82. Except where otherwise indicated, German words in brackets are the terminology used in the German original, inserted by the editor in addition to their renderings in the translation. The second volume of Jaspers's three-volume *Philosophie* (1932), *Existenzerhellung* (*Elucidation of Existenz*) is his most important contribution to existential philosophy.

MARTIN BUBER
(1878 – 1965)

Buber is generally regarded as a religious thinker in the Jewish tradition rather than as a philosopher. It is certainly true that he was one of the most significant and influential religious thinkers of the twentieth century, who not only has long been held in high regard by theologians from many religions but is read and admired by a very broad audience beyond as well as within the Jewish community (in which he is revered, both in Israel and elsewhere). Yet he was also a philosopher—or rather, like KIERKE-GAARD, a philosophically sophisticated religious thinker whose thought has philosophical as well as religious dimensions and significance. Many of his writings are devoted to his other concerns, which included Israel and the kind of society it ought to be; but some are of general philosophical and human interest. His best-known book, *I and Thou* (1923), from which our selection is drawn, is a case in point.

Martin (Mordechai) Buber ("BOO-ber") was born in Vienna. When his parents separated four years later, he went to live with his paternal grandparents in Lemberg (Lvov), a city now in Ukraine (and called Lviv) that was then part of the Austro-Hungarian Empire. His grandfather was a Jewish scholar and successful businessman, whose wealth made Buber financially independent until the family estates and businesses were appropriated by the Nazis in 1939. He was homeschooled by his grandparents to the age of 10. When he was 9 he began to spend summers in the town of Bukovina with his father, with whom he came to live at 14. His father often took him to a nearby village, Sadagora, whose large Hasidic population helped introduce him to that Jewish movement. From 1888 to 1896 he attended the Franz Joseph Gymnasium, a school in which

the language of instruction was Polish. Fascinated by languages at an early age, he had a gift for them, learning—in addition to the Polish, German, and Yiddish he heard around him—French, Hebrew, Greek, Latin, Italian, and English. The earliest philosophical influences on him were KANT's *Prolegomena* and NIE-TZSCHE's *Zarathustra*, which he read as a schoolboy. The influence on him of both of these very different philosophers remained strong throughout his life.

From 1896 to 1899 Buber attended a succession of universities (Vienna, Leipzig, Berlin, and Zurich), without completing degree requirements at any of them, as was common at the time. During these years he also became significantly involved in the Zionist movement. He edited the leading Zionist weekly *Die Welt* (*The World*) at the invitation of Theodor Herzl (though their serious differences concerning the future of Palestine made his tenure there brief), and he developed a relationship with Chaim Weizmann, whose more democratic and cultural vision of Zionism was more congenial to him. Around 1904 he became actively interested in Hasidism and for a time withdrew from Zionist politics; but in 1916 he began publishing a cultural and political Zionist journal called *Der Jude* (*The Jew*), which he edited until 1924. In the debates in the late 1920s about whether Jewish settlers in Palestine should be armed he took the pacifist side. He also argued that the new state should be binational rather than Jewish.

In 1899, while studying in Zurich, Buber met Paula Winkler, who became his partner and eventually his wife. In 1900 they moved to Berlin, where their two children were born (in 1900 and 1901). In 1916, the family moved from the suburbs of Berlin (where they had been living since 1906) to Heppenheim, near Frankfurt on the Main, where Buber devoted himself to editorial work, writing, and—at the initiative of his philosopher-friend Franz Rosenzweig—teaching at a new institution for Jewish adult education called the Freies jüdisches Lehrhaus (Free Jewish Teaching Center). In 1923, again with the assistance of Rosenzweig, Buber took a position at the University of Frankfurt as a high-profile lecturer in Jewish studies. In 1930 he was awarded an honorary title by the university. In 1933, however, all Jews were barred from lecturing at any German university. He remained director of the Lehrhaus in Frankfurt until 1937, when all such activities were forbidden to Jews, at which point he (fortunately) emigrated to Jerusalem.

When the Hebrew University in Jerusalem was established, Buber became a professor there, and was one of its most illustrious faculty members. He soon became active politically as well, involving himself in the effort to achieve a two-state solution to the problem of the political reorganization of Palestine. During the 1950s he made frequent trips to Europe and North America, giving numerous lectures at many universities and in other venues. He received many honors, including the Hanseatic Goethe Prize awarded by the City of Hamburg (1951), the Peace Prize from the German Booksellers' Association (1953), and the Erasmus Award awarded by a Dutch foundation (1963). His wife died in Venice in 1958; and he himself died seven years later, in Jerusalem.

Buber's philosophical thinking centers upon human reality and, more specifically, upon genuinely human existing. In approach, sensibility, and even manner of expression, it is similar to that of JASPERS's version of existential philosophy, sounding similar themes and attempting a similar sort of elucidation of the kind of human possibility Jaspers calls *Existenz*. Yet Buber chose to characterize his general philosophical project as a form of "philosophical anthropology"—for example, in his 1938 essay "What Is Man?"—

perhaps to distance himself from HEIDEGGER, and in any event associating himself with that rival movement and its inaugurator MAX SCHELER (see below), whose emphasis on the concept of the human *person* he shared.

Buber was deeply influenced by his early encounters with Kant and Nietzsche, and subsequently with Kierkegaard, each of whom he found both compelling and lacking. He was convinced of the cardinal human importance of relating in deeply personal ways with what is *other* than ourselves and yet not merely an object of some sort—other human beings first and foremost, but not exclusively. (Buber has God in mind, but also other sorts of realities we encounter within the world—natural, artistic, even mundane.) He characterizes such relations in terms of "dialogue," which may take a variety of forms. The exploration and differentiation of "dialogue" in contrast to other possible sorts of relations—the task he pursues in the following selection—is for him the key to understanding what is most distinctive and important in our humanity.

The word "Thou" in the selection's title translates Buber's "*Du*," one of the words for "you" in German that the translator renders as "You" (capitalized), when a personal relationship of the sort Buber has in mind is meant. It contrasts with the signifiers "I" (*Ich*) and "It" (*Es*)—as well as with "*Sie*," the German word used to address others formally. Buber contends that there are two fundamental types of relation in which an "I" can stand to other realities: an impersonal relation to something other as an "It" that is a mere object of some sort for that "I," and as a "You" or something that is more than that; and that the kind of "I" one is depends significantly upon that "I" relating to encountered other realities in the latter sort of way as well as the former.

Buber's philosophical thinking is sometimes referred to as a "philosophy of dialogue." It is that and more: a philosophical exploration of *relations*—a multifaceted reflection upon different ways in which human beings do and can relate to each other, themselves, and the many sorts of realities that may be encountered in the world of human life and experience; and upon associated sorts of selfhood, personhood, community, and spirituality. It is a kind of phenomenological anthropology. In the following excerpts Buber develops some of its fundamental themes. His style is more suggestive than argumentative. His aim is simply to develop these themes and thereby invite the reader to consider whether they ring true.

From I and Thou

From *First Part*

The world is twofold for man in accordance with his twofold attitude.

The attitude of man is twofold in accordance with the two basic words he can speak.

The basic words are not single words but word pairs.

One basic word is the word pair I-You.[1]

The other basic word is the word pair I-It; but this basic word is not changed when He or She takes the place of It.

Thus the I of man is also twofold.

For the I of the basic word I-You is different from that in the basic word I-It.

*

Basic words do not state something that might exist outside them; by being spoken they establish a mode of existence.

Basic words are spoken with one's being.[2]

When one says You, the I of the word pair I-You is said, too.

When one says It, the I of the word pair I-It is said, too.

The basic word I-You can only be spoken with one's whole being.

The basic word I-It can never be spoken with one's whole being.

*

There is no I as such but only the I of the basic word I-You and the I of the basic word I-It.

When a man says I, he means one or the other. The I he means is present when he says I. And when he says You or It, the I of one or the other basic word is also present.

Being I and saying I are the same. Saying I and saying one of the two basic words are the same.

Whoever speaks one of the basic words enters into the word and stands in it.

---

1. German has both a formal second-person singular, *Sie*, and a familiar pronoun, *du*, used when addressing family members, close friends, and God in prayer. *Du* is sometimes translated as "thou," the archaic English familiar (as in this book's title) to emphasize and clarify that the intimate sort of relationship is meant. The word *es* (it) is used to refer to objects, and also to human beings in categories that are grammatically neuter in gender—e.g., "child" (*das Kind*) and "maiden" or "young girl" (*das Mädchen*). The contrast that Buber has in mind is between the intimacy of "I-

you" (*ich–du*) and an impersonal or depersonalized relation of "I-it" (*ich–es*) that treats others as if they were things or objects. Buber capitalizes these and other pronouns when using them to specify categories of (personalized and depersonalized) reference, and the translator does the same to reflect this special usage.

2. That is, with one's fundamental human reality (*Wesen*), which is capable of relating to other encountered realities (things, other people, etc.) in different ways.

*

The life of a human being does not exist merely in the sphere of goal-directed verbs. It does not consist merely of activities that have something for their object.

I perceive something. I feel something. I imagine something. I want something. I sense something. I think something. The life of a human being does not consist merely of all this and its like.

All this and its like is the basis of the realm of It.

But the realm of You has another basis.

*

Whoever says You does not have something for his object. For wherever there is something there is also another something; every It borders on other Its; It is only by virtue of bordering on others. But where You is said there is no something. You has no borders.

Whoever says You does not have something; he has nothing. But he stands in relation.

*

We are told that man experiences his world. What does this mean?

Man goes over the surfaces of things and experiences them. He brings back from them some knowledge of their condition—an experience. He experiences what there is to things.

But it is not experiences alone that bring the world to man.

For what they bring to him is only a world that consists of It and It and It, of He and He and She and She and It.

I experience something.

All this is not changed by adding "inner" experiences to the "external" ones, in line with the non-eternal distinction that is born of mankind's craving to take the edge off the mystery of death. Inner things like external things, things among things!

I experience something.

And all this is not changed by adding "mysterious" experiences to "manifest" ones, self-confident in the wisdom that recognizes a secret compartment in things, reserved for the initiated, and holds the key. O mysteriousness without mystery, O piling up of information! It, it, it!

*

Those who experience do not participate in the world. For the experience is "in them" and not between them and the world.

The world does not participate in experience. It allows itself to be experienced, but it is not concerned, for it contributes nothing, and nothing happens to it.

*

The world as experience belongs to the basic word I-It. The basic word I-You establishes the world of relation.

*

Three are the spheres in which the world of relation arises.

The first: life with nature. Here the relation vibrates in the dark and remains below language. The creatures stir across from us, but they are unable to come to us, and the You we say to them sticks to the threshold of language.

The second: life with men.[3] Here the relation is manifest and enters language. We can give and receive the You.

The third: life with spiritual beings. Here the relation is wrapped in a cloud but reveals itself, it lacks but creates language. We hear no You and yet feel addressed; we answer—creating, thinking, acting: with our being we speak the basic word, unable to say You with our mouth.

But how can we incorporate into the world of the basic word what lies outside language?

In every sphere, through everything that becomes present to us, we gaze toward the train of the eternal You; in each we perceive a breath of it; in every You we address the eternal You, in every sphere according to its manner.

*

*　*　*

When I confront a human being as my You and speak the basic word I-You to him,[4] then he is no thing among things nor does he consist of things.

He is no longer He or She, limited by other Hes and Shes, a dot in the world grid of space and time, nor a condition that can be experienced and described, a loose bundle of named qualities. Neighborless and seamless, he is You and fills the firmament. Not as if there were nothing but he; but everything else lives in *his* light.

Even as a melody is not composed of tones, nor a verse of words, nor a statue of lines—one must pull and tear to turn a unity into a multiplicity—so it is with the human being to whom I say You. I can abstract from him the color of his hair or the color of his speech or the color of his graciousness; I have to do this again and again; but immediately he is no longer You.

And even as prayer is not in time but time in prayer, the sacrifice not in space but space in the sacrifice—and whoever reverses the relation annuls the reality—I do not find the human being to whom I say You in any Sometime and Somewhere. I can place him there and have to do this again and again, but immediately he becomes a He or a She, an It, and no longer remains my You.

As long as the firmament of the You is spread over me, the tempests of causality cower at my heels, and the whirl of doom congeals.

The human being to whom I say You I do not experience. But I stand in relation to him, in the sacred basic word. Only when I step out of this do I experience him again. Experience is remoteness from You.[5]

---

3. That is, life with fellow human beings (*Menschen*).

4. That is, to "that person" (rather than either "him" or "her"). For Buber, "He" and "She" (capitalized) are modalities of "it"; here and in other such contexts, by "he" or "him" (lowercase) Buber means the individual *person* (Mensch) encountered. But capitalization signifies that a word is being used to specify a category of either sort (per-

sonalized or depersonalized); thus "You" (capitalized) is the category term for the personalized other (*du*).

5. Buber is contrasting "experience" (here to be understood in the sense of impersonal perception of and dealings with things) with "relation" (two people *relating* to each other on a genuinely personal level).

The relation can obtain even if the human being to whom I say You does not hear it in his experience. For You is more than It knows. You does more, and more happens to it, than It knows. No deception reaches this far: here is the cradle of actual life.

*

* * *

—What, then, does one experience of the You?
—Nothing at all. For one does not experience it.
—What, then, does one know of the You?
—Only everything. For one no longer knows particulars.

*

The You encounters me by grace—it cannot be found by seeking. But that I speak the basic word to it is a deed of my whole being, is my essential deed.

The You encounters me. But I enter into a direct relationship to it. Thus the relationship is election and electing, passive and active at once[.] An action of the whole being must approach passivity, for it does away with all partial actions and thus with any sense of action, which always depends on limited exertions.

The basic word I-You can be spoken only with one's whole being. The concentration and fusion into a whole being can never be accomplished by me, can never be accomplished without me. I require a You to become; becoming I, I say You.

All actual life is encounter.

*

The relation to the You is unmediated. Nothing conceptual intervenes between I and You, no prior knowledge and no imagination; and memory itself is changed as it plunges from particularity into wholeness. No purpose intervenes between I and You, no greed and no anticipation; and longing itself is changed as it plunges from the dream into appearance. Every means is an obstacle. Only where all means have disintegrated encounters occur.[6]

*

Before the immediacy of the relationship everything mediate becomes negligible. It is also trifling whether my You is the It of other I's ("object of general experience") or can only become that as a result of my essential deed. For the real boundary, albeit one that floats and fluctuates, runs not between experience and non-experience, nor between the given and the not-given, nor between the world of being and the world of value, but across all the regions between You and It: between presence and object.

*

6. That is, (genuinely personal) encounters occur between two people only if "means" (i.e., means–ends relations between those involved) are no longer the issue, motivation, and primary substance of their dealings with each other.

The present—not that which is like a point and merely designates whatever our thoughts may posit as the end of "elapsed" time, the fiction of the fixed lapse, but the actual and fulfilled present—exists only insofar as presentness, encounter, and relation exist. Only as the You becomes present does presence come into being.

The I of the basic word I-It, the I that is not bodily confronted by a You but surrounded by a multitude of "contents," has only a past and no present. In other words: insofar as a human being makes do with the things that he experiences and uses, he lives in the past, and his moment has no presence. He has nothing but objects; but objects consist in having been.

Presence is not what is evanescent and passes but what confronts us, waiting and enduring. And the object is not duration but standing still, ceasing, breaking off, becoming rigid, standing out, the lack of relation, the lack of presence.

What is essential is lived in the present, objects in the past.

*

* * *

This, however, is the sublime melancholy of our lot that every You must become an It in our world. However exclusively present it may have been in the direct relationship—as soon as the relationship has run its course or is permeated by *means*, the You becomes an object among objects, possibly the noblest one and yet one of them, assigned its measure and boundary. The actualization of the work involves a loss of actuality. Genuine contemplation never lasts long; the natural being that only now revealed itself to me in the mystery of reciprocity has again become describable, analyzable, classifiable— the point at which manifold systems of laws intersect. And even love cannot persist in direct relation; it endures, but only in the alternation of actuality and latency. The human being who but now[7] was unique and devoid of qualities, not at hand but only present, not experienceable, only touchable, has again become a He or She, an aggregate of qualities, a quantum with a shape. Now I can again abstract from him the color of his hair, of his speech, of his graciousness; but as long as I can do that he is my You no longer and not yet again.

Every You in the world is doomed by its nature to become a thing or at least to enter into thinghood again and again. In the language of objects: every thing in the world can—either before or after it becomes a thing—appear to some I as its You. But the language of objects catches only one corner of actual life.

The It is the chrysalis, the You the butterfly. Only it is not always as if these states took turns so neatly; often it is an intricately entangled series of events that is tortuously dual.

*

* * *

In the history of the primitive mind the fundamental difference between the two basic words appears in this: even in the original relational event, the primitive man speaks the basic word I-You in a natural, as it were still unformed

7. That is, who just now; just a moment ago.

manner, not yet having recognized himself as an I; but the basic word I-It is made possible only by this recognition, by the detachment of the I.

The former word splits into I and You, but it did not originate as their aggregate, it antedates any I. The latter originated as an aggregate of I and It, it postdates the I.

Owing to its exclusiveness, the primitive relational event includes the I. For by its nature this event contains only two partners, man and what confronts him, both in their full actuality, and the world becomes a dual system; and thus man begins to have some sense of that cosmic pathos of the I without as yet realizing this.

In the natural fact, on the other hand, that will give way to the basic word I-It and I-related experience, the I is not yet included. This fact is the discreteness of the human body as the carrier of its sensations, from its environment. In this particularity the body learns to know and discriminate itself, but this discrimination remains on the plane where things are next to each other, and therefore it cannot assume the character of implicit I-likeness.[8]

But once the I of the relation has emerged and has become existent in its detachment, it somehow etherializes and functionalizes itself and enters into the natural fact of the discreteness of the body from its environment, awakening I-likeness in it. Only now can the conscious I-act, the first form of the basic word I-It, of experience by an I, come into being. The I that has emerged proclaims itself as the carrier of sensations and the environment as their object. Of course, this happens in a "primitive" and not in an "epistemological" manner; yet once the sentence "I see the tree" has been pronounced in such a way that it no longer relates a relation between a human I and a tree You but the perception of the tree object by the human consciousness, it has erected the crucial barrier between subject and object; the basic word I-It, the word of separation, has been spoken.

*

* * *

Even if we could fully understand the life of the primitive, it would be no more than a metaphor for that of the truly primal man. Hence the primitive affords us only brief glimpses into the temporal sequence of the two basic words. More complete information we receive from the child.

Here it becomes unmistakably clear how the spiritual reality of the basic words emerges from a natural reality: that of the basic word I-You from a natural association, that of the basic word I-It from a natural discreteness.

* * *

The innateness of the longing for relation is apparent even in the earliest and dimmest stage. Before any particulars can be perceived, dull glances push into the unclear space toward the indefinite; and at times when there is obviously no desire for nourishment, soft projections of the hands reach, aimlessly to all appearances, into the empty air toward the indefinite. Let anyone call

---

8. That is, having the sort of reality that the "I" has (*Ichhaftigkeit*).

this animalic: that does not help our comprehension. For precisely these glances will eventually, after many trials, come to rest upon a red wallpaper arabesque and not leave it until the soul of red has opened up to them. Precisely this motion will gain its sensuous form and definiteness in contact with a shaggy toy bear and eventually apprehend lovingly and unforgettably a complete body: in both cases not experience of an object but coming to grips with a living, active being that confronts us, if only in our "imagination." (But this "imagination" is by no means a form of "panpsychism"; it is the drive to turn everything into a You, the drive to pan-relation—and where it does not find a living, active being that confronts it but only an image or symbol of that, it supplies the living activity from its own fullness.) Little inarticulate sounds still ring out senselessly and persistently into the nothing; but one day they will have turned imperceptibly into a conversation—with what? Perhaps with a bubbling tea kettle, but into a conversation. Many a motion that is called a reflex is a sturdy trowel for the person building up his world. It is not as if a child first saw an object and then entered into some relationship with that. Rather, the longing for relation is primary, the cupped hand into which the being that confronts us nestles; and the relation to that, which is a wordless anticipation of saying You, comes second. But the genesis of the thing is a late product that develops out of the split of the primal encounters, out of the separation of the associated partners—as does the genesis of the I. In the beginning is the relation—as the category of being, as readiness, as a form that reaches out to be filled, as a model of the soul; the *a priori* of relation; *the innate You.*

In the relationships through which we live, the innate You is realized in the You we encounter: that this, comprehended as a being we confront and accepted as exclusive, can finally be addressed with the basic word, has its ground in the *a priori* of relation.

In the drive for contact (originally, a drive for tactile contact, then also for optical contact with another being) the innate You comes to the fore quite soon, and it becomes ever clearer that the drive aims at reciprocity, at "tenderness." But it also determines the inventive drive which emerges later (the drive to produce things synthetically or, where that is not possible, analytically— through taking or tearing apart), and thus the product is "personified" and a "conversation" begins. The development of the child's soul is connected indissolubly with his craving for the You, with the fulfillments and disappointments of this craving, with the play of his experiments and his tragic seriousness when he feels at a total loss. Any real understanding of these phenomena is compromised by all attempts to reduce them to narrower spheres and can be promoted only when in contemplating and discussing them we recall their cosmic-metacosmic origin. We must remember the reach beyond that undifferentiated, not yet formed primal world from which the corporeal individual that was born into the world has emerged completely, but not yet the bodily, the actualized being that has to evolve from it gradually through entering into relationships.[9]

9. Buber is here contrasting the (thinglike) corporeal (*körperliche*) human being with the embodied (*leibliche*) human person—both of which are real and significant dimensions of human reality.

*

Man becomes an I through a You.[1] What confronts us comes and vanishes, relational events take shape and scatter, and through these changes crystallizes, more and more each time, the consciousness of the constant partner, the I-consciousness. To be sure, for a long time it appears only woven into the relation to a You, discernible as that which reaches for but is not a You; but it comes closer and closer to the bursting point until one day the bonds are broken and the I confronts its detached self for a moment like a You—and then it takes possession of itself and henceforth enters into relations in full consciousness.

Only now can the other basic word be put together. For although the You of the relation always paled again, it never became the It of an I—an object of detached perception and experience, which is what it will become henceforth—but as it were an It for itself, something previously unnoticed that was waiting for the new relational event. Of course, the maturing body as the carrier of its sensations and the executor of its drives stood out from its environment, but only in the next-to-each-other where one finds one's way, not yet in the absolute separation of I and object. Now, however, the detached I is transformed—reduced from substantial fullness to the functional one-dimensionality of a subject that experiences and uses objects—and thus approaches all the "It for itself," overpowers it and joins with it to form the other basic word. The man who has acquired an I and says I-It assumes a position before things but does not confront them in the current of reciprocity. He bends down to examine particulars under the objectifying magnifying glass of close scrutiny, or he uses the objectifying telescope of distant vision to arrange them as mere scenery. In his contemplation he isolates them without any feeling for the exclusive or joins them without any world feeling. The former could be attained only through relation, and the latter only by starting from that. Only now he experiences things as aggregates of qualities. Qualities, to be sure, had remained in his memory after every encounter, as belonging to the remembered You; but only now things seem to him to be constructed of their qualities. Only by drawing on his memory of the relation—dreamlike, visual, or conceptual, depending on the kind of man he is—he supplements the core that revealed itself powerfully in the You, embracing all qualities: the substance. Only now does he place things in a spatio-temporal-causal context; only now does each receive its place, its course, its measurability, its conditionality. The You also appears in space, but only in an exclusive confrontation in which everything else can only be background from which it emerges, not its boundary and measure. The You appears in time, but in that of a process that is fulfilled in itself—a process lived through not as a piece that is a part of a constant and organized sequence but in a "duration"[2] whose purely intensive dimension can be determined only by starting from the You. It appears simultaneously as acting on and as acted upon, but not as if it had been fitted into a causal chain; rather as, in its reciprocity with the I, the beginning and end of the event. This is part of the basic truth of the

---

1. This is one of Buber's central claims: being an "I" is inherently bound up with "I-you" relatedness.
2. A reference to BERGSON's conception of the "duration" of "lived" time in human reality (see above).

human world: only It can be put in order. Only as things cease to be our You and become our It do they become subject to coordination. The You knows no system of coordinates.

But having got this far, we must also make another pronouncement without which this piece of the basic truth would remain an unfit fragment: an ordered world is not the world order. There are moments of the secret ground in which world order is beheld as present. Then the tone is heard all of a sudden whose uninterpretable score the ordered world is. These moments are immortal; none are more evanescent. They leave no content that could be preserved, but their force enters into the creation and into man's knowledge, and the radiation of its force penetrates the ordered world and thaws it again and again. Thus the history of the individual, thus the history of the race.

*

The world is twofold for man in accordance with his twofold attitude.

He perceives the being that surrounds him, plain things and beings as things; he perceives what happens around him, plain processes and actions as processes, things that consist of qualities and processes that consist of moments, things recorded in terms of spatial coordinates and processes recorded in terms of temporal coordinates, things and processes that are bounded by other things and processes and capable of being measured against and compared with those others—an ordered world, a detached world. This world is somewhat reliable; it has density and duration; its articulation can be surveyed; one can get it out again and again; one recounts it with one's eyes closed and then checks with one's eyes open. There it stands—right next to your skin if you think of it that way, or nestled in your soul if you prefer that: it is your object and remains that, according to your pleasure—and remains primally alien both outside and inside you. You perceive it and take it for your "truth"; it permits itself to be taken by you, but it does not give itself to you. It is only *about* it that you can come to an understanding with others; although it takes a somewhat different form for everybody, it is prepared to be a common object for you; but you cannot encounter others in it. Without it you cannot remain alive; its reliability preserves you; but if you were to die into it, then you would be buried in nothingness.

Or man encounters being and becoming as what confronts him—always only *one* being and every thing only as a being. What is there reveals itself to him in the occurrence, and what occurs there happens to him as being. Nothing else is present but this one, but this one cosmically. Measure and comparison have fled. It is up to you how much of the immeasurable becomes reality for you. The encounters do not order themselves to become a world, but each is for you a sign of the world order. They have no association with each other, but every one guarantees your association with the world. The world that appears to you in this way is unreliable, for it appears always new to you, and you cannot take it by its word. It lacks density, for everything in it permeates everything else. It lacks duration, for it comes even when not called and vanishes even when you cling to it. It cannot be surveyed: if you try to make it surveyable, you lose it. It comes—comes to fetch you—and if it does not reach you or encounter you it vanishes, but it comes again, transformed. It does not stand outside you, it touches your ground; and if you say "soul of my soul" you have not said too much. But beware of trying to transpose it into your soul—that way you destroy it. It is your present; you have a present only insofar as you have it; and you can make it into an object for you and experience and use it—you must do that again and again—and then you have no present any more. Between you and it there is a reciprocity of giving: you say You to it and give yourself to it; it says You to you and gives itself to you. You cannot come to an understanding *about* it with others; you are lonely with it; but it teaches you to encounter others and to stand your ground in such encounters; and through the grace of its advents and the melancholy of its departures it leads you to that You in which the lines of relation, though parallel, intersect. It does not help you to survive; it only helps you to have intimations of eternity.

The It-world hangs together in space and time.

The You-world does not hang together in space and time.

The individual You *must* become an It when the event of relation has run its course.

The individual It *can* become a You by entering into the event of relation.

These are the two basic privileges of the It-world. They induce man to consider the It-world as the world in which one has to live and also can live comfortably—and that even offers us all sorts of stimulations and excitements, activities and knowledge. In this firm and wholesome chronicle the You-moments appear as queer lyric-dramatic episodes. Their spell may be seductive, but they pull us dangerously to extremes, loosening the well-tried structure, leaving behind more doubt than satisfaction, shaking up our security—altogether uncanny, altogether indispensable. Since one must after all return into "the world," why not stay in it in the first place? Why not call to order that which confronts us and send it home into objectivity? And when one cannot get around saying You, perhaps to one's father, wife, companion—why not say You and mean It? After all, producing the sound "You" with one's vocal cords does not by any means entail speaking the uncanny basic word. Even whispering an amorous You with one's soul is hardly dangerous as long as in all seriousness one means nothing but experiencing and using.

One cannot live in the pure present: it would consume us if care were not taken that it is overcome quickly and thoroughly. But in pure past one can live; in fact, only there can a life be arranged. One only has to fill every moment with experiencing and using, and it ceases to burn.

And in all the seriousness of truth, listen: without It a human being cannot live. But whoever lives only with that is not human.

SOURCE: From Martin Buber, *I and Thou*, trans. Walter Kaufmann (New York: Charles Scribner's Sons, 1970), pp. 53–57, 59–64, 68–69, 73–85. Originally published in 1923 as *Ich und Du*.

SIMONE WEIL
(1909 – 1943)

Simone Weil was many things—brilliant, troubled, driven, intense, passionate, introverted, sickly, ascetic, initially politically radical, later deeply and mystically religious, eccentric, and a thinker and writer of extraordinary and uncompromising personal and philosophical moral fervor. During her brief life Europe was wracked by a series of devastating crises of increasing severity, which weighed very heavily on her; the world seemed to be spiraling into the abyss at the time of her early tuberculosis-related death, possibly hastened by virtual self-starvation. She made an extraordinary impression on those who knew her and on others who read her. (She may be the first and only philosopher ever to be the subject of an oratorio—*La Passion de Simone*, by the Finnish composer Kaija Saariaho, which had its American premiere in New York in August 2008.) Her burning spirituality made her more akin to a mystic and martyr from another time and place than to a French philosopher of the twentieth century; but it found expression in her unique philosophical thought in a way that is as riveting as it is discomforting.

Weil (pronounced "Vay") was born in Paris into a secular Jewish family. Her father was French; her mother was from Russia. Her only sibling, a brother, was a mathematical prodigy. As a child she herself, though intellectually precocious, was regarded by her family and others as strange, inept, weak, and sickly. There was some truth in these descriptions, but they also became self-fulfilling prophecies and contributed to severe bouts of depression. In 1925 she began studying at the Lycée Henri IV to prepare for the entrance exams for the prestigious École Normale Supérieure, to which women had not previously been admitted. At the Lycée she studied with the philosopher Alain (Émile Chartier), who strongly influenced and encouraged her. She passed the examination and entered the École in 1928. SIMONE DE BEAUVOIR began studying there at the same time, although she was not formally enrolled. Two more different personalities can hardly be imagined, and they were never on good terms.

From her childhood onward Weil was very politically sensitive and active, displaying great concern with the issues of egalitarianism, labor, and justice. Her intensity expressed itself in combativeness, cutting humor, and political radicalism (she proclaimed herself to be a Bolshevik at the age of 10, at the time of the Russian Revolution), making her few friends and many enemies among her fellow students. Initially strongly leftist as well as austerely moralistic, she came to be referred to as "the Red Virgin" and "the Categorical Imperative in skirts." Undaunted, she passed her *agrégation* exams (required of those desiring to teach) in 1931.

Her desire for solidarity with the working classes led Weil to engage in manual labor during breaks from school, and her increasingly intense interest in their plight came to border on fanaticism. After obtaining her diploma she contemplated going to work in a factory; but she instead took a teaching position, first at a girls' school in Le Puy and then at a series of other schools. Beloved by her students, she was reviled by their parents and her administrative superiors. Her radical politics and her students' lack of success in their state examinations led to repeated dismissals. In 1934 she chose to work in an auto factory for a year, damaging her health, before returning to teaching. In 1936, her frailty and poor health notwithstanding, she went to Spain to participate in the Spanish Civil War. By that point she had become highly skeptical of the communist ideology of the main leftist forces, and so she joined an allied group of anarcho-syndicalists. Soon thereafter she was badly burned in a cooking accident, and she left her unit to recuperate. In 1937 she went back to teaching, but after only one semester she left for health reasons and never taught again.

Weil had begun attending Catholic church services in 1935; and in 1937 and 1938 she had two transformative mystical religious experiences, after which her thought took a profoundly religious turn. With the defeat of France by Germany and the Nazi occupation of much of the country in 1940, she and her parents fled to the nominally unoccupied south, where she both wrote and worked on a farm for a time. In 1942 they were able to travel to the United States; but, hoping to join the French Resistance, she returned to England, where she threw herself into her writing. In 1943 she developed tuberculosis but continued working. Seeking solidarity with her French compatriots, she also reduced her diet to the level of what she believed was their official ration under Nazi rule. Radical to the end, she supposed that to be next to nothing, and so ate next to nothing herself. Her health declined further, and she died of heart failure in August of that year.

Weil published very little, but she left a good deal of writing in notebook and manuscript form as well as in her letters, and their posthumous publication attracted considerable attention. She was intensely concerned with the plight of the poor, and of all who suffer; but she came to distrust and reject all forms of ideology and all ordinary political and governmental ways of attempting to address such problems. Her ethical thought emphasized solidarity and compassion; and yet she was strongly attracted to a kind of affirmation of suffering, especially in the more extreme sorts of affliction to which human life is susceptible. She related its acceptance and embrace both to the idea of the possibility of death as something holy and to the attainment of unity with the divine even in this life. The kind of spirituality she envisioned and sought to attain involved relinquishing attachment to everything worldly, and had nothing to do with improving the conditions of human life in any ordinary sense.

Weil might seem to be the very opposite of an existentialist—if one conceives of an existentialist as someone who is "self-preoccupied" in the extreme. As she makes startlingly clear in the following essay, she is a radical critic of the celebration of individuality and personality, and a passionate proponent of their transcendence. It is goodness, truth, and beauty that she holds to be sacred—and she considers them all to be utterly impersonal. But she opposes the "collectivity" in which human beings submerge themselves in the "we" of social community even more strongly than the individuality that is its apparent opposite. "The whole effort of the mystic has always been to become such that there is no part left in his soul to say 'I,'" she approvingly writes. "But the part of the soul which says 'We' is infinitely more dangerous still."

As her reference to "the mystic" suggests, Weil conceives of true spirituality as something completely different from both of these alternative human possibilities. She might seem to be a kind of humanist, since she begins by apparently claiming that what is sacred is the whole human being: "It is this man [i.e., human being]; no more and no less." But she actually is saying something else: not that every person qua human being (or even human life as such) is what is sacred, but rather that there is sacredness "in every man." And for her the true locus of all sacredness—and so the source of the sacredness "in every man"—radically transcends all that makes us who and what we are, or that we might make of ourselves.

In taking that position, Weil parts company not with Existenz-philosophy altogether but only with certain of its most familiar variants. In fact, she invites comparison with Heidegger (who was himself no stranger to the kind of mysticism of which Weil speaks), and more specifically with the thought of the later Heidegger. Weil's version of authenticity does not revolve around a radical conception of autonomy and strongly individuated selfhood. Indeed, it provides a powerful alternative to such a conception. Yet it is an alternative that shares a deep kinship with it in one respect: both depart radically from most conceptions of "the good life" previously envisioned in the Western philosophical tradition.

Weil is as passionately concerned with the question of what it does mean and can mean to exist as a human being as KIERKEGAARD was, and her approach to that question is as existential and as phenomenological as that of any figure who is more commonly so characterized. Her vision of truly human existing, however, revolves around the ideal of a kind of selfless selfhood purified of every sort of identity—whether individual or collective—that would compromise that purity of heart and mind. Its focus is something like that in each and all of us that harm violates, that is sensitive to such violation wherever it may occur, and that is responsive to such supra-personal realities as love, beauty, and truth. It is this in our humanity that she calls sacred, both within ourselves and in our relations with others.

It is difficult to know what to make of Weil and her thought. Her writing is vividly clear on the surface and yet almost impossible to make sense of when one goes beneath that surface. Her thinking is at once strongly appealing and profoundly disturbing—both because of the strangeness of some of her central ideas and because her certainty about them, combined with her brilliance and her passion, makes it impossible to simply dismiss them. The light she shines on the questions that concern her is almost blinding in its intensity, leaving the reader wishing to look away and yet unable to ignore what it so searingly illuminates. It is small wonder that she had such an impact on those whom she encountered, for interactions with her must have been as unforgettable as they were challenging. By any ordinary standard, she was an impossible thinker, and a nearly invisible and fleeting presence. But one cannot read her seriously without being compelled to take her seriously.

Human Personality

'You do not interest me.' No man[1] can say these words to another without committing a cruelty and offending against justice.

'Your person[2] does not interest me.' These words can be used in an affectionate conversation between close friends, without jarring upon even the tenderest nerve of their friendship.

In the same way, one can say without degrading oneself, 'My person does not count', but not 'I do not count'.

This proves that something is amiss with the vocabulary of the modern trend of thought known as Personalism.[3] And in this domain, where there is

---

1. That is, human being (like the German *Mensch*). The word "man" should be understood in this way throughout the essay.
2. The implications of the French *personne* cannot be conveyed completely by a single word in English. What Simone Weil meant by "person" in this context will become clearer as the essay proceeds, as also will the pejorative sense in which she uses the word "personality" [translator's note].
3. A way of thinking that accords critical importance to each of us as a "person," or to the extent that we become true "persons," rather than to each of us simply as "human" or as a "human being." It has affinities both with the philosophy of KANT and with a strand of Roman Catholic thought. As a movement it is associated most explicitly with the French philosopher Emmanuel Mounier (1905–1950), MAX SCHELER (see below), and the Catholic existentialist Gabriel Marcel (1889–1973); it is also often connected, at least loosely, to MARTIN BUBER and KARL JASPERS (see above).

a grave error of vocabulary it is almost certainly the sign of a grave error of thought.

There is something sacred in every man, but it is not his person. Nor yet is it the human personality. It is this man; no more and no less.

I see a passer-by in the street. He has long arms, blue eyes, and a mind whose thoughts I do not know, but perhaps they are commonplace.

It is neither his person, nor the human personality in him, which is sacred to me. It is he. The whole of him. The arms, the eyes, the thoughts, everything. Not without infinite scruple would I touch anything of this.

If it were the human personality in him that was sacred to me, I could easily put out his eyes. As a blind man he would be exactly as much a human personality as before. I should not have touched the person in him at all. I should have destroyed nothing but his eyes.

It is impossible to define what is meant by respect for human personality. It is not just that it cannot be defined in words. That can be said of many perfectly clear ideas. But this one cannot be conceived either; it cannot be defined nor isolated by the silent operation of the mind.

To set up as a standard of public morality a notion which can neither be defined nor conceived is to open the door to every kind of tyranny.

The notion of rights, which was launched into the world in 1789,[4] has proved unable, because of its intrinsic inadequacy, to fulfil the role assigned to it.

To combine two inadequate notions, by talking about the rights of human personality, will not bring us any further.

What is it, exactly, that prevents me from putting that man's eyes out if I am allowed to do so and if it takes my fancy?

Although it is the whole of him that is sacred to me, he is not sacred in all respects and from every point of view. He is not sacred in as much as he happens to have long arms, blue eyes, or possibly commonplace thoughts. Nor as a duke, if he is one; nor as a dustman, if that is what he is. Nothing of all this would stay my hand.

What would stay it is the knowledge that if someone were to put out his eyes, his soul would be lacerated by the thought that harm was being done to him.

At the bottom of the heart of every human being, from earliest infancy until the tomb, there is something that goes on indomitably expecting, in the teeth of all experience of crimes committed, suffered, and witnessed, that good and not evil will be done to him. It is this above all that is sacred in every human being.

The good is the only source of the sacred. There is nothing sacred except the good and what pertains to it.

This profound and childlike and unchanging expectation of good in the heart is not what is involved when we agitate for our rights. The motive which prompts a little boy to watch jealously to see if his brother has a slightly larger piece of cake arises from a much more superficial level of the soul. The word justice means two very different things according to whether it refers to the one or the other level. It is only the former one that matters.

---

4. In the Declaration of the Rights of Man (one of the basic documents of the French Revolution, adopted by the French National Assembly in August 1789).

Every time that there arises from the depths of a human heart the childish cry which Christ himself could not restrain, 'Why am I being hurt?', then there is certainly injustice. For if, as often happens, it is only the result of a misunderstanding, then the injustice consists in the inadequacy of the explanation.

Those people who inflict the blows which provoke this cry are prompted by different motives according to temperament or occasion. There are some people who get a positive pleasure from the cry; and many others simply do not hear it. For it is a silent cry, which sounds only in the secret heart.

These two states of mind are closer than they appear to be. The second is only a weaker mode of the first; its deafness is complacently cultivated because it is agreeable and it offers a positive satisfaction of its own. There are no other restraints upon our will than material necessity and the existence of other human beings around us. Any imaginary extension of these limits is seductive, so there is a seduction in whatever helps us to forget the reality of the obstacles. That is why upheavals like war and civil war are so intoxicating; they empty human lives of their reality and seem to turn people into puppets. That is also why slavery is so pleasant to the masters.

In those who have suffered too many blows, in slaves for example, that place in the heart from which the infliction of evil evokes a cry of surprise may seem to be dead. But it is never quite dead; it is simply unable to cry out any more. It has sunk into a state of dumb and ceaseless lamentation.

And even in those who still have the power to cry out, the cry hardly ever expresses itself, either inwardly or outwardly, in coherent language. Usually, the words through which it seeks expression are quite irrelevant.

That is all the more inevitable because those who most often have occasion to feel that evil is being done to them are those who are least trained in the art of speech. Nothing, for example, is more frightful than to see some poor wretch in the police court stammering before a magistrate who keeps up an elegant flow of witticisms.

Apart from the intelligence, the only human faculty which has an interest in public freedom of expression is that point in the heart which cries out against evil. But as it cannot express itself, freedom is of little use to it. What is first needed is a system of public education capable of providing it, so far as possible, with means of expression; and next, a régime in which the public freedom of expression is characterized not so much by freedom as by an attentive silence in which this faint and inept cry can make itself heard; and finally, institutions are needed of a sort which will, so far as possible, put power into the hands of men who are able and anxious to hear and understand it.

Clearly, a political party busily seeking, or maintaining itself in, power can discern nothing in these cries except a noise. Its reaction will be different according to whether the noise interferes with or contributes to that of its own propaganda. But it can never be capable of the tender and sensitive attention which is needed to understand its meaning.

The same is true to a lesser degree of organizations contaminated by party influences; in other words, when public life is dominated by a party system, it is true of all organizations, including, for example, trade unions and even churches.

Naturally, too, parties and similar organizations are equally insensitive to intellectual scruples.

So when freedom of expression means in fact no more than freedom of propaganda for organizations of this kind, there is in fact no free expression for the only parts of the human soul that deserve it. Or if there is any, it is infinitesimal; hardly more than in a totalitarian system.

And this is how it is in a democracy where the party system controls the distribution of power; which is what we call democracy in France, for up to now we have known no other. We must therefore invent something different.

Applying the same criterion in the same way to any public institution we can reach equally obvious conclusions.

It is not the person which provides this criterion. When the infliction of evil provokes a cry of sorrowful surprise from the depth of the soul, it is not a personal thing. Injury to the personality and its desires is not sufficient to evoke it, but only and always the sense of contact with injustice through pain. It is always, in the last of men as in Christ himself, an impersonal protest.

There are also many cries of personal protest, but they are unimportant; you may provoke as many of them as you wish without violating anything sacred.

*

So far from its being his person, what is sacred in a human being is the impersonal in him.

Everything which is impersonal in man is sacred, and nothing else.

In our days, when writers and scientists have so oddly usurped the place of priests, the public acknowledges, with a totally unjustified docility, that the artistic and scientific faculties are sacred. This is generally held to be self-evident, though it is very far from being so. If any reason is felt to be called for, people allege that the free play of these faculties is one of the highest manifestations of the human personality.

Often it is, indeed, no more than that. In which case it is easy to see how much it is worth and what can be expected from it.

One of its results is the sort of attitude which is summed up in Blake's horrible saying: 'Sooner murder an infant in its cradle than nurse unacted desires',[5] or the attitude which breeds the idea of the 'gratuitous act.' Another result is a science in which every possible standard, criterion, and value is recognized except truth.

Gregorian chant, Romanesque architecture, the *Iliad*, the invention of geometry were not, for the people through whom they were brought into being and made available to us, occasions for the manifestation of personality.

When science, art, literature, and philosophy are simply the manifestation of personality they are on a level where glorious and dazzling achievements are possible, which can make a man's name live for thousands of years. But above this level, far above, separated by an abyss, is the level where the highest things are achieved. These things are essentially anonymous.

---

5. It seems possible that Simone Weil took Blake to mean: *If you desire to murder an infant you should do so*, instead of: *If you stifle your desires, you are doing something similar to murdering an infant.* But her point does not depend upon this illustration [translator's note]. William Blake (1757–1827), British engraver, poet, and visionary. The quotation is from "Proverbs of Hell" in *The Marriage of Heaven and Hell* (1790–93).

It is pure chance whether the names of those who reach this level are preserved or lost; even when they are remembered they have become anonymous. Their personality has vanished.

Truth and beauty dwell on this level of the impersonal and the anonymous. This is the realm of the sacred; on the other level nothing is sacred, except in the sense that we might say this of a touch of colour in a picture if it represented the Eucharist.

What is sacred in science is truth; what is sacred in art is beauty. Truth and beauty are impersonal. All this is too obvious.

If a child is doing a sum and does it wrong, the mistake bears the stamp of his personality. If he does the sum exactly right, his personality does not enter into it at all.

Perfection is impersonal. Our personality is the part of us which belongs to error and sin. The whole effort of the mystic has always been to become such that there is no part left in his soul to say 'I'.

But the part of the soul which says 'We' is infinitely more dangerous still.

*

Impersonality is only reached by the practice of a form of attention which is rare in itself and impossible except in solitude; and not only physical but mental solitude. This is never achieved by a man who thinks of himself as a member of a collectivity, as part of something which says 'We'.

Men as parts of a collectivity are debarred from even the lower forms of the impersonal. A group of human beings cannot even add two and two. Working out a sum takes place in a mind temporarily oblivious of the existence of any other minds.

Although the personal and the impersonal are opposed, there is a way from the one to the other. But there is no way from the collective to the impersonal. A collectivity must dissolve into separate persons before the impersonal can be reached.

This is the only sense in which the person has more of the sacred than the collectivity.

The collectivity is not only alien to the sacred, but it deludes us with a false imitation of it.

Idolatry is the name of the error which attributes a sacred character to the collectivity; and it is the commonest of crimes, at all times, at all places. The man for whom the development of personality is all that counts has totally lost all sense of the sacred; and it is hard to know which of these errors is the worst. They are often found combined, in various proportions, in the same mind. But the second error is much less powerful and enduring than the first.

Spiritually, the struggle between Germany and France in 1940[6] was in the main not a struggle between barbarism and civilization or between evil and good, but between the first of these two errors and the second. The victory of the former is not surprising; it is by nature the stronger.

There is nothing scandalous in the subordination of the person to the collectivity; it is a mechanical fact of the same order as the inferiority of a gram

6. In the Second World War; the German occupation of France began in June 1940.

to a kilogram on the scales. The person is in fact always subordinate to the collectivity, even in its so-called free expression.

For example, it is precisely those artists and writers who are most inclined to think of their art as the manifestation of their personality who are in fact the most in bondage to public taste. Hugo had no difficulty in reconciling the cult of the self with his role of 'resounding echo';[7] and examples like Wilde, Gide, and the Surrealists[8] are even more obvious. Scientists of the same class are equally enslaved by fashion, which rules over science even more despotically than over the shape of hats. For these men the collective opinion of specialists is practically a dictatorship.

The person, being subordinate to the collective both in fact and by the nature of things, enjoys no natural rights which can be appealed to on its behalf.

It is said, quite correctly, that in antiquity there existed no notion of respect for the person. The ancients thought far too clearly to entertain such a confused idea.

The human being can only escape from the collective by raising himself above the personal and entering into the impersonal. The moment he does this, there is something in him, a small portion of his soul, upon which nothing of the collective can get a hold. If he can root himself in the impersonal good so as to be able to draw energy from it, then he is in a condition, whenever he feels the obligation to do so, to bring to bear without any outside help, against any collectivity, a small but real force.

There are occasions when an almost infinitesimal force can be decisive. A collectivity is much stronger than a single man; but every collectivity depends for its existence upon operations, of which simple addition is the elementary example, which can only be performed by a mind in a state of solitude.

This dependence suggests a method of giving the impersonal a hold on the collective, if only we could find out how to use it.

Every man who has once touched the level of the impersonal is charged with a responsibility towards all human beings: to safeguard, not their persons, but whatever frail potentialities are hidden within them for passing over to the impersonal.

It is primarily to these men that the appeal to respect the sacredness of the human being should be addressed. For such an appeal can have no reality unless it is addressed to someone capable of understanding it.

It is useless to explain to a collectivity that there is something in each of the units composing it which it ought not to violate. To begin with, a collectivity is not someone, except by a fiction; it has only an abstract existence and can only be spoken to fictitiously. And, moreover, if it were someone it would be someone who was not disposed to respect anything except himself.

Further, the chief danger does not lie in the collectivity's tendency to circumscribe the person, but in the person's tendency to immolate himself in the collective. Or perhaps the first danger is only a superficial and deceptive aspect of the second.

---

7. A quotation from "This Century Was Two Years Old . . ." (1831), by the French Romantic poet and novelist Victor Hugo (1802–1885).
8. Members of an experimental literary and artistic movement founded in France in 1924; inspired in part by the psychoanalytic theories of Sigmund Freud, surrealists sought to express subconscious thought and feeling. Oscar Wilde (1854–1900), Irish author and wit; André Gide (1869–1951), French writer.

Just as it is useless to tell the collectivity that the person is sacred, it is also useless to tell the person so. The person cannot believe it. It does not feel sacred. The reason that prevents the person from feeling sacred is that actually it is not.

If there are some people who feel differently, who feel something sacred in their own persons and believe they can generalize and attribute it to every person, they are under a double illusion.

What they feel is not the authentic sense of the sacred but its false imitation engendered by the collective; and if they feel it in respect of their own person it is because it participates in collective prestige through the social consideration bestowed upon it.

So they are mistaken in thinking they can generalize from their own case. Their motive is generous, but it cannot have enough force to make them really see the mass of people as anything but mere anonymous human matter. But it is hard for them to find this out, because they have no contact with the mass of people.

The person in man is a thing in distress; it feels cold and is always looking for a warm shelter.

But those in whom it is, in fact or in expectation, warmly wrapped in social consideration are unaware of this.

That is why it was not in popular circles that the philosophy of personalism originated and developed, but among writers, for whom it is part of their profession to have or hope to acquire a name and a reputation.

Relations between the collectivity and the person should be arranged with the sole purpose of removing whatever is detrimental to the growth and mysterious germination of the impersonal element in the soul.

This means, on the one hand, that for every person there should be enough room, enough freedom to plan the use of one's time, the opportunity to reach ever higher levels of attention, some solitude, some silence. At the same time the person needs warmth, lest it be driven by distress to submerge itself in the collective.

*

If this is the good, then modern societies, even democratic ones, seem to go about as far as it is possible to go in the direction of evil. In particular, a modern factory reaches perhaps almost the limit of horror. Everybody in it is constantly harassed and kept on edge by the interference of extraneous wills while the soul is left in cold and desolate misery. What man needs is silence and warmth; what he is given is an icy pandemonium.

Physical labour may be painful, but it is not degrading as such. It is not art; it is not science; it is something else, possessing an exactly equal value with art and science, for it provides an equal opportunity to reach the impersonal stage of attention.

To take a youth who has a vocation for this kind of work and employ him at a conveyor-belt or as a piece-work machinist is no less a crime than to put out the eyes of the young Watteau[9] and make him turn a grindstone. But the painter's vocation can be discerned and the other cannot.

9. Antoine Watteau (1684–1721), French painter.

Exactly to the same extent as art and science, though in a different way, physical labour is a certain contact with the reality, the truth, and the beauty of this universe and with the eternal wisdom which is the order in it.

For this reason it is sacrilege to degrade labour in exactly the same sense that it is sacrilege to trample upon the Eucharist.

If the workers felt this, if they felt that by being the victim they are in a certain sense the accomplice of sacrilege, their resistance would have a very different force from what is provided by the consideration of personal rights. It would not be an economic demand but an impulse from the depth of their being, fierce and desperate like that of a young girl who is being forced into a brothel; and at the same time it would be a cry of hope from the depth of their heart.

This feeling, which surely enough exists in them, is so inarticulate as to be indiscernible even to themselves; and it is not the professionals of speech who can express it for them.

Usually, when addressing them on their conditions, the selected topic is wages; and for men burdened with a fatigue that makes any effort of attention painful it is a relief to contemplate the unproblematic clarity of figures.

In this way, they forget that the subject of the bargain, which they complain they are being forced to sell cheap and for less than the just price, is nothing other than their soul.

Suppose the devil were bargaining for the soul of some poor wretch and someone, moved by pity, should step in and say to the devil: 'It is a shame for you to bid so low; the commodity is worth at least twice as much.'

Such is the sinister farce which has been played by the working-class movement, its trade unions, its political parties, its leftist intellectuals.

This bargaining spirit was already implicit in the notion of rights which the men of 1789 so unwisely made the keynote of their deliberate challenge to the world. By so doing, they ensured its inefficacy in advance.

*

The notion of rights is linked with the notion of sharing out, of exchange, of measured quantity. It has a commercial flavour, essentially evocative of legal claims and arguments. Rights are always asserted in a tone of contention; and when this tone is adopted, it must rely upon force in the background, or else it will be laughed at.

There is a number of other notions, all in the same category, which are themselves entirely alien to the supernatural but nevertheless a little superior to brute force. All of them relate to the behaviour of the collective animal, to use Plato's[1] language, while it still exhibits a few traces of the training imposed on it by the supernatural working of grace. If they are not continually revived by a renewal of this working, if they are merely survivals of it, they become necessarily subject to the animal's caprice.

To this category belong the notion of rights, and of personality, and of democracy. As Bernanos[2] had the courage to point out, democracy offers no defence against dictatorship. By the nature of things, the person is subdued

---

1. Greek philosopher (ca. 427–ca. 347 B.C.E.).
2. Georges Bernanos (1888–1948), French novelist and writer of political polemics.

to the collectivity, and rights are dependent upon force. The lies and misconceptions which obscure this truth are extremely dangerous because they prevent us from appealing to the only thing which is immune to force and can preserve us from it: namely, that other force which is the radiance of the spirit. It is only in plants, by virtue of the sun's energy caught up by the green leaves and operating in the sap, that inert matter can find its way upward against the law of gravity. A plant deprived of light is gradually but inexorably overcome by gravity and death.

Among the lies in question is the eighteenth-century materialists' notion of natural right. We do not owe this to Rousseau,[3] whose lucid and powerful spirit was of genuinely Christian inspiration, but to Diderot and the Encyclopedists.[4]

It was from Rome that we inherited the notion of rights, and like everything that comes from ancient Rome, who is the woman full of the names of blasphemy in the Apocalypse,[5] it is pagan and unbaptizable. The Romans, like Hitler, understood that power is not fully efficacious unless clothed in a few ideas, and to this end they made use of the idea of rights, which is admirably suited to it. Modern Germany has been accused of flouting the idea; but she invoked it *ad nauseam* in her role of deprived, proletarian nation. It is true, of course, that she allows only one right to her victims: obedience. Ancient Rome did the same.

It is singularly monstrous that ancient Rome should be praised for having bequeathed to us the notion of rights. If we examine Roman law in its cradle, to see what species it belongs to, we discover that property was defined by the *jus utendi et abutendi*.[6] And in fact the things which the property owner had the right to use or abuse at will were for the most part human beings.

The Greeks had no conception of rights. They had no words to express it. They were content with the name of justice.

It is extraordinary that Antigone's unwritten law should have been confused with the idea of natural right.[7] In Creon's eyes there was absolutely nothing that was natural in Antigone's behaviour. He thought she was mad.

And we should be the last people to disagree with him; we who at this moment are thinking, talking, and behaving exactly as he did. One has only to consult the text.

Antigone says to Creon: 'It was not Zeus[8] who published that edict; it was not Justice, companion of the gods in the other world, who set such laws among men.'[9] Creon tries to convince her that his orders were just; he accuses her of having outraged one of her brothers by honouring the other, so that the same

---

3. Jean-Jacques Rousseau (1712–1778), Swiss-born French writer and political theorist; he argued that through a kind of "social contract," we give up our natural rights in return for civil rights.
4. French philosophers who worked together to produce the *Encyclopedia, or a Systematic Dictionary of the Sciences, Arts, and Trades* (1751–72), a major work of the Enlightenment whose chief editor was the man of letters and philosopher Denis Diderot (1713–1784).
5. That is, the New Testament book of Revelation; see 17:3.
6. Right to use and abuse (Latin).
7. Weil here draws on and quotes from the Greek

tragedy *Antigone* (ca. 441 B.C.E.), by Sophocles. In the myth, Antigone had two brothers, both of whom felt entitled to rule the city of Thebes. One had died attacking the city to seize it from the other, who had held it and had died defending it (and his rule of it). Antigone defies the order of Creon, her uncle and now the king, that the brother who had attacked the city be left unburied. Her defense was that she was obliged to give him burial by the "unwritten and immovable laws of the gods" (lines 454–55).
8. In Greek mythology, king of the gods.
9. We have translated the author's own versions of the Greek [translator's note].

honour has been paid to the impious and the loyal, to the one who died in the attempt to destroy his own country and the one who died defending it.

She answers: 'Nevertheless the other world demands equal laws.' To which he sensibly objects: 'There can be no equal sharing between a brave man and a traitor', and she has only the absurd reply: 'Who knows whether this holds in the other world?'

Creon's comment is perfectly reasonable: 'A foe is never a friend, not even in death.' And the little simpleton can only reply: 'I was born to share, not hate, but love.'

To which Creon, ever more reasonable: 'Pass, then, to the other world, and if thou must love, love those who dwell there.'

And, truly, this was the right place for her. For the unwritten law which this little girl obeyed had nothing whatsoever in common with rights, or with the natural; it was the same love, extreme and absurd, which led Christ to the Cross.

It was Justice, companion of the gods in the other world, who dictated this surfeit of love, and not any right at all. Rights have no direct connexion with love.

Just as the notion of rights is alien to the Greek mind, so also it is alien to the Christian inspiration whenever it is pure and uncontaminated by the Roman, Hebraic, or Aristotelian heritage. One cannot imagine St. Francis of Assisi[1] talking about rights.

If you say to someone who has ears to hear: 'What you are doing to me is not just', you may touch and awaken at its source the spirit of attention and love. But it is not the same with words like 'I have the right . . .' or 'you have no right to . . .' They evoke a latent war and awaken the spirit of contention. To place the notion of rights at the centre of social conflicts is to inhibit any possible impulse of charity on both sides.

Relying almost exclusively on this notion, it becomes impossible to keep one's eyes on the real problem. If someone tries to browbeat a farmer to sell his eggs at a moderate price, the farmer can say: 'I have the right to keep my eggs if I don't get a good enough price.' But if a young girl is being forced into a brothel she will not talk about her rights. In such a situation the word would sound ludicrously inadequate.

Thus it is that the social drama, which corresponds to the latter situation, is falsely assimilated, by the use of the word 'rights', to the former one.

Thanks to this word, what should have been a cry of protest from the depth of the heart has been turned into a shrill nagging of claims and counter-claims, which is both impure and unpractical.

*

The notion of rights, by its very mediocrity, leads on naturally to that of the person, for rights are related to personal things. They are on that level.

It is much worse still if the word 'personal' is added to the word 'rights', thus implying the rights of the personality to what is called full expression. In that case the tone that colours the cry of the oppressed would be even meaner than bargaining. It would be the tone of envy.

1. Italian saint (1181/82–1226), founder of the Franciscan orders.

For the full expression of personality depends upon its being inflated by social prestige; it is a social privilege. No one mentions this to the masses when haranguing them about personal rights. They are told the opposite; and their minds have not enough analytic power to perceive this truth clearly for themselves. But they feel it; their everyday experience makes them certain of it.

However, this is not a reason for them to reject the slogan. To the dimmed understanding of our age there seems nothing odd in claiming an equal share of privilege for everybody—an equal share in things whose essence is privilege. The claim is both absurd and base; absurd because privilege is, by definition, inequality; and base because it is not worth claiming.

But the category of men who formulate claims, and everything else, the men who have the monopoly of language, is a category of privileged people. They are not the ones to say that privilege is unworthy to be desired. They don't think so and, in any case, it would be indecent for them to say it.

Many indispensable truths, which could save men, go unspoken for reasons of this kind; those who could utter them cannot formulate them and those who could formulate them cannot utter them. If politics were taken seriously, finding a remedy for this would be one of its more urgent problems.

In an unstable society the privileged have a bad conscience. Some of them hide it behind a defiant air and say to the masses: 'It is quite appropriate that I should possess privileges which you are denied.' Others benevolently profess: 'I claim for all of you an equal share in the privileges I enjoy.'

The first attitude is odious. The second is silly, and also too easy.

Both of them equally encourage the people down the road of evil, away from their true and unique good, which they do not possess, but to which, in a sense, they are so close. They are far closer than those who bestow pity on them to an authentic good, which could be a source of beauty and truth and joy and fulfilment. But since they have not reached it and do not know how to, this good might as well be infinitely far away. Those who speak for the people and to them are incapable of understanding either their distress or what an overflowing good is almost within their reach. And, for the people, it is indispensable to be understood.

Affliction is by its nature inarticulate. The afflicted silently beseech to be given the words to express themselves. There are times when they are given none; but there are also times when they are given words, but ill-chosen ones, because those who choose them know nothing of the affliction they would interpret.

Usually, they are far removed from it by the circumstances of their life; but even if they are in close contact with it or have recently experienced it themselves, they are still remote from it because they put it at a distance at the first possible moment.

Thought revolts from contemplating affliction, to the same degree that living flesh recoils from death. A stag advancing voluntarily step by step to offer itself to the teeth of a pack of hounds is about as probable as an act of attention directed towards a real affliction, which is close at hand, on the part of a mind which is free to avoid it.

But that which is indispensable to the good and is impossible naturally is always possible supernaturally.

*

Supernatural good is not a sort of supplement to natural good, as we are told, with support from Aristotle,[2] for our greater comfort. It would be nice if this were true, but it is not. In all the crucial problems of human existence the only choice is between supernatural good on the one hand and evil on the other.

To put into the mouth of the afflicted words from the vocabulary of middle values, such as democracy, rights, personality, is to offer them something which can bring them no good and will inevitably do them much harm.

These notions do not dwell in heaven; they hang in the middle air, and for this very reason they cannot root themselves in earth.

It is the light falling continually from heaven which alone gives a tree the energy to send powerful roots deep into the earth. The tree is really rooted in the sky.

It is only what comes from heaven that can make a real impress on the earth.

In order to provide an armour for the afflicted, one must put into their mouths only those words whose rightful abode is in heaven, beyond heaven, in the other world. There is no fear of its being impossible. Affliction disposes the soul to welcome and avidly drink in everything which comes from there. For these products it is not consumers but producers who are in short supply.

The test for suitable words is easily recognized and applied. The afflicted are overwhelmed with evil and starving for good. The only words suitable for them are those which express nothing but good, in its pure state. It is easy to discriminate. Words which can be associated with something signifying an evil are alien to pure good. We are criticizing a man when we say: 'He puts his person forward'; therefore the person is alien to good. We can speak of an abuse of democracy; therefore democracy is alien to good. To possess a right implies the possibility of making good or bad use of it; therefore rights are alien to good. On the other hand, it is always and everywhere good to fulfil an obligation. Truth, beauty, justice, compassion are always and everywhere good.

For the aspirations of the afflicted, if we wish to be sure of using the right words, all that is necessary is to confine ourselves to those words and phrases which always, everywhere, in all circumstances express only the good.

This is one of the only two services which can be rendered to the afflicted with words. The other is to find the words which express the truth of their affliction, the words which can give resonance, through the crust of external circumstances, to the cry which is always inaudible: 'Why am I being hurt?'

For this, they cannot count upon men of talent, personality, celebrity, or even genius in the sense in which the word is usually employed, which assimilates it to talent. They can count only upon men of the very highest genius: the poet of the *Iliad*, Aeschylus, Sophocles, Shakespeare as he was when he wrote *Lear*, or Racine when he wrote *Phèdre*.[3] There are not very many of them.

---

2. Greek philosopher (384–322 B.C.E.); Weil found his emphasis on "natural good" and the good life conceived accordingly to be not only uncongenial but also obtuse, neglecting what she considered to be the far greater importance of "supernatural good."

3. Weil lists these great writers chronologically: the Greek poet Homer (ca. 8th century B.C.E.) and the tragedians Aeschylus (ca. 525–456 B.C.E.) and Sophocles (ca. 496–406 B.C.E.), the English dramatist and poet William Shakespeare (1564–1616; *King Lear* was first performed in 1605), and the French dramatist Jean Racine (1639–1699; *Phèdre* was first performed in 1677).

But there are many human beings only poorly or moderately endowed by nature, who seem infinitely inferior not merely to Homer, Aeschylus, Sophocles, Shakespeare, and Racine but also to Virgil, Corneille, and Hugo,[4] but who nevertheless inhabit the realm of impersonal good where the latter poets never set foot.

A village idiot in the literal sense of the word, if he really loves truth, is infinitely superior to Aristotle in his thought; even though he never utters anything but inarticulate murmurs. He is infinitely closer to Plato than Aristotle ever was. He has genius, while only the word talent applies to Aristotle. If a fairy offered to change his destiny for one resembling Aristotle's he would be wise to refuse unhesitatingly. But he does not know this. And nobody tells him. Everybody tells him the contrary. But he must be told. Idiots, men without talent, men whose talent is average or only a little more, must be encouraged if they possess genius. We need not be afraid of making them proud, because love of truth is always accompanied by humility. Real genius is nothing else but the supernatural virtue of humility in the domain of thought.

What is needed is to cherish the growth of genius, with a warm and tender respect, and not, as the men of 1789 proposed, to encourage the flowering of talents. For it is only heroes of real purity, the saints and geniuses, who can help the afflicted. But the help is obstructed by a screen which is formed between the two by the men of talent, intelligence, energy, character, or strong personality. The screen must not be damaged, but put aside as gently and imperceptibly as possible. The far more dangerous screen of the collective must be broken by abolishing every part of our institutions and customs which harbours the party spirit in any form whatsoever. Neither a personality nor a party is ever responsive either to truth or to affliction.

*

There is a natural alliance between truth and affliction, because both of them are mute suppliants, eternally condemned to stand speechless in our presence.

Just as a vagrant accused of stealing a carrot from a field stands before a comfortably seated judge who keeps up an elegant flow of queries, comments, and witticisms while the accused is unable to stammer a word, so truth stands before an intelligence which is concerned with the elegant manipulation of opinions.

It is always language that formulates opinions, even when there are no words spoken. The natural faculty called intelligence is concerned with opinion and language. Language expresses relations; but it expresses only a few, because its operation needs time. When it is confused and vague, without precision or order, when the speaker or listener is deficient in the power of holding a thought in his mind, then language is empty or almost empty of any real relational content. When it is perfectly clear, precise, rigorous, ordered, when it is addressed to a mind which is capable of keeping a thought present while it adds another to it and of keeping them both present while it adds a third, and so on, then in such a case language can hold a fairly rich content of relations.

---

4. Three writers often ranked as slightly less great than those in the first group. Virgil (70–17 B.C.E.), Roman poet; Pierre Corneille (1606–1684), French poet and dramatist.

But like all wealth, this relative wealth is abject poverty compared with the perfection which alone is desirable.

At the very best, a mind enclosed in language is in prison. It is limited to the number of relations which words can make simultaneously present to it; and remains in ignorance of thoughts which involve the combination of a greater number. These thoughts are outside language, they are unformulable, although they are perfectly rigorous and clear and although every one of the relations they involve is capable of precise expression in words. So the mind moves in a closed space of partial truth, which may be larger or smaller, without ever being able so much as to glance at what is outside.

If a captive mind is unaware of being in prison, it is living in error. If it has recognized the fact, even for the tenth of a second, and then quickly forgotten it in order to avoid suffering, it is living in falsehood. Men of the most brilliant intelligence can be born, live, and die in error and falsehood. In them, intelligence is neither a good, nor even an asset. The difference between more or less intelligent men is like the difference between criminals condemned to life imprisonment in smaller or larger cells. The intelligent man who is proud of his intelligence is like a condemned man who is proud of his large cell.

A man whose mind feels that it is captive would prefer to blind himself to the fact. But if he hates falsehood, he will not do so; and in that case he will have to suffer a lot. He will beat his head against the wall until he faints. He will come to again and look with terror at the wall, until one day he begins afresh to beat his head against it; and once again he will faint. And so on endlessly and without hope. One day he will wake up on the other side of the wall.

Perhaps he is still in a prison, although a larger one. No matter. He has found the key; he knows the secret which breaks down every wall. He has passed beyond what men call intelligence, into the beginning of wisdom.

The mind which is enclosed within language can possess only opinions. The mind which has learned to grasp thoughts which are inexpressible because of the number of relations they combine, although they are more rigorous and clearer than anything that can be expressed in the most precise language, such a mind has reached the point where it already dwells in truth. It possesses certainty and unclouded faith. And it matters little whether its original intelligence was great or small, whether its prison cell was narrow or wide. All that matters is that it has come to the end of its intelligence, such as it was, and has passed beyond it. A village idiot is as close to truth as a child prodigy. The one and the other are separated from it only by a wall. But the only way into truth is through one's own annihilation; through dwelling a long time in a state of extreme and total humiliation.

It is the same barrier which keeps us from understanding affliction. Just as truth is a different thing from opinion, so affliction is a different thing from suffering. Affliction is a device for pulverizing the soul; the man who falls into it is like a workman who gets caught up in a machine. He is no longer a man but a torn and bloody rag on the teeth of a cog-wheel.

The degree and type of suffering which constitutes affliction in the strict sense of the word varies greatly with different people. It depends chiefly upon the amount of vitality they start with and upon their attitude towards suffering.

Human thought is unable to acknowledge the reality of affliction. To acknowledge the reality of affliction means saying to oneself: 'I may lose at any moment, through the play of circumstances over which I have no control, anything whatsoever that I possess, including those things which are so intimately mine that I consider them as being myself. There is nothing that I might not lose. It could happen at any moment that what I am might be abolished and replaced by anything whatsoever of the filthiest and most contemptible sort.'

To be aware of this in the depth of one's soul is to experience non-being. It is the state of extreme and total humiliation which is also the condition for passing over into truth. It is a death of the soul. This is why the naked spectacle of affliction makes the soul shudder as the flesh shudders at the proximity of death.

We think piously of the dead when we evoke them in memory, or when we walk among graves, or when we see them decently laid out on a bed. But the sight of corpses lying about as on a battlefield can sometimes be both sinister and grotesque. It arouses horror. At the stark sight of death, the flesh recoils.

When affliction is seen vaguely from a distance, either physical or mental, so that it can be confused with simple suffering, it inspires in generous souls a tender feeling of pity. But if by chance it is suddenly revealed to them in all its nakedness as a corrosive force, a mutilation or leprosy of the soul, then people shiver and recoil. The afflicted themselves feel the same shock of horror at their own condition.

To listen to someone is to put oneself in his place while he is speaking. To put oneself in the place of someone whose soul is corroded by affliction, or in near danger of it, is to annihilate oneself. It is more difficult than suicide would be for a happy child. Therefore the afflicted are not listened to. They are like someone whose tongue has been cut out and who occasionally forgets the fact. When they move their lips no ear perceives any sound. And they themselves soon sink into impotence in the use of language, because of the certainty of not being heard.

That is why there is no hope for the vagrant as he stands before the magistrate. Even if, through his stammerings, he should utter a cry to pierce the soul, neither the magistrate nor the public will hear it. His cry is mute. And the afflicted are nearly always equally deaf to one another; and each of them, constrained by the general indifference, strives by means of self-delusion or forgetfulness to become deaf to his own self.

Only by the supernatural working of grace can a soul pass through its own annihilation to the place where alone it can get the sort of attention which can attend to truth and to affliction. It is the same attention which listens to both of them. The name of this intense, pure, disinterested, gratuitous, generous attention is love.

Because affliction and truth need the same kind of attention before they can be heard, the spirit of justice and the spirit of truth are one. The spirit of justice and truth is nothing else but a certain kind of attention, which is pure love.

Thanks to an eternal and providential decree, everything produced by a man in every sphere, when he is ruled by the spirit of justice and truth, is endowed with the radiance of beauty.

Beauty is the supreme mystery of this world. It is a gleam which attracts the attention and yet does nothing to sustain it. Beauty always promises, but never gives anything; it stimulates hunger but has no nourishment for the part of the soul which looks in this world for sustenance. It feeds only the part of the soul that gazes. While exciting desire, it makes clear that there is nothing in it to be desired, because the one thing we want is that it should not change. If one does not seek means to evade the exquisite anguish it inflicts, then desire is gradually transformed into love; and one begins to acquire the faculty of pure and disinterested attention.

In proportion to the hideousness of affliction is the supreme beauty of its true representation. Even in recent times one can point to *Phèdre*, *L'École des femmes*,[5] *Lear*, and the poems of Villon;[6] but far better examples are the plays of Aeschylus and Sophocles, and far better still, the *Iliad*, the book of Job and certain folk poems; and far beyond these again are the accounts of the Passion in the Gospels. The radiance of beauty illumines affliction with the light of the spirit of justice and love, which is the only light by which human thought can confront affliction and report the truth of it.

And it sometimes happens that a fragment of inexpressible truth is reflected in words which, although they cannot hold the truth that inspired them, have nevertheless so perfect a formal correspondence with it that every mind seeking that truth finds support in them. Whenever this happens a gleam of beauty illumines the words.

Everything which originates from pure love is lit with the radiance of beauty.

Beauty can be perceived, though very dimly and mixed with many false substitutes, within the cell where all human thought is at first imprisoned. And upon her rest all the hopes of truth and justice, with tongue cut out. She, too, has no language; she does not speak; she says nothing. But she has a voice to cry out. She cries out and points to truth and justice who are dumb, like a dog who barks to bring people to his master lying unconscious in the snow.

Justice, truth, and beauty are sisters and comrades. With three such beautiful words we have no need to look for any others.

*

Justice consists in seeing that no harm is done to men. Whenever a man cries inwardly: 'Why am I being hurt?' harm is being done to him. He is often mistaken when he tries to define the harm, and why and by whom it is being inflicted on him. But the cry itself is infallible.

The other cry, which we hear so often: 'Why has somebody else got more than I have?', refers to rights. We must learn to distinguish between the two cries and to do all that is possible, as gently as possible, to hush the second one, with the help of a code of justice, regular tribunals, and the police. Minds capable of solving problems of this kind can be formed in a law school.

But the cry 'Why am I being hurt?' raises quite different problems, for which the spirit of truth, justice, and love is indispensable.

In every soul the cry to be delivered from evil is incessant. The Lord's Prayer[7] addresses it to God. But God has power to deliver from evil only the eternal

5. *School for Wives* (1662), by Molière.
6. François Villon (1431–after 1463), French lyric poet.

7. Matthew 6:9–13; the phrase "deliver us from evil" appears in the last verse.

part of the soul of those who have made real and direct contact with him. The rest of the soul, and the entire soul of whoever has not received the grace of real and direct contact with God, is at the mercy of men's caprice and the hazards of circumstance.

Therefore it is for men to see that men are preserved from harm.

When harm is done to a man, real evil enters into him; not merely pain and suffering, but the actual horror of evil. Just as men have the power of transmitting good to one another, so they have the power to transmit evil. One may transmit evil to a human being by flattering him or giving him comforts and pleasures; but most often men transmit evil to other men by doing them harm.

Nevertheless, eternal wisdom does not abandon the soul entirely to the mercy of chance and men's caprice. The harm inflicted on a man by a wound from outside sharpens his thirst for the good and thus there automatically arises the possibility of a cure. If the wound is deep, the thirst is for good in its purest form. The part of the soul which cries 'Why am I being hurt?' is on the deepest level and even in the most corrupt of men it remains from earliest infancy perfectly intact and totally innocent.

To maintain justice and preserve men from all harm means first of all to prevent harm being done to them. For those to whom harm has been done, it means to efface the material consequences by putting them in a place where the wound, if it is not too deep, may be cured naturally by a spell of well-being. But for those in whom the wound is a laceration of the soul it means further, and above all, to offer them good in its purest form to assuage their thirst.

Sometimes it may be necessary to inflict harm in order to stimulate this thirst before assuaging it, and that is what punishment is for. Men who are so estranged from the good that they seek to spread evil everywhere can only be reintegrated with the good by having harm inflicted upon them. This must be done until the completely innocent part of their soul awakens with the surprised cry 'Why am I being hurt?' The innocent part of the criminal's soul must then be fed to make it grow until it becomes able to judge and condemn his past crimes and at last, by the help of grace, to forgive them. With this the punishment is completed; the criminal has been reintegrated with the good and should be publicly and solemnly reintegrated with society.

That is what punishment is. Even capital punishment, although it excludes reintegration with society in the literal sense, should be the same thing. Punishment is solely a method of procuring pure good for men who do not desire it. The art of punishing is the art of awakening in a criminal, by pain or even death, the desire for pure good.

*

But we have lost all idea of what punishment is. We are not aware that its purpose is to procure good for a man. For us it stops short with the infliction of harm. That is why there is one, and only one, thing in modern society more hideous than crime—namely, repressive justice.

To make the idea of repressive justice the main motive of war or revolt is inconceivably dangerous. It is necessary to use fear as a deterrent against the criminal activity of cowards; but that repressive justice, as we ignorantly conceive it today, should be made the motive of heroes is appalling.

All talk of chastisement, punishment, retribution, or punitive justice nowadays always refers solely to the basest kind of revenge.

The treasure of suffering and violent death, which Christ chose for himself and which he so often offers to those he loves, means so little to us that we throw it to those whom we least esteem, knowing that they will make nothing of it and having no intention of helping them to discover its value.

For criminals, true punishment; for those whom affliction has bitten deep into the soul, such help as may bring them to quench their thirst at the supernatural springs; for everyone else, some well-being, a great deal of beauty, and protection from those who would harm him; in every sphere, a strict curb upon the chatter of lies, propaganda, and opinion, and the encouragement of a silence in which truth can germinate and grow; this is what is due to men.

To ensure that they get it, we can only count upon those who have passed beyond a certain barrier, and it may be objected that they are too few in number. Probably there are not many of them, but they are no object for statistics, because most of them are hidden. Pure good from heaven only reaches the earth in imperceptible quantities, whether in the individual soul or in society. The grain of mustard seed is 'the least of all seeds'.[8] Persephone ate only one grain of the pomegranate.[9] A pearl buried deep in a field is not visible; neither is the yeast in dough.

But just as the catalysts or bacteria, such as yeast, operate by their mere presence in chemical reactions, so in human affairs the invisible seed of pure good is decisive when it is put in the right place.

How is it to be put there?

Much could be done by those whose function it is to advise the public what to praise, what to admire, what to hope and strive and seek for. It would be a great advance if even a few of these makers of opinion were to resolve in their hearts to eschew absolutely and without exception everything that is not pure good, perfection, truth, justice, love.

It would be an even greater advance if the majority of those who possess today some fragments of spiritual authority were aware of their obligation never to hold up for human aspiration anything but the real good in its perfect purity.

*

By the power of words we always mean their power of illusion and error. But, thanks to a providential arrangement, there are certain words which possess, in themselves, when properly used, a virtue which illumines and lifts up towards the good. These are the words which refer to an absolute perfection which we cannot conceive. Since the proper use of these words involves not trying to make them fit any conception, it is in the words themselves, as words, that the power to enlighten and draw upward resides. What they express is beyond our conception.

God and *truth* are such words; also *justice*, *love*, and *good*.

It is dangerous to use words of this kind. They are like an ordeal. To use them legitimately one must avoid referring them to anything humanly conceivable

8. A reference to the parable of the mustard seed, which "indeed is the least of all seeds: but when it is grown, it is greatest among herbs, and becometh a tree" (Matthew 13:32, KJV).
9. In Greek mythology, Persephone, the daughter of Demeter (goddess of agriculture), was abducted by Hades, god of the underworld; Demeter won her release, but because she had eaten while captive she had to return to Hades for part of the year.

and at the same time one must associate with them ideas and actions which are derived solely and directly from the light which they shed. Otherwise, everyone quickly recognizes them for lies.

They are uncomfortable companions. Words like *right, democracy* and *person* are more accommodating and are therefore naturally preferred by even the best intentioned of those who assume public functions. Public functions have no other meaning except the possibility of doing good to men, and those who assume them with good intentions do in fact want to procure good for their contemporaries; but they usually make the mistake of thinking they can begin by getting it at bargain prices.

Words of the middle region, such as *right, democracy, person*, are valid in their own region, which is that of ordinary institutions. But for the sustaining inspiration of which all institutions are, as it were, the projection, a different language is needed.

The subordination of the person to the collectivity is in the nature of things, like the inferiority of a gram to a kilogram on the scales. But there can be a scales on which the gram outweighs the kilogram. It is only necessary for one arm to be more than a thousand times as long as the other. The law of equilibrium easily overcomes an inequality of weight. But the lesser will never outweigh the greater unless the relation between them is regulated by the law of equilibrium.

In the same way, there is no guarantee for democracy, or for the protection of the person against the collectivity, without a disposition of public life relating it to the higher good which is impersonal and unrelated to any political form.

It is true that the word person is often applied to God. But in the passage where Christ offers God himself as an example to men of the perfection which they are told to achieve, he uses not only the image of a person but also, above all, that of an impersonal order: 'That ye may be like the children of your Father which is in heaven; for he maketh his sun to rise on the evil and on the good, and sendeth rain on the just and on the unjust.'[1]

Justice, truth, and beauty are the image in our world of this impersonal and divine order of the universe. Nothing inferior to them is worthy to be the inspiration of men who accept the fact of death.

Above those institutions which are concerned with protecting rights and persons and democratic freedoms, others must be invented for the purpose of exposing and abolishing everything in contemporary life which buries the soul under injustice, lies, and ugliness.

They must be invented, for they are unknown, and it is impossible to doubt that they are indispensable.

SOURCE: Simone Weil, *Selected Essays, 1934–1943*, chosen and trans. Richard Rees (London: Oxford University Press, 1962), pp. 9–34. Translator's note: "This essay appeared in *La Table Ronde* (December 1950) with the title 'La Personnalité humaine, le juste et l'injuste [Human Personality, Justice and Injustice],' and in *Écrits de Londres* with the title 'La Personne et le sacré [The Person and the Sacred].'" The essay was written in 1943, the year of Weil's death.

1. Matthew 5:45 (KJV).

EMMANUEL LÉVINAS
(1905 – 1995)

Lévinas began as a student of HUSSERL and his kind of phenomenology, and as an admirer of HEIDEGGER and his kind of phenomenological *Existenz*-philosophy. Yet his thought became perhaps the most radical rival to both—and to SARTRE's "phenomenological ontology" in *Being and Nothingness* (1943) as well—in the philosophical movement to which they all have contributed so importantly. MARTIN BUBER, KARL JASPERS, and SIMONE WEIL are among his kindred spirits in this rivalry, but it is Lévinas who has done the most to provide a substantial counterbalance to the ways in which those three figures have dealt with—or failed to deal with—the significance of the experience of other human beings in giving their accounts of consciousness and human reality. Lévinas's many writings are really one long, continuing phenomenological meditation on the meaning of "the Other" as we seek to understand ourselves and what it means to exist as a truly human being.

Emmanuel (originally Emanuelis) Lévinas ("Lay-vee-NAS") was born into a Jewish family in Kovno (Kaunas), Lithuania, which was then a part of Russia. Russian was thus the language of his education. In 1915 the Jews were exiled from Lithuania and his family relocated to Ukraine in 1916, returning to Lithuania in 1920. In 1923 Lévinas attended the University of Strasbourg in France, where he met and became the lifelong friend of fellow student and philosopher-to-be Maurice Blanchot. His chief philosophical influences at the time were HENRI BERGSON and Husserl, with whom he hoped to study. He therefore spent 1928–29 in Freiburg, Germany, and attended the last lecture course given by Husserl before he retired. Lévinas also attended the first course of Husserl's successor, Heidegger, on the just-published *Being and Time* (1927). In 1929 he attended the famous Davos meeting and debate between Heidegger and ERNST CASSIRER. His dissertation, on Husserl's theory of intuition, was published in 1930; Sartre later said that it was this book that introduced him to phenomenology.

During the 1930s Lévinas taught in a private Jewish school in Paris (the École Normale Israélite Orientale), attended the lectures of Léon Brunschvicg and Alexandre Kojève, and became acquainted with a number of the emerging young French philosophers of the day, including Sartre, Jean Hyppolite, and Gabriel Marcel. In 1931 he published a French translation of Husserl's important *Cartesian Meditations*, which Husserl had first presented in 1929 as a series of lectures at the Sorbonne. In 1932 Lévinas married Raïssa Levi, whom he had known since childhood; their first child, a daughter, was born in 1935. By that time he had become a French citizen; and in 1939, at the outbreak of the war, he was drafted into the French army, serving as a Russian and German translator. Captured in June 1940, he spent the rest of the war in a prisoner of war labor camp in northern Germany (his Jewish ethnicity remaining undetected), while his Jewish wife and daughter lived in hiding in France. (Most of the rest of his family, who had remained in Lithuania, died in the Holocaust.) He returned to them after his liberation. A second daughter was born but lived only a few months, and a son was born in 1949.

After the war Lévinas resumed his position in the Jewish school in Paris at which he had taught previously, eventually becoming its director. He also began studying Jewish thought and traditions more deeply. In 1957 he co-founded the Colloque des intellectuels juifs de langue française (Colloquy of Jewish Intellectuals in the French Language), with which he was involved until the early 1990s.

Though he had published a number of significant books, he did not obtain a university teaching position until his mid-50s, joining the University of Poitiers in 1961. In that same year, *Totality and Infinity*—the book which made his importance clear—was published. In 1967 he at long last became a professor of philosophy, at the branch of the University of Paris at Nanterre. His colleagues there included Mikel Dufrenne, PAUL RICOEUR, JEAN-FRANÇOIS LYOTARD, and Henri Lefebvre. In 1973, at the age of 67, he was appointed to a professorship at the Sorbonne. In 1980, Lévinas met Pope John Paul II and later took part in his summer retreats for selected intellectuals in 1983 and 1985. In 1989 Lévinas was a recipient of the Balzan Prize, awarded for outstanding academic and humanitarian achievements. He died in 1995.

For Lévinas it is not metaphysics, epistemology, or logic that should be considered "first philosophy"—that is, the central focus and guiding concern of philosophical thinking. Rather, that central focus and concern is (or should be) ethics—but an "ethics" of an unusual kind. Lévinas's kind of ethics has nothing to do with rules or principles of conduct in our dealings with others. Instead, it is an ethics in which "the Other"—other human beings in their full, individually existing humanity—is at the center of philosophical attention, phenomenological description, and existential analysis. And for Lévinas, a particular sort of experience of the Other deserves priority in this endeavor: "the face-to-face encounter," when that encounter is not distorted by the many ways in which we can manage to avoid looking each other in the eye and taking each other seriously.

The reality of the other, for Lévinas, is concealed by the many forms of impersonal interaction that make up much of everyday life. It begins to come into focus only in the experience of being appealed to by another in a personal way, and of being responsible for responding to such an appeal in an equally personal way. Personal appeal and responsible response are for him the fundamental elements of intersubjectivity, of the possibility of genuine human communication and community, and of truly human selfhood. They also are key to Lévinas's conception of "transcendence." His central philosophical project in his writings from the 1960s onward is a kind of interpretive (rather than merely descriptive) phenomenological exploration and illumination of the experiences relating to these humanly possible phenomena.

The following selection is the concluding chapter of what is perhaps the most important of Lévinas's books, in which this project received its fullest articulation and initial development: *Totality and Infinity*. His later writings largely pursue themes and ideas that are already present in it. In this chapter from it he attempts a kind of summary of what he has tried to do and to say in the book. His writing style is as challenging to the reader as is his thought. But for him, as for Jaspers and for the later Heidegger, they are inseparable.

Totality and Infinity is as much an exemplar of existential phenomenology and of *Existenz*-philosophy as are *Being and Time* and *Being and Nothingness*; and Lévinas's other-centered thinking, like that of Jaspers, makes clear the importance of conceiving of existential philosophy in a way that does not reduce it to Sartrean "existentialism," or even to Heidegger's "analytic of Dasein." Lévinas also demonstrates that existential philosophy did not come to an end when Heidegger and Sartre moved on. His insistence on the centrality to human existence of positive experience of "the Other," and on the centrality to human authenticity of an ethic of "the Other," has made it impossible to dismiss existential philosophy on the grounds that it is oblivious to both points. It would be difficult to think of any philosopher for whom these themes have been more important. Lévinas provides powerful reinforcement for the view—once associated primarily with Jaspers—that they are inseparable both from each other and from the very project of a phenomenological *Existenzerhellung* (elucidation of human existing).

From Totality and Infinity:
An Essay on Exteriority

Conclusions

1. From the Like to the Same

This work has not sought to describe the psychology of the social relation, beneath which the eternal play of the fundamental categories reflected definitively in formal logic would be maintained. On the contrary the social relation, the idea of infinity, the presence in a container of a content exceeding its capacity, was described in this book as the logical plot of being. The specification of a concept the moment it issues in its individuation is not produced by adjunction of an ultimate specific difference, not even if it originates in matter. The individualities thus obtained within the ultimate species would be indiscernible. The Hegelian dialectic is all powerful to reduce this individuality of the τόδε τί[1] to the concept, since the act of pointing to a here and a now implies references to the *situation*, in which the finger's movement is identified from the outside. The identity of the individual does not consist in being like to itself, and in letting itself be identified *from the outside* by the finger that points to it; it consists in being the *same*—in being oneself, in identifying oneself from within. There exists a logical passage from the like to the same; singularity logically arises from the logical sphere *exposed to the gaze* and organized into a totality by the reversion of this sphere into the interiority of the I, the reversion, so to speak, of convexity into concavity. And the entire analysis of interiority pursued in this work describes the conditions of this reversion. Relations such as the idea of infinity, which the formal logic of the gaze cannot let show through without absurdity, and which it prompts us to interpret in theological or psychological terms (as a miracle or as an illusion), have a place in the logic of interiority—in a sort of micro-logic—in which logic is pursued beyond the τόδε τί. Social relations do not simply present us with a superior empirical matter, to be treated in terms of the logic of genus and species. They are the original deployment of the relationship that is no longer open to the gaze that would encompass its terms, but is *accomplished* from me to the other in the face to face.

2. Being Is Exteriority

Being is exteriority. This formula does not only mean to denounce the illusions of the subjective, and claim that objective forms alone, in opposition to the sands in which arbitrary thought is mired and lost, merit the name of being. Such a conception would in the end destroy exteriority, since subjectivity itself would be absorbed into exteriority, revealing itself to be a moment of a panoramic play. Exteriority would then no longer mean anything, since it would encompass the very interiority that justified this appellation.

But exteriority is not yet maintained if we affirm a subject insoluble into objectivity, and to which exteriority would be opposed. This time exteriority would acquire a relative meaning, as the great by relation to the small. But in the absolute the subject and the object would still be parts of the same system,

---

1. This something (Greek, *tode ti*); sometimes translated "thisness."

would be enacted and revealed panoramically. Exteriority, or, if one prefers, alterity, would be converted into the same. And over and beyond the relation between the interior and the exterior there would be room for the perception of this relation by a lateral view that would take in and perceive (or penetrate) their play, or would provide an ultimate stage on which this relation would be enacted, on which its being would be effected *truly*.

Being is exteriority: the very exercise of its being consists in exteriority, and no thought could better obey being than by allowing itself to be dominated by this exteriority. Exteriority is true not in a lateral view apperceiving it in its opposition to interiority; it is true in a face to face that is no longer entirely vision, but goes further than vision. The face to face is established starting with a point separated from exteriority so radically that it maintains itself of itself, is me; every other relation that would not part from this separated and therefore arbitrary point (but whose arbitrariness and separation are produced in a positive mode as me), would miss the—necessarily subjective—field of truth. The true essence of man is presented in his face, in which he is infinitely other than a violence like unto mine, opposed to mine and hostile, already at grips with mine in a historical world where we participate in the same system. He arrests and paralyzes my violence by his call, which does not do violence, and comes from on high. The truth of being is not the *image* of being, the *idea* of its nature; it is the being situated in a subjective field which *deforms* vision, but precisely thus allows exteriority to state itself, entirely command and authority: entirely superiority. This curvature of the intersubjective space inflects distance into elevation; it does not falsify being, but makes its truth first possible.

One cannot "allow for" this refraction "produced" by the subjective field, so as to thus "correct" it; it constitutes the very mode in which the exteriority of being is effectuated-in its truth. The impossibility of "total reflection" is not due to a flaw in subjectivity. The so-called "objective" nature of the entities that would appear outside of this "curvature of space"—the phenomenon—would, on the contrary, indicate the loss of metaphysical truth, the superior truth—in the literal sense of the term. This "curvature" of the intersubjective space in which exteriority is effectuated (we do not say "in which it appears") as superiority must be distinguished from the arbitrariness of "points of view" taken upon objects that appear. But the latter, source of errors and opinions, issued from the violence opposed to exteriority, is the price of the former.

This "curvature of space" expresses the relation between human beings. That the Other is placed higher than me would be a pure and simple error if the welcome I make him consisted in "perceiving" a nature. Sociology, psychology, physiology are thus deaf to exteriority. Man as Other comes to us from the outside, a separated—or holy—face. His exteriority, that is, his appeal to me, is his truth. My response is not added as an accident to a "nucleus" of his objectivity, but first *produces* his truth (which his "point of view" upon me can not nullify). This surplus of truth over being and over its idea, which we suggest by the metaphor of the "curvature of intersubjective space," signifies the divine intention of all truth. This "curvature of space" is, perhaps, the very presence of God.

The face to face is a final and irreducible relation which no concept could cover without the thinker who thinks that concept finding himself forthwith before a new interlocutor; it makes possible the pluralism of society.

3. The Finite and the Infinite

Exteriority, taken as the essence of being, signifies the resistance of the social multiplicity to the logic that totalizes the multiple. For this logic, multiplicity is a fall of the One or the Infinite, a diminution in being which each of the multiple beings would have to surmount so as to return from the multiple to the One, from the finite to the Infinite. Metaphysics, the relation with exteriority, that is, with superiority, indicates, on the contrary, that the relation between the finite and the infinite does not consist in the finite being absorbed in what faces him, but in remaining in his own being, maintaining himself there, acting here below. The austere happiness of goodness would invert its meaning and would be perverted if it confounded us with God. In understanding being as exteriority, in breaking with the panoramic existing of being and the totality in which it is produced, we can understand the meaning of the *finite* without its limitation, occurring within the infinite, requiring an incomprehensible fall of the infinite, without finitude consisting in a nostalgia for infinity, a longing for return. To posit being as exteriority is to apperceive infinity as the Desire for infinity, and thus to understand that the production of infinity calls for separation, the production of the absolute arbitrariness of the I or of the origin.

The traits of limitation and finitude, which separation takes on, do not sanction a simple "less," intelligible on the basis of the "infinitely more" and the unfailing plenitude of infinity; they ensure the very overflowing of infinity, or, to speak concretely, the very overflowing of all the surplus over being—all the Good—that is produced in the social relation. The negativeness of the finite is to be understood on the basis of this Good. The social relation engenders this surplus of the Good over being, multiplicity over the One. It does not consist in reconstituting the wholeness of the perfect being which Aristophanes speaks of in the myth of the *Symposium*,[2] nor in being immersed again in the whole and abdicating into the intemporal, nor in gaining the whole through history. The adventure separation opens is absolutely new with regard to the beatitude of the One and its famous freedom, which consists in negating or in absorbing the other, so as to encounter nothing. The concept of a Good beyond Being and beyond the beatitude of the One announces a rigorous concept of creation, which would be neither a negation nor a limitation nor an emanation of the One. Exteriority is not a negation, but a marvel.

4. Creation

Theology imprudently treats the idea of the relation between God and the creature in terms of ontology. It presupposes the logical privilege of totality, as a concept adequate to being. Thus it runs up against the difficulty of understanding that an infinite being would border on or tolerate something outside of itself, or that a free being would send its roots into the infinity of a God. But transcendence precisely refuses totality, does not lend itself to a view that would encompass it from the outside. Every "comprehension" of transcendence

---

2. The dialogue by Plato (ca. 427–ca. 347 B.C.E.). One of the characters is the comic dramatist Aristophanes (ca. 450–ca. 385 B.C.E.), who explains love as humans' attempt to re-create a lost original wholeness: according to the myth he recounts, we were originally four-legged, four-armed, two-faced beings that were divided by the gods into our present form.

leaves the transcendent outside, and is enacted before its face. If the notions of totality and being are notions that cover one another, the notion of the transcendent places us beyond categories of being. We thus encounter, in our own way, the Platonic idea[3] of the Good, beyond Being. The transcendent is what can not be encompassed. This is an essential precision of the notion of transcendence, utilizing no theological notion. What embarrasses the traditional theology, which treats of creation in terms of ontology—God leaving his eternity, in order to create—is incumbent as a first truth in a philosophy that begins with transcendence: nothing could better distinguish totality and separation than the difference between eternity and time. But then the Other, in his signification prior to my initiative, resembles God. This signification precedes my *Sinngebung*[4] initiative.

For the idea of totality, in which ontological philosophy veritably reunites— or comprehends—the multiple, must be substituted the idea of a separation resistant to synthesis. To affirm origin from nothing by creation is to contest the prior community of all thing within eternity, from which philosophical thought, guided by ontology, makes things arise as from a common matrix. The absolute gap of separation which transcendence implies could not be better expressed than by the term creation, in which the kinship of beings among themselves is affirmed, but at the same time their radical heterogeneity also, their reciprocal exteriority coming from nothingness. One may speak of creation to characterize entities situated in the transcendence that does not close over into a totality. In the face to face the I has neither the privileged position of the subject nor the position of the thing defined by its place in the system; it is apology, discourse *pro domo*,[5] but discourse of justification before the Other. The Other is the prime intelligible, since he is capable of justifying my freedom, rather than awaiting a *Sinngebung* or a meaning from it. In the conjuncture of creation the I is for itself, without being *causa sui*.[6] The will of the I affirms itself as infinite (that is, free), and as limited, as subordinated. It does not get its limits from the proximity of the other, who, being transcendent, does not *define* it. The I's form no totality; there exists no privileged plane where these I's could be grasped in their principle. There is an anarchy essential to multiplicity. In the absence of a plane common to the totality (which one persists in seeking, so as to relate the multiplicity to it) one will never know which will, in the free play of the wills, pulls the strings of the game; one will not know who is playing with whom. But a principle breaks through all this trembling and vertigo when the face presents itself, and demands justice.

5. EXTERIORITY AND LANGUAGE

We have begun with the resistance of beings to totalization, with an untotaled multiplicity they constitute, the impossibility of their conciliation in the same.

This impossibility of conciliation among beings, this radical heterogeneity, in fact indicates a mode of being produced and an ontology that is not

3. In Plato, ideas (or forms) are fundamental, timeless universals, in whose reality objects in the natural world (their less than perfect copies) participate or share.

4. That is, "meaning- (or 'sense-,' *Sinn*-)giving."
5. For [one's] home (Latin); that is, for one's own cause or benefit.
6. Cause of itself (Latin).

equivalent to panoramic existence and its disclosure. For common sense but also for philosophy, from Plato to Heidegger, panoramic existence and its disclosure are equivalent to the very production of being, since truth or disclosure is at the same time the work or the essential virtue of being, the *Sein* of the *Seiendes*[7] and of every human behavior it would in the last analysis govern. The Heideggerian thesis that every human attitude consists in "bringing to light" (modern technology itself would be but a mode of extracting things or producing them in the sense of "fully bringing to light") rests on this primacy of the panoramic. The break-up of totality, the denunciation of the panoramic structure of being, concerns the very existing of being and not the collocation or configuration of entities refractory to system. Correlatively, the analysis that tends to show intentionality as an aiming at the visible, at the *idea*, expresses this domination of the panoramic as the ultimate virtue of being, the Being of the existent. This trait is maintained in the modern analysis of affectivity, practice, and existence, despite all the suppleness forced upon the notion of contemplation. One of the principal theses of this work is that the noesis-noema structure is not the primordial structure of intentionality[8] (which is not equivalent to interpreting intentionality as a logical relation or as causality).

The exteriority of being does not, in fact, mean that multiplicity is without relation. However, the relation that binds this multiplicity does not fill the abyss of separation; it confirms it. In this relation we have recognized language, produced only in the face to face; and in language we have recognized teaching. Teaching is a way for truth to be produced such that it is not my work, such that I could not derive it from my own interiority. In affirming such a production of truth we modify the original meaning of truth and the noesis-noema structure, taken as the meaning of intentionality.

In effect, the being who speaks to me and to whom I respond or whom I interrogate does not offer himself to me, does not *give* himself so that I could assume this manifestation, measure it to my own interiority, and receive it as come from myself. Vision operates in this manner, totally impossible in discourse. For vision is essentially an adequation of exteriority with interiority: in it exteriority is reabsorbed in the contemplative soul and, as an *adequate idea*, revealed to be a priori, the result of a *Sinngebung*. The exteriority of discourse cannot be converted into interiority. The interlocutor can have no place in an inwardness; he is forever outside. The relationship between separated beings does not totalize them; it is a "unrelating relation," which no one can encompass or thematize. Or more exactly, he who would think it, who would totalize it, would by this "reflection" mark a new scission in being, since he would still tell this total to someone. The relation between the "fragments" of separated being is a face to face, the irreducible and ultimate relation.[9] An

---

7. The being (or be-ing) of the beings (or entities) (German), terminology associated with HEIDEGGER.
8. Lévinas is challenging HUSSERL's contention that "the noesis-noema structure," or the "act-object" (literally, "thinking-thought") structure of consciousness (the notion that seeing as a form of consciousness or experience involves something being seen), *is* the primordial structure of inten-

tionality (i.e., "consciousness of X").
9. If "face to face" is "the irreducible and ultimate relation," then Lévinas's challenge to the noesis-noema structure is understandable. For as he goes on to say several sentences later, "the face to face proper to discourse does not connect a subject with an object."

interlocutor arises again behind him whom thought has just apprehended—
as the certitude of the *cogito*[1] arises behind every negation of certitude. The
description of the face to face which we have attempted here is told to the
other, to the reader who appears anew behind my discourse and my wisdom.
Philosophy is never a wisdom, for the interlocutor whom it has just encompassed has already escaped it. Philosophy, in an essentially liturgical sense,
invokes the Other to whom the "whole" is told, the master or student. It is
precisely for this that the face to face proper to discourse does not connect a
subject with an object, and differs from the essentially adequate thematization. For no concept lays hold of exteriority.

The object thematized remains in itself, but it belongs to its essence to be
known by me; and the surplus of the in itself over my knowledge is progressively absorbed by knowledge. The difference between the knowing that bears
on the object and the knowing that bears on the in itself or the solidity of the
object dwindles in the course of a development of thought which, according
to Hegel, would be history itself.[2] Objectivity is absorbed in absolute knowledge, and the being of the thinker, the humanity of man, is therewith con-
formed to the perpetuity of the solid in itself, within a totality where the
humanity of man and the exteriority of the object are at the same time conserved and absorbed. Would the transcendence of exteriority simply indicate
an unfulfilled thought, and would it be overcome in the totality? Would exteriority have to be inverted into interiority? Is it evil?

We have broached the exteriority of being not as a form that being would
eventually or provisionally take on in dispersion or in its fall, but as its very
existing—inexhaustible, infinite exteriority. Such an exteriority opens in the
Other; it recedes from thematization. But it refuses thematization positively
because it is produced in a being who expresses himself. In contradistinction
to plastic manifestation or disclosure, which manifests something *as* something, and in which the disclosed renounces its originality, its hitherto unpublished existence, in expression the manifestation and the manifested coincide;
the manifested attends its own manifestation and hence remains exterior to
every image one would retain of it, presents itself in the sense that we say of
someone that he presents himself by stating his name, which permits evoking
him, even though he remains always the source of his own presence. A presentation which consists in saying "It's me"[3]—and nothing else to which one
might be tempted to assimilate me. This presentation of the exterior being
nowise referred to in our world is what we have called the face. And we have
described the relation with the face that presents itself in speech as desire—
goodness and justice.

Speech refuses vision, because the speaker does not deliver images of himself only, but is personally present in his speech, absolutely exterior to every
image he would leave. In language exteriority is exercised, deployed, brought
about. Whoever speaks attends his manifestation, is non-adequate to the
meaning that the hearer would like to retain of it as a result acquired outside
of the very relationship of discourse, as though this presence in speech were

---

1. I think (Latin); a term associated with the
French philosopher René Descartes (1596–1650)
and with Husserl, who used it to refer to first-
person experience.

2. See "On History and *Geist*" in the HEGEL selections, above.
3. "Moi, c'est moi" [translator's note].

reducible to the *Sinngebung* of him who listens. Language is the incessant surpassing of the *Sinngebung* by the signification. This presence whose format exceeds the measure of the I is not reabsorbed into my vision. The overflowing of exteriority, non-adequate to the vision which still measures it, precisely constitutes the dimension of height or the divinity of exteriority. Divinity keeps its distances. Discourse is discourse with God and not with equals, according to the distinction established by Plato in the *Phaedrus*.[4] Metaphysics is the essence of this language with God; it leads above being.

6. Expression and Image

The presence of the Other, or expression, source of all signification, is not contemplated as an intelligible essence, but is heard as language, and thereby is effectuated exteriorly. Expression, or the face, overflows images, which are always immanent to my thought, as though they came from me. This overflowing, irreducible to an image of overflowing, is produced commensurate with—or in the inordinateness of—Desire and goodness, as the moral dissymmetry of the I and the other. The distance of this exteriority immediately extends to height. The eye can conceive it only by virtue of position which, as an above-below disposition, constitutes the elementary fact of morality. Because it is the presence of exteriority the face never becomes an image or an intuition. Every intuition depends on a signification irreducible to intuition; it comes from further than intuition, and it alone comes from afar. Signification, irreducible to intuitions, is measured by Desire, morality, and goodness—the infinite exigency with regard to oneself, or Desire of the other, or relation with infinity.

The presence of the face, or expression, is not to be ranked among other meaningful manifestations. The works of man all have meaning, but the human being absents himself from them immediately, and is divined across them; he too is given in the articulation of the "as."[5] There is an abyss between labor, which results in works having a meaning for other men, and which others can acquire—already merchandise reflected in money—and language, in which I attend my manifestation, irreplaceable and vigilant. But this abyss gapes open because of the energy of the vigilant presence which does not *quit* the expression. It is not to expression what the will is to its work; the will withdraws from its work, delivering it over to its fate, and is found to have willed "a lot of things" it had not willed. For the absurdity of these works is not due to a defect of the thought that formed them; it is due to the anonymity into which this thought immediately falls, to the unrecognition of the worker that results from this essential anonymity. Jankélévitch is right to say that labor is not an expression.[6] In acquiring the work I desacralize the neighbor who produced it. Man is really apart, non-encompassable, only in expression, where he can "bring aid" to his own manifestation.

---

4. This is Lévinas's reading of the dialogue, not a reference to any specific passage.
5. That is, "in the articulation of the *'en tant que.'*" The translation as published has "in the articulation of the 'qas,'" which is clearly a typographical error. The French *en tant que* means "as" in the sense of our expression "qua," and it is possible that

the translator intended to write *"quas"*; but "in the articulation of the 'as'" clearly renders the French.
6. V. Jankélévitch, *L'Austérité et la vie morale* (Paris, 1956), p. 34 [Lévinas's note]. Vladimir Jankélévitch (1903–1985), French philosopher and musicologist.

In political life, taken unrebuked, humanity is understood from its works—a humanity of interchangeable men, of reciprocal relations. The substitution of men for one another, the primal disrespect, makes possible exploitation itself. In history—the history of States—the human being appears as the sum of his works; even while he lives he is his own heritage. Justice consists in again making possible expression, in which in non-reciprocity the person presents himself as unique. Justice is a right to speak. It is perhaps here that the perspective of a religion opens. It diverges from political life, to which philosophy does not lead necessarily.

7. Against the Philosophy of the Neuter

We have thus the conviction of having broken with the philosophy of the Neuter: with the Heideggerian Being of the existent whose impersonal neutrality the critical work of Blanchot[7] has so much contributed to bring out, with Hegel's impersonal reason, which shows to the personal consciousness only its ruses. The movements of ideas of the philosophy of the Neuter, so different in their origins and their influences, agree in announcing the end of philosophy. For they exalt the obedience that no face commands. Desire in the spell of the Neuter, said to have been revealed to the Presocratics, or desire interpreted as need, and thus bound to the essential violence of action, dismisses philosophy and is gratified only in art or in politics. The exaltation of the Neuter may present itself as the anteriority of the We with respect to the I, of the situation with respect to the beings in situation. This book's insistence on the separation of enjoyment was guided by the necessity of liberating the I from the situation into which little by little philosophers have dissolved it as totally as reason swallows up the subject in Hegelian idealism. Materialism does not lie in the discovery of the primordial function of the sensibility, but in the primacy of the Neuter. To place the Neuter dimension of Being above the existent which unbeknown to it this Being would determine in some way, to make the essential events unbeknown to the existents, is to profess materialism. Heidegger's late philosophy becomes this faint materialism. It posits the revelation of Being in human inhabitation between Heavens and Earth, in the expectation of the gods and in the company of men, and sets up the landscape or the "still life" as an origin of the human. The Being of the existent is a *Logos*[8] that is the word of no one. To begin with the face as a source from which all meaning appears, the face in its absolute nudity, in its destitution as a head that does not find a place to lay itself, is to affirm that being is enacted in the relation between men, that Desire rather than need commands acts. Desire, an aspiration that does not proceed from a lack—metaphysics— is the desire of a person.

8. Subjectivity

Being is exteriority, and exteriority is produced in its truth in a subjective field, for the separated being. Separation is accomplished positively as the interiority

---

7. Maurice Blanchot (1907–2003), French philosopher and critical theorist who anticipated and contributed to the development of poststructuralism.

8. Word; reason (Greek); here used in the sense of "a meaning."

of a being referring to itself and maintaining itself of itself—all the way to atheism! This self-reference is concretely constituted or accomplished as enjoyment or happiness. It is an essential sufficiency, which in its expansion—in knowledge, whose ultimate essence critique (the recapturing of its own condition) develops—is even in possession of its own origin.

To metaphysical thought, where a finite has the idea of infinity—where radical separation and relationship with the other are produced simultaneously—we have reserved the term intentionality, consciousness of. . . . It is attention to speech or welcome of the face, hospitality and not thematization. Self-consciousness is not a dialectical rejoinder of the metaphysical consciousness that I have of the other. Nor is its relation with itself a *representation* of itself. Prior to every vision of self it is accomplished by holding *oneself* up [*se tenant*]; it is *implanted in itself* as a body and it keeps itself [*se tient*][9] in its interiority, in its home. It thus accomplishes separation positively, without being reducible to a negation of the being from which it separates. But thus precisely it can welcome that being. The subject is a host.

Subjective existence derives its features from separation. Individuation—an inner *identification* of a being whose essence is exhausted in identity, an identification of the same—does not come to strike the terms of some relation called separation. Separation is the very act of individuation, the possibility in general for an entity which is posited in being to be posited not by being defined by its references to a whole, by its place within a system, but starting from itself. The fact of starting from oneself is equivalent to separation. But the act of starting from oneself and separation itself can be produced in being only by opening the dimension of interiority.

9. THE MAINTENANCE OF SUBJECTIVITY
THE REALITY OF THE INNER LIFE AND THE REALITY OF THE STATE
THE MEANING OF SUBJECTIVITY

Metaphysics, or the relation with the other, is accomplished as service and as hospitality. In the measure that the face of the Other relates us with the third party, the metaphysical relation of the I with the Other moves into the form of the We, aspires to a State, institutions, laws, which are the source of universality. But politics left to itself bears a tyranny within itself; it deforms the I and the other who have given rise to it, for it judges them according to universal rules, and thus as in absentia. In welcoming the Other I welcome the On High to which my freedom is subordinated. But this subordination is not an absence: it is brought about in all the personal work of my moral initiative (without which the truth of judgment cannot be produced), in the attention to the Other as unicity[1] and face (which the visibleness of the political leaves invisible), which can be produced only in the unicity of an I. Subjectivity is thus rehabilitated in the work of truth, and not as an egoism refusing the system which offends it. Against this egoist protestation of the subjectivity, against this protestation in the first person, the universalism of Hegelian reality will perhaps prevail. But how could universal, that is, visible principles be opposed with this same pride to the face of the other, without recoiling before

---

9. Translator's brackets, in both instances here.   1. That is, a kind of uniqueness.

the cruelty of this impersonal justice! And then how could the subjectivity of the I not be introduced as the sole possible source of goodness?

Metaphysics therefore leads us to the accomplishment of the I as unicity by relation to which the work of the State must be situated, and which it must take as a model.

The irreplaceable unicity of the I which is maintained against the State is accomplished by fecundity. It is not to purely subjective events, losing themselves in the sands of interiority which the rational reality mocks, that we appeal to in insisting on the irreducibility of the personal to the universality of the State; we appeal to a dimension and a perspective of transcendence as real as the dimension and perspective of the political and more true than it, because in it the apology of the ipseity[2] does not disappear. The interiority opened up by separation is not the ineffable of the clandestine or the subterranean—but the infinite time of fecundity. Fecundity permits the assuming of the actual as the vestibule of a future. It opens the subterranean, where a life called inward or merely subjective seemed to take refuge, upon being.

The subjectivity present to the judgment of truth is therefore not reducible simply to an impotent, clandestine, unforeseeable, and from the outside invisible protestation against totality and objective totalization. And yet its entry into being is not wrought as an integration into a totality the separation had broken up. Fecundity and the perspectives it opens evince the ontological character of separation. But fecundity does not join together the fragments of a broken totality into a subjective history. Fecundity opens up an infinite and discontinuous time. It liberates the subject from his facticity by placing him beyond the possible which presupposes and does not surpass facticity; it lifts from the subject the last trace of fatality, by enabling him to be an other. In eros the fundamental exigencies of the subjectivity are maintained—but in this alterity the ipseity is graceful, lightened of egoist unwieldiness.

10. BEYOND BEING

Thematization does not exhaust the meaning of the relationship with exteriority. Thematization or objectification is not to be described only as an impassive contemplation, but is to be described as a relation with the solid, with the thing, since Aristotle the term of the analogy of being.[3] The solid is not reducible to the structures imposed by the impassibility of the look that contemplates it; it is to be understood in terms of the structures imposed by its relation with time—which it traverses. The being of the object is perduration, a filling of the time which is empty and inconsolable against death as an end. If exteriority consists not in being presented as a theme but in being open to desire, the existence of the separated being which desires exteriority no longer consists in caring for Being. To exist has a meaning in another dimension than that of the perduration of the totality; it can go beyond being. Contrary to the Spinozist tradition,[4] this going beyond death is produced not in the universality of thought but in the pluralist relation, in the goodness of being for

2. Individual identity, selfhood.
3. A reference to *Metaphysics* 7.4, by the Greek philosopher Aristotle (384–322 B.C.E.).

4. The tradition of the Dutch philosopher Benedict (Baruch) de Spinoza (1632–1677).

the Other, in justice. The surpassing of being starting from being—the relation with exteriority—is not measured by duration. Duration itself becomes visible in the relation with the Other, where being is surpassed.

11. Freedom Invested

The presence of exteriority in language, which commences with the presence of the face, is not produced as an affirmation whose formal meaning would remain without development. The relation with the face is produced as goodness. The exteriority of being is morality itself. Freedom, the event of separation in arbitrariness which constitutes the I, at the same time maintains the relation with the exteriority that morally resists every appropriation and every totalization in being. If freedom were posited outside of this relation, every relation within multiplicity would enact but the *grasp* of one being by another or their common participation in reason, where no being looks at the face of the other, but all beings negate one another. Knowledge or violence would appear in the midst of the multiplicity as events that realize being. The common knowledge proceeds toward unity, either toward the apparition in the midst of a multiplicity of beings of a rational system in which these beings would be but objects, and in which they would find their being—or toward the brutal conquest of beings outside of every system by violence. Whether in scientific thought or in the object of science, or in history understood as a manifestation of reason, where violence reveals itself to be reason, philosophy presents itself as a realization of being, that is, as its liberation by the suppression of multiplicity. Knowledge would be the suppression of the other by the grasp, by the hold, or by the vision that grasps before the grasp. In this work metaphysics has an entirely different meaning. If its movement leads to the transcendent as such, transcendence means not appropriation of *what is*, but its respect. Truth as a respect for being is the meaning of metaphysical truth.

If, in contradistinction to the tradition of the primacy of freedom, taken as the measure of being, we contest vision its primacy in being, and contest the pretension of human emprise[5] to gain access to the rank of *logos*, we take leave neither of rationalism, nor of the ideal of freedom. One is not an irrationalist nor a mystic nor a pragmatist for questioning the identification of power and *logos*. One is not against freedom if one seeks for it a justification. Reason and freedom seem to us to be founded on prior structures of being whose first articulations are delineated by the metaphysical movement, or respect, or justice—identical to truth. The terms of the conception making truth rest on freedom must be inverted. What justification there is in truth does not rest on freedom posited as independence in regard to all exteriority. It would be so, to be sure, if justified freedom would simply express the necessities rational order imposes on the subject. But true exteriority is metaphysical; it does not weigh on the separated being and commands him as free. The present work has sought to describe metaphysical exteriority. One of the consequences that follows from its very notion is that freedom is posited as requiring justification. The founding of truth on freedom would imply a freedom justified by itself. There would have been for freedom no greater scandal than to dis-

---

5. That is, enterprise, undertaking.

cover itself to be finite. To not have chosen one's freedom would be the supreme absurdity and the supreme tragic of existence; this would be the irrational. The Heideggerian *Geworfenheit*[6] marks a finite freedom and thus the irrational. The encounter with the Other in Sartre[7] threatens my freedom, and is equivalent to the fall of my freedom under the gaze of another freedom. Here perhaps is manifested most forcefully being's incompatibility with what remains veritably exterior. But to us here there rather appears the problem of the justification of freedom: does not the presence of the Other put in question the naïve legitimacy of freedom? Does not freedom appear to itself as a shame for itself? And, reduced to itself, as a usurpation? The irrational in freedom is not due to its limits, but to the infinity of its arbitrariness. Freedom must justify itself; reduced to itself it is accomplished not in sovereignty but in arbitrariness. Precisely through freedom—and not because of its limitation—the being freedom is to express in its plentitude appears as not having its reason in itself. Freedom is not justified by freedom. To account for being or to be in truth is not to comprehend nor to take hold of . . . , but rather to encounter the Other without allergy, that is, in justice.

To approach the Other is to put into question my freedom, my spontaneity as a living being, my emprise over the things, this freedom of a "moving force," this impetuosity of the current to which everything is permitted, even murder. The "You shall not commit murder" which delineates the face in which the Other is produced submits my freedom to judgment. Then the free adherence to truth, an activity of knowledge, the free will which, according to Descartes, in certitude adheres to a clear idea, seeks a reason which does not coincide with the radiance of this clear and distinct idea itself. A clear idea which imposes itself by its clarity calls for a strictly personal work of a freedom, a solitary freedom that does not put itself in question, but can at most suffer a failure. In morality alone it is put in question. Morality thus presides over the work of truth.

It will be said that the radical questioning of certitude reduces itself to the search for another certitude: the justification of freedom would refer to freedom. Indeed that is so, in the measure that justification cannot result in noncertitude. But in fact, the moral justification of freedom is neither certitude nor incertitude. It does not have the status of a result, but is accomplished as movement and life; it consists in addressing an infinite exigency to one's freedom, in having a radical non-indulgence for one's freedom. Freedom is not justified in the consciousness of certitude, but in an infinite exigency with regard to oneself, in the overcoming of all good conscience. But this infinite exigency with regard to oneself, precisely because it puts freedom in question, places me and maintains me in a situation in which I am not alone, in which I am judged. This is the primary sociality: the personal relation is in the rigor of justice which judges me and not in love that excuses me. For this judgment does not come to me from a Neuter; before the Neuter I am spontaneously free. In the infinite exigency with regard to oneself is produced the duality of the face to face. One does not prove God thus, since this is a situation that precedes proof, and is metaphysics itself. The ethical, beyond vision

6. Thrownness (German). See the selection from Heidegger's *Being and Time* (1927), above, section 38.

7. See the selection from SARTRE's *Being and Nothingness* (1943), below.

and certitude, delineates the structure of exteriority as such. Morality is not a branch of philosophy, but first philosophy.[8]

12. BEING AS GOODNESS—THE I—PLURALISM—PEACE

We have posited metaphysics as Desire. We have described Desire as the "measure" of the Infinite which no term, no satisfaction arrests (Desire opposed to Need). The discontinuity of generations, that is, death and fecundity, releases Desire from the prison of its own subjectivity and puts an end to the monotony of its identity. To posit metaphysics as Desire is to interpret the production of being—desire engendering Desire—as goodness and as beyond happiness; it is to interpret the production of being as being for the Other.

But "being for the Other" is not the negation of the I, engulfed in the universal. The universal law itself refers to a face to face position which refuses every exterior "viewing." To say that universality refers to the face to face position is (against a whole tradition of philosophy) to deny that being is produced as a panorama, a coexistence, of which the face to face would be a modality. This whole work opposes this conception. The face to face is not a modality of coexistence nor even of the knowledge (itself panoramic) one term can have of another, but is the primordial production of being on which all the possible collocations of the terms are founded. The revelation of the third party, ineluctable in the face, is produced only through the face. Goodness does not radiate over the anonymity of a collectivity presenting itself panoramically, to be absorbed into it. It concerns a being which is revealed in a face, but thus it does not have eternity without commencement. It has a principle, an origin, issues from an I, is subjective. It is not regulated by the principles inscribed in the nature of a particular being that manifests it (for thus it would still proceed from universality and would not respond to the face), nor in the codes of the State. It consists in going where no clarifying—that is, panoramic—thought precedes, in going without knowing where. An absolute adventure, in a primal imprudence, goodness is transcendence itself. Transcendence is the transcendence of an I. Only an I can respond to the injunction of a face.

The I is conserved then in goodness, without its resistance to system manifesting itself as the egoist cry of the subjectivity, still concerned for happiness or salvation, as in Kierkegaard.[9] To posit being as Desire is to decline at the same time the ontology of isolated subjectivity and the ontology of impersonal reason realizing itself in history.

To posit being as Desire and as goodness is not to first isolate an I which would then tend toward a beyond. It is to affirm that to apprehend oneself from within—to produce oneself as I—is to apprehend oneself with the same gesture that already turns toward the exterior to extra-vert and to manifest—to respond for what it apprehends—to express; it is to affirm that the becoming-conscious is already language, that the essence of language is goodness, or

---

8. That is, the most fundamental and central part of philosophy. Descartes called metaphysics "first philosophy" (the full title of his famous *Medita-* *tions* [1641] is *Meditations on First Philosophy*).
9. For KIERKEGAARD, see above.

again, that the essence of language is friendship and hospitality. The other is not the negation of the same, as Hegel would like to say. The fundamental fact of the ontological scission into same and other is a non-allergic relation of the same with the other.

Transcendence or goodness is produced as pluralism. The pluralism of being is not produced as a multiplicity of a constellation spread out before a possible gaze, for thus it would be already totalized, joined into an entity. Pluralism is accomplished in goodness proceeding from me to the other, in which first the other, as absolutely other, can be produced, without an alleged lateral view upon this movement having any right to grasp of it a truth superior to that which is produced in goodness itself. One does not enter into this pluralist society without always remaining outside by speech (in which goodness is produced)—but one does not leave it in order to simply *see oneself* inside. The unity of plurality is peace, and not the coherence of the elements that constitute plurality. Peace therefore cannot be identified with the end of combats that cease for want of combatants, by the defeat of some and the victory of the others, that is, with cemetaries or future universal empires. Peace must be my peace, in a relation that starts from an I and goes to the other, in desire and goodness, where the I both maintains itself and exists without egoism. It is conceived starting from an I assured of the convergence of morality and reality, that is, of an infinite time which through fecundity is its time. It will remain a personal I before the judgment in which truth is stated, and this judgment will come from outside of it without coming from an impersonal reason, which uses ruse with persons and is pronounced in their absence.

The situation in which the I thus posits itself before truth in placing its subjective morality in the infinite time of its fecundity—a situation in which the instant of eroticism and the infinity of paternity are conjoined—is concretized in the marvel of the family. The family does not only result from a rational arrangement of animality; it does not simply mark a step toward the anonymous universality of the State. It identifies itself outside of the State, even if the State reserves a framework for it. As source of human time it permits the subjectivity to place itself under a judgment while retaining speech. This is a metaphysically ineluctable structure which the State would not dismiss, as in Plato, nor make exist in view of its own disappearance, as Hegel would have it. The biological structure of fecundity is not limited to the biological fact. In the biological fact of fecundity are outlined the lineaments of fecundity in general as a relation between man and man and between the I and itself not resembling the structures constitutive of the State, lineaments of a reality that is not subordinated to the State as a means and does not represent a reduced model of the State.

Situated at the antipodes of the subject living in the infinite time of fecundity is the isolated and heroic being that the State produces by its virile virtues. Such a being confronts death out of pure courage and whatever be the cause for which he dies. He assumes finite time, the death-end or the death-transition, which do not arrest the continuation of a being without discontinuity. The heroic existence, the isolated soul, can gain its salvation in seeking an eternal life for itself, as though its subjectivity, returning to itself in a continuous time, could not be turned against it—as though in this continuous time identity itself would not be affirmed obsessively, as though in the identity that remains in the midst of the most extravagant avatars[,] "tedium, fruit of the mournful incuriosity that takes on the proportions of immortality"[1] did not triumph.

SOURCE: From Emmanuel Lévinas, *Totality and Infinity: An Essay on Exteriority*, trans. Alphonso Lingis (Pittsburgh: Duquesne University Press, 1969), pp. 289–307. Originally published in 1961 as *Totalité et infini: Essai sur l'extériorité*.

1. A quotation from a poem by the French poet Charles Baudelaire (1821–1867) titled "Spleen."

JEAN-PAUL SARTRE
(1905 – 1980)

Sartre made "existentialism" a household word. Through his lectures, essays, plays, and novels, he gave great numbers of people who knew little about philosophy and its history a variety of forms of ready access to it. And he did so in a way that made both his version of existentialism and the idea of existentialism enormously popular, particularly with students and in the literary and theatrical communities. Other talented French writers were assisting in the cause—Albert Camus and Sartre's longtime companion SIMONE DE BEAUVOIR in particular—but it was Sartre's version that shaped the understanding of it throughout the Western world in the decades following the Second World War.

His version triumphed in part because of Sartre's extensive "existentialist" literary output and its rapid translation, and in part because he was something of an intellectual celebrity with a knack for publicity and a talent for coming up with quotable quotes on controversial topics. Moreover, his appealing and readily understandable essay "Existentialism Is a Humanism" (1946; see below) was nearly everyone's introduction to "existentialism" as a kind of philosophical position—and that essay and his other pronouncements on the topic were grounded in the weight and authority of a massive treatise, *Being and Nothingness* (1943). Inspired by his reading of HEIDEGGER's *Being and Time* (1927), and (perhaps deliberately) every bit as dense and formidable, it quickly became the bible of existentialism.

The pronunciation of Sartre's name is a problem for English speakers, who have difficulty with the glottal articulation of the French "-re." Probably the best course for those who also cannot be bothered to give the "r" an unvoiced trip of the tongue after "Sart-" (a marginally acceptable alternative) is to leave the last letters silent and simply rhyme the name with "start."

Jean-Paul Charles Aymard Sartre was born in Paris, just a year before the death of his father, an officer in the French navy. The boy was raised by his mother, Anne-Marie Schweitzer (a cousin of Albert Schweitzer), who was from the Alsace region, in which German and French influences were both strong. Her father, a German language and literature teacher who assisted in Sartre's home education, soon became convinced that he was a child prodigy. He learned to read and write at a very early age. As a child he much preferred the company of words to that of other children, or of people other than family more generally. When he did eventually begin attending school, however, he made the adjustment (with some difficulty) and was an outstanding student, qualifying for admission to the prestigious École Normale Supérieure. There he met Simone de Beauvoir and Albert Camus, becoming very close to both of them. He and Camus subsequently broke with each other (over Camus's rejection of communism, to which Sartre was—in his own way—attracted); but he and Beauvoir became lifelong lovers and companions, maintaining an open relationship that was sometimes strained by their many affairs with others.

Sartre was drawn to philosophy when he read one of HENRI BERGSON's books in his teens. He pursued his interest in it at the École, studying Descartes, KANT, and HEGEL and also becoming aware of HUSSERL in Germany. After his graduation in 1929 he was conscripted into the French army, serving two years in a noncombatant role. He then obtained a teaching position in philosophy at Le Havre in 1931, leaving after a year for Germany to pursue his growing interests in Husserlian phenomenology. He returned to Le Havre two years later, but soon moved on to other teaching positions in Lyon and at the Lycée Pasteur in Paris.

After Germany invaded Poland in 1939, Sartre was recalled to the French army, and was captured by the Germans in June 1940. While a prisoner of war, he first read Heidegger's *Being and Time*. After he was released in March 1941, he resumed teaching and became involved in a resistance group, writing and distributing underground material. But he focused mainly on his philosophical and literary efforts, completing not only his primary contribution to existential philosophy—*Being and Nothingness*—but also two of his most famous plays, *The Flies* (produced 1943) and *No Exit* (produced 1944). His works were ignored by the German censors, perhaps because they dealt not with the Germans but with the human condition.

After the liberation of Paris (and France) in the summer of 1944, Sartre founded the monthly review *Les Temps modernes* (*Modern Times*) and entered on a period of great productivity, becoming something of a literary and philosophical celebrity. From that time on he found it possible to support himself (modestly) through his writings, and so he stopped teaching. He became a strident critic of Western European and (especially) American social, cultural, and political developments, opposing first French colonial rule in North Africa and Southeast Asia and then U.S. involvement in Vietnam. He joined with Bertrand Russell and other leading public intellectuals in their attempt to organize a tribunal to convict the United States of war crimes in Vietnam and elsewhere. He was also an outspoken critic of Israel and a supporter of the Algerian, Cuban, Vietcong, Palestinian, and student radical causes. He was awarded the 1964 Nobel Prize in Literature, but—as he had done earlier when offered the Légion d'honneur (Legion of Honor) in recognition of his wartime work for the French resistance—he declined it, less on political grounds than out of a deep anti-establishmentarianism.

Sartre lived to the end of his life as a kind of perpetual radical, resisting all forms of institutionalization even as he philosophically recognized their inevitability in human life. During his long flirtation with communism, he embraced its revolutionary opposition to bourgeois, capitalist, and imperialist institutions and powers—but he was never willing to submit to party discipline. In his later years he was a kind of French institution in his own right, revered even as he continued his protests and feuds with other public intellectuals (including many former allies). When he was arrested for civil disobedience in 1968 during the student revolutionary strikes in Paris, he was pardoned by President Charles de Gaulle himself—the very embodiment of almost everything to which Sartre was opposed—who explained his pardon with a simple and grand compliment: "One doesn't arrest Voltaire."

Sartre had a double advantage over Heidegger in the postwar Western world. He had the best of credentials with respect to National Socialism and the war, while Heidegger's were among the worst of anyone of significance in philosophy; and in another marked contrast to Heidegger, he was a brilliant writer when he chose to be—with a very extensive readership who could not get enough of him. Publishers in Britain and America rushed to meet the growing demand for his literary and popular writings, which usually were translated soon after their original publication in French. There was thus an eager audience for his *Being and Nothingness*, which appeared in English in 1956, long before Heidegger's *Being and Time* (or KARL JASPERS's main contributions to existential philosophy). As a result, Sartre—together with Camus and other kindred spirits—had nearly a decade in which to establish the "French existentialist" version(s) of existential philosophy in the minds (and anthologies) of English-speaking readers and teachers attentive to the latest developments in European philosophy.

Their spectacular success in doing so, at the expense of most of their philosophical rivals, has long been and remains a problem for the understanding of existential philosophy more generally, which by no means entails commitment to Sartre's views. For related reasons, both Heidegger and Jaspers emphatically rejected the label "existentialist" for themselves and their writings, insisting that their "*Existenz*-philosophies" had nothing to do with (Sartrean) "existentialism." But it also underscores the importance of looking closely at what Sartre does in *Being and Nothingness* and how he does it (rather than examining only his "Humanism" essay and his literary writings), to see what sort of philosophical project and thinking underlie his more accessible writings from this period that generated so much excitement.

In Sartre's later writings, he (like Heidegger) moved in several different directions, the most significant of which (very much *un*like Heidegger) was toward a kind of Marxism that incorporated elements of his earlier existentialism. This development culminated in his *Critique of Dialectical Reason* (2 vols., 1960–85), an even more formidable work than *Being and Nothingness*. He wrote much more as well, in the course of his long and extraordinarily productive life; but he remains best known and respected philosophically for that earlier classic of existential philosophy.

Sartre began his philosophical career as a kind of phenomenologist and ended it as a kind of Marxist, but its peak was at its existential-philosophical midpoint. Most of the following discussion will pertain to his thought during that middle period. His existentialism grew out of his phenomenological thinking in his early books *The Transcendence of the Ego* (1936) and *The Imaginary* (1940), in which he developed his version of Husserl's radical distinction between consciousness and its objects. Like Heidegger, and under Heidegger's influence, Sartre wanted to reconsider human reality in the light of this distinction, which appeared to rule out any naturalistic

attempt to conceive and explain consciousness as a feature or function of the causal order of things and of natural phenomena. Unlike Heidegger, he was quite content to say that the kind of reality he is talking about is "human"; but like Heidegger, he was prepared to call his analysis of it both methodologically "phenomenological" and substantively a kind of "ontology." He also had considerable sympathy for Kant, however; and in his "Existentialism Is a Humanism," he attempted to make existentialism out to be a kind of radicalized version of Kantian thinking with respect to human freedom, responsibility, and dignity.

For Sartre as for Descartes, Kant, and Husserl, consciousness is something fundamentally different from the kinds of *things* that we encounter as objects of experience, in ways that make it not subject to the kinds of laws and causal necessities that obtain among them. If they are considered to be paradigmatic or definitive of types of "beings," then consciousness is not another such *being*, for it is "no thing" at all—and so "nothing," a kind of "nothingness." Hence the title of *Being and Nothingness*. While human reality does not consist merely of consciousness, it is no mere type of thing. It somehow involves both being and nothingness—that is, the special sort of "no-thing-ness" that consciousness is or that pertains to human reality because consciousness is at the heart of human reality. And it does this in a way that alters the status of those features of human reality that *do* have the character of types of determinate being, such as our bodies and our pasts and our situations in the world, in relation both to things and to others.

Sartre's concern, in his existential-literary writings (from *Nausea* [1938] onward) as well as in his existential-philosophical writings, was to illuminate this peculiar kind of reality and enable it to be comprehended—and to consider what the normative implications are of what we thus can and should comprehend about ourselves and about our human condition. Like KIERKEGAARD and Heidegger, he focuses on the question of what it means to *exist* as a particular human being, living one's life in the first-person singular. What this means, for him, is first of all existing in the mode of consciousness and self-consciousness (which, following Hegel, he calls being "for-itself"), rather than in the mode of a mere thing or object (which he calls being "in-itself"). The reality of a mere thing is not mediated by consciousness of itself or of anything else (it has no "being for-itself"); it simply "is what it is"—even though that may well be what it is, when considered not all by itself or as some sort of metaphysical "thing-in-itself" but rather in its relatedness to other things. The world in which we find ourselves, for Sartre, is nothing more than a vast expanse and array of that sort of reality. Heidegger's talk about "being" and "the meaning of being" has no interest or meaning for Sartre, for whom this very prosaic and mundane state of affairs is all that such talk comes down to. There is something more to reality than mere things of this sort—but it is only *our own* different sort of reality, in the "for-itself" mode of consciousness and self-consciousness.

Sartre has no answer to the question of how or why this sort of reality could come to exist in a world that otherwise contains nothing but mere things, from which he insists the for-itself could not possibly have arisen. For him it simply happens to be the case, however astonishing or absurd that may seem to us to be; and the task of the philosopher as phenomenological ontologist is to describe and analyze these different sorts of evident reality as carefully, clearly, and completely as possible, not to undertake the futile quest for an ultimate explanation of how they might have come to be. He would appear to think that the possibility of such ultimate explanations has vanished along with the idea of a God who could have grounded them.

Like NIETZSCHE, Sartre takes as his point of departure not only the existence of two sorts of being or reality—our con-

sciousness and self-consciousness, and the sorts of things and objectivities with which we find ourselves consciously and self-consciously confronted—but also what Nietzsche had called "the death of God": the demise of the viability of the idea of any type of transcendent being or reality by reference to which our human reality and the reality of our world might be understood, explained, justified, evaluated, or normatively guided. Sartre's primary philosophical task in his existential-philosophical writings is to carry out a phenomenological-ontological analysis of human reality; but an associated task, which comes to the fore in his literary and more popular philosophical writings, is that of taking the death of God seriously and working out its consequences to the end—consequences that Sartre considers to be quite radical.

The nonsubstantiality of the for-itself is taken by Sartre as rendering it independent of the "causal order" of the in-itself, thereby showing the idea that we are subject to that causal order in our choices to be false, however externally constrained our actions might be. In short, he sees it as establishing our radical freedom—at least up to the point that our choices and attempts to act on those choices run up against circumstances thwarting them; and even then, for Sartre, we still have the freedom to determine the meaning of such situations for us. Moreover, the absence of any "God" or other transcendent ground of meaning, value, and normativity means that there is no standard beyond human reality by reference to which our determinations can and should be either assessed or guided. Our capacity to act is constrained by the contingencies that we confront, but those contingencies have no authority or normative significance that we are bound to accept. Within their limitations, our freedom is absolute—and our responsibility for ourselves and what we do with our lives is likewise absolute.

For Sartre as for Kant, this freedom and responsibility for ourselves set us apart from all mere things, making us self-legislating agents deserving of self-respect and mutual respect as such. And for Sartre as for Kant, this unique status is the key to the postreligious understanding of human dignity and worth. It is the basis of Sartre's contention that existentialism (or his version of existentialism, at any rate) is a kind of humanism. Yet it is a humanism that does not accord equal dignity and worth to all human life as such, however it might be lived. Rather, it lays great stress on Sartre's version of integrity or authenticity—of existing in a genuinely or truly human manner. Sartre vehemently denies that this notion has anything essentialistic or idealistic about it, rejecting the very idea of any conception of a human "essence" that dictates what an ideal human life would look like. Instead, authenticity is presented as something like Kierkegaard's idea of what it is to exist as a human being (or to exist "subjectively") *in truth*. For Sartre it means existing in a manner that takes full account of the fundamental "truth" with respect to human reality: namely, that our freedom and our responsibility for ourselves are absolute within whatever constraints upon us may exist; there is no higher authority, standard, or law to which we are subject in the exercise of that freedom and responsibility—to which we are "condemned" but by which we are also distinguished from all mere things and challenged to acknowledge and embrace.

Sartre does not hesitate to use harsh language to characterize those who flee from this challenge (e.g., "cowards"). In his view, their failing is not "immoral" or "wrong" in any ordinary sense; but in refusing to face up to the truth of the matter, they display their lack of truthfulness, honesty, intellectual integrity, and courage. Sartre does not use the terms "authenticity" and "inauthenticity," but he does use the expression *mauvaise foi*, meaning "self-deception" (literally, "bad faith"), to somewhat the same effect as the latter. He contends that its opposite is not to be conceived as "good faith" or "sincerity," nor characterized as "being true to oneself," since

these concepts too involve forms of "self-deception" (that is, supposing that one *has* some sort of substantial "self" or fundamental identity that one ought to be "true to"). Sartre has no standard term for his preferred alternative to *mauvaise foi*, though "integrity" may best capture what he has in mind.

Perhaps in imitation of Nietzsche, Sartre has a penchant for catchy—and also for paradoxical-sounding—phrases. They can be helpful, but they require careful explication if they are not to be misunderstood. A good example is his assertion that an existentialist is one for whom "Existence precedes essence." His point is that a human being has no predetermined substantial nature that specifies either what human beings generally or what any of us in particular ought to do or be. Instead, for a human being the formation of a determinate identity (an "essence") is something that occurs (to the extent that it does) in the course of "existing," making choices as one does so. Moreover, it is a point of great significance for the Sartre of *Being and Nothingness* that even as a human being does come to acquire a personal identity in this manner, that identity acquires no genuine authority or normativity concerning an individual's future choices and decisions. One's freedom is freedom with respect to it as well as to everything else: it neither causes nor mandates anything whatsoever relating to what one goes on to do.

Another seeming paradox is the contention that human reality "is what it is not and is not what it is"—as opposed to the reality of a mere thing, which simply is what it is and is not what it is not. Sartre's point is that a human being is not *merely* "what it is" (that is, the sum total of facts about it at any particular point) but rather is *also* "what it is not" (that is, its possibilities and its freedom with respect to them, which are both indefinite at any particular point). This, he contends, is the basic structure of human reality or "existing"; and when he says that "man alone exists," what he means is that (as far as we know) human reality is the only type of reality that has this structure.

Sartre relishes opportunities to make his points in striking and memorable language. When he proclaims our existence and our choices to be "absurd," he is simply denying that there is any ultimate reason for them. In calling human existence a "futile" and "useless passion," his point is that although the synthesis of the in-itself and the for-itself—a kind of being that would combine the features of both types of being (which is his analysis of the idea of God)—is a contradiction in terms, this utter impossibility is nonetheless something to which human reality is compelled by the very nature and dynamics of the for-itself to aspire. When he says, "Life begins on the far side of despair," the despair of which he speaks is the hopelessness that tends initially to accompany the loss of belief in absolutes that previously have given life meaning and value. And when he says that "my freedom is the unique foundation of values," his point is that values do not exist in the world apart from the choices that establish and sustain them, and that such choices are always and only the choices of subjects who are free in making them.

Sartre makes much of experiential phenomena—someone's absence, something's being disappointing, something having been destroyed—that turn out to have a kind of "negativity" as part of their very structure, and that cannot be analyzed in terms of purely positive features of the situation. He draws on such phenomena to argue that they must have a kind of "nothingness" as their origin, and that that nothingness must be a structure of our own reality. According to Sartre, more complex sorts of phenomena—for example, the phenomenon of "bad faith"—require certain more complex structures of human reality as conditions of their possibility. That is the type of "transcendental" argument he had learned from Heidegger (deriving from Husserl and ultimately from Kant), around which his entire phenomenological ontology in *Being and Nothingness* revolves.

This kind of argument takes on a particular richness and intricacy in *Being and Nothingness* in Sartre's discussion of various experiential phenomena involving others, which are taken to be importantly revealing of yet other structures of human reality relating our identities to our relations with others and to our own bodies in ways mediated by others. A salient example is what he calls "the Look," in which one becomes aware of being seen while in the act of watching someone else. One of the striking features of this discussion is that it presents "being with others" as at once a fundamental dimension of human reality and inherently conflictual. We may come to know ourselves more fully through the kinds of relations with others that Sartre discusses; but he sees such relations generally as being more conducive to self-deception and the abdication of freedom and responsibility than to personal integrity, because they prompt us to identify ourselves with objectifications of ourselves that are merely expressions of our agency rather than that agency itself.

For Kierkegaard true subjectivity (and thus authentic selfhood) is an isolated, inward affair, essentially involving only one's relation to oneself and to God; our relations to others are at best incidental to it—and all too often draw us insidiously toward other untrue forms of selfhood. For Sartre much the same can be said—except that for him there is no God-relationship. We exist in a world of things and others, but we are each very much on our own insofar as freedom, responsibility, and integrity are concerned. Others are inescapable; but for Sartre genuine subject–subject relations are impossible, because consciousness can be conscious of something only by objectifying it. We are all embodied subjects, and in our relations with others we can get past the struggle to remain subjects by objectifying each other only through more complicated conflicts in which some are thrown together in dealings with yet others. (The most famous line of *No Exit*, Sartre's best-known play, is: "Hell is other people.")

In his later writings Sartre continued to regard relations with others as a major complication of human reality, but his attention (in a manner no doubt influenced by his reckoning with MARX) shifted to the problem of how to understand human social structures and groups and the kinds of difference they can and do make for the ways in which human life is concretely lived. His encounter with Marx's thought led him to a fundamental methodological broadening of his approach to human reality, supplementing his earlier "first-person-centered" phenomenological orientation by recognizing the need for a kind of social theory that would be more structural, historical, and "third-person" oriented. The very title of the book-length essay that he used as an introduction to his massive *Critique of Dialectical Reason*— namely, *Search for a Method*—indicates his recognition that such a modification is required. In that essay the outlines of his modified thinking with respect to human reality can also be seen (considerably more clearly than in the *Critique* itself, a short sampling of which is provided below).

In *Search* Sartre attempts to integrate some of the main ideas of his earlier existential-phenomenological analysis of human existence into the larger framework of what he himself is now prepared to call a "philosophical anthropology." Indeed, here he has moved some distance from his earlier existentialism. In the preface he observes: "I do not like to talk about existentialism. It is the nature of an intellectual quest to be undefined. To name it and define it is to wrap it up and tie the knot. What is left? A finished, already outdated mode of culture, something like a brand of soap—in other words, an idea." He considers phenomenological analysis and existentialism itself to have a place *within* such a philosophical anthropology, in order to ensure that it remains connected with and true to human existence at the individual, first-person level; but he now contends further that a kind of social-structural perspective and analysis are needed in order to deal with the context within which such existence occurs. The sought-for "method" is to be one that moves back and forth between these approaches and perspectives, and between the more general and more particular levels of human reality that its comprehension requires— from the social-theoretical analysis of social groups, structures, and processes to the exploration of individual relationships and projects.

Sartre credits Marx with having understood this, going so far as to locate his own position and efforts within Marxist thought even as he also criticizes contemporary Marxism for having become abstract, rigid, and forgetful of "what it means to exist as a human being" (as both Marx and Kierkegaard had taken Hegel's "system" of "Idealism" to be). He thus might be seen as attempting two kinds of reformation simultaneously: using existentialism to reform the Marxism of his time, to make it more faithful to the spirit and insights of Marx's own Marxism (as Sartre understands it), and also using Marxism to reform the existential philosophy of his time, to enable it to do greater justice to human reality than phenomenology can.

The centrality given to "freedom" in the earlier Sartre's analysis of human existence is now bestowed on the Marxist concept of "praxis" (that is, human action as Marx conceived of it). The concept of the "project" (as a chosen course of action) remains fundamental; but "objectification" rather than "choice" is now the issue around which everything revolves. And now Sartre presents self-realization through "objectification" as what matters most in and about human life, rather than integrity in making one's choices, however limited one's possibilities might be. There can and should be more to human life than choosing freely in clear recognition of one's freedom and responsibility for one's choices: the character and quality of the identity one is able to fashion for oneself matters as well—and therefore the constraints on one's "field of possibilities" become a matter of major concern.

The kind of freedom that matters most to the "later Sartre" is the freedom to objectify—and thereby realize—oneself without being subject to coercion, deprivation, and alienation. Human existence is no longer characterized in terms of "nothingness" and "absurdity," and as a "futile passion," even though the points Sartre used such language to make still apply; instead, more positive themes regarding human possibility are emphasized. And Sartre now explicitly recognizes the interpretive (rather than straightforwardly analytical) character of the kind of philosophical inquiry needed to work toward an understanding of human reality that does justice to it; that is the point of his repeated references (in translation) to "comprehensive" thinking—that is, thinking that "comprehends."

In short: one can see an important "turn" in the thinking of the later Sartre no less than in the thinking of the later Heidegger, but Sartre's turn takes a quite different direction—one that has affinities with several of the developments that will be encountered in the next part of this volume. *Search* reveals both the con-tinuities and the modifications quite clearly, and the excerpts from it (and from the *Critique*) that follow those from *Being and Nothingness* should be read with an eye to both.

Existential philosophy would have existed without Heidegger (owing to Jaspers), but it was Heidegger who made it more—much more—than a minor development on the fringe of phenomenology. Sartre, more than anyone else, was the thinker who broke Heidegger's near-monopoly on it and showed that one didn't have to be German (or even think in German) to engage in it and pursue it. He popularized it and sold that popularization of it to the world, though that was a problematic "contribution" to its development. His greater and more genuine contribution was to provide and elaborate a significantly different existential-philosophical analysis of human reality—and also (albeit inadvertently, through its own limitations and inadequacies) to make it clear that his was no more the last word with respect to human "existence" than was Heidegger's.

Existentialism Is a Humanism

I should like on this occasion to defend existentialism against some charges which have been brought against it.

First, it has been charged with inviting people to remain in a kind of desperate quietism because, since no solutions are possible, we should have to consider action in this world as quite impossible. We should then end up in a philosophy of contemplation; and since contemplation is a luxury, we come in the end to a bourgeois philosophy. The communists[1] in particular have made these charges.

On the other hand, we have been charged with dwelling on human degradation, with pointing up everywhere the sordid, shady, and slimy, and neglecting the gracious and beautiful, the bright side of human nature; for example, according to Mlle. Mercier,[2] a Catholic critic, with forgetting the smile of the child. Both sides charge us with having ignored human solidarity, with con-

1. A powerful force intellectually as well as politically and socially in postwar France on the left, as was the Roman Catholic establishment on the right. The two were rivals, and Sartrean "existentialism" was emerging as a new adversary to both.
2. Jeanne Mercier (1896–1991), a teacher of philosophy who provided a Christian critique of Sartrean existentialism in "Le ver dans le fruit: A propos de l'oeuvre de M. J.-P. Sartre [The Worm in the Fruit: Concerning the Work of Mr. J.-P. Sartre]," *Études*, February 1945, pp. 232–49.

sidering man as an isolated being. The communists say that the main reason for this is that we take pure subjectivity, the Cartesian I think,[3] as our starting point; in other words, the moment in which man becomes fully aware of what it means to him to be an isolated being; as a result, we are unable to return to a state of solidarity with the men who are not ourselves, a state which we can never reach in the cogito.

From the Christian standpoint, we are charged with denying the reality and seriousness of human undertakings, since, if we reject God's commandments and the eternal verities, there no longer remains anything but pure caprice, with everyone permitted to do as he pleases and incapable, from his own point of view, of condemning the points of view and acts of others.

I shall try today to answer these different charges. Many people are going to be surprised at what is said here about humanism. We shall try to see in what sense it is to be understood. In any case, what can be said from the very beginning is that by existentialism we mean a doctrine which makes human life possible and, in addition, declares that every truth and every action implies a human setting and a human subjectivity.

As is generally known, the basic charge against us is that we put the emphasis on the dark side of human life. Someone recently told me of a lady who, when she let slip a vulgar word in a moment of irritation, excused herself by saying, "I guess I'm becoming an existentialist." Consequently, existentialism is regarded as something ugly; that is why we are said to be naturalists; and if we are, it is rather surprising that in this day and age we cause so much more alarm and scandal than does naturalism, properly so called. The kind of person who can take in his stride such a novel as Zola's The Earth[4] is disgusted as soon as he starts reading an existentialist novel; the kind of person who is resigned to the wisdom of the ages—which is pretty sad—finds us even sadder. Yet, what can be more disillusioning than saying "true charity begins at home" or "a scoundrel will always return evil for good?"

We know the commonplace remarks made when this subject comes up, remarks which always add up to the same thing: we shouldn't struggle against the powers-that-be; we shouldn't resist authority; we shouldn't try to rise above our station; any action which doesn't conform to authority is romantic; any effort not based on past experience is doomed to failure; experience shows that man's bent is always toward trouble, that there must be a strong hand to hold him in check[;] if not, there will be anarchy. There are still people who go on mumbling these melancholy old saws, the people who say, "It's only human!" whenever a more or less repugnant act is pointed out to them, the people who glut themselves on chansons réalistes;[5] these are the people who accuse existentialism of being too gloomy, and to such an extent that I wonder whether they are complaining about it not for its pessimism, but much rather its optimism. Can it be that what really scares them in the doctrine I shall try to present here is that it leaves to man a possibility of choice? To answer this

---

3. That is, the cogito (Latin), the starting point of the French philosopher and mathematician René Descartes (1596–1650).
4. The 1887 novel by Émile Zola (1840–1902), the most prominent member of the naturalist movement (which blended realism with the perceived determinism of natural science); it focuses on the brutality of peasant life.
5. Realist songs (French), a genre of music especially popular in France in the first part of the 20th century.

question, we must re-examine it on a strictly philosophical plane. What is meant by the term *existentialism*?

Most people who use the word would be rather embarrassed if they had to explain it, since, now that the word is all the rage, even the work of a musician or painter is being called existentialist. A gossip columnist in *Clartés* signs himself *The Existentialist*, so that by this time the word has been so stretched and has taken on so broad a meaning, that it no longer means anything at all. It seems that for want of an advance-guard doctrine analogous to surrealism, the kind of people who are eager for scandal and flurry turn to this philosophy which in other respects does not at all serve their purposes in this sphere.

Actually, it is the least scandalous, the most austere of doctrines. It is intended strictly for specialists and philosophers. Yet it can be defined easily. What complicates matters is that there are two kinds of existentialist; first, those who are Christian, among whom I would include Jaspers and Gabriel Marcel,[6] both Catholic; and on the other hand the atheistic existentialists, among whom I class Heidegger, and then the French existentialists and myself. What they have in common is that they think that existence precedes essence,[7] or, if you prefer, that subjectivity must be the starting point.

Just what does that mean? Let us consider some object that is manufactured, for example, a book or a paper-cutter: here is an object which has been made by an artisan whose inspiration came from a concept. He referred to the concept of what a paper-cutter is and likewise to a known method of production, which is part of the concept, something which is, by and large, a routine. Thus, the paper-cutter is at once an object produced in a certain way and, on the other hand, one having a specific use; and one can not postulate[8] a man who produces a paper-cutter but does not know what it is used for. Therefore, let us say that, for the paper-cutter, essence—that is, the ensemble of both the production routines and the properties which enable it to be both produced and defined—precedes existence. Thus, the presence of the paper-cutter or book in front of me is determined. Therefore, we have here a technical view of the world whereby it can be said that production precedes existence.

When we conceive God as the Creator, He is generally thought of as a superior sort of artisan. Whatever doctrine we may be considering, whether one like that of Descartes or that of Leibnitz,[9] we always grant that will more or less follows understanding or, at the very least, accompanies it, and that when God creates He knows exactly what He is creating. Thus, the concept of man in the mind of God is comparable to the concept of paper-cutter in the mind of the manufacturer, and, following certain techniques and a conception, God produces man, just as the artisan, following a definition and a technique, makes a paper-cutter. Thus, the individual man is the realisation of a certain concept in the divine intelligence.

---

6. French philosopher and leading representative of French Catholic existentialism (1889–1973). For KARL JASPERS, see above.
7. A formula significantly different from Heidegger's thesis in *Being and Time* (1927) that "the essence of Dasein (human reality) lies in its Existenz," despite sounding similar. Sartre's point is that human reality has no preestablished nature or sub-

stantive "essence" that determines how it must or ought to be: instead, it first "exists" and determines subsequently what it is to be and do (by its own radically free and self-responsible choices).
8. That is, concieve of, imagine that there could be.
9. Gottfried Wilhelm Leibniz (1646–1716), German rationalist philosopher.

In the eighteenth century, the atheism of the *philosophes*[1] discarded the idea of God, but not so much for the notion that essence precedes existence. To a certain extent, this idea is found everywhere; we find it in Diderot, in Voltaire, and even in Kant. Man has a human nature; this human nature, which is the concept of the human, is found in all men, which means that each man is a particular example of a universal concept, man. In Kant, the result of this universality is that the wild-man, the natural man, as well as the bourgeois, are circumscribed by the same definition and have the same basic qualities. Thus, here too the essence of man precedes the historical existence that we find in nature.

Atheistic existentialism, which I represent, is more coherent. It states that if God does not exist, there is at least one being in whom existence precedes essence, a being who exists before he can be defined by any concept, and that this being is man, or, as Heidegger says, human reality.[2] What is meant here by saying that existence precedes essence? It means that, first of all, man exists, turns up, appears on the scene, and, only afterwards, defines himself. If man, as the existentialist conceives him, is indefinable, it is because at first he is nothing. Only afterward will he be something, and he himself will have made what he will be. Thus, there is no human nature, since there is no God to conceive it. Not only is man what he conceives himself to be, but he is also only what he wills himself to be after this thrust toward existence.

Man is nothing else but what he makes of himself. Such is the first principle of existentialism. It is also what is called subjectivity, the name we are labeled with when charges are brought against us. But what do we mean by this, if not that man has a greater dignity than a stone or table? For we mean that man first exists, that is, that man first of all is the being who hurls himself toward a future and who is conscious of imagining himself as being in the future. Man is at the start a plan which is aware of itself, rather than a patch of moss, a piece of garbage, or a cauliflower; nothing exists prior to this plan; there is nothing in heaven; man will be what he will have planned to be. Not what he will want to be. Because by the word "will" we generally mean a conscious decision, which is subsequent to what we have already made of ourselves. I may want to belong to a political party, write a book, get married; but all that is only a manifestation of an earlier, more spontaneous choice that is called "will." But if existence really does precede essence, man is responsible for what he is. Thus, existentialism's first move is to make every man aware of what he is and to make the full responsibility of his existence rest on him. And when we say that a man is responsible for himself, we do not only mean that he is responsible for his own individuality, but that he is responsible for all men.[3]

The word subjectivism has two meanings, and our opponents play on the two. Subjectivism means, on the one hand, that an individual chooses and makes himself; and, on the other, that it is impossible for man to transcend human subjectivity. The second of these is the essential meaning of existentialism.

1. Philosophers (French); that is, the rationalist thinkers of the French Enlightenment, including Denis Diderot (1713–1784) and Voltaire (François-Marie Arouet, 1694–1778).
2. That is, Heidegger's conception of human reality as "Dasein."

3. This highly problematic generalization represents Sartre's strategic attempt to link himself to KANT's "categorical imperative"—a moral law that is absolute for all rational agents, requiring each to act in a way that he or she would be prepared to will as a universal law.

When we say that man chooses his own self, we mean that every one of us does likewise; but we also mean by that that in making this choice he also chooses all men. In fact, in creating the man that we want to be, there is not a single one of our acts which does not at the same time create an image of man as we think he ought to be. To choose to be this or that is to affirm at the same time the value of what we choose, because we can never choose evil. We always choose the good, and nothing can be good for us without being good for all.[4]

If, on the other hand, existence precedes essence, and if we grant that we exist and fashion our image at one and the same time, the image is valid for everybody and for our whole age. Thus, our responsibility is much greater than we might have supposed, because it involves all mankind. If I am a working-man and choose to join a Christian trade-union rather than be a communist, and if by being a member I want to show that the best thing for man is resignation, that the kingdom of man is not of this world, I am not only involving my own case—I want to be resigned for everyone. As a result, my action has involved all humanity. To take a more individual matter, if I want to marry, to have children; even if this marriage depends solely on my own circumstances or passion or wish, I am involving all humanity in monogamy and not merely myself. Therefore, I am responsible for myself and for everyone else. I am creating a certain image of man of my own choosing. In choosing myself, I choose man.

This helps us understand what the actual content is of such rather grandiloquent words as anguish, forlornness, despair. As you will see, it's all quite simple.

First, what is meant by anguish? The existentialists say at once that man is anguish. What that means is this: the man who involves himself and who realizes that he is not only the person he chooses to be, but also a law-maker who is, at the same time, choosing all mankind as well as himself, can not help escape the feeling of his total and deep responsibility. Of course, there are many people who are not anxious; but we claim that they are hiding their anxiety, that they are fleeing from it. Certainly, many people believe that when they do something, they themselves are the only ones involved, and when someone says to them, "What if everyone acted that way?" they shrug their shoulders and answer, "Everyone doesn't act that way." But really, one should always ask himself, "What would happen if everybody looked at things that way?" There is no escaping this disturbing thought except by a kind of double-dealing. A man who lies and makes excuses for himself by saying "not everybody does that," is someone with an uneasy conscience, because the act of lying implies that a universal value is conferred upon the lie.

Anguish is evident even when it conceals itself. This is the anguish that Kierkegaard called the anguish of Abraham.[5] You know the story: an angel has ordered Abraham to sacrifice his son; if it really were an angel who has come and said, "You are Abraham, you shall sacrifice your son," everything

---

4. Sartre here attempts to align himself with another philosophical icon, Socrates, who is represented in Plato's dialog *Laches* as maintaining that, in making our choices, we always mean to be choosing the good (rather than its opposite)—not just for ourselves but more generally (and so for all). Sartre's actual position, however, is that this is so only in the sense that it is our choices that endow what we choose with value. (See his *Being and Nothingness*, below.)

5. The biblical patriarch Abraham, who was ordered by God to offer his son Isaac as a burnt offering (Genesis 22:1–19), as discussed in KIERKEGAARD's *Fear and Trembling* (1843); see above.

would be all right. But everyone might first wonder, "Is it really an angel, and am I really Abraham? What proof do I have?"

There was a madwoman who had hallucinations; someone used to speak to her on the telephone and give her orders. Her doctor asked her, "Who is it who talks to you?" She answered, "He says it's God." What proof did she really have that it was God? If an angel comes to me, what proof is there that it's an angel? And if I hear voices, what proof is there that they come from heaven and not from hell, or from the subconscious, or a pathological condition? What proves that they are addressed to me? What proof is there that I have been appointed to impose my choice and my conception of man on humanity? I'll never find any proof or sign to convince me of that. If a voice addresses me, it is always for me to decide that this is the angel's voice; if I consider that such an act is a good one, it is I who will choose to say that it is good rather than bad.

Now, I'm not being singled out as an Abraham, and yet at every moment I'm obliged to perform exemplary acts. For every man, everything happens as if all mankind had its eyes fixed on him and were guiding itself by what he does. And every man ought to say to himself, "Am I really the kind of man who has the right to act in such a way that humanity might guide itself by my actions?" And if he does not say that to himself, he is masking his anguish.

There is no question here of the kind of anguish which would lead to quietism, to inaction. It is a matter of a simple sort of anguish that anybody who has had responsibilities is familiar with. For example, when a military officer takes the responsibility for an attack and sends a certain number of men to death, he chooses to do so, and in the main he alone makes the choice. Doubtless, orders come from above, but they are too broad; he interprets them, and on this interpretation depend the lives of ten or fourteen or twenty men. In making a decision he can not help having a certain anguish. All leaders know this anguish. That doesn't keep them from acting; on the contrary, it is the very condition of their action. For it implies that they envisage a number of possibilities, and when they choose one, they realize that it has value only because it is chosen. We shall see that this kind of anguish, which is the kind that existentialism describes, is explained, in addition, by a direct responsibility to the other men whom it involves. It is not a curtain separating us from action, but is part of action itself.

When we speak of forlornness [*délaissement*],[6] a term Heidegger was fond of, we mean only that God does not exist and that we have to face all the consequences of this. The existentialist is strongly opposed to a certain kind of secular ethics which would like to abolish God with the least possible expense. About 1880, some French teachers tried to set up a secular ethics which went something like this: God is a useless and costly hypothesis; we are discarding it; but, meanwhile, in order for there to be an ethics, a society, a civilization, it is essential that certain values be taken seriously and that they be considered as having an *a priori* existence. It must be obligatory, *a priori*, to be honest, not to lie, not to beat your wife, to have children, etc.,

---

6. That is, abandonment, aloneness (i.e., Godlessness)—but not (as this rendering suggests) sad, miserable. (Pronounced "day-less-MAW.") Sartre's version of Heidegger's concept of "thrownness" (*Geworfenheit*; see the selection from *Being and Time*, above), signifying the absence of any underlying intent.

etc. So we're going to try a little device which will make it possible to show that values exist all the same, inscribed in a heaven of ideas, though otherwise God does not exist. In other words—and this, I believe, is the tendency of everything called reformism in France—nothing will be changed if God does not exist. We shall find ourselves with the same norms of honesty, progress, and humanism, and we shall have made of God an outdated hypothesis which will peacefully die off by itself.

The existentialist, on the contrary, thinks it very distressing that God does not exist, because all possibility of finding values in a heaven of ideas disappears along with Him; there can no longer be an *a priori* Good, since there is no infinite and perfect consciousness to think it. Nowhere is it written that the Good exists, that we must be honest, that we must not lie; because the fact is we are on a plane where there are only men. Dostoievsky said, "If God didn't exist, everything would be possible."[7] That is the very starting point of existentialism. Indeed, everything is permissible if God does not exist, and as a result man is forlorn,[8] because neither within him nor without does he find anything to cling to. He can't start making excuses for himself.

If existence really does precede essence, there is no explaining things away by reference to a fixed and given human nature. In other words, there is no determinism, man is free, man is freedom. On the other hand, if God does not exist, we find no values or commands to turn to which legitimize our conduct. So, in the bright realm of values, we have no excuse behind us, nor justification before us. We are alone, with no excuses.

That is the idea I shall try to convey when I say that man is condemned to be free. Condemned, because he did not create himself, yet, in other respects is free; because, once thrown into the world, he is responsible for everything he does. The existentialist does not believe in the power of passion. He will never agree that a sweeping passion is a ravaging torrent which fatally leads a man to certain acts and is therefore an excuse. He thinks that man is responsible for his passion.

The existentialist does not think that man is going to help himself by finding in the world some omen by which to orient himself. Because he thinks that man will interpret the omen to suit himself. Therefore, he thinks that man, with no support and no aid, is condemned every moment to invent man. Ponge,[9] in a very fine article, has said, "Man is the future of man." That's exactly it. But if it is taken to mean that this future is recorded in heaven, that God sees it, then it is false, because it would really no longer be a future. If it is taken to mean that, whatever a man may be, there is a future to be forged, a virgin future before him, then this remark is sound. But then we are forlorn.[1]

To give you an example which will enable you to understand forlornness [*délaissement*] better, I shall cite the case of one of my students who came to see me under the following circumstances: his father was on bad terms with his mother, and, moreover, was inclined to be a collaborationist; his older brother had been killed in the German offensive of 1940,[2] and the young

---

7. That is, "everything would be permitted." Quoted from a character in the novel *The Brothers Karamazov* (1880), by the Russian writer Fyodor Dostoevsky (1821–1881).
8. That is, abandoned, on his own.
9. Francis Ponge (1899–1988), French poet; Sartre

quotes from his "Notes premières de l'"Homme' [First notes on the 'Man']," *Les Temps modernes* 1 (October 1945): 14.
1. That is, entirely on our own.
2. That is, Germany's invasion of France, which resulted in the occupation.

man, with somewhat immature but generous feelings, wanted to avenge him. His mother lived alone with him, very much upset by the half-treason of her husband and the death of her older son; the boy was her only consolation.

The boy was faced with the choice of leaving for England and joining the Free French forces—that is, leaving his mother behind—or remaining with his mother and helping her to carry on. He was fully aware that the woman lived only for him and that his going-off—and perhaps his death—would plunge her into despair. He was also aware that every act that he did for his mother's sake was a sure thing, in the sense that it was helping her to carry on, whereas every effort he made toward going off and fighting was an uncertain move which might run aground and prove completely useless; for example, on his way to England he might, while passing through Spain, be detained indefinitely in a Spanish camp; he might reach England or Algiers and be stuck in an office at a desk job. As a result, he was faced with two very different kinds of action: one, concrete, immediate, but concerning only one individual; the other concerned an incomparably vaster group, a national collectivity, but for that very reason was dubious, and might be interrupted en route. And, at the same time, he was wavering between two kinds of ethics. On the one hand, an ethics of sympathy, of personal devotion; on the other, a broader ethics, but one whose efficacy was more dubious. He had to choose between the two.

Who could help him choose? Christian doctrine? No. Christian doctrine says, "Be charitable, love your neighbor, take the more rugged path, etc., etc." But which is the more rugged path? Whom should he love as a brother? The fighting man or his mother? Which does the greater good, the vague act of fighting in a group, or the concrete one of helping a particular human being to go on living? Who can decide *a priori*? Nobody. No book of ethics can tell him. The Kantian ethics says, "Never treat any person as a means, but as an end."[3] Very well, if I stay with my mother, I'll treat her as an end and not as a means; but by virtue of this very fact, I'm running the risk of treating the people around me who are fighting, as means; and, conversely, if I go to join those who are fighting, I'll be treating them as an end, and, by doing that, I run the risk of treating my mother as a means.

If values are vague, and if they are always too broad for the concrete and specific case that we are considering, the only thing left for us is to trust our instincts.[4] That's what this young man tried to do; and when I saw him, he said, "In the end, feeling is what counts. I ought to choose whichever pushes me in one direction. If I feel that I love my mother enough to sacrifice everything else for her—my desire for vengeance, for action, for adventure— then I'll stay with her. If, on the contrary, I feel that my love for my mother isn't enough, I'll leave."

But how is the value of a feeling determined? What gives his feeling for his mother value? Precisely the fact that he remained with her. I may say that I like so-and-so well enough to sacrifice a certain amount of money for him, but I may say so only if I've done it. I may say "I love my mother well enough to remain with her" if I have remained with her. The only way to determine the value of this affection is, precisely, to perform an act which confirms and

3. A misquotation of Kant's *Groundwork of the Metaphysics of Morals* (1785): "Never treat humanity (whether in ourselves or in others) as a means *only*, but always as an end *also*."
4. That is, *one might think* this is "the only thing left for us."

defines it. But, since I require this affection to justify my act, I find myself caught in a vicious circle.

On the other hand, Gide[5] has well said that a mock feeling and a true feeling are almost indistinguishable; to decide that I love my mother and will remain with her, or to remain with her by putting on an act, amount somewhat to the same thing. In other words, the feeling is formed by the acts one performs; so, I can not refer to it in order to act upon it. Which means that I can neither seek within myself the true condition which will impel me to act, nor apply to a system of ethics for concepts which will permit me to act. You will say, "At least, he did go to a teacher for advice." But if you seek advice from a priest, for example, you have chosen this priest; you already knew, more or less, just about what advice he was going to give you. In other words, choosing your adviser is involving yourself. The proof of this is that if you are a Christian, you will say, "Consult a priest." But some priests are collaborating, some are just marking time, some are resisting. Which to choose? If the young man chooses a priest who is resisting or collaborating, he has already decided on the kind of advice he's going to get. Therefore, in coming to see me he knew the answer I was going to give him, and I had only one answer to give: "You're free, choose, that is, invent." No general ethics can show you what is to be done; there are no omens in the world. The Catholics will reply, "But there are." Granted—but, in any case, I myself choose the meaning they have.

When I was a prisoner,[6] I knew a rather remarkable young man who was a Jesuit. He had entered the Jesuit order in the following way: he had had a number of very bad breaks; in childhood, his father died, leaving him in poverty, and he was a scholarship student at a religious institution where he was constantly made to feel that he was being kept out of charity; then, he failed to get any of the honors and distinctions that children like; later on, at about eighteen, he bungled a love affair; finally, at twenty-two, he failed in military training, a childish enough matter, but it was the last straw.

This young fellow might well have felt that he had botched everything. It was a sign of something, but of what? He might have taken refuge in bitterness or despair. But he very wisely looked upon all this as a sign that he was not made for secular triumphs, and that only the triumphs of religion, holiness, and faith were open to him. He saw the hand of God in all this, and so he entered the order. Who can help seeing that he alone decided what the sign meant?

Some other interpretation might have been drawn from this series of setbacks; for example, that he might have done better to turn carpenter or revolutionist. Therefore, he is fully responsible for the interpretation. Forlornness [délaissement] implies that we ourselves choose our being. Forlornness [délaissement] and anguish go together.

As for despair,[7] the term has a very simple meaning. It means that we shall confine ourselves to reckoning only with what depends upon our will, or on

---

5. André Gide (1869–1951), French writer; Sartre paraphrases an observation from his novel *The Counterfeiters* (1925).
6. While serving in the French army, Sartre was captured by Germans in 1940 and spent 9 months as a prisoner of war.
7. *Désespoir*, a concept that figures importantly in

Sartre's existentialism. It has no real counterpart in Heidegger but corresponds to what Kierkegaard calls "the sickness unto death"; for Sartre, however, it is a badge of honor, and something that neither warrants nor is overcome by any religious "leap of faith."

the ensemble of probabilities which make our action possible. When we want something, we always have to reckon with probabilities. I may be counting on the arrival of a friend. The friend is coming by rail or street-car; this supposes that the train will arrive on schedule, or that the street-car will not jump the track. I am left in the realm of possibility; but possibilities are to be reckoned with only to the point where my action comports with the ensemble of these possibilities, and no further. The moment the possibilities I am considering are not rigorously involved by my action, I ought to disengage myself from them, because no God, no scheme, can adapt the world and its possibilities to my will. When Descartes said, "Conquer yourself rather than the world,"[8] he meant essentially the same thing.

The Marxists to whom I have spoken reply, "You can rely on the support of others in your action, which obviously has certain limits because you're not going to live forever. That means: rely on both what others are doing elsewhere to help you, in China, in Russia, and what they will do later on, after your death, to carry on the action and lead it to its fulfillment, which will be the revolution. You even *have* to rely upon that, otherwise you're immoral." I reply at once that I will always rely on fellow-fighters insofar as these comrades are involved with me in a common struggle, in the unity of a party or a group in which I can more or less make my weight felt; that is, one whose ranks I am in as a fighter and whose movements I am aware of at every moment. In such a situation, relying on the unity and will of the party is exactly like counting on the fact that the train will arrive on time or that the car won't jump the track. But, given that man is free and that there is no human nature for me to depend on, I can not count on men whom I do not know by relying on human goodness or man's concern for the good of society. I don't know what will become of the Russian revolution; I may make an example of it to the extent that at the present time it is apparent that the proletariat plays a part in Russia that it plays in no other nation. But I can't swear that this will inevitably lead to a triumph of the proletariat.[9] I've got to limit myself to what I see.

Given that men are free and that tomorrow[1] they will freely decide what man will be, I can not be sure that, after my death, fellow-fighters will carry on my work to bring it to its maximum perfection. Tomorrow, after my death, some men may decide to set up Fascism, and the others may be cowardly and muddled enough to let them do it. Fascism will then be the human reality, so much the worse for us.

Actually, things will be as man will have decided they are to be. Does that mean that I should abandon myself to quietism? No. First, I should involve myself; then, act on the old saw, "Nothing ventured, nothing gained." Nor does it mean that I shouldn't belong to a party, but rather that I shall have no illusions and shall do what I can. For example, suppose I ask myself, "Will socialization,[2] as such, ever come about?" I know nothing about it. All I know is that I'm going to do everything in my power to bring it about. Beyond that, I can't count on anything. Quietism is the attitude of people who say, "Let others

---

8. Paraphrased from Descartes, *Discourse on Method* (1637), part 3.
9. Predicted in chapter 1 of the *Manifesto of the Communist Party* (1848), by KARL MARX and

FRIEDRICH ENGELS.
1. That is, *every* tomorrow.
2. That is, collectivism (*collectivisation*).

do what I can't do." The doctrine I am presenting is the very opposite of quietism, since it declares, "There is no reality except in action." Moreover, it
goes further, since it adds, "Man is nothing else than his plan; he exists only
to the extent that he fulfills himself; he is therefore nothing else than the
ensemble of his acts, nothing else than his life."

According to this,[3] we can understand why our doctrine horrifies certain
people. Because often the only way they can bear their wretchedness is to
think, "Circumstances have been against me. What I've been and done doesn't
show my true worth. To be sure, I've had no great love, no great friendship,
but that's because I haven't met a man or woman who was worthy. The books
I've written haven't been very good because I haven't had the proper leisure.
I haven't had children to devote myself to because I didn't find a man with
whom I could have spent my life. So there remains within me, unused and
quite viable, a host of propensities, inclinations, possibilities, that one wouldn't
guess from, the mere series of things I've done."

Now, for the existentialist there is really no love other than one which manifests itself in a person's being in love. There is no genius other than one
which is expressed in works of art; the genius of Proust is the sum of Proust's
works; the genius of Racine[4] is his series of tragedies. Outside of that, there
is nothing. Why say that Racine could have written another tragedy, when he
didn't write it? A man is involved in life, leaves his impress on it, and outside
of that there is nothing. To be sure, this may seem a harsh thought to someone whose life hasn't been a success. But, on the other hand, it prompts people
to understand that reality alone is what counts, that dreams, expectations,
and hopes warrant no more than to define a man as a disappointed dream, as
miscarried hopes, as vain expectations. In other words, to define him negatively and not positively. However, when we say, "You are nothing else than
your life," that does not imply that the artist will be judged solely on the basis
of his works of art; a thousand other things will contribute toward summing
him up. What we mean is that a man is nothing else than a series of undertakings, that he is the sum, the organization, the ensemble of the relationships which make up these undertakings.[5]

When all is said and done, what we are accused of, at bottom, is not our
pessimism, but an optimistic toughness. If people throw up to us our works
of fiction in which we write about people who are soft, weak, cowardly, and
sometimes even downright bad, it's not because these people are soft, weak,
cowardly, or bad; because if we were to say, as Zola did, that they are that
way because of heredity, the workings of environment, society, because of biological or psychological determinism, people would be reassured. They would
say, "Well, that's what we're like, no one can do anything about it." But when
the existentialist writes about a coward, he says that this coward is responsible for his cowardice. He's not like that because he has a cowardly heart or

---

3. That is, in view of what Sartre has just asserted.
4. Jean Racine (1639–1699), preeminent writer of
French classical tragedy. Marcel Proust (1871–
1922), French novelist and master of modern
fiction.
5. That is: this, for Sartre, is what one (a human
being) *is* insofar as one is a particular determinate
being; but there is something else that is a part of

one's human reality as well that is of the greatest
importance—one's consciousness, and with it, one's
freedom and transcendence (even if not independence) of all such specificity. This duality of human
reality is the central topic of *Being and Nothingness*,
and is that about our human reality to which its
title refers. (See below.)

lung or brain; he's not like that on account of his physiological makeup; but he's like that because he has made himself a coward by his acts. There's no such thing as a cowardly constitution; there are nervous constitutions; there is poor blood, as the common people say, or strong constitutions. But the man whose blood is poor is not a coward on that account, for what makes coward-ice is the act of renouncing or yielding. A constitution is not an act; the coward is defined on the basis of the acts he performs. People feel, in a vague sort of way, that this coward we're talking about is guilty of being a coward, and the thought frightens them. What people would like is that a coward or a hero be born that way.

One of the complaints most frequently made about *The Ways of Freedom*[6] can be summed up as follows: "After all, these people are so spineless, how are you going to make heroes out of them?" This objection almost makes me laugh, for it assumes that people born heroes. That's what people really want to think. If you're born cowardly, you may set your mind perfectly at rest; there's nothing you can do about it; you'll be cowardly all your life, whatever you may do. If you're born a hero, you may set your mind just as much at rest; you'll be a hero all your life; you'll drink like a hero and eat like a hero. What the existentialist says is that the coward makes himself cowardly, that the hero makes himself heroic. There's always a possibility for the coward not to be cowardly any more and for the hero to stop being heroic. What counts is total involvement; some one particular action or set of circumstances is not total involvement.

Thus, I think we have answered a number of the charges concerning exis-tentialism. You see that it can not be taken for a philosophy of quietism, since it defines man in terms of action; nor for a pessimistic description of man— there is no doctrine more optimistic, since man's destiny is within himself; nor for an attempt to discourage man from acting, since it tells him that the only hope is in his acting and that action is the only thing that enables a man to live. Consequently, we are dealing here with an ethics of action and involvement.

Nevertheless, on the basis of a few notions like these, we are still charged with immuring man in his private subjectivity. There again we're very much misunderstood. Subjectivity of the individual is indeed our point of departure, and this for strictly philosophic reasons. Not because we are bourgeois, but because we want a doctrine based on truth and not a lot of fine theories, full of hope but with no real basis. There can be no other truth to take off from than this: *I think; therefore, I exist.*[7] There we have the absolute truth of con-sciousness becoming aware of itself. Every theory which takes man out of the moment in which he becomes aware of himself is, at its very beginning, a the-ory which confounds truth, for outside the Cartesian *cogito*, all views are only probable, and a doctrine of probability which is not bound to a truth dis-solves into thin air. In order to describe the probable, you must have a firm hold on the true. Therefore, before there can be any truth whatsoever, there

---

6. A projected tetralogy of novels begun by Sartre in 1945 (*Les Chemins de la liberté,* more often translated as *The Roads to Freedom*). This comment refers to *The Age of Reason* (1945), *The Reprieve* (1945), and *Troubled Sleep* (1947); the fragmentary fourth volume, *The Last Chance,* was not published until 1981.
7. The famous declaration of Descartes' *Medita-tions* (in Latin, *cogito, ergo sum*).

must be an absolute truth; and this one is simple and easily arrived at; it's on everyone's doorstep; it's a matter of grasping it directly.

Secondly, this theory is the only one which gives man dignity, the only one which does not reduce him to an object. The effect of all materialism is to treat all men, including the one philosophizing, as objects, that is, as an ensemble of determined reactions in no way distinguished from the ensemble of qualities and phenomena which constitute a table or a chair or a stone. We definitely wish to establish the human realm as an ensemble of values distinct from the material realm. But the subjectivity that we have thus arrived at, and which we have claimed to be truth, is not a strictly individual subjectivity, for we have demonstrated that one discovers in the *cogito* not only himself, but others as well.

The philosophies of Descartes and Kant to the contrary, through the *I think* we reach our own self in the presence of others, and the others are just as real to us as our own self. Thus, the man who becomes aware of himself through the *cogito* also perceives all others, and he perceives them as the condition of his own existence. He realizes that he can not be anything (in the sense that we say that someone is witty or nasty or jealous) unless others recognize it as such. In order to get any truth about myself, I must have contact with another person. The other is indispensable to my own existence, as well as to my knowledge about myself.[8] This being so, in discovering my inner being I discover the other person at the same time, like a freedom placed in front of me which thinks and wills only for or against me. Hence, let us at once announce the discovery of a world which we shall call inter-subjectivity; this is the world in which man decides what he is and what others are.

Besides, if it is impossible to find in every man some universal essence which would be human nature, yet there does exist a universal human condition. It's not by chance that today's thinkers speak more readily of man's condition than of his nature. By condition they mean, more or less definitely, the *a priori* limits which outline man's fundamental situation in the universe. Historical situations vary; a man may be born a slave in a pagan society or a feudal lord or a proletarian. What does not vary is the necessity for him to exist in the world, to be at work there, to be there in the midst of other people, and to be mortal there.[9] The limits are neither subjective or objective, or, rather, they have an objective and a subjective side. Objective because they are to be found everywhere and are recognizable everywhere; subjective because they are *lived* and are nothing if man does not live them, that is, freely determine his existence with reference to them. And though the configurations may differ, at least none of them are completely strange to me, because they all appear as attempts either to pass beyond these limits or recede from them or deny them or adapt to them. Consequently, every configuration, however individual it may be, has a universal value.[1]

---

8. This is an important point in Hegel (see above), with whom Sartre is in agreement more often than one might suppose from the common depiction of existential philosophy as a comprehensive rejection of everything Hegelian.
9. This is a quick, basic summary of Heidegger's analysis of Dasein (in his view, the "being" or character of human reality), here characterized as the "universal human condition." For Sartre, this is not at all the idea of "human nature" or of "some universal essence (of man)," because he thinks that those concepts are by their very nature normative ideals and that no such ideal can be true or binding on all in the absence of a God who could mandate it.
1. That is, a general significance (another significant Hegelian point that Sartre expresses in a manner suggestive of a further kinship with Kant).

Every configuration, even the Chinese, the Indian, or the Negro, can be understood by a Westerner. "Can be understood" means that by virtue of a situation that he can imagine, a European of 1945 can, in like manner, push himself to his limits and reconstitute within himself the configuration of the Chinese, the Indian, or the African. Every configuration has universality in the sense that every configuration can be understood by every man. This does not at all mean that this configuration defines man forever, but that it can be met with again. There is always a way to understand the idiot, the child, the savage, the foreigner, provided one has the necessary information.

In this sense we may say that there is a universality of man; but it is not given, it is perpetually being made. I build the universal in choosing myself; I build it in understanding the configuration of every other man, whatever age he might have lived in. This absoluteness of choice does not do away with the relativeness of each epoch. At heart, what existentialism shows is the connection between the absolute character of free involvement, by virtue of which every man realizes himself in realizing a type of mankind, an involvement always comprehensible in any age whatsoever and by any person whosoever, and the relativeness of the cultural ensemble which may result from such a choice; it must be stressed that the relativity of Cartesianism and the absolute character of Cartesian involvement go together. In this sense, you may, if you like, say that each of us performs an absolute act in breathing, eating, sleeping, or behaving in any way whatever. There is no difference between being free, like a configuration, like an existence which chooses its essence, and being absolute. There is no difference between being an absolute temporarily localised, that is, localised in history, and being universally comprehensible.

This does not entirely settle the objection to subjectivism. In fact, the objection still takes several forms. First, there is the following: we are told, "So you're able to do anything, no matter what!" This is expressed in various ways. First we are accused of anarchy; then they say, "You're unable to pass judgment on others, because there's no reason to prefer one configuration to another"; finally they tell us, "Everything is arbitrary in this choosing of yours. You take something from one pocket and pretend you're putting it into the other."

These three objections aren't very serious. Take the first objection. "You're able to do anything, no matter what" is not to the point. In one sense choice is possible, but what is not possible is not to choose. I can always choose, but I ought to know that if I do not choose, I am still choosing. Though this may seem purely formal, it is highly important for keeping fantasy and caprice within bounds. If it is true that in facing a situation, for example, one in which, as a person capable of having sexual relations, of having children, I am obliged to choose an attitude, and if I in any way assume responsibility for a choice which, in involving myself, also involves all mankind, this has nothing to do with caprice, even if no *a priori* value determines my choice.

If anybody thinks that he recognizes here Gide's theory of the arbitrary act,[2] he fails to see the enormous difference between this doctrine and Gide's. Gide does not know what a situation is. He acts out of pure caprice. For us, on the contrary, man is in an organized situation in which he himself is involved.

---

2. The *acte gratuit*, illustrated in Gide's novel *Laf-cadio's Adventures* (1914, *Les Caves du Vatican*), which features a deliberately gratuitous murder.

Through his choice, he involves all mankind, and he can not avoid making a choice: either he will remain chaste, or he will marry without having children, or he will marry and have children; anyhow, whatever he may do, it is impossible for him not to take full responsibility for the way he handles this problem. Doubtless, he chooses without referring to pre-established values, but it is unfair to accuse him of caprice. Instead, let us say that moral choice is to be compared to the making of a work of art. And before going any further, let it be said at once that we are not dealing here with an aesthetic ethics, because our opponents are so dishonest that they even accuse us of that. The example I've chosen is a comparison only.

Having said that, may I ask whether anyone has ever accused an artist who has painted a picture of not having drawn his inspiration from rules set up *a priori*? Has anyone ever asked, "What painting ought he to make?" It is clearly understood that there is no definite painting to be made, that the artist is engaged in the making of his painting, and that the painting to be made is precisely the painting he will have made. It is clearly understood that there are no *a priori* aesthetic values, but that there are values which appear subsequently in the coherence of the painting, in the correspondence between what the artist intended and the result. Nobody can tell what the painting of tomorrow will be like. Painting can be judged only after it has once been made. What connection does that have with ethics? We are in the same creative situation. We never say that a work of art is arbitrary. When we speak of a canvas of Picasso,[3] we never say that it is arbitrary; we understand quite well that he was making himself what he is at the very time he was painting, that the ensemble of his work is embodied in his life.

The same holds on the ethical plane. What art and ethics have in common is that we have creation and invention in both cases. We can not decide *a priori* what there is to be done. I think that I pointed that out quite sufficiently when I mentioned the case of the student who came to see me, and who might have applied to all the ethical systems, Kantian or otherwise, without getting any sort of guidance. He was obliged to devise his law himself. Never let it be said by us that this man—who, taking affection, individual action, and kindheartedness toward a specific person as his ethical first principle, chooses to remain with his mother, or who, preferring to make a sacrifice, chooses to go to England—has made an arbitrary choice. Man makes himself. He isn't ready made at the start. In choosing his ethics, he makes himself, and force of circumstances is such that he can not abstain from choosing one. We define man only in relationship to involvement. It is therefore absurd to charge us with arbitrariness of choice.

In the second place, it is said that we are unable to pass judgment on others. In a way this is true, and in another way, false. It is true in this sense, that, whenever a man sanely and sincerely involves himself and chooses his configuration, it is impossible for him to prefer another configuration,[4] regard-

---

3. Pablo Picasso (1881–1973), Spanish artist who was one of the great innovators of the 20th century; he spent most of his life in France.
4. He cannot *prefer* another configuration (though another might have been chosen or may be chosen in the future) because, for Sartre, it is meaningless to speak of a real preference that is at odds with a choice in which one has "sanely and sincerely involved oneself"—for in that case one's "preferences" (properly understood or conceived) simply *are* what one chooses.

less of what his own may be in other respects. It is true in this sense, that we do not believe in progress. Progress is betterment. Man is always the same. The situation confronting him varies. Choice always remains a choice in a situation. The problem has not changed since the time one could choose between those for and those against slavery, for example, at the time of the Civil War, and the present time, when one can side with the Maquis Resistance Party,[5] or with the Communists.

But, nevertheless, one can still pass judgment, for, as I have said, one makes a choice in relationship to others. First, one can judge (and this is perhaps not a judgment of value, but a logical judgment) that certain choices are based on error and others on truth. If we have defined man's situation as a free choice, with no excuses and no recourse, every man who takes refuge behind the excuse of his passions, every man who sets up a determinism, is a dishonest man.

The objection may be raised, "But why mayn't he choose himself dishonestly?" I reply that I am not obliged to pass moral judgment on him, but that I do define his dishonesty as an error. One can not help considering the truth of the matter. Dishonesty is obviously a falsehood because it belies the complete freedom of involvement. On the same grounds, I maintain that there is also dishonesty if I choose to state that certain values exist prior to me; it is self-contradictory for me to want them and at the same time state that they are imposed on me. Suppose someone says to me, "What if I want to be dishonest?" I'll answer, "There's no reason for you not to be, but I'm saying that that's what you are, and that the strictly coherent attitude is that of honesty."

Besides, I can bring moral judgment to bear. When I declare that freedom in every concrete circumstance can have no other aim than to want itself, if man has once become aware that in his forlornness [délaissement] he imposes values, he can no longer want but one thing, and that is freedom,[6] as the basis of all values.[7] That doesn't mean that he wants it in the abstract. It means simply that the ultimate meaning of the acts of honest men is the quest for freedom as such. A man who belongs to a communist or revolutionary union wants concrete goals; these goals imply an abstract desire for freedom; but this freedom is wanted in something concrete. We want freedom for freedom's sake and in every particular circumstance. And in wanting freedom we discover that it depends entirely on the freedom of others, and that the freedom of others depends on ours. Of course, freedom as the definition of man does not depend on others, but as soon as there is involvement, I am obliged to want others to have freedom at the same time that I want my own freedom. I can take freedom as my goal only if I take that of others as a goal as well. Consequently, when, in all honesty, I've recognized that man is a being in whom existence precedes essence, that he is a free being who, in various circumstances, can want only his freedom, I have at the same time recognized that I can want only the freedom of others.

---

5. Guerrilla fighters in the French underground who opposed the Germans.
6. That is, "he can no longer want anything other than freedom."
7. Sartre appears to believe that if it is the case both that freedom "can have no other aim than to want itself" and that freedom that has become aware of itself *must* "want itself," then this internal imperative within the very nature of freedom is sufficient to justify "moral judgment" with respect to freedom, and to mandate an integrity that will brook no compromise of freedom.

Therefore, in the name of this will for freedom, which freedom itself implies, I may pass judgment on those who seek to hide from themselves the complete arbitrariness and the complete freedom of their existence. Those who hide their complete freedom from themselves out of a spirit of seriousness or by means of deterministic excuses, I shall call cowards; those who try to show that their existence was necessary, when it is the very contingency of man's appearance on earth, I shall call stinkers [salauds].[8] But cowards or stinkers [salauds] can be judged only from a strictly unbiased point of view.[9]

Therefore though the content of ethics is variable, a certain form of it is universal. Kant says that freedom desires both itself and the freedom of others. Granted. But he believes that the formal and the universal are enough to constitute an ethics. We, on the other hand, think that principles which are too abstract run aground in trying to decide action. Once again, take the case of the student. In the name of what, in the name of what great moral maxim do you think he could have decided, in perfect peace of mind, to abandon his mother or to stay with her? There is no way of judging. The content is always concrete and thereby unforeseeable; there is always the element of invention. The one thing that counts is knowing whether the inventing that has been done, has been done in the name of freedom.

For example, let us look at the following two cases. You will see to what extent they correspond, yet differ. Take *The Mill on the Floss*.[1] We find a certain young girl, Maggie Tulliver, who is an embodiment of the value of passion and who is aware of it. She is in love with a young man, Stephen, who is engaged to an insignificant young girl. This Maggie Tulliver, instead of heedlessly preferring her own happiness, chooses, in the name of human solidarity, to sacrifice herself and give up the man she loves. On the other hand, Sanseverina, in *The Charterhouse of Parma*,[2] believing that passion is man's true value, would say that a great love deserves sacrifices; that it is to be preferred to the banality of the conjugal love that would tie Stephen to the young ninny he had to marry. She would choose to sacrifice the girl and fulfill her happiness; and, as Stendhal shows, she is even ready to sacrifice herself for the sake of passion, if this life demands it. Here we are in the presence of two strictly opposed moralities. I claim that they are much the same thing; in both cases what has been set up as the goal is freedom.

You can imagine two highly similar attitudes: one girl prefers to renounce her love out of resignation; another prefers to disregard the prior attachment of the man she loves out of sexual desire. On the surface these two actions resemble those we've just described. However, they are completely different. Sanseverina's attitude is much nearer that of Maggie Tulliver, one of heedless rapacity.

Thus, you see that the second charge is true and, at the same time, false. One may choose anything if it is on the grounds of free involvement.[3]

---

8. That is, bastards (a slang expression indicative of contempt). Best left untranslated and understood accordingly. (Pronounced "sa-LOW.")
9. That is, as descriptive epithets (perhaps in the spirit of Heidegger's similar claim that "inauthenticity" and "falling" in his usage are simply descriptive terms).
1. The English novel (1860) by George Eliot (Mar-

ian Evans, 1819–1880).
2. The French novel (1839) by Stendhal (Marie-henri Beyle, 1783–1842).
3. That is, the only normative restriction on choice is that it be made "with no excuses" and in full recognition of one's freedom and responsibility for it (precisely as an exercise and concrete realization of one's freedom).

The third objection is the following: "You take something from one pocket and put it into the other. That is, fundamentally, values aren't serious, since you choose them." My answer to this is that I'm quite vexed that that's the way it is; but if I've discarded God the Father, there has to be someone to invent values. You've got to take things as they are. Moreover, to say that we invent values means nothing else but this: life has no meaning *a priori*. Before you come alive, life is nothing; it's up to you to give it a meaning, and value is nothing else but the meaning that you choose. In that way, you see, there is a possibility of creating a human community.[4]

I've been reproached for asking whether existentialism is humanistic. It's been said, "But you said in *Nausea*[5] that the humanists were all wrong. You made fun of a certain kind of humanist. Why come back to it now?" Actually, the word humanism has two very different meanings. By humanism one can mean a theory which takes man as an end and as a higher value. Humanism in this sense can be found in Cocteau's tale *Around the World in Eighty Hours*[6] when a character, because he is flying over some mountains in an airplane, declares, "Man is simply amazing." That means that I, who did not build the airplanes, shall personally benefit from these particular inventions, and that I, as man, shall personally consider myself responsible for, and honored by, acts of a few particular men. This would imply that we ascribe a value to man on the basis of the highest deeds of certain men. This humanism is absurd, because only the dog or the horse would be able to make such an over-all judgment about man, which they are careful not to do, at least to my knowledge.

But it can not be granted that a man may make a judgment about man.[7] Existentialism spares him from any such judgment. The existentialist will never consider man as an end because he is always in the making. Nor should we believe that there is a mankind to which we might set up a cult in the manner of Auguste Comte.[8] The cult of mankind ends in the self-enclosed humanism of Comte, and, let it be said, of fascism. This kind of humanism we can do without.

But there is another meaning of humanism. Fundamentally it is this: man is constantly outside of himself; in projecting himself, in losing himself outside of himself, he makes for man's existing; and, on the other hand, it is by pursuing transcendent goals that he is able to exist; man, being this state of passing-beyond, and seizing upon things only as they bear upon this passing-beyond, is at the heart, at the center of this passing-beyond. There is no universe other than a human universe, the universe of human subjectivity. This connection between transcendency, as a constituent element of man—not in the sense that God is transcendent, but in the sense of passing beyond—and subjectivity, in the sense that man is not closed in on himself but is always present in a human universe, is what we call existentialist humanism.[9]

4. That is, a community of people who either have chosen the same meanings (and thus share the same values) or have chosen to respect each other as "choosers of meanings" and "inventors of values" (whether similar or different).
5. Sartre's 1938 novel.
6. That is, *Around the World in 80 Days* (1936, *Mon premier voyage*), a compilation of articles by the French writer and film director Jean Cocteau

(1889–1963).
7. That is, about "man" or humanity in general.
8. French positivist philosopher (1798–1857), a founder of sociology.
9. Asked to comment on this conception of "existentialist humanism," Heidegger produced his very critical and disdainful "Letter on Humanism" (1947; see above).

Humanism, because we remind man that there is no law-maker other than himself, and that in his forlornness [*délaissement*] he will decide by himself; because we point out that man will fulfill himself as man, not in turning toward himself, but in seeking outside of himself a goal which is just this liberation, just this particular fulfillment.

From these few reflections it is evident that nothing is more unjust than the objections that have been raised against us. Existentialism is nothing else than an attempt to draw all the consequences of a coherent atheistic position. It isn't trying to plunge man into despair at all. But if one calls every attitude of unbelief despair, like the Christians, then the word is not being used in its original sense. Existentialism isn't so atheistic that it wears itself out showing that God doesn't exist. Rather, it declares that even if God did exist, that would change nothing. There you've got our point of view. Not that we believe that God exists, but we think that the problem of His existence is not the issue. In this sense existentialism is optimistic, a doctrine of action, and it is plain dishonesty for Christians to make no distinction between their own despair and ours and then to call us despairing.

SOURCE: Jean-Paul Sartre, "Existentialism," in *Existentialism*, trans. Bernard Frechtman (New York: Philosophical Library, [1947]), pp. 11–61. Except where otherwise indicated, French words in brackets are the terminology used in the French original, inserted by the editor in addition to their renderings in the translation. Originally published as "L'Existentialisme est un humanisme" (1946); this essay originated as a lecture (delivered in 1945) that was intended to explain "existentialism" to a general audience and to show that it was not as outrageous and offensive to human values as it was widely thought to be. When HEIDEGGER was asked to comment on it, his response was "Letter on Humanism" (1947; see above).

From Being and Nothingness: An Essay in Phenomenological Ontology

From *Part One* The Problem of Nothingness

FROM CHAPTER ONE THE ORIGIN OF NEGATION

FROM 1. THE QUESTION

* * *

* * * The concrete can be only the synthetic totality of which consciousness, like the phenomenon, constitutes only moments. The concrete is man within the world in that specific union of man with the world which Heidegger, for example, calls "being-in-the-world."[1] We deliberately begin with the abstract if we question "experience" as Kant does, inquiring into the conditions of its possibility—or if we effect a phenomenological reduction like Husserl, who would reduce the world to the state of the noema-correlate of consciousness.[2]

---

1. That is, Dasein; see the introduction to and selections from HEIDEGGER, above.

2. By "noema," HUSSERL meant the object of phenomenologically reduced consciousness; see above.

But we will no more succeed in restoring the concrete by the summation or organization of the elements which we have abstracted from it than Spinoza[3] can reach substance by the infinite summation of its modes.

The relation of the regions of being is an original emergence and is a part of the very structure of these beings. But we discovered this in our first observations. It is enough now to open our eyes and question ingenuously this totality which is man-in-the-world.[4] It is by the description of this totality that we shall be able to reply to these two questions: (1) What is the synthetic relation which we call being-in-the-world? (2) What must man and the world be in order for a relation between them to be possible? In truth, the two questions are interdependent, and we can not hope to reply to them separately. But each type of human conduct, being the conduct of man in the world, can release for us simultaneously man, the world, and the relation which unites them, only on condition that we envisage these forms of conduct as realities objectively apprehensible and not as subjective affects which disclose themselves only in the face of reflection.

We shall not limit ourselves to the study of a single pattern of conduct. We shall try on the contrary to describe several and[,] proceeding from one kind of conduct to another, attempt to penetrate into the profound meaning of the relation "man-world." But first of all we should choose a single pattern which can serve us as a guiding thread in our inquiry.

Now this very inquiry furnishes us with the desired conduct; this man that *I am*—if I apprehend him such as he is at this moment in the world, I establish that he stands before being in an attitude of interrogation.[5] At the very moment when I ask, "Is there any conduct which can reveal to me the relation of man with the world?" I pose a question. This question I can consider objectively, for it matters little whether the questioner is myself or the reader who reads my work and who is questioning along with me. But on the other hand, the question is not simply the objective totality of the words printed on this page; it is indifferent to the symbols which express it. In a word, it is a human attitude filled with meaning. What does this attitude reveal to us?

In every question we stand before a being[6] which we are questioning. Every question presupposes a being who questions and a being which is questioned. This is not the original relation of man to being-in-itself, but rather it stands within the limitations of this relation and takes it for granted. On the other hand, this being which we question, we question *about* something. That *about which* I question the being participates in the transcendence of being. I question being about its ways of being or about its being. From this point of view the question is a kind of expectation; I expect a reply from the being questioned. That is, on the basis of a pre-interrogative familiarity with being, I expect from this being a revelation of its being or of its way of being. The reply will be a "yes" or a "no." It is the existence of these two equally objective and contradictory possibilities which on principle distinguishes the question from

---

3. Benedict (Baruch) de Spinoza (1632–1677), Dutch philosopher, who conceived of God (the one substance in the universe) as consisting of an infinity of attributes.
4. Sartre treats "being-in-the-world" and "man-in-the-world" as more or less synonymous expres-
sions; he also prefers to speak directly about "man" rather than relying on a French version of Heidegger's Dasein (his designation of human reality).
5. That is, asking questions.
6. That is, before *something or other* (although not necessarily *an entity* of some sort).

affirmation or negation. There are questions which on the surface do not permit a negative reply—like, for example, the one which we put earlier, "What does this attitude reveal to us?" But actually we see that it is always possible with questions of this type to reply, "Nothing" or "Nobody" or "Never." Thus at the moment when I ask, "Is there any conduct which can reveal to me the relation of man with the world?" I admit *on principle* the possibility of a negative reply such as, "No, such a conduct does not exist." This means that we admit to being faced with the transcendent fact[7] of the non-existence of such conduct.

One will perhaps be tempted not to believe in the objective existence of a non-being; one will say that in this case the fact simply refers me to my subjectivity; I would learn from the transcendent being that the conduct sought is a pure fiction. But in the first place, to call this conduct a pure fiction is to disguise the negation without removing it. "To be pure fiction" is equivalent here to "to be only a fiction." Consequently to destroy the reality of the negation is to cause the reality of the reply to disappear. This reply, in fact, is the very being which gives it to me; that is, reveals the negation to me. There exists then for the questioner the permanent objective possibility of a negative reply. In relation to this possibility the questioner by the very fact that he is questioning, posits himself as in a state of indetermination; he *does not know* whether the reply will be affirmative or negative. Thus the question is a bridge set up between two non-beings: the non-being[8] of knowing in man, the possibility of non-being of being in transcendent being. Finally the question implies the existence of a truth. By the very question the questioner affirms that he expects an objective reply, such that we can say of it, "It is thus and not otherwise." In a word the truth, as differentiated from being, introduces a third non-being as determining the question—the non-being of limitation. This triple non-being conditions every question and in particular the metaphysical question, which is our question.

We set out upon our pursuit of being, and it seemed to us that the series of our questions had led us to the heart of being. But behold, at the moment when we thought we were arriving at the goal, a glance cast on the question itself has revealed to us suddenly that we are encompassed with nothingness. The permanent possibility of non-being, outside us and within, conditions our questions about being. Furthermore it is non-being which is going to limit the reply. What being *will be* must of necessity arise on the basis of what *it is not*. Whatever being is, it will allow this formulation: "Being is *that* and outside of that, *nothing*."[9]

* * *

FROM V. THE ORIGIN OF NOTHINGNESS

It would be well at this point to cast a glance backward and to measure the road already covered. We raised first the question of being. Then examining

7. That is, with the possibility.
8. That is, the actual absence or real nonexistence (of knowledge of the answer to the question being asked).
9. By offering a simpler conception of "being" than Heidegger's *Sein*, Sartre makes room for a different and more concretely meaningful conception than

Heidegger's of "nothing" (and the "nothingness" of his title), relating it to the nature of consciousness as something radically different from its objects, with a kind of reality that Sartre takes to be the very opposite of the "being" of the world of things in which we find ourselves.

this very question conceived as a type of human conduct, we questioned this in turn. We next had to recognize that no question could be asked, in particular not that of being, if negation did not exist. But this negation itself when inspected more closely referred us back to Nothingness as its origin and foundation. In order for negation to exist in the world and in order that we may consequently raise questions concerning Being, it is necessary that in some way Nothingness be given. We perceived then that Nothingness can be conceived neither *outside of* being, nor as a complementary, abstract notion, nor as an infinite milieu where being is suspended. Nothingness must be given at the heart of Being, in order for us to be able to apprehend that particular type of realities which we have called *négatités*.[1] But this intra-mundane Nothingness cannot be produced by Being-in-itself; the notion of Being as full positivity does not contain Nothingness as one of its structures. We can not even say that Being excludes it. Being lacks all relation with it. Hence the question which is put to us now with a particular urgency: if Nothingness can be conceived neither outside of Being, nor in terms of Being, and if on the other hand, since it is non-being, it can not derive from itself the necessary force to "nihilate itself," *where does Nothingness come from?*

If we wish to pursue the problem further, we must first recognize that we can not grant to nothingness the property of "nihilating itself." For although the expression "to nihilate itself" is thought of as removing from nothingness the last semblance of being, we must recognize that only *Being* can nihilate itself; however it comes about, in order to nihilate itself, it must *be*. But Nothingness *is not*. If we can speak of it, it is only because it possesses an appearance of being, a borrowed being, as we have noted above. Nothingness is not, Nothingness "is made-to-be," Nothingness does not nihilate itself; Nothingness "is nihilated." It follows therefore that there must exist a Being (this can not be the In-itself) of which the property is to nihilate Nothingness, to support it in its being, to sustain it perpetually in its very existence, *a being by which nothingness comes to things*. But how can this Being be related to Nothingness so that through it Nothingness comes to things? We must observe first that the being postulated can not be passive in relation to Nothingness, can not receive it; Nothingness could not come to this being except through another Being—which would be an infinite regress. But on the other hand, the Being by which Nothingness comes to the world can not produce Nothingness while remaining indifferent to that production—like the Stoic cause which produces its effect without being itself changed. It would be inconceivable that a Being which is full positivity should maintain and create outside itself a Nothingness or transcendent being, for there would be nothing in Being by which Being could surpass itself toward Non-Being. The Being by which Nothingness arrives in the world must nihilate Nothingness in its Being, and even so it still runs the risk of establishing Nothingness as a transcendent in the very heart of immanence unless it nihilates Nothingness in its being *in connection with its own being*. The Being by which Nothingness arrives in the world is a being such that in its Being, the Nothingness of its Being is in question. *The being by which Nothingness comes to the world must*

---

1. That is, negativities (a term coined by Sartre)— i.e., realities of a sort that are not *things* or positive states of affairs with definite characteristics, but rather the absence of any such substantiality or positive content.

be its own Nothingness.[2] By this we must understand not a nihilating act, which would require in turn a foundation in Being, but an ontological characteristic of the Being required. It remains to learn in what delicate, exquisite region of Being we shall encounter that Being which is its own Nothingness.

We shall be helped in our inquiry by a more complete examination of the conduct which served us as a point of departure. We must return to the question. We have seen, it may be recalled, that every question in essence posits the possibility of a negative reply. In a question we question a being about its being or its way of being. This way of being or this being is veiled; there always remains the possibility that it may unveil itself as a Nothingness. But from the very fact that we presume that an Existent can always be revealed as *nothing*, every question supposes that we realize a nihilating withdrawal in relation to the given, which becomes a simple *presentation*, fluctuating between being and Nothingness.

It is essential therefore that the questioner have the permanent possibility of dissociating himself from the causal series which constitutes being and which can produce only being. If we admitted that the question is determined in the questioner by universal determinism, the question would thereby become unintelligible and even inconceivable. A real cause, in fact, produces a real effect and the caused being is wholly engaged by the cause in positivity; to the extent that its being depends on the cause, it can not have within itself the tiniest germ of nothingness. Thus in so far as the questioner must be able to effect in relation to the questioned a kind of nihilating withdrawal, he is not subject to the causal order of the world;[3] he detaches himself from Being. This means that by a double movement of nihilation, he nihilates the thing questioned in relation to himself, by placing it in a *neutral* state, between being and non-being—and that he nihilates himself in relation to the thing questioned by wrenching himself from being in order to be able to bring out of himself the possibility of a non-being. Thus in posing a question, a certain negative element is introduced into the world. We see nothingness making the world irridescent, casting a shimmer over things. But at the same time the question emanates from a questioner who in order to motivate himself in his being as one who questions, disengages himself from being. This disengagement is then by definition a human process. Man presents himself at least in this instance as a being who causes Nothingness to arise in the world, inasmuch as he himself is affected with non-being to this end.

These remarks may serve as guiding thread as we examine the *négatités* of which we spoke earlier. There is no doubt at all that these are transcendent realities; distance, for example, is imposed on us as something which we have to take into account, which must be cleared with effort. However these realities are of a very peculiar nature; they all indicate immediately an essential relation of human reality to the world. They derive their origin from an act, an expectation, or a project of the human being; they all indicate an aspect of being as it appears to the human being who is engaged in the world. The relations of man in the world, which the *négatités* indicate, have nothing in

---

2. That is, if there are realities that have the character of "nothingness" (no-thing-ness, not-a-thing-ness, the absence of positive being), they must originate in something that is itself of an essentially contentless "negative" or "nothing-like" nature.

3. Sartre's entire position ultimately rests on this radically important inference.

common with the relations *a posteriori* which are brought out by empirical activity. We are no longer dealing with those relations of *instrumentality* by which, according to Heidegger, objects in the world disclose themselves to "human reality." Every *négatité* appears rather as one of the essential conditions of this relation of instrumentality. In order for the totality of being to order itself around us as instruments, in order for it to parcel itself into differentiated complexes which refer one to another and which can *be used*, it is necessary that negation rise up not as a thing among other things but as the rubric of a category which presides over the arrangement and the redistribution of great masses of being in things. Thus the rise of man in the midst of the being which "invests" him causes a world to be discovered. But the essential and primordial moment of this rise is the negation. Thus we have reached the first goal of this study. Man is the being through whom nothingness comes to the world. But this question immediately provokes another: What must man be in his being in order that through him nothingness may come to being?[4]

Being can generate only being and if man is inclosed in this process of generation, only being will come out of him. If we are to assume that man is able to question this process—*i.e.*, to make it the object of interrogation—he must be able to hold it up to view as a totality. He must be able to put himself *outside of* being and by the same stroke weaken the structure of the being of being. Yet it is not given to "human reality" to annihilate even provisionally the mass of being which it posits before itself. Man's *relation* with being is that he can modify it. For man to put a particular existent out of circuit is to put himself out of circuit in relation to that existent. In this case he is not subject to it; he is out of reach; it can not act on him, for he has retired *beyond a nothingness*. Descartes[5] following the Stoics has given a name to this possibility which human reality has to secrete a nothingness which isolates it— it is *freedom*. But freedom here is only a name. If we wish to penetrate further into the question, we must not be content with this reply and we ought to ask now, What is human freedom if through it nothingness comes into the world?

It is not yet possible to deal with the problem of freedom in all its fullness. In fact the steps which we have completed up to now show clearly that freedom is not a faculty of the human soul to be envisaged and described in isolation. What we have been trying to define is the being of man in so far as he conditions the appearance of nothingness, and this being has appeared to us as freedom. Thus freedom as the requisite condition for the nihilation of nothingness is not a *property* which belongs among others to the essence of the human being. We have already noticed furthermore that with man the relation of existence to essence is not comparable to what it is for the things of

---

4. This is the first major instance of Sartre's method of "phenomenological ontology" in this book. That method involves his version of a kind of Kantian "transcendental argument." Having first established the reality of phenomena involving the kind of "nothingness" he is talking about, and having shown that "man is the being through whom nothingness comes into the world," his strategy is then to consider what the underlying *conditions of the possibility of* these phenomena—their ontological presuppositions—must be. In this way, aspects of the basic structure of human reality may

come to light.
5. René Descartes (1596–1650), French philosopher and mathematician. For Sartre, Descartes shows that as thinking subject, human reality distances itself from all that merely exists and so has a kind of freedom in relation to it, even though that distance is nothing substantial. Stoicism, a philosophical school founded in 3rd century B.C.E. Greece, stressed freedom but conceived of it in a fundamentally external way, as freedom from dependence on things beyond one's control.

the world. Human freedom precedes essence in man and makes it possible,[6] the essence of the human being is suspended in his freedom. What we call freedom is impossible to distinguish from the *being* of "human reality." Man does not exist *first* in order to be free *subsequently*; there is no difference between the being of man and his *being-free*. This is not the time to make a frontal attack on a question which can be treated exhaustively only in the light of a rigorous elucidation of the human being. Here we are dealing with freedom in connection with the problem of nothingness and only to the extent that it conditions the appearance of nothingness.

* * *

Thus the condition on which human reality can deny all or part of the world is that human reality carry nothingness within itself as the *nothing* which separates its present from all its past. But this is still not all, for the *nothing* envisaged would not yet have the sense of nothingness; a suspension of being which would remain unnamed, which would not be consciousness of suspending being would come from outside consciousness and by reintroducing opacity into the heart of this absolute lucidity, would have the effect of cutting it in two. Furthermore this nothing would by no means be negative. Nothingness, as we have seen above, is the ground of the negation because it conceals the negation within itself, because it is the negation as being. It is necessary then that conscious being constitute itself in relation to its past as separated from this past by a nothingness. It must necessarily be conscious of this cleavage in being, but not as a phenomenon which it experiences, rather as a structure of consciousness which it is. Freedom is the human being putting his past out of play by secreting his own nothingness.[7] Let us understand indeed that this original necessity of being its own nothingness does not belong to consciousness intermittently and on the occasion of particular negations. This does not happen just at a particular moment in psychic life when negative or interrogative attitudes appear; consciousness continually experiences itself as the nihilation of its past being.

But someone doubtless will believe that he can use against us here an objection which we have frequently raised ourselves: if the nihilating consciousness exists only as consciousness of nihilation, we ought to be able to define and describe a constant mode of consciousness, present *qua* consciousness, which would be consciousness of nihilation. Does this consciousness exist? Behold a new question has been raised here: if freedom is the being of consciousness, consciousness ought to exist [as] a consciousness of freedom. What form does this consciousness of freedom assume? In freedom the human being *is* his own past (as also his own future) in the form of nihilation. If our analysis has not led us astray, there ought to exist for the human being, in so far as he is conscious of being, a certain mode of standing opposite his past and his future, as being both this past and this future and as not being them. We shall

6. Sartre's initial formulation of the slogan that "existence precedes essence." "Essence" here has the sense of "determinate being" rather than abstract and general "human nature": the determination of that nature occurs through a person's prior existence and exercise of human freedom, which thus must be conceived to be presupposed by it and therefore to "precede" it, both conceptually and in reality.

7. This is one of the most famous sentences in *Being and Nothingness*.

be able to furnish an immediate reply to this question; it is in anguish that man gets the consciousness of his freedom, or if you prefer, anguish[8] is the mode of being of freedom as consciousness of being; it is in anguish that freedom is, in its being, in question for itself.

* * *

Now as we have seen, consciousness of being is the being of consciousness.[9] There is no question here of a contemplation which I could make after the event, of an honor already constituted; it is the very being of horror to appear to itself as "not being the cause" of the conduct it calls for. In short, to avoid fear, which reveals to me a transcendent future strictly determined, I take refuge in reflection, but the latter has only an undetermined future to offer. This means that in establishing a certain conduct as a possibility and precisely because it is *my* possibility, I am aware that *nothing* can compel me to adopt that conduct. Yet I am indeed already there in the future; it is for the sake of that being which I will be there at the turning of the path that I now exert all my strength, and in this sense there is already a relation between my future being and my present being. But a nothingness has slipped into the heart of this relation; I *am* not the self which I will be. First I am not that self because time separates me from it. Secondly, I am not that self because what I am is not the foundation of what I will be. Finally I am not that self because no actual existent can determine strictly what I am going to be. Yet as I am already what I will be (otherwise I would not be interested in any one being more than another), *I am the self which I will be, in the mode of not being it.*[1] It is through my horror that I am carried toward the future and the horror nihilates itself in that it constitutes the future as possible.[2] Anguish is precisely my consciousness of being my own future, in the mode of not-being. To be exact, the nihilation of horror as a *motive*, which has the effect of reinforcing horror as a *state*, has as its positive counterpart the appearance of other forms of conduct (in particular that which consists in throwing myself over the precipice) as *my* possible *possibilities.* If *nothing* compels me to save my life, *nothing* prevents me from precipitating myself into the abyss. The decisive conduct will emanate from a self which I am not yet. Thus the self which I am depends on the self which I am not yet to the exact extent that the self which I am not yet does not depend on the self which I am. Vertigo appears as the apprehension of this dependence. I approach the precipice, and my scrutiny is searching for myself in my very depths. In terms of this moment, I play with my possibilities. My eyes, running over the abyss from top to bottom, imitate the possible fall and realize it symbolically; at the same time suicide, from the fact that it becomes a *possibility* possible for *me*, now causes to appear possible motives for adopting it (suicide would cause anguish to cease). Fortunately these motives in their turn, from the sole fact that they are motives of a possibility, present themselves as ineffective, as non-determinant; they can no

---

8. *L'angoisse,* Sartre's counterpart to Heidegger's *Angst* (anxiety).
9. Sartre's version of Husserl's principle of the "intentionality of consciousness" (i.e., consciousness is always consciousness *of something*).
1. That is, "of not (*yet*) being it."

2. That is, this nihilation is productive, bringing something important about the self I am into reality "in the mode of not-being" (i.e., as something other than a positive state of affairs of any sort). Sartrean nihilation is not *an*nihilation.

more *produce* the suicide than my horror of the fall can *determine* me to avoid it. It is this counter-anguish which generally puts an end to anguish by transmuting it into indecision. Indecision in its turn, calls for decision. I abruptly put myself at a distance from the edge of the precipice and resume my way.

The example which we have just analyzed has shown us what we could call "anguish in the face of the future." There exists another: anguish in the face of the past. It is that of the gambler who has freely and sincerely decided not to gamble any more and who when he approaches the gaming table, suddenly sees all his resolutions melt away. This phenomenon has often been described as if the sight of the gaming table reawakened in us a tendency which entered into conflict with our former resolution and ended by drawing us in spite of this. Aside from the fact that such a description is done in materialistic terms and peoples the mind with opposing forces (there is, for example, the moralists' famous "struggle of reason with the passions"), it does not account for the facts. In reality—the letters of Dostoevsky[3] bear witness to this—there is nothing in us which resembles an inner *debate* as if we had to weigh motives and incentives before deciding. The earlier resolution of "not playing anymore" is always *there*, and in the majority of cases the gambler when in the presence of the gaming table, turns toward it as if to ask it for help; for he does not wish to play, or rather having taken his resolution the day before, he thinks of himself still as not wishing to play anymore; he believes in the effectiveness of this resolution. But what he apprehends then in anguish is precisely the total inefficacy of the past resolution. It is there doubtless but fixed, ineffectual, surpassed by the very fact that I am conscious *of* it. The resolution is still *me* to the extent that I realize constantly my identity with myself across the temporal flux, but it is no longer *me*—due to the fact that it has become an object *for* my consciousness. I am not subject to it, it fails in the mission which I have given it. The resolution is there still, I *am* it in the mode of not-being. What the gambler apprehends at this instant is again the permanent rupture in determinism; it is nothingness which separates him from himself; I should have liked so much not to gamble anymore; yesterday I even had a synthetic apprehension of the situation (threatening ruin, disappointment of my relatives) as *forbidding* me to play. It seemed to me that I had established a *real barrier* between gambling and myself, and now I suddenly perceive that my former understanding of the situation is no more than a memory of an idea, a memory of a feeling. In order for it to come to my aid once more, I must remake it *ex nihilo*[4] and freely. The not-gambling is only one of my possibilities, as the fact of gambling is another of them, neither more nor less. *I must rediscover* the fear of financial ruin or of disappointing my family, *etc.*, I must re-create it as experienced fear. It stands behind me like a boneless phantom. It depends on me alone to lend it flesh. I am alone and naked before temptation as I was the day before. After having patiently built up barriers and walls, after enclosing myself in the magic circle of a resolution, I perceive with anguish that *nothing* prevents me from gambling. The anguish *is me* since by the very fact of taking my position in existence as consciousness of being, I make myself *not to be* the past of good resolutions *which I am*.

---

3. Fyodor Dostoevsky (1821–1881), Russian writer of fiction and essays; many of his letters touch on his compulsive gambling.
4. From (or out of) nothing (Latin).

It would be in vain to object that the sole condition of this anguish is igno-rance of the underlying psychological determinism. According to such a view my anxiety would come from lack of knowing the real and effective incen-tives which in the darkness of the unconscious determine my action. In reply we shall point out first that anguish has not appeared to us as a *proof* of human freedom; the latter was given to us as the necessary condition for the ques-tion. We wished only to show that there exists a specific consciousness of free-dom, and we wished to show that this consciousness is anguish. This means that we wished to established anguish in its essential structure as conscious-ness of freedom. Now from this point of view the existence of a psychologi-cal determinism could not invalidate the results of our description. Either indeed anguish is actually an unrealized ignorance of this determinism—and then anguish apprehends itself in fact as freedom—or else one may claim that anguish is consciousness of being ignorant of the real causes of our acts. In the latter case anguish would come from that of which we have a presenti-ment, a screen deep within ourselves for monstrous motives which would suddenly release guilty acts. But in this case we should suddenly appear to ourselves as *things in the world*; we should be to ourselves our own transcen-dent situation. Then anguish would disappear to give away to *fear*, for fear is a synthetic apprehension of the transcendent as dreadful.

This freedom which reveals itself to us in anguish can be characterized by the existence of that *nothing* which insinuates itself between motives and act. It is not *because* I am free that my act is not subject to the determination of motives; on the contrary, the structure of motives as ineffective is the condi-tion of my freedom.[5] If someone asks what this *nothing* is which provides a foundation for freedom, we shall reply that we can not describe it since it *is not*, but we can at least hint at its meaning by saying that this nothing is made-to-be by the human being in his relation with himself. The nothing here cor-responds to the necessity for the motive to appear as motive only as a correlate of a consciousness *of* motive. In short, as soon as we abandon the hypothesis of the contents of consciousness, we must recognize that there is never a motive *in* consciousness; motives are only *for* consciousness. And due to the very fact that the motive can arise only as appearance, it constitutes itself as ineffective. Of course it does not have the externality of a temporal-spatial thing; it always belongs to subjectivity and it is apprehended as *mine*. But it is by nature transcendence in immanence, and consciousness is not subject to it because of the very fact that consciousness posits it; for consciousness has now the task of conferring on the motive its meaning and its importance. Thus the *nothing* which separates the motive from consciousness character-izes itself as transcendence in immanence. It is by arising as immanence that consciousness nihilates the nothing which makes consciousness exist for itself as transcendence. But we see that the nothingness which is the condition of all transcendent negation can be elucidated only in terms of two other origi-nal nihilations: (1) Consciousness *is not* its own motive inasmuch as it is *empty* of all content. This refers us to a nihilating structure of the pre-reflective *cogito*.[6] (2) Consciousness confronts its past and its future as facing a self

---

5. Sartre here offers a very distinctive line of argu-ment against determinism and in favor of the idea of human freedom in what we do with ourselves.

6. I think (Latin), Descartes' starting point.

which it is in the mode of not-being. This refers us to a nihilating structure of temporality.

There can be for us as yet no question of elucidating these two types of nihilation; we do not at the moment have the necessary techniques at our disposal. It is sufficient to observe here that the definitive explanation of negation can not be given without a description of self-consciousness and of temporality.

What we should note at present is that freedom, which manifests itself through anguish, is characterized by a constantly renewed obligation to remake the *Self* which designates the free being. As a matter of fact when we showed earlier that my possibilities were filled with anguish because it depended on *me* alone to sustain them in their existence, that did not mean that they derived from a *Me* which to itself at least, would first be given and would then pass in the temporal flux from one consciousness to another consciousness. The gambler who must realize anew the synthetic apperception of a *situation* which would forbid him to play, must rediscover at the same time the *self* which can appreciate that situation, which "is in situation." This *self* with its *a priori* and historical content is the *essence* of man. Anguish as the manifestation of freedom in the face of self means that man is always separated by a nothingness from his essence. We should refer here to Hegel's statement: "*Wesen ist was gewesen ist.*" Essence is what has been.[7] Essence is everything in the human being which we can indicate by the words—that *is*. Due to this fact it is the totality of characteristics which *explain* the act. But the act is always beyond that essence; it is a human act only in so far as it surpasses every explanation which we can give of it, precisely because the very application of the formula "that is" to man causes all that is designated, *to have-been*. Man continually carries with him a pre-judicative comprehension of his essence, but due to this very fact he is separated from it by a nothingness. Essence is all that human reality apprehends in itself as *having been*.[8] It is here that anguish appears as an apprehension of self inasmuch as its exists in the perpetual mode of detachment from what is; better yet, in so far as it makes itself exist as such. For we can never apprehend an *Erlebnis*[9] as a living consequence of that nature which is ours. The overflow of our consciousness progressively constitutes that nature, but it remains always behind us and it dwells in us as the permanent object of our retrospective comprehension. It is in so far as this nature is a demand without being a recourse that it is apprehended in anguish.

* * *

Now at each instant we are thrust into the world and engaged there. This means that we act before positing our possibilities and that these possibilities which are disclosed as realized or in process of being realized refer to meanings which necessitate special acts in order to be put into question. The alarm which rings in the morning refers to the possibility of my going to work, which

7. An adaptation of HEGEL's famous quip, perhaps most aptly rendered as "What is is what was": that is, to be (in some specific way) is to have been (in some specific way). *Wesen* can mean "essence"; but that English word is suggestive of something abstractly general, which is not at all what either Hegel or Sartre had in mind.
8. A further elaboration of the concept of "essence," as it is to be understood here, that helps clarify what Sartre means by claiming that for a human being, "existence precedes essence."
9. Experience (German).

is *my* possibility. But to apprehend the summons of the alarm as a summons is to get up. Therefore the very act of getting up is reassuring, for it eludes the question, "Is work *my* possibility?" Consequently it does not put me in a position to apprehend the possibility of quietism, of refusing to work, and finally the possibility of refusing the world and the possibility of death. In short, to the extent that I apprehend the meaning of the ringing, I am already up at its summons; this apprehension guarantees me against the anguished intuition that it is I who confer on the alarm clock its exigency—I and I alone.

In the same way, what we might call everyday morality is exclusive of ethical anguish. There is ethical anguish when I consider myself in my original relation to values.[1] Values in actuality are demands which lay claim to a foundation. But this foundation can in no way be *being*, for every value which would base its ideal nature on its being would thereby cease even to be a value and would realize the heteronomy of my will. Value derives its being from its exigency and not its exigency from its being. It does not deliver itself to a contemplative intuition which would apprehend it as *being* value and thereby would remove from it its right over my freedom. On the contrary, it can be revealed only to an active freedom which makes it exist as value by the sole fact of recognizing it as such. It follows that my freedom is the unique foundation of values and that *nothing*, absolutely nothing, justifies me in adopting this or that particular value, this or that particular scale of values. As a being by whom values exist, I am unjustifiable. My freedom is anguished at being the foundation of values while itself without foundation. It is anguished in addition because values, due to the fact that they are essentially revealed to a freedom, can not disclose themselves without being at the same time "put into question," for the possibility of overturning the scale of values appears complementarily as *my* possibility. It is anguish before values which is the recognition of the ideality of values.

Ordinarily, however, my attitude with respect to values is eminently reassuring. In fact I am engaged in a world of values. The anguished apperception of values as sustained in being by my freedom is a secondary and mediated phenomenon. The immediate is the world with its urgency; and in this world where I engage myself, my acts cause values to spring up like partridges.[2] My indignation has given to me the negative value "baseness," my admiration has given the positive value "grandeur." Above all my obedience to a multitude of tabus,[3] which is real, reveals these tabus to me as existing in fact. The bourgeois who call themselves "respectable citizens" do not become respectable as the result of contemplating moral values. Rather from the moment of their arising in the world they are thrown into a pattern of behavior the meaning of which is respectability. Thus respectability acquires a being; it is not put into question. Values are sown on my path as thousands of little real demands, like the signs which order us to keep off the grass.

Thus in what we shall call the world of the immediate, which delivers itself to our unreflective consciousness, we do not first appear to ourselves, to be

---

1. That is, anguished recognition and acceptance of my freedom and responsibility for my choices in ethical matters pertain to my fundamental relation to values rather than to "everyday morality"—an important distinction.
2. One of the book's most memorable images.
3. That is, taboos.

thrown subsequently into enterprises. Our being is immediately "in situation"; that is, it arises in enterprises and knows itself first in so far as it is reflected in those enterprises. We discover ourselves then in a world peopled with demands, in the heart of projects "in the course of realization." I write. I am going to smoke. I have an appointment this evening with Pierre. I must not forget to reply to Simon. I do not have the right to conceal the truth any longer from Claude. All these trivial passive expectations of the real, all these commonplace, everyday values, derive their meaning from an original projection of myself which stands as my choice of myself in the world. But to be exact, this projection of myself toward an original possibility, which causes the existence of values, appeals, expectations, and in general a world, appears to me only beyond the world as the meaning and the abstract, logical significa-tion of my enterprises. For the rest, there exist concretely alarm clocks, sign-boards, tax forms, policemen, so many guard rails against anguish. But as soon as the enterprise is held at a distance from me, as soon as I am referred to myself because I must await myself in the future, then I discover myself suddenly as the one who gives its meaning to the alarm clock, the one who by a signboard forbids himself to walk on a flower bed or on the lawn, the one from whom the boss's order borrows its urgency, the one who decides the inter-est of the book which he is writing, the one finally who makes the values exist in order to determine his action by their demands. I emerge alone and in anguish confronting the unique and original project which constitutes my being; all the barriers, all the guard rails collapse, nihilated by the conscious-ness of my freedom. I do not have nor can I have recourse to any value against the fact that it is I who sustain values in being. Nothing can ensure me against myself, cut off from the world and from my essence by this nothingness which I am. I have to realize the meaning of the world and of my essence;[4] I make my decision concerning them—without justification and without excuse.

* * *

FROM CHAPTER TWO
BAD FAITH

FROM 1. BAD FAITH AND FALSEHOOD

The human being is not only the being by whom *négatités* are disclosed in the world; he is also the one who can take negative attitudes with respect to him-self. In our Introduction we defined consciousness as "a being[5] such that in its being, its being is in question in so far as this being implies a being other than itself." But now that we have examined the meaning of "the question," we can at present also write the formula thus: "Consciousness is a being, the nature of which is to be conscious of the nothingness of its being." In a pro-hibition or a veto, for example, the human being denies a future transcen-dence. But this negation is not explicative. My consciousness is not restricted to *envisioning* a *négatité*. It constitutes itself in its own flesh as the nihilation

---

4. That is, my essence as my specific determinate nature, described earlier in the paragraph as "an *original projection of myself* which stands *as my*   *choice of myself* in the world" (emphasis added).
5. That is, a reality (but not a thing or substantial entity of any sort).

of a possibility which another human reality projects as *its* possibility. For that reason it must arise in the world as a *Not*; it is as a Not that the slave first apprehends the master, or that the prisoner who is trying to escape sees the guard who is watching him. There are even men (*e.g.*, caretakers, overseers, gaolers[6]), whose social reality is uniquely that of the Not, who will live and die, having forever been only a Not upon the earth. Others so as to make the Not a part of their very subjectivity, establish their human personality as a perpetual negation. This is the meaning and function of what Scheler calls "the man of resentment"[7]—in reality, the Not. But there exist more subtle behaviors, the description of which will lead us further into the inwardness of consciousness. Irony is one of these. In irony a man annihilates what he posits within one and the same act; he leads us to believe in order not to be believed; he affirms to deny and denies to affirm; he creates a positive object but it has no being other than its nothingness. Thus attitudes of negation toward the self permit us to raise a new question: What are we to say is the being of man who has the possibility of denying himself? But it is out of the question to discuss the attitude of "self-negation" in its universality. The kinds of behavior which can be ranked under this heading are too diverse; we risk retaining only the abstract form of them. It is best to choose and to examine one determined attitude which is essential to human reality[8] and which is such that consciousness instead of directing its negation outward turns it toward itself. This attitude, it seems to me, is *bad faith* [*mauvaise foi*].[9]

Frequently this is identified with falsehood. We say indifferently of a person that he shows signs of bad faith or that he lies to himself. We shall willingly grant that bad faith is a lie to oneself, on condition that we distinguish the lie to oneself from lying in general. Lying is a negative attitude, we will agree to that. But this negation does not bear on consciousness itself; it aims only at the transcendent. The essence of the lie implies in fact that the liar actually is in complete possession of the truth which he is hiding. A man does not lie about what he is ignorant of; he does not lie when he spreads an error of which he himself is the dupe; he does not lie when he is mistaken. The ideal description of the liar would be a cynical consciousness, affirming truth within himself, denying it in his words, and denying that negation as such. Now this doubly negative attitude rests on the transcendent; the fact expressed is transcendent since it does not exist, and the original negation rests on a *truth*; that is, on a particular type of transcendence. As for the inner negation which I effect correlatively with the affirmation for myself of the truth, this rests on *words*; that is, on an event in the world. Furthermore the inner disposition of the liar is positive; it could be the object of an affirmative judgment. The liar intends to deceive and he does not seek to hide this intention

---

6. That is, jailers.
7. The French title of MAX SCHELER's *Das Ressentiment im Aufbau der Moralen* (1915, *The Role of Ressentiment in the Makeup of Morals*).
8. A statement that shows Sartre ready to ascribe something like Heidegger's "structures" of Dasein's being to what he is calling "human reality," thereby suggesting that it has a kind of general structural "essence" or *Wesen* after all (as Heidegger had proclaimed)—in the manner of its "existence," even if

not in the way in which that existence is or ought to be lived.
9. An accurate literal translation of the French expression *mauvaise foi*; but its ordinary use, in French as in English, is in connection with someone's deception of *others*. Sartre retains its basic meaning but shifts its focus to one's relation to *oneself*, adopting it as his name for the kind of *self-deception* that is the topic of this chapter.

from himself nor to disguise the translucency of consciousness; on the contrary, he has recourse to it when there is a question of deciding secondary behavior. It explicitly exercises a regulatory control over all attitudes. As for his flaunted intention of telling the truth ("I'd never want to deceive you! This is true! I swear it!")—all this, of course, is the object of an inner negation, but also it is not recognized by the liar as *his* intention. It is played, imitated, it is the intention of the character which he plays in the eyes of his questioner, but this character, precisely because he *does not exist*, is a transcendent. Thus the lie does not put into the play the inner structure of present consciousness; all the negations which constitute it bear on objects which by this fact are removed from consciousness. The lie then does not require special ontological foundation,[1] and the explanations which the existence of negation in general requires are valid without change in the case of deceit. Of course we have described the ideal lie; doubtless it happens often enough that the liar is more or less the victim of his lie, that he half persuades himself of it. But these common, popular forms of the lie are also degenerate aspects of it; they represent intermediaries between falsehood and bad faith. The lie is a behavior of transcendence.

The lie is also a normal phenomenon of what Heidegger calls the *"Mit-sein."*[2] It presupposes my existence, the existence of the *Other*, my existence *for* the Other, and the existence of the Other *for* me. Thus there is no difficulty in holding that the liar must make the project of the lie in entire clarity and that he must possess a complete comprehension of the lie and of the truth which he is altering. It is sufficient that an over-all opacity hide his intentions from the *Other*; it is sufficient that the Other can take the lie for truth. By the lie consciousness affirms that it exists by nature as *hidden from the Other*; it utilizes for its own profit the ontological duality of myself and myself in the eyes of the Other.

The situation can not be the same for bad faith if this, as we have said, is indeed a lie to oneself. To be sure, the one who practices bad faith is hiding a displeasing truth or presenting as truth a pleasing untruth. Bad faith then has in appearance the structure of falsehood. Only what changes everything is the fact that in bad faith it is from myself that I am hiding the truth. Thus the duality of the deceiver and the deceived does not exist here. Bad faith on the contrary implies in essence the unity of a *single* consciousness. This does not mean that it can not be conditioned by the *Mit-sein* like all other phenomena of human reality, but the *Mit-sein* can call forth bad faith only by presenting itself as *a situation* which bad faith permits surpassing; bad faith does not come from outside to human reality. One does not undergo his bad faith; one is not infected with it; it is not a *state*. But consciousness affects itself with bad faith. There must be an original intention and a project of bad faith; this project implies a comprehension of bad faith as such and a pre-reflective apprehension (of) consciousness as affecting itself with bad faith.

---

1. A phrase indicating that Sartre intends to employ a version of KANT's kind of "transcendental argument," examining certain indisputable phenomena of human experience and asking what they presuppose about the nature and structure of human reality. In this regard, the ontological pre-suppositions of self-deception are much more interesting and philosophically significant than those of mere lying.

2. That is, "being-with (others in the world)," as explored in *Being and Time* (1927; see above).

It follows first that the one to whom the lie is told and the one who lies are one and the same person, which means that I must know in my capacity as deceiver the truth which is hidden from me in my capacity as the one deceived. Better yet I must know the truth very exactly *in order* to conceal it more carefully—and this not at two different moments, which at a pinch would allow us to reestablish a semblance of duality—but in the unitary structure of a single project. How then can the lie subsist if the duality which conditions it is suppressed?

* * *

FROM II. PATTERNS OF BAD FAITH

If we wish to get out of this difficulty, we should examine more closely the patterns of bad faith and attempt a description of them. This description will permit us perhaps to fix more exactly the conditions for the possibility of bad faith; that is, to reply to the question we raised at the outset: "What must be the being of man if he is to be capable of bad faith?"

Take the example of a woman who has consented to go out with a particular man for the first time. She knows very well the intentions which the man who is speaking to her cherishes regarding her. She knows also that it will be necessary sooner or later for her to make a decision. But she does not want to realize the urgency; she concerns herself only with what is respectful and discreet in the attitude of her companion. She does not apprehend this conduct as an attempt to achieve what we call "the first approach"; that is, she does not want to see possibilities of temporal development which his conduct presents. She restricts this behavior to what is in the present; she does not wish to read in the phrases which he addresses to her anything other than their explicit meaning. If he says to her, "I find you so attractive!" she disarms this phrase of its sexual background; she attaches to the conversation and to the behavior of the speaker, the immediate meanings, which she imagines as objective qualities. The man who is speaking to her appears to her sincere and respectful as the table is round or square, as the wall coloring is blue or gray. The qualities thus attached to the person she is listening to are in this way fixed in a permanence like that of things, which is no other than the projection of the strict present of the qualities into the temporal flux. This is because she does not quite know what she wants. She is profoundly aware of the desire which she inspires, but the desire cruel and naked would humiliate and horrify her. Yet she would find no charm in a respect which would be only respect. In order to satisfy her, there must be a feeling which is addressed wholly to her *personality*—i.e., to her full freedom—and which would be a recognition of her freedom. But at the same time this feeling must be wholly desire; that is, it must address itself to her body as object. This time then she refuses to apprehend the desire for what it is; she does not even give it a name; she recognizes it only to the extent that it transcends itself toward admiration, esteem, respect and that it is wholly absorbed in the more refined forms which it produces, to the extent of no longer figuring anymore as a sort of warmth and density. But then suppose he takes her hand. This act of her companion risks changing the situation by calling for an immediate decision. To leave the hand there is to consent in herself to flirt, to engage herself. To withdraw it is to break the troubled and unstable harmony which gives the hour its charm. The aim is to postpone the moment of decision as long as possible. We know what happens next; the young woman leaves her hand there, but she *does not notice* that she is leaving it. She does not notice because it happens by chance that she is at this moment all intellect. She draws her companion up to the most lofty regions of sentimental speculation; she speaks of Life, of her life, she shows herself in her essential aspect—a personality, a consciousness. And during this time the divorce of the body from the soul is accomplished; the hand rests inert between the warm hands of her companion—neither consenting nor resisting—a thing.

We shall say that this woman is in bad faith. But we see immediately that she uses various procedures in order to maintain herself in this bad faith. She has disarmed the actions of her companion by reducing them to being only what they are; that is, to existing in the mode of the in-itself. But she permits herself to enjoy his desire, to the extent that she will apprehend it as not being what it is, will recognize its transcendence. Finally while sensing profoundly the presence of her own body—to the degree of being disturbed perhaps— she realizes herself as *not being* her own body, and she contemplates it as though from above as a passive object to which events can *happen* but which can neither provoke them nor avoid them because all its possibilities are out- side of it. What unity do we find in these various aspects of bad faith? It is a certain art of forming contradictory concepts which unite in themselves both an idea and the negation of that idea. The basic concept which is thus engen- dered, utilizes the double property of the human being, who is at once a *fac- ticity* and a *transcendence*.[3] These two aspects of human reality are and ought to be capable of a valid coordination. But bad faith does not wish either to coordinate them nor to surmount them in a synthesis. Bad faith seeks to affirm their identity while preserving their differences. It must affirm facticity as *being* transcendence and transcendence as *being* facticity, in such a way that at the instant when a person apprehends the one, he can find himself abruptly faced with the other.

* * *

We can see the use which bad faith can make of these judgments which all aim at establishing that I am not what I am. If I were only what I *am*, I could, for example, seriously consider an adverse criticism which someone makes of me, question myself scrupulously, and perhaps be compelled to recognize the truth in it. But thanks to transcendence, I am not subject to all that I am. I do not even have to discuss the justice of the reproach. As Suzanne says to Figaro, "To prove that I am right would be to recognize that I can be wrong."[4] I am on a plane where no reproach can touch me since what I really am is my transcendence. I flee from myself, I escape myself, I leave my tattered gar- ment in the hands of the fault-finder. But the ambiguity necessary for bad faith comes from the fact that I affirm here that I *am* my transcendence in the mode of being of a thing. It is only thus, in fact, that I can feel that I escape all

3. This is the complex ontological structure that Sartre contends is presupposed by the phenome- non of bad faith (self-deception).

4. Quoted from the play *The Marriage of Figaro* (1778), by Pierre-Augustin Caron de Beaumarchais.

reproaches. It is in the sense that our young woman purifies the desire of anything humiliating by being willing to consider it only as pure transcendence, which she avoids even naming. But inversely "I Am Too Great for Myself,"[5] while showing our transcendence changed into facticity, is the source of an infinity of excuses for our failures or our weaknesses. Similarly the young coquette maintains transcendence to the extent that the respect, the esteem manifested by the actions of her admirer are already on the plane of the transcendent. But she arrests this transcendence, she glues it down with all the facticity of the present; respect is nothing other than respect, it is an arrested surpassing which no longer surpasses itself toward anything.

But although this *metastable* concept of "transcendence-facticity" is one of the most basic instruments of bad faith, it is not the only one of its kind. We can equally well use another kind of duplicity derived from human reality which we will express roughly by saying that its being-for-itself implies complementarily a being-for-others. Upon any one of my conducts it is always possible to converge two looks, mine and that of the Other. The conduct will not present exactly the same structure in each case. But as we shall see later, as each look perceives it, there is between these two aspects of my being, no difference between appearance and being—as if I were to my self the truth of myself and as if the Other possessed only a deformed image of me. The equal dignity of being, possessed by my being-for-others and by my being-for-myself, permits a perpetually disintegrating synthesis and a perpetual game of escape from the for-itself to the for-others and from the for-others to the for-itself. We have seen also the use which our young lady made of our being-in-the-midst-of-the-world—i.e., of our inert presence as a passive object among other objects—in order to relieve herself suddenly from the functions of her being-in-the-world—that is, from the being which causes there to be a world by projecting itself beyond the world toward its own possibilities. Let us note finally the confusing syntheses which play on the nihilating ambiguity of these temporal ekstases,[6] affirming at once that I am what I have been (the man who deliberately *arrests himself*[7] at one period in his life and refuses to take into consideration the later changes) and that I am not what I have been (the man who in the face of reproaches or rancor dissociates himself from his past by insisting on his freedom and on his perpetual re-creation). In all these concepts, which have only a transitive role in the reasoning and which are eliminated from the conclusion (like hypochondriacs in the calculations of physicians), we find again the same structure. We have to deal with human reality as a being which is what it is not and which is not what it is.[8]

But what exactly is necessary in order for these concepts of disintegration to be able to receive even a pretence of existence, in order for them to be able to appear for an instant to consciousness, even in a process of evanescence? A quick examination of the idea of sincerity, the antithesis of bad faith, will

---

5. The title of a popular 1924 comedy by the French playwright Jean Sarment.
6. That is, dimensions of the temporality of human reality in which we may be said to stand outside of ourselves (a phrase that echoes Heidegger).
7. That is, curtails his own development.
8. A famous formula that sums up Sartre's discus-

sion. Human reality *is* what-it-is-not (freedom, which has no determinate content) and *is not* (merely) what-it-is (its facticity). Because both statements are true, human reality is neither pure transcendence (what-it-is-not) nor merely its facticity, but rather is both at once.

be very instructive in this connection. Actually sincerity presents itself as a demand and consequently is not a *state*. Now what is the ideal to be attained in this case? It is necessary that a man be *for himself* only what he *is*. But is this not precisely the definition of the in-itself—or if you prefer—the principle of identity? To posit as an ideal the being of things, is this not to assert by the same stroke that this being does not belong to human reality and that the principle of identity, far from being a universal axiom universally applied, is only a synthetic principle enjoying a merely regional universality? Thus in order that the concepts of bad faith can put us under illusion at least for an instant, in order that the candor of "pure hearts" (*cf.* Gide, Kessel[9]) can have validity for human reality as an ideal, the principle of identity must not represent a constitutive principle of human reality and human reality must not be necessarily what it is but must be able to be what it is not. What does this mean?

If man is what he is, bad faith is for ever impossible and candor ceases to be his ideal and becomes instead his being. But is man what he is? And more generally, how can he *be* what he is when he exists as consciousness of being? If candor or sincerity is a universal value, it is evident that the maxim "one must be what one is" does not serve solely as a regulating principle for judgments and concepts by which I express what I am. It posits not merely an ideal of knowing but an ideal of *being*; it proposes for us an absolute equivalence of being with itself as a prototype of being. In this sense it is necessary that we *make ourselves* what we are. But what *are we* then if we have the constant obligation to make ourselves what we are, if our mode of being is having the obligation to be what we are?

Let us consider this waiter in the café. His movement is quick and forward, a little too precise, a little too rapid. He comes toward the patrons with a step a little too quick. He bends forward a little too eagerly; his voice, his eyes express an interest a little too solicitous for the order of the customer. Finally there he returns, trying to imitate in his walk the inflexible stiffness of some kind of automaton while carrying his tray with the recklessness of a tight-rope-walker by putting it in a perpetually unstable, perpetually broken equilibrium which he perpetually reestablishes by a light movement of the arm and hand. All his behavior seems to us a game. He applies himself to chaining his movements as if they were mechanisms, the one regulating the other; his gestures and even his voice seem to be mechanisms; he gives himself the quickness and pitiless rapidity of things. He is playing, he is amusing himself. But what is he playing? We need not watch long before we can explain it: he is playing at *being* a waiter in a café. There is nothing there to surprise us. The game is a kind of marking out and investigation. The child plays with his body in order to explore it, to take inventory of it; the waiter in the café plays with his condition in order to *realize* it. This obligation is not different from that which is imposed on all tradesmen. Their condition is wholly one of ceremony. The public demands of them that they realize it as a ceremony; there is the dance of the grocer, of the tailor, of the auctioneer, by which they

9. Two French writers, André Gide (1869–1951) and Joseph Kessel (1898–1979).

endeavour to persuade their clientele that they are nothing but a grocer, an auctioneer, a tailor. A grocer who dreams is offensive to the buyer, because such a grocer is not wholly a grocer. Society demands that he limit himself to his function as a grocer, just as the soldier at attention makes himself into a soldier-thing with a direct regard which does not see at all, which is no longer meant to see, since it is the rule and not the interest of the moment which determines the point he must fix his eyes on (the sight "fixed at ten paces"). There are indeed many precautions to imprison a man in what he is, as if we lived in perpetual fear that he might escape from it, that he might break away and suddenly elude his condition.

In a parallel situation, from within, the waiter in the café can not be immediately a café waiter in the sense that this inkwell *is* an inkwell, or the glass is a glass. It is by no means that he can not form reflective judgments or concepts concerning his condition. He knows well what it "means:" the obligation of getting up at five o'clock, of sweeping the floor of the shop before the restaurant opens, of starting the coffee pot going, *etc.* He knows the rights which it allows: the right to the tips, the right to belong to a union, *etc.* But all these concepts, all these judgments refer to the transcendent. It is a matter of abstract possibilities, of rights and duties conferred on a "person possessing rights." And it is precisely this person *who I have to be* (if I am the waiter in question) and who I am not. It is not that I do not wish to be this person or that I want this person to be different. But rather there is no common measure between his being and mine. It is a "representation" for others and for myself, which means that I can be he only in *representation*. But if I represent myself as him, I am not he; I am separated from him as the object from the subject, separated *by nothing*, but this nothing isolates me from him. I can not be he, I can only play *at being* him; that is, imagine to myself that I am he. And thereby I affect him with nothingness. In vain do I fulfill the functions of a café waiter. I can be he only in the neutralized mode, as the actor is Hamlet, by mechanically making the *typical gestures* of my state and by aiming at myself as an imaginary café waiter through those gestures taken as an "analogue."[1] What I attempt to realize is a being-in-itself of the café waiter, as if it were not just in my power to confer their value and their urgency upon my duties and the rights of my position, as if it were not my free choice to get up each morning at five o'clock or to remain in bed, even though it meant getting fired. As if from the very fact that I sustain this role in existence I did not transcend it on every side, as if I did not constitute myself as one *beyond* my condition. Yet there is no doubt that I *am* in a sense a café waiter—otherwise could I not just as well call myself a diplomat or a reporter? But if I am one, this can not be in the mode of being in-itself. I am a waiter in the mode of *being what I am not.*

* * *

Furthermore the being of my own consciousness does not appear to me as the consciousness of the Other. It *is* because it makes itself, since its being is

---

1. Cf. [Sartre,] *L'Imaginaire* [1936, *The Imagination*]. Conclusion [Sartre's note].

consciousness of being. But this means that making sustains being; consciousness has to be its own being, it is never sustained by being; it sustains being in the heart of subjectivity, which means once again that it is inhabited by being but that it is not being: *consciousness is not what it is.*

Under these conditions what can be the significance of the ideal of sincerity except as a task impossible to achieve, of which the very meaning is in contradiction with the structure of my consciousness. To be sincere, we said, is to be what one is. That supposes that I am not originally what I am. But here naturally Kant's "You ought, therefore you can"[2] is implicitly understood. I can *become* sincere; this is what my duty and my effort to achieve sincerity imply. But we definitely establish that the original structure of "not being what one is" renders impossible in advance all movement toward being in itself or "being what one is." And this impossibility is not hidden from consciousness; on the contrary, it is the very stuff of consciousness; it is the embarrassing constraint which we constantly experience; it is our very incapacity to recognize ourselves, to constitute ourselves as being what we are. It is this necessity which means that, as soon as we posit ourselves as a certain being, by a legitimate judgment, based on inner experience or correctly deduced from *a priori* or empirical premises, then by that very positing we surpass this being—and that not toward another being but toward emptiness, toward *nothing.*

How then can we blame another for not being sincere or rejoice in our own sincerity since this sincerity appears to us at the same time to be impossible? How can we in conversation, in confession, in introspection, even attempt sincerity since the effort will by its very nature be doomed to failure and since at the very time when we announce it we have a pre-judicative comprehension of its futility? In introspection I try to determine exactly what I am, to make up my mind to be my true self without delay—even though it means consequently to set about searching for ways to change myself. But what does this mean if not that I am constituting myself as a thing? Shall I determine the ensemble of purposes and motivations which have pushed me to do this or that action? But this is already to postulate a causal determinism which constitutes the flow of my states of consciousness as a succession of physical states. Shall I uncover in myself "drives," even though it be to affirm them in shame? But is this not deliberately to forget that these drives are realized with my consent, that they are not forces of nature but that I lend them their efficacy by a perpetually renewed decision concerning their value. Shall I pass judgment on my character, on my nature? Is this not to veil from myself at that moment what I know only too well, that I thus judge a past to which by definition my present is not subject? The proof of this is that the same man who in sincerity posits that he is what in actuality he was, is indignant at the reproach of another and tries to disarm it by asserting that he can no longer be what he was. We are readily astonished and upset when the penalties of the court affect a man who in his new freedom *is no longer* the guilty person he was. But at the same time we require of this man that he recognize himself as *being* this guilty one. What then is sincerity except precisely a phenome-

2. That is, if it is true that one is obligated to do something, then it must also be true that it is possible for one to do it. See Kant, *Critique of Pure Reason* (1781; 2nd ed., 1787), A548 / B576.

non of bad faith? Have we not shown indeed that in bad faith human reality is constituted as a being which is what it is not and which is not what it is?

* * *

Thus the essential structure of sincerity does not differ from that of bad faith since the sincere man constitutes himself as what he is *in order not to be it*. This explains the truth recognized by all that one can fall into bad faith through being sincere. As Valéry[3] pointed out, this is the case with Stendhal. Total, constant sincerity as a constant effort to adhere to oneself is by nature a constant effort to dissociate oneself from oneself. A person frees himself from himself by the very act by which he makes himself an object for himself. To draw up a perpetual inventory of what one is means constantly to redeny oneself and to take refuge in a sphere where one is no longer anything but a pure, free regard. The goal of bad faith, as we said, is to put oneself out of reach; it is an escape. Now we see that we must use the same terms to define sincerity. What does this mean?

In the final analysis the goal of sincerity and the goal of bad faith are not so different. To be sure, there is a sincerity which bears on the past and which does not concern us here; I am sincere if I confess *having had* this pleasure or that intention. We shall see that if this sincerity is possible, it is because in his fall into the past, the being of man is constituted as a being-in-itself. But here our concern is only with the sincerity which aims at itself in present immanence. What is its goal? To bring me to confess to myself what I am in order that I may finally coincide with my being; in a word, to cause myself to be, in the mode of the in-itself,[4] what I am in the mode of "not being what I am." Its assumption is that fundamentally I am already, in the mode of the in-itself, what I have to be. Thus we find at the base of sincerity a continual game of mirror and reflection, a perpetual passage from the being which is what it is, to the being which is not what it is and inversely from the being which is not what it is to the being which is what it is. And what is the goal of bad faith? To cause me to be what I am, in the mode of "not being what one is," or not to be what I am in the mode of "being what one is." We find here the same game of mirrors. In fact in order for me to have an intention of sincerity, I must at the outset simultaneously be and not be what I am. Sincerity does not assign to me a mode of being or a particular quality, but in relation to that quality it aims at making me pass from one mode of being to another mode of being. This second mode of being, the ideal of sincerity, I am prevented by nature from attaining; and at the very moment when I struggle to attain it, I have a vague prejudicative comprehension that I shall not attain it. But all the same, in order for me to be able to conceive an intention in bad faith, I must have such a nature that within my being I escape from my being. If I were sad or cowardly in the way in which this inkwell is an inkwell, the

---

3. Paul Valéry (1871–1945), French writer, public intellectual, and philosopher. In a 1927 preface to the unfinished novel *Lucien Leuwen* (1894), he criticized its author, the writer Stendhal (Marie-henri Beyle, 1783–1842), for having thought it possible to achieve "the natural."
4. That is, the mode of being of a mere thing, which simply is what it is and has no transcendence of "what it is" as a part of its being: it is merely determinate content. The mode of the *for*-itself (the subject of the book's next part), in contrast, is the mode of consciousness, which has the character of a transcendence of all determinate content.

possibility of bad faith could not even be conceived. Not only should I be unable to escape from my being; I could not even imagine that I could escape from it. But if bad faith is possible by virtue of a simple project, it is because so far as my being is concerned, there is no difference between being and non-being if I am cut off from my project.

Bad faith is possible only because sincerity is conscious of missing its goal inevitably, due to its very nature. I can try to apprehend myself as "*not being cowardly*," when I *am* so, only on condition that the "being cowardly" is itself "in question" at the very moment when it exists, on condition that it is itself *one* question, that at the very moment when I wish to apprehend it, it escapes me on all sides and annihilates itself. The condition under which I can attempt an effort in bad faith is that in one sense, I *am not* this coward which I do not wish to be. But if I were not cowardly in the simple mode of not-being-what-one-is-not, I would be "in good faith" by declaring that I am not cowardly. Thus this inapprehensible coward is evanescent; in order for me not to be cowardly, I must in some way also be cowardly. That does not mean that I must be "a little" cowardly, in the sense that "a little" signifies "to a certain degree cowardly—and not cowardly to a certain degree." No. I must at once both be and not be totally and in all respects a coward. Thus in this case bad faith requires that I should not be what I am; that is, that there be an imponderable difference separating being from non-being in the mode of being of human reality.

But bad faith is not restricted to denying the qualities which I possess, to not seeing the being which I am. It attempts also to constitute myself as being what I am not. It apprehends me positively as courageous when I am not so. And that is possible, once again, only if I am what I am not; that is, if non-being in me does not have being even as non-being. Of course necessarily I *am not* courageous; otherwise bad faith would not be *bad* faith. But in addition my effort in bad faith must include the ontological comprehension that even in my usual being what I *am*, I am not it really and that there is no such difference between the being of "being-sad," for example—which I *am* in the mode of not being what I am—and the "non-being" of not-being-courageous which I wish to hide from myself. Moreover it is particularly requisite that the very negation of being should be itself the object of a perpetual nihilation, that the very meaning of "non-being" be perpetually in question in human reality. If I *were not* courageous in the way in which this inkwell is not a table; that is, if I were isolated in my cowardice, propped firmly against it, incapable of putting it in relation to its opposite, if I were not capable of *determining* myself as cowardly—that is, to deny courage to myself and thereby to escape my cowardice in the very moment that I posit it—if it were not on principle *impossible* for me to coincide with my *not-being-courageous* as well as with my being-courageous—then any project of bad faith would be prohibited me. Thus in order for bad faith to be possible, sincerity itself must be in bad faith. The condition of the possibility for bad faith is that human reality, in its most immediate being, in the intra-structure of the pre-reflective *cogito*, must be what it is not and not be what it is.

* * *

From *Part Two*
Being-for-Itself

FROM CHAPTER ONE
IMMEDIATE STRUCTURES OF THE FOR-ITSELF

FROM III. THE FOR-ITSELF AND THE BEING OF VALUE

* * *

The for-itself,[5] as the foundation of itself, is the upsurge of the negation. The for-itself founds itself in so far as it denies *in relation to itself* a certain being or a mode of being. What it denies or nihilates, as we know, is being-in-itself. But no matter *what* being-in-itself: human reality is before all else its own nothingness. What it denies or nihilates *in relation to* itself as for-itself can be only *itself*. The meaning of human reality as nihilated is constituted by this nihilation and this presence in it of what it nihilates; hence the self-as-being-in-itself is what human reality lacks and what makes its meaning. Since human reality in its primitive relation to itself is not what it is, its relation to itself is not primitive and can derive its meaning only from an original relation which is the *null relation*[6] or identity. It is the self which would be[7] what it is which allows the for-itself to be apprehended as not being what it is; the relation denied in the definition of the for-itself—which as such should be first posited—is a relation (given as perpetually absent) between the for-itself and itself in the mode of identity. The meaning of the subtle confusion by which thirst escapes and is not thirst (in so far as it is consciousness of thirst), is a thirst which would be thirst and which haunts it. What the for-itself lacks is the self—or itself as in-itself.[8]

Nevertheless we must not confuse this missing in-itself (the lacked), with that of facticity. The in-itself of facticity in its failure to found itself is reabsorbed in pure presence in the world on the part of the for-itself. The missing in-itself, on the other hand, is pure absence. Moreover the failure of the act to found the in-itself has caused the for-itself to rise up from the in-itself as the foundation of its own nothingness. But the meaning of the missing act of founding remains as transcendent. The for-itself in its being is failure because it is the foundation only of itself as nothingness. In truth this failure is its very being, but it has meaning only if the for-itself apprehends itself as failure *in the presence* of the being which it has failed to be; that is, of the being which would be the foundation of its being and no longer merely the foundation of its nothingness—or, to put it another way, which would be its foundation as coincidence with itself. By nature the *cogito* refers to the lacking and to the lacked, for the *cogito* is haunted by being, as Descartes well realized.

Such is the origin of transcendence. Human reality is its own surpassing toward what it lacks; it surpasses itself toward the particular being which it

---

5. See the previous note on p. 1253.
6. That is, no relation at all (to anything else).
7. That is, wants to be.
8. That is, because the for-itself (consciousness) has no inherent, essential determinate content, it craves nonfleeting, determinate content so that it can *be* something—a substantial self. But such determinate content would give it the character of a kind of *thing*. This, for Sartre, is what human reality both inherently lacks and inherently craves, thereby explaining the disposition to bad faith (self-deception with respect to having such an identity).

would be if it were what it is. Human reality is not something which exists first in order afterwards to lack this or that; it exists first as lack and in immediate, synthetic connection with what it lacks. Thus the pure event by which human reality rises as a presence in the world is apprehended by itself as *its own lack*. In its coming into existence human reality grasps itself as an incomplete being. It apprehends itself as being in so far as it is not, in the presence of the particular totality which it lacks and which it is in the form of not being it and which is what it is. Human reality is a perpetual surpassing toward a coincidence with itself which is never given. If the *cogito reaches* toward being, it is because by its very thrust it surpasses itself toward being by qualifying itself in its being as the being to which coincidence with self is lacking in order for it to be what it is. The *cogito* is indissolubly linked to being-in-itself, not as a thought to its object—which would make the in-itself relative—but as a lack to that which defines its lack. In this sense the second Cartesian proof[9] is rigorous. Imperfect being surpasses itself toward perfect being; the being which is the foundation only of its nothingness surpasses itself toward the being which is the foundation of its being. But the being toward which human reality surpasses itself is not a transcendent God; it is at the heart of human reality; it is only human reality itself as totality.

This totality is not the pure and simple contingent in-itself of the transcendent. If what consciousness apprehends as the being toward which it surpasses itself were the pure in-itself, it would coincide with the annihilation of consciousness. But consciousness does not surpass itself toward its annihilation; it does not want to lose itself in the in-itself of identity at the limit of its surpassing. It is for the for-itself as such that the for-itself lays claim to being-in-itself.

Thus this perpetually absent being which haunts the for-itself is itself fixed in the in-itself. It is the impossible synthesis of the for-itself and the in-itself,[1] it would be its own foundation not as nothingness but as being and would preserve within it the necessary translucency of consciousness along with the coincidence with itself of being-in-itself. It would preserve in it that turning back upon the self which conditions every necessity and every foundation. But this return to the self would be without distance; it would not be presence to itself, but identity with itself. In short, this being would be exactly the *self* which we have shown can exist only as a perpetually evanescent relation, but it would be this self as substantial being. Thus human reality arises as such in the presence of its own totality or self as a lack of that totality. And this totality can not be given by nature, since it combines in itself the incompatible characteristics of the in-itself and the for-itself.

Let no one reproach us with capriciously inventing a being of this kind; when by a further movement of thought the being and absolute absence of this totality are hypostasized as transcendence beyond the world, it takes on the name of God. Is not God a being who is what he is—in that he is all positivity and the foundation of the world—and at the same time a being who is not what he is and who is what he is not—in that he is self-consciousness and the necessary foundation of himself? The being of human reality is suffering

---

9. Descartes' second proof of God's existence in his *Meditations* (because God is a perfect being, and existence is a perfection, God exists).
1. Because of this impossibility, Sartre refers to human reality as "a futile passion"—and also characterizes the idea of God, who would be precisely such a synthesis writ large, as an impossible contradiction in terms.

because it rises in being as perpetually haunted by a totality which it is without being able to be it, precisely because it could not attain the in-itself without losing itself as for-itself. Human reality therefore is by nature an unhappy consciousness with no possibility of surpassing its unhappy state.

* * *

Furthermore this being need not be conceived as present to consciousness with only the abstract characteristics which our study has established. The concrete consciousness arises in situation, and it is a unique, individualized consciousness *of* this situation and (of) itself in situation. It is to this concrete consciousness that the self is present, and all the concrete characteristics of consciousness have their correlates in the totality of the self. The self is individual; it is the individual completion of the self which haunts the for-itself.

* * *

Now we can ascertain more exactly what is the being of the self: it is value. Value is affected with the double character, which moralists have very inadequately explained, of both being unconditionally and not being. Qua value indeed, value has being, but this normative existent does not have to be precisely as reality. Its being is to be value; that is, not-to-be being. Thus the being of value qua value is the being of what does not have being. Value then appears inapprehensible. To take it as being is to risk totally misunderstanding its unreality and to make of it, as sociologists do, a requirement of fact among other facts. In this case the contingency of being destroys value. But conversely if one looks only at the ideality of values, one is going to extract being from them, and then for lack of being, they dissolve. Of course, as Scheler has shown,[2] I can achieve an intuition of values in terms of concrete exemplifications; I can grasp nobility in a noble act. But value thus apprehended is not given as existing on the same level of being as the act on which it confers value—in the way, for example, that the essence "red" is in relation to a particular red. Value is given as a beyond of the acts confronted, as the limit, for example, of the infinite progression of noble acts. Value is beyond being. Yet if we are not to be taken in by fine words, we must recognize that this being which is beyond being possesses being in some way at least.

These considerations suffice to make us admit that human reality is that by which value arrives in the world. But the meaning of being for value is that it is that toward which a being surpasses its being; every value-oriented act is a wrenching away from its own being toward—. Since value is always and everywhere the beyond of all surpassings, it can be considered as the unconditioned unity of all surpassings of being. Thereby it makes a dyad with the reality which originally surpasses its being and by which surpassing comes into being—*i.e.*, with human reality. We see also that since value is the unconditioned beyond of all surpassings, it must be originally the beyond of the very being which surpasses, for that is the only way in which value can be the original beyond of all possible surpassings. If every surpassing must be able to be surpassed, it is necessary that the being which surpasses should be *a*

---

2. See SCHELER below (first selection).

priori surpassed *in so far* as it is the very source of surpassings. Thus value taken in its origin, or the supreme value, is the beyond and the *for* of transcendence. It is the beyond which surpasses and which provides the foundation for all my surpassings but toward which I can never surpass myself, precisely because my surpassings presuppose it.

In all cases of lack value is "the lacked"; it is not "the lacking." Value is the self in so far as the self haunts the heart of the for-itself as that for which the for-itself *is*. The supreme value toward which consciousness at every instant surpasses itself by its very being is the absolute being of the self with its characteristics of identity, of purity, of permanence, *etc.*, and as its own foundation. This is what enables us to conceive why value can simultaneously be and not be. It *is* as the meaning and the beyond of all surpassing; it *is* as the absent in-itself which haunts being-for-itself. But as soon as we consider value, we see that it is itself a surpassing of this being-in-itself, since value *gives being to itself*. It is beyond its own being since with the type of being of coincidence with self, it immediately surpasses this being, its permanence, its purity, its consistency, its identity, its silence, by reclaiming these qualities by virtue of presence to itself. And conversely if we start by considering it as presence to itself, this presence immediately is solidified, fixed in the in-itself. Moreover it is in its being the missing totality toward which a being makes itself be. It arises for a being, not as this being is what it is in full contingency, but as it is the foundation of its own nihilation. In this sense value haunts being as being founds itself but not as being *is*. Value haunts *freedom*. This means that the relation of value to the for-itself is very particular: it is the being which has to be in so far as it is the foundation of its nothingness of being. Yet while it has to be this being, this is not because it is under the pressure of an external constraint, nor because value, like the Unmoved Mover of Aristotle,[3] exercises over it an attraction of fact, nor is it because its being has been received; but it is because in its being it makes itself be as having to be this being. In a word the *self*, the for-itself, and their inter-relation stand within the limits of an unconditioned freedom—in the sense that *nothing* makes value exist—unless it is that freedom which by the same stroke makes me myself exist—and also within the limits of concrete facticity—since as the foundation of its nothingness, the for-itself can not be the foundation of its being. There is then a total contingency of being-for-value (which will come up again in connection with morality to paralyze and relativize it) and at the same time a free and absolute necessity.

Value in its original upsurge is not *posited* by the for itself; it is consubstantial with it—to such a degree that there is no consciousness which is not haunted by *its* value[,] and that human-reality in the broad sense includes both the for-itself and value.

* * *

---

3. Greek philosopher (384–322 B.C.E.); in his *Metaphysics* (12.7), he argues that all causation in the universe is attributable to an eternal unmoved mover that is the object of love.

From *Part Three*
Being-for-Others[4]

FROM CHAPTER ONE
THE EXISTENCE OF OTHERS

FROM IV. THE LOOK

* * *

* * * There is no one who has not at some time been surprised in an attitude which was guilty or simply ridiculous. The abrupt modification then experienced was in no way provoked by the irruption of knowledge. It is rather in itself a solidification and an abrupt stratification of myself which leaves intact my possibilities and my structures "for-myself," but which suddenly pushes me into a new dimension of existence—the dimension of the *unrevealed*. Thus the appearance of the look is apprehended by me as the upsurge of an ekstatic relation of being,[5] of which one term is the "me" as for-itself which is what it is not and which is not what it is, and of which other term is still the "me" but outside my reach, outside my action, outside my knowledge.[6] This term, since it is directly connected with the infinite possibilities of a free Other, is itself an infinite and inexhaustible synthesis of unrevealed properties. Through the Other's look I *live* myself as fixed in the midst of the world, as in danger, as irremediable. But I *know* neither what I am nor what is my place in the world, not what face this world in which I am turns toward the Other.

Now at last we can make precise the meaning of this upsurge of the Other in and through his look. The Other is in no way given to us as an object. The objectivation of the Other would be the collapse of his being-as-a-look. Furthermore as we have seen, the Other's look is the disappearance of the Other's *eyes* as objects which manifest the look. The Other can not even be the object aimed at emptily at the horizon of my being for the Other. The objectivation of the Other, as we shall see, is a defence on the part of my being which, precisely by conferring on the Other a being for-me, frees me from my being-for the Other. In the phenomenon of the look, the Other is on principle that which can not be an object. At the same time we see that he can not be a *limiting term* of that relation of myself to myself which makes me arise for myself as the *unrevealed*. Neither can the Other be the goal of my *attention;* if in the upsurge of the Other's look, I *paid attention* to the look or to the Other, this could be only as to objects, for attention is an intentional direction toward objects. But it is not necessary to conclude that the Other is an abstract condition, a conceptual structure of the ekstatic relation; there is here in fact no object really thought, of which the Other could be a universal, formal structure. The Other is, to be sure, the condition of my being-unrevealed.

---

4. In the previous part of the book Sartre was concerned to develop an account of that ontological dimension of human reality that has the character of self-conscious "being-for-itself." In this part he turns to an account of that dimension of human reality that comes to light in the context of "being-for-others."

5. That is, the experience of "the look" of another when I am in a compromising situation that does not merely lead me to *infer* that I am in the presence of another "for-itself" but also makes me *directly aware* both of the reality of the "other" as a "for-itself" (rather than a mere "in-itself") and of a dimension of my own reality that has the character of "object" for that consciousness.

6. That is, "me" as an object, rather than "'me' as for-itself" (a subject).

But he is the concrete, particular condition of it. He is not engaged in my being in the midst of the world as one of its integral parts since he is precisely that which transcends this world in the midst of which I am as non-revealed; as such he can therefore be neither an object nor the formal, constituent element of an object. He can not appear to me, as we have seen, as a unifying or regulative category of my experience since he comes to me through an encounter. Then what is the Other?

In the first place, he is the being toward whom I do not turn my attention. He is the one who looks at me and at whom I am not yet looking, the one who delivers me to myself as *unrevealed* but without revealing himself, the one who is present to me as directing at me but never as the object of my direction; he is the concrete pole (though out of reach) of my flight, of the alienation of my possibles, and of the flow of the world toward another world which is the *same* world and yet lacks all communication with it. But he can not be distinct from this same alienation and flow; he is the meaning and the direction of them; he haunts this flow not as a *real or categorical* element but as a presence which is fixed and made part of the world if I attempt to "make-it-present" and which is never more present, more urgent than when I am not aware of it. For example if I am wholly engulfed in my shame, the Other is the immense, invisible presence which supports this shame and embraces it on every side; he is the supporting environment of my being-unrevealed. Let us see what it is which the Other manifests as *unrevealable* across my lived experience of the unrevealed.

First, the *Other's look* as the necessary condition of my objectivity is the destruction of all objectivity for me. The Other's look touches me across the world and is not only a transformation of myself but a total metamorphosis of the *world*. I am looked-at in a world which is looked-at. In particular the Other's look, which is a look-looking and not a look-looked-at, denies my distances from objects and unfolds its own distances. This look of the Other is given immediately as that by which distance comes to the world at the heart of a presence without distance. I withdraw; I am stripped of my distanceless presence to my world, and I am provided with a distance from the Other. There I am fifteen paces from the door, six yards from the window. But the Other comes searching for me so as to constitute me at a certain distance from him. As the Other constitutes me as at six yards from him, it is necessary that he be present to me without distance. Thus within the very experience of my distance from things and from the Other, I experience the distanceless presence of the Other to me.

Anyone may recognize in this abstract description that immediate and burning presence of the Other's look which has so often filled him with shame. In other words, in so far as I experience myself as looked-at there is realized for me a trans-mundane presence of the Other.[7] The Other looks at me not as he is "in the midst of" *my* world but as he comes toward the world and toward me from all his transcendence; when he looks at me, he is separated from me by no distance, by no object of the world—whether real or ideal—by no body in the world, but the sole fact of his nature as Other. Thus the appearance of

---

7. That is, the experience of "myself as looked-at" does not merely *warrant the inference* of the "presence [and thus the reality] of the Other" but rather *includes* this—perhaps in the same way as my knowledge of the "things" that are present to me experientially.

the Other's look is not an appearance *in the world*—neither in "mine" nor in the "Other's"—and the relation which unites me to the Other cannot be a relation of exteriority inside the world. By the Other's look I effect the concrete proof that there is a "beyond the world." The Other is present to me without any intermediary as a transcendence *which is not mine*. But this presence is not reciprocal. All of the world's density is necessary in order that I may myself be present to the Other. An omnipresent and inapprehensible transcendence, posited upon me without intermediary as I am my being-unrevealed, a transcendence separated from me by the infinity of being, as I am plunged by this look into the heart of a world complete with its distances and its instruments—such is the Other's look when first I experience it as a look.

Furthermore by fixing my possibilities[8] the Other reveals to me the impossibility of my being an object except for another freedom. I can not be an object for myself, for I am what I am; thrown back on its own resources, the reflective effort toward a dissociation results in failure; I am always reapprehended by myself. And when I naively assume that it is possible for me to be an objective being without being responsible for it, I thereby implicitly suppose the Other's existence; for how could I be an object if not for a subject. Thus for me the Other is first the being for whom I am an object; that is, the being *through whom* I gain my object-ness. If I am to be able to conceive of even one of my properties in the objective mode, then the Other is already given. He is given not as a being of my universe but as a pure subject. Thus this pure subject which by definition I am unable to know—*i.e.*, to posit as object—is always *there* out of reach and without distance whenever I try to grasp myself as object. In experiencing the look, in experiencing myself as an unrevealed object-ness, I experience the inapprehensible subjectivity of the Other directly and with my being.

At the same time I experience the Other's infinite freedom. It is for and by means of a freedom and only for and by means of it that my possibles can be limited and fixed. A material obstacle can not fix my possibilities; it is only the occasion for my projecting myself toward other possibles and can not confer upon them an *outside*. To remain at home because it is raining and to remain at home because one has been forbidden to go out are by no means the same thing. In the first case I myself determine to stay inside in consideration of the consequences of my acts; I surpass the obstacle "rain" toward myself and I make an instrument of it. In the second case it is my very possibilities of going out of or staying inside which are presented to me as surpassed and fixed and which a freedom simultaneously foresees and prevents. It is not mere caprice which causes us often to do very naturally and without annoyance what would irritate us if another commanded it. This is because the order and the prohibition cause us to experience the Other's freedom across our own slavery. Thus in the look the death of my possibilities causes me to experience the Other's freedom. This death is realized only at the heart of that freedom; I am inaccessible to myself and yet myself, thrown, abandoned at the heart of the Other's freedom. In connection with this

---

8. That is, freezing my possibilities, and thereby temporarily stripping me of my transcendence.

experience my belonging to universal time can appear to me only as contained and realized by an autonomous temporalization; only a for-itself which temporalizes itself can throw me into time.

Thus through the look I experience the Other concretely as a free, conscious subject who causes there to be a world by temporalizing himself toward his own possibilities. That subject's presence without intermediary is the necessary condition of all thought which I would attempt to form concerning myself. The Other is that "myself" from which nothing separates me, absolutely nothing except his pure and total freedom; that is, that indetermination of himself which he has to be for and through himself.

We know enough at present to attempt to explain that unshakable resistance which common sense has always opposed to the solipsistic argument. This resistance indeed is based on the fact that the Other is given to me as a concrete evident presence which I can in no way derive from myself and which can in no way be placed in doubt nor made the object of a phenomenological reduction or of any other ἐποχή.[9]

If someone looks at me, I am conscious *of being* an object. But this consciousness can be produced only in and through the existence of the Other. In this respect Hegel was right. However *that other* consciousness and *that other* freedom are never *given* to me;[1] for if they were, they would be *known* and would therefore be an object, which would cause me to cease being an object.

* * *

Thus myself-as-object is neither knowledge nor a unity of knowledge but an uneasiness, a lived wrenching away from the ekstatic unity of the for-itself, a limit which I can not reach and which yet I am. The Other through whom this Me *comes to me* is neither knowledge nor category but the fact of the presence of a strange freedom.[2] In fact my wrenching away from myself and the upsurge of the Other's freedom are one; I can feel them and live them only as an ensemble; I cannot even try to conceive of one without the other. The fact of the Other is incontestable and touches me to the heart. I realize him through *uneasiness*; through him I am perpetually *in danger* in a world which is *this* world and which nevertheless I can only glimpse. The Other does not appear to me as a being who is constituted first so as to encounter me later; he appears as a being who arises in an original relation of being with me and whose indubitability and *factual necessity* are those of my own consciousness.

* * *

We are able now to apprehend the nature of the look. In every look there is the appearance of an Other-as-object as a concrete and probable presence in

---

9. *Epochē* (a technical term in Greek philosophy, meaning "suspension of judgment"); Husserl's term for the "bracketing out" of any questions pertaining to causes or explanations of the contents of consciousness external to that consciousness or experience. See §§31–32 of Husserl's *Ideas* (1913), above.
1. That is, that "other consciousness" and "other freedom" cannot be (perceptually or cognitively

"given") *contents* of my consciousness, because consciousness and freedom are not objects at all, and so cannot be directly present to my object-requiring consciousness. My awareness of them can only be indirect, mediated by my consciousness of "being an object"—which I realize I can be only for an objectifying consciousness other than my own.
2. That is, an alien freedom, the freedom of an Other.

my perceptive field; on the occasion of certain attitudes of that Other I determine myself to apprehend—through shame, anguish, *etc.*—my being-looked-at. This "being-looked-at" is presented as the pure probability that I am at present this concrete *this*—a probability which can derive its meaning and its very nature as probable, only from a fundamental certainty that the Other is always present to me inasmuch as I am always *for-others.* The proof of my condition as man, as an object for *all* other living men, as thrown in the arena beneath millions of looks and escaping myself millions of times—this proof I realize concretely on the occasion of the upsurge of an object into *my* universe if this object indicates to me that I am probably an object at present functioning as a *differentiated this* for a consciousness. The proof is the ensemble of the phenomenon which we call the *look.* Each look makes us prove[3] concretely—and in the indubitable certainty of the *cogito*—that we exist for all living men; that is, that there are (some) consciousnesses for whom I exist. We put "some" between parentheses to indicate that the Other-as-subject present to me in this look is not given in the form of plurality any more than as unity (save in its concrete relation to *one* particular Other-as-object). Plurality, in fact, belongs only to objects; it comes into being through the appearance of a world-making For-itself. Being-looked-at, by causing (some) subjects to arise for us, puts us in the presence of an unnumbered reality.

By contrast, as soon as I *look* at those who are looking at me, the *other* consciousnesses are isolated in multiplicity. On the other hand if I turn away from the look as the occasion of concrete proof and seek to think *emptily* of the infinite indistinction of the human presence and to unify it under the concept of the infinite subject which is never an object, then I obtain a purely formal notion which refers to an infinite series of mystic experiences of the presence of the Other, the notion of God as the omnipresent, infinite subject *for whom* I exist. But these two objectivations, the concrete, enumerating objectivation and the unifying, abstract objectivation, both lack proved reality—that is, the prenumerical presence of the Other.

* * *

FROM CHAPTER TWO
THE BODY

* * *

FROM III. THE THIRD ONTOLOGICAL DIMENSION OF THE BODY

I exist my body:[4] this is its first dimension of being. My body is utilized and known by the Other: this is its second dimension. But in so far as I *am for others,* the Other is revealed to me as the subject for whom I am an object. Even there the question, as we have seen, is of my fundamental relation with the Other. I exist therefore for myself as known by the Other—in particular in my very facticity. I exist for myself as a body known by the Other. This is

3. That is, proves to us.
4. That is, my sense of myself from the standpoint of the first-person-singular for-itself that finds itself embodied and situated in the world in some particular way and circumstances.

the third ontological dimension of my body. This is what we are going to study next; with it we shall have exhausted the question of the body's modes of being.

With the appearance of the Other's look I experience the revelation of my being-as-object; that is, of my transcendence as transcended. A me-as-object is revealed to me as an unknowable being, as the flight into an Other which I am with full responsibility. But while I can not know nor even conceive of this "Me" in its reality, at least I am not without apprehending certain of its formal structures. In particular I feel myself touched by the Other in my factual existence; it is my being-there-for-others for which I am responsible. This *being-there* is precisely the body. Thus the encounter with the Other does not only touch me in my transcendence: in and through the transcendence which the Other surpasses, the facticity which my transcendence nihilates and transcends exists for the Other; and to the extent that I am conscious of existing for the Other I apprehend my own facticity, not only in its non-thetic[5] nihilation, not only in *the existent*, but in its flight towards a being-in-the-midst-of-the-world. The shock of the encounter with the Other is for me a revelation in emptiness of the existence of my body outside as an in-itself for the Other. Thus my body is not given merely as that which is purely and simply lived; rather this "lived experience" becomes—in and through the contingent, absolute fact of the Other's existence—extended outside in a dimension of flight which escapes me. My body's depth of being is for me this perpetual "outside" of my most intimate "inside."

To the extent that the Other's omnipresence is the fundamental fact, the objectivity of my being-there is a constant dimension of my facticity; I exist my contingency in so far as I surpass it toward my possibles and in so far as it surreptitiously flees me toward an irremediable. My body is there not only as the point of view which I am but again as a point of view on which are actually brought to bear points of view which I could never take; my body escapes me on all sides. This means first that this ensemble of *senses*, which themselves can not be apprehended, is given as apprehended elsewhere and by others. This apprehension which is thus emptily manifested does not have the character of an ontological necessity; its existence can not be derived even from my facticity, but it is an evident and absolute fact. It has the character of a factual necessity. Since my facticity is pure contingency and is revealed to me non-thetically as a factual necessity, the being-for-others of this facticity comes to increase the contingency of this facticity, which is lost and flees from me in an infinity of contingency which escapes me. Thus at the very moment when I *live* my senses as this inner point of view on which I can take no point of view, their being-for-others haunts me: they *are*. For the Other, my senses are as this table or as this tree is for me. They are in the midst of *a world*; they are in and through the absolute flow of *my* world toward the Other. Thus the relativity of my senses, which I can not think abstractly without destroying *my* world, is at the same time perpetually made present to me through the Other's existence; but it is a pure and inapprehensible appresentation.

In the same way my body is for me the instrument which I am and which can not be utilized by any instrument. But to the extent that the Other in the original encounter transcends my being-there toward his possibilities, this

---

5. Pre-reflective.

instrument which I am is made-present to me as an instrument submerged in an infinite instrumental series, although I can in no way view this series by "surveying" it. My body as alienated escapes me toward a being-a-tool-among-tools, toward a being-a-sense-organ-apprehended-by-sense-organs, and this is accompanied by an alienating destruction and a concrete collapse of *my* world which flows toward the Other and which the Other will reapprehend in *his* world. When, for example, a doctor listens to my breathing, I *perceive his ear.* To the extent that the objects of the world indicate me as an absolute center of reference, this perceived ear indicates certain structures as forms which I exist on my body-as-a-ground. These structures—in the same upsurge with my being—belong with the purely lived; they are that which I exist and which I nihilate. Thus we have here in the first place the original connection between designation and the lived. The things perceived designate that which I subjectively exist. But I apprehend—on the collapse of the sense object "ear"—the doctor as listening to the sounds in my body, feeling my body with his body, and immediately the lived-designated becomes designated as a *thing outside my subjectivity,* in the midst of a world which is not mine. My body is designated as alienated.[6]

The experience of my alienation is made in and through affective structures such as, for example, *shyness.* To "feel oneself blushing," to "feel oneself sweating," *etc.,* are inaccurate expressions which the shy person uses to describe his state; what he really means is that he is vividly and constantly conscious of his body not as it is for him but as it is *for the Other.* This constant uneasiness, which is the apprehension of my body's alienation as irremediable, can determine psychoses such as ereutophobia (a pathological fear of blushing); these are nothing but the horrified metaphysical apprehension of the existence of my body for the Others. * * *

The explanation here is that we in fact attribute to the body-for-the-Other as much reality as to the body-for-us. Better yet, the body-for-the-Other *is* the body-for-us, but inapprehensible and alienated.

* * *

From *Part Four*
Having, Doing, and Being

FROM CHAPTER ONE
BEING AND DOING: FREEDOM

FROM I. FREEDOM: THE FIRST CONDITION OF ACTION

* * *

In our attempt to reach to the heart of freedom we may be helped by the few observations which we have made on the subject in the course of this work and which we must summarize here. In the first chapter we established the fact that if negation comes into the world through human-reality, the latter must be a being who can realize a nihilating rupture with the world and with himself; and we established that the permanent possibility of this

---

6. That is, it has become something "alien" to me in that (and to the extent that) I experience it as having been incorporated into the projects of others.

rupture is the same as freedom. But on the other hand, we stated that this permanent possibility of nihilating what I am in the form of "having-been" implies for man a particular type of existence. We were able then to determine by means of analyses like that of bad faith that human reality is its own nothingness. For the for-itself, to be is to nihilate the in-itself which it is. Under these conditions freedom can be nothing other than this nihilation. It is through this that the for-itself escapes its being as its essence; it is through this that the for-itself is always something other than what can be *said* of it. For in the final analysis the For-itself is the one which escapes this very denomination, the one which is already beyond the name which is given to it, beyond the property which is recognized in it. To say that the for-itself has to be what it is, to say that it is what it is not while not being what it is, to say that in it existence precedes and conditions essence or inversely according to Hegel, that for it "Wesen ist was gewesen ist"—all this is to say one and the same thing: to be aware that man is free.[7] Indeed by the sole fact that I am conscious of the causes which inspire my action, these causes are already transcendent objects for my consciousness; they are outside. In vain shall I seek to catch hold of them; I escape them by my very existence. I am condemned to exist forever beyond my essence, beyond the causes and motives of my act. I am condemned to be free. This means that no limits to my freedom can be found except freedom itself or, if you prefer, that we are not free to cease being free. To the extent that the for-itself wishes to hide its own nothingness from itself and to incorporate the in-itself as its true mode of being, it is trying also to hide its freedom from itself.

The ultimate meaning of determinism is to establish within us an unbroken continuity of existence in itself. The motive conceived as a psychic fact—i.e., as a full and given reality—is, in the deterministic view, articulated without any break with the decision and the act, both of which are equally conceived as psychic givens. The in-itself has got hold of all these "data"; the motive provokes the act as the physical cause its effect; everything is real, everything is full. Thus the refusal of freedom can be conceived only as an attempt to apprehend oneself as being-in-itself; it amounts to the same thing. Human reality may be defined as a being such that in its being its freedom is at stake because human reality perpetually tries to refuse to recognize its freedom. Psychologically in each one of us this amounts to trying to take the causes and motives as *things*. We try to confer permanence upon them. We attempt to hide from ouselves that their nature and their weight depend each moment on the meaning which I give to them; we take them for constants. This amounts to considering the meaning which I gave to them just now or yesterday—which is irremediable because it is *past*—and extrapolating from it a character fixed still in the present. I attempt to persuade myself that the cause *is* as it was. Thus it would pass whole and untouched from my past consciousness to my present consciousness. It would inhabit my consciousness. This amounts to trying to give an essence to the for-itself. In the same way people will posit ends as transcendences, which is not an error. But

---

7. A summation of Sartre's position at this point. (The following three sentences provide the essential elements of Sartre's argument for it.)

instead of seeing that the transcendences there posited are maintained in their being by my own transcendence, people will assume that I encounter them upon my surging up in the world; they come from God, from nature, from "my" nature, from society. These ends ready made and pre-human will therefore define the meaning of my act even before I conceive it, just as causes as pure psychic givens will produce it without my even being aware of them.

Cause, act, and end constitute a *continuum*, a *plenum*.[8] These abortive attempts to stifle freedom under the weight of being (they collapse with the sudden upsurge of anguish before freedom) show sufficiently that freedom in its foundation coincides with the nothingness which is at the heart of man. Human-reality is free because it *is not enough*. It is free because it is perpetually wrenched away from itself and because it has been separated by a nothingness from what it is and from what it will be. It is free, finally, because its present being is itself a nothingness in the form of the "reflection-reflecting." Man is free because he is not himself but *presence to* himself. The being which is what it is can not be free. Freedom is precisely the nothingness which *is made-to-be* at the heart of man and which forces human-reality *to make itself* instead of *to be*. As we have seen, for human reality, to be is to *choose oneself*; nothing comes to it either from the outside or from within which it can *receive or accept*. Without any help whatsoever, it is entirely abandoned to the intolerable necessity of making itself be—down to the slightest detail. Thus freedom is not *a* being; it is *the being* of man—i.e., his nothingness of being. If we start by conceiving of man as a plenum, it is absurd to try to find in him afterwards moments or psychic regions in which he would be free. As well look for emptiness in a container which one has filled beforehand up to the brim! Man can not be sometimes slave and sometimes free; he is wholly and forever free or he is not free at all.

* * *

* * * Human reality can not receive its ends, as we have seen, either from outside or from a so-called inner "nature." It chooses them and by this very choice confers upon them a transcendent existence as the external limit of its projects. From this point of view—and if it is understood that the existence of the *Dasein* precedes and commands its essence—human reality in and through its very upsurge decides to define its own being by its ends. It is therefore the positing of my ultimate ends which characterizes my being and which is identical with the sudden thrust of the freedom which is mine. And this thrust is an *existence*; it has nothing to do with an essence or with a property of a being which would be engendered conjointly with an idea.

Thus since freedom is identical with my existence, it is the foundation of ends whch I shall attempt to attain either by the will or by passionate efforts. Therefore it can not be limited to voluntary acts. Volitions, on the contrary, like passions are certain subjective attitudes by which we attempt to attain the ends posited by original freedom. By original freedom, of course, we should not understand a freedom which would be *prior* to the voluntary or passionate act but rather a foundation which is strictly contemporary with the will or

8. Fullness (Latin); that is, a continuum of being, a fullness of being.

the passion and which these *manifest*, each in its own way. Neither should we oppose freedom to the will or to passion as the "profound self" of Bergson is opposed to the superficial self;[9] the for-itself is wholly selfness and can not have a "profound self," unless by this we mean certain transcendent structures of the psyche. Freedom is nothing but the *existence* of our will or of our passions in so far as this existence is the nihilation of facticity; that is, the existence of a being which is its being in the mode of having to be it. We shall return to this point. In any case let us remember that the will is determined within the compass of motives and ends already posited by the for-itself in a transcendent projection of itself toward its possibles. If this were not so, how could we understand deliberation, which is an evaluation of means in relation to already existing ends?

If these ends are already posited, then what remains to be decided at each moment is the way in which I shall conduct myself with respect to them; in other words, the attitude which I shall assume. Shall I act by volition or by passion? Who can decide except me?

* * *

* * * My ultimate and initial project—for these are but one—is, as we shall see, always the outline of a solution of the problem of being. But this solution is not first conceived and then realized; we *are* this solution. We make it exist by means of our very engagement, and therefore we shall be able to apprehend it only by living it. Thus we are always wholly present to ourselves; but precisely because we are wholly present, we can not hope to have an analytical and detailed consciousness of what we are. Moreover this consciousness can be only non-thetic.

On the other hand, the world by means of its very articulation refers to us exactly the image of what we are. Not, as we have seen so many times, that we can decipher this image—*i.e.*, break it down and subject it to analysis—but because the world necessarily appears to us as we are. In fact, it is by surpassing the world toward ourselves that we make it appear such as it is. We choose the world, not in its contexture as in-itself but in its meaning, by choosing ourselves. Through the internal negation by denying that we are the world, we make the world appear as world, and this internal negation can exist only if it is at the same time a projection toward a possible. It is the very way in which I entrust myself to the inanimate, in which I abandon myself to my body (or, on the other hand, the way in which I resist either one of these) which causes the appearance of both my body and the inanimate world with their respective value. Consequently there also I enjoy a full consciousness of myself and of my fundamental projects, and this time the consciousness is positional.[1] Nevertheless, precisely because it is positional, what it releases to me is the transcendent image of what I am. The value of things, their instrumental role, their proximity and real distance (which have no relation to their spatial proximity and distance) do nothing more than to outline my image—that is, my choice. My clothing (a uniform or a lounge suit, a soft or a starched shirt) whether neglected or cared for, carefully chosen or ordinary, my furniture, the street on which I live, the city in which I reside, the books with which I surround myself, the recreation which I enjoy, everything which is mine (that is, finally, the world of which I am perpetually conscious, at least by way of a meaning implied by the object which I look at or use): all this informs me of my choice—that is, my being.

* * *

The anguish which, when this possibility is revealed, manifests our freedom to our consciousness is witness of this perpetual modifiability of our initial project. In anguish we do not simply apprehend the fact that the possibles which we project are perpetually eaten away by our freedom-to-come; in addition we apprehend our choice—*i.e.,* ourselves—*as unjustifiable.* This means that we apprehend our choice as not deriving from any prior reality but rather as being about to serve as foundation for the ensemble of significations which constitute reality. Unjustifiability is not only the subjective recognition of the absolute contingency of our being but also that of the interiorization and recovery of this contingency on our own account. For the choice—as we shall see—issues from the contingency of the in-itself which it nihilates and transports it to the level of the gratuitous determination of the for-itself by itself. Thus we are perpetually engaged in our choice and perpetually conscious of the fact that we ourselves can abruptly invert this choice and "reverse steam"; for we project the future by our very being, but our existential freedom perpetually eats it away as we make known to ourselves what we are by means of the future but without getting a grip on this future which remains always possible without ever passing to the rank of the *real.* Thus we are perpetually *threatened* by the nihilation of our actual choice and perpetually threatened with choosing ourselves—and consequently with becoming—other than we are. By the sole fact that our choice is absolute, it is *fragile;* that is, by positing our freedom by means of it, we posit by the same stroke the perpetual possibility that the choice may become a "here and now" which has been made-past in the interests of a "beyond" which I shall be.

* * *

* * * But since this freedom is neither a given nor a property, it can be only by choosing itself. The freedom of the for-itself is always *engaged;* there is no question here of a freedom which could be undetermined and which would pre-exist its choice. We shall never apprehend ourselves except as a choice in the making. But freedom is simply the fact that this choice is always unconditioned.

Such a choice made without base of support and dictating its own causes to itself, can very well appear *absurd,* and in fact it is absurd.[2] This is because freedom is a *choice* of its being but not the *foundation* of its being. We shall return to this relation between freedom and facticity in the course of this

---

2. "Absurd" here means neither "ridiculous" (the word's common sense) nor "irrational" (in the sense of *contrary to* reason) but simply nonrational— unjustifiable in terms of good and sufficient reasons *for the person making the choice* (or, as Sartre says later in this paragraph, "beyond all reasons").

chapter. For the moment it will suffice us to say that human-reality can choose itself as it intends but is not able not to choose itself. It can not even refuse to be; suicide, in fact, is a choice and affirmation—of being. By this being which is *given* to it, human reality participates in the universal contingency of being and thereby in what we may call absurdity. This choice is absurd, not because it is without reason but because there has never been any possibility of not choosing oneself. Whatever the choice may be, it is founded and reapprehended by being, for it is choice which *is*. But what must be noted here is that this choice is not absurd in the sense in which in a rational universe a phenomenon might arise which would not be bound to others by any *reasons*. It is absurd in this sense—that the choice is that by which all foundations and all reasons come into being, that by which the very notion of the absurd receives a meaning. It is absurd as being beyond all reasons. Thus freedom is not pure and simple contingency in so far as it turns back toward its being in order to illuminate its being in the light of its end. It is the perpetual escape from contingency; it is the interiorization, the nihilation, and the subjectivizing of contingency, which thus modified passes wholly, into the gratuity of the choice.

* * *

III. FREEDOM AND RESPONSIBILITY

Although the considerations which are about to follow are of interest primarily to the ethicist, it may nevertheless be worthwhile after these descriptions and arguments to return to the freedom of the for-itself and to try to understand what the fact of this freedom represents for human destiny.

The essential consequence of our earlier remarks is that man being condemned to be free carries the weight of the whole world on his shoulders; he is responsible for the world and for himself as a way of being. We are taking the word "responsibility" in its ordinary sense as "consciousness (of) being the incontestable author of an event or of an object." In this sense the responsibility of the for-itself is overwhelming since he[3] is the one by whom it happens that *there is* a world,[4] since he is also the one who makes himself be, then whatever may be the situation in which he finds himself, the for-itself must wholly assume this situation with its peculiar coefficient of adversity, even though it be insupportable. He must assume the situation with the proud consciousness of being the author of it, for the very worst disadvantages or the worst threats which can endanger my person have meaning only in and through my project; and it is on the ground of the engagement which I am that they appear. It is therefore senseless to think of complaining since nothing foreign[5] has decided what we feel, what we live, or what we are.

Furthermore this absolute responsibility is not resignation; it is simply the

---

3. I am shifting to the personal pronoun here since Sartre is describing the for-itself in concrete personal terms rather than as a metaphysical entity. Strictly speaking, of course, this is his position throughout, and the French "*il*" is indifferently "he" or "it" [translator's note].
4. A "world" here in the sense of a meaningful totality (i.e., in Heidegger's sense). Sartre's point is that the entire "responsibility" for that world ulti-

mately comes down to individuals and their choices (not, of course, to a single individual, despite the translator's use of "he"), since it comes down to human reality, and human reality is in every instance individual. The sweeping consequences that Sartre draws in the following paragraphs are the more remarkable given that he was writing during the German occupation of France.
5. That is, alien or external to me.

logical requirement of the consequences of our freedom. What happens to me happens through me, and I can neither affect myself with it nor revolt against it nor resign myself to it. Moreover everything which happens to me is *mine*. By this we must understand first of all that I am always equal to what happens to me *qua* man, for what happens to a man through other men and through himself can be only human. The most terrible situations of war, the worst tortures do not create a non-human state of things; there is no non-human situation. It is only through fear, flight, and recourse to magical types of conduct that I shall decide on the non-human, but this decision is human, and I shall carry the entire responsibility for it. But in addition the situation is *mine* because it is the image of my free choice of myself, and everything which it presents to me is *mine* in that this represents me and symbolizes me. Is it not I who decide the coefficient of adversity in things and even their unpredictability by deciding myself?

Thus there are no *accidents* in a life; a community event which suddenly bursts forth and involves me in it does not come from the outside. If I am mobilized in a war, this war is *my* war; it is in my image and I deserve it. I deserve it first because I could always get out of it by suicide or by desertion; these ultimate possibles are those which must always be present for us when there is a question of envisaging a situation. For lack of getting out of it, I have *chosen* it.[6] This can be due to inertia, to cowardice in the face of public opinion, or because I prefer certain other values to the value of the refusal to join in the war (the good opinion of my relatives, the honor of my family, *etc.*). Anyway you look at it, it is a matter of a choice. This choice will be repeated later on again and again without a break until the end of the war. Therefore we must agree with the statement by J. Romains, "In war there are no innocent victims."[7] If therefore I have preferred war to death or to dishonor, everything takes place as if I bore the entire responsibility for this war. Of course others have declared it, and one might be tempted perhaps to consider me as a simple accomplice. But this notion of complicity has only a juridical sense, and it does not hold here. For it depended on me that for me and by me this war should not exist, and I have decided that it does exist. There was no compulsion[8] here, for the compulsion could have got no hold on a freedom. I did not have any excuse; for as we have said repeatedly in this book, the peculiar character of human-reality is that it is without excuse. Therefore it remains for me only to lay claim to this war.

But in addition the war is *mine* because by the sole fact that it arises in a situation which I cause to be and that I can discover it there only by engaging myself for or against it, I can no longer distinguish at present the choice which I make of myself from the choice which I make of the war. To live this war is to choose myself through it and to choose it through my choice of myself. There can be no question of considering it as "four years of vacation" or as a "reprieve," as a "recess," the essential part of my responsibilities being elsewhere in my married, family, or professional life. In this war which I have chosen I choose

---

6. That is, even in a situation such as this one, in which my options are incredibly tightly constrained and extreme, I still am able to choose (and the meaning of it all still depends on such choices). 7. J. Romains: *Les hommes de bonne volonté*; "Prélude à Verdun" [Sartre's note]. *Prelude to Verdun* (1938) is vol. 15 of the 27-volume novel cycle *Men*

of Good Will, by Jules Romains (pseudonym of Louis-henri-jean Farigoule, 1885–1972). Verdun (1916) was the longest single battle of the First World War, with hundreds of thousands of French and German casualties. 8. That is, no causal necessity that made it literally impossible to do otherwise.

myself from day to day, and I make it mine by making myself. If it is going to be four empty years, then it is I who bear the responsibility for this.

Finally, as we pointed out earlier, each person is an absolute choice of self from the standpoint of a world of knowledges and of techniques which this choice both assumes and illumines; each person is an absolute upsurge at an absolute date and is perfectly unthinkable at another date. It is therefore a waste of time to ask what I should have been if this war had not broken out, for I have chosen myself as one of the possible meanings of the epoch which imperceptibly led to war. I am not distinct from this same epoch; I could not be transported to another epoch without contradiction. Thus I *am* this war which restricts and limits and makes comprehensible the period which preceded it. In this sense we may define more precisely the responsibility of the for-itself if to the earlier quoted statement, "There are no innocent victims," we add the words, "We have the war we deserve." Thus, totally free, undistinguishable from the period for which I have chosen to be the meaning, as profoundly responsible for the war as if I had myself declared it, unable to live without integrating it in my situation, engaging myself in it wholly and stamping it with my seal, I must be without remorse or regrets as I am without excuse; for from the instant of my upsurge into being, I carry the weight of the world by myself alone without anything or any person being able to lighten it.

Yet this responsibility is of a very particular type. Someone will say, "I did not ask to be born." This is a naive way of throwing greater emphasis on our facticity. I am responsible for everything, in fact, except for my very responsibility, for I am not the foundation of my being. Therefore everything takes place as if I were compelled to be responsible. I am *abandoned* [*délaissé*][9] in the world, not in the sense that I might remain abandoned and passive in a hostile universe like a board floating on the water, but rather in the sense that I find myself suddenly alone and without help, engaged in a world for which I bear the whole responsibility without being able, whatever I do, to tear myself away from this responsibility for an instant. For I am responsible for my very desire of fleeing responsibilities. To make myself passive in the world, to refuse to act upon things and upon Others is still to choose myself, and suicide is one mode among others of being-in-the-world. Yet I find an absolute responsibility for the fact that my facticity (here the fact of my birth) is directly inapprehensible and even inconceivable, for this fact of my birth never appears as a brute fact but always across a projective reconstruction of my for-itself. I am ashamed of being born or I am astonished at it or I rejoice over it, or in attempting to get rid of my life I affirm that I live and I assume this life as bad. Thus in a certain sense I *choose* being born. This choice itself is integrally affected with facticity since I am not able not to choose, but this facticity in turn will appear only in so far as I surpass it toward my ends. Thus facticity is everywhere but inapprehensible; I never encounter anything except my responsibility. That is why I can not ask, "*Why* was I born?" or curse the day of my birth or declare that I did not ask to be born, for these various attitudes toward my birth—i.e., toward the *fact* that I realize a presence in the world—are absolutely nothing else but ways of assuming this birth in full responsibility and of making it *mine*. Here again I encounter only myself and

9. That is, entirely on my own. Sartre goes on to elaborate. (A more apt translation than "forlorn," its rendering in the translation of the "Humanism" essay above.)

my projects so that finally my abandonment—*i.e.*, my facticity—consists simply in the fact that I am condemned to be wholly responsible for myself. I am the being which *is* in such a way that in its being its being is in question. And this "is" of my being *is* as present and inapprehensible.

Under these conditions since every event in the world can be revealed to me only as an *opportunity* (an opportunity made use of, lacked, neglected, *etc.*), or better yet since everything which happens to us can be considered as a *chance* (*i.e.*, can appear to us only as a way of realizing this being which is in question in our being) and since others as transcendences-transcended are themselves only *opportunities* and *chances*, the responsibility of the for-itself extends to the entire world as a peopled-world. It is precisely thus that the for-itself apprehends itself in anguish; that is, as a being which is neither the foundation of its own being nor of the Other's being nor of the in-itselfs which form the world, but a being which is compelled to decide the meaning of being—within it and everywhere outside of it.[1] The one who realizes in anguish his condition as *being* thrown into a responsibility which extends to his very abandonment has no longer either remorse or regret or excuse; he is no longer anything but a freedom which perfectly reveals itself and whose being resides in this very revelation. But as we pointed out at the beginning of this work, most of the time we flee anguish in bad faith.

* * *

From *Conclusion*

* * *

FROM II. ETHICAL IMPLICATIONS

Ontology itself can not formulate ethical precepts. It is concerned solely with what is, and we can not possibly derive imperatives from ontology's indicatives. It does, however, allow us to catch a glimpse of what sort of ethics will assume its responsibilities when confronted with a *human reality in situation*. Ontology has revealed to us, in fact, the origin and the nature of *value*; we have seen that value is the *lack* in relation to which the for-itself determines its being as *a lack*. By the very fact that the for-itself *exists*, as we have seen, value arises to haunt its being-for-itself. It follows that the various tasks of the for-itself can be made the object of an existential psychoanalysis, for they all aim at producing the missing synthesis of consciousness and being in the form of value or self-cause. Thus existential psychoanalysis is *moral description*, for it releases to us the ethical meaning of various human projects. It indicates to us the necessity of abandoning the psychology of interest along with any utilitarian interpretation of human conduct—by revealing to us the *ideal* meaning of all human attitudes. These meanings are beyond egoism and altruism, beyond also any behavior which is called *disinterested*. Man makes himself man in order to be God, and selfness considered from this point of view can appear to be an egoism; but precisely because there is no common measure

---

1. Here Sartre differs radically from Heidegger on the very question that matters most to Heidegger: the question of "the meaning of being"—how that question is to be understood, and how it is to be dealt with. For Sartre the only "meaning of being" it makes any sense to speak of is the kind of "meaning" we give things by our choices and projects.

between human reality and the self-cause which it wants to be, one could just as well say that man loses himself in order that the self-cause may exist. We will consider then that all human existence is a passion, the famous *self-interest* being only one way freely chosen among others to realize this passion.

* * *

But ontology and existential psychoanalysis (or the spontaneous and empirical application which men have always made of these disciplines) must reveal to the moral agent that he is *the being by whom values exist*. It is then that his freedom will become conscious of itself and will reveal itself in anguish as the unique source of value and the nothingness by which the *world* exists. As soon as freedom discovers the quest for being and the appropriation of the in-itself as *its own possibles*, it will apprehend by and in anguish that they are possibles only on the ground of the possibility of other possibles. But hitherto although possibles could be chosen and rejected *ad libitum*,[2] the theme which made the unity of all choices of possibles was the value or the ideal presence of the *ens causa sui*.[3] What will become of freedom if it turns its back upon this value? Will freedom carry this value along with it whatever it does and even in its very turning back upon the in-itself-for-itself? Will freedom be reapprehended from behind by the value which it wishes to contemplate? Or will freedom by the very fact that it apprehends itself as a freedom in relation to itself, be able to put an end to the reign of this value? In particular is it possible for freedom to take itself for a value as the source of all value, or must it necessarily be defined in relation to a transcendent value which haunts it? And in case it could will itself as its own possible and its determining value, what would this mean? A freedom which wills itself freedom is in fact a being-which-is-not-what-it-is and which-is-what-it-is-not, and which chooses as the ideal of being, being-what-it-is-not and not-being-what-it-is.[4]

This freedom chooses then not to *recover* itself but to flee itself, not to coincide with itself but to be always at a distance *from* itself. What are we to understand by this being which wills to hold itself in awe, to be at a distance from itself? Is it a question of bad faith or of another fundamental attitude? And can one *live* this new aspect of being? In particular[,] will freedom by taking itself for an end escape all *situation*? Or on the contrary, will it remain situated? Or will it situate itself so much the more precisely and the more individually as it projects itself further in anguish as a conditioned freedom and accepts more fully its responsibility as an existent by whom the world comes into being. All these questions, which refer us to a pure and not an accessory reflection, can find their reply only on the ethical plane. We shall devote to them a future work.[5]

SOURCE: From Jean-Paul Sartre, *Being and Nothingness: An Essay on Phenomenological Ontology*, trans. Hazel E. Barnes (New York: Philosophical Library, 1956), pp. 3–5, 21–25,

2. In accordance with one's desire (Latin); that is, at will.
3. The being [that is] the cause of itself [i.e., of its own existence] (Latin).
4. A restatement of the seeming paradox that human reality is "a being which is what it is not and which is not what it is"; see p. 1218, n. 8, above.
5. Sartre never published this promised "future work" on ethics. However, his "Existentialism is a Humanism" (above), written not long after this book, does offer a sketch of the sort of ethics he may have had in mind here; and Sartre also made extensive notes on the matter shortly thereafter in 1947–48 that have been published as *Notebooks for an Ethics*.

28–29, 31–35, 37–39, 47–49, 55–60, 62–63, 65–67, 88–94, 268–71, 275, 280–81, 351–53, 439–41, 443–44, 463–65, 479, 553–56, 625–28. Except where otherwise indicated, French words in brackets are the terminology used in the French original, inserted by the editor in addition to their renderings in the translation. Originally published in 1943 as *L'Être et le néant, essai d'ontologie phénoménologique.*

From Search for a Method

From *Preface*

* * *

[T]here is *one* question which I am posing—only one: Do we have today the means to constitute a structural, historical anthropology?[1] It finds its place within Marxist philosophy because—as will be seen further on—I consider Marxism the one philosophy of our time which we cannot go beyond[,] and because I hold the ideology of existence[2] and its "comprehensive" method[3] to be an enclave inside Marxism, which simultaneously engenders it and rejects it.

From Marxism, which gave it a new birth, the ideology of existence inherits two requirements which Marxism itself derives from Hegelianism: if such a thing as a Truth can exist in anthropology, it must be a truth that has *become,*[4] and it must make itself a *totalization.*[5] It goes without saying that this double requirement defines that movement of being and of knowing (or of comprehension) which since Hegel is called "dialectic." Also, in *Search for a Method* I have taken it for granted that such a totalization is perpetually in process as History and as historical Truth. Starting from this fundamental postulate, I have attempted to bring to light the internal conflicts of philosophical anthropology, and in certain cases I have been able to outline—upon the methodological ground which I have chosen—the provisional solutions of these difficulties.

From *III. The Progressive-Regressive Method*[6]

I have said that we accept without reservation the thesis set forth by Engels in his letter to Marx: "Men themselves make their history but in a given

---

1. That is, a philosophical anthropology—a comprehensive philosophical account of human reality—that would be structural and historical (rather than abstractly metaphysical, primarily biological, or merely cultural), and so deserving of a place on the agenda of contemporary philosophy. (At the time, such a project was of considerable interest in Western European philosophy as well as in the liberal or "neo-Marxist" wing of Eastern European Marxism. Sartre here associates himself with the Marxist version of this project and development, other versions of which are represented in the fourth part of this volume below.)

2. That is, "existentialism," as characterized by the Marxism then current (which labeled as "ideologies" all philosophies and religions that advanced interpretive or evaluative positions of any sort).

3. That is, the method that aims at the "comprehension" or "understanding" (in German, *Verstehen*) of human phenomena, in contrast to the paradigm of knowledge associated with the scientific model of "explanation" (*Erklären*). Better: comprehending.

4. That is, a truth with respect to a *reality* (namely, human reality) that has "become"—and that continues to do so.

5. That is, human reality must be dealt with as a whole rather than piecemeal, because any part of it is what it is only in its relation to all the rest.

6. This is the "method" to which Sartre's title refers—a movement of going back and forth between the more general and the more particular levels of analysis, and between the more fundamental and the more elaborated or overtly manifested dimensions of human reality.

environment which conditions them."[7] However, this text is not one of the clearest, and it remains open to numerous interpretations. How are we to understand that man makes History if at the same time it is History which makes him? Idealist Marxism[8] seems to have chosen the easiest interpretation: entirely determined by prior circumstances—that is, in the final analysis, by economic conditions—man is a passive product, a sum of conditioned reflexes. Being inserted in the social world amidst other equally conditioned inertias, this inert object, with the nature which it has received, contributes to precipitate or to check the "course of the world." It changes society in the way that a bomb, without ceasing to obey the principle of inertia, can destroy a building. In this case there would be no difference between the human agent and the machine.

* * *

From The Project

* * * We refuse to confuse the alienated man with a thing or alienation with the physical laws governing external conditions. We affirm the specificity of the human act, which cuts across the social milieu while still holding on to its determinations, and which transforms the world on the basis of given conditions. For us man is characterized above all by his going beyond a situation, and by what he succeeds in making of what he has been made—even if he never recognizes himself in his objectification. This going beyond we find at the very root of the human—in *need*. It is need which, for example, links the scarcity of women in the Marquesas,[9] as a structural fact of the group, and polyandry as a matrimonial institution. For this scarcity is not a simple lack; in its most naked form it expresses a situation in society and contains already an effort to go beyond it. The most rudimentary behavior must be determined both in relation to the real and present factors which condition it and in relation to a certain object, still to come, which it is trying to bring into being. This is what we call *the project*.[1]

Starting with the project, we define a double simultaneous relationship. In relation to the given, the *praxis*[2] is negativity; but what is always involved is the negation of a negation. In relation to the object aimed at, *praxis* is positivity, but this positivity opens onto the "non-existent," to what *has not yet* been. A flight and a leap ahead, at once a refusal and a realization, the project retains and unveils the surpassed reality which is refused by the very movement which surpassed it. Thus knowing is a moment of *praxis*, even its most fundamental

---

7. Quoted from a letter of January 25, 1894, written by ENGELS not to MARX but to the German political economist and individual anarchist Walther Borgius; it paraphrases an observation by Marx in *The Eighteenth Brumaire of Louis Napoleon* (1852).
8. Here, dogmatic economic-determinist Marxism.
9. Islands in French Polynesia, in the central South Pacific Ocean.
1. The idea that human reality has a "project" character—that human existing involves a kind of "projecting" toward future possibilities—is the central concept of Sartre's analysis of it here (as it had also been central to both his and HEIDEGGER's earlier existential-philosophical accounts of human existence).
2. That is, practical concrete (human) activity—a term used by the early Marx to characterize and designate human activity. It became a key concept in neo-Marxist philosophy, which sought a humanistic alternative within Marxism to the orthodoxy of "economic determinism" and "dialectical materialism."

one; but this knowing does not partake of an absolute Knowledge. Defined by the negation of the refused reality in the name of the reality to be produced, it remains the captive of the action which it clarifies, and disappears along with it. Therefore it is perfectly accurate to say that man is the product of his product. The structures of a society which is created by human work define for each man an objective situation as a starting point; the truth of a man[3] is the nature of his work, and it is his wages. But this truth defines him just insofar as he constantly goes beyond it in his practical activity. (In a popular democracy this may be, for example, by working a double shift or by becoming an "activist" or by secretly resisting the raising of work quotas. In a capitalist society it may be by joining a union, by voting to go on strike, etc.) Now this surpassing is conceivable only as a relation of the existent to its possibles. Furthermore, to say what man "is" is also to say what he can be—and vice versa. The material conditions of his existence circumscribe the field of his possibilities (his work is too hard, he is too tired to show any interest in union or political activity). Thus the field of possibles is the goal toward which the agent surpasses his objective situation. And this field in turn depends strictly on the social, historical reality. For example, in a society where everything is bought, the possibilities of culture are practically eliminated for the workers if food absorbs 50 per cent or more of their budget. The freedom of the bourgeois, on the contrary, consists in the possibility of his allotting an always increasing part of his income to a great variety of expenditures. Yet the field of possibles, however reduced it may be, always exists, and we must not think of it as a zone of indetermination, but rather as a strongly structured region which depends upon all of History and which includes its own contradictions.[4] It is by transcending the given toward the field of possibles and by realizing one possibility from among all the others that the individual objectifies himself and contributes to making History. The project then takes on a reality which the agent himself may not know, one which, through the conflicts it manifests and engenders, influences the course of events.

Therefore we must conceive of the possibility as doubly determined. On the one side, it is at the very heart of the particular action, the presence of the future as *that which is lacking* and that which, by its very absence, reveals reality. On the other hand, it is the real and permanent future which the collectivity forever maintains and transforms. When common needs bring about the creation of new offices (for example, the multiplication of physicians in a society which is becoming industrialized), these offices, not yet filled—or vacant as the result of retirement or death—constitute for certain people a real, concrete, and *possible* future. These persons *can* go into medicine. This career is not closed to them; at this moment their life lies open before them until death. All things being equal, the professions of army doctor, country doctor, colonial doctor, etc., are characterized by certain advantages and certain obligations which they will quickly know. This future, to be sure, is only partly true; it presupposes a *status quo* and a minimum of order (barring

---

3. That is, the reality of a human being (conceived by Marx to be a matter of that human being's life activity).
4. This sentence encapsulates the text's blending of Sartre's then-current version of existentialism and his newly developing version of Marxism, in which social dimensions of human reality loom much larger than they had in his earlier thought.

accidents) which is contradicted precisely by the fact that our societies are in constant process of making history. But neither is it false, since it is this—in other words, the interests of the profession, of class, etc., the ever-increasing division of labor, etc.—which first manifests the present contradictions of society. The future is presented, then, as a schematic, always open possibility and as an immediate action on the present.

Conversely, this future defines the individual in his present reality; the conditions which the medical students must fulfill in a bourgeois society *at the same time* reveal the society, the profession, and the social situation of the one who will meet these conditions. If it is still necessary for parents to be well-off, if the practice of giving scholarships is not widespread, then the future doctor appears in his own eyes as a member of the moneyed classes. In turn, he becomes aware of his class by means of the future which it makes possible for him; that is, through his chosen profession. In contrast, for the man who does not meet the required conditions, medicine becomes his *lack*, his *non-humanity* (all the more so as many other careers are "closed" to him at the same time). It is from this point of view, perhaps, that we ought to approach the problem of relative pauperism. Every man is defined negatively by the sum total of possibles which are impossible for him; that is, by a future more or less blocked off. For the underprivileged classes, each cultural, technical, or material enrichment of society represents a diminution, an impoverishment; the future is almost entirely barred. Thus, both positively and negatively, the social possibles are lived as schematic determinations of the individual future. And the most individual possible is only the internalization and enrichment of a social possible.[5]

* * *

I cannot describe here the true dialectic of the subjective and the objective. One would have to demonstrate the joint necessity of "the internalization of the external" and "the externalization of the internal." *Praxis*, indeed, is a passage, from objective to objective through internalization.[6] The project, as the subjective surpassing of objectivity toward objectivity, and stretched between the objective conditions of the environment and the objective structures of the field of possibles, represents *in itself* the moving unity of subjectivity and objectivity, those cardinal determinants of activity. The subjective appears then as a necessary moment in the objective process. If the material conditions which govern human relations are to become real conditions of *praxis*, they must be lived in the particularity of particular situations. The diminution of buying power would never provoke the workers to make economic demands if they did not feel the diminution in their flesh in the form of a need or of a fear based on bitter experiences. The practice of union action can increase the importance and the efficacy of objective significations among the experienced party militants; the wage scale and the price index can by themselves clarify or motivate their action. But all this objectivity refers ultimately

5. These last two sentences articulate major features of Sartre's emerging conception of the human condition and human reality, and major "Marxist" themes that he has now incorporated into that account.

6. That is, the mediation of a human agent, who does some internal processing in response to one objective state of affairs and proceeds to do something that brings about another.

to a lived reality. The worker knows what he has resented and what others will resent. Now, to resent is already to go beyond, to move toward the possibility of an objective transformation. In the *lived experience*, the subjectivity turns back upon itself and wrenches itself from despair by means of *objectification*. Thus the subjective contains within itself the objective, which it denies and which it surpasses toward a new objectivity; and this new objectivity by virtue of *objectification* externalizes the internality of the project as an objectified subjectivity.[7] This means *both* that the lived as such finds its place in the result[,] and that the projected meaning of the action appears in the reality of the world that it may get its truth in the process of totalization.

Only the project, as a mediation between two moments of objectivity, can account for history; that is, for human *creativity*.[8] It is necessary to choose. In effect: either we reduce everything to identity (which amounts to substituting a mechanistic materialism for dialectical materialism)—or we make of dialectic a celestial law which imposes itself on the Universe, a metaphysical force which by itself engenders the historical process (and this is to fall back into Hegelian idealism)—or we restore to the individual man his power to go beyond his situation by means of work and action.[9] This solution alone enables us to base the movement of totalization *upon the real*.

* * *

Man defines himself by his project. This material being perpetually goes beyond the condition which is made for him; he reveals and determines his situation by transcending it in order to objectify himself—by work, action, or gesture.[1] The project must not be confused with the will, which is an abstract entity, although the project can assume a voluntary form under certain circumstances. This immediate relation with the Other than oneself, beyond the given and constituted elements, this perpetual production of oneself by work and *praxis*, is our peculiar structure. It is neither a will nor a need nor a passion, but our needs—like our passions or like the most abstract of our thoughts—participate in this structure. They are always *outside of themselves toward* . . . This is what we call existence,[2] and by this we do not mean a stable substance which rests in itself, but rather a perpetual disequilibrium, a wrenching away from itself with all its body. As this impulse toward objectification assumes various forms according to the individual, as it projects us across a field of possibilities, some of which we realize to the exclusion of others, we call it also choice or freedom. But it would be a mistake to accuse us of introducing the irrational here, of inventing a "first beginning" unconnected

---

7. The second "moment" of *praxis*, in which what has become internalized by the human subject prompts a response that is expressed externally in some accessible objective medium. That such objectification enables human selfhood or personal identity to be attained and developed is a major Hegelian as well as Marxian theme, and it is the key to Sartre's new idea of human self-realization.
8. That is, for the transformations of human reality through which (in Sartre's phrase) "man makes himself"—in history (socially and culturally), as Sartre is now prepared to acknowledge, and, at least potentially, at the level of individual human

life as well.
9. This third alternative is Sartre's hybrid of genuine Marxism and genuine existentialism.
1. Such "self-objectification" is at once the distinctive structure of human reality and the basic formula for human self-realization. Here Sartre's concern shifts from the integrity with which choices are made (the focus of his earlier work) to the quality of such self-realization that is actually possible in specific historical circumstances and that is achieved through one's "project" in those circumstances.
2. That is, human *existing*; its basic character.

with the world, or of giving to man a freedom-fetish. This criticism, in fact, could only issue from a mechanist philosophy; those who would direct it at us do so because they would like to *reduce praxis*, creation, invention, to the simple reproduction of the elementary given of our life. It is because they would like to *explain* the work, the act, or the attitude by the factors which condition it; their desire for explanation is a disguise for the wish to assimilate the complex to the simple, to deny the specificity of structures, and to reduce change to identity. This is to fall back again to the level of scientistic determinism. The dialectical method, on the contrary, refuses to *reduce*; it follows the reverse procedure. It surpasses by conserving, but the terms of the surpassed contradiction cannot account for either the transcending itself or the subsequent synthesis; on the contrary, it is the synthesis which clarifies them and which enables us to understand them. For us the basic contradiction is only one of the factors which delimit and structure the field of possibles; it is the choice which must be interrogated if one wants to explain them in their detail, to reveal their singularity (that is, the particular aspect in which *in this case* generality is presented), and to understand how they have been lived. It is the work or the act of the individual which reveals to us the secret of his conditioning. Flaubert[3] by his choice of writing discloses to us the meaning of his childish fear of death—not the reverse. By misunderstanding these principles, contemporary Marxism has prevented itself from understanding significations and values. For it is as absurd to reduce the signification of an object to the pure inert materiality of that object itself as to want to deduce the law from the fact. The meaning of a conduct and its value can be grasped only in perspective by the movement which realizes the possibles as it reveals the given.

Man is, for himself and for others, a signifying being, since one can never understand the slightest of his gestures without going beyond the pure present and explaining it by the future. Furthermore, he is a creator of signs to the degree that—always ahead of himself—he employs certain objects to designate other absent or future objects. But both operations are reduced to a pure and simple surpassing. To surpass present conditions toward their later change and to surpass the present object toward an absence are one and the same thing. Man constructs signs because in his very reality he is signifying; and he is signifying because he is a dialectical surpassing of all that is simply given. What we call freedom is the irreducibility of the cultural order to the natural order.[4]

* * *

* * * It was legitimate for the natural sciences to free themselves from the anthropomorphism which consists in bestowing human properties on inanimate objects. But it is perfectly absurd to assume by analogy the same scorn for anthropomorphism where anthropology is concerned. When one is studying man, what can be more exact or more rigorous than to *recognize human properties in him*? The simple inspection of the social field ought to have led

---

3. Gustave Flaubert (1821–1880), French realist novelist.
4. A strikingly different conception of and argument for "freedom" than those found in *Being and Nothingness* (1943); see above.

to the discovery that the relation to ends is a permanent structure of human enterprises and that it is *on the basis of this relation* that real men evaluate actions, institutions, or economic constructions. It ought to have been established that our comprehension of the other is necessarily attained through ends.[5] A person who from a distance watches a man at work and says: "I don't understand what he is doing," will find that clarification comes when he can unify the disjointed moments of this activity, thanks to the anticipation of the result aimed at. A better example—in order to fight, to outwit the opponent, a person must have at his disposal several systems of ends at once. In boxing, one will grant to a feint its true finality (which is, for example, to force the opponent to lift his guard) if one discovers and rejects at the same time its pretended finality (to land a left hook on the forehead). The double, triple systems of ends which others employ condition our activity as strictly as our own. A positivist who held on to his teleological color blindness in practical life would not live very long.

* * *

The dialectical movement, which proceeds from the objective conditioning to objectification,[6] enables us to understand that the ends of human activity are not mysterious entities added on to the act itself; they represent simply the surpassing and the maintaining of the given in an act which goes from the present toward the future. The end is the objectification itself[7] inasmuch as it constitutes the dialectical law of a human conduct and the unity of its internal contradictions. The presence of the future at the heart of the present will not be surprising if one stops to consider that the end is enriched at the same time as the action itself; it surpasses this action inasmuch as it makes the unity of the action, but the content of this unity is never more concrete nor more explicit than the unified enterprise is at the same instant.

* * *

Conclusion

Since Kierkegaard,[8] a certain number of ideologists, in their attempt to distinguish between being (*être*) and knowing (*savoir*), have succeeded in describing better what we might call "the ontological region" of existences. Without prejudice to the givens of animal psychology and psychobiology, it is evident that the *presence-in-the-world* described by these ideologists characterizes a sector—or perhaps even the whole—of the animal world. But within this living universe, man occupies, *for us*, a privileged place. First, because he is able to be historical; that is, he can continually define himself by his own

---

5. That is, by reference to "ends" (intentions, goals, purposes, objectives), and thus to various sorts of "projects." "Our comprehension": that is, our understanding.
6. That is, from the objective states of affairs that set and condition the contexts in which we find ourselves to the results of our actions in these circumstances, through which we pursue our objectives and so express (and realize) ourselves.

7. That is, the larger meaning or point of human reality, to the extent that there is one, is simply self-realization as self-objectification. (This is a strikingly different theme from the idea of radically free and responsible choice put forth in *Being and Nothingness*, where all that matters is that it be exercised "for the sake of freedom.")
8. For KIERKEGAARD, see above.

praxis by means of changes suffered or provoked and their internalization, and then by the very surpassing of the internalized relations.[9] Second, because he is characterized as *the existent which we are*. In this case the questioner finds himself to be precisely the questioned, or, if you prefer, human reality is the existent whose being is in question in its being. It is evident that this "being-in-question" must be taken as a determination of *praxis* and that the theoretical questioning comes in only as an abstract moment of the total process. Moreover, knowing is inevitably practical; it changes the known. Not in the sense of classical rationalism. But in the way that an experiment in microphysics necessarily transforms its object.

In choosing as the object of our study, within the ontological sphere, that privileged existent which is man (privileged *for us*), it is evident that existentialism poses to itself the question of its fundamental relations with those disciplines which are grouped under the general heading of *anthropology*. And—although its field of application is theoretically larger—existentialism is anthropology too insofar as anthropology seeks to give itself a foundation.[1] Let us note, in fact, that the problem is the same one which Husserl defined apropos of sciences in general:[2] classical mechanics, for example, *uses* space and time as being each one a homogeneous and continuous milieu, but it never *questions* itself about time or space or motion. In the same way, the sciences of man *do not question themselves* about man; they study the development and the relation of human facts, and man appears as a signifying milieu (determinable by significations) in which particular facts are constituted (such as the structures of a society or a group, the evolution of institutions, etc.). Thus if we take it for granted that experience will give us the complete collection of facts concerning any group whatsoever and that the anthropological disciplines will bind together these facts by means of objective, strictly defined relations, then "human reality" as such will be no more accessible for us than the space of geometry or mechanics—for this fundamental reason, that our research is not aimed at revealing but at constituting laws and at bringing to light functional relations or processes.

But to the degree that anthropology at a certain point in its development perceives that it is denying man (by the systematic rejection of anthropomorphism) or that it takes him for granted (as the ethnologist does at every moment), it implicitly demands to know what is the *being* of human reality. Between an ethnologist or a sociologist—for whom history is too often only the movement which disarranges the lines of division—and a historian—for whom the very permanence of structures is a perpetual change—the essential difference and opposition are derived much less from the diversity of methods than from a more profound contradiction which touches on the very meaning of human reality. If anthropology is to be an organized whole, it must

---

9. That is, Sartre rejects the ideas of a "human essence" and of "human nature" because he conceives of them as necessarily taking the form of a fixed collection of determinations, of a kind and degree of specificity that would be incompatible with the diversity of groups of human beings at any given time and across time. (See also next page.)
1. That is, while Sartre continues to agree with Heidegger that the philosophical analysis of our manner of "existing" is more fundamental than

(because "foundational" in relation to) the various "disciplines which are grouped under the general heading of *anthropology*," he (unlike Heidegger) is now prepared to conceive of existential philosophy as a part of a more comprehensive (philosophical) anthropology that includes this foundational sort of inquiry.
2. See HUSSERL's *Philosophy and the Crisis of European Man* (1935; excerpted above).

surmount this contradiction—the origin of which does not reside in a Knowledge but in reality itself—and it must on its own constitute itself as a structural, historical anthropology.

This task of integration would be easy if one could bring to light some sort of *human essence*; that is, a fixed collection of determinations in terms of which one could assign a definite place to the objects studied. But the majority of anthropologists agree that the diversity of groups—considered from the synchronic point of view—and the diachronic evolution of societies forbid us to found anthropology upon a conceptual knowledge. It would be impossible to find a "human nature" which is common to the Murians,[3] for example, and to the historical man of our contemporary societies. But, conversely, a real communication and in certain situations a reciprocal comprehension are established or can be established between existents thus distinct (for example, between the ethnologist and the young Murians who speak of their *gothul*[4]). It is in order to take into account these two opposed characteristics (no common *nature* but an always possible communication) that the movement of anthropology once again and in a new form gives rise to the "ideology" of existence.

This ideology, in fact, considers that human reality eludes direct knowledge[5] to the degree that it *makes itself*. The determinations of the person appear only in a society which constantly constructs itself by assigning to each of its members a specific work, a relation to the product of his work, and relations of production with the other members—all of this in a never-ceasing movement of totalization. But these determinations are themselves sustained, internalized, and lived (whether in acceptance or refusal) by a *personal project* which has two fundamental characteristics: first, it cannot under any circumstances be defined by concepts; second, as a *human* project it is always *comprehensible* (theoretically if not actually). To make this comprehension *explicit* does not by any means lead us to discover abstract notions, the combination of which could put the comprehension back into conceptual Knowledge; rather it reproduces the dialectic movement which starts from simply existing givens and is raised to signifying activity. This comprehension, which is not distinguished from *praxis*, is at once both immediate existence (since it is produced as the movement of action) and the foundation of an indirect knowing of existence (since it comprehends the ex-istence of the other).

By indirect knowing we mean the result of reflection on existence.[6] This knowing is indirect in this sense—that it is presupposed by all the concepts of anthropology, whatever they may be, without being itself made the object of concepts. Whatever the discipline considered, its most elementary notions would be *incomprehensible* without the *immediate comprehension* of the *project* which underlies them, of negativity as the basis of the project, of transcendence as the existence outside-of-itself in relation with the Other-than-itself

<hr/>

3. The Muria, an aboriginal people of central India.
4. The dormitories in which unmarried young men and women of the Muria live together.
5. That is, "conceptual knowledge," which Sartre takes to be the norm in empirical/theoretical disciplines centering on description and explanation; it cannot yield the kind of "comprehension" or understanding that alone can do justice to human reality, or the "signifying activity" involved in the "projects" that are so central to it.
6. That is, drawing on one's general store of experience and understanding of how actions and expressions relate to the kinds of ends, purposes, intentions, and meanings that people can have for doing things; direct knowledge, in contrast, relies exclusively on empirical observation.

and the Other-than-man, of the surpassing as a mediation between the given that is simply there and the practical signification, of *need*, finally, as the being-outside-of-itself-in-the-world on the part of a practical organism. It is useless to try to disguise this comprehension of the project by a mechanistic positivism, a materialist "Gestaltism." It remains, and it supports the discussion. The dialectic itself—which could not be made the object of concepts because its movement engenders and dissolves them all—appears as History and as historical Reason only upon the foundation of existence; for it is the development of *praxis*, and *praxis* is inconceivable without *need, transcendence*, and the *project*. The very employment of these vocables to designate existence in the structures of its unveiling indicate to us that it is capable of *denotation*. But the relation of the sign or signified cannot be conceived of here in the form of an empirical signification. The signifying movement—inasmuch as language is at once an immediate attitude of each person in relation to all and a human product—is itself a project. This means that the existential project will be in the word which will denote it, not as the signified—which on principle is *outside*—but as its original foundation and its very structure. And of course the very word "language" has a conceptual signification; one part of the language can designate the whole conceptually. But the language is not in the word as the reality providing the basis for all nomination; the contrary is true, and every word is the whole language. The word "project" originally designates a certain human attitude (one "makes" projects) which supposes as its foundation the pro-ject, an existential structure. And this word, as a word, is possible only as a particular effectuation of human reality inasmuch as it is a pro-ject. In this sense the word by itself manifests the project from which it derives only in the way in which the piece of merchandise retains in itself and passes on to us the human work which has produced it.

Yet what is involved is an entirely rational process. In fact the word, although it regressively designates its act, refers to the fundamental comprehension of human reality in each one and in all. This comprehension, always actual, is given in all *praxis* (individual or collective) although not in systematic form. Thus words—even those which do not try to refer regressively to the fundamental, dialectical act—contain a regressive indication referring to the comprehension of that act. And those which try to unveil the existential structures explicitly, are limited to denoting regressively the reflective act inasmuch as it is a structure of existence and a practical operation which existence performs upon itself. The original irrationalism of the Kierkegaardian attempt disappears entirely to give place to anti-intellectualism. The concept, indeed, aims at the object (whether this object be outside man or in him), and precisely for this reason, it is an intellectual *Knowledge*.[7] In language, man designated himself insofar as he is the object of man. But in the effort to recover the source of every sign and consequently of all objectivity, language turns back upon itself to indicate the moments of a comprehension forever in process, since it is nothing other than existence itself. In giving names to these

---

7. That is, the kind of concept employed in cognition on the scientific model. Sartre adds a footnote here: "It would be an error to believe that comprehension refers to the *subjective*. For *subjective* and *objective* are two opposed and complementary characteristics of man *as an object of knowledge*. In fact, the question concerns action itself *qua action*; that is, distinct on principle from the results (objective and subjective) which it engenders."

moments, one does not transform them into *Knowledge*—since this concerns the internal, and what we shall in *Critique of Dialectical Reason*, call the "practico-inert."[8] But one stakes out the comprehensive actualization by means of indications which refer simultaneously to reflective practice and to the content of comprehensive reflection. Need, negativity, surpassing, project, transcendence, form a synthetic totality in which each one of the moments designated contains all the others. Thus the reflective operation—as a particular, dated act—can be indefinitely repeated. Thereby the dialectic develops indefinitely and wholly in each dialectic process, whether it be individual or collective.

But this reflective operation would not need to be repeated and would be transformed into a formal knowledge if its content could exist by itself and be separated from concrete, historical actions, strictly defined by the situation. The true role of the "ideologies of existence" is not to describe an abstract "human reality" which has never existed, but constantly to remind anthropology of the existential dimension of the processes studied. Anthropology studies only objects. Now man is the being by whom becoming-an-object comes to man. Anthropology will deserve its name only if it replaces the study of human objects by the study of the various processes of becoming-an-object. Its role is to found its *knowledge* on rational and comprehensive *non-knowledge*;[9] that is, the historical totalization will be possible only if anthropology understands itself instead of ignoring itself. To understand itself, to understand the other, to exist, to act, are one and the same movement which founds direct, conceptual knowledge upon indirect, comprehensive knowledge but without ever leaving the concrete—that is, history or, more precisely, the one who *comprehends what he knows*.[1] This perpetual dissolution of intellection in comprehension and, conversely, the perpetual redescent which introduces comprehension into intellection as a dimension of *rational non-knowledge* at the heart of knowledge is the very ambiguity of a discipline in which the questioner, the question, and the questioned are one.

These considerations enable us to understand why we can at the same time declare that we are in profound agreement with Marxist philosophy and yet for the present maintain the autonomy of the existential ideology. There is no doubt, indeed, that Marxism appears today to be the only possible anthropology which can be at once historical and structural. It is the only one which at the same time takes man in his totality—that is, in terms of the materiality of his condition. Nobody can propose to it another point of departure, for this would be to offer to it *another man* as the object of its study. It is *inside* the movement of Marxist thought that we discover a flaw of such a sort that despite itself Marxism tends to eliminate the questioner from his investigation and to make of the questioned the object of an absolute Knowledge.[2] The very notions which Marxist research employs to describe our historical society—exploitation, alienation, fetishizing, reification, etc.—are precisely those which most immediately refer to existential structures. The very notion of *praxis* and that of dialectic—inseparably bound together—are contradictory to the intellectualist idea of a knowledge. And to come to the most important point, *labor*, as man's reproduction of his life, can hold no meaning if its fundamental structure is not to pro-ject. In view of this default—which pertains to the historical development and not to the actual principles of the doctrine—existentialism, at the heart of Marxism and taking the same givens, the same Knowledge, as its point of departure, must attempt in its turn—at least as an experiment—the dialectical interpretation of History. It puts nothing in question except a mechanistic determinism which is not exactly Marxist and which has been introduced from the outside into this total philosophy. Existentialism, too, wants to situate man in his class and in the conflicts which oppose him to other classes, starting with the mode and the relations of production. But it can approach this "situation" in terms of *existence*—that is, of comprehension. It makes itself the questioned and the question as questioner; it does not, as Kierkegaard did apropos of Hegel, set the irrational singularity of the individual in opposition to universal Knowledge. But into this very Knowledge and into the universality of concepts, it wants to reintroduce the unsurpassable singularity of the human adventure.

Thus the comprehension of existence[3] is presented as the human foundation of Marxist anthropology. Nevertheless, we must beware here of a confusion heavy with consequences. In fact, in the order of Knowledge, what we know concerning the principle or the foundations of a scientific structure, even when it has come—as is ordinarily the case—later than the empirical determinations, is set forth first; and one deduces from it the determinations of Knowledge in the same way that one constructs a building after having secured its foundations. But this is because the foundation is itself a knowing: and if one can deduce from it certain propositions already guaranteed by experience, this is because one has induced it in terms of them as the most general hypothesis. In contrast, the foundation of Marxism, as a historical, structural anthropology, is man himself inasmuch as human existence and the comprehension of the human are inseparable. Historically Marxist Knowledge produces its foundation at a certain moment of its development, and this foundation is presented in a disguised form. It does not appear as the practical foundations of the theory, but as that which, on principle, pushes forward all theoretical knowing. Thus the singularity of existence is presented in Kierkegaard as that which on principle is kept outside the Hegelian system (that is, outside total Knowledge), as that which can in no way be *thought* but only *lived* in the act of faith. The dialectical procedure to reintegrate existence (which is never *known*) as a foundation at the heart of Knowledge could

---

2. That is, even at its best, "scientific" Marxism suffers from the same defect as other conceptual disciplines: it is too "scientific" and thus "knows" too much but "comprehends" too little of the human reality it is talking about (which includes itself, as a human endeavor).
3. That is, human existing. This endeavor is what

Sartre is here calling "existentialism," but what might better be called (following JASPERS) *Existenzerhellung*—"the elucidation of *Existenz*"— or "existential philosophy," pursued in a manner that is guided by historical understanding as well as lived sensitivity to the first-person-singular character of what it means to exist as a human being.

not be attempted then, since neither of the current attitudes—an idealist Knowledge, a spiritual existence—could lay claim to concrete actualization. These two terms outlined abstractly the future contradiction. And the development of anthropological knowing could not lead then to the synthesis of these formal positions: the movement of ideas—as the movement of society— had first to produce Marxism as the only possible form of a really concrete Knowledge. And as we indicated at the beginning, Marx's own Marxism, while indicating the dialectical opposition between knowing and being, contained implicitly the demand for an existential foundation for the theory. Furthermore, in order for notions like reification and alienation to assume their full meaning, it would have been necessary for the questioner and the questioned to be made one. What must be the nature of human relations in order for these relations to be capable of appearing in certain definite societies as the relations of things to each other? If the reification of human relations is possible, it is because these relations, even if reified, are fundamentally distinct from the relations of things. What kind of practical organism is this which reproduces its life by its work so that its work and ultimately its very reality are alienated; that is, so that they, *as others*, turn back upon him and determine him? But before Marxism, itself a product of the social conflict, could turn to these problems, it had to assume fully its role as a practical philosophy—that is, as a theory clarifying social and political *praxis*. The result is a profound *lack* within contemporary Marxism; the use of the notions mentioned earlier— and many others—refers to a comprehension of human reality which is missing. And this lack is not—as some Marxists declare today—a localized void, a hole in the construction of Knowledge. It is inapprehensible and yet everywhere present; it is a general anemia.

Doubtless this *practical* anemia becomes an anemia in the Marxist man— that is, in us, men of the twentieth century, inasmuch as the unsurpassable framework of Knowledge is Marxism; and inasmuch as this Marxism clarifies our individual and collective *praxis*, it therefore determines us in our existence. About 1949 numerous posters covered the walls in Warsaw: "Tuberculosis slows down production." They were put there as the result of some decision on the part of the government, and this decision originated in a very good intention. But their content shows more clearly than anything else the extent to which man has been eliminated from an anthropology which wants to be pure knowledge. Tuberculosis is an object of a practical Knowledge: the physician learns to know it in order to cure it; the Party determines its importance in Poland by statistics. Other mathematical calculations connecting these with production statistics (quantitative variations in production for each industrial group in proportion to the number of cases of tuberculosis) will suffice to obtain a law of the type $y=f(x)$, in which tuberculosis plays the role of independent variable. But this law, the same one which could be read on the propaganda posters, reveals a new and double alienation by totally eliminating the tubercular man, by refusing to him even the elementary role of *mediator* between the disease and the number of manufactured products. In a socialist society, at a certain moment in its development, the worker is alienated from his production; in the theoretical-practical order, the human foundation of anthropology is submerged in Knowledge.

It is precisely this expulsion of man, his exclusion from Marxist Knowledge, which resulted in the renascence of existentialist thought outside the historical totalization of Knowledge. Human science is frozen in the non-human, and human-reality seeks to understand itself outside of science. But this time the opposition comes from those who directly demand their synthetic transcendence. Marxism will degenerate into a non-human anthropology if it does not reintegrate man into itself as its foundation. But this comprehension, which is nothing other than existence itself, is disclosed at the same time by the historical movement of Marxism, by the concepts which indirectly clarify it (alienation, etc.), and by the new alienations which give birth to the contradictions of socialist society and which reveal to it its abandonment; that is, the incommensurability of existence and practical Knowledge. The movement can *think* itself only in Marxist terms and can *comprehend* itself only as an alienated existence, as a human-reality made into a thing. The moment which will surpass this opposition must reintegrate comprehension into Knowledge as its non-theoretical foundation.

In other words, the foundation of anthropology is man himself, not as the object of practical Knowledge, but as a practical organism producing Knowledge as a moment of its *praxis*. And the reintegration of man as a concrete existence into the core of anthropology, as its constant support, appears necessarily as a stage in the process of philosophy's "becoming-the-world." In this sense the foundation of anthropology cannot precede it (neither historically nor logically). If *existence*, in its free comprehension of itself, preceded the awareness of alienation or of exploitation, it would be necessary to suppose that the free development of the practical organism historically preceded its present fall and captivity. (And if this were established, the historical precedence would scarcely advance us in our comprehension, since the retrospective study of vanished societies is made today with the enlightenment furnished by techniques for reconstruction and by means of the alienations which enchain us.) Or, if one insisted on a logical priority, it would be necessary to suppose that the freedom of the project could be recovered in its full reality *underneath* the alienations of our society and that one could move dialectically from the concrete existence which understands its freedom to the various alterations which distort it in present society. This hypothesis is absurd. To be sure, man can be enslaved only if he is free. But for the historical man who *knows* himself and *comprehends* himself, this practical freedom is grasped only as the permanent, concrete condition of his servitude; that is, across that servitude and by means of it as that which makes it possible, as its foundation. Thus Marxist Knowledge bears on the alienated man; but if it doesn't want to make a fetish of its knowing and to dissolve man in the process of knowing his alienations, then it is not enough to describe the working of capital or the system of colonization. It is necessary that the questioner understand how the questioned—that is, himself—*exists his alienation*, how he surpasses it and is alienated in this very surpassing. It is necessary that his very thought should at every instant surpass the intimate contradiction which unites the comprehension of man-as-agent with the knowing of man-as-object and that it forge new concepts, new determinations of Knowledge which emerge from the existential comprehension and which regulate the movement of their contents by its dialectical procedure. Yet this comprehension—as a living movement of the practical organism—can take place

only within a concrete situation, insofar as theoretical Knowledge illuminates and interprets this situation.

Thus the autonomy of existential studies[4] results necessarily from the negative qualities of Marxists (and not from Marxism itself). So long as the doctrine does not recognize its anemia, so long as it founds its Knowledge upon
a dogmatic metaphysics (a dialectic[s] of Nature) instead of seeking its support
in the comprehension of the living man, so long as it rejects as irrational those
ideologies which wish, as Marx did, to separate being from Knowledge and,
in anthropology, to found the knowing of man on human existence, existentialism will follow its own path of study. This means that it will attempt to
clarify the givens of Marxist Knowledge by indirect knowing (that is, as we
have seen, by words which regressively denote existential structures), and to
engender within the framework of Marxism a veritable *comprehensive knowing* which will rediscover man in the social world and which will follow him
in his *praxis*—or, if you prefer, in the project which throws him toward the
social possibles in terms of a defined situation. Existentialism will appear
therefore as a fragment of the system, which has fallen outside of Knowledge.
From the day that Marxist thought will have taken on the human dimension
(that is, the existential project) as the foundation of anthropological Knowledge, existentialism will no longer have any reason for being. Absorbed, surpassed and conserved by the totalizing movement of philosophy, it will cease
to be a particular inquiry and will become the foundation of all inquiry. The
comments which we have made in the course of the present essay are
directed—to the modest limit of our capabilities—toward hastening the
moment of that dissolution.

SOURCE: From Jean-Paul Sartre, *Search for a Method*, trans. Hazel E. Barnes (New York:
Alfred A. Knopf, 1963), pp. xiv–xxxv, 85, 91–95, 97–99, 150–52, 157, 159, 167–81. Asked to
contribute an article to a Polish journal on "the situation of existentialism in 1957" for a special issue on French culture, Sartre instead wrote "Existentialism and Marxism," situating
"existentialism" in relation to the kind of Marxism that was then the dominant ideology in
Poland and elsewhere in Eastern Europe (and seeking to express the contradictions in that
Marxism). A revised version was published in *Les Temps modernes*, and then incorporated into
his *Critique of Dialectical Reason* (1960) as a "prefatory essay" titled "Question de méthode."
This essay is the version translated by Barnes.

From Critique of Dialectical Reason

From *Introduction*

* * *

THE PLAN OF THIS WORK

If History is totalisation and if individual practices are the sole ground of totalising temporalisation, it is not enough to reveal the totalisation developing in

---

4. That is, of philosophical inquiry into human existing.

everyone, and consequently in our critical investigations, through the contradictions which both express and mask it.[1] Our critical investigation must also show us *how* the practical multiplicity (which may be called 'men' or 'Humanity' according to taste) realises, in its very dispersal, its interiorisation. In addition, we must exhibit the dialectical necessity of this totalising process. Indeed, the multiplicity of dialectical agents (that is, of individuals producing a *praxis*) seems at first sight to involve a second-order atomism, through the multiplicity of totalisations. If this were so, we should return on a new level, to the atomism of analytical Reason. But since our starting point is individual *praxis*, we must carefully follow up every one of those threads of Ariadne[2] which lead from this *praxis*, to the various forms of human ensembles;[3] and in each case we shall have to determine the structures of these ensembles, their real mode of formation out of their elements, and finally their totalising action upon the elements which formed them. But it will never be sufficient to show the production of ensembles by individuals or by one another, nor, conversely, to show how individuals are produced by the ensembles which they compose. It will be necessary to show the dialectical intelligibility of these transformations in every case.

Of course, this is a matter of *formal* intelligibility. By this I mean that we must understand the bonds between *praxis*, as self-conscious, and all the complex multiplicities which are organised through it and in which it loses itself as *praxis* in order to become *praxis-process*. However—and I shall have occasion to repeat this still more emphatically—it is no part of my intention to determine the concrete history of these incarnations of *praxis*. In particular, as we shall see later, the practical individual enters into ensembles of very different kinds, for example, into what are called *groups* and what I shall call *series*.[4] It is no part of our project to determine whether series precede groups or vice versa, either originally or in a particular moment of History. On the contrary: as we shall see, groups are born of series and often end up by realising themselves in their turn. So the *only* thing which matters to us is to display the transition from series to groups and from groups to series as constant incarnations of our practical multiplicity, and to test the dialectical intelligibility of these reversible processes. In the same way, when we study class and class-being (*l'être de classe*) we shall find ourselves drawing examples from the history of the working class. But the purpose will not be to define the particular class which is known as the proletariat: our sole aim will be to seek the constitution of a class in these examples, its totalising (and detotalising) function and its dialectical intelligibility (bonds of interiority and of exteriority,

---

1. Sartre had already begun to use the term "totalisation" (spelled the same way in his French) in *Search for a Method* (above), and uses it extensively in this work, applying it on many levels of human reality—individual, social, and even (as here) historical. Human history is a totalisation phenomenon for him because human reality is itself such a phenomenon, through and through. Totalisation here refers to the internal and objective processes associated with complex human entities and formations of various sorts (e.g., individuals, groups, institutions, cultural phenomena) through which their diverse component elements are coordinated and integrated into functional (and functioning) units or "totalities."
2. In Greek mythology, the daughter of Minos; the

hero Theseus was able to escape the labyrinth of the Minotaur because she had given him a ball of thread to unroll as he went. *Praxis*: practical concrete (human) activity.
3. That is, human groups and collectivities of various sorts; part I of this work focuses on the "theory" of human ensembles.
4. Sartre uses the term "series" to refer to the sort of human ensemble or collection of human beings who do not share a group identity and self-identification but do share a set of circumstances and understandings in loosely rule-governed situations that structures their actions and interactions, giving their ensemble a merely external sort of unity and identity.

interior structures, relations to other classes, etc.). In short, we are dealing with neither human history, nor sociology, nor ethnography. To parody a title of Kant's, we would claim, rather, to be laying the foundations for 'Prolegomena to any future anthropology'.[5]

If our critical investigation actually yields positive results, we shall have established *a priori*—and not, as the Marxists *think* they have done, *a posteriori*—the heuristic value of the dialectical method when applied to the human sciences, and the necessity, with any fact, provided it is *human*, of reinserting it within the developing totalisation and understanding it on this basis. Thus the critical investigation will always present itself as a double investigation: *if* totalisation exists, the investigation will supply us with, *on the one hand* (and in the regressive order), all the *means* brought into play by the totalisation, that is to say the partial totalisations, detotalisations and retotalisations in their functions and abstract structures and, *on the other hand*, it must enable us to see how these forms dialectically generate one another in the full intelligibility of *praxis*. Moreover, in so far as our investigation proceeds from the simple to the complex, from the abstract to the concrete, from the constituting to the constituted, we must be able to settle, without reference to concrete history, the incarnations of individual *praxis*, the formal structural conditions of its alienations[6] and the abstract circumstances which encourage the constitution of a common *praxis*. This leads to the principal divisions of this first volume: *the constituent dialectic* (as it grasps itself in its abstract translucidity in individual *praxis*) finds its limit within its own work and is transformed into an *anti-dialectic*. This anti-dialectic, or dialectic against the dialectic (dialectic *of passivity*), must reveal *series* to us as a type of human gathering and alienation as a mediated relation to the other and to the objects of labour in the element of seriality and as a serial mode of co-existence.[7] At this level we will discover an equivalence between alienated *praxis* and worked inertia, and we shall call the domain of this equivalence the *practico-inert*.[8] And we shall see the group emerge as a second type of dialectical gathering, in opposition both to the *practico-inert* and to impotence. But I shall distinguish, as will be seen, between the constituted dialectic and the constituent dialectic to the extent that the group has to constitute its common *praxis* through the individual *praxis* of the agents of whom it is composed. Therefore, if there is to be any such thing as totalisation, the intelligibility of constituted dialectical Reason (the intelligibility of common actions

5. That is, any future study of human reality (whether social-scientific or philosophical). Sartre is playing off the title of KANT's *Prolegomena to Any Future Metaphysics* (1783).
6. This means: the dialectical investigations of alienation as an *a priori possibility* of human *praxis* on the basis of the *real* alienations to be found in concrete History. It would indeed be inconceivable that human activity should be *alienated* or that human relations should be capable of being *reified* if there were no such thing as alienation and reification in the *practical* relation of the agent to the object of his act and to other agents. Neither the unsituated freedom of certain idealists, nor the Hegelian relation of consciousness to itself, nor the mechanistic determinism of certain pseudo-Marxists can account for it. It is in the concrete and synthetic relation of the agent to the other

through the mediation of the thing, and to the thing through the mediation of the other, that we shall be able to discover the foundations of all possible alienation [Sartre's note].
7. Obviously alienation is a much more complex phenomenon and its conditions, as we shall see, are present at all levels of experience. Nevertheless we must here indicate its ground. For example, alienation exists as a constant danger within the practical group. But this is intelligible only in so far as the most lively and united group is always in danger of relapsing into the series from which it came [Sartre's note].
8. Sartre's coinage, referring to the material world as worked matter (the product of earlier praxis), which includes features reflecting the human structures involved.

and of *praxis*-process) must be based on constituent dialectical reason (the abstract and individual *praxis* of man at work). Within the context of our critical investigation, we shall be able at this point to define the limits of dialectical intelligibility and, by the same token, the specific meaning of totalisation. It may then appear that realities such as class, for example, do not have a unique and homogeneous kind of being, but rather that they exist and they create themselves on all levels at once, through a more complex totalisation than we expected (since the anti-dialectic must be integrated and totalised, but not destroyed, by the constituted dialectic which, in turn, can totalise only on the basis of a constituent dialectic).

At this level, it will become evident that the regressive investigation has reached bedrock. In other words, we shall have grasped our individual depth in so far as, through the movement of groups and series, our roots reach down to fundamental materiality. Every moment of the regress will seem more complex and general than the isolated, superficial moment of our individual *praxis*, yet from another point of view, it remains completely abstract, that is, it is still no more than a *possibility*. Indeed, whether we consider the relations between group and series formally, in so far as each of these ensembles may produce the other, or whether we grasp the individual, within our investigation, as the practical ground of an ensemble and the ensemble as producing the individual in his reality as historical agent, this formal procedure will lead us to a dialectical circularity. This circularity exists; it is even (for Engels as much as for Hegel[9]) characteristic of the dialectical order and of its intelligibility. But the fact remains that reversible circularity is in contradiction with the irreversibility of History, as it appears to investigation. Though it is true in the abstract that groups and series can indifferently produce each other, it is also true that historically a particular group, through its serialisation, produces a given serial ensemble (or conversely) and that, if a new group originated in the serial ensemble, then, whatever it might be, it would be irreducible to the serial ensemble. Moreover, such a regressive investigation, though it brings certain conflicts into play, only reveals our underlying structures and their intelligibility, without revealing the dialectical relations between groups and series, between different series or between different groups.

Thus, dialectical investigation in its regressive moment will reveal to us no more than the static conditions of the possibility of a totalisation, that is to say, of a history. We must therefore proceed to the opposite and complementary investigation: by progressively recomposing the historical process on the basis of the shifting and contradictory relations of the formations in question, we shall experience History; and this dialectical investigation should be able to show us whether the contradictions and social struggles, the communal and individual *praxis*, labour as producing tools, and tools as producing men and as regulator of human labour and human relations, etc., make up the unity of an intelligible (and thus directed) totalising movement. But above all, though these discoveries have to be made and consolidated in relation to these particular examples, our critical investigation aims to recompose the intelligibility of the historical movement within which the different ensembles are defined by their conflicts. On the basis of synchronic structures and

9. For ENGELS and for HEGEL, see above.

their contradictions, it seeks the diachronic intelligibility of historical transformations, the order of their conditionings and the intelligible reason for the irreversibility of History, that is to say, for its direction. This synthetic progression, though merely formal, must fulfil[l] several functions: by recomposing instances in terms of process, it must lead us, if not to the absolute concrete, which can only be individual (*this* event at *this* date of *this* history), at least to the absolute system of conditions for applying the determination '*concrete* fact' to the fact of *one* history.

In this sense it could be said that the aim of the critical investigation is to establish a structural and historical anthropology, that the regressive moment of the investigation is the basis of the intelligibility of sociological Knowledge (without prejudging any of the individual components of this Knowledge), and that the progressive moment must be the basis of the intelligibility of historical Knowledge (without prejudging the real individual unfolding of the totalised facts). Naturally, the progression will deal with the same structures as those brought to light by regressive investigation. Its sole concern will be to rediscover the moments of their inter-relations, the ever vaster and more complex movement which totalises them and, finally, the very direction of the totalisation, that is to say, the 'meaning of History' and its Truth. The multiple, fundamental bonds between the constituent dialectic and the constituted dialectic and vice versa through the constant mediation of the anti-dialectic, will become clear to us in the course of these new investigations. If the results of the investigation are positive, we shall finally be in a position to define dialectical Reason as the constituent and constituted reason of practical multiplicities. We shall then understand the meaning of totalisation—a totalising meaning, or a de-totalised totalisation—and we shall finally be able to prove the strict equivalence between *praxis* with its particular articulations and the dialectic as the logic of creative action, that is to say, in the final analysis, as the logic of freedom.

Volume I of the *Critique of Dialectical Reason* stops as soon as we reach the 'locus of history'; it is solely concerned with finding the intelligible foundations for a structural anthropology—to the extent, of course, that these synthetic structures are the condition of a directed, developing totalisation. Volume II, which will follow shortly,[1] will retrace the stages of the critical progression: it will attempt to establish that there is *one* human history, with *one* truth and *one* intelligibility—not by considering the material content of this history, but by demonstrating that a practical multiplicity, whatever it may be, must unceasingly totalise itself through interiorising its multiplicity at all levels.

THE INDIVIDUAL AND HISTORY

The locus of our critical investigation is none other than the fundamental identity between an individual life and human history (or, from the methodological point of view, the 'reciprocity of their perspectives'). Strictly speaking, the identity of these two totalising processes must itself be proved. But

1. It was never completed; the unfinished volume was published after Sartre's death as *The Intelligibility of History* (1985).

in fact critical investigation proceeds from exactly this hypothesis and each moment of the regression (and, later, of the progression) directly calls it into question. The continuity of the regression would be interrupted at every level if ontological identity and methodological reciprocity did not in fact always appear both as fact and as necessary and intelligible Truth. In reality, the hypothesis which makes the critical investigation feasible is precisely the one which the investigation aims to prove. If there is a dialectic we must submit to it as the unavoidable discipline of the totalisation which totalises *us* and grasp it, in its free practical spontaneity, as the totalising *praxis* which we are; at each stage in our investigation we must rediscover, within the intelligible unity of the synthetic movement, the contradiction and indissoluble connection between necessity and freedom, though, at each moment, this connection appears in different forms. In any case, if my life, as it deepens, becomes History, it must reveal itself, at a deep level of its free development, as the strict necessity of the historical process so as to rediscover itself at an even deeper level, as the freedom of this necessity and, finally, as the necessity of freedom.

The critical investigation will reveal this interplay of aspects in so far as the totaliser is always also the totalised, even if, as we shall see, he is the Prince in person. And, if the investigation is successful, and we reveal the rocky sub-soil of necessity beneath the translucidity of free individual *praxis*, we will be able to hope that we have taken the right track. Then we shall be able to glimpse what these two volumes together will try to prove: that *necessity*, as the apodictic structure of dialectical investigation, resides neither in the free development of interiority nor in the inert dispersal of exteriority; it asserts itself, as an inevitable and irreducible moment, in the interiorisation of the exterior and in the exteriorisation of the interior. This double movement will be that of our entire regressive investigation: a thorough examination of individual *praxis* will show us that it interiorises the exterior (in delimiting, through action itself, a practical field); but conversely, we shall grasp in the tool and in objectification through labour an intentional exteriorisation of interiority (of which a *seal* is both the symbol and the example); similarly, the movement by which the practical life of the individual must, in the course of the investigation, dissolve itself into sociological or historical totalisations, does not preserve the translucid interiority of the totalising agent in the new form, which appears as the objective reality of life (series, group, system, process). To put it more vividly if less precisely, it is *initially within itself* that free subjectivity discovers its objectivity as the intelligible necessity of being a perspective within totalisations which totalise it (which integrate it in synthetic developing forms). Subjectivity then appears, in all its abstraction, as the verdict which compels us to carry out, freely and through ourselves, the sentence that a 'developing' society has pronounced upon us and which defines us *a priori* in our being. This is the level at which we shall encounter the practico-inert.

However, it must be understood that *praxis* presupposes a material agent (the organic individual) and the material organisation of an operation on and by matter. Thus we shall never find men who are not mediated by matter at the same time as they mediate different material regions. A practical multiplicity is a certain relation of matter to itself through the mediation of the *praxis* which transforms the inert into worked matter, just as the collection of objects which surrounds us imposes its mediation on the practical multiplicity which totalises us. Thus, the history of man is an adventure of nature, not only because man is a material organism with material needs, but also because worked matter, as an exteriorisation of interiority, produces man, who produces or uses this worked matter in so far as he is forced to re-interiorise the exteriority of his product, in the totalising movement of the multiplicity which totalises it. The *external* unification of the inert, whether by the seal or by law, and the introduction of inertia at the heart of *praxis* both result, as we have seen, in producing necessity as a strict determination at the heart of human relations. And the totalisation which controls me, in so far as I discover it within my free lived totalisation, only takes the form of necessity for two fundamental reasons: first, the totalisation which totalises me has to make use of the mediation of inert products of labour; second, a practical multiplicity must *always* confront its own external inertia, that is to say, its character as a discrete quantity. We shall see that the interiorisation of number is not always possible and that, when it does take place, quantity produces in each member of a group a thick layer of inertia (exteriority within interiority), though it is lived dialectically in interiority. Consequently, the problem of necessity, which is immediately given as a structure of our critical investigation, necessarily leads us to the fundamental problem of anthropology, that is, to the relations of practical organisms to inorganic matter. We must never lose sight of the fact that exteriority, (that is to say, quantity, or, in other words, Nature), is, for every multiplicity of agents, a threat both from without and from within (we shall see its role in the anti-dialectic), and that it is both the permanent means and the profound occasion for totalisation. We shall also see that it is the *essence* of man in the sense that essence, as transcended past, is inert and becomes the transcended objectification of the practical agent (thus producing within everyone and within every multiplicity the continually resolved and constantly renewed contradiction between man-as-producer and man-as-product).[2] In the second volume we will also learn that exteriority is the inert motive force of History in that it is the only possible basis for the *novelty* which places its seal on it and which it preserves both as an irreducible moment and as a memory of Humanity. Whether as inert motive force or as creative memory, inorganic matter (always organised by us) is never absent from the history of our organic materialities; it is the condition of exteriority, interiorised so as to make history possible, and this fundamental condition is the absolute requirement *that there must be* a necessity in History at the very heart of intelligibility—and perpetually dissolved in the movement of practical understanding. Thus, our critical investigation must present us with apodicticity as the indissoluble unity—at every totalising and totalised level—of the organic and the inorganic through all the forms that this connection can assume (from the presence of the inorganic within the organism itself and all around it, up to and including the organisation of the inorganic

2. The objectification of man places a seal on the inert. Thus, a transcended objectification, in so far as it is the space of the practical man, is, in the last analysis, a robot. In the strange world which we are describing the robot is the essence of man: he freely transcends himself towards the future, but he thinks of himself as a robot as soon as he looks back on his past. He *comes to know himself in the inert* and is therefore a victim of his reified image, even prior to all alienation [Sartre's note].

and the presence of number as pure exteriority within number interiorised by organised practical multiplicity). It is in this way that we rediscover the schema of the critical investigation. In the regressive moment, we shall find the constituent dialectic, the anti-dialectic and the constituted dialectic. And in the moment of synthetic progression, we shall trace the totalising movement which integrates these three partial movements within a total totalisation. On this basis we shall be able to put the question of *possibility* in history (and, in general, in *praxis*), and of historical *necessity* in its true light. It is thus in this progressive moment that we shall finally understand our original problem: what is Truth as the *praxis* of synthetic unification, and what is History? Why is there such a thing as human history (ethnography having acquainted us with societies with no history)? And what is the *practical* meaning of historical totalisation in so far as it can reveal itself today to a (totalising and totalised) agent situated within History in development?

* * *

SOURCE: From Jean-Paul Sartre, *Critique of Dialectical Reason: Theory of Practical Ensembles*, trans. Alan Sheridan-Smith, ed. Jonathan Rée (London: NLB; Atlantic Highlands, N.J.: Humanities Press, 1976), pp. 64–74. First published in 1960 as *Critique de la raison dialectique*, vol. 1, *Théorie des ensembles pratiques*. This introduction was preceded by the "prefatory essay" translated separately as *Search for a Method* (see the previous selection).

MAURICE MERLEAU-PONTY
(1908 – 1961)

Merleau-Ponty is often assumed to be an existentialist in the mold of SARTRE because he was closely associated with Sartre for a considerable time, and both were French phenomenologists centrally interested in human reality. But he was by no means a Sartrean existentialist, and their phenomenologies and analyses of human reality differed greatly from the outset.

Maurice Merleau-Ponty ("Mare-LOW-pawn-TEE") was born in Rochefort-sur-Mer, France. He was very young when his father was killed in the First World War. His education began in the lycées (French secondary schools) Janson-de-Sailly and Louis-le-Grande, and continued (1926–30) at the École Normale Supérieure. Sartre was one of his classmates there, but they were not particularly close. Unlike Sartre, who was vehemently anti-religious, Merleau-Ponty was an active Catholic. The professors most important to him were the Neo-Kantian Léon Brunschvicg and the sociologist Georges Gurvitch; he also attended Alexandre Kojève's famous lectures on HEGEL and worked on a Catholic journal. Following his graduation he taught for nearly a decade at lycées in Beauvais, Chartres, and Paris, and then briefly served in the French infantry at the outset of the Second World War.

After France fell and the Franco-German Armistice was signed in June 1940, Merleau-Ponty returned to teaching—and he also became active in the resistance to the German occupation. He (along with Sartre and Albert Camus) belonged to a resistance group called "Socialism and Liberty"; and though its activities were mainly of the pen rather than the sword, they nevertheless were at risk. During these years, Merleau-Ponty wrote two of his most important books: The Structure of Behav-ior (1942) and Phenomenology of Perception (1945). On the strength of the former, he obtained a faculty appointment at the University of Lyons after the liberation of France. The publication of the latter established him as one of the leading French philosophers of his generation, along with Sartre, whose Being and Nothingness had appeared just two years earlier.

Their association during the German occupation had drawn Merleau-Ponty and Sartre together, and from 1945 to 1952 they were co-editors of Les Temps modernes (Modern Times), a journal founded by Sartre. In 1948 they helped establish a new political party, the Rassemblement Démocratique Révolutionnarie (Democratic Revolutionary Rally). In 1949 Merleau-Ponty was offered and accepted a position at the Sorbonne in Paris as a professor of child psychology and pedagogy, and in 1952 he became the youngest person to hold the chair of philosophy at the distinguished Collège de France. During the next few years his relations with Sartre became increasingly strained. They differed greatly in political temperament, as Merleau-Ponty's 1947 book Humanism and Terror had already made clear; and their heated differences over Marxism and the Communist Party, recounted in his book Adventures of the Dialectic (1955), led to a complete and enduring break.

Though not a disciple, Merleau-Ponty was strongly influenced by HUSSERL, and in particular by his reading of Husserl's voluminous late manuscripts, to which he obtained early access. He was deeply interested in issues and empirical research relating to human development (as his first appointment at the Sorbonne demonstrates), as well as in social, cultural, and linguistic theory. He also influenced the development of structuralism in France through his personal connections to Claude Lévi-Strauss and Ferdinand de Saussure. The arts were another of his interests, both aesthetically and as forms of expression and experience. His sudden and unexpected death in 1961, at the age of only 53, was a great blow to the development of French philosophy in the 1960s—a critical decade for it and for the interpretive tradition more generally.

Merleau-Ponty began by focusing primarily on human reality, seeking to work out an account that would do greater justice to it than either the naturalisms and empiricisms or the idealisms and intellectualisms that he took to be the dominant tendencies in the European philosophical world in the 1930s. He was attracted by the idea of a phenomenology that would be guided by the principle of fidelity to the character and content of our experience as human beings living our lives in the world—an attraction shared by HEIDEGGER and Sartre, and in his view by the late Husserl as well. However, he believed that a different way of conceptualizing and approaching this task was needed in order to bring our human reality properly into focus. The works excerpted below were steps in that direction. Toward the end of his life he was expanding and adjusting his focus further as he sought to fashion a new kind of account of the larger reality in which we experientially find ourselves, but his untimely death left that task barely begun.

Merleau-Ponty's version of phenomenology is distinguished from many others by his readiness to take empirical studies of human phenomena very seriously, even as he resists the scientistic naturalism so often associated with them. In developing his rich and distinctive conceptions of *embodiment* and *perception*—ideas that figure centrally in his thinking—he draws on both empirical and experiential perspectives. His concern is to avoid and overcome mind–body dualisms without succumbing to reductionism in either direction. Scientistic naturalism fails to do justice to the

subjectivity of human embodiment, while what Merleau-Ponty calls "intellectualism" (which would seem to include the position of Husserl, at least in his published writings, as well as that of the Neo-Kantians) fails to do justice to the embodiment of human subjectivity.

Human reality for Merleau-Ponty is not only "being-in-the-world" (even though it certainly has that character); it is also "being-in-the-body-in-the-world." In fact, even that characterization does not go far enough: it would be better to say that for him our embodiment is less a matter of "being-in-the-body" than of "being-the-body"—and yet not being identical with the body as an empirically analyzable object. The body as the medium of our embodied being-in-the-world is the *lived* body—the body that is our ways of perceiving, feeling, moving, acting, expressing, being with others, and doing and experiencing everything else that we do and experience. The body of our embodiment is reducible to neither subjectivity nor objectivity, and to neither consciousness nor physicality: it is the nexus of all such abstract conceptualizations of our living human reality.

Merleau-Ponty conceives of perception in a similar way. His "phenomenology of perception" is in effect his phenomenology of human reality as it is lived, experienced, and carried on in movement, action, and expression. Though nominally in the new tradition of Husserl, it actually is more strongly suggestive of the tradition of Hegel's "phenomenology of *Geist*" and of Hegel's reinterpretation of human reality in his work of that title. For Merleau-Ponty, perception is not simply one type of process or relation involving our senses and our minds. Rather, it is our presence to our world and its presence to us, in all of the modes of engagement and detachment of which we are capable. Far from being just a mental or conscious phenomenon that goes on in our heads, it is the basic form of all embodied subjectivity, and thus is inseparable from Merleau-Ponty's conception of embodiment. Like embodiment, perception is more fundamental than all reflection, cognition, and linguistic articulation, although the development of the latter capacities affects how embodiment and perception play out in human life and cannot be reduced to a mere elaboration of their primordial practical character and structure.

The body thus looms much larger in Merleau-Ponty's thinking than it does in the phenomenological and existential thought of Husserl, Heidegger, and Sartre (not to mention KIERKEGAARD and JASPERS). In this respect he is closer than any of them to NIETZSCHE. And like Nietzsche, he recognized that "the body" needs to be fundamentally reconsidered even as it is being moved to the center of our thinking about ourselves, just as the status of everything else about ourselves— including everything "mental" and "spiritual"—needs to be reconsidered in their relation to it. He further recognized, again like Nietzsche, that to this end a great many perspectives on the body and the bodily need to be cultivated and brought into play. In company with Husserl and the existential phenomenologists he had inspired, on the other hand, Merleau-Ponty accorded interpretive primacy to those perspectives that are attuned to the perceptual-practical experiential character of the "lived body."

These very themes and priorities posed challenges for Merleau-Ponty, owing to the need to work out their implications for our understanding of the interpersonal, linguistic, cultural, social, and historical dimensions of human reality, and of their significance for the kind of account he was developing around the conceptions of perception and embodiment. He was all the more sensitive to this question because it had posed the greatest of difficulties for Husserl and for the version of phenomenology developed in his published writings. In his own later writings, Merleau-Ponty appeared to have been modifying his commitment to "the primacy of perception," to the centrality of the model of "embodied subjectivity" in the understanding of human reality, and to a phe-

nomenological account of it, as he sought to find a more satisfactory way of dealing with these matters. Had he lived to complete The Visible and the Invisible (only a few of its chapters had been drafted at the time of his death), we would have a better sense of those changes. As in the cases of Heidegger and Sartre, however, his earlier thought might still be regarded as his greatest and most enduring accomplishment.

His indebtedness to Husserlian phenomenology notwithstanding, Merleau-Ponty could just as appropriately be grouped with the adherents of the project of a "philosophical anthropology" with whom the next part of this volume begins. Like its two founding figures MAX SCHELER and HELMUTH PLESSNER, he began as a Husserlian phenomenologist— and he kept one foot on phenomenological ground even as he stepped beyond it with the other (toward the human sciences in particular) in an attempt to develop an account of human reality informed by the perspectives and conceptual-methodological tools of the latter as well as the former. For this reason he might be regarded as a transitional thinker, between the other figures in this part of the volume and those in the next, who are further beyond or outside of the phenomenological movement.

Phenomenology began as a reaction against the naturalistic ways of conceiving of human experience, knowledge, and value that were becoming increasingly popular in European philosophy in the late nineteenth and early twentieth centuries. That reaction led to existential philosophy, while those naturalistic tendencies led to the positivism and scientism with which it came to be locked in mortal combat. In Merleau-Ponty we can see the bridging and healing process already under way— or at least foreshadowed, since yet another chasm was about to open, as existential philosophy gave way to poststructuralism and related developments. But the path he tried to walk remained and remains open, even if new bridges may need to be built along the way.

From The Structure of Behavior

From *Introduction*

Our goal is to understand the relations of consciousness and nature: organic, psychological or even social. By nature we understand here a multiplicity of events external to each other and bound together by relations of causality.

* * *

Thus, among contemporary thinkers in France, there exist side by side a philosophy, on the one hand, which makes of every nature an objective unity constituted vis-à-vis consciousness and, on the other, sciences which treat the organism and consciousness as two orders of reality and, in their reciprocal relation, as "effects" and as "causes." Is the solution to be found in a pure and simple return to critical thought? And once the criticism of realistic analysis and causal thinking has been made, is there nothing justified in the naturalism of science—nothing which, "understood" and transposed, ought to find a place in a transcendental philosophy?[1]

We will come to these questions by starting "from below" and by an analysis of the notion of behavior. This notion seems important to us because, taken in itself, it is neutral with respect to the classical distinctions between the "mental" and the "physiological" and thus can give us the opportunity of defining them anew. It is known that in Watson,[2] following the classical antinomy, the negation of consciousness as "internal reality" is made to the benefit of physiology; behavior is reduced to the sum of reflexes and conditioned reflexes between which no intrinsic connection is admitted. But precisely this atomistic interpretation fails even at the level of the theory of the reflex (Chapter I) and all the more so in the psychology—even the objective psychology—of higher levels of behavior (Chapter II), as Gestalt theory[3] has clearly shown. By going through behaviorism, however, one gains at least in being able to introduce consciousness, not as psychological reality or as cause, but as structure. It will remain for us to investigate (Chapter III) the meaning and the mode of existence of these structures.

---

1. Merleau-Ponty saw himself as taking up the project of a Husserlian phenomenology, which HUSSERL had characterized as a "transcendental" philosophy in opposition both to the various forms of materialism and naturalism that were gaining a considerable following and to the forms of speculative and historicist philosophy in the Hegelian tradition that continued to find favor. Merleau-Ponty here invokes KANT's idea of the transcendence of the subject of experience in relation to all actual and possible objects and modes of experience, and its Husserlian elaboration into a philoso-phy that treats all conceivable reality as what he later calls in this book an "object of consciousness" (see below, "Is There Not a Truth of Naturalism?").

2. John B. Watson (1878–1958), American psychologist; he was largely responsible for the dominance of the behaviorist school of psychological theory and research in the United States in the 1920s and '30s.

3. A school of psychology, developed in the early 20th century, that made use of phenomenology in emphasizing the whole rather than its parts.

From *Chapter III*
The Physical Order; the Vital Order; the Human Order

* * *

FROM THE HUMAN ORDER[4]

In describing the physical or organic individual and its milieu, we have been led to accept the fact that their relations were not mechanical, but dialectical.[5] A mechanical action, whether the word is taken in a restricted or looser sense, is one in which the cause and the effect are decomposable into real elements which have a one-to-one correspondence. In elementary actions, the dependence is uni-directional; the cause is the necessary and sufficient condition of the effect considered in its existence and its nature; and, even when one speaks of reciprocal action between two terms, it can be reduced to a series of uni-directional determinations. On the contrary, as we have seen, physical stimuli act upon the organism only by eliciting a global response which will vary qualitatively when the stimuli vary quantitatively; with respect to the organism they play the role of occasions rather than of cause; the reaction depends on their vital significance rather than on the material properties of the stimuli. Hence, between the variables upon which conduct actually depends and this conduct itself there appears a relation of meaning, an intrinsic relation. One cannot assign a moment in which the world acts on the organism, since the very effect of this "action" expresses the internal law of the organism. The mutual exteriority of the organism and the milieu is surmounted along with the mutual exteriority of the stimuli. Thus, two correlatives must be substituted for these two terms defined in isolation: the "milieu" and the "aptitude," which are like two poles of behavior and participate in the same structure.

It is this intrinsic connection which Bergson expresses when he finds in instinct a relation of "sympathy" with its object,[6] or Koehler[7] when he writes that each part of a form "dynamically knows" the other parts. In speaking here of knowledge and consequently of consciousness, we are not constructing a metaphysics of nature; we are limiting ourselves to denominating the relations of the milieu and the organism as science itself defines them as they should be denominated. In recognizing that behavior has a meaning and depends upon the vital significance of situations, biological science is prohibited from conceiving of it as a thing in-itself (*en soi*) which would exist, *partes extra partes*,[8] *in* the nervous system or *in* the body; rather it sees in behavior an embodied dialectic which radiates over a milieu immanent to it.

There is no question—as we have said often enough—of returning to any form whatsoever of vitalism or animism, but simply of recognizing that the

---

4. Merleau-Ponty takes the appropriate and central focus of phenomenological analysis to be "the human order," rather than the phenomenologically "reduced" forms of experiences produced by Husserl's "bracketing" of all assumptions regarding their origins and status.
5. That is, interactive and mutually influencing (rather than either being the "cause" of the other).
6. An idea expressed by BERGSON in *Creative Evolution* (1907); see above.
7. Wolfgang Köhler (1887–1967), German-born psychologist who came to the United States as a refugee in 1934; he was a key figure in the founding of Gestalt psychology, which argues that sense experience has a holistic and dynamic character.
8. Parts outside of parts (Latin); that is, one inside the other.

object of biology cannot be grasped without the unities of signification which a consciousness finds and sees unfolding in it. "The mind of nature is a hidden mind. It is not produced in the form of mind itself; it is only mind for the mind which knows it: it is mind in itself, but not for itself."[9] In reality then we have already introduced consciousness and what we have designated under the name of life was already the consciousness of life. "The concept is only the interior of nature," says Hegel;[1] and already it has seemed to us that the notion of the living body could not be grasped without this internal unity of signification which distinguishes a gesture from a sum of movements. The phenomenon of life appeared therefore at the moment when a piece of extension, by the disposition of its movements and by the allusion that each movement makes to all the others, turned back upon itself and began to express something, to manifest an interior being externally.

If now we continue our description—always from the point of view of the "outside spectator"—and if we consider the human order, we will at first see in it only the production of new structures. If life is the manifestation of an "interior" in the "exterior," consciousness is nothing at first but the projection onto the world of a new "milieu"—irreducible to the preceding ones, it is true—and humanity nothing but a new species of animal. In particular, perception should be integrated in its turn into the dialectic of actions and reactions. While a physical system equilibrates itself in respect to the given forces of the milieu and the animal organism constructs a stable milieu for itself corresponding to the monotonous *a prioris* of need and instinct, human work inaugurates a third dialectic. For, between man and the physico-chemical stimuli, it projects "use-objects" (*Gebrauchobjekts*)[2]—clothing, tables, gardens—and "cultural objects"[3]—books, musical instruments, language— which constitute the proper milieu of man and bring about the emergence of new cycles of behavior. Just as it seemed to us to be impossible to reduce the pair: vital situation-instinctive reaction, to the pair: stimulus-reflex, just so it will doubtless be necessary to recognize the originality of the pair: perceived situation-work.

It is by design that, instead of speaking of action as do most contemporary psychologists, we choose the Hegelian term "work," which designates the ensemble of activities by which man transforms physical and living nature. For, although nothing is more common than to link consciousness and action, it is rare that human action is taken with its original meaning and its concrete content. * * *

Properly human acts—the act of speech, of work, the act of clothing oneself, for example—have no significance in their own right. They are understood in reference to the aims of life: clothing is an artificial skin, an instrument

9. Hegel, *Jenenser Logik* [*The Jena System*], in G. Lasson (ed.), *Hegels Sämtliche Werke Kritische Ausgabe*, Leipzig, Meiner [(1923)], p. 113. Cf. Hyppolite, "Vie et prise de conscience de la vie dans la philosophie hégélienne d'Iena [Life and Consciousness of Life in Hegel's Philosophy at Jena]," *Revue de Métaphysique et de Morale*, January 1938, p. 47 [Merleau-Ponty's note]. Jean Hyppolite (1907–1968), French philosopher who helped disseminate HEGEL's ideas in France.

1. Cited by Hyppolite without reference, *ibid.* [Merleau-Ponty's note].
2. Husserl, "Ideen zu einer reinen Phänomenologie und phänomenologische Philosophie," *passim* [Merleau-Ponty's note]. For Husserl's *Ideas* (1913), see above.
3. E. Husserl, *Méditations cartésiennes* [*Cartesian Meditations*; excerpted above], Paris, Colin, 1931, *passim* [Merleau-Ponty's note].

replaces an organ, language is a means of adaptation to the "unorganized mass."

* * *

It has been clearly shown that animal perception is sensitive only to certain concrete stimulus wholes, the form of which is prescribed by instinct itself; and, rightly, a lived abstraction by means of which what does not correspond to the structure of the animal's instinct is left purely and simply outside its sensory field has been discussed.[4] But the thought of relating the content of human perception to the structure of human action in the same way does not occur. Of course it is said that our "needs," our "tendencies," and our attention oriented by them make the objects of our actual perception emerge from the possible sensory field. But what is ordinarily implicitly understood by this is an ensemble of qualities—color, weight, flavor—among which attention chooses; and it is from a mosaic of preconscious sensations that one tries to rejoin the actual content of infantile or original perception. The analysis is made following the same postulates which we encountered in the theory of the reflex: one tries to make a determinate content of consciousness correspond to each partial stimulus—a luminous vibration, for example— exactly as reflex theory tried to decompose the instinctive act into a sum of elementary reactions each one of which would correspond to an elementary stimulus. And just as instinctual activity unfolds, as we have seen, according to the structures prescribed by the organism itself, one could show likewise that sensations cannot be supposed, even ideally, behind the concrete unities of original perception. But then the needs, tendencies and acts of spontaneous attention—the forces, in a word, which are also preconscious—which must be introduced in order to reconstruct the original syncretism on the basis of pure qualities[,] appear in turn as hypothetical constructions, as "faculties," which are rendered indispensable only by the myth of sensations. They are abstract ideas which are formed in order to explain the discrepancy between our *de facto* perception and a perception which is in principle wholly conventional. Two abstractions together do not make a concrete description. There are not these impersonal forces on the one hand and, on the other, a mosaic of sensations which they would transform; there are melodic unities, significant wholes experienced in an indivisible manner as poles of action and nuclei of knowledge. Primitive knowledge is not comparable to the result of an energic process in which the tendencies and needs would be released over a mosaic of pure qualities and would give directions to an impartial thinking subject which it will docilely execute. Perception is a moment of the living dialectic of a concrete subject; it participates in its total structure and, correlatively, it has as its original object, not the "unorganized mass," but the actions of other human subjects.

* * *

From this new point of view one realizes that, although all actions permit an adaptation to life, the word "life" does not have the same meaning in

4. "C'est l'herbe en général qui attire l'herbivore [It is plants in general that attract the plant-eating animal]" (H. Bergson, *Matière et mémoire* [1896, *Matter and Memory*]) [Merleau-Ponty's note].

animality and humanity; and the conditions of life are defined by the proper essence of the species. Doubtless, clothing and houses serve to protect us from the cold; language helps in collective work and in the analysis of the "unorganized mass." But the act of dressing becomes the act of adornment or also of modesty and thus reveals a new attitude toward oneself and others. Only men see that they are nude. In the house that he builds for himself, man projects and realizes his preferred values. Finally, the act of speaking expresses the fact that man ceases to adhere immediately to the milieu, that he elevates it to the status of spectacle and takes possession of it mentally by means of knowledge properly so called.[5]

* * *

* * * What defines man is not the capacity to create a second nature—economic, social or cultural—beyond biological nature; it is rather the capacity of going beyond created structures in order to create others. And this movement is already visible in each of the particular products of human work. A nest is an object which has a meaning only in relation to the possible behavior of the organic individual; if a monkey picks a branch in order to reach a goal, it is because it is able to confer a functional value on an object of nature. But monkeys scarcely succeed at all in constructing instruments which would serve only for preparing others; we have seen that, having become a stick for the monkey, the tree branch is eliminated as such—which is the equivalent of saying that it is never possessed as an instrument in the full sense of the word. Animal activity reveals its limits in the two cases: it loses itself in the real transformations which it accomplishes and cannot reiterate them. For man, on the contrary, the tree branch which has become a stick will remain precisely a tree-branch-which-has-become-a-stick, the same *thing* in two different functions and visible *for him* under a plurality of aspects.

This power of choosing and varying points of view permits man to create instruments, not under the pressure of a *de facto* situation, but for a virtual use and especially in order to fabricate others. The meaning of human work therefore is the recognition, beyond the present milieu, of a world of things visible for each "I" under a plurality of aspects, the taking possession of an indefinite time and space; and one could easily show that the signification of speech or that of suicide and of the revolutionary act is the same. These acts of the human dialectic all reveal the same essence: the capacity of orienting oneself in relation to the possible, to the mediate, and not in relation to a limited milieu; they all reveal what we called above, with Goldstein, the categorial attitude.[6] Thus, the human dialectic is ambiguous: it is first manifested by the social or cultural structures, the appearance of which it brings about and in which it imprisons itself. *But its use-objects and its cultural objects would*

---

5. This paragraph (and this section of the book more broadly) shows Merleau-Ponty's affinities with the "philosophical anthropology" of MAX SCHELER, HELMUTH PLESSNER, ARNOLD GEHLEN, and ERNST CASSIRER (see below), no less than the phenomenology of Husserl and the existential philosophies of HEIDEGGER and SARTRE.
6. That is, the ability to view an object and the

word naming it as representatives of a category; Merleau-Ponty earlier cited "Über Farbennamen-amnesie" (1925, "On Color Name Amnesia"), an article co-written by Adhémar Gelb and Kurt Goldstein (1878–1965), a pioneering German neuro-psychologist who influenced Gestalt psychology; he left Germany in 1933 and emigrated to the United States in 1935.

not be what they are if the activity which brings about their appearance did not also have as its meaning to reject them and to surpass them.

* * *

But neither the psychological with respect to the vital nor the rational (*spirituel*) with respect to the psychological can be treated as substances or as new worlds. The relation of each order to the higher order is that of the partial to the total. A normal man is not a body bearing certain autonomous instincts joined to a "psychological life" defined by certain characteristic processes— pleasure and pain, emotion, association of ideas—and surmounted with a mind which would unfold its proper acts over this infrastructure. The advent of higher orders, to the extent that they are accomplished, eliminate the autonomy of the lower orders and give a new signification to the steps which constitute them. This is why we have spoken of a human order rather than of a mental or rational order. The so frequent distinction of the mental and the somatic has its place in pathology but cannot serve for the knowledge of normal man, that is, of integrated man, since in him the somatic processes do not unfold in isolation but are integrated into a cycle of more extensive action. It is not a question of two *de facto* orders external to each other, but of two types of relations, the second of which integrates the first. The contrast between what is called mental life and what are called bodily phenomena is evident when one has in view the body considered part by part and moment by moment.

But, as we have seen, biology already refers to the phenomenal body, that is, to the center of vital actions which are extended over a segment of time, respond to certain concrete stimulus wholes and effect the collaboration of the whole organism. These modes of behavior do not even subsist as such in man. Reorganized in its turn in new wholes, vital behavior as such disappears. This is what is signified, for example, by the periodicity and monotony of sexual life in animals, by its constancy and its variations in man. Thus, one cannot speak of the body and of life in general, but only of the animal body and animal life, of the human body and of human life; and the body of the normal subject—if it is not detached from the spatio-temporal cycles of behavior of which it is the support—is not distinct from the psychological.

Remarks of the same kind would be possible concerning the notion of mind. We are not defending a mentalism which would distinguish mind and life or mind and the psychological as two "powers of being."[7] It is a question of a "functional opposition" which cannot be transformed into a "substantial opposition."[8] Mind is not a specific difference which would be added to vital or psychological being in order to constitute a man. Man is not a rational animal. The appearance of reason and mind does not leave intact a sphere of self-enclosed instincts in man. Cognitive disorders which affect the categorial attitude are expressed by a loss of sexual initiatives. The alteration of higher functions reaches as far as the so-called instinctive structures; the ablation of

7. Goldstein, *Der Aufbau des Organismus* [The Hague: Martinus Nijhoff, 1934], p. 213 (cf. *The Organism* [New York: American Book, 1938], pp. 322 sqq.) [Merleau-Ponty's note].

8. E. Cassirer, "Geist und Leben in der Philosophie der Gegenwart ['Spirit' and 'Life' in Contemporary Philosophy]," *Die neue Rundschau*, 41 [1930], pp. 244 sqq. [Merleau-Ponty's note].

the higher centers entails death, although decerebrate animals can subsist after a fashion. "If man had the senses of an animal, he would not have reason."[9] Man can never be an animal: his life is always more or less integrated than that of an animal. But if the alleged instincts of man do not exist *apart* from the mental dialectic, correlatively, this dialectic is not conceivable outside of the concrete situations in which it is embodied. One does not act with mind alone. Either mind is nothing, or it constitutes a real and not an ideal transformation of man. Because it is not a new sort of being but a new form of unity, it cannot stand by itself.

* * *

CONCLUSION

In the preceding chapters we have considered the birth of behavior in the physical world and in an organism; that is, we have pretended to know nothing of man by reflection and have limited ourselves to developing what was implied in the scientific representation of his behavior. Aided by the notion of structure or form, we have arrived at the conclusion that both mechanism and finalism should be rejected and that the "physical," the "vital" and the "mental" do not represent three powers of being, but three dialectics.[1] Physical nature in man is not subordinated to a vital principle, the organism does not conspire to actualize an idea, and the mental is not a motor principle *in* the body; but what we call nature is already consciousness of nature, what we call life is already consciousness of life and what we call mental is still an object vis-à-vis consciousness. Nevertheless, while establishing the ideality of the physical form, that of the organism, and that of the "mental," and *precisely because we did it,* we could not simply superimpose these three orders; not being a new substance, each of them had to be conceived as a retaking and a "new" structuration of the preceding one.[2] From this comes the double aspect of the analysis which both liberated the higher from the lower and founded the former on the latter. It is this double relation which remains obscure and which now induces us to situate our results with respect to the classical solutions and in particular with respect to critical idealism. At the beginning we considered consciousness as a region of being and as a particular type of behavior. Upon analysis one finds it presupposed everywhere as the place of ideas and everywhere interconnected as the integration of existence. What then is the relation between consciousness as universal milieu and consciousness enrooted in the subordinated dialectics? Must the point of view of the "outside spectator" be abandoned as illegitimate to the benefit of an unconditioned reflection?

---

9. Herder, cited by Goldstein, *Der Aufbau des Organismus*, p. 305 (cf. *The Organism*, p. 478) [Merleau-Ponty's note]. Johann Herder (1744–1803), an important and influential German philosopher, linguistic theorist, critic, and theologian, associated with the rise of historical studies, German Roman-

ticism, and German nationalism.
1. A summary of Merleau-Ponty's position: this sentence could be regarded as the central thesis of the book.
2. This process recalls the Hegelian conception of *Aufhebung* (see the Hegel glossary, p.144).

From *Chapter IV*
The Relations of the Soul and the Body
and the Problem of Perceptual Consciousness

* * *

FROM IS THERE NOT A TRUTH OF NATURALISM?

Are we compelled in this direction by the preceding analyses? At least they lead to the transcendental attitude, that is, to a philosophy which treats all conceivable reality as an object of consciousness. It has seemed to us that matter, life, and mind could not be defined as three orders of reality or three sorts of beings, but as three planes of signification or three forms of unity. In particular, life would not be a force which is added to physico-chemical processes; its originality would be that of modes of connection without equivalent in the physical domain, that of phenomena gifted with a proper structure and which bind each other together according to a special dialectic. In a living being, bodily movements and moments of behavior can be described and understood only in a specially tailored language and in accordance with the categories of an original experience. And it is in this same sense that we have recognized a psychological order and a mental order. But these distinctions then are those of different regions of experience. We have been moved from the idea of a *nature* as *omnitudo realitatis*[3] to the idea of objects which could not be conceived in-themselves (*en soi*), *partes extra partes*, and which are defined only by an idea in which they participate, by a signification which is realized in them. Since the relations of the physical system and the forces which act upon it and those of the living being and its milieu are not the external and blind relations of juxtaposed realities, but dialectical relations in which the effect of each partial action is determined by its signification for the whole, the human order of consciousness does not appear as a third order superimposed on the two others, but as their condition of possibility and their foundation.

The problem of the relations of the soul and the body seems to disappear from the point of view of this absolute consciousness, milieu of the universe, as it did from the critical point of view. There can be no question of a causal operation between three planes of signification. One says that the soul "acts" on the body when it happens that our conduct has a rational signification, that is, when it cannot be understood by any play of physical forces or by any of the attitudes which are characteristic of the vital dialectic. In reality the expression is improper: we have seen that the body is not a self-enclosed mechanism on which the soul could act from the outside. It is defined only by its functioning, which can present all degrees of integration. To say that the soul acts on the body is wrongly to suppose a univocal notion of the body and to add to it a second force which accounts for the rational signification of certain conducts. In this case it would be better to say that bodily functioning is

3. The wholeness of reality (Latin); the phrase is taken from Kant's *Critique of Pure Reason* (1781; 2nd ed., 1787), where it is identified with "a transcendental substrate that contains . . . the whole store of material from which all possible predicates of things must be taken" (A575 / B603; trans. Norman Kemp Smith).

integrated with a level which is higher than that of life and that the body has truly become a human body. Inversely one will say that the body has acted on the soul if the behavior can be understood without residue in terms of the vital dialectic or by known psychological mechanisms.

Here again one does not, properly speaking, have the right to imagine a transitive action from substance to substance, as if the soul were a constantly present force whose activity would be held in check by a more powerful force. It would be more exact to say that the behavior had become disorganized, leaving room for less integrated structures. In brief, the alleged reciprocal action is reducible to an alternation or a substitution of dialectics. Since the physical, the vital and the mental individual are distinguished only as different degrees of integration, to the extent that man is completely identified with the third dialectic, that is, to the extent that he no longer allows systems of isolated conduct to function in him, his soul and his body are no longer distinguished.

* * *

There is always a duality which reappears at one level or another: hunger or thirst prevents thought or feelings; the properly sexual dialectic ordinarily reveals itself through a passion; integration is never absolute and it always fails—at a higher level in the writer, at a lower level in the aphasic. There always comes a moment when we divest ourselves of a passion because of fatigue or self-respect. This duality is not a simple fact; it is founded in principle—all integration presupposing the normal functioning of subordinated formations, which always demand their own due.

But it is not a duality of substances; or, in other words, the notions of soul and body must be relativized: there is the body as mass of chemical components in interaction, the body as dialectic of living being and its biological milieu, and the body as dialectic of social subject and his group; even all our habits are an impalpable body for the ego of each moment. Each of these degrees is soul with respect to the preceding one, body with respect to the following one. The body in general is an ensemble of paths already traced, of powers already constituted; the body is the acquired dialectical soil upon which a higher "formation" is accomplished, and the soul is the meaning which is then established. The relations of the soul and the body can indeed be compared to those of concept and word, but on the condition of perceiving, beneath the separated products, the constituting operation which joins them and of rediscovering, beneath the empirical languages—the external accompaniment or contingent clothing of thought—the living *word* which is its unique actualization, in which the meaning is formulated for the first time and thus establishes itself as meaning and becomes available for later operations.[4]

* * *

The distinction which we are introducing is rather that of the lived and the known. The problem of the relations of the soul and body is thus transformed instead of disappearing: now it will be the problem of the relations of con-

4. This paragraph is another summary of central ideas in Merleau-Ponty's thinking.

sciousness as flux of individual events, of concrete and resistant structures, and that of consciousness as tissue of ideal significations. The idea of a transcendental philosophy, that is, the idea of consciousness as constituting the universe before it and grasping the objects themselves in an indubitable external experience, seems to us to be a definitive acquisition as the first phase of reflection. But is one not obliged to re-establish a duality within consciousness which is no longer accepted between it and external realities? The objects as ideal unities and as significations are grasped through individual perspectives. When I look at a book placed in front of me, its rectangular form is a concrete and embodied structure. What is the relation between this rectangular "physiognomy" and the signification, "rectangle," which I can make explicit by a logical act?

Every theory of perception tries to surmount a well-known contradiction: on the one hand, consciousness is a function of the body—thus it is an "internal" event dependent upon certain external events; on the other hand, these external events themselves are known only by consciousness. In another language, consciousness appears on one hand to be part of the world and on the other to be co-extensive with the world. In the development of methodical knowledge, of science, that is, the first observation seems initially to be confirmed: the subjectivity of the secondary qualities seems to have as a counterpart the reality of the primary qualities. But a deeper reflection on the objects of science and on physical causality finds relations in them which cannot be posited in-themselves (*en soi*) and which have meaning only before the inspection of mind.

The antinomy of which we are speaking disappears along with its realistic thesis at the level of reflexive thought (*la pensée réfléchie*); it is in perceptual knowledge that it has its proper location. Until now critical thought[5] seemed to us to be incontestable. It shows marvelously that the problem of perception does not exist for a consciousness which adheres to objects of reflexive thought, that is, to significations. It is subsequently that it seems necessary to leave it. Having in this way referred the antinomy of perception to the order of life, as Descartes[6] says, or to the order of confused thought, one pretends to show that it has no consistency there: if perception conceptualizes itself ever so little and knows what it is saying, it reveals that the experience of passivity is also a construction of the mind. Realism is not even based on a coherent appearance, it is an *error*. One wonders then what can provide consciousness with the very notion of passivity and why this notion is confused with its body if these natural errors rest on no authentic experience and *possess strictly no meaning whatsoever*. We have tried to show that, as a matter of fact, to the extent that the scientific knowledge of the organism becomes more precise, it becomes impossible to give a coherent meaning to the alleged action of the world on the body and of the body on the soul. The body and the soul are significations and have meaning, then, only with regard to a consciousness.[7]

From our point of view also, the realistic thesis of common sense disappears at the level of reflexive thought, which encounters only significations

---

5. That is, Kant's "critical" philosophy, or the "critical" analysis of perception and theoretical reason in his *Critique of Pure Reason*.
6. René Descartes (1596–1650), French mathema-
tician and philosopher; he discusses perception in his *Meditations* (1641).
7. Such language recalls Husserl.

in front of it. The experience of passivity *is not explained* by an actual passivity. But it should have a meaning and be able *to be understood*. As philosophy, realism is an error because it transposes into dogmatic thesis an experience which it deforms or renders impossible by that very fact. But it is a motivated error; it rests on an authentic phenomenon which philosophy has the function of making explicit. The proper structure of perceptual experience, the reference of partial "profiles" to the total signification which they "present," would be this phenomenon. Indeed, the alleged bodily conditioning of perception, taken in its actual meaning, requires nothing more—and nothing less—than this phenomenon in order to be understood. We have seen that excitations and nerve influxes are abstractions and that science links them to a total functioning of the nervous system in the definition of which the phenomenal is implied. The perceived is not an effect of cerebral functioning; it is its signification.

All the consciousnesses which we know present themselves in this way through a body which is their perspectival aspect. But, after all, each individual dialectic has cerebral stages, as it were, of which it itself knows nothing; the signification of nerve functioning has organic bases which do not figure in it. Philosophically, this fact admits of the following translation: each time that certain sensible phenomena are actualized in my field of consciousness, a properly placed observer would see certain other phenomena in my brain which cannot be given to me myself in the mode of actuality. In order to understand these phenomena, he would be led to grant them (as we did in Chapter II[8]) a signification which would concur with the content of my perception. Inversely, I can represent for myself in the virtual mode, that is, as pure significations, certain retinal and cerebral phenomena which I localize in a virtual image of my body on the basis of the actual view which is given to me. The fact that the spectator and myself are both bound to our bodies comes down in sum to this: that that which can be given to me in the mode of actuality, as a concrete perspective, is given to him only in the mode of virtuality, as a signification, and conversely. In sum, my total psycho-physical being (that is, the experience which I have of myself, that which others have of me, and the scientific knowledge which they and I apply to the knowledge of myself) is an interlacing of significations such that, when certain among them are perceived and pass into actuality, the others are only virtually intended. But this structure of experience is similar to that of external objects. Even more, they mutually presuppose each other. If there are things for me, that is, perspectival beings, reference to a point from which I see them is included in their perspectival character itself.

* * *

All the sciences situate themselves in a "complete" and real world without realizing that perceptual experience is constituting with respect to this world. Thus we find ourselves in the presence of a field of lived perception which is prior to number, measure, space and causality and which is nonetheless given only as a perspectival view of objects gifted with stable properties, a perspec-

8. Not included here.

tival view of an objective world and an objective space. The problem of perception consists in trying to discover how the intersubjective world, the determinations of which science is gradually making precise, is grasped through this field. The antinomy of which we spoke above is based upon this ambiguous structure of perceptual experience. The thesis and the antithesis express the two aspects of it: it is true to say that my perception is always a flux of individual events and that what is radically contingent in the lived perspectivism of perception accounts for the realistic appearance. But it is also true to say that my perception accedes to things themselves, for these perspectives are articulated in a way which makes access to inter-individual significations possible; they "present" a world.

Thus there are things *exactly in the sense in which I see them,* in my history and outside it, and inseparable from this double relation. I perceive things directly without my body forming a screen between them and me; it is a phenomenon just as they are, a phenomenon (gifted, it is true, with an original structure) which precisely presents the body to me as an intermediary between the world and myself although it *is not* as a matter of fact. I see with my eyes, which are not an ensemble of transparent or opaque tissues and organs, but the instruments of my looking. The retinal image, to the extent that I know it, is not yet produced by the light waves issuing from the object; but these two phenomena resemble and correspond to each other in a magical way across an interval which is not yet space.

We are returning to the givens of naive consciousness which we were analyzing at the beginning of this chapter. The philosophy of perception is not ready made in life: we have just seen that it is natural for consciousness to misunderstand itself precisely because it is consciousness of things. The classical discussions centering around perception are a sufficient testimony to this natural error. The constituted world is confronted with the perceptual experience of the world and one either tries to engender perception from the world, as realism does, or else to see in it only a commencement of the science of the world, as critical thought does. To return to perception as to a type of original experience in which the real world is constituted in its specificity is to impose upon oneself an inversion of the natural movement of consciousness; on the other hand every question has not been eliminated: it is a question of understanding, without confusing it with a logical relation, the lived relation of the "profiles" to the "things" which they present, of the perspectives to the ideal significations which are intended through them. * * *

FROM CONCLUSION

* * *

If one understands by perception the act which makes us know existences, all the problems which we have just touched on are reducible to the problem of perception. It resides in the duality of the notions of structure and signification. A "form," such as the structure of "figure and ground," for example, is a whole which has a meaning and which provides therefore a base for intellectual analysis. But at the same time it is not an idea: it constitutes, alters and reorganizes itself before us like a spectacle. The alleged bodily, social and psychological "causalities" are reducible to this contingency of lived perspectives which limit our access to eternal significations. The "horizontal localizations" of cerebral functioning, the adhesive structures of animal behavior and those of pathological behavior are only particularly striking examples of this. "Structure" is the philosophical truth of naturalism and realism. * * *

SOURCE: From Maurice Merleau-Ponty, *The Structure of Behavior*, trans. Alden L. Fischer (Boston: Beacon Press, 1963), pp. 3–5, 160–63, 165–66, 174–76, 180–81, 184, 201–3, 210, 215–17, 219–20, 224. Originally published in 1942 as *La Structure du comportement*; the manuscript was completed in 1938.

From Phenomenology of Perception

From *Preface*

What is phenomenology? It may seem strange that this question has still to be asked half a century after the first works of Husserl. The fact remains that it has by no means been answered. Phenomenology is the study of essences; and according to it, all problems amount to finding definitions of essences: the essence of perception, or the essence of consciousness, for example. But phenomenology is also a philosophy which puts essences back into existence, and does not expect to arrive at an understanding of man and the world from any starting point other than that of their 'facticity'.[1] It is a transcendental philosophy which places in abeyance the assertions arising out of the natural attitude, the better to understand them; but it is also a philosophy for which the world is always 'already there' before reflection begins—as an inalienable presence; and all its efforts are concentrated upon re-achieving a direct and primitive contact with the world, and endowing that contact with a philosophical status. It is the search for a philosophy which shall be a 'rigorous science', but it also offers an account of space, time and the world as we 'live' them.[2] It tries to give a direct description of our experience as it is, without taking account of its psychological origin and the causal explanations which the scientist, the historian or the sociologist may be able to provide. Yet Husserl in his last works mentions a 'genetic phenomenology',[3] and even a 'constructive phenomenology'.[4] One may try to do away with these contradictions by making a distinction between Husserl's and Heidegger's phenomenologies; yet the whole of *Sein und Zeit*[5] springs from an indication given by Husserl and amounts to no more than an explicit account of the 'natürlicher Weltbegriff' or the 'Lebenswelt'[6] which Husserl, towards the end of his life, identified as

---

1. An accurate description of the existential phenomenologies of HEIDEGGER and SARTRE, but not of HUSSERL (at least in his published writings). Not everyone agrees with Merleau-Ponty's view that Husserl was moving in this direction toward the end of his life.
2. A description that recalls BERGSON as well as Husserl and the early Heidegger.
3. [Husserl,] *Méditations cartésiennes* [*Cartesian*

Meditations (Paris: Colin, 1931); see above], pp. 120ff. [Merleau-Ponty's note].
4. See the unpublished *6th Méditation cartésienne*, edited by Eugen Fink [Merleau-Ponty's note]. Translated as *Sixth Cartesian Meditation* (1995).
5. *Being and Time* (1927), by Heidegger; see above.
6. "The 'natural world-concept' or the 'life-world'" (German).

the central theme of phenomenology, with the result that the contradiction reappears in Husserl's own philosophy. The reader pressed for time will be inclined to give up the idea of covering a doctrine which says everything, and will wonder whether a philosophy which cannot define its scope deserves all the discussion which has gone on around it, and whether he is not faced rather by a myth or a fashion.

Even if this were the case, there would still be a need to understand the prestige of the myth and the origin of the fashion, and the opinion of the responsible philosopher must be that *phenomenology can be practised and identified as a manner or style of thinking, that it existed as a movement before arriving at complete awareness of itself as a philosophy*. It has been long on the way, and its adherents have discovered it in every quarter, certainly in Hegel and Kierkegaard, but equally in Marx, Nietzsche and Freud.[7] A purely linguistic examination of the texts in question would yield no proof; we find in texts only what we put into them, and if ever any kind of history has suggested the interpretations which should be put on it, it is the history of philosophy. We shall find in ourselves, and nowhere else, the unity and true meaning of phenomenology. It is less a question of counting up quotations than of determining and expressing in concrete form this *phenomenology for ourselves* which has given a number of present-day readers the impression, on reading Husserl or Heidegger, not so much of encountering a new philosophy as of recognizing what they had been waiting for. Phenomenology is accessible only through a phenomenological method. Let us, therefore, try systematically to bring together the celebrated phenomenological themes as they have grown spontaneously together in life. Perhaps we shall then understand why phenomenology has for so long remained at an initial stage, as a problem to be solved and a hope to be realized.

It is a matter of describing, not of explaining or analysing. Husserl's first directive to phenomenology, in its early stages, to be a 'descriptive psychology', or to return to the 'things themselves', is from the start a rejection of science.[8] I am not the outcome or the meeting-point of numerous causal agencies which determine my bodily or psychological make-up. I cannot conceive myself as nothing but a bit of the world, a mere object of biological, psychological or sociological investigation. I cannot shut myself up within the realm of science. All my knowledge of the world, even my scientific knowledge, is gained from my own particular point of view, or from some experience of the world without which the symbols of science would be meaningless. The whole universe of science is built upon the world as directly experienced, and if we want to subject science itself to rigorous scrutiny and arrive at a precise assessment

---

7. Sigmund Freud (1856–1939), Austrian neurologist and founder of psychoanalysis. For HEGEL, KIERKEGAARD, MARX, and NIETZSCHE, see above.
8. That is, a rejection of *scientism*, the view that the natural sciences have the final word on all questions of truth and knowledge with respect to reality. Husserl's exhortation here rendered as "To

the things themselves!" (*An den Sachen selbst!*) refers *not* to "things *in* themselves" but rather to the contents of experience; it therefore is better translated as "To the *matters* themselves!" and understood to mean: "To the *phenomena* themselves!"; see the introduction to Husserl, above.

of its meaning and scope, we must begin by reawakening the basic experience of the world of which science is the second-order expression. Science
has not and never will have, by its nature, the same significance *qua* form of
being as the world which we perceive, for the simple reason that it is a rationale or explanation of that world. I am, not a 'living creature' nor even a 'man',
nor again even 'a consciousness' endowed with all the characteristics which
zoology, social anatomy or inductive psychology recognize in these various
products of the natural or historical process—I am the absolute source, my
existence does not stem from my antecedents, from my physical and social
environment; instead it moves out towards them and sustains them, for I alone
bring into being for myself (and therefore into being in the only sense that
the word can have for me) the tradition which I elect to carry on, or the horizon whose distance from me would be abolished—since that distance is not
one of its properties—if I were not there to scan it with my gaze. Scientific
points of view, according to which my existence is a moment of the world's,
are always both naïve and at the same time dishonest, because they take for
granted, without explicitly mentioning it, the other point of view, namely that
of consciousness, through which from the outset a world forms itself round
me and begins to exist for me. To return to things themselves is to return to
that world which precedes knowledge, of which knowledge always *speaks*, and
in relation to which every scientific schematization is an abstract and derivative sign-language, as is geography in relation to the countryside in which we
have learnt beforehand what a forest, a prairie or a river is.

This move is absolutely distinct from the idealist return to consciousness,
and the demand for a pure description excludes equally the procedure of analytical reflection on the one hand, and that of scientific explanation on the
other. Descartes[9] and particularly Kant *detached* the subject, or consciousness, by showing that I could not possibly apprehend anything as existing
unless I first of all experienced myself as existing in the act of apprehending
it. They presented consciousness, the absolute certainty of my existence for
myself, as the condition of there being anything at all; and the act of relating
as the basis of relatedness. It is true that the act of relating is nothing if
divorced from the spectacle of the world in which relations are found; the
unity of consciousness in Kant is achieved simultaneously with that of the
world. And in Descartes methodical doubt does not deprive us of anything,
since the whole world, at least in so far as we experience it, is reinstated in
the *Cogito*, enjoying equal certainty, and simply labelled 'thought about . . .'.
But the relations between subject and world are not strictly bilateral: if they
were, the certainty of the world would, in Descartes, be immediately given
with that of the *Cogito*, and Kant would not have talked about his 'Copernican revolution'.[1] Analytical reflection starts from our experience of the world
and goes back to the subject as to a condition of possibility distinct from that
experience, revealing the all embracing synthesis as that without which there
would be no world. To this extent it ceases to remain part of our experience

9. René Descartes (1596–1650), French mathematician and philosopher, whose "procedure of analytical reflection" began with *cogito* (Latin, "I think").
1. The reversal of the traditional picture of the
relationship between the basic *features of the world*
and the basic *structures of the mind* that cognizes
that world, according primacy to the latter rather
than the former (and thus analogous to the original Copernican reversal that accorded centrality
to the sun rather than the earth).

and offers, in place of an account, a reconstruction. It is understandable, in view of this, that Husserl, having accused Kant of adopting a 'faculty psychologism',[2] should have urged, in place of a noetic analysis which bases the world on the synthesizing activity of the subject, his own *'noematic reflection'* which remains within the object and, instead of begetting it, brings to light its fundamental unity.

The world is there before any possible analysis of mine, and it would be artificial to make it the outcome of a series of syntheses which link, in the first place sensations, then aspects of the object corresponding to different perspectives, when both are nothing but products of analysis, with no sort of prior reality. Analytical reflection believes that it can trace back the course followed by a prior constituting act and arrive, in the 'inner man'—to use Saint Augustine's expression[3]—at a constituting power which has always been identical with that inner self. Thus reflection itself is carried away and transplanted in an impregnable subjectivity, as yet untouched by being and time. But this is very ingenuous, or at least it is an incomplete form of reflection which loses sight of its own beginning. When I begin to reflect my reflection bears upon an unreflective experience; moreover my reflection cannot be unaware of itself as an event, and so it appears to itself in the light of a truly creative act, of a changed structure of consciouness, and yet it has to recognize, as having priority over its own operations, the world which is given to the subject, because the subject is given to himself. The real has to be described, not constructed or formed. Which means that I cannot put perception into the same category as the syntheses represented by judgements, acts or predications. My field of perception is constantly filled with a play of colours, noises and fleeting tactile sensations which I cannot relate precisely to the context of my clearly perceived world, yet which I nevertheless immediately 'place' in the world, without ever confusing them with my daydreams. Equally constantly I weave dreams round things. I imagine people and things whose presence is not incompatible with the context, yet who are not in fact involved in it: they are ahead of reality, in the realm of the imaginary. If the reality of my perception were based solely on the intrinsic coherence of 'representations', it ought to be forever hesitant and, being wrapped up in my conjectures on probabilities, I ought to be ceaselessly taking apart misleading syntheses, and reinstating in reality stray phenomena which I had excluded in the first place. But this does not happen. The real is a closely woven fabric. It does not await our judgement before incorporating the most surprising phenomena, or before rejecting the most plausible figments of our imagination. Perception is not a science of the world, it is not even an act, a deliberate taking up of a position; it is the background from which all acts stand out, and is presupposed by them. The world is not an object such that I have in my possession the law of its making; it is the natural setting of, and field for, all my thoughts and all my explicit perceptions. Truth does not 'inhabit' only 'the inner man', or more accurately, there is no inner man, man is in the world,

---

2. [Husserl,] *Logische Untersuchungen: Prolegomena zur reinen Logik* [*Logical Investigations: Prolegomena to a Pure Logic*, 4th ed. (Halle: Niemeyer, 1928)], p. 93 [Merleau-Ponty's note].

3. See *On the Trinity* (12.1) and the *Confessions* (10.6) by St. Augustine (354–430); later in the paragraph Merleau-Ponty quotes a reference to the "inner man" from his *On True Religion* 39.72.

and only in the world does he know himself. When I return to myself from an excursion into the realm of dogmatic common sense or of science, I find, not a source of intrinsic truth, but a subject destined to be in the world.

* * *

Probably the chief gain from phenomenology is to have united extreme subjectivism and extreme objectivism in its notion of the world or of rationality. Rationality is precisely measured by the experiences in which it is disclosed. To say that there exists rationality is to say that perspectives blend, perceptions confirm each other, a meaning emerges. But it should not be set in a realm apart, transposed into absolute Spirit, or into a world in the realist sense. The phenomenological world is not pure being, but the sense which is revealed where the paths of my various experiences intersect, and also where my own and other people's intersect and engage each other like gears. It is thus inseparable from subjectivity and intersubjectivity, which find their unity when I either take up my past experiences in those of the present, or other people's in my own. For the first time the philosopher's thinking is sufficiently conscious not to anticipate itself and endow its own results with reified form in the world. The philosopher tries to conceive the world, others and himself and their interrelations. But the meditating Ego, the 'impartial spectator' (*uninteressierter Zuschauer*) do not rediscover an already given rationality, they 'establish themselves',[4] and establish it, by an act of initiative which has no guarantee in being, its justification resting entirely on the effective power which it confers on us of taking our own history upon ourselves.

The phenomenological world is not the bringing to explicit expression of a pre-existing being, but the laying down of being. Philosophy is not the reflection of a pre-existing truth, but, like art, the act of bringing truth into being. One may well ask how this creation is *possible*, and if it does not recapture in things a pre-existing Reason. The answer is that the only pre-existent Logos is the world itself, and that the philosophy which brings it into visible existence does not begin by being *possible*; it is actual or real like the world of which it is a part, and no explanatory hypothesis is clearer than the act whereby we take up this unfinished world in an effort to complete and conceive it. Rationality is not a *problem*. There is behind it no unknown quantity which has to be determined by deduction, or, beginning with it, demonstrated inductively. We witness every minute the miracle of related experiences, and yet nobody knows better than we do how this miracle is worked, for we are ourselves this network of relationships. The world and reason are not problematical. We may say, if we wish, that they are mysterious, but their mystery defines them: there can be no question of dispelling it by some 'solution', it is on the hither side of all solutions. True philosophy consists in re-learning to look at the world, and in this sense a historical account can give meaning to the world quite as 'deeply' as a philosophical treatise. We take our fate in our hands, we become responsible for our history through reflection, but equally by a decision on which we stake our life, and in both cases what is involved is a violent act which is validated by being performed.

---

4. [Husserl,] *6th Méditation cartésienne* (unpublished) [Merleau-Ponty's note].

Phenomenology, as a disclosure of the world, rests on itself, or rather provides its own foundation.[5] All knowledge is sustained by a 'ground' of postulates and finally by our communication with the world as primary embodiment of rationality. Philosophy, as radical reflection, dispenses in principle with this resource. As, however, it too is in history, it too exploits the world and constituted reason. It must therefore put to itself the question which it puts to all branches of knowledge, and so duplicate itself infinitely, being, as Husserl says, a dialogue or infinite meditation, and, in so far as it remains faithful to its intention, never knowing where it is going. The unfinished nature of phenomenology and the inchoative atmosphere which has surrounded it are not to be taken as a sign of failure[;] they were inevitable because phenomenology's task was to reveal the mystery of the world and of reason. If phenomenology was a movement before becoming a doctrine or a philosophical system, this was attributable neither to accident, nor to fraudulent intent. It is as painstaking as the works of Balzac, Proust, Valéry or Cézanne[6]—by reason of the same kind of attentiveness and wonder, the same demand for awareness, the same will to seize the meaning of the world or of history as that meaning comes into being. In this way it merges into the general effort of modern thought.

From *Part One*
The Body

Experience and Objective Thought. The Problem of the Body

Our perception ends in objects, and the object once constituted, appears as the reason for all the experiences of it which we have had or could have.[7] For example, I see the next-door house from a certain angle, but it would be seen differently from the right bank of the Seine,[8] or from the inside, or again from an aeroplane: the house *itself* is none of these appearances; it is, as Leibnitz[9] said, the flat projection of these perspectives and of all possible perspectives, that is, the perspectiveless position from which all can be derived, the house seen from nowhere. But what do these words mean? Is not to see always to see from somewhere? To say that the house itself is seen from nowhere is surely to say that it is invisible! Yet when I say that I see the house with my own eyes, I am saying something that cannot be challenged: I do not mean that my retina and crystalline lens, my eyes as material organs, go into action and cause me to see it: with only myself to consult, I can know nothing about this. I am trying to express in this way a certain manner of approaching the object, the 'gaze' in short, which is as indubitable as my own thought, as directly known by me. We must try to understand how vision can be brought into being from somewhere without being enclosed in its perspective.

5. In a note here Merleau-Ponty quotes the phrase from Husserl's then-unpublished *Sixth Cartesian Meditation* that he is echoing.
6. That is, works of art, by the novelists Honoré de Balzac (1799–1850) and Marcel Proust (1871–1922), the poet and critic Paul Valéry (1871–1945), and the painter Paul Cézanne (1839–1905), all French.
7. This section serves as the introduction of part I, "The Body."
8. One of the longest rivers in France, and the main river of Paris.
9. Gottfried Wilhelm Leibniz (1646–1716), German philosopher and mathematician; he often used the metaphor of perspective.

To see an object is either to have it on the fringe of the visual field and be able to concentrate on it, or else respond to this summons by actually concentrating upon it. When I do concentrate my eyes on it, I become anchored in it, but this coming to rest of the gaze is merely a modality of its movement: I continue inside one object the exploration which earlier hovered over them all, and in one movement I close up the landscape and open the object. The two operations do not fortuitously coincide: it is not the contingent aspects of my bodily make-up, for example the retinal structure, which force me to see my surroundings vaguely if I want to see the object clearly. Even if I knew nothing of rods and cones, I should realize that it is necessary to put the surroundings in abeyance the better to see the object, and to lose in background what one gains in focal figure, because to look at the object is to plunge oneself into it, and because objects form a system in which one cannot show itself without concealing others. More precisely, the inner horizon of an object cannot become an object without the surrounding objects' becoming a horizon, and so vision is an act with two facets. For I do not identify the detailed object which I now have with that over which my gaze ran a few minutes ago, by expressly comparing these details with a memory of my first general view. When, in a film, the camera is trained on an object and moves nearer to it to give a close-up view, we can *remember* that we are being shown the ash tray or an actor's hand, we do not actually identify it. This is because the screen has no horizons. In normal vision, on the other hand, I direct my gaze upon a sector of the landscape, which comes to life and is disclosed, while the other objects recede into the periphery and become dormant, while, however, not ceasing to be there. Now with them I have at my disposal their horizons, in which there is implied, as a marginal view, the object on which my eyes at present fall. The horizon, then, is what guarantees the identity of the object throughout the exploration; it is the correlative of the impending power which my gaze retains over the objects which it has just surveyed, and which it already has over the fresh details which it is about to discover. No distinct memory and no explicit conjecture could fill this rôle: they would give only a probable synthesis, whereas my perception presents itself as actual. The object-horizon structure, or the perspective, is no obstacle to me when I want to see the object: for just as it is the means whereby objects are distinguished from each other, it is also the means whereby they are disclosed. To see is to enter a universe of beings which *display themselves*, and they would not do this if they could not be hidden behind each other or behind me. In other words: to look at an object is to inhabit it, and from this habitation to grasp all things in terms of the aspect which they present to it. But in so far as I see those things too, they remain abodes open to my gaze, and, being potentially lodged in them, I already perceive from various angles the central object of my present vision. Thus every object is the mirror of all others. When I look at the lamp on my table, I attribute to it not only the qualities visible from where I am, but also those which the chimney, the walls, the table can 'see'; the back of my lamp is nothing but the face which it 'shows' to the chimney. I can therefore see an object in so far as objects form a system or a world, and in so far as each one treats the others [a]round it as spectators of its hidden aspects which guarantee the permanence of those aspects by their presence. Any seeing of an object by me is instantaneously repeated between all those objects in the world which are apprehended as co-existent, because each of them is all that the others 'see' of it. Our previous formula must therefore be modified; the house itself is not the house seen from nowhere, but the house seen from everywhere. The completed object is translucent, being shot through from all sides by an infinite number of present scrutinies which intersect in its depths leaving nothing hidden.

What we have just said about the spatial perspective could equally be said about the temporal. If I contemplate the house attentively and with no thought in my mind, it has something eternal about it, and an atmosphere of torpor seems to be generated by it. It is true that I see it from a certain point in my 'duration', but it is the same house that I saw yesterday when it was a day younger; it is the same house that either an old man or a child might behold. It is true, moreover, that age and change affect it, but even if it should collapse tomorrow, it will remain for ever true that it existed today: each moment of time calls all the others to witness; it shows by its advent 'how things were meant to turn out' and 'how it will all finish'; each present permanently underpins a point of time which calls for recognition from all the others, so that the object is seen at all times as it is seen from all directions and by the same means, namely the structure imposed by a horizon. The present still holds on to the immediate past without positing it as an object, and since the immediate past similarly holds its immediate predecessor, past time is wholly collected up and grasped in the present. The same is true of the imminent future which will also have its horizon of imminence. But with my immediate past I have also the horizon of futurity which surrounded it, and thus I have my actual present seen as the future of that past. With the imminent future, I have the horizon of past which will surround it, and therefore my actual present as the past of that future. Thus, through the double horizon of retention and protention,[1] my present may cease to be a factual present quickly carried away and abolished by the flow of duration, and become a fixed and identifiable point in objective time.[2]

But, once more, my human gaze[3] never *posits* more than one facet of the object, even though by means of horizons it is directed towards all the others. It can never come up against previous appearances or those presented to other people otherwise than through the intermediary of time and language. If I conceive in the image of my own gaze those others which, converging from all directions, explore every corner of the house and define it, I have still only a harmonious and indefinite set of views of the object, but not the object in its plenitude. In the same way, although my present draws into itself time past and time to come, it possesses them only in intention, and even if, for example, the consciousness of my past which I now have seems to me to cover exactly the past as it was, the past which I claim to recapture is not the real past, but my past as I now see it, perhaps after altering it. Similarly in the future I may

---

1. Extension of the consciousness of some present act or event into the future (a term from Husserl).
2. These paragraphs emphasize the experiential character of (spatial) perception and (temporal) duration, as the basic forms of space and time (phenomenologically speaking), in relation to which "objective space" and "objective time" are derivative artificial abstractions (as both Bergson and Heidegger had previously argued).
3. Merleau-Ponty constantly emphasizes that for him the subject is the embodied, perceiving, acting human being—myself as an existing human being. (For Husserl the phenomenological subject of experience is the Ego [*das Ich*].)

have a mistaken idea about the present which I now experience. Thus the synthesis of horizons is no more than a presumptive synthesis, operating with certainty and precision only in the immediate vicinity of the object. The remoter surrounding is no longer within my grasp; it is no longer composed of still discernible objects or memories; it is an anonymous horizon now incapable of bringing any precise testimony, and leaving the object as incomplete and open as it is indeed, in perceptual experience. Through this opening, indeed, the substantiality of the object slips away. If it is to reach perfect density, in other words if there is to be an absolute object, it will have to consist of an infinite number of different perspectives compressed into a strict co-existence, and to be presented as it were to a host of eyes all engaged in one concerted act of seeing. The house *has its* water pipes, *its* floor, perhaps its cracks which are insidiously spreading in the thickness of its ceilings. We never see them, but it *has them* along with its chimneys and windows which we can see. We shall forget our present perception of the house: every time we are able to compare our memories with the objects to which they refer, we are surprised, even allowing for other sources of error, at the changes which they owe to their own duration. But we still believe that there is a truth about the past; we base our memory on the world's vast Memory, in which the house has its place as it really was on that day, and which guarantees its *being* at this moment. Taken in itself—and as an object it demands to be taken thus— the object has nothing cryptic about it; it is completely displayed and its parts co-exist while our gaze runs from one to another, its present does not cancel its past, nor will its future cancel its present. The positing of the object therefore makes us go beyond the limits of our actual experience which is brought up against and halted by an alien being, with the result that finally experience believes that it extracts all its own teaching from the object. It is this *ek-stase*[4] of experience which causes all perception to be perception of something.

Obsessed with being, and forgetful of the perspectivism of my experience, I henceforth treat it as an object and deduce it from a relationship between objects. I regard my body, which is my point of view upon the world, as one of the objects of that world. My recent awareness of my gaze as a means of knowledge I now repress, and treat my eyes as bits of matter. They then take their place in the same objective space in which I am trying to situate the external object and I believe that I am producing the perceived perspective by the projection of the objects on my retina. In the same way I treat my own perceptual history as a result of my relationships with the objective world; my present, which is my point of view on time, becomes one moment of time among all the others, my duration a reflection or abstract aspect of universal time, as my body is a mode of objective space. In the same way, finally, if the objects which surround the house or which are found in it remained what they are in perceptual experience, that is, acts of seeing conditioned by a certain perspective, the house would not be posited as an autonomous being. Thus the positing of one single object, in the full sense, demands the composi-

---

4. Active transcendence of the subject in relation to the world. The author uses either the French word *extase*, or Heidegger's form *ek-stase*. The lat-ter is the one used throughout this translation [translator's note].

tive bringing into being of all these experiences in one act of manifold creation. Therein it exceeds perceptual experience and the synthesis of horizons—as the notion of a *universe*, that is to say, a completed and explicit totality, in which the relationships are those of reciprocal determination, exceeds that of a *world*, or an open and indefinite multiplicity of relationships which are of reciprocal implication.[5] I detach myself from my experience and pass to the *idea*. Like the object, the idea purports to be the same for everybody, valid in all times and places, and the individuation of an object in an objective point of time and space finally appears as the expression of a universal positing power. I am no longer concerned with my body, nor with time, nor with the world, as I experience them in antepredicative knowledge, in the inner communion that I have with them. I now refer to my body only as an idea, to the universe as idea, to the idea of space and the idea of time. Thus 'objective' thought (in Kierkegaard's sense) is formed—being that of common sense and of science—which finally causes us to lose contact with perceptual experience, of which it is nevertheless the outcome and the natural sequel. The whole life of consciousness is characterized by the tendency to posit objects, since it is consciousness, that is to say self-knowledge, only in so far as it takes hold of itself and draws itself together in an identifiable object. And yet the absolute positing of a single object is the death of consciousness, since it congeals the whole of existence, as a crystal placed in a solution suddenly crystallizes it.

We cannot remain in this dilemma of having to fail to understand either the subject or the object. We must discover the origin of the object at the very centre of our experience; we must describe the emergence of being and we must understand how, paradoxically, there is *for us* an *in-itself*. In order not to prejudge the issue, we shall take objective thought on its own terms and not ask it any questions which it does not ask itself. If we are led to rediscover experience behind it, this shift of ground will be attributable only to the difficulties which objective thought itself raises. Let us consider it then at work in the constitution of our body as object since this is a crucial moment in the genesis of the objective world.[6] It will be seen that one's own body evades, even within science itself, the treatment to which it is intended to subject it. And since the genesis of the objective body is only a moment in the constitution of the object, the body, by withdrawing from the objective world, will carry with it the intentional threads linking it to its surrounding and finally reveal to us the perceiving subject as the perceived world.[7]

* * *

5. Husserl, *Umsturz der kopernikanischen Lehre: die Erde als Ur-Arche bewegt sich nicht [Overthrow of the Copernican Doctrine: The Earth as Primordial Origin Does Not Move]* (unpublished) [Merleau-Ponty's note]. An important distinction: "a universe" for Merleau-Ponty is a totality of *causal* relations ("determination"), whereas "a world" is a totality of *meaning* relations ("implication").

6. That is, the experience of an "objective world" (the counterpart to that of "our body as object").

7. That is, the perceiving subject and the perceived world are inseparable: they can be revealed only together, as a mutually implicating totality (see the following excerpt).

From *Part Two*
The World as Perceived

The Theory of the Body Is Already a Theory of Perception[8]

Our own body is in the world as the heart is in the organism: it keeps the visible spectacle constantly alive, it breathes life into it and sustains it inwardly, and with it forms a system. When I walk round my flat,[9] the various aspects in which it presents itself to me could not possibly appear as views of one and the same thing if I did not know that each of them represents the flat seen from one spot or another, and if I were unaware of my own movements, and of my body as retaining its identity through the stages of those movements. I can of course take a mental bird's eye view of the flat, visualize it or draw a plan of it on paper, but in that case too I could not grasp the unity of the object without the mediation of bodily experience, for what I call a plan is only a more comprehensive perspective: it is the flat 'seen from above', and the fact that I am able to draw together in it all habitual perspectives is dependent on my knowing that one and the same embodied subject can view successively *from* various positions. It will perhaps be objected that by restoring the object to bodily experience as one of the poles of that experience, we deprive it of precisely that which constitutes its objectivity. From the point of view of my body I never see as equal the six sides of the cube, even if it is made of glass, and yet the word 'cube' has a meaning; the cube itself, the cube in reality, beyond its sensible appearances, has *its* six equal sides. As I move round it, I see the front face, hitherto a square, change its shape, then disappear, while the other sides come into view and one by one become squares. But the successive stages of this experience are for me merely the opportunity of conceiving the whole cube with its six equal and simultaneous faces, the intelligible structure which provides the explanation of it. And it is even necessary, for my tour of inspection of the cube to warrant the judgement: 'here is a cube', that my movements themselves be located in objective space and, far from its being the case that the experience of my own movement conditions the position of an object, it is, on the contrary, by conceiving my body itself as a mobile object that I am able to interpret perceptual appearance and construct the cube as it truly is. The experience of my own movement would therefore appear to be more than a psychological circumstance of perception and to make no contribution to determining the significance of the object. The object and my body, it will be alleged, certainly form a system, but what we have then is a nexus of objective correlations and not, as we have just said, a collection of lived-through correspondences. The unity of the object is thus conceived, and not experienced, as the correlative of our body's unity.

But can the object be thus detached from the actual conditions under which it is presented to us? One can bring together discursively the notion of the number six, the notion of 'side' and that of equality, and link them together in a formula which is the definition of the cube. But this definition rather puts a question to us than offers us something to conceive. One emerges from

---

8. This section serves as the introduction of Part Two, "The World as Perceived."   9. Apartment.

blind, symbolic thought only by perceiving the particular spatial entity which bears these predicates all together. It is a question of visualizing that particular form which encloses a fragment of space between six equal faces. Now, if the words 'enclose' and 'between' have a meaning for us, it is because they derive it from our experience as embodied subjects.[1] In space *itself* independently of the presence of a psycho-physical subject, there is no direction, no inside and no outside. A space is 'enclosed' between the sides of a cube as we are enclosed between the walls of our room. In order to be able to conceive the cube, we take up a position in space, either on its surface, or in it, or outside it, and from that moment we see it in perspective. The cube with six equal sides is not only invisible, but inconceivable; it is the cube as it would be for itself; but the cube is not for itself, since it is an object. There is a first order dogmatism, of which analytical reflection rids us, and which consists in asserting that the object is in itself, or absolutely, without wondering what it is. But there is another, which consists in affirming the ostensible significance of the object, without wondering how it enters into our experience. Analytical reflection puts forward, instead of the absolute existence of the object, the thought of an absolute object, and, through trying to dominate the object and think of it from no point of view, it destroys the object's internal structure. If there is, for me, a cube with six equal sides, and if I can link up with the object, this is not because I constitute it from the inside: it is because I delve into the thickness of the world by perceptual experience. The cube with six equal sides is the limiting idea whereby I express the material presence of the cube which is there before my eyes, under my hands, in its perceptual self-evidence. The sides of the cube are not projections of it, but precisely sides. When I perceive them successively, with the appearance they present in different perspectives, I do not construct the idea of the flat projection which accounts for these perspectives; the cube is already there in front of me and reveals itself through them. I do not need to take an objective view of my own movement, or take it into account, in order to reconstitute the true form of the object behind its appearance; the account is already taken, and already the new appearance has compounded itself with the lived-through movement and presented itself as an appearance of a cube. The thing, and the world, are given to me along with the parts of my body, not by any 'natural geometry', but in a living connection comparable, or rather identical, with that existing between the parts of my body itself.

External perception and the perception of one's own body vary in conjunction because they are the two facets of one and the same act. The attempt has long been made to explain Aristotle's celebrated illusion[2] by allowing that the unaccustomed position of the fingers makes the synthesis of their perceptions impossible: the right side of the middle finger and the left side of the index do not ordinarily 'work' together, and if both are touched at once, then there must be two marbles. In reality, the perceptions of the two fingers are not only disjoined, they are inverted: the subject attributes to the index what

---

1. This principle of meaning and of the way that meaning is engendered is fundamental to Merleau-Ponty's thought.
2. The illusory perception of two objects when a single small object is held between two crossed fingers, noted by the Greek philosopher Aristotle (384–322 B.C.E.) in several texts, including his *Metaphysics* (4.6).

is touched by the middle finger and *vice versa*, as can be shown by applying two distinct stimuli to the fingers, a point and a ball, for example. Aristotle's illusion is primarily a disturbance of the body image. What makes the synthesis of the two tactile perceptions in one single object impossible, is not so much that the position of the fingers is unaccustomed or statistically rare, it is that the right face of the middle finger and the left face of the index cannot combine in a joint exploration of the object, that the crossing of the fingers, being a movement which has to be imposed on them, lies outside the motor possibilities of the fingers themselves and cannot be aimed at in a project towards movement. The synthesis of the object is here effected, then, through the synthesis of one's own body, it is the reply or correlative to it, and it is literally the same thing to perceive one single marble, and to use two fingers as one single organ. The disturbance of the body image may even be directly translated into the external world without the intervention of any stimulus. In heautoscopy,[3] before seeing himself, the subject always passes through a state akin to dreaming, musing or disquiet, and the image of himself which appears outside him is merely the counterpart of this depersonalization. The patient has the feeling of being in the double outside himself, just as, in a lift[4] which goes upwards and suddenly stops, I feel the substance of my body escaping from me through my head and overrunning the boundaries of my objective body. * * * Every external perception is immediately synonymous with a certain perception of my body, just as every perception of my body is made explicit in the language of external perception. If, then, as we have seen to be the case, the body is not a transparent object, and is not presented to us in virtue of the law of its constitution, as the circle is to the geometer, if it is an expressive unity which we can learn to know only by actively taking it up, this structure will be passed on to the sensible world. The theory of the body image is, implicitly, a theory of perception. We have relearned to feel our body; we have found underneath the objective and detached knowledge of the body that other knowledge which we have of it in virtue of its always being with us and of the fact that we are our body. In the same way we shall need to reawaken our experience of the world as it appears to us in so far as we are in the world through our body, and in so far as we perceive the world with our body. But by thus remaking contact with the body and with the world, we shall also rediscover ourself, since, perceiving as we do with our body, the body is a natural self and, as it were, the subject of perception.

SOURCE: From Maurice Merleau-Ponty, *Phenomenology of Perception*, trans. Colin Smith (London: Routledge and Kegan Paul; New York: Humanities Press, 1962), pp. vii–xi, xix–21, 67–72, 203–6. Originally published in 1945 as *Phénoménologie de la perception*.

3. That is, "autoscopy," or self-examination; specifically, a visual hallucination of one's own body image.
4. Elevator.

Part IV

Cross-Currents: Rethinking Human Reality and Possibility

The emergence of phenomenology and existential philosophy in the first third of the twentieth century was not the only significant development in the interpretive tradition at that time. It was during that period that interest in the thought of BERGSON and DILTHEY (see Part II, above) was at its height, and that NIETZSCHE began (posthumously) to receive serious attention. The triumph of National Socialism in Germany in the early 1930s and its horrific consequences wreaked havoc with philosophy—as with so much else—in Europe. Yet both before and after that traumatic time, and to some extent even during it, the tradition continued to develop further, in new as well as already-established directions, both in Europe and (especially after 1933) in the English-speaking world.

Twentieth-century existential philosophers are often associated—and often associated themselves—not only with KIERKEGAARD but also with Nietzsche. The approaches of these two thinkers to the understanding of human reality (as well as to religion and its relevance to human life) were radically different, however; and Nietzsche is arguably related more closely to two other subsequent developments, at odds with each other as well as with existential philosophy: philosophical anthropology and what has come to be called "poststructuralism." That all three movements (although emphatically *not* Husserlian phenomenology) claim Nietzsche as a major precursor and inspiration says something about the openness of his thought to differing interpretations.

The fourth and final part of this volume begins with selections from the writings of a number of figures associated with philosophical anthropology and poststructuralism. They are followed by selections indicative of two other notable developments, which pose challenges to the ways of thinking about human reality typical of philosophical anthropology that are of a different sort from those raised by poststructuralism. These challenges are associated with ways in which those on different sides of long-established and much-emphasized demarcation lines of sex and race have come to experience significantly differing human realities. Part IV concludes with selections exemplifying several other important recent varieties of interpretive theory, including the movement known as "hermeneutics." Nietzsche figures in the genealogies of some of these movements, while others have other heritages and affinities, drawing on MARX, Dilthey, and even HEGEL. As different as they are from each other, they have at least one thing in common that differentiates them fundamentally from phenomenology and existential philosophy: while they may avail themselves of first-person experiential perspectives on human reality, they also rely on others (biological, historical, social, cultural) and view them as no less important, or even as more important, for comprehending that reality.

These developments are by no means the only ones that a complete history of philosophy in the interpretive tradition (or in Europe) in the twentieth century would need to mention. Marxist philosophy, for example, loomed large for a time; and so did other approaches, including positivism and both neo-Hegelian and Catholic philosophy. Moreover, other developments that are represented in this volume could certainly be treated more fully (such as the sort of "critical social theory" associated with the Frankfurt School, here exemplified only by its latest and most important figure, JÜRGEN HABERMAS). But the selections that follow provide a sense of several of the most significant cross-currents that emerged at the same time as and after phenomenology and existential philosophy.

Philosophical anthropology, which originated in German-speaking Europe between the world wars (and has been largely eclipsed in the English-speaking world by other developments with greater popular appeal), is akin to some of the "naturalisms" encountered in Part II, supplemented to some extent by phenomenological strategies. Its focus is on "man" or humankind (*der Mensch*, in German), conceived as a type of living creature that must as a first step be approached and comprehended as such, with attention to developmental biology and physiology—but that also needs to be understood in ways that take account of other aspects of human reality that have come to characterize it very centrally and pervasively, including human social, cultural, behavioral, linguistic, and intellectual life.

Philosophical anthropology thus involves attempting to make comprehensive sense of the full range of human reality on display in human life—including its plasticity and historical character, and thus its variability and diversity. Like philosophical psychology and philosophy of mind in the analytic tradition, it presupposes no commitment to any sort of "essentialist" conception of "human nature" (let alone one with normative content), or even to the idea that human nature is characterized by anything fixed and unchanging at all. Its guiding idea is simply the supposition that there may well be something about *der Mensch* (or human reality) that is not only very distinctively biological but more than merely biological, that relates to human social and cultural dimensions and behavioral and intellectual capacities, and that is likely to require not only human-scientific investigation but also a kind of philosophical interpretation to make comprehensive sense of it all. But as will be seen, there is room within these broad parameters for considerable divergence, both methodological and substantive.

The idea and project of a philosophical anthropology can be traced back to KANT's and Hegel's provision for an empirically oriented type of philosophical inquiry into that about ourselves which is specifically "human," and to FEUERBACH's call for the "anthropological reduction" of Hegel's speculative philosophy of *Geist* (spirit) to a naturalistic philosophy of "man" (*der Mensch*). As it emerged out of *Lebensphilosophie* (life philosophy) in the second quarter of the twentieth century, however, it was more specifically and directly a response to and continuation of the kind of postreligious and post metaphysical, scientifically informed, and developmentally minded reinterpretation of "the type *Mensch*" that Nietzsche had called for and initiated, involving both "translating man back into nature" and seeking to understand the ways in which our original merely natural humanity has been "dis-animalized" and transformed. Nietzsche had insisted that any such reinterpretation needed to be "historical" rather than metaphysical or essentialist, bringing many sorts of inquiry—biological, physiological, psychological, social, cultural, and linguistic, among others—to bear on its subject.

Those who took up this task emphasized different elements of the mix; some were content to focus on certain parts of the picture, while others sought to develop more comprehensive interpretations. In general, they tended to focus on structural or functional features of human reality that are capable of being realized in quite different ways, rather than on particular human qualities, traits, or behaviors. The first four thinkers included in this section— MAX SCHELER (1874–1928), ARNOLD GEHLEN (1904–1976), HELMUTH PLESSNER (1892–1985), and ERNST CASSIRER (1874–1945)—all explicitly embrace the idea and program of a philosophical anthropology. A number of the others—Jürgen Habermas (b. 1929), HANS-GEORG GADAMER (1900–2002), PAUL RICOEUR (1913–2005), and CHARLES TAYLOR (b. 1931)—can be read as contributing to it as well, as several of them acknowledge. This can even be said of those among them who are attempting to come to grips with issues relating to race and color lines—W. E. B. DU BOIS (1868–1963) and FRANTZ FANON (1925–1961).

The same can by no means be said of MICHEL FOUCAULT (1926–1984), JACQUES DERRIDA (1930–2004), JEAN-FRANÇOIS LYOTARD (1924–1998), and GILLES DELEUZE (1925–1994) and FÉLIX GUATTARI (1930–1992), who loom large in one of the most radical of this tradition's many divergences in the twentieth century. (JUDITH BUTLER, in her basic orientation, may be associated with this "cross-current" in the postexistential era.) That development, which came to be even more polarizing in the philosophical world (and popular in other interpretive disciplines) than existentialism had been, has been designated and described in a number of (not very illuminating) ways, including most notably "poststructuralism," "postmodernism," and "deconstruction."

It is striking, and of some significance, that each of these notions and designations is framed negatively, in terms of some contrast or opposition. Each of them presupposes as well as opposes some development in philosophy (and perhaps also in related areas of thought, inquiry, and debate—especially in the arts and humanities and other kindred cultural and intellectual activities). Their oppositional relations thus contribute to their somewhat distinctive characters.

"Poststructuralism" is actually no substantive position or orientation at all, as other "-isms" in philosophy (such as "empiricism" and "existentialism") have tended to be. The expression itself conveys little more than the idea of a kind of philosophical (or quasi-philosophical) thinking that is critical (or simply dismissive) of structuralism, which had emerged as an alternative and successor to existentialism, particularly in French philosophy. The interpretive tradition in general had moved away from metaphysical conceptions of reality in terms of "substances" of some kind(s) from its very outset; and one of the prime candidates for their replacement in thinking about reality—from Hegel and Marx to HEIDEGGER and SARTRE—was the idea of "structures" of one sort or another.

Structure was also a central concept in the linguistics of Ferdinand de Saussure earlier in the twentieth century; and his structuralist linguistics subsequently inspired others to employ a similar approach in interpreting other social and cultural phenomena. A prime example is the structuralist anthropology of Claude Lévi-Strauss. The method was taken up by Marxist and other philosophers in the 1960s, as attention shifted from first-person perspectives on human "existing" to human reality viewed as a social phenomenon. Sartre himself came to advocate a philosophical anthropology that would be both historical and structural, dealing at great length with the structural character of human social reality in his *Critique of Dialectical Reason* (1960).

"Structure" thus was becoming the organizing concept in an increasingly broad range of domains of inquiry—and it has remained widely popular beyond French-oriented philosophical circles, seeming to be an attractive substitute for "substance" both in philosophy and in the social and humanistic disciplines. Linguistic structures are something real, possessing an evident kind of objectivity, and the same is arguably true of many other social and cultural formations—as Hegel had insisted, in his philosophy of "objective *Geist* (spirit)." Poststructuralists might be thought of not as abandoning the idea of structure for some other organizing concept, but rather as rejecting the ahistoricity and rather rigid formalism of structuralist analyses modeled on those of Saussure. More generally, they display a kind of disillusionment with the structuralist program for analyzing things human; for further reflection on the contingently historical character of everything structural in and about human reality seemed to deprive discernible structures of any sort of substantiality or even objectivity, not to mention of necessity, meaning, and value.

Yet poststructuralism cannot be said to dissolve the objectivity of structure into *subjectivity*; for in it the subjectivity of the subject is dissolved as well, into the historical contingencies of the social-relational and cultural-formational complexities of our existence. Thus poststructuralism has tended toward a kind of radical historicism, for which all "knowledges" (or ways of thinking that lay claim to be knowledge) are interpretational, all interpretations are perspectival, all perspectives are contingently historical, and all master narratives about historical contingencies are untenable. This, in a nutshell, is essentially the standpoint of what has come to be called postmodernism in philosophy.

The label "postmodernism" is used so often, in so many ways and contexts, that it is often more confusing than helpful. The term "modern" is of course a moving target; but in philosophy the target was fixed in a lasting way by Hegel, who was enormously influential in shaping how we think about the history of Western philosophy, and indeed in establishing the idea of philosophy as *having* a "history" that is significantly related to the nature of the enterprise. Hegel divided the history of philosophy (as he did so many things) into three—in this case, three parts or periods: ancient, medieval, and "modern." The "modern" period began, for him, with Descartes (1596–1650) and some of his contemporaries, and extended to Hegel's present—that is, to Kant and his immediate successors (FICHTE and SCHELLING). And the label stuck.

Thus one might say that at least in a nominal sense, Hegel was the first "postmodern" philosopher—and that the entire interpretive tradition is in effect the history of "postmodern" philosophy. This unusual characterization of both is actually surprisingly apt, because that tradition has differed more significantly from what is sometimes called "classical modern" philosophy from Descartes to Kant than has the analytic tradition. Hegel began a reconsideration of *ways* of conceiving of truth, knowledge, morality, our own reality and reality more generally (including what has traditionally been called "God"), and *paradigms* of reason and rationality—both of which had been matters of sufficient general agreement to make disputes about them possible.

Hegel intended to salvage these elements, insofar as that was possible, by recasting and reinterpreting them in a way that would reconcile them with his conception of the historically developmental character of everything human and spiritual—up to and including the very nature of knowledge and the fundamental nature of reality. By the end of the nineteenth century, however, the break with the classical modern tradition on these matters had become more radical—particularly in the thought of Nietzsche, who therefore is commonly viewed as either the first truly postmodern philosopher or the herald of postmodern philosophy. "The crisis of modernity" had been building during his century, and now that crisis was dawning. It had to do with what he called "the death of God" (and the demise of all other absolutes), and with the implications of the kind of historical-developmental thinking begun by Hegel, in conjunction with scientific ways of thinking that were no less corrosive (even if problematic in their own right). So Nietzsche proclaimed "the advent of nihilism" to be at hand, as modes of interpretation and evaluation associated with traditional philosophical as well as religious thought lost first their self-evidence, then their viability, and finally their very believability.

Postmodernism might be thought of as the realization and elaboration of that vision—pursued by some through the strategy of "deconstruction." Heidegger had spoken of the need for a "destruction" of all of the fundamental concepts of metaphysical thinking, which he believed to hinder rather than aid our comprehension of "the meaning of being." This idea and project were taken up by Jacques Derrida, albeit without Heidegger's larger hopes and expectations. He approached the kinds of concepts that philosophers traditionally have employed (and continue to employ) by showing that they undermine themselves, and that the kinds of distinctions and dichotomies on which logical reasoning depends cannot be sustained. Deconstruction is thus akin to Hegel's method of attempting, in his *Phenomenology of Spirit* (1807), to show the untenability of such concepts—before their reinterpretation and integration into his philosophical system—as candidates for a knowledge of reality that would be absolute and final. But here we find no such Hegelian-style happy ending to the story, for *this* story's moral is meant to be the opposite of Hegel's: to wit, the entire quest is a mistake.

Postmodernism does not stop with its negative verdict on the basic tenets of the classical modern philosophical tradition that culminates in Kant. It extends that verdict to all subsequent attempts that might be made to develop, modify, or even replace those tenets so that strong validity claims of a cognitive or evaluative nature could be warranted and justified. This extension encompasses much of philosophy after Kant, in both the interpretive and analytical traditions. It also covers thought in the social and even natural sciences, as well as judgments pertaining to all aspects of social and cultural life. As the crisis of modernity is thus expanded to what might be called "late modernity," all confidence in the past two centuries' developments in philosophical, scientific, and social thought is eroded. The fundamental thesis of postmodernism is that this crisis is no mere "transitional stage," as Nietzsche had suggested of the "nihilism" he saw coming, but rather is here to stay, as the final word and the only real truth of the matter.

Because this stance is taken by many associated with postmodernism to be the upshot of Nietzsche's thinking—even if perhaps something about which he was deeply ambivalent—he is often regarded as the movement's precursor and inspiration. That, however, is a matter of much debate. Nietzsche can also be read as seeing the great challenge and task of the "philosophy of the future" that he calls for to be finding a way *beyond* this crisis, which he was by no means prepared to view as the last word. He, as well as other figures encountered here and in earlier parts of this volume, can and should be revisited to consider whether they may point the way to kinds of alternative philosophical thinking that may actually prove capable of withstanding the challenge of poststructuralist deconstructionist postmodernism. Habermas, Gadamer, Ricoeur, and Taylor were no strangers to its philosophical literature during the decades of its greatest celebrity, for example, and yet did not hesitate to pursue their philosophical projects and contests in poststructuralism's wake.

They and many of the others encountered here are primarily interested in human phenomena that are significantly (even if not entirely) contingent and variable—not only because of their importance for understanding the aspects of human reality to which they pertain but also because of their impact on the character and quality of human life. HANNAH ARENDT (1906–1975) made political life (broadly conceived) her focus, in her social-theoretical reflections in *The Human Condition* (1958), while SIMONE DE BEAUVOIR (1908–1986) gave powerful impetus to the emergence of modern feminist theory in her analysis and critique of the identity phenomenon she sought to illuminate and problematize in *The Second Sex* (1949).

Feminist theory itself has developed in a number of strikingly different interpretive and programmatic directions, two of which are on display in the selections by Judith Butler (b. 1956) and MARTHA NUSSBAUM (b. 1947), which follow excerpts from Beauvoir's classic study. Set against *The Second Sex*, the very titles of their books—*Gender Trouble* (1990) and *Sex and Social Justice* (1990), respectively—show the diversity of approaches to these issues: Beauvoir and Butler are both addressing themselves to gender theory, whereas the focus of Nussbaum's "conception of feminism" is closer to the earlier concern of MARY WOLLSTONECRAFT (and JOHN STUART MILL, in his final selection above) with the human flourishing of women. Taken together, these selections also show that there are a multiplicity of human possibilities and realities relating to these topics that need to be sorted out and examined, requiring differing modes of analysis, interpretation, and assessment. Moreover, little if anything about any of them is determined or can be settled—interpretively, evaluatively, or normatively—by apparently simple circumstances of human biology. Rather: they are just the sorts of humanly emergent phenomena that belong on the agenda of the interpretive tradition as it goes forward.

Much the same may be said of matters of color and race, which are no more merely biological affairs than are matters of sex and gender. The former, like the latter, long seemed to many philosophers to raise only general moral and ethical issues; but Du Bois and Fanon championed more expansive views, which reflect their differing links to the interpretive tradition. Rather like Beauvoir, both are concerned with the dynamics of group oppression, examining the consequences that an imposed identity conceived as "inferior" has for the kind of human reality available to those on the receiving end of this process, and exploring the question of what might be done about it. Du Bois, as an African American, initially had in mind primarily black Americans and their social situation, but he eventually expanded his focus to all populations on what he called the "dark" side of the "color line." Fanon, as an Afro-Caribbean from a French colony, had a double focus, on the dynamics and consequences of both racism and colonialism. Both advocated radical social as well as cultural transformation, in the name of a better humanity; but as their selections show, Du Bois's version was evolutionary while Fanon's was revolutionary.

Both Du Bois and Fanon might be said to be deeply engaged in the kind of interpretive and evaluative inquiry—represented most saliently in this volume by Habermas—that has come to be called "critical social theory," but with a relatively specific focus. Habermas stands in the tradition of the Frankfurt School—thinkers inspired by Marx's program of historically informed social critique, who also drew on Kant, Hegel, Nietzsche, Freud, and others in their critical analyses of social and cultural phenomena; and he has provided this distinctive strand of interpretive theory with its most impressive comprehensive elaboration and systematic articulation. In his hands social theory becomes constructive as well as "critical," on a scale comparable to the treatments of human social reality by Marx, Dilthey, and even Hegel, and in rivalry with Foucault's radically historicist opposition to the very idea that there is such a reality about which anything of significance can be said.

Gadamer and Ricoeur are associated with yet another such strand: the development of hermeneutics from the study of theories and procedures of textual interpretation (initially focused specifically on the Bible and other religious texts) into a more general and deeper conception of interpretation as a central feature of human thought and life. This is a development to which Nietzsche, Dilthey, and Heidegger all contributed. Indeed, it is rooted in the Hegelian beginnings of the tradition dealt with in this volume, as the volume's very title underscores. In the hands of Gadamer and Ricoeur it becomes a form of reflection on the phenomenon of meaning in human language and life that brings the interpretive tradition within bridging distance of the analytical tradition, in one of their most significant areas of convergence. The same may also be said of Taylor; but he and Ricoeur are also drawn to the idea and project of philosophical anthropology, which they see hermeneutics—as well as social theory and the philosophy of action (both interpretive and analytic)—as assisting.

————————

This part begins with Max Scheler, who was at the forefront of the emergence of philosophical anthropology as an explicit philosophical movement and project. Like existential philosophy, it takes human reality as its focus; but it construes human reality as a form of life that is undeniably biological, social, and cultural—and that therefore must be comprehended in a way that takes these dimensions and perspectives of analysis into account, as well as from the inside out. So Scheler begins by comparing human life with other forms of life, both vegetable and animal, before moving on to consider the respects in which human spiritual life differs significantly from them, and to examine how "spirit" (*Geist*) is related to "life" as a natural phenomenon. His moral and value theory reflects his insistence that the content of spiritual reality cannot be reduced to merely natural vitality or anything deriving developmentally from the world of mere nature.

Arnold Gehlen was equally committed to the project of a philosophical anthropology; but he was convinced that there is nothing about human reality that cannot be understood in terms of the development of its distinctive form of vitality and the imperatives of our biological existence. In this sense, his interpretation of human reality is uncompromisingly naturalizing. Yet he emphatically opposes the idea that human life is merely a variation on themes common to animal life more generally, arguing that man (*der Mensch*) has come to have a nature radically different from the natures of other forms of animal life, in that very little of what we do is instinctive or biologically determined in any specific way, and everything depends (for better or worse) on social institutions and cultural practices.

Helmuth Plessner, like Gehlen, developed a philosophical anthropology that dispensed with Scheler's concept of *Geist* in its account of human reality and possibility. But unlike Gehlen's, his own account emphasizes and explores the multiple transformations of human life that have made it so different from other forms of life on their own terms. He writes in the spirit of a phenomenologist (the stance with which he began), whose concerns are primarily descriptive, rather than of a scientist, concerned with explanation. He too considers human life to differ in a fundamental way from other forms of life, but his emphasis is on the radical difference of the structure of our consciousness of ourselves and our world from those of other sentient creatures.

Ernst Cassirer's central interest was in human culture, and more specifically in the various types of symbol systems and symbolic forms—linguistic, artistic, mythological, religious, and scientific—that figure prominently in it. He regarded his kind of "philosophy of culture" and "philosophy of symbolic forms" as the key to understanding what makes human reality more than just another type of animality, and so as an essential and critically important part of philosophical anthropology. Viewing both the classical conception of man as the "rational animal" and the more recent conception of man as the "tool-making and -using animal" as too narrow, he proposed that man might better be characterized as *homo symbolicum*—"man the symbol maker and user."

Michel Foucault rightly resisted identification with any of the disciplines (history, sociology, philosophy) or developments (historicism, structuralism, poststructuralism, postmodernism) with which he has been associated. His thought may with some justice be characterized in any of these ways; but it reduces neither to any of them nor simply to their sum. He considered the ideas of "man" and "human nature" to be mere artifacts of a certain cultural-historical epoch whose time has come and gone; but while his work was devoted largely to examining various historically specific cultural formations and social institutions, his reflections on their underlying dynamics apply with critical significance and interpretive suggestiveness to human reality and possibility more generally.

Jacques Derrida was one of the most provocative, controversial, and per-plexing figures associated with the interpretive tradition in the second half of the twentieth century. Beginning as a Husserlian phenomenologist, he became one of the most notable and highly visible representatives and architects of the poststructuralist and postmodernist tendencies that took hold in philoso-phy and in humanistic disciplines more broadly in that period. He was par-ticularly closely identified with the (originally Heideggerian) idea and project of a "deconstruction" of the basic concepts, distinctions, and dichotomies of classical metaphysics and of the Western philosophical tradition more gener-ally, and thus with the attempt to subvert them in favor of a kind of postphi-losophical thinking no longer governed and guided by traditional aims, values, and norms of thought.

Jean-François Lyotard developed and popularized the ideas both of the untenability of all "grand [sense-making] narratives," such as Hegel's, to inter-pret human history and reality, and of "the postmodern condition" resulting from the collapse of the classically "modern" picture of life and the world. Instead, in the spirit of the nihilism whose advent Nietzsche had heralded, he purported to discern (and also held) a growing conviction of that unten-ability and of the artificiality and inadequacy of human rationality in the face of the singularity and irrationality of events.

Gilles Deleuze, often writing with Félix Guattari, subscribed to the basic tenets of postmodernism, and had affinities with deconstructionist poststruc-turalism. Nonetheless, he sought to develop and advance a kind of vitalist meta-physical interpretation of human reality, which he took to be in the spirit of both Spinoza (1632–1677) and Nietzsche. His conception of philosophy was likewise unconventional, yet it was fundamentally positive rather than entirely deconstructionist in its aspirations as well as in its relation to the philosophi-cal tradition.

W. E. B. Du Bois was a prominent African American public intellectual who brought his training as a historian and sociologist and his exposure to American (pragmatist) and German philosophy to bear on race, racism, Afri-can American life and experience, education, and public policy. He took strong objection to racism and racial discrimination but had a positive view of race conceived along the primarily ethnic and cultural lines of Hegel's idea of a "people" (*Volk*), with its distinctive spirit and contribution to make to humanity (an affinity underscored in the title of his most famous book, *The Souls of Black Folk* [1903]).

Frantz Fanon, an Afro-Caribbean from the French territory of Martinique, came to know and detest French colonialism and the racism he encountered both there and in the course of his experiences in France. Educated there in both philosophy (Hegel, Marx, Sartre, MERLEAU-PONTY) and medicine, he became a psychiatrist. His first book, *Black Skin, White Masks* (1952), was a study of the kind of "self-alienated" self-consciousness that he took colonialism and racism to produce in blacks like himself. He became involved in the Algerian revolt against French colonial rule, which he saw as paradigmatic of the colonialist system that was the target of his last and most famous book, *The Wretched of the Earth* (1961).

Simone de Beauvoir was closely associated with Jean-Paul Sartre both philosophically and personally throughout her adult life, and she contributed significantly to the literature of existentialism. The book for which she is best known, however, is *The Second Sex*, one of the founding texts of modern feminist thought. It not only opened the way for issues relating to "woman" to be discussed and taken seriously in philosophical inquiry into human reality, but helped make clear the necessity of such discussion. Availing herself of ideas articulated in Sartre's *Being and Nothingness* (1943) and Mill's *The Subjection of Women* (1869; both excerpted above), Beauvoir developed and employed them in ways that influenced not only philosophy but also contemporary thought and social critique more broadly.

Judith Butler has been an important contributor to feminist and gender theory throughout her career—not least through her intimate familiarity with developments in French philosophy and feminist theory during the past century. Through her *Gender Trouble* and other writings she has played a major role in articulating and developing the idea of "gender" as a form of identity that is to be understood culturally rather than naturalistically, and moreover "performatively" rather than either descriptively or (even self-) ascriptively. She also has done important work on the phenomenon of "subjection."

Martha Nussbaum began her career as a classicist and has been broadening her scope ever since. Her work in feminist philosophy is itself wide-ranging, and its linkages to her work in other areas—from social justice to the emotions to ethics and "quality of life" issues—anchor it even more substantially in a comprehensive view of things that matter in human life. The selections from her writings included here illustrate a number of her philosophical and human interests, her conception of feminism and its application in real-world contexts among them; and they provide hints of others of her interests, while also exemplifying her distinctive ways of doing philosophy.

Hannah Arendt moved beyond her early intimate philosophical and personal relationship with Martin Heidegger to become an astute observer and analyst of some of the most vexing political developments of her time, as well as a political thinker of considerable importance. Although she was reluctant to call herself a philosopher, her reflections on the political and "action"-centered character of human life in *The Human Condition* and other writings enriched both political philosophy and philosophical anthropology.

Jürgen Habermas developed perspectives that derived from his early interests in the kind of critical social theory associated with the Frankfurt School and in philosophical anthropology, and molded them into one of the most impressive recent contributions to the interpretive tradition. He has become a leading social, political, and moral philosopher, and also may be regarded as a significant contributor to the philosophical reconsideration of human reality. In his work the distinction between the interpretive and analytical traditions becomes a distinction without any fundamental difference.

Hans-Georg Gadamer expanded the project of a philosophical hermeneutics as a philosophy of language and meaning in ways anticipated and suggested by Dilthey and Heidegger. In his hands it became an approach to the understanding of human reality that is guided by sensitivity to its historical, cultural, and linguistic character. His hermeneutic philosophy is both a reflection on the idea and practice of interpretation and an attempt to deal with human reality in a manner that is self-consciously interpretive, taking that reflection into account. This and his essay therefore have a particular aptness and relevance to this volume and its tradition.

Paul Ricoeur attempted to extend and develop the interpretive tradition in a way that not only draws on and combines approaches advocated in different strands of that tradition in the twentieth century but also brings it within bridging distance of counterparts in the recent analytic tradition. Human reality was his fundamental concern; and he was equally insistent that its comprehension is an interpretive affair and that a variety of interpretive approaches are helpful, drawing upon contributions within both traditions.

Finally, Charles Taylor exemplifies the possibility of combining elements of the general interpretive programs and procedures of many of the seemingly disparate figures and developments in this volume—Hegel, Heidegger, and Habermas; phenomenology, philosophical anthropology, and hermeneutics—not only with each other but also with the sensibility of an analytic philosopher, in work that is newly insightful. That combination characterizes his masterful *Sources of the Self* (1989), and it can be seen on a smaller scale in the selection from his work with which this part concludes.

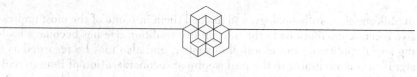

MAX SCHELER
(1874 – 1928)

Many of Scheler's most formidable rivals—notably HEIDEGGER and, somewhat later, SARTRE—are best known and are likely to be best remembered for their first major works. Scheler's most important work may well prove to be his last—*Die Stellung des Menschen im Kosmos* (1928, *The Place of Man in the Cosmos*; published in English as *Man's Place in Nature*)—which actually is only a sketch and preview of a major treatise that he did not live to complete. In it, Scheler announced and inaugurated the project of a "philosophical anthropology," which would counter his arch-rival Heidegger's program of an existential phenomenology of our human type of "being," set out in *Being and Time* (1927).

Scheler's early death (at the age of only 54), shortly after his book's publication, precluded any further elaboration of his position in print, and so this contest was a very unequal one. This slender book was no match for *Being and Time*. Yet it proved to be a rallying point for others who shared or were persuaded to share Scheler's conviction that to comprehend human reality, the approach of HUSSERL (and of Heidegger and JASPERS as well) must be supplemented with attention to what we can discern from the broad range of developing human-scientific perspectives—from the evolutionary-biological and physiological to the social, cultural, and historical. Scheler and Heidegger both

had been drawn to Husserl's phenomenology, and both had aspired to be his successor at Freiburg (a competition won by Heidegger). Yet both were moving beyond Husserl, though in quite different directions. Whereas Heidegger basically followed KIERKEGAARD's lead (focusing on the character of human "existing"), Scheler combined elements of NIETZSCHE, HEGEL, the emerging life sciences, and the *Lebensphilosophie* (philosophy of life) with which Husserl had taken issue.

Max Ferdinand Scheler ("SHAY-ler") was born in Munich. Though he was raised and baptized a Protestant, his writings were suppressed by the Nazis because his mother was Jewish. Scheler began his university career in Munich, studying medicine, psychology, and philosophy, and then studied briefly in Berlin with WILHELM DILTHEY and Georg Simmel. He completed his education in Jena, where he earned his doctorate in 1887 and his second doctorate ("habilitation") in 1899, under the guidance of one of the leading Idealist philosophers of the day, Rudolf Eucken. That same year he converted to Catholicism and married his first wife, Amelie Ottilie Wollman.

Scheler met Husserl in January 1902. Though he was attracted by Husserl's phenomenological program, he was not a follower and even was critical of Husserl (which may partly explain why Heidegger rather than Scheler succeeded Husserl at

Freiburg in 1928). Husserl was support-ive of him, however. Scheler had begun to lecture at Jena in 1900 as a *Privat-dozent* (unsalaried instructor), and when he decided to seek a position at Munich in 1905, he asked for and received a letter of support from Husserl.

Scheler began teaching at Munich in 1907, where the Husserlians he met deepened his interest in phenomenology; but he was obliged to resign from his position at that conservative Catholic university in 1910 following his separa-tion from his wife and accusations of adultery. For the next nine years he made his living as a private scholar and writer. During that period he wrote many of his most important books, including *Ressentiment* (1912), a critique of Nietzsche's analysis of this concept and defense of a nonnaturalistic concep-tion of moral values; and *Formalism in Ethics and Non-Formal Ethics of Values* (1913–16), a critique of Kantian "formal-ism in ethics" and advocacy of a substan-tive values-based ethics, from which the first selection below is taken. (It might better have been titled *Against Formal-ism in Ethics: Toward a Substantive Value-Ethics*.)

Scheler lectured in Göttingen in 1910 and 1911, but without a formal aca-demic appointment. In 1912 he married his second wife, Märit Furtwängler (whom he would divorce in 1924). When Husserl's journal *Jahrbuch für Philoso-phie und phänomenologische Forschung* (*Yearbook for Philosophy and Phenome-nological Research*) was founded in 1913, Scheler became one of its several co-editors. He did little actual editorial work on it; but a number of his own writings appeared in it. Scheler was passionately supportive of the German cause at the outset of the First World War (even pub-lishing a book lauding it in 1915, titled *The Genius of War and the German War*), but came to find the war itself increas-ingly distressing. During its course he served in the German Foreign Office and went on diplomatic missions to Swit-zerland and the Netherlands.

In 1919 Scheler finally obtained a for-mal academic position, as professor of philosophy and sociology at the Univer-sity of Cologne, and as director of its new Sociological Institute. (Sociology and philosophy were closely related disci-plines in German-speaking Europe from the emergence of sociology as a form of social theory in the nineteenth century until the middle of the twentieth cen-tury.) Scheler had developed a strong interest in and commitment to religion in the aftermath of the war, whose hor-rors deeply affected him; but after pub-lishing his major work on religion (*On the Eternal in Man*, 1921), Scheler became dissatisfied with Catholicism. He turned to a non-Christian form of personalism combined with a kind of spiritualism that finds expression in *Man's Place in Nature* (from which our second selection is taken) in the concep-tion of *Geist* (spirit)—there invoked in connection with his call for a "philo-sophical anthropology." Nonetheless, his thought has been influential in Catholic circles; Karol Wojtyla, the future Pope John Paul II, wrote his 1953 doctoral dissertation on Catholicism and Sche-ler's ethics.

In 1924 Scheler married his third wife, Maria Scheu. In 1927, their rivalry not-withstanding, Scheler invited Heidegger to Cologne to give a lecture on KANT. The two then spent three days discussing *Being and Time* and Scheler's conception of phenomenology. In that same year, Scheler was called to a professorship at Frankfurt—but he died in 1928, before he could take up his new position. After his death, his wife—assisted by an edi-torial board that included Heidegger—began to oversee an authoritative collection of his published and unpub-lished works. Though the project was halted soon after the Nazis came to power, it resumed after their defeat, and she continued to work on it until her own death in 1969.

Scheler did not leave his earlier views and interests behind when he conceived of the need for a philosophical anthro-pology. Rather, he folded them into it, and even regarded them as well served by it. He previously had been a leading figure in phenomenological ethics and value theory; and the book from which the first selection is drawn was a significant contribution to it. He also had been a strong proponent of personalism and a defender of a conception of spirituality that in his view was necessary to do justice not only to human reality but to reality more generally. As the second selection shows, he makes important provision for these concerns and convictions in (and in association with) his philosophical anthropology. His broader philosophical position thus differs significantly from those of many others of a more naturalistic persuasion who rallied to the banner of a philosophical anthropology (a number of whom appear below). He was not alone in his resistance to the naturalistic turn that was finding increasing favor, however; and his ideas concerning spirituality have been as influential within subsequent religious thought as his general anthropological program was in the secular European philosophical tradition he initiated. It is no doubt for this reason that the project of a philosophical anthropology is best known in the English-speaking world within the tradition of Catholic philosophy.

Scheler's interests both in value theory and in a philosophical anthropology were stimulated and influenced by his conviction that there are philosophical as well as religious reasons for rejecting the claims of all materialisms, naturalisms, and historicisms to be complete, adequate, and definitive in accounting for the character and status of value and of human reality. Already beginning to develop under the influence of his Idealist mentor Eucken during his Jena years, this conviction was reinforced by his introduction to Husserlian phenomenology, which likewise strongly opposed such naturalistic claims. But Scheler also was dissatisfied with Kantian formalism, which was his primary target in the most important of his books on this subject, *Formalism in Ethics and Substantive Value-Ethics*, the latter being his preferred alternative to it.

His phenomenological approach to values enabled him to present them as having a kind of reality and truth that answer to and are attested to by our experience of them as objective and valid for all who are capable of being aware of them. The consciousness of value and values is for him both key and guide to knowledge of their structures and relations, which is of a different kind than (and in no way inferior to or derivative of) the knowledge of natural and historical phenomena. Indeed, for Scheler the reality of value transcends that of the natural and historical and is quite independent of them, even though values can achieve concrete embodiment in the experience of beings like ourselves only in the realms of the natural and the historical. Moreover, our capacity for such experience, and for action that is value-guided rather than merely impelled by natural causes, differentiates us from the rest of nature: it is a hallmark of the spirituality that gives human life its special meaning and significance. The selection from *Formalism in Ethics and Substantive Value-Ethics* indicates the kind of account of value and of a value-based ethics that Scheler elaborates at length and in great detail in this classic of phenomenological value theory.

In turning to a philosophical anthropology, Scheler was no doubt motivated at least in part by his recognition that an interpretation of human reality that is both persuasive in its own right and plausible in the context of his value theory would greatly strengthen the case for that theory. His earlier work makes clear that had his life not been cut short, he would have developed and elaborated his version of a philosophical anthropology into something far more substantial and significant than the introduction provided by *The Place of Man in the Cosmos*. That introduction was an intriguing one, however; and while few embraced his version entirely, it was a powerful stimulus and challenge to others attracted by the idea. It also threw down the gauntlet to those who would attempt to carry out the program of a philosophical anthropology in a purely naturalistic manner, without recourse to anything like his conception of spirituality (*Geist*).

For Scheler, as for Kant, there is more to human reality than that dimension of it which is a part of the world of nature and is subject to nature's laws. In their view, human reality has to do with our capacity to experience and be responsive to the moral law, which is no part of that world, and which raises us and our dignity and worth above everything that is merely natural. Indeed, for Scheler there is more than mere nature not only to human reality but to reality more generally—the realm of nonnaturalistic value, for example; and because we are so constituted as to be capable of responding to it, we are capable of becoming something more than mere creatures of nature ourselves.

Scheler readily grants that there *is* a naturalistic story to be told with respect to human reality; but he contends that there is also a *non*naturalistic one to be told about it—or, at any rate, about human possibility. And while it is made possible and plausible by the naturalistic story, it is not a mere extension of that story. He discusses this further dimension of human reality under the same rubric of *Geist* that had been employed extensively by Kant's successors in their attempt to bring into focus that about us which is more than merely natural. *Geist*, for Scheler, is not some sort of entity that can and does exist concretely apart from living creatures like ourselves. Rather, it refers to a kind of spirituality that is no less fundamental to reality than is all materiality, by which life can be infused and transformed in ways that raise it above merely natural existence.

Scheler's strategy is to consider the characteristics of various forms of organic existence other than human life, and then to examine forms of human experience and activity, in an attempt to ascertain both similarities and differences—in particular, with a view to ascertaining whether there are some phenomena that cannot be explained (either in their

characteristics or in their functions) as biologically or vitally purposive. He poses the question of what these different sorts of characteristics or functions suggest about our nature, and his answer involves not only our biology but also our capacity for various forms of "spiritual" experience and activity. He then attempts to develop a model of human nature that would make comprehensible their relations and the manner in which our vital nature connects with and contributes to the realization of our spiritual possibilities.

Thus the first parts of *The Place of Man in the Cosmos* deal with forms or modes of existence *in nature*: physical, vegetable, and animal. Scheler contends that human reality involves elements of each of them. He then argues that many things of which human beings are capable transcend those elements—and some not only diverge from and operate differently from those elements but can result in their denial and negation. We are capable of behavior that is independent of vital drives and environmental conditions; of objectifying ourselves and our surroundings; of obtaining purely theoretical as well as practically significant knowledge; of insight into the essential natures of things; of the redirection, modification, or suppression of our drives; and even of saying No to life itself. We can become—and relate to each other as—*persons*, respecting and caring for each other as "ends" and individuals rather than as mere means to our own ends. We are capable of reason, emotion, volition, decision, and commitment.

In all these cases Scheler sees the substitution of nonnatural norms and values for those associated with mere "life," biologically conceived, even when the biological model of life is extended to include forms of social existence and institutionally structured practices related to practical purposes. They all transcend the standpoint of "utility" or "value for life." Much of his discussion is devoted to arguing that there really are qualitative differences between what transpires in human life on the level of mere vitality and its social elaborations, on the one hand, and the various forms of "spirituality" he identifies, on the other. He thus contrasts animal immersion in the here and now with the human capacity to detach oneself and think objectively about oneself and the world; the playfulness of animality with the creativity that expresses itself in art; biological drives with human emotions and will; practical intelligence with the capacity and desire to attain theoretical and intuitive knowledge for its own sake; and unreflective, unquestioning immersion in the flow of life with the possibility of the choice of selective or general asceticism. His point is not that human reality is opposed to animal vitality completely and in every respect, but rather that what he calls *Geist* contrasts with animal vitality in these and other such respects, and that human reality must be conceived not only as a particular configuration of animal vitality (which it is) but *also* as the capacity to reduce its dominance and attain these and other such forms of "spirituality."

Making the case for this distinction and conception leaves Scheler with the question of the relation between human vitality and spirituality; and it is that question in particular with which he is concerned in our second selection. Here he borrows a concept from Nietzsche (who, as a "naturalizing" reinterpreter of human reality, was both an inspiration and a provocation for him): *sublimation.* Nietzsche had introduced and employed this concept in the same context; but for him the very content and character as well as the possibility of human spirituality result from the sublimation of the drives and impulses of our natural human reality. For Scheler, in contrast, sublimation is simply the process whereby vital energies are redirected from merely vital functions to the realization of spiritual possibilities in human life.

These possibilities have an objective reality anchored in what Scheler calls the very "Ground of Being," awaiting the infusion of energy deriving from vital nature required to bring them to life—as can and does happen in human lives. We may first be introduced to them by our educators; but he suggests that once spirituality awakens and gains a foothold in our lives, it can strategically expand and focus the sublimation process. Although the competition within us between vitality and spirituality may never cease, human life may in this way be genuinely enhanced in the direction of a developing spirituality, to which Scheler believes that he does greater interpretive justice than had Nietzsche.

Scheler's contributions to ethics and value theory alone would have earned him a place in this volume; but he went on to give focus, identity, and impetus to one of the most important developments in the interpretive tradition in the twentieth century: philosophical anthropology. And he made it clear that, as is also true of existential philosophy, its idea and program leave open the issue of the reality or possibility of some sort of spirituality—human, transcendent, or both—even though most of its principal proponents were decidedly postreligious in their thinking.

From Formalism in Ethics and Non-Formal Ethics of Values

From I. *Non-Formal Value-Ethics and Ethics of Goods and Purposes*

* * *

FROM I. GOODS AND VALUES

No more than the names of colors refer to mere properties of corporeal things—notwithstanding the fact that appearances of colors in the natural standpoint come to our attention only insofar as they function as a means for distinguishing various corporeal, thinglike unities—do the names of values refer to mere properties of the thinglike given unities that we call *goods* [*Güte*]. Just as I can bring to givenness a red color as a mere extensive quale, e.g., as a pure color of the spectrum, without regarding it as covering a corporeal surface or as something spatial, so also are such *values* [*Werte*] as agreeable, charming, lovely, friendly, distinguished, and noble in principle accessible to me without my having to represent them as properties belonging to things or men.

Let us first attempt to demonstrate this by considering the simplest of values taken from the sphere of sensory agreeableness, where the relation of the value-quality to its concrete bearer is no doubt the most intimate that *can* be conceived. Every savory fruit always has its particular *kind* of pleasant taste. It is therefore not the case that one and the same savor of a fruit, e.g., a cherry, an apricot, or a peach, is only an amalgamation of various sensations given in tasting, seeing, or touching. Each of these fruits has a savor that is *qualitatively* distinct from that of the others; and what determines the qualitative difference of the savor consists neither in the complexes of sensations of taste, touch, and sight, which are in such cases allied with the savor, nor in the diverse properties of these fruits, which are manifested in the perception of them. The value-qualities, which in these cases "sensory agreeableness"[1] possesses, are *authentic* qualities of a value *itself*. And insofar as we have the ability to grasp these qualities, there is no doubt that we can distinguish fruits without reference to the optical, tactile, or any other *image* except that given by taste; of course it is difficult to effect such a distinction without the function of scent, for example, when we are accustomed to such a function. For the amateur it may be difficult to distinguish red wine from white while in the dark. However, this and many similar facts, such as decreased ability to distinguish among flavors when scent is set aside, show only the very many degrees of competence found among the men in question and their particular habituation to the ways in which they *take* and *grasp* a particular flavor.

What is valid in the sphere of sensory agreeableness is even more so in value-realms outside it. For in the sphere of sensory agreeableness, values are undoubtedly bound most intimately to the vacillations of our states and at the same time to those things which provoke these vacillations in us. It is therefore readily understandable that in most cases language has developed no special names to designate these value-qualities. Rather, language distinguishes them either according to their concrete bearer (e.g., the agreeableness of the scent of a rose) or according to their sensory bases (e.g., the agreeableness of sweetness, the disagreeableness of bitterness).

It is entirely certain that, for example, the aesthetic values which correspond to the terms *pleasant, charming, sublime, beautiful,* etc., are not simple conceptual terms that find their fulfillment in the common qualities of the things which are bearers of these values. This is shown by the simple fact that each time we attempt to determine such "common properties," we find our hands *empty*. Only when we have already classified things according to a non-axiological concept[2] can an attempt to grasp such common properties—of pleasant vases or flowers or noble horses, for example—have success. Values

---

1. That is, pleasantness to the senses.
2. That is, a value-neutral concept. (Axiology is the study or theory of value and values.)

of this kind are not definable. Despite their indubitable objectlike character, we must necessarily have *already* brought them to givenness with things in order for such things to be characterized as "beautiful," "lovely," or "charming." Each of these words brings together, in the unity of an axiological concept, a series of qualitatively discrete value-phenomena; however, they do not include axiologically indifferent properties, which, by way of their constant conjunction, feign an independent value-object.

The above also applies to values belonging to the ethical sphere. That a man or a deed is "noble" or "base," "courageous" or "cowardly," "innocent" or "guilty," "good" or "evil," is not made certain for us by constant characteristics which can be discerned in such things and events; nor do such values *consist* in such characteristics. In certain circumstances a *single* deed or a *single* person is all that we need to grasp the *essence* of the value in question. On the other hand, if the sphere of values is excluded in attempting to establish a common characteristic of, for example, good or evil men, we are theoretically led not only into an epistemological error but also into a moral illusion of the gravest kind. Anyone who has presumed to bind good and evil to self-sufficient *criteria* from outside the domain of values—whether such criteria are demonstrable bodily or psychic predispositions and properties of men or whether they are those of membership in a class or party—and has accordingly spoken of the "good and just" or the "evil and unjust" as if they were an objectively determinable and definable class, has necessarily succumbed to a kind of "pharisaism," confounding possible bearers of the "good" and *their* common characteristics (as simple bearers) with the corresponding *values themselves* and with the essence of these values for which they function only as bearers. * * * In correctly determining a value, it never suffices to attempt to derive it from characteristics and properties which do not belong to the sphere of value-phenomena.[3] The value itself always must be *intuitively given* or must refer back to that kind of givenness. Just as it is senseless to ask for the common properties of all blue or red things, since they have nothing in common except their blueness or redness, so is it senseless to ask for the common properties of good or evil deeds, moral tenors [*Gesinnungen*], men,[4] etc.

From the above it follows that there are *authentic* and *true* value-qualities and that they constitute a special domain of objectivities, have their own *distinct* relations and correlations, and, as value-*qualities*, can be, for example, higher or lower. This being the case, there can be among these value-qualities an *order* and an *order of ranks*, both of which are independent of the presence of a *realm of goods* in which they appear, entirely independent of the movement and changes of these goods in history, and "*a priori*" to the experience of this realm of goods.

* * *

All values (including the values "good" and "evil") are non-formal[5] *qualities* of contents possessing a determinate order of ranks with respect to "higher"

---

3. Nevertheless, there are factors of consistency and contradiction as well as many types of connections among valuations. These, however, are not of a logical nature but belong to autonomous laws in the realm of values and have their foundation in essential interconnections and essential disagreements among values [Scheler's note].

4. That is, human beings (*Menschen*). In German, *der Mensch* is generic in its application; a different word (*Mann*) is gendered male. "Moral tenors [*Gesinnungen*]": that is, moral sensibilities.

5. That is, substantive (i.e., not *merely* formal).

and "lower." This order is independent of the form of being into which values enter—no matter, for instance, if they are present to us as purely objective qualities, as members of value-complexes (e.g., the being-agreeable or being-beautiful of something), or as values that "a thing has."

The ultimate independence of the being of values with regard to things, goods, and states of affairs appears clearly in a number of facts. We know of a stage in the grasping of values wherein the *value* of an object is already very clearly and evidentially given *apart from* the givenness of the *bearer* of the value. Thus, for example, a man can be distressing and repugnant, agreeable, or sympathetic to us without our being able to indicate *how* this comes about; in like manner we can for the longest time consider a poem or another work of art "beautiful" or "ugly," "distinguished" or "common," without knowing in the least which properties of the contents of the work prompt this. Again, a landscape or a room in a house can appear "friendly" or "distressing," and the same holds for a sojourn in a room, without our knowing the *bearers* of such values. This applies equally to physical and psychical realities. Clearly, neither the experience of values nor the degree of the adequation[6] and the evidence (adequation in a full sense plus evidence constitutes the "self-givenness" of a value) depends in any way on the experience of the bearer of the values. Further, the *meaning* of an object in regard to "what" it is (whether, for example, a man is more "poet" or "philosopher") may *fluctuate* to any degree *without* its *value* ever fluctuating. In such cases the extent to which values are, in their *being, independent* of their bearer clearly reveals itself. This applies equally to things and to states of affairs. Distinguishing the values of wines in *no* sense presupposes a knowledge of their composition, the origin of this or that grape, or the method of pressing. Nor are "*value-complexes*" [*Wertverhalte*] mere values *of* states of affairs. The grasping of states of affairs is not the condition under which they are given to us. It can be given to me that a certain day in August last year "was beautiful" without its being given to me that at that time I visited a friend who is especially dear to me. Indeed, it is as if the *axiological nuance* of an object (whether it be remembered, anticipated, represented, or perceived) were the *first* factor that came upon us, and it is as if the value of the totality of which this object is a member or part constituted a "medium," as it were, in which the value comes to develop its content or (conceptual) meaning. A value precedes its object; it is the first "messenger" of its particular nature. An object may be vague and unclear while its value is already distinct and clear. In any comprehension of our milieu, for example, we immediately grasp the unanalyzed totality and its value; but, again, in the value of the totality we grasp partial values in which individual represented objects [*Bildgegenstände*] are "situated."

* * *

But how do value-qualities and value-complexes relate to *things* and *goods*?

It is not merely as *goods* that values differ from the feelings-states and desires which we experience in their presence. They are already different in terms of the most elementary *qualities*. Apart from the erroneous theory of a "thing" as a mere "order in the sequence of appearances," there is the error

6. That is, adequateness (of the bearer of a value to the full character of the value itself).

made by positivistic philosophers who attempt to relate values to factual desires and feelings in the same way that they relate things to their appearances. As value-phenomena (no matter if in the order of appearance or reality), values are *true objects*[7] and are different from all *states* of feeling. In a single given case a completely unrelated "agreeable" is distinct from the pleasure in it. A single case of pleasure in the agreeable—not a series of cases—is sufficient for us to discern the difference between pleasure and being-agreeable.[8]

* * *

A *good* is related to a *value*-quality as a thing is to the qualities that fulfill its "properties." This implies that we must distinguish between goods, i.e., "*value-things*," and mere values which things "have" and which "belong" to things, i.e., "*thing-values*." Goods have no foundation in things such that in order for them to be goods they must first be things. Rather, a good represents a "thinglike" unity of value-qualities or value-complexes which is founded in a specific basic value. "*Thinglikeness*," not "the" thing, is present in a good. (If we are concerned with a "material" good, it is not matter but the phenomenon of *materiality* which is present.) A natural thing of perception may be a bearer of certain values, and in this sense a valuable thing. But insofar as its unity as "thing" is constituted not by the unity of a value-quality but by a value that we fortuitously find on the thing, it is not yet a "good." It may be called a "*complex*" [*Sache*],[9] a word that we use to designate things insofar as they are objects of a lived relation, itself founded in a value, to an ability to dispose of such things by a volitional faculty. Thus the concept of property presupposes neither mere things nor goods, but "complexes" [*Sachen*]. A *good*, however, is a *value-thing*.

The difference between unities of things and goods becomes clear when we consider that a good is destructible, for instance, apart from the destruction of the thing representing the same real object, e.g., a work of art (a painting) whose colors fade. Also, a thing can be divided, but the same real object as a "good" is not divided but annihilated; or it may be that such a division does not affect the object's character as a good, namely, when the division pertains only to unessential factors. Thus, changes in goods are not identical with changes in the same real objects as things and vice versa.

It is only in goods that values become "real." They are not yet real in valuable things. In a good, however, a value is *objective* (whatever the value may be) *and real* at the same time. There is a *genuine* increase of value in the real world with any new good. Value-qualities, however, are "*ideal objects*,"[1] as qualities of colors and sounds.

* * *

7. That is, genuine objective realities (though of a different sort than physical things or living creatures).
8. That is, between pleasure and agreeableness in the sense of pleasantness (a difference that may not be quite the same for these pairs of terms in English and in German).
9. "Complex" is an odd and misleading translation of *Sache*, which means "matter" in the sense of "subject under consideration." That sense should be kept in mind when "complex" occurs later in this context.
1. That is, objects whose status is like that of meanings or concepts rather than that of physical or social or even psychological objectivities or phenomena.

From II. *Formalism and Apriorism*

* * *

From 3. "Higher" and "Lower" Values

In the *totality* of the realm of values there exists a singular order, an *"order of ranks"* that all values possess among themselves. It is because of this that a value is *"higher"* or *"lower"* than another one. This order lies in the *essence* of values themselves, as does the difference between "positive" and "negative" values. It does not belong simply to "values known" by us.

The fact that one value is "higher" than another is apprehended in a special act of value-cognition: the act of *preferring*. One must not assume that the height of a value is *"felt"* in the same manner as the value itself, and that the higher value is *subsequently* "preferred" or "placed after." Rather, the height of a value is "given," by virtue of its essence, only *in* the act of preferring. Whenever this is denied, one falsely equates this preferring with *"choosing"* in general, i.e., an act of conation. Without doubt, choosing must be grounded in the cognition of a higher value, for we choose that purpose among others which has its foundation in a higher value. But "preferring" occurs in the absence of all conation, choosing, and willing. For instance, we can say, "I prefer roses to carnations," *without* thinking of a choice. All "choosing" takes place between different deeds. By contrast, preferring also occurs with regard to any of the goods and values. This first kind of preferring (i.e., the preferring between different *goods*) may also be called *empirical* preferring.

On the other hand "preferring" is *a priori* if it occurs between different *values themselves*—independent of "goods." Such preferring always encompasses whole (and indefinitely wide) complexes of goods. He who "prefers" the noble to the agreeable will end up in an (inductive) experience of a *world of goods* very different from the one in which he who does not do so will find himself. The "height [highness] of a value" is "given" not "prior" to preferring, but *in* preferring. Hence, whenever we choose an end founded in a lower value, there must exist a *deception of preferring*. But this is not the place to discuss the possibility of such a deception.

But one may not say that the "being-higher" of a value only "means" that it is the value "preferred." For if the height of a value is given "in" preferring, this height is nevertheless a relation in the *essence* of the values concerned. Therefore, the *"ordered ranks of values"* are themselves absolutely *invariable*, whereas the "rules of preferring" are, in principle, variable throughout history (a variation which is very different from the apprehension of new values).

When an act of preferring takes place, it is not necessary that a multiplicity of values be given in feeling, nor is it necessary that such a multiplicity serve as a "foundation" for the act of preferring.

Concerning the former point, there are those cases where, for example, a deed is given as preferable to others *without* our thinking of these other deeds or our representing them in detail. It is only the consciousness of "being able to prefer something else" that must accompany the act.[2] Also, the

---

2. The same obtains in the case of choosing [Scheler's note].

consciousness of height can accompany a felt value in the absence of the *factual givenness* of the related value with respect to which the felt value is higher.[3] It suffices that this other value is indicated in a specific "consciousness of direction." This is precisely the case when preferring is most *definitive* (without there having been any prior indeterminate attitude), and when at the same time the height of a felt value is given in maximal degrees of evidence. Moreover, there may be given, in the act of preferring, the fact that "there exists a value higher than the one given in feeling" without the givenness of this value *itself* in feeling.[4] The height of a value B, in contrast to a value A, can be "given" in *preferring B to A, as well as* in the act of placing A *after B.* Nevertheless, these two methods of apprehending the same relation of value-ranks are basically different. True, it is an a priori interconnection that both types of acts can lead to the same relation of ranks. The difference exists nonetheless. It is distinctly manifest in human characters! For there are moral characters who are specifically "critical"; they may, in extreme cases, become "ascetics." These persons realize the height of a value principally in the act of "placing after." In contrast to these persons, there are positive types of characters who principally "prefer," and to whom the "lower" value shows itself only from the "platform" that they ascended in the act of preferring. Whereas the former strive for "virtue" by means of a battle against "vice," the latter bury and cover vices under newly acquired virtues.

As an act, "preferring" must be sharply distinguished from its kinds of realization. The realization may consist in the special activity that we experience in its execution. This is the case in a clearly *conscious* preferring, accompanied by a "*deliberation,*" among several values given in feeling. The realization may also occur, however, quite "*automatically,*" so that we are not at all aware of any "activity." In this case a higher value comes to us as if it were coming "by itself," as in "instinctive" preferring. Whereas in the former case we must labor to reach this value, in the latter this higher value "draws" us toward it, as it were. Such is the case in "enthusiastically" devoting oneself to a higher value. The act of preferring is in both cases the same.

Since all values stand essentially in an order of ranks—i.e., since all values are, in relation to each other, higher or lower—and since these relations are comprehensible only "in" preferring or rejecting them, the "feeling" of values has its foundation, by essential necessity, in "preferring" and "placing after." The feeling of values is by no means a "foundation" for the manner of preferring, as though preferring were "added" to the values comprehended in a primary intention of feeling as only a secondary act. Rather, all *widening* of the value-range (e.g., of an individual) takes place only "in" preferring and placing after. Only those values which are originally "given" in these acts can *secondarily* be "felt." Hence, the *structure of preferring and placing after circumscribes* the value-qualities that we feel.

Therefore the order of the ranks of values can *never be deduced or derived.* Which value is "higher" can be comprehended only through the acts of pre-

---

3. It is characteristic of "determined" preferring, in contrast to "wavering" preferring, that the other values belonging to the same series are barely given [Scheler's note].
4. Thus we often realize that we could have done something "better" than we did without this "better" being given to us [Scheler's note]—that is, without having any clear idea of what this "something 'better'" would actually be.

ferring and placing after. There exists here an *intuitive "evidence of prefer-ence"* that cannot be replaced by logical deduction.

But we can and must ask whether or not there are *a priori essential inter-connections* between the *higher* and *lower levels* of a value and its *other* essential properties.

We can find, in this respect, different characters of values—already to be found in everyday experiences—with which their "height" seems to grow. But these may be traced back to *one* factor.

It appears that values are "higher" the *more* they *endure* and the *less* they partake in *"extension"* and *divisibility.* They are higher the *less they are "founded"* through other values and the *"deeper"* the *"satisfaction"* connected with feeling them. Moreover, they are higher the *less* the feeling of them is *relative* to the *positing* of a specific bearer of "feeling" and "preferring."

* * *

* * * I maintain that *absolute values* are those that exist in "pure" feeling (and preferring and loving), i.e., they exist in a type of feeling that is *independent* of the *nature* of sensibility and of life as such.[5] This feeling possesses its own functional characteristics and laws. Among the values belonging to this feeling are *moral* values. In *pure* feeling we may be able to "understand" the feeling of sensible values (i.e., in a feeling manner) without performing sensible feeling-functions through which we (or others) enjoy the agreeable, but we cannot feel them in this manner. From this we infer that God can "understand" pain, for instance, but that he does so without feeling pain.

Such relativity of the being of *kinds* of values has, of course, *nothing* to do with another relativity: that of the *kinds of goods* that are the *bearers* of such values. For kinds of goods are, *in addition*, relative to the special factual psy-chophysical constitution of the real being that has such goods. The fact that the same object can be poisonous for one species and nutritious for another, for instance, or that something may be agreeable to the perverted drives of one living being and "disagreeable" or "harmful" to the normal drives of another being of the same species, determines only a relativity of values *in relation to* the *goods* in question. But this relativity in no way represents an ontic relativity of the values themselves. It is one of a "second order" only, which has nothing to do with the relativity of the above-mentioned "first order." One cannot reduce this relativity of *kinds* of values to that of goods (*in relation* to kinds of values). Both orders are essentially different. There are even "a priori" interconnections holding among relative values, but there are none holding among goods.[6]

Taking the words *relative* and *absolute* in *this* sense, I assert it to be an essen-tial interconnection that values given in immediate intuition *"as higher"* are values that are given as *nearer* to *absolute* values *in* feeling and preferring (and not by way of deliberation). Entirely outside the sphere of "judgment" or "delib-eration" there is an *immediate* feeling of the "relativity" of a value.[7] And for

---

5. That is, of life (*Leben*) considered as a vital or biological form of existence and reality (i.e., "life" as a part of nature).
6. That there must be "goods" for *all* values is the one *absolute* interconnection here [Scheler's note].

7. That is, its relation to other goods or other val-ues. (This has nothing to do with any kind of sub-jectivist "relativism" with respect to values, which Scheler rejects.)

this feeling the variability of a relative value in comparison with the concomitant constancy of a less "relative" value (no matter if variability and constancy pertain to "endurance," "divisibility," "depth of contentment") is a *confirmation*, but not a *proof*. Thus the value of the cognition of a truth, or the value of the silent beauty of a work of art, has a *phenomenal detachment* from the concomitant feeling of our *life*[8]—above all, from our sensible feeling-states. Such a value is also quite independent of an estimative deliberation about the permanence of such beauty or truth with regard to the "experiences of life," which tend more to detract us from true absolute values than to bring us nearer to them. In living an act of pure love toward a person,[9] the *value* of this person is detached from all simultaneously felt value-levels of our own personal world of values when we experience these as connected with our sense and feeling of life. Again, this value is also quite independent of any estimative deliberation about the permanence that an act of pure loving may have through happiness and sorrow, the inherent or accidental fate of life. *Implicit* in the very kind of the given value-experience there is a *guarantee* (and not a "conclusion") that there is here an absolute value. This *evidence* of an absolute value stems neither from an estimative deliberation about the permanence it may have in practical life nor from the universality of a judgment which holds that "this value is absolute in *all* moments of our lives." Rather, it is the *felt absoluteness* of this value that makes us feel that a defection from it in favor of other values constitutes "*possible* guilt" as well as a "falling away" from the height of value-existence which we had just reached.

Whereas the "relativity" of values to goods (and therefore also to our psychophysical constitution) is found by judgment and syllogism—by comparisons and induction—*this kind of relativity* and *absoluteness* is *given in emotive immediacy*. In this area judgments and the allied acts of comparing and induction tend more to cover the immediacy of the fact of the self-given "relativity" or "absoluteness" of a felt value than to make it clear to us. There is a *depth* in man that always silently tells him what the "relativity" of felt values is, no matter how much he may seek to cover it up by means of judgments, comparisons, and induction.

The essential (i.e., *original*) characteristic of a "higher value" is, then, its being less "*relative*"; of the "highest" value, its being an "*absolute*" value. All other essential interconnections among values are grounded in these criteria.

* * *

FROM 5. A PRIORI RELATIONS OF RANK AMONG VALUE-MODALITIES

The most important and most fundamental a priori relations obtain as an *order of ranks* among the systems of qualities of non-formal values which we call *value-modalities*. They constitute the *non-formal a priori* proper in the intuition of values and the intuition of preferences. The facts of these

---

8. That is, our vital reality as living creatures (see p. 1347, n. 5).
9. That is, someone who is encountered and respected as an autonomous, spiritual (more than merely natural and social), distinctively individual human self and subject. "Person" is a term and concept that had been central to KANT's understanding of human reality and morality; and it figures so prominently and centrally in Scheler's thought that he is often associated with the development known as "personalism" (see p. 1171, n. 3).

modalities present the *strongest* refutation of Kant's formalism. The ultimate divisions of value-qualities that are presupposed for these essential interconnections must be as independent of all factual goods and the special organizations of living beings that feel values as is the order of the ranks of the value-modalities.

Rather than giving a full development and establishment of these systems of qualities and their implicit laws of preferring, the following presents an explanation through examples of the kinds of a priori orders of ranks among values.

1. The values ranging from *the agreeable to the disagreeable* represent a sharply delineated value-modality (Aristotle already mentions them in his division of the ἡδύ, the χρήσιμον, and the καλόν[1]). The function of *sensible feeling* (with its modes of enjoying and suffering) is correlative to this modality. The respective feeling-states, the so-called feelings of sensation, are pleasure and pain. As in all value-modalities, there are values of *things* [*Sachwerte*],[2] values of *feeling-functions*, and values of *feeling-states*.

This modality is "*relative*" to beings endowed with sensibility in general. But it is relative *neither* to a specific species, e.g., man, *nor* to specific things or events of the real world that are "agreeable" or "disagreeable" to a being of a particular species. Although one type of event may be agreeable to one man[3] and disagreeable to another (or agreeable and disagreeable to different animals), the difference between the values of agreeable and disagreeable as such is an *absolute* difference, clearly given prior to any cognition of things.

The proposition that the agreeable is preferable to the disagreeable (*ceteris paribus*[4]) is not based on observation and induction. The preference lies in the essential contents of these values as well as in the nature of sensible feelings. If a traveler or a historian or a zoologist were to tell us that this preference is reversed in a certain kind of animal, we would "a priori" disbelieve his story. We would say that this is impossible unless it is only *things* different from ours that this animal feels are disagreeable and agreeable, or unless its preferring the disagreeable to the agreeable is based on a value of a *modality* (perhaps unknown to us) that is "higher" than that of the agreeable and the disagreeable. In the latter case the animal would only "put up with" the disagreeable in preferring the value of the extra modality. There may also be cases of perverted drives in this animal, allowing it to experience as agreeable those things that are *detrimental* to life. The state of affairs in all of these examples, as well as that which our proposition expresses, namely, that the agreeable is preferable to the disagreeable, also serves as a *law of understanding* external expressions of life and concrete (e.g., historical) valuation (even one's *own*, e.g., in remembering); our proposition is a *presupposition* of all observation and induction, and it is "a priori" to all ethnological experience.

Nor can this proposition and its respective facts be "explained" by way of evolutionary theories. It is nonsense to say that values (and their laws of preference) "developed" as *signs* of kinetic combinations that proved purposeful

---

1. In Greek, the pleasant (*hēdu*), the useful (*chrēsimon*), and the beautiful or noble (*kalon*). In *Nicomachean Ethics* 8.2, 1155b18–19, Aristotle (384–322 B.C.E.) divides things that are "lovable" (*philēton*) into the good (*agathon*), the pleasant,

and the useful.
2. That is, "*thing*-values."
3. That is, one human being (*Mensch*).
4. Other things being equal (Latin).

for the individual or its species. Such a theory can explain only the accompanying feeling-states that are connected with impulsive actions directed toward things. But *the values themselves* and their *laws of preferring* could *never* be thus explained. For the latter are independent of all specific organizations of living beings.

Certain groups of consecutive values (technical values[5] and symbolic values) correspond to these self-values of the modality of the agreeable and the disagreeable. But they do not concern us here.

2. The essence of values correlated to *vital feeling* differs sharply from the above modality. Its thing-values, insofar as they are self-values, are such qualities as those encompassed by the "*noble*" and the "*vulgar*" (and by the "*good*" in the pregnant sense of "excellent" [*tüchtig*] as opposed to "bad" rather than "evil").[6] All corresponding consecutive values (technical and symbolic) belong to the sphere denoted by "*weal*," or "*well-being*."[7] They are *subordinated* to the noble and its opposite. The feeling-states of this modality include all modes of the feelings of life (e.g., the feelings of "quickening" and "declining" life, the feelings of health and illness, the feeling of aging and oncoming death, the feelings of "weakness," "strength," etc.). Certain emotional reactions also belong to this modality—(a certain kind of) "being glad about" or "being sad about," drive reactions such as "courage," "anxiety," revengeful impulses, ire, etc. Here we cannot even indicate the tremendous richness of these value-qualities and their correlates.

Vital values form an entirely *original* modality. They cannot be "reduced" to the values of the agreeable and the useful, nor can they be reduced to spiritual values. Previous ethical theories made a *basic mistake* in ignoring this fact. Even Kant tacitly presupposes that these values can be reduced to mere hedonistic ones when he tries to divide all values in terms of good-evil on the one hand and agreeable-disagreeable on the other.[8] This division, however, is not applicable even to values of "well-being," let alone the vital self-value of the noble.

The particular character of this modality lies in the fact that "*life*" is a *genuine essence* and not an "empirical generic conception" that contains only "common properties" of all living organisms. When this fact is misconceived, the uniqueness of vital values is overlooked. We will not go into this in further detail here.

3. The realm of *spiritual values* is distinct from that of vital values as an

---

5. They are in part technical values concerning the *production* of agreeable things and are unified in the concept of the "useful" (*values of civilization*), and in part values concerning the enjoyment of agreeable things (*luxury values*) [Scheler's note]. Scheler is drawing a contrast between *Kollektivwerte* (here translated "consecutive values," but better rendered "collective/connected values") and *Individualwerte* (here translated "self-values," but better rendered "individual/independent values"). Like the latter, the former are genuine "phenomenal values" or "value-facts," rather than mere instrumental values that have no value at all other than as means to realize genuine values; but unlike "self-values," "consecutive values" do not stand entirely on their own as values.
6. One also uses "noble" and its opposite with respect to vital values ("noble horse," "noble tree,"

"noble race," "nobility," etc.) [Scheler's note].
7. "Weal" and "well-being" therefore do not coincide with vital values in general; the value of well-being is determined by the extent to which the individual or the community, which can be in a good or a bad state, is *noble* or *base*. On the other hand, "weal" is superior as a vital value to mere "usefulness" (and "agreeableness"), and the well-being of a community is superior to the sum of its interests (as a society) [Scheler's note].
8. See *Critique of Practical Reason* [1788], pt. I, bk. II, chap. 2. The hedonists and the utilitarians, like Kant, make the mistake of reducing this value-modality to the agreeable and the useful; the rationalists make the (equally erroneous) mistake of reducing it to spiritual [*geistig*] values (especially the rational ones) [Scheler's note].

original modal unity. In the kind of their *givenness*, spiritual values have a peculiar detachment from and independence of the spheres of the lived body and the environment. Their unity reveals itself in the clear evidence that vital values "ought" to be sacrificed for them. The functions and acts in which they are apprehended are functions of *spiritual* feeling and acts of *spiritual* preferring, loving, and hating. They are set off from like-named *vital* functions and acts by pure phenomenological evidence as well as by their *own proper lawfulness* (which *cannot be reduced* to any "*biological*" lawfulness).

The main types of spiritual values are the following: (1) the values of "*beautiful*" and "*ugly*," together with the whole range of purely aesthetic values; (2) the values of "*right*" and "*wrong*" [*des Rechten und Unrechten*], objects that are "values" and wholly different from what is "correct" and "incorrect" according to a law, which form the ultimate phenomenal basis of the idea of the objective *order of right* [*Rechtsordnung*], an order that is independent of the idea of "law," the idea of the state, and the idea of the life-community on which the state rests (it is especially independent of all positive legislation);[9] (3) the values of the "*pure cognition of truth*," whose realization is sought in *philosophy* (in contrast to positive "science," which is guided by the aim of controlling natural appearances).[1] Hence "*values of science*" are consecutive values of the values of the cognition of truth. So-called *cultural values* in general are the consecutive (technical and symbolic) values of *spiritual* values and belong to the value-sphere of *goods* (e.g., art treasures, scientific institutions, positive legislation, etc.). The correlative feeling-states of spiritual values—for instance, the feeling-states of spiritual joy and sorrow (as opposed to the vital "being gay" and "not being gay")—possess the phenomenal quality of appearing *without mediation*. That is to say, they do not appear on an "ego" as its states, nor does an antecedent givenness of the lived body of a person serve as a condition of their appearance. Spiritual feeling-states vary *independent* of changes in vital feeling-states (and, of course, sensible feeling-states). Their variations are directly dependent upon the variations of the values of the *objects themselves* and occur according to their own proper laws.

Finally, there are the reactions belonging to this modality, including "pleasing" and "displeasing," "approving" and "disapproving," "respect" and "disrespect," "retributive conation" (as opposed to the vital impulses of revenge) and "spiritual sympathy" (which is the foundation of friendship, for instance).

4. Values of the last modality are those of the *holy* and the *unholy*. This modality differs sharply from the above modalities. It forms a unit of value-qualities not subject to further definition. Nevertheless, these values have *one* very definite condition of their givenness: they appear only in objects that are given in intention as "absolute objects." This expression, however, refers *not* to a specific or definable *class* of objects, but (in principle) to *any* object given in the "absolute sphere." Again, this modality is quite independent of all that has been considered "holy" by different peoples at various times, such as holy things, powers, persons, institutions, and the like (i.e., from ideas of fetishism to the purest conceptions of God). These latter problems do not belong

---

9. "Law" is only a consecutive value for the self-value of the "order of right": positive law (of a state) is the consecutive value for the (objective) "order of right" which is valid in the state and which lawmakers *and* judges must realize [Scheler's note].

"Positive law" is established by government, in contrast to natural law.
1. We speak of the value of "cognition," not of the value of "truth." Truth does *not* belong among the values [Scheler's note].

to an *a priori phenomenology of values* [*apriorische Wertlehre*] and the theory of ordered ranks of values. They concern the *positive representations of goods* within this value-sphere. With regard to the values of the holy, however, *all* other values are at the same time given as symbols for these values.

The feeling-states belonging to this modality range from "blissfulness" to "despair"; they are independent of "happiness" and "unhappiness," whether it be in occurrence, duration, or change. In a certain sense these feeling-states indicate the "nearness" or the "remoteness" of the divine in experience.

"Faith" and "lack of faith," "awe," "adoration," and analogous attiudes are specific reactions in this modality.

However, the act through which we *originally* apprehend the value of the holy is an act of a specific kind of *love* (whose value-direction *precedes* and *determines* all pictorial representations and concepts of holy objects); that is to say, in essence the act is directed toward persons, or toward something of the *form of a personal being*, no matter what content or what "conception" of personhood is implied. The self-value in the sphere of the values of the "holy" is therefore, by essential necessity, a "*value of the person.*"

* * *

SOURCE: From Max Scheler, *Formalism in Ethics and Non-Formal Ethics of Values: A New Attempt toward the Foundation of an Ethical Personalism*, trans. Manfred S. Frings and Roger L. Funk (Evanston, Ill.: Northwestern University Press, 1973), pp. 12–15, 17–21, 86–90, 98–100, 104–9. Except where otherwise indicated, German words in brackets are the terminology used in the German original, inserted in addition to their renderings in the translation. Originally published in installments as *Der Formalismus in der Ethik und die materiale Wertethik* (1913–16); the translation is from the 5th ed. (1966). The title chosen by the translators is an attempt to improve upon the original but is misleading, since Scheler actually is criticizing (Kantian) "formalism in ethics" and advocating an alternative sort of ethics that would be substantive and value-based.

From Man's Place in Nature[1]

Introduction: The Concept of Man

If we ask an educated person in the Western world what he means by the word "man,"[2] three irreconcilable ways of thinking are apt to come into conflict in his mind. The first is the Jewish-Christian tradition of Adam and Eve,[3] including creation, paradise and fall. The second is the Greek tradition in which, for the first time, man's self-consciousness raised him to a unique place on the grounds that he is endowed with "reason."[4] Closely bound up with this view is the doctrine that there is a superhuman "reason" in the total universe

1. This translates "*Kosmos*." This translation is very misleading; by "*Kosmos*," Scheler means not simply "nature" (or even "the universe") as conceived in ordinary usage and in the natural sciences—as the totality of spatio-temporal phenomena—but rather the whole of reality (all of "being") more generally.
2. That is, "the concept of human being" (*das Begriff des Menschen*). In German, *der Mensch* is generic in its application; a different word (*Mann*)

designates a gendered male.
3. That is, the idea that human beings are created by God in God's own image, and for that reason have a very special significance and place in the world.
4. That is, the classical conception of man as "the rational animal"—a type of living creature distinguished from others by virtue of possessing the capacity for "rationality" in thought and action.

in which man alone of all creatures participates.[5] The third idea is that of modern science and genetic psychology, which also has a tradition of its own. According to this view, man is a very recent product of evolution on our planet, a creature distinguished from its antecedents in the animal world only by the degree of complexity of energies and capacities already present on a subhuman level. These three ideas are not compatible with each other. Thus we have a scientific, a philosophical and a theological anthropology in complete separation from each other. We do not have a unified idea of man.

The increasing multiplicity of the special sciences [*Wissenschaften*] that deal with man, valuable as they are, tend to hide his nature more than they reveal it. Moreover, since the status of these three traditional ideas is severely impaired, in particular the Darwinian theory of the origin of man,[6] we may say that at no time in his history has man been so much of a problem to himself as he is now. For this reason I have tried to give an outline of a new philosophical anthropology based on as broad a foundation as possible. In the following essay, however, I want to raise only a few issues and suggest a few conclusions that deal with the nature of man in relation to animal and plant and with man's unique metaphysical place in the universe [*Kosmos*].[7]

In setting out upon this inquiry, we must be aware that the word "man" has a deceptive ambiguity. In one sense, it signifies the particular morphological characteristics of man as a subclass of the vertebrates and mammals. It is perfectly clear that, regardless of the specific form of this conceptual model, the living being described as man is not only subordinate to the concept "animal," but occupies a relatively very small corner of the animal kingdom. This is the case even if we say with Linnaeus[8] that man is the "pinnacle" of the vertebrate-mammal kingdom—an assertion, in itself highly debatable, since this pinnacle, like any other, still belongs to the line of development of which it is the highest point. This view derives a unified concept of man from the upright posture, the transformation of the vertebral column, equilibration of the brain pan, the big increase in the relative size of the brain and the organic changes resulting from the upright posture: the grasping hand with opposable thumb, the recession of the jawbone and the teeth.

Yet, the same word "man," in ordinary language and among all civilized peoples, means something so totally different that it is difficult to find another word in our language with the same ambiguity. The word "man," in the second sense, signifies a set of characteristics which must be sharply distinguished from the concept "animal"—including all mammals and vertebrates. In this sense, it is as much opposed to *infusorium stentor*[9] as to the chimpanzee, although it is obvious that man resembles the chimpanzee in his morphological, physiological and psychological characteristics much more than both man and chimpanzee resemble infusoria.

Thus, this second concept of man must have an entirely different meaning and an entirely different origin from the first, which refers only to a very small section of the vertebrate world. Let us call the second concept the essential

5. Presumably a reference to HEGEL—which would have been clearer had Scheler written "in which man alone of all creatures self-consciously, conceptually, and cognitively participates."
6. The theory of evolution by natural selection, put forth by the English naturalist Charles Darwin (1809–1882).
7. That is, in the whole of reality.
8. Carl Linnaeus (Carl von Linné, 1707–1778), Swedish naturalist who devised the basic system used to classify all organisms.
9. A genus of trumpet-shaped Protista (a kingdom of mostly one-cell organisms); "infusoria" is a class of minute organisms.

nature of man in contrast to the first concept defined within the context of natural science.[1] The theme of this essay is to inquire whether this second concept can be justified, that is to say, whether we can assign to man unique characteristics not comparable to those of any other species.

* * *

From II. The Essence of Spirit [Geist][2]

We have now come to the problem that is crucial for our inquiry. If the animal has intelligence, does this mean there is only a difference in degree between man and animal—or is there still an essential difference?[3] Is there still in man, beyond the stages of life discussed heretofore, something that is quite different and unique, something that is not yet defined by, or included in, the capacity for choice and intelligence?

Here the paths divide sharply. One side would reserve intelligence and choice for man and deny them to the animal. This view, in fact, affirms that there is an essential, qualitative difference, but locates it at a point where in my opinion it does not exist. The other side, especially the evolutionists of the Darwinian-Lamarckian[4] school, deny that there is an essential difference between man and animal precisely because the animal does have intelligence. These writers adhere, in one way or another, to a unified conception of man which I have called the theory of "Homo faber."[5] Accordingly, they do not recognize any distinctive metaphysical or ontological status of man.

For my own part, I reject both views. I assert that the nature of man, or that which may be called his unique place in nature, goes far beyond the capacity for choice and intelligence and would not be reached even if we were to enlarge these powers, in a quantitative sense, to infinity.[6] But it would also be a mistake to think that the new element which gives man his unique characteristics is nothing but a new essential form of being added to the previous stages of psychic life—the vital impulse, instinct, associative memory, intelligence and choice; in other words, an element which still belongs to the psychic and vital functions and capacities, and which falls into the province of psychology and biology.

The new principle transcends what we call "life" in the most general sense. It is not a stage of life, especially not a stage of the particular mode of life

1. That is, the "first concept" is the (vital) nature of "man" as a type of living creature, biologically and physiologically considered, in contrast to the "essential nature of man," elaborated in terms of forms of experience and activity that are qualitatively different from anything of which other types of creature known to us are capable.
2. On *Geist*, see the glossary in the introduction to Hegel, p. 144. This term (best left untranslated) has figured importantly in the interpretive tradition from SCHILLER and Hegel onward. Scheler considers it to be of continuing usefulness and importance in the interpretation of human reality, serving to draw attention to those forms of possible human experience and activity that must be recognized to be more than merely natural, and that defy analysis in merely naturalistic terms.
3. In Part I (not included here), Scheler distinguishes and discusses the basic types of functioning of the various forms of life (both vegetable and

animal) found in nature as we know it. In nonhuman living creatures he identifies not only instinctive and memory-assisted associative forms of behavior but also (in at least some other species) forms of (practical) intelligence and the ability to make choices—all of which he views as relating to and serving "vital functions and capacities."
4. Jean-Baptiste Lamarck (1744–1829), French biologist who believed that species evolved but (unlike Darwin) held that changes occur when animals alter their habits to respond to new environments and that such acquired characteristics are inheritable.
5. Man the maker (Latin)—that is, the maker and user of tools (with "tool" construed as any sort of device that facilitates activities).
6. Between the clever chimpanzee and an Edison, taking the latter only as a technician, there is only a difference in degree—though a great one to be sure [Scheler's note]. Thomas Alva Edison (1847–1931), American inventor.

called psyche, but a principle opposed to life as such, even to life in man.[7] Thus it is a genuinely new phenomenon which cannot be derived from the natural evolution of life, but which, if reducible to anything, leads back to the ultimate Ground of Being of which "life" is a particular manifestation.[8]

The Greeks affirmed the existence of such a principle and called it reason. We will use a more inclusive term and call it "spirit [Geist]"—a term which includes the concept of reason, but which, in addition to conceptual thought, also includes the intuition of essences and a class of voluntary and emotional acts such as kindness, love, remorse, reverence, wonder, bliss, despair and free decision. The center of action in which spirit appears within a finite mode of being we call "person" in sharp contrast to all functional vital centers which, from an inner perspective, may be called "psychic centers."[9]

What, then, is this spirit [Geist], this new crucial principle? Seldom has a word been more abused so that it hardly has a clear meaning for anybody. If we put at the head of this concept of spirit a special function of knowledge which it alone can provide, then the essential characteristic of the spiritual being, regardless of its psychological make-up, is its existential liberation from the organic world—its freedom and detachability from the bondage and pressure of life, from its dependence upon all that belongs to life,[1] including its own drive-motivated intelligence.

The spiritual being, then, is no longer subject to its drives and its environment. Instead, it is "free from the environment" or, as we shall say, "open to the world."[2] Such a being has a "world." Moreover, such a being is capable of transforming the primary centers of resistance and reaction into "objects." (The animal remains immersed in them "ecstatically."[3]) Such a being is capable of grasping the qualities of objects without the restriction imposed upon this thing-world by the system of vital drives and the mediating functions and organs of the sensory apparatus.

Thus, spirit [Geist] is objectivity, or the determination of the objective nature of things. Spirit only belongs to a being capable of strict objectivity. More precisely: in order to be a bearer of spirit [Geist], the being must have *reversed*, dynamically and in principle, its relationship both to external reality and to itself as compared with the animal, including its intelligence. What is this reversal?

In the case of the animal, whether it is highly organized or not, every action and reaction, even that which is "intelligent," proceeds from a physiological condition of the nervous system with which are coordinated, on the psychic

---

7. That is, it is a principle that revolves around the pursuit of a set of values different from those of life as a merely vital phenomenon ("life as such").
8. Scheler had already argued in *Formalism in Ethics and Substantive Value-Ethics* (1913–16; see above) that values have a kind of reality that is fundamentally different from (and not derivable from) anything about the world of physical and biological phenomena and processes—and therefore that, since neither is reducible to the other, the ultimate "ground" (foundation or basis) of all existence, reality, and value can itself *be* of neither sort. Rather, he supposed, it must be something of which both are (different) "manifestations" or expressions.
9. That is, centers of vital activity that have a rudimentary "psychological" as well as biological character, conceived in terms of organized sets of

dispositions relating to vital requirements of different types of living creature.
1. That is, "life" in the sense of vitality (biological and psychological) and its extension into those forms of social and cultural life that remain governed by such vital values and imperatives.
2. That is, able to relate to the reality in which it finds itself in ways that are "open" to it to work out, experiment with, develop and modify. The manner in which it does so for Scheler is not predetermined by its vital nature and associated causalities. This concept of "world-openness" is a crucial feature of Scheler's conception of human reality.
3. That is, is focused not within itself but rather entirely "outside of itself" in the surrounding world and its objects.

side, certain instincts, drives and sensory perceptions. What does not interest the instinct or drive is not given.[4] What is given is given only as a center of resistance to attraction and repulsion, that is, to the animal as a biological unit. Thus the impetus from a physiological-psychological condition is always the first act in the drama of an animal's behavior toward the environment. The structure of the environment is precisely adapted to the physiological peculiarities of the animal, and indirectly to its morphological characteristics as well, and to its instincts and sensory structure, which form a strictly functional unity. Animals only notice and grasp those things which fall into the secure boundaries of their environmental structure. The second act of the drama of animal behavior consists in making some actual changes in the environment as a result of the animal's free action with respect to a dominant goal set by its drives. The third act consists in a concomitant change of its physiological-psychological condition. The course of animal behavior therefore always has this form:

$$A \text{ (animal)} \rightleftarrows E \text{ (environment)}$$

The situation is altogether different in the case of a being that has spirit [*Geist*].[5] Such a being is capable of behavior (at least in so far as it makes use of spirit) that runs a diametrically opposed course. The first act of this new and human drama is this: Its behavior is "motivated" by a complex of sensations and ideas raised to the status of an object. It is, in principle, independent of the drives and the sensuous surfaces in the environment conditioned by the system of drives that appear in the visual and auditory fields. The second act of the drama consists in the voluntary inhibition, or release, of a drive and of the corresponding reaction. The third act consists of a final and intrinsic change with regard to the objective nature of a thing. The course of such behavior is "world-openness," and such behavior, once it appears, is capable of unlimited expansion—as far as the "world" of existing things extends.

$$M \text{ (man)} \rightleftarrows W \text{ (world)} \longrightarrow \longrightarrow$$

Man, then, is a being that can exhibit, to an unlimited degree, behavior which is open to the world. To become human is to acquire this openness to the world by virtue of spirit.[6]

The animal has no "object." It lives, as it were, ecstatically immersed in its environment which it carries along as a snail carries its shell. It cannot transform the environment into an object. It cannot perform the peculiar act of detachment and distance by which man transforms an "environment" into the "world," or into a symbol of the world. It cannot perform the act by which man transforms the centers of resistance determined by drives and affects into "objects."

Objective being or objectification, therefore, is the most formal category of the logical aspect of spirit [*Geist*]. I might say the animal is involved too deeply in the actualities of life which correspond to its organic needs and conditions ever to experience and grasp them as objects. The animal, to be sure, no lon-

---

4. That is, does not come to its attention.
5. That is, that has the character or capacity of operating on the level of *Geist*.

6. That is, by virtue of realizing the human capacity for the kind of "spirituality" Scheler is talking about.

ger lives in quite the same ecstatic[7] state as the plant does, that is to say, subject to nothing but the vital impulse without sensation, representation, consciousness, and without any reporting back of the particular states of the organism to an inner center. Owing to the separation of the sensory and the motor system, and owing to its continuously holding back of specific sensory contents, the animal, as it were, owns itself.[8] It does have a "body schema."[9] But in relation to the environment, the animal still behaves "ecstatically"— even when it acts "intelligently." Its intelligence remains strictly within the bounds of organic drives and practical needs. The spiritual act[1] in man, in contrast to the simple reporting back of the animal's body schema and its contents, is essentially linked with the second dimension stage of the reflexive act. We call this act "concentration,"[2] and if we bring the act together with the goal at which concentration aims, we have "self-consciousness," by which is meant the consciousness that the spiritual center of action has of itself. The animal has consciousness as distinguished from the plant, but, as Leibniz[3] knew, it has no self-consciousness. It does not "own itself," it is not its own master; hence, it is not conscious of itself.

Concentration, self-consciousness and the capacity to objectify the original centers of resistance encountered by the drives—these characteristics form a single indivisible structure which, as such, is peculiar only to man. Self-consciousness, or the new act of centering its existence, is the second essential characteristic of man. By virtue of spirit [Geist],[4] man is capable of expanding the environment into the dimension of a world and of objectifying resistance. He is also capable—and this is most remarkable—of objectifying his own physiological and psychological states, every psychic experience and every vital function. It is for this reason that this being can also throw his life away freely.

The animal hears and sees—without knowing that it does so. The psyche of the animal functions and works, but the animal is not a potential psychologist or physiologist. We must single out very exceptional ecstatic states in man; for example, the state of emerging from hypnosis or the state induced by drugs— techniques that in certain cases, as in orgiastic cults of all kinds, render the spirit inactive—in order to imagine the normal condition of the animal. The animal does not even experience its drives as its own, but as dynamic pushes and pulls that emanate from the things in the environment. Primitive man, who in certain psychic characteristics is still close to the animal, does not say, "I avoid this thing," but "This thing is taboo." For the animal there are only those factors in the environment that are determined by attraction and repulsion. The monkey who jumps hither and yonder lives, as it were, in successive states of ecstasy (comparable to the pathological flights of ideas in man). It does not have a "will" that outlasts the drives and their changing states, and that preserves a kind of continuity in the variations of the psycho-physical conditions. An animal always arrives, as it were, elsewhere than at

---

7. Externally absorbed.
8. That is, it has at least a measure of self-possession or control of itself.
9. That is, a functional "body image," by means of which it is (unself-consciously) able to operate effectively in its environment.
1. That is, activity mediated by spirituality.

2. That is, the mental "act" of seeing things in relation to itself, or in a "self-centered" (con-centric) way.
3. Gottfried Wilhelm Leibniz (1646–1716), German philosopher and mathematician.
4. That is, by virtue of developing the kind of "spirituality" discussed in the previous paragraph.

the destination at which it originally aimed. Nietzsche made a profound and correct remark when he said, "Man is an animal that can make promises."[5]

There are four essential stages in which all existence manifests itself with regard to inner being. *Inorganic* forms have no such inner state or self-being whatsoever. They have no center that is their own; hence, no medium, no environment in which they live. What we designate as unities in this world, down to the world of molecules, atoms and electrons depends entirely upon our power to divide bodies, whether we do so in actual practice or in conceptual thought. Every inorganic body is a unity only within a specific context of causal action relative to other bodies. The nonspatial centers of energy, which give the appearance of extension through time and which we attribute to the images of bodies on metaphysical grounds, are mutually interacting points of energy in which the lines of an energy field run together.

An organism, on the other hand, is always an ontic center. It invariably forms "its own" spatiotemporal unity and individuality. These are not produced, as in the case of inorganic unities, by virtue of our capacity to synthesize, which is itself conditioned biologically. An organism is self-limiting. It has individuality. To dissect it means to murder it, that is, to destroy its essence and being. To the vital impulse of the plant there corresponds a center and a medium into which the plant, relatively open in its growth, is placed without any reporting back of its varying states to its center. Yet the plant does have an "inner being" or a kind of soul.[6] In the animal, however, we find both sensation and consciousness and, together with them, a central organization for the reporting back of changing conditions in the organism and the capacity of modifying the central organization on the basis of these reports. It is thus given to itself a second time. Man, however, by virtue of spirit [*Geist*], is given to himself a third time: in self-consciousness and in the capacity to objectify psychic states and his sensory and motor system. "Person," as applied to man, therefore, must be envisaged as the center of acts raised beyond the interaction and contrast between organism and environment.[7] Does this hierarchy of forms not appear as if there were different levels in the structure of being in which the ultimate Ground of Being bends back more and more upon itself to become more and more conscious of itself on higher levels and new dimensions—until it comes to possess and grasp itself completely in man?[8]

The structure of man—his self-consciousness and his capacity to objectify both the environment and his own physiological and psychic states and the causal relations existing in both—helps to explain a number of specific human characteristics. I shall mention a few of them.

————

Only in man do we find the fully developed categories of thing and substance. The animal does not have them. The spider waiting for prey will rush imme-

5. See the first two sections of the second essay of NIETZSCHE's *On the Genealogy of Morals* (1887), above.
6. That is, a kind of centered organization associated with its kind of animation. Scheler is here clearly following Aristotle, for whom the soul (*psyche*) is the form of a living thing (i.e., that in virtue of which it is a specific kind of living thing).

It thus is not an immaterial essence or any kind of thing separate from or in addition to the creature's living body.
7. This sentence indicates what Scheler means by "person" (and how that dimension of human reality relates to what he calls "soul").
8. This is a strikingly Hegelian formulation and speculation.

diately after an insect that is caught in its web and whose presence is probably communicated through the tactile sense by a faint pull. But if the insect is put into such proximity that the spider can see it, the spider will run away. Thus the thing that is seen is quite different from the thing that is felt by touch. The spider is incapable of coordinating visual space with kinaesthetic space, or the respective objects disclosed in each. Even the highest animals do not have a fully developed thing-category. The ape that is handed a half-peeled banana will again run away from it, whereas he will eat it if it is completely peeled, and he will peel and eat it if it is not peeled at all. The thing called "banana" has not changed for the animal; rather, the thing has changed into something else. The animal lacks a center which would relate all the psychophysical functions of seeing, hearing, smelling and grasping, and the different things coordinated with them, into a unity belonging to one and the same concrete object.

Next, man has, from the start, a unified space. For example, a person born blind whose sight is restored through an operation does not learn to synthesize different spaces—such as tactile space, visual space, auditory space, and kinaesthetic space—into a unified intuition of space. What he learns is only how to identify sensory data as symbols and qualities of the same thing occupying one place. The animal again lacks the central function which provides a unified space as a fixed form prior to the particular things and their perception in it. More importantly, it lacks the capacity of self-reference to a center by means of which man combines all sensory data, and the drives coordinated with them, and relates them to a single world as an ordered field composed of different substances. The animal lacks a "world space" which persists as a stable background independent of the animal's movements. It also lacks the empty forms of space and time into which man is placed and in which he originally encounters things and events. These forms are possible only for a being in whom the frustration of drives always exceeds their gratification. For "empty" means, to begin with, an expectation that is not satisfied. The original "emptiness" is, as it were, the emptiness of our hearts.

The basis for the human intuitions of space and time preceding all external sensations is the capacity for spontaneous movement and action according to a definite order. The fact (apparent in certain pathological deficiencies) that tactile space is not directly coordinated with visual space, but that this coordination is possible only through the mediation of kinaesthetic sensations, also indicates that the empty form of space, at least in the sense of an unformed "spatiality," is experienced prior to any conscious sensations. In other words, it is first experienced merely on the basis of motor impulses and the capacity to produce such impulses, for it is these very motor impulses that are followed by kinaesthetic sensations. This primitive "movement-space," this "consciousness-of-being-around-and/or-surrounded," remains with us even when visual space in which the uniform manifold of extension is given, is completely removed.

Although the higher animals do have spatial manifolds (in the most primitive animals we probably find only temporal impressions) these spaces are not homogeneous. There is no fixed, prior ordering system of places in the visual sphere from which the qualities and movements of things in the environment are sharply separated. Only the highest visual organization in man (with erect posture!) has such a system, but he can lose it in pathological cases so that only the primitive space remains. The animal can no more separate the empty forms of space and time from specific objects in the environment than it can isolate the concept of "number" from the notion of plurality, the notion of more or less inherent in the things outside. It lives wholly in the concrete actuality of its immediate present. Only in man do we find the strange phenomenon that both spatial and temporal emptiness appears prior to, and is the basis of, all possible perceptions in the world of objects. This is possible only because the drive expectations converted into motor impulses outweigh the actual gratification of drives in sensation. Thus, without suspecting it, man takes his own emptiness of heart for the "infinite emptiness" of space and time—as if the latter could exist without objects. Science has corrected the serious illusion of the natural world view only very late by showing that space and time are nothing but forms of ordering things, possibilities for relations and successions among things, and that they have no independent reality apart from these things.

The animal, as I said, has no world space. A dog may have lived for years in a garden, and may have frequently visited every place in it, yet he will not be able to form an over-all picture of the garden, no matter how large or small it may be, or of the arrangements of the trees and bushes independent of his own position. He has only "environmental spaces" that vary with his movements, and he is not able to coordinate these with the garden space that is independent of the position of his own body. The reason is that he cannot objectify his own body and its movements so as to include them as variable features in his intuition of space and to reckon instinctively, as it were, with the accident of his own position as man is able to do even without science.

This achievement is but the beginning of what man continues in science [*Wissenschaft*]. For the greatness of science is this: by means of science, man learns to reckon on a more and more comprehensive scale with his own accidental position in the universe, and with himself or his whole physical and psychical apparatus, as if it were an external object linked in strict causal relations with other things. In this way, he gradually constructs a picture of the world, the objects and laws of which are completely independent of his own psychophysical organism, of his senses, their thresholds, of his needs and their interests in things. Thus the objective world and its laws remain constant throughout the changing conditions of man's place in the universe.

Man alone—in so far as he is a person—is able to go beyond himself as an organism and to transform, from a center beyond the spatiotemporal world, everything (himself included) into an object of knowledge. Thus man as a spiritual [*geistig*] being is a being that surpasses himself in the world.[9] As such he is also capable of irony and humor which always indicate the transcendence of actual existence (*Dasein*). The center, however, from which man performs the acts by means of which he objectifies body, psyche and world in its spatial and temporal abundance cannot itself be part of this world. It cannot be located in space or in time: it can only be located in the highest Ground of Being itself. In his profound theory of the transcendental apperception, Kant clarified this new unity of the *cogito*[1] as the "condition of all possible experi-

---

9. Here, man's surpassing himself relates to the capacity for detached objective knowledge, reflecting Scheler's close early association with HUSSERL (and kinship with the tradition of Kant, Hegel, and, in this respect SCHOPENHAUER); it is strikingly different from the kind of "self-surpassing" or "self-transcendence" of which SARTRE makes so much.

1. I think (Latin), the starting point of the French philosopher René Descartes (1596–1650). See Kant's "Transcendental Deduction" in *Critique of Pure Reason* (1781; 2nd ed., 1787), A115ff. / B131ff.

ence and, therefore, also of all objects in experience," both outer and inner, by which our own inner life becomes accessible to us. He was thus the first to raise "spirit [Geist]" above "psyche" and expressly denied that spirit was nothing but a group of functions belonging to a so-called mental substance, or soul, which owes its fictitious status merely to an unjustified reification of the actual unity of the spirit.

Thus, we have come to a third important characteristic of spirit [Geist]. Spirit is the only being incapable of becoming an object. It is pure actuality. It has its being only in and through the execution of its acts. The center of spirit, the person, is not an object or a substantial kind of being, but a continuously self-executing, ordered structure of acts. The person is only in and through his acts.[2] The psychic act is not self-contained. It is an event "in" time which, in principle, we can observe from the center of spirit and which we can objectify through introspection. Psychic acts are capable of objectification, but not the spiritual [geistig] act—the intentionality itself which makes the psychic process visible. We can only "collect" ourselves with regard to our being as a person: we can concentrate upon it; we cannot objectify it. Other people, too, as *persons* cannot become objects. (In this sense Goethe[3] said of Lili Schönemann that he "loved her too much" to be able to "observe" her.) We can come to "know" them only by participating in, or by entering into, their free acts, through the kind of "understanding" possible in an attitude of empathetic love, the very opposite of objectification—in short, by "identifying," as we say, with the will and love of another person and thereby with himself.

In the acts of a superindividual spirit [Geist], too, we can participate only by some kind of identification. We postulate such spirit on the basis of the essential bond between fact and idea in so far as we assume that there is a self-realizing order of ideas independent of human consciousness, and in so far as we ascribe this order to the ultimate Ground of Being as one of its attributes.[4] We participate in such an order in three respects: in an order of essences, in so far as spirit is intellect; in an objective order of values in so far as spirit expresses itself in love and in a teleological order of the world in so far as spirit expresses itself in action. The traditional type of philosophical idealism, prevailing since St. Augustine,[5] held that "ideas were prior to things" (*ideae ante res*), that there was providence and a *plan* of creation before the *act* of creation. But ideas do not exist "before," "in" or "after" things, but *with* them. They are created by the eternal spirit in the act of continuous world-realization (*creatio continua*). Therefore our own participation in these acts is not simply a matter of discovering or of disclosing some being or essence that exists independently of us. It is, rather, a genuine co-creation of the essences, ideas, values and goals coordinated with the eternal logos, the eternal love and the eternal will.

---

2. "The person" (as Scheler uses this term) is thus the individuated "self" of a human being: that is, the center of its "spirituality," or the full range of spiritual acts and experiences of which it is capable.
3. Johann Wolfgang von Goethe (1749–1832), the preeminent German literary figure of his time; in 1775 he became engaged to marry Anne Elisabeth (Lili) Schönemann (1758–1817), the daughter of a

Frankfurt banker, but he broke off the engagement within months.
4. Here Scheler is both characterizing and summarizing his reasons for postulating the higher sort of spiritual reality that is his version of God.
5. Bishop and highly influential early Christian (and late Roman) philosopher (354–430); for Augustine, universals exist *ante res* as ideas in the mind of God.

If we wish to clarify the special and unique quality of what we call "spirit" it is best to begin with a special [*geistig*] act—the act of ideation.[6] This is an act completely different from all technical intelligence and from the inferential kind of thinking, the beginnings of which we find in animals. Practical intelligence would set itself a problem such as this: I now have a pain in my arm. What caused it? How can it be removed? This would be a task for such sciences as physiology, psychology or medicine. But I can also take the same experience in a more detached and contemplative attitude, as a "case" disclosing the strange and surprising essential condition that this world is polluted by pain, evil and sorrow. Then I would ask another question: What is "pain itself" apart from the fact that I experience it here and now? What must be the nature of things that such a thing as "pain itself" is possible?

A striking example of such an act of ideation is the well-known conversion of the Buddha.[7] The prince encounters one poor man, one sick person, one dead man after having been protected from such experiences for years in his father's palace. But he immediately grasps these three chance occurrences as signs for an essential condition of the world. Descartes tried to grasp the essence or essential structure of bodies, by examining a piece of wax[8]—which is quite different from the chemist who analyzes the ingredients of a certain substance. The whole field of mathematics provides impressive evidence for essences of this kind. The animal has a vague conception of plurality which is completely attached to things perceived in their shapes and arrangements. Man alone is able to separate the concept or class of "threeness," as a "collection" of three things from these things themselves, and to operate with the "number" 3 as an independent object according to formal rules for producing a series of such objects. Yet, what mathematics discovers about the relations of nonsensible entities in an axiomatic system is, strange to say, capable of being applied, if not today, then tomorrow with great precision to the world of real things. These are the achievements of spirit, not of a practical, inferential intelligence. The animal cannot do anything like this.

Ideation, therefore, means to grasp the essential modes and formal structures of the world through a single case only, independent of the number of observations and inductive inferences which belong to intelligence. The knowledge so gained is then universally valid for all possible cases of the same essential nature, and for all possible subjects who think about the same case, quite independent of the accidents of the senses and the manner and degree of their stimulation. Insights so gained, therefore, are valid beyond the limits of sensory experience. They are valid not only for this world, but for all possible worlds. In technical language, we call them a priori.

This knowledge of essences fulfills two different functions. On the one hand, it provides the presuppositions, or fundamental axioms, for the positive sciences whose field of research is strictly delimited by methods of proof through observation and measurement. There are different groups of such axioms in different areas within the general system of logic, and they give direction to fruitful observation and inferences, both inductive and deductive. For

---

6. On the possibility and significance of this special kind of essential knowledge, Scheler follows Husserl.
7. Siddhartha Gautama (active ca. 5th c. B.C.E.),
the founder of Buddhism; he was born the prince of a kingdom in northeastern India.
8. See Descartes's *Meditations on First Philosophy* (1641), Meditation II.

metaphysics, on the other hand, whose goal is the knowledge of absolute being, the essences are, as Hegel said appropriately, "windows into the absolute." For each genuine essence which reason discovers in the world cannot be reduced to causes of a finite kind, nor can the existence of "something" characterized by such an essence be so reduced. It can only be ascribed *qua* essence to a superindividual spirit as an attribute of the superindividual being in itself (*ens a se*). And the existence of such an essence can only be understood as a secondary attribute inherent in the nature of the eternal vital impulse.

The capacity to distinguish between essence and existence is a basic characteristic of the human spirit. Not that man's capability of knowledge in general is his essential characteristic, as Leibniz observed, but that he is capable of a priori knowledge. This does not mean that there is a constant, permanent structure of reason, as Kant believed. On the contrary, this structure is always subject to historical change. What is constant is reason as a disposition and capacity to create and to shape, through the actualization of new essential insights, new forms of thought, intuition, love and value. (These forms first take shape in the minds of the leading pioneers and then are shared by the rest of mankind through participation.)[9]

If we wish to probe more deeply into the nature of man, we must try to deal with the structure of processes which lead to the act of ideation. Whether consciously or unconsciously, man employs a technique which may be described as a tentative experimental suspension of reality. In this experimental technique the essence is peeled off, as it were, from the concrete sensory object. The animal, as we saw, still lives entirely within the domain of concrete reality. The notion of reality involves, partly, a place in space and time, a here and now and, partly, an adventitious quality as it is disclosed through sense perception from a particular perspective.

To be human means to oppose this reality with an emphatic "No." Buddha knew this when he said that it is wonderful to look upon the things of this world and terrible to be them, and when he developed his technique of de-actualizing the world and the self. Plato knew this when he envisaged the intuition of forms as a turning away of the soul from the sensory world,[1] and the return of the soul to itself, in order to go back to the original nature and source of things. And Husserl meant the same thing when he based the intuition of essences upon a phenomenological reduction, a "canceling" or "bracketing" of the accidental coefficients of things in the world in order to bring out their essences. While I do not go along with Husserl's theory of reduction in its details, I do believe that it refers to the essential act by which the human spirit must be defined.

If we wish to know how this act of reduction takes place, we must first ask what our experience of reality is. There is no specific sensory experience that conveys the impression of reality, nor do the senses in general do so, or memory or thought. They can convey some quality (*Sosein*) of things, not their existence (*Dasein*). Existence, or a sense of reality, is derived from the experience of resistance in a world already present as given, and this experience of resistance is

---

9. This is an important point of divergence from Husserl (in a direction that may owe something to BERGSON).

1. In the dialogues of the Greek philosopher Plato

(ca. 427–ca. 347 B.C.E.), the Forms or Ideas are fundamental, timeless universals, in whose reality objects in the natural world (their less than perfect copies) participate or share.

inherent in the vital drive, in the central life impulse of our being. The reality of the external world (which is present even in dreams) is not a matter of inference, is not a perceptual experience, is not associated with an experience of objects (which occurs even in fantasy) or with a fixed position in space, arresting our attention. Reality is always a sense of resistance experienced on the lowest and most primitive stage of psychic life, or in the very center of our vital drives constantly active even in sleep and in a state of unconsciousness. In the strict organization of the characteristics of a physical thing, including color, shape and extension—an organization which we can study in pathological deficiencies of perception—there is nothing more immediate than the sense of reality. Suppose we let all colors and sensory qualities, all forms and relations of a physical thing dissolve in our consciousness[;] what remains naked, as it were, and without qualitative characteristics, is the powerful impression of reality itself, the impression of the reality of the world.

This original experience of reality as an experience of resistance precedes any consciousness, conception and perception. Even the strongest sensory experience is never a function of the stimulus and the normal processes of the nervous system only. A drive-attitude, whether attraction or repulsion, must also be present if there is to be even the simplest perception. A drive-attitude is an indispensable accessory condition for all possible perceptions. This explains why the resistances which the centers and fields of forces behind the physical images in the environment exercise upon the vital impulse—the images themselves are ineffective—can be experienced at a point in the temporal process of an incipient perception when it has not yet become a conscious image. Experience of reality, therefore, does not come after, but before any representation of the world.

What, then, is meant by this radical "No" of which I just spoke? What does it mean to "de-actualize" the world or to "ideate" it? It does not mean, as Husserl believed, to suspend the existential judgment which is inherent in every natural act of perception. The judgment "A is real" presupposes, as far as the predicate is concerned, the content of experience, if "real" is not to be an empty word. No, what it means is to suspend, at least tentatively, the experience of reality itself, or to annihilate the entire, indivisible, powerful impression of reality together with its affective corollates. What it means is to remove the "anguish of earthly existence" which, as Schiller wrote, is overcome only "in those regions where the pure forms dwell."[2] For all reality, because it is reality, and regardless of what it is, is a kind of inhibiting, constraining pressure for every living being. Its corollate is "pure" anxiety, an anxiety without an object. If reality means resistance, the canceling of reality can only be the kind of ascetic act by which we suspend the operation of the vital impulse in relation to which the world appears as resistance, and which is the precondition for all sensory experience and its accidental qualities. Drives and senses belong together. This is the reason why Plato said that philosophy is a process of "dying" (to the body), and this is the reason why every type of extreme rationalism is ultimately founded upon an "ascetic ideal."[3]

2. Quoted from Schiller's poem "The Ideal and Life" (1795).
3. An expression used by Nietzsche in *On the Genealogy of Morals* to characterize "life-denying" or "life-negating" ideals he considered to be profoundly pathological; Scheler employs it to emphasize opposition to Nietzsche and his attempt to reinterpret all human spirituality in purely naturalistic terms. Plato discusses the philosopher's asceticism and "dying" in life in *Phaedo* 64b–68b.

This act of de-actualization, or de-realizing the world, can be performed only by a being which we have called "spirit [*Geist*]." Only spirit [*Geist*] in its form as pure will can, by an act of will—an act of inhibition—put out of action that center of vital impulses which we recognized as the key to reality.

Man is the kind of being who, by means of spirit, can take an ascetic attitude toward life. He can suppress and repress his own vital drives and deny them the nourishment of perceptual images and representations. Compared with the animal that always says "Yes," to reality, even when it avoids it and flees from it, man is the being who can say "No," the "ascetic of life," the protestant par excellence, against mere reality. This has nothing to do with any question of value or *Weltanschauung*.[4] It does not matter whether we follow Buddha and say that this ascent of spirit into the unreal sphere of essence is the ultimate goal and good of man because reality is inherently evil (*omne ens est malum*)[5] or whether, as I believe, we must try to return from the sphere of essences to the reality of the world in order to improve it (in this case existence is, to begin with, neutral with respect to good and evil) and whether we envisage the true life and destiny of man in terms of an eternal rhythmic movement between idea and reality, spirit and instinct—and in the reconciliation of this constant tension.

At any rate, as compared with the animal whose existence is as it were, Philistinism incarnate, man is the eternal Faust,[6] the creature always seeking and desiring (*bestia cupidissima rerum novarum*[7]), never at peace with his environment, always anxious to break through the barriers of his life here and now, always striving to transcend his environment, including his own state of being. For Freud,[8] too, man is the being who represses his instincts.

Only because man has this capacity for repression, not now and then, but as a permanent capacity, does he accomplish two things. First, he erects a superstructure of ideas above the world of sensory experience. Secondly, by this very means, he makes accessible to his spirit [*Geist*] the latent energy of the repressed drives. In other words, man is capable of sublimating his instinctual energy into spiritual activity.[9]

From III. Spirit and Life[1]

Another crucial question arises at this point: Is spirit [*Geist*] the product of asceticism, repression and sublimation, or does spirit merely receive its energy by these means? Is the technique of repression—which, in turn, is conditioned by the inhibiting act of the will—simply a means for manifesting spirit in man, or is spirit itself, in its very nature, principles and laws, a product of repression and sublimation? In my opinion, the negative acts, the "No," thrown against reality, the cancellation and repression of drives, do not determine the being of spirit. They only determine the supply of energy available to

---

4. Worldview (German).
5. All being is evil (Latin).
6. The title character of Goethe's two-part greatest work (1808, 1832), inspired by the German legend of a magician or astrologer whose desire for knowledge and power led him to sell his soul to the devil to achieve them.
7. Beast most desirous of new things (Latin).

8. Sigmund Freud (1856–1939), the Austrian father of psychoanalysis and psychoanalytic theory.
9. Scheler here joins both Nietzsche and Freud in considering "sublimation" to be the key to the existence and development (and comprehension) of human spirituality.
1. That is, "Spirituality and Vitality" (*Geist und Leben*).

spirit and thus its power to manifest itself in the word. Spirit [*Geist*] is, as we said, ultimately an attribute of Being itself which becomes manifest in man, in the unity of self-concentration characteristic of the person. But in its pure form spirit is originally without power, energy or activity. In order to gain the smallest degree of energy and activity, asceticism, the repression and sublimation of instincts must be added to the pure form of spirit.

From this perspective, we gain an insight into two conceptions of spirit [*Geist*] which have played an important role in the history of the idea of man. The first theory, developed by the Greeks, attributes to spirit not only a unique nature and autonomy, but also energy and activity—yes, the highest degree of power. This is the classical theory of man. It is part of a total world view according to which the permanent nature of the universe, remaining unchanged throughout its historical development, is so constructed that the higher forms of being from the Godhead to brute matter are also the more powerful ones, the causal agents and creative modes of being. The apex of such a world then is a spiritual and omnipotent God, a God who is omnipotent because he is spirit [*Geist*].

The second theory—which we may call the negative theory—takes the opposite point of view: spirit [*Geist*] (if this be an admissible term) or, at least all culture-producing activities of man, including all logical, moral, aesthetic and creative acts, are possible only as a result of man's capacity to repress his impulses.[2]

I reject both theories. Instead, I claim that spirit [*Geist*] has its own nature and autonomy, but lacks an original energy of its own. The negative acts of inhibition, which originate in the spiritual act of willing, provide energy for spirit which, to begin with, is impotent and consists only of a group of pure "intentions." They do not produce spirit itself.

* * *

Spirit is originally devoid of power and efficacy, and the more this is so, the purer it is. The original order of relations holding between the higher and lower forms of being and categories of value, on the one hand, and the forces and energies in which these forms are realized, on the other, may be expressed as follows: "To begin with, the lowest forms are the most powerful, and the highest the most impotent." Every higher form of being is relatively impotent with respect to the lower: it is realized, not through its own power, but through the energy of the lower forms. The process of life has its own structure unfolding in time, but it is realized exclusively through the material substance and energy of the inorganic world.

Spirit and life are related in the same way. It is true that spirit can *acquire* energy through the process of sublimation. It is true that the vital impulses can enter into the autonomous and meaningful structure of spirit [*Geist*] and, in so doing, lend power to spirit in the individual and in history. But, to begin with and inherently, spirit has no energy of its own. The higher forms of being may determine the essence or the essential regions of the world, but these essences are realized only through another principle that belongs to Ground

---

2. Scheler has in mind not just Freud (named in an omitted passage) but, more important, Nietzsche.

of Being as intimately as the spiritual principle. This is the principle which we have called vital impulse, or the image-producing "vital fantasy" out of which a sense of reality emerges.

The most powerful forces are the centers of energy in the inorganic world which represent the most primitive manifestations of this vital impulse. They are "blind," as it were, to any idea, form or meaning. According to contemporary physics, it is likely that these centers are not even subject to a strict causal order in their interaction, but only to the accidental order of statistical regularity. Only man as a living being introduces law and order into nature, not from a rational, but from a biological necessity (that is, in order to be able to act) by virtue of the fact that the sensory organs or functions indicate more the regular than the irregular processes in the world. Later, reason interprets this regularity as a natural law.[3]

It is not lawfulness in the ontological sense which is behind the chaos of chance and caprice, but it is chaos which is to be found behind the laws in the formal mechanical sense. If this view that all natural laws are ultimately statistical laws only, that all natural processes (including those on a submicroscopic level) are total processes resulting from the interaction of energy centers governed by chance—if this view should prevail, it would mean a complete transformation of our conception of nature. The true natural laws would then be so-called structural laws (Gestaltgesetze), laws which prescribe a certain temporal rhythm in natural processes and, following from these, certain static structures of physical objects. Now, since within the sphere of life, in its physiological and psychic aspects, only laws of a structural kind are valid, although not necessarily the material laws of physics only, this new view would again make possible a unified conception of lawfulness in nature.

From this point of view it might be possible to extend the concept of sublimation to all natural processes. Sublimation would then designate the natural process by which energies of a lower sphere of being, in the course of evolution, are made available to higher forms of being and becoming. For example, the energy exchange among electrons would give rise to the structure of the atom, or, the energies in the inorganic world would be pressed into service on behalf of life. The evolution of man would then represent the last act of sublimation in nature, at least until now. It manifests itself in two ways: in the channeling of more and more external energy absorbed by the organism into the most complicated processes we know (the stimulation of the cerebral cortex) and, at the same time, in the analogous psychic process of sublimation as the transformation of instinctual energy into spiritual activity.

We encounter the same relationship of spirit [Geist] and life in the field of history. Hegel's thesis that history is an unfolding of mere ideas is surely untenable. On the contrary, Marx was right: ideas which do not have interests and passions behind them, that is, energies derived from the vital and instinctual sphere of man, invariably tend to make fools of themselves in history.[4] Nonetheless, history does show, on the whole and in general, an increasing scope in the power of reason. But this is the case only by virtue of the fact that ideas and values tend to become appropriated by the great instinctual tendencies

3. These last two sentences summarize some ideas of Nietzsche's, not "contemporary physics."
4. Scheler here misrepresents Hegel, who not only did not hold this "mere ideas" thesis, but actually held precisely the view that Scheler attributes to MARX. See p. 229 ff above.

in social groups and by the common interests that link them. Here, too, we must be much more modest in our view of the influence of the human spirit and will upon the course of history.

Spirit [Geist] and will never mean anything else but guidance and direction. And this means that spirit as such presents ideas to the drives and that the will supplies to, or withdraws from, the drives (which must always be present first) such images and representations as may lead to the complete realization of these ideas. The central spiritual will, therefore, originally has no guiding power over the drives themselves, but only over the modification of their (psychic) representations.[5] A direct struggle of the pure will against the instinct is impossible—a struggle without the representation of ideas or without interference of ideas that are presented or withheld. Whenever the struggle is put in such direct terms, it only strengthens the tendency of the drives to go in their own direction. That was the experience of St. Paul when he said that the law was running around like a roaring lion in order to attack men with sin.[6] In more recent times, William James[7] has made some profound observations on this point. The will always achieves the opposite of what it intends when, instead of aiming at a higher value, the realization of which attracts the impulse and makes us forget what is "bad," it is directed merely toward inhibiting and at struggling against the impulse whose goal is condemned as "bad" by our conscience. Thus, man must learn to live with himself and to tolerate even those inclinations which he recognizes as bad and perverse. He must not fight them directly, but he must learn to overcome them indirectly by investing his energies in worthwhile tasks which are accessible to him and which his conscience recognizes as good and decent. There is, as Spinoza[8] saw with great insight, a deep truth in the doctrine of the "nonresistance" to evil.

The process of becoming human represents the highest sublimation known to us and, at the same time, the most intimate fusion of all the essential stages of nature. For man unifies within himself all the essential stages of existence, especially of life—at least in their *essential* aspects, not in their accidental variations and still less in their quantitative distribution. The world view sketched here cuts through the dualism that has prevailed for so many centuries: the dualism between a teleological and a mechanistic explanation of reality.

This train of thought, obviously, cannot stop short of the highest form of Being—the world-ground. Even the Being which is its own cause (*causa sui*) and upon which everything else depends cannot, in so far as the attribute of spirit applies to it, possess any original power of energy. Instead, it is the other attribute—the *natura naturans*[9] in the highest Being, the all-powerful drive charged with infinite images—which must account for reality and for

---

5. This is a key feature of Scheler's theory of sublimation and spirituality.
6. Scheler seems to be combining Paul's discussion of sin and the law in Romans 7 with the "roaring lion" (the devil) mentioned in 1 Peter 5:8.
7. American psychologist and pragmatist philosopher (1842–1910); see this anthology's companion volume, *The Analytic Tradition*.

8. Benedict (Baruch) de Spinoza (1632–1677), Dutch philosopher; see his *Ethics* (1677), part 4, §46.
9. Nature naturing (Latin); that is, nature doing what nature does. Spinoza distinguished this nature (self-causing, which he identified with God) from its product, *natura naturata* (nature natured).

the contingent qualities of this reality which are never determined unequivo-cably by the essential laws and ideas. If we call the spiritual attributes of the highest Ground of Being *deitas*,[1] then we cannot impute any positive, creative power to what we call spirit [*Geist*] or Godhead in this highest ground. Thus, the idea of a creation *ex nihilo* is untenable. If there is in the highest Ground of Being this tension between spirit and drive, then the relationship of this Being to the world must be different.

We put this relationship as follows: In order to realize its *deitas*, or its inher-ent plenitude of ideas and values, the Ground of Being was compelled to release the world-creative drive. It was compelled, as it were, to pay the price of this world process in order to realize its own essence in and through this temporal process. And this Being would deserve to be called divine being only to the degree to which it realizes its eternal *deitas* in the processes of world history and in or through man. In fact, this process, essentially timeless, but manifesting itself in time for our finite experience, can approach its goal— the self-realization of the Godhead—only to the degree to which what we call "world" becomes the perfect body of the eternal substance.[2]

An assimilation of the forms of being and value with the actual, effective energies can take place only in the raging tempest of the world. Yes, in the course of this development there may even occur a gradual reversal in the origi-nal relationship, according to which the higher forms of being are the weaker, the lower forms the stronger. To put it differently: spirit [*Geist*], originally impotent, and the demonic drive originally blind to all spiritual ideas and values, may fuse in the growing process of ideation, or spiritualization, in the sublimation of the drives and in the simultaneous actualization, or vitaliza-tion, of spirit. This interaction and exchange represent the goal of finite being and becoming. Theism[3] erroneously puts this goal at the beginning.

———————

We have climbed rather high. Let us return to the problem of human nature which is closer to our experience.

In modern times, the classical theory found its most effective exponent in Descartes. We are only now in the process of discarding it. By dividing all substances into two, a thinking substance (mind) and an extended substance (matter), and by arguing that man alone consisted of the mutual interaction of these two substances, Descartes is responsible for a host of the most seri-ous fallacies about human nature. * * *

That there is no such a thing as a substantial soul located, as Descartes believed, in the pineal gland is perfectly obvious because there is no central point, neither in the brain nor elsewhere in the body, where all sensitive nerve filaments run together, or where all nerve processes meet. It is also false to assume, as Descartes did, that psychic life consists of nothing but conscious-ness and is exclusively bound up with the cerebral cortex. * * * It is the entire body, and not only the brain, which has become the physiological field

———————

1. Deity, divinity (Latin).
2. This paragraph is a virtual paraphrase of Hegel.
3. Belief in a transcendent God who created the world.

corresponding to psychic processes. Nobody today would take seriously the kind of superficial connection between a mental substance and a physical substance as Descartes envisaged it.

Philosophers, medical men and natural scientists concerned with the mind-body problem converge more and more toward a unified conception. It is one and the same life which, in its inwardness, has a psychic structure and which, in its being for others, has a physical structure. * * * The physiological and psychic processes of life are strictly identical in an ontological sense. They differ only as phenomena. But even as phenomena they are strictly identical in their structural laws and in the rhythm of their processes. Both processes are nonmechanical, the physiological as well as the psychic. Both are oriented toward a goal and toward wholeness (teleoclitic[4] and holistic). The physiological processes are all the more the lower (not the higher), as are the segments of the nervous system in which they take place. The psychic processes are also more unified and goal-directed the more primitive they are. Both processes are but two aspects of the process of life, which is one and nonmechanical in its structure and in the interaction of its functions.

* * *

The gap which Descartes opened up with his dualism of extension and consciousness as essential attributes of body and soul is now being closed almost to a point where we can grasp the unity of life.

* * *

SOURCE: From Max Scheler, *Man's Place in Nature*, trans. Hans Meyerhoff (Boston: Beacon Press, 1961), pp. 5–7, 35–57, 66–75. Except where otherwise indicated, German words in brackets are the terminology used in the German original, inserted by the editor in addition to their renderings in the translation. Originally published in 1928 as *Die Stellung des Menschen im Kosmos* (*The Place of Man in the Cosmos*). It was intended to be a mere introductory announcement and sketch of a far more substantial treatment of the book's topic that Scheler was planning.

4. A term coined by Scheler; it means "oriented toward a goal" (as defined here), without requiring that the goal be explicitly represented.

ARNOLD GEHLEN
(1904 – 1976)

There is a German saying that reflects a widely held and deeply felt German sentiment: *"Ordnung muss sein!"* (There must be order!). It aptly captures one of the central themes of Arnold Gehlen's philosophical anthropology and social philosophy, as well as the social, cultural, and political conservatism that he displayed as a very prolific and high-profile public intellectual and cultural critic during the last third of his life. It also was reflected, far more dismayingly, in his decision to join the Nazi Party in 1933, and to remain a member through the war—for which he was in effect later excluded from mainstream German academic life. Yet he, like HEIDEGGER, should not be disqualified from being read and taken seriously as a philosopher because of those choices (although there are some who would say otherwise in both cases).

Gehlen ("GAY-len") was as important a contributor to the development of philosophical anthropology as Heidegger and SARTRE were to the development of existential philosophy. The formidable interpretation of human reality that Gehlen developed, which some have seen as an attempt to rationalize and justify his social and political tendencies and choices, could actually have motivated them instead. But even if so, the conclusion that he drew from that interpretation is not the only one possible: and the question of its practical consequences in fact remains open and is well worth considering.

Arnold Gehlen was born in Leipzig, to a family whose roots were in northwest Germany. His father was a publisher. He attended school in Leipzig and in 1923 entered the university there, studying with the philosophical biologist Hans Driesch before transferring to Cologne. At both universities he pursued interests in the sciences (biology, zoology, physics) as well as the humanities (philosophy, German studies, art history). At Cologne he studied with MAX SCHELER and Nicolai Hartmann, both of whom had interests in philosophy and the life sciences that were developing in the direction of a philosophical anthropology. He received his doctorate in 1927, writing a dissertation on Driesch's conception of the role of "positing" in the "positive" sciences. Continuing his studies in both the sciences and philosophy as an assistant to Driesch at Leipzig, he completed his habilitation (second doctorate) in 1933 with a dissertation under Driesch's supervision on *Geist* (spirit).

With an early burst of publication, Gehlen's career advanced rapidly during the next few years. He had the dubious distinction of replacing the philosopher-theologian Paul Tillich at Frankfurt for a semester in 1933 when Tillich, an outspoken critic of Hitler and the Nazis, fled after Hitler came to power. Gehlen, who had just joined the Nazi Party, had the right political and academic credentials. He then returned to Leipzig, taught for a year as an instructor in the sociological institute, and published his first book (*The Theory of Free Will*, 1933) and a monograph on existential philosophy and idealism. In 1934 Gehlen succeeded Driesch as professor of philosophy—at the surprisingly early age (by German standards) of 30. Though his Nazi Party membership and his publication of *The State and Philosophy* (1935) may have hastened his advancement, his work merited the position. In 1938 he was offered and accepted the Kant Professorship in Philosophy at KANT's university in Königsberg. Two years later, in 1940, he moved again—this time to the University of Vienna, where he became acquainted with the evolutionary biologist Konrad Lorenz.

This would be the last in Gehlen's series of distinguished professorships in philosophy. His high academic position and party membership notwithstanding, he was drafted into the German army in 1943, and he served as an officer on the Eastern Front until he was seriously wounded in January 1945. After the war, he—like Heidegger and all other academics who had been associated with the Nazi Party and regime—was forbidden to teach in any German university. In difficult straits, Gehlen obtained an appointment in 1947 at a new business-oriented *Hochschule* (an institute of higher education typically organized around some type of research program) in the small town of Speyer in northwest Germany, teaching philosophy and sociology. It was only in 1962 that he obtained a somewhat more appropriate academic appointment— professor of philosophy and sociology at the respected technical Hochschule Aachen, which was a university in all but name. It remained his academic base for the rest of his life (he retired from teaching in 1969).

Despite these professionally difficult conditions, Gehlen maintained a remarkably high rate of philosophical productivity as well as a high profile as a public intellectual until shortly before his death in 1976. He was unapologetic to the end for having chosen to join the Nazi Party when he did, and for remaining committed to it as a political party and to his perceived duty as a citizen of Germany—while condemning the war that was its ruin, and the Holocaust that was its greatest horror and disgrace. Though he bore his academic exile stoically, he lamented that the kind of philosophical program he had sought to foster had suffered lasting harm from being associated by many in postwar Germany and elsewhere with his personal views and decisions.

Gehlen's book *Man: His Nature and Place in the World* (*Der Mensch: Seine Natur und seine Stellung in der Welt*, 1940) appeared at nearly the same time as Sartre's *Being and Nothingness* (1943), and it is to philosophical anthropology

what that book is to existential philosophy. Both men were following paths that had been blazed by very significant figures before them (Heidegger and JASPERS in Sartre's case, Scheler and PLESSNER in Gehlen's); and in the eyes of many, both superseded their predecessors, owing to the impressiveness and incisiveness of their very different but similarly substantial and comprehensive treatments of human reality. Gehlen's book is more closely akin to MAURICE MERLEAU-PONTY's *The Structure of Behavior* (1942); together, they are two of the most important "second-generation" contributions to philosophical anthropology.

But Gehlen was much more strongly oriented toward a biological perspective on human nature than was Merleau-Ponty, or any other major figure associated with philosophical anthropology. Scheler and Plessner both came to the project of a philosophical anthropology from phenomenology, prompted by their growing acquaintance with and respect for biological perspectives relating to human and other forms of life. Gehlen, in contrast, came to it from the biologically centered *Lebensphilosophie* ("philosophy of life," or philosophical biology) of his mentor Driesch. Scheler's influence on him was significant as a stimulus—but one more negative than positive, for he disdained Scheler's personalism and preoccupation with a conception of *Geist* that he deemed much too religiously metaphysical. In the early 1930s, Gehlen went through a period of interest in the idealisms of FICHTE, HEGEL, and SCHELLING and in Heideggerian existential philosophy, but it left few traces on his subsequent thinking about human reality.

There is one respect in which Gehlen is in agreement with all these figures: he too contends that human reality differs fundamentally from the reality of other forms of life and types of living creature. For Gehlen, however, this fundamental difference does not arise from anything irreducibly different about *Geist* or *Existenz* in relation to "life" as it occurs in other forms in nature (and in ourselves). He points instead to the fact (in his view) that human life has come to have a radically different structure (*Bauplan*) from that of any other form of life. Man, he contends, is a *biological* "exception," and so a special problem (*Sonderproblem*) both for biology and for philosophy, both of which are needed to comprehend our nature and bring it into focus. Human reality does not simply have a extra "level" added to or developed on top of nonhuman biological reality; but it also is not just one type of biological reality among others, differentiated merely by its own distinctive set of drives and instincts.

Gehlen's initial approach to human reality, in *Man*, is comparative; and his initial characterization of our nature is framed in comparative terms. Compared to other species, man is said to be a "deficient being" (*Mängelwesen*): for rather than having a characteristic set of instincts and natural weapons and abilities that are structured to secure our survival, we lack anything of the sort. Our development has sacrificed specific instincts and weapons to a radical *plasticity* and openness to our environment, combined with an extraordinary ability to learn and to process information. But in the process, the burden of strategizing for survival and regulating behavior has shifted from our nature to our cultural and social practices and institutions. Gehlen therefore agrees with NIETZSCHE that man is the animal that has strayed the farthest from the security and reliability of instinct, and is thus the "unfixed" animal—and also the "most endangered" one—even if also now open to the most extraordinary range of possibilities.

Gehlen thus makes much of the importance of developing an account of human reality in language that is anthropomorphic, rather than borrowed from the consideration of other types of creature or thing. A prime example is the central concept of his entire anthropology: "action" (*Handlung*). Human action, for him, is fundamentally different from animal behavior (as well as the varieties

of motion found both in nature and in mechanisms). His philosophical anthropology is a kind of extensively developed "philosophy of action"—a characterization he considers much more appropriate than either "philosophy of mind" or "philosophy of *Geist*." Man, he contends, is "an acting being": a being whose entire constitution is structured around the necessity of action and its facilitation.

Action for Gehlen may be characterized as bodily, purposive, learned, linguistically mediated, and social. Though it is fundamentally directed at meeting practical needs, it is also capable of being directed at pursuing other sorts of ends and intentions. His analysis of it deals extensively with everything it involves, from the levels of human biology, physiology, and ontogeny to those of our perceptual apparatus, motor system, impulse structure, expressive capacities, language, cognitive capacities, and social structures. In the human *Bauplan* they are interconnected and have developed in ways that enhance that interconnection, giving them all a distinctively human character.

Action demands plasticity, versatility, openness to the unexpected, and the ability to be responsive and opportunistic. It thus requires a perceptual apparatus that yields an excess of sensory stimulation and an affective system that produces an excess of motor impulses—both of which must be channeled, developed, and coordinated, if purposive action is to be possible and effective. This leads Gehlen to another central concept: the practical necessity of "relief" or "disburdenment" (*Entlastung*) from what would otherwise be the overwhelming profusion and confusion of these excesses. To avoid the strain of greater complexity than can be handled, ways must be developed of ordering, simplifying, and streamlining our lives. Many features of human life—perceptual, psychological, cognitive, linguistic, cultural, and institutional—perform this "disburdening" function, as well as enabling particular types of action and interaction that are necessary or advantageous to be developed or refined.

This line of thought leads Gehlen to a third key concept: there must be a "hiatus" or break between our impulses and the initiation of action sequences so that things other than whatever happens to be going on in the here and now may come into play. This hiatus is a crucial feature of human action, but—like everything else about ourselves—its origins lie in the interaction of aspects of human reality that have developed in purely mundane ways. In this sense, Gehlen's philosophical anthropology is entirely naturalistic. He disavows that characterization, but only because he conceives of "naturalism" as a simplistic scientistic way of thinking, involving a kind of biological determinism that he rejects. Although his position does emphasize our biology, one of his basic aims is precisely to show that our biology has been reshaped in unique ways that supersede the biological determinism that reigns in other forms of life—even though our development has been a response to very practical necessities.

These necessities, for Gehlen, are surprisingly simple and basic. They relate to nothing more than survival, in a world in which human survival is possible but difficult. Human beings come into the world completely incapable of surviving on their own and lacking any internally determinate dispositions that might ensure their subsequent development of survival skills. The entire human *Bauplan* has become geared to the presupposition that human beings will enter a social world that has sufficient order and structure not only to keep them alive but to supply them with the content and interaction necessary for them to thrive—and to maintain it.

Gehlen has no answer to the question of why human societies seem rarely to stop at the archaic level he distinguishes

from the type of society characteristic of the modern world, other than to hint that the latter may be a kind of pathological mutation of the former that is all too likely to fail. In his most important book after *Man*, titled *Urmensch und Spätkultur* (1956, *Early Man and Late Culture*), he considers the differences between them and poses that disturbing question. In the first of the following excerpts from *Man*, which summarizes many of its main ideas, he in effect sets the stage for that book and question.

If Gehlen is right about human nature, then there are powerful reasons for concluding that the German saying mentioned at the outset expresses a well-founded concern, reflecting a deep problem for which at times there may be no easy solution. If human life depends for its very survival as well as for its flourishing on social order, and if our human biology has come to be devoid of any instincts or dispositions that can be counted on to ensure that human beings will establish and maintain such order, then there is no viable substitute for strong traditions and institutions that can sustain social order. And if the only real alternative to chaos on some occasions is a set of institutions that leave much to be desired, it nevertheless would be folly to reject or subvert them—unless they lead to (and persist in presenting) a kind of fate worse than death.

These are hard questions, and certainty about such matters and situations is problematic. Gehlen may be faulted for his reading of the situation in which he and Germany found themselves in the 1930s, or for the values that informed his choices; but even so, these reflections would seem to lend urgency to his project of a philosophical anthropology. Its merit, whatever that may be, is its own. And that assessment applies to the account of human nature that he advances as well.

From Man: His Nature and Place in the World

From *Introduction*

I. MAN[1] AS A SPECIAL BIOLOGICAL PROBLEM

The need felt by reflective persons for an interpretation of human existence is not simply a theoretical need. Depending on the decisions that such an interpretation entails, certain concerns become evident while others are concealed. Whether man sees himself as a creature of God or as a highly evolved ape will make a distinct difference in his attitude toward concrete facts; in each case as well, he will respond to very different inner callings.

Of course, religions, world views, and the sciences are not exclusively devoted to answering the question of man's nature. They do, however, tend to offer some answers or at least points of view from which an answer may be drawn. There is no guarantee of finding an agreement among these, however, because, as is the case above, the answers may be mutually exclusive.

Precisely these circumstances should be considered in determining the nature of the human being; that is to say, there is a living being, one of whose most significant characteristics is the need for self-explanation, for which an "image," an interpretative formula, is necessary. This self-explanation must include not only the individual's own perceived motivations and characteristics, but also those of other humans, since treatment of others will depend on how the individual views them and how he views himself. However, it is not as easy to explain what it means to say that man *must* interpret his existence and, based on this interpretation, must actively formulate opinions about himself and others.

Nonetheless, an answer is necessary because one could otherwise mistakenly assume that it is possible to remain neutral in this issue and refrain from choosing one of the conflicting interpretations of the meaning of man's existence.

The first of these interpretations sees man as descended from God, the second from animals. The first is not a scientific approach and the second, as we shall see, is scientifically ambiguous. It is striking that both points of view do share one common assumption—that man cannot be understood in and of himself but that it is necessary to employ categories above and beyond man to describe and explain him. It is here that the particular interest of this book comes into focus, for I contend that this assumption is *not* necessary, but instead, that it is possible to develop an understanding of man's nature that would make use of very specific concepts, applicable only to the subject of man. This line of examination opens up when one considers the following question: What does man's need to interpret his existence mean?

We could answer this question if we viewed man as a being whose very nature and existence poses a problem, which man must seek to understand and clarify through his self-interpretation. It all depends on whether or not it is possible to develop this point of view within a scientific, that is to say empirical,

---

1. That is, "the human being" (*der Mensch*). In German, *der Mensch* is generic (not gendered) in its application; a different word (*Mann*) is gendered male. In its use as a mass noun (as in "Man is mortal"), "man" is often the most natural translation; readers of English must always keep in mind that human reality is the topic.

analysis of man. Man would be, according to this understanding, not only a being who must, for a variety of peculiarly human reasons, seek explanations, but also, in a certain sense, would be unequipped to do so. In other words, man is a being whose very existence poses problems for which no ready solutions are provided. If this view is correct, then man has to develop an understanding of himself, for he can make something of himself only after he has formed a self-concept. The problems man faces must indeed be a part of his very existence and must, therefore, lie in the very fact of his identity as "man [*Mensch*]." Nietzsche recognized precisely this at one point when he referred to man as "the not yet determined animal."[2] The phrase "not yet determined" is apt and has two meanings. First, it is as yet undetermined exactly what man is; second, the human being is somehow "unfinished," not firmly established. We can accept both statements as true.

The above discussion has given a preliminary indication of the contents of this book. These will be elaborated upon further in the following pages.

This work is a philosophical and scientific one. It will remain firmly within the bounds of experience, of analysis of facts or processes that are accessible to or verifiable for everyone.

In view of the advances in modern technology, metaphysical statements possess only a very limited persuasive power and, above all, little true ability to motivate and influence the actions of real people. Lofty statements formulated as abstract truths can hardly hold their own against the broad range of attainable factual knowledge, which is indeed often subject to internal contradictions. Such statements necessarily prompt the further question: What internal and external experiences are they based upon and therefore limited by, and in what traditions or revolutions do they appear logical? Empirical-analytical science, on the other hand, does have the advantage that it can rely upon a consciousness that is, even today, self-evident and self-sufficient, but it pays for this advantage with its fragmentary statements. Even the presentation in this book may be one-sided, at best many-sided, and in any event in need of critique or, better yet, elaboration. In any case, it is apparent that the facts described here can be realized only with the precondition of a technical abstention from metaphysics. Man is an area of research in which, even today, an indefinite number of unseen and unnamed phenomena exist.

The first topic that calls for a metaphysical explanation is that of the "mind [*Geist*]." The problems attendant to taking a stance on this subject are so complex, many-layered, and difficult that any simplified position necessarily appears naïve. Who are to be convinced by global theses about the mind, which may, for example, ignore the problem of ideology or of relativism? These great questions are not directly a concern of this book so I will reserve them for later examination. The final section of this book will be devoted to an exposition of these fundamental questions to the extent that I am able to undertake at this time.

To turn back now to the original theme of this introduction, we are attempting to describe the "special place [*Sonderstellung*]" of man. It would be advantageous if, in the course of this discussion, the general, popular view that characterizes everything that is not man, from a worm to a chimpanzee, as

---

2. Nietzsche, *Beyond Good and Evil* (1886), §62.

"animal" and thereby sets it apart from man, could be upheld. But what truth is there in this distinction, and is it possible to maintain this view when one takes into account the basic principles of evolutionary theory?

Just as anatomy is a general science of the structure of the human body, so must a comprehensive theory of man be possible. Since we are never in doubt as to whether or not a being is a man [*ein Mensch*][3] and since, furthermore, man [*der Mensch*] does actually constitute a true species, we are justified in our expectation that a general anthropology should have a clear, well-defined subject. Logically, such an anthropology would be ranked above every specialized anthropology, certainly above a theory of races, but also above psychology, as well as any other science that focuses on a particular aspect of man. It would therefore not expressly treat the problems of these specialized disciplines, just as general anatomy does not treat particular anatomical features of race.

When one speaks of the special position of man, one must first make clear from what man is being distinguished. For this reason, no small amount of space has been devoted to comparing human characteristics and abilities with those of animals. It is only in recent times, however, that these comparisons have been carried out with the preconceived purpose of tracing the descent of man from animals by using the ever-handy concept of "development," which all too easily grows from a hypothetical construct to a metaphysical one. Quasi-empirical concepts, too, which were originally developed in opposition to metaphysical ones, such as creation, may become "metaphysical" if they take on the latter's functions. The derivation of human traits from those of animals succeeds perhaps in cases of individual characteristics or complexes of characteristics, but not when "the whole man" is taken into account; the problem of explaining man is very difficult—often attempted but not yet achieved.

This challenge has not been met for several reasons. The main reason is that the "external" and the "internal" have not been brought together; morphology and psychology, body and soul, have always been treated as separate worlds. In addition, the general claim that man is a unity of body, soul, and mind [*Geist*] must necessarily remain abstract. This claim is no doubt correct, but logically speaking it is a negation because a rejection of abstract dualism is expressed therein. Nothing is said, on the other hand, of the positive side of this claim. As does every universal statement it remains abstract—too true to be correct—and can offer no answers to concrete questions. To use concepts from Nicolai Hartmann's[4] new ontology, it is up to us, in spite of the admitted impossibility of deriving "mind [*Geist*]" from "life," to find those categories that are common to both and that therefore make their coexistence possible.

A further reason for the failure of universal anthropological theories of man is that in any such effort several single scientific disciplines must be combined: biology, psychology, cognitive theory, linguistics, physiology, sociology, and so forth. Simply becoming oriented in such widely different disciplines would not be easy; even more questionable is the possibility of forming a point of

---

3. That is, an instance of the type *Mensch*, a human being.
4. German philosopher educated in the Neo-Kantian tradition (1882–1950); he developed inter-

ests in both biological and existential perspectives on human reality and sought to work out a general ontology that unified them.

view from which all these sciences could be applied to *one* subject. The bound-aries between these sciences would have to be torn down, but in a productive way. Out of this destruction, material for the creation of a new single science [*Wissenschaft*][5] must be obtained. I wish to propose such a unifying point of view, which cannot be derived from any one of the single disciplines involved, but which is instead a philosophical one. This book will detail the applica-tion of this one fundamental thought, this one simple viewpoint.

Until now, the development of a philosophical anthropology was prevented by the following difficulty: Although individual distinguishing features or characteristics were identified in man, none of these was found to be uniquely human. Human beings [*Menschen*] do indeed have a very unusual physical structure but the anthropoids (great apes) have one quite similar. In addition, there are many animals, from ants to beavers, that form living quarters or artificial dwellings or that are social. Like man [*der Mensch*], elephants are also clever, and acoustical communication similar to our language definitely exists in many species. Later, we will take a look in greater detail at Köhler's[6] interesting studies of intelligence in chimpanzees. If, in addition to such spe-cific observations, we add into account evolutionary theory, then anthropology would seem at best to be the last chapter in zoology. As long as there is no universal theory of man, we must be content with simply considering and comparing individual features. As long as this is the case, there will be no truly independent anthropology because there is no independent being "man."

If one wishes to adhere to the latter view, one must acknowledge the "totality" of man. The theory of the unity of body and soul does not, however, actually overcome the dualism of body and soul, of the "external" and "inter-nal." It only avoids the problems contained within it. Why did it occur to Nature to fashion a being who, by reason of his consciousness, so often falls prey to error and disturbance? Why, instead of "soul [*Seele*]" and "mind [*Geist*],"[7] did she[8] not supply him with a few unerring instincts? Furthermore, if such a unity does exist, where then are the concepts and philosophical categories necessary for understanding the "soul" and the "mind" in terms of the "body," or for understanding the "body" in terms of the "soul" and "mind," which should the-oretically be possible if such a unity does exist? No answer has been provided to this question and therefore the right to try anew is incontestable.

It could be that there is a hitherto unrecognized connection between all external and internal human traits and capabilities which becomes clear only from *one* particular point of view. While this train of thought might neces-sitate choosing concepts that would be directly opposed to those prevalent in zoology and animal psychology, this would help solve the anthropological problem of defining man and thereby contribute to an understanding of man's special place in nature and to the formulation of a universal[9] theory of man. This single point of view would have to be a central one or, in any case, make

---

5. For Gehlen, as for most German-speaking phi-losophers, a *Wissenschaft* is a cognitive discipline, which may or may not be among or similar to the natural sciences. The "new single *Wissenschaft*" of which he is speaking here is his kind of philosophi-cal anthropology that is to be scientifically informed but differs in character from the natural sciences.
6. Wolfgang Köhler (1887–1967), German psy-chologist who emigrated to America in 1935; he is famous both for his primate studies and as one of

the founders of Gestalt psychology.
7. Gehlen here uses the traditional terms *Seele* (soul) and *Geist* (spirit) informally, but he will be reinterpreting these aspects of human reality in a thoroughly naturalistic—or at any rate, nonmeta-physical and nonreligious—way.
8. That is, Nature (in German, grammatically fem-inine: *die Natur*).
9. That is, general (*allgemein*).

it impossible to declare any one distinguishing characteristic of man—such as his intelligence, upright gait, use of hands, language, or anything else—to be the "whole." Such an approach never succeeds, for any one of these isolated characteristics can be found somewhere in the animal kingdom and hence, if taken on its own, becomes ambiguous.

Strictly speaking, I am proposing only an *elementary anthropology*, but one that, as far as man is concerned, is far-reaching and probably even unlimited in its implications. For this purpose, many facts from various scientific [*wissenschaftlich*] disciplines must become easily accessible; to accomplish this by employing a universal theory is the real philosophical challenge. Philosophy is concerned with specific existing facts and objects (even when these are processes, such as actions) and thus "man" is a theme of philosophy. None of the single sciences that are also concerned with man—morphology, psychology, linguistics, etc.—has "man" as its principal subject; however, there can be no science [*Wissenschaft*] of man[1] that does not take into consideration findings from these various disciplines.

This book takes issue with another view as well—the widespread "naturalistic"[2] and so-called "biological" interpretation of man as descended from animals, whether it be in the form of the classical—or, as one may also call it, naïve—theory of evolution, or in any other approach that claims to be "biological" and reduces everything to physiology. I will evaluate these approaches from a scientific perspective in the body of this work and would like just to foreshadow my argument here: I assert that it is precisely this type of approach that is *not* biological when it is applied to man and, further, that it discredits biological thought. I claim in addition to have developed a biological approach to man that contradicts almost all current views. If one were to accept the hypothesis, which will be supported throughout this work, that in man there is a unique, unprecedented, all-encompassing plan of Nature, then any direct derivation of man from animal—that is from the great apes, chimpanzees, etc.—would immediately rule out this line of inquiry. In fact, even an attempt to seek such a derivation would scatter all kernels of truly anthropological thought. Thus, an important dialectic becomes evident in what we call "biological thought."

If one considers man from an external perspective—in terms of his physical structure—and if one is well-versed in the history of zoological development, and perhaps also in fossils, then a definite theory will present itself, particularly if one yields to the intellectual instinct to simplify and unify—the theory of man's evolution from the anthropoids. This theory claims to be a biological approach because it proceeds from the corporal, from physical structure, from the laws of development of organic life. Precisely for this reason it never touches upon the "inner side" of man at all, and thus has to place great importance on Köhler's experiments with chimpanzees, according to which anthropoid apes also possess intelligence, even creative intelligence.

---

1. That is, "no discipline of man." In German, *Wissenschaft* refers not simply to the sciences but to cognitive disciplines of any sort—philosophical as well as natural-scientific, social-scientific, historical, and mathematical—including the "humanities."
2. Gehlen associates the term "naturalistic" with the kind of biologically reductionist interpretation of human reality that he goes on to describe

and reject. Yet his own interpretation might be considered a different and broader sort of "naturalism"—one that is strongly "emergentist," not only allowing for but insisting on the idea that *der Mensch* as a species has developed in a way that renders it fundamentally different in important ways even from those other species to which it is most closely related.

Thus, a schema for a general theory of man does exist, and it is currently dominant; but this has resulted in the quite inconsiderate neglect of the inner life of man or at best in rather child-like representations of the nature of this inner life. What is language? What is imagination? What is will? Is there such a thing as cognition? And, if so, what is perceived and what is not? Why one and not the other? What are "morals" and why do they exist? With the concepts of the theory of evolution,[3] these questions cannot even be posed, let alone answered.

I would like to argue that one can come closer to answering these questions by examining the possibility of impartial, purely descriptive concept formation. The difficulty here lies primarily in the casting aside of stubborn habits of thought. If man does indeed represent a "special plan" of Nature, then any nonspecific consideration of him necessarily falls short. I will prove, on the contrary, that there is an "anthropobiological" view that brings together the peculiar physical structure of man and his complex and complicated inner life. This is accomplished by means of special fundamental concepts that can yield insights even where the nexus of body and soul is probably permanently obscured from direct observation.

An objective analysis of a living being from a biological perspective is possible only if it treats the spiritual and intellectual aspects of life as facts in relation to other facts. Such an approach should not be restricted to an examination of the somatic or to a comparison of certain of man's intellectual or physical achievements with those of animals. A biological approach can succeed only if it can discover specifically human laws, which can be documented in all areas of the human constitution. It thus makes sense for now to turn away from all current theories, to "bracket" them, even the theory of man's direct descent from the anthropoids. It is also necessary to bracket the belief that there are "transitions" from animal to human intelligence or language, from animal societies or symbiotic arrangements to human institutions. This holds true as well for many familiar psychological concepts. This bracketing is by no means an unreasonable suggestion since these theories have in any case not yet succeeded in coming up with a satisfactory universal theory of man, even within the boundaries of what can be achieved. A new approach is needed.

As far as man is concerned, any biological consideration should not confine itself to the somatic or physical. What then constitutes the anthropobiological approach? It consists of answering the question of what are the necessary conditions for man's existence.[4] Let us consider this strange and incomparable being who lacks the conditions for survival which animals possess and ask ourselves what problems does such a being face in simply staying alive and surviving. It will soon become apparent from our study of this difficult question that what is clearly at stake here is nothing less than the whole spectrum of man's inner life—his thought and language, imagination, unique structure of drives, unique motor skills, and mobility. Each of these features will be considered in turn and will serve to shed light on and clarify the others. A highly complex, marvelous array of skills is necessary for a being

3. That is, a simplistic and dogmatic version of evolutionary theory.
4. That is (for Gehlen), the conditions necessary for the survival of human beings, both individually and collectively.

with this particular physical constitution to survive until tomorrow, next week, and next year. This is what a biological approach to man should involve.

It was stated above that man is the "not yet determined animal"; he is somehow not "firmly established." I also claimed that he finds his existence a challenge and therefore needs to develop an interpretation of himself—a matter that has always been of crucial importance. We can now expand upon these statements: Nature has accorded a special position to man, or—to put it differently—in man she has pursued a unique, hitherto untrodden path of development; she has created a new organizational principle.[5] A consequence of this principle is that man's existence poses a difficult problem; his survival becomes his greatest challenge and greatest accomplishment. Quite simply, it is a considerable feat for man to survive from one year to the next, and all his abilities are employed toward this end. To say that man is not "firmly established" means that he draws upon his own aptitudes and talents to survive; of necessity, he relates to himself in a way that no animal does. I would say that he does not so much *live* as *lead* his life. He does this not for reasons of enjoyment, not for the luxury of contemplation, but out of sheer desperation.

There must be a good reason for Nature to expose a being to all the dangers of disturbance and aberration that are intrinsic to man's existence as an "undetermined" being, to his compulsion to understand himself and exercise control over his life. The reason can be found in the risks posed by a physical structure that contradicts the organic laws in strong evidence among animals. If any approach can be called biological, then it is the following one: to ask by what means a given being is able to exist. By adopting this approach, the ground work is laid for a new science [*Wissenschaft*]—a universal [*allgemein*] science of man. We will learn that man's unique biological—indeed anatomical,—structure makes his particular form of intelligence necessary. We will also see how language is an extension of a system of deeply rooted interrelationships of movement and sensation, how thought and imagination are developed, and how man's perceptual world harmonizes with all this. An unprecedented structure of drives, unknown among animal species, is also evident in man. Finally, there is one system of thought that can enable us to organize the wealth of factual knowledge we have accumulated about man. We would like to create a system of relationships encompassing all the essential features of man, from his upright gait to his morals. These features do form a system, because each presupposes the other; a single error, a deviation in one point would render the whole system incapable of life. It is impossible to identify "causes" here because there are no causal relationships between these features; intelligence did not bring about language, an erect posture did not "cause" intelligence, and so on. Precisely these characteristics in precisely this system of interrelationships permit man to exist. In part 1, I will demonstrate that this special position of man poses an insoluble problem for the classical theory of evolution and I will draw on other theories to document this.

Again, in terms of methodology, it is necessary to keep in mind here that the notion of "cause" should be discarded. This concept has a meaning only

5. Both ways of speaking are figurative; but the latter is less problematic than the former, which seems to impute a deliberateness, intention, or teleology to "Nature" that Gehlen does not intend.

in those cases in which single relationships can be isolated—that is, only within the bounds of experimental science. Otherwise, it is of limited value and usually indicates that one feature has been isolated from an entire system and designated as the "cause" of that very system. Examples of this include the claim that the use of the hands caused strong brain development which, in turn, led to the emergence of man or the argument that the disappearance of the jungles during the late Tertiary Period[6] caused the famous descent from the trees which then caused man to walk upright, and so forth.

Another approach exists which avoids the pitfalls of such questions of cause and which is firmly in keeping with our biological orientation. This involves determining the relationship between conditions and can be formulated as follows: without A there is no B; without B, no C; without C, no D; and so on. If this sequence ultimately circles back upon itself—without N, no A—then we will have arrived at a total understanding of the system in question without having to resort to the metaphysics of a single cause.

It should be immediately clear that this method alone is appropriate for investigating the "totality" of man, if such does indeed exist. Conversely, this totality can be proven only if this method, which we will adopt, is successful.

The fundamental theses that I have been emphasizing in an unchanged form since the first edition have not protected this book from misunderstandings; these have usually stemmed from a narrow, popular understanding of the term "biological." I have become sensitized to this term because it is so frequently misused. It is difficult, however, to come up with a satisfactory alternative. I wish, therefore, to stress again that I am not proposing to derive consciousness, imagination, and language from bodily processes nor am I claiming that art, religion, and law should be understood as mere outgrowths of organic life. Instead, the method of observation I have chosen and termed biological consists of examining in process the higher functions of imagination, language, thought, and so forth. Parallel to this, I will document the unique position of man from a morphological or, in a narrower sense, biological, perspective. At this point, the question arises: how can such a vulnerable, needy, exposed being possibly manage to survive? The answer then suggests itself that the higher functions must be necessary for survival, that they are necessary determinants of man's unique morphological position. Both lines of inquiry share the important concept of *action*,[7] a close empirical analysis of which reveals true structures or categories, which express the relationship between the physical and spiritual and limit this relationship to certain areas of concentration. This relationship itself transcends our understanding. As Heisenberg wrote: "As we perceive it, reality is separated into distinct layers which, as it were, are only united in an abstract space behind phenomena" so that "all knowledge is, in a certain sense, suspended over a bottomless abyss."[8] On the other hand, this relationship between mind and body is, of course, continually expressed in every voluntary arm movement

6. About 7 to 1.8 million years ago (the Tertiary, also known as the age of mammals, began around 65 million years ago).
7. This concept is central to Gehlen's interpretation of human reality. His philosophical anthropology might be characterized as a biologically framed anthropological elaboration of his philosophy of action.
8. *Die Einheit des naturwissenschaftlichen Weltbildes* [*The Unity of the Natural-Scientific World Picture* (Leipzig: J. A. Barth, 1942)], p. 32 [Gehlen's note]. Werner Heisenberg (1901–1976), German theoretical physicist.

and is therefore a fact and an experience. An analysis of man's actions as they are carried out might possibly shed some light, however slight, on this darkest of all "abstract spaces."

Here I would like to give an example involving the fundamental category of "relief" (Entlastung).[9] Thought, representation, and imagination rest—as will become apparent—upon a broad base of "sensorimotor" functions expressed through the hands, eyes, and in language. It would, however, be an inexcusable simplification to attempt to attribute the former to the latter or to claim one evolved from the other. On the other hand, there can be no doubt that the former are based upon the latter. The category of relief employed in this discussion means that the functions of thought and imagination have achieved their level of versatility through primary visual and tactile experiences interwoven with language, that they develop the experiences gained through sight and touch in an easier, or freer, form. Further, certain structures in both areas can be proven to be identical. These higher functions can, as Hartmann explained in his review of this book, "surpass and leave behind the speech apparatus but could also for this very reason first gain their range of freedom through it."[1] In Bergson, there is a tendency in a similar direction, also employing the category of relief: "In man . . . the motor habit can hold other motor habits in check, and thereby, in overcoming automatism, set consciousness free."[2] According to this scheme, then, the problems of thought and language, of language and action, are formulated in such a way as to leave them open for analytical study as long as such study retains action as its focal point.

To return to the more general issues at hand, the higher functions are understood here as belonging to the conditions that enable a vulnerable being such as man to survive. Although this "biological" viewpoint is elementary, few objections can be raised against it. As one cannot treat all problems at the same time, we shall later see how this viewpoint must be modified when it is applied to the intellectual [geistig] superstructure of an entire society. Even now it should be apparent that our viewpoint is actually the opposite of one that seeks to explain the intellectual and spiritual [geistig] aspects through the organic. Indeed, it becomes obvious again and again that what is commonly attributed and relegated solely to the area of intellectual [geistig] achievement is often actually already presaged in the vital functions. The vegetative, sensory, and motor functions apparently work more ingeniously than Idealism has been willing to or than Materialism was able to admit. Precisely for this reason, one cannot conceive of those higher functions as existing in an arbitrarily structured organism and they will never be clearly understood if they are not seen in relation to the organically unique position of man.

If, in comparison to animals, man appears as a "deficient being,"[3] then this designation expresses a comparative relationship and is therefore of limited value and not a concept of real substance. In this respect, this concept attempts precisely what H. Freyer criticizes it for: "One envisions man fictitiously as animal only to discover that he makes an imperfect and indeed impossible

9. More literally, "disburdenment": that is, lightening a "burden" of some sort (and thereby alleviating a difficulty). This is a key concept in Gehlen's analysis of human reality.
1. Nicolai Hartmann, Blätter für deutsche Philosophie 15, 1941 [Gehlen's note].

2. Henri Bergson, Creative Evolution (Westport, Conn.: Greenwood Press, 1975), p. 201 [translators' note]. On BERGSON and this work, see above.
3. Mängelwesen: that is, a being that is significantly deficient in certain respects. This is a key concept for Gehlen.

animal."[4] The designation "deficient being" is intended to convey the following: From a biological point of view, in comparison to animals, the structure of the human body appears to be a paradox and stands out sharply. This designation does not, of course, completely define man but it does serve to point out his special position from a morphological perspective.

* * *

From 3. A Preliminary Definition of Man

* * *

Man is an acting being. In a narrower sense, he is also "undetermined"—he presents a challenge to himself. One might also say that he is a being who must form attitudes. Actions are the expression of man's need to develop an attitude toward the outside world. To the extent that he presents a problem to himself, he must also develop an attitude toward himself and make something of himself. This process is not a luxury which man could forego; rather, his "unfinishedness" is a basic part of his physical condition, of his very nature. In this sense man must become a being of discipline: self-discipline, training, self-correction in order to achieve a certain state of being and maintain it are necessary to the survival of an "undetermined" being.

Because man, dependent on his own initiative, may fail to meet this vital challenge, he is an endangered being facing a real chance of perishing. Man is ultimately an *anticipatory (vorsehend)* being. Like Prometheus, he must direct his energies toward what is removed,[5] what is not present in time and space. Unlike animals, he lives for the future and not in the present. This disposition is one of the preconditions for an acting existence, and human consciousness must be understood from this point of view. Indeed, all the aspects of man, which should be kept in mind through the ensuing discussion, are actually elaborations of the basic defining characteristic of man—action. We shall see that many of the isolated statements about man are really developments of one basic point of view—that man represents Nature's experiment with an acting being.

In Germany, I believe it was in the classical period that a tendency in this direction of thought was first proposed, although not ardently pursued. Evidence of this tendency can be found in the works of Schiller and Herder.[6] In his essay "On Grace and Dignity" Schiller writes: "With the animal and plant, Nature did not only specify their dispositions but she also carried these out herself. With man, however, she merely provided the disposition and left its execution up to him. . . . Among all known beings, man alone as a person has the privilege of breaking the bonds of necessity, to which all creatures of nature are subject, with his will and can begin in himself a completely new series of phenomena. (This is a Kantian definition of Freedom.) The act,

---

4. Hans Freyer, *Weltgeschichte Europas* [*Europe's World History*] (Weisbaden: Dieterich, 1948), 1:169 [Gehlen's note]. Freyer (1887–1969), German sociologist.
5. That is, what is distant, not the here and now.

Prometheus: in Greek mythology, a pre-Olympian god whose name literally means "forethought."
6. Johann Gottfried Herder (1744–1803), German critic and philosopher. On SCHILLER, see above.

through which he accomplishes this, is called an *action*."[7] Herder, whom I will discuss in greater depth in later chapters, writes, "no longer an infallible machine in the hands of Nature, [man] himself becomes a purpose and an objective of his own efforts."[8] These are valuable insights into the problem of the undetermined animal, of the being who is its own challenge, but these thoughts were not developed further in the philosophy of the times, because the prevailing philosophical orientation then favored the old understanding of man as an intellectual [*geistig*] being—a view that was too narrow to permit consideration of the abovementioned ideas.

This characterization of man, somewhat sketchily described for now, permits us to account for his special morphological position. This is of great importance, for only by pursuing this concept of an acting, undetermined being can man's peculiar physical constitution be explained. The definition of man as an intellectual [*geistig*] being does not in itself bring to light the relationship between the peculiar human bodily structure and the human mind [*Geist*]. In terms of morphology, man is, in contrast to all other higher mammals, primarily characterized by deficiencies, which, in an exact, biological sense, qualify as lack of adaptation, lack of specialization, primitive states, and failure to develop, and which are therefore essentially negative features. Humans have no natural protection against inclement weather; we have no natural organs for defense and attack but yet neither are our bodies designed for flight. Most animals surpass man as far as acuity of the senses is concerned. Man has what could even be termed a dangerous lack of true instincts and needs an unusually long period of protection and care during his infancy and childhood. In other words, under natural conditions, among dangerous predators, man would long ago have died out.

The tendency in natural development is for organically highly specialized forms to adapt to their specific environments, for the infinitely diverse "milieus" in nature to serve as living spaces for creatures adapted to survive in them. The shallow shores of tropical waters as well as the depths of the oceans, the bare precipices of the northern Alps as well as the underbrush of a forest are all equally specific environments for specialized animals that are capable of surviving only in them. The skin of warm-blooded animals serves the same function for parasites; countless examples are possible. Man, however, from a morphological point of view, has practically no specializations. He exhibits an absence of specialization that appears primitive from a developmental, biological stand-point. His bite, for example, shows a primitive lack of gaps between the teeth and an undetermined structure, making him neither a herbivore nor a carnivore. Compared to the great apes—highly specialized arboreal animals with overdeveloped arms for swinging, feet designed for climbing, body hair, and powerful canine teeth—man appears hopelessly unadapted. Man is characterized by a singular lack of biological means—a fact that we will examine more closely in part 1. He compensates for this deficiency with his ability to work and his disposition toward action, that is, with

---

7. Schiller, "On Grace and Dignity," in *Essays Aesthetical and Philosophical* (London: G. Bell, 1884) [translators' note].

8. Herder, *Essay on the Origin of Language* [1772] (New York: Ungar, 1996), p. 109 [translators' note].

his hands and intelligence; precisely for this reason, he stands erect, has cir-cumspect vision,[9] and a free use of his hands.

Again, as I will go into later, it was Herder who first put forth this idea, though, because of the limited knowledge available in his time, he was able to do so only with a certain vagueness. Kant, too, expressed a similar intu-ition in 1784 in his paper "Idee zu einer allgemeinen Geschichte in welt-bürgerlicher Absicht."[1] He wrote that nothing in Nature is superfluous and that while she gave man reason and freedom of will, she denied him instinct and the means of looking after himself through "ready knowledge." "Instead, man must obtain all that he needs from himself. Everything, food, shelter, security, and self-defense (for which she did not provide him with the horns of a bull or the claws of a lion, or the fangs of a dog but rather only with two hands), all the pleasures to make his life comfortable, even his power of insight, his cleverness, and his good disposition were all left up to him. Nature seems to have been pleased with her extreme economy here and to have measured her supply of animals exactly so as to meet the great needs of a new existence. It is almost as if once man had managed to pull himself up from a crude exis-tence to the greatest level of skill, to inner perfection of thought and, as much as is possible on earth, to happiness, Nature wanted him to receive all the credit for this achievement and owe it all to his own efforts." In these important sentences, Kant has brilliantly characterized man as lacking the organic means and instincts, as dependent upon himself to develop his poten-tial, and as facing the challenge of interpreting his own existence. Kant's insight is a product of his times only in that he narrows man's challenge to the "acquisition of rational morality."

Recent biological findings have allowed us to place the exposed and vul-nerable human constitution in a larger context. For most animals, particu-larly for the higher mammals, the environment is an unchanging milieu to which the specialized organ structure of the animal is adapted and within which equally specific, innate, instinctive behavior is carried out. Specialized organic structure and environment are mutually dependent concepts. Man's "world," in which the perceivable is clearly not limited to what is necessary for basic survival, may at first seem to be a disadvantage. To say that man is "world-open" means that he foregoes an animal adaptation to a specific envi-ronment.[2] Man's unusual receptivity to perceptions that do not have an innate function as signals definitely constitutes a great burden to him which he must overcome in special ways.[3] The lack of physical specialization, his vulnerabil-ity, as well as his astonishing lack of true instincts together form a coherent whole which is manifested in his "world-openness" (Scheler) or, what amounts to the same thing, in his lack of ties to a specific environment. In animals, organ specialization, the repertory of instincts, and the ties of the environ-ment correspond to each other. This is an important point. We have now for-mulated a structural definition of man, which does not rely solely on the characteristic of reason or the mind [Geist]. We can move beyond the alter-

---

9. That is, is able to look around (humans have ste-reoscopic vision, whereas prey animals have eyes on the sides of the head).

1. "Idea for a General History with Cosmopolitan Intent." For KANT, see above.

2. On SCHELER's concept of "world-openness," see

the excerpt from *Man's Place in Nature* (1928), above, with p. 1355, n. 2.

3. An example of the kind of "burden" (*Last*) to which Gehlen's concept of "relief" or "disburden-ment" (*Entlastung*) is meant to apply.

natives mentioned above of assuming a gradual differentiation of man from the higher animals or of arguing that the basic difference lies with the mind [*Geist*]. We have proposed that man is organically a deficient being and is for this reason world-open; in other words, his survival is not strictly dependent upon a specific environment. It is now clear in what sense man is "undetermined" and a "challenge" to himself. The survival of such a being is highly questionable; simply getting by poses great problems which he must face alone and solve through his own efforts. He is therefore an acting being. Since man is obviously able to survive, it logically follows that the necessary conditions for solving his problems must lie within himself; if existence alone is a serious problem and man's greatest achievement, then this must be evidenced throughout his entire structure. All special human capabilities must be examined in light of the question: How is such a strange being able to survive? Our biological approach is hereby justified. It does not consist of comparing man's physique to that of chimpanzees, but rather rests in the answer to the question of how the being, essentially incomparable with any other animal, is viable.

In light of the above, man's world-openness might appear to be a great burden. He is flooded with stimulation, with an abundance of impressions, which he somehow must learn to cope with. He cannot rely upon instincts for understanding his environment. He is confronted with a "world" that is surprising and unpredictable in its structure and that must be worked through with care and foresight, must be experienced. By relying on his own means and efforts, man must find *relief* [*Entlastung*] from the burden of overwhelming stimulation; he must transform his deficiencies into opportunities for survival.

At this point, the deeper, scientific [*wissenschaftlich*] problem surfaces which this book will address. We could continue to orient ourselves in the scheme described by touching on various researchers, but real proof of the validity of this scheme, including the particulars of the interrelationships between human functions, has never been provided. This is so because the principle of relief [*Entlastung*] has not been recognized. This principle is the key to understanding the structural law governing the development of all human skills; the second and third parts of this book are devoted to substantiating this. The underlying thesis is that all the deficiencies in the human constitution, which under natural conditions would constitute grave handicaps to survival, become for man, through his own initiative and action, the very means of his survival; this is the foundation for man's character as an acting being and for his unique place in the world.

The acts through which man meets the challenge of survival should always be considered from two angles: They are *productive* acts of overcoming the deficiencies and obtaining relief, on the one hand, and, on the other, they are completely new means for conducting life drawn from within man himself.

All human actions are twofold: First, man actively masters the world around him by transforming it to serve his purposes. Second, to accomplish this, he draws upon a highly complex hierarchy of skills and establishes within himself a developmental order of abilities; this order is based on potential usefulness of the skills and must be constructed singlehandedly by man, sometimes overcoming internal resistance to do so. Thus, the essence of human skills, from the most elementary to the most sophisticated, is their development by man through a process of coming to terms with the world, the purpose of which is to set up a ranking order of skills in which a true ability to survive is achieved only after a long time. Later sections of this book will go into the particulars of this process so for now I will try to make it clear by focusing on a few special points.

Man is incapable of surviving in truly natural and primitive conditions because of his organic primitiveness and lack of natural means. He must make up for this loss of means on his own by actively transforming the world to suit his own ends. He must create weapons for defense and attack to compensate for those that have been denied him; he must obtain food that is not readily available to him. To this end, he develops through experience techniques of objective ways of coping with particular situations. He must devise his own shelter against the weather, care for and raise his offspring during their abnormally long period of dependence; to accomplish these things, he needs to learn to cooperate and communicate with others. In order to survive, he must master and re-create nature, and for this reason must *experience* the world. He acts because he is unspecialized and deprived of a natural environment to which he is adapted. The epitome of nature restructured to serve his needs is called *culture* and the culture world[4] is the human world. There are no "natural men" in a strict sense—that is, no human society without weapons, without fire, without prepared, artificial food, without shelter, and without systems of cooperation. Culture is therefore the "second nature"— man's restructured nature, within which he can survive. "Unnatural" culture is the product of a unique being, itself of an "unnatural" construction in comparison to animals. The cultural world exists for man in exactly the same way in which the environment exists for an animal. For this reason alone, it is wrong to speak of an environment, in a strictly biological sense, for man. His world-openness is directly related to his unspecialized structure; similarly, his lack of physical means corresponds directly to his self-created "second nature." Furthermore, this explains why man, in contrast to almost all animal species, does not have natural, geographically defined territories. Almost every animal species is adapted to a specific milieu with a consistent climate and ecology. Man alone is capable of existing anywhere on earth, from the polar to equatorial regions, on water and on land, in forests, swamps, on mountains and plains. He is able to survive in these places if he can create the possibilities for constructing a second nature in which he can live.

The cultural realm of man, that is, of any particular group or community of man, contains the conditions necessary for his existence such as weapons and agricultural tools. In contrast to this, the conditions necessary for animals to survive are already given in the environment to which they are adapted. The difference between cultural men and natural men can easily be understood. No human population can exist in real wilderness; every society has some form of hunting techniques, weapons, fire, tools. Accordingly, I do not agree with the familiar distinction between culture and civilization.[5] In my understanding, culture is the epitome of natural conditions actively mastered,

4. That is, the sociocultural world.
5. The opposition of culture and civilization—on the view that they represent conflicting values and tendencies—had long been common in Europe and was a favorite theme of Romanticism.

reworked, and used by man and it includes the more qualified, *relieved* skills and abilities which become possible only with this foundation.

Now that this has been established, one of the most important aspects of the above mentioned principle comes to light—namely, man's "world-openness," his exposure, foreign to animal species, to an overwhelming abundance of perceptions and impressions which he is not organically equipped to handle;[6] this first poses a tremendous burden, but is also a necessary condition for man's survival, providing, of course, that he can successfully come to terms with this openness. The abundance and diversity of the world accessible to man and streaming in upon him harbor the possibility of unexpected and unpredictable experiences which man may possibly be able to use in his struggle for survival, in taking the next step to secure his existence. To put this another way, the world-openness of man is so limitless and undifferentiated in its variety precisely because man must choose from this chaos those experiences that he can use to his own advantage, as a tool to survive. This immediate handicap is thus productively turned into an opportunity for prolonging existence. We will see in detail how the process of coping with the abundance of impressions is always simultaneously a process of obtaining relief, a way of reducing immediate contact with the world; we will learn how man is thereby able to orient himself, to order his impressions, to understand them, and above all to gain control of them. As we are now touching on an area in which little research has been conducted, I should provide a certain preparatory and orienting introduction.

In the first place, it should be noted that the perceivable world around us is undeniably the result of human activity. From a purely visual point of view, this world is highly symbolic, that is, a realm of *suggested experiences* which conveys to us the nature and usefulness of the objects around us. Exposure to an unchecked flood of impressions presents man, even at the earliest age, with the problem of coping with it, of relieving himself of this burden, of taking action against the world sensuously impinging upon him. This action consists of *communicative*, manipulative activities involving experiencing objects and then setting them aside and these activities have no immediate value for gratifying drives.[7] The world is thereby "processed" in communicative, relieved movements;[8] its open abundance is experienced, "realized," and subsequently absorbed. This process, which occupies the majority of childhood, results in our perceptual world in which symbols convey the potential usefulness of objects. A superficial visual impression gives us symbols which impart the utility and specific properties of an object (its form, weight, texture, hardness, density, etc.). The profound cooperation between eye and hand and the communicative, manipulative activities culminate in the achievement that the eye alone oversees a world teeming with symbols of experienced objects always readily available to man. The existence of such a system in which certain skills

6. Gehlen's idea here is that our senses are not restricted to input tied directly to specific needs and modes of behavior to which we are innately disposed, but rather are "open" to a profusion of sensory input that we must learn to select, organize, and relate to our needs and purposes as well as our motor and manipulative abilities.

7. That is, in infancy and childhood, a great deal of human activity is *exploratory*; and this experi-

mentation with ways of coordinating sensory inputs and motor activities goes on in a *communicative* environment, in which the child receives guidance and is given linguistic means of organizing it all.

8. That is, movements that involve communication and "relief" (or "disburdenment") from the "burden" of being overwhelmed by a chaotic profusion of unfiltered sensory input.

are dominant and others subordinate, in which hand and body movements gradually disassociate themselves from the task of initiating experiences and thereby become free for other tasks—namely, planned work—while the eye alone is able to undertake "trial experiences," provides further substantiation for the law of the development and relief of human skills. A variety of functions come into play here: the senses of near and far (which to some extent regulate each other), language, thought, imagination, and highly complex "deferred" needs, oriented toward potential, not given, situations. All of these react to each other and occupy varying positions of dominance and subordination within the system.

4. Continuation of the Same Approach

Man's world-openness is actually expedient in the sense that it provides him with a truly infinite range of real and possible experiences, a realm of creativity in which there is such great diversity that, no matter what the circumstances may be, man is always able to find and employ some means of effecting changes that will enable him to survive; thus he is able to compensate in some manner for the deficiencies in his organic structure. By his own efforts, he transforms what was a handicap into something productive.

In general, these efforts consist of the "movements" that occupy man's childhood, movements through which man gradually experiences the world around him. In this process, objects are seen, touched, moved, handled in communicative movements of interaction, which we will study more closely. This process involves the coordination of all types of movement, particularly between the hand and the senses (above all, the eyes). As a result, the world is "worked through" with an eye toward its potential availability and usefulness to man. In succession, objects are experienced by man and then set aside; the objects are thereby unwittingly endowed with a high degree of symbolism such that, eventually, the eye alone (an effortless sense) can take them in and quickly assess their potential usefulness and value. The problem of orientation in the face of a deluge of stimulation is thus solved in that man is both able to manipulate objects and also to put them aside and dispense with them until the irrational abundance of impressions is finally reduced to a series of easily manageable centers (things). Each of these centers holds suggestions for potentially fruitful interaction, for changes that might be effected and for potential usefulness. When described in this manner, the relief that these processes provide is readily apparent. Man can, while immobile, look around him and oversee a wide range of highly symbolic visual suggestions of the ends to which certain things and situations may be used. He has achieved this through his own initiative alone, through a laborious process of actively accumulating experiences. Clearly, only a being who is not adapted to a specific environment, a being who is "unspecialized," would have to resort to this behavior.[9] Furthermore, only such a being would have to rely on its own initiative, finding itself confronted with a flood of stimula-

---

9. This captures the central feature of Gehlen's conception of man's "world-openness": our sensorimotor "being in the world" is "open" in the sense that it is "not adapted" exclusively to specific features of the environment, lacking any specialization inherent to our very nature. For Gehlen, this world-openness is both a liability and a potential opportunity.

tion amidst which it must try to orient itself. This process of self-orientation thus entails a reduction of the incoming impressions to certain productive centers, thereby providing relief [*Entlastung*] from the pressure of the direct flood of impressions. Whereas an animal is subject to the pressures of an immediate situation and changes in that situation, man is able to draw back and establish distance.

Directly involved in this process of orientation is another series of problems posed by the immaturity of a child's motor skills. As is well known, animals gain command of their range of movement after only a few hours or days and this range is then set. Human movements, on the other hand, are characterized by an enormous potential diversity, by a wealth of possible combinations that exceeds imagination. One need only consider the number of precise movements used in one single motion of the hands, not to mention what is involved in the complexity of an entire industrial system. Movements are, therefore, incredibly "plastic," that is, able to be coordinated and combined in an unlimited variety of ways. Each new combination of movements is self-directed, developed on the basis of a more or less conscious plan of coordination. Consider the difficult changes in movement necessary when learning a new sport. Remarkably, this incredible abundance of possible movements (used by artists, athletes, and all the numerous professions) and of arbitrary combinations of movements has rarely been seen in contrast to the monotony of animal forms of movement.

If we ask ourselves why man has available to him such a wide diversity of movements, then the answer can only be because his range of movement is unspecialized. The unlimited plasticity of human movement and action can thus only be understood in view of the similarly unlimited abundance of facts that confronts such a world-open being from which it must select and utilize certain ones.

The immaturity of a child's motor skills is a handicap, when compared to the situation with animals. It is also a challenge, a challenge to develop possibilities for movement through one's own efforts, through a difficult learning process involving failure, inner resistance, and self-mastery. The immature motor skills are qualitatively different from those of animals, which are established very early but then become monotonous and purely self-serving. Human movements are undeveloped because they contain an infinite number of possible variations, which the human being must work through in his interaction with his surroundings. He does this in such a way that each experience of movement opens up new combinations of imagined movements, so that ultimately man has at his disposal an infinite number of possible movements and variations involving the dominance of certain movements, coordination of movements, reversals, etc. This range of motor skills differs from that of animals in two additional respects:

1. It can be developed only through the same process of interaction with the surroundings that we described above from another angle. The experiences of movement in the unlimited, open sphere in which man must orient himself are at the same time solutions to the problem of developing a broad and refined range of motor skills equal to the infinite range of situations man might encounter in life. A being with such unnatural conditions for survival needs to be able to vary his movements in accordance with the demands of

each particular situation because it must change an unanticipated situation to meet its needs. To accomplish this, *controlled variations in movement* are necessary. They are developed in the same actions through which man orients himself in the world. Thus, these two achievements, orientation and controlled variations in movement, can be described as follows.

A defenseless being, overcome by stimulation and incapable of movement, transforms this double handicap into the basis for an existence totally foreign to the animal kingdom. The world is mastered and ordered through communicative actions unrelated to the gratification of needs. Only in a controllable, manageable world can incentives be found to enact those changes which will help an organically defenseless being survive. Through this same process, a wealth of experienced, controlled, and variable actions is developed to form initially immature movements, by carefully honing the ability to cope with unpredictable, changeable circumstances. From a philosophical perspective, it is vitally important to expose *the common root of knowledge and action*, for orientation in the world and the control of actions are the primary laws of human life. The immaturity of motor skills leads to a personal experience of the ability to move, and this in turn provides an incentive for the further development of the potentially unlimited diversity of movement.

2. An important factor in the development of these skills is the great sensitivity toward things and toward oneself in human actions. Human motor skills involve an acute tactile sensitivity; in addition, the actions themselves are seen as they are carried out along with the changes they effect. It is exceedingly important, as we shall see, that all movements be re-experienced through visual and tactile sensations, so that the movements are not engaged solely in responding to new impressions from the surroundings, but can also react *to themselves* and *to each other*. We shall later learn that this is a prerequisite for developing the ability to imagine movements. All human sensorimotor skills are *self-perceived*, that is, capable of reacting to themselves and to each other. This facilitates the forming of an "inner world," composed of imagined interactions and movements, ideas of possible outcomes, and anticipated impressions. This world can be constructed and developed *independently of the actual situation* and represents a high, but by no means the ultimate, level of relief. In relation to man's ability to observe his own movements and re-experience them through touch and sight, one must also consider his erect posture, the variety of perceptual axes, and his hairlessness (which makes the entire body a sensory surface).

To sum all this up in a few words: The existence of an unspecialized, world-open being depends upon action, upon anticipatory practical changes in things in order to use them as means. Making sense of the reality streaming in upon him and developing an unlimited, variable ability to act comes about through special, relieved, communicative processes of experience and interaction which are not in evidence among animals; above all, this is achieved through cooperation between the hands, eyes, and the sense of touch. Hand and arm movements, with their visible relation to the behavior of things, permit the broadest range of variation; given man's orientation toward the future, these may also appear as imagined movements, as images of outcome of actions, and as expectations (see part 2).

Adolph Portmann[1] has studied man's unique position from an ontogenetic viewpoint. Such lower mammals as many insect eaters, rodents, and martens, with their short gestation periods and high number of young, come into the world as "nestlings"—that is, in a completely helpless condition, hairless, and with sensory organs not yet functioning. In contrast, among the higher mammals, a much greater degree of differentiation is achieved in order to form a central organ that to some extent, as far as its functions are concerned, corresponds to a mature state. Among these species we find a marked reduction in the number of young (usually limited to one or two) and a lengthening of the gestation period, during which time the embryo/fetus undergoes a functionally meaningless phase of closing the eyelids, organs of hearing, and so forth, which are then reopened right before birth.

The young thus pass through a stage in the womb that corresponds in form to the condition at birth of a nestling, such that their development at birth is already comparable in many respects to the mature form. They can command the species-specific patterns of movement and means of communication—in a sense, they have already left the nest.[2]

Human ontogenesis, however, is unique among vertebrates. Man's brain at birth weighs approximately three times more than that of newborn anthropoids, and man also has a correspondingly higher body weight at birth (roughly 3200 grams compared to 100 grams among orangutans). The characteristic erect posture and the rudiments of communication (words) are usually established a year after birth. "After one year, man has achieved a level of development which a true mammal must effect at birth. For man's situation to correspond to that of true mammals, pregnancy would have to continue a year longer than it actually does; it would have to last approximately 21 months."[3]

The newborn is thus a type of "physiological," or normalized, premature infant, a "secondary nestling," and is the "only example of this category among vertebrates." The great increase in length and mass during the first year has long been recognized as having a fetal character.[4] This "extra-uterine year"[5] has a fundamental significance: in it, processes of maturation, which as such would also be fostered inside the uterus, are combined with experiences of countless sources of stimulation; in the course of working through these experiences, the processes of maturation, as well as the acquisition of an erect posture and of the rudiments of language and movement, first get underway.

"Thus, natural processes take place in man in the first year of life under unique conditions instead of under the generally favorable conditions within the mother's body," or "it is man's lot to go through critical phases in his behavioral and physical development in a close reciprocal relationship with psychic and corporal events outside the mother's body."[6] The special status of human

---

1. Adolf Portmann (1897–1982), Swiss zoologist and biological theorist; he was a pioneer in philosophical biology and anthropology.
2. This contrast—between "nestlings" (or "nest needers," *Nesthöcker*) and "nest fleers," or creatures born sufficiently well developed to require little or no nest-bound (or mother-bound) period—is important to what follows, because (according to Portmann and Gehlen) humans have in effect reverted to the former type, in marked contrast

with other higher mammals.
3. Adolf Portmann, *Biologische Fragmente*, [*zu einer Lehre vom Menschen* (*Biological Fragments to a Study of Mankind*), 2nd ed. (Basel: Schwabe, 1951)], p. 45 [Gehlen's note].
4. Ibid., p. 47 [Gehlen's note].
5. That is, "extra-uterine preemie-year" (*Extrauterin Frühjahr*)—a premature year outside the womb.
6. Portmann, *Biologische Fragmente*, pp. 79, 81 [Gehlen's note].

ontogenesis, with its marked morphological peculiarities (high birth weight and brain weight, high sensory receptivity coupled with immature motor skills, and an unusually late development of mature physical proportions) can therefore be understood only in relation to the "world-open behavior of the mature-form," which again is directly connected to the "early contact with the richness of the world, accorded to man alone."[7] To put this in another way, the mode of existence and laws of behavior of the mature form are prefigured in the embryology of man. Consequently, "a series of ontogenetic peculiarities, such as the duration of gestation, the early physical growth, the level of development at birth, can only be understood in relation to the manner in which our social behavior is formed."[8]

To clarify this astonishing fact, it is useful to draw a comparison with the condition of a nestling from the group of higher birds. In these groups (as Portmann has shown)[9] a longer period of dependency is necessary because of the great degree of differentiation needed for the development of the central nerve organs; this is then compensated for by involving the older birds in the process of development. "The older bird becomes an obligatory component in the entire ontogenesis," and the "staggered process" between the older and younger birds, in particular, of course, the coordination of their instincts (feeding, on the one hand, and opening the jaws on the other) is one of the laws of the ontogenesis of the nestling. If we agree with Portmann's description of man as a "secondary nestling," then we must further say that not only maternal care, but also communicative contact with other humans, and indeed, even the indefinite open stimulation from the surroundings, all become "obligatory functions of the entire ontogenesis."

5. Action and Language

By now a framework has been established within which the uniqueness of the human constitution is represented in man's achievements. These achievements arise from man's active attempts to solve the problem of orientation in the world in order to make it accessible to him and bring it under his control. Man obtains relief [Entlastung] and thereby breaks the spell of immediacy under which animals remain captive because of their direct sensory suggestiveness and immediate responses. The human being[1] singlehandedly creates an "empty space" around him, a world that he can oversee, that is readily available for his use, and that contains a wealth of suggestions for ways in which it can be used. He creates this in the course of his experiences and movements, in which, without the pressure of fulfilling drives, but instead in more of a playful manner, the things around him are experienced, communicatively explored, and then set aside, until eventually the eye alone reigns over an ordered, neutralized world. Through these laborious, self-experienced processes, in which man also discovers the impetus for further variations, he matures and develops a faculty for action which, in its controlled flexibility,

7. Ibid., p. 80 [Gehlen's note].
8. Ibid., p. 12 [Gehlen's note].
9. Portmann, "Die Ontogenese des Menschen [als Problem der Evolutionsforschung" ("The Ontogenesis of Man as a Problem of Evolution Research"), *Verhandlungen der Schweizer Naturforschenden Gesellschaft* 125 (1945)], p. 2 [Gehlen's note].
1. That is, as a species or type; or the individual acting in the manner characteristic of the species or type.

reflects the diversity of his world. Because man has refined and developed these movements on his own, he is able to build up a rich reserve of variable movements that can then be called into play whenever the eye spots a promising possibility for their use. Here we are not speaking of some sudden impression that calls forth an immediate response, as, for example, an unfamiliar stimulus would provoke flight in an animal; instead, by his own doing, man has reduced *the points of contact with an immediate situation* to a minimum, as far as his senses and motor skills are concerned.

It is precisely in the context of this development, interwoven with these processes, that language evolves. Language springs from several roots which at first function independently of each other; as part 2 will examine this more closely, I will not treat it in depth here. It can be established here, however, that the following are developed to a high degree in language: communicative, interactive behavior; the creation of "indicators," or symbols; self-perceived activity reexperienced through the senses; and, finally, reduced, relieved [*entlastet*] contact with the world. These are not, however, solely confined to language; indeed, they are, as has been stated previously, features of man's relieved [*entlastet*][2] existence in general and are already present in prelinguistic behavior.

If these statements hold up under closer scrutiny, as I intend to demonstrate, then it will be clear that the fundamental law of the structure of human sensorimotor behavior is continued in language and that it ultimately explains the uniqueness of human intelligence. In other words, the task man faces of transforming his basic handicaps into means of securing his survival result from his morphology. To meet this challenge, man creates a surveyable perceptual world and orients himself within it, in the process of which objects become accessible to him. Man also develops a highly flexible ability to act. The *direction* of these sensorimotor processes is clearly taken over by language and there perfected. It is here that the transition to "thought" can be located. This anthropological model is distinguished from others by the fact that it can, by using the concept of a structure of skills, find the level on which a transition from the "physical" to the "intellectual [*geistig*]" can be carried out, reconstructed, and understood. Under the pressure of a vital challenge, a hierarchy of skills is developed throughout which a single law can be documented.

In order to show how language continues the described law of the structure of skills, I would like to raise the following points for consideration:

Even among animals, there exists the "primal phenomenal" (*urphanomenal*) ability of *intention*, which cannot be further reduced. This is an active self-orientation by means of a perceived signal toward a "whole" that is manifested therein. The development of a "conditioned reflex," in particular, means that an entire situation has been restructured in perception such that a precise initial signal is confirmed in behavior through the subsequent development of the situation. *Symbols*, on the other hand, are essentially formed through communicative interaction. The symbols of the infinitely open world in which man exists were created in the course of his interaction with his surroundings. If, for example, the front of an object, its shadows, and its highlights

2. That is, disburdened (because simplified, and thereby facilitated). In some contexts, as Gehlen uses them, the terms *Entlastung* and *entlastet* imply facilitation.

are sufficient to suggest to us a heavy, metallic, round object, then behind this highly concentrated symbolic structure lies a long period of practice, of manipulation of objects, and of learning. The self-developed symbolism of things around us creates a world of implications of availability even when automatic gestalt-psychological processes are also involved. The laws of the forms of perception, which are aimed at establishing an overview of a situation and at facilitating classification, formation of points of emphasis, and the transposability of forms, are designed to make "changes" and "interventions" possible. These processes are involved in creating the symbolic structure of things, which is developed in the course of our interaction with our surroundings and which culminates in an implied world of potential availability.

Analogous to tactile movements, movements of sound articulation have the extraordinary quality of being reexperienced—in this case, through the sense of hearing. A sound is, for the time being, to be considered simply as a movement, and belongs in the category of movements that are reexperienced. Such movements play an important role for man because, above all, they make possible the experience of movement and thus promote self-directed, self-controlled improvements in skills.

Within the realm of communicative, sensitive movements of interaction, "movements of sound" arise from several roots; the "heard" aspect of these movements is experienced as a sensation, as originating from the outside world. The articulation of the sound resounds back from the world to the ear. When specifically these sound movements are employed in ways which I will detail later as means of communicating with seen things, it then becomes possible to direct oneself toward something in a specific, free, and effortless movement; in other words, man is able simultaneously to intend the movement and to perceive it. This unusual ability represents a very high degree of relief. This intention, that is, directing oneself in a communicative manner toward things, is the vital basis for thought.

In language (as will be more closely analyzed in part 2), we again find sensorimotor communication within an unrestricted sphere which culminates in the active development of concentrated symbols and in the ready availability of these symbols (or what they represent). The act of intending, as it occurs within movements of sound articulation, directly creates a symbol, the heard sound, which it receives from a thing in the course of interaction. This intention simultaneously perceives itself and hears the sound. This type of communication is highly creative, because it actually *increases* what can be perceived in the world; it is also the most effortless, most relieved form of communication. The perceivable abundance of the world is actively increased through this communication, only then to be condensed and concentrated in specific, easily used symbols which are themselves actions.[3] This is the masterpiece of human skill: the maximal ability to orient oneself and create symbols with the freest access to what is perceived—a process that, through words, is involved in man's self-awareness of his own actions.

It is perhaps already apparent from what has been said that the process just described logically carries the anthropological challenge to the furthest

---

3. Such "condensation" illustrates *Entlastung* as disburdenment; the increase in the world's "perceivable abundance" illustrates *Entlastung* as facilitation.

extreme. This should become even clearer if the following points are considered:

1. It is possible to concentrate in symbols even that which is removed from direct experience and thereby gain an overview of it. Man's ability to organize his world and create symbols extends as far as his eye can see.

2. Now a form of active behavior becomes possible that extends beyond direct interaction with the surroundings. This does not actually change objects, but in fact leaves them untouched. As far as the infinite range of the perceivable is concerned, there is a type of communication, experienced only in itself, that effects no actual changes in the world. This is, of course, the basis for all *theoretical behavior* which, however, invariably remains oriented toward things so that it may, at any time, through a simple inner transformation of the form of movement, become practical behavior. Between perception and the active treatment of what is perceived, there is positioned an intermediate phase of interaction with things which brings about no changes (planning).

3. All movements of sound are readily available and reproducible. Thus, to the extent that these sound movements can express an intention toward things, such intentions may be *independent from the actual presence* of the things or situations represented through symbols. The sound symbol perceived from a thing is distinct from the thing itself. It thereby represents the thing even in absentia. This is the basis for imagination. It is thereby possible to direct oneself beyond the actual situation toward circumstances and realities that are not given. As Schopenhauer once said, through language, man acquires an overview of the past and future as well as of that which is absent. The biological necessity of this skill is clear for man. If man were restricted to the here and now, as animals are, he would not be able to survive. Man must possess the ability to break through the boundaries of an immediate situation, to direct himself toward the future and what is not present and to act accordingly, as well as to turn then back to the present, employing its resources as means for coping with future circumstances. Man thereby becomes "Prometheus," simultaneously planning ahead and taking action.

4. Because sounds may also symbolize actions in general and even one's own actions (as in verbs), any movement or action can be intended through language along with the subject it concerns, and can accordingly be represented through symbols and communicated independently of the actual situation.

5. The importance of this fact for man's particular challenge in life hardly needs clarification, as is also true of this final point: language allows man to *communicate* intentions, whereby he is directly *freed from his own realm of experiences* and becomes able to act based on *those of others*.

To summarize all this: Language leads and closes the entire structural order of human sensorimotor functions in its incomparable, unique structure. In language, man's progress toward obtaining relief from the pressure of responding to the immediate present reaches completion. The experiential processes of communication reach their peak in language, man's world-openness is productively mastered, and an infinite number of models for action and plans become possible. Language facilitates agreement between men toward the direction of common activity, a common world, and a common future.

6. ACTION AND IMPULSES

The basic challenges man faces are liberating himself in order to pursue circumspect and anticipatory activities and obtaining relief from the pressures of the immediate present. To meet these challenges, he perfects difficult skills through a lengthy, laborious process of coming to terms with the world and with himself. In view of man's deficiencies, it is clear that he must perceive in order to act and must act in order to survive. This simple formula becomes more complicated, however, once one sees that this perception is itself very limited. At first, nothing can be perceived amidst the chaos of overwhelming stimulation; only with the gradual mastering of this chaos through interaction with the surroundings and accumulation of experiences do the comprehensive symbols evolve that make what we call knowledge possible. Immediate perceptions are always just the beginning of the process through which man acquires an overview of a situation and becomes able to take advantage of whatever it may offer. Language grows from this structure of achievements and is employed within it; and accurate memory and keen foresight are bound up with language for, without these, there can be no planned, directed activity, as well as no possibility of communication or understanding. Again, it is easy to see how the problem of survival for man is such that an individual can never solve it alone.

In contrast, an animal exists in the here and now and hence does not encounter the problems man faces. An order and harmony (expressed by the concept of biocenosis[4]) of which it is not aware and which it cannot influence in any way ensures that the means for its survival are accessible to the animal. For example, the restlessness accompanying hunger results in searching movements and, guided by a highly specialized sense of smell, permits the animal to find its prey. An animal lives *with* time. Man, whom "even future hunger makes hungry"[5] has "no time"—unless he prepares for tomorrow, he will not be able to survive. Because of this, man has knowledge of time. It is important for him to remember and to anticipate, while remaining active in a state of suspenseful alertness.

In part 3 of this book, we will examine the question of the nature of the needs and drives of such a being as man. The answer, in brief, is quite simple: it is crucial for man's survival that his needs and impulses function in the direction of action, knowledge, and anticipation. It would present an untenable situation if man's impulses were concerned simply with the here and now, directed only toward what is perceived, and running their course within the confines of the immediate situation while his consciousness and actions were oriented beyond the immediate toward the future. Human needs must become objectified and long-term; they must become removed interests in specific, experienced things and related specific activities. The hunger drive must smoothly lead into the need to search for food in, for example, a certain place proven successful earlier and the need to exercise those practical skills necessary to reach this end. To put it another way, the basic, minimal needs for relieving physical distress must be able to be augmented to include needs

4. An association of organisms forming a biotic community.
5. Hobbes, *De homine* [*On Man* (1658)] 10.3

[Gehlen's note]. Thomas Hobbes (1588–1679), English political philosopher.

for the means of satisfaction and the means of obtaining these means; that is, the needs must become clear, specific interests, which must arise from actions and encompass the activities necessary for their gratification.

Many peculiarities in man's system of impulses can be explained from this point of view, including, above all, his awareness of his own impulses. Not without good reason would Nature have made man aware of his own motivational life, thereby exposing him to possible disturbance of it. Man must be conscious of his impulses; they must incorporate images of goals, of situations in which fulfillment was achieved, and the specific steps for obtaining gratification. They must also allow even the most indirect actions toward the desired end. The boundary must therefore be fluid between basic, short-term drives, such as hunger and sex, and the more sophisticated interests in concrete, objective situations and activities in order to obtain lasting and successful fulfillment. For this reason, I always propose the formula of "needs and interests," because interests are conscious, long-term needs that have been *adapted to action*. Clearly, two unique aspects of human motivation come to light here: the ability to *inhibit* and the ability to *defer* gratification of needs and interests. Again, inhibition and deferment can only be possible when needs and interests are conscious. Man must be able to inhibit spontaneous instinctive actions in the immediate present whenever long-term interests are vital to his survival. Long-term interests can surface only when immediate needs have been suppressed. For example, if a child were unable to suppress his occasionally strong destructive urges, he could not develop an objective interest in the properties of things, which is a necessary prerequisite to the ability to manipulate objects. A need, in addition to being conscious, can also be suppressed or deferred; this even holds true for hunger. The ability to defer gratification of needs is, of course, necessary if these needs are to become substantial and goal-oriented. The needs must be able to vary along with any changes in external conditions or new constellations of facts. This is possible only if the needs are conscious, that is, imbued with mental images of content.

In an acting being, therefore, impulses present a unique structure. Above all, they can be oriented—that is, they can encompass not only certain vital needs but also the particular steps necessary to satisfying them. In addition, because the means of attaining gratification are so changeable, the impulses can vary accordingly. Awareness of the nature of the impulses, mental images of the situation of gratification, and the necessary procedures for achieving gratification guarantee the proper orientation. Deferment of gratification is therefore of the utmost importance and must extend so far that even the most qualified and inconvenient actions can have a motivational interest; otherwise, one would not bother with such actions or would carry them out haphazardly. Thus, the key to understanding the structure of human impulses is *action*.

Man's *lack of instincts*,[6] often remarked upon and bemoaned, does have a positive side and brings up a fact of great significance. Between elemental needs and their external gratification (which varies according to unpredictable and random circumstances) is interpolated the entire system of world orientation and action; that is, the intermediate world of conscious praxis and

---

6. A key point for Gehlen (with which many other biologically oriented reinterpreters of human nature strongly disagree). He takes it to be a mark of human biological deficiency (see p. 1383, n. 3, on *Mängelwesen*) and uniqueness in nature (for better or for worse).

objective experience, which is conveyed through the hands, eyes, sense of touch, and language. Finally, the entire social context inserts itself between first-hand needs of the individual and their gratification, thereby connecting these. It is this reduction of instincts[7] which, on the one hand, dismantles the direct automatism that, given sufficient internal stimulus, will evoke an innate response if the appropriate releaser appears, and which, on the other hand, establishes a new system of behavior, relieved of the pressure of instincts. This new system is the one I have just described, in which perception, language, thought, and variable action patterns (not innate but learned), can respond to variations in the *external world*, in the behavior of *other people*, and, importantly, can even react to *each other*. To express this differently, man's actions and his perceiving and thinking consciousness are to a great extent independent of his own elemental needs and drives. Man has the ability to disjoin or "unhinge" these aspects from each other and thereby create a "hiatus."[8]

This behavior, which is not manifested by animals, can definitely not be categorized as "appetitive behavior," if one understands thereby a behavior that can vary while maintaining a constant goal or consummatory action. Ever since Tolman,[9] however, animal psychology has held fast to this notion of purposeful behavior, of behavior directed toward a goal. In fact, as far as man is concerned, it is this hiatus that opens up the extraordinary possibility of a *change in the direction of the drive*. Although our rational behavior naturally includes the goal of procuring daily sustenance, it can, at times, ignore this altogether and bring about a *purely subjective state* on this side of the hiatus. For example, all primitive cultures possess some means of inducing a state of intoxication, trance, rapture, or ecstasy usually achieved through drugs. This is on the whole a collective process: through feasting, music, and dancing, man becomes transported beyond himself; these are social intoxications which, biologically speaking, are just as irrational as the self-mutilation and ascetism (ascetism as a stimulus, not as a discipline or sacrifice) often accompanying them. In many cases, the acts that usually appear as the final phase or consummatory action (such as eating, drinking, or sexual intercourse) take place on the same level where otherwise the rational, expedient behavior would occur; that is, they are used as the *means* of symbolically expressing an inner, ecstatic relationship among men. One finds this in numerous cults. This "change in the direction of the impulse" can be understood as a progressive increase in the ability to contain one's drives. Indeed, in the advanced forms of ascetism, it can be viewed as a continuation of instinct reduction itself, that is, of the process of becoming human.

I would like to clarify the independence of actions from impulses or the ability to "unhinge" these and create a hiatus. The cycle of action—that is, the cooperation of action, perception, thought, etc.—in changing a situation,

---

7. That is, the breaking down into their basic elements of whatever instinct structures our proto-human ancestors may once have had.

8. This gap or separation, in which language plays an essential role, is another central concept in Gehlen's anthropology. It enables our consciousness and

actions to be largely independent of our "elemental needs and drives," and even to oppose as well as master and redirect them.

9. Edward C. Tolman (1886–1959), American psychologist; his best-known work was *Purposive Behavior in Animals and Men* (1932).

can, now that it is relieved [*entlastet*], function alone and develop its own motives and goals. It is obliged to follow the laws of objective reality, to investigate facts, and to develop them. On the other hand, objectivity of behavior toward random facts encourages the suppression of needs—these needs must be set aside or deferred, must be prevented from prematurely disrupting invention or orientation, particularly when such activity is designed to serve *future* needs. The ability to contain impulses, to vary behavior independently of them, first creates an "inner life." This hiatus is, to be exact, the vital basis for the phenomenon of the soul.[1] The containment of impulses is infinitely important for man's existence and is impressed upon even the smallest child, in that the immaturity of his movements and actions, as total inhibitions of his needs, cause his needs to be dammed up and hence perceivable.

If, as I have proposed, elemental needs are not adapted to established releasers but rather have a looser relationship to the objects of gratification, it then becomes obvious why it is necessary to *orient* these needs to experience, to "imprint" them in their initially formless openness, to give them substance. The ability to inhibit impulses, to give them substance, and to defer gratification as well as the plasticity of impulses are all aspects of the same thing; we commonly call that level of impulses that manifests itself in images and ideas, that level of conscious needs and of oriented interests, the "soul." Only in this hiatus can needs and actions continuously be oriented to each other; needs must be formed, must be tempered by experience, and must become subject to differentiated expectations, in order to remain equal to the widening range of man's activity in the world, which is constantly increased and "opened up" through his knowledge and action. Finally, man can entertain a specific "objective interest" in, even a need for, a specific activity while the image of and the motivation toward the goal of this activity lie in his soul and outlast any immediate changes. This is precisely the purpose of such a structure of drives.

Human impulses should thus be considered from the point of view of their role in the context of action; one can then identify a series of clearly related characteristics. I would like to propose the following series of schematic statements that encompasses the general structure of man's drives and within which other special features function which still remain to be considered:

(1.) Impulses can be inhibited and contained, thereby creating a "hiatus" between them and action.

(2.) They are first formed through the accumulation of experiences, thus are systematically developed through experience.

(3.) They can be invested with mental images and "memories" of their content and nature. If suppressed, they then become conscious along with these images as specific needs and interests.

(4.) They are plastic and variable, can adjust to changes in experience and circumstance, can grow from actions.

(5.) For this reason, there is no sharp boundary between elemental needs and qualified interests.

---

1. A deliberate close echo of Nietzsche's explanation of the evolution of the soul in *On the Genealogy of Morals* (1887), second essay, §16 (see above).

(6.) Higher needs can grow from inhibited ones; these "enduring interests" sustain action into the future and, in contrast to the changeable
needs of the present, remain internalized. They are always the subjective correlates of objective institutions.

(7.) All needs and interests, as soon as they are awakened by experience and thereby given substance, are also the *object* toward which
other virtual interests are directed and may then be put aside or
deemphasized.

The teleology of this arrangement is clear for a being who acts in anticipation of the future, governed by internal impulses as well as by the changing
demands of a changing world. On the one hand, it is vital that man's needs,
which can be acute because of his lack of organ specialization, remain world-
open, that they be developed in a close relationship with active experience, and
that they become, without sharp demarcation, interests in specific situations
and activities. The changes that such a vulnerable being must effect in the
world in order to survive are themselves, however qualified and complex they
may be, important for his basic drives. For this reason, all intermediate
activities to accomplish these changes also turn into needs—perception, language, variations in movement, instrumental actions. On the other hand,
enduring interests must also be cultivated, oriented, and retained and must
remain conscious as inner invariants which control and outlast any changes
in activities and circumstances of the present. Organizing this architectonic
and well-oriented system of impulses is one of the problems man faces, perhaps even the most difficult one. Testament to this is provided by the often
very limited stability of *institutions*, only through which or beyond which can
this organization be carried out.[2]

The approach, developed from the study of animals, which seeks to attribute all human behavior to instincts (McDougall's[3] method, for instance)
shows as little regard for the special conditions of man as does the abstract
view that considers his inner life without regard to action and that has fostered the chaos in the various branches of psychology.

SOURCE: From Arnold Gehlen, *Man: His Nature and Place in the World*, trans. Clare McMillan
and Karl Pillemer (New York: Columbia University Press, 1988), pp. 3–13, 24–48. Except where
otherwise indicated, German words in brackets are the terminology used in the German original, inserted by the editor in addition to their renderings in the translation. First published in
1940 as *Der Mensch: Seine Natur und seine Stellung in der Welt*, the work went through numerous editions; its most significant revisions were for the 4th ed. (1950), and the translation is
from the 10th ed. (1974). Gehlen's title deliberately echoes—but also significantly departs
from—the title of SCHELER's pioneering *Die Stellung des Menschen im Kosmos* (1928, *The Place
of Man in the Universe*; see above), which was both Gehlen's inspiration and his provocation.

2. That is, it requires stable institutions. Gehlen's
later thought emphasizes this crucial role played
by sociocultural institutions in human life.

3. William McDougall (1871–1938), British-born
American psychologist.

HELMUTH PLESSNER
(1892 – 1985)

Plessner deserves as much credit for the launching of the project of a "philosophical anthropology" in central Europe as does MAX SCHELER. The appearance of Scheler's *Man's Place in Nature* (1928; see above) attracted more attention at the time, but in the same year Plessner published a much more substantial book, *The Levels of the Organic and Man*, that also deals with the general characteristics of nonhuman as well as human forms of life. Despite the profound disruptions of his life and work in the two decades that followed (he was of German Jewish origin), Plessner continued to make contributions, but on a lesser scale. It is one of the great injustices of the reception of European philosophy in the twentieth century that he has been and remains so little known and appreciated in the English-speaking world. Had there been no HEIDEGGER and no Hitler, the history of philosophy in the twentieth century would have been a very different story, in which Plessner undoubtedly would have figured much more prominently on both sides of the English Channel.

Helmuth Plessner ("PLESS-ner") was born in Wiesbaden, in southwestern Germany on the Rhine River, into a secular family. His early interests led him in the direction of the sciences; and when he first entered the university in Freiburg, in 1910, he focused on medicine and zoology. He continued his university education at Göttingen and at Heidelberg, where he was taught by the famous vitalist biologist and Kantian Hans Driesch. There he also developed and began to pursue an interest in philosophy. He had the good fortune to study both with the eminent Neo-Kantian philosopher Wilhelm Windelband and the phenomenologist EDMUND HUSSERL, and he published his first paper—on the "form" of well-formed "ideas" in the cognitive disciplines—in 1913, at the age of only 21. In 1916 he received his doctorate at Erlangen, with a dissertation on the Kantian topic of "transcendental truth." Four years later he completed his habilitation (second doctoral level) at the university in Cologne, under the supervision of Driesch and Max Scheler, with a dissertation on another Kantian topic, "philosophical judgment."

During the next few years Plessner held an appointment as an instructor at Cologne; and in 1923 his first book appeared, *The Unity of the Senses*. This examination of the relation between the senses and *Geist* (human mentality and spirituality) signaled the beginning of his interest and work in what was to become the project of a philosophical anthropology. A year later he published his second book (one of his only two books translated into English), on a completely different topic that reflected both the tumultuous times and another of his strong interests: *The Limits of Community: A Critique of Social Radicalism*. In 1926 he was given an appointment as professor at Cologne, becoming Scheler's colleague. Just two years later, in the year of Scheler's departure for Heidelberg and sudden death (1928), he published *The Levels of the Organic and Man*, which he subtitled *Introduction to Philosophical Anthropology*. (Scheler rushed his own introduction, *Man's Place in Nature*, into print at almost the same time—in part, one suspects, to avoid allowing the student to beat the teacher to the punch.) Plessner thus established himself as Scheler's peer in this new philosophical enterprise; and with Scheler's death, Plessner became its leading figure.

In 1931 Plessner published another significant book that brought together his social/political and anthropological interests: *Power and Human Nature*. As the storm clouds gathered over Germany, he sought to put the political power struggle into philosophical-anthropological perspective. But when the Nazis assumed power in 1933, he lost his academic position (owing to his Jewish ancestry) and emigrated—first to Istanbul and then, with the help of a Dutch colleague who shared his philosophical-anthropological interests, to Groningen in the Netherlands, where he was given an appointment in sociology. His book *The Fate of the German Spirit* (1935) soon followed, and then the second of his two books translated into English, from which our selection is taken: *Laughing and Crying: An Investigation of the Limits of Human Behavior* (1941).

Shortly before this book's appearance, however, the Netherlands were occupied by Germany, and in 1943 it became necessary for Plessner to flee once again. This time he took refuge in New York, in the community of German intellectual refugees who established the New School for Social Research—where Plessner would later hold an emeritus appointment. After the war he returned to Groningen as a professor of philosophy. In 1951 he began teaching at Göttingen, as professor first of sociology and then of philosophy as well; in 1952 he married. He remained at Göttingen until 1961, serving in its administration as rector during his final year there. After a year at the New School in New York, he took a position at the University of Zurich, which he held until 1972. He remained in Switzerland during his retirement, continuing to publish until shortly before his death in 1985.

Like Scheler, Plessner began as a phenomenologist, with a Neo-Kantian philosophical background. He came to philosophy after initially focusing on medicine and zoology, however, and after continuing his studies with an eminent philosophically-minded biologist. Not surprisingly, therefore, it seemed obvious to him that if human reality is to be properly understood, it must be recognized to be first and foremost a form of *life* or biological reality and must—at least as a starting point—be considered in relation to other types and forms of life. So,

while he retained his phenomenological sensitivity to experiential fine points while analyzing and interpreting various sorts of human phenomena, he also understood the importance of adopting and employing external perspectives—biological and physiological as well as social, cultural, and interpersonal—in developing a philosophical-anthropological account of them and of ourselves. (Significantly, one of his last essays is titled "With Other Eyes.") These strategies as well as his general program are both clearly displayed in the following selection.

As the title of Plessner's most substantial and systematic contribution to this project indicates (*The Levels of the Organic and Man*), his preliminary approach to human reality was comparative. Indeed, one of his central concepts emerged through such a comparison to other forms and levels of animate reality: human beings are "positioned" or situated and related to their lives and the world in which they exist in a fundamentally different way than are plants and other animals. He calls this positioning "ex-centric" (*exzentrisch*), meaning something like "decentered." Plants are organized as functional units; but their "positionality" in relation to their lives and environments is "open" in the sense that their structures are not organized around central organs that coordinate their functioning. The positionality of nonhuman animals is "centric" in the sense that their structures and functioning *are* organized in that "centered" manner, at and as the centers of their worlds, in which they are immersed. Our human positionality in relation to our lives and world differs from both: it is *ex-centric*, for we are capable of stepping back from and out of the here and now, of adopting reflective standpoints, of becoming aware of ourselves and the world under a variety of objectifying descriptions, and of acting in ways that have nothing to do with our immediate internal and external circumstances.

A particularly important instance of this ex-centric positionality pertains to our embodiment. An animal's relation to its body is one of complete identity. Its body is simply what it is. Our relation to our bodies, on the other hand, has a "double aspect": my body is both *me* and *mine*—what I *am* and something I *have*. Not only is human existing "being in the world ex-centrically"; it also is both to *be* a body and to *have* a body. That double relation is one of the most basic and important structures of human reality, for Plessner; and it is a prime example of the kind of thing he considers it to be the task of a philosophical anthropology to look for, to illuminate, and to explore. When Plessner discusses "man's nature" or "human nature" or "the human condition," the topic is structural features of this sort—rather than anything that might simply be a kind of coded cultural or ideological norm or value. The idea that this sort of philosophical anthropology is somehow inherently and untenably "essentialist" is thus a serious and unfortunate misunderstanding.

Our ex-centric positionality and our double relation to our bodies are related to a number of further important features of our human reality that Plessner identifies and discusses. One is that we are capable of *expression*, and of "expressing ourselves," in diverse ways that admit of seemingly limitless variations. The three most basic general modes of human expression, he suggests, are speech, action, and what he calls "variable shaping"—that is, making or producing things of different sorts in different ways, guided by many different kinds of intentions. Two others, quite different from these three but also of considerable philosophical-anthropological interest and importance, are the title subjects of *Laughing and Crying*.

All these forms of human expression involve our bodies; but all also involve meanings and intentions that we use our bodies to express and pursue. Their almost infinite variety is related to the *plasticity* made possible by the ways in which our whole psychosomatic system has become de-specialized. In this context, as elsewhere, Plessner draws heavily on insights relating to the evolution of both our bodily structure and our behav-ioral capacities ("the two aspects of human existence") that he gleans from recent developments in the biological and physiological sciences.

Plessner further identifies what he calls three "basic anthropological laws" or derivative structural features of human reality. One is the "law" of "natural artificiality": that is, it is "natural" for human beings to use culturally developed (rather than instinctive) means of expressing ourselves and doing things—and to master them so completely that they become second nature. Another is the law of "mediated immediacy": that is, rather than immediately and directly mirroring their objects, our consciousness and self-consciousness involve the mediation of linguistic and cultural forms, and depend heavily on them—and those forms tend to be so completely internalized that they become invisible, resulting in a kind of experiential immediacy. The third is the (oddly named) law of the "utopian standpoint": that is, we experience the way things are through the lenses of values and meanings that inflect them; and although those lenses tend to be invisible to us, they contribute significantly to whether those things strike us positively or negatively, and to precisely how they do so.

Plessner further pays close attention to the layerings and structurings that are aspects of the very fabric of human reality as it has come to be constituted, beginning with the ways in which the senses connect and interact (the topic of his first book), and continuing with the way in which the "eye-hand field" and its enormous significance for human action are to be understood. That dimension of experience and activity in turn has been superseded and transformed by the development of language—which itself has become increasingly complex and refined as an alternative means of representation and symbolization, making it possible for human life to be pervaded by cultural norms that expand experience in some ways even while narrowing it in others.

Social and cultural life requires repression, which thus has become a "natural"

part of human life; for without it socialization and acculturation would not be
possible. Plessner pursues this line of
inquiry as he discusses the institutionalization of group relationships, as well as
such issues as the relation between naming, norms, and social roles in the formation of human identity, personality, and
selfhood. They too may be conceived as
forms of human "embodiment," as it comes
to transcend the confines of our individual
bodily existence. The historicality of
human life—both developmentally (and
therefore contingently) and interpretively
(and so experientially)—is a further feature of it, raising questions about the conditions of its possibility and also about its
own extent in relation to these other
dimensions and structures of human reality. (Plessner here makes common cause
with DILTHEY, while diverging from Heidegger, to whose entire "phenomenological ontological" approach to human reality
he was deeply unsympathetic.)

Through his whole discussion, Plessner attempts to attain and retain a clear
anthropological optic, resisting the temptation to adopt models appropriate for
characterizing other forms of animate
and inanimate existence in interpreting
the more distinctive aspects of human
reality. His discussion begins comparatively; but once comparative consider-

ations have set the stage, he pursues a
course guided by the aim of doing justice
to the full range of human reality in language attuned to it, refined in ways that
this inquiry itself seems to require. His
starting point is that, as NIETZSCHE
observed, man is both an animal and no
longer merely an animal, spiritual and
yet never purely so. And like Nietzsche,
Plessner remains fundamentally naturalistic in the account he develops, making no appeal to anything transcending
this life in this world. His account turns
out to be one that is richly nuanced, in
places more so than Nietzsche's, as well
as differing from Nietzsche's in important respects. Yet it could well be seen as
the kind of reinterpretation of human
reality that Nietzsche had called for and
had sought to begin—and, in its social
and cultural sophistication, a better
example of it than GEHLEN's.

Plessner's work makes evident how
narrow, incomplete, and unjust the common generalizations about and stereotypes of "twentieth-century European
philosophy" and "Continental philosophy" are. It also exemplifies one of the
most philosophically interesting developments within the interpretive tradition,
and makes a strong case for taking the
task of a philosophical anthropology very
seriously.

From Laughing and Crying:
A Study of the Limits of Human Behavior

From *Preface to the Second Edition*

* * *

Our idea of what is common to all men [*Menschen*][1] and differentiates them
from other beings adheres—within the framework of familiar types of physical appearance and posture—to certain modes of behavior which are capable of development and which facilitate the intellectual [*geistig*][2] and historical

1. That is, "human beings." In German, *die Menschen* and *der Mensch* are terms that are generic in
their application; a different word (*Mann*) designates the gendered male.
2. The adjective *geistig* and the corresponding noun
Geist mean much more than "intellectual"/"intellect"
or "mental"/"mind," encompassing also "spiritual"/

"spirit" and "cultural"/"culture." At least from HEGEL
onward (see the glossary to his terms, p. 144), in the
interpretive tradition *Geist* comprises everything in
and about human life, both individually and collectively, that is more than merely biological and has
been developed historically. These terms are best
left untranslated.

existence of man on whatever level or interpretation of culture you will: *speaking, acting methodically*, and *shaping things in various ways* [*variables Gestalten*].[3] Strange to say, however, our conception of the human monopolies deals as well with two forms or, indeed, outbursts, of an elementary character, incapable of higher development: *laughing* and *crying*. No reference to their lack of utility and the various ways in which we may find them offensive can dissuade us from thinking that a creature without the possibility of laughing and crying is not human. No attempt, however ingenious, to find instances of laughing and crying among animals can overcome our mistrust of them and release us from the duty of clarifying what laughing and crying really mean.

For this, as with all specifically human utterances, man himself must be heard. Only his grasp of these utterances, the interpretation which he gives them, the significance which he confers on them in the management of his life, reveals them in their full extent, and, what is more, all this belongs to them internally as their formative and impelling power. Any external registration of sound stimuli, of gesture and expressive movement [*Gebärde*], misses the significance of laughing and crying, just as with speaking, acting, and shaping. Indeed, in the very selection of these particular kinds of behavior, which, however natural and innate in every human creature, distinguish this creature from nature, from animal existence—perhaps to its detriment and certainly with honor to another mode of existence—there already appears an interpretation of man by himself. In this interpretation, man lays claim to a special position which observation, directed merely to the externals of behavior by seemingly objective methods, can neither confirm nor contest.

Not only does the interpretation of man by himself enhance (or weaken), the gifts of speaking, acting, and shaping,[4] as well as laughing and crying; not only does this interpretation give them different rank and significance (sacred or profane, for example); more to the point, it also singles them out from the rich store of human capability, elicits them from this store, is their first condition, the principle of their articulation and differentiation, and sees to it that they remain gifts which can be cultivated. Naturally, to the extent that human nature is corporeal, it admits of being determined by external characteristics, behind man's back, so to speak, and untroubled by any interpretation which man has of himself. But what is the significance of such characteristics as shape of the teeth, angle of vision, development of the cerebrum, differentiation of hands and feet, sparseness of body hair, or late puberty, irrespective of what a being so constituted does with these characteristics, irrespective, that is, of his behavior in the world? *Only behavior explains the body*, and only modes of behavior such as speaking, acting, shaping, and laughing and crying, all of which are peculiar to man in conformity with his apprehension and positing of goals, make the human body intelligible, complete its anatomy.

It is an obvious error, suggested to us by our everyday habits, to believe that types of behavior are in themselves as differentiated from one another and as

3. By "acting methodically" Plessner means conducting oneself in accordance with norms, rules, intentions, ideas of means to desired ends, and the like (i.e., in the way that distinguishes human *action* from animal *behavior*). By "shaping things in various ways" he means *making* in that kind of methodical way.

4. That is, "making."

neatly structured as the organs by which they are brought about. This holds true neither for the differentiated kinds of specifically human behavior nor for those kinds common to both men and animals, such as running, jumping, sitting, lying down, grasping, attacking, fleeing, resting, waiting, lurking, etc., which are located in the vital sphere because they can take place over long periods even without conscious control. We must not forget that the names at our disposal for denoting actual modes of behavior, the situations and objectives in and for the sake of which they take place, and the fixed image of the parts of the body of which we make use entice us to the assumption of modes of behavior, articulated in themselves but entirely void of significance.

Physiology, which is an analytic science, speaks of the functions which characterize relatively isolated organs such as the heart, blood vessels, kidneys, intestines, and lungs. And physiology must speak in this way if it is to gain insight into the way such organs affect one another. To this extent, therefore, provisionally, it makes good sense to differentiate an effect bound to two or more organs as their function from behavior in which the *whole* organism, even though under the particular influence of definite organs, enters into association with the environment. But in both cases the principle of the division into particular, differentiated functions or kinds of behavior is to be assigned neither to the organism alone nor to the environment alone but to the bond between the two. In view of this, the fact that it is not always clear what is function and what is behavior should not astonish us. There must be transitions here. To which shall we assign, e.g., sleeping, yawning, breathing, blushing, and turning pale? We will meet this situation again with laughing and crying.

Nevertheless, in the case of human behavior, if it is not a question of merely biological modes of behavior but of those specifically reserved to man, we find in addition a peculiar dependence not found among animals, a dependence which goes beyond that holding between the environment and the organism. Animal behavior is composed of a chain of functions of which the animal makes use, but yet does not coincide with this. It is a reciprocal bond between the whole organism and its milieu. Human behavior is also all this but, beyond it, is at the same time a reciprocal bond between man and himself.

It is the self-interpretation of man by himself as man—and we should not confuse this with personal self-evaluation—which differentiates behavior in this instance and therewith assigns to particular types their locus and significance.

The ability to speak, to act, and to shape means having, not merely definite organs, but a meaning as well at our disposal, and also relying on this power. A self-disclosure, an appreciation of meaning, always precedes and guides mouth and hand, the "relation" of a person to his body and to the world in which he finds himself. As we shall see, speaking, acting, and shaping, also laughing and crying, are not rigid faculties which do their work secretly and exert power over a man whether he will or not. They are faculties only to the extent that man is completely at home with them and consents to them. A basic discovery, a basic invention, always precedes: a sustaining conception, that of being human—self-determining, responsible, capable of acknowledgment.[5] Whatever is to be reckoned among the specific endowments of human

5. That is, recognition.

nature does not lie in back of[6] human freedom but in its domain, which every single individual must always take possession of anew if he would be a man [*ein Mensch*].

Without this insight, we would never arrive at a theory of human behavior but would always be slipping back into the errors of the anthropologists and natural law theorists of those periods which thought abstractly, absolutistically, and unhistorically. Not only do men change; what is human is also altered in the changing course of time.[7] All those fine catalogues and models of hereditary factors, faculties, and drives, by means of which we try to capture man and his behavior, from the point of view of social psychology, characterology, or typology, remain only makeshift jobs. For such catalogues have too little grasp of the dependence of their concepts and types on the idea which they, the investigators, and they, their objects, have of themselves: the dependence of behavior on the sense which awakens it to life and form.

Nevertheless, man does not form himself according to his own image or according to that of a superior being alone; "Es bleibt ein Erdenrest / Zu tragen peinlich": "An earthly part remains, painful to bear."[8] Here, in the conflicts with his corporeality, man experiences a limit which defies all spiritual and historical change. As far as man's altercation with his body extends, and there is no speaking, acting, or shaping without this, it remains in the shadow of his cumbersome anatomy, as the compass of the universally[9] human. The how, what, or whereof of our speaking, acting, or shaping: that changes because it belongs to the spirit [*Geist*], which, in historical action, must be constantly reconquered; it belongs to comprehension, to goal-setting, to appraisal. But the modes of speaking, acting, and shaping, often overlapping and uniting in a common task, are preserved in all change.

So also laughing and crying. If it is correct, and if the following investigation succeeds in demonstrating, that laughing and crying are forms of expression of a crisis precipitated in certain situations by the relation of a man to his body (a relation which is a form of behavior as well and not a piece of fixed machinery on which one need only rely), then laughing and crying are revealed as genuine, basic possibilities of the universally human, despite all historical change, all varieties of jest, wit, drollery, humor, irony, pain, and tragedy. Laughing and crying are sensitive reagents, which literary artists, their true masters and teachers, know how to use. Our analysis has much to learn from them. And yet, to comprehend the origin of laughing and crying, we must look to the basic form of human existence under the spell of the body. As Stendhal suggested (he mentions only laughter, we add crying), "le problème du rire doit être écrit en style d'anatomie et non en style d'académie."[1]

Introduction

Much has been written about laughing, little about crying. The theme laughing *and* crying is among the exceptions. This asymmetrical division of interests

6. That is, underlie.
7. Plessner's kind of philosophical anthropology and conception of human nature are compatible with (and indeed are intended to allow for and make comprehensible) a very considerable amount of alteration in the contours of "what is human."
8. Goethe, *Faust*, Pt. II [1832], lines 11954–55

[Grene's note].
9. That is, generally (*allgemein*).
1. The problem of laughing should be written about in the style of anatomy and not in the style of the academy (French). Stendhal (pseudonym of Marie-henri Beyle, 1783–1842), French novelist.

in an obviously symmetrical association of phenomena has traditional grounds. Neither laughing nor crying itself was a matter of discussion, but its motive, not the form of expression in its singularity compared to other forms of expression such as speech, gesture, and expressive movement, but its occasion. For the most part, theoretical writers have directed their attention to the question of what we laugh at and why we cry, toward the aesthetic and psychological laws of the amusing and the sad, the comic and the tragic. In their studies, laughing and crying played the role of indicators which report the course of a reaction. Their analysis is concerned with the reaction and treats the indicators only as means.

Those familiar with the history of psychology and aesthetics will better understand the asymmetrical division of interest, the preference for laughter, and the neglect of crying. Both these disciplines throughout their history, i.e., since they developed a consciousness of the interrelation of their problems (and this consciousness hardly extends beyond[2] the eighteenth century), have labored, inquired, and found answers under the thralldom of the concept of the mental image [*Vorstellung*]. This model of the mind as the stage for magic-lantern displays and peep shows accommodates itself more naturally to laughter, which is bound to images, than to crying, which is bound to feeling. The theory of crying, like the theory of feelings in general, necessarily suffered from the fact that the disciplines in question tried to adapt them to their model of the mind and were not capable of breaking free of the spell of consciousness as a so-called horizon of all experience.

Only in the last decades has the truth begun to be appreciated that the theory of knowledge does not enjoy a commanding position, that accordingly the perspective of consciousness and of mental images [*Vorstellungen*] is only one among the many ways in which man moves in and with the real world. The originality of feeling, intuition, and conduct thus demands that they receive their own mode of interpretation. Philosophy and psychology share equally in this truth. What is more, this truth is the result of a revolution in the domain of all the disciplines concerned with man. The study of history and society has made them suspicious of rigid models and dissatisfied with an out-of-date theory of science. Thus they want to see the essence of human nature with new eyes. The revolution is directed against two dogmatic systems: idealism (primarily of the Kantian-Hegelian stamp), which is at home in the old world, and positivism of the Darwinian-Spencerian variety,[3] which the Americans especially abandon only with reluctance. The work of Nietzsche, Bergson, and Dilthey is slowly being reabsorbed and forms, if not a new point of view, at least a new readiness to understand man spontaneously and radically as a living reality, or, what amounts to the same thing, to learn to see man with his own eyes.

An important, if not the most important, means to this end is the *theory of human expression*. The romantics had already recognized its significance, although by coupling it with speculative metaphysics they hampered its free

---

2. Earlier than.
3. That is, the 20th-century version of the scientistic positivism of Auguste Comte (1798–1857) in which particular emphasis is accorded to explanations inspired by the evolutionary theory of the

English naturalist Charles Darwin (1809–1882) and popularized and expanded by the English sociologist and philosopher Herbert Spencer (1820–1903).

development. With the energetic rejection of romanticism on the part of science, the turn to experiment, and—not to be overlooked—the development of comparative philology as an independent discipline, the theory of expression languished. However, there is one movement characteristic of the last decades which has awakened the theory to a new and promising life: that is the movement associated with the name of Klages,[4] a movement opposed to the dominance of positivism and idealism. To Klages, in particular, is due the rehabilitation of and fresh impetus for the theory of expression, an impetus which has wider implications than his own theory and metaphysics.

Our study is in line with a theory of human expression. We wish to interpret laughing and crying as forms of expression. Their analysis no longer serves the aesthetics of the comic, of wit [*Witz*],[5] of tragedy; it is not concerned with the psychology of humor and feeling but with the theory of human nature. The question reads: how are we to understand that a living creature of flesh and blood, which has speech and sign-making at its disposal—and thereby differs from animals—yet at the same time in its mimic expression documents its vital bondage and its kinship with animal nature? How is it possible that such a dual and intermediate creature can laugh and cry? How is it possible, in other words, what conditions must be given in order that such reactions can take place, reactions which, in the full sense at least, are reserved to man?

To assert that this study serves the theory of human expression means, then, that it aims at knowledge of human nature, provided, of course, that man's expression betrays something of this nature. And as long as we do not limit the concept of human nature to regions of man's existence which are foreign to expression, i.e., to an inwardness inaccessible to everything external and to all utterance, we should expect expression to be a mirror, indeed a revelation, of human nature. It certainly is such for the interplay of man with his body.[6]

In our analysis of laughing and crying, the emphasis is on this interplay. Just as this analysis must necessarily occupy itself with the occasions of laughing and crying, whether emotional or conceptual, so it must also keep the interplay of the human person with his body constantly in view. Although the effect cannot be understood without the cause, the cause lies, not in the actual occasion alone, but just as much in the relation of man to his body, which always determines his existence in the world.

Our study does not, as is customary, evade the question of the physical form of expression of laughing and crying with a philosophical obeisance to physiology, and declare itself to be incompetent, but makes this form of expression the cardinal question and subordinates everything to its solution. With this approach it is continuing the line of my earlier efforts. The first had as its object the interplay of the functions of communication or understanding and the senses; the second, the relation between organism, body, and environment

---

4. Ludwig Klages (1872–1956), German philosopher and central figure in the development of the movement known as *Lebensphilosophie*, or the "philosophy of 'life'" (both human life and life more generally); the philosophical anthropology of SCHELER, Plessner, and GEHLEN developed out of it, and (as Plessner indicates in the previous paragraph) in German-speaking Europe NIETZSCHE, BERGSON, and DILTHEY are commonly associated with it.

5. That is, the joke, the funny.

6. Elsewhere Plessner frequently notes that our human relation to our bodies is unique in that my body is something that I experientially both *have* and *am*, that these very different relations are in a tension with each other, and that that tension itself is an important feature of human reality.

on the different levels of plant, animal, and human existence.[7] It is no accident, then, if we consider the phenomena of human expression from the point of view of the relation between man and his body in order to understand these phenomena from this point of view and conversely, from the phenomena, to learn something about this relation.

With this, we assert once more our conviction that an understanding of human nature, if it is to press radically on into man's fundamental constitution—one may call it anthropology or existential philosophy or what you will—must (1) proceed from an understanding of expression in the richness of its various possibilities, and (2) make intelligible the intermeshing of the components of expression in their whole breadth, from the mental [geistig] to the physical.

But does this imply a psychophysics of laughing and crying? Surely not, if the concept "psychophysical" is taken in the Weber-Fechner sense.[8] This classical psychophysics proceeds from a strict and, as people long believed, clearcut separation between physical and mental events, events which on closer examination turn out to be artifacts of an experimental arrangement. Now artifacts can still assert something about the reality from which they have been wrested by our intervention, if we are in a position to correct what they assert, i.e., to compare the assertion with reality. To inquire about the relations between the magnitude of a stimulus and the magnitude of the corresponding sensation—taking careful note of the ambiguities of the word "magnitude"—surely has its value. It is not directed to thin air; it is concerned with something. But what it is concerned with, and artificially isolates, on the side of the "stimuli" as well as of the "sensations," we know only from the reality to which the inquiry is directed.

Experiments of this kind are useful and instructive. But they constitute, not the upshot of our knowledge of the interplay of physical and mental [geistig] factors, but a means, desirable under certain circumstances and for certain purposes, by which to learn something about this interplay. We can make allowances for the artificiality of the results, due to the question itself, to experimental interference, and to the unavoidable fictions arising from causal analyses, but we must remain conscious of this artificiality as measured against the original context of life.

This original context falls victim to every type of cognition which pledges itself to a determinate method of observation, be it physiological, psychological, or psychophysical. Methodological procedure always follows the path of isolation. Isolation, in turn, implies abstraction. If one knows what he has abstracted from in order to attain the isolation of particular "factors," this isolation will not conceal the original context. But science has frequently made the mistake of taking the abstraction on which it rests for ready cash, for reality itself, as if its basic concepts and fictions were themselves set like building

---

7. Plesner's first effort was *The Unity of the Senses* (1923); the second, *The Levels of the Organic and Man* (1928). He cites both.
8. In the view of the German experimental psychologists and physiologists Ernst Heinrich Weber (1795–1878) and Gustav Theodor Fechner (1801–1889), the physical and the experiential are directly

correlated (the latter being presumably a function of the former). Plessner refers below to the "law" proposed by Weber (and refined by Fechner) that quantified the correlation between the physical magnitudes of stimuli and the experienced intensity of their effects.

blocks in the original context itself. Physiology, psychology, and, not least, "quantitative" psychophysics are constantly exposed to such illusions and succumb to them when they set up the requirement that knowledge of the object under investigation must begin with their methodology. Such science then forgets the original context from which the object in its very character as open to investigation had been extracted, in which it had been interrogated [*abgefragt*], and must be interrogated again and again. It then neglects a contact in and with the immediate reality which objectively precedes every methodologically isolating "specialized" science.

To understand laughing and crying as expressive phenomena, therefore, does not mean that we subject them first to the isolating techniques of psychological and physiological methodology and then to a subsequent correlative unification according to the principle of psychophysics. On the contrary; it means first and foremost to put them back into their original living context. It means first of all to keep them free from the usual separations into sharply contrasted regions of physical and psychological objectivity, in order to cultivate perception of and understanding for the fact that it is here a matter of human affairs, which take place in the domain of the human experience of life, of the behavior of man to man and of man to world. Those who would criticize us because in this study we do not dance attendance with tables, curves, and series of experiments and who would see in the dearth of questionnaires and photographs a dearth of exactitude should consider—as should the disillusioned lover of exact definitions—that the reason for this was not a deficiency but rather an excess of accuracy, something which many authors in this difficult field have neglected, to the detriment of the subject.

That physiology and psychology have a share in our question goes without saying, but as to how great this share is only vague notions prevail. Expression, as the transition from inner to outer, presents a problem to sciences which have after all been established by the separation of the outer (bodily) from the inner (mental). If, misusing the concept of psychology, one interprets the mind from the beginning *as* external expression [*Äusserung*], then, to be sure, the problem vanishes—for psychology. But not so for physiology. Precisely as the physiology of expression, it will always see to it that consciousness of the "unfathomable" in all external expression and embodiment of the "inner" does not disappear. Such concern is motivated, not by comprehension of this fundamental category of life, but by incomprehension, by a very wholesome and necessary restriction of the range of physiology to bodily processes as such.

To whatever -ology one assigns the theory of expression, moreover, whether to psychology, anthropology, or sociology, it should not be overlooked that the treatment of questions of the nature and possibility of types of expression is, methodologically speaking, unaffected. A consideration of the concepts employed in the study of expressive phenomena must precede any investigation of these phenomena in their actual multiplicity. Typology, characterology, graphology, physiognomies, and mimetics cannot facilitate or take the place of such a consideration. They will not put to the phenomena the question which interests us. This is their privilege, just as it is ours to ask the question of the essence and possibility of expression, a question which has been overlooked or made trivial by many, if indeed, through arbitrary extensions of the concept of mind or through metaphysical theses, it is not lost sight of altogether.

———————

Can we escape such theses? Does not our question as to the character and possibility of expression—in this case of laughing and crying—arise only by reason of a definite metaphysical conviction? We speak of "essence" or "nature," of expression as a mirror, a revelation of the "essence" of man (at least as regards the domain of the interplay of man with his body). We stress that man's existence in the world is determined by the relation to his body, that the understanding of human nature is bound to the possibility of expression as a unity of intellectual, affective, and physical components.

In the eyes of the reader, the warning advanced against the usual appeal to the empirical sciences naturally makes us liable to be suspected of some kind of metaphysical purpose. Thus, he will read into the use of terms like "intellectual [geistig]" and "affective," in contrast to "physical," an avowal of triadism[9] and will expect an explicit declaration in favor of this triple-essence theory of human nature, as opposed to dualism and monism. He will suppose that in the concept "possibility" (of expression) lies a potency, the knowledge of which would be crucial. He will take exception to the concept of "essence" or "nature." In short, he will detect an appeal to occult sources in our keeping a distance from the empirical. How simple it is to brand someone a follower of some metaphysical theory if he does not explicitly declare himself against it!

There is no occasion for this. Our questioning is dedicated to no metaphysics; it appeals to none for an answer. We entrust our inquiry to experience, to which its object and its cognitive sources belong. In this context experience suffers no restriction in order to oblige a method, but requires complete openness in the everyday commerce of man with man and man with world. If (in resisting the monopolistic claims of psychophysics, physiology, and psychology to the problem of laughing and crying) we argued above that our endeavor was first and foremost aimed at restoring the phenomena in their original living context as befits human affairs, the same also holds in the defense against the monopolistic claims of metaphysics. Phrases like "relation of man to his body," "physical," "affective," "intellectual," appeal to the average understanding and should not be used to express more than they assert within this horizon.

Granted, without strict conceptual limitations. Of itself, this is a broad field. But if we entrust ourselves to everyday experience, we must put up with uncertainty. Loyalty to everyday intuition is paid for only with an elasticity in linguistic usage. "Definitionists" who take umbrage at this should never forget what price terminological clarity exacts. We are convinced that exactitude of definition—not exactitude of inquiry—at least in human affairs (in which

9. That is, a theory of the reality and mutual irreducibility of three different sorts of reality: the physical, the affective, and the geistig (the spiritual, intellectual, cultural), in place of the dualism of mind and body.

we include laughing and crying), brings with it the danger of impairment of vision, of one-sidedness, and of distortion.

"Man" is not a being who understands himself in the same way among all peoples and at all times; he is historically bound, precisely in his original, everyday understanding. The idioms of the language that shapes his thought, poetic or prosaic, the language in which he "expounds" himself,[1] spring from no timeless ground. They are products of history, deposits of dead religions and metaphysical systems, as much as they are the apparel of living beliefs. And yet it is impossible to demand of knowledge that is oriented to the enduring-in-change, to the non- and trans-historical, that it should not entrust itself to the idioms of common speech, but should take refuge, for the sake of terminological clarity and stability, in an artificial language.

Antiquity and Christendom alike have contributed to words of common speech like "mind [Geist]," "soul," "body," and "human being [Mensch]." Tracing the changes in their significance,[2] however, can never replace the analysis of what is reflected in them. The organization of the stimuli and motives of our conscious life into categories like cheerful and sad, comic and tragic, ironic and satiric, humorous and witty, and so on, does not come about by chance but has its own history. But what these words mean and where they have their roots is revealed only in living social understanding. Thus the analysis of all human expression remains, despite its historical stamp, directed to "everyday experience," to the province of man's behavior to his world and to his like.[3] Thus the analysis can never call the concepts and schemata of a metaphysic to its aid.

In our case, this reserve relative to metaphysical theories does not spring from hostility toward, or devaluation of, metaphysical thinking but only from the concern to free ourselves from prejudices which stand in the way of a solution to problems of expression. The worst enemy of the sciences[4] is the laziness which justifies itself with a tradition or an allegedly definitive, well-established doctrine. For centuries the alternative of parallelism and interactionism in the doctrine of mind-body relations barricaded[5] the analysis of expression. Antimetaphysical agnosticism had an equally inhibitory effect. Today, metaphysics is concealed behind evolutionary ideas and tries, in line with the positivists' program, to comprehend the phenomena of expression in particular, like all human affairs, in terms of historical development.

For the analysis of expression, the evolutionary point of view undoubtedly has a stimulating power. As long as it remains a point of view, the disciplines dealing with expression will derive benefit from it; historical linguistics in itself proves this. But development as a controllable alteration from germ to the mature form, and evolution as progress (according to naturalistic criteria if possible) are two different things. Empirical study of the development of a human mode of expression through all stages of personal maturation unearths facts without bringing us nearer to an understanding of the mode of expression itself. On the other hand, the interpretation of the stages and series of

---

1. In German, *sich auslegt*. Figuratively (and commonly) *Auslegen* means "to interpret"; literally (and not infrequently), it means "to lay out or display." In this pun, Plessner suggests that the use of language is at once self-revealing and self-interpreting.
2. That is, meanings.

3. That is, his kind (other human beings).
4. That is, the cognitive disciplines (*Wissenschaften*), whether natural-scientific, social-scientific, humanistic, or philosophical.
5. That is, obstructed.

phases within the framework of any given idea of evolution or development—whether it derives from Hegel, Darwin, or Bergson—subjects them to the selection of metaphysical criteria before the interpretation itself has become clear about what it is that passes through these stages and phases. In order to understand how something develops, one must first have understood what it is supposed to be developing *into*.[6]

On this account, every observation of the genesis of human expression—whether with purely empirical or metaphysical intent (and the latter can be given a biological or psychoanalytical, in any case a naturalistic or "anti-metaphysical," complexion)—must proceed from an understanding of the expression in question itself. What use are derivations, e.g., verbal speech from cries, from expressive movements and gestures of particular emotions, from tendencies to onomatopeia, from communication drives, if we ourselves are not clear about the expressive significance of language, its possibilities and its limits? What use is the finest exposition or interpretation of the phase-sequence of laughing and crying if their own expressive significance remains obscure? It is certainly not a matter of indifference to know when and under what circumstances these reactions first appear in infants and how they are differentiated in the course of development. But it is certainly an illusion to consider the germinal forms and first stages more informative than the fully developed forms of maturity.

Equating the elementary in the sense of the initial with the elementary in the sense of the fundamental has always made for confusion. What is first in time is not necessarily first in substantive importance. Evolutionary metaphysics believes it can set aside this simple thought, especially since Darwinism presented it with a suitable instrument to shape its metaphysical conception scientifically and to connect individual development with phylogeny. A great part of the science [*Wissenschaft*] of man still lives by this conception, even that part which believes it has nothing more in common with Darwinism and naturalism. Especially in Anglo-Saxon countries, it is difficult for investigators to free themselves from this perspective. And because, now as much as formerly, the problem of laughing (and crying) has attracted the greatest number of workers in those countries—even more than in France—this methodological side of the subject deserves to be vigorously stressed.

It has been said often enough: the program of so-called behaviorism, with its rigid restriction of behavior to visible movements and series of movements, and the mechanistic interpretation of these as reflexes, has hindered more than furthered the investigation of behavior. Scarcely less harmful has been the dogma of evolution. For "primitive" forms of expression like laughing and crying it is especially natural to attempt an explanation in terms of "archaic" reactions like screaming, terror, shock, etc., and to reduce them to comparatively elementary drives for shelter or communication, to affective reflex mechanisms, or directly to sensory excitations. Thus the investigation is directed from the first into unsuitable paths. Even if laughing and crying are forms expressing a disorganization of the human person, with which a lowering of level, a breakdown of differentiation, and a general coarsening is naturally

---

6. This point is central to Plessner's kind of philosophical anthropology.

connected, still, the presumption that, in laughing and crying, archaic strata of existence are breaking through remains completely speculative.

———————

To understand laughing and crying as forms of expression means to proceed from man as a whole, and not some particular aspect which can be detached from the whole in quasi-independent fashion, like body, soul, mind, or social unit. Man is accessible to us as a whole, that is, as our fellow man, and we are accessible to ourselves, in the context of behavior, in commerce with our own kind and with the environment. We live in and by this context; it is, though of course in various historical forms, the basis of all experience. Thus forms of expression are forms of behavior toward others, toward oneself, toward things, events, and everything that people can encounter. These forms do not lie within the fenced-off area of a consciousness providing isolation from external reality, not in the inner or outer aspect of human existence, but rather athwart all these antitheses. For dogmatists of some "ism" or other, this may be a reason to consider them secondary structures, conglomerates, or fictions of subsidiary importance.

Such people are not to be convinced. We are addressing only those who are ready to face experience without prejudice, experience which has neither passed through the sieve of some special science nor asks what different philosophies of experience think about it. Such lack of bias, to be sure, is found all too infrequently. Even the reader who is bound to no particular scientific[7] system is usually inclined to ask about the standpoint, the method, in a word, the rubric, under which he can classify the book. He doesn't reckon with the possibility of being brought by a book to independence of thought and vision. He wants "contributions to" something which already exists. A book about laughing and crying? Well, a "contribution to" psychology, anthropology, existential philosophy, philosophy of life![8] He sees trends, schools, relations of dependence, or of master and disciple. But he sees neither the thing itself nor the originality.

* * *

1. The Relation of Man to His Body

1. THE PROBLEMATIC NATURE OF LAUGHING AND CRYING

Laughing and crying are forms of expression which, in the full sense of the words, only man [der Mensch] has at his disposal. At the same time, these forms of expression are of a kind to which this monopolistic situation is in strange contrast. For one thing, they have nothing in common with language and expressive movement, by which man shows himself superior to other living creatures and which provide his thoughts, feelings, and intentions with an expression that mediates by pointing, that is objective and subject to discussion. Laughing and crying are not found in the same stratum, are not on

———————

7. That is, disciplinary (wissenschaftlich). For Plessner too, a Wissenschaft is simply a cognitive discipline of some sort.

8. That is, Lebensphilosophie (see p. 1411, n. 4, above).

the same level, as language and expressive movement. To laugh or cry is in a sense to lose control; when we laugh or cry, the objective manipulation of the situation is, for the time being, over.

The eruptive character of laughing and crying links them closely with movements that express emotion. Just as, when we are mastered and deeply stirred by feelings, their force is stamped on facial expression and gesture, so here also the cheerful or the sad, the laughable or the touching and affecting occasion gains the ascendancy and must discharge itself. Closer to the inarticulate cry than to disciplined, articulate speech, laughing and crying surge up from the depths of life bound to feeling.

Nevertheless, their form of expression separates them from emotional expressive movements. While anger or joy, love and hate, sympathy and envy, etc., acquire in the body a symbolic stamp which allows the emotion to appear in the expressive movement, the expressive form of laughing and crying remains opaque and, for all its capacity for modulation, is largely fixed in its course. From this point of view, laughing and crying belong to the same range of processes as blushing, turning pale, vomiting, coughing, sneezing, and other vegetative processes, largely removed from voluntary influences.

Again, in comparison to the reactions just mentioned, eruptivity and compulsiveness of the form of expression, coupled with a lack of symbolic character, also appear to be especially prominent in laughing and crying. As vocal expressions, they cannot well be overlooked in social life. They are not mere reactions to the actual situation like blushing, turning pale, and so on (which are limited primarily to the person who is ashamed or alarmed); but they direct themselves to the situation, even if perhaps involuntarily, and interrupt the normal course of life. Nor should we overlook the fact, perhaps also of significance here, that laughing and (to a lesser extent) crying are easier to induce voluntarily than are the reactions controlled chiefly by the sympathetic and parasympathetic nervous systems.

Further, if simply as uniquely human forms of expression of an opaque character, falling outside the circle of intelligibly transparent expressions in speech, expressive movement, and mime, laughing and crying naturally arouse attention, then this interest deepens when we look at the diverse situations that induce them. Like the expressive form itself, they too are strange and go beyond the limits of the ordinary. It accords with learned tradition to be especially concerned with these diversities. Philosophers have been enthralled since antiquity by the phenomena of the comic and the tragic, of the joke and of the sublime. The expression, in itself somewhat insignificant, of the living creature, man, moves here into the technical, and therefore truly humane, perspective of the laws of aesthetics. Only since psychology and physiology have existed have the other aspects of laughing and crying come into view: the sustaining or releasing emotions of cheerfulness, sadness, regret, shame, commiseration and compassion, embarrassment; the bodily expressive movements performed in accordance with their muscular coordination, their nervous and presumably also hormonal regulation.

Thus the disclosure of many-sidedness and its elaboration in different disciplines, methodologically distinct from one another, raises the counterquestion of the unity of the phenomena of laughing and crying. In contrast to the specialized approach of the aesthetician, the psychologist, and the physiologist, this unity also necessitates a methodologically unique approach. For here it is not a question of the product of a synthesis to be attained a posteriori, but of the original unity in which we live, a unity always kept in view by the aesthetician, psychologist, and physiologist, even if—according to the special interest of each discipline—in a biased way. Starting from this unity, we can then understand the interaction of the physical, psychic, and mental dimensions; but from the dimensions, mutually isolated, we cannot understand the mechanism of their unity.

About it we know. The statement made at the beginning, that evidently only man has laughing and crying at his disposal, but not the lower animals, states no hypothesis which can one day be disproved by observation, but a certainty. For we know that the concepts laughing and crying lay claim to the widest range of human behavior, to the context in which indeed the words "mind," "soul," and "body" are once and for all at our disposal. We say, indeed, that tickling can produce laughter, and we find the smile, for example, among chimpanzees: the mouth drawn wide, the giggling sound characteristic of pleasure. These, although perhaps not the products of reflex action, still, as expressive motions remaining in the sensory, vital sphere, are no more to be considered genuine laughter than the compulsive laughter of sufferers from certain brain disorders. To laughing (and to crying) belongs—and if not, the concepts are misplaced—the significant and conscious relating of an expression to its occasion, an expression which breaks out eruptively, runs its course compulsively, and lacks definite symbolic form. It is not my body but I who laugh and cry, and for a reason, "about something." Whereas in bearing and expressive movement I immediately assimilate the occasion in a symbolic expression and thus dispose of it by a direct reaction, in laughing and crying I keep my distance from it: I reply to it.

Thus our problem is not to derive these specifically human forms of expression from the essence of human nature, for whatever is hidden in that essence is also contained in laughing and crying and gives us assurance of their humanity. Our problem looks different: it asks how their form of expression can be joined with human nature, as displayed in other specifically human powers, e.g., language and work. The relation to intelligible order which man lays claim to and attests by his activity must somehow also make laughing and crying possible; otherwise, the comic and the tragic, the funny and the sorrowful, could not have the effects they do. The matter under discussion is not whether laughing and crying are human monopolies, but how. The strangely opaque mode of expression of the human body must be understood from the relation of man to his body (and not, for example, from the problematic "relation" of mind to matter, of soul to body, as isolated entities).

Naturally, this task demands just as much a specific conception of human nature as a specific characterization of its bodily situation. Usually, if human monopolies are in question—language, the invention and use of tools, clothing, habitation, and custom—we are satisfied with a reference to rationality or intellectuality and somehow or other try to ground the human in these. Even our permanently erect posture, with its liberation of the hands, unburdening of the head, and broadening of the field of vision and distance to the environment, fits into this context. Everyone knows what man has in this monopoly and understands the link with the traditional criterion of his uniqueness: reason, mind [*Geist*]. But what laughing and crying have to do with man and why exactly they are denied to other creatures remain obscure. In itself, their eruptive, compulsive, and inarticulate character resists any connection with reason and mind and points in the direction of the subhuman, which is nourished by affective sources alone. On the other hand, if laughing and crying were only affective utterances and emotional expressive movements, it would be incomprehensible why at least those animals most closely related to man cannot also laugh and cry.

Knowledge of the reasons which, under certain circumstances, dispose man to express himself in one way and not another also provides the answer to the question why only he and no other creature can so express himself. The presupposition of such knowledge is, above all, an unprejudiced view of the phenomenon in the wealth of all its aspects: the mental, the psychic, and the physical, and also, as far as method goes, a unique approach to it. We will not reach our goal via the well-trodden paths of biological interpretation or those of motivational or social psychology. Let us leave undecided whether laughing and crying are processes which serve a hidden purpose. Nature, the life of instinct, and society doubtless have a share in them. But we are, unfortunately, unacquainted with it, and hence it appears to us basically absurd to entrust the problem wholly to one of these anonymous powers. Nor do we get very far with causal explanations: we seem at once to be stuck fast in the breach between psychic or mental motive and physical effect.

Before one tries to interpret phenomena by reference to their elements or their goals, it is advisable at least to try to understand them in the sphere of experience from which they spring. Laughing and crying are forms of human expression and statement, modes of conduct, kinds of behavior. This fact brings difficulties, but also possibilities of understanding, in its wake. Theories which overlook this fact out of metaphysical or scientific prejudice are certain to go astray. Again and again, an answer to the question of why we laugh and cry has been frustrated because of such prejudices.

2. Against the Prejudice of a Dualistic Interpretation of Man, and the False Alternatives

In order to obtain a complete picture of the bodily state of a person who is laughing or crying, we would have to correlate the changes in musculature, breathing, and glandular secretion with changes in the central nervous system. This follows from the assumption that there are certain release mechanisms of the central nervous system for the characteristic forms of expression in the domain of animal as well as vegetative vital activity. If there is central regulation of breathing, body temperature, and circulation, as well as of special processes such as swallowing, blushing and turning pale, yawning, and vomiting, for example, then there is reason to suppose a central regulatory mechanism for laughing and crying. To this end, the attempt is made to evaluate specific brain diseases associated with compulsive laughing and crying.

It is not necessary to think immediately of "centers" in this connection. Laughing and crying seem rather to rest on interruptions of the normal sequence of functions than to be processes which have their "seat" (always within the limits within which it makes sense to speak of a function in general as being able to have a seat, a locus) in definite parts of the brain. Granted that physiology might have advanced so far as to arrive at clear decisions in this area, what would have been gained for the problem of laughing and crying?

An idea of the mechanism of laughing or crying, of the means of inducing these expressions: not less, but also not more. Insight into the cooperation of the physical components of the process, however, remains unrelated to the total process of the laughing or weeping individual as long as we do not obtain from the "sense" of the total process an indication of how just these and no other physical components become effective. Why do we laugh at a joke and not weep? Why do we weep from remorse and not laugh? Even precise knowledge of the mechanism of laughing and crying cannot answer these questions. Joking and remorse may evoke a precisely localized physical excitation in the brain—there are only quite vague limits to our conjectures here—and proceeding from these specific excitations, their physical representatives, so to speak, call laughter or weeping into action. But plainly this physiological characterization of something which is nothing physical, but a system of meaning or a psychic event, is not even wishful thinking but mere nonsense.

Jokes appeal to men[9] with a gift of reason and intellect; remorse is experienced by men with conscience and heart. It is always the *whole man*[1] who is implicated, now more superficially, now more deeply, when he laughs or cries. The body as the seat of physiological mechanisms is not affected, and moved to react, by joking or remorse, but again only by physical "stimuli" which—if words are involved—are acoustical or optical in nature. But where reason and intellect, conscience and heart, are wanting, words, although heard or read, do not become "stimuli." In that case the configuration appropriate to release them does not arise "in the brain." Why not? Physiology knows no answer to this question; the inquiry is stuck fast in the breach between the physical and the psychical aspect.

Beyond this breach, in the domain of the internal aspect, psychology has its area of competence. Here is disclosed the understanding of joy and pain, cheerfulness and sorrow, of sensuous and intellectual feelings, emotions, moods, and thoughts. Here no limits are fixed to the analysis of complex states such as remorse and grief, commiseration and compassion, logically or aesthetically relevant contents of consciousness and combinations of ideas. But the competence of psychology ends in the area of bodily reaction. It is not in a position to comprehend the physical phenomenon of expression.

Here a typical difficulty becomes evident for the entire realm of conduct and behavior, one which is not to be overcome with our scientific resources, split as they are into physiology and psychology. As act, gesture, or mimic expression, a physical occurrence is, to be sure, stamped by the psychical and related to the physical. But this stamp and this relatedness hover, as it were, between the realm of the body, physiologically interpreted, and the realm of the mind, which is interpreted psychologically. As physical occurrences, act, gesture, and expression do not reside in the inner realm of the psychical. But if we try to lay hold of them in the play of joints and muscles, we are looking only at physical events, and their characteristic stamp is lost.

As long as science[2] remains bound to the alternatives of the physiological versus the psychological method, the realm of behavior in the full profusion

---

9. That is, people, human beings (*Menschen*).
1. That is, the whole human being (*Mensch*).

2. That is, cognitive inquiry (*Wissenschaft*).

of its forms remains closed to it. In order to obtain access to this realm, we need an original method of approach to the phenomena themselves and a new confidence in everyday experience, in which we perceive our own behavior and that of others, respond to it, and come to terms with it. This confidence runs up against a crucial prejudice which constantly finds fresh sustenance from the exact natural sciences: the belief that human nature must be experienced and investigated under two fundamentally irreducible aspects because it is composed of two substances, the body (as extended thing) and the mind (as thinking thing).

This model, fashioned by Descartes,[3] prevented the reconciliation between man as a natural thing and man as a moral and intellectual being. Physics was not to be sacrificed to the claims of theology and morality, nor theology and morality to those of physics. The strength of the model rests on this concern for two absolutely different spheres of lawfulness. Time after time, this model has prevailed against all philosophical doubts, and especially in times of rapid scientific development. Attempts have been made to soften or reinterpret its metaphysical rigor. But the dualistic conception of man has persisted, with its compulsion to separate the physical from the psychical and with its fatal possibility of playing off one against the other. Nothing in this schema is basically altered if the internal aspect in turn acquires differential avenues of access to the "psychical" and the "mental" or "intellectual," respectively. Every time, the development of scientific specialization has followed the Cartesian model. Not until the nineteenth century did the new sciences dealing with life and man—biology, sociology, and the historical disciplines dealing with culture [*die historischen Geisteswissenschaften*]—reveal the artificiality of this model and its inapplicability to experience.

The most obvious course, naturally, is to replace the ontology of Cartesianism by a monistic counterontology. This can be, and has been, done, whether on the basis of physical or mental existence or, ultimately, on the basis of a third reality, life perhaps, which then encompasses them both. Monistic constructions of this kind, frequently with reference to Spinoza,[4] had their heyday in the nineteenth century but proved unable to influence the course of scientific development.[5] On the contrary, the monistic principle was reduced to a hypothesis which respected the details of empirical knowledge obtained in the usual ways and sought "only" metaphysically to unify them.

Against this development, the theory of knowledge mounted its assault. Yet it was not philosophical considerations which proved decisive but the deepening and enrichment of the range of human experience, for which we are indebted to the nineteenth century. In history, ethnology, sociology, psychology, and psychopathology, men confront human beings of other times and cultures, with other attitudes toward life and other forms of self-interpretation. The obviousness of one's own familiar existence itself becomes questionable, and its interpretation, followed and acknowledged as valid for centuries, loses its persuasive power. In consequence, old models of human nature lost their value, but the readiness to replace them by new ones was weakened by relativism.

---

3. René Descartes (1596–1650), French mathematician and philosopher.
4. Benedict (Baruch) de Spinoza (1632–1677), Dutch philosopher.
5. That is, of the development of cognitive inquiry (*Wissenschaft*).

Out of this characteristic attitude of our time, a time marked by the lack of confidence in reason, another type of opposition to Cartesianism has arisen, which differs from the monistic. This new opposition wishes, not simply to replace the dualistic model of human nature by another, but to render it superfluous. It does not take up the mind-body problem at all, but attempts to do away with it as an artificial difficulty, an unnecessary construction, a misconception. In truth, this attitude evades the problem by going back to an allegedly unproblematic, primordial level of existence, which coincides with the level of conduct or behavior in its *niveau*[6] but not in its inner structure. By a technique which, as we shall point out in greater detail, is always feasible, the forms of behavior are so characterized from the start that the cleft between "inner" and "outer" does not appear at all. In this way, the semblance of a primordial problem-free human condition is produced—at any rate, with regard to the relation of the psyche, i.e., man, to the body.

In the face of such irresponsibility and carelessness in the treatment of nature, which marks the fashionable anti-Cartesianism, phenomena like laughing and crying force us to show our true colors and stand up for the real difficulty of human existence. Speaking, acting, shaping, and expressive movement do not of themselves necessitate this. In these instances, the human body accommodates itself to impulses and intentions of a psychological nature. The body goes along with, allows itself to be molded by, sustains, and, just because it is so tractable, also demands no other role than that of matter, embodying stuff, the compliant means of presentation. As stuff and medium, it means that from which intelligible content can emancipate itself. This aspect fits the interpretation of man which has become traditional under the dominance of the dualistic schema: the body is the enveloping layer, indispensable to life and unavoidable for the purpose of expression, of a being which in its true nature knows itself to be emancipated from this envelope and has command over it to the limits[7] of sickness and death.

Laughing and crying provide another view of the relation of man to his body. Their form of utterance, whether expressive or expressionless, whether full or empty of meaning, reveals as such no symbolic form. Although initially motivated by us, laughing and crying make their appearance as uncontrolled and unformed eruptions of the body, which acts, as it were, autonomously. Man falls into their power; he breaks—out laughing, and lets himself break— into tears. He responds to something by laughing and crying, but not with a form of expression which could be appropriately compared with verbal utterance, expressive movement, gesture, or action. He responds—with his body as body, as if from the impossibility of being able to find an answer himself. And in the loss of control over himself and his body, he reveals himself at the same time as a more than bodily being who lives in a state of tension with regard to his physical existence yet is wholly and completely bound to it.[8]

From this impenetrability in the relation of man to his body, earlier analysis has recoiled. Even where it rose above the prejudices of a dualistic psychophysics (for example, in the direction influenced by Klages, as well as in many existential psychologists and pathologists) it was limited to the sphere of the

6. Level (French).
7. That is, up to (within) the limits of.

8. See p. 1411, n. 6, above.

rationally significant, to symbolically formed kinds of behavior, i.e., to actions, expressive movements, and gestures. Such analyses emphasized on principle the cooperation and interaction of the psychical and the physical from the point of view of their greatest possible convergence, indeed, their unity. Whatever disturbs this image, or at any rate does not immediately fit in with it, whatever, in its motoric and static aspects, is not derivable from motivational theory, was put aside, and turned over to a physiology presumably competent to deal with it.

It was overlooked that man has, not a univocal, but an equivocal relation to his body, that his existence imposes on him the ambiguity of being an "embodied" [leibhaften] creature and a creature "in the body" [im Körper], an ambiguity that means an actual break in his way of existing. It is this broken-ness that distinguishes what phenomena like laughter and tears suggest: the impenetrability of man's relation to his body.

It will be the task of the following study to show that man's ambiguous posi-tion as living body in a physical body [Leib im Körper] constitutes the basis of laughing and crying—a position which is also present in his other monopo-lies, like speech, expressive movement, the use of clothing and tools. To this end, the inquiry must free itself from the bias inherent in the Cartesian inter-pretation of human existence. The two-substance theory, which survives as a double-aspect theory, in the rigid and seemingly self-evident alternative: phys-ical or mental, is not capable of understanding the phenomena of laughing and crying. Hence it would be a crude misunderstanding to reduce the "ambi-guity" of physical existence to a duality of interpretation, that is, to conscious-ness. The brokenness of man's relation to his body is rather the basis of his existence, the source, but also the limit, of his power.

3. The Eccentric[9] Position

Beginning with man in the original concreteness of his existence, laughing and crying are to be comprehended as physical reactions. In the appended phrase "as physical reactions," however, we are not expressing any abandon-ment of understanding from the unitary perspective of man as a being who rejoices and sorrows and with heart and mind is bound to a whole world. On the other hand, with respect to physiology, the limits of its competence have convinced us that the problem can no more be left to this science than to psychology or the double-aspect science of psychophysics. With the phrase "as physical reactions," we only mean to emphasize that this study does not recoil from the genuine difficulty of understanding bodily events, as is else-where the practice of philosophy, because it allegedly has nothing to do with them. The cleverly chosen perspective of existential analysis[1] bypasses the true problems of human existence and consequently a real knowledge of it.

Compared with speech, gesture, and mimic expressive movements, laugh-ing and crying attest to an incalculable emancipation of bodily events from

9. That is, "ex-centric" (exzentrisch): i.e., "not (sim-ply) centric." Like (other) animals, for Plessner, human beings are centered in their active relation to their environing world ("centric"), as the living bodies they are; but human beings also are posi-tioned differently, in that they are aware of their bodies as something that they have, positioned in a world of other entities of which they are only parts rather than the center. Plessner calls that double relation or "position" exzentrisch, here rendered as "eccentric." (This term should be so understood throughout the rest of this selection.)
1. That is, the first-person-singular perspective on what it means to exist as a human being.

the person. In this disproportion and willfulness, we surmise, lies what is truly revelatory in the phenomena. In no other form of expression is the secret composition of human nature more directly disclosed than in these.

Speaking and acting show man in his mastery at the height of the free power of control given to him through reason. If he loses mastery here, he sinks below his proper level. To be sure, this sinking testifies to the height originally occupied, but it does not disclose the way in which man is bound to his body.

We learn just as little of this type of bond when a man loses control over himself in cases of the narrowing, clouding, or blacking-out of his consciousness, as through overpowering emotion or the use of narcotics. For in such cases the human unity of the person is destroyed.

And finally, nothing of this bond is revealed by partially reflexive reactions such as blushing, turning pale, sweating, vomiting, coughing, and sneezing—all dependent for their identity on a more or less artificial separation. For these reactions can indeed be psychologically induced in situations involving shame, anxiety, terror, repugnance, and disgust—embarrassment and excitement generally. But they lack the character of being conscious responses. Their symbolism—to which psychoanalytically oriented medicine pays even more attention today than thirty years ago—is not something for which the subject directly knows himself to be responsible. As in cases of psychosomatic illness, the process here reflects only symptomatically a disturbance of personal existence.

On the other hand, with laughing and crying the person does indeed lose control, but he remains a person, while the body, so to speak, takes over the answer for him. With this is disclosed a possibility of cooperation between the person and his body, a possibility which usually remains hidden because it is not usually invoked.

Usually, in unequivocal situations which can be unequivocally answered and controlled, man responds *as* a person and makes use of his body for that purpose: as an instrument of speech, as a grasping, thrusting, supporting, and conveying organ, as a means of locomotion, as a means of signaling, as the sounding board of his emotions. He controls his body, or learns to control it.

This control, individually fluctuating, is subject to certain limits, probably not rigid, and which certainly do not coincide with the boundaries between voluntary and involuntary regulation. Nor is the distribution of nervous processes among the partly consciously, partly unconsciously operative system of animal functions (the sensorimotor system) and the unconsciously operative system of vegetative functions (which regulates the processes of circulation, metabolism, and internal secretion and is important for the *milieu interne*[2] and for internal equilibrium, for mood and emotional state) decisive in determining the extent of man's control over his body.

(If certain reports are to be believed, many people can exercise control over circulation, breathing, and even the regulation of body temperature. The autonomic processes—and anyone who practices a bit of training in will power can convince himself of this—are in any event more susceptible to influence by the total human attitude than present-day physiology generally assumes,

---

2. Internal environment (French), a phrase used both in biology and in sociology.

since it has civilized man in view. Training in the field of sport is wholly oriented toward the sensorimotor, animal system. While it does indeed master many autonomic processes, it intervenes from without and does not follow the path of the classical techniques of self-control through self-submergence.)

The goal of mastery—either in the service of the affirmation of man's bodily existence, in which case it is oriented now to maximum performance, now to complete relaxation, i.e., grace, or in the service of the denial of the body, i.e., asceticism and escape—is set to man by his physical existence: lived body *in* a physical body [*als Leib im* Körper]. From the day of his birth on, everyone must come to terms with this double role. Every kind of learning, e.g., grasping and the correlation of its effects with visual distance, standing, running, and so on, takes place on the basis and within the framework of this double role. The frame itself is never broken. A human being always and conjointly *is* a living body (head, trunk, extremities, with all that these contain)—even if he is convinced of his immortal soul, which somehow exists "therein"—and *has* this living body as this physical thing.

The possibility of using such different verbal expressions to refer to physical existence is rooted in the ambiguous character of this existence itself. A man has it, and he is it. He confronts his physical existence as something which he masters or sets aside, something which he uses as a means, an instrument; he is in it *and* (to a given extent) coincides with it. Thus bodily existence for man is a *relation*, in itself not unequivocal, but ambiguous, a relation of himself to himself [*sich . . . sich*] (or, to put it precisely, of him to himself). *Who* it is that stands in this relation can remain open. Nor do verbal expressions like "mind [*Geist*]," "I," "soul"—if we take them without a dogmatic religious sense—say more than everyday social experience convincingly reveals of our confrontation with the body and yet inclusion by it.

Convincingly and fundamentally, because our behavior toward the environment, both in its practical execution and in its interpretation by our fellow man, is shaped by this double role. Since it is usually taken for granted, only a reflective person can take cognizance of it as such. For we have come to terms with our double role, even theoretically, in such a fashion as to conjure away its immediacy.

Everyone speaks of his "I," his "self," whose domain extends in each case no further than the confining surfaces of his own body, but yet, as nonspatial, stands in its turn over against this domain. It asserts itself within, now in the region of the breast as the subject of sympathy, feeling, and desire, now in the region of the head as the subject of reflection, observation, and attention. "Within," at the level of breast or head, and "inside one's own body" are again descriptions which, though contradicting the nonspatial nature of the self, nevertheless persist and appeal to everyone's self-experience. We can enhance this paradoxical insight by thought experiments, but we cannot overcome it: behind eyes and ears, I sit as the center of my consciousness; between breast and back live disposition and "heart." My thoughts and desires, hidden to others, seem, lying within and surrounded by the body, to belong to a spaceless deep.

This internal location of myself in my body is enmeshed, in a way entirely obvious to common sense, in an immediate location of myself within the space of things. Here I am separated from the "outer" world, not by an intermediate layer, which I, as a separate entity, live through and "comprehend" from within, but as myself a piece of the external world, somewhere in a room or on the street. Here stands my body *qua* content of my visual or tactile field, of my locomotor, attentional, and visceral sensations, on the same line with other physical things which appear within the horizon of my perception. Regardless of whether I move about and do something or quietly let the images of the external world, including my own body as a part of it, act on me, the situation of my existence is ambiguous: *as* physical lived body—*in* the physical lived body.

Both orders[3] are entwined in each other and form a remarkable unity. Each can indeed be observed and characterized in itself, but they cannot be separated. I go walking *with* my consciousness, my body is its bearer, on whose momentary position the selective content and perspective of my consciousness depend; and I go walking *in* my consciousness, and my own body with its changes of position appears as the content of its sphere.

To wish to make a decision between these two orders would mean to misunderstand the necessity of their mutual interlacing. But with the same justification, I must hold firm to two mutually exclusive orders; that is, I must insist on the absolute focal reference of all things in the environment to my body, or to the center of perception, thinking, initiative, and sympathy persisting "in" it, i.e., to me or the "self" in me; *and* I must give up this absolute focal reference in favor of the relative localization of all things, including my body (together with my consciousness). Both orders are evident in the dual role of man as body and in the body. Both suggest powerful motives and arguments for the idealistic as well as the realistic theories of consciousness or nature, theories whose polemics can no more easily be settled than prevented, since the situation to which they appeal is necessarily ambiguous.

In this situation, the human position can be understood as *eccentric*. Just as the world and my own body are revealed to me, and can be controlled by me, only insofar as they appear in relation to me as a central "I," so, on the other hand, they retain their ascendancy over their subjection in this perspective as an order indifferent to me and including me in a nexus of mutual neighborhoods.

Even if man can come to no decision between these two orders, the one related to a center and the other not, he must nevertheless find a relation to them. For he is totally merged in neither. Neither *is* he just living body, nor does he just *have* a body. Every requirement of physical existence demands a reconciliation between being and having, outside and inside.

In the normal course of life, with its attachment to accustomed goals, this pressure for reconciliation is not conspicuous. In unusual situations, on the other hand, it meets with difficulties. These may involve questions of spatial orientation, of the estimation of size and distance in the perceptual field, or of the coordination of bodily movements with external things and with one's own body. Everyone knows from his own experience how easy it is to become confused in matters involving symmetry, mirror images, and the relations of

---

3. That is, the dimension in which I relate to my "physically lived body" as *something* I *have* and *am in* and the dimension in which I relate to my body as *what I am* (it is *me*).

left and right. Moreover, in recent times, clinical experiments in the areas of aphasia, ataxia, and apraxia have brought to light a wealth of material on disturbances to which the relation of man to his body can be subject. Among the basic insights which we owe to these studies is precisely the knowledge that it is here a question of the relation to the body or, more accurately, of the reconciliation between being a body and having a body in particular situations, and not merely a question of deficiencies occasioned by disturbances of the nervous system.

Moreover, we need only demand of our body some unaccustomed activity to find ourselves again faced with problems like those of a child learning to walk. The pressure for reconciliation between the two kinds of physical existence then presents itself, for example, as a problem of balance or of weight distribution. Thus expressions like "he has to have it in his bones" mean, not simply that a movement consciously brought about and controlled must become a reflex, but that the reconciliation between having a body and being one must take place readily and quickly. Each individual must come to terms with this in his own way—and in a certain sense can never come to terms with it.

In this respect man is inferior to the animal since the animal does not experience itself as shut off from its physical existence, as an inner self or I, and in consequence does not have to overcome a break between itself and itself, itself and its physical existence. The fact of an animal's being a body does not cut it off from its having one. It does indeed live in this separation—no movement, no leap (which an appraisal of distance must precede) would be possible without it. The animal too must put its body into action, employ it according to the given situation; otherwise, it does not reach its goal. But the switch from being to having, from having to being, which the animal constantly performs, does not in its turn present itself to him, nor, consequently, does it present any difficulty to him.

The lack of inhibition which makes the animal superior to man in control determines at the same time its restriction to the role that happens to be biologically assigned to it. It cannot come upon the idea (nor, in general, on any idea) to try out with its body something not immediately prescribed by its motor functions and instincts. Things may go ever so well with real donkeys; yet they never venture out on the ice.[4]

Only man is impersonally *and* personally aware of his physical situation, a constant restraint but also a constant incentive to overcome it. From the first, man's relation to himself as living body has an instrumental character, because he experiences his body as "means." In the compulsion ever again to find a new accommodation between the physical thing which he somehow happens to be and the body which he inhabits and controls—and not only by artificial abstraction—man comes to discover the mediated character, the instrumental character, of his concrete physical existence.

---

4. From the proverb: *Wenn dem Esel zu wohl wird, geht er aufs Eis*: "The overconfident jackass tries to skate." Its counterpart in English is "Pride goeth before a fall" [Churchill's note]. More literally translated, the proverb is "When a donkey gets to feeling too good, it goes out on the ice."

4. Mediateness and Explicitness. Face and Voice

It would seem that our last observations on man's special position, his specific mode of being, have taken us away from our theme. In reality, they provide the foundation for its discussion. If laughing and crying are human monopolies, then they must be understood through human nature. For this purpose, the usual characterization through concepts like soul and mind [*Geist*] is insufficient. Apart from the ambiguity and incomprehensibility which cling to them because of their theological and metaphysical past, these concepts leave us in the lurch in questions of the relation to the body. If it is objected to our observations that they convey nothing which could not be understood through the nature of man as a person, distinguished by selfhood [*Ichhaftigkeit*] and rationality [*Geistigkeit*],[5] such an objection misunderstands what they have been attempting. They seek, from the first, to secure the determination of man's physical existence and within its horizon to outline the specific character of human life as "being-there" [*Da-sein*].

On this account, we have deliberately chosen to introduce a neutral concept like that of "eccentric position," which refrains from every interpretation of what is essentially human and authentic. In conscious avoidance of loaded, ambiguous words, which conceal the intuitively obvious, basic facts, this concept points to those facts as the constitution and manner of embodied human existence. It also preserves neutrality of aspect against the temptation to espouse now the external, now the internal side of the dualistic model of man: the temptation to determine the constitution of human existence according to physical or psychological categories and then afterwards, in order to make up for the damage of this one-sidedness, to arrange a compromise between outer and inner. To the shift of viewpoint to which, incipiently, all living existence, but in its full development only human existence, compels us, the concept of "eccentricity" is, not indifferent, but neutral. As the formal designation of a "standing in . . . ," it encompasses the double aspect of outer and inner and thus makes possible the differentiated apprehension of the human relation to one's own body.

If, in this concept, we have caught the human manner of embodied being in the world, then it must be possible to develop from it those essential characteristics which are specifically human, such as speech, the use of tools, dress, religiosity, social organization, the development of power, art: in short, the regions of expression and representation peculiar to man. As necessary possibilities, which a being of eccentric position can have at its command, they can be reduced in a number of respects.

In my *Stufen des Organischen und der Mensch*,[6] which introduced the concept of eccentric position and substantiated it by a theory of organic categories, I summarized these necessary possibilities from a threefold point of view: from the standpoint of the natural-artificial, the immediate-mediated, and the rooted-groundless. The basic anthropological laws[7] of natural artificiality, mediated immediacy, and utopian standpoint thus mediate between

5. Better translated as "spirituality."
6. *The Levels of the Organic and Man.*

7. That is, the basic general structures or features of human reality.

the fundamental constitution of the eccentric position and the typical modes of human activity. They are linked to the historically attested interpretation of human being without claiming to exhaust all the possibilities implicit in it. The points of view under which these laws are summarized are not presented as the only ones conceivable, although they were not chosen arbitrarily but with a view to the great areas of human production.[8]

Eccentric position makes possible in like manner, for example, the gift of speech and the need for clothing (thus, conceptualization and the consciousness of nakedness); or upright posture and religious consciousness; or the use of tools and interest in decoration. Physical and mental "properties," in which man shows himself to be man, as tendencies, capacities, abilities, or however we wish to designate the modes of self-interpretation and presentation of human existence: all these are grounded equally radically in this concept.

To be sure, we should not conceive of this foundation as a single source from which everything springs, as if all possible properties put in their appearance from a single basic constitution. For these specifically human gifts are connected most intimately together and have need of one another, or at least evoke one another. For example, since standing upright freed the hands for grasping, the use of tools and an upright gait form a unity, quite apart from the other advantages that resulted from the achievement of upright posture: advantages for the extension of the perceptual field, the emancipation from the immediate environment, the development of the cerebrum—and with the latter, again, the differentiation of intelligence—or, in another direction, for the understanding of one's own body as an instrument and thus the gift of speech.

In the eccentric position, the formal condition is given under which man's essential characteristics and monopolies appear in their indissoluble unity (indissoluble in meaning), quite apart from the question, to what aspect of human existence they are ascribed, whether to the physical, psychic, or mental. Consequently, provided that they belong among the human monopolies, laughing and crying must likewise be intelligible, along with the other essential characters, under the formal condition of the eccentric position.

The problem will be to hit upon the right spot in the web of reciprocal connections. As forms of expression adjacent to speech and mime, laughing and crying belong to the sphere of expressivity. It will become evident that this sphere is closely connected with the situation of imprisonment in one's own body which we have already outlined. Thus the analysis takes up the thread of the discussion again and begins with what was last said about the instrumental, or means, character of the body.

Only to man, so we said, is his situation as body given at once impersonally and personally. He experiences himself *as* a thing and *in* a thing: but a thing which differs absolutely from all other things because he himself is that thing, because it obeys his intentions or at least responds to them. He is borne by it, encompassed by it, developed to effectiveness with and by it, yet at the same time it forms a resistance never to be wholly overcome. In this unity, of the relation to his physical existence as impersonally and personally given, a unity which he must constantly renew, man's living body is disclosed to him as a

---

8. That is, with a view to what is characteristic of broad areas of human experience and activity.

means, i.e., as something he can utilize to move about, carry loads, sit, lie, grasp, strike, and so on. This adaptability, together with its independent, objective thinghood, makes the living body an instrument.

The same also holds true of animals, but with the limitation that they achieve this instrumentality without being aware of it and without first having to find a relation to it. In the singular withdrawal [*Abgehobenheit*] from his physical existence which makes it possible for man to say "I" to himself, his situation in the world is presented to him as a *mediated* immediacy. By means of my body, I am in immediate contact, experienced as immediate, with the things in my environment. Seeing, hearing, touching, every sensation, visualization, and perception, has the import of being fulfilled in an immediate presentation of the colors and shapes, the sounds, surface configurations, and solidity of the things themselves. Granted, consideration of the fact that intervening processes in the sense organs, nerves, and central nervous system are necessary for such presentation complicates the substantiation of this truth, but it does not nullify it. The image of the object on the retina is admittedly inverted, but "I" do not need to reinvert it in my head in order that the correct impression, as I really have it, should occur. For I do not see the retinal image, and my brain does not see it either. The latter is a piece of protoplasm, which cannot see.

Such facts, among which one must also reckon the sense-specific energies of the nerves themselves, give rise, understandably, to the basic mistrust of the objectivity and inherent accuracy of our sensations and perceptions. First the secondary qualities of sense and then even the primary qualities were subjectivized, and the further development of subjective idealism went so far as to absorb completely even the ultimate describability and self-presence of the real in consciousness. Consciousness itself remained as a mere conjuror's stage and so lost all significance. With the one-sided exaggeration of the mediating and mediated aspect, its immediacy, the contact of I and world in knowing and acting, was bound to perish.

It makes no sense to oppose the fact of mediated immediacy and to keep trying to put simpler models in its place, be they models of immanence or of transcendence, of closure from or openness to what there is [*das Seiende*]. Those times of epistemology should be over. Only in the entwining of withdrawal and presence, remoteness and proximity, does the immanence of consciousness fulfill its function of disclosing reality. Only in the mediation by my body, which I myself bodily am (although I also possess it), is the I with things, looking and acting. As in all analysis, the demonstrable existence of connecting links such as chemical processes, contents of consciousness, images, and psychical processes interrupts, for our conception of it, the significance of this very mediation, just as an isolated presentation of individual notes cancels out their musical significance. In the course of the mediation, on the other hand, their significance is realized: to cancel one another in order to produce an immediate relation between the terms related.

Mediated immediacy is just as little to be "explained" as other "lower" modes of living. It is itself a basis for the explanation of the role of spatial, material processes in the structure of consciousness, for example, of its illusions and their corrections. If we take mediated immediacy as basic, then we can get further in questions pertaining to brain and mind, consciousness and object, than was possible up to now under the guidance of worn-out theories involving bisubstantial, double-aspect, two-component models.

Within the framework of mediated immediacy, i.e., of the eccentric position, as presented in terms of the relation of I and body, problems can be stated with greater precision and lead to a future solution, where within the old framework, with its crude alternatives, we at once struck the boundaries of all knowledge. As a mode of life, the eccentric position is reducible to, and so intelligible in terms of, certain laws of structure governing all living things—and that not only more or less, but exactly. But it is not to be explained in terms, say, of matter. Certain elemental and radical modes of being must be accepted, among them life and its positional character, i.e., its modes of relation to the environment. One of these is the eccentric position of man, with the perplexities and monopolies, infirmities and strengths, that belong to it specifically.

We have already argued that the possibility, particularly reserved to man, of controlling nature objectively in knowing and doing, is rooted in mediated immediacy. Indeed, in terms of the problems arising from the immanence of consciousness, i.e., from the standpoint of cognition alone, this insight has long been familiar to us. Corresponding to this character is the *instrumentality* of the body, which, however, again emphasizes only one side of the relation to physical existence (but an important one, since to a substantial degree the use of tools, inventive intelligence, and *Homo faber*[9] are anchored in it).

A no less important side of this relation is the *expressivity* of the body, which manifests itself in very diverse ways in gesture, mime, posture, speech, and naturally also in forms of expression like laughing and crying. But its nature is not exhausted in any of its characteristic forms. Nor do phrases like "drive to expression," "tendency toward vocal expression" (or even "communication") render it without distortion. Expression is a fundamental trait of mediated immediacy and, like the instrumentality of the body or the objectivity of knowledge, corresponds to that tension and entwinement which we are always having to adjust, between being a body and having a body. Expressivity is a fundamental way of coming to terms with the fact that man occupies a body and yet is a body.

Again, this also holds true for animals—with the restriction that they achieve expressivity without being aware of it and without having to find a position to take to it. They live in it, and hence their body mirrors the change of excitation in typical expressive movements (change of color, ruffling of feathers, erection of crest, sound) but with complete absence of gesture, speech, or laughing and crying. In expressive movement and posture, the "inner" becomes visible, it moves outward. This externalization occurs on the animal level as the direct radiation from the center of excitation to the periphery of the bodily surfaces. To the extent that man also lives on the animal level—and the eccentric position includes the centric position of the animal, by encircling it—he deports himself expressively in ways not basically different from animals. Many expressive gestures in the spheres of mime and sound are common to men and animals. Greed, fear, terror, surprise, pleasure, depres-

9. Man the maker (Latin)—that is, the maker and user of tools (a concept associated with Max Scheler; see the selection from *Man's Place in Nature* [1928], above).

sion, joy, restlessness and repose, rage, hesitation, watchfulness, and many other kinds of dispositional states in the behavior linked to vital sources show the same dynamic morphology in animal and man.

For the creature gripped by excitement, expression, as the outward movement and shaping of the "internal," takes place immediately on the level of expressive movement. But that this can occur bears witness to a relation of inner and outer that is ambiguous, since inner and outer are reciprocally interrelated. In animals, too, the body as expressive surface is no passive envelope and external layer into which excitations boil over from within, but a felt boundary surface over against the environment. Although external, it belongs from the very first with the internal. Animals live this relation, and—to the extent that he exists on this level—so does man. But only he knows of it.

This "knowing of it" is no occasional act of reflection which leaves the expressive relation untouched, taking place only beyond and apart from it. It is a luminosity and a distance into which our own expressive life is displaced. In this way, it can become the basis of an autonomous expressive system (in gesture and speech). Apart from this, however, body surface and voice, the natural sounding boards of expression, acquire throughout the character of being "organs of expression." Thus, expressivity is set free to become a power more or less at the disposal of the individual, which permits the individual, under certain conditions, to assume an artificial mask and posture, as the actor shows. That man must constantly take this power into account in order to find a balanced relation to his physical existence, he learns at every hand; for it is difficult to remain natural, to speak and behave spontaneously. Everyone is predisposed (and needs) to assume the attitude of his social position, his home, his calling, and his ideal. Naturalness is a task which appears to man in many guises when, in his personal or social development, he penetrates the artificiality of his existence.

Body surface and voice, the primal sounding boards of expression, have for the power or "faculty" of expressivity the character of organs of expression. That is, they appear as means and fields of expression, with and in which it becomes externally perceptible. In this process, that part of the body which is naturally outside the range of self-perception, i.e., the *face*, takes the lead and (with certain limits) becomes its representative. As the posture of the whole body mirrors in itself the mental state, so the face—and, again in a concentrated way, the look—becomes the mirror, indeed the "window," of the soul. As the area of sight and vocal utterance, a man's face is at once imperceptible and open. He looks out of and sounds forth from it, and by means of it captures the glances of others, the vistas of the world. Concealment and overtness make the face the front, the boundary and mediating surface of one's own against the other, the inner against the outer. So, even on the animal level, the outer is no mere containing wall which encloses something inner, but it is incorporated into the inner and, conversely, implicates the inner— becoming a true boundary through the autonomy of this double outer-inner relation. This relation not only expresses and subsists on a "reciprocity of perspectives"; it *gives expression to* them. Thus eyes, mouth, and nose as such do not make up the face, for, if this were true, animals too would have faces. Only the eccentric position toward the world gives these features this sense of unity, to the deployment of which the upright posture, the development of forehead, chin, and nose, and the free mobility of the head contribute, each in its way.

Like the face with its unmistakable cast of features, the *voice* is also a primal sounding board for expression—for man: his organ. In and with his voice, man stretches out and lays hold on the other, as he himself is attuned and held. If concealment from oneself and overtness toward the world are characteristic of the face, so that through his face the individual is completely exposed and delivered over to every counterreaction before he can protect himself by facial mime, the voice is the ideal medium of deployment from the internal to the external. It can be graduated according to strength, pitch, and emotional and persuasive force; it can be modulated and articulated, whether as sung or spoken sound, as "bearer" of musical or linguistic communication.

The self-control and self-transparency of the voice supplement the frontal openness to the outside, the inner concealment, through which, in two directions, but without gradual transition, the face confronts men with one another and with the world, as observing-observable. In it we step, constantly hearing ourselves, open and exposed from within as well as without, in a gradual transition of regulable deployment into the communal system of informing and being informed.

This also holds—within the limits mentioned above—for the air-breathing animals. Inhaling and exhaling govern the possibilities of giving voice and serve as the basis for the many species-specific sounds of warning and enticement which accompany the biologically important situations as signals or purely expressive attitudes. They guarantee a contact which occasionally evokes the appearance of speech and mutual understanding, or even of song (as with birds), although (and this is also true of anthropoid apes) they never lose their vital connection and in no wise achieve autonomy from emotion. Animals "give cry," and the wealth of their vocalizations reveals many kinships with the vocalizations of man. Shrieking and moaning, groaning and sighing, jabbering and yowling: molds evoked under strong internal pressure, by pain, confinement, frustration, fatigue, already appear among the higher vertebrates. Less frequent are sounds indicative of ease, of pleasure, in states of satiation and relaxation; more frequent, on the other hand, are sounds of delight, of physical surprise, of aggressiveness, in which the internal pressure increases with such force as to relieve itself.

Such sudden release also marks the vital-functional side of the higher forms of expression reserved to man, such as gesture, speech, and laughing and crying, especially at times when, as in the last case, strong emotion and tension compel their discharge. The repression of an excitation, which is manifested in an appropriately sudden breakdown, we find widely distributed in the animal world. In order that such repression may be relieved through laughing and crying, both occasion and possibilities of release must be given, which only man, in his eccentric position toward the world and his own physical existence, has at his disposal. The specific occasions we will treat separately. On the other hand, the possibilities of release can be correctly understood only against the background of these forms of expression as a whole. In everyday life, the human modes of expression constantly overlap one another, supplement one another, and have grown so close together that speech, gesture, mime, and facial expressive movement cannot be sharply recognized in themselves. Nevertheless, such a characterization of the modes of expression is the only way to arrive at a clear demarcation of the unique nature of laughing and crying.

The uncertainty of the situation in this respect is revealed by the mere fact that in professional treatment the theme of laughing far outweighs that of crying. So pronounced is this ascendancy that we must ask ourselves seriously whether, in general, laughing and crying really form a pair of expressions and present a true contrast in the way that people generally believe. Our analysis of these modes of human expression will always keep in mind the question of their coordinate relationship.

SOURCE: From Helmuth Plessner, *Laughing and Crying: A Study of the Limits of Human Behavior*, trans. James Spencer Churchill and Marjorie Grene (Evanston, Ill.: Northwestern University Press, 1970), pp. 7–47. Except where otherwise indicated, German words in brackets are the terminology used in the German original, inserted by the editor in addition to their renderings in the translation. Originally published in 1941 as *Lachen und Weinen: Eine Untersuchung nach den Grenzen menschlichen Verhaltens*; the translation is from the 3rd ed. (1961).

ERNST CASSIRER
(1874 – 1945)

Ernst Cassirer began his philosophical career in late nineteenth-century Germany as a Neo-Kantian interested primarily in the theory of knowledge and philosophy of science. He ended it in the United States as a refugee from the Nazis with the publication of *An Essay on Man* (1945) and *The Myth of the State* (1946), written in English and intended to contribute to our understanding both of ourselves as human beings and of the political madness that had threatened the very civilization and culture he so cherished. He was an enormously prolific writer, whose interests and works spanned much of the history of philosophy (including the often-neglected Renaissance and Enlightenment periods) and classic modern literature. His "philosophy of symbolic forms" was actually much more than that: it was an entire philosophy of culture and of human nature, making him one of the most important contributors to the development of the philosophical anthropology movement.

Born in Silesia in eastern Germany into a wealthy Jewish family, Cassirer ("Cah-SIH-rer") studied at Berlin, Leipzig, and Heidelberg before earning his doctorate in 1899 at Marburg, a leading center of Neo-Kantianism. He taught for some time at Berlin before the First World War, and then took a position at Hamburg in 1919, becoming rector there in 1930. When Hitler came to power he fled, first to England (teaching at Oxford, 1933–35), then to Sweden (teaching at Göteborg, 1935–41), and finally to the United States, where he taught at Yale (1941–44) and Columbia (1944–45). It was during his years at Yale that he wrote *An Essay on Man*, from which the following selection was taken. He died in New York in 1945.

Cassirer's initial philosophical focus, reflecting the emphasis at Marburg on the development and extension of KANT's thinking with respect to knowledge in general and science in particular, was on the philosophy of science. His interests soon broadened, however, encompassing other forms of human thought and experience. His philosophical orientation and sensibility shifted, as he moved toward a comprehensive cultural conception of human mental and spiritual life more akin to HEGEL's than to Kant's, and toward an appreciation of the historical-developmental character of its various elements.

Scientific thought remained significant in Cassirer's thinking; but he came to see it as only one instance of a much broader phenomenon that is of central importance in human life, and indeed is the key to our very humanity: *symbolism*. This takes many different forms, only some of which are properly conceived as having to do with attaining knowledge and cultivating rationality. Symbol use is both a mental function and a cultural phenomenon, and it became the guiding concept for Cassirer in his understanding of human culture and human nature alike. In his massive work *Philosophy of Symbolic Forms* (3 vols., 1923–29), he examined the different sorts of symbolic forms operative in language, myth, and various types of knowledge (of which scientific thinking is an instance); and he went on to interpret religion, art, and history similarly, as further forms of symbolizing activity.

Symbolic forms differ from mere signs and signals, according to Cassirer, in that they do more than convey information and practical imperatives. They (and through them, human consciousness) are expressive, complexly representational, and—most importantly—significative. That is, they generate as well as communicate forms of *meaning* that endow human cultures (and thereby human life) with a developing richness that amounts to a whole new dimension of human reality, grounded in but transcending all merely physical, biological, and socially functional reality. Cassirer's conception of this new dimension of human reality is at once thoroughly naturalistic—in the sense of invoking no higher powers and appealing to no metaphysical or teleological principles—and strongly emergentist, emphasizing the creatively dynamic character of symbol systems. They have a radically novel kind of life of their own, transforming human reality into something more than merely biological and emancipating human life from complete determination by merely natural causes. Symbolic forms make it possible for human beings to act in ways that are culturally meaningful rather than merely biologically needful; and they also make possible myriad forms of differentiation and division among human beings—while at the same time making possible compensating forms of human unity.

In *An Essay on Man*, written near the end of his life, Cassirer spells out the approach to a philosophical anthropology that he believed to be most appropriate to its topic and provides a sketch of his own interpretation of our fundamental human nature as *homo symbolicum*, the human symbol creator and user. Explicitly agreeing with MAX SCHELER about the need for a philosophical anthropology, and finding existential philosophy—particularly

in HEIDEGGER's version of it—to be both inadequate in its approach to human reality and deeply problematic in its seeming upshot and implications, Cassirer sought to support and advance this alternative approach to doing justice philosophically to what it means to be human.

Cassirer has virtually nothing to say about the biological and physiological dimensions of human reality, leaving that to others. He focuses instead on its cultural dimension and the kinds of experience and activity made possible by the various symbolic forms associated with it. It is the latter, he contends, that make human life human, supplying the means of everything about ourselves that is more than merely biological. A place exists in a philosophical anthropology for inquiry into human biology and physiology but it is secondary, explaining what it is about our constitution that makes the symbolic activities of human cultural life biologically and neurologically possible. Their comprehension, however, requires a different sort of inquiry: the study of these symbolic forms and activities themselves. There likewise is a place in Cassirer's kind of philosophical anthropology for an existential-philosophical consideration of the experiential character of individual human existence; but for him as for Hegel, that can be properly understood only in terms of the cultural conditions of its possibility, in any particular human form it may take.

From An Essay on Man

From *Part I. What is Man?*[1]

From Chapter I. The Crisis in Man's Knowledge of Himself[2]

* * *

* * * No former age was ever in such a favorable position with regard to the sources of our knowledge of human nature. Psychology, ethnology,

---

1. Although he wrote this book in English, Cassirer has in mind the German word *Mensch*—a generic that has the sense "human being" or "humankind" and "human," not "male"—when he uses "man."
2. To provide context for the "crisis" in this knowl-

edge, in the immediately preceding paragraph Cassirer quoted from SCHELER's *Die Stellung des Menschen im Kosmos* (1928; see *Man's Place in Nature*, above), a founding text of philosophical anthropology that had not yet been translated into English.

anthropology, and history have amassed an astoundingly rich and constantly increasing body of facts. Our technical instruments for observation and experimentation have been immensely improved, and our analyses have become sharper and more penetrating. We appear, nevertheless, not yet to have found a method for the mastery and organization of this material. When compared with our own abundance the past may seem very poor. But our wealth of facts is not necessarily a wealth of thoughts. Unless we succeed in finding a clue of Ariadne[3] to lead us out of this labyrinth, we can have no real insight into the general character of human culture,[4] we shall remain lost in a mass of disconnected and disintegrated data which seem to lack all conceptual unity.

CHAPTER II. A CLUE TO THE NATURE OF MAN: THE SYMBOL

The biologist Johannes von Uexküll[5] has written a book in which he undertakes a critical revision of the principles of biology. Biology, according to Uexküll, is a natural science which has to be developed by the usual empirical methods—the methods of observation and experimentation. Biological thought, on the other hand, does not belong to the same type as physical or chemical thought. Uexküll is a resolute champion of vitalism; he is a defender of the principle of the autonomy of life. Life is an ultimate and self-dependent reality. It cannot be described or explained in terms of physics or chemistry. From this point of view Uexküll evolves a new general scheme of biological research. As a philosopher he is an idealist or phenomenalist. But his phenomenalism is not based upon metaphysical or epistemological considerations; it is founded rather on empirical principles. As he points out, it would be a very naïve sort of dogmatism to assume that there exists an absolute reality of things which is the same for all living beings. Reality is not a unique and homogeneous thing; it is immensely diversified, having as many different schemes and patterns as there are different organisms. Every organism is, so to speak, a monadic being. It has a world of its own because it has an experience of its own. The phenomena that we find in the life of a certain biological species are not transferable to any other species. The experiences—and therefore the realities—of two different organisms are incommensurable with one another. In the world of a fly, says Uexküll, we find only "fly things"; in the world of a sea urchin we find only "sea urchin things."

From this general presupposition Uexküll develops a very ingenious and original scheme of the biological world. Wishing to avoid all psychological interpretations, he follows an entirely objective or behavioristic method. The only clue to animal life, he maintains, is given us in the facts of comparative anatomy. If we know the anatomical structure of an animal species, we possess all the necessary data for reconstructing its special mode of experience. A careful study of the structure of the animal body, of the number, the quality,

---

3. In Greek mythology, the daughter of Minos, king of Crete; she provided the Greek hero Theseus with the help he needed to escape the Minotaur's labyrinth.
4. The "philosophy of culture" for Cassirer is inseparable from and central to a philosophical anthropology or philosophy of human nature, just

as it had previously been central to HEGEL's "philosophy of Geist."
5. An important Estonian-born German biological theorist (1864–1944); his research and thought figured significantly in the early development of philosophical anthropology up to the middle of the 20th century.

and the distribution of the various sense organs, and the conditions of the nervous system, gives us a perfect image of the inner and outer world of the organism. Uexküll began his investigations with a study of the lowest organisms; he extended them gradually to all the forms of organic life. In a certain sense he refuses to speak of lower or higher forms of life. Life is perfect everywhere; it is the same in the smallest as in the largest circle. Every organism, even the lowest, is not only in a vague sense adapted to (*angepasst*) but entirely fitted into (*eingepasst*) its environment. According to its anatomical structure it possesses a certain *Merknetz* and a certain *Wirknetz*—a receptor system and an effector system. Without the coöperation and equilibrium of these two systems the organism could not survive. The receptor system by which a biological species receives outward stimuli and the effector system by which it reacts to them are in all cases closely interwoven. They are links in one and the same chain which is described by Uexküll as the *functional circle (Funktionskreis)* of the animal.[6]

I cannot enter here upon a discussion of Uexküll's biological principles. I have merely referred to his concepts and terminology in order to pose a general question. Is it possible to make use of the scheme proposed by Uexküll for a description and characterization of the *human world*? Obviously this world forms no exception to those biological rules which govern the life of all the other organisms. Yet in the human world we find a new characteristic which appears to be the distinctive mark of human life. The functional circle of man is not only quantitively enlarged; it has also undergone a qualitative change. Man has, as it were, discovered a new method of adapting himself to his environment. Between the receptor system and the effector system, which are to be found in all animal species, we find in man a third link which we may describe as the *symbolic system*. This new acquisition transforms the whole of human life. As compared with the other animals man lives not merely in a broader reality; he lives, so to speak, in a new *dimension* of reality. There is an unmistakable difference between organic reactions and human responses. In the first case a direct and immediate answer is given to an outward stimulus; in the second case the answer is delayed. It is interrupted and retarded by a slow and complicated process of thought. At first sight such a delay may appear to be a very questionable gain. Many philosophers have warned man against this pretended progress. "L'homme qui médite," says Rousseau, "est un animal dépravé":[7] it is not an improvement but a deterioration of human nature to exceed the boundaries of organic life.

Yet there is no remedy against this reversal of the natural order. Man cannot escape from his own achievement. He cannot but adopt the conditions of his own life. No longer in a merely physical universe, man lives in a symbolic universe. Language, myth, art, and religion are parts of this universe. They are the varied threads which weave the symbolic net, the tangled web of human experience. All human progress in thought and experience refines upon and strengthens this net. No longer can man confront reality immediately;

6. See Johannes von Uexküll, *Theoretische Biologie* [*Theoretical Biology*] (2nd ed., Berlin, 1938); *Umwelt und Innenwelt der Tiere* [*The Environment and Inner World of Animals*] (1909; 2nd ed. Berlin, 1921) [Cassirer's note].

7. The human being who meditates [reflects] is a depraved animal (French); quoted from part 1 of *Discourse on the Origin and Foundation of Inequality among Mankind* (1755), by the Swiss-born French philosopher Jean-Jacques Rousseau (1712–1778).

he cannot see it, as it were, face to face. Physical reality seems to recede in proportion as man's symbolic activity advances. Instead of dealing with the things themselves man is in a sense constantly conversing with himself. He has so enveloped himself in linguistic forms, in artistic images, in mythical symbols or religious rites that he cannot see or know anything except by the interposition of this artificial medium. His situation is the same in the theoretical as in the practical sphere. Even here man does not live in a world of hard facts, or according to his immediate needs and desires. He lives rather in the midst of imaginary emotions, in hopes and fears, in illusions and disillusions, in his fantasies and dreams. "What disturbs and alarms man," said Epictetus, "are not the things, but his opinions and fancies about the things."[8]

From the point of view at which we have just arrived we may correct and enlarge the classical definition of man. In spite of all the efforts of modern irrationalism this definition of man as an *animal rationale*[9] has not lost its force. Rationality is indeed an inherent feature of all human activities. Mythology itself is not simply a crude mass of superstitions or gross delusions. It is not merely chaotic, for it possesses a systematic or conceptual form.[1] But, on the other hand, it would be impossible to characterize the structure of myth as rational. Language has often been identified with reason, or with the very source of reason. But it is easy to see that this definition fails to cover the whole field. It is a *pars pro toto*;[2] it offers us a part for the whole. For side by side with conceptual language there is an emotional language; side by side with logical or scientific language there is a language of poetic imagination. Primarily language does not express thoughts or ideas, but feelings and affections. And even a religion "within the limits of pure reason" as conceived and worked out by Kant[3] is no more than a mere abstraction. It conveys only the ideal shape, only the shadow, of what a genuine and concrete religious life is. The great thinkers who have defined man as an *animal rationale* were not empiricists, nor did they ever intend to give an empirical account of human nature. By this definition they were expressing rather a fundamental moral imperative. Reason is a very inadequate term with which to comprehend the forms of man's cultural life in all their richness and variety. But all these forms are symbolic forms. Hence, instead of defining man as an *animal rationale*, we should define him as an *animal symbolicum*.[4] By so doing we can designate his specific difference, and we can understand the new way open to man—the way to civilization.

FROM CHAPTER III. FROM ANIMAL REACTIONS TO HUMAN RESPONSES

By our definition of man as an *animal symbolicum* we have arrived at our first point of departure for further investigations. But it now becomes imperative that we develop this definition somewhat in order to give it greater precision.

8. Paraphrased from §5 of the *Enchiridion* (or *Manual*) by the Greek Stoic philosopher Epictetus (ca. 55—ca. 135 C.E.): "Men are disturbed not by the occurrences, but by the opinions about the occurrences."
9. Rational animal (Latin); this definition is deduced from the writings of Aristotle (384–322 B.C.E.).

1. See Cassirer, *Die Begriffsform im mythischen Denken* [*The Form of Concepts in Mythical Thinking*] (Leipzig, 1921) [Cassirer's note].
2. Part in place of the whole (Latin).
3. See KANT, *Religion within the Limits of Reason Alone* (1793).
4. Symbolizing [or symbol-creating and -using] animal (Latin).

That symbolic thought and symbolic behavior are among the most character-istic features of human life, and that the whole progress of human culture is based on these conditions, is undeniable. But are we entitled to consider them as the special endowment of man to the exclusion of all other organic beings? Is not symbolism a principle which we may trace back to a much deeper source, and which has a much broader range of applicability? If we answer this question in the negative we must, as it seems, confess our ignorance con-cerning many fundamental questions which have perennially occupied the center of attention in the philosophy of human culture. The question of the *origin* of language, of art, of religion becomes unanswerable, and we are left with human culture as a given fact which remains in a sense isolated and, therefore, unintelligible.

It is understandable that scientists[5] have always refused to accept such a solution. They have made great efforts to connect the fact of symbolism with other well-known and more elementary facts. The problem has been felt to be of paramount importance, but unfortunately it has very rarely been approached with an entirely open mind. From the first it has been obscured and confused by other questions which belong to a quite different realm of discourse. Instead of giving us an unbiased description and analysis of the phenomena themselves the discussion of this problem has been converted into a metaphysical dispute. It has become the bone of contention between the different metaphysical systems: between idealism and materialism, spiritual-ism and naturalism. For all these systems the question of symbolism has become a crucial problem, on which the future shape of science and meta-physics has seemed to hinge.

With this aspect of the problem we are not concerned here, having set for ourselves a much more modest and concrete task. We shall attempt to describe the symbolic attitude of man in a more accurate manner in order to be able to contradistinguish it from other modes of symbolic behavior found through-out the animal kingdom.

* * *

* * * Speech is not a simple and uniform phenomenon. It consists of differ-ent elements which, both biologically and systematically, are not on the same level. We must try to find the order and interrelationships of the constituent elements; we must, as it were, distinguish the various geological strata of speech. The first and most fundamental stratum is evidently the language of the emotions. A great portion of all human utterance still belongs to this stratum. But there is a form of speech that shows us quite a different type. Here the word is by no means a mere interjection; it is not an involuntary expression of feeling, but a part of a sentence which has a definite syntactical and logical structure. It is true that even in highly developed, in theoretical language the connection with the first element is not entirely broken off. Scarcely a sentence can be found—except perhaps the pure formal sentences of mathematics—without a certain affective or emotional tinge. Analogies and parallels to emotional language may be found in abundance in the animal

5. That is, scholars and theorists in the various cognitive disciplines (including philosophy) that deal with such matters. Cassirer has in mind the German term *Wissenschaftler*, which is much broader in scope than "[natural] scientists."

world. As regards chimpanzees Wolfgang Koehler[6] states that they achieve a considerable degree of expression by means of gesture. Rage, terror, despair, grief, pleading, desire, playfulness, and pleasure are readily expressed in this manner. Nevertheless one element, which is characteristic of and indispensable to all human language, is missing: we find no signs which have an objective reference or meaning. * * *

Here we touch upon the crucial point in our whole problem. The difference between *propositional language* and *emotional language* is the real landmark between the human and the animal world. All the theories and observations concerning animal language are wide of the mark if they fail to recognize this fundamental difference.[7] In all the literature of the subject there does not seem to be a single conclusive proof of the fact that any animal ever made the decisive step from subjective to objective, from affective to propositional language. * * * The logical analysis of human speech always leads us to an element of prime importance which has no parallel in the animal world. The general theory of evolution in no sense stands in the way of the acknowledgment of this fact. Even in the field of the phenomena of organic nature we have learned that evolution does not exclude a sort of original creation. The fact of sudden mutation and of emergent evolution has to be admitted. Modern biology no longer speaks of evolution in terms of earlier Darwinism;[8] nor does it explain the causes of evolution in the same way. We may readily admit that the anthropoid apes, in the development of certain symbolic processes, have made a significant forward step. But again we must insist that they did not reach the threshold of the human world. They entered, as it were, a blind alley.

For the sake of a clear statement of the problem we must carefully distinguish between *signs* and *symbols*. That we find rather complex systems of signs and signals in animal behavior seems to be an ascertained fact. We may even say that some animals, especially domesticated animals, are extremely susceptible to signs. A dog will react to the slightest changes in the behavior of his master; he will even distinguish the expressions of a human face or the modulations of a human voice. But it is a far cry from these phenomena to an understanding of symbolic and human speech. The famous experiments of Pavlov[9] prove only that animals can easily be trained to react not merely to direct stimuli but to all sorts of mediate or representative stimuli. A bell, for example, may become a "sign for dinner," and an animal may be trained not to touch its food when this sign is absent. But from this we learn only that the experimenter, in this case, has succeeded in changing the food-situation of the animal. He has complicated this situation by voluntarily introducing into it a new element. All the phenomena which are commonly described as conditioned reflexes are not merely very far from but even opposed to the essential character of human symbolic thought. Symbols—in the proper sense

---

6. German psychologist (1887–1967), who emigrated to America in 1935; he is famous both for his primate studies and as one of the founders of Gestalt psychology. In the omitted passage below, Cassirer quotes Köhler's *The Mentality of Apes* (1921; trans. 1925).
7. See Cassirer, *Philosophie der symbolischen Formen* [*Philosophy of Symbolic Forms* (1929)], III,

chap. 6, pp. 237–323 [Cassirer's note].
8. That is, the evolutionary theory of the English naturalist Charles Darwin (1809–1882) himself.
9. Ivan Pavlov (1848–1936), Russian physiologist; in his most famous experiment, he showed that a dog could be conditioned to salivate at the sound of a bell that had become associated with food.

of this term—cannot be reduced to mere signals. Signals and symbols belong to two different universes of discourse: a signal is a part of the physical world of being; a symbol is a part of the human world of meaning. Signals are "operators"; symbols are "designators."[1] Signals, even when understood and used as such, have nevertheless a sort of physical or substantial being; symbols have only a functional value.

Bearing this distinction in mind, we can find an approach to one of the most controverted problems. The question of the *intelligence of animals* has always been one of the greatest puzzles of anthropological philosophy. Tremendous efforts, both of thought and observation, have been expended on answers to this question. But the ambiguity and vagueness of the very term "intelligence" has always stood in the way of a clear solution. How can we hope to answer a question whose import we do not understand? * * * If by intelligence we understand either adjustment to the immediate environment or adaptive modification of environment, we must certainly ascribe to animals a comparatively highly developed intelligence. It must also be conceded that not all animal actions are governed by the presence of an immediate stimulus. The animal is capable of all sorts of detours in its reactions. It may learn not only to use implements but even to invent tools for its purposes. Hence some pyschobiologists do not hesitate to speak of a creative or constructive imagination in animals.[2] But neither this intelligence nor this imagination is of the specifically human type. In short, we may say that the animal possesses a practical imagination and intelligence whereas man alone has developed a new form: a *symbolic imagination and intelligence*.

Moreover, in the mental development of the individual mind the transition from one form to the other—from a merely practical attitude to a symbolic attitude—is evident. But here this step is the final result of a slow and continuous process. * * *

* * *

The principle of symbolism, with its universality, validity, and general applicability, is the magic word, the Open Sesame! giving access to the specifically human world, to the world of human culture. Once man is in possession of this magic key further progress is assured. Such progress is evidently not obstructed or made impossible by any lack in the sense material. The case of Helen Keller,[3] who reached a very high degree of mental development and intellectual culture, shows us clearly and irrefutably that a human being in the construction of his human world is not dependent upon the quality of his sense material. If the theories of sensationalism were right, if every idea were nothing but a faint copy of an original sense impression, then the condition of a blind, deaf, and dumb child would indeed be desperate. For it would be deprived of the very sources of human knowledge; it would be, as it were, an exile from reality. But if we study Helen Keller's autobiography we are at once

---

1. See Charles Morris, "The Foundation of the Theory of Signs," *Encyclopedia of the Unified Sciences* [i.e., *Foundations of the Theory of Signs*, vol. 1, no. 2, of *International Encyclopedia of Unified Science*] (1938) [Cassirer's note].
2. See R. M. and A. W. Yerkes, *The Great Apes* (New Haven: Yale University Press, 1929), pp. 368ff.,

520ff. [Cassirer's note].
3. Deaf and blind American author and educator (1880–1968); she suddenly came to understand the symbolic nature of language at age 6. Her autobiography, *The Story of My Life* (1903), was a best-seller.

aware that this is untrue, and at the same time we understand why it is untrue. Human culture derives its specific character and its intellectual and moral values, not from the material of which it consists, but from its form, its architectural structure. And this form may be expressed in any sense material. Vocal language has a very great technical advantage over tactile language; but the technical defects of the latter do not destroy its essential use. The free development of symbolic thought and symbolic expression is not obstructed by the use of tactile signs in the place of vocal ones. If the child has succeeded in grasping the meaning of human language, it does not matter in which particular material this meaning is accessible to it. As the case of Helen Keller proves, man can construct his symbolic world out of the poorest and scantiest materials. The thing of vital importance is not the individual bricks and stones but their general *function* as architectural form. In the realm of speech it is their general symbolic function which vivifies the material signs and "makes them speak." Without this vivifying principle the human world would indeed remain deaf and mute. With this principle, even the world of a deaf, dumb, and blind child can become incomparably broader and richer than the world of the most highly developed animal.

Universal applicability, owing to the fact that everything has a name, is one of the greatest prerogatives of human symbolism. But it is not the only one. There is still another characteristic of symbols which accompanies and complements this one, and forms its necessary correlate. A symbol is not only universal but extremely variable. I can express the same meaning in various languages; and even within the limits of a single language a certain thought or idea may be expressed in quite different terms. A sign or signal is related to the thing to which it refers in a fixed and unique way. Any one concrete and individual sign refers to a certain individual thing. In Pavlov's experiments the dogs could easily be trained to reach for food only upon being given special signs; they would not eat until they heard a particular sound which could be chosen at the discretion of the experimenter. But this bears no analogy, as it has often been interpreted, to human symbolism; on the contrary, it is in opposition to symbolism. A genuine human symbol is characterized not by its uniformity but by its versatility. It is not rigid or inflexible but mobile.

* * *

Another important aspect of our general problem now emerges—the problem of the *dependence of relational thought upon symbolic thought*. Without a complex system of symbols relational thought cannot arise at all, much less reach its full development. It would not be correct to say that the mere *awareness* of relations presupposes an intellectual act, an act of logical or abstract thought. Such an awareness is necessary even in elementary acts of perception. The sensationalist theories used to describe perception as a mosaic of simple sense data. Thinkers of this persuasion constantly overlooked the fact that sensation itself is by no means a mere aggregate or bundle of isolated impressions. Modern Gestalt psychology has corrected this view. It has shown that the very simplest perceptual processes imply fundamental structural elements, certain patterns or configurations. This principle holds both for the human and the animal world. Even in comparatively low stages of animal life the presence of these structural elements—especially of spatial and optical structures—has been experimentally proved. The mere awareness of relations cannot, therefore, be regarded as a specific feature of human consciousness. We do find, however, in man a special type of relational thought which has no parallel in the animal world. In man an ability to isolate relations—to consider them in their abstract meanings—has developed. In order to grasp this meaning man is no longer dependent upon concrete sense data, upon visual, auditory, tactile, kinesthetic data. He considers these relations "in themselves[.]" * * * Geometry is the classic example of this turning point in man's intellectual life. Even in elementary geometry we are not bound to the apprehension of concrete individual figures. We are not concerned with physical things or perceptual objects, for we are studying universal spatial relations for whose expression we have an adequate symbolism. Without the preliminary step of human language such an achievement would not be possible. * * *

The first thinker to have clear insight into this problem was Herder.[4] He spoke as a philosopher of humanity who wished to pose the question in entirely "human" terms. Rejecting the metaphysical or theological thesis of a supernatural or divine origin of language, Herder begins with a critical revision of the question itself. Speech is not an object, a physical thing for which we may seek a natural or a supernatural cause. It is a process, a general function of the human mind. Psychologically we cannot describe this process in the terminology which was used by all the psychological schools of the eighteenth century. According to Herder speech is not an artificial creation of reason, nor is it to be accounted for by a special mechanism of associations. In his own attempt to set forth the nature of language Herder lays the whole stress upon what he calls "*reflection*." Reflection or reflective thought is the ability of man to single out from the whole undiscriminated mass of the stream of floating sensuous phenomena certain fixed elements in order to isolate them and to concentrate attention upon them.

> Man evinces reflection when the power of his soul acts so freely that it can segregate from the whole ocean of sensation surging through all his senses *one* wave, as it were; and that it can stay this wave, draw attention to it, and be aware of this attention. He evinces reflection when from the whole wavering dream of images rushing through his senses he can collect himself into a moment of waking, dwell on *one* image spontaneously, observe it clearly and more quietly, and abstract characteristics showing him that *this* and no other is the object. Thus he evinces reflection when he can not only perceive all the qualities vividly or clearly but when he can *recognize* one or several of them as distinctive qualities. . . . Now by what means did this recognition come about? Through a characteristic which he had to abstract, and which, as an element of consciousness, presented itself clearly. Well then, let us exclaim: Eureka! This initial character of consciousness was the language of the soul. With this, human language is created.[5]

---

4. Johann Herder (1744–1803), important German philosopher of language and history, as well as linguist and historian.

5. Herder, *Über den Ursprung der Sprache* ["(Essay) on the Origin of Language"] (1772), *Werke* [*Works*], ed. Suphan, V, 34f. [Cassirer's note].

This has more the appearance of a poetical portrait than of a logical analysis of human speech. Herder's theory of the origin of language remained entirely speculative. It did not proceed from a general theory of knowledge, nor from an observation of empirical facts. It was based on his ideal of humanity and on his profound intuition of the character and development of human culture. Nevertheless it contains logical and psychological elements of the most valuable sort. All the processes of generalization or abstraction in animals that have been investigated and described with accuracy clearly lack the distinctive mark emphasized by Herder. Later on, however, Herder's view found a rather unexpected clarification and confirmation from a quite different quarter. Recent research in the field of the *psychopathology of language* has led to the conclusion that the loss, or severe impairment, of speech caused by brain injury is never an isolated phenomenon. Such a defect alters the whole character of human behavior. Patients suffering from aphasia or other kindred diseases have not only lost the use of words but have undergone corresponding changes in personality. Such changes are scarcely observable in their outward behavior, for here they tend to act in a perfectly normal manner. They can perform the tasks of everyday life; some of them even develop considerable skill in all tests of this sort. But they are at a complete loss as soon as the solution of the problem requires any specific theoretical or reflective activity. They are no longer able to think in general concepts or categories. Having lost their grip on universals, they stick to the immediate facts, to concrete situations. Such patients are unable to perform any task which can be executed only by means of a comprehension of the abstract.[6] All this is highly significant, for it shows us to what degree that type of thought which Herder called reflective is dependent on symbolic thought. Without symbolism the life of man would be like that of the prisoners in the cave of Plato's famous simile.[7] Man's life would be confined within the limits of his biological needs and his practical interests; it could find no access to the "ideal world" which is opened to him from different sides by religion, art, philosophy, science.

* * *

From *Part II. Man and Culture*

FROM CHAPTER VI. THE DEFINITION OF MAN IN TERMS OF HUMAN CULTURE

It was a turning point in Greek culture and Greek thought when Plato interpreted the maxim "Know thyself"[8] in an entirely new sense. This interpretation introduced a problem which was not only alien to pre-Socratic thought but also went far beyond the limits of the Socratic method. In order to obey

6. A detailed and highly interesting account of these phenomena will be found in various publications of K. Goldstein and A. Gelb. Goldstein has given a general survey of his theoretical views in *Human Nature in the Light of Psychopathology*, the William James Lectures delivered at Harvard University, 1937–38 (Cambridge, Mass.: Harvard University Press, 1940). I have discussed the question from a general philosophical point of view in *Philosophie der symbolischen Formen*, III, chap. 6, pp. 237–323 [Cassirer's note].

7. In his *Republic* (7.514a–517c), the Greek philosopher Plato (ca. 427–ca. 347 B.C.E.) compares the situation of uneducated men to prisoners who believe that the shadows they see cast on the walls in front of them are reality.

8. A Greek maxim carved into the temple of Apollo at Delphi (4th c. B.C.E.), home of the god's oracle.

the demand of the Delphic god, in order to fulfill the religious duty of self-examination and self-knowledge, Socrates[9] had approached the individual man. Plato recognized the limitations of the Socratic way of inquiry. In order to solve the problem, he declared, we must project it upon a larger plan. The phenomena we encounter in our individual experience are so various, so complicated and contradictory that we can scarcely disentangle them. Man is to be studied not in his individual life but in his political and social life. Human nature, according to Plato, is like a difficult text, the meaning of which has to be deciphered by philosophy. But in our personal experience this text is written in such small characters that it becomes illegible. The first labor of philosophy must be to enlarge these characters. Philosophy cannot give us a satisfactory theory of man until it has developed a theory of the state. The nature of man is written in capital letters in the nature of the state. Here the hidden meaning of the text suddenly emerges, and what seemed obscure and confused becomes clear and legible.

But political life is not the only form of a communal human existence. In the history of mankind the state, in its present form, is a late product of the civilizing process. Long before man had discovered this form of social organization he had made other attempts to organize his feelings, desires, and thoughts. Such organizations and systematizations are contained in language, in myth, in religion, and in art.[1] We must accept this broader basis if we wish to develop a theory of man. The state, however important, is not all. It cannot express or absorb all the other activities of man. To be sure these activities in their historical evolution are closely connected with the development of the state; in many respects they are dependent upon the forms of political life. But, while not possessing a separate historical existence, they have nevertheless a purport and value of their own.

* * *

After this brief survey of the different methods that have hitherto been employed in answering the question: What is man? we now come to our central issue. Are these methods sufficient and exhaustive? Or is there still another approach to an anthropological philosophy? Is any other way left open besides that of psychological introspection, biological observation and experiment, and of historical investigation? I have endeavored to discover such an alternative approach in my *Philosophy of Symbolic Forms*.[2] The method of this work is by no means a radical innovation. It is not designed to abrogate but to complement former views. The philosophy of symbolic forms starts from the presupposition that, if there is any definition of the nature or "essence" of man, this definition can only be understood as a functional one, not a substantial one. We cannot define man by any inherent principle which constitutes his metaphysical essence—nor can we define him by any inborn faculty or instinct that may be ascertained by empirical observation. Man's outstanding characteristic,

9. Plato's teacher (469–399 B.C.E.), and the main speaker in most of his dialogues. His method was to use questions to lead his interlocutors to recognize their ignorance of the matter being discussed.
1. Topics treated at length in Cassirer's *Philosophy*

of Symbolic Forms (3 vols., 1923–29).
2. *Philosophie der symbolischen Formen*. Vol. I, *Die Sprache* [*Language*] (1923); Vol. II, *Das mythische Denken* [*Mythical Thinking*] (1925); Vol. III, *Phänomenologie der Erkenntnis* [*Phenomenology of Knowledge*] (1929) [Cassirer's note].

his distinguishing mark, is not his metaphysical or physical nature—but his work.[3] It is this work, it is the system of human activities, which defines and determines the circle of "humanity." Language, myth, religion, art, science, history are the constituents, the various sectors of this circle. A "philosophy of man" would therefore be a philosophy which would give us insight into the fundamental structure of each of these human activities, and which at the same time would enable us to understand them as an organic whole. Language, art, myth, religion are no isolated, random creations. They are held together by a common bond. But this bond is not a *vinculum substantiale*,[4] as it was conceived and described in scholastic thought; it is rather a *vinculum functionale*.[5] It is the basic function of speech, of myth, of art, of religion that we must seek far behind their innumerable shapes and utterances, and that in the last analysis we must attempt to trace back to a common origin.

It is obvious that in the performance of this task we cannot neglect any possible source of information. We must examine all the available empirical evidence, and utilize all the methods of introspection, biological observation, and historical inquiry. These older methods are not to be eliminated but referred to a new intellectual center, and hence seen from a new angle. In describing the structure of language, myth, religion, art, and science, we feel the constant need of a psychological terminology. We speak of religious "feeling," of artistic or mythical "imagination," of logical or rational thought. And we cannot enter into all these worlds without a sound scientific psychological method. Child psychology gives us valuable clues for the study of the general development of human speech. Even more valuable seems to be the help we get from the study of general sociology. We cannot understand the form of primitive mythical thought without taking into consideration the forms of primitive society. And more urgent still is the use of historical methods. The question as to what language, myth, and religion "are" cannot be answered without a penetrating study of their historical development.

But even if it were possible to answer all these psychological, sociological, and historical questions, we should still be in the precincts of the properly "human" world; we should not have passed its threshold. All human works arise under particular historical and sociological conditions. But we could never understand these special conditions unless we were able to grasp the general structural principles underlying these works. In our study of language, art, and myth the problem of meaning takes precedence over the problem of historical development. And here too we can ascertain a slow and continuous change in the methodological concepts and ideals of empirical science. In linguistics, for instance, the conception that the history of language covers the whole field of linguistic studies was for a long time an accepted dogma. This dogma left its mark upon the whole development of linguistics during the nineteenth century. Nowadays, however, this one-sidedness appears to have been definitely overcome.

The necessity of independent methods of descriptive analysis is generally recognized. We cannot hope to measure the depth of a special branch of

---

3. That is, the activities of humankind that revolve around its greatest collective product: human culture, in its various historically emergent forms.

4. Substantial bond (Latin).
5. Functional bond (Latin).

human culture unless such measurement is preceded by a descriptive analysis. This structural view of culture must precede the merely historical view. History itself would be lost in the boundless mass of disconnected facts if it did not have a general structural scheme by means of which it can classify, order, and organize these facts. * * *

* * * Philosophy cannot be content with analyzing the individual forms of human culture. It seeks a universal synthetic view which includes all individual forms. But is not such an all-embracing view an impossible task, a mere chimera? In human experience we by no means find the various activities which constitute the world of culture existing in harmony. On the contrary, we find the perpetual strife of diverse conflicting forces. Scientific thought contradicts and suppresses mythical thought. Religion in its highest theoretical and ethical development is under the necessity of defending the purity of its own ideal against the extravagant fancies of myth or art. Thus the unity and harmony of human culture appear to be little more than a *pium desiderium*[6]—a pious fraud—which is constantly frustrated by the real course of events.

But here we must make a sharp distinction between a material and a formal point of view. Undoubtedly human culture is divided into various activities proceeding along different lines and pursuing different ends. If we content ourselves with contemplating the results of these activities—the creations of myth, religious rites or creeds, works of art, scientific theories—it seems impossible to reduce them to a common denominator. But a philosophic synthesis means something different. Here we seek not a unity of effects but a unity of action; not a unity of products but a unity of the *creative process*. If the term "humanity" means anything at all it means that, in spite of all the differences and oppositions existing among its various forms, these are, nevertheless, all working toward a common end. In the long run there must be found an outstanding feature, a universal character, in which they all agree and harmonize. If we can determine this character the divergent rays may be assembled and brought into a focus of thought. As has been pointed out, such an organization of the facts of human culture is already getting under way in the particular sciences—in linguistics, in the comparative study of myth and religion, in the history of art. All of these sciences are striving for certain principles, for definite "categories," by virtue of which to bring the phenomena of religion, of art, of language into a systematic order. Were it not for this previous synthesis effected by the sciences themselves philosophy would have no starting point. Philosophy cannot, on the other hand, stop here. It must seek to achieve an even greater condensation and centralization. In the boundless multiplicity and variety of mythical images, of religious dogmas, of linguistic forms, of works of art, philosophic thought reveals the unity of a general function by which all these creations are held together. Myth, religion, art, language, even science, are now looked upon as so many variations on a common theme—and it is the task of philosophy to make this theme audible and understandable.

* * *

---

6. Pious desire (Latin).

From Chapter VIII. Language

* * *

In order to find a clue of Ariadne to guide us through the complicated and baffling labyrinth of human speech we may proceed in a twofold manner. We may attempt to find a logical and systematic or a chronological and genetic order. In the second case we try to trace the individual idioms and the various linguistic types back to a former comparatively simple and amorphous stage. Attempts of this sort were often made by linguists of the nineteenth century when the opinion became current that human speech, before it could attain its present form, had had to pass through a state in which there were no definite syntactical or morphological forms. Languages at first consisted of simple elements, of monosyllabic roots. Romanticism favored this view. * * * We know of no language devoid of formal or structural elements, [however,] although the expression of formal relations, such as the difference between subject and object, between attribute and predicate, varies widely from language to language. Without form language has the appearance of being not merely a highly questionable historical construct but a contradiction in terms. The languages of the most uncivilized nations are by no means formless; on the contrary they exhibit in most cases a very complicated structure. * * * All forms of human speech are perfect in so far as they succeed in expressing human feelings and thoughts in a clear and appropriate manner. The so-called primitive languages are as much in congruity with the conditions of primitive civilization and with the general tendency of the primitive mind as our own languages are with the ends of our refined and sophisticated culture. * * *

* * * In an analysis of human culture we must accept the facts in their concrete shape, in all their diversity and divergence. The philosophy of language is here confronted with the same dilemma as appears in the study of every symbolic form. The highest, indeed the only, task of all these forms is to unite men.[7] But none of them can bring about this unity without at the same time dividing and separating men. Thus what was intended to secure the harmony of culture becomes the source of the deepest discords and dissensions. This is the great antinomy, the dialectic of the religious life. The same dialectic appears in human speech. Without speech there would be no community of men. Yet there is no more serious obstacle to such community than the diversity of speech. Myth and religion refuse to regard this diversity as a necessary and unavoidable fact. They attribute it rather to a fault or guilt of man than to his original constitution and the nature of things. * * *

Yet the true unity of language, if there is such a unity, cannot be a substantial one; it must rather be defined as a functional unity. Such a unity does not presuppose a material or formal identity. Two different languages may represent opposite extremes both with respect to their phonetic systems and to their parts-of-speech systems. This does not prevent them from accomplishing the same task in the life of the speaking community. The important thing here is not the variety of means but their fitness for and congruity with the end.

* * *

7. This very important sentence (despite the lack of fanfare) sums up Cassirer's answer to the all-important question he poses at the end of the previous excerpt (and oddly poses again at the end of the book): What is the "common theme" or function of all types of symbolic forms that it is "the task of philosophy" to identify?

Chapter XII. Summary and Conclusion

If at the end of our long road we look back at our point of departure we may be uncertain whether we have attained our end. A philosophy of culture begins with the assumption that the world of human culture is not a mere aggregate of loose and detached facts. It seeks to understand these facts as a system, as an organic whole. For an empirical or historical view it would seem to be enough to collect the data of human culture. Here we are interested in the breadth of human life. We are engrossed in a study of the particular phenomena in their richness and variety; we enjoy the polychromy and the polyphony of man's nature. But a philosophical analysis sets itself a different task. Its starting point and its working hypothesis are embodied in the conviction that the varied and seemingly dispersed rays may be gathered together and brought into a common focus. The facts here are reduced to forms, and these forms themselves are supposed to possess an inner unity. But have we been able to prove this essential point? Did not all our individual analyses show us just the opposite? For we have had to stress all along the specific character and structure of the various symbolic forms—of myth, language, art, religion, history, science. Bearing in mind this aspect of our investigation we may perhaps feel inclined to favor the converse thesis, the thesis of the discontinuity and radical heterogeneity of human culture.

From a merely ontological or metaphysical point of view it would be very difficult indeed to refute this thesis. But for a critical philosophy the problem assumes another face. Here we are under no obligation to prove the substantial unity of man. Man is no longer considered as a simple substance which exists in itself and is to be known by itself. His unity is conceived as a functional unity. Such a unity does not presuppose a homogeneity of the various elements of which it consists. Not merely does it admit of, it even requires, a multiplicity and multiformity of its constituent parts. For this is a dialectic unity, a coexistence of contraries.

"Men do not understand," said Heraclitus, "how that which is torn in different directions comes into accord with itself—harmony in contrariety, as in the case of the bow and the lyre."[8] In order to demonstrate such a harmony we need not prove the identity or similarity of the different forces by which it is produced. The various forms of human culture are not held together by an identity in their nature but by a conformity in their fundamental task. If there is an equipoise in human culture it can only be described as a dynamic, not as a static equilibrium; it is the result of a struggle between opposing forces. This struggle does not exclude that "hidden harmony" which, according to Heraclitus, "is better than that which is obvious."[9]

Aristotle's definition of man as a "social animal"[1] is not sufficiently comprehensive. It gives us a generic concept but not the specific difference. Sociability as such is not an exclusive characteristic of man, nor is it the privilege of man alone. In the so-called animal states, among bees and ants, we find a

---

8. Heraclitus, Fragment 51, in Diels, *Die Fragmente der Vorsokratiker* [*The Fragments of the Pre-Socratics*] (5th ed.). English trans. by Charles M. Bakewell, *Source Book in Ancient Philosophy* (New York: Charles Scribner's Sons, 1907), p. 81 [Cassirer's note]. Heraclitus (active ca. 500 B.C.E.), pre-

Socratic Greek philosopher who famously declared that all things are in flux.
9. Heraclitus, Fragment 54, in Bakewell, op. cit., p. 81 [Cassirer's note].
1. Literally, in Aristotle, a "political animal" (a member of a city-state, or *polis*): *Politics* 1.1253a.

clear-cut division of labor and a surprisingly complicated social organization. But in the case of man we find not only, as among animals, a society of action but also a society of thought and feeling. Language, myth, art, religion, science are the elements and the constitutive conditions of this higher form of society. They are the means by which the forms of social life that we find in organic nature develop into a new state, that of social consciousness. Man's social consciousness depends upon a double act, of identification and discrimination. Man cannot find himself, he cannot become aware of his individuality, save through the medium of social life. But to him this medium signifies more than an external determining force. Man, like the animals, submits to the rules of society but, in addition, he has an active share in bringing about, and an active power to change, the forms of social life. In the rudimentary stages of human society such activity is still scarcely perceptible; it appears to be at a minimum. But the farther we proceed the more explicit and significant this feature becomes. This slow development can be traced in almost all forms of human culture.

It is a well-known fact that many actions performed in animal societies are not only equal but in some respects superior to the works of man. It has often been pointed out that bees in the construction of their cells act like a perfect geometer, achieving the highest precision and accuracy. Such activity requires a very complex system of coördination and collaboration. But in all these animal performances we find no individual differentiation. They are all produced in the same way and according to the same invariable rules. No latitude remains for individual choice or ability. It is only when we arrive at the higher stages of animal life that we meet the first traces of a certain individualization. Wolfgang Koehler's observations of anthropoid apes seem to prove that there are many differences in the intelligence and skill of these animals. One of them may be able to solve a task which for another remains insoluble. And here we may even speak of individual "inventions." For the general structure of animal life, however, all this is irrelevant. This structure is determined by the general biological law according to which acquired characters are not capable of hereditary transmission. Every perfection that an organism can gain in the course of its individual life is confined to its own existence and does not influence the life of the species. Even man is no exception to this general biological rule. But man has discovered a new way to stabilize and propagate his works. He cannot live his life without expressing his life. The various modes of this expression constitute a new sphere. They have a life of their own, a sort of eternity by which they survive man's individual and ephemeral existence. In all human activities we find a fundamental polarity, which may be described in various ways. We may speak of a tension between stabilization and evolution, between a tendency that leads to fixed and stable forms of life and another tendency to break up this rigid scheme. Man is torn between these two tendencies, one of which seeks to preserve old forms whereas the other strives to produce new ones. There is a ceaseless struggle between tradition and innovation, between reproductive and creative forces. This dualism is to be found in all the domains of cultural life. What varies is the proportion of the opposing factors. Now the one factor, now the other, seems to preponderate. This preponderance to a high degree determines the character of the single forms and gives to each of them its particular physiognomy.

In myth and in primitive religion the tendency to stabilization is so strong that it entirely outweighs the opposite pole. These two cultural phenomena seem to be the most conservative powers in human life. Mythical thought is, by its origin and by its principle, traditional thought. For myth has no means of understanding, explaining, and interpreting the present form of human life other than to reduce it to a remote past. What has its roots in this mythical past, what has been ever since, what has existed from immemorial times, is firm and unquestionable. To call it into question would be a sacrilege. For the primitive mind there is no more sacred thing than the sacredness of age. It is age that gives to all things, to physical objects and to human institutions, their value, their dignity, their moral and religious worth. In order to maintain this dignity it becomes imperative to continue and to preserve the human order in the same unalterable shape. Any breach of continuity would destroy the very substance of mythical and religious life. From the point of view of primitive thought the slightest alteration in the established scheme of things is disastrous. The words of a magic formula, of a spell or incantation, the single phases of a religious act, of a sacrifice or a prayer, all this must be repeated in one and the same invariable order. Any change would annihilate the force and efficiency of the magical word or religious rite. Primitive religion can therefore leave no room for any freedom of individual thought. It prescribes its fixed, rigid, inviolable rules not only for every human action but also for every human feeling. The life of man is under a constant pressure. It is enclosed in the narrow circle of positive and negative demands, of consecrations and prohibitions, of observances and taboos. Nevertheless the history of religion shows us that this first form of religious thought by no means expresses its real meaning and its end. Here too we find a continuous advance in the opposite direction. The ban under which human life was put by primitive mythical and religious thought is gradually relaxed, and at last it seems to have lost its binding force. There arises a new dynamic form of religion that opens a fresh perspective of moral and religious life. In such a dynamic religion the individual powers have won the preponderance over the mere powers of stabilization. Religious life has reached its maturity and its freedom; it has broken the spell of a rigid traditionalism.

If from the field of mythical and religious thought we pass to language we find here, in a different shape, the same fundamental process. Even language is one of the firmest conservative powers in human culture. Without this conservatism it could not fulfil its principal task, communication. Communication requires strict rules. Linguistic symbols and forms must have a stability and constancy in order to resist the dissolving and destructive influence of time. Nevertheless phonetic change and semantic change are not only accidental features in the development of language. They are inherent and necessary conditions of this development. One of the principal reasons for this continual change is the fact that language has to be transmitted from one generation to another. This transmission is not possible by mere reproduction of fixed and stable forms. The process of the acquisition of language always involves an active and productive attitude. Even the child's mistakes are very characteristic in this respect. Far from being mere failures that arise from an insufficient power of memory or reproduction, they are the best proofs of activity and spontaneity on the part of the child. In a comparatively early stage of its development the child seems to have gained a certain feeling of the general structure of its mother tongue without, of course, possessing any abstract consciousness of linguistic rules. It uses words or sentences that it never has heard and that are infractions of the morphologic or syntactic rules. But it is in these very attempts that the child's keen sense for analogies appears. In these he proves his ability to grasp the form of language instead of merely reproducing its matter. The transference of a language from one generation to another is, therefore, never to be compared to a simple transfer of property by which a material thing, without altering its nature, only changes possession. In his *Prinzipien der Sprachgeschichte* Hermann Paul laid special stress upon this point. He showed by concrete examples that the historical evolution of a language depends to a large degree on those slow and continual changes that take place in the transference of words and linguistic forms from parents to children. According to Paul this process is to be regarded as one of the principal reasons for the phenomena of sound shift and semantic change.[2] In all this we feel very distinctly the presence of two different tendencies—the one leading to the conservation, the other to the renovation and rejuvenation of language. We can, however, scarcely speak of an opposition between these two tendencies. They are in perfect equipoise; they are the two indispensable elements and conditions of the life of language.

A new aspect of the same problem is given us in the development of art. Here, however, the second factor—the factor of originality, individuality, creativeness—seems definitely to prevail over the first. In art we are not content with the repetition or reproduction of traditional forms. We sense a new obligation; we introduce new critical standards. "Mediocribus esse poetis non di, non homines, non concessere columnae," says Horace[3] in his *Ars Poetica* ("Mediocrity of poets is not allowed, either by the gods, or men, or the pillars which sustain the booksellers' shops"). To be sure even here tradition still plays a paramount role. As in the case of language the same forms are transmitted from one generation to another. The same fundamental motives of art recur over and over again. Nevertheless every great artist in a certain sense makes a new epoch. We become aware of this fact when comparing our ordinary forms of speech with poetical language. No poet can create an entirely new language. He has to adopt the words and he has to respect the fundamental rules of his language. To all this, however, the poet gives not only a new turn but also a new life. In poetry the words are not only significant in an abstract way; they are no mere pointers by which we wish to designate certain empirical objects. Here we meet with a sort of metamorphosis of all our common words. Every verse of Shakespeare, every stanza of Dante or Ariosto, every lyrical poem of Goethe[4] has its peculiar sound. Lessing said that it is just as impossible to steal a verse of Shakespeare as to steal the club of Hercules.[5]

---

2. H. Paul, *Prinzipien der Sprachgeschichte* [*Principles of the History of Language*] (4th ed. 1909), p. 63 [Cassirer's note]. Paul (1846–1921), German linguist and lexicographer.
3. Roman poet (65–8 B.C.E.); he wrote his *Art of Poetry* around 10 B.C.E. (the slightly misquoted lines are 372–73).
4. All supreme masters of their respective languages: English for William Shakespeare (1564–

1616), Italian for Dante Alighieri (1265–1321) and Ludovico Ariosto (1474–1533), and German for Johann Wolfgang von Goethe (1749–1832).
5. See *Hamburgische Dramaturgie* (1767–69, *Hamburg Dramaturgy*; translated as *Dramatic Notes*), no. 73, by the German dramatist and philosopher Gotthold Lessing (1729–1781). Hercules, the greatest hero of classical mythology, was frequently portrayed with his club.

And what is even more astounding is the fact that a great poet never repeats himself. Shakespeare spoke a language that had never been heard before—and every Shakespearean character speaks his own incomparable and unmistakable language. In Lear and Macbeth, in Brutus or Hamlet, in Rosalind or Beatrice we hear this personal language which is the mirror of an individual soul. In this manner alone poetry is able to express all those innumerable nuances, those delicate shades of feeling, that are impossible in other modes of expression. If language in its development is in need of constant renovation there is no better and deeper source for this than poetry. Great poetry always makes a sharp incision, a definite caesura, in the history of language. The Italian language, the English language, the German language were not the same at the death of Dante, of Shakespeare, of Goethe as they had been at the day of their birth.

In our aesthetic theories the difference between the conservative and the productive powers on which the work of art depends was always felt and expressed. At all times there has been a tension and conflict between the theories of imitation and inspiration. The first declares that the work of art has to be judged according to fixed and constant rules or according to classical models. The second rejects all standards or canons of beauty. Beauty is unique and incomparable, it is the work of the genius. It was this conception which, after a long struggle against theories of classicism and neoclassicism, became prevalent in the eighteenth century and which paved the way for our modern aesthetic. "*Genius*," says Kant in his *Critique of Judgment*, "is the innate mental disposition (*ingenium*) *through which* Nature gives the rule to Art." It is "a *talent* for producing that for which no definite rule can be given; it is not a mere aptitude for what can be learnt by a rule. Hence *originality* must be its first property." This form of originality is the prerogative and distinction of art; it cannot be extended to other fields of human activity. "Nature by the medium of genius does not prescribe rules to Science, but to Art; and to it only in so far as it is to be beautiful Art." We may speak of Newton[6] as a scientific genius; but in this case we speak only metaphorically. "Thus we can readily learn all that *Newton* has set forth in his immortal work on the Principles of Natural Philosophy, however great a head was required to discover it; but we cannot learn to write spirited poetry, however express may be the precepts of the art and however excellent its models."[7]

The relation between subjectivity and objectivity, individuality and universality, is indeed not the same in the work of art as it is in the work of the scientist.[8] It is true that a great scientific discovery also bears the stamp of the individual mind of its author. In it we find not merely a new objective aspect of things but also an individual attitude of mind and even a personal style. But all this has only a psychological, not a systematic relevance. In the objective content of science [*Wissenschaft*] these individual features are forgotten and effaced, for one of the principal aims of scientific thought is the elimination of all personal and anthropomorphic elements. In the words of

---

6. Isaac Newton (1643–1727), English mathematician and scientist; his *Mathematical Principles of Natural Philosophy* (1687) was hugely influential.
7. Kant, *Critique of Judgment* [1790], secs. 46, 47.

English trans. by J. H. Bernard (London: Macmillan, 1892), pp. 188–90 [Cassirer's note].
8. See p. 1441, n. 5, above.

Bacon, science strives to conceive the world *"ex analogia universi,"* not *"ex analogia hominis."*[9]

Human culture taken as a whole may be described as the process of man's progressive self-liberation.[1] Language, art, religion, science, are various phases in this process. In all of them man discovers and proves a new power—the power to build up a world of his own, an "ideal" world. Philosophy cannot give up its search for a fundamental unity in this ideal world. But it does not confound this unity with simplicity. It does not overlook the tensions and frictions, the strong contrasts and deep conflicts between the various powers of man. These cannot be reduced to a common denominator. They tend in different directions and obey different principles. But this multiplicity and disparateness does not denote discord or disharmony. All these functions complete and complement one another. Each one opens a new horizon and shows us a new aspect of humanity. The dissonant is in harmony with itself; the contraries are not mutually exclusive, but interdependent: "harmony in contrariety, as in the case of the bow and the lyre."

SOURCE: From Ernst Cassirer, *An Essay on Man: An Introduction to a Philosophy of Human Culture* (New Haven, Conn.: Yale University Press, 1944), pp. 21–27, 29–33, 35–36, 38–41, 63–64, 67–71, 128–30, 222–28.

9. Cf. Bacon, *Novum Organum* [1620], Liber I, Aphor. XLI [Cassirer's note]. Francis Bacon (1561–1626), English statesman and philosopher; his Latin translates as "'according to the analogy of the universe,' not 'according to the analogy of man.'"
1. That is, the progressive collective self-emancipation of human life from subjection to the merely natural and the laws that broadly govern it.

MICHEL FOUCAULT
(1926 – 1984)

Foucault is the only French philosopher of the twentieth century whose importance and impact rival SARTRE's. The influence of his thought is visible throughout the humanities, the social sciences, and many other disciplines, applied as well as interpretive. His historical studies of madness, medicine, incarceration, and sexuality brought to light many previously overlooked complexities and problematic aspects of modern institutions and power relations. Although often seen through the narrow lens of the antihumanist proclamation of "the death of man" (a seemingly odd notion that does have a point), Foucault's work is broad and rich, constantly evolving until his untimely death. His early works were focused on the social structures that have codified and systematized knowledge and language. It was not until the final decade or so of his life that he began to articulate an explicit theory of power, its constitutive and normalizing operations on and through bodies, and its linkage with truth.

One result of this analysis was a questioning of traditional liberal and leftist political approaches to political action, which tend to see power as merely repressive. Foucault, on the other hand, argued that power was constitutive; in his later writings, he seemed to suggest that it could even be constructive, by categorizing and proliferating desire into discourse and by creating both a myth of the repressed and an ethos of confessional truth. For Foucault, this deployment of discourse—through which the interiority of subjects and a desire to overcome repression by articulating that interior life are constructed—is not external to power (and therefore powerless) but rather is a significant way in which power may function. It is not surprising, therefore, that Foucault's work has had particular impact on areas of philosophy and other humanities and sciences concerned with social reform, political action, and ethics.

Michel Foucault ("Foo-KOH"), who happens to share a birthday with NIETZSCHE (October 15), was born in Poitiers. As the son of a doctor, he enjoyed a relatively privileged childhood; but the times were challenging for all, especially during the war and the German occupation of France. The young Foucault attended the public school in Poitiers until 1940, when he was enrolled at the Collège Saint-Stanislas, a nearby Catholic boarding school for boys. After graduating in 1943, he returned to Poitiers to prepare for admission to the École Normale Supérieure in Paris. Unable to pass the entrance examination in 1945, he enrolled for a year at the Lycée Henri-IV in Paris, where he studied with the HEGEL scholar Jean Hyppolite.

Foucault was finally admitted to the École Normale in 1946. There he became friends with the future Marxist philosopher Louis Althusser and took courses from MAURICE MERLEAU-PONTY. He earned a degree in philosophy in 1948, and another in psychology in 1949. In 1952 he obtained his *agrégation* certification, which qualified him to teach. He then spent the next year doing research at the Fondation Thiers, before taking his first teaching position at the University of Lille. In 1955 Foucault taught French and French literature at the University of Uppsala in Sweden, where he also became a cultural attaché— work that he continued in Warsaw (Poland) and Hamburg (Germany) in 1958 and 1959.

Foucault returned to France in 1960 with a French translation he had made of KANT's *Anthropology* (which undoubtedly influenced his thinking about philosophical conceptions of "man" and of "human nature") and a thousand-page

graduate thesis that earned him his doctorate and became his first book, *History
of Madness* (1961). He began teaching
psychology at the University of Clermont-
Ferrand and was awarded a permanent
appointment after obtaining his degree.
By 1965, however, he had become dissatisfied with this position; and after a summer in Brazil, he moved to Tunisia and
began teaching at the University of
Tunis. In 1968 he returned to France,
becoming professor of philosophy and
department head at the University at
Vincennes. In 1970 he finally settled
into an institutional home: he was
elected to succeed his former teacher
Jean Hyppolite at the prestigious Collège
de France, where he had no responsibilities other than to do his research and
annually present lectures on it.

In the years that followed Foucault
became increasingly involved in political activism. He co-founded the Prison
Information Group, which sought to
improve the treatment of prisoners, and
became engaged with a host of other
issues, including the Vietnam War, the
treatment of immigrants, and sexual politics. In 1978 he was nearly killed when a
car struck him as he crossed a street,
and the accident's effects lingered for
the rest of his life. Later that year he
traveled to Iran to report on the uprising
against the shah for an Italian newspaper. He lectured around the world, and
through the 1970s spent longer stints in
the United States, mainly on the East and
West Coasts and especially at Berkeley.
In 1983 he agreed to teach regularly
there; but in 1984 he developed AIDS,
and died that year in Paris.

Foucault's early works focused on the
psychiatric and medical practices that
were prevalent at the time (and remain
common models of treatment). As part
of the larger antipsychiatry movement,
and also as a critique of a scientific
humanism, he investigated both the
historical emergence and the contingencies of development of these institutions, exploring the eras when the
analytical codification and institutionalization of persons was not yet in place.

These works leave the reader with questions concerning the humaneness of
our seeming enlightened and benevolent
modern institutions and our ways of
dealing with their populations. They
convey a sense that modern practices
are dehumanizing—although such a
judgment would seem to presuppose
the idea (famously repudiated by Foucault) of some sort of true human
nature that is being violated, alienated,
or repressed. While certainly critical of
liberal humanist theories of the self and
the social practices predicated on that
idea, these early works do not articulate
an alternative post-, non-, or antihumanist conception of human reality that is
sufficient to the task at hand (or to
appropriately framing the task at hand).
Structuralism simply lacked the philosophical resources suited to Foucault's
needs.

One important step along Foucault's
way was taken in the first of the following selections, from *The Order of Things*
(1966). Here he analyzes three (Europe-
centered) historical epochs through
their *"epistemes"*—that is, their structuring conceptual frameworks and epistemological assumptions—which he
considers to be radically incommensurable. He examines the Renaissance
(roughly the sixteenth century), the
period of what he calls classical thought
(the seventeenth and eighteenth centuries), and the modern period (beginning
at the end of the eighteenth century).
During the Renaissance, knowledge and
language were interwoven in a system of
resemblances and correspondences to
reality. Foucault identifies this model of
thought as the proliferation or play of
"simulacra." The Renaissance lacked
the idea of analysis or penetration to the
inner nature or heart of things. That
idea came to characterize the period of
classical thought, in which a notion of
mathematical reason and a use of language for taxonomy and classification
became dominant. Foucault, particularly in his early works, made much of
this use of language and its role in constituting knowledge and truth. In the

classical *episteme*, on his account, language was conceived as the transparent means of arriving at truth. The "subject" was a thorn in the side of the classical *episteme*, because it eludes representation.

This "subject," on Foucault's analysis, became the object that has been the central focus and organizing idea of the modern *episteme* (now already losing its sway). Characterized by the conception and study of "man," the modern period became an epoch of anthropological sciences. The focus of the modern *episteme* is the anthropological trinity of *life*, *labor*, and *language*—three notions that are treated as transcendental structures of reality and representation, thereby exposing the limits of representation in the classical *episteme*. Foucault's basic target in the modern period is clearly Kant, whose *Anthropology* (1798) was the first work on "man" (*der Mensch*) and "human nature" by a major modern philosopher to bear such a title, and who instantiated a kind of thinking that he considers to have extended through German Idealism well into the twentieth century.

This period features an "analytic of finitude" that construes the nature of man (often in terminological disguises) in terms of certain dualities. So man is seen as both an empirical and a transcendental being; as both an apodictic *cogito* (a conscious subject capable of certain knowledge) and an unknown unconscious agency; and as the transcendence of his origin and also as impelled by a longing to return to or recover it. These dualities, Foucault contends, are fracturing, and it is with this breakdown of the modern *episteme* and its central idea of "man" in mind that he famously proclaims "the death of man" (which might better have been written as "the death of 'man'"). He envisions a liberation of the power of discourse from anthropological analysis, invoking the Nietzschean themes of the "*Übermensch*," "the death of God," and the "eternal return of the same" as heralding the demise of the anthropological *episteme*.

After *The Order of Things*, Foucault produced his most abstract philosophical work, *The Archaeology of Knowledge* (1969), which is devoted to an analysis of the notion of discourse. Discourse and what Foucault calls "statements" must not be thought of simply as everyday language use, speech acts, or language in general. He is specifically concerned here with language that has been invested with power or institutional justification, and with the radical shifts or ruptures that fracture it. At this point his method was that of (attempted) pure description; but it sufficed for him to formulate an antihumanist position in which "the subject" disappears into the fields and folds of discourse. It also was during this transitional period, in the wake of the student-led revolt of May 1968 that nearly brought down the French government, that Foucault's philosophy became more overtly political.

The second of the following selections is from the 1970 lecture "The Discourse of Language," which represents an important development in Foucault's thought. His thinking at this point was clearly turning away from structuralism. In its place he proposes a quasi-Nietzschean kind of analysis that is to be called "genealogy." Here Foucault analyzes "the will to truth" and "the will to knowledge" in terms of institutional power relations that drive and direct discourse. He appropriates the Nietzschean ideas of a breakdown of "the will to truth" through its own activity, its turn upon itself, and its own investment with desire and power. The external, institutional forces that control discourse are seen as being in league with internal practices of control—assumptions about authorship, the production of textual analysis, and the division of knowledge into disciplines. Foucault further contends that involvement in discursive communities significantly affects language and knowledge.

Thus the remnants of the formalism of structuralism give way to a Nietzsche-inspired materialism that locates discourse in "practices" and "bodies." It is the materiality of language and discourse that explains its deep connection to power and desire. This is often overlooked, Foucault suggests, because we see the subject as the autonomous ground of discourse, which he argues is displaced (hence his "antihumanism," or hostility to the reality and central significance of the idea of "the subject" in the interpretation of human reality). His genealogical method contains an element that was at best inchoate in his earlier historical analyses—namely, the means of making critical or deconstructive moves. Rather than simply mapping historical knowledge systems, Foucault now undertakes to disrupt their divisions, dichotomies, and hierarchies. This methodological shift (which may or may not be consistent with his earlier positions) quite obviously reflects a more explicitly critical stance with respect to all matters metaphysical and anything suggestive of essentialism, in what he conceives to be a Nietzschean mode of metaphysical skepticism and intellectual playfulness. But he continues to attach little significance to the question of how to label his emerging and highly individual approach to philosophy, loosely (and playfully) calling it both structuralist and positivist.

The third selection below comes from the second lecture of a series that Foucault delivered in 1976 at the Collège de France (recently translated as "Society Must Be Defended," 2003). These lectures followed on the heels of one of his best-known books, *Discipline and Punish* (1975), in which he first articulated his theory of biopower (or micro-power). More than simply an impressive analysis of prisons, that book further examines how disciplinary technologies are deployed throughout social space—for example, in the organization of schools, factories, and towns. Foucault sees this spatial and material organization of the world as going beyond facilitating the objective of "repression" or making people (bodies) docile or normalized. He proposes as its paradigmatic expression the Panopticon, a prison designed to allow complete surveillance of all inmates by a single guard. As such it is the optimal model of power. The constituting gaze of power aims at bringing to light or articulating all things—a process that at the same time employs the disciplinary technologies institutionalized within in society. This model raises the question of whether the controlling power can be escaped or resisted at all. One of the most interesting and important questions about Foucault's thought is whether he ever came to conceive of that as a real possibility.

The third selection offers a remarkable analysis of war, racism, and biopower. This examination of power rejects a traditional liberal model of sovereign state power and individuals with sovereign rights within it. In such a model, law and legislation are the primary manifestations of power. Foucault admits that to some extent his own model had been that of struggle and repression, as the play of multiple forces at the local level gives rise to reified juridical structures of rights, law, the state, and the subject. To keep us from simplifying its nature, he proposes a variety of methodological restrictions and barriers to traditional assumptions about power. Dismissing both Marxist and psychoanalytic conceptions of the working of power, he argues that what is left to us is careful scrutiny of the materialization of power in bodies and the material world.

This period of Foucault's work thus is marked by an important methodological shift. His strategy of "genealogy," analyzing institutions and power in the light of the "knowledges" and localized discourses associated with them that resist generalization, now supplants the earlier historical, epistemic analysis ("archaeology") that was concerned with instances in which discourse and knowledge break down. The attempt to introduce multiplicity and difference into knowledge, which is the core of Foucauldian genealogy, is also well paired with the ethical and political direction of Foucault's later thought.

The first volume of *The History of*

Sexuality, his last major work, is similar in theme and historical focus to the meditations on biopower just discussed. The second and third volumes, which were rushed into publication in the final year of his life, are quite different. They proceed by way of a reflection on sexual practices and discourses in ancient Greece and Rome to suggest the possibility of a kind of ethics conceived as "care for the self," and so center on the self's relation to itself. Here the notion of a style of existence—a notion found in both Nietzsche and Merleau-Ponty—now dominates Foucault's thinking on ethics. This quasi-aesthetic notion of style and self-cultivation may seem disappointingly familiar, with its obvious kinship with the tradition of perfectionist thought in the history of ethics and with existentialist concerns with authenticity. However, it is of considerable interest to see that and how such an aesthetic ethics (or ethical aesthetics) not only is not precluded by the kinds of attention to power relations that Foucault's earlier work exemplifies and advocates but also can actually be joined with them—as they turn out to be, in the end, in his thought. This connection between power-analysis and self-cultivation is evident in his late essay "What Is Enlightenment?," with which this volume concludes (as its "Epilogue," below).

From The Order of Things

From *Preface*

* * *

When we establish a considered classification, when we say that a cat and a dog resemble each other less than two greyhounds do, even if both are tame or embalmed, even if both are frenzied, even if both have just broken the water pitcher, what is the ground on which we are able to establish the validity of this classification with complete certainty? On what 'table', according to what grid of identities, similitudes, analogies, have we become accustomed to sort out so many different and similar things? What is this coherence—which, as is immediately apparent, is neither determined by an *a priori* and necessary concatenation, nor imposed on us by immediately perceptible contents? For it is not a question of linking consequences, but of grouping and isolating, of analysing, of matching and pigeon-holing concrete contents; there is nothing more tentative, nothing more empirical (superficially, at least) than the process of establishing an order among things; nothing that demands a sharper eye or a surer, better-articulated language; nothing that more insistently requires that one allow oneself to be carried along by the proliferation of qualities and forms. And yet an eye not consciously prepared might well group together certain similar figures and distinguish between others on the basis of such and such a difference: in fact, there is no similitude and no distinction, even for the wholly untrained perception, that is not the result of a precise operation and of the application of a preliminary criterion. A 'system of elements'—a definition of the segments by which the resemblances and differences can be shown, the types of variation by which those segments can be affected, and, lastly, the threshold above which there is a difference and below which there is a similitude—is indispensable for the establishment of even the simplest form of order. Order is, at one and the same time, that which is given in things as their inner law, the hidden network that determines the way they confront one another, and also that which has no existence except in the grid created by a glance, an examination, a language; and it is only in the blank spaces of this grid that order manifests itself in depth as though already there, waiting in silence for the moment of its expression.

The fundamental codes of a culture—those governing its language, its schemas of perception, its exchanges, its techniques, its values, the hierarchy of its practices—establish for every man, from the very first, the empirical orders with which he will be dealing and within which he will be at home. At the other extremity of thought, there are the scientific theories or the philosophical interpretations which explain why order exists in general, what universal law it obeys, what principle can account for it, and why this particular order has been established and not some other. But between these two regions, so distant from one another, lies a domain which, even though its role is mainly an intermediary one, is nonetheless fundamental: it is more confused, more obscure, and probably less easy to analyse. It is here that a culture, imperceptibly deviating from the empirical orders prescribed for it by its primary codes, instituting an initial separation from them, causes them to lose their original transparency, relinquishes its immediate and invisible powers, frees itself sufficiently to discover that these orders are perhaps not the only possible ones or the best ones; this culture then finds itself faced with the stark fact that there exists, below the level of its spontaneous orders, things that are in themselves capable of being ordered, that belong to a certain unspoken order; the fact, in short, that order *exists*. As though emancipating itself to some extent from its linguistic, perceptual, and practical grids, the culture superimposed on them another kind of grid which neutralized them, which by this superimposition both revealed and excluded them at the same time, so that the culture, by this very process, came face to face with order in its primary state. It is on the basis of this newly perceived order that the codes of language, perception, and practice are criticized and rendered partially invalid. It is on the basis of this order, taken as a firm foundation, that general theories as to the ordering of things, and the interpretation that such an ordering involves, will be constructed. Thus, between the already 'encoded' eye and reflexive knowledge there is a middle region which liberates order itself: it is here that it appears, according to the culture and the age in question, continuous and graduated or discontinuous and piecemeal, linked to space or constituted anew at each instant by the driving force of time, related to a series of variables or defined by separate systems of coherences, composed of resemblances which are either successive or corresponding, organized around increasing differences, etc. This middle region, then, in so far as it makes manifest the modes of being of order, can be posited as the most fundamental of all: anterior to words, perceptions, and gestures, which are then taken to be more or less exact, more or less happy, expressions of it (which is why this experience of order in its pure primary state always plays a critical role); more solid, more archaic, less dubious, always more 'true' than the theories that attempt to give those expressions explicit form, exhaustive application, or philosophical foundation. Thus, in every culture, between the use of what one might call the ordering codes and reflections upon order itself, there is the pure experience of order and of its modes of being.

The present study is an attempt to analyse that experience. I am concerned to show its developments, since the sixteenth century, in the mainstream of a culture such as ours: in what way, as one traces—against the current, as it were—language as it has been spoken, natural creatures as they have been perceived and grouped together, and exchanges as they have been practised; in what way, then, our culture has made manifest the existence of order, and how, to the modalities of that order, the exchanges owed their laws, the living beings their constants, the words their sequence and their representative value; what modalities of order have been recognized, posited, linked with space and time, in order to create the positive basis of knowledge as we find it employed in grammar and philology, in natural history and biology, in the study of wealth and political economy. Quite obviously, such an analysis does not belong to the history of ideas or of science: it is rather an inquiry whose aim is to rediscover on what basis knowledge and theory became possible; within what space of order knowledge was constituted; on the basis of what historical *a priori*, and in the element of what positivity, ideas could appear, sciences be established, experience be reflected in philosophies, rationalities be formed, only, perhaps, to dissolve and vanish soon afterwards. I am not concerned, therefore, to describe the progress of knowledge towards an objectivity in which today's science can finally be recognized; what I am attempting to bring to light is the epistemological field, the *episteme*[1] in which knowledge, envisaged apart from all criteria having reference to its rational value or to its objective forms, grounds its positivity and thereby manifests a history which is not that of its growing perfection, but rather that of its conditions of possibility; in this account, what should appear are those configurations within the *space* of knowledge which have given rise to the diverse forms of empirical science. Such an enterprise is not so much a history, in the traditional meaning of that word, as an 'archaeology.'

* * *

In this way, analysis has been able to show the coherence that existed, throughout the Classical age, between the theory of representation and the theories of language, of the natural orders, and of wealth and value. It is this configuration that, from the nineteenth century onward, changes entirely; the theory of representation disappears as the universal foundation of all possible orders; language as the spontaneous *tabula*,[2] the primary grid of things, as an indispensable link between representation and things, is eclipsed in its turn; a profound historicity penetrates into the heart of things, isolates and defines them in their own coherence, imposes upon them the forms of order implied by the continuity of time; the analysis of exchange and money gives way to the study of production, that of the organism takes precedence over the search for taxonomic characteristics, and, above all, language loses its privileged position and becomes, in its turn, a historical form coherent with the density of its own past. But as things become increasingly reflexive, seeking the principle of their intelligibility only in their own development, and abandoning the space of representation, man enters in his turn,[3] and for the first

---

1. A technical term in Foucault: an epoch's conceptual framework, or its unconscious structures that organize knowledge (*epistēmē* means "knowledge" in Greek).

2. Writing tablet (Latin).
3. The idea of "man" (conceived as the type of being we are) is Foucault's culminating topic in this book (on which the remainder of this selection focuses).

time, the field of Western knowledge. Strangely enough, man—the study of whom is supposed by the naïve to be the oldest investigation since Socrates[4]—is probably no more than a kind of rift in the order of things, or, in any case, a configuration whose outlines are determined by the new position he has so recently taken up in the field of knowledge. Whence all the chimeras of the new humanisms, all the facile solutions of an 'anthropology' understood as a universal reflection on man, half-empirical, half-philosophical. It is comforting, however, and a source of profound relief to think that man is only a recent invention, a figure not yet two centuries old, a new wrinkle in our knowledge, and that he will disappear again as soon as that knowledge has discovered a new form.

* * *

From *Chapter 9. Man and His Doubles*

* * *

VIII. The Anthropological Sleep

Anthropology as an analytic of man has certainly played a constituent role in modern thought, since to a large extent we are still not free from it. It became necessary at the moment when representation lost the power to determine, on its own and in a single movement, the interplay of its syntheses and analyses. It was necessary for empirical syntheses to be performed elsewhere than within the sovereignty of the 'I think'.[5] They had to be required at precisely the point at which that sovereignty reached its limit, that is, in man's finitude—a finitude that is as much that of consciousness as that of the living, speaking, labouring individual. This had already been formulated by Kant in his *Logic*, when to his traditional trilogy of questions he added an ultimate one: the three critical questions (What can I know? What must I do? What am I permitted to hope?) then found themselves referred to a fourth, and inscribed, as it were, 'to its account': *Was ist der Mensch?*[6]

This question, as we have seen, runs through thought from the early nineteenth century: this is because it produces, surreptitiously and in advance, the confusion of the empirical and the transcendental, even though Kant had demonstrated the division between them. By means of this question, a form of reflection was constituted which is mixed in its levels and characteristic of modern philosophy. The concern it has for man, which it lays claim to not only in its discourse but in its pathos, the care with which it attempts to define him as a living being, an individual at work, or a speaking subject, herald the long-awaited return of a human reign only to the high-minded few; in fact, it concerns, rather more prosaically and less morally, an empirico-critical reduplication by means of which an attempt is made to make the man of nature, of exchange, or of discourse,[7] serve as the foundation of his own finitude. In

4. Greek philosopher (469–399 B.C.E.); his professed aim was to urge men to care about the perfection of their souls (Plato, *Apology* 30b).
5. The *cogito* (Latin), which was the starting point of the French philosopher René Descartes (1596–1650), and thus the starting point of modern philosophy.
6. Kant, *Logik* [1800] (*Werke*, ed. Cassirer, vol. VIII, p. 343) [Foucault's note]. The German means

"What is man?" This edition's volume of Kant's *Works* was published in 1923.
7. That is, man conceived in biological terms, or as an economic agent, or as a language user. These correspond to the three "disciplines in search of an object" that had emerged in the 19th century and that Foucault had analyzed earlier in the book.

this Fold,[8] the transcendental function is doubled over so that it covers with its dominating network the inert, grey space of empiricity; inversely, empirical contents are given life, gradually pull themselves upright, and are immediately subsumed in a discourse which carries their transcendental presumption into the distance. And so we find philosophy falling asleep once more in the hollow of this Fold; this time not the sleep of Dogmatism,[9] but that of Anthropology. All empirical knowledge, provided it concerns man, can serve as a possible philosophical field in which the foundation of knowledge, the definition of its limits, and, in the end, the truth of all truth must be discoverable. The anthropological configuration of modern philosophy consists in doubling over dogmatism, in dividing it into two different levels each lending support to and limiting the other: the pre-critical analysis of what man is in his essence becomes the analytic of everything that can, in general, be presented to man's experience.

In order to awaken thought from such a sleep—so deep that thought experiences it paradoxically as vigilance, so wholly does it confuse the circularity of a dogmatism folded over upon itself in order to find a basis for itself within itself with the agility and anxiety of a radically philosophical thought—in order to recall it to the possibilities of its earliest dawning, there is no other way than to destroy the anthropological 'quadrilateral'[1] in its very foundations. We know, in any case, that all efforts to think afresh are in fact directed at that obstacle: whether it is a matter of crossing the anthropological field, tearing ourselves free from it with the help of what it expresses, and rediscovering a purified ontology or a radical thought of being; or whether, rejecting not only psychologism and historicism, but all concrete forms of the anthropological prejudice, we attempt to question afresh the limits of thought, and to renew contact in this way with the project for a general critique of reason. Perhaps we should see the first attempt at this uprooting of Anthropology—to which, no doubt, contemporary thought is dedicated—in the Nietzschean experience: by means of a philological critique, by means of a certain form of biologism, Nietzsche rediscovered the point at which man and God belong to one another, at which the death of the second is synonymous with the disappearance of the first, and at which the promise of the superman signifies first and foremost the imminence of the death of man.[2] In this, Nietzsche, offering this future to us as both promise and task, marks the threshold beyond which contemporary philosophy can begin thinking again; and he will no doubt continue for a long while to dominate its advance. If the discovery of the Return is indeed the end of philosophy, then the end of man, for its part, is the return of the beginning of philosophy. It is no longer possible to think in our day other than in the void left by man's disappearance. For this void does not create a

---

8. A term explained in the remainder of this paragraph (especially the last sentence).
9. An allusion to Kant, who had famously remarked in his introduction to *Prolegomena to Any Future Metaphysics* (1783) that the empiricist David Hume (1711–1776) had awakened him from his dogmatic slumbers (an uncritical acceptance of what he came to see as a deeply problematic way of thinking).
1. Originally a Roman four-sided fortification (blockhouse or fort), subsequently a four-cornered

area with fortresses at each corner, long thought to be impregnable—here, the discipline of anthropology as "the science of man."
2. Foucault here suggests that just as (in his view) NIETZSCHE had maintained that we must come to terms with "the death of God," where God is a kind of absolute principle of meaning, truth, and value, so we must now also come to terms with "the death of 'man,'" understood as the foundation of any possible humanism or normatively significant philosophical anthropology.

deficiency; it does not constitute a lacuna that must be filled. It is nothing more, and nothing less, than the unfolding of a space in which it is once more possible to think.

Anthropology constitutes perhaps the fundamental arrangement that has governed and controlled the path of philosophical thought from Kant until our own day. This arrangement is essential, since it forms part of our history; but it is disintegrating before our eyes, since we are beginning to recognize and denounce in it, in a critical mode, both a forgetfulness of the opening that made it possible and a stubborn obstacle standing obstinately in the way of an imminent new form of thought. To all those who still wish to talk about man, about his reign or his liberation, to all those who still ask themselves questions about what man is in his essence, to all those who wish to take him as their starting-point in their attempts to reach the truth, to all those who, on the other hand, refer all knowledge back to the truths of man himself, to all those who refuse to formalize without anthropologizing, who refuse to mythologize without demystifying, who refuse to think without immediately thinking that it is man who is thinking, to all these warped and twisted forms of reflection we can answer only with a philosophical laugh—which means, to a certain extent, a silent one.

From *Chapter 10. The Human Sciences*[3]

FROM I. THE THREE FACES OF KNOWLEDGE

Man's mode of being as constituted in modern thought enables him to play two roles: he is at the same time at the foundation of all positivities and present, in a way that cannot even be termed privileged, in the element of empirical things. This fact—it is not a matter here of man's essence in general, but simply of that historical *a priori* which, since the nineteenth century, has served as an almost self-evident ground for our thought—this fact is no doubt decisive in the matter of the status to be accorded to the 'human sciences', to the body of knowledge (though even that word is perhaps a little too strong: let us say, to be more neutral still, to the body of discourse) that takes as its object man as an empirical entity.

The first thing to be observed is that the human sciences did not inherit a certain domain, already outlined, perhaps surveyed as a whole, but allowed to lie fallow, which it was then their task to elaborate with positive methods and with concepts that had at last become scientific; the eighteenth century did not hand down to them, in the name of man or human nature, a space, circumscribed on the outside but still empty, which it was then their role to cover and analyse. The epistemological field traversed by the human sciences was not laid down in advance: no philosophy, no political or moral option, no empirical science of any kind, no observation of the human body, no analysis of sensation, imagination, or the passions, had ever encountered, in the seventeenth or eighteenth century, anything like man; for man did not exist (any more than life, or language, or labour);[4] and the human sciences did not appear

---

3. It is crucial to Foucault's argument that after HEGEL, these disciplines (the *Geisteswissenschaften*) were reconceived in a more naturalistic way, as the *Wissenschaften* that deal with "man"
(*der Mensch*) and "human (*menschlich*) life."
4. That is, prior to the 19th century, there was nothing like a *science* of man.

when, as a result of some pressing rationalism, some unresolved scientific problem, some practical concern, it was decided to include man (willy-nilly, and with a greater or lesser degree of success) among the objects of science—among which it has perhaps not been proved even yet that it is absolutely possible to class him; they appeared when man constituted himself in Western culture as both that which must be conceived of and that which is to be known. There can be no doubt, certainly, that the historical emergence of each one of the human sciences was occasioned by a problem, a requirement, an obstacle of a theoretical or practical order: the new norms imposed by industrial society upon individuals were certainly necessary before psychology, slowly, in the course of the nineteenth century, could constitute itself as a science; and the threats that, since the French Revolution,[5] have weighed so heavily on the social balances, and even on the equilibrium established by the bourgeoisie, were no doubt also necessary before a reflection of the sociological type could appear. But though these references may well explain why it was in fact in such and such a determined set of circumstances and in answer to such and such a precise question that these sciences were articulated, nevertheless, their intrinsic possibility, the simple fact that man, whether in isolation or as a group, and for the first time since human beings have existed and have lived together in societies, should have become the object of science—that cannot be considered or treated as a phenomenon of opinion: it is an event in the order of knowledge.

* * *

FROM II.   THE FORM OF THE HUMAN SCIENCES

* * *

In fact, the human sciences are addressed to man in so far as he lives, speaks, and produces. It is as a living being that he grows, that he has functions and needs, that he sees opening up a space whose movable coordinates meet in him; in a general fashion, his corporeal existence interlaces him through and through with the rest of the living world; since he produces objects and tools, exchanges the things he needs, organizes a whole network of circulation along which what he is able to consume flows, and in which he himself is defined as an intermediary stage, he appears in his existence immediately interwoven with others; lastly, because he has a language, he can constitute a whole symbolic universe for himself, within which he has a relation to his past, to things, to other men, and on the basis of which he is able equally to build something like a body of knowledge (in particular, that knowledge of himself, of which the human sciences outline one of the possible forms). The site of the sciences of man may therefore be fixed in the vicinity, on the immediate frontiers, and along the whole length of those sciences that deal with life, labour, and language. Were they not formed, after all, at precisely that period when, for the first time, man offered himself to the possibility of a positive knowledge? Nevertheless, biology, economics, and philology must not be regarded as the first human sciences, or the most fundamental. This is easily

5. The revolt against the monarchy (1787–99), which initiated a new political order.

recognized in the case of biology, since it is addressed to many other living beings besides man; but it is more difficult to accept in the cases of economics and philology, which have as their particular and exclusive domain activities that are specific to man. But we do not ask ourselves why human biology or physiology, why the anatomy of the cortical centres of language, cannot in any way be considered as sciences of man. This is because the object of those sciences is never posited in the mode of being of a biological function (or even in that of its particular form, and, as it were, its extension into man); it is rather its reverse, or the hollow it would leave; it begins at the point, not where the action or the effects stop, but where that function's own being stops—at that point where representations are set free, true or false, clear or obscure, perfectly conscious or rooted in some deep sleep, observable directly or indirectly, presented within what man himself expresses, or discoverable only from the outside; research into the intracortical connections between the different centres of linguistic integration (auditive, visual, motor) is not the province of the human sciences; but those sciences will find their field of action as soon as we question that space of words, that presence or that forgetfulness of their meaning, that hiatus between what one wishes to say and the articulation in which that aim is invested, whose subject may not be conscious, but which would have no assignable mode of being if that subject did not have representations.

In a more general fashion, man for the human sciences is not that living being with a very particular form (a somewhat special physiology and an almost unique autonomy); he is that living being who, from within the life to which he entirely belongs and by which he is traversed in his whole being, constitutes representations by means of which he lives, and on the basis of which he possesses that strange capacity of being able to represent to himself precisely that life. Similarly, even though man is, if not the only species in the world that works, at least the one in whom the production, distribution, and consumption of goods have taken on so great an importance and acquired so many and such differentiated forms, economics is still not a human science. It may perhaps be objected that in order to define certain laws, even though they are interior to the mechanics of production (such as the accumulation of capital or the relations between wage rates and prices), economics has recourse to human behaviour patterns and a representation that provide its foundation (interest, the search for maximum profit, the tendency to accumulate savings); but, in doing so, it is utilizing representations as the requisite of a function (which occurs, in effect, within an explicitly human activity); on the other hand, there will be no science of man unless we examine the way in which individuals or groups represent to themselves the partners with whom they produce or exchange, the mode in which they clarify or ignore or mask this function and the position they occupy in it, the manner in which they represent to themselves the society in which it takes place, the way in which they feel themselves integrated with it or isolated from it, dependent, subject, or free; the object of the human sciences is not that man who, since the dawn of the world, or the first cry of his golden age, is doomed to work; it is that being who, from within the forms of production by which his whole existence is governed, forms the representation of those needs, of the society by which, with which, or against which he satisfies them, so that upon that basis he can finally provide himself with a representation of economics itself.

The same is true of language: although man is the only being in the world who speaks, inquiry into phonetic mutations, relationships between languages, and semantic shifts, does not constitute a human science; on the other hand, it will be possible to speak of human science when an attempt is made to define the way in which individuals or groups represent words to themselves, utilize their forms and their meanings, compose real discourse, reveal and conceal in it what they are thinking or saying, perhaps unknown to themselves, more or less than they wish, but in any case leave a mass of verbal traces of those thoughts, which must be deciphered and restored as far as possible to their representative vivacity. The object of the human sciences is not language (though it is spoken by men alone); it is that being which, from the interior of the language by which he is surrounded, represents to himself, by speaking, the sense of the words or propositions he utters, and finally provides himself with a representation of language itself.

The human sciences are not, then, an analysis of what man is by nature; but rather an analysis that extends from what man is in his positivity (living, speaking, labouring being) to what enables this same being to know (or seek to know) what life is, in what the essence of labour and its laws consist, and in what way he is able to speak. The human sciences thus occupy the distance that separates (though not without connecting them) biology, economics, and philology from that which gives them possibility in the very being of man. It would therefore be wrong to see the human sciences as an extension, interiorized within the human species, within its complex organism, within its behaviour and consciousness, of biological mechanisms; and it would be no less wrong to place within the human sciences the science of economics or the science of language (whose irreducibility to the human sciences is expressed in the effort to constitute a pure economics and a pure linguistics). In fact, the human sciences are no more within these sciences than they give them interiority by deflecting them towards man's subjectivity; if they take them up again in the dimension of representation, it is rather by re-apprehending them upon their outer slope, by leaving them their opacity, by accepting as things the mechanisms and functions they isolate, by questioning those functions and mechanisms not in terms of what they are but in terms of what they cease to be when the space of representation is opened up; and upon that basis they show how a representation of what they are can come into being and be deployed. Surreptitiously, they lead the sciences of life, labour, and language back to that analytic of finitude which shows how man, in his being, can be concerned with the things he knows, and know the things that, in positivity, determine his mode of being. But what the analytic requires in the inferiority, or at least in the profound kinship, of a being who owes his finitude only to himself, the human sciences develop in the exteriority of knowledge. This is why what characterizes the human sciences is not that they are directed at a certain content (that singular object, the human being); it is much more a purely formal characteristic: the simple fact that, in relation to the sciences in which the human being is given as object (exclusive in the case of economics and philology, or partial in that of biology), they are in a position of duplication, and that this duplication can serve *a fortiori* for themselves.

* * *

FROM III. THE THREE MODELS

* * *

* * * It is useless, then, to say that the 'human sciences' are false sciences; they are not sciences at all; the configuration that defines their positivity and gives them their roots in the modern *episteme* at the same time makes it impossible for them to be sciences; and if it is then asked why they assumed that title, it is sufficient to recall that it pertains to the archaeological definition of their roots that they summon and receive the transference of models borrowed from the sciences. It is therefore not man's irreducibility, what is designated as his invincible transcendence, nor even his excessively great complexity, that prevents him from becoming an object of science. Western culture has constituted, under the name of man, a being who, by one and the same interplay of reasons, must be a positive domain of *knowledge* and cannot be an object of *science*.

FROM IV. HISTORY

* * *

* * * Will the history of man ever be more than a sort of modulation common to changes in the conditions of life (climate, soil fertility, methods of agriculture, exploitation of wealth), to transformations in the economy (and consequently in society and its institutions), and to the succession of forms and usages in language? But, in that case, man is not himself historical: since time comes to him from somewhere other than himself, he constitutes himself as a subject of history only by the superimposition of the history of living beings, the history of things, and the history of words. He is subjected to the pure events those histories contain. But this relation of simple passivity is immediately reversed; for what speaks in language, what works and consumes in economics, what lives in human life, is man himself; and, this being so, he too has a right to a development quite as positive as that of beings and things, one no less autonomous—and perhaps even more fundamental: is it not a historicity proper to man, one inscribed in the very depths of his being, that enables him to adapt himself like any living being, and to evolve like any living being (though with the help of tools, techniques, and organizations belonging to no other living being), that enables him to invent forms of production, to stabilize, prolong, or abridge the validity of economic laws by means of the consciousness he attains of them and by means of the institutions he constructs upon or around them, and that enables him to exercise upon language, with every word he speaks, a sort of constant interior pressure which makes it shift imperceptibly upon itself at any given moment in time. Thus, behind the history of the positivities,[6] there appears another, more radical, history, that of man himself—a history that now concerns man's very being, since he now realizes that he not only 'has history' all around him, but is himself, in his own historicity, that by means of which a history of human life, a history of economics, and a history of languages are given their form. In which case,

---

6. That is, definite and concrete specificities and particularities of the sort that may be considered to determine the natures of other types of creature.

at a very deep level, there exists a historicity of man which is itself its own history but also the radical dispersion that provides a foundation for all other histories. It was just this primary erosion that the nineteenth century sought in its concern to historicize everything, to write a general history of everything, to go back ceaselessly through time, and to place the most stable of things in the liberating stream of time. Here again, we should no doubt revise the way in which we traditionally write the history of History; we are accustomed to saying that the nineteenth century brought an end to the pure chronicle of events, the simple memory of a past peopled only by individuals and accidents, and that it began the search for the general laws of development. In fact, no history was ever more 'explanatory', more preoccupied with general laws and constants, than were the histories of the Classical age—when the world and man were inextricably linked in a single history. What first comes to light in the nineteenth century is a simple form of human historicity—the fact that man as such is exposed to the event. Hence the concern either to find laws for this pure form (which gives us philosophies such as that of Spengler[7]) or to define it on the basis of the fact that man lives, works, speaks, and thinks: and this gives us interpretations of history from the standpoint of man envisaged as a living species, or from the standpoint of economic laws, or from that of cultural totalities.

In any case, this arrangement of history within the epistemological space is of great importance for its relation with the human sciences. Since historical man is living, working, and speaking man, any content of History is the province of psychology, sociology, or the sciences of language. But, inversely, since the human being has become historical, through and through, none of the contents analysed by the human sciences can remain stable in itself or escape the movement of History. And this for two reasons: because psychology, sociology, and philosophy, even when applied to objects—that is, men—which are contemporaneous with them, are never directed at anything other than synchronological patternings within a historicity that constitutes and traverses them; and because the forms successively taken by the human sciences, the choice of objects they make, and the methods they apply to them, are all provided by History, ceaselessly borne along by it, and modified at its pleasure. The more History attempts to transcend its own rootedness in historicity, and the greater the efforts it makes to attain, beyond the historical relativity of its origin and its choices, the sphere of universality, the more clearly it bears the marks of its historical birth, and the more evidently there appears through it the history of which it is itself a part (and this, again, is to be found in Spengler and all the philosophers of history); inversely, the more it accepts its relativity, and the more deeply it sinks into the movement it shares with what it is recounting, then the more it tends to the slenderness of the narrative, and all the positive content it obtained for itself through the human sciences is dissipated.

History constitutes, therefore, for the human sciences, a favourable environment which is both privileged and dangerous. To each of the sciences of man it offers a background, which establishes it and provides it with a fixed

---

7. Oswald Spengler (1880–1936), German philosopher; in *The Decline of the West* (1918–22), he argued that in their histories, civilizations pass through life cycles.

ground and, as it were, a homeland; it determines the cultural area—the chronological and geographical boundaries—in which that branch of knowledge can be recognized as having validity; but it also surrounds the sciences of man with a frontier that limits them and destroys, from the outset, their claim to validity within the element of universality. It reveals in this way that though man—even before knowing it—has always been subjected to the determinations that can be expressed by psychology, sociology, and the analysis of language, he is not therefore the intemporal[8] object of a knowledge which, at least at the level of its rights, must itself be thought of as ageless. Even when they avoid all reference to history, the human sciences (and history may be included among them) never do anything but relate one cultural episode to another (that to which they apply themselves as their object, and that in which their existence, their mode of being, their methods, and their concepts have their roots); and though they apply themselves to their own synchronology, they relate the cultural episode from which they emerged to itself. Man, therefore, never appears in his positivity and that positivity is not immediately limited by the limitlessness of History.

* * *

In modern thought, historicism and the analytic of finitude confront one another. Historicism is a means of validating for itself the perpetual critical relation at play between History and the human sciences. But it establishes it solely at the level of the positivities: the positive knowledge of man is limited by the historical positivity of the knowing subject, so that the moment of finitude is dissolved in the play of a relativity from which it cannot escape, and which itself has value as an absolute. To be finite, then, would simply be to be trapped in the laws of a perspective which, while allowing a certain apprehension—of the type of perception or understanding—prevents it from ever being universal and definitive intellection. All knowledge is rooted in a life, a society, and a language that have a history; and it is in that very history that knowledge finds the element enabling it to communicate with other forms of life, other types of society, other significations: that is why historicism always implies a certain philosophy, or at least a certain methodology, of living comprehension (in the element of the *Lebenswelt*[9]), and of interhuman communication (against a background of social structures), and of hermeneutics (as the re-apprehension through the manifest meaning of the discourse of another meaning at once secondary and primary, that is, more hidden but also more fundamental). By this means, the different positivities formed by History and laid down in it are able to enter into contact with one another, surround one another in the form of knowledge, and free the content dormant within them; it is not, then, the limits themselves that appear, in their absolute rigour, but partial totalities, totalities that turn out to be limited by fact, totalities whose frontiers can be made to move, up to a certain point, but which will never extend into the space of a definitive analysis, and will never raise themselves to the status of absolute totality.

* * *

8. Timeless.
9. Life-world (German), a central concept in HUSSERL's late philosophy.

FROM V. PSYCHOANALYSIS AND ETHNOLOGY

* * *

And yet the impression of fulfilment and of end, the muffled feeling that carries and animates our thought, and perhaps lulls it to sleep with the facility of its promises, and makes us believe that something new is about to begin, something we glimpse only as a thin line of light low on the horizon—that feeling and that impression are perhaps not ill founded. It will be said that they exist, that they have never ceased to be formulated over and over again since the early nineteenth century; it will be said that Hölderlin, Hegel, Feuerbach, and Marx[1] all felt this certainty that in them a thought and perhaps a culture were coming to a close, and that from the depths of a distance, which was perhaps not invincible, another was approaching—in the dim light of dawn, in the brilliance of noon, or in the dissension of the falling day. But this close, this perilous imminence whose promise we fear today, whose danger we welcome, is probably not of the same order. Then, the task enjoined upon thought by that annunciation was to establish for man a stable sojourn upon this earth from which the gods had turned away or vanished. In our day, and once again Nietzsche indicated the turning-point from a long way off, it is not so much the absence or the death of God that is affirmed as the end of man (that narrow, imperceptible displacement, that recession in the form of identity, which are the reason why man's finitude has become his end); it becomes apparent, then, that the death of God and the last man[2] are engaged in a contest with more than one round: is it not the last man who announces that he has killed God, thus situating his language, his thought, his laughter in the space of that already dead God, yet positing himself also as he who has killed God and whose existence includes the freedom and the decision of that murder? Thus, the last man is at the same time older and yet younger than the death of God; since he has killed God, it is he himself who must answer for his own finitude; but since it is in the death of God that he speaks, thinks, and exists, his murder itself is doomed to die; new gods, the same gods, are already swelling the future Ocean; man will disappear. Rather than the death of God—or, rather, in the wake of that death and in a profound correlation with it—what Nietzsche's thought heralds is the end of his murderer; it is the explosion of man's face in laughter, and the return of masks; it is the scattering of the profound stream of time by which he felt himself carried along and whose pressure he suspected in the very being of things; it is the identity of the Return of the Same with the absolute dispersion of man. Throughout the nineteenth century, the end of philosophy and the promise of an approaching culture were no doubt one and the same thing as the thought of finitude and the appearance of man in the field of knowledge; in our day, the fact that philosophy is still—and again—in the process of coming to an end, and the fact that in it perhaps, though even more outside and against it, in literature as well as in formal reflection, the question of language is being posed, prove no doubt that man is in the process of disappearing.

For the entire modern *episteme*—that which was formed towards the end

---

1. For MARX and FEUERBACH, see above. Friedrich Hölderin (1770–1843), German poet.
2. That is, the final form of degenerate humanity that Nietzsche envisions; this image and much else in this paragraph derive from Nietzsche's *Thus Spoke Zarathustra* (1883–85; excerpted above).

of the eighteenth century and still serves as the positive ground of our knowledge, that which constituted man's particular mode of being and the possibility of knowing him empirically—that entire *episteme* was bound up with the disappearance of Discourse and its featureless reign, with the shift of language towards objectivity, and with its reappearance in multiple form. If this same language is now emerging with greater and greater insistence in a unity that we ought to think but cannot as yet do so, is this not the sign that the whole of this configuration is now about to topple, and that man[3] is in the process of perishing as the being of language continues to shine ever brighter upon our horizon? Since man was constituted at a time when language was doomed to dispersion, will he not be dispersed when language regains its unity? And if that were true, would it not be an error—a profound error, since it could hide from us what should now be thought—to interpret our actual experience as an application of the forms of language to the human order? Ought we not rather to give up thinking of man, or, to be more strict, to think of this disappearance of man—and the ground of possibility of all the sciences of man—as closely as possible in correlation with our concern with language? Ought we not to admit that, since language is here once more, man will return to that serene non-existence in which he was formerly maintained by the imperious unity of Discourse? Man had been a figure occurring between two modes of language; or, rather, he was constituted only when language, having been situated within representation and, as it were, dissolved in it, freed itself from that situation at the cost of its own fragmentation: man composed his own figure in the interstices of that fragmented language. Of course, these are not affirmations; they are at most questions to which it is not possible to reply; they must be left in suspense, where they pose themselves, only with the knowledge that the possibility of posing them may well open the way to a future thought.

SOURCE: From Michel Foucault, *The Order of Things: An Archaeology of the Human Sciences*, trans. Alan Sheridan-Smith (New York: Pantheon Books, 1971), pp. xix–xxiii, 340–45, 351–54, 366–67, 369–73, 384–86. Originally published in 1966 as *Les Mots et les choses* [*Words and Things*]: *Une archéologie des sciences humaines*. According to the publisher's note, the English title was chosen to avoid confusion with two existing books titled *Words and Things*; but in fact, *The Order of Things* was Foucault's original preference.

Orders of Discourse

I would really like to have slipped imperceptibly into this lecture, as into all the others I shall be delivering, perhaps over the years ahead. I would have preferred to be enveloped in words, borne way beyond all possible beginnings. At the moment of speaking, I would like to have perceived a nameless voice, long preceding me, leaving me merely to enmesh myself in it, taking up its cadence, and to lodge myself, when no one was looking, in its interstices as if it had paused an instant, in suspense, to beckon to me. There would have been no beginnings: instead, speech would proceed from me, while I stood in its path—a slender gap—the point of its possible disappearance.

3. That is, the *concept of* "man" as a being with a certain sort of determinate general nature.

Behind me, I should like to have heard (having been at it long enough already, repeating in advance what I am about to tell you) the voice of Molloy, beginning to speak thus: "I must go on; I can't go on; I must go on; I must say words as long as there are words, I must say them until they find me, until they say me—heavy burden, heavy sin; I must go on; maybe it's been done already; maybe they've already said me; maybe they've already borne me to the threshold of my story, right to the door opening onto my story; I'd be surprised if it opened".[1]

A good many people, I imagine, harbour a similar desire to be freed from the obligation to begin, a similar desire to find themselves, right from the outside, on the other side of discourse, without having to stand outside it, pondering its particular, fearsome, and even devilish features. To this all too common feeling, institutions have an ironic reply, for they solemnise beginnings, surrounding them with a circle of silent attention; in order that they can be distinguished from far off, they impose ritual forms upon them.

Inclination speaks out: "I don't want to have to enter this risky world of discourse; I want nothing to do with it insofar as it is decisive and final; I would like to feel it all around me, calm and transparent, profound, infinitely open, with others responding to my expectations, and truths emerging, one by one. All I want is to allow myself to be borne along, within it, and by it, a happy wreck". Institutions reply: "But you have nothing to fear from launching out; we're here to show you discourse is within the established order of things, that we've waited a long time for its arrival, that a place has been set aside for it—a place which both honours and disarms it; and if it should happen to have a certain power, then it is we, and we alone, who give it that power".

Yet, maybe this institution and this inclination are but two converse responses to the same anxiety: anxiety as to just what discourse is, when it is manifested materially, as a written or spoken object; but also, uncertainty faced with a transitory existence, destined for oblivion—at any rate, not belonging to us; uncertainty at the suggestion of barely imaginable powers and dangers behind this activity, however humdrum and grey it may seem; uncertainty when we suspect the conflicts, triumphs, injuries, dominations and enslavements that lie behind these words, even when long use has chipped away their rough edges.

What is so perilous, then, in the fact people speak, and that their speech proliferates? Where is the danger in that?

Here then is the hypothesis I want to advance, tonight, in order to fix the terrain—or perhaps the very provisional theatre—within which I shall be working. I am supposing that in every society the production of discourse is at once controlled, selected, organised and redistributed according to a certain number of procedures, whose role is to avert its powers and its dangers, to cope with chance events, to evade its ponderous, awesome materiality.

In a society such as our own we all know the rules of *exclusion*. The most obvious and familiar of these concerns what is *prohibited*. We know perfectly well that we are not free to say just anything, that we cannot simply speak of anything, when we like or where we like; not just anyone, finally, may speak

---

1. Slightly misquoted from the end of Samuel Beckett's *L'Innommable* (1953, *The Unnamable*), the third volume of his Molloy trilogy (which famously concludes, "I'll go on").

of just anything. We have three types of prohibition, covering objects, ritual with its surrounding circumstances, the privileged or exclusive right to speak of a particular subject; these prohibitions interrelate, reinforce and complement each other, forming a complex web, continually subject to modification. I will note simply that the areas where this web is most tightly woven today, where the danger spots are most numerous, are those dealing with politics and sexuality. It is as though discussion, far from being a transparent, neutral element, allowing us to disarm sexuality and to pacify politics, were one of those privileged areas in which they exercised some of their more awesome powers. In appearance, speech may well be of little account, but the prohibitions surrounding it soon reveal its links with desire and power. This should not be very surprising, for psychoanalysis has already shown us that speech is not merely the medium which manifests—or dissembles—desire; it is also the object of desire. Similarly, historians have constantly impressed upon us that speech is no mere verbalisation of conflicts and systems of domination, but that it is the very object of man's conflicts.

But our society possesses yet another principle of exclusion; not another prohibition, but a division and a rejection. I have in mind the opposition: reason and folly.[2] From the depths of the Middle Ages, a man was mad if his speech could not be said to form part of the common discourse of men. His words were considered nul and void, without truth or significance, worthless as evidence, inadmissible in the authentification of acts or contracts, incapable even of bringing about transubstantiation—the transformation of bread into flesh— at Mass. And yet, in contrast to all others, his words were credited with strange powers, of revealing some hidden truth, of predicting the future, of revealing, in all their naivete, what the wise were unable to perceive. It is curious to note that for centuries, in Europe, the words of a madman were either totally ignored or else were taken as words of truth. They either fell into a void— rejected the moment they were proferred—or else men deciphered in them a naive or cunning reason, rationality more rational than that of a rational man. At all events, whether excluded or secretly invested with reason, the madman's speech did not strictly exist. It was through his words that one recognised the madness of the madman; but they were certainly the medium within which this division became active; they were neither heard nor remembered. No doctor before the end of the 18th century had ever thought of listening to the content—how it was said and why—of these words; and yet it was these which signalled the difference between reason and madness. Whatever a madman said, it was taken for mere noise; he was credited with words only in a symbolic sense, in the theatre, in which he stepped forward, unarmed and reconciled, playing his role: that of masked truth.

Of course people are going to say all that is over and done with, or that it is in the process of being finished with, today; that the madman's words are no longer on the other side of this division; that they are no longer nul and void, that, on the contrary, they alert us to the need to look for a sense behind them, for the attempt at, or the ruins of some "œuvre"; we have even come to notice these words of madmen in our own speech, in those tiny pauses when we forget what we are talking about. But all this is no proof that the old division is not just as active as before; we have only to think of the systems by

2. That is, madness, craziness.

which we decipher this speech; we have only to think of the network of institutions established to permit doctors and psychoanalists to listen to the mad and, at the same time, enabling the mad to come and speak, or, in desperation, to withhold their meagre words; we have only to bear all this in mind to suspect that the old division is just as active as ever, even if it is proceeding along different lines and, via new institutions, producing rather different effects. Even when the role of the doctor consists of lending an ear to this finally liberated speech, this procedure still takes place in the context of a hiatus between listener and speaker. For he is listening to speech invested with desire, crediting itself—for its greater exultation or for its greater anguish—with terrible powers. If we truly require silence to cure monsters, then it must be an attentive silence, and it is in this that the division lingers.

It is perhaps a little risky to speak of the opposition between true and false as a third system of exclusion, along with those I have mentioned already. How could one reasonably compare the constraints of truth with those other divisions, arbitrary in origin if not developing out of historical contingency—not merely modifiable but in a state of continual flux, supported by a system of institutions imposing and manipulating them, acting not without constraint, nor without an element, at least, of violence?

Certainly, as a proposition, the division between true and false is neither arbitrary, nor modifiable, nor institutional, nor violent. Putting the question in different terms, however—asking what has been, what still is, throughout our discourse, this will to truth which has survived throughout so many centuries of our history; or if we ask what is, in its very general form, the kind of division governing our will to knowledge—then we may well discern something like a system of exclusion (historical, modifiable, institutionally constraining) in the process of development.

It is, undoubtedly, a historically constituted division. For, even with the 6th century Greek poets, true discourse—in the meaningful sense—inspiring respect and terror, to which all were obliged to submit, because it held sway over all and was pronounced by men who spoke as of right, according to ritual, meted out justice and attributed to each his rightful share; it prophesied the future, not merely announcing what was going to occur, but contributing to its actual event, carrying men along with it and thus weaving itself into the fabric of fate. And yet, a century later, the highest truth no longer resided in what discourse *was*, nor in what it *did*: it lay in what was *said*. The day dawned when truth moved over from the ritualised act—potent and just—of enunciation to settle on what was enunciated itself: its meaning, its form, its object and its relation to what it referred to. A division emerged between Hesiod and Plato,[3] separating true discourse from false; it was a new division for, henceforth, true discourse was no longer considered precious and desirable, since it had ceased to be discourse linked to the exercise of power. And so the Sophists[4] were routed.

This historical division has doubtless lent its general form to our will to knowledge. Yet it has never ceased shifting: the great mutations of science may well sometimes be seen to flow from some discovery, but they may equally

3. Greek philosopher (ca. 427–ca. 327 B.C.E.); Hesiod (active ca. 700 B.C.E.) was one of the earliest Greek poets.
4. Greek proto-philosophers of the 5th century B.C.E., expert in reasoning and rhetoric and often characterized as more concerned with success than with truth in argument.

be viewed as the appearance of new forms of the will to truth. In the 19th century there was undoubtedly a will to truth having nothing to do, in terms of the forms examined, of the fields to which it addressed itself, nor the techniques upon which it was based, with the will to knowledge which characterised classical culture. Going back a little in time, to the turn of the 16th and 17th centuries—and particularly in England—a will to knowledge emerged which, anticipating its present content, sketched out a schema of possible, observable, measurable and classifiable objects; a will to knowledge which imposed upon the knowing subject—in some ways taking precedence over all experience—a certain position, a certain viewpoint, and a certain function (look rather than read, verify rather than comment), a will to knowledge which prescribed (and, more generally speaking, all instruments determined) the technological level at which knowledge could be employed in order to be verifiable and useful (navigation, mining, pharmacopoeia). Everything seems to have occurred as though, from the time of the great Platonic division onwards, the will to truth had its own history, which is not at all that of the constraining truths: the history of a range of subjects to be learned, the history of the functions of the knowing subject, the history of material, technical and instrumental investment in knowledge.

But this will to truth, like the other systems of exclusion, relies on institutional support: it is both reinforced and accompanied by whole strata of practices such as pedagogy—naturally—the book-system, publishing, libraries, such as the learned societies in the past, and laboratories today. But it is probably even more profoundly accompanied by the manner in which knowledge is employed in a society, the way in which it is exploited, divided and, in some ways, attributed. It is worth recalling at this point, if only symbolically, the old Greek adage, that arithmetic should be taught in democracies, for it teaches relations of equality, but that geometry alone should be reserved for oligarchies, as it demonstrates the proportions within inequality.[5]

Finally, I believe that this will to knowledge, thus reliant upon institutional support and distribution, tends to exercise a sort of pressure, a power of constraint upon other forms of discourse—I am speaking of our own society. I am thinking of the way Western literature has, for centuries, sought to base itself in nature, in the plausible, upon sincerity and science—in short, upon true discourse. I am thinking, too, of the way economic practices, codified into precepts and recipes—as morality, too—have sought, since the 18th century, to found themselves, to rationalise and justify their currency, in a theory of wealth and production; I am thinking, again, of the manner in which such prescriptive ensembles as the Penal Code[6] have sought their bases or justifications. For example, the Penal Code started out as a theory of Right; then, from the time of the 19th century, people looked for its validation in sociological, psychological, medical and psychiatric knowledge. It is as though the very words of the law had no authority in our society, except insofar as they are derived from true discourse. Of the three great systems of exclusion governing discourse—prohibited words, the division of madness and the will to truth—I have spoken at greatest length concerning the third. With good

5. See Plutarch, *Moralia* 719a–c (ca. 100 C.E.).
6. Adopted in France in 1791, during the French Revolution.

reason: for centuries, the former have continually tended toward the latter; because this last has, gradually, been attempting to assimilate the others in order both to modify them and to provide them with a firm foundation. Because, if the two former are continually growing more fragile and less certain to the extent that they are now invaded by the will to truth, the latter, in contrast, daily grows in strength, in depth and implacability.

And yet we speak of it least. As though the will to truth and its vicissitudes were masked by truth itself and its necessary unfolding. The reason is perhaps this: if, since the time of the Greeks, true discourse no longer responds to desire or to that which exercises power in the will to truth, in the will to speak out in true discourse, what, then, is at work, if not desire and power? True discourse, liberated by the nature of its form from desire and power, is incapable of recognising the will to truth which pervades it; and the will to truth, having imposed itself upon us for so long, is such that the truth it seeks to reveal cannot fail to mask it.

Thus, only one truth appears before our eyes: wealth, fertility and sweet strength in all its insidious universality. In contrast, we are unaware of the prodigious machinery of the will to truth, with its vocation of exclusion. All those who, at one moment or another in our history, have attempted to remould this will to truth and to turn it against truth at that very point where truth undertakes to justify the taboo, and to define madness; all those, from Nietzsche to Artaud and Bataille,[7] must now stand as (probably haughty) signposts for all our future work.

There are, of course, many other systems for the control and delimitation of discourse. Those I have spoken of up to now are, to some extent, active on the exterior; they function as systems of exclusion; they concern that part of discourse which deals with power and desire.

I believe we can isolate another group: internal rules, where discourse exercises its own control; rules concerned with the principles of classification, ordering and distribution. It is as though we were now involved in the mastery of another dimension of discourse: that of events and chance.

In the first place, commentary. I suppose, though I am not altogether sure, there is barely a society without its major narratives, told, retold and varied; formulae, texts, ritualised texts to be spoken in well-defined circumstances; things said once, and conserved because people suspect some hidden secret or wealth lies buried within. In short, I suspect one could find a kind of gradation between different types of discourse within most societies: discourse "uttered" in the course of the day and in casual meetings, and which disappears with the very act which gave rise to it; and those forms of discourse that lie at the origins of a certain number of new verbal acts, which are reiterated, transformed or discussed; in short, discourse which *is spoken* and remains spoken, indefinitely, beyond its formulation, and which remains to be spoken. We know them in our own cultural system: religious or juridical texts, as well as some curious texts, from the point of view of their status, which we term "literary"; to a certain extent, scientific texts also.

What is clear is that this gap is neither stable, nor constant, nor absolute.

7. Georges Bataille (1897–1962), French writer fascinated with eroticism, transgression, and the irrational. For NIETZSCHE, see above. Antonin Artaud (1895–1948), French playwright, poet, actor, and theoretician of the surrealist movement.

There is no question of there being one category, fixed for all time, reserved for fundamental or creative discourse, and another for those which reiterate, expound and comment. Not a few major texts become blurred and disappear, and commentaries sometimes come to occupy the former position. But while the details of application may well change, the function remains the same, and the principle of hierarchy remains at work. The radical denial of this gradation can never be anything but play, utopia or anguish. Play, as Borges[8] uses the term, in the form of commentary that is nothing more than the reappearance, word for word (though this time it is solemn and anticipated) of the text commented on; or again, the play of a work of criticism talking endlessly about a work that does not exist. It is a lyrical dream of talk reborn, utterly afresh and innocent, at each point; continually reborn in all its vigour, stimulated by things, feelings or thoughts. Anguish, such as that of Janet[9] when sick, for whom the least utterance sounded as the "word of the Evangelist", concealing an inexhaustible wealth of meaning, worthy to be broadcast, rebegun, commented upon indefinitely: "When I think", he said on reading or listening; "When I think of this phrase, continuing its journey through eternity, while I, perhaps, have only incompletely understood it . . ."

But who can fail to see that this would be to annul one of the terms of the relationship each time, and not to suppress the relationship itself? A relationship in continual process of modification; a relationship taking multiple and diverse forms in a given epoch: juridical exegesis is very different—and has been for a long time—from religious commentary; a single work of literature can give rise, simultaneously, to several distinct types of discourse. The Odyssey, as a primary text, is repeated in the same epoch, in Berard's translation, in infinite textual explanations and in Joyce's Ulysses.[1]

For the time being, I would like to limit myself to pointing out that, in what we generally refer to as commentary, the difference between primary text and secondary text plays two interdependent roles. On the one hand, it permits us to create new discourses ad infinitum: the top-heaviness of the original text, its permanence, its status as discourse ever capable of being brought up to date, the multiple or hidden meanings with which it is credited, the reticence and wealth it is believed to contain, all this creates an open possibility for discussion. On the other hand, whatever the techniques employed, commentary's only role is to say *finally*, what has silently been articulated *deep down*. It must—and the paradox is ever-changing yet inescapable—say, for the first time, what has already been said, and repeat tirelessly what was, nevertheless, never said. The infinite rippling of commentary is agitated from within by the dream of masked repetition: in the distance there is, perhaps, nothing other than what was there at the point of departure: simple recitation. Commentary averts the chance element of discourse by giving it its due: it gives us the opportunity to say something other than the text itself, but on condition that it is the text itself which is uttered and, in some ways, finalised. The open multiplicity, the fortuitousness, is transferred, by the

8. Jorge Luis Borges (1899–1986), Argentine poet, essayist, and short story writer who was a major figure of 20th-century literature; Foucault alludes to his stories "Pierre Menard, Author of the Quixote" (1939) and "The Approach to Al-Mu'tasim" (1936).

9. Pierre Janet (1859–1947), French psychologist and neurologist.
1. The 1922 novel by the Irish author James Joyce (1882–1941) reimagines Homer's Odyssey; the French diplomat and Hellenist Victor Bérard (1864–1931) translated the Greek epic in 1924.

principle of commentary, from what is liable to be said to the number, the form, the masks and the circumstances of repetition. The novelty lies no longer in what is said, but in its reappearance.

I believe there is another principle of rarefaction, complementary to the first: the author. Not, of course, the author in the sense of the individual who delivered the speech or wrote the text in question, but the author as the unifying principle in a particular group of writings or statements, lying at the origins of their significance, as the seat of their coherence. This principle is not constant at all times. All around us, there are sayings and texts whose meaning or effectiveness has nothing to do with any author to whom they might be attributed: mundane remarks, quickly forgotten; orders and contracts that are signed, but have no recognisable author; technical prescriptions anonymously transmitted. But even in those fields where it is normal to attribute a work to an author—literature, philosophy, science—the principle does not always play the same role; in the order of scientific discourse, it was, during the Middle Ages, indispensable that a scientific text be attributed to an author, for the author was the index of the work's truthfulness. A proposition was held to derive its scientific value from its author. But since the 17th century this function has been steadily declining; it barely survives now, save to give a name to a theorem, an effect, an example or a syndrome. In literature, however, and from about the same period, the author's function has become steadily more important. Now, we demand of all those narratives, poems, dramas and comedies which circulated relatively anonymously throughout the Middle Ages, whence they come, and we virtually insist they tell us who wrote them. We ask authors to answer for the unity of the works published in their names; we ask that they reveal, or at least display the hidden sense pervading their work; we ask them to reveal their personal lives, to account for their experiences and the real story that gave birth to their writings. The author is he who implants, into the troublesome language of fiction, its unities, its coherence, its links with reality.

I know what people are going to say: "But there you are speaking of the author in the same way as the critic reinvents him after he is dead and buried, when we are left with no more than a tangled mass of scrawlings. Of course, then you have to put a little order into what is left, you have to imagine a structure, a cohesion, the sort of theme you might expect to arise out of an author's consciousness or his life, even if it is a little fictitious. But all that cannot get away from the fact the author existed, irrupting into the midst of all the words employed, infusing them with his genius, or his chaos".

Of course, it would be ridiculous to deny the existence of individuals who write, and invent. But I think that, for some time, at least, the individual who sits down to write a text, at the edge of which lurks a possible *œuvre*, resumes the functions of the author. What he writes and does not write, what he sketches out, even preliminary sketches for the work, and what he drops as simple mundane remarks, all this interplay of differences is prescribed by the author-function. It is from his new position, as an author, that he will fashion—from all he might have said, from all he says daily, at any time—the still shaky profile of his *œuvre*.

Commentary limited the hazards of discourse through the action of an *identity* taking the form of *repetition* and *sameness*. The author principle limits this same chance element through the action of an *identity* whose form is that of *individuality* and the *I*.

But we have to recognise another principle of limitation in what we call, not sciences, but "disciplines". Here is yet another relative, mobile principle, one which enables us to construct, but within a narrow framework.

The organisation of disciplines is just as much opposed to the commentary-principle as it is to that of the author. Opposed to that of the author, because disciplines are defined by groups of objects, methods, their corpus of propositions considered to be true, the interplay of rules and definitions, of techniques and tools: all these constitute a sort of anonymous system, freely available to whoever wishes, or whoever is able to make use of them, without there being any question of their meaning or their validity being derived from whoever happened to invent them. But the principles involved in the formation of disciplines are equally opposed to that of commentary. In a discipline, unlike in commentary, what is supposed at the point of departure is not some meaning which must be rediscovered, nor an identity to be reiterated; it is that which is required for the construction of new statements. For a discipline to exist, there must be the possibility of formulating—and of doing so ad infinitum—fresh propositions.

But there is more, and there is more, probably, in order that there may be less. A discipline is not the sum total of all the truths that may be uttered concerning something; it is not even the total of all that may be accepted, by virtue of some principle of coherence and systematisation, concerning some given fact or proposition. Medicine does not consist of all that may be truly said about disease; botany cannot be defined by the sum total of the truths one could say about plants. There are two reasons for this, the first being that botany and medicine, like other disciplines, consist of errors as well as truths, errors that are in no way residuals, or foreign bodies, but having their own positive functions and their own valid history, such that their roles are often indissociable from that of the truths. The other reason is that, for a proposition to belong to botany or pathology, it must fulfil certain conditions, in a stricter and more complex sense than that of pure and simple truth: at any rate, other conditions. The proposition must refer to a specific range of objects; from the end of the 17th century, for example, a proposition, to be "botanical", had to be concerned with the visible structure of plants, with its system of close, and not so close resemblances or with the behaviour of its fluids; (but it could no longer retain, as had still been the case in the 16th century, references to its symbolic value or to the virtues and properties accorded it in antiquity). But without belonging to any discipline, a proposition is obliged to utilize conceptual instruments and techniques of a well-defined type; from the 19th century onwards, a proposition was no longer medical—it became "non-medical", becoming more of an individual fantasy or item of popular imagery—if it employed metaphorical or qualitative terms or notions of essence (congestion, fermented liquids, dessicated solids); in return, it could—it had to—appeal to equally metaphorical notions, though constructed according to a different functional and physiological model (concerning irritation, inflamation or the decay of tissue). But there is more still, for in order to belong to a discipline, a proposition must fit into a certain type of theoretical field. Suffice it to recall that the quest for primitive language, a perfectly acceptable theme up to the 18th century, was enough, in the second half of the 19th century, to throw any discourse into, I hesitate to say error, but into a world of chimera and reverie—into pure and simple linguistic monstrosity.

Within its own limits, every discipline recognises true and false propositions, but it repulses a whole teratology of learning. The exterior of a science is both more, and less, populated than one might think: certainly, there is immediate experience, imaginary themes bearing on and continually accompanying immemorial beliefs; but perhaps there are no errors in the strict sense of the term, for error can only emerge and be identified within a well-defined process; there are monsters on the prowl, however, whose forms alter with the history of knowledge. In short, a proposition must fulfil some onerous and complex conditions before it can be admitted within a discipline; before it can be pronounced true or false it must be, as Monsieur Canguilhem might say, "within the true".[2]

People have often wondered how on earth 19th-century botanists and biologists managed not to see the truth of Mendel's[3] statements. But it was precisely because Mendel spoke of objects, employed methods and placed himself within a theoretical perspective totally alien to the biology of his time. But then, Naudin[4] had suggested that hereditary traits constituted a separate element before him; and yet, however novel or unfamiliar the principle may have been, it was nevertheless reconcilable, if only as an enigma, with biological discourse. Mendel, on the other hand, announced that hereditary traits constituted an absolutely new biological object, thanks to a hitherto untried system of filtrage:[5] he detached them from species, from the sex transmitting them, the field in which he observed being that infinitely open series of generations in which hereditary traits appear and disappear with statistical regularity. Here was a new object, calling for new conceptual tools, and for fresh theoretical foundations. Mendel spoke the truth, but he was not *dans le vrai* (within the true) of contemporary biological discourse: it simply was not along such lines that objects and biological concepts were formed. A whole change in scale, the deployment of a totally new range of objects in biology was required before Mendel could enter into the true and his propositions appear for the most part, exact. Mendel was a true monster, so much so that science could not even properly speak of him. And yet Schleiden,[6] for example, thirty years earlier, denying, at the height of the 19th century, vegetable sexuality, was committing no more than a disciplined error.

It is always possible one could speak the truth in a void; one would only be in the true, however, if one obeyed the rules of some discursive "policy" which would have to be reactivated every time one spoke.

Disciplines constitute a system of control in the production of discourse, fixing its limits through the action of an identity taking the form of a permanent reactivation of the rules.

2. That is, posed in terms of concepts already recognized by the discourse. Georges Canguilhem (1904–1995), French physician and philosopher specializing in epistemology and the history and philosophy of science; Foucault was one of his students.
3. Gregor Mendel (1822–1884), Austrian monk and botanist who discovered the principles of heredity.
4. Charles Naudin (1815–1899), French botanist who experimented with hybridization.
5. Filtering.
6. Matthias Schleiden (1804–1881), German botanist; he studied microscopic plant structure.

We tend to see, in an author's fertility, in the multiplicity of commentaries and in the development of a discipline so many infinite resources available for the creation of discourse. Perhaps, so, but they are nonetheless principles of constraint, and it is probably impossible to appreciate their positive, multiplicatory role without first taking into consideration their restrictive, constraining role.

There is, I believe, a third group of rules serving to control discourse. Here, we are no longer dealing with the mastery of the powers contained within discourse, nor with averting the hazards of its appearance; it is more a question of determining the conditions under which it may be employed, of imposing a certain number of rules upon those individuals who employ it, thus denying access to everyone else. This amounts to a rarefaction among speaking subjects: none may enter into discourse on a specific subject unless he has satisfied certain conditions or if he is not, from the outset, qualified to do so. More exactly, not all areas of discourse are equally open and penetrable; some are forbidden territory (differentiated and differentiating) while others are virtually open to the winds and stand, without any prior restrictions, open to all.

Here, I would like to recount a little story so beautiful I fear it may well be true. It encompasses all the constraints of discourse: those limiting its powers, those controlling its chance appearances and those which select from among speaking subjects. At the beginning of the 17th century, the Shogun[7] heard tell of European superiority in navigation, commerce, politics and the military arts, and that this was due to their knowledge of mathematics. He wanted to obtain this precious knowledge. When someone told him of an English sailor possessed of this marvellous discourse, he summoned him to his palace and kept him there. The Shogun took lessons from the mariner in private and familiarised himself with mathematics, after which he retained power and lived to a very old age. It was not until the 19th century that there were *Japanese* mathematicians. But that is not the end of the anecdote, for it has its European aspect as well. The story has it that the English sailor, Will Adams, was a carpenter and an autodidact. Having worked in a shipyard he had learnt geometry. Can we see in this narrative the expression of one of the great myths of European culture? To the monopolistic, secret knowledge of oriental tyranny, Europe opposed the universal communication of knowledge and the infinitely free exchange of discourse.

This notion does not, in fact, stand up to close examination. Exchange and communication are positive forces at play within complex, but restrictive systems; it is probable that they cannot operate independently of these. The most superficial and obvious of these restrictive systems is constituted by what we collectively refer to as ritual; ritual defines the qualifications required of the speaker (of who in dialogue, interrogation or recitation, should occupy which position and formulate which type of utterance); it lays down gestures to be made, behaviour, circumstances and the whole range of signs that must accompany discourse; finally, it lays down the supposed, or imposed significance of the words used, their effect upon those to whom they are addressed,

7. Tokugawa Ieyasu (1543–1616), who in 1603 founded Japan's last shogunate; as shogun, he was authorized to command the army in the emperor's name. The English pilot in the story, William Adams, died in Japan in 1620.

the limitations of their constraining validity. Religious discourse, juridical and therapeutic as well as, in some ways, political discourse are all barely dissociable from the functioning of a ritual that determines the individual properties and agreed roles of the speakers.

A rather different function is filled by "fellowships of discourse", whose function is to preserve or to reproduce discourse, but in order that it should circulate within a closed community, according to strict regulations, without those in possession being dispossessed by this very distribution. An archaic model of this would be those groups of Rhapsodists,[8] possessing knowledge of poems to recite or, even, upon which to work variations and transformations. But though the ultimate object of this knowledge was ritual recitation, it was protected and preserved within a determinate group, by the, often extremely complex, exercises of memory implied by such a process. Apprenticeship gained access both to a group and to a secret which recitation made manifest, but did not divulge. The roles of speaking and listening were not interchangeable.

Few such "fellowships of discourse" remain, with their ambiguous interplay of secrecy and disclosure. But do not be deceived; even in true discourse, even in the order of published discourse, free from all ritual, we still find secret-appropriation and non-interchangeability at work. It could even be that the act of writing, as it is institutionalised today, with its books, its publishing system and the personality of the writer, occurs within a diffuse, yet constraining, "fellowship of discourse". The separateness of the writer, continually opposed to the activity of all other writing and speaking subjects, the intransitive character he lends to his discourse, the fundamental singularity he has long accorded to "writing", the affirmed dissymmetry between "creation" and any use of linguistic systems—all this manifests in its formulation (and tends moreover to accompany the interplay of these factors in practice) the existence of a certain "fellowship of discourse". But there are many others, functioning according to entirely different schemas of exclusivity and disclosure: one has only to think of technical and scientific secrets, of the forms of diffusion and circulation in medical discourse, of those who have appropriated economic or political discourse.

At first sight, "doctrine" (religious, political, philosophical) would seem to constitute the very reverse of a "fellowship of discourse"; for among the latter, the number of speakers were, if not fixed, at least limited, and it was among this number that discourse was allowed to circulate and be transmitted. Doctrine, on the other hand, tends to diffusion: in the holding in common of a single ensemble of discourse that individuals, as many as you wish, could define their reciprocal allegiance. In appearance, the sole requisite is the recognition of the same truths and the acceptance of a certain rule—more or less flexible—of conformity with validated discourse. If it were a question of just that, doctrines would barely be any different from scientific disciplines, and discursive control would bear merely on the form or content of what was uttered, and not on the speaker. Doctrinal adherence, however, involves both speaker and the spoken, the one through the other. The speaking subject is involved through, and as a result of, the spoken, as is demonstrated by the

8. In ancient Greece, reciters of poems (often accompanied by music).

rules of exclusion and the rejection mechanism brought into play when a speaker formulates one, or many, inassimilable utterances; questions of heresy and unorthodoxy in no way arise out of fanatical exaggeration of doctrinal mechanisms; they are a fundamental part of them. But conversely, doctrine involves the utterances of speakers in the sense that doctrine is, permanently, the sign, the manifestation and the instrument of a prior adherence— adherence to a class, to a social or racial status, to a nationality or an interest, to a struggle, a revolt, resistance or acceptance. Doctrine links individuals to certain types of utterance while consequently barring them from all others. Doctrine effects a dual subjection, that of speaking subjects to discourse, and that of discourse to the group, at least virtually, of speakers.

Finally, on a much broader scale, we have to recognise the great cleavages in what one might call the social appropriation of discourse. Education may well be, as of right, the instrument whereby every individual, in a society like our own, can gain access to any kind of discourse. But we well know that in its distribution, in what it permits and in what it prevents, it follows the well-trodden battle-lines of social conflict. Every educational system is a political means of maintaining or of modifying the appropriation of discourse, with the knowledge and the powers it carries with it.

I am well aware of the abstraction I am performing when I separate, as I have just done, verbal rituals, "fellowships of discourse", doctrinal groups and social appropriation. Most of the time they are linked together, constituting great edifices that distribute speakers among the different types of discourse, and which appropriate those types of discourse to certain categories of subject. In a word, let us say that these are the main rules for the subjection of discourse. What is an educational system, after all, if not a ritualisation of the word; if not a qualification of some fixing of roles for speakers; if not the constitution of a (diffuse) doctrinal group; if not a distribution and an appropriation of discourse, with all its learning and its powers? What is "writing" (that of "writers") if not a similar form of subjection, perhaps taking rather different forms, but whose main stresses are nonetheless analogous? May we not also say that the judicial system also, as well as institutionalised medicine, constitute similar systems for the subjection of discourse?

I wonder whether a certain number of philosophical themes have not come to conform to this activity of limitation and exclusion and perhaps even to reinforce it.

They conform, first of all, by proposing an ideal truth as a law of discourse, and an immanent rationality as the principle of their behaviour. They accompany, too, an ethic of knowledge, promising truth only to the desire for truth itself and the power to think it.

They then go on to reinforce this activity by denying the specific reality of discourse in general.

Ever since the exclusion of the activity and commerce of the sophists, ever since their paradoxes were muzzled, more or less securely, it would seem that Western thought has seen to it that discourse be permitted as little room as possible between thought and words. It would appear to have ensured that to discourse should appear merely as a certain interjection between speaking and thinking; that it should constitute thought, clad in its signs and rendered visible by words or, conversely, that the structures of language themselves should be brought into play, producing a certain effect of meaning.

This very ancient elision[9] of the reality of discourse in philosophical thought has taken many forms in the course of history. We have seen it quite recently in the guise of many themes now familiar to us.

It seems to me that the theme of the founding subject permits us to elide the reality of discourse. The task of the founding subject is to animate the empty forms of language with his objectives; through the thickness and inertia of empty things, he grasps intuitively the meanings lying within them. Beyond time, he indicates the field of meanings, leaving history to make them explicit, and in which propositions, sciences, and deductive ensembles ultimately find their foundation. In this relationship with meaning, the founding subject has signs, marks, tracks, letters at his disposal. But he does not need to demonstrate these passing through the singular instance of discourse.

The opposing theme, that of originating experience, plays an analogous role. This asserts, in the case of experience, that even before it could be grasped in the form of a *cogito*,[1] prior significations, in some ways already spoken, were circulating in the world, scattering it all about us, and from the outset made possible a sort of primitive recognition. Thus, a primary complicity with the world founds, for us, a possibility of speaking of experience, in it, to designate and name it, to judge it and, finally, to know it in the form of truth. If there is discourse, what could it legitimately be if not a discrete reading? Things murmur meanings our language has merely to extract; from its most primitive beginnings, this language was already whispering to us of a being of which it forms the skeleton.

The theme of universal mediation is, I believe, yet another manner of eliding the reality of discourse. And this despite appearances. At first sight it would seem that, to discover the movement of a logos[2] everywhere elevating singularities into concepts, finally enabling immediate consciousness to deploy all the rationality in the world, is certainly to place discourse at the centre of speculation. But, in truth, this logos is really only another discourse already in operation, or rather, it is things and events themselves which *insensibly* become discourse in the unfolding of the essential secrets. Discourse is no longer much more than the shimmering of a truth about to be born in its own eyes; and when all things come eventually to take the form of discourse, when everything may be said and when anything becomes an excuse for pronouncing a discourse, it will be because all things having manifested and exchanged meanings, they will then all be able to return to the silent interiority of self-consciousness.

Whether it is the philosophy of a founding subject, a philosophy of originating experience or a philosophy of universal mediation, discourse is really only an activity, of writing in the first case, of reading in the second and exchange in the third. This exchange, this writing, this reading never involve

---

9. Omission; specifically, in linguistics, the suppression of a vowel or syllable that results in two words running together. Here, "thoughts and words" are the elements brought together.
1. I think (Latin); that is, the thinking subject,

which was the starting point of the French philosopher René Descartes (1596–1650).
2. That is, an underlying rationality or structure (literally, "utterance, reason"; Greek).

anything but signs. Discourse thus nullifies itself, in reality, in placing itself at the disposal of the signifier.

What civilization, in appearance, has shown more respect towards discourse than our own? Where has it been more and better honoured? Where have men depended more radically, apparently, upon its constraints and its universal character? But, it seems to me, a certain fear hides behind this apparent supremacy accorded, this apparent logophilia.[3] It is as though these taboos, these barriers, thresholds and limits were deliberately disposed in order, at least partly, to master and control the great proliferation of discourse, in such a way as to relieve its richness of its most dangerous elements; to organise its disorder so as to skate round its most uncontrollable aspects. It is as though people had wanted to efface all trace of its irruption into the activity of our thought and language. There is undoubtedly in our society, and I would not be surprised to see it in others, though taking different forms and modes, a profound logophobia,[4] a sort of dumb fear of these events, of this mass of spoken things, of everything that could possibly be violent, discontinuous, querulous, disordered even and perilous in it, of the incessant, disorderly buzzing of discourse.

If we wish—I will not say to efface this fear—but to analyse it in its conditions, its activity and its effects, I believe we must resolve ourselves to accept three decisions which our current thinking rather tends to resist, and which belong to the three groups of function I have just mentioned: to question our will to truth; to restore to discourse its character as an event; to abolish the sovereignty of the signifier.

These are the tasks, or rather, some of the themes which will govern my work in the years ahead.[5] One can straight away distinguish some of the methodological demands they imply.

A principle of *reversal*, first of all. Where, according to tradition, we think we recognise the source of discourse, the principles behind its flourishing and continuity, in those factors which seem to play a positive role, such as the author discipline, will to truth, we must rather recognise the negative activity of the cutting-out and rarefaction of discourse.

But, once we have distinguished these principles of rarefaction, once we have ceased considering them as a fundamental and creative action, what do we discover behind them? Should we affirm that a world of uninterrupted discourse would be virtually complete? This is where we have to bring other methodological principles into play.

Next, then, the principle of *discontinuity*. The existence of systems of rarefaction does not imply that, over and beyond them lie great vistas of limitless discourse, continuous and silent, repressed and driven back by them, making it our task to abolish them and at last to restore it to speech. Whether talking in terms of speaking or thinking, we must not imagine some unsaid thing, or an unthought, floating about the world, interfacing with all its forms and events. Discourse must be treated as a discontinuous activity, its different manifestations sometimes coming together, but just as easily unaware of, or excluding each other.

3. Love of words.
4. Abhorrence of words.
5. This lecture was a clear announcement of the agenda that Foucault pursued throughout the rest of his career.

The principle of *specificity* declares that a particular discourse cannot be resolved by a prior system of significations; that we should not imagine that the world presents us with a legible face, leaving us merely to decipher it; it does not work hand in glove with what we already know; there is no pre-discursive fate disposing the word in our favour. We must conceive discourse as a violence that we do to things, or, at all events, as a practice we impose upon them; it is in this practice that the events of discourse find the principle of their regularity.

The fourth principle, that of *exteriority*, holds that we are not to burrow to the hidden core of discourse, to the heart of the thought or meaning manifested in it; instead, taking the discourse itself, its appearance and its regularity, that we should look for its external conditions of existence, for that which gives rise to the chance series of these events and fixes its limits.

As the regulatory principles of analysis, then, we have four notions: event, series, regularity and the possible conditions of existence. Term for term we find the notion of event opposed to that of creation, the possible conditions of existence opposing signification. These four notions (signification, originality, unity, creation) have, in a fairly general way, dominated the traditional history of ideas; by general agreement one sought the point of creation, the unity of a work, of a period or a theme, one looked also for the mark of individual originality and the infinite wealth of hidden meanings.

I would like to add just two remarks, the first of which concerns history. We frequently credit contemporary history with having removed the individual event from its privileged position and with having revealed the more enduring structures of history. That is so. I am not sure, however, that historians have been working in this direction alone. Or, rather, I do not think one can oppose the identification of the individual event to the analysis of long term trends quite so neatly. On the contrary, it seems to me that it is in squeezing the individual event, in directing the resolving power of historical analysis onto official price-lists (*mercuriales*), title deeds, parish registers, to harbour archives analysed year by year and week by week, that we gradually perceive— beyond battles, decisions, dynasties and assemblies—the emergence of those massive phenomena of secular[6] or multi-secular importance. History, as it is practised today, does not turn its back on events; on the contrary, it is continually enlarging the field of events, constantly discovering new layers—more superficial as well as more profound—incessantly isolating new ensembles— events, numerous, dense and interchangeable or rare and decisive: from daily price fluctuations to secular inflations. What is significant is that history does not consider an event without defining the series to which it belongs, without specifying the method of analysis used, without seeking out the regularity of phenomena and the probable limits of their occurrence, without enquiring about variations, inflexions and the slope of the curve, without desiring to know the conditions on which these depend. History has long since abandoned its attempts to understand events in terms of cause and effect in the formless unity of some great evolutionary process, whether vaguely homogeneous or rigidly hierarchised. It did not do this in order to seek out structures anterior to, alien or hostile to the event. It was rather in order to establish those diverse

6. Century-long (*séculaire*).

converging, and sometimes divergent, but never autonomous series that enable us to circumscribe the "locus" of an event, the limits to its fluidity and the conditions of its emergence.

The fundamental notions now imposed upon us are no longer those of consciousness and continuity (with their correlative problems of liberty and causality), nor are they those of sign and structure. They are notions, rather, of event and of series, with the group of notions linked to these; it is around such an ensemble that this analysis of discourse I am thinking of is articulated, certainly not upon those traditional themes which the philosophers of the past took for "living" history, but on the effective work of historians.

But it is also here that this analysis poses some, probably awesome philosophical or theoretical problems. If discourses are to be treated first as ensembles of discursive events, what status are we to accord this notion of event, so rarely taken into consideration by philosophers? Of course, an event is neither substance, nor accident, nor quality nor process; events are not corporeal. And yet, an event is certainly not immaterial; it takes effect, becomes effect, always on the level of materiality. Events have their place; they consist in relation to, coexistence with, dispersion of, the cross-checking accumulation and the selection of material elements; it occurs as an effect of, and in, material dispersion. Let us say that the philosophy of event should advance in the direction, at first sight paradoxical, of an incorporeal materialism. If, on the other hand, discursive events are to be dealt with as homogeneous, but discontinuous series, what status are we to accord this discontinuity? Here we are not dealing with a succession of instants in time, nor with the plurality of thinking subjects; what is concerned are those caesurae[7] breaking the instant and dispersing the subject in a multiplicity of possible positions and functions. Such a discontinuity strikes and invalidates the smallest units, traditionally recognised and the least readily contested: the instant and the subject. Beyond them, independent of them, we must conceive—between these discontinuous series of relations which are not in any order of succession (or simultaneity) within any (or several) consciousnesses—and we must elaborate—outside of philosophies of time and subject—a theory of discontinuous systematisation. Finally, if it is true that these discursive, discontinuous series have their regularity, within certain limits, it is clearly no longer possible to establish mechanically causal links or an ideal necessity among their constitutive elements. We must accept the introduction of chance as a category in the production of events. There again, we feel the absence of a theory enabling us to conceive the links between chance and thought.

In the sense that this slender wedge I intend to slip into the history of ideas consists not in dealing with meanings possibly lying behind this or that discourse, but with discourse as regular series and distinct events, I fear I recognise in this wedge a tiny (odious, too, perhaps) device permitting the introduction, into the very roots of thought, notions of *chance*, *discontinuity* and *materiality*. This represents a triple peril which one particular form of history attempts to avert by recounting the continuous unfolding of some ideal necessity. But they are three notions which ought to permit us to link the his-

---

7. Breaks, interruptions.

tory of systems of thought to the practical work of historians; three directions to be followed in the work of theoretical elaboration.

Following these principles, and referring to this overall view, the analyses I intend to undertake fall into two groups. On the one hand, the "critical" group which sets the reversal-principle to work. I shall attempt to distinguish the forms of exclusion, limitation and appropriation of which I was speaking earlier; I shall try to show how they are formed, in answer to which needs, how they are modified and displaced, which constraints they have effectively exercised, to what extent they have been worked on. On the other hand, the "genealogical" group, which brings the three other principles into play: how series of discourse are formed, through, in spite of, or with the aid of these systems of constraint: what were the specific norms for each, and what were their conditions of appearance, growth and variation.

Taking the critical group first, a preliminary group of investigations could bear on what I have designated functions of exclusion. I have already examined one of these for a determinate period: the disjunction of reason and madness in the classical age.[8] Later, we could attempt an investigation of a taboo system in language, that concerning sexuality from the 16th to the 19th century. In this, we would not be concerned with the manner in which this has progressively—and happily—disappeared, but with the way it has been altered and rearticulated, from the practice of confession, with its forbidden conduct, named, classified, hierarchised down to the smallest detail, to the belated, timid appearance of the treatment of sexuality in 19th-century psychiatry and medicine. Of course, these only amount to somewhat symbolic guidelines, but one can already be pretty sure that the stresses will not fall where we expect, and that taboos are not always to be found where we imagine them to be.

For the time being, I would like to address myself to the third system of exclusion. I will envisage it in two ways. Firstly, I would like to try to visualise the manner in which this truth within which we are caught, but which we constantly renew, was selected, but at the same time, was repeated, extended and displaced. I will take first of all the age of the Sophists and its beginning with Socrates,[9] or at least with Platonic philosophy, and I shall try to see how effective, ritual discourse, charged with power and peril, gradually arranged itself into a disjunction between true and false discourse. I shall next take the turn of the 16th and 17th centuries and the age which, above all in England, saw the emergence of an observational, affirmative science, a certain natural philosophy inseparable, too, from religious ideology—for this certainly constituted a new form of the will to knowledge. In the third place, I shall turn to the beginning of the 19th century and the great founding acts of modern science, as well as the formation of industrial society and the accompanying positivist ideology. Three slices out of the morphology of our will to knowledge; three staging posts in our philistinism.

I would also like to consider the same question from quite another angle. I would like to measure the effect of a discourse claiming to be scientific—

8. See *Folie et déraison: Histoire de la folie à l'âge classique* (1961, *Madness and Unreason: A History of Madness in the Classical Age*), translated into English as *History of Madness* (2006; abridged translation published in 1965 as *Madness and Civilization: A History of Insanity in the Age of Reason*).
9. Greek philosopher (469–399 B.C.E.), Plato's teacher and the protagonist in most of his dialogues.

medical, psychiatric or sociological—on the ensemble of practices and pre-scriptive discourse of which the penal code consists. The study of psychiatric skills and their role in the penal system will serve as a point of departure and as basic material for this analysis.

It is within this critical perspective, but on a different level, that the analy-sis of the rules for the limitation of discourse should take place, of those among which I earlier designated the author principle, that of commentary and that of discipline. One can envisage a certain number of studies in this field. I am thinking, for example, of the history of medicine in the 18th and 19th centu-ries; not so much an account of discoveries made and concepts developed, but of grasping—from the construction of medical discourse, from all its sup-porting institutions, from its transmission and its reinforcement, but also the constraint—to transform itself—how the principles of author, commentary and discipline worked in practice; of seeking to know how the great author principle, whether Hippocrates, Galen, Paracelsus and Sydenham, or Boer-haave,[1] became a principle of limitation in medical discourse; how, even late into the 19th century, the practice of aphorism and commentary retained its currency and how it was gradually replaced by the emphasis on case-histories and clinical training on actual cases; according to which model medicine sought to constitute itself as a discipline, basing itself at first on natural his-tory and, later, on anatomy and biology.

One could also envisage the way in which 18th and 19th-century literary criticism and history have constituted the character of the author and the form of the work, utilising, modifying and altering the procedures of religious exe-gesis, biblical criticism, hagiography, the "lives" of historical or legendary fig-ures, of autobiography and memoirs. One day, too, we must take a look at Freud's role in psychoanalytical knowledge, so different from that of Newton in physics, or from that an author might play in the field of philosophy (Kant, for example, who originated a totally new way of philosophizing).[2]

These then, are some of the projects falling within the critical aspect of the task, for the analysis of instances of discursive control. The genealogical aspect concerns the effective formation of discourse, whether within the lim-its of control, or outside of them, or as is most frequent, on both sides of the delimitation. Criticism analyses the processes of rarefaction, consolidation and unification in discourse; genealogy studies their formation, at once scattered, discontinuous and regular. To tell the truth, these two tasks are not always exactly complementary. We do not find, on the one hand, forms of rejection, exclusion, consolidation or attribution, and, on a more profound level, the spontaneous pouring forth of discourse, which immediately before or after its manifestation, finds itself submitted to selection and control. The regular formation of discourse may, in certain conditions and up to a certain

---

1. All considered to be crucial figures in medicine: Hippocrates (ca. 460–ca. 377 B.C.E.), Greek physi-cian viewed as the father of medicine; Galen (129–ca. 199 C.E.), Greek physician whose writings dominated European medicine from the Middle Ages until the 17th century; Theophrastus von Hohenheim (Paracelsus, 1493–1541), German-Swiss physician and alchemist who brought chem-istry into medicine; Thomas Sydenham (1624–1689), English physician who was a founder of clinical medicine and epidemiology; and Herman Boerhaave (1668–1738), Dutch physician credited with the modern system of teaching medicine.

2. Three foundational figures: Sigmund Freud (1856–1939), Austrian founder of psychoanalysis; Isaac Newton (1643–1727), English mathemati-cian and physicist viewed as one of the most important figures in modern science; and IMMAN-UEL KANT.

point, integrate control procedures (this is what happens, for example, when a discipline takes on the form and status of scientific discourse). Conversely, modes of control may take on life within a discursive formation (such as literary criticism as the author's constitutive discourse) even though any critical task calling instances of control into play must, at the same time, analyse the discursive regularities through which these instances are formed. Any genealogical description must take into account the limits at play within real formations. The difference between the critical and the genealogical enterprise is not one of object or field, but of point of attack, perspective and delimitation.

Earlier on I mentioned one possible study, that of the taboos in discourse on sexuality. It would be difficult, and in any case abstract, to try to carry out this study, without at the same time analysing literary, religious and ethical, biological and medical as well as juridical discursive ensembles: wherever sexuality is discussed, wherever it is named or described, metaphorised, explained or judged. We are a very long way from having constituted a unitary, regular discourse concerning sexuality; it may be that we never will, and that we are not even travelling in that direction. No matter. Taboos are homogeneous neither in their forms nor their behaviour whether in literary or medical discourse, in that of psychiatry or of the direction of consciousness. Conversely, these different discursive regularities do not divert or alter taboos in the same manner. It will only be possible to undertake this study, therefore, if we take into account the plurality of series within which the taboos, each one to some extent different from all the others, are at work.

We could also consider those series of discourse which, in the 16th and 17th centuries, dealt with wealth and poverty, money, production and trade. Here, we would be dealing with some pretty heterogeneous ensembles of enunciations, formulated by rich and poor, the wise and the ignorant, protestants and catholics, royal officials, merchants or moralists. Each one has its forms of regularity and, equally, its systems of constraint. None of them precisely prefigures that other form of regularity that was to acquire the momentum of a discipline and which was later to be known, first as "the study of wealth" and, subsequently, "political economy". And yet, it was from the foregoing that a new regularity was formed, retrieving or excluding, justifying or rejecting, this or that utterance from these old forms.

One could also conceive a study of discourse concerning heredity, such as it can be gleaned, dispersed as it was until the beginning of the 20th century, among a variety of disciplines, observations, techniques and formulae; we would be concerned to show the process whereby these series eventually became subsumed under the single system, now recognised as epistemologically coherent, known as genetics. This is the work François Jacob[3] has just completed, with unequalled brilliance and scholarship.

It is thus that critical and genealogical descriptions are to alternate, support and complete each other. The critical side of the analysis deals with the systems enveloping discourse; attempting to mark out and distinguish the principles of ordering, exclusion and rarity in discourse. We might, to play

---

3. French biologist (1920–2013), a researcher in cellular genetics who shared the 1965 Nobel Prize for Physiology or Medicine. In 1970 he published a book titled *The Logic of Life: A History of Heredity*.

with our words, say it practises a kind of studied casualness. The genealogical side of discourse, by way of contrast, deals with series of effective formation of discourse: it attempts to grasp it in its power of affirmation, by which I do not mean a power opposed to that of negation, but the power of constituting domains of objects, in relation to which one can affirm or deny true or false propositions. Let us call these domains of objects positivist and, to play on words yet again, let us say that, if the critical style is one of studied casualness, then the genealogical mood is one of felicitous positivism.

At all events, one thing at least must be emphasised here: that the analysis of discourse thus understood, does not reveal the universality of a meaning, but brings to light the action of imposed rarity, with a fundamental power of affirmation. Rarity and affirmation; rarity, in the last resort of affirmation—certainly not any continuous outpouring of meaning, and certainly not any monarchy of the signifier.

And now, let those who are weak on vocabulary, let those with little comprehension of theory call all this—if its appeal is stronger than its meaning for them—structuralism.[4]

I am well aware that I could never have begun to undertake these researches I have just outlined to you, were I not able to benefit from the aid of certain models and props. I believe I owe much to Monsieur Dumézil,[5] for it was he who encouraged me to work at an age when I still thought writing a pleasure. But I owe a lot, too, to his work; may he forgive me if I have wandered from the meaning and rigour of his texts, which dominate us today. It is he who taught me to analyse the internal economy of discourse quite differently from the traditional methods of exegesis or those of linguistic formalism. It is he who taught me to refer the system of functional correlations from one discourse to another by means of comparison. It was he, again, who taught me to describe the transformations of a discourse, and its relations to the institution. If I have wished to apply a similar method to discourse quite other than legendary or mythical narratives, it is because before me lay the works of the historians of science, above all, that of Monsieur Canguilhem. I owe it to him that I understood that the history of science did not necessarily involve, either an account of discoveries, or descriptions of the ideas and opinions bordering science either from the side of its doubtful beginnings, or from the side of its fall-out; but that one could—that one should—treat the history of science as an ensemble, at once coherent, and transformable into theoretical models and conceptual instruments.

A large part of my indebtedness, however, is to Jean Hyppolite.[6] I know that, for many, his work is associated with that of Hegel, and that our age, whether through logic or epistemology, whether through Marx or through Nietzsche, is attempting to flee Hegel: and what I was attempting to say earlier concerning discourse was pretty disloyal to Hegel.

But truly to escape Hegel involves an exact appreciation of the price we have to pay to detach ourselves from him. It assumes that we are aware of the extent

4. Note Foucault's scorn for those who would call his position and program "structuralist."
5. Georges Dumézil (1898–1986), prominent French philologist and analyst of cultural phenomena; he supported and was helpful to Foucault early in his career.

6. French philosopher (1907–1968), who did much to encourage other French philosophers to pay attention not only to Kant but also to German philosophers after him (for HEGEL and MARX, see above). He preceded Foucault as professor at the Collège de France.

to which Hegel, insidiously perhaps, is close to us; it implies a knowledge, in that which permits us to think against Hegel, of that which remains Hegelian. We have to determine the extent to which our anti-Hegelianism is possibly one of his tricks directed against us, at the end of which he stands, motionless, waiting for us.

If, then, more than one of us is indebted to Jean Hyppolite, it is because he has tirelessly explored, for us, and ahead of us, the path along which we may escape Hegel, keep our distance, and along which we shall find ourselves brought back to him, only from a different angle, and then, finally, be forced to leave him behind, once more.

First, Hyppolite took the trouble to give some presence to this great, slightly phantomlike shadow that was Hegel, prowling through the 19th century, with whom men struggled in the dark. He gave Hegel this presence with his translation of the *Phenomenology of the mind*;[7] proof of the extent to which Hegel came to life in this text was the number of Germans who came to consult this text in order to understand what, for a moment at least, had become the German version.

From this text, Hyppolite sought out and explored all the issues, as though his chief concern had become: can one still philosophize where Hegel is no longer possible? Can any philosophy continue to exist that is no longer Hegelian? Are the non-Hegelian elements in our thought necessarily non-philosophical? Is that which is antiphilosophical necessarily non-Hegelian? As well as giving us this Hegelian presence, he sought not merely a meticulous historical description: he wanted to turn Hegel into a schema for the experience of modernity (is it possible to think of the sciences, politics and daily suffering as a Hegelian?) and he wanted, conversely, to make modernity the test of Hegelianism and, beyond that, of philosophy. For Hyppolite, the relationship with Hegel was the scene of an experiment, of a confrontation in which it was never certain that philosophy would come out on top. He never saw the Hegelian system as a reassuring universe; he saw in it the field in which philosophy took the ultimate risk.

From this stem, I believe, the alterations he worked, not within Hegelian philosophy, but upon it, and upon philosophy as Hegel conceived it; from this also, a complete inversion of themes. Instead of conceiving philosophy as a totality ultimately capable of dispersing and regrouping itself in the movement of the concept, Jean Hyppolite transformed it into an endless task, against the background of an infinite horizon. Because it was a task without end, it was also a task in process of continuous recommencement, given over to the forms and paradoxes of repetition. For Hyppolite, philosophy, as the thought of the inaccessible totality, was that which could be rejected in the extreme irregularity of experience; it was that which presents and reveals itself as the continually recurring question in life, death and in memory. Thus he transformed the Hegelian theme of the end of self-consciousness into one of repeated interrogation. But because it consisted in repetition, this philosophy did not lie beyond concepts; its task was not that of abstraction, it was, rather, to maintain a certain reticence, to break with acquired generalisations and continually to reestablish contact with the non-philosophical; it was to

---

7. That is, *Phenomenology of Geist*. This was the first French translation (1939).

draw as close as possible, not to its final fulfilment, but to that which precedes it, that which has not yet stirred its uncertainty. In order not to reduce
them, but to think them, this philosophy was to examine the singularity of
history, the regional rationalities of science, the depths of memory in consciousness; thus arose the notion of a philosophy that was present, uncertain, mobile all along its line of contact with non-philosophy, existing on its
own, however, and revealing the meaning this non-philosophy has for us. But,
if it is in repeated contact with non-philosophy, where then lies the beginning of philosophy? Is it already there, secretly present in that which is not
philosophy, beginning to formulate itself half under its breath, amid the mur-
muring of things? But, perhaps, from that point on, philosophy has no *raison
d'être*,[8] or, maybe, philosophy should start out on a priori foundations? We see,
thus, the theme of the foundations of discourse and its formal structure substituting itself for the Hegelian one of present movement.

The final alteration Jean Hyppolite worked upon Hegelian philosophy was
this: if philosophy really must begin as absolute discourse, then what of history,
and what is this beginning which starts out with a singular individual, within
a society and a social class, and in the midst of struggle?

These five alterations, leading to the very extremities of Hegelian philosophy, doubtless forcing it to spill over its own limits, evoke by turns the great
figures of modern philosophy Jean Hyppolite ceaselessly opposed to Hegel:
Marx, with his questions of history; Fichte, and the problem of the absolute
beginnings of philosophy; Bergson's theme of contact with non-philosophy;
Kierkegaard, with the problem of repetition and truth; Husserl, and the theme
of philosophy as an infinite task, linked to the history of our rationality.[9]
Beyond these philosophical figures we can perceive all those fields of knowledge Hyppolite invoked around his own questions: psychoanalysis, with its
strange logic of desire; mathematics and the formalisation of discourse; information theory and its application to the analysis of life—in short, all those
fields giving rise to questions of logic and existence, continually intertwining
and unravelling their links.

I think this work, articulated in a small number of major books, but, even
more, invested in research, teaching, in a perpetual attentiveness, in an everyday alertness and generosity, in its apparently administrative and pedagogic
responsibilities (*i.e.*, doubly political), has traversed and formulated the most
fundamental problems of our age. Many of us are infinitely indebted to him.

It is because I have borrowed both the meaning and the possibility of what
I am doing from him; because, often, he enlightened me when I struck out
blindly; because I would like to dedicate my work to him, that I end this presentation of my projected work by invoking the name of Jean Hyppolite. It is
towards him, towards that hiatus—where I feel at once his absence and my
failings—that the questions I now ask myself are pointing.

Because I owe him so much, I well understand that your choice, in inviting
me to teach here is, in good part, a homage to Jean Hyppolite. I am profoundly
grateful to you for the honour you have done me, but I am no less grateful for
the honour your choice does to Jean Hyppolite. If I do not feel equal to the
challenge of succeeding him, I know nonetheless that, if that happiness should

8. Reason to exist (French).
9. For all of these "great figures," see above.

have been granted us, I should have been encouraged by his indulgence this evening.

I now understand better why I experienced so much difficulty when I began speaking, earlier on. I now know which voice it was I would have wished for, preceding me, supporting me, inviting me to speak and lodging within my own speech. I know now just what was so awesome about beginning; for it was here, where I speak now, that I listened to that voice, and where its possessor is no longer, to hear me speak.

SOURCE: Michel Foucault, "Orders of Discourse," trans. Rupert Swyer, *Social Science Information* 10.2 (April 1971): 7–30. Originally delivered in 1970 as Foucault's inaugural lecture at the Collège de France, then published as *L'ordre du discours* (1971, *The Order of Discourse*). This essay is commonly referred to as Foucault's "Discourse on Language."

[Power, Right, Truth]

The course of study that I have been following until now—roughly since 1970/71—has been concerned with the *how* of power. I have tried, that is, to relate its mechanisms to two points of reference, two limits: on the one hand, to the rules of right that provide a formal delimitation of power; on the other, to the effects of truth that this power produces and transmits, and which in their turn reproduce this power. Hence we have a triangle: power, right, truth.

Schematically, we can formulate the traditional question of political philosophy in the following terms: how is the discourse of truth, or quite simply, philosophy as that discourse which *par excellence* is concerned with truth, able to fix limits to the rights of power? That is the traditional question. The one I would prefer to pose is rather different. Compared to the traditional, noble and philosophic question it is much more down to earth and concrete. My problem is rather this: what rules of right are implemented by the relations of power in the production of discourses of truth? Or alternatively, what type of power is susceptible of producing discourses of truth that in a society such as ours are endowed with such potent effects? What I mean is this: in a society such as ours, but basically in any society, there are manifold relations of power which permeate, characterise and constitute the social body, and these relations of power cannot themselves be established, consolidated nor implemented without the production, accumulation, circulation and functioning of a discourse. There can be no possible exercise of power without a certain economy of discourses of truth which operates through and on the basis of this association. We are subjected to the production of truth through power and we cannot exercise power except through the production of truth. This is the case for every society, but I believe that in ours the relationship between power, right and truth is organised in a highly specific fashion. If I were to characterise, not its mechanism itself, but its intensity and constancy, I would say that we are forced to produce the truth of power that our society demands, of which it has need, in order to function: we *must* speak the truth; we are constrained or condemned to confess or to discover the truth. Power never ceases its interrogation, its inquisition, its registration of truth: it institutionalises, professionalises and rewards its pursuit. In the last analysis, we must produce truth as we must produce wealth, indeed we must produce truth in order to produce wealth in the first place. In another way, we are also subjected to truth in the sense in which it is truth that makes the laws, that produces the true discourse which, at least partially, decides, transmits and itself extends upon the effects of power. In the end, we are judged, condemned, classified, determined in our undertakings, destined to a certain mode of living or dying, as a function of the true discourses which are the bearers of the specific effects of power.

So, it is the rules of right, the mechanisms of power, the effects of truth or if you like, the rules of power and the powers of true discourses, that can be said more or less to have formed the general terrain of my concern, even if, as I know full well, I have traversed it only partially and in a very zig-zag fashion. I should like to speak briefly about this course of research, about what I have considered as being its guiding principle and about the methodological imperatives and precautions which I have sought to adopt. As regards the general principle involved in a study of the relations between right and power, it seems to me that in Western societies since Medieval times it has been royal power that has provided the essential focus around which legal thought has been elaborated. It is in response to the demands of royal power, for its profit and to serve as its instrument or justification, that the juridical edifice of our own society has been developed. Right in the West is the King's right. Naturally everyone is familiar with the famous, celebrated, repeatedly emphasised role of the jurists in the organisation of royal power. We must not forget that the re-vitalisation of Roman Law in the twelfth century was the major event around which, and on whose basis, the juridical edifice which had collapsed after the fall of the Roman Empire was reconstructed. This resurrection of Roman Law had in effect a technical and constitutive role to play in the establishment of the authoritarian, administrative, and, in the final analysis, absolute power of the monarchy. And when this legal edifice escapes in later centuries from the control of the monarch, when, more accurately, it is turned against that control, it is always the limits of this sovereign power that are put in question, its prerogatives that are challenged. In other words, I believe that the King remains the central personage in the whole legal edifice of the West. When it comes to the general organisation of the legal system in the West, it is essentially with the King, his rights, his power and its eventual limitations, that one is dealing. Whether the jurists were the King's henchmen or his adversaries, it is of royal power that we are speaking in every case when we speak of these grandiose edifices of legal thought and knowledge.

There are two ways in which we do so speak. Either we do so in order to show the nature of the juridical armoury that invested royal power, to reveal the monarch as the effective embodiment of sovereignty, to demonstrate that his power, for all that it was absolute, was exactly that which befitted his fundamental right. Or, by contrast, we do so in order to show the necessity of imposing limits upon this sovereign power, of submitting it to certain rules of right, within whose confines it had to be exercised in order for it to remain legitimate. The essential role of the theory of right, from medieval times onwards, was to fix the legitimacy of power; that is the major problem around which the whole theory of right and sovereignty is organised.

When we say that sovereignty is the central problem of right in Western societies, what we mean basically is that the essential function of the discourse and techniques of right has been to efface the domination intrinsic to power in order to present the latter at the level of appearance under two different aspects: on the one hand, as the legitimate rights of sovereignty, and on the other, as the legal obligation to obey it. The system of right is centred entirely upon the King, and it is therefore designed to eliminate the fact of domination and its consequences.

My general project over the past few years has been, in essence, to reverse the mode of analysis followed by the entire discourse of right from the time of the Middle Ages. My aim, therefore, was to invert it, to give due weight, that is, to the fact of domination, to expose both its latent nature and its brutality. I then wanted to show not only how right is, in a general way, the instrument of this domination—which scarcely needs saying—but also to show the extent to which, and the forms in which, right (not simply the laws but the whole complex of apparatuses, institutions and regulations responsible for their application) transmits and puts in motion relations that are not relations of sovereignty, but of domination. Moreover, in speaking of domination I do not have in mind that solid and global kind of domination that one person exercises over others, or one group over another, but the manifold forms of domination that can be exercised within society. Not the domination of the King in his central position, therefore, but that of his subjects in their mutual relations: not the uniform edifice of sovereignty, but the multiple forms of subjugation that have a place and function within the social organism.

The system of right, the domain of the law, are permanent agents of these relations of domination, these polymorphous techniques of subjugation. Right should be viewed, I believe, not in terms of a legitimacy to be established, but in terms of the methods of subjugation that it instigates.

The problem for me is how to avoid this question, central to the theme of right, regarding sovereignty and the obedience of individual subjects in order that I may substitute the problem of domination and subjugation for that of sovereignty and obedience. Given that this was to be the general line of my analysis, there were a certain number of methodological precautions that seemed requisite to its pursuit. In the very first place, it seemed important to accept that the analysis in question should not concern itself with the regulated and legitimate forms of power in their central locations, with the general mechanisms through which they operate, and the continual effects of these. On the contrary, it should be concerned with power at its extremities, in its ultimate destinations, with those points where it becomes capillary, that is, in its more regional and local forms and institutions. Its paramount concern, in fact, should be with the point where power surmounts the rules of right which organise and delimit it and extends itself beyond them, invests itself in institutions, becomes embodied in techniques, and equips itself with instruments and eventually even violent means of material intervention. To give an example: rather than try to discover where and how the right of punishment is founded on sovereignty, how it is presented in the theory of monarchical right or in that of democratic right, I have tried to see in what ways punishment and the power of punishment are effectively embodied in a certain number of local, regional, material institutions, which are concerned with torture or imprisonment, and to place these in the climate—at once institutional and physical, regulated and violent—of the effective apparatuses of punishment. In other words, one should try to locate power at the extreme points of its exercise, where it is always less legal in character.

A second methodological precaution urged that the analysis should not concern itself with power at the level of conscious intention or decision; that it should not attempt to consider power from its internal point of view and that it should refrain from posing the labyrinthine and unanswerable question: 'Who then has power and what has he in mind? What is the aim of someone who possesses power?' Instead, it is a case of studying power at the point where its intention, if it has one, is completely invested in its real and effective practices. What is needed is a study of power in its external visage, at the point where it is in direct and immediate relationship with that which we can provisionally call its object, its target, its field of application, there—that is to say—where it installs itself and produces its real effects.

Let us not, therefore, ask why certain people want to dominate, what they seek, what is their overall strategy. Let us ask, instead, how things work at the level of on-going subjugation, at the level of those continuous and uninterrupted processes which subject our bodies, govern our gestures, dictate our behaviours etc. In other words, rather than ask ourselves how the sovereign appears to us in his lofty isolation, we should try to discover how it is that subjects are gradually, progressively, really and materially constituted through a multiplicity of organisms, forces, energies, materials, desires, thoughts etc. We should try to grasp subjection in its material instance as a constitution of subjects. This would be the exact opposite of Hobbes' project in Leviathan,[1] and of that, I believe, of all jurists for whom the problem is the distillation of a single will—or rather, the constitution of a unitary, singular body animated by the spirit of sovereignty—from the particular wills of a multiplicity of individuals. Think of the scheme of Leviathan: insofar as he is a fabricated man, Leviathan is no other than the amalgamation of a certain number of separate individualities, who find themselves reunited by the complex of elements that go to compose the State; but at the heart of the State, or rather, at its head, there exists something which constitutes it as such, and this is sovereignty, which Hobbes says is precisely the spirit of Leviathan. Well, rather than worry about the problem of the central spirit, I believe that we must attempt to study the myriad of bodies which are constituted as peripheral subjects as a result of the effects of power.

A third methodological precaution relates to the fact that power is not to be taken to be a phenomenon of one individual's consolidated and homogeneous domination over others, or that of one group or class over others. What, by contrast, should always be kept in mind is that power, if we do not take too distant a view of it, is not that which makes the difference between those who exclusively possess and retain it, and those who do not have it and submit to it. Power must by analysed as something which circulates, or rather as something which only functions in the form of a chain. It is never localised here or there, never in anybody's hands, never appropriated as a commodity or piece of wealth.

1. The masterpiece of political philosophy (1651) by the English historian and philosopher Thomas Hobbes (1588–1679).

Power is employed and exercised through a net-like organisation. And not only do individuals circulate between its threads; they are always in the position of simultaneously undergoing and exercising this power. They are not only its inert or consenting target; they are always also the elements of its articulation. In other words, individuals are the vehicles of power, not its points of application.

The individual is not to be conceived as a sort of elementary nucleus, a primitive atom, a multiple and inert material on which power comes to fasten or against which it happens to strike, and in so doing subdues or crushes individuals. In fact, it is already one of the prime effects of power that certain bodies, certain gestures, certain discourses, certain desires, come to be identified and constituted as individuals. The individual, that is, is not the *vis-à-vis* of power; it is, I believe, one of its prime effects. The individual is an effect of power, and at the same time, or precisely to the extent to which it is that effect, it is the element of its articulation. The individual which power has constituted is at the same time its vehicle.

There is a fourth methodological precaution that follows from this: when I say that power establishes a network through which it freely circulates, this is true only up to a certain point. In much the same fashion we could say that therefore we all have a fascism in our heads, or, more profoundly, that we all have a power in our bodies. But I do not believe that one should conclude from that that power is the best distributed thing in the world, although in some sense that is indeed so. We are not dealing with a sort of democratic or anarchic distribution of power through bodies. That is to say, it seems to me—and this then would be the fourth methodological precaution—that the important thing is not to attempt some kind of deduction of power starting from its centre and aimed at the discovery of the extent to which it permeates into the base, of the degree to which it reproduces itself down to and including the most molecular elements of society. One must rather conduct an *ascending* analysis of power, starting, that is, from its infinitesimal mechanisms, which each have their own history, their own trajectory, their own techniques and tactics, and then see how these mechanisms of power have been—and continue to be—invested, colonised, utilised, involuted, transformed, displaced, extended etc., by ever more general mechanisms and by forms of global domination. It is not that this global domination extends itself right to the base in a plurality of repercussions: I believe that the manner in which the phenomena, the techniques and the procedures of power enter into play at the most basic levels must be analysed, that the way in which these procedures are displaced, extended and altered must certainly be demonstrated; but above all what must be shown is the manner in which they are invested and annexed by more global phenomena and the subtle fashion in which more general powers or economic interests are able to engage with these technologies that are at once both relatively autonomous of power and act as its infinitesimal elements. In order to make this clearer, one might cite the example of madness. The descending type of analysis, the one of which I believe one ought to be wary, will say that the bourgeoisie has, since the sixteenth or seventeenth century, been the dominant class; from this premise, it will then set out to deduce the internment of the insane. One can always make this deduction, it is always easily done and that is precisely what I would hold against it. It is in fact a simple matter to show that since lunatics are precisely those persons who are useless to industrial production, one is obliged to dispense with them. One could argue similarly in regard to infantile sexuality—and several thinkers, including Wilhelm Reich[2] have indeed sought to do so up to a certain point. Given the domination of the bourgeois class, how can one understand the repression of infantile sexuality? Well, very simply—given that the human body had become essentially a force of production from the time of the seventeenth and eighteenth century, all the forms of its expenditure which did not lend themselves to the constitution of the productive forces—and were therefore exposed as redundant—were banned, excluded and repressed. These kinds of deduction are always possible. They are simultaneously correct and false. Above all they are too glib, because one can always do exactly the opposite and show, precisely by appeal to the principle of the dominance of the bourgeois class, that the forms of control of infantile sexuality could in no way have been predicted. On the contrary, it is equally plausible to suggest that what was needed was sexual training, the encouragement of a sexual precociousness, given that what was fundamentally at stake was the constitution of a labour force whose optimal state, as we well know, at least at the beginning of the nineteenth century, was to be infinite: the greater the labour force, the better able would the system of capitalist production have been to fulfil and improve its functions.

I believe that anything can be deduced from the general phenomenon of the domination of the bourgeois class. What needs to be done is something quite different. One needs to investigate historically, and beginning from the lowest level, how mechanisms of power have been able to function. In regard to the confinement of the insane; for example, or the repression and interdiction of sexuality, we need to see the manner in which, at the effective level of the family, of the immediate environment, of the cells and most basic units of society, these phenomena of repression or exclusion possessed their instruments and their logic, in response to a certain number of needs. We need to identify the agents responsible for them, their real agents (those which constituted the immediate social *entourage*, the family, parents, doctors etc.), and not be content to lump them under the formula of a generalised bourgeoisie. We need to see how these mechanisms of power, at a given moment, in a precise conjuncture and by means of a certain number of transformations, have begun to become economically advantageous and politically useful. I think that in this way one could easily manage to demonstrate that what the bourgeoisie needed, or that in which its system discovered its real interests, was not the exclusion of the mad or the surveillance and prohibition of infantile masturbation (for, to repeat, such a system can perfectly well tolerate quite opposite practices), but rather, the techniques and procedures themselves of such an exclusion. It is the mechanisms of that exclusion that are necessary, the apparatuses of surveillance, the medicalisation of sexuality, of madness, of delinquency, all the micro-mechanisms of power, that came, from a certain moment in time, to represent the interests of the bourgeoisie. Or even better, we could say that to the extent to which this view of the bourgeoisie and of its interests appears to lack content, at least in regard to the problems with which we are here concerned, it reflects the fact that it was not the bour-

2. Viennese psychiatrist (1897–1957), who believed that orgasms were essential to human psychological health.

geoisie itself which thought that madness had to be excluded or infantile sexuality repressed. What in fact happened instead was that the mechanisms of the exclusion of madness, and of the surveillance of infantile sexuality, began from a particular point in time, and for reasons which need to be studied, to reveal their political usefulness and to lend themselves to economic profit, and that as a natural consequence, all of a sudden, they came to be colonised and maintained by global mechanisms and the entire State system. It is only if we grasp these techniques of power and demonstrate the economic advantages or political utility that derives from them in a given context for specific reasons, that we can understand how these mechanisms come to be effectively incorporated into the social whole.

To put this somewhat differently: the bourgeoisie has never had any use for the insane; but the procedures it has employed to exclude them have revealed and realised—from the nineteenth century onwards, and again on the basis of certain transformations—a political advantage, on occasion even a certain economic utility, which have consolidated the system and contributed to its overall functioning. The bourgeoisie is interested in power, not in madness, in the system of control of infantile sexuality, not in that phenomenon itself. The bourgeoisie could not care less about delinquents, about their punishment and rehabilitation, which economically have little importance, but it is concerned about the complex of mechanisms with which delinquency is controlled, pursued, punished and reformed etc.

As for our fifth methodological precaution: it is quite possible that the major mechanisms of power have been accompanied by ideological productions. There has, for example, probably been an ideology of education, an ideology of the monarchy, an ideology of parliamentary democracy etc.; but basically I do not believe that what has taken place can be said to be ideological. It is both much more and much less than ideology. It is the production of effective instruments for the formation and accumulation of knowledge—methods of observation, techniques of registration, procedures for investigation and research, apparatuses of control. All this means that power, when it is exercised through these subtle mechanisms, cannot but evolve, organise and put into circulation a knowledge, or rather apparatuses of knowledge, which are not ideological constructs.

By way of summarising these five methodological precautions, I would say that we should direct our researches on the nature of power not towards the juridical edifice of sovereignty, the State apparatuses and the ideologies which accompany them, but towards domination and the material operators of power, towards forms of subjection and the inflections and utilisations of their localised systems, and towards strategic apparatuses. We must eschew the model of Leviathan in the study of power. We must escape from the limited field of juridical sovereignty and State institutions, and instead base our analysis of power on the study of the techniques and tactics of domination.

This, in its general outline, is the methodological course that I believe must be followed, and which I have tried to pursue in the various researches that we have conducted over recent years on psychiatric power, on infantile sexuality, on political systems, etc. Now as one explores these fields of investigation, observing the methodological precautions I have mentioned, I believe that what then comes into view is a solid body of historical fact, which will ultimately bring us into confrontation with the problems of which I want to speak this year.

This solid, historical body of fact is the juridical-political theory of sovereignty of which I spoke a moment ago, a theory which has had four roles to play. In the first place, it has been used to refer to a mechanism of power that was effective under the feudal monarchy. In the second place, it has served as instrument and even as justification for the construction of the large scale administrative monarchies. Again, from the time of the sixteenth century and more than ever from the seventeenth century onwards, but already at the time of the wars of religion,[3] the theory of sovereignty has been a weapon which has circulated from one camp to another, which has been utilised in one sense or another, either to limit or else to re-inforce royal power: we find it among Catholic monarchists and Protestant anti-monarchists, among Protestant and more-or-less liberal monarchists, but also among Catholic partisans of regicide or dynastic transformation. It functions both in the hands of aristocrats and in the hands of parliamentarians. It is found among the representatives of royal power and among the last feudatories. In short, it was the major instrument of political and theoretical struggle around systems of power of the sixteenth and seventeenth centuries. Finally, in the eighteenth century, it is again this same theory of sovereignty, re-activated through the doctrine of Roman Law, that we find in its essentials in Rousseau[4] and his contemporaries, but now with a fourth role to play: now it is concerned with the construction, in opposition to the administrative, authoritarian and absolutist monarchies, of an alternative model, that of parliamentary democracy. And it is still this role that it plays at the moment of the Revolution.[5]

Well, it seems to me that if we investigate these four roles there is a definite conclusion to be drawn: as long as a feudal type of society survived, the problems to which the theory of sovereignty was addressed were in effect confined to the general mechanisms of power, to the way in which its forms of existence at the higher level of society influenced its exercise at the lowest levels. In other words, the relationship of sovereignty, whether interpreted in a wider or a narrower sense, encompasses the totality of the social body. In effect, the mode in which power was exercised could be defined in its essentials in terms of the relationship sovereign–subject. But in the seventeenth and eighteenth centuries, we have the production of an important phenomenon, the emergence, or rather the invention, of a new mechanism of power possessed of highly specific procedural techniques, completely novel instruments, quite different apparatuses, and which is also, I believe, absolutely incompatible with the relations of sovereignty.

This new mechanism of power is more dependent upon bodies and what they do than upon the Earth and its products. It is a mechanism of power which permits time and labour, rather than wealth and commodities, to be extracted from bodies. It is a type of power which is constantly exercised by means of surveillance rather than in a discontinuous manner by means of a system of levies or obligations distributed over time. It presupposes a tightly knit grid of material coercions rather than the physical existence of a sovereign. It is ultimately dependent upon the principle, which introduces a genuinely new economy of power, that one must be able simultaneously both to increase the subjected forces and to improve the force and efficacy of that which subjects them.

3. Bloody conflicts in France between Protestants and Roman Catholics (1562–98).
4. Jean-Jacques Rousseau (1712–1778), Swiss-born
French philosopher and political theorist.
5. That is, the French Revolution (1787–99).

This type of power is in every aspect the antithesis of that mechanism of power which the theory of sovereignty described or sought to transcribe. The latter is linked to a form of power that is exercised over the Earth and its products, much more than over human bodies and their operations. The theory of sovereignty is something which refers to the displacement and appropriation on the part of power, not of time and labour, but of goods and wealth. It allows discontinuous obligations distributed over time to be given legal expression but it does not allow for the codification of a continuous surveillance. It enables power to be founded in the physical existence of the sovereign, but not in continuous and permanent systems of surveillance. The theory of sovereignty permits the foundation of an absolute power in the absolute expenditure of power. It does not allow for a calculation of power in terms of the minimum expenditure for the maximum return.

This new type of power, which can no longer be formulated in terms of sovereignty, is, I believe, one of the great inventions of bourgeois society. It has been a fundamental instrument in the constitution of industrial capitalism and of the type of society that is its accompaniment. This non-sovereign power, which lies outside the form of sovereignty, is disciplinary power.[6] Impossible to describe in the terminology of the theory of sovereignty from which it differs so radically, this disciplinary power ought by rights to have led to the disappearance of the grand juridical edifice created by that theory. But in reality, the theory of sovereignty has continued not only to exist as an ideology of right, but also to provide the organising principle of the legal codes which Europe acquired in the nineteenth century, beginning with the Napoleonic Code.[7]

Why has the theory of sovereignty persisted in this fashion as an ideology and an organising principle of these major legal codes? For two reasons, I believe. On the one hand, it has been, in the eighteenth and again in the nineteenth century, a permanent instrument of criticism of the monarchy and of all the obstacles that can thwart the development of disciplinary society. But at the same time, the theory of sovereignty, and the organisation of a legal code centred upon it, have allowed a system of right to be superimposed upon the mechanisms of discipline in such a way as to conceal its actual procedures, the element of domination inherent in its techniques, and to guarantee to everyone, by virtue of the sovereignty of the State, the exercise of his proper sovereign rights. The juridical systems—and this applies both to their codification and to their theorisation—have enabled sovereignty to be democratised through the constitution of a public right articulated upon collective sovereignty, while at the same time this democratisation of sovereignty was fundamentally determined by and grounded in mechanisms of disciplinary coercion.

To put this in more rigorous terms, one might say that once it became necessary for disciplinary constraints to be exercised through mechanisms of domination and yet at the same time for their effective exercise of power to be disguised, a theory of sovereignty was required to make an appearance at the level of the legal apparatus, and to re-emerge in its codes. Modern society,

---

6. That is, the power of those complex structures that Foucault calls "disciplines." The conceptualization of this historically relatively new type of structure, and of its "new type of power," is central to Foucault's philosophical project, pursued in conjunction with the historical project that he has been articulating.

7. Civil code enacted in 1804 in France (and the basis of French law today).

then, from the nineteenth century up to our own day, has been characterised on the one hand, by a legislation, a discourse, an organisation based on public right, whose principle of articulation is the social body and the delegative status of each citizen; and, on the other hand, by a closely linked grid of disciplinary coercions whose purpose is in fact to assure the cohesion of this same social body. Though a theory of right is a necessary companion to this grid, it cannot in any event provide the terms of its endorsement. Hence these two limits, a right of sovereignty and a mechanism of discipline, which define, I believe, the arena in which power is exercised. But these two limits are so heterogeneous that they cannot possibly be reduced to each other. The powers of modern society are exercised through, on the basis of, and by virtue of, this very heterogeneity between a public right of sovereignty and a polymorphous disciplinary mechanism. This is not to suggest that there is on the one hand an explicit and scholarly system of right which is that of sovereignty, and, on the other hand, obscure and unspoken disciplines which carry out their shadowy operations in the depths, and thus constitute the bedrock of the great mechanism of power. In reality, the disciplines have their own discourse. They engender, for the reasons of which we spoke earlier, apparatuses of knowledge (*savoir*) and a multiplicity of new domains of understanding. They are extraordinarily inventive participants in the order of these knowledge-producing apparatuses. Disciplines are the bearers of a discourse, but this cannot be the discourse of right. The discourse of discipline has nothing in common with that of law, rule, or sovereign will. The disciplines may well be the carriers of a discourse that speaks of a rule, but this is not the juridical rule deriving from sovereignty, but a natural rule, a norm. The code they come to define is not that of law but that of normalisation. Their reference is to a theoretical horizon which of necessity has nothing in common with the edifice of right. It is human science which constitutes their domain, and clinical knowledge their jurisprudence.

In short, what I have wanted to demonstrate in the course of the last few years is not the manner in which at the advance front of the exact sciences the uncertain, recalcitrant, confused dominion of human behaviour has little by little been annexed to science: it is not through some advancement in the rationality of the exact sciences that the human sciences are gradually constituted. I believe that the process which has really rendered the discourse of the human sciences possible is the juxtaposition, the encounter between two lines of approach, two mechanisms, two absolutely heterogeneous types of discourse: on the one hand there is the re-organisation of right that invests sovereignty, and on the other, the mechanics of the coercive forces whose exercise takes a disciplinary form. And I believe that in our own times power is exercised simultaneously through this right and these techniques and that these techniques and these discourses, to which the disciplines give rise[,] invade the area of right so that the procedures of normalisation come to be ever more constantly engaged in the colonisation of those of law. I believe that all this can explain the global functioning of what I would call a *society of normalisation*. I mean, more precisely, that disciplinary normalisations come into ever greater conflict with the juridical systems of sovereignty: their incompatibility with each other is ever more acutely felt and apparent; some kind of arbitrating discourse is made ever more necessary, a type of power and of knowledge that the sanctity of science would render neutral. It is precisely in the extension of medicine that we see, in some sense, not so much the linking as the perpetual exchange or encounter of mechanisms of discipline with the principle of right. The developments of medicine, the general medicalisation of behaviours, conducts, discourses, desires etc., take place at the point of intersection between the two heterogeneous levels of discipline and sovereignty. For this reason, against these usurpations by the disciplinary mechanisms, against this ascent of a power that is tied to scientific knowledge, we find that there is no solid recourse available to us today, such being our situation, except that which lies precisely in the return to a theory of right organised around sovereignty and articulated upon its ancient principle. When today one wants to object in some way to the disciplines and all the effects of power and knowledge that are linked to them, what is it that one does, concretely, in real life, what do the Magistrates Union[8] or other similar institutions do, if not precisely appeal to this canon of right, this famous, formal right, that is said to be bourgeois, and which in reality is the right of sovereignty? But I believe that we find ourselves here in a kind of blind alley: it is not through recourse to sovereignty against discipline that the effects of disciplinary power can be limited, because sovereignty and disciplinary mechanisms are two absolutely integral constituents of the general mechanism of power in our society.

If one wants to look for a non-disciplinary form of power, or rather, to struggle against disciplines and disciplinary power, it is not towards the ancient right of sovereignty that one should turn, but towards the possibility of a new form of right, one which must indeed be anti-disciplinarian, but at the same time liberated from the principle of sovereignty.[9] It is at this point that we once more come up against the notion of repression, whose use in this context I believe to be doubly unfortunate. On the one hand, it contains an obscure reference to a certain theory of sovereignty, the sovereignty of the sovereign rights of the individual, and on the other hand, its usage introduces a system of psychological reference points borrowed from the human sciences, that is to say, from discourses and practices that belong to the disciplinary realm. I believe that the notion of repression remains a juridical-disciplinary notion[,] whatever the critical use one would make of it. To this extent the critical application of the notion of repression is found to be vitiated and nullified from the outset by the two-fold juridical and disciplinary reference it contains to sovereignty on the one hand and to normalisation on the other.

SOURCE: Michel Foucault, "Lecture Two: 14 January 1976," trans. Kate Soper, in *Power/Knowledge: Selected Interviews and Other Writings, 1972–1977*, ed. Colin Gordon (New York: Pantheon; Brighton, Sussex: Harvester Press, 1980), pp. 92–108. This untitled lecture was the second delivered by Foucault that term at the Collège de France. He never published it, but it was transcribed and translated into Italian by Alessandro Fontana and Pasquale Pasquino, appearing in a collection of his works that they edited: *Microfisica del Potere* (1977, *Short Writings on Power*).

8. This Union, established after 1968, has adopted a radical line on civil rights, the law and the prisons [Gordon's note].
9. This is one of the few places where Foucault hints at the possibility of a new kind of power through which contemporary humanity might be able to be liberated or emancipated from the grip and domination of human life by "disciplinary power." What that "new form of right" and of power might be, however, remains unarticulated.

JACQUES DERRIDA
(1930 – 2004)

Derrida began his philosophical career interested in issues and problems relating to Husserlian phenomenology. He ended it as the epitome of post-phenomenological, post-existential, poststructuralist, postmodern, deconstructionist rebellion against the Western philosophical tradition and its various extensions and developments in the first half of the twentieth century. In the course of this trajectory he became one of the most controversial figures in twentieth-century philosophy, inspiring off-the-charts responses at both ends—lionized by many, reviled by many others—to his apparent delight. He seems to have deliberately made it difficult for mainstream philosophers to know what to make of him—or rather, he made it easy for them, by making it so difficult for them to take him seriously. It is impossible to say at this point whether Derrida will be judged by posterity to have been a significant figure in the history of philosophy in (or against) any of its traditions. But during the last decades of his life, he was impossible to ignore. For some he was philosophy's court jester and clown prince, the reductio ad absurdum of deconstructionism. For others he was philosophy's joyful liberator, a whistle-blower on its past and the herald of its only possible (postmodern) future. And for others still, whose judgment is more mixed, he matters because he was onto something important. At this juncture the jury is still out.

Jacques Derrida ("Derry-DAH") was born in Algeria (then under French colonial rule). His family, though not actively religious, was ethnically Jewish, and he therefore was expelled from school in 1942, under the anti-Jewish regulations imposed on the Vichy French government by the Germans. He received his baccalaureate degree in 1948 and in the following year moved to France, where he attended the Lycée Louis-le-Grand in Paris. He had already become interested in philosophy, and (supposedly upon hearing a radio broadcast about Albert Camus, who like him was born in Algeria) conceived a desire to take philosophy classes at the École Normale Supérieure. He failed his entrance examination twice before being admitted in 1952 on his third try. On his first day he met Louis Althusser, who would become a leading Marxist philosopher and a lifelong friend, to whom Derrida remained true even after Althusser murdered his wife (and spent the rest of his life in and out of mental hospitals).

In Derrida's student years, Sartrean existentialism and Hegelianism were ascendant in French philosophy; but he soon shifted his focus to HUSSERL, HEIDEGGER, and phenomenology, writing his master's thesis (1954) on Husserl. He then studied with the prominent HEGEL scholar Jean Hyppolite, who was to have directed the dissertation he planned to write on the ideality of the literary object. But Derrida's attention began to be attracted by the growing French appropriation of NIETZSCHE and by the movement of structuralism in the social sciences. He also won a scholarship to study at Harvard for a year (in 1956–57), during which he met and married his first wife, Marguerite Aucouturier, a psychoanalyst.

Upon returning to France, during the Algerian War, Derrida spent two years teaching English and French to the children of soldiers in lieu of military service. He then taught at the lycée in Le Mans (1959–60) and at the Sorbonne (1960–64), before becoming a professor of philosophy at the École Normale (in 1965), where he remained for twenty years. In 1966, he participated in a seminar on structuralism at Johns Hopkins University (presenting the paper that is the second of the selections below); there he met Paul de Man, a prominent Yale deconstructionist literary theorist, with whom he formed a close relationship and who helped launch the American part of his career. In 1968 he had his first visiting appointment at Yale, which was followed by frequent appointments at both Yale and Johns Hopkins.

Yet Derrida still had no academic qualifications beyond his 1954 master's degree and 1956 *agrégation* exam (the competitive test required for advanced teaching positions). Finally, in 1980, at the age of 50, after he had already published seven books and become one of the world's best-known philosophers, he submitted already published works as his *thèse d'état* (advanced doctoral thesis) and was awarded his doctorate by the École Normale. EMMANUEL LÉVINAS was one of his examiners. In 1983 he helped found the Collège International de Philosophie, and in 1984 he assumed the post—which he held until his death—of director at the School for Advanced Studies in the Social Sciences in Paris. In 1987 he became professor of philosophy at the University of California at Irvine, which from that time served as his American academic base and residence. He died in France of pancreatic cancer in 2004. He had three sons—two with his wife Marguerite, and one with Sylviane Agacinski, a philosopher and feminist (and future wife of Lionel Jospin, who after their marriage became prime minister of France).

Derrida had a flair for publicity. He and the American analytic philosopher John Searle had a long-running philosophical debate that entertained the profession for years. He also was involved in several movies, including a 2002 documentary about himself and his work (called, appropriately enough, *Derrida*) and the 1983 film *Ghost Dance*, in which he also appeared (as himself). His stage management of his career helped make him a legend in his own time. And this status was achieved at least in part by the flair with which he tried to subvert philosophy itself as we

know it. Though he was neither the first nor the last figure in the recent history of philosophy featured in these volumes to make such an attempt, he was second to none in the playfulness with which he carried on his campaign.

Derrida's philosophical rebellion began with what might seem to be a marginal idea in the philosophical tradition: the difference between writing and speaking. He sought to develop this distinction into a powerful tool with which to undermine the entire Western philosophic tradition—a metaphysical tradition, as he construed it, in which the idea of truth as "self-presence" is privileged, while writing is seen as, a best, a necessary evil. This tradition is centered on the Greek notion of *logos*—a notoriously challenging word to translate—which Derrida took to mean the essence, law, principle, or self-same truth of a thing. He then proceeded to show how supposedly self-present truth and self-evident meaning are in fact not immediately "present" at all, and indeed can never be made present, as he investigated Western philosophy's failure to articulate such a truth. Plato (ca. 427– ca. 347 B.C.E.) resorts to metaphor and myth, for example; Descartes (1596– 1650) dismisses the hypotheses of madness and the evil deceiver but remains haunted by their conceivability; and the transcendental ego is all-important, for Husserl, but must remain empty. Such internal conflicts suggest the illusory nature of the certainty that the tradition affirms. Derrida then proceeded to propose that *writing* in fact had priority, in that it is the location of the traces and ruptures that inhabit language and that are ignored by the Western tradition, which is preoccupied with the idea and ideal of the immediate self-presence of truth and meaning in consciousness and their supposedly direct transference through the *spoken* word.

As the first selection below—on *différance*—shows, Derrida attempts to think about and describe something that is by definition a paradox (an "aporia"), and thus logically should be quite simply impossible. This impossibility, which he designates "*différance*," is a production that is neither passive nor active, an "origin" that is neither a *genetic* origin nor a metaphysical one, in any sense. It might be thought of, he suggests, as a gap that disrupts all identity, and that can never be made articulate or intelligible. It is a mind-bending concept; and one of the points at issue between those who are sympathetic to Derrida and those who are not is whether it is important or even appropriate *to ask* whether the very idea of something of this sort is meaningful, what sort of case can be made for invoking it, or how one can know whether the concept has been grasped. Derrida and those sympathetic to him regard all such questions—and even the desire to ask them—as symptoms of a misguided way of thinking, of which they hope to cure those afflicted by it.

Différance, a term created by inserting an "a" into the ordinary French word *différence* in place of its second "e," is one of Derrida's many neologisms that resist translation. But significantly, this modification cannot be heard or spoken in the French language: it is perceptible only in writing. By making (inscribing) this difference on the written page, Derrida wants to keep it from being taken up as a concept or a (spoken) word in a language system. It remains a reminder and a remainder, indicating the "play of intertextuality" or the fact that all attempts to achieve perfect meaning and absolute truth suffer from a textual slippage—an infection (as it were) by *différance* that enables deconstruction to trace the traces of subversive meanings within a text.

Différance has a double meaning for Derrida: it indicates the notions both of difference and of deferral. This double meaning is perhaps more evident to the English-speaker in another crucial Derridian notion—that of a "supplement" (*supplément*), which in his usage indicates both an addition to something and its being supplanted. Such duality is also found in the notion of a "trace"— something that is at once present and absent—and indeed is a virtual hallmark

of Derrida's key terms. His *différance* remains a mere mark through which we try to name the unnamable: a mark that acts as a spur turning us toward the ceaseless play of differences in language.

In the 1970s Derrida worked out these ideas through applications, in various styles, of "deconstruction" to a multitude of texts. In the 1980s deconstruction blossomed as a method of literary criticism. Many of his writings during this decade were attempts to respond both to legitimate criticisms and to what he considered to be distortions of his positions. In the 1990s his interest turned toward questions of ethics, politics, and institutions, on which he wrote profusely. Derrida has often been deemed an irresponsible skeptic who subverts all distinctions merely for the fun of it—a representation that makes talk of the ethics and politics of deconstruction seem like an absurdity. He claimed to the contrary that the impetus behind his kind of deconstruction, its focus on the texts of the tradition, and its subversion of the hegemonic discourse of the Western (logocentric) tradition is a demand for justice.

The second selection below is the earlier of the two selections. "Structure, Sign and Play in the Discourse of the Human Sciences"—Derrida's 1966 lecture given at "The Languages of Criticism and the Sciences of Man," a landmark conference at Johns Hopkins University in Baltimore—is a vivid statement of his critique of structuralism. The development of poststructuralism did not occur overnight, and his lecture was certainly not the first statement of his criticism of structuralist thought, but it might be seen as the occasion on which the movement crystallized. MICHEL FOUCAULT (three years Derrida's senior) had already written his first three books, which Foucault himself would later call imperfect and too heavily influenced by structuralism (an influence removed in 1969 in his methodological work *The Archaeology of Knowledge*). GILLES DELEUZE's writing to that point had been largely historical, though his 1963 work on Nietzsche and the themes of affirmation, play, laughter, and eternal recurrence undoubtedly influenced Derrida's thinking and texts. Developments beyond structuralism were present in these early works, just as the elements of the criticisms of immediate self-presence—the traces of *différance*—can be found scattered throughout the history of recent thought (in KIERKEGAARD, Nietzsche, Heidegger, and Freud, among others); but in the early and mid-1960s, structuralism remained the dominant intellectual paradigm in France. Derrida's criticisms and development of the notion of *différance* arguably mark the break that has come to be known as poststructuralism.

That being said, Derrida not only is paradigmatic of poststructuralism but also stands apart from its less nuanced practitioners and advocates, because he did not believe a simple inversion of the tradition to be possible. One cannot simply elevate oneself out of "logocentric" discourse—discourse that privileges "logically rigorous" argument and accepts the "metaphysics of presence"—by recovering "minority voices." Derrida believed rather that language remains forever bound to the notions of presence, being, and origin. There is no location outside this discourse for him. The trace of *différance* is forever that—a trace that can never be made present. Thus he suggests that both Heidegger (a critic of Western metaphysics and humanism) and structuralists—and even some poststructuralists—still display a nostalgia for presence and a lingering hope of finding a way to capture some sort of ultimate Reality, Truth, and Being. Derrida, however, can fairly be said to have lived and written with no such hope.

Différance

I will speak, therefore, of a letter.

Of the first letter, if the alphabet, and most of the speculations which have ventured into it, are to be believed.

I will speak, therefore, of the letter *a*, this initial letter which it apparently has been necessary to insinuate, here and there, into the writing of the word *difference*; and to do so in the course of a writing on writing, and also of a writing within writing whose different trajectories thereby find themselves, at certain very determined points, intersecting with a kind of gross spelling mistake, a lapse in the discipline and law which regulate writing and keep it seemly. One can always, de facto or de jure, erase or reduce this lapse in spelling, and find it (according to situations to be analyzed each time, although amounting to the same), grave or unseemly, that is, to follow the most ingenuous hypothesis, amusing. Thus, even if one seeks to pass over such an infraction in silence, the interest that one takes in it can be recognized and situated in advance as prescribed by the mute irony, the inaudible misplacement, of this literal permutation. One can always act as if it made no difference. And I must state here and now that today's discourse will be less a justification of, and even less an apology for, this silent lapse in spelling, than a kind of insistent intensification of its play.

On the other hand, I will have to be excused if I refer, at least implicitly, to some of the texts I have ventured to publish. This is precisely because I would like to attempt, to a certain extent, and even though in principle and in the last analysis this is impossible, and impossible for essential reasons, to reassemble in a *sheaf* the different directions in which I have been able to utilize what I would call provisionally the word or concept of *différance*, or rather to let it impose itself upon me in its neographism,[1] although as we shall see, *différance* is literally neither a word nor a concept. And I insist upon the word *sheaf* for two reasons. On the one hand, I will not be concerned, as I might have been, with describing a history and narrating its stages, text by text, context by context, demonstrating the economy that each time imposed this graphic disorder; rather, I will be concerned with the *general system of this economy*. On the other hand, the word *sheaf* seems to mark more appropriately that the assemblage to be proposed has the complex structure of a weaving, an interlacing which permits the different threads and different lines of meaning—or of force—to go off again in different directions, just as it is always ready to tie itself up with others.

Therefore, preliminarily, let me recall that this discreet graphic intervention, which neither primarily nor simply aims to shock the reader or the grammarian, came to be formulated in the course of a written investigation of a question about writing. Now it happens, I would say in effect, that this graphic difference (*a* instead of *e*), this marked difference between two apparently vocal notations, between two vowels, remains purely graphic: it is read, or it is written, but it cannot be heard.[2] It cannot be apprehended in speech, and we will see why it also bypasses the order of apprehension in general. It is offered by a mute mark, by a tacit monument, I would even say by a pyramid, thinking not only of the form of the letter when it is printed as a capital, but also of the text in Hegel's *Encyclopedia* in which the body of the sign is compared to the Egyptian Pyramid.[3] The *a* of *différance*, thus, is not heard; it remains silent, secret and discreet as a tomb: *oikēsis*.[4] And thereby let us anticipate the delineation of a site, the familial residence and tomb of the proper[5] in which is produced, by *différance*, the *economy of death*. This stone—provided that one knows how to decipher its inscription—is not far from announcing the death of the tyrant.[6]

And it is a tomb that cannot even be made to resonate. In effect, I cannot let you know through my discourse, through the speech being addressed at this moment to the French Society of Philosophy, what difference I am talking about when I talk about it. I can speak of this graphic difference only through a very indirect discourse on writing, and on the condition that I spec-

---

1. That is, novel written expression. Derrida's spelling of the term in question is deliberate, and is a matter of which he makes much in the essay.
2. A statement perhaps more true in French than in English.
3. See HEGEL, *Encyclopedia of the Philosophical Sciences*, part 3, *The Philosophy of Geist* (1830), §458.
4. Tomb (Greek).
5. Throughout this book I will translate *le proper* as "the proper." Derrida most often intends all the senses of the word at once: that which is correct, as in *le sens propre* (proper, literal meaning), and that which is one's own, that which may be owned, that which is legally, correctly owned—all the links between proper, property, and propriety [translator's note].
6. The last three sentences refer elliptically and playfully to the following ideas. Derrida first plays on the "silence" of the *a* in *différance* as being like a silent tomb, like a pyramid, like the pyramid to

which Hegel compares the body of the sign. "Tomb" in Greek is *oikēsis*, which is akin to the Greek *oikos*—house—from which the word "economy" derives (*oikos*—house—and *nemein*—to manage). Thus Derrida speaks of the "economy of death" as the "familial residence and tomb of the proper." Further, and more elliptically still, Derrida speaks of the tomb, which always bears an inscription in stone, announcing the death of the tyrant. This seems to refer to Hegel's treatment of the Antigone story in the *Phenomenology* [1807; see excerpt, above]. It will be recalled that Antigone defies the tyrant Creon by burying her brother Polynices. Creon retaliates by having Antigone entombed. There she cheats the slow death that awaits her by hanging herself. The tyrant Creon has a change of heart too late, and—after the suicides of his son and his wife, his *family*—kills himself. Thus family, death, inscription, tomb, law, economy [translator's note]. This analysis illustrates some typical features of Derrida's way of writing (and thinking).

ify, each time, whether I am referring to difference with an *e* or *différance* with an *a*. Which will not simplify things today, and will give us all, you and me, a great deal of trouble, if, at least, we wish to understand each other. In any event, the oral specifications that I will provide—when I say "with an *e*" or "with an *a*"—will refer uncircumventably to a *written text* that keeps watch over my discourse, to a text that I am holding in front of me, that I will read, and toward which I necessarily will attempt to direct your hands and your eyes. We will be able neither to do without the passage through a written text, nor to avoid the order of the disorder produced within it—and this, first of all, is what counts for me.

The pyramidal silence of the graphic difference between the *e* and the *a* can function, of course, only within the system of phonetic writing, and within the language and grammar which is as historically linked to phonetic writing as it is to the entire culture inseparable from phonetic writing. But I would say that this in itself—the silence that functions within only a so-called phonetic writing—quite opportunely conveys or reminds us that, contrary to a very widespread prejudice, there is no phonetic writing. There is no purely and rigorously phonetic writing. So-called phonetic writing, by all rights and in principle, and not only due to an empirical or technical insufficiency, can function only by admitting into its system nonphonetic "signs" (punctuation, spacing, etc.). And an examination of the structure and necessity of these nonphonetic signs quickly reveals that they can barely tolerate the concept of the sign itself. Better, the play of difference, which, as Saussure[7] reminded us, is the condition for the possibility and functioning of every sign, is in itself a silent play. Inaudible is the difference between two phonemes which alone permits them to be and to operate as such. The inaudible opens up the apprehension of two present phonemes such as they present themselves. If there is no purely phonetic writing, it is that there is no purely phonetic *phōnē*.[8] The difference which establishes phonemes and lets them be heard remains in and of itself inaudible, in every sense of the word.

It will be objected, for the same reasons, that graphic difference itself vanishes into the night, can never be sensed as a full term, but rather extends an invisible relationship, the mark of an inapparent relationship between two spectacles. Doubtless. But, from this point of view, that the difference marked in the "differ( )nce" between the *e* and the *a* eludes both vision and hearing perhaps happily suggests that here we must be permitted to refer to an order which no longer belongs to sensibility. But neither can it belong to intelligibility, to the ideality which is not fortuitously affiliated with the objectivity of *theōrein* or understanding.[9] Here, therefore, we must let ourselves refer to an order that resists the opposition, one of the founding oppositions of philosophy,

7. Ferdinand de Saussure (1857–1913), Swiss linguist whose work was foundational for structuralism in philosophy and social theory as well as in linguistics; he viewed language as a system of signs, with each element in a language defined by its differences from other elements in that language.
8. Sound (Greek).
9. ". . . not fortuitously affiliated with the objectivity of *theōrein* or understanding." A play on words has been lost in translation here, a loss that makes this sentence difficult to understand. In the previous sentence Derrida says that the difference between the *e* and the *a* of *différence/différance* can neither be seen nor heard. It is not a sensible— that is, relating to the senses—difference. But, he goes on to explain, neither is this an intelligible difference, for the very names by which we conceive of objective intelligibility are already in complicity with sensibility. *Theōrein*—the Greek origin of "theory"—literally means "to look at," *see*; and the word Derrida uses for "understanding" here is *entendement*, the noun form of *entendre*, to *hear* [translator's note].

between the sensible and the intelligible. The order which resists this opposition, and resists it because it transports it, is announced in a movement of *différance* (with an *a*) between two differences or two letters, a *différance* which belongs neither to the voice nor to writing in the usual sense, and which is located, as the strange space that will keep us together here for an hour, *between* speech and writing, and beyond the tranquil familiarity which links us to one and the other, occasionally reassuring us in our illusion that they are two.

What am I to do in order to speak of the *a* of *différance*? It goes without saying that it cannot be *exposed*. One can expose only that which at a certain moment can become *present*, manifest, that which can be shown, presented as something present, a being-present in its truth, in the truth of a present or the presence of the present. Now if *différance* i̶s̶ (and I also cross out the "i̶s̶") what makes possible the presentation of the being-present, it is never presented as such. It is never offered to the present. Or to anyone. Reserving itself, not exposing itself, in regular fashion it exceeds the order of truth at a certain precise point, but without dissimulating itself as something, as a mysterious being, in the occult of a nonknowledge or in a hole with indeterminable borders (for example, in a topology of castration). In every exposition it would be exposed to disappearing as disappearance. It would risk appearing: disappearing.

So much so that the detours, locutions, and syntax in which I will often have to take recourse will resemble those of negative theology, occasionally even to the point of being indistinguishable from negative theology. Already we have had to delineate *that différance is not*, does not exist, is not a present-being (*on*) in any form; and we will be led to delineate also everything *that* it *is not*, that is, *everything*; and consequently that it has neither existence nor essence. It derives from no category of being, whether present or absent. And yet those aspects of *différance* which are thereby delineated are not theological, not even in the order of the most negative of negative theologies, which are always concerned with disengaging a superessentiality beyond the finite categories of essence and existence, that is, of presence, and always hastening to recall that God is refused the predicate of existence, only in order to acknowledge his superior, inconceivable, and ineffable mode of being. Such a development is not in question here, and this will be confirmed progressively. *Différance* is not only irreducible to any ontological or theological—ontotheological—reappropriation, but as the very opening of the space in which ontotheology—philosophy—produces its system and its history, it includes ontotheology, inscribing it and exceeding it without return.

For the same reason there is nowhere to *begin* to trace the sheaf or the graphics of *différance*. For what is put into question is precisely the quest for a rightful beginning, an absolute point of departure, a principal responsibility. The problematic of writing is opened by putting into question the value *arkhē*.[1] What I will propose here will not be elaborated simply as a philosophical discourse, operating according to principles, postulates, axioms or definitions, and proceeding along the discursive lines of a linear order of reasons.

1. The Greek *arkhē* combines the values of a founding principle and of government by a controlling principle (e.g. *arche*ology, mon*arch*y) [translator's note].

In the delineation of *différance* everything is strategic and adventurous. Strategic because no transcendent truth present outside the field of writing can govern theologically the totality of the field. Adventurous because this strategy is not a simple strategy in the sense that strategy orients tactics according to a final goal, a *telos* or theme of domination, a mastery and ultimate reappropriation of the development of the field. Finally, a strategy without finality, what might be called blind tactics, or empirical wandering if the value of empiricism did not itself acquire its entire meaning in its opposition to philosophical responsibility. If there is a certain wandering in the tracing of *différance*, it no more follows the lines of philosophical-logical discourse than that of its symmetrical and integral inverse, empirical-logical discourse. The concept of *play* keeps itself beyond this opposition, announcing, on the eve of philosophy and beyond it, the unity of chance and necessity in calculations without end.

Also, by decision and as a rule of the game, if you will, turning these propositions back on themselves, we will be introduced to the thought of *différance* by the theme of strategy or the strategem. By means of this solely strategic justification, I wish to underline that the efficacity of the thematic of *différance* may very well, indeed must, one day be superseded, lending itself if not to its own replacement, at least to enmeshing itself in a chain that in truth it never will have governed. Whereby, once again, it is not theological.

I would say, first off, that *différance*, which is neither a word nor a concept, strategically seemed to me the most proper one to think, if not to master—thought, here, being that which is maintained in a certain necessary relationship with the structural limits of mastery—what is most irreducible about our "era." Therefore I am starting, strategically, from the place and the time in which "we" are, even though in the last analysis my opening is not justifiable, since it is only on the basis of *différance* and its "history" that we can allegedly know who and where "we" are, and what the limits of an "era" might be.

Even though *différance* is neither a word nor a concept, let us nevertheless attempt a simple and approximate semantic analysis that will take us to within sight of what is at stake.

We know that the verb *différer* (Latin verb *differre*) has two meanings which seem quite distinct,[2] for example in Littré[3] they are the object of two separate articles. In this sense the Latin *differre* is not simply a translation of the Greek *diapherein*,[4] and this will not be without consequences for us, linking our discourse to a particular language, and to a language that passes as less philosophical, less originally philosophical than the other. For the distribution of meaning in the Greek *diapherein* does not comport one of the two motifs of the Latin *differre*, to wit, the action of putting off until later, of taking into account, of taking account of time and of the forces of an operation that implies an economical calculation, a detour, a delay, a relay, a reserve, a representation—concepts that I would summarize here in a word I have never used but that could be inscribed in this chain: *temporization*. *Différer* in this

---

2. In English the two distinct meanings of the Latin *differre* have become two separate words: to defer and to differ [translator's note].
3. A monumental French dictionary compiled by the French lexicographer Paul-Émile Littré

(1801–1881).
4. Literally, "to carry over or across"; intransitively, "to differ" (the verb is cognate with the Latin *differre*).

sense is to temporize, to take recourse, consciously or unconsciously, in the temporal and temporizing mediation of a detour that suspends the accomplishment or fulfillment of "desire" or "will," and equally effects this suspension in a mode that annuls or tempers its own effect. And we will see, later, how this temporization is also temporalization and spacing, the becoming-time of space and the becoming-space of time, the "originary constitution" of time and space, as metaphysics or transcendental phenomenology would say, to use the language that here is criticized and displaced.

The other sense of *différer* is the more common and identifiable one: to be not identical, to be other, discernible, etc. When dealing with *differen(ts)(ds)*, a word that can be written with a final *ts* or a final *ds*, as you will, whether it is a question of dissimilar otherness or of allergic and polemical otherness, an interval, a distance, *spacing*, must be produced between the elements other, and be produced with a certain perseverence in repetition.[5]

Now the word *différence* (with an *e*) can never refer either to *différer* as temporization or to *différends* as *polemos*.[6] Thus the word *différance* (with an *a*) is to compensate—economically—this loss of meaning, for *différance* can refer simultaneously to the entire configuration of its meanings. It is immediately and irreducibly polysemic,[7] which will not be indifferent to the economy of my discourse here. In its polysemia this word, of course, like any meaning, must defer to the discourse in which it occurs, its interpretive context; but in a way it defers itself, or at least does so more readily than any other word, the *a* immediately deriving from the present participle (*différant*), thereby bringing us close to the very action of the verb *différer*, before it has even produced an effect constituted as something different or as *différence* (with an *e*).[8] In a conceptuality adhering to classical strictures "*différance*" would be said to designate a constitutive, productive, and originary causality, the process of scission and division which would produce or constitute different things or differences. But, because it brings us close to the infinitive and active kernel of *différer*, *différance* (with an *a*) neutralizes what the infinitive denotes as simply active, just as *mouvance* in our language does not simply mean the fact of moving, of moving oneself or of being moved. No more is resonance the act of resonating. We must consider that in the usage of our language the ending *-ance* remains undecided *between* the active and the passive. And we will see why that which lets itself be designated *différance* is neither simply active nor simply passive, announcing or rather recalling something like the middle voice,[9] saying an operation that is not an operation, an operation that cannot

5. The next few sentences will require some annotation, to be found in this note and the next [notes 6 and 8]. In this sentence Derrida is pointing out that two words that sound exactly alike in French (*différents*, *différends*) refer to the sense of *différer* that implies spacing, otherness—difference in its usual English sense. *Les différents* are different things; *les différends* are differences of opinion, grounds for dispute—whence the references to *allergy* (from the Greek *allos*, other) and polemics [translator's note].

6. However, to continue the last note, *différence* (in French) does not convey the sense of active putting off, of deferring (*différance* in what would be its usual sense in French, if it were a word in common usage), or the sense of active polemical difference, actively differing with someone or

something. ("Active" here, though, is not really correct, for reasons that Derrida will explain below.) The point is that there is no noun-verb, no gerund for either sense in French [translator's note]. *Polemos*: war; battle (Greek).

7. That is, has multiple meanings.

8. Such a gerund would normally be constructed from the present participle of the verb: *différant*. Curiously then, the noun *différance* suspends itself between the two senses of *différant*—deferring, differing. We might say that it defers differing, and differs from deferring, in and of itself [translator's note].

9. In classical Greek, the form of the verb that signifies that the subject is acting upon itself or for its own benefit.

be conceived either as passion or as the action of a subject on an object, or on the basis of the categories of agent or patient, neither on the basis of nor moving toward any of these *terms*. For the middle voice, a certain nontransitivity, may be what philosophy, at its outset, distributed into an active and a passive voice, thereby constituting itself by means of this repression.

Différance as temporization, *différance* as spacing. How are they to be joined?

Let us start, since we are already there, from the problematic of the sign and of writing. The sign is usually said to be put in the place of the thing itself, the present thing, "thing" here standing equally for meaning or referent. The sign represents the present in its absence. It takes the place of the present. When we cannot grasp or show the thing, state the present, the being-present, when the present cannot be presented, we signify, we go through the detour of the sign. We take or give signs. We signal. The sign, in this sense, is deferred presence. Whether we are concerned with the verbal or the written sign, with the monetary sign, or with electoral delegation and political representation, the circulation of signs defers the moment in which we can encounter the thing itself, make it ours, consume or expend it, touch it, see it, intuit its presence. What I am describing here in order to define it is the classically determined structure of the sign in all the banality of its characteristics—signification as the *différance* of temporization. And this structure presupposes that the sign, which defers presence, is conceivable only on the *basis* of the presence that it defers and *moving toward* the deferred presence that it aims to reappropriate. According to this classical semiology, the substitution of the sign for the thing itself is both *secondary* and *provisional*: secondary due to an original and lost presence from which the sign thus derives; provisional as concerns this final and missing presence toward which the sign in this sense is a movement of mediation.

In attempting to put into question these traits of the provisional secondariness of the substitute, one would come to see something like an originary *différance*; but one could no longer call it originary or final in the extent to which the values of origin, archi-, *telos*, *eskhaton*, etc. have always denoted presence—*ousia*, *parousia*.[1] To put into question the secondary and provisional characteristics of the sign, to oppose to them an "originary" *différance*, therefore would have two consequences.

1. One could no longer include *différance* in the concept of the sign, which always has meant the representation of a presence, and has been constituted in a system (thought or language) governed by and moving toward presence.

2. And thereby one puts into question the authority of presence, or of its simple symmetrical opposite, absence or lack. Thus one questions the limit which has always constrained us, which still constrains us—as inhabitants of a language and a system of thought—to formulate the meaning of Being in general as presence or absence, in the categories of being or beingness (*ousia*). Already it appears that the type of question to which we are redirected is, let us say, of the Heideggerian type, and that *différance* seems to lead back to the ontico-ontological difference. I will be permitted to hold off on this reference. I will note only that between difference as temporization-temporalization,

---

1. *Ousia* and *parousia* imply presence as both origin and end, the founding principle (*arkhē*-) as that toward which one moves (*telos*, *eskhaton*) [translator's note].

which can no longer be conceived within the horizon of the present, and what Heidegger says in *Being and Time* about temporalization as the transcendental horizon of the question of Being,[2] which must be liberated from its traditional, metaphysical domination by the present and the now, there is a strict communication, even though not an exhaustive and irreducibly necessary one.

But first let us remain within the semiological problematic in order to see *différance* as temporization and *différance* as spacing conjoined. Most of the semiological or linguistic researches that dominate the field of thought today, whether due to their own results or to the regulatory model that they find themselves acknowledging everywhere, refer genealogically to Saussure (correctly or incorrectly) as their common inaugurator. Now Saussure first of all is the thinker who put the *arbitrary character of the sign* and the *differential character* of the sign at the very foundation of general semiology, particularly linguistics. And, as we know, these two motifs—arbitrary and differential—are inseparable in his view. There can be arbitrariness only because the system of signs is constituted solely by the differences in terms, and not by their plenitude. The elements of signification function due not to the compact force of their nuclei but rather to the network of oppositions that distinguishes them, and then relates them one to another. "Arbitrary and differential," says Saussure, "are two correlative characteristics."

Now this principle of difference, as the condition for signification, affects the *totality* of the sign, that is the sign as both signified and signifier. The signified is the concept, the ideal meaning; and the signifier is what Saussure calls the "image," the "psychical imprint" of a material, physical—for example, acoustical—phenomenon. We do not have to go into all the problems posed by these definitions here. Let us cite Saussure only at the point which interests us: "The conceptual side of value is made up solely of relations and differences with respect to the other terms of language, and the same can be said of its material side . . . Everything that has been said up to this point boils down to this: in language there are only differences. Even more important: a difference generally implies positive terms between which the difference is set up; but in language there are only differences *without positive terms*. Whether we take the signified or the signifier, language has neither ideas nor sounds that existed before the linguistic system, but only conceptual and phonic differences that have issued from the system. The idea or phonic substance that a sign contains is of less importance than the other signs that surround it."[3]

The first consequence to be drawn from this is that the signified concept is never present in and of itself, in a sufficient presence that would refer only to itself. Essentially and lawfully, every concept is inscribed in a chain or in a system within which it refers to the other, to other concepts, by means of the systematic play of differences. Such a play, *différance*, is thus no longer simply a concept, but rather the possibility of conceptuality, of a conceptual process and system in general. For the same reason, *différance*, which is not a

2. In the introduction to *Being and Time* (1927), §8, HEIDEGGER describes the task of part 1 of that book as "the explication of time as the transcendental horizon of the question of being" (trans. Joan Stambaugh).

3. Ferdinand de Saussure, *Course in General Lin-* *guistics*, trans. Wade Baskin (New York: Philosophical Library, 1959), pp. 117–18, 120 [translator's note]. These ideas are Derrida's points of departure in this essay. (For the quotation that ends the previous paragraph, see p. 118, where the translation replaces "characteristics" with "qualities.")

concept, is not simply a word, that is, what is generally represented as the calm, present, and self-referential unity of concept and phonic material. Later we will look into the word in general.

The difference of which Saussure speaks is itself, therefore, neither a concept nor a word among others. The same can be said, a fortiori, of *différance*. And we are thereby led to explicate the relation of one to the other.

In a language, in the *system* of language, there are only differences. Therefore a taxonomical operation can undertake the systematic, statistical, and classificatory inventory of a language. But, on the one hand, these differences *play*: in language, in speech too, and in the exchange between language and speech. On the other hand, these differences are themselves *effects*. They have not fallen from the sky fully formed, and are no more inscribed in a *topos noētos*,[4] than they are prescribed in the gray matter of the brain. If the word "history" did not in and of itself convey the motif of a final repression of difference, one could say that only differences can be "historical" from the outset and in each of their aspects.

What is written as *différance*, then, will be the playing movement that "produces"—by means of something that is not simply an activity—these differences, these effects of difference. This does not mean that the *différance* that produces differences is somehow before them, in a simple and unmodified— in-different—present. *Différance* is the non-full, non-simple, structured and differentiating origin of differences. Thus, the name "origin" no longer suits it.

Since language, which Saussure says is a classification, has not fallen from the sky, its differences have been produced, are produced effects, but they are effects which do not find their cause in a subject or a substance, in a thing in general, a being that is somewhere present, thereby eluding the play of *différance*. If such a presence were implied in the concept of cause in general, in the most classical fashion, we then would have to speak of an effect without a cause, which very quickly would lead to speaking of no effect at all. I have attempted to indicate a way out of the closure of this framework via the "trace," which is no more an effect than it has a cause, but which in and of itself, outside its text, is not sufficient to operate the necessary transgression.

Since there is no presence before and outside semiological difference, what Saussure has written about language can be extended to the sign in general: "Language is necessary in order for speech to be intelligible and to produce all of its effects; but the latter is necessary in order for language to be established; historically, the fact of speech always comes first."[5]

Retaining at least the framework, if not the content, of this requirement formulated by Saussure, we will designate as *différance* the movement according to which language, or any code, any system of referral in general, is constituted "historically" as a weave of differences. "Is constituted," "is produced," "is created," "movement," "historically," etc., necessarily being understood beyond the metaphysical language in which they are retained, along with all their implications. We ought to demonstrate why concepts like *production*, constitution, and history remain in complicity with what is at issue here. But this would take me too far today—toward the theory of the representation of

4. Intelligible region (Greek), a phrase taken from the allegory of the cave in Plato's *Republic* 7.517b; it refers to the Platonic realm of Forms or Ideas (fundamental, timeless universals).

5. Saussure, *Course in General Linguistics*, p. 18 [translator's note].

the "circle" in which we appear to be enclosed—and I utilize such concepts, like many others, only for their strategic convenience and in order to undertake their deconstruction at the currently most decisive point.[6] In any event, it will be understood, by means of the circle in which we appear to be engaged, that as it is written here, *différance* is no more static than it is genetic, no more structural than historical. Or is no less so; and to object to this on the basis of the oldest of metaphysical oppositions (for example, by setting some generative point of view against a structural-taxonomical point of view, or vice versa) would be, above all, not to read what here is missing from orthographical ethics. Such oppositions have not the least pertinence to *différance*, which makes the thinking of it uneasy and uncomfortable.

Now if we consider the chain in which *différance* lends itself to a certain number of nonsynonymous substitutions, according to the necessity of the context, why have recourse to the "reserve," to "archi-writing," to the "archi-trace," to "spacing," that is, to the "supplement," or to the *pharmakon*, and soon to the hymen, to the margin-mark-march, etc.[7]

Let us go on. It is because of *différance* that the movement of signification is possible only if each so-called "present" element, each element appearing on the scene of presence, is related to something other than itself, thereby keeping within itself the mark of the past element, and already letting itself be vitiated by the mark of its relation to the future element, this trace being related no less to what is called the future than to what is called the past, and constituting what is called the present by means of this very relation to what it is not: what it absolutely is not, not even a past or a future as a modified present. An interval must separate the present from what it is not in order for the present to be itself, but this interval that constitutes it as present must, by the same token, divide the present in and of itself, thereby also dividing, along with the present, everything that is thought on the basis of the present, that is, in our metaphysical language, every being, and singularly substance or the subject. In constituting itself, in dividing itself dynamically, this interval is what might be called *spacing*, the becoming-space of time or the becoming-time of space (*temporization*). And it is this constitution of the present, as an "originary" and irreducibly nonsimple (and therefore, *stricto sensu*[8] nonoriginary) synthesis of marks, or traces of retentions and protentions (to reproduce analogically and provisionally a phenomenological and transcendental language that soon will reveal itself to be inadequate), that I propose to call archi-writing, archi-trace, or *différance*. Which (is) (simultaneously) spacing (and) temporization.

---

6. An important disclaimer that applies to Derrida's writings generally (making it nearly impossible to state his "position" or "theory" or even "view" on any matter clearly and precisely).

7. All these terms refer to writing and inscribe *différance* within themselves, as Derrida says, according to the context. The supplement (*supplément*) is Rousseau's word to describe writing (analyzed in [Derrida's] *Of Grammatology*, trans. Gayatri Spivak [Baltimore: Johns Hopkins University Press, 1976]). It means *both* the missing piece and the extra piece. The *pharmakon* is Plato's word for writing (analyzed in [Derrida's] "Plato's Pharmacy" in *Dissemination*, trans. Barbara Johnson [Chicago: University of Chicago Press, 1981]), meaning *both*

remedy and poison; the hymen (*l'hymen*) comes from Derrida's analysis of Mallarmé's writing and Mallarmé's reflections on writing ("The Double Session" in *Dissemination*) and refers *both* to virginity and to consummation; *marge-marque-marche* is the series *en différance* that Derrida applies to Sollers's *Nombres* ("Dissemination" in *Dissemination*) [translator's note]. Derrida discussed *supplément* in Jean-Jacques Rousseau, *Confessions* (1781–88); *pharmakon* in Plato, *Phaedrus* 230d–e, 274e; *l'hymen* in Stéphane Mallarmé, "Mimique" (1886); and *marge-marque-marche* in Philippe Sollers, *Nombres* (1966).

8. In a strict or narrow sense (Latin)

Could not this (active) movement of (the production of) *différance* without origin be called simply, and without neographism, *differentiation*? Such a word, among other confusions, would have left open the possibility of an organic, original, and homogeneous unity that eventually would come to be divided, to receive difference as an event. And above all, since it is formed from the verb "to differentiate," it would negate the economic signification of the detour, the temporizing delay, "deferral." Here, a remark in passing, which I owe to a recent reading of a text that Koyré[9] (in 1934, in *Revue d'histoire et de philosophie réligieuse*, and reprinted in his *Etudes d'histoire de la pensée philosophique*) devoted to "Hegel in Jena." In this text Koyré gives long citations, in German, of the Jena *Logic*, and proposes their translation. On two occasions he encounters the expression *differente Beziehung* in Hegel's text. This word (*different*), with its Latin root, is rare in German and, I believe, in Hegel, who prefers *verschieden* or *ungleich*, calling difference *Unterschied* and qualitative variety *Verschiedenheit*. In the Jena *Logic* he uses the word *different* precisely where he treats of time and the present. Before getting to a valuable comment of Koyré's, let us look at some sentences from Hegel, such as Koyré translates them: "The infinite, in this simplicity, is, as a moment opposed to the equal-to-itself, the negative, and in its moments, although it is (itself) presented to and in itself the totality, (it is) what excludes in general, the point or limit; but in its own (action of) negating, it is related immediately to the other and negates itself by itself. The limit or moment of the present (*der Gegen-wart*), the absolute 'this' of time, or the now, is of an absolutely negative simplicity, which absolutely excludes from itself all multiplicity, and, by virtue of this, is absolutely determined; it is not whole or a *quantum* which would be extended in itself (and) which, in itself, also would have an undetermined moment, a diversity which, as indifferent (*gleichgultig*) or exterior in itself, would be related to an other (*auf ein anderes bezöge*), but in this is a relation absolutely different from the simple (*sondern es ist absolut differente Beziehung*)." And Koyré most remarkably specifies in a note: "different Relation: *differente Beziehung*. One might say: 'differentiating relation.'" And on the next page, another text of Hegel's in which one can read this: "*Diese Beziehung ist Gegenwart, als eine differente Beziehung* (This relationship is [the] present as a different relationship)." Another note of Koyré's: "The term *different* here is taken in an active sense."[1]

Writing "*différant*"[2] or "*différance*" (with an *a*) would have had the advantage of making it possible to translate Hegel at that particular point—which is also an absolutely decisive point in his discourse—without further notes or specifications. And the translation would be, as it always must be, a transformation of one language by another. I contend, of course, that the word *différance* can also serve other purposes: first, because it marks not only the

9. Alexandre Koyré (1892–1964), Russian-born French philosopher who specialized in the history and philosophy of science; the publications named are *Review of History and Religious Philosophy* and *Studies of the History of Philosophic Thought*.
1. Alexandre Koyré, "Hegel à Iena," in *Etudes d'histoire de la pensé philosophique* (Paris: Armand Colin, 1961), pp. 153–54 [translator's note].
2. The point here, which cannot be conveyed in English, is that Koyré's realization that Hegel is describing a "differentiating relation," or "different" in an active sense, is precisely what the formation of *différance* from the participle *différant* describes, as explained in notes 6 and 8 [on p. 1516] above. And that it is the *present* that is described as differing from and deferring itself helps clarify Derrida's argument (at the end of the essay) that presence is to be rethought as the trace of the trace, as *différance* differed-and-deferred [translator's note].

activity of "originary" difference, but also the temporizing detour of deferral; and above all because *différance* thus written, although maintaining relations of profound affinity with Hegelian discourse (such as it must be read), is also, up to a certain point, unable to break with that discourse (which has no kind of meaning or chance); but it can operate a kind of infinitesimal and radical displacement of it, whose space I attempt to delineate elsewhere but of which it would be difficult to speak briefly here.

Differences, thus, are "produced"—deferred—by *différance*. But *what* defers or *who* defers? In other words, *what is différance?* With this question we reach another level and another resource of our problematic.

What differs? Who differs? What is *différance?*

If we answered these questions before examining them as questions, before turning them back on themselves, and before suspecting their very form, including what seems most natural and necessary about them, we would immediately fall back into what we have just disengaged ourselves from. In effect, if we accepted the form of the question, in its meaning and its syntax ("what is?" "who is?" "who is it that?"), we would have to conclude that *différance* has been derived, has happened, is to be mastered and governed on the basis of the point of a present being, which itself could be some thing, a form, a state, a power in the world to which all kinds of names might be given, a *what*, or a present being as a *subject*, a *who*. And in this last case, notably, one would conclude implicitly that this present being, for example a being present to itself, as consciousness, eventually would come to defer or to differ: whether by delaying and turning away from the fulfillment of a "need" or a "desire," or by differing from itself. But in neither of these cases would such a present being be "constituted" by this *différance*.

Now if we refer, once again, to semiological difference, of what does Saussure, in particular, remind us? That "language [which only consists of differences][3] is not a function of the speaking subject." This implies that the subject (in its identity with itself, or eventually in its consciousness of its identity with itself, its self-consciousness) is inscribed in language, is a "function" of language, becomes a *speaking* subject only by making its speech conform—even in so-called "creation," or in so-called "transgression"—to the system of the rules of language as a system of differences, or at very least by conforming to the general law of *différance*, or by adhering to the principle of language which Saussure says is "spoken language minus speech." "Language is necessary for the spoken word to be intelligible and so that it can produce all of its effects."[4]

If, by hypothesis, we maintain that the opposition of speech to language is absolutely rigorous, then *différance* would be not only the play of differences within language but also the relation of speech to language, the detour through which I must pass in order to speak, the silent promise I must make; and this is equally valid for semiology in general, governing all the relations of usage to schemata, of message to code, etc. (Elsewhere I have attempted to suggest that this *différance* in language, and in the relation of speech and language, forbids the essential dissociation of speech and language that Saussure, at

3. Brackets in the original.
4. Saussure, *Course in General Linguistics*, p. 37 [translator's note].

another level of his discourse, traditionally wished to delineate. The practice of a language or of a code supposing a play of forms without a determined and invariable substance, and also supposing in the practice of this play a retention and protention[5] of differences, a spacing and a temporization, a play of traces—all this must be a kind of writing before the letter, an archi-writing without a present origin, without archi-. Whence the regular erasure of the archi-, and the transformation of general semiology into grammatology, this latter executing a critical labor on everything within semiology, including the central concept of the sign, that maintained metaphysical presuppositions incompatible with the motif of *différance*.)

One might be tempted by an objection: certainly the subject becomes a *speaking* subject only in its commerce with the system of linguistic differences; or yet, the subject becomes a *signifying* (signifying in general, by means of speech or any other sign) subject only by inscribing itself in the system of differences. Certainly in this sense the speaking or signifying subject could not be present to itself, as speaking or signifying, without the play of linguistic or semiological *différance*. But can one not conceive of a presence, and of a presence to itself of the subject before speech or signs, a presence to itself of the subject in a silent and intuitive consciousness?

Such a question therefore supposes that, prior to the sign and outside it, excluding any trace and any *différance*, something like consciousness is possible. And that consciousness, before distributing its signs in space and in the world, can gather itself into its presence. But what is consciousness? What does "consciousness" mean? Most often, in the very form of meaning, in all its modifications, consciousness offers itself to thought only as self-presence, as the perception of self in presence. And what holds for consciousness holds here for so-called subjective existence in general. Just as the category of the subject cannot be, and never has been, thought without the reference to presence as *hupokeimenon* or as *ousia*[6] etc., so the subject as consciousness has never manifested itself except as self-presence. The privilege granted to consciousness therefore signifies the privilege granted to the present; and even if one describes the transcendental temporality of consciousness, and at the depth at which Husserl does so, one grants to the "living present" the power of synthesizing traces, and of incessantly reassembling them.

This privilege is the ether of metaphysics, the element of our thought that is caught in the language of metaphysics. One can delimit such a closure today only by soliciting[7] the value of presence that Heidegger has shown to be the ontotheological determination of Being; and in thus soliciting the value of presence, by means of an interrogation whose status must be completely exceptional, we are also examining the absolute privilege of this form or epoch of presence in general that is consciousness as meaning[8] in self-presence.

Thus one comes to posit presence—and specifically consciousness, the being beside itself of consciousness—no longer as the absolutely central form

5. Extension into the future.
6. As substance (or matter) or as being (Greek).
7. The French *solliciter*, as the English *solicit*, derives from an Old Latin expression meaning to shake the whole, to make something tremble in its entirety. Derrida comments on this later, but is already using "to solicit" in this sense here [trans-

lator's note].
8. "Meaning" here is the weak translation of *vouloir-dire*, which has a strong sense of willing (*voluntas*) to say, putting the attempt to mean in conjunction with speech, a crucial conjunction for Derrida [translator's note].

of Being but as a "determination" and as an "effect." A determination or an effect within a system which is no longer that of presence but of *différance*, a system that no longer tolerates the opposition of activity and passivity, nor that of cause and effect, or of indetermination and determination, etc., such that in designating consciousness as an effect or a determination, one continues—for strategic reasons that can be more or less lucidly deliberated and systematically calculated—to operate according to the lexicon of that which one is de-limiting.

Before being so radically and purposely the gesture of Heidegger, this gesture was also made by Nietzsche and Freud,[9] both of whom, as is well known, and sometimes in very similar fashion, put consciousness into question in its assured certainty of itself. Now is it not remarkable that they both did so on the basis of the motif of *différance*?

Différance appears almost by name in their texts, and in those places where everything is at stake. I cannot expand upon this here; I will only recall that for Nietzsche "the great principal activity is unconscious,"[1] and that consciousness is the effect of forces whose essence, byways, and modalities are not proper to it. Force itself is never present; it is only a play of differences and quantities. There would be no force in general without the difference between forces; and here the difference of quantity counts more than the content of the quantity, more than absolute size itself. "Quantity itself, therefore, is not separable from the difference of quantity. The difference of quantity is the essence of force, the relation of force to force. The dream of two equal forces, even if they are granted an opposition of meaning, is an approximate and crude dream, a statistical dream, plunged into by the living but dispelled by chemistry."[2] Is not all of Nietzsche's thought a critique of philosophy as an active indifference to difference, as the system of adiaphoristic[3] reduction or repression? Which according to the same logic, according to logic itself, does not exclude that philosophy lives *in* and *on* *différance*, thereby blinding itself to the *same*, which is not the identical. The same, precisely, is *différance* (with an *a*) as the displaced and equivocal passage of one different thing to another, from one term of an opposition to the other. Thus one could reconsider all the pairs of opposites on which philosophy is constructed and on which our discourse lives, not in order to see opposition erase itself but to see what indicates that each of the terms must appear as the *différance* of the other, as the other different and deferred in the economy of the same (the intelligible as differing-deferring the sensible, as the sensible different and deferred; the concept as different and deferred, differing-deferring intuition; culture as nature different and deferred, differing-deferring; all the others of *physis—tekhnē, nomos, thesis*,[4] society, freedom, history, mind, etc.—as *physis* different and deferred, or as *physis* differing and deferring. *Physis* in *différance*. And in this we may see the site of a reinterpretation of *mimēsis*[5] in its alleged opposition

9. Sigmund Freud (1856–1939), Austrian founder of psychoanalysis. For NIETZSCHE, see above.
1. While presented as a quotation, this would seem to be an attempt by Derrida to invoke or encapsulate a number of things Nietzsche says along these lines, e.g., in *The Gay Science*, §§ 354 and 357 (see above), and in his late notebooks (see also above) in notes that were selected and published posthumously under the title *Der Wille zur Macht* (*The Will to Power*, trans. Walter Kaufmann

and R. J. Hollingdale), such as the note numbered 479.
2. Gilles Deleuze, *Nietzsche et la philosophie* [*Nietzsche and Philosophy*] (Paris: Presses Universitaires de France, 1970), p. 49 [translator's note]. For DELEUZE, see below.
3. In Derrida's usage, "indifferent to difference."
4. That is, all realities other than nature—craft, law, position (Greek terms).
5. Imitation (Greek).

to *physis*). And on the basis of this unfolding of the same as *différance*, we see announced the sameness of *différance* and repetition in the eternal return. Themes in Nietzsche's work that are linked to the symptomatology that always diagnoses the detour or ruse of an agency disguised in its *différance*; or further, to the entire thematic of active interpretation, which substitutes incessant deciphering for the unveiling of truth as the presentation of the thing itself in its presence, etc. Figures without truth, or at least a system of figures not dominated by the value of truth, which then becomes only an included, inscribed, circumscribed function.

Thus, *différance* is the name we might give to the "active," moving discord of different forces, and of differences of forces, that Nietzsche sets up against the entire system of metaphysical grammar, wherever this system governs culture, philosophy, and science.

It is historically significant that this diaphoristics,[6] which, as an energetics or economics of forces, commits itself to putting into question the primacy of presence as consciousness, is also the major motif of Freud's thought: another diaphoristics, which in its entirety is both a theory of the figure (or of the trace) and an energetics. The putting into question of the authority of consciousness is first and always differential.

The two apparently different values of *différance* are tied together in Freudian theory: to differ as discernibility, distinction, separation, diastem,[7] *spacing*; and to defer as detour, relay, reserve, *temporization*.

1. The concepts of trace (*Spur*), of breaching (*Bahnung*),[8] and of the forces of breaching, from the *Project* on, are inseparable from the concept of difference. The origin of memory, and of the psyche as (conscious or unconscious) memory in general, can be described only by taking into account the difference between breaches. Freud says so overtly. There is no breach without difference and no difference without trace.

2. All the differences in the production of unconscious traces and in the processes of inscription (*Niederschrift*) can also be interpreted as moments of *différance*, in the sense of putting into reserve. According to a schema that never ceased to guide Freud's thought, the movement of the trace is described as an effort of life to protect itself by *deferring* the dangerous investment, by constituting a reserve (*Vorrat*). And all the oppositions that furrow Freudian thought relate each of his concepts one to another as moments of a detour in the economy of *différance*. One is but the other different and deferred, one differing and deferring the other. One is the other in *différance*, one is the *différance* of the other. This is why every apparently rigorous and irreducible *opposition* (for example the opposition of the secondary to the primary) comes to be qualified, at one moment or another, as a "theoretical fiction." Again, it is thereby, for example (but such an example governs, and communicates with, everything), that the difference between the pleasure principle and the reality principle is only *différance* as detour. In *Beyond the Pleasure Principle* Freud writes: "Under the influence of the ego's instincts of self-preservation, the pleasure principle is replaced by the reality principle. This latter principle does

6. A theory of differences.
7. An interval (in ancient Greek music); a separation.
8. Derrida is referring here to his essay "Freud and the Scene of Writing" in *Writing and Difference*

[1967]. * * * The *Project* Derrida refers to here is the *Project for a Scientific Psychology* (1895), in which Freud attempted to cast his psychological thinking in a neurological framework [translator's note].

not abandon the intention of ultimately obtaining pleasure, but it nevertheless demands and carries into effect the postponement of satisfaction, the abandonment of a number of possibilities of gaining satisfaction and the temporary toleration of unpleasure as a step on the long indirect road (*Aufschub*) to pleasure."[9]

Here we are touching upon the point of greatest obscurity, on the very enigma of *différance*, on precisely that which divides its very concept by means of a strange cleavage. We must not hasten to decide. How are we to think *simultaneously*, on the one hand, *différance* as the economic detour which, in the element of the same, always aims at coming back to the pleasure or the presence that have been deferred by (conscious or unconscious) calculation, and, on the other hand, *différance* as the relation to an impossible presence, as expenditure without reserve, as the irreparable loss of presence, the irreversible usage of energy, that is, as the death instinct, and as the entirely other relationship that apparently interrupts every economy? It is evident—and this is the evident itself—that the economical and the noneconomical, the same and the entirely other, etc., cannot be thought *together*. If *différance* is unthinkable in this way, perhaps we should not hasten to make it evident, in the philosophical element of evidentiality which would make short work of dissipating the mirage and illogicalness of *différance* and would do so with the infallibility of calculations that we are well acquainted with, having precisely recognized their place, necessity, and function in the structure of *différance*. Elsewhere, in a reading of Bataille,[1] I have attempted to indicate what might come of a rigorous and, in a new sense, "scientific" *relating* of the "restricted economy" that takes no part in expenditure without reserve, death, opening itself to nonmeaning, etc., to a general economy that *takes into account* the nonreserve, that keeps in reserve the nonreserve, if it can be put thus. I am speaking of a relationship between a *différance* that can make a profit on its investment and a *différance* that misses its profit, the *investiture* of a presence that is pure and without loss here being confused with absolute loss, with death. Through such a relating of a restricted and a general economy the very project of philosophy, under the privileged heading of Hegelianism, is displaced and reinscribed. The *Aufhebung*[2]—*la relève*—is constrained into writing itself otherwise. Or perhaps simply into writing itself. Or, better, into taking account of its consumption of writing.[3]

---

9. *The Standard Edition of the Complete Psychological Works* (London: Hogarth Press, 1950), vol. 18, p. 10 [translator's note]. *Beyond the Pleasure Principle* was originally published in 1920.
1. Georges Bataille (1897–1962), French writer fascinated with eroticism, transgression, and the irrational. See Derrida's "From Restricted to General Economy" (1967).
2. Supersession (German)—for Hegel, negation, preservation and transcendence all at once.
3. Derrida is referring here to the reading of Hegel he proposed in "From Restricted to General Economy: A Hegelianism Without Reserve," in *Writing and Difference*. In that essay Derrida began his consideration of Hegel as the great philosophical *speculator*; thus all the economic metaphors of the previous sentences. For Derrida the deconstruction of metaphysics implies an endless confrontation with Hegelian concepts, and the move from a

restricted, "speculative" philosophical economy— in which there is nothing that cannot be made to make sense, in which there is nothing *other* than meaning—to a "general" economy—which affirms that which exceeds meaning, the excess of meaning from which there can be no speculative profit— involves a reinterpretation of the central Hegelian concept: the *Aufhebung*. *Aufhebung* literally means "lifting up"; but it also contains the double meaning of conservation and negation. For Hegel, dialectics is a process of *Aufhebung*: every concept is to be negated and lifted up to a higher sphere in which it is thereby conserved. In this way, there is nothing from which the *Aufhebung* cannot profit. However, as Derrida points out, there is always an effect of *différance* when the same word has two contradictory meanings. Indeed it is this effect of *différance*—the excess of the trace *Aufhebung* itself—that is precisely what the *Aufhebung* can

For the economic character of *différance* in no way implies that the deferred presence can always be found again, that we have here only an investment that provisionally and calculatedly delays the perception of its profit or the profit of its perception. Contrary to the metaphysical, dialectical, "Hegelian" interpretation of the economic movement of *différance*, we must conceive of a play in which whoever loses wins, and in which one loses and wins on every turn. If the displaced presentation remains definitively and implacably postponed, it is not that a certain present remains absent or hidden. Rather, *différance* maintains our relationship with that which we necessarily misconstrue, and which exceeds the alternative of presence and absence. A certain alterity—to which Freud gives the metaphysical name of the unconscious— is definitively exempt from every process of presentation by means of which we would call upon it to show itself in person. In this context, and beneath this guise, the unconscious is not, as we know, a hidden, virtual, or potential self-presence. It differs from, and defers, itself; which doubtless means that it is woven of differences, and also that it sends out delegates, representatives, proxies; but without any chance that the giver of proxies might "exist," might be present, be "itself" somewhere, and with even less chance that it might become conscious. In this sense, contrary to the terms of an old debate full of the metaphysical investments that it has always assumed, the "unconscious" is no more a "thing" than it is any other thing, is no more a thing than it is a virtual or masked consciousness. This radical alterity as concerns every possible mode of presence is marked by the irreducibility of the aftereffect, the delay. In order to describe traces, in order to read the traces of "unconscious" traces (there are no "conscious" traces), the language of presence and absence, the metaphysical discourse of phenomenology, is inadequate. (Although the phenomenologist is not the only one to speak this language.)

The structure of delay (*Nachträglichkeit*) in effect forbids that one make of temporalization (temporization) a simple dialectical complication of the living present as an originary and unceasing synthesis—a synthesis constantly directed back on itself, gathered in on itself and gathering—of retentional traces and protentional openings. The alterity of the "unconscious" makes us concerned not with horizons of modified—past or future—presents, but with a "past" that has never been present, and which never will be, whose future to come will never be a *production* or a reproduction in the form of presence. Therefore the concept of trace is incompatible with the concept of retention, of the becoming-past of what has been present. One cannot think the

---

never *aufheben*: lift up, conserve, and negate. This is why Derrida wishes to constrain the *Aufhebung* to write itself otherwise, or simply to write itself, to take into account its consumption of writing. Without writing, the trace, there could be no words with double, contradictory meanings.

As with *différance*, the translation of a word with a double meaning is particularly difficult, and touches upon the entire problematics of writing and *différance*. The best translators of Hegel usually cite Hegel's own delight that the most speculative of languages, German, should have provided this most speculative of words as the vehicle for his supreme speculative effort. Thus *Aufhebung* is

usually best annotated and left untranslated. * * * Derrida, however, in his attempt to make *Aufhebung* write itself otherwise, has proposed a new translation of it that *does* take into account the effect of *différance* in its double meaning. Derrida's translation is *la relève*. The word comes from the verb *relever*, which means to lift up, as does *Aufheben*. But *relever* also means to relay, to relieve, as when one soldier on duty relieves another. Thus the conserving-and-negating lift has become *la relève*, a "lift" in which is inscribed an effect of substitution and difference, the effect of substitution and difference inscribed in the double meaning of *Aufhebung* [translator's note].

trace—and therefore, *différance*—on the basis of the present, or of the presence of the present.

A past that has never been present: this formula is the one that Emmanuel Levinas uses, although certainly in a nonpsychoanalytic way, to qualify the trace and enigma of absolute alterity: the Other.[4] Within these limits, and from this point of view at least, the thought of *différance* implies the entire critique of classical ontology undertaken by Levinas. And the concept of the trace, like that of *différance* thereby organizes, along the lines of these different traces and differences of traces, in Nietzsche's sense, in Freud's sense, in Levinas's sense—these "names of authors" here being only indices—the network which reassembles and traverses our "era" as the delimitation of the ontology of presence.

Which is to say the ontology of beings and beingness. It is the domination of beings that *différance* everywhere comes to solicit, in the sense that *sollicitare*, in old Latin, means to shake as a whole, to make tremble in entirety. Therefore, it is the determination of Being as presence or as beingness that is interrogated by the thought of *différance*. Such a question could not emerge and be understood unless the difference between Being and beings were somewhere to be broached. First consequence: *différance* is not. It is not a present being, however excellent, unique, principal, or transcendent. It governs nothing, reigns over nothing, and nowhere exercises any authority. It is not announced by any capital letter. Not only is there no kingdom of *différance*, but *différance* instigates the subversion of every kingdom. Which makes it obviously threatening and infallibly dreaded by everything within us that desires a kingdom, the past or future presence of a kingdom. And it is always in the name of a kingdom that one may reproach *différance* with wishing to reign, believing that one sees it aggrandize itself with a capital letter.

Can *différance*, for these reasons, settle down into the division of the ontico-ontological difference, such as it is thought, such as its "epoch" in particular is thought, "through," if it may still be expressed such, Heidegger's uncircumventable meditation?

There is no simple answer to such a question.

In a certain aspect of itself, *différance* is certainly but the historical and epochal *unfolding* of Being or of the ontological difference. The *a* of *différance* marks the *movement* of this unfolding.

And yet, are not the thought of the *meaning* or *truth* of Being, the determination of *différance* as the ontico-ontological difference, difference thought within the horizon of the question *of Being*, still intrametaphysical effects of *différance*? The unfolding of *différance* is perhaps not solely the truth of Being, or of the epochality of Being. Perhaps we must attempt to think this unheard-of thought, this silent tracing: that the history of Being, whose thought engages the Greco-Western *logos* such as it is produced via the ontological difference, is but an epoch of the *diapherein*. Henceforth one could no longer even call this an "epoch," the concept of epochality belonging to what is within history as the history of Being. Since Being has never had a "meaning," has never been thought or said as such, except by dissimulating itself in

---

4. The translator here cites Derrida's essay on EMMANUEL LÉVINAS, "Violence and Metaphysics," in *Writing and Difference*, and his own note to the English translation ([London: Routledge and Kegan Paul, 1978], n. 6), where he explains that Lévinas's term "*autrui*' (the personal Other, the you)" is translated by "Other," and *autre* is translated by "other."

beings, then *différance*, in a certain and very strange way, (is) "older" than the ontological difference or than the truth of Being. When it has this age it can be called the play of the trace. The play of a trace which no longer belongs to the horizon of Being, but whose play transports and encloses the meaning of Being: the play of the trace, or the *différance*, which has no meaning and is not. Which does not belong. There is no maintaining, and no depth to, this bottomless chessboard on which Being is put into play.

Perhaps this is why the Heraclitean play of the *hen diapheron heautōi*,[5] of the one differing from itself, the one in difference with itself, already is lost like a trace in the determination of the *diapherein* as ontological difference.

To think the ontological difference doubtless remains a difficult task, and any statement of it has remained almost inaudible. Further to prepare, beyond our *logos*, for a *différance* so violent that it can be interpellated[6] neither as the epochality of Being nor as ontological difference, is not in any way to dispense with the passage through the truth of Being, or to "criticize," "contest," or misconstrue its incessant necessity. On the contrary, we must stay within the difficulty of this passage, and repeat it in the rigorous reading of metaphysics, wherever metaphysics normalizes Western discourse, and not only in the texts of the "history of philosophy." As rigorously as possible we must permit to appear/disappear the trace of what exceeds the truth of Being. The trace (of that) which can never be presented, the trace which itself can never be presented: that is, appear and manifest itself, as such, in its phenomenon. The trace beyond that which profoundly links fundamental ontology and phenomenology. Always differing and deferring, the trace is never as it is in the presentation of itself. It erases itself in presenting itself, muffles itself in resonating, like the *a* writing itself, inscribing its pyramid in *différance*.

The annunciating and reserved trace of this movement can always be disclosed in metaphysical discourse, and especially in the contemporary discourse which states, through the attempts to which we just referred (Nietzsche, Freud, Levinas), the closure of ontology. And especially through the Heideggerean text.

This text prompts us to examine the essence of the present, the presence of the present.

What is the present? What is it to think the present in its presence?

Let us consider, for example, the 1946 text entitled *Der Spruch des Anaximander* ("The Anaximander Fragment").[7] In this text Heidegger recalls that the forgetting of Being forgets the difference between Being and beings: ". . . to be the Being *of* beings is the matter of Being (*die Sache des Seins*). The grammatical form of this enigmatic, ambiguous genitive indicates a genesis (*Genesis*), the emergence (*Herkunft*) of what is present from presencing (*des Anwesenden aus dem Anwesen*). Yet the essence (*Wesen*) of this emergence remains concealed (*verbogen*)[8] along with the essence of these two words. Not

5. An allusion to fragment 51 by the Greek pre-Socratic philosopher Heraclitus (active ca. 500 B.C.E.); Derrida glosses its meaning in the next two phrases.
6. That is, constituted.
7. Martin Heidegger, *Holzwege* [*Off the Beaten Track*] (Frankfurt: V. Klostermann, 1957). English translation ("The Anaximander Fragment") in

Early Greek Thinking, trans. David Farrell Krell and Frank Capuzzi (New York: Harper and Row, 1975). All further references in the text [translator's note]. The fragment of Anaximander (ca. 610–540 B.C.E.) is the earliest surviving writing in Greek philosophy.
8. Should be "verborgen."

only that, but even the very relation between presencing and what is present (*Anwesen und Anwesendem*) remains unthought. From early on it seems as though presencing and what is present were each something for itself. Presencing itself unnoticeably becomes something present . . . The essence of presencing (*Das Wesen des Anwesens*), and with it the distinction between presencing and what is present, remains forgotten. *The oblivion of Being is oblivion of the distinction between Being and beings*" (p. 50).

In recalling the difference between Being and beings (the ontological difference) as the difference between presence and the present, Heidegger advances a proposition, a body of propositions, that we are not going to use as a subject for criticism. This would be foolishly precipitate; rather, what we shall try to do is to return to this proposition its power to provoke.

Let us proceed slowly. What Heidegger wants to mark is this: the difference between Being and beings, the forgotten of metaphysics, has disappeared without leaving a trace. The very trace of difference has been submerged. If we maintain that *différance* (is) (itself) other than absence and presence, if it *traces*, then when it is a matter of the forgetting of the difference (between Being and beings), we would have to speak of a disappearance of the trace of the trace. Which is indeed what the following passage from "The Anaximander Fragment" seems to imply: "Oblivion of Being belongs to the self-veiling essence of Being. It belongs so essentially to the destiny of Being that the dawn of this destiny rises as the unveiling of what is present in its presencing. This means that the history of Being begins with the oblivion of Being, since Being—together with its essence, its distinction from beings—keeps to itself. The distinction collapses. It remains forgotten. Although the two parties to the distinction, what is present and presencing (*das Anwesende und das Anwesen*), reveal themselves, they do not do so as distinguished. Rather, even the early trace (*die frühe Spur*) of the distinction is obliterated when presencing appears as something present (*das Anwesen wie ein Anwesendes erscheint*) and finds itself in the position of being the highest being present (*in einem höchsten Anwesenden*)" (pp. 50–51).

Since the trace is not a presence but the simulacrum of a presence that dislocates itself, displaces itself, refers itself, it properly has no site—erasure belongs to its structure. And not only the erasure which must always be able to overtake it (without which it would not be a trace but an indestructible and monumental substance), but also the erasure which constitutes it from the outset as a trace, which situates it as the change of site, and makes it disappear in its appearance, makes it emerge from itself in its production. The erasure of the early trace (*die frühe Spur*) of difference is therefore the "same" as its tracing in the text of metaphysics. This latter must have maintained the mark of what it has lost, reserved, put aside. The paradox of such a structure, in the language of metaphysics, is an inversion of metaphysical concepts, which produces the following effect: the present becomes the sign of the sign, the trace of the trace. It is no longer what every reference refers to in the last analysis. It becomes a function in a structure of generalized reference. It is a trace, and a trace of the erasure of the trace.

Thereby the text of metaphysics is *comprehended*. Still legible; and to be read. It is not surrounded but rather traversed by its limit, marked in its interior by the multiple furrow of its margin. Proposing *all at once* the monument and the mirage of the trace, the trace simultaneously traced and erased, simultaneously living and dead, and, as always, living in its simulation of life's preserved inscription. A pyramid. Not a stone fence to be jumped over but itself stonelike, on a wall, to be deciphered otherwise, a text without voice.

Thus one can think without contradiction, or at least without granting any pertinence to such a contradiction, what is perceptible and imperceptible in the trace. The "early trace" of difference is lost in an invisibility without return, and yet its very loss is sheltered, retained, seen, delayed. In a text. In the form of presence. In the form of the proper. Which itself is only an effect of writing.

Having stated the erasure of the early trace, Heidegger can therefore, in a contradiction without contradiction, consign, countersign, the sealing of the trace. A bit further on: "However, the distinction between Being and beings, as something forgotten, can invade our experience only if it has already unveiled itself with the presencing of what is present (*mit dem Anwesen des Anwesenden*); only if it has left a trace (*eine Spur geprägt hat*) which remains preserved (*gewahrt bleibt*) in the language to which Being comes" (p. 51).

Still further on, while meditating on Anaximander's *to khreon*,[9] which he translates as *Brauch* (usage), Heidegger writes this: "Enjoining order and reck (*Fug und Ruch verfügend*), usage delivers to each present being (*Anwesende*) the while into which it is released. But accompanying this process is the constant danger that lingering will petrify into mere persistence (*in das blosse Beharren verhärtet*). Thus usage essentially remains at the same time the distribution (*Aushändigung*: dis-maintenance) of presencing (*des Anwesens*) into disorder (*in den Un-fug*). Usage conjoins the dis (*Der Brauch fügt das Un-*)" (p. 54).

And it is at the moment when Heidegger recognizes *usage* as *trace* that the question must be asked: can we, and to what extent, think this trace and the *dis* of *différance* as *Wesen des Seins*?[1] Does not the *dis* of *différance* refer us beyond the history of Being, and also beyond our language, and everything that can be named in it? In the language of Being, does it not call for a necessarily violent transformation of this language by an entirely other language?

Let us make this question more specific. And to force the "trace" out of it (and has anyone thought that we have been tracking something down, something other than tracks themselves to be tracked down?), let us read this passage: "The translation of *to khreon* as 'usage' has not resulted from a preoccupation with etymologies and dictionary meanings. The choice of the word stems from a prior crossing *over* (*Über-setzen*; trans-lation) of a thinking which tries to think the distinction in the essence of Being (*im Wesen des Seins*) in the fateful beginning of Being's oblivion. The word 'usage' is dictated to thinking in the experience (*Erfahrung*) of Being's oblivion. What properly remains to be thought in the word 'usage' has presumably left a trace (*Spur*) in *to khreon*. This trace quickly vanishes (*alsbald verschwindet*) in the destiny of Being which unfolds in world history as Western metaphysics" (p. 54).

How to conceive what is outside a text? That which is more or less than a text's *own, proper* margin? For example, what is other than the text of Western

9. The usual meaning of this phrase is "necessity,"   1. The essence of Being.
"fate," "that which must be."

metaphysics? It is certain that the trace which "quickly vanishes in the destiny of Being (and) which unfolds . . . as Western metaphysics" escapes every determination, every name it might receive in the metaphysical text. It is sheltered, and therefore dissimulated, in these names. It does not appear in them as the trace "itself." But this is because it could never appear itself, *as such*. Heidegger also says that difference cannot appear as such: "Lichtung des Unterschiedes kann deshalb auch nicht bedeuten, dass der Unterschied als der Unterschied erscheint." There is no essence of *différance*; it (is) that which not only could never be appropriated in the *as such* of its name or its appearing, but also that which threatens the authority of the *as such* in general, of the presence of the thing itself in its essence. That there is not a proper essence[2] of *différance* at this point, implies that there is neither a Being nor truth of the play of writing such as it engages *différance*.

For us, *différance* remains a metaphysical name, and all the names that it receives in our language are still, as names, metaphysical. And this is particularly the case when these names state the determination of *différance* as the difference between presence and the present (*Anwesen/Anwesend*), and above all, and is already the case when they state the determination of *différance* as the difference of Being and beings.

"Older" than Being itself, such a *différance* has no name in our language. But we "already know" that if it is unnameable, it is not provisionally so, not because our language has not yet found or received this *name*, or because we would have to seek it in another language, outside the finite system of our own. It is rather because there is no *name* for it at all, not even the name of essence or of Being, not even that of "*différance*," which is not a name, which is not a pure nominal unity, and unceasingly dislocates itself in a chain of differing and deferring substitutions.

"There is no name for it": a proposition to be read in its *platitude*. This unnameable is not an ineffable Being which no name could approach: God, for example. This unnameable is the play which makes possible nominal

---

2. *Différance* is not a "species" of the genus *ontological difference*. If the "gift of presence is the property of Appropriating" (*Die Gabe von Anwesen ist Eigentum des Ereignens*)" ["Time and Being," in *On Time and Being*, trans. Joan Stambaugh (New York: Harper and Row, 1972), p. 22], *différance* is not a process of propriation in any sense whatever. It is neither position (appropriation) nor negation (expropriation), but rather other. Hence it seems—but here, rather, we are marking the necessity of a future itinerary—that *différance* would be no more a species of the genus *Ereignis* than Being. Heidegger: ". . . then Being belongs into Appropriating (*Dann gehört das Sein in das Ereignen*). Giving and its gift receive their determination from Appropriating. In that case, Being would be a species of Appropriation (*Ereignis*), and not the other way around. To take refuge in such an inversion would be too cheap. Such thinking misses the matter at stake (*Sie denkt am Sachverhalt vorbei*). Appropriation (*Ereignis*) is not the encompassing general concept under which Being and time could be subsumed. Logical classifications mean nothing here. For as we think Being itself and follow what is its own (*seinem Eigenen folgen*), Being proves to be destiny's gift or presence (*gewahrte Gabe des*

Geschickes von Anwesenheit), the gift granted by the giving (*Reichen*) or time. The gift of presence is the property of Appropriating (*Die Gabe von Anwesen ist Eigentum des Ereignens*)." (*On Time and Being*, pp. 21–22.)

Without a displaced reinscription of this chain (Being, presence, -propriation, etc.) the relation between general or fundamental onto-logy and whatever ontology masters or makes subordinate under the rubric of a regional or particular science will never be transformed rigorously and irreversibly. Such regional sciences include not only political economy, psychoanalysis, semiolinguistics—in all of which, and perhaps more than elsewhere, the value of the *proper* plays an irreducible role—but equally all spiritualist or materialist metaphysics. The analyses articulated in this volume aim at such a preliminary articulation. It goes without saying that such a reinscription will never be contained in theoretical or philosophical discourse, or generally in any discourse or writing, but only on the scene of what I have called elsewhere the text in general (1972) [Derrida's note; translator's brackets]. On "the text in general," see Derrida's *Positions*, trans. Allan Bass (Chicago: University of Chicago Press, 1981), p. 44.

effects, the relatively unitary and atomic structures that are called names, the chains of substitutions of names in which, for example, the nominal effect *différance* is itself *enmeshed*, carried off, reinscribed, just as a false entry or a false exit is still part of the game, a function of the system.

What we know, or what we would know if it were simply a question here of something to know, is that there has never been, never will be, a unique word, a master-name. This is why the thought of the letter *a* in *différance* is not the primary prescription or the prophetic annunciation of an imminent and as yet unheard-of nomination. There is nothing kerygmatic[3] about this "word," provided that one perceives its decapita(liza)tion. And that one puts into question the name of the name.

There will be no unique name, even if it were the name of Being. And we must think this without *nostalgia*, that is, outside of the myth of a purely maternal or paternal language, a lost native country of thought. On the contrary, we must *affirm* this, in the sense in which Nietzsche puts affirmation into play, in a certain laughter and a certain step of the dance.

From the vantage of this laughter and this dance, from the vantage of this affirmation foreign to all dialectics, the other side of nostalgia, what I will call Heideggerian *hope*, comes into question. I am not unaware how shocking this word might seem here. Nevertheless I am venturing it, without excluding any of its implications, and I relate it to what still seems to me to be the metaphysical part of "The Anaximander Fragment": the quest for the proper word and the unique name. Speaking of the first word of Being (*das frühe Wort des Seins: to khreon*), Heidegger writes: "The relation to what is present that rules in the essence of presencing itself is a unique one (*ist eine einzige*), altogether incomparable to any other relation. It belongs to the uniqueness of Being itself (*Sie gehört zur Einzigkeit des Seins selbst*). Therefore, in order to name the essential nature of Being (*das wesende Seins*), language would have to find a single word, the unique word (*ein einziges, das einzige Wort*). From this we can gather how daring every thoughtful word (*denkende Wort*) addressed to Being is (*das dem Sein zugesprochen wird*). Nevertheless such daring is not impossible, since Being speaks always and everywhere throughout language" (p. 52).

Such is the question: the alliance of speech and Being in the unique word, in the finally proper name. And such is the question inscribed in the simulated affirmation of *différance*. It bears (on) each member of this sentence: "Being / speaks / always and everywhere / throughout / language."

SOURCE: Jacques Derrida, *Margins of Philosophy*, trans. Alan Bass (Chicago: University of Chicago Press, 1982), pp. 1–27. This essay, collected in *Marges de la philosophie* (1972), was first published in 1968. It originally was an address delivered that year to the French Society of Philosophy.

3. Proclamatory (especially of religious faith); in the New Testament, "the Word" (*Logos*) is God (John 1:1).

From Structure, Sign and Play
in the Discourse of the Human Sciences

We need to interpret interpretations more than to interpret things.
(Montaigne)[1]

Perhaps something has occurred in the history of the concept of structure
that could be called an "event," if this loaded word did not entail a meaning
which it is precisely the function of structural—or structuralist—thought to
reduce or to suspect. Let us speak of an "event," nevertheless, and let us use
quotation marks to serve as a precaution. What would this event be then? Its
exterior form would be that of a *rupture* and a redoubling.

It would be easy enough to show that the concept of structure and even
the word "structure" itself are as old as the *epistēmē*[2]—that is to say, as old as
Western science and Western philosophy—and that their roots thrust deep
into the soil of ordinary language, into whose deepest recesses the *epistēmē*
plunges in order to gather them up and to make them part of itself in a metaphorical displacement. Nevertheless, up to the event which I wish to mark
out and define, structure—or rather the structurality of structure—although
it has always been at work, has always been neutralized or reduced, and this
by a process of giving it a center or of referring it to a point of presence, a
fixed origin. The function of this center was not only to orient, balance, and
organize the structure—one cannot in fact conceive of an unorganized
structure—but above all to make sure that the organizing principle of the
structure would limit what we might call the *play* of the structure. By orienting and organizing the coherence of the system, the center of a structure permits the play of its elements inside the total form. And even today the notion
of a structure lacking any center represents the unthinkable itself.

Nevertheless, the center also closes off the play which it opens up and makes
possible. As center, it is the point at which the substitution of contents, elements, or terms is no longer possible. At the center, the permutation or the
transformation of elements (which may of course be structures enclosed
within a structure) is forbidden. At least this permutation has always remained
interdicted (and I am using this word deliberately). Thus it has always been
thought that the center, which is by definition unique, constituted that very
thing within a structure which while governing the structure, escapes structurality. This is why classical thought concerning structure could say that the
center is, paradoxically, *within* the structure and *outside it*. The center is at
the center of the totality, and yet, since the center does not belong to the totality (is not part of the totality), the totality *has its center elsewhere*. The center
is not the center. The concept of centered structure—although it represents
coherence itself, the condition of the *epistēmē* as philosophy or science—is
contradictorily coherent. And as always, coherence in contradiction expresses

---

1. Michel de Montaigne (1533–1592), French
writer and philosopher; the quotation is from his
essay "Of Experience."

2. Knowledge (Greek); Derrida provides his definition in the following phrase.

the force of a desire.[3] The concept of centered structure is in fact the concept of a play based on a fundamental ground, a play constituted on the basis of a fundamental immobility and a reassuring certitude, which itself is beyond the reach of play. And on the basis of this certitude anxiety can be mastered, for anxiety is invariably the result of a certain mode of being implicated in the game, of being caught by the game, of being as it were at stake in the game from the outset. And again on the basis of what we call the center (and which, because it can be either inside or outside, can also indifferently be called the origin or end, *archē* or *telos*), repetitions, substitutions, transformations, and permutations are always *taken* from a history of meaning [*sens*][4]—that is, in a word, a history—whose origin may always be reawakened or whose end may always be anticipated in the form of presence. This is why one perhaps could say that the movement of any archaeology, like that of any eschatology, is an accomplice of this reduction of the structurality of structure and always attempts to conceive of structure on the basis of a full presence which is beyond play.

If this is so, the entire history of the concept of structure, before the rupture of which we are speaking, must be thought of as a series of substitutions of center for center, as a linked chain of determinations of the center. Successively, and in a regulated fashion, the center receives different forms or names. The history of metaphysics, like the history of the West, is the history of these metaphors and metonymies. Its matrix—if you will pardon me for demonstrating so little and for being so elliptical in order to come more quickly to my principal theme—is the determination of Being as *presence* in all senses of this word. It could be shown that all the names related to fundamentals, to principles, or to the center have always designated an invariable presence— *eidos, archē, telos, energeia, ousia* (essence, existence, substance, subject) *alētheia*,[5] transcendentality, consciousness, God, man, and so forth.

The event I called a rupture, the disruption I alluded to at the beginning of this paper, presumably would have come about when the structurality of structure had to begin to be thought, that is to say, repeated, and this is why I said that this disruption was repetition in every sense of the word. Henceforth, it became necessary to think both the law which somehow governed the desire for a center in the constitution of structure, and the process of signification which orders the displacements and substitutions for this law of central presence—but a central presence which has never been itself, has always already been exiled from itself into its own substitute. The substitute does not substitute itself for anything which has somehow existed before it. Henceforth, it was necessary to begin thinking that there was no center, that the center could not be thought in the form of a present-being, that the center had no natural site, that it was not a fixed locus but a function, a sort of nonlocus in which an infinite number of sign-substitutions came into play.

3. The reference, in a restricted sense, is to the Freudian theory of neurotic symptoms and of dream interpretation in which a given symbol is understood contradictorily as both the desire to fulfill an impulse and the desire to suppress the impulse. In a general sense the reference is to Derrida's thesis that logic and coherence themselves can only be understood contradictorily, since they presuppose the suppression of *différance*, "writing" in the sense of the general economy [translator's note]. For Derrida's term *différance*, see the previous selection.

4. Translator's brackets.

5. Truth (Greek). *Eidos*: form. *Energeia*: actuality.

This was the moment when language invaded the universal problematic, the moment when, in the absence of a center or origin, everything became discourse—provided we can agree on this word—that is to say, a system in which the central signified, the original or transcendental signified, is never absolutely present outside a system of differences. The absence of the transcendental signified extends the domain and the play of signification infinitely.

Where and how does this decentering, this thinking the structurality of structure, occur? It would be somewhat naïve to refer to an event, a doctrine, or an author in order to designate this occurrence. It is no doubt part of the totality of an era, our own, but still it has always already begun to proclaim itself and begun to *work*. Nevertheless, if we wished to choose several "names," as indications only, and to recall those authors in whose discourse this occurrence has kept most closely to its most radical formulation, we doubtless would have to cite the Nietzschean critique of metaphysics, the critique of the concepts of Being and truth, for which were substituted the concepts of play, interpretation, and sign (sign without present truth); the Freudian critique of self-presence, that is, the critique of consciousness, of the subject, of self-identity and of self-proximity or self-possession; and, more radically, the Heideggerean destruction of metaphysics, of onto-theology, of the determination of Being as presence. But all these destructive discourses and all their analogues are trapped in a kind of circle. This circle is unique. It describes the form of the relation between the history of metaphysics and the destruction of the history of metaphysics. There is no sense in doing without the concepts of metaphysics in order to shake metaphysics. We have no language—no syntax and no lexicon—which is foreign to this history; we can pronounce not a single destructive proposition which has not already had to slip into the form, the logic, and the implicit postulations of precisely what it seeks to contest. To take one example from many: the metaphysics of presence is shaken with the help of the concept of *sign*. But, as I suggested a moment ago, as soon as one seeks to demonstrate in this way that there is no transcendental or privileged signified and that the domain or play of signification henceforth has no limit, one must reject even the concept and word "sign" itself—which is precisely what cannot be done. For the signification "sign" has always been understood and determined, in its meaning, as sign-of, a signifier referring to a signified, a signifier different from its signified. If one erases the radical difference between signifier and signified, it is the word "signifier" itself which must be abandoned as a metaphysical concept. When Lévi-Strauss says in the preface to *The Raw and the Cooked* that he has "sought to transcend the opposition between the sensible and the intelligible by operating from the outset at the level of signs,"[6] the necessity, force, and legitimacy of his act cannot make us forget that the concept of the sign cannot in itself surpass this opposition between the sensible and the intelligible. The concept of the sign, in each of its aspects, has been determined by this opposition throughout the totality of its history. It has lived only on this opposition and its system. But

---

6. *The Raw and the Cooked* [1964], trans. John and Doreen Wightman (New York: Harper and Row, 1969), p. 14 [Derrida's note]. Claude Lévi-Strauss (1908–2009), French anthropologist; a central figure in the development of structuralism in the social sciences and social theory.

we cannot do without the concept of the sign, for we cannot give up this metaphysical complicity without also giving up the critique we are directing against this complicity, or without the risk of erasing difference in the self-identity of a signified reducing its signifier into itself or, amounting to the same thing, simply expelling its signifier outside itself. For there are two heterogenous ways of erasing the difference between the signifier and the signified: one, the classic way, consists in reducing or deriving the signifier, that is to say, ultimately in *submitting* the sign to thought; the other, the one we are using here against the first one, consists in putting into question the system in which the preceding reduction functioned: first and foremost, the opposition between the sensible and the intelligible. For the *paradox* is that the metaphysical reduction of the sign needed the opposition it was reducing. The opposition is systematic with the reduction. And what we are saying here about the sign can be extended to all the concepts and all the sentences of metaphysics, in particular to the discourse on "structure." But there are several ways of being caught in this circle. They are all more or less naïve, more or less empirical, more or less systematic, more or less close to the formulation— that is, to the formalization—of this circle. It is these differences which explain the multiplicity of destructive discourses and the disagreement between those who elaborate them. Nietzsche, Freud, and Heidegger,[7] for example, worked within the inherited concepts of metaphysics. Since these concepts are not elements or atoms, and since they are taken from a syntax and a system, every particular borrowing brings along with it the whole of metaphysics. This is what allows these destroyers to destroy each other reciprocally—for example, Heidegger regarding Nietzsche, with as much lucidity and rigor as bad faith and misconstruction, as the last metaphysician, the last "Platonist." One could do the same for Heidegger himself, for Freud, or for a number of others. And today no exercise is more widespread.

———

What is the relevance of this formal schema when we turn to what are called the "human sciences"?[8] One of them perhaps occupies a privileged place— ethnology. In fact one can assume that ethnology could have been born as a science only at the moment when a decentering had come about: at the moment when European culture—and, in consequence, the history of metaphysics and of its concepts—had been *dislocated*, driven from its locus, and forced to stop considering itself as the culture of reference. This moment is not first and foremost a moment of philosophical or scientific discourse. It is also a moment which is political, economic, technical, and so forth. One can say with total security that there is nothing fortuitous about the fact that the critique of ethnocentrism—the very condition for ethnology—should be systematically and historically contemporaneous with the destruction of the history of metaphysics. Both belong to one and the same era. Now, ethnology—like any science—comes about within the element of discourse.

7. For NIETZSCHE and HEIDEGGER, see above. Sigmund Freud (1856–1939), Austrian founder of psychoanalysis.

8. That is, the cluster of disciplines in the humanities and social sciences known in German as the *Geisteswissenschaften*.

And it is primarily a European science employing traditional concepts, however much it may struggle against them. Consequently, whether he wants to or not—and this does not depend on a decision on his part—the ethnologist accepts into his discourse the premises of ethnocentrism at the very moment when he denounces them. This necessity is irreducible; it is not a historical contingency. We ought to consider all its implications very carefully. But if no one can escape this necessity, and if no one is therefore responsible for giving in to it, however little he may do so, this does not mean that all the ways of giving in to it are of equal pertinence. The quality and fecundity of a discourse are perhaps measured by the critical rigor with which this relation to the history of metaphysics and to inherited concepts is thought. Here it is a question both of a critical relation to the language of the social sciences and a critical responsibility of the discourse itself. It is a question of explicitly and systematically posing the problem of the status of a discourse which borrows from a heritage the resources necessary for the deconstruction of that heritage itself. A problem of *economy* and *strategy*.

* * *

Besides the tension between play and history, there is also the tension between play and presence. Play is the disruption of presence. The presence of an element is always a signifying and substitutive reference inscribed in a system of differences and the movement of a chain. Play is always play of absence and presence, but if it is to be thought radically, play must be conceived of before the alternative of presence and absence. Being must be conceived as presence or absence on the basis of the possibility of play and not the other way around. If Lévi-Strauss, better than any other, has brought to light the play of repetition and the repetition of play, one no less perceives in his work a sort of ethic of presence, an ethic of nostalgia for origins, an ethic of archaic and natural innocence, of a purity of presence and self-presence in speech—an ethic, nostalgia, and even remorse, which he often presents as the motivation of the ethnological project when he moves toward the archaic societies which are exemplary societies in his eyes. These texts are well known.[9]

Turned towards the lost or impossible presence of the absent origin, this structuralist thematic of broken immediacy is therefore the saddened, *negative*, nostalgic, guilty, Rousseauistic side of the thinking of play whose other side would be the Nietzschean *affirmation*, that is the joyous affirmation of the play of the world and of the innocence of becoming, the affirmation of a world of signs without fault, without truth, and without origin which is offered to an active interpretation. *This affirmation then determines the noncenter otherwise than as loss of the center.* And it plays without security. For there is a *sure* play: that which is limited to the *substitution* of *given* and *existing, present*, pieces. In absolute chance, affirmation also surrenders itself to *genetic* indetermination, to the *seminal* adventure of the trace.

There are thus two interpretations of interpretation, of structure, of sign, of play. The one seeks to decipher, dreams of deciphering a truth or an origin

9. The reference is to *Tristes tropiques* [1955], trans. John Russell (London: Hutchinson and Co., 1961) [translator's note].

which escapes play and the order of the sign, and which lives the necessity of interpretation as an exile. The other, which is no longer turned toward the origin, affirms play and tries to pass beyond man and humanism, the name of man being the name of that being who, throughout the history of metaphysics or of ontotheology—in other words, throughout his entire history—has dreamed of full presence, the reassuring foundation, the origin and the end of play. The second interpretation of interpretation, to which Nietzsche pointed the way, does not seek in ethnography, as Lévi-Strauss does, the "inspiration of a new humanism" (again citing the "Introduction to the Work of Marcel Mauss").[1]

There are more than enough indications today to suggest we might perceive that these two interpretations of interpretation—which are absolutely irreconcilable even if we live them simultaneously and reconcile them in an obscure economy—together share the field which we call, in such a problematic fashion, the social sciences.

For my part, although these two interpretations must acknowledge and accentuate their difference and define their irreducibility, I do not believe that today there is any question of *choosing*—in the first place because here we are in a region (let us say, provisionally, a region of historicity) where the category of choice seems particularly trivial; and in the second, because we must first try to conceive of the common ground, and the *différance* of this irreducible difference. Here there is a kind of question, let us still call it historical, whose *conception, formation, gestation,* and *labor* we are only catching a glimpse of today. I employ these words, I admit, with a glance toward the operations of childbearing—but also with a glance toward those who, in a society from which I do not exclude myself, turn their eyes away when faced by the as yet unnamable which is proclaiming itself and which can do so, as is necessary whenever a birth is in the offing, only under the species of the nonspecies, in the formless, mute, infant, and terrifying form of monstrosity.

SOURCE: From Jacques Derrida, "Structure, Sign and Play in the Discourse of the Human Sciences," in *Writing and Difference,* trans. Alan Bass (Chicago: University of Chicago Press, 1978), pp. 278–82, 292–93. This essay was first published in the French version of this collection, *L'Écriture et la différence* (1967); it was originally delivered as a lecture in 1966.

1. Cited by Derrida in a passage not included here: Lévi-Strauss, "Introduction à l'oeuvre de Marcel Mauss," in Marcel Mauss, *Sociologie et anthropol-* *ogie* [*Sociology and Anthropology*] (Paris: P.U.F., 1950).

JEAN-FRANÇOIS LYOTARD
(1924 – 1998)

Lyotard's writing must be viewed in light of his life as a radical political activist. His thought cannot be separated from his determination to confront and overcome Marxism, Freudianism, and structuralism. Nor can his thinking be separated from the social and political conflicts of the historical events and times through which he lived—in particular, the Second World War, the Algerian battle for independence from France, and the radical leftist politics of 1960s France. Along with the philosophy of GILLES DELEUZE, Lyotard's thought is one of the most vivid encapsulations of the political spirit that infused students, workers, and academics in the massive demonstrations of 1968.

Lyotard's work is often thought to be more aesthetic and literary-theoretic than philosophical; but this is a misconception. His understanding of art is that, at least in its avant-garde forms, it can be a militant, political act. His analyses of aesthetic experience, feeling and sensation, the sublime, language, and representation are deeply philosophical and even coherently constructive, notwithstanding his attacks on theory, the ability of language and knowledge to capture the singularity of "the event" and difference, and his methodology—which he likens to picking through ruins and fragments. He is best known for his analysis of the social phenomenon of postmodernism, which can be most aptly summarized in terms of the loss of "metanarratives," or big-picture stories of universal values and rules that cut across and unify different groups within the multitude of modern, late-capitalist social, political, historical, linguistic, and epistemic communities.

Jean-François Lyotard ("Lee-oh-TAR") was born in Versailles. After being educated at the Lycée Buffon and Henri-le-Grand, he studied at the Sorbonne and the École Normale Supérieure, writing his master's thesis on the notion of indifference as an ethical concept. He took part in the 1944 fight to liberate Paris from Nazi control by aiding the wounded, and later wrote on his experiences for the journal *Les Temps Modernes* (*Modern Times*). In 1948 he married Andrée May, with whom he had two children.

Lyotard obtained a teaching position at a French secondary school in Constantine, Algeria, in 1950, and became politically active in support of Algerian independence. Returning to France in 1952, he taught (until 1959) at La Flèche. In 1954 he joined a radical socialist movement calling itself "Socialism or Barbarism," contributing to and editing its journal of the same name (*Socialisme ou barbarie*). Internal politics splintered the group, and Lyotard eventually gave up the underlying Marxist-socialist theory that had motivated his affiliation with it. Between 1959 and 1966, he taught at the Sorbonne, where he also attended Jacques Lacan's seminars. In 1967 he began to teach at the new campus of the University of Paris at Nanterre. There he helped organize the protests of May 1968. During this period he was also a researcher at the National Center for Scientific Research.

In 1971 Lyotard received his doctorate and joined the faculty at the University of Paris campus at Vincennes, where he taught until he retired to emeritus status in 1987. He subsequently held professorships at the University of California at Irvine and at Emory University, and visiting appointments elsewhere in the Americas, including at Yale, the University of Minnesota, Johns Hopkins University, the University of Montreal, and the University of São Paulo. He helped found the Collège Internationale de Philosophie in Paris. In 1993 he married his second wife, Dolorès Djidzek, with whom he had a son. He died in Paris in 1998 of leukemia.

Lyotard's work from the 1970s shares much with the materialist metaphysics, anti-capitalist politics, and anti-representationalist epistemology of Deleuze and FÉLIX GUATTARI. Although this work (in tune with the times) is against theory and in favor of practice, it attempts to rethink the notion of theory itself as an enactment of desire. Lyotard's account of the "libidinal economy" expands a post-Freudian theory of desire and energy into a large-scale theory of society and reality. The main elements of this libidinal economy are "intensities," the libidinal surface or body, and the figure or "disposition." The body or libidinal surface is thought of abstractly and as reaching far beyond the physical body: it is the site where intensities, feelings, or affects occur. An "intensity" or event is a material, sensory phenomenon that exceeds representation and knowledge. It can be thought of as a locus of powers and unstable energies. Attempts to direct this energy, to capture it, or to exploit it are called "figures." Figures and representations are themselves manifestations of desire, but are by nature restrictive: they impose order and predictability on the "intensity." This idea of an intensity as featuring a multitude of incompossible figures—that is, equally legitimate but incommensurable representations with their origin in the same event—led Lyotard to a politics of a radical leftist, anarchist sort. Politics, so construed, is the enactment of desire.

Lyotard is rightly thought of as a poststructuralist. He leaves behind the structuralist theory of signs and their meanings, which operates on the model of interdependence and the relation of negation, and he radically alters the structuralist model by infusing it with this notion of desire. Desire and the intensities that manifest it are for him paradoxical singularities capable of interacting with a multitude of possible structures or models, but necessarily remaining outside any such representation.

At the end of the 1970s and through the 1980s, Lyotard became known as the leading theorist of the "postmodern." Lyotard's most famous analysis of the postmodern, from which the following selection is taken, employs Ludwig Wittgenstein's notion of a "language game" rather than his own theory of a "libidinal economy." This change in imagery tends to hide the deep similarity in Lyotard's work in these two periods. His theory of the postmodern begins as an examination of the state of knowledge in the late twentieth century but then enlarges its focus to the general condition and character of society. Knowledge in "modernity" is accompanied by "foundational narratives," or self-legitimating theories of the validity of the discourse within a particular language game. These narratives of legitimacy exceed the rules or allowable moves within a language game: they thereby become "metanarratives" that purport to link an individual language game with a set of universal values and truths.

The postmodern condition in knowledge is that of metanarrative breakdown, which Lyotard diagnoses as necessary given the incommensurability of language games. The terminology used to explain this condition shifts in his late work *The Differend* (1983), but the analysis remains consistent. There the notion of a language game is called a "phrase regime"; and the rules that govern a language game and its "linkages" between phrases are called "genres." Lyotard models society on language; but his model is quite different from that of the structuralists. The "differend" is the point of conflict between language games—that which cannot be represented, the unsayable, the *event* that stands beyond all representation and language. The event is rooted in matter, feeling, and the sensory. Conflict inevitably results, as different language games attempt to do justice to that which is unable to be captured in any of them.

The outcome of this analysis is a theory of the subject that is fragmented and caught within various language games.

But this fragmentation, for Lyotard, is actually the result of the forces of late capitalism, which attempts to erase all difference and to unite all forms of life into one mold. Classical "alienation" from the fruits of our labor or from those universal values and metanarratives may exist; but our true alienation, he suggests, is our separation from the fundamental sources of the differend or the event. The politics that operates within the field of absolute difference and incommensurable language games, therefore, does not attempt to make progress through reconciliation. Such attempts are misguided and dangerous. Postmodern political action emerges from careful study of the actual, concrete situation in society and from attention to the freeing experience of difference. Lyotard's postmodern politics avoids employing universal values and makes no promise of certainty of the success of its action. It rather is a creative and risky response to an exigency or desire—often to a barrier in society that silences, controls, or exploits that desire.

Not surprisingly, art looms large in Lyotard's thinking. The conflict of incommensurable language games is not resolved; but the creative act of art can transform our encounter with the differend. The feeling of anxiety and loss of meaning in the face of those irreconcilable attempts to do justice to the event can be transformed into enthusiastic and overpowering feeling—a recognition of the sublime. Being caught up in that experience of intense feeling can galvanize action, spark creation, and perhaps transform the situation and partially liberate difference. Postmodern politics is tempered, however, with a pessimistic realization that this experience itself will give rise to new language games and new conflict. The unrepresentable event cannot be perfectly represented even in avant-garde art, which in fact does not even aim at something like representation. But for Lyotard, such creative resistance to the attempt to cancel out difference remains a disrupting and disquieting force that can stimulate difference in the phrase regimes that structure our lives.

From The Postmodern Condition: A Report on Knowledge

Introduction

The object of this study is the condition of knowledge in the most highly developed societies. I have decided to use the word *postmodern* to describe that condition. The word is in current use on the American continent among sociologists and critics; it designates the state of our culture following the transformations which, since the end of the nineteenth century, have altered the game rules for science, literature, and the arts. The present study will place these transformations in the context of the crisis of narratives.

Science has always been in conflict with narratives. Judged by the yardstick of science, the majority of them prove to be fables. But to the extent that science does not restrict itself to stating useful regularities and seeks the truth, it is obliged to legitimate the rules of its own game. It then produces a discourse of legitimation with respect to its own status, a discourse called philosophy. I will use the term *modern* to designate any science that legitimates itself with reference to a metadiscourse of this kind making an explicit appeal to some grand narrative, such as the dialectics of Spirit, the hermeneutics of meaning, the emancipation of the rational or working subject, or the creation of wealth. For example, the rule of consensus between the sender and addressee of a statement with truth-value is deemed acceptable if it is cast in terms of a possible unanimity between rational minds: this is the Enlightenment narrative, in which the hero of knowledge works toward a good ethico-political end—universal peace. As can be seen from this example, if a metanarrative implying a philosophy of history is used to legitimate knowledge, questions are raised concerning the validity of the institutions governing the social bond: these must be legitimated as well. Thus justice is consigned to the grand narrative in the same way as truth.

Simplifying to the extreme, I define *postmodern* as incredulity toward metanarratives. This incredulity is undoubtedly a product of progress in the sciences: but that progress in turn presupposes it. To the obsolescence of the metanarrative apparatus of legitimation corresponds, most notably, the crisis of metaphysical philosophy and of the university institution which in the past relied on it. The narrative function is losing its functors, its great hero, its great dangers, its great voyages, its great goal. It is being dispersed in clouds of narrative language elements—narrative, but also denotative, prescriptive, descriptive, and so on. Conveyed within each cloud are pragmatic valencies specific to its kind. Each of us lives at the intersection of many of these. However, we do not necessarily establish stable language combinations, and the properties of the ones we do establish are not necessarily communicable.

Thus the society of the future falls less within the province of a Newtonian anthropology (such as structuralism or systems theory) than a pragmatics of language particles. There are many different language games[1]—a heterogeneity of elements. They only give rise to institutions in patches—local determinism.

The decision makers, however, attempt to manage these clouds of sociality according to input/output matrices, following a logic which implies that their elements are commensurable and that the whole is determinable. They allocate our lives for the growth of power. In matters of social justice and of scientific truth alike, the legitimation of that power is based on its optimizing the system's performance—efficiency. The application of this criterion to all of our games necessarily entails a certain level of terror, whether soft or hard: be operational (that is, commensurable) or disappear.

The logic of maximum performance is no doubt inconsistent in many ways, particularly with respect to contradiction in the socioeconomic field: it demands both less work (to lower production costs) and more (to lessen the social burden of the idle population). But our incredulity is now such that we no longer expect salvation to rise from these inconsistencies, as did Marx.[2]

Still, the postmodern condition is as much a stranger to disenchantment as it is to the blind positivity of delegitimation. Where, after the metanarratives, can legitimacy reside? The operativity criterion is technological; it has no relevance for judging what is true or just. Is legitimacy to be found in consensus obtained through discussion, as Jürgen Habermas thinks?[3] Such consensus does violence to the heterogeneity of language games. And invention

1. That is, cases in which language is used to structure human social practices; this concept is discussed in *Philosophical Investigations* (1953), by the Austrian-born British philosopher Ludwig Wittgenstein (1889–1951; see this anthology's companion volume, *The Analytic Tradition*).
2. On KARL MARX, who believed that the contradictions of capitalism would lead to its collapse (and the salvation of the working class), see above.
3. For HABERMAS, see above.

is always born of dissension. Postmodern knowledge is not simply a tool of the authorities; it refines our sensitivity to differences and reinforces our ability to tolerate the incommensurable. Its principle is not the expert's homology, but the inventor's paralogy.[4]

Here is the question: is a legitimation of the social bond, a just society, feasible in terms of a paradox analogous to that of scientific activity? What would such a paradox be?

The text that follows is an occasional one. It is a report on knowledge in the most highly developed societies and was presented to the Conseil des Universités of the government of Quebec at the request of its president.[5] I would like to thank him for his kindness in allowing its publication.

It remains to be said that the author of the report is a philosopher, not an expert. The latter knows what he knows and what he does not know: the former does not. One concludes, the other questions—two very different language games. I combine them here with the result that neither quite succeeds.

The philosopher at least can console himself with the thought that the formal and pragmatic analysis of certain philosophical and ethico-political discourses of legitimation, which underlies the report, will subsequently see the light of day. The report will have served to introduce that analysis from a somewhat sociologizing slant, one that truncates but at the same time situates it.

Such as it is, I dedicate this report to the Institut Polytechnique de Philosophie of the Université de Paris VIII (Vincennes)—at this very postmodern moment that finds the University nearing what may be its end, while the Institute may just be beginning.

1. The Field: Knowledge in Computerized Societies

Our working hypothesis is that the status of knowledge is altered as societies enter what is known as the postindustrial age and cultures enter what is known as the postmodern age. This transition has been under way since at least the end of the 1950s, which for Europe marks the completion of reconstruction.[6] The pace is faster or slower depending on the country, and within countries it varies according to the sector of activity: the general situation is one of temporal disjunction which makes sketching an overview difficult. A portion of the description would necessarily be conjectural. At any rate, we know that it is unwise to put too much faith in futurology.

Rather than painting a picture that would inevitably remain incomplete, I will take as my point of departure a single feature, one that immediately defines our object of study. Scientific knowledge is a kind of discourse. And it is fair to say that for the last forty years the "leading" sciences and technologies have had to do with language: phonology and theories of linguistics,

---

4. That is, the movement beyond or against an established way of reasoning—a different way to legitimate science. "Homology" (correspondence) literally means "agreement."
5. Perhaps because this text is a report (whether to meet or to parody the expectations raised), Lyotard provides a great many endnotes; they are not included here but can be found in the source text.
6. That is, reconstruction after the Second World War.

problems of communication and cybernetics, modern theories of algebra and informatics, computers and their languages, problems of translation and the search for areas of compatibility among computer languages, problems of information storage and data banks, telematics and the perfection of intelligent terminals, paradoxology.[7] The facts speak for themselves (and this list is not exhaustive).

These technological transformations can be expected to have a considerable impact on knowledge. Its two principal functions—research and the transmission of acquired learning—are already feeling the effect, or will in the future. With respect to the first function, genetics provides an example that is accessible to the layman: it owes its theoretical paradigm to cybernetics. Many other examples could be cited. As for the second function, it is common knowledge that the miniaturization and commercialization of machines is already changing the way in which learning is acquired, classified, made available, and exploited. It is reasonable to suppose that the proliferation of information-processing machines is having, and will continue to have, as much of an effect on the circulation of learning as did advancements in human circulation (transportation systems) and later, in the circulation of sounds and visual images (the media).

The nature of knowledge cannot survive unchanged within this context of general transformation. It can fit into the new channels, and become operational, only if learning is translated into quantities of information. We can predict that anything in the constituted body of knowledge that is not translatable in this way will be abandoned and that the direction of new research will be dictated by the possibility of its eventual results being translatable into computer language. The "producers" and users of knowledge must now, and will have to, possess the means of translating into these languages whatever they want to invent or learn. Research on translating machines is already well advanced. Along with the hegemony of computers comes a certain logic, and therefore a certain set of prescriptions determining which statements are accepted as "knowledge" statements.

We may thus expect a thorough exteriorization of knowledge with respect to the "knower," at whatever point he or she may occupy in the knowledge process. The old principle that the acquisition of knowledge is indissociable from the training (*Bildung*) of minds, or even of individuals, is becoming obsolete and will become ever more so. The relationship of the suppliers and users of knowledge to the knowledge they supply and use is now tending, and will increasingly tend, to assume the form already taken by the relationship of commodity producers and consumers to the commodities they produce and consume—that is, the form of value. Knowledge is and will be produced in order to be sold, it is and will be consumed in order to be valorized in a new production: in both cases, the goal is exchange. Knowledge ceases to be an end in itself, it loses its "use-value."[8]

It is widely accepted that knowledge has become the principal force of production over the last few decades; this has already had a noticeable effect on

---

7. Use of paradoxes. "Telematics": the merging of telecommunications and computerized information.
8. A term from Marxian economics: a commodity's usefulness in fulfilling human needs. (Its exchange value, which is abstracted from its use value, is the rate at which it can be traded for other commodities.)

the composition of the work force of the most highly developed countries and constitutes the major bottleneck for the developing countries. In the postindustrial and postmodern age, science will maintain and no doubt strengthen its preeminence in the arsenal of productive capacities of the nation-states. Indeed, this situation is one of the reasons leading to the conclusion that the gap between developed and developing countries will grow ever wider in the future.

But this aspect of the problem should not be allowed to overshadow the other, which is complementary to it. Knowledge in the form of an informational commodity indispensable to productive power is already, and will continue to be, a major—perhaps *the* major—stake in the worldwide competition for power. It is conceivable that the nation-states will one day fight for control of information, just as they battled in the past for control over territory, and afterwards for control of access to and exploitation of raw materials and cheap labor. A new field is opened for industrial and commercial strategies on the one hand, and political and military strategies on the other.

However, the perspective I have outlined above is not as simple as I have made it appear. For the mercantilization of knowledge is bound to affect the privilege the nation-states have enjoyed, and still enjoy, with respect to the production and distribution of learning. The notion that learning falls within the purview of the State, as the brain or mind of society, will become more and more outdated with the increasing strength of the opposing principle, according to which society exists and progresses only if the messages circulating within it are rich in information and easy to decode. The ideology of communicational "transparency," which goes hand in hand with the commercialization of knowledge, will begin to perceive the State as a factor of opacity and "noise." It is from this point of view that the problem of the relationship between economic and State powers threatens to arise with a new urgency.

Already in the last few decades, economic powers have reached the point of imperiling the stability of the State through new forms of the circulation of capital that go by the generic name of *multinational corporations*. These new forms of circulation imply that investment decisions have, at least in part, passed beyond the control of the nation-states. The question threatens to become even more thorny with the development of computer technology and telematics. Suppose, for example, that a firm such as IBM is authorized to occupy a belt in the earth's orbital field and launch communications satellites or satellites housing data banks. Who will have access to them? Who will determine which channels or data are forbidden? The State? Or will the State simply be one user among others? New legal issues will be raised, and with them the question: "who will know?"

Transformation in the nature of knowledge, then, could well have repercussions on the existing public powers, forcing them to reconsider their relations (both de jure and de facto) with the large corporations and, more generally, with civil society. The reopening of the world market, a return to vigorous economic competition, the breakdown of the hegemony of American capitalism, the decline of the socialist alternative, a probable opening of the Chinese market—these and many other factors are already, at the end of the 1970s, preparing States for a serious reappraisal of the role they have been accustomed to playing since the 1930s: that of guiding, or even directing investments. In this light, the new technologies can only increase the urgency of such a reexamination, since they make the information used in decision making (and therefore the means of control) even more mobile and subject to piracy.

It is not hard to visualize learning circulating along the same lines as money, instead of for its "educational" value or political (administrative, diplomatic, military) importance; the pertinent distinction would no longer be between knowledge and ignorance, but rather, as is the case with money, between "payment knowledge" and "investment knowledge"—in other words, between units of knowledge exchanged in a daily maintenance framework (the reconstitution of the work force, "survival") versus funds of knowledge dedicated to optimizing the performance of a project.

If this were the case, communicational transparency would be similar to liberalism. Liberalism does not preclude an organization of the flow of money in which some channels are used in decision making while others are only good for the payment of debts. One could similarly imagine flows of knowledge traveling along identical channels of identical nature, some of which would be reserved for the "decision makers," while the others would be used to repay each person's perpetual debt with respect to the social bond.

2. THE PROBLEM: LEGITIMATION

That is the working hypothesis defining the field within which I intend to consider the question of the status of knowledge. This scenario, akin to the one that goes by the name "the computerization of society" (although ours is advanced in an entirely different spirit), makes no claims of being original, or even true. What is required of a working hypothesis is a fine capacity for discrimination. The scenario of the computerization of the most highly developed societies allows us to spotlight (though with the risk of excessive magnification) certain aspects of the transformation of knowledge and its effects on public power and civil institutions—effects it would be difficult to perceive from other points of view. Our hypothesis, therefore, should not be accorded predictive value in relation to reality, but strategic value in relation to the question raised.

Nevertheless, it has strong credibility, and in that sense our choice of this hypothesis is not arbitrary. It has been described extensively by the experts and is already guiding certain decisions by the governmental agencies and private firms most directly concerned, such as those managing the telecommunications industry. To some extent, then, it is already a part of observable reality. Finally, barring economic stagnation or a general recession (resulting, for example, from a continued failure to solve the world's energy problems), there is a good chance that this scenario will come to pass: it is hard to see what other direction contemporary technology could take as an alternative to the computerization of society.

This is as much as to say that the hypothesis is banal. But only to the extent that it fails to challenge the general paradigm of progress in science and technology, to which economic growth and the expansion of sociopolitical power seem to be natural complements. That scientific and technical knowledge is cumulative is never questioned. At most, what is debated is the form that accumulation takes—some picture it as regular, continuous, and unanimous, others as periodic, discontinuous, and conflictual.

But these truisms are fallacious. In the first place, scientific knowledge does not represent the totality of knowledge; it has always existed in addition to, and in competition and conflict with, another kind of knowledge, which I will call narrative in the interests of simplicity (its characteristics will be described later). I do not mean to say that narrative knowledge can prevail over science, but its model is related to ideas of internal equilibrium and conviviality next to which contemporary scientific knowledge cuts a poor figure, especially if it is to undergo an exteriorization with respect to the "knower" and an alienation from its user even greater than has previously been the case. The resulting demoralization of researchers and teachers is far from negligible; it is well known that during the 1960s, in all of the most highly developed societies, it reached such explosive dimensions among those preparing to practice these professions—the students—that there was noticeable decrease in productivity at laboratories and universities unable to protect themselves from its contamination. Expecting this, with hope or fear, to lead to a revolution (as was then often the case) is out of the question: it will not change the order of things in postindustrial society overnight. But this doubt on the part of scientists must be taken into account as a major factor in evaluating the present and future status of scientific knowledge.

It is all the more necessary to take it into consideration since—and this is the second point—the scientists' demoralization has an impact on the central problem of legitimation. I use the word in a broader sense than do contemporary German theorists in their discussions of the question of authority.[9] Take any civil law as an example: it states that a given category of citizens must perform a specific kind of action. Legitimation is the process by which a legislator is authorized to promulgate such a law as a norm. Now take the example of a scientific statement: it is subject to the rule that a statement must fulfill a given set of conditions in order to be accepted as scientific. In this case, legitimation is the process by which a "legislator" dealing with scientific discourse is authorized to prescribe the stated conditions (in general, conditions of internal consistency and experimental verification) determining whether a statement is to be included in that discourse for consideration by the scientific community.

The parallel may appear forced. But as we will see, it is not. The question of the legitimacy of science has been indissociably linked to that of the legitimation of the legislator since the time of Plato.[1] From this point of view, the right to decide what is true is not independent of the right to decide what is just, even if the statements consigned to these two authorities differ in nature. The point is that there is a strict interlinkage between the kind of language called science and the kind called ethics and politics: they both stem from the same perspective, the same "choice" if you will—the choice called the Occident.

When we examine the current status of scientific knowledge—at a time when science seems more completely subordinated to the prevailing powers

---

9. Lyotard specifically has in mind Habermas. 1. Greek philosopher (ca. 427–ca. 347 B.C.E.).

than ever before and, along with the new technologies, is in danger of becoming a major stake in their conflicts—the question of double legitimation, far from receding into the background, necessarily comes to the fore. For it appears in its most complete form, that of reversion, revealing that knowledge and power are simply two sides of the same question: who decides what knowledge is, and who knows what needs to be decided? In the computer age, the question of knowledge is now more than ever a question of government.

3. THE METHOD: LANGUAGE GAMES

The reader will already have noticed that in analyzing this problem within the framework set forth I have favored a certain procedure: emphasizing facts of language and in particular their pragmatic aspect. To help clarify what follows it would be useful to summarize, however briefly, what is meant here by the term *pragmatic*.

A denotative utterance such as "The university is sick," made in the context of a conversation or an interview, positions its sender (the person who utters the statement), its addressee (the person who receives it), and its referent (what the statement deals with) in a specific way: the utterance places (and exposes) the sender in the position of "knower" (he knows what the situation is with the university), the addressee is put in the position of having to give or refuse his assent, and the referent itself is handled in a way unique to denotatives, as something that demands to be correctly identified and expressed by the statement that refers to it.

If we consider a declaration such as "The university is open," pronounced by a dean or rector at convocation, it is clear that the previous specifications no longer apply. Of course, the meaning of the utterance has to be understood, but that is a general condition of communication and does not aid us in distinguishing the different kinds of utterances or their specific effects. The distinctive feature of this second, "performative," utterance[2] is that its effect upon the referent coincides with its enunciation. The university is open because it has been declared open in the above-mentioned circumstances. That this is so is not subject to discussion or verification on the part of the addressee, who is immediately placed within the new context created by the utterance. As for the sender, he must be invested with the authority to make such a statement. Actually, we could say it the other way around: the sender is dean or rector—that is, he is invested with the authority to make this kind of statement—only insofar as he can directly affect both the referent, (the university) and the addressee (the university staff) in the manner I have indicated.

A different case involves utterances of the type, "Give money to the university"; these are prescriptions. They can be modulated as orders, commands, instructions, recommendations, requests, prayers, pleas, etc. Here, the sender is clearly placed in a position of authority, using the term broadly (including the authority of a sinner over a god who claims to be merciful): that is, he expects the addressee to perform the action referred to. The pragmatics of

2. A concept introduced by the English philosopher of language J. L. Austin (1911–1960); see this anthology's companion volume, *The Analytic Tradition*.

prescription entail concomitant changes in the posts of addressee and referent.

Of a different order again is the efficiency of a question, a promise, a literary description, a narration, etc. I am summarizing. Wittgenstein, taking up the study of language again from scratch, focuses his attention on the effects of different modes of discourse; he calls the various types of utterances he identifies along the way (a few of which I have listed) *language games*. What he means by this term is that each of the various categories of utterance can be defined in terms of rules specifying their properties and the uses to which they can be put—in exactly the same way as the game of chess is defined by a set of rules determining the properties of each of the pieces, in other words, the proper way to move them.

It is useful to make the following three observations about language games. The first is that their rules do not carry within themselves their own legitimation, but are the object of a contract, explicit or not, between players (which is not to say that the players invent the rules). The second is that if there are no rules, there is no game, that even an infinitesimal modification of one rule alters the nature of the game, that a "move" or utterance that does not satisfy the rules does not belong to the game they define. The third remark is suggested by what has just been said: every utterance should be thought of as a "move" in a game.

This last observation brings us to the first principle underlying our method as a whole: to speak is to fight, in the sense of playing, and speech acts fall within the domain of a general agonistics.[3] This does not necessarily mean that one plays in order to win. A move can be made for the sheer pleasure of its invention: what else is involved in that labor of language harassment undertaken by popular speech and by literature? Great joy is had in the endless invention of turns of phrase, of words and meanings, the process behind the evolution of language on the level of *parole*.[4] But undoubtedly even this pleasure depends on a feeling of success won at the expense of an adversary—at least one adversary, and a formidable one: the accepted language, or connotation.

This idea of an agonistics of language should not make us lose sight of the second principle, which stands as a complement to it and governs our analysis: that the observable social bond is composed of language "moves." An elucidation of this proposition will take us to the heart of the matter at hand.

4. The Nature of the Social Bond: The Modern Alternative

If we wish to discuss knowledge in the most highly developed contemporary society, we must answer the preliminary question of what methodological representation to apply to that society. Simplifying to the extreme, it is fair to say that in principle there have been, at least over the last half-century, two basic representational models for society: either society forms a functional whole, or it is divided in two. An illustration of the first model is suggested by

3. A theory of conflict and competition.
4. An individual's everyday language use, as opposed to language as an abstract structure (*langue*, another French term); the distinction was first drawn by the Swiss linguist Ferdinand de Saussure (1857–1913).

Talcott Parsons[5] (at least the postwar Parsons) and his school, and of the second, by the Marxist current (all of its component schools, whatever differences they may have, accept both the principle of class struggle and dialectics as a duality operating within society).

This methodological split, which defines two major kinds of discourse on society, has been handed down from the nineteenth century. The idea that society forms an organic whole, in the absence of which it ceases to be a society (and sociology ceases to have an object of study), dominated the minds of the founders of the French school. Added detail was supplied by functionalism; it took yet another turn in the 1950s with Parsons's conception of society as a self-regulating system. The theoretical and even material model is no longer the living organism; it is provided by cybernetics, which, during and after the Second World War, expanded the model's applications.

In Parsons's work, the principle behind the system is still, if I may say so, optimistic: it corresponds to the stabilization of the growth economies and societies of abundance under the aegis of a moderate welfare state. In the work of contemporary German theorists, *Systemtheorie* is technocratic, even cynical, not to mention despairing: the harmony between the needs and hopes of individuals or groups and the functions guaranteed by the system is now only a secondary component of its functioning. The true goal of the system, the reason it programs itself like a computer, is the optimization of the global relationship between input and output—in other words, performativity. Even when its rules are in the process of changing and innovations are occurring, even when its dysfunctions (such as strikes, crises, unemployment, or political revolutions) inspire hope and lead to belief in an alternative, even then what is actually taking place is only an internal readjustment, and its result can be no more than an increase in the system's "viability." The only alternative to this kind of performance improvement is entropy, or decline.

Here again, while avoiding the simplifications inherent in a sociology of social theory, it is difficult to deny at least a parallel between this "hard" technocratic version of society and the ascetic effort that was demanded (the fact that it was done in name of "advanced liberalism" is beside the point) of the most highly developed industrial societies in order to make them competitive—and thus optimize their "rationality"—within the framework of the resumption of economic world war in the 1960s.

Even taking into account the massive displacement intervening between the thought of a man like Comte and the thought of Luhmann,[6] we can discern a common conception of the social: society is a unified totality, a "unicity." Parsons formulates this clearly: "The most essential condition of successful dynamic analysis is a continual and systematic reference of every problem to the state of the system as a whole. . . . A process or set of conditions either 'contributes' to the maintenance (or development) of the system or it is 'dysfunctional' in that it detracts from the integration, effectiveness, etc., of the system."[7] The "technocrats" also subscribe to this idea. Whence its credibility:

5. American sociologist (1902–1979), whose work in the mid-twentieth century helped shape modern American sociology.
6. Niklas Luhmann (1927–1998), German philosopher and prominent thinker in social systems theory. Auguste Comte (1798–1857), French philosopher

and leading figure in the emergence of sociology and of positivism in the social sciences.
7. Talcott Parsons, "The Present Position and Prospects of Systematic Theory in Sociology" (1945), in *Essays in Sociological Theory*, rev. ed. (Glencoe, Ill.: Free Press, 1954), pp. 216, 218.

it has the means to become a reality, and that is all the proof it needs. This is what Horkheimer[8] called the "paranoia" of reason.

But this realism of systemic self-regulation, and this perfectly sealed circle of facts and interpretations, can be judged paranoid only if one has, or claims to have, at one's disposal a viewpoint that is in principle immune from their allure. This is the function of the principle of class struggle in theories of society based on the work of Marx.

"Traditional" theory is always in danger of being incorporated into the programming of the social whole as a simple tool for the optimization of its performance; this is because its desire for a unitary and totalizing truth lends itself to the unitary and totalizing practice of the system's managers. "Critical" theory,[9] based on a principle of dualism and wary of syntheses and reconciliations, should be in a position to avoid this fate. What guides Marxism, then, is a different model of society, and a different conception of the function of the knowledge that can be produced by society and acquired from it. This model was born of the struggles accompanying the process of capitalism's encroachment upon traditional civil societies. There is insufficient space here to chart the vicissitudes of these struggles, which fill more than a century of social, political, and ideological history. We will have to content ourselves with a glance at the balance sheet, which is possible for us to tally today now that their fate is known: in countries with liberal or advanced liberal management, the struggles and their instruments have been transformed into regulators of the system; in communist countries, the totalizing model and its totalitarian effect have made a comeback in the name of Marxism itself, and the struggles in question have simply been deprived of the right to exist. Everywhere, the Critique of political economy (the subtitle of Marx's *Capital*) and its correlate, the critique of alienated society, are used in one way or another as aids in programming the system.

Of course, certain minorities, such as the Frankfurt School or the group *Socialisme ou barbarie*,[1] preserved and refined the critical model in opposition to this process. But the social foundation of the principle of division, or class struggle, was blurred to the point of losing all of its radicality; we cannot conceal the fact that the critical model in the end lost its theoretical standing and was reduced to the status of a "utopia" or "hope," a token protest raised in the name of man or reason or creativity, or again of some social category—such as the Third World or the students—on which is conferred in extremis the henceforth improbable function of critical subject.

The sole purpose of this schematic (or skeletal) reminder has been to specify the problematic in which I intend to frame the question of knowledge in advanced industrial societies. For it is impossible to know what the state of knowledge is—in other words, the problems its development and distribution are facing today—without knowing something of the society within which it

---

8. Max Horkheimer (1895–1973), German philosopher and sociologist who was a founder of the Frankfurt School of critical social theory. He and Theodor Adorno discuss the link between modernity and paranoia in *Dialectic of Enlightenment* (1947).
9. That is, critical social theory of the sort associated with the Institute for Social Research established at Frankfurt University in 1930, directed by

Horkheimer. He and Adorno were among the first generation of the Frankfurt School, whose interests in Marx, Freud, social theory, and cultural criticism were both sociological and philosophical. Habermas and Herbert Marcuse were among its second generation.
1. Socialism or Barbarism (French), a postwar French libertarian socialist group to which Lyotard belonged in the 1950s.

is situated. And today more than ever, knowing about that society involves first of all choosing what approach the inquiry will take, and that necessarily means choosing how society can answer. One can decide that the principal role of knowledge is as an indispensable element in the functioning of society, and act in accordance with that decision, only if one has already decided that society is a giant machine.

Conversely, one can count on its critical function, and orient its development and distribution in that direction, only after it has been decided that society does not form an integrated whole, but remains haunted by a principle of opposition. The alternative seems clear: it is a choice between the homogeneity and the intrinsic duality of the social, between functional and critical knowledge. But the decision seems difficult, or arbitrary.

It is tempting to avoid the decision altogether by distinguishing two kinds of knowledge. One, the positivist kind, would be directly applicable to technologies bearing on men and materials, and would lend itself to operating as an indispensable productive force within the system. The other—the critical, reflexive, or hermeneutic kind—by reflecting directly or indirectly on values or aims, would resist any such "recuperation."

5. THE NATURE OF THE SOCIAL BOND: THE POSTMODERN PERSPECTIVE

I find this partition solution unacceptable. I suggest that the alternative it attempts to resolve, but only reproduces, is no longer relevant for the societies with which we are concerned and that the solution itself is still caught within a type of oppositional thinking that is out of step with the most vital modes of postmodern knowledge. As I have already said, economic "redeployment" in the current phase of capitalism, aided by a shift in techniques and technology, goes hand in hand with a change in the function of the State: the image of society this syndrome suggests necessitates a serious revision of the alternate approaches considered. For brevity's sake, suffice it to say that functions of regulation, and therefore of reproduction, are being and will be further withdrawn from administrators and entrusted to machines. Increasingly, the central question is becoming who will have access to the information these machines must have in storage to guarantee that the right decisions are made. Access to data is, and will continue to be, the prerogative of experts of all stripes. The ruling class is and will continue to be the class of decision makers. Even now it is no longer composed of the traditional political class, but of a composite layer of corporate leaders, high-level administrators, and the heads of the major professional, labor, political, and religious organizations.

What is new in all of this is that the old poles of attraction represented by nation-states, parties, professions, institutions, and historical traditions are losing their attraction. And it does not look as though they will be replaced, at least not on their former scale. The Trilateral Commission[2] is not a popular pole of attraction. "Identifying" with the great names, the heroes of contemporary history, is becoming more and more difficult. Dedicating oneself

---

2. A private organization founded in 1974 by the American banker and philanthropist David Rockefeller to address the problems of globalization by bringing together leaders within the private sector from Europe, North American, and Asia.

to "catching up with Germany," the life goal the French president[3] seems to be offering his countrymen, is not exactly exciting. But then again, it is not exactly a life goal. It depends on each individual's industriousness. Each individual is referred to himself. And each of us knows that our *self* does not amount to much.

This breaking up of the grand Narratives (discussed below, sections 9 and 10) leads to what some authors analyze in terms of the dissolution of the social bond and the disintegration of social aggregates into a mass of individual atoms thrown into the absurdity of Brownian motion.[4] Nothing of the kind is happening: this point of view, it seems to me, is haunted by the paradisaic representation of a lost "organic" society.

A *self* does not amount to much, but no self is an island; each exists in a fabric of relations that is now more complex and mobile than ever before. Young or old, man or woman, rich or poor, a person is always located at "nodal points" of specific communication circuits, however tiny these may be. Or better: one is always located at a post through which various kinds of messages pass. No one, not even the least privileged among us, is ever entirely powerless over the messages that traverse and position him at the post of sender, addressee, or referent. One's mobility in relation to these language game effects (language games, of course, are what this is all about) is tolerable, at least within certain limits (and the limits are vague); it is even solicited by regulatory mechanisms, and in particular by the self-adjustments the system undertakes in order to improve its performance. It may even be said that the system can and must encourage such movement to the extent that it combats its own entropy; the novelty of an unexpected "move," with its correlative displacement of a partner or group of partners, can supply the system with that increased performativity it forever demands and consumes.

It should now be clear from which perspective I chose language games as my general methodological approach. I am not claiming that the *entirety* of social relations is of this nature—that will remain an open question. But there is no need to resort to some fiction of social origins to establish that language games are the minimum relation required for society to exist: even before he is born, if only by virtue of the name he is given, the human child is already positioned as the referent in the story recounted by those around him, in relation to which he will inevitably chart his course. Or more simply still, the question of the social bond, insofar as it is a question, is itself a language game, the game of inquiry. It immediately positions the person who asks, as well as the addressee and the referent asked about: it is already the social bond.

On the other hand, in a society whose communication component is becoming more prominent day by day, both as a reality and as an issue, it is clear that language assumes a new importance. It would be superficial to reduce its significance to the traditional alternative between manipulatory speech and the unilateral transmission of messages on the one hand, and free expression and dialogue on the other.

A word on this last point. If the problem is described simply in terms of communication theory, two things are overlooked: first, messages have quite

---

3. [Valéry] Giscard d'Estaing at the time this book was published in France [translator's note]. Giscard d'Estaing was the founder and head of a conservative party, and he believed in strengthening

European union.
4. The random motion of microscopic particles suspended in a liquid or gas.

different forms and effects depending on whether they are, for example, denotatives, prescriptives, evaluatives, performatives, etc. It is clear that what is important is not simply the fact that they communicate information. Reducing them to this function is to adopt an outlook which unduly privileges the system's own interests and point of view. A cybernetic machine does indeed run on information, but the goals programmed into it, for example, originate in prescriptive and evaluative statements it has no way to correct in the course of its functioning—for example, maximizing its own performance. How can one guarantee that performance maximization is the best goal for the social system in every case? In any case the "atoms" forming its matter are competent to handle statements such as these—and this question in particular.

Second, the trivial cybernetic version of information theory misses something of decisive importance, to which I have already called attention: the agonistic aspect of society. The atoms are placed at the crossroads of pragmatic relationships, but they are also displaced by the messages that traverse them, in perpetual motion. Each language partner, when a "move" pertaining to him is made, undergoes a "displacement," an alteration of some kind that not only affects him in his capactiy as addressee and referent, but also as sender. These "moves" necessarily provoke "countermoves"—and everyone knows that a countermove that is merely reactional is not a "good" move. Reactional countermoves are no more than programmed effects in the opponent's strategy; they play into his hands and thus have no effect on the balance of power. That is why it is important to increase displacement in the games, and even to disorient it, in such a way as to make an unexpected "move" (a new statement).

What is needed if we are to understand social relations in this manner, on whatever scale we choose, is not only a theory of communication, but a theory of games which accepts agonistics as a founding principle. In this context, it is easy to see that the essential element of newness is not simply "innovation." Support for this approach can be found in the work of a number of contemporary sociologists, in addition to linguists and philosophers of language.

This "atomization" of the social into flexible networks of language games may seem far removed from the modern reality, which is depicted, on the contrary, as afflicted with bureaucratic paralysis. The objection will be made, at least, that the weight of certain institutions imposes limits on the games, and thus restricts the inventiveness of the players in making their moves. But I think this can be taken into account without causing any particular difficulty.

In the ordinary use of discourse—for example, in a discussion between two friends—the interlocutors use any available ammunition, changing games from one utterance to the next: questions, requests, assertions, and narratives are launched pell-mell into battle. The war is not without rules, but the rules allow and encourage the greatest possible flexibility of utterance.

From this point of view, an institution differs from a conversation in that it always requires supplementary constraints for statements to be declared admissible within its bounds. The constraints function to filter discursive potentials, interrupting possible connections in the communication networks: there are things that should not be said. They also privilege certain classes of statements (sometimes only one) whose predominance characterizes the discourse of the particular institution: there are things that should be said, and there are ways of saying them. Thus: orders in the army, prayer in church, denotation in the schools, narration in families, questions in philosophy, performativity in businesses. Bureaucratization is the outer limit of this tendency.

However, this hypothesis about the institution is still too "unwieldy": its point of departure is an overly "reifying" view of what is institutionalized. We know today that the limits the institution imposes on potential language "moves" are never established once and for all (even if they have been formally defined). Rather, the limits are themselves the stakes and provisional results of language strategies, within the institution and without. Examples: Does the university have a place for language experiments (poetics)? Can you tell stories in a cabinet meeting? Advocate a cause in the barracks? The answers are clear: yes, if the university opens creative workshops; yes, if the cabinet works with prospective scenarios; yes, if the limits of the old institution are displaced. Reciprocally, it can be said that the boundaries only stabilize when they cease to be stakes in the game.

This, I think, is the appropriate approach to contemporary institutions of knowledge.

* * *

SOURCE: From Jean-François Lyotard, *The Postmodern Condition: A Report on Knowledge*, trans. Geoff Bennington and Brian Massumi (Minneapolis: University of Minnesota Press, 1984), pp. xxiii–xxv, 3–17. Originally published in 1979 as *La condition postmoderne: Rapport sur le savoir*.

GILLES DELEUZE
(1925 – 1995)

FÉLIX GUATTARI
(1930 – 1992)

MICHEL FOUCAULT is said to have asserted that one day the twentieth century would be known as Deleuzian. The basic tenets of Gilles Deleuze's thinking remained consistent throughout his career, his constant shifting of models of thought and terminology notwithstanding. His focus never strayed from the attempt to create a metaphysics centered on difference, multiplicity, and the singular event, in opposition to one that favors identity, substance, possibility, representation, and dialectic; and he persisted in applying that metaphysics to politics and aesthetics. The real challenges of his writing are the level of extreme abstraction at which it operates and the immense wealth of knowledge of both the sciences and the humanities that informs his terminology and substantial ideas.

By far the most theoretically sophisticated and philosophically comprehensive of the antihumanist responses to the revolutionary ideas of the 1960s, Deleuze's thought extends to aesthetics, theory of language, epistemology, metaphysics, ethics, and politics. Each of his major theoretical works, moreover, requires readers to immerse themselves in its vocabulary. This makes the price of admission to the substance of his thought a high one. The best way into it may be through his creative interpretations of Hume, KANT, Spinoza, Leibniz, NIETZSCHE, and BERGSON. His work with Félix Guattari is also a paradigmatic philosophical expression of the revolutionary spirit of France in the late 1960s. Foucault summarized the task of their work in his introduction to their *Anti-Oedipus* (1972): "the tracking down of all varieties of fascism, from the enormous ones that surround and crush us to the petty ones that constitute the tyrannical bitterness of our everyday lives."

Gilles Deleuze ("Dih-LOSE") was born in Paris, where he lived most of his life. He and his brother Georges briefly attended a secondary school in Deauville in Normandy, where his lifelong interest in literature was inspired. Upon returning to Paris at the outset of the war, he finished his secondary schooling at the Lycées Carnot and Henri-IV. His brother, arrested for participating in the French resistance, died while being transported to a concentration camp. After the liberation of France, Deleuze entered the Sorbonne and studied philosophy (with the HEGEL scholar Jean Hyppolyte, among others). In 1948 he graduated and passed his *agrégation* examination, which qualified him to teach. He taught at several secondary and college preparatory schools before finally obtaining a position at the Sorbonne in 1957. He married Denise Paul Grandjouan in 1956, and they had two children (one of whom, their daughter Emilie, became a film director).

Between 1960 and 1964 Deleuze was a researcher at the National Center for Scientific Research. It was at that time that he met Foucault, and the two men remained friends for the rest of their lives. He taught from 1964 to 1969 at the University of Lyon and then, until his retirement in 1987, at the University of Paris. It was there that he began his collaboration with Guattari. He was active in a number of political groups concerned with such causes as prison conditions in France, the rights of homosexuals, and the Israel-Palestine conflict. In 1968, however, he contracted a severe case of tuberculosis, which affected his health for the rest of his life. In his later years he suffered from lung cancer and severe respiratory problems, making almost any activity impossible for him. Finding his condition intolerable, he ended his life in 1995 by throwing himself from a window of his Paris apartment.

Pierre-Félix Guattari ("Gwa-TAR-y") was born in Villeneuve-les-Sablons (Oise), France. He abandoned his undergraduate studies in pharmacology and philosophy at the Sorbonne to pursue a career in psychoanalysis. When he was 15 he met Jean Oury, and they became radical political activists after the Second World War ended. After participating in the youth movement of the French Communist Party, Guattari joined the party in 1950. In 1953 he assisted Oury—who by then had become a student and follower of the prominent Freudian psychoanalyst Jacques Lacan—in founding a nontraditional private psychiatric clinic. Their effort was part of a larger antipsychiatric movement, then gaining political as well as theoretical force in France, critical of how mental health institutions were structured and how they treated patients.

In 1960 Guattari helped found a radical group known as Opposition de Gauche (Opposition of the Left), which was very active in the May 1968 protests. It was then that he met Deleuze. In the early 1960s he also became interested in Lacan; and when Lacan founded the École Freudienne de Paris in 1964 Guattari enrolled, studied with him, and even underwent analysis by him, but subsequently developed doubts about his views and diverged from him. In the 1970s and 1980s Guattari was involved in "action groups" on almost every political issue and international crisis of note. This pattern of organizing and working within collectives and groups around the world was central to both his philosophy and his life. He died of a heart attack in 1992.

What Deleuze calls his "transcendental empiricism"—and explores with Guattari in the following selection (from one of their most notable collaborations)—consists of several interrelated ideas that flow from his interpretation of the history of philosophy. Following the example of Kant, he and Guattari begin with an analysis of our faculties; but whereas Kant saw a harmony between sensibility and understanding that he attributed to

a "common sense," they see it as forced through a dogmatic image of thought. Within this original conflict of the faculties is rooted an alternative image of thought, modeled in part on schizophrenia. This fragmentation of the faculties radicalizes the Humean "bundle theory" of the self, in effect unbundling the bundle.

In the spirit of Hume, Deleuze also accepts a methodological focus on the sensory and the concrete. Yet his focus on the sensory—and his reaction against representation through universal *concepts*—should not be seen as a sort of anti-intellectualism that is hostile to thinking altogether. Rather, he contends that we must rethink the notion of the "concept," and in so doing provide a new image of thought. He holds that part of empiricism is to see concepts as living *reactions to the sensory*—a sort of moving scaffolding—that are constantly being created and altered. This vital, experimental, and creative vision of thought emerged from Deleuze's reading of Nietzsche and Bergson. He proceeded to develop an ontology of force, power, drive, and conatus (Spinoza's term for the impulse of all things to continue to exist), drawing creatively on Hume and psychoanalytic sources as well as on Spinoza, Nietzsche, and Bergson. In spite of (or perhaps because of) this multiplicity of historical influences, the end product—Deleuze's own philosophy—is highly original.

The originality of that thought is seen particularly in his magnum opus, *Difference and Repetition* (1968). "Difference" is opposed by Deleuze to identity and is prior to individualization. Furthermore, it is opposed to the Hegelian notion of "negation," which necessarily rests on the logic of the identical: the two opposing terms each presuppose an identity. To think and philosophize about difference, we must use notions such as movement, action, affirmation, and expression, which lead us back to what is most concrete: sensory experience. Deleuze's metaphysics of difference is based on the idea of pre-individual singularities—undifferentiated but differentiating mechanisms. Perhaps the best way to understand this idea is through the notion of the *virtual*. Mere possibility is unreal, whereas the virtual is the full potentiality of the real—a potentiality that can be actualized in situations or points of view. Deleuze uses the notion of an "Idea"—in the Kantian sense of an illusion or antinomy, rather than in the Platonic or Hegelian sense— to designate a *problem*, which one might think of as a vortex of difference. In his theory of difference he also draws on the Leibnizian notion of a "monad" as a sort of infinite, vital potential world unto itself.

The other term in this work's title is "repetition." This theme derives from the Nietzschean notion of the "eternal recurrence of the same," understood as a cyclical notion of time. Repetition is opposed to "generality" and that which can be exchanged in a general economy: it is an expression of *singularity*, construed as an effect of the flux internal to being. Repetition and the model of time that emerges from it are at the core of Deleuze's vitalism. This notion owes much to KIERKE-GAARD's criticism of Hegel's dialectic as being unable to capture the real movement of life. Deleuze is also critical of Plato and believes that the relationship between model and image, which Plato invokes in his critique of art, must be inverted. Repetition expresses itself in symbols and "simulacra"—that is, copies or images that lack an origin, a model, or a foundation. The virtual (conceived as the differently actualizable potentiality of the real), like its pure difference, is not a Platonic idea copied imperfectly in human reality. It is nothing of which there can be copies; and so simulacra stand in a different sort of relation to it, and have another sort of status. They rather are "events," expressions of difference, and intensive qualities or sensory intensities that reflect the play of the manifold, complex, and conflicting nature of difference.

An "event," for Deleuze, is no corporeal entity that "exists" as bodies do; but

neither is it merely a function of sentences, relations among sentences, relations of sentences to the world, or the relation of sentences to mental states or beliefs of the subject. It is something with meaning or "sense"; and "sense" is ultimately tied to "expression." In his investigation of the genesis of sense and expression, Deleuze makes use of results of experimental psychologists. Their studies of children suggest that the origin of sense and expression ("the actual") is in "non-sense"—that is, in the sort of paradoxes of conflicting qualities and states that motivated Plato's search for the Forms. Non-sense is in the first instance the fluctuating sensory intensities that infants and schizophrenics seem to experience at a physical level. At the level of language, non-sense is essentially a made-up or stipulated word that in fact designates nothing; Deleuze uses the example of Lewis Carroll's nonsense words. At the same time, however, it acts as an organizational linchpin in our system of meanings.

The following selection brings together the opening and conclusion of Deleuze's final work, written with Guattari, which provides a vision of how philosophy, science, and art do or could operate in human experience. Despite the level of abstraction at which Deleuze operates, he constantly returns to the practical and the political. *What Is Philosophy?* (1991) is as much an account of the positive or affirmative role of truly creative thinking as it is a criticism of the democratic value of "communication" (as promoted by JÜRGEN HABERBAS) and the relativistic reduction of everything into mere "opinion." Deleuze's antihumanist politics does not value consensus; rather, it is a theory of radical and revolutionary political action that takes place through a creative event. He thus sees any self-protective attempt to avoid chaos, change, and the unsettling nature of difference and multiplicity as the enemy of such creativity.

In this last work, as in his others, Deleuze seeks to achieve an "image of thought" (or conception of both language and thought) that does not falsify or reify the infinite variability of difference and multiplicity. Instead, he envisions thought as an "infinite movement." The philosophical creation of concepts at the same time institutes what he calls "the plane of immanence." Each historical epoch—and with it each truly creative philosophical thought—can be seen as a different plane, whose matrix is made up of concepts. The plane stretches across what he calls chaos, the multiplicity of differentials or infinitely realizable organizations of the virtual.

Philosophy, for Deleuze, uses concepts that still resonate with the variability of pure difference but have imposed a consistent plane on it. Science creates abstract functions that map out determinate relations and enable us to get our bearings and find our way through the multiple. Art operates by creating sensible being that in its infinity gives us a sensible vision of the chaotic. Deleuze argues that art, science, and philosophy interweave to constitute the subject—a notion that is radically material, vital, and affective. Therefore, we should not think of philosophy, art, and science as manifestations of anything like "mind" or Hegelian absolute *Geist*. For Deleuze, they remain vital and sensory—uniting us with the chaotic material multiplicity rather than separating us from it.

From What Is Philosophy?

Introduction: The Question Then . . .

The question *what is philosophy?* can perhaps be posed only late in life, with the arrival of old age and the time for speaking concretely. In fact, the bibliography on the nature of philosophy is very limited. It is a question posed in a moment of quiet restlessness, at midnight, when there is no longer anything to ask. It was asked before; it was always being asked, but too indirectly or obliquely; the question was too artificial, too abstract. Instead of being seized by it, those who asked the question set it out and controlled it in passing. They were not sober enough. There was too much desire to *do* philosophy to wonder what it was, except as a stylistic exercise. That point of nonstyle where one can finally say, "What is it I have been doing all my life?" had not been reached. There are times when old age produces not eternal youth but a sovereign freedom, a pure necessity in which one enjoys a moment of grace between life and death, and in which all the parts of the machine come together to send into the future a feature that cuts across all ages: Titian, Turner, Monet.[1] In old age Turner acquired or won the right to take painting down a deserted path of no return that is indistinguishable from a final question. *Vie de Rancé* could be said to mark both Chateaubriand's old age and the start of modern literature.[2] Cinema too sometimes offers us its gifts of the third age, as when Ivens,[3] for example, blends his laughter with the witch's laughter in the howling wind. Likewise in philosophy, Kant's *Critique of Judgment*[4] is an unrestrained work of old age, which his successors have still not caught up with: all the mind's faculties overcome their limits, the very limits that Kant had so carefully laid down in the works of his prime.

---

1. Three great painters: the Italian Tiziano Vecelli (1488/90–1576), the English Joseph Mallord William Turner (1775–1851), and the French Claude Monet (1840–1926).
2. In 1844 the French author and diplomat François-Auguste-René, vicomte de Chateaubriand (1768–1848), published his final work, *The Life of Rancé* (a biography).
3. Joris Ivens (1898–1989), Dutch film director.
4. Published in 1790, when KANT was 66.

We cannot claim such a status. Simply, the time has come for us to ask what philosophy is. We had never stopped asking this question previously, and we already had the answer, which has not changed: philosophy is the art of forming, inventing, and fabricating concepts. But the answer not only had to take note of the question, it had to determine its moment, its occasion and circumstances, its landscapes and personae, its conditions and unknowns. It had to be possible to ask the question "between friends," as a secret or a confidence, or as a challenge when confronting the enemy, and at the same time to reach that twilight hour when one distrusts even the friend. It is then that you say, "That's what it was, but I don't know if I really said it, or if I was convincing enough." And you realize that having said it or been convincing hardly matters because, in any case, that is what it is now.

We will see that concepts need conceptual personae [*personnages conceptuels*] that play a part in their definition. *Friend* is one such persona that is even said to reveal the Greek origin of philo-sophy:[5] other civilizations had sages, but the Greeks introduce these "friends" who are not just more modest sages. The Greeks might seem to have confirmed the death of the sage and to have replaced him with philosophers—the friends of wisdom, those who seek wisdom but do not formally possess it. But the difference between the sage and the philosopher would not be merely one of degree, as on a scale: the old oriental sage thinks, perhaps, in Figures, whereas the philosopher invents and thinks the Concept. Wisdom has changed a great deal. It is even more difficult to know what *friend* signifies, even and especially among the Greeks. Does it designate a type of competent intimacy, a sort of material taste and potentiality, like that of the joiner with wood—is the potential of wood latent in the good joiner; is he the friend of the wood? The question is important because the friend who appears in philosophy no longer stands for an extrinsic persona, an example or empirical circumstance, but rather for a presence that is intrinsic to thought, a condition of possibility of thought itself, a living category, a transcendental lived reality [*un vécu transcendantal*]. With the creation of philosophy, the Greeks violently force the friend into a relationship that is no longer a relationship with an other but one with an Entity, an Objectality [*Objectité*], an Essence—Plato's friend,[6] but even more the friend of wisdom, of truth or the concept, like Philalethes and Theophilus.[7] The philosopher is expert in concepts and in the lack of them. He knows which of them are not viable, which are arbitrary or inconsistent, which ones do not hold up for an instant. On the other hand, he also knows which are well formed and attest to a creation, however disturbing or dangerous it may be.

What does *friend* mean when it becomes a conceptual persona, or a condition for the exercise of thought? Or rather, are we not talking of the lover? Does not the friend reintroduce into thought a vital relationship with the Other that was supposed to have been excluded from pure thought? Or again, is it not a matter of someone other than the friend or lover? For if the philosopher is the friend or lover of wisdom, is it not because he lays claim to wisdom,

---

5. Literally, "friend" or lover (*philos*) and "wisdom" (*sophia*).
6. "Essence" is the "friend" of the Greek philosopher Plato (ca. 427–ca. 347 B.C.E.) because Plato's epistemology centrally features fundamental time-

less universals or essences (the "Forms" or "Ideas"), in whose reality objects in the natural world (their less than perfect copies) participate or share.
7. These names literally mean "friend of truth" and "friend of God."

striving for it potentially rather than actually possessing it? Is the friend also the claimant then, and is that of which he claims to be the friend the Thing to which he lays claim but not the third party who, on the contrary, becomes a rival? Friendship would then involve competitive distrust of the rival as much as amorous striving toward the object of desire. The basic point about friendship is that the two friends are like claimant and rival (but who could tell them apart?). It is in this first aspect that philosophy seems to be something Greek and coincides with the contribution of cities: the formation of societies of friends or equals but also the promotion of relationships of rivalry between and within them, the contest between claimants in every sphere, in love, the games, tribunals, the judiciaries, politics, and even in thought, which finds its condition not only in the friend but in the claimant and the rival (the dialectic Plato defined as *amphisbetesis*[8]). It is the rivalry of free men, a generalized athleticism: the agon.[9] Friendship must reconcile the integrity of the essence and the rivalry of claimants. Is this not too great a task?

Friend, lover, claimant and rival are transcendental determinations that do not for that reason lose their intense and animated existence, in one persona or in several. When again today Maurice Blanchot,[1] one of the rare thinkers to consider the meaning of the word *friend* in philosophy, takes up this question internal to the conditions of thought as such, does he not once more introduce new conceptual personae into the heart of the purest Thought? But in this case the personae are hardly Greek, arriving from elsewhere as if they had gone through a catastrophe that draws them toward new living relationships raised to the level of a priori characteristics—a turning away, a certain tiredness, a certain distress between friends that converts friendship itself to thought of the concept as distrust and infinite patience? The list of conceptual personae is never closed and for that reason plays an important role in the evolution or transformations of philosophy. The diversity of conceptual personae must be understood without being reduced to the already complex unity of the Greek philosopher.

The philosopher is the concept's friend; he is potentiality of the concept. That is, philosophy is not a simple art of forming, inventing, or fabricating concepts, because concepts are not necessarily forms, discoveries, or products. More rigorously, philosophy is the discipline that involves *creating* concepts. Does this mean that the friend is friend of his own creations? Or is the actuality of the concept due to the potential of the friend, in the unity of creator and his double? The object of philosophy is to create concepts that are always new. Because the concept must be created, it refers back to the philosopher as the one who has it potentially, or who has its power and competence. It is no objection to say that creation is the prerogative of the sensory and the arts, since art brings spiritual entities into existence while philosophical concepts are also "sensibilia." In fact, sciences, arts, and philosophies are all equally creative, although only philosophy creates concepts in the strict sense. Concepts are not waiting for us ready-made, like heavenly bodies. There is no heaven for concepts. They must be invented, fabricated, or rather created and would be nothing without their creator's signature. Nietzsche laid

8. Controversy, dispute (Greek); see, e.g., Plato, *Philebus* 15a; *Republic* 7.533e. As a legal term, it means a claim (particularly to an inheritance).

9. Contest (Greek).
1. French philosopher, novelist, and literary theorist (1907–2003).

down the task of philosophy when he wrote, "[Philosophers] must no longer accept concepts as a gift, nor merely purify and polish them, but first *make* and *create* them, present them and make them convincing. Hitherto one has generally trusted one's concepts as if they were a wonderful dowry from some sort of wonderland,"[2] but trust must be replaced by distrust, and philosophers must distrust most those concepts they did not create themselves (Plato was fully aware of this, even though he taught the opposite).[3] Plato said that Ideas must be contemplated, but first of all he had to create the concept of Idea. What would be the value of a philosopher of whom one could say, "He has created no concepts; he has not created his own concepts"?

We can at least see what philosophy is not: it is not contemplation, reflection, or communication. This is the case even though it may sometimes believe it is one or other of these, as a result of the capacity of every discipline to produce its own illusions and to hide behind its own peculiar smokescreen. It is not contemplation, for contemplations are things themselves as seen in the creation of their specific concepts. It is not reflection, because no one needs philosophy to reflect on anything. It is thought that philosophy is being given a great deal by being turned into the art of reflection, but actually it loses everything. Mathematicians, as mathematicians, have never waited for philosophers before reflecting on mathematics, nor artists before reflecting on painting or music. So long as their reflection belongs to their respective creation, it is a bad joke to say that this makes them philosophers. Nor does philosophy find any final refuge in communication, which only works under the sway of opinions in order to create "consensus" and not concepts. The idea of a Western democratic conversation between friends has never produced a single concept. The idea comes, perhaps, from the Greeks, but they distrusted it so much, and subjected it to such harsh treatment, that the concept was more like the ironical soliloquy bird that surveyed [*survolait*] the battlefield of destroyed rival opinions (the drunken guests at the banquet). Philosophy does not contemplate, reflect, or communicate, although it must create concepts for these actions or passions. Contemplation, reflection and communication are not disciplines but machines for constituting Universals in every discipline. The Universals of contemplation, and then of reflection, are like two illusions through which philosophy has already passed in its dream of dominating the other disciplines (objective idealism and subjective idealism). Moreover, it does no credit to philosophy for it to present itself as a new Athens by falling back on Universals of communication that would provide rules for an imaginary mastery of the markets and the media (intersubjective idealism). Every creation is singular, and the concept as a specifically philosophical creation is always a singularity. The first principle of philosophy is that Universals explain nothing but must themselves be explained.

To know oneself, to learn to think, to act as if nothing were self-evident—wondering, "wondering that there is being"—these, and many other determinations of philosophy create interesting attitudes, however tiresome they may

---

2. An entry from 1885 in one of the notebooks of FRIEDRICH NIETZSCHE, selected along with others by his sister and a friend who published them in his name after his death as *Der Wille zur Macht*; see *The Will to Power*, trans. Walter Kaufmann and R. J. Hollingdale, ed. Walter Kaufmann (1967), §409. Retranslated above, p. 835.
3. Plato, *The Statesman*, 268a, 279a [Deleuze and Guattari's note].

be in the long run, but even from a pedagogical point of view they do not constitute a well-defined occupation or precise activity. On the other hand, the following definition of philosophy can be taken as being decisive: knowledge through pure concepts. But there is no reason to oppose knowledge through concepts and the construction of concepts within possible experience on the one hand and through intuition on the other. For, according to the Nietzschean verdict, you will know nothing through concepts unless you have first created them—that is, constructed them in an intuition specific to them: a field, a plane, and a ground that must not be confused with them but that shelters their seeds and the personae who cultivate them. Constructivism requires every creation to be a construction on a plane that gives it an autonomous existence. To create concepts is, at the very least, to make something. This alters the question of philosophy's use or usefulness, or even of its harmfulness (to whom is it harmful?).

Many problems hurry before the hallucinating eyes of an old man who sees all sorts of philosophical concepts and conceptual personae confronting one another. First, concepts are and remain signed: Aristotle's substance, Descartes's cogito, Leibniz's monad, Kant's condition, Schelling's power, Bergson's duration [*durée*].[4] But also, some concepts must be indicated by an extraordinary and sometimes even barbarous or shocking word, whereas others make do with an ordinary, everyday word that is filled with harmonics so distant that it risks being imperceptible to a nonphilosophical ear. Some concepts call for archaisms, and others for neologisms, shot through with almost crazy etymological exercises: etymology is like a specifically philosophical athleticism. In each case there must be a strange necessity for these words and for their choice, like an element of style. The concept's baptism calls for a specifically philosophical *taste* that proceeds with violence or by insinuation and constitutes a philosophical language within language—not just a vocabulary but a syntax that attains the sublime or a great beauty. Although concepts are dated, signed, and baptized, they have their own way of not dying while remaining subject to constraints of renewal, replacement, and mutation that give philosophy a history as well as a turbulent geography, each moment and place of which is preserved (but in time) and that passes (but outside time). What unity remains for philosophies, it will be asked, if concepts constantly change? Is it the same for the sciences and arts that do not work with concepts? And what are their respective histories the histories of? If philosophy is this continuous creation of concepts, then obviously the question arises not only of what a concept is as philosophical Idea but also of the nature of the other creative Ideas that are not concepts and that are due to the arts and sciences, which have their own history and becoming and which have their own variable relationships with one another and with philosophy. The exclusive right of concept creation secures a function for philosophy, but it does not give it any preeminence or privilege since there are other ways of thinking and creating, other modes of ideation that, like scientific thought,

---

4. Each philosopher is paired with his foundational concept: the Greek philosopher Aristotle (384–322 B.C.E.) stated that substance is the primary category of being; the French philosopher and mathematician René Descartes (1596–1650) took "I think" (*cogito*, Latin) as the starting point of his philosophy; and the German philosopher and mathematician Gottfried Wilhelm Leibniz (1646–1716) called the basic substances that are immaterial but make up all of reality "monads." For Kant, SCHELLING, and BERGSON, see above.

do not have to pass through concepts. We always come back to the question of the use of this activity of creating concepts, in its difference from scientific or artistic activity. Why, through what necessity, and for what use must concepts, and always new concepts, be created? And in order to do what? To say that the greatness of philosophy lies precisely in its not having any use is a frivolous answer that not even young people find amusing any more. In any case, the death of metaphysics or the overcoming of philosophy has never been a problem for us: it is just tiresome, idle chatter. Today it is said that systems are bankrupt, but it is only the concept of system that has changed. So long as there is a time and a place for creating concepts, the operation that undertakes this will always be called philosophy, or will be indistinguishable from philosophy even if it is called something else.

We know, however, that the friend or lover, as claimant, does not lack rivals. If we really want to say that philosophy originates with the Greeks, it is because the city, unlike the empire or state, invents the agon as the rule of a society of "friends," of the community of free men as rivals (citizens). This is the invariable situation described by Plato: if each citizen lays claim to something, then we need to be able to judge the validity of claims. The joiner lays claim to wood, but he comes up against the forester, the lumberjack, and the carpenter, who all say, "I am the friend of wood." If it is a matter of the care of men, then there are many claimants who introduce themselves as man's friend: the peasant who feeds people, the weaver who clothes them, the doctor who nurses them, and the warrior who protects them. In all these cases the selection is made from what is, after all, a somewhat narrow circle of claimants. But this is not the case in politics where, according to Plato, anyone can lay claim to anything in Athenian democracy. Hence the necessity for Plato to put things in order and create authorities for judging the validity of these claims: the Ideas as philosophical concepts. But, even here, do we not encounter all kinds of claimants who say. "I am the true philosopher, the friend of Wisdom or of the Well-Founded"? This rivalry culminates in the battle between philosopher and sophist,[5] fighting over the old sage's remains. How, then, is the false friend to be distinguished from the true friend, the concept from the simulacrum?[6] The simulator and the friend: this is a whole Platonic theater that produces a proliferation of conceptual personae by endowing them with the powers of the comic and the tragic.

Closer to our own time, philosophy has encountered many new rivals. To start with, the human sciences, and especially sociology, wanted to replace it. But because philosophy, taking refuge in universals, increasingly misunderstood its vocation for creating concepts, it was no longer clear what was at stake. Was it a matter of giving up the creation of concepts in favor of a rigorous human science or, alternatively, of transforming the nature of concepts by turning them into the collective representations or worldviews created by the vital, historical, and spiritual forces of different peoples? Then it was the turn of epistemology, of linguistics, or even of psychoanalysis and logical analysis. In

---

5. One of the largely itinerant Greek teachers of philosophy and rhetoric in the 5th century B.C.E., often characterized as more concerned with success than with truth in argument; frequently in Plato's dialogues, a sophist was bested by Socrates.

6. That is, simulation, copy, imitation. The concept of the "simulacrum" is important for them and for other postmodern thinkers; see especially Jean Baudrillard's *Simulacres et simulation* (1981, *Simulacra and Simulation*).

successive challenges, philosophy confronted increasingly insolent and calamitous rivals that Plato himself would never have imagined in his most comic moments. Finally, the most shameful moment came when computer science, marketing, design, and advertising, all the disciplines of communication, seized hold of the word *concept* itself and said: "This is our concern, we are the creative ones, we are the *ideas men!* We are the friends of the concept, we put it in our computers." Information and creativity, concept and enterprise: there is already an abundant bibliography. Marketing has preserved the idea of a certain relationship between the concept and the event. But here the concept has become the set of product displays (historical, scientific, artistic, sexual, pragmatic), and the event has become the exhibition that sets up various displays and the "exchange of ideas" it is supposed to promote. The only events are exhibitions, and the only concepts are products that can be sold. Philosophy has not remained unaffected by the general movement that replaced Critique with sales promotion. The simulacrum, the simulation of a packet of noodles, has become the true concept; and the one who packages the product, commodity, or work of art has become the philosopher, conceptual persona, or artist. How could philosophy, an old person, compete against young executives in a race for the universals of communication for determining the marketable form of the concept, *Merz*?[7] Certainly, it is painful to learn that *Concept* indicates a society of information services and engineering. But the more philosophy comes up against shameless and inane rivals and encounters them at its very core, the more it feels driven to fulfill the task of creating concepts that are aerolites rather than commercial products. It gets the giggles, which wipe away its tears. So, the question of philosophy is the singular point where concept and creation are related to each other.

Philosophers have not been sufficiently concerned with the nature of the concept as philosophical reality. They have preferred to think of it as a given knowledge or representation that can be explained by the faculties able to form it (abstraction or generalization) or employ it (judgment). But the concept is not given, it is created; it is to be created. It is not formed but posits itself in itself—it is a self-positing. Creation and self-positing mutually imply each other because what is truly created, from the living being to the work of art, thereby enjoys a self-positing of itself, or an autopoetic[8] characteristic by which it is recognized. The concept posits itself to the same extent that it is created. What depends on a free creative activity is also that which, independently and necessarily, posits itself in itself: the most subjective will be the most objective. The post-Kantians, and notably Schelling and Hegel, are the philosophers who paid most attention to the concept as philosophical reality in this sense.[9] Hegel powerfully defined the concept by the Figures of its creation and the Moments of its self-positing. The figures become parts of the concept because they constitute the aspect through which the concept is created by and in consciousness, through successive minds; whereas the Moments form the other aspect according to which the concept posits itself and unites minds in the absolute of the Self. In this way Hegel showed that the concept has nothing

7. *Merz* is the term coined by the [German] artist Kurt Schwitters to refer to the aesthetic combination of any kind of material, and the equal value of these different materials, in his collages and assemblages. The term itself came from a fragment of a word in one of his assemblages, the whole phrase being "*Kommerz und Privatbank*" [the kind of bank that has both commercial and private accounts and does both sorts of business; translators' note].
8. Able to maintain and renew itself.
9. See above, especially *Begriff* (concept) in the HEGEL glossary, p. 144.

whatever to do with a general or abstract idea, any more than with an uncreated Wisdom that does not depend on philosophy itself. But he succeeded in doing this at the cost of an indeterminate extension of philosophy that, because it reconstituted universals with its own moments and treated the personae of its own creation as no more than ghostly puppets, left scarcely any independent movement of the arts and sciences remaining. The post-Kantians concentrated on a universal *encyclopedia* of the concept that attributed concept creation to a pure subjectivity rather than taking on the more modest task of a *pedagogy* of the concept, which would have to analyze the conditions of creation as factors of always singular moments. If the three ages of the concept are the encyclopedia, pedagogy, and commercial professional training, only the second can safeguard us from falling from the heights of the first into the disaster of the third—an absolute disaster for thought whatever its benefits might be, of course, from the viewpoint of universal capitalism.

* * *

Conclusion: From Chaos to the Brain

We require just a little order to protect us from chaos. Nothing is more distressing than a thought that escapes itself, than ideas that fly off, that disappear hardly formed, already eroded by forgetfulness or precipitated into others that we no longer master. These are infinite *variabilities*, the appearing and disappearing of which coincide. They are infinite speeds that blend into the immobility of the colorless and silent nothingness they traverse, without nature or thought. This is the instant of which we do not know whether it is too long or too short for time. We receive sudden jolts that beat like arteries. We constantly lose our ideas. That is why we want to hang on to fixed opinions so much. We ask only that our ideas are linked together according to a minimum of constant rules. All that the association of ideas has ever meant is providing us with these protective rules—resemblance, contiguity, causality—which enable us to put some order into ideas, preventing our "fantasy" (delirium, madness) from crossing the universe in an instant, producing winged horses and dragons breathing fire. But there would not be a little order in ideas if there was not also a little order in things or states of affairs, like an objective antichaos: "If cinnabar were sometimes red, sometimes black, sometimes light, sometimes heavy . . . , my empirical imagination would never find opportunity when representing red color to bring to mind heavy cinnabar."[1] And finally, at the meeting point of things and thought, the sensation must recur—that of heaviness whenever we hold cinnabar in our hands, that of red whenever we look at it—as proof or evidence of their agreement with our bodily organs that do not perceive the present without imposing on it a conformity with the past. This is all that we ask for in order to *make an opinion* for ourselves, like a sort of "umbrella," which protects us from chaos.

Our opinions are made up from all this. But art, science, and philosophy require more: they cast planes over the chaos. These three disciplines are not like religions that invoke dynasties of gods, or the epiphany of a single god, in

1. Immanuel Kant, *Critique of Pure Reason* [1781; 2nd ed., 1787], Transcendental Analytic, "The Synthesis of Reproduction in Imagination" [Deleuze and Guattari's note]. The translators here quote the English translation of N. Kemp-Smith (London: Macmillan, 1929), p. 132 (A 100–101).

order to paint a firmament on the umbrella, like the figures of an *Urdoxa*[2] from which opinions stem. Philosophy, science, and art want us to tear open the firmament and plunge into the chaos. We defeat it only at this price. And thrice victorious I have crossed the Acheron.[3] The philosopher, the scientist, and the artist seem to return from the land of the dead. What the philosopher brings back from the chaos are *variations* that are still infinite but that have become inseparable on the absolute surfaces or in the absolute volumes that lay out a secant[4] [*sécant*] plane of immanence: these are not associations of distinct ideas, but reconnections through a zone of indistinction in a concept. The scientist brings back from the chaos *variables* that have become independent by slowing down, that is to say, by the elimination of whatever other variabilities are liable to interfere, so that the variables that are retained enter into determinable relations in a function: they are no longer links of properties in things, but finite coordinates on a secant plane of reference that go from local probabilities to a global cosmology. The artist brings back from the chaos *varieties* that no longer constitute a reproduction of the sensory in the organ but set up a being of the sensory, a being of sensation, on an anorganic[5] plane of composition that is able to restore the infinite. The struggle with chaos that Cézanne and Klee[6] have shown in action in painting, at the heart of painting, is found in another way in science and in philosophy: it is always a matter of defeating chaos by a secant plane that crosses it. Painters go through a catastrophe, or through a conflagration, and leave the trace of this passage on the canvas, as of the leap that leads them from chaos to composition.[7] Mathematical equations do not enjoy a tranquil certainty, which would be like the sanction of a dominant scientific opinion, but arise from an abyss that makes the mathematician "readily skip over calculations," in anticipation of not being able to bring about or arrive at the truth without "colliding here and there."[8] And philosophical thought does not bring its concepts together in friendship without again being traversed by a fissure that leads them back to hatred or disperses them in the coexisting chaos where it is necessary to take them up again, to seek them out, to make a leap. It is as if one were casting a net, but the fisherman always risks being swept away and finding himself in the open sea when he thought he had reached port. The three disciplines advance by crises or shocks in different ways, and in each case it is their succession that makes it possible to speak of "progress." It is as if the *struggle against chaos* does not take place without an affinity with the enemy, because another struggle develops and takes on more importance—the struggle *against opinion*, which claims to protect us from chaos itself.

In a violently poetic text, Lawrence[9] describes what produces poetry: people are constantly putting up an umbrella that shelters them and on the under-

---

2. That is, a basic belief; this coinage (mixing German and Greek) was popularized by HUSSERL.
3. In classical mythology, one of the rivers of the underworld. (Line from Virgil's *Aeneid*, Bk. 6.)
4. Intersecting (the precise geometry being described here is unclear).
5. Inorganic.
6. Two major painters: the French Paul Cézanne (1839–1906) and the Swiss Paul Klee (1879–1940).
7. On Cézanne and chaos, see [Joachim] Gasquet, *Cézanne* [1921]; on Klee and chaos, see Paul Klee,

"Note on the Gray Point," in *Théorie de l'art moderne* [*Theory of Modern Art*] (Paris: Gonthier, 1963) [Deleuze and Guattari's note].
8. Galois, in [André] Dalmas, *Evariste Galois* [*revolutionnaire et géómetre* (Paris: Fasquelle, 1956)], pp. 121, 130 [Deleuze and Guattari's note].
9. D. H. (David Herbert) Lawrence (1885–1930), English writer of prose, plays, and poetry. The reference is to "Chaos in Poetry" (1929), later printed as his introduction to Harry Crosby's *Chariots of the Sun* (1931).

side of which they draw a firmament and write their conventions and opinions. But poets, artists, make a slit in the umbrella, they tear open the firmament itself, to let in a bit of free and windy chaos and to frame in a sudden light a vision that appears through the rent—Wordsworth's spring or Cézanne's apple, the silhouettes of Macbeth or Ahab.[1] Then come the crowd of imitators who repair the umbrella with something vaguely resembling the vision, and the crowd of commentators who patch over the rent with opinions: communication. Other artists are always needed to make other slits, to carry out necessary and perhaps ever-greater destructions, thereby restoring to their predecessors the incommunicable novelty that we could no longer see. This is to say that artists struggle less against chaos (that, in a certain manner, all their wishes summon forth) than against the "clichés" of opinion.[2] The painter does not paint on an empty canvas, and neither does the writer write on a blank page; but the page or canvas is already so covered with preexisting, preestablished clichés that it is first necessary to erase, to clean, to flatten, even to shred, so as to let in a breath of air from the chaos that brings us the vision. When Fontana[3] slashes the colored canvas with a razor, he does not tear the color in doing this. On the contrary, he makes us see the area of plain, uniform color, of pure color, through the slit. Art indeed struggles with chaos, but it does so in order to bring forth a vision that illuminates it for an instant, a Sensation. Even houses: Soutine's[4] drunken houses come from chaos, knocking up against one another and preventing one another from falling back into it; Monet's house also rises up like a slit through which chaos becomes the vision of roses. Even the most delicate pink opens on to chaos, like flesh on the flayed body. A work of chaos is certainly no better than a work of opinion; art is no more made of chaos than it is of opinion. But if art battles against chaos it is to borrow weapons from it that it turns against opinion, the better to defeat it with tried and tested arms. Because the picture starts out covered with clichés, the painter must confront the chaos and hasten the destructions so as to produce a sensation that defies every opinion and cliché (how many times?). Art is not chaos but a composition of chaos that yields the vision or sensation, so that it constitutes, as Joyce says, a chaosmos,[5] a composed chaos—neither foreseen nor preconceived. Art transforms chaotic variability into *chaoid* variety, as in El Greco's black and green-gray conflagration, for example, or Turner's golden conflagration, or de Staël's[6] red conflagration. Art struggles with chaos but it does so in order to render it sensory, even through the most charming character, the most enchanted landscape (Watteau[7]).

Science is perhaps inspired by a similar sinuous, reptilian movement. A struggle against chaos seems to be an essential part of science when it puts slow variability under constants or limits, when it thereby refers it to centers of equilibrium, when it subjects it to a selection that retains only a small number

1. All major artistic creations: the English poet William Wordsworth (1770–1850) wrote of spring in "Lines Written in Early Spring" (1798) and "I wandered lonely as a cloud" (1807); Cézanne famously painted apples in his still lifes; Macbeth is the protagonist of Shakespeare's *Macbeth* (1606); and Ahab is a central figure in Herman Melville's *Moby-Dick* (1851).
2. Lawrence, "Chaos in Poetry," in D. H. Lawrence, *Selected Literary Criticism*, ed. A. Beal (London: Heinemann, 1955) [Deleuze and Guattari's note].
3. Lucio Fontana (1899–1968), Italian painter and sculptor.
4. Chaim Soutine (1893–1943), Russian-born French painter.
5. Chaos+cosmos, a word coined by the Irish novelist James Joyce (1882–1941) in *Finnegans Wake* (1939) to describe the structure of that book and of reality.
6. Nicolas de Staël (1914–1955), Russian-born French painter. El Greco (Doménikos Theotokópoulos, 1541–1614), Cretan-born Spanish painter.
7. Antoine Watteau (1684–1721), French painter.

of independent variables within coordinate axes, and when between these variables it installs relationships whose future state can be determined on the basis of the present (determinist calculus) or, alternatively, when it introduces so many variables at once that the state of affairs is only statistical (calculus of probabilities). In this sense we speak of a specifically scientific opinion won from chaos, as we do of a communication defined sometimes by initial pieces of information, sometimes by large-scale pieces of information, which usually go from the elementary to the composite, or from the present to the future, or from the molecular to the molar. But, here again, science cannot avoid experiencing a profound attraction for the chaos with which it battles. If slowing down is the thin border that separates us from the oceanic chaos, science draws as close as it can to the nearest waves by positing relationships that are preserved with the appearance and disappearance of variables (differential calculus). The difference between the chaotic state where the appearance and disappearance of a variability blend together, and the semichaotic state that manifests a relationship as the limit of the variables that appear or disappear becomes ever smaller. As Michel Serres says of Leibniz, "There would be two infraconsciousnesses: the deeper would be structured like any set whatever, a pure multiplicity or possibility in general, an aleatory mixture of signs; the less deep would be covered by combinatory schemas of this multiplicity."[8] One could conceive of a series of coordinates or phase spaces as a succession of filters, the earlier of which would be in each case a relatively chaotic state, and the later a chaoid state, so that we would cross chaotic thresholds rather than go from the elementary to the composite. Opinion offers us a science that dreams of unity, of unifying its laws, and that still searches today for a community of the four forces.[9] Nevertheless, the dream of capturing a bit of chaos is more insistent, even if the most diverse forces stir restlessly within it. Science would relinquish all the rational unity to which it aspires for a little piece of chaos that it could explore.

Art takes a bit of chaos in a frame in order to form a composed chaos that becomes sensory, or from which it extracts a chaoid sensation as variety; but science takes a bit of chaos in a system of coordinates and forms a referenced chaos that becomes Nature, and from which it extracts an aleatory function and chaoid variables. In this way one of the most important aspects of modern mathematical physics appears in the action of "strange" or chaotic attractors: two neighboring trajectories in a determinate system of coordinates do not remain so and diverge in an exponential manner before coming together through operations of stretching and folding that are repeated and intersect with chaos. If equilibrium attractors (fixed points, limit cycles, cores) express science's struggle with chaos, strange attractors reveal its profound attraction to chaos, as well as the constitution of a chaosmos internal to modern science (everything that, in one way or another, was misrepresented in earlier periods, notably in the fascination for turbulences). We thus come back to a conclusion to which art led us: the struggle with chaos is only the instrument of a more profound struggle against opinion, for the misfortune of people comes from opinion. Science turns against opinion, which lends to it a reli-

---

8. Michel Serres, *Le système de Leibniz [et ses modèles mathématiques* (*Leibniz's System and Mathematical Models*) (1968; reprint,] Paris: P.U.F., 1990), vol. I, p. 111 [Deleuze and Guattari's note]. Serres (b. 1930), French philosopher. Leibniz was one of the inventors of differential calculus.

9. The four fundamental interactions in physics on the atomic level (strong, electromagnetic, weak, and gravitational).

gious taste for unity or unification. But it also turns within itself against properly scientific opinion as *Urdoxa*, which consists sometimes in determinist prediction (Laplace's God[1]) and sometimes in probabilistic evaluation (Maxwell's demon[2]): by releasing itself from initial pieces of information and large-scale pieces of information, science substitutes for communication the conditions of creativity defined by singular effects and minimal fluctuations. Creation is the aesthetic varieties or scientific variables that emerge on a plane that is able to crosscut chaotic variability. As for pseudosciences that claim to study the phenomena of opinion, the artificial intelligences of which they make use maintain as their models probabilistic processes, stable attractors, an entire logic of the recognition of forms; but they must achieve chaoid states and chaotic attractors to be able to understand both thought's struggle against opinion and its degeneration into opinion (one line in the development of computers is toward the assumption of a chaotic or chaoticizing system).

This is what confirms the third case, which is no longer sensory variety or functional variable but conceptual variation as it appears in philosophy. Philosophy struggles in turn with the chaos as undifferentiated abyss or ocean of dissemblance. But this does not mean that philosophy ranges itself on the side of opinion, nor that opinion can take its place. A concept is not a set of associated ideas like an opinion. Neither is it an order of reasons, a series of ordered reasons that could rigorously constitute a kind of rationalized *Urdoxa*. To reach the concept it is not even enough for phenomena to be subject to principles analogous to those that associate ideas or things, or to principles that order reasons. As Michaux[3] says, what suffices for "current ideas" does not suffice for "vital ideas"—those that must be created. Ideas can only be associated as images and can only be ordered as abstractions; to arrive at the concept we must go beyond both of these and arrive *as quickly as possible* at mental objects determinable as real beings. This is what Spinoza or Fichte have already shown: we must make use of fictions and abstractions, but only so far as is necessary to get to a plane where we go from real being to real being and advance through the construction of concepts.[4] We have seen how this result can be achieved to the extent that variations become inseparable according to zones of neighborhood or indiscernibility: they then cease being associable according to the caprice of imagination, or discernible and capable of being ordered according to the exigencies of reason, in order to form genuine conceptual blocs. A concept is a set of inseparable variations that is produced or constructed on a plane of immanence insofar as the latter crosscuts the chaotic variability and gives it consistency (reality). A concept is therefore a chaoid state par excellence; it refers back to a chaos rendered consistent, become Thought, mental chaosmos. And what would *thinking* be if it did not constantly confront chaos? Reason shows us its true face only when it "thunders

1. An intellect (*une intelligence*) capable of analyzing all existing data; according to the French mathematician and scientist Pierre-Simon Laplace (1749–1827), such an intellect could rely on causal determinism to see with certainty everything that had been and would be.
2. A being hypothesized by the Scottish physicist James Clerk Maxwell (1831–1879) that would be capable of violating the second law of thermodynamics (i.e., that total entropy in a system can never decrease); he intended to show that the "law" had only a very high probability.
3. Henri Michaux (1899–1984), Belgian-born French lyric poet and painter.
4. See Martial Guéroult, *L'évolution et la structure de la doctrine de la science chez Fichte* [(*Evolution and Structure of the Doctrine of Science in Fichte*) (1930; reprint,] Paris: Belles Lettres, 1982), vol. I, p. 174 [Deleuze and Guattari's note]. Benedict (Baruch) de Spinoza (1632–1677), Dutch rationalist philosopher. For FICHTE, see above.

in its crater."[5] Even the cogito is only an opinion, an *Urdoxa* at best, if we do not extract from it the inseparable variations that make it a concept, if we do not give up finding an umbrella or shelter in it, unless we stop presupposing an immanence that would be accommodated *to itself,* so that, on the contrary, it can set itself up on a plane of immanence to which it belongs that which takes it back to the open sea. In short, chaos has three daughters, depending on the plane that cuts through it: these are the *Chaoids*—art, science, and philosophy—as forms of thought or creation. We call *Chaoids* the realities produced on the planes that cut through the chaos in different ways.

The brain is the junction—not the unity—*of the three planes.* Certainly, when the brain is considered as a determinate function it appears as a complex set both of horizontal connections and of vertical integrations reacting on one another, as is shown by cerebral "maps." The question, then, is a double one: are the connections preestablished, as if guided by rails, or are they produced and broken up in fields of forces? And are the processes of integration localized hierarchical centers, or are they rather forms (*Gestalten*) that achieve their conditions of stability in a field on which the position of center itself depends? In this respect the importance of Gestalt theory concerns the theory of the brain just as much as the conception of perception, since it is directly opposed to the status of the cortex as it appears from the point of view of conditioned reflexes. But, whatever point of view is considered, it is not difficult to show that similar difficulties are encountered whether paths are ready-made or self-producing, and whether centers are mechanical or dynamical. Ready-made paths that are followed step by step imply a preestablished track, but trajectories constituted within a field of forces proceed through resolution of tensions also acting step by step (for example, the tension of reconciliation between the fovea and the luminous point projected on the retina, the latter having a structure analogous to a cortical area): both schemas presuppose a "plane," not an end or a program, but a *survey of the entire field.* This is what Gestalt theory does not explain, any more than mechanism explains preassembly [*prémontage*].

It is not surprising that the brain, treated as a constituted object of science, can be an organ only of the formation and communication of opinion: this is because step-by-step connections and centered integrations are still based on the limited model of recognition (gnosis[6] and praxis; "this is a cube"; "this is a pencil"), and the biology of the brain is here aligned on the same postulates as the most stubborn logic. Opinions are pregnant forms, like soap bubbles according to the Gestalt, with regard to milieus, interests, beliefs, and obstacles. Thus it seems difficult to treat philosophy, art, and even science as "mental objects," simple assemblages of neurones in the objectified brain, since the derisory model of recognition confines these latter within the *doxa.* If the mental objects of philosophy, art, and science (that is to say, vital ideas) have a place, it will be in the deepest of the synaptic fissures, in the hiatuses, intervals, and meantimes of a nonobjectifiable brain, in a place where to go in search of them will be to create. It will be a bit like tuning a television screen whose intensities would bring out that which escapes the power of objective definition.[7] That is to say, thought, even in the form it actively assumes in

5. A phrase from "The Internationale" (1871), a poem written by Eugène Pottier that was set to music and became a Communist anthem.
6. The act of knowing.

7. Jean-Clet Martin's forthcoming *Variations* [Deleuze and Guattari's note]. *Variations: La philosophie de Gilles Deleuze* (1993, *Variations: The Philosophy of Gilles Deleuze*).

science, does not depend upon a brain made up of organic connections and integrations: according to phenomenology, thought depends on man's relations with the world—with which the brain is necessarily in agreement because it is drawn from these relations, as excitations are drawn from the world and reactions from man, including their uncertainties and failures. "Man thinks, not the brain"; but this ascent of phenomenology beyond the brain toward a Being in the world, through a double criticism of mechanism and dynamism, hardly gets us out of the sphere of opinions. It leads us only to an *Urdoxa* posited as original opinion, or meaning of meanings.[8]

Will the turning point not be elsewhere, in the place where the brain is "subject," where it becomes subject? It is the brain that thinks and not man— the latter being only a cerebral crystallization. We will speak of the brain as Cézanne spoke of the landscape: man absent from, but completely within the brain. Philosophy, art, and science are not the mental objects of an objectified brain but the three aspects under which the brain becomes subject, Thought-brain. They are the three planes, the rafts on which the brain plunges into and confronts the chaos. What are the characteristics of this brain, which is no longer defined by connections and secondary integrations? It is not a brain behind the brain but, first of all, a state of survey without distance, at ground level, a self-survey that no chasm, fold, or hiatus escapes. It is a primary, "true form" as Ruyer defined it: neither a Gestalt nor a perceived form but a *form in itself* that does not refer to any external point of view, any more than the retina or striated area of the cortex refers to another retina or cortical area; it is an absolute consistent form that surveys *itself* independently of any supplementary dimension, which does not appeal therefore to any transcendence, which has only a single side whatever the number of its dimensions, which remains copresent to all its determinations without proximity or distance, traverses them at infinite speed, without limit-speed, and which makes of them so many *inseparable variations* on which it confers an equipotentiality without confusion.[9] We have seen that this was the status of the concept as pure event or reality of the virtual. And doubtless concepts are not limited to just one and the same brain since each one of them constitutes a "domain of survey," and the transitions from one concept to another remain irreducible insofar as a new concept does not render its copresence or equipotentiality of determinations necessary in turn. Nor will we say that every concept is a brain. But the brain, under its first aspect of absolute form, appears as the faculty of concepts, that is to say, as the faculty of their creation, at the same time that it sets up the plane of immanence on which concepts are placed, move, change order and relations, are renewed, and never cease being created. The brain is the *mind* itself. At the same time that the brain becomes subject—or rather "superject," as Whitehead[1] puts it—the concept becomes object as created, as event or creation itself; and philosophy becomes the plane of immanence that supports the concepts and that the brain lays out. Cerebral movements also give rise to conceptual personae.

8. Erwin Straus, *Du sens des sens* [1989], part 3 [Deleuze and Guattari's note]. Originally published as *Vom Sinn der Sinn* (1935), and translated into English as *The Primary World of Senses* (1963). Straus (1891–1975) was a German-born American phenomenologist and neurologist.
9. Raymond Ruyer, *Néo-finalisme* (Paris: P.U.F., 1952). Throughout his work Ruyer has directed a double critique against mechanism and dynamism (Gestalt), which differs from the critique made by phenomenology [Deleuze and Guattari's note]. Ruyer (1902–1987), French philosopher.
1. Alfred North Whitehead (1861–1947), English mathematician and philosopher; he distinguished between an entity as subject (in the process of realizing itself) and as superject (as actually realized).

It is the brain that says *I*, but *I* is an other. It is not the same brain as the brain of connections and secondary integrations, although there is no transcendence here. And this *I* is not only the "I conceive" of the brain as philosophy, it is also the "I feel" of the brain as art. Sensation is no less brain than the concept. If we consider the nervous connections of excitation-reaction and the integrations of perception-action, we need not ask at what stage on the path or at what level sensation appears, for it is presupposed and withdrawn. The withdrawal is not the opposite but a correlate of the survey. Sensation is excitation itself, not insofar as it is gradually prolonged and passes into the reaction but insofar as it is preserved or preserves its vibrations. Sensation contracts the vibrations of the stimulant on a nervous surface or in a cerebral volume: what comes before has not yet disappeared when what follows appears. This is its way of responding to chaos. Sensation itself vibrates because it contracts vibrations. It preserves itself because it preserves vibrations: it is Monument. It resonates because it makes its harmonics resonate. Sensation is the contracted vibration that has become quality, variety. That is why the brain-subject is here called *soul* or *force*, since only the soul preserves by contracting that which matter dissipates, or radiates, furthers, reflects, refracts, or converts. Thus the search for sensation is fruitless if we go no farther than reactions and the excitations that they prolong, than actions and the perceptions that they reflect: this is because the soul (or rather, the force), as Leibniz said, does nothing, or does not act, but is only present; it preserves. Contraction is not an action but a pure passion, a contemplation that preserves the before in the after.[2] Sensation, then, is on a plane that is different from mechanisms, dynamisms, and finalities: it is on a plane of composition where sensation is formed by contracting that which composes it, and by composing itself with other sensations that contract it in turn. Sensation is pure contemplation, for it is through contemplation that one contracts, contemplating oneself to the extent that one contemplates the elements from which one originates. Contemplating is creating, the mystery of passive creation, sensation. Sensation fills out the plane of composition and is filled with itself by filling itself with what it contemplates: it is "enjoyment" and "self-enjoyment."[3] It is a subject, or rather an *inject*. Plotinus[4] defined all things as contemplations, not only people and animals but plants, the earth, and rocks. These are not Ideas that we contemplate through concepts but the elements of matter that we contemplate through sensation. The plant contemplates by contracting the elements from which it originates—light, carbon, and the salts—and it fills itself with colors and odors that in each case qualify its variety, its composition: it is sensation in itself. It is as if flowers smell themselves by smelling what composes them, first attempts of vision or of sense of smell, before being perceived or even smelled by an agent with a nervous system and a brain.

Of course, plants and rocks do not possess a nervous system. But, if nerve connections and cerebral integrations presuppose a brain-force as faculty of feeling coexistent with the tissues, it is reasonable to suppose also a faculty

---

2. David Hume defines imagination by this passive contemplation-contraction: A *Treatise of Human Nature* (Oxford: Clarendon Press, 1978), book I, part 3, p. 14 [Deleuze and Guattari's note]. Hume (1711–1776), Scottish empiricist philosopher; the *Treatise* was originally published in 1739–40.
3. In English in the original [translators' note].
4. Founder of Neoplatonic philosophy (205–270 C.E.).

of feeling that coexists with embryonic tissues and that appears in the Species as a collective brain; or with the vegetal tissues in the "small species." Chemical affinities and physical causalities themselves refer to primary forces capable of preserving their long chains by contracting their elements and by making them resonate: no causality is intelligible without this subjective instance. Not every organism has a brain, and not all life is organic, but everywhere there are forces that constitute microbrains, or an inorganic life of things. We can dispense with Fechner's or Conan Doyle's[5] splendid hypothesis of a nervous system of the earth only because the force of contracting or of preserving, that is to say, of feeling appears only as a global brain in relation to the elements contracted directly and to the mode of contraction, which differ depending on the domain and constitute precisely irreducible varieties. But, in the final analysis, the same ultimate elements and the same withdrawn force constitute a single plane of composition bearing all the varieties of the universe. Vitalism has always had two possible interpretations: that of an Idea that acts, but is not—that acts therefore only from the point of view of an external cerebral knowledge (from Kant to Claude Bernard[6]); or that of a force that is but does not act—that is therefore a pure internal Awareness (from Leibniz to Ruyer). If the second interpretation seems to us to be imperative it is because the contraction that preserves is always in a state of detachment in relation to action or even to movement and appears as a pure contemplation without knowledge. This can be seen even in the cerebral domain par excellence of apprenticeship or the formation of habits: although everything seems to take place by active connections and progressive integrations, from one test to another, the tests or cases, the occurrences, must, as Hume showed, be contracted in a contemplating "imagination" while remaining distinct in relation to actions and to knowledge. Even when one is a rat, it is through contemplation that one "contracts" a habit. It is still necessary to discover, beneath the noise of actions, those internal creative sensations or those silent contemplations that bear witness to a brain.

These first two aspects or layers of the brain-subject, sensation as much as the concept, are very fragile. Not only objective disconnections and disintegrations but an immense weariness results in sensations, which have now become woolly, letting escape the elements and vibrations it finds increasingly difficult to contract. Old age is this very weariness: then, there is either a fall into mental chaos outside of the plane of composition or a falling-back on ready-made opinions, on cliches that reveal that an artist, no longer able to create new sensations, no longer knowing how to preserve, contemplate, and contract, no longer has anything to say. The case of philosophy is a bit different, although it depends upon a similar weariness. In this case, weary thought, incapable of maintaining itself on the plane of immanence, can no longer bear the infinite speeds of the third kind that, in the manner of a vortex, measure the concept's copresence to all its intensive components at once (consistency). It falls back on the relative speeds that concern only the succession of movement from one point to another, from one extensive component to another, from one idea to another, and that measure simple associations without being

5. Sir Arthur Conan Doyle (1859–1930), Scottish author; his story "When the World Screamed" (1929) portrays the world as a living organism.

Gustav Theodor Fechner (1801–1887), German physicist who believed in an animistic universe.
6. French physiologist (1813–1878).

able to reconstitute any concept. No doubt these relative speeds may be very great, to the point of simulating the absolute, but they are only the variable speeds of opinion, of discussion or "repartee," as with those untiring young people whose mental quickness is praised, but also with those weary old ones who pursue slow-moving opinions and engage in stagnant discussions by speaking all alone, within their hollowed head, like a distant memory of their old concepts to which they remain attached so as not to fall back completely into the chaos.

No doubt, as Hume says, causalities, associations, and integrations inspire opinions and beliefs in us that are ways of expecting and recognizing something (including "mental objects"): it will rain, the water will boil, this is the shortest route, this is the same figure from a different view. But, although such opinions frequently slip in among scientific propositions, they do not form part of them; and science subjects these processes to operations of a different nature, which constitute an activity of knowing and refer to a faculty of knowledge as the third layer of a brain-subject that is no less creative than the other two. Knowledge is neither a form nor a force but a *function*: "I function." The subject now appears as an "eject,"[7] because it extracts elements whose principal characteristic is distinction, discrimination: limits, constants, variables, and functions, all those functives and prospects that form the terms of the scientific proposition. Geometrical projections, algebraic substitutions and transformations consist not in recognizing something through variations but in distinguishing variables and constants, or in progressively discriminating the terms that tend toward successive limits. Hence, when a constant is assigned in a scientific operation, it is not a matter of contracting cases or moments in a single contemplation but one of establishing a necessary relation between factors that remain independent. The fundamental actions of the scientific faculty of knowledge appear to us in this sense to be the following: setting limits that mark a renunciation of infinite speeds and lay out a plane of reference; assigning variables that are organized in series tending toward these limits; coordinating the independent variables in such a way as to establish between them or their limits necessary relations on which distinct functions depend, the plane of reference being a coordination in actuality; determining mixtures or states of affairs that are related to the coordinates and to which functions refer. It is not enough to say that these operations of scientific knowledge are functions of the brain; the functions are themselves the folds of a brain that lay out the variable coordinates of a plane of knowledge (reference) and that dispatch partial observers everywhere.

There is still an operation that clearly shows the persistence of chaos, not only around the plane of reference or coordination but in the detours of its variable surface, which are always put back into play. These are operations of branching and individuation: if states of affairs are subject to them it is because they are inseparable from the potentials they take from chaos itself and that they do not actualize without risk of dislocation or submergence. It is therefore up to science to make evident the chaos into which the brain itself, as subject of knowledge, plunges. The brain does not cease to constitute limits that determine functions of variables in particularly extended areas; relations between these variables (connections) manifest all the more an uncertain and

---

7. An inferred mental object.

hazardous characteristic, not only in electrical synapses, which show a statistical chaos, but in chemical synapses, which refer to a deterministic chaos. There are not so much cerebral centers as points, concentrated in one area and disseminated in another, and "oscillators," oscillating molecules that pass from one point to another. Even in a linear model like that of the conditioned reflex, Erwin Straus has shown that it was essential to understand the intermediaries, the hiatuses and gaps. Arborized paradigms give way to rhizomatic figures,[8] acentered systems, networks of finite automatons, chaoid states. No doubt this chaos is hidden by the reinforcement of opinion generating facilitating paths, through the action of habits or models of recognition; but it will become much more noticeable if, on the contrary, we consider creative processes and the bifurcations they imply. And individuation, in the cerebral state of affairs, is all the more functional because it does not have the cells themselves for variables, since the latter constantly die without being renewed, making the brain a set of little deaths that puts constant death within us. It calls upon a potential that is no doubt actualized in the determinable links that derive from perceptions, but even more in the free effect that varies according to the creation of concepts, sensations, or functions themselves.

The three planes, along with their elements, are irreducible: *plane of immanence of philosophy, plane of composition of art, plane of reference or coordination of science; form of concept, force of sensation, function of knowledge; concepts and conceptual personae, sensations and aesthetic figures, figures and partial observers.* Analogous problems are posed for each plane: in what sense and how is the plane, in each case, one or multiple—what unity, what multiplicity? But what to us seem more important now are the problems of interference between the planes that join up in the brain. A first type of interference appears when a philosopher attempts to create the concept of a sensation or a function (for example, a concept peculiar to Riemannian space[9] or to irrational number); or when a scientist tries to create functions of sensations, like Fechner or in theories of color or sound, and even functions of concepts, as Lautman[1] demonstrates for mathematics insofar as the latter actualizes virtual concepts; or when an artist creates pure sensations of concepts or functions, as we see in the varieties of abstract art or in Klee. In all these cases the rule is that the interfering discipline must proceed with its own methods. For example, sometimes we speak of the intrinsic beauty of a geometrical figure, an operation, or a demonstration, but so long as this beauty is defined by criteria taken from science, like proportion, symmetry, dissymmetry, projection, or transformation, then there is nothing aesthetic about it: this is what Kant demonstrated with such force.[2] The function must be grasped within a sensation that gives it percepts and affects composed exclusively by art, on a specific plane of creation that wrests it from any reference (the intersection of two black lines or the thickness of color in the right angles in Mondrian;

8. Deleuze and Guattari begin Anti-Oedipus (1972) by arguing that the traditional model of knowledge, drawn from ramifying plants with roots ("arborized paradigms"), should be replaced with a model of fungal "rhizomes"—a network that can send out growth from anywhere.
9. The non-Euclidean geometry of the universe described by general relativity, developed by the German mathematician Bernhard Riemann (1826–1866).
1. Albert Lautman (1908–1944), French mathematical philosopher.
2. Immanuel Kant, *Critique of Judgement* [(1790); [Deleuze and Guattari's note]. The translators here cite the English translation of J. H. Bernard (New York: Macmillan, 1951), p. 62.

or the approach of chaos through the sensation of strange attractors in Noland or Shirley Jaffe[3]).

These, then, are extrinsic interferences, because each discipline remains on its own plane and utilizes its own elements. But there is a second, intrinsic type of interference when concepts and conceptual personae seem to leave a plane of immanence that would correspond to them, so as to slip in among the functions and partial observers, or among the sensations and aesthetic figures, on another plane; and similarly in the other cases. These slidings are so subtle, like those of Zarathustra in Nietzsche's philosophy or of Igitur in Mallarmé's[4] poetry, that we find ourselves on complex planes that are difficult to qualify. In turn, partial observers introduce into science sensibilia that are sometimes close to aesthetic figures on a mixed plane.

Finally, there are interferences that cannot be localized. This is because each distinct discipline is, in its own way, in relation with a negative: even science has a relation with a nonscience that echoes its effects. It is not just a question of saying that art must form those of us who are not artists, that it must awaken us and teach us to feel, and that philosophy must teach us to conceive, or that science must teach us to know. Such pedagogies are only possible if each of the disciplines is, on its own behalf, in an essential relationship with the No that concerns it. The plane of philosophy is prephilosophical insofar as we consider it in itself independently of the concepts that come to occupy it, but nonphilosophy is found where the plane confronts chaos. *Philosophy needs a nonphilosophy that comprehends it; it needs a nonphilosophical comprehension just as art needs nonart and science needs nonscience.*[5] They do not need the No as beginning, or as the end in which they would be called upon to disappear by being realized, but at every moment of their becoming or their development. Now, if the three Nos are still distinct in relation to the cerebral plane, they are no longer distinct in relation to the chaos into which the brain plunges. In this submersion it seems that there is extracted from chaos the shadow of the "people to come" in the form that art, but also philosophy and science, summon forth: mass-people, world-people, brain-people, chaos-people—nonthinking thought that lodges in the three, like Klee's nonconceptual concept or Kandinsky's[6] internal silence. It is here that concepts, sensations, and functions become undecidable, at the same time as philosophy, art, and science become indiscernible, as if they shared the same shadow that extends itself across their different nature and constantly accompanies them.

SOURCE: From Gilles Deleuze and Félix Guattari, *What Is Philosophy?*, trans. Hugh Tomlinson and Graham Burchell (New York: Columbia University Press, 1994), pp. 1–12, 201–18. Originally published in 1991 as *Qu'est-ce que la philosophie?* The brackets in the text are the translators'.

3. Three abstract painters: Piet Mondrian (Pieter Cornelis Mondriaan, 1872–1944), born in the Netherlands; Kenneth Noland (1924–2010), an American; and Jaffe (b. 1923), born in the United States.
4. Stéphane Mallarmé (1842–1898), French poet; Igitur is the hero of his prose-poem *Igitur; or, Elbehnon's Folly* (1925). For Nietzsche's Zarathustra, see above.

5. François Laruelle proposes a comprehension of nonphilosophy as the "real (of) science," beyond the object of knowledge: *Philosophie et nonphilosophie* (Liege: Mardage, 1989). But we do not see why this real of science is not nonscience as well [Deleuze and Guattari's note].
6. Wassily Kandinsky (1866–1944), Russian-born abstract artist.

W. E. B. DU BOIS
(1868 – 1963)

W. E. B. Du Bois was a phenomenon in American social and intellectual history. Born less than three years after Lincoln's assassination, he died just months before Kennedy's. His long lifetime of activity and productivity on an extraordinary range of fronts rivaled and closely tracked that of his fellow American pragmatic thinker and doer John Dewey (1859–1952; see this anthology's companion volume, *The Analytic Tradition*), with whose philosophical sensibility his own resonated. Academically trained and accomplished, Du Bois was a trailblazing African American pioneer in his main academic disciplines, history and sociology; but his social and political activism was even more impressive and influential than his astonishing array of publications. His efforts of both sorts challenged philosophical thinking about human reality to take serious account of the African American reality to which he vividly called attention in *The Souls of Black Folk* (1903) and many other writings. His connection with the interpretive tradition was also direct: the influence of HEGEL (to whose ideas he was exposed during several years of study in Berlin) can be discerned in his early thinking about race; and the influence of MARX is evident in his social and political thought.

William Edward Burghardt Du Bois (doo-BOYS) was born and raised by his mother (whom his father left two years after his birth) in Great Barrington, Massachusetts. The community was accepting of them, and he fared well in its schools. In 1885 (the year of his mother's death), with financial support from the community, he enrolled at Fisk University in Nashville, Tennessee, from which he graduated in 1888. He then enrolled again, this time at Harvard, where he studied with William James (see *The Analytic Tradition*); he received a second bachelor's degree (concentrat-

ing in history) in 1890. In the following year, he won a scholarship to pursue graduate work in sociology at Harvard. In 1892, supported by a fellowship, he went to Europe; he remained there for several years, attending the university in Berlin and traveling extensively. Upon his return, he completed his doctoral program and became the first African American to receive a Harvard PhD.

In the years that followed Du Bois held a series of academic appointments: at Wilberforce University in Ohio, a historically black university (where he married one of his students, Nina Gomer, in 1896); at the University of Pennsylvania, where he held a sociology field research appointment; and from 1897 to 1910 at Atlanta University, another black institution. The expression "Afro-American" was already coming into vogue, as was the term "Negro" (which Du Bois initially seems to have identified with "African"); and he undertook a campaign to advance both knowledge about the populations so designated and the improvement of their condition. He took the lead in making an issue of the whole matter, insisting that it not only could but should be openly confronted and discussed, and proclaiming what he called "the color line" to be a human problem of the utmost importance, practically as well as intellectually.

These concerns came increasingly to preoccupy Du Bois, in both his writings and his many social and political activities; but for some time he also continued to pursue his broader intellectual and academic interests. One such interest had to do with the conception of sociology itself; and that in turn required a consideration of the character of human reality with which sociology must deal. His thinking on these fundamentally philosophical issues is displayed in an early essay, "Sociology Hesitant" (written in 1905), which is among the selections below. Its intellectual sensibility shows the influence not only of Du Bois's study with William James at Harvard but also of his extended period of study at Berlin, where these same issues were being debated in its philosophical community, and where similar views were being espoused by DILTHEY and others. Thus in both content and circumstance, it links him with the philosophical tradition with which this volume is concerned.

Another selection, "The Conservation of Races" (1897), is one of Du Bois's early attempts to come to grips with the problem of race. In his first important book, *The Philadelphia Negro* (1899), based on his field research at the University of Pennsylvania (and something of a landmark in the emerging discipline of research-based sociology), he considered the possibility that race problems may reflect deeply rooted human traits and dispositions that must be reckoned with both theoretically and practically. (He had previously presented an early sketch of his general conception of the task of investigating African American history and culture—a task broadly sociological, but also philosophical and anthropological—in his 1898 essay "The Study of the Negro Problems.")

A few years later Du Bois published *The Souls of Black Folk* (excerpted below), which is perhaps the most significant and enduring of his many books. It joins a profound humanism with powerful revelations about the circumstances and experience of "black folk" at the turn of the century. One of its themes is the prevalence and complexity of what Du Bois calls the "double consciousness" of African American identity, as both "Negro" and "American"—each element essential in a positive way, even as they also are and must remain in tension.

The Souls of Black Folk instantly made Du Bois a national figure comparable to Booker T. Washington, whose "accommodationist" approach to the betterment of African Americans in American society the book sharply criticized. In 1905 Du Bois convened a meeting of prominent African Americans opposed to Washing-

ton's embrace of the so-called Atlanta Compromise, which involved acceptance of segregation and discriminatory practices, the exclusion of African Americans from political life in the wider society, and an emphasis on vocational training in their education, in exchange for the help of white society in improving their social and economic conditions. Gathering at Niagara Falls, the group formed what became known as the "Niagara Movement," and their manifesto opposed all of these concessions, calling for full political, civil, and social rights for black people. The organization they formed did not garner much support, but its core joined in the formation of the National Association for the Advancement of Colored People (NAACP), founded in 1909 by Du Bois and others. (It was at his suggestion that they used the term "colored" in its name, to include all peoples on the "dark-skinned" side of the "color line.") In 1910 Du Bois left Atlanta University and moved to New York to become editor of the NAACP's new journal, *The Crisis*, whose influence and importance grew quickly.

Because he was a historian as well as a sociologist, Du Bois attracted the attention of the American Historical Association, and in 1909 he was the first African American invited to address its annual meeting. In his book *The Negro* (1915), he attempted the first comprehensive history of Africans from ancient times to the age of colonialization. It was a topic to which he would return several times, in works such as *Black Folk: Then and Now* (1939) and *The World and Africa* (1947). Du Bois's writings became increasingly multidisciplinary. *Darkwater: Voices from within the Veil* (1920) continued his effort to draw back the "veil" that conceals African American life and experience, both to enlighten white readers and to encourage his black peers, mixing autobiography, sociology, history, philosophy, literature, politics, and criticism (a style he often favored). In *The Gift of Black Folk* (1924, later subtitled *The Negroes in the Making of America*), Du Bois sought to draw attention to the cultural as well as economic contributions of African Americans to American society. He also occasionally wrote fiction, including two utopian novels, *The Quest for the Silver Fleece* (1911) and *Dark Princess* (1928). His literary-political efforts culminated in the *Black Flame* trilogy, published late in his life (1957–61).

Du Bois became more politically engaged during these years, as he sought—in *The Crisis* and other venues— to expose racially charged incidents and practices and to rally responses to them, and his focus expanded to international issues. He helped organize the first Pan-African Congress in 1919, and his activities in opposition to the European domination of Africa led to his later being celebrated in postcolonial Africa, where he spent the last years of his life. Also attracted to socialism, Du Bois took a great interest in developments in post-revolutionary Russia. In 1926 he traveled to the young Soviet Union, which impressed him and which in turn appreciated him. That experience reinforced his socialist convictions, which became more pronounced in his subsequent writings—as, for example, in "Of the Ruling of Men" (1940), excerpted below. He found Marx's completely secular (and atheistic) humanism very congenial. Yet despite his increasingly explicit Marxist leanings, Du Bois, like SARTRE, was never entirely comfortable with communism, either in theory or in twentieth-century practice. Among other things, he was skeptical of the faux universalism of assimilationist and integrationist policies, whose shortcomings he saw communism as exacerbating rather than resolving.

Nonetheless, Du Bois's interest in the Soviet Union, together with turmoil within the NAACP and disagreement over the role of *The Crisis*, led to strains in his relationship with the organization's leadership. Matters reached a breaking point when he published editorials defending segregation that does not involve discrimination—a position that was viewed as heretical by that leadership. In 1934 Du Bois resigned as editor and returned to Atlanta University, where he resumed his academic career. An important work during his second tenure there was *Black Reconstruction* (1935), which challenged the dominant idea that the federal government's interventions in the South after the Civil War were a total failure, for which African Americans were largely to blame. In 1940 he published *Dusk of Dawn*, a work partly autobiographical but also partly philosophical. Its middle chapters— "The Concept of Race" (excerpted below) and "The White World"—deal interestingly with race and his evolving conception of it.

In 1944, at the age of 76, Du Bois was summarily dismissed from the faculty of Atlanta University. In response to public outcry he was given emeritus status and a lifetime annuity. He then rejoined the NAACP, directing its "Special Research" department. From that base, he became increasingly active in a variety of causes both nationally and internationally, while also continuing to publish extensively. His books issued during this period range from a polemic against colonialism (*Color and Democracy: Colonies and Peace*, 1945) to more books on Africa and its place in history and the modern world, as well as a number of books promoting world peace and opposing nuclear armament. In 1950, at the age of 82, he ran (unsuccessfully) for political office in New York, as the American Labor Party's candidate for the U.S. Senate. A harder loss was that of his wife, who died that year.

Also in that year, Du Bois agreed to become chairman of a new Peace Information Center, which was focused on publicizing the Stockholm Peace Appeal for nuclear disarmament. When the U.S. Justice Department demanded that the organization register as an agent of a foreign state, it disbanded—but Du Bois was indicted and put on trial. Although the case was dismissed, his passport was confiscated for eight years. The experience contributed to his estrangement not only from the American political establishment but once again from the NAACP, which declined to stand by him and support him at his trial. And even though he had expressed his misgivings and reservations about communism, criticized the Communist Party USA in the 1930s, and repudiated it in the 1940s, he drew harsh treatment as a purported "communist sympathizer" in the anti-communist hysteria and witch hunts of the early 1950s. This vilification only intensified his sense of persecution, and heightened his negative feelings about his country.

The confiscation of his passport made it impossible for the increasingly internationally minded Du Bois to travel to the many conferences to which he was invited. When it was returned in 1958, he and his second wife (whom he had married in 1951) set off on a world tour that lasted almost a year. In the course of it they spent considerable time in the Soviet Union and China, which treated them as celebrities. In 1961, when the U.S. Supreme Court upheld legislation requiring communist organizations to register with the government, Du Bois in effect gave up on the United States. He very publicly joined the Communist Party USA and departed with his wife for Ghana, accepting the invitation of Kwame Nkrumah, the president of the newly independent country (whom Du Bois had met in 1945), to relocate to its capital, Accra. His new task there was to supervise the government-supported project of an *Encyclopedia Africana* cov-

ering all things (and populations) African and of African origin. Du Bois remained in Ghana until his death two years later, at the age of 95, and was buried there.

Du Bois was a public intellectual of the first rank, whose intellect and activity both reflected and transcended the African American "double consciousness" he identified and claimed. They also both reflected and transcended the various specific disciplinary specializations and turns of mind that he acquired and drew on as he moved between theory and practice. The philosophical dimension of his thinking often accords with elements of the interpretive tradition; but the relevance of his writing to that tradition is perhaps more a matter of what it illuminates—what it calls into question and calls to our attention—than of its sustained reflective treatment. Some of these issues are normative and evaluative as well as interpretive, relating to the character of genuinely human individual and interpersonal life as well as to human possibilities and realities that are deeply and significantly problematic in different ways. Du Bois illuminates and compels us to come to terms—both philosophically and practically—with a range of these possibilities and realities that are too important and too pervasive to be overlooked or ignored. Although he may not have a ready set of answers, he has a set of passionate concerns and wields a powerful searchlight.

Sociology Hesitant

The Congress of Arts and Sciences at St. Louis last summer[1] served to emphasize painfully the present plight of Sociology; for the devotee of the cult made the strange discovery that the further following of his bent threatened violent personal dismemberment.[2] His objects of interest were distributed quite impartially under some six of the seven grand divisions of Science: economics, here; ethnology, there; a thing called "Sociology" hidden under Mental

1. That is, the summer of 1904.
2. A joking reference to the number of sessions that the devotee would have to attend simulta-

neously to pursue all the "divisions of Science" with which the emerging discipline of sociology might be associated.

Science, and the things really sociological ranged in a rag-bag and labeled "Social Regulation." And so on.

A part of this confusion of field was inevitable to any attempt at classifying knowledge, but the major part pointed to a real confusion of mind as to the field and method of Sociology. For far more than forty years we have wandered in this sociological wilderness, lisping a peculiar *patois*, uttering fat books and yet ever conscious of a fundamental confusion of thought at the very foundations of our science—something so wrong that while a man boasts himself an Astronomer, and acknowledges himself a biologist, he owns to Sociology[3] only on strict compulsion and with frantic struggles.

And yet three things at the birth of the New Age bear weighty testimony to an increased and increasing interest in human deeds: the Novel, the Trust[4] and the Expansion of Europe; the study of individual life and motive, the machine-like organizing of human economic effort, and the extension of all organization to the ends of the earth. Is there a fairer field than this for the Scientist? Did not the Master Comte[5] do well to crown his scheme of knowledge with Knowledge of Men?

Yet this was not exactly what he did, it was rather what he meant to do, what he and we long assumed he had done. For, steering curiously by the Deeds of Men[6] as objects of scientific study and induction, he suggested a study of Society. And Society? The prophet really had a vision of two things, the vast and bewildering activities of men and the lines of rhythm that coordinate certain of these actions. So he said: "Now in the inorganic sciences, the elements are much better known to us than the Whole which they constitute; so that in that case we must proceed from the simple to the compound. But the reverse method is necessary in the study of Man and of Society: Man and Society as a whole being better known to us, and more accessible subjects of study than the parts which constitute them."[7] And on this dictum has been built a science—not of Human Action but of "Society," a Sociology. Did Comte thus mean to fix scientific thought on the study of an abstraction? Probably not—rather he meant to call attention to the fact that amid the bewildering complexities of human life ran great highways of common likenesses and agreements in human thoughts and action, which world-long observation had already noted and pondered upon. Here we must start the new science, said the Pioneer, this is the beginning. Once having emphasized this point, however, and Comte was strangely hesitant as to the real elements of Society which must some time be studied—were they men or cells or atoms or something subtler than any of these? Apparently he did not answer but wandered on quickly to a study of "Society." And yet "Society" was but an abstraction. It was as though Newton[8] noticing falling as characteristic of matter and explaining this phenomenon as gravitation had straightaway

3. He admits to being a sociologist.
4. The monopolistic concentration of corporate power, attacked by Theodore Roosevelt early in his presidency (1901–09).
5. Auguste Comte (1798–1857), French philosopher and social scientist; the originator of the doctrine of "positivism" (a kind of radical empiricism) in intellectual inquiry. He is generally viewed as the founding father of sociology.
6. That is, guided by the idea of treating human

actions.
7. Comte, *Cours de philosophie positive* (1830–42, *Course in Positive Philosophy*), trans. Harriet Martineau as *The Positive Philosophy of Auguste Comte* (1853), book 6, chap. 3.
8. Isaac Newton (1642–1727), English physicist and mathematician who made foundational discoveries in optics, mechanics, and mathematics, including the law of universal gravitation.

sought to study some weird entity known as Falling instead of soberly investigating Things which fall. So Comte and his followers noted the grouping of men, the changing of government, the agreement in thought, and then, instead of a minute study of men grouping, changing, and thinking proposed to study the Group, the Change, and the Thought, and call this new created Thing, Society.

Mild doubters as to this method were cavalierly hushed by Spencer's verbal jugglery: "we consistently regard a society as an entity, because though formed of discreet units, a certain concreteness in the aggregate of them is implied by the general persistence of the arrangements among them throughout the area occupied."[9]

Thus were we well started toward metaphysical wanderings—studying not the Things themselves but the mystical whole which it was argued bravely they did form because they logically must. And to prove this imperative there was begun that bulky essay in descriptive sociology which has been the stock in trade of formal treatises in this science ever since. And what is Descriptive Sociology? It is a description of those Thoughts, and Thoughts of Things, and Things, that go to make human life—an effort to trace in the deeds and actions of men great underlying principles of harmony and development—a philosophy of history with modest and mundane ends, rather than eternal, teleological purpose. In this line Spencer and his imitators have done good inspiring but limited work. Limited because their data were imperfect—woefully imperfect: depending on hearsay, rumor and tradition, vague speculations, traveler's tales, legends and imperfect documents, the memory of memories and historic error. All our knowledge of the past lay to be sure, before them. But what is our knowledge of the past as a basis for scientific induction? Consequently the Spencerian Sociologists could only limn a shadowy outline of the meaning and rhythm of human deed to be filled in when scientific measurement and deeper study came to the rescue. Yet here, they lovingly lingered changing and arranging, expressing old thoughts anew, invent[ing] strange terms and yet withal adding but little to our previous knowledge.

This sociologists were not slow to see and they looked for means of escaping their vicious logical circle but looked only in the direction of their going and not backward toward the initial mistakes. So they came to the essay of two things: they sought the help of biological analogy as a suggestive aid to further study; they sought a new analysis in search of the Sociological Element. The elaborate attempt to compare the social and animal organism failed because analogy implies knowledge but does not supply it—suggests but does not furnish lines of investigation—And who was able to investigate "Society?" Nor was the search for the ultimate Sociological element more successful. Instead of seeking men as the natural unit of associated men it strayed further in metaphysical lines, and confounding Things with Thoughts of Things they sought not the real element of Society but the genesis of our social ideas. Society became for them a mode of mental action and its germ

---

9. Quoted from *The Principles of Sociology*, vol. 1 (1876), §212, by Herbert Spencer (1820–1903), English philosopher, influential advocate of Dar- win's theory of evolution, and an early prominent sociologist. Spencer's text has "discrete units."

was—according to their ingenuity—"Consciousness of Kind," "Imitation," the "Social Imperative" and the like.

All this was straying into the field of psychology and fifty years ago these wanderers might have been welcomed. But today psychology has left behind the fruitless carvings up of consciousness and begun a new analysis and a new mode of measurement. This new psychology has scant welcome for sociological novices. It might be historically interesting to know whether our social thinking began with this idea or that, or proceeded by that combination of thoughts or this—but how shall we ever know? And knowing what is such knowledge worth?

But enough of this. Let us go back a bit and ask frankly, Why did Comte hesitate so strangely at the "parts which constitute" Society and why have men so strangely followed his leading? Is it not very clear that the object of sociology is to study the deeds of men? Yes it is clear—clear to us, clear to our predecessors and yet the very phrasing of such an attempt to reduce human action to law, rule, and rythm [sic] show how audacious was the plan and why scientists have quailed before it and veiling their words in phrases half dimmed the intent of their science.[1]

For the Great Assumption of real life is that in the deeds of men there lies along with rule and rhythm—along with physical law and biological habit, a something incalculable. This assumption is ever with us—it pervades all our thinking, all our science, all our literature; it lies at the bottom of our conception of legal enactments, philanthropy, crime, education and ethics; and language has crystallized the thought and belief in Ought and May and Choice. Now in the face of this to propose calmly the launching of a science which would discover and formulate the exact laws of human action and parallel "Heat as a mode of motion" with a mathematical formula of "Shakespeare as pure Energy" or "Edison[2] as electrical force"—simply to propose such a thing seemed to be and was preposterous.

And yet how much so even the formulation of such a science seemed unthinkable, just as insistently came the call for scientific knowledge of men. The new Humanism of the 19th century was burning with new interest in human deeds; Law, Religion, Education—all call men to study of that singular unit of highest interest—the Individual Man. A Categorical Imperative[3] pushed through all thought toward the Paradox.

    1. The evident rhythm of human action.
    2. The evident incalculability of human action.

What then, is Sociology? Simply an attempt to discover the laws underlying the conduct of men.

Why then is it called Sociology? It ought not be, but it is, and "what is in a name?"

Why do not Sociologists state their object simply and plainly?

For fear of criticism.

---

1. That is, their elaborate phrases have half-obscured the aim of their science.
2. Thomas Alva Edison (1847–1931), American inventor; many of his best-known inventions (including the incandescent lightbulb) involved electricity.
3. A moral law that is absolute for all agents (KANT's fundamental principle of morality).

The criticism of whom?

Of the physical scientists on the one hand who say: the laws of men's deeds are physical laws, and physics studies them; of the Mass of men on the other hand who say: Man is not wholly a creature of unchanging law, he is in some degree a free agent and so outside the realm of scientific law. Now whatever one's whims and predilections no one can wholly ignore either of these criticisms: if this is a world of absolute unchanging physical laws, then the laws of physics and chemistry are the laws of all action—of stones and stars and Newtons and Nortons.[4] On the other hand for a thousand and a thousand years, and today as strongly as, and even more strongly than ever, men after experiencing the facts of life have almost universally assumed that in among physical forces stalk self-directing Wills, which modify, restrain and re-direct the ordinary laws of nature. The assumption is tremendous in its import. It means that from the point of view of Science this is a world of Chance as well as Law; that the conservation of energy and correlation of forces are not universally true, but that out of some unknown Nowhere burst miraculously now and then controlling Energy. So utterly inexplicable are the facts thus assumed that they are seldom flatly and plainly stated. Protagonists of "free" will are found to be horrified deniers of "Chance." And strenuous defenders of orthodox Science are found talking as though the destinies of this universe lay largely in undetermined human action—indeed they could not avoid such talk and continue talking.

Why not then flatly face the Paradox? frankly state the Hypothesis of Law and the Assumption of Chance and seek to determine by study and measurement the limits of each?[5]

This is what the true students of sociology are and have been doing now a half century and more. They have adopted the speech and assumption of humanity in regard to human action and yet studied those actions with all possible scientific accuracy. They have refused to cloud their reason with metaphysical entities undiscovered and undiscoverable, and they have also refused to neglect the greatest possible field of scientific investigation because they are unable to find laws similar to the law of gravitation. They have assumed a world of physical law peopled by beings capable in some degree of actions Inexplicable and Uncalculable according to these laws. And their object has been to determine as far as possible the limits of the Uncalculable— to measure if you will, the Kantian Absolute and the Undetermined Ego. In this way our knowledge of human life has been vastly increased by Statisticians, Ethnologists, Political Scientists, Economists, Students of Finance and Philanthropy, Criminologists, Educators, Moral Philosophers, and critics of art and literature. These men have applied statistical measurement and historical research to the study of physical manhood and the distribution of population by dwelling, age, and sex; they have compared and followed the trend of systems of government and political organization; they have given long and minute study to the multitudinous phenomena of the production and dis-

---

4. "Norton" has not been identified, but he evidently was a natural scientist of some sort.
5. This proposal, with its following elaboration, is very much in the spirit of much of the interpretive tradition. Du Bois calls for an approach to human

reality that rejects dogmatic positivism and scientism as well as antiscientific thinking, is both scientifically and humanistically informed and sophisticated, and embraces the seeming "Paradox" as a reality we must learn to comprehend.

tribution of wealth and work; they have sought to reduce philanthropy to a system by a study of dependents and delinquents and especially by a study of the social outcast called the criminal. Even in higher and more difficult regions of human training and Taste something of systematic investigation has been carried on.

In all this work the unit of investigation has frankly been made the Individual Man. There have been attempts to replace this troublesome element with something more tractable as in the case of the pliable law abiding "Economic Man"[6] where a being warranted to act from one motive without erratic by-play was created. But common sense prevailed and real men were studied—not metaphysical lay figures. Again these students of human nature have repeatedly refused to be thrown into utter confusion by the question: Is this a science? Where are your natural laws? What sort of a science is a science without laws? Without undertaking to answer these disturbing questions or to falsify the facts for sake of a glib rejoinder, these students have been content with pointing out bare facts, general rules and principles, and moral advice; they have neither accepted human life as chaotic nor have they lightly assumed laws, the existence of which they could not prove. They have insisted that we must study men because men are the greatest things in the known universe and they have also fearlessly accepted the fact that the "ought" is the greatest thing in human life.

Not that their work has been perfect. It has been open to two great criticisms; lack of adequate recognition of the essential unity in the various studies of human activity and of effort to discover and express that unity, and a hesitancy in attacking the great central problem of scientific investigation today—the relation of the science of man and physical science.

What then is the future path open before Sociology? It must seek a working hypothesis which will include Sociology and physics. To do this it must be provisionally assumed that this is a world of Law and Chance. That in time and space, Law covers the major part of the universe but that in significance the area left in that world to Chance is of tremendous import. In the last analysis Chance is as explicable as law: just as the Voice of God may sound behind physical law, so behind Chance we place free human wills capable of undetermined choices, frankly acknowledging that in both these cases we front the humanly inexplicable. This assumption does not in the least hinder the search of natural law, it merely suspends as unproved and improbable its wilder hypotheses; nay, considering some of the phenomena of radio-active matter, electrical energy and biological development, perhaps the incubus of the assumed Conservation of all Energy would be removed to the great relief of future Physics.

On the side of Sociology this proposed hypothesis would clear away forever the metaphysical cobwebs that bind us and open the way for a new unified conception of human deeds. We would no longer have two separate realms of knowledge, speaking a mutually unintelligible language, but one realm and in it physical science studying the manifestations of force and natural law, and the other, sociology, assuming the data of physics and studying within

6. One who makes purely rational decisions, objectively calculating the value and cost of their choices; the label came into use in the 19th century.

these that realm where determinate force is acted on by human wills, by indeterminate force.

Some such reconciliation of the two great wings of Science must come. It is inconceivable that the present dualism in classified knowledge can continue much longer. Mutual understanding must come under a working hypothesis which will give scope to historian as well as biologist.

Finally, it remains to point out that such a restatement of hypothesis involves a restatement of the bases of Sociology.

Suppose now we frankly assume a realm of Chance. What then is the programme of Science?

Looking over the world we see evidence of the reign of law; as we rise however from the physical to the human there comes not simply complication and interaction of forces but traces of indeterminate force until in the realm of higher human action we have chance—that is actions undetermined by and independent of actions gone before. The duty of science then is to measure carefully the limits of this Chance in human conduct.

That there are limits is shown by the rhythm in birth and death rates and the distribution by sex; it is found further in human customs and laws, the form of government, the laws of trade and even in charity and ethics. As however we rise in the realm of conduct we note a primary and a secondary rythm [sic]. A primary rythm depending as we have indicated on physical forces and physical law; but within this appears again and again a secondary rythm which while presenting nearly the same uniformity as the first, differs from it in its more or less sudden rise at a given tune, in accordance with prearranged plan and prediction and in being liable to stoppage and change according to similar plan. An example of primary uniformity is the death rate; of secondary uniformity, [an example is] the operation of a woman's club; to confound the two sorts of human uniformity is fatal to clear thinking; to explain them we must assume Law and Chance working in conjunction— Chance being the scientific side of inexplicable Will. Sociology then, is the Science that seeks the limits of Chance in human conduct.

SOURCE: From W. E. B. Du Bois, *The Problem of the Color Line at the Turn of the Twentieth Century: The Essential Early Essays*, ed. Nahum Dimitri Chandler (New York: Fordham University Press, 2015), pp. 271–78. This essay, written in 1905, was first published in 2000, as transcribed by Ronald A. T. Judy.

From The Conservation of Races

The American Negro has always felt an intense personal interest in discussions as to the origins and destinies of races: primarily because back of most discussions of race with which he is familiar, have lurked certain assumptions as to his natural abilities, as to his political, intellectual and moral status, which he felt were wrong. He has, consequently, been led to deprecate and minimize race distinctions, to believe intensely that out of one blood God created all nations, and to speak of human brotherhood as though it were the possibility of an already dawning to-morrow.

Nevertheless, in our calmer moments we must acknowledge that human beings are divided into races; that in this country the two most extreme types of the world's races have met, and the resulting problem as to the future relations of these types is not only of intense and living interest to us, but forms an epoch in the history of mankind.

It is necessary, therefore, in planning our movements, in guiding our future development, that at times we rise above the pressing, but smaller questions of separate schools and cars, wage-discrimination and lynch law, to survey the whole question of race in human philosophy and to lay, on a basis of broad knowledge and careful insight, those large lines of policy and higher ideals which may form our guiding lines and boundaries in the practical difficulties of every day. For it is certain that all human striving must recognize the hard limits of natural law, and that any striving, no matter how intense and earnest, which is against the constitution of the world, is vain.[1] The question, then, which we must seriously consider is this: What is the real meaning of Race; what has, in the past, been the law of race development, and what lessons has the past history of race development to teach the rising Negro people?

When we thus come to inquire into the essential difference of races we find it hard to come at once to any definite conclusion. Many criteria of race differences have in the past been proposed, as color, hair, cranial measurements and language. And manifestly, in each of these respects, human beings differ widely. They vary in color, for instance, from the marble-like pallor of the Scandinavian to the rich, dark brown of the Zulu, passing by the creamy Slav, the yellow Chinese, the light brown Sicilian and the brown Egyptian. Men vary, too, in the texture of hair from the obstinately straight hair of the Chinese to the obstinately tufted and frizzled hair of the Bushman. In measurement of heads, again, men vary; from the broad-headed Tartar to the medium-headed European and the narrow-headed Hottentot;[2] or, again in language, from the highly-inflected Roman tongue to the monosyllabic Chinese. All these physical characteristics are patent enough, and if they agreed with each other it would be very easy to classify mankind. Unfortunately for scientists, however, these criteria of race are most exasperatingly intermingled. Color does not agree with texture of hair, for many of the dark races have straight hair; nor does color agree with the breadth of the head, for the yellow Tartar has a broader head than the German; nor, again, has the science of language as yet succeeded in clearing up the relative authority of these various and contradictory criteria. The final word of science, so far, is that we have at least two, perhaps three, great families of human beings—the whites and Negroes, possibly the yellow race. That other races have arisen from the intermingling of the blood of these two. This broad division of the world's races which men like Huxley and Raetzel[3] have introduced as more nearly true than the old five-race scheme of Blumenbach,[4] is nothing more than an

---

1. Futile.
2. A Khoikhoi, a people of southern Africa; "Hottentot" (like some other terms used here that were in common usage at the time of this writing) is now considered a pejorative.
3. Friedrich Ratzel (1844–1904), German geographer and ethnographer. Thomas Huxley (1825–

1895), English biologist and prominent advocate of Darwin's theory of evolution.
4. Johann Friedrich Blumenbach (1752–1840), German anthropologist and comparative anatomist. On the basis of his research on craniums, he divided humanity into five families: Caucasian, Mongolian, Malayan, Ethiopian, and American.

acknowledgment that, so far as purely physical characteristics are concerned, the differences between men do not explain all the differences of their history. It declares, as Darwin[5] himself said, that great as is the physical unlikeness of the various races of men their likenesses are greater, and upon this rests the whole scientific doctrine of Human Brotherhood.[6]

Although the wonderful developments of human history teach that the grosser physical differences of color, hair and bone go but a short way toward explaining the different roles which groups of men have played in Human Progress, yet there are differences—subtle, delicate and elusive, though they may be—which have silently but definitely separated men into groups. While these subtle forces have generally followed the natural cleavage of common blood, descent and physical peculiarities, they have at other times swept across and ignored these. At all times, however, they have divided human beings into races, which, while they perhaps transcend scientific definition, nevertheless, are clearly defined to the eye of the Historian and Sociologist.

If this be true, then the history of the world is the history, not of individuals, but of groups, not of nations, but of races, and he who ignores or seeks to override the race idea in human history ignores and overrides the central thought of all history. What, then, is a race? It is a vast family of human beings, generally of common blood and language, always of common history, traditions and impulses, who are both voluntarily and involuntarily striving together for the accomplishment of certain more or less vividly conceived ideals of life.

Turning to real history, there can be no doubt, first, as to the widespread, nay, universal, prevalence of the race idea, the race spirit, the race ideal, and as to its efficiency as the vastest and most ingenious invention of human progress.[7] We, who have been reared and trained under the individualistic philosophy of the Declaration of Independence and the laissez-faire philosophy of Adam Smith,[8] are loath to see and loath to acknowledge this patent fact of human history. We see the Pharaohs, Caesars, Toussaints and Napoleons[9] of history and forget the vast races of which they were but epitomized expressions. We are apt to think in our American impatience, that while it may have been true in the past that closed race groups made history, that here in conglomerate America *nous avons changé tout cela*—we have changed all that,[1] and have no need of this ancient instrument of progress. This assumption of which the Negro people are especially fond, can not be established by a careful consideration of history.

5. Charles Darwin (1809–1882), English naturalist who developed the theory of evolution by natural selection.
6. That is, the doctrine that all human beings are of the same species or natural kind.
7. It is this striking (and perhaps surprising) conviction that underlies Du Bois's argument for "the conservation of races."
8. Scottish Enlightenment philosopher and economic theorist (1723–1790), most famous for arguing that economic markets are self-regulating and thus require minimal government interference.

9. That is, the rulers and emperors. Pharaohs, supposedly divine rulers in ancient Egypt; Julius Caesar (100–44 B.C.E.), Roman general who replaced the Roman Republic with his own rule (and whose name came to signify "supreme ruler"); Toussaint Louverture (ca. 1743–1803), black Haitian general and leader of the slave revolution that resulted in the Haitian slaves' emancipation and the temporary independence of Haiti from France, with him as governor-general; and Napoleon Bonaparte (1769–1821), French general who became emperor of the French.
1. A translation of the preceding French.

We find upon the world's stage today eight distinctly differentiated races, in the sense in which History tells us the word must be used. They are, the Slavs of eastern Europe, the Teutons of middle Europe, the English of Great Britain and America, the Romance nations of Southern and Western Europe, the Negroes of Africa and America, the Semitic people of Western Asia and Northern Africa, the Hindoos of Central Asia and the Mongolians of Eastern Asia. There are, of course, other minor race groups, as the American Indians, the Esquimaux and the South Sea Islanders; these larger races, too, are far from homogeneous; the Slav includes the Czech, the Magyar, the Pole and the Russian; the Teuton includes the German, the Scandinavian and the Dutch; the English include the Scotch, the Irish and the conglomerate American. Under Romance nations the widely-differing Frenchman, Italian, Sicilian and Spaniard are comprehended. The term Negro is, perhaps, the most indefinite of all, combining the Mulattoes and Zamboes[2] of America and the Egyptians, Bantus and Bushmen of Africa. Among the Hindoos are traces of widely differing nations, while the great Chinese, Tartar, Corean and Japanese families fall under the one designation—Mongolian.

The question now is: What is the real distinction between these nations? Is it the physical differences of blood, color and cranial measurements? Certainly we must all acknowledge that physical differences play a great part, and that, with wide exceptions and qualifications, these eight great races of to-day follow the cleavage of physical race distinctions; the English and Teuton represent the white variety of mankind; the Mongolian, the yellow; the Negroes, the black. Between these are many crosses and mixtures, where Mongolian and Teuton have blended into the Slav, and other mixtures have produced the Romance nations and the Semites. But while race differences have followed mainly physical race lines, yet no mere physical distinctions would really define or explain the deeper differences—the cohesiveness and continuity of these groups. The deeper differences are spiritual, psychical, differences—undoubtedly based on the physical, but infinitely transcending them. The forces that bind together the Teuton nations are, then, first, their race identity and common blood; secondly, and more important, a common history, common laws and religion, similar habits of thought and a conscious striving together for certain ideals of life. The whole process which has brought about these race differentiations has been a growth, and the great characteristic of this growth has been the differentiation of spiritual and mental differences between great races of mankind and the integration of physical differences.[3]

The age of nomadic tribes of closely related individuals represents the maximum of physical differences. They were practically vast families, and there were as many groups as families. As the families came together to form cities the physical differences lessened, purity of blood was replaced by the requirement of domicile, and all who lived within the city bounds became gradually to be regarded as members of the group; i.e., there was a slight and slow

---

2. "Sambos," those who are half mulatto (of mixed European and black parentage) and half black ("zambos" are also those of mixed indigenous and African parentage).
3. That is, race is a kind of human differentiation that has itself evolved or developed, from one that

was originally "physical" to one that is, more importantly, also "spiritual and mental"—and so is now more an ethnic than a biological differentiation. Du Bois's idea is reminiscent of HEGEL's concepts of a *Volk* and its *Volksgeist*.

breaking down of physical barriers. This, however, was accompanied by an increase of the spiritual and social differences between cities. This city became husbandmen, this, merchants, another warriors, and so on. The *ideals of life* for which the different cities struggled were different. When at last cities began to coalesce into nations there was another breaking down of barriers which separated groups of men. The larger and broader differences of color, hair and physical proportions were not by any means ignored, but myriads of minor differences disappeared, and the sociological and historical races of men began to approximate the present division of races as indicated by physical researches. At the same time the spiritual and physical differences of race groups which constituted the nations became deep and decisive. The English nation stood for constitutional liberty and commercial freedom; the German nation for science and philosophy; the Romance nations stood for literature and art, and the other race groups are striving, each in its own way, to develop for civilization its particular message, its particular ideal, which shall help to guide the world nearer and nearer that perfection of human life for which we all long, that

"one far off Divine event."[4]

This has been the function of race differences up to the present time. What shall be its function in the future? Manifestly some of the great races of today—particularly the Negro race—have not as yet given to civilization the full spiritual message which they are capable of giving. I will not say that the Negro-race has yet given no message to the world, for it is still a mooted question among scientists as to just how far Egyptian civilization was Negro in its origin; if it was not wholly Negro, it was certainly very closely allied. Be that as it may, however, the fact still remains that the full, complete Negro message of the whole Negro race has not as yet been given to the world: that the messages and ideal of the yellow race have not been completed, and that the striving of the mighty Slavs has but begun. The question is, then: How shall this message be delivered; how shall these various ideals be realized? The answer is plain: By the development of these race groups, not as individuals, but as races.[5] For the development of Japanese genius, Japanese literature and art, Japanese spirit, only Japanese, bound and welded together, Japanese inspired by one vast ideal, can work out in its fullness the wonderful message which Japan has for the nations of the earth. For the development of Negro genius, of Negro literature and art, of Negro spirit, only Negroes bound and welded together, Negroes inspired by one vast ideal, can work out in its fullness that great message we have for humanity. We cannot reverse history; we are subject to the same natural laws as other races, and if the Negro is ever to be a factor in the world's history—if among the gaily-colored banners that deck the broad ramparts of civilizations is to hang one uncompromising black, then it must be placed there by black hands, fash-

---

4. Alfred, Lord Tennyson, *In Memoriam* (1850), "Epilogue," line 143. The suggestion that "the perfection of human-spiritual self-realization), in which each race participates and has a distinctive contribution to make, is the most "Divine" of events humanly possible and attainable is another echo of Hegel's philosophy of history and *Geist*.
5. In Hegel, not as individuals, but as peoples (*Völker*).

ioned by black heads and hallowed by the travail of 200,000,000[6] black hearts beating in one glad song of jubilee.

For this reason, the advance guard of the Negro people—the 8,000,000 people of Negro blood in the United States of America—must soon come to realize that if they are to take their just place in the van of Pan-Negroism, then their destiny is NOT absorption by the white Americans. That if in America it is to be proven for the first time in the modern world that not only Negroes are capable of evolving individual men like Toussaint, the Saviour, but are a nation stored with wonderful possibilities of culture, then their destiny is not a servile imitation of Anglo-Saxon culture, but a stalwart originality which shall unswervingly follow Negro ideals.

It may, however, be objected here that the situation of our race in America renders this attitude impossible; that our sole hope of salvation lies in our being able to lose our race identity in the commingled blood of the nation; and that any other course would merely increase the friction of races which we call race prejudice, and against which we have so long and so earnestly fought.

Here, then, is the dilemma, and it is a puzzling one, I admit. No Negro who has given earnest thought to the situation of his people in America has failed, at some time in life, to find himself at these cross-roads; has failed to ask himself at some time: What, after all, am I? Am I an American or am I a Negro? Can I be both? Or is it my duty to cease to be a Negro as soon as possible and be an American? If I strive as a Negro, am I not perpetuating the very cleft that threatens and separates Black and White America? Is not my only possible practical aim the subduction of all that is Negro in me to the American? Does my black blood place upon me any more obligation to assert my nationality than German, or Irish or Italian blood would?

It is such incessant self-questioning and the hesitation that arises from it, that is making the present period a time of vacillation and contradiction for the American Negro; combined race action is stifled, race responsibility is shirked, race enterprises languish, and the best blood, the best talent, the best energy of the Negro people cannot be marshalled to do the bidding of the race. They stand back to make room for every rascal and demagogue who chooses to cloak his selfish deviltry under the veil of race pride.

Is this right? Is it rational? Is it good policy? Have we in America a distinct mission as a race—a distinct sphere of action and an opportunity for race development, or is self-obliteration the highest end to which Negro blood dare aspire?

If we carefully consider what race prejudice really is, we find it, historically, to be nothing but the friction between different groups of people; it is the difference in aim, in feeling, in ideals of two different races; if, now, this difference exists touching territory, laws, language, or even religion, it is manifest that these people cannot live in the same territory without fatal collision; but if, on the other hand, there is substantial agreement in laws, language and religion; if there is a satisfactory adjustment of economic life, then there is no reason why, in the same country and on the same street, two or

6. Du Bois's approximation of the world's total black population at the time.

three great national ideals might not thrive and develop, that men of different races might not strive together for their race ideals as well, perhaps even better, than in isolation. Here, it seems to me, is the reading of the riddle that puzzles so many of us. We are Americans, not only by birth and by citizenship, but by our political ideals, our language, our religion. Farther than that, our Americanism does not go. At that point, we are Negroes, members of a vast historic race that from the very dawn of creation has slept, but half awakening in the dark forests of its African fatherland.[7] We are the first fruits of this new nation, the harbinger of that black to-morrow which is yet destined to soften the whiteness of the Teutonic to-day. We are that people whose subtle sense of song has given America its only American music, its only American fairy tales, its only touch of pathos and humor amid its mad money-getting plutocracy. As such, it is our duty to conserve our physical powers, our intellectual endowments, our spiritual ideals; as a race we must strive by race organization, by race solidarity, by race unity to the realization of that broader humanity which freely recognizes differences in men, but sternly deprecates inequality in their opportunities of development.

For the accomplishment of these ends we need race organizations: Negro colleges, Negro newspapers, Negro business organizations, a Negro school of literature and art, and an intellectual clearing house, for all these products of the Negro mind, which we may call a Negro Academy. Not only is all this necessary for positive advance, it is absolutely imperative for negative defense. Let us not deceive ourselves at our situation in this country. Weighted with a heritage of moral iniquity from our past history, hard pressed in the economic world by foreign immigrants and native prejudice, hated here, despised there and pitied everywhere; our one haven of refuge is ourselves, and but one means of advance, our own belief in our great destiny, our own implicit trust in our ability and worth. There is no power under God's high heaven that can stop the advance of eight thousand thousand honest, earnest, inspired and united people. But—and here is the rub—they *must* be honest, fearlessly criticising their own faults, zealously correcting them; they must be *earnest*. No people that laughs at itself, and ridicules itself, and wishes to God it was anything but itself ever wrote its name in history; it *must* be inspired with the Divine faith of our black mothers, that out of the blood and dust of battle will march a victorious host, a mighty nation, a peculiar people, to speak to the nations of earth a Divine truth that shall make them free. And such a people must be united; not merely united for the organized theft of political spoils, not united to disgrace religion with whoremongers and ward-heelers; not united merely to protest and pass resolutions, but united to stop the ravages of consumption among the Negro people, united to keep black boys from loafing, gambling and crime; united to guard the purity of black women and to reduce the vast army of black prostitutes that is today marching to hell; and united in serious organizations, to determine by careful conference and thoughtful interchange of opinion the broad lines of policy and action for the American Negro.

7. This is an early articulation of Du Bois's idea of the "double consciousness" of those who are both American and black: while not (and not becoming) a distinct race, in his estimation, they are set apart from those who are just the one or just the other.

* * *

SOURCE: From *The Problem of the Color Line at the Turn of the Twentieth Century: The Essential Early Essays*, ed. Nahum Dimitri Chandler (New York: Fordham University Press, 2015), pp. 51–59, 62; originally a pamphlet published by the American Negro Academy in 1897. The second of the academy's "occasional papers," it began with the following "Announcement":

The American Negro Academy believes that upon those of the race who have had the advantage of higher education and culture, rests the responsibility of taking concerted steps for the employment of these agencies to uplift the race to higher planes of thought and action.

Two great obstacles to this consummation are apparent: (a) The lack of unity, want of harmony, absence of a self-sacrificing spirit, and no well-defined line of policy seeking definite aims; and (b) The persistent, relentless, at times covert opposition employed to thwart the Negro at every step of his upward struggles to establish the justness of his claim to the highest physical, intellectual and moral possibilities.

The Academy will, therefore, from time to time, publish such papers as in their judgment aid, by their broad and scholarly treatment of the topics discussed the dissemination of principles tending to the growth and development of the Negro along right lines, and the vindication of that race against vicious assaults.

From The Souls of Black Folk

From I. *Of Our Spiritual Strivings*

O water, voice of my heart, crying in the sand,
   All night long crying with a mournful cry,
As I lie and listen, and cannot understand
     The voice of my heart in my side or the voice of the sea,
O water, crying for rest, is it I, is it I?
   All night long the water is crying to me.

Unresting water, there shall never be rest
   Till the last moon droop and the last tide fail,
And the fire of the end begin to burn in the west;
     And the heart shall be weary and wonder and cry like the sea,
  All life long crying without avail,
    As the water all night long is crying to me.

ARTHUR SYMONS.[1]

1. British poet and critic (1865–1945). His poem is titled "The Crying of Water" (1902). The music below is the opening bars of "Nobody Knows the Trouble I've Seen," a well-known Negro spiritual.

Between me and the other world[2] there is ever an unasked question: unasked by some through feelings of delicacy; by others through the difficulty of rightly framing it. All, nevertheless, flutter round it. They approach me in a half-hesitant sort of way, eye me curiously or compassionately, and then, instead of saying directly, How does it feel to be a problem? they say, I know an excellent colored man in my town; or, I fought at Mechanicsville;[3] or, Do not these Southern outrages make your blood boil? At these I smile, or am interested, or reduce the boiling to a simmer, as the occasion may require. To the real question, How does it feel to be a problem? I answer seldom a word.

And yet, being a problem is a strange experience,—peculiar even for one who has never been anything else, save perhaps in babyhood and in Europe. It is in the early days of rollicking boyhood that the revelation first bursts upon one, all in a day, as it were. I remember well when the shadow swept across me. I was a little thing, away up in the hills of New England, where the dark Housatonic winds between Hoosac and Taghkanic[4] to the sea. In a wee wooden schoolhouse, something put it into the boys' and girls' heads to buy gorgeous visiting-cards—ten cents a package—and exchange.[5] The exchange was merry, till one girl, a tall newcomer, refused my card,—refused it peremptorily, with a glance.[6] Then it dawned upon me with a certain suddenness that I was different from the others; or like, mayhap, in heart and life and longing, but shut out from their world by a vast veil.[7] I had thereafter no desire to tear down that veil, to creep through; I held all beyond it in common contempt, and lived above it in a region of blue sky and great wandering shadows. That sky was bluest when I could beat my mates at examination-time, or beat them at a foot-race, or even beat their stringy heads. Alas, with the years all this fine contempt began to fade; for the worlds I longed for, and all their dazzling opportunities, were theirs, not mine. But they should not keep these prizes, I said; some, all, I would wrest from them. Just how I would do it I could never decide: by reading law, by healing the sick, by telling the wonderful tales that swam in my head,—some way. With other black boys the strife was not so fiercely sunny: their youth shrunk into tasteless sycophancy, or into silent hatred of the pale world about them and mocking distrust of everything white; or wasted itself in a bitter cry, Why did God make me an outcast and a stranger in mine own house? The shades of the prison-house closed round about us all:[8] walls strait and stubborn to the whitest, but relentlessly narrow, tall, and unscalable to sons of night who must plod darkly on in resignation, or beat unavailing palms against the stone, or steadily, half hopelessly, watch the streak of blue above.

After the Egyptian and Indian, the Greek and Roman, the Teuton and Mongolian, the Negro is a sort of seventh son, born with a veil,[9] and gifted with

---

2. That is, the white world.
3. A town near Richmond, Virginia; the site of a Civil War battle (1862).
4. A river and two ranges of hills in the Berkshires, close to Du Bois's childhood home in western Massachusetts.
5. Visiting cards were an important part of middle-class American and European social etiquette in the 19th century, with elaborate rules for their use.
6. Du Bois's family lived in a white community,

where generally they were made to feel welcome.
7. A common image in Du Bois's writing for the separation between black and white worlds (as in the 1920 book from which the last selection below is taken, *Darkwater: Voices from within the Veil*).
8. An echo of William Wordsworth, "Ode: Intimations of Immortality" (1807), lines 67–68.
9. In folklore, babies born with their heads covered by a caul, or membrane that is part of the amniotic sac, have psychic powers; seventh sons are believed to be similarly gifted.

second-sight in this American world,—a world which yields him no true self-consciousness, but only lets him see himself through the revelation of the other world. It is a peculiar sensation, this double-consciousness,[1] this sense of always looking at one's self through the eyes of others, of measuring one's soul by the tape of a world that looks on in amused contempt and pity. One ever feels his two-ness,—an American, a Negro; two souls, two thoughts, two unreconciled strivings; two warring ideals in one dark body, whose dogged strength alone keeps it from being torn asunder.

The history of the American Negro is the history of this strife,—this longing to attain self-conscious manhood, to merge his double self into a better and truer self. In this merging he wishes neither of the older selves to be lost. He would not Africanize America, for America has too much to teach the world and Africa. He would not bleach his Negro soul in a flood of white Americanism, for he knows that Negro blood has a message for the world. He simply wishes to make it possible for a man to be both a Negro and an American, without being cursed and spit upon by his fellows, without having the doors of Opportunity closed roughly in his face.

This, then, is the end of his striving: to be a co-worker in the kingdom of culture, to escape both death and isolation, to husband and use his best powers and his latent genius. These powers of body and mind have in the past been strangely wasted, dispersed, or forgotten. The shadow of a mighty Negro past flits through the tale of Ethiopia the Shadowy and of Egypt the Sphinx. Throughout history, the powers of single black men flash here and there like falling stars, and die sometimes before the world has rightly gauged their brightness. Here in America, in the few days since Emancipation, the black man's turning hither and thither in hesitant and doubtful striving has often made his very strength to lose effectiveness, to seem like absence of power, like weakness. And yet it is not weakness,—it is the contradiction of double aims. The double-aimed struggle of the black artisan—on the one hand to escape white contempt for a nation of mere hewers of wood and drawers of water, and on the other hand to plough and nail and dig for a poverty-stricken horde—could only result in making him a poor craftsman, for he had but half a heart in either cause. By the poverty and ignorance of his people, the Negro minister or doctor was tempted toward quackery and demagogy; and by the criticism of the other world, toward ideals that made him ashamed of his lowly tasks. The would-be black *savant*[2] was confronted by the paradox that the knowledge his people needed was a twice-told tale to his white neighbors, while the knowledge which would teach the white world was Greek to his own flesh and blood. The innate love of harmony and beauty that set the ruder souls of his people a-dancing and a-singing raised but confusion and doubt in the soul of the black artist; for the beauty revealed to him was the soul-beauty of a race which his larger audience despised, and he could not articulate the message of another people. This waste of double aims, this seeking to satisfy two unreconciled ideals, has wrought sad havoc with the courage

---

1. A reference both to "the two-ness" of thinking of oneself as at once "an American, a Negro" (in the next sentence) and also to a special case of the phenomenon later made much of by SARTRE: having a consciousness of oneself that is derived from an awareness of how one is seen by others (in this case, whites). In this sentence Du Bois emphasizes the second, more complex meaning that makes double-consciousness itself multiple.
2. Intellectual.

and faith and deeds of ten thousand thousand people,—has sent them often wooing false gods and invoking false means of salvation, and at times has even seemed about to make them ashamed of themselves.

Away back in the days of bondage they thought to see in one divine event the end of all doubt and disappointment; few men ever worshipped Freedom with half such unquestioning faith as did the American Negro for two centuries. To him, so far as he thought and dreamed, slavery was indeed the sum of all villainies, the cause of all sorrow, the root of all prejudice; Emancipation was the key to a promised land of sweeter beauty than ever stretched before the eyes of wearied Israelites.[3] In song and exhortation swelled one refrain—Liberty; in his tears and curses the God he implored had Freedom in his right hand. At last it came,—suddenly, fearfully, like a dream. With one wild carnival of blood and passion came the message in his own plaintive cadences:—

> "Shout, O children!
> Shout, you're free!
> For God has bought your liberty!"[4]

Years have passed away since then,—ten, twenty, forty; forty years of national life, forty years of renewal and development, and yet the swarthy spectre[5] sits in its accustomed seat at the Nation's feast. In vain do we cry to this our vastest social problem:—

> "Take any shape but that and my firm nerves
> Shall never tremble!"[6]

The Nation has not yet found peace from its sins; the freedman has not yet found in freedom his promised land. Whatever of good may have come in these years of change, the shadow of a deep disappointment rests upon the Negro people,—a disappointment all the more bitter because the unattained ideal was unbounded save by the simple ignorance of a lowly people.

The first decade was merely a prolongation of the vain search for freedom, the boon that seemed ever barely to elude their grasp,—like a tantalizing will-o'-the-wisp, maddening and misleading the headless host. The holocaust of war, the terrors of the Ku-Klux Klan,[7] the lies of carpet-baggers,[8] the disorganization of industry, and the contradictory advice of friends and foes, left the bewildered serf[9] with no new watchword beyond the old cry for freedom. As the time flew, however, he began to grasp a new idea. The ideal of liberty demanded for its attainment powerful means, and these the Fifteenth Amendment gave him.[1] The ballot, which before he had looked upon as a visible sign of freedom, he now regarded as the chief means of gaining and perfect-

---

3. That is, the land of Canaan (named below; see Numbers 34:2), reached by the Israelites 40 years after they were freed from their bondage in Egypt.
4. From a Negro spiritual.
5. That is, the "Negro problem."
6. Shakespeare, *Macbeth* (1606), 3.4.101–2.
7. Originally a social organization formed in 1866 by Confederate veterans, the Klan quickly became a secret organization intent on restoring white supremacy in the South. That first version of the Klan largely disappeared by 1880 (the modern Klan was not revived until 1915).

8. Northerners seen as descending on the South after the Civil War to pursue opportunities to enrich themselves.
9. That is, the freed American slave, hardly better off than Russian serfs—peasants bound to a hereditary plot of land owned by a noble (the serfs themselves were freed in 1861).
1. The amendment to the U.S. Constitution, ratified in 1870, granting voting rights to men regardless of "race, color, or previous condition of servitude."

ing the liberty with which war had partially endowed him. And why not? Had not votes made war and emancipated millions? Had not votes enfranchised the freedmen? Was anything impossible to a power that had done all this? A million black men started with renewed zeal to vote themselves into the kingdom. So the decade flew away, the revolution of 1876 came,[2] and left the half-free serf weary, wondering, but still inspired. Slowly but steadily, in the following years, a new vision began gradually to replace the dream of political power,—a powerful movement, the rise of another ideal to guide the unguided, another pillar of fire by night after a clouded day. It was the ideal of "book-learning"; the curiosity, born of compulsory ignorance, to know and test the power of the cabalistic letters[3] of the white man, the longing to know. Here at last seemed to have been discovered the mountain path to Canaan; longer than the highway of Emancipation and law, steep and rugged, but straight, leading to heights high enough to overlook life.

Up the new path the advance guard toiled, slowly, heavily, doggedly; only those who have watched and guided the faltering feet, the misty minds, the dull understandings, of the dark pupils of these schools know how faithfully, how piteously, this people strove to learn. It was weary work. The cold statistician wrote down the inches of progress here and there, noted also where here and there a foot had slipped or some one had fallen. To the tired climbers, the horizon was ever dark, the mists were often cold, the Canaan was always dim and far away. If, however, the vistas disclosed as yet no goal, no resting-place, little but flattery and criticism, the journey at least gave leisure for reflection and self-examination; it changed the child of Emancipation to the youth with dawning self-consciousness, self-realization, self-respect. In those sombre forests of his striving his own soul rose before him, and he saw himself,—darkly as through a veil;[4] and yet he saw in himself some faint revelation of his power, of his mission. He began to have a dim feeling that, to attain his place in the world, he must be himself, and not another. For the first time he sought to analyze the burden he bore upon his back, that deadweight of social degradation partially masked behind a half-named Negro problem.[5] He felt his poverty; without a cent, without a home, without land, tools, or savings, he had entered into competition with rich, landed, skilled neighbors. To be a poor man is hard, but to be a poor race in a land of dollars is the very bottom of hardships. He felt the weight of his ignorance,—not simply of letters, but of life, of business, of the humanities; the accumulated sloth and shirking and awkwardness of decades and centuries shackled his hands and feet. Nor was his burden all poverty and ignorance. The red stain of bastardy, which two centuries of systematic legal defilement of Negro women had stamped upon his race, meant not only the loss of ancient African chastity, but also the hereditary weight of a mass of corruption from white adulterers, threatening almost the obliteration of the Negro home.

A people thus handicapped ought not to be asked to race with the world, but rather allowed to give all its time and thought to its own social problems.

2. In 1876, to resolve a disputed election and respond to the threat of secession by some Southern states, Republicans agreed to reduce federal support of former slaves in the South.
3. That is, the seeming magic of literacy. The Kabbalah is a system of esoteric Jewish mysticism.

4. An echo of 1 Corinthians 13:12, "For now we see through a glass, darkly," but using Du Bois's favored image of a veil.
5. "Half-named," because it should really be called the "white-and-Negro problem."

But alas! while sociologists gleefully count his bastards and his prostitutes, the very soul of the toiling, sweating black man is darkened by the shadow of a vast despair. Men call the shadow prejudice, and learnedly explain it as the natural defence of culture against barbarism, learning against ignorance, purity against crime, the "higher" against the "lower" races. To which the Negro cries Amen! and swears that to so much of this strange prejudice as is founded on just homage to civilization, culture, righteousness, and progress, he humbly bows and meekly does obeisance.[6] But before that nameless prejudice that leaps beyond all this he stands helpless, dismayed, and well-nigh speechless; before that personal disrespect and mockery, the ridicule and systematic humiliation, the distortion of fact and wanton license of fancy, the cynical ignoring of the better and the boisterous welcoming of the worse, the all-pervading desire to inculcate disdain for everything black, from Toussaint[7] to the devil,—before this there rises a sickening despair that would disarm and discourage any nation save that black host to whom "discouragement" is an unwritten word.

But the facing of so vast a prejudice could not but bring the inevitable self-questioning, self-disparagement, and lowering of ideals which ever accompany repression and breed in an atmosphere of contempt and hate. Whisperings and portents came borne upon the four winds: Lo! we are diseased and dying, cried the dark hosts; we cannot write, our voting is vain; what need of education, since we must always cook and serve? And the Nation echoed and enforced this self-criticism, saying: Be content to be servants, and nothing more; what need of higher culture for half-men? Away with the black man's ballot, by force or fraud,—and behold the suicide of a race! Nevertheless, out of the evil came something of good,—the more careful adjustment of education to real life, the clearer perception of the Negroes' social responsibilities, and the sobering realization of the meaning of progress.

So dawned the time of *Sturm und Drang*: storm and stress[8] to-day rocks our little boat on the mad waters of the world-sea; there is within and without the sound of conflict, the burning of body and rending of soul; inspiration strives with doubt, and faith with vain questionings. The bright ideals of the past,—physical freedom, political power, the training of brains and the training of hands,—all these in turn have waxed and waned, until even the last grows dim and overcast. Are they all wrong,—all false? No, not that, but each alone was over-simple and incomplete,—the dreams of a credulous race-childhood, or the fond imaginings of the other world which does not know and does not want to know our power. To be really true, all these ideals must be melted and welded into one. The training of the schools we need to-day more than ever,—the training of deft hands, quick eyes and ears, and above all the broader, deeper, higher culture of gifted minds and pure hearts. The power of the ballot we need in sheer self-defence,—else what shall save us from a second slavery? Freedom, too, the long-sought, we still seek,—the freedom of life and limb, the freedom to work and think, the free-

<hr />

6. Acknowledges its superiority.
7. Toussaint Louverture (ca. 1743–1803), black Haitian general and leader of the slave revolution that resulted in the slaves' emancipation and the temporary independence of Haiti from France, with

him as governor-general.
8. A translation of the preceding German, a phrase associated with German Romanticism: the basic idea is that of turmoil.

dom to love and aspire. Work, culture, liberty,—all these we need, not singly but together, not successively but together, each growing and aiding each, and all striving toward that vaster ideal that swims before the Negro people, the ideal of human brotherhood, gained through the unifying ideal of Race; the ideal of fostering and developing the traits and talents of the Negro, not in opposition to or contempt for other races, but rather in large conformity to the greater ideals of the American Republic, in order that some day on American soil two world-races may give each to each those characteristics both so sadly lack. We the darker ones come even now not altogether empty-handed: there are to-day no truer exponents of the pure human spirit of the Declaration of Independence than the American Negroes; there is no true American music but the wild sweet melodies of the Negro slave; the American fairy tales and folk-lore are Indian and African; and, all in all, we black men seem the sole oasis of simple faith and reverence in a dusty desert of dollars and smartness. Will America be poorer if she replace her brutal dyspeptic blundering with light-hearted but determined Negro humility? or her coarse and cruel wit with loving jovial good-humor? or her vulgar music with the soul of the Sorrow Songs?[9]

Merely a concrete test of the underlying principles of the great republic is the Negro Problem, and the spiritual striving of the freedmen's sons is the travail of souls whose burden is almost beyond the measure of their strength, but who bear it in the name of an historic race, in the name of this the land of their fathers' fathers, and in the name of human opportunity.

* * *

From W. E. B. Du Bois, *The Souls of Black Folk*, ed. Henry Louis Gates Jr. and Terri Hume Oliver (New York: W. W. Norton, 1999), pp. 9–16. This book, a collection of essays, was first published in 1903.

From Dusk of Dawn

From *Chapter I.*
The Plot

* * *

What now was this particular social problem which, through the chances of birth and existence, became so peculiarly mine? At bottom and in essence it was as old as human life. Yet in its revelation, through the nineteenth century, it was significantly and fatally new: the differences between men; differences in their appearance, in their physique, in their thoughts and customs; differences so great and so impelling that always from the beginning of time, they thrust themselves forward upon the consciousness of all living things. Culture among human beings came to be and had to be built upon knowledge and recognition of these differences.

But after the scientific method had been conceived in the seventeenth century it came toward the end of the eighteenth century to be applied to man

9. Negro spirituals, the subject of chap. 14 of *The Souls of Black Folk*.

and to man as he appeared then, with no wide or intensive inquiry into what he had been or how he had lived in the past. In the nineteenth century however came the revolution of conceiving the world not as permanent structure but as changing growth and then the study of man as changing and developing physical and social entity had to begin.

But the mind clung desperately to the idea that basic racial differences between human beings had suffered no change; and it clung to this idea not simply from inertia and unconscious action but from the fact that because of the modern African slave trade a tremendous economic structure and eventually an industrial revolution had been based upon racial differences between men; and this racial difference had now been rationalized into a difference mainly of skin color. Thus in the latter part of the nineteenth century when I was born and grew to manhood, color had become an abiding unchangeable fact chiefly because a mass of self-conscious instincts and unconscious prejudices had arranged themselves rank on rank in its defense. Government, work, religion and education became based upon and determined by the color line.[1] The future of mankind was implicit in the race and color of men.

Already in my boyhood this matter of color loomed significantly. My skin was darker than that of my schoolmates. My family confined itself not entirely but largely to people of this same darker hue. Even when in fact the color was lighter, this was an unimportant variation from the norm. As I grew older, and saw the peoples of the land and of the world, the problem changed from a simple thing of color, to a broader, deeper matter of social condition: to millions of folk born of dark slaves, with the slave heritage in mind and home; millions of people spawned in compulsory ignorance; to a whole problem of the uplift of the lowly who formed the darker races.

This social condition pictured itself gradually in my mind as a matter of education, as a matter of knowledge; as a matter of scientific procedure in a world which had become scientific in concept. Later, however, all this frame of concept became blurred and distorted. There was evidently evil and hindrance blocking the way of life. Not science alone could settle this matter, but force must come to its aid. The black world must fight for freedom. It must fight with the weapons of Truth, with the sword of the intrepid, uncompromising Spirit, with organization in boycott, propaganda and mob frenzy. Upon this state of mind after a few years of conspicuous progress fell the horror of World War—of ultimate agitation, propaganda and murder.

The lesson of fighting was unforgettable; it was eternal loss and cost in victory or defeat. And again my problem of human difference, of the color line, of social degradation, of the fight for freedom became transformed. First and natural to the emergence of colder and more mature manhood from hot youth, I saw that the color bar could not be broken by a series of brilliant immediate assaults. Secondly, I saw defending this bar not simply ignorance and ill will; these to be sure; but also certain more powerful motives less open to reason or appeal. There were economic motives, urges to build wealth on the backs of black slaves and colored serfs; there followed those unconscious acts and

---

1. The "color line"—with the white population of the Western world on one side and people of "color" generally ("the darker races," in the next paragraph) on the other—became Du Bois's favored way of characterizing the social problem of which the "Negro problem" was only one part.

irrational reactions, unpierced by reason, whose current form depended on the long history of relation and contact between thought and idea. In this case not sudden assault but long siege was indicated; careful planning and subtle campaign with the education of growing generations and propaganda.

For all this, time was needed to move the resistance in vast areas of unreason and especially in the minds of men where conscious present motive had been built on false rationalization. Meantime the immediate problem of the Negro was the question of securing existence, of labor and income, of food and home, of spiritual independence and democratic control of the industrial process. It would not do to concenter all effort on economic well-being and forget freedom and manhood and equality. Rather Negroes must live and eat and strive, and still hold unfaltering commerce with the stars.

Finally, I could see that the scientific task of the twentieth century would be to explore and measure the scope of chance and unreason in human action, which does not yield to argument but changes slowly and with difficulty after long study and careful development.[2]

* * *

From Chapter V.
The Concept of Race

* * * The history of the development of the race concept in the world and particularly in America, was naturally reflected in the education offered me. In the elementary school it came only in the matter of geography when the races of the world were pictured: Indians, Negroes and Chinese, by their most uncivilized and bizarre representatives; the whites by some kindly and distinguished-looking philanthropist. In the elementary and high school, the matter was touched only incidentally, due I doubt not to the thoughtfulness of the teachers; and again my racial inferiority could not be dwelt upon because the single representative of the Negro race in the school did not happen to be in any way inferior to his fellows. In fact it was not difficult for me to excel them in many ways and to regard this as quite natural.

At Fisk,[3] the problem of race was faced openly and essential racial equality asserted and natural inferiority strenuously denied. In some cases the teachers expressed this theory; in most cases the student opinion naturally forced it. At Harvard, on the other hand, I began to face scientific race dogma:[4] first of all, evolution and the "Survival of the Fittest."[5] It was continually stressed in the community and in classes that there was a vast difference in the development of the whites and the "lower" races; that this could be seen in the physical development of the Negro. I remember once in a museum, coming face to face with a demonstration: a series of skeletons arranged from a little monkey to a tall well-developed white man, with a Negro barely outranking a

---

2. These last three paragraphs spell out the larger strategic plan to which the title of this chapter refers, as well his plan for the project of the book itself, intended to help set the stage—autobiographically, but also reflectively—for that campaign.

3. A historically black university in Nashville, Tennessee (incorporated in 1867), from which Du Bois graduated in 1888.
4. That is, putatively "scientific" race dogma.
5. The theory of natural selection, proposed by the English naturalist Charles Darwin (1809–1882).

chimpanzee. Eventually in my classes stress was quietly transferred to brain weight and brain capacity, and at last to the "cephalic index."

In the graduate school at Harvard and again in Germany, the emphasis again was altered, and race became a matter of culture and cultural history. The history of the world was paraded before the observation of students. Which was the superior race? Manifestly that which had a history, the white race; there was some mention of Asiatic culture, but no course in Chinese or Indian history or culture was offered at Harvard, and quite unanimously in America and Germany, Africa was left without culture and without history. * * *

The first thing which brought me to my senses in all this racial discussion was the continuous change in the proofs and arguments advanced. I could accept evolution and the survival of the fittest, provided the interval between advanced and backward races was not made too impossible. I balked at the usual "thousand years." But no sooner had I settled into scientific security here, than the basis of race distinction was changed without explanation, without apology. I was skeptical about brain weight; surely much depended upon what brains were weighed. I was not sure about physical measurements and social inquiries. For instance, an insurance actuary published in 1890 incontrovertible statistics showing how quickly and certainly the Negro race was dying out in the United States through sheer physical inferiority. I lived to see every assumption of Hoffman's "Race Traits and Tendencies"[6] contradicted; but even before that, I doubted the statistical method which he had used. When the matter of race became a question of comparative culture, I was in revolt. I began to see that the cultural equipment attributed to any people depended largely on who estimated it; and conviction came later in a rush as I realized what in my education had been suppressed concerning Asiatic and African culture.

It was not until I was long out of school and indeed after the World War that there came the hurried use of the new technique of psychological tests, which were quickly adjusted so as to put black folk absolutely beyond the possibility of civilization. By this time I was unimpressed. I had too often seen science made the slave of caste and race hate. And it was interesting to see Odum, McDougall and Brigham[7] eventually turn somersaults from absolute scientific proof of Negro inferiority to repudiation of the limited and questionable application of any test which pretended to measure innate human intelligence.

So far I have spoken of "race" and race problems quite as a matter of course without explanation or definition. That was our method in the nineteenth century. Just as I was born a member of a colored family, so too I was born a member of the colored race. That was obvious and no definition was needed. Later I adopted the designation "Negro" for the race to which I belong. It seemed more definite and logical. At the same time I was of course aware that

6. *Race Traits and Tendencies of the American Negro* (1896), by Frederick Hoffman (1865–1946), a German-born statistician whose focus was on public health issues. The book was published just five years after he emigrated from Germany to the United States.

7. Three American social scientists: Howard W. Odum (1884–1954), a sociologist specializing in the social problems of the South; William McDougall (1871–1938), a British-born social psychologist who developed a Darwinian theory of human behavior; and Carl Brigham (1890–1943), a psychologist who developed intelligence tests (notably, the SAT).

all members of the Negro race were not black and that the pictures of my race which were current were not authentic nor fair portraits. But all that was incidental. The world was divided into great primary groups of folk who belonged naturally together through heredity of physical traits and cultural affinity.

I do not know how I came first to form my theories of race. The process was probably largely unconscious. The differences of personal appearance between me and my fellows, I must have been conscious of when quite young. Whatever distinctions came because of that did not irritate me; they rather exalted me because, on the whole, while I was still a youth, they gave me exceptional position and a chance to excel rather than handicapping me.

Then of course, when I went South to Fisk, I became a member of a closed racial group with rites and loyalties, with a history and a corporate future, with an art and philosophy. I received these eagerly and expanded them so that when I came to Harvard the theory of race separation was quite in my blood. I did not seek contact with my white fellow students. On the whole I rather avoided them. I took it for granted that we were training ourselves for different careers in worlds largely different. There was not the slightest idea of the permanent subordination and inequality of my world. Nor again was there any idea of racial amalgamation. I resented the assumption that we desired it. I frankly refused the possibility while in Germany and even in America gave up courtship with one "colored" girl because she looked quite white, and I should resent the inference on the street that I had married outside my race.

All this theory, however, was disturbed by certain facts in America, and by my European experience. Despite everything, race lines were not fixed and fast. Within the Negro group especially there were people of all colors. Then too, there were plenty of my colored friends who resented my ultra "race" loyalty and ridiculed it. They pointed out that I was not a "Negro," but a mulatto;[8] that I was not a Southerner but a Northerner, and my object was to be an American and not a Negro; that race distinctions must go. I agreed with this in part and as an ideal, but I saw it leading to inner racial distinction in the colored group. I resented the defensive mechanism of avoiding too dark companions in order to escape notice and discrimination in public. As a sheer matter of taste I wanted the color of my group to be visible. I hotly championed the inclusion of two black school mates whose names were not usually on the invitation list to our social affairs. In Europe my friendships and close contact with white folk made my own ideas waver. The eternal walls between races did not seem so stern and exclusive. I began to emphasize the cultural aspects of race.

* * *

* * * But as I grew older the matter became more serious and less capable of jaunty settlement. I not only met plenty of persons equal in ability to myself but often with greater ability and nearly always with greater opportunity. Racial identity presented itself as a matter of trammels and impediments as "tightening bonds about my feet." As I looked out into my racial world the whole thing verged on tragedy. My "way was cloudy" and the approach to its high goals by no means straight and clear. I saw the race problem was not as

8. A person of mixed European and black parentage.

I conceived, a matter of clear, fair competition, for which I was ready and eager. It was rather a matter of segregation, of hindrance and inhibitions, and my struggles against this and resentment at it began to have serious repercussions upon my inner life.

* * *

Practically, this group imprisonment within a group has various effects upon the prisoner. He becomes provincial and centered upon the problems of his particular group. He tends to neglect the wider aspects of national life[9] and human existence. On the one hand he is unselfish so far as his inner group is concerned. He thinks of himself not as an individual but as a group man, a "race" man. His loyalty to this group idea tends to be almost unending and balks at almost no sacrifice. On the other hand, his attitude toward the environing race congeals into a matter of unreasoning resentment and even hatred, deep disbelief in them and refusal to conceive honesty and rational thought on their part. This attitude adds to the difficulties of conversation, intercourse, understanding between groups.

This was the race concept which has dominated my life, and the history of which I have attempted to make the leading theme of this book. It had as I have tried to show all sorts of illogical trends and irreconcilable tendencies. Perhaps it is wrong to speak of it at all as "a concept" rather than as a group of contradictory forces, facts and tendencies. At any rate I hope I have made its meaning to me clear. It was for me as I have written first a matter of dawning realization, then of study and science; then a matter of inquiry into the diverse strands of my own family; and finally consideration of my connection, physical and spiritual, with Africa and the Negro race in its homeland. All this led to an attempt to rationalize the racial concept and its place in the modern world.

SOURCE: From W. E. B. Du Bois, *Dusk of Dawn: An Essay toward an Autobiography of a Race Concept*, ed. Henry Louis Gates Jr. (New York: Oxford University Press, 2007), pp. 1–3, 49–51, 66–67. First published in 1940.

From Darkwater: Voices from Within the Veil

From *Chapter VI.*
Of the Ruling of Men

The ruling of men is the effort to direct the individual actions of many persons toward some end. This end theoretically should be the greatest good of all, but no human group has ever reached this ideal because of ignorance and selfishness. The simplest object would be rule for the Pleasure of One, namely the Ruler; or of the Few—his favorites; or of many—the Rich, the Privileged, the Powerful. Democratic movements inside groups and nations are always taking place and they are the efforts to increase the number of beneficiaries of the ruling. In 18th century Europe, the effort became so broad and sweeping that an attempt was made at universal expression and

9. That is, public life.

the philosophy of the movement said that if All ruled they would rule for All and thus Universal Good was sought through Universal Suffrage.

* * *

The real argument for democracy is * * * that in the people we have the source of that endless life and unbounded wisdom which the rulers of men must have. A given people today may not be intelligent, but through a democratic government that recognizes, not only the worth of the individual to himself, but the worth of his feelings and experiences to all, they can educate, not only the individual unit, but generation after generation, until they accumulate vast stores of wisdom. Democracy alone is the method of showing the whole experience of the race[1] for the benefit of the future and if democracy tries to exclude women or Negroes or the poor or any class because of innate characteristics which do not interfere with intelligence, then that democracy cripples itself and belies its name.

* * *

The addition of the new wisdom, the new points of view, and the new interests must, of course, be from time to time bewildering and confusing. Today those who have a voice in the body politic have expressed their wishes and sufferings. The result has been a smaller or greater balancing of their conflicting interests. The appearance of new interests and complaints means disarrangement and confusion to the older equilibrium. It is, of course, the inevitable preliminary step to that larger equilibrium in which the interests of no human soul will be neglected. These interests will not, surely, be all fully realized, but they will be recognized and given as full weight as the conflicting interests will allow. The problem of government thereafter would be to reduce the necessary conflict of human interests to the minimum.

* * *

Great as are our human differences and capabilities there is not the slightest scientific reason for assuming that a given human being of any race or sex cannot reach normal, human development if he is granted a reasonable chance. This is, of course, denied. It is denied so volubly and so frequently and with such positive conviction that the majority of unthinking people seem to assume that most human beings are not human and have no right to human treatment or human opportunity. All this goes to prove that human beings are, and must be, woefully ignorant of each other. It always startles us to find folks thinking like ourselves. We do not really associate with each other, we associate with our ideas of each other, and few people have either the ability or courage to question their own ideas. None have more persistently and dogmatically insisted upon the inherent inferiority of women than the men with whom they come in closest contact. It is the husbands, brothers, and sons of women whom it has been most difficult to induce to consider women seriously or to acknowledge that women have rights which men are bound to respect. So, too, it is those people who live in closest contact with black folk who have most unhesitatingly asserted the utter impossibility of living beside

1. Here, the human race.

Negroes who are not industrial or political slaves or social pariahs. All this proves that none are so blind as those nearest the thing seen, while, on the other hand, the history of the world is the history of the discovery of the common humanity of human beings among steadily-increasing circles of men.

* * *

The world has long since awakened to a realization of the evil which a privileged few may exercise over the majority of a nation. So vividly has this truth been brought home to us that we have lightly assumed that a privileged and enfranchised majority cannot equally harm a nation. Insane, wicked, and wasteful as the tyranny of the few over the many may be, it is not more dangerous than the tyranny of the many over the few. Brutal physical revolution can, and usually does, end the tyranny of the few. But the spiritual losses from suppressed minorities may be vast and fatal and yet all unknown and unrealized because idea and dream and ability are paralyzed by brute force.

If, now, we have a democracy with no excluded groups, with all men and women enfranchised, what is such a democracy to do? How will it function? What will be its field of work?

The paradox which faces the civilized world today is that democratic control is everywhere limited in its control of human interests. Mankind is engaged in planting, forestry, and mining, preparing food and shelter, making clothes and machines, transporting goods and folk, disseminating news, distributing products, doing public and private personal service, teaching, advancing science, and creating art.

In this intricate whirl of activities, the theory of government has been hitherto to lay down only very general rules of conduct, marking the limits of extreme anti-social acts, like fraud, theft, and murder.

The theory was that within these bounds was Freedom—the Liberty to think and do and move as one wished. The real realm of freedom was found in experience to be much narrower than this in one direction and much broader in another. In matters of Truth and Faith and Beauty, the Ancient Law was inexcusably strait and modern law unforgivably stupid. It is here that the future and mighty fight for Freedom must and will be made. Here in the heavens and on the mountaintops, the air of Freedom is wide, almost limitless, for here, in the highest stretches, individual freedom harms no man, and, therefore, no man has the right to limit it.

On the other hand, in the valleys of the hard, unyielding laws of matter and the social necessities of time production, and human intercourse, the limits on our freedom are stern and unbending if we would exist and thrive. This does not say that everything here is governed by incontrovertible "natural" law which needs no human decision as to raw materials, machinery, prices, wages, news-dissemination, education of children, etc.; but it does mean that decisions here must be limited[2] by brute facts and based on science and human wants.

Today the scientific and ethical boundaries of our industrial activities are not in the hands of scientists, teachers, and thinkers; nor is the intervening opportunity for decision left in the control of the public whose welfare such

2. That is, constrained.

decisions guide. On the contrary, the control of industry is largely in the hands of a powerful few, who decide for their own good and regardless of the good of others. The making of the rules of Industry, then, is not in the hands of All, but in the hands of the Few. The Few who govern industry envisage, not the wants of mankind, but their own wants. They work quietly, often secretly, opposing Law, on the one hand, as interfering with the "freedom of industry"; opposing, on the other hand, free discussion and open determination of the rules of work and wealth and wages, on the ground that harsh natural law brooks no interference by Democracy.

These things today, then, are not matters of free discussion and determination. They are strictly controlled. Who controls them? Who makes these inner, but powerful, rules? Few people know. Others assert and believe these rules are "natural"—a part of our inescapable physical environment. Some of them doubtless are; but most of them are just as clearly the dictates of self-interest laid down by the powerful private persons who today control industry. Just here it is that modern men demand that Democracy supplant skilfully concealed, but all too evident, Monarchy.

* * *

That the problem of the democratization of industry is tremendous, let no man deny. We must spread that sympathy and intelligence which tolerates the widest individual freedom despite the necessary public control; we must learn to select for public office ability rather than mere affability. We must stand ready to defer to knowledge and science and judge by result rather than by method; and finally we must face the fact that the final distribution of goods— the question of wages and income is an ethical and not a mere mechanical problem and calls for grave public human judgment and not secrecy and closed doors. All this means time and development. It comes not complete by instant revolution of a day, nor yet by the deferred evolution of a thousand years—it comes daily, bit by bit and step by step, as men and women learn and grow and as children are trained in Truth.

These steps are in many cases clear: the careful, steady increase of public democratic ownership of industry, beginning with the simplest type of public utilities and monopolies, and extending gradually as we learn the way[.]³ * * *

But beyond all this must come the Spirit—the Will to Human Brotherhood of all Colors, Races, and Creeds; the Wanting of the wants of All. Perhaps the finest contribution of current Socialism to the world is neither its light nor its dogma, but the idea back of its one mighty word—Comrade!⁴

SOURCE: From W. E. B. Du Bois, *Darkwater: Voices from within the Veil* (1920; reprint, Mineola, N.Y.: Dover, 1999), pp. 78, 84–86, 89–92. This essay is Du Bois's most succinct statement of his political philosophy.

3. Though Du Bois had strong Marxist leanings, he here restricts himself to proclaiming the desirability of a thoroughgoing democratic socialism, guided by due deference to "knowledge and science."
4. The reference to "current Socialism" makes clear that Du Bois is nodding to the Soviet Union and its version of Marxism; but significantly, what he finds commendable is its (nominal) emphasis on the ideal of "comradeship" or social and human solidarity, community, and fellowship, as articulated in the previous sentence.

FRANTZ FANON
(1925 – 1961)

Fanon's life was short, but his shadow has been long; and his thinking has at least the air of paradox. Like MARX, he was a subtle and deeply humanistic thinker, to whom nothing mattered more than human dignity and flourishing—and whose passionate commitment to those values impelled him to champion extreme measures when seemingly required to break the grip of a social reality that denies them to an oppressed population. The original and primary target of his wrath was the racist colonial system that prevailed during his lifetime in much of the non-Western world. The reasoning he articulated, however, particularly in the polemical *The Wretched of the Earth* (1961) from the last year of his life, can easily be—and often has been—applied to other contexts of entrenched systemic oppression and degradation. Fanon himself, at the end of that work, extended the scope of his critique from the colonial system to the broad economic, technological, cultural, and intellectual as well as military dominance of "Europe" (meaning the Western world); and he concludes it with a call for the "Third World" to go its own way, to create its own (new and superior) humanity. He does not say what that might be; but his critical depictions of the reality of the European type (and its American outgrowth) are indirectly suggestive. There also is much in his earlier *Black Skin, White Masks* (1952) that at least hints at aspects of his idea of a far more genuinely human way of being a human being than he saw among colonized and colonizers (and their European templates) alike. His subsequent revolutionary fervor may well have sprung from a determination to eliminate what he took to be the real-world conditions that made any realization of this vision impossible.

Frantz Fanon (fa-NOH) was born in Fort-de-France on the island of Marti-nique, then a colony and now a department of France in the Lesser Antilles island chain in the Caribbean. His father was a customs inspector of African descent, while his mother, a woman of means, was of mixed European and African ancestry. As was common among the Afro-Caribbean middle class in French territories, they thought of themselves as French, and were well assimilated socially and linguistically into the island's French culture. Since they were economically comfortable and socially aspiring, their son attended the best schools on the island. One of his high school teachers happened to be Aimé Césaire, a well-known writer who strongly opposed the cultural assimilation of colonized subjects and advocated difference-affirming "Negritude." Césaire influenced the young Fanon powerfully, and they formed a lasting bond. From that time on Fanon became ever more convinced not only that true assimilation on a basis of genuine equality and mutual respect was an impossible dream, but also that it was not even desirable, because the dominant society and culture were themselves deeply flawed.

The racism of the French, from which Fanon had been protected in his early life, was a case in point. Césaire drew his attention to it, and events on Martinique after France fell to the Germans in 1940 underscored it: the Vichy French naval forces who found themselves blockaded there established a governing authority that tolerated abusive behavior by the French military personnel and dealt unfairly and harshly with the Afro-Caribbean population. At 18, Fanon managed to escape from the island. He joined the Free French army in North Africa, and soon was in France fighting to expel the Germans. Wounded in a battle in 1944, he was awarded a military decoration. However, the many instances of racist treatment that he and his fellow Afro-Caribbean soldiers experienced while their units were in France increasingly embittered him.

After the war Fanon returned briefly to Martinique to finish his secondary education. While there he reconnected with Césaire, and helped in Césaire's successful campaign (as a Communist) for a seat representing Martinique in the new French National Assembly. He then went to France for a university education, moving from Paris to Lyon to pursue a degree in medicine. He also studied literature and philosophy (attending lectures by MAURICE MERLEAU-PONTY, among others). In 1951 he qualified to practice as a psychiatrist; and to his dismay and further disillusionment, he found as much blatant institutional as well as interpersonal racism in that field as elsewhere in French society.

Fanon's philosophical studies at Lyon included extensive readings in Marx, HEGEL, phenomenology, and existential philosophy (SARTRE in particular); and he drew on these philosophical resources as his own thinking developed. An early result was a manuscript he titled "Essay on the Disalienation of the Black," which he hoped to use as his doctoral dissertation. Although he was not allowed to do so, a revised version became his first book, *Black Skin, White Masks*. The revision reflects the influence of his residency supervisor, the psychiatrist François Tosquelles, who emphasized the significance of culture in psychopathology. It is the most richly and interestingly philosophical of his books, and the longer of the selections below consists of excerpts from it.

Following his residency Fanon practiced psychiatry for a year in France, and then sought and obtained a position at a psychiatric hospital in Blida, Algeria. He began serving as its chief of service in 1953. In late 1954, the Algerian revolution began, and soon thereafter Fanon joined the Algerian National Liberation Front (Front de Libération Nationale, or FLN). He resigned from the hospital in 1956, unable to reconcile himself to

treating not only the victims of torture by the French forces attempting to suppress the revolution but also their torturers (some of whom were psychologically stressed by what they were doing), to whose activities he was profoundly opposed. (His letter of resignation appears in *Toward the African Revolution* [1964], a posthumously published collection of his activist essays.) He then joined the revolutionaries, and was deported from Algeria in January 1957.

Following his expulsion, Fanon resided for the most part in Tunisia, doing what he could in support of the cause of Algerian independence from French colonial rule. In 1960 the fledgling Algerian provisional government made him ambassador to Ghana (one of its most important supporters). While there, he was diagnosed with leukemia. He devoted his remaining time and strength, in steadily worsening health, to writing his polemic against colonialism, *The Wretched of the Earth*, living just long enough to know of its publication. He had been persuaded very late in his illness that his only hope was to obtain treatment in a country he despised: in October 1961 he arrived at the National Institutes of Health in Bethesda, Maryland (rather ironically, escorted and assisted by a CIA case officer). He died just two months later. He was survived by his French wife, Josie, whom he married in 1952; their son; and a daughter from an earlier relationship.

Fanon's published work thus was the issue of a single fraught decade. It nonetheless constitutes a significant achievement and contribution to the interpretive tradition. His book *Black Skin* is a classic of Africana phenomenology, existential psychology, postcolonial studies, and critical race theory. It explores how colonization, at least as exemplified in the French world of Fanon's experience, results in the inauthentic striving of the colonized to be what they are not: in this case, French and white. At the same time it also seeks an alternative to the no less inauthentic determination to suppose that the truth of the matter is that they are simply Afro-Caribbean and black.

In *Black Skin* Fanon attempts a form of consciousness-raising, aimed both at the subjects of colonization who strive to replicate the colonizers and at those within the culture who ridicule them for trying to rise above their station. Each group is operating without an understanding of the dynamics and consequences of colonization, and each suffers from what Sartre calls "bad faith." Those among the colonized population who aspire to be French can never be French enough and so are humiliated, believing themselves to be less than human. For them, being fully human is identified with being French, European, white. And by disparaging those who strive to acquire Western education, manners, and language, cynical fellow subjects of colonization perform the task of the colonizer, reaffirming that no matter what airs they put on, colonized subjects will still be less than human. Fanon's aim is to help the colonized understand this situation and recognize that the operating image of "being human" is a tool of the colonial power.

Fanon here is obviously offering a critical depiction of the colonizers' racism (both overt and covert) and inhuman behavior, together with a phenomenological and psychological analysis of their effects. But he also is challenging the humanism of classical liberalism insofar as it retains a single standard of human rationality, experience, and value. Sartre, in *Anti-Semite and Jew* (1946), had similarly criticized the liberal (and anti-anti-Semite) who calls for assimilation of Jews under the banner of universal humanity and thereby hinders the development of a conception of authentic ways of being Jewish. But Fanon differentiates his analysis of racism from Sartre's analysis of anti-Semitism, because in the dynamic he is discussing blacks are reduced to the "absolute density" of their racial identity—an identity entirely immanent and immutable—not only in the eyes and at the hands of whites but also (derivatively) in their own attained "black conscious-

ness." The result of combining such an identity with an unattainable ideal is shame and self-loathing, which Fanon discusses in psychoanalytic terms as an "inferiority complex."

It is tempting to view Fanon's diagnosis of the insidiousness of colonialism, racism, and the pathologies to which they give rise as pointing the way toward a new humanism. But because he is intent on radically problematizing traditional European humanism, he expresses his own differently humanistic convictions and longings in other language. So he says in his introduction to *Black Skin* (included in the excerpts from it below) that he is not attempting in the book to "shape the iron" of a new identity and ideal, but rather is merely stoking the fire to make possible the revolutionary act of the invention of "new values" (a phrase of NIETZSCHE's, whom he invokes). Yet his project here of the "disalienation" of the black man has a profoundly practical aim. Beyond consciousness-raising, Fanon aspires to redirect the efforts of colonized peoples into action to get at "the real source of the conflict—that is, toward the social structures" of the colonial order—and to achieve their transformation. Here one hears an echo of the last of Marx's "Theses on Feuerbach" (see above): "The philosophers have only interpreted the world in various ways; the point is to change it."

Fanon's *The Wretched of the Earth* has a very different sort of agenda, sensibility, and temperament, and it has had considerable influence on revolutionary thinking—both theoretical and practical— around the world. It ends with a call to "reexamine the question of man"—and to do so from a non-Eurocentric perspective, in order to "make a new start, develop a new way of thinking, and endeavor to create a new man" to replace the "European" versions that Fanon deemed fatally flawed, as well as the alternatives offered (such as that of the colonial subject). The middle chapters attempt a kind of sociology of revolutionary groups and of national identity. Infused with Marxian terminology, this discussion invites comparison with Sartre's *Critique of Dialectical Reason* (2 vols., 1960–85) and its logic of revolutionary collectives. But it is the opening long chapter (excerpted below), in which Fanon addresses the subject of violence in situations like that of colonial oppression, that has made this work so appealing and compelling to many.

Fanon can easily be read here— and often is, by both admirers and detractors—as legitimizing, advocating, and even celebrating violence against oppressor populations as not only practically but also spiritually liberating. That reading is supported by Sartre's famous preface to the book, which is itself something of a paean to violence: "Offspring of violence," Sartre writes of Fanon's "new man," "he draws every moment of his humanity from it" and thus is "a man of higher quality" than "we" are. But while this may be the later Sartre's own view, it conflates Fanon's idea of a possible postcolonial new humanity with his portrait of the self-liberating dehumanized colonial subject and his assessment of what the decolonization process requires, both socially and psychologically, given the human consequences of how the colonial system was established and how it functions. He does take the position, however, disturbingly but unflinchingly, that the fundamental principle that all human subjects are deserving of respect does not rule out doing violence to them, even if they have committed no overt acts of violence against specific others and show no signs of being so inclined. Respect and respectful treatment, for Fanon, have a mutuality requirement. Those who disrespect others, as individuals or as a group, deserve no respect from them—and if they are active *or complicit* in the blighting of the lives of the disrespected, the (violent) blighting of their own lives by those who have been disrespected and blighted is their just desert. Marx would seem to have reasoned similarly.

From Fanon's perspective, and perhaps from any objective one, colonialization was a crime against humanity comparable to slavery and other such atrocities perpetrated by some human beings upon others. An important reason that his work continues to resonate today is that some see variants of the dynamic and phenomenology that he discerns in colonialism in many other arenas and phenomena in the postcolonial world. There is a kind of progression of scope in Fanon's thought. Starting from the perspective of Martinique and its relation to France, he brought his analytical and critical attention to bear on Algeria, then on all the French colonies, subsequently on the continent of Africa, on the colonized world as a whole, and ultimately on the system of global capitalism itself—the culmination, in his eyes, of what "Europe" and its American extension came to mean to him.

Fanon's revolutionary passion, like Marx's, developed out of the depth of his commitment to his humanistic convictions regarding the respect and opportunity to flourish authentically that human beings equally deserve and owe each other—and out of his outrage upon becoming increasingly and vividly aware of the barriers that have been erected to deny that respect and opportunity to so much of humanity. His passion was channeled—again, as in Marx's case— into a determination to do whatever it will take to sweep away those barriers, undo their damage, and make it possible for a new humanity to emerge that would have a better chance than now exists to make human flourishing the general rule. Fanon's own humanity is very much in evidence in *Black Skin* (as is Marx's in his early writings). It may still animate his thinking in *Wretched of the Earth*, whose difficult circumstances of composition must be kept in mind. But it may also have changed in the intervening years, as his life certainly had.

Fanon's conclusion to that book—his last words on the subject—makes clear his ultimate repudiation of the Western world, its values, and its version of humanity, calling for their rejection in favor of the attempt "to create a new man" and to "start over a new history of man." The difficult question this raises, even for those who share his concerns, is whether the practical outcome of so radical a preparatory housecleaning can be counted on to be anything more than a dehumanized humanity—without the resources and aspiration to rehumanize itself—that even he would not recognize and deem deserving of respect. Fanon must have faced this question, and his actions gave his answer. To reach that answer, the astute and probing author of *Black Skin* seems to have made a very considerable leap of faith.

From Black Skin, White Masks

Introduction

> *I am talking about millions of men whom they have knowingly instilled with fear and a complex of inferiority, whom they have infused with despair and trained to tremble, to kneel and behave like flunkeys.*

—A. Césaire, *Discourse on Colonialism*[1]

Don't expect to see any explosion today. It's too early . . . or too late.

I'm not the bearer of absolute truths.

No fundamental inspiration has flashed across my mind.

I honestly think, however, it's time some things were said.

Things I'm going to say, not shout. I've long given up shouting.

A long time ago . . .

Why am I writing this book? Nobody asked me to.

Especially not those for whom it is intended.

So? So in all serenity my answer is that there are too many idiots on this earth. And now that I've said it, I have to prove it.

Striving for a New Humanism.

Understanding Mankind.

Our Black Brothers.

I believe in you, Man.

Racial Prejudice.

Understanding and Loving.

I'm bombarded from all sides with hundreds of lines that try to foist themselves on me. A single line, however, would be enough. All it needs is one simple answer and the black question would lose all relevance.

What does man want?

What does the black man want?

---

1. An essay first published in 1950 (*Discours sur le colonialisme*) by Aimé Césaire (1913–2008), poet and politician of Martinique, Fanon's native island in the French Caribbean. He was a critic of colonialism, one of the founders of the Negritude movement (which opposed French colonial rule and celebrated the distinctiveness of "blackness" and of African heritage), and Fanon's early teacher, inspiration, and mentor.

Running the risk of angering my black brothers, I shall say that a Black is not a man.

There is a zone of nonbeing, an extraordinarily sterile and arid region, an incline stripped bare of every essential from which a genuine new departure can emerge. In most cases, the black man cannot take advantage of this descent into a veritable hell.

Man is not only the potential for self-consciousness or negation.[2] If it be true that consciousness is transcendental, we must also realize that this transcendence is obsessed with the issue of love and understanding. Man is a "yes" resonating from cosmic harmonies. Uprooted, dispersed, dazed, and doomed to watch as the truths he has elaborated vanish one by one, he must stop projecting his antinomy into the world.

Blacks are men who are black; in other words, owing to a series of affective disorders they have settled into a universe from which we have to extricate them.

The issue is paramount. We are aiming at nothing less than to liberate the black man from himself.[3] We shall tread very carefully, for there are two camps: white and black.

We shall inquire persistently into both metaphysics and we shall see that they are often highly destructive.

We shall show no pity for the former colonial governors or missionaries. In our view, an individual who loves Blacks is as "sick" as someone who abhors them.

Conversely, the black man who strives to whiten his race is as wretched as the one who preaches hatred of the white man.

The black man is no more inherently amiable than the Czech; the truth is that we must unleash the man.

This book should have been written three years ago. But at the time the truths made our blood boil. Today the fever has dropped and truths can be said without having them hurled into people's faces. They are not intended to endorse zealousness. We are wary of being zealous.

Every time we have seen it hatched somewhere it has been an omen of fire, famine, and poverty, as well as contempt for man.

Zealousness is the arm par excellence of the powerless. Those who heat the iron to hammer it immediately into a tool. We would like to heat the carcass of man and leave. Perhaps this would result in Man's keeping the fire burning by self-combustion.

Man freed from the springboard embodying the resistance of others and digging into his flesh in order to find self-meaning.

Only some of you will guess how difficult it was to write this book.

In an age of skepticism when, according to a group of *salauds*,[4] sense can no longer be distinguished from nonsense, it becomes arduous to

2. Fanon is using the language of SARTRE's account of human reality in *Being and Nothingness* (1943; see above).
3. That is, from a demeaning interpretation of himself imposed by whites.
4. "Salaud" is what Sartre abusively calls someone

who refuses to take responsibility for his acts and demonstrates his bad faith, a form of self-deception, a denial of human freedom, and an abdication of responsibility toward oneself and others [translator's note]. The term *salaud* is best translated as something like "bastard" (as a derogative).

descend to a level where the categories of sense and nonsense are not yet in use.

The black man wants to be white. The white man is desperately trying to achieve the rank of man.

This essay will attempt to understand the Black-White relationship.

The white man is locked in his whiteness.

The black man in his blackness.

We shall endeavor to determine the tendencies of this double narcissism and the motivations behind it.

At the beginning of our reflections it seemed inappropriate to clarify our conclusions.

Our sole concern was to put an end to a vicious cycle.

Fact: some Whites consider themselves superior to Blacks.

Another fact: some Blacks want to prove at all costs to the Whites the wealth of the black man's intellect and equal intelligence.

How can we break the cycle?

We have just used the word "narcissism." We believe, in fact, that only a psychoanalytic interpretation of the black problem can reveal the affective disorders responsible for this network of complexes. We are aiming for a complete lysis of this morbid universe. We believe that an individual must endeavor to assume the universalism inherent in the human condition. And in this regard, we are thinking equally of men like Gobineau or women like Mayotte Capécia.[5] But in order to apprehend this we urgently need to rid ourselves of a series of defects inherited from childhood.

Man's misfortune, Nietzsche said, was that he was once a child.[6] Nevertheless, we can never forget, as Charles Odier[7] implies, that the fate of the neurotic lies in his own hands.

As painful as it is for us to have to say this: there is but one destiny for the black man. And it is white.

Before opening the proceedings, we would like to say a few things. The analysis we are undertaking is psychological. It remains, nevertheless, evident that for us the true disalienation of the black man[8] implies a brutal awareness of the social and economic realities. The inferiority complex can be ascribed to a double process:

First, economic.

Then, internalization or rather epidermalization of this inferiority.

Reacting against the constitutionalizing trend at the end of the nineteenth century, Freud[9] demanded that the individual factor be taken into account in psychoanalysis. He replaced the phylogenetic theory by an ontogenetic approach. We shall see that the alienation of the black man is not an indi-

5. Francophone novelist from Martinique (1916–1955), author of *I Am a Martinican Woman* (1948) and *The White Negress* (1950). Joseph-Arthur, comte de Gobineau (1816–1862), French diplomat and writer, best known for the racist theory of racial determinism set forth in *Essay on the Inequality of Human Races* (4 vols., 1853–55).

6. For FRIEDRICH NIETZSCHE, see above.
7. Swiss psychoanalyst (1886–1954).
8. A phrase that describes the project of this book, which in its initial version was titled "Essay on the Disalienation of the Black."
9. Sigmund Freud (1856–1939), Austrian founder of psychoanalysis.

vidual question. Alongside phylogeny and ontogeny, there is also sociogeny.[1] In a way, in answer to the wishes of Leconte and Damey,[2] let us say that here it is a question of sociodiagnostics.

What is the prognosis?

Society, unlike biochemical processes, does not escape human influence. Man is what brings society into being. The prognosis is in the hands of those who are prepared to shake the worm-eaten foundations of the edifice.

The black man must wage the struggle on two levels: whereas historically these levels are mutually dependent, any unilateral liberation is flawed, and the worst mistake would be to believe their mutual dependence automatic. Moreover, such a systematic trend goes against the facts. We will demonstrate this.

For once, reality requires total comprehension. An answer must be found on the objective as well as the subjective level.

And there's no point sidling up crabwise with a mea culpa look, insisting it's a matter of salvation of the soul.

Genuine disalienation will have been achieved only when things, in the most materialist sense, have resumed their rightful place.

It is considered appropriate to preface a work on psychology with a methodology. We shall break with tradition. We leave methods to the botanists and mathematicians. There is a point where methods are resorbed.[3]

That is where we would like to position ourselves. We shall attempt to discover the various mental attitudes the black man adopts in the face of white civilization.

The "savage" will not be included here. Certain elements have not yet had enough impact on him.

We believe the juxtaposition of the black and white races has resulted in a massive psycho-existential complex. By analyzing it we aim to destroy it.[4]

Many Blacks will not recognize themselves in the following pages.

Likewise many Whites.

But the fact that I feel alien to the world of the schizophrenic or of the sexually impotent in no way diminishes their reality.

The attitudes I propose describing are true. I have found them any number of times.

I identified the same aggressiveness and passivity in students, workers, and the pimps of Pigalle or Marseille.[5]

This book is a clinical study. Those who recognize themselves in it will, I believe, have made a step in the right direction. My true wish is to get my brother, black or white, to shake off the dust from that lamentable livery built up over centuries of incomprehension.

The structure of the present work is grounded in temporality. Every human problem cries out to be considered on the basis of time, the ideal being that the present always serves to build the future.

---

1. The origin and development of society.
2. M. Leconte and A. Damey, "Essai critique des nosographies psychiatriques actuelles" [Fanon's note]. *Critical Essay on Current Practices of Naming Psychiatric Phenomena* (1949), by Maurice Leconte and Alfred Damey.

3. That is, dissolved and assimilated (biology).
4. This paragraph expresses both Fanon's conception of the nature of the problem and his practical and intellectual project.
5. Port city in southern France. Pigalle: a neighborhood in Paris.

And this future is not that of the cosmos, but very much the future of my century, my country, and my existence. In no way is it up to me to prepare for the world coming after me. I am resolutely a man of my time.

And that is my reason for living. The future must be a construction supported by man in the present. This future edifice is linked to the present insofar as I consider the present something to be overtaken.

The first three chapters deal with the black man in modern times. I take the contemporary black man and endeavor to determine his attitudes in a white world. The last two chapters focus on an attempt to explain psychopathologically and philosophically the *being* of the black man.

The analysis is above all regressive.

The fourth and fifth chapters are situated at a fundamentally different level.

In the fourth chapter, I make a critical study of a book[6] that I consider dangerous. Moreover, the author, O. Mannoni, is aware of the ambiguity of his position. There lies perhaps one of the merits of his testimony. He has attempted to give an account of a situation. We are entitled to be dissatisfied with it. It is our duty to convey to the author the instances in which we disagree with him.

The fifth chapter, which I have called "The Lived Experience of the Black Man," is important for more than one reason. It shows the black man confronted with his race. Note that there is nothing in common between the black man in this chapter and the black man who wants to sleep with the white woman. The latter wants to be white. Or has a thirst for revenge, in any case. In this chapter, on the contrary, we are witness to the desperate efforts of a black man striving desperately to discover the meaning of black identity. White civilization and European culture have imposed an existential deviation on the black man. We shall demonstrate furthermore that what is called the black soul is a construction by white folk.

The educated black man, slave of the myth of the spontaneous and cosmic Negro, feels at some point in time that his race no longer understands him.

Or that he no longer understands his race.

He is only too pleased about this, and by developing further this difference, this incomprehension and discord, he discovers the meaning of his true humanity. Less commonly he wants to feel a part of his people. And with feverish lips and frenzied heart he plunges into the great black hole. We shall see that this wonderfully generous attitude rejects the present and future in the name of a mystical past.

As those of an Antillean, our observations and conclusions are valid only for the French Antilles[7]—at least regarding the black man *on his home territory*. A study needs to be made to explain the differences between Antilleans and Africans. One day perhaps we shall conduct such a study. Perhaps it will no longer be necessary, in which case we can but have reason for applause.

---

6. O. Mannoni, *Psychologie de la colonisation* (*Prospero and Caliban: The Psychology of Colonization*), Éditions du Seuil, 1950 [Fanon's note]. Dominique-Octave Mannoni (1899–1989), French psychoanalyst. Fanon's chapter 4, "The So-Called Dependency Complex of the Colonized," is not included here.

7. The islands in the Caribbean (including Martinique) that are overseas departments of France.

From *Chapter One*
The Black Man and Language

We attach a fundamental importance to the phenomenon of language and consequently consider the study of language essential for providing us with one element in understanding the black man's dimension of being-for-others,[7] it being understood that to speak is to exist absolutely for the other.

The black man possesses two dimensions: one with his fellow Blacks, the other with the Whites. A black man behaves differently with a white man than he does with another black man. There is no doubt whatsoever that this fissiparousness[8] is a direct consequence of the colonial undertaking. Nobody dreams of challenging the fact that its principal inspiration is nurtured by the core of theories which represent the black man as the missing link in the slow evolution from ape to man. These are objective facts that state reality.

But once we have taken note of the situation, once we have understood it, we consider the job done. How can we possibly not hear that voice again tumbling down the steps of History: "It's no longer a question of knowing the world, but of transforming it."[9]

This question is terribly present in our lives.

To speak means being able to use a certain syntax and possessing the morphology of such and such a language, but it means above all assuming a culture and bearing the weight of a civilization.

Since the situation is not one-sided, the study should reflect this. We would very much like to be given credit for certain points that, however unacceptable they may appear early on, will prove to be factually accurate.

The problem we shall tackle in this chapter is as follows: the more the black Antillean assimilates the French language, the whiter he gets—i.e., the closer he comes to becoming a true human being. We are fully aware that this is one of man's attitudes faced with Being. A man who possesses a language possesses as an indirect consequence the world expressed and implied by this language. You can see what we are driving at: there is an extraordinary power in the possession of a language. Paul Valéry knew this, and described language as "The god gone astray in the flesh."[1]

In a work in progress[2] we propose to study this phenomenon. For the time being we would like to demonstrate why the black Antillean, whoever he is, always has to justify his stance in relation to language. Going one step farther, we shall enlarge the scope of our description to include every colonized subject.

All colonized people—in other words, people in whom an inferiority complex has taken root, whose local cultural originality has been committed to the grave—position themselves in relation to the civilizing language: i.e.,

---

7. One of the dimensions of human reality identified and analyzed by Sartre in *Being and Nothingness*.
8. Tendency to divide.
9. A paraphrase of the last of MARX's twelve "Theses on Feuerbach" (written 1845; see above), which Fanon echoes in his introduction (see especially the text at p. 514, n. 4).

1. *Charmes*, "La Pythie" ["The Pythia"; Fanon's note]. Valéry (1871–1945), French critic and poet. *Charms* was published in 1922; the Pythia was the god Apollo's oracle at Delphi.
2. "Language and Aggressiveness" [Fanon's note]. No writings connected with this study have been found.

the metropolitan culture. The more the colonized has assimilated the cultural values of the metropolis, the more he will have escaped the bush.[3] The more he rejects his blackness and the bush, the whiter he will become. In the colonial army, and particularly in the regiments of Senégalese soldiers, the "native" officers are mainly interpreters. They serve to convey to their fellow soldiers the master's orders, and they themselves enjoy a certain status.

There is the town, there is the country. There is the capital, there are the provinces. Apparently, the problem is the same. Take an inhabitant of Lyon in Paris. He will boast of how calm his city is, how bewitchingly beautiful are the banks of the Rhône, how magnificent are the plane trees, and so many other things that people with nothing to do like to go on about. If you meet him on his return from Paris, and especially if you've never been to the capital, he'll never stop singing its praises: Paris, City of Light; the Seine; the riverside dance cafés; see Paris and die.[4]

* * *

There is a dramatic conflict in what is commonly called the human sciences. Should we postulate a typical human reality and describe its psychic modalities, taking into account only the imperfections, or should we not rather make a constant, solid endeavor to understand man in an ever-changing light?

When we read that a man loses his affective faculties starting at the age of twenty-nine and he has to wait until he is forty-nine to regain them, we feel the ground give way beneath our feet. Our only hope[5] of getting out of the situation is to pose the problem correctly, for all these findings and all this research have a single aim: to get man to admit he is nothing, absolutely nothing—and get him to eradicate this narcissism whereby he thinks he is different from the other "animals."

This is nothing more nor less than the *capitulation of man*.

All in all, I grasp my narcissism with both hands and I reject the vileness of those who want to turn man into a machine. If the debate cannot be opened up on a philosophical level—i.e., the fundamental demands of human reality—I agree to place it on a psychoanalytical level: in other words, it "misfires,"[6] just as we talk about an engine misfiring.

* * *

We have said that the black man was the missing link between the ape and man—the white man, of course—and only on page 108 of his book[7] does Sir Alan Burns come to the conclusion, "We are unable to accept as scientifically proven the theory that the black man is inherently inferior to the white, or that he comes from a different stock." Let us add it would be easy to prove the absurdity of such statements as: "The Bible says that the black and white races shall be separated in Heaven as they are on earth, and the natives admitted to the Kingdom of Heaven will find themselves separated to certain of

---

3. The back country.
4. A famous saying, whose point is that nothing is left to experience after one sees the glories of Paris.
5. That is, the only hope according to the received wisdom that Fanon is challenging.

6. That is, the debate misfires.
7. *Colour Prejudice* (London: Allen and Unwin, 1948), just cited by Fanon in a passage omitted here. Burns (1887–1980), British colonial governor (mainly in African posts) and historian.

our Father's mansions mentioned in the New Testament." Or else: "We are the chosen people; look at the color of our skin; others are black or yellow because of their sins."

By appealing, therefore, to our humanity—to our feelings of dignity, love, and charity—it would be easy to prove and have acknowledged that the black man is equal to the white man. But that is not our purpose. What we are striving for is to liberate the black man from the arsenal of complexes that germinated in a colonial situation.

* * *

From Chapter Five
The Lived Experience of the Black Man

"Dirty nigger!" or simply "Look! A Negro!"

I came into this world anxious to uncover the meaning of things, my soul desirous to be at the origin of the world, and here I am an object among other objects.

Locked in this suffocating reification, I appealed to the Other so that his liberating gaze, gliding over my body suddenly smoothed of rough edges, would give me back the lightness of being I thought I had lost, and taking me out of the world put me back in the world. But just as I get to the other slope I stumble, and the Other fixes me with his gaze, his gestures and attitude, the same way you fix a preparation with a dye.[8] I lose my temper, demand an explanation. . . . Nothing doing. I explode. Here are the fragments put together by another me.

As long as the black man remains on his home territory, except for petty internal quarrels, he will not have to experience his being for others. There is in fact a "being for other," as described by Hegel, but any ontology is made impossible in a colonized and acculturated society. Apparently, those who have written on the subject have not taken this sufficiently into consideration. In the weltanschauung of a colonized people, there is an impurity or a flaw that prohibits any ontological explanation. Perhaps it could be argued that this is true for any individual, but such an argument would be concealing the basic problem. Ontology does not allow us to understand the being of the black man, since it ignores the lived experience. For not only must the black man be black; he must be black in relation to the white man.[9] Some people will argue that the situation has a double meaning. Not at all. The black man has no ontological resistance in the eyes of the white man. From one day to the next, the Blacks have had to deal with two systems of reference. Their metaphysics, or less pretentiously their customs and the agencies to which they refer, were abolished because they were in contradiction with a new civilization that imposed its own.

In the twentieth century the black man on his home territory is oblivious of the moment when his inferiority is determined by the Other. Naturally, we

8. Fanon here is drawing mainly on Sartre (specifically, Being and Nothingness), supplemented by ideas from HEGEL and Marx.

9. A key point, because it means that for Fanon "the being of the black man" is not unalterable.

have had the opportunity to discuss the black problem with friends and, less often, with African-Americans. Together we proclaimed loud and clear the equality of man in the world. In the Antilles there is also that minor tension between the cliques of white Creoles, Mulattoes,[1] and Blacks. But we were content to intellectualize these differences. In fact, there was nothing dramatic about them. And then . . .

And then we were given the occasion to confront the white gaze. An unusual weight descended on us. The real world robbed us of our share. In the white world, the man of color encounters difficulties in elaborating his body schema. The image of one's body is solely negating. It's an image in the third person. All around the body reigns an atmosphere of certain uncertainty. I know that if I want to smoke, I shall have to stretch out my right arm and grab the pack of cigarettes lying at the other end of the table. As for the matches, they are in the left drawer, and I shall have to move back a little. And I make all these moves, not out of habit, but by implicit knowledge. A slow construction of my self as a body in a spatial and temporal world—such seems to be the schema. It is not imposed on me; it is rather a definitive structuring of my self and the world—definitive because it creates a genuine dialectic between my body and the world.[2]

For some years now, certain laboratories have been researching for a "denegrification" serum. In all seriousness they have been rinsing out their test tubes and adjusting their scales and have begun research on how the wretched black man could whiten himself and thus rid himself of the burden of this bodily curse. Beneath the body schema I had created a historical-racial schema. The data I used were provided not by "remnants of feelings and notions of the tactile, vestibular, kinesthetic, or visual nature"[3] but by the Other, the white man, who had woven me out of a thousand details, anecdotes, and stories. I thought I was being asked to construct a physiological self, to balance space and localize sensations, when all the time they were clamoring for more.

"Look! A Negro!" It was a passing sting. I attempted a smile.

"Look! A Negro!" Absolutely. I was beginning to enjoy myself.

"Look! A Negro!" The circle was gradually getting smaller. I was really enjoying myself.

"Maman,[4] look, a Negro; I'm scared!" Scared! Scared! Now they were beginning to be scared of me. I wanted to kill myself laughing, but laughter had become out of the question.

I couldn't take it any longer, for I already knew there were legends, stories, history, and especially the *historicity* that Jaspers[5] had taught me. As a result, the body schema, attacked in several places, collapsed, giving way to an epidermal racial schema. In the train, it was a question of being aware of my body, no longer in the third person but in triple. In the train, instead of one seat, they left me two or three. I was no longer enjoying myself. I was unable to discover the feverish coordinates of the world. I existed in triple: I was tak-

---

1. Individuals of mixed black and European parentage. "Creoles": descendants of French settlers, who speak a language derived from but distinct from French.
2. That is, to change the construction of the self, the "dialectic" must be changed.

3. Jean Lhermitte, *L'image de notre corps* [*The Image of Our Body*], Éditions de la Nouvelle Revue Critique [Paris, 1939], p. 17 [Fanon's note].
4. Mama (French).
5. For KARL JASPERS, see above.

ing up room. I approached the Other . . . and the Other, evasive, hostile, but not opaque, transparent and absent, vanished. Nausea.[6]

I was responsible not only for my body but also for my race and my ancestors. I cast an objective gaze over myself, discovered my blackness, my ethnic features; deafened by cannibalism, backwardness, fetishism, racial stigmas, slave traders, and above all, yes, above all, the grinning *Y a bon Banania*.[7]

Disoriented, incapable of confronting the Other, the white man, who had no scruples about imprisoning me, I transported myself on that particular day far, very far, from myself, and gave myself up as an object. What did this mean to me? Peeling, stripping my skin, causing a hemorrhage that left congealed black blood all over my body. Yet this reconsideration of myself, this thematization, was not my idea. I wanted quite simply to be a man among men. I would have liked to enter our world young and sleek, a world we could build together.

I refused, however, any affective tetanization.[8] I wanted to be a man, and nothing but a man. There were some who wanted to equate me with my ancestors, enslaved and lynched: I decided that I would accept this. I considered this internal kinship from the universal level of the intellect—I was the grandson of slaves the same way President Lebrun[9] was the grandson of peasants who had been exploited and worked to the bone.

The alert was soon over, in fact.

In the United States, Blacks are segregated. In South America, they are whipped in the streets and black strikers are gunned down. In West Africa, the black man is a beast of burden. And just beside me there is this student colleague of mine from Algeria who tells me, "As long as the Arab is treated like a man, like one of us, there will be no viable answer."

"You see, my dear fellow, color prejudice is totally foreign to me." "But do come in, old chap, you won't find any color prejudice here." "Quite so, the Black is just as much a man as we are." "It's not because he's black that he's less intelligent than we are." "I had a Senegalese colleague in the regiment, very smart guy."

Where do I fit in? Or, if you like, where should I stick myself?

"Martinican, a native from one of our 'old' colonies."[1]

Where should I hide?

"Look, a Negro! *Maman*, a Negro!"

"Ssh! You'll make him angry. Don't pay attention to him, monsieur, he doesn't realize you're just as civilized as we are."

My body was returned to me spread-eagled, disjointed, redone, draped in mourning on this white winter's day. The Negro is an animal, the Negro is bad, the Negro is wicked, the Negro is ugly; look, a Negro; the Negro is trembling, the Negro is trembling because he's cold, the small boy is trembling because

6. A reference to Sartre's novel *Nausea* (1938) and to the experience of the world as meaningless and absurd that it explores.
7. "This is good Banania," the slogan (in invented pidgin French) used for decades to advertise the chocolate breakfast drink popular in France; its packaging featured a smiling black man (originally an Antillean).

8. That is, immunization.
9. Albert Lebrun (1871–1950), the last president of France's Third Republic (1932–40).
1. A French settlement was established in Martinique in 1635; France's newer colonies, beginning with Algeria (1830), were in Africa, Indochina, and the South Pacific.

he's afraid of the Negro, the Negro is trembling with cold, the cold that chills the bones, the lovely little boy is trembling because he thinks the Negro is trembling with rage, the little white boy runs to his mother's arms: "*Maman*, the Negro's going to eat me."

The white man is all around me; up above the sky is tearing at its navel; the earth crunches under my feet and sings white, white. All this whiteness burns me to a cinder.

I sit down next to the fire and discover my livery for the first time. It is in fact ugly. I won't go on because who can tell me what beauty is?

Where should I put myself from now on? I can feel that familiar rush of blood surge up from the numerous dispersions of my being. I am about to lose my temper. The fire had died a long time ago, and once again the Negro is trembling.

"Look how handsome that Negro is."

"The handsome Negro says, 'Fuck you,' madame."

Her face colored with shame. At last I was freed from my rumination. I realized two things at once: I had identified the enemy and created a scandal. Overjoyed. We could now have some fun.

The battlefield had been drawn up; I could enter the lists.[2]

I don't believe it! Whereas I was prepared to forget, to forgive, and to love, my message was flung back at me like a slap in the face. The white world, the only decent one, was preventing me from participating. It demanded that a man behave like a man. It demanded of me that I behave like a black man— or at least like a Negro. I hailed the world, and the world amputated my enthusiasm. I was expected to stay in line and make myself scarce.

I'll show them! They can't say I didn't warn them. Slavery? No longer a subject of discussion, just a bad memory. My so-called inferiority? A hoax that it would be better to laugh about. I was prepared to forget everything, provided the world integrated me. My incisors were ready to go into action. I could feel them, sharp. And then . . .

I don't believe it! Whereas I had every reason to vent my hatred and loathing, they were rejecting me? Whereas I was the one they should have begged and implored, I was denied the slightest recognition? I made up my mind, since it was impossible to rid myself of an *innate complex*, to assert myself as a BLACK MAN. Since the Other was reluctant to recognize me, there was only one answer: to make myself known.

In *Anti-Semite and Jew*[3] Sartre writes: "They [the Jews] have allowed themselves to be poisoned by the stereotype that others have of them, and they live in fear that their acts will correspond to this stereotype. . . . We may say that their conduct is perpetually overdetermined from the inside" (p. 95).

The Jewishness of the Jew, however, can go unnoticed. He is not integrally what he is. We can but hope and wait. His acts and behavior are the determining factor. He is a white man, and apart from some debatable features, he can pass undetected. He belongs to the race that has never practiced cannibalism. What a strange idea, to eat one's father! Serves them right; they

---

2. The arena of combat.
3. Published in 1946; the quotation is from

George J. Becker's translation (New York: Schocken, 1948).

shouldn't be black. Of course the Jews have been tormented—what am I say-ing? They have been hunted, exterminated, and cremated, but these are just minor episodes in the family history. The Jew is not liked as soon as he has been detected. But with me things take on a *new* face. I'm not given a second chance. I am overdetermined from the outside. I am a slave not to the "idea" others have of me, but to my appearance.

I arrive slowly in the world; sudden emergences are no longer my habit. I crawl along. The white gaze, the only valid one, is already dissecting me. I am *fixed*. Once their microtomes are sharpened, the Whites objectively cut sec-tions of my reality. I have been betrayed. I sense, I see in this white gaze that it's the arrival not of a new man, but of a new type of man, a new species. A Negro, in fact!

* * *

The proof was there, implacable. My blackness was there, dense and undeni-able. And it tormented me, pursued me, made me uneasy, and exasperated me.

Negroes are savages, morons, and illiterates. But I knew personally that in my case these assertions were wrong. There was this myth of the Negro that had to be destroyed at all costs. We were no longer living in an age when people marveled at a black priest. We had doctors, teachers, and statesmen. OK, but there was always something unusual about them. "We have a Sene-galese history teacher. He's very intelligent. . . . Our physician's black. He's very gentle."

Here was the Negro teacher, the Negro physician; as for me, I was becom-ing a nervous wreck, shaking at the slightest alert. I knew for instance that if the physician made one false move, it was over for him and for all those who came after him. What, in fact, could one expect from a Negro physician? As long as everything was going smoothly, he was praised to the heavens; but watch out—there was no room whatsoever for any mistake. The black physi-cian will never know how close he is to being discredited. I repeat, I was walled in: neither my refined manners nor my literary knowledge nor my understand-ing of the quantum theory could find favor.

I insisted on, I demanded an explanation. Speaking softly, as if addressing a child, they explained to me that some people have adopted a certain opin-ion, but, they added, "We can only hope it will soon disappear." And what was that? Color prejudice.

It [color prejudice] is nothing more than the unreasoning hatred of one race for another, the contempt of the stronger and richer peoples for those whom they consider inferior to themselves and the bitter resentment of those who are kept in subjection and are so frequently insulted. As colour is the most obvious outward manifestation of race it has been made the criterion by which men are judged, irrespective of their social or educational attain-ments. The light-skinned races have come to despise all those of a darker colour, and the dark-skinned peoples will no longer accept without protest the inferior position to which they have been relegated.[4]

4. Sir Alan Burns, *Colour Prejudice*, p. 16 [Fanon's note].

I was not mistaken. It was hatred; I was hated, detested, and despised, not by my next-door neighbor or a close cousin, but by an entire race. I was up against something irrational. The psychoanalysts say that there is nothing more traumatizing for a young child than contact with the rational. I personally would say that for a man armed solely with reason, there is nothing more neurotic than contact with the irrational.

I felt the knife blades sharpening within me. I made up my mind to defend myself. Like all good tacticians I wanted to rationalize the world and show the white man he was mistaken.

* * *

I had rationalized the world, and the world had rejected me in the name of color prejudice. Since there was no way we could agree on the basis of reason, I resorted to irrationality. It was up to the white man to be more irrational than I. For the sake of the cause, I had adopted the process of regression, but the fact remained that it was an unfamiliar weapon; here I am at home; I am made of the irrational; I wade in the irrational. Irrational up to my neck.

* * *

* * * Black magic, primitive mentality, animism and animal eroticism—all this surges toward me. All this typifies people who have not kept pace with the evolution of humanity. Or, if you prefer, they constitute third-rate humanity. Having reached this point, I was long reluctant to commit myself. Then even the stars became aggressive. I had to choose. What am I saying? I had no choice.

Yes, we niggers are backward, naive, and free. For us the body is not in opposition to what you call the soul. We are in the world. And long live the bond between Man and the Earth! * * *

So here we have the Negro rehabilitated, "standing at the helm," governing the world with his intuition, rediscovered, reappropriated, in demand, accepted; and it's not a Negro, oh, no, but the Negro, alerting the prolific antennae of the world, standing in the spotlight of the world, spraying the world with his poetical power, "porous to every breath in the world." I embrace the world! I am the world! The white man has never understood this magical substitution. The white man wants the world; he wants it for himself. He discovers he is the predestined master of the world. He enslaves it. His relationship with the world is one of appropriation. But there are values that can be served only with my sauce. As a magician I stole from the white man a "certain world," lost to him and his kind. When that happened the white man must have felt an aftershock he was unable to identify, being unused to such reactions. The reason was that above the objective world of plantations and banana and rubber trees, I had subtly established the real world. The essence of the world was my property. Between the world and me there was a relation of coexistence. I had rediscovered the primordial One. * * *

So here I was poet of the world. The white man had discovered poetry that had nothing poetic about it. The soul of the white man was corrupted, and as a friend who taught in the United States told me: "The Blacks represent a kind of insurance for humanity in the eyes of the Whites. When the Whites feel they have become too mechanized, they turn to the Coloreds and request a little human sustenance." At last I had been recognized; I was no longer a nonentity.

I was soon to become disillusioned. Momentarily taken aback, the white man explained to me that genetically I represented a phase. "Your distinctive qualities have been exhausted by us. We have had our back-to-nature mystics such as you will never have. Take a closer look at our history and you'll understand how far this fusion has gone." I then had the feeling things were repeating themselves. My originality had been snatched from me. I wept for a long time, and then I began to live again. But I was haunted by a series of corrosive stereotypes: the Negro's sui generis smell . . . the Negro's sui generis good nature . . . the Negro's sui generis naïveté.

I tried to escape without being seen, but the Whites fell on me and hamstrung me on the left leg. I gauged the limits of my essence; as you can guess, it was fairly meager. It was here I made my most remarkable discovery, which in actual fact was a rediscovery.

In a frenzy I excavated black antiquity. What I discovered left me speechless. In his book on the abolition of slavery Schoelcher[5] presented us with some compelling arguments. Since then, Frobenius, Westermann, and Delafosse,[6] all white men, have voiced their agreement: Segu, Djenné,[7] cities with over 100,000 inhabitants; accounts of learned black men (doctors of theology who traveled to Mecca to discuss the Koran). Once this had been dug up, displayed, and exposed to the elements, it allowed me to regain a valid historic category. The white man was wrong, I was not a primitive or a subhuman; I belonged to a race that had already been working silver and gold 2,000 years ago. * * *

I put the white man back in his place; emboldened, I jostled him and hurled in his face: accommodate me as I am; I'm not accommodating anyone. I snickered to my heart's delight. The white man was visibly growling. His reaction was a long time coming. I had won. I was overjoyed.

"Lay aside your history, your research into the past, and try to get in step with our rhythm. In a society such as ours, industrialized to the extreme, dominated by science, there is no longer room for your sensitivity. You have to be tough to be able to live. It is no longer enough to play ball with the world; you have to master it with integrals and atoms. Of course, they will tell me, from time to time when we are tired of all that concrete, we will turn to you as our children, our naive, ingenuous, and spontaneous children. We will turn to you as the childhood of the world. You are so authentic in your life, so playful. Let us forget for a few moments our formal, polite civilization and bend down over those heads, those adorable expressive faces. In a sense, you reconcile us with ourselves."

So they were countering my irrationality with rationality, my rationality with the "true rationality." I couldn't hope to win. I tested my heredity. I did a complete checkup of my sickness. I wanted to be typically black—that was out of the question. I wanted to be white—that was a joke. And when I tried to claim

5. Victor Schoelcher (1804–1893), French journalist and advocate of ending slavery in France's empire; his books on the subject include *Abolition of Slavery* (1840).
6. Maurice Delafosse (1870–1926), French ethnographer and linguist who worked in Africa in the colonial service. Leo Frobenius (1873–1938), German explorer and ethnologist. Diedrich Westermann (1875–1956), German scholar of African languages and culture.
7. An ancient city in southern Mali that was a center of Islamic scholarship. Segu: Ségou, a historic town in south-central Mali.

my negritude intellectually as a concept, they snatched it away from me. They proved to me that my reasoning was nothing but a phase in the dialectic[.]

*   *   *

In terms of consciousness, black consciousness claims to be an absolute density, full of itself, a stage preexistent to any opening, to any abolition of the self by desire. In his essay[8] Jean-Paul Sartre has destroyed black impulsiveness. He should have opposed the unforeseeable to historical destiny. I needed to lose myself totally in negritude. Perhaps one day, deep in this wretched romanticism . . .

In any case I *needed* not to know. This struggle, this descent once more, should be seen as a completed aspect. There is nothing more disagreeable than to hear: "You'll change, my boy; I was like that too when I was young. . . . You'll see, you'll get over it."

The dialectic that introduces necessity as a support for my freedom expels me from myself. It shatters my impulsive position. Still regarding consciousness, black consciousness is immanent in itself. I am not a potentiality of something; I am fully what I am. I do not have to look for the universal. There's no room for probability inside me. My black consciousness does not claim to be a loss. It *is*. It merges with itself.

*   *   *

The black man is a toy in the hands of the white man. So in order to break the vicious circle, he explodes. I can't go to the movies without encountering myself. I wait for myself. Just before the film starts, I wait for myself. Those in front of me look at me, spy on me, wait for me. A black bellhop is going to appear. My aching heart makes my head spin.

The crippled soldier from the Pacific war tells my brother: "Get used to your color the way I got used to my stump. We are both casualties."[9]

Yet, with all my being, I refuse to accept this amputation. I feel my soul as vast as the world, truly a soul as deep as the deepest of rivers; my chest has the power to expand to infinity. I was made to give and they prescribe for me the humility of the cripple. When I opened my eyes yesterday I saw the sky in total revulsion. I tried to get up but the eviscerated silence surged toward me with paralyzed wings. Not responsible for my acts, at the crossroads between Nothingness and Infinity, I began to weep.

*   *   *

8. *Black Orpheus*, cited by Fanon in a note not included here: Jean-Paul Sartre, *Orphée noir*, preface to Léopold Sédar Senghor's *Anthologie de la nouvelle poésie nègre et malgache de langue française* (1948), translated by S. W. Allen as *Black Orpheus* (Paris: Présence Africaine, 1963).
9. *Home of the Brave* [Fanon's note]. A 1949 film, directed by Mark Robson.

From *Chapter Seven*
The Black Man and Recognition

* * *

B. THE BLACK MAN AND HEGEL

Self-consciousness exists *in itself* and *for itself*, in that and by the fact that it exists for another self-consciousness; that is to say, it *is* only by being acknowledged or recognized.[1]

Man is human only to the extent to which he tries to impose himself on another man in order to be recognized by him. As long as he has not been effectively recognized by the other, it is this other who remains the focus of his actions. His human worth and reality depend on this other and on his recognition by the other. It is in this other that the meaning of his life is condensed.

There is no open conflict between White and Black.

One day the white master recognized *without a struggle* the black slave.

But the former slave wants to *have himself recognized*.

There is at the basis of Hegelian dialectic an absolute reciprocity that must be highlighted.

It is when I go beyond my immediate existential being that I apprehend the being of the other as a natural reality, and more than that. If I shut off the circuit, if I make the two-way movement unachievable, I keep the other within himself. In an extreme degree, I deprive him even of this being-for-self.

The only way to break this vicious circle that refers me back to myself is to restore to the other his human reality, different from his natural reality, by way of mediation and recognition. The other, however, must perform a similar operation. "Action from one side only would be useless, because what is to happen can only be brought about by means of both. . . . *They recognize themselves as mutually recognizing each other.*"[2]

In its immediacy, self-consciousness is simply being-for-self. In order to achieve certainty of oneself, one has to integrate the concept of recognition. Likewise, the other is waiting for our recognition so as to blossom into the universal self-consciousness. Each consciousness of self is seeking absoluteness. It wants to be recognized as an essential value outside of life, as transformation of subjective certainty (*Gewissheit*) into objective truth (*Wahrheit*).

Encountering opposition from the other, self-consciousness experiences *desire*, the first stage that leads to the dignity of the mind. It agrees to risk life, and consequently threatens the other in his physical being. "It is solely by risking life that freedom is obtained; only thus is it tried and proved that the essential nature of self-consciousness is not *bare existence*, is not the merely immediate form in which it at first makes its appearance, is not its mere absorption in the expanse of life."[3]

Only conflict and the risk it implies can, therefore, make human reality, in-itself-for-itself, come true. This risk implies that I go beyond life toward an

1. Hegel, *Phenomenology of Mind* [1807; Fanon's note].
2. G. W. F. Hegel, *The Phenomenology of Mind*, translated by J. B. Baillie, 2nd rev. ed., Allen and Unwin, 1949, pp. 230, 231 [translator's note].
3. Ibid., p. 233 [translator's note].

ideal which is the transformation of subjective certainty of my own worth into a universally valid objective truth.

I ask that I be taken into consideration on the basis of my desire. I am not only here-now, locked in thinghood. I desire somewhere else and something else. I demand that an account be taken of my contradictory activity insofar as I pursue something other than life, insofar as I am fighting for the birth of a human world, in other words, a world of reciprocal recognitions.

He who is reluctant to recognize me is against me. In a fierce struggle I am willing to feel the shudder of death, the irreversible extinction, but also the possibility of impossibility.

* * *

The I posits itself by opposing, said Fichte.[4] Yes and no.

We said in our introduction that man was an *affirmation*. We shall never stop repeating it.

Yes to life. Yes to love. Yes to generosity.

But man is also a *negation*. No to man's contempt. No to the indignity of man. To the exploitation of man. To the massacre of what is most human in man: freedom.

Man's behavior is not only reactional. And there is always resentment in *reaction*. Nietzsche had already said it in *The Will to Power*.[5]

To induce man to be *actional*, by maintaining in his circularity the respect of the fundamental values that make the world human, that is the task of utmost urgency for he who, after careful reflection, prepares to act.

Chapter Eight
By Way of Conclusion

The social revolution cannot draw its poetry from the past, but only from the future. It cannot begin with itself before it has stripped itself of all its superstitions concerning the past. Earlier revolutions relied on memories out of world history in order to drug themselves against their own content. In order to find their own content, the revolutions of the nineteenth century have to let the dead bury the dead. Before, the expression exceeded the content; now the content exceeds the expression.

—Karl Marx, *The Eighteenth Brumaire*[6]

I can already see the faces of those who will ask me to clarify such and such a point or condemn such and such behavior.

It is obvious—and I can't say this enough—that the motivations for dis-alienating a physician from Guadeloupe are essentially different from those for the African construction worker in the port at Abidjan.[7] For the former, alien-ation is almost intellectual in nature. It develops because he takes European

4. For J. G. FICHTE, see above.
5. It is not clear what Fanon is referring to here; perhaps he had in mind Nietzsche's discussion of *ressentiment* in *On the Genealogy of Morals* (1887; see above).
6. An essay published in 1852 on the establishment

of a dictatorship in France on November 9, 1799 ("Eighteenth Brumaire," in the French revolution-ary calendar).
7. The main port of Côte d'Ivoire (the Ivory Coast), on the coast of western Africa. Guadeloupe: a group of islands in the Antilles, under French control.

culture as a means of detaching himself from his own race. For the latter, it develops because he is victim to a system based on the exploitation of one race by another and the contempt for one branch of humanity by a civilization that considers itself superior.

We would not be so naive as to believe that the appeals for reason or respect for human dignity can change reality. For the Antillean working in the sugarcane plantations in Le Robert,[8] to fight is the only solution. And he will undertake and carry out this struggle not as the result of a Marxist or idealistic analysis but because quite simply he cannot conceive his life otherwise than as a kind of combat against exploitation, poverty, and hunger.

It would never occur to us to ask these men to rethink their concept of history. Besides, we are convinced that, without knowing it, they share our views, since they are so used to speaking and thinking in terms of the present. The few worker comrades I have had the opportunity to meet in Paris have never bothered to ask themselves about discovering a black past. They knew they were black, but, they told me, that didn't change a thing.

And damn right they were.

On this subject, I shall remark on something I have found in many writers: intellectual alienation is a creation of bourgeois society. And for me bourgeois society is any society that becomes ossified in a predetermined mold, stifling any development, progress, or discovery. For me bourgeois society is a closed society where it's not good to be alive, where the air is rotten and ideas and people are putrefying. And I believe that a man who takes a stand against this living death is in a way a revolutionary.

The discovery that a black civilization existed in the fifteenth century does not earn me a certificate of humanity. Whether you like it or not, the past can in no way be my guide in the actual state of things.

It should be clear by now that the situation I have studied is not a conventional one. Scientific objectivity had to be ruled out, since the alienated and the neurotic were my brother, my sister, and my father. I constantly tried to demonstrate to the black man that in a sense he abnormalizes himself, and to the white man that he is both mystifier and mystified.

At certain moments the black man is locked in his body. And yet "for a being who has acquired the consciousness of self and body, who has achieved the dialectic of subject and object, the body is no longer a cause of the structure of consciousness; it has become an object of consciousness."[9]

The black man, however sincere, is a slave to the past. But I am a man, and in this sense the Peloponnesian War[1] is as much mine as the invention of the compass. Confronted with the white man, the black man has to set a high value on his own past, to take his revenge; confronted with the black man, today's white man feels a need to recall the age of cannibalism. A few years ago, the Association for Overseas Students in Lyon asked me to respond to an article that literally likened jazz to cannibalism irrupting into the modern world. Knowing full well where I was going, I rejected the article's premise

---

8. A commune of Martinique [Fanon's note]. "Commune": a small administrative district.
9. Merleau-Ponty, *Phénoménologie de la perception* [Paris: Gallimard, 1945], p. 277 [Fanon's note]. For MAURICE MERLEAU-PONTY and excerpts from *Phe-*

nomenology of Perception, see above.
1. The war fought between the two leading city-states in ancient Greece, Sparta and Athens (431–404 B.C.E.).

and asked the defender of European purity to cure himself of a spasm that had nothing cultural about it. Some men want the whole world to know who they are. One German philosopher described the process as the pathology of freedom.[2] In the case in point, I didn't have to defend black music against white music; rather, I had to help my brother get rid of an unhealthy attitude.

The problem considered here is located in temporality. Disalienation will be for those Whites and Blacks who have refused to let themselves be locked in the substantialized "tower of the past." For many other black men disalienation will come from refusing to consider their reality as definitive.

I am a man, and I have to rework the world's past from the very beginning. I am not just responsible for the slave revolt in Saint Domingue.[3]

Every time a man has brought victory to the dignity of the spirit, every time a man has said no to an attempt to enslave his fellow man, I have felt a sense of solidarity with his act.

In no way does my basic vocation have to be drawn from the past of peoples of color.

In no way do I have to dedicate myself to reviving a black civilization unjustly ignored. I will not make myself the man of any past. I do not want to sing the past to the detriment of my present and my future.

It is not because the Indo-Chinese discovered a culture of their own that they revolted. Quite simply this was because it became impossible for them to breathe, in more than one sense of the word.

When we recall how the old colonial hands in 1938 described Indochina as the land of piastres and rickshaws, of houseboys and cheap women, we understand only too well the fury of the Vietminh's struggle.[4]

A friend of mine, who had fought alongside me during the last war,[5] recently came back from Indochina. He enlightened me on many things—for example, on the serenity with which the sixteen- or seventeen-year-old Vietnamese fell in front of the firing squad. Once, he told me, we had to kneel down to fire: the soldiers, confronted with such young "fanatics," were shaking. To sum up, he added: "The war we fought together was child's play compared with what is going on out there."

Seen from Europe, such things are incomprehensible. Some people claim there is a so-called Asian attitude toward death. But nobody is convinced by these third-rate philosophers. It wasn't so long ago that this Asian serenity could be seen in the "vandals" of Vercors[6] and the "terrorists" of the Resistance.

The Vietnamese who die in front of a firing squad don't expect their sacrifice to revive a forgotten past. They accept death for the sake of the present and the future.

2. Günther Anders (1902–1992) published an essay (in French) with this title in 1936.
3. The portion of the Caribbean island of Hispaniola that later became Haiti; the slave revolt against the French colonialists began in 1791.
4. The Viet Minh was a nationalist group founded in 1941 to fight for independence from France, which had made Vietnam a colony in 1862 (it became part of the larger "Indochinese Union" in 1887). The First Indochina War, with France,

began in 1946; French rule of Vietnam collapsed in 1954.
5. World War II, in which Fanon served in the Free French army.
6. A plateau in southeastern France where members of the French resistance openly rose against the Germans in 1944, after the D-Day invasion; many were executed and the town of Vassieux-en-Vercors was destroyed.

If the question once arose for me about showing solidarity with a given past, it was because I was committed to myself and my fellow man, to fight with all my life and all my strength so that never again would people be enslaved on this earth.

It is not the black world that governs my behavior. My black skin is not a repository for specific values. The starry sky that left Kant in awe has long revealed its secrets to us. And moral law has doubts about itself.[7]

As a man, I undertake to risk annihilation so that two or three truths can cast their essential light on the world.

Sartre has shown that the past, along the lines of an inauthentic mode, catches on and "takes" en masse, and, once solidly structured, then *gives form* to the individual. It is the past transmuted into a thing of value. But I can also revise my past, prize it, or condemn it, depending on what I choose.

The black man wants to be like the white man. For the black man, there is but one destiny. And it is white.[8] A long time ago the black man acknowledged the undeniable superiority of the white man, and all his endeavors aim at achieving a white existence.

Haven't I got better things to do on this earth than avenge the Blacks of the seventeenth century?

Is it my duty to confront the problem of black truth on this earth, this earth which is already trying to sneak away?

Must I confine myself to the justification of a facial profile?

I have not the right as a man of color to research why my race is superior or inferior to another.

I have not the right as a man of color to wish for a guilt complex to crystallize in the white man regarding the past of my race.

I have not the right as a man of color to be preoccupied with ways of trampling on the arrogance of my former master.

I have neither the right nor the duty to demand reparations for my subjugated ancestors.

There is no black mission; there is no white burden.[9]

I find myself one day in a world where things are hurtful; a world where I am required to fight; a world where it is always a question of defeat or victory.

I find myself, me, a man, in a world where words are fringed with silence; in a world where the other hardens endlessly.

No, I have not the right to come and shout my hatred at the white man. It is not my duty to murmur my gratitude to the white man.

Here is my life caught in the noose of existence. Here is my freedom, which sends back to me my own reflection. No, I have not the right to be black.

It is not my duty to be this or that.

If the white man challenges my humanity I will show him by weighing down on his life with all my weight of a man that I am not this grinning *Y a bon Banania* figure that he persists in imagining I am.

---

7. KANT declares his awe at the starry sky above him and the moral law within him in the Conclusion of his *Critique of Practical Reason* (1788); see above.
8. This is part of the colonial subject mentality that Fanon considers dominant and is seeking to analyze

and overcome.
9. A reference to Rudyard Kipling's "The White Man's Burden" (1899), a poem in praise of imperialism.

I find myself one day in the world, and I acknowledge one right for myself: the right to demand human behavior from the other.

And one duty: the duty never to let my decisions renounce my freedom.

I do not want to be the victim of the Ruse of a black world.

My life must not be devoted to making an assessment of black values.

There is no white world; there is no white ethic—any more than there is a white intelligence.

There are from one end of the world to the other men who are searching.

I am not a prisoner of History. I must not look for the meaning of my destiny in that direction.

I must constantly remind myself that the real *leap* consists of introducing invention into life.

In the world I am heading for, I am endlessly creating myself.

I show solidarity with humanity provided I can go one step further.

And we see that through a specific problem there emerges one of action. Placed in this world, in a real-life situation, "embarked" as Pascal[1] would have it, am I going to accumulate weapons?

Am I going to ask today's white men to answer for the slave traders of the seventeenth century?

Am I going to try by every means available to cause guilt to burgeon in their souls?

And grief, when they are confronted with the density of the past? I am a black man, and tons of chains, squalls of lashes, and rivers of spit stream over my shoulders.

But I have not the right to put down roots. I have not the right to admit the slightest patch of being into my existence. I have not the right to become mired by the determinations of the past.

I am not a slave to slavery that dehumanized my ancestors.

For many black intellectuals European culture has a characteristic of exteriority. Furthermore, in human relationships, the western world can feel foreign to the black man. Not wanting to be thought of as a poor relation, an adopted son, or a bastard child, will he feverishly try to discover a black civilization?

Above all, let there be no misunderstanding. We are convinced that it would be of enormous interest to discover a black literature or architecture from the third century before Christ. We would be overjoyed to learn of the existence of a correspondence between some black philosopher and Plato.[2] But we can absolutely not see how this fact would change the lives of eight-year-old kids working in the cane fields of Martinique or Guadeloupe.

There should be no attempt to fixate man, since it is his destiny to be unleashed.

The density of History determines none of my acts.

I am my own foundation.

And it is by going beyond the historical and instrumental given that I initiate my cycle of freedom.

---

1. Blaise Pascal (1623–1662), French philosopher and mathematician; in his *Pensées* (1670, *Thoughts*), he uses the phrase "You are embarked" to empha-size the necessity of making a choice (in his case, wagering on whether God exists).
2. Greek philosopher (ca. 427–ca. 347 B.C.E.).

The misfortune of the man of color is having been enslaved.

The misfortune and inhumanity of the white man are having killed man[3] somewhere.

And still today they are organizing this dehumanization rationally. But I, a man of color, insofar as I have the possibility of existing absolutely, have not the right to confine myself in a world of retroactive reparations.

I, a man of color, want but one thing:

May man never be instrumentalized. May the subjugation of man by man— that is to say, of me by another—cease. May I be allowed to discover and desire man wherever he may be.

The black man is not. No more than the white man.

Both have to move away from the inhuman voices of their respective ances-tors so that a genuine communication can be born. Before embarking on a positive voice, freedom needs to make an effort at disalienation. At the start of his life, a man is always congested, drowned in contingency. The misfor-tune of man is that he was once a child.

It is through self-consciousness and renunciation, through a permanent ten-sion of his freedom, that man can create the ideal conditions of existence for a human world.

Superiority? Inferiority?

Why not simply try to touch the other, feel the other, discover each other?

Was my freedom not given me to build the world of *you*, man?

At the end of this book we would like the reader to feel with us the open dimension of every consciousness.

My final prayer:

O my body, always make me a man who questions!

SOURCE: From Frantz Fanon, *Black Skin, White Masks*, trans. Richard Philcox (New York: Grove Press, 2008), pp. xi–xviii, 1–3, 6–7, 13–14, 89–98, 102, 105–11, 113–14, 119, 191–93, 197–206. Originally published in 1952 as *Peau noire, masques blancs*. Some of Fanon's notes have been adjusted by his translator to conform to English editions of the works cited.

From The Wretched of the Earth

From *I. On Violence*

National liberation, national reawakening, restoration of the nation to the people or Commonwealth, whatever the name used, whatever the latest expres-sion, decolonization is always a violent event. At whatever level we study it— individual encounters, a change of name for a sports club, the guest list at a cocktail party, members of a police force or the board of directors of a state or private bank—decolonization is quite simply the substitution of one "spe-cies" of mankind by another. The substitution is unconditional, absolute, total, and seamless. We could go on to portray the rise of a new nation, the establishment of a new state, its diplomatic relations and its economic and

3. That is, in having dehumanized man.

political orientation. But instead we have decided to describe the kind of tabula rasa which from the outset defines any decolonization. What is singularly important is that it starts from the very first day with the basic claims of the colonized. In actual fact, proof of success lies in a social fabric that has been changed inside out. This change is extraordinarily important because it is desired, clamored for, and demanded. The need for this change exists in a raw, repressed, and reckless state in the lives and consciousness of colonized men and women. But the eventuality of such a change is also experienced as a terrifying future in the consciousness of another "species" of men and women: the *colons*, the colonists.

*

Decolonization, which sets out to change the order of the world, is clearly an agenda for total disorder. But it cannot be accomplished by the wave of a magic wand, a natural cataclysm, or a gentleman's agreement. Decolonization, we know, is an historical process: In other words, it can only be understood, it can only find its significance and become self coherent insofar as we can discern the history-making movement which gives it form and substance. Decolonization is the encounter between two congenitally antagonistic forces that in fact owe their singularity to the kind of reification secreted and nurtured by the colonial situation. Their first confrontation was colored by violence and their cohabitation—or rather the exploitation of the colonized by the colonizer—continued at the point of the bayonet and under cannon fire. The colonist and the colonized are old acquaintances. And consequently, the colonist is right when he says he "knows" them. It is the colonist who *fabricated* and *continues to fabricate* the colonized subject. The colonist derives his validity, i.e., his wealth, from the colonial system.

———————

Decolonization never goes unnoticed, for it focuses on and fundamentally alters being, and transforms the spectator crushed to a nonessential state into a privileged actor, captured in a virtually grandiose fashion by the spotlight of History. It infuses a new rhythm, specific to a new generation of men, with a new language and a new humanity. Decolonization is truly the creation of new men. But such a creation cannot be attributed to a supernatural power: The "thing" colonized becomes a man through the very process of liberation.

Decolonization, therefore, implies the urgent need to thoroughly challenge the colonial situation. Its definition can, if we want to describe it accurately, be summed up in the well-known words: "The last shall be first."[1] Decolonization is verification of this. At a descriptive level, therefore, any decolonization is a success.

*

In its bare reality, decolonization reeks of red-hot cannonballs and bloody knives. For the last can be the first only after a murderous and decisive confrontation between the two protagonists. This determination to have the last

———————

1. Matthew 19:30, 20:16.

move up to the front, to have them clamber up (too quickly, say some) the famous echelons of an organized society, can only succeed by resorting to every means, including, of course, violence.

———————

You do not disorganize a society, however primitive it may be, with such an agenda if you are not determined from the very start to smash every obstacle encountered. The colonized, who have made up their mind to make such an agenda into a driving force, have been prepared for violence from time immemorial. As soon as they are born it is obvious to them that their cramped world, riddled with taboos, can only be challenged by out and out violence.

The colonial world is a compartmentalized world. It is obviously as superfluous to recall the existence of "native" towns and European towns, of schools for "natives" and schools for Europeans, as it is to recall apartheid in South Africa. Yet if we penetrate inside this compartmentalization we shall at least bring to light some of its key aspects. By penetrating its geographical configuration and classification we shall be able to delineate the backbone on which the decolonized society is reorganized.

The colonized world is a world divided in two. The dividing line, the border, is represented by the barracks and the police stations. In the colonies, the official, legitimate agent, the spokesperson for the colonizer and the regime of oppression, is the police officer or the soldier. In capitalist societies, education, whether secular or religious, the teaching of moral reflexes handed down from father to son, the exemplary integrity of workers decorated after fifty years of loyal and faithful service, the fostering of love for harmony and wisdom, those aesthetic forms of respect for the status quo, instill in the exploited a mood of submission and inhibition which considerably eases the task of the agents of law and order. In capitalist countries a multitude of sermonizers, counselors, and "confusion-mongers" intervene between the exploited and the authorities. In colonial regions, however, the proximity and frequent, direct intervention by the police and the military ensure the colonized are kept under close scrutiny, and contained by rifle butts and napalm. We have seen how the government's agent uses a language of pure violence. The agent does not alleviate oppression or mask domination. He displays and demonstrates them with the clear conscience of the law enforcer, and brings violence into the homes and minds of the colonized subject.

* * *

This compartmentalized world, this world divided in two, is inhabited by different species. The singularity of the colonial context lies in the fact that economic reality, inequality, and enormous disparities in lifestyles never manage to mask the human reality. Looking at the immediacies of the colonial context, it is clear that what divides this world is first and foremost what species, what race one belongs to. In the colonies the economic infrastructure is also a superstructure. The cause is effect: You are rich because you are white, you are white because you are rich. This is why a Marxist analysis should always be slightly stretched when it comes to addressing the colonial issue. It is not just the concept of the precapitalist society, so effectively studied by

Marx,[2] which needs to be reexamined here. The serf is essentially different from the knight, but a reference to divine right is needed to justify this difference in status. In the colonies the foreigner imposed himself using his cannons and machines. Despite the success of his pacification, in spite of his appropriation, the colonist always remains a foreigner. It is not the factories, the estates, or the bank account which primarily characterize the "ruling class." The ruling species is first and foremost the outsider from elsewhere, different from the indigenous population, "the others."

The violence which governed the ordering of the colonial world, which tirelessly punctuated the destruction of the indigenous social fabric, and demolished unchecked the systems of reference of the country's economy, lifestyles, and modes of dress, this same violence will be vindicated and appropriated when, taking history into their own hands, the colonized swarm into the forbidden cities. To blow the colonial world to smithereens is henceforth a clear image within the grasp and imagination of every colonized subject. To dislocate the colonial world does not mean that once the borders have been eliminated there will be a right of way between the two sectors. To destroy the colonial world means nothing less than demolishing the colonist's sector, burying it deep within the earth or banishing it from the territory.

* * *

As soon as the colonized begin to strain at the leash and to pose a threat to the colonist, they are assigned a series of good souls who in the "Symposiums on Culture" spell out the specificity and richness of Western values. But every time the issue of Western values crops up, the colonized grow tense and their muscles seize up. During the period of decolonization the colonized are called upon to be reasonable. They are offered rock-solid values, they are told in great detail that decolonization should not mean regression, and that they must rely on values which have proved to be reliable and worthwhile. Now it so happens that when the colonized hear a speech on Western culture they draw their machetes or at least check to see they are close to hand. The supremacy of white values is stated with such violence, the victorious confrontation of these values with the lifestyle and beliefs of the colonized is so impregnated with aggressiveness, that as a counter measure the colonized rightly make a mockery of them whenever they are mentioned. In the colonial context the colonist only quits undermining the colonized once the latter have proclaimed loud and clear that white values reign supreme. In the period of decolonization the colonized masses thumb their noses at these very values, shower them with insults and vomit them up.

Such an occurrence normally goes unseen because, during decolonization, certain colonized intellectuals have established a dialogue with the bourgeoi-

2. For KARL MARX, see above.

sie of the colonizing country. During this period the indigenous population is seen as a blurred mass. The few "native" personalities whom the colonialist bourgeois have chanced to encounter have had insufficient impact to alter their current perception and nuance their thinking. During the period of liberation, however, the colonialist bourgeoisie frantically seeks contact with the colonized "elite." It is with this elite that the famous dialogue on values is established. When the colonialist bourgeoisie realizes it is impossible to maintain its domination over the colonies it decides to wage a rearguard campaign in the fields of culture, values, and technology, etc. But what we should never forget is that the immense majority of colonized peoples are impervious to such issues. For a colonized people, the most essential value, because it is the most meaningful, is first and foremost the land: the land, which must provide bread and, naturally, dignity. But this dignity has nothing to do with "human" dignity. The colonized subject has never heard of such an ideal. All he has ever seen on his land is that he can be arrested, beaten, and starved with impunity; and no sermonizer on morals, no priest has ever stepped in to bear the blows in his place or share his bread. For the colonized, to be a moralist quite plainly means silencing the arrogance of the colonist, breaking his spiral of violence, in a word ejecting him outright from the picture.

* * *

Wherever an authentic liberation struggle has been fought, wherever the blood of the people has been shed and the armed phase has lasted long enough to encourage the intellectuals to withdraw to their rank and file base, there is an effective eradication of the superstructure borrowed by these intellectuals from the colonialist bourgeois circles. In its narcissistic monologue the colonialist bourgeoisie, by way of its academics, had implanted in the minds of the colonized that the essential values—meaning Western values—remain eternal despite all errors attributable to man. The colonized intellectual accepted the cogency of these ideas and there in the back of his mind stood a sentinel on duty guarding the Greco-Roman pedestal. But during the struggle for liberation, when the colonized intellectual touches base again with his people, this artificial sentinel is smashed to smithereens. All the Mediterranean values, the triumph of the individual, of enlightenment and Beauty turn into pale, lifeless trinkets. All those discourses appear a jumble of dead words. Those values which seemed to ennoble the soul prove worthless because they have nothing in common with the real-life struggle in which the people are engaged.

And first among them is individualism. The colonized intellectual learned from his masters that the individual must assert himself. The colonialist bourgeoisie hammered into the colonized mind the notion of a society of individuals where each is locked in his subjectivity, where wealth lies in thought. But the colonized intellectual who is lucky enough to bunker down with the people during the liberation struggle, will soon discover the falsity of this theory. Involvement in the organization of the struggle will already introduce him to a different vocabulary. "Brother," "sister," "comrade" are words outlawed by the colonialist bourgeoisie because in their thinking my brother is my wallet and my comrade, my scheming. In a kind of auto-da-fé, the colonized intellectual witnesses the destruction of all his idols: egoism, arrogant recrimination, and the idiotic, childish need to have the last word. This colonized intellectual, pulverized by colonialist culture, will also discover the strength of the village assemblies, the power of the people's commissions and the extraordinary productiveness of neighborhood and section committee meetings. Personal interests are now the collective interest because in reality *everyone* will be discovered by the French legionnaires and consequently massacred or else *everyone* will be saved. In such a context, the "every man for himself" concept, the atheist's form of salvation, is prohibited.

* * *

* * * The Third World has no intention of organizing a vast hunger crusade against Europe. What it does expect from those who have kept it in slavery for centuries is to help it rehabilitate man, and ensure his triumph everywhere, once and for all.

But it is obvious we are not so naive as to think this will be achieved with the cooperation and goodwill of the European governments. This colossal task, which consists of reintroducing man into the world, man in his totality, will be achieved with the crucial help of the European masses who would do well to confess that they have often rallied behind the position of our common masters on colonial issues. In order to do this, the European masses must first of all decide to wake up, put on their thinking caps and stop playing the irresponsible game of Sleeping Beauty.

* * *

From *Conclusion*

Now, comrades, now is the time to decide to change sides. We must shake off the great mantle of night which has enveloped us, and reach for the light. The new day which is dawning must find us determined, enlightened and resolute.

We must abandon our dreams and say farewell to our old beliefs and former friendships. Let us not lose time in useless laments or sickening mimicry. Let us leave this Europe which never stops talking of man yet massacres him at every one of its street corners, at every corner of the world.

For centuries Europe has brought the progress of other men to a halt and enslaved them for its own purposes and glory; for centuries it has stifled virtually the whole of humanity in the name of a so-called "spiritual adventure." Look at it now teetering between atomic destruction and spiritual disintegration.

* * *

When I look for man in European lifestyles and technology I see a constant denial of man, an avalanche of murders.

Man's condition, his projects and collaboration with others on tasks that strengthen man's totality, are new issues which require genuine inspiration.

Let us decide not to imitate Europe and let us tense our muscles and our brains in a new direction. Let us endeavor to invent a man in full, something which Europe has been incapable of achieving.

* * *

The Third World must start over a new history of man which takes account of not only the occasional prodigious theses maintained by Europe but also its crimes, the most heinous of which have been committed at the very heart of man, the pathological dismembering of his functions and the erosion of his unity, and in the context of the community, the fracture, the stratification and the bloody tensions fed by class, and finally, on the immense scale of humanity, the racial hatred, slavery, exploitation and, above all, the bloodless genocide whereby one and a half billion men have been written off.

So comrades, let us not pay tribute to Europe by creating states, institutions, and societies that draw their inspiration from it.

Humanity expects other things from us than this grotesque and generally obscene emulation.

If we want to transform Africa into a new Europe, America into a new Europe, then let us entrust the destinies of our countries to the Europeans. They will do a better job than the best of us.

But if we want humanity to take one step forward, if we want to take it to another level than the one where Europe has placed it, than we must innovate, we must be pioneers.

If we want to respond to the expectations of our peoples, we must look elsewhere besides Europe.

Moreover, if we want to respond to the expectations of the Europeans we must not send them back a reflection, however ideal, of their society and their thought that periodically sickens even them.

For Europe, for ourselves and for humanity, comrades, we must make a new start, develop a new way of thinking, and endeavor to create a new man.

SOURCE: From Frantz Fanon, *The Wretched of the Earth*, trans. Richard Philcox (New York: Grove Press, 2004), pp. 1–6, 8–12, 61–62, 235–36, 238–39. Originally published in 1961 as *Damnées de la terre*.

SIMONE DE BEAUVOIR
(1908 – 1986)

Beauvoir made a difference, in several ways. One that is well known is in fulfilling the promise made by SARTRE, at the end of *Being and Nothingness* (1943), of a book on ethics that would develop the ethical implications of that work. Though he never delivered the promised book himself, four years later Beauvoir published *The Ethics of Ambiguity* (1947)—an elaboration of her version of an existentialist ethics that is in fundamental accord with Sartre's thinking. A minor classic of the literature of existential philosophy, it remains one of the best statements of and introductions to such an ethics.

That book is the clearest example among her many books of Beauvoir's intellectual partnership with Sartre. Because most of her books were either novels or memoirs, the extent of her considerable contributions to that partnership is not easy to see and remains a matter of speculation. Yet her novels, which easily surpass Sartre's as literature, did much to establish the literary context that prepared the way for the reception and impact of *Being and Nothingness*, particularly in the English-speaking world. More importantly, she quite probably made substantial contributions to the development of Sartre's thinking as he wrote that book and moved beyond it.

But Beauvoir truly came into her own as a philosopher in her two studies of aspects of human reality that were entirely overlooked by Sartre, HEIDEGGER, and other leading figures in existential philosophy—and in the interpretive tradition in the first half of the twentieth century more generally: *The Second Sex* (1949) and *The Coming of Age* (1970). Indeed, *The Second Sex*, which became a foundational document of second-wave feminism, has had a particularly profound impact beyond as well as within philosophical discussion of human real-

ity. It drew on her phenomenological sensitivity and existential-philosophical sensibility; and while making use of some ideas familiar from *Being and Nothingness*, it departed from them in important ways that clearly established her own formidable philosophical identity.

Simone Lucie Ernestine Marie Bertrand de Beauvoir ("Bow-VWAR") was born in Paris, two years before her sister Hélène (who was to become a painter). Her mother, whose father was the president of a major bank and was quite wealthy, was a devout Catholic and raised her children accordingly. Her father, who at one time had been a lawyer, was devoted to the theater and acting, which the family's comfortable circumstances allowed him to pursue as an amateur. Though he had wished for sons, he recognized Simone's precocious brilliance and encouraged her in her studies, at which she excelled. He gave her the self-confidence that she would need in the future to compete—and hold her own—in an almost entirely male intellectual world (and in her lifelong relationship with Sartre). She also came to share her father's love of the theater and literature, in ways that would find expression in her remarkably diverse works of both literature and philosophy.

The family's circumstances changed dramatically when her grandfather's bank failed after the First World War. He was disgraced and impoverished, and times were hard for them all. The young Simone nonetheless received a good education at a private Catholic school for girls, and resolved while in her early teens to become a writer. She rejected Catholicism at about the same time, becoming a resolute atheist, but after graduation in 1925 she continued her education at postsecondary Catholic schools for several years. To prepare for an attempt to gain admission to the École Normale Supérieure or the Sorbonne—institutions that few women were allowed to enter—she focused her studies on mathematics, literature, and languages.

Though Beauvoir (unlike SIMONE WEIL) was not formally admitted to the virtually all-male École, she was allowed to study there; and she was admitted to the Sorbonne in 1928. Sartre, MERLEAU-PONTY, Weil, and Henri Lefebvre were among her fellow students. She wrote a thesis on Leibniz in 1929 under the eminent French rationalist and idealist philosopher Léon Brunschvicg. She also was permitted to take the philosophy *agrégation* (the rigorous national examination to teach in an upper-level secondary school), and at 21 she became the youngest person ever to pass it. (On some accounts, she passed it with the second-highest score, just behind Sartre—who, at 24, was taking it for the second time; on others, they tied.)

Beauvoir and Sartre began an affair that year that turned into a lifelong bond. Their relationship was unusual for what it was not (they never married or even lived under the same roof, and other relationships were permitted), and also for what it was—an alliance embodying genuine commitment and companionship on many levels, both intellectual and personal. They became an extraordinary philosophical, literary, and political power couple of a kind rarely seen, and a living legend in French intellectual life.

From 1931 to 1943 Beauvoir held a string of teaching positions at Montgrand in Marseille, Jeanne d'Arc in Rouen, Molière at Passy, and Camille-Sée in Paris. She was dismissed from the last after she was accused of sleeping with a (female) student, and her teaching permit was suspended. Deeply angered, she never again taught in the French educational system.

In 1941, under the German occupation, Beauvoir helped organize a (ineffectual) French resistance group with Sartre and Merleau-Ponty. The three would also work together after the war to found the journal *Les Temps Modernes* (*Modern Times*). In 1943 her first novel appeared, followed after the war by a steady stream of publications and lectures around the world. In 1947 she did a lecture tour in the United States, which resulted in the book *America Day by Day* (1948). She also met the writer Nelson Algren, with whom she began a romantic affair lasting nearly two decades (her continuing relationship with Sartre notwithstanding).

In 1948 Beauvoir helped Sartre to found a political party (which, not surprisingly, was unsuccessful). In 1955 she and Sartre spent considerable time in Russia and China—to whose regimes they tended to be well disposed, owing to their radical-left leanings—in an attempt to understand what was happening there. Similar motives brought them in 1960 to Cuba, where they spent several days with Fidel Castro. Beauvoir was very active politically throughout the 1950s and 1960s, agitating for Algerian independence from France and participating in political activities focused on the war in Vietnam, the May 1968 student protests in France, and women's rights, especially to contraception and abortion. She was a founder and (in 1974) became the president of France's League of Women's Rights. In 1975 she was awarded the Jerusalem Prize, given to writers whose work addresses and promotes individual freedom. She helped found the journal *Questions féministes* (*Feminist Questions*) in 1979.

Beauvoir was deeply affected by the death of her mother in 1964, about which she wrote movingly. The death of Sartre in 1980 was even more difficult for her, but she marked the occasion with another memorable testimonial: her last book, *Adieux: A Farewell to Sartre* (1981), which presents conversations between them and her account of his final decade. She herself died six years after Sartre, and was buried in the same grave with him in Paris.

It is an oversimplification to call Sartre's thinking in *Being and Nothingness* the basis of Beauvoir's philosophical orientation, and the point of departure for her ethical meditation *Pyrrhus et Cinéas* (1944) and for *Ethics of Ambiguity*. They had been thinking together for some time about the themes and ideas elaborated in those works. They shared a preoccupation with the freedom and responsibility of the human subject at the level that matters most—the level of choice at which meaning is determined—regardless of external circumstances. They also shared a conception of the deep "ambiguity" of human reality, as consciousness always transcends the determinateness of its content and yet cannot escape that determinateness even in transcending it. They further shared a vivid appreciation of the complications arising from human existing not only at the level of a subject relating to an object but also at the level of a subject mediated in its self-conception by the tendency to internalize the ways in which others objectify us (as they perceive us to be—and want us to be). And they shared a recognition that that tendency is very commonly and readily reinforced by the burdens of freedom and responsibility.

Beauvoir's *Ethics of Ambiguity* draws out the implications of these ideas for existing in a world that she (like Sartre) sees as devoid of anything divine or metaphysical to supply life with meaning and direction. Her great insight—which surely went well beyond anything suggested by Sartre—was that the dynamic of internalizing an objectifying identity that comes from someone "other" than oneself could be discerned not only on an interpersonal level, or in the context of a phenomenon such as anti-Semitism (which Sartre had discussed), but also at the level of relations between the sexes. That became the topic and driving idea of *The Second Sex*—whose backdrop was the existential ethic of freedom, responsibility, intellectual integrity, and authenticity, providing the resources for the critique of all things (internal and external) that contribute to and reinforce the perpetuation of an identity and existence as a "second sex."

The "other" that is the source and ongoing reinforcement of that identity, however, required a kind of analysis that took Beauvoir well into philosophically new and different territory. Like Sartre, she rejects any essentialism that would reach beyond biological fact to the content of what it has come to mean—both descriptively and normatively—to be a woman. So, in her famous opening line of the second part of the book, she flatly asserts: "One is not born, but rather becomes, woman." But while she continues to hold to the radical existentialist position that nothing makes it impossible for one who has accepted the identity of a woman to reject it, she also recognizes and argues that such rejection is almost overwhelmingly difficult, for reasons of internal compulsion as well as external constraint. She thus contends that for all practical purposes, most women in the world she is describing have been deprived of the possibility of realizing their freedom: they have so firmly acquired the identity of "woman"—as a kind of object—that one can hardly expect them to throw it off. They may in a sense be complicit in their "objectification"; but it is neither their doing nor simply a choice that they continue to embrace (in the manner that Sartre excoriates as cowardice and "bad faith," or self-deception).

What is both needed and possible, Beauvoir suggests, and what her book is intended to foster, is a liberating process, beginning with an analysis of the cultural and social fabric of myths, values, ideals, expectations, roles, and sanctions that has been woven and used—both coercively and seductively—to ensure that women's lives conform to that identity and are lived within it. She takes a somewhat similar approach to the human phenomenon of "coming of age," or aging, and has a similar emancipatory agenda. Her analyses make so strong a case for the power of the array of elements in culture and society that work to effect the kinds of identity formation she discusses that it is difficult to imagine how it would be humanly possible for anyone to be able to avoid succumbing to them.

In that respect, *The Second Sex* might seem to anticipate—and perhaps even to provide a template for—the writings of

MICHEL FOUCAULT, rather than appropriating and further developing certain ideas of the early Sartre. (Foucault's first book appeared five years after *The Second Sex*; *Discipline and Punish*, more than twenty-five years later.) Unlike Foucault, however, Beauvoir held resolutely to the conviction she shared with the Sartre of that period: that the freedom of every human being to opt into or opt out of any such state of affairs is not merely potential but real.

Moreover, in *Search for a Method* (1957), and then *Critique of Dialectical Reason* (1960), Sartre himself turned in the direction of a reinterpretation of human reality that took the social and cultural context in which human action and choice occur much more seriously than he had in *Being and Nothingness*, though without abandoning the idea of such freedom altogether. That development in his thought might be seen as his response to the challenge Beauvoir had posed—no doubt in person as well as in that book—to reconsider his earlier picture and account of the human subject. And perhaps his "search" was for a "method" more comprehensive and better suited to the purpose than the phenomenological one—a method along the lines of what we see already at work in her book, capable of coming to grips with those features of human reality that make her goal both a very real and a very fraught human possibility.

Beauvoir is commonly—and rightly—credited with having written a brilliant and penetrating critique of the subtleties of the sexism that has resulted in women's being made into a "second sex," the phenomenon she so astutely frames and explores in her book of that name. She deserves credit for having made a similar, though less spectacular, contribution to changing attitudes toward aging and ageism in *The Coming of Age*. These two books are also important for significantly helping to develop the kind of agenda that needs to be pursued—and strategies for pursuing it—if the philosophical consideration of human reality is to do interpretive and practical justice to it. They provide grist for the mills of both philosophical anthropology and normative theory.

From The Second Sex

From *Volume I. Facts and Myths*

FROM INTRODUCTION

I hesitated a long time before writing a book on woman. The subject is irritating, especially for women; and it is not new. Enough ink has flowed over the quarrel about feminism; it is now almost over: let's not talk about it anymore. Yet it is still being talked about. And the volumes of idiocies churned out over this past century do not seem to have clarified the problem. Besides, is there a problem? And what is it? Are there even women? True, the theory of the eternal feminine[1] still has its followers; they whisper, "Even in Russia, *women* are still very much women"; but other well-informed people—and also at times those same ones—lament, "Woman is losing herself, woman is lost." It is hard to know any longer if women still exist, if they will always exist, if there should be women at all, what place they hold in this world, what place

---

1. An allusion to the last line of Goethe's *Faust*, part 2 (1832)—"die ewige Weibliche zieht uns hinan" (the eternal feminine draws us ever upward). At the time when Beauvoir wrote *The Second Sex*, "the eternal feminine" had become a code phrase for the idea that there is some sort of sublime immutable essence of femininity possessing that power of attraction.

they should hold. "Where are the women?" asked a short-lived magazine recently.[2] But first, what is a woman? *"Tota mulier in utero:*[3] she is a womb," some say. Yet speaking of certain women, the experts proclaim, "They are not women," even though they have a uterus like the others. Everyone agrees there are females in the human species; today, as in the past, they make up about half of humanity; and yet we are told that "femininity is in jeopardy"; we are urged, "Be women, stay women, become women." So not every female human being is necessarily a woman; she must take part in this mysterious and endangered reality known as femininity. Is femininity secreted by the ovaries? Is it enshrined in a Platonic heaven?[4] Is a frilly petticoat enough to bring it down to earth? Although some women zealously strive to embody it, the model has never been patented. It is typically described in vague and shimmering terms borrowed from a clairvoyant's vocabulary. In Saint Thomas's[5] time it was an essence defined with as much certainty as the sedative quality of a poppy. But conceptualism has lost ground: biological and social sciences no longer believe there are immutably determined entities that define given characteristics like those of the woman, the Jew, or the black; science considers characteristics as secondary reactions to a *situation.* If there is no such thing today as femininity, it is because there never was. Does the word "woman," then, have no content? It is what advocates of Enlightenment philosophy, rationalism, or nominalism vigorously assert: women are, among human beings, merely those who are arbitrarily designated by the word "woman"; American women in particular are inclined to think that woman as such no longer exists. If some backward individual still takes herself for a woman, her friends advise her to undergo psychoanalysis to get rid of this obsession. Referring to a book—a very irritating one at that—*Modern Woman: The Lost Sex*, Dorothy Parker[6] wrote: "I cannot be fair about books that treat women as women. My idea is that all of us, men as well as women, whoever we are, should be considered as human beings." But nominalism is a doctrine that falls a bit short; and it is easy for antifeminists to show that women *are* not men. Certainly woman like man is a human being; but such an assertion is abstract; the fact is that every concrete human being is always uniquely situated. To reject the notions of the eternal feminine, the black soul, or the Jewish character is not to deny that there are today Jews, blacks, or women: this denial is not a liberation for those concerned but an inauthentic flight. Clearly, no woman can claim without bad faith[7] to be situated beyond her sex. A few years ago, a well-known woman writer refused to have her portrait appear in a series of photographs devoted specifically to women writers. She wanted to be included in the men's category; but to get this privilege, she used her husband's influence. Women who assert they are men still claim masculine consideration and respect.

2. Out of print today, titled *Franchise* [Beauvoir's note].
3. Woman is entirely in the womb (Latin); this statement is attributed to the Flemish chemist and doctor Jan Baptista van Helmont (1580–1644).
4. That is, the realm of Forms or Ideas—the fundamental, timeless universals in which objects in the natural world (their less than perfect copies) participate or share—of the Greek philosopher Plato

(ca. 427–ca. 327 B.C.E.).
5. Thomas Aquinas (1224/25–1274), Italian theologian and philosopher.
6. American short story writer, poet, and wit (1893–1967). *Modern Woman* (1947) was written by Ferdinand Lundberg and Marynia F. Farnham.
7. That is, "self-deception" (*mauvaise foi*); see the introduction to SARTRE, above.

I also remember a young Trotskyite standing on a platform during a stormy meeting, about to come to blows in spite of her obvious fragility. She was denying her feminine frailty; but it was for the love of a militant man she wanted to be equal to. The defiant position that American women occupy proves they are haunted by the feeling of their own femininity. And the truth is that anyone can clearly see that humanity is split into two categories of individuals with manifestly different clothes, faces, bodies, smiles, movements, interests, and occupations; these differences are perhaps superficial; perhaps they are destined to disappear. What is certain is that for the moment they exist in a strikingly obvious way.

If the female function is not enough to define woman, and if we also reject the explanation of the "eternal feminine," but if we accept, even temporarily, that there are women on the earth, we then have to ask: What is a woman?

Merely stating the problem suggests an immediate answer to me. It is significant that I pose it. It would never occur to a man to write a book on the singular situation of males in humanity.[8] If I want to define myself, I first have to say, "I am a woman"; all other assertions will arise from this basic truth. A man never begins by positing himself as an individual of a certain sex: that he is a man is obvious. The categories masculine and feminine appear as symmetrical in a formal way on town hall records or identification papers. The relation of the two sexes is not that of two electrical poles: the man represents both the positive and the neuter to such an extent that in French *hommes* designates human beings, the particular meaning of the word *vir* being assimilated into the general meaning of the word "homo."[9] Woman is the negative, to such a point that any determination is imputed to her as a limitation, without reciprocity. I used to get annoyed in abstract discussions to hear men tell me: "You think such and such a thing because you're a woman." But I know my only defense is to answer, "I think it because it is true," thereby eliminating my subjectivity; it was out of the question to answer, "And you think the contrary because you are a man," because it is understood that being a man is not a particularity; a man is in his right by virtue of being man; it is the woman who is in the wrong. In fact, just as for the ancients there was an absolute vertical that defined the oblique, there is an absolute human type that is masculine. Woman has ovaries and a uterus; such are the particular conditions that lock her in her subjectivity; some even say she thinks with her hormones. Man vainly forgets that his anatomy also includes hormones and testicles. He grasps his body as a direct and normal link with the world that he believes he apprehends in all objectivity, whereas he considers woman's body an obstacle, a prison, burdened by everything that particularizes it. "The female is female by virtue of a certain *lack* of qualities," Aristotle[1] said. "We should regard women's nature as suffering from natural defectiveness." And Saint Thomas in his turn decreed that woman was an "incomplete man," an "incidental" being.[2] This is what the Genesis story symbolizes,

8. The Kinsey Report, for example, confines itself to defining the sexual characteristics of the American man, which is completely different [Beauvoir's note]. *Sexual Behavior in the Human Male* (1948), a statistical study compiled by the American zoologist and sexologist Alfred Charles Kinsey (1894–1956) and his colleagues Wardell B. Pomeroy and Clyde E. Martin.

9. In Latin, *vir* means "male human," while *homo* is a generic term, "human being."

1. Greek philosopher (384–322 B.C.E.); these ideas appear in *On the Generation of Animals*, book 2.

2. See *Summa Theologica* (ca. 1265–73), Ia, question 92, article 1, objection 1 (and reply).

where Eve appears as if drawn from Adam's "supernumerary" bone, in Bossuet's[3] words. Humanity is male, and man defines woman, not in herself, but in relation to himself; she is not considered an autonomous being. "Woman, the relative being," writes Michelet.[4] Thus Monsieur Benda[5] declares in *Le rapport d'Uriel* (Uriel's Report): "A man's body has meaning by itself, disregarding the body of the woman, whereas the woman's body seems devoid of meaning without reference to the male. Man thinks himself without woman. Woman does not think herself without man." And she is nothing other than what man decides; she is thus called "the sex," meaning that the male sees her essentially as a sexed being; for him she is sex, so she is it in the absolute. She is determined and differentiated in relation to man, while he is not in relation to her; she is the inessential in front of the essential. He is the Subject; he is the Absolute. She is the Other.[6]

The category of *Other* is as original as consciousness itself. The duality between Self and Other can be found in the most primitive societies, in the most ancient mythologies; this division did not always fall into the category of the division of the sexes, it was not based on any empirical given: this comes out in works like Granet's on Chinese thought, and Dumézil's[7] on India and Rome. In couples such as Varuna–Mitra, Uranus–Zeus,[8] Sun–Moon, Day–Night, no feminine element is involved at the outset; neither in Good–Evil, auspicious and inauspicious, left and right, God and Lucifer; alterity is the fundamental category of human thought. No group ever defines itself as One without immediately setting up the Other opposite itself.[9] It only takes three travelers brought together by chance in the same train compartment for the rest of the travelers to become vaguely hostile "others." Village people view anyone not belonging to the village as suspicious "others." For the native of a country inhabitants of other countries are viewed as "foreigners"; Jews are the "others" for anti-Semites, blacks for racist Americans, indigenous people for colonists, proletarians for the propertied classes. After studying the diverse forms of primitive society in depth, Lévi-Strauss could conclude: "The passage from the state of Nature to the state of Culture is defined by

---

3. Jacques-Bénigne Bossuet (1627–1704), French bishop. See Genesis 2:21–23.
4. Jules Michelet (1798–1874), French historian; in *Woman* (1860), he wrote, "Woman cannot live without man."
5. Julien Benda (1867–1956), French novelist and philosopher; *Uriel's Report* (1946) was a commentary on contemporary France.
6. This idea has been expressed in its most explicit form by E. Levinas in his [1947] essay *Le temps et l'autre* (*Time and the Other*). He expresses it like this: "Is there not a situation where alterity would be borne by a being in a positive sense, as essence? What is the alterity that does not purely and simply enter into the opposition of two species of the same genus? I think that the absolutely contrary contrary, whose contrariety is in no way affected by the relationship that can be established between it and its correlative, the contrariety that permits its terms to remain absolutely other, is the feminine. Sex is not some specific difference . . . Neither is the difference between the sexes a contradiction . . . Neither is the difference between the sexes the duality of two complementary terms, for two complementary terms presuppose a pre-

existing whole . . . [A]lterity is accomplished in the feminine. The term is on the same level as, but in meaning opposed to, consciousness." I suppose Mr. Levinas is not forgetting that woman also is consciousness for herself. But it is striking that he deliberately adopts a man's point of view, disregarding the reciprocity of the subject and the object. When he writes that woman is mystery, he assumes that she is mystery for man. So this apparently objective description is in fact an affirmation of masculine privilege [Beauvoir's note]. On LÉVINAS, see above.
7. Georges Dumézil (1898–1986), French comparative philologist and scholar of religious studies. Marcel Granet (1884–1940), French sociologist and sinologist.
8. In Greek mythology, two sky gods: Uranus, as the heavens, was husband of the Earth; Zeus, his grandson, was the ruler of the Olympian gods. "Varuna–Mitra": in Vedic Hindu mythologies, deities paired as guardian of the cosmic order and guardian of the human order, respectively.
9. A point made by Sartre in *Being and Nothingness* (1943).

man's ability to think biological relations as systems of oppositions; duality, alternation, opposition, and symmetry, whether occurring in defined or less clear form, are not so much phenomena to explain as fundamental and immediate givens of social reality."[1] These phenomena could not be understood if human reality were solely a *Mitsein*[2] based on solidarity and friendship. On the contrary, they become clear if, following Hegel,[3] a fundamental hostility to any other consciousness is found in consciousness itself; the subject posits itself only in opposition; it asserts itself as the essential and sets up the other as inessential, as the object.

But the other consciousness has an opposing reciprocal claim: traveling, a local is shocked to realize that in neighboring countries locals view him as a foreigner; between villages, clans, nations, and classes there are wars, potlatches, agreements, treaties, and struggles that remove the absolute meaning from the idea of the *Other* and bring out its relativity; whether one likes it or not, individuals and groups have no choice but to recognize the reciprocity of their relation. How is it, then, that between the sexes this reciprocity has not been put forward, that one of the terms has been asserted as the only essential one, denying any relativity in regard to its correlative, defining the latter as pure alterity? Why do women not contest male sovereignty? No subject posits itself spontaneously and at once as the inessential from the outset; it is not the Other who, defining itself as Other, defines the One; the Other is posited as Other by the One positing itself as One. But in order for the Other not to turn into the One, the Other has to submit to this foreign point of view. Where does this submission in woman come from?

There are other cases where, for a shorter or longer time, one category has managed to dominate another absolutely. It is often numerical inequality that confers this privilege: the majority imposes its law on or persecutes the minority. But women are not a minority like American blacks, or like Jews: there are as many women as men on the earth. Often, the two opposing groups concerned were once independent of each other; either they were not aware of each other in the past, or they accepted each other's autonomy; and some historical event subordinated the weaker to the stronger: the Jewish Diaspora, slavery in America, and the colonial conquests are facts with dates. In these cases, for the oppressed there was a *before*: they share a past, a tradition, sometimes a religion, or a culture. In this sense, the parallel Bebel[4] draws between women and the proletariat would be the best founded: proletarians are not a numerical minority either, and yet they have never formed a separate group. However, not *one* event but a whole historical development explains their existence as a class and accounts for the distribution of *these* individuals in this class. There have not always been proletarians: there have always been women; they are women by their physiological structure; as far back as history can be traced, they have always been subordinate to men; their dependence is not the consequence of an event or a becoming, it did not *happen*. Alterity here

1. See Claude Lévi-Strauss, *Les Structures élémentaires de la parenté* (*The Elementary Structures of Kinship*). I thank Claude Lévi-Strauss for sharing the proofs of his thesis, which I drew on heavily, particularly in the second part, pp. 76–89 [Beauvoir's note]. Lévi-Strauss (1908–2009), French social anthropologist; *Elementary Structures* (1949) was his first major work.
2. Being with (German). This is not a reference to HEIDEGGER or JASPERS: neither uses this expression in connection with such "fellowship."
3. For HEGEL, see above.
4. August Bebel (1840–1913), German socialist; he draws the parallel in *Woman and Socialism* (1883).

appears to be an absolute, partly because it falls outside the accidental nature of historical fact. A situation created over time can come undone at another time—blacks in Haiti for one are a good example;[5] on the contrary, a natural condition seems to defy change. In truth, nature is no more an immutable given than is historical reality. If woman discovers herself as the inessential and never turns into the essential, it is because she does not bring about this transformation herself. Proletarians say "we." So do blacks. Positing themselves as subjects, they thus transform the bourgeois or whites into "others." Women—except in certain abstract gatherings such as conferences—do not use "we"; men say "women," and women adopt this word to refer to themselves; but they do not posit themselves authentically as Subjects. The proletarians made the revolution in Russia, the blacks in Haiti, the Indo-Chinese are fighting in Indochina.[6] Women's actions have never been more than symbolic agitation; they have won only what men have been willing to concede to them; they have taken nothing; they have received. It is that they lack the concrete means to organize themselves into a unit that could posit itself in opposition. They have no past, no history, no religion of their own; and unlike the proletariat, they have no solidarity of labor or interests; they even lack their own space that makes communities of American blacks, the Jews in ghettos, or the workers in Saint-Denis[7] or Renault factories. They live dispersed among men, tied by homes, work, economic interests, and social conditions to certain men—fathers or husbands—more closely than to other women. As bourgeois women, they are in solidarity with bourgeois men and not with women proletarians; as white women, they are in solidarity with white men and not with black women. The proletariat could plan to massacre the whole ruling class; a fanatic Jew or black could dream of seizing the secret of the atomic bomb and turning all of humanity entirely Jewish or entirely black: but a woman could not even dream of exterminating males. The tie that binds her to her oppressors is unlike any other. The division of the sexes is a biological given, not a moment in human history. Their opposition took shape within an original *Mitsein*, and she has not broken it. The couple is a fundamental unit with the two halves riveted to each other: cleavage of society by sex is not possible. This is the fundamental characteristic of woman: she is the Other at the heart of a whole whose two components are necessary to each other.

One might think that this reciprocity would have facilitated her liberation; when Hercules spins wool at Omphale's[8] feet, his desire enchains him. Why was Omphale unable to acquire long-lasting power? Medea,[9] in revenge against Jason, kills her children: this brutal legend suggests that the bond attaching the woman to her child could have given her a formidable upper hand. In *Lysistrata*, Aristophanes[1] lightheartedly imagined a group of women who, uniting

---

5. In Haiti, blacks successfully revolted against French colonial rule, gaining independence in 1804.

6. That is, Vietnam, Cambodia, and Laos, which were French protectorates; Vietnam's war for independence from France began in 1945.

7. A northern suburb of Paris; it became an industrial center in the 19th century.

8. Legendary queen of Lydia (in modern Turkey); according to Greek myth, Hercules was forced to serve as her slave to be cleansed of accidental murder, and she made him wear women's clothing and hold wool for their spinning.

9. In classical mythology, the sorceress who helped Greek hero Jason with his quest and married him; but when he decided to leave her for the daughter of the king of Corinth, she killed their two children and his new bride.

1. Greek comic dramatist (ca. 450–ca. 385 B.C.E.); in *Lysistrata* (411 B.C.E.), the women of Athens and Sparta refuse to have sex with their husbands until the men end their war.

together for the social good, tried to take advantage of men's need for them: but it is only a comedy. The legend that claims that the ravished Sabine women resisted their ravishers[2] with obstinate sterility also recounts that by whipping them with leather straps, the men magically won them over into submission. Biological need—sexual desire and desire for posterity—which makes the male dependent on the female, has not liberated women socially. Master and slave are also linked by a reciprocal economic need that does not free the slave. That is, in the master-slave relation, the master does not *posit* the need he has for the other; he holds the power to satisfy this need and does not mediate it; the slave, on the other hand, out of dependence, hope, or fear, internalizes his need for the master; however equally compelling the need may be to them both, it always plays in favor of the oppressor over the oppressed: this explains the slow pace of working-class liberation, for example. Now, woman has always been, if not man's slave, at least his vassal; the two sexes have never divided the world up equally; and still today, even though her condition is changing, woman is heavily handicapped. In no country is her legal status identical to man's, and often it puts her at a considerable disadvantage. Even when her rights are recognized abstractly, long-standing habit keeps them from being concretely manifested in customs. Economically, men and women almost form two castes; all things being equal, the former have better jobs, higher wages, and greater chances to succeed than their new female competitors; they occupy many more places in industry, in politics, and so forth, and they hold the most important positions. In addition to their concrete power, they are invested with a prestige whose tradition is reinforced by the child's whole education: the present incorporates the past, and in the past all history was made by males. At the moment that women are beginning to share in the making of the world, this world still belongs to men: men have no doubt about this, and women barely doubt it. Refusing to be the Other, refusing complicity with man, would mean renouncing all the advantages an alliance with the superior caste confers on them. Lord-man will materially protect liege-woman and will be in charge of justifying her existence: along with the economic risk, she eludes the metaphysical risk of a freedom that must invent its goals without help. Indeed, beside every individual's claim to assert himself as subject—an ethical claim—lies the temptation to flee freedom and to make himself into a thing: it is a pernicious path because the individual, passive, alienated, and lost, is prey to a foreign will, cut off from his transcendence, robbed of all worth. But it is an easy path: the anguish and stress of authentically assumed existence are thus avoided. The man who sets the woman up as an *Other* will thus find in her a deep complicity. Hence woman makes no claim for herself as subject because she lacks the concrete means, because she senses the necessary link connecting her to man without positing its reciprocity, and because she often derives satisfaction from her role as *Other*.

But a question immediately arises: How did this whole story begin? It is understandable that the duality of the sexes, like all duality, be expressed in conflict. It is understandable that if one of the two succeeded in imposing its superiority, it had to establish itself as absolute. It remains to be explained

---

2. The Romans; according to legend, the founder of Rome invited the neighboring Sabines to a religious celebration and then his men carried off their women to help populate his new city.

how it was that man won at the outset. It seems possible that women might have carried off the victory, or that the battle might never be resolved. Why is it that this world has always belonged to men and that only today things are beginning to change? Is this change a good thing? Will it bring about an equal sharing of the world between men and women or not?

These questions are far from new; they have already had many answers; but the very fact that woman is *Other* challenges all the justifications that men have ever given: these were only too clearly dictated by their own interest. "Everything that men have written about women should be viewed with suspicion, because they are both judge and party," wrote Poulain de la Barre,[3] a little-known seventeenth-century feminist. Males have always and everywhere paraded their satisfaction of feeling they are kings of creation. "Blessed be the Lord our God, and the Lord of all worlds that has not made me a woman," Jews say in their morning prayers; meanwhile, their wives resignedly murmur: "Blessed be the Lord for creating me according to his will." Among the blessings Plato thanked the gods for was, first, being born free and not a slave and, second, a man and not a woman.[4] But males could not have enjoyed this privilege so fully had they not considered it as founded in the absolute and in eternity: they sought to make the fact of their supremacy a right. "Those who made and compiled the laws, being men, favored their own sex, and the jurisconsults have turned the laws into principles," Poulain de la Barre continues. Lawmakers, priests, philosophers, writers, and scholars have gone to great lengths to prove that women's subordinate condition was willed in heaven and profitable on earth. Religions forged by men reflect this will for domination: they found ammunition in the legends of Eve and Pandora.[5] They have put philosophy and theology in their service, as seen in the previously cited words of Aristotle and Saint Thomas. Since ancient times, satirists and moralists have delighted in depicting women's weaknesses. The violent indictments brought against them all through French literature are well-known: Montherlant, with less verve, picks up the tradition from Jean de Meung.[6] This hostility seems sometimes founded but is often gratuitous; in truth, it covers up a more or less skillfully camouflaged will to self-justification. "It is much easier to accuse one sex than to excuse the other," says Montaigne.[7] In certain cases, the process is transparent. It is striking, for example, that the Roman code limiting a wife's rights invokes "the imbecility and fragility of the sex" just when a weakening family structure makes her a threat to male heirs. It is striking that in the sixteenth century, to keep a married woman under wardship, the authority of Saint Augustine[8] affirming "the wife is an animal neither reliable nor stable" is called on, whereas the unmarried woman is recognized as capable of managing her own affairs.

3. François Poullain de la Barre (1647–1725), French priest and social philosopher. Beauvoir quotes from his *On the Equality of the Two Sexes* (1673).
4. This saying or one similar to it has long been attributed to Plato or to his teacher Socrates, but it is not found in his writings.
5. In Greek mythology, the first woman; she is blamed for opening the jar containing all evils. Eve, the first woman in the Judeo-Christian and Islamic traditions, is likewise blamed for the loss of an earthly paradise.

6. French poet (ca. 1240–ca. 1305); his poems are often satiric and antifeminist. Henry de Montherlant (1895–1972), French novelist and dramatist; his major work, a tetralogy written in the 1930s, was notably misogynist.
7. Michel de Montaigne (1533–1592), French writer and philosopher; the quotations here and below are from his essay "Upon Some Verses of Virgil," in the 3rd volume of his *Essays* (1588).
8. Bishop and highly influential theologian (354–430).

Montaigne well understood the arbitrariness and injustice of the lot assigned to women: "Women are not wrong at all when they reject the rules of life that have been introduced into the world, inasmuch as it is the men who have made these without them. There is a natural plotting and scheming between them and us." But he does not go so far as to champion their cause. It is only in the eighteenth century that deeply democratic men begin to consider the issue objectively. Diderot,[9] for one, tries to prove that, like man, woman is a human being. A bit later, John Stuart Mill ardently defends women.[1] But these philosophers are exceptional in their impartiality. In the nineteenth century the feminist quarrel once again becomes a partisan quarrel; one of the consequences of the Industrial Revolution is that women enter the labor force: at that point, women's demands leave the realm of the theoretical and find economic grounds; their adversaries become all the more aggressive; even though landed property is partially discredited, the bourgeoisie clings to the old values where family solidity guarantees private property: it insists all the more fiercely that woman's place be in the home as her emancipation becomes a real threat; even within the working class, men tried to thwart women's liberation because women were becoming dangerous competitors—especially as women were used to working for low salaries. To prove women's inferiority, antifeminists began to draw not only, as before, on religion, philosophy, and theology but also on science: biology, experimental psychology, and so forth. At most they were willing to grant "separate but equal status" to the *other* sex. That winning formula is most significant: it is exactly that formula the Jim Crow laws put into practice with regard to black Americans; this so-called egalitarian segregation served only to introduce the most extreme forms of discrimination. This convergence is in no way pure chance: whether it is race, caste, class, or sex reduced to an inferior condition, the justification process is the same. "The eternal feminine" corresponds to "the black soul" or "the Jewish character." However, the Jewish problem on the whole is very different from the two others: for the anti-Semite, the Jew is more an enemy than an inferior, and no place on this earth is recognized as his own; it would be preferable to see him annihilated. But there are deep analogies between the situations of women and blacks: both are liberated today from the same paternalism, and the former master caste wants to keep them "in their place," that is, the place chosen for them; in both cases, they praise, more or less sincerely, the virtues of the "good black," the carefree, childlike, merry soul of the resigned black, and the woman who is a "true woman"—frivolous, infantile, irresponsible, the woman subjugated to man. In both cases, the ruling caste bases its argument on the state of affairs it created itself. The familiar line from George Bernard Shaw[2] sums it up: The white American relegates the black to the rank of shoe-shine boy, and then concludes that blacks are only good for shining shoes. The same vicious circle can be found in all analogous circumstances: when an individual or a group of individuals is kept in a situation of inferiority, the fact is that he or they *are* inferior. But the scope of the verb *to be* must be understood; bad faith means giving it a substantive value,

9. Denis Diderot (1713–1784), French man of letters and philosopher.
1. See MILL's *The Subjection of Women* (1869), excerpted above.
2. Irish dramatist, critic, and socialist polemicist (1856–1950).

when in fact it has the sense of the Hegelian dynamic: *to be* is to have become, to have been made as one manifests oneself. Yes, women in general *are* today inferior to men; that is, their situation provides them with fewer possibilities: the question is whether this state of affairs must be perpetuated.

* * *

But how, then, will we ask the question? And in the first place, who are we to ask it? Men are judge and party: so are women. Can an angel be found? In fact, an angel would be ill qualified to speak, would not understand all the givens of the problem; as for the hermaphrodite, it is a case of its own: it is not both a man and a woman, but neither man nor woman. I think certain women are still best suited to elucidate the situation of women. It is a sophism to claim that Epimenides[3] should be enclosed within the concept of Cretan and all Cretans within the concept of liar: it is not a mysterious essence that dictates good or bad faith to men and women; it is their situation that disposes them to seek the truth to a greater or lesser extent. Many women today, fortunate to have had all the privileges of the human being restored to them, can afford the luxury of impartiality: we even feel the necessity of it. We are no longer like our militant predecessors; we have more or less won the game; in the latest discussions on women's status, the UN has not ceased to imperiously demand equality of the sexes, and indeed many of us have never felt our femaleness to be a difficulty or an obstacle; many other problems seem more essential than those that concern us uniquely: this very detachment makes it possible to hope our attitude will be objective. Yet we know the feminine world more intimately than men do because our roots are in it; we grasp more immediately what the fact of being female means for a human being, and we care more about knowing it. I said that there are more essential problems; but this one still has a certain importance from our point of view: How will the fact of being women have affected our lives? What precise opportunities have been given us, and which ones have been denied? What destiny awaits our younger sisters, and in which direction should we point them? It is striking that most feminine literature is driven today by an attempt at lucidity more than by a will to make demands; coming out of an era of muddled controversy, this book is one attempt among others to take stock of the current state.

But it is no doubt impossible to approach any human problem without partiality: even the way of asking the questions, of adopting perspectives, presupposes hierarchies of interests; all characteristics comprise values; every so-called objective description is set against an ethical background. Instead of trying to conceal those principles that are more or less explicitly implied, we would be better off stating them from the start; then it would not be necessary to specify on each page the meaning given to the words "superior," "inferior," "better," "worse," "progress," "regression," and so on. If we examine some of the books on women, we see that one of the most frequently held points of view is that of public good or general interest: in reality, this is taken to mean the interest of society as each one wishes to maintain or establish it.

---

3. Cretan religious teacher (active 6th c. B.C.E.?), credited with creating the liar's paradox by making the claim that all Cretans are liars.

In our opinion, there is no public good other than one that assures the citizens' private good; we judge institutions from the point of view of the concrete opportunities they give to individuals. But neither do we confuse the idea of private interest with happiness: that is another frequently encountered point of view; are women in a harem not happier than a woman voter? Is a housewife not happier than a woman worker? We cannot really know what the word "happiness" means, and still less what authentic values it covers; there is no way to measure the happiness of others, and it is always easy to call a situation that one would like to impose on others happy: in particular, we declare happy those condemned to stagnation, under the pretext that happiness is immobility. This is a notion, then, we will not refer to. The perspective we have adopted is one of existentialist morality. Every subject posits itself as a transcendence concretely, through projects; it accomplishes its freedom only by perpetual surpassing toward other freedoms; there is no other justification for present existence than its expansion toward an indefinitely open future. Every time transcendence lapses into immanence, there is degradation of existence into "in-itself," of freedom into facticity; this fall is a moral fault if the subject consents to it; if this fall is inflicted on the subject, it takes the form of frustration and oppression; in both cases it is an absolute evil. Every individual concerned with justifying his existence experiences his existence as an indefinite need to transcend himself. But what singularly defines the situation of woman is that being, like all humans, an autonomous freedom, she discovers and chooses herself in a world where men force her to assume herself as Other: an attempt is made to freeze her as an object and doom her to immanence, since her transcendence will be forever transcended by another essential and sovereign consciousness. Woman's drama lies in this conflict between the fundamental claim of every subject, which always posits itself as essential, and the demands of a situation that constitutes her as inessential. How, in the feminine condition, can a human being accomplish herself? What paths are open to her? Which ones lead to dead ends? How can she find independence within dependence? What circumstances limit women's freedom and can she overcome them? These are the fundamental questions we would like to elucidate. This means that in focusing on the individual's possibilities, we will define these possibilities not in terms of happiness but in terms of freedom.

Clearly this problem would have no meaning if we thought that a physiological, psychological, or economic destiny weighed on woman. So we will begin by discussing woman from a biological, psychoanalytical, and historical materialist point of view. We will then attempt to positively demonstrate how "feminine reality" has been constituted, why woman has been defined as Other, and what the consequences have been from men's point of view. Then we will describe the world from the woman's point of view such as it is offered to her, and we will see the difficulties women are up against just when, trying to escape the sphere they have been assigned until now, they seek to be part of the human *Mitsein*.

* * *

FROM PART THREE. MYTHS
CHAPTER 3

The myth of woman plays a significant role in literature; but what is its importance in everyday life? To what extent does it affect individual social customs and behavior? To reply to this question, we will need to specify the relation of this myth to reality.

There are different kinds of myths. This one, sublimating an immutable aspect of the human condition—that is, the "division" of humanity into two categories of individuals—is a static myth; it projects into a Platonic heaven a reality grasped through experience or conceptualized from experience; for fact, value, significance, notion, and empirical law, it substitutes a transcendent Idea, timeless, immutable, and necessary. This idea escapes all contention because it is situated beyond the given; it is endowed with an absolute truth. Thus, to the dispersed, contingent, and multiple existence of *women*, mythic thinking opposes the Eternal Feminine, unique and fixed; if the definition given is contradicted by the behavior of real flesh-and-blood women, it is women who are wrong: it is said not that Femininity is an entity but that women are not feminine. Experiential denials cannot do anything against myth. Though in a way, its source is in experience. It is thus true that woman is other than man, and this alterity is concretely felt in desire, embrace, and love; but the real relation is one of reciprocity; as such, it gives rise to authentic dramas: through eroticism, love, friendship, and their alternatives of disappointment, hatred, and rivalry, the relation is a struggle of consciousnesses, each of which wants to be essential, it is the recognition of freedoms that confirm each other, it is the undefined passage from enmity to complicity. To posit the Woman is to posit the absolute Other, without reciprocity, refusing, against experience, that she could be a subject, a peer.

In concrete reality, women manifest themselves in many different ways; but each of the myths built around woman tries to summarize her as a whole; each is supposed to be unique; the consequence of this is a multiplicity of incompatible myths, and men are perplexed before the strange inconsistencies of the idea of Femininity; as every woman enters into many of these archetypes, each of which claims to incarnate its Truth alone, men also find the same old confusion before their companions as did the Sophists,[4] who had difficulty understanding how a person could be light and dark at the same time. The transition to the absolute shows up in social representations: relations are quickly fixed in classes, and roles in types, just as, for the childlike mentality, relations are fixed in things. For example, patriarchal society, focused on preserving the patrimony, necessarily implies, in addition to individuals who hold and transmit goods, the existence of men and women who wrest them from their owners and circulate them; men—adventurers, crooks, thieves, speculators—are generally repudiated by the group; women using their sexual attraction can lure young people and even family men into dissipating their patrimony, all within the law; they appropriate men's fortunes or seize their inheritance; this role being considered bad, women who play it are called "bad women." But in other families—those of their fathers,

4. Professional teachers of 5th-century B.C.E. Greece, including a number of philosophers.

brothers, husbands, or lovers—they can in fact seem like guardian angels; the courtesan who swindles rich financiers is a patroness of painters and writers. The ambiguity of personalities like Apasia and Mme de Pompadour[5] is easy to understand as a concrete experience. But if woman is posited as the Praying Mantis, the Mandrake,[6] or the Demon, then the mind reels to discover in her the Muse, the Goddess Mother, and Beatrice[7] as well.

As group representation and social types are generally defined by pairs of opposite terms, ambivalence will appear to be an intrinsic property of the Eternal Feminine. The saintly mother has its correlation in the cruel step-mother, the angelic young girl has the perverse virgin: so Mother will be said sometimes to equal Life and sometimes Death, and every virgin is either a pure spirit or flesh possessed by the devil.

It is obviously not reality that dictates to society or individuals their choices between the two opposing principles of unification; in every period, in every case, society and individual decide according to their needs. Very often they project the values and institutions to which they adhere onto the myth they adopt. Thus paternalism that calls for woman to stay at home defines her as sentiment, inferiority, and immanence; in fact, every existent is simultaneously immanence and transcendence; when he is offered no goal, or is prevented from reaching any goal, or denied the victory of it, his transcendence falls uselessly into the past, that is, it falls into immanence; this is the lot assigned to women in patriarchy; but this is in no way a vocation, any more than slavery is the slave's vocation. The development of this mythology is all too clear in Auguste Comte.[8] To identify Woman with Altruism is to guarantee man absolute rights to her devotion; it is to impose on women a categorical must-be.

The myth must not be confused with the grasp of a signification; signification is immanent in the object; it is revealed to consciousness in a living experience, whereas the myth is a transcendent Idea that escapes any act of consciousness. When Michel Leiris in L'âge d'homme (Manhood)[9] describes his vision of female organs, he provides significations and does not develop a myth. Wonder at the feminine body and disgust for menstrual blood are apprehensions of a concrete reality. There is nothing mythical in the experience of discovering the voluptuous qualities of feminine flesh, and expressing these qualities by comparisons to flowers or pebbles does not turn them into myth. But to say that Woman is Flesh, to say that Flesh is Night and Death, or that she is the splendor of the cosmos, is to leave terrestrial truth behind and spin off into an empty sky. After all, man is also flesh for woman; and woman is other than a carnal object; and for each person and in each experience the

5. Jeanne-Antoinette Poisson, marquise de Pompadour (1721–1764), influential mistress (from 1745 on) of the French king Louis XV; she was also a patron of literature and the arts. Aspasia: mistress (ca. 445–429 B.C.E.) of the Athenian statesman Pericles and a woman of considerable learning.
6. A plant long used both as a narcotic and as an aphrodisiac. "Praying Mantis": in the first paragraph of chapter 1 (not included here), Beauvoir notes that the word "female" evokes the image of "the praying mantis and the spider, gorged on love, crushing their partners and gobbling them up."
7. Beatrice Portinari (1266–1290), the Italian

noblewoman idealized by Dante as the inspiration for much of his poetry. "Muse": in Greek mythology, one of the 9 daughters of Memory who preside over the arts and all intellectual pursuits.
8. French philosopher (1798–1857), known as the founder of positivism and of sociology; he idealized the role of women in society.
9. That is, The Age of Man (1939), an autobiographical work translated into English as Manhood: A Journey from Childhood into the Fierce Order of Virility (1962). The French writer Leiris (1901–1990) was also an anthropologist.

flesh is takes on singular significations. It is likewise perfectly true that woman—like man—is a being rooted in nature; she is more enslaved to the species than the male is, her animality is more manifest; but in her as in him, the given is taken on by existence; she also belongs to the human realm. Assimilating her with Nature is simply a prejudice.

Few myths have been more advantageous to the ruling master caste than this one: it justifies all its privileges and even authorizes taking advantage of them. Men do not have to care about alleviating the suffering and burdens that are physiologically women's lot since they are "intended by Nature"; they take this as a pretext to increase the misery of the woman's condition—for example, by denying woman the right to sexual pleasure, or making her work like a beast of burden.[1]

Of all these myths, none is more anchored in masculine hearts than the feminine "mystery." It has numerous advantages. And first it allows an easy explanation for anything that is inexplicable; the man who does not "understand" a woman is happy to replace his subjective deficiency with an objective resistance; instead of admitting his ignorance, he recognizes the presence of a mystery exterior to himself: here is an excuse that flatters his laziness and vanity at the same time. An infatuated heart thus avoids many disappointments: if the loved one's behavior is capricious, her remarks stupid, the mystery serves as an excuse. And thanks to the mystery, this negative relation that seemed to Kierkegaard infinitely preferable to positive possession is perpetuated;[2] faced with a living enigma, man remains alone: alone with his dreams, hopes, fears, love, vanity; this subjective game that can range from vice to mystical ecstasy is for many a more attractive experience than an authentic relation with a human being. Upon what bases does such a profitable illusion rest?

Surely, in a way, woman is mysterious, "mysterious like everyone," according to Maeterlinck.[3] Each one is subject only for himself; each one can grasp only his own self in his immanence; from this point of view, the other is always mystery. In men's view, the opacity of the for-itself[4] is more flagrant in the feminine other; they are unable to penetrate her unique experience by any effect of sympathy; they are condemned to ignorance about the quality of woman's sexual pleasure, the discomforts of menstruation, and the pains of childbirth. The truth is that mystery is reciprocal: as another, and as a masculine other, there is also a presence closed on itself and impenetrable to woman in the heart of every man; she is without knowledge of male eroticism. But according to a universal rule already mentioned, the categories in which men think the world are constituted from *their point of view as absolutes*: they fail to understand reciprocity here as everywhere. As she is mystery for man, woman is regarded as mystery in herself.

1. Cf. Balzac, *Physiology of Marriage*: "Do not trouble yourself in any way about her murmurings, her cries, her pains; nature has made her for your use, made her to bear all: the children, the worries, the blows, and the sorrows of man. But do not accuse us of harshness. In the codes of all the so-called civilised nations, man has written the laws which rule the destiny of woman beneath this bloody inscription: *Vae victis!* Woe to the vanquished!" [Beauvoir's note]. Honoré de Balzac (1799–1850), French novelist renowned for his depiction of French middle-class society; *Physiology of Marriage* (1830) is a satirical essay on marital infidelity.
2. KIERKEGAARD notoriously broke off his engagement, though he deeply loved his fiancée.
3. Maurice Maeterlinck (1862–1949), Belgian poet, playwright, and essayist.
4. An expression often used by Sartre in *Being and Nothingness* to refer to the sort of reality (or aspect of human reality) that has the character of self-consciousness.

It is true that her situation especially disposes her to be seen in this image. Her physiological destiny is very complex; she herself endures it as a foreign story; her body is not for her a clear expression of herself; she feels alienated from it; the link that for every individual joins physiological to psychic life—in other words, the relation between the facticity of an individual and the freedom that assumes it—is the most difficult enigma brought about by the human condition: for woman, this enigma is posed in the most disturbing way.

But what is called mystery is not the subjective solitude of consciousness, or the secret of organic life. The word's true meaning is found at the level of communication: it cannot be reduced to pure silence, to obscurity, to absence; it implies an emerging presence that fails to appear. To say that woman is mystery is to say not that she is silent but that her language is not heard; she is there, but hidden beneath veils; she exists beyond these uncertain appearances. Who is she? An angel, a demon, an inspiration, an actress? One supposes that either there are answers impossible to uncover or none is adequate because a fundamental ambiguity affects the feminine being; in her heart she is indefinable for herself: a sphinx.

The fact is, deciding *who* she *is* would be quite awkward for her; the question has no answer; but it is not that the hidden truth is too fluctuating to be circumscribed: in this area there is no truth. An existent *is* nothing other than what he does;[5] the possible does not exceed the real, essence does not precede existence: in his pure subjectivity, the human being *is nothing*. He is measured by his acts. It can be said that a peasant woman is a good or bad worker, that an actress has or does not have talent: but if a woman is considered in her immanent presence, absolutely nothing can be said about that, she is outside of the realm of qualification. Now, in amorous or conjugal relations and in all relations where woman is the vassal, the Other, she is grasped in her immanence. It is striking that the woman friend, colleague, or associate is without mystery; on the other hand, if the vassal is male and if, in front of an older and richer man or woman, a young man, for example, appears as the inessential object, he also is surrounded in mystery. And this uncovers for us an infrastructure of feminine mystery that is economic. A sentiment cannot *be* something, either. "In the domain of feeling, what is real is indistinguishable from what is imaginary," writes Gide.[6] "And it is sufficient to imagine one loves, in order to love, so it is sufficient to say to oneself that when one loves one imagines one loves, in order to love a little less." There is no discriminating between the imaginary and the real except through behavior. As man holds a privileged place in this world, he is the one who is able actively to display his love; very often he keeps the woman, or at least he helps her out; in marrying her, he gives her social status; he gives her gifts; his economic and social independence permits his endeavors and innovations: separated from Mme de Villeparisis, M. de Norpois[7] takes twenty-four-hour trips to be with her; very often he is busy and she is idle: he *gives* her the time he spends with her; she takes it: with pleasure, passion, or simply for entertainment?

---

5. That is, "what *it* does"; an "existent" is the kind of being, male or female, that *exists* in the manner in which a human being "exists."
6. André Gide (1869–1951), French writer and humanist; the quotation is from his novel *The Counterfeiters* (1926).
7. Two characters (lovers) in Marcel Proust's multi-volume *À la recherche du temps perdu* (1913–27, *In Search of Lost Time*).

Does she accept these benefits out of love or out of one interest? Does she love husband or marriage? Of course, even the proof man gives is ambiguous: Is such a gift given out of love or pity? But while normally woman finds numerous advantages in commerce with man, commerce with woman is profitable to man only inasmuch as he loves her. Thus, the degree of his attachment to her can be roughly estimated by his general attitude, while woman barely has the means to sound out her own heart; according to her moods she will take different points of view about her own feelings, and as long as she submits to them passively, no interpretation will be truer than another. In the very rare cases where it is she who holds the economic and social privileges, the mystery is reversed: this proves that it is not linked to *this* sex rather than to the other but to a situation. For many women, the roads to transcendence are blocked: because they *do* nothing, they do not make themselves *be* anything; they wonder indefinitely what they *could have* become, which leads them to wonder what they *are*: it is a useless questioning; if man fails to find that secret essence, it is simply because it does not exist. Kept at the margins of the world, woman cannot be defined objectively through this world, and her mystery conceals nothing but emptiness.

Furthermore, like all oppressed people, woman deliberately dissimulates her objective image; slave, servant, indigent, all those who depend upon a master's whims have learned to present him with an immutable smile or an enigmatic impassivity; they carefully hide their real feelings and behavior. Woman is also taught from adolescence to lie to men, to outsmart, to sidestep them. She approaches them with artificial expressions; she is prudent, hypocritical, playacting.

But feminine Mystery as recognized by mythical thinking is a more profound reality. In fact, it is immediately implied in the mythology of the absolute Other. If one grants that the inessential consciousness is also a transparent subjectivity, capable of carrying out the cogito,[8] one grants that it is truly sovereign and reverts to the essential; for all reciprocity to seem impossible, it is necessary that the Other be another for itself, that its very subjectivity be affected by alterity; this consciousness, which would be alienated as consciousness, in its pure immanent presence, would obviously be a Mystery; it would be a Mystery in itself because it would be it for itself; it would be absolute Mystery. It is thus that, beyond the secrecy their dissimulation creates, there is a mystery of the Black, of the Yellow, insofar as they are considered absolutely as the inessential Other. It must be noted that the American citizen who deeply confounds the average European is nonetheless not considered "mysterious": one more modestly claims not to understand him; likewise, woman does not always "understand" man, but there is no masculine mystery; the fact is that rich America and the male are on the side of the Master, and Mystery belongs to the slave.

Of course, one can only dream about the positive reality of the Mystery in the twilight of bad faith; like certain marginal hallucinations, it dissolves once one tries to pin it down. Literature always fails to depict "mysterious" women; they can only appear at the beginning of a novel as strange and enigmatic;

---

8. "I think" (Latin), the starting point of the French philosopher and mathematician René Descartes (1596–1650).

but unless the story remains unfinished, they give up their secret in the end and become consistent and translucent characters. The heroes in Peter Cheyney's[9] books, for example, never cease to be amazed by women's unpredictable caprices; one can never guess how they will behave, they confound all calculations; in truth, as soon as the workings of their actions are exposed to the reader, they are seen as very simple mechanisms: this one is a spy or that one a thief; however clever the intrigue, there is always a key, and it could not be otherwise, even if the author had all the talent, all the imagination possible. Mystery is never more than a mirage; it vanishes as soon as one tries to approach it.

Thus we see that myths are explained in large part by the use man makes of them. The myth of the woman is a luxury. It can appear only if man escapes the imperious influence of his needs; the more relations are lived concretely, the less idealized they are. The fellah in ancient Egypt, the bedouin peasant, the medieval artisan, and the worker of today, in their work needs and their poverty, have relations with the particular woman who is their companion that are too basic for them to embellish her with an auspicious or fatal aura. Eras and social classes that had the leisure to daydream were the ones who created the black-and-white statues of femininity. But luxury also has its usefulness; these dreams were imperiously guided by interest. Yes, most myths have their roots in man's spontaneous attitude to his own existence and the world that invests it: but the move to surpass experience toward the transcendent Idea was deliberately effected by patriarchal society for the end of self-justification; through myths, this society imposed its laws and customs on individuals in an imagistic and sensible way; it is in a mythical form that the group imperative insinuated itself into each consciousness. By way of religions, traditions, language, tales, songs, and film, myths penetrate even into the existence of those most harshly subjected to material realities. Everyone can draw on myth to sublimate his own modest experiences: betrayed by a woman he loves, one man calls her a slut; another is obsessed by his own virile impotence: this woman is a praying mantis; yet another takes pleasure in his wife's company: here we have Harmony, Repose, Mother Earth. The taste for eternity at bargain prices and for a handy, pocket-sized absolute, seen in most men, is satisfied by myths. The least emotion, a small disagreement, become the reflection of a timeless Idea; this illusion comfortably flatters one's vanity.

The myth is one of those traps of false objectivity into which the spirit of seriousness falls headlong. It is once again a matter of replacing lived experience and the free judgments of experience it requires by a static idol. The myth of Woman substitutes for an authentic relationship with an autonomous existent the immobile contemplation of a mirage. "Mirage! Mirage! Kill them since we cannot seize them; or else reassure them, instruct them, help them give up their taste for jewelry, make them real equal companions, our intimate friends, associates in the here and now, dress them differently, cut their hair, tell them everything," cried Laforgue.[1] Man would have nothing to lose, quite the contrary, if he stopped disguising woman as a symbol. Dreams, when collective and controlled—clichés—are so poor and monotonous compared

9. English writer of crime fiction (1896–1951).
1. Jules Laforgue (1860–1887), French symbolist poet; here and later in the chapter, Beauvoir quotes his "Sur la Femme" ("On Woman"), in *Mélanges posthumes* (1903, *Posthumous Assortment*).

to living reality: for the real dreamer, for the poet, living reality is a far more generous resource than a worn-out fantasy. The times when women were the most sincerely cherished were not courtly feudal ones, nor the gallant nineteenth century; they were the times—the eighteenth century, for example—when men regarded women as their peers; this is when women looked truly romantic: only read *Les liaisons dangereuses* (*Dangerous Liaisons*), *Le rouge et le noir* (*The Red and the Black*), or *A Farewell to Arms*[2] to realize this. Laclos' heroines like Stendhal's and Hemingway's are without mystery: and they are no less engaging for it. To recognize a human being in a woman is not to impoverish man's experience: that experience would lose none of its diversity, its richness, or its intensity if it was taken on in its intersubjectivity; to reject myths is not to destroy all dramatic relations between the sexes, it is not to deny the significations authentically revealed to man through feminine reality; it is not to eliminate poetry, love, adventure, happiness, and dreams: it is only to ask that behavior, feelings, and passion be grounded in truth.[3]

"Woman is lost. Where are the women? Today's women are not women"; we have seen what these mysterious slogans mean. In the eyes of men—and of the legions of women who see through these eyes—it is not enough to have a woman's body or to take on the female function as lover and mother to be a "real woman"; it is possible for the subject to claim autonomy through sexuality and maternity; the "real woman" is one who accepts herself as Other. The duplicitous attitude of men today creates a painful split for women; they accept, for the most part, that woman be a peer, an equal; and yet they continue to oblige her to remain the inessential; for her, these two destinies are not reconcilable; she hesitates between them without being exactly suited to either, and that is the source of her lack of balance. For man, there is no hiatus between public and private life: the more he asserts his grasp on the world through action and work, the more virile he looks; human and vital characteristics are merged in him; but women's own successes are in contradiction with her femininity since the "real woman" is required to make herself object, to be the Other. It is very possible that on this point even men's sensibility and sexuality are changing. A new aesthetic has already been born. Although the fashion for flat chests and narrow hips—the boyish woman—only lasted a short while,[4] the opulent ideal of past centuries has nevertheless not returned. The feminine body is expected to be flesh, but discreetly so; it must be slim and not burdened with fat; toned, supple, robust, it has to suggest transcendence; it is preferred tanned, having been bared to a universal sun like a worker's torso, not white like a hothouse plant. Woman's clothes, in becoming more practical, have not made her look asexual: on the contrary, short skirts have shown off her legs and thighs more than before. There is no reason for work to deprive her of her erotic appeal. To see woman as both a social person and carnal prey can be disturbing: in a recent series of drawings by Peynet,[5] there is a young fiancé deserting his fiancée because he was

---

2. Novels by, respectively, Pierre Chonderlos de Laclos (1741–1803), Stendhal (Marie-henri Beyle, 1783–1842), and Ernest Hemingway (1899–1961).
3. Laforgue goes on to say about woman: "As she has been left in slavery, idleness, without arms other than her sex, she has overdeveloped it and has become the Feminine . . . we have permitted

her to overdevelop; she is on the earth for us . . . Well, that is all wrong . . . we have played doll with the woman until now. This has gone on too long!" [Beauvoir's note].
4. The 1920s.
5. November 1948 [Beauvoir's note]. Raymond Peynet (1908–1999), French artist and designer.

seduced by the pretty mayoress about to celebrate the marriage; that a woman could hold a "man's office" and still be desirable has long been a subject of more or less dirty jokes; little by little, scandal and irony have lost their bite and a new form of eroticism seems to be coming about: perhaps it will produce new myths.

What is certain is that today it is very difficult for women to assume both their status of autonomous individual and their feminine destiny; here is the source of the awkwardness and discomfort that sometimes leads them to be considered "a lost sex." And without doubt it is more comfortable to endure blind bondage than to work for one's liberation; the dead, too, are better suited to the earth than the living. In any case, turning back is no more possible than desirable. What must be hoped is that men will assume, without reserve, the situation being created; only then can women experience it without being torn. Then will Laforgue's wish be fulfilled: "O young women, when will you be our brothers, our closest brothers without ulterior motives of exploitation? When will we give to each other a true handshake?" Then "Melusina, no longer under the burden of the fate unleashed on her by man alone, Melusina rescued," will find "her human base."[6] Then will she fully be a human being, "when woman's infinite servitude is broken, when she lives for herself and by herself, man—abominable until now—giving her her freedom."[7]

SOURCE: From Simone de Beauvoir, *The Second Sex*, trans. Constance Borde and Sheila Malovany-Chevallier (New York: Alfred A. Knopf, 2010), pp. 3–13, 15–17, 266–74. Originally published in 1949 as *Le deuxième sexe* in two volumes, *Les faits et les mythes* (*The Facts and the Myths*) and *L'expérience vécue* (*The Lived Experience*).

6. Breton, *Arcanum 17* [Beauvoir's note]. André Breton (1896–1966), French symbolist poet and essayist. In western European folklore, Melusina is a water spirit, half woman and half serpent.

7. Rimbaud, to Paul Demeny, May 15, 1871 [Beauvoir's note]. Arthur Rimbaud (1854–1891), French symbolist poet; Demeny (1844–1918), French poet.

JUDITH BUTLER
(b. 1956)

Butler has played a major role in the development of feminist and gender theory since the mid-1980s, working at the confluence of multiple disciplines, philosophical traditions, and concerns—both theoretical and practical. Her interests in a variety of developments in the interpretive tradition from HEGEL through phenomenology and on into poststructuralism and postmodernism have enabled her to bring an array of philosophical resources to bear on issues in feminist theory, gender and sexuality theory, and also moral and political philosophy, in striking and interesting ways. Among the most notable of her contributions is her idea of the "performativity"—and so contingency and instability—of gender identities and concepts. This idea has significant consequences for how we both conceive of and deal with gender.

Judith Butler was born in Cleveland, Ohio, into a Jewish family. Her early education included Hebrew school, where she had her first introduction to the kind of thinking and argument that goes on in ethics and moral philosophy, to which she was strongly attracted. She studied first at Bennington College and then at Yale, receiving a BA in 1978 and a PhD in philosophy in 1984.

Butler's first teaching position was at Wesleyan University. In 1993, after positions in several other institutions, she arrived at the University of California at Berkeley. She is now the Maxine Elliot Professor in the Department of Comparative Literature, with another appointment in Berkeley's Program of Critical Theory (which she helped establish). Her various visiting appointments have included the University of Amsterdam's Spinoza Chair of Philosophy (in 2002). She also holds the Hannah Arendt Chair at the recently founded international European Graduate School, headquartered in Switzerland. Butler has received many awards and honors, including the insignia of the French Chevalier in the Order of Arts and Letters from the French Cultural Ministry. She and her partner Wendy Brown, a professor of political science at Berkeley, are the parents of a son.

Butler's first book, an outgrowth of her dissertation, was *Subjects of Desire: Hegelian Reflections in Twentieth-Century France* (1987). Its thesis is that philosophy has had to tame and rationalize desire in order to arrive at a notion of the metaphysically secure, unified subject. Butler shows how Hegel's thought profoundly shaped late twentieth-century French theory, through lectures and works on Hegel by Alexandre Kojève (1902–1968) and Jean Hyppolite (1907–1968) that influenced their generation (including JEAN-PAUL SARTRE and SIMONE DE BEAUVOIR). She also shows how the notion of desire came to figure significantly in the theory of the subject as a kind of plurality, in the work of GILLES DELEUZE, MICHEL FOUCAULT, and JACQUES DERRIDA.

Her second book was the now classic *Gender Trouble: Feminism and the Subversion of Identity* (1990; 2nd ed., 1999), whose opening chapter is reprinted below. Here Butler put the idea of performativity to work in the analysis of gender. In her analysis, the notion of the "performative"—also found in analytic ordinary language philosophy and speech act theory—conveys the thought that gender categories are constituted by their being *performed*. Her approach is quite Foucauldian (with an echo of Sartre's thought in *Being and Nothingness* [1943]), in that it provides a "genealogy" of the structure of power and language that reifies the gendered categories— man, woman, heterosexual, homosexual, and so on—that we perform or act out. Butler's project is to "denaturalize" and "politicize" the body. Her notion of gender "trouble" is intentionally ambiguous, underscoring first that the traditional dichotomies in gender terms and concepts are problematic (and thus troubling) because of their bias toward the heteronormative and the masculine; and, second, that the cracks in the seemingly definite and objective gender identities show them to be performances and capable of deconstruction (and thus to be in trouble).

Butler's next work was *Bodies That Matter: On the Discursive Limits of "Sex"* (1993). It is a response to critics of her theory of the performativity of gender who hold that the materiality of the body sets limits on the indefiniteness of sex and gender. As the title of the work suggests, Butler argues that the normativity and even the materiality of the body, far from being immutable, are culturally, linguistically, and politically determined. What matters in the materiality of the body therefore supports Butler's thesis rather than supporting a critique of it. She continues this line of argument in her contribution to a volume that she co-wrote with Seyla Benhabib, Drucilla Cornell, and Nancy Fraser, *Feminist Contentions: A Philosophical Exchange* (1995).

These works are to a large extent theoretically oriented. They were followed by *Excitable Speech: A Politics of the Performative* (1997), which is more practical and political, exploring the implications of her theory for acts of speech and representation—in the media, the culture at large, politics, and the military—that are often hateful and harmful. In *The Psychic Life of Power: Theories in Subjection* (1997) Butler returned to her theory of the constitution and construction of subjectivity, which in *Subjects of Desire* had been explained in terms of desire. Taking her lead from NIETZSCHE, Freud, and Foucault, Butler here explores the ambiguity of "subjection"—that is, both being *subjected to* power and being *made into a subject by* power. Thus it is not just facets of identity (like gender) that are

performed, but also *being a subject* itself. Such performance results in a subject that is "haunted by an unassimilable remainder"—that is, by the impossible dream of being or becoming an authentic or radically free subjectivity—and yet a subject that nonetheless affects itself by transfiguring language, practices, and other cultural forms.

Between *The Psychic Life of Power* and her next major work, *Precarious Life: The Powers of Mourning and Violence* (2004), Butler contributed essays to a number of volumes, including *Contingency, Hegemony, Universality: Contemporary Dialogues on the Left*, co-written with Ernesto Laclau and Slavoj Žižek (2000); *Prejudicial Appearances: The Logic of American Antidiscrimination Law*, by Robert C. Post and others (2002); and *Women and Social Transformation*, co-written with Elizabeth Beck-Gernsheim and Lídia Puigver (2003). *Precarious Life*, which was written in response to the terrorist attacks of 9/11, explores how grief and anger over those 2001 attacks led to censorship, the violation of civil liberties, war, and torture. She continued this analysis in *Frames of War: When Is Life Grievable?* (2009).

Butler's major work in the field of moral theory is *Giving an Account of Oneself* (2005). Much of postmodern political theorizing has to contend with charges of moral relativism, nihilism, and aestheticism. Butler does not: she boldly ventures an account of the narrative nature of the self and its moral life as that self addresses itself, other people, and the world. This social and dialectical conception of the morally responsible subject shows her profound debt to Sartre, Theodor Adorno (1903–1969), and Foucault, yet also shows her originality in going beyond them. Butler's most recent work is *Notes toward a Performative Theory of Assembly* (2015), which explores the political power and possibilities of collective action.

From Gender Trouble

From *1. Subjects of Sex/Gender/Desire*

One is not born a woman, but rather becomes one.

—Simone de Beauvoir[1]

Strictly speaking, "women" cannot be said to exist.

—Julia Kristeva[2]

Woman does not have a sex.

—Luce Irigaray[3]

The deployment of sexuality . . . established this notion of sex.

—Michel Foucault[4]

The category of sex is the political category that founds society as heterosexual.

—Monique Wittig[5]

I. "Women" as the Subject of Feminism

For the most part, feminist theory has assumed that there is some existing identity, understood through the category of women, who not only initiates feminist interests and goals within discourse, but constitutes the subject for whom political representation is pursued. But *politics* and *representation* are controversial terms. On the one hand, *representation* serves as the operative term within a political process that seeks to extend visibility and legitimacy to women as political subjects; on the other hand, representation is the normative function of a language which is said either to reveal or to distort what is assumed to be true about the category of women. For feminist theory, the development of a language that fully or adequately represents women has seemed necessary to foster the political visibility of women. This has seemed obviously important considering the pervasive cultural condition in which women's lives were either misrepresented or not represented at all.

Recently, this prevailing conception of the relation between feminist theory and politics has come under challenge from within feminist discourse. The very subject of women is no longer understood in stable or abiding terms. There is a great deal of material that not only questions the viability of "the subject" as the ultimate candidate for representation or, indeed, liberation, but there is very little agreement after all on what it is that constitutes, or ought to constitute, the category of women. The domains of political and linguistic "representation" set out in advance the criterion by which subjects

1. For BEAUVOIR, see above; the quotation is from *The Second Sex* (1949) [editor's note].
2. Bulgarian-born French feminist, philosopher, psychoanalyst, and literary critic (b. 1941); the quotation is from *The Power of Horror* (1980) [editor's note].
3. Belgian-born French feminist, philosopher, and psychoanalyst (b. 1930); the quotation is from *This Sex Which Is Not One* (1977) [editor's note].
4. For FOUCAULT, see above; the quotation is from *The History of Sexuality*, vol. 1 (1976) [editor's note].
5. French feminist theorist and novelist (1935–2003); the quotation is from "The Category of Sex" (1976) [editor's note].

themselves are formed, with the result that representation is extended only to what can be acknowledged as a subject. In other words, the qualifications for being a subject must first be met before representation can be extended.

Foucault points out that juridical systems of power *produce* the subjects they subsequently come to represent.[6] Juridical notions of power appear to regulate political life in purely negative terms—that is, through the limitation, prohibition, regulation, control, and even "protection" of individuals related to that political structure through the contingent and retractable operation of choice. But the subjects regulated by such structures are, by virtue of being subjected to them, formed, defined, and reproduced in accordance with the requirements of those structures. If this analysis is right, then the juridical formation of language and politics that represents women as "the subject" of feminism is itself a discursive formation and effect of a given version of representational politics. And the feminist subject turns out to be discursively constituted by the very political system that is supposed to facilitate its emancipation. This becomes politically problematic if that system can be shown to produce gendered subjects along a differential axis of domination or to produce subjects who are presumed to be masculine. In such cases, an uncritical appeal to such a system for the emancipation of "women" will be clearly self-defeating.

The question of "the subject" is crucial for politics, and for feminist politics in particular, because juridical subjects are invariably produced through certain exclusionary practices that do not "show" once the juridical structure of politics has been established. In other words, the political construction of the subject proceeds with certain legitimating and exclusionary aims, and these political operations are effectively concealed and naturalized by a political analysis that takes juridical structures as their foundation. Juridical power inevitably "produces" what it claims merely to represent; hence, politics must be concerned with this dual function of power: the juridical and the productive. In effect, the law produces and then conceals the notion of "a subject before the law"[7] in order to invoke that discursive formation as a naturalized foundational premise that subsequently legitimates that law's own regulatory hegemony. It is not enough to inquire into how women might become more fully represented in language and politics. Feminist critique ought also to understand how the category of "women," the subject of feminism, is produced and restrained by the very structures of power through which emancipation is sought.

Indeed, the question of women as the subject of feminism raises the possibility that there may not be a subject who stands "before" the law, awaiting representation in or by the law. Perhaps the subject, as well as the invocation of a temporal "before," is constituted by the law as the fictive foundation of

6. See Michel Foucault, "Right of Death and Power over Life," in *The History of Sexuality, Volume I, An Introduction*, trans. Robert Hurley (New York: Vintage, 1980), originally published as *Histoire de la sexualité 1: La volonté de savoir* (Paris: Gallimard, 1976). In that final chapter, Foucault discusses the relation between the juridical and productive law. His notion of the productivity of the law is clearly derived from Nietzsche, although not identical with Nietzsche's "will to power." The use of Foucault's notion of productive power is not meant as a simple-minded "application" of Foucault to gender issues. [Where not otherwise indicated, notes are the author's. For FRIEDRICH NIETZSCHE, see above— editor's note.]

7. References throughout this work to a subject before the law are extrapolations of Derrida's reading of Kafka's parable "Before the Law," in *Kafka and the Contemporary Critical Performance: Centenary Readings*, ed. Alan Udoff (Bloomington: Indiana University Press, 1987). [For JACQUES DERRIDA, see above. The fable "Before the Law" (1914) was incorporated into Franz Kafka's novel *The Trial* (1925)—editor's note.]

its own claim to legitimacy. The prevailing assumption of the ontological integrity of the subject before the law might be understood as the contemporary trace of the state of nature hypothesis, that foundationalist fable constitutive of the juridical structures of classical liberalism. The performative invocation of a nonhistorical "before" becomes the foundational premise that guarantees a presocial ontology of persons who freely consent to be governed and, thereby, constitute the legitimacy of the social contract.

Apart from the foundationalist fictions that support the notion of the subject, however, there is the political problem that feminism encounters in the assumption that the term *women* denotes a common identity. Rather than a stable signifier that commands the assent of those whom it purports to describe and represent, *women*, even in the plural, has become a troublesome term, a site of contest, a cause for anxiety. As Denise Riley's title suggests, *Am I That Name?* is a question produced by the very possibility of the name's multiple significations.[8] If one "is" a woman, that is surely not all one is; the term fails to be exhaustive, not because a pregendered "person" transcends the specific paraphernalia of its gender, but because gender is not always constituted coherently or consistently in different historical contexts, and because gender intersects with racial, class, ethnic, sexual, and regional modalities of discursively constituted identities. As a result, it becomes impossible to separate out "gender" from the political and cultural intersections in which it is invariably produced and maintained.

The political assumption that there must be a universal basis for feminism, one which must be found in an identity assumed to exist cross-culturally, often accompanies the notion that the oppression of women has some singular form discernible in the universal or hegemonic structure of patriarchy or masculine domination. The notion of a universal patriarchy has been widely criticized in recent years for its failure to account for the workings of gender oppression in the concrete cultural contexts in which it exists. Where those various contexts have been consulted within such theories, it has been to find "examples" or "illustrations" of a universal principle that is assumed from the start. That form of feminist theorizing has come under criticism for its efforts to colonize and appropriate non-Western cultures to support highly Western notions of oppression, but because they tend as well to construct a "Third World" or even an "Orient" in which gender oppression is subtly explained as symptomatic of an essential, non-Western barbarism. The urgency of feminism to establish a universal status for patriarchy in order to strengthen the appearance of feminism's own claims to be representative has occasionally motivated the shortcut to a categorial or fictive universality of the structure of domination, held to produce women's common subjugated experience.

Although the claim of universal patriarchy no longer enjoys the kind of credibility it once did, the notion of a generally shared conception of "women," the corollary to that framework, has been much more difficult to displace. Certainly, there have been plenty of debates: Is there some commonality among "women" that preexists their oppression, or do "women" have a bond by vir-

---

8. See Denise Riley, *Am I That Name?: Feminism and the Category of 'Women' in History* (New York: Macmillan, 1988). [Riley (b. 1948), English feminist, poet, and philosopher—editor's note.]

tue of their oppression alone? Is there a specificity to women's cultures that is independent of their subordination by hegemonic, masculinist cultures? Are the specificity and integrity of women's cultural or linguistic practices always specified against and, hence, within the terms of some more dominant cultural formation? If there is a region of the "specifically feminine," one that is both differentiated from the masculine as such and recognizable in its difference by an unmarked and, hence, presumed universality of "women"? The masculine/feminine binary constitutes not only the exclusive framework in which that specificity can be recognized, but in every other way the "specificity" of the feminine is once again fully decontextualized and separated off analytically and politically from the constitution of class, race, ethnicity, and other axes of power relations that both constitute "identity" and make the singular notion of identity a misnomer.[9]

My suggestion is that the presumed universality and unity of the subject of feminism is effectively undermined by the constraints of the representational discourse in which it functions. Indeed, the premature insistence on a stable subject of feminism, understood as a seamless category of women, inevitably generates multiple refusals to accept the category. These domains of exclusion reveal the coercive and regulatory consequences of that construction, even when the construction has been elaborated for emancipatory purposes. Indeed, the fragmentation within feminism and the paradoxical opposition to feminism from "women" whom feminism claims to represent suggest the necessary limits of identity politics. The suggestion that feminism can seek wider representation for a subject that it itself constructs has the ironic consequence that feminist goals risk failure by refusing to take account of the constitutive powers of their own representational claims. This problem is not ameliorated through an appeal to the category of women for merely "strategic" purposes, for strategies always have meanings that exceed the purposes for which they are intended. In this case, exclusion itself might qualify as such an unintended yet consequential meaning. By conforming to a requirement of representational politics that feminism articulate a stable subject, feminism thus opens itself to charges of gross misrepresentation.

Obviously, the political task is not to refuse representational politics—as if we could. The juridical structures of language and politics constitute the contemporary field of power; hence, there is no position outside this field, but only a critical genealogy of its own legitimating practices. As such, the critical point of departure is *the historical present*, as Marx put it.[1] And the task is to formulate within this constituted frame a critique of the categories of identity that contemporary juridical structures engender, naturalize, and immobilize.

Perhaps there is an opportunity at this juncture of cultural politics, a period that some would call "postfeminist," to reflect from within a feminist perspective on the injunction to construct a subject of feminism. Within feminist political practice, a radical rethinking of the ontological constructions of

9. See Sandra Harding, "The Instability of the Analytical Categories of Feminist Theory," in *Sex and Scientific Inquiry*, eds. Sandra Harding and Jean F. O'Barr (Chicago: University of Chicago Press, 1987), pp. 283–302.

1. For KARL MARX, see above [editor's note].

identity appears to be necessary in order to formulate a representational politics that might revive feminism on other grounds. On the other hand, it may be time to entertain a radical critique that seeks to free feminist theory from the necessity of having to construct a single or abiding ground which is invariably contested by those identity positions or anti-identity positions that it invariably excludes. Do the exclusionary practices that ground feminist theory in a notion of "women" as subject paradoxically undercut feminist goals to extend its claims to "representation"?[2]

Perhaps the problem is even more serious. Is the construction of the category of women as a coherent and stable subject an unwitting regulation and reification of gender relations? And is not such a reification precisely contrary to feminist aims? To what extent does the category of women achieve stability and coherence only in the context of the heterosexual matrix?[3] If a stable notion of gender no longer proves to be the foundational premise of feminist politics, perhaps a new sort of feminist politics is now desirable to contest the very reifications of gender and identity, one that will take the variable construction of identity as both a methodological and normative prerequisite, if not a political goal.

To trace the political operations that produce and conceal what qualifies as the juridical subject of feminism is precisely the task of *a feminist genealogy* of the category of women. In the course of this effort to question "women" as the subject of feminism, the unproblematic invocation of that category may prove to *preclude* the possibility of feminism as a representational politics. What sense does it make to extend representation to subjects who are constructed through the exclusion of those who fail to conform to unspoken normative requirements of the subject? What relations of domination and exclusion are inadvertently sustained when representation becomes the sole focus of politics? The identity of the feminist subject ought not to be the foundation of feminist politics, if the formation of the subject takes place within a field of power regularly buried through the assertion of that foundation. Perhaps, paradoxically, "representation" will be shown to make sense for feminism only when the subject of "women" is nowhere presumed.

II. The Compulsory Order of Sex/Gender/Desire

Although the unproblematic unity of "women" is often invoked to construct a solidarity of identity, a split is introduced in the feminist subject by the dis-

---

2. I am reminded of the ambiguity inherent in Nancy Cott's title, *The Grounding of Modern Feminism* (New Haven: Yale University Press, 1987). She argues that the early twentieth-century U.S. feminist movement sought to "ground" itself in a program that eventually "grounded" that movement. Her historical thesis implicitly raises the question of whether uncritically accepted foundations operate like the "return of the repressed"; based on exclusionary practices, the stable political identities that found political movements may invariably become threatened by the very instability that the foundationalist move creates.

3. I use the term *heterosexual matrix* throughout the text to designate that grid of cultural intelligibility through which bodies, genders, and desires

are naturalized. I am drawing from Monique Wittig's notion of the "heterosexual contract" and, to a lesser extent, on Adrienne Rich's notion of "compulsory heterosexuality" to characterize a hegemonic discursive/epistemic model of gender intelligibility that assumes that for bodies to cohere and make sense there must be a stable sex expressed through a stable gender (masculine expresses male, feminine expresses female) that is oppositionally and hierarchically defined through the compulsory practice of heterosexuality. [See Wittig, "The Straight Mind" (1978), and "Compulsory Heterosexuality and Lesbian Existence" (1980) by Rich (1929–2012), an American poet and feminist critic—editor's note.]

tinction between sex and gender. Originally intended to dispute the biology-is-destiny formulation, the distinction between sex and gender serves the argument that whatever biological intractability sex appears to have, gender is culturally constructed: hence, gender is neither the causal result of sex nor as seemingly fixed as sex. The unity of the subject is thus already potentially contested by the distinction that permits of gender as a multiple interpretation of sex.[4]

If gender is the cultural meanings that the sexed body assumes, then a gender cannot be said to follow from a sex in any one way. Taken to its logical limit, the sex/gender distinction suggests a radical discontinuity between sexed bodies and culturally constructed genders. Assuming for the moment the stability of binary sex, it does not follow that the construction of "men" will accrue exclusively to the bodies of males or that "women" will interpret only female bodies. Further, even if the sexes appear to be unproblematically binary in their morphology and constitution (which will become a question), there is no reason to assume that genders ought also to remain as two.[5] The presumption of a binary gender system implicitly retains the belief in a mimetic relation of gender to sex whereby gender mirrors sex or is otherwise restricted by it. When the constructed status of gender is theorized as radically independent of sex, gender itself becomes a free-floating artifice, with the consequence that *man* and *masculine* might just as easily signify a female body as a male one, and *woman* and *feminine* a male body as easily as a female one.

This radical splitting of the gendered subject poses yet another set of problems. Can we refer to a "given" sex or a "given" gender without first inquiring into how sex and/or gender is given, through what means? And what is "sex" anyway? Is it natural, anatomical, chromosomal, or hormonal, and how is a feminist critic to assess the scientific discourses which purport to establish such "facts" for us? Does sex have a history?[6] Does each sex have a different history, or histories? Is there a history of how the duality of sex was established, a genealogy that might expose the binary options as a variable construction? Are the ostensibly natural facts of sex discursively produced by various scientific discourses in the service of other political and social interests? If the immutable character of sex is contested, perhaps this construct called "sex" is as culturally constructed as gender; indeed, perhaps it was always already gender, with the consequence that the distinction between sex and gender turns out to be no distinction at all.[7]

It would make no sense, then, to define gender as the cultural interpretation of sex, if sex itself is a gendered category. Gender ought not to be conceived merely as the cultural inscription of meaning on a pregiven sex (a

4. For a discussion of the sex/gender distinction in structuralist anthropology and feminist appropriations and criticisms of that formulation, see chapter 2, section i, "Structuralism's Critical Exchange" [not included here—editor's note].
5. For an interesting study of the *berdache* and multiple-gender arrangements in Native American cultures, see Walter L. Williams, *The Spirit and the Flesh: Sexual Diversity in American Indian Culture* (Boston: Beacon Press, 1988). See also, Sherry B. Ortner and Harriet Whitehead, eds., *Sexual Meanings: The Cultural Construction of Sexuality* (New York: Cambridge University Press, 1981).

6. Clearly Foucault's *History of Sexuality* offers one way to rethink the history of "sex" within a given modern Eurocentric context. For a more detailed consideration, see Thomas Laqueur and Catherine Gallagher, eds., *The Making of the Modern Body: Sexuality and Society in the 19th Century* (Berkeley: University of California Press, 1987), originally published as an issue of *Representations*, No. 14, Spring 1986.
7. See my "Variations on Sex and Gender: Beauvoir, Wittig, Foucault," in *Feminism as Critique*, eds. Seyla Benhabib and Drucilla Cornell (Basil Blackwell, dist. by University of Minnesota Press, 1987).

juridical conception); gender must also designate the very apparatus of production whereby the sexes themselves are established. As a result, gender is not to culture as sex is to nature; gender is also the discursive/cultural means by which "sexed nature" or "a natural sex" is produced and established as "prediscursive," prior to culture, a politically neutral surface *on which* culture acts. This construction of "sex" as the radically unconstructed will concern us again in the discussion of Lévi-Strauss[8] and structuralism in chapter 2. At this juncture it is already clear that one way the internal stability and binary frame for sex is effectively secured is by casting the duality of sex in a prediscursive domain. This production of sex as the prediscursive ought to be understood as the effect of the apparatus of cultural construction designated by *gender*. How, then, does gender need to be reformulated to encompass the power relations that produce the effect of a prediscursive sex and so conceal that very operation of discursive production?

III. Gender: The Circular Ruins of Contemporary Debate

Is there "a" gender which persons are said to *have*, or is it an essential attribute that a person is said to *be*, as implied in the question "What gender are you?" When feminist theorists claim that gender is the cultural interpretation of sex or that gender is culturally constructed, what is the manner or mechanism of this construction? If gender is constructed, could it be constructed differently, or does its constructedness imply some form of social determinism, foreclosing the possibility of agency and transformation? Does "construction" suggest that certain laws generate gender differences along universal axes of sexual difference? How and where does the construction of gender take place? What sense can we make of a construction that cannot assume a human constructor prior to that construction? On some accounts, the notion that gender is constructed suggests a certain determinism of gender meanings inscribed on anatomically differentiated bodies, where those bodies are understood as passive recipients of an inexorable cultural law. When the relevant "culture" that "constructs" gender is understood in terms of such a law or set of laws, then it seems that gender is as determined and fixed as it was under the biology-is-destiny formulation. In such a case, not biology, but culture, becomes destiny.

On the other hand, Simone de Beauvoir suggests in *The Second Sex* that "one is not born a woman, but, rather, becomes one."[9] For Beauvoir, gender is "constructed," but implied in her formulation is an agent, a *cogito*,[1] who somehow takes on or appropriates that gender and could, in principle, take on some other gender. Is gender as variable and volitional as Beauvoir's account seems to suggest? Can "construction" in such a case be reduced to a form of choice? Beauvoir is clear that one "becomes" a woman, but always under a cultural compulsion to become one. And clearly, the compulsion does not come from "sex." There is

---

8. Claude Lévi-Strauss (1908–2009), French anthropologist; he was a central figure in the development of structuralism in the social sciences and social theory. Butler's discussion of him is not included here [editor's note].

9. Simone de Beauvoir, *The Second Sex*, trans. E. M. Parshley (New York: Vintage, 1973), p. 301.
1. Literally, "I think" (Latin): the thinking or experiencing mind [editor's note].

nothing in her account that guarantees that the "one" who becomes a woman is necessarily female. If "the body is a situation,"[2] as she claims, there is no recourse to a body that has not always already been interpreted by cultural meanings; hence, sex could not qualify as a prediscursive anatomical facticity. Indeed, sex, by definition, will be shown to have been gender all along.[3]

The controversy over the meaning of *construction* appears to founder on the conventional philosophical polarity between free will and determinism. As a consequence, one might reasonably suspect that some common linguistic restriction on thought both forms and limits the terms of the debate. Within those terms, "the body" appears as a passive medium on which cultural meanings are inscribed or as the instrument through which an appropriative and interpretive will determines a cultural meaning for itself. In either case, the body is figured as a mere *instrument* or *medium* for which a set of cultural meanings are only externally related. But "the body" is itself a construction, as are the myriad "bodies" that constitute the domain of gendered subjects. Bodies cannot be said to have a signifiable existence prior to the mark of their gender; the question then emerges: To what extent does the body *come into being* in and through the mark(s) of gender? How do we reconceive the body no longer as a passive medium or instrument awaiting the enlivening capacity of a distinctly immaterial will?[4]

Whether gender or sex is fixed or free is a function of a discourse which, it will be suggested, seeks to set certain limits to analysis or to safeguard certain tenets of humanism as pre-suppositional to any analysis of gender. The locus of intractability, whether in "sex" or "gender" or in the very meaning of "construction," provides a clue to what cultural possibilities can and cannot become mobilized through any further analysis. The limits of the discursive analysis of gender presuppose and preempt the possibilities of imaginable and realizable gender configurations within culture. This is not to say that any and all gendered possibilities are open, but that the boundaries of analysis suggest the limits of a discursively conditioned experience. These limits are always set within the terms of a hegemonic cultural discourse predicated on binary structures that appear as the language of universal rationality. Constraint is thus built into what that language constitutes as the imaginable domain of gender.

Although social scientists refer to gender as a "factor" or a "dimension" of an analysis, it is also applied to embodied persons as "a mark" of biological, linguistic, and/or cultural difference. In these latter cases, gender can be understood as a signification that an (already) sexually differentiated body assumes, but even then that signification exists only *in relation* to another, opposing signification. Some feminist theorists claim that gender is "a relation," indeed, a set

2. Beauvoir, *The Second Sex*, p. 38.
3. See my "Sex and Gender in Beauvoir's *Second Sex*," *Yale French Studies, Simone de Beauvoir: Witness to a Century*, No. 72, Winter 1986.
4. Note the extent to which phenomenological theories such as Sartre's, Merleau-Ponty's, and Beauvoir's tend to use the term *embodiment*. Drawn as it is from theological contexts, the term tends to figure "the" body as a mode of incarnation and, hence, to preserve the external and dualistic relationship between a signifying immateriality and the materiality of the body itself. [For JEAN-PAUL SARTRE and MAURICE MERLEAU-PONTY, see above—editor's note.]

of relations, and not an individual attribute. Others, following Beauvoir, would argue that only the feminine gender is marked, that the universal person and the masculine gender are conflated, thereby defining women in terms of their sex and extolling men as the bearers of a body-transcendent universal personhood.

In a move that complicates the discussion further, Luce Irigaray argues that women constitute a paradox, if not a contradiction, within the discourse of identity itself. Women are the "sex" which is not "one." Within a language pervasively masculinist, a phallogocentric language,[5] women constitute the *unrepresentable*. In other words, women represent the sex that cannot be thought, a linguistic absence and opacity. Within a language that rests on univocal signification, the female sex constitutes the unconstrainable and undesignatable. In this sense, women are the sex which is not "one," but multiple.[6] In opposition to Beauvoir, for whom women are designated as the Other, Irigaray argues that both the subject and the Other are masculine mainstays of a closed phallogocentric signifying economy that achieves its totalizing goal through the exclusion of the feminine altogether. For Beauvoir, women are the negative of men, the lack against which masculine identity differentiates itself; for Irigaray, that particular dialectic constitutes a system that excludes an entirely different economy of signification. Women are not only represented falsely within the Sartrian frame of signifying-subject and signified-Other, but the falsity of the signification points out the entire structure of representation as inadequate. The sex which is not one, then, provides a point of departure for a criticism of hegemonic Western representation and of the metaphysics of substance that structures the very notion of the subject.

What is the metaphysics of substance, and how does it inform thinking about the categories of sex? In the first instance, humanist conceptions of the subject tend to assume a substantive person who is the bearer of various essential and nonessential attributes. A humanist feminist position might understand gender as an *attribute* of a person who is characterized essentially as a pregendered substance or "core," called the person, denoting a universal capacity for reason, moral deliberation, or language. The universal conception of the person, however, is displaced as a point of departure for a social theory of gender by those historical and anthropological positions that understand gender as a relation among socially constituted subjects in specifiable contexts. This relational or contextual point of view suggests that what the person "is," and, indeed, what gender "is," is always relative to the constructed relations in which it is determined.[7] As a shifting and contextual phenomenon, gender does not denote a substantive being, but a relative point of convergence among culturally and historically specific sets of relations.

Irigaray would maintain, however, that the feminine "sex" is a point of linguistic *absence*, the impossibility of a grammatically denoted substance,

---

5. That is, language that privileges the masculine (the phallus) and the word (the logos) in constructing meaning; the term was coined by Derrida [editor's note].

6. See Luce Irigaray, *This Sex Which Is Not One*, trans. Catherine Porter with Carolyn Burke (Ithaca: Cornell University Press, 1985), originally published as Ce *sexe qui n'en est pas un* (Paris: Éditions de Minuit, 1977).

7. See Joan Scott, "Gender as a Useful Category of Historical Analysis," in *Gender and the Politics of History* (New York: Columbia University Press, 1988), pp. 28–52, repr. from *American Historical Review*, Vol. 91, No. 5, 1986.

and, hence, the point of view that exposes that substance as an abiding and foundational illusion of a masculinist discourse. This absence is not marked as such within the masculine signifying economy—a contention that reverses Beauvoir's argument (and Wittig's) that the female sex is marked, while the male sex is not. For Irigaray, the female sex is not a "lack" or an "Other" that immanently and negatively defines the subject in its masculinity. On the contrary, the female sex eludes the very requirements of representation, for she is neither "Other" nor the "lack," those categories remaining relative to the Sartrian subject, immanent to that phallogocentric scheme. Hence, for Irigaray, the feminine could never be the *mark of a subject*, as Beauvoir would suggest. Further, the feminine could not be theorized in terms of a determinate *relation* between the masculine and the feminine within any given discourse, for discourse is not a relevant notion here. Even in their variety, discourses constitute so many modalities of phallogocentric language. The female sex is thus also *the subject* that is not one. The relation between masculine and feminine cannot be represented in a signifying economy in which the masculine constitutes the closed circle of signifier and signified. Paradoxically enough, Beauvoir prefigured this impossibility in *The Second Sex* when she argued that men could not settle the question of women because they would then be acting as both judge and party to the case.[8]

The distinctions among the above positions are far from discrete; each of them can be understood to problematize the locality and meaning of both the "subject" and "gender" within the context of socially instituted gender asymmetry. The interpretive possibilities of gender are in no sense exhausted by the alternatives suggested above. The problematic circularity of a feminist inquiry into gender is underscored by the presence of positions which, on the one hand, presume that gender is a secondary characteristic of persons and those which, on the other hand, argue that the very notion of the person, positioned within language as a "subject," is a masculinist construction and prerogative which effectively excludes the structural and semantic possibility of a feminine gender. The consequence of such sharp disagreements about the meaning of gender (indeed, whether *gender* is the term to be argued about at all, or whether the discursive construction of *sex* is, indeed, more fundamental, or perhaps *women* or *woman* and/or *men* and *man*) establishes the need for a radical rethinking of the categories of identity within the context of relations of radical gender asymmetry.

For Beauvoir, the "subject" within the existential analytic of misogyny is always already masculine, conflated with the universal, differentiating itself from a feminine "Other" outside the universalizing norms of personhood, hopelessly "particular," embodied, condemned to immanence. Although Beauvoir is often understood to be calling for the right of women, in effect, to become existential subjects and, hence, for inclusion within the terms of an abstract universality, her position also implies a fundamental critique of the very disembodiment of the abstract masculine epistemological subject.[9] That subject is abstract to the extent that it disavows its socially marked embodiment and, further, projects that disavowed and disparaged embodiment on to

---

8. Beauvoir, *The Second Sex*, p. xxvi.

9. See my "Sex and Gender in Beauvoir's *Second Sex*."

the feminine sphere, effectively renaming the body as female. This association of the body with the female works along magical relations of reciprocity
whereby the female sex becomes restricted to its body, and the male body,
fully disavowed, becomes, paradoxically, the incorporeal instrument of an
ostensibly radical freedom. Beauvoir's analysis implicitly poses the question:
Through what act of negation and disavowal does the masculine pose as a
disembodied universality and the feminine get constructed as a disavowed corporeality? The dialectic of master-slave,[1] here fully reformulated within the
non-reciprocal terms of gender asymmetry, prefigures what Irigaray will later
describe as the masculine signifying economy that includes both the existential subject and its Other.

Beauvoir proposes that the female body ought to be the situation and
instrumentality of women's freedom, not a defining and limiting essence.[2]
The theory of embodiment informing Beauvoir's analysis is clearly limited
by the uncritical reproduction of the Cartesian distinction between freedom
and the body. Despite my own previous efforts to argue the contrary, it appears
that Beauvoir maintains the mind/body dualism, even as she proposes a synthesis of those terms.[3] The preservation of that very distinction can be read
as symptomatic of the very phallogocentrism that Beauvoir underestimates. In the philosophical tradition that begins with Plato and continues through Descartes, Husserl,[4] and Sartre, the ontological distinction
between soul (consciousness, mind) and body invariably supports relations of political and psychic subordination and hierarchy. The mind not
only subjugates the body, but occasionally entertains the fantasy of fleeing its embodiment altogether. The cultural associations of mind with
masculinity and body with femininity are well documented within the
field of philosophy and feminism.[5] As a result, any uncritical reproduction
of the mind/body distinction ought to be rethought for the implicit gender
hierarchy that the distinction has conventionally produced, maintained,
and rationalized.

1. A reference to HEGEL's discussion in the "Self-
Consciousness" section of his *Phenomenology of
Geist* (1807); see above [editor's note]
2. The normative ideal of the body as both a "situation" and an "instrumentality" is embraced by
both Beauvoir with respect to gender and Frantz
Fanon with respect to race. Fanon concludes his
analysis of colonization through recourse to the
body as an instrument of freedom, where freedom
is, in Cartesian fashion, equated with a consciousness capable of doubt: "O my body, make of me
always a man who questions!" (Frantz Fanon, *Black
Skin, White Masks* [New York: Grove Press, 1967]
p. 323, originally published as *Peau noire, masques
blancs* [Paris: Éditions de Seuil, 1952]). [This passage from FANON is included above—editor's note.]
3. The radical ontological disjunction in Sartre
between consciousness and the body is part of the
Cartesian inheritance of his philosophy. Significantly, it is Descartes' distinction that Hegel
implicitly interrogates at the outset of the "Master-
Slave" section of *The Phenomenology of Spirit*.
Beauvoir's analysis of the masculine Subject and
the feminine Other is clearly situated in Hegel's
dialectic and in the Sartrian reformulation of that
dialectic in the section on sadism and masochism

in *Being and Nothingness*. Critical of the very possibility of a "synthesis" of consciousness and the
body, Sartre effectively returns to the Cartesian
problematic that Hegel sought to overcome. Beauvoir insists that the body can be the instrument and
situation of freedom and that sex can be the occasion for a gender that is not a reification, but a
modality of freedom. At first this appears to be a
synthesis of body and consciousness, where consciousness is understood as the condition of freedom. The question that remains, however, is
whether this synthesis requires and maintains the
ontological distinction between body and mind of
which it is composed and, by association, the hierarchy of mind over body and of masculine over
feminine.
4. For EDMUND HUSSERL, see above. Plato (ca.
427–ca. 347 B.C.E.), Greek philosopher. René
Descartes (1596–1650), French mathematician
and philosopher who argued that mind and body
are fundamentally different substances [editor's
note].
5. See Elizabeth V. Spelman, "Woman as Body:
Ancient and Contemporary Views," *Feminist Studies*, Vol. 8, No. 1, Spring 1982.

The discursive construction of "the body" and its separation from "freedom" in Beauvoir fails to mark along the axis of gender the very mind-body distinction that is supposed to illuminate the persistence of gender asymmetry. Officially, Beauvoir contends that the female body is marked within masculinist discourse, whereby the masculine body, in its conflation with the universal, remains unmarked. Irigaray clearly suggests that both marker and marked are maintained within a masculinist mode of signification in which the female body is "marked off," as it were, from the domain of the signifiable. In post-Hegelian terms, she is "cancelled," but not preserved. On Irigaray's reading, Beauvoir's claim that woman "is sex" is reversed to mean that she is not the sex she is designated to be, but, rather, the masculine sex *encore* (and *en corps*[6]) parading in the mode of otherness. For Irigaray, that phallogocentric mode of signifying the female sex perpetually reproduces phantasms of its own self-amplifying desire. Instead of a self-limiting linguistic gesture that grants alterity or difference to women, phallogocentrism offers a name to eclipse the feminine and take its place.

IV. THEORIZING THE BINARY, THE UNITARY, AND BEYOND

Beauvoir and Irigaray clearly differ over the fundamental structures by which gender asymmetry is reproduced; Beauvoir turns to the failed reciprocity of an asymmetrical dialectic, while Irigaray suggests that the dialectic itself is the monologic elaboration of a masculinist signifying economy. Although Irigaray clearly broadens the scope of feminist critique by exposing the epistemological, ontological, and logical structures of a masculinist signifying economy, the power of her analysis is undercut precisely by its globalizing reach. Is it possible to identify a monolithic as well as a monologic masculinist economy that traverses the array of cultural and historical contexts in which sexual difference takes place? Is the failure to acknowledge the specific cultural operations of gender oppression itself a kind of epistemological imperialism, one which is not ameliorated by the simple elaboration of cultural differences as "examples" of the selfsame phallogocentrism? The effort to *include* "Other" cultures as variegated amplifications of a global phallogocentrism constitutes an appropriative act that risks a repetition of the self-aggrandizing gesture of phallogocentrism, colonizing under the sign of the same those differences that might otherwise call that totalizing concept into question.[7]

Feminist critique ought to explore the totalizing claims of a masculinist signifying economy, but also remain self-critical with respect to the totalizing

6. In body (French). Butler is punning on *encore* (once again), pronounced the same in French [editor's note].

7. Gayatri Spivak most pointedly elaborates this particular kind of binary explanation as a colonizing act of marginalization. In a critique of the "self-presence of the cognizing supra-historical self," which is characteristic of the epistemic imperialism of the philosophical cogito, she locates politics in the production of knowledge that creates and censors the margins that constitute, through exclusion, the contingent intelligibility of that subject's given knowledge-regime: "I call 'politics as such' the prohibition of marginality that is implicit in the production of any explanation. From that point of view, the choice of particular binary oppositions . . . is no mere intellectual strategy. It is, in each case, the condition of the possibility for centralization (with appropriate apologies) and, correspondingly, marginalization" (Gayatri Chakravorty Spivak, "Explanation and Culture: Marginalia," in *In Other Worlds: Essays in Cultural Politics* [New York: Routledge, 1987], p. 113).

gestures of feminism. The effort to identify the enemy as singular in form is a reverse-discourse that uncritically mimics the strategy of the oppressor instead of offering a different set of terms. That the tactic can operate in feminist and antifeminist contexts alike suggests that the colonizing gesture is not primarily or irreducibly masculinist. It can operate to effect other relations of racial, class, and heterosexist subordination, to name but a few. And clearly, listing the varieties of oppression, as I began to do, assumes their discrete, sequential coexistence along a horizontal axis that does not describe their convergences within the social field. A vertical model is similarly insufficient; oppressions cannot be summarily ranked, causally related, distributed among planes of "originality" and "derivativeness."[8] Indeed, the field of power structured in part by the imperializing gesture of dialectical appropriation exceeds and encompasses the axis of sexual difference, offering a mapping of intersecting differentials which cannot be summarily hierarchized either within the terms of phallogocentrism or any other candidate for the position of "primary condition of oppression." Rather than an exclusive tactic of masculinist signifying economies, dialectical appropriation and suppression of the Other is one tactic among many, deployed centrally but not exclusively in the service of expanding and rationalizing the masculinist domain.

The contemporary feminist debates over essentialism raise the question of the universality of female identity and masculinist oppression in other ways. Universalistic claims are based on a common or shared epistemological standpoint, understood as the articulated consciousness or shared structures of oppression or in the ostensibly transcultural structures of femininity, maternity, sexuality, and/or *écriture feminine*.[9] The opening discussion in this chapter argued that this globalizing gesture has spawned a number of criticisms from women who claim that the category of "women" is normative and exclusionary and is invoked with the unmarked dimensions of class and racial privilege intact. In other words, the insistence upon the coherence and unity of the category of women has effectively refused the multiplicity of cultural, social, and political intersections in which the concrete array of "women" are constructed.

Some efforts have been made to formulate coalitional politics which do not assume in advance what the content of "women" will be. They propose instead a set of dialogic encounters by which variously positioned women articulate separate identities within the framework of an emergent coalition. Clearly, the value of coalitional politics is not to be underestimated, but the very form of coalition, of an emerging and unpredictable assemblage of positions, cannot be figured in advance. Despite the clearly democratizing impulse that motivates coalition building, the coalitional theorist can inadvertently reinsert herself as sovereign of the process by trying to assert an ideal form for coalitional structures in *advance*, one that will effectively guarantee unity as the outcome. Related efforts to determine what is and is not the true shape of a dialogue, what constitutes a subject-position, and, most importantly, when

---

8. See the argument against "ranking oppressions" in Cherríe Moraga, "La Güera," in *This Bridge Called My Back: Writings of Radical Women of Color*, eds. Gloria Anzaldúa and Cherríe Moraga (New York: Kitchen Table, Women of Color Press,

1982).
9. Feminine writing (French), a term coined by Hélène Cixous in "The Laugh of the Medusa" (1975) [editor's note].

"unity" has been reached, can impede the self-shaping and self-limiting dynamics of coalition.

The insistence in advance on coalitional "unity" as a goal assumes that solidarity, whatever its price, is a prerequisite for political action. But what sort of politics demands that kind of advance purchase on unity? Perhaps a coalition needs to acknowledge its contradictions and take action with those contradictions intact. Perhaps also part of what dialogic understanding entails is the acceptance of divergence, breakage, splinter, and fragmentation as part of the often tortuous process of democratization. The very notion of "dialogue" is culturally specific and historically bound, and while one speaker may feel secure that a conversation is happening, another may be sure it is not. The power relations that condition and limit dialogic possibilities need first to be interrogated. Otherwise, the model of dialogue risks relapsing into a liberal model that assumes that speaking agents occupy equal positions of power and speak with the same presuppositions about what constitutes "agreement" and "unity" and, indeed, that those are the goals to be sought. It would be wrong to assume in advance that there is a category of "women" that simply needs to be filled in with various components of race, class, age, ethnicity, and sexuality in order to become complete. The assumption of its essential incompleteness permits that category to serve as a permanently available site of contested meanings. The definitional incompleteness of the category might then serve as a normative ideal relieved of coercive force.

Is "unity" necessary for effective political action? Is the premature insistence on the goal of unity precisely the cause of an ever more bitter fragmentation among the ranks? Certain forms of acknowledged fragmentation might facilitate coalitional action precisely because the "unity" of the category of women is neither presupposed nor desired. Does "unity" set up an exclusionary norm of solidarity at the level of identity that rules out the possibility of a set of actions which disrupt the very borders of identity concepts, or which seek to accomplish precisely that disruption as an explicit political aim? Without the presupposition or goal of "unity," which is, in either case, always instituted at a conceptual level, provisional unities might emerge in the context of concrete actions that have purposes other than the articulation of identity. Without the compulsory expectation that feminist actions must be instituted from some stable, unified, and agreed-upon identity, those actions might well get a quicker start and seem more congenial to a number of "women" for whom the meaning of the category is permanently moot.

This antifoundationalist approach to coalitional politics assumes neither that "identity" is a premise nor that the shape or meaning of a coalitional assemblage can be known prior to its achievement. Because the articulation of an identity within available cultural terms instates a definition that forecloses in advance the emergence of new identity concepts in and through politically engaged actions, the foundationalist tactic cannot take the transformation or expansion of existing identity concepts as a normative goal. Moreover, when agreed-upon identities or agreed-upon dialogic structures, through which already established identities are communicated, no longer constitute the theme or subject of politics, then identities can come into being and dissolve depending on the concrete practices that constitute them. Certain political practices institute identities on a contingent basis in order to accomplish whatever aims are in view. Coalitional politics requires neither an expanded category of "women" nor an internally multiplicitous self that offers its complexity at once.

Gender is a complexity whose totality is permanently deferred, never fully what it is at any given juncture in time. An open coalition, then, will affirm identities that are alternately instituted and relinquished according to the purposes at hand; it will be an open assemblage that permits of multiple convergences and divergences without obedience to a normative telos of definitional closure.

V. IDENTITY, SEX, AND THE METAPHYSICS OF SUBSTANCE

What can be meant by "identity," then, and what grounds the presumption that identities are self-identical, persisting through time as the same, unified and internally coherent? More importantly, how do these assumptions inform the discourses on "gender identity"? It would be wrong to think that the discussion of "identity" ought to proceed prior to a discussion of gender identity for the simple reason that "persons" only become intelligible through becoming gendered in conformity with recognizable standards of gender intelligibility. Sociological discussions have conventionally sought to understand the notion of the person in terms of an agency that claims ontological priority to the various roles and functions through which it assumes social visibility and meaning. Within philosophical discourse itself, the notion of "the person" has received analytic elaboration on the assumption that whatever social context the person is "in" remains somehow externally related to the definitional structure of personhood, be that consciousness, the capacity for language, or moral deliberation. Although that literature is not examined here, one premise of such inquiries is the focus of critical exploration and inversion. Whereas the question of what constitutes "personal identity" within philosophical accounts almost always centers on the question of what internal feature of the person establishes the continuity or self-identity of the person through time, the question here will be: To what extent do *regulatory practices* of gender formation and division constitute identity, the internal coherence of the subject, indeed, the self-identical status of the person? To what extent is "identity" a normative ideal rather than a descriptive feature of experience? And how do the regulatory practices that govern gender also govern culturally intelligible notions of identity? In other words, the "coherence" and "continuity" of "the person" are not logical or analytic features of personhood, but, rather, socially instituted and maintained norms of intelligibility. Inasmuch as "identity" is assured through the stabilizing concepts of sex, gender, and sexuality, the very notion of "the person" is called into question by the cultural emergence of those "incoherent" or "discontinuous" gendered beings who appear to be persons but who fail to conform to the gendered norms of cultural intelligibility by which persons are defined.

"Intelligible" genders are those which in some sense institute and maintain relations of coherence and continuity among sex, gender, sexual practice, and desire. In other words, the spectres of discontinuity and incoherence, themselves thinkable only in relation to existing norms of continuity and coherence, are constantly prohibited and produced by the very laws that seek to establish causal or expressive lines of connection among biological sex, culturally constituted genders, and the "expression" or "effect" of both in the manifestation of sexual desire through sexual practice.

The notion that there might be a "truth" of sex, as Foucault ironically terms it, is produced precisely through the regulatory practices that generate coherent identities through the matrix of coherent gender norms. The heterosexualization of desire requires and institutes the production of discrete and asymmetrical oppositions between "feminine" and "masculine," where these are understood as expressive attributes of "male" and "female." The cultural matrix through which gender identity has become intelligible requires that certain kinds of "identities" cannot "exist"—that is, those in which gender does not follow from sex and those in which the practices of desire do not "follow" from either sex or gender. "Follow" in this context is a political relation of entailment instituted by the cultural laws that establish and regulate the shape and meaning of sexuality. Indeed, precisely because certain kinds of "gender identities" fail to conform to those norms of cultural intelligibility, they appear only as developmental failures or logical impossibilities from within that domain. Their persistence and proliferation, however, provide critical opportunities to expose the limits and regulatory aims of that domain of intelligibility and, hence, to open up within the very terms of that matrix of intelligibility rival and subversive matrices of gender disorder.

Before such disordering practices are considered, however, it seems crucial to understand the "matrix of intelligibility." Is it singular? Of what is it composed? What is the peculiar alliance presumed to exist between a system of compulsory heterosexuality and the discursive categories that establish the identity concepts of sex? If "identity" is an *effect* of discursive practices, to what extent is gender identity, construed as a relationship among sex, gender, sexual practice, and desire, the effect of a regulatory practice that can be identified as compulsory heterosexuality? Would that explanation return us to yet another totalizing frame in which compulsory heterosexuality merely takes the place of phallogocentrism as the monolithic cause of gender oppression?

Within the spectrum of French feminist and poststructuralist theory, very different regimes of power are understood to produce the identity concepts of sex. Consider the divergence between those positions, such as Irigaray's, that claim there is only one sex, the masculine, that elaborates itself in and through the production of the "Other," and those positions, Foucault's, for instance, that assume that the category of sex, whether masculine or feminine, is a production of a diffuse regulatory economy of sexuality. Consider also Wittig's argument that the category of sex is, under the conditions of compulsory heterosexuality, always feminine (the masculine remaining unmarked and, hence, synonymous with the "universal"). Wittig concurs, however paradoxically, with Foucault in claiming that the category of sex would itself disappear and, indeed, *dissipate* through the disruption and displacement of heterosexual hegemony.

The various explanatory models offered here suggest the very different ways in which the category of sex is understood depending on how the field of power is articulated. Is it possible to maintain the complexity of these fields of power and think through their productive capacities together? On the one hand, Irigaray's theory of sexual difference suggests that women can never

be understood on the model of a "subject" within the conventional representational systems of Western culture precisely because they constitute the
fetish of representation and, hence, the unrepresentable as such. Women can
never "be," according to this ontology of substances, precisely because they
are the relation of difference, the excluded, by which that domain marks
itself off. Women are also a "difference" that cannot be understood as the
simple negation or "Other" of the always-already-masculine subject. As discussed earlier, they are neither the subject nor its Other, but a difference from
the economy of binary opposition, itself a ruse for a monologic elaboration
of the masculine.

Central to each of these views, however, is the notion that sex appears
within hegemonic language as a *substance*, as, metaphysically speaking, a self-
identical being. This appearance is achieved through a performative twist of
language and/or discourse that conceals the fact that "being" a sex or a gender is fundamentally impossible. For Irigaray, grammar can never be a true
index of gender relations precisely because it supports the substantial model
of gender as a binary relation between two positive and representable terms.[1]
In Irigaray's view, the substantive grammar of gender, which assumes men
and women as well as their attributes of masculine and feminine, is an example
of a binary that effectively masks the univocal and hegemonic discourse of
the masculine, phallogocentrism, silencing the feminine as a site of subversive
multiplicity. For Foucault, the substantive grammar of sex imposes an artificial
binary relation between the sexes, as well as an artificial internal coherence
within each term of that binary. The binary regulation of sexuality suppresses
the subversive multiplicity of a sexuality that disrupts heterosexual, reproductive, and medicojuridical hegemonies.

For Wittig, the binary restriction on sex serves the reproductive aims of a
system of compulsory heterosexuality; occasionally, she claims that the overthrow of compulsory heterosexuality will inaugurate a true humanism of "the
person" freed from the shackles of sex. In other contexts, she suggests that
the profusion and diffusion of a non-phallocentric erotic economy will dispel
the illusion of sex, gender, and identity. At yet other textual moments it
seems that "the lesbian" emerges as a third gender that promises to transcend
the binary restriction on sex imposed by the system of compulsory heterosexuality. In her defense of the "cognitive subject," Wittig appears to have no
metaphysical quarrel with hegemonic modes of signification or representation; indeed, the subject, with its attribute of self-determination, appears to
be the rehabilitation of the agent of existential choice under the name of the
lesbian: "the advent of individual subjects demands first destroying the categories of sex . . . the lesbian is the only concept I know of which is beyond
the categories of sex."[2] She does not criticize "the subject" as invariably
masculine according to the rules of an inevitably patriarchal Symbolic, but
proposes in its place the equivalent of a lesbian subject as language-user.

---

1. For a fuller elaboration of the unrepresentabil-
ity of women in phallogocentric discourse, see Luce
Irigaray, "Any Theory of the 'Subject' Has Always
Been Appropriated by the Masculine," in *Speculum
of the Other Woman*, trans. Gillian C. Gill (Ithaca:
Cornell University Press, 1985). Irigaray appears to
revise this argument in her discussion of "the feminine gender" in *Sexes et parentés* (Paris: Éditions
de Minuit, 1987).

2. Monique Wittig, "One Is Not Born a Woman,"
Feminist Issues, Vol. 1, No. 2, Winter 1981, p. 53.
Also in *The Straight Mind and Other Essays* (Bos-
ton: Beacon Press, 1992), pp. 9–20.

The identification of women with "sex," for Beauvoir as for Wittig, is a conflation of the category of women with the ostensibly sexualized features of their bodies and, hence, a refusal to grant freedom and autonomy to women as it is purportedly enjoyed by men. Thus, the destruction of the category of sex would be the destruction of an *attribute*, sex, that has, through a misogynist gesture of synecdoche,[3] come to take the place of the person, the self-determining *cogito*. In other words, only men are "persons," and there is no gender but the feminine:

> Gender is the linguistic index of the political opposition between the sexes. Gender is used here in the singular because indeed there are not two genders. There is only one: the feminine, the "masculine" not being a gender. For the masculine is not the masculine, but the general.[4]

Hence, Wittig calls for the destruction of "sex" so that women can assume the status of a universal subject. On the way toward that destruction, "women" must assume both a particular and a universal point of view.[5] As a subject who can realize concrete universality through freedom, Wittig's lesbian confirms rather than contests the normative promise of humanist ideals premised on the metaphysics of substance. In this respect, Wittig is distinguished from Irigaray, not only in terms of the now familiar oppositions between essentialism and materialism,[6] but in terms of the adherence to a metaphysics of substance that confirms the normative model of humanism as the framework for feminism. Where it seems that Wittig has subscribed to a radical project of lesbian emancipation and enforced a distinction between "lesbian" and "woman," she does this through the defense of the pregendered "person," characterized as freedom. This move not only confirms the presocial status of human freedom, but subscribes to that metaphysics of substance that is responsible for the production and naturalization of the category of sex itself.

The *metaphysics of substance* is a phrase that is associated with Nietzsche within the contemporary criticism of philosophical discourse. In a commentary on Nietzsche, Michel Haar[7] argues that a number of philosophical ontologies have been trapped within certain illusions of "Being" and "Substance" that are fostered by the belief that the grammatical formulation of subject and predicate reflects the prior ontological reality of substance and attribute. These constructs, argues Haar, constitute the artificial philosophical means by which simplicity, order, and identity are effectively instituted. In no sense, however, do they reveal or represent some true order of things.

---

3. Use of a part to represent a whole (a figure of speech) [editor's note].

4. Monique Wittig, "The Point of View: Universal or Particular?" *Feminist Issues*, Vol. 3, No. 2, Fall 1983, p. 64. Also in *The Straight Mind and Other Essays*, pp. 59–67.

5. "One must assume both a particular *and* a universal point of view, at least to be part of literature" (Monique Wittig, "The Trojan Horse," *Feminist Issues*, Vol. 4, No. 2, Fall 1984, p. 68. Also in *The Straight Mind and Other Essays*, pp. 68–75).

6. The journal, *Questions Féministes*, available in English translation as *Feminist Issues*, generally defended a "materialist" point of view which took

practices, institution, and the constructed status of language to be the "material grounds" of the oppression of women. Wittig was part of the original editorial staff. Along with Monique Plaza, Wittig argued that sexual difference was essentialist in that it derived the meaning of women's social function from their biological facticity, but also because it subscribed to the primary signification of women's bodies as maternal and, hence, gave ideological strength to the hegemony of reproductive sexuality.

7. French philosopher and translator of Nietzsche (1937–2003) [editor's note].

For our purposes, this Nietzschean criticism becomes instructive when it is applied to the psychological categories that govern much popular and theoretical thinking about gender identity. According to Haar, the critique of the metaphysics of substance implies a critique of the very notion of the psychological person as a substantive thing:

> The destruction of logic by means of its genealogy brings with it as well the ruin of the psychological categories founded upon this logic. All psychological categories (the ego, the individual, the person) derive from the illusion of substantial identity. But this illusion goes back basically to a superstition that deceives not only common sense but also philosophers— namely, the belief in language and, more precisely, in the truth of grammatical categories. It was grammar (the structure of subject and predicate) that inspired Descartes' certainty that "I" is the subject of "think," whereas it is rather the thoughts that come to "me": at bottom, faith in grammar simply conveys the will to be the "cause" of one's thoughts. The subject, the self, the individual, are just so many false concepts, since they transform into substances fictitious unities having at the start only a linguistic reality.[8]

Wittig provides an alternative critique by showing that persons cannot be signified within language without the mark of gender. She provides a political analysis of the grammar of gender in French. According to Wittig, gender not only designates persons, "qualifies" them, as it were, but constitutes a conceptual episteme by which binary gender is universalized. Although French gives gender to all sorts of nouns other than persons, Wittig argues that her analysis has consequences for English as well. At the outset of "The Mark of Gender" (1984), she writes:

> The mark of gender, according to grammarians, concerns substantives. They talk about it in terms of function. If they question its meaning, they may joke about it, calling gender a "fictive sex." . . . as far as the categories of the person are concerned, both [English and French] are bearers of gender to the same extent. Both indeed give way to a primitive ontological concept that enforces in language a division of beings into sexes. . . . As an ontological concept that deals with the nature of Being, along with a whole nebula of other primitive concepts belonging to the same line of thought, gender seems to belong primarily to philosophy.[9]

For gender to "belong to philosophy" is, for Wittig, to belong to "that body of self-evident concepts without which philosophers believe they cannot develop a line of reasoning and which for them go without saying, for they exist prior to any thought, any social order, in nature."[1] Wittig's view is corroborated by that popular discourse on gender identity that uncritically

8. Michel Haar, "Nietzsche and Metaphysical Language," *The New Nietzsche: Contemporary Styles of Interpretation*, ed. David Allison (New York: Delta, 1977), pp. 17–18.

9. Monique Wittig, "The Mark of Gender," *Feminist Issues*, Vol. 5, No. 2, Fall 1985, p. 4. Also in *The Straight Mind and Other Essays*, pp. 76–89.
1. Ibid., p. 3.

employs the inflectional attribution of "being" to genders and to "sexualities." The unproblematic claim to "be" a woman and "be" heterosexual would be symptomatic of that metaphysics of gender substances. In the case of both "men" and "women," this claim tends to subordinate the notion of gender under that of identity and to lead to the conclusion that a person is a gender and is one in virtue of his or her sex, psychic sense of self, and various expressions of that psychic self, the most salient being that of sexual desire. In such a prefeminist context, gender, naively (rather than critically) confused with sex, serves as a unifying principle of the embodied self and maintains that unity over and against an "opposite sex" whose structure is presumed to maintain a parallel but oppositional internal coherence among sex, gender, and desire. The articulation "I feel like a woman" by a female or "I feel like a man" by a male presupposes that in neither case is the claim meaninglessly redundant. Although it might appear unproblematic to be a given anatomy (although we shall later consider the way in which that project is also fraught with difficulty), the experience of a gendered psychic disposition or cultural identity is considered an achievement. Thus, "I feel like a woman" is true to the extent that Aretha Franklin's invocation of the defining Other is assumed: "You make me feel like a natural woman."[2] This achievement requires a differentiation from the opposite gender. Hence, one is one's gender to the extent that one is not the other gender, a formulation that presupposes and enforces the restriction of gender within that binary pair.

Gender can denote a *unity* of experience, of sex, gender, and desire, only when sex can be understood in some sense to necessitate gender—where gender is a psychic and/or cultural designation of the self—and desire—where desire is heterosexual and therefore differentiates itself through an oppositional relation to that other gender it desires. The internal coherence or unity of either gender, man or woman, thereby requires both a stable and oppositional heterosexuality. That institutional heterosexuality both requires and produces the univocity of each of the gendered terms that constitute the limit of gendered possibilities within an oppositional, binary gender system. This conception of gender presupposes not only a causal relation among sex, gender, and desire, but suggests as well that desire reflects or expresses gender and that gender reflects or expresses desire. The metaphysical unity of the three is assumed to be truly known and expressed in a differentiating desire for an oppositional gender—that is, in a form of oppositional heterosexuality. Whether as a naturalistic paradigm which establishes a causal continuity among sex, gender, and desire, or as an authentic-expressive paradigm in which some true self is said to be revealed simultaneously or successively in

---

2. Aretha's song, originally written by Carole King, also contests the naturalization of gender. "Like a natural woman" is a phrase that suggests that "naturalness" is only accomplished through analogy or metaphor. In other words, "You make me feel like a metaphor of the natural," and without "you," some denaturalized ground would be revealed. For a further discussion of Aretha's claim in light of Simone de Beauvoir's contention that "one is not born, but rather becomes a woman," see my "Beauvoir's Philosophical Contribution," in eds. Ann Garry and Marilyn Pearsall, *Women, Knowledge, and Reality* (Boston: Unwin Hyman, 1989): 2nd ed. (New York: Routledge, 1996). [Franklin (b. 1942), American soul singer; King (b. 1942), American singer and songwriter who co-wrote "(You Make Me Feel Like) A Natural Woman," a hit song of 1967—editor's note.]

sex, gender, and desire, here "the old dream of symmetry,"[3] as Irigaray has called it, is presupposed, reified, and rationalized.

This rough sketch of gender gives us a clue to understanding the political reasons for the substantializing view of gender. The institution of a compulsory and naturalized heterosexuality requires and regulates gender as a binary relation in which the masculine term is differentiated from a feminine term, and this differentiation is accomplished through the practices of heterosexual desire. The act of differentiating the two oppositional moments of the binary results in a consolidation of each term, the respective internal coherence of sex, gender, and desire.

The strategic displacement of that binary relation and the metaphysics of substance on which it relies presuppose that the categories of female and male, woman and man, are similarly produced within the binary frame. Foucault implicitly subscribes to such an explanation. In the closing chapter of the first volume of The History of Sexuality and in his brief but significant introduction to Herculine Barbin, Being the Recently Discovered Journals of a Nineteenth-Century Hermaphrodite,[4] Foucault suggests that the category of sex, prior to any categorization of sexual difference, is itself constructed through a historically specific mode of sexuality. The tactical production of the discrete and binary categorization of sex conceals the strategic aims of that very apparatus of production by postulating "sex" as "a cause" of sexual experience, behavior, and desire. Foucault's genealogical inquiry exposes this ostensible "cause" as "an effect," the production of a given regime of sexuality that seeks to regulate sexual experience by instating the discrete categories of sex as foundational and causal functions within any discursive account of sexuality.

Foucault's introduction to the journals of the hermaphrodite, Herculine Barbin, suggests that the genealogical critique of these reified categories of sex is the inadvertent consequence of sexual practices that cannot be accounted for within the medicolegal discourse of a naturalized heterosexuality. Herculine is not an "identity," but the sexual impossibility of an identity. Although male and female anatomical elements are jointly distributed in and on this body, that is not the true source of scandal. The linguistic conventions that produce intelligible gendered selves find their limit in Herculine precisely because she/he occasions a convergence and disorganization of the rules that govern sex/gender/desire. Herculine deploys and redistributes the terms of a binary system, but that very redistribution disrupts and proliferates those terms outside the binary itself. According to Foucault, Herculine is not categorizable within the gender binary as it stands; the disconcerting convergence of heterosexuality and homosexuality in her/his person are only occasioned, but never caused, by his/her anatomical discontinuity. Foucault's appropriation of Herculine is suspect, but his analysis implies the interesting belief that sexual heterogeneity (paradoxically foreclosed by a naturalized "hetero"-

---

3. The first section of Irigaray's Speculum of the Other Woman is titled "The Blind Spot of an Old Dream of Symmetry" [editor's note].
4. Michel Foucault, ed., Herculine Barbin, Being the Recently Discovered Memoirs of a Nineteenth-Century Hermaphrodite, trans. Richard McDou-

gall (New York: Colophon, 1980), originally published as Herculine Barbin, dite Alexina B. presenté par Michel Foucault (Paris: Gallimard, 1978). The French version lacks the introduction supplied by Foucault with the English translation.

sexuality) implies a critique of the metaphysics of substance as it informs the identitarian categories of sex. Foucault imagines Herculine's experience as "a world of pleasures in which grins hang about without the cat."[5] Smiles, happinesses, pleasures, and desires are figured here as qualities without an abiding substance to which they are said to adhere. As free-floating attributes, they suggest the possibility of a gendered experience that cannot be grasped through the substantializing and hierarchizing grammar of nouns (*res extensa*[6]) and adjectives (attributes, essential and accidental). Through his cursory reading of Herculine, Foucault proposes an ontology of accidental attributes that exposes the postulation of identity as a culturally restricted principle of order and hierarchy, a regulatory fiction.

If it is possible to speak of a "man" with a masculine attribute and to understand that attribute as a happy but accidental feature of that man, then it is also possible to speak of a "man" with a feminine attribute, whatever that is, but still to maintain the integrity of the gender. But once we dispense with the priority of "man" and "woman" as abiding substances, then it is no longer possible to subordinate dissonant gendered features as so many secondary and accidental characteristics of a gender ontology that is fundamentally intact. If the notion of an abiding substance is a fictive construction produced through the compulsory ordering of attributes into coherent gender sequences, then it seems that gender as substance, the viability of *man* and *woman* as nouns, is called into question by the dissonant play of attributes that fail to conform to sequential or causal models of intelligibility.

The appearance of an abiding substance or gendered self, what the psychiatrist Robert Stoller refers to as a "gender core,"[7] is thus produced by the regulation of attributes along culturally established lines of coherence. As a result, the exposure of this fictive production is conditioned by the deregulated play of attributes that resist assimilation into the ready made framework of primary nouns and subordinate adjectives. It is of course always possible to argue that dissonant adjectives work retroactively to redefine the substantive identities they are said to modify and, hence, to expand the substantive categories of gender to include possibilities that they previously excluded. But if these substances are nothing other than the coherences contingently created through the regulation of attributes, it would seem that the ontology of substances itself is not only an artificial effect, but essentially superfluous.

In this sense, *gender* is not a noun, but neither is it a set of free-floating attributes, for we have seen that the substantive effect of gender is performatively produced and compelled by the regulatory practices of gender coherence. Hence, within the inherited discourse of the metaphysics of substance, gender proves to be performative—that is, constituting the identity it is purported to be. In this sense, gender is always a doing, though not a doing by a subject who might be said to preexist the deed. The challenge for rethinking gender categories outside of the metaphysics of substance will have to consider the relevance of Nietzsche's claim in *On the Genealogy of Morals* that "there is no

---

5. Foucault, ed., *Herculine Barbin*, p. x. [A reference to the Cheshire Cat in chap. 6 of *Alice's Adventures in Wonderland* (1865), by Lewis Carroll—editor's note.]
6. Extended thing (Latin); that is, corporeal substance [editor's note].
7. Robert Stoller, *Presentations of Gender* (New Haven: Yale University Press, 1985), pp. 11–14. [Stoller (1924–1991), American psychiatrist and researcher into gender identity—editor's note.]

'being' behind doing, effecting, becoming; 'the doer' is merely a fiction added to the deed—the deed is everything."[8] In an application that Nietzsche himself would not have anticipated or condoned, we might state as a corollary: There is no gender identity behind the expressions of gender; that identity is performatively constituted by the very "expressions" that are said to be its results.

VI. LANGUAGE, POWER, AND THE STRATEGIES OF DISPLACEMENT

A great deal of feminist theory and literature has nevertheless assumed that there is a "doer" behind the deed. Without an agent, it is argued, there can be no agency and hence no potential to initiate a transformation of relations of domination within society. Wittig's radical feminist theory occupies an ambiguous position within the continuum of theories on the question of the subject. On the one hand, Wittig appears to dispute the metaphysics of substance, but on the other hand, she retains the human subject, the individual, as the metaphysical locus of agency. While Wittig's humanism clearly presupposes that there is a doer behind the deed, her theory nevertheless delineates the performative construction of gender within the material practices of culture, disputing the temporality of those explanations that would confuse "cause" with "result." In a phrase that suggests the intertextual space that links Wittig with Foucault (and reveals the traces of the Marxist notion of reification in both of their theories), she writes:

> A materialist feminist approach shows that what we take for the cause or origin of oppression is in fact only the *mark* imposed by the oppressor; the "myth of woman," plus its material effects and manifestations in the appropriated consciousness and bodies of women. Thus, this mark does not preexist oppression . . . sex is taken as an "immediate given," a "sensible given," "physical features," belonging to a natural order. But what we believe to be a physical and direct perception is only a sophisticated and mythic construction, an "imaginary formation."[9]

Because this production of "nature" operates in accord with the dictates of compulsory heterosexuality, the emergence of homosexual desire, in her view, transcends the categories of sex: "If desire could liberate itself, it would have nothing to do with the preliminary marking by sexes."[1]

Wittig refers to "sex" as a mark that is somehow applied by an institutionalized heterosexuality, a mark that can be erased or obfuscated through practices that effectively contest that institution. Her view, of course, differs radically from Irigaray's. The latter would understand the "mark" of gender to be part of the hegemonic signifying economy of the masculine that operates through the self-elaborating mechanisms of specularization that have virtually

---

8. Friedrich Nietzsche, *On the Genealogy of Morals*, trans. Walter Kaufmann (New York: Vintage, 1969), p. 45.
9. Wittig, "One Is Not Born a Woman," p. 48. * * * The "Myth of Woman" is a chapter of Beauvoir's *The Second Sex*.
1. Monique Wittig, "Paradigm," in *Homosexualities and French Literature: Cultural Contexts/Critical Texts*, eds. Elaine Marks and George Stambolian (Ithaca: Cornell University Press, 1979), p. 114.

determined the field of ontology within the Western philosophical tradition. For Wittig, language is an instrument or tool that is in no way misogynist in its structures, but only in its applications. For Irigaray, the possibility of another language or signifying economy is the only chance at escaping the "mark" of gender which, for the feminine, is nothing but the phallogocentric erasure of the female sex. Whereas Irigaray seeks to expose the ostensible "binary" relation between the sexes as a masculinist ruse that excludes the feminine altogether, Wittig argues that positions like Irigaray's reconsolidate the binary between masculine and feminine and recirculate a mythic notion of the feminine. Clearly drawing on Beauvoir's critique of the myth of the feminine in *The Second Sex*, Wittig asserts, "there is no 'feminine writing.'"[2]

Wittig is clearly attuned to the power of language to subordinate and exclude women. As a "materialist," however, she considers language to be "another order of materiality,"[3] an institution that can be radically transformed. Language ranks among the concrete and contingent practices and institutions maintained by the choices of individuals and, hence, weakened by the collective actions of choosing individuals. The linguistic fiction of "sex," she argues, is a category produced and circulated by the system of compulsory heterosexuality in an effort to restrict the production of identities along the axis of heterosexual desire. In some of her work, both male and female homosexuality, as well as other positions independent of the heterosexual contract, provide the occasion either for the overthrow or the proliferation of the category of sex. In *The Lesbian Body* and elsewhere, however, Wittig appears to take issue with genitally organized sexuality *per se* and to call for an alternative economy of pleasures which would both contest the construction of female subjectivity marked by women's supposedly distinctive reproductive function.[4] Here the proliferation of pleasures outside the reproductive economy suggests both a specifically feminine form of erotic diffusion, understood as a counterstrategy to the reproductive construction of genitality. In a sense, *The Lesbian Body* can be understood, for Wittig, as an "inverted" reading of Freud's *Three Essays on the Theory of Sexuality*,[5] in which he argues for the developmental superiority of genital sexuality over and against the less restricted and more diffuse infantile sexuality. Only the "invert," the medical classification invoked by Freud for "the homosexual," fails to "achieve" the genital norm. In waging a political critique against genitality, Wittig appears to deploy "inversion" as a critical reading practice, valorising precisely those features of an undeveloped sexuality designated by Freud and effectively inaugurating a "post-genital politics."[6] Indeed, the notion of development can be read only as normalization within the heterosexual matrix. And yet, is this the only reading of Freud possible? And to what extent is Wittig's practice of "inversion" committed to the very model of normalization that she seeks to dismantle? In other words, if the model of a more diffuse and antigenital sexuality serves as the singular, oppositional alternative

2. Monique Wittig, "The Point of View: Universal or Particular?" p. 63.
3. Monique Wittig, "The Straight Mind," *Feminist Issues*, Vol. 1, No. 1, Summer 1980, p. 108. Also in *The Straight Mind and Other Essays*, pp. 21–32.
4. Monique Wittig, *The Lesbian Body*, trans. Peter

Owen (New York: Avon, 1976), originally published as *Le corps lesbien* (Paris: Éditions de Minuit, 1973).
5. Published in 1905. Freud (1856–1939), Austrian founder of psychoanalysis [editor's note].
6. I am grateful to Wendy Owen for this phrase.

to the hegemonic structure of sexuality, to what extent is that binary relation fated to reproduce itself endlessly? What possibility exists for the disruption of the oppositional binary itself?

Wittig's oppositional relationship to psychoanalysis produces the unexpected consequence that her theory presumes precisely that psychoanalytic theory of development, now fully "inverted," that she seeks to overcome. Polymorphous perversity, assumed to exist prior to the marking by sex, is valorised as the telos of human sexuality.[7] One possible feminist psychoanalytic response to Wittig might argue that she both under-theorizes and underestimates the meaning and function of *the language* in which "the mark of gender" occurs. She understands that marking practice as contingent, radically variable, and even dispensable. The status of a primary *prohibition* in Lacanian theory operates more forcefully and less contingently than the notion of a *regulatory practice* in Foucault or a materialist account of a system of heterosexist oppression in Wittig.

In Lacan,[8] as in Irigaray's post-Lacanian reformulation of Freud, sexual difference is not a simple binary that retains the metaphysics of substance as its foundation. The masculine "subject" is a fictive construction produced by the law that prohibits incest and forces an infinite displacement of a heterosexualizing desire. The feminine is never a mark of the subject; the feminine could not be an "attribute" of a gender. Rather, the feminine is the signification of lack, signified by the Symbolic, a set of differentiating linguistic rules that effectively create sexual difference. The masculine linguistic position undergoes individuation and heterosexualization required by the founding prohibitions of the Symbolic law, the law of the Father. The incest taboo that bars the son from the mother and thereby instates the kinship relation between them is a law enacted "in the name of the Father." Similarly, the law that refuses the girl's desire for both her mother and father requires that she take up the emblem of maternity and perpetuate the rules of kinship. Both masculine and feminine positions are thus instituted through prohibitive laws that produce culturally intelligible genders, but only through the production of an unconscious sexuality that reemerges in the domain of the imaginary.

The feminist appropriation of sexual difference, whether written in opposition to the phallogocentrism of Lacan (Irigaray) or as a critical reelaboration of Lacan, attempts to theorize the feminine, not as an expression of the metaphysics of substance, but as the unrepresentable absence effected by (masculine) denial that grounds the signifying economy through exclusion. The feminine as the repudiated/excluded within that system constitutes the possibility of a critique and disruption of that hegemonic conceptual scheme. The works of Jacqueline Rose[9] and Jane Gallop[1] underscore in different ways the constructed status of sexual difference, the inherent instability of that con-

7. Of course, Freud himself distinguished between "the sexual" and "the genital," providing the very distinction that Wittig uses against him. See, for instance, "The Development of the Sexual Function" in Freud, *Outline of a Theory of Psychoanalysis* [1940], trans. James Strachey (New York: Norton, 1979).

8. Jacques Lacan (1901–1981), French psychologist and psychoanalyst who reinterpreted Freud in the terms of structural linguistics [editor's note].

9. Jacqueline Rose, *Sexuality in the Field of Vision* (London: Verso, 1987). [Rose (b. 1949), British feminist theorist and literary critic—editor's note.]

1. Jane Gallop, *Reading Lacan* (Ithaca: Cornell University Press, 1985); *The Daughter's Seduction: Feminism and Psychoanalysis* (Ithaca: Cornell University Press, 1982). [Gallop (b. 1952), American feminist theorist and literary critic—editor's note.]

struction, and the dual consequentiality of a prohibition that at once institutes a sexual identity and provides for the exposure of that construction's tenuous ground. Although Wittig and other materialist feminists within the French context would argue that sexual difference is an unthinking replication of a reified set of sexed polarities, these criticisms neglect the critical dimension of the unconscious which, as a site of repressed sexuality, reemerges within the discourse of the subject as the very impossibility of its coherence. As Rose points out very clearly, the construction of a coherent sexual identity along the disjunctive axis of the feminine/masculine is bound to fail;[2] the disruptions of this coherence through the inadvertent reemergence of the repressed reveal not only that "identity" is constructed, but that the prohibition that constructs identity is inefficacious (the paternal law ought to be understood not as a deterministic divine will, but as a perpetual bumbler, preparing the ground for the insurrections against him).

The differences between the materialist and Lacanian (and post-Lacanian) positions emerge in a normative quarrel over whether there is a retrievable sexuality either "before" or "outside" the law in the mode of the unconscious or "after" the law as a postgenital sexuality. Paradoxically, the normative trope of polymorphous perversity is understood to characterize both views of alternative sexuality. There is no agreement, however, on the manner of delimiting that "law" or set of "laws." The psychoanalytic critique succeeds in giving an account of the construction of "the subject"—and perhaps also the illusion of substance—within the matrix of normative gender relations. In her existential-materialist mode, Wittig presumes the subject, the person, to have a presocial and pregendered integrity. On the other hand, "the paternal Law" in Lacan, as well as the monologic mastery of phallogocentrism in Irigaray, bear the mark of a monotheistic singularity that is perhaps less unitary and culturally universal than the guiding structuralist assumptions of the account presume.

But the quarrel seems also to turn on the articulation of a temporal trope of a subversive sexuality that flourishes *prior* to the imposition of a law, *after* its overthrow, or during its reign as a constant challenge to its authority. Here it seems wise to reinvoke Foucault who, in claiming that sexuality and power are coextensive, implicitly refutes the postulation of a subversive or emancipatory sexuality which could be free of the law. We can press the argument further by pointing out that "the before" of the law and "the after" are discursively and performatively instituted modes of temporality that are invoked within the terms of a normative framework which asserts that subversion, destabilization, or displacement requires a sexuality that somehow escapes the hegemonic prohibitions on sex. For Foucault, those prohibitions are invariably and inadvertently productive in the sense that "the subject" who is supposed to be founded and produced in and through those prohibitions does not have access to a sexuality that is in some sense "outside," "before," or "after" power itself. Power, rather than the law, encompasses both the juridical

2. "What distinguishes psychoanalysis from sociological accounts of gender (hence for me the fundamental impasse of Nancy Chodorow's work) is that whereas for the latter, the internalisation of norms is assumed roughly to work, the basic premise and indeed starting point of psychoanalysis is that it does not. The unconscious constantly reveals the 'failure' of identity" (Jacqueline Rose, *Sexuality in the Field of Vision*, p. 90).

(prohibitive and regulatory) and the productive (inadvertently generative) functions of differential relations. Hence, the sexuality that emerges within the matrix of power relations is not a simple replication or copy of the law itself, a uniform repetition of a masculinist economy of identity. The productions swerve from their original purposes and inadvertently mobilize possibilities of "subjects" that do not merely exceed the bounds of cultural intelligibility, but effectively expand the boundaries of what is, in fact, culturally intelligible.

The feminist norm of a postgenital sexuality became the object of significant criticism from feminist theorists of sexuality, some of whom have sought a specifically feminist and/or lesbian appropriation of Foucault. This utopian notion of a sexuality freed from heterosexual constructs, a sexuality beyond "sex," failed to acknowledge the ways in which power relations continue to construct sexuality for women even within the terms of a "liberated" heterosexuality or lesbianism.[3] The same criticism is waged against the notion of a specifically feminine sexual pleasure that is radically differentiated from phallic sexuality. Irigaray's occasional efforts to derive a specific feminine sexuality from a specific female anatomy have been the focus of anti-essentialist arguments for some time.[4] The return to biology as the ground of a specific feminine sexuality or meaning seems to defeat the feminist premise that biology is not destiny. But whether feminine sexuality is articulated here through a discourse of biology for purely strategic reasons,[5] or whether it is, in fact, a feminist return to biological essentialism, the characterization of female sexuality as radically distinct from a phallic organization of sexuality remains problematic. Women who fail either to recognize that sexuality as their own or understand their sexuality as partially constructed within the terms of the phallic economy are potentially written off within the terms of that theory as "male-identified" or "unenlightened." Indeed, it is often unclear within Irigaray's text whether sexuality is culturally constructed, or whether it is only culturally constructed within the terms of the phallus. In other words, is specifically feminine pleasure "outside" of culture as its prehistory or as its utopian future? If so, of what use is such a notion for negotiating the contemporary struggles of sexuality within the terms of its construction?

The pro-sexuality movement within feminist theory and practice has effectively argued that sexuality is always constructed within the terms of discourse and power, where power is partially understood in terms of heterosexual and phallic cultural conventions. The emergence of a sexuality constructed (not determined) in these terms within lesbian, bisexual, and heterosexual contexts is, therefore, *not* a sign of a masculine identification in some reductive sense. It is not the failed project of criticizing phallogocentrism or heterosexual hegemony, as if a political critique could effectively undo the cultural

---

3. See Gayle Rubin, "Thinking Sex: Notes for a Radical Theory of the Politics of Sexuality," in *Pleasure and Danger*, ed. Carole S. Vance (Boston: Routledge and Kegan Paul, 1984), pp. 267–319. Also in *Pleasure and Danger*, see Carole S. Vance, "Pleasure and Danger: Towards a Politics of Sexuality," pp. 1–28; Alice Echols, "The Taming of the Id: Feminist Sexual Politics, 1968–83," pp. 50–72; Amber Hollibaugh, "Desire for the Future: Radical Hope in Pleasure and Passion," pp. 401–410.

4. Irigaray's perhaps most controversial claim has been that the structure of the vulva as "two lips touching" constitutes the nonunitary and auto-erotic pleasure of women prior to the "separation" of this doubleness through the pleasure-depriving act of penetration by the penis. See Irigaray, *Ce sexe qui n'en est pas un*.

5. See a compelling argument for precisely this interpretation by Diana J. Fuss, *Essentially Speaking* (New York: Routledge, 1989).

construction of the feminist critic's sexuality. If sexuality is culturally constructed within existing power relations, then the postulation of a normative sexuality that is "before," "outside," or "beyond" power is a cultural impossibility and a politically impracticable dream, one that postpones the concrete and contemporary task of rethinking subversive possibilities for sexuality and identity within the terms of power itself. This critical task presumes, of course, that to operate within the matrix of power is not the same as to replicate uncritically relations of domination. It offers the possibility of a repetition of the law which is not its consolidation, but its displacement. In the place of a "male-identified" sexuality in which "male" serves as the cause and irreducible meaning of that sexuality, we might develop a notion of sexuality constructed in terms of phallic relations of power that replay and redistribute the possibilities of that phallicism precisely through the subversive operation of "identification" that are, within the power field of sexuality, inevitable. If "identifications," following Jacqueline Rose, can be exposed as phantasmatic, then it must be possible to enact an identification that displays its phantasmatic structure. If there is no radical repudiation of a culturally constructed sexuality, what is left is the question of how to acknowledge and "do" the construction one is invariably in. Are there forms of repetition that do not constitute a simple imitation, reproduction, and, hence, consolidation of the law (the anachronistic notion of "male identification" that ought to be discarded from a feminist vocabulary)? What possibilities of gender configurations exist among the various emergent and occasionally convergent matrices of cultural intelligibility that govern gendered life?

Within the terms of feminist sexual theory, it is clear that the presence of power dynamics within sexuality is in no sense the same as the simple consolidation or augmentation of a heterosexist or phallogocentric power regime. The "presence" of so-called heterosexual conventions within homosexual contexts as well as the proliferation of specifically gay discourses of sexual difference, as in the case of "butch" and "femme" as historical identities of sexual style, cannot be explained as chimerical representations of originally heterosexual identities. And neither can they be understood as the pernicious insistence of heterosexist constructs within gay sexuality and identity. The repetition of heterosexual constructs within sexual cultures both gay and straight may well be the inevitable site of the denaturalization and mobilization of gender categories. The replication of heterosexual constructs in non-heterosexual frames brings into relief the utterly constructed status of the so-called heterosexual original. Thus, gay is to straight *not* as copy is to original, but, rather, as copy is to copy. The parodic repetition of "the original," discussed in the final sections of chapter 3 of this text,[6] reveals the original to be nothing other than a parody of the *idea* of the natural and the original. Even if heterosexist constructs circulate as the available sites of power/discourse from which to do gender at all, the question remains: What possibilities of recirculation exist? Which possibilities of doing gender repeat and displace through hyperbole, dissonance, internal confusion, and proliferation the very constructs by which they are mobilized?

6. Not included here [editor's note].

Consider not only that the ambiguities and incoherences within and among heterosexual, homosexual, and bisexual practices are suppressed and redescribed within the reified framework of the disjunctive and asymmetrical binary of masculine/feminine, but that these cultural configurations of gender confusion operate as sites for intervention, exposure, and displacement of these reifications. In other words, the "unity" of gender is the effect of a regulatory practice that seeks to render gender identity uniform through a compulsory heterosexuality. The force of this practice is, through an exclusionary apparatus of production, to restrict the relative meanings of "heterosexuality," "homosexuality," and "bisexuality" as well as the subversive sites of their convergence and resignification. That the power regimes of heterosexism and phallogocentrism seek to augment themselves through a constant repetition of their logic, their metaphysic, and their naturalized ontologies does not imply that repetition itself ought to be stopped—as if it could be. If repetition is bound to persist as the mechanism of the cultural reproduction of identities, then the crucial question emerges: What kind of subversive repetition might call into question the regulatory practice of identity itself?

If there is no recourse to a "person," a "sex," or a "sexuality" that escapes the matrix of power and discursive relations that effectively produce and regulate the intelligibility of those concepts for us, what constitutes the possibility of effective inversion, subversion, or displacement within the terms of a constructed identity? What possibilities exist *by virtue of* the constructed character of sex and gender? Whereas Foucault is ambiguous about the precise character of the "regulatory practices" that produce the category of sex, and Wittig appears to invest the full responsibility of the construction to sexual reproduction and its instrument, compulsory heterosexuality, yet other discourses converge to produce this categorial fiction for reasons not always clear or consistent with one another. The power relations that infuse the biological sciences are not easily reduced, and the medicolegal alliance emerging in nineteenth-century Europe has spawned categorial fictions that could not be anticipated in advance. The very complexity of the discursive map that constructs gender appears to hold out the promise of an inadvertent and generative convergence of these discursive and regulatory structures. If the regulatory fictions of sex and gender are themselves multiply contested sites of meaning, then the very multiplicity of their construction holds out the possibility of a disruption of their univocal posturing.

Clearly this project does not propose to lay out within traditional philosophical terms an *ontology* of gender whereby the meaning of *being* a woman or a man is elucidated within the terms of phenomenology. The presumption here is that the "being" of gender is *an effect*, an object of a genealogical investigation that maps out the political parameters of its construction in the mode of ontology. To claim that gender is constructed is not to assert its illusoriness or artificiality, where those terms are understood to reside within a binary that counterposes the "real" and the "authentic" as oppositional. As a genealogy of gender ontology, this inquiry seeks to understand the discursive production of the plausibility of that binary relation and to suggest that certain cultural configurations of gender take the place of "the real" and consolidate and augment their hegemony through that felicitous self-naturalization.

If there is something right in Beauvoir's claim that one is not born, but rather *becomes* a woman, it follows that *woman* itself is a term in process, a becoming, a constructing that cannot rightfully be said to originate or to end. As an ongoing discursive practice, it is open to intervention and resignification. Even when gender seems to congeal into the most reified forms, the "congealing" is itself an insistent and insidious practice, sustained and regulated by various social means. It is, for Beauvoir, never possible finally to become a woman, as if there were a *telos* that governs the process of acculturation and construction. Gender is the repeated stylization of the body, a set of repeated acts within a highly rigid regulatory frame that congeal over time to produce the appearance of substance, of a natural sort of being. A political genealogy of gender ontologies, if it is successful, will deconstruct the substantive appearance of gender into its constitutive acts and locate and account for those acts within the compulsory frames set by the various forces that police the social appearance of gender. To expose the contingent acts that create the appearance of a naturalistic necessity, a move which has been a part of cultural critique at least since Marx, is a task that now takes on the added burden of showing how the very notion of the subject, intelligible only through its appearance as gendered, admits of possibilities that have been forcibly foreclosed by the various reifications of gender that have constituted its contingent ontologies.

* * *

SOURCE: From Judith Butler, *Gender Trouble: Feminism and the Subversion of Identity*, 2nd ed. (1999; reprint, New York: Routledge, 2006), pp. 1–46. The first edition was published in 1990. Except as indicated, all notes are Butler's; some of her notes have been omitted and some have been shortened.

MARTHA C. NUSSBAUM
(b. 1947)

Nussbaum is remarkable. In addition to publishing books and articles as impressive in their interest and quality as in their quantity, she has distinguished herself among contemporary American philosophers through the frequency and range of her interventions in public discourse, in a variety of venues. She has contributed significantly in a number of areas of both long-standing and emerging importance in philosophy; and she has contributed no less significantly to contemporary debates on higher education and on the humanities in our society and in the world more generally, as well as on issues of social justice, sexual orientation, the status and rights of women globally, sex and gender issues, religious tolerance, and more. Now the Ernst Freund Distinguished Service Professor of Law and Ethics at the University of Chicago, she has emerged as one of the staunchest and most articulate defenders and extenders of a classically liberal stance and outlook in philosophy today. Hers is a modern-day Enlightenment liberalism without apology, without illusions, and without timidity. Though she is an ardent feminist, her feminism is of an unusual sort on the contemporary scene—one that has a certain resonance with the spirit and sensibility of MARY WOLLSTONECRAFT and JOHN STUART MILL.

Born Martha Craven in New York City, Nussbaum had a privileged childhood in the Philadelphia area, where her father was a prosperous lawyer. She first attended Wellesley College, where she majored in classics, and then left to join a repertory company specializing in Greek drama. Returning to school at New York University to study acting, she also resumed her classics studies, and received her BA in 1969. That year she also married a fellow classicist, Alan Nussbaum (they would divorce in 1987), and converted to Judaism, which she has contin-

ued to engage actively throughout her life. She went on to graduate school at Harvard, where her initial focus on classics expanded to include first ancient philosophy and then other areas of philosophy. She received her MA in 1972 and her PhD in 1975, after which she was the first female Junior Fellow in the Harvard Society of Fellows (writing what became her first book during that appointment). She then began teaching courses in classics and philosophy at Harvard.

Nussbaum's Harvard years were difficult. While receiving strong support from some senior faculty, she also encountered widespread sexism. As a junior faculty member, she was faced with the challenge of being the only woman on regular faculty appointment in her two departments (Philosophy and Classics). She published her first book during that period—Aristotle's *"De Motu Animalium"* (1978), a translation of and commentary on *On the Movement of Animals* together with five analytical and interpretive essays discussing Aristotle's epistemology and philosophy of science more broadly. At the time, however, Harvard rarely awarded tenure to its own assistant professors, and Nussbaum was no exception. (She was on a split appointment, and only the Philosophy Department supported her tenure.) She accepted a tenured appointment at Brown University and began teaching there in 1984, after a year in a visiting position at Wellesley.

By the time she left Brown for the University of Chicago in 1995, Nussbaum was a University Professor. At Chicago, where she remains, her primary appointments are in the Law School and the Philosophy Department, with further appointments in Political Science and Classics. That has proven to be an ideal situation and arrangement from which to pursue her multifaceted and numerous academic and other interests.

Nussbaum published four significant books while at Brown. Her second book, *The Fragility of Goodness: Luck and Ethics in Greek Tragedy and Philosophy* (1986; rev. ed., 2001), which combined her interests in the classics and philosophy, won considerable attention and admiration. *Love's Knowledge: Essays on Philosophy and Literature* (1990) collected fifteen essays, all but two of which had been previously published. *The Quality of Life* (1993), co-edited with Amartya Sen, was the beginning of Nussbaum's impressive stream of writings at the conjunction of philosophy and public policy (and of a long and fruitful collaboration with Sen; for Sen, see this anthology's companion volume, *The Analytic Tradition*). It was followed by *The Therapy of Desire: Theory and Practice in Hellenistic Ethics* (1994), a major contribution to the understanding of the main strands of ethical thought in late ancient philosophy.

The Fragility of Goodness is an examination of the ways in which the ideas of chance and events outside of human control figured in the works and thought of Aeschylus, Sophocles, Plato, Aristotle, and Euripides. Tragedy, fate, conflict, madness, the affects, the body, and history itself show human beings to be "fragile" creatures dependent on much more than their own will. Ethical treatment of others and self-development, for the Greeks, needed to be conceived in a way that takes account of this fragility and what is beyond our power.

Love's Knowledge is Nussbaum's first extended treatment of a specific emotion, as it is explored in works of literature. Her general theme, to which she would later return, is that the emotions and our ethical and rational selves are intertwined. An emotion—love being the paradigmatic example—is a sort of ethical vision; but it is not a vision that is complete unto itself, and it cannot be relied upon alone. Emotions are cognitive and evaluative, but they are not trustworthy guides in social, political, and ethical life. Nevertheless, they are essential to the quality of that life: without them, our ethical considerations would be lacking in humanity and goodness. In her subsequent writings Nussbaum subjects a considerable range of emotions to extended philosophical examination.

In *The Therapy of Desire* Nussbaum explores an important aspect of the ethical thought of the three main Hellenistic schools of philosophy: Stoic, Skeptic, and Epicurean. She considers the ways in which the body, the emotions, and medicine informed the philosophical and ethical theories of these late ancient thinkers, who saw thought itself as a sort of medicine or therapy. She also emphasizes the importance of separating the philosophical naturalism of their thinking about life and ethics from the doctrine of ascetic detachment and freedom from the body that some of them espoused. She takes something of a neo-Stoic approach to the emotions and to ethics, although she finds the roots of modern liberal conceptions of personhood and respect for persons as such (to which she is favorably disposed as well) in these ancient sources.

Another emotion of interest to Nussbaum, here and in later work, is anger, which figures centrally in her most recent book, *Anger and Forgiveness: Resentment, Generosity, Justice* (2016), and is the topic of the third selection below. In it she criticizes the notion of forgiveness, in a manner akin to NIETZSCHE's in his analysis of the phenomena of forgiveness and *ressentiment*. Anger too is subjected to criticism, particularly insofar as it underlies ideas of retribution through punishment rather than a more enlightened notion of justice.

In *Poetic Justice: The Literary Imagination and Public Life* (1995) Nussbaum pursues the theme explored and illustrated in *Love's Knowledge* of the importance of literature in activating the imagination and emotions and aiding thought. It is the first work in which she focuses explicitly on the actual character of contemporary legal and political thought, and aspires to influence the sphere of public discourse and practice. It thus marks a widening of the scope and character of her thought, as she took on and embraced the role of public intellectual.

This expansion of Nussbaum's agenda can also be seen in her article "Patriotism and Cosmopolitanism" (1994), collected in *For Love of Country? Debating the Limits of Patriotism* (1996) with sixteen responses to it. Similarly, in *Cultivating Humanity: A Classical Defense of Reform in Liberal Education* (1997), which examines higher education in America, she considers how the humanities can instill intellectual and ethical virtues in students and public life.

In view of the significance of Nussbaum's work in feminist philosophy, it may seem surprising that her first book in this area, *Sex and Social Justice*, did not appear until 1999. But she had been publishing on feminist topics and issues for some time, and this volume brings together fifteen essays written in the 1990s (including several on gay and lesbian rights). The second selection below, "A Conception of Feminism," is from her introduction to it. The naturalistic ethics that Nussbaum had been developing culminates in the "capabilities" approach to the ethical and political problem of human equality and diversity that she and Sen first developed in the 1980s, and that is the topic of the first selection below. She defends an Aristotelian conception of *eudaimonia*—of human flourishing as well as happiness—as a way of assessing how any human life is going and what any human being needs to flourish.

The capabilities approach is also a central element of Nussbaum's kind of feminism—which (like Wollstonecraft's and Mill's) is driven by a passion for human flourishing, commitment to social justice, and a conviction that differentiations in both contexts based on sex and gender differences are human wrongs. These passions and this conviction find concrete critical expression in *Women and Human Development: The Capabilities Approach* (2000), which extensively investigates the plight of women around the world.

Upheavals of Thought: The Intelligence of Emotions (2001), in which Nussbaum works out her neo-Stoic philosophy of emotion in detail (with particular attention to grief and compassion), may be her most imposing work. She develops the cognitivist thesis that emotions are a sort of judgment by analyzing the emotional intelligence of animals and human infants. Her theory of love and its ethical significance, first advanced a decade earlier, is here given a complex genealogy with ancient, Christian, modern, and literary sources.

Nussbaum's next two books, *Hiding from Humanity: Disgust, Shame, and the Law* (2004) and *Frontiers of Justice: Disability, Nationality, Species Membership* (2006), can be viewed as elaborations and applications of ideas from *Upheavals of Thought*. Her aim in *Hiding from Humanity* is twofold: both to show how the negative emotions of shame and disgust figure into law, public policy, and social norms, and to make the case that they ought not to play such a role in our liberal society. This discussion is continued and extended in *From Disgust to Humanity: Sexual Orientation and Constitutional Law* (2010), which focuses specifically on gay rights. *Frontiers of Justice* examines the limits of moral concern and the propriety of the granting of lesser status (morally speaking) to animals, people from other nations, and the mentally or physically impaired. In it Nussbaum mounts a sustained critique of social contract views that limit the sphere of moral concern to beings that can enter into contracts, are members of our society, and are able to enter into what JÜRGEN HABERMAS calls the "discourse community."

In recent years Nussbaum has expanded her attention to include a variety of national and international issues of great practical importance, reflected in such works as *The Clash Within: Democracy, Religious Violence, and India's Future* (2007), *Liberty of Conscience: In Defense of America's Tradition of Religious Equality* (2008), *Not for Profit: Why Democracy Needs the Humanities* (2010), and *The New Religious Intolerance: Overcoming the Politics of Fear in an Anxious Age* (2012). In them she promotes a new ethics and politics of compassion that are not driven by negative emotions such as fear, and have a bedrock commitment to the moral principle of equality. Her latest venture of this sort (with Saul Levmore) is *Aging Thoughtfully: Philosophical, Legal, and Economic Perspectives* (2017).

Even while pursuing these many concerns, Nussbaum has continued to develop the philosophical position that grounds them and her efforts to address them. She offers an impressive statement, elaboration, and defense of her thinking on human flourishing, development, and capabilities in *Creating Capabilities: The Human Development Approach* (2011), from which the first selection is taken. And she presents her grand social-philosophical vision in *Political Emotions: Why Love Matters for Justice* (2013), which combines political philosophy, philosophical anthropology, legal philosophy, aesthetics, and ethics. Aristotle's idea that humans are "political animals" has perhaps never had a more engaging philosophical articulation than she has given it. And EMERSON's idea of "the American scholar" may never have had a more vivid exemplar than Nussbaum herself.

From Creating Capabilities

[*Introduction*]¹ From *Conclusion*

We are living in an era dominated by the profit motive and by anxiety over national economic achievements. Economic growth, however, while a part of wise public policy, is just a part, and a mere instrument at that. It is people who matter ultimately; profits are only instrumental means to human lives. The purpose of global development, like the purpose of a good domestic national policy, is to enable people to live full and creative lives, developing their potential and fashioning a meaningful existence commensurate with their equal human dignity. In other words, the real purpose of development is *human development;* other approaches and measures are at best a proxy for the development of human lives, and most don't reflect human priorities in a rich, accurate, or nuanced way. The widespread use of average GDP² as a measure of quality of life persists despite a growing consensus that it is not even a good proxy for human life quality.

Most nations, operating domestically, have understood that respect for people requires a richer and more complicated account of national priorities than that provided by GDP alone. On the whole, they have offered a more adequate account in their constitutions and other founding documents. But the theories that dominate policy-making in the new global order have yet to attain the respectful complexity embodied in good national constitutions, and these theories, defective as they are, have enormous power. Unfortunately, they greatly influence not just international bodies but also the domestic priorities of nations—and many nations today are pursuing economic growth in ways that shortchange other commitments they have made to their people. The use of incomplete theories is only one part of the story behind this narrowness of focus, but it is a part that can be and is being resourcefully addressed.

---

1. In the book as published this short section is its "conclusion"; but it serves here to introduce the chapter from *Creating Capabilities* that follows.
2. Gross domestic product.

A new theoretical paradigm is evolving, one that is the ally of people's demands for a quality of life that their equal human dignity requires. Unlike the dominant approaches, it begins from a commitment to the equal dignity of all human beings, whatever their class, religion, caste, race, or gender, and it is committed to the attainment, for all, of lives that are worthy of that equal dignity. Both a comparative account of the quality of life and a theory of basic social justice, it remedies the major deficiencies of the dominant approaches. It is sensitive to distribution, focusing particularly on the struggles of traditionally excluded or marginalized groups. It is sensitive to the complexity and the qualitative diversity of the goals that people pursue. Rather than trying to squeeze all these diverse goals into a single box, it carefully examines the relationships among them, thinking about how they support and complement one another. It also takes account of the fact that people may need different quantities of resources if they are to come up to the same level of ability to choose and act, particularly if they begin from different social positions.

For all these reasons, the Capabilities Approach is attracting attention all over the world, as an alternative to dominant approaches to development in development economics and public policy. It is also attracting attention as an approach to basic social justice, within nations and between nations—in some ways agreeing with other philosophical theories of social justice, in some ways departing from them—for example, by giving greater support to the struggles of people with disabilities than a social contract model seems to permit.

Our world needs more critical thinking and more respectful argument. The distressingly common practice of arguing by sound bite urgently needs to be replaced by a mode of public discourse that is itself more respectful of our equal human dignity. The Capabilities Approach is offered as a contribution to national and international debate, not as a dogma that must be swallowed whole. It is laid out to be pondered, digested, compared with other approaches—and then, if it stands the test of argument, to be adopted and put into practice. What this means is that you, the readers of this book, are the authors of the next chapter in this story of human development.

* * *

Chapter Two
The Central Capabilities

The approach we are investigating is sometimes called the *Human Development Approach* and sometimes the *Capability* or *Capabilities Approach*. Occasionally the terms are combined, as in *Journal of Human Development and Capabilities*, the current name of the former *Journal of Human Development*—a title reflecting its new status as the official journal of the HDCA.[3] To some extent these titles are used as mere verbal variants, and many people make no distinction among them. Insofar as there are any significant differences, "Human Development Approach" is associated, historically, with the Human Development Report Office of the United Nations Development Programme and its annual Human Development Reports. These reports use the

3. The Human Development and Capability Association, of which Nussbaum was (with Amartya Sen) co-founder.

notion of capabilities as a comparative measure rather than as a basis for normative political theory. Amartya Sen[4] had a major intellectual role in framing them, but they do not incorporate all aspects of his (pragmatic and result-oriented) theory; they simply aim to package comparative information in such a way as to reorient the development and policy debate, rather than to advance a systematic economic or political theory.

"Capability Approach" and "Capabilities Approach" are the key terms in the political/economic program Sen proposes in works such as *Inequality Reexamined* and *Development as Freedom*,[5] where the project is to commend the capability framework as the best space within which to make comparisons of life quality, and to show why it is superior to utilitarian and quasi-Rawlsian approaches.[6] I typically use the plural, "Capabilities," in order to emphasize that the most important elements of people's quality of life are plural and qualitatively distinct: health, bodily integrity, education, and other aspects of individual lives cannot be reduced to a single metric without distortion. Sen, too, emphasizes this idea of plurality and nonreducibility, which is a key element of the approach.

I prefer the term "Capabilities Approach," at least in many contexts, to the term "Human Development Approach," because I am concerned with the capabilities of nonhuman animals as well as human beings. The approach provides a fine basis for a theory of justice and entitlement for both nonhuman animals and humans. Sen shares this interest, although he has not made it a central focus of his work.

The Capabilities Approach can be provisionally defined as an approach to comparative quality-of-life assessment and to theorizing about basic social justice. It holds that the key question to ask, when comparing societies and assessing them for their basic decency or justice, is, "What is each person able to do and to be?" In other words, the approach takes *each person as an end*, asking not just about the total or average well-being but about the opportunities available to each person. It is *focused on choice or freedom*, holding that the crucial good societies should be promoting for their people is a set of opportunities, or substantial freedoms, which people then may or may not exercise in action: the choice is theirs. It thus commits itself to respect for people's powers of self-definition. The approach is resolutely *pluralist about value*: it holds that the capability achievements that are central for people are different in quality, not just in quantity; that they cannot without distortion be reduced to a single numerical scale; and that a fundamental part of understanding and producing them is understanding the specific nature of each. Finally, the approach is *concerned with entrenched social injustice and inequality*, especially capability failures that are the result of discrimination or marginalization. It ascribes an urgent *task to government and public policy*—namely, to improve the quality of life for all people, as defined by their capabilities.

These are the essential elements of the approach. It has (at least) two versions, in part because it has been used for two different purposes. My own version, which puts the approach to work in constructing a theory of basic social justice, adds other notions in the process (those of *human dignity*, the

---

4. Prominent India-born economist and philosopher (b. 1933), winner of the 1998 Nobel Prize in Economic Sciences; for more on Sen, see this anthology's companion volume, *The Analytic Tradition*.

5. Published in 1992 and 1999, respectively.
6. For the American moral and political philosopher John Rawls (1921–2002), see this anthology's companion volume *The Analytic Tradition*.

threshold, political liberalism). As a theory of fundamental political entitlements, my version of the approach also employs a specific list of the *Central Capabilities*. Compared with many familiar theories of welfare, my approach also subtracts: my capability-based theory of justice refrains from offering a comprehensive assessment of the quality of life in a society, even for comparative purposes, because the role of *political liberalism* in my theory requires me to prescind from offering any comprehensive account of value. Sen's primary concern has been to identify capability as the most pertinent space of comparison for purposes of quality-of-life assessment, thus changing the direction of the development debate. His version of the approach does not propose a definite account of basic justice, although it is a normative theory and does have a clear concern with issues of justice (focusing, for example, on instances of capability failure that result from gender or racial discrimination). In consequence, Sen does not employ a threshold or a specific list of capabilities, although it is clear that he thinks some capabilities (for example, health and education) have a particular centrality. Nor does he make central theoretical use of the concept of *human dignity*, though he certainly acknowledges its importance. At the same time, Sen does propose that the idea of capabilities can be the basis for a comprehensive quality-of-life assessment in a nation, in that sense departing from the deliberately limited aims of my political liberalism.

These differences will occupy us further in Chapter 4.[7] At this point, however, we may continue to treat the approach as a single, relatively unified approach to a set of questions about both quality of life and basic justice. The story of Vasanti[8] and what is salient in her situation could have been told by either Sen or me, and the same essential features would have been recognized—although Sen would not formalize them as a list or make assessments of minimal social justice, choosing instead to focus on quality-of-life issues. Enough has been said, I hope, to draw attention to the shared contours of the approach and its guiding concepts, as well as to some specific concepts of my own version that will also be defined in this chapter, even though they do not figure centrally in Sen's theory.

What are *capabilities*? They are the answers to the question, "What is this person able to do and to be?" In other words, they are what Sen calls "substantial freedoms," a set of (usually interrelated) opportunities to choose and to act. In one standard formulation by Sen, "a person's 'capability' refers to the alternative combinations of functionings that are feasible for her to achieve. Capability is thus a kind of freedom: the substantive freedom to achieve alternative functioning combinations."[9] In other words, they are not just abilities residing inside a person but also the freedoms or opportunities created by a combination of personal abilities and the political, social, and economic environment. To make the complexity of capabilities clear, I refer to these "substantial freedoms" as *combined capabilities*. Vasanti's combined capabilities are the totality of the opportunities she has for choice and action in her specific political, social, and economic situation.

---

7. "Fundamental Entitlements," not included in this volume.
8. Related in chapter 1 ("A Woman Seeking Justice"), where the difficult circumstances and responses to them of Vasanti, a young lower-class woman in India, are used to illustrate the need for and importance of measures to foster the "capabilities" discussed in this chapter.
9. Amartya Sen, *Development as Freedom* (New York: Knopf, 1999), p. 75.

Of course the characteristics of a person (personality traits, intellectual and emotional capacities, states of bodily fitness and health, internalized learning, skills of perception and movement) are highly relevant to his or her "combined capabilities," but it is useful to distinguish them from combined capabilities, of which they are but a part. I call these states of the person (not fixed, but fluid and dynamic) *internal capabilities*. They are to be distinguished from innate equipment: they are trained or developed traits and abilities, developed, in most cases, in interaction with the social, economic, familial, and political environment. They include such traits as Vasanti's learned political skill, or her skill in sewing; her newfound self-confidence and her freedom from her earlier fear. One job of a society that wants to promote the most important human capabilities is to support the development of internal capabilities—through education, resources to enhance physical and emotional health, support for family care and love, a system of education, and much more.

Why is it important to distinguish internal capabilities from combined capabilities? The distinction corresponds to two overlapping but distinct tasks of the decent society. A society might do quite well at producing internal capabilities but might cut off the avenues through which people actually have the opportunity to function in accordance with those capabilities. Many societies educate people so that they are capable of free speech on political matters—internally—but then deny them free expression in practice through repression of speech. Many people who are internally free to exercise a religion do not have the opportunity to do so in the sense of combined capability, because religious free exercise is not protected by the government. Many people who are internally capable of participating in politics are not able to choose to do so in the sense of combined capability: they may be immigrants without legal rights, or they may be excluded from participation in some other manner. It is also possible for a person to live in a political and social environment in which she could realize an internal capability (for example, criticizing the government) but lack the developed ability to think critically or speak publicly.

Because combined capabilities are defined as internal capabilities plus the social/political/economic conditions in which functioning can actually be chosen, it is not possible conceptually to think of a society producing combined capabilities without producing internal capabilities. We could, however, imagine a society that does well in creating contexts for choice in many areas but does not educate its citizens or nourish the development of their powers of mind. Some states in India are like this: open to those who want to participate but terrible at delivering the basic health care and education that would enable them to do so. Here, terminologically, we would say that neither internal nor combined capabilities were present, but that the society had done at least some things right. (And of course in such a society many people do have combined capabilities, just not the poor or the marginalized.) Vasanti's Gujarat[1] has a high rate of political participation, like all Indian states: so it has done well in extending political capabilities to all. (Notice that here we infer the presence of the capability from the actual functioning: it seems hard to do otherwise empirically, but conceptually we ought to remember that a person might be fully capa-

---

1. Vasanti's home state, in western India.

ble of voting and yet choose not to vote.) Gujarat has not done similarly well in promoting related internal capabilities, such as education, adequate information, and confidence, for the poor, women, and religious minorities.

The distinction between internal and combined capabilities is not sharp, since one typically acquires an internal capability by some kind of functioning, and one may lose it in the absence of the opportunity to function. But the distinction is a useful heuristic in diagnosing the achievements and shortcomings of a society.

Internal capabilities are not innate equipment. The idea of innate equipment does, however, play a role in the Human Development Approach. After all, the term "human development" suggests the unfolding of powers that human beings bring into the world. Historically, the approach is influenced by philosophical views that focus on human flourishing or self-realization, from Aristotle to John Stuart Mill in the West and Rabindranath Tagore[2] in India. And the approach in many ways uses the intuitive idea of waste and starvation to indicate what is wrong with a society that thwarts the development of capabilities. Adam Smith wrote that deprivation of education made people "mutilated and deformed in a[n] . . . essential part of the character of human nature."[3] This captures an important intuitive idea behind the capabilities project. We therefore need a way to talk about these innate powers that are either nurtured or not nurtured, and for that we may use the term *basic capabilities*. We now know that the development of basic capabilities is not hardwired in the DNA[4]: maternal nutrition and prenatal experience play a role in their unfolding and shaping. In that sense, even after a child is born we are always dealing with very early internal capabilities, already environmentally conditioned, not with a pure potential. Nonetheless, the category is a useful one, so long as we do not misunderstand it. Basic capabilities are the innate faculties of the person that make later development and training possible.

The concept of basic capabilities must be used with much caution, since we can easily imagine a theory that would hold that people's political and social entitlements should be proportional to their innate intelligence or skill. This approach makes no such claim. Indeed, it insists that the political goal for all human beings in a nation ought to be the same: all should get above a certain threshold level of combined capability, in the sense not of coerced functioning but of substantial freedom to choose and act. That is what it means to treat all people with equal respect. So the attitude toward people's basic capabilities is not a meritocratic one—more innately skilled people get better treatment—but, if anything, the opposite: those who need more help to get above the threshold get more help. In the case of people with cognitive disabilities, the goal should be for them to have the same capabilities as "normal" people, even though some of those opportunities may have to be exercised through a surrogate, and the surrogate may in some cases supply part of the internal capability if the person is unable to develop sufficient choice capability on her own, for example, by voting on that person's behalf even if the person

2. Bengali writer in all genres (including songs), as well as a painter (1861–1941); the first non-European awarded the Noble Prize in Literature (1913), Tagore was one of the foremost humanists and creative artists of modern India. Aristotle (384–322 B.C.E.), Greek philosopher. For MILL, see above.
3. From *The Wealth of Nations* (1776), 1.1.3.2, by the Scottish moral philosopher and political economist Smith (1723–1790).
4. That is, in our genes.

is unable to make a choice. The one limitation is that the person has to be a child of human parents and capable of at least some sort of active striving: thus a person in a permanent vegetative condition or an anencephalic person would not be qualified for equal political entitlements under this theory. But the notion of basic capability is still appropriate in thinking about education: if a child has innate cognitive disabilities, special interventions are justified.

On the other side of capability is *functioning*. A functioning is an active realization of one or more capabilities. Functionings need not be especially active or, to use the term of one critic, "muscular." Enjoying good health is a functioning, as is lying peacefully in the grass. Functionings are beings and doings that are the outgrowths or realizations of capabilities.

In contrasting capabilities with functionings, we should bear in mind that capability means opportunity to select. The notion of *freedom to choose* is thus built into the notion of capability. To use an example of Sen's, a person who is starving and a person who is fasting have the same type of functioning where nutrition is concerned, but they do not have the same capability, because the person who fasts is able not to fast, and the starving person has no choice.[5]

In a sense, capabilities are important because of the way in which they may lead to functionings. If people never functioned at all, in any way, it would seem odd to say that the society was a good one because it had given them lots of capabilities. The capabilities would be pointless and idle if they were never used and people slept all through life. In that limited way, the notion of functioning gives the notion of capability its end-point. But capabilities have value in and of themselves, as spheres of freedom and choice. To promote capabilities is to promote areas of freedom, and this is not the same as making people function in a certain way. Thus the Capabilities Approach departs from a tradition in economics that measures the real value of a set of options by the best use that can be made of them. Options are freedoms, and freedom has intrinsic value.

Some political views deny this: they hold that the right thing for government to do is to make people lead healthy lives, do worthwhile activities, exercise religion, and so on. We deny this: we say that capabilities, not functionings, are the appropriate political goals, because room is thereby left for the exercise of human freedom. There is a huge moral difference between a policy that promotes health and one that promotes health capabilities—the latter, not the former, honors the person's lifestyle choices.

The preference for capabilities is connected to the issue of respect for a plurality of different religious and secular views of life, and thus to the idea of political liberalism (defined in Chapter 4).

Children, of course, are different; requiring certain sorts of functioning of them (as in compulsory education) is defensible as a necessary prelude to adult capability.

Some people who use the Capabilities Approach think that in a few specific areas government is entitled to promote functionings rather than just capabilities. Richard Arneson,[6] for example, has defended paternalistic function-oriented policies in the area of health: government should use its power to make people take up healthy lifestyles. Sen and I do not agree with this position because of the high value we ascribe to choice. There is one exception:

5. See Sen, *Inequality Re-examined* (Oxford: Clarendon, 1992), p. 52.   6. American political philosopher (b. 1945).

government, I hold, should not give people an option to be treated with respect and nonhumiliation. Suppose, for example, that the U.S. government gave every citizen a penny that they could then choose to pay back to "purchase" respectful treatment. But if the person chose to keep the penny, the government would humiliate them. This is unacceptable. Government must treat all people respectfully and should refuse to humiliate them. I make this exception because of the centrality of notions of dignity and respect in generating the entire capabilities list. Similarly, virtually all users of the approach would agree that slavery should be prohibited, even if favored by a majority, and even if by voluntary contract.

Another area of reasonable disagreement involves the right to do things that would appear to destroy some or all capabilities. Should people be permitted to sell their organs? To use hard drugs? To engage in a wide range of risky sports? Typically we make compromises in such areas, and these compromises do not always make sense: thus alcohol, an extremely destructive drug, remains legal while marijuana is for the most part illegal. We regulate most sports for safety, but we do not have an organized public debate about which areas of freedom it makes sense to remove for safety's sake. We can certainly agree that capability-destruction in children is a particularly grave matter and as such should be off-limits. In other cases, reasonable safety regulation seems plausible—unless debate reveals that the removal of an option (boxing without gloves, say) is really an infringement of freedom so grave as to make people's lives incompatible with human dignity. Usually situations are not so grave, and thus in many such cases the approach has little to say, allowing matters to be settled through the political process.

This issue will be further illuminated if we turn to a related and crucial question: Which capabilities are the most important? The approach makes this valuational question central rather than concealing it. This is one of its attractive features. Other approaches always take some sort of stand on questions of value, but often without explicitness or argument. Sen and I hold that it is crucial to face this question head on, and to address it with pertinent normative arguments.

Sen takes a stand on the valuational issue by emphasis, choice of examples, and implication, but he does not attempt anything like a systematic answer, an issue to which we will return in Chapter 4. It is reasonable for him not to attempt a systematic answer, insofar as he is using the idea of capabilities merely to frame comparisons. Insofar as he is using it to construct a theory of democracy and of justice, it is less clear that his avoidance of commitments on substance is wise. Any use of the idea of capabilities for the purposes of normative law and public policy must ultimately take a stand on substance, saying that some capabilities are important and others less important, some good, and some (even) bad.

Returning to the idea of basic capabilities will help us grasp this point. Human beings come into the world with the equipment for many "doings and beings" (to use a common phrase of Sen's), and we have to ask ourselves which ones are worth developing into mature capabilities. Adam Smith, thinking of children deprived of education, said that their human powers were "mutilated and deformed." Imagine, instead, a child whose capacity for cruelty and the humiliation of others is starved and thwarted by familial and social development. We would not describe such a child as "mutilated and deformed," even if we granted that these capacities have their basis in innate human nature. Again, suppose we were told that a particular child was never taught to be capable of whistling *Yankee Doodle Dandy*[7] while standing on her head. We would not say that this child's human powers had been "mutilated and deformed" because, even though the capability in question is not—unlike the capacity for cruelty—bad, and even though it is probably grounded in human nature, it is just not very important.

The Capabilities Approach is not a theory of what human nature is, and it does not read norms off from innate human nature. Instead, it is evaluative and ethical from the start: it asks, among the many things that human beings might develop the capacity to do, which ones are the really valuable ones, which are the ones that a minimally just society will endeavor to nurture and support? An account of human nature tells us what resources and possibilities we have and what our difficulties may be. It does not tell us what to value.

Nonhuman animals are less malleable than human animals, and they may not be able to learn to inhibit a harmful capacity without painful frustration. They are also hard to "read," since their lives are not ours. Observing their actual capacities and having a good descriptive theory of each species and its form of life will thus rightly play a larger role in creating a normative theory of animal capabilities than it does in the human case. Still, the normative exercise is crucial, difficult though it may be.

How would we begin selecting the capabilities on which we want to focus? Much depends on our purpose. On the one hand, if our intention is simply comparative, all sorts of capabilities suggest interesting comparisons across nations and regions, and there is no reason to prescribe in advance: new problems may suggest new comparisons. On the other hand, if our aim is to establish political principles that can provide the grounding for constitutional law and public policy in a nation aspiring to social justice (or to propose goals for the community of nations), selection is of the utmost importance. We cannot select, however, using only the notion of capabilities. The title "Capabilities Approach" should not be read as suggesting that the approach uses only a single concept and tries to squeeze everything out of it.

At this point I invoke the notion of human dignity and of a life worthy of it—or, when we are considering other animal species, the dignity appropriate to the species in question. Dignity is an intuitive notion that is by no means utterly clear. If it is used in isolation, as if it is completely self-evident, it can be used capriciously and inconsistently. Thus it would be mistaken to use it as if it were an intuitively self-evident and solid foundation for a theory that would then be built upon it. My approach does not do this: dignity is one element of the theory, but all of its notions are seen as interconnected, deriving illumination and clarity from one another. (This idea of a holistic and non-foundational type of justification will be elaborated in Chapter 4.) In the case of dignity, the notion of respect is a particularly important relative, and the political principles themselves illuminate what we take human dignity

---

7. "Yankee Doodle" is a well-known American song, versions of which date from Revolutionary War days. "(I'm a) Yankee Doodle Dandy" is an American patriotic song inspired by (and partially incorporating) "Yankee Doodle," from a popular 1904 Broadway musical by George M. Cohan that became even more popular as the title song of the hit Hollywood film *Yankee Doodle Dandy* (1942), a biographical musical about Cohan himself. It does not matter which is meant.

(and its absence) to mean. But the basic idea is that some living conditions deliver to people a life that is worthy of the human dignity that they possess, and others do not. In the latter circumstance, they retain dignity, but it is like a promissory note whose claims have not been met. As Martin Luther King, Jr., said of the promises inherent in national ideals: dignity can be like "a check that has come back marked 'insufficient funds.'"[8]

Although dignity is a vague idea that needs to be given content by placing it in a network of related notions, it does make a difference. A focus on dignity is quite different, for example, from a focus on satisfaction. Think about debates concerning education for people with severe cognitive disabilities. It certainly seems possible that satisfaction, for many such people, could be produced without educational development. The court cases that opened the public schools to such people used, at crucial junctures, the notion of dignity: we do not treat a child with Down syndrome in a manner commensurate with that child's dignity if we fail to develop the child's powers of mind through suitable education. In a wide range of areas, moreover, a focus on dignity will dictate policy choices that protect and support agency, rather than choices that infantilize people and treat them as passive recipients of benefit.

The claims of human dignity can be denied in many ways, but we may reduce them all to two, corresponding to the notions of internal capability and combined capability. Social, political, familial, and economic conditions may prevent people from choosing to function in accordance with a developed internal capability: this sort of thwarting is comparable to imprisonment. Bad conditions can, however, cut deeper, stunting the development of internal capabilities or warping their development. In both cases, basic human dignity remains: the person is still worthy of equal respect. In the former case, however, dignity has been more deeply violated. Think of the difference between rape and simple robbery. Both damage a person; neither removes the person's equal human dignity. Rape, however, can be said to violate a woman's dignity because it invades her internal life of thought and emotion, changing her relationship to herself.

The notion of dignity is closely related to the idea of active striving. It is thus a close relative of the notion of basic capability, something inherent in the person that exerts a claim that it should be developed. But whereas there is room to argue about whether innate potential differs across people, human dignity, from the start, is equal in all who are agents in the first place (again, excluding those in a permanent vegetative state and those who are anencephalic, thus without agency of any kind). All, that is, deserve equal respect from laws and institutions. If people are considered as citizens, the claims of all citizens are equal. Equality holds a primitive place in the theory at this point, although its role will be confirmed by its fit with the rest of the theory. From the assumption of equal dignity, it does not follow that all the centrally important capabilities are to be equalized. Treating people as equals may not entail equalizing the living conditions of all. The question of what treating people as equals requires must be faced at a later stage, with independent arguments.

In general, then, the Capabilities Approach, in my version, focuses on the protection of areas of freedom so central that their removal makes a life not

8. From the "I Have a Dream" speech, delivered in Washington, D.C., on August 28, 1963, by King (1929–1968), the preeminent African American religious and civil rights leader of his time.

worthy of human dignity. When a freedom is not that central, it will be left to the ordinary workings of the political process. Sometimes it is clear that a given capability is central in this way: the world has come to a consensus, for example, on the importance of primary and secondary education. It seems equally clear that the ability to whistle *Yankee Doodle Dandy* while standing on one's head is not of central importance and does not deserve a special level of protection. Many cases may be unclear for a long time: for example, it was not understood for many centuries that a woman's right to refuse her husband intercourse was a crucial right of bodily integrity. What must happen here is that the debate must take place, and each must make arguments attempting to show that a given liberty is implicated in the idea of human dignity. This cannot be done by vague intuitive appeals to the idea of dignity all by itself: it must be done by discussing the relationship of the putative entitlement to other existing entitlements, in a long and detailed process— showing, for example, the relationship of bodily integrity inside the home to women's full equality as citizens and workers, to their emotional and bodily health, and so forth. But there will be many unclear cases. What about the right to plural marriages? The right to homeschooling? Because the approach does not derive value from people's existing preferences (which may be distorted in various ways), the quality of the argument, not the number of supporters, is crucial. But it is evident that the approach will leave many matters as optional, to be settled by the political process.

Considering the various areas of human life in which people move and act, this approach to social justice asks, What does a life worthy of human dignity require? At a bare minimum, an ample threshold level of ten Central Capabilities is required. Given a widely shared understanding of the task of government (namely, that government has the job of making people able to pursue a dignified and minimally flourishing life), it follows that a decent political order must secure to all citizens at least a threshold level of these ten Central Capabilities:

1. *Life*. Being able to live to the end of a human life of normal length; not dying prematurely, or before one's life is so reduced as to be not worth living.
2. *Bodily health*. Being able to have good health, including reproductive health; to be adequately nourished; to have adequate shelter.
3. *Bodily integrity*. Being able to move freely from place to place; to be secure against violent assault, including sexual assault and domestic violence; having opportunities for sexual satisfaction and for choice in matters of reproduction.
4. *Senses, imagination, and thought*. Being able to use the senses, to imagine, think, and reason—and to do these things in a "truly human" way, a way informed and cultivated by an adequate education, including, but by no means limited to, literacy and basic mathematical and scientific training. Being able to use imagination and thought in connection with experiencing and producing works and events of one's own choice, religious, literary, musical, and so forth. Being able to use one's mind in ways protected by guarantees of freedom of expression with respect to both political and artistic speech, and freedom of religious exercise. Being able to have pleasurable experiences and to avoid non-beneficial pain.

5. *Emotions.* Being able to have attachments to things and people outside ourselves; to love those who love and care for us, to grieve at their absence; in general, to love, to grieve, to experience longing, gratitude, and justified anger. Not having one's emotional development blighted by fear and anxiety. (Supporting this capability means supporting forms of human association that can be shown to be crucial in their development.)

6. *Practical reason.* Being able to form a conception of the good and to engage in critical reflection about the planning of one's life. (This entails protection for the liberty of conscience and religious observance.)

7. *Affiliation.* (A) Being able to live with and toward others, to recognize and show concern for other human beings, to engage in various forms of social interaction; to be able to imagine the situation of another. (Protecting this capability means protecting institutions that constitute and nourish such forms of affiliation, and also protecting the freedom of assembly and political speech.) (B) Having the social bases of self-respect and nonhumiliation; being able to be treated as a dignified being whose worth is equal to that of others. This entails provisions of nondiscrimination on the basis of race, sex, sexual orientation, ethnicity, caste, religion, national origin.

8. *Other species.* Being able to live with concern for and in relation to animals, plants, and the world of nature.

9. *Play.* Being able to laugh, to play, to enjoy recreational activities.

10. *Control over one's environment.* (A) *Political.* Being able to participate effectively in political choices that govern one's life; having the right of political participation, protections of free speech and association. (B) *Material.* Being able to hold property (both land and movable goods), and having property rights on an equal basis with others; having the right to seek employment on an equal basis with others; having the freedom from unwarranted search and seizure. In work, being able to work as a human being, exercising practical reason and entering into meaningful relationships of mutual recognition with other workers.

Although this list pertains to human life, its general headings provide a reasonable basis for beginning to think more adequately about what we owe to nonhuman animals, a topic to be pursued in the final chapter.[9]

Capabilities belong first and foremost to individual persons, and only derivatively to groups. The approach espouses a principle of *each person as an end.*[1] It stipulates that the goal is to produce capabilities for each and every person, and not to use some people as a means to the capabilities of others or of the whole. This focus on the person makes a huge difference for policy, since many nations have thought of the family, for example, as a homogeneous unit to be supported by policy, rather than examining and promoting the separate capabilities of each of its members. At times group-based policies (for example, affirmative action) may be effective instruments in the creation of individual capabilities, but that is the only way they can be justified. This normative focus on the individual cannot be dislodged by pointing to the

9. Chapter 8, "Capabilities and Contemporary Issues" (not included here).

1. A basic principle of Kantian moral philosophy.

obvious fact that people at times identify themselves with larger collectivities, such as the ethnic group, the state, or the nation, and take pride in the achievements of that group. Many poor residents of Gujarat identify with that state's overall development achievements, even though they themselves don't gain much from them. The approach, however, considers each person worthy of equal respect and regard, even if people don't always take that view about themselves. The approach is not based on the satisfaction of existing preferences.

The irreducible heterogeneity of the Central Capabilities is extremely important. A nation cannot satisfy the need for one capability by giving people a large amount of another, or even by giving them some money. All are distinctive, and all need to be secured and protected in distinctive ways. If we consider a constitution that protects capabilities as essential rights of all citizens, we can see how this works in practice: people have a claim against government if their constitution protects religious freedom and that freedom has been violated—even though they may be comfortable, well-fed, and secure with respect to every other capability that matters.

The basic claim of my account of social justice is this: respect for human dignity requires that citizens be placed above an ample (specified) threshold of capability, in all ten of those areas. (By mentioning citizens, I do not wish to deny that resident aliens, legal and illegal, have a variety of entitlements: I simply begin with the core case.)

The list is a proposal: it may be contested by arguing that one or more of the items is not so central and thus should be left to the ordinary political process rather than being given special protection. Let's suppose someone asks why play and leisure time should be given that sort of protection. I would begin by pointing out that for many women all over the world, "the double day"—working at a job and then coming home to do all the domestic labor, including child care and elder care, is a crushing burden, impeding access to many of the other capabilities on the list: employment opportunities, political participation, physical and emotional health, friendships of many kinds. What play and the free expansion of the imaginative capacities contribute to a human life is not merely instrumental but partly constitutive of a worthwhile human life. That's the sort of case that needs to be made to put something on the list.

Sometimes social conditions make it seem impossible to deliver a threshold amount of all ten capabilities to everyone: two or more of them may be in competition. For example, poor parents in Vasanti's state may feel that they need to keep their children out of school in order to survive at all, since they need the wages from the child's labor to eke out an existence. In such a case, the economist's natural question is, "How do we make trade-offs?" However, when capabilities have intrinsic value and importance (as do the ten on my list), the situation produced when two of them collide is tragic: any course we select involves doing wrong to someone.

This situation of *tragic choice* is not fully captured in standard cost-benefit analysis: the violation of an entitlement grounded in basic justice is not just a large cost; it is a cost of a distinctive sort, one that in a fully just society no person has to bear.

Sen has argued that such tragic situations show a defect in standard economic approaches, which typically demand a complete ordering over all states of affairs. In tragic cases, he insists, we cannot rank one alternative above the other, and thus any good ordering will remain incomplete. Here there is a nuance of difference between his critique and mine. I would hold that not all tragic situations involve an inability to rank one state of affairs as better than another. We should distinguish between the presence of a tragic dilemma— any choice involves wrongdoing—and the impossibility of a ranking. Sometimes one choice may be clearly better than another in a tragic situation, even though all available choices involve a violation of some sort. (For the tragic hero Eteocles, in Aeschylus' play *Seven against Thebes*,[2] it was a horrible wrong to choose to kill his brother, even though the alternative, which involved the destruction of the entire city, was clearly worse.) Sen is probably right that the demand for a complete ordering is misguided, but he is mistaken if he holds that all tragic dilemmas are cases in which no overall ordering is possible.

When we see a tragic choice—assuming that the threshold level of each capability has been correctly set—we should think, "This is very bad. People are not being given a life worthy of their human dignity. How might we possibly work toward a future in which the claims of all the capabilities can be fulfilled?" If the whole list has been wisely crafted and the thresholds set at a reasonable level, there usually will be some answer to that question. To return to India, the dilemma faced by poor parents was resolved by the state of Kerala, which pioneered a program of flexible school hours and also offered a nutritious midday meal that more than offset children's lost wages. The program has virtually wiped out illiteracy in the state. Seeing that it was possible for a relatively poor state to solve the problem by ingenuity and effort, the Supreme Court of India has made the midday meal mandatory for all government schools in the nation.

Such tragic choices abound in richer countries as well. In the United States, for example, a poor single mother may frequently be forced to choose between high-quality care for her child and a decent living standard, since some welfare rules require her to accept full-time work even when no care of high quality is available to her. Many women in the United States are forced to forgo employment opportunities in order to care for children or elderly relations; policies of family and medical leave, together with public provision of child and elder care, might address such dilemmas. One tragic choice ubiquitous in the United States is that between leisure time and a decent living standard (together with related health care benefits). It is widely known that Americans work longer hours than people in most other wealthy nations, and it is understood that family relations suffer in consequence, but the full measure of this tragic situation has not yet been taken. The capabilities perspective helps us see what is amiss here.

In other words, when we note a tragic conflict, we do not simply wring our hands: we ask what the best intervention point is to create a future in which this sort of choice does not confront people. We must also consider how to move people closer to the capability threshold right away, even if we can't immediately get them above it: thus, for example, equalizing access to primary edu-

2. First performed in 467 B.C.E. In this Greek myth, the twins Eteocles and Polyneices agreed to rule Thebes in alternate years; but when Eteocles refused to give up the throne, his brother marched against the city with seven champions.

cation for all when we are not yet in a position to give everyone access to secondary education.

The Central Capabilities support one another in many ways. Two, however, appear to play a distinctive *architectonic* role: they organize and pervade the others. These two are *affiliation* and *practical reason*. They pervade the others in the sense that when the others are present in a form commensurate with human dignity, they are woven into them. If people are well-nourished but not empowered to exercise practical reason and planning with regard to their health and nutrition, the situation is not fully commensurate with human dignity: they are being taken care of the way we take care of infants. Good policy in the area of each of the capabilities is policy that respects an individual's practical reason; this is just another way of alluding to the centrality of choice in the whole notion of capability as freedom. What is meant by saying that the capability of practical reason organizes all the others is more obvious: the opportunity to plan one's own life is an opportunity to choose and order the functionings corresponding to the various other capabilities.

As for affiliation, the point is similar: it pervades the other capabilities in the sense that when they are made available in a way that respects human dignity, affiliation is part of them—the person is respected as a social being. Making employment options available without considering workplace relationships would not be adequate; nor would forms of health care that neglect, for example, people's needs to protect zones of intimacy by provisions for personal privacy. Affiliation organizes the capabilities in that deliberation about public policy is a social matter in which relationships of many kinds (familial, friendly, group-based, political) all play a structuring role.

The capabilities on the list are rather abstract: who specifies them further? For the most part, the answer is given by each nation's system of constitutional law, or its basic principles if it lacks a written constitution. There is room for nations to elaborate capabilities differently to some extent, given their different traditions and histories. The world community poses unique problems of specification because there is no overarching government, accountable to the people as a whole, that would supply the specification.

Part of the conception of the capabilities list, as we have already seen, is the idea of a *threshold*. The approach, in my version, is a partial theory of social justice: it does not purport to solve all distributional problems; it just specifies a rather ample social minimum. Delivering these ten capabilities to all citizens is a necessary condition of social justice. Justice may well require more: for example, the approach as developed thus far does not make any commitment about how inequalities above the minimum ought to be handled. Many approaches to social justice hold that an ample threshold is not sufficient. Some demand strict equality; John Rawls insists that inequalities can be justified only where they raise the level of the worst-off. The Capabilities Approach does not claim to have answered these questions, although it might tackle them in the future.

The threshold does, however, require equality in some cases. It is a difficult question how far adequacy of capability requires equality of capability. Such a question can be answered only by detailed thought about each capability, by asking what respect for equal human dignity requires. I argue, for example, that respect for equal human dignity requires equal voting rights and equal rights to religious freedom, not simply an ample minimum. A system that allotted to women one-half of the votes it allots to men would be manifestly disrespectful, as would a system that gave members of minority religions some freedom but not the same degree of freedom as is given to the majority. (For example, if Christians could celebrate their holy day without penalty because work days are arranged that way, but Jews and Seventh Day Adventists[3] would be fired for refusing to work on a Saturday, that system would raise manifest problems of justice.) All the political entitlements, I argue, are such that inequality of distribution is an insult to the dignity of the unequal. Similarly, if some children in a nation have educational opportunities manifestly unequal to those of other children, even though all get above a minimum, this seems to raise an issue of basic fairness—as Justice Thurgood Marshall[4] famously argued in a case concerning the Texas public schools. Either equality or something near to it may be required for adequacy.

But the same may not be true of entitlements in the area of material conditions. Having decent, ample housing may be enough: it is not clear that human dignity requires that everyone have exactly the same type of housing. To hold that belief might be to fetishize possessions too much. The whole issue needs further investigation.

Setting the threshold precisely is a matter for each nation, and, within certain limits, it is reasonable for nations to do this differently, in keeping with their history and traditions. Some questions will remain very difficult: in such cases, the Capabilities Approach tells us what to consider salient, but it does not dictate a final assignment of weights and a sharp-edged decision. (The contours of an abortion right, for example, are not set by the approach, although it does tell us what to think about in debating this divisive issue.) Even at the level of threshold-drawing, the ordinary political process of a well-functioning democracy plays, rightly, an ineliminable role.

Another question raised by the idea of a threshold is that of utopianism. At one extreme, we might specify such a high threshold that no nation could meet it under current world conditions. Tragic conflicts would be ubiquitous, and even ingenuity and effort would not be able to resolve them. At the other end of the spectrum is lack of ambition: we might set the threshold so low that it is easy to meet, but less than what human dignity seems to require. The task for the constitution-maker (or, more often, for courts interpreting an abstract constitution and for legislators proposing statutes) is to select a level that is aspirational but not utopian, challenging the nation to be ingenious and to do better.

Many questions remain about how to do this: for example, should the threshold be the same in every nation, despite the fact that nations begin with very different economic resources? To say otherwise would seem to be disrespectful to people who by sheer chance are born in a poorer nation; to say yes, however, would require nations to meet some of their obligations at least par-

---

3. Members of a Protestant Christian denomination who, like Jews, celebrate the Sabbath on Saturday.
4. The first African American justice of the U.S. Supreme Court (1908–1993); the reference is to Marshall's dissent in *San Antonio Independent School District v. Rodriguez* (1973), where the Court upheld a school-funding mechanism that resulted in large disparities between districts in per-pupil expenditures.

tially through redistribution from richer to poorer nations. It might also be too dictatorial, denying nations a right to specify things somewhat differently, given their histories and situations.

The Capabilities Approach has recently been enriched by Jonathan Wolff and Avner De-Shalit's important book *Disadvantage*.[5] In addition to providing support for the list of the ten Central Capabilities, and in addition to developing strong arguments in favor of recognizing irreducibly heterogeneous goods, Wolff and De-Shalit introduce some new concepts that enhance the theoretical apparatus of the Capabilities Approach. The first is that of *capability security*. They argue, plausibly, that public policy must not simply give people a capability, but give it to them in such a way that they can count on it for the future. Consider Vasanti: when she had a loan from her brothers, she had a range of health- and employment related capabilities, but they were not secure, since her brothers could call in the loan at any point, or turn her out of the house. The SEWA loan[6] gave her security: so long as she worked regularly, she could make the payments and even build up some savings.

Working with new immigrant groups in their respective countries (Britain and Israel), Wolff and De-Shalit find that security about the future is of overwhelming importance in these people's ability to use and enjoy all the capabilities on the list. (Notice that a feeling of security is one aspect of the capability of "emotional health," but they are speaking of both emotions and reasonable expectations—capability security is an objective matter and has not been satisfied if government bewitches people into believing they are secure when they are not.) The security perspective means that for each capability we must ask how far it has been protected from the whims of the market or from power politics. One way nations often promote capability security is through a written constitution that cannot be amended except by a laborious supramajoritarian process. But a constitution does not enforce itself, and a constitution contributes to security only in the presence of adequate access to the courts and justified confidence in the behavior of judges.

Thinking about capability security makes us want to think about political procedure and political structure: What form of political organization promotes security? How much power should courts have, and how should their role be organized? How should legislatures be organized, what voting procedures should they adopt, and how can the power of interest groups and lobbies to disrupt the political process be constrained? What are the roles of administrative agencies and expert knowledge in promoting citizens' capabilities? We shall return to these issues—as yet underexplored in the Capabilities Approach—in the final chapter.

Wolff and De-Shalit introduce two further concepts of great interest: *fertile functioning* and *corrosive disadvantage*. A fertile functioning is one that tends to promote other related capabilities. (At this point they do not distinguish as clearly as they might between functioning and capability, and I fear that alliteration has superseded theoretical clarity.) They argue plausibly that

---

5. Published in 2007.
6. A loan from the Self-Employed Women's Association; offering microloans is one of the ways in which that organization helps poor women.

affiliation is a fertile functioning, supporting capability-formation in many areas. (Do they really mean that it is the functioning associated with affiliation, or is it the capability to form affiliations that has the good effect? This is insufficiently clear in their analysis.) Fertile functionings are of many types, and which functionings (or capabilities) are fertile may vary from context to context. In Vasanti's story, we can see that access to credit is a fertile capability, for the loan enabled her to protect her bodily integrity (not returning to her abusive husband), to have employment options, to participate in politics, to have a sense of emotional well-being, to form valuable affiliations, and to enjoy enhanced self-respect. In other contexts, education plays a fertile role, opening up options of many kinds across the board. Landownership can sometimes have a fertile role, protecting a woman from domestic violence, giving her exit options, and generally enhancing her status. Corrosive disadvantage is the flip side of fertile capability: it is a deprivation that has particularly large effects in other areas of life. In Vasanti's story, subjection to domestic violence was a corrosive disadvantage: this absence of protection for her bodily integrity jeopardized her health, emotional well-being, affiliations, practical reasoning, and no doubt other capabilities as well.

The point of looking for fertile capabilities/functionings and corrosive disadvantages is to identify the best intervention points for public policy. Each capability has importance on its own, and all citizens should be raised above the threshold on all ten capabilities. Some capabilities, however, may justly take priority, and one reason to assign priority would be the fertility of the item in question, or its tendency to remove a corrosive disadvantage. This idea helps us think about tragic choices, for often the best way of preparing a tragedy-free future will be to select an especially fertile functioning and devote our scarce resource to that.

SOURCE: From Martha C. Nussbaum, *Creating Capabilities: The Human Development Approach* (Cambridge, Mass.: Belknap Press of Harvard University Press, 2011), pp. 185–87, 17–45.

From Sex and Social Justice

From *Introduction: Feminism, Internationalism, Liberalism*

A CONCEPTION OF FEMINISM

* * * The feminism defended here has five salient features: It is *internationalist, humanist, liberal, concerned with the social shaping of preference and desire*, and, finally, *concerned with sympathetic understanding*. These five elements are not usually found together, and some of them are widely thought to be at odds with others. I shall argue, however, that a coherent and powerful picture emerges from their combination. Among the advantages of the combination is an opportunity to link feminist inquiry closely to the important progress that has been made during the past few decades in articulating the elements of a theory of both national and global justice.

INTERNATIONALISM

Feminism begins from the real lives of women, and the lives of women are highly varied. It is myopic to focus only on conditions and problems that are shared by a local or national group while neglecting the very different gender-related problems that may be faced by women in very different political and economic circumstances. Feminists in the United States have long acknowledged that arguments based on the experiences of white middle-class women are incomplete without the insights and experiences of women from other racial and ethnic groups. Too often, however, this admirable curiosity has not extended to the world outside the United States. The isolationist habits of our nation lead us to focus inward rather than on urgent needs at a distance. Thus, by now there is a rich feminist literature on questions such as rape and sexual harassment, which are common concerns of women all over the world. Much less is known and said about women's hunger, about sex-selective infanticide and abortion, about the denial of the right to work, about sex discrimination in religious courts of family law.

This volume takes its start from such urgent questions and from the experiences of women who are grappling with them in many places. It has been important to me to work in close partnership with women and men who do empirical fieldwork and to hear, through these partnerships, the voices of women fighting against hunger and illiteracy and inherently unequal legal systems. This volume contains far more empirical material than is common in a work of political philosophy because one of its central aims is to let reality speak for itself. I present both statistical material about the situation of women and also case studies of particular women and groups and their legal and political struggles.

The internationalism of this volume's method is linked to views about global justice that I do not develop fully here. I believe that individuals have moral obligations to promote justice for people outside their national boundaries and that their governments do also. In this volume I focus on the obligations of each nation to secure a basic level of functioning for its citizens, and also on universal obligations to protect and promote human dignity through the international human rights movement and through support for international agencies. I do not articulate principles of international distributive justice for material resources, although I think this immensely important and necessary to a complete account of justice for the world's women. That is a large question that goes beyond the scope of the present inquiry. But at least a beginning of the larger inquiry is made by thinking about the facts of human inequality in basic life chances, and by attempting to remedy some of these through domestic and private strategies. When we become able to conceive of the humanity of distant human beings, of their dignity and their needs, we at least begin to ask the hard questions about the contingency that affects people's lives more than any other, the contingency of birth location. Although I shall be focusing on differences in life chances between the sexes, we should never forget that the difference in life expectancy at birth between Iceland (78.2) and Sierra Leone (39.0) is enormously greater than that between females and males in any nation,[1] and so it goes for all the indicators of quality of life. One might therefore feel that the biggest question of distributive justice is lurking around the edges of these essays and is not addressed within them. True, and yet I hope that the method of my inquiry makes it at least audible.

Because many of these essays take their start from experiences of women in developing countries, and because economics is the intellectual discipline that has so far had the largest public impact on the lives of such women, development economics is an important part of this volume. My coworkers and I have been highly critical of conventional approaches in development economics. Convinced that development is a normative notion and that normative argument can be rational rather than merely subjective, we have also been concerned to develop that normative structure and to criticize irrationalist approaches that dismiss it—both those deriving from neoclassical economics, with its subjectivism about value, and those that derive from postmodernism. * * * But it is very important for feminist philosophers to care about and to study economics because no normative project, however valuable, can be pursued and implemented without adequate formal models. For philosophers to turn in disdain from economic modeling on the grounds that the foundations of existing models are philosophically crude is one way of guaranteeing that their work will have no impact on the real world.

HUMANISM

The view developed here seeks justice for human beings as such, believing all human beings to be fundamentally equal in worth. It also holds that human beings have common resources and common problems wherever they live, and that their special dilemmas can best be seen as growing out of special circumstances, rather than out of a nature or identity that is altogether unlike that of other humans. This is not to say that historical, social, political, and natural circumstances do not shape extremely different lives for people in different parts of the world. But it is to say that there is likely to be a good deal of overlap of problems within those lives, and also a good deal of commonness about what people must have if they are to be capable of living well.

The problems people face wherever they live include scarce resources, competition for resources, and the shortness of life. These have been called "the circumstances of justice,"[2] circumstances that make it incumbent upon us to develop an account of what is due to people and to their dignity. We might

---

1. Women on average live somewhat longer than men, although this is not the case in many parts of the world. See chapter 1 [included in this volume—editor's note]. Thus the greatest life expectancy for any discrete group, according to the 1996 Human Development Report (United Nations Development Program) is that for women in Japan, 82.5 years. With respect to many other indicators of quality of life women do systematically worse than men. See

chapter 1.
2. See John Rawls, *A Theory of Justice* (hereafter TJ) (Cambridge, MA: Harvard University Press, 1971), referring to Hume. [The phrase appears as a subheading to chap. 3 of TJ. For the American philosopher Rawls (1921–2002), see this anthology's companion volume, *The Analytic Tradition*. David Hume (1711–1776), Scottish empiricist philosopher—editor's note.]

hold that people share common problems but that the solutions that are proper vary from region to region and group to group. To some extent, we should hold this, in the sense that any good solution to a problem must be responsive to the concrete circumstances for which it is designed. But it is a long step from that sensible interest in specificity to a normative cultural relativism, according to which the ultimate standard of what is right for an individual or group must derive from that group's internal traditions. The approach defended here refuses to take that step, arguing that an account of the central human capacities and functions, and of the basic human needs and rights, can be given in a fully universal manner, at least at a high level of generality, and that this universal account is what should guide feminist thought and planning. The essays are strongly critical of forms of both descriptive and normative relativism deriving from postmodernism. They try to show that a universal account of human justice need not be insensitive to the variety of traditions or a mere projection of narrow Western values onto groups with different concerns.

One crucial step in defending a universalist project is to point to the variety within groups, cultures, and traditions. The relativist move of deferring to "local knowledge" is not very plausible even initially: For why shouldn't we think from the start that traditions can be evil as well as good, a view most people hold about their own traditions? But it begins to lose whatever appeal it had once we begin to reflect that traditions are not monoliths. Any living culture contains plurality and argument; it contains relatively powerful voices, relatively silent voices, and voices that cannot speak at all in the public space. Often some of these voices would speak differently, too, if they had more information or were less frightened—so part of a culture, too, is what its members *would* say if they were freer or more fully informed. When women are at issue, we should be especially skeptical of deferring to the most powerful voices in local tradition. In most parts of the world, that voice is especially likely to be a male voice, and that voice may not be all that attentive to the needs and interests of women. One may also find that a voice that is in some sense foreign proves to be essential to the self-expression of a marginalized or oppressed group: for people often appropriate good ideas from outside and vindicate their dignity by pointing to examples of respect elsewhere.

A vivid example of this last point occurred at a conference in Beijing in June 1995, which brought Western feminist philosophers together with Chinese scholars in women's studies. Most of the Chinese scholars were harshly critical of the Confucian tradition as a tradition that subordinates women. One paper was different. Presented by a young scholar from Hong Kong, it argued that one could mine the Confucian tradition for values of community and solidarity that could be used in building a Chinese feminism. The Chinese women reacted with unanimous negativity, saying that this was a "Western paper." She could not have said that, they said, had she not been from Hong Kong. For these women, the Confucian tradition was a living source of humiliation and disempowerment. It was not their voice, and it spoke politically against them even in 1995, defending the "women go home" policy that is responsible for many layoffs of female workers. Where did they locate their tradition? In their own critical thought and work, in the efforts of women to win respect within history—but also in John Stuart Mill, whose *The Subjection of Women*, translated into Chinese early in the twentieth century, is a primary source of the Chinese feminist tradition.[3]

What is East and what is West? What is the tradition of a person who is fighting for freedom and empowerment? Why should one's group be assumed to be the ethnic or religious group of one's birth? Might it not, if one so chooses, be, or become, the international group of women—or of people who respect the equality and dignity of women?

In an important sense, the views expressed in this volume are not really about women at all but about human beings and about women seen as fully human. The focus on women is justified, it seems to me, by the urgency of the problems facing women in today's world and by the sorry record of our dealings with (and evasions of) these problems. But no theory of justice could plausibly call itself such if it did select out one group for favorable treatment on the basis of a contingency of birth. This, then, is a theory of human justice, and of feminism as a humanism.[4] It ought to prompt reflection about hunger more generally, about the relief of poverty and misery more generally. As I said, it leaves a tremendous question, that of the global redistribution of wealth, waiting in the wings.

Universalist views, applied to women, are frequently suspected of being the projections of a male view onto women, or of the views of well-educated Western white women onto women of diverse backgrounds and cultures. I try to answer this concern through my method, which lets the voices of many women speak and which seeks collaboration with women and men from many different regions in the process of forming a view. The universals defended here are the fruit of many years of collaborative international work. I also try to answer it in the details of my proposal, with its emphasis on a positive role for knowledge of local circumstances. Nonetheless, another most important way to answer this worry is to insist on the universal importance of protecting spheres of choice and freedom, within which people with diverse views of what matters in life can pursue flourishing according to their own lights. We can hardly be charged with imposing a foreign set of values upon individuals or groups if what we are doing is providing support for basic capacities and opportunities that are involved in the selection of any flourishing life and then leaving people to choose for themselves how they will pursue flourishing. Any universalism that has a chance to be persuasive in the modern world must, it seems to me, be a form of political liberalism.

LIBERALISM

The liberal tradition in political philosophy has frequently been thought to be inadequate for the goals of feminism. One central purpose of the volume is to answer that charge, defending a form of liberalism (deriving, in different ways, from Kant, Mill, and Aristotle[5]) that can answer the feminist charges that are legitimate and show why other charges are not legitimate. The version of liberalism here begins from the idea of the equal worth of human

---

3. On the complexity of "Asian values," see Amartya Sen, "Human Rights and Asian Values," *New Republic*, July 14/21, 1997, 33–40. [MILL's *The Subjection of Women* (1869) is excerpted above—editor's note.]

4. See, in a similar vein, Susan Moller Okin, *Justice, Gender, and the Family* (New York: Basic Books, 1989), chap. 8.
5. Greek philosopher (384–322 B.C.E.). For IMMANUEL KANT, see above [editor's note].

beings as such, in virtue of their basic human capacities for choice and reasoning. All, in virtue of those human capacities, are worthy of equal concern and respect: Thus; the view is at its core antifeudal, opposed to the political ascendancy of hierarchies of rank, caste, and birth. The crucial addition liberal feminism makes to the tradition is to add sex to that list of morally irrelevant characteristics. It should have been there all along, for no liberal thinker ever presented a cogent argument to justify the subordination of women to men while opposing feudalism and monarchy. Subordination by sex was simply seen as natural, and the entire topic was basically ignored in theories of political justice. This was a profound inconsistency in the liberal tradition, as J. S. Mill powerfully showed already in 1869, but we have had to wait until the present decade for serious and sustained work on the justice of family arrangements that is beginning to make the promise of liberalism real for the world's women.

The basic argument I make, then, is that the liberal tradition of equal concern and respect should, and in all consistency must, be extended to women and to the relations between women and men in the family. In the process, we should not be quick to dismiss the often-criticized individualism of the liberal tradition. I argue that liberal individualism does not entail egoism or a preference for the type of person who has no deep need of others. Many liberal thinkers have made compassion, care, and love an essential part of their normative program. What does distinguish liberalism from other political traditions is its insistence on the separateness of one life from another, and the equal importance of each life, seen on its own terms rather than as part of a larger organic or corporate whole. Each human being should be regarded as an end rather than as a means to the ends of others. The liberal insists that the goal of politics should be the amelioration of lives taken one by one and seen as separate ends, rather than the amelioration of the organic whole or the totality. I argue that this is a very good position for women to embrace, seeing that women have all too often been regarded not as ends but as means to the ends of others, not as sources of agency and worth in their own right but as reproducers and caregivers.

The form of liberalism endorsed here is fully compatible with ascribing great importance to care and love. But it suggests a way in which the commitment to care should be qualified. Emotions of love and care, like other emotions, have in part a social origin, but this means that they are only as reliable as the social norms that give rise to them. The common propensity of women to subordinate themselves to others and to sacrifice their well-being for that of a larger unit may in many cases be morally admirable, but this should by no means be taken for granted. Such dispositions have been formed, often, in unjust conditions and may simply reflect the low worth society itself has placed on women's well-being. My view urges that all such emotions be valued with the constraints of a life organized by critical reasoning. The same, I argue, is true of sexual desire and emotion: Insofar as these are shaped by unjust social conditions, they should not be relied on as unproblematic guides to a flourishing life. The norm, here as elsewhere, should be the idea of being treated as an end rather than a means, a person rather than an object.

Liberalism concerns itself with freedom and with spheres of choice. As I conceive it, this does not mean maximizing the sheer numbers of choices people get to make for themselves. The idea of liberty should be understood in close conjunction with the idea of equal worth and respect: The choices that liberal politics should protect are those that are deemed of central importance to the development and expression of personhood. In this sense, liberalism has to take a stand about what is good for people, and I argue that it needs a somewhat more extensive conception of the basic human functions and capacities than many liberal thinkers have used if it is to provide sufficient remedies for entrenched injustice and hierarchy. But the goal should always be to put people into a position of agency and choice, not to push them into functioning in ways deemed desirable. I argue that this is no mere parochial Western ideology but the expression of a sense of agency that has deep roots all over the world; it expresses the joy most people have in using their own bodies and minds. * * * It is this experiential idea of choice on which I rely in defending choice as goal, and no argument has yet shown that there is any human being who does not desire choice so construed.

CONCERN WITH THE SOCIAL SHAPING OF PREFERENCE AND DESIRE

Among the most significant charges feminists have made against the liberal tradition is its neglect of the social formation and deformation of preference, emotion, and desire. It is indeed true that some offshoots of the tradition, in particular neoclassical economics (until recent years), have indeed treated people's subjective preferences and desires as simply given, a bedrock external to law and public policy. Economists have typically understood the goal of public policy to be the satisfaction of preference, regarded as antecedently given and more or less impervious to policy.

Such a view is exceedingly myopic and ultimately indefensible. Empirically, it has been amply demonstrated that people's desires and preferences respond to their beliefs about social norms and about their own opportunities. Thus people usually adjust their desires to reflect the level of their available possibilities: They can get used to having luxuries and mind the absence of these very much, and they can also fail to form desires for things their circumstances have placed out of reach. People from groups that have not traditionally had access to education, or employment outside the home, may be slow to desire these things because they may not know what they are like or what they could possibly mean in lives like theirs. Even at the level of simple bodily health and nutrition, people who have been malnourished all their lives may not know what it would be like to feel strong. Especially if they have been told that women are weaker than men, they may not be able to form a desire for the health and strength of which they are capable. The absence of such a desire should not convince policymakers that health and strength are not important goals to be promoted for these people.

Conceptually, the traditional economic picture is also naive. For centuries philosophers and others have debated about the nature of experiences such as emotion, desire, and pleasure. A considerable consensus has emerged that emotions, at any rate, are at least in part made up out of evaluative judgments; these judgments are likely to have been learned in society and shaped by that society's norms of appropriateness. It was on this basis, for example, that the

Greek and Roman Stoics criticized the prevalence of anger in their society, holding that a change in social norms could make people less obsessed with slights to their honor and therefore less prone to rage. As for desire and pleasure, arguments of great power, beginning with Plato[6] if not earlier, urge us to see these experiences, too, as infused by judgments of value and appropriateness, and thus responsive in at least some measure to changes in social norms. (Acceptance of such a view need not involve denying that emotions are grounded in biological tendencies; societies deal in many different ways with the tendencies in their members' biology, shaping expression and choice of objects, and at times either repressing or encouraging the entire emotion category.)

If these arguments are sound, they mean a good deal for justice between the sexes. For they suggest that appeals to an unchanging human nature, in the context of defending a traditional pattern of family love and fear, may posit an immutable bedrock where reality presents us with many possibilities for change. If many actual women are fearful and dependent, it may in part be because they have been formed to be that way. If many men are possessive and tyrannical, it may be less because of unchanging male aggression than because society gives permission to males to form and to express such attitudes. The philosophical tradition suggests that even something as apparently deepseated as the character of a person's erotic desire may contain a socially learned component. It may therefore be not too utopian to imagine a culture in which men's sexual desire for women will not commonly be associated with projects of possession and control, and in which female sexual agency will not inspire fear and suspicion.

Some feminists have thought the recognition of a social dimension in desire alien to the liberal tradition of political philosophy; it is not. Following the Roman Stoics, Adam Smith developed a powerful critique of socially learned greed and excessive anger, proposing norms of rational self-scrutiny that should move each person nearer to an appropriate balance in passion.[7] The contemporary Kantian tradition represented in John Rawls's A Theory of Justice focuses intently on the social origins of envy and fear, insisting that mutable social conditions are in large part responsible for the genesis of these destructive passions.[8] John Stuart Mill anticipated the arguments of leading modern feminists such as Catharine MacKinnon and Andrea Dworkin[9] when he argued that the nature of both male and female sexuality has been shaped by long habits of domination and subordination. To call women's sexual personalities "natural" is about as plausible, he says, as to put a tree one half in a vapor bath and the other half in the snow—and then, seeing that one half is withered and the other half luxuriant, to declare that it is the "nature" of the tree to grow that way.[1]

6. Greek philosopher (ca. 427–ca. 347 B.C.E.) [editor's note].

7. Adam Smith, The Theory of Moral Sentiments (6th ed., 1790), ed. D. D. Raphael and A. L. Mackie (Indianapolis: Liberty Press, 1979), esp. Part I. [Smith (1723–1790), Scottish social philosopher and political economist—editor's note.]

8. TJ; and also J. Rawls, "Fairness to Goodness," Philosophical Review 84 (1975), 536–54.

9. American feminist and activist (1946–2005); she collaborated with the American feminist and legal theorist MacKinnon (b. 1946) in attacking pornography [editor's note].

1. John Stuart Mill, The Subjection of Women (1869), ed. Susan M. Okin (Indianapolis: Hackett, 1988).

Mill understood, too, that a moral critique of deformed desire and preference is not antithetical to liberal democracy; it is actually essential to its success. Children learn how to be good citizens in families; what they see in the demeanor of those closest to them shapes their citizenship powerfully for good or for ill. At present, he argues, the family is "a school of despotism," where male children learn that just in virtue of being born male they are the superiors of one half of the human race. This cannot be a good preparation for political equality in the rest of life. "The family, justly constituted," he concludes, "would be the real school of the virtues of freedom." But the just constitution of the family requires a reform of moral education on a large scale, and this reform must be facilitated by at least some changes in laws and institutions, especially those concerning marital rape, domestic violence, and women's legal rights over children.

It therefore seems crucial for an inquiry into gender justice to investigate the social origins of desire, preference, and emotion, both through refined conceptual analysis and through empirical study, drawing on the excellent work that has recently been done in these areas in cognitive psychology and in anthropology. Liberalism cannot make sense of its own subject matter unless it looks deeper into these questions than some liberal thinkers have.

CONCERN WITH SYMPATHETIC UNDERSTANDING

Women are often valued as creatures of care and sympathy. Often they are devalued for the same characteristics. Sometimes, too, women's propensity to care for others veers over into an undignified self-abnegation in which a woman subordinates her humanity utterly to the needs of another or others. It is tempting to praise women for their ability to care and to sympathize and to suggest that men have a great deal to learn from their example. It is also tempting to criticize women for their frequent passivity and lack of autonomy and to suggest that they have at least something to learn from the example of men. Some feminists deeply concerned with women's dignity and agency, for example, Catharine MacKinnon and Claudia Card,[2] have questioned the validity of women's instincts of care, suggesting that those "instincts" are actually constructs of women's subordination, which frequently serve male interests and work against women. Other feminists, such as Carol Gilligan and Virginia Held,[3] have suggested that women's ability to love and care for others is at the core of morality, and should be emulated by all. To Gilligan's claim that women speak in a "different voice," the voice of care, MacKinnon responds with skepticism: "If you will take your foot off our necks, then you will hear in what voice women speak."[4]

Anyone who believes, as I do, that emotions are in part made up out of socially learned beliefs is likely to share MacKinnon's suspiciousness of emotions formed under conditions of injustice. It seems wrong to observe the way women are under injustice and to conclude directly from this that they should and must be that way. Nonetheless, duly scrutinized and

---

2. American philosopher (1940–2015) [editor's note].

3. American social and political philosopher (b. 1929). Gilligan (b. 1936), American ethicist and psychologist; her best-known work is In a Different

Voice: Psychological Theory and Women's Development (1982) [editor's note].

4. Catharine MacKinnon, Feminism Unmodified (Cambridge, MA: Harvard University Press, 1987), 45.

assessed, emotions of care and sympathy lie at the heart of the ethical life. No society can afford not to cultivate them, and certainly a society that is struggling to overcome a legacy of great injustice needs all the love and sympathy it can muster. Many feminists have believed that the record of injustice erodes, practically speaking, all possibility of sympathy, trust, and love between women and men. Or at least—as few real women actually believe something so extreme—many feminists feel that it is politically valuable to call for the repudiation of trust and the refusal of sympathy and mercy. I dispute this claim.

I try here, however uneasily, to combine a radical feminist critique of sex relations with an interest in the possibilities of trust and understanding. Each reader must judge in the light of his or her own sense of life the odd combination that results—of Kant with D. H. Lawrence, of MacKinnon with Virginia Woolf.[5] To some the moral interest in sympathy and forgiveness will seem like a kind of collaboration with oppression. And indeed, who knows at what point patience becomes masochism or sympathy self-torment. These questions are rightly pressed by MacKinnon and Dworkin. It would be naive to claim to have definitive answers. But one important ingredient of a response is the reminder that cultures are not monoliths; people are not stamped out like coins by the power machine of social convention. They are constrained by social norms, but norms are plural and people are devious. Even in societies that nourish problematic roles for men and women, real men and women can also find spaces in which to subvert those conventions, resourcefully creating possibilities of love and joy. (And some societies offer their members more space than others: Mill's England is not 1999 America, and we should be clear about these differences.)

SOURCE: From Martha C. Nussbaum, *Sex and Social Justice* (New York: Oxford University Press, 1999), pp. 6–14, 29–54, 375–84. Except as indicated, all notes are Nussbaum's; some of her notes have been omitted and some have been shortened.

Transitional Anger

We feel calm toward those who humble themselves before us and do not talk back. For they seem to acknowledge that they are our inferiors. . . . That our anger ceases toward those who humble themselves before us is shown even by dogs, who do not bite people when they sit down.

—Aristotle,[1] *Rhetoric*, 1380a21–25

The idea that anger is a central threat to decent human interactions runs through the Western philosophical tradition—as do various claims about its usefulness and value. Nonetheless, recent philosophers, at least, spend little

---

5. English writer (1882–1941); her fiction and criticism have had great influence on later feminists. The English poet and novelist D. H. Lawrence (1885–1930) has been attacked as misogynist by some feminist critics [editor's note].

1. Greek philosopher (384–322 B.C.E.). Here and later, Nussbaum cites only the Bekker numbers (based on the page numbers and columns of an 1831 edition) used almost universally in citing Aristotle's works; the epigraph is from book 2, chapter 3.

time analyzing the emotion. Typical, and highly influential, are Peter Strawson's reference to a class of 'reactive attitudes', including guilt, resentment, and indignation, all of which track the relation of another's will to us;[2] and R. Jay Wallace's highly abstract, albeit valuable, characterization of a class of 'reactive emotions'.[3] But anger is a specific emotion, distinct from disgust and guilt, and it seems crucial to analyze it closely, examining its general cognitive content and distinguishing its varieties.

Agreeing with most traditional philosophical definitions of anger, I shall argue that the idea of payback or retribution—in some form, however subtle—is a conceptual part of anger. I shall then argue that the payback idea is normatively problematic, and anger, therefore, with it. There are two possibilities. Either anger focuses on some significant injury, such as a murder or a rape, or it focuses only on the significance of the wrongful act for the victim's relative status—what Aristotle calls a 'down-ranking'. In the first case, the idea of payback makes no sense, since inflicting pain on the offender does not remove or constructively address the victim's injury. In the second, it makes all too much sense—payback may successfully effect a reversal of positions—but only because the values involved are distorted: relative status should not be so important. In the process of defending these contentions, I shall recognize a borderline species of anger that is free from these defects, and I shall describe, and recommend, a transition from anger to constructive thinking about future good.

Let me begin by simply stipulating three parts of my framework for which I argue in other writing. Like all the major emotions, anger has a cognitive/intentional content, including appraisals or evaluations of several distinct types. Often, it involves not simply value-laden appraisals, but also beliefs.

Second, the appraisals and beliefs involved in anger are what I call 'eudaimonistic':[4] as is the case with all the major emotions, they are made from the point of view of the agent, and register the agent's own view of what matters for life, rather than some detached or impersonal table of values.

Third, anger is typically accompanied by a wide range of bodily changes and subjective feeling-states. But these bodily changes and subjective feelings, though important in their way, have too little constancy for them to be included in the definition of anger as necessary conditions of that emotion.[5] For one thing some anger isn't felt at all, like a fear of death that lurks beneath the surface of awareness.

---

2. Peter F. Strawson, "Freedom and Resentment," originally published in *Proceedings of the British Academy* 48 (1962): 1–25, and reprinted in Strawson, *Studies in the Philosophy of Thought and Action* (Oxford: Oxford University Press, 1968), pp. 71–96, page numbers from the latter. Strawson does mention distinct emotions, including resentment, indignation, and "moral disapprobation," which may or may not be conceived as an emotion. He does not define them or investigate their internal structure, however [Nussbaum's note].

3. Wallace, *Responsibility and the Moral Sentiments* (Cambridge, Mass.: Harvard University Press, 1994) [Nussbaum's note].

4. A term that echoes Aristotle, who argues in the *Nicomachean Ethics* that human *eudaimonia* (happiness) results from an activity of the human soul in accordance with excellence or virtue (see book 1, especially 1098a12–16).

5. On all these claims, see Martha Nussbaum, *Upheavals of Thought: The Intelligence of Emotions* (New York: Cambridge University Press, 2001), chapters 1 and 2; on the role of feelings, see also Martha Nussbaum, "Précis" and "Responses," in book symposium on Nussbaum, *Upheavals of Thought*, [in] *Philosophy and Phenomenological Research* 68 (2004): 443–49, 473–86 [Nussbaum's note].

What is anger's distinctive content? A good starting point is Aristotle's definition. Although it will turn out to be too narrow to cover all cases and varieties of anger, it helps us dissect its elements, as contemporary cognitive psychologists acknowledge.

Anger, Aristotle holds, is: 'a desire accompanied by pain for an imagined retribution on account of an imagined slighting inflicted by people who have no legitimate reason to slight oneself or one's own' (1378a31–3).[6] Anger, then, involves:

1. slighting or down-ranking (*oligôria*)
2. of the self or people close to the self
3. wrongfully or inappropriately done (*më prosêkontôn*)
4. accompanied by pain
5. and linked to a desire for retribution

By twice repeating 'imagined' (*phainomenês*), Aristotle emphasizes that what is relevant to the emotion is the way the situation is seen from the angry person's viewpoint, not the way it really is, which could, of course, be different.

Anger is an unusually complex emotion since it involves both pain and pleasure: Aristotle shortly says that the prospect of retaliation is pleasant. He does not clarify the causal relationships involved, but we can easily see that the pain is supposed to be produced by the injury, and the desire for retaliation somehow responds to the injury. Moreover, anger also involves a double reference—to a person or people and to an act. To use non-Aristotelian terminology that makes explicit an issue that remains implicit in his discussion: the *target* of anger is typically a person, the one who is seen as having inflicted damage—and as having done so wrongfully. 'I am angry *at* so-and-so'. And the *focus* of anger is an act imputed to the target, which is taken to be a wrongful damage.

Injuries may be the focus in grief as well. But whereas grief focuses on the loss or damage itself, anger focuses on the act that inflicted the damage, seeing it as wrongfully inflicted by the target. Anger, then, requires causal thinking, and ideas of right and wrong. The damage may be inflicted on the person who, as a result, feels anger, or it may be inflicted on some other person or thing within that person's circle of concern.

From the vantage point of contemporary intuitions, the least puzzling parts of Aristotle's definition are its emphasis on pain and its emphasis on wrongful damage. How exactly does the wrongful act of another cause pain to the self? Well, says Aristotle, the person sees (or believes) that something about which she cares deeply has been damaged. In other words, the item damaged has to be seen as significant and not trivial, and that is why pain is a consequence. This pain is, up to a point, not dissimilar to the pain felt in grief. It tracks the perceived 'size' of the damage. Nonetheless, the pain of anger typically also makes internal reference to the (believed) wrongful act of another person: the pain of seeing one's child murdered just feels different from that of losing a child to accidental death. In numerous texts, Aristotle emphasizes that pleasure and pain themselves have an intentional content:

6. *Rhetoric* 2.2.

the pain, then, is pain *at* the injury that has (as the person believes) been inflicted. It's that specific sort of pain.

As for wrongful injury: even though we experience frustration when someone inadvertently damages us, we only become angry when we believe (rightly or wrongly) that the damage was inflicted by a person or persons, and in a manner that was illegitimate or wrongful. Contemporary psychologist Richard Lazarus gives the example of a store clerk who ignores a customer because he is busy talking on the phone. The customer will feel wrongly slighted. But if she learns that the reason for the phone call was a medical emergency involving the clerk's child, she will no longer be angry, because she will see that it was legitimate to give the phone call priority.[7] We aren't always so reasonable, of course, but what matters is how we see the situation: we are angry only if we *see* the damage as illegitimate or wrongful.

Notoriously, however, people sometimes get angry when they are frustrated by inanimate objects, which presumably cannot act wrongfully. This sort of behavior was reported already by the Stoic philosopher Chrysippus,[8] who spoke of people biting their keys and kicking their door when it doesn't open right away, all the while 'saying the most inappropriate things' (*Stoicorum Veterum Fragmenta*[9] III.478). In 1988, the *Journal of the American Medical Association* published an article on 'vending machine rage': fifteen injuries, three of them fatal, as a result of angry men,[1] kicking or rocking machines that had taken their money without dispensing the drink. The fatal injuries were caused by machines falling over on the men and crushing them.[2] Do such familiar reactions show that anger does not require the perception that there is wrongful damage? I see no reason to think this. We irrationally think that we have a right to expect 'respect' and cooperation from the inanimate objects that assist us. So we react as if they were bad people, since they clearly are not doing 'their job' for us. We quickly realize that this doesn't make sense—most of the time.

More problematic, at least initially, is Aristotle's restriction to 'oneself or one's own'; surely we may have anger when a cause or principle we care about has been wrongfully assailed or when a stranger is the victim of an unjust aggression. Yes, indeed, we may, but that (claims the Aristotelian) is because in that case the cause or stranger has become part of our circle of concern. In other words, 'oneself or one's own' is just a way of alluding to the eudaimonistic structure that anger shares with other emotions. This response seems correct: just as we grieve not about every death in the world, but only the deaths of those who are dear to us, so we get angry not at any and every instance of wrongdoing in the world, but only those that touch on core values of the self. As with other emotions, a vivid episode may jump-start the response by moving a distant object into the circle of concern. If, instead of

---

7. Richard Lazarus, *Emotion and Adoption* (New York: Oxford University Press, 1991), pp. 219, 223 [Nussbaum's note].
8. Greek philosopher (ca. 280–207 B.C.E.).
9. The standard edition of "fragments of the earlier Stoics" (1903–24), edited by Hans von Arnim.
1. It does appear to be a male phenomenon, at least in this study. Or perhaps women who reacted

angrily did not kick the machine hard enough to topple it over. Or perhaps they did not want to ruin their shoes [Nussbaum's note].
2. See Carol Tavris, *Anger: The Misunderstood Emotion* (New York: Simon and Schuster, 1982), p. 164, cf. p. 72; cf. also James Averill, *Anger and Aggression* (New York: Springer, 1982), p. 166 [Nussbaum's note].

Adam Smith's tale of an earthquake in China,[3] which jump-starts compassion, we hear a vivid tale of genocide in a distant country, then we may be aroused to anger on behalf of the slaughtered people, even if they were not antecedently of concern. But Smith's point holds: the emotion lasts only as long as those people are of concern to us. If the concern ceases (because, for example, we are diverted by pressing concerns closer to home), so does the emotion.

Far more problematic, at least initially, is Aristotle's reference to a 'slighting' or 'down-ranking'. We immediately associate that emphasis with the values of an honor culture, in which people are always ranking themselves against one another and in which the central case of wrongdoing is a down-ranking. Surely, we are inclined to say, many cases of wrongdoing involve cherished projects without being seen as diminutions of status.

Has Aristotle simply made a mistake here? I shall argue that he has, but not as large a mistake as one might think: he has captured a style of thinking that is very common in anger though not omnipresent.

The narrower sense of *oligôria* as involving down-ranking proves more explanatorily fertile, however, than we might at first suppose. There is something comical in the self-congratulatory idea that honor cultures are in another time or at least another place (such as, putatively, the Middle East), given the obsessive attention paid by Americans (and perhaps Europeans, too) to competitive ranking in terms of status, money, and other qualities. Empirical psychologist Carol Tavris's wide-ranging study of anger in America finds ubiquitous reference to 'insults', 'slights', 'condescension', 'being treated as if I were of no account'.[4] People remain intensely concerned about their standing, and they find endless occasions for anger in acts that seem to threaten it.

From now on I shall call this sort of perceived down-ranking a *status-injury.* The very idea of a status-injury already includes the idea of culpability, for, as Aristotle notes, diminution of status is always voluntary: if someone acted accidentally, I won't perceive that as diminishing my status. (Remember the store clerk who had an urgent phone call.) Anger is not always, but very often, about status injury. And status-injury has a narcissistic flavor: rather than focusing on the wrongfulness of the act as such, a focus that might lead to concern for wrongful acts of the same type more generally, the status-angry person focuses obsessively on her own standing vis-à-vis others.

In connection with such injuries, both Aristotle and Lazarus emphasize the relevance of personal insecurity or vulnerability: we are prone to anger to the extent that we feel insecure or lacking in control with respect to the aspect of our goals that has been assailed—and to the extent that we expect or desire control. Anger aims at restoring lost control and often achieves at least an illusion of control.[5] To the extent that a culture encourages people to feel vulnerable to affront and down-ranking in a wide variety of situations, to that extent it encourages the roots of status-focused anger.

What is anger's aim? The philosophical tradition concurs in holding that there is a double movement in the emotion; this double movement, from pain

3. In *The Theory of Moral Sentiments* (1759), 3.3, the Scottish moral philosopher and political economist Smith (1723–1790) imagines the limited effect on the feelings of a cultured European man of the news that an earthquake had suddenly killed all the inhabitants of China.
4. Tavris, *Anger*, pp. 72, 94 [Nussbaum's note].
5. Tavris, *Anger*, pp. 152–53 [Nussbaum's note].

inflicted to striking back, is so prominent that ancient taxonomies classify anger as an emotion that looks forward to a future good, rather than as one that responds to a present bad—although, once they say more, they acknowledge that anger has both aspects. Aristotle emphasizes that the outward movement characteristic of anger is pleasant, and that anger is in that sense constructive and linked to hope. The imagined retaliation or payback is seen as somehow assuaging the pain or making good the damage.

But how exactly does this work? How does pain lead to the sort of lashing out, or striking back, that we associate with anger in many, if not all, cases? And why would someone who has been gravely wounded look forward with hope to doing something unwelcome to the offender? If we had a noncognitive account of anger, there would be nothing further to say: that is just the way hard-wired mechanisms work. But ours is not that type of account, so we must try to understand this puzzle. For it is a puzzle. Doing something to the offender does not bring dead people back to life, heal a broken limb, or undo a sexual violation. So why do people somehow believe that it does? Or what, exactly, do they believe that makes even a little sense of their retaliatory project?

First, however, we had better make sure that the philosophical tradition is correct in holding that a wish for payback is a conceptual part of anger. It is pretty impressive that so many first-rate thinkers, from Aristotle and the Stoics to Butler[6] and Smith to recent empirical psychologists such as Richard Lazarus and James Averill should agree on this. They have thought long and hard about the concept, and it would be surprising if they had made an obvious error. Still, let us think again. Anger is not the only emotion that contains a double movement. Many emotions involve a backward-looking appraisal of what has occurred, as well as associated action tendencies oriented toward a future goal. Grief contains pain at a loss but also often involves a wish for restoration. The grieved person fantasizes about bringing back the loved one. Despite the fact that this is impossible if the person is dead (rather than lost or merely ill), the fantasy can be very persistent and can organize long stretches of the bereaved person's life. When the person is not, or not known to be, dead, the restoration idea is even more central to grief. Parents of an abducted child often respond with obsessive recreation of the child's room, clothing, etc., and obsessive pursuit of any hope for restoration. As grief runs its course, the fantasy of restoration is typically transmuted into a dream of substitution, which can be enacted by finding a new lover to replace the lost one, having another child to replace the lost one.

But even though these action tendencies are closely associated with grief, it is interesting to observe that no standard philosophical or psychological analysis of grief makes them an intrinsic part of grief, a necessary element in its definition. And this corresponds, I believe, to our usage. We typically think that grief and mourning can take people in many directions, even if restoration is a powerful element in many of them.

Compassion too has an associated future-directed action tendency, which has been the focus of a lot of psychological research. When I feel compassion for a person who is suffering, I often imagine helping that person, and in many cases

6. Joseph Butler (1692–1752), English bishop and religious philosopher

I do it. C. Daniel Batson's empirical research shows that this tendency toward helping is powerful if the helpful action is ready at hand and not very costly.[7] But that connection is typically understood as contingent and causal, rather than conceptual, even if the causality is pretty robust. I think this is probably correct.

With anger, however, the future-oriented aim is standardly thought to be part of the emotion, something without which there is pain of some sort, but not anger. (Butler holds that anger's internal goal is the misery of our fellow humans.[8]) We must figure out, first, whether this is correct—whether there really is a conceptual connection in this case, and not simply a causal connection as in the others. Second, we must figure out precisely how the pain is connected to the strike-back response.

First, let's be clear about what the claim is. The claim is not that anger conceptually involves a wish for violent revenge; nor is it that anger involves the wish to inflict suffering upon the offender. For I may not want to get involved in revenge myself; I may want someone else, or the law, or life itself, to do it for me. I just want the doer to suffer. And the suffering can be quite subtle. One might wish for a physical injury; one might wish for psychological unhappiness; one might wish for unpopularity; one might merely wish for the perpetrator's future (your ex's new marriage, for example) to turn out badly. And one can even imagine as a type of punishment the sheer continued existence of the person as the bad and benighted person he or she is; that is how Dante imagines hell.[9] All I am investigating here (and ultimately accepting, with one significant exception) is that anger involves, conceptually, a wish for things to go badly, somehow, for the offender in a way that is envisaged, somehow, however vaguely, as a payback for the offense.

So let's investigate this further, considering a range of different cases. And let us start from a basic scenario: Offender O has raped Angela's close friend Rebecca on the campus where both Angela and Rebecca are students. Angela has true beliefs about what has occurred, about how seriously damaging it is, and about the wrongful intentions involved: O, she knows, is mentally competent, understood the wrongfulness of his act, etc. (I choose rape rather than murder in order to leave Angela with a wider range of possible actions and wishes than would typically be the case with murder. And I choose a friend in order to give Angela more latitude about how to position herself.)

Case 1. Angela feels pain at Rebecca's rape. She feels that her circle of concern, what she deeply cares about, has been severely damaged, and she believes, correctly, that the damage was wrongful. She now takes steps to mitigate the damage: she spends time with Rebecca, she makes efforts to support her in therapy, she devotes a great deal of energy to mending Rebecca's life—and thus to mending the breach in her own circle of concern. So far, Angela's emotion appears to be grief and/or compassion, and I think the standard definitions are correct when they suggest that it is not anger, even though the occasion for the grief is a wrongful act. We should notice that in this case the primary focus of Angela's emotion is the loss and pain caused to Rebecca, rather than

7. Batson's research is summarized in *Altruism in Humans* (New York: Oxford University Press, 2011) [Nussbaum's note].
8. See Sermon VIII in Butler's *Fifteen Sermons*

Preached at the Rolls Chapel (1726).
9. In *Inferno*, the first section of the *Divine Comedy* (1308–21), the epic poem by the Italian writer Dante Alighieri (1265–1321).

the criminal act itself, and to that extent her emotion would seem to have Rebecca, not the rapist, as its target.

Case 2. Angela feels pain at Rebecca's rape, etc. She does all the things that she did in Case 1, thus expressing her compassion. But she also focuses on the wrongfulness of the act, and her pain includes a special pain directed at the wrongful act—to some extent distinct from her pain at Rebecca's suffering. This additional pain leads her to want to do something about that wrongfulness. So Angela forms a group to support rape victims, and she gives money to such groups. She also campaigns for better public safety measures to prevent rape. Should we call Angela's emotion anger because it focuses not only on Rebecca's pain but also on the wrongfulness of the act, and has an outward movement aimed at something like a righting of the wrong? It is an interesting case, but I think that we typically would not call Angela's emotion anger. I am inclined to see it as a type of morally inflected compassion—not very different, really, from compassion for one hungry acquaintance that leads me to campaign for better welfare support for all. As in Case 1, the emotion does not have the offender as its target; its target is Rebecca, and other women in Rebecca's position. The offender comes into it only because stopping similar harms is Angela's goal for the future, so she will want to deter or incapacitate O and people like O.

Case 3. Angela feels pain, etc., as in Cases 1 and 2. As in Case 2, she focuses on the wrongfulness of O's act, comforts Rebecca, and she may campaign for general measures to prevent that sort of damage in future. But this time she also focuses on O. She seeks to mend the damage *by making the offender suffer.* *Because* her circle of concern is damaged, she wants something to happen to O (whether through legal or extralegal means). Here we finally have arrived at anger as the philosophical tradition understands it: a retributive and hopeful outward movement that seeks the pain of the offender *because of and as a way of compensating for* one's own damage.

The question now is, why? Why would an intelligent person think that inflicting pain on the offender assuages or cancels her own harm? There seems to be some type of magical thinking going on. In reality, harsh punishment of the offender rarely repairs a damage. Adding O's pain to Rebecca's does not do anything to ameliorate Rebecca's situation, as far as one can see. In a TV interview after his father's murder, Michael Jordan[1] was asked whether, if they ever caught the murderer, Jordan would want him executed. Jordan sadly replied, 'Why? That wouldn't bring him back'. This eminently sensible reply is rare is rare, however, and perhaps only someone whose credentials in the area of masculinity are as impeccable as Jordan's would dare to think and say it.[2] The fantasy that payback restores is magical thinking, abetted by ideas of cosmic balance that are deeply engrained in many cultures, but not the less irrational for that.

This brings us back to Aristotle's idea of down-ranking, which, it emerges, is a likely abettor of this type of magical thinking.

Case 4. Angela is pained, etc. She believes that O's bad act is not only a wrongful act that seriously damaged someone dear to her, but also an insult

---

1. One of the greatest American basketball players of all time (b. 1963); his father was murdered in 1993 (two men were convicted of the crime in 1996).

2. See the similar critique of payback in Thom Brooks, *Punishment* (New York: Routledge, 2012) [Nussbaum's note].

or denigration of her. She thinks something like, 'This guy thinks that he can insult my friend's dignity with impunity, and, insofar as he thinks this, he thinks that he can push me around—that I'll just sit by while my friend is insulted. So he diminishes me and insults my self-respect'. Here, the connection between pain and retaliation is made through the Aristotelian idea that the damage O has inflicted is a kind of humiliation or down-ranking. No matter how implausible it is to read O's act as a down-ranking of Angela (given that O doesn't know Angela, or even Rebecca), Angela sees O's harm to her friend as an ego-wound that lessens Angela's status. She therefore thinks that lowering O through pain and even humiliation will right the balance.[3]

Modern western cultures think this way all the time. In most major sports we find an emphasis on retaliation for injury, and players are thought unmanly if they do not strike back to the extent the rules permit (and a little beyond). Even though it is obvious that injuring one player does not take away the *injury* to another, it is a different story if one focuses not on injury but on ranking and humiliation: the retaliatory hit is plausibly seen as taking away the humiliation of the first hit. Slighting in the sense of diminution reaches a broad class of cases, even if not all cases, where anger is involved. It is very easy for people to shift mentally from a eudaimonistic concern (this is part of my circle of concern, what I care about) to a narrower status-focused concern (this is all about me and my pride or rank). In such cases, a retaliatory strike back is thought to restore the balance of status, manliness, or whatever. And often it does.

Jean Hampton,[4] whose analysis is very close to mine, puts it this way: if people are secure in their dignity, they won't see an injury as a diminishment; but people are rarely this secure. They secretly fear that the offense has revealed a real lowness or lack of value in themselves, and that putting the offender down will prove that the offender has made a mistake.[5] I feel her account does not cover all the cases: more straightforwardly, people may simply care a lot about public standing, and they can see quite clearly that to be pushed around has indeed diminished that. Even in Hampton's cases, the fear she describes is much more plausible if the value people care about is status, which is easily damaged, than if it is human dignity, which is not.

Now the retaliatory tendency makes sense and is no longer merely magical. To someone who thinks this way, in terms of diminution and status-ranking, it is not only plausible to think that retaliation atones for or annuls the damage, it is often true. If Angela retaliates successfully (whether through law or in some other way, but always focusing on status-injury), the retaliation really does effect a reversal that annuls the injury, *seen as an injury of down-ranking*. Angela is victorious, and the previously powerful offender is suffering in prison. Insofar as the salient feature of O's act is its down-ranking of Angela, the turnabout effected by the retaliation really does put him down and her (relatively) up.

---

3. See the similar analysis in chapter 1 of Jeffrie Murphy, "Forgiveness and Resentment," in *Forgiveness and Mercy*, ed. Jeffrie Murphy and Jean Hampton (New York: Cambridge University Press, 1988), and in Murphy's other writings on this topic [Nussbaum's note].

4. American moral and political philosopher (1954–1996).

5. Jean Hampton, "Forgiveness, Resentment, and Hatred," in Murphy and Hampton, eds., *Forgiveness and Mercy*, pp. 54–59 [Nussbaum's note].

Notice that things make sense only if the focus is *purely* on relative status, rather than on some intrinsic attribute (health, safety, bodily integrity, friendship, love, wealth, good academic work) that has been jeopardized by the wrongful act. Retaliation does not confer or restore those things. It's only if Angela thinks purely in terms of relative status that she can plausibly hope to effect a reversal through a strike-back that inflicts pain of some type on the offender. Thus, for example, people in academic life who love to diss scholars who have criticized them and who believe that this does them some good, have to be focusing only on reputation and status, since it's obvious that injuring someone else's reputation does not make one's own *work* better than it was before, or correct whatever flaws the other person has found in it.

It's clear that Angela need not think that the injury she has suffered is a down-ranking. That is why Aristotle's definition is too narrow. Indeed, in this case it seems odd for her to think in those terms, given that O is a stranger who does not know her connection with Rebecca. But this way of seeing injury is very common, and it is very common even in cases where people are eager to deny that this is really what is going on.[6] That is why Aristotle's definition is helpful.

Suppose Angela does not think this way, but stops at Case 3. Then, insofar as her emotion is anger and not simply some combination of grief and compassion, she does initially wish some sort of bad result for the offender, and she does initially think (magically) that this will set things right, somehow counterbalancing or even annulling the offense. It is human to think this way. However, if she is really focusing on Rebecca and not on her own status-injury, she is likely to think this way only briefly. Magical fantasies of replacement can be very powerful, but in most sane people they prove short-lived. Instead, Angela is likely to take a mental turn toward a different set of future-directed attitudes. Insofar as she really wants to help Rebecca and women in Rebecca's position, she will focus on the responses characteristic of Cases 1 and 2: helping Rebecca get on with her life, but also setting up help groups, trying to publicize the problem of campus rape and to urge the authorities to deal with it better.

One of these future-directed projects may well involve the punishment of O. But notice that insofar as Angela is thinking rationally about what will make the world a better place for rape victims, she will view the punishment of O very differently from the way she viewed it in case 4. There she saw punishment as 'payback' or retribution—or, more specifically, as a down-ranking of O, which effected a reversal of positions between her and O: women (and Angela above all) on top, bad men (and O in particular) on the bottom. Now, however, she is likely to view the punishment of O in the light of the future good that could be achieved by punishment. This can take several forms: specific deterrence, general deterrence, and, possibly, the reform of O. But it might also take the form of creating a better society with better educational institutions and less poverty.[7]

---

6. See Averill (*Anger and Aggression*, p. 177), reporting a survey in which subjects were asked about their motives in becoming angry. The two most common were "To assert your authority" and "To get back at, or gain revenge on, the instigator"

[Nussbaum's note].

7. I discuss this issue in chapter 6 of my forthcoming book [*Anger and Forgiveness* (2016)], dealing with the criminal justice system and larger issues of social failure [Nussbaum's note].

In short, an Angela who is really angry, seeking to strike back, soon arrives, I claim, at a fork in the road. Three paths lie before her. Either she goes down the path of status-focus, seeing the event as all about her and her rank, or she focuses on payback and imagines that the offender's suffering would actually make things better, a thought that doesn't make sense. Or, if she is rational, after exploring and rejecting these two roads, she will notice that a third path is open to her, which is the best of all: she can focus on doing what would make sense in the situation and be really helpful. This may include the punishment of O, but in a spirit that is ameliorative rather than retaliatory.[8]

What is really wrong with the first path, the path of status? Many societies do encourage people to think of all injuries as essentially about them and their own ranking. Life involves perpetual status-anxiety, and more or less everything that happens to one either raises one's rank or lowers it. Aristotle's society, as he depicts it, was to a large extent like this, and he was very critical of this tendency on the grounds that obsessive focus on honor impedes the pursuit of intrinsic goods. The error involved in the first path is not silly or easily dismissed. Still, the tendency to see everything that happens as about oneself and one's own rank seems very narcissistic, and ill-suited to a society in which many aspects of human welfare have intrinsic value. This way of seeing things loses the sense that actions have intrinsic moral worth: that rape is bad because of the suffering it inflicts, and not because of the way it humiliates the friends of the victim. If rape were primarily a down-ranking, it could be rectified by the humiliation of the offender, and many people, certainly, believe something like this. But isn't this thought a red herring, diverting us from the reality of the victim's pain and trauma, which need to be constructively addressed? All sorts of bad acts—murder, assault, theft—need to be addressed as the specific acts they are, and their victims (or the victims' families) need constructive attention. None of this will be likely to happen if one thinks of the offense as all about relative status rather than injury and pain.

There is an instructive exception. Discrimination, for example, on grounds of race or gender, is often conceived as an injury that really does consist in down-ranking, and there is truth to this, just in this special sense: discrimination involves a denial of a special status of equal dignity, and this status has intrinsic value. But the idea that denials of equal dignity can be rectified by bringing the injurer low is a false lure. What is wanted is equal respect for human dignity. What is wrong with discrimination is its denial of equality. Reversing positions through payback does not create equality. It just substitutes one inequality for another. As we shall see shortly, Martin Luther King Jr.[9] wisely eschewed this way of framing the racial issue.

So the first path, the path of status, makes payback intelligible and useful, but it seems morally flawed. This path converts all injuries into problems of

---

8. When the Stoics said that animals are not rational, their opponents pointed to an ingenious dog allegedly belonging to Chrysippus, who came to a three-fork crossing, following a rabbit. He sniffed down the first path; no scent. He sniffed down the second; no scent. Without sniffing further, he galloped off down the third path—thus showing, they said, that he had mastered the disjunctive syllogism. Angela might be like that dog, but as I've imagined here she is not quite as smart, since she goes partway down the second path before turning back [Nussbaum's note]. "Disjunctive syllogism": an argument of the form "P or Q. Not P, therefore Q."

9. The preeminent African American religious and civil rights leader of his time (1929–1968).

relative rank, thus making the world revolve around the desire of vulnerable selves for domination and control. Because this wish is at the heart of infantile narcissism, I think of this as a *narcissistic error*, but we can also ignore that label and just call it the *status error*. If Angela takes the first path, then, payback makes sense, but she commits a (ubiquitous) moral error.

If Angela chooses the second path, by contrast, the *path of payback*, she remains focused on the intrinsic good of bodily integrity, but thinks the suffering of the offender somehow counterbalances or assuages the damage to that intrinsic good. In focusing on this good, she does not make a moral error, but in thinking that payback helps, she engages in magical thinking, which is normatively objectionable in a different way since we all want to make sense to ourselves and to be rational. If she cares about rationality, she will soon see little point in payback, and she will soon backtrack and shift, very likely, to a third path—a focus on promoting future welfare.

This third path, which I recommend, seems, and is, very Utilitarian, and this may be surprising. But sympathy with the Utilitarian idea of punishment arises as the more or less inexorable conclusion of some thoughts about why anger is problematic—irrational in some cases, morally objectionable (because hooked on one's own status) in others. I began working on anger with little sympathy with Utilitarian views of punishment, having criticized them in print numerous times. I find it hard to avoid the conclusion that Bentham[1] had a deep insight about the defects of his society, suffused as it was with status-consciousness and a virulent payback mentality.

I am hereby renouncing a range of things I said in earlier work about the constructive role of anger, and I am now saying something very radical: that in a sane and not excessively anxious and status-focused person, anger's idea of retribution or payback is a brief dream or cloud, soon dispelled by saner thoughts of personal and social welfare. So anger (if we understand it to involve, internally, a wish for retributive suffering) quickly puts itself out of business, in that even the residual focus on punishing the offender is soon seen as part of a set of projects for improving both offenders and society—and the emotion that has this goal is not so easy to see as anger. It looks more like compassionate hope. When anger does not put itself out of business in this way—and we all know that in a multitude of cases it does not—its persistence and power, I claim, owes much, even perhaps everything, to an underlying competitive obsession, which is the only thing that really makes sense of retribution as ordinarily conceived.

To put my radical claim succinctly: when anger makes sense, it is normatively problematic (focused on status); when it is normatively reasonable (focused on the injury), it doesn't make good sense, and is normatively problematic in that different way. In a rational person, anger, realizing that, soon laughs at itself and goes away. From now on, I shall call this healthy segue into forward-looking thoughts of welfare and, accordingly, from anger into compassionate hope, *the Transition*.

I have imagined the Transition in personal terms, and there is much more to say about these cases.[2] But to clarify further what I mean by the Transi-

---

1. English philosopher (1748–1832), the founder of utilitarianism.

2. See chapter 4 of my *Anger and Forgiveness* [Nussbaum's note].

tion, let us consider a case in which it takes a political form. For it has often been thought (including by me, in many earlier writings) that anger provides an essential motivation for work to correct social injustice. Let us look carefully at just one case, the sequence of emotions in Martin Luther King Jr.'s speech 'I Have a Dream'.[3] King begins, indeed, with an Aristotelian summons to anger: he points to the wrongful injuries of racism, which have failed to fulfill the nation's implicit promises of equality. One hundred years after the Emancipation Proclamation, 'the life of the Negro is still sadly crippled by the manacles of segregation and the chains of discrimination'.

The next move King makes is significant: for instead of demonizing white Americans, or portraying their behavior in terms apt to elicit murderous rage, he calmly compares them to people who have defaulted on a financial obligation: 'America has given the Negro people a bad check, a check which has come back marked "insufficient funds"'. This begins the Transition: for it makes us think ahead in non-retributive ways: the question is not how whites can be humiliated, but how can this debt be paid, and in the financial metaphor the thought of humiliating the debtor is not likely to be central. Indeed, humiliation looks counterproductive, for how will such a debtor be in a position to pay?

The Transition then gets underway in earnest, as King focuses on a future in which all may join together in pursuing justice and honoring obligations: 'But we refuse to believe that the bank of justice is bankrupt. We refuse to believe that there are insufficient funds in the great vaults of opportunity of this nation'. No mention, again, of torment or payback, only of determination to ensure payment of what is owed, at last. King reminds his audience that the moment is urgent, and that there is a danger of rage spilling over, but he repudiates that behavior in advance. 'In the process of gaining our rightful place, we must not be guilty of wrongful deeds. Let us not seek to satisfy our thirst for freedom by drinking from the cup of bitterness and hatred. . . . Again and again, we must rise to the majestic heights of meeting physical force with soul force'.

Here, the payback is reconceived as the paying of a debt, a process that unites black and white in a quest for freedom and justice. Everyone benefits: as many white people already recognize, 'their freedom is inextricably bound to our freedom'.

King next repudiates a despair that could lead either to violence or to the abandonment of effort. It is at this point that the most famous section of the speech, 'I have a dream', takes flight. And of course, this dream is one not of torment or retributive punishment but of equality, liberty, and brotherhood. In pointed terms, King invites the African-American members of his audience to imagine brotherhood even with their former tormentors:

> I have a dream that one day on the red hills of Georgia, the sons of former slaves and the sons of former slave owners will be able to sit down together at the table of brotherhood.

3. See my longer analysis in Martha Nussbaum, *Political Emotions: Why Love Matters for Justice* (Cambridge, Mass.: Harvard University Press, 2013), chapter 8 [Nussbaum's note]. King delivered his "I Have a Dream" speech in Washington, D.C., on August 28, 1963.

I have a dream that one day even the state of Mississippi, a state sweltering with the heat of injustice, sweltering with the heat of oppression, will
be transformed into an oasis of freedom and justice. . . .

I have a dream that one day, down in Alabama, with its vicious racists,
with its governor having his lips dripping with the words "interposition"
and "nullification"—one day right there in Alabama little black boys and
black girls will be able to join hands with little white boys and white
girls as sisters and brothers.

There is indeed anger in this speech, and the anger summons up a vision
of rectification, which naturally takes a retributive form initially. But King
gets busy right away reshaping retributivism into work and hope. For how,
sanely and really, could injustice be made good by retributive payback? Only
an intelligent and imaginative effort toward justice can do that. This is what
I mean by the 'Transition'.

We notice something else: once the Transition gets underway, there is no
room for forgiveness as classically conceived in transactional terms, namely,
as a waiving of resentment because of an expression of contrition.[4] The payback mentality wants groveling. The Transition mentality wants justice and
brotherhood. If what we want is a racially just society, it would do no more
good for Governor Wallace[5] to moan and grovel than for him to burn in hell:
these things do not produce justice, and they are restorative only in the magical
thinking characteristic of anger's initial pre-Transition phase. In the Transition, one comes to see that the real issue is how to produce justice. Rituals of
forgiveness might possibly be thought useful to this end. But King has no room
for them: he wants reconciliation and shared effort.

It is here that I introduce a major exception to my thesis that anger always
involves, conceptually, a thought of payback. There are many cases in which
one gets standardly angry first, thinking about some type of payback, and then,
in a cooler moment, heads for the Transition. But there are at least a few cases
in which one is there already: the *entire* content of one's emotion is, 'How
outrageous! Something must be done about this.' I shall call this emotion
Transition-Anger, since it is anger, or quasi-anger, already heading down the
third fork in Angela's road. One might give it some ordinary-language name,
such as Hampton's 'indignation',[6] but I prefer to segment it cleanly from other
cases, since I think a lot of cases of 'indignation' involve some thought of payback. So I prefer the clearly made-up term. Transition-Anger does not focus
on status; nor does it want, even briefly, the suffering of the offender as a type
of payback for the injury. It never gets involved in that type of magical thinking. It focuses on future welfare from the start. Saying 'Something should be
done about this', Transition-Anger commits itself to a search for strategies,
but it remains an open question whether the suffering of the offender will be
a strong candidate.

---

4. This conception of forgiveness is discussed in
chapter 3 of *Anger and Forgiveness* and contrasted
both with unconditional forgiveness and unconditional generosity [Nussbaum's note].
5. George C. Wallace (1919–1998), who as governor of Alabama in the 1960s led the fight against
court-ordered integration in the South. In the
1980s, he renounced his segregationist views.
6. See Hampton, "Forgiveness, Resentment, and
Hatred," p. 56.

Is Transition-Anger a species of anger? I really don't care how we answer this question. Such special borderline cases are rarely handled well by conceptual analysis. It's certainly an emotion: the person is really upset. And it appears distinct, though subtly, from compassionate hope, since the focus is on outrage and the target is the offender. The person says, 'How outrageous', not 'How sad', and entertains forward-looking projects focused on diminishing or preventing wrongful acts. What is important is how rare and exceptional this pure forward-looking emotion is. Angry people very rarely think in this way from the start. It is much more common to get angry first and then head to the Transition, than to be there already, focused on social welfare, because the retaliatory instinct is, as Butler observed, deeply human, no doubt through both evolutionary tendency and cultural reinforcement. It is only exceptional individuals who are there already, in major issues affecting their welfare. Such presence of mind typically requires long self-discipline. Thus, one could imagine that King's own emotion was Transition-Anger, while the emotion constructed in his speech, for his audience, is brief (standard) anger and then a turn to the Transition.

How might someone become less prone to the errors of anger, and more likely to make the Transition? Aristotle offers a suggestive insight. He says that the person who manages anger well is likely to be good at sympathetic understanding of the positions and motives of other people. How does this work? The idea is, I think, that seeing the situation from the other person's viewpoint helps steer one toward a balanced focus on harm and correction of harm, rather than toward the often unbalanced wishes and motives of anger. To put things in my terms: if you see the other person's point of view, by that very act you are no longer exclusively focused on your own status, and therefore you are less prone to make the status error. You are also less prone to make the payback error, for you will see the future as one involving other people, and your tendency to think of welfare in general social terms will be assisted.

What good can be said of (garden-variety) anger, in the end? First, it may serve as a *signal* that something is amiss. Anger embodies the idea of significant wrongdoing targeting a person or thing that is of deep concern to the self. While one could have that idea of significant injury without anger—with, and through, grief and compassion—those two emotions do not contain the idea of wrongfulness, which is anger's specific focus. It is for that reason that Bishop Butler, for all his animadversions against the passion, nonetheless concedes that it is 'one of the common bonds, by which society is held together; a fellow feeling which each individual has in behalf of the whole species, as well as of himself' (Sermon VIII). Nor, importantly, do those two emotions contain the thought that something needs to be done, which, as I've argued, is a conceptual part of anger. The signal anger sends is pretty misleading, since it embodies an idea of payback that is primitive. So it is a false lead to that extent, and the angry person is always well advised to begin moving beyond anger as soon as possible, in the direction of the Transition. Still, anger can be a useful wake-up call. We see this in King's speech, where he does express anger at the behavior of white America, and urges his audience to feel anger as well, acknowledging the magnitude of the wrongs done and the way in which they affect everyone's well-being. But then he immediately turns the audience away from the payback thought that inevitably surfaces, toward a different picture of the future. Managed by such a skillful entrepreneur, anger can be useful, and King always conceived of his project as active and militant, pitted against complacency. Perhaps it's even more useful in cases where the wrongdoing might have slid along barely noticed, beneath the surface of daily life, and only the emotion directs people's attention to its presence.

Anger can also be a source of *motivation*. The Greek Stoics were often charged with robbing society of motives to pursue justice by their insistence that anger is always mistaken. This charge is even more pertinent to my own view, since, according to my non-Stoic view of damage and loss, anger is often appropriate in its underlying values: the loss or damage can be major, and something really ought to be done about it. The problem comes with the idea of payback. The payback idea is, I argued, a conceptual part of anger (except in the borderline case of Transition-Anger), and no doubt it is part of what motivates people, at least initially. The intensity of the emotion, and perhaps, too, its magical fantasy of retribution are part of what get people going when otherwise at least some people might simply fail to act (or, without anger's signal, even fail to notice the wrongdoing). So in fact Dr. King acknowledged in other writings.

But once people get going, they had better not follow anger's lure all the way to fantasized retribution. King's audience might have imagined a future of payback, in which African-Americans would attain power and inflict retributive pain and humbling on white Americans. Society abounded with such ideas. King's altogether superior stance was that the Transition is only a heartbeat away, since only cooperation will really solve the nation's problems. Still, anger was a useful motivational step along the road—for a very brief time, and carefully managed.

Anger has a very limited but real utility, which derives, very likely, from its evolutionary role as a 'fight-or-flight' mechanism. We may retain this limited role for anger while insisting that its payback fantasy is profoundly misleading and that to the extent that it makes sense, it does so against the background of diseased values. The emotion, in consequence, is highly likely to lead us astray.

Finally, anger may be a deterrent. People who are known to get angry often thereby deter others from infringing their rights. Here one can only say that the way anger deters is not likely to lead to a future of stability or peace; instead, it is all too likely to lead to more aggression. And there are many ways of deterring wrongdoing, some of which are much more attractive than inspiring fear of an explosion.

The tendency to anger is deeply rooted in human psychology. Believers in a providential deity, like Butler, find this fact difficult to explain, given its irrationality and destructiveness.[7] For those who do not share Butler's framework, however, it is much less difficult to understand. Anger brings some benefits that may have been valuable at one stage in human prehistory. Even

---

7. See Butler, Sermon VIII: "Since perfect goodness in the Deity is the principle from whence the universe was brought into being, and by which it is preserved; and since general benevolence is the great law of the whole moral creation; it is a question which immediately occurs, 'Why had man implanted in him a principle, which appears the direct contrary to benevolence?'" [Nussbaum's note].

today, vestiges of its useful role remain. As Aeschylus[8] notes, however, forward-looking systems of justice have to a great extent made this emotion unnecessary, whether in personal or in public life. Like Athena's citizens,[9] we are now free to attend to its irrationality and destructiveness, and we should do so, focusing first on intimate personal relations, and then on the political realm.

References

Averill, James. (1982) *Anger and Aggression.* New York: Springer.

Brooks, Thom. (2012) *Punishment.* New York: Routledge.

Chrysippus. *Stoicorum Veterum Fragmenta,* III.478.

Lazarus, Richard. (1991) *Emotion and Adaptation.* New York: Oxford University Press.

Murphy, Jeffrie. (1988) 'Forgiveness and Resentment'. In Jeffrie Murphy and Jean Hampton, *Forgiveness and Mercy* (New York: Cambridge University Press), ch. 1.

Murphy, Jeffrie, and Jean Hampton. (1988) *Forgiveness and Mercy.* New York: Cambridge University Press.

Nussbaum, Martha. (2013) *Political Emotions: Why Love Matters for Justice.* Cambridge, MA: Harvard University Press.

Strawson, Peter F. ([1962] 1968) 'Freedom and Resentment'. Repr. in *Studies in the Philosophy of Thought and Action* (Oxford: Oxford University Press), 71–96.

Tavris, Carol. (1982) *Anger: The Misunderstood Emotion.* New York: Simon & Schuster.

Wallace, R. Jay. (1994) *Responsibility and the Moral Sentiments.* Cambridge, MA: Harvard University Press.

SOURCE: Martha C. Nussbaum, "Transitional Anger," *Journal of the American Philosophical Association* 1 (2015): 41–56. Based on Lecture 2 of Nussbaum's John Locke Lectures in Philosophy at Oxford University, May–June 2014, which, in turn, is a much shorter version of the second chapter of *Anger and Forgiveness: Resentment, Generosity, Justice* (New York: Oxford University Press, 2016). Except as indicated, notes are the editor's.

8. Greek tragedian (ca. 525–456 B.C.E.). Nussbaum begins *Anger and Forgiveness* with a discussion of the transformation of the Furies (Greek spirits of vengeance) into the Eumenides (literally, the Kindly Ones) at the end of his *Oresteia,* as blood vengeance is replaced by legal institutions.

9. That is, the citizens of the ancient Greek city-state of Athens, whose patron was Athena, goddess of both war and wisdom. In Aeschylus's play, she is responsible for instituting the rule of law as well as for giving the Eumenides a place of honor in the city.

HANNAH ARENDT
(1906 – 1975)

Arendt is widely and deservedly known and esteemed as one of the most prominent public intellectuals of the mid-twentieth century, owing particularly to her attempts to understand the appeal of totalitarianism and the phenomenon of Nazism. One of her best-known works, *Eichmann in Jerusalem: A Report on the Banality of Evil* (1963), focuses on the case of a leading architect of the Holocaust. But she was a political thinker of much broader scope and depth, and also (though she long shied away from the label) a philosopher of the human condition, from the beginning of her career to its end. She initially was strongly attracted to the existential philosophy of MARTIN HEIDEGGER and KARL JASPERS; but she moved beyond it to a distinctive kind of philosophical thinking that centers on a broad and rich conception of political life, thereby throwing a different light on human reality.

Hannah Arendt ("ARE-ent") was born in Hanover, in northern Germany, to secular Jewish parents. She began her university education at the University of Berlin in 1922 at the age of just 16, focusing on classical studies. But she soon discovered philosophy and transferred to Marburg University in 1924, where she encountered and studied with Heidegger, several years before he published *Being and Time* (1927) and rose to prominence. Though still in her teens, she and the married Heidegger became romantically involved. In 1925 she ended the affair and went to Heidelberg University, where Jaspers, another rising existential philosopher, became her teacher and mentor. It was under Jaspers's direction that she wrote her doctoral dissertation, on Augustine's concept of love. Her estrangement from Heidegger deepened as he associated himself with the Nazis in the early 1930s, but his philosophical influence on her remained profound. Long after the war she reestablished an intellectual and personal relationship with him that attested to the strength of their earlier bond. Her relationship with Jaspers, though less intense, was close and constant to the end.

Arendt's dissertation was published in 1929; but because of her Jewish parentage and her political activism she had to flee when the Nazis came to power in 1933. She settled first in France, but in 1941 she again fled the Nazis, this time (with her husband, Heinrich Blücher) to the United States, where she remained for the rest of her life. She made English her new language and found work as an editor at Schocken Books, a New York publishing house. After the war she focused her attention for a time on trying to understand what had happened in her native Germany, writing *The Origins of Totalitarianism* (1951). It established her reputation as a political theorist and opened the way to an academic career.

Arendt held appointments at a number of American universities, including Princeton, Berkeley, the University of Chicago, and finally the New School for Social Research in New York, where she was a professor of political philosophy from 1967 until her death. In 1961 the *New Yorker* magazine sent her to Jerusalem to report on the trial of Adolf Eichmann, who had been captured in Argentina by Israeli agents and was being tried for his role in the Holocaust. The resulting book, published two years later, made her something of an intellectual celebrity. She died in New York in 1975, after having completed the first two of the projected three volumes—on "thinking," "willing," and "judging"—of what was to be her philosophical masterwork, *The Life of the Mind*.

That the three topics of this work correspond to the topics of IMMANUEL KANT's three critiques was no coincidence. Arendt was attempting to provide a new treatment of these three fundamental dimensions of human experience and activity from the different perspective of her own philosophical orientation toward and understanding of human reality. She had previously expressed that understanding most extensively in *The Human Condition* (1958), from which the following selections are taken. It reflects phenomenological attentiveness to the character of lived human experience in the spirit of Heidegger and Jaspers; but by assigning a special significance to what she conceives as the "political" dimension of human existence, it also significantly broadens the first-person singular (and, in Jaspers's case, second-person singular) perspective associated with their versions of existential philosophy. There is nothing comparable to it in Heidegger and Jaspers, who had conceived of attainable human authenticity in a way that emphasized individuation, in contrast to (and in tension with) impersonally social forms of human life (though both allow for the human possibility of authentic relatedness with others). *The Human Condition* combines Arendt's emphasis on the con-

cept of *action* as central to the understanding of human reality—reflected in her characterization of that reality in terms of the idea of *vita activa* ("active life" or "life as activity")—with her insistence on the fundamentally *social* character of that reality.

Arendt's reluctance to present herself as a philosopher and to write in a recognizably philosophical manner makes it difficult to assess her thought and work in relation to the philosophical debates that were occurring in her own time and that continue today in Europe and in the English-speaking world. Yet she has been an inspiration to many readers both within and beyond the philosophical community, because the topics on which she wrote and the manner in which she dealt with them have many dimensions, and because what she had to say about them was so insightful and provocative on so many levels. There are clearly aspects of her thought that deserve to be taken seriously by philosophers and nonphilosophers alike, as the following reflections illustrate, from *The Human Condition*, in which she sets forth and develops her conception of human reality as *vita activa*.

From The Human Condition

From *Chapter 1. The Human Condition*

1. *VITA ACTIVA*[1] AND THE HUMAN CONDITION

With the term *vita activa*, I propose to designate three fundamental human activities: labor, work, and action. They are fundamental because each corresponds to one of the basic conditions under which life on earth has been given to man.[2]

Labor is the activity which corresponds to the biological process of the human body, whose spontaneous growth, metabolism, and eventual decay are bound to the vital necessities produced and fed into the life process by labor. The human condition of labor is life itself.

Work is the activity which corresponds to the unnaturalness of human existence, which is not imbedded in, and whose mortality is not compensated by,

---

1. Active life (Latin); beginning with the Greeks and continuing into medieval times, philosophers were expected instead to value most highly and attempt to live the *vita contemplativa* (contemplative life).

2. When she uses "man," Arendt has in mind the German word *Mensch*—a generic that has the sense "human being" or "humankind" and "human," not "male."

the species' ever-recurring life cycle. Work provides an "artificial" world of things, distinctly different from all natural surroundings. Within its borders each individual life is housed, while this world itself is meant to outlast and transcend them all. The human condition of work is worldliness.

Action, the only activity that goes on directly between men without the intermediary of things or matter, corresponds to the human condition of plurality, to the fact that men, not Man, live on the earth and inhabit the world. While all aspects of the human condition are somehow related to politics,[3] this plurality is specifically *the* condition—not only the *conditio sine qua non*, but the *conditio per quam*[4]—of all political life. Thus the language of the Romans, perhaps the most political people we have known, used the words "to live" and "to be among men" (*inter homines esse*) or "to die" and "to cease to be among men" (*inter homines esse desinere*) as synonyms. But in its most elementary form, the human condition of action is implicit even in Genesis ("Male and female created He *them*"[5]), if we understand that this story of man's creation is distinguished in principle from the one according to which God originally created Man (*adam*[6]), "him" and not "them," so that the multitude of human beings becomes the result of multiplication. Action would be an unnecessary luxury, a capricious interference with general laws of behavior, if men were endlessly reproducible repetitions of the same model, whose nature or essence was the same for all and as predictable as the nature or essence of any other thing. Plurality is the condition of human action because we are all the same, that is, human, in such a way that nobody is ever the same as anyone else who ever lived, lives, or will live.

All three activities and their corresponding conditions are intimately connected with the most general condition of human existence: birth and death, natality and mortality.[7] Labor assures not only individual survival, but the life of the species. Work and its product, the human artifact, bestow a measure of permanence and durability upon the futility of mortal life and the fleeting character of human time. Action, in so far as it engages in founding and preserving political bodies, creates the condition for remembrance, that is, for history. Labor and work, as well as action, are also rooted in natality in so far as they have the task to provide and preserve the world for, to foresee and reckon with, the constant influx of newcomers who are born into the world as strangers. However, of the three, action has the closest connection with the human condition of natality; the new beginning inherent in birth can make itself felt in the world only because the newcomer possesses the capacity of beginning something anew, that is, of acting. In this sense of initiative, an element of action, and therefore of natality, is inherent in all human activities. Moreover, since action is the political activity par excellence, natality, and not mortality, may be the central category of political, as distinguished from metaphysical, thought.

---

3. In the classical sense, living in a community (the Greek *polis*, or city).
4. Condition through which (Latin); that is, the enabling condition. *Conditio sine qua non*: condition without which not (Latin); that is, the necessary condition.
5. Genesis 1:27 (KJV).

6. That is, "human being" or "mankind" (Hebrew).
7. That is, "being from birth" and "being toward death." Arendt here echoes her mentor MARTIN HEIDEGGER's similar characterization of *Dasein*—human reality—in *Being and Time* (1927), excerpted above.

The human condition comprehends more than the conditions under which life has been given to man. Men are conditioned beings because everything they come in contact with turns immediately into a condition of their existence. The world in which the *vita activa* spends itself consists of things produced by human activities; but the things that owe their existence exclusively to men nevertheless constantly condition their human makers. In addition to the conditions under which life is given to man on earth, and partly out of them, men constantly create their own, self-made conditions, which, their human origin and their variability notwithstanding, possess the same conditioning power as natural things. Whatever touches or enters into a sustained relationship with human life immediately assumes the character of a condition of human existence. This is why men, no matter what they do, are always conditioned beings. Whatever enters the human world of its own accord or is drawn into it by human effort becomes part of the human condition. The impact of the world's reality upon human existence is felt and received as a conditioning force. The objectivity of the world—its object- or thing-character—and the human condition supplement each other; because human existence is conditioned existence, it would be impossible without things, and things would be a heap of unrelated articles, a non-world, if they were not the conditioners of human existence.

To avoid misunderstanding: the human condition is not the same as human nature, and the sum total of human activities and capabilities which correspond to the human condition does not constitute anything like human nature. For neither those we discuss here nor those we leave out, like thought and reason, and not even the most meticulous enumeration of them all, constitute essential characteristics of human existence in the sense that without them this existence would no longer be human.[8] The most radical change in the human condition we can imagine would be an emigration of men from the earth to some other planet. Such an event, no longer totally impossible, would imply that man would have to live under man-made conditions, radically different from those the earth offers him. Neither labor nor work nor action nor, indeed, thought as we know it would then make sense any longer. Yet even these hypothetical wanderers from the earth would still be human; but the only statement we could make regarding their "nature" is that they still are conditioned beings, even though their condition is now self-made to a considerable extent.

The problem of human nature, the Augustinian[9] *quaestio mihi factus sum* ("a question have I become for myself"), seems unanswerable in both its individual psychological sense and its general philosophical sense. It is highly unlikely that we, who can know, determine, and define the natural essences of all things surrounding us, which we are not, should ever be able to do the same for ourselves—this would be like jumping over our own shadows. Moreover, nothing entitles us to assume that man has a nature or essence in the same sense as other things. In other words, if we have a nature or essence, then

---

8. That is, what Arendt means by "the human condition": the general contours of our human reality in all of the contingency of its origins, circumstances, and sociohistorical character, rather than any conception of "human nature" such as those

mentioned.
9. St. Augustine (354–430), bishop and highly influential Christian philosopher who lived in the late Roman Empire; Arendt provides the citation for the quotation in her note that follows.

surely only a god could know and define it, and the first prerequisite would be that he be able to speak about a "who" as though it were a "what."[1] The perplexity is that the modes of human cognition applicable to things with "natural" qualities, including ourselves to the limited extent that we are specimens of the most highly developed species of organic life, fail us when we raise the question: And *who* are we? This is why attempts to define human nature almost invariably end with some construction of a deity, that is, with the god of the philosophers, who, since Plato,[2] has revealed himself upon closer inspection to be a kind of Platonic idea of man. Of course, to demask such philosophic concepts of the divine as conceptualizations of human capabilities and qualities is not a demonstration of, not even an argument for, the non-existence of God; but the fact that attempts to define the nature of man lead so easily into an idea which definitely strikes us as "superhuman" and therefore is identified with the divine may cast suspicion upon the very concept of "human nature."

On the other hand, the conditions of human existence—life itself, natality and mortality, worldliness, plurality, and the earth—can never "explain" what we are or answer the question of who we are for the simple reason that they never condition us absolutely. This has always been the opinion of philosophy, in distinction from the sciences—anthropology, psychology, biology, etc.—which also concern themselves with man. But today we may almost say that we have demonstrated even scientifically that, though we live now, and probably always will, under the earth's conditions, we are not mere earth-bound creatures. Modern natural science owes its great triumphs to having looked upon and treated earth-bound nature from a truly universal viewpoint, that is, from an Archimedean standpoint[3] taken, wilfully and explicitly, outside the earth.

2. The Term *Vita Activa*

The term *vita activa* is loaded and overloaded with tradition. It is as old as (but not older than) our tradition of political thought. And this tradition, far

---

1. Augustine, who is usually credited with having been the first to raise the so-called anthropological question in philosophy, knew this quite well. He distinguishes between the questions of "Who am I?" and "What am I?"—the first being directed at man himself ("And I directed myself at myself and said to me: You, who are you? And I answered: A man"—*tu, quis es?* [*Confessiones* x. 6]) and the second being addressed to God ("What then am I, my God? What is my nature?"—*Quid ergo sum, Deus meus? Quae natura sum?* [x.17]). For in the "great mystery," the *grande profundum*, which man is (iv.14), there is "something of man [*aliquid hominis*] which the spirit of man which is in him itself knoweth not. But Thou, Lord, who has made him [*fecisti eum*] knowest everything of him [*eius omnia*]" (x.5). Thus, the most familiar of these phrases which I quoted in the text, the *quaestio mihi factus sum*, is a question raised in the presence of God, "in whose eyes I have become a question for myself" (x.33). In brief, the answer to the question "Who am I?" is simply: "You are a man—whatever that may be"; and the answer to the question "What am I?" can be given only by God who made man. The question about the nature of man is no less a theological question than the question about the nature of God; both can be settled only within the framework of a divinely revealed answer [Arendt's note, and her brackets].

This claim assumes that "human nature" is a concept very much like "human purpose," which makes sense only on the supposition that "man" is the work of a divine creator by whom it could be established; and that supposition is by no means beyond dispute.
2. Greek philosopher (ca. 427–ca. 347 B.C.E.); his Forms (referred to by Arendt here as "Platonic ideas") are fundamental, timeless universals, in whose reality objects in the natural world (their less than perfect copies) participate or share.
3. A leverage (and so also vantage) point in relation to the earth that is beyond it; the metaphor is derived from a famous remark attributed to the Greek mathematician and inventor Archimedes (ca. 287–212 B.C.E.), who said of the lever, "Give me a place to stand and I will move the earth."

from comprehending and conceptualizing all the political experiences of Western mankind, grew out of a specific historical constellation: the trial of Socrates and the conflict between the philosopher and the *polis*.[4] It eliminated many experiences of an earlier past that were irrelevant to its immediate political purposes and proceeded until its end, in the work of Karl Marx,[5] in a highly selective manner. The term itself, in medieval philosophy the standard translation of the Aristotelian *bios politikos*,[6] already occurs in Augustine, where, as *vita negotiosa* or *actuosa*,[7] it still reflects its original meaning: a life devoted to public-political matters.[8]

Aristotle distinguished three ways of life (*bioi*) which men might choose in freedom,[9] that is, in full independence of the necessities of life and the relationships they originated. This prerequisite of freedom ruled out all ways of life chiefly devoted to keeping one's self alive—not only labor, which was the way of life of the slave, who was coerced by the necessity to stay alive and by the rule of his master, but also the working life of the free craftsman and the acquisitive life of the merchant. In short, it excluded everybody who involuntarily or voluntarily, for his whole life or temporarily, had lost the free disposition of his movements and activities. The remaining three ways of life have in common that they were concerned with the "beautiful," that is, with things neither necessary nor merely useful: the life of enjoying bodily pleasures in which the beautiful, as it is given, is consumed; the life devoted to the matters of the *polis*, in which excellence produces beautiful deeds; and the life of the philosopher devoted to inquiry into, and contemplation of, things eternal, whose everlasting beauty can neither be brought about through the producing interference of man nor be changed through his consumption of them.

The chief difference between the Aristotelian and the later medieval use of the term is that the *bios politikos* denoted explicitly only the realm of human affairs, stressing the action, *praxis*, needed to establish and sustain it. Neither labor nor work was considered to possess sufficient dignity to constitute a *bios* at all, an autonomous and authentically human way of life; since they served and produced what was necessary and useful, they could not be free, independent of human needs and wants. That the political way of life escaped this verdict is due to the Greek understanding of *polis* life, which to them denoted a very special and freely chosen form of political organization and by no means just any form of action necessary to keep men together in an orderly fashion. Not that the Greeks or Aristotle were ignorant of the fact that human life always demands some form of political organization and that ruling over subjects might constitute a distinct way of life; but the despot's way of life, because it was "merely" a necessity, could not be considered free and had no relationship with the *bios politikos*.

With the disappearance of the ancient city-state—Augustine seems to have been the last to know at least what it once meant to be a citizen—the term

4. It was the city-state of Athens that condemned the Greek philosopher Socrates (469–399 B.C.E.) to death for impiety and corrupting the youth with his teachings; later polities became much larger.
5. For MARX, see above.
6. Political life (Greek), or engagement in the *polis*, which the philosopher Aristotle (384–322 B.C.E.) conceived on the model of the modestly sized Greek city-state and praised as the optimal sort of sociopolitical entity in his *Politics* and *Nicomachean Ethics*.
7. Life full of business (literally, "non-idleness" or "busyness") or activity (Latin).
8. See Augustine *De civitate Dei* [*The City of God*] xix.2, 19 [Arendt's note].
9. See *Nicomachean Ethics* 1.5.

vita activa lost its specifically political meaning and denoted all kinds of active engagement in the things of this world. To be sure, it does not follow that work and labor had risen in the hierarchy of human activities and were now equal in dignity with a life devoted to politics. It was, rather, the other way round: action was now also reckoned among the necessities of earthly life, so that contemplation (the *bios theōrētikos*, translated into the *vita contemplativa*) was left as the only truly free way of life.[1]

However, the enormous superiority of contemplation over activity of any kind, action not excluded, is not Christian in origin. We find it in Plato's political philosophy, where the whole utopian reorganization of *polis* life is not only directed by the superior insight of the philosopher but has no aim other than to make possible the philosopher's way of life. Aristotle's very articulation of the different ways of life, in whose order the life of pleasure plays a minor role, is clearly guided by the ideal of contemplation (*theōria*). To the ancient freedom from the necessities of life and from compulsion by others, the philosophers added freedom and surcease from political activity (*skholē*),[2] so that the later Christian claim to be free from entanglement in worldly affairs, from all the business of this world, was preceded by and originated in the philosophic *apolitia* of late antiquity. What had been demanded only by the few was now considered to be a right of all.

The term *vita activa*, comprehending all human activities and defined from the viewpoint of the absolute quiet of contemplation, therefore corresponds more closely to the Greek *askholia* ("unquiet"), with which Aristotle designated all activity, than to the Greek *bios politikos*. As early as Aristotle the distinction between quiet and unquiet, between an almost breathless abstention from external physical movement and activity of every kind, is more decisive than the distinction between the political and the theoretical way of life, because it can eventually be found within each of the three ways of life. It is like the distinction between war and peace: just as war takes place for the sake of peace, thus every kind of activity, even the processes of mere thought, must culminate in the absolute quiet of contemplation. Every movement, the movements of body and soul as well as of speech and reasoning, must cease before truth. Truth, be it the ancient truth of Being or the Christian truth of the living God, can reveal itself only in complete human stillness.

Traditionally and up to the beginning of the modern age, the term *vita activa* never lost its negative connotation of "un-quiet," *nec-otium, a-skholia*. As such it remained intimately related to the even more fundamental Greek distinction between things that are by themselves whatever they are and things which owe their existence to man, between things that are *physei* and things that are *nomō*.[3] The primacy of contemplation over activity rests on the conviction that no work of human hands can equal in beauty and truth the physical *kosmos*, which swings in itself in changeless eternity without any interference or assistance from outside, from man or god. This eternity discloses itself to mortal eyes only when all human movements and activities are at perfect rest.

---

1. See Aquinas *Summa theologica* ii.2.179, especially article 2 [Arendt's note]. Saint Thomas Aquinas (1224/25–1274), Italian theologian and the most important of the medieval Scholastic philosophers.

2. The Greek word *skholē*, like the Latin *otium*, means primarily freedom from political activity and not simply leisure time, although both words are also used to indicate freedom from labor and life's necessities. In any event, they always indicate a condition free from worries and cares [Arendt's note].

3. "By nature" and "by custom" (Greek).

Compared with this attitude of quiet, all distinctions and articulations within the *vita activa* disappear. Seen from the viewpoint of contemplation, it does not matter what disturbs the necessary quiet, as long as it is disturbed.

Traditionally, therefore, the term *vita activa* receives its meaning from the *vita contemplativa*; its very restricted dignity is bestowed upon it because it serves the needs and wants of contemplation in a living body.[4] Christianity, with its belief in a hereafter whose joys announce themselves in the delights of contemplation, conferred a religious sanction upon the abasement of the *vita activa* to its derivative, secondary position; but the determination of the order itself coincided with the very discovery of contemplation (*theōria*) as a human faculty, distinctly different from thought and reasoning, which occurred in the Socratic school and from then on has ruled metaphysical and political thought throughout our tradition.[5] It seems unnecessary to my present purpose to discuss the reasons for this tradition. Obviously they are deeper than the historical occasion which gave rise to the conflict between the *polis* and the philosopher and thereby, almost incidentally, also led to the discovery of contemplation as the philosopher's way of life. They must lie in an altogether different aspect of the human condition, whose diversity is not exhausted in the various articulations of the *vita activa* and, we may suspect, would not be exhausted even if thought and the movement of reasoning were included in it.

If, therefore, the use of the term *vita activa*, as I propose it here, is in manifest contradiction to the tradition, it is because I doubt not the validity of the experience underlying the distinction but rather the hierarchical order inherent in it from its inception. This does not mean that I wish to contest or even to discuss, for that matter, the traditional concept of truth as revelation and therefore something essentially given to man, or that I prefer the modern age's pragmatic assertion that man can know only what he makes himself. My contention is simply that the enormous weight of contemplation in the traditional hierarchy has blurred the distinctions and articulations within the *vita activa* itself and that, appearances notwithstanding, this condition has not been changed essentially by the modern break with the tradition and the eventual reversal of its hierarchical order in Marx and Nietzsche.[6] It lies in the very nature of the famous "turning upside down" of philosophic systems or currently accepted values, that is, in the nature of the operation itself, that the conceptual framework is left more or less intact.

The modern reversal shares with the traditional hierarchy the assumption that the same central human preoccupation must prevail in all activities of men, since without one comprehensive principle no order could be established. This assumption is not a matter of course, and my use of the term *vita activa*

---

4. Aquinas is quite explicit on the connection between the *vita activa* and the wants and needs of the human body which men and animals have in common (*Summa theologica* ii.2.182.1) [Arendt's note].

5. The time-honored resentment of the philosopher against the human condition of having a body is not identical with the ancient contempt for the necessities of life; to be subject to necessity was only one aspect of bodily existence, and the body, once freed of this necessity, was capable of that pure appearance the Greeks called beauty. The philosophers since Plato added to the resentment of being forced by bodily wants the resentment of movement of any kind. It is because the philosopher lives in complete quiet that it is only his body which, according to Plato, inhabits the city. Here lies also the origin of the early reproach of busybodiness (*polypragmosynē*) leveled against those who spent their lives in politics [Arendt's note].

6. Marx and NIETZSCHE, according to Arendt, valued the *vita activa* above the *vita contemplativa*.

presupposes that the concern underlying all its activities is not the same as and is neither superior nor inferior to the central concern of the *vita contemplativa*.

* * *

From *Chapter VI. The* Vita Activa *and the Modern Age*

* * *

43. The Defeat of *Homo Faber*[7] and the Principle of Happiness

If one considers only the events that led into the modern age and reflects solely upon the immediate consequences of Galileo's discovery,[8] which must have struck the great minds of the seventeenth century with the compelling force of self-evident truth, the reversal of contemplation and fabrication, or rather the elimination of contemplation from the range of meaningful human capacities, is almost a matter of course. It seems equally plausible that this reversal should have elevated *homo faber*, the maker and fabricator, rather than man the actor or man as *animal laborans*,[9] to the highest range of human possibilities.

And, indeed, among the outstanding characteristics of the modern age from its beginning to our own time we find the typical attitudes of *homo faber*: his instrumentalization of the world, his confidence in tools and in the productivity of the maker of artificial objects; his trust in the all-comprehensive range of the means-end category, his conviction that every issue can be solved and every human motivation reduced to the principle of utility; his sovereignty, which regards everything given as material and thinks of the whole of nature as of "an immense fabric from which we can cut out whatever we want to resew it however we like";[1] his equation of intelligence with ingenuity, that is, his contempt for all thought which cannot be considered to be "the first step . . . for the fabrication of artificial objects, particularly of tools to make tools, and to vary their fabrication indefinitely";[2] finally, his matter-of-course identification of fabrication with action.

It would lead us too far afield to follow the ramifications of this mentality, and it is not necessary, for they are easily detected in the natural sciences, where the purely theoretical effort is understood to spring from the desire to create order out of "mere disorder," the "wild variety of nature,"[3] and where therefore *homo faber*'s predilection for patterns for things to be produced replaces the older notions of harmony and simplicity. It can be found in

---

7. Man the maker (Latin)—that is, the maker and user of tools.
8. That is, the telescope, which the astronomer Galileo (1564–1642) improved and used to demonstrate that the earth revolves around the sun.
9. Laboring animal (Latin).
1. Henri Bergson, *Évolution creatrice* [*Creative Evolution* (1907); excerpted above] ([Paris: Presses Universitaires de France,] 1948), p. 157. An analysis of Bergson's position in modern philosophy would lead us too far afield. But his insistence on the priority of *homo faber* over *homo sapiens* [man the wise or knowing] and on fabrication as the source of human intelligence, as well as his emphatic

opposition of life to intelligence, is very suggestive. Bergson's philosophy could easily be read like a case study of how the modern age's earlier conviction of the relative superiority of making over thinking was then superseded and annihilated by its more recent conviction of an absolute superiority of life over everything else. It is because Bergson himself still united both of these elements that he could exert such a decisive influence on the beginnings of labor theories in France [Arendt's note].
2. Bergson, op. cit., p. 140 [Arendt's note].
3. J. Bronowski, "Science and Human Values," *Nation*, December 29, 1956 [Arendt's note].

classical economics, whose highest standard is productivity and whose prejudice against non-productive activities is so strong that even Marx could
justify his plea for justice for laborers only by misrepresenting the laboring,
non-productive activity in terms of work and fabrication. It is most articulate,
of course, in the pragmatic trends of modern philosophy, which are not
only characterized by Cartesian world alienation[4] but also by the unanimity
with which English philosophy from the seventeenth century onward and
French philosophy in the eighteenth century adopted the principle of utility
as the key which would open all doors to the explanation of human motivation and behavior. Generally speaking, the oldest conviction of homo faber—
that "man is the measure of all things"[5]—advanced to the rank of a universally
accepted commonplace.

What needs explanation is not the modern esteem of homo faber but the
fact that this esteem was so quickly followed by the elevation of laboring to
the highest position in the hierarchical order of the vita activa. This second
reversal of hierarchy within the vita activa came about more gradually and
less dramatically than either the reversal of contemplation and action in general or the reversal of action and fabrication in particular. The elevation of
laboring was preceded by certain deviations and variations from the traditional
mentality of homo faber which were highly characteristic of the modern age
and which, indeed, arose almost automatically from the very nature of the
events that ushered it in. What changed the mentality of homo faber was
the central position of the concept of process in modernity. As far as homo faber
was concerned, the modern shift of emphasis from the "what" to the "how,"
from the thing itself to its fabrication process, was by no means an unmixed
blessing. It deprived man as maker and builder of those fixed and permanent
standards and measurements which, prior to the modern age, have always
served him as guides for his doing and criteria for his judgment. It is not only
and perhaps not even primarily the development of commercial society that,
with the triumphal victory of exchange value over use value,[6] first introduced
the principle of interchangeability, then the relativization, and finally the
devaluation, of all values. For the mentality of modern man, as it was determined by the development of modern science and the concomitant unfolding
of modern philosophy, it was at least as decisive that man began to consider
himself part and parcel of the two superhuman, all-encompassing processes
of nature and history, both of which seemed doomed to an infinite progress
without ever reaching any inherent telos[7] or approaching any preordained idea.

Homo faber, in other words, as he arose from the great revolution of modernity, though he was to acquire an undreamed-of ingenuity in devising instruments to measure the infinitely large and the infinitely small, was deprived of
those permanent measures that precede and outlast the fabrication process
and form an authentic and reliable absolute with respect to the fabricating

---

4. That is, the fundamental split between mind
and the world (including the body) as two wholly
different kinds of substance (one whose essence is
"thinking" or consciousness and the other whose
essence is extension, which each exist essentially
independent of the other), as maintained by the
French philosopher and mathematician René Descartes (1596–1650).

5. A claim made by the Greek philosopher Protag-
oras (5th c. B.C.E.).
6. Terms especially associated with Marxian economics: a commodity's exchange value (the rate at
which it can be traded for other commodities) is
abstracted from its use value (its usefulness in fulfilling human needs).
7. End, goal, purpose (Greek).

activity. Certainly, none of the activities of the *vita activa* stood to lose as much through the elimination of contemplation from the range of meaningful human capacities as fabrication. For unlike action, which partly consists in the unchaining of processes, and unlike laboring, which follows closely the metabolic process of biological life, fabrication experiences processes, if it is aware of them at all, as mere means toward an end, that is, as something secondary and derivative. No other capacity, moreover, stood to lose as much through modern world alienation and the elevation of introspection into an omnipotent device to conquer nature as those faculties which are primarily directed toward the building of the world and the production of worldly things.

Nothing perhaps indicates clearer the ultimate failure of *homo faber* to assert himself than the rapidity with which the principle of utility, the very quintessence of his world view, was found wanting and was superseded by the principle of "the greatest happiness of the greatest number."[8] When this happened it was manifest that the conviction of the age that man can know only what he makes himself—which seemingly was so eminently propitious to a full victory of *homo faber*—would be overruled and eventually destroyed by the even more modern principle of process, whose concepts and categories are altogether alien to the needs and ideals of *homo faber*. For the principle of utility, though its point of reference is clearly man, who uses matter to produce things, still presupposes a world of use objects by which man is surrounded and in which he moves. If this relationship between man and world is no longer secure, if worldly things are no longer primarily considered in their usefulness but as more or less incidental results of the production process which brought them into being, so that the end product of the production process is no longer a true end and the produced thing is valued not for the sake of its predetermined usage but "for its production of something else," then, obviously, the objection can be "raised that . . . its value is secondary only, and a world that contains no primary values can contain no secondary ones either."[9] This radical loss of values within the restricted frame of reference of *homo faber* himself occurs almost automatically as soon as he defines himself not as the maker of objects and the builder of the human artifice who incidentally invents tools, but considers himself primarily a toolmaker and "particularly [a maker] of tools to make tools" who only incidentally also produces things. If one applies the principle of utility in this context at all, then it refers primarily not to use objects and not to usage but to the production process. Now what helps stimulate productivity and lessens pain and effort is useful. In other words, the ultimate standard of measurement is not utility and usage at all, but "happiness," that is, the amount of pain and pleasure experienced in the production or in the consumption of things.

Bentham's invention of the "pain and pleasure calculus" combined the advantage of seemingly introducing the mathematical method into the moral sciences with the even greater attraction of having found a principle which resided entirely on introspection. His "happiness," the sum total of pleasures

---

8. The necessary object of all legislation, according to Jeremy Bentham in *An Introduction to the Principles of Morals and Legislation* (1789). The English philosopher and economist Bentham (1748–1832) was the first expounder of utilitarianism.

9. Laurence J. Lafleur, introduction to the Hafner edition [(New York: Hafner Publishing, 1948)] of Bentham's *An Introduction to the Principles of Morals and Legislation*, p. xi [Arendt's note].

minus pains, is as much an inner sense which senses sensations and remains unrelated to worldly objects as the Cartesian consciousness that is conscious of its own activity. Moreover, Bentham's basic assumption that what all men have in common is not the world but the sameness of their own nature, which manifests itself in the sameness of calculation and the sameness of being affected by pain and pleasure, is directly derived from the earlier philosophers of the modern age. For this philosophy, "hedonism" is even more of a misnomer than for the epicureanism of late antiquity, to which modern hedonism is only superficially related. The principle of all hedonism, as we saw before, is not pleasure but avoidance of pain, and Hume, who in contradistinction to Bentham was still a philosopher, knew quite well that he who wants to make pleasure the ultimate end of all human action is driven to admit that not pleasure but pain, not desire but fear, are his true guides. "If you . . . inquire, why [somebody] desires health, he will readily reply, because sickness is painful. If you push your inquiries further and desire a reason why he hates pain, it is impossible he can ever give any. This is an ultimate end, and is never referred to by any other object."[1] The reason for this impossibility is that only pain is completely independent of any object, that only one who is in pain really senses nothing but himself; pleasure does not enjoy itself but something besides itself. Pain is the only inner sense found by introspection which can rival in independence from experienced objects the self-evident certainty of logical and arithmetical reasoning.

While this ultimate foundation of hedonism in the experience of pain is true for both its ancient and modern varieties, in the modern age it acquires an altogether different and much stronger emphasis. For here it is by no means the world, as in antiquity, that drives man into himself to escape the pains it may inflict, under which circumstance both pain and pleasure still retain a good deal of their worldly significance. Ancient world alienation in all its varieties—from stoicism to epicureanism down to hedonism and cynicism—had been inspired by a deep mistrust of the world and moved by a vehement impulse to withdraw from worldly involvement, from the trouble and pain it inflicts, into the security of an inward realm in which the self is exposed to nothing but itself. Their modern counterparts—puritanism, sensualism, and Bentham's hedonism—on the contrary, were inspired by an equally deep mistrust of man as such; they were moved by doubt of the adequacy of the human senses to receive reality, the adequacy of human reason to receive truth, and hence by the conviction of the deficiency or even depravity of human nature.

This depravity is not Christian or biblical either in origin or in content, although it was of course interpreted in terms of original sin, and it is difficult to say whether it is more harmful and repulsive when puritans denounce man's corruptness or when Benthamites brazenly hail as virtues what men always have known to be vices. While the ancients had relied upon imagination and memory, the imagination of pains from which they were free or the memory of past pleasures in situations of acute painfulness, to convince themselves

---

1. Quoted from Élie Halévy, *The Growth of Philosophical Radicalism* (Beacon Press, 1955), p. 13 [Arendt's note and brackets]. Halévy is quoting "Concerning Moral Sentiment," an appendix to *Enquiry Concerning the Principles of Morals* (1751) by the Scottish philosopher David Hume (1711–1776).

of their happiness, the moderns needed the calculus of pleasure or the puritan moral bookkeeping of merits and transgressions to arrive at some illusory mathematical certainty of happiness or salvation. (These moral arithmetics are, of course, quite alien to the spirit pervading the philosophic schools of late antiquity. Moreover, one need only reflect on the rigidity of self-imposed discipline and the concomitant nobility of character, so manifest in those who had been formed by ancient stoicism or epicureanism, to become aware of the gulf by which these versions of hedonism are separated from modern puritanism, sensualism, and hedonism. For this difference, it is almost irrelevant whether the modern character is still formed by the older narrow-minded, fanatic self-righteousness or has yielded to the more recent self-centered and self-indulgent egotism with its infinite variety of futile miseries.) It seems more than doubtful that the "greatest happiness principle" would have achieved its intellectual triumphs in the English-speaking world if no more had been involved than the questionable discovery that "nature has placed mankind under the governance of two sovereign masters, pain and pleasure,"[2] or the absurd idea of establishing morals as an exact science by isolating "in the human soul that feeling which seems to be the most easily measurable."[3]

Hidden behind this as behind other, less interesting variations of the sacredness of egoism and the all-pervasive power of self-interest, which were current to the point of being commonplace in the eighteenth and early nineteenth centuries, we find another point of reference which indeed forms a much more potent principle than any pain-pleasure calculus could ever offer, and that is the principle of life itself. What pain and pleasure, fear and desire, are actually supposed to achieve in all these systems is not happiness at all but the promotion of individual life or a guaranty of the survival of mankind. If modern egoism were the ruthless search for pleasure (called happiness) it pretends to be, it would not lack what in all truly hedonistic systems is an indispensable element of argumentation—a radical justification of suicide. This lack alone indicates that in fact we deal here with life philosophy in its most vulgar and least critical form. In the last resort, it is always life itself which is the supreme standard to which everything else is referred, and the interests of the individual as well as the interests of mankind are always equated with individual life or the life of the species as though it were a matter of course that life is the highest good.

The curious failure of *homo faber* to assert himself under conditions seemingly so extraordinarily propitious could also have been illustrated by another, philosophically even more relevant, revision of basic traditional beliefs. Hume's radical criticism of the causality principle, which prepared the way for the later adoption of the principle of evolution, has often been considered one of the origins of modern philosophy. The causality principle with its twofold central axiom—that everything that is must have a cause (*nihil sine causa*)[4] and that the cause must be more perfect than its most perfect effect—obviously relies entirely on experiences in the realm of fabrication, where the maker is superior to his products. Seen in this context, the turning point in the intellectual history of the modern age came when the image of organic life development—where the evolution of a lower being, for instance the ape, can cause the appearance of a higher being, for instance man—appeared in the place of the image of the watchmaker who must be superior to all watches whose cause he is.

Much more is implied in this change than the mere denial of the lifeless rigidity of a mechanistic world view. It is as though in the latent seventeenth-century conflict between the two possible methods to be derived from the Galilean discovery, the method of the experiment and of making on one hand and the method of introspection on the other, the latter was to achieve a somewhat belated victory. For the only tangible object introspection yields, if it is to yield more than an entirely empty consciousness of itself, is indeed the biological process. And since this biological life, accessible in self-observation, is at the same time a metabolic process between man and nature, it is as though introspection no longer needs to get lost in the ramifications of a consciousness without reality, but has found within man—not in his mind but in his bodily processes—enough outside matter to connect him again with the outer world. The split between subject and object, inherent in human consciousness and irremediable in the Cartesian opposition of man as a *res cogitans* to a surrounding world of *res extensae*,[5] disappears altogether in the case of a living organism, whose very survival depends upon the incorporation, the consumption, of outside matter. Naturalism, the nineteenth-century version of materialism, seemed to find in life the way to solve the problems of Cartesian philosophy and at the same time to bridge the ever-widening chasm between philosophy and science.[6]

FROM 44. LIFE AS THE HIGHEST GOOD

Tempting as it may be for the sake of sheer consistency to derive the modern life concept from the self-inflicted perplexities of modern philosophy, it would be a delusion and a grave injustice to the seriousness of the problems of the modern age if one looked upon them merely from the viewpoint of the development of ideas. The defeat of *homo faber* may be explainable in terms of the initial transformation of physics into astrophysics, of natural sciences into a "universal" science. What still remains to be explained is why this defeat ended with a victory of the *animal laborans*; why, with the rise of the *vita activa*, it was precisely the laboring activity that was to be elevated to the highest rank of man's capacities or, to put it another way, why within the diversity of the

---

5. Extended things or substance (Latin). *Res cogitans*: thinking thing or substance.

6. The greatest representatives of modern life philosophy [i.e., *Lebensphilosophie*] are Marx, Nietzsche, and Bergson, inasmuch as all three equate Life and Being. For this equation, they rely on introspection, and life is indeed the only "being" [i.e., "reality"] man can possibly be aware of by looking merely into himself. The difference between these and the earlier philosophers of the modern age is that life appears to be more active and more productive than consciousness, which seems to be still too closely related to contemplation and the old ideal of truth. This last stage of modern philosophy is perhaps best described as the rebellion of the philosophers against philosophy, a rebellion which, beginning with Kierkegaard and ending in existentialism, appears at first glance to emphasize action as against contemplation. Upon closer inspection, however, none of these philosophers is actually concerned with action as such. We may leave aside here Kierkegaard and his non-worldly, inward-directed acting. Nietzsche and Bergson describe action in terms of fabrication—*homo faber* instead of *homo sapiens*—just as Marx thinks of acting in terms of making and describes labor in terms of work. But their ultimate point of reference is not work and worldliness any more than action; it is life and life's fertility [Arendt's note]. For KIERKEGAARD, see above.

human condition with its various human capacities it was precisely life that overruled all other considerations.

The reason why life asserted itself as the ultimate point of reference in the modern age and has remained the highest good of modern society is that the modern reversal operated within the fabric of a Christian society whose fundamental belief in the sacredness of life has survived, and has even remained completely unshaken by, secularization and the general decline of the Christian faith. In other words, the modern reversal followed and left unchallenged the most important reversal with which Christianity had broken into the ancient world, a reversal that was politically even more far-reaching and, historically at any rate, more enduring than any specific dogmatic content or belief. For the Christian "glad tidings"[7] of the immortality of individual human life had reversed the ancient relationship between man and world and promoted the most mortal thing, human life, to the position of immortality, which up to then the cosmos had held.

Historically, it is more than probable that the victory of the Christian faith in the ancient world was largely due to this reversal, which brought hope to those who knew that their world was doomed, indeed a hope beyond hope, since the new message promised an immortality they never had dared to hope for. This reversal could not but be disastrous for the esteem and the dignity of politics. Political activity, which up to then had derived its greatest inspiration from the aspiration toward worldly immortality, now sank to the low level of an activity subject to necessity, destined to remedy the consequences of human sinfulness on one hand and to cater to the legitimate wants and interests of earthly life on the other. Aspiration toward immortality[8] could now only be equated with vainglory; such fame as the world could bestow upon man was an illusion, since the world was even more perishable than man, and a striving for worldly immortality was meaningless, since life itself was immortal.

It is precisely individual life which now came to occupy the position once held by the "life" of the body politic, and Paul's statement that "death is the wages of sin,"[9] since life is meant to last forever, echoes Cicero's statement that death is the reward of sins committed by political communities which were built to last for eternity.[1]

* * *

The reason why Christianity, its insistence on the sacredness of life and on the duty to stay alive notwithstanding, never developed a positive labor philosophy lies in the unquestioned priority given to the *vita contemplativa* over all kinds of human activities. *Vita contemplativa simpliciter melior est quam vita activa* ("the life of contemplation is simply better than the life of action"), and whatever the merits of an active life might be, those of a life devoted to contemplation are "more effective and more powerful."[2] This conviction, it is true, can hardly be found in the preachings of Jesus of Nazareth, and it is certainly due to the influence of Greek philosophy; yet even if medieval

---

7. See Luke 8:1; Acts 13:32.
8. That is, "toward worldly immortality" (i.e., everlasting fame and honor), as Arendt had written in the previous sentence..
9. Romans 6:23.

1. See *On the Republic* 3.34, by the Roman statesman and scholar Cicero (106–43 B.C.E.).
2. Aquinas *Summa theologica* ii.2.182.1, 2 [Arendt's note].

philosophy had kept closer to the spirit of the Gospels, it could hardly have found there any reason for a glorification of laboring. The only activity Jesus of Nazareth recommends in his preachings is action, and the only human capacity he stresses is the capacity "to perform miracles."

However that may be, the modern age continued to operate under the assumption that life, and not the world, is the highest good of man; in its boldest and most radical revisions and criticisms of traditional beliefs and concepts, it never even thought of challenging this fundamental reversal which Christianity had brought into the dying ancient world. No matter how articulate and how conscious the thinkers of modernity were in their attacks on tradition, the priority of life over everything else had acquired for them the status of a "self-evident truth," and as such it has survived even in our present world, which has begun already to leave the whole modern age behind and to substitute for a laboring society the society of jobholders. But while it is quite conceivable that the development following upon the discovery of the Archimedean point would have taken an altogether different direction if it had taken place seventeen hundred years earlier, when not life but the world was still the highest good of man, it by no means follows that we still live in a Christian world. For what matters today is not the immortality of life, but that life is the highest good. And while this assumption certainly is Christian in origin, it constitutes no more than an important attending circumstance for the Christian faith. Moreover, even if we disregard the details of Christian dogma and consider only the general mood of Christianity, which resides in the importance of faith, it is obvious that nothing could be more detrimental to this spirit than the spirit of distrust and suspicion of the modern age. Surely, Cartesian doubt has proved its efficiency nowhere more disastrously and irretrievably than in the realm of religious belief, where it was introduced by Pascal[3] and Kierkegaard, the two greatest religious thinkers of modernity. (For what undermined the Christian faith was not the atheism of the eighteenth century or the materialism of the nineteenth—their arguments are frequently vulgar and, for the most part, easily refutable by traditional theology—but rather the doubting concern with salvation of genuinely religious men, in whose eyes the traditional Christian content and promise had become "absurd.")

Just as we do not know what would have happened if the Archimedean point had been discovered before the rise of Christianity, we are in no position to ascertain what the destiny of Christianity would have been if the great awakening of the Renaissance had not been interrupted by this event. Before Galileo, all paths still seemed to be open. If we think back to Leonardo,[4] we may well imagine that a technical revolution would have overtaken the development of humanity in any case. This might well have led to flight, the realization of one of the oldest and most persistent dreams of man, but it hardly would have led into the universe; it might well have brought about the unification of the earth, but it hardly would have brought about the transformation of matter into energy and the adventure into the microscopic universe. The only thing we can be sure of is that the coincidence of the reversal of doing

3. Blaise Pascal (1623–1662), French scientist and philosopher. "Cartesian doubt": Descartes began his *Meditations on First Philosophy* (1641) by methodically doubting everything he previously thought he knew.

4. Leonardo da Vinci (1452–1519), Italian artist, architect, and engineer; among his sketches were designs for flying machines.

and contemplating with the earlier reversal of life and world became the point of departure for the whole modern development. Only when the *vita activa* had lost its point of reference in the *vita contemplativa* could it become active life in the full sense of the word; and only because this active life remained bound to life as its only point of reference could life as such, the laboring metabolism of man with nature, become active and unfold its entire fertility.

45. The Victory of the *Animal Laborans*

The victory of the *animal laborans* would never have been complete had not the process of secularization, the modern loss of faith inevitably arising from Cartesian doubt, deprived individual life of its immortality, or at least of the certainty of immortality. Individual life again became mortal, as mortal as it had been in antiquity, and the world was even less stable, less permanent, and hence less to be relied upon than it had been during the Christian era. Modern man, when he lost the certainty of a world to come, was thrown back upon himself and not upon this world; far from believing that the world might be potentially immortal, he was not even sure that it was real. And in so far as he was to assume that it was real in the uncritical and apparently unbothered optimism of a steadily progressing science, he had removed himself from the earth to a much more distant point than any Christian otherworldliness had ever removed him. Whatever the word "secular" is meant to signify in current usage, historically it cannot possibly be equated with worldliness; modern man at any rate did not gain this world when he lost the other world, and he did not gain life, strictly speaking, either; he was thrust back upon it, thrown into the closed inwardness of introspection, where the highest he could experience were the empty processes of reckoning of the mind, its play with itself. The only contents left were appetites and desires, the senseless urges of his body which he mistook for passion and which he deemed to be "unreasonable" because he found he could not "reason," that is, not reckon with them. The only thing that could now be potentially immortal, as immortal as the body politic in antiquity and as individual life during the Middle Ages, was life itself, that is, the possibly everlasting life process of the species mankind.

We saw before that in the rise of society it was ultimately the life of the species which asserted itself. Theoretically, the turning point from the earlier modern age's insistence on the "egoistic" life of the individual to its later emphasis on "social" life and "socialized man" (Marx) came when Marx transformed the cruder notion of classical economy—that all men, in so far as they act at all, act for reasons of self-interest—into forces of interest which inform, move, and direct the classes of society, and through their conflicts direct society as a whole. Socialized mankind is that state of society where only one interest rules, and the subject of this interest is either classes or mankind, but neither man nor men.[5] The point is that now even the last trace of

---

5. That is, either classes (and so particular subsets or groups) of human beings or humankind as a whole in a classless world, but neither "man" (*der Mensch*) as a form of life and existing collective human reality nor a multiplicity of individual human beings.

action in what men were doing, the motive implied in self-interest, disappeared. What was left was a "natural force," the force of the life process itself, to which all men and all human activities were equally submitted ("the thought process itself is a natural process")[6] and whose only aim, if it had an aim at all, was survival of the animal species man. None of the higher capacities of man was any longer necessary to connect individual life with the life of the species; individual life became part of the life process, and to labor, to assure the continuity of one's own life and the life of his family, was all that was needed. What was not needed, not necessitated by life's metabolism with nature, was either superfluous or could be justified only in terms of a peculiarity of human as distinguished from other animal life—so that Milton[7] was considered to have written his *Paradise Lost* for the same reasons and out of similar urges that compel the silkworm to produce silk.

If we compare the modern world with that of the past, the loss of human experience involved in this development is extraordinarily striking. It is not only and not even primarily contemplation which has become an entirely meaningless experience. Thought itself, when it became "reckoning with consequences," became a function of the brain, with the result that electronic instruments are found to fulfil these functions much better than we ever could. Action was soon and still is almost exclusively understood in terms of making and fabricating, only that making, because of its worldliness and inherent indifference to life, was now regarded as but another form of laboring, a more complicated but not a more mysterious function of the life process.

Meanwhile, we have proved ingenious enough to find ways to ease the toil and trouble of living to the point where an elimination of laboring from the range of human activities can no longer be regarded as utopian. For even now, laboring is too lofty, too ambitious a word for what we are doing, or think we are doing, in the world we have come to live in. The last stage of the laboring society, the society of jobholders, demands of its members a sheer automatic functioning, as though individual life had actually been submerged in the over-all life process of the species and the only active decision still required of the individual were to let go, so to speak, to abandon his individuality, the still individually sensed pain and trouble of living, and acquiesce in a dazed, "tranquilized," functional type of behavior. The trouble with modern theories of behaviorism is not that they are wrong but that they could become true, that they actually are the best possible conceptualization of certain obvious trends in modern society. It is quite conceivable that the modern age—which began with such an unprecedented and promising outburst of human activity—may end in the deadliest, most sterile passivity history has ever known.

But there are other more serious danger signs that man may be willing and, indeed, is on the point of developing into that animal species from which, since Darwin,[8] he imagines he has come. If, in concluding, we return once

---

6. In a letter Marx wrote to Kugelmann in July, 1868 [Arendt's note]. Ludwig Kugelmann (1828–1902), German physician and friend of Marx's.
7. John Milton (1608–1674), English writer of prose tracts and poetry; *Paradise Lost* (1667, 1674)

is widely considered to be the greatest epic poem written in English.
8. Charles Darwin (1809–1882), English naturalist who formulated the theory of evolution by natural selection.

more to the discovery of the Archimedean point and apply it, as Kafka[9] warned us not to do, to man himself and to what he is doing on this earth, it at once becomes manifest that all his activities, watched from a sufficiently removed vantage point in the universe, would appear not as activities of any kind but as processes, so that, as a scientist recently put it, modern motorization would appear like a process of biological mutation in which human bodies gradually begin to be covered by shells of steel. For the watcher from the universe, this mutation would be no more or less mysterious than the mutation which now goes on before our eyes in those small living organisms which we fought with antibiotics and which mysteriously have developed new strains to resist us. How deep-rooted this usage of the Archimedean point against ourselves is can be seen in the very metaphors which dominate scientific thought today. The reason why scientists can tell us about the "life" in the atom—where apparently every particle is "free" to behave as it wants and the laws ruling these movements are the same statistical laws which, according to the social scientists, rule human behavior and make the multitude behave as it must, no matter how "free" the individual particle may appear to be in its choices— the reason, in other words, why the behavior of the infinitely small particle is not only similar in pattern to the planetary system as it appears to us but resembles the life and behavior patterns in human society is, of course, that we look and live in this society as though we were as far removed from our own human existence as we are from the infinitely small and the immensely large which, even if they could be perceived by the finest instruments, are too far away from us to be experienced.

Needless to say, this does not mean that modern man has lost his capacities or is on the point of losing them. No matter what sociology, psychology, and anthropology will tell us about the "social animal," men persist in making, fabricating, and building, although these faculties are more and more restricted to the abilities of the artist, so that the concomitant experiences of worldliness escape more and more the range of ordinary human experience.

Similarly, the capacity for action, at least in the sense of the releasing of processes, is still with us, although it has become the exclusive prerogative of the scientists, who have enlarged the realm of human affairs to the point of extinguishing the time-honored protective dividing line between nature and the human world. In view of such achievements, performed for centuries in the unseen quiet of the laboratories, it seems only proper that their deeds should eventually have turned out to have greater news value, to be of greater political significance, than the administrative and diplomatic doings of most so-called statesmen. It certainly is not without irony that those whom public opinion has persistently held to be the least practical and the least political members of society should have turned out to be the only ones left who still know how to act and how to act in concert. For their early organizations, which they founded in the seventeenth century for the conquest of nature and in which they developed their own moral standards and their own code of honor, have not only survived all vicissitudes of the modern age, but they have become

9. Frank Kafka (1883–1924), Prague-born German-language writer of novels and short stories; the epigraph to this chapter (not included here) is his aphorism: "He found the Archimedean point, but he used it against himself; it seems that he was permitted to find it only under this condition."

one of the most potent power-generating groups in all history. But the action of the scientists, since it acts into nature from the standpoint of the universe and not into the web of human relationships, lacks the revelatory character of action as well as the ability to produce stories and become historical, which together form the very source from which meaningfulness springs into and illuminates human existence. In this existentially most important aspect, action, too, has become an experience for the privileged few, and these few who still know what it means to act may well be even fewer than the artists, their experience even rarer than the genuine experience of and love for the world.

Thought, finally—which we, following the premodern as well as the modern tradition, omitted from our reconsideration of the *vita activa*—is still possible, and no doubt actual, wherever men live under the conditions of political freedom. Unfortunately, and contrary to what is currently assumed about the proverbial ivory-tower independence of thinkers, no other human capacity is so vulnerable, and it is in fact far easier to act under conditions of tyranny than it is to think. As a living experience, thought has always been assumed, perhaps wrongly, to be known only to the few. It may not be presumptuous to believe that these few have not become fewer in our time. This may be irrelevant, or of restricted relevance, for the future of the world; it is not irrelevant for the future of man. For if no other test but the experience of being active, no other measure but the extent of sheer activity were to be applied to the various activities within the *vita activa*, it might well be that thinking as such would surpass them all. Whoever has any experience in this matter will know how right Cato[1] was when he said: *Numquam se plus agere quam nihil cum ageret, numquam minus solum esse quam cum solus esset*—"Never is he more active than when he does nothing, never is he less alone than when he is by himself."

SOURCE: From Hannah Arendt, *The Human Condition* (Chicago: University of Chicago Press, 1958), pp. 7–17, 305–14, 308–25.

1. Cato the Elder (234–149 B.C.E.), Roman statesman and prose writer; his saying is related by Cicero in *On the Republic* 1.27.

JÜRGEN HABERMAS
(b. 1929)

Habermas is arguably the most prominent figure in German philosophy since HEIDEGGER. He is best known in the English-speaking world as the leading German counterpart to the major American moral and political philosopher John Rawls, because he seeks to develop and defend a somewhat Kantian moral-philosophical position rivaling that of Rawls. Habermas's version is commonly known as "communicative" or "discourse ethics"; in it, moral norms are determined through an ongoing dialogue among "reasonable" social subjects rather than in some more abstractly rational fashion. His larger project is even more ambitious: to develop a comprehensive theory of contemporary society, relating it to the historical contingencies and constitution of our humanity.

Born in Düsseldorf, Jürgen Habermas ("YOU'RE-gen HAH-ber-mahs") studied at the universities of Göttingen, Bonn, Frankfurt, and finally Marburg, at which he took his second doctoral (habilitation) degree in political science in 1961. His experience at Frankfurt, as a student of Max Horkheimer and Theodor Adorno, was particularly important in his development; and this philosophical lineage places him in the tradition of the Frankfurt School, with its emphasis on the need to subject all aspects of modern society to radical social and philosophical critique. After only a year of teaching at Marburg, he was appointed to a professorship in philosophy at Heidelberg in 1962. Even more remarkably, he was offered a chaired professorship in philosophy and sociology at Frankfurt just two years later. In 1971 he assumed the directorship of the Max Planck Institute in Starnberg, and then returned to Frankfurt in 1983 as a professor. He retired in 1994 and subsequently divided his time between Germany and the United States, where he became a "permanent visiting professor" at Northwestern University.

The title of Habermas's first book, *The Absolute and History: On the Dichotomy in Schelling's Thinking* (1954), foreshadowed the development of his own interests. In it he identified a tension in SCHELLING's work between his recognition of the pervasiveness of historical contingency in all things human and his desire to identify some sort of transcultural but nonmetaphysical principle to which normative thinking can appeal and by which it can be guided. A similar tension characterizes Habermas's own thought.

Like many others of his generation, Habermas's thinking developed through engagement with Martin Heidegger's existential philosophy, and through confrontation with both Marxist thought and the philosophical anthropology of ARNOLD GEHLEN and HELMUTH PLESSNER. These influences and challenges are reflected in many of his writings. Indeed, his own work can be seen not only as making a major contribution to normative and social theory but also as continuing the project of a philosophical anthropology whose theme is "human reality" rather than "human nature," sensitive at once to the pervasively social and historical character of human life and to the persistence of certain fundamental interests as general features of the profile of human reality.

Habermas's early philosophical work culminated in *Knowledge and Human Interests* (1968; trans. 1987), which analyzes KANT, HEGEL, MARX, C. S. Peirce's pragmatism, DILTHEY's hermeneutics, and NIETZSCHE (among other figures and developments) as it examines responses to the problem of the objectivity of knowledge. In essence, it identifies the major doctrines of and divisions between positivist scientific thought and historicist or hermeneutic thought. Habermas's aim is to develop an alternative to these two schools. His guiding idea is that because knowers have a self-reflective stance and are existing human agents who as such have the aims of achieving mutual understanding and consensus, we can conclude that there is a "knowledge-constitutive" human interest. The aims or interests of human activity and work and their historical development cannot be eliminated from the analysis of human knowledge, he argues; and yet historicism must not be taken to the point of eliminating objectivity and truth, for to do so would make the human activity of knowing unintelligible. His thinking on these matters was undoubtedly influenced by his encounters and interaction—at first sharp, subsequently amicable—with the much more historicist HANS-GEORG GADAMER. (Its most notable public moment was his critical 1967 review of Gadamer's *Truth and Method* [1960], to which Gadamer in effect replied vigorously in one of the selections from his writings included below.)

Habermas's magnum opus is *The Theory of Communicative Action*, published in two volumes: *Reason and the Rationalization of Society* (1981; trans. 1984) and *Lifeworld and System: A Critique of Functionalist Reason* (1981; trans. 1987). In these books Habermas provides illuminating critical discussions of Max Weber, Western Marxism, and the Frankfurt School. The first volume aims to eliminate Cartesianism from the theory of rationality: no longer should the analysis of knowledge and reason take place from the perspective of the solitary thinker. The twentieth-century shift known as the "linguistic turn" does not sufficiently overcome Cartesianism, insofar as it fails to consider language as a social act of communication. The shared situation of acting and living in the world is what constitutes the pragmatic and universal foundation of the norms of rationality. In the second volume, Habermas wants to preserve the perspective of the social-theoretical "observer" employing the concept and framework of social systems or structures to perform social analysis. But

he further contends that this inquiry must be balanced with social analysis undertaken from the perspective of a living member of the community, which takes into consideration the agent's aims and intentions. Hence the title of that volume features two contrasting notions, "system" and "lifeworld."

After developing his theory of communicative action in the late 1970s, Habermas turned his attention to the field of ethics, in which his most important book is *Moral Consciousness and Communicative Action* (1983; trans. 1990). Habermas's ethics is basically Kantian, but it involves no appeal to a transcendental-rational justification of morality that imposes the moral law on all persons. Instead, he attempts a transcendental-pragmatic justification for morality. From the pragmatic norms that govern how individuals argue and offer reasons to one another, Habermas derives a "universalization principle": all persons who are affected by a controversial norm must b[e] able to accept its consequences and s[ide] effects, and only norms that pass su[ch] test are valid. But he rejects the ide[a] a meaningful basic categorical norm can be derived from the n[…] the communicative situation it[…] ethical system is ultimately base[d] idea of a shared lifeworld and matics of the situation of co[…] tion, rather than on some fu[…] moral and rational principle.

Habermas's ethical theo[…] naturally to engage with pol[…] the theory of democracy, an[…] ophy of law. His major work[…] *Between Facts and Norms:* to a Discourse Theory of La[…] racy (1992; trans. 1996). [...] theory of discourse, wit[…] on reason giving, to argu[…] cratic process, which fo[…] will of a people throug[…] public reason, legitima[…] This is the internal o[…] tion between law an[…] Habermas wishes to[…] he holds is best ex[…] "discourse-theoretic[…]

The following two selections, from two of Habermas's most important works, reflect his thinking on several of these large and fundamental issues. The first is from *Knowledge and Human Interests*, and the second is from *The Theory of Communicative Action*. In his early work, as was observed above, he was keenly concerned to make and pursue the point that cognitive inquiry is affected by the pervasive influence on human thought of social, cultural, economic, and other such historical circumstances and human interests. Yet he also sought a way to place human inquiry on firmer ground, arguing that knowledge need not be thought to dissolve into historical contingency once absolutist assumptions and commitments are abandoned. In his later work he has attempted to salvage significant notions of knowledge, truth, and rationality from the philosophy of language, and to extend those notions into the domain of ethics and normativity.

In this way, Habermas is attempting to give a new lease on life to some of the most fundamental aspirations and concerns of the Western philosophical tradition, in opposition to those who call for their abandonment, by providing them with a different sort of basis and warrant than many philosophers have long supposed were necessary to retain them. But this strategy requires us to reconsider very fundamentally what the concepts in question can and do amount to in human life and thought. For some, Habermas gives up too little as he seeks to preserve revised versions of these themes; for others, he gives up too much. In the eyes of his many admirers, however, he is showing the possibility of a genuinely viable alternative to the "all or nothing" approaches to these matters advocated by the philosophical conservatives and radicals among us.

Knowledge and Human Interests: *A General Perspective*

I

In 1802, during the summer semester at Jena, Schelling gave his Lectures on the Method of Academic Study. In the language of German Idealism he emphatically renewed the concept of theory that has defined the tradition of great philosophy since its beginnings.

> The fear of speculation, the ostensible rush from the theoretical to the practical, brings about the same shallowness in action that it does in knowledge. It is by studying a strictly theoretical philosophy that we become most immediately acquainted with Ideas, and only Ideas provide action with energy and ethical significance.[1]

: *only* knowledge that can truly orient action is knowledge that frees itself
 ı mere human interests and is based on Ideas—in other words, knowl-
  that has taken a theoretical attitude.
  ε word "theory" has religious origins. The *theoros* was the representa-
  ent by Greek cities to public celebrations.[2] Through *theoria*, that is

∷h W. J. von Schelling, *Werke* [*Works*], Manfred Schröter (Munich: Beck, 1958–) [Habermas's note]. On SCHELLING, see

ınell, "Theorie und Praxis [Theory and in *Die Entdeckung des Geistes* [The *Geist* (Spirit)], 3rd ed. (Hamburg: Claas-

sen, 1955), pp. 401ff.; Georg Picht, "Der Sinn der Unterscheidung von Theorie und Praxis in der griechischen Philosophie [The Meaning of the Distinction of Theory and Practice in Greek Philosophy]," in *Evangelische Ethik* (1964), 8:321ff. [Habermas's note].

through looking on, he abandoned himself to the sacred events. In philosophical language, theoria was transferred to contemplation of the cosmos. In this form, theory already presupposed the demarcation between Being and time that is the foundation of ontology. This separation is first found in the poem of Parmenides and returns in Plato's *Timaeus*.[3] It reserves to *logos* a realm of Being purged of inconstancy and uncertainty and leaves to *doxa*[4] the realm of the mutable and perishable. When the philosopher views the immortal order, he cannot help bringing himself into accord with the proportions of the cosmos and reproducing them internally. He manifests these proportions, which he sees in the motions of nature and the harmonic series of music, within himself; he forms himself through *mimesis*.[5] Through the soul's likening itself to the ordered motion of the cosmos, theory enters the conduct of life. In *ethos*[6] theory molds life to its form and is reflected in the conduct of those who subject themselves to its discipline.

This concept of theory and of life in theory has defined philosophy since its beginnings. The distinction between theory in this traditional sense and theory in the sense of critique was the object of one of Max Horkheimer's most important studies.[7] Today, a generation later, I should like to reexamine this theme;[8] starting with Husserl's *The Crisis of the European Sciences*, which appeared at about the same time as Horkheimer's.[9] Husserl used as his frame of reference the very concept of theory that Horkheimer was countering with that of critical theory. Husserl was concerned with crisis: not with crises in the sciences, but with their crisis as science. For "in our vital state of need this science has nothing to say to us." Like almost all philosophers before him, Husserl, without second thought, took as the norm of his critique an idea of knowledge that preserves the Platonic connection of pure theory with the conduct of life. What ultimately produces a scientific culture is not the information content of theories but the formation among theorists themselves of a thoughtful and enlightened mode of life. The evolution of the European mind [*Geist*] seemed to be aiming at the creation of a scientific culture of this sort. After 1933,[1] however, Husserl saw this historical tendency endangered. He was convinced that the danger was threatening not from without but from within. He attributed the crisis to the circumstance that the most advanced disciplines, especially physics, had degenerated from the status of true theory.

---

3. A dialogue on cosmology by the Greek philosopher Plato (ca. 427–ca. 327 B.C.E.). "The poem of Parmenides": a long didactic poem by the Greek philosopher (b. ca. 515 B.C.E.), some fragments of which survive under the title "On Nature."
4. Belief, opinion (Greek). *Logos*: reason (Greek).
5. Imitation (Greek).
6. Custom, moral character (Greek); here, ethics understood as proper character formation.
7. "Traditionelle und kritische Theorie" [1937, "Traditional and Critical Theory"], in *Zeitschrift für Sozialforschung*, 6:245ff. Reprinted in Max Horkheimer, *Kritische Theorie*, edited by Alfred Schmidt (Frankfurt am Main: Fischer, 1968), pp. 137–91 [Habermas's note]. Horkheimer (1895–

1973), German philosopher and sociologist, and one of the founders of the Frankfurt School of critical social theory.
8. The appendix was the basis of my inaugural lecture at the University of Frankfurt am Main on June 28, 1965 [Habermas's note].
9. *Die Krisis der europäischen Wissenschaften und die transzendentale Phänomenologie* [1954, *The Crisis of the European Wissenschaften (Cognitive Disciplines) and Transcendental Phenomenology*], in *Gesammelte Schriften* [*Collected Writings*] (The Hague: Martinus Nijhoff, 1950), vol. 6 [Habermas's note]. On HUSSERL, see above.
1. When the Nazis came to power in Germany.

II

Let us consider this thesis. There is a real connection between the positivistic self-understanding of the sciences [*Wissenschaften*] and traditional ontology. The *empirical-analytic* sciences develop their theories in a self-understanding that automatically generates continuity with the beginnings of philosophical thought. For both are committed to a theoretical attitude that frees those who take it from dogmatic association with the natural interests of life and their irritating influence; and both share the cosmological intention of describing the universe theoretically in its lawlike order, just as it is. In contrast, the *historical-hermeneutic* sciences, which are concerned with the sphere of transitory things and mere opinion, cannot be linked up so smoothly with this tradition—they have nothing to do with cosmology. But they, too, comprise a *scientistic consciousness*,[2] based on the model of science. For even the symbolic meanings of tradition seem capable of being brought together in a cosmos of facts in ideal simultaneity. Much as the cultural sciences[3] may comprehend their facts through understanding and little though they may be concerned with discovering general laws, they nevertheless share with the empirical-analytic sciences the methodological consciousness of describing a structured reality within the horizon of the theoretical attitude. Historicism has become the positivism[4] of the cultural and social sciences.

Positivism has also permeated the self-understanding of the *social sciences*, whether they obey the methodological demands of an empirical-analytic behavioral science or orient themselves to the pattern of normative-analytic sciences, based on presuppositions about maxims of action.[5] In this field of inquiry, which is so close to practice, the concept of value-freedom[6] (or ethical neutrality) has simply reaffirmed the ethos that modern science owes to the beginnings of theoretical thought in Greek philosophy: psychologically an unconditional commitment to theory and epistemologically the severance of knowledge from interest. This is represented in logic by the distinction between descriptive and prescriptive statements, which makes grammatically obligatory the filtering out of merely emotive from cognitive contents.

Yet the very term "value freedom" reminds us that the postulates associated with it no longer correspond to the classical meaning of theory. To dissociate values from facts means counter posing an abstract Ought to pure Being. Values are the nominalistic by-products of a centuries-long critique of the emphatic concept of Being to which theory was once exclusively oriented. The very term "values," which neo-Kantianism brought into philosophical currency, and in relation to which science is supposed to preserve neutrality, renounces the connection between the two that theory originally intended.

2. That is, a consciousness that is "scientific" (*wissenschaftlich*) not merely in the sense of being scientifically informed and sophisticated but also taking scientific—and more specifically natural-scientific—thinking, proceeding, and knowing to be paradigmatic and unproblematic with respect to thought, inquiry, and comprehension more generally.
3. Here and throughout this essay, the term being translated as "science(s)" is "*Wissenschaft(en)*," which should be understood as "(cognitive) discipline(s)."
4. The doctrine that the only true knowledge is "positive" knowledge, defined as knowledge based on clear and objective data (as in physics and chemistry). The acceptable data were originally restricted to sense experience, then expanded to include empirical data more generally and ultimately logic as well.
5. See Gérard Gäfgen, *Theorie des wirtschaftlichen Entscheidung* [*Theory of Economic Decision*] (Tübingen: Mohr, 1963) [Habermas's note].
6. That is, freedom from value biases (judgments, presuppositions, commitments).

Thus, although the sciences share the concept of theory with the major tradition of philosophy, they destroy its classical claim. They borrow two elements from the philosophical heritage: the methodological meaning of the theoretical attitude and the basic ontological assumption of a structure of the world independent of the knower. On the other hand, however, they have abandoned the connection of *theoria* and *kosmos*, of *mimesis* and *bios theoretikos*[7] that was assumed from Plato through Husserl. What was once supposed to comprise the practical efficacy of theory has now fallen prey to methodological prohibitions. The conception of theory as a process of cultivation of the person has become apocryphal. Today it appears to us that the mimetic conformity of the soul to the proportions of the universe, which seemed accessible to contemplation, had only taken theoretical knowledge into the service of the internalization of norms and thus estranged it from its legitimate task.

III

In fact the sciences had to lose the specific significance for life that Husserl would like to regenerate through the renovation of pure theory. I shall reconstruct his critique in three steps. It is directed in the first place against the objectivism of the sciences, for which the world appears objectively as a universe of facts whose lawlike connection can be grasped descriptively. In truth, however,[8] knowledge of the apparently objective world of facts has its transcendental basis in the prescientific world. The possible objects of scientific analysis are constituted a priori in the self-evidence of our primary life-world. In this layer phenomenology discloses the products of a meaning-generative subjectivity. Second, Husserl would like to show that this productive subjectivity disappears under the cover of an objectivistic self-understanding, because the sciences have not radically freed themselves from interests rooted in the primary life-world. Only phenomenology breaks with the naive attitude in favor of a rigorously contemplative one and definitively frees knowledge from interest. Third, Husserl identifies transcendental self-reflection, to which he accords the name of phenomenological description, with theory in the traditional sense. The philosopher owes the theoretical attitude to a transposition that liberates him from the fabric of empirical interests. In this regard theory is "unpractical." But this does not cut it off from *practical* life. For, according to the traditional concept, it is precisely the consistent abstinence of theory that produces action-orienting culture. Once the theoretical attitude has been adopted, it is capable in turn of being mediated with the practical attitude:

> This occurs in the form of a novel practice . . . , whose aim is to elevate mankind to all forms of veridical norms through universal scientific reason, to transform it into a fundamentally new humanity, capable of absolute self-responsibility on the basis of absolute theoretical insight.[9]

7. The contemplative life (Greek).
8. That is, in Husserl's view: this paragraph presents his position.

9. Husserl, *The Crisis of the European Sciences* (*Wissenschaften*).

If we recall the situation of thirty years ago, the prospect of rising barbarism, we can respect this invocation of the therapeutic power of phenomenological description; but it is unfounded. At best, phenomenology grasps transcendental norms in accordance with which consciousness necessarily operates. It describes (in Kantian terms) laws of pure reason, but not norms of a universal legislation derived from practical reason, which a free will could obey. Why, then, does Husserl believe that he can claim practical efficacy for phenomenology as pure theory? He errs because he does not discern the connection of positivism, which he justifiably criticizes, with the ontology from which he unconsciously borrows the traditional concept of theory.

Husserl rightly criticizes the objectivist illusion that deludes the sciences with the image of a reality-in-itself consisting of facts structured in a lawlike manner; it conceals the constitution of these facts, and thereby prevents consciousness of the interlocking of knowledge with interests from the life-world. Because phenomenology brings this to consciousness, it is itself, in Husserl's view, free of such interests. It thus earns the title of pure theory unjustly claimed by the sciences. It is to this freeing of knowledge from interest that Husserl attaches the expectation of practical efficacy. But the error is clear. Theory in the sense of the classical tradition only had an impact on life because it was thought to have discovered in the cosmic order an ideal world structure, including the prototype for the order of the human world. Only as cosmology was *theoria* also capable of orienting human action. Thus Husserl cannot expect self-formative processes to originate in a phenomenology that, as transcendental philosophy, purifies the classical theory of its cosmological contents, conserving something like the theoretical attitude only in an abstract manner. Theory had educational and cultural implications not because it had freed knowledge from interest. To the contrary, it did so because it derived *pseudonormative*[1] *power* from *the concealment of its actual interest*. While criticizing the objectivist self-understanding of the sciences, Husserl succumbs to another objectivism, which was always attached to the traditional concept of theory.

IV

In the Greek tradition, the same forces that philosophy reduces to powers of the soul still appeared as gods and superhuman powers. Philosophy domesticated them and banished them to the realm of the soul as internalized demons. If from this point of view we regard the drives and affects that enmesh man in the empirical interests of his inconstant and contingent activity, then the attitude of pure theory, which promises *purification* from these very affects, takes on a new meaning: disinterested contemplation then obviously signifies emancipation. The release of knowledge from interest was not supposed to purify theory from the obfuscations of subjectivity but inversely to provide the subject with an ecstatic purification from the passions. What indicates the new stage of emancipation is that catharsis is now no longer attained through mystery cults[2] but established in the will of individuals themselves

---

1. That is, quasi-normative; covertly (and problematically) normative.

2. Secret religions, often of an ecstatic nature, in the Greco-Roman world.

by means of theory. In the communication structure of the polis, individuation has progressed to the point where the identity of the individual ego as a stable entity can only be developed through identification with abstract laws of cosmic order. Consciousness, emancipated from archaic powers, now anchors itself in the unity of a stable cosmos and the identity of immutable Being.

Thus it was only by means of ontological distinctions that theory originally could take cognizance of a self-subsistent world purged of demons. At the same time, the illusion of pure theory served as a protection against regression to an earlier stage that had been surpassed. Had it been possible to detect that the identity of pure Being was an objectivistic illusion, ego identity would not have been able to take shape on its basis. The repression of interest appertained to this interest itself.

If this interpretation is valid, then the two most influential aspects of the Greek tradition, the theoretical attitude and the basic ontological assumption of a structured, self-subsistent world, appear in a connection that they explicitly prohibit: the connection of knowledge with human interests. Hence we return to Husserl's critique of the objectivism of the sciences. But this connection turns *against* Husserl. Our reason for suspecting the presence of an unacknowledged connection between knowledge and interest is not that the sciences have abandoned the classical concept of theory, but that they have not completely abandoned it. The suspicion of objectivism exists because of the *ontological illusion of pure theory* that the sciences still deceptively share with the philosophical tradition *after casting off its practical content*.

With Husserl we shall designate as objectivistic an attitude that naively correlates theoretical propositions with matters of fact. This attitude presumes that the relations between empirical variables represented in theoretical propositions are self-existent. At the same time, it suppresses the transcendental framework that is the precondition of the meaning of the validity of such propositions. As soon as these statements are understood in relation to the prior frame of reference to which they are affixed, the objectivist illusion dissolves and makes visible a knowledge-constitutive interest.

There are three categories of processes of inquiry for which a specific connection between logical-methodological rules and knowledge-constitutive interests can be demonstrated. This demonstration is the task of a critical philosophy of science that escapes the snares of positivism.[3] The approach of the empirical-analytic sciences incorporates a *technical* cognitive interest; that of the historical-hermeneutic sciences incorporates a practical one; and the approach of critically oriented sciences incorporates the *emancipatory* cognitive interest that, as we saw, was at the root of traditional theories. I should like to clarify this thesis by means of a few examples.

V

In the *empirical-analytic sciences* the frame of reference that prejudges the meaning of possible statements establishes rules both for the construction of

3. This path has been marked out by Karl-Otto Apel. See Apel, *Analytic Philosophy of Language and the Geisteswissenschaften*, translated by Harald Holstelitie (Dordrecht: D. Reidel, 1967), and "Szientifik, Hermeneutik, Ideologiekritik [Scientificity, Hermeneutics, Ideology Critique]," in *Man and World* I (1968), pp. 37ff. [Habermas's note].

theories and for their critical testing.[4] Theories comprise hypothetico-deductive connections of propositions, which permit the deduction of lawlike hypotheses with empirical content. The latter can be interpreted as statements about the covariance of observable events; given a set of initial conditions, they make predictions possible. Empirical-analytic knowledge is thus possible predictive knowledge. However, the *meaning* of such predictions, that is their technical exploitability, is established only by the rules according to which we apply theories to reality.

In controlled observation, which often takes the form of an experiment, we generate initial conditions and measure the results of operations carried out under these conditions. Empiricism attempts to ground the objectivist illusion in observations expressed in basic statements. These observations are supposed to be reliable in providing immediate evidence without the admixture of subjectivity. In reality basic statements are not simple representations of facts in themselves, but express the success or failure of our operations. We can say that facts and the relations between them are apprehended descriptively. But this way of talking must not conceal that as such the facts relevant to the empirical sciences are first constituted through an a priori organization of our experience in the behavioral system of instrumental action.

Taken together, these two factors, that is the logical structure of admissible systems of propositions and the type of conditions for corroboration suggest that theories of the empirical sciences disclose reality subject to the constitutive interest in the possible securing and expansion, through information, of feedback-monitored action. This is the cognitive interest in technical control over objectified processes.

The *historical-hermeneutic* sciences gain knowledge in a different methodological framework. Here the meaning of the validity of propositions is not constituted in the frame of reference of technical control. The levels of formalized language and objectified experience have not yet been divorced. For theories are not constructed deductively and experience is not organized with regard to the success of operations. Access to the facts is provided by the understanding of meaning, not observation. The verification of lawlike hypotheses in the empirical-analytic sciences has its counterpart here in the interpretation of texts. Thus the rules of hermeneutics determine the possible meaning of the validity of statements of the cultural sciences.[5]

Historicism has taken the understanding of meaning, in which mental facts[6] are supposed to be given in direct evidence, and grafted onto it the objectivist illusion of pure theory. It appears as though the interpreter transposes himself into the horizon of the world or language from which a text derives its meaning. But here, too, the facts are first constituted in relation to the standards that establish them. Just as positivist self-understanding does not take into account explicitly the connection between measurement operations and feedback control, so it eliminates from consideration the interpreter's pre-understanding. Hermeneutic knowledge is always mediated through this

4. See [Karl] Popper's *The Logic of Scientific Discovery* [1959], and my paper "Analytische Wissenschaftstheorie [Analytic Theory of *Wissenschaft*]," in *Zeugnisse* (Frankfurt am Main: Europäische Verlagsanstalt, 1963), pp. 473ff. [Habermas's note].
5. I concur with the analyses in Part II of Hans-

Georg Gadamer, *Wahrheit und Methode* [Habermas's note]. For GADAMER and his *Truth and Method* (1960), see below.
6. That is, facts relating to various (cultural) forms of *Geist*.

pre-understanding, which is derived from the interpreter's initial situation. The world of traditional meaning discloses itself to the interpreter only to the extent that his own world becomes clarified at the same time. The subject of understanding establishes communication between both worlds. He comprehends the substantive content of tradition by *applying* tradition to himself and his situation.

If, however, methodological rules unite interpretation and application in this way, then this suggests that hermeneutic inquiry discloses reality subject to a constitutive interest in the preservation and expansion of the intersubjectivity of possible action-orienting mutual understanding. The understanding of meaning is directed in its very structure toward the attainment of possible consensus among actors in the framework of a self-understanding derived from tradition. This we shall call the *practical* cognitive interest, in contrast to the technical.

The systematic *sciences of social action*, that is economics, sociology, and political science, have the goal, as do the empirical-analytic sciences, of producing nomological knowledge.[7] A critical social science, however, will not remain satisfied with this. It is concerned with going beyond this goal to determine when theoretical statements grasp invariant regularities of social action as such and when they express ideologically frozen relations of dependence that can in principle be transformed. To the extent that this is the case, the *critique of ideology*, as well, moreover, as *psychoanalysis*, take into account that information about lawlike connections sets off a process of reflection in the consciousness of those whom the laws are about. Thus the level of unreflected consciousness, which is one of the initial conditions of such laws, can be transformed. Of course, to this end a critically mediated knowledge of laws cannot through reflection alone render a law itself inoperative, but it can render it inapplicable.

The methodological framework that determines the meaning of the validity of critical propositions of this category is established by the concept of *self-reflection*. The latter releases the subject from dependence on hypostatized powers. Self-reflection is determined by an emancipatory cognitive interest. Critically oriented sciences share this interest with philosophy.

However, as long as philosophy remains caught in ontology, it is itself subject to an objectivism that disguises the connection of its knowledge with the human interest in autonomy and responsibility (*Mündigkeit*). There is only one way in which it can acquire the power that it vainly claims for itself in virtue of its seeming freedom from presuppositions: by acknowledging its dependence on this interest and turning against its own illusion of pure theory the critique it directs at the objectivism of the sciences.[8]

VI

The concept of knowledge-constitutive human interests already conjoins the two elements whose relation still has to be explained: knowledge and interest.

7. Ernst Topitsche, editor, *Logik der Sozialwissenschaften* [*Logic of the Social Science*] (Cologne: 1965) [Habermas's note]. "Nomological knowledge": knowledge that takes the form of laws or lawlike generalizations and correlations.

8. Theodor W. Adorno, *Zur Metakritik der Erkenntnistheorie* [Habermas's note]. Literally, *Toward the Metacriticism of Epistemology* (1956); translated as *Against Epistemology: A Metacritique* (1982).

From everyday experience we know that ideas serve often enough to furnish our actions with justifying motives in place of the real ones. What is called rationalization at this level is called ideology at the level of collective action. In both cases the manifest content of statements is falsified by consciousness' unreflected tie to interests, despite its illusion of autonomy. The discipline of trained thought thus correctly aims at excluding such interests. In all the sciences routines have been developed that guard against the subjectivity of opinion, and a new discipline, the sociology of knowledge, has emerged to counter the uncontrolled influence of interests on a deeper level, which derive less from the individual than from the objective situation of social groups. But this accounts for only one side of the problem. Because science must secure the objectivity of its statements against the pressure and seduction of particular interests, it deludes itself about the fundamental interests to which it owes not only its impetus but *the conditions of possible objectivity* themselves.

Orientation toward technical control, toward mutual understanding in the conduct of life, and toward emancipation from seemingly "natural" constraint establish the specific viewpoints from which we can apprehend reality as such in any way whatsoever. By becoming aware of the impossibility of getting beyond these transcendental limits, a part of nature acquires, through us, autonomy in nature. If knowledge could ever outwit its innate human interest, it would be by comprehending that the mediation of subject and object that philosophical consciousness attributes exclusively to *its own* synthesis is produced originally by interests. The mind can become aware of this natural basis reflexively. Nevertheless, its power extends into the very logic of inquiry.

Representations and descriptions are never independent of standards. And the choice of these standards is based on attitudes that require critical consideration by means of arguments, because they cannot be either logically deduced or empirically demonstrated. Fundamental methodological decisions, for example such basic distinctions as those between categorial and noncategorial being, between analytic and synthetic statements, or between descriptive and emotive meaning, have the singular character of being neither arbitrary nor compelling.[9] They prove appropriate or inappropriate. For their criterion is the metalogical necessity of interests that we can neither prescribe nor represent, but with which we must instead *come to terms.* Therefore my first thesis is this: *The achievements of the transcendental subject have their basis in the natural history of the human species.*

Taken by itself this thesis could lead to the misunderstanding that reason is an organ of adaptation for men just as claws and teeth are for animals. True, it does serve this function. But the human interests that have emerged in man's natural history, to which we have traced back the three knowledge-constitutive interests, derive both from nature and *from the cultural break* with nature. Along with the tendency to realize natural drives they have incorporated the tendency toward release from the constraint of nature. Even the interest in self-preservation, natural as it seems, is represented by a social system that compensates for the lacks in man's organic equipment and secures

---

9. Morton White, *Toward Reunion in Philosophy* (Cambridge: Harvard University Press, 1956) [Habermas's note].

his historical existence *against* the force of nature threatening from without. But society is not only a system of self-preservation. An enticing natural force, present in the individual as libido, has detached itself from the behavioral system of self-preservation and urges toward utopian fulfillment.[1] These individual demands, which do not initially accord with the requirement of collective self-preservation, are also absorbed by the social system. That is why the cognitive processes to which social life is indissolubly linked function not only as means to the reproduction of life; for in equal measure they themselves determine the definitions of this life. What may appear as naked survival is always in its roots a historical phenomenon. For it is subject to the criterion of what a society intends for itself as *the good life*. My *second thesis* is thus that *knowledge equally serves as an instrument and transcends mere self-preservation.*[2]

The specific viewpoints from which, with transcendental necessity, we apprehend reality ground three categories of possible knowledge: information that expands our power of technical control; interpretations that make possible the orientation of action within common traditions; and analyses that free consciousness from its dependence on hypostatized powers. These viewpoints originate in the interest structure of a species that is linked in its roots to definite means of social organization: work, language, and power. The human species secures its existence in systems of social labor and self-assertion through violence, through tradition-bound social life in ordinary-language communication, and with the aid of ego identities that at every level of individuation reconsolidate the consciousness of the individual in relation to the norms of the group. Accordingly the interests constitutive of knowledge are linked to the functions of an ego that adapts itself to its external conditions through learning processes, is initiated into the communication system of a social life-world by means of self-formative processes, and constructs an identity in the conflict between instinctual aims and social constraints. In turn these achievements become part of the productive forces accumulated by a society, the cultural tradition through which a society interprets itself, and the legitimations that a society accepts or criticizes. My *third thesis* is thus that *knowledge-constitutive interests take form in the medium*[3] *of work, language, and power.*

However, the configuration of knowledge and interest is not the same in all categories. It is true that at this level it is always illusory to suppose an autonomy, free of presuppositions, in which knowing first grasps reality theoretically, only to be taken subsequently into the service of interests alien to it. But the mind can always reflect back upon the interest structure that joins subject and object a priori: this is reserved to self-reflection. If the latter cannot cancel out interest, it can to a certain extent make up for it.

It is no accident that the standards of self-reflection are exempted from the singular state of suspension in which those of all other cognitive processes require critical evaluation. They possess theoretical certainty. The human interest in autonomy and responsibility is not mere fancy, for it can be apprehended

---

1. This sentence points to the kind of philosophical anthropology that underlies Habermas's discussion.
2. Here Habermas takes issue with ARNOLD GEHLEN, whose kind of philosophical anthropology he took

seriously, and for whom the fundamental human interest was survival.
3. More accurately "media," since each "medium" differs significantly from the others.

a priori. What raises us out of nature is the only thing whose nature we can know: *language*. Through its structure, autonomy and responsibility are posited for us.[4] Our first sentence expresses unequivocally the intention of universal and unconstrained consensus. Taken together, autonomy and responsibility constitute the only Idea [that] we possess a priori in the sense of the philosophical tradition. Perhaps that is why the language of German Idealism, according to which "reason" contains both will and consciousness as its elements, is not quite obsolete. Reason also means the will to reason. In self-reflection knowledge for the sake of knowledge attains congruence with the interest in autonomy and responsibility. The emancipatory cognitive interest aims at the pursuit of reflection as such. My *fourth thesis* is thus that *in the power of self-reflection, knowledge and interest are one.*

However, only in an emancipated society, whose members' autonomy and responsibility had been realized,[5] would communication have developed into the non-authoritarian and universally practiced dialogue from which both our model of reciprocally constituted ego identity and our idea of true consensus are always implicitly derived. To this extent the truth of statements is based on anticipating the realization of the good life. The ontological illusion of pure theory behind which knowledge-constitutive interests become invisible promotes the fiction that Socratic dialogue is possible everywhere and at any time. From the beginning philosophy has presumed that the autonomy and responsibility posited with the structure of language are not only anticipated but real. It is pure theory, wanting to derive everything from itself, that succumbs to unacknowledged external conditions and becomes ideological. Only when philosophy discovers in the dialectical course of history the traces of violence that deform repeated attempts at dialogue and recurrently close off the path to unconstrained communication does it further the process whose suspension it otherwise legitimates: mankind's evolution toward autonomy and responsibility. My *fifth thesis* is thus that *the unity of knowledge and interest proves itself in a dialectic that takes the historical traces of suppressed dialogue and reconstructs what has been suppressed.*

VII

The sciences have retained one characteristic of philosophy: the illusion of pure theory. This illusion does not determine the practice of scientific research but only its self-understanding. And to the extent that this self-understanding reacts back upon scientific practice, it even has its point.

The glory of the sciences is their unswerving application of their methods without reflecting on knowledge-constitutive interests. From knowing not what they do methodologically, they are that much surer of their discipline, that is of methodical progress within an unproblematic framework. False consciousness[6] has a protective function. For the sciences lack the means of dealing with the risks that appear once the connection of knowledge and human interest has been comprehended on the level of self-reflection. It was

4. An important claim for Habermas's philosophical anthropology.
5. An idea that echoes the selection above from MARX's *Capital*, vol. 3.

6. A Marxist term referring to the tendency to view reality in ways congruent with the interests of the dominant orthodoxy rather than in ways that reflect one's own class interest.

possible for fascism to give birth to the freak of a national physics and Stalin-ism to that of a Soviet Marxist genetics[7] (which deserves to be taken more seriously than the former) only because the illusion of objectivism was lack-ing. It would have been able to provide immunity against the more dangerous bewitchments of misguided reflection.

But the praise of objectivism has its limits. Husserl's critique was right to attack it, if not with the right means. As soon as the objectivist illusion is turned into an affirmative *Weltanschauung*,[8] methodologically unconscious necessity is perverted to the dubious virtue of a scientistic profession of faith. Objectivism in no way prevents the sciences from intervening in the conduct of life, as Husserl thought it did. They are integrated into it in any case. But they do not of themselves develop their practical efficacy in the direction of a growing rationality of action.

Instead, the positivist self-understanding of the *nomological sciences* lends countenance to the substitution of technology for enlightened action. It directs the utilization of scientific information from an illusory viewpoint, namely that the practical mastery of history can be reduced to technical control of objectified processes. The objectivist self-understanding of the *hermeneutic sciences* is of no lesser consequence. It defends sterilized knowledge against the reflected appropriation of active traditions and locks up history in a museum. Guided by the objectivist attitude of theory as the image of facts, the nomological and hermeneutical sciences reinforce each other with regard to their practical consequences. The latter displace our connection with tra-dition into the realm of the arbitrary, while the former, on the levelled-off basis of the repression of history, squeeze the conduct of life into the behavioral system of instrumental action. The dimension in which acting subjects could arrive rationally at agreement about goals and purposes is surrendered to the obscure area of mere decision among reified value systems and irrational beliefs.[9] When this dimension, abandoned by all men of good will, is subjected to reflection that relates to history objectivistically, as did the philosophical tradition, then positivism triumphs at the highest level of thought, as with Comte.[1] This happens when critique uncritically abdicates its own connection with the emancipatory knowledge-constitutive interest in favor of pure theory. This sort of high-flown critique projects the undecided process of the evolution of the human species onto the level of a philosophy of history that dogmati-cally issues instructions for action. *A delusive philosophy of history, however, is only the obverse of deluded decisionism.* Bureaucratically prescribed partisan-ship goes only too well with contemplatively misunderstood value freedom.

These practical consequences of a restricted, scientistic consciousness of the sciences[2] can be countered by a critique that destroys the illusion of objectiv-ism. Contrary to Husserl's expectations, objectivism is eliminated not through

---

7. The Soviet leader Joseph Stalin (1878–1953) effec-tively outlawed scientific research in standard gene-tics, favoring instead a theory that stressed environ-mentally acquired inheritance. "National physics": in the 1930s, under the Nazis, there was a movement to ban the teaching of relativity and quantum phys-ics in Germany for ideological reasons.
8. Worldview (German).
9. See my essay "Dogmatismus, Vernunft und

Entscheidung" (Dogmatism, Reason, and Deci-sion) in *Theorie und Praxis* [*Theory and Practice* (1963); Habermas's note].
1. Auguste Comte (1798–1857), French philosopher and social theorist who was a leading figure in developing a positivist theory of knowledge into a positivist social theory and discipline (sociology).
2. In *One-Dimensional Man* (Boston: Beacon, 1964) Herbert Marcuse has analyzed the dangers of the

the power of renewed *theoria* but through demonstrating what it conceals: the connection of knowledge and interest. Philosophy remains true to its classic tradition by renouncing it. The insight that the truth of statements is linked in the last analysis to the intention of the good and true life can be preserved today only on the ruins of ontology. However even this philosophy remains a specialty alongside of the sciences and outside public consciousness as long as the heritage that it has critically abandoned lives on in the positivistic self-understanding of the sciences.

SOURCE: Jürgen Habermas, appendix to *Knowledge and Human Interests*, trans. Jeremy J. Shapiro (Boston: Beacon Press, 1971), pp. 301–17. Except where otherwise indicated, German words in brackets are the terminology used in the German original, inserted by the editor in addition to their renderings in the translation. This essay was originally published separately as "Erkenntnis und Interesse" in the journal *Merkur* (1965), then reprinted in *Technik und Wissenschaft als "Ideologie"* (1968, *Technology and Science as "Ideology"*); it was not included in the original version of the book published under the title *Erkenntnis und Interesse* in 1968.

From The Theory of Communicative Action, Volume 1
Reason and the Rationalization of Society

From *1. Introduction: Approaches to the Problem of Rationality*

The rationality of beliefs and actions is a theme usually dealt with in philosophy. One could even say that philosophical thought originates in reflection on the reason embodied in cognition, speech, and action; and reason remains its basic theme.[1] From the beginning philosophy has endeavored to explain the world as a whole, the unity in the multiplicity of appearances, with principles to be discovered in reason—and not in communication with a divinity beyond the world nor, strictly speaking, even in returning to the ground of a cosmos encompassing nature and society. Greek thought did not aim at a theology nor at an ethical cosmology, as the great world religions did, but at an ontology. If there is anything common to philosophical theories, it is the intention of thinking being or the unity of the world by way of explicating reason's experience of itself.

---

reduction of reason to technical rationality and the reduction of society to the dimension of technical control. In another context, Helmut Schelsky has made the same diagnosis:

> With a scientific civilization that man himself creates according to plan, a new peril has entered the world: the danger that man will develop himself only in external actions of altering the environment, and keep and deal with everything, himself and other human beings, at this object level of constructive action. This new self-alienation of man, which can rob him of his own and others' identity . . . is the danger of the creator losing himself in his work, the constructor in his creation. Man may recoil from completely transcending himself toward self-produced objectivity, toward constructed being; yet he

works incessantly at extending this process of scientific self-objectification.

See Schelsky's *Einsamkeit und Freiheit* [*Solitude and Freedom*] (Hamburg: 1963), p. 299 [Habermas's note]. Marcuse (1898–1979), German-born American political philosopher. Schelsky (1912–1984), German sociologist.

1. See Bruno Snell, *Die Entdeckung des Geistes* [*The Discovery of Geist*] (Hamburg, 1946); Hans-Georg Gadamer, "Platon und die Vorsokraticker [Plato and the Presocratics]," in *Kleine Schriften* (Tübingen, 1977), 4:14ff. and "Mythos und Vernunft [Myth and Reason]," 4:48ff.; W. Schadewalt, *Die Anfänge der Philosophie bei den Griechen* [*The Beginnings of Philosophy among the Greeks*] (Frankfurt, 1978) [Habermas's note]. FOR GADAMER, see below.

In speaking this way, I am drawing upon the language of modern philosophy. But the philosophical tradition, insofar as it suggests the possibility of a philosophical worldview, has become questionable.[2] Philosophy can no longer refer to the whole of the world, of nature, of history, of society, in the sense of a totalizing knowledge. Theoretical surrogates for worldviews have been devalued, not only by the factual advance of empirical science but even more by the reflective consciousness accompanying it. With this consciousness philosophical thought has withdrawn self-critically behind itself; in the question of what it can accomplish with its reflective competence *within the framework* of scientific conventions, it has become metaphilosophy.[3] Its theme has thereby changed, and yet it remains the same. In contemporary philosophy, wherever coherent argumentation has developed around constant thematic cores—in logic and the theory of science, in the theory of language and meaning, in ethics and action theory, even in aesthetics—interest is directed to the formal conditions of rationality in knowing, in reaching understanding through language, and in acting, both in everyday contexts and at the level of methodically organized experience or systematically organized discourse. The theory of argumentation thereby takes on a special significance; to it falls the task of reconstructing the formal-pragmatic presuppositions and conditions of an explicitly rational behavior.

If this diagnosis points in the right direction, if it is true that philosophy in its postmetaphysical, post-Hegelian currents is converging toward the point of a *theory of rationality*, how can sociology[4] claim any competence for the rationality problematic? We have to bear in mind that philosophical thought, which has surrendered the relation to totality, also loses its self-sufficiency. To the goal of formally analyzing the conditions of rationality, we can tie neither ontological hopes for substantive theories of nature, history, society, and so forth, nor transcendental-philosophical hopes for an aprioristic reconstruction of the equipment of a nonempirical species subject, of consciousness in general. All attempts at discovering ultimate foundations, in which the intentions of First Philosophy live on, have broken down.[5] In this situation, the way is opening to a new constellation in the relationship of philosophy and the sciences. As can be seen in the case of the history and philosophy of science, formal explication of the conditions of rationality and empirical analysis of the embodiment and historical development of rationality structures mesh in a peculiar way. Theories of modern empirical science, whether along the lines of logical empiricism, critical rationalism, or constructivism, make a normative and at the same time universalistic claim that is no longer

2. See Jürgen Habermas, "Does Philosophy Still Have a Purpose?," in *Philosophical-Political Profiles* (MIT Press, forthcoming [1983]) [Habermas's note].
3. See Richard Rorty, ed., *The Linguistic Turn* (Chicago, 1967) and *Philosophy and the Mirror of Nature* (Princeton, N.J., 1979) [Habermas's note]. For Rorty, see this anthology's companion volume, *The Analytic Tradition*.
4. In Germany, sociology has long been a theoretical discipline closely related to the interpretive tradition in philosophy. Habermas is thinking and writing from a standpoint that bridges them, as had WILHELM DILTHEY and the Frankfurt School of critical social theory that significantly influenced him.

5. On the critique of First Philosophy, see Theodor Adorno, *Against Epistemology* (Cambridge, Mass., 1983); for an opposed view, see Karl-Otto Apel, "Das Problem der philosophischen Letztbegründung im Lichte einer transzendentalen Sprachpragmatik [The Problem of Fundamental Grounding in Philosophy in the Light of a Transcendental Pragmatics of Language]," in B. Kanitschneider, ed., *Sprache und Erkenntnis* (Innsbruck, 1976), pp. 55ff. [Habermas's note]. "First Philosophy": originally metaphysics (the study of "being as such"), but the influence of Descartes' *Meditations on First Philosophy* (1641) gave epistemology primacy in philosophy.

covered by fundamental assumptions of an ontological or transcendental-philosophical nature. This claim can be tested only against the evidence of counterexamples, and it can hold up in the end only if reconstructive theory proves itself capable of distilling internal aspects of the history of science and systematically explaining, in conjunction with empirical analyses, the actual, narratively documented history of science in the context of social development.[6] What is true of so complex a configuration of cognitive rationality as modern science holds also for other forms of objective spirit, that is, other embodiments of rationality, be they cognitive and instrumental or moral-practical, perhaps even aesthetic-practical.

Empirically oriented sciences of this kind must, as regards their basic concepts, be laid out in such a way that they can link up with rational reconstructions of meaning constellations and problem solutions.[7] Cognitive developmental psychology provides an example of that. In the tradition of Piaget,[8] cognitive development in the narrow sense, as well as socio-cognitive and moral development, is conceptualized as internally reconstructible sequences of stages of competence.[9] On the other hand, if the validity claims against which we measure problem solutions, rational-action orientations, learning levels, and the like are reinterpreted in an empiricist fashion and defined away—as they are in behaviorism—processes of embodying rationality structures cannot be interpreted as learning processes in the strict sense, but at best as an increase in adaptive capacities.

Among the social sciences sociology is most likely to link its basic concepts to the rationality problematic. There are historical and substantive reasons for this, as a comparison with other disciplines will show. *Political science* had to free itself from rational natural law; even modern natural law started from the old-European view that represented society as a politically constituted community integrated through legal norms. The new concepts of bourgeois formal law made it possible to proceed constructively and, from normative points of view, to project the legal-political order as a rational mechanism.[1] An empirically oriented political science had to dissociate itself radically from that view. It concerned itself with politics as a societal subsystem and absolved itself of the task of conceiving society as a whole. In opposition to natural-law normativism, it excluded moral-practical questions of legitimacy from scientific consideration, or it treated them as empirical questions about descriptively ascertainable beliefs in legitimacy. It thereby broke off relations to the rationality problematic.

6. See the discussions in connection with Thomas Kuhn's *The Structure of Scientific Revolutions* ([1960; 2nd ed.,] Chicago, 1972) [Habermas's note]. For Kuhn, see this anthology's companion volume, *The Analytic Tradition*.

7. See Ulrich Oevermann, "Programmatische Überlegungen zu einer Theorie der Bildungsprozesse und einer Strategie der Socialisationsforschung" ["Programmatic Reflections toward a Theory of Educational Processes and a Strategy of Socialization Research"], in K. Hurrelmann, ed., *Socialisation und Lebenslauf* (Hamburg, 1976), pp. 34ff. [Habermas's note].

8. Jean Piaget (1896–1980), Swiss psychologist and a major figure in 20th-century developmental psychology.

9. See R. Döbert, J. Habermas, and G. Nunner-Winkler, eds., *Entwicklung des Ichs* [*Development of the I*] (Köln, 1977) [Habermas's note].

1. See W. Hennis, *Politik und praktische Philosophie* [*Politics and Practical Philosophy*] (Neuwied, 1963); H. Maier, *Die ältere deutsche Staats- und Verwaltungslehre* [*Traditional German Political and Administrative Theory*] (Neuwied, 1966); and J. Habermas, "The Classical Doctrine of Politics in Relation to Social Philosophy," in *Theory and Practice* (Boston, 1973), pp. 41–81 [Habermas's note].

The situation is somewhat different in *political economy*. In the eighteenth century it entered into competition with rational natural law and brought out the independence of an action system held together through functions and not primarily through norms.[2] As political economy, economics still held fast at the start to the relation to society as a whole that is characteristic of crisis theories. It was concerned with questions of how the dynamic of the economic system affected the orders through which society was normatively integrated. Economics as a specialized science has broken off that relation. Now it too concerns itself with the economy as a subsystem of society and absolves itself from questions of legitimacy. From this perspective it can tailor problems of rationality to considerations of economic equilibrium and questions of rational choice.

In contrast, *sociology* originated as a discipline responsible for the problems that politics and economics pushed to one side on their way to becoming specialized sciences.[3] Its theme was the changes in social integration brought about within the structure of old-European societies by the rise of the modern system of national states and by the differentiation of a market-regulated economy. Sociology became the science of crisis par excellence; it concerned itself above all with the anomic aspects of the dissolution of traditional social systems and the development of modern ones.[4] Even under these initial conditions, sociology could have confined itself to one subsystem, as the other social sciences did. From the perspective of the history of science, the sociologies of religion and law formed the core of the new discipline in any case.

If I may—for illustrative purposes and, for the time being, without further elaboration—refer to the schema of functions proposed by Parsons,[5] the correlations between *social-scientific disciplines* and *subsystems of society* readily emerge (*see* Figure 1).

Figure 1

	A		G	
Economics	Economy		Polity	Political Science
Cultural Anthropology	Culture		Societal Community	Sociology
	L		I	

A: adaptation, G: goal-attainment,
I: integration, L: pattern-maintenance

2. See F. Jonas, "Was heisst ökonomische Theorie? Vorklassisches und klassisches Denken [What Is Economic Theory? Preclassical and Classical Thinking]," in *Schmollers Jahrbuch* 78 (1958); and H. Neuendorff, *Der Begriff des Interesses [The Concept of Interest]* (Frankfurt, 1973) [Habermas's note].

3. See F. Jonas, *Geschichte der Soziologie [History of Sociology]*, vols. I–IV (Reinbek, 1968/69); R. W. Friedrichs, *A Sociology of Sociology* (New York, 1970); and T. Bottomore and R. Nisbet, *A History of Sociological Analysis* (New York, 1978) [Habermas's note]. Habermas is describing sociology in German-speaking Europe; it is not clear that his claim was ever true in the English-speaking world.

4. Jürgen Habermas, "Kritische und konservativen Aufgaben der Soziologie" [Critical and Conservative Tasks of Sociology]," in *Theorie und Praxis* (Frankfurt, 1971), pp. 290–306 [Habermas's note].

5. Talcott Parsons (1902–1979), the leading American sociologist of the mid-20th century. He first proposed this scheme in *Working Papers in the Theory of Action* (1953), co-written with Robert Bales and Edward Shils.

To be sure, there has been no lack of attempts to make sociology a specialized science for social integration. But it is no accident—rather a symptom—that the great social theorists I shall discuss are fundamentally sociologists. Alone among the disciplines of social science, sociology has retained its relations to problems of society as a whole. Whatever else it has become, it has always remained a theory of society as well. As a result, sociology could not, as other disciplines could, shove aside questions of rationalization, redefine them, or cut them down to small size. As far as I can see, there are two reasons for that.

The first concerns *cultural anthropology* and sociology equally. The correlation of basic functions with social subsystems conceals the fact that social interactions in the domains important to cultural reproduction, social integration, and socialization are not at all specialized in the same way as interactions in the economic and political domains of action. Both sociology and cultural anthropology are confronted with the whole spectrum of manifestations of social action and not with relatively clear-cut types of action that can be stylized to variants of purposive-rational action with regard to problems of maximizing profit or acquiring and using political power. Both disciplines are concerned with everyday practice in lifeworld contexts and must, therefore, take into account *all* forms of symbolic interaction. It is not so easy for them to push aside the basic problem of action theory and of interpretation. They encounter structures of a lifeworld that underlie the other subsystems, which are functionally specified in a different way. We shall take up below the question of how the paradigmatic conceptualizations "lifeworld" and "system" relate to one another.[6] Here I would like only to stress that the investigation of societal community and culture cannot be as easily detached from the lifeworld paradigm as the investigation of the economic and political subsystems can. That explains the stubborn connection of sociology to the theory of society.

Why it is sociology and not cultural anthropology that has shown a particular willingness to take up the problem of rationality can be understood only if we take into consideration a circumstance mentioned above. Sociology arose as the theory of bourgeois society; to it fell the task of explaining the course of the capitalist modernization of traditional societies and its anomic side effects.[7] This problem, a result of the objective historical situation, formed the reference point from which sociology worked out its foundational problems as well. On a *metatheoretical level* it chose basic concepts that were tailored to the growth of rationality in the modern lifeworld. Almost without exception, the classical figures of sociological thought attempted to lay out their action theory in such a way that its basic categories would capture the most important aspects of the transition from "community" to "society."[8] On a *methodological level* the problem of gaining access to the object domain of symbolic objects through "understanding" was dealt with correspondingly;

---

6. See Chap. VI, Vol. 2 [Habermas's note]. "Intermediate Reflections: System and Lifeworld," in *Lifeworld and System: A Critique of Functionalist Reason* (1981), the second volume of *The Theory of Communicative Action*.
7. See H. Neuendorff, "Soziologie," in *Evangelisches Staatslexikon* (Stuttgart, 1975), pp. 2424ff.

[Habermas's note].
8. On the paired concepts of the older sociology, see J. Habermas, "Technology and Science as 'Ideology,'" in *Toward a Rational Society* (Boston, 1970), pp. 81–122; and C. W. Mills, *The Sociological Imagination* (Oxford, 1959) [Habermas's note].

understanding rational orientations of action became the reference point for understanding all action orientations.

This connection between (a) the *metatheoretical* question of a framework for action theory conceived with a view to the rationalizable aspects of action, and (b) the *methodological* question of a theory of interpretive understanding [*Sinnverstehen*] that clarifies the internal relation between meaning and validity (between explicating the meaning of a symbolic expression and taking a position on its implicit validity claim), was connected with (c) the *empirical* question—whether and in what sense the modernization of a society can be described from the standpoint of cultural and societal rationalization. This connection emerged with particular clarity in the work of Max Weber.[9] His hierarchy of concepts of action is designed with an eye to the type of purposive-rational action, so that all other actions can be classified as specific deviations from this type. Weber also analyzes the method of *Sinnverstehen* in such a way that complex cases can be related to the limit case of understanding purposive-rational action; understanding action that is subjectively oriented to success requires at the same time that it be objectively evaluated as to its correctness (according to standards of *Richtigkeitstrationalität*[1]). Finally, the connection of these conceptual and methodological decisions with Weber's central theoretical question—how Occidental rationalism can be explained—is evident.

This connection could, of course, be contingent; it could indicate merely that Weber was personally preoccupied with these problems and that this—from a theoretical point of view—contingent interest affected his theory construction down to its foundations. One has only to detach modernization processes from the concept of rationalization and to view them in *other* perspectives, so it seems, in order to free the foundations of action theory from connotations of the rationality of action and to free the methodology of interpretive understanding from a problematic intertwining of questions of meaning with questions of validity. Against that, I would like to defend the thesis that there were compelling reasons for Weber to treat the historically contingent question of Occidental rationalism, as well as the question of the meaning of modernity and the question of the causes and side effects of the capitalist modernization of society, from the perspectives of rational action, rational conduct of life, and rationalized worldviews. I want to defend the thesis that there are systematic reasons for the interconnection of the precisely three rationality themes one finds in his work. To put it a different way, *any* sociology that claims to be a theory of society has to face the problem of rationality simultaneously on the *metatheoretical, methodological,* and *empirical* levels.

I shall begin (1) with a provisional discussion of the concept of rationality, and then (2) place this concept in the evolutionary perspective of the rise of a modern understanding of the world. After these preliminaries, I shall point out the internal connection between the theory of rationality and social theory: on the one hand, at the metatheoretical level (3) by demonstrating the rationality implications of sociological concepts of action current today; on the other hand, at the methodological level (4) by showing that similar implications

9. German philosopher and social theorist (1864–1920); he was a key figure in the development of sociology and social philosophy.

1. Correctness rationality (German).

follow from approaching the object domain by way of interpretive understanding. This argumentation sketch is meant to demonstrate the need for a
theory of communicative action that arises when we want to take up once
again, and, in a suitable way, the problematic of societal rationalization,
which was largely ousted from professional sociological discussion after Weber.

* * *

3. Relations to the World and Aspects of Rationality in Four Sociological Concepts of Action

The concept of communicative rationality[2] that emerged from our provisional
analysis of the use of the linguistic expression "rational" and from our review
of the anthropological debate concerning the status of the modern understanding of the world is in need of a more precise explication. I shall pursue
this task only indirectly, by way of a formal-pragmatic clarification of the concept of communicative action, and only within the limits of a systematic look
at certain positions in the history of social theory. We can begin with the claim
that the concept of communicative rationality has to be analyzed in connection with achieving understanding in language. The concept of reaching an
understanding suggests a rationally motivated agreement among participants
that is measured against criticizable validity claims. The validity claims (propositional truth, normative rightness, and subjective truthfulness) characterize different categories of a knowledge embodied in symbolic expressions.
These expressions can be more closely analyzed in two ways—with respect to
how they can be defended and with respect to how actors relate through them
to something in a world. The concept of communicative rationality points,
on the one side, to different forms of discursively redeeming validity claims
(thus Wellmer[3] speaks also of discursive rationality); on the other side, it points
to relations to the world that communicative actors take up in raising validity
claims for their expressions. Thus the decentration of our understanding of
the world proved to be the most important dimension of the development of
worldviews. I shall pursue no further the discussion of the theory of argumentation. However, if we return to the thesis introduced at the outset—that
every sociology with theoretical pretensions faces the problem of rationality
on both the metatheoretical and methodological planes—we come upon the
path of examining formal concepts of the world.

I would like to support the first part of my thesis by drawing out the "ontological"—in the broader sense—presuppositions of *four action concepts* relevant to theory formation in the social sciences. I shall analyze the rationality
implications of these concepts in connection with the *relations between actor
and world* presupposed by each. Generally the connection between social
action and actor-world relations is not explicitly established in sociological

2. The kind of rationality that is implicit in and
presupposed by the very phenomenon or practice
of "communication" between and among creatures like ourselves (and the central concept of
Habermas's later thought). The "provisional analysis" of the term "rational" and the "review of the
anthropological debate" occupied sections 1

and 2, not included here.
3. Albrecht Wellmer (b. 1933), German philosopher; in the previous section (not included here),
Habermas notes his indebtedness to an unpublished
manuscript by Wellmer, "On Rationality," vols.
I–IV (1977).

theories of action. One exception is I. C. Jarvie, who makes interesting use of Popper's three-world theory.[4] In order to clarify the concepts of the objective, social, and subjective worlds that I have introduced in a provisional way, I shall (a) examine Popper's theory of the third world, and then (b) analyze the concepts of teleological, normatively regulated, and dramaturgical action in terms of actor-world relations. This reconstruction will then make it possible to (c) introduce the concept of communicative action.

A.—In his 1967 address, "Epistemology Without a Knowing Subject," Popper makes an unexpected proposal:

> We may distinguish the following three worlds or universes: first the world of physical objects or physical states; secondly, the world of states of consciousness, or of mental states, or perhaps of behavioral dispositions to act; and thirdly, the world of *objective contents of thought*, especially of scientific and poetic thoughts and of works of art.[5]

Later Popper speaks generally about the world of "the products of the human mind."[6] He stresses that those internal relations between symbolic formations that still wait for discovery and explication by the human mind also have to be included in the third world.[7] In the present context we are not interested in the special epistemological considerations that induced Popper to fasten on to Frege's concept of *Gedanken*,[8] to take up Husserl's critique of psychologism, and to claim a status independent of mental acts and states for the semantic contents of symbolic—as a rule, linguistically objectivated—productions of the human mind; nor are we interested in the proposed solution to the problem of the relation between mind and body that he develops with the help of the concept of the third world.[9] It is, however, of interest that in both cases Popper is criticizing the fundamental empiricist conception of a subject that confronts the world in an unmediated way, receives impressions from it through sense perceptions, or influences states in it through actions.

This problem context explains why he understands his doctrine of objective mind [*Geist*] as a critical extension of the empiricist concept and introduces both objective and subjective mind [*Geist*] as "worlds," that is, as special totalities of entities. The older theories of objective mind or spirit [*Geist*] developed in the historicist and neo-Hegelian traditions from Dilthey to Theodor

---

4. I. C. Jarvie, *Concepts and Society* (London, 1972), pp. 147ff. [Habermas's note]. Ian Charles Jarvie (b. 1937), British-born philosopher who studied with Karl Popper (1902–1994), a prominent British philosopher of science. For Popper, see this anthology's second volume, *The Analytic Tradition*.
5. K. R. Popper, *Objective Knowledge* (Oxford, 1972), p. 106 [Habermas's note]. Popper here figures as a surprising latter-day counterpart in the analytic tradition to MAX SCHELER, whose idea of a realm of *Geist* transcending the world of nature he here parallels (see above).
6. K. R. Popper and J. C. Eccles, *The Self and Its*

Brain (New York, 1977), p. 38 [Habermas's note].
7. K. R. Popper, "Reply to My Critics," in P. A. Schilpp, ed., *The Philosophy of Karl Popper* (La Salle, Ill., 1974), p. 1050 [Habermas's note].
8. Thoughts (German). Gottlob Frege (1848–1925), German mathematician and philosopher who was a founder of modern mathematical logic; see this anthology's companion volume, *The Analytic Tradition*. His essay "The Thought" (1918) was very influential in that tradition.
9. Popper and Eccles, *The Self and Its Brain*, pp. 100ff. [Habermas's note].

Litt and Hans Freyer[1] start from an active mind [*Geist*] that expounds itself in the worlds it constitutes. By contrast, Popper holds fast to the primacy of the world in relation to mind and construes the second and third worlds analogously to the first, in *ontological* terms. In this regard, his construction of the third world is reminiscent of Nicolai Hartmann's theory of mental being [*geistigen Sein*].[2]

The world counts as[3] the totality of what is the case; and what is the case can be stated in the form of true propositions. Starting from this general concept of the world, Popper specifies the concepts of the first, second, and third worlds by the way in which states of affairs exist. The entities belonging to each of these three worlds have a specific mode of being: physical objects and events, mental states and episodes, and semantic contents of symbolic formations.

As Nicolai Hartmann distinguished between objectivated and objective *Geist*, Popper distinguishes between explicit semantic contents that are already *embodied* in phonemes and written signs, in color or stone, in machines, and so forth, on the one hand, and those implicit semantic contents that are not yet "discovered," not yet objectified in carrier objects of the first world, but are simply inherent in already embodied meanings.

These "unembodied world 3 objects"[4] are an important indicator of the independence of the world of objective mind. Symbolic formations are, it is true, generated by the productive human mind; but though they are themselves products, they confront subjective mind with the objectivity of a problematic, uncomprehended complex of meaning that can be opened up only through intellectual labor. The *products* of the human mind immediately turn against it as *problems*.

These problems are clearly autonomous. They are in no sense made by us; rather, they are discovered by us; and in this sense they exist, undiscovered, before their discovery. Moreover, at least some of these unsolved problems may be insoluble. In our attempts to solve these or other problems we may invent new theories. These theories, again, are produced by us: they are the product of our critical and creative thinking in which we are greatly helped by other established theories inhabiting the third world. Yet the moment we have produced these theories, they create new, unintended and unexpected problems, autonomous problems, problems to be discovered. This explains why the third world, which in its origin is our product, is *autonomous* in what may be called its ontological status. It explains why we can act upon it and add to it or help its growth, even though no one can master even a small corner of this world. All of us contribute to its growth, but almost all of our individual contributions are vanishingly small. All of us try to grasp it, and none of us could live without being in contact with it, for all of us make use of speech, without which we would hardly be human. Yet the third world has grown far

---

1. German sociologist and philosopher (1887–1969). Litt (1880–1962), German cultural and social philosopher.
2. Nicolai Hartmann, *Das Problem des geistigen Seins* [*The Problem of Mental Being*] (Berlin, 1932) [Habermas's note]. Hartmann (1882–1950), Baltic German philosopher who divided *Geist* into the

personal (the *Geist* of the individual), the objective (the *Geist* of communities), and the objectivated (the realization of *Geist* in objective existence).
3. That is, may be considered to consist of.
4. Popper and Eccles, *The Self and Its Brain*, pp. 41ff. [Habermas's note].

beyond the grasp not only of any individual but even of all individuals (as shown by the existence of insoluble problems).[5]

Two noteworthy consequences follow from this description of the third world. The first concerns *interaction between the worlds*, the second *the cognitivistically abridged interpretation of the third world*. In Popper's view the first and second worlds are in immediate interchange, as are the second and third. By contrast, the first and third worlds interact only through the mediation of the second. This entails a renunciation of two fundamental empiricist conceptions. On the one hand, the entities of the third world cannot be reduced—as forms of expression of subjective mind—to mental states, that is, to entities of the second world. On the other hand, the relations between entities of the first and second worlds cannot be conceived exclusively in terms of the causal model that holds for relations between entities of the first world themselves. Popper bars the way both to a psychologistic conception of objective mind and to a physicalistic conception of subjective mind. The autonomy of the third world guarantees instead that knowledge of, as well as intervention into, states of the objective world are mediated through discovery of the independence of internal meaning connections. "And [thus] it is impossible to interpret either the third world as a mere expression of the second, or the second as the mere reflection of the third."[6]

In other respects Popper remains tied to the empiricist context from which he is distancing himself. Cognitive-instrumental relations between the knowing and acting subject on the one hand, and things and events appearing in the world on the other, are so much the center of his attention that they dominate the exchange between subjective and objective mind. The process of bringing forth, externalizing, penetrating, and assimilating products of the human mind primarily serves the growth of *theoretical knowledge* and the expansion of *technically utilizable knowledge*. The development of science, which Popper understands as a cumulative feedback process involving initial problems, creative formation of hypotheses, critical testing, revision, and discovery of new problems, not only serves as the model for subjective mind's grasp of the world of objective mind; according to Popper, the third world is *essentially made up* of problems, theories, and arguments. He does also mention, in addition to theories and tools, social institutions and works of art as examples of entities in the third world; but he sees in them only variant forms of embodiment of propositional contents. Strictly speaking, the third world is the totality of Fregian *Gedanken*, whether true or false, embodied or not: "Theories, or propositions, or statements are the most important third-world linguistic entities."[7]

Popper not only conceives of the third world in ontological terms as a totality of entities with a specific mode of being; within this framework he also understands it in a one-sided manner, from the conceptual perspective of the development of science: the third world encompasses the scientifically processed, cognitive components of the cultural traditon.[8]

---

5. Popper, *Objective Knowledge*, pp. 180–81 [Habermas's note].
6. Ibid., pp. 168–69 [Habermas's note and brackets].
7. Ibid., p. 157 [Habermas's note].

8. This is an oversimplification, because Popper states that the "third world" also encompasses the "objective contents" of "poetic thoughts and of works of art."

Both aspects prove to be severe restrictions in the attempt to make Popper's concept of the third world useful for the foundations of sociology. I. C. Jarvie starts from the phenomenological sociology of knowledge inspired by Alfred Schutz, which conceives of society as a social construction of the everyday world that issues from the interpretive processes of acting subjects and congeals to objectivity.[9] But he analyzes the ontological status of the social life-context, which is produced by the human mind and yet preserves a relative independence in relation to it, on the model of the third world.

> We have argued, then, that the social is an independent realm between the hard physical world and soft mental world: This realm, reality, world, whatever we choose to call it, is very diverse and complex and people in society are constantly striving by trial and error to come to terms with it; to map it; to coordinate their maps of it. Living in an unmanageably large and changing society permits neither perfect mapping, nor perfect coordination of maps. This means that the members of the society are constantly learning about it; both the society and its members are in a constant process of self-discovery and of self-making.[1]

This proposal throws light on the interesting connection between a sociological concept of action and the relations of actor to world presupposed therein. On the other hand, carrying Popper's three-world theory over from epistemological to action-theoretic contexts makes the weaknesses of the construction visible. In adopting Popper's concept of the third world to characterize social relations and institutions, Jarvie has to represent socially acting subjects on the model of theory-forming and problem-solving scientists: in the lifeworld everyday theories compete in a way similar to scientific theories in the community of investigators.

> People living in a society have to find their way around it, both to accomplish what they want and to avoid what they do not want. We might say that to do this they construct in their minds a conceptual map of the society and its features, of their own location among them, of the possible paths which will lead them to their goals, and of the hazards along each path. The maps are in a way "softer" than geographic maps—like dream maps they create the terrain they are mapping. Yet in a way this is a harder reality: geographical maps are never real but sometimes reflect real terrains, yet social maps *are* terrains to be studied and mapped by other people.[2]

There are at least three difficulties with this proposal.

a) In the first place, Jarvie blurs the distinction between a performative and a hypothetical-reflective attitude toward cultural tradition. In communicative everyday practice, the agent draws on the available cultural store of background knowledge to arrive at situation definitions capable of consensus.

---

9. Peter Berger and Thomas Luckmann, *The Social Construction of Reality* (New York, 1966) [Habermas's note]. Schutz (1899–1959), Austrian-born philosopher and sociologist who emigrated to the United States in 1939; he was the leading proponent of a form of Husserlian-phenomenological approach to analyzing human social reality.
1. Jarvie, *Concepts and Society*, p. 165 [Habermas's note].
2. Ibid., p. 161 [Habermas's note].

In the process, disagreements can arise that make it necessary to revise individual interpretive patterns; but the application of traditional knowledge from the backround is not equivalent to the hypothetical treatment of knowledge that is systematically questioned. Under the pressure for decision in a given action situation, the layman takes part in interactions with the intention of coordinating the actions of participants through a process of reaching understanding, that is, by employing common cultural knowledge. Certainly the scientist takes part in interactions as well; but in his case the cooperative processes of interpretation serve the end of testing the validity of *problematic* items of knowledge. The aim is not the coordination of actions, but the criticism and growth of knowledge.

b) Further, Jarvie neglects the elements of cultural tradition that cannot be reduced to *Gedanken* or propositions admitting of truth. He limits the objective complexes of meaning that acting subjects both produce and discover to *cognitive interpretations* in the narrow sense. In this respect Popper's model of the third world is particularly implausible, for the action-orienting power of cultural values is at least as important for interactions as that of theories.[3] Either the status of societal entities is assimilated to that of theories—and then we can't explain how social structures can shape motives for action; or, in view of the fact that descriptive, normative, and evaluative meanings interpenetrate in everyday theories, the model of scientific theories is not meant to be taken so seriously—and then we can conceive an interrelation between motives and third-world concepts; however this approach would make it necessary to expand Popper's version of the third world in such a way that the normative reality of society would owe its independence vis-a-vis subjective mind not—and not even primarily—to the autonomy of truth claims, but to the binding character of values and norms. That raises the question of how the components of cultural tradition that are relevant to social integration can be understood as systems of knowledge and connected with validity claims *analogous* to truth.

c) In my view, the most serious weakness in Jarvie's proposal is that it permits no distinction between cultural values and the institutional embodiment of values in norms. Institutions are supposed to issue from processes of reaching understanding among acting subjects (and to solidify as objective meaning complexes in relation to them) in a way similar to that in which, on Popper's view, problems, theories, and arguments issue from cognitive processes. With this model we can, it is true, explain the conceptual nature and the relative independence of social reality, but not the specific resistance and *coercive* character of established norms and existing institutions through which societal formations are distinguished from cultural. Jarvie himself remarks at one point: "Unlike a true idea the status of which is not threatened even by universal disbelief, social entities can be jeopardized by universal disbelief—a widespread disinclination to treat them seriously."[4] Thus it makes sense to distinguish, as Parsons does, the domain of institutionalized values from the domain of free-floating cultural values. The latter do not have the same obligatory character as legitimate norms of action.

---

3. It is arguable that Popper himself opened the door of his "third world" concept in that direction by making reference to the "objective contents" of aesthetic thoughts and objects in the statement Habermas cites at the outset of "A."
4. Ibid., p. 153 [Habermas's note].

Jarvie's strategy of employing Popper's three-world theory is instructive in that it reveals the ontological presuppositions that enter into sociological concepts of action. If we wish to avoid the weaknesses in Jarvie's proposal, it will be necessary, however, to revise the three-world theory on which he bases it. It is indeed true that cultural objectivations can be reduced neither to the generative activity of knowing, speaking, and acting subjects, nor to spatio-temporal, causal relations between things and events. For this reason Popper conceives the semantic contents of symbolic formations as entities of a "third world." He bases this concept on the ontological concept of "world" introduced to refer to a totality of entities. Before the concept of a world can become fruitful for action, it has to be modified in the three respects mentioned above.

(ad⁵ a) To begin with, I would like to replace the ontological concept of "world" with one derived from the phenomenological tradition and to adopt the pair of concepts "world" and "life-world." Sociated subjects, when participating in cooperative processes of interpretation, themselves employ the concept of the world in an implicit way. Cultural tradition, which Popper introduces under the catchphrase "products of the human mind," plays different roles depending on whether it functions from behind as a cultural stock of knowledge from which the participants in interaction draw their interpretations or is itself made the topic of intellectual endeavor. *In the first case*, the cultural tradition shared by a community is constitutive of the lifeworld which the individual member finds already interpreted. This intersubjectively shared *lifeworld* forms the background for communicative action. Thus phenomenologists like Alfred Schutz speak of the lifeworld as the unthematically given horizon within which participants in communication move in common when they refer thematically to something in the *world*. *In the second case*, individual elements of the cultural tradition are themselves made thematic. The participants must thereby adopt a reflective attitude toward cultural patterns of interpretation that ordinarily *make possible* their interpretive accomplishments. This change in attitude means that the validity of the thematized interpretive pattern is suspended and the corresponding knowledge rendered problematic; at the same time, the problematic element of the cultural tradition is brought under the category of a state of affairs to which one can refer in an objectivating manner. Popper's theory of the third world explains how cultural semantic contents and symbolic objects can be understood as something in the world, and can at the same time be distinguished as higher-level objects from (observable) physical and (experienciable) mental episodes.

(ad b) Further, I would like to replace the one-sidedly cognitivistic interpretation of the concept "objective mind [*Geist*]" with a concept of cultural knowledge differentiated according to several validity claims. Popper's third world encompasses higher-level entities, which are accessible in a reflective attitude and which retain a relative autonomy in relation to subjective mind because they form, on the basis of their relation to truth, a network of problem complexes open to investigation. We could say in the language of neo-Kantianism that the third world enjoys the independence of a sphere of validity. The entities of this world that admit of truth stand in a peculiar relation to the first world. The problems, theories, and arguments attributed

5. To (Latin); that is, with regard to.

to the third world serve in the final analysis to describe and explain events and persons within the first world. And both are mediated in turn through the world of subjective mind, through acts of knowing and doing. The noncognitive elements of culture thereby slip into a peculiar marginal position. But precisely these elements are of significance for a sociological theory of action. From the perspective of action theory, the activities of the human mind are not easily limited to the cognitive-instrumental confrontation with external nature; social actions are oriented to cultural values and these do not have a truth relation. Thus we are faced with the following alternative: either we deny to the noncognitive elements of the cultural tradition the status that third world entities occupy by virtue of being embedded in a sphere of validity connections, and classify them in an empiricist manner as forms of expression of subjective mind, or we seek equivalents for the missing truth relation.

As we shall see, Max Weber chose the second way. He distinguishes several cultural spheres of value—science and technology, law and morality, as well as art and criticism. The noncognitive spheres of value are also spheres of validity. Legal and moral representations can be criticized and analyzed from the standpoint of normative rightness and works of art from that of authenticity (or beauty); that is, they can be treated as autonomous problem domains. Weber understands cultural tradition *in toto* as a store of knowledge out of which special spheres of value and systems of knowledge are formed under different validity claims. He would thus include in the third world the evaluative and expressive components of culture as well as the cognitive-instrumental. If one adopts this alternative, one must of course explain what "validity" and "knowledge" can mean in regard to the noncognitive components of culture. They cannot be correlated in the same way as theories and statements with entities of the first world. Cultural values do not fulfill a representational function.

(*ad c*) These shifts provide us with an opportunity to rid the concept of world from its narrow ontological connotations. Popper introduces different world concepts to demarcate regions of being *within* the one objective world. In his later works he deems it important to speak not of different worlds, but of *one* world with the indices "1," "2," and "3."[6] I would like, on the contrary, to continue speaking of three worlds (which are in turn to be distinguished from the lifeworld). Of these, only one, namely the objective world, can be understood as the correlate of the totality of true propositions; only this concept retains the strictly ontological significance of a totality of entities. On the other hand, taken together the worlds form a reference system that is mutually presupposed in communication processes. With this reference system participants lay down what there can possibly be understanding about *at all*. Participants in communication who are seeking to come to an understanding with one another about something do not take up a relation only to the one objective world, as is suggested by the precommunicative model dominant in empiricism. They by no means refer only to things that happen or could happen or could be made to happen in the objective world, but to things

6. Popper, "Reply to My Critics," p. 1050. Popper takes this terminology from J. C. Eccles, *Facing Realities* (New York, 1970) [Habermas's note].

in the social and subjective worlds as well. Speakers and hearers operate with a *system* of several equally primordial worlds. That is, with propositionally differentiated speech they have mastered not only a level on which they can describe states of affairs—as is suggested by Popper's classification into lower and higher functions of language; rather, all three functions—the "descriptive," the "signalling" and the "self-expressive"—lie in one and the same evolutionary plane.

B.—In what follows I shall no longer employ the Popperian terminology. My purpose in reviewing Jarvie's action-theoretic translation of Popper's three-world theory was only to prepare the way for the thesis that with the choice of a specific sociological concept of action we generally make specific "ontological" assumptions. And the aspects of possible rationality of an agent's actions depend, in turn, on the world relations that we thereby impute to him. The profusion of action concepts employed (for the most part, implicitly) in social-scientific theories can be reduced in essence to four basic, analytically distinguishable concepts.

Since Aristotle the concept of *teleological action* has been at the center of the philosophical theory of action.[7] The actor attains an end or brings about the occurrence of a desired state by choosing means that have promise of being succesful in the given situation and applying them in a suitable manner. The central concept is that of a *decision* among alternative courses of action, with a view to the realization of an end, guided by maxims, and based on an interpretation of the situation.

The teleological model of action is expanded to a *strategic* model when there can enter into the agent's calculation of success the anticipation of decisions on the part of at least one additional goal-directed actor. This model is often interpreted in utilitarian terms; the actor is supposed to choose and calculate means and ends from the standpoint of maximizing utility or expectations of utility. It is this model of action that lies behind decision-theoretic and game-theoretic approaches in economics, sociology, and social psychology.[8]

The concept of *normatively regulated action* does not refer to the behavior of basically solitary actors who come upon other actors in their environment, but to members of a social group who orient their action to common values. The individual actor complies with (or violates) a norm when in a given situation the conditions are present to which the norm has application. Norms express an agreement that obtains in a social group. All members of a group for whom a given norm has validity may expect of one another that in certain situations they will carry out (or abstain from) the actions commanded (or proscribed). The central concept of *complying with a norm* means fulfilling a generalized expectation of behavior. The latter does not have the cognitive

---

7. R. Bubner, *Handlung, Sprache und Vernunft* [*Action, Language, and Reason*] (Frankfurt, 1976) [Habermas's note]. The Greek philosopher Aristotle (284–322 B.C.E.) emphasized teleology both in his physics (the "final cause" is one of four causes; see, e.g., *Metaphysics* 5.2) and his ethics (*Nicomachean Ethics* 1.1).

8. On decision theory, see H. Simon, *Models of Man* (New York, 1957). *** On game theory, see R. D. Luce and H. Raiffa, *Games and Decisions* (New York, 1957). *** On exchange-theoretical approaches in social psychology, see P. P. Ekeh, *Social Exchange Theory* (London, 1964) [Habermas's note].

sense of expecting a predicted event, but the normative sense that members are *entitled* to expect a certain behavior. This normative model of action lies behind the role theory that is widespread in sociology.[9]

The concept of *dramaturgical action* refers primarily neither to the solitary actor nor to the member of a social group, but to participants in interaction constituting a public for one another, before whom they present themselves. The actor evokes in his public a certain image, an impression of himself, by more or less purposefully disclosing his subjectivity. Each agent can monitor public access to the system of his own intentions, thoughts, attitudes, desires, feelings, and the like, to which only he has privileged access. In dramaturgical action, participants make use of this and steer their interactions through regulating mutual access to their own subjectivities. Thus the central concept of *presentation of self* does not signify spontaneous expressive behavior but stylizing the expression of one's own experiences with a view to the audience. The dramaturgical model of action is used primarily in phenomenologically oriented descriptions of interaction; but it has not yet been developed into a theoretically generalizing approach.[1]

Finally the concept of *communicative action* refers to the interaction of at least two subjects capable of speech and action who establish interpersonal relations (whether by verbal or by extra-verbal means). The actors seek to reach an understanding about the action situation and their plans of action in order to coordinate their actions by way of agreement. The central concept of *interpretation* refers in the first instance to negotiating definitions of the situation which admit of consensus. As we shall see, language is given a prominent place in this model.[2]

The teleological concept of action was first rendered fruitful for an economic theory of choice by the founders of neoclassical economics, and then for a theory of strategic games by Von Neumann and Morgenstern.[3] The concept of normatively regulated action gained paradigmatic significance for theory formation in the social sciences through Durkheim and Parsons, that of dramaturgical action through Goffman, that of communicative action through Mead and later Garfinkel.[4] I cannot carry out a detailed explication of these concepts here. My concern is rather with the rationality implications of the corresponding conceptual strategies. At first glance, only the teleological concept of action seems to open up an aspect of the rationality of action. Action represented as purposeful activity can be viewed under the aspect of purposive-rationality. This is a point of view from which actions can be more or less rationally planned and carried out, or can be judged by a third person

9. T. R. Sarbin, "Role Theory," in G. Lindsey, ed., *Handbook of Social Psychology*, vol. 1 (Cambridge, Mass., 1954), pp. 223–58; Talcott Parsons, "Social Interaction," in *International Encyclopedia of Social Science*, 7:1429–41 [Habermas's note].

1. G. J. McCall and J. L. Simmons, *Identity and Interactions* (New York, 1966); E. Goffman, *Frame Analysis* (Harmondsworth, Eng., 1975), *Relations in Public* (Harmondsworth, 1971), *Interaction Ritual* (Harmondsworth, 1957); R. Harré and P. F. Secord, *Explanation of Behavior* (Totowa, N.J., 1972); R. Harré, *Social Being* (Oxford, 1979) [Habermas's note].

2. One can get an overview of symbolic interactionism and ethnomethodology from, for instance, [the collection] *Alltagswissen, Interaktion und gesellschaftliche Wirklichkeit* [*Everyday Knowledge, Interaction, and Social Reality*], 2 vols. (Hamburg, 1973) [Habermas's note].

3. Oskar Morgenstern (1902–1977), German-born American economist; with the Hungarian-born American mathematician John von Neumann (1903–1957), he wrote *Theory of Games and Economic Behavior* (1944).

4. Harold Garfinkel (1917–2011), American sociologist. Émile Durkheim (1858–1917), French pioneer of sociology. Erving Goffman (1922–1982), Canadian-born American sociologist. George Herbert Mead (1863–1931), American philosopher and social psychologist.

to be more or less rational. In elementary cases of purposeful activity the plan of action can be represented in the form of a practical syllogism.[5] The other three models of action appear at first not to place action in the perspective of rationality and possible rationalization. That this appearance is deceiving becomes evident when we represent to ourselves the "ontological"—in the broad sense—presuppositions that are, as a matter of conceptual necessity, connected with these models of action. In the sequence teleological, normative, dramaturgical, the presuppositions not only become increasingly complex; they reveal at the same time stronger and stronger implications for rationality.

(a) The concept of teleological action presupposes relations between an actor and a world of existing states of affairs. This objective world is defined as the totality of states of affairs that either obtain or could arise or could be brought about by purposeful intervention. The model equips the agent with a "cognitive-volitional complex," so that he can, on the one hand, form *beliefs* about existing states of affairs through the medium of perception, and can, on the other hand, develop *intentions* with the aim of bringing desired states of affairs into existence. At the semantic level such states of affairs are represented as propositional contents of sentences expressing beliefs or intentions. Through his beliefs and intentions the actor can take up basically two types of rational relation to the world. I call these relations rational because they are open to objective appraisal depending on the "direction of fit."[6] In one direction the question arises whether the actor has succeeded in bringing his perceptions and beliefs into agreement with what is the case in the world; in the other direction the question is whether he succeeds in bringing what is the case in the world into agreement with his desires and intentions. In both instances the actor can produce expressions susceptible of being judged by a third person in respect to "fit and misfit"; he can make assertions that are *true* or *false* and carry out goal-directed interventions that succeed or fail, that *achieve* or *fail to achieve* the intended effect in the world. These relations between actor and world allow then for expressions that can be judged according to criteria of *truth* and *efficacy*.

With regard to ontological presuppositions, we can classify *teleological* action as a concept that presupposes *one* world, namely the objective world. The same holds for the concept of *strategic action*. Here we start with at least two goal-directed acting subjects who achieve their ends by way of an orientation to, and influence on, the decisions of other actors.[7] Success in action is also dependent on other actors, each of whom is oriented to his own success and behaves cooperatively only to the degree that this fits with his egocentric calculus of utility.[8] Thus strategically acting subjects must be cognitively so

5. G. H. von Wright, *Explanation and Understanding* (London, 1971), pp. 96ff. Von Wright's point of departure is G. E. M. Anscombe, *Intention* (Oxford, 1957) [Habermas's note]. For Anscombe, see this anthology's companion volume, *The Analytic Tradition*.

6. J. L. Austin speaks of the "direction of fit" or the "onus of match," which Anthony Kenny elaborates [in] *Will, Freedom and Power* (Oxford, 1975), p. 38. If we conceive of intention sentences as imperatives that a speaker addresses to himself, then assertoric and intention sentences represent

the two possibilities of agreement between sentence and state of affairs that are open to objective appraisal [Habermas's note]. For Austin, see this anthology's companion volume, *The Analytic Tradition*.

7. G. Gaefgen, "Formale Theorie des strategischen Handelns [Formal Theory of Strategic Action]," in H. Lenk, ed., *Handlungstheorien*, 1 (Munich, 1980): 249ff. [Habermas's note].

8. Compare Otfried Höffe, *Strategien der Humanität* [*Strategies of Humanity*] (Munich, 1975), pp. 77–78 [Habermas's note].

equipped that for them not only physical objects but decision-making systems can appear in the world. They must expand their conceptual apparatus for what can be the case; but they do not need any richer *ontological presuppositions*. The concept of the objective world does not itself become more complex with the growing complexity of innerworldly entities. Even purposeful activity differentiated to include strategic action remains, as regards its ontological presuppositions, a *one-world concept*.

(b) By contrast, the concept of normatively regulated action presupposes relations between an actor and exactly two worlds. Besides the objective world of existing states of affairs there is the social world to which the actor belongs as a role-playing subject, as do additional actors who can take up normatively regulated interactions among themselves. A social world consists of a normative context that lays down which interactions belong to the totality of legitimate interpersonal relations. And all actors for whom the corresponding norms have force (by whom they are accepted as valid) belong to the same social world. As the meaning of the objective world can be elucidated with reference to the existence [*Existieren*] of states of affairs, the meaning of the social world can be elucidated with reference to the "existence" [*Bestehen*][9] of norms. It is important here that we do *not* understand the "existence" of norms in the sense of existence sentences stating that there are social facts of the type: normative regulations. The sentence "It is the case that *q* is commanded" obviously has a different meaning than the sentence "It is commanded that *q*." The latter sentence expresses a norm or a specific command when it is uttered in suitable form with the claim to normative rightness, that is, such that it claims *validity* for a circle of addressees. And we say that a norm exists, is in force, or enjoys social currency [*Geltung*] when it is recognized as valid [*gültig*] or justified by those to whom it is addressed. Existing states of affairs are represented by true statements, existing norms by general ought-sentences or commands that count as justified among the addressees. That a norm is ideally *valid* means that it *deserves* the assent of all those affected because it regulates problems of action in their common interest. That a norm is *de facto established* means by contrast that the validity claim with which it appears is recognized by those affected, and this intersubjective recognition grounds the *social force or currency* of the norm.

We do not attach such a normative validity claim to cultural values; but values are candidates for embodiment in norms—they *can* attain a general binding force with respect to a matter requiring regulation. In the light of cultural values the needs [*Bedürfnisse*] of an individual appear as plausible to other individuals standing in the same tradition. However, plausibly interpreted needs are transformed into legitimate motives of action only when the corresponding values become, for a circle of those affected, normatively binding in regulating specific problem situations. Members can then expect of one another that in corresponding situations each of them will orient his action to values normatively prescribed for all concerned.

This consideration is meant to make comprehensible the fact that the normative model of action equips the agent not only with a "cognitive" but also

---

9. That is, the establishment.

with a "motivational complex" that makes norm-conformative behavior possible. Moreover this model of action is connected with a learning model of value internalization.[1] According to this model, existing norms gain action-motivating force to the degree that the values embodied in them represent the standards according to which, in the circle of addressees, needs are interpreted and developed through learning processes into need dispositions.

Under these presuppositions the actor can again take up relations to the world, here to the social world, which are open to objective evaluation according to the "direction of fit." In one direction the question is whether the motives and actions of an agent are in accord with existing norms or deviate from these. In the other direction the question is whether the existing norms themselves embody values that, in a particular problem situation, give expression to generalizable interests of those affected and thus deserve the assent of those to whom they are addressed. In the one case, actions are judged according to whether they are in accord with or deviate from an existing normative context, that is, whether or not they are right with respect to a normative context recognized as legitimate. In the other case, norms are judged according to whether they can be justified, that is, whether they deserve to be recognized as legitimate.[2]

With regard to its ontological—in the broad sense—presuppositions, we can classify *normatively regulated action* as a concept that presupposes *two worlds*, the objective world and a social world. Norm-conformative action presupposes that the agent can distinguish the factual from the normative elements of an action situation, that is, conditions and means from values. The point of departure for the normative model of action is that participants can simultaneously adopt both an objectivating attitude to something that is or is not the case, and a norm-conformative attitude to something that is commanded (whether rightly or not). But as in the teleological model, action is represented *primarily* as a relation between the actor and a world—there, as a relation to the objective world over against which the actor as knower stands and in which he can goal-directly intervene; here, as a relation to the social world to which the actor in his role as a norm-addressee belongs and in which he can take up legitimately regulated interpersonal relations. Neither here nor there is the actor *himself* presupposed as a world toward which he

---

1. H. Gerth and C. W. Mills, *Character and Social Structure* (New York, 1953) [Habermas's note].
2. This does not prejudge the question of whether we, as social scientists and philosophers, adopt a cognitive or a sceptical position in regard to moral-practical questions; that is, whether we hold a justification of action norms that is not relative to given ends to be possible. For example, Talcott Parsons shares with Weber a position of value scepticism; but when we use the concept of normatively regulated action we have to describe the actors *as if* they consider the legitimacy of action norms to be basically open to objective appraisal, no matter in which metaphysical, religious, or theoretical framework. Otherwise they would not take the concept of a world of legitimately regulated interpersonal relations as the basis of their action and could not orient themselves to valid norms but only to social facts. Acting in a norm-conformative attitude requires an intuitive understanding of normative validity; and this concept presupposes

some possibility or other of normative grounding. It cannot be a priori excluded that this conceptual necessity is a deception embedded in linguistic meaning conventions and thus calls for enlightenment—for example, by reinterpreting the concept of normative validity in emotivist or decisionistic terms and redescribing it with the help of other concepts like expressions of feeling, appeals, or commands. But the action of agents to whom such categorically "purified" action orientations can be ascribed could no longer be described in concepts of normatively regulated action [Habermas's note].
Habermas thus takes the position that genuine normativity, normative validity, and normatively regulated action require and presuppose the possibility of "normative grounding." That Kantian position is one of the central questions at issue in the interpretive tradition, for which KANT's proposed solution to the problem of normative grounding is not deemed to have settled the matter.

can behave reflectively. It is the concept of dramaturgical action that requires the additional presupposition of a subjective world to which the actor relates when in acting he puts himself "on stage."

(c) The concept of dramaturgical action is less clearly developed in social-science literature than are those of teleological and normatively guided action. Goffman first explicitly introduced it in 1956 in his investigation of "the presentation of self in everyday life."[3] From the perspective of dramaturgical action we understand social action as an encounter in which participants form a visible public for each other and perform for one another. "Encounter" and "performance" are the key concepts. The performance of a troop before the eyes of third persons is only a special case. A performance enables the actor to present himself to his audience in a certain way; in bringing something of his subjectivity to appearance, he would like to be seen by his public in a particular way.

The dramaturgical qualities of action are in a certain way parasitic; they rest on a structure of goal-directed action.

> For certain purposes people control the style of their actions . . . and superimpose this upon other activities. For instance work may be done in a manner in accordance with the principles of dramatic performance in order to project a certain impression of the people working to an inspector or manager . . . In fact what people are doing is rarely properly described as *just* eating, or *just* working, but has stylistic features which have certain conventional meanings associated with recognized types of personae.[4]

Of course, there are special roles tailored to virtuoso self-staging: "The roles of prizefighters, surgeons, violinists, and policemen are cases in point. These activities allow so much dramatic self-expression that exemplary practitioners—whether real or fictional—become famous and are given special places in the commercially organized fantasies of the nation."[5] The trait that is here stylized into an element of the professional role, namely the reflective character of self-presentation before others, is, however, constitutive for social interactions in general insofar as they are regarded only under the aspect of persons encountering one another.

In dramaturgical action the actor, in presenting a view of himself, has to behave toward his own subjective world. I have defined this as the totality of subjective experiences to which the actor has, in relation to others, a privileged access.[6] To be sure, this domain of subjectivity deserves to be called a "world" only if the significance of the subjective world can be explicated in a way similar to that in which I explained the significance of the social world,

---

3. E. Goffman, *The Presentation of Self in Everyday Life* (New York, 1959) [Habermas's note].
4. Harré and Secord, *Explanation of Behavior*, pp. 215–16 [Habermas's note].
5. Goffman, *Presentation of Self*, p. 31 [Habermas's note].
6. For the sake of simplicity, I am confining myself to *intentional* experiences (including weakly intentional moods) in order not to have to deal with the complicated limit case of sensations. The complication consists in the fact that here the misleading assimilation of experiential sentences to propositions is particularly tempting. Experiential sentences that express a sensation have almost the same meaning as propositional sentences that refer to a corresponding inner state brought about by stimulation of the senses [Habermas's note].

Habermas uses the term *intentional experience* in the way that Husserl does, but without wanting thereby to subscribe to the phenomenological concept of intentionality [translator's note].

through referring to an "existence" of norms analogous to the existence of states of affairs. Perhaps one can say that the subject is represented by truthfully uttered experiential sentences in nearly the same way as are existing states of affairs by true statements and valid norms by justified ought-sentences. We should not understand subjective experiences as mental states or inner episodes, for we would thereby assimilate them to entities, to elements of the objective world. We can comprehend having subjective experiences as something analogous to the existence of states of affairs without assimilating the one to the other. A subject capable of expression does not "have" or "possess" desires and feelings in the same sense as an observable object has extension, weight, color, and similar properties. An actor has desires and feelings in the sense that he can at will express these experiences before a public, and indeed in such a way that this public, if it trusts the actor's expressive utterances, attributes to him, as something subjective, the desires and feelings expressed.

Desires and feelings have a paradigmatic status in this connection. Of course, cognitions, beliefs, and intentions also belong to the subjective world; but they stand in internal relation to the objective world. Beliefs and intentions come to consciousness *as* subjective only when there is in the objective world no corresponding state of affairs that exists or is brought to exist. It becomes a question of "mere," that is, "mistaken" belief as soon as the corresponding statement turns out to be untrue. It is a matter merely of "good," that is, of "ineffectual" intentions as soon as it turns out that the corresponding action was either left undone or failed. In a similar way, feelings of, say, obligation, shame, or guilt stand in internal relation to the social world. But in general feelings and desires can *only* be expressed as something subjective. They cannot be expressed *otherwise*, cannot enter into relation with the external world, whether the objective or the social. For this reason the expression of desires and feelings is measured only against the reflexive relation of the speaker to his inner world.

Desires and feelings are two aspects of a partiality rooted in needs.[7] Needs have two faces. They are differentiated on the volitional side into inclinations and desires; and on the other side, the intuitive, into feelings and moods. Desires are directed toward situations of need satisfaction; feelings "perceive" situations in the light of possible need satisfaction. Needs are, as it were, the background of a partiality that determines our subjective attitudes in relation to the external world. Such predilections express themselves both in the active striving for goods and in the affective perception of situations (so long as the latter are not objectivated into something in the world and thus lose their situational character). The partiality of desires and feelings is expressed at the level of language in the interpretation of needs, that is, in evaluations for which evaluative expressions are available. One can gain clarity about the meaning of value judgments by examining the dual, descriptive-prescriptive content of these evaluative, need-interpreting expressions. They serve to make predilection understandable. This component of justification[8] is the bridge between the subjectivity of experience and that intersubjective

7. Compare the analysis of desires and feelings by Charles Taylor, "Explaining Action," *Inquiry* 13 (1970): 54–89 [Habermas's note].

8. Richard Norman, *Reasons for Actions* (New York, 1971), pp. 65ff. [Habermas's note].

transparency that experience gains in being truthfully expressed and, on this basis, attributed to an actor by onlookers. For example, in characterizing an object or a situation as splendid, ample, elevating, auspicious, dangerous, forbidding, dreadful, and so forth, we are trying to express a predilection and at the same time to justify it, in the sense of making it plausible by appeal to general standards of evaluation that are widespread at least in our own culture. Evaluative expressions or standards of value have justificatory force when they characterize a need in such a way that addressees can, in the framework of a common cultural heritage, recognize in these interpretations their own needs. This explains why attributes of style, aesthetic expression, formal qualities in general, have such great weight in dramaturgical action.

In the case of dramaturgical action the relation between actor and world is also open to objective appraisal. As the actor is oriented to his own subjective world in the presence of his public, there can be *one* direction of fit: In regard to a self-presentation, there is the question whether at the proper moment the actor is expressing the experiences he has, whether he *means* what he *says*, or whether he is merely feigning the experiences he expresses. So long as we are dealing here with beliefs or intentions, that is, with cognitive acts, the question of whether someone says what he means is clearly a question of truthfulness or sincerity. With desires and feelings this is not always the case. In situations in which accuracy of expression is important, it is sometimes difficult to separate questions of sincerity from those of authenticity. Often we lack the words to say what we feel; and this in turn places the feelings themselves in a questionable light.

According to the dramaturgical model of action, a participant can adopt an attitude to his own subjectivity in the role of an actor and to the expressive utterances of another in the role of a public, but only in the awareness that ego's inner world is bounded by an external world. In this external world the actor can certainly distinguish between normative and nonnormative elements of the action situation; but Goffman's model of action does not provide for his behaving toward the social world in a norm-conformative attitude. He takes legitimately regulated interpersonal relations into account only as social facts. Thus it seems to me correct also to classify *dramaturgical action* as a concept that presupposes *two worlds*, the internal world and the external. Expressive utterances present subjectivity in demarcation from the external world; the actor can in principle adopt only an objectivating attitude toward the latter. And in contrast to the case of normatively regulated action, this holds not only for physical but for social objects as well.

In virtue of this option, dramaturgical action can take on latently strategic qualities to the degree that the actor treats his audience as *opponents* rather than as a public. The scale of self-presentations ranges from sincere communication of one's own intentions, desires, moods, etc., to cynical management of the impressions the actor arouses in others.

> At one extreme, one finds that the performer can be fully taken in by his own act; he can be sincerely convinced that the impression of reality which he stages is the real reality. When his audience is also convinced in this way about the show he puts on—and this seems to be the typical case—then for the moment at least, only the sociologist or the socially

disgruntled will have doubts about the "realness" of what is presented. At the other extreme . . . the performer may be moved to guide the conviction of his audience only as a means to other ends, having no ultimate concern with the beliefs of his audience; we may call him cynical, reserving the term "sincere" for individuals who believe in the impression fostered by their own performance.[9]

The manipulative production of false impressions—Goffman investigates techniques of "impression management," from harmless segmentation to long-term information control—is by no means identical with strategic action. It too remains dependent on a public that takes itself to be present at a performance and fails to recognize its strategic character. Even a strategically intended self-presentation has to be capable of being understood as an expression that appears with the claim to subjective truthfulness. As soon as it is judged only according to criteria of success by the audience as well, it no longer falls under the description of dramaturgical action. We then have a case of strategic interaction in which participants have conceptually enriched their objective world in such a way that opponents can appear in it who are capable not only of purposive-rational action but of subjective expressions as well.

C.—With the concept of communicative action there comes into play the additional presupposition of a *linguistic medium* that reflects the actor's relations to the world as such. At this level of concept formation the rationality problematic, which until now has arisen only for the social scientist, moves into the perspective of the agent himself. We have to make clear in what sense achieving understanding in language is thereby introduced as a mechanism for coordinating action; Even the strategic model of action *can* be understood in such a way that participants' actions, directed through egocentric calculations of utility and coordinated through interest situations, are mediated through speech acts. In the cases of normatively regulated and dramaturgical action we even *have to* suppose a consensus formation among participants that is in principle of a linguistic nature. Nevertheless, in these three models of action language is conceived *one-sidedly* in different respects.

The teleological model of action takes language as one of several media through which speakers oriented to their own success can influence one another in order to bring opponents to form or to grasp beliefs and intentions that are in the speakers' own interest. This concept of language—developed from the limit case of indirect communication aimed at *getting* someone to form a belief, an intention, or the like—is, for instance, basic to intentionalist semantics.[1] The normative model of action presupposes language as a medium that transmits cultural values and carries a consensus that is merely reproduced with each additional act of understanding. This culturalist con-

9. Goffman, *Presentation of Self*, pp. 17–18 [Habermas's note].
1. I shall come back to the nominalistic theory of language developed by H. P. Grice in Chapter III ["Intermediate Reflections: Social Action, Purposive Activity, and Communication"; Habermas's note].

Paul Grice (1913–1988), British philosopher who attempted to analyze sentence and word meaning entirely in terms of the intention of the speaker (see this anthology's companion volume, *The Analytic Tradition*).

cept of language is widespread in cultural anthropology and content-oriented linguistics.[2] The dramaturgical model of action presupposes language as a medium of self-presentation; the cognitive significance of the propositional components and the interpersonal significance of the illocutionary components are thereby played down in favor of the expressive functions of speech acts. Language is assimilated to stylistic and aesthetic forms of expression.[3] Only the communicative model of action presupposes language as a medium of uncurtailed communication whereby speakers and hearers, out of the context of their preinterpreted lifeworld, refer simultaneously to things in the objective, social, and subjective worlds in order to negotiate common definitions of the situation. This interpretive concept of language lies behind the various efforts to develop a formal pragmatics.[4]

The one-sidedness of the first three concepts of language can be seen in the fact that the corresponding types of communication singled out by them prove to be limit cases of communicative action: *first*, the indirect communication of those who have only the realization of their own ends in view; *second*, the consensual action of those who simply actualize an already existing normative agreement; and *third*, presentation of self in relation to an audience. In each case only one function of language is thematized: the release of perlocutionary effects,[5] the establishment of interpersonal relations, and the expression of subjective experiences. By contrast, the communicative model of action, which defines the traditions of social science connected with Mead's symbolic interactionism, Wittgenstein's[6] concept of language games, Austin's theory of speech acts, and Gadamer's hermeneutics, takes all the functions of language equally into consideration. As can be seen in the ethnomethodological and hermeneutic approaches, there is a danger here of reducing social *action* to the interpretive accomplishments of participants in communication, of assimilating action to speech, interaction to conversation. In the present context I can introduce this concept of communicative action only in a provisional way. I shall restrict myself to remarks concerning: (a) the character of independent actions; and (b) the reflective relation to the world of actors in processes of understanding.

(a) In order to avoid mislocating the concept of communicative action from the start, I would like to characterize the level of complexity of speech acts that simultaneously express a propositional content, the offer of an interpersonal relationship, and the intention of the speaker. In the course of the analysis it will become evident how much this concept owes to investigations in the philosophy of language stemming from Wittgenstein. Precisely for this reason it might be well to point out that the concept of following a rule with which analytic philosophy of language begins does not go far enough. If one grasps linguistic conventions only from the perspective of rule following, and explains them by means of a concept of intentions based on rule consciousness,

2. Benjamin Lee Whorf, *Language, Thought and Reality* (Cambridge, Mass., 1956); H. Gipper, *Gibt es ein sprachliches Relativitätsprinzip? [Is There a Linguistic Relativity Principle?]* (Frankfurt, 1972); P. Henle, ed., *Sprache, Denken, Kultur [Language, Thought, Culture]* (Frankfurt, 1969) [Habermas's note].

3. Harré and Secord, *Explanation of Behavior*, pp. 215ff.; see especially Charles Taylor, *Language and Human Nature* (Carleton, Montreal, 1978) [Habermas's note].

4. F. Schütze, *Sprache [Language]*, 2 vols. (Munich, 1975) [Habermas's note].

5. That is, effects produced by speech acts designed to have such effects on an audience.

6. Ludwig Wittgenstein (1889–1951), Austrian-born British philosopher of immense influence (see this anthology's companion volume, *The Analytic Tradition*); "language games," discussed in his *Philosophical Investigations* (1953), are cases in which language is used to structure human social practices.

one loses that aspect of the *threefold relation to the world* of communicative agents that is important to me.[7]

I shall use the term "action" only for those symbolic expressions with which the actor takes up a relation to at least one world (but always to the objective world *as well*)—as is the case in the previously examined models of teleological, normatively regulated, and dramaturgical action. I shall distinguish from actions the bodily movements and operations that are *concomitantly executed* and can acquire the independence of actions only *secondarily*, through being *embedded, for instance, in play or teaching* practices. This can easily be shown through the example of bodily movements. Under the aspect of observable events in the world, actions appear as bodily movements of an organism. Controlled by the central nervous system, these movements are the substratum in which actions are carried out. With his actions the agent changes something in the world. We can, of course, distinguish the movements with which a subject intervenes in the world (acts instrumentally) from those with which a subject embodies a meaning (expresses himself communicatively). In both cases the bodily movements bring about a physical change in the world; in the one case this is of causal relevance, in the other of semantic relevance. Examples of causally relevant bodily movements are straightening the body, spreading the hand, lifting the arm, bending the leg, and so forth. Examples of semantically relevant bodily movements are movements of the larynx, tongue, lips, etc. in the generation of phonetic sounds; nodding the head; shrugging the shoulders; finger movements while playing the piano; hand movements while writing, drawing; and so on.

Arthur Danto has analyzed these movements as "basic actions."[8] This has given rise to a broad discussion which is biased by the idea that bodily movements do not represent the substratum through which actions enter into the world but are themselves primitive actions.[9] In this view, a complex action is characterized by the fact that it is performed "through" carrying out another action: "through" flicking the light switch I turn on the light; "through" raising my right arm I greet someone; "through" forcefully kicking a ball I score a goal. These are examples of actions performed "through" a basic action. A basic action is characterized in turn by the fact that it cannot be performed by means of an additional act. I regard this conceptual strategy as misleading. In a certain sense, actions are realized through movements of the body, but only in such a way that the actor, in following a technical or social rule, *concomitantly executes* these movements. Concomitant execution means that the actor intends an action but not the bodily movements with the help of which he realizes it.[1] *A bodily movement is an element of an action but not an action.*

---

7. For similar reasons, M. Roche insists on the distinction between linguistic and social conventions[; see] "Die Philosophische Schule der Begriffsanalyse [The Philosophical School of Concept Analysis]," in R. Wiggershaus, ed., *Sprachanalyse und Soziologie* (Frankfurt, 1975), p. 187 [Habermas's note].

8. Arthur C. Danto, "Basic Actions," *American Philosophical Quarterly* 2 (1965): 141–48, and *Analytic Philosophy of Action* (Cambridge, 1973) [Habermas's note]. Danto (1924–2013), American philosopher and art critic.

9. The false impression that bodily movements coordinated with actions are themselves basic actions might be sustained perhaps by looking to certain exercises in which we intend nonindependent actions *as such.* * * * But the fact that such bodily movements can be carried out intentionally does not contradict the thesis that they represent nonindependent actions [Habermas's note].

1. A. I. Goldman, *A Theory of Action* (Englewood Cliffs, N.J., 1970) [Habermas's note].

As far as their status as nonindependent actions is concerned, *bodily* movements are similar to just those *operations* from which Wittgenstein developed
his concepts of rules and rule following. Operations of thought and speech
are always only executed concomitantly in *other* actions. If need be, they can
be *rendered independent* within the framework of a training exercise—for
instance, when a Latin teacher, in the course of a lesson, demonstrates the
passive transformation with a sample sentence formed in the active voice. This
explains the special heuristic utility of the model of social games. Wittgenstein preferred to elucidate operational rules with reference to chess. He did
not see that this model has only limited value. We can certainly understand
speaking or doing sums as practices constituted by the grammar of a particular language or the rules of arithmetic, in a way similar to that in which chess
playing is constituted by the familiar rules of the game. But the two cases are
as distinct as is the concomitantly executed arm movement from the gymnas-
tic exercise that is carried out by means of the same movement. In applying
arithmetical or grammatical rules we generate symbolic objects such as sums
or sentences; but they do not lead an independent existence. We normally
carry out *other* actions by means of sums and sentences—for example, school-
work or commands. Operatively generated structures can, taken by themselves, be judged as more or less correct, in conformity with a rule, or
well-formed; but they are not, as are actions, open to criticism from the standpoints of truth, efficacy, rightness, or sincerity, for they acquire relations to
the world only as the infrastructure of other actions. *Operations do not concern the world.*

This can be seen in the fact that operational rules can serve to identify an
operatively generated structure as more or less well formed, that is, to make
it *comprehensible* but not to *explain* its appearance. They permit an answer
to the question of whether certain scrawled-out symbols are sentences, measurements, computations, etc.; and if they are, say, a computation, just which
one it is. To show that someone has calculated, and indeed correctly, does
not, however, explain *why* he carried out this computation. If we wish to
answer *this* question, we must have recourse to a rule of *action*; for example,
to the fact that a pupil used this sheet of paper to solve a mathematical problem. With the help of arithmetic rules, we can, it is true, state the reason why
he continues the number series 1,3,6,10,15 . . . with 21,28,36, and so forth;
but we cannot *explain* why he writes this series on a piece of paper. We are
explicating the meaning of a symbolic structure and not giving a rational
explanation for its coming to be. Operational rules do not have explanatory
power; following them does not mean, as does following rules of action, that
the actor is relating to something in the world and is thereby oriented to validity claims connected with action-motivating reasons.

(*b*) This should make clear why we cannot analyze communicative utterances in the same way as we do the grammatical sentences with the help of
which we carry them out. For the communicative model of action, language
is relevant only from the pragmatic viewpoint that speakers, in employing sentences with an orientation to reaching understanding, take up relations to
the world, not only directly as in teleological, normatively regulated, or dramaturgical action, but in a reflective way. Speakers integrate the three formal world-concepts, which appear in the other models of action either singly

or in pairs, into a system and presuppose this system in common as a framework of interpretation within which they can reach an understanding. They no longer relate *straightaway* to something in the objective, social, or subjective worlds; instead they relativize their utterances against the possibility that their validity will be contested by other actors. Reaching an understanding functions as a mechanism for coordinating actions only through the participants in interaction coming to an agreement concerning the claimed *validity* of their utterances, that is, through intersubjectively recognizing the *validity claims* they reciprocally raise. A speaker puts forward a criticizable claim in relating with his utterance to at least one "world"; he thereby uses the fact that this relation between actor and world is in principle open to objective appraisal in order to call upon his opposite number to take a rationally motivated position. The concept of communicative action presupposes language as the medium for a kind of reaching understanding, in the course of which participants, through relating to a world, reciprocally raise validity claims that can be accepted or contested.

With this model of action we are supposing that participants in interaction can now mobilize the rationality potential—which according to our previous analysis resides in the actor's three relations to the world—expressly for the cooperatively pursued goal of reaching understanding. If we leave to one side the well-formedness of the symbolic expressions employed, an actor who is oriented to understanding in this sense must raise at least three validity claims with his utterance, namely:

(1.) That the statement made is true (or that the existential presuppositions of the propositional content mentioned are in fact satisfied);
(2.) That the speech act is right with respect to the existing normative context (or that the normative context that it is supposed to satisfy is itself legitimate); and
(3.) That the manifest intention of the speaker is meant as it is expressed.

Thus the speaker claims truth for statements or existential presuppositions, rightness for legitimately regulated actions and their normative context, and truthfulness or sincerity for the manifestation of subjective experiences. We can easily recognize therein the three relations of actor to world presupposed *by the social scientist* in the previously analyzed concepts of action; but in the concept of communicative action they are ascribed to the perspective of *the speakers and hearers themselves*. It is the actors themselves who seek consensus and measure it against truth, rightness, and sincerity, that is, against the "fit" or "misfit" between the speech act, on the one hand, and the three worlds to which the actor takes up relations with his utterance, on the other. Such relations hold between an utterance and;

(1.) The objective world (as the totality of all entities about which true statements are possible);
(2.) The social world (as the totality of all legitimately regulated interpersonal relations);
(3.) The subjective world (as the totality of the experiences of the speaker to which he has privileged access).

Every process of reaching understanding takes place against the background of a culturally ingrained preunderstanding. This background knowledge remains unproblematic as a whole; only that part of the stock of knowledge that participants make use of and thematize at a given time is put to the test. To the extent that definitions of situations are negotiated by participants *themselves*, this thematic segment of the lifeworld is at their disposal with the negotiation of each new definition of the situation.

A definition of the situation establishes an order. Through it, participants in communication assign the various elements of an action situation to one of the three worlds and thereby incorporate the actual action situation into their preinterpreted lifeworld. A definition of the situation by another party that prima facie diverges from one's own presents a problem of a peculiar sort; for in cooperative processes of interpretation no participant has a monopoly on correct interpretation. For both parties the interpretive task consists in incorporating the other's interpretation of the situation into one's own in such a way that in the revised version "his" external world and "my" external world can—against the background of "our" lifeworld—be relativized in relation to "the" world, and the divergent situation definitions can be brought to coincide sufficiently. Naturally this does not mean that interpretation must lead in every case to a stable and unambiguously differentiated assignment. Stability and absence of ambiguity are rather the exception in the communicative practice of everyday life. A more realistic picture is that drawn by ethnomethodologists—of a diffuse, fragile, continuously revised and only momentarily successful communication in which participants rely on problematic and unclarified presuppositions and feel their way from one occasional commonality to the next.

To avoid misunderstanding I would like to repeat that the communicative model of action does not equate action with communication. Language is a medium of communication that serves understanding, whereas actors, in coming to an understanding with one another so as to coordinate their actions, pursue their particular aims. In this respect the teleological structure is fundamental to *all* concepts of action.[2] Concepts of *social action* are distinguished, however, according to how they specify the *coordination* among the goal-directed actions of different participants: as the interlacing of egocentric calculations of utility (whereby the degree of conflict and cooperation varies with the given interest positions); as a socially integrating agreement about values and norms instilled through cultural tradition and socialization; as a consensual relation between players and their publics; or as reaching understanding in the sense of a cooperative process of interpretation. In all cases the teleological structure of action is presupposed, inasmuch as the capacity for goal-setting and goal-directed action is ascribed to actors, as well as an interest in carrying out their plans of action. But only the strategic model of action *rests content* with an explication of the features of action oriented directly to success; whereas the other models of action specify conditions under which the actor pursues his goals—conditions of legitimacy, of self-presentation, or of agreement arrived at in communication, under which alter can "link up" his actions with those of ego. In the

---

2. R. Bubner, *Handlung, Sprache und Vernunft*, pp. 168ff. [Habermas's note].

case of communicative action the interpretive accomplishments on which cooperative processes of interpretation are based represent the mechanism for *coordinating* action; communicative action is *not exhausted* by the act of reaching understanding in an interpretive manner. If we take as our unit of analysis a simple speech act carried out by S, to which at least one participant in interaction can take up a "yes" or "no" position, we can clarify the conditions for the communicative coordination of action by stating what it means for a hearer to understand what is said. But communicative action designates a type of interaction that is *coordinated through* speech acts and does *not coincide with* them.

SOURCE: From Jürgen Habermas, The *Theory of Communicative Action*, vol. 1, *Reason and the Rationalization of Society*, trans. Thomas McCarthy (Boston: Beacon Press, 1984), pp. 1–7, 75–101. Except where otherwise indicated, German words in brackets are the terminology used in the German original, inserted by the editor in addition to their renderings in the translation. Originally published in 1981 as *Theorie des Kommunikativen Handelns*, vol. 1, *Handlungsrationalität und gesellschaftliche Rationalizierung*.

HANS-GEORG GADAMER
(1900 – 2002)

Although the philosophy of Gadamer is often thought to be virtually synonymous with hermeneutics, it is in fact a radical transformation of the hermeneutic tradition—a transformation to which the title of his major work, *Truth and Method*, alludes. Hermeneutics originally was conceived as having to do with the theory and practice of interpretation: its purpose was to guide those engaged with religious texts and similar matters by providing them with a grasp of sound truth-yielding interpretive procedures or methods. But Gadamer's hermeneutic philosophy revolves around rejecting "method" in the conception as well as the practice of interpretive endeavor—or at least rejecting the idea that there is any sort of interpretive method that is necessary, desirable, or even useful for achieving true understanding. In matters interpretive, for him, there are no reliable methods or rules—easy or otherwise—to guide us to truth. Instead, he contends that understanding must always operate within contexts and with self-understanding armed only with a kind of "practical wisdom" (Aristotelian *phronēsis*).

Gadamer's work is sometimes called an application of HEIDEGGER's philosophy to the hermeneutic enterprise, but that characterization sells it short. To be sure, his work is deeply Heideggerian, taking as its point of departure the notion of a "hermeneutics of suspicion" that attempts to uncover deep ontological truths that have been hidden by various scientific, technological, and social features of modern life that are conducive to inauthenticity. He also shares Heidegger's conception of our kind of "being" (or *Dasein*) as being-in-the-world, deeply historical, linguistic, truth-disclosing, and creative. But while these similarities are worth noting when characterizing his thought, they should not be allowed to obscure Gadamer's significant departures from Heidegger.

Hans-Georg Gadamer ("GAH-dahmer") was born in Marburg, Germany. His family was from a region then part of Germany but now in Poland; and they returned there, to Breslau (now Wroclaw), in 1902. His childhood was not easy, though the family was socially respected and well-to-do. His father was a professor of pharmaceutical chemistry, but his mother died when he was four years old and his one brother had chronic epilepsy. Gadamer attended the Heiligen Geist Gymnasium in Breslau; and while his father urged him in the direction of the natural sciences, it was the humanities (languages and literature) that attracted and held his interest.

Gadamer began his university studies in 1918–19 at the University of Breslau, where he was first introduced to philosophy by the Neo-Kantian Richard Hönigswald. In 1919 he returned to Marburg with his father, who had accepted a position at its university (eventually becoming rector). There Gadamer pursued his studies in philosophy, with the Neo-Kantians Paul Natorp and Nicolai Hartmann in particular, temporarily relegating his literary interests to a secondary position. He defended his doctoral dissertation on Plato in 1922, at the remarkably early age of 22.

That very year there was a polio epidemic, and Gadamer contracted a nearly fatal case of the disease. During the many months while he was bedridden, he read HUSSERL and a manuscript of Heidegger's early lectures on Aristotle that Natorp sent him. In early 1923 he married Frida Kratz (a daughter was born to them in 1926), and then went to Freiburg to study with Husserl and with Heidegger, who was still only an instructor. He attended several of Heidegger's lecture courses, including one on "the herme-neutics of facticity" and another on Aris-totle's ethics, and also had a private tutorial with him on Aristotle's *Meta-physics*. Gadamer even was extended (and accepted) an invitation by Heidegger to spend four weeks with him in his cabin in Todnauberg.

In the fall of 1923, Heidegger relocated to the university at Marburg. Gadamer followed him there to be his assistant, and he became a part of the circle of advanced students who soon gathered around Heidegger, which included Karl Löwith, Leo Strauss, HANNAH ARENDT, and Hans Jonas. Gadamer also came to know MAX SCHELER there, and studied with the theologian Rudolf Bultmann as well. He soon left his earlier Neo-Kantian tendencies behind him. Within a few years, however, he began to move away from phenomenology as well; and by 1925 his focus had shifted to ancient philosophy, literature, and languages. In 1927 he took his state-administered qualifying examination in classical phi-lology, and a year later defended his sec-ond (habilitation) dissertation on Plato's *Philebus*, written under the supervision of Heidegger and the classicist Paul Fried-lander. This qualified him for university teaching positions, but he was unable to obtain one for almost a decade. He lec-tured at Marburg and Kiel until 1938, when he succeeded ARNOLD GEHLEN in Leipzig (after Gehlen's departure for Königsberg), remaining there through the war. During this period his first mar-riage ended. He later (in 1950) married Käte Lekebusch, who during the war had been his student and assistant; and they had a daughter in 1956.

Unlike Heidegger and Gehlen, Gadamer never joined the Nazi Party; indeed, he was quietly critical of it. After the war an American tribunal judged him to be untainted by Nazism, and he became the rector of the University of Leipzig. Since Leipzig was in what was to become East Germany, this administrative position required him to be in close contact with Russian authorities as well as with the nascent East German government, both of which were deeply uncongenial to him. After a brief attempt to learn to live with and under the new regime, Gadamer relocated to the west, taking a position at Frankfurt in 1947. Two years later he became JASPERS's successor at Heidelberg, which remained his primary appoint-ment (eventually as professor emeritus) and residence for the remainder of his long life. He retired from his regular fac-ulty appointment in 1968 but continued teaching, for decades dividing his time between Heidelberg and North America (with his final and longest visiting appointment at Boston College).

During the 1950s Gadamer devoted himself to what was to become his mas-terwork, *Truth and Method* (1960). The 1970s and 1980s were marked by much-publicized encounters and debates first with JÜRGEN HABERMAS (with whom he came to have a warm relationship) and then with JACQUES DERRIDA (with whom he did not). He enjoyed high esteem and many honors to the end of his days, dying in Heidelberg in 2002 at the age of 102.

Gadamer's work is a challenge for many non-German readers in part because they lack familiarity with the debates in which he was so often engaged. One such debate had to do with the nature of hermeneutics itself, which in turn related to its history as a self-conscious endeavor. Its founding father, the theo-logian and philosopher Friedrich Schlei-ermacher (1786–1834), thought of hermeneutics as a teachable method that was needed to deal with religious texts such as the Bible but also had wide application in humanistic inquiry. In his view, purely formal modes of textual analysis were inadequate for understand-ing many important sorts of texts, and he sought to bring psychological and other broader considerations to bear on and within aesthetic and historical interpre-tation. WILHELM DILTHEY then expanded the scope of hermeneutics by attempting to develop it rigorously so that it could act as the method and foundation through which the *Geisteswissenschaften* (human-ities and other disciplines that study human social and cultural life) might become true *Wissenschaften* (cognitive disciplines). Gadamerian hermeneutics is in constant dialogue with this history.

Gadamer was educated during a time when Neo-Kantianism still dominated academic philosophy in German-speaking Europe but was being challenged from a number of directions. Neo-Kantianism had revived KANT's central concern with knowledge and the conditions of its possibility, took the sciences to provide paradigmatic instances of knowledge, and tended toward a conception of the human subject that emphasized its cognitive capacities and the formal structures associated with them. (Husserlian phenomenology was more closely related to Neo-Kantianism—both in its spirit and in its actual contours—than it was to the various developing challenges to that movement.)

Neo-Kantianism was of no use to Gadamer insofar as his interests in literature and in Greek philosophy were concerned. He was attracted by Heidegger's developing program of existential philosophy, as well as by Dilthey's renewal of Hegelianism and hermeneutics. Moreover, perhaps influenced in part by his metaphysically minded teacher Nicolai Hartmann, he had a strong interest in fundamental questions (relating to truth and reality) that were alien to the formalism and methodological orientation of Neo-Kantianism. His writing not only reflects these many and diverse influences but also is a part of his own dialogue with them. And because he insists in *Truth and Method* on the need to take context into account in the act of interpretation—especially when what one is interpreting is a text from a time and place other than one's own—understanding him is a challenge.

Yet Gadamer's goals are clear enough. He wishes to transform hermeneutics into a general account of the most distinctively human and truth-disclosing form of understanding. Indeed, he wants to develop the idea (found both in HEGEL—albeit in different terms—and in Heidegger) that "understanding" is

fundamental to the very nature of human reality and is an essential feature of the human way of being-in-the-world—from which it follows that hermeneutics ultimately deals (and must deal) with the basic structure or character of human reality itself. This can be called Gadamer's ontological account of hermeneutics. Gadamerian hermeneutics is no longer merely a method that the subject applies to the world: it is the subject's way of existing, in the world and in history.

The starting point of *Truth and Method*—an account of truth as it emerges in our encounter with art—may seem odd for several reasons. First, the notion of truth may seem to have no place in art. This, however, is one of many common (and also both Kantian and Nietzschean) ideas about art that Gadamer rejects. In so doing, he is clearly drawing on Heidegger's concept of art and its relation to truth. Gadamer disputes Kant's description of aesthetic experience and judgment as "disinterested." He also dismisses the subjectivist reduction of aesthetic experience to a mere play of feelings, because such a view is incapable of doing justice to the important phenomenon of truth in art. Art has a central place in Gadamer's hermeneutics because he believes that aesthetic experience is in fact paradigmatic of hermeneutic understanding and the disclosure of truth as a whole. Thus the dialogic interpretive process by which we encounter art is not seen as some special domain of experience: it is an element of all truly human encounters. Rather than being something marginal to human life, it indicates something central to human reality.

Gadamer's aesthetics also draws on FRIEDRICH SCHILLER's notion of "play" (see above), but transforms it from a subjective notion into an ontological one. It is not the experiencing subject who alone plays, in isolation and internally. Play is externalized objectively in the world, like a game into which we enter. Similarly, the art object is something like an unfinished event, which is what it truly is only within a temporal process and which opens a unique horizon into which our own activity enters. The removal of art from our everyday lives and general experience, to be isolated in museums, is antithetical to Gadamer's aesthetics. The philosophy of art's traditional concerns with representation are replaced in *Truth and Method* by an account of the artwork as an autonomous presentation and entity with its own complex horizon, tradition, and language.

Gadamer advances and defends his claim that art is paradigmatic in and for human experience in the second major portion of *Truth and Method*, where he develops his own unique approach to hermeneutics. Hermeneutic consciousness is always embedded in the concrete situation. It has what Gadamer (following Heidegger) calls a "fore-structure"—a pre-thematic, prescientific grasp of the structure of being and the world. This tends to be covered up by the abstractions and distortions of scientific, objective ways of thinking and conceptualization, which are oblivious to the historically configured character of understanding. Prompted by an awareness of that tendency, the "hermeneutics of suspicion" is a constant questioning that attempts to counter it.

The hermeneutics of suspicion is no method of textual analysis at all; rather, it is the self-consciously critical process of developing and employing historical consciousness in the world. It is aided by the multifariousness of that consciousness. How a particular consciousness encounters other traditions and horizons is founded on prejudgings or preconceptions that are products of its own history and tradition. Through this encounter, its prejudgings are both retained and transformed (*aufgehoben*, in a Hegelian manner of speaking). This process does not elevate us above and beyond history altogether, or eliminate preconceptions entirely, because preconceivings are essential to there being any understanding at all. The historically embedded but sensitive consciousness that reckons with the world is transformed by the

world with which it reckons, as part of the very price and process of attaining understanding.

Gadamer's hermeneutics arguably derives more from Aristotle's moral philosophy than from Heidegger. For the Heidegger of *Being and Time* (1927), self-knowledge of *Dasein* (our human kind of "being") is merely preparatory, paving the way to asking the larger and more fundamental "question of Being" generally: and in that context, it turns out (for the later Heidegger) that "man" matters only as a kind of means to Being's end. For Gadamer, on the other hand, "man" remains at the center of the picture; and self-knowing is an essential and ongoing process by which we achieve moral knowledge and the virtues, culminating in wisdom. But this is no advocacy of self-absorption, for in Gadamer's view self-understanding in one's concrete situation is essentially bound up with the ability to engage in dialogue with horizons other than our own, in a responsible and moral way.

The second, longer selection below from *Truth and Method* is taken from its final major section, an analysis of language. Gadamer turns to language because it alone makes possible the connection of horizons, and has a transformative power. Gadamer has little interest in the sort of formal linguistic analysis that investigates universal grammar. He likewise has little in common with those who hold that language and our grammar are self-enclosed, incommensurable forms of life. His idea is that human beings who find themselves together in some situation spontaneously create a shared language and understanding that becomes their world. He does not suppose that there is some absolute fixed meaning in texts. Meaning emerges through the encounter. Art and great texts are wellsprings of meaning from which repeated encounters across time will always draw something new, rather as if one were conversing with a person. The written text is the hermeneutic object par excellence: it is language in its pure form detached from psychology, from the speaker, and turned into an independent object.

Gadamer ends *Truth and Method* with an account of the ontological nature of language. Language is considered a "life process." To exist as a historical being is to exist as a linguistic one, because tradition is transmitted through and encountered by way of language. Language as our way of being is factual and world-disclosing, in a way quite different from the objective, scientific employment of language. Inasmuch as language is the being of historically effected consciousness, it is as much a listening to the world and to other languages as a simple transmission of thoughts. This position leads Gadamer to contend that the interplay of question and answer is what is primary in hermeneutics. One might say that something like the attitude that Heidegger called "dwelling," as opposed to a technological manner of existence, is essential to Gadamer's account of language and hermeneutics.

Gadamer thus returns to art, beauty, and play, drawing heavily on the Platonic connection between beauty, goodness, and truth. *Truth and Method* ends with the Platonic twist that truth and goodness radiate through beauty. But rather than seeing these as eternal and immutable Forms, as Plato did, he argues that truth and beauty are essentially historical events with which we connect.

The first selection is an essay written by Gadamer in 1967 in response to a critical review of *Truth and Method* by Habermas, which serves nicely as an introduction to the book. In that review Habermas had questioned Gadamer's separation of methodological concerns from the hermeneutic experience, supposing (with Dilthey) that hermeneutics should still operate as the methodological foundation of the social sciences. For him the point of hermeneutic reflection is to make possible a Hegelian attainment of critical distance from the hegemonic forces of language, culture, and tradition, facilitating an Enlightenment-inspired striving toward Kantian cosmopolitanism or Hegelian universalism.

Gadamer's response begins with an analysis of the historical connections between hermeneutics and rhetoric. In this context he thinks of the practical power of hermeneutics as persuasion. He reiterates his concept of hermeneutic experience as a fundamental *prescientific* ontological knowing. Although he sounds Heideggerian, his inspiration is in part the Platonic dialectic and Plato's theory of recollection—the idea that knowledge is innate and can and must be elicited through dialogue. Thus, rejecting an Enlightenment model of ascension out of the particular to the universal, Gadamer charges Habermas with a "dogmatic objectivism" that falsifies the hermeneutic experience by abstracting understanding out of history. Whereas Habermas accuses Gadamer of failing to recognize the power of reflection to transform language and science into a critique of ideology, Gadamer argues that Habermas seems to forget that this act of critique is already conditioned by and within language and history.

Gadamer thus questions Habermas's Enlightenment assumptions, contending that the hermeneutic problem of differing experiential horizons is inescapable for all interhuman experience. Yet he also insists that it does not render hermeneutics practically ineffective or politically impotent, as Habermas claims. On the contrary: the dialogic encounter and its alteration of horizons can serve such engagement—indeed, it can do so without having to rely on either the (illusory) ideal of complete, intersubjective reciprocity and understanding or the (false and distorting) belief in one's independence from prejudice and tradition.

Gadamer replaced the quasi-mystical, creative act of the poet celebrated by Heidegger in his late writings with the labor of dialogue. With his recognition of the importance of dialogue and community, he moved past the late Heidegger's quietism (as well as his early political ineptitude). Gadamer had little patience with or sympathy for Heidegger's grandiose pronouncements concerning such things as the history of Western metaphysics,

the truth of Being, and the end of philosophy itself. Instead, Gadamer proposed
that although our history, language, prejudices, and traditions surround us like
a horizon, we can achieve truth and
understanding through the practical, dialogic encounter and fusion of our horizon

with that of others, insisting that this is a
real human possibility. And for him something like such dialogue also can and
should characterize our encounter with
the history of philosophy—a tradition
that he finds it unnecessary, undesirable,
and in any event impossible to overcome.

From On the Scope and Function of Hermeneutical Reflection

Philosophical hermeneutics takes as its task the opening up of the hermeneutical dimension in its full scope, showing its fundamental significance for
our entire understanding of the world and thus for all the various forms in
which this understanding[1] manifests itself: from interhuman communication
to manipulation of society; from personal experience by the individual in society to the way in which he encounters society; and from the tradition as it is
built of religion and law, art and philosophy, to the revolutionary consciousness that unhinges the tradition through emancipatory reflection.

Despite this vast scope and significance, however, individual explorations
necessarily start from the very limited experiences and fields of experience.
My own effort, for instance, went back to Dilthey's philosophical development
of the heritage of German romanticism,[2] in that I too made the theory of the
Geisteswissenschaften (humanistic sciences[3] and social sciences) my theme.
But I hope to have placed it on a new and much broader footing linguistically, ontologically, and aesthetically; for the experience of art can answer the
prevailing presumption of historical alienation in the humanistic disciplines,
I believe, with its own overriding and victorious claim to contemporaneousness, a claim that lies in its very essence. It should be evident already from
the essential linguisticality of all human experience of the world, which has
as its own way of fulfillment a constantly self-renewing contemporaneousness.
I maintain that precisely this contemporaneousness and this linguisticality
point to a truth that goes questioningly behind all knowledge and anticipat-
ingly before it.

And so it was unavoidable that in my analysis of the universal linguisticality of man's relation to the world, the limitations of the fields of experience
from which the investigation took its start would unwittingly predetermine
the result. Indeed, it paralleled what happened in the historical development
of the hermeneutical problem. It came into being in encounter with the written tradition that demanded translation, for the tradition had become
estranged from the present as a result of such factors as temporal distance,
the fixity of writing, and the sheer inertia of permanence. Thus it was that

1. "Understanding" (*Verstehen*) is the focus of philosophical "hermeneutics"; it is the kind of comprehension that this tradition considers to be essential
in all matters historical, cultural, and human.

2. WILHELM DILTHEY is a key figure in the emergence of philosophical hermeneutics; see above.
3. That is, disciplines.

the many-layered problem of translation became for me the model for the linguisticality of all human behavior in the world. From the structure of translation was indicated the general problem of making what is alien our own. Yet further reflection on the universality of hermeneutics eventually made clear that the model of translation does not, as such, fully come to grips with the manifoldness of what language means in man's existence. Certainly in translation one finds the tension and release that structure all understanding and understandability, but it ultimately derives from the universality of the hermeneutical problem. It is important to realize that this phenomenon is not secondary in human existence, and hermeneutics is not to be viewed as a mere subordinate discipline within the arena of the *Geisteswissenschaften*.

The universal phenomenon of human linguisticality also unfolds in other dimensions than those which would appear to be directly concerned with the hermeneutical problem, for hermeneutics reaches into all the contexts that determine and condition the linguisticality of the human experience of the world. Some of those have been touched upon in my *Truth and Method;*[4] for instance, the *wirkungsgeschichtliches Bewusstsein* (consciousness of effective history,[5] or the consciousness in which history is ever at work) was presented in a conscious effort to shed light on the idea of language in some phases of its history. And of course linguisticality extends into many different dimensions not mentioned in *Truth and Method.*

* * *

Because of [the] historical development of hermeneutics hermeneutical theory oriented itself to the task of interpreting expressions of life that are fixed in writing, although Schleiermacher's[6] theoretical working out of hermeneutics included understanding as it takes place in the oral exchange of conversation. Rhetoric, on the other hand, concerned itself with the impact of *speaking* in all its immediacy. It did of course also enter into the realm of effective *writing*, and thus it developed a body of teaching on style and styles. Nevertheless, it achieved its authentic realization not in the act of reading but in speaking. The phenomenon of the orally read speech occupies an in-between, a hybrid, position: already it displays a tendency to base the art of speaking on the techniques of expression inherent in the medium of writing, and thus it begins to abstract itself from the original situation of speaking. Thus begins the transformation into poetics, whose linguistic objects are so wholly and completely art that their transformation from the oral sphere into writing and back is accomplished without loss or damage.

Rhetoric as such, however, is tied to the immediacy of its effect. Now the arousing of emotions, which is clearly the essence of the orator's task, is effectual to a vastly diminished degree in written expression, which is the traditional object of hermeneutical investigation. And this is precisely the difference that matters: the orator carries his listeners away with him; the convincing power of his arguments overwhelms the listener. While under the persuasive

4. Published in 1960; see the following selection.
5. More literally, "consciousness of the history of influences."
6. Friedrich Schleiermacher (1768–1834), German theologian and philologist; he championed the idea of "interpretation" as basic to theology and biblical studies, literary studies, and the *Geisteswissenschaften* (humanities and social sciences) more generally.

spell of speech, the listener for the moment cannot and ought not to indulge in critical examination. On the other hand, the reading and interpreting of what is written is so distanced and detached from its author—from his mood, intentions, and unexpressed tendencies—that the grasping of the meaning of the text takes on something of the character of an independent productive act, one that resembles more the art of the orator than the process of mere listening. Thus it is easy to understand why the theoretical tools of the art of interpretation (hermeneutics) have been to a large extent borrowed from rhetoric.

Where, indeed, but to rhetoric should the theoretical examination of interpretation turn? Rhetoric from oldest tradition has been the only advocate of a claim to truth that defends the probable, the *eikós* (verisimile), and that which is convincing to the ordinary reason, against the claim of science to accept as true only what can be demonstrated and tested! Convincing and persuading, without being able to prove—these are obviously as much the aim and measure of understanding and interpretation as they are the aim and measure of the art of oration and persuasion. And this whole wide realm of convincing "persuasions" and generally reigning views has not been gradually narrowed by the progress of science,[7] however great it has been; rather, this realm extends to take in every new product of scientific endeavor, claiming it for itself and bringing it within its scope.

The ubiquity of rhetoric, indeed, is unlimited. Only through it is science a sociological factor of life, for all the representations of science that are directed beyond the mere narrow circle of specialists (and, perhaps one should say, insofar as they are not limited in their impact to a very small circle of initiates) owe their effectiveness to the rhetorical element they contain. Even Descartes,[8] that great and passionate advocate of method and certainty, is in all his writings an author who uses the means of rhetoric in a magnificent fashion. There can be no doubt, then, about the fundamental function of rhetoric within social life. But one may go further, in view of the ubiquity of rhetoric, to defend the primordial claims of rhetoric over against modern science, remembering that all science that would wish to be of practical usefulness at all is dependent on it.

No less universal is the function of hermeneutics. The lack of immediate understandability of texts handed down to us historically or their proneness to be misunderstood is really only a special case of what is to be met in all human orientation to the world as the *atopon* (the strange), that which does not "fit" into the customary order of our expectation based on experience. Hermeneutics has only called our attention to this phenomenon. Just as when we progress in understanding the *mirabilia*[9] lose their strangeness, so every successful appropriation of tradition is dissolved into a new and distinct familiarity in which it belongs to us and we to it. They both flow together into one owned and shared world, which encompasses past and present and which receives its linguistic articulation in the speaking of man with man.

The phenomenon of understanding, then, shows the universality of human linguisticality as a limitless medium that carries *everything* within it—not only the "culture" that has been handed down to us through language, but abso-

---

7. *Wissenschaft*: that is, intellectual inquiry in the various cognitive disciplines, from the natural sciences to the humanities (and including philosophy).

8. René Descartes (1596–1650), French mathematician and rationalist philosopher.

9. Wonders; miracles (Latin).

lutely everything—because everything (in the world and out of it) is included in the realm of "understandings" and understandability in which we move. Plato was right when he asserted that whoever regards things in the mirror of speech becomes aware of them in their full and undiminished truth. And he was profoundly correct when he taught that all cognition is only what it is as re-cognition, for a "first cognition" is as little possible as a first word.[1] In fact, a cognition in the very recent past, one whose consequences appear as yet unforeseeable, becomes what it truly is for us only when it has unfolded into its consequences and into the medium of intersubjective understanding.

And so we see that the rhetorical and hermeneutical aspects of human linguisticality completely interpenetrate each other. There would be no speaker and no art of speaking if understanding and consent were not in question, were not underlying elements; there would be no hermeneutical task if there were no mutual understanding that has been disturbed and that those involved in a conversation must search for and find again together.

* * *

My thesis is—and I think it is the necessary consequence of recognizing the operativeness of history in our conditionedness and finitude—that the thing which hermeneutics teaches us is to see through the dogmatism of asserting an opposition and separation between the ongoing, natural "tradition" and the reflective appropriation of it. For behind this assertion stands a dogmatic objectivism that distorts the very concept of hermeneutical reflection itself. In this objectivism the understander is seen—even in the so-called sciences of understanding like history—not in relationship to the hermeneutical situation and the constant operativeness of history in his own consciousness, but in such a way as to imply that his own understanding does not enter into the event.

But this is simply not the case. Actually, the historian, even the one who treats history as a "critical science," is so little separated from the ongoing traditions (for example, those of his nation) that he is really *himself engaged in* contributing to the growth and development of the national state. He is one of the "nation's" historians; he belongs to the nation. And for the epoch of national states, one must say: the more he may have reflected on his hermeneutical conditionedness, the more national he knows himself to be. J. F. Droysen,[2] for instance, who saw through the "eunuch-like objectivity" of the historian in all its methodological naïvete, was himself tremendously influential for the national consciousness of bourgeois nineteenth-century culture. He was, in any case, more effective than the epical consciousness of Ranke,[3] which was inclined to foster the nonpoliticality appropriate to an authoritarian state. To understand, we may say, is itself a kind of happening. Only a naïve and unreflective historicism in hermeneutics would see the historical-hermeneutical sciences as something absolutely new that would do away with the power of "tradition." On the contrary, I have tried to present in *Truth and Method*, through the aspect of linguisticality that operates in all

1. The Greek philosopher Plato (ca. 427–ca. 347 B.C.E.) compared speech to a mirror in *Theaetetus* 206d; he argued in the *Meno* and other dialogues that knowledge is acquired through a process of recollection.
2. Johann Gustav Droysen (1808–1884), German

historian; the quoted phrase is from his *Outlines of the Principles of History* (1858).
3. Leopold von Ranke (1795–1886), leading German historian of the 19th century; he advocated the impartiality and neutrality rejected by Droysen.

understanding, an unambiguous demonstration of the continual process of mediation by which that which is societally transmitted (the tradition) lives on. For language is not only an object in our hands, it is the reservoir of tradition and the medium in and through which we exist and perceive our world.

* * *

* * * With [the] area of what lies outside the realm of human understanding and human understandings (our world) hermeneutics is not concerned.[4] Certainly I affirm the hermeneutical fact that the world is the medium of human understanding or not understanding,[5] but it does not lead to the conclusion that cultural tradition should be absolutized and fixed. To suppose that it does have this implication seems to me erroneous. The principle of hermeneutics simply means that we should try to understand everything that can be understood. This is what I meant by the sentence: "Being that can be understood is language."[6]

This does not mean that there is a world of meanings that is narrowed down to[7] the status of secondary objects of knowledge and mere supplements to the economic and political realities that fundamentally determine the life of society. Rather, it means that the mirror of language is reflecting everything that is. In language, and only in it, can we meet what we never "encounter" in the world, because we are ourselves it (and not merely what we mean or what we know of ourselves). But the metaphor of a mirror is not fully adequate to the phenomenon of language, for in the last analysis language is not simply a mirror. What we perceive in it is not merely a "reflection" of our own and all being; it is the living out of what it is with us—not only in the concrete interrelationships of work and politics but in all the other relationships and dependencies that comprise our world.

Language, then, is not the finally found anonymous subject of all social-historical processes and action, which presents the whole of its activities as objectivations to our observing gaze; rather, it is by itself the game of interpretation that we all are engaged in every day. In this game nobody is above and before all the others; everybody is at the center, is "it" in this game. Thus it is always his turn to be interpreting. This process of interpretation takes place whenever we "understand," especially when we see through prejudices or tear away the pretenses that hide reality. There, indeed, understanding comes into its own. This idea recalls what we said about the *atopon*, the strange, for in it we have "seen through" something that appeared odd and unintelligible: we have brought it into our linguistic world. To use the analogy of chess, everything is "solved," resembling a difficult chess problem where only the definitive solution makes understandable (and then right down to the last piece) the necessity of a previous absurd position.

* * *

* * * If the hermeneutical problematic wishes to maintain itself in the face of the ubiquity and universality of rhetoric, as well as the obvious topicality

---

4. Better translated: "Hermeneutics is not concerned with what lies outside the realm of human understanding [as a phenomenon and capacity] and human understandings."

5. That is, misunderstanding.
6. *Wahrheit und Methode* [*Truth and Method*] (Tübingen, 1960), p. 450 [Gadamer's note].
7. That is, reduced or confined to.

of critiques of ideology, it must establish its own universality.[8] And it must do so especially over against the claims of modern science to universality, and thus to its tendency to absorb hermeneutical reflection into itself and render it serviceable to science (as in the concept, for instance, of the "methodical development of intelligence" Habermas has in mind[9]). Still, it will be able to do so only if it does not become imprisoned in the impregnable immanence of transcendental reflection but rather gives account of what its own kind of reflection achieves. And it must do it not only within the realm of modern science but also over against this realm, in order to show a universality that transcends that of modern science.

Hermeneutical reflection fulfills the function that is accomplished in all bringing of something to a conscious awareness. Because it does, it can and must manifest itself in all our modern fields of knowledge, and especially science. Let us reflect a bit on this hermeneutical reflection. Reflection on a given preunderstanding brings before me something that otherwise happens *behind my back*. Something—but not everything, for what I have called the *wirkungsgeschichtliches Bewusstsein* is inescapably more *being* than consciousness, and being is never fully manifest. Certainly I do not mean that such reflection could escape from ideological ossification if it does not engage in constant self-reflection and attempts at self-awareness. Thus only through hermeneutical reflection am I no longer unfree over against myself but rather can deem freely what in my preunderstanding may be justified and what unjustifiable.

And also only in this manner do I learn to gain a new understanding of what I have seen through eyes conditioned by prejudice. But this implies, too, that the prejudgments that lead my preunderstanding are also constantly at stake, right up to the moment of their surrender—which surrender could also be called a transformation. It is the untiring power of *experience*, that in the process of being instructed, man is ceaselessly forming a new preunderstanding.

In the fields that were the starting points of my hermeneutical studies— the study of art and the philological-historical sciences—it is easy to demonstrate how hermeneutical reflection is at work. For instance, consider how the autonomy of viewing art from the vantage point of the history of style has been shaken up by hermeneutical reflection (1) on the concept of art itself, and (2) on concepts of individual styles and epochs. Consider how iconography has pressed from the periphery to the forefront, and how hermeneutical reflection on the concepts of experience and expression has had literary-critical consequences (even in cases where it becomes only a more conscious carrying forward of tendencies long favored in literary criticism). While it is of course evident how the shake-up of fixed presuppositions promises scientific progress by making new questions possible, it should be equally evident that this applies in the history of artistic and literary styles. And we constantly experience what historical research can accomplish through becoming

8. That is, generality (*Allgemeinheit*).
9. In an earlier passage not included here, Gadamer cited this quote to JÜRGEN HABERMAS's "Zur Logik der Sozialwissenschaften [On the Logic of the Social Sciences]," *Philosophische Rundschau* 14, supplement 5 (1966–67): 172–74.

conscious of the history of ideas. In *Truth and Method* I believe I have been able to show how historical alienation is mediated in the form of what I call the "fusion of horizons."

The overall significance of hermeneutical reflection, however, is not exhausted by what it means for and in the sciences[1] themselves. For all the modern sciences possess a deeply rooted alienation that they impose on the natural consciousness and of which we need to be aware. This alienation has already reached reflective awareness in the very beginning stages of modern science in the concept of *method*. Hermeneutical reflection does not desire to change or eliminate this situation; it can, in fact, indirectly serve the methodological endeavor of science by making transparently clear the guiding preunderstandings in the sciences and thereby open new dimensions of questioning. But it must also bring to awareness, in this regard, the price that methods in science have paid for their own progress: the toning down and abstraction they demand, through which the natural consciousness still always must go along as the consumer of the inventions and information attained by science. One can with Wittgenstein[2] express this insight as follows: The language games of science remain related to the metalanguage presented in the mother tongue. All the knowledge won by science enters the societal consciousness through school and education, using modern informational media, though maybe sometimes after a great—too great—delay. In any case, this is the way that new sociolinguistic realities are articulated.

For the *natural* sciences, of course, this gap and the methodical alienation of research are of less consequence than for social sciences. The true natural scientist does not have to be told how very particular is the realm of knowledge of his science in relation to the whole of reality. He does not share in the deification of his science that the public would press upon him. All the more, however, the public (and the researcher who must go before the public) needs hermeneutical reflection on the presuppositions and limits of science. The so-called "humanities," on the other hand, are still easily mediated to the common consciousness, so that insofar as they are accepted at all, their objects belong immediately to the cultural heritage and the realm of traditional education. But the modern social sciences stand in a particularly strained relationship to their object, the social reality, and this relationship especially requires hermeneutical reflection. For the methodical alienation to which the social sciences owe their progress is related here to the human-societal world as a whole. These sciences increasingly see themselves as marked out for the purpose of scientific ordering and control of society. They have to do with "scientific" and "methodical" planning, direction, organization, development— in short, with an infinity of functions that, so to speak, determine from outside the whole of the life of each individual and each group. Yet this social engineer, this scientist who undertakes to look after the functioning of the machine of society, appears himself to be methodically alienated and split off from the society to which, at the same time, he belongs.

---

1. That is, the cognitive disciplines (*Wissenschaften*).
2. Ludwig Wittgenstein (1889–1951), Austrian-born British philosopher of immense influence (see this anthology's companion volume, *The Ana-* lytic Tradition*); "language games," discussed in his *Philosophical Investigations* (1953), are cases in which language is used to structure human social practices.

But is man as a political being the mere object of the techniques of making public opinion? I think not: he is a member of society, and only in playing his role with free judgment and politically real effectiveness can he conserve freedom. It is the function of hermeneutical reflection, in this connection, to preserve us from naïve surrender to the experts of social technology.

* * *

SOURCE: From Hans-Georg Gadamer, "On the Scope and Function of Hermeneutical Reflection (1967)," trans. G. B. Hess and R. E. Palmer, in his *Philosophical Hermeneutics*, ed. David E. Linge (Berkeley: University of California Press, 1976), pp. 18–20, 23–25, 28–29, 31–32, 37–40. Originally published in 1967 as "Rhetorik, Hermeneutik und Ideologiekritik"; this translation was first published in slightly different form in 1970.

From Truth and Method

From *Chapter 5. Language and Hermeneutics*

FROM 1. LANGUAGE AS THE MEDIUM OF HERMENEUTIC EXPERIENCE

We say that we "conduct" a conversation, but the more genuine a conversation is, the less its conduct lies within the will of either partner. Thus a genuine conversation is never the one that we wanted to conduct. Rather, it is generally more correct to say that we fall into conversation, or even that we become involved in it. The way one word follows another, with the conversation taking its own twists and reaching its own conclusion, may well be conducted in some way, but the partners conversing are far less the leaders of it than the led. No one knows in advance what will "come out" of a conversation. Understanding or its failure is like an event that happens to us. Thus we can say that something was a good conversation or that it was ill fated. All this shows that a conversation has a spirit of its own, and that the language in which it is conducted bears its own truth within it—i.e., that it allows something to "emerge" which henceforth exists.

In our analysis of romantic hermeneutics we have already seen that understanding is not based on transposing oneself into another person, on one person's immediate participation with another. To understand what a person says is, as we saw, to come to an understanding about the subject matter, not to get inside another person and relive his experiences (Erlebnisse). We emphasized that the experience (Erfahrung) of meaning that takes place in understanding always includes application. Now we are to note *that this whole process is verbal*. It is not for nothing that the special problematic of understanding and the attempt to master it as an art—the concern of hermeneutics—belongs traditionally to the sphere of grammar and rhetoric. Language is the medium in which substantive understanding and agreement take place between two people.

In situations where coming to an understanding is disrupted or impeded, we first become conscious of the conditions of all understanding. Thus the verbal process whereby a conversation in two different languages is made possible through translation is especially informative. Here the translator must translate the meaning to be understood into the context in which the other speaker lives. This does not, of course, mean that he is at liberty to falsify the meaning of what the other person says. Rather, the meaning must be preserved, but since it must be understood within a new language world, it must establish its validity within it in a new way. Thus every translation is at the same time an interpretation. We can even say that the translation is the culmination of the interpretation that the translator has made of the words given him.

The example of translation, then, makes us aware that language as the medium of understanding must be consciously created by an explicit mediation. This kind of explicit process is undoubtedly not the norm in a conversation. Nor is translation the norm in the way we approach a foreign language. Rather, having to rely on translation is tantamount to two people giving up their independent authority. Where a translation is necessary, the gap between the spirit of the original words and that of their reproduction must be taken into account. It is a gap that can never be completely closed. But in these cases understanding does not really take place between the partners of the conversation, but between the interpreters, who can really have an encounter in a common world of understanding. (It is well known that nothing is more difficult than a dialogue in two different languages in which one person speaks one and the other person the other, each understanding the other's language but not speaking it. As if impelled by a higher force, one of the languages always tries to establish itself over the other as the medium of understanding.)

Where there is understanding, there is not translation but speech. To understand a foreign language means that we do not need to translate it into our own. When we really master a language, then no translation is necessary—in fact, any translation seems impossible. Understanding how to speak is not yet of itself real understanding and does not involve an interpretive process; it is an accomplishment of life. For you understand a language by living in it—a statement that is true, as we know, not only of living but dead languages as well. Thus the hermeneutical problem concerns not the correct mastery of language but coming to a proper understanding about the subject matter, which takes place in the medium of language. Every language can be learned so perfectly that using it no longer means translating from or into one's native tongue, but thinking in the foreign language. Mastering the language is a necessary precondition for coming to an understanding in a conversation. Every conversation obviously presupposes that the two speakers speak the same language. Only when two people can make themselves understood through language by talking together can the problem of understanding and agreement even be raised. Having to depend on an interpreter's translation is an extreme case that doubles the hermeneutical process, namely the conversation: there is one conversation between the interpreter and the other, and a second between the interpreter and oneself.

Conversation is a process of coming to an understanding. Thus it belongs to every true conversation that each person opens himself to the other, truly accepts his point of view as valid and transposes himself into the other to such an extent that he understands not the particular individual but what he says.

What is to be grasped is the substantive rightness of his opinion, so that we can be at one with each other on the subject. Thus we do not relate the other's opinion to him but to our own opinions and views. Where a person is concerned with the other as individuality—e.g., in a therapeutic conversation or the interrogation of a man accused of a crime—this is not really a situation in which two people are trying to come to an understanding.[1]

Everything we have said characterizing the situation of two people coming to an understanding in conversation has a genuine application to hermeneutics, which is concerned with *understanding texts*. Let us again start by considering the extreme case of translation from a foreign language. Here no one can doubt that the translation of a text, however much the translator may have dwelt with and empathized with his author, cannot be simply a re-awakening of the original process in the writer's mind; rather, it is necessarily a re-creation of the text guided by the way the translator understands what it says. No one can doubt that what we are dealing with here is interpretation, and not simply reproduction. A new light falls on the text from the other language and for the reader of it. The requirement that a translation be faithful cannot remove the fundamental gulf between the two languages. However faithful we try to be, we have to make difficult decisions. In our translation if we want to emphasize a feature of the original that is important to us, then we can do so only by playing down or entirely suppressing other features. But this is precisely the activity that we call interpretation. Translation, like all interpretation, is a highlighting. A translator must understand that highlighting is part of his task. Obviously he must not leave open whatever is not clear to him. He must show his colors. Yet there are borderline cases in the original (and for the "original reader") where something is in fact unclear. But precisely these hermeneutical borderline cases show the straits in which the translator constantly finds himself. Here he must resign himself. He must state clearly how he understands. But since he is always in the position of not really being able to express all the dimensions of his text, he must make a constant renunciation. Every translation that takes its task seriously is at once clearer and flatter than the original. Even if it is a masterly re-creation, it must lack some of the overtones that vibrate in the original. (In rare cases of masterly re-creation the loss can be made good or even mean a gain—think, for example, of how Baudelaire's *Les fleurs du mal*[2] seems to acquire an odd new vigor in Stefan George's version.)

The translator is often painfully aware of his inevitable distance from the original. His dealing with the text is like the effort to come to an understanding in conversation. But translating is like an especially laborious process of understanding, in which one views the distance between one's own opinion and its contrary as ultimately unbridgeable. And, as in conversation, when there are such unbridgeable differences, a compromise can sometimes be achieved in the to and fro of dialogue, so in the to and fro of weighing and

1. If one transposes oneself into the position of another with the intent of understanding not the truth of what he is saying, but him, the questions asked in such a conversation are marked by the inauthenticity described above (pp. 362f.) [Gadamer's note]. The page numbers refer to the source text (a passage not included here).
2. *The Flowers of Evil* (1857), a collection of poems by the French poet Charles Baudelaire (1821–1867); it was translated into German in 1901 by George (1868–1933), a German lyric poet.

balancing possibilities, the translator will seek the best solution—a solution that can never be more than a compromise. As one tries in conversation to transpose oneself into the other person in order to understand his point of view, so also does the translator try to transpose himself completely into his author. But doing so does not automatically mean that understanding is achieved in a conversation, nor for the translator does such transposition mean success in re-creating the meaning. The structures are clearly analogous. Reaching an understanding in conversation presupposes that both partners are ready for it and are trying to recognize the full value of what is alien and opposed to them. If this happens mutually, and each of the partners, while simultaneously holding on to his own arguments, weighs the counterarguments, it is finally possible to achieve—in an imperceptible but not arbitrary reciprocal translation of the other's position (we call this an exchange of views)—a common diction and a common dictum. Similarly, the translator must preserve the character of his own language, the language into which he is translating, while still recognizing the value of the alien, even antagonistic character of the text and its expression. Perhaps, however, this description of the translator's activity is too truncated. Even in these extreme situations where it is necessary to translate from one language into another, the subject matter can scarcely be separated from the language. Only that translator can truly re-create who brings into language the subject matter that the text points to; but this means finding a language that is not only his but is also proportionate to the original.[3] The situation of the translator and that of the interpreter are fundamentally the same.

In bridging the gulf between languages, the translator clearly exemplifies the reciprocal relationship that exists between interpreter and text, and that corresponds to the reciprocity involved in reaching an understanding in conversation. For every translator is an interpreter. The fact that a foreign language is being translated means that this is simply an extreme case of hermeneutical difficulty—i.e., of alienness and its conquest. In fact all the "objects" with which traditional hermeneutics is concerned are alien in the same unequivocally defined sense. The translator's task of re-creation differs only in degree, not in kind, from the general hermeneutical task that any text presents.

This is not to say, of course, that the hermeneutic situation in regard to texts is exactly the same as that between two people in conversation. Texts are "enduringly fixed expressions of life"[4] that are to be understood; and that means that one partner in the hermeneutical conversation, the text, speaks only through the other partner, the interpreter. Only through him are the written marks changed back into meaning. Nevertheless, in being changed back by understanding, the subject matter of which the text speaks itself finds expression. It is like a real conversation in that the common subject matter is what binds the two partners, the text and the interpreter, to each other. When a translator interprets a conversation, he can make mutual understanding

---

3. We have here the problem of "alienation," on which Schadewaldt has important things to say in the appendix to his translation of the *Odyssey* (RoRoRo-Klassiker, 1958), p. 324 [Gadamer's note]. Wolfgang Schadewaldt (1900–1974), Ger-

man classical philologist and translator.
4. [J. G.] Droysen, *Historik* [i.e., *Grundriss der Historik* (1858, *Outlines of the Principles of History*)], ed. Hübner (1937), p. 63 [Gadamer's note].

possible only if he participates in the subject under discussion; so also in relation to a text it is indispensable that the interpreter participate in its meaning.

Thus it is perfectly legitimate to speak of a *hermeneutical conversation*. But from this it follows that hermeneutical conversation, like real conversation, finds a common language, and that finding a common language is not, any more than in real conversation, preparing a tool for the purpose of reaching understanding but, rather, coincides with the very act of understanding and reaching agreement. Even between the partners of this "conversation" a communication like that between two people takes place that is more than mere accommodation. The text brings a subject matter into language, but that it does so is ultimately the achievement of the interpreter. Both have a share in it.

Hence the meaning of a text is not to be compared with an immovably and obstinately fixed point of view that suggests only one question to the person trying to understand it, namely how the other person could have arrived at such an absurd opinion. In this sense understanding is certainly not concerned with "understanding historically"—i.e., reconstructing the way the text came into being. Rather, one intends to *understand the text itself*. But this means that the interpreter's own thoughts too have gone into re-awakening the text's meaning. In this the interpreter's own horizon is decisive, yet not as a personal standpoint that he maintains or enforces, but more as an opinion and a possibility that one brings into play and puts at risk, and that helps one truly to make one's own what the text says. I have described this above[5] as a "fusion of horizons." We can now see that this is what takes place in conversation, in which something is expressed that is not only mine or my author's, but common.

We are indebted to German romanticism for disclosing the systematic significance of the verbal nature of conversation for all understanding. It has taught us that understanding and interpretation are ultimately the same thing. As we have seen, this insight elevates the idea of interpretation from the merely occasional and pedagogical significance it had in the eighteenth century to a systematic position, as indicated by the key importance that the problem of language has acquired in philosophical inquiry.

Since the romantic period we can no longer hold the view that, in the absence of immediate understanding, interpretive ideas are drawn, as needed, out of a linguistic storeroom where they are lying ready. *Rather, language is the universal medium in which understanding occurs. Understanding occurs in interpreting.* This statement does not mean that there is no special problem of expression. The difference between the language of a text and the language of the interpreter, or the gulf that separates the translator from the original, is not merely a secondary question. On the contrary, the fact is that the problems of verbal expression are themselves problems of understanding. All understanding is interpretation, and all interpretation takes place in the medium of a language that allows the object to come into words and yet is at the same time the interpreter's own language.

Thus the hermeneutical phenomenon proves to be a special case of the general relationship between thinking and speaking, whose enigmatic intimacy conceals the role of language in thought. Like conversation, interpretation is

---

5. In a passage not included here (the same is true of other references to points made "above").

a circle closed by the dialectic of question and answer. It is a genuine histori-cal life comportment achieved through the medium of language, and we can call it a conversation with respect to the interpretation of texts as well. The linguisticality of understanding is *the concretion of historically effected consciousness*.

The essential relation between language and understanding is seen primar-ily in the fact that the essence of tradition is to exist in the medium of lan-guage, so that the preferred *object* of interpretation is a verbal one.

(A) LANGUAGE AS DETERMINATION OF THE HERMENEUTIC OBJECT

The fact that tradition is essentially verbal in character has consequences for hermeneutics. The understanding of verbal tradition retains special priority over all other tradition. Linguistic tradition may have less perceptual imme-diacy than monuments of plastic art. Its lack of immediacy, however, is not a defect; rather, this apparent lack, the abstract alienness of all "texts," uniquely expresses the fact that everything in language belongs to the process of under-standing. Linguistic tradition is tradition in the proper sense of the word—i.e., something handed down.[6] It is not just something left over, to be investigated and interpreted as a remnant of the past. What has come down to us by way of verbal tradition is not left over but given to us, told us—whether through direct retelling, in which myth, legend, and custom have their life, or through written tradition, whose signs are, as it were, immediately clear to every reader who can read them.

The full hermeneutical significance of the fact that tradition is essentially verbal becomes clear in the case of a *written* tradition. The detachability of language from speaking derives from the fact that it can be written. In the form of writing, all tradition is contemporaneous with each present time. Moreover, it involves a unique co-existence of past and present, insofar as present consciousness has the possibility of a free access to everything handed down in writing. No longer dependent on retelling, which mediates past knowl-edge with the present, understanding consciousness acquires—through its immediate access to literary tradition—a genuine opportunity to change and widen its horizon, and thus enrich its world by a whole new and deeper dimen-sion. The appropriation of literary tradition even surpasses the experience connected with the adventure of traveling and being immersed in the world of a foreign language. At every moment the reader who studies a foreign lan-guage and literature retains the possibility of free movement back to himself, and thus is at once both here and there.

A written tradition is not a fragment of a past world, but has already raised itself beyond this into the sphere of the meaning that it expresses. The ideal-ity of the word is what raises everything linguistic beyond the finitude and transience that characterize other remnants of past existence. It is not this document, as a piece of the past, that is the bearer of tradition but the conti-nuity of memory. Through it tradition becomes part of our own world, and thus what it communicates can be stated immediately. Where we have a writ-ten tradition, we are not just told a particular thing; a past humanity itself

---

6. In German, "tradition" is *Überlieferung*, a compound of *liefern* (to deliver) and *über* (over).

becomes present to us in its general relation to the world. That is why our understanding remains curiously unsure and fragmentary when we have no written tradition of a culture but only dumb monuments, and we do not call this information about the past "history." Texts, on the other hand, always express a whole. Meaningless strokes that seem strange and incomprehensible prove suddenly intelligible in every detail when they can be interpreted as writing—so much so that even the arbitrariness of a corrupt text can be corrected if the context as a whole is understood.

Thus written texts present the real hermeneutical task. Writing is self-alienation.[7] Overcoming it, reading the text, is thus the highest task of understanding. Even the pure signs of an inscription can be seen properly and articulated correctly only if the text can be transformed back into language. As we have said, however, this transformation always establishes a relationship to what is meant, to the subject matter being discussed. Here the process of understanding moves entirely in a sphere of meaning mediated by the verbal tradition. Thus in the case of an inscription the hermeneutical task starts only after it has been deciphered (presumably correctly). Only in an extended sense do non-literary monuments present a hermeneutical task, for they cannot be understood of themselves. What they mean is a question of their interpretation, not of deciphering and understanding the wording of a text.

In writing, language gains its true ideality, for in encountering a written tradition understanding consciousness acquires its full sovereignty. Its being does not depend on anything. Thus reading consciousness is in potential possession of its history. It is not for nothing that with the emergence of a literary culture the idea of "philology," "love of speech,"[8] was transferred entirely to the all-embracing art of reading, losing its original connection with the cultivation of speech and argument. A reading consciousness is necessarily a historical consciousness and communicates freely with historical tradition. Thus it is historically legitimate to say with Hegel that history begins with the emergence of a will to hand things down, "to make memory last."[9] Writing is no mere accident or mere supplement that qualitatively changes nothing in the course of oral tradition. Certainly, there can be a will to make things continue, a will to permanence, without writing. But only a written tradition can detach itself from the mere continuance of the vestiges of past life, remnants from which one human being can by inference piece out another's existence.

The tradition of inscriptions has never shared in the free form of tradition that we call literature, since it depends on the existence of the remains, whether of stone or whatever material. But it is true of everything that has come down to us by being written down that here a will to permanence has created the unique forms of continuance that we call literature. It does not present us with only a stock of memorials and signs. Rather, literature

7. That is, the objectification of oneself in an external medium that does or can distance what one expresses from the thought, intention, or meaning that one sought to convey. Gadamer is appropriating and applying the concept of *Entfremdung*, which HEGEL developed and used broadly and significantly in his account of the nature, development, and self-realization of *Geist*.

8. A literal rendering of the Greek roots *philo-* (love) and *logos* (speech, word).

9. Hegel, *Die Vernunft in der Geschichte* [*Reason in History*], ed. Lasson [in *Sämtliche Werke* (*Complete Works*), vol. 8], p. 145 [Gadamer's note].

has acquired its own contemporaneity with every present. To understand it does not mean primarily to reason one's way back into the past, but to have a present involvement in what is said. It is not really a relationship between persons, between the reader and the author (who is perhaps quite unknown), but about sharing in what the text shares with us. The meaning of what is said is, when we understand it, quite independent of whether the tradition-ary text gives us a picture of the author and of whether or not we want to interpret it as a historical source.

Let us here recall that the task of hermeneutics was first and foremost the understanding of texts. Schleiermacher[1] was the first to downplay the impor-tance of writing for the hermeneutical problem because he saw that the prob-lem of understanding was raised—and perhaps in its fullest form—by oral utterance too. We have outlined above how the psychological dimension he gave hermeneutics concealed its historical dimension. In actual fact, writing is central to the hermeneutical phenomenon insofar as its detachment both from the writer or author and from a specifically addressed recipient or reader gives it a life of its own. What is fixed in writing has raised itself into a public sphere of meaning in which everyone who can read has an equal share.

Certainly, in relation to language, writing seems a secondary phenomenon. The sign language of writing refers to the actual language of speech. But that language is capable of being written is by no means incidental to its nature. Rather, this capacity for being written down is based on the fact that speech itself shares in the pure ideality of the meaning that communicates itself in it. In writing, the meaning of what is spoken exists purely for itself, completely detached from all emotional elements of expression and communication. A text is not to be understood as an expression of life but with respect to what it says. Writing is the abstract ideality of language. Hence the meaning of something written is fundamentally identifiable and repeatable. What is iden-tical in the repetition is only what was actually deposited in the written record. This indicates that "repetition" cannot be meant here in its strict sense. It does not mean referring back to the original source where something is said or written. The understanding of something written is not a repetition of something past but the sharing of a present meaning.

Writing has the methodological advantage of presenting the hermeneuti-cal problem in all its purity, detached from everything psychological. How-ever, what is from our point of view and for our purpose a methodological advantage is at the same time the expression of a specific weakness that is even more characteristic of writing than of speaking. The task of understand-ing is presented with particular clarity when we recognize the weakness of all writing. We need only recall what Plato said, namely that the specific weak-ness of writing was that no one could come to the aid of the written word if it falls victim to misunderstanding, intentional or unintentional.[2]

In the helplessness of the written word Plato discerned a more serious weak-ness than the weakness of speech (to asthenes ton logon[3]) and when he calls

1. Friedrich Schleiermacher (1768–1834), German theologian and philologist; he championed the idea of "interpretation" as basic to theology and biblical studies, literary studies, and the *Geisteswissen-schaften* (humanities and social sciences) more generally.
2. Plato [ca. 427–ca. 347 B.C.E.], *Seventh Letter,* 341c, 344c, and *Phaedrus,* 275 [Gadamer's note].
3. A near-quote of Plato's Greek (*Letter 7,* 343a).

on dialectic to come to the aid of the weakness of speech, while declaring the condition of the written word beyond hope, this is obviously an ironic exaggeration with which to conceal his own writing and his own art. In fact, writing and speech are in the same plight. Just as in speech there is an art of appearances and a corresponding art of true thought—sophistry and dialectic—so in writing there are two arts, one serving sophistic, the other dialectic. There is, then, an art of writing that comes to the aid of thought, and it is to this that the art of understanding—which affords the same help to what is written—is allied.

As we have said, all writing is a kind of alienated speech, and its signs need to be transformed back into speech and meaning. Because the meaning has undergone a kind of self-alienation through being written down, this transformation back is the real hermeneutical task. The meaning of what has been said is to be stated anew, simply on the basis of the words passed on by means of the written signs. In contrast to the spoken word there is no other aid in interpreting the written word. Thus in a special sense everything depends on the "art" of writing.[4] The spoken word interprets itself to an astonishing degree, by the manner of speaking, the tone of voice, the tempo, and so on, and also by the circumstances in which it is spoken.[5]

But there is also such a thing as writing that, as it were, reads itself. A remarkable debate on the spirit and the letter in philosophy between two great German philosophical writers, Schiller and Fichte,[6] starts from this fact. It is interesting that the dispute cannot be resolved with the aesthetic criteria used by the two men. Fundamentally this is not a question of the aesthetics of good style, but a hermeneutical question. The "art" of writing in such a way that the thoughts of the reader are stimulated and held in productive movement has little to do with the conventional rhetorical or aesthetic means. Rather, it consists entirely in one's being drawn into the course of thought. The "art" of writing does not try to be understood and noticed as such. The art of writing, like the art of speaking, is not an end in itself and therefore not the fundamental object of hermeneutical effort. Understanding is drawn on entirely by the subject matter. Hence unclear thinking and "bad" writing are not exemplary cases where the art of hermeneutics can show itself in its full glory but, on the contrary, limiting cases which undermine the basic presupposition of all hermeneutical success, namely the clear unambiguity of the intended meaning.

All writing claims it can be awakened into spoken language, and this claim to autonomy of meaning goes so far that even an authentic reading—e.g., a poet's reading of his poem—becomes questionable when we are listening to something other than what our understanding should really be directed toward. Because the important thing is communicating the text's true meaning,

---

4. This is the reason for the enormous difference that exists between what is spoken and what is written, between the style of spoken material and the far higher demands of style that something fixed as literature has to satisfy [Gadamer's note].
5. Kippenberg relates that Rilke once read one of his *Duino Elegies* aloud in such a way that the listeners were not at all aware of the difficulty of the poetry [Gadamer's note]. Anton Kippenberg (1874–1950), the publisher of the Austro-German poet Rainer Maria Rilke (1875–1926); the *Duino Elegies* (1923), a series of 10 poems composed over 10 years, is considered a masterpiece.
6. Cf. the correspondence that followed Fichte's essay "Über Geist und Buchstabe in der Philosophie [On Spirit and Letter in Philosophy]" (Fichte, *Briefwechsel* [*Correspondence* (1925)], II, ch. 5) [Gadamer's note]. For SCHILLER and FICHTE, see above.

interpreting it is already subject to the norm of the subject matter. This is the requirement that the Platonic dialectic makes when it tries to bring out the logos as such and in doing so often leaves behind the actual partner in the conversation. In fact, the particular weakness of writing, its greater helplessness as compared to speech, has another side to it, in that it demonstrates with redoubled clarity the dialectical task of understanding. As in conversation, understanding here too must try to strengthen the meaning of what is said. What is stated in the text must be detached from all contingent factors and grasped in its full ideality, in which alone it has validity. Thus, precisely because it entirely detaches the sense of what is said from the person saying it, the written word makes the understanding reader the arbiter of its claim to truth. The reader experiences what is addressed to him and what he understands in all its validity. What he understands is always more than an unfamiliar opinion: it is always possible truth. This is what emerges from detaching what is spoken from the speaker and from the permanence that writing bestows. This is the deeper hermeneutical reason for the fact, mentioned above, that it does not occur to people who are not used to reading that what is written down could be wrong, since to them anything written seems like a self-authenticating document.

Everything written is, in fact, the paradigmatic object of hermeneutics. What we found in the extreme case of a foreign language and in the problems of translation is confirmed here by the autonomy of reading: understanding is not a psychic transposition. The horizon of understanding cannot be limited either by what the writer originally had in mind or by the horizon of the person to whom the text was originally addressed.

It sounds at first like a sensible hermeneutical rule—and is generally recognized as such—that nothing should be put into[7] a text that the writer or the reader could not have intended. But this rule can be applied only in extreme cases. For texts do not ask to be understood as a living expression of the subjectivity of their writers. This, then, cannot define the limits of a text's meaning. However, it is not only limiting a text's meaning to the "actual" thoughts of the *author* that is questionable. Even if one tries to determine the meaning of a text objectively by regarding it as a contemporary document and in relation to its original *reader*, as was Schleiermacher's basic procedure, one does not get beyond an accidental delimitation. The idea of the contemporary addressee can claim only a restricted critical validity. For what is contemporaneity? Listeners of the day before yesterday as well as of the day after tomorrow are always among those to whom one speaks as a contemporary. Where are we to draw the line that excludes a reader from being addressed? What are contemporaries and what is a text's claim to truth in the face of this multifarious mixture of past and future? The idea of the original reader is full of unexamined idealization.

Furthermore, our conception of the nature of literary tradition contains a fundamental objection to the hermeneutical legitimacy of the idea of the original reader. We saw that literature is defined by the will to hand on.[8] But a person who copies and passes on is doing it for his own contemporaries. Thus the reference to the original reader, like that to the meaning of the author,

---

7. That is, imputed to, read into.   8. That is, pass on, hand down.

seems to offer only a very crude historico-hermeneutical criterion that cannot really limit the horizon of a text's meaning. What is fixed in writing has detached itself from the contingency of its origin and its author and made itself free for new relationships. Normative concepts such as the author's meaning or the original reader's understanding in fact represent only an empty space that is filled from time to time in understanding.

(B) LANGUAGE AS DETERMINATION OF THE HERMENEUTIC ACT

This brings us to the second aspect of the relationship between language and understanding. Not only is the special object of understanding, namely tradition, of a verbal nature; understanding itself has a fundamental connection with language. We started from the proposition that understanding is already interpretation because it creates the hermeneutical horizon within which the meaning of a text comes into force. But in order to be able to express a text's meaning and subject matter, we must translate it into our own language. However, this involves relating it to the whole complex of possible meanings in which we linguistically move. We have already investigated the logical structure of this in relation to the special place of the *question* as a hermeneutical phenomenon. In now considering the verbal nature of all understanding, we are expressing from another angle what we already saw in considering the dialectic of question and answer.

Here we are emphasizing a dimension that is generally ignored by the dominant conception that the historical sciences [*Wissenschaften*] have of themselves. For the historian usually chooses concepts to describe the historical particularity of his objects without expressly reflecting on their origin and justification. He simply follows his interest in the material and takes no account of the fact that the descriptive concepts he chooses can be highly detrimental to his proper purpose if they assimilate what is historically different to what is familiar and thus, despite all impartiality, subordinate the alien being of the object to his own preconceptions. Thus, despite his scientific method,[9] he behaves just like everyone else—as a child of his time who is unquestioningly dominated by the concepts and prejudices of his own age.

Insofar as the historian does not admit this naivete to himself, he fails to reach the level of reflection that the subject matter demands. But his naivete becomes truly abysmal when he starts to become aware of the problems it raises and so demands that in understanding history one must leave one's own concepts aside and think only in the concepts of the epoch one is trying to understand. This demand, which sounds like a logical implementation of historical consciousness is, as will be clear to every thoughtful reader, a naive illusion. The naivete of this claim does not consist in the fact that it goes unfulfilled because the interpreter does not sufficiently attain the ideal of leaving himself aside. This would still mean that it was a legitimate ideal, and one should strive to reach it as far as possible. But what the legitimate demand of the historical consciousness—to understand a period in terms of its own concepts—really means is something quite different. The call to leave aside the concepts of the present does not mean a naive transposition into the past.

9. That is, despite the historian's adherence to the *wissenschaftlich* method appropriate to a rigorous cognitive discipline.

It is, rather, an essentially relative demand that has meaning only in relation to one's own concepts. Historical consciousness fails to understand its own nature if, in order to understand, it seeks to exclude what alone makes understanding possible. *To think historically* means, in fact, *to perform the transposition that the concepts of the past undergo* when we try to think in them. To think historically always involves mediating between those ideas and one's own thinking. To try to escape from one's own concepts in interpretation is not only impossible but manifestly absurd. To interpret means precisely to bring one's own preconceptions[1] into play so that the text's meaning can really be made to speak for us.

In our analysis of the hermeneutical process we saw that to acquire a horizon of interpretation requires a fusion of horizons. This is now confirmed by the verbal aspect of interpretation. The text is made to speak through interpretation. But no text and no book speaks if it does not speak a language that reaches the other person. Thus interpretation must find the right language if it really wants to make the text speak. There cannot, therefore, be any single interpretation that is correct "in itself," precisely because every interpretation is concerned with the text itself. The historical life of a tradition depends on being constantly assimilated and interpreted. An interpretation that was correct in itself would be a foolish ideal that mistook the nature of tradition. Every interpretation has to adapt itself to the hermeneutical situation to which it belongs.

Being bound by a situation does not mean that the claim to correctness that every interpretation must make is dissolved into the subjective or the occasional. We must not here abandon the insights of the romantics, who purified the problem of hermeneutics from all its occasional elements. Interpretation is not something pedagogical for us either; it is the act of understanding itself, which is realized—not just for the one for whom one is interpreting but also for the interpreter himself—in the explicitness of verbal interpretation. Thanks to the verbal nature of all interpretation, every interpretation includes the possibility of a relationship with others. There can be no speaking that does not bind the speaker and the person spoken to. This is true of the hermeneutic process as well. But this relationship does not determine the interpretative process of understanding—as if interpreting were a conscious adaptation to a pedagogical situation; rather, this process is simply *the concretion of the meaning itself.* Let us recall our emphasis on the element of application, which had completely disappeared from hermeneutics. We saw that to understand a text always means to apply it to ourselves and to know that, even if it must always be understood in different ways, it is still the same text presenting itself to us in these different ways. That this does not in the least relativize the claim to truth of every interpretation is seen from the fact that all interpretation is essentially verbal. The verbal explicitness that understanding achieves through interpretation does not create a second sense apart from that which is understood and interpreted. The interpretive concepts are not, as such, thematic in understanding. Rather, it is their nature to disappear behind what they bring to speech in interpretation. Paradoxically, an interpretation is right when it is capable of disappearing in this

---

1. That is, the concepts one already has at one's disposal (conceptual resources, not prejudices).

way. And yet at the same time it must be expressed as something that is supposed to disappear. The possibility of understanding is dependent on the possibility of this kind of mediating interpretation.

This is also true in those cases when there is immediate understanding and no explicit interpretation is undertaken. For in these cases too interpretation must be possible. But this means that interpretation is contained potentially within the understanding process. It simply makes the understanding explicit. Thus interpretation is not a means through which understanding is achieved; rather, it enters into the content of what is understood. Let us recall that this means not only that the sense of the text can be realized as a unity but that the subject matter of which the text speaks is also expressed. The interpretation places the object, as it were, on the scales of words. There are a few characteristic variations on this general statement that indirectly confirm it. When we are concerned with understanding and interpreting verbal texts, interpretation in the medium of language itself shows what understanding always is: assimilating what is said to the point that it becomes one's own. Verbal interpretation is the form of all interpretation, even when what is to be interpreted is not linguistic in nature—i.e., is not a text but a statue or a musical composition. We must not let ourselves be confused by forms of interpretation that are not verbal but in fact presuppose language. It is possible to demonstrate something by means of contrast—e.g., by placing two pictures alongside each other or reading two poems one after the other, so that one is interpreted by the other. In these cases demonstration seems to obviate verbal interpretation. But in fact this kind of demonstration is a modification of verbal interpretation. In such demonstration we have the reflection of interpretation, and the demonstration is used as a visual shortcut. Demonstration is interpretation in much the same sense as is a translation that embodies an interpretation, or the correct reading aloud of a text that has already decided the questions of interpretation, because one can only read aloud what one has understood. Understanding and interpretation are indissolubly bound together.

Obviously connected with the fact that interpretation and understanding are bound up with each other is that the concept of *interpretation* can be applied not only to scholarly interpretation but to artistic *reproduction*—e.g., musical or dramatic performance. We have shown above that this kind of reproduction is not a second creation re-creating the first; rather, it makes the work of art appear as itself for the first time. It brings to life the signs of the musical or dramatic text. Reading aloud is a similar process, in that it awakens a text and brings it into new immediacy.

From this it follows that the same thing must be true of understanding in silent reading. Reading fundamentally involves interpretation. This is not to say that understanding as one reads is a kind of inner production in which the work of art would acquire an independent existence—as in a production visible to all—although remaining in the intimate sphere of one's own inner life. Rather, we are stating the contrary, namely that a production that takes place in the external world of space and time does not in fact have any existence independent of the work itself and can acquire such only through a secondary aesthetic differentiation. Interpreting music or a play by performing it is not basically different from understanding a text by reading it: understanding always includes interpretation. The work of the philologist too consists in making texts readable and intelligible—i.e., safeguarding a text against misunderstandings. Thus there is no essential difference between the interpretation that a work undergoes in being performed and that which the scholar produces. A performing artist may feel that justifying his interpretation in words is very secondary, rejecting it as inartistic, but he cannot want to deny that such an account can be given of his reproductive interpretation. He too must want his interpretation to be correct and convincing, and it will not occur to him to deny that it is tied to the text he has before him. But this text is the same one that presents the scholarly interpreter with his task. Thus the performing artist will be unable to deny that his own understanding of a work, expressed in his reproductive interpretation, can itself be understood—i.e., interpreted and justified—and this interpretation will take place in verbal form. But even this is not a new creation of meaning. Rather, it too disappears again as an interpretation and preserves its truth in the immediacy of understanding.

This insight into the way interpretation and understanding are bound together will destroy that false romanticism of immediacy that artists and connoisseurs have pursued, and still do pursue, under the banner of the aesthetics of genius. Interpretation does not try to replace the interpreted work. It does not, for example, try to draw attention to itself by the poetic power of its own utterance. Rather, it remains *fundamentally* accidental. This is true not only of the interpreting word but also of performative interpretation. The interpreting word always has something accidental about it insofar as it is motivated by the hermeneutic question, not just for the pedagogical purposes to which it was limited in the Enlightenment but because understanding is always a genuine event. Similarly, performative interpretation is accidental in a fundamental sense—i.e., not just when something is played, imitated, translated, or read aloud for didactic purposes. These cases—where performance is interpretation in a special demonstrative sense, where it includes demonstrative exaggeration and highlighting—in fact differ only in degree, and not in kind, from other sorts of reproductive interpretation. However much it is the literary work or musical composition itself that acquires its mimic presence through the performance, every performance still has its own emphasis. There is little difference between this emphasis and using emphasis for didactic ends. All performance is interpretation. All interpretation is highlighting.

It is only because the performance has no permanent being of its own and disappears in the work which it reproduces that this fact does not emerge clearly. But if we take a comparable example from the plastic arts—e.g., drawings after old masters made by a great artist—we find the same interpretive highlighting in them. The same effect is experienced in watching revivals of old films or seeing for a second time a film that one has just seen and remembers clearly: everything seems overplayed. Thus it is wholly legitimate for us to speak of the interpretation that lies behind every reproduction, and it must be possible to give a fundamental account of it. The interpretation as a whole is made up of a thousand little decisions which all claim to be correct. Argumentative justification and interpretation do not need to be the artist's proper concern. Moreover, an explicit interpretation in language would only approximate correctness and fall short of the rounded concreteness achieved by an "artistic" reproduction. But this precludes neither the fact that all understanding has an intrinsic relation to interpretation nor the basic possibility of an interpretation in words.

We must rightly understand the fundamental priority of language asserted here. Indeed, language often seems ill suited to express what we feel. In the face of the overwhelming presence of works of art, the task of expressing in words what they say to us seems like an infinite and hopeless undertaking. The fact that our desire and capacity to understand always go beyond any statement that we can make seems like a critique of language. But this does not alter the fundamental priority of language. The possibilities of our knowledge seem to be far more individual than the possibilities of expression offered by language. Faced with the socially motivated tendency toward uniformity with which language forces understanding into particular schematic forms which hem us in, our desire for knowledge tries to escape from these schematizations and predecisions. However, the critical superiority which we claim over language pertains not to the conventions of verbal expression but to the conventions of meaning that have become sedimented in language. Thus that superiority says nothing against the essential connection between understanding and language. In fact it confirms this connection. For all critique that rises above the schematism of our statements in order to understand finds its expression in the form of language. Hence language always forestalls any objection to its jurisdiction. Its universality[2] keeps pace with the universality of reason. Hermeneutical consciousness only participates in what constitutes the general relation between language and reason. If all understanding stands in a necessary relation of equivalence to its possible interpretation, and if there are basically no bounds set to understanding, then the verbal form in which this understanding is interpreted must contain within it an infinite dimension that transcends all bounds. Language is the language of reason itself.

One says this, and then one hesitates. For this makes language so close to reason—which means, to the things it names—that one may ask why there should be different languages at all, since all seem to have the same proximity to reason and to objects. When a person lives in a language, he is filled with the sense of the unsurpassable appropriateness of the words he uses for the subject matter he is talking about. It seems impossible that other words in other languages could name the things equally well. The suitable word always seems to be one's own and unique, just as the thing referred to is always unique. The agony of translation consists ultimately in the fact that the original words seem to be inseparable from the things they refer to, so that to make a text intelligible one often has to give an interpretive paraphrase of it rather than translate it. The more sensitively our historical consciousness reacts, the more it seems to be aware of the untranslatability of the unfamiliar. But this makes the intimate unity of word and thing a hermeneutical scandal. How can we possibly understand anything written in a foreign language if we are thus imprisoned in our own?

2. That is, "generality" (*Allgemeinheit*).

It is necessary to see the speciousness of this argument. In actual fact the sensitivity of our historical consciousness tells us the opposite. The work of understanding and interpretation always remains meaningful. This shows the superior universality with which reason rises above the limitations of any given language. The hermeneutical experience is the corrective by means of which the thinking reason escapes the prison of language, and it is itself verbally constituted.[3]

From this point of view the problem of language does not present itself in the same way as *philosophy of language* raises it. Certainly the variety of languages in which linguistics is interested presents us with a question. But this question is simply how every language, despite its difference from other languages, can say everything it wants. Linguistics teaches us that every language does this in its own way. But we then ask how, amid the variety of these forms of utterance, there is still the same unity of thought and speech, so that everything that has been transmitted in writing can be understood. Thus we are interested in the opposite of what linguistics tries to investigate.

The intimate unity of language and thought is the premise from which linguistics too starts. It is this alone that has made it a science [*Wissenschaft*]. For only because this unity exists is it worthwhile for the investigator to make the abstraction which causes language to be the object of his research. Only by breaking with the conventionalist prejudices of theology and rationalism could Herder and Humboldt[4] learn to see languages as views of the world. By acknowledging the unity of thought and language they could envision the task of comparing the various forms of this unity. We are starting from the same insight but going, as it were, in the opposite direction. Despite the multiplicity of ways of speech, we are trying to keep in mind the indissoluble unity of thought and language as we encounter it in the hermeneutical phenomenon, namely as the unity of understanding and interpretation.

Thus the question that concerns us is *the conceptual character* of all understanding. This only appears to be a secondary question. We have seen that conceptual interpretation is the realization of the hermeneutical experience itself. That is why our problem is so difficult. The interpreter does not know that he is bringing himself and his own concepts into the interpretation. The verbal formulation is so much part of the interpreter's mind that he never becomes aware of it as an object. Thus it is understandable that this side of the hermeneutic process has been wholly ignored. But there is the further point that the situation has been confused by incorrect *theories of language*. It is obvious that an instrumentalist theory of signs which sees words and concepts as handy tools has missed the point of the hermeneutical phenomenon. If we stick to what takes place in speech and, above all, in every dialogue with tradition carried on by the human sciences, we cannot fail to see that here concepts are constantly in the process of being formed. This does not mean that the interpreter is using new or unusual words. But the capacity to use

---

3. Here Gadamer sets forth one of the cardinal tenets of his position, in direct opposition to the contrary position associated with his poststructuralist rivals (and sometimes—questionably—attributed to NIETZSCHE).
4. Wilhelm von Humboldt (1767–1835), an impor-

tant philosopher of language, of education, and of culture; he was a leading figure of the German Enlightenment. Johann Gottfried von Herder (1744–1803), linguist, historian, and important German philosopher of language and of history; he is associated with Romanticism and historicism.

familiar words is not based on an act of logical subsumption, through which a particular is placed under a universal concept. Let us remember, rather, that understanding always includes an element of application and thus produces an ongoing process of concept formation. We must consider this now if we want to liberate the verbal nature of understanding from the presuppositions of philosophy of language. The interpreter does not use words and concepts like a craftsman who picks up his tools and then puts them away. Rather, we must recognize that all understanding is interwoven with concepts and reject any theory that does not accept the intimate unity of word and subject matter.

Indeed, the situation is even more difficult. It is doubtful that the *concept of language* that modern linguistics and philosophy of language take as their starting point is adequate to the situation. It has recently been stated by some linguists—and rightly so—that the modern concept of language presumes a verbal consciousness that is itself a product of history and does not apply to the beginning of the historical process, especially to what language was for the Greeks.[5] From the complete unconsciousness of language that we find in classical Greece, the path leads to the instrumentalist devaluation of language that we find in modern times. This process of increasing consciousness, which also involves a change in the attitude to language, makes it possible for "language" as such—i.e., its form, separated from all content—to become an independent object of attention.

We can doubt whether this view's characterization of the relation between language behavior and language theory is correct, but there is no doubt that the science [*Wissenschaft*] and philosophy of language operate on the premise that their only concern is the *form* of language. Is the idea of form still appropriate here? Is language a symbolic form, as Cassirer calls it? Does this take account of the fact that language is unique in embracing everything—myth, art, law, and so on—that Cassirer also calls symbolic form?[6]

In analyzing the hermeneutical phenomenon we have stumbled upon the universal function of language. In revealing the verbal nature of the hermeneutical phenomenon, we see that it has a universal significance. Understanding and interpretation are related to verbal tradition in a specific way. But at the same time they transcend this relationship not only because all the creations of human culture, including the nonverbal ones, can be understood in this way, but more fundamentally because everything that is intelligible must be accessible to understanding and to interpretation. What is true of understanding is just as true of language. Neither is to be grasped simply as a fact that can be empirically investigated. Neither is ever simply an object but instead comprehends everything that can ever be an object.[7]

If we recognize this basic connection between language and understanding, we will not be able to view the development from unconsciousness of language

---

5. Johannes Lohmann in *Lexis* III and elsewhere [Gadamer's note]. Lohmann (1895–1983), German philosopher and linguist; the reference is to his book *Das Verhältnis des abendländischen Menschen zur Sprache* (1952, *The Relation of Western Man to Language*).
6. Cf. Ernst Cassirer, *Wesen und Wirkung des Symbolbegriffs* [*The Nature and Influence of the Concept of Symbol*] (1956), which chiefly contains the essays published in the Warburg Library Series. R. Hönigswald, *Philosophie und Sprach* [*Philosophy and Language*] (1937), starts his critique here [Gadamer's note]. For CASSIRER, see above.
7. Hönigswald puts it in this way: "Language is not only a fact, but a principle" (op. cit., p. 448) [Gadamer's note].

via consciousness of language to the devaluation of language[8] even as an unequivocally correct description of the historical process. This schema does not seem to me to be adequate even for the history of theories of language, as we shall see, let alone for the life of language. The language that lives in speech—which comprehends all understanding, including that of the interpreter of texts—is so much bound up with thinking and interpretation that we have too little left if we ignore the actual content of what languages hand down to us and try to consider language only as form.

* * *

SOURCE: From Hans-Georg Gadamer, *Truth and Method*, trans. Joel Weinsheimer and Donald G. Marshall, 2nd rev. ed. (New York: Crossroad, 1989), pp. 383–404. Except where otherwise indicated, German words in brackets are the terminology used in the German original, inserted by the editor in addition to their renderings in the translation. Originally published in 1960 as *Wahrheit und Methode*; this translation is based on the expanded 5th German edition (1986), published as vol. 1 of Gadamer's *Gesammelte Werke* (*Collected Works*).

8. This is how Lohmann, op. cit., describes the development [Gadamer's note].

PAUL RICOEUR
(1913 – 2005)

Ricoeur thought of his work as a kind of existentially, phenomenologically, and hermeneutically sensitive philosophical anthropology. He sought to achieve a penetrating and comprehensive view of the richness, complexities, and deep conflicts of human existence, as well as an understanding of how it is humanly possible to live meaningfully in the face of them. He opposed himself to simplistic forms of reductionist thinking that fail to provide accounts capable of doing justice to this breadth of human reality, and resisted seductive forms of interpretation that neglect or give up prematurely on what he saw as the second part of the task. These stances made him one of the most attractively and deeply humanistic thinkers of the twentieth century— and a welcome ambassador representing developments in the interpretive tradition in Europe to the English-speaking philosophical community, in which he came to be very much at home.

Jean Paul Gustave Ricoeur ("Ree-COOR") was born in Valence, France. His mother died when he was seven months old, and his father was killed a year into the First World War, in the fall of 1915. He and his sister were raised by their devout Protestant grandparents, in the town of Rennes. He became interested in philosophy while in secondary school, and studied it at the university there, earning an undergraduate degree in 1933 and a master's degree in philosophy in 1934. He also developed an interest in theology, particularly in the thought of Friedrich Schleiermacher (1768–1834), the philosopher-theologian father of hermeneutics, and of the neo-orthodox Protestant theologian Karl Barth (1886–1968). His master's dissertation was "The Problem of God in Lachelier and Langneau."

In 1934–35 Ricoeur studied at the Sorbonne, where he met the existential-ist philosopher Gabriel Marcel, who had recently converted to Catholicism. (Ricoeur did not follow suit, but his work came to be of considerable interest to Catholic theologians and philosophers.) The year was marred for him by the death of his sister, to whom he had been close. In 1935 he passed the *agrégation* examination that qualified him to find employment as a teacher. That year he also married a young woman named Simone Lejas, whom he had known since childhood and to whom he had been engaged since 1931. Two sons were born to them in 1936 and 1938, followed by a daughter in 1940. Between 1935 and 1940 (interrupted in 1936 by a year of military service), he held a number of teaching positions in advanced secondary schools and began writing papers, primarily on "Christian socialism" and pacifism.

Following the outbreak of war with Germany, Ricoeur was again called into military service and complied, his pacifist inclinations notwithstanding. Captured in 1940, he spent the next five years as a prisoner of war in detainment camps in eastern Germany. There he was imprisoned with a number of other intellectuals, including the philosopher Mikel Dufrenne, and together they studied the writings of the existential philosopher KARL JASPERS, to whom he was strongly attracted. Indeed, after the war his first publication was a book on Jaspers, co-authored with Dufrenne.

During his detention, Ricoeur also read and translated some of HUSSERL's work—a labor that subsequently satisfied the "minor thesis" requirement for his doctorate degree. In addition, he began drafting his first major work, *Freedom and Nature*, the first part of which would ultimately satisfy the "major thesis" requirement. Upon his release at the war's end he returned to his family (his fourth child was born in 1947, followed by a fifth in 1953), his friendship with Marcel, and his work toward his doctorate, which he was awarded in 1950. He taught in a secondary school at Le Chambon from 1945 to 1948, when he at long last obtained a university-level academic appointment at Strasbourg, where he remained until 1955.

In 1956, Ricoeur began to teach at the Sorbonne. He met Jacques Lacan in 1960 and attended some of Lacan's famous seminars in the early 1960s, but their friendship effectively ended when Ricoeur published his 1965 book on Freud. During this period JACQUES DERRIDA was briefly his assistant. Ricoeur left the Sorbonne in 1967 to become dean of the Faculty of Letters at the new Nanterre branch of the University of Paris, hoping there to overcome some of the problems he saw in the French academic system. But the political chaos of the late 1960s soon ended those hopes and in fact prompted him to abandon French academic life altogether. He left France in 1970, and spent the next few years teaching at the University of Louvain in Belgium. He taught at the University of Chicago from 1971 until 1991, named to a chair previously held by Paul Tillich. Twice in the 1980s and again in 1994 he was invited (along with several other intellectuals) to spend several days in retreat with Pope John Paul II. He died in France at age 92 in 2005.

Initially, Ricoeur undertook to achieve an existential understanding of human freedom. This concern broadened into a phenomenological interest in forms of experience associated with freedom, related to matters such as the passions, the body, and habits. The trajectory of his work then carried him into analyses of symbol, myth, and metaphor, as they relate to and help elucidate some of our most fundamental experiences of ourselves. He attempted a kind of balancing act in which psychoanalysis, hermeneutic investigation of meaning, and structuralist analysis of language mutually illuminate the living, vital nature of language. A recurring theme of Ricoeur's work is that distinctly human forms of experience are made possible through the multiple levels of meaning made available in words, sentences, texts, symbols, and myths. His approach to hermeneutical understanding moved from the study of texts and symbols to the study of life, and he explored narrative and how it figures in the construction of time, the self, and the world. He also found himself drawn to issues relating to ethics and justice.

Ricoeur's early work was influenced by his interpretations of Husserl, Marcel, and Jaspers. He completed only two-thirds of the projected three volumes of *Freedom and Nature: The Voluntary and the Involuntary* (1950) and the two parts of *Finitude and Guilt—Fallible Man* (1960) and *The Symbolism of Evil* (1960). Its unrealized final volume was to be on the poetics of the will. Ricoeur's early thinking can be characterized as existential phenomenology, having much in common with the theories of embodiment and freedom found in Marcel and MAURICE MERLEAU-PONTY. The fundamental thrust of the work is to give a pure description of acts of the will: the act of choosing or deciding to act, the act of moving or performance of what was decided, and the completion of the act of will that Ricoeur calls "consent," or our embracing of necessity and the involuntary. This pure description is intended as a corrective to the existentialist tendency to glorify transcendence and freedom as a kind of absolute act, failing to recognize the essential involuntary, necessary (or "unfree") foundations on which human freedom is built. Ricoeur's larger goal here is to arrive at a human (and non-idealist, non-absolutist) conception of freedom.

In *Fallible Man* Ricoeur attempts to insert the pure description of freedom and necessity into an account of human weakness and fragility. He argues that there is a "fault" in the core of human being—an interruption, an absurdity, a kind of fall. Human existence contains a fundamental ambiguity. Human beings are neither finite nor infinite: neither entirely free nor entirely subject, they are also not completely unfree or mere objects. This "disproportion," which is an element of the very nature of our being, is experienced by way of a *pathétique*, or pathos of misery. In investigating this fracture within human being and our affective (feeling) natures, Ricoeur ends up taking a position similar to that of KANT in *Religion within the Limits of Reason Alone* (1793): moral evil is inherent in human nature. There are multiple conflicts within human nature, and the one between the infinite promise of happiness and our finite character is particularly important. Ricoeur concludes that these conflicts or faults, although they cannot be overcome, need not lead us to despair and guilt if we make the most of the possibility of the affirmative attitudes of love and hope.

In the third work of this series, *The Symbolism of Evil*, Ricoeur makes his move to hermeneutics. Obviously influenced by the "demythologizing" theology of Rudolf Bultmann (1884–1976), he attempts to recover the living nature of symbols, whose dynamic being and wellspring of meaning can be captured only through the circular interpretive process traditionally associated with hermeneutics. He explores the notion of evil by progressively developing the idea of the "servile will" through the symbols of defilement, sin, and guilt. These symbols afford us access to the reality of evil, which is why phenomenology must give way to hermeneutics.

One path from phenomenology to hermeneutics is that of HEIDEGGER and GADAMER, who construe hermeneutical understanding as a part of the very nature of human existence. Rejecting this direct route, Ricoeur argues that the analysis of language and symbol enables us to arrive at a similar place without dismissing a host of significant issues. His encounter with Lacan may have encouraged him to see the symbolic as central to understanding human existence. In any event, it was at this juncture that he turned to Freud—though primarily as a hermeneutic-legitimizing foil.

Freud gives an account of symbols (both religious and otherwise) that is opposed to Ricoeur's. Symbols for Freud are illusory, and so are not truthful. For Ricoeur, in contrast, symbols are complex, overdetermined loci of meaning. Furthermore, Freud's conception of the self is starkly opposed to Ricoeur's. For Freud the unconscious, the Id, and desire become primary—and while this usurpation of the Ego is in a sense liberating, it also contains elements of the nihilistic, pessimistic attitudes that Ricoeur had found objectionable and had rejected within existentialism. Ricoeur treats Freudian psychoanalysis as a competing hermeneutic method. He accepts the idea of a hermeneutic treatment of the subject as text but rejects the resort to the supposition of a realistically conceived unconscious, focusing on the subject conceived not as a quasi-metaphysical myth of deep structure but rather as a complex nexus of meanings and symbolic structures.

Ricoeur's next move was to begin to examine the nature of hermeneutics more carefully, while extending it beyond the study of symbol, myth, and metaphor. It is in this period that the following selection was written. In "The Model of the Text" (1971), Ricoeur investigates the paradigmatic nature of textual interpretation for the sort of inquiry that makes up the human disciplines (this, of course, was essentially the project of WILHELM DILTHEY). He begins by considering the nature of speech acts, the nature of discourse, and the way that meaning is constituted not merely in the propositions of language but also in the larger linguistic situation of speaker and utterance. However, the text breaks free from this context. The notions of a world and text are intertwined, because a text carries with it a system of meanings or references that designate a general mode of being-in-the-world that was once tied to a situation but now floats free.

Ricoeur believes that hermeneutics may be the model of the sort of inquiry that is called for in the human sciences— understood as the disciplines that study meaningful behavior or action—because he finds a strong analogy between meaningful behavior and texts. The problem that he hopes to solve is how the human disciplines can be more than merely descriptive, going beyond simply elucidating facts to help us achieve an understanding that can effectively move inside human "worlds" and their meanings, intentions, and values. Ricoeur thinks that a subjective discerning of meaning that is then justified through a process of textual validation can realize this goal. His juridical model of reading extends to both texts and behavior. He maintains that texts contain a multiplicity of possible interpretations, some of which can be justified more fully than others. At the same time, Ricoeur believes a more abstract, formalist, or structuralist approach can lead or contribute significantly to understanding, by showing how it is possible to grasp the deep meanings of a text and to make it one's own.

Ricoeur's next work was his monumental three-volume *Time and Narrative* (1983–85), which is an investigation of human self-understanding and self-construction through the process of narration. There is a problem at the heart of our notion of time, because it can be viewed in two different ways: subjectively and objectively. An Augustinian account of time as the activity of the soul is set against an Aristotelian account of time as the objective structure of motions in the world. At least for the purpose of human (self-)understanding, the conflict between them is overcome (although not dissipated completely) through the notion of narrative as a process that weaves a history, or a "human-time." We can understand this work as extending the notion of hermeneutics of the text even further, to the domain of the self and to history. Ricoeur's path from existential phenomenology to hermeneutics

in effect circles back to the theory of action and the will with which he began. This exploration of the fictional and poetic elements of narrative may fill the gap that "Poetics of the Will" was originally intended to address, perhaps explaining why that projected work was never written: it was no longer thought to be needed.

In Ricoeur's final works ethics and the question of justice come to the fore, in a manner prepared for by his earlier writings. He had never had much sympathy with either Kantian deontology or consequentialism. In approaching ethics (which he contrasts with "morality," defined as norms regarded as obligatory), he begins, as did classical philosophers, with the question of how to pursue the good life. That idea, for Ricoeur, is tied to the nature of human life as necessarily constructive and narrative—though its narrative is not radically free but always responds to the exigencies of the world. The good life is already prestructured by the demand for justice in and through relations to others. Therefore the interpersonal and dialogic nature of the self and of the aim of the good life ultimately both require that we recognize moral norms and the dignity of others. The "ethical aim" toward the good life has a hermeneutic structure that responds to the solicitude or demands of others. Ricoeur's ethics thus focuses on the interconnectedness of self and other and the hermeneutical process of recognition. In extending this account of hermeneutical understanding to understanding how we reason practically in new and challenging situations, he draws heavily on Aristotle's theory of practical wisdom (*phronēsis*). His discussion of justice grows out of what he sees as a forgetting of the place of the juridical, and of how law and its institutions mediate our relations to others.

The Model of the Text:
Meaningful Action Considered as a Text

My aim in this essay is to test an hypothesis which I shall expound briefly.

I assume that the primary sense of the word 'hermeneutics' concerns the rules required for the interpretation of the written documents of our culture. In assuming this starting point I am remaining faithful to the concept of *Auslegung* as it was stated by Wilhelm Dilthey;[1] whereas *Verstehen* (understanding, comprehension) relies on the recognition of what a foreign subject means or intends on the basis of all kinds of signs in which psychic life expresses itself (*Lebensäusserungen*), *Auslegung* (interpretation, exegesis) implies something more specific: it covers only a limited category of signs, those which are fixed by writing, including all the sorts of documents and monuments which entail a fixation similar to writing.

Now my hypothesis is this: if there are specific problems which are raised by the interpretation of texts because they are texts and not spoken language, and if these problems are the ones which constitute hermeneutics as such, then the human sciences[2] may be said to be hermeneutical (1) inasmuch as their *object* displays some of the features constitutive of a text as text, and (2) inasmuch as their *methodology* develops the same kind of procedures as those of *Auslegung* or text-interpretation.

Hence the two questions to which my essay will be devoted are: (1) To what extent may we consider the notion of text as a good paradigm for the so-called object of the social sciences? (2) To what extent may we use the methodology of text-interpretation as a paradigm for interpretation in general in the field of the human sciences?

I. THE PARADIGM OF TEXT

In order to justify the distinction between spoken and written language, I want to introduce a preliminary concept, that of *discourse*. It is as discourse that language is either spoken or written.

Now what is discourse? We shall not seek the answer from the logicians, not even from the exponents of linguistic analysis, but from the linguists themselves. Discourse is the counterpart of what linguists call language-systems or linguistic codes. Discourse is language-event or linguistic usage. [. . .]

If the sign (phonological or lexical) is the basic unit of language, the sentence is the basic unit of discourse. Therefore it is the linguistics of the sentence which supports the theory of speech as an event. I shall retain four traits from this linguistics of the sentence which will help me to elaborate the hermeneutics of the event and of discourse.

First trait: Discourse is always realised temporally and in the present, whereas the language system is virtual and outside of time. Emile Benveniste[3] calls this the 'instance of discourse'.

Second trait: Whereas language lacks a subject—in the sense that the question 'Who is speaking?' does not apply at its level—discourse refers back to

---

1. See DILTHEY, above.
2. That is, the *Geisteswissenschaften*, the range of disciplines that include the humanities, social sciences, history, and philosophy itself.

3. French structuralist linguist (1902–1976); he makes this point in his *Problems in General Linguistics*, vol. 1 (1966).

its speaker by means of a complex set of indicators such as the personal pronouns. We shall say that the 'instance of discourse' is self-referential.

Third trait: Whereas the signs in language only refer to other signs within the same system, and whereas language therefore lacks a world just as it lacks temporality and subjectivity, discourse is always about something. It refers to a world which it claims to describe, to express, or to represent. It is in discourse that the symbolic function of language is actualised.

Fourth trait: Whereas language is only the condition for communication for which it provides the codes, it is in discourse that all messages are exchanged. In this sense, discourse alone has not only a world, but an other, another person, an interlocutor to whom it is addressed.

These four traits taken together constitute speech as an event. [. . .] Let us see how differently these four traits are actualised in spoken and written language.

(1) Discourse, as we said, only exists as a temporal and present instance of discourse. This first trait is realised differently in living speech and in writing. In living speech, the instance of discourse has the character of a fleeting event. The event appears and disappears. This is why there is a problem of fixation, of inscription. What we want to fix is what disappears. If, by extension, we can say that one fixes language—inscription of the alphabet, lexical inscription, syntactical inscription—it is for the sake of that which alone has to be fixed, discourse. Only discourse is to be fixed, because discourse disappears. The atemporal system neither appears nor disappears; it does not happen. Here is the place to recall the myth in Plato's *Phaedo*.[4] Writing was given to men to 'come to the rescue' of the 'weakness of discourse', a weakness which was that of the event. The gift of the *grammata*—of that 'external' thing, of those 'external marks', of that materialising alienation—was just that of a 'remedy' brought to our memory. The Egyptian king of Thebes could well respond to the god Theuth that writing was a false remedy in that it replaced true reminiscence by material conservation, and real wisdom by the semblance of knowing. This inscription, in spite of its perils, is discourse's destination. What in effect does writing fix? Not the event of speaking, but the 'said' of speaking, where we understand by the 'said' of speaking that intentional exteriorisation constitutive of the aim of discourse thanks to which the *sagen*—the saying—wants to become *Aus-sage*—the enunciation, the enunciated. In short, what we write, what we inscribe, is the *noema*[5] of the speaking. It is the meaning of the speech event, not the event as event.

What, in effect, does writing fix? If it is not the speech *event*, it is speech itself insofar as it is *said*. But what is said?

Here I should like to propose that hermeneutics has to appeal not only to linguistics (linguistics of discourse versus linguistics of language) as it does above, but also to the theory of the speech-act such as we find it in Austin and Searle.[6] The act of speaking, according to these authors, is constituted

---

4. The following myth about writing as the gift of Theuth is actually found in *Phaedrus* 274d–275b; Plato (ca. 427–ca. 347 B.C.E.) gives the king of Thebes the stronger argument.

5. That is, the experiential object. EDMUND HUSSERL borrowed the nouns *noema* and *noesis* from the Greek words for "mind" (*nous*), "to think" (*noein*), and "perception" (*noēsis*) to refer to the

objects (*noemata*) and modes (*noeses*) of phenomenologically reduced consciousness; see the selection from *Ideas* (1913), above.

6. John Searle (b. 1932), American analytic philosopher of language and of mind. J. L. (John Langshaw) Austin (1911–1960), British analytic philosopher of language. For both, see this anthology's companion volume, *The Analytic Tradition*.

by a hierarchy of subordinate acts which are distributed on three levels: (1) the level of the locutionary or propositional act, the act *of* saying; (2) the level of the illocutionary act or force, that which we do *in* saying; and (3) the level of the perlocutionary act, that which we do *by* saying. [. . .]

What is the implication of these distinctions for our problem of the intentional exteriorisation by which the event surpasses itself in the meaning and lends itself to material fixation? The locutionary act exteriorises itself in the sentence. The sentence can in effect be identified and reidentified as being the same sentence. A sentence becomes an utterance (*Aus-sage*) and thus is transferred to others as being such-and-such a sentence with such-and-such a meaning. But the illocutionary act can also be exteriorised through grammatical paradigms (indicative, imperative, and subjunctive modes, and other procedures expressive of the illocutionary force) which permit its identification and reidentification. Certainly, in spoken discourse, the illocutionary force leans upon mimicry and gestural elements and upon the non-articulated aspects of discourse, what we call prosody. In this sense, the illocutionary force is less completely inscribed in grammar than is the propositional meaning. In every case, its inscription in a syntactic articulation is itself gathered up in specific paradigms which in principle make possible fixation by writing. Without a doubt we must concede that the perlocutionary act is the least inscribable aspect of discourse and that by preference it characterises spoken language. But the perlocutionary action is precisely what is the least discourse in discourse. It is the discourse as stimulus. It acts, not by my interlocutor's recognition of my intention, but sort of energetically, by direct influence upon the emotions and the affective dispositions. Thus the propositional act, the illocutionary force, and the perlocutionary action are apt, in a decreasing order, for the intentional exteriorisation which makes inscription in writing possible.

Therefore it is necessary to understand by the meaning of the speech-act, or by the noema of the saying, not only the sentence, in the narrow sense of the propositional act, but also the illocutionary force and even the perlocutionary action in the measure that these three aspects of the speech-act are codified, gathered into paradigms, and where, consequently, they can be identified and reidentified as having the same meaning. Therefore I am here giving the word 'meaning' a very large acceptation which covers all the aspects and levels of the intentional exteriorisation that makes the inscription of discourse possible.

The destiny of the other three traits of discourse in passing from discourse to writing will permit us to make more precise the meaning of this elevation of saying to what is said.

(2) In discourse, we said—and this was the second differential trait of discourse in relation to language—the sentence designates its speaker by diverse indicators of subjectivity and personality. In spoken discourse, this reference by discourse to the speaking subject presents a character of immediacy that we can explain in the following way. The subjective intention of the speaking subject and the meaning of the discourse overlap each other in such a way that it is the same thing to understand what the speaker means and what his discourse means. The ambiguity of the French expression *vouloir-dire*, the German *meinen*, and the English 'to mean', attests to this overlapping. It is almost the same thing to ask 'What do you mean?' and 'What does that mean?'

With written discourse, the author's intention and the meaning of the text cease to coincide. This dissociation of the verbal meaning of the text and the mental intention is what is really at stake in the inscription of discourse. Not that we can conceive of a text without an author; the tie between the speaker and the discourse is not abolished, but distended and complicated. The dissociation of the meaning and the intention is still an adventure of the reference of discourse to the speaking subject. But the text's career escapes the finite horizon lived by its author. What the text says now matters more than what the author meant to say, and every exegesis unfolds its procedures within the circumference of a meaning that has broken its moorings to the psychology of its author. Using Plato's expression again, written discourse cannot be 'rescued' by all the processes by which spoken discourse supports itself in order to be understood—intonation, delivery, mimicry, gestures. In this sense, the inscription in 'external marks' which first appeared to alienate discourse, marks the actual spirituality of discourse. Henceforth, only the meaning 'rescues' the meaning, without the contribution of the physical and psychological presence of the author. But to say that the meaning rescues the meaning is to say that only interpretation is the 'remedy' for the weakness of discourse which its author can no longer 'save'.

(3) The event is surpassed by the meaning a third time. Discourse, we said, is what refers to the world, to *a* world. In spoken discourse this means that what the dialogue ultimately refers to is the *situation* common to the interlocutors. This situation in a way surrounds the dialogue, and its landmarks can all be shown by a gesture, or by pointing a finger, or designated in an ostensive manner by the discourse itself through the oblique reference of those other indicators which are the demonstratives, the adverbs of time and place, and the tense of the verb. In oral discourse, we are saying, reference is *ostensive*. What happens to it in written discourse? Are we saying that the text no longer has a reference? This would be to confound reference and monstration,[7] world and situation. Discourse cannot fail to be about something. In saying this, I am separating myself from any ideology of an absolute text. Only a few sophisticated texts satisfy this ideal of a text without reference. They are texts where the play of the signifier breaks away from the signified. But this new form is only valuable as an exception and cannot give the key to all other texts which in one manner or another speak about the world. But what then is the subject of texts when nothing can be shown? Far from saying that the text is then without a world, I shall now say without paradox that only man *has a world* and not just a situation. In the same manner that the text frees its meaning from the tutelage of the mental intention, it frees its reference from the limits of ostensive reference. For us, the world is the ensemble of references opened up by the texts. Thus we speak about the 'world' of Greece, not to designate any more what were the situations for those who lived them, but to designate the non-situational references which outlive the effacement of the first and which henceforth are offered as possible modes of being, as symbolic dimensions of our being-in-the-world. For me, this is the referent of all literature; no longer the *Umwelt*[8] of the ostensive references of

---

7. Demonstration, proof.
8. Environment, surroundings (German). In contrast, the *Welt* (world) is (for Ricoeur as for HEI-

DEGGER) an experiential totality structured by meanings of the sort that texts and their references make possible.

dialogue, but the *Welt* projected by the non-ostensive references of every text that we have read, understood, and loved. To understand a text is at the same time to light up our own situation, or, if you will, to interpolate among the predicates of our situation all the significations which make a *Welt* of our *Umwelt*. It is this enlarging of the *Umwelt* into the *Welt* which permits us to speak of the references *opened up* by the text—it would be better to say that the references *open up* the world. Here again the spirituality of discourse manifests itself through writing, which frees us from the visibility and limitation of situations by opening up a world for us, that is, new dimensions of our being-in-the-world.

In this sense, Heidegger rightly says—in his analysis of *verstehen* in *Being and Time*[9]—that what we understand first in a discourse is not another person, but a project, that is, the outline of a new being-in-the-world. Only writing, in freeing itself, not only from its author, but from the narrowness of the dialogical situation, reveals this destination of discourse as projecting a world.

In thus tying reference to the projection of a world, it is not only Heidegger whom we rediscover, but Wilhelm von Humboldt[1] for whom the great justification of language is to establish the relation of man to the world. If you suppress this referential function, only an absurd game of errant signifiers remains.

(4) But it is perhaps with the fourth trait that the accomplishment of discourse in writing is most exemplary. Only discourse, not language, is addressed to someone. This is the foundation of communication. But it is one thing for discourse to be addressed to an interlocutor equally present to the discourse situation, and another to be addressed, as is the case in virtually every piece of writing, to whoever knows how to read. The narrowness of the dialogical relation explodes. Instead of being addressed just to you, the second person, what is written is addressed to the audience that it creates itself. This, again, marks the spirituality of writing, the counterpart of its materiality and of the alienation which it imposes upon discourse. The *vis-à-vis* of the written is just whoever knows how to read. The co-presence of subjects in dialogue ceases to be the model for every 'understanding'. The relation writing-reading ceases to be a particular case of the relation speaking-hearing. But at the same time, discourse is revealed as discourse in the universality of its address. In escaping the momentary character of the event, the bounds lived by the author, and the narrowness of ostensive reference, discourse escapes the limits of being face to face. It no longer has a visible auditor. An unknown, invisible reader has become the unprivileged addressee of the discourse.

To what extent may we say that the object of the human sciences conforms to the paradigm of the text? Max Weber[2] defines this object as *sinnhaft orientiertes Verhalten*, as meaningfully oriented behaviour. To what extent may we replace the predicate 'meaningfully oriented' by what I should like to call *readability-characters* derived from the preceding theory of the text?

Let us try to apply our four criteria of what a text is to the concept of meaningful action.

9. Published in 1927 (excerpted above); on *Verstehen* (understanding), see especially §§31–32.
1. An important philosopher of language, of education, and of culture (1767–1835); he was a leading figure of the German Enlightenment.

2. An important German social theorist (1864–1920); he was one of the founders of the discipline of sociology as a *Wissenschaft* of social structures and social phenomena.

1. THE FIXATION OF ACTION

Meaningful action is an object for science[3] only under the condition of a kind of objectification which is equivalent to the fixation of a discourse by writing. This trait presupposes a simple way to help us at this stage of our analysis. In the same way that interlocution is overcome in writing, interaction is overcome in numerous situations in which we treat action as a fixed text. These situations are overlooked in a theory of action for which the discourse of action is itself a part of the situation of transaction which flows from one agent to another, exactly as spoken language is caught in the process of interlocution, or, if we may use the term, of translocution. This is why the understanding of action at the prescientific level is only 'knowledge without observation', or as E. Anscombe[4] says, 'practical knowledge' in the sense of 'knowing how' as opposed to 'knowing that'. But this understanding is not yet an *interpretation* in the strong sense which deserves to be called scientific interpretation.

My claim is that action itself, action as meaningful, may become an object of science, without losing its character of meaningfulness, through a kind of objectification similar to the fixation which occurs in writing. By this objectification, action is no longer a transaction to which the discourse of action would still belong. It constitutes a delineated pattern which has to be interpreted according to its inner connections.

This objectification is made *possible* by some inner traits of the action which are similar to the structure of the speech-act and which make doing a kind of utterance. In the same way as the fixation by writing is made possible by a dialectic of intentional exteriorisation immanent to the speech-act itself, a similar dialectic within the process of transaction prepares the detachment of the *meaning* of the action from the *event* of the action.

First an action has the structure of a locutionary act. It has a *propositional* content which can be identified and reidentified as the same. This 'propositional' structure of the action has been clearly and demonstratively expounded by Anthony Kenny in *Action, Emotion and Will*.[5] The verbs of action constitute a specific class of predicates which are similar to relations and which, like relations, are irreducible to all the kinds of predicates which may follow the copula 'is'. The class of action predicates, in its turn, is irreducible to the relations and constitutes a specific set of predicates. Among other traits, the verbs of action allow a plurality of 'arguments' capable of complementing the verb, ranging from no argument (Plato taught) to an indeterminate number of arguments (Brutus killed Caesar in the Curia,[6] on the Ides of March, with a . . . , with the help of . . .). This variable polydicity[7] of the predicative structure of the action-sentences is typical of the propositional structure of action. Another trait which is important for the transposition of the concept of fixation from the sphere of discourse to the sphere of action concerns the

---

3. That is, for *wissenschaftlich* (disciplined and methodologically refined cognitive) analysis.
4. G. E. M. (Elizabeth) Anscombe (1919–2001), English philosopher of language, mind, and action; she wrote on "practical knowledge" in *Intention* (1957). See this anthology's companion volume, *The Analytic Tradition*.
5. Anthony Kenny, *Action, Emotion and Will* (London: Routledge and Kegan Paul, 1963) [Ricoeur's note]. Kenny (b. 1931), British philosopher of mind and action.
6. The Curia of Pompey, in a meeting hall in the complex in Rome called Pompey's Theater; Julius Caesar was killed there in 44 B.C.E.
7. That is, polyadicity, the ability of action verbs to be filled out in a variety of meaningful ways (as just described).

ontological status of the 'complements' of the verbs of action. Whereas relations hold between terms equally existing (or non-existing), certain verbs of action have a topical subject which is identified as existing and to which the sentence refers, and complements which do not exist. Such is the case with the 'mental acts' (to believe, to think, to will, to imagine, etc.).

Anthony Kenny describes some other traits of the propositional structure of actions derived from the description of the functioning of the verbs of action. For example, the distinction between states, activities, and performances can be stated according to the behaviour of the tenses of the verbs of action which fix some specific temporal traits of the action itself. The distinction between the formal and the material object of an action (let us say the difference between the notion of all inflammable things and this letter which I am now burning) belongs to the logic of action as mirrored in the grammar of the verbs of action. Such, roughly described, is the propositional content of action which gives a basis to a dialectic of *event* and *meaning* similar to that of the speech-act. I should like to speak here of the noematic structure of action. It is this noematic structure which may be fixed and detached from the process of interaction and become an object to interpret.

Moreover, this noema has not only a propositional content, but also presents 'illocutionary' traits very similar to those of the complete speech-act. The different classes of performative acts of discourse described by Austin at the end of *How to do Things with Words* may be taken as paradigms not only for the speech-acts themselves, but for the actions which fulfil the corresponding speech-acts.[8] A typology of action, following the model of illocutionary acts, is therefore possible. Not only a typology, but a criteriology, inasmuch as each type implies *rules*, more precisely 'constitutive rules' which, according to Searle in *Speech Acts*, allow the construction of 'ideal models' similar to the 'ideal types' of Max Weber.[9] For example, to understand what a promise is, we have to understand what the 'essential condition' is according to which a given action 'counts as' a promise. Searle's 'essential condition' is not far from what Husserl called *Sinngehalt*,[1] which covers both the 'matter' (propositional content) and the 'quality' (the illocutionary force).

We may now say that an action, like a speech-act, may be identified not only according to its propositional content, but also according to its illocutionary force. Both constitute its 'sense-content'. Like the speech-act, the action-event (if we may coin this analogical expression) develops a similar dialectic between its temporal status as an appearing and disappearing event, and its logical status as having such-and-such identifiable meaning or 'sense-content'. But if the 'sense-content' is what makes possible the 'inscription' of the action-event, what makes it real? In other words, what corresponds to writing in the field of action?

Let us return to the paradigm of the speech-act. What is fixed by writing, we said, is the noema of the speaking, the saying as *said*. To what extent may we say that what is *done* is inscribed? Certain metaphors may be helpful at this point. We say that such-and-such event *left its mark* on its time. We speak

8. J. L. Austin, *How to Do Things with Words* (Oxford: Oxford University Press, 1962) [Ricoeur's note].

9. John R. Searle, *Speech Acts* (Cambridge: Cambridge University Press, 1969), p. 56 [Ricoeur's note].
1. Sense content (German).

of marking events. Are not there 'marks' on time, the kind of thing which calls for a reading, rather than for a hearing? But what is meant by this metaphor of the printed mark?

The three other criteria of the text will help us to make the nature of this fixation more precise.

2. THE AUTONOMISATION OF ACTION

In the same way that a text is detached from its author, an action is detached from its agent and develops consequences of its own. This autonomisation of human action constitutes the *social* dimension of action. An action is a social phenomenon not only because it is done by several agents in such a way that the role of each of them cannot be distinguished from the role of the others, but also because our deeds escape us and have effects which we did not intend. One of the meanings of the notion of 'inscription' appears here. The kind of distance which we found between the intention of the speaker and the verbal meaning of a text occurs also between the agent and its action. It is this distance which makes the ascription of responsibility a specific problem. We do not ask, who smiled? who raised his hand? The doer is present to his doing in the same way as the speaker is present to his speech. With simple actions like those which require no previous action in order to be done, the meaning (noema) and the intention (noesis) coincide or overlap. With complex actions some segments are so remote from the initial simple segments, which can be said to express the intention of the doer, that the ascription of these actions or action-segments constitutes a problem as difficult to solve as that of authorship in some cases of literary criticism. The assignation of an author becomes a mediate inference well known to the historian who tries to isolate the role of an historical character in the course of events.

We just used the expression 'the course of events'. Could we not say that what we call the course of events plays the role of the material thing which 'rescues' the vanishing discourse when it is written? As we said in a metaphorical way, some actions are events which imprint their mark on their time. But on what did they imprint their mark? Is it not in something spatial that discourse is inscribed? How could an event be printed on something temporal? Social time, however, is not only something which flees; it is also the place of durable effects, of persisting patterns. An action leaves a 'trace', it makes its 'mark' when it contributes to the emergence of such patterns which become the *documents* of human action.

Another metaphor may help us to delineate this phenomenon of the social 'imprint': the metaphor of the 'record' or of the 'registration'. Joel Feinberg, in *Reason and Responsibility*, introduces this metaphor in another context, that of responsibility, in order to show how an action may be submitted to blame. Only actions, he says, which can be 'registered' for further notice, placed as an entry on somebody's 'record', can be blamed.[2] And when there are no formal records (such as those which are kept by institutions like employment offices, schools, banks, and the police), there is still an informal analogue of these formal records which we call reputation and which constitutes a basis

---

2. Joel Feinberg, *Reason and Responsibility* (Belmont, Calif.: Dickenson Pub. Co., 1965) [Ricoeur's note]. Feinberg (1926–2004), American social, political, and moral philosopher.

for blaming. I should like to apply this interesting metaphor of a record and reputation to something other than the quasi-judicial situations of blaming, charging, crediting, or punishing. Could we not say that history is itself the record of human action? History is this quasi-'thing' *on* which human action leaves a 'trace', puts its mark. Hence the possibility of 'archives'. Before the archives which are intentionally written down by the memorialists, there is this continuous process of 'recording' human action which is history itself as the sum of 'marks', the fate of which escapes the control of individual actors. Henceforth history may appear as an autonomous entity, as a play with players who do not know the plot. This hypostasis of history may be denounced as a fallacy, but this fallacy is well entrenched in the process by which human action becomes social action when written down in the archives of history. Thanks to this sedimentation in social time, human deeds become 'institutions', in the sense that their meaning no longer coincides with the logical intentions of the actors. The meaning may be 'depsychologised' to the point where the *meaning* resides in the work itself. In the words of P. Winch, in *The Idea of a Social Science*, the object of the social sciences is a 'rule-governed behaviour'.[3] But this rule is not superimposed; it is the meaning as articulated from within these sedimented or instituted works.

Such is the kind of 'objectivity' which proceeds from the 'social fixation' of meaningful behaviour.

3. RELEVANCE AND IMPORTANCE

According to our third criterion of what a text is, we could say that a meaningful action is an action the *importance* of which goes 'beyond' its *relevance* to its initial situation. This new trait is very similar to the way in which a text breaks the ties of discourse to all the ostensive references. As a result of this emancipation from the situational context, discourse can develop non-ostensive references which we called a 'world', in the sense in which we speak of the Greek 'world', not in the cosmological sense of the word, but as an ontological dimension. What would correspond in the field of action to the non-ostensive references of a text?

We opposed, in introducing the present analysis, the *importance* of an action to its *relevance* as regards the situation to which it wanted to respond. An important action, we could say, develops meanings which can be actualised or fulfilled in situations other than the one in which this action occurred. To say the same thing in different words, the meaning of an important event exceeds, overcomes, transcends, the social conditions of its production and may be re-enacted in new social contexts. Its importance is its durable relevance and, in some cases, its omni-temporal relevance.

This third trait has important implications as regards the relation between cultural phenomena and their social conditions. Is it not a fundamental trait of the great works of culture to overcome the conditions of their social production, in the same way as a text develops new references and constitutes new 'worlds'? It is in this sense that Hegel spoke, in *The Philosophy of Right*,

3. Peter Winch, *The Idea of a Social Science and Its Relation to Philosophy* (London: Routledge and Kegan Paul, 1958) [Ricoeur's note]. Winch (1926– 1997), British moral and social philosopher and philosopher of action, of language, and of social science.

of the institutions (in the largest sense of the word) which 'actualise' freedom as a *second nature* in accordance with freedom.[4] This 'realm of actual freedom' is constituted by the deeds and works capable of receiving relevance in new historical situations. If this is true, this way of overcoming one's own conditions of production is the key to the puzzling problem raised by Marxism concerning the status of the 'superstructures'.[5] The autonomy of superstructures as regards their relation to their own infrastructures has its paradigm in the non-ostensive references of a text. A work does not only mirror its time, but it opens up a world which it bears within itself.

4. HUMAN ACTION AS AN 'OPEN WORK'

Finally, according to our fourth criterion of the text as text, the meaning of human action is also something which is *addressed* to an indefinite range of possible 'readers'. The judges are not the contemporaries, but, as Hegel said, history itself. *Weltgeschichte ist Weltgericht.*[6] That means that, like a text, human action is an open work, the meaning of which is 'in suspense'. It is because it 'opens up' new references and receives fresh relevance from them, that human deeds are also waiting for fresh interpretations which decide their meaning. All significant events and deeds are, in this way, opened to this kind of practical interpretation through present *praxis*. Human action, too, is opened to anybody who *can read*. In the same way that the meaning of an event is the sense of its forthcoming interpretations, the interpretation by the contemporaries has no particular privilege in this process.

This dialectic between the work and its interpretations will be the topic of the *methodology* of interpretation that we shall now consider.

II. THE PARADIGM OF TEXT-INTERPRETATION

I want now to show the fruitfulness of this analogy of the text at the level of methodology.

The main implication of our paradigm, as concerns the methods of the social sciences, is that it offers a fresh approach to the question of the relation between *erklären* (explanation) and *verstehen* (understanding, comprehension) in the human sciences. As is well known, Dilthey gave this relation the meaning of a dichotomy. For him, any model of explanation is borrowed from a different region of knowledge, that of the natural sciences with their inductive logic. Thereafter, the autonomy of the so-called *Geisteswissenschaften* is preserved only by recognising the irreducible factor of understanding a foreign psychic life on the basis of the signs in which this life is immediately exteriorised. But if *verstehen* is separated from *erklären* by this logical gap, how can the human sciences be scientific at all? Dilthey kept wrestling with this paradox. He discovered more and more clearly, mainly after having read Husserl's *Logical Investigations*,[7] that the *Geisteswissenschaften* are sciences inasmuch as the expressions of life undergo a kind of objectification which

4. For HEGEL and excerpts from *The Philosophy of Right* (1821; rev. ed., 1833), see above.
5. That is, those social, cultural, and ideological structures that are built on what MARX viewed as society's base, its economic relations of production;

see the selection from *The German Ideology*, above.
6. World history is the world's court (German)— that is, for Hegel, the supreme court, from which there is no higher appeal.
7. Published 1900–01.

makes possible a scientific approach somewhat similar to that of the natural sciences, in spite of the logical gap between *Natur* and *Geist*, factual knowledge and knowledge by signs. In this way the mediation offered by these objectifications appeared to be more important, for a scientific purpose than the immediate meaningfulness of the expressions of life for everyday transactions.

My own interrogation starts from this last perplexity in Dilthey's thought. And my hypothesis is that the kind of objectification implied in the status of discourse as text provides a better answer to the problem raised by Dilthey. This answer relies on the dialectical character of the relation between *erklären* and *verstehen* as it is displayed in reading. Our task therefore will be to show to what extent the paradigm of reading, which is the counterpart of the paradigm of writing, provides a solution for the methodological paradox of the human sciences.

The dialectic involved in reading expresses the originality of the relation between writing and reading and its irreducibility to the dialogical situation based on the immediate reciprocity between speaking and hearing. There is a dialectic between explaining and comprehending *because* the writing-reading situation develops a problematic of its own which is not merely an extension of the speaking-hearing situation constitutive of dialogue.

It is here, therefore, that our hermeneutics is most critical as regards the Romantic tradition in hermeneutics which took the dialogical situation as the standard for the hermeneutical operation applied to the text. My contention is that it is this operation, on the contrary, which reveals the meaning of what is already hermeneutical in dialogical understanding. So if the dialogical relation does not provide us with the paradigm of reading, we have to build it as an original paradigm, as a paradigm of its own.

This paradigm draws its main features from the status of the text itself as characterised by (1) the fixation of the meaning, (2) its dissociation from the mental intention of the author, (3) the display of non-ostensive references, and (4) the universal range of its addressees. These four traits taken together constitute the 'objectivity' of the text. From this 'objectivity' derives a possibility of *explaining* which is not derived in any way from another field, that of natural events, but which is congenial to this kind of objectivity. Therefore there is no transfer from one region of reality to another—let us say, from the sphere of facts to the sphere of signs. It is within the same sphere of signs that the process of objectification takes place and gives rise to explanatory procedures. And it is within the same sphere of signs that explanation and comprehension are confronted.

I propose that we consider this dialectic in two different ways: (1) as proceeding from comprehension to explanation, and (2) as proceeding from explanation to comprehension. The exchange and the reciprocity between both procedures will provide us with a good approximation of the dialectical character of the relation. At the end of each half of this demonstration I shall try to indicate briefly the possible extension of the paradigm of reading to the whole sphere of the human sciences.

1. FROM UNDERSTANDING TO EXPLANATION

This first dialectic—or rather this first figure of a unique dialectic—may be conveniently introduced by our contention that to understand a text is not to rejoin the author. The disjunction of the meaning and the intention creates an absolutely original situation which engenders the dialectic of *erklären* and *verstehen*. If the objective meaning is something other than the subjective intention of the author, it may be construed in various ways. The problem of the right understanding can no longer be solved by a simple return to the alleged intention of the author.

This construction necessarily takes the form of a process. As Hirsch says in his book *Validity in Interpretation*, there are no rules for making good guesses. But there are methods for validating guesses.[8] This dialectic between guessing and validating constitutes one figure of our dialectic between comprehension and explanation.

In this dialectic both terms are decisive. Guessing corresponds to what Schleiermacher[9] called the 'divinatory', validation to what he called the 'grammatical'. My contribution to the theory of this dialectic will be to link it more tightly to the theory of the text and text-reading.

Why do we need an art of guessing? Why do we have to 'construe' the meaning? Not only—as I tried to say a few years ago—because language is metaphorical and because the double meaning of metaphorical language requires an art of deciphering which tends to unfold the several layers of meaning. The case of the metaphor is only a particular case for a general theory of hermeneutics. In more general terms, a text has to be construed because it is not a mere sequence of sentences, all on an equal footing and separately understandable. A text is a whole, a totality. The relation between whole and parts—as in a work of art or in an animal—requires a specific kind of 'judgement' for which Kant gave the theory in the third *Critique*.[1] Correctly, the whole appears as a hierarchy of topics, or primary and subordinate topics. The reconstruction of the text as a whole necessarily has a circular character, in the sense that the presupposition of a certain kind of whole is implied in the recognition of the parts. And reciprocally, it is in construing the details that we construe the whole. There is no necessity and no evidence concerning what is important and what is unimportant, what is essential and what is unessential. The judgement of importance is a guess.

To put the difficulty in other terms, if a text is a whole, it is once more an individual like an animal or a work of art. As an individual it can only be reached by a process of narrowing the scope of generic concepts concerning the literary genre, the class of text to which this text belongs, the structures of different kinds which intersect in this text. The localisation and the individualisation of this unique text is still a guess.

8. Eric D. Hirsch, Jr., *Validity in Interpretation* (New Haven: Yale University Press, 1967), p. 25 [Ricoeur's note]. E. D. Hirsch (b. 1928), American literary critic and educational theorist.
9. Friedrich Schleiermacher (1768–1834), German theologian and philologist; he championed the idea of "interpretation" as basic to theology and biblical studies, literary studies, and the *Geisteswis-senschaften* (humanities and social sciences) more generally. On the "divinatory" and the "grammatical," see, e.g., his *Hermeneutics: The Handwritten Manuscripts*, ed. Heinz Kimmerle, trans. James Duke and Jack Forstman (Missoula, Mont.: Scholars Press, for the American Academy of Religion, 1977), p. 192.
1. KANT's *Critique of Judgment* (1790).

Still another way of expressing the same enigma is that as an individual the text may be reached from different sides. Like a cube, or a volume in space, the text presents a 'relief'. Its different topics are not at the same altitude. Therefore the reconstruction of the whole has a perspectivist aspect similar to that of perception. It is always possible to relate the same sentence in different ways to this or that sentence considered as the cornerstone of the text. A specific kind of onesidedness is implied in the act of reading. This onesidedness confirms the guess character of interpretation.

For all these reasons there is a problem of interpretation not so much because of the incommunicability of the psychic experience of the author, but because of the very nature of the verbal intention of the text. This intention is something other than the sum of the individual meanings of the individual sentences. A text is more than a linear succession of sentences. It is a cumulative, holistic process. This specific structure of the text cannot be derived from that of the sentence. Therefore the kind of plurivocity which belongs to texts as texts is something other than the polysemy[2] of individual words in ordinary language and the ambiguity of individual sentences. This plurivocity is typical of the text considered as a whole, open to several readings and to several constructions.

As concerns the procedures of validation by which we test our guesses, I agree with Hirsch that they are closer to a logic of probability than to a logic of empirical verification. To show that an interpretation is more probable in the light of what is known is something other than showing that a conclusion is true. In this sense, validation is not verification. Validation is an argumentative discipline comparable to the juridical procedures of legal interpretation. It is a logic of uncertainty and of qualitative probability. In this sense we may give an acceptable sense to the opposition between *Geisteswissenschaften* and *Naturwissenschaften* without conceding anything to the alleged dogma of the ineffability of the individual. The method of conveyance of indices, typical of the logic of subjective probability, gives a firm basis for a science of the individual deserving the name of science.[3] A text is a quasi-individual, and the validation of an interpretation applied to it may be said, with complete legitimacy, to give a scientific knowledge of the text.

Such is the balance between the genius of guessing and the scientific character of validation which constitutes the modern complement of the dialectic between *verstehen* and *erklären*.

At the same time, we are prepared to give an acceptable meaning to the famous concept of a *hermeneutical circle*. Guess and validation are in a sense circularly related as subjective and objective approaches to the text. But this circle is not a vicious circularity. It would be a cage if we were unable to escape the kind of 'self-confirmability' which, according to Hirsch,[4] threatens this relation between guess and validation. To the procedures of validation also belong procedures of invalidation similar to the criteria of falsifiability emphasised by Karl Popper in his *Logic of Scientific Discovery*.[5] The role of falsification

---

2. Multiplicity of meaning. "Plurivocity": plurality of meaning or interpretation.
3. That is, a cognitive discipline or *Wissenschaft*.
4. Hirsch, *Validity in Interpretation*, pp. 164ff. [Ricoeur's note].

5. Published in 1959. Popper (1902–1994), Austrian-born British philosopher of natural and social science (see this anthology's companion volume, *The Analytic Tradition*).

is played here by the conflict between competing interpretations. An interpretation must not only be probable, but more probable than another. There are criteria of relative superiority which may easily be derived from the logic of subjective probability.

In conclusion, if it is true that there is always more than one way of construing a text, it is not true that all interpretations are equal and may be assimilated to so-called 'rules of thumb'. The text is a limited field of possible constructions. The logic of validation allows us to move between the two limits of dogmatism and scepticism. It is always possible to argue for or against an interpretation, to confront interpretations, to arbitrate between them, and to seek for an agreement, even if this agreement remains beyond our reach.

To what extent is this dialectic between guessing and validating paradigmatic for the whole field of the human sciences?

That the meaning of human actions, of historical events, and of social phenomena may be *construed* in several different ways is well known by all experts in the human sciences. What is less known and understood is that this methodological perplexity is founded in the nature of the object itself and, moreover, that it does not condemn the scientist to oscillate between dogmatism and scepticism. As the logic of text-interpretation suggests, there is a *specific plurivocity* belonging to the meaning of human action. Human action, too, is a limited field of possible constructions.

A trait of human action which has not yet been emphasised in the preceding analysis may provide an interesting link between the specific plurivocity of the text and the analogical plurivocity of human action. This trait concerns the relation between the purposive and the motivational dimensions of action. As many philosophers in the new field of action theory have shown, the purposive character of an action is fully recognised when the answer to the question 'what' is explained in terms of an answer to the question 'why'. I *understand* what you intended to do, if you are able to *explain* to me why you did such-and-such an action. Now, what kinds of answer to the question 'why' make sense? Only those answers which afford a motive understood as a reason for . . . and not as a cause. And what is a reason for . . . which is not a cause? It is, in the terms of E. Anscombe and A.I. Melden, an expression, or a phrase, which allows us to consider the action *as* this or that.[6] If you tell me that you did this or that because of jealousy or in a spirit of revenge, you are asking me to put your action in the light of this category of feelings or dispositions. By the same token, you claim to make sense of your action. You claim to make it understandable for others and for yourself. This attempt is particularly helpful when applied to what Anscombe calls the 'desirability-character' of wanting. Wants and beliefs have the character not only of being *forces* which make people act in such-and-such ways, but of making sense as a result of the apparent good which is the correlate of their desirability-character. I may have to answer the question, *as* what do you want this? On the basis of these desirability-characters and the apparent good which corresponds to them, it is possible to *argue* about the meaning of an action, to argue for or against this or that interpretation. In this way the account of

6. G.E.M. Anscombe, *Intention* (Oxford: Basil Blackwell, 1972); A.I. Melden, *Free Action* (London: Routledge and Kegan Paul, 1961) [Ricoeur's note]. Abraham I. Melden (1910–1991), American philosopher of mind, action, and ethics.

motives already foreshadows a logic of argumentation procedures. Could we not say that what can be (and must be) *construed* in human action is the motivational basis of this action, i.e., the set of desirability-characters which may explain it? And could we not say that the process of *arguing* linked to the explanation of action by its motives unfolds a kind of plurivocity which makes action similar to a text?

What seems to legitimate this extension from guessing the meaning of a text to guessing the meaning of an action is that in arguing about the meaning of an action I put my wants and my beliefs at a distance and submit them to a concrete dialectic of confrontation with opposite points of view. This way of putting my action at a distance in order to make sense of my own motives paves the way for the kind of distanciation which occurs with what we called the social *inscription* of human action and to which we applied the metaphor of the 'record'. The same actions which may be put into 'records' and henceforth 'recorded' may also be *explained* in different ways according to the multivocity of the arguments applied to their motivational background.

If we are correct in extending to action the concept of 'guess' which we took as a synonym for *verstehen*, we may also extend to the field of action the concept of 'validation' in which we saw an equivalent of *erklären*. Here, too, the modern theory of action provides us with an intermediary link between the procedures of literary criticism and those of the social sciences. Some thinkers have tried to elucidate the way in which we *impute* actions to agents in the light of the juridical procedures by which a judge or a tribunal validates a decision concerning a contract or a crime. In a famous article, 'The ascription of responsibility and rights', H.L.A. Hart shows in a very convincing way that juridical reasoning does not at all consist in applying general laws to particular cases, but each time in construing uniquely referring decisions.[7] These decisions terminate a careful refutation of the excuses and defences which could 'defeat' the claim or the accusation. In saying that human actions are fundamentally 'defeasible' and that juridical reasoning is an argumentative process which comes to grips with the different ways of 'defeating' a claim or an accusation, Hart has paved the way for a general theory of validation in which juridical reasoning would be the fundamental link between validation in literary criticism and validation in the social sciences. The intermediary function of juridical reasoning clearly shows that the procedures of validation have a polemical character. In front of the court, the plurivocity common to texts and to actions is exhibited in the form of a conflict of interpretations, and the final interpretation appears as a verdict to which it is possible to make appeal. Like legal utterances, all interpretations in the field of literary criticism and in the social sciences may be challenged, and the question 'what can defeat a claim' is common to all argumentative situations. Only in the tribunal is there a moment when the procedures of appeal are exhausted. But it is because the decision of the judge is implemented by the force of public power. Neither in literary criticism, nor in the social sciences, is there such a last word. Or, if there is any, we call that violence.

---

7. H.L.A. Hart, "The ascription of responsibility and rights," *Proceedings of the Aristotelian Society*, 49 (1948), pp. 171–94 [Ricoeur's note]. Herbert Lionel Adolphus Hart (1907–1992), English social, legal, and political philosopher (see this anthology's companion volume, *The Analytic Tradition*).

2. FROM EXPLANATION TO UNDERSTANDING

The same dialectic between comprehension and explanation may receive a new meaning if taken in the reverse way, from explanation to understanding. This new *Gestalt* of the dialectic proceeds from the nature of the referential function of the text. This referential function, as we said, exceeds the mere ostensive designation of the situation common to both speaker and hearer in the dialogical situation. This abstraction from the surrounding world gives rise to two opposite attitudes. As readers, we may either remain in a kind of state of suspense as regards any kind of referred-to world, or we may actualise the potential non-ostensive references of the text in a new situation, that of the reader. In the first case, we treat the text as a worldless entity; in the second, we create a new ostensive reference through the kind of 'execution' which the art of reading implies. These two possibilities are equally entailed by the act of reading, conceived as their dialectical interplay.

The first way of reading is exemplified today by the different *structural* schools of literary criticism. Their approach is not only possible, but legitimate. It proceeds from the suspension, the *epoché*,[8] of the ostensive reference. To read, in this way, means to prolong this suspension of the ostensive reference to the world and to transfer oneself into the 'place' where the text stands, within the 'enclosure' of this worldless place. According to this choice, the text no longer has an outside, it has only an inside. Once more, the very constitution of the text as text and of the system of texts as literature justifies this conversion of the literary thing into a closed system of signs, analogous to the kind of closed system which phonology discovered at the root of all discourse, and which de Saussure[9] called *la langue*. Literature, according to this working hypothesis, becomes an *analogon*[1] of *la langue*.

On the basis of this abstraction, a new kind of explanatory attitude may be extended to the literary object, which, contrary to the expectation of Dilthey, is no longer borrowed from the natural sciences, i.e., from an area of knowledge alien to language itself. The opposition between *Natur* and *Geist* is no longer operative here. If some model is borrowed, it comes from the same field, from the semiological field. It is henceforth possible to treat texts according to the elementary rules which linguistics successfully applied to the elementary systems of signs that underlie the use of language. We have learned from the Geneva school, the Prague school, and the Danish school, that it is always possible to abstract *systems* from *processes* and to relate these systems— whether phonological, lexical, or syntactical—to units which are merely defined by their opposition to other units of the same system. This interplay of merely distinctive entities within finite sets of such units defines the notion of structure in linguistics.

It is this structural model which is now applied to *texts*, i.e., to sequences of signs longer than the sentence, which is the last kind of unit that linguistics takes into account. In his *Structural Anthropology*, Claude Lévi-Strauss

8. Husserl's term for phenomenological bracketing, borrowed from the Greek.
9. Ferdinand de Saussure (1857–1913), Swiss linguist whose work was foundational for structuralism in philosophy and social theory as well as in linguistics. He also introduced the distinction between *langue* (language system) and *parole* (an individual's speech), and was a founder of semiotics or semiology (the study of signs).
1. A proportionate thing (Greek); that is, an analog.

formulates this working hypothesis in regard to one category of texts, that of myths.[2]

By means of this working hypothesis, the large units which are at least the same size as the sentence and which, put together, form the narrative proper of the myth, will be able to be treated according to the same rules as the smallest units known to linguistics. [. . . In this way,] we can indeed say that we have explained a myth, but not that we have interpreted it. We can, by means of structural analysis, bring out the logic of it, the operations which relate the 'bundles of relations' among themselves. This logic constitutes 'the structural law of the myth under consideration'.[3] This law is pre-eminently an object of reading and not at all of speaking, in the sense of a recitation where the power of the myth would be re-enacted in a particular situation. Here the text is only a text, thanks to the suspension of its meaning for us, to the postponement of all actualisation by present speech.

I want now to show in what way 'explanation' (*erklären*) requires 'understanding' (*verstehen*) and brings forth in a new way the inner dialectic which constitutes 'interpretation' as a whole.

As a matter of fact, nobody stops with a conception of myths and of narratives as formal as this algebra of constitutive units. This can be shown in different ways. First, even in the most formalised presentation of myths by Lévi-Strauss, the units which he calls 'mythemes' are still expressed as sentences which bear meaning and reference. Can anyone say that their meaning as such is neutralised when they enter into the 'bundle of relations' which alone is taken into account by the 'logic' of the myth? Even this bundle of relations, in its turn, must be written in the form of a sentence. Finally, the kind of language-game which the whole system of oppositions and combinations embodies, would lack any kind of significance if the oppositions themselves, which, according to Lévi-Strauss, the myth tends to mediate, were not meaningful oppositions concerning birth and death, blindness and lucidity, sexuality and truth. Beside these existential conflicts there would be no contradictions to overcome, no logical function of the myth as an attempt to solve these contradictions. Structural analysis does not exclude, but presupposes, the opposite hypothesis concerning the myth, i.e., that it has a meaning as a narrative of origins. Structural analysis merely represses this function. But it cannot suppress it. The myth would not even function as a logical operator if the propositions which it combines did not point toward boundary situations. Structural analysis, far from getting rid of this radical questioning, restores it at a level of higher radicality.

If this is true, could we not say that the function of structural analysis is to lead from a surface semantics, that of the narrated myth, to a depth semantics, that of the boundary situations which constitute the ultimate 'referent' of the myth?

I really believe that if such were not the function of structural analysis, it would be reduced to a sterile game, a divisive algebra, and even the myth

2. Claude Lévi-Strauss, *Anthropologie structurale* (Paris: Plon, 1958) [English translation: *Structural Anthropology*, translated by Claire Jacobson and Brooke Grundfest Schoepf (Harmondsworth: Penguin Books, 1968)] [Ricoeur's note, with translator's brackets]. Lévi-Strauss (1908–2009), French anthropologist; he was a central figure in the development of structuralism in the social sciences and social theory.

3. Ibid., p. 241 [p. 217] [Ricoeur's note, with translator's brackets].

would be bereaved of the function which Lévi-Strauss himself assigns to it, that of making men aware of certain oppositions and of tending toward their progressive mediation. To eliminate this reference to the *aporias*[4] of existence around which mythic thought gravitates would be to reduce the theory of myth to the necrology of the meaningless discourses of mankind. If, on the contrary, we consider structural analysis as a stage—and a necessary one— between a naive interpretation and a critical interpretation, between a surface interpretation and a depth interpretation, then it would be possible to locate explanation and understanding at two different stages of a unique *hermeneutical arc*. It is this depth semantics which constitutes the genuine object of understanding and which requires a specific affinity between the reader and the kind of things the text is *about*.

But we must not be misled by this notion of personal affinity. The depth semantics of the text is not what the author intended to say, but what the text is about, i.e., the non-ostensive reference of the text. And the non-ostensive reference of the text is the kind of world opened up by the depth semantics of the text. Therefore what we want to understand is not something hidden behind the text, but something disclosed in front of it. What has to be understood is not the initial situation of discourse, but what points toward a possible world. Understanding has less than ever to do with the author and his situation. It wants to grasp the proposed worlds opened up by the references of the text. To understand a text is to follow its movement from sense to reference, from what it says, to what it talks about. In this process the *mediating* role played by structural analysis constitutes both the justification of this objective approach and the rectification of the subjective approach. We are definitely prevented from identifying understanding with some kind of intuitive grasping of the intention underlying the text. What we have said about the depth semantics which structural analysis yields invites us rather to think of the sense of the text as an injunction starting from the text, as a new way of looking at things, as an injunction to think in a certain manner. [. . .]

This second figure or *Gestalt* of the dialectic between explanation and comprehension has a strong paradigmatic character which holds for the whole field of the human sciences. I want to emphasise three points.

First, the structural model, taken as a paradigm for explanation, may be extended beyond textual entities to all social phenomena because it is not limited in its application to linguistic signs, but applies to all kinds of signs which are analogous to linguistic signs. The intermediary link between the model of the text and social phenomena is constituted by the notion of semiological systems. A linguistic system, from the point of view of semiology, is only a species within the semiotic genre, although this species has the privilege of being a paradigm for the other species of the genre. We can say therefore that a structural model of explanation can be generalised as far as all social phenomena which may be said to have a semiological character, i.e., as far as it is possible to define the typical relations of a semiological system at their level: the general relation between code and message, relations among the specific units of the code, the relation between signifier and signified, the

4. Difficulties, logical impasses, seemingly unresolvable uncertainties: a term often used in deconstructive criticism to indicate a gap or dilemma— the point in a text where internal contradictions render interpretation undecidable.

typical relation within and among social messages, the structure of communication as an exchange of messages, etc. Inasmuch as the semiological model holds, the semiotic or symbolic function, i.e., the function of substituting signs for things and of representing things by the means of signs, appears to be more than a mere effect in social life. It is its very foundation. We should have to say, according to this generalised function of the semiotic, not only that the symbolic function is social, but that social reality is fundamentally symbolic.

If we follow this suggestion, then the kind of explanation which is implied by the structural model appears to be quite different from the classical causal model, especially if causation is interpreted in Humean terms as a regular sequence of antecedents and consequents with no inner logical connection between them.[5] Structural systems imply relations of a quite different kind, correlative rather than sequential or consecutive. If this is true, the classical debate about motives and causes which has plagued the theory of action these last decades loses its importance. If the search for correlations within semiotic systems is the main task of explanation, then we have to reformulate the problem of motivation in social groups in new terms. But it is not the aim of this essay to develop this implication.

Secondly, the second paradigmatic factor in our previous concept of text-interpretation proceeds from the role which we assigned to depth semantics *between* structural analysis and appropriation. This mediating function of depth semantics must not be overlooked, since the appropriation's losing its psychological and subjective character and receiving a genuine epistemological function depends on it.

Is there something similar to the depth semantics of a text in social phenomena? I should tend to say that the search for correlations within and between social phenomena treated as semiotic entities would lose importance and interest if it did not yield *something like* a depth semantics. In the same way as language-games are forms of life, according to the famous aphorism of Wittgenstein,[6] social structures are also attempts to cope with existential perplexities, human predicaments and deep-rooted conflicts. In this sense, these structures, too, have a referential dimension. They point toward the *aporias* of social existence, the same *aporias* around which mythical thought gravitates. And this analogical function of reference develops traits very similar to what we called the non-ostensive reference of a text, i.e., the display of a *Welt* which is no longer an *Umwelt*, the projection of a world which is more than a situation. May we not say that in social science, too, we proceed from naive interpretations to critical interpretations, from surface interpretations to depth interpretations *through* structural analysis? But it is depth interpretation which gives meaning to the whole process.

This last remark leads us to our third and last point. If we follow the paradigm of the dialectic between explanation and understanding to its end, we must say that the meaningful patterns which a depth interpretation wants to grasp cannot be understood without a kind of personal commitment similar

5. The Scottish empiricist philosopher David Hume (1711–1776) concluded that it is impossible to give meaningful empirical content (beyond that of constant conjunction) to the idea of causality; see *An Enquiry Concerning Human Understanding* (1748).

6. Ludwig Wittgenstein (1889–1951), Austrian-born Cambridge philosopher of immense influence (see this anthology's companion volume, *The Analytic Tradition*); for the identification of "language-games" with "forms of life," see *Philosophical Investigations* (1953), §23.

to that of the reader who grasps the depth semantics of the text and makes it his 'own'. Everybody knows the objection which an extension of the concept of appropriation to the social sciences is exposed to. Does it not legitimate the intrusion of personal prejudices, of subjective bias into the field of scientific inquiry? Does it not introduce all the paradoxes of the hermeneutical circle into the human sciences? In other words, does not the paradigm of disclosure *plus* appropriation destroy the very concept of a human science? The way in which we introduced this pair of terms within the framework of text-interpretation provides us not only with a paradigmatic problem, but with a paradigmatic solution. This solution is not to deny the role of personal commitment in understanding human phenomena, but to qualify it.

As the model of text-interpretation shows, understanding has nothing to do with an *immediate* grasping of a foreign psychic life or with an *emotional* identification with a mental intention. Understanding is entirely *mediated* by the whole of explanatory procedures which precede it and accompany it. The counterpart of this personal appropriation is not something which can be *felt*, it is the dynamic meaning released by the explanation which we identified earlier with the reference of the text, i.e., its power of disclosing a world.

The paradigmatic character of text-interpretation must be applied down to this ultimate implication. This means that the conditions of an authentic appropriation, as they were displayed in relation to texts, are themselves paradigmatic. Therefore we are not allowed to exclude the final act of personal commitment from the whole of objective and explanatory procedures which mediate it.

This qualification of the notion of personal commitment does not eliminate the 'hermeneutical circle'. This circle remains an insuperable structure of knowledge when it is applied to human things, but this qualification prevents it from becoming a vicious circle.

Ultimately, the correlation between explanation and understanding, between understanding and explanation, is the 'hermeneutical circle'.

SOURCE: Paul Ricoeur, *Hermeneutics and the Human Sciences: Essays on Language, Action, and Interpretation*, ed. and trans. John B. Thompson (Cambridge: Cambridge University Press; Paris: Éditions de la Maison des Sciences de l'Homme, 1981), pp. 197–221. This essay first appeared (in this English translation) in *Social Research* 38 (1971); bracketed ellipses here mark Thompson's deletions from that earlier version.

CHARLES TAYLOR
(b. 1931)

Taylor has long been both one of the interpretive tradition's most prominent Anglophone champions and one of its foremost North American figures. It is entirely fitting that he and JÜRGEN HABERMAS were selected to share the prestigious 2015 John W. Kluge Prize for Achievement in the Study of Humanity. Taylor made his first major contribution through two substantial books on HEGEL, which helped rekindle not only interest in but also respect for Hegel as a philosopher whose thought is of continuing philosophical importance (particularly in social and political philosophy). In these and many other writings Taylor has made ideas of a number of often forbidding European figures in the interpretive tradition more comprehensible and engaging to English-speaking readers (and analytically inclined philosophers), by recasting them in an idiom more familiar and congenial to such audiences than that found in their straightforward translations. But he has been much more than a lucid intermediary for noteworthy ideas advanced by others. His *Sources of the Self: The Making of the Modern Identity* (1989) is one of the most substantial and significant late twentieth-century contributions to the interpretive tradition. And it was followed by a remarkable array of other important writings, ranging from *The Ethics of Authenticity* (1991) to studies of contemporary forms of religiousness and secularism. In the sweep, subtlety, and power of his interpretive thought, Taylor has had few peers in the Anglophone philosophical literature during the past half century.

Charles Margrave Taylor is a Canadian, born in Montreal to an English, Anglophone, and Protestant father and a French, Francophone, and Catholic mother. He thus was accustomed from childhood on to moving easily between two traditions, much as he would later negotiate the differing Anglo-American and European traditions that he encountered in philosophy. After attending an elite private English-speaking school for boys, he earned an undergraduate degree as a history major at McGill University (1952). He then went as a Rhodes Scholar to Balliol College at Oxford University, where he took another undergraduate degree in philosophy, politics, and economics (1955). He stayed at Oxford for graduate studies, supervised by eminent figures associated with each of philosophy's post-Kantian traditions: Isaiah Berlin (who might well have been included in this volume) and G. E. M. Anscombe (who is in its companion volume, *The Analytic Tradition*). He received his DPhil in 1961. In 2012 Oxford awarded him the honorary degree of Doctor of Letters.

When he returned to Canada Taylor took a position at McGill University, first in political science and then, in 1973, in philosophy as well. He held a simultaneous appointment in philosophy at the Université de Montréal until 1971. Between 1976 and 1981 he was Chichele Professor of Social and Political Theory at Oxford, after which he returned to McGill. Following his retirement to emeritus status in 1998, he accepted an appointment at Northwestern University in 2002 as Board of Trustees Professor of Law and Philosophy. In addition to the Kluge Prize, he has received many other honors, notably the $1.5 million Templeton Prize (2007) given in support of research relating to "spiritual realities" (Taylor has written extensively on religion and is a practicing Roman Catholic), and the Kyoto Prize (often called the "Japanese Nobel"), awarded for "significant contributions to the scientific, cultural, or spiritual betterment of humankind" (2008).

Taylor's involvements and activities have not been confined to academia. He has been actively involved in Canadian politics, running (albeit unsuccessfully) four times in the 1960s for a seat in the federal parliament as a candidate of Canada's social-democratic New Democratic Party. He subsequently served in a number of appointed positions dealing with various Canadian social and cultural issues, primarily in Quebec, his home province. In recognition of his services, in 1996 he was made a Companion of the Order of Canada, and in 2000 he was awarded the title of Grand Officer of the National Order of Quebec.

Taylor's philosophical training was largely in the analytic tradition; but finding that tradition to be inadequate to his developing interests and concerns, he began to draw on the thought of a considerable number of figures in the interpretive tradition—not only Hegel but also MARTIN HEIDEGGER, MAURICE MERLEAU-PONTY, and HANS-GEORG GADAMER. He also became acquainted with European philosophical anthropology, and (unlike many recent philosophers in both traditions) has no reluctance to talk in a positive way about "human nature." His own thinking does not fall neatly under any single rubric. It is perhaps best described as having connections with Hegelian *Geist*-philosophy, Heideggerian *Existenz*-philosophy, Merleau-Ponty's kind of phenomenology, WILHELM DILTHEY's and Gadamer's kinds of hermeneutics, and HELMUTH PLESSNER's (and even MAX SCHELER's) kind of philosophical anthropology—as well as with a number of strands of analytic philosophy, including the thought of Ludwig Wittgenstein (see *The Analytic Tradition*).

A central theme of Taylor's thinking is the fundamental inadequacy and misguidedness of positivistic, scientistic, and biologistic materialisms and naturalisms, on the one hand, and of historicist and deconstructionist relativisms, on the other. In his view they all are hopelessly simplistic and superficial, and do not do justice to human reality and to human phenomena such as the self,

community, meaning, worth, and obligation. Because all such phenomena involve interpretation and self-interpretation, all involve relations that must be understood hermeneutically and phenomenologically. Taylor is critical of the human disciplines in general and the "social sciences" in particular for their failure to appreciate this point, and to take account of it both conceptually and methodologically. For him as for Heidegger, human selves are interpreters and self-interpreters through and through. For him as for the philosophical anthropologists, human beings are "self-interpreting animals" (the title of the following selection, in which he makes his case for and elaborates on this thesis). For him as for the hermeneuticists Dilthey and Gadamer, we are language- and meaning-creating self-interpreting animals. And for Taylor as for all those named above, including Hegel and Wittgenstein, all of this needs to be conceived in a communitarian manner. One of his important contributions has been to update Hegel's idea of the social character—institutional, interpersonal, and cultural—of much of human spirituality, according centrality to "forms of life" in its realization and development, even in the case of the seemingly individual human "self."

This description captures an important feature of Taylor's thought, which is an important feature of philosophical thinking in the interpretive tradition more generally: it builds and draws on previous efforts, even as it goes beyond them. In many of his best and most interesting writings, Taylor both sets forth an account and reconstruction of ideas that he finds—and finds promising—in the analytical and interpretive work of others (in both traditions), and develops his own versions and extensions of them. The following selection is a good example. Another, "Interpretation and the Sciences of Man" (1971), is one of the best arguments in the literature for the kind of approach to the understanding of human reality that makes the interpretive tradition what it is.

Self-Interpreting Animals

I

Human beings are self-interpreting animals. This is a widely echoing theme of contemporary philosophy. It is central to a thesis about the sciences of man, and what differentiates them from the sciences of nature, which passes through Dilthey[1] and is very strong in the late twentieth century. It is one of the basic ideas of Heidegger's philosophy,[2] early and late. Partly through his influence, it has been made the starting point for a new skein of connected conceptions of man, self-understanding and history, of which the most prominent protagonist has been Gadamer.[3] At the same time, this conception of man as self-interpreting has been incorporated into the work of Habermas,[4] the most important successor of the post-Marxist line of thought known somewhat strangely as critical theory.

And one could go on. Through all this cross-talk about 'hermeneutics', the question of what one means by this basic thesis, that man is a self-interpreting animal, and how one can show that it is so, may still go unanswered. These are of course tightly related questions; and I would like to try to fumble my way towards an answer to them.

It may turn out to be a mistake, but I am tempted to try to put together the full picture that this thesis means to convey by stages; to lay out, in other words, a series of claims, where the later ones build on the earlier ones, and in that sense form a connected picture. But to talk of claims implies that what is said at each stage is controversial, and that it will have to be established against opposition. So before starting it may be useful to say a word about who or what is opposing, or what the argument is all about.

The thesis that man is a self-interpreting being cannot just be stated flatly, or taken as a truism without argument, because it runs against one of the fundamental prejudices or, to sound less negative, leading ideas of modern thought and culture. It violates a paradigm of clarity and objectivity.

According to this, thinking clearly about something, with a view to arriving at the truth about it, requires that we think of it objectively, that is, as an object among other objects. This means that we avoid attributing to it properties, or describing it in terms of properties, which are 'subjective' in the sense that they are only properties of the object in our experience of it.

This was one of the basic components of the seventeenth-century revolution in scientific thought, which we still see rightly as the foundation of modern science, and indeed of modern thought in general. And perhaps the best illustrative example to take is that paradigm of the seventeenth-century discussion, the distinction between primary and secondary qualities.[5]

Secondary qualities could not be integrated into a science of nature in the same way as the primary, because they were subjective in the above sense.

---

1. For WILHELM DILTHEY, see above.
2. For MARTIN HEIDEGGER, see above.
3. For HANS-GEORG GADAMER, see above.
4. For JÜRGEN HABERMAS, see above.
5. That is, between qualities that belong to things themselves (extension, size, shape, mass, number, and motion or rest) and qualities that occur in our perceptual experience (such as color, heat, sound, and taste). Two of the main originators of this discussion were the French philosopher and mathematician René Descartes (1596–1650) and the English philosopher John Locke (1632–1704).

That is, they were properties of the objects concerned only in our experience of them. Only in the experience of creatures endowed with the particular form of sensibility we call sight can things be coloured. Should these creatures cease to exist, the light that objects give off would indeed go on being of a certain wave-length, but there would no longer be what we think of as colour. Secondary properties were sometimes objected to on the grounds that they were variable, or not susceptible to inter-subjective validation—the water that feels cold to me now may feel warm later, or warm to you now. But the ultimate ground of objection was that they were subjective. Even if we were somehow guaranteed in fact against variations in our perceptions over time and between persons, such properties were still suspect because they cannot make good a claim to be independently part of the furniture of things. The assurance against variation could always only be *de facto*,[6] because these properties are in their nature dependent on our sensibility.

The distinction could be put in terms of a contemporary science-fiction fable if we say that the primary, the objective, is what we could agree about with Alpha Centaurans,[7] who as everybody knows are large gaseous clouds, somehow endowed with sapience, but unrecognizable by us as living beings, lacking what we think of as sense organs, lacking our notion of individuality (they agglomerate and redivide in all sorts of ways). When we finally managed to establish communication with them, and learnt each other's conventions of measurement, we could presumably come to agreement with them in attributing wave-lengths to the light reflecting off different objects. But what we experience as colour would remain quite incommunicable. With Alpha Centaurans, we shall have to be completely Democritean:[8] by convention, coloured and sweet; by nature, atoms, quarks, pi-mesons, and wave-lengths.

Following this line of thought, colour, sweetness, felt heat, and so on, are not banished altogether—how could they be considered as nothing? But they are placed ontologically not in things but in our sensibility, or in our experience of things. And this was one of the roots of the notorious theory of perception as made up of 'ideas' or 'impressions', which has wreaked such havoc in philosophical psychology down the centuries. This theory of experience has turned out to be an embarrassment for everyone, and in recent times this same basic objectivist orientation rather expresses itself in the perspective of a reductive explanation of human action and experience in physiological and ultimately in physical and chemical terms. In this way we shall be able to treat man, like everything else, as an object among other objects, characterizing him purely in terms of properties which are independent of his experience— in this case, his self-experience; and treat the lived experience of, for example, sensation as epiphenomenon, or perhaps as a misdescription of what is really a brain-state.

This view gets a little incoherent around the edges; but I do not want to argue that now. I wanted only to articulate somewhat the standard of clarity

---

6. That is, ascertained as a matter of fact (rather than of principle).
7. Imagined inhabitants of a planet in Alpha Centauri, the star system closest to us. (Taylor's "as everybody knows" is said in jest.)

8. That is, followers of the Greek philosopher Democritus (ca. 460–ca. 370 B.C.E.), a founder of ancient atomist theory (a materialist account of the natural world).

and objectivity, that is, of a clear account of what things objectively are, against which the conception of man as self-interpreting must contend all the way. For it essentially resists the reduction of experience to a merely subjective view on reality, or an epiphenomenon, or a muddled description. On the contrary, the claim is that our interpretation of ourselves and our experience is constitutive of what we are, and therefore cannot be considered as merely a view on reality, separable from reality, nor as an epiphenomenon, which can be by-passed in our understanding of reality.

II

1

With the background established, I turn to the claims. The first is that many of our feelings, emotions, desires, in short much of our experienced motivation, are such that saying properly what they are like involves expressing or making explicit a judgement about the object they bear on.

This point has often been made in contemporary philosophy in the form of a thesis that (to put it in capsule form) emotions are essentially related to certain objects. To experience fear is to experience some object as terrifying or dangerous; to experience shame is to experience some object or situation as shameful or humiliating, and so on.

The obvious counter-examples that one is tempted to bring forward to this thesis serve to entrench it and at the same time to clarify it. People are tempted to invoke as an objection such 'objectless' emotions as nameless dread, or unfocussed anxiety. But the point about these, one might reply, is just that there is no object where there should be one. The very structure of fear is that it is of something; what marks out nameless fear, or in a different way, unfocussed anxiety, is that we cannot designate an object. But this does not show that the emotions are not essentially related to objects; for it is not just that there is no object here, rather there is a felt absence of object. The empty slot where the object of fear should be is an essential phenomenological feature of this experience. But an essential phenomenological feature of an *experience* is equivalent to an essential feature of it *tout court*.[9]

To put the point in different terms, to have a sense of nameless dread is to have a sense of threat for which I can not find any (rational) focus in this situation. The inability to find a focus is itself an aspect of my sense of my situation. But even in this unfocussed way, the sense I have is one of *threat*, or that something *harmful* is impending, that something terrible might *happen*. Without something of this range, it cannot be *dread* that we experience. The emotion is not 'objectless' *simpliciter*,[1] because it is of something terrible impending; it is just that I cannot say what. But perhaps for this reason, it is better not to put the point in terms of an essential relation to objects, and speak rather of these emotions as essentially involving a sense of our situation. They are affective modes of awareness of situation. And we can rephrase our first claim and say that describing properly what these emotions are like

---

9. And nothing else (French).   1. Simply (Latin).

involves making explicit the sense of the situation they essentially incorporate, making explicit some judgement about the situation which gives the emotion its character.

We could put it this way: that experiencing a given emotion involves experiencing our situation as being of a certain kind or having a certain property. But this property cannot be neutral, cannot be something to which we are indifferent, or else we would not be moved. Rather, experiencing an emotion is to be aware of our situation as humiliating, or shameful, or outrageous, or dismaying, or exhilarating, or wonderful; and so on.

Each of these adjectives defines what I would like to call an import, if I can introduce this as a term of art. By 'import' I mean a way in which something can be relevant or of importance to the desires or purposes or aspirations or feelings of a subject; or otherwise put, a property of something whereby it is a matter of non-indifference to a subject.

But the 'whereby' in the previous clause is meant in a strong sense. In identifying the import of a given situation we are picking out what in the situation gives the grounds or basis of our feelings, or what could give such grounds, or perhaps should give such grounds, if we feel nothing or have inappropriate feelings. We are not just stating in other terms that we experience a certain feeling in this situation.

That is, it could not be a sufficient condition of our ascribing what I am calling an import to a given situation that we experience a certain feeling or desire in it or relative to it. Some predicates do have this logic. Louis XV was 'le bien aimé'[2] just because he was in fact loved by many of his subjects. A situation is painful, just because we feel pain in it. A certain place at the table is much coveted just because many people desire it. But we are saying something different when we say that someone is lovable, or that a position is enviable. Whether these properties are correctly ascribed does not turn on whether many love the person or envy the position, although their being popular or much sought after can be good evidence for the ascription.

But imports have a different logic. And my first claim, therefore, can be put this way: that experiencing a given emotion involves experiencing our situation as bearing a certain import, where for the ascription of the import it is not sufficient just that I feel this way, but rather the import gives the grounds or basis for the feeling. And that is why saying what an emotion is like involves making explicit the sense of the situation it incorporates, or, in our present terms, the import of the situation as we experience it.

Thus it is essential to an emotion like fear or shame that we experience it as a response to the situation's bearing the relevant import—its being menacing or shameful. These emotions are defined by the imports they relate to: fear is the affective response to the menacing, anger to the provoking, indignation to the flagrantly wrongful, and so on. We might say: fear is the affect which belongs to our experience of our situation as menacing; and so on for the other emotions.

That is why we can experience emotions like shame and fear mistakenly or unwarrantedly, whereas we cannot in the same sense love mistakenly—although we can love unwisely, which is quite a different matter—nor, for instance, feel

2. "The Well-Beloved" (French), the nickname of this king of France (1710–1774; reigned 1715–74).

pain mistakenly. And, for the same reason, it is possible to feel shame or fear irrationally, where for instance, we are intellectually convinced that the situation is not menacing or shameful, but we cannot help feeling afraid or ashamed. There would be no room for the notion of irrationality, if we were not in some sense affirming the import in feeling the emotion that we are intellectually agreeing to deny. There can be no irrational pain.

But in what sense affirming it?

It cannot simply be that experiencing the emotion is ascribing the import. Because a prominent feature of those situations we consider as paradigmatic of irrational emotion is where the person sees and admits that the import does not apply, but goes on feeling that way anyway. I feel ashamed, even though I see perfectly that it's absurd, that there is nothing shameful in having succumbed to a bout of anger in such trying circumstances. So having the feeling plainly is not equivalent to ascribing the import, particularly if we think of this as equvalent to making the judgement that the situation bears the import. For in the case I am imagining, I am precisely withholding the intellectual assent which is essential to my being said to have judged that p.[3] It is just that I cannot help going on feeling ashamed.

So the relation is not one of simple equivalence, where feeling the emotion is ascribing the import. But nor can it be true that there is no relation at all, as with physical pain. Rather it is that experiencing the emotion is experiencing our situation as bearing a certain import, where this is compatible in some cases with recognizing that the situation does not bear this import, and withholding intellectual assent from the judgement that it does.

Saying what an emotion is like therefore involves making explicit the import-ascription, a judgement which is not thereby affirmed, it is true, but experienced as holding the sense of the situation which it incorporates.

This first claim does not sit well with the modern conception of objectivity. That is, emotions understood as having this logical structure do not fit easily into an account of men and human behaviour as objects among objects. Such an account should be able to explain what men do in terms of objective factors in the meaning of this term sketched above, that is, in terms of factors which are not experience-dependent. Properties are experience-dependent when they hold of things only in human experience (or the experience of other sentient beings), like the secondary properties of the classical distinction.

Thus we should be able to explain human motivation in terms, say, of certain underlying physiological states, which are certainly identifiable in terms independent of experience. In addition to this a role is certainly played by the environment, but this can surely be coped with if we can characterize this 'input' to the system itself in experience-independent terms: either as 'receptor impulses', or in terms of physical features of our field.

Of course, the ideally simple theory of this objective kind would be a behaviourist one, where we would correlate physical features of the environment with movements of the organism; and this helps account for the strange continuing obsession with this wildly implausible approach to the science of man. But once this breaks down, and one has to admit some inner motivational

---

3. "p" signifies "some proposition or other."

states, the least disturbing are those, like physical pain, which involve no import-ascription at all. Someone moves his finger on the blackboard,[4] and I wince and shudder. This is a bit of experienced motivation which involves no judgement or import-ascription at all. It is sufficient that I take in the squeak for me to react. The same can be said for the leap and curse that escape me in the dentist's chair when he touches a nerve suddenly.

But what I have called imports are quite essentially experience-dependent properties, or appear to be. For they characterize things in their relevance to our desires and purposes, or in their role in our emotional life. If we now claim that reference to an import is essential to making clear what is involved in certain emotions, and if in turn we have recourse to these emotions in order to explain the behaviour they motivate, then the ideal of an objective account will have been breached.

That is why those who aim for an objective account would rather propose reductive explanations of our emotions. One can do this, presumably, through an account of human behaviour at a neurophysiological level, by-passing the psychological level altogether. But we are very far from even the beginnings of such a theory of neurophysiological function, let alone any idea of how to characterize the 'input' of, say, humiliating or threatening situations in physiological terms.

The hope for a reductive account must surely lie in another direction. And one can see another possibility: that one can give an objective account of the imports involved. To take a plausible example, when we are physically afraid we experience our situation as importing menace to life and limb. A tiger is prowling in the garden, or a hostile mob seems about to attack. Now presumably we could give an account of what this import involves in objective terms. We fear, you might say, injury which will cause severe pain, or malfunction of our limbs or organs, or death. For all of these states, we can set out the conditions in a medical language which invokes only experience-independent properties. However difficult it may be to define bone fracture, and especially the distinction life/death, in medical terms, the difficulties surely do not arise from our having to use experience-dependent terms. The heart's ceasing, or the decay of certain brain cells, can be characterized in a language which does not depend for its meaning on our experiencing things the way we do. We could presumably communicate about these distinctions with Alpha Centaurans, even though they might have some trouble understanding how it was that our function as sapient beings depended on the condition of these brain cells.

Now the import of a menacing situation could be defined in terms of these medically defined states: it would be a situation which in virtue of well-understood causal mechanisms had a certain probability of bringing about one of these states; hungry tigers are likely to sink their teeth in nearby flesh, angry human beings in the mass are likely to beat whoever provokes them unrelentingly. Our model of human beings as capable of experiencing fear would then see them as beings capable of recognizing situations with these causal properties, that is correlated with a high degree of probability with the

4. That is, scrapes a fingernail on the slate writing surface once common in classrooms and thereby produces a very unpleasant sound and feeling.

negative medically defined states. And there seems to be no obstacle in principle to our giving an objective account of a system capable of such recognition. We could imagine building a machine, with receptors attached to a computer and memory-bank, which could presumably recognize a tiger, search in the bank for facts about tigers, and recognize danger accordingly.[5]

On recognizing danger, the machine could print out instructions to some locomotion mechanism to take evasive action. We would then have, it seems, a complete structural analogue of fear, including the import-recognition of danger and the flight. What would be missing would be the actual feeling of fear, and indeed the sense of self-awareness itself. But this, as we have seen, has to be treated as epiphenomenon in an objective account. Whether it is ultimately coherent to treat it so, I very much doubt. But I do not want to pursue that now. The whole enterprise has another flaw.

The crucial flaw with this as a general formula for a reductive account of emotions is that it breaks down for the key cases in its first step: the objective explication of the import. And this is the substance of my second claim.

The explication seemed to work well enough for the physically menacing. But let us look at the shameful. Shame is an emotion that a subject experiences in relation to a dimension of his existence as a subject. What we can be ashamed of are properties which are essentially properties of a subject. This may not be immediately evident, because I may be ashamed of my shrill voice, or my effeminate hands. But of course it only makes sense to see these as objects of shame if they have for me or my culture an expressive dimension: a shrill voice is (to me, to my culture) something unmanly, betokens hysteria, not something solid, strong, macho, self-contained. It does not radiate a sense of strength, capacity, superiority. Effeminate hands are—effeminate. Both voice and hands clash with what I aspire to be, feel that my dignity demands that I be, as a person, a presence among others.

These properties are thus only demeaning for a subject for whom things can have this kind of meaning. But things can have this kind of meaning only for a subject in whose form of life there figures an aspiration to dignity, to be a presence among men which commands respect.

In a world in which there were no beings of this kind the concept 'shameful' could not be given a sense. But a subject with this kind of aspiration must be a subject of awareness, of experience. This is not to say that I am always aware of what is shameful in my life. I may be lamentably insensitive to it. The point is rather that a subject with this aspiration must be capable of experiencing the whole range of imports connected with shame, dignity, respect, however insensitive he may be in certain cases. A world without beings capable of this kind of experience would be one without any aspiration to dignity. In this kind of world—say, to take an extreme case, a world without sentient beings—the concept 'shameful' could get no grip whatever.

Thus the import shameful can be explicated only by reference to a subject who experiences his world in a certain way. And in this the shameful is quite unlike the physically menacing which we discussed earlier.

5. Actually this is much more problematic than it sounds, as work on the limitation of computers—especially H. L. Dreyfus, *What Computers Can't Do* (New York, 1979)—has shown; but I want to set this aside for the sake of the discussion here [Taylor's note].

What is emerging here is not the banal truism that nothing has the import shameful except for a subject for whom there are imports. This is a tautology, valid for any import, including the physically menacing. Rather the point is that the term 'shameful' has no sense outside of a world in which there is a subject for whom things have certain (emotional) meanings. For the (linguistic) meaning of 'shameful' can only be explicated with reference to a subject for whom these (emotional) meanings have weight, and if there were no such subjects, the term itself would lack sense.

We could put the point in this way: the import term 'shameful' only has sense in a world in which there are subjects who experience it as an import. For we can explicate the term only with reference to such subjects and their experience. By contrast the physically menacing can be given a sense quite independent of any subject's experience of it. It can be given a meaning even for animate beings who have no sense of it, and could be given a meaning even if all animate beings lacked such a sense. We can give its meaning, we argued above, in purely medical terms. That is why the Alpha Centaurans could understand what we meant by menacing, but they will never be able to grasp this human business of shame and humiliation.

To go into this further, an import defines a way in which our situation is of relevance to our purposes or desires, or aspirations. Consequently, no sense can be given to an import term except in a world in which there are beings which are taken to have purposes. (These may be external purposes, like the purposes our instruments have in our lives; so that there can be imports for my car: sand in the petrol is a menace; or they may be 'internal' purposes, those of animate organisms.) But it may still be that some of these imports can be explicated independently of the experience, if any, of animate beings. This seemed to be the case with our medically defined states of danger to life and limb.

An objectifying science would even aspire to define the crucial properties— for example, the heart's beating/stopping—independently of their status as imports (as Alpha Centaurans would understand it: they would be able to see that the heart stopped, but they would not quite understand why it mattered).

But with the shameful, this pattern of explication breaks down. For the shameful is not a property which can hold of something quite independent of the experience subjects have of it. Rather, the very account of what shame means involves reference to things—like our sense of dignity, of worth, of how we are seen by others—which are essentially bound up with the life of a subject of experience.

I should like to call properties of which this is true, like shameful, 'subject-referring' properties. These are properties which can only exist in a world in which there are subjects of experience, because they concern in some way the life of the subject *qua* subject.

Subject-referring properties are experience-dependent, since these properties are what they are only in relation to the experience of subjects. The relation may not be a simple one, as is that of secondary qualities, viz., that they are only what they are in the ordinary experience of human subjects. It may be something that is presupposed by this experience, or gives it its shape; like an aspiration to dignity or, even less immediately, one to integrity, or wholeness, or fulfilment, about which we can only speculate or offer controvertible interpretations. But in either case we are dealing with factors which can only be explicated with reference to human experience, and hence for all of these a reductive account along the lines of the physically menacing above is impossible.

That is why, as has frequently been noticed for emotion terms like shame, an explication cannot be found which does not invoke other meanings for the subject. Why is this situation shameful? Because something shows me up to be base, or to have some unavowable and degrading property, or to be dishonourable. In this account, however long we carry it on, other words appear, like 'base', 'dishonourable', 'degrading', or a host of moral terms: 'cheat', 'liar', 'coward', 'fraud', which involve other meanings that things have for us. We cannot escape from these terms into an objective account, because in fact shame is about an aspect of the life of the subject *qua* subject.

Subject-referring properties do not fit into an objectivist's view of the world. This allows for an account of things in terms of objective properties, and then also perhaps for a subjective reaction to or view of things on the part of the subject. Emotions like shame do not fit into either slot. They cannot take a place, unamended, in the objective account of things, because they can only be explicated in experience-dependent terms. But nor can they just be classed as a subjective view on things. To feel shame is related to an import-ascription, in the way described above. But to ascribe an import is to make a judgement about the way things are, which cannot simply be reduced to the way we feel about them, as we saw earlier. Beyond the question whether I feel ashamed is the question whether the situation is really shameful, whether I am rightly or wrongly, rationally or irrationally, ashamed.

It is this quality of the shameful, like the other crucial imports of our emotional life, which will not fit into the objectivist's grid. According to the logic of the concept, there is a truth of the matter, what is shameful, irreducible to me or you feeling this or that way about it. But the truth of this matter has no place in the objectivist's ontology.

This is the kind of matter, to return to our fable, that one could not explain to the Alpha Centaurans. But we could not blame them for not understanding the fuss we humans make about shame, dignity, and the like. For all this relates to our lives *qua* subjects, and the kind of subjects that we are. We can only explicate these things in terms which again only make sense to us. With Alpha Centaurans, we shall have a radical communication gap. But this is hardly surprising; on these matters, we have quite a communication gap among ourselves, when we come from different cultures, and sometimes even when we are from the same culture. For our human experience differs, and this helps shape the language that will be meaningful to us in this area.

2

There are two further points, before going on. The first is that it is this irreducibility of our emotion terms which is essentially linked to their playing the role they do in our language. For one of the things they do is to enable us to characterize our feelings in a richer way. One way we can characterize our feelings is in terms of the things we want to do or have or experience, the consummations desired: I want to eat, to sleep, to be at home again. These provide alternative ways of saying that I am hungry, sleepy, home-sick (but the equivalence fails in the last case).

But we can sometimes go deeper into our feelings, make more articulate what is involved in our desires, if we can express the imports which underlie them and give them their point. When I am ashamed, I want to hide, or conceal, or perhaps undo what is shameful. But the vocabulary of shame and the shameful allows us to articulate to a considerable degree what it is which makes me want to hide. I could try to say what I feel purely in terms of a consummation desired, by saying something like: 'I want my pride back', or 'I want my self-respect back'. But these terms would not be understood, either, without a grasp of the import which is articulated in the whole vocabulary of shame, the shameful, dignity, pride, respect.

A language which enables us to talk of imports as well allows a much fuller and richer articulation of feelings than one which only deals with consummations desired. Our understanding of the consummations we desire is deepened by our grasp of the imports things have for us, and vice versa, and a language in which we can speak of both enables us to be more articulate.

Now our emotion vocabulary describes our experience of the import things have for us, and of the consummations we correspondingly desire. Where we are dealing with an import which is objectively specifiable, we can say what is involved in language which makes no reference to experience, as we saw above, that is in language other than that of feeling and emotion. But where the meaning of the import is bound up with the nature of our experience, we can only articulate import and consummation in emotion language. Thus, to return to our fable again, we could explain the imports and goals involved in our fear for our physical safety to Alpha Centaurans, but not our outrage at our wounded dignity. Our emotion language is indispensable precisely because it is irreducible. It becomes an essential condition of articulacy; and import and goal, the language of feelings and consummations desired, form a skein of mutual referrals, from which there is no escape into objectified nature.

3

The second point concerns the use of the term 'subject-referring'. The choice of this term, as well as the examples above—shame and wounded dignity—may mislead. But subject-referring does not necessarily mean self-referring. The shameful or humiliating is subject-referring, because something is only humiliating for me by virtue of the way I understand myself—or better (as I hope to expound below), because of the way I see myself and aspire to appear in public space. Something only offends my dignity because it upsets or challenges the way I present, project or express myself in this public space. So one might gather from these examples that subject-referring imports only arise in connection with emotions which are self-concerned, not to say self-absorbed; that only our narcissistic side is engaged in this analysis.

But what about the experience of coming across someone in trouble and feeling called on to help, the experience the good Samaritan had (and presumably also the priest and the Levite, but they somehow rationalized it away)?[6] Here the import surely does not concern the self. We see the man lying bleeding in the road, and feel that we cannot pass by on the other side, but must bind his wounds. The import concerns the needs of this wounded man, not ourselves. Indeed, we may feel that there is something morally inferior, and tainted, about a motivation here which is self-regarding.

We are always painfully reminded that self-regarding motivations are all too possible even in this kind of situation. We go to help because we will look bad otherwise. What will others say? Or perhaps, more subtly, because we have a certain self-image we must keep up. But we are usually aware that such 'narcissistic' motivations reflect badly on us, and that the truly good man is focussed on the needs of the wounded person.

What of his motivation? This too is subject-referring in the above sense, even though not self-regarding. It is subject-referring, because the full recognition of this import involves reference to a subject. Of course, in this example, there is also irrelevantly reference to a subject because the being in need of help is a human being. But this is not the point I am making; and we could alter the example to exclude it: I might feel an obligation to succour animals, or to leave the world-order as it ought to be.

The crucial reference to the subject is, however, to the addressee of this felt obligation. For I do not just feel desire to help this man. Indeed, I might feel no such desire in the usual sense of the term. But I feel called upon to help him. And I feel called upon *qua* rational being, or moral being, or creature made by God in his image, in other words capable of responding to this like God, that is, out of agape.[7] The obligation does not lie on an animal nor, in another way, on an idiot, nor on an infant.

In other words, implicit in this import is a reference to the subject; because the import this situation bears is that it lays an obligation of strong kind on me—what we call a moral obligation or an obligation of charity. And a full understanding of what this means involves reference to the kind of being on whom this obligation is laid. The situation bears this import for me, in virtue of the kind of being I am; and this is a logical truth, internal to the meaning of the import.

For the import is not just that the situation provokes some impulse to go help. This would indeed happen, if it did, in virtue of the kind of being I am—a truism of the flattest. But that I am a being of the appropriate kind would not be part of the meaning of the import. But in this case, the import is that we are *called upon* to act. And we are called upon in virtue of being a certain kind of creature. Even though we may not be very sure in virtue of what we are called on, we know that the obligation lies on us, not on animals, stones, or idiots. The kind of being we are enters into the definition of this import.

It is true, of course, that the needs of the wounded man could be accounted for in objective terms. The import of the situation for him is perhaps objectively accountable. He needs to have his wounds bound. To explain this we need consider him only as a living being, not as a human subject (but this would not allow very satisfactory treatment, as we know, alas, from the many

6. In the New Testament parable (Luke 10:30–37), a priest and member of the tribe of Levi (who commonly fulfilled lesser temple functions) passed by a seemingly dead man who had been beaten and robbed, while a native of Samaria (the central region of ancient Palestine) helped him.
7. Selflessly caring love.

doctors who relate in this way to their patients). But to explain the import for us, we have to bring in the notion of an obligation; and this involves reference to the subject as proper addressee.

Hence the class of subject-referring imports is much wider than that of self-referring or self-regarding imports. To speak of subject-referring imports is not to see all motivation as narcissistic. On the contrary, these imports can have a very different structure, very different foci of attribution, as it were.

4

I can sum up the first two claims in the jargon I have developed in these pages:

1. that some of our emotions or experienced motivations involve import-ascriptions, and
2. that some of these imports are subject-referring.

Jointly, these two claims run very much against the bent of the objectivist ideal in that they show our important motivations to be irreducible to an objective account. This helps to account for the great resistance which the view incorporating these two claims encounters. But it seems to me clear nevertheless that these claims are valid. For these claims alone seem to make sense of our emotions as we live them, or, otherwise put, to be compatible with the logic of our language of the emotions.

III

1

Our subject-referring emotions are especially worth examining. For since they refer us to the life of the subject *qua* subject, they offer an insight into what this life amounts to.

In speaking of subject-referring emotions, I include all those which involve ascribing imports which are subject-referring, our sense of shame, of dignity, of guilt, or pride, our feelings of admiration and contempt, or moral obligation, of remorse, of unworthiness and self-hatred, and (less frequently) of self-acceptance, certain of our joys and anxieties. But we might also include some feelings which are not import-ascribing, at least which we do not understand to be such, but where we have some reason to believe that any adequate explanation of why we experience them would involve subject-referring imports. It may seem that our finding a given landscape, or someone's style, attractive, or our being sexually attracted to some people and not to others, are all examples of what we might call immediate reactions, and involve no import-ascription. We might be tempted therefore to class them with our fingernail-on-blackboard example, or the stab of pain in the tooth. But when we examine them more closely, it appears more than plausible that these feelings are related to, or shaped by, a host of subject-referring imports, of which we are only partially aware. Indeed, part of what is involved in growing insight is coming to see more clearly what these are. With time and greater self-understanding we can sometimes come to see what it is that draws us to certain places and people. A great number of our seemingly immediate desires and feelings are nevertheless partially constituted by a skein of subject-referring imports, which resonate through our psychic life.

Now all of these offer potential insight into our lives as subjects. They incorporate a sense of what is important to us *qua* subjects, or to put it slightly differently, of what we value, or what matters to us, in the life of the subject. We also value other things, for instance going on living, which pertain to us *qua* living organisms. But our feelings of shame, remorse, pride, dignity, moral obligations, aspirations to excel—just because the imports they involve are essentially those of a subject—all incorporate a sense of what is important for us in our lives as subjects.

If we think of this reflexive sense of what matters to us as subjects as being distinctively human—and it is clearly central to our notion of ourselves that we are such reflexive beings; this is what underlies the traditional definition of man as a rational animal—we could say that our subject-referring feelings incorporate a sense of what it is to be human, that is, of what matters to us as human subjects.

Now I want to claim—and this is my third claim—that this sense is crucial to our understanding of what it is to be human. This might not be immediately evident, because we also see ourselves as being aware of what is important to us as humans in other ways. Our society and tradition present us with moral rules, standards of excellence, pictures of good and bad lifeforms, which go beyond, may even run against, what we sense in our feelings of shame, remorse, pride, aspiration, etc. We should distinguish what we feel as important or valuable, we often are led to say, from what we know rationally to be so.

But putting the distinction this way is misleading. If I want to say that I know certain things to be truly important: that one should be generous even to blackguards; or that the only thing one should really be ashamed of is being untrue to oneself; or that acting out of spite is always bad—even though my gorge rises at the thought of helping that cad, I feel ashamed at not making the football team, and I cannot resist lashing out at my successful rival— I am not just opposing feeling to reason. For I would not 'know' that one should be generous, and so on, unless I was moved in some way: perhaps I feel remorse when I have delivered myself of a spiteful attack; or feel self-contempt at my lack of autonomy when I allow myself to feel shame at not making the football team; or feel morally inspired by the ideal of universal generosity. If I were quite impervious to any such feelings, these norms and ideals would carry no weight with me; I would not even be tempted to subscribe to them, and I would not describe myself as 'knowing' that they were true/valid.

It is of course true that these insights can be 'recollected in tranquillity'.[8] I may have a clear sense now that one should not be ashamed of any such unimportant thing, even though the insight is not now accompanied by any feeling; rather my only feeling at present is that ridiculous shame over not making the team. But I would not have this sense of the proper object of shame if I *never* felt any self-reproach, or self-contempt, or self-dissatisfaction, as a result

8. In his preface to *Lyrical Ballads* (2nd ed., 1800), William Wordsworth wrote that the origin of poetry is "emotion recollected in tranquillity."

of my continued unwarranted sense of humiliation. I have this sense of the proper object of shame through these feelings.

We often say 'I know that X, but I feel that Y', or 'I know that X, but I don't feel it'. But it would be wrong to conclude that knowing can be simply opposed to feeling. What I know is also grounded in certain feelings. It is just that I understand these feelings to incorporate a deeper, more adequate sense of our moral predicament. If feeling is an affective awareness of situation, I see these feelings as reflecting my moral situation as it truly is; the imports they attribute truly apply.

But are there not cases where our knowing is quite abstracted from feeling? Take this case, for instance. Someone is an instinctive racist, that is, he only feels a sense of moral solidarity with members of his own race; it is only towards them that he feels bound to act with respect, concerning them that he feels repugnance at killing or harming; in short, towards others he is like a contemporary carnivorous liberal towards animals. But then we reason with him, and argue that race should not make any difference; that what is to be valued and respected in people is nothing to do with race; and he is thus led to assent to the proposition that the respect for life and well-being ought to be extended to everyone. But we can easily imagine him saying that he knows this to be so, but does not feel it.

This does seem like a case of reasoning against feeling. But consider. What we built on was his sense of obligation to respect others, in his case, his compatriots. This sense is grounded in his feelings, for example, of repugnance at harming them. We then induced him to make explicit the sense of his compatriots that these feelings incorporate: what is it about them that gives them this claim to respect? We may not bring him so far as to accept some philosophical formulation, for instance that they are rational animals; but we bring him far enough to recognize that whatever it is race has nothing to do with it. He is thus forced to consent to our universalism.

Reasoning there certainly is here; but it is reasoning out of insight embedded in feeling, and in the absence of such feeling we could never have led our racist to the conclusion that he *ought* to respect all men. This is because our argument had to start from an awareness of import on his part. But there cannot be an awareness of subject-referring imports which is not grounded in feelings. This really flows from the point made in the previous section, that our subject-referring feelings attribute imports which cannot be reductively explained, but which involve reference to a subject who is aware of them. They are essentially imports for a subject. But this must mean a subject who has intuitive experience of them. For the awareness could not be exclusively that which comes from grasping an explanation of the imports; for in this case, *ex hypothesi*[9] the subject-referring emotions would not exist at all prior to their being explained. But then they would never come to exist, since prior to the explanation there would be nothing to explain.

Now our direct, intuitive experience of import is through feeling. And thus feeling is our mode of access to this entire domain of subject-referring imports, of what matters to us *qua* subjects, or of what it is to be human. We may come to feel the force of some imports through having explained to us their rela-

---

9. That is, by hypothesis.

tions to others, but these we must experience directly, through feeling. The chain of explanations must be anchored somewhere in our intuitive grasp of what is at stake.

It is only through our feelings that we are capable of grasping imports of this range at all. The fact that we are sometimes dispassionately aware of an import should not induce us to think that we could always be so aware. That supposition is absurd. This is a domain to which there is no dispassionate access.

But if feeling is our mode of access, the feelings are import-attributing. They incorporate a certain understanding of our predicament, and of the imports it bears. Thus we can feel entitled to say on the strength of certain feelings, or inferences from what we sense through certain feelings, that we know that X is right, or good, or worthy, or valuable; and this even when other feelings and reactions fail to concur, or even have an opposing purport! 'I know that X, but I feel that Y' does not oppose knowing to feeling, but rather reflects our conviction that what we sense through certain feelings is valid or adequate, while it devalues others as shallow, blind, distorting or perverse.

2

Our subject-referring feelings therefore open us on to the domain of what it is to be human; for we can have no dispassionate awareness of the human good; and the quality of our awareness of the good is a function of the alignment of our feelings. But if being divided we can know that certain feelings, for instance this remorse or that élan of aspiration, incorporate a deeper insight than others, for instance that sense of repulsion or this feeling of spite, it is because these feelings are articulated. That is, the sense of imports that they incorporate has been articulated into a picture of our moral predicament, according to which some goods are higher than others, while still others are false or illusory.

And this is where it begins to make sense to speak of man as a self-interpreting animal. For these articulations are in a sense interpretations. But it is not as though we started off with a raw material of repulsions and attractions, élans and uneases, which were then interpreted as higher and lower, élans towards some deep good, or uneases before some discreditable trait. On the contrary, human life is never without interpreted feeling; the interpretation is constitutive of the feeling.

That is, the feeling is what it is in virtue of the sense of the situation it incorporates. But a given sense may presuppose a certain level of articulacy, that the subject understand certain terms or distinctions. For example, a feeling cannot be one of remorse unless there is a sense of my having done wrong. Some understanding of right/wrong is built into remorse, is essential to its attributing the import that it does.

Thus certain feelings involve a certain level of articulation, in that the sense of things they incorporate requires the application of certain terms. But at the same time, they can admit of further articulation, in that the sense of things can yet be further clarified and made articulate. Thus while a feeling of remorse implies our sense that our act was wrong, and while it may be hard to imagine our having a feeling less articulate than this, which would only subsequently be clarified as one of remorse by our realizing that we see this act as wrong (though there are circumstances in which something like this could happen), it is quite a common experience for us to feel remorse without being able fully to articulate what is wrong about what we have done. In these cases we may seek to understand further. And if we succeed, our feelings may alter. The remorse may dissipate altogether, if we come to see that our sense of wrong-doing is unfounded; or it may alter in other ways, as we come to understand what is wrong; perhaps it will be more acute as we see how grave the offence was; perhaps it will be less as we see how hard it was to avoid.

Hence we can see that our feelings incorporate a certain articulation of our situation, that is, they presuppose that we characterize our situation in certain terms. But at the same time they admit of [1]—and very often we feel that they call for—further articulation, the elaboration of finer terms permitting more penetrating characterization. And this further articulation can in turn transform the feelings.

On closer examination, we can see that these two sides, that feelings incorporate an articulation, and that they call for further articulation, are related. Our subject-referring feelings have to incorporate a certain degree of articulation in order to open us to the imports involved. For instance, as we saw above, remorse presupposes that we can apply the terms 'right' and 'wrong'; shame requires that we have terms like 'worthy' and 'unworthy' in our lexicon. These feelings are essentially articulated; that is, they cannot be without a certain degree of articulation.

But these feelings attribute imports, indeed they open us to the domain of what it is to be human. And because they are articulated they purport to give a characterization of these imports, and hence to offer insight into this domain. One might say, they ascribe a form to what matters to us. For example, in feeling remorse for some act of self-affirmation, I experience this act as a violation, or a betrayal, or as evil.

But in offering a characterization, these feelings open the question whether this characterization is adequate, whether it is not incomplete or distortive. And so from the very fact of their being articulated, the question cannot but arise whether we have properly articulated our feelings, that is, whether we have properly explicated what the feeling gives us a sense of.

In an important sense, this question once opened can never be closed. For unlike the non-subject-referring imports like physical danger, which can ultimately be grounded on external criteria, the articulations of these emotions have to be self-validating. The adequate insight would just show itself to be so by its intrinsic clarity and the access to reality it opens. There could be no appeal to some unchallengeable external mark.

That our feelings are thus bound up with a process of articulation is my fourth claim. And it is this feature on top of the other three which justifies our talking of self-interpretation. For the joint result of the first three claims is that our subject-referring emotions open us to the domain of what it is to be human. And now we see them as giving articulation to this domain.

But we can speak of these attempted articulations as interpretations; for although they are constitutive of our feelings, these cannot just be shaped at

---

1. Allow.

will by the account we offer of them. On the contrary, an articulation purports to characterize a feeling; it is meant to be faithful to what it is that moves us. There is a getting it right and getting it wrong in this domain. Articulations are like interpretations in that they are attempts to make clearer the imports things have for us.

But then we must speak of man as a self-interpreting being, because this kind of interpretation is not an optional extra, but is an essential part of our existence. For our feelings always incorporate certain articulations; while just because they do so they open us on to a domain of imports which call for further articulation. The attempt to articulate further is potentially a life-time process. At each stage, what we feel is a function of what we have already articulated and evokes the puzzlement and perplexities which further understanding may unravel. But whether we want to take the challenge or not, whether we seek the truth or take refuge in illusion, our self-(mis)understandings shape what we feel. This is the sense in which man is a self-interpreting animal.

Reference to 'articulation' poses the question of the role of language in our emotions, something which has been implicitly evoked in the above discussion. More should be said about this.

IV

But before saying more, I should like to examine something else which was implicit in the above discussion. Our subject-referring emotions open us to a sense of what it is to be human, and this sense, as we saw, involves our interpreting some of our feelings as offering valid insight into what really matters and others as shallow, or even blind and distorted. Our emotions make it possible for us to have a sense of what the good life is for a subject; and this sense involves in turn our making qualitative discriminations between our desires and goals, whereby we see some as higher and others as lower, some as good and others as discreditable, still others as evil, some as truly vital and others as trivial, and so on. This kind of discrimination is an essential part of the articulations of our emotions.

I should like briefly to examine this discrimination by means of the notion of strong evaluation. I want to speak of strong evaluation where we 'evaluate', that is, consider good/bad, desirable/despicable, our desires themselves. Of course, what we frequently articulate as good or bad are actions, or even ways of life. We condemn running away from the danger, or gross self-indulgence, or spiteful speech or action without utilitarian purpose; or else we condemn a slothful life-form. But to speak of strong evaluation as an evaluation of desires, or motivations, brings out something important here.

It is not just that these actions/ways of life incorporate as part of their definition certain motivations: the running away concerned is out of fear, the self-indulgence is only that if one is indulging in things desired for pleasure, spiteful action specifies its own motivation, and so on. It is also that the condemnation here is in spite of, or even sometimes because of, the motivation.

The essence of strong evaluation comes out when we consider what it is to condemn an act in spite of our motivation to it. For the fact that we desired to do it is at least an embryonic justification, a prima facie ground for calling it good, following the precedent of the ancients. To condemn the act is to over-ride the embryonic justification in the name of another good which is thus judged higher or more worthy. It is to introduce a class difference between motivations, here between that turned to the good sought in the condemned act and that turned to the more worthy end.

The man who flees seeks a good, safety. But we condemn him: he ought to have stood.[2] For there is a higher good, the safety of the polis,[3] which was here at stake. The judgement involves ranking goods, hence ranking motivations (since these are defined by their consummations, which is what we are calling 'goods' in this context).

It is because this involves ranking motivations that I speak of it as strong evaluation. It means that we are not taking our *de facto* desires as the ultimate in justification, but are going beyond that to their worth. We are evaluating not just objects in the light of our desires, but also the desires themselves. Hence strong evaluation has also been called 'second-order' evaluation.[4]

The dimension of strong evaluation is even more evident where we condemn the action not in spite of but because of the motivation. The spite case above is a good example. Acting out of that motivation is base, mean, unworthy. Indeed, a man is the better for not experiencing such a motivation at all, though being human we often find it hard not to, however successfully we may keep it from influencing our conduct. Here we have not just a comparative ranking of motivations, but the judging of one as intrinsically bad. Hence we have once more an evaluation of desires themselves, so strong evaluation, or 'second-order' evaluation.

In the cases of both comparison and intrinsic judgement we have a qualitative assessment of motivations, where some are judged higher or lower, others as intrinsically bad. Because it weighs motivations, hence ends, this kind of assessment bites deeper than one which might, for instance, condemn certain actions in the name of the desires they are meant to fulfil, as being inefficacious, or confused, or ill-directed, for instance.

I have spoken of these strong evaluations as assessments, but they are anchored in feelings, emotions, aspirations; and could not motivate us unless they were. Such are our moral and aesthetic intuitions about given acts and possibilities, our remorse or sense of worthiness, our longings to be good, noble, pure, or whatever. In giving the strongly evaluative assessment, we are giving the import to which the feeling relates. Our moral revulsion before an act of spite is our affective awareness of the act as having an import of moral baseness.

And this is where we connect with the topic of subject-referring feelings. Strong evaluations involve subject-referring imports because they involve discriminating our motivations as higher or lower, or intrinsically good or bad. They are thus, one might say, inherently reflexive, and explicating the imports concerned involves referring to the life of the subject. It involves, one might say, attributing to different motivations their place in the life of the subject. When I hold back a certain reaction, because it springs from spite, and I see this as base, petty, or bad; or when I feel remorse for not having held it back, or perhaps contempt or disapproval for you when you have

2. That is, stood fast.
3. That is, the community.
4. Cf. Harry Frankfurt, "Freedom of the Will and the Concept of a Person," *Journal of Philosophy* 67, no. 1 (Jan. 1971): 5–20 [Taylor's note].

acted spitefully; what is involved is a strong evaluation. And the tenor of this evaluation is perhaps something like this: that spite, revenge, returning evil for evil, is something we are prone to, but that there is a higher way of seeing our relations with others; which is higher not just in producing happier consequences—less strife, pain, bad blood—but also in that it enables us to see ourselves and others more broadly, more objectively, more truly. One is a bigger person, with a broader, more serene vision, when one can act out of this higher standpoint.

Implicit in this strong evaluation is thus a placing of our different motivations relative to each other, the drawing, as it were, of a moral map of ourselves; we contrast a higher, more clairvoyant, more serene motivation, with a baser, more self-enclosed and troubled one, which we can see ourselves as potentially growing beyond, if and when we can come to experience things from the higher standpoint. The drawing of a moral map puts us squarely in the domain of the subject-referring, since this touches quintessentially on the life of the subject *qua* subject. It is in fact an attempt to give shape to our experience.

This drawing a moral map of the subject is an intrinsic part of what I referred to earlier as discerning the good or higher life, or the shape of our aspirations, or the shape of our life as subject. It involves defining what it is we really are about, what is really important to us; it involves entering the problematic area of our self-understanding and self-interpretation. We can see from the above example how the strong evaluations which are woven into our emotional experience place us in this problematic domain, for they refer us to a map of our motivations which we have yet to draw clearly, and will never complete.

The only reminder we need in connection with the example above about spite is that strong evaluation involves all qualitative discriminations between motives or ends, not just those we call moral. We (almost) all have an important set of strong evaluations concerning what we could call personal style. Some people feel that it is more worthy, or dignified, or admirable, to be 'cool' in their style, for instance. But most of them would repudiate any suggestion that they were making a moral issue out of this. We also think that some people are more sensitive in their tastes and others more gross, and we unquestionably admire the first and are perhaps mildly contemptuous of the second; but our praise and blame are not moral. And so on. All this enters into the (unfinished) map of goals and motivations which defines what we have been calling the good life.

These strong evaluations involve, as we have seen, subject-referring imports, and reciprocally our subject-referring feelings are or involve strong evaluations. And this is why they refer us to the central issues about our lives as subjects.

V

1

Now we may return to the question posed above: what is the role of language in our subject-referring emotions? Following what was said in section III about articulations, it would seem to be absolutely central. For these articulations surely require language. Language would thus be essential to these emotions, indeed constitutive of them. This fits in with a common intuition, or prejudice. But some challenge this as species chauvinism. We think that we, the language animals, are the only ones to have feelings of shame, wounded dignity, even right and wrong. But we just assume this, it is said, because we neglect to examine other species.

But look at baboons. The top ones swagger around with a sense of—dignity? And they react with anger when this is challenged. All-too-human behaviour. Is there not at least a proto-sense of dignity?

One answer to this kind of challenge has been to question how one really can know whether the big baboon is experiencing indignation at his offended dignity or just anger, or indeed anything that we could give a sense to. For it is our being in the same community of discourse, potentially or actually, with people which allows us to make these judgements in their case, often with certainty.

But suppose we hold this point in suspense for a moment, and concede for the sake of argument that baboons have a sense of dignity. Nevertheless this must be *toto caelo*[5] different from ours, because our sense of dignity, and shame, and moral remorse, and so on, are all shaped by language.

To see this we have to examine more closely what we barely invoked in section III.2, the way in which our feelings are shaped by articulations. Let us look at common experiences, and see how our experience of these emotions has been changed by our coming to accept different terms, or a new vocabulary, in which to talk about them. Thus consider someone who has been ashamed of his background. This is what we say (and also he says) retrospectively; at the time, this was not at all clear to him. He feels unease, lack of confidence, a vague sense of unworthiness. Then he is brought to reflect on this. He comes to feel that being ashamed for what you are, apologizing for your existence, is senseless. That on the contrary, there is something demeaning precisely about feeling such shame, something degrading, merely supine, craven. So he goes through a revolution like that expressed in the phrase 'black is beautiful'.[6]

Now the shame disappears; or sinks to a merely residual unease like the craving for a cigarette after meals of the ex-smoker; and is judged as merely another such nagging emotional kink, not as a voice telling him something about his predicament. What he can now feel ashamed of is having felt such shame. At the same time, the various features of himself and his background which were formerly objects of shame undergo a transvaluation. They too are seen under different concepts and experienced differently. Let us say there is some property very common in his group, a kind of tenacity. This was formerly seen as a kind of stupid obstinacy, and was one of the objects of shame. Now it is seen as a kind of admirable tenacity, a courage of one's own convictions and right.

In this example of transvaluation, we can see two kinds of conceptual revolution going on. The first is when he comes to say to himself: 'What I am

---

5. By the entire extent of the heavens (Latin); that is, completely.

6. A catchphrase of the 1960s and '70s that originated in the U.S. black power movement.

doing is apologizing for my own existence'; that is, he comes to see his set of attitudes as a personal stance towards himself, a kind of cringing. The second is the one involved in the transvaluation of the different typical features, like the tenacity above. Now it is clear that the changes in outlook connected with coming to see that the new concepts are appropriate (coming to see that I am apologizing for my existence, coming to see that this stubbornness really is tenacity) are essential to the transvaluation. In order to deny an essential, constitutive role for language, one would have to be able to envisage a non-conceptual analogue for such changes in outlook.

This is already quite hard to do; but another example might quite dispel the temptation even to try. Let us imagine that we are very drawn to someone, we have a kind of love–fascination–attraction to him—but precisely the right term is hard, because we are dealing with an emotion that has not yet become fixed. Then we come, perhaps under his influence, to think very highly of certain qualities or causes or achievements; and these are qualities which he exhibits, causes he has espoused, achievements he has realized. Our feeling now takes shape as admiration. And we come to be able to apply this term to it.

Here again we can see two phases. We come to recognize certain qualities, achievements, and so on; and this can often mean that we have a vocabulary we did not have before. Let us say we are taught by this man what a refined sensibility is. We did not really know before, as we might put it in retrospect. This is one change intrinsically related to language; not of course, our finding a use for the term 'refined sensibility', but our finding a sense for all the terms which, used in judgements about things, express such a sensibility. And the second change comes when we disambiguate our feeling for this person, at least partly, by seeing it as admiration. This recognition helps to shape the feeling itself.

Similar self-shaping recognitions come when one realizes, for example: I deeply love her; or, I am jealous; or, I don't really care.

Why should it be that coming to see (or feel) that certain terms properly describe our emotions often involves shaping (reshaping) those emotions? This is because our subject-referring feelings are given their character by the sense of the import they incorporate; when this sense alters in an important way, then the feeling changes. But because of the problematic nature of our self-understanding, a number of different accounts are possible; and these, by changing our understanding of the import, also change the emotions we can experience.

(Of course, this is not to say that we can change our emotions arbitrarily by applying different names to them. We are not talking about a process which could be arbitrarily undertaken. It is not just applying the name that counts, but coming to 'see–feel' that this is the right description; this is what makes the difference. Language is essential here because it articulates insight, or it makes insight possible.

It follows from this that our thesis here that language is constitutive of our subject-referring emotions says nothing about the order of causation. It is not a thesis to the effect that people change because their ideas about themselves change. Sometimes this is (part of) a good explanation, as in varying degrees in our two examples above. But it is also common experience that our insight grows or changes because of what we have suffered or what we have been forced to become. To say that language is constitutive of emotion is to say that experiencing an emotion essentially involves seeing that certain descriptions apply; or a given emotion involves some (degree of) insight. Nothing is said about how this emotion-insight comes into being or develops.)

This was what happened with our transvaluer above. And the same is also true of our admirer; only here the change is not a revolution negating the past, but rather the move from a confused, inchoate understanding of his imports to a clearer, more articulate view of the same. In both cases, the emotions themselves are transformed. We do not experience the same things, we do not have the same feelings. We can even say we cannot have the same feelings before and after such breaks.

To deny a role for language here is to want to claim that we can have such import-redefining revolutions without language. And this is just what our second group of cases is meant to show up as unbelievable. For here we have a move from the inchoate to the articulate. But this is precisely the change which language brings about. One might argue that it is this that only language (in the widest sense) can bring about. Language articulates our feelings, makes them clearer and more defined; and in this way transforms our sense of the imports involved; and hence transforms the feeling.

The reason why coming to recognize that 'I love her' or 'I'm jealous' alters the emotion is that this kind of self-articulacy is essential to *that* kind of love and jealousy. The avowal is constitutive of *this* feeling.

Thus the emotional lives of human beings from different cultures, who have been brought up with very different import vocabularies, differ very greatly. And even within one culture, people with different vocabularies have different experiences. Consider two people, one with a single love/lust dichotomy for the possible types of sexual feeling, the other with a very variegated vocabulary of different kinds of sexual relations. The experience of sexual emotions of these two men differs. And even if it is the case that one finds that his own vocabulary is distortive, and that the other's is much truer to his real experience, and so comes to adopt it, there will still be a change when he does, and comes to recognize and identify more clearly what he has been feeling, allegedly, all along.

Thus because our subject-referring import-attributing emotions are shaped by the way we see the imports, and the way we see the imports is shaped by the language we come to be able to deploy, language shapes these emotions. We can see this if we contrast them to our immediate feelings. What we experience in the dentist's chair, or when the fingernail is rubbed along the blackboard, is in a sense quite independent of language. That is, all sorts of terrible things we have learnt to be apprehensive about in our teeth can add to our panic. But we feel that this pain is language-independent; and we have no trouble imagining an animal having *this* experience.

Something similar might be said for non-subject-referring imports. Take fear. Here language can enter in because we may need to be apprised in language of the danger. But the import of physical danger is language-independent, in that different descriptions and understandings of the danger do not fundamentally alter for us the imports of bodily integrity or life. Thus we have the sense that there is something continuous here between what we felt before language, would feel without language, what animals feel, and what we feel now as fully developed language beings.

But with our subject-referring imports, the situation is different. As we articulate the imports, the emotions change. On this level, our experience is transformed by language.

What it is transformed by is the changed understanding of the imports which language makes possible. Our understanding of the imports that impinge on us is accepting a certain conception of ourselves. We are coming now once again to the point behind the claim that man is a self-interpreting animal. *Verstehen* is a *Seinsmodus*.[7] We are language animals, we are stuck with language, as it were. And through the language we have come to accept, we have a certain conception of the imports that impinge on us. This conception helps constitute our experience; it plays an essential role in making us what we are. To say that man is a self-interpreting animal is not just to say that he has some compulsive tendency to form reflexive views of himself, but rather that as he is, he is always partly constituted by self-interpretation, that is, by his understanding of the imports which impinge on him.

But to finish first with the baboons: we can happily concede to the ape-protagonists that the baboons do have some analogue of human dignity. Only it cannot be the human experience, for reasons similar to, although multiplied by an untold factor, those which make it impossible for me to experience the emotions of a seventeenth-century Samurai[8] who has just suffered an unanswerable affront, the emotions immediately preceding his decision to kill himself; or to share the experience of a Homeric hero which could be characterized poetically as having power breathed into him by a god.[9] The fact that there are animal analogues should not obscure for us the language-dependence of what we experience.

But when this is said, there are some human imports for which even an analogue in animal life seems implausible, indeed puzzling. Take that of moral obligation; take the kind of experience of the man who sees the wounded victim lying in the road and feels called upon to help. Here the sense of being called on, quite distinct from desiring to help, though that may also be there, depends on a sense of the subject as a moral agent. For this demand is one that essentially is directed to him as an autonomous moral agent. In order to feel this range of emotions, for example, *Achtung*[1] before the moral law, we have to have some idea of different dimensions in ourselves as subjects, that as moral subjects we have demands which are incomparable with those of desire.

But how could there be any such distinction without language? Of course, there do not need to be specific words in language meaning 'moral' or 'moral subject'. It can be that the distinction is carried in our language for something else, for instance deeds, or even in some of our ritual. This gets us into the wider question of what is language, which cannot be resolved here. But

7. "Understanding" is a "mode of being." Taylor is here using the German terminology of Heidegger.
8. A member of a Japanese warrior caste that developed in the 12th century; in their traditional code of conduct, ritual suicide was the only honorable response in this sort of situation.
9. See, e.g., *Iliad* 20.110, where the god Apollo "breathes great might" into the Trojan warrior Aeneas.
1. Respect (German). Taylor uses the term because it has a particular weight in German, and in German moral philosophy (especially as derived from KANT).

without some symbolic medium of expression, how could this distinction be articulated? How could it become a distinction for the agents concerned?

Does this necessity for language not apply to the whole range of strong evaluations? How can there be a sense of some goals or desires as higher and others as lower without a symbolic medium in which this can be articulated? For without this articulation, how can a higher (or more fulfilling, or moral, or worthy) desire be identified? What could discriminate it as higher, as against just stronger, or prepotent?[2] And if it were not prepotent, what grounds would there be for calling it higher, except perhaps its functional importance?

What may obscure this for us is our experience of inarticulate emotion. We all know what it is like to have feelings which we only identify properly afterwards. Thus while it is clear that the *articulate understanding* of certain goals and desires as higher and others as lower depends on language, we may think of the pre-articulate sense as being language-independent. And thus we might be tempted to think of animals as experiencing inarticulately what we give names to.

But of course *our* pre-articulate sense of our feelings is *not* language-independent. For they are the feelings of a language being, who therefore can and does say something about them, for example, that he feels something disturbing and perplexing, which baffles him, and to which he cannot give a name. *We* experience our pre-articulate emotion as perplexing, as raising a question. And *this* is an experience that no non-language animal can have.

But it makes no sense to ascribe strong evaluation to a being who could not even have inarticulate emotion in our sense, for whom the question of what quality of feeling he is experiencing *could not arise*.

Thus for us language-animals our language is constitutive of our emotions, not just because *de facto* we have articulated some of them, but also *de jure*[3] as the medium in which all our emotions, articulate and inarticulate, are experienced. Only a language-animal could have our emotions: and that means, inter alia, emotions which involve strong evaluations. This is my fifth claim.

What emerges from the five together is a picture of man as a self-interpreting animal. This is an animal whose emotional life incorporates a sense of what is really important to him, of the shape of his aspirations, which asks to be understood, and which is never adequately understood. His understanding is explicated at any time in the language he uses to speak about himself, his goals, what he feels, and so on; and in shaping his sense of what is important it also shapes what he feels.

But why does it ask to be understood? (This question can represent a real longing, a nostalgia, as the myths of the age of Kronos[4] testify.) Because as language-animals we are already engaged in understanding; we already have incorporated into our language an interpretation of what is really important. And it is this articulation, as we saw just a minute ago, which makes our inarticulate feelings into questions. Without language we could not have a sense of this distinction between what is really important and what we just from time to time desire. In our language we have already opened the issue by giving a first, fumbling answer.

---

2. Preeminent in power; predominant.
3. By right; that is, rightly.
4. In classical mythology, the golden age before the rule of the Olympian gods, when there was no war among humans and spring was everlasting.

It is language which lies behind the feature mentioned in section III.2, that our feelings are always open to further articulation just because they already involve articulation. It is because we are language-animals that we have articulated feelings, and hence that none of our subject-referring feelings can exist out of the range of articulation.

Because our language gives expression to qualitative distinctions, by which we can have a sense of higher goals, and hence have an emotional experience with strong evaluation, we open an issue which can never be definitively closed. Or otherwise put, man by his existence gives an answer to a question which *thereby* is posed and can never be finally answered. Our language is not just that in which we frame our answers, but that whereby there is a question about the truly worthy or good. Human language and language-constituted emotion opens this problematic area, which can never be decisively circumscribed because it can never be specified in objectified terms.

Now our attempted definitions of what is really important can be called interpretations, as we have suggested, and we can therefore say that the human animal not only finds himself impelled from time to time to interpret himself and his goals, but that he is always already in some interpretation, constituted as human by this fact. To be human is to be already engaged in living an answer to the question, an interpretation of oneself and one's aspirations.

The paradox of human emotions is that although only an articulated emotional life is properly human, all our articulations are open to challenge from our inarticulate sense of what is important, that is, we recognize that they ought to be faithful articulations of something of which we have as yet only fragmentary intimations. If one focusses only on the first point, one can believe that human beings are formed arbitrarily by the language they have accepted. If one focusses only on the second, one can think that we ought to be able to isolate scientifically the pure, uninterpreted basis of human emotion that all these languages are about. But neither of these is true. There is no human emotion which is not embodied in an interpretive language; and yet all interpretations can be judged as more or less adequate, more or less distortive. What a given human life is an interpretation of cannot exist uninterpreted; for human emotion is only what it is refracted as in human language.

Human emotion is interpreted emotion, which is nevertheless seeking its adequate form. This is what is involved in seeing man as a self-interpreting animal. It means that he cannot be understood simply as an object among objects, for his life incorporates an interpretation, an expression of what cannot exist unexpressed, because the self that is to be interpreted is essentially that of a being who self-interprets.

2

I want at the close to list in summary form my five claims. They are:

1. that some of our emotions involve import-ascriptions;
2. that some of these imports are subject-referring;
3. that our subject-referring feelings are the basis of our understanding of what it is to be human;

4. that these feelings are constituted by the articulations we come to accept of them; and

5. that these articulations, which we can think of as interpretations, require language.

Together these five claims, each of which builds on its predecessors, offer a picture of man as a self-interpreting being. This is a picture in which interpretation plays no secondary, optional role, but is essential to human existence. This is the view, I believe, which was adumbrated by Heidegger,[5] and which has justly been immensely influential in contemporary thought.

SOURCE: From Charles Taylor, *Human Agency and Language: Philosophical Papers I* (Cambridge: Cambridge University Press, 1985), pp. 45–76. This essay was written in 1977.

5. Specifically, in *Being and Time* (1927), excerpted above.

Epilogue

MICHEL FOUCAULT
(1926 – 1984)

Foucault wrote the following essay shortly before his death. It is his own response both to Kant's short essay "What Is Enlightenment?," which opens this volume, and to the question itself. Foucault's take on Kant here is undeniably mischievous. The Kantian notion of "critique"—an investigation of the necessary limits and structure of reason—is turned into a critical, political encounter with power, authority, and reason. An even more radical change is in the notion of reason itself, which for Foucault is the dominant discursive deployment of power. That stark difference is emblematic of the dramatic and fundamental transformations that occurred within the interpretive tradition in the two centuries separating the two philosophers.

These changes can be seen with respect not only to "reason" but also to ethics. Kant's notion of Enlightenment as overcoming "self-incurred tutelage" certainly contains an ethical element, but it remains politically conservative: Kantian Enlightenment is the achievement of reason and autonomy and is the pathway to Kant's utopian Kingdom of Ends. Foucault, by contrast, understands "enlightenment" as an attitude of constant investigation of the present and a permanent critique of ourselves. He appears to suppose that this investigation is (or can be) motivated by something like an impulse for liberation, which—if it can avoid certain naïvetés—may have positive results. Therefore, in a fundamental departure from Kant, Foucault rejects the search for universal value and rights, as well as for their prerequisite structures of knowledge and judgment. He puts in its place a historical investigation of the sort in which he had been engaged throughout his career, and a consideration of the human possibilities that remain or thereby come to light.

Although Foucault questions the Enlightenment ideal of the autonomous subject, he does take the ongoing process of critique to be a way in which the subject as an effect of power is able to question and challenge power. The self can take itself as a project—not of self-discovery, as if it had some hidden identity or essence, but rather of self-creation, seeing itself as a canvas that could become a painting. This (rather Nietzschean) ascetic/aesthetic practice becomes possible for those who—with the "death of man" (as well as of God) behind them—dispense with the myths of essence and interiority, reject both repression and confession, and become who they might be. (For more on Foucault, see pp. 1457–61 above).

From What Is Enlightenment?

(*Was ist Aufklärung?*)

I.

Today when a periodical asks its readers a question, it does so in order to collect opinions on some subject about which everyone has an opinion already; there is not much likelihood of learning anything new. In the eighteenth century, editors preferred to question the public on problems that did not yet have solutions. I don't know whether or not that practice was more effective; it was unquestionably more entertaining.

In any event, in line with this custom, in November 1784 a German periodical, *Berlinische Monatschrift*, published a response to the question: *Was ist Aufklärung?* And the respondent was Kant.

A minor text, perhaps. But it seems to me that it marks the discreet entrance into the history of thought of a question that modern philosophy has not been capable of answering, but that it has never managed to get rid of, either. And one that has been repeated in various forms for two centuries now. From Hegel through Nietzsche or Max Weber to Horkheimer or Habermas,[1] hardly any philosophy has failed to confront this same question, directly or indirectly. What, then, is this event that is called the *Aufklärung* and that has determined, at least in part, what we are, what we think, and what we do today? Let us imagine that the *Berlinische Monatschrift* still exists and that it is asking its readers the question: What is modern philosophy?[2] Perhaps we could respond with an echo: modern philosophy is the philosophy that is attempting to answer the question raised so imprudently two centuries ago: *Was ist Aufklärung?*

* * *

I shall not go into detail here concerning this text, which is not always very clear despite its brevity. I should simply like to point out three or four features that seem to me important if we are to understand how Kant raised the philosophical question of the present day.

Kant indicates right away that the "way out" that characterizes Enlightenment is a process that releases us from the status of "immaturity." And by "immaturity," he means a certain state of our will that makes us accept someone else's authority to lead us in areas where the use of reason is called for. Kant gives three examples: we are in a state of "immaturity" when a book takes the place of our understanding, when a spiritual director takes the place of our conscience, when a doctor decides for us what our diet is to be. (Let us note in passing that the register of these three critiques is easy to recognize, even though the text does not make it explicit.) In any case, Enlightenment is defined by a modification of the preexisting relation linking will, authority, and the use of reason.

---

1. For HEGEL, NIETZSCHE, and HABERMAS, see above. Weber (1864–1920), German political economist and influential figure in the history of sociology. Max Horkheimer (1895–1973), German philosopher who was a founder of the Frankfurt School of critical social theory.
2. More specifically, for Foucault: What is modern philosophy (in what is here being called the post-Kantian "interpretive tradition")?

We must also note that this way out is presented by Kant in a rather ambiguous manner. He characterizes it as a phenomenon, an ongoing process; but he also presents it as a task and an obligation. From the very first paragraph, he notes that man himself is responsible for his immature status. Thus it has to be supposed that he will be able to escape from it only by a change that he himself will bring about in himself. Significantly, Kant says that this Enlightenment has a *Wahlspruch*: now a *Wahlspruch* is a heraldic device, that is, a distinctive feature by which one can be recognized, and it is also a motto, an instruction that one gives oneself and proposes to others. What, then, is this instruction? *Aude sapere*: "dare to know," "have the courage, the audacity, to know." Thus Enlightenment must be considered both as a process in which men participate collectively and as an act of courage to be accomplished personally. Men are at once elements and agents of a single process. They may be actors in the process to the extent that they participate in it; and the process occurs to the extent that men decide to be its voluntary actors.

A third difficulty appears here in Kant's text, in his use of the word "mankind," *Menschheit*. The importance of this word in the Kantian conception of history is well known. Are we to understand that the entire human race is caught up in the process of Enlightenment? In that case, we must imagine Enlightenment as a historical change that affects the political and social existence of all people on the face of the earth. Or are we to understand that it involves a change affecting what constitutes the humanity of human beings? But the question then arises of knowing what this change is. Here again, Kant's answer is not without a certain ambiguity. In any case, beneath its appearance of simplicity, it is rather complex.

Kant defines two essential conditions under which mankind can escape from its immaturity. And these two conditions are at once spiritual and institutional, ethical and political.

The first of these conditions is that the realm of obedience and the realm of the use of reason be clearly distinguished. Briefly characterizing the immature status, Kant invokes the familiar expression: "Don't think, just follow orders"; such is, according to him, the form in which military discipline, political power, and religious authority are usually exercised. Humanity will reach maturity when it is no longer required to obey, but when men are told: "Obey, and you will be able to reason as much as you like." We must note that the German word used here is *räsonieren*; this word, which is also used in the *Critiques*,[3] does not refer to just any use of reason, but to a use of reason in which reason has no other end but itself: *räsonieren* is to reason for reasoning's sake. And Kant gives examples, these too being perfectly trivial in appearance: paying one's taxes, while being able to argue as much as one likes about the system of taxation, would be characteristic of the mature state; or again, taking responsibility for parish service, if one is a pastor, while reasoning freely about religious dogmas.

We might think that there is nothing very different here from what has been meant, since the sixteenth century, by freedom of conscience: the right to think as one pleases so long as one obeys as one must. Yet it is here that Kant

---

3. Kant's *Critique of Pure Reason* (1781; 2nd ed., 1787), *Critique of Practical Reason* (1788), and *Critique of Judgment* (1790).

brings into play another distinction, and in a rather surprising way. The distinction he introduces is between the private and public uses of reason. But he adds at once that reason must be free in its public use, and must be submissive in its private use. Which is, term for term, the opposite of what is ordinarily called freedom of conscience.

But we must be somewhat more precise. What constitutes, for Kant, this private use of reason? In what area is it exercised? Man, Kant says, makes a private use of reason when he is "a cog in a machine"; that is, when he has a role to play in society and jobs to do: to be a soldier, to have taxes to pay, to be in charge of a parish, to be a civil servant, all this makes the human being a particular segment of society; he finds himself thereby placed in a circumscribed position, where he has to apply particular rules and pursue particular ends. Kant does not ask that people practice a blind and foolish obedience, but that they adapt the use they make of their reason to these determined circumstances; and reason must then be subjected to the particular ends in view. Thus there cannot be, here, any free use of reason.

On the other hand, when one is reasoning only in order to use one's reason, when one is reasoning as a reasonable being (and not as a cog in a machine), when one is reasoning as a member of reasonable humanity, then the use of reason must be free and public. Enlightenment is thus not merely the process by which individuals would see their own personal freedom of thought guaranteed. There is Enlightenment when the universal, the free, and the public uses of reason are superimposed on one another.

Now this leads us to a fourth question that must be put to Kant's text. We can readily see how the universal use of reason (apart from any private end) is the business of the subject himself as an individual; we can readily see, too, how the freedom of this use may be assured in a purely negative manner through the absence of any challenge to it; but how is a public use of that reason to be assured? Enlightenment, as we see, must not be conceived simply as a general process affecting all humanity; it must not be conceived only as an obligation prescribed to individuals: it now appears as a political problem. The question, in any event, is that of knowing how the use of reason can take the public form that it requires, how the audacity to know can be exercised in broad daylight, while individuals are obeying as scrupulously as possible. And Kant, in conclusion, proposes to Frederick II,[4] in scarcely veiled terms, a sort of contract—what might be called the contract of rational despotism with free reason: the public and free use of autonomous reason will be the best guarantee of obedience, on condition, however, that the political principle that must be obeyed itself be in conformity with universal reason.

Let us leave Kant's text here. I do not by any means propose to consider it as capable of constituting an adequate description of Enlightenment; and no historian, I think, could be satisfied with it for an analysis of the social, political, and cultural transformations that occurred at the end of the eighteenth century.

4. King of Prussia (1712–1786; r. 1740–86) at the time of Kant's essay.

Nevertheless, notwithstanding its circumstantial nature, and without intending to give it an exaggerated place in Kant's work, I believe that it is necessary to stress the connection that exists between this brief article and the three *Critiques*. Kant in fact describes Enlightenment as the moment when humanity is going to put its own reason to use, without subjecting itself to any authority; now it is precisely at this moment that the critique is necessary, since its role is that of defining the conditions under which the use of reason is legitimate in order to determine what can be known, what must be done, and what may be hoped. Illegitimate uses of reason are what give rise to dogmatism and heteronomy, along with illusion; on the other hand, it is when the legitimate use of reason has been clearly defined in its principles that its autonomy can be assured. The critique is, in a sense, the handbook of reason that has grown up in Enlightenment; and, conversely, the Enlightenment is the age of the critique.

It is also necessary, I think, to underline the relation between this text of Kant's and the other texts he devoted to history. These latter, for the most part, seek to define the internal teleology of time and the point toward which history of humanity is moving. Now the analysis of Enlightenment, defining this history as humanity's passage to its adult status, situates contemporary reality with respect to the overall movement and its basic directions. But at the same time, it shows how, at this very moment, each individual is responsible in a certain way for that overall process.

The hypothesis I should like to propose is that this little text is located in a sense at the crossroads of critical reflection and reflection on history. It is a reflection by Kant on the contemporary status of his own enterprise. No doubt it is not the first time that a philosopher has given his reasons for undertaking his work at a particular moment. But it seems to me that it is the first time that a philosopher has connected in this way, closely and from the inside, the significance of his work with respect to knowledge, a reflection on history and a particular analysis of the specific moment at which he is writing and because of which he is writing. It is in the reflection on "today" as difference in history and as motive for a particular philosophical task that the novelty of this text appears to me to lie.

And, by looking at it in this way, it seems to me we may recognize a point of departure: the outline of what one might call the attitude of modernity.

II.

I know that modernity is often spoken of as an epoch, or at least as a set of features characteristic of an epoch; situated on a calendar, it would be preceded by a more or less naive or archaic premodernity, and followed by an enigmatic and troubling "postmodernity." And then we find ourselves asking whether modernity constitutes the sequel to the Enlightenment and its development, or whether we are to see it as a rupture or a deviation with respect to the basic principles of the eighteenth century.

Thinking back on Kant's text, I wonder whether we may not envisage modernity rather as an attitude than as a period of history. And by "attitude," I mean a mode of relating to contemporary reality; a voluntary choice made by certain people; in the end, a way of thinking and feeling; a way, too, of acting and behaving that at one and the same time marks a relation of belonging and presents itself as a task. A bit, no doubt, like what the Greeks called an *ethos*. And consequently, rather than seeking to distinguish the "modern era" from the "premodern" or "postmodern," I think it would be more useful to try to find out how the attitude of modernity, ever since its formation, has found itself struggling with attitudes of "countermodernity."

To characterize briefly this attitude of modernity, I shall take an almost indispensable example, namely, Baudelaire;[5] for his consciousness of modernity is widely recognized as one of the most acute in the nineteenth century.

1.   Modernity is often characterized in terms of consciousness of the discontinuity of time: a break with tradition, a feeling of novelty, of vertigo in the face of the passing moment. And this is indeed what Baudelaire seems to be saying when he defines modernity as "the ephemeral, the fleeting, the contingent."[6] But, for him, being modern does not lie in recognizing and accepting this perpetual movement; on the contrary, it lies in adopting a certain attitude with respect to this movement; and this deliberate, difficult attitude consists in recapturing something eternal that is not beyond the present instant, nor behind it, but within it. Modernity is distinct from fashion, which does no more than call into question the course of time; modernity is the attitude that makes it possible to grasp the "heroic" aspect of the present moment. Modernity is not a phenomenon of sensitivity to the fleeting present; it is the will to "heroize" the present.

I shall restrict myself to what Baudelaire says about the painting of his contemporaries. Baudelaire makes fun of those painters who, finding nineteenth-century dress excessively ugly, want to depict nothing but ancient togas. But modernity in painting does not consist, for Baudelaire, in introducing black clothing onto the canvas. The modern painter is the one who can show the dark frock-coat as "the necessary costume of our time," the one who knows how to make manifest, in the fashion of the day, the essential, permanent, obsessive relation that our age entertains with death. "The dress-coat and frock-coat not only possess their political beauty, which is an expression of universal equality, but also their poetic beauty, which is an expression of the public soul—an immense cortège of undertaker's mutes (mutes in love, political mutes, bourgeois mutes . . .). We are each of us celebrating some funeral."[7] To designate this attitude of modernity, Baudelaire sometimes employs a litotes[8] that is highly significant because it is presented in the form of a precept: "You have no right to despise the present."

5. Charles Baudelaire (1821–1867), French poet and critic; his *Les Fleurs du mal* (1857, *The Flowers of Evil*) was one of the most notable collections of poems in the 19th century.
6. Charles Baudelaire, *The Painter of Modern Life and Other Essays*, trans. Jonathan Mayne (London: Phaidon, 1964), p. 3 [Rabinow's note]. Quoted from "The Painter of Modern Life" (1863).

7. Charles Baudelaire, "On the Heroism of Modern Life" [1846], in *The Mirror of Art: Critical Studies by Charles Baudelaire*, trans. Jonathan Mayne (London: Phaidon, 1955), p. 127 [Rabinow's note].
8. An understated affirmation through the negation of its contrary. The quotation is from "The Painter of Modern Life."

2. This heroization is ironical, needless to say. The attitude of modernity does not treat the passing moment as sacred in order to try to maintain or perpetuate it. It certainly does not involve harvesting it as a fleeting and interesting curiosity. That would be what Baudelaire would call the spectator's posture. The *flâneur*, the idle, strolling spectator, is satisfied to keep his eyes open, to pay attention and to build up a storehouse of memories. In opposition to the *flâneur*, Baudelaire describes the man of modernity: "Away he goes, hurrying, searching. . . . Be very sure that this man . . . —this solitary, gifted with an active imagination, ceaselessly journeying across the great human desert—has an aim loftier than that of a mere *flâneur*, an aim more general, something other than the fugitive pleasure of circumstance. He is looking for that quality which you must allow me to call 'modernity.' . . . He makes it his business to extract from fashion whatever element it may contain of poetry within history." As an example of modernity, Baudelaire cites the artist Constantin Guys.[9] In appearance a spectator, a collector of curiosities, he remains "the last to linger wherever there can be a glow of light, an echo of poetry, a quiver of life or a chord of music; wherever a passion can *pose* before him, wherever natural man and conventional man display themselves in a strange beauty wherever the sun lights up the swift joys of the *depraved animal.*"[1]

But let us make no mistake. Constantin Guys is not a *flâneur*; what makes him the modern painter *par excellence* in Baudelaire's eyes is that, just when the whole world is falling asleep, he begins to work, and he transfigures that world. His transfiguration does not entail an annulling of reality, but a difficult interplay between the truth of what is real and the exercise of freedom; "natural" things become "more than natural," "beautiful" things become "more than beautiful," and individual objects appear "endowed with an impulsive life like the soul of [their] creator."[2] For the attitude of modernity, the high value of the present is indissociable from a desperate eagerness to imagine it, to imagine it otherwise than it is, and to transform it not by destroying it but by grasping it in what it is. Baudelairean modernity is an exercise in which extreme attention to what is real is confronted with the practice of a liberty that simultaneously respects this reality and violates it.

3. However, modernity for Baudelaire is not simply a form of relationship to the present; it is also a mode of relationship that has to be established with oneself. The deliberate attitude of modernity is tied to an indispensable asceticism. To be modern is not to accept oneself as one is in the flux of the passing moments; it is to take oneself as object of a complex and difficult elaboration; what Baudelaire, in the vocabulary of his day, calls *dandysme.*[3] Here I shall not recall in detail the well-known passages on "vulgar, earthy, vile nature"; on man's indispensable revolt against himself; on the "doctrine of elegance" which imposes "upon its ambitious and humble disciples" a discipline more

---

9. French artist who worked in ink and watercolors (1802–1892), best known as a cartoonist and comic illustrator. He is the main figure in "The Painter of Modern Life" (as "Monsieur G.").
1. Baudelaire, *Painter*, pp. 12, 11 [Rabinow's note].

2. Ibid., p. 12 [Rabinow's note; translator's brackets].
3. Dandyism (French), the artificiality and excessive refinement in dress and behavior affected by some in the late 19th century.

despotic than the most terrible religions; the pages, finally, on the asceticism of the dandy who makes of his body, his behavior, his feelings and passions, his very existence, a work of art. Modern man, for Baudelaire, is not the man who goes off to discover himself, his secrets and his hidden truth; he is the man who tries to invent himself. This modernity does not "liberate man in his own being"; it compels him to face the task of producing himself.

4. Let me add just one final word. This ironic heroization of the present, this transfiguring play of freedom with reality, this ascetic elaboration of the self—Baudelaire does not imagine that these have any place in society itself, or in the body politic. They can only be produced in another, a different place, which Baudelaire calls art.

I do not pretend to be summarizing in these few lines either the complex historical event that was the Enlightenment, at the end of the eighteenth century, or the attitude of modernity in the various guises it may have taken on during the last two centuries.

I have been seeking, on the one hand, to emphasize the extent to which a type of philosophical interrogation—one that simultaneously problematizes man's relation to the present, man's historical mode of being, and the constitution of the self as an autonomous subject—is rooted in the Enlightenment. On the other hand, I have been seeking to stress that the thread that may connect us with the Enlightenment is not faithfulness to doctrinal elements, but rather the permanent reactivation of an attitude—that is, of a philosophical ethos that could be described as a permanent critique of our historical era. I should like to characterize this ethos very briefly.

A. NEGATIVELY

1. This ethos implies, first, the refusal of what I like to call the "blackmail" of the Enlightenment. I think that the Enlightenment, as a set of political, economic, social, institutional, and cultural events on which we still depend in large part, constitutes a privileged domain for analysis. I also think that as an enterprise for linking the progress of truth and the history of liberty in a bond of direct relation, it formulated a philosophical question that remains for us to consider. I think, finally, as I have tried to show with reference to Kant's text, that it defined a certain manner of philosophizing.

But that does not mean that one has to be "for" or "against" the Enlightenment. It even means precisely that one has to refuse everything that might present itself in the form of a simplistic and authoritarian alternative: you either accept the Enlightenment and remain within the tradition of its rationalism (this is considered a positive term by some and used by others, on the contrary, as a reproach); or else you criticize the Enlightenment and then try to escape from its principles of rationality (which may be seen once again as good or bad). And we do not break free of this blackmail by introducing "dialectical" nuances while seeking to determine what good and bad elements there may have been in the Enlightenment.

We must try to proceed with the analysis of ourselves as beings who are historically determined, to a certain extent, by the Enlightenment. Such an analysis implies a series of historical inquiries that are as precise as possible; and these inquiries will not be oriented retrospectively toward the "essential kernel of rationality" that can be found in the Enlightenment and that would have to be preserved in any event; they will be oriented toward the "contemporary limits of the necessary," that is, toward what is not or is no longer indispensable for the constitution of ourselves as autonomous subjects.[4]

2. This permanent critique of ourselves has to avoid the always too facile confusions between humanism and Enlightenment.

We must never forget that the Enlightenment is an event, or a set of events and complex historical processes, that is located at a certain point in the development of European societies. As such, it includes elements of social transformation, types of political institution, forms of knowledge, projects of rationalization of knowledge and practices, technological mutations that are very difficult to sum up in a word, even if many of these phenomena remain important today. The one I have pointed out and that seems to me to have been at the basis of an entire form of philosophical reflection concerns only the mode of reflective relation to the present.

Humanism is something entirely different.[5] It is a theme or, rather, a set of themes that have reappeared on several occasions, over time, in European societies; these themes, always tied to value judgments, have obviously varied greatly in their content, as well as in the values they have preserved. Furthermore, they have served as a critical principle of differentiation. In the seventeenth century, there was a humanism that presented itself as a critique of Christianity or of religion in general; there was a Christian humanism opposed to an ascetic and much more theocentric humanism. In the nineteenth century, there was a suspicious humanism, hostile and critical toward science, and another that, to the contrary, placed its hope in that same science. Marxism has been a humanism; so have existentialism and personalism; there was a time when people supported the humanistic values represented by National Socialism, and when the Stalinists themselves said they were humanists.

From this, we must not conclude that everything that has ever been linked with humanism is to be rejected, but that the humanistic thematic is in itself too supple, too diverse, too inconsistent to serve as an axis for reflection. And it is a fact that, at least since the seventeenth century, what is called humanism has always been obliged to lean on certain conceptions of man borrowed from religion, science, or politics. Humanism serves to color and to justify the conceptions of man to which it is, after all, obliged to take recourse.

Now, in this connection, I believe that this thematic, which so often recurs and which always depends on humanism, can be opposed by the principle of a critique and a permanent creation of ourselves in our autonomy: that is, a principle that is at the heart of the historical consciousness that the Enlight-

---

4. This last phrase concisely expresses Foucault's fundamental concern—which also (in a sense) was Kant's.

5. Foucault presumably has in mind SARTRE's "Existentialism Is a Humanism" (1946; see above), among others.

enment has of itself. From this standpoint, I am inclined to see Enlightenment and humanism in a state of tension rather than identity.

In any case, it seems to me dangerous to confuse them; and further, it seems historically inaccurate. If the question of man, of the human species, of the humanist, was important throughout the eighteenth century, this is very rarely, I believe, because the Enlightenment considered itself a humanism. It is worthwhile, too, to note that throughout the nineteenth century, the historiography of sixteenth-century humanism, which was so important for people like Saint-Beuve or Burckhardt,[6] was always distinct from and sometimes explicitly opposed to the Enlightenment and the eighteenth century. The nineteenth century had a tendency to oppose the two, at least as much as to confuse them.

In any case, I think that, just as we must free ourselves from the intellectual blackmail of "being for or against the Enlightenment," we must escape from the historical and moral confusionism that mixes the theme of humanism with the question of the Enlightenment. An analysis of their complex relations in the course of the last two centuries would be a worthwhile project, an important one if we are to bring some measure of clarity to the consciousness that we have of ourselves and of our past.

B.   POSITIVELY

Yet while taking these precautions into account, we must obviously give a more positive content to what may be a philosophical ethos consisting in a critique of what we are saying, thinking, and doing, through a historical ontology of ourselves.

1.   This philosophical ethos may be characterized as a *limit-attitude*. We are not talking about a gesture of rejection. We have to move beyond the outside-inside alternative; we have to be at the frontiers. Criticism indeed consists of analyzing and reflecting upon limits. But if the Kantian question was that of knowing what limits knowledge has to renounce transgressing, it seems to me that the critical question today has to be turned back into a positive one: in what is given to us as universal, necessary, obligatory, what place is occupied by whatever is singular, contingent, and the product of arbitrary constraints? The point, in brief, is to transform the critique conducted in the form of necessary limitation into a practical critique that takes the form of a possible transgression.

This entails an obvious consequence: that criticism is no longer going to be practiced in the search for formal structures with universal value, but rather as a historical investigation into the events that have led us to constitute ourselves and to recognize ourselves as subjects of what we are doing, thinking, saying. In that sense, this criticism is not transcendental, and its goal is not that of making a metaphysics possible: it is genealogical in its design and archaeological in its method. Archaeological—and not transcendental—in the sense that it will not seek to identify the universal structures of all knowledge or of all possible moral action, but will seek to treat the instances

---

6. Jacob Burckhardt (1818–1897), Swiss historian of art and culture. Charles-Augustin Saint-Beuve (1804–1869), French literary historian and critic.

of discourse that articulate what we think, say, and do as so many historical events. And this critique will be genealogical in the sense that it will not deduce from the form of what we are what it is impossible for us to do and to know; but it will separate out, from the contingency that has made us what we are, the possibility of no longer being, doing, or thinking what we are, do, or think. It is not seeking to make possible a metaphysics that has finally become a science; it is seeking to give new impetus, as far and wide as possible, to the undefined work of freedom.[7]

2. But if we are not to settle for the affirmation or the empty dream of freedom, it seems to me that this historico-critical attitude must also be an experimental one. I mean that this work done at the limits of ourselves must, on the one hand, open up a realm of historical inquiry and, on the other, put itself to the test of reality, of contemporary reality, both to grasp the points where change is possible and desirable, and to determine the precise form this change should take. This means that the historical ontology of ourselves must turn away from all projects that claim to be global or radical. In fact we know from experience that the claim to escape from the system of contemporary reality so as to produce the overall programs of another society, of another way of thinking, another culture, another vision of the world, has led only to the return of the most dangerous traditions.

I prefer the very specific transformations that have proved to be possible in the last twenty years in a certain number of areas that concern our ways of being and thinking, relations to authority, relations between the sexes, the way in which we perceive insanity or illness; I prefer even these partial transformations that have been made in the correlation of historical analysis and the practical attitude, to the programs for a new man that the worst political systems have repeated throughout the twentieth century.

I shall thus characterize the philosophical ethos appropriate to the critical ontology of ourselves as a historico-practical test of the limits that we may go beyond, and thus as work carried out by ourselves upon ourselves as free beings.

3. Still, the following objection would no doubt be entirely legitimate: if we limit ourselves to this type of always partial and local inquiry or test, do we not run the risk of letting ourselves be determined by more general structures of which we may well not be conscious, and over which we may have no control?

To this, two responses. It is true that we have to give up hope of ever acceding to a point of view that could give us access to any complete and definitive knowledge of what may constitute our historical limits. And from this point of view the theoretical and practical experience that we have of our limits and of the possibility of moving beyond them is always limited and determined; thus we are always in the position of beginning again.

But that does not mean that no work can be done except in disorder and

---

7. This is a hint at the positive direction in which Foucault believes it may be possible, at this human-historical juncture, for us to move.

contingency. The work in question has its generality, its systematicity, its homogeneity, and its stakes.

(a) *Its Stakes*

These are indicated by what might be called "the paradox of the relations of capacity and power." We know that the great promise or the great hope of the eighteenth century, or a part of the eighteenth century, lay in the simultaneous and proportional growth of individuals with respect to one another. And, moreover, we can see that throughout the entire history of Western societies (it is perhaps here that the root of their singular historical destiny is located—such a peculiar destiny, so different from the others in its trajectory and so universalizing, so dominant with respect to the others), the acquisition of capabilities and the struggle for freedom have constituted permanent elements. Now the relations between the growth of capabilities and the growth of autonomy are not as simple as the eighteenth century may have believed. And we have been able to see what forms of power relation were conveyed by various technologies (whether we are speaking of productions with economic aims, or institutions whose goal is social regulation, or of techniques of communication): disciplines, both collective and individual, procedures of normalization exercised in the name of the power of the state, demands of society or of population zones, are examples. What is at stake, then, is this: How can the growth of capabilities be disconnected from the intensification of power relations?

(b) *Homogeneity*

This leads to the study of what could be called "practical systems." Here we are taking as a homogeneous domain of reference not the representations that men give of themselves, not the conditions that determine them without their knowledge, but rather what they do and the way they do it. That is, the forms of rationality that organize their ways of doing things (this might be called the technological aspect) and the freedom with which they act within these practical systems, reacting to what others do, modifying the rules of the game, up to a certain point (this might be called the strategic side of these practices). The homogeneity of these historico-critical analyses is thus ensured by this realm of practices, with their technological side and their strategic side.

(c) *Systematicity*

These practical systems stem from three broad areas: relations of control over things, relations of action upon others, relations with oneself. This does not mean that each of these three areas is completely foreign to the others. It is well known that control over things is mediated by relations with others; and relations with others in turn always entail relations with oneself, and vice versa. But we have three axes whose specificity and whose interconnections have to be analyzed: the axis of knowledge, the axis of power, the axis of ethics. In other terms, the historical ontology of ourselves has to answer an open series of questions; it has to make an indefinite number of inquiries which may be multiplied and specified as much as we like, but which will all address the questions systematized as follows: How are we constituted as subjects of our own knowledge? How are we constituted as subjects who exercise or submit to power relations? How are we constituted as moral subjects of our own actions?

(d) *Generality*

Finally, these historico-critical investigations are quite specific in the sense that they always bear upon a material, an epoch, a body of determined practices and discourses. And yet, at least at the level of the Western societies from which we derive, they have their generality, in the sense that they have continued to recur up to our time: for example, the problem of the relationship between sanity and insanity, or sickness and health, or crime and the law; the problem of the role of sexual relations; and so on.

But by evoking this generality, I do not mean to suggest that it has to be retraced in its metahistorical continuity over time, nor that its variations have to be pursued. What must be grasped is the extent to which what we know of it, the forms of power that are exercised in it, and the experience that we have in it of ourselves constitute nothing but determined historical figures, through a certain form of problematization that defines objects, rules of action, modes of relation to oneself. The study of [modes of][8] problematization (that is, of what is neither an anthropological constant nor a chronological variation) is thus the way to analyze questions of general import in their historically unique form.

A brief summary, to conclude and to come back to Kant.

I do not know whether we will ever reach mature adulthood. Many things in our experience convince us that the historical event of the Enlightenment did not make us mature adults, and we have not reached that stage yet. However, it seems to me that a meaning can be attributed to that critical interrogation on the present and on ourselves which Kant formulated by reflecting on the Enlightenment. It seems to me that Kant's reflection is even a way of philosophizing that has not been without its importance or effectiveness during the last two centuries. The critical ontology of ourselves has to be considered not, certainly, as a theory, a doctrine, nor even as a permanent body of knowledge that is accumulating; it has to be conceived as an attitude, an ethos, a philosophical life in which the critique of what we are is at one and the same time the historical analysis of the limits that are imposed on us and an experiment with the possibility of going beyond them.

This philosophical attitude has to be translated into the labor of diverse inquiries. These inquiries have their methodological coherence in the at once archaeological and genealogical study of practices envisaged simultaneously as a technological type of rationality and as strategic games of liberties; they have their theoretical coherence in the definition of the historically unique forms in which the generalities of our relations to things, to others, to ourselves, have been problematized. They have their practical coherence in the care brought to the process of putting historico-critical reflection to the test of concrete practices. I do not know whether it must be said today that the critical task still entails faith in Enlightenment; I continue to think

8. Translator's brackets.

that this task requires work on our limits, that is, a patient labor giving form to our impatience for liberty.

SOURCE: From Michel Foucault, "What Is Enlightenment?," trans. Catherine Porter, in *The Foucault Reader*, ed. Paul Rabinow (New York: Pantheon, 1984), pp. 32, 34–50. Based on an unpublished French manuscript that Rabinow prepared for publication, this essay first appeared 200 years after the publication in the *Berlin Monthly* of KANT's "What Is Enlightenment? [*Was ist Aufklärung?*]," the first selection in this anthology. That year (1984) also was the year of Foucault's death.

Afterword

This volume is bookended by Kant's 1784 essay "What Is Enlightenment?" at its beginning and Foucault's (1984) essay of the same title at its close. It deals with developments and associated figures from the intervening two centuries of the interpretive tradition in the history of Western philosophy after Kant— a period that, as was suggested in the Preface, is as much of that tradition as now must be recognized to be a part of that history. That tradition of course did not end with the death of Foucault in 1984. Others of his generation remained active, and a new generation has taken the stage. But subsequent interests and efforts and their relation to that tradition are ongoing matters that remain to be further pursued and determined, rather than already part of that history as well. The developments surveyed from that recent history contributed in major ways to the setting of the stage for these subsequent and ongoing further ones, and in some instances and respects continue to be a living presence in them. Philosophy will always be a work in progress; and its history will always be following in its wake. The span of the interpretive tradition surveyed here is best thought of as both the inheritance and the point of departure for what becomes of it and for those through whom that happens.

But whither the interpretive tradition? And what remains of it? It no longer has the geographical base it once did; for philosophy in most of the European universities that once served as its institutional home has become much more loosely related to its past, and more connected with broader currents in the Western philosophical community. And the same would seem to be true of philosophy in most of the Anglophone universities that once were its strongholds in North America, Britain, and elsewhere. The separation between the analytic and interpretive traditions may be coming to an end, as the stark oppositions that once fueled their hostility become an increasingly remote memory. Or rather: the difference in philosophical sensibility that was reflected in and intensified by their divergence and antagonism has mutated, taking different forms and expressing itself in different ways that are more difficult to map and follow.

Some of the most interesting and promising developments in philosophy in recent decades exemplify what might be called the straddling of the two traditions, reflecting and drawing upon elements of both of them. A tendency in that direction has been noted in a number of the figures featured in this volume (Habermas among them); and it is also observable in some of those included in its companion volume, several of whom (like Mill) would not have been out of place in this volume as well. And there are a good many notable presences in the contemporary philosophical community whose thought has affinities with (as well as differences from) both traditions in their various recent and earlier incarnations. That is a promising development, the strengthening of which would be welcome.

In one sense, therefore, it would be a mistake to attempt to maintain the distinctness of these two traditions, as we move forward in the present century. Yet it would also be a mistake to regard it as a mere artifact of philosophy's past that can now safely be ignored—and not only because there is some truth to the saying that those who neglect history are doomed to repeat it. Each tradition developed as a response to something important not only in the philosophy of Kant but also in the nature of philosophy itself, which is at its best when there is a creative tension and interaction between two impulses of the human mind and spirit that drive philosophy in different directions. On the one hand, we wish to get things clear, precise, definite, and beyond dispute. On the other, we try more broadly to make sense of what's going on, do justice to what things and their possibilities have become, and discern the kinds of meanings and matterings associated with them.

Each impulse is more readily satisfied in some areas of experience and inquiry than in others; and each expresses itself in different ways of looking at things, framing questions about them, and developing ways of pursuing those questions. Moreover, it seems, each impulse (as Nietzsche would put it) wants to be master. Yet it also seems that each must be balanced by the other if we are to gain as much comprehension as is humanly possible—especially concerning human reality and the human world, but also regarding life and the world in which we find ourselves more generally. Kant attempted to find that balance but did not succeed to anyone's satisfaction; and so, after him, it tipped in both of the broadly different ways reflected in the two *After Kant* volumes of this *Norton Anthology of Western Philosophy*.

It remains to be seen whether a better balance can be achieved and sustained in the years to come, and whether a new tradition of creative tension between the two impulses—honoring both parent traditions in equal measure and to constructive effect—can be the next chapter of philosophy's story. The spirit of the interpretive tradition is to focus on the importance of pursuing its characteristic concerns rather than to worry about the thinness of the ice when they are pursued in intellectually adventuresome ways. It may be vital for that spirit to live on in the philosophical community in some form, letting the results sort themselves out as interpretations are elaborated and contested. But that form need not entail the continued existence of distinct traditions, each with its own institutional embodiments.

To the dynamic just described another must be added, related but distinct: the rise of the sciences, in the centuries before and after Kant, and of a worldview in which the natural sciences are deemed paradigmatic in their modes of analysis, explanation, and cognition (formal logic and mathematics aside). Kant was prepared to allow the sciences to be authoritative concerning much of reality—but not all. He drew the line at what he called "practical reason" and its proper domain: moral experience and agency, and what they might reasonably be taken to presuppose, involve, and imply. And with this august precedent, the interpretive tradition was off and running; for Kant's answer to the question of where the authoritativeness of science ends was not the only one possible (his supposition to the contrary notwithstanding).

We might think of the interpretive tradition as a variety of attempts to identify and reflect on things about human reality and possibility, and about life and the world more generally, that the scientific and formal disciplines (and ways of thinking modeled on them) either tend to miss altogether or fail to do justice. It thus has opposed itself to the idea that "scientific" thinking does or should have the last word with respect to everything whatsoever. The analytic tradition has by no means unanimously embraced that idea; but the generalization is understandable. One result has been the common but erroneous impression that the interpretive tradition is characterized by hostility to the sciences and logic—which is no more true of this tradition in general than it is of Kant himself.

The interpretive tradition is not (on the whole) unfriendly to science; but it has sought to make sure that philosophy does not become so impressed by the scientific and formal disciplines that it is content to be little more than their champions and analysts, allowing them to define and determine what is real, what is true—and so also, by implication, what really matters. It has sought to make sure that philosophy does not make the mistake of supposing that what things really are is what they are made of or what they were in the first place, or of taking it for granted that what is really going on in the world of human life and human reality is neither more nor less than the scientifically identifiable and analyzable processes that undergird and enable it. Such efforts will continue to be necessary, for the sake of the health of the discipline (and of philosophical education).

The interpretive tradition further stands as a rich resource of interpretive experiments that can be learned from, drawn on, and responded to—as challenges, inspirations, or provocations—as we continue to attempt to comprehend ourselves and our world, discern and assess our possibilities, and consider what to do with ourselves and each other. It may have settled nothing, but it has much to offer beyond what can be found and encountered in the previous history of philosophy—or in the world of the present moment. And it can help anyone who is so inclined to think about whether there are things concerning human reality that our sciences leave out, what they are, and what to make of them.

The interpretive tradition may or may not have a future that continues to be recognizable as a tradition. However, its past is rich enough to convey what it can mean to engage in this sort of interpretive philosophical activity—and should help ensure that, in one way or another, it will continue to be a vital part both of philosophy and of human reality. This volume is meant to be a step in that direction, looking not only to philosophy's past but also toward its future.

Timeline

The following chart is intended to help readers situate the thinkers and selections in this volume in their times, and in relation to some of the many other figures, developments, creations, and events that contributed to the character of their times. It begins in the year of the birth of Kant, with whom this volume opens. Its entries are primarily European, British, and American, reflecting the predominantly European cast of characters represented in the volume and the Anglo-American tradition most familiar to its anticipated readership. Its basic purpose is to indicate what was going on in European, British, and American history, society, and culture during the formative years and adult lifetimes of Hegel, Mill, Nietzsche, Heidegger, Foucault, and the rest, by way of specific examples amplifying on the account of the times at the beginning of the general introduction.

Some of the names, titles, and events mentioned will be recognized by all readers, while others will be familiar to only a few—as in some cases was true even for their contemporaries. But they, like the writings collected in this volume, are all notable parts of the rich tapestry of the past several centuries of Western civilization; and those who are curious enough to find out more about the less well known will benefit not only by learning something new but also by gaining a deeper understanding of the settings in which the philosophical concerns and ideas encountered in this volume emerged and developed.

Brevity is a necessity as well as a virtue in timelines of this sort, which are meant to help the reader literally see many different things together. To that end, usually only last names are given—except in the first column, which lists the years of birth and death of all of the figures included in this volume (named in boldface), as well as of other notable philosophers and intellectual and cultural figures (many of whom appear in the second and third columns). The second column lists—by year of publication or completion—most of the texts presented or excerpted in this volume (in boldface), together with other writings by the authors represented here (names only in boldface) and titles of representative writings by other philosophers and various important literary figures.

The third column features significant contributions of other sorts—artistic, musical, scientific, technological—to modern Western culture and civilization in this period, as well as some of the most notable individuals responsible for such contributions. Only a sampling of the works for which they are known and admired can be given here. Finally, the fourth column provides general political-historical context.

The selection of people and things in this timeline (beyond the volume's figures and texts) admittedly says as much about the editor's sensibility, experience, education, and ideas about who and what in the Western world is relevant to the volume and worth mentioning as it does about this period itself. Some of them (such as American presidents and various European monarchs and political leaders) are included mainly as historical signposts. The others are by no means the only writers, composers, artists, scientists, texts, musical compositions, inventions, and events that matter in this period; nor do they all matter equally or in the same way. This is simply one among many possible timelines; other choices could well have been made. Those that have been made simply reflect the editor's sense of some of what is worth knowing of and knowing something about if one cares enough about our intellectual history generally—and about the last several centuries of the history of philosophy more particularly—to be reading this volume.

Year	Intellectual/ Cultural Figures	Significant Texts	Cultural/Social Events	Historical Events and Figures
1724	• Immanuel Kant born		• Bach's *St. John Passion*	
1725		• Vico's *New Science*		• Peter the Great dies (Russia)
1726		• Swift's *Gulliver's Travels*		
1727	• Isaac Newton dies		• Bach's *St. Matthew Passion*	• King George I (Britain) dies • George II becomes king
1729	• Gotthold Lessing born	• Swift's *A Modest Proposal*	• Electrical conductivity discovered	
1732	• Joseph Haydn born			• George Washington born
1733		• Franklin's *Poor Richard's Almanac* begins • Voltaire's *Letters Concerning the English*		
1739		• Hume's *Treatise on Human Nature*, vols. 1 & 2		• Britain declares war on Spain
1740				• Frederick II ("the Great") becomes king (Prussia)
1741			• Handel's *Messiah*	
1746	• Francesco Goya born			
1747		• La Mettrie's *Man a Machine*	• First controlled trials prove citrus prevents scurvy	
1748	• Jeremy Bentham born	• Montesquieu's *Spirit of Laws*		
1749	• J. W. v. Goethe born	• Fielding's *Tom Jones*	• Bach's *Mass in B Minor* • Handel's *Music for the Royal Fireworks*	
1750	• Johann Seb. Bach dies			
1751	• Julien de La Mettrie dies	• Diderot and d'Alembert begin publishing their *Encyclopedia*		

Year	Intellectual/ Cultural Figures	Significant Texts	Cultural/Social Events	Historical Events and Figures
1753	• George Berkeley dies			
1755		• Johnson's *Dictionary of the English Language* • Rousseau's *Second and Third Discourses*		• Lisbon earthquake • Marie Antoinette born
1756	• Wolfgang A. Mozart born			• The Seven Years' War begins
1757	• William Blake born	• Burke's *On the Sublime and Beautiful*		
1759	• **Friedrich Schiller** born • **Mary Wollstonecraft** born • George F. Handel dies	• Voltaire's *Candide* • Smith's *Theory of Moral Sentiments*	• The British Museum opens • Haydn's Symphony #1	• British defeat French at Quebec
1760				• George III king (Britain)
1762	• **J. G. Fichte** born	• Rousseau's *The Social Contract* and *Emile*		• Catherine II empress (Russia)
1763				• Treaty of Paris; France cedes Canadian territories to Britain
1764		• Voltaire's *Philosophical Dictionary*	• Mozart's first symphony (age 8)	
1766	• Thomas Malthus born	• Lessing's *Laocoon*	• Haydn's *Cecilia* mass • Hydrogen discovered	
1768	• Schleiermacher born		• Mozart's first opera (age 12)	
1769	• A. von Humboldt born		• Watt patents steam engine	• Napoleon born
1770	• Ludwig v. Beethoven born • **G. W. F. Hegel** born	• d'Holbach's *System of Nature* • **Kant's** *Inaugural Dissertation* • Rousseau's *Confessions* written (published 1782)	• Spinning jenny patented	
1772	• Friedrich Schlegel born • Samuel Coleridge born	• Herder's *Treatise on the Origin of Language* • Final volume of Diderot and d'Alembert's 28-volume *Encyclopedia*	• Nitrogen discovered • Oxygen discovered	

Year	Intellectual/ Cultural Figures	Significant Texts	Cultural/Social Events	Historical Events and Figures
1773				• Boston Tea Party
1774		• Goethe's *Sorrows of the Young Werther*		• Louis XV dies; Louis XVI becomes king (France) • First Continental Congress
1775	• **Friedrich Schelling** born			• American Revolutionary War (War of Independence) begins
1776	• David Hume dies	• Smith's *Wealth of Nations* • Paine's *Common Sense* • Gibbon's *Decline and Fall of the Roman Empire*, first of 6 vols. (the last in 1788)		• Declaration of Independence (of "the 13 Colonies") from Britain
1777		• Five more vols. added to Diderot and d'Alembert's *Encyclopedia*		
1778	• J.-J. Rousseau dies • Voltaire dies			
1779		• Hume's *Dialogues Concerning Natural Religion* • Lessing's *Nathan the Wise*	• Goethe's *Iphigenia in Tauris*	
1781	• Gotthold Lessing dies	• **Kant's *Critique of Pure Reason*** • Schiller's *The Robbers*	• Uranus discovered	• Ratification of Articles of Confederation (future US) • Joseph II abolishes serfdom in Austrian Empire
1782		• Rousseau's *Confessions*, vol. 1	• Mozart's *Haffner* Symphony	
1783		• **Kant's *Prolegomena to Any Future Metaphysics***	• Hot-air balloon invented • Mozart's Mass in C Minor	• American colonies achieve independence from Britain • Treaty of Peace with Britain
1784	• Samuel Johnson dies • Denis Diderot dies	• Herder's *Ideas on the Philosophy of the History of Humanity*, vol. 1 • **Kant's "What Is Enlightenment?"**	• Beaumarchais's *Marriage of Figaro*	

Year	Intellectual/ Cultural Figures	Significant Texts	Cultural/Social Events	Historical Events and Figures
1785		• Jacobi's *Spinoza Conversations* • **Kant's** *Groundwork of the Metaphysics of Morals* • de Sade's *The 120 Days of Sodom*	• Power loom patented • *The Times* (London) launched	
1786	• Moses Mendelssohn dies		• Mozart's *Marriage of Figaro*	• Frederick "the Great" (Prussia) dies
1787		• The Federalist Papers begin publication • **Kant's** *Critique of Pure Reason*, **2nd ed.** • **Wollstonecraft's** *Thoughts on the Education of Daughters*	• Mozart's *Don Giovanni* • David's *Death of Socrates* • Steamboat invented	• US Constitution written (ratified 1788)
1788	• **Arthur Schopenhauer born**	• **Kant's** *Critique of Practical Reason*	• Mozart's last symphony (#41, the *Jupiter*)	
1789		• Bentham's *Introduction to the Principles of Morals & Legislation*		• French Revolution begins • France's "Declaration of the Rights of Man" • Washington 1st US president
1790	• Benjamin Franklin dies	• **Kant's** *Critique of Judgment* • Burke's *On the Revolution in France* • **Wollstonecraft's** *A Vindication of the Rights of Men* • Reinhold's *Letters on the Kantian Philosophy*	• Mozart's *Così fan tutte*	• Joseph II (Austria) dies
1791	• W. A. Mozart dies	• Paine's *Rights of Man* • Radcliffe's *The Romance of the Forest* • Franklin's *Autobiography*, part 1 (in French)	• Mozart's *Magic Flute* • Mozart's *Requiem* • Haydn's *Surprise* Symphony	• US Bill of Rights ratified
1792	• Gioachino Rossini born • Percy B. Shelley born	• **Wollstonecraft's** *Vindication of the Rights of Woman*	• Gas lighting invented	• First French Republic established
1793		• **Kant's** *Religion within the Limits of Reason Alone*	• Cotton gin invented • David's *Death of Marat*	• French Reign of Terror begins • Louis XVI and Marie Antoinette (France) executed by guillotine

Year	Intellectual/ Cultural Figures	Significant Texts	Cultural/Social Events	Historical Events and Figures
1794		• Schiller's *Aesthetic Education of Man* • Fichte's *Wissenschaftslehre* • Wollstonecraft's *A Historical and Moral View of the Origin and Progress of the French Revolution* • Blake's *Songs of Innocence and Experience*, including "The Tyger"		• Conservative "Thermidor Reaction" (France)
1795	• John Keats born • Thomas Carlyle born	• Goethe's *Wilhelm Meister's Apprenticeship*	• Haydn's last symphony (#104)	• Directorate established (France)
1796	• Thomas Reid dies	• Diderot's *Jacques the Fatalist* • Fichte's *Foundations of Natural Right*, vol. 1	• Jenner discovers smallpox vaccine	• Napoleon marries Josephine • Catherine II (Russia) dies
1797	• Franz Schubert born • Mary Shelley born • **Mary Wollstonecraft** dies • Heinrich Heine born	• Kant's *Metaphysics of Morals* • Hölderlin's *Hyperion*, vol. 1 • Schelling's *Ideas for a Philosophy of Nature*		• J. Adams 2nd US president
1798	• Auguste Comte born	• Fichte's *System of Ethics* • Malthus's *Essay on the Principle of Population* • Wordsworth and Coleridge's *Lyrical Ballads* • Coleridge's "Rime of the Ancient Mariner"	• Whitney (US) develops mass production of firearms • Lithography invented • Haydn's *The Creation*	
1799	• Alexander Pushkin born	• Hölderlin's *Hyperion*, vol. 2 • Schlegel's *Lucinde* • Schleiermacher's *On Religion*	• First income tax (Britain)	• Consulate established (French government) • Napoleon made First Counsel • Washington dies
1800		• Schelling's *System of Transcendental Idealism* • Fichte's *The Vocation of Man*	• The battery invented • Beethoven's First Symphony • US Library of Congress founded	

Year	Intellectual/ Cultural Figures	Significant Texts	Cultural/Social Events	Historical Events and Figures
1801	• Novalis dies	• **Schiller's** *Maid of Orleans* • **Hegel's** *The Difference between Fichte's and Schelling's Systems of Philosophy* • Lamarck's *System of Animals*	• Young's wave theory of light (first two-slit experiment) • Haydn's *The Seasons*	• Jefferson 3rd US president • Alexander I emperor (Russia)
1802		• **Schelling's** *Bruno* • **Hegel's** *Faith and Knowledge*		
1803	• **Ralph W. Emerson** born • **Johann G. Herder** dies	• **Schiller's** *The Bride from Messina*	• Dalton proposes atomic theory	• The Louisiana Purchase (by US, from France)
1804	• **Immanuel Kant** dies • **Ludwig Feuerbach** born	• **Schiller's** *Wilhelm Tell*	• First steam locomotive • Lewis and Clark Expedition begins	• Napoleon crowns himself emperor (France)
1805	• **Friedrich Schiller** dies		• Beethoven's Third Symphony • Beethoven's *Fidelio* (original)	
1806	• **John Stuart Mill** born	• Webster's first English dictionary		• Battle of Jena; French victory • Holy Roman Empire ends
1807	• Henry W. Longfellow born	• **Hegel's** *Phenomenology of Spirit* • Wordsworth's "Ode: Intimations of Immortality"	• First internal combustion engine	• Britain ends African slave trade
1808		• **Fichte's** *Addresses to the German Nation* • Goethe's *Faust*, Part I	• Beethoven's Fifth Symphony	• US ends African slave trade
1809	• Joseph Haydn dies • Edgar Allan Poe born • Charles Darwin born	• Goethe's *Elective Affinities* • **Schelling's** *Philosophical Inquiries into the Essence of Human Freedom* • Lamarck's *Zoological Philosophy*		• Madison 4th US president • Lincoln born
1810	• Frédéric Chopin born			• Mexican War of Independence
1811	• Franz Liszt born	• Austen's *Sense and Sensibility*	• Luddite riots begin in England	

Year	Intellectual/ Cultural Figures	Significant Texts	Cultural/Social Events	Historical Events and Figures
1812	• Charles Dickens born	• Hegel's *Science of Logic*, Part 1		• French invasion of Russia (fails) • War of 1812 (US/UK)
1813	• Søren Kierke-gaard born • Richard Wagner born • Guiseppe Verdi born	• Austen's *Pride and Prejudice* • Schopenhauer's *On the Fourfold Root of the Principle of Suffi-cient Reason*		• Battle of Leipzig (Battle of the Nations); major French defeat
1814	• Johann Fichte dies • Marquis de Sade dies	• Austen's *Mansfield Park* • Scott's *Waverley*	• Goya's *The Second of May* • Beethoven's *Fidelio* (revised)	• Napoleon abdicates, is exiled
1815		• Austen's *Emma*		• War of 1812 ends • Napoleon returns: defeated at Waterloo; second exile • Treaty of Congress of Vienna
1816		• Coleridge's "Kubla Khan"	• Rossini's *The Bar-ber of Seville*	
1817	• Henry D. Thoreau born	• Hegel's *Encyclopedia* • Byron's *Manfred* • Scott's *Rob Roy*		• Monroe 5th US president
1818	• Karl Marx born • Frederick Doug-lass born	• Mary Shelley's *Frankenstein* • Percy Shelley's "Ozymandias" • Schopenhauer's *The World as Will and Representation*		
1819	• Friedrich Jacobi dies • Herman Melville born • Walt Whitman born	• Scott's *Ivanhoe* • Irving's "Rip Van Winkle"	• Ship first employs steam power in Atlantic crossings	
1820	• Friedrich Engels born • Herbert Spencer born	• Keats's "Ode on a Gre-cian Urn" • Shelley's *Prometheus Unbound*	• Ørsted discovers electromagnetism	• George IV king (UK)
1821	• Gustave Flaubert born • Baudelaire born • Dostoevsky born	• Hegel's *Philosophy of Right* • Goethe's *Wilhelm Meister's Journeyman Years*		• Napoleon dies in St. Helena • Mexican independence • War of Greek Indepen-dence (from Ottoman Empire) begins

Year	Intellectual/ Cultural Figures	Significant Texts	Cultural/Social Events	Historical Events and Figures
1822	• Percy Shelley dies		• Schubert's Symphony #8	• Brazilian independence
1824	• Byron dies in Greece	• Heine's "Die Lorelei" • Byron's *Don Juan* completed	• Beethoven's 9th Symphony • Mendelssohn's 1st Symphony • David's *Mars Disarmed*	
1825	• Johann Strauss born		• First public steam-engine passenger train	• J. Q. Adams 6th US president • Nicholas I emperor (Russia)
1826		• Heine's "Die Harzreise"	• Mendelssohn's *Overture to A Midsummer Night's Dream*	• Jefferson dies • J. Adams dies
1827	• Beethoven dies		• Schubert's *Winterreise*	
1828	• Leo Tolstoy born		• Schubert's last symphony (#9)	
1829			• Rossini's *William Tell*	• Jackson 7th US president • Slavery abolished in Mexico
1830	• Emily Dickinson born	• Lyell's *Principles of Geology*, vol. 1 • Stendhal's *The Red and the Black*	• First US railroad opens • Delacroix's *Liberty* • Mendelssohn's *Fingal's Cave* • Berlioz's *Symphonie fantastique*	• Charles X (France) deposed in July Revolution • Simón Bolívar dies
1831	• **G. W. F. Hegel** dies	• Hugo's *Hunchback of Notre Dame*	• Darwin's *Beagle* voyage begins • Electromagnetic induction discovered	• Nat Turner leads slave rebellion (US)
1832	• Goethe dies • Jeremy Bentham dies • Édouard Manet born	• Goethe's *Faust*, Part II • Balzac conceives of "The Human Comedy" • Pushkin's *Eugene Onegin* completed		• Greek independence
1833	• **Wilhelm Dilthey** born • Johannes Brahms born	• Carlyle's *Sartor Resartus* begins publication		
1834				• Slavery abolished throughout the British Empire

Year	Intellectual/ Cultural Figures	Significant Texts	Cultural/Social Events	Historical Events and Figures
1835	• Samuel Clemens (Mark Twain) born	• de Tocqueville's *Democracy in America* • Balzac's *Père Goriot*	• Darwin visits the Galapagos • Colt revolver invented	• Ferdinand I emperor (Austria)
1836		• **Emerson's "Nature"** • **Schopenhauer's *On the Will in Nature***		• Battle of the Alamo • Texas attains independence from Mexico, becomes republic
1837	• Aleksandr Pushkin dies	• **Emerson's "The American Scholar"**	• Electrical telegraph invented • Babbage describes "analytical engine" (early computer)	• Victoria queen (UK) • Van Buren 8th US president
1838		• **Emerson's "Divinity School Address"**	• Schumann's *Kinderszenen*	
1839	• Charles S. Peirce born • Paul Cézanne born • Modest Mussorgsky born	• Poe's "The Fall of the House of Usher" • Stendhal's *The Charterhouse of Parma*	• Berlioz's *Roméo et Juliette* • Invention of the daguerrotype announced	• First Anglo-Afghan War begins
1840	• Claude Monet born • Émile Zola born • Pyotr Tchaikovsky born	• **Schopenhauer's "On The Basis of Morality"** • James Fenimore Cooper's *Pathfinder*	• First postage stamp (UK)	
1841	• Antonín Dvořák born	• **Emerson's *Essays* (1st series)** • **Kierkegaard's *The Concept of Irony*** • **Feuerbach's *The Essence of Christianity*** • Carlyle's *On Heroes, Hero-Worship, and the Heroic in History*	• **Schelling's** lectures on revelation and myth • Schumann's Symphony #1	• W. H. Harrison 9th US president, dies • Tyler 10th US president
1842	• William James born • Stendhal dies	• **Emerson's "The Transcendentalist"**	• The Doppler effect discovered • Verdi's *Nabucco*	• Hong Kong ceded to Britain
1843	• Henry James born	• **Kierkegaard's *Either/ Or* and *Fear and Trembling*** • **Mill's *System of Logic*** • **Feuerbach's *Philosophy of the Future*** • Dickens's *Christmas Carol*	• Joule publishes work that leads to law of conservation of energy • Mendelssohn's Symphony #3	

Year	Intellectual/ Cultural Figures	Significant Texts	Cultural/Social Events	Historical Events and Figures
1844	• Friedrich Nietzsche born	• Schopenhauer's *The World as Will and Representation*, 2nd ed. • Emerson's *Essays* (2nd series) • Kierkegaard's *Philosophical Fragments* • Marx's "1844 Manuscripts"	• Telegraph using Morse code introduced	
1845	• Georg Cantor born	• Stirner's *The Ego and Its Own* • Poe's "The Raven" • Marx's *The German Ideology* written • Dumas's *The Count of Monte-Cristo*	• Thoreau moves to Walden Pond • Wagner's *Tannhäuser*	• Polk 11th US president • Texas's annexation to US approved • Irish Potato Famine begins
1846	• F. H. Bradley born	• Kierkegaard's *Concluding Unscientific Postscript*	• Neptune discovered • Mendelssohn's *Elijah* • Berlioz's *Damnation of Faust*	• Mexican-American War begins
1847	• Thomas Edison born	• C. Brontë's *Jane Eyre* • E. Brontë's *Wuthering Heights*		
1848	• Gottlob Frege born • Paul Gauguin born	• Marx and Engels's *Communist Manifesto* • Mill's *Principles of Political Economy* • Comte's *A General View of Positivism*	• Feuerbach's lectures on religion	• Revolutions across Europe fail • Franz Josef I emperor (Austria) • Second Republic in France • Mexico cedes the American Southwest and California to US
1849	• Edgar Allan Poe dies	• Thoreau's "Civil Disobedience" • Kierkegaard's *Sickness unto Death*	• Marx settles in London	• California Gold Rush • Taylor 12th US president
1850		• Hawthorne's *Scarlet Letter* • Kierkegaard's *Practice in Christianity* • Dickens's *David Copperfield* • Elizabeth Browning's "How do I love thee"	• Telegraph cable laid across the English Channel • Wagner's *Lohengrin* • Schumann's Symphony #3	• Fillmore 13th US president • Fugitive Slave Act (US)

Year	Intellectual/ Cultural Figures	Significant Texts	Cultural/Social Events	Historical Events and Figures
1851	• James F. Cooper dies	• Melville's *Moby-Dick* • **Schopenhauer's** *Parerga und Paralipomena*	• Foucault uses pendulum to show rotation of the earth • *New York Times* launched • Verdi's *Rigoletto* • Foster's "Swanee River"	
1852	• Nikolay Gogol dies	• Stowe's *Uncle Tom's Cabin* • **Marx's** *The 18th Brumaire of Louis Bonaparte*	• Schumann's *Mass* and *Requiem*	
1853	• Vincent van Gogh born		• Verdi's *La Traviata*	• Pierce 14th US president • Crimean War begins
1854	• **Friedrich Schelling** dies	• Thoreau's *Walden* • Tennyson's "Charge of the Light Brigade"	• Liszt's *Les Préludes*	
1855	• **Søren Kierkegaard** dies • Josiah Royce born	• **Kierkegaard's "Unchangeableness of God"** • Whitman's *Leaves of Grass*		• Alexander II emperor (Russia)
1856	• Sigmund Freud born • Heinrich Heine dies		• Bessemer patents steelmaking process	• The Crimean War ends
1857	• Auguste Comte dies	• Baudelaire's *Flowers of Evil* • Flaubert's *Madame Bovary*	• Dred Scott decision denies citizenship to free US blacks • Liszt's *Faust Symphony*, revised	• Buchanan 15th US president
1859	• **Henri Bergson** born • **Edmund Husserl** born • John Dewey born	• Dickens's *Tale of Two Cities* • Tennyson's *Idylls of the King* (first version) • Darwin's *On the Origin of Species* • **Mill's** *On Liberty* • **Marx's** *A Contribution to the Critique of Political Economy*	• Pasteur disproves theory of spontaneous generation	• John Brown raids Harpers Ferry
1860	• **Arthur Schopenhauer** dies • Gustav Mahler born • Anton Chekhov born	• **Emerson's** *The Conduct of Life* • Eliot's *The Mill on the Floss*		• Garibaldi takes Naples; unification of Italy

Year	Intellectual/ Cultural Figures	Significant Texts	Cultural/Social Events	Historical Events and Figures
1861	• Alfred N. White-head born	• **Mill's *Utilitarianism*** • Dickens's *Great Expectations* • Eliot's *Silas Marner*	• Broca finds brain speech center • Delacroix's *Lion Hunt* • First US income tax	• Wilhelm I king of Prussia • Kingdom of Italy proclaimed • Lincoln 16th US president • US Civil War begins • Serfdom abolished in Russia
1862	• Henry Thoreau dies • Claude Debussy born	• Hugo's *Les Misérables*		• Bismarck minister-president of Prussia
1863	• George Santayana born • Edvard Munch born		• Manet's *Luncheon on the Grass* • Pasteurization process invented	• Emancipation Proclamation (US) • Battle of Gettysburg
1864	• Max Weber born • Richard Strauss born	• Dostoevsky's *Notes from Underground* • Verne's *Journey to the Center of the Earth*	• Maxwell presents unified theory of electromagnetism • Yosemite made a park (in 1906, a national park)	
1865	• W. B. Yeats born	• Carroll's *Alice's Adventures in Wonderland* • **Mill's *Sir William Hamilton's Philosophy***	• Wagner's *Tristan und Isolde* • Mendel provides evidence for genetic inheritance	• Slavery abolished in US • Lincoln assassinated • A. Johnson 17th US president • US Civil War ends
1866	• Wassily Kandinsky born	• Lange's *History of Materialism* • Dostoevsky's *Crime and Punishment*	• Trans-Atlantic cable laid • Tchaikovsky's first symphony	• Austro-Prussian War
1867	• Frank Lloyd Wright born • Charles Baudelaire dies • Wilbur Wright born	• **Marx's *Capital*, vol. I** • Arnold's "Dover Beach" • Ibsen's *Peer Gynt*	• Mussorgsky's *Bald Mountain* • Verdi's *Don Carlos* • Typewriter invented • J. Strauss Jr.'s "Blue Danube"	• Alaska purchased from Russia • Canada becomes autonomous
1868	**W. E. B. Du Bois born**		• Brahms's *Deutsches Requiem*	
1869	• André Gide born • Henri Matisse born	• Alcott's *Little Women* • Tolstoy's *War and Peace* • **Mill's *The Subjection of Women*** • Dostoyevsky's *The Idiot*	• Transcontinental railroad (US) • First Vatican Council begins • Tchaikovsky's *Romeo and Juliet*	• Suez Canal opens • Grant 18th US president • Mahatma Gandhi born

Year	Intellectual/ Cultural Figures	Significant Texts	Cultural/Social Events	Historical Events and Figures
1870				• Franco-Prussian War begins
1871	• Marcel Proust born • Orville Wright born	• Carroll's *Through the Looking-Glass* • Darwin's *Descent of Man*	• Verdi's *Aida*	• The Paris Commune • The Great Chicago Fire • German Unification; empire proclaimed, with Wilhelm I kaiser, Bismarck chancellor
1872	• Bertrand Russell born • Ludwig Feuerbach dies	• **Nietzsche's *The Birth of Tragedy*** • **Nietzsche's "Truth and Lie" written** • Eliot's *Middlemarch*	• Yellowstone National Park created (first US national park) • Monet's *Sunrise*	
1873	• **John Stuart Mill dies** • **G. E. Moore born**	• Verne's *Around the World in 80 Days* • Rimbaud's *A Season in Hell*	• Dye sensitization makes color photography possible	
1874	• **Max Scheler born** • **Ernst Cassirer born** • Arnold Schoenberg born	• Wundt's *Physiological Psychology* • Brentano's *Psychology from an Empirical Standpoint* • **Nietzsche's "Schopenhauer as Educator"** • Sidgwick's *Method of Ethics* • Twain's *Adventures of Tom Sawyer*	• Mussorgsky's *Pictures at an Exhibition* • First of Cantor's papers that create modern set theory • Bruckner's Symphony #4 • Verdi's *Requiem*	• Churchill born
1875	• Carl Jung born • Albert Schweitzer born	• **Marx's *Critique of the Gotha Program* written**	• Eakins's *Gross Clinic* • Bizet's *Carmen*	
1876		• Twain's *The Adventures of Tom Sawyer* • George Eliot's *Daniel Deronda*	• Bell patents the telephone • First Wagner *Ring* in Bayreuth • Renoir's *Dance at Le Moulin*	• Custer's defeat at Little Bighorn
1877	• Hermann Hesse born	• Tolstoy's *Anna Karenina* • Engels's *Anti-Dühring*, vol. 1	• Mars's 2 moons discovered • Edison invents the phonograph • Brahms's Symphony #2 • Tchaikovsky's *Swan Lake*	• Hayes 19th US president

Year	Intellectual/ Cultural Figures	Significant Texts	Cultural/Social Events	Historical Events and Figures
1878	• **Martin Buber** born	• Thomas Hardy's *The Return of the Native* • **Nietzsche's** *Human, All Too Human*	• Carbon filament electric lightbulb invented • Tchaikovsky's Symphony #4 • Gilbert and Sullivan's *Pinafore*	
1879	• Albert Einstein born • Paul Klee born	• Frege's *Begriffsschrift*	• Ibsen's *A Doll House* • Tchaikovsky's *Eugene Onegin*	• Stalin born
1880		• Dostoevsky's *The Brothers Karamazov*	• Rodin's *Thinker* • Edison patents the lightbulb • Tchaikovsky's *1812 Overture*	
1881	• Béla Bartók born • Pablo Picasso born	• Henry James's *Portrait of a Lady*	• Brahms's *Academic Festival Overture* • Pasteur creates anthrax vaccine • Degas' *Little Dancer*	• Czar Alexander II (Russia) assassinated; succeeded by Alexander III • Garfield 20th US president • Garfield assassinated • Arthur 21st US president
1882	• **Ralph W. Emerson** dies • Charles Darwin dies • Igor Stravinsky born • Jacques Maritain born	• **Nietzsche's** *The Gay Science*, first edition	• Wagner's *Parsifal*	
1883	• **Karl Marx** dies • **Karl Jaspers** born • Wagner dies • Franz Kafka born	• Dilthey's *Introduction to the Human Sciences* • **Nietzsche's** *Thus Spoke Zarathustra, I & II*		• Krakatoa volcano erupts • Mussolini born
1884	• Gaston Bachelard born • Rudolf Bultmann born	• **Nietzsche's** *Zarathustra, Part III* • Twain's *Huckleberry Finn* • Engels's *The Origin of the Family* • Frege's *The Foundations of Arithmetic*	• Gilbert and Sullivan's *Mikado*	

Year	Intellectual/ Cultural Figures	Significant Texts	Cultural/Social Events	Historical Events and Figures
1885		• Nietzsche's *Zarathustra*, Part IV written • Zola's *Germinal*	• First skyscraper (in Chicago) • Brahms's Symphony #4 • Renoir's *In the Garden* • Pasteur develops rabies vaccine	• Cleveland 22nd US president
1886	• Emily Dickinson dies • Paul Tillich born • Karl Barth born	• Nietzsche's *Beyond Good and Evil* • Hardy's *The Mayor of Casterbridge* • Engels's *Ludwig Feuerbach and the End of Classical German Philosophy*	• Seurat's *A Sunday Afternoon* • Freud opens practice in Vienna • Benz patents first practical gasoline-powered automobile • Rodin's *The Kiss* • Statue of Liberty dedicated	
1887	• Georgia O'Keeffe born • Marcel Duchamp born	• Nietzsche's *The Gay Science*, second edition • Nietzsche's *On the Genealogy of Morals* • Husserl's *On the Concept of Number*	• Van Gogh's *Sunflowers* • Renoir's *The Large Bathers* • Michelson and Morley establish constancy of speed of light • Debussy's *Printemps* in E major • Verdi's *Otello*	
1888	• T. S. Eliot born	• Nietzsche's *Twilight of the Idols* written • Nietzsche's *Ecce Homo* written	• Jack the Ripper murders • Tchaikovsky's Symphony #5 • Mahler's Symphony #1 • Van Gogh's *Starry Night*	• Wilhelm I (Germany) dies; Wilhelm II becomes kaiser
1889	• **Nietzsche** suffers terminal collapse • **Martin Heidegger** born • Ludwig Wittgenstein born • Gabriel Marcel born • Charlie Chaplin born	• **Bergson's** *Time and Free Will* • Brentano's *The Origin of Our Knowledge of Right and Wrong*	• Dvořák's Symphony #8 • Eiffel Tower completed • *Wall Street Journal* launched • Van Gogh's *Irises* • Rodin's *Burghers of Calais*	• B. Harrison 23rd US president • Hitler born in Austria

Year	Intellectual/ Cultural Figures	Significant Texts	Cultural/Social Events	Historical Events and Figures
1890		• W. James's *Principles of Psychology* • Zola's *The Human Beast* • Kipling's "Gunga Din" • Dickinson's "Because I could not stop for Death" (posthumous)	• Tchaikovsky's *Sleeping Beauty* • Fauré's *Requiem* • Van Gogh's *Wheatfield* • Proofs to verify germ theory of disease published	• Bismarck dismissed as German chancellor
1891	• Rudolf Carnap born	• Wilde's *The Picture of Dorian Gray*	• Monet's *Haystacks*	
1892	• **Helmuth Plessner** born • Walt Whitman dies • Walter Benjamin born	• Frege's "On Sense and Reference" • **Nietzsche's Zarathustra, Part IV** published	• Tchaikovsky's *Nutcracker* • Cézanne's *Card Players* • Toulouse-Lautrec's *Two Women Waltzing*	
1893		• Blondel's *Action*	• Dvořák's 9th Symphony (*New World*) • Verdi's *Falstaff* • Oscar Wilde's *A Woman of No Importance* • Munch's *The Scream*	• Cleveland 24th US president • Mao Zedong born • New Zealand is first country to give women vote
1894		• Kipling's *Jungle Book*	• Debussy's *Prelude to the Afternoon of a Faun* • Mahler's Symphony #2 • Bruckner's Symphony #9	• Nicolas II (last) czar of Russia
1895	• **Friedrich Engels** dies • Carl Orff born • Max Horkheimer born	• **Nietzsche's Antichrist** and "Nietzsche *Contra* Wagner" published • Breuer and Freud's *Studies on Hysteria* • Durkheim's *Rules of Sociological Method* • Wells's *The Time Machine* • Hardy's *Jude the Obscure*	• First movie (Lumière brothers) • X-rays discovered • Dvořák's Cello Concerto	
1896	• Jean Piaget born • Antoine Artaud born	• **Bergson's Matter and Memory**	• Puccini's *La Bohème* • R. Strauss's *Also sprach Zarathustra* • Seurat's *Sunday Afternoon* • Chekhov's *The Seagull* • Sullivan's Guaranty Building • Ford's first car built	• First modern Olympic Games

Year	Intellectual/ Cultural Figures	Significant Texts	Cultural/Social Events	Historical Events and Figures
1897	• William Faulkner born	• **Du Bois's "The Conservation of Races"** • **Du Bois's** The Philadelphia Negro • Durkheim's Suicide • Bram Stoker's Dracula	• The electron is discovered • Tesla files basic radio patents • Gauguin's Where Do We Come From? • Sousa's "Stars and Stripes" • Chekhov's Uncle Vanya	• McKinley 25th US president
1898	• Herbert Marcuse born • C. S. Lewis born	• Wells's The War of the Worlds • H. James's Turn of the Screw	• Cézanne's Bathers begun	• Spanish-American War
1899	• Victor Nabokov born • Ernest Hemingway born	• Freud's Interpretation of Dreams • Kate Chopin's The Awakening • Conrad's "The Heart of Darkness"	• Debussy's Nocturnes • Elgar's Enigma Variations • Gauguin's Two Tahitian Women • Hilbert's axiomatization of geometry • Joplin's "Maple Leaf Rag"	• Boer War (South Africa) begins • Boxer Rebellion in China
1900	• **Friedrich Nietzsche** dies • Oscar Wilde dies • **Hans-Georg Gadamer** born • Henry Sidgwick dies	• **Husserl's** Logical Investigations, vol. 1 • Dewey's School and Society • Conrad's Lord Jim	• Puccini's Tosca	
1901	• Jacques Lacan born • Alfred Tarski born • Margaret Mead born	• Selections from **Nietzsche's** 1883–88 notebooks posthumously assembled and published as The Will to Power • Freud's Psychopathology of Everyday Life • Mann's Buddenbrooks • Washington's Up from Slavery	• US Steel Corporation formed • Nobel Prizes first awarded • Picasso's Blue period begins • Elgar's first two "Pomp and Circumstance" marches • Picasso's Absinthe Drinker	• Queen Victoria dies, Edward VII becomes king (UK) • McKinley assassinated • T. Roosevelt 26th US president
1902		• Lenin's "What Is to Be Done?" • Gide's The Immoralist • William James's The Varieties of Religious Experience	• Mahler's Symphony #5	• Boer War ends

Year	Intellectual/ Cultural Figures	Significant Texts	Cultural/Social Events	Historical Events and Figures
1903	• Theodor Adorno born	• Russell's *Principles of Mathematics* • Moore's *Principia Ethica* • **Bergson's *Introduction to Metaphysics*** • **Du Bois's *Souls of Black Folk*** • London's *Call of the Wild* • H. James's *The Ambassadors* • Shaw's *Man and Superman*	• Pavlov reports on conditioned responses and reflexes • Wright brothers' first flight • The Curies share Nobel Prize • First World Series (baseball)	
1904	• **Arnold Gehlen born** • Salvador Dalí born	• H. James's *The Golden Bowl* • Chekhov's *The Cherry Orchard* • Weber's *The Protestant Ethic and the Spirit of Capitalism*	• Picasso's Rose period begins • Puccini's *Madame Butterfly* • Barrie's *Peter Pan*	• US receives Panama Canal Zone
1905	• **Jean-Paul Sartre born** • Ayn Rand born	• **Du Bois's "*Sociology Hesitant*"** • Freud's *Essays on the Theory of Sexuality* • Wharton's *House of Mirth* • Lenin's *Two Tactics of Social-Democracy*	• Einstein proposes theory of special relativity • Matisse and Fauvism exhibition • R. Strauss's *Salome* • Cassatt's *Mother and Child* • Shaw's *Major Barbara*	• First Russian Revolution
1906	• **Emmanuel Lévinas born** • **Hannah Arendt born** • Samuel Beckett born	• **Cassirer's *The Problem of Knowledge*** • Sinclair's *The Jungle*	• Monet's *Water Lilies* • First radio broadcast	• Susan B. Anthony dies • Great San Francisco earthquake
1907	• **Maurice Merleau-Ponty born**	• **Bergson's *Creative Evolution***	• First commercially marketed color photography • Picasso's *Les Demoiselles d'Avignon*	
1908	• **Simone de Beauvoir born** • Claude Lévi-Strauss born • W. V. Quine born	• **Nietzsche's *Ecce Homo* published** • Sorel's *Reflections on Violence* • Forster's *Room with a View*	• Klimt's *The Kiss* • Rachmaninoff's Symphony #2	

Year	Intellectual/ Cultural Figures	Significant Texts	Cultural/Social Events	Historical Events and Figures
1909	• **Simone Weil** born • Isaiah Berlin born	• Lenin's *Materialism and Empirio-Criticism*	• Matisse's *The Dance* • NAACP founded • Mahler's *Song of the Earth*	• Taft 27th US president
1910	• Mark Twain dies • Leo Tolstoy dies • William James dies • Jean Genet born • Mother Teresa born • A. J. Ayer born	• **Cassirer's** *Substance and Function* • **Dilthey's** *Construction of the Historical World* • **Husserl's** "Philosophy as Rigorous Science" • Russell and Whitehead's *Principia Mathematica*, vol. 1	• Mahler's 8th Symphony (*Symphony of a Thousand*) • Stravinsky's *Firebird* • Matisse's *The Dance*	• George V king (UK)
1911	• **Wilhelm Dilthey** dies • J. L. Austin born	• **Dilthey's** "Types of Worldviews"	• Kandinsky begins his series of pure abstract compositions • Chagall's *I and the Village* • R. Strauss's *Rosenkavalier*	
1912	• Jackson Pollock born • John Cage born • Alan Turing born	• **Husserl's** *Ideas* • **Scheler's** *Ressentiment* • Durkheim's *Forms of Religious Life* • Jung's *Psychology of the Unconscious* • Shaw's *Pygmalion* • Mann's *Death in Venice* • Rilke writes first 2 *Duino Elegies*	• Schoenberg's *Pierrot Lunaire* • Duchamp's *Nude Descending a Staircase, No. 2*	
1913	• **Paul Ricoeur** born • Albert Camus born • Ferdinand de Saussure dies	• **Jaspers's** *General Psychopathology* • Proust's *In Search of Lost Time* begins • Freud's *Totem and Taboo* • Lawrence's *Sons and Lovers*	• Stravinsky's *Rite of Spring* • Kandinsky's *Composition VII*	• Wilson 28th US president
1914	• Charles Peirce dies • Octavio Paz born	• Russell's *Our Knowledge of the External World*	• First Chaplin "Tramp" movie • Panama Canal opens	• Archduke Franz Ferdinand assassinated in Sarajevo • Gandhi returns to India from South Africa • The Great War (WWI) begins

Year	Intellectual/ Cultural Figures	Significant Texts	Cultural/Social Events	Historical Events and Figures
1915	• Roland Barthes born	• Kafka's "Metamorphosis" • **Du Bois's** *The Negro* • Maugham's *Of Human Bondage*	• Einstein proposes theory of general relativity • Griffith's *Birth of a Nation* • Rachmaninoff's *Vespers*	
1916		• **Scheler's** *Formalism in Ethics* • Joyce's *Portrait of the Artist as a Young Man* • Saussure's *Course in General Linguistics* • Dewey's *Democracy and Education* • Frost's "Road Not Taken"	• Dadaist group forms in Zürich	• Emperor Franz Josef (Austria) dies
1917	• Franz Brentano dies • Donald Davidson born • Heinrich Böll born	• Edith Stein's *On the Problem of Empathy*	• Duchamp's *Fountain*	• US enters World War I • Russian (Bolshevik) Revolution • Bolshevik government led by Lenin established in Russia
1918	• Leonard Bernstein born • Louis Althusser born • Claude Debussy dies	• **Cassirer's** *Kant's Life and Thought* • Brecht's *Baal* written (first play) • Spengler's *Decline of the West*, vol. 1 • Russell's "Philosophy of Logical Atomism" • Lenin's *State and Revolution*	• Holst's *The Planets* • Planck awarded Nobel Prize • Stravinsky's *Soldier's Tale* • Miró's *The Guitar*	• World War I ends • Russian Civil War begins • German revolution attempted
1919	• Iris Murdoch born • G. E. M. Anscombe born	• **Jaspers's** *Psychology of Worldviews* • Hesse's *Demian* • Mencken's *The American Language*	• Bauhaus School (architecture) founded by Gropius in Weimar • Elgar's *Cello Concerto* • Klee's *Moonshine*	• T. Roosevelt dies • Treaty of Versailles • German, Austro-Hungarian, Russian, and Ottoman Empires all cease to exist • Weimar Republic (Germany)
1920	• Max Weber dies • Paul Celan born • Ray Bradbury born	• **Du Bois's** *Darkwater: Voices from Within the Veil* • Freud's *Beyond the Pleasure Principle* • Dewey's *Reconstruction in Philosophy* • Colette's *Chéri* • Lukács's *The Theory of the Novel* • Yeats's "Second Coming"	• Mamie Smith first records blues songs • Mondrian creates his grid-style abstract paintings • Prohibition begins in US	• League of Nations established (US Senate never ratifies) • Women get the vote in US

Year	Intellectual/ Cultural Figures	Significant Texts	Cultural/Social Events	Historical Events and Figures
1921	• John Rawls born	• **Scheler's** *On the Eternal in Man* • Benjamin's "Critique of Violence" • Wittgenstein's *Tractatus*	• Schoenberg discovers 12-tone technique • Einstein awarded Nobel Prize • Picasso's *Three Musicians*	• Harding 29th US president
1922	• Marcel Proust dies • Jack Kerouac born • Thomas Kuhn born	• T. S. Eliot's *The Waste Land* • Joyce's *Ulysses* • Hesse's *Siddhartha* • Rilke's *Sonnets to Orpheus*	• Bohr awarded Nobel Prize • Klee's *Red Balloon*	• Lenin establishes USSR • Mussolini and Fascists take power in Italy
1923	• Roy Lichtenstein born	• **Scheler's** *The Nature of Sympathy* • **Cassirer's** *Philosophy of Symbolic Forms*, vol. 1 • **Buber's** *I and Thou* • Lukács's *History and Class Consciousness* • Frost's "Stopping by Woods"	• First movies with sound • Hubble discovers other galaxies • *Time* launched (first weekly magazine of world news) • Kandinsky's *On White II*	• Hitler's Beer Hall Putsch • Harding dies • Coolidge 30th US president • Hyperinflation in Germany
1924	• **Jean-François Lyotard** born • Franz Kafka dies	• **Plessner's** *The Limits of Community* • Mann's *The Magic Mountain* • **Du Bois's** *The Gift of Black Folk* • Melville's *Billy Budd* (posthumous) • Neruda's *Twenty Poems of Love*	• Breton's *Surrealist Manifesto* • Gershwin's *Rhapsody in Blue* • O'Neill's *Desire under the Elms*	• Lenin dies
1925	• **Gilles Deleuze** born • **Frantz Fanon** born • Gottlob Frege dies • Malcolm X born	• **Cassirer's** *Philosophy of Symbolic Forms II* • Moore's "A Defense of Common Sense" • Dewey's *Experience and Nature* • Kafka's *The Trial* • Fitzgerald's *The Great Gatsby* • Dreiser's *American Tragedy*	• Heisenberg develops modern (matrix) quantum mechanics • Berg's *Wozzeck* • The Scopes "Monkey Trial"	• Hitler's *Mein Kampf*, vol. 1
1926	• **Michel Foucault** born • Hilary Putnam born • Stanley Cavell born • Claude Monet dies	• Hartmann's *Ethics* • **Scheler's** *Sociology of Knowledge* • Kafka's *The Castle* • Hemingway's *The Sun Also Rises*	• Bartók's *Miraculous Mandarin* • Gropius's Bauhaus building • First public TV transmission	• Gramsci imprisoned

Year	Intellectual/ Cultural Figures	Significant Texts	Cultural/Social Events	Historical Events and Figures
1927	• Günter Grass born	• **Heidegger's** *Being and Time* • Husserl's *Britannica* entry "Phenomenology" • Marcel's *Metaphysical Journal* • Proust's *In Search*, final vol. (7) • Woolf's *To the Lighthouse* • Hesse's *Steppenwolf*	• Heisenberg proposes "uncertainty principle" • Stravinsky's *Oedipus Rex* • O'Keeffe's *Poppy* • Babe Ruth hits 60 home runs	• Stalin consolidates power in USSR
1928	• **Max Scheler dies** • Andy Warhol born • Noam Chomsky born	• **Plessner's** *Levels of the Organic and of Man* • **Scheler's** *Man's Place in Nature* • Carnap's *Logical Structure of the World* • Lawrence's *Lady Chatterley's Lover* • Yeats's "Sailing to Byzantium"	• Stravinsky's *Apollo* ballet • Ravel's *Boléro* • Brecht's *Threepenny Opera* • Discovery of penicillin	
1929	• **Jürgen Habermas born** • Bernard Williams born • Jean Baudrillard born • Martin Luther King born	• Husserl's *Formal and Transcendental Logic* • **Heidegger's** *Kant and the Problem of Metaphysics* and "What Is Metaphysics?" • **Cassirer's** *Philosophy of Symbolic Forms*, vol. 3 • Whitehead's *Process and Reality* • Woolf's *A Room of One's Own* • Faulkner's *The Sound and the Fury* • Remarque's *All Quiet on the Western Front*	• The Davos debate between **Heidegger** and **Cassirer** • Mother Teresa arrives in India	• Hoover 31st US president • Stock Market Crash • The Great Depression begins
1930	• **Jacques Derrida born** • **Félix Guattari born**	• Freud's *Civilization and Its Discontents* • Ross's *The Right and the Good* • Faulkner's *As I Lay Dying*	• Schoenberg's *Von Heute auf Morgan* (first 12-tone opera) • Pluto is discovered • Wood's *American Gothic*	• Nazi Party makes strong showing in German elections • Dust Bowl drought begins • Gandhi's Salt March protest
1931	• **Charles Taylor born** • Richard Rorty born	• **Husserl's** *Cartesian Meditations* • Jaspers's *Man in the Modern Age*	• Dalí's *Persistence of Memory* • Gödel proves incompleteness theorem • Empire State Building built	

Year	Intellectual/ Cultural Figures	Significant Texts	Cultural/Social Events	Historical Events and Figures
1932	• Luce Irigaray born • Sylvia Plath born • John Searle born	• **Jaspers's** *Philosophy* • Maritain's *The Degrees of Knowledge* • Huxley's *Brave New World*	• Neutron is discovered • Heisenberg awarded Nobel Prize • O'Keeffe's *Jimson Weed*	• Nazi Party wins plurality (but not majority) in Reichstag
1933		• Malraux's *Man's Fate*	• Wittgenstein begins "Blue and Brown Books" seminars • Prohibition repealed in US • First comic books	• Hitler appointed German chancellor by last president • Third Reich proclaimed • F. Roosevelt 32nd US president
1934		• Toynbee's *Study of History*, vol. 1 • H. Miller's *Tropic of Cancer*	• Rachmaninoff's *Paganini Rhapsody*	
1935	• Nietzsche's sister dies • Elvis Presley born • Luciano Pavarotti born • T. E. Lawrence dies	• **Husserl's "Philosophy and the Crisis of European Man"** • **Lévinas's** *On Escape* • Marcel's *Being and Having* • **Jaspers's** *Reason and Existenz* • **Du Bois's** *Black Reconstruction* • T. S. Eliot's *Murder in the Cathedral*	• Hoover Dam dedicated • First color photographic film • Riefenstahl's *Triumph of the Will* (Nazi rally at Nuremberg) • Prokofiev's *Romeo and Juliet* • Gershwin's *Porgy and Bess*	• Italy invades Ethiopia • Roosevelt's "Second New Deal" • Social Security Act passed (US)
1936		• **Heidegger's** *Contributions to Philosophy* • Benjamin's *The Work of Art in the Age of Mechanical Reproduction* • Horkheimer's *Authority and the Family* • Bernanos's *Diary of a Country Priest*	• Turing machine proposed • Prokofiev's *Peter and the Wolf*	• Spanish Civil War begins • Edward VIII becomes king (UK), then abdicates • George VI becomes king
1937	• Alain Badiou born • Hélène Cixous born • Philip Glass born	• **Sartre's** *The Transcendence of the Ego* • Bonhoeffer's *The Cost of Discipleship* • Malraux's *L'Espoir* (*Man's Hope*)	• Picasso's *Guernica* • Dalí's *Narcissus* • Shostakovich's Symphony #5 • Golden Gate Bridge completed • Volkswagen founded • F. L. Wright's Fallingwater completed	• Sino-Japanese War begins • "Rape of Nanking" by Japanese

Year	Intellectual/ Cultural Figures	Significant Texts	Cultural/Social Events	Historical Events and Figures
1938	• Edmund Husserl dies	• Sartre's *Nausea* • Kazantzakis's *Odyssey: A Modern Sequel*	• Magritte's *Time Transfixed* • Copland's *Billy the Kid* • First Superman comic (*Action Comics #1*) • Riefenstahl's *Olympia* (Berlin summer Olympics of 1936)	• Austria absorbed into Germany • Munich Agreement gives Germany the Czech Sudetenland • "Night of Broken Glass" (anti-Jewish pogrom) in Germany
1939	• Sigmund Freud dies	• Sartre's *Sketch for a Theory of the Emotions* • Joyce's *Finnegan's Wake* • Steinbeck's *The Grapes of Wrath*	• Scheduled TV broadcasts begin • The Manhattan Project (named 1942) is proposed • First jet aircraft (German) • Kandinsky's *Composition X*	• Spanish Civil War ends in Franco's dictatorship • German-Soviet Non-aggression Pact • Germany invades Poland • World War II begins
1940	• Saul Kripke born • F. Scott Fitzgerald dies • Paul Klee dies	• **Gehlen's *Man*** • Freud's *Outline of Psycho-Analysis* • **Du Bois's *Dusk of Dawn*** • Wright's *Native Son* • Hemingway's *For Whom the Bell Tolls*		• France surrenders to Germany • Italy allies with Germany • Churchill prime minister (UK)
1941	• **Henri Bergson dies** • Julia Kristeva born • Richard Schacht born	• **Plessner's *Laughing and Crying*** • Marcuse's *Reason and Revolution* • Brecht's *Mother Courage*	• Mount Rushmore sculptures completed	• Germany attacks USSR • Japan attacks Pearl Harbor • US declares war against Japan and Germany
1942	• John McDowell born • Stephen Hawking born • Muhammad Ali born • Edith Stein dies	• **Merleau-Ponty's *The Structure of Behavior*** • Camus' *Stranger* and *Myth of Sisyphus*	• Hopper's *Nighthawks* • German V-2 rocket reaches space • Copland's *Rodeo*	• Gandhi's "Quit India" campaign for Indian independence begins
1943	• **Simone Weil dies**	• **Sartre's *Being and Nothingness*** • **Weil's "Human Personality"** • **Beauvoir's *She Came to Stay*** • Bonhoeffer's *Ethics* written • Hesse's *The Glass Bead Game*		• Allies invade Sicily and Italy • Battle of Stalingrad ends in crucial German defeat

Year	Intellectual/ Cultural Figures	Significant Texts	Cultural/Social Events	Historical Events and Figures
1944	• Edvard Munch dies • Wasily Kandinsky dies	• **Cassirer's** *An Essay on Man* • Anouilh's *Antigone* • Marcel's *Homo Viator*	• **Sartre's** *No Exit* • Bernstein's *On the Town* • Copland's *Appalachian Spring*	• D-Day (invasion of Normandy) • Soviet armies enter Germany • Battle of the Bulge (last German offensive)
1945	• **Ernst Cassirer dies** • Dietrich Bonhoeffer dies • Béla Bartók dies	• **Sartre's** *The Age of Reason* and *The Reprieve* • **Merleau-Ponty's** *The Phenomenology of Perception* • **Du Bois's** *Color and Democracy*	• "Trinity": first detonation of a nuclear weapon • Prokofiev's *Cinderella*	• F. Roosevelt dies • Truman 33rd US president • Hitler commits suicide • Atomic bombs dropped on Hiroshima and Nagasaki • World War II ends • United Nations established
1946		• **Sartre's "Existentialism Is a Humanism"** • Sartre's *Anti-Semite and Jew* • Beauvoir's *All Men Are Mortal* • **Cassirer's** *The Myth of the State* • Kazantzakis's *Zorba the Greek*	• ENIAC computer built	• "Iron Curtain" divides Europe, separating Soviet client states from the West
1947		• **Heidegger's "Letter on Humanism"** • **Beauvoir's** *The Ethics of Ambiguity* • **Jaspers's** *On Truth* • **Lévinas's** *Time and the Other* and *Existence and Existents* • Adorno and Horkheimer's *Dialectic of Enlightenment* • Camus' *The Plague*	• Rothko's abstract expressionism • Matisse's *Jazz* (cutouts) • Pollock pioneers drip technique	• Cold War begins • Independence of India and its partition into India and Pakistan • UN divides Palestine into an Arab and a Jewish state
1948	• Babe Ruth dies	• **Buber's** *The Way of Man* • **Wittgenstein writes part II of** *Philosophical Investigations* • Mailer's *The Naked and the Dead*	• International law against genocide approved by the UN • Pollock's *Number 5* • Wyeth's *Christina's World*	• Israel declares independence • First Arab–Israeli War • Communist coup in Czechoslovakia • The Berlin Blockade: first international crisis of Cold War

Year	Intellectual/ Cultural Figures	Significant Texts	Cultural/Social Events	Historical Events and Figures
1949	• Richard Strauss dies	• **Beauvoir's *The Second Sex*** • Ryle's *The Concept of Mind* • Orwell's *1984* • **Sartre's *Troubled Sleep*** • Genet's *The Thief's Journal*	• A. Miller's *Death of a Salesman* • First Volkswagen sold in US	• NATO established • Mao Zedong proclaims the People's Republic of China • Apartheid made official policy in South Africa • Indonesian independence
1950	• Nicolai Hartmann dies	• **Jaspers's *The Way to Wisdom*** • Marcel's Gifford Lectures (published as *The Mystery of Being*) • **Ricoeur's *Freedom and Nature*** • Ionesco's *The Bald Soprano*	• Mother Teresa founds the Missionaries of Charity • Chagall's *The Bride* • Picasso's *She-Goat* • Pollock's *Number 1, 1950*	• The Korean War begins • China invades Tibet
1951	• Arnold Schoenberg dies • Ludwig Wittgenstein dies	• Marcel's *Man Against Mass Society* • **Heidegger's "Building Dwelling Thinking"** • **Arendt's *Origins of Totalitarianism*** • Camus' *The Rebel* • Salinger's *Catcher in the Rye*		
1952	• John Dewey dies • George Santayana dies	• **Sartre's *Saint Genet*** • **Fanon's *Black Skin, White Masks*** • **Buber's *Images of Good and Evil*** • Hemingway's *The Old Man and the Sea*	• First commercial jet airplanes • Matisse's *Blue Nude II* cutout	• Elizabeth II queen (UK) • American hydrogen bomb tested
1953		• **Deleuze's *Empiricism and Subjectivity*** • Baldwin's *Go Tell It on the Mountain* • Thomas's "Do Not Go Gentle" • Bellow's *Adventures of Augie March* • Skinner's *Science and Human Behavior*	• Structure of DNA discovered • Prokofiev's *War and Peace* • Beckett's *Waiting for Godot* • A. Miller's *The Crucible*	• Eisenhower 34th US president • Korean War ends • Stalin dies • Soviet hydrogen bomb tested
1954	• Enrico Fermi dies • Henri Matisse dies	• **Beauvoir's *The Mandarins*** • Golding's *Lord of the Flies* • Thomas's *Under Milk Wood*	• *Brown v. Board of Education* orders US school desegregation • Copland's *The Tender Land* • First color TVs sold • Bannister's sub–4-minute mile (first)	• French leave Indochina • Vietnam split into North and South

Year	Intellectual/ Cultural Figures	Significant Texts	Cultural/Social Events	Historical Events and Figures
1955	• Thomas Mann dies • José Ortega y Gasset dies	• Lévi-Strauss's *Tristes Tropiques* • **Merleau-Ponty's** *Adventures of the Dialectic* • Marcuse's *Eros and Civilization* • Kazantzakis's *The Last Temptation of Christ* • Nabokov's *Lolita* • Baldwin's *Notes of a Native Son*	• The Montgomery bus boycott starts • Austin gives William James Lectures at Harvard, "How to Do Things with Words"	
1956	• **Judith Butler** born	• Camus' *The Fall* • Ginsberg's *Howl* • Genet's *The Balcony*	• The neutrino is detected • Bernstein's *Candide* • O'Neill's *Long Day's Journey into Night*	• Hungarian uprising; crushed by Soviet invasion
1957	• Nikos Kazantzakis dies	• **Sartre's** *Search for a Method* • **Gehlen's** *Man in the Age of Technology* • Lonergan's *Insight* • Bataille's *Eroticism* • Pasternak's *Doctor Zhivago* • Kerouac's *On the Road*	• Sputnik launched by USSR • Beckett's *Endgame* • Bernstein's *West Side Story* • First Japanese cars sold in US	• Common Market created in Europe • British hydrogen bomb tested • Communist insurgency in South Vietnam begins
1958	• **Martha Nussbaum** born • G. E. Moore dies	• **Arendt's** *The Human Condition* • Lévi-Strauss's *Structural Anthropology* • Polanyi's *Personal Knowledge* • Genet's *The Blacks*	• Van der Rohe's Seagram Building	• De Gaulle president (France) • Khrushchev premier (USSR) • Military coup in Iraq ends monarchy
1959	• Frank Lloyd Wright dies	• Grass's *The Tin Drum* • Fanon's *A Dying Colonialism*	• Anouilh's *Becket* • Wright's Guggenheim Museum • Earliest case of AIDS in Africa	• Cuban Revolution • Castro becomes Cuba's premier
1960	• Albert Camus dies • J. L. Austin dies	• **Gadamer's** *Truth and Method* • **Sartre's** *Critique of Dialectical Reason* • **Ricoeur's** *Fallible Man & Symbolism of Evil* • Quine's *Word and Object* • Lee's *To Kill a Mockingbird*	• Birth control pill approved by FDA	

Year	Intellectual/ Cultural Figures	Significant Texts	Cultural/Social Events	Historical Events and Figures
1961	• **Maurice Merleau-Ponty** dies • **Frantz Fanon** dies • Ernest Hemingway dies	• **Foucault's** *Madness and Civilization* • **Lévinas's** *Totality and Infinity* • **Fanon's** *The Wretched of the Earth* • Heller's *Catch-22* • Updike's *Rabbit, Run* • Toynbee's *Study of History*, final vol. (12)	• First human space flight (USSR)	• Kennedy 35th US president • Bay of Pigs invasion (by US of Cuba) • Berlin Wall built to halt East Germans' access to West Berlin
1962	• Hermann Hesse dies • William Faulkner dies • Georges Bataille dies	• **Deleuze's** *Nietzsche and Philosophy* • Austin's *Sense and Sensibilia* • Lévi-Strauss's *The Savage Mind* • Rachel Carson's *Silent Spring* • Solzhenitsyn's *A Day in the Life of Ivan Denisovich* • Borges's *Labyrinths*	• Second Vatican Council begins • Shostakovich's Symphony #13 • Warhol's *Campbell's Soup Cans*	• US/USSR Cuban missile crisis
1963	• **W. E. B. Du Bois** dies • Sylvia Plath dies	• **Foucault's** *The Birth of the Clinic* • **Arendt's** *Eichmann in Jerusalem* • Plath's *The Bell Jar*	• King's "I Have a Dream" speech • Beatlemania begins in UK • Bernstein's Symphony #3 • Lichtenstein's *Drowning Girl*	• Kennedy assassinated • L. Johnson 36th US president
1964		• **Heidegger's** "The End of Philosophy" • **Taylor's** *The Explanation of Behavior* • Marcuse's *One-Dimensional Man* • McLuhan's *Understanding Media*	• King awarded Nobel Peace Prize • **Sartre** awarded (but refuses) Nobel Prize in Literature • Civil Rights Act (US)	• Gulf of Tonkin Resolution (authorizing US military action in Vietnam)
1965	• **Martin Buber** dies • T. S. Eliot dies • Paul Tillich dies	• **Ricoeur's** *Freud and Philosophy* • Capote's *In Cold Blood*	• Saarinen's Gateway Arch built	• Medicare enacted (US) • Malcolm X assassinated
1966		• Lacan's *Écrits* • **Derrida's** "Structure, Sign, and Play" lecture • Lorenz's *On Aggression* • Anais Nin's *Diary*		• China's Cultural Revolution begins

Year	Intellectual/ Cultural Figures	Significant Texts	Cultural/Social Events	Historical Events and Figures
1967		• Gadamer's "On the Scope and Function of Hermeneutical Understanding" • Derrida's *Of Grammatology* • Horkheimer's *Critique of Instrumental Reason* • Márquez's *One Hundred Years of Solitude*	• "Summer of Love" (US) • Picasso's "Chicago" sculpture	• Chinese hydrogen bomb tested • Che Guevara killed • Israel captures Gaza and the West Bank in Six-Day War
1968	• Marcel Duchamp dies	• Habermas's *Knowledge and Human Interests* • Derrida's "Différance" lecture • Deleuze's *Difference and Repetition* and *Expressionism in Philosophy* • Solzhenitsyn's *The First Circle*	• May '68 in France (student protests and general strike) • Picasso's *Nude with Necklace*	• French hydrogen bomb tested • M. L. King assassinated • R. Kennedy assassinated
1969	• **Karl Jaspers** dies • Jack Kerouac dies	• Foucault's *The Archaeology of Knowledge* • Deleuze's *The Logic of Sense* • Vonnegut's *Slaughterhouse-Five*	• Men land on the moon (US) • Woodstock music festival • Stonewall riots (New York) • First death from AIDS in US	• De Gaulle resigns French presidency • Arafat chairman of PLO • Nixon 37th US president
1970	• Bertrand Russell dies • Rudolf Carnap dies	• Taylor's *The Patterns of Politics*	• The first Earth Day	
1971	• Georg Lukács dies • Igor Stravinsky dies	• Habermas's *Theory and Practice* • Murdoch's *The Sovereignty of the Good* • Rawls's *A Theory of Justice* • Gadamer's *Hegel's Dialectic* • Ricoeur's "The Model of the Text"	• Soft contact lenses marketed in US	
1972		• Derrida's *Margins of Philosophy* and *Dissemination* • Deleuze and Guattari's *Anti-Oedipus*		• Nixon visits China • Watergate break-in (Nixon scandal)
1973	• Pablo Picasso dies • Gabriel Marcel dies	• Habermas's *Legitimation Crisis* • Solzhenitsyn's *Gulag Archipelago*, vol. 1 • Pynchon's *Gravity's Rainbow*	• *Roe v. Wade* establishes right to abortion (US)	• Yom Kippur War (Arab–Israeli) • US oil crisis

Year	Intellectual/ Cultural Figures	Significant Texts	Cultural/Social Events	Historical Events and Figures
1974		• **Lévinas's** *Otherwise Than Being* • **Lyotard's** *Libidinal Economy* • **Nozick's** *Anarchy, State and Utopia* • Irigaray's *Speculum of the Other Woman*	• Personal computer invented	• Nixon resigns • Ford 38th US president • First nuclear test by India
1975	• **Hannah Arendt** dies	• **Foucault's** *Discipline and Punish* • **Ricoeur's** *The Rule of Metaphor* • **Taylor's** *Hegel* • Cixous & Clément's *The Newly Born Woman* • Solzhenitsyn's *Gulag*, final vol. (3)		• Indonesia invades and occupies East Timor • Khmer Rouge rule begins in Cambodia
1976	• **Martin Heidegger** dies • **Arnold Gehlen** dies • Gilbert Ryle dies	• **Foucault's** *The History of Sexuality*, vol. 1 • **Habermas's** *Communication and the Evolution of Society* • **Gadamer's** *Reason in the Age of Science*		
1977				• Carter 39th US president
1978		• **Arendt's** *The Life of the Mind* (posthumous) • **Derrida's** *The Truth in Painting*		
1979	• Herbert Marcuse dies	• **Lyotard's** *The Postmodern Condition* • **Taylor's** *Hegel and Modern Society*	• Mother Teresa awarded Nobel Peace Prize	• Iranian Revolution • US oil crisis • Saddam Hussein president (Iraq) • Thatcher first female prime minister (UK) • Soviet Union invades Afghanistan
1980	• **Jean-Paul Sartre** dies • Roland Barthes dies • John Lennon assassinated	• **Derrida's** *The Post Card* • **Deleuze & Guattari's** *A Thousand Plateaus* • Eco's *The Name of the Rose*		
1981	• **Jacques Lacan** dies • John Paul II shot	• **Habermas's** *Theory of Communicative Action*	• The **Derrida–Gadamer** debate	• Reagan 40th US president

Year	Intellectual/ Cultural Figures	Significant Texts	Cultural/Social Events	Historical Events and Figures
1982			• AIDS named	
1983	• Joan Miró dies • Tennessee Williams dies	• **Ricoeur's** *Time and Narrative*, vol. 1 • **Habermas's** *Moral Consciousness and Communicative Action* • **Lyotard's** *The Differend*		
1984	• **Michel Foucault** dies	• **Foucault's** *History of Sexuality*, vols. 2 & 3 • **Foucault's "What Is Enlightenment?"**		
1985	• **Helmuth Plessner** dies	• **Habermas's** *Discourse of Modernity* • **Taylor's** *Philosophical Papers* • Williams's *Ethics and the Limit of Philosophy* • García Márquez's *Love in the Time of Cholera*		• Reagan's 2nd term • Gorbachev general secretary (USSR)
1986	• **Simone de Beauvoir** dies • Jean Genet dies • Georgia O'Keeffe dies	• **Nussbaum's** *The Fragility of Goodness* • Dawkins's *The Blind Watchmaker* • Nancy's *The Inoperative Community*	• Wiesel awarded Nobel Peace Prize • Space shuttle *Challenger* explodes	• Iran-Contra affair (Reagan scandal)
1987	• Andy Warhol dies	• **Butler's** *Subjects of Desire* • **Derrida's** *Of Spirit* • Morrison's *Beloved*		• US Stock Market Crash
1988		• **Lyotard's** *The Inhuman* • **Deleuze's** *The Fold* • Badiou's *Being and Event*	• First World AIDS Day	• Kurdish genocide in Iraq • Iran-Iraq war ends
1989	• Samuel Beckett dies • A. J. Ayer dies	• Rorty's *Contingency, Irony, and Solidarity* • **Taylor's** *Sources of the Self*		• G. H. W. Bush 41st US president • The Berlin Wall falls
1990	• Louis Althusser dies	• **Ricoeur's** *Oneself as Another* • **Butler's** *Gender Trouble* • **Nussbaum's** *Love's Knowledge* • **Habermas's** *The Discourse of Modernity*	• Human genome project begins	• German reunification • Iraq invades Kuwait • Russia declares independence

Year	Intellectual/ Cultural Figures	Significant Texts	Cultural/Social Events	Historical Events and Figures
1991		• Lyotard's *On the Analytic of the Sublime* • Habermas's *Justification and Application* • **Deleuze and Guattari's *What Is Philosophy?*** • Habermas's *The Structural Transformation of the Public Sphere*	• Christo's *Umbrellas*	• The Persian Gulf War • Apartheid ends in South Africa • USSR dissolves; former Soviet republics achieve independence • Yeltsin 1st president of Russian Republic
1992	• **Félix Guattari** dies	• Habermas's *Between Facts and Norms* • Taylor's *The Ethics of Authenticity* • Derrida's *The Gift of Death* • Guattari's *Chaosmosis*	• Rodney King riots (Los Angeles)	• Bosnian war begins • European Union created
1993		• Gadamer's *The Enigma of Health* • Butler's *Bodies That Matter*	• Mandela awarded Nobel Peace Prize	• Clinton 42nd US president
1994		• Derrida's *The Politics of Friendship* • Nussbaum's *The Theory of Desire*		• Rwandan genocide
1995	• **Gilles Deleuze** dies • **Emmanuel Lévinas** dies	• Ricoeur's *The Just* • Taylor's *Philosophical Arguments*		• Bosnian genocide • Oklahoma City bombing • US budget crisis
1996	Thomas Kuhn dies	• **Wallace's *Infinite Jest***		
1997	• Mother Teresa dies	• Nussbaum's *Cultivating Humanity* • Butler's *The Psychic Life of Power*	• Rowling's first *Harry Potter* book • US rover lands on Mars	• Clinton's 2nd term • Hong Kong returns to Chinese rule
1998	• Frank Sinatra dies • Octavio Paz dies		• Space station assembly begins • Viagra approved by US FDA • *Seinfeld* (TV series) ends	• EU members agree to common currency (Euro) • US House impeaches Clinton
1999	• Stanley Kubrick dies	• **Nussbaum's *Sex and Social Justice***	• 2nd *Star Wars* trilogy begins • First human hand transplant with long-term success	• NATO intervenes in Kosovo war; Belgrade is bombed • US Senate acquits Clinton

Year	Intellectual/ Cultural Figures	Significant Texts	Cultural/Social Events	Historical Events and Figures
2000	• Charles Schulz dies • John Gielgud dies • Alec Guinness dies		• Human genome draft published • Abortion pill approved by USDA	• Putin 2nd president of Russian Republic • US presidential election decided in Supreme Court (in favor of Bush) • Global concern over "mad cow" disease
2001	• G. E. M. Anscombe dies • George Harrison dies	• **Nussbaum's** *Upheavals of Thought*	• First *Lord of the Rings* and *Harry Potter* movies	• G. W. Bush 43rd US president • 9/11 terrorist attacks ("Twin Towers") • US and UK intervene in Afghanistan
2002	• John Rawls dies • Stephen Jay Gould dies • Princess Margaret dies		• Debut of *The Osbournes* (TV reality show)	• AIDS is leading cause of death worldwide among those aged 15–59
2003	• Bernard Williams dies • Donald Davidson dies • Johnny Cash dies		• Space shuttle *Columbia* breaks up on reentry • DNA sequence of Y chromosome published • Age of universe calculated (13.7 billion years)	• Yugoslavia breaks up • NATO assumes control of support mission in Afghanistan
2004	• Yasir Arafat dies • Marlon Brando dies • Julia Child dies	• **Taylor's** *Modern Social Imaginaries* • **Nussbaum's** *Hiding from Humanity* • **Butler's** *Precarious Life*	• First gay marriages recognized in US (in Mass.) • Evidence of water found on Mars • Google goes public	• Reagan dies • US transfers political power in Iraq to interim civilian government
2005	• John Paul II dies • Saul Bellow dies • Arthur Miller dies	• **Butler's** *Giving an Account of Oneself*	• *Brokeback Mountain* (movie)	• Benedict XVI becomes pope • Merkel first female German chancellor • G. W. Bush's 2nd term
2006	• Betty Friedan dies	• **Nussbaum's** *Frontiers of Justice*	• Pluto reclassified: no longer a planet	• Gerald Ford dies • Saddam Hussein is executed
2007	• Art Buchwald dies • Kurt Vonnegut dies • Norman Mailer dies	• **Taylor's** *A Secular Age*	• UN report ties global warming to human activity	• Yeltsin dies • Pelosi 1st female Speaker of the House (US)

Year	Intellectual/ Cultural Figures	Significant Texts	Cultural/Social Events	Historical Events and Figures
2008	• David Foster Wallace dies • Aleksandr Solzhenitsyn dies		• Large Hadron Collider tested • Collins's first *Hunger Games* book	• Bill Gates begins transition out of leadership of Microsoft
2009	• Michael Jackson dies • Ted Kennedy dies • Walter Cronkite dies	• **Butler's** *Frames of War*	• Fossil skeleton of oldest known human ancestor found: 4.4 million years old	• Sotomayor 1st Hispanic Supreme Court justice (US) • Obama 44th US president
2010	• J. D. Salinger dies			• Largest oil spill in history in Gulf of Mexico (caused by BP-leased oil rig)
2011	• Václav Havel dies • Elizabeth Taylor dies	• **Butler, Habermas, Taylor,** and Cornel West, *The Power of Religion in the Public Sphere*	• 135th and last US space shuttle flight	• Osama bin Laden killed • "Arab Spring" protests spread • Libyan civil war ousts Gaddafi, who is killed
2012	• Dave Brubeck dies • Neil Armstrong dies		• Higgs boson found • Two Mars rovers land • First *Hunger Games* movie	• Putin's 3rd term (Russia)
2013	• Nelson Mandela dies		• Human embryonic stem cells cloned	• Obama's 2nd term • Edward Snowden leaks NSA secrets • Thatcher dies • Benedict XVI resigns; Francis I becomes pope
2014	• Robin Williams dies		• First probe landed on a comet	• ISIS proclaims caliphate • Ebola outbreak in West Africa • Crimea incorporated into Russian Federation
2015	• Günter Grass dies • Oliver Sacks dies • Yogi Berra dies	• **Taylor** and Dreyfus's *Retrieving Realism* • **Butler's** *Senses of the Subject* • **Butler's** *Notes toward a Performative Theory of Assembly* • **Nussbaum's** "Transitional Anger"	• Evidence of flowing water found on Mars	• First legally binding global climate accord (Paris) • Iran agrees to curb its nuclear program • US Supreme Court strikes down bans on same-sex marriage
2016	• Hilary Putnam dies • Muhammad Ali dies	• **Nussbaum's** *Anger and Forgiveness*		

Selected Bibliographies

General Bibliographies: Periods, Movements, and Areas

I. SURVEYS

NINETEENTH AND TWENTIETH CENTURIES

One of the most accessible surveys of nineteenth- and early twentieth-century European philosophy is Frederick Copleston's *A History of Philosophy*, vol. 7, *Fichte to Nietzsche* (1963). It treats Fichte, Schelling, Friedrich Schliermacher, Hegel, critics of Hegel such as Johann Herbart, Schopenhauer, Feuerbach and left-Hegelianism, Marx, Friedrich Albert Lange and materialism, Neo-Kantianism, Nietzsche, and the emergence of twentieth-century movements such as phenomenology, *Lebensphilosophie* ("life-philosophy," or the philosophy of human and other forms of life), and hermeneutics.

William R. Schroeder's *Continental Philosophy: A Critical Approach* (2005), David West's *An Introduction to Continental Philosophy* (1996), and Andrew Cutrofello's *Continental Philosophy: A Contemporary Introduction* (2005) provide broad surveys—each with its own merits—of nineteenth- and twentieth-century Continental philosophy (in the interpretive tradition). Robert C. Solomon's *Continental Philosophy since 1750: The Rise and Fall of the Self* (1988), less expansive and complete, tells the story of Continental philosophy from Kant to structuralism and poststructuralism through the theme of the self. Richard Schacht's *Hegel and After: Studies in Continental Philosophy between Kant and Sartre* (1975) attempts to bridge the analytic/interpretive divide in essays dealing with figures from Hegel to Sartre. Essays in *The Cambridge History of Philosophy, 1870–1945*, edited by Thomas Baldwin (2003), discuss developments in both Continental and analytic philosophy in the nineteenth century (positivism, Neo-Kantianism, Anglo-American Idealism, Nietzsche, Marxism, and a variety of themes) and twentieth century (Bergson, pragmatism, Neo-Thomism, phenomenology, Heidegger, and Western Marxism).

Major figures of German philosophy during the past several centuries are examined in Andrew Bowie, *Introduction to German Philosophy: From Kant to Habermas* (2003), and Julian Roberts, *German Philosophy: An Introduction* (1988). Herbart Schnädelbach, *Philosophy in Germany, 1831–1933* (1983; trans. 1984), is an important discussion of the nineteenth-century roots of hermeneutics, existentialism and phenomenology—in particular, the movements of Neo-Kantianism and *Lebensphilosophie*, which flourished in the aftermath of absolute idealism. Joseph M. Bochenski, *Contemporary European Philosophy* (1947; trans. 1956), endeavors to trace a return to realism in the major movements of the first half of the twentieth century (in particular, positivism, dialectical materialism, *Lebensphilosophie*, phenomenology, and existentialism), examining the nineteenth-century roots of these movements as well as the return to metaphysics in Nicolai Hartmann, Alfred North Whitehead, and the Neo-Thomists. Three interesting works by Robert B. Pippin examine nineteenth- and twentieth-century Continental philosophy through the lens of Kant, Hegel, Nietzsche, and a host of cultural and philosophical issues surrounding modernity, postmodernity, nihilism, and the loss of meaning: *Modernism as a Philosophical Problem: On the Dissatisfactions of European High Culture* (2nd ed., 1999), *Idealism as Modernism: Hegelian Variations* (1997), and *The Persistence of Subjectivity: On the Kantian Aftermath* (2005).

Volumes of essays surveying both nineteenth- and twentieth-century philosophy include *A Companion to Continental Philosophy*, edited by Simon Critchley and William Schroeder (1998); *The Oxford Handbook of Continental Philosophy*, edited by Brian Leiter and Michael Rosen (2007); *German Philosophy Since Kant*, edited by Anthony O'Hear (1999); *The Blackwell Guide to Continental Philosophy*, edited by Robert C. Solomon and David Sherman (2003); and Roger Scruton, *A Short History of Modern Philosophy: From Descartes to Wittgenstein* (2nd ed., 1995).

NINETEENTH CENTURY

A comprehensive and diverse treatment of the nineteenth century can be found in W. T. Jones's *A History of Western Philosophy*, vol. 4, *Kant and the Nineteenth Century* (2nd ed., 1969), which deals not only with Kant, Hegel, Schopenhauer, Kierkegaard, and Nietzsche but also with Hans Driesch's vitalism, the positivism of Auguste Comte and Ernst Mach, the materialism of Ernst Haeckel, the pragmatism of C. S. Peirce and William James, and the idealism of F. H. Bradley.

A classic German survey of this period in the history of philosophy is Wilhelm Windelband's *A History of Philosophy: With Especial Reference to the Formation and Development of Its Problems and Conceptions* (1892; trans., 2nd ed., 1901). The first half of the book ranges over Enlightenment and Renaissance thought in Germany, Britain, and France; the latter half surveys Kantian philosophy, German Idealism, and the plethora of realist, Idealist, and materialist movements that emerged in Europe in the latter half of the nineteenth century, as well as the concurrent development of value theory.

Karl Löwith's *From Hegel to Nietzsche: The Revolution in Nineteenth-Century Thought* (1941; trans. 1964) is another classic German study of developments beginning with Goethe and Hegel and proceeding through the "Young Hegelians" and the criticisms of Hegelianism by Marx and Kierkegaard. It also contains an interesting discussion of Nietzsche, as well as an analysis of several important themes in nineteenth-century philosophy, particularly work, Christianity, and bourgeois society.

Charles Taylor's *Sources of the Self: The Making of the Modern Identity* (1989) tells the larger story of the development of modern thought and culture in the nineteenth century and its influence on how the self has come to be conceived. An earlier work of similar breadth and focus is George Herbert Mead's *Movements of Thought in the Nineteenth Century* (1936), which explores the relation of industrialization, science, psychology, and technology to the development of modern consciousness. Mead discusses vitalism, pragmatism, and positivistic philosophy.

Terry Pinkard's *German Philosophy, 1760–1860: The Legacy of Idealism* (2002) begins with Kant and his immediate reception by Friedrich Jacobi, Karl Reinhold, and Fichte; discusses Romanticism in the philosophies of Friedrich Hölderlin, Novalis, Friedrich Schlegel, and Schelling; and treats Hegel and the reactions against Hegelianism in Schelling, Kierkegaard, and Schopenhauer.

Other useful books dealing with European philosophy in the nineteenth century include Robert C. Solomon, *History and Human Nature: A Philosophical Review of European Philosophy and Culture, 1750–1850* (1979); *The Edinburgh Critical History of Nineteenth-Century Philosophy*, edited by Alison Stone (2011); *The Nineteenth Century*, edited by C. L. Ten (1994); *German Philosophers: Kant, Hegel, Schopenhauer, and Nietzsche* (1997), containing essays by Roger Scruton (Kant), Peter Singer (Hegel), Christopher Janaway (Schopenhauer), and Michael Tanner (Nietzsche); *The Routledge Companion to Nineteenth Century Philosophy*, edited by Dean Moyar (2010); and *Nineteenth-Century Philosophy: Revolutionary Responses to the Existing Order*, edited by Alan Schrift and Daniel Conway (2013).

TWENTIETH CENTURY AND BEYOND

A classic survey of twentieth-century thought is Frederick Copleston's *A History of Philosophy*, vol. 9, *Maine de Biran to Sartre* (1974). It begins with positivism and *Lebensphilosophie* and goes on to discuss twentieth-century Neo-Thomism, personalism, developments in the philosophy of science, existentialism, and phenomenology. Three helpful resources for thinking about twentieth-century philosophy in general are *One Hundred Twentieth-Century Philosophers*, edited by Stuart Brown, Diané Collinson, and Robert Wilkinson (1998); Simon Glendinning, *The Idea of Continental Philosophy: A Philosophical Chronicle* (2006); and *The Edinburgh Dictionary of Continental Philosophy*, edited by John Proteri (2006).

Helpful general surveys of the major movements of twentieth-century philosophy include Robert D'Amico, *Contemporary Continental Philosophy* (1999); Peter Dews, *The Limits of Disenchantment: Essays on Contemporary European Philosophy* (1995); Richard Kearney, *Modern Movements in European Philosophy* (2nd ed., 1994); John McCumber, *Philosophy and Freedom: Derrida, Rorty, Habermas, Foucault* (2000); William Ralph Schroeder, *Sartre and His Predecessors: The Self and the Other* (1984), and Richard Wolin, *The Terms of Cultural Criticism: The Frankfurt School, Existentialism, Poststructuralism* (1992).

The major movements and themes in both the analytic and interpretive traditions are the subject of essays in *Columbia Companion to Twentieth-Century Philosophies*, edited by Constantin V. Boundas (2007), and *The Routledge Companion to Twentieth-Century Philosophy*, edited by Dermot Moran (2008). Christian Delacampagne, in *A History of Philosophy in the Twentieth Century* (1995; trans. 1999), also discusses developments in both Continental and analytic philosophy. *Continental Philosophy in the 20th Century*, edited by Richard Kearney (1994), collects essays by leading scholars on the major figures and movements of Continental philosophy. Several recent surveys of the field are Lee Braver, *A Thing of This World: A History of Continental Anti-realism* (2007); David West, *Continental Philosophy: An Introduction* (2nd ed., 2010); John McCumber, *Time and Philosophy: A History of Continental Thought* (2011); and Leonard Lawlor, *Early Twentieth-Century Continental Philosophy* (2012).

Three works focusing on German thinkers are Rüdiger Bubner, *Modern German Philosophy* (1981); Paul Gorner, *Twentieth Century German Philosophy* (2000); and Richard Wolin, *Heidegger's Children: Hannah Arendt, Karl Löwith, Hans Jonas, and Herbert Marcuse* (2001). Recent works focusing on French thought include Vincent Descombes, *Modern French Philosophy* (1979; trans. 1980); Gary Gutting, *French Philosophy in the Twentieth Century* (2001) and *Thinking the Impossible: French Philosophy since 1960* (2011); *The Columbia History of Twentieth-Century French Thought*, edited by Lawrence D. Kritzman (2006); Eric Matthews, *Twentieth-Century French Philosophy* (1996); Tom Rockmore, *Heidegger and French Philosophy: Humanism, Antihumanism and Being* (1995); Alan D. Schrift, *Twentieth-Century French Philosophy: Key Themes and Thinkers* (2006), which offers short biographies of all the major and minor French thinkers of the twentieth century and an extensive bibliography of their works; Hugh Silverman, *Inscriptions: After Phenomenology and Structuralism* (2nd ed., 1997); and Robert Wicks, *Modern French Philosophy: From Existentialism to Postmodernism* (2003).

II. NINETEENTH-CENTURY MOVEMENTS

GERMAN IDEALISM

Frederick C. Beiser's *The Fate of Reason: German Philosophy from Kant to Fichte* (1987) is a study of the major debates and controversy that sprang up in Kant's wake. It includes discussions of Johann Georg Hamann, Friedrich Jacobi, Johann Herder, Karl Reinhold, G. E. Schulze, and Solomon Maimon. Beiser's *German Idealism: The Struggle against Subjectivism, 1781–1801* (2002) is a sophisticated treatment of Kant's Idealism as it developed over time, followed by a significant study of Fichte and the development of absolute idealism in Friedrich Hölderlin, Novalis, Friedrich Schlegel, and Schelling.

Other useful works that focus on major figures of post-Kantian German Idealism are Josiah Royce, *Lectures on Modern Idealism* (1919), an early twentieth-century classic; Karl Ameriks, *Kant and the Fate of Autonomy: Problems in the Appropriation of the Critical Philosophy* (2000); *The Cambridge Companion to German Idealism*, edited by Karl Ameriks (2000); Lewis White Beck, *Early German Philosophy: Kant and His Predecessors* (1969); Rüdiger Bubner, *The Innovations of Idealism* (1995; trans. 2003); Will Dudley, *Understanding German Idealism* (2007); Dieter Henrich, *Between Kant and Hegel: Lectures on German Idealism* (2003); *The Routledge Handbook to German Idealism*, edited by Brian O'Connor et al. (2015); and *The Impact of Idealism: The Legacy of Post-Kantian German Thought*, edited by Nicholas Boyle, Liz Disley, and Karl Ameriks (4 vols., 2013).

David James's *Rousseau and German Idealism: Freedom, Dependence and Necessity* (2013) explores the deep influences of Rousseau's thought on this movement. Among works that examine Kantian and post-Kantian Idealism from an "analytic-philosophical" perspective are Paul W. Franks, *All or Nothing: Systematicity, Transcendental Arguments, and Skepticism in German Idealism* (2005); Tom Rockmore, *Hegel, Idealism, and Analytic Philosophy* (2005) and *Kant and Idealism* (2007); and *German Idealism: Contemporary Perspectives*, edited by Espen Hammer (2007). Other useful volumes of recent essays on German Idealism include *The Modern Subject: Conceptions of the Self in Classical German Philosophy*, edited by Karl Ameriks and Dieter Sturma (1995); Dieter Henrich, *The Course of Remembrance and Other Essays on Hölderlin* (trans. 1997); *The Emergence of German Idealism*, edited by Michael Baur and Daniel O. Dahlstrom (1999); *Figuring the Self: Subject, Absolute, and Others in Classical German Philosophy*, edited by David E. Klemm and Günter Zöller (1997); *The Reception of Kant's Critical Philosophy: Fichte, Schelling, and Hegel*, edited by Sally Sedgwick (2000); and *The Age of German Idealism*, edited by Robert Solomon and Kathleen Higgins, vol. 6 of the *Routledge History of Philosophy* (1993).

ROMANTICISM

Useful discussions of the development of Romantic philosophy and culture can be found in Frederick C. Beiser, *The Romantic Imperative: The Concept of Early German Romanticism* (2003) and *Enlightenment, Revolution, and Romanticism: The Genesis of German Political Thought, 1790–1800* (1992), as well as in Isaiah Berlin, *The Roots of Romanticism* (1999) and *Three Critics of the Enlightenment: Vico, Hamann, Herder* (2000; 2nd ed., 2013). Robert J. Richards's *The Romantic Conception of Life: Science and Philosophy in the Age of Goethe* (2002) is a magisterial examination of the philosophy of Romanticism and, in particular, its relation to science. It is the most complete study available of the roots of *Lebensphilosophie* within the philosophies and science of the late Enlightenment and Romantic periods. Other good studies are George S. Williamson, *The Longing for Myth in Germany: Religion and Aesthetic Culture from Romanticism to Nietzsche* (2004); Manfred Frank, *The Philosophical Foundations of Early German Romanticism* (1997; trans. 2004); Elizabeth Millán-Zaibert, *Friedrich Schlegel and the Emergence of Romantic Philosophy* (2007); and Dalia Nassar, *The Romantic Absolute: Being and Knowing in Early German Romantic Philosophy, 1795–1804* (2013).

Selections from Romantic thinkers are becoming more widely available. Writings of Schlegel, Schleiermacher, and Novalis are translated in *The Early Political Writings of the German Romantics*, edited by Frederick C. Beiser (1996); and *Classic and Romantic German Aesthetics*, edited by J. M. Bernstein (2003), contains selections from Schiller, Hölderlin, Lessing, Novalis, Schlegel, and others.

LEFT-HEGELIANISM AND MARXISM

Hegelianism itself was an important movement that influenced a series of thinkers, including David Strauss, Feuerbach, Bruno Bauer and Edgar Bauer, Arnold Ruge, Marx and Engels, Max Stirner, and Karl Schmidt. Selections from their writings are collected in *The Young Hegelians: An Anthology*, edited by Lawrence S. Stepelevich (1983). Notable secondary works on these early transformations of Hegelian thought and its development toward and into Marxism include the classic studies Sidney Hook, *From Hegel to Marx: Studies in the Intellectual Development of Karl Marx* (1936); Herbert Marcuse, *Reason and Revolution: Hegel and the Rise of Social Theory* (1941; 2nd ed., 1954); Louis Dupré, *The Philosophical Foundations of Marxism* (1966); and David McLellan, *The Young Hegelians and Karl Marx* (1969), as well as Christopher J. Arthur, *Dialectics of Labour: Marx and His Relation to Hegel* (1986) and *The New Dialectic and Marx's "Capital"* (2002); Warren Breckman, *Marx, The Young Hegelians, and the Origins of Radical Social Theory: Dethroning the Self* (1999); and David Leopold, *The Young Karl Marx: German Philosophy, Modern Politics, and Human Flourishing* (2007).

The literature of and on Marxism as philosophy is vast, though much of it is of little interest and value, other than for the light it sheds on one of the stranger chapters in modern European intellectual history. One exception among the largely stultifying writings of the "orthodox" Marxist theorists is *Fundamental Problems of Marxism* (1908; trans. 1969), by Georgi V. Ple-khanov, one the best of them. Leszek Kolakowski's *Main Currents of Marxism: Its Rise, Growth, and Dissolution* (3 vols., 1976–78; trans. 1978) is perhaps the best secondary source on Marx and Western Marxism in general. Kolakowski, a prominent Polish philosopher and Oxford don, has also published in English several volumes of essays relating to his own Marxist-philosophical views—most notably *Toward a Marxist Humanism: Essays on the Left Today* (1968).

Adam Schaff, another prominent Polish Marxist-humanist philosopher worth reading, is best known in the English-speaking world for his *Marxism and the Human Individual* (1965; trans. 1970), *A Philosophy of Man* (1961; trans. 1963), and *Alienation as a Social Phenomenon* (1977; trans. 1980). Gajo Petrović, a Yugoslavian philosopher, provided an important reinterpretation and reassessment of Marx—emphasizing his early (but very belatedly discovered and published) writings—in *Marx in the Mid-Twentieth Century* (1965; trans. 1967). Selections from the writings of a number of Austrian Marxists—Max Adler, Otto Bauer, and Karl Renner—are collected in *Austro-Marxism*, edited by Tom Bottomore and Patrick Goode (1978).

The writings of the Hungarian-born philosopher György (Georg) Lukács (1885–1971) are among the most significant contributions to the literature of Western Marxism. Many focus on literary analysis and criticism; but Lukács also wrote several important theoretical works, such as *History and Class Consciousness: Studies in Marxist Dialectics* (1923; trans. 1971) and *The Ontology of Social Being* (3 vols., 1971–73; trans. 1978–80). Another foundational thinker for Western European Marxism is Antonio Gramsci, a leader of the Italian Communist Party who was imprisoned in the 1920s. He wrote an enormous amount in prison (published in 4 vols., 1975), some of which has been translated into English in *Selections from the Prison Notebooks of Antonio Gramsci* (1971) and in *Further Selections from the Prison Notebooks* (1995). A wider range of his writings is available in *An Antonio Gramsci Reader: Selected Writings, 1916–1935*, edited by David Forgacs (1988).

France has produced many notable Marxist thinkers. Louis Althusser, who resisted the humanist interpretation of Marx, was among the best and most formidable of the "neo-orthodox" Marxist philosophers; his main works are *For Marx* (1965; trans. 1969); with Étienne Balibar, *Reading Capital* (1968; trans. 1970); and *Lenin and Philosophy and Other Essays* (1969; trans. 1971). Alain Badiou follows in the footsteps of Althusser's anti-humanist Marxist position; see his *Metapolitics* (1998; trans. 2005), *Ethics: An Essay on the Understanding of Evil* (1993; trans. 2001), *Polemics* (2003–04; trans. 2006), *The Communist Hypothesis* (2009, trans. 2010), and the title essay of the collection *The Idea of Communism* (2 vols., 2010–13). Other important works of or relating to French philosophical Marxism include Jean-Paul Sartre, *Critique of Dialectical Reason* (2 vols., 1960–85; trans. 1976–90) and *Search for a Method* (1960; trans. 1963); Maurice Merleau-Ponty, *Adventures of the Dialectic* (1955; trans. 1973); André Gorz, *Critique of Economic Reason* (1988; trans. 1989); and Henri Lefebvre, *Sociology of Marx* (1966; trans. 1968), *Dialectical Materialism* (1939; trans. 1968), and *Critique of Everyday Life* (3 vols., 2nd ed., 1958–81; trans. 1991–2005).

Marxist thought also lived on in the Frankfurt School in Germany, through the Marx-influenced cultural and political analyses of twentieth-century capitalism by those associated with this "school" of critical social theorists—who, however, often deviated significantly from the letter of Marx's writings and from "orthodox" Marxist doctrine. See "Frankfurt School/Critical Social Theory" in section III, below.

BRITISH IDEALISM AND AMERICAN TRANSCENDENTALISM

The influence of Idealism (and Hegelianism in particular) in Great Britain and America, in and through the thought of Anglophone philosophers such as T. H. Green, F. H. Bradley, and Josiah Royce, is examined in *Anglo-American Idealism, 1865–1927*, edited by W. J. Mander (2000). Frederick Copleston's *A History of Philosophy*, vol. 8, *Bentham to Russell* (1966), also deals with the development of Idealism among thinkers such Green, Bradley, and Bernard Bosanquet in Britain and the Transcendentalists, Royce, and other figures in the United States, as well as with positivism and naturalism in Britain after John Stuart Mill, and with pragmatism in the United States. Two recent works on British Idealism are David Boucher and Andrew Vincent, *British Idealism: A Guide for the Perplexed* (2012), and W. J. Mander, *British Idealism: A History* (2011). Writings by the British Idealists mentioned above, as well as Henry Jones, Edward Caird, and David Ritchie, are collected in *The British Idealists*, edited by David Boucher (1997). For secondary works devoted to this movement, see David Boucher and Andrew Vincent, *British Idealism and Political Theory* (2000), and Sandra M. den Otter, *British Idealism and Social Explanation: A Study in Late Victorian Thought* (1996).

On Emerson and the history of American Transcendentalism in general, see Paul F. Boller Jr., *American Transcendentalism, 1830–1860: An Intellectual Inquiry* (1974); Carlos Baker, *Emerson among the Eccentrics: A Group Portrait* (1996); Philip L. Gura, *American Transcendentalism: A History* (2007); and Barbara L. Packer, *The Transcendentalists* (2007). For histories of the Transcendentalists, see Susan Cheever, *American Bloomsbury: Louisa May Alcott, Ralph Waldo Emerson, Margaret Fuller, Nathaniel Hawthorne, and Henry David Thoreau: Their Lives, Their Loves, Their Work* (2006), and Samuel A. Schreiner Jr., *The Concord Quartet: Alcott, Emerson, Hawthorne, Thoreau, and the Friendship That Freed the American Mind* (2006).

NEO-KANTIANISM

Frederick C. Beiser's *Late German Idealism: Trendelenburg and Lotze* (2013) is a study of two thinkers who, reacting against Hegel, returned to and modified Kantian and Fichtean philosophy, thereby creating what is now known as Neo-Kantianism. Thomas E. Willey's *Back to Kant: The Revival of Kantianism in German Social and Historical Thought, 1860–1914* (1978) is an even-handed discussion of the Neo-Kantians (Hermann Lotze, Kuno Fischer, Friedrich Albert Lange, Hermann Cohen, Wilhelm Windelband, and Heinrich Rickert) with an emphasis on the social-political context in which they were working and the consequences of their thought for the cultural and political development of Germany. Klaus Köhnke's *The Rise of Neo-Kantianism: German Academic Philosophy between Idealism and Positivism* (1986; trans. 1991), a much more polemical work, focuses more on the historical conflicts between and philosophies of these thinkers. Essays in *Neo-Kantianism in Contemporary Philosophy*, edited by Rudolf A. Makkreel and Sebastian Luft (2009), examine how Neo-Kantianism is influencing current trends in philosophy, and Luft has also edited a volume of primary sources, *The Neo-Kantian Reader* (2015).

MATERIALISM AND POSITIVISM

Frederick Gregory's *Scientific Materialism in Nineteenth Century Germany* (1977) examines the post-Feuerbachian materialisms of Karl Vogt, Jacob Moleschott, Ludwig Büchner, and Heinrich Czolbe. Friedrich Albert Lange's *The History of Materialism and Criticism of Its Present Importance* (1866, 2-vol. 2nd ed. 1873–75; 3 vols., trans. 1877–81) is a classic examination of the developments of materialist philosophy. Volume 1 deals with materialism from antiquity up to Kant; volume 2 concerns Kant and materialist thinkers after Kant (including Feuerbach), and surveys contemporary developments in science; and volume 3 discusses Darwinism and the extensive developments in anthropology, physiology, and psychology and their intersection with materialist philosophies in Germany in the nineteenth century.

Maurice Mandelbaum's *History, Man, and Reason: A Study in Nineteenth-Century Thought* (1971), another classic study, focuses on the overlooked threads of materialism, historicism, organicism, and positivism in both the British and Continental traditions. In addition to the towering figures of Hegel, Marx, Schopenhauer, and Nietzsche, Mandelbaum discusses Auguste Comte, Herbert Spencer, Ernst Mach, Hermann Helmholtz, and others. A recent historical study of nineteenth-century positivism is Andrew Wernick, *Auguste Comte and the Religion of Humanity: The Post-theistic Program of French Social Theory* (2001).

III. TWENTIETH-CENTURY MOVEMENTS

PHENOMENOLOGY

Herbert Spiegelberg's *The Phenomenological Movement: A Historical Introduction* (2 vols., 1960; 3rd ed., 1984) is a monumental study of this development that is unlikely ever to be surpassed. Spiegelberg discusses crucial, founding figures such as Franz Brentano and Carl Stumpf as well as those who are better known, including Husserl, Heidegger, and Scheler. He examines the Göttingen and Munich circles of phenomenology and figures associated with them such as Alexander Pfänder, Adolf Reinach, Moritz Geiger, and Edith Stein. He also assesses the contributions to the phenomenological movement of French thinkers such as Sartre, Merleau-Ponty, Ricoeur, and Gabriel Marcel.

Other important studies of phenomenology include David Carr, *Phenomenology and the Problem of History: A Study of Husserl's Transcendental Philosophy* (1974); Marvin Farber, *Phenomenology and Existence: Toward a Philosophy within Nature* (1967); Gerhard Funke, *Phenomenology, Metaphysics or Method?* (1966; trans. 1987); Quentin Lauer, *Phenomenology: Its Genesis and Prospect* (1958); *Readings in Existential Phenomenology*, edited by Nathaniel Lawrence and Daniel O'Connor (1967); William A. Luijpen, *Existential Phenomenology* (1963); William A. Luijpen and Henry J. Koren, *A First Introduction to Existential Phenomenology* (1969); and Pierre Thévenaz, *What Is Phenomenology? And Other Essays* (1962).

The early influence of phenomenology in American can be seen in Samuel Todes's *Body and World* (rev. ed., 2001; first published 1990 as *The Human Body as Material Subject of the World*), and in two collections of essays edited by James M. Edie, *Phenomenology in America: Studies in the Philosophy of Experience* (1967) and *New Essays in Phenomenology: Studies in the Philosophy of Experience* (1969). Recent studies of phenomenology include David R. Cerbone, *Understanding Phenomenology* (2006); Robert Denoon Cumming, *Phenomenology and Deconstruction* (4 vols., 1991–2001); Simon Glendinning, *In the Name of Phenomenology* (2007); Reinhardt Grossmann, *Phenomenology and Existentialism: An Introduction* (1984); Christopher E. Macann, *Four Phenomenological Philosophers: Husserl, Heidegger, Sartre, Merleau-Ponty* (1993); J. N. Mohanty, *Phenomenology: Between Essentialism and Transcendental Philosophy* (1997); Dermot Moran, *Introduction to Phenomenology* (2000); and Robert Sokolowski, *Introduction to Phenomenology* (2000).

Two collections of essays surveying the subject are *Understanding Phenomenology*, edited by Michael Hammond, Jane Howarth, and Russell Keat (1991), and *A Companion to Phenomenology and Existentialism*, edited by Hubert L. Dreyfus and Mark A. Wrathall (2006). Volumes that survey respects in which phenomenology and analytic philosophy do or could intersect include *Phenomenology and Philosophy of Mind*, edited by David Woodruff Smith and Amie L. Thomasson (2005); Paul Gilbert and Kathleen Lennon, *The World, the Flesh, and the Subject: Continental Themes in the Philosophy of Mind and Body* (2005); and Shaun Gallagher and Dan Zahavi, *The Phenomenological Mind* (2nd ed., 2012). Some recent works in the field are Robert Sokolowski, *Phenomenology of the Human Person* (2008); *The Routledge Companion to Phenomenology*, edited by Sebastian Luft and Søren Overgaard (2012); Michael Lewis and Tanja Staehler, *Phenomenology: An Introduction* (2010); Shaun Gallagher, *Phenomenology* (2012); *The Oxford Handbook of Contemporary Phenomenology*, edited by Dan Zahavi (2013); and David Detmer, *Phenomenology Explained: From Experience to Insight* (2013).

EXISTENZ-PHILOSOPHY AND EXISTENTIALISM

The classic collection that introduced English-speaking readers to existential philosophy by way of samples of the work of those associated with it is *Existentialism from Dostoevsky to*

Sartre, edited by Walter Kaufmann (1956; rev. ed., 1975). A helpful early collection of essays on many of these figures is *Existential Philosophers: Kierkegaard to Merleau-Ponty*, edited by George Alfred Schrader Jr. (1967). A good recent collection is *Situating Existentialism: Key Texts in Context*, edited by Jonathan Judaken and Robert Bernasconi (2012). In *From Rationalism to Existentialism: The Existentialists and Their Nineteenth-Century Backgrounds* (1972), and again in *From Hegel to Existentialism* (1987), Robert C. Solomon describes the development of existentialism, out of and in response to such earlier sources as Kant, Hegel, Kierkegaard, and Nietzsche. An excellent recent guide to the movement is *The Cambridge Companion to Existentialism*, edited by Steven Crowell (2012).

During the period of existentialism's greatest popularity, numerous surveys of its basic ideas were published. The best of them include such classics as Hazel Barnes, *The Literature of Possibility: Studies in Humanistic Existentialism* (1959; reprinted in 1967 as *Humanistic Existentialism: The Literature of Possibility*); William Barrett, *Irrational Man: A Study in Existential Philosophy* (1958) and *What Is Existentialism?* (1964); H. J. Blackham, *Six Existentialist Thinkers* (1952); Ernst Breisach, *Introduction to Modern Existentialism* (1962); James Collins, *The Existentialists: A Critical Study* (1952); Marjorie Grene, *Dreadful Freedom* (1948; reprinted in 1959 and later as *Introduction to Existentialism*); and Mary Warnock, *Existentialism* (1970; rev. ed., 1996).

Other useful discussions include Francis J. Lescoe, *Existentialism: With or Without God* (1974); John Macquarrie, *Existentialism* (1972); Fernando Molina, *Existentialism as Philosophy* (1962); Robert Olson, *An Introduction to Existentialism* (1962); Patricia F. Sanborn, *Existentialism* (1968); Jean Wahl, *Philosophies of Existence: An Introduction to the Basic Thought of Kierkegaard, Heidegger, Jaspers, Marcel, Sartre* (1954; trans. 1969) and *A Short History of Existentialism* (1949); John Wild, *The Challenge of Existentialism* (1955) and *Existence and the World of Freedom* (1963); and David E. Cooper *Existentialism: A Reconstruction* (2nd ed., 1999).

Among recent discussions of existential philosophy are Steven Earnshaw, *Existentialism: A Guide for the Perplexed* (2007); *Dictionary of Existentialism*, edited by Haim Gordon (1999); and Jack Reynolds, *Understanding Existentialism* (2006). Ann Fulton's *Apostles of Sartre: Existentialism in America, 1945–1963* (1999) and George Cotkin's *Existential America* (2003) are interesting examinations of the influence of existentialism on American culture, arts, and philosophy.

LEBENSPHILOSOPHIE

The movement that came to be known in German-speaking Europe as *Lebensphilosophie* (literally, "life philosophy") had the phenomenon of "life" as its central focus—which for some of its central figures meant forms of life generally and for others primarily meant human life more specifically. There are no surveys of this movement in English. Although it has many historical antecedents (Schopenhauer and Nietzsche are clearly among them, and Nietzsche is often associated with it), the movement proper dates from the debate surrounding the *Geisteswissenshaften* (disciplines that deal with *Geist* [spirit]: that is, the humanities and social sciences) in Germany in the late nineteenth century—around the time of the flourishing of Neo-Kantianism, and to some extent in response to it. Dilthey was another of its initiators, who viewed scientific thinking as ill suited to the comprehension of much of human "life" (experience and activity, particularly as it has developed historically at the sociocultural level); it therefore should not be emulated by *Geisteswissenschaften*. The second major factor in the development of *Lebensphilosophie* as a philosophical movement at the turn of the century was the gradual dissemination of the philosophies of Schopenhauer and Nietzsche into the German intellectual and academic worlds.

Georg Simmel, a colleague of Dilthey's in Berlin, was another leading early figure in the movement (and also in the development of sociology as a discipline—the work for which he is best known in the English-speaking world). His *Schopenhauer and Nietzsche* (1907; trans. 1986) was one of the earliest scholarly German treatments of these figures. His major contribution to *Lebensphilosophie* remains untranslated: *Lebensanschauung: Vier metaphysische Kap-*

itel (1918, *Life Interpretation*). A discussion of Simmel's *Lebensphilosophie* can be found in Rudolph Weingartner, *Experience and Culture: The Philosophy of Georg Simmel* (1962).

The German scientist and philosopher Hans Driesch contributed to the movement of *Lebensphilosophie* as well as to philosophical anthropology and biology. His 1907 and 1908 Gifford lecture series, *The Science and Philosophy of the Organism*, was published (1908); also available in English are his *Mind and Body: A Critique of Psychophysical Parallelism* (1916, 3rd ed. 1923; trans. 1927) and *The History and Theory of Vitalism* (1914). Michael Polanyi, who himself was at the juncture of science and philosophical anthropology, deals with the concept of life (and the ideas of Hans Driesch) in his two main works, *Knowing and Being: Essays* (1969) and *Personal Knowledge: Towards a Post-critical Philosophy* (1958). Perhaps the best-known figure associated with *Lebensphilosophie* other than Nietzsche is Henri Bergson, who won it significant attention (under a different name, in his revival of vitalism) both in academia and in popular culture, in the United States as well as Europe. From the late 1920s onward, however, *Lebensphilosophie* gradually gave way to philosophical anthropology.

PHILOSOPHICAL ANTHROPOLOGY

Only a few surveys of the tradition of philosophical anthropology exist in English: Michael Landmann, *Philosophical Anthropology* (1955; 3rd ed., 1969; trans. 1974) and *Fundamental Anthropology* (1974; trans. 1985), and Gerd Haeffner, *The Human Situation: A Philosophical Anthropology* (1982; trans. 1989). A classic work at the intersection of philosophy and biology that influenced the development of philosophical anthropology is Jacob von Uexküll's *Theoretical Biology* (1920; trans. 1926); see also his *A Foray into the Worlds of Humans and Animals* (1934; trans. 2010). The work of Adolf Portmann, another zoologist, has also been important not just for philosophical anthropology but also in the study of human beings, sociality, and animal behavior more generally; a representative work in English is *New Paths in Biology* (1964). Kurt Goldstein's *The Organism: A Holistic Approach to Biology Derived from Pathological Data in Man* (1934; trans. 1939) and *Human Nature in the Light of Psychopathology* (1940), important works on the nature of living beings, may also be considered a part of the literature of philosophical anthropology. In this connection see also Erwin Straus's *Man, Time, and World: Two Contributions to Anthropological Psychology* (1978; trans. 1982), *The Primary World of Senses: A Vindication of Sensory Experience* (1935; trans. 1963), and the selected papers translated in *Phenomenological Psychology* (1966).

Many of these works are discussed in Marjorie Grene's *Approaches to a Philosophical Biology* (1968); she was one of the first American philosophers to attempt to bring philosophical anthropology to the attention of English-speaking philosophers and readers. Her other works on similar topics are *The Understanding of Nature: Essays in the Philosophy of Biology* (1974) and, with David Depew, *The Philosophy of Biology: An Episodic History* (2004). Suzanne K. Langer's *Mind: An Essay on Human Feeling* (3 vols., 1967–82)—also situated at the intersection of biology, anthropology, and philosophy—was intended to be a work of philosophical anthropology.

A number of other works are at least tangentially related to philosophical anthropology. Hans Jonas's *The Phenomenon of Life: Toward a Philosophical Biology* (1966) examines the facts of human biology from an existentialist-Heideggerian perspective. Axel Honneth and Hans Joas, in *Social Action and Human Nature* (1980; trans. 1988), briefly discuss the roots of philosophical anthropology in Feuerbach and Marx, then provide a substantial analysis of the thought of Plessner and Gehlen and discuss current developments concerning human nature and the Foucault/Habermas debate. David J. Levy's *Political Order: Philosophical Anthropology, Modernity, and the Challenge of Ideology* (1987) and *The Measure of Man: Incursions in Philosophical and Political Anthropology* (1993) collect his historical and critical essays that discuss Gehlen, Scheler, Plessner, Heidegger, Nicolai Hartmann, Hans Jonas, Hans Freyer, and Carl Schmitt. A recent work that explores classic themes in philosophical anthropology is Giorgio Agamben's *The Open: Man and Animal* (2002; trans. 2004).

An extensive treatment of philosophical anthropology as it influenced Christian (and more specifically Catholic) thought is J. F. Donceel's *Philosophical Anthropology* (3rd ed.,

1967; originally titled *Philosophical Psychology*, 1955). Other influential works that engage the philosophical tradition from both a Christian and a philosophical anthropological perspective include Karol Wojtyla (Pope John Paul II), *The Acting Person* (1969; trans. 1979); Joseph Endres, *Man as the Ontological Mean* (1956; trans. 1965); John Macquarrie, *In Search of Humanity: A Theological and Philosophical Approach* (1982); and Reinhold Niebuhr, *The Nature and Destiny of Man: A Christian Interpretation* (2 vols., 1941–43), the published version of his 1939 Gifford Lectures.

HERMENEUTICS

Surveys of the history of hermeneutics can be found in Maurizio Ferraris, *History of Hermeneutics* (1988; trans. 1996); Jean Grondin, *Sources of Hermeneutics* (1995); Robert S. Leventhal, *The Disciplines of Interpretation: Lessing, Herder, Schlegel and Hermeneutics in Germany, 1750–1800* (1994); Richard E. Palmer, *Hermeneutics: Interpretation Theory in Schleiermacher, Dilthey, Heidegger, and Gadamer* (1969); and Yvonne Sherratt, *Continental Philosophy of Social Science: Hermeneutics, Genealogy, and Critical Theory from Greece to the Twenty-First Century* (2006). The birth of hermeneutics within the philosophy of the German Enlightenment and Counter-Enlightenment is discussed in Frederick C. Beiser's *The German Historicist Tradition* (2011).

More topical and thematic surveys of the field can be found in Jean Grondin, *Introduction to Philosophical Hermeneutics* (1991; trans. 1994); Michael Kelly, *Hermeneutics and Critical Theory in Ethics and Politics* (1990); Thomas M. Seebohm, *Hermeneutics: Method and Methodology* (2004); Hans-Herbert Kögler, *The Power of Dialogue: Critical Hermeneutics after Gadamer and Foucault* (1992; trans. 1996); Cristina Lafont, *The Linguistic Turn in Hermeneutic Philosophy* (1993; trans. 1999); and Lawrence K. Schmidt, *Understanding Hermeneutics* (2006). Collections of essays on hermeneutics include *Hermeneutics: Questions and Prospects*, edited by Gary Shapiro and Alan Sica (1984), and *Hermeneutics and Modern Philosophy*, edited by Brice R. Wachterhauser (1986). Two recent introductory surveys of the field are Anthony C. Thiselton, *Hermeneutics: An Introduction* (2009), and Stanley E. Porter and Jason C. Robinson, *Hermeneutics: An Introduction to Interpretive Theory* (2011).

FRANKFURT SCHOOL/CRITICAL SOCIAL THEORY

The Frankfurt School was an important center for studies in "critical social theory" at Frankfurt University for a few years before Hitler came to power in Germany; it then in effect relocated to New York, and was to some extent reconstituted again at Frankfurt after the Second World War ended. Jürgen Habermas is its most famous and important product. Its most prominent earlier figures were Max Horkheimer, Theodor Adorno, and Herbert Marcuse. They sought to develop Marxist thought in response to the unique social and political situations of their times. Among their significant works are Horkheimer's *Eclipse of Reason* (1947), Adorno's *Negative Dialectics* (1966; trans. 1973), Adorno and Horkheimer's *Dialectic of Enlightenment* (1969; trans. 1972), and Marcuse's *One-Dimensional Man: Studies in the Ideology of Advanced Industrial Society* (1964), *Negations: Essays in Critical Theory* (1968), and *Counterrevolution and Revolt* (1972). The psychologist Erich Fromm was also associated with the Frankfurt School; like many socialist thinkers of the time, he turned to the works of early Marx for inspiration, as is most evident in his analysis of Marx in *Marx's Concept of Man* (1961). Selections from the writings of associated figures may be found in *An Anthology of Western Marxism: From Lukács and Gramsci to Socialist-Feminism*, edited by Roger S. Gottlieb (1989), and *Interpretations of Marx*, edited by Tom Bottomore (1988).

The development of critical social theory in Germany reflected both the Hegelian background and the Marxian sensibility of many in the German academic community in the late nineteenth and the early twentieth centuries. Harry Liebersohn's *Fate and Utopia in German Sociology, 1870–1923* (1988) is an important discussion of the foundational thinkers in German social thinking, such as Ferdinand Tonnies, Ernst Troeltsch, Max Weber, Georg Simmel, and György (Georg) Lukács. They strongly influenced the thought of the figures associated with the founding and early years of the Frankfurt School.

The most complete study and intellectual history of this movement is Rolf Wiggershaus, *The Frankfurt School: Its History, Theories, and Political Significance* (1986; trans. 1994). Other important studies are Helmut Dubiel, *Theory and Politics: Studies in the Development of Critical Theory* (1978; trans. 1985); John Abromeit, *Max Horkheimer and the Foundations of the Frankfurt School* (2011); Martin Jay, *The Dialectical Imagination: A History of the Frankfurt School and the Institute for Social Research, 1923–1950* (1973); and Thomas Wheatland, *The Frankfurt School in Exile* (2009).

On the Frankfurt School and its type of critical social theory, see also Stephen Bronner, *Of Critical Theory and Its Theorists* (1994; 2nd ed., 2002); David Held, *An Introduction to Critical Theory: Horkheimer to Habermas* (1980); Alan How, *Critical Theory* (2003); David Couzens Hoy and Thomas McCarthy, *Critical Theory* (1994); David Ingram, *Critical Theory and Philosophy* (1990); *The Handbook of Critical Theory*, edited by David M. Rasmussen (1996); *The Cambridge Companion to Critical Theory*, edited by Fred Rush (2004); William E. Scheuerman, *Between the Norm and the Exception: The Frankfurt School and the Rule of Law* (1994); and *From Kant to Lévi-Strauss: The Background to Contemporary Critical Theory*, edited by Jon Simmons (2002).

STRUCTURALISM

The most complete analysis of the development of the structuralist movement in France is François Dosse's *History of Structuralism* (2 vols., 1991–92; trans. 1997). Its prominent figures include Claude Lévi-Strauss, Louis Althusser, Henri Lefebvre, Ricoeur, Jacques Lacan, Jean Piaget, Roland Barthes, and Foucault. The many surveys of the movement include Eve Tavor Bannet, *Structuralism and the Logic of Dissent: Barthes, Derrida, Foucault, Lacan* (1989); Peter Caws, *Structuralism: The Art of the Intelligible* (1988; reprinted in 1997 as *Structuralism: A Philosophy for the Human Sciences*); *Structuralism*, edited by Jacques Ehrmann (1966); Howard Gardner, *The Quest for Mind: Piaget, Lévi-Strauss, and the Structuralist Movement* (1972); Terence Hawkes, *Structuralism and Semiotics* (1977); Edith Kurzweil, *The Age of Structuralism: Lévi-Strauss to Foucault* (1980); Jean Piaget, *Structuralism* (1968; trans. 1970); and John Sturrock, *Structuralism* (2nd ed., 1993).

POSTSTRUCTURALISM, POSTMODERNISM, AND DECONSTRUCTION

The terms "poststructuralism," "postmodernism," and "deconstruction" are all used—rather loosely, and often almost interchangeably—to refer to a cluster of developments that emerged in France in the 1960s and '70s and that tend to be grouped and often discussed together. The literature on them is considerable. Useful comprehensive discussions include Luc Ferry and Alain Renaut, *French Philosophy of the Sixties: An Essay on Antihumanism* (1985; trans. 1990); John Lechte, *Fifty Key Contemporary Thinkers: From Structuralism to Post-Humanism* (2nd ed., 2008); Richard Harland, *Superstructuralism: The Philosophy of Structuralism and Post-structuralism* (1987); David Couzens Hoy, *Critical Resistance: From Poststructuralism to Post-Critique* (2004); Madan Sarup, *An Introductory Guide to Post-structuralism and Postmodernism* (2nd ed., 1993); Alan D. Schrift, *Nietzsche's French Legacy: A Genealogy of Poststructuralism* (1995); *Structuralism and Since: From Lévi-Strauss to Derrida*, edited by John Sturrock (1979); *Reading Material Culture: Structuralism, Hermeneutics, and Post-structuralism*, edited by Christopher Tilley (1990); James Williams, *Understanding Poststructuralism* (2005); and Colin Davis, *After Poststructuralism: Reading, Stories and Theory* (2004). An intellectual-historical study that tells the story of how poststructuralism influenced American academia is François Cusset's *French Theory: How Foucault, Derrida, Deleuze, & Co. Transformed the Intellectual Life of the United States* (2003; trans. 2008).

Works on the movement and themes of postmodernism as a more general phenomenon (of which philosophical postmodernism is a special and not altogether typical instance) are legion. Among them are Perry Anderson, *The Origins of Postmodernity* (1998); Richard J. Bernstein, *The New Constellation: The Ethical-Political Horizons of Modernity/Postmodernity* (1991); Hans Bertens, *The Idea of the Postmodern: A History* (1995); *Postmodernism: The Key Figures*, edited by Hans Bertens and Joseph Natoli (2002); *The Cambridge Companion to Postmodernism*, edited by Steven Connor (2004); Steven Connor, *Postmodernist Culture: An Introduction to Theories of the Contemporary* (2nd ed., 1997); Kevin Hart, *Postmodernism: A Beginner's Guide* (2004); Fredric Jameson, *Postmodernism, or, The Cultural Logic of Late Capitalism* (1991) and *The Cultural Turn: Selected Writings on the Postmodern, 1983–1988* (1998); Simon Malpas, *The Postmodern* (2005); *Postmodernism and Continental Philosophy*, edited by Hugh J. Silverman and Donn Welton (1988); *The Routledge Critical Dictionary of Postmodern Thought* (1998) and *The Routledge Companion to Postmodernism* (2nd ed., 2005), both edited by Stuart Sim; Gianni Vattimo, *The End of Modernity: Nihilism and Hermeneutics in Post-modern Culture* (1985; trans. 1988); and Tim Woods, *Beginning Postmodernism* (1999).

Studies that focus on the idea of "deconstruction" include Art Berman, *From the New Criticism to Deconstruction: The Reception of Structuralism and Post-structuralism* (1988); Jonathan Culler, *On Deconstruction: Theory and Criticism after Structuralism* (1982) and *The Pursuit of Signs: Semiotics, Literature, Deconstruction* (1981); Mark Currie, *Difference* (2004); Herman Rapaport, *The Theory Mess: Deconstruction in Eclipse* (2001); Robert C. Holub, *Crossing Borders: Reception Theory, Poststructuralism, Deconstruction* (1992); Christopher Norris, *Deconstruction: Theory and Practice* (1982; 3rd ed., 2002) and *Deconstruction and the 'Unfinished Project of Modernity'* (2000); *Deconstruction in Context: Literature and Philosophy*, edited by Mark C. Taylor (1986); Tilottama Rajan, *Deconstruction and the Remainders of Phenomenology: Sartre, Derrida, Foucault, Baudrillard* (2002); *Deconstructions: A User's Guide*, edited by Nicholas Royle (2000); Samuel C. Wheeler, *Deconstruction as Analytic Philosophy* (2000); and Peter V. Zima, *Deconstruction and Critical Theory* (1994; trans. 2002).

FEMINIST PHILOSOPHY AND FRENCH FEMINISM

Modern feminist theory might be traced back to the works of Mary Wollstonecraft (and John Stuart Mill) excerpted above, and to Simone de Beauvoir's extraordinarily influential *The Second Sex* (1949; also excerpted above). In recent years, it has developed into a massive and diverse interdisciplinary field. We here suggest a small selection of useful introductory texts, important contemporary scholarship, and wide-ranging anthologies that together provide a sense of both the history and recent trends of feminist philosophical thought. Feminist interpretations of thinkers from Hegel to Foucault are mentioned in the individual bibliographies.

This volume might have included selections from the work of such major theorists of French feminism as Luce Irigaray, Hélène Cixous, Michèle Le Doeuff, and Julia Kristeva. However, because their thought has ties not only to certain developments in recent French philosophy but also to areas beyond philosophy (notably linguistics, semiotics, and psychoanalysis, especially as grounded in the writings of Ferdinand de Saussure, Roland Barthes, Sigmund Freud, and Jacques Lacan), giving the background needed to understand them would have required considerable expansion of the scope of this volume. The selection from Judith Butler, above, in which she comments on these figures, provides a sense of the kinds of issues that this literature addresses.

Irigaray's works available in English include *This Sex Which Is Not One* (1977; trans. 1985), *Speculum of the Other Woman* (1974; trans. 1985), *Ethics of Sexual Difference* (1984; trans. 1993), and *To Be Two* (1994; trans. 2000). Kristeva's works include *Desire in Language: A Semiotic Approach to Literature and Art* (1969, 1977; trans. 1980), *Powers of Horror: An Essay on Abjection* (1980; trans. 1982), *Strangers to Ourselves* (1988; trans. 1991), and *The Kristeva Reader* (1986). Among Cixous's many books are *The Book of Promethea* (1983; trans. 1991), *Three Steps on the Ladder of Writing* (1993), *Stigmata: Escaping Texts* (1998), and *The Third Body* (1970; trans. 1999). Le Doeuff's writings include *The Philosophical Imaginary* (1980; trans. 1989), *Hipparchia's Choice: An Essay Concerning Women, Philosophy, Etc.* (1989; trans. 1990), and *The Sex of Knowing* (1998; trans. 2003). *French Feminism Reader*, edited by Kelly Oliver (2000), and *Contemporary French Feminism*, edited by Kelly Oliver and Lisa Walsh (2004), are useful collections.-

Studies of their (and others') thought and of its intersection with the interpretive tradition include *Revaluing French Feminism: Critical Essays on Difference, Agency, and Culture*, edited by Nancy Fraser and Sandra Lee Bartky (1992); Dani Cavallaro, *French Feminist Theory: An*

Introduction (2003); *French Women Philosophers: A Contemporary Reader: Subjectivity, Identity, Alterity,* edited by Christina Howells (2004); *Resistance, Flight, Creation: Feminist Enactments of French Philosophy,* edited by Dorothea Olkowski (2000); and Kelly Ives, *Cixous, Irigaray, Kristeva: The Jouissance of French Feminism* (1996; 5th ed., 2013). See also Sara Heinämaa's *Toward a Phenomenology of Sexual Difference: Husserl, Merleau-Ponty, Beauvoir* (2003).

There are many introductory surveys and anthologies of feminist philosophy more generally. See Lorna Finlayson, *An Introduction to Feminism* (2016); *The Cambridge Companion to Feminism in Philosophy,* edited by Miranda Fricker and Jennifer Hornsby (2000); Georgia Warnke, *Debating Sex and Gender* (2011); bell hooks, *Feminism Is for Everybody: Passionate Politics* (2000); Jennifer Mather Saul, *Feminism: Issues and Arguments* (2003); *Continental Feminism Reader,* edited by Ann J. Cahill and Jennifer Hansen (2003); *Theorizing Feminisms: A Reader,* edited by Elizabeth Hackett and Sally Anne Haslanger (2005); *The Feminist Philosophy Reader,* edited by Alison Bailey and Chris Cuomo (2007); Alison Stone, *An Introduction to Feminist Philosophy* (2007); and *Feminism and Philosophy: Essential Readings in Theory, Reinterpretation, and Application,* edited by Nancy Tuana and Rosemarie Tong (1995).

The works of Catharine A. MacKinnon are foundational in the literature on feminism, political theory, and the law: see especially *Feminism Unmodified: Discourses on Life and Law* (1987), *Toward a Feminist Theory of the State* (1989), and *Women's Lives, Men's Laws* (2005). Also important in the field of political philosophy are the works of Carole Pateman: see *The Sexual Contract* (1988) and *The Disorder of Women: Democracy, Feminism, and Political Theory* (1989). Nancy Fraser's works of feminist theory range into political philosophy; see *Unruly Practices: Power, Discourse, and Gender in Contemporary Social Theory* (1989), *Justice Interruptus: Critical Reflections on the "Postsocialist" Condition* (1997), *Scales of Justice: Reimagining Political Space in a Globalizing World* (2009), and *Fortunes of Feminism: From State-Managed Capitalism to Neoliberal Crisis* (2013). Other noteworthy studies include Sandra Lee Bartky's *Femininity and Domination: Studies in the Phenomenology of Oppression* (1990) and Rosi Braidotti's *Patterns of Dissonance: A Study of Women in Contemporary Philosophy* (trans. 1991) and *Nomadic Subjects: Embodiment and Sexual Difference in Contemporary Feminist Theory* (1994; 2nd ed., 2011). Marilyn Frye's *The Politics of Reality: Essays in Feminist Theory* (1983) is among the most influential works of lesbian feminism.

The theory of care ethics, which has been an influential strand of feminist theory, was largely developed by two women working in the fields of developmental psychology and education, respectively: see Carol Gilligan, *In a Different Voice: Psychological Theory and Women's Development* (1982), and Nel Noddings, *Caring: A Feminine Approach to Ethics and Moral Education* (1984; updated 2nd ed., 2013, subtitled *A Relational Approach to Ethics and Moral Education*). This kind of ethical theory has been elaborated by Virginia Held in *Feminist Morality: Transforming Culture, Society, and Politics* (1993) and *The Ethics of Care* (2007). Among other significant additions to feminist ethics are Margaret Walker's *Moral Understandings: A Feminist Study in Ethics* (1998; 2nd ed., 2007) and the works of Iris Young, including *On Female Body Experience: "Throwing Like a Girl" and Other Essays* (2005), *Justice and the Politics of Difference* (1990), and *Responsibility for Justice* (2011). And of course Martha Nussbaum and Judith Butler have made major contributions to it; see their individual bibliographies.

A useful overview of the significance of feminist theory in the area of epistemology can be found in Alessandra Tanesini, *An Introduction to Feminist Epistemologies* (1999). Two noteworthy collections of essays in this field are *Feminist Epistemologies,* edited by Linda Alcoff and Elizabeth Potter (1993), and *A Mind of One's Own: Feminist Essays on Reason and Objectivity,* edited by Louise M. Antony and Charlotte Witt (1993; 2nd ed., 2002).

A few classic works at the intersection of feminism and critical race theory (see below) are Patricia Hill Collins, *Black Feminist Thought: Knowledge, Consciousness, and the Politics of Empowerment* (1990; 2nd ed., 2000); Angela Y. Davis, *Women, Race and Class* (1981); and the works of bell hooks, such as *Ain't I a Woman: Black Women and Feminism* (1981), *Feminist Theory from Margin to Center* (1984), and *Talking Back: Thinking Feminist, Thinking Black* (1989; new ed., 2014).

CRITICAL RACE THEORY AND AFRICANA PHILOSOPHY

This short bibliography focuses on the works of major thinkers and leading scholars in the fields of critical race theory and Africana philosophy, as they relate to the compass of the general scope of this volume. Though its scope does not extend beyond the post-Kantian interpretive tradition to cover philosophies rooted in the religions and indigenous cultures of the African and Asian continents, it does include several anthologies that offer introductions to and examples of work of philosophers within those other traditions.

Critical race theory typically refers to a focus on race within the interdisciplinary field of cultural studies, also known as "critical theory." Here it refers more narrowly to the analysis of the topic of race in the various subdisciplinary fields as they have emerged within the Anglo-American and European philosophical traditions. Africana philosophy also has a broad meaning, encompassing all philosophy rooted in African traditions or in the African diaspora: thus, so understood, it essentially includes critical race theory. Some of the works and anthologies mentioned below suggest ways of expanding the philosophical conversation beyond the dialogue between the Enlightenment and counter-Enlightenment thinkers focused on in this volume. We list some of the most significant works in the field, as well as informative surveys and anthologies that offer more extensive bibliographies of the full range of interdisciplinary research on race and African thought, which was one of the major developments in twentieth-century scholarship. The long tradition of racially focused social reformers from Frederick Douglass to the Reverend Dr. Martin Luther King Jr. constitutes one significant strand of critical race theory and is one of the most original and important features of American thought as a whole.

Of first importance is the philosophy of Alain Locke, who taught at Howard University between 1912 and 1953. For collections of his works and works about him, see *The Works of Alain Locke*, edited by Charles Molesworth (2012); *The Critical Pragmatism of Alain Locke: A Reader on Value Theory, Aesthetics, Community, Culture, Race, and Education* (1999) and *The Philosophy of Alain Locke: Harlem Renaissance and Beyond* (1989), both edited by Leonard Harris; and Harris and Molesworth, *Alain L. Locke: The Biography of a Philosopher* (2008). Bernard R. Boxill—in *Blacks and Social Justice* (1984; rev. ed., 1992), his edited volume *Race and Racism* (2001), and his numerous essays—has made a significant contribution to political theory. The many works by Cornel West span an impressive range of topics from the history of philosophy, the philosophy of religion, the philosophy of race, and political theory: see *The American Evasion of Philosophy: A Genealogy of Pragmatism* (1989), *Prophesy Deliverance! An Afro-American Revolutionary Christianity* (1982), *Race Matters* (1993), *Democracy Matters: Winning the Fight against Imperialism* (2004), *The Ethical Dimensions of Marxist Thought* (1991), and *Keeping Faith: Philosophy and Race in America* (1993). Charles Mills's works, such as *The Racial Contract* (1997), *Blackness Visible: Essays on Philosophy and Race* (1998), and *From Class to Race: Essays in White Marxism and Black Radicalism* (2003), have been groundbreaking in their analysis of how race has been systematically overlooked by the philosophical tradition and what its theoretical implications are.

Kwame Anthony Appiah (included in this anthology's companion volume, *The Analytic Tradition*) has published a remarkable series of books that draw extensively both on the tradition of European thought after Kant and on insights from the African continent. His works—such as *Cosmopolitanism: Ethics in a World of Strangers* (2006), *The Honor Code: How Moral Revolutions Happen* (2000), *The Ethics of Identity* (2005), *In My Father's House: Africa in the Philosophy of Culture* (1992), and *Color Conscious: The Political Morality of Race* (1996)—have been on (and perhaps have even defined) the cutting edge of the philosophy of race and identity; they offer an important model of how this kind of philosophy can be done. Also recommended is the work of Sylvia Wynter, as found in her *We Must Learn to Sit Down Together and Talk about a Little Culture: Decolonizing Essays, 1967–1984* (2012); on her work, see *Sylvia Wynter: On Being Human as Praxis*, edited by Katherine McKittrick (2015), and *After Man, Towards the Human: Critical Essays on Sylvia Wynter*, edited by Anthony Bogues (2005).

The Routledge series Africana Thought: The World of Black Philosophy is notable for the diversity of its many volumes. In particular, see Anthony Bogues, *Black Heretics, Black Prophets: Radical Political Intellectuals* (2003); Lewis R. Gordon, *Existentia Africana: Understanding*

Africana Existential Thought (2000); and Paget Henry, *Caliban's Reason: Introducing Afro-Caribbean Philosophy* (2000). Some works by Gordon are mentioned in the Frantz Fanon bibliography; others worth noting include *Bad Faith and Antiblack Racism* (1995), *An Introduction to Africana Philosophy* (2008), *Her Majesty's Other Children: Sketches of Racism from a Neocolonial Age* (1997), and *Disciplinary Decadence: Living Thought in Trying Times* (2006).

A number of volumes survey the philosophies of Africa, the African diaspora, and critical race theory, including *African Philosophy: An Anthology*, edited by Emmanuel Chukwudi Eze (1998); *A Companion to African Philosophy*, edited by Kwasi Wiredu (2004); *The African Philosophy Reader*, edited by P. H. Coetzee and A. P. J. Roux (1998); *Critical Race Theory*, edited by Kimberlé Crenshaw et al. (1995); and *Critical Race Theory: The Cutting Edge*, edited by Richard Delgado and Jean Stefancic (1995, ed. by Delgado only; 3rd ed., 2013). A classic introductory work designed for classroom use is Delgado and Stefancic's *Critical Race Theory: An Introduction* (2001; 2nd ed., 2012).

There are a growing number of works on the philosophy of race. Among the most helpful for providing an overview of the wide-ranging issues are Paul Taylor, *Race: A Philosophical Introduction* (2004; 2nd ed., 2013); Albert Atkin, *The Philosophy of Race* (2012); Lucius T. Outlaw, *On Race and Philosophy* (1996); *Race and Epistemologies of Ignorance*, edited by Shannon Sullivan and Nancy Tuana (2007); Linda Martín Alcoff, *Visible Identities: Race, Gender, and the Self* (2005); and two collections edited by Robert Bernasconi, *Race* (2001) and *Race and Racism in Continental Philosophy* (2003).

Author Bibliographies

In what follows the dates of translation indicated are those of the publication of what we regard as the best of the alternatives currently available.

Arendt, Hannah

The Origins of Totalitarianism (1951; 3rd ed., 1973) is perhaps Arendt's most widely read work; each of its three parts was also published separately in 1968, under the titles *Antisemitism*, *Imperialism*, and *Totalitarianism*. Also well known are *Eichmann in Jerusalem: A Report on the Banality of Evil* (1963; rev. ed., 1964) and *Men in Dark Times* (1968). Other important works on politics and ethics are *Crises of the Republic* (1972), a collection of essays, including "Lying in Politics: Reflections on the Pentagon Papers," "Civil Disobedience," "On Violence," and "Thoughts on Politics and Revolution: A Commentary"; *On Revolution* (1963; rev. ed., 1965); *The Jew as Pariah: Jewish Identity and Politics in the Modern Age* (1978), a collection of writings (1942–66), some of which were originally written in German; and *The Promise of Politics* (2005), another collection, of greatest interest for its "Introduction *into* Politics" (written 1956–60). Three excellent collections of essays that address the intersections of philosophy, ethics, politics, and practical problems of the times are *Between Past and Future* (1961; rev. ed., 1968); *Responsibility and Judgment* (2003), containing writings of the 1960s; and *Essays in Understanding, 1930–1954* (1994). Her two major works of theoretical philosophy are *The Human Condition* (1958; 2nd ed., 1998) and *The Life of the Mind* (2 vols., 1977–78). Her *Lectures on Kant's Political Philosophy* (1982) and *Love and Saint Augustine* (1929; trans. 1996), which began as her dissertation, are essential reading on those topics and thinkers. Several interviews with Arendt are available in *Hannah Arendt: The Last Interview* (2013).

For collections of her letters, see *Letters, 1925–1975* (1998; trans. 2004), to Heidegger; *Hannah Arendt/Karl Jaspers Correspondence, 1926–1969* (1985; trans. 1992); *Within Four Walls: The Correspondence between Hannah Arendt and Heinrich Blücher, 1936–1968* (1996; trans. 2000); and *Between Friends: The Correspondence of Hannah Arendt and Mary McCar-*

thy, 1949–1975 (1995). The intersection of her life and thought with Martin Heidegger is examined in several works: Dana R. Villa, *Arendt and Heidegger: The Fate of the Political* (1996); Elżbieta Ettinger, *Hannah Arendt/Martin Heidegger* (1995); Jacques Taminiaux, *The Thracian Maid and the Professional Thinker: Arendt and Heidegger* (1992; trans. 1997); and Daniel Maier-Katkin, *Strangers from Abroad: Hannah Arendt, Martin Heidegger, Friendship, and Forgiveness* (2010).

The diverse issues and concerns in Arendt's thought are surveyed in a number of collections of critical essays: see *The Cambridge Companion to Hannah Arendt*, edited by Dana Villa (2000); *Hannah Arendt: Critical Essays*, edited by Lewis P. Hinchman and Sandra K. Hinchman (1994); *Feminist Interpretations of Hannah Arendt*, edited by Bonnie Honig (1995); *Hannah Arendt: Twenty Years Later*, edited by Larry May and Jerome Kohn (1996); and *Thinking in Dark Times: Hannah Arendt on Ethics and Politics*, edited by Roger Berkowitz, Thomas Keenan, and Jeffrey Katz (2010). Introductions to her ideas include Karin Fry, *Arendt: A Guide for the Perplexed* (2009); Elisabeth Young-Bruehl, *Why Arendt Matters* (2006); Finn Bowring, *Hannah Arendt: A Critical Introduction* (2011); and Simon Swift, *Hannah Arendt* (2009). Julia Kristeva's *Hannah Arendt* (1999; trans. 2001) is a significant study of Arendt's life and thought. For other intellectual autobiographies, see Elisabeth Young-Bruehl, *Hannah Arendt: For Love of the World* (1982; 2nd ed., 2004), and Derwent May, *Hannah Arendt* (1986).

There are many works on Arendt's political thought. Among them are Lisa Jane Disch, *Hannah Arendt and the Limits of Philosophy* (1994; 2nd ed., 1996); Dana R. Villa, *Politics, Philosophy, Terror: Essays on the Thought of Hannah Arendt* (1999); Margaret Canovan, *Hannah Arendt: A Reinterpretation of Her Political Thought* (1992); George Kateb, *Hannah Arendt, Politics, Conscience, Evil* (1983); Seyla Benhabib, *The Reluctant Modernism of Hannah Arendt* (1996; 2nd ed., 2003); *Politics in Dark Times: Encoun-*

ters with Hannah Arendt, edited by Seyla Benhabib (2010); Michael G. Gottsegen, The Political Thought of Hannah Arendt (1994); Robert C. Pirro, Hannah Arendt and the Politics of Tragedy (2000); Mary G. Dietz, Turning Operations: Feminism, Arendt, and Politics (2002); Phillip Hansen, Hannah Arendt: Politics, History and Citizenship (1993); Shiraz Dossa, The Public Realm and the Public Self: The Political Theory of Hannah Arendt (1989); and Maurizio Passerin d'Entrèves, The Political Philosophy of Hannah Arendt (1993).

More recently, see Patricia Owens, Between War and Politics: International Relations and the Thought of Hannah Arendt (2007); Steve Buckler, Hannah Arendt and Political Theory: Challenging the Tradition (2011); Hannah Arendt and the Law, edited by Marco Goldoni and Christopher McCorkindale (2012); Action and Appearance: Ethics and the Politics of Writing in Hannah Arendt, edited by Anna Yeatman, Phillip Hansen, Magdalena Zolkos, and Charles Barbour (2011); Serena Parekh, Hannah Arendt and the Challenge of Modernity: A Phenomenology of Human Rights (2008); Hannah Arendt and International Relations: Readings across the Lines, edited by Anthony F. Lang and John Williams (2005); and Michael H. McCarthy, The Political Humanism of Hannah Arendt (2012). The following two collections of critical essays also deserve mentioning: Hannah Arendt and the Meaning of Politics, edited by Craig Calhoun and John McGowan (1997), and Judgment, Imagination, and Politics: Themes from Kant and Arendt, edited by Ronald Beiner and Jennifer Nedelsky (2001).

Among the works examining Arendt's life and thought in relation to politics, history, and Judaism are Bernard J. Bergen, The Banality of Evil: Hannah Arendt and "The Final Solution" (1998); Jennifer Ring, The Political Consequences of Thinking: Gender and Judaism in the Work of Hannah Arendt (1997); Hannah Arendt in Jerusalem, edited by Steven E. Aschheim (2001); and Richard J. Bernstein, Hannah Arendt and the Jewish Question (1996).

Beauvoir, Simone de

Beauvoir's novels are a significant contribution to twentieth-century literature. They include She Came to Stay (1943; trans. 1954), The Blood of Others (1945; trans. 1948), Who Shall Die? (1945; trans. 1983), All Men Are Mortal (1946; trans. 1955), The Mandarins (1954; trans. 1956), and The Woman Destroyed (1967; trans. 1969).

The book for which Beauvoir is best known today, both among philosophers and more broadly, is The Second Sex (1949; 1952 and 2010)—a founding document of feminist thought. No less courageous, penetrating, and pathbreaking in its analysis of social norms and attitudes is

her examination of aging in The Coming of Age (1970; trans. 1972). The Ethics of Ambiguity (1947; trans. 1948) remains among the most precise and clear statements of the tenets of existentialism and their ethical import. Many of her shorter philosophical writings have recently been gathered and published in Philosophical Writings (2004); this is part of the Beauvoir Series, edited by Margaret A. Simons and Sylvie Le Bon de Beauvoir, which is making much of her work available in English for the first time, in scholarly editions. The other volumes to date are Political Writings (2012); Diary of a Philosophy Student, vol. 1, 1926–27 (2006); Wartime Diary (2009); and "The Useless Mouths," and Other Literary Writings (2011).

Beauvoir's massive autobiography, which chronicles her life up to 1972, may be one of the most complete and insightful ever produced. The volumes are Memoirs of a Dutiful Daughter (1958; trans. 1959); The Prime of Life (1960; trans. 1962); The Force of Circumstances (1963), translated in two volumes as After the War, 1944–1952 (1964) and Hard Times, 1952–1962 (1965); and All Said and Done (1972, trans. 1974). A Very Easy Death (1964; trans. 1965), a brief account of her mother's death, can also be considered a part of this series.

Among Beauvoir's other nonfiction works are her account of her travels in America, America Day by Day (1948; trans. 1952), and her long essay that accompanies the interviews with Sartre in Adieux: A Farewell to Sartre (1981; trans. 1984). Two sets of her letters—to the loves of her life—have been published: Letters to Sartre (1990; trans. 1991) and A Transatlantic Love Affair: Letters to Nelson Algren (1997; trans. 1998).

As one might expect, there are many biographies of Beauvoir, no few of which focus on her relation to Sartre. See Hazel Rowley, Tête-à-tête: Simone de Beauvoir and Jean-Paul Sartre (2005); Deirdre Bair, Simone de Beauvoir: A Biography (1990); Lisa Appignanesi, Simone de Beauvoir (1988; new ed., 2005); Claude Francis and Fernande Gontier, Simone de Beauvoir: A Life, a Love Story (1985; trans. 1987); Carol Ascher, Simone de Beauvoir: A Life of Freedom (1981); Kate Fullbrook and Edward Fullbrook, Simone de Beauvoir and Jean-Paul Sartre: The Remaking of a Twentieth-Century Legend (1994); and Carole Seymour-Jones, A Dangerous Liaison: A Revelatory New Biography of Simone de Beauvoir and Jean-Paul Sartre (2008). More philosophical in nature are Toril Moi, Simone de Beauvoir: The Making of an Intellectual Woman (1994; 2nd ed., 2008), and Edward Fullbrook and Kate Fullbrook, Sex and Philosophy: Rethinking de Beauvoir and Sartre (2008).

Ursula Tidd's Simone de Beauvoir (2009) provides an introduction to Beauvoir's thinking.

For philosophical secondary literature, see *The Cambridge Companion to Simone de Beauvoir*, edited by Claudia Card (2003); *The Legacy of Simone de Beauvoir*, edited by Emily R. Grosholz (2004); *Simone de Beauvoir: A Critical Reader*, edited by Elizabeth Fallaize (1998); *Simone de Beauvoir's Political Thinking*, edited by Lori Jo Marso and Patricia Moynagh (2006); *The Philosophy of Simone de Beauvoir: Critical Essays*, edited by Margaret A. Simons (2006); and *Beauvoir and Sartre: The Riddle of Influence*, edited by Christine Daigle and Jacob Golomb (2009).

Books that look specifically at the intersection of Beauvoir's thought and feminism include Nancy Bauer, *Simone de Beauvoir, Philosophy, and Feminism* (2001); Toril Moi, *Feminist Theory and Simone de Beauvoir* (1990); Margaret A. Simons, *Beauvoir and "The Second Sex": Feminism, Race, and the Origins of Existentialism* (1999); *Feminist Interpretations of Simone de Beauvoir*, edited by Margaret A. Simons (1995); and *Simone de Beauvoir's "The Second Sex": New Interdisciplinary Essays*, edited by Ruth Evans (1998).

Significant works that consider Beauvoir's existentialist ethics are Fredrika Scarth, *The Other Within: Ethics, Politics, and the Body in Simone de Beauvoir* (2004); Kristana Arp, *The Bonds of Freedom: Simone de Beauvoir's Existential Ethics* (2001); *The Contradictions of Freedom: Philosophical Essays on Simone de Beauvoir's "The Mandarins,"* edited by Sally J. Scholz and Shannon M. Mussett (2005); and Debra B. Bergoffen, *The Philosophy of Simone de Beauvoir: Gendered Phenomenologies, Erotic Generosities* (1997). See also Anne Whitmarsh, *Simone de Beauvoir and the Limits of Commitment* (1981); Eleanore Holveck, *Simone de Beauvoir's Philosophy of Lived Experience: Literature and Metaphysics* (2002); Karen Vintges, *Philosophy as Passion: The Thinking of Simone de Beauvoir* (1992; trans. 1996), which analyzes Beauvoir's work in relation to that of Foucault; *Contingent Loves: Simone de Beauvoir and Sexuality*, edited by Melanie C. Hawthorne (2000); *The Existential Phenomenology of Simone de Beauvoir*, edited by Wendy O'Brien and Lester Embree (2001); and Penelope Deutscher, *The Philosophy of Simone de Beauvoir: Ambiguity, Conversion, Resistance* (2008).

Bergson, Henri

Bergson produced two doctoral theses in 1888: in Latin, "Aristotle's Concept of Place," and in French, published in 1889, *Time and Free Will: An Essay on the Immediate Data of Consciousness* (trans. 1910). His next major work was *Matter and Memory* (1896; 5th ed., 1908; trans. 1911). *Laughter: An Essay on the Meaning of the Comic* (1900; trans. 1911) was followed by the substantial essays "Dreams" (1901; trans. 1914)

and "Introduction to Metaphysics" (1903; trans. 1912). A selection of shorter essays written between 1903 and 1907 and developing ideas initially set forth in *Matter and Memory* was published as *Mind-Energy: Lectures and Essays* (*L'Energie spirituelle: Essais et conférences*, 1919; trans. 1920).

That collection appeared after what is generally considered to be Bergson's masterwork, *Creative Evolution* (1907; trans. 1911). In 1914, he gave the Gifford Lectures at Edinburgh University, titled "The Problem of Personality." His lectures delivered the same year at the Academie des Sciences Morales et Politiques were translated and published as *The Meaning of the War: Life and Matter in Conflict* (1915). In 1922 he published his next major work, *Duration and Simultaneity: With Reference to Einstein's Theory* (1922; trans. 1965). Relatively little further work appeared in print before *The Two Sources of Morality and Religion* (1932; trans. 1935). His last book, *The Creative Mind* (*La Pensée et le mouvant*, 1934; trans. 1946), contained two new introductory essays together with articles and lectures produced between 1903 and 1923, including "Introduction to Metaphysics" and "The Possible and the Real" (delivered at Oxford in 1920).

Several important recent works on Bergson are A. R. Lacey, *Bergson* (1989); Suzanne Guerlac, *Thinking in Time: An Introduction to Henri Bergson* (2006); Leszek Kolakowski, *Bergson* (1985); Keith Ansell Pearson, *Philosophy and the Adventure of the Virtual: Bergson and the Time of Life* (2002); F. C. T. Moore, *Bergson: Thinking Backwards* (1996); Leonard Lawlor, *The Challenge of Bergsonism: Phenomenology, Ontology, Ethics* (2003); John Mullarkey, *Bergson and Philosophy* (1999); *The New Bergson*, edited by John Mullarkey (1999); *Bergson, Politics, and Religion*, edited by Alexandre Lefebvre and Melanie White (2012); Alexandre Lefebvre, *Human Rights as a Way of Life: On Bergson's Political Philosophy* (2013); *Bergson and Phenomenology*, edited by Michael R. Kelly (2010); and G. William Barnard, *Living Consciousness: The Metaphysical Vision of Henri Bergson* (2011).

A fair amount of philosophical writing was inspired by Gilles Deleuze's use of Bergson and adaptation of his vitalism in his *Bergsonism* (1966; trans. 1988); for example, see Valentine Moulard-Leonard, *Deleuze-Bergson Encounters: Transcendental Experience and the Thought of the Virtual* (2008). Mark Antliff's *Inventing Bergson: Cultural Politics and the Parisian Avant-garde* (1993) relates Bergson to the artistic and cultural movements of his time. There are also several works on Bergson's relation to modernism in the arts, such as *Understanding Bergson, Understanding Modernism*, edited by Paul Ardoin, S. E. Gontarski, and Laci Mattison

(2012). Earlier works that remain useful include *Bergson and the Evolution of Physics*, edited by P. A. Y. Gunter (1969), and A. E. Pilkington, *Bergson and His Influence: A Reassessment* (1976). A spate of works about Bergson emerged at the start of the twentieth century; now in the public domain, they are widely available in reprints.

More sources containing discussions of Bergson can be found in the sections on *Lebensphilosophie* and philosophical anthropology in General Bibliographies (above).

Buber, Martin

Many English-language translations of Buber's writings are books that collect essays and lectures drawn from various original sources rather than a single corresponding German-language volume. One exception is Buber's masterwork *I and Thou* (1923; trans. 1937). The volume *Good and Evil* (1953) contains two works, *Images of Good and Evil* (1952) and *Right and Wrong: An Interpretation of Some Psalms* (1952), both intended by Buber to contribute to founding an ontological ethics. *Between Man and Man* (1947) contains five essays: "Dialogue" (1929), "The Question to the Single One" (1936), "Education" (1926), "The Education of Character" (1939), and "What Is Man?" (1938). *The Knowledge of Man: Selected Essays* (1965) contains six essays originally published between 1951 and 1963. *The Martin Buber–Carl Rogers Dialogue: A New Transcript with Commentary* (1997) prints the transcripts of the 1957 meeting of these two thinkers, excerpted in *The Knowledge of Man*. Also noteworthy is Buber's early poetic-philosophical work *Daniel: Dialogues on Realization* (1913; trans. 1964), which set the stage for *I and Thou*.

Buber had a strong interest in the pietistic-mystical eastern European strain of Judaism called Hasidism. *The Way of Man, According to the Teaching of Hasidism* (1948; trans. 1950) contains six short essays that interpret Hasidic stories. *Mamre: Essays in Religion* (1946) contains essays selected from two books, one on the Israel question (*Kampf um Israel*, 1933) and one on Hasidism (*Deutung des chassidismus*, 1935). The translated essay collections *Hasidism* (1948) and *The Origin and Meaning of Hasidism* (1960) both draw on that 1935 volume, and overlap considerably in their contents. The contents of the latter volume and *Hasidism and Modern Man* (1958), which collects translations of other writings on this topic, were initially intended to be published together under the title *Hasidism and the Way of Man*. *Tales of the Hasidim*, published in German in 1949 and originally translated in two volumes—*The Early Masters* (1947) and *The Later Masters* (1948)—is now available in English in a single volume (1991). The brief volume *Ten Rungs* (1962; in some editions subtitled *Collected Hasidic Sayings*) is drawn from the same source. *Tales of the Hasidim* contains translations of revised forms of such earlier works as *The Hidden Light* (1924) and *The Great Maggid and His Succession* (1922). Still earlier works in this same area are *The Legend of the Baal-Shem* (1908; trans. 1955) and *The Tales of Rabbi Nachman* (1906; trans. 1956), Buber's adaptation of an early nineteenth-century work published in Yiddish and Hebrew. *Ecstatic Confessions: The Heart of Mysticism* (1909; trans. 1985), which he edited and introduced, collects descriptions of ecstatic, mystical experience from various religious sources.

Buber's short monograph *Meetings: Autobiographical Fragments* (3rd ed., 2002) was first published in the 1967 volume dedicated to him in the Library of Living Philosophers series. Also of a somewhat autobiographical nature is *Believing Humanism: My Testament, 1902–1965* (1965; trans. 1967). *The Letters of Martin Buber: A Life of Dialogue* (1991) translates selected letters from the three-volume German edition (1972–75).

Eclipse of God: Studies in the Relation between Religion and Philosophy (1952) consists primarily of talks given by Buber in the United States in 1951. *Pointing the Way: Collected Essays* (1957) translates essays and lectures written between 1909 and 1954 (many of which had been collected in *Hinweise*, 1953). *Paths in Utopia* (1946; trans. 1949) collects a series of lectures delivered in Hebrew. *On Judaism* (1967) translates two sets of addresses, delivered 1909–18 and 1939–51. *The Prophetic Faith* (1949; trans. 1949) and *Two Types of Faith* (1950; trans. 1951) explore Judaism and Christianity. *Kingship of God* (1932, 3rd. ed. 1956; trans. 1967) and *On the Bible: Eighteen Studies* (1968) are works of biblical scholarship. The latter contains chapters from *Moses: The Revelation and the Covenant* (1945; trans. 1946). A novel by Buber (1943/44) has appeared in English under two different titles: *For the Sake of Heaven: A Chronicle* (1945) and *Gog and Magog: A Novel* (1999).

The First Buber: Youthful Zionist Writings of Martin Buber (1999) translates writings from 1898 to 1902. Other writings on Israel in English translation are *A Land of Two Peoples: Martin Buber on Jews and Arabs* (1983; trans. 1983), which contains various letters and addresses of 1918 to 1965 in support of a two-nation solution; *Israel and the World: Essays in a Time of Crisis* (1948), a selection of essays and lectures written and published between 1920 and the early 1940s; *On Zion: The History of an Idea* (1945; trans. 1973 [trans. 1952 as *Israel and Palestine: The History of an Idea*]), lectures of 1944; *At the Turning: Three Addresses on Juda-*

ism (1952), delivered in New York in 1951 (all reprinted in *On Judaism*); and, co-written with Judah Magnes, *Arab–Jewish Unity* (1947).

Martin Buber on Psychology and Psychotherapy: Essays, Letters, and Dialogue (1999) contains essays published in German between 1950 and 1960, as well as letters between Buber and Hans Trüb. Other anthologies in English are *The Writings of Martin Buber* (1956), *To Hallow This Life: An Anthology* (1958), *On Intersubjectivity and Cultural Creativity* (1992), and *The Martin Buber Reader: Essential Writings* (2002). Maurice Friedman's *My Friendship with Martin Buber* (2013) contains some of Buber's letters.

Several excellent surveys of Buber's thought are available: see Maurice S. Friedman, *Martin Buber: The Life of Dialogue* (1955; 4th ed., 2002); Nathan Rotenstreich, *Immediacy and Its Limits: A Study in Martin Buber's Thought* (1991); Dan Avnon, *Martin Buber: The Hidden Dialogue* (1998); Avraham Shapira, *Hope for Our Time: Key Trends in the Thought of Martin Buber* (1994; trans. 1999); *The Philosophy of Martin Buber*, edited by Paul Arthur Schilpp (1967), in the Library of Living Philosophers series; *Martin Buber: A Contemporary Perspective*, edited by Paul Mendes-Flohr (2002); Paul R. Mendes-Flohr, *From Mysticism to Dialogue: Martin Buber's Transformation of German Social Thought* (1989); and *Martin Buber and the Human Sciences*, edited by Maurice Friedman et al. (1996), also on social thought.

Works that emphasize *I and Thou* and its philosophical and ethical implications include Kenneth Paul Kramer with Mechthild Gawlick, *Martin Buber's "I and Thou": Practicing Living Dialogue* (2003); Robert E. Wood, *Martin Buber's Ontology: An Analysis of "I and Thou"* (1969); Maurice Friedman, *Martin Buber and the Eternal* (1986); and Alexander S. Kohanski, *Martin Buber's Philosophy of Interhuman Relation: A Response to the Human Problematic of Our Time* (1982) and *An Analytical Interpretation of Martin Buber's "I and Thou"* (1975). Among works devoted to the ethical and sociopolitical implications of Buber's thought are James W. Walters, *Martin Buber and Feminist Ethics: The Priority of the Personal* (2003); *Levinas and Buber: Dialogue and Difference*, edited by Peter Atterton, Matthew Calarco, and Maurice Friedman (2004); Laurence J. Silberstein, *Martin Buber's Social and Religious Thought: Alienation and the Quest for Meaning*; and Bernard Susser, *Existence and Utopia: The Social and Political Thought of Martin Buber* (1989).

Works that focus on Buber and religious thought include Pamela Vermes, *Buber on God and the Perfect Man* (1980); Roy Oliver [Walker], *The Wanderer and the Way: The Hebrew Tradition in the Writings of Martin Buber* (1968); Donald J. Moore, *Martin Buber: Prophet of Religious Secularism* (1974; 2nd ed., 1996); Grete Schaeder, *The Hebrew Humanism of Martin Buber* (1966; trans. 1973); John M. Oesterreicher, *The Unfinished Dialogue: Martin Buber and the Christian Way* (1986); Steven Kepnes, *The Text as Thou: Martin Buber's Dialogical Hermeneutics and Narrative Theology* (1992); Martina Urban, *Aesthetics of Renewal: Martin Buber's Early Representation of Hasidism as Kulturkritik* (2008); and Kenneth Paul Kramer, *Martin Buber's Spirituality: Hasidic Wisdom for Everyday Life* (2012). Two series on the thought of modern theologians contain volumes titled *Martin Buber*, one by Ronald Gregor Smith (1966) and the other by Stephen M. Panko (1976).

Buber figures significantly in Walter Kaufmann's *Nietzsche, Heidegger, and Buber*, vol. 2 of *Discovering the Mind* (1980). Other works that focus on Buber's intersection with other thinkers include Haim Gordon, *The Heidegger–Buber Controversy: The Status of the I–Thou* (2001); Sylvain Boni, *The Self and the Other in the Ontologies of Sartre and Buber* (1982); Paul E. Pfuetze, *Self, Society, Existence: Human Nature and Dialogue in the Thought of George Herbert Mead and Martin Buber* (1954); Kenneth N. Cissna and Rob Anderson, *Moments of Meeting: Buber, Rogers, and the Potential for Public Dialogue* (2002); and Alexander Even-Chen and Ephraim Meir, *Between Heschel and Buber: A Comparative Study* (2012).

For biographical works, see Maurice S. Friedman, *Martin Buber's Life and Work* (3 vols., 1981–83), abridged as *Encounter on the Narrow Ridge: A Life of Martin Buber* (1991); *The Other Martin Buber: Recollections of His Contemporaries*, edited by Haim Gordon (1988); and Gilya Gerda Schmidt, *Martin Buber's Formative Years: From German Culture to Jewish Renewal, 1897–1909* (1995).

Butler, Judith

Butler's books are listed and discussed in her headnote, above. Many of her essays have been collected in *Who Sings the Nation-State? Language, Politics, Belonging*, co-written with Gayatri Chakravorty Spivak (2007); *Is Critique Secular? Blasphemy, Injury, and Free Speech*, co-written with Talal Asad, Wendy Brown, and Saba Mahmood (2009); *The Power of Religion in the Public Sphere*, co-written with Jürgen Habermas, Charles Taylor, and Cornel West (2011); and, most recently, *Senses of the Subject* (2015). For a representative selection, see *The Judith Butler Reader*, edited by Sara Salih, with Judith Butler (2004).

Butler's work is extensively discussed in the philosophical literature on sex and sexuality, gender, politics, selfhood, power, and language. Studies devoted specifically to Butler's thought include Sara Salih, *Judith Butler* (2002); Anita Brady and Tony Schirato, *Understanding Judith Butler* (2011); Gill Jagger, *Judith Butler: Sexual Politics, Social Change and the Power of the Performative* (2008); Moya Lloyd, *Judith Butler: From Norms to Politics* (2007); Samuel Chambers and Terrell Carver, *Judith Butler and Political Theory: Troubling Politics* (2008); Annika Thiem, *Unbecoming Subjects: Judith Butler, Moral Philosophy, and Critical Responsibility* (2008); and Birgit Schippers, *The Political Philosophy of Judith Butler* (2014).

Cassirer, Ernst

Cassirer's masterwork is *The Philosophy of Symbolic Forms*. Three volumes were published in his lifetime: 1, *Language* (1923; trans. 1955); 2, *Mythical Thought* (1925; trans. 1955); and 3, *The Phenomenology of Knowledge* (1929; trans. 1957). (Cassirer had originally intended the title of the third volume—*Phänomenologie der Erkenntnis*, echoing Hegel's *Phänomenologie des Geistes*—to be the title of the entire project and work.) After his death a fourth volume was published (as the first volume of his *Nachgelassene Manuskripte und Texte*): *The Metaphysics of Symbolic Forms* (1995; trans. 1996), containing unpublished manuscripts dating from 1928 to 1940. In 1925 Cassirer also published *Language and Myth* (trans. 1946), a short introduction to some of his central ideas on those matters.

Cassirer wrote *An Essay on Man: An Introduction to a Philosophy of Human Culture* (1944) in English, late in his life, to introduce English-speaking readers to his thinking about symbolic forms and human culture, and to elaborate on their significance for understanding our human nature. In *The Myth of the State* (1946), also written in English, Cassirer extended his philosophy of culture into the arena of political life. The works translated in *Symbol, Myth and Culture: Essays and Lectures of Ernst Cassirer, 1935–1945* (1979) help fill out the picture of his thinking during this last period of his life. Finally, a valuable general account of what it is to study cultural or, more broadly, human phenomena is offered in *The Logic of the Humanities* (1942; trans. 1961).

Before *Language and Myth* was translated and Cassirer himself began writing in English in the mid-1940s, his only works available in English were two early books in the philosophy of science, *Substance and Function* (1910) and *Einstein's Theory of Relativity* (1921), translated and published in a single volume in 1923. It was thus as a philosopher of science that he first became known in the English-speaking world. Another work in this area is *Determinism and Indeterminism in Modern Physics: Historical and Systematic Studies of the Problem of Causality* (1937; trans. 1956). Other early writings are translated in *The Warburg Years (1919–1933): Essays on Language, Art, Myth, and Technology* (2013).

Cassirer is now perhaps best and most widely known as an outstanding and prodigious intellectual historian. *Das Erkenntnisproblem in der Philosophie und Wissenschaft der neueren Zeit* (*The Problem of Knowledge in Modern Philosophy and Science*), much of which remains untranslated, is an impressive 4-volume work that spans his entire career. Volume 1 (1906) covers the period from the Renaissance to Descartes, 2 (1907) continues the story up to Kant, and 3 (1920) is concerned with Kant and post-Kantian thought through Hegel. A fourth volume, compiled after Cassirer's death from his manuscripts written in the 1940s, is the only one that has been translated into English, as *The Problem of Knowledge: Philosophy, Science, and History Since Hegel* (1957; trans. 1950). *The Philosophy of the Enlightenment* (1932; trans. 1951) and *The Individual and the Cosmos in Renaissance Philosophy* (1927; trans. 1963) are further contributions to Cassirer's sweeping intellectual history of Western philosophy.

Three other works provide more detailed studies of major figures of the Enlightenment: *Kant's Life and Thought* (1918, 2nd ed. 1921; trans. 1981); *The Question of Jean-Jacques Rousseau* (1932; trans. 1954); and *Rousseau, Kant, Goethe* (1945), which collects two essays. *Platonic Renaissance in England* (1932; trans. 1953) is another work of intellectual history. Cassirer's studies of Descartes and Leibniz—*Descartes' Critique of the Foundations of Mathematics and the Sciences* (1899), *Descartes: Teachings, Personality, and Impact* (1939), and *Leibniz's System in Its Scientific Foundations* (1902)—have not yet been translated.

Perhaps the most useful secondary source on Cassirer is the volume devoted to him in the Library of Living Philosophers series, *The Philosophy of Ernst Cassirer*, edited by Paul Arthur Schilpp (1949); it also contains Cassirer's essay "'Spirit' and 'Life' in Contemporary Philosophy" (1930), originally a 1929 lecture, in which he discusses Max Scheler. Steve G. Lofts, *Ernst Cassirer: A "Repetition" of Modernity* (2000), and Seymour W. Itzkoff, *Ernst Cassirer: Philosopher of Culture* (1977) and *Ernst Cassirer: Scientific Knowledge and the Concept of Man* (1971; 2nd ed., 1997), offer helpful introductions to Cassirer's thought.

Secondary works focusing on *The Philosophy of Symbolic Forms* include John Michael Krois, *Cassirer: Symbolic Forms and History* (1987); Carl H. Hamburg, *Symbol and Reality: Studies in the Philosophy of Ernst Cassirer* (1956); and Thora Ilin Bayer, *Cassirer's Metaphysics of Symbolic Forms: A Philosophical Commentary* (2001). William Schultz, *Cassirer and Langer on*

Myth: An Introduction (2000), and *Symbolic Forms and Cultural Studies: Ernst Cassirer's Theory of Culture*, edited by Cyrus Hamlin and John Michael Krois (2004), are also recommended. Excellent recent works on Cassirer include Edward Skidelsky, *Ernst Cassirer: The Last Philosopher of Culture* (2008); Donald Phillip Verene, *The Origins of the Philosophy of Symbolic Forms: Kant, Hegel, and Cassirer* (2011); *Ernst Cassirer on Form and Technology: Contemporary Readings*, edited by Aud Sissel Hoel and Ingvild Folkvord (2012); *The Symbolic Construction of Reality: The Legacy of Ernst Cassirer*, edited by Jeffrey Andrew Barash (2008); and *The Persistence of Myth as Symbolic Form*, edited by Paul Bishop and R. H. Stephenson (2008).

For more biographical books, see David R. Lipton, *Ernst Cassirer: The Dilemma of a Liberal Intellectual in Germany, 1914–1933* (1978); Emily J. Levine, *Dreamland of Humanists: Warburg, Cassirer, Panofsky, and the Hamburg School* (2013); and Gregory B. Moynahan, *Ernst Cassirer and the Critical Science of Germany, 1899–1919* (2013). Michael Friedman's *A Parting of the Ways: Carnap, Cassirer, and Heidegger* (2000) and Peter E. Gordon's *Continental Divide: Heidegger, Cassirer, Davos* (2010) both shed light on Cassirer's interaction with Heidegger.

Deleuze, Gilles and Guattari, Félix

Deleuze's early works are primarily studies of other thinkers. He first examined Hume in *Empiricism and Subjectivity: An Essay on Hume's Theory of Human Nature* (1953; trans. 1991), and then Nietzsche in *Nietzsche and Philosophy* (1962; trans. 1983, rev. ed. 2006). This was followed by *Kant's Critical Philosophy: The Doctrine of the Faculties* (1963; trans. 1984) and *Bergsonism* (1966; trans. 1988). Deleuze wrote two books on Spinoza: *Expressionism in Philosophy: Spinoza* (1968; trans. 1990) and *Spinoza: Practical Philosophy* (1981; trans. 1988). He also wrote *Foucault* (1986; trans. 1988) and *The Fold: Leibniz and the Baroque* (1988; trans. 1993). The collection *Pure Immanence: Essays on Life* (trans. 2005) contains an early essay on Nietzsche (1965) and an essay on Hume (1972). It also contains his final essay, "Immanence: A Life" (1995), written shortly before he committed suicide. *Gilles Deleuze from A to Z* (2011), a DVD set of a rather unconventional series of interviews given late in his life, is also available.

Deleuze's major works are *Difference and Repetition* (1968; trans. 1994) and *The Logic of Sense* (1969; trans. 1990). Also significant are the books that he co-wrote with Guattari: the two volumes of *Anti-Oedipus: Capitalism and Schizophrenia* (1972; trans. 1977) and *A Thousand Plateaus* (1980; trans. 1987), and *What Is Philosophy?* (1991; trans. 1994), the source of the selection above.

Deleuze is one of the few philosophers who have thought deeply about film, and his writings on this subject—*Cinema 1: The Movement-Image* (1983; trans. 1986) and *Cinema 2: The Time-Image* (1985; trans. 1989)—have had enormous impact. He also wrote extensively on other arts, in his books *Proust and Signs* (1964; trans. 2000); with Guattari, *Kafka: Toward a Minor Literature* (1975; trans. 1986); *Francis Bacon: The Logic of Sensation* (1981; trans. 2003); and *Masochism: Coldness and Cruelty* (1967, trans. 1989). Several collections of his essays and interviews are available in English, including *Desert Islands and Other Texts, 1953–1974* (2004); *Essays Critical and Clinical* (1993; trans. 1997); with Claire Parnet, *Dialogues* (1977; trans. 1987); *Negotiations, 1972–1990* (1990; trans. 1995); and *Two Regimes of Madness: Texts and Interviews, 1975–1995* (2006).

In addition to his collaborations with Deleuze, Guattari's works available in English translation are *The Anti-Oedipus Papers* (2004; trans. 2006), texts written between 1969 and 1973; *Molecular Revolution: Psychiatry and Politics* (1984), which translates selected chapters from two books, *Psychanalyse et transversalité* (1972, *Psychoanalysis and Transversality*) and *La révolution moléculaire* (1977, *Molecular Revolution*); *Chaosophy: Texts and Interviews, 1972–1977* (2009); *Soft Subversions: Texts and Interviews, 1977–1985* (2009); *The Machinic Unconscious: Essays in Schizoanalysis* (1979; trans. 2011); *The Three Ecologies* (1989; trans. 2000); *Schizoanalytic Cartographies* (1989; trans. 2013); and *Chaosmosis: An Ethico-Aesthetic Paradigm* (1992; trans. 1995).

Several studies that introduce and survey Deleuze's work are Michael Hardt, *Gilles Deleuze: An Apprenticeship in Philosophy* (1993); Patrick Hayden, *Multiplicity and Becoming: The Pluralist Empiricism of Gilles Deleuze* (1998); John Marks, *Gilles Deleuze: Vitalism and Multiplicity* (1998); Dorothea Olkowski, *Gilles Deleuze and the Ruin of Representation* (1999); John Rajchman, *The Deleuze Connections* (2000); Manuel De Landa, *Intensive Science and Virtual Philosophy* (2002); Todd May, *Gilles Deleuze: An Introduction* (2005); François Dosse, *Gilles Deleuze and Félix Guattari: Intersecting Lives* (2007; trans. 2010); Joe Hughes, *Philosophy after Deleuze* (2012); François Zourabichvili, *Deleuze: A Philosophy of the Event; together with The Vocabulary of Deleuze* (1994, 2003; trans. 2012); and Eugene B. Young, *The Deleuze and Guattari Dictionary* (2013).

A number of edited volumes of essays provide overviews of Deleuze's thought as a whole. See *Deleuze: A Critical Reader*, edited by Paul Patton (1996); *The Deleuze Dictionary*, edited by Adrian Parr (2005); *Gilles Deleuze: Key Concepts*, edited by Charles J. Stivale (2005); *Gilles*

Deleuze: The Intensive Reduction, edited by Constantin V. Boundas (2009); *Demystifying Deleuze: An Introductory Assemblage of Crucial Concepts*, edited by Rob Shields and Mickey Vallee (2012); and *The Cambridge Companion to Deleuze*, edited by Daniel W. Smith and Henry Somers-Hall (2012).

Two significant works on the philosophy of Deleuze are Alain Badiou, *Deleuze: The Clamor of Being* (1997; trans. 2000), and Slavoj Žižek, *Organs without Bodies: On Deleuze and Consequences* (2004). Badiou's interpretation is challenged by Clayton Crockett in *Deleuze beyond Badiou: Ontology, Multiplicity, and Event* (2013). Several works by Claire Colebrook are deserving of mention: *Gilles Deleuze* (2002), *Understanding Deleuze* (2002), and *Deleuze and the Meaning of Life* (2010). Ian Buchanan has written *Deleuzism: A Metacommentary* (2000), and has edited *A Deleuzian Century?* (1999). Together, Buchanan and Colebrook have edited *Deleuze and Feminist Theory* (2000).

For other useful and important studies, see Keith Ansell-Pearson, *Germinal Life: The Difference and Repetition of Deleuze* (1999); *Deleuze and Philosophy: The Difference Engineer*, edited by Ansell-Pearson (1997); and Daniel W. Smith, *Essays on Deleuze* (2012). Several other significant interpretations are Levi R. Bryant, *Difference and Givenness: Deleuze's Transcendental Empiricism and the Ontology of Immanence* (2008); James Williams, *Gilles Deleuze's Philosophy of Time: A Critical Introduction and Guide* (2011); Eleanor Kaufman, *Deleuze, The Dark Precursor: Dialectic, Structure, Being* (2012); and Miguel de Beistegui, *Immanence: Deleuze and Philosophy* (2010).

Analyses of Deleuze's relation to other significant figures in the history of philosophy are also plentiful. They include *Hegel and Deleuze: Together Again for the First Time*, edited by Karen Houle and Jim Vernon (2013); Henry Somers-Hall, *Hegel, Deleuze, and the Critique of Representation: Dialectics of Negation and Difference* (2012); Jeffrey Bell, *Deleuze's Hume: Philosophy, Culture and the Scottish Enlightenment* (2009); *Thinking between Deleuze and Kant: A Strange Encounter*, edited by Edward Willatt and Matt Lee (2009); *Deleuze's Philosophical Lineage*, edited by Graham Jones and Jon Roffe (2009); and Joe Hughes, *Deleuze and the Genesis of Representation* (2008).

Several studies of *Difference and Repetition* are available: James Williams, *Gilles Deleuze's "Difference and Repetition": A Critical Introduction and Guide* (2003); Joe Hughes, *Deleuze's "Difference and Repetition": A Reader's Guide* (2009); and Henry Somers-Hall, *Deleuze's "Difference and Repetition": An Edinburgh Philosophical Guide* (2013). On *Logic of Sense*, see James Williams, *Gilles Deleuze's "Logic of Sense": A Critical Introduction and Guide* (2008; 2nd ed., 2013), and Sean Bowden, *The Priority of Events: Deleuze's "Logic of Sense"* (2011). *Deleuze and "The Fold": A Critical Reader*, edited by Sjoerd van Tuinen and Niamh McDonnell (2010), deals with Deleuze's debt to Leibniz.

Deleuze's co-authored works with Guattari have also received much attention. See Ronald Bogue, *Deleuze and Guattari* (1989); Brian Massumi, *A User's Guide to "Capitalism and Schizophrenia": Deviations from Deleuze and Guattari* (1992); Philip Goodchild, *Deleuze and Guattari: An Introduction to the Politics of Desire* (1996); Charles J. Stivale, *The Two-Fold Thought of Deleuze and Guattari: Intersections and Animations* (1998); *Deleuze & Guattari: New Mappings in Politics, Philosophy, and Culture*, edited by Eleanor Kaufman and Kevin Jon Heller (1998); Eugene W. Holland, *Deleuze and Guattari's "Anti-Oedipus": Introduction to Schizoanalysis* (1999) and *Deleuze and Guattari's "A Thousand Plateaus": A Reader's Guide* (2013); *A Shock to Thought: Expressions after Deleuze and Guattari*, edited by Brian Massumi (2002); Eric Alliez, *The Signature of the World, or, What Is Deleuze and Guattari's Philosophy?* (1993; trans. 2004); Ian Buchanan, *Deleuze and Guattari's "Anti-Oedipus": A Reader's Guide* (2008); Gregg Lambert, *Who's Afraid of Deleuze and Guattari?* (2006); and Rodolphe Gasché, *Geophilosophy: On Gilles Deleuze and Felix Guattari's "What Is Philosophy?"* (2014). One of the few secondary sources concerned solely with Guattari is Gary Genosko's *Félix Guattari: An Aberrant Introduction* (2002).

Essays on the ethical implications of Deleuze's thought are collected in *Deleuze/Guattari & Ecology*, edited by Bernd Herzogenrath (2009); *Deleuze and Ethics*, edited by Nathan Jun and Daniel W. Smith (2011); and *Revisiting Normativity with Deleuze*, edited by Rosi Braidotti and Patricia Pisters (2012). Also of note is Gordon C. F. Bearn, *Life Drawing: A Deleuzean Aesthetics of Existence* (2013). Works that focus on the political aspects of Deleuze's thought, as expressed individually and with Guattari, include Paul Patton, *Deleuze and the Political* (2000) and *Deleuzian Concepts: Philosophy, Colonization, Politics* (2010), and Iain Mackenzie and Robert Porter, *Dramatizing the Political: Deleuze and Guattari* (2011).

Secondary works that focus on Deleuze, film, literature, and aesthetics in general include *The Brain Is the Screen: Deleuze and the Philosophy of Cinema*, edited by Gregory Flaxman (2000); Laura U. Marks, *The Skin of the Film: Intercultural Cinema, Embodiment, and the Senses* (2000); Barbara M. Kennedy, *Deleuze and Cinema: The Aesthetics of Sensation* (2000); Patricia Pisters, *The Matrix of Visual Culture: Working with Deleuze in Film Theory* (2003); Ronald

Bogue, *Deleuze on Cinema* (2003) and *Deleuze on Music, Painting, and the Arts* (2003); and *Deleuze and Literature*, edited by Ian Buchanan and John Marks (2000). More recent studies are Paola Marrati, *Gilles Deleuze: Cinema and Philosophy* (2003; trans. 2008); *Deleuze and the Schizoanalysis of Cinema*, edited by Ian Buchanan and Patricia MacCormack (2008); *Deleuze and Contemporary Art*, edited by Stephen Zepke and Simon O'Sullivan (2010); *Afterimages of Gilles Deleuze's Film Philosophy*, edited by D. N. Rodowick (2010); Felicity Colman, *Deleuze and Cinema: The Film Concepts* (2011); and Nadine Boljkovac, *Untimely Affects: Gilles Deleuze and an Ethics of Cinema* (2013).

Derrida, Jacques

Derrida was an extraordinarily prolific writer. In addition to the books mentioned here, he also wrote a vast number of essays and other short pieces. *The Problem of Genesis in Husserl's Philosophy* (1990; trans. 2003) was Derrida's master's degree thesis from 1954. Much of his early work focuses on Husserl, notably *Edmund Husserl's "Origin of Geometry": An Introduction* (1962; trans. 1978) and *Speech and Phenomena, and Other Essays on Husserl's Theory of Signs* (1967; trans. 1973). An early collection of important essays written between 1959 and 1967 is *Writing and Difference* (1967; trans. 1978), which includes discussions of Lévinas, Freud, phenomenology, Foucault, Descartes, and Hegel. Derrida's major early theoretical work is *Of Grammatology* (1967; trans. 1976, corrected ed. 1997). *Limited Inc* (1988) gathers Derrida's engagement with John Searle on language: two essays (1972, 1977), first published in English in 1977, and an afterword original to the volume. The earlier essay is also found in *Margins of Philosophy* (1972; trans. 1982), which contains in addition important essays on figures such as Hegel and Heidegger, as well as key essays on language and *différance*. Volumes that collect and translate essays on literature, politics, the history of philosophy, and autobiography (among other topics) are *Psyche: Inventions of the Other* (1987, 2 vols. 1998–2003; trans. 2007–08) and *Signature Derrida* (2013).

Another important theoretical work from this period is *Dissemination* (1972; trans. 1981)—a major treatise on, among other things, Plato. One of Derrida's primary encounters with Heidegger is found in *Of Spirit: Heidegger and the Question* (1987; trans. 1989), which some scholars view as a major turning point in his ethical and political thinking. His main discussion of Nietzsche is found in the early work *Spurs: Nietzsche's Styles* (1978; trans. 1979). *The Ear of the Other: Otobiography, Transference, Translation* (1982; trans. 1985) contains "Otobiographies: The Teaching of Nietzsche and the

Politics of the Proper Name" as well as an interview with Derrida and two roundtable discussions on autobiography and translation. *Raising the Tone of Philosophy: Late Essays by Immanuel Kant, Transformative Critique by Jacques Derrida* (1993) translates two late essays by Kant and Derrida's 1982 essay on them. One of Derrida's most stylistically challenging works is his encounter with Hegel in *Glas* (1974; trans. 1986).

An unusual work in the history of philosophy, which is in part an epistolary novel, is *The Post Card: From Socrates to Freud and Beyond* (1980; trans. 1987). Derrida discusses Freud, Lacan, and Foucault in *Resistances of Psychoanalysis* (1996; trans. 1998). His interest in psychoanalysis, as well as in writing, books, memory, forgetting, machines, and technology, is pursued in *Archive Fever: A Freudian Impression* (1995; trans. 1995) and in its companion piece, *Paper Machine* (2001; trans. 2005). A related work, containing essays from 2000 and 2001 discussing language, speech acts, psychoanalysis, globalization, and technology, is *Without Alibi* (2002). It extends these discussions to the themes of lying and forgiveness and so serves as a bridge to his thought on ethics and religion.

Derrida wrote two books about the French feminist theorist Hélène Cixous: *Geneses, Genealogies, Genres, and Genius: The Secrets of the Archive* (2003; trans. 2006) and *H.C. for Life, That Is to Say . . .* (2002; trans. 2006). He also co-authored a book with her, *Veils* (1998; trans. 2001). *The Instant of My Death/Demeure: Fiction and Testimony* (1998; trans. 2000) contains and responds to a short text by another of his friends and colleagues, Maurice Blanchot. *Mémoires: For Paul de Man* (1986), published originally in English, contains Derrida's response to the controversy surrounding his friend Paul de Man, whose youthful fascist writings caused an uproar when discovered after his death. Derrida analyzes Jean-Luc Nancy and the sense of touch in the history of philosophy in *On Touching: Jean-Luc Nancy* (2000; trans. 2005). *The Work of Mourning* (2001) collects translated writings occasioned by the deaths of various philosophers and friends. One of those essays is found as well in *Adieu to Emmanuel Levinas* (1997; trans. 1999), which also contains an analysis of Lévinas's ethics.

Aporias (1996; trans. 1993) is a work that reflects on death. Concerns with death prompted Derrida's first extended studies of religion, beginning with his encounter with Kierkegaard in *The Gift of Death* (1992; trans. 1995). See also the essays translated in *Acts of Religion* (2002), including "Hospitality" and "The Eyes of Language," and Derrida's essay in a collection that he co-edited, *Religion* (1996; trans. 1998). *Given Time: I, Counterfeit Money* (1991; trans. 1992) is an important text for understanding the central notions of giving and the gift, largely via a meditation on a story by Baudelaire. *A Taste for the Secret*, with Maurizio Ferraris (1997; trans. 2001), is a reflection on the themes around which Derrida sees his entire corpus as being organized.

An important work bridging Derrida's political and religious thinking is *Of Hospitality: Anne Dufourmantelle Invites Jacques Derrida to Respond* (1997; trans. 2000). *Specters of Marx: The State of the Debt, the Work of Mourning, and the New International* (1993; trans. 1994) sheds light on the nexus of concepts that dominate Derrida's ethical and political thought. Two important works on politics are *Politics of Friendship* (1994; trans. 1997) and *Rogues: Two Essays on Reason* (2003; trans. 2005). *On the Name* (1995) collects three short works, originally published separately—one on Plato's *Timaeus* and two that deal with issues in politics, religion, and language. *On Cosmopolitanism and Forgiveness* (1997; trans. 2001) is a meditation on the political issues of the rights of refugees, reconciliation after crimes against humanity, and the nature of our political duties and capacity to forgive others. Derrida's final works are available in the volumes *The Animal That Therefore I Am* (2006; trans. 2008), *The Beast and the Sovereign* (2 vols., 2008–10; trans. 2009–11), and *The Death Penalty*, vol. 1 (2012; trans. 2014).

Monolingualism of the Other; or, The Prosthesis of Origin (1996; trans. 1998) deals with membership in linguistic and cultural communities; *The Other Heading: Reflections on Today's Europe* (1991; trans. 1992) discusses threats to Europe from fundamentalism. A work that ties Derrida's study of education and philosophy to his views on politics, containing a lecture that he gave in 1991 as well as a roundtable discussion, is *Ethics, Institutions, and the Right to Philosophy* (1997; trans. 2002). Derrida's *Right to Philosophy* (1990), a massive work on education and philosophy (particularly the teaching of and institutionalization of philosophy) has been translated in two volumes: *Who's Afraid of Philosophy? Right to Philosophy 1* (2002) and *Eyes of the University: Right to Philosophy 2* (2004).

The Truth in Painting (1978; trans. 1987) is an early book in philosophical aesthetics and art criticism. *Memoirs of the Blind: The Self-Portrait and Other Ruins* (1990; trans. 1993) discusses representation, art, and vision. Derrida examines the drawings and portraits of the French writer Antonin Artaud in *The Secret Art of Antonin Artaud* (1986; trans. 1998). Two works of literary criticism are *Sovereignties in Question: The Poetics of Paul Celan* (2005), which collects essays originally published in French between 1986 and 2005, and *Acts of Literature* (1992), which gathers a range of essays and excerpts.

Finally, a number of volumes in English contain interviews with Derrida: see *Positions* (1972; trans. 1981, rev. ed. 2004), *Negotiations: Interventions and Interviews, 1971–2001* (2002), *Philosophy in a Time of Terror: Dialogues with Jürgen Habermas and Jacques Derrida* (2003), *For What Tomorrow . . . : A Dialogue* (2001; trans. 2004), *Echographies of Television: Filmed Interviews* (1996; trans. 2002), *Points . . . : Interviews, 1974–1994* (1992; trans. 1995), and *Learning to Live Finally: An Interview with Jean Birnbaum* (2005; trans. 2007).

As one might expect, the secondary literature on Derrida is considerable. Among the biographical works on his life and thought are Benoit Peeters, *Derrida: A Biography* (2010; trans. 2013); David Mikics, *Who Was Jacques Derrida? An Intellectual Biography* (2009); and Edward Baring, *The Young Derrida and French Philosophy, 1945–1968* (2011). Helpful introductory works include Jeff Collins, *Introducing Derrida* (1996); Penelope Deutscher, *How to Read Derrida* (2005); Nicholas Royle, *Jacques Derrida* (2003); Simon Glendinning, *Derrida: A Very Short Introduction* (2011); *Jacques Derrida: Key Concepts*, edited by Claire Colebrook (2014); Simon Morgan Wortham, *The Derrida Dictionary* (2010); K. Malcolm Richards, *Derrida Reframed: Interpreting Key Thinkers for the Arts* (2008); Sean Gaston, *Starting with Derrida: Plato, Aristotle and Hegel* (2007); and Barry Stocker, *Routledge Philosophy Guidebook to Derrida on Deconstruction* (2006). There are several studies of two of his major works: see in particular Arthur Bradley, *Derrida's "Of Grammatology"* (2008); *Reading Derrida's "Of Grammatology,"* edited by Sean Gaston and Ian Maclachlan (2011); and Sarah Wood, *Derrida's 'Writing and Difference': A Reader's Guide* (2009).

General surveys of Derrida's thought include Christopher Norris, *Derrida* (1987); James K. A. Smith, *Jacques Derrida: Live Theory* (2005); Christina Howells, *Derrida: Deconstruction from Phenomenology to Ethics* (1999); Rodolphe Gasché, *Inventions of Difference: On Jacques Derrida* (1994); and Geoffrey Bennington, *Interrupting Derrida* (2000) and *Jacques Derrida* (1993), the latter of which contains an extended commentary by Derrida. Collections of essays providing overviews of the key issues in the study of Derrida include *Understanding Derrida*, edited by Jack Reynolds and Jonathan Roffe (2004); *Working through Derrida*, edited by Gary B. Madison (1993); *Arguing with Derrida*, edited by Simon Glendinning (2001); *Derrida: A Critical Reader*, edited by David Wood (1992); *Derrida and "Différance,"* edited by David Wood and Robert Bernasconi (1985); *Derrida's Legacies: Literature and Philosophy*, edited by Simon Glendinning and Robert Eaglestone (2008); and

Derrida Now: Current Perspectives in Derrida Studies, edited by John Phillips (2014). Two works that provide overviews of the applications of Derrida's thought to the humanities in general are *Jacques Derrida and the Humanities: A Critical Reader*, edited by Tom Cohen (2001), and *Deconstructing Derrida: Tasks for the New Humanities*, edited by Peter Pericles Trifonas and Michael A. Peters (2005). Recent works, appearing after Derrida's death and engaging with his late thought, are Nicholas Royle, *In Memory of Jacques Derrida* (2009); J. Hillis Miller, *For Derrida* (2009); David Farrell Krell, *Derrida and Our Animal Others: Derrida's Final Seminar, "The Beast and the Sovereign"* (2013); Michael Naas, *Derrida from Now On* (2008); and Michael Marder, *The Event of the Thing: Derrida's Post-Deconstructive Realism* (2009).

There are many useful studies analyzing Derrida in relation to various figures in the history of philosophy. See *Deconstruction and Philosophy: The Texts of Jacques Derrida*, edited by John Sallis (1987); Rodolphe Gasché, *The Tain of the Mirror: Derrida and the Philosophy of Reflection* (1986); Irene E. Harvey, *Derrida and the Economy of "Différance"* (1986); and *Derrida and Deconstruction*, edited by Hugh J. Silverman (1989). Works comparing Derrida and eighteenth- and nineteenth-century philosophy include *Hegel after Derrida*, edited by Stuart Barnett (1998); Michael Ryan, *Marxism and Deconstruction: A Critical Articulation* (1982); and Ulrike Oudée Dünkelsbühler, *Reframing the Frame of Reason: "Trans-Lation" in and beyond Kant and Derrida* (1991; trans. 2002). His thought is examined in relation to various thinkers and movements in twentieth-century Continental thought in Leonard Lawlor, *Imagination and Chance: The Difference between the Thought of Ricoeur and Derrida* (1992); Todd May, *Reconsidering Difference: Nancy, Derrida, Levinas, and Deleuze* (1997); Steve Martinot, *Forms in the Abyss: A Philosophical Bridge between Sartre and Derrida* (2006); and *Deconstruction and Pragmatism*, edited by Chantal Mouffe (1996), to which Derrida contributed.

Discussions of Derrida's relation to Husserl and phenomenology include Leonard Lawlor, *Derrida and Husserl: The Basic Problem of Phenomenology* (2002); Joshua Kates, *Essential History: Jacques Derrida and the Development of Deconstruction* (2005); David Wood, *The Deconstruction of Time* (1989); and Paola Marrati, *Genesis and Trace: Derrida Reading Husserl and Heidegger* (1998; trans. 2005). Heidegger and Derrida are examined in Ernst Behler, *Confrontations: Derrida/Heidegger/Nietzsche* (1988; trans. 1991); Giuseppe Stellardi, *Heidegger and Derrida on Philosophy and Metaphor: Imperfect Thought* (2000); Herman Rapaport, *Heidegger and Derrida: Reflections on Time and Language*

(1989); and *Of Derrida, Heidegger, and Spirit*, edited by David Wood (1993). Two works that examine Derrida and Merleau-Ponty are Jack Reynolds, *Merleau-Ponty and Derrida: Intertwining Embodiment and Alterity* (2004), and *Écart & Différance: Merleau-Ponty and Derrida on Seeing and Writing*, edited by M. C. Dillon (1997). Derrida is related to Wittgenstein and themes in analytic philosophy in *Derrida & Wittgenstein*, edited by Newton Garver and Seung-Chong Lee (1994); Henry Staten, *Wittgenstein and Derrida* (1984); and Samuel C. Wheeler, *Deconstruction as Analytic Philosophy* (2000).

Derrida's thinking on ethics is explored in *Deconstruction and the Possibility of Justice*, edited by Drucilla Cornell, Michel Rosenfeld, and David Gray Carlson (1992), and in Sean Gaston, *Derrida and Disinterest* (2005). His ethical thought is compared to that of Lévinas in Martin C. Srajek, *In the Margins of Deconstruction: Jewish Conceptions of Ethics in Emmanuel Levinas and Jacques Derrida* (1998); Simon Critchley, *The Ethics of Deconstruction: Derrida and Levinas* (1992; 3rd ed., 2014); and John Llewelyn, *Appositions of Jacques Derrida and Emmanuel Levinas* (2002). The intersection of Derrida's thought and political philosophy is considered in Richard Beardsworth, *Derrida and the Political* (1996); A. J. P. Thomson, *Deconstruction and Democracy: Derrida's Politics of Friendship* (2005); *Living Together: Jacques Derrida's Communities of Violence and Peace*, edited by Elisabeth Weber (2013); *Re-reading Derrida: Perspectives on Mourning and Its Hospitalities*, edited by Tony Thwaites and Judith Seaboyer (2013); *Derrida and the Time of the Political*, edited by Pheng Cheah and Suzanne Guerlac (2009); Judith Still, *Derrida and Hospitality: Theory and Practice* (2010); Jacques de Ville, *Jacques Derrida: Law as Absolute Hospitality* (2011); and *Europe after Derrida: Crisis and Potentiality*, edited by Agnes Czajka and Bora Isyar (2014).

The influence of Derridian deconstruction on religion is explored in *Derrida and Negative Theology*, edited by Harold Coward and Toby Foshay (1992); *Derrida and Religion: Other Testaments*, edited by Yvonne Sherwood and Kevin Hart (2005); John D. Caputo, *The Prayers and Tears of Jacques Derrida: Religion without Religion* (1997); Theodore W. Jennings, *Reading Derrida/Thinking Paul: On Justice* (2006); *Questioning God*, edited by John D. Caputo, Mark Dooley, and Michael J. Scanlon (2001); and Robyn Horner, *Rethinking God as Gift: Marion, Derrida, and the Limits of Phenomenology* (2001).

Dilthey, Wilhelm
The contents of Dilthey's *Gesammelte Schriften* (19 vols., 1914–82; 26 vols., 1961–2006) demonstrate the range of his writings, both published

and unpublished. A single-volume anthology of Dilthey's works in English translation was published in 1976 as *Selected Writings*, drawing from volumes 1, 5, 7, 8, 13, and 26. Volume 1 (1922) is Dilthey's *Einleitung in die Geisteswissenschaften: Versuch einer Grundlegung für das Studium der Gesellschaft und der Geschichte* (*Introduction to the Spiritual/Human Disciplines: Attempt at a Foundation for the Study of Society and of History*, 1883). In a 6-volume edition of Dilthey's major writings titled *Selected Works* (5 vols. to date, 1989–), it is volume 1, *Introduction to the Human Sciences*, and contains drafts from late in Dilthey's life when he returned to and attempted to complete the project (originally planned as 3 volumes).

Volume 2 (1914) of the *Gesammelte Schriften*, *Weltanschauung und Analyse des Menschen seit Renaissance und Reformation* (*Worldview and the Analysis of Humanity since the Renaissance and Reformation*), consists of essays on intellectual history written in the 1890s. Volume 3 (1921), *Studien zur Geschichte des deutschen Geistes* (*Studies on the History of German Spirit*), contains essays written in the early 1900s on such figures in intellectual history as Leibniz and Frederick the Great. Some of them are translated in *Selected Works*, vol. 4, *Hermeneutics and the Study of History* (1996), which also contains selections from volumes 5, 11, 14, 16, and 22.

Volume 4 (1921) in the German edition, *Die Jugendgeschichte Hegels und andere Abhandlungen zur Geschichte des Deutschen Idealismus* (*The History of the Young Hegel and Other Essays on the History of German Idealism*), is another volume of intellectual history.

Volumes 5 and 6 (1924) are a two-volume set, each titled *Die geistige Welt: Einleitung in die Philosophie des Lebens* (*The Spiritual World: Introduction to the Philosophy of Life*) and subtitled *Abhandlungen zur Grundlegung der Geisteswissenschaften* (*Essays on the Grounding of the Human Sciences*) and *Abhandlungen zur Poetik, Ethik und Pädagogik* (*Essays on Poetics, Ethics, and Pedagogy*), respectively. Both volumes contain essays published between 1864 and 1911. Some of the essays in volume 5 are translated in *Selected Works*, vol. 5, *Poetry and Experience* (1985). Other essays are translated in *Selected Works*, vol. 2, *Understanding the Human World* (2010); an earlier partial translation of volume 5 of the *Gesammelte Schriften* was published as *The Essence of Philosophy* (1954).

Der Aufbau der geschichtlichen Welt in den Geisteswissenschaften (1910) makes up volume 7 of the *Gesammelte Schriften* (1927). It is translated as *The Formation of the Historical World in the Human Sciences* in *Selected Works*, vol. 3 (2002), which also contains "Studies Toward the Foundation of the Human Sciences" and Dil-

they's drafts for the continuation of this work. An excerpt from it was translated in 1961 as *Pattern and Meaning in History: Thoughts on History and Society*; another partial translation (drawn on for the selections in this volume) is included in *Selected Writings* (1976), where the title is rendered *The Construction of the Historical World in the Human Studies*.

Volume 8 of the *Gesammelte Schriften* (1931), titled *Weltanschauungslehre: Abhandlungen zur Philosophie der Philosophie* (*The Theory of Worldviews: Essays on the Philosophy of Philosophy*), contains the important essay "The Types of Worldviews and Their Development in Metaphysical Systems" (1911). It will be included in *Selected Works*, vol. 6, *Philosophy and Life* (forthcoming), and has already been translated as *Dilthey's Philosophy of Existence: Introduction to "Weltanschauungslehre"* (1959). The remaining 18 volumes of the *Gesammelte Schriften* contain other published and unpublished writings, lectures, and letters.

Two of the best and most helpful books in English on Dilthey are Rudolf Makkreel, *Dilthey: Philosopher of the Human Studies* (1975), and *Dilthey and Phenomenology*, edited by Rudolf A. Makkreel and John Scanlon (1987). Other useful discussions can be found in Charles R. Bambach, *Heidegger, Dilthey, and the Crisis of Historicism: History and Metaphysics in Heidegger, Dilthey, and the Neo-Kantians* (1995); Jacob Owensby, *Dilthey and the Narrative of History* (1994); Jos de Mul, *The Tragedy of Finitude: Dilthey's Hermeneutics of Life* (1993; trans. 2004); Ilse Nina Bulhof, *Wilhelm Dilthey: A Hermeneutic Approach to the Study of History and Culture* (1980); H. P. Rickman, *Dilthey Today: A Critical Appraisal of the Contemporary Relevance of His Work* (1988) and *Wilhelm Dilthey: Pioneer of the Human Studies* (1979); and Theodore Plantinga, *Historical Understanding in the Thought of Wilhelm Dilthey* (1980).

Earlier studies of Dilthey's thought include H. A. Hodges, *Wilhelm Dilthey: An Introduction* (1944) and *The Philosophy of Wilhelm Dilthey* (1952); William Kluback, *Wilhelm Dilthey's Philosophy of History* (1956), which also contains a translation of an essay by Dilthey; Howard N. Tuttle, *Wilhelm Dilthey's Philosophy of Historical Understanding: A Critical Analysis* (1969); Kurt Mueller-Vollmer, *Towards a Phenomenological Theory of Literature: A Study of Wilhelm Dilthey's Poetik* (1963); Michael Ermarth, *Wilhelm Dilthey: The Critique of Historical Reason* (1978); and Richard E. Palmer, *Hermeneutics: Interpretation Theory in Schleiermacher, Dilthey, Heidegger, and Gadamer* (1969).

More sources containing discussions of Dilthey can be found in the bibliography section on hermeneutics in General Bibliographies (above).

Du Bois, W. E. B.

The Autobiography of W. E. B. Du Bois was published posthumously in 1968. Throughout his life, Du Bois constantly gave speeches, published essays, and wrote for magazines. Many of these writings have been published in numerous collections and readers over the years. Several volumes of his correspondence have also been published.

The best biography of Du Bois may be David Levering Lewis, *W. E. B. Du Bois: A Biography, 1868–1963* (2008), a condensed and updated one-volume edition of his *W. E. B. Du Bois: Biography of a Race, 1868–1919* (1993) and *W. E. B. Du Bois: The Fight for Equality and the American Century, 1919–1963* (2000). See also Shawn Leigh Alexander, *W. E. B. Du Bois: An American Intellectual and Activist* (2015); Gerald Horne, *W. E. B. Du Bois: A Biography* (2010); Edward J. Blum, *W. E. B. Du Bois, American Prophet* (2007); and Manning Marable, *W. E. B. Du Bois: Black Radical Democrat*, new updated ed. (2005).

An excellent resource for the whole of his thought is *W. E. B. Du Bois: An Encyclopedia*, edited by Gerald Horne and Mary Young (2001). On individual works, see *W. E. B. Du Bois, Race, and the City: "The Philadelphia Negro" and Its Legacy*, edited by Michael B. Katz and Thomas J. Sugrue (1998); Stephanie J. Shaw, *W. E. B. Du Bois and "The Souls of Black Folk"* (2013); and Alford A. Young Jr., Jerry G. Watts, Manning Marable, Charles Lemert, and Elizabeth Higginbotham, *The Souls of W. E. B. Du Bois* (2006). For essays providing a fine introduction to his work more generally, see *The Cambridge Companion to W. E. B. Du Bois*, edited by Shamoon Zamir (2008); *W. E. B. Du Bois and Race: Essays Celebrating the Centennial Publication of "The Souls of Black Folk,"* edited by Chester J. Fontenot and Mary Alice Morgan (2002); and *Recognizing W. E. B. Du Bois in the Twenty-First Century*, edited by Mary Keller and Chester J. Fontenot (2007).

The major philosophical works on Du Bois's thought are Kwame Anthony Appiah, *Lines of Descent: W. E. B. Du Bois and the Emergence of Identity* (2014), and Shamoon Zamir, *Dark Voices: W. E. B. Du Bois and American Thought, 1888–1903* (1995). Two works on Du Bois and political philosophy are Adolph L. Reed Jr., *W. E. B. Du Bois and American Political Thought: Fabianism and the Color Line* (1997), and Lawrie Balfour, *Democracy's Reconstruction: Thinking Politically with W. E. B. Du Bois* (2011).

Works focusing on Du Bois's thought and its intersection with religion include Gary Dorrien, *The New Abolition: W. E. B. Du Bois and the Black Social Gospel* (2015); Jonathon S. Kahn, *Divine Discontent: The Religious Imagination of W. E. B. Du Bois* (2009); and Brian Johnson, *W. E. B. Du Bois: Toward Agnosticism, 1868–1934* (2008). For an edited volume of essays dealing with his thought and religion, see *The Souls of W. E. B. Du Bois: New Essays and Reflections*, edited by Edward J. Blum and Jason R. Young (2009). Works on Du Bois's sociology include Aldon D. Morris, *The Scholar Denied: W. E. B. Du Bois and the Birth of Modern Sociology* (2015); Reiland Rabaka, *Against Epistemic Apartheid: W. E. B. Du Bois and the Disciplinary Decadence of Sociology* (2010); and Rabaka, *W. E. B. Du Bois and the Problems of the Twenty-First Century: An Essay on Africana Critical Theory* (2007).

On Du Bois's philosophy of education, see Derrick P. Alridge, *The Educational Thought of W. E. B. Du Bois: An Intellectual History* (2008). The bearing of his thought on art is discussed in Amy Helene Kirschke, *Art in Crisis: W. E. B. Du Bois and the Struggle for African American Identity and Memory* (2007), and Samuel O. Doku, *Cosmopolitanism in the Fictive Imagination of W. E. B. Du Bois: Toward the Humanization of a Revolutionary Art* (2015). Two works on Du Bois's late writings are Bill Mullen, *Un-American: W. E. B. Du Bois and the Century of World Revolution* (2015), and Eric Porter, *The Problem of the Future World: W. E. B. Du Bois and the Race Concept at Mid-century* (2010).

Emerson, Ralph Waldo

In 1836 Emerson published his first major essay, "Nature." In 1841 the first series of his *Essays* was published, and in 1844 the second series was published. These two collections contain many of his best-known essays, including "The Over-Soul" and "Self-Reliance." In 1849 *Nature; Addresses, and Lectures* was published; it contains "Nature" along with many now classic lectures, such as "The American Scholar" (1837), "The Divinity School Address" (1838), and "The Transcendentalist" (1842). Other prose works are *Representative Men* (1850), containing discussions of Plato, Swedenborg, Montaigne, Shakespeare, Goethe, and Napoleon; *English Traits* (1856); *Conduct of Life* (1860), which in such essays as "Fate" conveys the loss of his earlier characteristic optimism; *Society and Solitude* (1870), containing lectures turned into essays; and *Letters and Social Aims* (1875), produced collaboratively with two of Emerson's children and his literary executor. He published three collections of poetry in his lifetime: *Poems* (1846), *May-Day and Other Pieces* (1867), and *Selected Poems* (1876).

Emerson also published extensively in newspapers and the magazines of the day, including *The Dial*, the magazine of the Transcendentalist movement. Many of these miscellaneous writings are available in volumes of the numerous editions of his complete works, and also in such collections as *Emerson's Antislavery Writings* (1995). Other collections include *The Complete Sermons of Ralph Waldo Emerson* (4 vols., 1989–93); drafts and notes for lectures from 1833 to 1842 (which were often incorporated into his early essays), published as *Early Lectures of Ralph Waldo Emerson* (3 vols., 1959–72); his letters from 1813 to 1881, *The Letters of Ralph Waldo Emerson* (10 vols., 1939–95); previously unpublished notebooks from 1819 to 1882, *Journals and Miscellaneous Notebooks* (16 vols., 1960–82); and previously unpublished lectures, *The Later Lectures of Ralph Waldo Emerson, 1843–1871* (2 vols., 2001).

Useful biographical works include Robert D. Richardson Jr., *Emerson: The Mind on Fire* (1995); Lawrence Buell, *Emerson* (2003); Donald Yannella, *Ralph Waldo Emerson* (1982); Joel Porte, *Representative Man: Ralph Waldo Emerson in His Time* (1979; with new preface, 1988); O. W. Firkins, *Ralph Waldo Emerson* (2000); and Maurice York and Rick Spaulding, *Ralph Waldo Emerson: The Infinitude of the Private Man* (2008). For intellectual biographies of Emerson, see Kenneth S. Sacks, *Understanding Emerson: "The American Scholar" and His Struggle for Self-Reliance* (2003), and Mary Kupiec Cayton, *Emerson's Emergence: Self and Society in the Transformation of New England, 1800–1845* (1989).

Harmon Smith's *My Friend, My Friend: The Story of Thoreau's Relationship with Emerson* (1999) is a biographical work. Thoreau and Emerson are studied from a more philosophical and literary perspective in Sam McGuire Worley, *Emerson, Thoreau, and the Role of the Cultural Critic* (2001); Joel Porte, *Consciousness and Culture: Emerson and Thoreau Reviewed* (2004) and *Emerson and Thoreau: Transcendentalists in Conflict* (1966); James R. Guthrie, *Above Time: Emerson's and Thoreau's Temporal Revolutions* (2001); and *Emerson and Thoreau: Figures of Friendship*, edited by John T. Lysaker and William Rossi (2010). Two important studies of Emerson's influence on Nietzsche have also been published: George J. Stack, *Nietzsche and Emerson: An Elective Affinity* (1992), and David Mikics, *The Romance of Individualism in Emerson and Nietzsche* (2003).

Some of the best recent philosophical scholarship on Emerson can be found in *The Cambridge Companion to Ralph Waldo Emerson*, edited by Joel Porte and Saundra Morris (1999); Stanley Cavell, *Emerson's Transcendental Etudes* (2003); George Kateb, *Emerson and Self-Reliance* (1995); *Ralph Waldo Emerson: A Collection of Critical Essays*, edited by Lawrence Buell (1993); B. L. Packer, *Emerson's Fall: A New Interpretation of the Major Essays* (1982); *Emerson: Bicentennial Essays*, edited by Ronald A. Bosco and Joel

Myerson (2006); John T. Lysaker, *Emerson and Self-Culture* (2008); Christopher J. Windolph, *Emerson's Nonlinear Nature* (2007); *The Other Emerson*, edited by Branka Arsić and Cary Wolfe (2010); Branka Arsić, *On Leaving: A Reading in Emerson* (2010); and Richard G. Geldard, *God in Concord: Ralph Waldo Emerson's Awakening to the Infinite* (1998) and *Emerson and Universal Mind* (2013). Also of note are David Van Leer, *Emerson's Epistemology: The Argument of the Essays* (1986); Laura Dassow Walls, *Emerson's Life in Science: The Culture of Truth* (2003); *Emerson for the Twenty-First Century: Global Perspectives on an American Icon*, edited by Barry Tharaud (2013); and *Emerson in Context*, edited by Wesley T. Mott (2013).

A number of recent studies focus on Emerson's concept of individualism and its ethical, social, and political implications; their perspectives range from philosophical to literary and historical. They include Christopher Newfield, *The Emerson Effect: Individualism and Submission in America* (1996); Charles E. Mitchell, *Individualism and Its Discontents: Appropriations of Emerson, 1880–1950* (1997); Gustaaf Van Cromphout, *Emerson's Ethics* (1999); *The Emerson Dilemma: Essays on Emerson and Social Reform*, edited by T. Gregory Garvey (2000); Maurice Gonnaud, *An Uneasy Solitude: Individual and Society in the Work of Ralph Waldo Emerson* (1964; trans. 1987); Len Gougeon, *Virtue's Hero: Emerson, Antislavery, and Reform* (1990) and *Emerson and Eros: The Making of a Cultural Hero* (2007); David M. Robinson, *Emerson and the Conduct of Life: Pragmatism and Ethical Purpose in the Later Work* (1993); Neal Dolan, *Emerson's Liberalism* (2009); *A Political Companion to Ralph Waldo Emerson*, edited by Alan M. Levine and Daniel S. Malachuk (2011); Alex Zakaras, *Individuality and Mass Democracy: Mill, Emerson, and the Burdens of Citizenship* (2009); and James M. Albrecht, *Reconstructing Individualism: A Pragmatic Tradition from Emerson to Ellison* (2012).

For more sources relating to Emerson, see the bibliography section on British and American idealism in the surveys of movements and periods.

Engels, Friedrich (see Marx)

Fanon, Frantz
Fanon's major works are *Black Skin, White Masks* (1952; trans. 1967), *A Dying Colonialism* (1959; trans. 1965), *The Wretched of the Earth* (1961; trans. 1963), and *Toward the African Revolution: Political Essays* (1964; trans. 1967).

Several excellent biographies of Fanon's interesting life are available: see David Macey, *Frantz Fanon: A Biography*, 2nd ed. (2012); Peter Hudis,

Frantz Fanon: Philosopher of the Barricades (2015); Christopher J. Lee, *Frantz Fanon: Toward a Revolutionary Humanism* (2015); and Alice Cherki, *Frantz Fanon: A Portrait* (2000; trans. 2006). After decades of neglect, Fanon's work has been receiving more attention in recent years. Books that engage his thought at a high level of philosophical sophistication include Lewis R. Gordon, *Fanon and the Crisis of European Man: An Essay on Philosophy and the Human Sciences* (1995) and *What Fanon Said: A Philosophical Introduction to His Life and Thought* (2015); Nigel C. Gibson, *Fanon: The Postcolonial Imagination* (2003); Ato Sekyi-Out, *Fanon's Dialectic of Experience* (1996); Pramod K. Nayar, *Frantz Fanon* (2013); Reiland Rabaka, *Forms of Fanonism: Frantz Fanon's Critical Theory and the Dialectics of Decolonization* (2010); Anthony C. Alessandrini, *Frantz Fanon and the Future of Cultural Politics: Finding Something Different* (2014); and Vivaldi Jean-Marie, *Fanon: Collective Ethics and Humanism* (2007).

For readily available collections of essays on Fanon, see *Fanon and the Decolonization of Philosophy*, edited by Elizabeth A. Hoppe and Tracey Nicholls (2010); *Fanon: A Critical Reader*, edited by Lewis R. Gordon, T. Denean Sharpley-Whiting, and Renée T. White (1996); *Fanon: Critical Perspectives*, edited by Anthony C. Alessandrini (1999); *Frantz Fanon's "Black Skin, White Masks": New Interdisciplinary Essays*, edited by Max Silverman (2005); and *Rethinking Fanon: The Continuing Dialogue* (1999) and *Living Fanon: Global Perspectives* (2011), both edited by Nigel C. Gibson.

Feuerbach, Ludwig

Feuerbach's early, anonymously published work *Thoughts on Death and Immortality* (1830; trans. 1980) cost him his teaching position at Erlangen when his authorship of it became known. It is contained in volume 1 of his *Gesammelte Werke* (*Collected Works*, 2nd ed. [*GW*]; 21 vols., 1981–96), along with other writings from 1828 to 1834. Volumes 2, 3, and 4 of *GW* are devoted to his analyses from the 1830s of Bacon, Hobbes, Gassendi, Descartes, Malebranche, Spinoza, Leibniz, and Bayle, among others. None of Feuerbach's historical research has been translated into English.

Feuerbach's most famous and widely read work is *The Essence of Christianity* (*Das Wesen des Christentums*, 1841 [vol. 5 of *GW*]; trans. 1854). He returned to this general subject in a series of thirty lectures given in 1848–49, which were published two years later as *Lectures on the Essence of Religion* (1851 [vol. 6 of *GW*]; trans. 1967).

Feuerbach's *Principles of the Philosophy of the Future* (1843; trans. 1966) is one of many short writings on philosophical and religious topics

from 1839 to 1846 gathered in volume 9 of *GW*. Volumes 10 and 11 contain other briefer essays and articles published throughout his life, a number of which have been translated and published in the collection *The Fiery Brook: Selected Writings of Ludwig Feuerbach* (1972), including "Towards a Critique of Hegel's Philosophy," "The Beginning of Philosophy," and "Preliminary Theses on the Reform of Philosophy."

Among the relatively few secondary works on Feuerbach in English are several very good ones, such as William B. Chamberlain, *Heaven Wasn't His Destination: The Philosophy of Ludwig Feuerbach* (1941; reprint, 2013); Van A. Harvey, *Feuerbach and the Interpretation of Religion* (1995); Marx W. Wartofsky, *Feuerbach* (1977); Charles A. Wilson, *Feuerbach and the Search for Otherness* (1989); Larry Johnston, *Between Transcendence and Nihilism: Species-Ontology in the Philosophy of Ludwig Feuerbach* (1995); and Eugene Kamenka, *The Philosophy of Ludwig Feuerbach* (1970). *The Fiery Brook*, the collection of Feuerbach's writings mentioned above, contains a helpful introductory essay by the translator, Zawar Hanfi.

The most famous writings on Feuerbach are those of Karl Marx and Friedrich Engels. They include Engels's *Ludwig Feuerbach and the End of Classical German Philosophy* (published in 1886, but based on notes that he and Marx had made 40 years earlier; trans. 1934); Marx's brief 1845 "Theses on Feuerbach" (which Engels included as an appendix to *Ludwig Feuerbach*); and Marx and Engels's *The German Ideology* (written 1845–46, published 1932; partial trans., 1947), which contains an essay relating to Feuerbach and their differences from him.

For more sources on Feuerbach and other thinkers in the first generation after Hegel, see the bibliography section on Left-Hegelianism and Marxism in General Bibliographies (above).

Fichte, Johann Gottlieb

Fichte's first published work was *Attempt at a Critique of All Revelation* (1792; trans. 1978). His primary philosophical work is known as the *Wissenschaftslehre* or *Science of Knowledge*. Its first version (or "presentation") dates from 1794–95; in 1797, Fichte added two new introductions (trans. 1970). A second version of the *Wissenschaftslehre* (1796–99), which was unpublished in Fichte's lifetime, is known as the *Nova Methodo* (*New Method*); it has been translated as *Foundations of Transcendental Philosophy* (*Wissenschaftslehre*) *nova methodo* (1992). Both versions were written when Fichte was at Jena (1794–99), before he lost his position there. A collection of short works, essays, and letters from this period has been published in English under the title *Fichte: Early Philosophical Writings* (1988). Two works by Fichte representative of his *nova methodo*, but dealing with what he took to be the ethical and political consequences of the *Wissenschaftslehre* rather than with its theoretical exposition and development, are *Foundations of Natural Right* (1796–97; trans. 2000) and *System of Ethics* (1798; trans. 2005).

Publications and letters related to his dismissal from Jena in 1799 (on the charge of atheism) can be found in *J. G. Fichte and the Atheism Dispute (1798–1800)*, edited by Yolanda Estes and Curtis Bowman (2010). Arguably Fichte's greatest literary work is his presentation of his ideas intended for a wider audience published in 1800 under the title *The Vocation of Man* (*Die Bestimmung des Menschen*; trans. 1987 [first trans. 1848]). *The Closed Commercial State* (trans. 2012), also written in 1800, advances Fichte's thoughts on history, the state, and economy. In 1801 he published a shorter work whose very title shows his exasperation with the bewildered reception of his *Wissenschaftslehre*: "A Crystal Clear Report to the General Public Concerning the Actual Essence of the Newest Philosophy: An Attempt to Force the Reader to Understand"; it has been translated in a collection titled *Philosophy of German Idealism*, edited by Ernst Behler (1987).

Some of Fichte's correspondence and philosophical writings from this era have been published under the title *The Philosophical Rupture between Fichte and Schelling* (2012). A final presentation of the *Wissenschaftslehre* has been translated from transcripts of his late Berlin lectures and published as *The Science of Knowing: J. G. Fichte's 1804 Lectures on the Wissenschaftslehre* (2005). A two-volume collection of translations from the nineteenth century, *Popular Works of Johann Gottlieb Fichte* (4th ed., 1889), is now available at the Internet Archive (archive.org). Several of Fichte's works, such as *Guide to the Blessed Life* and *The Characteristics of the Present Age* (both originally published in 1806), are available in translation only in this collection.

Fichte's collected works in German have appeared in four series. The first series of works contains everything Fichte published himself; the second, unpublished works; the third, his correspondence; and the fourth, transcriptions of his lectures by auditors. Most of the first series has been translated, but much of the others has not.

Hegel's own first published philosophical work, *The Difference between Fichte's and Schelling's System of Philosophy* (1801; trans. 1977), offers insight into Fichte's thought as well as some criticism. The poet known as Novalis (Friedrich von Hardenberg) wrote a work of fragments and aphorisms in 1795 to 1796 that is critical of Fichte's early philosophy: it has

been translated as *Fichte Studies* (2003). Two highly recommended studies are Günter Zöller's *Fichte's Transcendental Philosophy: The Original Duplicity of Intelligence and Will* (1998) and Frederick Neuhouser's *Fichte's Theory of Subjectivity* (1990). Daniel Breazeale and Tom Rockmore have edited a number of volumes of essays on Fichte: see *Rights, Bodies and Recognition: New Essays on Fichte's "Foundations of Natural Right"* (2006), *New Essays on Fichte's Later Jena "Wissenschaftslehre"* (2002), *New Essays in Fichte's "Foundation of the Entire Doctrine of Scientific Knowledge"* (2001), *Fichte: Historical Contexts/Contemporary Controversies* (1994), *Fichte's "Vocation of Man": New Interpretative and Critical Essays* (2013), *After Jena: New Essays on Fichte's Later Philosophy* (2008), *Fichte and the Phenomenological Tradition* (2010, with Violetta L. Waibel), and *Fichte, German Idealism, and Early Romanticism* (2010). The influence of the philosophy of Spinoza on Fichte and German idealism in general is discussed in Alexandre Guilherme's *Fichte and Schelling: The Spinoza Connection* (2009) and in *Spinoza and German Idealism*, edited by Eckart Förester and Yitzhak Y. Melamed (2012).

Several studies focusing on Fichte's Jena period are Wayne M. Martin, *Idealism and Objectivity: Understanding Fichte's Jena Project* (1997); George J. Seidel's *"Wissenschaftslehre" of 1794* (1993); David Wood, *"Mathesis of the Mind": A Study of Fichte's "Wissenschaftslehre" and Geometry* (2012); T. P. Hohler, *Imagination and Reflection: Intersubjectivity: Fichte's "Grundlage" of 1794* (1982); and Daniel Breazeale, *Thinking through the "Wissenschaftslehre": Themes from Fichte's Early Philosophy* (2013). Fichte's political philosophy and moral philosophy are discussed in David James, *Fichte's Social and Political Philosophy: Property and Virtue* (2011), and in Gunnar Beck, *Fichte and Kant on Freedom, Rights, and Law* (2008). Two works that deal with his thinking on intersubjectivity and language are Robert R. Williams, *Recognition: Fichte and Hegel on the Other* (1992), and Jere Paul Surber, *Language and German Idealism: Fichte's Linguistic Philosophy* (1996). The latter also contains some translations of Fichte's work.

For a biography of Fichte through his Jena period, see Anthony J. La Vopa's *Fichte: The Self and the Calling of Philosophy, 1762–1799* (2001).

For more discussion of Fichte, see the bibliography section on German idealism in the General Bibliographies (above).

Foucault, Michel

Three of Foucault's earliest books are *Mental Illness and Psychology* (1954; trans. 1976 [and in 2011 as *Madness: The Invention of an Idea*]), *History of Madness* (1961; trans. 2006 [abridged trans. 1965, *Madness and Civilization: A History of Insanity in the Age of Reason*), and *Birth of the Clinic: An Archaeology of Medical Perception* (1963; trans. 1973). The two works that followed are more conscious of questions of method, reacting against while still under the influence of structuralism: *The Order of Things: An Archaeology of the Human Sciences* (1966; trans. 1970) and *The Archaeology of Knowledge* (1969; trans. 1972), a translation that also contains *The Order of Discourse* (1971, here titled *The Discourse on Language*). His primary later works, in which he develops his influential theory of power, are *Discipline and Punish: The Birth of the Prison* (1975; trans. 1977) and the three volumes of *The History of Sexuality*: vol. 1, *An Introduction* (1976 [French title, *The Will to Knowledge*]; trans. 1978); vol. 2, *The Use of Pleasure* (1984; trans. 1985); and vol. 3, *The Care of the Self* (1984; trans. 1986). *The Essential Works of Foucault, 1954–1984* collects articles, interviews, and course descriptions—some published earlier in English, some first translated here: vol. 1, *Ethics: Subjectivity and Truth* (1994; trans. 1997); vol. 2, *Aesthetics, Method and Epistemology* (1994; trans. 1998); and vol. 3, *Power* (1994; trans. 2001).

Foucault's lectures from the Collège de France are gradually becoming available in English (projected to 13 vols.). Available to date—all of which bear the series title *Lectures at the Collège de France*, and show the years in which the lectures were delivered—are: *Lectures on the Will to Know, 1970–1971* (2013); *Psychiatric Power, 1973–1974* (2006); *Abnormal, 1974–1975* (2003); "*Society Must Be Defended," 1975–1976* (2003); *Security, Territory, Population, 1975–1976* (2007); *The Birth of Biopolitics, 1978–1979* (2008); *The Hermeneutics of the Subject, 1981–1982* (2005); *The Government of Self and Others, 1982–1983* (2010); and *The Courage of Truth: The Government of Self and Others II, 1983–1984* (2011).

Wrong-Doing, Truth-Telling: The Function of Avowal in Justice (2012; trans. 2014) is a series of lectures from 1981. Six short lectures delivered in English in 1983 have been gathered under the title *Fearless Speech* (2001). Four important collections of articles, lectures, and interviews available in English are *Language, Counter-Memory, Practice: Selected Essays and Interviews* (1977), *Power/Knowledge: Selected Interviews and Other Writings, 1972–1977* (1980), *Foucault Live: Interviews, 1961–84* (1989), and *Politics, Philosophy, Culture: Interviews and Other Writings, 1977–1984* (1988). Volumes containing both critical essays and work by Foucault are *The Final Foucault*, edited by James Bernauer and David Rasmussen (1988); *Technologies of the Self: A Seminar with Michel Foucault*, edited by Luther H. Martin,

Huck Gutman, and Patrick H. Hutton (1988); *Critique and Power: Recasting the Foucault/Habermas Debate*, edited by Michael Kelly (1994); and *Foucault and His Interlocutors*, edited by Arnold Davidson (1998).

Biographical works on Foucault include Didier Eribon, *Michel Foucault* (1989; trans. 1991); David Macey, *The Lives of Michel Foucault* (1993); James Miller, *The Passion of Michel Foucault* (1993); and David Halperin, *Saint Foucault: Towards a Gay Hagiography* (1995).

There is a large body of secondary literature on Foucault. For general introductory overviews of his thought, see Sara Mills, *Michel Foucault* (2003); Lisa Downing, *The Cambridge Introduction to Michel Foucault* (2008); *Michel Foucault: Key Concepts*, edited by Dianna Taylor (2011); Tony Schirato, Geoff Danaher, and Jen Webb, *Understanding Foucault: A Critical Introduction* (2000; 2nd ed., 2012); Johanna Oksala, *How to Read Foucault* (2008); Todd May, *The Philosophy of Foucault* (2006); Paul Veyne, *Foucault: His Thought, His Character* (2010); and David A. Harbour, *Understanding Foucault, a Primer for Beginners: With Appendices on Figuring and Indexing* (2013). For early studies of his thought in English, see Alan Sheridan, *Foucault: The Will to Truth* (1980); Hubert Dreyfus and Paul Rabinow, *Michel Foucault: Beyond Structuralism and Hermeneutics* (2nd ed., 1983); Pamela Major-Poetzl, *Michel Foucault's Archaeology of Western Culture: Toward a New Science of History* (1983); Gilles Deleuze, *Foucault* (1986; trans. 1988); J. G. Merquior, *Foucault* (1987); Gary Gutting, *Michel Foucault's Archaeology of Scientific Reason* (1989); and James W. Bernauer, *Michel Foucault's Force of Flight* (1990). More recent studies include Joseph J. Tanke, *Foucault's Philosophy of Art: A Genealogy of Modernity* (2009); Johanna Oksala, *Foucault on Freedom* (2005); and Colin Koopman, *Genealogy as Critique: Foucault and the Problems of Modernity* (2013).

Useful collections of critical essays include *The Cambridge Companion to Foucault*, edited by Gary Gutting (2nd ed., 2005); *Foucault: A Critical Reader*, edited by David Couzens Hoy (1986); *After Foucault: Humanistic Knowledge, Postmodern Challenges*, edited by Jonathan Arac (1988); *Michel Foucault: Critical Assessments*, edited by Barry Smart (7 vols., 1994–95); *Foucault and Philosophy*, edited by Timothy O'Leary and Christopher Falzon (2010); *Foucault's Legacy*, edited by C. G. Prado (2009); and *A Companion to Foucault*, edited by Christopher Falzon, Timothy O'Leary, and Jana Sawicki (2013).

The secondary literature on Foucault's political thought is extensive. Useful studies include Mark Poster, *Foucault, Marxism, and History: Mode of Production versus Mode of Information*

(1984); Jon Simons, *Foucault and the Political* (1995); Michèle Barrett, *The Politics of Truth: From Marx to Foucault* (1991); Christopher Falzon, *Foucault and Social Dialogue: Beyond Fragmentation* (1998); Richard Marsden, *The Nature of Capital: Marx after Foucault* (1999); Barry Smart, *Foucault, Marxism, and Critique* (1983); and *The Later Foucault: Politics and Philosophy*, edited by Jeremy Moss (1998).

For more recent works that bring Foucault's thought to bear on recent geopolitical events, see *Foucault in an Age of Terror: Essays on Biopolitics and the Defence of Society*, edited by Stephen Morton and Stephen Bygrave (2008); *Foucault on Politics, Security and War*, edited by Michael Dillon and Andrew W. Neal (2008); and Johanna Oksala, *Foucault, Politics, and Violence* (2011). Works that examine Foucault's politics and ethics in relation to questions of gender, race, and sex include Jana Sawicki, *Disciplining Foucault: Feminism, Power, and the Body* (1991); Lois McNay, *Foucault and Feminism: Power, Gender, and the Self* (1992); Ladelle McWhorter, *Bodies and Pleasures: Foucault and the Politics of Sexual Normalization* (1999); Ann Laura Stoler, *Race and the Education of Desire: Foucault's "History of Sexuality" and the Colonial Order of Things* (1995); Margaret A. McLaren, *Feminism, Foucault, and Embodied Subjectivity* (2002); *Feminism & Foucault: Reflections on Resistance*, edited by Irene Diamond and Lee Quinby (1988); *Feminist Interpretations of Michel Foucault*, edited by Susan J. Hekman (1996); *Rethinking Sexuality: Foucault and Classical Antiquity*, edited by David H. J. Larmour, Paul Allen Miller, and Charles Platter (1997); and *Feminism and the Final Foucault*, edited by Dianna Taylor and Karen Vintges (2004).

Although many of the books mentioned above engage in some fashion and to some extent with Foucault's ethics, other works focus more explicitly on his ethics and theory of the subject as an effect of power; see John S. Ransom, *Foucault's Discipline: The Politics of Subjectivity* (1997); Michael Mahon, *Foucault's Nietzschean Genealogy: Truth, Power, and the Subject* (1992); Timothy O'Leary, *Foucault: The Art of Ethics* (2002); Charles E. Scott, *The Question of Ethics: Nietzsche, Foucault, Heidegger* (1990); and Wolfgang Detel, *Foucault and Classical Antiquity: Power, Ethics and Knowledge* (1998; trans. 2005).

Studies attentive to Foucault's methodology include John Rajchman, *Michel Foucault: The Freedom of Philosophy* (1985); Charles L. Lemert and Garth Gillan, *Michel Foucault: Social Theory as Transgression* (1982); Rudi Visker, *Michel Foucault: Genealogy as Critique* (1991; trans. 1995); Mitchell Dean, *Critical and Effective Histories: Foucault's Methods and Historical Sociology* (1994); Todd May, *Between Genealogy and Epistemology: Psychology, Politics, and Knowledge in the Thought of Michel Foucault* (1993); and Béatrice Han, *Foucault's Critical Project: Between the Transcendental and the Historical* (1998; trans. 2002).

Gadamer, Hans-Georg

Gadamer's magnum opus is *Truth and Method* (1960; trans. 1975, 2nd ed. 1989). *Philosophical Hermeneutics*, a collection of translated essays written between 1967 and 1972 (1976), helps situate the theory presented in *Truth and Method* within the philosophical tradition. Also helpful in that regard are his studies of two of his influential predecessors, Hegel and Heidegger: *Hegel's Dialectic: Five Hermeneutical Studies* (1971; trans. 1976) and *Heidegger's Ways* (1983; trans. 1994). Other collections of essays, interviews, and lectures in which Gadamer applies his philosophical approach to various practical topics are *Hans-Georg Gadamer on Education, Poetry and History: Applied Hermeneutics* (1992), which translates pieces written 1947–88; *The Enigma of Health: The Art of Healing in a Scientific Age* (1993; trans. 1996); *Hermeneutics, Religion and Ethics* (1999), which translates essays written 1941–89; *Praise of Theory: Speeches and Essays* (1983; trans. 1999); and *Reason in the Age of Science* (1976 [with two added essays, 1978, 1979]; trans. 1981).

Gadamer's work on ancient Greek philosophy is extensive. It includes two monographs: *The Idea of the Good in Platonic-Aristotelian Philosophy* (1978; trans. 1986) and *Plato's Dialectical Ethics: Phenomenological Interpretations Relating to the "Philebus"* (1983; trans. 1991). The essays translated in *Dialogue and Dialectic: Eight Hermeneutical Studies on Plato* (1983) were written between 1934 and 1978. Other collections of essays are *The Beginning of Knowledge* (1999; trans. 2001), containing essays on Heraclitus, Plato, and pre-Socratic science, and *The Beginning of Philosophy* (1996; trans. 1998), which has essays on Plato, Aristotle, and Parmenides.

Gadamer's many publications in aesthetics include *The Relevance of the Beautiful and Other Essays* (1967–80; trans. 1986); *Literature and Philosophy in Dialogue: Essays in German Literary Theory* (1994), translating essays published mostly between the 1940s and 1960s; and *Gadamer on Celan: 'Who Am I and Who Are You?' and Other Essays* (1997), translating essays published 1977–91. Three collections of interviews are available in translation: *Gadamer in Conversation: Reflections and Commentary* (1993, 3rd ed. 2000; trans. 2001), *A Century of Philosophy: A Conversation with Ricardo Dot-*

tori (2000; trans. 2003), and *Hermeneutics and the Humanities: Dialogues with Hans-Georg Gadamer* (2013).

Gadamer wrote an illuminating intellectual autobiography: *Philosophical Apprenticeships* (1977; trans. 1985). An overview of Gadamer's life and work can be found in Donatella Di Cesare's *Gadamer: A Philosophical Portrait* (2007; trans. 2013). See also Jean Grondin's *Hans-Georg Gadamer: A Biography* (1999; trans. 2003).

Helpful introductory resources include Chris Lawn and Niall Keane, *The Gadamer Dictionary* (2011), and Karl Simms, *Hans-Georg Gadamer* (2015). Among the more important studies of Gadamer are Jean Grondin, *The Philosophy of Gadamer* (1999; trans. 2003) and *Sources of Hermeneutics* (1995); Brice R. Wachterhauser, *Beyond Being: Gadamer's Post-Platonic Hermeneutic Ontology* (1999); Georgia Warnke, *Gadamer: Hermeneutics, Tradition and Reason* (1987); Joel Weinsheimer, *Gadamer's Hermeneutics: A Reading of "Truth and Method"* (1985); P. Christopher Smith, *Hermeneutics and Human Finitude: Toward a Theory of Ethical Understanding* (1991); and James Risser, *Hermeneutics and the Voice of the Other: Re-reading Gadamer's "Philosophical Hermeneutics"* (1997). More recent studies include Kristin Gjesdal, *Gadamer and the Legacy of German Idealism* (2009); Lauren Swayne Barthold, *Gadamer's Dialectical Hermeneutics* (2009); John Arthos, *The Inner Word in Gadamer's Hermeneutics* (2009); Monica Vilhauer, *Gadamer's Ethics of Play: Hermeneutics and the Other* (2010); Stefano Marino, *Gadamer and the Limits of the Modern Techno-Scientific Civilization* (2011); John Arthos, *Gadamer's Poetics: A Critique of Modern Aesthetics* (2013); and Nicholas Davey, *Unfinished Worlds: Hermeneutics, Aesthetics and Gadamer* (2013).

A number of studies discuss Gadamer's thought in relation to that of others (Heidegger in particular): see Jerald Wallulis, *The Hermeneutics of Life History: Personal Achievement and History in Gadamer, Habermas, and Erikson* (1990); Richard E. Palmer, *Hermeneutics: Interpretation Theory in Schleiermacher, Dilthey, Heidegger, and Gadamer* (1969); Ingrid Scheibler, *Gadamer: Between Heidegger and Hermeneutics* (2000); Rodney R. Coltman, *The Language of Hermeneutics: Gadamer and Heidegger in Dialogue* (1998); Hans Herbert Kögler, *The Power of Dialogue: Critical Hermeneutics after Gadamer and Foucault* (1992; trans. 1996); and Thomas K. Carr, *Newman and Gadamer: Toward a Hermeneutics of Religious Knowledge* (1996).

There are several good collections of critical essays on Gadamer: *The Cambridge Companion to Gadamer*, edited by Robert J. Dostal (2002);

The Philosophy of Hans-Georg Gadamer, edited by Lewis Edwin Hahn (1997), which includes an intellectual biography by Gadamer; *Gadamer's Century: Essays in Honour of Hans-Georg Gadamer*, edited by Jeff Malpas, Ulrich Arnswald, and Jens Kertscher (2002); *Feminist Interpretations of Hans-Georg Gadamer*, edited by Lorraine Code (2003); *Festivals of Interpretation: Essays on Hans-Georg Gadamer's Work*, edited by Kathleen Wright (1990); *Gadamer's Repercussions: Reconsidering Philosophical Hermeneutics*, edited by Bruce Krajewski (2003); *Gadamer and Hermeneutics*, edited by Hugh J. Silverman (1991), with an essay by Gadamer; *Consequences of Hermeneutics: Fifty Years after Gadamer's "Truth and Method,"* edited by Jeff Malpas and Santiago Zabala (2010); and two collections edited by Brice R. Wachterhauser, *Hermeneutics and Modern Philosophy* (1986) and *Hermeneutics and Truth* (1994).

Each of the following collections of essays contains work by Gadamer himself: *Language and Linguisticality in Gadamer's Hermeneutics*, edited by Lawrence K. Schmidt (2001); *Dialogue and Deconstruction: The Gadamer–Derrida Encounter*, edited by Diane P. Michelfelder and Richard E. Palmer (1989); and *The Hermeneutic Tradition: From Ast to Ricoeur*, edited by Gayle L. Ormiston and Alan D. Schrift (1990)—a volume that contains a number of writings by Gadamer and others relevant to his debates with Habermas and the eminent Italian theologian, philosopher and jurist Emilio Betti. The debate between Gadamer and Habermas is examined in Alan How, *The Habermas–Gadamer Debate and the Nature of the Social: Back to Bedrock* (1995); Demetrius Teigas, *Knowledge and Hermeneutic Understanding: A Study of the Habermas–Gadamer Debate* (1995); and Austin Harrington, *Hermeneutical Dialogue and Social Science: A Critique of Gadamer and Habermas* (2001).

Gehlen, Arnold

Only two of Gehlen's books have been translated into English: *Man: His Nature and Place in the World* (1940, *Der Mensch: Seine Natur und seine Stellung in der Welt*; trans. 1988) and a collection of essays, *Man in the Age of Technology* (1957, *Die Seele im technischen Zeitalter: Sozialpsychologische Probleme in der industriellen Gesellschaft*; trans. 1980), a revised version of a volume originally published as *Sozialpsychologische Probleme in der industriellen Gesellschaft* (1949, *Social-psychological Problems in Industrialized Society*). A few of Gehlen's essays of have been published in translation in journals: "Epochs of Painting" (1975), "On Politics and Freedom: Depoliticized Revolution" (1974), and "An Anthropological Model" (1968).

Gehlen wrote his doctoral dissertation, *Zur Theorie der Setzung und des setzungshaften Wissens bei Driesch* (1927, *On the Theory of Positioning and Positional Knowledge in Driesch*), on the thought of his adviser, Hans Driesch. His *Habilitationsschrift* (postdoctoral thesis) was *Wirklicher und unwirklicher Geist: Eine philosophische Untersuchung in der Methode absoluter Phänomenologie* (1931, *Actual and Non-actual Spirit: A Philosophical Investigation of the Method of Absolute Phenomenology*). Other works from the 1930s are *Theorie der Willensfreiheit* (1933, *Theory of Freewill*), *Idealismus und Existentialphilosophie* (1933, *Idealism and Existential Philosophy*), and *Der Staat und die Philosophie* (1935, *The State and Philosophy*); they are found in the first two volumes (1978–80) of his *Gesamtausgabe* (*Complete Edition*), which also contain essays on tragedy, Fichte, Descartes, and Schelling.

Gehlen's main works from the 1950s and 1960s are quite diverse. The most important of them are *Urmensch und Spätkultur: Philosophische Ergebnisse und Aussagen* (1956, *Early Man and Late Culture: Philosophical Conclusions and Assertions*) and *Moral und Hypermoral: Eine pluralistische Ethik* (1969, *Morality and Hypermorality: A Pluralistic Ethic*). Others include *Macht einmal anders gesehen* (1954, *Power Viewed Differently for Once*), *Zeit-Bilder: Zur Soziologie und Ästhetik der modernen Malerei* (1960, *Time-Images: Toward the Sociology and Aesthetic of Modern Painting*), *Über kulturelle Kristallisation* (1961, *On Cultural Crystallization*), and two volumes of essays, most already published: *Anthropologische Forschung: Zur Selbstbegegnung und Selbstentdeckung des Menschen* (1961, *Anthropological Research: On the Self-encountering and Self-discovery of Man*) and *Studien zur Anthropologie und Soziologie* (1963, *Studies in Anthropology and Sociology*).

Volume 4 of Gehlen's collected works (1983) contains his miscellaneous writings between 1936 and 1975 on topics in philosophical anthropology. Volumes 6 (2004) and 7 (1978) contain essays published between 1950 and 1975 on industrialized society, the state, technology, personality, sociology, and business and the public. His collected works are still being published.

The literature on Gehlen in German is considerable, but to date no monographs in English or English translation are devoted exclusively to him. His thought has begun to find its way into the secondary literature via the recent interest in vitalism (and in particular Deleuze) in Europe: see, for example, Tim Scott, *Organization Philosophy: Gehlen, Foucault, Deleuze* (2010). Gehlen's ideas have also been making their way into English-language works through the translations of several Italian philosophers, in particular Giorgio Agamben, Roberto Esposito, and Paolo Virno. For more information on Gehlen and the movement of which his thought is a part, see the bibliography section on philosophical anthropology in General Bibliographies (above).

Guattari, Félix (see Deleuze)

Habermas, Jürgen
Habermas's first book, *Das Absolute und das Geschichte* (1954, *The Absolute and History*), shows his philosophical rootedness in nineteenth-century German philosophy. As the intellectual climate shifted after the Second World War, however, much of his subsequent work for some time had a distinctively contemporary and Marx-influenced political character. *The Structural Transformation of the Public Sphere: An Inquiry into a Category of Bourgeois Society* (1962; trans. 1989) is an analysis of public opinion, the public–private distinction, and many practical issues such as consumerism, voting, journalism, and the family. The essays translated in *Toward a Rational Society: Student Protest, Science and Politics* (1970), originally published in German books of 1968 and 1969, reflect on the role of the university in modern democracy, student protest movements in Germany, and the role of technology and science as ideologies in modern society. *Theory and Practice* (1963, 4th ed. 1971; trans. 1973) contains important assessments of Marx and Hegel, and ultimately argues that politics has suffered because of the theory/practice divide. *Legitimation Crisis* (1973; trans. 1976) analyzes the problems associated with "advanced" or "late" capitalism.

In addition to *Knowledge and Human Interests* (1968; trans. 1971), another early work concerned with epistemological questions is *On the Logic of the Social Sciences* (1967; trans. 1988). It also contains a survey of the major theories of social analysis and their tension with traditional scientific aims and methods. Habermas returned to these epistemic issues in *Truth and Justification* (1999; trans. 2003), where he engaged the realism/antirealism debate and the appropriation of Kant and Hegel in analytic philosophy.

Two of Habermas's works from the 1970s laid the foundation for his mature thought. In *On the Pragmatics of Social Interaction: Preliminary Studies in the Theory of Communicative Action* (1984; trans. 2001), a series of lectures from 1971, he examines the nature of language; *Communication and the Evolution of Society* (1976; trans. 1979) is an essential work in the development of his theory of communication, speech acts, and their sociopolitical implications.

Habermas pursued ideas set forth in his masterwork *The Theory of Communicative Action* (2 vols., 1981; trans. 1984–87) in essays translated together in *On the Pragmatics of Communication* (1998), reflecting further on the structural features of meaningful communication. His communicative or discourse ethics is set forth in *Moral Consciousness and Communicative Action* (1983; trans. 1990), and worked out in further detail in *Justification and Application: Remarks on Discourse Ethics* (1990 and 1991; trans. 1993). He also discusses his discourse theories of ethics, law, and politics not only in *Between Facts and Norms: Contributions to a Discourse Theory of Law and Democracy* (1992; trans. 1996) but also in *The Inclusion of the Other: Studies in Political Theory* (1996; trans. 1998) and *Between Naturalism and Religion: Philosophical Essays* (2005; trans. 2008). In these works Habermas carries on his side of his long-running debate with John Rawls.

Habermas critically engages the history of philosophy and the twentieth-century trends to which he is largely unsympathetic in *Philosophical-Political Profiles* (1971, 3rd ed. 1981; trans. 1983), *Postmetaphysical Thinking* (1988; trans. 1992), and *The Philosophical Discourse of Modernity* (1985; trans. 1987). Lastly, numerous smaller works extend his thought in different areas; many contain occasional pieces written in Habermas's lifelong role as one of Europe's leading cultural critics. These collections include *The New Conservatism* (from *Kleine politische Schriften* [*Minor Political Writings*] 5 and 7, 1985 and 1987; trans. 1989), *The Past as Future* (1990; trans. 1994), *The Liberating Power of Symbols: Philosophical Essays* (1997; trans. 2001), *The Postnational Constellation: Political Essays* (1998; trans. 2001), *The Crisis of the European Union: A Response* (2011; trans. 2012), and *An Awareness of What Is Missing: Faith and Reason in a Post-secular Age* (2008; trans. 2010). *Habermas: A Critical Reader,* edited by Peter Dews (1999), is a useful volume.

The secondary literature on Habermas is substantial. For introductory works, see William Outhwaite, *Habermas: A Critical Introduction* (1994; 2nd ed., 2009); Uwe Steinhoff, *The Philosophy of Jürgen Habermas: A Critical Introduction* (2009); Lasse Thomassen, *Habermas: A Guide for the Perplexed* (2010); and David Ingram, *Habermas: Introduction and Analysis* (2010). For his biography, see Matthew G. Specter's *Habermas: An Intellectual Biography* (2010).

There are many edited volumes of critical essays on Habermas's thought and work, including *Jürgen Habermas: Key Concepts,* edited by Barbara Fultner (2011); *Habermas and the Public Sphere,* edited by Craig Calhoun (1992); *The Cambridge Companion to Habermas,* edited by Stephen K. White (1995); *Habermas and the Unfinished Project of Modernity: Critical Essays on "The Philosophical Discourse of Modernity,"* edited by Maurizio Passerin d'Entrèves and Seyla Benhabib (1997); and *Communicative Action: Essays on Jürgen Habermas's "The Theory of Communicative Action,"* edited by Axel Honneth and Hans Joas (1986; trans. 1991). See also two companion volumes of critical essays edited by Axel Honneth, Thomas McCarthy, Claus Offe, and Albrecht Wellmer, *Cultural-Political Interventions in the Unfinished Project of Enlightenment* (1992) and *Philosophical Interventions in the Unfinished Project of Enlightenment* (1992).

Major studies of Habermas include Raymond Geuss, *The Idea of a Critical Theory: Habermas and the Frankfurt School* (1981); Joseph Heath, *Communicative Action and Rational Choice* (2001); David M. Rasmussen, *Reading Habermas* (1990); Stephen K. White, *The Recent Work of Jürgen Habermas: Reason, Justice and Modernity* (1988); and Thomas A. McCarthy, *The Critical Theory of Jürgen Habermas* (1978) and *Ideals and Illusions: On Reconstruction and Deconstruction in Contemporary Critical Theory* (1991). A work critical of Habermas is Nicholas Rescher's *Pluralism: Against the Demand for Consensus* (1993). Two works that focus on epistemology and the philosophy of language are James Swindal, *Reflection Revisited: Jürgen Habermas's Discursive Theory of Truth* (1999), and Maeve Cooke, *Language and Reason: A Study of Habermas's Pragmatics* (1994).

Studies that focus on Habermas's discourse ethics are J. M. Bernstein, *Recovering Ethical Life: Jürgen Habermas and the Future of Critical Theory* (1995), and Ricardo Blaug, *Democracy, Real and Ideal: Discourse Ethics and Radical Politics* (1999). On Habermas's political philosophy and its consequences, see George Trey, *Solidarity and Difference: The Politics of Enlightenment in the Aftermath of Modernity* (1998); J. Craig Hanks, *Refiguring Critical Theory: Jürgen Habermas and the Possibilities of Political Change* (2002); Jane Braaten, *Habermas's Critical Theory of Society* (1991); and David S. Owen, *Between Reason and History: Habermas and the Idea of Progress* (2002).

Much of the recent work on Habermas has focused on his political philosophy. See Pauline Johnson, *Habermas: Rescuing the Public Sphere* (2006); Todd Hedrick, *Rawls and Habermas: Reason, Pluralism, and the Claims of Political Philosophy* (2010); Hugh Baxter, *Habermas: The Discourse Theory of Law and Democracy* (2011); Lasse Thomassen, *Habermas and Radical Democracy* (2012); *Deprovincializing Habermas:*

Global Perspectives, edited by Tom Bailey (2013); Miriam Bankovsky, *Perfecting Justice in Rawls, Habermas and Honneth: A Deconstructive Perspective* (2012); and *Beyond Habermas: Democracy, Knowledge, and the Public Sphere*, edited by Christian J. Emden and David Midgley (2012).

Hegel, Georg Wilhelm Friedrich

On Christianity: Early Theological Writings (trans. 1948) contains a number of Hegel's earliest writings from 1794 to 1800, first published in German in 1907. *Three Essays, 1793–1795* (1984) contains other writings from this period. *Miscellaneous Writings of G. W. F. Hegel* (2001) presents fragments, essays, poems, and reviews from Hegel's entire career, but mainly from his early years. *System of Ethical Life (1802/3) and First Philosophy of Spirit (Part III of the System of Speculative Philosophy 1803/4)* (1979) presents translations from two incomplete early texts on his ethical, social, and political philosophy and his concept of *Geist* (spirit), published in German as *Jenaer Systementwürfe I* (1975) and *System der Sittlichkeit* (1923). *The Jena System, 1804–5: Logic and Metaphysics* (1986) translates the German text *Jenaer Systementwürfe II* (1971).

Three of Hegel's most important early works are *The Difference between Fichte's and Schelling's System of Philosophy* (1801; trans. 1977), which was Hegel's first acknowledged publication; *Faith and Knowledge* (1802; trans. 1977); and *Natural Law* (1802; trans. 1975). Several other essays written in 1802 for the journal that Hegel co-edited with Schelling are available in *Between Kant and Hegel: Texts in the Development of Post-Kantian Idealism* (1985).

Hegel's *Phenomenologie des Geistes* (1807) was his first (and, in the opinion of many, his greatest) major work. It was first translated into English in 1910, as *The Phenomenology of Mind*, and then again in 1977, as *Phenomenology of Spirit*. The first version of his "Logic," his *Science of Logic* (or "Greater Logic"), was published in three parts in 1812, 1813, and 1816, then republished in revised second (1833) and third (1841) editions. It was first translated into English in 1929, and a new translation appeared in 2010. Writings from the period (1816–18) after the *Logic* appeared have recently been translated as *Heidelberg Writings: Journal Publications* (2009).

Hegel's *Encyclopedia of Philosophical Sciences*, first published in German in 1817, was expanded in subsequent editions of 1827 and 1830 (the last in his lifetime). After Hegel's death what are called *Zusätze* ("additions"— elucidating notes appended to specific passages) were added in each of its three volumes. These notes are drawn from Hegel's lectures— some written by Hegel, in his personal copies of the text, and some culled from students' notes. Part one of the *Encyclopedia*, *Logic* (also known as the "Lesser Logic"), was first translated into English in 1873 as *The Logic of Hegel*, then as *The Encyclopaedia Logic, with the Zusätze* (1991); the translation in the Cambridge Hegel series is titled *Encyclopedia of the Philosophical Sciences in Basic Outline*, part 1, *Science of Logic* (2010).

Part 2 of the *Encyclopedia* is available in English as *Hegel's Philosophy of Nature* (1970), translated from the 1830 edition together with the *Zusätze* added in 1847.

Part 3 of the *Encyclopedia* is translated into English as *Philosophy of Mind* (or *Spirit* [*Geist*]); it was originally translated in 1894 from the 1830 edition without the *Zusätze*, which were added in a 1971 edition. Those translations were substantially revised in 2010. Recently translated lectures, *Lectures on the Philosophy of Spirit, 1827–8* (2007), illuminate the *Encyclopedia*'s original outline of the philosophy of *Geist* far more fully than do the *Zusätze*. *Encyclopedia of the Philosophical Sciences in Outline, and Critical Writings* (1990) translates the complete three volumes of the *Encyclopedia*'s first edition (1817).

In 1821 Hegel published *Grundlinien der Philosophie des Rechts*, translated first as *Hegel's Philosophy of Right* (1896), and later under the same title (1942; rev. as *Outlines of the Philosophy of Right*, 2008) and as *Elements of the Philosophy of Right* (1991). This work also has *Zusätze* from student notes, first added in 1833. An early version of the philosophy of right is available in *Lectures on Natural Right and Political Science: The First Philosophy of Right: Heidelberg, 1817–1818, with Additions from the Lectures of 1818–1819* (1983; trans. 1995). *Hegel: Political Writings* (1999) collects and translates a number of briefer public writings, addresses, and lectures on political matters written between 1798 and 1831, including the "Natural Law" essay of 1802.

Hegel's Berlin lectures on history, religion, the history of philosophy, and aesthetics have resulted in a complicated set of manuscripts and translations. Despite their questionable construction from different manuscripts, older German editions and earlier translations have been quite influential. Only recently have more complete versions of these lectures and manuscripts become available.

Hegel's introductory lectures on aesthetics were first translated in 1886 as *The Introduction to Hegel's "Philosophy of Fine Art."* The complete series of lectures from the 1835–38 edition was translated as *The Philosophy of Fine Art* (4 vols., 1916–20) and more recently in *Aesthetics: Lectures on Fine Art* (2 vols., 1975).

Lectures on the Philosophy of Religion was first translated, in 3 volumes, in 1895 and then again in 1984–87; unlike its predecessor, the latter separates the lectures from 1821, 1824, 1827, and 1831. More recently, a lecture series from 1829, *Lectures on the Proofs of the Existence of God* (1995; trans. 2007), has become available.

Lectures on the History of Philosophy was first translated between 1892 and 1896 (3 vols.) as *Greek Philosophy to Plato, Plato and the Platonists*, and *Medieval and Modern Philosophy*. Like many of the old translations, these remain in print and in wide use. A newer translation of the lectures' introduction is available, *Introduction to the Lectures on the History of Philosophy* (1985). The most recent translation, *Lectures on the History of Philosophy 1825–6* (3 vols., 2006–09), groups the lectures as *Introduction and Oriental Philosophy, Greek Philosophy*, and *Medieval and Modern Philosophy*. Hegel's 1828 critical review of the thought of Johan George Hamann, a contemporary of Kant, can be found in *Hegel on Hamann* (2008).

Lectures on the Philosophy of History was first translated in 1857. That translation was reissued in 1956. A new translation, *Lectures on the Philosophy of World History*, is in process; to date, only vol. 1, *Manuscripts of the Introduction and the Lectures of 1822–1823* (2011), has been issued. Its famous introduction has been retranslated and published separately on a number of occasions, first as *Reason in History: A General Introduction to the Philosophy of History* (1953), and again as *Introduction to the Philosophy of History* (1988); both translations were based on the 1840 edition edited by Eduard Gans and Hegel's son Karl.

There are many introductions to Hegel. Recent ones include Allen Speight, *The Philosophy of Hegel* (2008); Craig B. Matarrese, *Starting with Hegel* (2010); Joseph McCarney, *Routledge Philosophy Guidebook to Hegel on History* (2000); Robert Stern, *The Routledge Guidebook to Hegel's "Phenomenology of Spirit"* (rev. ed., 2013); Dudley Knowles, *Routledge Philosophy Guidebook to Hegel and the "Philosophy of Right"* (2002); David James, *Hegel: A Guide for the Perplexed* (2007); Michael Allen Fox, *The Accessible Hegel* (2005); Stephen Houlgate, *An Introduction to Hegel: Freedom, Truth, and History* (2nd ed., 2005); and Howard P. Kainz, *Introduction to Hegel: Stages of Modern Philosophy* (1996) and *G. W. F. Hegel: The Philosophical System* (1996).

Two volumes that introduce Hegel by situating him within the history of philosophy are Tom Rockmore, *Before and After Hegel: A Historical Introduction to Hegel's Thought* (1993), and Richard Schacht, *Hegel and After: Studies in Continental Philosophy between Kant and Sartre* (1975). An anthology worth mentioning is *The Young Hegelians: An Anthology*, edited by

Robert Stepelevich (1993). It contains translations of writings from the generation after Hegel that was deeply influenced by him.

Recent collections of essays that explore diverse aspects of Hegel's thought include *A Companion to Hegel*, edited by Stephen Houlgate and Michael Baur (2011), and *The Cambridge Companion to Hegel* (1993) and *The Cambridge Companion to Hegel and Nineteenth-Century Philosophy* (2008), both edited by Frederick C. Beiser. The relation of Hegel's philosophy to Kant is discussed in many works. Some that focus on it are William F. Bristow, *Hegel and the Transformation of Philosophical Critique* (2007); Sally Sedgwick, *Hegel's Critique of Kant: From Dichotomy to Identity* (2012); Ido Geiger, *The Founding Act of Modern Ethical Life: Hegel's Critique of Kant's Moral and Political Philosophy* (2007); and John McCumber, *Understanding Hegel's Mature Critique of Kant* (2013).

Several historically important interpretations have influenced the way that Hegel is understood. Herbert Marcuse has contributed *Hegel's Ontology and the Theory of Historicity* (1932; trans. 1987) and *Reason and Revolution* (1941; 2nd ed., 1955). Alexandre Kojève's *Introduction to the Reading of Hegel* (1947; trans. 1969) contains his influential lectures given between 1934 and 1939 in France. Jean Hyppolite's works on Hegel have also had a tremendous impact on French thought: see his *Genesis and Structure of Hegel's Phenomenology of Spirit* (1946; trans. 1974), *Logic and Existence* (1953; trans. 1997), and *Introduction to Hegel's Philosophy of History* (1949; trans. 1996). Pierre Macherey's *Hegel or Spinoza* (1979; trans. 2011) is also a historically significant work.

Heidegger's interpretation of Hegel is available in *Hegel's Phenomenology of Spirit* (1971; trans. 1988). Hans-Georg Gadamer, *Hegel's Dialectic: Five Hermeneutical Studies* (1971; trans. 1976), shows Hegel's importance for hermeneutics. Georg Lukács's *The Young Hegel: Studies in the Relations between Dialectics and Economics* (1948; trans. 1975) and *Ontology of Social Being*, vol. 1, *Hegel* (1971; trans. 1978), are also significant and influential works. In the British idealist tradition, John McTaggart's *A Commentary on Hegel's Logic* (1910) and *Studies in the Hegelian Dialectic* (1896; 2nd ed., 1922) have been important.

In English-language Hegel scholarship there have been a number of classic interpretations of Hegel's thought, beginning with James Hutchison Stirling, *The Secret of Hegel: Being the Hegelian System in Origin, Principle, Form, and Matter* (2 vols., 1865). Others of more recent vintage include W. T. Stace, *The Philosophy of Hegel: A Systematic Exposition* (1924); J. N. Findlay, *Hegel: A Re-examination* (1958); G. R. G. Mure, *The Philosophy of Hegel* (1965);

Walter Kaufmann, *Hegel: Reinterpretation, Texts and Commentary* (1965); Charles Taylor, *Hegel* (1975); and M. J. Inwood, *Hegel* (1983). Other notable earlier studies are Stanley Rosen, *G. W. F. Hegel: An Introduction to the Science of Wisdom* (1974); Quentin Lauer, *Hegel's Idea of Philosophy: With a New Translation of Hegel's "Introduction to the History of Philosophy"* (1971); and Robert C. Solomon, *In the Spirit of Hegel: A Study of G. W. F. Hegel's "Phenomenology of Spirit"* (1983). In the two volumes of *Hegel's Development*, H. S. Harris explores Hegel's early thought: *Toward the Sunlight, 1770–1801* (1972) and *Night Thoughts: Jena, 1801–1806* (1983).

Significant works in recent Hegel scholarship include Frederick Beiser, *Hegel* (2005), and Michael N. Forster, *Hegel and Skepticism* (1989) and *Hegel's Idea of a Phenomenology of Spirit* (1998). Robert B. Pippin has contributed three studies: *Hegel's Idealism: The Satisfactions of Self-Consciousness* (1989), *Idealism as Modernism: Hegelian Variations* (1997), and *Hegel's Practical Philosophy: Rational Agency as Ethical Life* (2008). Terry Pinkard has contributed three as well: *Hegel's Dialectic: The Explanation of Possibility* (1988), *Hegel's Phenomenology: The Sociality of Reason* (1994), and *Hegel's Naturalism: Mind, Nature, and the Final Ends of Life* (2012). Further recent contributions are Brady Bowman, *Hegel and the Metaphysics of Absolute Negativity* (2013); Robert M. Wallace, *Hegel's Philosophy of Reality, Freedom, and God* (2005); Robert Stern, *Hegelian Metaphysics* (2009); and Béatrice Longuenesse, *Hegel's Critique of Metaphysics* (1981; trans. 2007).

Recent volumes of essays about Hegel include *Hegel: Myths and Legends*, edited by Jon Stewart (1996); *Essays on Hegel's Philosophy of Subjective Spirit*, edited by David S. Stern (2013); *Hegel and the Analytic Tradition* (2010) and *Hegel on Religion and Politics* (2013), both edited by Angelica Nuzzo; *Hegel: New Directions*, edited by Katerina Deligiorgi (2006); *The Spirit of the Age: Hegel and the Fate of Thinking*, edited by Paul Ashton, Toula Nicolacopoulos, and George Vassilacopoulos (2008); *Hegel's Theory of the Subject*, edited by David Gray Carlson (2005); *Identity and Difference: Studies in Hegel's Logic, Philosophy of Spirit, and Politics*, edited by Philip T. Grier (2007); and *The Dimensions of Hegel's Dialectic*, edited by Nectarios G. Limnatis (2010).

The following works examine Hegel in relation to twentieth-century Continental thought or are creative explorations of Hegel in that vein of philosophizing: Judith Butler, *Subjects of Desire: Hegelian Reflections in Twentieth-Century France* (1987); Catherine Malabou, *The Future of Hegel: Plasticity, Temporality and Dialectic* (1996; trans. 2005); Rebecca Comay, *Mourning Sickness: Hegel and the French Rev-olution* (2011); Slavoj Žižek, *Tarrying with the Negative: Kant, Hegel and the Critique of Ideology* (1993) and *Less Than Nothing: Hegel and the Shadow of Dialectical Materialism* (2012); *Hegel and Contemporary Continental Philosophy*, edited by Dennis King Keenan (2004); *Hegel and His Critics: Philosophy in the Aftermath of Hegel*, edited by William Desmond (1989); Michael S. Roth, *Knowing and History: Appropriations of Hegel in Twentieth-Century France* (1988); Theodore D. George, *Tragedies of Spirit: Tracing Finitude in Hegel's Phenomenology* (2006); *Hegel after Derrida*, edited by Stuart Barnett (1998); Frank Ruda, *Hegel's Rabble: An Investigation into Hegel's "Philosophy of Right"* (2011); and Jean-Luc Nancy, *Hegel: The Restlessness of the Negative* (1997; trans. 2002) and *The Speculative Remark: One of Hegel's Bons Mots* (1973; trans. 2001).

Recent studies from more analytic perspectives include Tom Rockmore, *Hegel, Idealism, and Analytic Philosophy* (2005); Michael Quante, *Hegel's Concept of Action* (1993; trans. 2004); Christopher Yeomans, *Freedom and Reflection: Hegel and the Logic of Agency* (2012); and two books by Kenneth R. Westphal, *Hegel's Epistemological Realism: A Study of the Aim and Method of Hegel's "Phenomenology of Spirit"* (1989) and *Hegel's Epistemology: A Philosophical Introduction to the "Phenomenology of Spirit"* (2003). Three works that discuss Hegel's philosophy of language are *Hegel and Language*, edited by Jere O'Neill Surber (2006); John McCumber, *The Company of Words: Hegel, Language, and Systematic Philosophy* (1993); and Jim Vernon, *Hegel's Philosophy of Language* (2007).

Two works that examine Hegel's theory of nature and natural science are *Hegel and the Philosophy of Nature*, edited by Stephen Houlgate (1998), and Alison Stone, *Petrified Intelligence: Nature in Hegel's Philosophy* (2005). Thomas A. Lewis, *Freedom and Tradition in Hegel: Reconsidering Anthropology, Ethics, and Religion* (2005), is an examination of Hegel from the perspective of philosophical anthropology, and themes relating to philosophical anthropology are discussed in Alfredo Ferrarin, *Hegel and Aristotle* (2001). Works that examine Hegel in relation to psychology include Jon Mills, *The Unconscious Abyss: Hegel's Anticipation of Psychoanalysis* (2002); Jennifer Ann Bates, *Hegel's Theory of Imagination* (2004); Molly Macdonald, *Hegel and Psychoanalysis: A New Interpretation of "Phenomenology of Spirit"* (2013); and Richard Dien Winfield, *Hegel and Mind: Rethinking Philosophical Psychology* (2010).

The following are works devoted to Hegel's 1807 *Phenomenology*: John Edward Russon, *Reading Hegel's "Phenomenology"* (2004); Merold Westphal, *History and Truth in Hegel's "Phenomenology"* (1979; 3rd ed., 1998); Howard P.

Kainz, Hegel's "Phenomenology," Part I: Analysis and Commentary (1976) and Part II: The Evolution of Ethical and Religious Consciousness to the Absolute Standpoint (1983); Donald Phillip Verene, Hegel's Recollection: A Study of Images in the "Phenomenology of Spirit" (1985); The "Phenomenology of Spirit" Reader: Critical and Interpretive Essays, edited by Jon Stewart (1998); Hegel's "Phenomenology of Spirit": New Critical Essays, edited by Alfred Denker and Michael Vater (2003); Quentin Lauer, A Reading of Hegel's "Phenomenology of Spirit" (1976); Jon Stewart, The Unity of Hegel's "Phenomenology of Spirit": A Systematic Interpretation (2000); Method and Speculation in Hegel's "Phenomenology," edited by Merold Westphal (1982); Philip J. Kain, Hegel and the Other: A Study of the "Phenomenology of Spirit" (2005); and Werner Marx, Hegel's "Phenomenology of Spirit," Its Point and Purpose: A Commentary on the Preface and Introduction (1971; trans. 1975). One of the most impressive studies of the Phenomenology is H. S. Harris's two-volume Hegel's Ladder (1997)—vol. 1, The Pilgrimage of Reason, and vol. 2, The Odyssey of Spirit—an expansion of Hegel: Phenomenology and System (1995).

In recent years, attention to the Phenomenology has, if anything, been increasing, with the appearance of such works as Stephen Houlgate, Hegel's "Phenomenology of Spirit": A Reader's Guide (2012); Ludwig Siep, Hegel's "Phenomenology of Spirit" (2000; trans. 2014); The Blackwell Guide to Hegel's "Phenomenology of Spirit," edited by Kenneth R. Westphal (2009); Robert B. Pippin, Hegel on Self-Consciousness: Desire and Death in the "Phenomenology of Spirit" (2010); Richard Dien Winfield, Hegel's "Phenomenology of Spirit": A Critical Rethinking in Seventeen Lectures (2013); Howard P. Kainz, Hegel's "Phenomenology of Spirit": Not Missing the Trees for the Forest (2008); Ardis Collins, Hegel's "Phenomenology": The Dialectical Justification of Philosophy's First Principles (2013); Hegel's "Phenomenology of Spirit": A Critical Guide, edited by Dean Moyar and Michael Quante (2008); Larry Krasnoff, Hegel's "Phenomenology of Spirit": An Introduction (2008); Donald Verene, Hegel's Absolute: An Introduction to Reading the "Phenomenology of Spirit" (2007); and Peter Kalkavage, The Logic of Desire: An Introduction to Hegel's "Phenomenology of Spirit" (2007).

The Philosophy of Right is the focus of the following works: Beyond Liberalism and Communitarianism: Studies in Hegel's "Philosophy of Right," edited by Robert R. Williams (2001); Thom Brooks, Hegel's Political Philosophy: A Systematic Reading of the "Philosophy of Right" (2007; 2nd ed., 2013); Hegel's "Philosophy of Right": Essays on Ethics, Politics, and Law, edited by Thom Brooks (2012); David Edward Rose, Hegel's "Philosophy of Right": A Reader's Guide (2007); and David James, Hegel's Philosophy of Right: Subjectivity and Ethical Life (2007). Hegel's political philosophy remains one of the most influential in the history of philosophy. The earlier literature on this work and its topics is massive, including Eric Weil, Hegel and the State (1950; trans. 1998); Charles Taylor, Hegel and Modern Society (1979); Shlomo Avineri, Hegel's Theory of the Modern State (1972); Paul Lakeland, The Politics of Salvation: The Hegelian Idea of the State (1984); Steven B. Smith, Hegel's Critique of Liberalism: Rights in Context (1989); Domenico Losurdo, Hegel and the Freedom of Moderns (1992; trans. 2004); Fred R. Dallmayr, G. W. F. Hegel: Modernity and Politics (1993; new ed., 2002); Lydia L. Moland, Hegel on Political Identity: Patriotism, Nationality, Cosmopolitanism (2011); Timothy C. Luther, Hegel's Critique of Modernity: Reconciling Individual Freedom and the Community (2009); Hegel on Ethics and Politics, edited by Robert B. Pippin and Otfried Höffe (2004); Eric Lee Goodfield, Hegel and the Metaphysical Frontiers of Political Theory (2013); Andrew Buchwalter, Dialectics, Politics, and the Contemporary Value of Hegel's Practical Philosophy (2012); and Thomas A. Lewis, Religion, Modernity, and Politics in Hegel (2011). A work on Hegel and the philosophy of law is William E. Conklin, Hegel's Laws: The Legitimacy of a Modern Legal Order (2008).

Works devoted in large part to Hegel's concept of freedom are Merold Westphal, Hegel, Freedom, and Modernity (1992); Renato Cristi, Hegel on Freedom and Authority (2005); Alan Patten, Hegel's Idea of Freedom (1999); Paul Franco, Hegel's Philosophy of Freedom (1999); Frederick Neuhouser, Foundations of Hegel's Social Theory: Actualizing Freedom (2000); Will Dudley, Hegel, Nietzsche, and Philosophy: Thinking Freedom (2002); and Axel Honneth, The Pathologies of Individual Freedom: Hegel's Social Theory (2001; trans. 2010). Michael O. Hardimon's Hegel's Social Philosophy: The Project of Reconciliation (1994) explores the pre-political human relations that constitute the foundation of society and ethics.

Works focused on Hegel's ethics and its key notion of recognition are Allen W. Wood, Hegel's Ethical Thought (1990); Robert R. Williams, Hegel's Ethics of Recognition (1997) and Recognition: Fichte and Hegel on the Other (1992); Sybol Cook Anderson, Hegel's Theory of Recognition: From Oppression to Ethical Liberal Modernity (2011); and Dean Moyar, Hegel's Conscience (2011).

Several works on Hegel and feminism are Feminist Interpretations of G. W. F. Hegel, edited by Patricia Jagentowicz Mills (1996); Kimberly Hutchings, Hegel and Feminist Philosophy

(2003); Jeffrey A. Gauthier, *Hegel and Feminist Social Criticism: Justice, Recognition, and the Feminine* (1997); Judith Butler, *Antigone's Claim: Kinship between Life and Death* (2000); and *Hegel's Philosophy and Feminist Thought: Beyond Antigone?*, edited by Kimberly Hutchings and Tuija Pulkkinen (2010).

A work devoted entirely to the third volume of the *Encyclopedia* is M. J. Inwood's *A Commentary on Hegel's "Philosophy of Mind"* (2007). Hegel's *Encyclopedia Logic* and the "greater Logic" are explored in the following works: Stephen Houlgate, *The Opening of Hegel's Logic: From Being to Infinity* (2006); John Burbidge, *On Hegel's Logic: Fragments of a Commentary* (1981) and *The Logic of Hegel's 'Logic': An Introduction* (2006); *Essays on Hegel's Logic*, edited by George di Giovanni (1990); Ermanno Bencivenga, *Hegel's Dialectical Logic* (2000); Justus Hartnack, *An Introduction to Hegel's Logic* (1995; trans. 1998); Clark Butler, *Hegel's Logic: Between Dialectic and History* (1996); Richard Dien Winfield, *Hegel's "Science of Logic": A Critical Rethinking in Thirty Lectures* (2012); and Stanley Rosen, *The Idea of Hegel's "Science of Logic"* (2013).

Studies of Hegel's philosophy of religion are available in Dale M. Schlitt, *Divine Subjectivity: Understanding Hegel's Philosophy of Religion* (1990); John W. Burbidge, *Hegel on Logic and Religion: The Reasonableness of Christianity* (1992); William Desmond, *Hegel and God: A Counterfeit Double?* (2003); Raymond Keith Williamson, *An Introduction to Hegel's Philosophy of Religion* (1984); Quentin Lauer, *Hegel's Concept of God* (1982); and Walter Jaeschke, *Reason in Religion: The Foundations of Hegel's Philosophy of Religion* (1986; trans. 1990).

Works devoted to Hegel's aesthetics include Kirk Pillow, *Sublime Understanding: Aesthetic Reflection in Kant and Hegel* (2000); William Desmond, *Art and the Absolute: A Study of Hegel's Aesthetics* (1986); Stephen Bungay, *Beauty and Truth: A Study of Hegel's Aesthetics* (1984); *Hegel and Aesthetics*, edited by William Maker (2000); Brian K. Etter, *Between Transcendence and Historicism: The Ethical Nature of the Arts in Hegelian Aesthetics* (2006); Andrew W. Hass, *Hegel and the Art of Negation: Hass, Creativity and Contemporary Thought* (2013); David James, *Art, Myth and Society in Hegel's Aesthetics* (2009); Beat Wyss, *Hegel's Art History and the Critique of Modernity* (1985; trans. 1999); *Hegel and the Arts*, edited by Stephen Houlgate (2007); Benjamin Rutter, *Hegel on the Modern Arts* (2010); and Robert B. Pippin, *After the Beautiful: Hegel and the Philosophy of Pictorial Modernism* (2013).

Several works on Hegel's theory of history are *Hegel, History and Interpretation*, edited by Shaun Gallagher (1997); George Dennis O'Brien, *Hegel on Reason and History: A Contemporary Interpretation* (1975); Daniel Berthold-Bond, *Hegel's Grand Synthesis: A Study of Being, Thought, and History* (1989); *Hegel and History*, edited by Will Dudley (2009); and Angelica Nuzzo, *Memory, History, Justice in Hegel* (2012). Three works that study Hegel in relation to Marx are *The Hegel–Marx Connection*, edited by Tony Burns and Ian Fraser (2000); *The New Hegelians: Politics and Philosophy in the Hegelian School*, edited by Douglas Moggach (2006); and Norman Levine, *Marx's Discourse with Hegel* (2012).

Two biographies of Hegel are available: Terry P. Pinkard, *Hegel: A Biography* (2000), and Horst Althaus, *Hegel: An Intellectual Biography* (1992; trans. 2000).

More sources containing discussions of Hegel can be found in the bibliography section on German idealism in General Bibliographies (above).

Heidegger, Martin

Heidegger published sixteen books in his lifetime, most of which were either collections of essays or reworked lectures. Yet there are at present 102 volumes in the critical edition, still in process, of his collected writings and other expressions of his thought (referred to as "the *Gesamtausgabe*"). Nearly half of them are devoted to lectures that he gave as a university professor at Marburg and Freiburg. (What makes this all the more remarkable is that Heidegger did not lecture between 1944 and 1951.) The focus in what follows will be on those of his writings and lectures that are available in English.

All of Heidegger's earliest lectures in Freiburg (1919–23) will soon be available in English translation. These works (vols. 56–63 of the *Gesamtausgabe*) offer insight into Heidegger's development prior to *Being and Time*. Already published are *Towards the Definition of Philosophy* (1987; trans. 2000), *The Basic Problems of Phenomenology: Winter Semester 1919/1920* (1993; trans. 2013), *The Phenomenology of Intuition and Expression: Theory of Philosophical Concept Formation* (1993; trans. 2010), *The Phenomenology of Religious Life* (1995; trans. 2004), *Phenomenological Interpretations of Aristotle: Initiation into Phenomenological Research* (1985; trans. 2001), and *Ontology: The Hermeneutics of Facticity* (1988; trans. 1999), which provides the first indications of some of the major themes that Heidegger would explore for the rest of his life.

Several collections of Heidegger's pre–*Being and Time* writings are now available, including *Becoming Heidegger: On the Trail of His Early Occasional Writings, 1910–1927*, edited by Theodore Kisiel and Thomas Sheehan (2007), and *Supplements: From the Earliest Essays to "Being and Time" and Beyond*, edited by John van Buren (2002). In 1924 Heidegger wrote but did not publish a long essay called *The Concept of Time* (2004; trans. 2011); also called the "Dilthey Review," it is commonly seen as a preliminary version of what became *Being and Time*. Much of its content is preserved in *Being and Time*, but in its original form it is a helpful 90-page introduction to Heidegger's major themes.

Heidegger's first major published work was *Being and Time* (1927; trans. 1962 and 1996). He originally envisioned a much larger work consisting of two parts, each divided into three sections. The published text contains only the first two sections of Part 1. The third section of Part 1 was to be on "time and Being," and further reflection on this theme may have been what subsequently led him far beyond the "analytic of Dasein" that is his focus in *Being and Time*. The lecture course from 1925, published as *History of the Concept of Time: Prolegomena* (1979; trans. 1985), can be thought of as a penultimate draft of *Being and Time*. It provides at least a sketch of the missing third section of Part 1, and also offers one of his more extensive analyses of phenomenology and Neo-Kantianism. Only the final half of *The Basic Problems of Phenomenology* ([lectures delivered 1927] 1975; trans. 1982) offers a glimpse at Heidegger's treatment of time itself during this period.

The other lectures from the Marburg era (1923–28, vols. 17–26 of the complete works) do provide an idea of the missing second part of *Being and Time*: it was to be "phenomenological destruction" of the history of ontology, with a focus on Plato, Aristotle, Descartes, Kant, and Husserl. These lecture courses are *Introduction to Phenomenological Research* (1994; trans. 2005), *Basic Concepts of Aristotelian Philosophy* (2002; trans. 2009), *Plato's "Sophist"* (1992; trans. 1997), *Logic: The Question of Truth* (1976; trans. 2010), *Basic Concepts of Ancient Philosophy* (1993; trans. 2007), *Phenomenological Interpretation of Kant's "Critique of Pure Reason"* (1977; trans. 1997), and *The Metaphysical Foundations of Logic* (1978; trans. 1984). Heidegger published *Kant and the Problem of Metaphysics* (trans. 1962; 5th ed., 1997) in 1929, which is a fitting close to the era of *Being and Time* and his time at Marburg.

The lectures from his time in Freiburg prior to his postwar ban from teaching constitute 28 volumes of the *Gesamtausgabe*. His initial lectures before he became rector in 1933 make up the volumes *The Fundamental Concepts of Metaphysics: World, Finitude, Solitude* (1983; trans. 1995), *The Essence of Human Freedom: An Introduction to Philosophy* (1982; trans. 2002), *Hegel's "Phenomenology of Spirit"* (1980; trans. 1988), *Aristotle's "Metaphysics" Θ 1–3: On the Essence and Actuality of Force* (1981; trans.

1995), and *The Essence of Truth: On Plato's Cave Allegory and "Theaetetus"* (1988; trans. 2002).

There are a number of collections of essays and lectures of a political nature from Heidegger's Nazi period (beginning in 1933), which make for disturbing reading. They include *Nature, History, State, 1933–1934* (2013), *The Heidegger Controversy: A Critical Reader* (1991), and *Martin Heidegger and National Socialism: Questions and Answers* (1988; trans. 1990).

One of the first translations of his lectures into English, *What Is a Thing?* ([delivered 1935–36] 1962; trans. 1967), continues and deepens his investigation of Kant. *Introduction to Metaphysics* ([delivered 1935] 1953; trans. 1959 and 2000) also has long been available in English. Although from the same year as *What Is a Thing?*, *Introduction to Metaphysics* can be seen, along with *Logic as the Question concerning the Essence of Language* ([delivered 1934] 1998; trans. 2009), as marking the transition to Heidegger's later philosophy, with its focus on Being, thought, language, and poetry. He was pursuing other interests during this period as well. In 1936 he gave a course on Schelling that has been published as *Schelling's Treatise on the Essence of Human Freedom* (1971; trans. 1985). He subsequently focused on Nietzsche in several lecture courses from the mid-1930s to the early 1940s. They became the basis of *Nietzsche* (2 vols., 1961; 4 vols., trans. 1979–87), a summation of his thinking on Nietzsche at that time.

The direction of Heidegger's late philosophy can be discerned in the manuscripts written between 1936 and 1938 that were published under the title *Contributions to Philosophy (Of the Event) (Beiträge zur Philosophie [Vom Ereignis])*, 1989; trans. 1999 and 2012). In private manuscripts, he continued to work out the ideas foreshadowed here. Two have been published so far: *Mindfulness (Besinnung*, 1997; trans. 2006) and *The Event (Das Ereignis*, 2009; trans. 2013).

Volumes deriving from Heidegger's lectures delivered after his "turn" include *Basic Questions of Philosophy: Selected "Problems" of "Logic"* (1984; trans. 1994), *Basic Concepts* (1981; trans. 1993); *Parmenides* (1982; trans. 1992); *Heraclitus* (1979; trans. 2007); and *On the Essence of Language: The Metaphysics of Language and the Essencing of the Word; Concerning Herder's Treatise "On the Origin of Language"* (1999; trans. 2004). Some of his most famous essays and lectures date from the transitional post–*Being and Time* period, and are contained in collections of essays published in German in his lifetime, including *Off the Beaten Track* (1950; trans. 2002), *Pathmarks* (1967; trans. 1998), *On the Way to Language* (1959; trans. 1971), and *Elucidations of Hölderlin's Poetry* (1981; trans. 2000). The following collections in English also contain essays and lectures appearing in some of these volumes, as well as other miscellaneous writings: *Early Greek Thinking* (1975), *Poetry, Language, Thought* (1971), *The End of Philosophy* (1973), *The Question Concerning Technology, and Other Essays* (1977), *Existence and Being* (1949, with a lengthy introduction by Werner Bock), and *Basic Writings: From "Being and Time" (1927) to "The Task of Thinking" (1964)* (1977).

Other lectures from the 1950s appear in *Bremen and Freiburg Lectures: "Insight into That Which Is" and "Basic Principles of Thinking"* ([delivered 1949, 1957] 1994; trans. 2012); *What Is Called Thinking?* ([delivered 1957] 1954; trans. 1968); *Discourse on Thinking: A Translation of "Gelassenheit"* (1959; trans. 1966), whose subtitle's memorial lecture was delivered in 1955; *What Is Philosophy?* ([delivered 1955] 1956; trans. 1956), and *The Principle of Reason* ([delivered 1955–56] 1957; trans. 1991). Several works collect lectures from the 1960s, including *Four Seminars: Le Thor 1966, 1968, 1969, Zähringen 1973* (1976 [French]; 1977 [German], trans. 2003); *On Time and Being (Zur Sache des Denkens* [delivered 1962–64], 1969; trans. 1972); and *Heraclitus Seminar, 1966/67* (1970; trans. 1979).

The primary biography of Heidegger available in English is Rüdiger Safranski's *Martin Heidegger: Between Good and Evil* (1994; trans. 1998). Heidegger's relation with Hannah Arendt is examined in Elżbieta Ettinger's *Hannah Arendt/Martin Heidegger* (1995), and their correspondence is collected in *Letters, 1925–1975* (1998; trans. 2004). For a more philosophical exploration of their relation, see Jacques Thaminiaux, *The Thracian Maid and the Professional Thinker: Arendt and Heidegger* (1992; trans. 1997). The *Heidegger–Jaspers Correspondence (1920–1963)* (1990; trans. 2003) is also available.

Recent useful general overviews of Heidegger's thought include Richard Polt, *Heidegger: An Introduction* (1999); Michael Inwood, *Heidegger* (1997; reprinted in 2000 as *Heidegger: A Very Short Introduction*); Timothy Clark, *Martin Heidegger* (2002; 2nd ed., 2011); Graham Harman, *Heidegger Explained: From Phenomenon to Thing* (2007); David R. Cerbone, *Heidegger: A Guide for the Perplexed* (2008); S. J. McGrath, *Heidegger: A (Very) Critical Introduction* (2008); *Martin Heidegger: Key Concepts*, edited by Bret W. Davis (2009); Tom Greaves, *Starting with Heidegger* (2010); Michael Watts, *The Philosophy of Heidegger* (2011); John Richardson, *Heidegger* (2012); and J. Jeremy Wisnewski, *Heidegger: An Introduction* (2012). Two overviews of the later works are Julian Young, *Heidegger's Later Philosophy* (2002), and George Pattison, *Routledge Philosophy Guidebook to the Later Heidegger* (2000).

Two helpful reference books are Michael Inwood, *A Heidegger Dictionary* (1999), and Daniel O. Dahlstrom, *The Heidegger Dictionary* (2013). Two classic collections of essays addressing general interpretative issues in Heidegger scholarship are *Cambridge Companion to Heidegger*, edited by Charles Guignon (1993), and *Heidegger: A Critical Reader*, edited by Hubert Dreyfus and Harrison Hall (1992).

There are many studies devoted to the analysis of Heidegger's *Being and Time*. See in particular Michael Gelven, *Commentary on Heidegger's "Being and Time"* (rev. ed., 1989); Gerald Prauss, *Knowing and Doing in Heidegger's "Being and Time"* (1977; trans. 1999); Theodore Kisiel, *The Genesis of Heidegger's "Being and Time"* (1993); Hubert L. Dreyfus, *Being-in-the-World: A Commentary on Heidegger's "Being and Time," Division I* (1991); Stephen Mulhall, *The Routledge Guidebook to Heidegger and "Being and Time"* (1996); Magda King, *A Guide to Heidegger's "Being and Time"* (2001); William D. Blattner, *Heidegger's Temporal Idealism* (1999) and *Heidegger's "Being and Time": A Reader's Guide* (2006); Richard M. McDonough, *Martin Heidegger's "Being and Time"* (2006); *Heidegger's "Being and Time": Critical Essays*, edited by Richard Polt (2005); Richard Sembera, *Rephrasing Heidegger: A Companion to "Being and Time"* (2007); Simon Critchley and Reiner Schürmann, *On Heidegger's "Being and Time"* (2008); William Large, *Heidegger's "Being and Time"* (2008); Paul Gorner, *Heidegger's "Being and Time": An Introduction* (2007); Taylor Carman, *Heidegger's Analytic: Interpretation, Discourse, and Authenticity in "Being and Time"* (2003); and *The Cambridge Companion to Heidegger's "Being and Time,"* edited by Mark A. Wrathall (2013).

Three recent works on the pre–*Being and Time* philosophy are James Luchte, *Heidegger's Early Philosophy: The Phenomenology of Ecstatic Temporality* (2008); Scott M. Campbell, *The Early Heidegger's Philosophy of Life: Facticity, Being, and Language* (2012); and Denis McManus, *Heidegger and the Measure of Truth: Themes from His Early Philosophy* (2012). Works focused on the transitional period directly after *Being and Time* include *A Companion to Heidegger's "Introduction to Metaphysics,"* edited by Richard Polt and Gregory Fried (2001); *Heidegger toward the Turn: Essays on the Work of the 1930s*, edited by James Risser (1999); Christopher Fynsk, *Heidegger: Thought and Historicity* (1986; 2nd ed., 1993); Bret W. Davis, *Heidegger and the Will: On the Way to "Gelassenheit"* (2007); and Mahon O'Brien, *Heidegger and Authenticity: From Resoluteness to Releasement* (2011).

Books dealing specifically with the major works of Heidegger's "turn" include *Companion* to Heidegger's "Contributions to Philosophy," edited by Charles E. Scott, Susan Schoenbohm, Daniela Vallega-Neu, and Alejandro Vallega (2001); Richard Polt, The Emergency of Being: On Heidegger's "Contributions to Philosophy" (2006); Daniela Vallega-Neu, Heidegger's "Contributions to Philosophy": An Introduction (2003); Lee Braver, Heidegger's Later Writings: A Reader's Guide (2009); and Richard Capobianco, Engaging Heidegger (2010).

An important work exploring the (too seldom considered) connection between Dilthey and the development of Heidegger's thought is Charles R. Bambach's Heidegger, Dilthey, and the Crisis of Historicism (1995). On Heidegger's connection with Husserl, see Timothy J. Stapleton, Husserl and Heidegger: The Question of a Phenomenological Beginning (1983); Steven Galt Crowell, Husserl, Heidegger, and the Space of Meaning: Paths toward Transcendental Phenomenology (2001) and Normativity and Phenomenology in Husserl and Heidegger (2013); Pierre Keller, Husserl and Heidegger on Human Experience (1999); Lilian Alweiss, The World Unclaimed: A Challenge to Heidegger's Critique of Husserl (2003); and Friedrich-Wilhelm von Herrmann, Hermeneutics and Reflection: Heidegger and Husserl on the Concept of Phenomenology (2000; trans. 2013).

Two collections of essays that explore Heidegger's connection to transcendental philosophy (and to Kant in particular) are Transcendental Heidegger, edited by Steven Crowell and Jeff Malpas (2007), and Heidegger, German Idealism, and Neo-Kantianism, edited by Tom Rockmore (2000). Heidegger's thinking with respect to Greek philosophy is explored in Werner Marx, Heidegger and the Tradition (1961; trans. 1971); The Presocratics after Heidegger, edited by David C. Jacobs (1999); Heidegger and the Greeks: Interpretive Essays, edited by Drew A. Hyland and John Panteleimon Manoussakis (2006); Walter Brogan, Heidegger and Aristotle: The Twofoldness of Being (2005); and Mark A. Ralkowski, Heidegger's Platonism (2009). Two works devoted to his thinking about Nietzsche are Paul Catanu, Heidegger's Nietzsche: Being and Becoming (2010), and The Movement of Nihilism: Heidegger's Thinking after Nietzsche, edited by Laurence Paul Hemming, Kostas Amiridis, and Bogdan Costea (2011).

Heidegger's relation to religious thought and theology is the topic of several studies, including three by John D. Caputo: The Mystical Element in Heidegger's Thought (1978), Heidegger and Aquinas: An Essay on Overcoming Metaphysics (1982), and Demythologizing Heidegger (1993). See also George Kovacs, The Question of God in Heidegger's Phenomenology (1990); Ben Vedder, Heidegger's Philosophy of Religion: From

God to the Gods (2007); and Benjamin D. Crowe, Heidegger's Religious Origins: Destruction and Authenticity (2006) and Heidegger's Phenomenology of Religion: Realism and Cultural Criticism (2007). A dissenting voice can be found in Laurence Paul Hemming, Heidegger's Atheism: The Refusal of a Theological Voice (2002).

Among works that discuss the range of Heidegger's thought are Miguel De Beistegui, The New Heidegger (2005); Appropriating Heidegger, edited by James E. Faulconer and Mark A. Wrathall (2000); Interpreting Heidegger: Critical Essays, edited by Daniel O. Dahlstrom (2011); John Haugeland, Dasein Disclosed: John Haugeland's Heidegger (2013); and The Bloomsbury Companion to Heidegger, edited by François Raffoul and Eric S. Nelson (2013). A monograph that takes Heidegger's analysis of tools, their functionality, and their breakdowns to be the core of his philosophy is Graham Harman's Tool-Being: Heidegger and the Metaphysics of Objects (2002). Among works that focus on Heidegger and epistemology are Charles B. Guignon, Heidegger and the Problem of Knowledge (1983); John Richardson, Existential Epistemology: A Heideggerian Critique of the Cartesian Project (1986); Daniel O. Dahlstrom, Heidegger's Concept of Truth (1994; trans. 2001); and Mark A. Wrathall, Heidegger and Unconcealment: Truth, Language, and History (2010). Heidegger's theory of language is discussed in Cristina Lafont, Heidegger, Language, and World-Disclosure (1994; trans. 2000); Joachim L. Oberst, Heidegger on Language and Death: The Intrinsic Connection in Human Existence (2009); and Heidegger and Language, edited by Jeffrey Powell (2013). Essays on Heidegger and contemporary work in the philosophy of mind are collected in Heidegger and Cognitive Science, edited by Julian Kiverstein and Michael Wheeler (2012). A work on the intersection of Heidegger and analytic philosophy is Michael Friedman's A Parting of the Ways: Carnap, Cassirer, and Heidegger (2000). Heidegger's meeting with Cassirer in 1929 is discussed in Peter E. Gordon's Continental Divide: Heidegger, Cassirer, Davos (2012).

William McNeill's The Time of Life: Heidegger and "Ēthos" (2006) examines Heidegger's conception of life and his ethics in relation to Aristotle and Foucault (among others). Another work on Heidegger's ethics, from a more applied perspective, is Gail Stenstad's Transformations: Thinking after Heidegger (2006). A collection of essays on Heidegger and ethics is Heidegger and Practical Philosophy, edited by François Raffoul and David Pettigrew (2002). Other works on Heidegger and ethics include Lawrence Vogel, The Fragile "We": Ethical Implications of Heidegger's "Being and Time" (1994); Frederick A. Olafson, Heidegger and the Ground of Ethics: A Study of "Mitsein" (1998); David Webb, Heidegger,

Ethics, and the Practice of Ontology (2009); Matthew King, *Heidegger and Happiness: Dwelling on Fitting and Being* (2009); Irene McMullin, *Time and the Shared World: Heidegger on Social Relations* (2013); and Michael Lewis, *Heidegger and the Place of Ethics: Being-with in the Crossing of Heidegger's Thought* (2005). Heidegger's aesthetics is discussed in Julian Young's *Heidegger's Philosophy of Art* (2001). Works focusing on Heidegger's thinking about technology include Richard Rojcewicz, *The Gods and Technology: A Reading of Heidegger* (2006), and Michael E. Zimmerman, *Heidegger's Confrontation with Modernity: Technology, Politics, Art* (1990).

Among works that discuss Heidegger's thought in relation to issues in environmental ethics are Frank Schalow, *The Incarnality of Being: The Earth, Animals and the Body in Heidegger's Thought* (2006); Bruce V. Foltz, *Inhabiting the Earth: Heidegger, Environment Ethics, and the Metaphysics of Nature* (1995); *Heidegger and the Earth: Essays in Environmental Philosophy*, edited by Ladelle McWhorter and Gail Stenstad (2nd ed., 2009); and Jeff Malpas, *Heidegger's Topology: Being, Place, World* (2006) and *Heidegger and the Thinking of Place: Explorations in the Topology of Being* (2012).

Considerations and assessments of the political consequences of Heidegger's thought include Miguel de Beistegui, *Heidegger and the Political: Dystopias* (1998); Pierre Bourdieu, *The Political Ontology of Martin Heidegger* (1988; trans. 1991); Gregory Fried, *Heidegger's "Polemos": From Being to Politics* (2000); and Reiner Schürmann, *Heidegger on Being and Acting: From Principles to Anarchy* (1982; trans. 1987).

For a discussion of Heidegger's connection to Nazism (along with some of his own lectures and addresses), see *The Heidegger Controversy: A Critical Reader*, edited by Richard Wolin (1991). The controversy was set into motion by Victor Farias's *Heidegger and Nazism* (1987; trans. 1989). Other works on this subject include Hans Sluga, *Heidegger's Crisis: Philosophy and Politics in Nazi Germany* (1993); Julian Young, *Heidegger, Philosophy, Nazism* (1997); and Richard Wolin, *The Politics of Being: The Political Thought of Martin Heidegger* (1990). A more recent addition to the debate is Emmanuel Faye's *Heidegger: The Introduction of Nazism into Philosophy in Light of the Unpublished Seminars of 1933–1935* (2005; trans. 2009).

Husserl, Edmund
Husserl's first major work, in which problems in the foundations of mathematics and logic led him to the creation of phenomenology, is *Logical Investigations* (2 vols., 1900–01; 2nd ed., 1913; trans. 1970). It is available in English both

unabridged and in an abridged form titled *The Shorter Logical Investigations* (2001). His later reflection on this groundbreaking work, written in 1913, has been published as *Introduction to the Logical Investigations: A Draft of a Preface to the "Logical Investigations"* (1939; trans. 1975). There is now an English-language translation of the transitional work *Introduction to Logic and Theory of Knowledge: Lectures 1906/07* (1984; trans. 2008). All three volumes of his monumental work *Ideas*, written in 1912, are available in English under the general title *Ideas Pertaining to a Pure Phenomenology and to a Phenomenological Philosophy*: vol. 1, *General Introduction to a Pure Phenomenology* (1913; trans. 1931, 1982); vol. 2, *Studies in the Phenomenology of Constitution* (1952; trans. 1989); and vol. 3, *Phenomenology and the Foundations of the Sciences* (1952; trans. 1980).

Ideas is based on lectures given in 1907. The five introductory lectures of that series have been published as *The Idea of Phenomenology* (1950; trans. 1964), and the remainder as *Thing and Space: Lectures of 1907* (1973; trans. 1997). A late work available in English is the important *Formal and Transcendental Logic* (1929; trans. 1969). Husserl's consideration of judgment and his development of a formal ontology and its relation to logic and mathematics are continued in the posthumously published *Experience and Judgment: Investigations in a Genealogy of Logic* (1939; trans. 1973).

Perhaps Husserl's best-known exposition of his phenomenology is *Cartesian Meditations: An Introduction to Phenomenology* (1931 [French trans.]; 1950 [German]; trans. 1960), which is based on two lectures delivered at the Sorbonne in 1929, published as *Paris Lectures* (1950; trans. 1964). The essay "Philosophy as Rigorous Science" (1911) and the late lecture "Philosophy and the Crisis of European Man" (1935) are both translated in *Phenomenology and the Crisis of Philosophy* (1965). Consonant with the latter lecture is Husserl's last major work, *The Crisis of European Sciences and Transcendental Phenomenology* (1936; trans. 1970). It is the most important source in English for his discussions of the significant and influential concept of the "life-world." A collection simply called *Husserl: Shorter Works* (1981) contains several articles originally published in *Encyclopaedia Britannica*: most notably "Phenomenology," as well as "Phenomenology and Anthropology" and "The Origin of Geometry." An excellent sampling of Husserl's works is available in *The Essential Husserl: Basic Writings in Transcendental Phenomenology* (1999).

Translations into English of several important volumes of Husserl's complete works have only recently appeared. A lecture series he gave a number of times in the 1920s, translated as *Analyses Concerning Passive and Active Synthesis: Lectures on Transcendental Logic* (2001), grounds and extends the lines of thought contained in *Formal and Transcendental Logic*. Husserl's considerations of time and its relation to consciousness may be found in *On the Phenomenology of the Consciousness of Internal Time (1893–1917)* (1966; trans. 1991). An earlier but incomplete edition of his writings on this subject was published in English in 1964. *Phantasy, Image Consciousness, and Memory (1898–1925)* (1980; trans. 2005) contains a variety of texts from different periods of Husserl's philosophical development, all of which concern the representational capacities of consciousness. Husserl's early work, prior to phenomenology, is found in *Philosophy of Arithmetic: Psychological and Logical Investigations* (1891; trans. 2003). The collection of writings translated as *Psychological and Transcendental Phenomenology and the Confrontation with Heidegger (1927–1931)* (1997) contains, among other things, the marginalia in his personal copy of Heidegger's *Being and Time*. The *Basic Problems of Phenomenology: From the Lectures, Winter Semester, 1910–1911* (1950; trans. 2006) is a set of lectures that begin to explore the notion of intersubjectivity and the life-world, which upcoming translations from Husserl's complete works will further illuminate.

Many philosophers of note have written works on or inspired by Husserl. Eugen Fink worked closely with him, and his reflections (written 1932) can be found in his *Sixth Cartesian Meditation*, vol. 1, *The Idea of a Transcendental Theory of Method* (1988; trans. 1994). Marvin Farber and Quentin Lauer were among the earliest proponents of Husserl's work in North America. Farber's works include *The Aims of Phenomenology: The Motives, Methods, and Impact of Husserl's Thought* (1966) and *The Foundation of Phenomenology: Edmund Husserl and the Quest for a Rigorous Science of Philosophy* (1943; 3rd ed., 1967). Lauer's works include *Phenomenology: Its Genesis and Prospect* (1958) and *The Triumph of Subjectivity: An Introduction to Transcendental Phenomenology* (1958). Aron Gurwitsch's work in psychology was deeply influenced by Husserl, as can be seen in articles collected in his *Studies in Phenomenology and Psychology* (1966). Emmanuel Lévinas has written two books on Husserl: *The Theory of Intuition in Husserl's Phenomenology* (1930; trans. 1973, 2nd ed. 1995) and *Discovering Existence with Husserl and Heidegger* (1949; partially trans. in *Discovering Existence with Husserl*, 1998). Paul Ricoeur also has written two books on Husserl: essays collected in *Husserl: An Analysis of His Phenomenology* (1967) and *A Key*

to *Husserl's "Ideas I"* (1950; trans. 1996). The Czech philosopher Jan Patočka has contributed *An Introduction to Husserl's Phenomenology* (1969; trans. 1996), and Leszek Kolakowski has published *Husserl and the Search for Certitude* (1975).

Maurice Merleau-Ponty's lecture notes outlining his unique utilization of Husserl's late work were published in English in *Husserl at the Limits of Phenomenology: Including Texts by Edmund Husserl* (2002). Jacques Derrida has written three books that focus on Husserl: his 1953–54 dissertation, *The Problem of Genesis in Husserl's Philosophy* (1990; trans. 2003); *Speech and Phenomena, and Other Essays on Husserl's Theory of Signs* (1967; trans. 1973); and *Edmund Husserl's Origin of Geometry: An Introduction* (1961; trans. 1978). Jean-Luc Marion has written a useful work defending Husserl against the challenges of Derrida and Heidegger: *Reduction and Givenness: Investigations of Husserl, Heidegger, and Phenomenology* (1989; trans. 1998).

Other important secondary literature on Husserl includes Maurice Natanson, *Edmund Husserl; Philosopher of Infinite Tasks* (1973); David Bell, *Husserl* (1990); and the valuable collection of critical essays *The Cambridge Companion to Husserl*, edited by Barry Smith and David Woodruff Smith (1995). An accessible introduction to Husserl's phenomenology via the *Cartesian Meditations* is A. D. Smith's *Routledge Philosophy Guidebook to Husserl and the "Cartesian Meditations"* (2003). Robert Sokolowski has written and edited several books specifically on Husserl, such as *Husserlian Meditations: How Words Present Things* (1974) and his helpful introduction to phenomenology from a roughly Husserlian perspective, *Introduction to Phenomenology* (2000). Other recent studies include Dan Zahavi, *Husserl and Transcendental Intersubjectivity: A Response to the Linguistic-Pragmatic Critique* (1996; trans. 2001) and *Husserl's Phenomenology* (1997; trans. 2003); Donn Welton, *The Other Husserl: The Horizons of Transcendental Phenomenology* (2000); *The New Husserl: A Critical Reader*, edited by Donn Welton (2003); and André de Muralt, *The Idea of Phenomenology: Husserlian Exemplarism* (1958; trans. 1974). See also Joseph J. Kockelmans, *Edmund Husserl's Phenomenology* (1994); Rudolf Bernet, Iso Kern, and Eduard Marbach, *An Introduction to Husserlian Phenomenology* (1989; trans. 1993); and James M. Edie, *Edmund Husserl's Phenomenology: A Critical Commentary* (1987).

Quite a number of works on Husserl have recently appeared, perhaps spurred by a growing interest in phenomenology among analytic philosophers of mind. Two introductory works are Dermot Moran, *Edmund Husserl: Founder of Phenomenology* (2005), and Matheson Russell, *Husserl: A Guide for the Perplexed* (2006). Works that provide overviews of Husserl's thought include Dermot Moran and Joseph Cohen, *The Husserl Dictionary* (2012); John J. Drummond, *The A to Z of Husserl's Philosophy* (2010); David Woodruff Smith, *Husserl* (2nd ed., 2013); J. N. Mohanty, *The Philosophy of Edmund Husserl: A Historical Development* (2008); and Burt C. Hopkins, *The Philosophy of Husserl* (2011). J. N. Mohanty's *Edmund Husserl's Freiburg Years: 1916–1938* (2011) focuses on the later stage of Husserl's life and thought. Dermot Moran's *Husserl's "Crisis of the European Sciences and Transcendental Phenomenology": An Introduction* (2012) offers an analysis of this important late work. Other books focused on the final stage of Husserl's thought are *Science and the Life-World: Essays on Husserl's "Crisis of European Sciences,"* edited by David Hyder and Hans-Jörg Rheinberger (2010), and Sebastian Luft, *Subjectivity and Lifeworld in Transcendental Phenomenology* (2011).

For recent scholarly research on Husserl's thought, see Brian Elliott, *Phenomenology and Imagination in Husserl and Heidegger* (2005); *Epistemology, Archaeology, Ethics: Current Investigations of Husserl's Corpus,* edited by Pol Vandevelde and Sebastian Luft (2010); Harry P. Reeder, *The Theory and Practice of Husserl's Phenomenology* (2nd ed., 2010); Victor Biceaga, *The Concept of Passivity in Husserl's Phenomenology* (2010); Bob Sandmeyer, *Husserl's Constitutive Phenomenology: Its Problem and Promise* (2009); Jon L. James, *Transcendental Phenomenological Psychology: Introduction to Husserl's Psychology of Human Consciousness* (2007); Steven Crowell, *Normativity and Phenomenology in Husserl and Heidegger* (2013); and Joona Taipale, *Phenomenology and Embodiment: Husserl and the Constitution of Subjectivity* (2014).

Works on the centrality of time to human subjectivity include James R. Mensch, *Husserl's Account of Our Consciousness of Time* (2010); Christian Lotz, *From Affectivity to Subjectivity: Husserl's Phenomenology Revisited* (2007); and Nicholas de Warren, *Husserl and the Promise of Time: Subjectivity in Transcendental Phenomenology* (2009). Although the several volumes on the topic of intersubjectivity in Husserl's complete works have not been translated into English, several secondary works deal with this topic; see Peter R. Costello, *Layers in Husserl's Phenomenology: On Meaning and Intersubjectivity* (2012); Eric Chelstrom, *Social Phenomenology: Husserl, Intersubjectivity, and Collective Intentionality* (2013); Joaquim Siles i Borràs, *The Ethics of Husserl's Phenomenology: Responsibility and Ethical Life* (2010); and Janet Donohoe,

Husserl on Ethics and Intersubjectivity: From Static to Genetic Phenomenology (2004).

Jaspers, Karl

Jaspers's dissertation, *Heimweh und Verbrechen* ("Homesickness and Crime"), was completed in 1909. His first major book was in psychology, *General Psychopathology* (1913; trans. 1963). His next book, *Psychologie der Weltanschauungen* (1919, *Psychology of Worldviews*), dealt with a topic bordering on philosophy, as he pursued Nietzsche's suggestion that worldviews are better understood as expressions of the psychologies of those who develop and are attracted to them than as conclusions based on evidence and reasoning. It was followed by a psychopathological case study of Strindberg and Van Gogh, *Strindberg und van Gogh: Versuch einer pathographischen Analyse unter vergleichender Heranziehung von Swedenborg und Hölderlin* (1922).

Jaspers wrote two essays on Max Weber, the first in 1921 and the second in 1932. The latter is translated as "Max Weber as Politician, Scientist, Philosopher" in *Three Essays* (1964), which also contains "Descartes and Philosophy" (1937) and "Leonardo as Philosopher" (1953). He wrote two long essays titled "The Idea of the University," the first in 1923 and the second in 1946; the latter was translated as a book in 1959. A book indicative of Jaspers's concerns as a public intellectual, *Man in the Modern Age* (1931; trans. 1933), written in the time of crisis that immediately preceded the Nazi takeover, diagnoses the problems facing individuals in relation to society, culture, the state, and the technological age.

Jaspers's most important philosophical work is *Philosophy* (3 vols., 1932; trans. 1969–71). One of his most widely read books, and an excellent introduction to his thought, is the collection *Reason and Existenz: Five Lectures* (*Vernunft und Existenz: Fünf Vorlesungen*, 1935; trans. 1955). It was followed by his influential work *Nietzsche: An Introduction to the Understanding of His Philosophical Activity* (1936; trans. 1965) and *The Philosophy of Existence* (1938; trans. 1971), which contains three lectures of 1937.

Jaspers resumed publication after the war with perhaps the greatest of his contributions as a public intellectual, addressing one of the most pressing questions of the time in a powerful and important way: his 1946 book *The Question of German Guilt* (trans. 1947). It was followed by his 1946 lecture translated as *The European Spirit* (1947; trans. 1948). In 1946 he also published a short work based on a 1938 lecture, *Nietzsche and Christianity* (trans. 1961). Another essay on Nietzsche from 1950 has been translated both as "Nietzsche and the Present"

(1952) and as "The Importance of Nietzsche" (1951). In 1947 he published his second major philosophical tome: the 1000-page *Von der Wahrheit*, vol. 1 of *Philosophischen Logik* (*On Truth*, vol. 1 of *Philosophical Logic*); small selections of it have been translated in *Tragedy Is Not Enough* (1952) and *Truth and Symbol* (1959). A useful English-language collection of his writings, *Karl Jaspers: Basic Philosophical Writings* (1986), also contains selections from *On Truth*.

Jaspers's next publications were a set of lectures, *The Perennial Scope of Philosophy* (1948; trans. 1949), and the single lecture "Philosophy and Science" (1948; trans. 1949). *The Origin and Goal of History* (1949; trans. 1953) appeared the following year. *The Way to Wisdom: An Introduction to Philosophy* (1950; trans. 1951) was originally 12 radio lectures and is an excellent introduction to his religious thought. A series of critical essays and exchanges between Jaspers and the important Protestant theologian Rudolf Bultmann are contained in *Myth and Christianity: An Inquiry into the Possibility of Religion without Myth* (1954; trans. 1958). *Philosophical Faith and Revelation* (1962; trans. 1967) and the shorter *Philosophie und Offenbarungsglaube* (1963, *Philosophy and Revealed Religion*) both concern faith and revelation. *Reason and Anti-Reason in Our Time* (1950; trans. 1952) was originally three lectures. Three essays relating to humanism have been published together in translation as *Existentialism and Humanism* (1952). A large work from this period on Schelling (*Schelling: Grösse und Verhängnis*, 1955) has not been translated.

Jaspers then published the first part of his monumental world history of philosophy, *The Great Philosophers* (1957, with another posthumous volume in 1981; trans., 4 vols., 1962–95). A number of volumes containing selections dealing with various philosophical and religious thinkers and figures have also been published. One volume of such essays, *Karl Jaspers on Philosophy of History and History of Philosophy*, edited by Joseph W. Koterski and Raymond J. Langley (2003), includes pieces on Aquinas, Kant, Hegel, and Kierkegaard. Other collections of Jaspers's essays, drawn from a variety of original sources, include *Philosophy and the World: Selected Essays and Lectures* (1958; trans. 1963); *Vernunft und Freiheit* (1959, *Reason and Freedom*); *Freiheit und Wiedervereinigung* (1960, *Freedom and Reunification*), eight political essays; *Lebensfragen der Deutschen Politik* (1963, *Vital Questions of German Politics*), twelve more political essays; *Wahrheit und Leben* (1965, *Truth and Life*), philosophical essays; *Hoffnung und Sorge* (1965, *Hope and Concern*), political essays; *Philosophische Aufsätze* (1967, *Philosophical Essays*); and *Schicksal und Wille* (1967,

Fate and Will), autobiographical essays. *Aneignung und Polemik* (1968, *Appropriation and Polemic*) and *Mitverantwortlich Provokationen* (1969, *Jointly Responsible Provocations*) contain interviews with Jaspers. A lecture series from 1964 was published as *Philosophy Is for Everyman: A Short Course in Philosophical Thinking* (1965; trans. 1967).

Two volumes of Jaspers's correspondence have been published: *Hannah Arendt/Karl Jaspers Correspondence, 1926–1969* (1985; trans. 1992), and *The Heidegger–Jaspers Correspondence (1920–1963)* (1990; trans. 2003).

A good biography is Suzanne Kirkbright's *Karl Jaspers: A Biography: Navigations in Truth* (2004).

The Jaspers volume in the Library of Living Philosophers series, *The Philosophy of Karl Jaspers*, edited by Paul Arthur Schilpp (1957), is an excellent collection of critical essays with Jaspers's response. Two particularly useful studies of Jaspers's thought are Elisabeth Young-Bruehl, *Freedom and Karl Jaspers's Philosophy* (1981), and *Heidegger and Jaspers*, edited by Alan M. Olsen (1994). Others include Chris Thornhill, *Karl Jaspers: Politics and Metaphysics* (2002); Alan M. Olson, *Transcendence and Hermeneutics: An Interpretation of the Philosophy of Karl Jaspers* (1979); *The Tasks of Truth: Essays on Karl Jaspers's Idea of the University*, edited by Gregory J. Walters (1996); and Ronny Miron, *Karl Jaspers: From Selfhood to Being* (2012). Recent collections of essays include *Karl Jaspers's Philosophy: Exposition and Interpretations*, edited by Kurt Salamun and Gregory J. Walters (2008), and *One Century of Karl Jaspers' "General Psychopathology,"* edited by Giovanni Stranghellini and Thomas Fuchs (2013).

Among important earlier studies of Jaspers thought are Charles F. Wallraff, *Karl Jaspers: An Introduction to His Philosophy* (1970); Sebastian Samay, *Reason Revisited: The Philosophy of Karl Jaspers* (1971); Oswald O. Schrag, *Existence, Existenz, and Transcendence: An Introduction to the Philosophy of Karl Jaspers* (1971); and E. L. Allen, *The Self and Its Hazards: A Guide to the Thought of Karl Jaspers* (1950). Earlier works that focus on Jaspers's religious thought include Leonard H. Ehrlich, *Karl Jaspers: Philosophy as Faith* (1975); Eugene Thomas Long, *Jaspers and Bultmann: A Dialogue between Philosophy and Theology in the Existentialist Tradition* (1968); and Bernard F. O'Connor, *A Dialogue between Philosophy and Religion: The Perspective of Karl Jaspers* (1988).

Kant, Immanuel

All of Kant's works have long been available in English translation. Kant's early or pre-critical philosophy has been collected in a volume titled

Theoretical Philosophy, 1755–1770 (1992). Kant was in his 50s when he discovered the approach that he called "critical philosophy," "critical idealism," or "transcendental idealism." The first major work of this "critical period" is his *Critique of Pure Reason* (major translations, 1929, 1998), first published in 1781 and revised in 1787. In 1783 Kant published a popularization of it titled *Prolegomena to Any Future Metaphysics*; and in 1786 he published another related work, *Metaphysical Foundations of Natural Science*. These monographs have been collected, along with a number of other short writings, in a volume titled *Theoretical Philosophy after 1781* (2002), but they can also be found individually. Together these three works constitute the core of what is known as his theoretical philosophy.

Kant's "practical" or moral philosophy began with his *Groundwork of the Metaphysics of Morals* (1785), followed by the *Critique of Practical Reason* (1788), and then by *The Metaphysics of Morals* (1797). These moral-philosophical writings, collected in a volume simply called *Practical Philosophy* (1996), are also available individually. In 1790 Kant published his third "critique," the *Critique of Judgment* (trans. as *Critique of the Power of Judgment*, 2000), which deals with judgments both aesthetic (beauty and the sublime) and teleological (purpose in nature). His main work on religion, *Religion within the Limits of Reason Alone* (1793), may be found separately or together with his other writings on the subject in *Religion and Rational Theology* (trans. as *Religion within the Limits of Mere Reason*, 1996). Other writings, including his *Anthropology in Pragmatic Perspective* (1798), his *Logic* (1800), and collections of student notes from his lectures, are also available in English translation.

The works of Paul Guyer provide a complete interpretation of Kant's philosophy; see in particular *Kant and the Claims of Knowledge* (1987), *Kant and the Experience of Freedom: Essays on Aesthetics and Morality* (1993), *Kant and the Claims of Taste* (2nd ed., 1997), *Kant's System of Nature and Freedom: Selected Essays* (2005), and the introductory work simply titled *Kant* (2006). For similar big-picture analysis, one can turn to the works of Henry E. Allison, including *Kant's Transcendental Idealism* (rev. ed., 2004), *Kant's Theory of Taste: A Reading of the "Critique of Aesthetic Judgment"* (2001), *Idealism and Freedom: Essays on Kant's Theoretical and Practical Philosophy* (1996), *Kant's Theory of Freedom* (1990), and *Essays on Kant* (2012).

Other useful studies and volumes that deal with both the theoretical and practical sides of Kant's philosophy include Karl Ameriks, *Interpreting Kant's Critiques* (2003) and *Kant's Elliptical Path* (2012); Arthur Melnick, *Themes in Kant's Metaphysics and Ethics* (2004); Allen W. Wood, *Kant* (2005); *The Cambridge Companion to Kant* (1992) and *The Cambridge Companion to Kant and Modern Philosophy* (2006), both edited by Paul Guyer; Susan Neiman, *The Unity of Reason: Rereading Kant* (1994); and *A Companion to Kant*, edited by Graham Bird (rev. ed., 2010).

Helpful recent introductions to Kant's theoretical philosophy include Jill Vance Buroker, *Kant's "Critique of Pure Reason": An Introduction* (2006); Sebastian Gardner, *The Routledge Philosophy Guidebook to Kant and the "Critique of Pure Reason"* (1999); *The Cambridge Companion to Kant's "Critique of Pure Reason,"* edited by Paul Guyer (2012); and Graham Bird, *The Revolutionary Kant: A Commentary on the "Critique of Pure Reason"* (2006).

For more detailed studies on specific topics, see Kenneth R. Westphal, *Kant's Transcendental Proof of Realism* (2004); James Van Cleve, *Problems from Kant* (1999); Rae Langton, *Kantian Humility: Our Ignorance of Things in Themselves* (1998); Béatrice Longuenesse, *Kant and the Capacity to Judge: Sensibility and Discursivity in the Transcendental Analytic of the "Critique of Pure Reason"* (1993; trans. 1998); Michael Friedman, *Kant and the Exact Sciences* (1992) and *Kant's Construction of Nature: A Reading of the "Metaphysical Foundations of Natural Science"* (2013); Pierre Keller, *Kant and the Demands of Self-Consciousness* (1998); Eric Watkins, *Kant and the Metaphysics of Causality* (2005); Patricia Kitcher, *Kant's Thinker* (2011); Michelle Greir, *Kant's Doctrine of Transcendental Illusion* (2001); and Robert Hanna, *Kant, Science, and Human Nature* (2006). Ernst Cassirer's *Kant's Life and Thought* (2nd ed., 1921; trans. 1981) remains valuable as an intellectual biography. A more recent biography is Manfred Kuehn's *Kant: A Biography* (2001).

The many excellent recent works on Kant's (and Kantian) moral philosophy include Onora O'Neill, *Constructions of Reason: Explorations of Kant's Practical Philosophy* (1989); Allen W. Wood, *Kant's Ethical Thought* (1999) and *Kantian Ethics* (2008); Thomas E. Hill Jr., *Dignity and Practical Reason in Kant's Moral Theory* (1992), *Respect, Pluralism, and Justice: Kantian Perspectives* (2000), *Human Welfare and Moral Worth: Kantian Perspectives* (2002), and *Virtue, Rules, and Justice: Kantian Aspirations* (2012); Christine M. Korsgaard, *The Sources of Normativity* (1996) and *Creating the Kingdom of Ends* (1996); Andrews Reath, *Agency and Autonomy in Kant's Moral Theory* (2006); Roger J. Sullivan, *Immanuel Kant's Moral Theory* (1989); Marcia W. Baron, *Kantian Ethics Almost without Apology* (1995); Barbara Herman, *The Practice of Moral Judgment* (1993); Jeanine Grenberg, *Kant and the Ethics of Humility: A Story of Dependence, Corruption, and Virtue* (2005) and *Kant's Defense of Common Moral Experience: A Phenomenological Account* (2013); *Kant on Moral Autonomy*, edited by Oliver Sensen (2013); Stephen Engstrom, *The Form of Practical Knowledge: A Study of the Categorical Imperative* (2009); *The Blackwell Guide to Kant's Ethics*, edited by Thomas E. Hill Jr. (2009); and Kristi Sweet, *Kant on Practical Life: From Duty to History* (2013).

One of the few works that focuses on Kant's work on history is Yirmiyahu Yovel's *Kant and the Philosophy of History* (1980). Kant's philosophical anthropology is discussed in *Essays on Kant's Anthropology*, edited by Brian Jacobs and Patrick Kain (2003); John H. Zammito, *Kant, Herder, and the Birth of Anthropology* (2002); Patrick R. Frierson, *Freedom and Anthropology in Kant's Moral Philosophy* (2003); and Robert Louden, *Kant's Human Being: Essays on His Theory of Human Nature* (2011). Kant's aesthetics can be explored through works such as *Kant's "Critique of the Power of Judgment": Critical Essays*, edited by Paul Guyer (2003); Robert Wicks, *Routledge Philosophy Guidebook to Kant on Judgment* (2007); John H. Zammito, *The Genesis of Kant's Critique of Judgment* (1992); Jane Kneller, *Kant and the Power of Imagination* (2007); *Aesthetics and Cognition in Kant's Critical Philosophy*, edited by Rebecca Kukla (2006); and Rachel Zuckert, *Kant on Beauty and Biology: An Interpretation of the "Critique of Judgment"* (2007).

Works that focus on Kant's thinking on religion are Allen W. Wood, *Kant's Moral Religion* (1970) and *Kant's Rational Theology* (1978); Gordon E. Michalson Jr., *Kant and the Problem of God* (1999); *Kant's Philosophy of Religion Reconsidered*, edited by Philip J. Rossi and Michael Wreen (1991); and *Kant's Anatomy of Evil*, edited by Sharon Anderson-Gold and Pablo Muchnik (2010). Finally, Kant's political philosophy is discussed in Allen D. Rosen, *Kant's Theory of Justice* (1993); Leslie Arthur Mulholland, *Kant's System of Rights* (1990); Otfried Höffe, *Kant's Cosmopolitan Theory of Law and Peace* (2001; trans. 2006); Pauline Kleingeld, *Kant and Cosmopolitanism: The Philosophical Ideal of World Citizenship* (2011); and Arthur Ripstein, *Force and Freedom: Kant's Legal and Political Philosophy* (2009).

See also the Kant bibliography in our companion volume, *The Analytic Tradition*.

Kierkegaard, Søren

A 25-volume edition of Kierkegaard's collected works is available in English (published by Princeton University Press), along with other translations of all of his major works. Each volume of that edition contains supplements from his journals relating to the work. The first volume, *Early Polemical Writings* (1990), collects writings from 1834 to 1838, when Kierkegaard was still a student. The second volume, *The Concept of Irony* (1841; trans. 1989), contains his dissertation (which he defended in 1841), as well as his notes on Schelling's 1841–42 lectures in Berlin. Kierkegaard's authorship proper begins with *Either/Or* (1843; trans. 1987), which also begins his use of pseudonyms. The companion piece to *Either/Or* is *Stages on Life's Way* (1845; trans. 1988), a text in the form of a series of articles supposedly written by various people. During this period Kierkegaard also published numerous religious writings in his own name. Texts in the first series of these "discourses," published between 1843 and 1844, are collected in *Eighteen Upbuilding Discourses* (1990). In 1845 he added to his signed authorship of Christian discourses with *Three Discourses on Imagined Occasions* (trans. 1993).

One of Kierkegaard's most famous works, *Fear and Trembling* (1843, by "Johannes de Silentio"), is collected with the contemporaneous work *Repetition* (attributed to "Constantin Constantius") in a single volume (trans. 1983); numerous other editions and translations are available. In 1844, under the name Nicolaus Notabene, Kierkegaard published *Prefaces* (trans. 1993), a satirical response to the critics of his pseudonymous works. An unpublished text from the same years, *Johannes Climacus or De omnibus dubitandum est*, is collected in a volume with *Philosophical Fragments* (1844; trans. 1985), purportedly written by Johannes Climacus and edited by Kierkegaard.

Perhaps the central work for understanding Kierkegaard's thought is his *Concluding Unscientific Postscript to "Philosophical Fragments"* (1846; trans. 1992), also said to be by Johannes Climacus, which dwarfs the text to which it is an alleged afterthought. As Vigilius Haufniensis, Kierkegaard published *The Concept of Anxiety: A Simple Psychologically Orienting Deliberation on the Dogmatic Issue of Hereditary Sin* (1844; trans. 1980). As Anti-Climacus, he published *The Sickness unto Death: A Christian Psychological Exposition for Upbuilding and Awakening* (1849; trans. 1980)—which might be regarded as a companion piece to *The Concept of Anxiety*—and *Practice in Christianity* (1850; trans. 1991).

Kierkegaard intended to end his authorship with *Concluding Unscientific Postscript* and become a pastor, but a public attack by *The Corsair*, a Danish newspaper, led him to change his mind. The documents from this dispute are collected in *The "Corsair" Affair* (1982). During the next few years (his "second authorship"), he published a greater number of positive Christian works and of negative critical analyses of culture under his own name, some of which were collected in *Upbuilding Discourses in Various Spirits* (1847; trans. 1993). Two further works, *Christian Discourses* (acknowledged as his own by Kierkegaard) and *The Crisis and a Crisis in the Life of an Actress* (by "Inter et Inter"), both written and published in 1848, are translated in a single volume (1997).

A work titled *The Book on Adler* (trans. 1995) was written in 1846–47 and extensively revised by Kierkegaard; but owing to his fear that it would harm the person who was its nominal topic (Adolph Peter Adler), he never published it. *Without Authority* (1997) contains five shorter works published between 1849 and 1851, all credited to Kierkegaard except for "Two Ethical-Religious Essays," said to be by "H.H." and incorporating some material from *The Book on Adler*. *Works of Love* (1847; trans. 1995) contains Kierkegaard's most sustained attempt at a positive Christian ethic.

In 1851 Kierkegaard published *On My Work as an Author*; it is translated in *The Point of View* (1994), which also contains *The Point of View for My Work as an Author* (written in 1848 and published posthumously in 1859) and *Armed Neutrality* (written in 1849 and published posthumously in 1880). *Two Ages: The Age of Revolution and the Present Age, A Literary Review* (1846; trans. 1978) is nominally a book review of a novel; its latter part was published in English as *The Present Age* (1940). Two works addressed to "the present age" are *For Self-Examination* (1851) and *Judge for Yourself!* (written in 1851 and published posthumously in 1876), which appear together in English (1990). After publishing *For Self-Examination*, Kierkegaard remained silent for almost four years. The pieces contained in *"The Moment" and Late Writings* (1993) were published earlier in a volume titled *Kierkegaard's Attack upon "Christendom," 1854–1855* (1944). The last volume of this edition of Kierkegaard's collected writings in translation is *Letters and Documents* (1978). His journals and papers have also been translated in *Søren Kierkegaard's Journals and Papers* (7 vols., 1967–78).

Each volume of the collected works is the subject of a volume in the International Kierkegaard Commentary series (1984–2010). Fifteen volumes to date have appeared in a series titled Kierkegaard Research: Sources, Reception, and Resources (2010–). For introductory overviews, see Frederick Sontag, *A Kierkegaard Handbook* (1979); Reidar Thomte, *Kierkegaard's Philosophy of Religion* (1948); Patrick Sheil, *Starting with Kierkegaard* (2011); Jamie Ferreira, *Kierkegaard* (2009); Daphne Hampson, *Kierkegaard: Exposition and Critique* (2013); and C. Stephen Evans, *Kierkegaard: An Introduction* (2009). A good resource for researching Kierkegaard is Julia Watkin's *Historical Dictionary of Kierkegaard's Philosophy* (2001; published in paperback as *The A to Z of Kierkegaard's Philosophy*, 2010).

Excellent volumes of essays on general topics in Kierkegaard's thought include *The Cambridge Companion to Kierkegaard*, edited by Alastair Hannay and Gordon D. Marino (1998); *Kierkegaard: A Critical Reader*, edited by Jona-than Rée and Jane Chamberlain (1998); *The Oxford Handbook of Kierkegaard*, edited by John Lippitt and George Pattison (2013); and Alastair Hannay, *Kierkegaard and Philosophy: Selected Essays* (2003).

Two works on the relation and influence of Hegel to and on Kierkegaard are Jon Stewart, *Kierkegaard's Relations to Hegel Reconsidered* (2003), and Mark C. Taylor, *Journeys to Selfhood: Hegel and Kierkegaard* (2nd ed., 2000). George Pattison's *Kierkegaard, Religion and the Nineteenth-Century Crisis of Culture* (2002) situates Kierkegaard's thought historically. Other significant secondary works include Merold Westphal, *Kierkegaard's Critique of Reason and Society* (1987); Theodor W. Adorno, *Kierkegaard: Construction of the Aesthetic* (1962; trans. 1989); Jacob Howland, *Kierkegaard and Socrates: A Study in Philosophy and Faith* (2008); and George Pattison, *Kierkegaard, the Aesthetic and the Religious: From the Magic Theatre to the Crucifixion of the Image* (2nd ed., 1999).

Three works on somewhat metaphysical questions are Gregor Malantschuk, *Kierkegaard's Concept of Existence* (1978; trans. 2003); David J. Kangas, *Kierkegaard's Instant: On Beginnings* (2007); and Ronald M. Green, *Kant and Kierkegaard on Time and Eternity* (2011). Monographs focused on epistemological themes include M. G. Piety, *Ways of Knowing: Kierkegaard's Pluralist Epistemology* (2010); Richard McCombs, *The Paradoxical Rationality of Søren Kierkegaard* (2013); Michelle Kosch, *Freedom and Reason in Kant, Schelling, and Kierkegaard* (2006); and Merigala Gabriel, *Subjectivity and Religious Truth in the Philosophy of Søren Kierkegaard* (2010). Kierkegaard's relevance to political philosophy is explored in Alison Assiter, *Kierkegaard, Metaphysics and Political Theory: Unfinished Selves* (2011), and *Kierkegaard and the Political*, edited by Alison Assiter and Margherita Tonon (2012).

C. Stephen Evans has written or edited a number of books with a focus on Kierkegaard's religion: *Kierkegaard's "Fragments" and "Postscript": The Religious Philosophy of Johannes Climacus* (1983), *Passionate Reason: Making Sense of Kierkegaard's Philosophical Fragments* (1992), *Kierkegaard's Ethic of Love: Divine Commands and Moral Obligations* (2004), *Kierkegaard on Faith and the Self: Collected Essays* (2006); *Faith beyond Reason: A Kierkegaardian Account* (1998), and *Foundations of Kierkegaard's Vision of Community: Religion, Ethics, and Politics in Kierkegaard*, edited by Evans and George Connell (1992). Numerous works on Kierkegaard and theology have been published recently, including George Pattison, *Kierkegaard and the Theology of the Nineteenth Century: The Paradox and the 'Point of Contact'* (2012); Murray Rae, *Kierkegaard and Theology* (2010); *Ethics, Love, and Faith in Kierkegaard: Philosophical Engagements*, edited by Edward F. Mooney (2008); Sylvia Walsh, *Kierkegaard: Thinking Christianly in an Existential Mode* (2009); Jack Mulder Jr., *Kierkegaard and the Catholic Tradition: Conflict and Dialogue* (2010); and Simon D. Podmore, *Kierkegaard and the Self before God: Anatomy of the Abyss* (2011).

Among the monographs focusing on individual works of Kierkegaard are Karsten Harries, *Between Nihilism and Faith: A Commentary on "Either/Or"* (2010); George Pattison, *Kierkegaard's Upbuilding Discourses: Philosophy, Theology, Literature* (2002); Tim Rose, *Kierkegaard's "Philosophical Fragments"* (2013); Merold Westphal, *Becoming a Self: A Reading of Kierkegaard's "Concluding Unscientific Postscript"* (1996); *Kierkegaard's "Concluding Unscientific Postscript": A Critical Guide*, edited by Rick Anthony Furtak (2012); Vivaldi Jean-Marie, *Kierkegaard: History and Eternal Happiness* (2008); John Lippitt, *The Routledge Philosophy Guidebook to Kierkegaard and "Fear and Trembling"* (2003); Clare Carlisle, *Kierkegaard's "Fear and Trembling": A Reader's Guide* (2010); Niels Nymann Eriksen, *Kierkegaard's Category of Repetition: A Reconstruction* (2000); Michael Theunissen, *Kierkegaard's Concept of Despair* (1993; trans. 2005); and Arne Grøn, *The Concept of Anxiety in Søren Kierkegaard* (1993; trans. 2008).

Ethical considerations are never far from any topic in Kierkegaard, but works devoted solely to this theme are George J. Stack, *Kierkegaard's Existential Ethics* (1977); Mark Dooley, *The Politics of Exodus: Søren Kierkegaard's Ethic of Responsibility* (2001); and W. Glenn Kirkconnell, *Kierkegaard on Ethics and Religion: From "Either/Or" to "Philosophical Fragments"* (2008) and *Kierkegaard on Sin and Salvation: From "Philosophical Fragments" through the "Two Ages"* (2010). Kierkegaard's ethics is based on his theory of love, making the following works essential for understanding it: Amy Laura Hall, *Kierkegaard and the Treachery of Love* (2002); M. Jamie Ferreira, *Love's Grateful Striving: A Commentary on Kierkegaard's "Works of Love"* (2001); Rick Anthony Furtak, *Wisdom in Love: Kierkegaard and the Ancient Quest for Emotional Integrity* (2005); and Sharon Krishek, *Kierkegaard on Faith and Love* (2009). There are several recent works on the connections between the ethical theories of Emmanuel Lévinas and Kierkegaard: Merold Westphal, *Levinas and Kierkegaard in Dialogue* (2008); Patrick Sheil, *Kierkegaard and Levinas: The Subjunctive Mood* (2010); Michael R. Paradiso-Michau, *The Ethical in Kierkegaard and Levinas* (2012); and *Kierkegaard and Levinas: Ethics, Politics, and Religion*, edited by J. Aaron Simmons and David Wood (2008).

Other studies that consider ethics in relation to classic existential problems concerning the self and meaning in the world include Sylvia Walsh, *Living Poetically: Kierkegaard's Existential Aesthetics* (1994); Peter J. Mehl, *Thinking through Kierkegaard: Existential Identity in a Pluralistic World* (2005); Arnold B. Come, *Kierkegaard as Humanist: Discovering My Self* (1995); Patrick Stokes, *Kierkegaard's Mirrors: Interest, Self and Moral Vision* (2010); John Lippitt, *Kierkegaard and the Problem of Self-Love* (2013); Thomas P. Miles, *Kierkegaard and Nietzsche on the Best Way of Life: A New Method of Ethics* (2013); George Pattison, *Kierkegaard and the Quest for Unambiguous Life: Between Romanticism and Modernism: Selected Essays* (2013); and Mark A. Tietjen, *Kierkegaard, Communication, and Virtue: Authorship as Edification* (2013).

A number of useful studies and collections deal with Kierkegaard in relation to modern trends in philosophy: see especially Michael Weston, *Kierkegaard and Modern Continental Philosophy: An Introduction* (1994); *Kierkegaard in Post/Modernity*, edited by Martin J. Matuštík and Merold Westphal (1995); Vasiliki Tsakiri, *Kierkegaard: Anxiety, Repetition and Contemporaneity* (2006); Michael Strawser, *Both/And: Reading Kierkegaard from Irony to Edification* (1997); *The New Kierkegaard*, edited by Elsebet Jegstrup (2004); *Feminist Interpretations of Søren Kierkegaard*, edited by Céline Léon and Sylvia Walsh (1997); Laura Llevadot, *Kierkegaard through Derrida: Toward a Postmetaphysical Ethics* (2013); and John Llewelyn, *Margins of Religion: Between Kierkegaard and Derrida* (2009).

Two important recent biographies are Alastair Hannay, *Kierkegaard: A Biography* (2001), and Joakim Garff, *Søren Kierkegaard: A Biography* (2000; trans. 2005). Walter Lowrie's *A Short Life of Kierkegaard* (1942) is a classic earlier biography. *Encounters with Kierkegaard: A Life as Seen by His Contemporaries*, edited by Bruce Kirmmse (1996), is a collection of biographical reflections on Kierkegaard by people who knew him.

Lévinas, Emmanuel

Much of Lévinas's work is available in English. His two early works on Husserl—*The Theory of Intuition in the Phenomenology of Husserl* (1930; trans. 1973) and *Discovering Existence with Husserl* (1949, 2nd ed. 1982; trans. 1998)—are important historical analyses that helped to greatly increase the influence of Husserl in France and elsewhere. Two small early works, *Existence and Existents* (1947; trans. 1978) and *Time and the Other* (1947; trans. 1987), contain the seeds of much of what was to be developed in Lévinas's mature works, and are helpful introductions to his thought. Another early essay is *On Escape* (1935; trans. 2003).

It is for his first major work, *Totality and Infinity: Essay on Exteriority* (1961; trans. 1969), that Lévinas is best known. It remains essential to any understanding of his thought. His other major work is *Otherwise Than Being, or Beyond Essence* (1974; trans. 1981), in which he develops and extends many of the ideas advanced in *Totality and Infinity*, adds an important discussion of language, and substantially develops his theory of ethics and justice.

Lévinas's work has been most influential in the field of ethics. Many of his essays (and some interviews) devoted specifically to his theory of "the Other" and intersubjectivity, as well as applications of his ideas on these subjects for social and political issues, can be found in the works *Entre Nous* [*Between Ourselves*]: *Thinking-of-the-Other* (1991; trans. 1998), which contains essays from as early as 1951, and *Alterity and Transcendence* (1995; trans. 1999). Two collections—*Proper Names* (1976; trans. 1996) and *Outside the Subject* (1987; trans. 1993)—include essays on such figures as Kierkegaard, Derrida, Merleau-Ponty, Blanchot, and Buber; other collections are *Humanism of the Other* (1972; trans. 2003), which is significant for understanding his ethics, and *Unforeseen History* (1994; trans. 2004). Many other essays are translated in *Collected Philosophical Papers* (1987). Several collections of illuminating and interesting interviews have also been published in English: *Ethics and Infinity* (1982; trans. 1985), *Is It Righteous to Be? Interviews with Emmanuel Lévinas* (2001), and *Conversations with Emmanuel Levinas, 1983–1994* (2010).

There are also several books containing lectures and essays by Lévinas on various aspects of the Talmud: see *Nine Talmudic Readings* (which combines *Quatre lectures talmudiques*, 1968, and *Du sacré au saint*, 1977; trans. 1990); *Beyond the Verse: Talmudic Readings and Lectures* (1982; trans. 1994); and *New Talmudic Readings* (1996; trans. 1999). An important work for understanding his influential theory of religion is *Of God Who Comes to Mind* (1982, 2nd ed. 1986; trans. 1998), whose thirteen essays are the clearest statement of the implications of his theory for religion; see also the collection *God, Death, and Time* (1993; trans. 2000).

The secondary literature on Lévinas is diverse and growing. The works of Adriaan Theodoor Peperzak are the standard by which other secondary work on him is generally judged; they include *To the Other: An Introduction to the Philosophy of Emmanuel Levinas* (1993), *Beyond:*

The Philosophy of Emmanuel Levinas (1997), and an edited volume, *Ethics as First Philosophy: The Significance of Emmanuel Levinas for Philosophy, Literature and Religion* (1995). For other useful overviews of Lévinas's thought, see Michael B. Smith, *Toward the Outside: Concepts and Themes in Emmanuel Levinas* (2005); Edith Wyschogrod, *Emmanuel Lévinas: The Problem of Ethical Metaphysics* (1974; 2nd ed., 2000); Robert John Sheffler Manning, *Interpreting Otherwise Than Heidegger: Emmanuel Levinas's Ethics as First Philosophy* (1993); and John E. Drabinski, *Sensibility and Singularity: The Problem of Phenomenology in Levinas* (2001). Several excellent introductions are Michael L. Morgan, *The Cambridge Introduction to Emmanuel Levinas* (2011) and *Discovering Levinas* (2008), and Seán Hand, *Emmanuel Lévinas* (2009).

Valuable collections of essays on Lévinas's thought include *Re-reading Levinas*, edited by Robert Bernasconi and Simon Critchley (1991); *The Cambridge Companion to Levinas*, edited by Simon Critchley and Robert Bernasconi (2002); *Addressing Levinas*, edited by Eric Sean Nelson, Antje Kapust, and Kent Still (2005); *Facing the Other: The Ethics of Emmanuel Lévinas*, edited by Seán Hand (1996); and *Radicalizing Levinas*, edited by Peter Atterton and Matthew Calarco (2010).

Three books that focus on questions of passivity and generosity from a psychological and interpersonal perspective are George Kunz, *The Paradox of Power and Weakness: Levinas and an Alternative Paradigm for Psychology* (1998); Rosalyn Diprose, *Corporeal Generosity: On Giving with Nietzsche, Merleau-Ponty, and Levinas* (2002); and Thomas Carl Wall, *Radical Passivity: Lévinas, Blanchot, and Agamben* (1999). Studies of Lévinas's ethics include Catherine Chalier, *What Ought I to Do? Morality in Kant and Levinas* (1998; trans. 2002); Bettina Bergo, *Levinas between Ethics and Politics: For the Beauty That Adorns the Earth* (1999); Roger Burggraeve, *The Wisdom of Love in the Service of Love: Emmanuel Levinas on Justice, Peace, and Human Rights* (2002); and Brian Schroeder, *Altared Ground: Levinas, History, and Violence* (1996).

Other recent works on Lévinas's ethics include Paul Marcus, *Being for the Other: Emmanuel Levinas, Ethical Living and Psychoanalysis* (2008); Joshua James Shaw, *Emmanuel Levinas on the Priority of Ethics: Putting Ethics First* (2008); Diane Perpich, *The Ethics of Emmanuel Levinas* (2008); Richard A. Cohen, *Levinasian Meditations: Ethics, Philosophy, and Religion* (2010); Anna Strhan, *Levinas, Subjectivity, Education: Towards an Ethics of Radical Responsibility* (2012); Hagi Kenaan, *The Ethics of Visuality: Levinas and the Contemporary Gaze*

(2013); and Aryeh Botwinick, *Emmanuel Lévinas and the Limits to Ethics: A Critique and a Re-appropriation* (2013).

Lévinas's work is often associated with the work of Derrida written after the latter's own "ethical turn." Derrida devotes several essays to him, most importantly "Violence and Metaphysics: An Essay on the Thought of Emmanuel Levinas" (1964), in *Writing and Difference* (1967; trans. 1978), as well as a book, *Adieu to Emmanuel Levinas* (1997; trans. 1999), containing his remarks at Lévinas's funeral and a long essay. John Llewelyn writes specifically on and from the intersection of Derrida and Lévinas in *Appositions of Jacques Derrida and Emmanuel Levinas* (2002) and *Emmanuel Levinas: The Genealogy of Ethics* (1995). Other useful studies include Simon Critchley, *The Ethics of Deconstruction: Derrida and Levinas* (1992) and *Ethics-Politics-Subjectivity: Essays on Derrida, Levinas and Contemporary French Thought* (1999); Martin C. Srajek, *In the Margins of Deconstruction: Jewish Conceptions of Ethics in Emmanuel Levinas and Jacques Derrida* (1998); Neal DeRoo, *Futurity in Phenomenology: Promise and Method in Husserl, Levinas, and Derrida* (2013); and Madeleine Fagan, *Ethics and Politics after Poststructuralism: Levinas, Derrida and Nancy* (2013).

The implications of Lévinas's thought for politics are discussed in Philip J. Harold, *Prophetic Politics: Emmanuel Levinas and the Sanctification of Suffering* (2009); Abi Doukhan, *Emmanuel Levinas: A Philosophy of Exile* (2012); John E. Drabinski, *Lévinas and the Postcolonial: Race, Nation, Other* (2013); Steven Shankman, *Other Others: Levinas, Literature, Transcultural Studies* (2011); Ernst Wolff, *Political Responsibility for a Globalised World: After Levinas' Humanism* (2011); Elisabeth Louise Thomas, *Emmanuel Levinas: Ethics, Justice, and the Human beyond Being* (2004); Claire Elise Katz, *Levinas and the Crisis of Humanism* (2012); Howard Caygill, *Levinas and the Political* (2002); and Victoria Tahmasebi-Birgani, *Emmanuel Lévinas and the Politics of Nonviolence* (2014).

Lévinas's religious thought is discussed in Nigel Zimmermann, *Levinas and Theology* (2013); *The Exorbitant: Emmanuel Lévinas between Jews and Christians*, edited by Kevin Hart and Michael A. Signer (2010); and Michael Fagenblat, *A Covenant of Creatures: Levinas's Philosophy of Judaism* (2010). The growing interest in the conjunction of the thought of Lévinas and Kierkegaard is evidenced by Merold Westphal, *Lévinas and Kierkegaard in Dialogue* (2008); Michael R. Paradiso-Michau, *The Ethical in Kierkegaard and Lévinas* (2012); and *Kierkegaard and Levinas: Ethics, Politics, and*

Religion, edited by J. Aaron Simmons and David Wood (2008).

Lyotard, Jean-François

Lyotard's first work was *Phenomenology* (1954, 10th ed. 1986; trans. 1991), a survey of phenomenology for the famous *Que sais-je?* (What Do I Know?) series. *Political Writings* (1993) collects and translates writings from 1948 on. His two early philosophical works are *Libidinal Economy* (1974; trans. 1993) and *Discourse, Figure* (1971; trans. 2011). Also belonging to this period is *Dérive à partir de Marx et Freud* (1973, *Starting from Marx and Freud*), translated in part as *Driftworks* (1984). *Toward the Postmodern* (1993) collects and translates essays representing both his early period and his later shift away from a Freudian idiom to a focus on language and the postmodern. *Postmodern Fables* (1993; trans. 1997) contains essays from 1970 to 1991.

Lyotard's thought from his mature (postmodern) period is on display in *The Postmodern Condition: A Report on Knowledge* (1979; trans. 1984), *Just Gaming* (1979, *Au Juste*; trans. 1985), *The Differend: Phrases in Dispute* (1983; trans. 1988), *The Postmodern Explained: Correspondence, 1982–1985* (1986; trans. 1992), and *The Inhuman: Reflections on Time* (1988; trans. 1991). *The Hyphen: Between Judaism and Christianity* (1993; trans. 1998), written with Eberhard Gruber, examines questions of a religious, political, and cultural nature.

Several of Lyotard's works are encounters with thinkers in the history of philosophy: *The Confession of Augustine* (1998; trans. 2000), *Heidegger and "the jews"* (1988; trans. 1990), *Lessons on the Analytic of the Sublime: Kant's "Critique of Judgment," 23–29* (1991; trans. 1994), and *Enthusiasm: The Kantian Critique of History* (1986; trans. 2009). He also wrote two books on the writer André Malraux, the first biographical and the second more analytical: *Signed, Malraux* (1996; trans. 1999) and *Soundproof Room: Malraux's Anti-Aesthetics* (1998; trans. 2001). Also available in English are *Peregrinations: Law, Form, Event* (1988), *Duchamp's TRANS/formers* (1977; trans. 1990), and *Pacific Wall* (1975; trans. 1990). A series of his writings on various artists and on aesthetics generally, each volume containing the French original and its English translation, has recently been published: *Jean-François Lyotard: Écrits sur l'art contemporain et les artistes / Writings on Contemporary Art and Artists* (7 vols., 2009–13). *Why Philosophize?* (2012; trans. 2013) is a series of lectures that serves as an introduction to philosophy and to Lyotard's own thought.

For studies that provide comprehensive accounts of Lyotard's philosophy, see Simon Malpas, *Jean-François Lyotard* (2003); Bill Readings, *Introducing Lyotard: Art and Politics* (1991); Geoffrey Bennington, *Lyotard: Writing the Event* (1988); Gary K. Browning, *Lyotard and the End of Grand Narratives* (2000); James Williams, *Lyotard: Towards a Postmodern Philosophy* (1998); Stuart Sim, *Jean-François Lyotard* (1995) and *Lyotard and the Inhuman* (2001); and *The Lyotard Dictionary*, edited by Sim (2011). Useful collections of essays on Lyotard include *Judging Lyotard*, edited by Andrew Benjamin (1992); *Afterwords: Essays in Memory of Jean-François Lyotard*, edited by Robert Harvey (2000); *Jean-François Lyotard: Time and Judgment*, edited by Robert Harvey and Lawrence R. Schehr (special issue of *Yale French Studies*, 2001); and *Rereading Jean-François Lyotard: Essays on His Later Works*, edited by Heidi Bickis and Rob Shields (2013).

Two works that examine Lyotard, postmodernism, and education are *Lyotard: Just Education*, edited by Pradeep A. Dhillon and Paul Standish (2000), and *Education and the Postmodern Condition*, edited by Michael Peters (1995). Studies dealing with Lyotard's political thought include *The Politics of Jean-François Lyotard*, edited by Chris Rojek and Bryan S. Turner (1998); *Lyotard: Philosophy, Politics and the Sublime*, edited by Hugh J. Silverman (2002); Stanley Raffel, *Habermas, Lyotard and the Concept of Justice* (1992); Honi Fern Haber, *Beyond Postmodern Politics: Lyotard, Rorty, Foucault* (1994); James Williams, *Lyotard and the Political* (2000); and Georges de Schrijver, *The Political Ethics of Jean-François Lyotard and Jacques Derrida* (2010).

Two works on Lyotard and aesthetics are Graham Jones, *Lyotard Reframed: Interpreting Key Thinkers for the Arts* (2014), and Kiff Bamford, *Lyotard and the Figural in Performance, Art and Writing* (2012). There also are a number of studies in which Lyotard is discussed in relation to other philosophers: see David Carroll, *Paraesthetics: Foucault, Lyotard, Derrida* (1987); Julian Pefanis, *Heterology and the Postmodern: Bataille, Baudrillard, and Lyotard* (1991); Emilia Steuerman, *The Bounds of Reason: Habermas, Lyotard, and Melanie Klein on Rationality* (2000); Manfred Frank, *The Boundaries of Agreement* (2005); and Keith Crome, *Lyotard and Greek Thought: Sophistry* (2004). Also discussing Lyotard in relation to major trends in poststructuralism are François Cusset, *French Theory: How Foucault, Derrida, Deleuze, & Co. Transformed the Intellectual Life of the United States* (2003; trans. 2008); Ashley Woodward, *Nihilism in Postmodernity: Lyotard, Baudrillard, Vattimo* (2009); and Simon Choat, *Marx through Post-structuralism: Lyotard, Derrida, Foucault, Deleuze* (2010).

Marx, Karl and Engels, Friedrich

Marx's first important post-dissertation philosophical effort is his "Critique of Hegel's Philosophy of Right" (1843), a commentary on paragraphs 261–313 of that work. Though it was not published in his lifetime, Marx's introduction to it, written later, was published in 1844 in the *Deutsch-Französische Jahrbücher*. In the same month and in the same journal, he published "On the Jewish Question," his earliest suggestion of socialism as the transcendence of the political state and the development of community in all aspects of life and work. Perhaps the most important of his early writings are found in *Economic and Philosophic Manuscripts of 1844*, along with his notebooks from that year. First published in 1932, they transformed perceptions about Marx's philosophy and its development. His well-known manifesto now known as "Theses on Feuerbach" was written in 1845 and first published, in a version edited by Engels, in 1888.

Written in 1844 and published in 1845, Marx's first collaboration with Engels was *The Holy Family*, which attacks the "Young Hegelian" Bruno Bauer and his brothers. *The German Ideology* (written 1845–46; published 1932), another collaborative effort, reflects their continued attempt to distance themselves from the Hegelians and from Feuerbach and presents a clear statement of Marx's "materialist" theory of history. It was not until Marx wrote and published *The Poverty of Philosophy* (1847, in French; trans. 1900)—a response to Proudhon's *The Philosophy of Poverty* (1847)—that his political, social, and historical philosophy first found its way into print.

Marx and Engels's *Manifesto of the Communist Party* (or *Communist Manifesto*, written 1847–48; published 1848) was intended to provide a catechism of communism for the various groups across Europe that had loosely organized as "the Communist League." From mid-1848 to 1849, Marx wrote for the *Neue Rheinische Zeitung*, which he founded in Germany; from these writings Engels later assembled a short work, *Wage Labour and Capital* (1891). After settling in London Marx established the *Neue Rheinische Zeitung-Revue*; some of the articles he contributed were collected and published by Engels as *The Class Struggles in France, 1848–1850* (1895; trans. 1924). *The Eighteenth Brumaire of Louis Bonaparte* (1852; trans. 1898) was first published in *Die Revolution*, a New York–based German-language journal.

Between 1857 and 1858 Marx drafted what amounts to an extensive outline of his political and economic theory; these notebooks were not published until 1939–41, as *Foundations [Grundrisse] of the Critique of Political Economy* (usually called simply the *Grundrisse*). The *Grundrisse* is much more expansive than volume 1 of *Capital*, which discusses only one of the six main parts it sketches, and also sheds light on the relation of the theories that would be developed there to the humanist philosophy found in Marx's early writings. However, it is a challenging work to read, because it was not systematically organized or revised by Marx.

A Contribution to the Critique of Political Economy (1859; trans. 1904) presents themes from the first part of the Grundrisse and introduces ideas that would be dealt with more completely in the opening of Capital. Its preface contains a sort of intellectual autobiography by Marx.

Marx's masterwork, Das Kapital (Capital), was drafted in the years 1862–66. Volume 1 (1867; trans. 1886)—the only section published during Marx's lifetime—contains an abstract account of the main ideas of Marx's theoretical orientation, followed by a very concrete account of the development of capitalism. Volumes 2 (1885; trans. 1907) and 3 (1894; trans. 1909) were edited and published by Engels from Marx's drafts and notes. A fourth volume was envisioned as an appendix, in which the economic theories of other thinkers were discussed; it was published, in two significantly different editions, as Theories of Surplus Value (3 vols., 1905–10/1977–79; trans. 1968/1989–91).

Two lectures given in English by Marx in 1865 were published under the title Value, Price and Profit (1898). Marx's English pamphlet The Civil War in France (1871) contains his reflections on the establishment of a communist commune in Paris after France's defeat in the Franco-Prussian War. The Critique of the Gotha Program was written by Marx in 1875 in response to the development of a common—and in Marx's eyes compromised—agenda by two political parties of workers in Germany. It was first published (abridged) by Engels in 1891 (trans. 1933).

Engels published many books on his own, beginning with Condition of the Working Class in England (1845; trans. 1887). The Peasant War in Germany (1850; trans. 1926) is primarily a historical study; The Housing Question (1872; trans. 1887) addresses Germany's housing shortage for workers. Herr Eugen Dühring's Revolution in Science (1877–78; trans. 1894), better known as Anti-Dühring, was Engels's response to the social and political influence of Eugen Dühring, a professor at the University of Berlin who became convinced of the truth of socialism and wrote several enormous works on it, in which he was quite critical of Marx. An extract from Anti-Dühring was published in French as Socialism: Utopian and Scientific (1880; trans. 1892). In order to write Anti-Dühring, Engels suspended work on his intended masterwork, now known as Dialectics of Nature, which was not published in its entirety (as he left it) until 1925 (trans. 1940), long after his death. The Origin of the Family, Private Property and the State (1884; trans. 1902) deals with early human history. The last of Engels's works is perhaps the most widely read: Ludwig Feuerbach and the End of Classical German Philosophy (1888; trans. 1934).

The complete works of Marx and Engels, including their correspondence, are available in English translation from International Publishers (50 vols., 1975–2004); more accessible are a number of single-volume collections of selected writings.

Intellectual biographies of Marx worth consulting include Isaiah Berlin, Karl Marx: His Life and Environment (1939; 4th ed., 1978); David McLellan, Karl Marx: A Biography (4th ed., 2006); Frank E. Manuel, A Requiem for Karl Marx (1995); Francis Wheen, Karl Marx: A Life (1999) and Marx's "Das Kapital": A Biography (2006); Jonathan Sperber, Karl Marx: A Nineteenth-Century Life (2013); and Rolf Hosfeld, Karl Marx: An Intellectual Biography (2009; trans. 2013). On Engels, see Tristram Hunt, Marx's General: The Revolutionary Life of Friedrich Engels (2009).

Helpful general introductions to Marx's thought include Ernest Mandel, Introduction to Marxist Economic Theory (1964; trans. 1970); Peter Singer, Marx: A Very Short Introduction (rev. ed., 2000); Peter Worsley, Marx and Marxism (1982); Jon Elster, An Introduction to Karl Marx (1986); Richard Schmitt, Introduction to Marx and Engels: A Critical Reconstruction (1987); Étienne Balibar, The Philosophy of Marx (1993; trans. 1995); Terry Eagleton, Marx (1997) and Why Marx Was Right (2011); and Jonathan Wolff, Why Read Marx Today? (2002). Three collections of essays by leading scholars in the field discussing main ideas and issues in Marxist philosophy are Marx: The First Hundred Years, edited by David McLellan (1983); The Cambridge Companion to Marx, edited by Terrell Carver (1991); and Karl Marx and Contemporary Philosophy, edited by Andrew Chitty and Martin McIvor (2009).

Works that act both as sophisticated and in-depth introductions to Marx and as important contributions to the interpretation and understanding of Marx include Jon Elster, Making Sense of Marx (1985); Allen Wood, Karl Marx (2nd ed., 2004); Robert Paul Wolff, Understanding Marx: A Reconstruction and Critique of "Capital" (1984); Daniel Brudney, Marx's Attempt to Leave Philosophy (1998); Tom Rockmore, Marx after Marxism: The Philosophy of Karl Marx (2002); Allan Megill, Karl Marx: The Burden of Reason (Why Marx Rejected Politics and the Market) (2002); Eric Hobsbawm, How to Change the World: Reflections on Marx and Marxism (2011); Sean Sayers, Marx and Alienation: Essays on Hegelian Themes (2011); and Thomas C. Patterson, Karl Marx, Anthropologist (2009).

David McLellan's Marxism after Marx: An Introduction (1979; 4th ed., 2007) discusses twentieth-century Marxism in general, and

Göran Therborn's *From Marxism to Post-Marxism?* (2008) examines how Marxism remains influential in twenty-first-century Continental philosophy. Kevin M. Brien's *Marx, Reason, and the Art of Freedom* (1987) examines Marx's theory of freedom. G. A. Cohen's *Karl Marx's Theory of History: A Defence* (1978; expanded ed., 2000) is a classic work on his materialist theory of history. Bertell Ollman's *Dance of the Dialectic: Steps in Marx's Method* (2003) focuses on methodological questions concerning the nature of dialectical thinking and analysis. Robert Tucker's *The Marxian Revolutionary Idea* (1969) examines Marx's theory of revolution as a moral and political idea. Among the works that deal helpfully with Marx's theory of alienation are Bertell Ollman, *Alienation: Marx's Conception of Man in Capitalist Society* (2nd ed., 1976); Ernest Mandel and George Novack, *The Marxist Theory of Alienation* (1970); and Richard Schacht, *Alienation* (1970).

The following works focus on Marx's early development and his relation to previous philosophers (especially Hegel and Feuerbach): Christopher J. Arthur, *Dialectics of Labour: Marx and His Relation to Hegel* (1986) and *The New Dialectic and Marx's "Capital"* (2002); David Leopold, *The Young Karl Marx: German Philosophy, Modern Politics, and Human Flourishing* (2007); David McLellan, *The Young Hegelians and Karl Marx* (1969); Warren Breckman, *Marx, the Young Hegelians, and the Origins of Radical Social Theory: Dethroning the Self* (1999); Louis Dupré, *The Philosophical Foundations of Marxism* (1966); Robert Tucker, *Philosophy and Myth in Karl Marx* (1961; 3rd ed., 2001), and Sidney Hook, *From Hegel to Marx: Studies in the Intellectual Development of Karl Marx* (1936). Among the titles devoted to Marx's masterwork are David Harvey, *A Companion to Marx's "Capital"* (2010) and *A Companion to Marx's "Capital," Volume 2* (2013); Michael Heinrich, *An Introduction to the Three Volumes of Karl Marx's "Capital"* (2004; trans. 2012); and Ben Fine and Alfredo Saad-Filho, *Marx's "Capital"* (5th ed., 2010).

For more on Marxism in Europe, see the bibliography section on Left-Hegelianism and Marxism in General Bibliographies (above).

Merleau-Ponty, Maurice

Merleau-Ponty's first book was *The Structure of Behavior* (1942; trans. 1963). It was followed by *Phenomenology of Perception* (1945; trans. 1962), which is one of the most important texts of the phenomenological movement, but which also stands at the junction of existentialism and philosophical anthropology. A series of 1948 radio lectures relating to it, translated as *The World of Perception* (2002; trans. 2004), was published after his death.

Three important collections of essays, containing his work on art and politics, as well as work relating to his phenomenological analysis of perception and the body, are available in translation: *Sense and Non-Sense* (1948; trans. 1964), *Signs* (1960; trans. 1964), and *The Primacy of Perception, and Other Essays on Phenomenological Psychology, the Philosophy of Art, History and Politics* (essays published 1947–61; trans. 1964). The incomplete, abandoned work *The Prose of the World* (1969; trans. 1973) is available; much of its content is presented more succinctly in "Indirect Language and the Voices of Silence," an essay in *Signs*. The short but interesting work *Consciousness and the Acquisition of Language* (1964; trans. 1973) marks the beginning of Merleau-Ponty's reflections on language and expression, which ultimately had major consequences in his thought. A lecture course from 1951–52, "The Experience of Others," is available in *Merleau-Ponty and Psychology* ([trans. 1982] 1993), which also contains several important essays from that period.

The Merleau-Ponty Aesthetics Reader: Philosophy and Painting (1993) brings together Merleau-Ponty's major essays on aesthetics, drawn from the three collections of essays mentioned above, together with critical and historical essays by scholars and philosophers. *The Debate between Sartre and Merleau-Ponty* (1998) gathers relevant documents from Sartre, Beauvoir, and Merleau-Ponty on their disagreement with one another, as well as scholarly essays on their intersections and divergences.

The actual break in the relationship between Sartre and Merleau-Ponty was caused largely by political disagreements. For Merleau-Ponty's main statements on his political thought, see *Humanism and Terror: An Essay on the Communist Problem* (1947; trans. 1969) and *Adventures of the Dialectic* (1955; trans. 1973).

Merleau-Ponty's late and important but fragmentary work *The Visible and the Invisible: Followed by Working Notes* (1964; trans. 1968) remains influential. Several other posthumously published works, containing some of his lecture notes, have also been translated: *Husserl at the Limits of Phenomenology: Including Texts by Edmund Husserl* (2002), which contains a course summary and course notes from 1960 (published in French in 1988 and 1998); *Nature: Course Notes from the Collège de France* (1995; trans. 2003); *Child Psychology and Pedagogy: The Sorbonne Lectures, 1949–1952* (2001; trans. 2010); and *Institution and Passivity: Course Notes from the Collège de France (1954–1955)* (2003; trans. 2010).

The secondary literature on Merleau-Ponty is not as large as one might expect. Introductions to his thought include Eric Matthews, *The Phi-*

losophy of Merleau-Ponty (2002); Stephen Priest, Merleau-Ponty (1998); Merleau-Ponty: Key Concepts, edited by Rosalyn Diprose and Jack Reynolds (2008); George J. Marshall, A Guide to Merleau-Ponty's "Phenomenology of Perception" (2008); Lawrence Hass, Merleau-Ponty's Philosophy (2008); Taylor Carman, Merleau-Ponty (2008); Komarine Romdenh-Romluc, Routledge Philosophy Guidebook to Merleau-Ponty and "Phenomenology of Perception" (2011); Katherine J. Morris, Starting with Merleau-Ponty (2012); and Donald A. Landes, The Merleau-Ponty Dictionary (2013). The Cambridge Companion to Merleau-Ponty, edited by Taylor Carman and Mark B. N. Hansen (2005), is helpful on various topics and aspects of his thought.

M. C. Dillon has written and edited several works on Merleau-Ponty—most importantly, Merleau-Ponty's Ontology (1988; 2nd ed., 1997). Renaud Barbaras, The Being of the Phenomenon: Merleau-Ponty's Ontology (1991; trans. 2004), also offers a detailed survey of his thought, with an emphasis on the later work. Samuel B. Mallin's Merleau-Ponty's Philosophy (1979) is an excellent but out-of-print analysis. Other worthwhile older surveys of Merleau-Ponty's thought are John Bannan, The Philosophy of Merleau-Ponty (1967), Gary Brent Madison, The Phenomenology of Merleau-Ponty: A Search for the Limits of Consciousness (1973; trans. 1981), and Ontology and Alterity in Merleau-Ponty, edited by Galen A. Johnson and Michael B. Smith (1990). Several useful recent works are Ted Toadvine, Merleau-Ponty's Philosophy of Nature (2009); Scott L. Marratto, The Intercorporeal Self: Merleau-Ponty on Subjectivity (2012); Justin Tauber, Invitations: Merleau-Ponty, Cognitive Science and Phenomenology (2008); and Kirk M. Besmer, Merleau-Ponty's Phenomenology: The Problem of Ideal Objects (2008).

James Schmidt's Maurice Merleau-Ponty: Between Phenomenology and Structuralism (1985) relates Merleau-Ponty to Hegel, Marx, Saussure, and Husserl. Two books by John O'Neill, Communicative Body: Studies in Communicative Philosophy, Politics, and Sociology (1989) and Perception, Expression, and History: The Social Phenomenology of Maurice Merleau-Ponty (1970), both focus on Merleau-Ponty's thinking on expression, the body, and language. James Edie also deals with Merleau-Ponty's theory of language and expression in Merleau-Ponty's Philosophy of Language: Structuralism and Dialectics (1987).

Useful discussions of Merleau-Ponty's politics include Barry Cooper, Merleau-Ponty and Marxism: From Terror to Reform (1979); Kerry H. Whiteside, Merleau-Ponty and the Foundation of an Existential Politics (1988); Sonia Kruks, The Political Philosophy of Merleau-Ponty (1987); James Miller, History and Human Existence: From Marx to Merleau-Ponty (1979); and Douglas Low, Merleau-Ponty in Contemporary Context: Philosophy and Politics in the Twenty-First Century (2013).

Discussions of Merleau-Ponty's aesthetics may be found in Eugene Kaelin, An Existentialist Aesthetic: The Theories of Sartre and Merleau-Ponty (1962); Merleau-Ponty: Difference, Materiality, Painting, edited by Véronique M. Fóti (1996); Rajiv Kaushik, Art and Institution: Aesthetics in the Late Works of Merleau-Ponty (2011); Merleau-Ponty at the Limits of Art, Religion, and Perception, edited by Kascha Semonovitch and Neal DeRoo (2010); Donald A. Landes, Merleau-Ponty and the Paradoxes of Expression (2013); Véronique M. Fóti, Tracing Expression in Merleau-Ponty: Aesthetics, Philosophy of Biology, and Ontology (2013); Galen A. Johnson, The Retrieval of the Beautiful: Thinking Through Merleau-Ponty's Aesthetics (2009); and Jessica Wiskus, The Rhythm of Thought: Art, Literature, and Music after Merleau-Ponty (2013).

Among the secondary works that focus primarily on The Visible and the Invisible are Mauro Carbone, The Thinking of the Sensible: Merleau-Ponty's A-Philosophy (2004); Chiasms: Merleau-Ponty's Notion of Flesh, edited by Fred Evans and Leonard Lawlor (2000); Douglas Low, Merleau-Ponty's Last Vision: A Proposal for the Completion of "The Visible and the Invisible" (2000); Merleau-Ponty's Later Works and Their Practical Implications: The Dehiscence of Responsibility, edited by Duane H. Davis (2001); and Sue L. Cataldi, Emotion, Depth, and Flesh: A Study of Sensitive Space: Reflections on Merleau-Ponty's Philosophy of Embodiment (1993).

Mill, John Stuart

Mill's collected works have been published in a monumental 33-volume edition (1963–91). Volume 1 contains Mill's autobiography, published in 1873. Volumes 2 and 3 contain his Principles of Political Economy (1848), which went through seven editions within Mill's lifetime. Volumes 4 and 5, Essays on Economics and Society, contain essays written and published throughout Mill's career on such topics as labor, class, taxes, property, and socialism. Volumes 7 and 8 contain A System of Logic: Ratiocinative and Inductive (1843). Volume 9 is An Examination of Sir William Hamilton's Philosophy (1865). Some of Mill's best-known shorter works—including Utilitarianism (1861), Auguste Comte and Positivism (1865), essays on Bentham and Sedgwick, and his Three Essays on Religion (1874)—are in volume 10, Essays on Ethics, Religion and Society. Mill's main shorter writings on society, politics, and rights—including On Liberty (1859),

Considerations on Representative Government (1861), and The Subjection of Women (1869)—are in volumes 18 (On Liberty) and 19 (Representative Government), titled Essays on Politics and Society (parts 1 and 2), and volume 21, Essays on Equality, Law, and Education (Subjection of Women). Many of these works are also readily available separately in relatively inexpensive editions.

The Cambridge Companion to Mill, edited by John Skorupski (1998), contains critical essays concerning many aspects of Mill's thought, as does Mill: A Collection of Critical Essays, edited by J. B. Schneewind (1968). Helpful surveys of Mill's thought include H. J. McCloskey, John Stuart Mill: A Critical Study (1971); Alan Ryan, The Philosophy of John Stuart Mill (2nd ed., 1987); Linda C. Raeder, John Stuart Mill and the Religion of Humanity (2002); Wendy Donner and Richard Fumerton, Mill (2009); and Dale E. Miller, J. S. Mill: Moral, Social and Political Thought (2010). For advanced scholarship on Mill's thought, see John Stuart Mill—Thought and Influence: The Saint of Rationalism, edited by Georgios Varouxakis and Paul Kelly (2010); John Stuart Mill and the Art of Life, edited by Ben Eggleston, Dale E. Miller, and David Weinstein (2011); Mill on Justice, edited by Leonard Kahn (2012); Georgios Varouxakis, Liberty Abroad: J. S. Mill and International Relations (2103); and Gregory Claeys, Mill and Paternalism (2013).

Useful monographs and collections of essays have been published on each of the works from which our selections are taken. On Mill's On Liberty, see Jonathan Riley, Routledge Philosophy Guidebook to Mill on Liberty (1998); J. S. Mill's "On Liberty" in Focus, edited by John Gray and G. W. Smith (1991); Mill's "On Liberty": Critical Essays, edited by Gerald Dworkin (1997); Liberty: Contemporary Responses to John Stuart Mill, edited by Andrew Pyle (2006); and K. C. O'Rourke, John Stuart Mill and Freedom of Expression: The Genesis of a Theory (2013). On Utilitarianism, see The Blackwell Guide to Mill's "Utilitarianism," edited by Henry R. West (2006); Roger Crisp, Routledge Philosophy Guidebook to Mill on Utilitarianism (1997); and Mill's "Utilitarianism": Critical Essays, edited by David Lyons (1997). On The Subjection of Women, see Mill's "The Subjection of Women": Critical Essays, edited by Maria H. Morales (2005); Gail Tulloch, Mill and Sexual Equality (1989); John Stuart Mill's "The Subjection of Women": His Contemporary and Modern Critics, edited by Lesley A. Jacobs and Richard VandeWetering (1999); and "The Subjection of Women": Contemporary Responses to John Stuart Mill, edited by Andrew Pyle (1995).

Useful studies of Mill's political theory include Maria H. Morales, Perfect Equality: John

Stuart Mill on Well-Constituted Communities (1996); Maurice Cowling, Mill and Liberalism (1963); John Gray, Mill on Liberty: A Defence (1983; 2nd ed., 1996); Ian Cook, Reading Mill: Studies in Political Theory (1998); and Gertrude Himmelfarb, On Liberty and Liberalism: The Case of John Stuart Mill (1974). Also worth noting are Graeme Duncan, Marx and Mill: Two Views of Social Conflict and Social Harmony (1973), and Samuel Hollander, The Economics of John Stuart Mill (2 vols., 1985).

Valuable studies and collections focusing more on Mill's moral philosophy include David Lyons, Rights, Welfare, and Mill's Moral Theory (1994); Utilitarianism and Beyond, edited by Amartya Sen and Bernard Williams (1982); Henry R. West, An Introduction to Mill's Utilitarian Ethics (2004); Candace A. Vogler, John Stuart Mill's Deliberative Landscape: An Essay in Moral Psychology (2001); Bernard Semmel, John Stuart Mill and the Pursuit of Virtue (1984); Fred R. Berger, Happiness, Justice and Freedom: The Moral and Political Philosophy of John Stuart Mill (1984); and Wendy Donner, The Liberal Self: John Stuart Mill's Moral and Political Philosophy (1991).

Biographies of Mill that are worth consulting include Bruce Mazlish, James and John Stuart Mill: Father and Son in the Nineteenth Century (1975); William Stafford, John Stuart Mill (1998); Nicholas Capaldi, John Stuart Mill: A Biography (2004); Richard Reeves, John Stuart Mill: Victorian Firebrand (2007); and Janice Carlisle, John Stuart Mill and the Writing of Character (2010). And anyone interested in Mill's life should also consult his Autobiography (1873), which Mill completed shortly before his death (see especially Jack Stillinger's 1969 edition).

Nietzsche, Friedrich

Most of the works Nietzsche published or intended for publication were translated into English in the early years of the twentieth century, and all of his major works now exist in multiple translations. Nietzsche published his first book, The Birth of Tragedy, in 1872 at the age of 27. He next published a series of four long essays—including On the Uses and Disadvantages of History for Life and Schopenhauer as Educator (both 1874)—that he later gathered together and republished under the title Unzeitgemässe Betrachtungen (usually translated Untimely Meditations). A useful translated collection of unpublished writings and notebook entries from that same period—including the essay "On Truth and Lie in a Nonmoral Sense"—is Philosophy and Truth, edited by Daniel Breazeale (1979).

Nietzsche's second book, Human, All Too Human, a collection of aphorisms, appeared in

1878. He published two further short collections of aphorisms in 1879 and 1880, the second of which first appeared under the title *The Wanderer and His Shadow*. They both were incorporated into a subsequent edition of *Human, All Too Human* as its second volume. *Daybreak* [or *Dawn*]: *Thoughts on the Prejudices of Morality* (1881) and *The Gay Science* (or *Joyful Wisdom*, 4-part [or "book"] version, 1882) are also aphoristic volumes. He referred to these books as his "free spirit series." They are commonly called the works of his "middle period."

Nietzsche's next publications, unlike anything he had written previously, were the first two parts (published separately) of his literary-philosophical masterpiece, *Thus Spoke Zarathustra* (1883), followed by a third part a year later (1884). Its fourth and final part was written and printed privately in the following year (1885). (It and the first four-part edition were not published publicly until 1892, after his collapse, by his sister.) Nietzsche then returned to a somewhat aphoristic prose style with *Beyond Good and Evil: Prelude to a Philosophy of the Future* (1886). In the same year he republished all of his pre-*Zarathustra* works, repackaging some of them into his books from that period as we know them (the four-essay *Untimely Meditations* and the two-volume *Human, All Too Human*), and supplying all volumes with substantial and significant new prefaces.

Nietzsche then published a second edition of *The Gay Science* with a new fifth "book" (part) and a new preface (1887), and *On the Genealogy of Morals* (1887). A final flurry of works were written in 1888—*Twilight of the Idols* (1888), *The Case of Wagner* (1888), *The Antichrist* (better, *The Antichristian*, published 1895), and the autobiographical *Ecce Homo* (published 1908). Another volume was published in Nietzsche's name after his death under the grand title *The Will to Power* (1901). He did contemplate writing such a masterwork—even announcing it (in *Genealogy*) as "a work in progress"—but never did so. This volume is merely a selection and rearrangement of material from his notebooks from 1883 onward (a small sampling of which is included in this volume). The standard German edition of Nietzsche's books and other writings (including those not published before his collapse in 1889) is the *Kritische Gesamtausgabe: Werke* (KGW; 30 vols., 1967–96), reprinted in paperback (the more commonly used version) as the *Kritische Studienausgabe* (KSA; 15 vols.).

The secondary literature on Nietzsche in English is vast. Works about Nietzsche began appearing at the turn of the twentieth century, shortly after his death. Journalists, poets, and radical political magazines began popularizing his ideas but did so with little scholarly rigor. The Nietzsche vogue from around 1900 to the

early 1930s came to an end with the rise of Nazism and, eventually, the Second World War. George Allen Morgan Jr.'s *What Nietzsche Means* (1941) and Walter Kaufmann's *Nietzsche: Philosopher, Psychologist, Antichrist* (1950; 4th ed., 1974) are two presentations of his thought that prepared the way for his post–World War II rehabilitation and remain useful introductions to his thought. Important studies that followed include Arthur C. Danto, *Nietzsche as Philosopher* (1967); Ruediger Hermann Grimm, *Nietzsche's Theory of Knowledge* (1977); Bernd Magnus, *Nietzsche's Existential Imperative* (1978); Richard Schacht, *Nietzsche* (1983); and Alexander Nehamas, *Nietzsche: Life as Literature* (1985). During this same period English translations of interpretations of Nietzsche by a number of important European philosophers also appeared: see Karl Jaspers, *Nietzsche: An Introduction to the Understanding of His Philosophical Activity* (1936; trans. 1965); Martin Heidegger, *Nietzsche* (2 vols., 1961; trans. 4 vols., 1979–87), based on lectures from the 1930s; Gilles Deleuze, *Nietzsche and Philosophy* (1962; trans. 1983); and Jacques Derrida, *Spurs: Nietzsche's Styles* (1978; trans. 1979).

Informative biographical studies include R. J. Hollingdale, *Nietzsche: The Man and His Philosophy* (1965; rev. ed., 1999); J. P. Stern, *Friedrich Nietzsche* (1978); Lesley Chamberlain, *Nietzsche in Turin: An Intimate Biography* (1996); Gary Elsner, *Nietzsche: A Philosophical Biography* (1992); Curtis Cate, *Friedrich Nietzsche* (2002); Rüdiger Safranski, *Nietzsche: A Philosophical Biography* (2000; trans. 2002); Thomas H. Brobjer, *Nietzsche's Philosophical Context: An Intellectual Biography* (2008); and Julian Young, *Friedrich Nietzsche: A Philosophical Biography* (2010). Two works on early influences on Nietzsche's thought are Thomas H. Brobjer, *Nietzsche and the "English": The Influence of British and American Thinking on His Philosophy* (2007), and Jessica N. Berry, *Nietzsche and the Ancient Skeptical Tradition* (2011). Jennifer Ratner-Rosenhagen's *American Nietzsche: A History of an Icon and His Ideas* (2012) is a historical account of Nietzsche's early reception in America.

There are many sorts of general introduction to Nietzsche: see, for example, Richard Schacht, *Making Sense of Nietzsche: Reflections Timely and Untimely* (1995); Robert Wicks, *Nietzsche: A Beginner's Guide* (2010); Ullrich Haase, *Starting with Nietzsche* (2008); Peter R. Sedgwick, *Nietzsche: The Key Concepts* (2009); Lucy Huskinson, *An Introduction to Nietzsche* (2009); Rebekah S. Peery, *Nietzsche for the 21st Century* (2009); and *Introductions to Nietzsche*, edited by Robert B. Pippin (2012), a collection of introductions to the works of Nietzsche in English translation. There are also introductory guides to almost all of Nietzsche's major works, including Douglas Burnham and Martin Jesinghausen, *Nietzsche's "The Birth of Tragedy": A Reader's Guide* (2010); Simon May, *Nietzsche's "On the Genealogy of Morality": A Critical Guide* (2011); Lawrence J. Hatab, *Nietzsche's "On the Genealogy of Morality": An Introduction* (2008); Clancy Martin and Daw-Nay Evans, *Nietzsche's 'Thus Spoke Zarathustra': A Reader's Guide* (2014); Christa Davis Acampora and Keith Ansell Pearson, *Nietzsche's "Beyond Good and Evil": A Reader's Guide* (2011); Daniel Conway, *Nietzsche's "On the Genealogy of Morals": A Reader's Guide* (2008); and Douglas Burnham and Martin Jesinghausen, *Nietzsche's "Thus Spoke Zarathustra"* (2010).

For more detailed studies of specific works, see Paul Raimond Daniels, *Nietzsche and "The Birth of Tragedy"* (2013); Jonathan R. Cohen, *Science, Culture, and Free Spirits: A Study of Nietzsche's "Human, All Too Human"* (2009); Monika M. Langer, *Nietzsche's "Gay Science": Dancing Coherence* (2010); Paul Franco, *Nietzsche's Enlightenment: The Free-Spirit Trilogy of the Middle Period* (2011); Ruth Abbey, *Nietzsche's Middle Period* (2000); James Luchte, *Nietzsche's "Thus Spoke Zarathustra": Before Sunrise* (2008); Kathleen Marie Higgins, *Nietzsche's "Zarathustra"* (rev. ed., 2010); Paul S. Loeb, *The Death of Nietzsche's Zarathustra* (2010); Maudemarie Clark and David Dudrick, *The Soul of Nietzsche's "Beyond Good and Evil"* (2012); Christopher Janaway, *Beyond Selflessness: Reading Nietzsche's "Genealogy"* (2007); and *Nietzsche's "Ecce Homo,"* edited by Duncan Large and Nicholas Martin (2013).

Nietzsche's postmoralist thinking with respect to a broad range of issues is explored in two volumes of essays edited by Richard Schacht: *Nietzsche's Postmoralism: Essays on Nietzsche's Prelude to Philosophy's Future* (2001) and *Nietzsche, Genealogy, Morality: Essays on Nietzsche's "On the Genealogy of Morals"* (1994). Other works that concentrate on ethics, values, and virtue theory include Brian Leiter, *Routledge Philosophy Guidebook to Nietzsche on Morality* (2002); Lester H. Hunt, *Nietzsche and the Origin of Virtue* (1991); Simon May, *Nietzsche's Ethics and His 'War on Morality'* (1999); E. E. Sleinis, *Nietzsche's Revaluation of Values: A Study in Strategies* (1994); Richard J. White, *Nietzsche and the Problem of Sovereignty* (1997); Leslie Paul Thiele, *Friedrich Nietzsche and the Politics of the Soul: A Study of Heroic Individualism* (1990); Peter Berkowitz, *Nietzsche: The Ethics of an Immoralist* (1995); Keith Ansell-Pearson, *Nietzsche contra Rousseau: A Study of Nietzsche's Moral and Political Thought* (1991); and Bernard Reginster, *The Affirmation of Life: Nietzsche on Overcoming Nihilism* (2006). Among more recent volumes on Nie-

tzsche's ethics are Paul E. Kirkland, *Nietzsche's Noble Aims: Affirming Life, Contesting Modernity* (2009); Michael Ure, *Nietzsche's Therapy: Self-Cultivation in the Middle Works* (2008); Craig M. Dove, *Nietzsche's Ethical Theory: Mind, Self and Responsibility* (2008); *Nietzsche and Morality*, edited by Brian Leiter and Neil Sinhababu (2009); Peter R. Sedgwick, *Nietzsche's Justice: Naturalism in Search of an Ethics* (2013); Paul Katsafanas, *Agency and the Foundations of Ethics: Nietzschean Constitutivism* (2013); and *Nietzsche, Naturalism, and Normativity*, edited by Christopher Janaway and Simon Robertson (2012).

Nietzsche's political thought is discussed in Keith Ansell-Pearson, *An Introduction to Nietzsche as Political Thinker: The Perfect Nihilist* (1994); Daniel W. Conway, *Nietzsche's Dangerous Game: Philosophy in the Twilight of the Idols* (2002) and *Nietzsche and the Political* (1997); Bruce Detwiler, *Nietzsche and the Politics of Aristocratic Radicalism* (1990); Fredrick Appel, *Nietzsche Contra Democracy* (1999); Peter Bergmann, *Nietzsche, "The Last Antipolitical German"* (1987); Lawrence J. Hatab, *A Nietzschean Defense of Democracy: An Experiment in Postmodern Politics* (1995); Alex McIntyre, *The Sovereignty of Joy: Nietzsche's Vision of Grand Politics* (1997); Mark Warren, *Nietzsche and Political Thought* (1988); and Tracy B. Strong, *Friedrich Nietzsche and the Politics of Transfiguration* (3rd ed., 2000).

This topic continues to generate significant scholarship; see Christian J. Emden, *Friedrich Nietzsche and the Politics of History* (2008); *Nietzsche and Political Thought*, edited by Keith Ansell-Pearson (2008); *Nietzsche, Power and Politics: Rethinking Nietzsche's Legacy for Political Thought*, edited by Herman W. Siemans and Vasti Roodt (2008); Tamsin Shaw, *Nietzsche's Political Skepticism* (2010); Alex McIntyre, *The Sovereignty of Joy: Nietzsche's Vision of Grand Politics* (1997); and Vanessa Lemm, *Nietzsche's Animal Philosophy: Culture, Politics, and the Animality of the Human Being* (2009).

Studies of the general character of Nietzsche's thought from analytic orientations include Maudemarie Clark, *Nietzsche on Truth and Philosophy* (1990); John Richardson, *Nietzsche's System* (1996) and *Nietzsche's New Darwinism* (2004); Peter Poellner, *Nietzsche and Metaphysics* (1995); Christoph Cox, *Nietzsche: Naturalism and Interpretation* (1999); and Steven D. Hales and Rex Welshon, *Nietzsche's Perspectivism* (2000). For recent works on topics of a metaphysical or epistemological nature, see *Nietzsche on Freedom and Autonomy*, edited by Ken Gemes and Simon May (2009); John Mandalios, *Nietzsche and the Necessity of Freedom* (2008); *Nietzsche on Time and History*, edited by Manuel Dries (2008); Anthony K. Jensen, *Nietzsche's Philosophy of History* (2013); Robin Small, *Time and Becoming in Nietzsche's Thought* (2010); Dirk Johnson, *Nietzsche's Anti-Darwinism* (2010); Manuel Dries, *Nietzsche on Consciousness and the Embodied Mind* (2013); Christian J. Emden, *Nietzsche on Language, Consciousness, and the Body* (2005); and Laird Addis, *Nietzsche's Ontology* (2012).

Examinations of Nietzsche from a feminist perspective include *Nietzsche, Feminism and Political Theory*, edited by Paul Patton (1993); Frances Nesbitt Oppel, *Nietzsche on Gender: Beyond Man and Woman* (2005); *Feminist Interpretations of Friedrich Nietzsche*, edited by Kelly Oliver and Marilyn Pearsall (1998); and Kelly Oliver, *Womanizing Nietzsche: Philosophy's Relation to the "Feminine"* (1994).

A growing number of noteworthy studies of Nietzsche by European authors have recently become available in English translation, including Karl Löwith, *Nietzsche's Philosophy of the Eternal Recurrence of the Same* (1935, 3rd ed. 1978; trans. 1997); Wolfgang Müller-Lauter, *Nietzsche: His Philosophy of Contradictions and the Contradictions of His Philosophy* (1971; trans. 1999); Sarah Kofman, *Nietzsche and Metaphor* (1972, 2nd ed. 1983; trans. 1993); Pierre Klossowski, *Nietzsche and the Vicious Circle* (1969; trans. 1997); Eric Blondel, *Nietzsche, the Body and Culture: Philosophy as a Philological Genealogy* (1986; trans. 1991); Eugen Fink, *Nietzsche's Philosophy* (1960; trans. 1999); and Mazzino Montinari, *Reading Nietzsche* (1982; trans. 2003).

Other useful volumes of essays on Nietzsche include *Nietzsche: A Collection of Critical Essays*, edited by Robert C. Solomon (1973); *Reading Nietzsche*, edited by Robert C. Solomon and Kathleen M. Higgins (1988); *The Cambridge Companion to Nietzsche*, edited by Bernd Magnus and Kathleen M. Higgins (1996); *Nietzsche: A Critical Reader*, edited by Peter R. Sedgwick (1995); *A Companion to Nietzsche*, edited by Keith Ansell Pearson (2006); *Nietzsche, Nihilism and the Philosophy of the Future*, edited by Jeffrey Metzger (2009); and *Exceedingly Nietzsche: Aspects of Contemporary Nietzsche-Interpretation*, edited by David Farrell Krell and David Wood (2010). Two recent volumes of particular interest and value are *A Companion to Nietzsche*, edited by Keith Ansell Pearson (2006), and *The Oxford Handbook of Nietzsche*, edited by Ken Gemes and John Richardson (2013).

Nussbaum, Martha

Nussbaum's written books are listed and discussed in her headnote, above. She also has co-edited a considerable number of books, including *The Quality of Life*, with Amartya Sen (1993); *Animal Rights: Current Debates and New Directions*, with Cass R. Sunstein (2004); *The Offensive Internet: Speech, Privacy, and Reputation*, with Saul Levmore (2012); *Rawls's "Political Liberalism*," with Thom Brooks (2015); *Pluralism and Democracy in India: Debating the Hindu Right*, with Wendy Doniger (2015); *Sexual Orientation and Human Rights in American Religious Discourse*, with Saul M. Olyan (1998); *Essays on Aristotle's "De Anima*," with Amélie Oksenberg Rorty (1995); *Clones and Clones: Facts and Fantasies about Human Cloning*, with Cass R. Sunstein (1998); *The Sleep of Reason: Erotic Experience and Sexual Ethics in Ancient Greece and Rome*, with Juha Sihvola (2013); *American Guy: Masculinity in American Law and Literature*, with Saul Levmore (2014); and *Capabilities, Gender, Equality: Towards Fundamental Entitlements*, with Flavio Comim (2014).

Many of the major secondary works on Nussbaum's thought consider her "capabilities approach" to assessing human life. They include John M. Alexander, *Capabilities and Social Justice: The Political Philosophy of Amartya Sen and Martha Nussbaum* (2008); Séverine Deneulin, *Wellbeing, Justice, and Development Ethics* (2014); Christopher A. Riddle, *Disability and Justice: The Capabilities Approach in Practice* (2014); Ashmita Khasnabish, *Negotiating Capability and Diaspora: A Philosophical Politics* (2014); and *An Aristotelian Feminism*, by Sarah Borden Sharkey (2016). Her work on philosophy and literature is discussed in Peter Johnson, *Moral Philosophers and the Novel: A Study of Winch, Nussbaum and Rorty* (2004). Her work on love is discussed in Robert J. Fitterer, *Love and Objectivity in Virtue Ethics: Aristotle, Lonergan, and Nussbaum on Emotions and Moral Insight* (2008), and in Ronald Hall, *The Human Embrace: The Love of Philosophy and the Philosophy of Love: Kierkegaard, Cavell, Nussbaum* (2000).

Plessner, Helmuth

Only two of Plessner's major works have been translated into English: *The Limits of Community: A Critique of Social Radicalism* (trans. 1999), originally published in 1924 as *Grenzen der Gemeinschaft: Ein Kritik des sozialen Radikalismus* (also in *Gesammelte Schriften* [*Collected Writings*], vol. 5, 1981), and *Laughing and Crying: A Study of the Limits of Human Behavior* (trans. 1970), originally published in 1941 as *Lachen und Weinen: Eine Untersuchung der Grenzen menschlichen Verhaltens* (in GS 7, 1982). A few of his essays—including "The Social Conditions of Modern Painting" (trans. 1970), "A Newton of a Blade of Grass?" (trans. 1969), "De homine abscondito" (trans. 1969), and "On Human Expression" (trans. 1964)—have been translated in various collections.

None of Plessner's early works (many of which focus on the philosophy of Kant) have been translated; they are contained in the GS 1–2 (1980–81). Among them are *Die Wissenschaftliche Idee: Ein Entwurf über ihre Form* (1913, *The Scientific Idea: An Outline of Its Form*); *Krisis der transzendentalen Wahrheit im Anfang* (1918, *Crisis Concerning the Origin of Transcendental Truth*); "Untersuchungen zu einer Kritik der philosophischen Urteilskraft" (1920, "Studies toward a Critique of the Philosophical Faculty of Judgment"); and "Kants System unter dem Gesichtspunkt einer Erkenntnistheorie der Philosophie" (1923, "Kant's System of Philosophy considered from the Viewpoint of a Theory of Knowledge"). Also untranslated are his two important early books on the nature of the senses, collected in GS 3 (1980): *Die Einheit der Sinne: Grundlinien einer Ästhesiologie des Geistes* (1923, *The Unity of the Senses: Grounding an Aesthesiology of Geist*), and *Anthropologie der Sinne* (1970, *Anthropology of the Senses*).

Most unfortunately, there is no English translation of Plessner's most important work, *Die Stufen des Organischen und der Mensch* (1928, *The Levels of the Organic and Man*), one of the foundational works of philosophical anthropology (reprinted as GS 4, 1981). The monograph *Macht und menschliche Natur* (1931, *Power and Human Nature*; in GS 5, 1981) extends his philosophical anthropology beyond its initial focus on the philosophy of biology to what he calls a political anthropology. His more political-historical writings are contained in GS 7 (1982) and have not been translated.

The last four volumes of Plessner's collected works (vols. 7–10, 1982–85) contain all of his shorter essays, written and published from the early 1920s up to the time of his death. They range over many different topics. Most important are those that continue his work in philosophical anthropology, including such monographs as "Das Lächeln" (1959, "The Smile") and *Conditio Humana* (1964, *The Human Condition*). His many essays on the philosophy of music—on its relation to the senses and its phenomenology, as well as an analysis of music from his anthropological perspective—also deserve attention. These volumes also contain essays on language, expression, animals, play, death, the theory of drives and passions, knowledge, art (particularly modern art), and the problem of modernity, as well as essays by Plessner on other thinkers, including Edmund Husserl, Nicolai Hartmann, and Adolf Portmann. The final volume of his collected works contains his various writings on sociology and social philosophy.

As lamentable as the unavailability of most of his writings in English translation is the neglect of Plessner in the English-language secondary literature. There are no complete studies of his thought, but his longtime American champion Marjorie Grene has written two excellent essays: "Helmuth Plessner," in her *Approaches to a Philosophical Biology* (1968), and "The Characters of Living Things III: Helmuth Plessner's Theory of Organic Models," in her *The Understanding of Nature: Essays in the Philosophy of Biology* (1974).

For more sources related to Plessner, see the bibliography section on philosophical anthropology in General Bibliographies (above).

Ricoeur, Paul

Ricoeur's first book was written with Mikel Dufrenne: *Karl Jaspers et la philosophie de l'existence* (1947, *Karl Jaspers and the Philosophy of Existence*). It has not been translated—nor, surprisingly, has his second, *Gabriel Marcel et Karl Jaspers: Philosophie du mystère et philosophie du paradoxe* (1947, *Gabriel Marcel and Karl Jaspers: Philosophy of Mystery and Philosophy of Paradox*). His earliest work available in English is *Philosophie de la volonté: Le volontaire et l'involontaire* (1949, *Philosophy of the Will: The Voluntary and the Involuntary*), translated as *Freedom and Nature: The Voluntary and the Involuntary* (1966; new ed., 2007). A lecture course given in 1953–54 was recently published as *Being, Essence and Substance in Plato and Aristotle* (2011; trans. 2013). His "philosophy of the will" is further developed in *Fallible Man* (1960; trans. 1965) and *The Symbolism of Evil* (1960; trans. 1967). *History and Truth* (1955; trans. 1965), a collection of essays, has appeared in several French editions.

Freud and Philosophy: An Essay on Interpretation (1965; trans. 1970), which grew out of the 1961 Terry Lectures delivered at Yale, remains one of Ricoeur's most popular works. *On Psychoanalysis*, vol. 1, *Writings and Lectures* (2008; trans. 2012), is a related collection of essays and lectures. *Husserl: An Analysis of His Phenomenology* (1967; new ed., 2007) is a translation collecting various articles that he published on Husserl, including his 1950 introduction to his French translation of Husserl's *Ideas*. His commentary that accompanied that translation is also available in English as *A Key to Husserl's Ideas I* (1996).

The Conflict of Interpretations: Essays in Hermeneutics (1969; trans. 1974, new ed. 2007) is an important book that extends the analyses of the previous works but makes Ricoeur's methodology clearer. Another collection of essays, *Hermeneutics: Writings and Lectures*, vol. 2 (2010; trans. 2013), is also available. *The Rule of Metaphor: Multi-Disciplinary Studies of the Creation of Meaning in Language* (1975; trans. 1977) marks the "linguistic turn" (or perhaps, better expressed, the "hermeneutic turn") in his philosophy. Another work of this period is *Interpretation Theory: Discourse and the Surplus of Meaning* (1976), which contains lectures originally written and delivered in English in 1973. *From Text to Action* (1986; trans. 1991), a supplement to *The Conflict of Interpretations*, contains a number of important essays on the history of philosophy, action theory, the imagination, and ethics. Two other important collections translating essays largely from the 1970s, originally published elsewhere, are *Political and Social Essays* (1974) and *Hermeneutics and the Human Sciences: Essays on Language, Action and Interpretation* (1981).

Ricoeur's monumental *Time and Narrative* was published in three volumes (1983–85; trans. 1984–88). Two sets of lectures that he gave around this time are also available in English: *Lectures on Ideology and Utopia* (1986), an impressive analysis of Marx, Althusser, Weber, and Habermas (among others), and *The Reality of the Historical Past* (1984). Ricoeur's important late works include *Oneself as Another* (1990; trans. 1992), *The Just* (1995; trans. 2000), *Reflections on the Just* (2001; trans. 2007), *Memory, History, Forgetting* (2000; trans. 2004), and *The Course of Recognition* (2004; trans. 2005). Two smaller works are *On Translation* (2004; trans. 2006) and, with Jean-Pierre Changeux, *What Makes Us Think? A Neuroscientist and a Philosopher Argue about Ethics, Human Nature, and the Brain* (1998; trans. 2000).

Ricoeur's main works on religion are *Evil: A Challenge to Philosophy and Theology* (1986; trans. 2007); *Figuring the Sacred: Religion, Narrative, and Imagination* (1995), which translates essays written between 1970 to 1995; *Essays on Biblical Interpretation* (1980), which translates essays published between 1974 and 1979; and, with André LaCocque, *Thinking Biblically: Exegetical and Hermeneutical Studies* (1998; trans. 1998). *Living Up to Death* (2007; trans. 2009), written in 1996, was not published until after his death.

For useful introductory overviews of Ricoeur's thought, see Karl Simms, *Paul Ricoeur* (2003); Mark Muldoon, *On Ricoeur* (2002); and David Pellauer, *Ricoeur: A Guide for the Perplexed* (2007). In the Library of Living Philosophers Series, *The Philosophy of Paul Ricoeur*, edited by Lewis Edwin Hahn (1995), contains many valuable scholarly essays on Ricoeur's thought as well as his response to them. Other collections of essays on Ricoeur (not all of which are still in print) include *On Paul Ricoeur: Narrative and Interpretation*, edited by David Wood (1991); *Studies in the Philosophy of Paul Ricoeur*, edited by Charles E. Reagan (1979); *The Narrative Path: The Later Works of Paul Ricoeur*, edited by T. Peter Kemp and David Rasmussen (1989); *Between Suspicion and Sympathy: Paul*

Ricoeur's Unstable Equilibrium, edited by Andrzej Wierciński (2003); *Paul Ricoeur and Narrative: Context and Contestation*, edited by Morny Joy (1997); and *Meanings in Texts and Action: Questioning Paul Ricoeur*, edited by David E. Klemm and William Schweiker (1993).

Several more recent volumes are *Ricoeur across the Disciplines*, edited by Scott Davidson (2010); *Reading Ricoeur*, edited by David M. Kaplan (2008); *A Passion for the Possible: Thinking with Paul Ricoeur*, edited by Brian Treanor and Henry Isaac Venema (2010); and *Paul Ricoeur: Honoring and Continuing the Work*, edited by Farhang Erfani (2011). *Paul Ricoeur: The Hermeneutics of Action*, edited by Richard Kearney (1996), contains three important essays by Ricoeur: "Reflections on a New Ethos for Europe" (1992), "Fragility and Responsibility" (1992), and "Love and Justice" (1990).

Substantial studies of Ricoeur's thought include S. H. Clark, *Paul Ricoeur* (1990); Don Ihde, *Hermeneutic Phenomenology: The Philosophy of Paul Ricoeur* (1971); Jeanne Evans, *Paul Ricoeur's Hermeneutics of the Imagination* (1995); Henry Isaac Venema, *Identifying Selfhood: Imagination, Narrative, and Hermeneutics in the Thought of Paul Ricoeur* (2000); David M. Kaplan, *Ricoeur's Critical Theory* (2003); Domenico Jervolino, *The Cogito and Hermeneutics: The Question of the Subject in Ricoeur* (1984; trans. 1990); Richard Kearney, *On Paul Ricoeur: The Owl of Minerva* (2004); and William C. Dowling, *Ricoeur on Time and Narrative: An Introduction to "Temps et récit"* (2011).

A number of studies deal with Ricoeur in the context of hermeneutics more generally: see *Gadamer and Ricoeur: Critical Horizons for Contemporary Hermeneutics*, edited by Francis J. Mootz III and George H. Taylor (2011); Bengt Kristensson Uggla, *Ricoeur, Hermeneutics, and Globalization* (2010); and Alison Scott-Baumann, *Ricoeur and the Hermeneutics of Suspicion* (2009). Works in which Ricoeur is discussed in relation to poststructuralism are Declan Sheerin, *Deleuze and Ricoeur: Disavowed Affinities and the Narrative Self* (2009); Eftichis Pirovlakis, *Reading Derrida and Ricoeur: Improbable Encounters between Deconstruction and Hermeneutics* (2010); and Gert-Jan van der Heiden, *The Truth (and Untruth) of Language: Heidegger, Ricoeur, and Derrida on Disclosure and Displacement* (2010). Ricoeur's work is discussed in relation to Habermas's in John B. Thompson, *Critical Hermeneutics: A Study in the Thought of Paul Ricoeur and Jürgen Habermas* (1981).

Ricoeur's ethical and political thought is explored in John Wall, *Moral Creativity: Paul Ricoeur and the Politics of Possibility* (2005), and W. David Hall, *Paul Ricoeur and the Poetic Imperative: The Creative Tension between Love and Justice* (2008). It is also discussed in *Paul Ricoeur and Contemporary Moral Thought*, edited by John Wall, William Schweiker, and W. David Hall (2002); Bernard P. Dauenhauer, *Paul Ricoeur: The Promise and Risk of Politics* (1998); *Ricoeur as Another: Ethics of Subjectivity*, edited by Richard A. Cohen and James L. Marsh (2002); Molly Harkirat Mann, *Ricoeur, Rawls, and Capability Justice: Civic Phronēsis and Equality* (2012); *Paul Ricoeur and the Task of Political Philosophy*, edited by Greg S. Johnson and Dan R. Stiver (2012); and *From Ricoeur to Action: The Socio-political Significance of Ricoeur's Thinking*, edited by Todd S. Mei and David Lewin (2012).

Works on Ricoeur's thought focusing on its relation to religion and theology include Gregory J. Laughery, *Living Hermeneutics in Motion: An Analysis and Evaluation of Paul Ricoeur's Contribution to Biblical Hermeneutics* (2002); Dan R. Stiver, *Theology after Ricoeur: New Directions in Hermeneutical Theology* (2001) and *Ricoeur and Theology* (2012); *Memory, Narrativity, Self and the Challenge to Think God: The Reception within Theology of the Recent Work of Paul Ricoeur*, edited by Maureen Junker-Kenny and Peter Kenny (2004); Boyd Blundell, *Paul Ricoeur between Theology and Philosophy: Detour and Return* (2010); Lance B. Pape, *The Scandal of Having Something to Say: Ricoeur and the Possibility of Postliberal Preaching* (2013); and Kenneth A. Reynhout, *Interdisciplinary Interpretation: Paul Ricoeur and the Hermeneutics of Theology and Science* (2013).

Ricoeur's *Critique and Conviction: Conversations with François Azouvi and Marc de Launay* (1995; trans. 1998) is a partially autobiographical and partially philosophical reflection on his life and work. Charles E. Reagan's *Paul Ricoeur: His Life and His Work* (1996) contains interviews with Ricoeur, as well as a biographical and interpretive essay.

Sartre, Jean-Paul

Sartre's philosophical work began with *The Imagination* (1936; trans. 1962 and 2012), *The Transcendence of the Ego: An Existentialist Theory of Consciousness* (1936; trans. 1957), *The Emotions: Outline of a Theory* (1939; trans. 1948), and *The Imaginary: A Phenomenological Psychology of the Imagination* (1940; trans. 2004 [trans. 1948 as *The Psychology of Imagination*]). These works were followed by *Being and Nothingness* (1943; trans. 1956). Sartre's own best introduction to his existentialist thought is his 1945 lecture "Existentialism and Humanism" (1946; trans. 1948), sometimes titled "Existentialism Is a Humanism" or simply "Existentialism." It was first published in *Existentialism*, a book that also contains a transcription of the question-and-answer period after his lecture.

This lecture, together with some selections from *Being and Nothingness*, has also been published in *Existentialism and Human Emotions* (1957). Sartre's *Anti-Semite and Jew* (1946; trans. 1948), an account of racism in postwar France, also illuminates his own thought on authentic and inauthentic ways of responding to one's situation. Essays from this time are translated in the recent collection *The Aftermath of the War* (2008).

Two other works, published posthumously, show Sartre continuing to explore and develop the ontology laid out in *Being and Nothingness*, before his philosophy underwent a dramatic change: *Truth and Existence* (1989; trans. 1992), written in 1948 as a response to Heidegger, and *Notebooks for an Ethics* (1983; trans. 1992), written in 1947 and 1948. Selections from Sartre's early and middle pre-Marxist period are collected in *Essays in Existentialism* (1965).

Sartre's second period begins with *Search for a Method* (1957; trans. 1963), in which existentialism is seen as merely a corrective to certain forms of misguided Marxism. This work is included as the introduction to his great late work *Critique of Dialectical Reason: Theory of Practical Ensembles* (1960; trans. 1976). The second, unfinished volume of the *Critique*, subtitled *The Intelligibility of History*, was published posthumously (1985; trans. 1991). Two collections of essays and interviews from this period of Sartre's authorship are quite helpful in understanding these imposing works: *Between Existentialism and Marxism* (*Situations* 8 and 9, 1972; trans. 1974) and *Life/Situations: Essays Written and Spoken* (*Situations* 10, 1976; trans. 1977). *Colonialism and Neo-colonialism* (*Situations* 5, 1964; trans. 2001) collects some of Sartre's political writings from this period, including his famous preface to Frantz Fanon's *The Wretched of the Earth* (1961)

Another collection of essays from Sartre's 10-volume *Situations* series is *We Only Have This Life to Live: Selected Essays of Jean-Paul Sartre, 1939–1975* (2013); see also *Critical Essays* (*Situations* 1, 1947; trans. 2010) and *Portraits: Situations IV* (1964; trans. 2009), a volume partially translated in *Situations* (1965). There are also two as-yet unpublished sets of lectures and notes devoted to the development of an ethics, one prepared for a 1964 lecture in Rome and the other intended for a 1965 lecture at Cornell University that was never delivered. Recently a series of interviews from the early 1970s has been made available as *Talking with Sartre* (2009); a final controversial interview was published as *Hope Now: The 1980 Interviews* (1991; trans. 1994).

Sartre's literary and philosophical interests came together in many works of both criticism and what might be thought of as philosophical-intellectual biographies of literary authors. A number of them are published in the *Situations* series; for translations, see *Literary Essays* (1955) and *Literary and Philosophical Essays* (1955), as well as *Situations* (1965). This conjunction of interests also finds significant expression in *What Is Literature?* (1948; trans. 1949 [also translated as *Literature and Existentialism*]). Sartre's literary biographies are *Baudelaire* (1946; trans. 1949); *Saint Genet, Actor and Martyr* (1952; trans. 1963), which provides much insight into his thinking on ethics in the late 1940s and early '50s; and *The Family Idiot: Gustave Flaubert, 1821–1857* (3 vols., 1971–72; trans., 5 vols., 1981–93). Sartre's first screenplay from the 1940s, the never-filmed *Typhus* (2007; trans. 2010), was recently discovered; another script discovered after Sartre's death was *The Freud Scenario* (1984; trans. 2013), written in the late 1950s.

The Words (1964; trans. 1964) is an autobiographical work; *The War Diaries: Notebooks from a Phoney War, November 1939–March 1940* (1983; trans. 1984) contains both autobiographical and philosophical writings. Similarly biographical and philosophical are the interviews with Sartre collected in Simone de Beauvoir's *Adieux: A Farewell to Sartre* (1981; trans. 1984). His letters to her are published in *Witness to My Life: The Letters of Jean-Paul Sartre to Simone de Beauvoir, 1926–1939* (1983; trans. 1992) and *Quiet Moments in a War: The Letters of Jean-Paul Sartre to Simone de Beauvoir, 1940–1963* (1983; trans. 1993).

Sartre's literary output began with his novel *Nausea* (1938; trans. 1949) and a volume of short stories, *The Wall, and Other Stories* (1939; trans. 1948). Several of Sartre's most famous plays, including *The Flies* (produced 1943), are collected in *No Exit and Three Other Plays* (1955, separately published 1942–48; trans. 1947–49). Sartre began a 4-volume novel series titled *Roads to Freedom*; he completed *The Age of Reason* (1945; trans. 1947), *The Reprieve* (1945; trans. 1947), and *Troubled Sleep* (1949; trans. 1950 in England as *Iron in the Soul* [the literal French title is "Death in the Soul"]). After his death the incomplete fourth volume appeared as *The Last Chance* (1981; trans. 2009); he himself published one chapter from it, "Strange Friendship," in 1949. Three important later plays are *The Devil and the Good Lord* (1951; trans. 1952 as *Lucifer and the Lord*), *The Condemned of Altona* (1960; trans. 1961), and *The Trojan Women* (1965; trans. 1967).

Sartre's life (including his relationship with Beauvoir) may be the best documented of any philosopher in history. For biographies, see Ronald Hayman, *Sartre: A Life* (1987); Annie Cohen-Solal, *Sartre: A Life* (1985; trans. 1987); John Gerassi, *Jean-Paul Sartre: Hated Conscience of His Century*, vol. 1, *Protestant or Protester?* (1989); Philip Thody, *Sartre: A Biographical Introduction* (1971); and David Drake, *Sartre* (2005). *Sartre and Camus: A Historic Confrontation*, edited by David A. Sprintzen and Adrian van den Hoven (2004), contains critical essays as well as work by both Sartre and Camus; the episode is chronicled by Ronald Aronson in *Camus and Sartre: The Story of a Friendship and the Quarrel That Ended It* (2004).

Introductory works include David Detmer, *Sartre Explained: From Bad Faith to Authenticity* (2008); Sebastian Gardner, *Sartre's "Being and Nothingness": A Reader's Guide* (2009); Katherine J. Morris, *Sartre* (2008); Jonathan Webber, *The Existentialism of Jean-Paul Sartre* (2009); Gail Linsenbard, *Starting with Sartre* (2010); Christine Daigle, *Jean-Paul Sartre* (2010); Anthony Hatzimoysis, *The Philosophy of Sartre* (2011); and *Jean-Paul Sartre: Key Concepts*, edited by Steven Churchill and Jack Reynolds (2013).

The Cambridge Companion to Sartre, edited by Christina Howells (1992), is an excellent philosophical survey of major topics in Sartre's work. *The Philosophy of Jean Paul-Sartre*, edited by Paul Arthur Schilpp (1981), in the Library of Living Philosophers series, contains an interview with Sartre and twenty-eight significant essays on his thought. *Sartre Alive*, edited by Ronald Aronson and Adrian van den Hoven (1991), also contains an interview with Sartre and many excellent critical essays. Important analyses of Sartre's thought include Peter Caws, *Sartre* (1979); Joseph S. Catalano, *Reading Sartre* (2010); and Christina Howells, *Sartre: The Necessity of Freedom* (1988). William Ralph Schroeder's *Sartre and His Predecessors: The Self and the Other* (1984) deals with Sartre's early existentialism and thinking on intersubjectivity. Among the works attempting to situate Sartre in relation to analytic philosophy are Kathleen Wider, *The Bodily Nature of Consciousness: Sartre and Contemporary Philosophy of Mind* (1997); Gregory McCulloch, *Using Sartre: An Analytical Introduction to Early Sartrean Themes* (1994); and Arthur C. Danto, *Jean-Paul Sartre* (1975), a classic study.

Wilfrid Desan's *The Tragic Finale: An Essay on the Philosophy of Jean-Paul Sartre* (1954; rev. ed., 1960) remains an excellent introduction to *Being and Nothingness*. Another work helpful in understanding this central text is Joseph S. Catalano, *A Commentary on Jean-Paul Sartre's "Being and Nothingness"* (1974). Classic criticisms of existentialism can be found in the works of Marjorie Grene, such as *Sartre* (1973) and *Dreadful Freedom: A Critique of Existentialism* (1948), and in such works by Iris Murdoch as *Sartre: Romantic Realist* (1953; 2nd ed., 1980). The work of Hazel E. Barnes, translator of several of Sartre's works, is also important; see especially *Sartre* (1973), *An Existentialist Ethics* (1967), and *Sartre and Flaubert* (1981). Gary Cox has written two helpful resources: *The Sartre Dictionary* (2008) and *Sartre and Fiction* (2009).

Many studies focus on the thought of the later Sartre. See Thomas R. Flynn, *Sartre and Marxist Existentialism: The Test Case of Collective Responsibility* (1984) and *Sartre, Foucault, and Historical Reason*, vol. 1, *Toward an Existentialist Theory of History* (1997), and vol. 2, *A Poststructuralist Mapping of History* (2005); R. D. Laing and D. G. Cooper, *Reason and Violence: A Decade of Sartre's Philosophy, 1950–1960* (1964); Joseph S. Catalano, *A Commentary on Jean-Paul Sartre's "Critique of Dialectical Reason," volume 1, "Theory of Practical Ensembles"* (1986); Raymond Aron, *History and the Dialectic of Violence: An Analysis of Sartre's "Critique de la raison dialectique"* (1975); and Wilfrid Desan, *The Marxism of Jean-Paul Sartre* (1965). Ronald Aronson's *Sartre's Second Critique* (1987) examines the second volume of the *Critique of Dialectical Reason*.

Other works on Sartre's political thought include Bill Martin, *The Radical Project: Sartrean Investigations* (2000); Andrew Dobson, *Jean-Paul Sartre and the Politics of Reason: A Theory of History* (1993); and Ronald E. Santoni, *Sartre on Violence: Curiously Ambivalent* (2003). The intersection of Sartre's political and philosophical thought with questions of race and colonialism is explored in Lewis R. Gordon, *Bad Faith and Antiblack Racism* (1995); *Race after Sartre: Antiracism, Africana Existentialism, Postcolonialism*, edited by Jonathan Judaken (2008); and Paige Arthur, *Unfinished Projects: Decolonization and the Philosophy of Jean-Paul Sartre* (2010).

One of the most significant works on Sartre's ethics is Thomas C. Anderson's *Sartre's Two Ethics: From Authenticity to Integral Humanity* (1993). Other works on this topic include Ronald E. Santoni, *Bad Faith, Good Faith, and Authenticity in Sartre's Early Philosophy* (1995); Linda A. Bell, *Sartre's Ethics of Authenticity* (1989); David Detmer, *Freedom as a Value: A Critique of the Ethical Theory of Jean-Paul Sartre* (1986); Joseph S. Catalano, *Good Faith and Other Essays: Perspectives on a Sartrean Ethics* (1996); T. Storm Heter, *Sartre's Ethics of Engagement: Authenticity and Civic Virtue* (2006); and Sorin Baiasu, *Kant and Sartre: Re-discovering Critical Ethics* (2011). Other works worth consulting include Robert C. Solomon, *Dark Feelings, Grim Thoughts: Experience and Reflection in Camus and Sartre* (2006), and Thomas Martin, *Oppression and the Human Condition: An Introduction to Sartrean Existentialism* (2002), as well as several edited volumes of critical essays on Sartre: *Sartre Today: A Centenary*

Celebration, edited by Andrew N. Leak and Adrian van den Hoven (2005); *Feminist Interpretations of Jean-Paul Sartre*, edited by Julien S. Murphy (1999); *The New Sartre: Explorations in Postmodernism*, edited by Nik Farrell Fox (2003); *Jean-Paul Sartre: Mind and Body, Word and Deed*, edited by Jean-Pierre Boulé and Benedict O'Donohoe (2011); *Sartre on the Body*, edited by Katherine J. Morris (2010); and *Reading Sartre: On Phenomenology and Existentialism*, edited by Jonathan Webber (2011).

Scheler, Max

Several of Scheler's most important works that have been translated were unavailable for some time, but have recently come back into print: *The Nature of Sympathy* (1923, and *Gesammelte Werke* [*Collected Works*] vol. 7, 1973; trans. 1954), his important work on intersubjectivity; *On the Eternal in Man* (1921 [*GW* 5, 1954]; trans. 1960), his most important work on religion; and *Man's Place in Nature* (1928 [*GW* 10, 1957]; trans. 1961), a founding work in the field of philosophical anthropology, which has also been translated as *The Human Place in the Cosmos* (2009). The English collection *Selected Philosophical Essays* (1973) contains some of his most important essays published between 1911 and 1927 (in *GW* 3, 1955; 9, 1976; and 10, 1957).

Two less well-known but equally important essays, one on shame and the other on virtue and exemplars (*GW* 10, 1957), are translated in *Person and Self-Value: Three Essays* (1987). A third essay in that volume is part of *On the Eternal in Man. Philosophical Perspectives* (1929 [*GW* 9, 1976]; trans. 1958) remains out of print; it contains various lectures and essays (1925–28) on topics including the nature of philosophy, Spinoza, and philosophical anthropology. Scheler's own theory of ethics is spelled out in relation to Kant's practical philosophy in the enormous work *Formalism in Ethics and Non-Formal Ethics of Values* [*materiale Wertethik*]: *A New Attempt toward the Foundation of an Ethical Personalism* (1913–16 [*GW* 2, 1954], 5th ed., 1966; trans. 1973). Also available are *Ressentiment* (1912 [*GW* 3, 1955]; trans. 1961) and *Problems of a Sociology of Knowledge* (1924, 1926 [*GW* 8, 1960]; trans. 1980). A collection of selections from his various writings has been published as *On Feeling, Knowing, and Valuing: Selected Writings*, edited by Harold J. Bershady (1992).

Many of Scheler's writings remain untranslated, including most of the writings in *GW* 4 (1982), on politics, war, education, and culture, as well as many of the essays in *GW* 1 (1971), his early writings, and in *GW* 6 (1963), on sociology and worldview theory. Finally, very little has been translated from the 6 volumes (*GW* 10–15, 1957–97) of his *Nachlass*, or manuscripts not published at the time of his death, which include substantial writings on philosophical anthropology, metaphysics, and history, as well as his university lectures on psychology and the history of philosophy. An exception is *The Constitution of the Human Being: From the Posthumous Works, Volumes 11 and 12* (2008).

Relatively few works on Scheler's philosophy are available in English. Manfred S. Frings has written several of the best known of them: *The Mind of Max Scheler: The First Comprehensive Guide Based on the Complete Works* (1997), *Max Scheler: A Concise Introduction into the World of a Great Thinker* (1965; 2nd ed., 1996), and *Lifetime: Max Scheler's Philosophy of Time: A First Inquiry and Presentation* (2003); he also edited *Max Scheler (1874–1928): Centennial Essays* (1974), which contains two essays by Scheler as well as critical essays on his work. Eugene Kelly has written two studies of Scheler, *Max Scheler* (1977) and *Structure and Diversity: Studies in the Phenomenological Philosophy of Max Scheler* (1997); he also discusses Scheler in *Material Ethics of Value: Max Scheler and Nicolai Hartmann* (2011).

For helpful examinations of Scheler's ethics, see Alfons Deeken, *Process and Permanence in Ethics: Max Scheler's Moral Philosophy* (1974); Ron Perrin, *Max Scheler's Concept of the Person: An Ethics of Humanism* (1991); Philip Blosser, *Scheler's Critique of Kant's Ethics* (1995); and Peter H. Spader, *Scheler's Ethical Personalism: Its Logic, Development, and Promise* (2002). A. R. Luther's *Persons in Love: A Study of Max Scheler's "Wesen und Formen der Sympathie"* (1972) is out of print. Other works of note are Stephen Frederick Schneck, *Person and Polis: Max Scheler's Personalism as Political Theory* (1986); Michael D. Barber, *Guardian of Dialogue: Max Scheler's Phenomenology, Sociology of Knowledge, and Philosophy of Love* (1993); and *Max Scheler's Acting Persons: New Perspectives*, edited by Stephen Schneck (2002).

Schelling, Friedrich

Schelling's complete works have been published in 14 volumes in German (1856–61). *The Unconditional in Human Knowledge: Four Early Essays (1794–96)* (1980) contains translations of "On the Possibility of a Form of All Philosophy" (1794), "On the I as Principle of Philosophy" (1795), "Philosophical Letters on Dogmatism and Criticism" (1795), and "New Deduction of Natural Right" (1796), all of which Schelling wrote before he was 22. Another early work, "Treatise Explicatory [*Abhandlungen zur Erläuterung*] of the Idealism in the Science of Knowledge [*Wissenschaftslehre*]" (1797), may be found in *Idealism and the Endgame of Theory: Three Essays* (1994).

Schelling's early philosophical development culminates in his *System of Transcendental Idealism* (1800; trans. 1978). All of his writings up to and including this work are often seen, and even came to be seen by Schelling himself, as being deeply indebted—to their detriment—to Fichte's system or *Wissenschaftslehre*. This is his own subsequent assessment of his thinking in a series of lectures given in Munich in 1833–34 (shortly after Hegel's death), which discuss Descartes, Spinoza, Leibniz, Kant, Fichte, and Hegel, among others; they are translated in *On the History of Modern Philosophy* (1994).

It is Schelling's philosophy of nature (*Naturphilosophie*) that initially was the clearest difference between his and Fichte's idealisms. His major work in this area is *Ideas for a Philosophy of Nature* (1797; 2nd ed., 1803, trans. 1988). "On the World Soul" (1798), a companion piece to it, has not yet been translated into English. *First Outline of a System of the Philosophy of Nature* (1799; trans. 2004) and the essay "System of the Whole of Philosophy and the Philosophy of Nature" (1804; trans. in *Idealism and the Endgame of Theory*, 1994) provide more of his philosophy of nature. Schelling's essay "On the True Concept of the Philosophy of Nature and the Right Way to Solve Its Problems" (1801) also remains untranslated, as do two works of aphorisms that concern the philosophy of nature (1806–07). (Hereafter, the absence of a date of translation indicates the lack of any English version.)

After 1800, Schelling began to move beyond Fichte, calling his new approach "the philosophy of identity" and considering himself to have discovered "dialectical" thought before Hegel. Schelling is known for having repeatedly changed and modified his thinking, and the development of his "identity philosophy" is a case in point. It is evident in the smaller works "Exhibition of My System of Philosophy" (1801) and "Further Exhibitions from the System of Philosophy" (1802). One work from this period available in English is the dialogue *Bruno, or, On the Divine and Natural Principle of Things* (1802; trans. 1984), which gives some insight into his philosophy at this stage of its development.

In 1804 Schelling published an essay titled *Philosophy and Religion* (trans. 2010), which sounds the themes that would fascinate him for the rest of his life: freedom, God, Being (or the Real), and history. During this time he also wrote the influential *On University Studies* (1803; trans. 1966); and he gave lectures on aesthetics that became his *The Philosophy of Art* (1802–03; trans. 1989) and "On the Relationship of the Fine Arts to Nature" (1807). He also wrote a fragment of a novel giving literary expression to some of his views, which attained considerable popularity following its posthumous publication in 1861: *Clara, or, On Nature's Connection to the Spirit World* (trans. 2002), probably written after the death of his first wife Caroline in 1809. One of his most important works, selections from which appear above, dates from the time of her illness: *Philosophical Inquiries into the Essence of Human Freedom* (1809; trans. 1936, 2006).

Schelling seems to have begun his intended masterwork, known as *Die Weltalter* or *The Ages of the World*, around 1810 and worked on it into the 1830s. His "Stuttgart Seminars" (1810), translated in *Idealism and the Endgame of Theory* (1994), can be seen as a bridge between the 1809 treatise on freedom and this project. There are three versions of what was conceived as its first part, from 1811, 1813, and 1815. The 1813 version has been published in English in a freestanding translation, *The Ages of the World* (2000), and in a work titled *The Abyss of Freedom/Ages of the World* (1996), which contains Slavoj Žižek's "The Abyss of Freedom" as well as the Schelling material. Also from this period is a 1815 work translated as *Schelling's Treatise on "The Deities of Samothrace"* (1977). During the 1820s Schelling continued to work on *Die Weltalter*, while also reconsidering the nature of philosophy itself in such manuscripts as *On the Nature of Philosophy as Wissenschaft* (1821).

In the last decades of his life, during which Schelling held the professorship that had been Hegel's in Berlin, he lectured extensively and influentially; many of his lecture series were published, some of which have been translated. Among them are *The Grounding of Positive Philosophy: The Berlin Lectures* (1832–33; trans. 2007), *Philosophy of Revelation* (1841–42, 1842–43), *Historical-Critical Introduction to the Philosophy of Mythology* (1842; partial trans. in *The Grounding of Positive Philosophy*, 2007), and *Introduction to the Philosophy of Mythology or Presentation of the Purely Rational Philosophy* (1847–52).

Several of the translated works mentioned above contain important critical essays on Schelling's work either by the editors or by other scholars, such as the essay by Žižek that accompanies *Ages of the World*. Žižek has also written *The Indivisible Remainder: An Essay on Schelling and Related Matters* (1996). As has been noted, some of Schelling's late lectures were attended by Kierkegaard; and his response to them has been published as "Notes of Schelling's Berlin Lectures" (1841–42) as an addendum to the 1989 translation of *The Concept of Irony*. Hegel's first published philosophical work was titled *The Difference between Fichte's and Schelling's System of Philosophy* (1801; trans. 1977). Also, Heidegger devoted a 1936 lecture to Schelling, *Schelling's Treatise: On the Essence of Human Freedom* (1971; trans. 1985).

Paul Tillich wrote on Schelling in *The Construction of the History of Religion in Schelling's Positive Principles: Its Presuppositions and Principles* (1910; trans. 1974). Other works that focus on Schelling's philosophy of religion are Friedemann Horn, *Schelling and Swedenborg: Mysticism and German Idealism* (1954; trans. 1997); Edward Allen Beach, *The Potencies of God(s): Schelling's Philosophy of Mythology* (1994); and Emil L. Fackenheim, *The God Within: Kant, Schelling, and Historicity*, edited by John W. Burbidge (1996).

Books and collections that relate Schelling to current trends and contemporary figures in European philosophy include Andrew Bowie, *Schelling and Modern European Philosophy: An Introduction* (1993); *The New Schelling*, edited by Judith Norman and Alistair Welchman (2004); Jason M. Wirth, *The Conspiracy of Life: Meditations on Schelling and His Time* (2003); Bernard Freydberg, *Schelling's Dialogical "Freedom Essay": Provocative Philosophy Then and Now* (2008); and *Schelling Now: Contemporary Readings*, edited by Jason M. Wirth (2005).

Two recent works explore Schelling's influence on psychology: S. J. McGrath, *The Dark Ground of Spirit: Schelling and the Unconscious* (2012), and Matt Ffytche, *The Foundation of the Unconscious: Schelling, Freud, and the Birth of the Modern Psyche* (2012). Other studies of note are Alan White, *Schelling: An Introduction to the System of Freedom* (1983); Dale E. Snow, *Schelling and the End of Idealism* (1996); Iain Hamilton Grant, *Philosophies of Nature after Schelling* (2006); Bruce Matthews, *Schelling's Organic Form of Philosophy: Life as the Schema of Freedom* (2011); and Devin Zane Shaw, *Freedom and Nature in Schelling's Philosophy of Art* (2010). Several works discuss Schelling in relation to Hegel, including Christopher Lauer, *The Suspension of Reason in Hegel and Schelling* (2010), and John Laughland, *Schelling versus Hegel: From German Idealism to Christian Metaphysics* (2007).

Several earlier books no longer in print that are worth noting are Joseph L. Esposito, *Schelling's Idealism and Philosophy of Nature* (1977); Werner Marx, *The Philosophy of F. W. J. Schelling: History, System, and Freedom* (1984); and Paul Collins Hayner, *Reason and Existence: Schelling's Philosophy of History* (1967).

More sources containing discussions of Schelling can be found in the bibliography section on German idealism in General Bibliographies (above).

Schiller, Friedrich

Schiller's writings are many and diverse—literary (in a variety of genres), historical, and philosophical. His primary plays are *The Robbers* (1781), *The Conspiracy of Genoa* (1783),

Love and Intrigue (1784), *Don Carlos* (1787), the three-part *Wallenstein* cycle (*Wallenstein's Camp*, *The Piccolomini*, and *The Death of Wallenstein*; 1789–99), *Maria Stuart* (1800), *The Maid of Orleans* (1801), *The Bride of Messina* (1803), *Wilhelm Tell* (1804), *Homage to the Arts* (1804), and *Demetrius* (1805). These are contained in volumes 3 through 11 of the *Nationalausgabe* of Schiller's work in German (1948–85). Volume 16 of the *Nationalausgabe* (1995) contains his stories, the best-known of which is the unfinished novel *The Ghost Seer* (1787–89). Volumes 1 and 2 (1943, 1983) of the *Nationalausgabe* contain Schiller's poems, divided into those written from 1776 to 1799 and those written between 1799 and 1805.

Schiller's works in history can be divided into three major groups: first, writings on the history of the Netherlands; second, writings on what he called "Universal History"; and, third, his work on the Thirty Years' War. The primary work of the first group is *History of the Revolt of the United Netherlands from Spanish Rule* (1788). The major works on "universal history" (human history generally) emerge from his lectures on the subject from 1789 onward. They are translated as *What Is and to What End Do We Study Universal History?*, *The Legislation of Lycurgus and Solon*, and *The Mission of Moses*. The third group consists of his *History of the Thirty Years' War* (1791–93). These works are all contained in volumes 17 and 18 of the *Nationalausgabe* (1970, 1976).

Schiller's aesthetic and philosophical works begin with his early works, prior to his encounter with Kantian philosophy. Among these are *The Philosophy of Physiology* (1779), *On the Relation between Man's Animal and Spiritual Nature* (1780), and *Philosophical Letters* (1786). The works of the 1790s contain his main philosophical and aesthetic works, written as he sought to come to terms with Kant's mature thought. His major theoretical works are *On Grace and Dignity* (1793), *On the Aesthetic Education of Man* (1794), and *On Naïve and Sentimental Poetry* (1795–96), collected into a single work in 1800. Numerous smaller pieces were also written during this period. *On the Sublime* and *On the Pathetic* (perhaps better translated as "On the Pathos-Inducing") were written in the early 1790s and published in 1794. *On the Moral Use of Aesthetic Manners* (1796), *On the Necessary Limits in the Use of Beautiful Forms* (1795; rev. 1800), and *On the Aesthetic Estimation of Magnitude* (1793) are interesting pieces that explore the implications and limitations of Kantian thought. These works are contained in volumes 20 and 21 of the *Nationalausgabe* (1962, 1963). Most of Schiller's major works exist in readily available English translations.

One of the earliest introductions of Schiller's work to English speakers is still in print: Thomas Carlyle's *The Life of Friedrich Schiller: Comprehending an Examination of His Works* (1825; 2nd ed., 1845). The existing secondary literature that examines Schiller's philosophical ideas are Deric Regin, *Freedom and Dignity: The Historical and Philosophical Thought of Schiller* (1965); Margaret C. Ives, *The Analogue of Harmony: Some Reflections on Schiller's Philosophical Essays* (1970); R. D. Miller, *Schiller and the Ideal of Freedom: A Study of Schiller's Philosophical Works with Chapters on Kant* (1970); Lesley Sharpe, *Friedrich Schiller: Drama, Thought, and Politics* (1991); David Pugh, *Dialectic of Love: Platonism in Schiller's Aesthetics* (1996); and Frederick Beiser, *Schiller as Philosopher: A Reexamination* (2005).

Secondary works that explore Schiller's theoretical work in relation to other philosophers and theorists include Michael John Kooy, *Coleridge, Schiller and Aesthetic Education* (2002); Nicholas Martin, *Nietzsche and Schiller: Untimely Aesthetics* (1996); Karin Schutjer, *Narrating Community after Kant: Schiller, Goethe, and Hölderlin* (2001); Juliet Sychrava, *Schiller to Derrida: Idealism in Aesthetics* (1989); Philip J. Kain, *Schiller, Hegel, and Marx: State, Society and the Aesthetic Ideal of Ancient Greece* (1982); Linda Marie Brooks, *The Menace of the Sublime to the Individual Self: Kant, Schiller, Coleridge, and the Disintegration of Romantic Identity* (1995); and D. C. Schindler, *The Perfection of Freedom: Schiller, Schelling, and Hegel between the Ancients and the Moderns* (2012).

A number of studies offer broad analyses and interpretations of all Schiller's work and of his historical significance. Among them are *A Schiller Symposium: In Observance of the Bicentenary of Schiller's Birth*, edited by A. Leslie Wilson (1960); Charles E. Passage, *Friedrich Schiller* (1975); John D. Simons, *Friedrich Schiller* (1981); T. J. Reed, *Schiller* (1991); Steven D. Martinson, *Harmonious Tensions: The Writings of Friedrich Schiller* (1996); Claudia Pilling, Diana Schilling, and Mirjam Springer, *Schiller* (2002; trans. 2005); and *A Companion to the Works of Friedrich Schiller*, edited by Steven D. Martinson (2005).

Both critical essays on Schiller and translations of some of his own works are contained in *Friedrich Schiller: Medicine, Psychology, and Literature: With the First English Edition of His Complete Medical and Psychological Writings*, edited by Kenneth Dewhurst and Nigel Reeves (1978), and *Schiller's "On Grace and Dignity" in Its Cultural Context: Essays and a New Translation*, edited by Jane V. Curran and Christophe Fricker (2005). The following works focus more on his literary and historical works: H. B. Garland, *Schiller, the Dramatic Writer: A Study of Style in the Plays* (1969); John Prudhoe, *The Theatre of Goethe and Schiller* (1973); Ilse Graham,

Schiller's Drama: Talent and Integrity (1974); Lesley Sharpe, *Schiller and the Historical Character: Presentation and Interpretation in the Historiographical Works and in the Historical Dramas* (1982); David Pugh, *Schiller's Early Dramas: A Critical History* (2000); and Gail K. Hart, *Friedrich Schiller: Crime, Aesthetics, and the Poetics of Punishment* (2005).

Schopenhauer, Arthur

Schopenhauer's first book, published when he was only 25, was *On the Fourfold Root of the Principle of Sufficient Reason* (1813; first trans. 1889, best trans. 1974). It was followed by the less well known *On Vision and Colors* (1816; trans. 1994) and then by his masterwork, *The World as Will and Representation* [*Vorstellung*] (1818; trans. 1883, 1958). In 1844 he published a second edition of *The World as Will* with a new second volume of essays elaborating on various ideas advanced in the first. Between the two editions several shorter works appeared: *On the Will in Nature* (1836; trans. 1889, 1992) and two important essays, "On the Freedom of the Human Will" (1839) and "On the Basis of Morality" (1840), which were subsequently published together as *The Two Fundamental Problems of Ethics* (1841) and have been translated into English several times. His only other book is an enormous collection of essays, *Parerga und Paralipomena* (1851; complete trans. 1974), various selections from which have appeared in English translation in numerous editions.

For Schopenhauer's life, see Rüdiger Safranski, *Schopenhauer and the Wild Years of Philosophy* (1987; trans. 1989); David E. Cartwright, *Schopenhauer: A Biography* (2010); and an earlier biography, V. J. McGill's *Schopenhauer: Pessimist and Pagan* (1931). Bryan Magee's *The Philosophy of Schopenhauer* (1983; rev. ed., 1997) is an excellent survey of Schopenhauer's thought, and his *Misunderstanding Schopenhauer* (1990) is also quite helpful. Three good introductions are Christopher Janaway, *Schopenhauer: A Very Short Introduction* (2002); Michael Tanner, *Schopenhauer* (1999); and Robert Wicks, *Schopenhauer's "The World as Will and Representation": A Reader's Guide* (2011). Christopher Janaway has also edited three commendable collections of essays: *The Cambridge Companion to Schopenhauer* (1999), *Willing and Nothingness: Schopenhauer as Nietzsche's Educator* (1998), and, with Alex Neill, *Better Consciousness: Schopenhauer's Philosophy of Value* (2009). Two other excellent resources are *A Companion to Schopenhauer,* edited by Bart Vandenabeele (2012), and David E. Cartwright, *The A to Z of Schopenhauer's Philosophy* (2010).

Useful comprehensive studies include D. W. Hamlyn, *Schopenhauer* (in Rutledge's "Argu-

ments" series, 1980); Christopher Janaway, *Schopenhauer* (1994); Julian Young, *Schopenhauer* (2005); Dale Jacquette, *The Philosophy of Schopenhauer* (2005); and Robert Wicks, *Schopenhauer* (2008). An early study that remains significant is Georg Simmel's *Schopenhauer and Nietzsche* (1907; trans. 1986). More detailed studies of Schopenhauer's thought include Christopher Janaway, *Self and World in Schopenhauer's Philosophy* (1989); John E. Atwell, *Schopenhauer: The Human Character* (1990) and *Schopenhauer on the Character of the World: The Metaphysics of Will* (1995); and Barbara Hannan, *The Riddle of the World: A Reconsideration of Schopenhauer's Philosophy* (2009).

One of the few studies to concentrate on Schopenhauer's early work is F. C. White's *On Schopenhauer's "Fourfold Root of the Principle of Sufficient Reason"* (1992). For Schopenhauer on ethics, religion, and aesthetics, see Gerard Mannion, *Schopenhauer, Religion and Morality: The Humble Path to Ethics* (2003); Christopher Ryan, *Schopenhauer's Philosophy of Religion: The Death of God and the Oriental Renaissance* (2010); Sophia Vasalou, *Schopenhauer and the Aesthetic Standpoint: Philosophy as a Practice of the Sublime* (2013); and *Schopenhauer, Philosophy, and the Arts,* edited by Dale Jacquette (1996).

Taylor, Charles

An excellent introduction to Taylor's thought is his two-volume collection titled *Philosophical Papers* (1985). The selection in this volume, "Self-Interpreting Animals," first appeared in *Human Agency and Action,* the collection's first volume; and the important essay "Interpretation and the Sciences of Man" (1971), singled out in the headnote above, is included in the second volume, *Philosophy and the Human Sciences.*

Taylor's first book, *The Explanation of Behaviour* (1964), derived from his dissertation. During the next ten years he published only one book, *The Patterns of Politics* (1970), but a large number of articles, including the just-mentioned "Sciences of Man." During that period he also was writing his very substantial study of Hegel, titled simply *Hegel* (1975). It was followed by many more articles and a second Hegel book, *Hegel and Modern Society* (1979). Both Hegel books have been translated into many other languages. In 1981 Taylor gave two lectures that were published as *Social Theory as Practice* (1983), his first major statement of his conception of social theory.

Taylor's next book, containing some of the same material in German translation, exists only in German: *Negative Freiheit? Zur Kritik des neuzeitlichen Individualismus* (1988, *Negative Freedom? Toward a Critique of Contemporary Individualism*). Its German publisher described it as a critique of the "reductionistic" and "atomistic conception of man in contemporary philosophy," and an argument instead for a "new 'philosophical anthropology'" of a "communitarian" sort. This campaign was carried forward in *Sources of the Self: The Making of the Modern Identity* (1989)—the magisterial work for which Taylor is now perhaps most highly esteemed. (It has been translated into 14 languages.) But he may be even more widely known for the book that followed: first published in Canada as *The Malaise of Modernity* (1991), it was republished in the United States as *The Ethics of Authenticity* (1992) and has been translated even more extensively.

In 1992 Taylor also wrote an essay to which four other philosophers responded in *Multiculturalism and "The Politics of Recognition"* (now translated into 11 other languages) and published *Reconciling the Solitudes: Essays on Canadian Federalism and Nationalism* (first in French, 1992; trans. 1993). He then came out with another collection of essays, *Philosophical Arguments* (1995), followed by two books on religious matters, in which he was becoming increasingly interested: *A Catholic Modernity?* (1996) and *Varieties of Religion Today: William James Revisited* (2002).

In *Modern Social Imaginaries* (2004) Taylor turned his attention to the complex of concepts, values, beliefs, practices, and institutions that gives human cultures and societies their distinctive identities and cohesion (an update of the Hegelian ideas of a *Volk* or "people," *Volksgeist*, and its "objective-spiritual" realization). And in *A Secular Age* (2007) he examined the profound transformation that has occurred in the Western world at a more fundamental level, as the religiousness that once permeated it has increasingly been replaced by a radical secularity. Another set of his philosophical papers was published in 2010: *Dilemmas and Connections: Selected Essays*. His most recent book, with Hubert Dreyfus, is *Retrieving Realism* (2015)—a radical critique of the Cartesian epistemic picture, intended to prepare the way for a fundamental rethinking of knowledge, ourselves, the world, and our relation to it.

The main secondary sources on the thought of Charles Taylor are Ian Fraser, *Dialectics of the Self: Transcending Charles Taylor* (2007); Mark Redhead, *Charles Taylor: Thinking and Living Deep Diversity* (2002); Ruth Abbey, *Charles Taylor* (2000); Nicholas H. Smith, *Charles Taylor: Meaning, Morals, and Modernity* (2002); and Arto Laitinen, *Strong Evaluation without Moral Sources: On Charles Taylor's Philosophical Anthropology and Ethics* (2008).

Taylor's *A Secular Age* has been the subject of considerable discussion: see especially James K. A. Smith, *How (Not) to Be Secular: Reading Charles Taylor* (2014); *Aspiring to Fullness in a Secular Age: Essays on Religion and Theology in the Work of Charles Taylor*, edited by Carlos D. Colorado and Justin D. Klassen (2014); *The Taylor Effect: Responding to a Secular Age*, edited by Ian Leask (2010); and *Varieties of Secularism in a Secular Age*, edited by Michael Warner, Jonathan VanAntwerpen, and Craig Calhoun (2010).

For a collection of essays on Taylor's thought as a whole, see *Philosophy in an Age of Pluralism: The Philosophy of Charles Taylor in Question*, edited by James Tully (1994), which also contains a full bibliography of Taylor's writings up to its date of publication. A number of works analyze his thought in relation to that of other philosophers and theologians, including Robert C. Sibley, *Northern Spirits: John Watson, George Grant, and Charles Taylor: Appropriations of Hegelian Thought* (2008); Andrew O'Shea, *Selfhood and Sacrifice: René Girard and Charles Taylor on the Crisis of Modernity* (2010); Robert Meynell, *Canadian Idealism and the Philosophy of Freedom: C. B. Macpherson, George Grant, and Charles Taylor* (2011); and Brian J. Braman, *Meaning and Authenticity: Bernard Lonergan and Charles Taylor on the Drama of Authentic Human Existence* (2008).

Weil, Simone

Weil's essay "The Iliad, or, The Poem of Force" (1940; trans. 1945) remains one of her best-known works. Her thoughts on religion became increasingly popular after her death. They are primarily found in *Gravity and Grace* (1947; trans. 1952), *Waiting for God* (1950; trans. 1951), and *Letter to a Priest* (1951; trans. 1953). Her political and ethical writings in translation include *The Need for Roots: Prelude to a Declaration of Duties toward Mankind* (1949; trans. 1952); *Oppression and Liberty* (1955; trans. 1958), and *Simone Weil on Colonialism: An Ethic of the Other* (2003), translations of articles and letters drawn from her entire literary career. Other writings of philosophical interest include *Intimations of Christianity among the Ancient Greeks* (1957), which consists of chapters from *Intuitions pré-chrétiennes* (1951) and *La source grecque* (1953), and *Lectures on Philosophy* (1959; trans. 1978).

The diversity of Weil's thought can be seen in the selections translated in *Selected Essays, 1934–1943* (1962); *On Science, Necessity, and the Love of God: Essays* (1968); and *Formative Writings, 1929–1941* (1987). See also *Seventy Letters: Some Hitherto Untranslated Texts from Published and Unpublished Sources* (1965); *The Notebooks of Simone Weil* (3 vols., 1951–56; 2 vols., trans. 1956); and *First and Last Notebooks* (1970), a translation that combines *Cahiers* (1970, *Notebooks*) and *La connaissance surnaturelle* (1950, *Supernatural Knowledge*).

The fascination that many have felt for Weil and her short but unique life is reflected in the many books about her that have been written in or translated into English. J. M. Perrin and G. Thibon's *Simone Weil as We Knew Her* (1952; trans. 1953) is a book of biographical reflections. Other biographical works include Francine du Plessix Gray, *Simone Weil* (2001); David McLellan, *Utopian Pessimist: The Life and Thought of Simone Weil* (1989); Simone Pétrement, *Simone Weil: A Life* (1973; trans. 1976); Gabriella Fiori, *Simone Weil: An Intellectual Biography* (1981; trans. 1989); Richard Rees, *Simone Weil: A Sketch for a Portrait* (1966); Thomas R. Nevin, *Simone Weil: Portrait of a Self-Exiled Jew* (1991); Robert Coles, *Simone Weil: A Modern Pilgrimage* (1987); Dorothy Tuck McFarland, *Simone Weil* (1983); *Simone Weil: Interpretations of a Life*, edited by George Abbott White (1981); and Palle Yourgrau, *Simone Weil* (2011).

Stephen Plant's *Simone Weil: A Brief Introduction* (2nd ed., 2007) provides an introduction to Weil's thought. Studies helpful in conveying a sense of the range and coherence of that thought include Vance G. Morgan, *Weaving the World: Simone Weil on Science, Mathematics, and Love* (2005); Henry Leroy Finch, *Simone Weil and the Intellect of Grace* (1999); Peter Winch, *Simone Weil: "The Just Balance"* (1989); and Robert Chenavier, *Simone Weil: Attention to the Real* (2009; trans. 2012). There are several excellent volumes in the Simone Weil Studies series published by the State University of New York Press, including Miklos Vetö, *The Religious Metaphysics of Simone Weil* (1971; trans. 1994); Rush Rhees, *Discussions of Simone Weil* (1999); Katherine T. Brueck, *The Redemption of Tragedy: The Literary Vision of Simone Weil* (1995); Joan Dargan, *Simone Weil: Thinking Poetically* (1999); and Diogenes Allen and Eric O. Springsted, *Spirit, Nature, and Community: Issues in the Thought of Simone Weil* (1994).

Two useful volumes of critical essays are *The Christian Platonism of Simone Weil*, edited by E. Jane Doering and Eric O. Springsted (2004), and *The Beauty That Saves: Essays on Aesthetics and Language in Simone Weil*, edited by John M. Dunaway and Eric O. Springsted (1996). More recent works include *The Relevance of the Radical: Simone Weil 100 Years Later*, edited by A. Rebecca Rozelle-Stone and Lucian Stone (2009); Marie Cabaud Meaney, *Simone Weil's Apologetic Use of Literature: Her Christological Interpretation of Classic Greek Texts* (2008); Desmond Avery, *Beyond Power: Simone Weil and the Notion of Authority* (2008); and E. Jane Doering, *Simone Weil and the Specter of Self-Perpetuating Force* (2010).

Several works that focus on Weil's political and ethical writings are Richard H. Bell, *Simone Weil: The Way of Justice as Compassion* (1998); *Simone Weil's Philosophy of Culture: Readings toward a Divine Humanity*, edited by

Richard H. Bell (1993); Athanasios Moulakis, *Simone Weil and the Politics of Self-Denial* (1981; trans. 1998); Mary G. Dietz, *Between the Human and the Divine: The Political Thought of Simone Weil* (1988); Lawrence A. Blum and Victor J. Seidler, *A Truer Liberty: Simone Weil and Marxism* (1989); and Louis Patsouras, *Simone Weil and the Socialist Tradition* (1992). But her ethical thought is inseparable from her religious thought; both are dealt with in Eric O. Springsted, *Simone Weil and the Suffering of Love* (1986) and *Christus Mediator: Platonic Mediation in the Thought of Simone Weil* (1983), and in Christopher Frost and Rebecca Bell-Metereau, *Simone Weil: On Politics, Religion and Society* (1998).

Wollstonecraft, Mary

Wollstonecraft's writings have been edited by Janet M. Todd and Marilyn Butler, *The Works of Mary Wollstonecraft* (7 vols., 1989). For other primary material, see *The Love Letters of Mary Wollstonecraft to Gilbert Imlay* (1908); *The Collected Letters of Mary Wollstonecraft*, edited by Todd (2003); and William Goodwin, *Memoirs of the Author of "A Vindication of the Rights of Woman"* (1798; reprint, 2001), a work whose scandalous revelations about Wollstonecraft's personal life damaged her reputation for decades. The philosophical monographs on Wollstonecraft's thought include Lena Halldenius, *Mary Wollstonecraft and Feminist Republicanism: Independence, Rights and the Experience of Unfreedom* (2015); Syndy Conger, *Mary Wollstonecraft and the Language of Sensibility* (1994); Barbara Taylor, *Mary Wollstonecraft and the Feminist Imagination* (2003); Gary Kelly, *Revolutionary Feminism: The Mind and Career of Mary Wollstonecraft* (1992); Virginia Sapiro, *A Vindication of Political Virtue: The Political Theory of Mary Wollstonecraft* (1992); Ashley Tauchert, *Mary Wollstonecraft and the Accent of the Feminine* (2002); Natalie Fuehrer Taylor, *The Rights of Woman as Chimera: The Political Philosophy of Mary Wollstonecraft* (2007); and Wendy Gunther-Canada, *Rebel Writer: Mary Wollstonecraft and Enlightenment Politics* (2001).

Two edited volumes of essays that are worthy of note are *The Cambridge Companion to Mary Wollstonecraft*, edited by Claudia L. Johnson (2002), and *Feminist Interpretations of Mary Wollstonecraft*, edited by Maria Falco (1996). Two works from the perspective of the philosophy of education are Kirstin Collins Hanley, *Mary Wollstonecraft, Pedagogy, and the Practice of Feminism* (2013), and Susan Laird, *Mary Wollstonecraft: Philosophical Mother of Coeducation* (2008). An intriguing edition of early and contemporary responses to Wollstonecraft's major work is *Mary Wollstonecraft's "A Vindication of the Rights of Woman": A Sourcebook*, edited by Adriana Craciun (2002). Many important essays on Wollstonecraft's thought have been collected in *Mary Wollstonecraft and the Critics, 1790–2001*, edited by Harriet Devine Jump (2 vols., 2003).

There are numerous biographies of Wollstonecraft. The more recent ones of note are Charlotte Gordon, *Romantic Outlaws: The Extraordinary Lives of Mary Wollstonecraft and Her Daughter Mary Shelley* (2015); Janet Todd, *Mary Wollstonecraft: A Revolutionary Life* (2000); Lyndall Gordon, *Vindication: A Life of Mary Wollstonecraft* (2005); Claire Tomalin, *The Life and Death of Mary Wollstonecraft*, rev. ed. (1992); Miriam Brody, *Mary Wollstonecraft: Mother of Women's Rights* (2000); Julie A. Carlson, *England's First Family of Writers: Mary Wollstonecraft, William Godwin, Mary Shelley* (2007); Diane Jacobs, *Her Own Woman: The Life of Mary Wollstonecraft* (2001); and Caroline Franklin, *Mary Wollstonecraft: A Literary Life* (2004). The notable biographies by the previous generation of scholars are Jean Detre, *A Most Extraordinary Pair: Mary Wollstonecraft and William Godwin* (1975); Eleanor Flexner, *Mary Wollstonecraft: A Biography* (1972); Edna Nixon, *Mary Wollstonecraft: Her Life and Times* (1971); Emily W. Sunstein, *A Different Face: The Life of Mary Wollstonecraft* (1975); and Ralph Martin Wardle, *Mary Wollstonecraft, a Critical Biography* (1951).

Permissions
Acknowledgments

Wilhelm Dilthey: From "The Construction of the Historical World" from W. DILTHEY SELECTED WRITINGS, ed. and trans. by H. P. Rickman is reprinted by permission of Cambridge University Press. Copyright © 1976 by Cambridge University Press.

W. E. B. Du Bois: "Sociology Hesitant" published in boundary 2 (2000) is reprinted by permission of The Permissions Company, Inc., on behalf of the David Graham Du Bois Trust. From DUSK OF DAWN: AN ESSAY TOWARD AN AUTOBIOGRAPHY OF RACE CONCEPT, ed. by Henry Louis Gates, Jr. (2007) by permission of Oxford University Press, USA. From THE SOULS OF BLACK FOLK, introduction by Donald B. Gibson, notes by Monica E. Elbert (Penguin Classics 1989). Copyright © the Estate of W. E. B. Du Bois 1903. Introduction copyright © Viking Penguin, a division of Penguin Books USA Inc., 1989. Reproduced by permission of Penguin Books Ltd.

Frantz Fanon: Excerpts from THE WRETCHED OF THE EARTH. English translation copyright © 1963 by Présence Africaine. Used by permission of Grove/Atlantic, Inc. Any third party use of this material, outside of this publication, is prohibited. Excerpts from BLACK SKIN, WHITE MASKS. English translation copyright © 2008 by Richard Philcox. Used by permission of Grove/Atlantic, Inc. Any third party use of this material, outside of this publication, is prohibited.

Ludwig Feuerbach: From "Principles of the Philosophy of the Future" from THE FIERY BROOK: SELECTED WRITINGS OF LUDWIG FEUERBACH, trans. by Zawar Hanfi. Translation and Introduction copyright © 1972 by Zawar Hanfi. Published in 2012 by Verso. Reprinted by permission of Verso.

Johann Gottlieb Fichte: From THE SCIENCE OF KNOWLEDGE, ed. & trans. by Peter Heath and John Lachs, is reprinted by permission of Cambridge University Press. Copyright © 1970 by Meredith Corporation. Copyright © 1982 by Cambridge University Press.

Michel Foucault: From THE ORDER OF THINGS: AN ARCHAEOLOGY OF THE HUMAN SCIENCES, trans. by Alan Sheridan-Smith. Copyright © 1970 by Random House, Inc., New York. Originally published in French as LES MOTS ET LES CHOSES. Copyright © 1966 by Editions Gallimard. Reprinted by permission of Georges Borchardt, Inc. for Editions Gallimard. Rights outside the U.S. by permission of Taylor & Francis Books UK. "What is Enlightenment?" from THE FOUCAULT READER, ed. by Paul Rabinow, trans. by Catherine Porter, (Pantheon Books 1984). Copyright © 1984 by Paul Rabinow. Reprinted by permission of Georges Borchardt, Inc. Rights outside the U.S. by permission of Editions Gallimard. Published in French as "Qu'est-ce que les lumières? From DITS ET ECRITS. Copyright © 1994 by Editions Gallimard, Paris. "Orders of Discourse" from Social Science Information, April 1971, trans. by Rupert Swyer, copyright © 1977 by Sage Publications & Foundation of the Maison des Science de l'Homme, reproduced by permission of Sage Publications Ltd. Lecture Two, 14 January 1976, trans. by Kate Soper, from POWER/KNOWLEDGE, ed. by Colin Gordon, copyright © 1972, 1975, 1976, 1977 by Michel Foucault. This collection © 1980 by The Harvester Press. Used by permission of Pantheon Books, an imprint of the Knopf Doubleday Publishing Group, a division of Random House LLC. All rights reserved.

Hans-Georg Gadamer: From "On the Scope and Function of Hermeneutical Reflection" trans. by G. B. Hess and R. E. Palmer from PHILOSOPHICAL HERMENEUTCS, ed. by David E. Linge (University of California Press, 1976) is reprinted by permission of the publisher via the Copyright Clearance Center. Copyright © 1976 by The Regents of the University of California. From TRUTH AND METHOD, rev. trans. by Joel Weinsheimer and Donald G. Marshall (The Continuum International Publishing Group, 1989) is reprinted by permission of the publisher via the Copyright Clearance Center. Second, rev. ed. copyright © 1989 by The Crossroad Publishing Co.

Arnold Gehlen: From MAN: HIS NATURE AND PLACE IN THE WORLD, trans. by Clare McMillan and Karl Pillemer (1988) is reprinted by permission of Columbia University Press. Copyright © 1988 by Columbia University Press.

Jurgen Habermas: From THE THEORY OF COMMUNICATIVE ACTION, Vol. 1, trans. by Thomas McCarthy. Introduction and English translation copyright © 1984 by Beacon Press. German Text Copyright © 1981 by Suhrkamp Verlag, Frankfurt am Main. Reprinted by permission of Beacon Press via the Copyright Clearance Center. From KNOWLEDGE AND HUMAN INTERESTS, trans. by Jeremy J. Shapiro, German Text Copyright © 1968 by Suhrkamp Verlag, Frankfurt am Main, English translation Copyright © 1971 by Beacon Press. Reprinted by permission of Beacon Press, via Copyright Clearance Center.

Georg Wilhelm Friedrich Hegel: From HEGEL'S PHILOSOPHY OF NATURE, pp. 1, 3–13, 20, 24, ed. and trans. by A. V. Miller (1970, 2005), is reprinted by permission of Oxford University Press. From HEGEL'S PHILOSOPHY OF MIND trans. by William Wallace and A. V. Miller and ed. by J. N. Findlay (1971); pp. 1–9; 11–22; 25–30; 51; 147; 151–55; 157–58; 165–167; 170–76; 179–180; 183–185; 228–229; 235–256; 238–240). Reprinted by permission of Oxford University Press.

Martin Heidegger: "Building Dwelling Thinking" from POETRY, LANGUAGE, THOUGHT, pp. 145–161, translation and introduction by Albert Hofstadter. Copyright © 1971 by Martin Heidegger. Reprinted by permission of HarperCollins Publishers. "The End of Philosophy and the Task of Thinking" from ON TIME AND BEING, pp. 55–73, trans. by Joan Stambaugh. English language translation copyright © 1972 by Harper & Row, Publishers, Inc. Reprinted by permission of HarperCollins Publishers. From BEING AND TIME: A TRANSLATION OF SEIN UND ZEIT, trans. by Joan Stambaugh, is reprinted by permission of the State University of New York Press, copyright © 1996 State University of New York. All rights reserved. From "Letter on Humanism" trans. by Edgar Lohner from PHILOSOPHY IN THE TWENTIETH CENTURY: AN ANTHOLOGY, v. 2, ed. by William Barrett and Henry D. Aiken published in 1962 by Random House.

Edmund Husserl: Reprinted with the permission of Scribner Publishing Group, from IDEAS: GENERAL INTRODUCTION TO PURE PHENOMENOLOGY by Edmund Husserl, trans. by W. R. Boyce-Gibson. Copyright © 1962 by Macmillan Publishing Company. All rights reserved. Rights outside the U.S. granted by

NACH DEN GRENZEN MENSCHLICHEN VERHALTENS, Third Edition, copyright © 1961 by A. Franke AG Verlag, Bern. Reprinted by permission of Northwestern University Press.

Paul Ricoeur: "The Model of the Text" from HERMENEUTICS AND THE HUMAN SCIENCES, trans. by John B. Thompson (1981) is reprinted by permission of Cambridge University Press. Copyright © 1981 by Maison des Sciences de l'Homme and Cambridge University Press.

Jean-Paul Sartre: From SEARCH FOR A METHOD by Jean Paul Sartre, trans. by Hazel E. Barnes, copyright © 1963 by Alfred A. Knopf, a division of Random House LLC. Used by permission of Alfred A. Knopf, an imprint of the Knopf Doubleday Publishing Group, a division of Random House LLC. All rights reserved. Any third party use of this material, outside of this publication, is prohibited. Interested parties must apply directly to Random House LLC for permission. Published in French as "Questions de Methode," copyright © Editions Gallimard, Paris, 1960. Reprinted by permission. From CRITIQUE OF DIALECTICAL REASON vol. 1, trans. by Alan Sheridan-Smith, ed. by Jonathan Ree (1976) is reprinted by permission of Verso. Copyright © 1976 NLB. From BEING AND NOTHINGNESS, trans. by Hazel E. Barnes. Translation copyright © 1956 by Philosophical Library. Copyright © renewed 1984. Originally appeared in French as "L'Être et le neant." Copyright © 1943 by Editions Gallimard. Reprinted by permission of Philosophical Library, Taylor & Francis Books, UK, and Georges Borchardt, Inc., for Editions Gallimard. "Existentialism is a Humanism" from EXISTENTIALISM, trans. by Bernard Frechtman. Translation copyright © 1947 by Philosophical Library. Copyright © renewed 1975. Originally a 1946 lecture in French entitled "L'Existentialisme est un humanisme." Copyright © 1996 by Editions Gallimard. Reprinted by permission of Philosophical Library, Taylor & Francis Books, UK, and Georges Borchardt, Inc., for Editions Gallimard. Rights outside North America by permission of Taylor & Francis Book UK.

Max Scheler: From MAN'S PLACE IN NATURE, trans. by Hans Meyerhoff, Copyright © 1961 by Beacon Press; originally published in German under the title of "Die Stellung des Menschen im Kosmos," copyright © 1928 by A, Francke A.G., Bern. Reprinted by permission of Beacon Press, Boston. From FORMALISM IN ETHICS AND NON-FORMAL ETHICS OF VALUES, fifth rev. ed., trans. by Manfred S. Frings and Roger L. Funk (1973). Copyright © 1973 by Northwestern University Press. All rights reserved. Originally published in German as DER FORMALISMUS IN DER ETHIK UND DIE MATERIALE WERTETHIK by A. Francke AG Verlag, Bern, 1966.

Friedrich Schelling: From IDEAS FOR A PHILOSOPHY OF NATURE, trans. by Errol E. Harris and Peter Heath, (1988), is reprinted by permission of Cambridge University Press. Copyright © 1988 by Cambridge University Press. From OF HUMAN FREEDOM, trans. by James Gutmann. Copyright 1936 by Carus Publishing Company. All Open Court Publishing material is copyrighted by Carus Publishing Company, d/b/a/ Cricket Media, and/or various authors and illustrators. Any commercial use or distribution without permission is strictly prohibited. Please visit http://www.cricketmedia.com/info/licensing2 for licensing and http://www.opencourtbooks.com/ for subscriptions.

Index of Authors and Works